The Oxford
Paperback Dictionary

The Oxford Paperback Dictionary

Compiled by Joyce M. Hawkins

SECOND EDITION

Oxford Toronto Melbourne

OXFORD UNIVERSITY PRESS

1983

Oxford University Press, Walton Street, Oxford OX2 6DP

London Glasgow New York Toronto
Delhi Bombay Calcutta Madras Karachi
Kuala Lumpur Singapore Hong Kong Tokyo
Nairobi Dar es Salaam Cape Town
Melbourne Auckland

and associates in
Beirut Berlin Ibadan Mexico City Nicosia

First published 1979
Second edition 1983

British Library Cataloguing in Publication Data

The Oxford paperback dictionary – New ed.
1. English language – Dictionaries
I. Hawkins, Joyce M.
423 PE1625
ISBN 0–19–281381–1

Printed in Great Britain by
Richard Clay (The Chaucer Press) Ltd,
Bungay, Suffolk

Preface to the Second Edition

In this new edition the *Oxford Paperback Dictionary* has been enlarged and updated, with the addition of a substantial number of terms in computer technology and an increased number of the notes on usage that were such a popular feature of the first edition.

I am grateful to my colleagues in the Oxford English Dictionary department, and particularly to the chief editor, Dr R. W. Burchfield CBE, for continued help and support.

J.M.H.
1983

Preface to the First Edition

This is an entirely new member of the Oxford family of dictionaries, and has been specially prepared for those who need a compact, up-to-date, and moderately priced guide to the English of today. It contains the words and phrases most likely to be met in everyday life, including a number of slang and colloquial expressions and a selection of technical terms. Names of countries of the world are included, together with the term used for the people of each, and names of the most important capital cities.

I am grateful to my colleagues in the Oxford English Dictionary department of the Oxford University Press for assistance of various kinds, particularly to Dr John Sykes, editor of the *Concise Oxford Dictionary*, who has given generous help at all stages of the work, and to A. J. Augarde, Mrs J. Coulson, D. J. Edmonds, Miss I. Macleod, and A. J. Spooner, who assisted with proof-reading.

J.M.H.

Introduction

Spelling

Some words have two or more spellings that are in common use, but few variants are given here. The aim is not to dictate the use of a particular spelling, but to offer a standard form to those who seek one. When two spellings are equally common the preferred one is given first. Similar principles are followed with regard to pronunciation.

Words ending in **-ize** and **-ization** (such as *realize* and *realization*) may also be speld with *s* instead of *z*. Words given in this dictionary with the spelling **-ise** (such as *advertise* and *surprise*) do not have an alternative spelling with *z*.

Derived forms

Plurals of nouns, comparatives in *-er* and superlatives in *-est* of adjectives and adverbs, and derived forms of verbs, are given if they are irregular or if there might be doubt about the spelling. When only two verb forms are given:

admit *v.* (admitted, admitting)

the first form is both the past tense (he *admitted* it) and the past participle (it was *admitted*). Where three forms are given:

come *v.* (came, come, coming)
freeze *v.* (froze, frozen, freezing)

the first is the past tense (he *came*; it *froze*) and the second is the past participle (he had *come*; it was *frozen*).

Notes on usage

These are introduced by the symbol ¶ and give comments about the meanings of words that are often confused (such as *gourmand* and *gourmet*), grammatical points (such as whether *data* and *media* are singular or plural), and information about the origin of expressions (such as *fifth column*, *sour grapes*) especially where this helps to a better understanding of why the words are used in this way.

Proprietary terms

This book includes some words which are or are asserted to be proprietary names. The presence or absence of such assertions should not be regarded as affecting the legal status of any proprietary name or trade mark.

Pronunciation

A guide to this is given for any word that is difficult to pronounce, or difficult to recognize when read, or is spelt the same as another word but pronounced differently. The pronunciation given represents the standard speech of southern England. It is shown in brackets, usually just after the word itself, and as a rule only one pronunciation is given (see the note on Spelling, above).

The letters *pr.* (= pronounced) are sometimes put in to make clear that it is the pronunciation that follows, not an alternative spelling.

Words are broken up into small units, usually of one syllable. The syllable that is spoken with most stress in a word of two or more syllables is shown in heavy letters, like **this.**

The sounds represented are as follows:

a *as in* cat	i *as in* pin	s *as in* sit
ă *as in* ago	ĭ *as in* pencil	sh *as in* shop
ah *as in* calm	I *as in* eye	t *as in* top
air *as in* hair	j *as in* jam	th *as in* thin
ar *as in* bar	k *as in* king	*th as in* this
aw *as in* law	l *as in* leg	u *as in* cup
ay *as in* say	m *as in* man	ŭ *as in* circus
b *as in* bat	n *as in* not	uu *as in* book
ch *as in* chin	ng *as in* sing, finger	v *as in* van
d *as in* day	nk *as in* thank	w *as in* will
e *as in* bed	o *as in* top	y *as in* yes
ě *as in* taken	ŏ *as in* lemon	or when preceded
ee *as in* meet	oh *as in* most	by a consonant = I
eer *as in* beer	oi *as in* join	*as in* cry, realize
er *as in* her	oo *as in* soon	yoo *as in* unit
ew *as in* few	oor *as in* poor	yoor *as in* Europe
ewr *as in* pure	or *as in* for	yr *as in* fire
f *as in* fat	ow *as in* cow	z *as in* zebra
g *as in* get	p *as in* pen	zh *as in* vision
h *as in* hat	r *as in* red	

A consonant is sometimes doubled, especially to help to show that the vowel just before it is short (like the vowels in *cat*, *bed*, *pin*, *top*, *cup*), or when without this the combination of letters might suggest a wrong pronunciation through looking misleadingly like a familiar word. The pronunciation of a word (or part of a word) is sometimes indicated by giving a well-known word that rhymes with it.

Abbreviations

abbrev.	abbreviation	*int.*	interjection
adj.	adjective	*n.*	noun
adjs.	adjectives	*ns.*	nouns
adv.	adverb	*pl.*	plural
advs.	adverbs	*pl. n.*	plural noun
Amer.	American	*pr.*	pronounced
Austral.	Australian	*prep.*	preposition
conj.	conjunction	*preps.*	prepositions
conjs.	conjunctions	*v.*	verb

Abbreviations that are in general use (such as ft.,
RC and UK) appear in the dictionary itself.

Aa

A the first letter of the alphabet. **A1**, (*informal*) in perfect condition; first-rate. **from A to Z**, from beginning to end.

a *adj.* (called the *indefinite article*) **1**. one person or thing but not any specific one, *I need a knife.* **2**. per, *we pay £40 a year*; *twice a day.*

Aaron's rod (air-ŏn) any of several tall flowering plants, especially mullein. ¶ In the Bible, Aaron's rod sprouted and blossomed as a sign that he was designated by God as high priest of the Hebrews.

aback *adv.* **taken aback**, disconcerted.

abacus (ab-ă-kŭs) *n.* (*pl.* abacuses) a frame containing parallel rods with beads that slide up and down, used for counting.

abaft *adv.* in the stern half of a ship. — *prep.* nearer to the stern than.

abandon *v.* **1**. to go away from (a person or thing or place) without intending to return; *abandon ship*, leave a sinking ship. **2**. to give up, to cease work on, *abandon the attempt.* **3**. to yield completely to an emotion or impulse, *abandoned himself to despair.* —*n.* careless freedom of manner. —**abandonment** *n.*

abandoned *adj.* (of behaviour) showing abandon, lacking restraint, depraved.

abase *v.* to humiliate, to degrade. **abasement** *n.*

abashed *adj.* embarrassed or ashamed.

abate *v.* to make or become less; *the storm abated*, died down. **abatement** *n.*

abattoir (ab-ă-twar) *n.* a slaughterhouse.

abbess (ab-ess) *n.* a woman who is head of an abbey of nuns.

abbey *n.* **1**. a building occupied by monks or nuns living as a community. **2**. the community itself. **3**. a church or house that was formerly an abbey; *the Abbey*, Westminster Abbey.

abbot *n.* a man who is head of an abbey of monks.

abbreviate *v.* to shorten (especially a word or title).

abbreviation *n.* **1**. abbreviating, being abbreviated. **2**. a shortened form of a word or title.

ABC *n.* **1**. the alphabet. **2**. the elementary facts of a subject, *the ABC of carpentry.*

abdicate *v.* to resign from a throne or other high office. **abdication** *n.*

abdomen (ab-dŏm-ĕn) *n.* **1**. the part of the body below the chest and diaphragm, containing most of the digestive organs.

2. the hindmost section of the body of an insect, spider, or crustacean, *head, thorax, and abdomen.* **abdominal** (ăb-dom-inăl) *adj.*, **abdominally** *adv.*

abduct *v.* to carry off (a person) illegally by force or fraud. **abduction** *n.*, **abductor** *n.*

Aberdeen Angus a Scottish breed of black hornless cattle.

Aberdonian (ab-er-doh-niăn) *adj.* of Aberdeen. —*n.* a native or inhabitant of Aberdeen.

aberration (ab-er-ay-shŏn) *n.* **1**. a deviation from what is normal. **2**. a mental or moral lapse. **3**. distortion, e.g. of an image produced through an imperfect lens.

abet *v.* (abetted, abetting) to encourage or assist in committing an offence. **abetter** (*or*, in legal use) **abettor** *n.*, **abetment** *n.*

abeyance (ă-bay-ăns) *n.* **in abeyance**, (of a right or rule or problem etc.) suspended for a time.

abhor (ăb-hor) *v.* (abhorred, abhorring) to detest.

abhorrent (*rhymes with* torrent) *adj.* detestable. **abhorrence** *n.* detestation.

abide *v.* (abided (in sense 1 abode), abiding) **1**. (*old use*) to remain, to dwell. **2**. to bear, to endure, *can't abide wasps.* □ **abide by**, to act in accordance with; *abide by a promise*, keep it; *abide by the consequences*, accept them.

abiding *adj.* long-lasting, permanent.

Abidjan (ab-i-jahn) the capital of the Ivory Coast.

ability *n.* **1**. the quality that makes an action or process possible, the capacity or power to do something. **2**. cleverness, talent.

abject (ab-jekt) *adj.* **1**. wretched, without resources, *abject poverty.* **2**. lacking all pride, *an abject coward*; *an abject apology*, very humble. **abjectly** *adv.*

ablaze *adj.* blazing.

able *adj.* **1**. having the ability to do something. **2**. having great ability, competent. **ably** *adv.* □ **able-bodied** *adj.* fit and strong.

ablutions (ă-bloo-shŏnz) *pl. n.* **1**. washing; *perform one's ablutions*, wash oneself. **2**. a place with facilities for washing oneself.

abnegation (abni-gay-shŏn) *n.* renunciation, self-denial.

abnormal *adj.* different from what is normal. **abnormally** *adv.*, **abnormality** (ab-nor-mal-iti) *n.*

1

aboard *adv. & prep.* on or into a ship or aircraft or train.

abode[1] *n.* (*old use*) a dwelling-place.

abode[2] *see* abide.

abolish *v.* to put an end to, *abolish slavery.* **abolition** (abŏ-**lish**-ŏn) *n.*

abolitionist *n.* a person who favours abolishing capital punishment.

A-bomb *n.* an atomic bomb.

abominable *adj.* 1. detestable, loathsome. 2. very bad or unpleasant, *abominable weather.* ☐ **Abominable Snowman**, a large man-like or bear-like animal said to exist in the Himalayas, a yeti.

abominate *v.* to detest, to loathe. **abomination** *n.* loathing, something loathed.

aboriginal *adj.* existing in a land from earliest times or from before the arrival of colonists, *aboriginal inhabitants* or *plants.* —*n.* an aboriginal inhabitant, especially (*Aboriginal*) of Australia.

aborigines (ab-er-**ij**-in-eez) *pl. n.* aboriginal inhabitants. **aborigine** *n.* (*informal*) an aboriginal inhabitant.

abort (ă-**bort**) *v.* 1. to cause or suffer abortion. 2. to end or cause to end prematurely and unsuccessfully.

abortion *n.* 1. the expulsion (either spontaneous or induced) of a foetus from the womb before it is able to survive, especially in the first 28 weeks of pregnancy. 2. a misshapen creature or thing.

abortionist *n.* a person who practises abortion illegally.

abortive *adj.* 1. producing abortion. 2. unsuccessful, *an abortive attempt.* **abortively** *adv.*

abound *v.* 1. to be plentiful, *fish abound in the river.* 2. to have in great quantities, *the river abounds in fish.*

about *prep. & adv.* 1. all around, *look about you.* 2. somewhere near, not far off, *he's somewhere about.* 3. here and there in (a place), *papers were lying about* or *about the room.* 4. on the move, in circulation, *will soon be about again.* 5. approximately, *about £10.* 6. in connection with, on the matter or subject of, *what is he talking about?* 7. so as to face in the opposite direction, *put the ship about.* 8. in rotation, *on duty week and week about.* ☐ **about-face, about-turn** *ns.* a complete reversal of previous actions or opinions. **be about to,** to be on the point or verge of doing something.

above *adv.* 1. at or to a higher point. 2. earlier in a book or article, *mentioned above.* —**above** *prep.* 1. over, higher than, more than. 2. upstream from. 3. beyond the level or reach of, *she is above suspicion;*

above himself, carried away by high spirits or conceit. 4. more important than, *this above all.* ☐ **above-board** *adv. & adj.* without deception or concealment, done honourably.

abracadabra (abră-kă-**dab**-ră) *n.* 1. a supposedly magic formula or spell. 2. gibberish.

abrade (ă-**brayd**) *v.* to scrape or wear away by rubbing.

abrasion (ă-**bray**-zhŏn) *n.* abrading, an abraded place.

abrasive (ă-**bray**-siv) *adj.* 1. causing abrasion. 2. harsh, causing angry feelings, *an abrasive personality.* —*n.* a substance used for grinding or polishing surfaces.

abreast *adv.* 1. side by side and facing the same way. 2. keeping up, not behind, *keep abreast of modern developments.*

abridge *v.* to shorten by using fewer words. **abridgement** *n.*

abroad *adv.* 1. away from one's own country. 2. far and wide, everywhere, *scattered the seeds abroad.* 3. out and about, *nothing was abroad.*

abrogate (**ab**-rŏ-gayt) *v.* to cancel or repeal, *abrogate a law.* **abrogation** *n.*

abrupt *adj.* 1. sudden, *came to an abrupt stop.* 2. disconnected, not smooth, *short abrupt sentences.* 3. curt. 4. (of a slope) very steep. **abruptly** *adv.,* **abruptness** *n.*

abscess (**ab**-sis) *n.* a collection of pus formed in the body.

abscond (ăb-**skond**) *v.* to go away secretly, especially after wrongdoing. **absconder** *n.*

abseil (**ab**-sayl) *v.* to descend a rock-face using a doubled rope that is fixed at a higher point. —*n.* this process.

absence *n.* 1. being away, the period of this. 2. lack, non-existence, *in the absence of proof.* 3. inattention, *absence of mind.*

absent[1] (**ab**-sĕnt) *adj.* 1. not present, *absent from school.* 2. non-existent. 3. with one's mind on other things, *stared in an absent way.* **absently** *adv.* ☐ **absent-minded** *adj.* with one's mind on other things; forgetful. **absent-mindedly** *adv.*

absent[2] (ăb-**sent**) *v.* to stay away, *absented himself from the meeting.*

absentee *n.* a person who is absent from work etc.; *absentee landlord,* one who seldom visits the premises he lets. **absenteeism** *n.* frequent absence from work or school.

absinthe (**ab**-sinth) *n.* a green liqueur made from brandy with wormwood and other herbs.

absolute *adj.* 1. complete, *absolute silence.* 2. unrestricted, *absolute power.* 3. independent, not relative, *there is no* *absolute standard for beauty.* **4.** (*informal*) utter, out-and-out, *it's an absolute miracle.* □ **absolute majority,** a majority over all rivals combined.

absolutely *adv.* **1.** completely. **2.** without restrictions, unconditionally. **3.** actually, *it absolutely exploded.* **4.** (*informal, pr.* ab-so-**loot**-li) quite so, yes.

absolution (absŏ-**loo**-shŏn) *n.* a priest's formal declaration of the forgiveness of penitents' sins.

absolve *v.* **1.** to clear of blame or guilt. **2.** to give absolution to (a person). **3.** to free from an obligation.

absorb *v.* **1.** to take in, to combine or merge into itself or oneself, *absorb fluid, food, knowledge*; *the large firm absorbed the smaller ones,* incorporated them. **2.** to reduce the effect of, *buffers absorbed most of the shock.* **3.** to occupy the attention or interest of; *an absorbing book,* holding one's interest. **absorber** *n.,* **absorption** *n.*

absorbable *adj.* able to be absorbed.

absorbent *adj.* able to absorb moisture etc. **absorbency** *n.*

absorptive *adj.* **1.** able to absorb liquids etc. **2.** engrossing.

abstain *v.* **1.** to keep oneself from some action or indulgence, especially from drinking alcohol. **2.** to refrain from using one's vote. **abstainer** *n.,* **abstention** *n.*

abstemious (ăb-**steem**-iŭs) *adj.* sparing in one's taking of food and drink, not self-indulgent. **abstemiously** *adv.,* **abstemiousness** *n.*

abstinence (**ab**-stin-ĕns) *n.* abstaining, especially from food or alcohol. **abstinent** *adj.*

abstract[1] (**ab**-strakt) *adj.* **1.** having no material existence, *beauty is an abstract quality.* **2.** theoretical rather than practical. —**abstract** *n.* **1.** an abstract quality or idea. **2.** a summary. **3.** an example of abstract art. **abstractly** *adv.,* **abstractness** *n.* □ **abstract art,** art which does not represent things pictorially but expresses the artist's ideas or sensations. **in the abstract,** regarded theoretically, *he favours economy in the abstract but refuses to economize.*

abstract[2] (ăb-**strakt**) *v.* **1.** to take out, to separate, to remove. **2.** to make a written summary. **abstractor** *n.*

abstracted *adj.* with one's mind on other things, not paying attention. **abstractedness** *n.*

abstraction *n.* **1.** abstracting, removing. **2.** an abstract idea. **3.** abstractedness.

abstruse (ăb-**strooss**) *adj.* hard to understand, profound. **abstrusely** *adv.,* **abstruseness** *n.*

absurd *adj.* **1.** not in accordance with common sense, very unsuitable. **2.** ridiculous, foolish. **absurdly** *adv.,* **absurdity** *n.*

abundance *n.* a quantity that is more than enough, plenty.

abundant *adj.* **1.** more than enough, plentiful. **2.** having plenty of something, rich, *a land abundant in minerals.* **abundantly** *adv.*

abuse[1] (ă-**bewss**) *n.* **1.** a misuse. **2.** an unjust or corrupt practice. **3.** abusive words, insults.

abuse[2] (ă-**bewz**) *v.* **1.** to make a bad or wrong use of, *abuse one's authority.* **2.** to ill-treat. **3.** to attack in words, to utter insults to or about.

abusive (ă-**bew**-siv) *adj.* insulting, criticizing harshly or angrily. **abusively** *adv.*

abut (ă-**but**) *v.* (abutted, abutting) to have a common boundary, to end or lean against, *their land abuts on ours*; *the garage abuts against the house.* **abutment** *n.*

abysmal (ă-**hiz**-măl) *adj.* **1.** extreme, *abysmal ignorance.* **2.** (*informal*) extremely bad, *their taste is abysmal.* **abysmally** *adv.*

abyss (ă-**biss**) *n.* a hole so deep that it appears bottomless.

AC or **a.c.** *abbrev.* alternating current.

acacia (ă-**kay**-shă) *n.* **1.** a tree or shrub from which gum arabic is obtained. **2.** a related tree (the false acacia or locust-tree) grown for ornament.

academic (akă-**dem**-ik) *adj.* **1.** of a school or college or university. **2.** scholarly as opposed to technical or practical, *academic subjects.* **3.** of theoretical interest only, with no practical application. —*n,* an academic person. —**academically** *adv.*

academician (ă-kad-ĕ-**mish**-ăn) *n.* a member of an Academy.

academy *n.* **1.** a school, especially for specialized training. **2.** (in Scotland) a secondary school. **3.** *Academy,* a society of scholars or artists.

acanthus *n.* a Mediterranean plant with large thistle-like leaves.

ACAS (**ay**-kass) *abbrev.* Advisory, Conciliation, and Arbitration Service.

accede (ăk-**seed**) *v.* **1.** to take office, to become monarch. **2.** to agree to what is proposed.

accelerate *v.* **1.** to cause to move faster or happen earlier, to increase the speed of a motor vehicle. **2.** to become faster, to move or happen more quickly. **acceleration** *n.*

accelerator *n.* **1.** a device for increasing

speed. **2.** the pedal or other device operating this.

accent¹ (ak-sĕnt) *n.* **1.** emphasis on a syllable or word. **2.** a mark indicating such emphasis or the quality of a vowel-sound. **3.** a national, local, or individual way of pronouncing words. **4.** the emphasis given to something, *the accent is on quality.*

accent² (ăk-**sent**) *v.* **1.** to pronounce with an accent. **2.** to emphasize.

accentuate (ăk-**sen**-tew-ayt) *v.* to emphasize. **accentuation** *n.*

accept *v.* **1.** to take (a thing offered) willingly, to say yes to an offer or invitation. **2.** to undertake (a responsibility); *we accept liability for the accident*, agree that we are legally responsible. **3.** to treat as welcome, *they were never really accepted by their neighbours.* **4.** to be willing to agree to, *we accept the proposed changes.* **5.** to take as true, *we do not accept your conclusions.* **acceptance** *n.*, **acceptor** *n.*

acceptable *adj.* **1.** worth accepting, welcome. **2.** tolerable, *an acceptable risk.* **acceptably** *adv.*, **acceptability** *n.*

access (ak-sess) *n.* **1.** a way in, a means of approaching or entering. **2.** the right or opportunity of reaching or using, *students need access to books.* **3.** an attack of emotion, *a sudden access of rage.* —*v.* to retrieve (information stored in a computer). ☐ **direct** *or* **random access,** the process of storing or retrieving information in a computer without having to read through items stored previously.

accessible *adj.* able to be reached or used. **accessibly** *adv.*, **accessibility** *n.*

accession (ăk-**sesh**-ŏn) *n.* **1.** reaching a rank or position, *the Queen's accession to the throne.* **2.** an addition, being added, *recent accessions to the library.*

accessory (ăk-**sess**-er-i) *adj.* additional, extra. —*n.* **1.** a thing that is extra or useful or decorative but not essential, a minor fitting or attachment. **2.** a person who helps another in a crime. ¶The spelling *accessary* is now disused.

accident *n.* **1.** an unexpected or undesirable event, especially one causing injury or damage. **2.** chance, fortune, *we met by accident.*

accidental *adj.* happening by accident. —*n.* a sign attached to a single note in music, showing temporary departure from the key signature. —**accidentally** *adv.*

acclaim (ă-**klaym**) *v.* to welcome with shouts of approval, to applaud enthusiastically. —*n.* a shout of welcome, applause.

acclamation (aklă-**may**-shŏn) *n.*

acclimatize *v.* to get used to a new climate or new conditions. **acclimatization** *n.*

accolade (ak-ŏ-**layd**) *n.* **1.** a ceremonial tap on the shoulder with the flat of a sword, given when a knighthood is conferred. **2.** praise, approval.

accommodate *v.* **1.** to provide or supply, *the bank will accommodate you with a loan.* **2.** to provide lodging or room for. **3.** to adapt, to make harmonize with, *I will accommodate my plans to yours.*

accommodating *adj.* willing to do as one is asked.

accommodation *n.* **1.** the process of accommodating or adapting. **2.** lodgings, living-premises. ☐ **accommodation address,** an address used on letters for a person who is unable or unwilling to give his permanent address.

accompaniment *n.* **1.** an accompanying thing. **2.** an instrumental part supporting a solo instrument or voice or a choir.

accompanist *n.* a person who plays a musical accompaniment.

accompany *v.* (accompanied, accompanying) **1.** to go with, to travel with as a companion or helper. **2.** to be present with, *the fever was accompanied by delirium.* **3.** to provide in addition. **4.** to play a musical accompaniment to.

accomplice (ă-**kum**-plis) *n.* a partner in wrongdoing.

accomplish (ă-**kum**-plish) *v.* to succeed in doing, to fulfil.

accomplished *adj.* skilled, having many accomplishments.

accomplishment *n.* **1.** accomplishing. **2.** skill in a social or domestic art.

accord *n.* consent, agreement. —*v.* **1.** to be in harmony or consistent. **2.** (*formal*) to give or grant, *he was accorded this privilege.* ☐ **of one's own accord,** without being asked or compelled. **with one accord,** all agreeing.

accordance *n.* agreement, conformity.

according *adv.* **according as,** in proportion as, in a manner depending on whether, *he was praised or blamed according as his work was good or bad.* **according to,** as stated by or in, *according to the Bible*; in a manner consistent with or in proportion to, *grouped according to size.*

accordingly *adv.* **1.** according to what is known or stated, *ask what they want and act accordingly.* **2.** therefore.

accordion *n.* a portable musical instrument with bellows, keys, and metal reeds.

accordionist *n.* a person who plays the accordion.

accost (ă-**kost**) *v.* **1.** to approach and speak to. **2.** (of a prostitute) to solicit.

account *n.* **1.** a statement of money paid or owed for goods or services. **2.** a credit arrangement with a bank or firm. **3.** importance, *that is of no account.* **4.** a description, a report. —*v.* to regard as, *a person is accounted innocent until proved guilty*. □ **account-book** *n.* a book for keeping accounts in. **account for,** to give a reckoning of (money received); to explain the cause of; to be the explanation of; to bring about the death or destruction etc. of; to supply or constitute (an amount). **by all accounts,** according to what everyone says. **give a good account of oneself,** to perform well. **keep accounts,** to keep a systematic record of money spent and received. **on account,** as an interim payment, *here is £10 on account*; debited to be paid for later, *bought it on account*. **on account of,** because of. **on no account,** under no circumstances, never. **on one's own account,** for one's own purposes and at one's own risk. **take into account,** to make allowances for. **turn to account,** to use profitably.

accountable *adj.* **1.** obliged to give a reckoning or explanation for one's actions etc., responsible. **2.** able to be explained. **accountability** *n.*

accountant *n.* one whose profession is to keep and examine business accounts. **accountancy** *n.* this profession.

accoutrements (ă-**koo**-trĕ-mĕnts) *pl. n.* equipment, a soldier's outfit other than weapons and clothes.

Accra (ă-**krah**) the capital of Ghana.

accredited (ă-**kred**-itid) *adj.* **1.** officially recognized, *our accredited representative*. **2.** generally accepted or believed. **3.** certified as being of a prescribed quality.

accretion (ă-**kree**-shŏn) *n.* **1.** a growth or increase by means of gradual additions. **2.** the growing of separate things into one.

accrue (ă-**kroo**) *v.* to come as a natural increase or advantage, to accumulate, *interest accrues on investments*. **accrual** *n.*

accumulate *v.* **1.** to acquire an increasing quantity of. **2.** to increase in quantity or amount. **accumulation** *n.*

accumulator *n.* **1.** a storage battery. **2.** a bet placed on a series of events, winnings from each being staked on the next.

accurate *adj.* **1.** free from error, conforming exactly to a standard or to truth. **2.** careful and exact, showing precision, *an accurate mind.* **accurately** *adv.,* **accuracy** *n.*

accursed (ă-**ker**-sid) *adj.* **1.** under a curse. **2.** (*informal*) detestable, hateful.

accusation *n.* **1.** accusing, being accused. **2.** a statement accusing a person of a fault or crime or wrongdoing.

accusative (ă-**kew**-ză-tiv) *n.* the objective

form of a word, e.g. *him* in *'we saw him'*.

accuse *v.* to state that one lays blame for a fault, crime, or wrongdoing etc. upon (a named person). **accuser** *n.,* **accusingly** *adv.* □ **the accused,** the person accused in a court of law.

accustom *v.* to make or become used to. **accustomed** *adj.* usual, customary, *in his accustomed seat.*

ace *n.* **1.** a playing-card with one spot. **2.** a person who excels at something, *an ace pilot.* **3.** (in tennis) a stroke that one's opponent cannot return. □ **have an ace up one's sleeve,** to have something effective kept secretly in reserve. **play one's ace,** to use one's best resource. **within an ace of,** on the verge of, *was within an ace of collapse.*

acerbity (ă-**serb**-iti) *n.* sharpness of speech or manner.

acetate (**ass**-it-ayt) *n.* **1.** a compound derived from acetic acid. **2.** a fabric made from cellulose acetate.

acetic (ă-**see**-tik) *adj.* of vinegar. **acetic acid,** the acid that gives vinegar its characteristic taste and smell.

acetone (**ass**-i-tohn) *n.* a colourless liquid used as a solvent.

acetylene (ă-**set**-i-leen) *n.* a gas that burns with a bright flame, used in cutting and welding metal.

ache *v.* **1.** to suffer a dull continuous physical or mental pain. **2.** to yearn. —*n.* a dull continuous pain. —**achy** *adj.*

achievable *adj.* able to be achieved.

achieve *v.* to accomplish, to gain or reach by effort, *we achieved success at last.* **achievement** *n.*

Achilles' heel (ă-**kil**-eez) a weak or vulnerable point. **Achilles tendon,** the tendon connecting the heel with the calf muscles. ¶ Named after a hero in Greek legend, who was invulnerable except in his heel.

acid *adj.* **1.** sharp-tasting, sour. **2.** looking or sounding bitter, *acid remarks.* —**acid** *n.* **1.** a sour substance. **2.** any of a class of substances containing hydrogen that can be replaced by a metal to form a salt. **3.** (*slang*) the drug LSD. —**acidly** *adv.* □ **acid test,** a severe or conclusive test. (¶ Acid is applied to a metal to test whether it is gold or not.)

acidic (ă-**sid**-ik) *adj.* of or like an acid.

acidify (ă-**sid**-i-fy) *v.* (acidified, acidifying) to make or become acid.

acidity (ă-**sid**-iti) *n.* **1.** being acid. **2.** an over-acid condition of the stomach.

acidosis (asid-**oh**-sis) *n.* an over-acid condition of the blood or body tissues.

acidulated (ă-**sid**-yoo-layt-id) *adj.* made slightly acid,

acknowledge *v.* **1.** to admit that something is true or valid. **2.** to report that one has received something, *acknowledge his letter.* **3.** to express thanks for, *acknowledge his services to the town.* **4.** to indicate that one has noticed or recognized, *acknowledged my presence with a sniff.* **acknowledgement** *n.*

acme (**ak**-mi) *n.* the highest point, the peak of perfection.

acne (**ak**-ni) *n.* inflammation of the oil-glands of the skin, producing red pimples.

acolyte (**ak**-ŏ-lyt) *n.* a person who assists a priest in certain church services.

aconite *n.* a perennial plant of the buttercup family, with a poisonous root.

acorn *n.* the fruit of the oak-tree, with a cup-like base.

acoustic (ă-**koo**-stik) *adj.* of sound or the sense of hearing, of acoustics. **acoustical** *adj.*, **acoustically** *adv.* □ **acoustics** *pl. n.* the properties of sound, the qualities of a hall etc. that make it good or bad for carrying sound.

acquaint *v.* to make aware or familiar, *acquaint him with the facts.* **be acquainted with**, to know slightly.

acquaintance *n.* **1.** being acquainted. **2.** a person one knows slightly.

acquiesce (akwi-**ess**) *v.* to agree without protest, to assent. **acquiesce in**, to accept as an arrangement.

acquiescent (akwi-**ess**-ĕnt) *adj.* acquiescing. **acquiescence** *n.*

acquire *v.* to gain possession of. **acquirement** *n.* □ **acquired taste**, a liking gained gradually.

acquisition (akwi-**zish**-ŏn) *n.* **1.** acquiring. **2.** something acquired.

acquisitive (ă-**kwiz**-itiv) *adj.* keen to acquire things. **acquisitively** *adv.*, **acquisitiveness** *n.*

acquit *v.* (acquitted, acquitting) to declare (a person) to be not guilty of the crime etc. with which he was charged. **acquit oneself**, to conduct oneself, to perform, *he acquitted himself well in the test.*

acquittal (ă-**kwi**-t'l) *n.* a judgement that a person is not guilty of the crime with which he was charged.

acre (**ay**-ker) *n.* **1.** a measure of land, 4840 sq. yds. **2.** a stretch of land, *broad acres.*

acreage (**ay**-ker-ij) *n.* the total number of acres.

acrid (**ak**-rid) *adj.* **1.** having a bitter smell or taste. **2.** bitter in temper or manner. **acridity** (ă-**krid**-iti) *n.*

acrimony (**ak**-ri-mŏni) *n.* bitterness of manner or words. **acrimonious** (akri-**moh**-niŭs) *adj.*, **acrimoniously** *adv.*

acrobat *n.* a performer of spectacular gymnastic feats. **acrobatic** *adj.*, **acrobatically** *adv.* □ **acrobatics** *pl. n.* acrobatic feats.

acronym (**ak**-rŏ-nim) *n.* a word formed from the initial letters of other words, e.g. *Ernie, Nato.*

acropolis (ă-**krop**-ŏ-lis) *n.* the citadel or upper fortified part of an ancient Greek city; *the Acropolis,* that of Athens.

across *prep. & adv.* **1.** from one side of a thing to the other. **2.** to or on the other side of. **3.** so as to be understood or accepted, *got his points across to the audience.* **4.** so as to form a cross or intersect, *laid across each other.* □ **across the board,** applying to all members or groups.

acrostic (ă-**kros**-tik) *n.* a word-puzzle or poem in which the first or last letters of each line form a word or words.

acrylic (ă-**kril**-ik) *adj.* of a synthetic material made from an organic acid. —*n.* an acrylic fibre, plastic, or resin.

act *n.* **1.** something done. **2.** the process of doing something, *caught in the act.* **3.** a decree or law made by a parliament. **4.** one of the main divisions of a play. **5.** one of a series of short performances in a programme, *a circus act.* **6.** (*informal*) a pose or pretence, *put on an act.* —**act** *v.* **1.** to perform actions, to behave, *you acted wisely.* **2.** to do what is required, to function, *act as umpire; the brakes did not act.* **3.** to have an effect on, *acid acts on metal.* **4.** to portray by actions, to perform a part in a play etc.; *act the fool,* to clown. □ **Act of God,** the operation of uncontrollable natural forces.

ACT *abbrev.* Australian Capital Territory.

acting *adj.* serving temporarily, especially as a substitute, *the acting headmaster.*

action *n.* **1.** the process of doing something, the exertion of energy or influence, *go into action; the action of acid on metal,* the way it affects metal. **2.** a thing done, *generous actions.* **3.** a series of events in a story or play, *the action is set in Spain.* **4.** a way or manner of moving or functioning, the mechanism of an instrument. **5.** a lawsuit. **6.** a battle, *was killed in action.* □ **out of action,** not working. **take action,** to do something in response to what has happened.

actionable *adj.* giving cause for a lawsuit.

activate *v.* to make active. **activation** *n.*, **activator** *n.*

active *adj.* **1.** moving about, characterized by energetic action. **2.** taking part in activities. **3.** functioning, in operation; *an active volcano,* one that erupts occasionally. **4.** having an effect, *the active in-*

gredients. **5.** radioactive. —*n.* the form of a verb used when the subject of the sentence is the doer of the action, e.g. *saw* in *'we saw him'.* —**actively** *adv.*, **activeness** *n.* □ **active service**, full-time service in the armed forces.

activist *n.* one who follows a policy of vigorous action, especially in politics.

activity *n.* **1.** being active, the exertion of energy. **2.** energetic action, being busy. **3.** actions, occupations, *outdoor activities.*

actor *n.* a performer in a stage play or a film. **actress** *n.*

actual *adj.* existing in fact, real, current. **actually** *adv.*

actuality (ak-tew-**al**-iti) *n.* reality. **actualities** *pl. n.* existing conditions.

actuary (ak-tew-er-i) *n.* an expert in statistics who calculates insurance risks and premiums. **actuarial** (ak-tew-**air**-iăl) *adj.*

actuate *v.* **1.** to activate (a movement or process). **2.** to be a motive for (a person's actions). **actuation** *n.*, **actuator** *n.*

acumen (ak-yoo-men) *n.* sharpness of mind, shrewdness.

acupuncture (ak-yoo-punk-cher) *n.* pricking the tissues of the body with fine needles to relieve pain or as a local anaesthetic. **acupuncturist** *n.* an expert in acupuncture.

acute *adj.* **1.** very perceptive, having a sharp mind **2.** sharp or severe in its effect, *acute pain; an acute shortage.* **3.** (of an illness) coming sharply to a crisis of severity, *acute appendicitis.* **acutely** *adv.*, **acuteness** *n.* □ **acute accent**, a mark over a vowel, as over *e* in *café.* **acute angle**, an angle of less than 90°.

ad *n.* (*informal*) an advertisement.

AD *abbrev.* of the Christian era. (¶ From the Latin *anno domini* = in the year of Our Lord.)

adage (**ad**-ij) *n.* a proverb, a saying.

adagio (ă-**dahj**-yoh) *adv.* (in music) slowly and gracefully. —*n.* (*pl.* adagios) a passage to be played in this way.

Adam (in Hebrew tradition) the first man; *I don't know him from Adam,* do not recognize him or know what he looks like. □ **Adam's apple,** the projection of cartilage at the front of the neck, especially in men.

adamant (**ad**-ă-mănt) *adj.* unyielding to requests, quite firm.

adapt *v.* to make or become suitable for a new use or situation. **adaptation** *n.*

adaptable *adj.* **1.** able to be adapted. **2.** able to adapt oneself. **adaptability** *n.*

adaptor *n.* a device that connects pieces of equipment that were not originally designed to be connected.

add *v.* **1.** to join (one thing to another) as an increase or supplement; *this adds to the expense,* increases it. **2.** to put numbers or amounts together to get a total. **3.** to make a further remark. □ **add up,** to find the total of; (*informal*) to seem consistent or reasonable, *his story doesn't add up.* **add up to,** to yield as a total; (*informal*) to result in, to be equivalent to.

addendum *n.* (*pl.* addenda) something added at the end of a book etc. ¶ The word *addenda* is used as a plural, and also as a collective noun with a singular verb, as in *the addenda contains new information.*

adder *n.* a small poisonous snake, a viper.

addict (**ad**-ikt) *n.* a person who is addicted to something, especially to drugs.

addicted (ă-**dik**-tid) *adj.* **1.** doing or using something as a habit or compulsively. **2.** devoted to something as a hobby or interest. **addiction** *n.*

addictive (ă-**dik**-tiv) *adj.* causing addiction.

Addis Ababa the capital of Ethiopia.

addition *n.* **1.** adding, being added. **2.** a thing added to something else. □ **in addition,** as an extra thing or circumstance.

additional *adj.* added, extra. **additionally** *adv.*

additive (**ad**-it-iv) *adj.* involving addition. —*n.* a substance added in small amounts for a special purpose.

addle *v.* **1.** to become rotten and produce no chick, *addled eggs.* **2.** to muddle or confuse, *addle one's brains.*

address *n.* **1.** the place where a person lives, particulars of where mail should be delivered to a person or firm. **2.** a speech delivered to an audience. **3.** the part of a computer instruction that specifies the location of a piece of stored information. —**address** *v.* **1.** to write directions for delivery on (an envelope or parcel). **2.** to make a speech to. **3.** to direct a remark or written statement to. **4.** to use a particular word or words in speaking or writing to, *how to address a bishop.* **5.** to apply (oneself) to a task or problem, to direct one's attention to (a problem). **6.** to take aim at (the ball) in golf. **7.** to store or retrieve (a piece of information) by using an address (see *n.* sense 3). □ **forms of address,** words (such as *Mr, Sir, Your Majesty*) used in addressing a person.

addressee (ad-ress-ee) *n.* a person to whom a letter etc. is addressed.

adduce (ă-**dewss**) *v.* to cite as an example or proof.

Aden (**ay**-d'n) the capital of the Democratic Republic of Yemen.

adenoids (**ad**-in-oidz) *pl. n.* enlarged

spongy tissue between the back of the nose and the throat, often hindering breathing. **adenoidal** *adj.*

adenoma (ad-in-**oh**-mă) *n.* a benign gland-like tumour.

adept (**ad**-ept) *adj.* very skilful. —*n.* one who is very skilful, *an adept at carpentry.*

adequate *adj.* **1.** sufficient, satisfactory. **2.** passable but not outstandingly good. **adequately** *adv.*, **adequacy** *n.*

adhere (ăd-**heer**) *v.* **1.** to stick when glued or by suction or as if by these. **2.** to remain faithful, to continue to give one's support (to a person or cause). **3.** to keep to and not alter, *we adhered to our plan.*

adherent *adj.* sticking, adhering. —*n.* a supporter of a party or doctrine. — **adherence** *n.*

adhesion (ăd-**hee**-*zh*ŏn) *n.* **1.** adhering. **2.** tissue formed when normally separate tissues of the body grow together as a result of inflammation or injury.

adhesive *adj.* causing things to adhere, sticky. —*n.* an adhesive substance. — **adhesiveness** *n.* □ **adhesive tape,** a strip of paper or transparent material coated with adhesive, used for fastening packages etc.

ad hoc for a specific purpose, *an ad hoc arrangement.* (¶ Latin, = for this.)

adieu (ă-**dew**) *int.* & *n.* (*pl.* adieus) goodbye.

ad infinitum (in-fin-**I**-tŭm) without limit, for ever. (¶ Latin, = to infinity.)

adipose (**ad**-i-pohs) *adj.* of animal fat, fatty. **adiposity** (ad-i-**poss**-iti) *n.*

adjacent *adj.* lying near, adjoining.

adjective (**aj**-ik-tiv) *n.* a word added to a noun to describe a quality or modify a meaning, e.g. *old, tall, Swedish, my, this.* **adjectival** (aj-ik-**ty**-văl) *adj.*, **adjectivally** *n.*

adjoin *v.* to be next or nearest to.

adjourn (ă-**jern**) *v.* **1.** to postpone, to break off temporarily. **2.** to break off and go elsewhere, *let's adjourn to the bar.* **adjournment** *n.*

adjudge *v.* to decide or award judicially, *he was adjudged to be guilty; the prize was adjudged to Charles.*

adjudicate (ă-**joo**-dik-ayt) *v.* **1.** to act as judge in a court, tribunal, or competition. **2.** to judge and pronounce a decision upon. **adjudication** *n.*, **adjudicator** *n.*

adjunct (**ad**-junkt) *n.* something added or attached but subordinate.

adjure (ă-**joor**) *v.* to command or urge solemnly, *I adjure you to tell the truth.* **adjuration** *n.*

adjust *v.* **1.** to arrange, to put into the proper position. **2.** to alter by a small amount so as to fit or be right for use, *the brakes need adjusting.* **3.** to be able to be

adjusted. **4.** to adapt or adapt oneself to new circumstances, *had difficulty in adjusting to civilian life.* **5.** to assess (loss or damages). **adjuster** *n.*, **adjustment** *n.*

adjustable *adj.* able to be adjusted.

adjutant (**aj**-oo-tănt) *n.* an army officer assisting a superior officer with administrative work. **adjutancy** *n.* □ **adjutant bird,** a large Indian stork.

ad lib as one pleases, without restraint (¶ From the Latin *ad libitum,* according to pleasure.) —**ad-lib** *adj.* said or done impromptu. —**ad-lib** *v.* (ad-libbed, ad-libbing) (*informal*) to speak impromptu, to improvise remarks or actions.

adman (**ad**-man) *n.* (*pl.* admen) (*informal*) a person who composes commercial advertisements.

admin (**ad**-min) *n.* (*informal*) administration.

administer *v.* **1.** to manage the business affairs of, to be an administrator, *administer a person's estate.* **2.** to give or hand out formally, to provide, *administer the sacrament; administer comfort* or *a rebuke; administer the oath to a person,* hear him swear it officially.

administrate *v.* to act as administrator.

administration *n.* **1.** administering. **2.** the management of public or business affairs.

administrative *adj.* of or involving administration.

administrator *n.* **1.** a person responsible for administration, one who has a talent for this. **2.** a person appointed to administer an estate.

admirable *adj.* worthy of admiration, excellent. **admirably** *adv.*

admiral *n.* a naval officer of high rank, commander of a fleet or squadron; *admiral of the Fleet, admiral, vice-admiral, rear-admiral,* the four grades of such officers. □ **red admiral, white admiral,** European species of butterfly.

Admiralty *n.* the former name for the department of State superintending the Royal Navy.

admire *v.* **1.** to regard with pleasure or satisfaction, to think highly of. **2.** to express admiration of, *don't forget to admire her cat.* **admiration** *n.*, **admirer** *n.*

admissible *adj.* capable of being admitted or allowed. **admissibly** *adv.*, **admissibility** *n.*

admission *n.* **1.** admitting, being admitted. **2.** the charge for this. **3.** a statement admitting something, a confession.

admit *v.* (admitted, admitting) **1.** to allow to enter. **2.** to accept into a school etc. as a pupil or into a hospital as a patient.

3. to accept as true or valid. **4.** to state reluctantly, *we admit that the task is difficult*. **5.** to leave room for, *the plan does not admit of improvement*.

admittance *n.* being allowed to enter, especially into a private place.

admittedly *adv.* as an acknowledged fact.

admixture *n.* something added as an ingredient.

admonish (ăd-**mon**-ish) *v.* **1.** to advise or urge seriously. **2.** to reprove mildly but firmly. **admonition** (admŏn-**ish**-ŏn) *n.*, **admonitory** (ăd-**mon**-it-er-i) *adj.*

ad nauseam (**naw**-si-am) to a sickening extent. (¶ Latin.)

ado (ă-**doo**) *n.* fuss, trouble, excitement.

adolescent (ad-ŏ-**less**-ĕnt) *adj.* between childhood and maturity. *—n.* an adolescent person. **adolescence** *n.*

Adonis (ă-**doh**-nis) *n.* a handsome young man. ¶ Named after a beautiful youth in mythology, loved by Venus.

adopt *v.* **1.** to take into one's family as a relation, especially as one's child with legal guardianship. **2.** to take (a person) as one's heir or representative, *adopt a candidate*. **3.** to take and use as one's own, *adopted this name* or *custom*. **4.** to accept responsibility for maintenance of (a road etc.). **5.** to approve or accept (a report or financial accounts). **adoption** *n.*

adoptive *adj.* related by adoption, *his adoptive parents*.

adorable *adj.* **1.** very lovable. **2.** (*informal*) delightful. **adorably** *adv.*

adore *v.* **1.** to love deeply. **2.** to worship as divine. **3.** (*informal*) to like very much. **adoration** *n.*, **adorer** *n.*

adorn *v.* **1.** to decorate with ornaments. **2.** to be an ornament to. **adornment** *n.*

adrenal (ă-**dree**-năl) *adj.* of the adrenal glands, ductless glands on top of the kidneys, secreting adrenalin. *—n.* an adrenal gland.

adrenalin (ă-**dren**-ă-lin) *n.* a hormone that stimulates the nervous system, secreted by a part of the adrenal glands or prepared synthetically.

Adriatic (ay-dri-**at**-ik) *adj.* of the Adriatic Sea, between Italy and Yugoslavia. *—n.* the Adriatic Sea.

adrift *adv.* & *adj.* **1.** drifting. **2.** (*informal*) unfastened, loose.

adroit (ă-**droit**) *adj.* skilful, ingenious. **adroitly** *adv.*, **adroitness** *n.*

adulation (ad-yoo-**lay**-shŏn) *n.* excessive flattery. **adulatory** (**ad**-yoo-layt-er-i) *adj.*

adult (**ad**-ult) *adj.* grown to full size or strength, mature. *—n.* an adult person. — **adulthood** *n.*

adulterant *n.* a substance added in adulterating something.

adulterate *v.* to make impure or poorer in quality by adding another substance, especially an inferior one. **adulteration** *n.*

adulterer *n.* a person who commits adultery. **adulteress** *n.*

adultery *n.* the act of being unfaithful to one's wife or husband by voluntarily having sexual intercourse with someone else. **adulterous** *adj.*

adumbrate *v.* to foreshadow.

advance *v.* **1.** to move or put forward, to make progress. **2.** to help the progress of, *advance someone's interests*. **3.** to bring forward or make, *advance a suggestion*. **4.** to bring (an event) to an earlier date. **5.** to lend (money), to pay before a due date, *advance her a month's salary*.— **advance** *n.* **1.** a forward movement, progress. **2.** an increase in price or amount. **3.** a loan, payment beforehand. *—adj.* going before others, done or provided in advance, *the advance party*; *advance bookings*. **—advancement** *n.* □ **advances** *pl. n.* attempts to establish a friendly relationship or a business agreement. **in advance**, ahead in place or time.

advanced *adj.* **1.** far on in progress or in life, *an advanced age*. **2.** not elementary, *advanced studies*. **3.** (of ideas etc.) new and not yet generally accepted. □ **Advanced level**, a GCE examination for university entrance qualification.

advantage *n.* **1.** a favourable condition or circumstance. **2.** benefit, profit; *the treaty is to their advantage*, benefits them; *turn it to your advantage*, use it profitably. **3.** the next point won after deuce in tennis. □ **take advantage of**, to make use of; to exploit. **to advantage**, making a good effect, *the painting shows to advantage here*.

advantageous (ad-van-**tay**-jŭs) *adj.* profitable, beneficial. **advantageously** *adv.*

Advent *n.* **1.** the coming of Christ; *Second Advent*, his coming at the Last Judgement. **2.** the season (with four Sundays) before Christmas Day. **3.** *advent*, the arrival of an important person, event, or development.

Adventist *n.* a member of a sect believing that Christ's second coming is very near.

adventure *n.* **1.** an exciting or dangerous experience. **2.** willingness to take risks, *the spirit of adventure*. **adventurous** *adj.*, **adventurously** *adv.*

adventurer *n.* **1.** a person who seeks adventures. **2.** a person who is ready to make gains for himself by risky or unscrupulous methods.

adverb *n.* a word that qualifies a verb, adjective, or other adverb and indicates how, when, or where, e.g. *gently, fully, soon.* **adverbial** *adj.,* **adverbially** *adv.*

adversary (**ad**-ver-ser-i) *n.* an opponent, an enemy.

adverse (**ad**-vers) *adj.* **1.** unfavourable, *an adverse report.* **2.** bringing misfortune or harm, *the drug has no adverse effects.* **adversely** *adv.*

adversity (ăd-**vers**-iti) *n.* misfortune, trouble.

advert *n.* (*informal*) an advertisement.

advertise *v.* **1.** to make generally or publicly known, *advertise a meeting.* **2.** to praise publicly in order to encourage people to buy or use something, *advertise soap.* **3.** to ask or offer by public notice, *advertise for a secretary.* **advertiser** *n.*

advertisement *n.* **1.** advertising. **2.** a public notice advertising something.

advice *n.* **1.** an opinion given about what to do or how to behave. **2.** a piece of information, *we received advice that the goods had been dispatched.* □ **advice note**, a document sent by supplier to customer stating that specified goods have been dispatched.

advisable *adj.* worth recommending as a course of action. **advisability** *n.*

advise *v.* **1.** to give advice to, to recommend. **2.** to inform, to notify. **adviser** *n.*

advisory *adj.* giving advice, having the power to advise, *an advisory committee.*

advocacy (**ad**-vŏk-ăsi) *n.* **1.** the advocating of a policy etc. **2.** the function of an advocate.

advocate [1] (**ad**-vŏ-kayt) *v.* to recommend, to be in favour of, *I advocate caution.*

advocate [2] (**ad**-vŏ-kăt) *n.* **1.** a person who advocates a policy, *an advocate of reform.* **2.** a person who pleads on behalf of another, a lawyer presenting a client's case in a lawcourt.

adze (*rhymes with* lads) *n.* a kind of axe with a blade at right angles to the handle, used for trimming large pieces of wood.

Aegean (i-**jee**-ăn) *adj.* of the Aegean Sea, between Greece and Turkey. —*n.* the Aegean Sea.

aegis (**ee**-jis) *n.* protection, sponsorship, *under the aegis of the Law Society.*

aeon (**ee**-ŏn) *n.* an immense time.

aerate (**air**-ayt) *v.* **1.** to expose to the chemical action of air, *aerate the soil by forking it.* **2.** to add carbon dioxide to (a liquid) under pressure, *aerated water.* **aeration** *n.,* **aerator** *n.*

aerial (**air**-iăl) *adj.* **1.** of or like air. **2.** existing in the air, suspended overhead, *an aerial railway.* **3.** by or from aircraft, *aerial bombardment.* —*n.* a wire or rod for transmitting or receiving radio waves.

□ **aerial piracy**, hijacking of aircraft.

aerobatics *pl. n.* spectacular feats of flying aircraft, especially for display. **aerobatic** *adj.*

aerodrome *n.* an airfield.

aerodynamics *n.* interaction between airflow and the movement of solid bodies (e.g. aircraft, bullets) through air. **aerodynamic** *adj.*

aerofoil *n.* an aircraft wing or fin or tailplane.

aeronautics *n.* the scientific study of the flight of aircraft. **aeronautic, aeronautical** *adjs.*

aeroplane *n.* a mechanically driven heavier-than-air aircraft with wings.

aerosol *n.* **1.** a substance sealed in a container under pressure, with a device for releasing it as a fine spray. **2.** the container itself.

aerospace *n.* **1.** earth's atmosphere and space beyond it. **2.** the technology of aviation in this region.

aesthete (**ees**-theet) *n.* a person who claims to have great understanding and appreciation of what is beautiful, especially in the arts.

aesthetic (iss-**thet**-ik) *adj.* **1.** belonging to the appreciation of beauty, *the aesthetic standards of the times.* **2.** having or showing such appreciation. **3.** artistic, tasteful. **aesthetically** *adv.* □ **aesthetics** *n.* a branch of philosophy dealing with the principles of beauty and tastefulness.

aetiology (ee-ti-**ol**-ŏji) *n.* **1.** the study of causes or reasons. **2.** a scientific account of the causes of any disease. **aetiological** *adj.,* **aetiologically** *adv.*

afar *adv.* far off, far away.

affable *adj.* polite and friendly. **affably** *adv.,* **affability** *n.*

affair *n.* **1.** a thing done or to be done, a matter, a concern. **2.** public or private business, *current affairs; put your affairs in order.* **3.** (*informal*) an event, a thing, *this camera is a complicated affair.* **4.** a temporary sexual relationship between two people who are not married to each other.

affect [1] *v.* **1.** to have an effect on, *the new tax laws affect us all.* **2.** to arouse sadness or sympathy in, *the news of his death affected us deeply.* **3.** (of a disease) to attack or infect, *tuberculosis affected his lungs.* **4.** to pretend to have or feel; *she affected ignorance,* pretended she did not know.

¶ The words *affect* and *effect* have totally different meanings and should not be confused.

affect [2] *v.* to like and make a display of

using or wearing, *he affects velvet jackets.*

affectation *n.* behaviour that is put on for display and not natural or genuine, pretence.

affected *adj.* **1.** full of affectation. **2.** pretended.

affecting *adj.* having an effect upon one's emotions, *an affecting appeal.*

affection *n.* **1.** love, a liking. **2.** a disease or diseased condition.

affectionate *adj.* showing affection, loving. **affectionately** *adv.*

affianced (ă-**fy**-ănst) *adj.* *(formal)* engaged to be married.

affidavit (af-i-**day**-vit) *n.* a written statement for use as legal evidence, sworn on oath to be true.

affiliate (ă-**fil**-i-ayt) *v.* to connect as a subordinate member or branch, *the club is affiliated to a national society.* **affiliation** *n.* □ **affiliation order,** an order compelling the father of an illegitimate child to help support it.

affinity (ă-**fin**-iti) *n.* **1.** relationship (especially by marriage) other than blood-relationship. **2.** similarity, close resemblance or connection, *affinities between different languages.* **3.** a strong natural liking or attraction. **4.** the tendency of certain substances to combine with others.

affirm *v.* **1.** to assert, to state as a fact. **2.** to make an affirmation instead of an oath.

affirmation (af-er-**may**-shŏn) *n.* **1.** affirming. **2.** a solemn declaration made instead of an oath by a person who has conscientious objections to swearing an oath or who has no religion.

affirmative (ă-**ferm**-ătiv) *adj.* affirming, agreeing; *an affirmative reply,* answering 'yes'. —*n.* an affirmative word or statement; *the answer is in the affirmative,* answer is 'yes'. **affirmatively** *adv.*

affix *v.* **1.** to stick on, to attach. **2.** to add in writing, *affix your signature.*

afflict *v.* to distress physically or mentally, *he is afflicted with rheumatism,* suffers from it.

affliction *n.* **1.** pain, distress, misery. **2.** something that causes this.

affluent (**af**-loo-ĕnt) *adj.* rich; *the affluent society,* in which most people are relatively wealthy. **affluently** *adv.,* **affluence** *n.*

afford *v.* **1.** to have enough money or means or time for a specified purpose, *we can afford to pay £50.* **2.** to be in a position to do something, *we can't afford to be critical.* **3.** *(formal)* to provide, *her diary affords no information.*

afforestation (ă-fo-ri-**stay**-shŏn) *n.* planting with trees to form a forest.

affray (ă-**fray**) *n.* a breach of the peace by fighting or rioting in public.

affront (ă-**frunt**) *v.* to insult deliberately, to offend or embarrass. —*n.* a deliberate insult or show of disrespect.

Afghan (**af**-gan) *n.* **1.** a native of Afghanistan. **2.** the language spoken there, Pushtu. **3.** *afghan,* a kind of loose sheepskin coat with shaggy fleece lining. □ **Afghan hound,** a dog of a breed with long silky hair.

Afghanistan (af-**gan**-i-stahn) a country in south-west Asia.

aficionado (ă-fis-yon-**ah**-doh) *n.* *(pl.* aficionados) a devotee of a particular sport or pastime.

afield *adv.* far away from home, to or at a distance.

afire *adv. & adj.* on fire.

aflame *adv. & adj.* in flames, burning.

afloat *adv. & adj.* **1.** floating. **2.** at sea, on board ship, *enjoying life afloat.* **3.** flooded.

afoot *adv. & adj.* progressing, in operation, *there's a scheme afoot to improve the roads.*

aforesaid *adj.* mentioned previously.

aforethought *adj.* premeditated, planned in advance, *with malice aforethought.*

afraid *adj.* **1.** alarmed, frightened, anxious about consequences. **2.** politely regretful, *I'm afraid there's none left.*

afresh *adv.* anew, beginning again.

Africa a continent south of the Mediterranean Sea between the Atlantic and Indian Oceans.

African *adj.* of Africa or its people or languages. —*n.* a native of Africa, especially a dark-skinned person. □ **African violet,** an East African plant with purple or pink or white flowers, grown as a house-plant.

Africanize *v.* to make African, to place under the control of African Negroes. **Africanization** *n.*

Afrikaans (af-ri-**kahns**) *n.* a language developed from Dutch, used in South Africa.

Afro (**af**-roh) *adj.* like the hair of some Negroes, bushy and frizzy.

Afro- *prefix* African; *Afro-Asian,* of Africa and Asia.

afrormosia (af-ror-**moh**-ziă) *n.* a wood like teak, used for furniture.

aft *adv.* in or near or towards the stern of a ship or the tail of an aircraft.

after *prep.* **1.** behind in place or order. **2.** at a later time than. **3.** in spite of, *after all I did for him he still ignored me.* **4.** as a result of, *after what he did to my family, I hate him.* **5.** in pursuit or search of, *run after him.* **6.** about, concerning; *he asked* *after you,* asked how you were. 7. in imitation of, *painted after the manner of Picasso*; *named after a person,* given this person's Christian name in honour of him. —**after** *adv.* 1. behind, *Jill came tumbling after.* 2. later, *twenty years after.* —*conj.* at or in a time later than, *they came after I left.* —**after** *adj.* 1. later, following, *in after years.* 2. nearer the stern in a boat, *the after cabins.* □ **after-care** *n.* further care or treatment of a patient who has left hospital, rehabilitation of a discharged prisoner. **after-effect** *n.* an effect that arises or persists after its cause has gone. **afters** *pl. n. (informal)* a course following the main course at a meal.

afterbirth *n.* the placenta and foetal membrane discharged from the womb after childbirth.

afterlife *n.* life in a later part of a person's lifetime or after death.

aftermath *n.* events or circumstances that follow and are a consequence of an event etc., *the aftermath of war.*

aftermost *adj.* furthest aft.

afternoon *n.* the time from noon to about 6 p.m. or sunset (if this is earlier).

aftershave *n.* a lotion for use after shaving.

afterthought *n.* something thought of or added later.

afterwards *adv.* at a later time. **afterward** *adv. (Amer.)* afterwards.

again *adv.* 1. another time, once more, *try again.* 2. as before, to or in the original place or condition, *you'll soon be well again.* 3. furthermore, besides. 4. on the other hand, *I might, and again I might not.*

against *prep.* 1. in opposition to; *his age is against him,* is a disadvantage to him. 2. in contrast to, *against a dark background.* 3. in preparation for, in anticipation of, *saved against a rainy day.* 4. opposite, so as to cancel or lessen, *allowances to be set against income.* 5. into collision or contact with, *lean against the wall.* □ **against the clock,** in order to finish by a certain time.

Aga Khan (ah-gă **kahn**) the spiritual leader of Ismaili Muslims.

agape *adj.* gaping, open-mouthed.

agaric (ag-er-ik) *n.* a fungus with a cap and stalk, e.g. the common mushroom.

agate (**ag**-ăt) *n.* a very hard stone with patches or concentric bands of colour.

age *n.* 1. the length of time a person has lived or a thing has existed. 2. the later part of life, old age. 3. a historical period, a time with special characteristics or events, *the Elizabethan Age*; *the atomic*

age. 4. *(informal)* a very long time, *it was ages before he came.* —**age** *v.* (aged, ageing) 1. to grow old, to show signs of age. 2. to become mature; *heavy wines age slowly.* 3. to cause to become old, *worry aged him rapidly.* 4. to allow to mature. □ **age-group** *n.* the people who are all of the same age. **age-limit** *n.* an age fixed as a limit for people taking part in an activity. **age-long, age-old** *adjs.* having existed for a very long time. **be your age!**, *(informal)* behave more sensibly. **of age,** having reached the age at which one has an adult's legal rights and obligations. **under age,** not yet of age.

aged *adj.* 1. *(pr.* ayjd) of the age of, *aged 10.* 2. *(pr.* **ay**-jid) very old, *an aged man.*

ageless *adj.* not growing or appearing old.

agency *n.* 1. the business or place of business of an agent, *a travel agency.* 2. the means of action through which something is done, *fertilized by the agency of bees.*

agenda (ă-**jen**-dă) *n.* a programme of items of business to be dealt with at a meeting, *the agenda is rather lengthy today.* ¶ This word is by origin a Latin plural, but is now always used with a singular verb; its plural is *agendas.*

agent *n.* 1. a person who does something or instigates some activity, *he is a mere instrument, not an agent.* 2. one who acts on behalf of another, *write to our agents in Rome.* 3. something that produces an effect or change, *soda is the active agent.* 4. a secret agent *(see* secret).

agent provocateur (azh-ahn prŏ-vok-ă-ter) *(pl.* agents provocateurs) a person employed to detect suspected offenders by tempting them to do something illegal openly.

ageratum (aj-er-**ah**-tŭm) *n.* a low-growing plant with soft blue flowers.

agglomerate[1] (ă-**glom**-er-ayt) *v.* to collect or become collected into a mass. **agglomeration** *n.*

agglomerate[2] (ă-**glom**-er-ăt) *n.* something composed of clustered fragments.

agglutination (ă-gloo-tin-**ay**-shŏn) *n.* sticking or fusing together.

aggrandizement (ă-**gran**-diz-měnt) *n.* an increase in power, wealth, or importance.

aggravate *v.* 1. to make worse or more serious. 2. *(informal)* to annoy. **aggravation** *n.*

aggregate[1] (**ag**-ri-găt) *adj.* combined, total, *the aggregate amount.* —*n.* 1. a total, a mass or amount brought together; *in the aggregate,* as a whole, collectively. 2. hard substances (sand, gravel, broken stone, etc.) mixed with cement to make concrete.

aggregate² (ag-ri-gayt) v. to collect or form into an aggregate, to unite. **2.** (*informal*) to amount to (a total). **aggregation** n.

aggression n. **1.** unprovoked attacking. **2.** a hostile action, hostile behaviour.

aggressive adj. **1.** apt to make attacks, showing aggression. **2.** self-assertive, forceful, *an aggressive salesman.* **aggressively** adv., **aggressiveness** n.

aggressor n. a person or country that attacks first or begins hostilities.

aggrieved (ă-**greevd**) adj. made resentful by unfair treatment.

aggro n. (*slang*) deliberate trouble-making.

aghast (ă-**gahst**) adj. filled with consternation.

agile adj. nimble, quick-moving. **agilely** adv., **agility** (ă-**jil**-iti) n.

agitate v. **1.** to shake or move briskly. **2.** to disturb, to cause anxiety to. **3.** to stir up public interest or concern. **agitation** n., **agitator** n.

agley (ă-**glay**) adv. (*Scottish*) askew, awry.

aglow adj. glowing. —adv. glowingly.

agnail (**ag**-nail) n. = hangnail.

agnostic (ag-**nos**-tik) n. a person who believes that nothing can be known about the existence of God or of anything except material things. —**agnosticism** n.

ago adv. in the past.

agog (ă-**gog**) adj. eager, expectant.

agonize v. **1.** to cause agony, to pain greatly; *agonized shrieks,* expressing agony. **2.** to suffer agony, to worry intensely, *agonizing over his mistakes.* **agonizingly** adv.

agony n. extreme mental or physical suffering.

agoraphobia (ag-er-ă-**foh**-biă) n. abnormal fear of crossing open spaces. **agoraphobic** n. a person who suffers from agoraphobia.

agree v. (agreed, agreeing) **1.** to consent, to say that one is willing; *agree to differ,* agree to cease trying to convince each other. **2.** to approve as correct or acceptable, *the tax inspector has agreed your allowances.* **3.** to hold or reach a similar opinion. **4.** to get on well together. **5.** to be consistent with, to harmonize, *your story agrees with what I've heard already.* **6.** to suit a person's health or digestion, *curry doesn't agree with me.* **7.** to correspond in grammatical case, number, gender, or person, *the pronoun 'she' agrees with the noun 'woman'; 'he' agrees with 'man'.*

agreeable adj. **1.** pleasing, giving pleasure, *an agreeable voice.* **2.** willing to agree, *we'll go if you are agreeable.* **agreeably** adv.

agreement n. **1.** agreeing. **2.** harmony in opinion or feeling. **3.** an arrangement agreed between people.

agriculture n. the science or practice of cultivating the land on a large scale. **agricultural** adj., **agriculturally** adv.

agronomy (ă-**gron**-ŏmi) n. the science of soil management and crop production.

aground adv. & adj. upon or touching the bottom in shallow water, *the ship is* or *ran aground.*

ah int. an exclamation of surprise, pity, admiration, etc.

aha int. an exclamation of surprise, triumph, or mockery.

ahead adv. further forward in space or time; *try to plan ahead,* plan for the future; *he is ahead of the others in mathematics,* has made more progress; *full speed ahead!,* go forward at full speed.

ahem int. the noise made when clearing one's throat, used to call attention or express doubt.

ahoy int. a cry used by seamen to call attention.

aid v. to help. —n. **1.** help; *what's all this fuss in aid of?,* (*informal*) what is its purpose? **2.** something that helps, *a hearing aid.* **3.** food, money, etc., sent to a country to help it, *overseas aid.*

aide n. **1.** an aide-de-camp. **2.** (*Amer.*) an assistant.

aide-de-camp (ayd-dĕ-**kahn**) n. (*pl.* aides-de-camp, *pr.* aydz-) a naval or military officer acting as assistant to a senior officer.

ail v. (*old use*) to make ill or uneasy, *what ails him?* **ailing** adj. unwell, in poor condition.

aileron (**ail**-er-ŏn) n. a hinged flap on an aeroplane wing, used to control balance.

ailment n. a slight illness.

aim v. **1.** to point or send towards a target, to direct (a blow, missile, remark, etc.) towards a specified object or goal; *aiming at a scholarship,* trying to win one; *aim high,* be ambitious. **2.** to attempt, to try, *we aim to please the customers.* —**aim** n. **1.** the act of aiming a weapon or missile at a target; *take aim,* aim a weapon. **2.** purpose, intention; *what is his aim?,* what does he want to achieve?

aimless adj. without a purpose. **aimlessly** adv., **aimlessness** n.

ain't = am not, is not, are not, has not, have not. ¶This word is avoided in standard speech except in humorous use, e.g. *she ain't what she used to be.*

13

air *n.* **1.** the mixture of gases surrounding the earth and breathed by all land animals and plants. **2.** the earth's atmosphere, open space in this. **3.** the earth's atmosphere as the place where aircraft operate; *air travel,* travel in aircraft. **4.** a light wind. **5.** an impression given, *an air of mystery.* **6.** an impressive manner, *he does things with such an air; put on airs,* behave in an affected haughty manner. **7.** a melody, a tune. —**air** *v.* **1.** to expose to the air, to ventilate (a room etc.) so as to cool or freshen it. **2.** to put (clothes etc.) into a warm place to finish drying. **3.** to express publicly, *air one's opinions.* □ **air-bed** *n.* an inflatable mattress. **air brake,** a brake worked by compressed air. **air-conditioned** *adj.* supplied with **air-conditioning,** a system controlling the humidity and temperature of the air in a room or building. **air force,** a branch of the armed forces equipped for attacking and defending by means of aircraft. **air freight,** freight carried by air. **air hostess,** a stewardess in a passenger aircraft. **air letter,** a folding sheet of light paper that may be sent cheaply by airmail. **air pocket,** a partial vacuum in the air causing aircraft in flight to drop suddenly. **air raid,** an attack by aircraft dropping bombs. **by air,** in or by aircraft. **in the air,** current, exerting an influence, *dissatisfaction is in the air;* uncertain; *these plans are still in the air.* **on the air,** broadcast or broadcasting by radio or television.

airborne *adj.* **1.** transported by the air, *airborne pollen.* **2.** in flight after taking off, *no smoking until the plane is airborne.* **3.** transported by aircraft, *airborne troops.*

airbrush *n.* a device for spraying paint by means of compressed air.

aircraft *n.* **1.** a machine or structure capable of flight in the air and regarded as a vehicle or carrier. **2.** such craft collectively, including aeroplanes, gliders, and helicopters. □ **aircraft-carrier** *n.* a ship that carries and acts as a base for aeroplanes.

aircraftman *n.* the lowest rank in the RAF.

aircraftwoman *n.* the lowest rank in the WRAF.

aircrew *n.* the crew of an aircraft.

Airedale (**air**-dayl) *n.* a large rough-coated terrier.

airer *n.* a structure on which clothes are aired.

airfield *n.* an area of open level ground equipped with hangars and runways for aircraft.

airflow *n.* a flow of air.

airgun *n.* a gun in which compressed air propels the missile.

airing *n.* **1.** exposing to air or to a drying heat. **2.** clothes being aired.

airless *adj.* **1.** stuffy. **2.** without a breeze, calm and still. **airlessness** *n.*

airlift *n.* large-scale transport of troops or supplies by aircraft, especially in an emergency. —*v.* to transport in this way.

airline *n.* a regular service of air transport for public use, a company providing this.

airliner *n.* a large passenger aircraft.

airlock *n.* **1.** a stoppage of the flow in a pump or pipe, caused by an air-bubble. **2.** a compartment with an airtight door at each end, providing access to a pressurized chamber.

airmail *n.* mail carried by air. —*v.* to send by airmail.

airman *n.* (*pl.* airmen) a member of the RAF, especially below the rank of a commissioned officer.

airport *n.* an airfield with facilities for passengers and goods.

airship *n.* an aircraft that is lighter than air.

airspace *n.* the atmosphere above a country and subject to its control.

air-strip *n.* a strip of ground prepared for aircraft to land and take off.

airtight *adj.* not allowing air to enter or escape.

airwoman *n.* (*pl.* airwomen) a member of the WRAF, especially below the rank of a commissioned officer.

airworthy *adj.* (of an aircraft) fit to fly. **airworthiness** *n.*

airy *adj.* (airier, airiest) **1.** well-ventilated. **2.** light as air. **3.** careless and light-hearted, *an airy manner.* **airily** *adv.,* **airiness** *n.* □ **airy-fairy** *adj.* fanciful, impractical.

aisle (*rhymes with* mile) *n.* **1.** a side part of a church. **2.** a gangway between rows of pews or seats.

aitchbone *n.* the rump-bone of an animal, a cut of beef lying over this.

ajar *adv. & adj.* slightly open.

akimbo (ă-**kim**-boh) *adv.* with hands on hips and elbows pointed outwards.

akin *adj.* related, similar, *a feeling akin to envy.*

Ala. *abbrev.* Alabama.

Alabama (al-ă-**bam**-ă) a State of the USA.

alabaster (**ăl**-ă-bah-ster) *n.* a translucent usually white form of gypsum, often carved into ornaments.

à la carte (ah lah **kart**) (of a restaurant meal) ordered as separate items from a menu.

alacrity (ă-**lak**-riti) *n.* prompt and eager readiness.

Aladdin's cave, a room or box etc. filled with wonderful things. ¶ Named after the hero of an Oriental tale.

alarm *n.* **1.** a warning sound or signal, an apparatus giving this. **2.** an alarm-clock. **3.** fear caused by expectation of danger. —*v.* to arouse to a sense of danger, to frighten. □ **alarm-clock** *n.* a clock with a device that rings at a set time.

alarmist *n.* a person who raises unnecessary or excessive alarm.

alas *int.* an exclamation of sorrow.

Alaska (ă-**las**-kă) a State of the USA, extending into the Arctic Circle. **baked Alaska,** a baked pudding containing ice cream between sponge cake and meringue covering.

alb *n.* a white robe reaching to the feet, worn by some Christian priests at church ceremonies.

Albania a country between Greece and Yugoslavia. **Albanian** *adj. & n.*

albatross *n.* a long-winged sea-bird related to the petrel.

Alberta (al-**ber**-tă) a province of Canada.

albino (al-**bee**-noh) *n.* (*pl.* albinos) a person or animal with no colouring pigment in the skin and hair (which are white) and the eyes (which are pink).

album *n.* **1.** a book in which a collection of autographs, photographs, postage stamps, etc., can be kept. **2.** a set of gramophone records, a holder for these. **3.** a long-playing record with several items by the same performer(s).

albumen (al-**bew**-min) *n.* white of egg.

alchemy (al-**kĕmi**) *n.* a medieval form of chemistry, the chief aim of which was to discover how to turn ordinary metals into gold. **alchemist** *n.*

alcohol *n.* **1.** a colourless inflammable liquid, the intoxicant present in wine, beer, whisky, etc. **2.** any liquor containing this. **3.** a chemical compound of this type.

alcoholic *adj.* **1.** of or containing alcohol. **2.** caused by drinking alcohol. —*n.* a person suffering from alcoholism.

alcoholism *n.* a diseased condition caused by continual heavy drinking of alcohol.

alcove *n.* **1.** a recess in a wall. **2.** a recess forming an extension of a room.

alder (**awl**-der) *n.* **1.** a tree of the birch family, usually growing in marshy places. **2.** a similar unrelated tree, *red, black,* and *white alder.*

alderman (**awl**-der-măn) *n.* (*pl.* aldermen). **1.** a co-opted member of an English county or borough council, next in dignity to the mayor. (¶ The office was abolished

in most cases in 1972.) **2.** an elected member of the municipal governing body in Australian and some American cities.

ale *n.* beer.

alert *adj.* watchful, observant. —*n.* **1.** a state of watchfulness or readiness. **2.** a warning of danger, notice to stand ready. —*v.* to warn of danger, to make alert. — **alertly** *adv.,* **alertness** *n.* □ **on the alert,** on the look-out, watchful.

A level Advanced level in GCE.

al fresco (al **fres**-koh) in the open air, *lunched al fresco.* —**alfresco** *adj.* taking place in the open air, *an alfresco lunch.*

alga (al-gă) *n.* (*pl.* algae, *pr.* al-jee) a water plant with no true stems or leaves.

algebra (al-jib-ră) *n.* a branch of mathematics in which letters and symbols are used to represent quantities. **algebraic** (alji-**bray**-ik) *adj.,* **algebraically** *adv.*

Algeria a country in North Africa. **Algerian** *adj. & n.*

Algiers (al-**jeerz**) the capital of Algeria.

algorithm (al ger-i*th*ĕm) *n.* a procedure or set of rules for solving a problem, especially by computer.

alias (ay-li-ăs) *n.* (*pl.* aliases) a false name, an assumed name, *Brown had several aliases.* —*adv.* also falsely called, *John Brown, alias Peter Harrison, alias James Finch.*

alibi (al-i-by) *n.* **1.** evidence that an accused person was elsewhere when the crime was committed. **2.** (*incorrect use*) an excuse, an answer to an accusation. — *v.* (alibied, alibiing) to provide an alibi for.

alien (ay-li-ĕn) *n.* **1.** a person who is not a subject of the country in which he is living. **2.** a being from another world. —**alien** *adj.* **1.** foreign, not one's own, unfamiliar, *alien customs.* **2.** of a different nature, contrary, *cruelty is alien to her character.*

alienate (ay-li-ĕn-ayt) *v.* to cause to become unfriendly or hostile. **alienation** *n.*

alight [1] *v.* **1.** to get down from a horse or a vehicle. **2.** to descend and settle, *the bird alighted on a branch.*

alight [2] *adj.* on fire, lit up.

align (ă-**lyn**) *v.* **1.** to place in line, to bring into line. **2.** to join as an ally, *they aligned themselves with the Liberals.* **alignment** *n.* □ **out of alignment,** not in line.

alike *adj. & adv.* like one another, in the same way.

alimentary canal (ali-**ment**-er-i) the tubular passage through which food passes from mouth to anus in the process of being digested and absorbed by the body.

alimony (al-i-mŏni) *n.* an allowance payable by a man to his wife or former wife pending or after a legal separation or divorce.

alive *adj.* 1. living. 2. alert, *he is alive to the possible dangers.* 3. active, lively; *look alive!,* hurry, get busy. 4. full of living or moving things, *river was alive with boats.*

alkali (al-kă-ly) *n.* (*pl.* alkalis) one of a class of substances (such as caustic soda, potash, and ammonia) that neutralize and are neutralized by acids, and form caustic or corrosive solutions in water. **alkaline** (al-kă-lyn) *adj.,* **alkalinity** (alkă-**lin**-iti) *n.*

all *adj.* the whole amount or number or extent of, *waited all day; beyond all doubt,* beyond any doubt whatever. —*n.* all persons concerned, everything, *all are agreed; all is lost; the score is four all,* four games or goals to each side. —*adv.* entirely, quite, *dressed all in white; an all-powerful dictator; ran all the faster,* even faster. □ **all but,** very little short of, *it is all but impossible.* **all-clear** *n.* a signal that a danger is over. **all for,** (*informal*) much in favour of. **all in,** (*informal*) exhausted. **all-in** *adj.* including everything, *the all-in price; all-in wrestling,* freestyle wrestling. **all in all,** of supreme importance; *taking it all in all,* as a whole. **all of a dither,** (*informal*) dithering. **all one to,** a matter of indifference to. **all out,** using all possible strength, energy, or speed. **all over,** in or on all parts of; *she was all over the captain,* (*slang*) excessively attentive or effusive towards him; *that's Jones all over,* is what one would expect of him. **all right,** as desired, satisfactorily; in good condition, safe and sound; yes, I consent. **all-round** *adj.* general, not specialized, *a good all-round education; an all-round athlete,* good at various forms of athletics. **all-rounder** *n.* a versatile person, especially in sport. **All Saints' Day,** 1 November. **all set,** (*informal*) ready to start. **All Souls' Day,** 2 November. **all-star** *adj.* with star performers for all the chief parts in an entertainment. **all there** (*informal*) mentally alert; *not quite all there,* mentally deficient. **all the same,** in spite of this; making no difference. **all-time** *adj.* unsurpassed, *an all-time record.* **be all eyes** *or* **ears,** to be watching or listening intently. **on all fours,** crawling on hands and knees; corresponding exactly, *this example is not on all fours with that one.* **with all speed,** as quickly as possible.

Allah (al-ă) the Muslim name of God.

allay (ă-lay) *v.* (allayed, allaying) to calm, to put at rest, *to allay suspicion.*

allegation (ali-gay-shŏn) *n.* a statement made without proof.

allege (ă-lej) *v.* to declare (especially to those doubting one's truthfulness) without being able to prove, *alleging that he was innocent; he alleged illness as the reason for his absence; the alleged culprit,* the person said to be the culprit. **allegedly** (ă-**lej**-idli) *adv.* according to allegation.

Alleghenies (ali-gay-niz) *pl. n.* the Allegheny Mountains, part of the Appalachians.

allegiance (ă-**lee**-jăns) *n.* support of a government or sovereign or cause, etc.

allegory (al-ig-er-i) *n.* a story or description in which the characters and events symbolize some deeper underlying meaning. **allegorical** (alig-o-ri-kăl) *n.,* **allegorically** *adv.*

allegro (ă-**lay**-groh) *adv.* (in music) fast and lively. —*n.* (*pl.* allegros) a passage to be played in this way.

alleluia *int.* & *n.* praise to God.

allergenic (al-er-**jen**-ik) *adj.* causing an allergic reaction.

allergic (ă-**ler**-jik) *adj.* 1. having an allergy. 2. caused by an allergy, *an allergic reaction.* 3. (*informal*) having a strong dislike, *allergic to hard work.*

allergy (**al**-er-ji) *n.* a condition producing an unfavourable reaction to certain foods, pollens, etc.

alleviate (ă-**lee**-vi-ayt) *v.* to lessen, to make less severe, *to alleviate pain.* **alleviation** *n.*

alley *n.* (*pl.* alleys) 1. a narrow passage or street between houses or other buildings. 2. a path bordered by hedges or shrubbery. 3. a long enclosure for games such as ten-pin bowling and skittles.

alliance *n.* a union or association formed for mutual benefit, especially of countries by treaty or families by marriage.

allied see ally². —*adj.* of the same general kind, similar.

alligator *n.* a reptile of the crocodile family, found especially in the rivers of tropical America and China.

alliteration (ă-lit-er-**ay**-shŏn) *n.* the occurrence of the same letter or sound at the beginning of several words in succession, e.g. *sing a song of sixpence.* **alliterative** (ă-**lit**-er-ătiv) *adj.*

allocate (**al**-ŏ-kayt) *v.* to allot. **allocation** *n.,* **allocator** *n.*

allot (ă-**lot**) *v.* (allotted, allotting) to distribute officially, to give as a share of things available or tasks to be done.

allotment *n.* 1. allotting. 2. a share allotted. 3. a small area of public land let out for cultivation.

allow *v.* 1. to permit; *dogs are not allowed in the park,* may not enter. 2. to permit to have, to give a limited quantity or sum, *allow him £200 a year*. **3.** to add or deduct in estimating, *allow 10% for inflation*; *allow for shrinkage*, provide for this when estimating. **4.** to agree that something is true or acceptable, *I allow that you have been patient*; *the judge allowed their claim for expenses*.

allowable *adj.* able to be allowed. **allowably** *adv.*

allowance *n.* **1.** allowing. **2.** an amount or sum allowed; *make allowances for him* or *for his youth*, be lenient towards him or because of this.

alloy¹ (**al**-oi) *n.* **1.** a metal formed of a mixture of metals or of metal and another substance. **2.** an inferior metal mixed with one of greater value.

alloy² (ă-**loi**) *v.* (alloyed, alloying) **1.** to mix with metal(s) of lower value. **2.** to weaken or spoil by something that reduces value or pleasure.

allspice *n.* spice made from the dried and ground berries of the pimento, a West Indian tree.

allude (ă-**lood**) *v.* to refer briefly or indirectly in speaking, *he alluded to the troubles in Ireland* **allusion** *n.*

allusive (ă-**loo**-siv) *adj.* containing allusions. **allusively** *adv.*

allure (ăl-**yoor**) *v.* to entice, to attract. — *n.* attractiveness. **allurement** *n.* □ **alluring** *adj.* attractive, charming.

alluvial (ă-**loo**-viăl) *adj.* made of soil and sand left by rivers or floods.

alluvium (ă-**loo**-viŭm) *n.* an alluvial deposit.

ally¹ (**al**-I) *n.* **1.** a country in alliance with another. **2.** a person who co-operates with another in some project.

ally² (ăl-**I**) *v.* (allied, allying) to form an alliance.

almanac (**awl**-măn-ak) *n.* **1.** an annual publication containing a calendar with times of sunrise and sunset, astronomical data, dates of anniversaries, and sometimes other information. **2.** a yearbook of sport, theatre, etc. ¶ Some publications use the older spelling *almanack* in their titles, e.g. *Whitaker's Almanack*.

almighty *adj.* **1.** all-powerful; *the Almighty*, God. **2.** (*informal*) very great, *an almighty nuisance*. —*adv.* (*slang*) very, *almighty glad*.

almond (**ah**-mŏnd) *n.* **1.** the kernel of the fruit of a tree related to the peach. **2.** this tree. □ **almond-eyed** *adj.* having eyes that appear to narrow and slant upwards at the outer corners. **almond paste**, edible paste made from ground almonds.

almost *adv.* all but, as the nearest thing to.

alms (*pr.* ahmz) *n.* (*old use*) money and gifts given to the poor. **almshouse** *n.* a house founded by charity for poor (usually elderly) people.

aloe *n.* a plant with thick sharp-pointed leaves and bitter juice. **aloes** *n.* this juice, used in medicine.

aloft *adv.* high up, up in the air.

alone *adj.* not with others, without the company or help of others or other things. —*adv.* only, exclusively, *you alone can help me*.

along *adv.* **1.** through part or the whole of a thing's length, *along by the hedge*; *knew it all along*, from the beginning. **2.** in company with oneself, in addition, *brought my sister along*; *I'll be along soon*, will come and join you. **3.** onward, into a more advanced state, *push it along*; *it is coming along nicely*. —*prep.* close to or parallel with the length of something, *along the wall*.

alongside *adv.* close to the side of a ship or pier or wharf. —*prep.* beside.

aloof *adv.* apart; *keep* or *hold aloof from*, deliberately take no part in. —*adj.* unconcerned, cool and remote in character, not friendly. —**aloofly** *adv.*, **aloofness** *n.*

aloud *adv.* in a voice loud enough to be heard, not silently or in a whisper.

alp *n.* pasture-land on mountains in Switzerland. **the Alps**, high mountains in Switzerland and adjacent countries.

alpenstock *n.* a long iron-tipped staff used in mountain-climbing.

alpha (**al**-fă) *n.* **1.** the first letter of the Greek alphabet, — a. **2.** *Alpha*, the chief star in a constellation.

alphabet *n.* **1.** the letters used in writing a language. **2.** a list of these in a set order. **3.** symbols or signs indicating letters but not written, *the Morse alphabet*.

alphabetize *v.* to put into alphabetical order. **alphabetization** *n.*

alphabetical *adj.* in the order of the letters of the alphabet. **alphabetically** *adv.*

alphanumeric (al-fă-new-**merr**ik) *adj.* containing letters of the alphabet and numerals.

alpine *adj.* **1.** of high mountains, growing on these. **2.** *Alpine*, of the Alps. —*n.* a plant suited to mountain regions or grown in rock-gardens.

already *adv.* **1.** before this time, *had already gone*. **2.** as early as this, *is he back already?*

alright *adv.* an incorrect form of *all right*.

Alsatian (al-**say**-shăn) *n.* a dog of a large strong smooth-haired breed, often trained as police dogs.

also *adv.* in addition, besides. **also-ran** *n.*

a horse or dog not among the first three to finish in a race; a person who fails to win distinction in his activities.

Alta. *abbrev.* Alberta.

altar *n.* **1.** the table on which bread and wine are consecrated in the Communion service. **2.** any structure on which offerings are made to a god.

alter *v.* to make or become different, to change in character, position, etc.; *alter a garment,* re-sew it in a different style or size; *alter the clock,* set it to show a different time, especially for daylight saving at the beginning or end of summer. **alteration** *n.*

altercation (ol-ter-**kay**-shŏn) *n.* a noisy dispute or quarrel.

alternate[1] (ol-ter-nāt) *adj.* happening or following in turns, first the one and then the other; *on alternate days,* every second day. **alternately** *adv.* ¶ Do not confuse with alternative.

alternate[2] (**ol**-ter-nayt) *v.* **1.** to arrange or perform or occur alternately. **2.** to consist of alternate things. **alternation** *n.* □ **alternating current,** electric current that reverses its direction at regular intervals.

alternative (ol-ter-nă-tiv) *adj.* available in place of something else. —*n.* one of two or more possibilities. (¶ A few people prefer not to use this word of more than two possibilities because it is derived from the Latin *alter* (= one or other of two), but the use is well established in standard English.) —**alternatively** *adv.*

alternator (**ol**-ter-nay-ter) *n.* a dynamo giving alternating current.

although *conj.* though.

altimeter (**al**-ti-meet-er) *n.* an instrument used especially in aircraft for showing the height above sea level.

altitude *n.* **1.** the height above sea level. **2.** the distance of a star etc. above the horizon, measured as an angle.

alto (**al**-toh) *n.* (*pl.* altos) **1.** the highest adult male singing-voice. **2.** a contralto. **3.** a singer with such a voice, a part written for it. **4.** a musical instrument with the second highest pitch in its group, *alto-saxophone.*

altogether *adv.* **1.** entirely, totally. **2.** on the whole. —*n.* (*informal*) a state of nudity; *in the altogether,* nude. ¶ Do not confuse with *all together.*

altruism (**al**-troo-izm) *n.* unselfishness. **altruist** *n.* an unselfish person. **altruistic** *adj.,* **altruistically** *adv.*

alum (**al**-ŭm) *n.* a white mineral salt used in medicine and in dyeing.

aluminium *n.* a lightweight silvery metal used either pure or as an alloy for making

utensils or fittings where lightness is an advantage.

aluminize (ă-**lew**-mi-nyz) *v.* to coat with aluminium.

always *adv.* **1.** at all times, on all occasions. **2.** whatever the circumstances, *you can always sleep on the floor.* **3.** repeatedly, *he is always complaining.*

alyssum (**al**-iss-ŭm) *n.* a plant with small usually yellow or white flowers.

am *see* be.

a.m. *abbrev.* before noon. (¶ From the Latin *ante meridiem.*)

amalgam *n.* **1.** an alloy of mercury and another metal. **2.** any soft pliable mixture.

amalgamate *v.* to mix, to combine. **amalgamation** *n.*

amaryllis (amă-**ril**-iss) *n.* a lily-like plant growing from a bulb.

amass (ă-**mass**) *v.* to heap up, to collect, *amassed a large fortune.*

amateur (**am**-ă-ter) *n.* a person who does something as a pastime rather than as a profession.

amateurish (am-ă-ter-ish) *adj.* inexpert, lacking professional skill. **amateurishly** *adv.,* **amateurishness** *n.*

amaze *v.* to overwhelm with wonder. **amazement** *n.*

amazon (**am**-ă-zŏn) *n.* a tall and strong or athletic woman. ¶ The *Amazons* were a race of female warriors in Greek mythology.

ambassador *n.* **1.** a diplomat sent by one country as a permanent representative or on a special mission to another. **2.** an official messenger. **ambassadorial** (am-bas-ă-**dor**-iăl) *adj.*

amber *n.* **1.** a hardened clear yellowish-brown resin used for making ornaments. **2.** a yellow traffic-light shown as a cautionary signal between red (=stop) and green (=go). —**amber** *adj.* **1.** made of amber. **2.** coloured like amber.

ambergris (**am**-ber-grees) *n.* a wax-like substance found floating in tropical seas and present in the intestines of sperm whales, used as a fixative in perfumes.

ambidextrous (ambi-**deks**-trŭs) *adj.* able to use either hand equally well.

ambience (**am**-bi-ĕns) *n.* environment, surroundings.

ambiguous (am-**big**-yoo-ŭs) *adj.* **1.** having two or more possible meanings. **2.** doubtful, uncertain, *the outcome is ambiguous.* **ambiguously** *adv.,* **ambiguity** (ambig-**yoo**-iti) *n.*

ambit *n.* the bounds, scope, or extent of something.

ambition *n.* **1.** a strong desire to achieve

something. 2. the object of this.

ambitious (am-**bish**-ŭs) *adj.* full of ambition. **ambitiously** *adv.*

ambivalent (am-**biv**-ălĕnt) *adj.* with mixed feelings towards a certain object or situation. **ambivalently** *adv.*, **ambivalence** *n.*

amble *v.* to walk at a slow easy pace. —*n.* a slow easy pace.

ambrosia (am-**broh**-ziă) *n.* something delicious.

ambulance *n.* a vehicle equipped to carry sick or injured people.

ambush *n.* 1. the placing of troops etc. in a concealed position to make a surprise attack on an enemy or victim who has approached. 2. such an attack. —*v.* to lie in wait for, to attack from an ambush.

ameliorate (ă-**mee**-li-er-ayt) *v.* to make or become better. **amelioration** *n.*

amen (ah-**men** *or* ay-**men**) *int.* (in prayers) so be it.

amenable (ă-**meen**-ăbŭl) *adj.* 1. subject to the legal authority of, *we are all amenable to the law.* 2. willing to be guided or controlled by some influence, *she is not amenable to discipline.*

amend *v.* to correct an error in, to make minor alterations in, *they amended the agreement.* **amendment** *n.* □ **make amends**, to compensate or make up for something.

amenity (ă-**meen**-iti *or* a-**men**-iti) *n.* 1. pleasantness of a place or circumstance. 2. a feature of a place etc. that makes life there easy or pleasant. □ **amenity bed**, a bed in a separate room in an NHS hospital, available for a small payment to a patient desiring privacy.

America 1. a continent of the western hemisphere (also called *the Americas*) consisting of the two great land-masses *North America* and *South America* joined by the narrow isthmus of *Central America.* 2. the USA.

American *adj.* 1. of the continent of America. 2. of the USA. —**American** *n.* 1. a native of America. 2. a citizen of the USA. 3. the English language as spoken in the USA.

Americanism *n.* a word or phrase used in American English but not in standard English in Britain.

Americanize *v.* to make American in form or character. **Americanization** *n.*

amethyst (am-i-thist) *n.* a precious stone, purple or violet quartz.

Amharic (am-**ha**-rik) *n.* the official and trade language of Ethiopia.

amiable (**aym**-i-ăbŭl) *adj.* feeling and inspiring friendliness, good-tempered. **amiably** *adv.*, **amiability** *n.*

amicable (**am**-ik-ăbŭl) *adj.* friendly. **amicably** *adv.*, **amicability** *n.*

amid, amidst *preps.* in the middle of, during, *amid shouts of dismay.*

amidships *adv.* in the middle of a ship.

amino acid (ă-mee-noh) an organic acid found in proteins.

amir (ă-**meer**) *n.* a title used by various Muslim rulers. **amirate** (ă-**meer**-ăt) *n.* the territory of an amir.

amiss *adj.* wrong, out of order, *what is amiss with it?* —*adv.* wrongly, faultily; *don't take his criticism amiss,* do not be offended by it.

Amman (ă-**mahn**) the capital of Jordan.

ammeter (**am**-it-er) *n.* an instrument that measures electric current, usually in amperes.

ammo *n.* (*informal*) ammunition.

ammonia *n.* 1. a colourless gas with a strong smell. 2. a solution of this in water.

ammonite (**am**-ŏ-nyt) *n.* the fossil of a coil-shaped shell.

ammunition *n.* 1. projectiles (bullets, shells, grenades, etc.) and their propellants. 2. facts and reasoning used to prove a point in an argument.

amnesia (am-**nee**-ziă) *n.* loss of memory.

amnesty (**am**-nis-ti) *n.* a general pardon, especially for offences against the State.

amniocentesis (amni-ŏ-sen-**tee**-sis) *n.* sampling of the fluid surrounding the foetus before birth by inserting a hollow needle into the surrounding membrane.

amoeba (ă-**mee**-bă) *n.* (*pl.* amoebae (*pr.* ă-mee-bee) *or* amoebas) a microscopic organism consisting of a single cell which changes shape constantly.

amok *adv.* on the rampage in murderous frenzy, *to run amok.*

among, amongst *preps.* 1. in an assembly of, surrounded by, *poppies amongst the corn.* 2. in the number of, *this is reckoned among his best works.* 3. within the limits of, between, *have only £5 amongst us; quarrelled among themselves,* with one another.

Amontillado (ă-mon-til-**ah**-doh) *n.* a medium dry sherry of a matured type.

amoral (ay-**mo**-răl) *adj.* not based on moral standards, neither moral nor immoral.

amorous (**am**-er-ŭs) *adj.* of or showing or readily feeling sexual love. **amorously** *adv.*, **amorousness** *n.*

amorphous (ă-**mor**-fŭs) *adj.* having no definite shape or form.

amount *n.* 1. the total of anything. 2. a quantity, *a small amount of salt* —**amount** *v.* 1. to add up to. 2. to be equivalent to.

amp *n.* (*informal*) **1.** an ampere. **2.** an amplifier.

ampere (**am**-pair) *n.* a unit for measuring electric current.

ampersand *n.* the sign & (= and).

amphetamine (am-**fet**-ămin) *n.* a drug used as a stimulant or to relieve congestion.

amphibian (am-**fib**-iăn) *n.* **1.** an animal able to live both on land and in water (e.g. a frog). **2.** an aircraft that can take off from and alight on both land and water. **3.** a vehicle that can move on both land and water.

amphibious (am-**fib**-iŭs) *adj.* **1.** living or operating both on land and in water. **2.** involving both sea and land forces, *amphibious operations.*

amphitheatre *n.* an oval or circular unroofed building with tiers of seats surrounding a central arena. ¶ This is not the same as a Greek or Roman *theatre*, which is semi-circular.

amphora (**am**-fer-ă) *n.* (*pl.* amphorae (*pr.* -ee) *or* amphoras) an ancient Greek or Roman jar with two handles, tapering at the base.

ample *adj.* **1.** plentiful, quite enough, *ample evidence.* **2.** large, of generous proportions. **amply** *adv.*

amplifier *n.* a device that increases the loudness of sounds or the strength of radio signals.

amplify *v.* (amplified, amplifying) **1.** to increase the strength of, *to amplify sound.* **2.** to make fuller, to add details to, *please amplify your story.* **amplification** *n.*

amplitude *n.* **1.** breadth. **2.** largeness, abundance.

ampoule (**am**-pool) a small sealed container holding a liquid, especially for injection.

amputate *v.* to cut off by surgical operation. **amputation** *n.* □ **amputee** *n.* a person who has had a limb amputated.

Amsterdam the capital of the Netherlands.

amuck *adv.* = amok.

amulet (**am**-yoo-lit) *n.* a thing worn as a charm against evil.

amuse *v.* **1.** to cause to laugh or smile. **2.** to make time pass pleasantly for. **amusement** *n.*

an *adj.* the form of *a* used before vowel sounds other than 'u' (*pr.* yoo), *an egg, an hour* (but *a unit*).

anachronism (ăn-ak-rŏn-izm) *n.* **1.** a mistake in placing something into a particular historical period. **2.** the thing wrongly placed. **3.** a person, custom, or idea regarded as out of date. **anachronistic** (ă-nak-rŏn-**ist**-ik) *adj.*

anaconda (ană-**kon**-dă) *n.* a large snake of tropical South America.

anaemia (ă-**nee**-miă) *n.* lack of red corpuscles, or of their haemoglobin in blood.

anaemic (ă-**nee**-mik) *adj.* **1.** suffering from anaemia. **2.** pale, weak in colour. **3.** lacking vigour or positive characteristics. **anaemically** *adv.*

anaesthesia (anis-**theez**-iă) *n.* loss of sensation, especially that induced by anaesthetics.

anaesthetic (anis-**thet**-ik) *n.* a substance that produces loss of sensation and of ability to feel pain. —*adj.* having this effect.

anaesthetist (ăn-**ees**-thĕt-ist) *n.* a person trained to administer anaesthetics.

anaesthetize (ăn-**ees**-thĕtyz) *v.* to administer an anaesthetic to (a person etc). **anaesthetization** *n.*

anagram (**an**-ă-gram) *n.* a word or phrase formed from the rearranged letters of another (*cart-horse* is an anagram of *orchestra*).

anal *adj.* of the anus.

analgesia (an-ăl-**jees**-iă) *n.* loss of ability to feel pain while still conscious.

analgesic (an-ăl-**jee**-sik) *adj.* relieving pain. —*n.* a drug that relieves pain.

analogous (ă-**nal**-ŏgŭs) *adj.* similar in certain respects. **analogously** *adv.*

analogue (**an**-ă-log) *n.* something that is analogous to something else. **analogue computer**, one that makes calculations with data represented by physical quantities such as length, weight, or voltage, *a slide rule is a simple analogue computer.*

analogy (ă-**nal**-ŏji) *n.* partial likeness between two things which are compared, *the analogy between the human heart and a pump.*

analyse *v.* **1.** to separate (a substance etc.) into its parts in order to identify it or study its structure. **2.** to examine and interpret, *tried to analyse the causes of their failure.* **3.** to psychoanalyse.

analysis *n.* (*pl.* analyses, *pr.* ă-**nal**-iseez) **1.** analysing. **2.** a statement of the result of this.

analyst (**an**-ă-list) *n.* **1.** a person who is skilled in analysis of chemical substances etc. **2.** a psychoanalyst.

analytic, analytical (ană-**lit**-ik-ăl) *adjs.* of or using analysis. **analytically** *adv.*

anarchist (**an**-er-kist) *n.* a person who believes that government and laws are undesirable and should be abolished. **anarchism** *n.,* **anarchistic** (an-er-**kist**-ik) *adj.*

anarchy (**an**-er-ki) *n.* **1.** absence of government or control, resulting in lawlessness. **2.** disorder, confusion. **anarchic** (ăn-**ar**-kik) *adj.*, **anarchical** *adj.*

anastigmatic (ană-stig-**mat**-ik) *adj.* free from astigmatism.

anathema (ăn-**ath**-imă) *n.* **1.** a formal curse of the Church, excommunicating someone or condemning something as evil. **2.** a detested person or thing, *blood sports are anathema to him.*

anatomy (ă-**nat**-ŏmi) *n.* **1.** the scientific study of bodily structures. **2.** the bodily structure of an animal or plant. **anatomical** (ană-**tom**-ikăl) *adj.*, **anatomically** *adv.*

ancestor (an-**sess**-ter) *n.* **1.** any of the persons from whom a person is descended, especially those more remote than grandparents. **2.** an early form of a machine etc. that in later years becomes more developed. **ancestral** (an-**sess**-trăl) *adj.*

ancestry (an-**sess**-tri) *n.* a line of ancestors.

anchor *n.* **1.** a heavy metal structure used to moor a ship to the sea-bottom or a balloon etc. to the ground; *at anchor,* moored by an anchor. **2.** anything that gives stability or security. —**anchor** *v.* **1.** to lower an anchor, to make secure with an anchor. **2.** to fix firmly. □ **anchor man,** a strong member of a sports team who plays a vital part (e.g. at the back of a tug-of-war team or a last runner in a relay race); the compère in a broadcast programme.

anchorage *n.* **1.** a place where ships may anchor safely. **2.** the charge for this.

anchovy (an-**chŏvi**) *n.* a small rich-flavoured fish of the herring family.

ancient *adj.* **1.** belonging to times long past; *the ancients,* people who lived in ancient times. □ **ancient history,** history of the period before the end of the Western Roman Empire in AD 476.

ancillary (an-**sil**-er-i) *adj.* helping in a subsidiary way, *ancillary services.*

and *conj.* **1.** together with, *cakes and buns.* **2.** then again repeatedly or increasingly, *gets better and better; miles and miles,* very many miles. **3.** added to, *two and two make four.* **4.** to, *go and buy one.* **5.** with this consequence; *move and I shoot,* if you move I shall shoot. □ **and/or,** together with or as an alternative; *A and/or B,* A or B or both.

andante (an-**dan**-ti) *adv.* (of music) in moderately slow time. —*n.* a passage to be played in this way.

Andean (an-**dee**-ăn) *adj.* of the Andes, a range of mountains in western South America.

andiron (**and**-I-ern) *n.* an iron support (usually one of a pair) for holding logs in a fireplace.

Andorra (and-o-ră) a semi-independent country in the Pyrenees. **Andorran** *adj.* & *n.*

android *n.* (in science fiction) a robot with human form.

anecdote (**an**-ik-doht) *n.* a short amusing or interesting story about a real person or event.

anemometer (anim-**om**-it-er) *n.* an instrument for measuring the force of wind.

anemone (ă-**nem**-ŏni) *n.* a plant related to the buttercup, with white, red, or purple flowers.

aneroid barometer (**an**-er-oid) a barometer that measures air-pressure by the action of air on the lid of a box containing a vacuum, not by the height of a fluid column.

aneurysm (**an**-yoor-izm) *n.* permanent abnormal dilatation of an artery.

anew *adv.* again, in a new or different way.

angel *n.* **1.** an attendant or messenger of God, usually shown in pictures as a being in human form with wings and dressed in long white robes. **2.** a very beautiful or kind person. □ **angel cake,** very light sponge cake. **angel-fish** *n.* a fish with wing-like fins.

angelic *adj.* of or like an angel. **angelically** *adv.*

angelica (an-**jel**-ikă) *n.* **1.** a fragrant plant used in cookery and medicine. **2.** its candied stalks.

angelus (**an**-jil-ŭs) *n.* (in the RC Church) **1.** a prayer to the Virgin Mary commemorating the Incarnation, said at morning, noon, and sunset. **2.** a bell rung as a signal for this.

anger *n.* the strong feeling caused by extreme displeasure. —*v.* to make angry.

angina pectoris (an-**jy**-nă **pek**-ter-iss) sharp pain in the chest caused by overexertion when the heart is diseased.

angle[1] *n.* **1.** the space between two lines or surfaces that meet. **2.** a point of view, *written from the woman's angle.* —**angle** *v.* **1.** to move or place in a slanting position. **2.** to present (news etc.) from a particular point of view.

angle[2] *v.* **1.** to fish with hook and bait. **2.** to try to obtain by hinting, *angling for an invitation.* **angler** *n.*

Anglican *adj.* of the Church of England or other Church in communion with it. —*n.* a member of the Anglican Church.

anglicize (**ang**-li-syz) *v.* to make English in form or character.

Anglo- *prefix* English, British; *an Anglo-French agreement,* an agreement between Britain and France.

Anglo-Catholic *adj.* of the section of the Church of England that stresses its unbroken connection with the early Christian Church and objects to being called Protestant. —*n.* a member of this section of the Church.

Anglophile (ang-loh-fyl) *n.* a person who loves England or English things.

Anglo-Saxon *n.* **1.** an English person of the period before the Norman Conquest. **2.** the English language of this period, also called *Old English.* **3.** a person of English descent. —*adj.* of the Anglo-Saxons or their language.

Angola (an-**goh**-lă) a country on the west coast of Africa. **Angolan** *adj.* & *n.*

angora *n.* **1.** yarn or fabric made from the hair of angora goats or rabbits. **2.** a long-haired variety of cat, goat, or rabbit.

angostura (angŏss-**tewr**-ă) *n.* the bitter bark of a South American tree.

angry *adj.* (angrier, angriest) **1.** feeling or showing anger. **2.** inflamed, *an angry sore.* **angrily** *adv.*

ångström (ang-strŏm) *n.* a unit of length used in measuring wavelengths.

anguish *n.* severe physical or mental pain. **anguished** *adj.* feeling anguish.

angular *adj.* **1.** having angles or sharp corners. **2.** lacking plumpness or smoothness. **3.** measured by angle, *the angular distance.* **angularity** (ang-yoo-**la**-riti) *n.*

Angus *n.* = Aberdeen Angus.

aniline (**an**-il-een) *n.* an oily liquid obtained from nitrobenzene, used in the manufacture of dyes and plastics.

animadversion (anim-ăd-**ver**-shŏn) *n.* hostile criticism.

animadvert (anim-ad-**vert**) *v.* to criticize in a hostile way.

animal *n.* **1.** a living thing that can feel and move voluntarily. **2.** such a being other than a human being. **3.** a four-footed animal distinguished from a bird or fish or reptile or insect. **4.** a brutish person. —*adj.* of or from or relating to animal life.

animate¹ (**an**-im-ăt) *adj.* living.

animate² (**an**-im-ayt) *v.* **1.** to give life or movement to, to make lively, *an animated discussion.* **2.** to motivate, *he was animated by loyalty.* **3.** to produce as an animated cartoon. **animator** *n.* □ **animated cartoon,** a film made by photographing a series of drawings, giving an illusion of movement.

animation *n.* **1.** animating. **2.** liveliness.

animism *n.* belief that all beings and things such as rocks, streams, and winds have a living soul. **animistic** *adj.*

animosity (anim-**os**-iti) *n.* a spirit of hostility.

animus (**an**-imŭs) *n.* animosity shown in speech or action.

anion (**an**-I-ŏn) *n.* an ion with a negative charge.

aniseed *n.* the sweet-smelling seed of the plant anise, used for flavouring.

Ankara (**ank**-er-ă) the capital of Turkey.

ankle *n.* **1.** the joint connecting the foot with the leg. **2.** the slender part between this and the calf. □ **ankle socks,** short socks just covering the ankles.

anklet *n.* an ornamental chain or band worn round the ankle.

annals (**an**-ălz) *pl. n.* a history of events year by year, historical records.

annex (ăn-**eks**) *v.* **1.** to add or join to a larger thing. **2.** to take possession of, *to annex territory.* **annexation** *n.*

annexe (**an**-eks) *n.* a building attached to a larger one or forming a subordinate part of a main building.

annihilate (ă-**ny**-hil-ayt) *v.* to destroy completely. **annihilation** *n.*, **annihilator** *n.*

anniversary *n.* the yearly return of the date of an event, a celebration of this.

Anno Domini (an-oh **dom**-in-I) **1.** in the year of Our Lord (usually shortened to AD). **2.** (*informal*) advancing age, *there's nothing wrong with him except Anno Domini.*

annotate (**an**-oh-tayt) *v.* to add notes of explanation to, *an annotated edition.* **annotation** *n.*

announce *v.* **1.** to make known publicly or to an audience. **2.** to make known the presence or arrival of. **announcement** *n.*

announcer *n.* a person who announces items in a broadcast.

annoy *v.* **1.** to cause slight anger to. **2.** to be troublesome to, to harass. **annoyance** *n.* □ **annoyed** *adj.* slightly angry.

annual *adj.* **1.** coming or happening once every year, *her annual visit.* **2.** of one year, reckoned by the year, *her annual income.* **3.** lasting only one year or season, *annual plants.* —**annual** *n.* **1.** a plant that lives for one year or one season. **2.** a book or periodical published in yearly issues. —**annually** *adv.*

annuity (ă-**new**-iti) *n.* a fixed annual allowance, especially one provided by a form of investment. **annuitant** (ă-**new**-i-tănt) *n.* one who receives an annuity.

annul (ă-**nul**) *v.* (annulled, annulling) to make null and void, to destroy the validity of, *the marriage was annulled.* **annulment** *n.*

annular (**an**-yoo-ler) *adj.* ring-like.

Annunciation *n.* **1.** the announcement by the angel Gabriel to the Virgin Mary that she was to be the mother of Christ. **2.** the festival commemorating this (25 March, also called *Lady Day*).

anode (an-ohd) *n.* the electrode by which current enters a device.

anodize (an-ŏ-dyz) *v.* to coat (metal) with a protective layer by electrolysis.

anodyne (an-ŏ-dyn) *n.* **1.** a drug that relieves pain. **2.** anything that relieves pain or distress.

anoint *v.* **1.** to apply ointment or oil to, especially as a sign of consecration. **2.** to smear or rub with grease.

anomaly (ă-nom-ăli) *n.* something that deviates from the general rule or the usual type, an irregularity or inconsistency, *the many anomalies in our tax system.* **anomalous** *adj.*

anon (ă-non) *adv.* (*old use*) soon, presently, *I will say more of this anon.*

anon. *abbrev.* anonymous (author).

anonymity (an-on-im-iti) *n.* being anonymous.

anonymous (ă-non-im-ŭs) *adj.* **1.** with a name that is not known or not made public, *an anonymous donor.* **2.** written or given by such a person, *an anonymous gift; an anonymous letter,* one that is not signed. **anonymously** *adv.*

anorak (an-er-ak) *n.* a jacket with a hood attached, worn as a protection against rain, wind, and cold.

anorexia (an-er-eks-iă) *n.* loss of appetite for food. **anorexic** *or* **anorectic** *n.* a person suffering from anorexia nervosa, a psychological condition causing reluctance to eat.

another *adj.* **1.** additional, one more; *he is another Solomon,* one like him. **2.** different, *fit another pipe, this one leaks.* **3.** some or any other, *will not do another man's work.* —*pronoun* another person or thing. □ **A. N. Other,** a player not named or not yet selected.

answer *n.* something said or written or needed or done to deal with a question, accusation, or problem. —*v.* **1.** to make an answer to, to say or write or do something in return; *answer the door,* go to it in response to a signal; *he answers to the name of Thomas,* is so called. **2.** to suffice or be suitable for, *this will answer the purpose.* **3.** to take responsibility for, to vouch for, *I will answer for his honesty; they must answer for their crimes,* must justify them or pay the penalty. **4.** to correspond, *this bag answers to the description of the stolen one.* □ **answer back,** to answer a rebuke cheekily.

answerable *adj.* **1.** able to be answered. **2.** having to account for something.

ant *n.* a very small insect of which there are many species, all of which form and live in highly organized groups. □ **anteater** *n.* an animal that feeds on ants and termites.

antacid (ant-ass-id) *n.* a substance that prevents or corrects acidity.

antagonism (an-tag-ŏn-izm) *n.* active opposition, hostility. **antagonist** *n.* an opponent, one who is hostile to something.

antagonistic (an-tag-ŏn-ist-ik) *adj.* showing or feeling antagonism. **antagonistically** *adv.*

antagonize *v.* to arouse antagonism in.

Antarctic *adj.* of the regions round the South Pole. —*n.* **1.** these regions. **2.** the Antarctic Ocean. □ **Antarctic Circle,** the line of latitude 66° 30′ S.

Antarctica the continent mainly within the Antarctic Circle.

ante (an-ti) *n.* a stake put up by a poker-player before drawing new cards. —*v.* to put up an ante, to pay up.

ante- (an-ti) *prefix* before.

antecedent (ant-i-seedn't) *n.* **1.** a preceding thing or circumstance, *the war and its antecedents; I know nothing of his antecedents,* of his ancestry or past life. **2.** a noun or clause or sentence to which a following pronoun refers (in *the book which I have,* 'book' is the antecedent of 'which'). —*adj.* previous.

antechamber *n.* an ante-room.

antedate *v.* to put an earlier date on (a document) than that on which it was issued.

antediluvian (anti-di-loo-viăn) *adj.* **1.** of the time before Noah's Flood. **2.** (*informal*) utterly out of date.

antelope *n.* a swift-running animal (e.g. chamois, gazelle) resembling a deer, found especially in Africa.

antenatal *adj.* **1.** before birth. **2.** before giving birth; *antenatal clinic,* for pregnant women.

antenna *n.* **1.** (*pl.* antennae, *pr.* an-ten-ee) one of a pair of flexible sensitive projections on the heads of insects, crustaceans, etc., a feeler. **2.** (*pl.* antennas) (*Amer.*) an aerial.

antepenultimate (anti-pin-ult-imăt) *adj.* last but two.

ante-post *adj.* (of bets) made before the runners' numbers are made known.

anterior *adj.* coming before in position or time.

ante-room *n.* a room leading to a more important one.

anthem *n.* a short musical composition to be sung in religious services, often with words taken from the Bible.

anther *n.* the part of a flower's stamen that contains pollen.

anthill *n.* a mound over an ants' nest.

anthologist *n.* a person who compiles an anthology.

anthologize *v.* to include in an anthology.

anthology (an-**thol**-ŏji) *n.* a collection of passages from literature, especially poems.

anthracite *n.* a hard form of coal that burns with little flame or smoke.

anthrax *n.* a disease of sheep and cattle that can be transmitted to people.

anthropoid (**an**-thrŏp-oid) *adj.* man-like in form. —*n.* an anthropoid ape such as a gorilla or chimpanzee.

anthropology (anthrŏ-**pol**-ŏji) *n.* the scientific study of mankind, especially of its origins, development, customs, and beliefs. **anthropological** (an-thrŏp-ŏ-**loj**-ikăl) *adj.*, **anthropologically** *adv.* □ **anthropologist** *n.* an expert in anthropology.

anthropomorphic (an-thrŏp-ŏ-**mor**-fik) *adj.* attributing human form or personality to a god or animal or object. **anthropomorphism** *n.*

anti *n.* (*pl.* antis) a person who opposes a certain policy etc. —*prep.* opposed to.

anti- *prefix* **1.** against, opposed to, *anti-slavery*. **2.** preventing, counteracting, *antiperspirant*.

anti-aircraft *adj.* used against enemy aircraft.

antibiotic (anti-by-**ot**-ik) *n.* a substance capable of destroying or preventing the growth of bacteria.

antibody (**an**-ti-bodi) *n.* a protein formed in the blood in reaction to certain substances which it then attacks and destroys.

antic *n.* **1.** absurd movements intended to cause amusement. **2.** odd or foolish behaviour.

anticipate *v.* **1.** to deal with or use before the proper time; *anticipate one's income,* spend it before receiving it. **2.** to take action before someone else has had time to do so, *others may have anticipated Columbus in the discovery of America.* **3.** to notice what needs doing and take action in advance; *anticipate someone's needs,* provide for them in advance; *boxer anticipated the blow,* saw it coming and blocked it. **4.** to expect, *we anticipate that it will rain.* (¶ Many people regard this use as unacceptable, but it is very common; it should be avoided in formal use.) **anticipation** *n.*

anticipatory (an-**tiss**-i-payt-er-i) *adj.* showing anticipation.

anticlimax *n.* a disappointing ending or outcome of events where a climax was expected.

anticlockwise *adv.* & *adj.* moving in a curve from right to left, as seen from the centre of the circle.

anticyclone *n.* an area in which atmospheric pressure is high, producing fine settled weather, with an outward flow of air.

antidepressant *n.* a drug that counteracts mental depression.

antidote (**an**-ti-doht) *n.* **1.** a substance that counteracts the effects of a poison or a disease. **2.** anything that counteracts unpleasant effects.

antifreeze *n.* a substance added to water to lower its freezing point and therefore make it less likely to freeze.

Antigua and Barbuda (an-**teeg**-ă, bar-**boo**-dă) a country consisting of two islands in the Caribbean Sea. **Antiguan** *adj.* & *n.,* **Barbudan** *adj.* & *n.*

antihistamine (anti-**hist**-ă-min) *n.* a substance that counteracts the effects of histamine, used in treating allergies.

anti-knock *adj.* preventing or reducing knock or pinking in internal combustion engines. **antiknock** *n.* a substance added to motor fuel to prevent or reduce knock.

antimacassar (anti-mă-**kas**-er) *n.* a small protective cover for the backs or arms of chairs etc.

antimony (**an**-ti-mŏni) *n.* a brittle silvery metal used in alloys.

antipathy (an-**tip**-ă-thi) *n.* **1.** a strong and settled dislike. **2.** the object of this.

antiperspirant (anti-**per**-spi-rănt) *n.* a substance that prevents or reduces sweating.

antiphon (**an**-ti-fŏn) *n.* a verse of a psalm etc. sung by part of a choir in response to one song by the other part. **antiphonal** (an-**tif**-ŏn-ăl) *adj.*

antipodes (an-**tip**-ŏ-deez) *pl. n.* places on opposite sides of the earth; *the antipodes,* the Australasian regions, diametrically opposite Europe. **antipodean** (antip-ŏ-**dee**-ăn) *adj.*

antiquary (**an**-tik-wer-i) *n.* one who studies or collects antiques or antiquities. **antiquarian** (anti-**kwair**-iăn) *adj.* & *n.*

antiquated (**an**-ti-kway-tid) *adj.* old-fashioned, out of date.

antique (an-**teek**) *adj.* belonging to the distant past, in the style of past times. —*n.* an antique object, especially furniture or a decorative object of a kind sought by collectors. —*v.* to make (furniture etc.) appear antique by artificial means.

antiquity (an-**tik**-witi) *n.* **1.** ancient times, especially before the Middle Ages; *it is of great antiquity,* is very old. **2.** an object dating from ancient times, *Greek and Roman antiquities.*

antirrhinum (anti-ry-nŭm) *n.* a garden flower commonly called snapdragon.

anti-Semitic (anti-sim-**it**-ik) *adj.* hostile to Jews. **anti-Semitism** (anti-**sem**-it-izm) *n.* hostility to Jews.

antiseptic *adj.* **1.** preventing the growth of bacteria etc. that cause things to become septic. **2.** thoroughly clean and free from germs. —*n.* a substance with an antiseptic effect. —**antiseptically** *adv.*

antisocial *adj.* **1.** opposed to the social institutions and laws of an organized community. **2.** interfering with amenities enjoyed by others, *it's antisocial to leave litter.* **3.** unsociable, withdrawing oneself from others. **antisocially** *adv.*

antistatic *adj.* counteracting the effects of static electricity.

antithesis (an-**tith**-i-sis) *n.* (*pl.* antitheses) **1.** the direct opposite of something, opposition or contrast, *slavery is the antithesis of freedom.* **2.** contrast of ideas emphasized by choice of words or by their arrangement. **antithetic** (anti-**thet** ik) *adj.*, **antithetical** *adj.*, **antithetically** *adv.*

antitoxin *n.* a substance that neutralizes a toxin and prevents it from having a harmful effect. **antitoxic** *adj.*

antivivisectionist *n.* a person who is opposed to making experiments on live animals.

antler *n.* a branched horn, one of a pair of these on a stag or other deer.

antonym (**ant**-ŏn-im) *n.* a word that is opposite in meaning to another.

Antrim a county of Northern Ireland.

anus (**ay**-nŭs) *n.* the opening at the end of the alimentary canal, through which waste matter passes out of the body.

anvil *n.* a block of iron on which a smith hammers metal into shape.

anxiety *n.* **1.** the state of being anxious. **2.** something causing this.

anxious *adj.* **1.** troubled and uneasy in mind. **2.** causing worry, filled with such feeling, *an anxious moment.* **3.** eager, *anxious to please.* **anxiously** *adv.*

any *adj.* **1.** one or some (but no matter which) from three or more or from a quantity. **2.** every, whichever you choose, *any fool knows that.* **3.** in a significant amount, *did not stay any length of time.* —*pronoun* any person or thing or amount, *can't find any of them; we haven't any.* —*adv.* at all, in some degree, *isn't any better.* □ **any amount** *or* **any number**, much, many. **not having any**, (*informal*) unwilling to take part in something or to agree with what is said.

anybody *n.* & *pronoun* **1.** any person. **2.** a person of importance, *is he anybody?*

□ **anybody's guess**, something no one can be sure about.

anyhow *adv.* **1.** anyway. **2.** not in an orderly manner, *work was done all anyhow.*

anymore *adv.* (*Amer.*) to any further extent, from now on. ¶ This is always written as two words in standard English.

anyone *n.* & *pronoun.* anybody.

anything *n.* & *pronoun* any thing, *anything will do; as easy as anything,* very easy. □ **anything but,** far from being, *it's anything but cheap.* **like anything,** with great intensity.

anyway *adv.* in any case. ¶ It is incorrect to write *anyway* as one word in sentences such as *do it any way you like.*

anywhere *adv.* in or to any place —*pronoun* any place.

Anzac *n.* **1.** a member of the Australian and New Zealand Army Corps (1914–18). (¶ The name is formed from the initial letters of the Corps.) **2.** an Australian or a New Zealander. □ **Anzac Day,** 25 April, commemorating the landings in Gallipoli (1915).

aorta (ay-**or**-tă) *n.* the great artery through which blood is carried from the left side of the heart.

apace *adv.* swiftly, *work proceeded apace.*

Apache (ă-**pach**-i) *n.* a member of a tribe of North American Indians inhabiting the south-western part of the USA.

apart *adv.* **1.** aside, separately, to or at a distance; *cannot tell them apart,* cannot distinguish one from the other. **2.** into pieces, *it came apart.* □ **apart from,** independently of, other than, *has no books apart from these.* **joking apart,** speaking seriously, without joking.

apartheid (ă-**part**-hayt) *n.* a policy in South Africa of racial segregation, separating Europeans and non-Europeans.

apartment *n.* **1.** a set of rooms. **2.** (*Amer.*) a flat.

apathy (**ap**-ă-thi) *n.* lack of interest or concern. **apathetic** (apă-**thet**-ik) *adj.*, **apathetically** *adv.*

ape *n.* any of the four primates (gorilla, chimpanzee, orang-utan, gibbon) most closely related to man. —*v.* to imitate, to mimic. □ **ape-man** *n,* an extinct creature intermediate between apes and men.

Apennines (**ap**-i-nynz) *pl. n.* a mountain range in Italy.

aperient (ă-**peer**-iĕnt) *adj.* laxative. —*n.* a laxative medicine.

aperitif (ă-**pe**-ri-teef) *n.* an alcoholic drink taken as an appetizer.

aperture *n.* an opening, especially one that admits light.

apex (**ay**-peks) *n.* (*pl.* apexes) the tip or highest point, the pointed end, *the apex of a triangle.*

aphid (**ay**-fid) *n.* a plant-louse such as a greenfly or blackfly.

aphis (**ay**-fiss) *n.* (*pl.* aphides, *pr.* **ay**-fid-eez) an aphid.

aphorism (**af**-er-izm) *n.* a short wise saying, a maxim.

aphrodisiac (afrŏ-**diz**-iak) *adj.* arousing sexual desire. —*n.* an aphrodisiac substance.

apiary (**ay**-pi-er-i) *n.* a place with a number of hives where bees are kept.

apiece *adv.* to each, for or by each one of a group, *cost a penny apiece.*

aplomb (ă-**plom**) *n.* dignity and confidence.

Apocalypse (ă-**pok**-ă-lips) *n.* the *Revelation of St. John the Divine,* the last book in the New Testament, containing a prophetic description of the end of the world.

apocalyptic (ă-pok-ă-**lip**-tik) *adj.* prophesying great and dramatic events like those described in the Apocalypse. **apocalyptically** *adv.*

Apocrypha (ă-**pok**-rif-ă) *n.* those books of the Old Testament that were not accepted by Jews as part of the Hebrew Scriptures and were excluded from the Protestant Bible at the Reformation.

apocryphal (ă-**pok**-rif-ăl) *adj.* **1.** untrue, invented, *an apocryphal account of his travels.* **2.** *Apocryphal,* of the Apocrypha. **apocryphally** *adv.*

apogee (**ap**-ŏ-jee) *n.* **1.** the point in the orbit of the moon or any planet when it is at its furthest point from earth. **2.** the highest or most distant point, a climax.

Apollo the sun god in Greek mythology. —*n.* (*pl.* Apollos) a young man of great physical beauty.

Apollyon (a-**pol**-yŏn) the Devil.

apologetic *adj.* making an apology. **apologetically** *adv.*

apologist *n.* a person who explains or defends a doctrine by reasoned argument.

apologize *v.* to make an apology.

apology *n.* **1.** a statement of regret for having done wrong or hurt someone's feelings. **2.** an explanation or defence of one's beliefs. **3.** a poor or scanty specimen, *this feeble apology for a meal.*

apoplectic (apŏ-**plek**-tik) *adj.* **1.** of apoplexy. **2.** suffering from apoplexy. **3.** (*informal*) liable to fits of rage in which the face becomes very red. **apoplectically** *adv.*

apoplexy (**ap**-ŏ-plek-si) *n.* sudden inability to feel and move, caused by blockage or rupture of an artery in the brain.

apostle *n.* **1.** *Apostle,* any of the twelve men sent forth by Christ to preach the Gospel. **2.** a leader or teacher of a new faith or movement. □ **apostle spoon,** a spoon with a figure of an Apostle on the handle.

apostolic (apŏ-**stol**-ik) *adj.* **1.** of the Apostles or their teaching. **2.** of the pope as successor to St. Peter; *apostolic succession,* transmission of spiritual authority from the Apostles through successive popes and other bishops.

apostrophe (ă-**pos**-trŏ-fi) *n.* **1.** the sign ' used to show that letters or numbers have been omitted (as in *can't* = cannot; '05 = 1905), or showing the possessive case (*the boy's book, the boys' books*), or the plurals of letters (*there are two l's in 'Bell'*). **2.** a passage in a speech or in a poem etc. addressing an absent person or an abstract idea.

apostrophize (ă-**pos**-trŏ-fyz) *v.* to address in an apostrophe.

apothecary (ă-**poth**-ik-eri) *n.* (*old use*) a pharmaceutical chemist. **apothecaries' weight,** a system of units formerly used in weighing drugs.

appal (ă-**pawl**) *v.* (appalled, appalling) to fill with horror or dismay, to shock deeply. **appalling** *adj.* (*informal*) shocking, unpleasant.

Appalachians (apă-**lay**-chi-ănz) *pl. n.* the Appalachian Mountains, in eastern North America.

apparatus *n.* **1.** the equipment used for doing something, the instruments etc. used in scientific experiments. **2.** the equipment (e.g. vaulting-horse, parallel bars, etc.) used in gymnastics. **3.** a group of bodily organs by which some natural process is carried out, *the digestive apparatus.*

apparel *n.* (*formal*) clothing.

apparent (ă-**pa**-rĕnt) *adj.* **1.** clearly seen or understood; *it became apparent,* became obvious. **2.** seeming but not real, *his reluctance was only apparent.* **apparently** *adv.* □ **heir apparent,** see heir.

apparition (apă-**rish**-ŏn) **1.** an appearance, something that appears, especially something remarkable or unexpected. **2.** a ghost.

appeal *v.* (appealed, appealing) **1.** to make an earnest request, *appealed for contributions.* **2.** to ask a person or go to a recognized authority for an opinion or for confirmation of what one says, *appealed to the umpire.* **3.** to take a question to a higher court for re-hearing and a new decision. **4.** to offer attraction, to seem pleasing, *cruises don't appeal to me.* —**appeal**

n. **1.** the act of appealing. **2.** attraction, pleasantness; *it has snob appeal,* appeals to people's snobbish feelings. **3.** a request for public donations to a cause.

appear *v.* **1.** to be or become visible. **2.** to present oneself, especially formally or publicly, *the Minstrels are appearing at the Victoria Theatre.* **3.** to act as counsel in a lawcourt, *I appear for the defendant.* **4.** to be published, *the story appeared in the newspapers.* **5.** to give a certain impression, *you appear to have forgotten.*

appearance *n.* **1.** appearing; *made its appearance,* appeared. **2.** an outward sign, what something appears to be, *has an appearance of prosperity.* □ **keep up appearances,** to keep an outward show of prosperity or good behaviour. **put in an appearance,** to be present, especially for only a short time. **to all appearances,** so far as can be seen, *he was to all appearances dead.*

appease *v.* to make calm or quiet by making concessions and by satisfying demands. **appeasement** *n.*

appellant (ă-**pel**-ănt) *n.* a person making an appeal to a higher court.

appellation (ap-ĕl-**ay**-shŏn) *n.* **1.** naming. **2.** name or title.

append *v.* **1** to attach. **2.** to add at the end, *append one's signature.*

appendage (ă-**pen**-dij) *n.* a thing added to or forming a natural part of something larger or more important.

appendicitis *n.* inflammation of the appendix of the intestine.

appendix *n.* **1.** (*pl.* appendices) a section with supplementary information at the end of a book or document. **2.** (*pl.* appendixes) a small blind tube of tissue attached to the intestine.

appertain (ap-er-**tayn**) *v.* **1.** to belong to. **2.** to be relevant to, *the facts appertaining to his dismissal.*

appetite *n.* **1.** physical desire, especially for food. **2.** a desire or liking, *an appetite for power.*

appetizer *n.* something eaten or drunk to stimulate the appetite.

appetizing *adj.* stimulating the appetite, *an appetizing smell.* **appetizingly** *adv.*

applaud *v.* **1.** to show approval of (a thing) by clapping one's hands. **2.** to praise, *we applaud your decision.*

applause *n.* **1.** hand-clapping by people applauding. **2.** warm approval.

apple *n.* a round fruit with firm juicy flesh. **apple of one's eye,** a cherished person or thing. **apple-pie order,** perfect order.

appliance *n.* a device, an instrument.

applicable (**ap**-lik-ăbŭl) *adj.* able to be applied, appropriate. **applicability** (ăplikă-**bil**-iti) *n.*

applicant (**ap**-lik-ănt) *n.* a person who applies, especially for a job.

application *n.* **1.** applying something, putting one thing on another, *ointment for external application only.* **2.** the thing applied. **3.** making a formal request, the request itself, *his application was refused.* **4.** bringing a rule into use, putting something to practical use. **5.** the ability to apply oneself.

applicator *n.* a device for applying something.

applied *see* apply. —*adj.* put to practical use; *applied science, applied mathematics,* these subjects used in a practical way (e.g. in engineering), not merely theoretical.

appliqué (ă-**plee**-kay) *n.* **1.** a piece of cut-out material sewn or fixed ornamentally to another. **2.** needlework of this kind. —*v.* (appliquéd, appliquéing) to ornament with appliqué.

apply *v.* (applied, applying) **1.** to put (a thing) into contact with another, to spread on a surface; *apply the brakes,* cause them to act on the wheels. **2** to bring into use or action, *apply economic sanctions; this name was applied to them,* was used in describing or referring to them. **3.** to put into effect, to be relevant, *the rules must be applied in every case; what I said does not apply to you.* **4.** to make a formal request, *to apply for a job.* □ **apply oneself,** to give one's attention and energy to a task.

appoint *v.* **1.** to fix or decide by authority, *they appointed a time for the next meeting.* **2.** to choose (a person) for a job, to set up by choosing members, *appoint a committee.* □ **appointee** *n.* the person appointed. **well-appointed** *adj.* well equipped or furnished.

appointment *n.* **1.** an arrangement to meet or visit at a particular time. **2.** appointing a person to a job. **3.** the job or position itself. □ **appointments** *pl. n.* equipment, furniture.

apportion (ă-**por**-shŏn) *v.* to divide into shares, to allot. **apportionment** *n.*

apposite (**ap**-ŏ-zit) *adj.* (of a remark) appropriate for a purpose or occasion. **appositely** *adv.,* **appositeness** *n.*

apposition (apŏ-**zish**-ŏn) *n.* **1.** placing side by side. **2.** a grammatical relationship in which a word or phrase is placed with another which it describes, e.g. in 'the reign of Elizabeth, our Queen', *our Queen* is in apposition to *Elizabeth.*

appraise *v.* to estimate the value or quality of. **appraisal** *n.*

appreciable (ă-**pree**-shă-bŭl) *adj.* able to be seen or felt, considerable, *an appreciable change in temperature.* **appreciably** *adv.*

appreciate *v.* **1.** to value greatly, to be grateful for. **2.** to enjoy intelligently, *to appreciate English poetry.* **3.** to understand, *we appreciate their reluctance to give details.* **4.** to increase in value, *the investments have appreciated greatly.* **appreciation** *n.*

appreciative (ă-**pree**-shă-tiv) *adj.* feeling or showing appreciation. **appreciatively** *adv.*

apprehend (apri-**hend**) *v.* **1.** to seize, to arrest. **2.** to grasp the meaning of, to understand. **3.** to expect with fear or anxiety.

apprehension (apri-**hen**-shŏn) *n.* **1.** a feeling of fear about a possible danger or difficulty. **2.** understanding. **3.** arrest.

apprehensive (apri-**hen**-siv) *adj.* feeling apprehension, anxious. **apprehensively** *adv.*

apprentice *n.* **1.** one who is learning a craft and is bound to an employer by legal agreement. **2.** a novice. —*v.* to bind (a person) legally as an apprentice. — **apprenticeship** *n.*

apprise (ă-**pryz**) *v.* (*formal*) to inform.

appro (**ap**-roh) *n.* (*informal*) **on appro,** on approval.

approach *v.* **1.** to come near or nearer in space or time. **2.** to set about doing or tackling, *approach the problem in a practical way.* **3.** to go to with a request or offer, *approach your bank for a loan.* **4.** to be similar to, *his liking for it approaches infatuation.* — **approach** *n.* **1.** approaching, *watched their approach.* **2.** a way of reaching a place. **3.** the final part of an aircraft's flight before landing. **4.** a method of doing or tackling something. **5.** an effort to establish an agreement or friendly relations. **6.** an approximation, *his nearest approach to a smile.*

approachable *adj.* able to be approached; *he is very approachable,* is friendly and easy to talk to. **approachability** *n.*

approbation (aprŏ-**bay**-shŏn) *n.* approval.

appropriate [1] (ă-**proh**-pri-ăt) *adj.* suitable, proper. **appropriately** *adv.,* **appropriateness** *n.*

appropriate [2] (ă-**proh**-pri-ayt) *v.* **1.** to take and use as one's own. **2.** to set aside for a special purpose, *£500 was appropriated to the sports fund.* **appropriation** *n.,* **appropriator** *n.*

approval *n.* feeling or showing or saying that one considers something to be good or acceptable. **on approval,** (of goods) taken by a customer for examination

without obligation to buy unless he is satisfied.

approve *v.* **1.** to say or feel that something is good or suitable. **2.** to sanction, to agree to, *the expenditure has been approved.*

approximate [1] (ă-**prok**-sim-ăt) *adj.* almost exact or correct but not completely so. **approximately** *adv.*

approximate [2] (ă-**prok**-sim-ayt) *v.* **1.** to be almost the same, *a story that approximated to the truth.* **2.** to make approximately the same. **approximation** *n.*

appurtenance (ă-**per**-tin-ăns) *n.* a minor piece of property, or a right or privilege, that goes with a more important one.

après-ski (ap-ray **skee**) *adj.* of or suitable for the evening period after skiing, at a resort. —*n.* this period.

apricot *n.* **1.** a juicy stone-fruit related to the plum and peach, orange-pink when ripe. **2.** this colour.

April the fourth month of the year. **April fool,** a person who is hoaxed on April Fool's Day (1 April).

apron *n.* **1.** a garment worn over the front part of the body to protect the wearer's clothes. **2.** a similar garment worn as part of his official dress by a bishop or freemason. **3.** anything resembling such a garment in shape or function. **4.** a hard-surfaced area on an airfield, where aircraft are manœuvred or loaded and unloaded. □ **tied to mother's apron-strings,** excessively dependent on or dominated by her.

apropos (aprŏ-**poh**) *adv.* appropriately, to the point. —*adj.* suitable or relevant to what is being said or done. □ **apropos of,** concerning, with reference to, *apropos of elections, who is to be our new candidate?*

apse *n.* a recess usually with an arched or domed roof, especially in a church.

apt *adj.* **1.** suitable, appropriate, *an apt quotation.* **2.** having a certain tendency, likely, *he is apt to be careless.* **3.** quick at learning. **aptly** *adv.,* **aptness** *n.*

aptitude *n.* a natural ability or skill.

aqua *n.* the colour aquamarine.

aqualung *n.* a diver's portable breathing-apparatus consisting of cylinders of compressed air connected to a face-mask.

aquamarine (akwă-mă-**reen**) *n.* **1.** a bluish-green beryl. **2.** its colour.

aquaplane *n.* a board, on which a person stands, to be towed by a speedboat. —*v.* **1.** to ride on such a board. **2.** to glide uncontrollably on the wet surface of a road.

aquarium (ă-**kwair**-iŭm) *n.* (*pl.* aquariums) **1.** an artificial pond or tank for keeping living fish and water animals and plants. **2.** a building containing such ponds or tanks.

Aquarius (ă-**kwair**-iŭs) a sign of the zodiac, the Water-carrier. **Aquarian** *adj.* & *n.*

aquatic (ă-**kwat**-ik) *adj.* **1.** growing or living in or near water, *aquatic plants.* **2.** taking place in or on water; *aquatic sports,* rowing, swimming, etc.

aquatint *n.* an etching made on copper by using nitric acid.

aqueduct (**ak**-wi dukt) *n.* an artificial channel carrying water across country, especially one built like a bridge above low ground.

aquilegia (akwi-**lee**-jă) *n.* a columbine.

aquiline (**ak**-wi-lyn) *adj.* hooked like an eagle's beak, *an aquiline nose.*

Arab *n.* a member of a Semitic people originally inhabiting the Arabian peninsula and neighbouring countries, now also other parts of the Middle East and North Africa. —*adj.* of Arabs.

arabesque (a-ră-**besk**) *n.* **1.** an elaborate design with intertwined leaves, branches, and scrolls. **2.** a ballet dancer's posture poised on one leg with the other stretched backwards horizontally.

Arabia a peninsula in the Middle East between the Red Sea and the Persian Gulf. **Arabian** *adj.*

Arabic *adj.* of the Arabs or their language. —*n.* the language of the Arabs. □ **arabic figures,** the symbols 1, 2, 3, 4, 5, etc.

arable (**a**-ră-bŭl) *adj* (of land) suitable for growing crops. —*n.* arable land.

arachnid (ă-**rak**-nid) *n.* a member of the class of animals including spiders, scorpions, and mites.

Aramaic (a-ră-**may**-ik) *n.* a Semitic language spoken in Syria and Palestine in New Testament times.

Aran *adj.* made in the knitted patterns traditional to the Aran Islands, off the west of Ireland, *Aran sweaters.*

arbiter (**ar** bit er) *n.* **1.** a person who has the power to decide what shall be done or accepted, one with entire control, *French designers are no longer the arbiters of fashion.* **2.** an arbitrator.

arbitrary (**ar**-bit-rer-i) *adj.* **1.** based on random choice or impulse, not on reason, *an arbitrary selection.* **2.** despotic, unrestrained, *arbitrary powers.* **arbitrarily** *adv.,* **arbitrariness** *n.*

arbitrate *v.* to act as an arbitrator.

arbitration *n.* settlement of a dispute by a person or persons acting as arbitrators.

arbitrator *n.* an impartial person chosen to settle a dispute between two parties.

arboreal (ar-**bor**-iăl) *adj.* **1.** of trees. **2.** living in trees.

arboretum (ar-bor-ee-tŭm) *n.* (*pl.* arboretums) a place where trees are grown for study and display.

arbour (**ar**-ber) *n.* a shady place among trees, often made in a garden with climbing plants growing over a framework.

arbutus (ar-**bew**-tŭs) *n.* **1.** an evergreen tree with strawberry-like fruits. **2.** (*Amer.*) a trailing plant that bears fragrant pink flowers in spring.

arc *n.* **1.** part of a curve. **2.** anything shaped like this. **3.** a luminous electric current passing across a gap between two terminals. —*v.* (arced, arcing) to form an electric arc. □ **arc lamp, arc light,** lighting using an electric arc. **arc welding,** welding by means of an electric arc.

arcade *n.* **1.** a covered passage or area, usually with shops on both sides; *amusement arcade,* one containing pintables and gambling machines etc. **2.** a series of arches supporting or along a wall.

arcane (ar **kayn**) *adj.* mysterious, secret.

arch[1] *n.* **1.** a curved structure supporting the weight of what is above it or used ornamentally. **2.** something shaped like this. **3.** the curved under-part of the foot. —*v.* to form into an arch.

arch[2] *adj.* consciously or affectedly playful, *an arch smile.* **archly** *adv.,* **archness** *n.*

archaeology (ar-ki-**ol**-ŏji) *n.* the scientific study of civilizations through their material remains. **archaeological** *adj.* □ **archaeologist** *n.* an expert in archaeology.

archaic (ar-**kay**-ik) *adj.* belonging to former or ancient times.

archangel *n.* an angel of the highest rank.

archbishop *n.* a bishop ranking above other bishops in a province of the Church.

archdeacon *n.* a priest ranking next below a bishop.

arch-enemy *n.* the chief enemy.

archer *n.* **1.** a person who shoots with bow and arrows. **2.** *the Archer,* a sign of the zodiac, Sagittarius.

archery *n.* the sport of shooting with bows and arrows.

archetype (**ar**-ki-typ) *n.* an original model from which others are copied. **archetypal** *adj.*

archipelago (arki-**pel**-ă-goh) *n.* (*pl.* archipelagos) a group of many islands, a sea containing such a group.

architect *n.* a designer of buildings.

architecture *n.* **1.** the art or science of designing buildings. **2.** the design or style of a building or buildings. **architectural** *adj.,* **architecturally** *adv.*

architrave (**ar**-ki-trayv) *n.* **1.** the horizontal piece resting on the columns of a building. **2.** the surround of a doorway or window.

archives (**ar**-kyvz) *pl. n.* the records or historical documents of an institution or community.

archivist (**ar**-kiv-ist) *n.* a person trained to deal with archives.

archway *n.* a passageway under an arch.

Arctic *adj.* **1.** of the regions round the North Pole. **2.** *arctic,* very cold, *the weather was arctic.* —**Arctic** *n.* **1.** the Arctic regions. **2.** the Arctic Ocean. □ **Arctic Circle,** the line of latitude 66° 30′ N.

ardent (**ar**-děnt) *adj.* full of ardour, enthusiastic. **ardently** *adv.*

ardour (**ar**-der) *n.* great warmth of feeling.

arduous (**ar**-dew-ŭs) *adj.* needing much effort, laborious. **arduously** *adv.*

are *see* be.

area *n.* **1.** the extent or measurement of a surface. **2.** a region; *picnic area,* a space set aside for this use. **3.** the field of an activity or subject, *in the area of finance.* **4.** a small sunken courtyard in front of the basement of a house.

arena (ǎ-**ree**-nǎ) *n.* the level area in the centre of an amphitheatre or a sports stadium.

aren't = are not. ¶ The phrase *aren't I* is a recognized colloquialism for *am I not?*

Argentina (ar-jěn-**teen**-ǎ) a country in South America. **Argentine** (**ar**-jěn-tyn) *adj. & n.,* **Argentinian** (ar-jěn-**tin**-iǎn) *adj. & n.*

arguable *adj.* **1.** able to be asserted. **2.** open to doubt or dispute, not certain. **arguably** *adv.*

argue *v.* **1.** to express disagreement, to exchange angry words. **2.** to give reasons for or against something, to debate. **3.** to persuade by talking, *argued him into going.* **4.** to indicate, *their life-style argues that they are well off.* □ **argue the toss,** to dispute about a choice.

argument *n.* **1.** a discussion involving disagreement, a quarrel. **2.** a reason put forward. **3.** a theme or chain of reasoning.

argumentation *n.* arguing.

argumentative (arg-yoo-**ment**-ǎtiv) *adj.* fond of arguing. **argumentatively** *adv.*

argy-bargy *n.* (*slang*) a heated argument.

aria (**ah**-riǎ) *n.* an operatic song for one voice.

arid (**a**-rid) *adj.* **1.** dry, parched; *arid regions,* deserts etc. **2.** uninteresting, *an arid discussion.* **aridly** *adv.,* **aridness** *n.,* **aridity** (ǎ-**rid**-iti) *n.*

Aries (**air**-eez) a sign of the zodiac, the Ram. **Arian** (**air**-iǎn) *adj. & n.*

aright *adv.* rightly.

arise *v.* (arose, arisen) **1.** to come into existence, to come to people's notice, *problems arose.* **2.** (*old use*) to get up, to stand up, to rise from the dead.

aristocracy (a-ri-**stok**-rǎsi) *n.* **1.** the hereditary upper classes of people in a country, the nobility. **2.** a country ruled by these.

aristocrat (**a**-ris-tǒ-krat) *n.* a member of the aristocracy, a noble.

aristocratic (a-ris-tǒ-**krat**-ik) *adj.* **1.** of the aristocracy. **2.** noble in style. **aristocratically** *adv.*

arithmetic (ǎ-**rith**-mě-tik) *n.* the science of numbers, calculating by means of numbers. **arithmetic** (a-rith-**met**-ik) *or* **arithmetical** *adjs.,* **arithmetically** *adv.*

Ariz. *abbrev.* Arizona.

Arizona (a-ri-**zoh**-nǎ) a State of the USA.

ark *n.* **1.** Noah's boat or a model of this. **2.** *the Ark of the Covenant,* a wooden chest in which the writings of Jewish Law were kept.

Ark. *abbrev.* Arkansas.

Arkansas (**ar**-kan-saw) a State of the USA.

arm[1] *n.* **1.** either of the two upper limbs of the human body, from the shoulder to the hand. **2.** a sleeve. **3.** something shaped like an arm or projecting from a main part, *an arm of a sea; the arms of a chair.* □ **arm in arm,** (of people) with the arm of one linked in the arm of another. **arm of the law,** the authority or power of the law. **at arm's length,** at the outside limit that the arm can reach; *kept people at arm's length,* avoided becoming too friendly with them. **in arms,** (of babies) too young to walk.

arm[2] *v.* **1.** to supply or fit with weapons; *the enemy is arming,* is preparing as if for war. **2.** to make (a bomb etc.) ready to explode, *the device was not yet armed.* —*n.* each of the kind of troops of which an army etc. is composed, *the Fleet Air Arm.* □ **armed forces** *or* **services,** military forces. **armed neutrality,** remaining neutral but prepared to defend itself against attack. **armed to the teeth,** fully or elaborately armed.

armada (ar-**mah**-dǎ) *n.* a fleet of warships; *the Spanish Armada,* that sent by Spain against England in 1588.

armadillo (ar-mǎ-**dil**-oh) *n.* (*pl.* armadillos) a small burrowing animal of South America with a body covered with a shell of bony plates.

Armageddon **1.** (in the Bible) the scene

of the final conflict between the forces of good and evil at the end of the world. **2.** any decisive conflict.

Armagh (ar-**mah**) a county of Northern Ireland.

armament *n.* **1.** the weapons with which an army or a ship, aircraft, or fighting vehicle is equipped. **2.** the process of equipping for war.

armature (**ar**-mă-choor) *n.* the wire-wound core of a dynamo or electric motor.

arm-band *n.* a band worn round the arm or sleeve.

armchair *n.* a chair with arms or raised sides; *armchair critics,* those who criticize without having practical experience; *armchair traveller,* one reading or hearing about travel.

Armenian *adj.* of Armenia, a republic of the USSR. —*n.* a native or inhabitant of Armenia.

armful *n.* as much as the arm can hold.

armhole *n.* an opening in a garment through which the arm is inserted.

armistice *n.* an agreement during a war or battle to stop fighting for a time.

armless *adj.* without arms.

armlet *n.* an arm-band.

armour *n.* **1.** a protective covering for the body, formerly worn in fighting. **2.** metal plates covering a warship, car, or tank to protect it from missiles. **3.** armoured fighting vehicles collectively. □ **armoured** *adj.* covered or protected with armour, *an armoured car;* equipped with armoured vehicles, *armoured divisions.*

armoury (**ar**-mer-i) *n.* a place where weapons and ammunition are stored.

armpit *n.* the hollow under the arm below the shoulder.

arms *pl. n.* **1.** weapons, *an arms depot.* **2.** a coat of arms (*see* coat). □ **arms race,** competition among nations in accumulating weapons. **up in arms,** protesting vigorously.

army *n.* **1.** an organized force equipped for fighting on land. **2.** a vast group, *an army of locusts.* **3.** a body of people organized for a particular purpose, *an army of helpers.*

aroma (ă-**roh**-mă) *n.* a smell, especially a pleasant one. **aromatic** (a-rŏ-**mat**-ik) *adj.*

arose *see* arise.

around *adv. & prep.* **1.** all round, on every side, in every direction. **2.** about, here and there; *he's somewhere around,* close at hand; *we shopped around,* going from place to place. **3.** (*Amer.*) about, approximately at, *be here around five o'clock.*

arouse *v.* to rouse.

arpeggio (ar-**pej**-i-oh) *n.* (*pl.* arpeggios)

the notes of a musical chord played in succession instead of simultaneously.

arrange *v.* **1.** to put into a certain order, to adjust; *arrange flowers,* place them attractively, especially in a vase. **2.** to form plans, to settle the details of, to prepare, *arrange to be there; arrange a meeting.* **3.** to adapt (a musical composition) for voices or instruments other than those for which it was written, to adapt (a play etc.) for broadcasting. **arrangement** *n.*

arrant (a-rănt) *adj.* downright, out-and-out, *this is arrant nonsense!*

array *v.* **1.** to arrange in order, *arrayed his forces along the river.* **2.** to dress, *arrayed in her coronation dress.* —*n.* **1.** an imposing series, a display, *a fine array of tools.* **2.** an arrangement of data in a computer, so constructed that a program can extract the items by means of a key.

arrears *pl. n.* **1.** money that is owing and ought to have been paid earlier, *arrears of rent.* **2.** work that should have been finished but is still waiting to be dealt with, *arrears of correspondence.* □ **in arrears,** behindhand with payment or work, not paid or done when it was due, *he is in arrears with his rent; the rent is in arrears.*

arrest *v.* **1.** to stop or check (a process or movement), *arrest attention,* catch and hold it. **2.** to seize by authority of the law. —*arrest n.* **1.** stoppage. **2.** seizure, legal arresting of an offender; *he is under arrest,* has been arrested.

arrestable *adj.* such that the offender may be arrested without a warrant, *an arrestable offence.*

arrival *n.* **1.** arriving. **2.** a person or thing that has arrived.

arrive *v.* **1.** to reach one's destination or a certain point on a journey; *arrived at an agreement,* reached it after discussion. **2.** to come at last, to make an appearance; *the great day arrived; the baby arrived on Tuesday,* was born. **3.** to be recognized as having achieved success in the world.

arrogant (a-rŏ-gănt) *adj.* proud and overbearing through an exaggerated feeling of one's superiority. **arrogantly** *adv.,* **arrogance** *n.*

arrow *n.* **1.** a straight thin pointed shaft to be shot from a bow. **2.** a line with an outward-pointing V at the end, used to show direction or position.

arrowhead *n.* the head of an arrow.

arrowroot *n.* an edible starch prepared from the root of an American plant.

arse *n.* (*vulgar*) the buttocks or rump.

arsenal *n.* a place where weapons and ammunition are stored or manufactured.

arsenic (ar-sĕn-ik) *n.* **1.** a brittle steel-grey chemical substance. **2.** a violently poisonous white compound of this. **arsenical** (ar-**sen**-ikăl) *adj.*

arson *n.* the act of setting fire to a house or other property intentionally and unlawfully, either from malice or in order to claim insurance money. **arsonist** *n.* a person guilty of arson.

art¹ *n.* **1.** the production of something beautiful, skill or ability in such work. **2.** works such as paintings or sculptures produced by skill. **3.** any practical skill, a knack, *the art of sailing.* —*adj.* involving artistic design, *art needlework.* □ **art gallery,** a gallery where paintings or pieces of sculpture are displayed. **arts** *pl. n.* subjects (e.g. languages, literature, history, etc.) in which sympathetic understanding plays a great part, as opposed to sciences where exact measurements and calculations are used. **arts and crafts,** decorative design and handicraft.

art² (*old use*) the present tense of be, used with *thou.*

artefact (**ar**-ti-fakt) *n.* a man-made object, a simple prehistoric tool or weapon.

arteriosclerosis (ar-teer-i-oh-skleer-**oh**-sis) *n.* a condition in which the walls of arteries become thicker and less elastic so that blood circulation is hindered.

artery *n.* **1.** any of the tubes carrying blood away from the heart to all parts of the body. **2.** an important transport route. **arterial** (ar-**teer**-iăl) *adj.* of an artery; *an arterial road,* an important main road.

artesian well (ar-**tee**-*zh*ăn) a well that is bored vertically into a place where a constant supply of water will rise to the earth's surface with little or no pumping.

artful *adj.* crafty, cunningly clever at getting what one wants. **artfully** *adv.,* **artfulness** *n.*

arthritis (arth-**ry**-tiss) *n.* a condition in which there is pain and stiffness in the joints. **arthritic** (arth-**rit**-ik) *adj. & n.*

artic (**ar**-tik) *n.* (*informal*) an articulated vehicle.

artichoke *n.* a plant related to the thistle, with a flower consisting of thick leaf-like scales used as a vegetable. **Jerusalem artichoke,** a kind of sunflower with tubers that are used as a vegetable. (¶ The name is taken from the Italian word *girasole* (= sunflower), which was altered to *Jerusalem*).

article *n.* **1.** a particular or separate thing; *articles of clothing, toilet articles,* things of the kind named. **2.** a piece of writing, complete in itself, in a newspaper or periodical, *an article on immigration.* **3.** a separate clause or item in an agreement, *articles of apprenticeship.* **4.** a word used before a noun to identify what it refers to; *the definite article* = 'the'; *the indefinite article* = 'a' or 'an'. —*v.* to bind by articles of apprenticeship.

articular (ar-**tik**-yoo-ler) *adj.* of the joints of the body.

articulate¹ (ar-**tik**-yoo-lăt) *adj.* **1.** spoken clearly, in words. **2.** able to express ideas clearly. **articulately** *adv.*

articulate² (ar-**tik**-yoo-layt) *v.* **1.** to say or speak distinctly, *articulating each word with care.* **2.** to form a joint, to connect by joints, *this bone articulates* or *is articulated with another.* **articulation** *n.* □ **articulated vehicle,** one that has sections connected by a flexible joint.

artifice (**ar**-ti-fiss) *n.* trickery, a clever trick intended to mislead someone.

artificer (ar-**tif**-i-ser) *n.* a skilled workman or mechanic.

artificial *adj.* not originating naturally, made by human skill in imitation of something natural. **artificially** *adv.,* **artificiality** (arti-fishi-**al**-iti) *n.* □ **artificial insemination,** injection of semen into the womb artificially so that conception may take place without sexual intercourse. **artificial respiration,** the process of forcing air into and out of the lungs to start natural breathing or stimulate it when it has failed.

artillery *n.* **1.** large guns used in fighting on land. **2.** a branch of an army that uses these. **artilleryman** *n.*

artisan (ar-ti-**zan**) *n.* a skilled workman in industry or trade, a mechanic.

artist *n.* **1.** a person who produces works of art, especially paintings. **2.** a person who does something with exceptional skill. **3.** a professional entertainer.

artiste (ar-**teest**) *n.* a professional entertainer.

artistic *adj.* **1.** showing or done with skill and good taste. **2.** of art or artists; *the artistic temperament,* impulsive and eccentric behaviour thought to be characteristic of artists. **artistically** *adv.*

artistry *n.* artistic skill.

artless *adj.* free from artfulness, simple and natural. **artlessly** *adv.,* **artlessness** *n.*

arty *adj.* (*informal*) with an exaggerated and often affected display of artistic style or interests. **artiness** *n.*

arty-crafty *adj.* (*informal*) of arts and crafts.

arum (**air**-ŭm) *n.* a plant with a flower consisting of a single petal-like part surrounding a central spike. **arum lily,** a cultivated white arum.

Aryan (air-iăn) *adj.* **1.** of the original Indo-European language, of its speakers or their descendants. **2.** (in Nazi Germany) of non-Jewish extraction. —*n.* an Aryan person.

as *adv.* **1.** in the same degree, equally; *I thought as much,* I thought so. **2.** similarly, like. **3.** in the character of, *Olivier as Hamlet.* —**as** *conj.* **1.** at the same time that, *they came as I left.* **2.** because, for the reason that, *as he refuses, we can do nothing.* **3.** in the way in which; *do as I do.* *rel. pronoun* that, who, which, *I had the same trouble as you*; *he was a foreigner, as I knew from his accent.* (¶ The use in *it was the manager as told me* is incorrect and should be avoided.) □ **as for**, with regard to, *as for you, I despise you.* **as from**, from the date stated, *your salary will be increased as from 1 April.* **as if**, as it would be if, *he said it as if he meant it.* **as it was**, in the actual circumstances. **as it were**, as if it was actually so, *he became, as it were, a man without a country.* **as of**, at the date mentioned, *that was the position as of last Monday.* **as though**, as if. **as to**, with regard to, *as to you, I despise you*; *said nothing as to holidays.* **as well**, in addition, too; desirable, *it might be as well to go*; desirably, *we might as well go.* **as well as**, in addition to. **as yet**, up to this time. **as you were!**, return to the previous position.

asbestos *n.* a soft fibrous mineral substance, made into fireproof material or used for heat insulation.

asbestosis (ass-best-**oh**-sis) *n.* a lung disease caused by inhaling asbestos particles.

ascend *v.* to go or come up. **ascend the throne**, to become king or queen.

ascendancy (ă-**sen**-dăn-si) *n.* the state of being dominant; *gain ascendancy*, win control.

ascendant *adj.* ascending, rising. **in the ascendant**, rising in power or influence.

ascension (ă-**sen**-shŏn) *n.* ascent; *the Ascension*, the taking up of Christ into heaven, witnessed by the Apostles. **Ascension Day**, the Thursday on which this is commemorated, the 40th day after Easter.

ascent *n.* **1.** ascending. **2.** a way up, an upward slope or path.

ascertain (ass-er-**tayn**) *v.* to find out by making enquiries. **ascertainable** *adj.* able to be ascertained.

ascetic (ă-**set**-ik) *adj.* self-denying, not allowing oneself pleasures and luxuries. —*n.* a person who leads a severely simple life without ordinary pleasures, often for religious reasons. —**ascetically** *adv.*, **asceticism** (ă-**set**-i-sizm) *n.*

ascorbic acid (ă-**skor**-bik) vitamin C, found especially in citrus fruits and in vegetables.

ascribable *adj.* able to be ascribed.

ascribe (ă-**skryb**) *v.* to attribute. **ascription** (ă-**skrip**-shŏn) *n.*

aseptic (ay-**sep**-tik) *adj.* free from bacteria that cause something to become septic, surgically clean. **aseptically** *adv.*

asexual (ay-**seks**-yoo-ăl) *adj.* without sex or sex organs. **asexually** *adv.*

ash[1] *n.* **1.** a tree with silver-grey bark and close-grained wood. **2.** this wood.

ash[2] *n.* the powder that remains after something has burnt. □ **ash-bin** *n.* a dustbin. **the ashes**, a trophy awarded as the symbol of victory in a set of Anglo-Australian cricket matches. **Ash Wednesday**, the first day of Lent.

ashamed *adj.* feeling shame.

ashen *adj.* **1.** of ashes. **2.** pale as ashes.

ashlar *n.* square-cut stones, masonry made of these.

ashore *adv.* to or on shore.

ashram *n.* an Indian place of religious retreat or sanctuary or hermitage.

ashtray *n.* a receptacle for tobacco ash.

ashy *adj.* **1.** ashen. **2.** covered with ash.

Asia (ay-shă) the largest of the continents, extending from Europe to the Pacific Ocean. **Asian** *adj.* & *n.* □ **Asia Minor**, a peninsula of western Asia between the Mediterranean and the Black Sea, including most of Turkey.

Asiatic (ay-shi-**at**-ik) *adj.* of Asia. —*n.* an Asian. ¶ *Asian* is the preferred word when used of people.

aside *adv.* **1.** to or on one side, away from the main part or group, *pull it aside*; *step aside*. **2.** away from one's thoughts or from consideration. **3.** in reserve, *put money aside for a holiday.* —*n.* words spoken so that only certain people will hear. □ **aside from**, (*Amer.*) apart from.

asinine (ass-i-nyn) *adj.* silly, stupid.

ask *v.* **1.** to call for an answer to or about, to address a question to (a person). **2.** to seek to obtain from another person, *ask a favour of him*; *asked £5 for the book.* **3.** to invite, *ask him to dinner.* □ **ask for**, to ask to be given, or to see or speak to, or to be directed to. **ask for it, ask for trouble,** to behave in such a way that trouble is likely. **asking price**, the price at which something is offered for sale. **I ask you!,** an exclamation of disgust.

askance (ă-**skanss**) *adv.* with distrust or disapproval, *looked askance at the new plan.*

askew *adv.* & *adj.* not straight or level.

asleep *adv.* & *adj.* **1.** in or into a state of sleep. **2.** numbed, *my foot is asleep.*

asp *n.* a small poisonous snake.

asparagus (ă-**spa**-ră-gŭs) *n.* **1.** a plant whose young shoots are cooked and eaten as a vegetable. **2.** these shoots.

aspect *n.* **1.** the look or appearance of a person or thing, *the forest had a sinister aspect*; *this aspect of the problem*, this feature of it. **2.** the direction a thing faces, a side facing this way, *the house has a southern aspect*. **3.** (in astrology) the relative position of a star or group of stars, regarded as having influence on events.

aspen *n.* a kind of poplar with leaves that move in the slightest wind.

asperity (ă-**spe**-riti) *n.* harshness or severity, especially of manner.

aspersions (ă-**sper**-shŏnz) *pl. n.* an attack on someone's reputation, *casting aspersions at his rivals*.

asphalt (**ass**-falt) *n.* **1.** a black sticky substance like coal-tar. **2.** a mixture of this with gravel etc. used for paving. —*v.* to surface with asphalt.

asphyxia (ă-**sfiks**-iă) *n.* a condition caused by lack of air in the lungs, suffocation.

asphyxiate (ă-**sfiks**-i-ayt) *v.* to suffocate. **asphyxiation** *n.*

aspic *n.* a savoury jelly used for coating meats, eggs, etc.

aspidistra *n.* a plant with broad tapering leaves, grown as a house-plant.

aspirant (**ass**-per-ănt) *n.* a person who aspires to something.

aspirate[1] (**ass**-per-ăt) *n.* the sound of 'h'.

aspirate[2] (**ass**-per-ayt) *v.* **1.** to pronounce with an h. **2.** to draw out with an aspirator.

aspiration (ass-per-**ay**-shŏn) *n.* **1.** aspirating. **2.** aspiring. **3.** a strong desire or ambition.

aspirator *n.* a device used to suck fluid from a cavity.

aspire *v.* to have a high ambition, *he aspires to become president, aspires to the presidency*.

aspirin *n.* a drug used to relieve pain and reduce fever, a tablet of this.

ass[1] *n.* **1.** a donkey. **2.** (*informal*) a stupid person. □ **make an ass of oneself**, to behave stupidly so that one is ridiculed.

ass[2] *n.* (*vulgar*) = arse.

assail (ă-**sayl**) *v.* to attack violently and persistently. **assailant** *n.* an attacker.

assassin *n.* a person, especially one hired by others, who assassinates another.

assassinate *v.* to kill (an important person) by violent means, usually from political or religious motives. **assassination** *n.*, **assassinator** *n.*

assault *n.* **1.** a violent attack. **2.** an unlawful personal attack on another person,

even if only with menacing words; *assault and battery*, an assault involving a blow or touch. —*v.* to make an assault upon.

assay (ă-**say**) *n.* testing of metals, especially those used for coin or bullion, for quality. —*v.* to make an assay of.

assemblage *n.* **1.** assembling. **2.** an assembly. **3.** things assembled.

assemble *v.* **1.** to bring or come together. **2.** to fit or put together. **3.** to translate by using an assembler.

assembler *n.* a computer program that translates instructions from a low-level language into a form that can be understood and executed by the computer.

assembly *n.* **1.** assembling. **2.** an assembled group, especially of people meeting for a specific purpose. □ **assembly line**, a sequence of machines and workers through which parts of a product move to be assembled in successive stages.

assent *v.* to consent, to express agreement. —*n.* consent or sanction.

assert *v.* **1.** to declare as true, to state, *asserted his innocence*. **2.** to use effectively, *asserted his authority*. □ **assert itself**, to become active, to make its effect felt. **assert oneself**, to take effective action, to use one's authority, to insist on one's rights.

assertion *n.* **1.** asserting. **2.** a statement that something is a fact.

assertive *adj.* asserting oneself, self-assertive. **assertively** *adv.*, **assertiveness** *n.*

assess *v.* **1.** to decide or fix the amount or value of. **2.** to estimate the worth or quality or likelihood of. **assessment** *n.*, **assessor** *n.*

asset (**ass**-et) *n.* **1.** any property that has money value, especially that which can be used or sold to pay debts. **2.** a useful or valuable quality or skill, a person regarded as useful.

asseverate (ă-**sev**-er-ayt) *v.* (*formal*) to assert solemnly. **asseveration** *n.*

assiduous (ă-**sid**-yoo-ŭs) *adj.* diligent and persevering. **assiduously** *adv.*, **assiduity** (ass-id-**yoo**-iti) *n.*

assign *v.* **1.** to allot, *rooms were assigned to us*. **2.** to appoint or designate to perform a task etc., *assign your best investigator to the job*. **3.** to ascribe, to regard as belonging to, *we cannot assign an exact date to Stonehenge*.

assignable *adj.* able to be assigned.

assignation (ass-ig-**nay**-shŏn) *n.* **1.** assigning. **2.** an arrangement to meet, an appointment.

assignment *n.* **1.** assigning, being assigned. **2.** a thing or task that is assigned to a person etc., a share.

assimilate *v.* **1.** to absorb into the body

or into a group or system, to become absorbed into something. **2.** to absorb into the mind as knowledge. **assimilation** *n.*

assist *v.* to help. **assistance** *n.*

assistant *n.* **1.** a person who assists, a helper. **2.** a person who serves customers in a shop. —*adj.* assisting, helping a senior and ranking next below him, *the assistant manager.*

associate[1] (ă-**soh**-si-ayt) *v.* **1.** to join or cause to join as a companion or colleague or supporter. **2.** to have frequent dealings, to be often in a certain company, *he associates with dishonest dealers.* **3.** to connect in one's mind, *we associate pyramids with Egypt.*

associate[2] *n.* **1.** a partner, colleague, or companion. **2.** one who has been admitted to a lower level of membership of an association without the status of a full member. —**associate** *adj.* **1.** associated. **2.** having subordinate membership.

association *n.* **1.** associating, being associated, companionship. **2.** a group of people organized for some common purpose, *the Automobile Association.* **3.** a mental connection between ideas. □ **Association football.** a form of football played with a spherical ball that may not be handled during play except by the goalkeeper.

assonance (**ass**-on-ăns) *n.* similarity of vowel sounds in syllables that do not form a complete rhyme, as in *vermin/furnish.*

assorted *adj.* **1.** of different sorts put together, *assorted chocolates*; *an ill-assorted couple,* not well matched.

assortment *n.* a collection composed of several sorts.

assuage (ă-**swayj**) *v.* to soothe, to make less severe; *to assuage one's thirst,* to satisfy it.

assume *v.* **1.** to take as true or sure to happen before there is proof, *we assume that we shall win.* **2.** to take on, to undertake, *he assumed the extra responsibility.* **3.** to put on, *assumed a serious expression.*

assuming *adj.* presumptuous.

assumption *n.* **1.** assuming. **2.** something taken for granted, something assumed but not proved; *on this assumption,* assuming this to be true or sure to happen. **3.** *the Assumption,* the reception of the Virgin Mary in bodily form into heaven, the festival commemorating this (15 August).

assurance *n.* **1.** a formal declaration or promise given to inspire confidence. **2.** a kind of life insurance. **3.** self-confidence.

¶ Insurance companies use the term *assurance* of policies where a sum is payable after a fixed number of years or on the death of the insured person, and *insurance* of policies relating to events such as fire, accident, or death within a limited period. In popular usage the word *insurance* is used in both cases.

assure (ă-**shoor**) *v.* **1.** to declare confidently, to promise, *I assure you there is no danger.* **2.** to cause to know for certain, *tried the door to assure himself that it was locked.* **3.** to make certain, to ensure, *this will assure your success.* **4.** to insure by means of an assurance policy.

assured (ă-**shoord**) *adj.* **1.** sure. **2.** confident, *has an assured manner.* **3.** payable under an assurance policy, *the sum assured.* **assuredly** (ă-**shoor**-idli) *adv.* certainly.

aster *n.* a garden plant with daisy-like flowers of various colours.

asterisk *n.* a star-shaped symbol * used in writing or printing to call attention to something or as a reference mark. —*v.* to mark with an asterisk.

astern *adv.* **1.** in or at or towards the stern of a ship or the tail of an aircraft, behind. **2.** backwards, *full speed astern!*

asteroid (**ass**-ter-oid) *n.* any of the small planets revolving round the sun, especially between the orbits of Mars and Jupiter.

asthma (**ass**-mă) *n.* a chronic condition causing difficulty in breathing.

asthmatic (ass-**mat**-ik) *adj.* **1.** of asthma. **2.** suffering from asthma. **asthmatically** *adv.*

astigmatism (ă-**stig**-mă-tizm) *n.* a defect in an eye or lens, preventing proper focusing. **astigmatic** (ass-tig-**mat**-ik) *adj.*, **astigmatically** *adv.*

astir *adv. & adj.* in motion, moving.

astonish *v.* to surprise very greatly. **astonishment** *n.*

astound *v.* to shock with surprise.

astrakhan (astră-**kan**) *n.* the dark tightly-curled fleece of lambs from Astrakhan in Russia, fabric imitating this.

astral (**ass**-trăl) *adj.* of or from the stars.

astray *adv. & adj.* away from the right path. **go astray,** to be led into error or wrongdoing; (of things) to be mislaid.

astride *adv.* **1.** with legs wide apart. **2.** with one leg on either side of something. —*prep.* astride of, extending across.

astringent (ă-**strin**-jĕnt) *adj.* **1.** causing skin or body tissue to contract. **2.** harsh, severe. —*n.* an astringent substance, used medically or in cosmetics. —**astringency** *n.*

astrologer *n.* an expert in astrology.

astrology (ă-**strol**-ŏji) *n.* study of the supposed influence of stars on human affairs. **astrological** *adj.*, **astrologically** *adv.*

astronaut *n.* a person trained to operate a spacecraft in which he travels.

astronautics *n.* the scientific study of space travel and its technology.

astronomer *n.* an expert in astronomy.

astronomical *adj.* **1.** of astronomy. **2.** enormous in amount, *an astronomical sum of money.* **astronomically** *adv.*

astronomy (ă-**stron**-ŏmi) *n.* the scientific study of the stars and planets and their movements.

astute (ă-**stewt**) *adj.* shrewd, quick at seeing how to gain an advantage. **astutely** *adv.,* **astuteness** *n.*

Asunción (ă-sŭn-si-**ohn**) the capital of Paraguay.

asunder (ă-**sun**-der) *adv.* apart, into pieces, *torn asunder.*

asylum *n.* **1.** refuge and safety, a place of refuge. **2.** (*old use*) a mental home or institution.

asymmetrical (ay-sim-et-rikăl) *adj.* not symmetrical. **asymmetrically** *adv.*

asynchronous (ay-**sink**-rŏn-ŭs) *adj.* not synchronous.

at *prep.* expressing position or state. **1.** of place or order or time of day, *at the top*; *came at midnight.* **2.** of condition or occupation, *at ease*; *they are at dinner.* **3.** of price or amount or age etc., *sold at £1 each*; *left school at 15.* **4.** of cause, *was annoyed at his failure.* **5.** of direction towards, *aimed at the target.* □ **at all,** in any way, to any extent, of any kind. **at home,** in one's home; relaxed and at ease; familiar with a subject; available to callers. **at-home** *n.* a reception for visitors between certain hours. **at it,** engaged in some activity, working. **at once,** immediately; simultaneously. **at one,** in agreement or in harmony with someone. **at risk,** undergoing a risk; in danger. **at that,** at that point; moreover.

atavistic (at-ă-**vis**-tik) *adj.* like a remote ancestor.

ate *see* eat.

atheist (**ayth**-ee-ist) *n.* a person who does not believe in the existence of a God or gods. **atheism** *n.,* **atheistic** (ayth-ee-**ist**-ik) *adj.*

Athens the capital of Greece.

athlete *n.* a person who is good at athletics. **athlete's foot,** a form of ringworm affecting the feet.

athletic *adj.* **1.** of athletes. **2.** physically strong and active, muscular in build. **athletically** *adv.* □ **athletics** *n.* physical exercises and sports, especially competitions in running, jumping, etc.

Atlantic *adj.* of the Atlantic Ocean. —*n.* the **Atlantic Ocean,** the ocean lying between the Americas and Europe/Africa.

atlas *n.* a book of maps.

atmosphere *n.* **1.** the mixture of gases surrounding the earth or any star or planet. **2.** the air in any place. **3.** a psychological environment, a feeling or tone conveyed by something, *an atmosphere of peace and calm.* **4.** a unit of pressure, equal to the pressure of the atmosphere at sea level. —**atmospheric** *adj.*

atmospherics *pl. n.* electrical disturbances in the atmosphere, crackling sounds or other interference in telecommunications caused by these.

atoll (**at**-ŏl) *n.* a ring-shaped coral reef enclosing a lagoon.

atom *n.* **1.** the smallest particle of a chemical element. **2.** this as a source of atomic energy. **3.** a very small quantity or thing, *there's not an atom of truth in it.* □ **atom bomb,** an atomic bomb.

atomic *adj.* of an atom or atoms. **atomic bomb,** a bomb that derives its destructive power from atomic energy. **atomic energy,** energy obtained as the result of nuclear fission. **atonement** *n.*

atomize *v.* to reduce to atoms or fine particles. **atomization** *n.* □ **atomizer** *n.* a device for reducing liquids to a fine spray.

atonal (ay-**toh**-năl) *adj.* (of music) not written in any particular key or scale-system.

atone *v.* to make amends, to make up for some error or deficiency. **atonement** *n.*

atrocious (ă-**troh**-shŭs) *adj.* **1.** extremely wicked, brutal. **2.** (*informal*) very bad or unpleasant. **atrociously** *adv.*

atrocity (ă-**tross**-iti) *n.* **1.** wickedness, a wicked or cruel act. **2.** a repellent thing.

atrophy (**at**-rŏ-fi) *n.* wasting away through under-nourishment or lack of use. —*v.* (atrophied, atrophying) to cause or suffer atrophy.

attaboy *int.* (*Amer. slang*) an exclamation of admiration or encouragement.

attach *v.* **1.** to fix to something else. **2.** to join as a companion or member, to assign (a person) to a particular group. **3.** to attribute, *we attach no importance to the matter.* **4.** to be ascribed, to be attributable, *no blame attaches to the company.* **5.** to make a legal attachment (of money or goods).

attaché (ă-**tash**-ay) *n.* a person who is attached to the staff of an ambassador in some specific field of activity, *the military attaché.* **attaché case,** a small rectangular case for carrying documents etc.

attached *adj.* **1.** fastened on. **2.** bound by affection or loyalty, *she is very attached to her cousin.*

attachment *n.* **1.** attaching, being attached. **2.** something attached, an extra part that fixes on. **3.** affection, devotion. □ **attachment of earnings,** legal seizure of a debtor's earnings before they are paid to him, in order to pay his debts.

attack v. **1.** to act violently against, to start a fight. **2.** to criticize strongly. **3.** to act harmfully on, *rust attacks metals.* **4.** to begin vigorous work on. —**attack** n. **1.** a violent attempt to hurt, overcome, or defeat. **2.** strong criticism. **3.** a sudden onset of illness, *an attack of flu.* — **attacker** n.

attain v. to succeed in doing or getting.

attainable adj. able to be attained.

attainment n. **1.** attaining. **2.** something attained, a personal achievement.

attar (at-er) n. fragrant oil obtained from flowers, *attar of roses.*

attempt v. to make an effort to accomplish, *that's attempting the impossible.* —n. **1.** an effort to accomplish something. **2.** an attack, an effort to overcome or surpass something.

attend v. **1.** to apply one's mind, to give care and thought; *attend to the matter,* deal with it. **2.** to take care of, to look after, *which doctor is attending you?* **3.** to be present at, to go regularly to, *to attend school.* **4.** to accompany as an attendant.

attendance n. **1.** attending. **2.** the number of people present.

attendant n. a person who is present as a companion or whose function is to provide service. —adj. accompanying.

attention n. **1.** applying one's mind to something, mental concentration; *the plug needs attention,* needs to be repaired. **2.** awareness, *it attracts attention.* **3.** consideration, care, *she shall have every attention.* **4.** a soldier's erect attitude of readiness with feet together and arms stretched downwards, *stand at attention.* —int. an exclamation used to call people to take notice or to assume an attitude of attention. ☐ **attentions** pl. n. small acts of kindness or courtesy.

attentive adj. **1.** paying attention, watchful. **2.** devotedly showing consideration or courtesy to another person. **attentively** adv., **attentiveness** n.

attenuate (ă-ten-yoo-ayt) v. **1.** to make slender or thin. **2.** to make weaker, to reduce the force or value of. **attenuation** n.

attest (ă-test) v. **1.** to provide clear proof of. **2.** to declare to be true or genuine. **attestation** (at-ess-tay-shŏn) n. ☐ **attested cattle,** cattle certified free from tuberculosis.

attic n. a room in the top storey of a house, immediately below the roof.

attire n. (*formal*) clothes. —v. (*formal*) to clothe.

attitude n. **1.** a position of the body or its parts. **2.** a way of thinking or behaving.

attorney (ăßter-ni) n. (*pl.* attorneys) **1.** a person who is appointed to act on behalf of another in business or legal matters; *power of attorney,* authority to act as attorney. **2.** (*Amer.*) a lawyer, especially one qualified to act for clients in legal proceedings. ☐ **Attorney-General** n. the chief legal officer in some countries, appointed by the Government holding office.

attract v. **1.** to draw towards itself by unseen force, *a magnet attracts iron.* **2.** to get the attention of. **3.** to arouse the interest or pleasure of.

attraction n. **1.** attracting. **2.** the ability to attract. **3.** something that attracts by arousing interest or pleasure.

attractive adj. able to attract, pleasing in appearance or effect. **attractively** adv., **attractiveness** n.

attribute[1] (ă-trib-yoot) v. to regard as belonging to or caused by or originated by; *this play is attributed to Shakespeare,* people say that he wrote it. **attribution** (at-rib-yoo-shŏn) n. ☐ **attributable** adj. able to be attributed.

attribute[2] (at-rib-yoot) n. **1.** a quality that is characteristic of a person or thing, *kindness is one of his attributes.* **2.** an object regularly associated with a person or thing, *keys are an attribute of St. Peter; a pair of scales is an attribute of Justice.*

attributive (ă-trib-yoo-tiv) adj. expressing an attribute and placed before the word it describes, e.g. 'old' in *the old dog* (but not in *the dog is old*). **attributively** adv.

attrition (ă-trish-ŏn) n. **1.** wearing something away by rubbing. **2.** a gradual wearing down of strength and morale by continuous harassment, *a war of attrition.*

aubergine (oh-ber-zheen) n. **1.** the deep-purple fruit of the egg-plant, used as a vegetable. **2.** its colour.

aubrietia (aw-bree-shă) n. a low-growing perennial rock-plant, flowering in spring. ¶ The spelling *aubretia* is incorrect.

auburn (aw-bern) adj. (of hair) reddish-brown.

auction n. a public sale in which articles are sold to the highest bidder. —v. to sell by auction. ☐ **auctioneer** n. a person who conducts an auction.

audacious (aw-day-shŭs) adj. bold, daring. **audaciously** adv., **audacity** (aw-dass-iti) n.

audible adj. loud enough to be heard. **audibly** adv., **audibility** n.

audience n. **1.** people who have gathered to hear or watch something. **2.** people within hearing. **3.** a formal interview with a ruler or other important person.

audio *n.* **1.** audible sound reproduced mechanically. **2.** its reproduction. □ **audio typist,** one who types from a recording.

audio-visual *adj.* (of teaching aids etc.) using both sight and sound.

audit *n.* an official examination of accounts to see that they are in order. —*v.* to make an audit of.

audition *n.* a trial to test the ability of a prospective performer. —*v.* **1.** to hold an audition. **2.** to be tested in an audition.

auditor *n.* a person who makes an audit.

auditorium (awdit-**or**-iŭm) *n.* the part of a building in which an audience sits.

auger (**awg**-er) *n.* a tool for boring holes in wood, like a gimlet but larger.

aught (*pr.* awt) *n.* (*old use*) anything, *for aught I know.*

augment (awg-**ment**) *v.* to add to, to increase. **augmentation** *n.*

au gratin (oh **grat**-an) cooked with a crisp crust of breadcrumbs or grated cheese.

augur (**awg**-er) *v.* to foretell, to be a sign of; *this augurs well for your future,* is a favourable sign.

august (aw-**gust**) *adj.* majestic, imposing.

August *n.* the eighth month of the year.

auk *n.* a northern sea-bird with small narrow wings.

auld lang syne days of long ago.

aunt *n.* **1.** a sister or sister-in-law of one's father or mother. **2.** (*children's informal*) an unrelated woman friend, *Aunt Jane.* □ **Aunt Sally,** a figure used as a target in a throwing-game; a target of general abuse or criticism.

aunty *n.* (*informal*) an aunt.

au pair (oh **pair**) a young woman from overseas helping with housework and receiving board and lodging in return.

aura (**or**-ă) *n.* the atmosphere surrounding a person or thing and thought to come from him or it, *an aura of happiness.*

aural (**or**-ăl) *adj.* of the ear. **aurally** *adv.*

au revoir (oh rĕ-**vwahr**) goodbye for the moment.

aurora (aw-**ror**-ă) *n.* bands of coloured light appearing in the sky at night and probably caused by electrical radiation from the North and South magnetic poles. **aurora borealis** (bor-i-**ay**-lis), also called the Northern Lights, in the northern hemisphere. **aurora australis,** similar lights in the southern hemisphere.

auspicious (aw-**spish**-ŭs) *adj.* showing signs that promise success. **auspiciously** *adv.*

Aussie (**oz**-i) *n.* (*informal*) an Australian.

austere (aw-**steer**) *adj.* severely simple and plain, without ornament or comfort. **austerely** *adv.*

austerity (aw-**ste**-riti) *n.* being austere, an austere condition, *the austerities of life in wartime.*

Australasia (oss-trăl-**ay**-shă) Australia, New Zealand, and neighbouring islands in the South Pacific. **Australasian** *adj.* & *n.*

Australia (oss-**tray**-liă) a continent between the Pacific and Indian Oceans. **Australian** *adj.* & *n.* □ **Australian Capital Territory,** the area of Australia containing Canberra.

Austria (**oss**-stri-ă) a country in Europe. **Austrian** *adj.* & *n.*

authentic *adj.* genuine, known to be true. **authentically** *adv.,* **authenticity** *n.*

authenticate *v.* to prove the truth or authenticity of. **authentication** *n.*

author *n.* **1.** the writer of a book or books etc. **2.** the originator of a plan or policy. **authoress** *n.,* **authorship** *n.*

authoritarian (awth-o-ri-**tair**-iăn) *adj.* favouring complete obedience to authority as opposed to individual freedom. —*n.* a supporter of such principles.

authoritative (awth-**o**-ri-tă-tiv) *adj.* having or using authority. **authoritatively** *adv.*

authority *n.* **1.** the power or right to give orders and make others obey, or to take specific action. **2.** a person or group with such power. **3.** a person with specialized knowledge, a book etc. that can supply reliable information, *he is an authority on spiders.*

authorize *v.* **1.** to give authority to. **2.** to give authority for, to sanction, *I authorized this payment.* **authorization** *n.* □ **Authorized Version,** the English translation of the Bible (1611) made by order of King James I and appointed to be read in churches.

autistic (aw-**tiss**-tik) *adj.* having a form of mental illness that causes a person to withdraw into a private world of fantasy and be unable to communicate with others or respond to his real environment, *autistic children.* **autism** (**aw**-tizm) *n.* this condition.

autobiography *n.* the story of a person's life written by himself. **autobiographical** *adj.*

autoclave (**aw**-tŏ-klayv) *n.* **1.** a strong vessel used for chemical reactions at high pressures and temperatures. **2.** a sterilizer using high-pressure steam.

autocracy (aw-**tok**-răsi) *n.* despotism.

autocrat (**aw**-tŏ-krat) *n.* a person with unlimited power, a dictatorial person.

autocratic (aw-tŏ-**krat**-ik) *adj.*, **auto-cratically** *adv.*

autocross *n.* motor-racing across country.

autograph *n.* **1.** a person's signature, his handwriting. **2.** a manuscript in an author's own handwriting. **3.** a document signed by its author. —*v.* to write one's name on or in, *the author will autograph copies of his book tomorrow.*

automate *v.* to control or operate by automation, *the process is fully automated.*

automatic *adj.* **1.** working of itself without direct human control, self-regulating. **2.** firing repeatedly until pressure on the trigger is released, *an automatic pistol.* **3.** done without thought, done from habit or routine, *made an automatic gesture of apology.* —**automatic** *n.* **1.** an automatic machine or tool or firearm. **2.** a vehicle with an automatic transmission system. —**automatically** *adv.*

automation *n.* the use of automatic equipment to save mental and manual labour.

automaton (aw-**tom**-ă-tŏn) *n.* a person who seems to act mechanically and without thinking.

automobile (**aw**-tŏm-ŏ-beel) *n.* (*Amer.*) a car.

automotive (aw-tŏm-**oh**-tiv) *adj.* concerned with motor vehicles.

autonomous (aw-**tonn**-ŏ-mŭs) *adj.* self-governing. **autonomy** *n.* self-government, independence.

autopsy (**aw**-top-si) *n.* a post-mortem.

autumn *n.* the season between summer and winter. **autumnal** (aw-**tum**-năl) *adj.*, **autumnally** *adv.*

auxiliary (awg-**zil**-yer-i) *adj.* giving help or support, *auxiliary services*; *an auxiliary verb,* one used in forming parts of other verbs, e.g. *have* in *I have finished.* —*n.* a helper. **auxiliaries** *pl. n.* auxiliary troops, foreign or allied troops employed by a country at war.

avail *v.* to be of help or advantage, *nothing availed against the storm*; *he availed himself of the opportunity,* made use of it. —*n.* effectiveness, advantage, *it was of no avail.*

available *adj.* ready or able to be used, obtainable. **availability** *n.*

avalanche (**av**-ă-lahnsh) *n.* **1.** a mass of snow or rock pouring down a mountain side. **2.** a great onrush, *an avalanche of letters.*

avant-garde (av-ahn **gard**) *adj.* using or favouring an ultra-modern style, especially in art or literature. —*n.* an avant-garde group.

avarice (**av**-er-iss) *n.* greed for gain. **avaricious** (av-er-**ish**-ŭs) *adj.*, **avariciously** *adv.*

Ave Maria (ah-vay mă-**ree**-ă) = Hail Mary.

avenge *v.* to take vengeance for. **avenger** *n.*

avenue *n.* **1.** a wide street or road. **2.** a way of approaching or making progress, *other avenues to fame.*

average *n.* **1.** the value arrived at by adding several quantities together and dividing the total by the number of quantities. **2.** the standard or level regarded as usual. —**average** *adj.* **1.** found by making an average, *the average age of the pupils is fifteen.* **2.** of the ordinary or usual standard, *people of average intelligence.* —**average** *v.* **1.** to calculate the average of. **2.** to amount to or produce as an average, *the car averaged 40 miles to the gallon.*

averse (ă-**verss**) *adj.* unwilling, disinclined, *he is averse to hard work.*

aversion (ă-**ver**-shŏn) *n.* **1.** a strong dislike. **2.** something disliked.

avert (ă-**vert**) *v.* **1.** to turn away, *people averted their eyes.* **2.** to prevent, to ward off, *managed to avert disaster.*

aviary (**ay**-vi-eri) *n.* a large cage or building for keeping birds.

aviation (ay-vi-ay-shŏn) *n.* the art of flying an aircraft.

aviator (**ay**-vi-ay-ter) *n.* a pilot or member of an aircraft crew in the early days of aviation.

avid (**av**-id) *adj.* eager, greedy. **avidly** *adv.*, **avidity** (ă-**vid**-iti) *n.*

avionics (ay-vi-on-iks) *n.* the application of electronics in aviation.

avocado (av-ŏ-**kah**-doh) *n.* (*pl.* avocados) a pear-shaped tropical fruit.

avoid *v.* **1.** to keep oneself away from (something dangerous or undesirable). **2.** to refrain from, *avoid making rash promises.* **avoidance** *n.*

avoidable *adj.* able to be avoided.

avoirdupois (av-er-dew-**poiz**) *n.* a system of weights based on the pound of 16 ounces or 7000 grains.

Avon a county of England.

avow *v.* (*formal*) to admit, to declare openly. **avowal** *n.*, **avowedly** (ă-**vow**-idli) *adv.*

avuncular (ă-**vunk**-yoo-ler) *adj.* of or like a kindly uncle.

await *v.* **1.** to wait for, *I await your reply.* **2.** to be waiting for, *a surprise awaits you.*

awake *v.* (awoke, awoken) to wake, to cease to sleep, to arouse from sleep. —*adj.* **1.** not yet asleep, no longer asleep. **2.** alert, aware, *he is awake to the possible danger.*

awaken v. to awake. **awakening** n.

award v. to give by official decision as a payment, penalty, or prize. —n. **1.** a decision of this kind. **2.** a thing awarded.

aware adj. having knowledge or realization, *I am aware of this possibility.* **awareness** n.

awash adj. washed over by water or waves.

away adv. **1.** to or at a distance. **2.** out of existence, *the water has boiled away.* **3.** constantly, persistently, *we worked away at it.* —adj. played on an opponent's ground, *an away match.* —n. an away match or (in football pools) victory in this.

awe n. respect combined with fear or wonder. —v. to fill with awe.

awesome adj. causing awe.

awestricken, awestruck adjs. suddenly filled with awe.

aweigh (ă-**way**) adv. hanging just clear of the sea bottom, *the anchor is aweigh.*

awful adj. **1.** extremely bad or unpleasant, *an awful accident.* **2.** (*informal*) extreme, very great, *that's an awful lot of money.* □ **awfully** adv. (*informal*) very; very much.

awhile adv. for a short time.

awkward adj. **1.** difficult to handle or use or deal with. **2.** clumsy, having little skill. **3.** inconvenient, *came at an awkward time.* **4.** embarrassed, *feel awkward about it.* **awkwardly** adv., **awkwardness** n.

awl n. a small pointed tool for making holes, especially in leather or wood.

awning n. a roof-like shelter of canvas etc., erected as a protection against sun or rain.

awoke see awake.

awry (ă-**ry**) adv. **1.** twisted towards one side. **2.** amiss, *plans went awry.* —adj. crooked, wrong.

axe n. **1.** a chopping-tool. **2.** (*informal*) removal, dismissal; *got the axe,* was dismissed. —v. to remove by abolishing or dismissing, *the project was axed.* □ **have an axe to grind,** to have some personal interest involved and be anxious to take care of it.

axil n. the angle where a leaf joins a stem.

axiom (**aks**-i-ŏm) n. an accepted general truth or principle.

axiomatic (aks-i-ŏm-**at**-ik) adj. **1.** of or like an axiom. **2.** self-evident.

axis n. (*pl.* axes) a line through the centre of an object, round which it rotates when spinning.

axle n. the bar or rod on which a wheel or wheels turn.

Axminster n. a tufted carpet with cut pile, named after a town in Devon.

ay (*pr.* I) adv. & n. (*pl.* ayes) = aye.

ayatollah (I-ă-**tol**-a) n. a senior Muslim religious leader in Iran.

aye [1] (*pr.* I) adv. yes. —n. a vote in favour of a proposal; *the ayes have it,* those in favour are in the majority.

aye [2] (*pr.* ay) adv. (*old use*) always.

Ayrshire n. an animal of a breed of mainly white dairy cattle.

azalea (ă-**zay**-liă) n. a shrub-like flowering plant.

azimuth (**az**-i-muth) n. **1.** an arc of the sky from the zenith to the horizon. **2.** the angle between this arc and the meridian.

Aztec n. a member of an Indian people of Mexico before the Spanish conquest.

azure (**az**-yoor) adj. & n. sky-blue.

Bb

BA abbrev. Bachelor of Arts.

baa n. the cry of a sheep or lamb. —v. to make this cry.

baba (**bah**-bah) n. a kind of sponge-cake served soaked in flavoured syrup, *rum baba.*

babble v. **1.** to chatter in a thoughtless or confused way. **2.** to make a continuous murmuring sound, *a babbling brook.* —n. babbling talk or sound.

babe n. (*formal*) a baby. **babes and sucklings,** very inexperienced people.

baboon n. a large African or Arabian monkey.

baby n. **1.** a very young child or animal. **2.** a babyish or timid person. **3.** (*Amer. slang*) a man's girl-friend. **4.** (*Amer. slang*) a person, *he's a tough baby.* **5.** something small of its kind; *a baby grand,* the smallest kind of grand piano. **6.** something that is one's creation or in one's care. —v. (babied, babying) to treat like a baby, to pamper. —**babyhood** n. □ **baby-sit** v. to be a baby-sitter. **baby-sitter** n. a person looking after a child in its home while its parents are out. **be left holding the baby,** (*informal*) to be left with an unwelcome responsibility.

babyish adj. like a baby.

baccarat (**bak**-er-ah) n. a gambling card-game.

bachelor n. **1.** an unmarried man; *a bachelor flat,* suitable for an unmarried person. **2.** *Bachelor,* a person who holds a university degree below that of Master, *Bachelor of Arts.* □ **bachelor girl,** a young unmarried woman living independently.

bacillus (bă-**sil**-ŭs) n. (*pl.* bacilli, *pr.* bă-**sil**-I) a rod-like bacterium.

back *n.* **1.** the hinder surface of the human body from neck to hip, the corresponding part of an animal's body. **2.** that part of a chair etc. against which a seated person's back rests. **3.** the part or surface of an object that is less used or less important, the part furthest from the front. **4.** the part of a garment covering the back. **5.** a defensive player near the goal in football etc., his position. —**back** *adj.* **1.** situated behind, *the back teeth*; *back streets,* remote and inferior. **2.** of or for a past time, *back pay.* —**back** *adv.* **1.** at or towards the rear, away from the front or centre. **2.** in check, *hold it back.* **3.** in or into a previous time or position or condition; *I'll be back at six,* shall return then. **4.** in return, *pay it back.* —**back** *v.* **1.** to go or cause to go backwards. **2.** (of wind) to change gradually in an anticlockwise direction. **3.** to give one's support to, to assist. **4.** to give financial support to, *he is backing the play.* **5.** to lay a bet on. **6.** to cover the back of, *the rug is backed with canvas.* — **backer** *n.* □ **at the back of,** giving (a person) help and support; being the underlying cause or motive of (a thing). **back-bencher** *n.* an MP who is not entitled to sit on the front benches (*see* front-bencher). **back boiler,** a boiler behind a domestic fire or cooking range. **back down,** to give up a claim; to withdraw one's argument. **back number,** an old issue of a periodical; an out-of-date person or idea. **back of beyond,** a very remote place. **back out,** to withdraw from an agreement. **back seat,** a seat at the back; *take a back seat,* to take a less prominent position; *back-seat driver,* a person who has no responsibility but is eager to give orders to one who has. **back to front,** with the back placed where the front should be. **back up,** to give one's support to. **back-up** *adj.* spare, reserve, supporting, (*n.*) a spare or reserve or supporting person or thing. **be on someone's back,** to be a burden or hindrance to him. **have one's back to the wall,** to be fighting for survival in a desperate situation. **put a person's back up,** to offend or antagonize him. **put one's back into something,** to use maximum effort on it.

backache *n.* a pain in one's back.

backbiting *n.* spiteful talk, especially about a person who is not present.

backbone *n.* **1.** the column of small bones down the centre of the back, the spine. **2.** strength of character.

backchat *n.* (*informal*) answering back.

backdate *v.* to declare that (a thing) is to be regarded as valid from some date in the past.

backfire *v.* **1.** to ignite or explode prematurely, especially in an internal combustion engine. **2.** to produce an undesired effect, especially upon the originators, *their plan backfired.*

backgammon *n.* a game played on a double board with draughts and dice.

background *n.* **1.** the back part of a scene or picture, the setting for the chief objects or people; *he was kept in the background,* in an inconspicuous position; *background music,* used as an accompaniment to a play or film etc.; *background heating,* giving mild general warmth. **2.** the conditions and events surrounding and influencing something; *a person's background,* his family life, education, experience, etc.

backhand *adj.* (of a stroke or blow) made with the back of the hand turned outwards. —*n.* a backhand stroke or blow.

backhanded *adj.* **1.** backhand. **2.** indirect; *a backhanded compliment,* one made with underlying sarcasm so that it is not a compliment at all.

backhander *n.* **1.** a backhanded stroke or blow or remark. **2.** (*slang*) a bribe, a reward for services rendered.

backing *n.* **1.** help, support; *he has a large backing,* many supporters. **2.** material used to cover a thing's back or to support it. **3.** a musical accompaniment to a pop singer.

backlash *n.* a violent and usually hostile reaction to some event.

backless *adj.* **1.** without a back. **2.** (of a dress) cut low at the back.

backlog *n.* arrears of work.

back-pedal *v.* (back-pedalled, back-pedalling) **1.** to work a pedal backwards. **2.** to back down from an argument or policy. **3.** to reverse one's previous action.

backside *n.* (*informal*) the buttocks.

backslide *v.* to slip back from good behaviour into bad.

backspace *v.* to cause a typewriter carriage (or 'golf ball') to move one space back.

backstage *adj.* & *adv.* behind the stage of a theatre, in the wings or dressing-rooms.

backstroke *n.* a swimming stroke in which the swimmer is lying on his back.

backtrack *v.* **1.** to go back the same way that one came. **2.** to back down from an argument or policy, to reverse one's previous action.

backward *adj.* **1.** directed towards the back or the starting-point. **2.** having made less than normal progress. **3.** diffident, not putting oneself forward. —*adv.* backwards. —**backwardness** *n.*

backwards *adv.* 1. away from one's front, towards the back. 2. with the back foremost, in a reverse direction or order. □ **backwards and forwards**, in each direction alternately. **know it backwards**, to know it thoroughly. **lean over backwards**, to do one's utmost.

backwash *n.* 1. a backward flow of water. 2. the after-effects of an action or event.

backwater *n.* 1. a stretch of stagnant water joining a stream. 2. a place unaffected by progress or new ideas.

bacon *n.* salted or smoked meat from the back or sides of a pig. **bring home the bacon**, (*informal*) to achieve something successfully. **save one's bacon**, (*informal*) to escape death or injury.

bacteriology *n.* the scientific study of bacteria. **bacteriological** *adj.*, **bacteriologist** *n.*

bacterium (bak-**teer**-iŭm) *n.* (*pl.* bacteria) a microscopic organism. **bacterial** *adj.*

bad *adj.* (worse, worst) 1. wicked, evil. 2. unpleasant. 3. serious, severe. 4. inferior, of poor quality, worthless, incorrect; *meat went bad*, decayed; *a bad business*, an unfortunate affair. 5. hurtful, unsuitable, *sweets are bad for the teeth*. 6. in ill health, diseased. —*adv.* (*Amer. informal*) badly, *is he hurt bad?* —**bad** *n.* 1. that which is bad or unfortunate; *I am £50 to the bad*, have lost this as the result of a deal. 2. *the bad*, wicked people. — **badly** *adv.* (worse, worst), **badness** *n.* □ **bad blood**, ill feeling, enmity. **bad debt**, one that will not be repaid. **bad language**, swear-words. **bad-tempered** *adj.* having or showing bad temper. **be in a bad way**, to be ill or in trouble. **feel bad about**, (*informal*) to feel upset or guilty about. **go to the bad**, to become completely immoral. **in bad with**, (*Amer. informal*) regarded with disapproval by. **not bad**, (*informal*) quite good.

baddy *n.* (*informal*) a villain.

bade see bid².

badge *n.* a thing worn to show one's rank, occupation, or membership of an organization.

badger *n.* an animal of the weasel family that burrows in the ground. —*v.* to pester.

badinage (**bad**-in-ah*zh*) *n.* banter.

badminton *n.* a game played with rackets and shuttlecocks across a high net.

baffle *v.* 1. to puzzle, to perplex. 2. to frustrate, *baffled their attempts*. —*n.* a screen placed so as to hinder or control the passage of sound, light, or fluid. — **bafflement** *n.*

bag *n.* 1. a container made of flexible material with an opening at the top, used for holding or carrying things. 2. this with its contents, the amount it contains. 3. something resembling a bag; *bags under the eyes*, folds of loose skin. 4. the amount of game shot by a sportsman. —**bag** *v.* (bagged, bagging) 1. to put into a bag or bags. 2. to kill or capture, *bagged a pheasant*. 3. (*informal*) to take possession of, to stake a claim to. 4. to hang loosely. □ **bag and baggage**, with all one's belongings. **bags** *pl. n.* (*slang*) trousers; plenty, *bags of room*. **be in the bag**, (*informal*) to be secured as one wished.

bagatelle (bag-ă-**tel**) *n.* 1. a game like billiards, played on a board with holes. 2. something small and unimportant.

bagful *n.* (*pl.* bagfuls) as much as a bag will hold.

baggage *n.* 1. luggage. 2. portable equipment. 3. (*humorous*) a lively or mischievous girl.

baggy *adj.* (baggier, baggiest) hanging in loose folds. **baggily** *adv.*, **bagginess** *n.*

Baghdad (bag-**dad**) the capital of Iraq.

bagpipes *pl. n.* a musical instrument with air stored in a bag and pressed out through pipes.

Bahamas (bă-**hah**-măz) a group of islands in the West Indies. **Bahamian** *adj. & n.*

Bahrain (bah-**rayn**) a sheikdom consisting of a group of islands on the Persian Gulf.

bail¹ *n.* 1. money or property pledged as security that a person accused of a crime will return, if he is released temporarily, to stand trial. 2. permission for a person's release on such security. —**bail** *v.* 1. to obtain or allow (a person's) release on bail. 2. to relieve by financial help in an emergency, *bail the firm out*. □ **go bail**, to pledge money etc. as bail. **out on bail**, released after bail is pledged.

bail² *n.* 1. either of the two cross-pieces resting on the three stumps in cricket. 2. a bar separating horses in an open stable. 3. a bar holding paper against the platen of a typewriter.

bail³ *v.* to scoop out (water that has entered a boat), to clear (a boat) in this way.

bailey *n.* the outer wall of a castle, a courtyard enclosed by this.

Bailey bridge a bridge made in prefabricated sections designed for rapid assembly.

bailie (**bay**-li) *n.* a Scottish municipal councillor serving as a magistrate.

bailiff *n.* 1. a law officer who helps a sheriff, serving writs and performing arrests. 2. a landlord's agent or steward.

bairn *n.* (*Scottish*) a child.

bait *n.* **1.** food (real or sham) placed to attract prey. **2.** an enticement. —**bait** *v.* **1.** to place bait on or in, *bait the trap.* **2.** to torment by jeering.

baize *n.* thick woollen green cloth, used for covering tables or doors.

bake *v.* **1.** to cook or be cooked by dry heat. **2.** to expose to great heat, to harden or be hardened by heat. □ **baking-hot** *adj.* very hot.

bakehouse *n.* a building or room for baking bread.

bakelite (**bay**-kĕ-lyt) *n.* a kind of plastic.

baker *n.* one who bakes and sells bread. **baker's dozen,** thirteen. (¶ From the former custom of allowing the retailer to receive thirteen loaves for each twelve he paid for.)

bakery *n.* a place where bread is baked for sale.

baking-powder *n.* a mixture of powders used as a raising-agent for cakes etc.

baking-soda *n.* sodium bicarbonate, used in baking.

Balaclava (bal-ă-**klah**-vă) *n.* a woollen helmet covering the head and neck.

balance *n.* **1.** a weighing-apparatus with two scales or pans hanging from a cross-bar. **2.** the regulating-apparatus of a clock. **3.** an even distribution of weight or amount, a steady position; *the balance of power,* a condition in which no country or group is much stronger than another; *the balance of one's mind,* one's sanity. **4.** the difference between credits and debits. **5.** money remaining after payment of a debt. —**balance** *v.* **1.** to consider by comparing, *balance one argument against another.* **2.** to be or put or keep (a thing) in a state of balance. **3.** to compare the debits and credits of an account and make the entry needed to equalize these, to have these equal. □ **balance of payments,** the difference between the amount paid to foreign countries for imports and services and the amount received from them for exports etc. in a given period. **balance of trade,** the difference in value between imports and exports. **balance sheet,** a written statement of assets and liabilities. **in the balance,** with the outcome still uncertain. **off balance,** in danger of falling. **on balance,** taking everything into consideration.

balcony (**bal**-kŏni) *n.* **1.** a platform with a rail or parapet, projecting outside an upper storey of a building. **2.** an upper floor of seats in a cinema or above the dress-circle in a theatre. **balconied** *adj.*

bald *adj.* **1.** with the scalp wholly or partly hairless. **2.** (of tyres) with the tread worn away. **3.** bare, without details, *bald facts.* **baldly** *adv.,* **baldness** *n.* □ **balding** *adj.* becoming bald.

balderdash *n.* nonsense.

bale[1] *n.* **1.** a large bundle of straw etc. bound with cord or wire. **2.** a large package of goods. —*v.* to make into a bale.

bale[2] *v.* **bale out,** to make a parachute descent from an aircraft in an emergency. ¶ Do not confuse with bail[1] and bail[3].

baleful *adj.* menacing, destructive, *a baleful influence.* **balefully** *adv.*

Balinese (bah-li-**neez**) *adj.* of Bali, an island of Indonesia. —*n.* (*pl.* Balinese) a native or inhabitant of Bali.

balk (*pr.* bawlk) *v.* **1.** to shirk, to jib at, *balked the problem.* **2.** to frustrate, *he was balked of his prey.*

Balkan (**bawl**-kăn) *adj.* of the peninsula in south-east Europe bounded by the Adriatic, Aegean, and Black Seas, or of its people or countries. **the Balkans,** the Balkan countries.

ball[1] *n.* **1.** a solid or hollow sphere. **2.** such a sphere used in games. **3.** a single delivery of the ball by the bowler in cricket or by the pitcher in baseball. **4.** material gathered or wound into a round mass, *a ball of string.* **5.** a rounded part; *the ball of the foot,* that under the foot at the base of the big toe. —**ball** *v.* **1.** to squeeze or wind so as to form a ball. **2.** to form a lump or lumps. □ **ball-bearing** *n.* a bearing using small steel balls, one of these balls. **ball-boy, ball-girl** *ns.* one who retrieves balls in a tennis match. **ball-cock** *n.* a device with a floating ball controlling the water-level in a cistern. **ball of fire,** a very lively spirited person. **ball-point** *n.* a pen with a tiny ball as its writing-point. **balls** *pl. n.* (*vulgar slang*) testicles. **balls-up** *n.* (*slang*) a muddle. **on the ball,** (*informal*) alert, competent. **start the ball rolling,** to start a discussion or activity.

ball[2] *n.* a social assembly for dancing. **have a ball,** (*slang*) to enjoy oneself.

ballad *n.* a simple song or poem, especially one telling a story.

ballast (**bal**-ăst) *n.* **1.** heavy material placed in a ship's hold to improve its stability; *ship is in ballast,* laden with ballast only. **2.** a device to stabilize current in an electric circuit.

ballerina (ba-ler-**ee**-nă) *n.* a female ballet dancer.

ballet (**bal**-ay) *n.* a form of dancing and mime to music, a performance of this.

ballistic (bă-**lis**-tik) *adj.* of projectiles such as bullets and missiles. **ballistics** *pl. n.*

the scientific study of projectiles or of firearms.

balloon *n.* a bag or envelope inflated with air or a lighter gas. —*v.* to swell out like a balloon. □ **balloonist** *n.* a person who travels by balloon.

ballot *n.* **1.** a paper or token used in secret voting. **2.** voting by means of such papers etc. —**ballot** *v.* (balloted, balloting) **1.** to vote by ballot. **2.** to cause to do this, *balloting their members.*

ballroom *n.* a large room where dances are held.

ballyhoo *n.* vulgar or misleading publicity.

balm (*pr.* bahm) *n.* **1.** (*old use*) an ointment that soothes or heals. **2.** a soothing influence. **3.** a fragrant herb.

balmy (**bah**-mi) *adj.* (balmier, balmiest) **1.** like balm, fragrant. **2.** soft and warm, *balmy air.* **3.** (*slang*) barmy.

baloney (bă-**loh**-ni) *n.* = boloney.

balsa (**bawl**-să) *n.* very lightweight wood from a tropical American tree.

balsam (**bawl**-săm) *n.* **1.** a soothing oil. **2.** a flowering plant.

Baltic (**bawl**-tik) *adj.* of the Baltic Sea, an almost land-locked sea of north-east Europe. —*n.* the Baltic Sea.

baluster (**bal**-ŭster) *n.* one of the short stone pillars in a balustrade.

balustrade (bal-ŭs-**trayd**) *n.* a row of short posts or pillars supporting a rail or stone coping round a balcony or terrace.

bamboo (bam-**boo**) *n.* a giant tropical grass with hollow stems.

bamboozle *v.* (*slang*) **1.** to mystify. **2.** to trick.

ban *v.* (banned, banning) to forbid officially. —*n.* an order that bans something.

banal (bă-**nahl**) *adj.* commonplace, uninteresting. **banality** *n.*

banana *n.* **1.** the finger-shaped fruit of a tropical tree. **2.** this tree. □ **banana republic**, (*contemptuous*) a small country dependent on its fruit exports and regarded as economically unstable. **go bananas**, (*slang*) to go crazy.

band *n.* **1.** a narrow strip, hoop, or loop. **2.** a range of values, wavelengths, etc. within a series. **3.** an organized group of people. **4.** a set of people playing music together, especially on wind or percussion instruments. —**band** *v.* **1.** to put a band on or round. **2.** to form into a league, *they banded together.*

bandage *n.* a strip of material for binding up a wound. —*v.* to bind up with this.

bandanna (ban-**dan**-ă) *n.* a large coloured handkerchief with yellow or white spots.

b. & b. *abbrev.* bed and breakfast.

bandit *n.* a member of a band of robbers.

bandstand *n.* a covered outdoor platform for a musical band.

bandwagon *n.* an imaginary vehicle thought of as carrying a thing that is heading for success. **climb** *or* **jump on the bandwagon**, to seek to join this thing or follow its example.

bandy[1] *v.* (bandied, bandying) to pass to and fro, *the story was bandied about*; *bandy words*, exchange remarks in quarrelling.

bandy[2] *adj.* (bandier, bandiest) curving apart at the knees. **bandiness** *n.*

bane *n.* a cause of trouble or misery or anxiety. **baneful** *adj.*, **banefully** *adv.*

bang *v.* **1.** to make a sudden loud noise like an explosion. **2.** to strike or shut noisily. —**bang** *n.* **1.** the sudden loud noise of or like an explosion. **2.** a sharp blow. — **bang** *adv.*, **1.** with a bang, abruptly; *bang go my chances*, they are suddenly destroyed. **2.** exactly, *bang in the middle*; *his estimate was bang on*, (*slang*) was exactly right. □ **go with a bang**, to be very successful or impressive.

banger *n.* **1.** a firework made to explode noisily. **2.** (*slang*) a noisy old car. **3.** (*slang*) a sausage.

Bangkok (bang-**kok**) the capital of Thailand.

Bangladesh (bang-lă-**desh**) a Muslim country in south-east Asia. **Bangladeshi** *adj.* & *n.* (*pl.* Bangladeshis)

bangle *n.* a bracelet of rigid material.

banian (**ban**-yăn) *n.* an Indian fig-tree with spreading branches from which roots grow downwards to the ground and form new trunks.

banish *v.* **1.** to condemn to exile. **2.** to dismiss from one's presence or one's mind, *banish care.* **banishment** *n.*

banister *n.* one of the uprights supporting the handrail of a stair. **banisters** *pl. n.* these uprights and the rail together.

banjo (**ban**-joh) *n.* (*pl.* banjos) a stringed instrument like a guitar.

bank[1] *n.* **1.** a slope, especially at the side of a river. **2.** a raised mass of sand etc. in a river bed. **3.** a long mass of cloud or snow or other soft substance. **4.** a row or series of lights, switches, etc. —**bank** *v.* **1.** to build or form a bank; *bank up the fire*, heap on coal-dust etc. so that it burns slowly. **2.** to tilt or be tilted sideways in rounding a curve.

bank[2] *n.* **1.** an establishment for keeping people's money etc. safely and paying it out on a customer's order. **2.** the money held by the keeper of a gaming-table. **3.** a place for storing a reserve supply, *a blood bank.* —**bank** *v.* **1.** to place or keep money in a bank. **2.** to base one's hopes, *we are banking on your success.* □ **bank-book** *n.* a book containing a customer's copy of his bank account. **bank holiday,** a day (other than Sunday) on which banks are officially closed, usually kept as a public holiday. **banking** *n.* the business of running a bank.

banker *n.* **1.** an expert in banking. **2.** the keeper of a gaming bank. **3.** a result selected for forecasting identically in a series of football-pool entries.

banknote *n.* a small strip of paper issued by a bank to serve as currency, printed with the amount for which it is valid.

bankrupt *n.* a person who is unable to pay his debts in full and whose estate is administered and distributed for the benefit of his creditors. —*adj.* **1.** declared by a lawcourt to be a bankrupt. **2.** financially ruined and in debt. —*v.* to make bankrupt. —**bankruptcy** *n.*

banner *n.* **1.** a flag. **2.** a strip of cloth bearing an emblem or slogan, hung up or carried on a crossbar or between two poles in a procession etc.

banns *pl. n.* a public announcement in church of a forthcoming marriage between two named people.

banquet *n.* an elaborate ceremonial public meal. —*v.* to take part in a banquet.

banshee (han-shee) *n.* (*Irish & Scottish*) a female spirit whose wail is superstitiously believed to foretell a death in a house.

bantam *n.* a small kind of fowl.

bantamweight *n.* a boxing-weight (54 kg) between featherweight and flyweight.

banter *n.* good-humoured teasing. —*v.* to joke in a good-humoured way.

Bantu (ban-too) *n.* (*pl.* Bantu *or* Bantus) one of a group of Black African peoples or their languages.

banyan *n.* = banian.

bap *n.* a large soft bread roll.

baptism *n.* the religious rite of sprinkling a person with water or immersing him in it to symbolize purification and (with Christians) admission to the Church. **baptismal** *adj.*

Baptist *n.* **1.** a member of a Protestant sect believing that baptism should be by immersion and performed at an age when the person is old enough to understand its meaning. **2.** *the Baptist,* St. John who baptized Christ.

baptistery (bap-tist-eri) *n.* a building or part of a church used for baptism.

baptize *v.* **1.** to perform baptism on. **2.** to name or nickname.

bar[1] *n.* **1.** a long piece of solid material.

2. a narrow strip, *bars of colour*; *DSO and bar,* a strip of silver given as an additional award. **3.** any barrier or obstacle, a sandbank. **4.** one of the vertical lines dividing a piece of music into equal units, a section contained by these. **5.** a partition (real or imaginary) across a court of justice separating the judge, jury, and certain lawyers from the public. **6.** *the bar,* barristers. **7.** a counter or room where alcohol is served. **8.** a place where refreshments are served across a counter, *a coffee bar.* **9.** a shop counter selling a single type of commodity or service. —**bar** *v.* (barred, barring) **1.** to fasten with a bar or bars. **2.** to keep in or out by this. **3.** to obstruct, *barred the way.* **4.** to prevent or prohibit. —*prep.* except, *it's all over bar the shouting.* □ **bar code,** a pattern of stripes (on packaging or on a library book etc.) containing information for processing by a computer. **be called to the bar,** to become a barrister. **behind bars,** in prison.

bar[2] *n.* a unit of pressure used in meteorology.

barathea (ba-rǎth-ee-ǎ) *n.* a kind of fine woollen cloth.

barb *n.* **1.** the backward-pointing part of an arrowhead or fish-hook etc. that makes it difficult to withdraw from what it has pierced. **2.** a wounding remark.

Barbados (bar-bay-dŏs) an island in the West Indies. **Barbadian** *adj. & n.*

barbarian *n.* an uncivilized person. —*adj.* of barbarians.

barbaric (bar-ba-rik) *adj.* suitable for barbarians, rough and wild. **barbarically** *adv.*

barbarity (bar-ba-riti) *n.* savage cruelty.

barbarous (bar-ber-ŭs) *adj.* uncivilized, cruel. **barbarously** *adv.*

barbecue (bar-bik-yoo) *n.* **1.** a metal frame for grilling food above an open fire. **2.** an open-air party at which food is cooked on this. **3.** the food itself. —*v.* to cook on a barbecue.

barbed *adj.* having a barb or barbs. **barbed wire,** wire with short sharp points at intervals.

barber *n.* a men's hairdresser.

barbiturate (bar-bit-yoor-ăt) *n.* a kind of sedative drug.

Barbuda *see* Antigua and Barbuda.

bard *n.* **1.** a Celtic minstrel. **2.** (*formal*) a poet; *the Bard of Avon,* Shakespeare.

bare *adj.* **1.** without clothing or covering; *trees were bare,* leafless; *with one's bare hands,* without tools or weapons. **2.** exposed, undisguised, *lay bare the truth.* **3.** plain, without detail, *the bare facts.* **4.** empty of stores, *cupboard was bare.* **5.** only just sufficient, *the bare necessities* *of life.* —*v.* to uncover, to reveal, *bared its teeth in a snarl.* —**barely** *adv.*, **bareness** *n.*

bareback *adv.* on a horse without a saddle.

barefaced *adj.* shameless, undisguised.

bareheaded *adj.* not wearing a hat.

bargain *n.* **1.** an agreement made with obligations on both or all sides. **2.** something obtained as a result of this, a thing got cheaply. —**bargain** *v.* **1.** to discuss the terms of an agreement. **2.** to be prepared for, to expect, *didn't bargain on his arriving so early; got more than he bargained for,* was unpleasantly surprised. □ **into the bargain**, in addition to other things.

barge *n.* a large flat-bottomed boat for use on canals or rivers, especially for carrying goods. —*v.* to move clumsily or heavily. □ **barge in**, to intrude. **barge-pole** *n.* a long pole used for fending from a barge; *I wouldn't touch it with a barge-pole,* I refuse to have anything to do with it.

bargee (bar-**jee**) *n.* a person in charge of a barge, a member of its crew.

baritone *n.* **1.** a male voice between tenor and bass. **2.** a singer with such a voice, a part written for this.

barium (**bair**-iŭm) *n.* **1.** a soft silvery-white metal. **2.** a chemical substance swallowed or injected into the digestive tract when this is to be X-rayed.

bark¹ *n.* the outer layer of tree trunks and branches. —*v.* **1.** to peel bark from. **2.** to scrape the skin off accidentally, *barked my knuckles.*

bark² *n.* the sharp harsh sound made by a dog or fox. —*v.* **1.** to make this sound. **2.** to speak in a sharp commanding voice, *barked out orders.* □ **bark up the wrong tree**, to direct one's effort or complaint in the wrong direction. **his bark is worse than his bite**, he speaks harshly but does not behave thus in this way.

barker *n.* a tout at an auction or sideshow.

barley *n.* a kind of cereal plant, its grain. **barley sugar**, a sweet made of boiled sugar, often shaped into twisted sticks. **barley-water** *n.* a drink made from pearl barley.

barmaid *n.* a female attendant at a bar serving alcohol.

barman *n.* (*pl.* **barmen**) a male attendant at a bar serving alcohol.

barmy *adj.* (*slang*) crazy.

barn *n.* a simple roofed building for storing grain or hay etc. on a farm. **barn owl**, an owl that often breeds and roosts in barns and other buildings.

barnacle *n.* a kind of shellfish that attaches itself to objects under water.

barnyard *n.* a yard beside a barn.

barometer (bă-**rom**-it-er) *n.* an instrument measuring atmospheric pressure, used for forecasting the weather. **barometric** (ba-rŏ-**met**-rik) *adj.*

baron *n.* **1.** a member of the lowest rank of the British peerage (called *Lord* —), or of foreign nobility (called *Baron* —). **2.** a man who held lands etc, from the king in the Middle Ages. **3.** a magnate; *a newspaper baron,* one controlling many newspapers. **baroness** *n.*

baronet *n.* a British nobleman ranking below a baron but above a knight, having the title 'Sir'. **baronetcy** *n.* the rank of a baronet.

baronial (bă-**roh**-niăl) *adj.* of or suitable for a baron.

barony *n.* the rank or lands of a baron.

baroque (bă-**rok**) *adj.* of the ornate architectural style of the 17th and 18th centuries. —*n.* this style or ornamentation.

barrack *v.* to shout protests or jeer at.

barracks *n.* **1.** a large building or group of buildings for soldiers to live in. **2.** a large plain and ugly building.

barrage (**ba**-rah*zh*) *n.* **1.** an artificial barrier, especially one damming a river. **2.** a heavy continuous bombardment by artillery. **3.** a rapid fire of questions or comments.

barre *n.* a horizontal bar used by dancers to steady themselves while exercising.

barred *see* **bar**¹.

barrel *n.* **1.** a large round container with flat ends. **2.** the amount this contains, (as a measure of mineral oil) 35 gallons (42 US gallons). **3.** a tube-like part, especially of a gun. —*v.* (**barrelled**, **barrelling**) to put into barrels. □ **over a barrel**, in a helpless position.

barrel-organ *n.* an instrument from which music is produced by turning a handle and so causing a pin-studded cylinder to act on keys.

barren *adj.* **1.** not fertile enough to produce crops, *barren land.* **2.** not producing fruit or seeds, *a barren tree.* **3.** unable to have young ones. **barrenness** *n.*

barricade *n.* a barrier, especially one hastily erected as a defence. —*v.* to block or defend with a barricade.

barrier *n.* something that prevents or controls advance, access, or progress. **barrier cream**, a cream used to protect a worker's skin from damage or infection. **barrier reef**, a coral reef with a channel between it and the land.

barrister (**ba**-riss-ter) *n.* a lawyer entitled to represent clients in the higher lawcourts.

barrow¹ *n.* **1.** a wheelbarrow. **2.** a

small cart with two wheels, pulled or pushed by hand. □ **barrow-boy** *n.* a person who sells goods from a barrow in the street.

barrow[2] *n.* a prehistoric burial mound.

Bart. *abbrev.* Baronet (*see* Bt).

barter *v.* to trade by exchanging goods etc. for other goods, not for money. —*n.* trading by exchange.

basalt (ba-sawlt) *n.* a kind of dark rock of volcanic origin.

base *n.* **1.** the lowest part of anything, the part on which it rests or is supported. **2.** a starting-point. **3.** the headquarters of an expedition or other enterprise, where its supplies are stored. **4.** a substance into which other things are mixed, *some paints have an oil base.* **5.** a cream or liquid applied to the skin as a foundation for make-up. **6.** a substance (e.g. an alkali) capable of combining with an acid to form a salt. **7.** one of the four stations to be reached by a runner in baseball. —*v.* to use as a base or foundation or as evidence for a forecast. —**base** *adj.* **1.** dishonourable, *base motives.* **2.** of inferior value, *base metals.* **3.** debased, not of acceptable quality, *base coins.* —**basely** *adv.*, **baseness** *n.*

baseball *n.* a team game in which runs are scored by hitting a ball and running round a series of four bases, the national game of the USA.

baseless *adj.* without foundation, *baseless rumours.*

basement *n.* the lowest storey of a building, below ground level.

bash *v.* **1.** to strike violently. **2.** to attack with blows or words or hostile actions. —*n.* a violent blow or knock. □ **have a bash,** (*informal*) to have a try.

bashful *adj.* shy and self-conscious. **bashfully** *adv.*, **bashfulness** *n.*

basic *adj.* forming a base or starting-point, fundamental, *basic principles*; *basic rates of pay*, calculated without including overtime etc. —**basically** *adv.* □ **basics** *pl. n.* basic facts or principles etc. **basic slag,** a by-product formed in steel manufacture, containing phosphates and used as a fertilizer.

BASIC *n.* a high-level computer language designed to be easy to learn. (¶ From the initials of Beginners' All-Purpose Symbolic Instruction Code.)

basil *n.* a sweet-smelling herb.

basilica (ba-zil-ikă) *n.* a large oblong hall or church with two rows of columns and an apse at one end.

basilisk (baz-il-isk) *n.* **1.** a small tropical American lizard. **2.** a mythical reptile said to cause death by its glance or breath.

basin *n.* **1.** a round open dish for holding liquids or soft substances. **2.** this with its contents, the amount it contains. **3.** a wash-basin. **4.** a sunken place where water collects; *a river basin*, the area drained by a river. **5.** an almost land-locked harbour, *a yacht basin.* **basinful** *n.*

basis *n.* (*pl.* bases) a foundation or support, a main principle.

bask *v.* **1.** to expose oneself comfortably to a pleasant warmth. **2.** to enjoy someone's approval.

basket *n.* **1.** a container for holding or carrying things, made of interwoven flexible material or wire. **2.** this with its contents. **basketful** *n.*

basketball *n.* a game resembling netball.

basketwork *n.* **1.** a structure of interwoven osiers etc. **2.** the art of making this.

Basque (*pr.* bahsk) *n.* **1.** a member of a people living in the western Pyrenees. **2.** their language.

bas-relief (bas-ri-leef) *n.* sculpture or carving in low relief.

bass[1] (*pr.* bas) *n.* (*pl.* bass) a fish of the perch family.

bass[2] (*pr.* bayss) *adj.* deep-sounding, of the lowest pitch in music. —*n.* **1.** the lowest male voice, a singer with such a voice, a part written for this. **2.** the lowest-pitched member of a group of similar musical instruments.

basset (bas-it) *n.* a short-legged hound used for hunting hares etc.

bassinet *n.* a hooded wicker cradle or pram for a baby.

bassoon (bă-soon) *n.* a deep-toned woodwind instrument.

bastard *n.* **1.** an illegitimate child. **2.** (*slang*) an unpleasant or difficult person or thing. **3.** (*slang*) a person. —**bastard** *adj.* **1.** of illegitimate birth. **2.** not considered a genuine specimen of its kind.

baste[1] (*pr.* bayst) *v.* to sew together temporarily with long loose stitches.

baste[2] (*pr.* bayst) *v.* **1.** to moisten with fat during cooking. **2.** to thrash.

bastinado (bas-tin-ay-doh) *n.* caning on the soles of the feet.

bastion (bas-ti-ŏn) *n.* **1.** a projecting part of a fortification. **2.** a fortified place near hostile territory. **3.** something serving as a stronghold, *a bastion of democracy.*

bat[1] *n.* **1.** a shaped wooden implement for striking the ball in games. **2.** a batsman, *he's a good bat.* —**bat** *v.* (batted, batting) **1.** to use a bat. **2.** to strike with a bat, to hit. □ **off one's own bat,** without prompting or help from another person.

bat[2] *n.* a flying animal with a mouse-like

body. **have bats in the belfry,** (*informal*) to be crazy or eccentric.

bat³ *v.* (batted, batting) to flutter, *it batted its wings; didn't bat an eyelid,* did not sleep a wink, did not show any surprise.

batch *n.* **1.** a number of loaves or cakes baked at the same time. **2.** a number of people or things dealt with as a group. —*v.* to group (data or programs) for batch processing by computer. □ **batch processing,** the processing by computer of similar transactions in batches in order to make economical use of computer time.

bated (**bay**-tid) *adj.* lessened. **with bated breath,** with breath held anxiously.

bath *n.* **1.** washing of the whole body by immersing it in water. **2.** water for this. **3.** a large container for water, in which one sits to wash all over. **4.** a liquid in which something is immersed, its container. —*v.* to wash in a bath. □ **baths** *pl. n.* a building with rooms where baths may be taken; a public swimming-pool.

bathe *v.* **1.** to apply liquid to, to immerse in liquid. **2.** to make wet or bright all over, *fields were bathed in sunlight.* **3.** to swim for pleasure. —*n.* a swim. —**bather** *n.* □ **bathing-suit** *n.* a garment worn for swimming.

bathos (**bay**-thoss) *n.* an anticlimax, descent from something important to something trivial.

bathroom *n.* a room containing a bath.

batik (**bat**-ik) *n.* **1.** a method of printing coloured designs on textiles by waxing the parts not to be dyed. **2.** fabric treated in this way.

batiste (bat-**eest**) *n.* a very soft fine woven fabric.

batman *n.* (*pl.* batmen) a soldier acting as an officer's personal servant.

baton (**bat**-ŏn) *n.* **1.** a short thick stick especially one serving as a symbol of authority, a truncheon. **2.** a thin stick used by the conductor of an orchestra for beating time. **3.** a short stick or tube carried in relay races.

bats *adj.* (*slang*) crazy.

batsman *n.* (*pl.* batsmen) a player who is batting in cricket or baseball, one who is good at this.

battalion *n.* an army unit made up of several companies and forming part of a regiment.

batten¹ *n.* a strip of wood or metal fastening or holding something in place. —*v.* to fasten with battens; *batten down the hatches,* close them securely.

batten² *v.* to feed greedily, to thrive or prosper at the expense of others or so as to injure them, *pigeons battening on the crops.*

batter *v.* to hit hard and often; *battered babies, battered wives,* those subjected to repeated violence. —*n.* a beaten mixture of flour, eggs, and milk, for cooking.

battering-ram *n.* an iron-headed beam formerly used in war to breach walls or gates.

battery *n.* **1.** a group of big guns on land or on a warship. **2.** an artillery unit of guns, men, and vehicles. **3.** a set of similar or connected units of equipment, or of cages for poultry etc. **4.** an electric cell or group of cells supplying current. **5.** unlawful blows or a menacing touch on a person or his clothes.

battle *n.* **1.** a fight between large organized forces. **2.** any contest, *a battle of wits.* **3.** victory, success; *confidence is half the battle,* a help towards success. —*v.* to engage in battle, to struggle. □ **battle-cry** *n.* a war-cry, a slogan.

battleaxe *n.* **1.** a heavy axe used as a weapon in ancient times. **2.** (*informal*) a formidable aggressive woman.

battlefield *n.* a place where a battle is or was fought.

battleground *n.* a battlefield.

battlements *pl. n.* **1.** a parapet with gaps at intervals, originally for firing from. **2.** the roof within this.

battleship *n.* the most heavily armed kind of warship.

batty *adj.* (*slang*) crazy. **battiness** *n.*

bauble *n.* a showy but valueless ornament or fancy article.

baud (*rhymes with* code) *n.* a unit for measuring speed in telegraphic signalling, corresponding to one dot or other signal per second.

baulk (*pr.* bawlk) *v.* = balk. —**baulk** *n.* **1.** a roughly-squared timber beam. **2.** a stumbling-block, a hindrance.

bauxite (**bawk**-syt) *n.* the clay-like substance from which aluminium is obtained.

bawdy *adj.* (bawdier, bawdiest) humorous in a coarse or indecent way. **bawdily** *adv.,* **bawdiness** *n.*

bawl *v.* to shout or cry loudly. **bawl a person out,** (*Amer. informal*) to scold him severely.

bay¹ *n.* a kind of laurel with deep-green leaves that are dried and used for seasoning.

bay² *n.* part of the sea or of a large lake within a wide curve of the shore.

bay³ *n.* **1.** one of a series of compartments in a building, structure, or area, *a parking bay.* **2.** a recess in a room or building. **3.** the cul-de-sac where a side-line terminates at a railway station. □ **bay window,** a window projecting from the outside wall of a house.

bay⁴ *n.* the deep drawn-out cry of a large dog or of hounds in pursuit of a hunted animal. —*v.* to make this sound. □ **at bay,** forced to face attackers and showing defiance in a desperate situation. **hold at bay,** to ward off.

bay⁵ *adj.* reddish-brown. —*n.* a bay horse.

bayonet (**bay**-ŏn-it) *n.* a dagger-like blade that can be fixed to the muzzle of a rifle and used in hand-to-hand fighting. —*v.* (bayoneted, bayoneting) to stab with a bayonet.

bazaar *n.* **1.** a series of shops or stalls in an Oriental country. **2.** a large shop selling a variety of cheap goods. **3.** a sale of goods to raise funds.

bazooka (bă-**zoo**-kă) *n.* a portable weapon for firing anti-tank rockets.

BBC *abbrev.* British Broadcasting Corporation.

BC *abbrev.* **1.** before Christ. **2.** British Columbia.

be *v.* (am, are, is; was, were; been, being) **1.** to exist, to occur, to live, to occupy a position. **2.** to have a certain identity or quality or condition; *how much is it?,* what does it cost? **3.** to become, *he wants to be a pilot.* —**be** *auxiliary verb,* used to form parts of other verbs, e.g. *it is rising; he was killed; I am to inform you,* it is my duty to inform you. □ **be-all and end-all,** the supreme purpose or essence. **be that as it may,** no matter what the facts about it may be. **have been,** to have come or gone as a visitor, *I have been to Cairo; has the postman been?* **let it be,** do not disturb it.

beach *n.* the shore between high and low water mark, covered with sand or waterworn pebbles. —*v.* to bring on shore from out of the water. □ **beach-head** *n.* a fortified position established on a beach by an invading army.

beachcomber (**beech**-koh-mer) *n.* **1.** a person who salvages stray articles along a beach. **2.** a loafer who lives on what he can earn casually on a waterfront. **beachcombing** *n.*

beacon *n.* **1.** a signal-fire on a hill. **2.** a light used as a signal or warning. **3.** a signal station such as a lighthouse. **4.** an amber globe on a pole, marking certain pedestrian crossings.

bead *n.* **1.** a small shaped piece of hard material pierced for threading with others on a string or wire, or for sewing on to fabric. **2.** a drop or bubble of liquid on a surface. □ **beads** *pl. n.* a necklace of beads; a rosary. **draw a bead on,** to take aim at.

beading *n.* **1.** a decoration of beads. **2.** a moulding or carving like a series of beads.

3. a strip of material with one side rounded, used as a trimming on edges of wood.

beady *adj.* like beads; *beady eyes,* small and bright. **beadily** *adv.*

beagle *n.* a small hound used for hunting hares. **beagling** *n.* hunting hares with beagles.

beak *n.* **1.** a bird's horny projecting jaws. **2.** any similar projection. **3.** (*slang*) magistrate. **beaked** *adj.*

beaker *n.* **1.** a small open glass vessel with straight sides and a lip for pouring liquids, used in laboratories. **2.** a tall narrow drinking-cup, often without a handle.

beam *n.* **1.** a long piece of squared timber or other solid material, supported at both ends and carrying the weight of part of a building or other structure. **2.** a ship's breadth at its widest part. **3.** the crosspiece of a balance, from which the scales hang. **4.** a ray or stream of light or other radiation, a radio signal used to direct the course of an aircraft. **5.** a bright look, a radiant smile. —**beam** *v.* **1.** to send out light or other radiation. **2.** to look or smile radiantly. □ **broad in the beam,** (*informal*) wide at the hips. **on one's beam-ends,** near the end of one's resources.

bean *n.* **1.** a plant bearing kidney-shaped seeds in long pods. **2.** its seed used as a vegetable. **3.** a similar seed of coffee and other plants. □ **bean-bag** *n.* a small bag filled with dried bean-seeds and used for throwing or carrying in games; a large bag with a circular base, filled with plastic granules and used as a chair. **full of beans,** (*informal*) in high spirits. **not a bean,** (*slang*) no money.

beano *n.* (*pl.* beanos) a jolly party.

beanpole *n.* (*informal*) a tall thin person.

bear¹ *n.* **1.** a large heavy animal with thick fur. **2.** a child's toy like this animal. **3.** a rough ill-mannered person. **4.** *the Great Bear, the Little Bear,* constellations near the North Pole. **5.** (*Stock Exchange*) a person who sells shares etc. in the hope that prices will fall and that he will be able to buy them back more cheaply very soon; *a bear market,* a situation where share prices are falling rapidly.

bear² *v.* (bore, borne, bearing; ¶ see the note under borne). **1.** to carry, to support; *bear oneself bravely,* to behave bravely. **2.** to have or show a certain mark or characteristic, *he still bears the scar; bears an honoured name,* has it as his own or a family name. **3.** to have in one's heart or mind, *bear a grudge; I will bear it in mind,* will remember it. **4.** to bring, to provide. **5.** to endure, to tolerate, *grin and bear it.*

6. to be fit for, *his language won't bear repeating.* **7.** to produce, to give birth to, *land bears crops*; *she had borne him two sons.* **8.** to turn, to diverge, *bear right when the road forks.* **9.** to exert pressure, to thrust. □ **bear down,** to press downwards. **bear down on,** to move rapidly or purposefully towards. **bear on,** to be relevant to, *matters bearing on public health.* **bear out,** to confirm. **bear up,** to be strong enough not to give way or despair. **bear with,** to tolerate patiently. **bear witness to,** to provide evidence of the truth of. **it was borne in upon him,** he was convinced.

bearable *adj.* able to be borne, endurable. **bearably** *adv.*

beard *n.* **1.** hair on and round a man's chin. **2.** a similar hairy or bristly growth of hair on an animal or plant. —*v.* to confront boldly; *beard the lion in his den,* confront and oppose someone in his own stronghold. —**bearded** *adj.*

bearer *n.* **1.** one who carries or bears something; *cheque is payable to bearer,* to the person who presents it at a bank. **2.** one who helps to carry something (e.g. a coffin to the grave, a stretcher).

beargarden *n.* a scene of uproar.

bearing *n.* **1.** deportment, behaviour, *soldierly bearing.* **2.** relationship, relevance, *it has no bearing on this problem.* **3.** a compass direction; *get one's bearings,* find out where one is by recognizing landmarks etc. **4.** a device reducing friction in a part of a machine where another part turns. **5.** a heraldic emblem.

bearskin *n.* a tall black fur headdress worn by the Guards.

beast *n.* **1.** a large four-footed animal. **2.** a cruel or disgusting person. **3.** a disliked person or thing, something difficult.

beastly *adj.* (beastlier, beastliest) **1.** like a beast or its ways. **2.** (*informal*) abominable, very unpleasant. —*adv.* (*informal*) very, unpleasantly, *it was beastly cold.*

beat *v.* (beat, beaten, beating) **1.** to hit repeatedly, especially with a stick; *we heard the drums beating,* being beaten. **2.** to strike; *the sun beat down,* shone with great heat. **3.** to shape or flatten by blows; *beat a path,* make it by trampling things down. **4.** to mix vigorously to a frothy or smooth consistency, *beat the eggs.* **5.** (of the heart) to expand and contract rhythmically. **6.** to overcome, to do better than; *someone beat me to it,* got there first; *it beats me,* is too difficult for me. **7.** to sail towards the direction from which the wind is blowing, by tacking in alternate directions. —**beat** *n.* **1.** a regular repeated

stroke, a sound of this. **2.** recurring emphasis marking rhythm in music or poetry, the strongly marked rhythm of pop music. **3.** the appointed course of a sentinel or policeman, the area covered by this. □ **beat about the bush,** to discuss a subject without coming to the point. **beat a person down,** to cause a seller to lower the price he is asking. **beat a retreat,** to go away defeated. **beaten track,** a well-worn path. **beat it,** (*slang*) to go away. **beat off,** to drive off by fighting. **beat time,** to mark or follow the rhythm of music by waving a stick or by tapping. **beat up,** to assault violently.

beater *n.* **1.** an implement for beating things. **2.** a person employed to drive game out of cover towards those waiting with guns to shoot it.

beatific (bee-ă-**tif**-ik) *adj.* showing great happiness, *a beatific smile.*

beatify (bee-**at**-i-fy) *v.* (beatified, beatifying) to honour by beatification. **beatification** *n.* the pope's official statement that a dead person is among the Blessed, the first step towards canonization.

beating *n.* **1.** the process of hitting or being hit with a stick etc. **2.** a defeat. □ **beating-up** *n.* a violent assault on a person.

beatitude (bee-**at**-i-tewd) *n.* blessedness. **the Beatitudes,** the declarations made by Christ in the Sermon on the Mount, beginning 'Blessed are . . .'.

Beaufort scale (**boh**-fert) a scale and description of wind velocity ranging from 0 (calm) to 12 (hurricane).

Beaujolais (**boh**-zhŏ-lay) *n.* a red or white burgundy wine from Beaujolais, France.

beaut *n.* (*slang*) a beauty.

beautician (bew-**tish**-ăn) *n.* a person whose job is to give beautifying treatments to the face or body.

beautiful *adj.* **1.** having beauty, giving pleasure to the senses or the mind. **2.** very satisfactory. **beautifully** *adv.*

beautify *v.* (beautified, beautifying) to make beautiful. **beautification** *n.*

beauty *n.* **1.** a combination of qualities that give pleasure to the sight or other senses or to the mind. **2.** a person or thing having this, a beautiful woman. **3.** a fine specimen, *here's a beauty.* **4.** a beautiful feature; *that's the beauty of it,* the point that gives satisfaction. □ **beauty parlour,** a beauty salon. **beauty queen,** a woman judged to be the most beautiful in a competition. **beauty salon,** an establishment for giving beautifying treatments to the face, body, etc. **beauty sleep,** sleep that is said to make or keep a person beautiful. **beauty spot,** a place with beautiful scenery; a birthmark or artificial patch on the face, said to heighten beauty.

beaver *n.* **1.** a soft-furred animal with strong teeth that lives both on land and in water. **2.** its brown fur. —*v.* to work hard, *beavering away at it.*

bebop *n.* a kind of jazz music.

becalmed (bi-**kahmd**) *adj.* unable to move because there is no wind.

became *see* become.

because *conj.* for the reason that, *did it because I was asked.* —*adv.* **because of,** by reason of, on account of, *because of his age.*

béchamel sauce (**besh**-ă-mel) a kind of white sauce.

beck [1] *n.* (*N. England*) a brook, a mountain stream.

beck [2] *n.* (*old use*) a gesture. **at someone's beck and call,** always ready and waiting to obey his orders.

beckon *v.* (beckoned, beckoning) to signal or summon by a gesture.

become *v.* (became, become, becoming) **1.** to come or grow to be, to begin to be, *he became a doctor; ask what has become of it,* ask what happened to it, or where it is. **2.** to suit, to be becoming to.

becoming *adj.* giving a pleasing appearance or effect, suitable. **becomingly** *adv.*

bed *n.* **1.** a thing to sleep or rest on, a piece of furniture with a mattress and coverings. **2.** a mattress, *a feather bed.* **3.** the use of a bed, being in bed, *price includes bed and breakfast; a quick drink and then bed; go to bed,* retire there to sleep; *go to bed with a person,* have sexual intercourse. **4.** a flat base on which something rests, a foundation. **5.** the bottom of the sea or a river etc. **6.** a layer, *a bed of clay.* **7.** a garden plot for plants. —**bed** *v.* (bedded, bedding) **1.** to provide with a place to sleep, to put to bed. **2.** to place or fix in a foundation, *the bricks are bedded in concrete.* **3.** to plant in a garden bed, *he was bedding out seedlings.* □ **no bed of roses,** not a pleasant or easy situation.

bedbug *n.* a bug infesting beds.

bedclothes *pl. n.* sheets, pillows, blankets, etc.

bedding *n.* mattresses and bedclothes.

bedfellow *n.* **1.** a person who shares one's bed. **2.** an associate; *it makes strange bedfellows,* obliges unlikely people to associate together.

Bedfordshire a county of England.

bedlam (**bed**-lăm) *n.* uproar.

Bedouin (**bed**-oo-in) *n.* (*pl.* Bedouin) a member of an Arab people living in tents in the desert.

bedpan *n.* a pan for use as a lavatory by a person confined to bed.

bedpost *n.* one of the upright supports of a bedstead.

bedraggled (bi-**drag**-ŭld) *adj.* hanging in a limp untidy way, especially when wet.

bedridden *n.* confined to bed through illness or weakness, especially permanently.

bedrock *n.* **1.** solid rock beneath loose soil. **2.** basic facts or principles.

bedroom *n.* a room for sleeping in.

Beds. *abbrev.* Bedfordshire.

bedside *n.* a position by a bed; *a bedside table,* one for placing by a bed.

bed-sitting-room *n.* a room used for both living and sleeping in. **bed-sit, bed-sitter** *ns.* (*informal*) a bed-sitting-room.

bedsore *n.* a sore developed by lying in bed for a long time.

bedspread *n.* a covering spread over a bed during the day.

bedstead *n.* a wooden or metal framework supporting the springs and mattress of a bed.

bedtime *n.* the hour for going to bed.

bee *n.* a four-winged stinging insect that produces wax and honey after gathering nectar from flowers. **have a bee in one's bonnet,** to have a particular idea that occupies one's thoughts continually. **make a bee-line for,** to go straight or rapidly towards.

Beeb *n.* (*informal*) the BBC.

beech *n.* **1.** a kind of tree with smooth bark and glossy leaves. **2.** its wood.

beef *n.* **1.** the flesh of ox, bull, or cow used as meat. **2.** muscular strength, brawn. **3.** (*slang*) a grumble —*v.* (*slang*) to grumble. □ **beef tea,** the juice from stewed beef, for invalids.

beefburger *n.* a flat round cake of minced beef, served fried.

beefeater *n.* a warder in the Tower of London, or a member of the Yeomen of the Guard, wearing Tudor dress as uniform.

beefsteak *n.* a slice of beef for grilling or frying.

beefy *adj.* (beefier, beefiest) having a solid muscular body. **beefiness** *n.*

beehive *n.* a hive.

beer *n.* an alcoholic drink made from malt and flavoured with hops.

beery *adj.* like beer, smelling of beer.

beeswax *n.* a yellowish substance secreted by bees, used for polishing wood.

beet *n.* a plant with a fleshy root used as a vegetable or for making sugar.

beetle *n.* an insect with hard wing-covers.

beetling *adj.* overhanging, projecting, *beetling brows.*

beetroot *n.* the fleshy root of beet, used as a vegetable.

befall (bi-**fawl**) *v.* (befell, befallen, befalling) (*formal*) to happen, to happen to.

befit (bi-**fit**) *v.* (befitted, befitting) to be right and suitable for.

before *adv., prep.,* & *conj.* **1.** at an earlier time, earlier than. **2.** ahead, ahead of, in front of; *they sailed before the wind,* under its impulse, with the wind behind them; *appeared before the magistrates,* in their presence for judgement. **3.** rather than, in preference to, *death before dishonour!* □ **before Christ,** before the birth of Christ.

beforehand *adv.* in advance, in readiness.

befriend *v.* to act as a friend to, to be kind and helpful to.

beg *v.* (begged, begging) **1.** to ask for as charity or as a gift, to obtain a living in this way. **2.** to request earnestly or humbly. **3.** to ask for formally, *I beg your pardon; beg to differ,* take the liberty of disagreeing. **4.** (of a dog) to sit up expectantly, as it has been trained, with forepaws off the ground. □ **beg off,** to ask to be excused from doing something; *beg a person off,* get him excused from a punishment. **beg the question,** to use circular reasoning (*see* circular sense 3). **go begging,** (of things) to be available but unwanted.

began *see* begin.

beget (bi-**get**) *v.* (begot, begotten, begetting) **1.** to be the father of. **2.** to give rise to, *war begets misery and ruin.*

beggar *n.* **1.** a person who lives by begging, a very poor person. **2.** (*informal*) a person, *you lucky beggar!* —**beggar** *v.* **1.** to reduce to poverty. **2.** to make seem poor or inadequate; *the scenery beggars description,* is so magnificent that any description is inadequate. —**beggary** *n.*

beggarly *adj.* mean and insufficient.

begin *v.* (began, begun, beginning) **1.** to perform the earliest or first part of some activity, to be the first to do something; *I can't begin to thank you,* cannot thank you enough. **2.** to come into existence, to arise. **3.** to have its first element or starting-point. □ **to begin with,** as the first thing.

beginner *n.* a person who is just beginning to learn a skill.

beginning *n.* **1.** the first part. **2.** the starting-point, the source or origin.

begone (bi-**gon**) *v.* to go away immediately, *begone dull care!*

begonia (bi-**goh**-niă) *n.* a garden plant with brightly coloured leaves and flowers.

begrudge *v.* to grudge.

beguile (bi-**gyl**) *v.* to deceive. **2.** to win the attention or interest of, to amuse. **beguilement** *n.*

begum (**bay**-gŭm) *n.* (in Pakistan and India) **1.** the title of a Muslim married woman, = Mrs. **2.** a Muslim woman of high rank.

behalf *n.* **on behalf of,** in aid or respect of; as the representative of, *speaking on behalf of his client.*

behave *v.* **1.** to act or react in some specified way. **2.** to function, *the car is behaving well.* **3.** to show good manners, *the child must learn to behave* or *to behave himself.* □ **well-behaved** *adj.* behaving well.

behaviour *n.* a way of behaving, treatment of others, manners. **behavioural** *adj.*

behead *v.* to cut the head from, to execute (a person) in this way.

behind *adv.* **1.** in or to the rear; *he was lagging behind,* did not keep up with the others; *stayed behind,* stayed after others had left. **2.** behindhand. —**behind** *prep.* **1.** in the rear of, on the further side of; *put the past behind you,* recognize that it is over and done with. **2.** causing or supporting; *ask what lies behind his refusal,* what causes it; *the man behind the project,* supporting or promoting it. **3.** having made less progress than, *some countries are behind others in development.* **4.** later than, *we are behind schedule; behind time,* unpunctual. □ **behind a person's back,** kept secret from him deceitfully. **behind the scenes,** backstage; hidden from public view or knowledge. **behind the times,** having out-of-date ideas or practices.

behindhand *adv.* & *adj.* **1.** in arrears. **2.** late, behind time, out of date.

behold *v.* (beheld, beholding) (*old use*) to see, to observe. **beholder** *n.*

beholden *adj.* owing thanks, *we don't want to be beholden to anybody.*

behove *v.* to be incumbent on, to befit.

behoove *v.* (*Amer.*) = behove.

beige (*pr.* bayzh) *n.* a light fawn colour.

Beijing (bay-**jing**) the capital of China (= Peking).

being *n.* **1.** existence; *come into being,* begin to exist; *the greatest army in being,* in existence. **2.** something that exists and has life, especially a person. **3.** *the Supreme Being,* God.

Beirut (bay-**root**) the capital of Lebanon.

belated (bi-**lay**-tid) *adj.* coming very late or too late. **belatedly** *adv.*

belch *v.* **1.** to send out wind from the stomach noisily through the mouth. **2.** to send out from an opening or funnel, to gush. —*n.* an act or sound of belching.

Belfast (bel-**fahst**) the capital of Northern Ireland.

belfry n. a bell tower, a space for bells in a tower.

Belgium a country in Europe. **Belgian** adj. & n.

Belgrade the capital of Yugoslavia.

belief n. 1. the feeling that something is real and true, trust, confidence. 2. something accepted as true, what one believes. 3. religion, something taught as part of this, *Christian beliefs.*

believable adj. able to be believed.

believe v. 1. to accept as true or as speaking or conveying truth. 2. to think, to suppose, *I believe it's raining.* □ **believe in,** to have faith in the existence of; to feel sure of the value or worth of.

believer n. a person who believes, one with religious faith.

Belisha beacon (bi-**lee**-shă) a beacon marking a pedestrian crossing.

belittle v. to imply that (a thing) is unimportant or of little value. **belittlement** n.

Belize (bĕl-**eez**) a country in Central America. **Belizian** (bĕl-**ee**-zhăn) adj. & n.

bell n. 1. a cup-shaped metal instrument that makes a ringing sound when struck 2. the sound of this, especially as a signal; *one* to *eight bells,* the strokes of a ship's bell, indicating the half hours of each four-hour watch; *eight bells,* 12, 4, or 8 o'clock. 3. a bell-shaped thing. □ **bell-bottomed** adj. widening from knee to ankle, *bell-bottomed trousers.* **bell-bottoms** pl. n. bell-bottomed trousers. **bell-push** n. a button pressed to operate an electric bell.

belle (*pr.* bel) n. a beautiful woman.

belligerent (bi-**lij**-er-ĕnt) adj. 1. waging a war, *the belligerent nations.* 2. aggressive, showing eagerness to fight, *a belligerent reply.* **belligerently** adv., **belligerence** n.

bellow n. 1. the loud deep sound made by a bull. 2. a deep shout. —v. to utter a bellow.

bellows pl. n. 1. an apparatus for driving air into or through something; *a pair of bellows,* two-handled bellows for blowing air into a fire. 2. a device or part that can be expanded or flattened in a series of folds.

belly n. 1. the abdomen. 2. the stomach. 3. a bulging or rounded part of something. —v. (bellied, bellying) to swell out, *the sails bellied out;* *wind bellied out the sails.* □ **belly-ache** n. pain in the belly, colic, (v.) (*slang*) to grumble. **belly-dance** n. an oriental dance by a woman, with erotic movement of the belly. **belly-dancer** n. one who performs this. **belly-flop** n. an

awkward dive in which the body hits the water almost horizontally. **belly-laugh** n. a deep loud laugh.

bellyful n. (*informal*) as much as one wants or rather more.

Belmopan (bel-moh-pan) the capital of Belize.

belong v. 1. to be rightly assigned as property or as a part or appendage or inhabitant etc., *the house belongs to me; that lid belongs to this jar; I belong to Glasgow.* 2. to be a member, *we belong to the club.* 3. to have a rightful or usual place, *the pans belong in the kitchen.* □ **belongings** pl. n. personal possessions.

Belorussian n. a native of Belorussia, a republic in western USSR. — adj. of Belorussia or its people.

beloved adj. (*pr.* bi-**luvd**) dearly loved, *she was beloved by all.* —adj. & n. (*pr.* bi-**luv**-id) darling, *my beloved wife.*

below adv. 1. at or to a lower position, downstream. 2. at the foot of a page, further on in a book or article, *see chapter 6 below.* —prep. 1. lower in position, amount, or rank etc. than. 2. downstream from, *the bridge is below the ford.*

belt n. 1. a strip of cloth or leather worn round the waist. 2. a continuous moving strap passing over pulleys and so driving machinery, *a fan-belt.* 3. a long narrow region or strip, *a belt of rain will move eastwards.* 4. (*slang*) a heavy blow. —**belt** v. 1. to put a belt round. 2. to attach with a belt. 3. to thrash with a belt, (*slang*) to hit. 4. (*slang*) to hurry, to rush. □ **belt out,** (*slang*) to sing or play loudly, *belting out pop songs.* **belt up,** (*informal*) to wear a seat-belt; (*slang*) to be quiet. **hit below the belt,** to give an unfair blow, to fight unfairly. **under one's belt,** (*informal*) eaten; obtained or achieved.

beluga (bi-**loo**-gă) n. 1. a large sturgeon. 2. caviare from this. 3. a white whale.

belvedere (**bel**-vi-deer) n. a raised turret or summer-house from which to view scenery.

bemused (bi-**mewzd**) adj. 1. bewildered. 2. lost in thought.

bench n. 1. a long seat of wood or stone. 2. a lawcourt; *the Queen's Bench,* a division of the High Court. 3. *the bench,* the judges or magistrates hearing a case. 4. a long working-table in certain trades or in a laboratory.

bend[1] v. (bent, bending) 1. to force out of straightness, to make curved or angular. 2. to become curved or angular. 3. to turn downwards, to stoop. 4. to turn in a new direction, *they bent their steps homeward; bend your mind to this,* give it your attention. **5.** (*slang*) to corrupt, to make dishonest. —**bend** *n.* **1.** a curve or turn. **2.** (*slang*) a spree. □ **bend the rules**, to interpret them loosely to suit oneself. **catch a person bending**, (*informal*) to catch him at a disadvantage, **on bended knees**, kneeling in prayer. **round the bend**, (*slang*) crazy.

bend² *n.* any of various knots. —*v.* (bent, bending) to attach (a rope or sail etc.) with a knot.

bender *n.* (*slang*) a spree.

beneath *adv.* & *prep.* **1.** below, under, underneath. **2.** not worthy of, not befitting; *beneath contempt*, not even worth despising.

Benedictine *n.* **1.** (*pr.* ben-i-**dik**-tin) a monk or nun following the monastic rule of St. Benedict. **2.** (*pr.* ben-i-**dik**-teen) a liqueur originally made by monks of this order.

benediction (ben-i-**dik**-shŏn) *n.* a spoken blessing.

benefactor *n.* a person who gives financial or other help. **benefactress** *n.*

benefice (**ben**-i-fiss) *n.* a position that provides a clergyman with a livelihood, charge of a parish.

beneficial *adj.* having a helpful or useful effect. **beneficially** *adv.*

beneficiary (ben-i-**fish**-er-i) *n.* a person who receives a benefit, one who is left a legacy under someone's will.

benefit *n.* **1.** something helpful, favourable, or profitable. **2.** an allowance of money etc. to which a person is entitled from an insurance policy or government funds. **3.** a performance or game held in order to raise money for a particular player, *a benefit match.* —**benefit** *v.* (benefited, benefiting) **1.** to do good to. **2.** to receive benefit. □ **benefit of the doubt**, the assumption that a person is innocent (or right) rather than guilty (or wrong) when nothing can be fully proved either way.

Benelux (**ben**-i-luks) Belgium, the Netherlands, and Luxemburg, considered as a group.

benevolent *adj.* **1.** wishing to do good to others, kindly and helpful. **2.** charitable, *a benevolent fund.* **benevolently** *adv.*, **benevolence** *n.*

Bengal (ben-**gawl**) a former province of north-east India, now divided into West Bengal (a State of India) and Bangladesh. **Bengali** *adj.* & *n.* (*pl.* Bengalis)

benign (bi-**nyn**) *adj.* **1.** kindly. **2.** mild and gentle in its effect! *a benign tumour*, one that is not malignant. **benignly** *adv.*

benignant (bi-**nig**-nănt) *adj.* kindly.

benignity (bi-**nig**-niti) *n.* kindliness.

Benin (ben-**een**) a country in West Africa.

bent *see* bend¹. —*n.* a natural skill or liking, *she has a bent for needlework.* —*adj.* (*slang*) dishonest. □ **bent on**, determined or seeking to do something, *bent on mischief.*

bentwood *n.* wood that has been artificially bent into a permanent curve, used for making chairs etc.

benzene (**ben**-zeen) *n.* a colourless liquid obtained from petroleum and coal-tar, used as a solvent, as fuel, and in the manufacture of plastics.

benzine (**ben**-zeen) *n.* a colourless liquid mixture of hydrocarbons obtained from petroleum and used as a solvent in dry-cleaning.

bequeath (bi-**kwee**th) *v.* to leave as a legacy.

bequest (bi-**kwest**) *n.* a legacy.

berate (bi-**rayt**) *v.* to scold.

berberis (**ber**-ber-iss) *n.* a prickly shrub with yellow flowers and red berries.

bereave *v.* to deprive, especially of a relative, by death; *the bereaved husband*, the man whose wife died. **bereavement** *n.*

bereft *adj.* deprived; *bereft of reason*, driven mad.

beret (**bair**-ay) *n.* a round flat cap with no peak.

bergamot (**ber**-gă-mot) *n.* a fragrant herb.

beriberi (*pr. as* berry-berry) *n.* a disease affecting the nervous system, caused by lack of vitamin B.

berk *n.* (*slang*) a stupid person.

Berks. *abbrev.* Berkshire.

Berkshire (**bark**-sher) a county of England.

Berlin the former German capital city.

Bermuda a group of islands in the West Atlantic. **Bermudian** *adj.*

Berne (*pr.* bern) the capital of Switzerland.

berry *n.* a small round juicy stoneless fruit.

berserk (ber-**zerk**) *adj.* frenzied. **go berserk**, to go into an uncontrollable and destructive rage.

berth *n.* **1.** a bunk or sleeping-place in a ship or train. **2.** a place for a ship to swing at anchor or tie up at a wharf. **3.** (*slang*) a job, employment. —*v.* to moor at a berth. □ **give a wide berth to**, to keep at a safe distance from.

beryl *n.* a transparent usually green precious stone.

beseech *v.* (besought, beseeching) to implore.

beset *v.* (beset, besetting) to hem in, to surround; *the temptations that beset people*, that face them on all sides. **besetting** *adj.* habitually affecting or troubling a person, *laziness is his besetting sin.*

beside *prep.* **1.** at the side of, close to. **2.** compared with, *his work looks poor beside yours.* **3.** wide of, having nothing to do with, *that's beside the point.* □ **be beside oneself**, to be at the end of one's self-control, *he was beside himself with rage.*

besides *prep.* in addition to, other than, *he has no income besides his pension.* —*adv.* also.

besiege *v.* **1.** to lay siege to. **2.** to crowd round with requests or questions. **besieger** *n.*

besom (**bee**-zŏm) *n.* a broom made by tying a bundle of twigs to a long handle.

besotted (bi-**sot**-id) *adj.* mentally stupefied, infatuated.

besought *see* beseech.

bespeak *v.* (bespoke, bespoken, bespeaking) **1.** to engage beforehand. **2.** to order (goods). **3.** to be evidence of.

bespoke *see* bespeak. —*adj.* (of clothes) made to order, (of a tailor etc.) making such clothes.

best *adj.* of the most excellent kind. —*adv.* **1.** in the best manner, to the greatest degree. **2.** most usefully; *we had best go*, would find it wisest to go. —*best n.* **1.** that which is best, the chief merit or advantage, *it brings out the best in us*; *dressed in his best*, in his best clothes. **2.** victory in a fight or argument; *we got the best of it*, son; *the best of three games*, the winning of two out of three; *give a person best*, admit that he has won. —*v.* to defeat, to outdo, to outwit. □ **as best one can**, as well as one is able under the circumstances. **at best**, taking the most hopeful view. **best end**, the rib end of lamb's neck for cooking, with more meat than scrag end. **best man**, the bridegroom's chief attendant at a wedding. **best part of**, most of. **best seller**, a book that sells in very large numbers. **make the best of**, to be as contented as possible with; to do what one can with. **put one's best foot forward**, to walk or work as fast as one can. **six of the best**, a vigorous caning. **to the best of one's ability**, using all one's ability. **to the best of one's knowledge**, so far as one knows. **with the best of them**, as well as anyone.

bestial (**best**-iăl) *adj.* of or like a beast, savage. **bestiality** (best-i-**al**-iti) *n.*

bestiary (**best**-i-er-i) *n.* a medieval collection of descriptions of animals, including legends and fables.

bestow *v.* to present as a gift. **bestowal** *n.*

bestride *v.* (bestrode, bestridden, bestriding) to sit or stand astride over.

bet *n.* **1.** an agreement pledging something that will be forfeited if one's forecast of some event proves to have been wrong. **2.** the money etc. pledged. **3.** a person or thing considered likely to be successful in something; *your best bet is to call tomorrow*, this is your best course of action. **4.** (*informal*) a prediction, *my bet is that he won't come.* —**bet** *v.* (bet *or* betted, betting) **1.** to make a bet, to pledge in a bet. **2.** (*informal*) to predict, to think most likely.

betake *v.* (betook, betaken, betaking) **betake oneself**, to go.

bête noire (bayt **nwahr**) a thing or person that one dislikes very much.

betide *v.* to happen to; *woe betide him*, trouble will come to him.

betray *v.* **1.** to give up or reveal disloyally to an enemy. **2.** to be disloyal to. **3.** to show unintentionally. **betrayal** *n.*, **betrayer** *n.*

betroth (bi-**troh**th) *v.* (*formal*) to engage with a promise to marry. **betrothal** *n.*

better[1] *adj.* **1.** of a more excellent kind; *one's better feelings*, more charitable feelings, conscience; *it's against my better judgement*, I feel it may be unwise. **2.** partly or fully recovered from an illness. —*adv.* in a better manner, to a better degree, more usefully; *we had better go*, would find it wiser to go. —*n.* that which is better. —*v.* to improve, to do better than. □ **better half**, (*humorous*) one's wife. **better oneself**, to get a better social position or status. **better part**, more than half. **betters** *pl. n.* people who are of higher status than oneself. **get the better of**, to overcome. **go one better**, to do better than someone else's effort.

better[2] *n.* a person who bets.

betterment *n.* making or becoming better.

betting-shop *n.* a bookmaker's office.

between *prep. & adv.* **1.** in the space bounded by two or more points, lines, or objects. **2.** intermediate to, especially in time or quantity or quality etc. **3.** separating, *the difference between right and wrong.* **4.** to and from, *liner sails between Naples and Haifa.* **5.** connecting, *the great love between them.* **6.** shared by, *divide the money between you; this is between you and me* or *between ourselves*, to be kept secret. (¶The phrase *between you and I* is incorrect.) **7.** taking one and rejecting the other, *choose between them.*

betwixt *prep. & adv.* (*old use*) between. **betwixt and between**, midway.

bevel (**bev**-ĕl) *n.* **1.** a sloping edge or surface. **2.** a tool for making such slopes. —*v.* (bevelled, bevelling) to give a sloping edge to.

beverage (bev-er-ij) *n.* any drink.

bevy (bev-i) *n.* a company, a large group.

beware *v.* to be on one's guard.

bewilder *v.* to puzzle, to confuse, *the questions bewildered him.* **bewilderment** *n.*

bewitch *v.* **1.** to put under a magic spell. **2.** to delight very much.

beyond *adv.* & *prep.* **1.** at or to the further side of, further on. **2.** outside, outside the range of, *this is beyond repair; it is beyond me,* too difficult for me to do or to understand; *he lives beyond his income,* spends more than he earns. **3.** besides, except. □ **beyond doubt,** quite certain, unquestionably.

b.f. *abbrev.* bloody fool.

b/f *abbrev.* brought forward.

Bhutan (boo-tahn) a country between India and Tibet. **Bhutanese** *adj.* & *n.* (*pl.* Bhutanese)

biannual *adj.* appearing or happening twice a year. **biannually** *adv.*

bias *n.* **1.** an opinion or feeling or influence that strongly favours one side in an argument or one item in a group or series. **2.** the slanting direction across threads of woven material; *skirt is cut on the bias,* cut with the threads running slantwise across the up-and-down line of the garment. **3.** the tendency of a ball in the game of bowls to swerve because of the way it is weighted. —*v.* (biased, biasing) to give a bias to, to influence. □ **bias binding,** a strip of fabric cut on the bias and used to bind edges.

bib *n.* **1.** a cloth or plastic covering put under a young child's chin to protect the front of its clothes, especially while it is feeding. **2.** the front part of an apron, above the waist. □ **best bib and tucker,** best clothes.

Bible *n.* **1.** the Christian scriptures. **2.** the Jewish scriptures. **3.** a copy of either of these. **4.** a book regarded as authoritative.

biblical *adj.* of or in the Bible.

bibliography (bibli-og-răfi) *n.* **1.** a list of books or articles about a particular subject or by a particular author. **2.** the study of the history of books and their production. **bibliographical** (bibli-ŏ-graf-ikăl) *adj.*

bicarbonate *n.* a kind of carbonate.

bicentenary (by-sen-teen-er-i) *n.* a 200th anniversary.

bicentennial (by-sen-ten-iăl) *adj.* of a bicentenary. —*n.* a bicentenary.

biceps (by-seps) *n.* the large muscle at the front of the upper arm, which bends the elbow.

bicker *v.* to quarrel constantly about unimportant things.

bicuspid (by-kusp-id) *adj.* having two cusps. —*n.* a bicuspid tooth.

bicycle *n.* a two-wheeled vehicle driven by pedals. —*v.* to ride on a bicycle. —**bicyclist** *n.* □ **bicycle clip,** one of a pair of clips for securing the trousers at the ankles while cycling.

bid ¹ *n.* **1.** an offer of a price in order to buy something, especially at an auction. **2.** a statement of the number of tricks a player proposes to win in a card-game. **3.** an effort to obtain something, *made a bid for popular support.* —*v.* (bid, bidding) to make a bid. —**bidder** *n.*

bid ² *v.* (bid, *old use* bade (*pr.* bad); bidden, bidding) **1.** to command, *do as you are bid* or *bidden.* **2.** to say as a greeting or farewell, *bidding them good night.*

biddable *adj.* willing to obey.

bidding *n.* a command. **do a person's bidding,** to do what he commands.

bide *v.* to wait. **bide one's time,** to wait for a good opportunity, **let it bide,** (*informal*) leave it without further action.

bidet (bee-day) *n.* a low narrow washing-basin that one can sit astride for washing the genital and anal regions.

biennial (by-en-iăl) *adj.* **1.** lasting or living for two years. **2.** happening every second year. —*n.* a plant that lives for two years, flowering and dying in the second. —**biennially** *adv.*

bier *n.* a movable stand on which a coffin or a dead body is placed before burial.

biff *v.* (*slang*) to hit. —*n.* (*slang*) a blow.

bifocals (by-foh-kălz) *pl. n.* spectacles with each lens made in two sections, the upper part for looking at distant objects and the lower part for reading and other close work.

big *adj.* (bigger, biggest) **1.** large in size or amount or intensity. **2.** more grown up, elder, *my big sister.* **3.** important, *the big match.* **4.** boastful, pretentious, *big talk.* **5.** (*slang*) generous, *that's big of you.* —**big** *adv.* (*Amer. slang*) **1.** on a large scale; *think big,* plan ambitiously. **2.** successfully, *it went over big.* □ **Big Ben,** the great bell, clock, and tower of the Houses of Parliament. **Big Brother,** an all-powerful dictator who exercises close supervision and control of everything while pretending to be kindly. **big business,** commerce on a large financial scale. **big deal!** (*Amer. slang*) I am not impressed. **big dipper,** a fairground switchback. **big end,** the end of a connecting-rod that encircles the crankshaft. **big game,** the larger animals hunted for sport. **big gun,** (*slang*) an important and powerful person. **big head,** (*slang*) a conceited person. **big-hearted** *adj.* very kind, generous. **big money**, a large amount of money. **big pot**, *(slang)* an important person. **big stick**, threat of force. **big-time** *adj. (slang)* of the highest or most important level. **big toe**, the first and largest toe. **big top**, the main tent at a circus. **have big ideas**, to be ambitious, **too big for one's boots**, *(slang)* conceited.

bigamy (**big**-ămi) *n.* the crime of going through a form of marriage while one's previous marriage is still valid. **bigamous** *adj.*, **bigamously** *adv.* ☐ **bigamist** *n.* a person guilty of bigamy.

bight (*rhymes with* kite) *n.* **1.** a long inward curve in a coast, *the Great Australian Bight*. **2.** a loop of rope.

bigot (**big**-ŏt) *n.* a person who holds an opinion or belief obstinately and is intolerant towards those who do not. **bigoted** *adj.* narrow-minded and intolerant. **bigotry** *n.* being a bigot or bigoted.

bigwig *n.* *(informal)* an important person.

bike *n.* *(informal)* a bicycle or motor cycle. —*v.* *(informal)* to travel on a bike.

bikini *n.* a woman's two-piece beach garment consisting of a very scanty bra and briefs. ¶ Named after *Bikini*, an atoll in the West Pacific, where an atomic bomb was tested in 1946.

bilateral (by-**lat**-er-ăl) *adj.* of two sides, having two sides; *a bilateral agreement*, made between two persons or groups. **bilaterally** *adv.*

bilberry *n.* the small round dark blue fruit of a shrub growing on heaths.

bile *n.* a bitter yellowish liquid produced by the liver and stored in the gall-bladder, aiding digestion of fats.

bilge (*pr.* bilj) *n.* **1.** a ship's bottom, inside and outside. **2.** the water that collects there. **3.** *(slang)* worthless ideas or talk.

bilingual (by-**ling**-wăl) *adj.* **1.** written in two languages. **2.** able to speak two languages.

bilious (**bil**-yŭs) *adj.* **1.** of biliousness, suffering from this. **2.** of a sickly yellowish colour or shade, *a bilious green*. ☐ **biliousness** *n.* sickness assumed to be caused by too much bile.

bilk *v.* to escape paying one's debts to, to defraud.

bill[1] *n.* **1.** a written statement of charges for goods supplied or services rendered. **2.** a poster or placard. **3.** a programme of entertainment. **4.** the draft of a proposed law, to be discussed by a parliament (and called an *Act* when passed). **4.** *(Amer.)* a banknote, *a ten-dollar bill*. **5.** a certificate; *a clean bill of health*, a declaration that there is no disease or defect. —**bill** *v.* **1.** to announce in a bill or poster, *Olivier was billed to appear as Hamlet*. **2.** to send a note of charges to, *we will bill you for these goods*. ☐ **bill of exchange**, a written order to pay a specified sum of money on a particular date to a named person or to the bearer. **bill of fare**, a menu. **bill of lading**, a list giving details of a ship's cargo. **fill the bill**, to be or do what is required.

bill[2] *n.* a bird's beak. —*v.* (of doves) to stroke each other with their bills.

billet *n.* **1.** a lodging for troops or evacuees, especially in a private house. **2.** *(informal)* a position, a job. —*v.* (billeted, billeting) to place in a billet.

billet-doux (bil-ay-**doo**) *n.* (*pl.* billets-doux, *pr.* bil-ay-**doo**) a love-letter.

billhook *n.* a long-handled tool with a curved blade for lopping trees.

billiards *n.* a game played with cues and 3 balls on a cloth-covered table. **bar billiards**, a form of billiards in which balls are struck into holes on a table.

billion *n.* **1.** a million million. **2.** a thousand million. **billionth** *adj. & n.* ¶ The sense 'a thousand million' was originally used in the USA but is now common in Britain and elsewhere.

billow *n.* a great wave. —*v.* to rise or roll like waves, *smoke billowed forth*.

billy *n.* a tin can or enamelled container with a lid, used by campers etc. as a kettle or cooking-pot.

billy-goat *n.* a male goat.

billy-o *n.* *(informal)* **like billy-o**, vigorously.

bimonthly *adj.* **1.** happening every second month. **2.** happening twice a month.

bin *n.* **1.** a large rigid container or enclosed space, usually with a lid, used for storing coal, grain, flour, etc. **2.** a receptacle for rubbish or litter.

binary (**by**-ner-i) *adj.* of a pair or pairs. **binary digit** *or* **number**, either of the two digits, 0 and 1, used in the binary scale. **binary scale**, a system of numbers using only the two digits 0 and 1. **binary star**, two stars that revolve round each other.

bind *v.* (bound, binding) **1.** to tie or fasten, to tie up. **2.** to hold together, to unite, *bound by ties of friendship*. **3.** to encircle with a strip or band of material; *bind up the wound*, bandage it. **4.** to cover the edge of (a thing) in order to strengthen it or as a decoration. **5.** to fasten the pages of (a book) into a cover. **6.** to stick together in a solid mass, *bind the mixture with egg-yolk*. **7.** to place under an obligation or a legal agreement; *he was bound over to keep the peace*, was ordered to do so by a judge. **8.** *(slang)* to grumble. **9.** *(slang)* to bore, to weary. —*n.* *(slang)* a bore, a nuisance.

binder *n*. **1**. a person or thing that binds. **2**. a bookbinder. **3**. a machine that binds harvested corn into sheaves or straw into bales. **4**. a loose cover for papers.

bindery *n*. a workshop where books are bound.

binding *n*. **1**. fabric used for binding edges. **2**. the strong covering holding the leaves of a book together. —*adj*. making a legal obligation, *the agreement is binding on both parties.*

bindweed *n*. wild convolvulus.

bine (*rhymes with* mine) *n*. the flexible stem of a climbing plant, especially of hops.

binge (*pr.* binj) *n*. (*slang*) a spree, eating and drinking and making merry.

bingo *n*. a gambling game played with cards on which numbered squares are covered as the numbers are called at random. —*int*. an exclamation at a sudden action or event.

binnacle (**bin**-ă-kŭl) *n*. a non-magnetic stand for a ship's compass.

binoculars *pl. n*. an instrument with lenses for both eyes, making distant objects seem nearer.

biochemistry (by-oh-**kem**-istri) *n*. chemistry of living organisms. **biochemical** *adj.*, **biochemist** *n*.

biodegradable (by-oh-di-**gray**-dă-bŭl) *adj*. able to be broken down by bacteria in the environment, *some plastics are not biodegradable.*

biography (by-**og**-răfi) *n*. the story of a person's life written by someone other than himself. **biographical** *adj*. ☐ **biographer** *n*. one who writes a biography.

biology (by-**ol**-ŏji) *n*. the scientific study of the life and structure of living things. **biological** *adj.*, **biologically** *adv*. ☐ **biological warfare**, the deliberate use of organisms to spread disease amongst an enemy. **biologist** *n*. an expert in biology.

bionic (by-**on**-ik) *adj*. **1**. of bionics. **2**. (of a person or his faculties) operated by electronic means, not naturally. ☐ **bionics** *n*. the study of mechanical systems that function like parts of living beings.

biopsy (**by**-op-si) *n*. examination of tissue cut from a living body.

biorhythm (**by**-ŏ-ri*th*m) *n*. any of the recurring cycles of physical, emotional, and intellectual activity said to occur in people's lives.

bipartisan (by-parti-**zan**) *adj*. of or involving two political or other parties.

bipartite (by-**par**-tyt) *adj*. having two parts, shared by or involving two groups.

biped (**by**-ped) *n*. a two-footed animal.

biplane (**by**-playn) *n*. an old type of aero-plane with two sets of wings, one above the other.

birch *n*. **1**. a deciduous tree with smooth bark and slender branches. **2**. its wood. **3**. a bundle of birch twigs used for flogging delinquents. —*v*. to flog with a birch.

bird *n*. **1**. a feathered animal with two wings and two legs. **2**. (*informal*) a person, *he's a cunning old bird.* **3**. (*slang*) a young woman. **3**. (*slang*) a prison sentence. ☐ **bird of paradise**, a New Guinea bird with brightly-coloured plumage. **bird's-eye view**, a general view from above. **bird-table** *n*. a platform on which food for birds is placed. **bird-watcher** *n*. one who studies the habits of birds in their natural surroundings. **get the bird**, (*slang*) to be hissed and booed, to be rejected. **strictly for the birds**, trivial, unimportant, to be regarded with contempt.

birdie *n*. **1**. (*informal*) a little bird. **2**. a score of one stroke under par for a hole at golf.

birdseed *n*. special seed used as food for caged birds.

biretta (bir-et-ă) *n*. a square cap worn by Roman Catholic and some Anglican clergymen.

Biro *n*. (*trade mark*) a ball-point pen.

birth *n*. **1**. the emergence of young from the mother's body. **2**. origin, parentage, *he is of noble birth.* ☐ **birth certificate**, an official document giving the date and place of a person's birth. **birth-control** *n*. prevention of unwanted pregnancy. **birth rate**, the number of births in one year for every 1000 persons. **give birth to**, to produce as young from the body.

birthday *n*. an anniversary of the day of one's birth. **birthday honours**, titles and other awards given on the sovereign's official birthday. **birthday suit**, a state of nakedness as at birth.

birthmark *n*. an unusual coloured mark on a person's skin at birth.

birthplace *n*. the house or district where one was born.

birthright *n*. a privilege or property to which a person has a right through being born into a particular family (especially as the eldest son) or country.

biscuit (**bis**-kit) *n*. **1**. a small flat thin piece of pastry baked crisp. **2**. (*Amer.*) a soft scone-like cake. **3**. light-brown.

bisect (by-**sekt**) *v*. to divide into two equal parts. **bisection** *n.*, **bisector** *n*.

bisexual (by-**seks**-yoo-ăl) *adj*. **1**. of two sexes. **2**. having both male and female sexual organs in one individual. **3**. sexually attracted by members of both sexes. **bisexuality** *n*.

bishop *n*. **1**. a clergyman of high rank with

authority over the work of the Church in a city or district (his *diocese*). **2.** a chess piece shaped like a mitre. □ **bishop sleeves,** long full sleeves gathered at the wrist.

bishopric *n.* the office or diocese of a bishop.

bismuth (**biz**-mŭth) *n.* **1.** a greyish-white metal used in alloys. **2.** a compound of this used in medicines.

bison (**by**-sŏn) *n.* (*pl.* **bison**) **1.** a wild ox of Europe. **2.** a wild ox of America (also called *buffalo*).

bistro (**bee**-stroh) *n.* a small bar or restaurant in Europe.

bit [1] *n.* **1.** a small piece or quantity or portion of anything; *I'm a bit puzzled,* slightly puzzled; *it's a bit of a nuisance,* rather a nuisance; *it takes a bit of doing,* is quite difficult. **2.** a short time or distance, *wait a bit.* □ **bit by bit,** gradually. **bit part,** (*informal*) a small part in a play or film. **bits and pieces,** odds and ends. **do one's bit,** (*informal*) to do one's due share.

bit [2] *n.* **1.** a metal bar forming the mouthpiece of a bridle. **2.** the part of a tool that cuts or grips when twisted, the boring-piece of a drill. □ **take the bit between one's teeth,** to get out of control.

bit [3] *n.* (in computers) a unit of information expressed as a choice between two possibilities. ¶ From *bi*nary dig*it*.

bit [4] *see* bite.

bitch *n.* **1.** a female dog, fox, or wolf. **2.** (*informal*) a spiteful woman. **3.** (*informal*) an unpleasant or difficult thing. — *v.* (*informal*) to speak spitefully, to grumble sourly. —**bitchy** *adj.,* **bitchiness** *n.*

bite *v.* (bit, bitten, biting) **1.** to cut into or nip with the teeth; *this dog bites,* is in the habit of biting people. **2.** (of an insect) to sting, (of a snake) to pierce with its fangs. **3.** to accept bait, *the fish are biting.* **4.** to grip or act effectively, *wheels can't bite on a slippery surface.* —**bite** *n.* **1.** an act of biting. **2.** a wound made by this. **3.** a mouthful cut off by biting. **4.** food to eat, a small meal. **5.** the taking of bait by a fish. **6.** a firm grip or hold, *this drill has no bite.* **7.** the way the teeth close in biting. — **biter** *n.* □ **bite a person's head off,** to reply angrily. **bite off more than one can chew,** to attempt more than one can manage. **bite the dust,** to fall wounded and die. **the biter bit,** the person who intended to cheat or harm someone was cheated or harmed himself. **what's biting you?,** (*informal*) what is worrying you?

biting *adj.* **1.** causing a smarting pain, *a biting wind.* **2.** (of remarks) sharp and critical.

bitten *see* bite.

bitter *adj.* **1.** tasting sharp like quinine or aspirin, not sweet; *bitter beer,* strongly flavoured with hops, not mild. **2.** unwelcome to the mind, causing sorrow. **3.** showing or feeling or caused by mental pain or resentment, *bitter remarks.* **4.** piercingly cold, *a bitter wind.* —*n.* bitter beer. —**bitterly** *adv.,* **bitterness** *n.* □ **bitters** *pl. n.* alcoholic liquor flavoured with bitter herbs to give a stimulating taste. **bitter-sweet** *adj.* sweet but with a bitter taste at the end; pleasant but with a mixture of something unpleasant. **to the bitter end,** until all that is possible has been done.

bittern *n.* a marsh bird related to the heron, especially the kind known for the male's booming note.

bitty *adv.* made up of unrelated bits.

bitumen (**bit**-yoo-měn) *n.* a black sticky substance obtained from petroleum, used for covering roads etc. **bituminous** (bit-**yoo**-min-ŭs) *adj.*

bivalve (**by**-valv) *n.* a shellfish with a hinged double shell.

bivouac (**biv**-oo-ak) *n.* a temporary camp without tents or other cover. —*v.* (bivouacked, bivouacking) to camp in a bivouac.

bi-weekly *adj.* **1.** happening every second week. **2.** happening twice a week.

biz *n.* (*informal*) business.

bizarre (biz-**ar**) *adj.* strikingly odd in appearance or effect.

blab *v.* (blabbed, blabbing) to talk indiscreetly, to let out a secret.

black *adj.* **1.** of the very darkest colour, like coal or soot. **2.** having a black skin. **3.** *Black,* of Negroes. **4.** soiled with dirt. **5.** dismal, sullen, hostile; *things look black,* not hopeful; *a black day,* disastrous. **6.** evil, wicked. **7.** not to be handled by trade unionists while others are on strike, *declared the cargo black.* —**black** *n.* **1.** black colour. **2.** a black substance or material, black clothes. **3.** the black ball in snooker etc. **4.** the black men in chess etc., the player using these. **5.** the credit side of an account; *in the black,* having a credit balance. **6.** *Black,* a Negro. —**black** *v.* **1.** to make black. **2.** to polish with blacking. **3.** to declare goods or work to be 'black'. —**blackly** *adv.,* **blackness** *n.* □ **black-beetle** *n.* a cockroach. **black box,** an electronic device in an aircraft recording information about its flight. **black coffee,** coffee without milk. **black comedy,** comedy presenting a tragic theme or situation in comic terms. **Black Country,** the smoky industrial area in the Midlands. **black economy,** an unofficial system of employing and paying people without observing legal requirements such as payment of income tax and National Insurance contributions. **black eye,** an eye with the skin round it darkened by a bruise. **Black Friars,** Dominicans. **black ice,** hard thin transparent ice on roads. **black list,** a list of persons who are disapproved of. **blacklist** v. to put into a black list. **black magic,** magic involving the invocation of devils. **Black Maria,** a secure van for taking prisoners to and from prison or into custody. **black mark,** a mark of disapproval placed against a person's name. **black market,** the illegal buying and selling of goods or currencies. **black marketeer,** one who trades in the black market. **black out,** to cover windows etc. so that no light can penetrate; to suffer temporary loss of consciousness or sight or memory. **blackout** n. a period of darkness when no light must be shown; the extinguishing of all lights; temporary loss of consciousness or sight or memory; prevention of the release of information. **Black Power,** a militant movement supporting civil rights of Blacks. **black pudding,** a large dark sausage containing blood, suet, etc. **Black Rod,** a gentleman usher so called from his ebony rod of office. **black sheep,** a bad character in an otherwise well-behaved group. **black spot,** a place where conditions are dangerous or difficult, one that has a bad record. **black tie,** a man's black bow-tie worn with a dinner-jacket. **Black Watch,** the Royal Highland Regiment whose uniform includes a dark-coloured tartan. **black widow,** a poisonous American spider. **in a person's black books,** having earned his disapproval. **in black and white,** recorded in writing or print.

blackball v. to prevent (a person) from being elected as a member of a club by voting against him at a secret ballot.

blackberry n. **1.** the bramble. **2.** its small dark berry. □ **blackberrying** n. picking blackberries.

blackbird n. a European songbird, the male of which is black.

blackboard n. a board usually coloured black, for writing on with chalk in front of a class in school etc.

blackcock n. a male black grouse.

blacken 1. to make or become black. **2.** to say unpleasant things about, *blackened his character.*

blackfly n. a kind of insect infesting plants.

blackguard (**blag**-erd) n. a scoundrel.

blackhead n. a small hard lump blocking a pore in the skin.

blackish adj. rather black.

blackleg n. a person who works while his fellow workers are on strike.

blackmail v. to demand payment or action from (a person) by threats especially of revealing a discreditable secret. —n. the crime of demanding payment in this way, the money itself. —**blackmailer** n.

blacksmith n. a smith who works in iron.

blackthorn n. a thorny shrub bearing white flowers and sloes.

bladder n. **1.** a sac in which urine collects in human and animal bodies. **2.** an inflatable bag e.g. in a football.

blade n. **1.** the flattened cutting-part of a knife, sword, chisel, etc. **2.** the flat wide part of an oar, spade, propeller, etc. **3.** a flat narrow leaf especially of grass and cereals. **4.** a broad flattish bone, *shoulder-blade.*

blame v. to hold responsible and criticize for a fault; *I don't blame you,* I feel your action was justified. —n. responsibility for a fault, criticism for doing wrong.

blameless adj. deserving no blame, innocent.

blanch v. to make or become white or pale; *blanch the almonds,* peel them.

blancmange (blă-**monj**) n. a flavoured jelly-like pudding made with milk.

bland adj. **1.** mild in flavour, *bland foods.* **2.** gentle and casual in manner, not irritating or stimulating. **blandly** adv., **blandness** n.

blandishments pl. n. flattering or coaxing words.

blank adj. **1.** not written or printed on, unmarked; *a blank wall,* without ornament or opening. **2.** without interest or expression, without result; *look blank,* to appear puzzled. —**blank** n. **1.** a blank space or paper, an empty surface; *his mind was a blank,* he could not remember anything. **2.** a blank cartridge. —**blankly** adv., **blankness** n. □ **blank cartridge,** one that contains no bullet. **blank cheque,** one with the amount left blank, to be filled in by the payee. **blank verse,** verse written in lines of usually ten syllables, without rhyme.

blanket n. a thick covering made of woollen or other fabric; *a blanket of fog,* a thick covering mass; *born on the wrong side of the blanket,* of illegitimate birth; *a blanket agreement,* an inclusive one, covering all cases. —v. (blanketed, blanketing) to cover with a blanket. □ **blanket bath,** the washing of a patient's body part by part while he remains in bed. **blanket stitch,** an embroidery stitch suitable for finishing a raw edge.

blare *n.* a harsh loud sound like that of a trumpet. —*v.* to make such a sound.

blarney *n.* smooth talk that flatters and deceives people.

blasé (**blah**-zay) *adj.* bored or unimpressed by things because one has already experienced or seen them so often.

blaspheme *v.* to utter blasphemies. **blasphemer** *n.*

blasphemy (**blas**-fĕmi) *n.* contemptuous or irreverent talk about God and sacred things. **blasphemous** *adj.*, **blasphemously** *adv.*

blast *n.* **1.** a sudden strong rush of wind or air, a wave of air from an explosion. **2.** the sound made by a wind-instrument or whistle or car horn etc. **3.** (*informal*) a severe reprimand. —**blast** *v.* **1.** to blow up with explosives. **2.** to cause to wither, to blight, to destroy. —*int.* damn. □ **at full blast**, at maximum power. **blast-furnace** *n.* a furnace for smelting ore, with compressed hot air driven in. **blast off**, to be launched by firing of rockets. **blast-off** *n.* the launching of a spacecraft.

blasted *adj.* (*informal*) damned.

blatant (**blay**-tănt) *adj.* attracting attention in a very obvious way; *a blatant lie,* very obvious and unashamed. **blatantly** *adv.*

blaze[1] *n.* **1.** a bright flame or fire. **2.** a bright light, a brightly-coloured display. **3.** an outburst, *a blaze of anger.* —**blaze** *v.* **1.** to burn or shine brightly. **2.** to have an outburst of intense feeling or anger. □ **blazes** *n.* hell, *go to blazes.* **like blazes,** very quickly, exceedingly.

blaze[2] *n.* **1.** a white mark on an animal's face. **2.** a mark chipped in the bark of a tree to mark a route. —*v.* to mark (a tree or route) with blazes; *blaze a trail,* to make such marks, to pioneer and show the way for others to follow.

blaze[3] *v.* to proclaim, *blazed the news abroad.*

blazer *n.* a loose-fitting jacket, often in the colours or bearing the badge of a school, club, or team.

blazon (**blay**-zŏn) *n.* a heraldic shield, a coat of arms.

bleach *v.* to whiten by sunlight or chemicals. —*n.* a bleaching substance.

bleak *adj.* cold and cheerless; *the future looks bleak,* unpromising. **bleakly** *adv.*, **bleakness** *n.*

bleary *adj.* watery and seeing indistinctly, *bleary eyes.*

bleat *n.* the cry of a sheep, goat, or calf. —*v.* **1.** to make this cry. **2.** to speak or say plaintively.

bleed *v.* (bled, bleeding) **1.** to leak blood or other fluid; *some dyes bleed,* come out in

water. **2.** to draw blood or fluid from. **3.** to extort money from.

bleeding *adj. & adv.* (*vulgar*) bloody, damned.

bleep *n.* a short high-pitched sound used as a signal. —*v.* to make this sound. — **bleeper** *n.*

blemish *n.* a flaw or defect that spoils the perfection of something. —*v.* to spoil with a blemish.

blench *v.* to flinch.

blend *v.* **1.** to mix in order to get a certain quality. **2.** to mingle, to become a mixture. **3.** to have no sharp or unpleasant contrast, *the colours blend well.* —*n.* a mixture of different sorts, *a blend of tea.*

blender *n.* **1.** something that blends things. **2.** a goblet for blending soft or liquid foods, with blades driven by an electric motor.

Blenheim (**blen**-im) *n.* a kind of apple. ¶ Named after *Blenheim Palace* at Woodstock, Oxfordshire.

bless *v.* **1.** to make sacred or holy with the sign of the Cross. **2.** to call holy, to praise, *to bless God.* **3.** to call God's favour upon, *Christ blessed the children; bless his heart!,* an exclamation of affection; *bless my soul!,* an exclamation of surprise. **4.** to curse, *she'll bless you for breaking that!* □ **be blessed with,** to be fortunate in having, *be blessed with good health.*

blessed (**bles**-id) *adj.* **1.** holy, sacred; *the Blessed Virgin,* the Virgin Mary. **2.** in paradise; *the Blessed,* people who are in paradise. **3.** (*old use*) fortunate, *blessed are the meek.* **4.** (*informal*) damned, *the blessed thing slipped.* **blessedness** *n.*

blessing *n.* **1.** God's favour, a prayer for this. **2.** a short prayer of thanks to God before or after a meal. **3.** something one is glad of; *a blessing in disguise,* something unwelcome that turns out to have a good effect.

blest *adj.* (*old use*) blessed, *our blest redeemer.* **well, I'm blest!,** an exclamation of surprise. **I'm blest if I know,** I do not know at all.

blether *v.* to talk nonsense.

blew see blow[1].

blight *n.* **1.** a disease that withers plants. **2.** a fungus or insect causing this disease. **3.** a malignant influence. **4.** an unsightly area. —**blight** *v.* **1.** to affect with blight. **2.** to spoil.

blighter *n.* (*slang*) a person or thing, especially an annoying one.

blimey (**bly**-mi) *int.* (*vulgar*) an exclamation of surprise.

blind *adj.* **1.** without sight; *a blind bend,* where road users cannot see what is approaching. **2.** without foresight or under-standing, without adequate information, *blind obedience*. **3.** concealed, *blind hem-ming*. **4.** (of a plant) failing to produce a flower. **5.** (in cookery) without filling, *bake it blind*. **6.** (*slang*) very drunk. —*adv.* blindly. —**blind** *v.* **1.** to make blind. **2.** to take away the power of judgement; *blinded with science*, overawed by a display of knowledge. **3.** (*slang*) to go along reck-lessly. —**blind** *n.* **1.** a screen, especially on a roller, for a window. **2.** a pretext. **3.** (*slang*) a heavy drinking-bout. —**blindly** *adv.*, **blindness** *n.* □ **blind alley,** an alley that is closed at one end; a job with no prospects of advancement. **blind date,** a date between persons of opposite sex who have not met before. **blind spot,** a point on the eye that is insensitive to light; an area where understanding is lacking; an area cut off from a motorist's vision. **not a blind bit of,** (*slang*) not the slightest. **turn a blind eye,** to pretend not to notice.

blinder *n.* (*slang*) a heavy drinking-bout.
blindfold *adj. & adv.* with the eyes covered with a cloth to block one's sight. —*n.* a cloth used for this. —*v.* to cover the eyes with a cloth.
blink *v.* **1.** to open and shut the eyes rapidly. **2.** to shine unsteadily. **3.** to ignore, to refuse to consider; *there's no blinking these facts*, we must consider them. —**blink** *n.* **1.** an act of blinking. **2.** a quick gleam. □ **on the blink,** (*slang*) failing from time to time.
blinker *v.* to obstruct the sight or under-standing of. **blinkers** *pl. n.* leather pieces fixed on a bridle to prevent a horse from seeing sideways.
blinking *adj.* (*informal*) damned.
blip *n.* a spot of light on a radar screen.
bliss *adj.* perfect happiness. **blissful** *adj.*, **blissfully** *adv.*
blister *n.* **1.** a bubble-like swelling on the skin, filled with watery liquid. **2.** a raised swelling e.g. on a painted surface. —**blister** *v.* **1.** to cause a blister, to be affected with blisters. **2.** to criticize severely. □ **blister pack,** a bubble pack.
blithe (*rhymes with* scythe) *adj.* casual and carefree. **blithely** *adv.*
blithering *adj.* (*informal*) absolute, con-temptible, *blithering idiot*.
blitz *n.* (also *blitzkrieg*) a violent attack, especially from aircraft. —*v.* to attack or damage in a blitz.
blizzard *n.* a severe snowstorm.
bloated *adj.* swollen with fat or gas or liquid.
bloater *n.* a salted smoked herring.

blob *n.* a drop of liquid, a round mass or spot.
bloc *n.* a group of parties or countries who unite to support a particular interest.
block *n.* **1.** a solid piece of wood or stone or other hard substance. **2.** a log of wood. **3.** a large piece of wood for chopping or hammering on; *the block,* that on which condemned people were beheaded. **4.** a pulley or pulleys mounted in a case; *block and tackle,* such pulleys and ropes used for lifting. **5.** the main part of a petrol engine, consisting of the cylinders and valves. **6.** a compact mass of buildings bounded by streets, *drive round the block.* **7.** a large building divided into separate flats or offi-ces. **8.** a large section of shares, seats, etc. as a unit. **9.** a pad of paper for drawing or writing on. **10.** an obstruction; *a mental block,* failure to understand etc., caused by emotional tension. —**block** *v.* **1.** to ob-struct, to prevent the movement or use of. **2.** to stop (a bowled ball) with the bat. □ **block-buster** *n.* (*slang*) a huge bomb able to destroy a whole block of buildings; some-thing very powerful. **block in,** to sketch in roughly. **block letters,** plain capital letters. **block vote,** a voting system in which each voter has influence according to the number of people he represents. **knock his block off,** (*slang*) clout his head.
blockade *n.* the blocking of access to a place in order to prevent the entry of goods etc. —*v.* to set up a blockade of.
blockage *n.* **1.** something that blocks. **2.** the state of being blocked.
blockhead *n.* a stupid person.
bloke *n.* (*slang*) a man.
blond, blonde *adjs.* fair-haired, *a blond man*; *a blonde woman*. —*ns.* a fair-haired man or woman.
blood *n.* **1.** the red oxygen-bearing liquid circulating in the bodies of animals. **2.** bloodshed, the guilt for this. **3.** temper, courage; *his blood is up,* he is in a fighting mood; *there's bad blood between them,* hatred. **4.** race, descent, parentage; *new blood,* new members admitted to a family or group; *a prince of the blood,* of royal descent; *they are my own blood,* rel-atives. —*v.* to give a first taste of blood to (a hound), to initiate. □ **blood-bath** *n.* a massacre. **blood-curdling** *adj.* horrifying. **blood group,** a class or type of human blood. **blood orange,** an orange with red-streaked pulp. **blood-poisoning** *n.* the con-dition that results when the bloodstream is infected with harmful micro-organisms that have entered the body, especially through a cut or wound. **blood pressure,** the pressure of blood within the arteries

and veins; abnormally high pressure of this kind. **blood-red** *adj.* as red as blood. **blood sports,** sports involving killing. **blood test,** an examination of a specimen of blood in medical diagnosis. **blood-vessel** *n.* a vein, artery, or capillary tube carrying blood.

bloodhound *n.* a large keen-scented dog formerly used in tracking.

bloodless *adj.* 1. having no blood. 2. looking pale, drained of blood. 3. without bloodshed.

bloodshed *n.* the killing or wounding of people.

bloodshot *adj.* (of eyes) red from dilated veins.

bloodstain *n.* a stain made by blood.

bloodstained *adj.* 1. stained with blood. 2. disgraced by bloodshed.

bloodstock *n.* thoroughbred horses.

bloodstream *n.* the blood circulating in the body.

bloodsucker *n.* 1. a creature that sucks blood. 2. a person who extorts money.

bloodthirsty *adj.* eager for bloodshed.

bloody *adj.* 1. blood-stained. 2. with much bloodshed, *a bloody battle.* 3. (in strong language) damned, very great —*adv* very, *bloody awful.* —*v.* (bloodied, bloodying) to stain with blood. —**bloodily** *adv.*, **bloodiness** *n.* □ **Bloody Mary,** a drink of mixed vodka and tomato juice (¶ the nickname of Mary Tudor, in whose reign many Protestants were executed). **bloody-minded** *adj.* (*informal*) deliberately un-cooperative. **bloody-mindedness** *n.*

bloom *n.* 1. a flower; *in bloom,* in flower. 2. beauty, perfection, *in the bloom of youth.* 3. fine powder on fresh ripe grapes etc. —**bloom** *v.* 1. to bear flowers, to be in bloom. 2. to be in full beauty.

bloomer *n.* (*slang*) a blunder.

bloomers *pl. n.* (*informal*) knickers with legs.

blooming *adj. & adv.* (*slang*) damned.

blossom *n.* 1. a flower, especially of a fruit-tree. 2. a mass of such flowers. —**blossom** *v.* 1. to open into flowers. 2. to develop and flourish.

blot *n.* 1. a spot of ink etc. 2. something ugly, *a blot on the landscape.* 3. a fault, a disgraceful act or quality. —**blot** *v.* (blotted, blotting) 1. to make a blot or blots on. 2. to dry with blotting paper, to soak up. □ **blot one's copybook,** to spoil one's good record. **blot out,** to cross out thickly; to obscure, *mist blotted out the view*; to destroy completely. **blotting-paper** *n.* absorbent paper for drying ink writing.

blotch *n.* a large irregular mark. **blotched** *adj.*, **blotchy** *adj.*

blotter *n.* a pad of blotting paper, a device holding this.

blotto *adj.* (*slang*) very drunk.

blouse *n.* 1. a shirt-like garment worn by women and children. 2. a waist-length coat forming part of a military uniform.

blow[1] *v.* (blew, blown, blowing) 1. to move or flow as a current of air does. 2. to send out a current of air or breath, to move or propel by this; *blow one's nose,* clear it by breathing out through it; *blow the whistle,* sound it. 3. to shape (molten glass) by blowing into it. 4. to be moved or carried by air, *door blew open.* 5. to puff and pant. 6. to swell; *tin of fruit has blown,* swollen from gas pressure inside. 7. to melt with too strong an electric current, *blow the fuse; a fuse has blown.* 8. to break with explosives. 9. (*slang*) to reveal; *the spy's cover was blown,* became known to the enemy. 10. (*slang*) to spend recklessly. —*int.* damn; *blow you Jack, I'm all right,* I don't care about you. —*n.* blowing; *go for a blow,* go outdoors for fresh air. □ **blow in,** (*informal*) to arrive casually or unexpectedly. **blow one's own trumpet,** to praise oneself. **blow one's top,** (*informal*) to show great anger. **blow over,** to die down without serious consequences. **blow the gaff,** (*slang*) to let out a secret. **blow the mind,** to produce hallucinations, or a very pleasurable or shocking sensation, in the mind. **blow up,** to inflate; to exaggerate; to make an enlargement of (a photograph); to explode; to shatter by an explosion; to lose one's temper, to reprimand severely; to become a crisis, *this problem has blown up recently.* **blow-up** *n.*

blow[2] *n.* 1. a stroke with a hand or weapon. 2. a shock, a disaster. □ **blow-by-blow** *adj.* telling all the details of an event in their order of occurrence.

blow-dry *v.* to use a hand-held drier to style (washed hair) while drying it.

blower *n.* 1. a person or thing that blows. 2. (*informal*) a telephone.

blowfly *n.* a fly that lays its eggs on meat.

blowlamp *n.* a portable burner producing a very hot flame that can be directed on a selected spot.

blown *see* blow[1]. —*adj.* breathless as the result of effort.

blow-out *n.* 1. a burst tyre. 2. a melted fuse. 3. a rapid uncontrolled upward rush of oil or gas from a well. 4. (*slang*) a large meal.

blowpipe *n.* 1. a tube through which air is blown. 2. a tube for sending out darts or pellets by blowing.

blowy *adj.* windy.

blowzy (*rhymes with* drowsy) *adj.* red-faced and coarse-looking.

blubber[1] *n.* whale fat.

blubber[2] *v.* to weep noisily.

bludgeon (**bluj**-ĕn) *n.* a short stick with a thickened end, used as a weapon. —*v.* **1.** to strike with a bludgeon. **2.** to compel forcefully.

blue[1] *adj.* **1.** of the colour of the sky on a cloudless day. **2.** unhappy, depressed. **3.** indecent, obscene, *blue jokes.* —**blue** *n.* **1.** blue colour. **2.** a blue substance or material, blue clothes. **3.** *the blue,* the clear sky, the sea. **4.** the distinction awarded to a member of Oxford or Cambridge University chosen to represent either of these against the other in a sport, a holder of this. —*v.* (blued, blueing) to make blue. — **blueness** *n.* □ **blue baby,** one with blueness of the skin from a heart defect. **blue-blooded** *adj.* of aristocratic descent. **Blue Book,** a parliamentary or Privy Council report. **blue cheese,** cheese with veins of blue mould. **blue-collar worker,** a manual or industrial worker. **blue funk,** (*slang*) a state of terror, **blue-pencil** *v.* (blue-pencilled, blue-pencilling) to cross out with a blue pencil, to censor. **Blue Peter,** a blue flat with a white square, hoisted by a ship about to sail. **blues** *n.* melancholy jazz melodies; *the blues,* a state of depression, **blue whale,** a rorqual, the largest known living animal. **once in a blue moon,** very rarely. **out of the blue,** unexpectedly. **true blue,** faithful, loyal.

blue[2] *v.* (blued, blueing) (*slang*) to spend recklessly.

Bluebeard's chamber a place containing gruesome things. ¶ Named after a character in a fairy-tale who murdered six wives and hid their bodies in a locked room.

bluebell *n.* a plant with blue bell-shaped flowers.

blueberry *n.* **1.** a shrub with edible blue berries. **2.** its fruit.

bluebottle *n.* a large fly with a bluish body.

blueprint *n.* **1.** a blue photographic print of building plans. **2.** a detailed plan or scheme.

bluestocking *n.* a learned woman.

bluetit *n.* a tit with a bright blue tail and blue wings.

bluey *adj.* rather blue, *bluey-green.*

bluff[1] *adj.* **1.** with a broad steep front, *a bluff headland.* **2.** abrupt, frank, and hearty in manner. —*n.* a bluff headland or cliff. —**bluffness** *n.*

bluff[2] *v.* to deceive someone by making a pretence especially of strength. —*n.* bluff-ing, a threat intended to get results without being carried out.

bluish *adj.* rather blue.

blunder *v.* **1.** to move clumsily and uncertainly. **2.** to make a blunder. —*n.* a mistake made especially through ignorance or carelessness. —**blunderer** *n.*

blunderbuss *n.* an old type of gun firing many balls at one shot.

blunt *adj.* **1.** with no sharp edge or point, not sharp. **2.** speaking or expressed in plain terms, *a blunt refusal.* —*v.* to make or become blunt. —**bluntly** *adv.*, **bluntness** *n.*

blur *n.* **1.** a smear. **2.** a confused or indistinct appearance. —*v.* (blurred, blurring) **1.** to smear. **2.** to make or become indistinct.

blurb *n.* a description of something praising it, e.g. in advertising matter.

blurt *v.* to utter abruptly or tactlessly, *blurted it out.*

blush *v.* to become red in the face from shame or embarrassment. —*n.* such reddening of the face. □ **blusher** *n.* a cosmetic used to give colour to the face.

bluster *v.* **1.** to be windy, to blow in gusts. **2.** to talk aggressively, especially with empty threats. —*n.* such talk. —**blustery** *adj.*

bo *int.* an exclamation intended to startle someone.

BO *abbrev.* (*informal*) body odour.

boa (**boh**-ă) *n.* a large non-poisonous South American snake that kills its prey by crushing it. **boa constrictor,** a Brazilian species of boa.

boar *n.* **1.** a male wild pig. **2.** an uncastrated domestic male pig.

board *n.* **1.** a long thin flat piece of wood. **2.** a flat piece of wood or stiff material for a special purpose, e.g. a notice-board, a diving-board, a chess-board. **3.** thick stiff paper used for book covers. **4.** daily meals obtained in return for payment or services, *board and lodging.* **5.** a committee e.g. the directors of a company, the members of a regional authority. —**board** *v.* **1.** to cover with boards. **2.** to go on board (a ship, aircraft, etc.). **3.** to receive or provide with meals and accommodation for payment. □ **board up,** to block with fixed boards. **go by the board,** to be ignored or rejected. **on board,** on or in a ship, aircraft, etc.

boarder *n.* **1.** a person who boards with someone. **2.** a resident pupil at a boarding-school.

boarding *n.* **1.** boards. **2.** material from which these are cut, a structure or covering made of this.

boarding-house *n.* a house at which board and lodging may be obtained for payment.

boarding-school *n.* a school in which pupils receive board and lodging.

boardroom *n.* a room where the meetings of the board of a company etc. are held.

boast *v.* 1. to speak with great pride and try to impress people, especially about oneself. 2. to possess as something to be proud of, *the town boasts a fine park.* **boast** *n.* 1. a boastful statement. 2. something one is proud of. —**boaster** *n.*

boastful *adj.* boasting frequently, full of boasting. **boastfully** *adv.,* **boastfulness** *n.*

boat *n.* 1. a vessel for travelling on water, the kind moved by oars or sails or an engine, a steamer; *a ship's boats,* lifeboats carried on board ship. 2. a boat-shaped serving dish for sauce or gravy. □ **boat drill,** practice in launching a ship's boats. **boat-house** *n.* a shed at the water's edge for housing boats. **boat people,** refugees leaving a country by sea. **boat race,** a race in rowing-boats. **boat-train** *n.* a train timed to carry passengers to or from a ship's docking-place. **In the same boat,** suffering the same troubles.

boater *n.* a hard flat straw hat.

boating *n.* going out in a rowing-boat for pleasure.

boatman *n.* (*pl.* boatmen) a man who rows or sails or rents out boats.

boatswain (**boh**-sün) *n.* a ship's officer in charge of rigging, boats, anchors, etc.

bob¹ *v.* (bobbed, bobbing) 1. to make a jerky movement, to move quickly up and down; *bob up,* to appear suddenly, to become active or conspicuous again; *bob a curtsy,* to curtsy quickly. 2. to cut (hair) short so that it hangs loosely. —**bob** *n.* 1. a bobbing movement. 2. the style of bobbed hair.

bob² *n.* **bob's your uncle,** (*slang*) success has been achieved.

bob³ *n.* (*pl.* bob) (*slang*) a shilling, 5p.

bobbin *n.* a small spool holding thread or wire in a machine.

bob-sleigh (**bob**-slay), **bob-sled** *ns.* a sledge with two sets of runners, especially with mechanical steering, used for tobogganning. **bob-sleighing** *n.*

bode *v.* to be a sign of, to promise, *it boded well for their future.*

bodice (**bod**-iss) *n.* the upper part of a woman's dress, down to the waist.

bodily *adj.* of the human body or physical nature. *adv.* 1. in person, physically. 2. as a whole, *the bridge was moved bodily 50 yards downstream.*

bodkin *n.* a blunt thick needle with a large eye, for drawing tape etc. through a hem.

body *n.* 1. the structure of bones, flesh, etc. of man or an animal, living or dead. 2. a corpse, a carcass. 3. the trunk, the main part of a body apart from the head and limbs. 4. the main part of anything; *a car body,* bodywork; *the body of a concert hall,* the central part where the seats are. 5. (*informal*) a person, *she's a cheerful old body.* 6. a group or quantity of people, things, or matter, regarded as a unit. 7. a distinct piece of matter, an object in space. 8. thick texture, strong quality, *this fabric has more body; this wine has no body.* □ **body-blow** *n.* a severe set-back. **body-odour,** the smell of the human body, especially when unpleasant. **In a body,** all together. **keep body and soul together,** to have just enough food etc. to remain alive.

bodyguard *n.* an escort or personal guard of an important person.

bodywork *n.* the shell of a motor vehicle.

Boer (**boh**-er) *n.* (*old use*) a South African of Dutch descent.

boffin *n.* (*slang*) a person engaged in technical research.

bog *n.* 1. an area of ground that is permanently wet and spongy, formed of decayed plants etc. 2. (*slang*) a lavatory. —*v.* (bogged, bogging) to be stuck fast in wet ground, to cause to be stuck and unable to make progress. —**boggy** *adj.*

bogey *n.* (*pl.* bogeys) 1. = bogy. 2. the number of strokes that a good golfer should take for a hole or course.

boggle *v.* to hesitate in fright, to raise objections, *the mind boggles at the idea.*

bogie (**boh**-gi) *n.* an undercarriage fitted below a railway vehicle, pivoted at the end for going round curves.

Bogotá (bog-ŏ-**tah**) the capital of Colombia.

bogus *adj.* sham, counterfeit.

bogy *n.* 1. an evil spirit. 2. something that causes fear.

bogyman *n.* an imaginary man feared by children, especially in the dark.

Bohemian *adj.* 1. of Bohemia, a province of Czechoslovakia. 2. very informal in one's way of living.

boil¹ *n.* an inflamed swelling under the skin, producing pus.

boil² *v.* 1. to bubble up and change into vapour through being heated. 2. to heat (a liquid or its container) so that the liquid boils, to cook or wash or process thus, to be heated or cooked etc. thus. 3. to seethe like a boiling liquid, to be hot with anger. —*n.* boiling-point; *on the boil,* boiling; *off* *the boil*, having just ceased to boil. □ **boil down**, to reduce or be reduced in quantity by boiling; (*informal*) to express or be expressed in fewer words. **boiled sweet**, a sweet made of boiled sugar. **boiling hot**, (*informal*) very hot, **boiling-point** *n.* the temperature at which a liquid boils; a state of great anger or excitement. **boil over**, to overflow when boiling. **the whole boiling**, (*slang*) the whole amount.

boiler *n.* 1. a container in which water is heated. 2. a water-tank in which a hot-water supply is stored. 3. a closed metal tub for boiling laundry. 4. a fowl too tough to roast but suitable for boiling. □ **boiler suit**, a one-piece garment combining overalls and shirt, worn for rough work.

boisterous *adj.* 1. windy, *boisterous weather*. 2. noisy and cheerful, *boisterous children*. **boisterously** *adv.*

bold *adj.* 1. confident and courageous. 2. without feelings of shame, impudent. 3. (of colours) strong and vivid. **boldly** *adv.*, **boldness** *n.*

bole *n.* the trunk of a tree.

bolero (*n.* (*pl.* boleros) 1. (*pr.* bŏ-**lair**-oh) a Spanish dance, the music for this. 2. (*pr.* **bol**-er-oh) a woman's short jacket with no front fastening.

Bolivia (bŏ-**liv**-iă) a country in South America. **Bolivian** *adj.* & *n.*

bollard (**bol**-erd) *n.* 1. a short thick post to which a ship's mooring rope may be tied. 2. a short post for keeping traffic off a path etc.

boloney (bŏ-**loh**-ni) *n.* = baloney.

Bolshie (**bol**-shi) *adj.* (*slang*) rebellious, refusing to co-operate with the authorities. ¶ The *Bolsheviks* were a Russian party favouring an extreme form of socialism.

bolster *n.* a long under-pillow for the head of a bed. —*v.* to support, to prop, *bolster up confidence.*

bolt *n.* 1. a sliding bar for fastening a door. 2. the sliding part of a rifle-breech. 3. a strong metal pin for fastening things together. 4. a shaft of lightening. 5. a roll of fabric. 6. the act of boiling. —**bolt** *v.* 1. to fasten with a bolt or bolts. 2. to run away, (of a horse) to run off out of control. 3. (of plants) to run to seed. 4. to gulp down (food) hastily. □ **a bolt from the blue**, a complete (usually unwelcome) surprise. **bolt-hole** *n.* a place into which one can escape. **bolt upright**, quite upright.

bomb *n.* 1. a container filled with explosive or incendiary material to be set off by impact or by a timing device. 2. *the bomb*, an atomic or hydrogen bomb, regarded as the supreme weapon. 3. (*slang*) a large sum of money. —*v.* to attack with bombs.

□ **go like a bomb**, (*slang*) to be very successful.

bombard *v.* 1. to attack with many missiles, especially from big guns. 2. to send a stream of high-speed particles against. 3. (to attack with questions or complaints. **bombardment** *n.*

bombardier *n.* a non-commissioned officer in the artillery.

bombastic (bom-**bas**-tik) *adj.* speaking pompously, using pompous words.

Bombay duck bummalo, eaten as a relish.

bomber *n.* 1. an aircraft that carries and drops bombs. 2. a person who throws or plants bombs. □ **bomber jacket**, a waist-length jacket gathered into a band at waist and cuffs.

bombshell *n.* something that comes as a great surprise and shock.

bona fide (boh-nă **fy**-di) genuine, without fraud, *bona fide customers.*

bona fides (boh-nă **fy**-deez) honest intention, sincerity, *he proved his bona fides.* ¶ This is not a plural form of *bona fide* and it is incorrect to say 'his bona fides *were* questioned'.

bonanza (bŏ-**nan**-ză) *n.* a source of sudden great wealth or luck, a windfall.

bon-bon *n.* a sweet.

bond *n.* 1. something that binds or attaches or restrains, e.g. a rope. 2. something that unites people. 3. a binding agreement, a document containing this. 4. money deposited as a guarantee. 5. a document issued by a government or public company acknowledging that money has been lent to it and will be repaid usually with interest. 5. writing-paper of high quality. —**bond** *v.* 1. to connect or unite with a bond, to link with an emotional bond. 2. to put into a Customs warehouse. 3. to insure a contract etc. by means of a financial bond. □ **bonded** *adj.* stored in bond, *bonded whisky*; storing bonded goods, *a bonded warehouse*. **in bond**, stored in a Customs warehouse until duties are paid.

bondage *n.* slavery, captivity.

bone *n.* 1. one of the hard parts that make up the skeleton of an animal's body. 2. a piece of bone with meat on it, as food. 3. the substance from which such parts are made, a similar hard substance. —*v.* to remove the bones from. □ **bone china**, fine china made of clay mixed with bone ash. **bone-dry** *adj.* quite dry. **bone idle**, very lazy. **bone of contention**, the subject of a dispute. **bone-shaker** *n.* a vehicle that jolts. **feel in one's bones**, to feel sure by intuition. **have a bone to pick**, to have something to argue or complain about. **make no bones about**, to raise no objection to, to speak frankly about. **to the bone,** thoroughly, completely.

bonehead *n.* a stupid person.

bonemeal *n.* crushed powdered bones used as a fertilizer.

bonfire *n.* a large fire built in the open air to destroy rubbish or as a celebration. **Bonfire Night,** 5 November, when bonfires are lit in memory of the Gunpowder Plot.

bongo *n.* (*pl.* bongos) one of a pair of small drums played with the fingers.

bonhomie (**bon**-ŏmi) *n.* a genial manner.

bonkers *adj.* (*slang*) crazy.

Bonn the capital of West Germany.

bonnet *n.* 1. a hat with strings that tie under the chin. 2. a Scotch cap. 3. a hinged cover over the engine etc. of a motor vehicle.

bonny *adj.* (bonnier, bonniest) 1. healthy-looking. 2. (*Scottish & N. England*) good-looking.

bonsai (**bon**-sy) *n.* 1. a plant or tree grown in miniature form in a pot by artificially restricting its growth. 2. the method of cultivating this.

bonus *n.* (*pl.* bonuses) a payment or benefit in addition to what is usual or expected.

bon vivant (bawn **vee**-vahn) a gourmand. (¶ French, = one who lives well.)

bon voyage (bawn vwah-**yah**zh) an expression of good wishes to someone starting a journey. (¶ French.)

bony *adj.* (bonier, boniest) 1. like bones. 2. having large or prominent bones, having bones with little flesh. 3. full of bones. **boniness** *n.*

boo *int.* 1. a sound made to show disapproval or contempt. 2. an exclamation used to startle someone. —*v.* to show disapproval by shouting 'boo'.

boob *n.* (*slang*) 1. a foolish person. 2. a stupid mistake. 3. *boobs,* a woman's breasts. —*v.* (*slang*) to make a stupid mistake.

booby *n.* a foolish person. **booby prize,** a prize given as a joke to the competitor with the lowest score. **booby trap,** a hidden trap rigged up for a practical joke; a hidden bomb placed so that it will explode when some apparently harmless object is touched or moved. **booby-trap** *v.* to place a booby trap in or on.

book *n.* 1. a series of written or printed or plain sheets of paper fastened together at one edge and enclosed in a cover. 2. a literary work that would fill such a book or books if printed, *he is working on his book.* 3. (*informal*) a magazine. 4. a number of cheques, stamps, tickets, matches, etc. fastened together in the shape of a book.

5. one of the main divisions of a written work. 6. a libretto. 7. a record of bets made; *make a book,* arrange a series of bets on an event. —**book** *v.* 1. to enter in a book or list; *the police booked him for speeding,* recorded a charge against him; *we booked in at the hotel,* registered our names there as guests. 2. to reserve (a seat or accommodation etc.), to buy (tickets) in advance. □ **book club,** a society whose members can buy certain books at a reduced price. **book-ends** *pl. n.* a pair of supports for keeping a row of books upright. **booking-office** *n.* an office where tickets are sold. **bring to book,** to make (a person) answer for his conduct. **by the book,** in accordance with the correct procedure. **in a person's good** (*or* bad) **books,** in favour (or not in favour) with him. **throw the book at,** *see* throw.

bookable *adj.* able to be booked.

bookcase *n.* a piece of furniture with shelves for books.

bookie *n.* (*informal*) a bookmaker.

bookish *adj.* fond of reading.

bookkeeping *n.* the systematic recording of business transactions.

booklet *n.* a small thin usually paper-covered book.

bookmaker *n.* a person whose business is taking bets.

bookmark *n.* a strip of paper or other material placed between the pages of a book to mark a place.

bookseller *n.* a person whose business is selling books.

bookshop *n.* a shop selling only (or chiefly) books.

bookstall *n.* a stall or kiosk at which books and newspapers are sold.

bookworm *n.* 1. a grub that eats holes in books. 2. a person who is very fond of reading.

boom[1] *v.* 1. to make a hollow deep resonant sound. 2. to have a period of prosperity or rapid economic growth. —**boom** *n.* 1. a booming sound. 2. a period of increased growth, prosperity, or value.

boom[2] *n.* 1. a long pole used to keep the bottom of a sail stretched. 2. a floating barrier or a heavy chain across a river or a harbour entrance. 3. a long pole carrying a microphone etc.

boomerang *n.* 1. a curved wooden missile used by Australian aborigines, especially one that can be thrown so that it returns to the thrower if it fails to hit anything. 2. something that causes unexpected harm to its originator. —*v.* to act as a boomerang.

boon[1] *n.* a benefit.

boon[2] *adj.* **boon companion,** a favourite sociable companion.

boor *n.* an ill-mannered person. **boorish** *adj.*, **boorishly** *adv.*, **boorishness** *n.*

boost *v.* **1.** to push upwards. **2.** to increase the strength, value, or good reputation of, to promote. —**boost** *n.* **1.** an upward thrust. **2.** an increase. —**booster** *n.*

boot *n.* **1.** a shoe or outer covering for the foot and ankle or leg. **2.** a compartment for luggage in a car. **3.** *the boot, (slang)* dismissal. —*v.* to kick. □ **boot-faced** *adj.* grim or expressionless. **put the boot in,** to kick brutally. **the boot is on the other foot** *or* **leg,** the situation has been reversed; the opposite is true.

bootee *n.* a baby's knitted or crocheted boot.

booth *n.* **1.** a small temporary shelter at a market or fair. **2.** an enclosure for a public telephone. **3.** a compartment in a large room, e.g. for voting at elections.

bootleg *v.* (bootlegged, bootlegging) **1.** to smuggle (alcohol). **2.** to make and sell illicitly. —*adj.* smuggled or sold illicitly. —**bootlegger** *n.*

booty *n.* loot.

booze *v.* (*informal*) to drink alcohol, especially in large quantities. —*n.* (*informal*) **1.** alcoholic drink. **2.** a drinking spree; *on the booze,* boozing. —**boozy** *adj.*

boozer *n.* **1.** (*informal*) a person who boozes. **2.** (*slang*) a public house.

boracic *adj.* = boric.

borage (*rhymes with* porridge) *n.* a plant with blue flowers and hairy leaves, used in salads.

borax *n.* a soluble white powder that is a compound of boron, used in making glass, enamels, and detergents.

Bordeaux (bor-**doh**) *n.* a red or white wine from Bordeaux in France, a similar wine from elsewhere.

border *n.* **1.** an edge or boundary, the part near this. **2.** the line dividing two countries, the area near this; *the Border,* that between England and Scotland. **3.** an edging. **4.** a strip of ground round a garden or a part of it, *a herbaceous border.* —*v.* to put or be a border to. □ **border on,** to be next to; come close to, *it borders on the absurd.* **border print,** printed fabric with a design based on one of its edges. **Borders,** a region of Scotland.

borderland *n.* the district near a boundary.

borderline *n.* the line that marks a boundary. —*adj.* on the borderline between different groups or categories.

bore[1] *see* bear[2].

bore[2] *v.* **1.** to make (a hole or well etc.) with a revolving tool or by digging out soil. **2.** to pierce or penetrate in this way; *bore one's way,* get through by pushing. —**bore** *n.* **1.** the hollow inside of a gun barrel or engine cylinder, its diameter. **2.** a hole made by boring.

bore[3] *v.* to make (a person) feel tired or uninterested by being dull or tedious. —*n.* a boring person or thing. —**boredom** *n.*, **boring** *adj.*

bore[4] *n.* a tidal wave with a steep front that moves up some estuaries, *the Severn bore.*

boric (**bor**-ik) *adj.* of boron. **boric acid,** a substance derived from boron, used as a mild antiseptic.

born (¶ See the note under borne.) **be born,** to be brought forth by birth; *born to suffer,* destined for this by birth; *their courage was born of despair,* originated from this. —*adj.* **1.** having a certain order or status or place of birth, *first-born; well-born; French-born.* **2.** having a certain natural quality or ability, *a born leader.* □ **in all one's born days,** (*informal*) in all one's lifetime. **not born yesterday,** experienced in people's ways and not easy to deceive.

borne *see* bear[2]. ¶ The word *borne* is used as part of the verb *to bear* only when it comes before *by* or after *have, has,* or *had,* e.g. *children borne by Eve, she had borne him a son.* The word *born* is used in *a son was born.*

boron (**bor**-on) *n.* a chemical element that is very resistant to high temperatures, used in metal working and in nuclear reactors.

borough (**burr**ă) *n.* **1.** (*old use*) a town with a corporation and with privileges (e.g. certain rights of self-government) conferred by royal charter or defined by statute. **2.** (since 1974) a town or district granted the status of a borough. **3.** an administrative area of Greater London.

borrow *v.* **1.** to get the temporary use of, on the understanding that the thing received is to be returned. **2.** to use without being the inventor; *borrow their methods,* copy them. **borrower** *n.* □ **borrowed time,** an extension of one's life beyond an illness or crisis which could have ended it.

Borstal *n.* an institution to which young offenders may be sent for reformative training.

borzoi (**bor**-zoi) *n.* a large hound with a narrow head and silky coat.

bosh *n.* & *int.* (*slang*) nonsense.

bo's'n (**boh**-sŭn) *n.* = boatswain.

bosom *n.* **1.** a person's breast. **2.** the part of a garment covering this. **3.** the centre or inmost part; *returned to the bosom of his family*, to a loving family circle. □ **bosom friend**, one who is dear and close.

bosomy *adj.* having large breasts.

boss¹ *n.* (*informal*) a person who controls or gives orders to workers. — *v.* (*slang*) to be the boss of, to give orders to; *boss someone about*, to order him about.

boss² *n.* a round projecting knob or stud.

boss³ *n.* (*slang*) a bungle, a muddle. **boss shot**, a bad shot or guess or attempt.

boss-eyed *adj.* (*slang*) 1. blind in one eye, cross-eyed. 2. crooked.

bossy *adj.* (bossier, bossiest) fond of ordering people about, doing this continually. **bossily** *adv.*, **bossiness** *n.*

bo'sun (boh-sŭn) *n.* = boatswain.

botanical (bŏ-tan-ikăl) *adj.* of botany. **botanical gardens**, gardens where plants and trees are grown for scientific study.

botany *n.* the scientific study of plants. **botanist** *n.* an expert in botany.

Botany wool wool from merino sheep, especially from Australia. ¶ Named after *Botany Bay* in New South Wales.

botch *v.* to spoil by poor or clumsy work. —*n.* a piece of spoilt work.

both *adj., pron., & adv.* the two, not only the one.

bother *v.* 1. to cause trouble or worry or annoyance to, to pester. 2. to take trouble, to feel concern. —*int.* an exclamation of annoyance. —*bother* *n.* 1. worry, minor trouble. 2. something causing this.

botheration *int. & n.* bother.

bothersome *adj.* causing bother.

Botswana (bot-swah-nă) a country in Africa north of the Republic of South Africa.

bottle *n.* 1. a narrow-necked glass or plastic container for storing liquid. 2. the amount contained in this. 3. a baby's feeding-bottle, milk from this. 4. a hot-water bottle. 5. *the bottle*, drinking alcoholic drinks, *too fond of the bottle*. 6. (*slang*) courage. —**bottle** *v.* 1. to store in bottles. 2. to preserve in glass jars, *bottled fruit*. □ **bottle-fed** *adj.* fed with milk from a feeding-bottle. **bottle-party** *n.* a party to which each guest brings a bottle of wine etc.

bottleneck *n.* 1. a narrow stretch of road where traffic cannot flow freely. 2. anything similarly obstructing progress.

bottom *n.* 1. the lowest part of anything, the part on which it rests, the lowest place; *the bottom of the garden*, the end furthest from the house; *the bottom fell out of the market*, trade fell dramatically.

2. the buttocks, the part of the body on which one sits. 3. the ground under a stretch of water. 4. bottom gear. —*adj.* lowest in position or rank or degree. □ **at bottom**, basically, really, **at the bottom of one's heart**, in one's most secret thoughts. **be at the bottom of**, to be the underlying cause or originator of. **bottom drawer**, a woman's store of clothes and linen etc. collected in preparation for marriage. **from the bottom of one's heart**, with deep feeling, sincerely. **get to the bottom of**, to find out the cause or origin of.

bottomless *adj.* extremely deep; *a bottomless purse*, an inexhaustible supply of money.

bottommost *adj.* lowest.

botulism (bot-yoo-lizm) *n.* a kind of food poisoning.

bouclé (boo-klay) *n.* 1. yarn with one of its strands looped at intervals. 2. fabric made from this.

boudoir (boo-dwahr) *n.* a woman's small private room.

bougainvillaea (boo-găn-vil-iă) *n.* a tropical shrub with red or purple bracts.

bough *n.* a large branch coming from the trunk of a tree.

bought *see* buy.

bouillon (boo-yawn) *n.* broth.

boulder (bohl-der) *n.* a large stone rounded by water or weather.

boulevard (boo-lĕ-vard) *n.* a wide street, often with trees on each side.

bounce *v.* 1. to spring back when sent against something hard, to cause to do this. 2. (*informal*) (of a cheque) to be sent back by the bank as worthless. 3. to jump suddenly, to move in a lively manner. —**bounce** *n.* 1. bouncing, the power of bouncing. 2. a lively manner.

bouncer *n.* 1. a bowled ball that bounces forcefully. 2. (*informal*) a person employed to expel troublesome people from a gathering.

bouncing *adj.* big and healthy, boisterous.

bouncy *adj.* full of bounce.

bound¹ *v.* to limit, to be the boundary of.

bound² *v.* to jump or spring, to run with jumping movements. —*n.* a bounding movement.

bound³ *adj.* going or heading towards, *bound for Spain*; *northbound traffic*.

bound⁴ *see* bind. —*adj.* obstructed or hindered by, *fog-bound*. □ **bound to**, certain to. **bound up with**, closely associated with. **I'll be bound**, I feel certain.

boundary *n.* 1. a line that marks a limit.

2. a hit to or over the boundary of the field in cricket.

bounden *adj.* obligatory. **one's bounden duty**, a duty dictated by one's conscience.

bounder *n.* (*slang*) a cad.

boundless *adj.* without limits.

bounds *pl. n.* limits. **out of bounds**, outside the areas one is allowed to enter.

bountiful *adj.* **1.** giving generously. **2.** abundant.

bounty *n.* **1.** generosity in giving. **2.** a generous gift. **3.** a reward or payment given as an inducement.

bouquet (boh-**kay**) *n.* **1.** a bunch of flowers for carrying in the hand. **2.** a compliment, praise. **3.** the perfume of wine. □ **bouquet garni** (**gar**-ni), a bunch of herbs used for flavouring.

bourbon (**boor**-bŏn) *n.* **1.** whisky made mainly from maize. **2.** a kind of chocolate-flavoured biscuit.

bourgeois (**boor**-zhwah) *adj.* (*contemptuous*) of the middle class, having conventional ideas and tastes.

bourgeoisie (**boor**-zhwah-zi) *n.* (*contemptuous*) the bourgeois class.

bout *n.* **1.** a period of exercise or work or illness. **2.** a boxing contest.

boutique (boo-**teek**) *n.* a small shop selling clothes etc. of the latest fashion.

bovine (**boh**-vyn) *adj.* **1.** of or like an ox. **2.** dull and stupid.

bow [1] (*rhymes with* go) *n.* **1.** a piece of wood curved by a tight string joining its ends, used as a weapon for shooting arrows. **2.** a rod with horse-hair stretched between its ends, used for playing the violin etc. **3.** a knot made with a loop or loops, ribbon etc. tied in this way. □ **bow-legged** *adj.* having **bow-legs**, bandy legs. **bow-tie** *n.* a man's necktie tied into a bow. **bow-window** *n.* a curved bay window.

bow [2] (*rhymes with* cow) *n.* bending of the head or body in greeting, respect, agreement, etc. —**bow** *v.* **1.** to make a bow, to bend in greeting etc. **2.** to bend downwards under a weight. **3.** to submit or give in, *must bow to the inevitable.* □ **bow and scrape**, to behave obsequiously.

bow [3] (*rhymes with* cow) *n.* **1.** the front or forward end of a boat or ship. **2.** the oarsman nearest the bow.

bowdlerize (**bowd**-ler-ryz) *v.* to censor words or scenes considered improper. ¶ Named after T. *Bowdler* who produced a censored version of Shakespeare's plays.

bowel *n.* the intestine. **bowels** *pl. n.* the intestines; the innermost parts.

bower (*rhymes with* flower) *n.* a leafy shelter.

bowl [1] *n.* **1.** a basin for holding food or liquid. **2.** this with its contents, the amount it contains. **3.** the hollow rounded part of a spoon, tobacco-pipe, etc.

bowl [2] *n.* **1.** a ball used in the game of bowls. **2.** a ball used in skittles etc. — **bowl** *v.* **1.** to send rolling along the ground. **2.** to be carried fast and smoothly by car etc., *bowling up the M4.* **3.** to send a ball to be played by a batsman, to dismiss by knocking down a wicket with this. □ **bowl over**, to knock down; to overwhelm with surprise or emotion. **bowls** *n.* a game played by rolling heavy balls that are weighted so that they roll in a curve.

bowler [1] *n.* **1.** a person who plays at bowls. **2.** a person who bowls in cricket.

bowler [2] *n.* a bowler hat. **bowler hat**, a hard felt hat with a rounded top.

bowline (**boh**-lin) *n.* a simple knot for forming a non-slipping loop at the end of a rope.

bowling *n.* playing bowls or skittles or a similar game. **bowling-alley** *n.* a long enclosure for playing skittles etc. **bowling-green** *n.* a lawn for playing bowls.

bowsprit (**boh**-sprit) *n.* a long pole projecting from the stem of a ship, to which ropes from the front mast and sails are fastened.

box [1] *n.* **1.** a container with a flat base and usually a lid, for holding solids. **2.** the amount it contains. **3.** a box-like receptacle, a money-box, pillar-box, etc. **4.** a compartment, e.g. with seats for several persons in a theatre, for a horse in a stable or vehicle, for the jury or witnesses in a lawcourt. **5.** a small hut or shelter, *sentry-box.* **6.** a box number (see below). — *v.* to put into a box. □ **box in** or **up**, to shut into a small space, preventing free movement. **box-junction** *n.* a road intersection marked with crossing yellow stripes on which vehicles must not be stationary, designed to prevent a stream of traffic from blocking the passage of one that crosses it. **box-kite** *n.* a kite with an open box-like frame. **box number**, a number used to identify a box in a newspaper office to which letters to an advertiser may be sent. **box-office** *n.* an office for booking seats at a theatre etc. **box-pleat** *n.* an arrangement of parallel pleats folding in alternate directions. **box-room** *n.* a room for storing empty boxes and trunks etc. **box-spring** *n.* one of a set of vertical springs in a mattress.

box [2] *v.* to fight with the fists, to engage in

boxing. —*n.* a slap with the open hand. □ **box a person's ears**, to slap them.
box³ *n.* **1.** a small evergreen shrub. **2.** its wood.
Box and Cox two people who take turns at doing the same thing. ¶ Named after two characters in a play to whom a landlady let the same room, one being at work all day and the other all night.
boxer *n.* **1.** a person who engages in boxing. **2.** a dog of a breed resembling the bulldog.
boxing *n.* the sport of fighting with the fists. **boxing-gloves** *pl. n.* a pair of padded leather mittens worn in boxing. **boxing-weights** *pl. n.* a series of weights used for grouping boxers to be matched against each other.
Boxing Day the first weekday after Christmas Day.
boy *n.* **1.** a male child. **2.** a young man. **3.** a young male employee, *a van boy.* **4.** (in some countries) a male servant. —*int.* an exclamation of surprise or joy. —**boyhood** *n.* □ **boy-friend** *n.* a woman's usual male companion.
boycott (**boy**-kot) *v.* to refuse to have anything to do with; *boycotted the goods,* refused to handle or buy them. —*n.* boycotting, treatment of this kind.
boyish *adj.* like a boy. **boyishly** *adv.,* **boyishness** *n.*
BP *abbrev.* **1.** British Petroleum. **2.** British Pharmacopoeia.
BPC *abbrev.* British Pharmaceutical Codex.
BR *abbrev.* British Rail.
bra *n.* a woman's undergarment worn to support the breasts, a brassière.
brace *n.* **1.** a device that clamps things together or holds and supports them in position. **2.** a pair, *five brace of partridge.* —*v.* to support, to give firmness to. —**bracer** *n.* □ **brace oneself, brace up,** to steady oneself in order to meet a blow or shock. **braces** *pl. n.* straps used to keep trousers up, fastened to the waistband and passing over the shoulders.
bracelet *n.* an ornamental band worn on the arm.
bracing *adv.* invigorating, stimulating.
bracken *n.* a large fern that grows on waste land, a mass of such ferns.
bracket *n.* **1.** a support projecting from an upright surface. **2.** any of the marks used in pairs for enclosing words or figures, (), []. **3.** a group bracketed together as similar or falling between certain limits, *an income bracket.* —**bracket** *v.* **1.** to enclose or join by brackets. **2.** to put together to imply connection or equality. **3.** to place

shots both short of the target and beyond it in order to find the range.
brackish *adj.* slightly salt, *brackish water.*
bract *n.* a leaf-like part of a plant, often highly coloured, e.g. in bougainvillea and poinsettia.
bradawl *n.* a small boring-tool.
brae (*pr.* bray) *n.* (*Scottish*) a hillside.
brag *v.* (bragged, bragging) to boast.
braggart (**brag**-ert) *n.* a person who brags.
brahmin (**brah**-min) *n.* a member of the Hindu priestly caste.
braid *n.* **1.** a woven ornamental trimming. **2.** a plait of hair. —**braid** *v.* **1.** to plait. **2.** to trim with braid.
Braille (*pr.* brayl) *n.* a system of representing letters etc. by raised dots which blind people can read by touch. —*v.* to represent in Braille. ¶ Named after its inventor, Louis Braille.
brain *n.* **1.** the organ that is the centre of the nervous system in animals, a mass of soft grey matter in the skull. **2.** the mind or intellect, intelligence. —*v.* to kill by a heavy blow on the head. □ **brain-child** *n.* a person's invention or plan. **brain drain,** the loss of clever and skilled people by emigration. **brains trust,** a group of people giving impromptu answers to questions as a form of entertainment.
brainless *adj.* stupid.
brainstorm *n.* **1.** a sudden violent mental disturbance. **2.** (*Amer.*) a sudden bright idea.
brainwash *v.* to force (a person) to reject old beliefs and accept new ones by subjecting him to great mental pressure.
brainwave *n.* **1.** an electrical impulse in the brain. **2.** a sudden bright idea.
brainy *adj.* (brainier, brainiest) clever, intelligent.
braise *v.* to cook slowly with very little liquid in a closed container.
brake¹ *n.* **1.** a device for reducing the speed of something or stopping its motion. **2.** the pedal etc. operating this. —*v.* to slow down by means of this.
brake² *n.* a thicket.
bramble *n.* a rough shrub with long prickly shoots, a blackberry-bush.
bran *n.* coarse meal consisting of the ground inner husks of grain, sifted out from flour. **bran tub,** a tub filled with bran into which children dip for concealed toys etc.
branch *n.* **1.** an arm-like part of a tree. **2.** a similar part of a river, road, railway, etc. **3.** a subdivision of a family or a group of languages or a subject. **4.** a local shop or office etc. belonging to a larger organization. —*v.* to send out branches, to

divide into branches. □ **branch off**, to leave a main route and take a minor one. **branch out**, to begin a new line of activity.

brand *n.* **1.** a trade mark, goods of a particular make. **2.** a mark of identification made with a hot iron, the iron used for this. **3.** a piece of burning or charred wood. —**brand** *v.* **1.** to mark with a hot iron, to label with a trade mark. **2.** to give a bad name to, *he was branded as a trouble-maker*. □ **brand-new** *adj.* completely new.

brandish *v.* to wave (a thing) in display or threateningly.

brandling *n.* a red earthworm with rings of brighter colour, used as bait.

brandy *n.* a strong alcoholic spirit distilled from wine or from fermented fruit-juice. **brandy-snap**, a thin crisp curled wafer of gingerbread.

brash *adj.* **1.** vulgarly self-assertive. **2.** reckless. **brashly** *adv.*, **brashness** *n.*

Brasilia the capital of Brazil.

brass *n.* **1.** a yellow alloy of copper and zinc. **2.** a thing or things made of this. **3.** the brass wind instruments of an orchestra. **4.** a brass memorial tablet in a church. **5.** (*slang*) money. **6.** (*slang*) impudence. **7.** (*slang*) high-ranking officers or officials, *the top brass*. —*adj.* made of brass. □ **brass band**, a band playing brass and percussion instruments only. **brass-rubbing** *n.* taking an impression of brass memorial tablets. **get down to brass tacks**, to start to consider the basic facts or practical details.

brasserie (**bras**-er-i) *n.* a beer saloon, a restaurant serving beer with food.

brassière (**bras**-i-air) *n.* a bra.

brassy *adj.* (brassier, brassiest) **1.** like brass in appearance or sound. **2.** bold and vulgar. **brassiness** *n.*

brat *n.* (*contemptuous*) a child.

bravado (bră-**vah**-doh) *n.* a show of boldness.

brave *adj.* **1.** able to face and endure danger or pain. **2.** spectacular, *a brave show of peonies.* —*n.* an American Indian warrior. —*v.* to face and endure with bravery. —**bravely** *adv.*, **bravery** *n.*

bravo *int.* well done!

brawl *n.* a noisy quarrel or fight. —*v.* to take part in a brawl.

brawn *n.* **1.** muscular strength. **2.** meat from a pig's or calf's head boiled, chopped, and pressed in a mould.

brawny *adj.* (brawnier, brawniest) strong and muscular.

bray *n.* the cry of a donkey, a sound like this. —*v.* to make this cry or sound.

brazen (**bray**-zĕn) *adj.* **1.** made of brass, like brass. **2.** shameless, impudent. —*v.* **brazen it out**, to behave, after doing wrong, as if one has nothing to be ashamed of.

brazier (**bray**-zi-er) *n.* a basket-like stand for holding burning coals.

Brazil a country in South America. —*n.* a Brazil-nut. —**Brazilian** *adj.* & *n.* □ **Brazil-nut** *n.* a large three-sided nut.

Brazzaville the capital of Congo.

breach *n.* **1.** the breaking or neglect of a rule or agreement etc. **2.** an estrangement. **3.** a broken place, a gap. —*v.* to break through, to make a gap in. □ **step into the breach**, to give help in a crisis.

bread *n.* **1.** a food made of flour and liquid, usually leavened by yeast, and baked. **2.** (*slang*) money. □ **breadcrumbs** *pl. n.* bread crumbled for use in cooking. **breaded** *adj.* coated with breadcrumbs. **bread-fruit** *n.* the fruit of a tropical tree, with white pulp like new bread. **bread-winner** *n.* the member of a family who earns the money to support the others. **on the breadline**, living in extreme poverty.

breadth *n.* width, broadness.

break *v.* (broke, broken, breaking) **1.** to fall into pieces, to cause to do this; *she broke her leg*, broke the bone in it. **2.** to damage, to make or become unusable. **3.** to fail to keep (a promise). **4.** to stop for a time, to make or become discontinuous, *broke the silence; we broke for coffee; broke into a run*, began to run; *broke the strike*, forced it to end by a means other than bargaining. **5.** to make a way suddenly or violently; *broke prison*, escaped from prison. **6.** to emerge or appear suddenly. **7.** to reveal (news etc.), to become known, *the story broke.* **8.** to surpass, *broke the world record.* **9.** to make or become weak, to overwhelm with grief etc., to destroy, *the scandal broke him.* **10.** (of a voice) to change its even tone, either with emotion or (of a boy's voice) by becoming suddenly deeper at puberty. **11.** (of a ball) to change direction after touching the ground. **12.** (of waves) to fall in foam. **13.** (of boxers) to come out of a clinch. —**break** *n.* **1.** breaking. **2.** an escape, a sudden dash. **3.** a gap, a broken place. **4.** an interval, e.g. between periods of work or exercise. **5.** points scored continuously in billiards. **6.** (*informal*) a piece of luck; *a bad break*, bad luck. **7.** a fair chance; *give him a break*, an opportunity. □ **break down**, to demolish; to cease to function because of mechanical failure; (of a person's health) to collapse;

to give way to emotion; to act upon chemically and reduce to constituent parts; to analyse, *break down the expenditure.* **break even,** to make gains and losses that balance exactly. **break fresh ground,** to deal with some aspect of a subject for the first time. **break in,** to force one's way into a building; to interrupt; to accustom to a new routine. **break-in** *n.* a forcible entry, especially by a thief. **breaking-point** *n.* the point at which a person or thing gives way under stress. **break in on,** to disturb, to interrupt. **break of day,** dawn. **break off,** to bring to an end; to stop speaking. **break one's neck,** to fracture or dislocate one's neck; (*informal*) to make a great effort, *we broke our necks to finish on time.* **break out,** to begin suddenly; to exclaim; to force one's way out; to develop (a rash etc.). **break service,** to win a game at tennis when one's opponent is serving. **break the bank,** to use up all its resources. **break the heart of,** to overwhelm with grief. **break the ice,** to overcome formality. **break up,** to bring or come to an end; to become weaker; to separate, (of schoolchildren) to begin holidays when school closes at the end of term. **breakup** *n.* breaking up. **break wind,** to expel wind from the bowels or stomach. **break with,** to give up; to end one's friendship with.

breakable *adj.* able to be broken.

breakage *n.* **1.** breaking. **2.** something broken.

breakaway *n.* **1.** becoming separate or free. **2.** an outside second-row forward in Rugby football. —*adj.* that breaks or has broken away, *a breakaway group.*

breakdown *n.* **1.** mechanical failure. **2.** weakening. **3.** a collapse of health or mental stability. **4.** an analysis.

breaker *n.* a heavy ocean-wave that breaks on the coast.

breakfast *n.* the first meal of the day. —*v.* to eat breakfast. ☐ **breakfast cup,** a large teacup.

breakneck *adj.* dangerously fast, *at breakneck speed.*

breakthrough *n.* a major advance in knowledge.

breakwater *n.* a wall built out into the sea to protect a harbour or coast against heavy waves.

bream *n.* a fish of the carp family.

breast *n.* **1.** either of the two milk-producing organs on the upper front of a woman's body. **2.** the upper front part of the human body or of a garment covering this. **3.** the corresponding part in animals. **4.** something shaped like this, *the chimney-*

breast. —*v.* to face and advance against, *breasted the waves.* ☐ **breast-feed** *v.* to feed (a baby) by allowing it to suck at the mother's breast. **breast-fed** *adj.* fed in this way. **breast-stroke** *n.* a swimming-stroke performed face downwards, with sweeping movements of the arms.

breastbone *n.* the flat vertical bone in the chest or breast, joined to the ribs.

breath (*pr.* breth) *n.* **1.** air drawn into and sent out of the lungs. **2.** breathing in, *take six deep breaths.* **3.** a gentle blowing, *a breath of wind.* **4.** a whisper, a trace, *not a breath of scandal.* ☐ **in the same breath,** immediately after saying something else. **out of breath,** panting after violent exercise. **save one's breath,** to refrain from useless discussion. **take one's breath away,** to make one breathless with surprise or delight. **under one's breath,** in a whisper.

breathalyse *v.* to test with a breathalyser.

breathalyser *n.* a device that measures the amount of alcohol in a person's breath as he breathes out.

breathe (*pr.* breeth) *v.* **1.** to draw air into the lungs and send it out again, (of plants) to respire. **2.** to take into or send out of the lungs, *breathing cigar smoke.* **3.** to utter; *don't breathe a word of it,* keep it secret. ☐ **breathe again,** to feel relieved of fear or anxiety. **breathing-space** *n.* room to breathe; a pause to recover from effort.

breather *n.* **1.** a pause for rest. **2.** a short period in the fresh air.

breathless *adj.* out of breath, panting. **breathlessly** *adv.*, **breathlessness** *n.*

breathtaking *adj.* very exciting, spectacular.

breathy (breth-i) *adj.* with a noticeable sound of breathing.

bred *see* breed.

breech *n.* the back part of a gun barrel. **breech birth,** a birth in which the baby's buttocks appear first.

breeches (brich-iz) *pl. n.* trousers reaching to just below the knee, worn for riding or as part of court costume etc.

breed *v.* (bred, breeding) **1.** to produce offspring. **2.** to keep (animals) for the purpose of producing young. **3.** to train, to bring up. **4.** to give rise to. —*n.* a variety of animals etc. within a species, having similar appearance.

breeder *n.* a person who breeds animals. **breeder reactor,** a nuclear reactor that produces more fissile material than it uses in operating.

breeding *n.* **1.** the production of young from animals, propagation. **2.** good manners resulting from training or background.

breeze *v.* a light wind. —*v.* (*informal*) to move in a lively manner, *they breezed in.*

breeze-blocks *pl. n.* light-weight building blocks made of cinders and cement.

breezy *adj.* (breezier, breeziest) 1. exposed to wind. 2. pleasantly windy. 3. lively, jovial. **breezily** *adv.*, **breeziness** *n.*

Bren gun a light-weight machine-gun.

brent-goose *n.* a small wild goose.

brethren *pl. n.* (*old use*) brothers.

Breton (**bret**-ŏn) *adj.* of Brittany or its people. —*n.* a native of Brittany.

breviary (**breev**-i-er-i) *n.* a book of prayers to be said daily by Roman Catholic priests.

brevity (**brev**-iti) *n.* shortness, briefness.

brew *v.* 1. to make (beer) by boiling and fermentation, to make (tea) by infusion. 2. to be being prepared in this way, *the tea is brewing.* 3. to bring about, to develop, *trouble is brewing.* —**brew** *n.* 1. liquid made by brewing. 2. an amount brewed.

brewer *n.* a person whose trade is brewing beer.

brewery *n.* a building in which beer is brewed.

Brewster Sessions magistrates' sessions for the issue of licenses to trade in alcoholic drinks.

briar *n.* = brier.

bribable *adj.* able to be bribed.

bribe *n.* something offered in order to influence a person to act in favour of the giver. —*v.* to persuade by a bribe. —**bribery** *n.*

bric-à-brac (**brik**-ă-brak) *n.* odd items of furniture, ornaments, etc. of no great value.

brick *n.* 1. a block of baked or dried clay or other substance used to build walls. 2. a child's toy building-block. 3. a rectangular block of something. 4. (*slang*) a kind-hearted person. —**brick** *adj.* 1. built of brick. 2. brick-red. —*v.* to block with brickwork. □ **brick-red** *adj.* of the red colour of bricks. **drop a brick,** (*slang*) to say something tactless or indiscreet.

brickbat *n.* a piece of brick, especially one used as a missile.

bricklayer *n.* a workman who builds with bricks.

brickwork *n.* a structure made of bricks.

bridal *adj.* of a bride or wedding.

bride *n.* a woman on her wedding-day, a newly married woman.

bridegroom *n.* a man on his wedding-day, a newly married man.

bridesmaid *n.* an unmarried woman or girl attending the bride at a wedding.

bridge¹ *n.* 1. a structure providing a way across something or carrying a road or railway etc. across. 2. the raised platform on a ship from which the captain and officers direct its course. 3. the bony upper part of the nose. 4. something that joins or connects or supports other parts. —*v.* to make or form a bridge over. □ **bridging loan,** a loan given for the period between two transactions, e.g. between buying a new house and selling one's own.

bridge² *n.* a card-game developed from whist. **bridge roll,** an oval soft bread roll.

bridgehead *n.* a fortified area established in enemy territory, especially on the far side of a river.

bridle *n.* the part of a horse's harness that goes on its head. —*v.* 1. to put a bridle on. 2. to restrain, to keep under control. 3. to draw one's head up in pride or scorn. □ **bridle-path** *n.* a path suitable for riders but not for vehicles.

Brie (*pr.* bree) *n.* a kind of soft cheese.

brief¹ *adj.* 1. lasting only for a short time. 2. concise. 3. short in length. **briefly** *adv.*, **briefness** *n.* □ **in brief,** in a few words.

brief² *n.* 1. a summary of the facts of a case, drawn up for a barrister. 2. a case given to a barrister. 3. instructions and information given in advance. —**brief** *v.* 1. to give a brief to. 2. to instruct or inform concisely in advance. □ **hold no brief for,** not to be obliged to support.

briefcase *n.* a flat case for carrying documents.

briefs *pl. n.* very short close-fitting pants or knickers.

brier *n.* 1. a thorny bush, the wild rose. 2. a bush with a hard woody root used for making tobacco pipes. 3. a pipe made of this.

brig¹ *n.* (*Scottish & N. England*) a bridge.

brig² *n.* a two-masted sailing-vessel.

brigade *n.* 1. an army unit forming part of a division. 2. a group of people organized for a particular purpose.

brigadier *n.* an officer commanding a brigade, a staff officer of similar status.

brigand (**brig**-ănd) *n.* a member of a band of robbers.

bright *adj.* 1. giving out or reflecting much light, shining. 2. cheerful. 3. quick-witted, clever. —*adv.* brightly. —**brightly** *adv.*, **brightness** *n.*

brighten *v.* to make or become brighter.

brill *n.* a flat-fish like a turbot.

brilliant *adj.* 1. very bright or sparkling. 2. very clever. —*n.* a cut diamond with many facets. —**brilliantly** *adv.*, **brilliance** *n.*

brilliantine *n.* a substance used to make the hair glossy.

brim *n.* **1.** the edge of a cup or hollow or channel. **2.** the projecting edge of a hat. — *v.* (brimmed, brimming) to fill or be full to the brim. □ **brim-full** *adj.* full to the brim. **brim over,** to overflow.

brimstone *n.* (*old use*) sulphur.

brindled (**brin**-d'ld) *adj.* brown with streaks of other colour, *the brindled cow.*

brine *n.* salt water.

bring *v.* (brought, bringing) **1.** to cause to come, especially with oneself by carrying or leading or attracting. **2.** to produce as profit or income. **3.** to result in, to cause, *war brought famine.* **4.** to put forward (charges etc.) in a lawcourt, *they brought an action for libel.* **5.** to cause to arrive at a particular state, *bring it to the boil.* □ **bring about,** to cause to happen. **bring-and-buy-sale,** a sale at which people contribute goods and buy things contributed by others. **bring back,** to restore; to make one remember. **bring down,** to cause to fall; *bring the house down,* to get loud applause in a theatre etc. **bring forth,** to give birth to; to cause; (*old use*) to produce. **bring forward,** to arrange for (a thing) to happen earlier than was intended; to call attention to (a matter); to transfer from a previous page or account. **bring in,** to initiate, to introduce; to produce as profit or income; to pronounce as a verdict in court. **bring into being,** to cause to exist. **bring off,** to do successfully. **bring on,** to cause to develop rapidly. **bring oneself to do something,** to cause oneself to do it in spite of reluctance. **bring out,** to cause to appear, to show clearly; to publish. **bring to bear,** to concentrate as an influence, *pressure was brought to bear on the dissenters.* **bring up,** to look after and train (growing children); to vomit; to cause to stop suddenly. **bring up the rear,** to come last in a line.

brink *n.* **1.** the edge of a steep place or of a stretch of water. **2.** the verge, the edge of something unknown or dangerous or exciting.

brinkmanship *n.* the art of pursuing a dangerous policy to the brink of war etc. before stopping.

briny *adj.* salty. —*n.* (*humorous*) the sea.

brioche (**bree**-osh) *n.* a small sweetened bread roll, circular in shape.

briquette (brik-et) *n.* a block of compressed coal-dust.

brisk *adj.* active, lively, moving quickly. **briskly** *adv.*, **briskness** *n.*

brisket (**brisk**-it) *n.* a joint of beef cut from the breast.

brisling (**briz**-ling) *n.* a small herring or sprat, processed like sardines.

bristle *n.* **1.** a short stiff hair. **2.** one of the stiff pieces of hair or wire etc. in a brush. —**bristle** *v.* **1.** (of an animal) to raise the bristles in anger or fear. **2.** to show indignation. **3.** to be thickly set with bristles. □ **bristle with,** to be full of, *the plan bristled with difficulties.*

bristly *adj.* full of bristles.

Britain England, Wales, and Scotland, also called *Great Britain.*

Britannia the personification of Britain, shown as a woman with a shield, helmet, and trident.

Britannic *adj.* of Britain, *Her Britannic Majesty.*

British *adj.* of Great Britain or its inhabitants; (as *n.*) *the British,* British people. **British Isles,** Britain and Ireland with the islands near their coasts. **British Columbia** a province of Canada.

Briton *n.* **1.** a native or inhabitant of southern Britain before the Roman conquest. **2.** a British person. *Britons never will be slaves.*

brittle *adj.* hard but easily broken. —*n.* a brittle sweet made of nuts and melted sugar. —**brittly** *adv.*, **brittleness** *n.*

broach *v.* **1.** to make a hole in and draw out liquid. **2.** to begin a discussion of, *broached the topic.*

broach spire an octagonal church-spire that rises from its tower without a parapet.

broad *adj.* **1.** large across, wide. **2.** measuring from side to side, *50 ft. broad.* **3.** full and complete, *broad daylight; a broad hint,* strong and unmistakable; *a broad Yorkshire accent,* strongly regional. **4.** in general terms, not detailed; *in broad outline,* without details. **5.** rather coarse, *broad humour.* —**broad** *n.* **1.** the broad part. **2.** (*Amer. slang*) a prostitute, a woman. —**broadly** *adv.,* **broadness** *n.* □ **broad bean,** an edible bean with large flat seeds. **broadly speaking,** speaking in a general way. **broad-minded** *adj.* having tolerant views.

broadcast *v.* (broadcast, broadcasting) **1.** to send out by radio or TV. **2.** to speak or appear in a radio or TV programme. **3.** to make generally known. **4.** to sow (seed) by scattering, not in drills. —*n.* a broadcast programme. —*adv.* scattered freely. —**broadcaster** *n.*

broaden *v.* to make or become broad.

broadloom *adj.* woven in broad widths.

broadside *n.* **1.** the firing of all guns on one side of a ship. **2.** a strong attack in words. □ **broadside on,** sideways on.

broadsword *n.* a sword with a broad

blade, used for cutting rather than thrusting.

brocade (brŏ-**kayd**) *n.* fabric woven with raised patterns. **brocaded** *adj.*

broccoli (**brok**-ŏli) *n.* (*pl.* broccoli) a hardy variety of cauliflower.

brochure (**broh**-shoor) *n.* a booklet or pamphlet containing information.

broderie anglaise (broh-dri ahn-**glayz**) fabric with a kind of openwork embroidery.

brogue (*rhymes with* rogue) *n.* **1.** a strong shoe with ornamental perforated bands. **2.** a dialectal accent, especially Irish.

broil *v.* **1.** to cook (meat) on a fire or gridiron. **2.** to make or be very hot, especially from sunshine.

broiler *n.* a young chicken suitable or specially reared for broiling or roasting. **broiler house**, a building for rearing broiler chickens in close confinement.

broke *see* break. —*adj.* (*slang*) having spent all one's money, bankrupt.

broken *see* break. **brokenly** *adv.* □ **broken English**, English spoken imperfectly by a foreigner. **broken-hearted** *adj.* crushed by grief. **broken home**, a family lacking one parent through divorce or separation. **broken reed**, a person or thing too weak to be depended upon.

broker *n.* **1.** an agent who buys and sells things on behalf of others, a stockbroker. **2.** an official licensed to sell the goods of someone unable to pay his debts. □ **brokerage** *n.* a broker's fee or commission.

brolly *n.* (*informal*) an umbrella.

bromide (**broh**-myd) *n.* a compound of bromine, used in medicine to calm the nerves.

bromine (**broh**-meen) *n.* a chemical element, compounds of which are used in medicine and photography.

bronchial (**bronk**-iăl) *adj.* of the branched tubes (*bronchi*) into which the windpipe divides before entering the lungs.

bronchitis (brong-**ky**-tiss) *n.* inflammation of the mucous membrane inside the bronchial tubes.

bronco (**brong**-koh) *n.* (*pl.* broncos) a wild or half-tamed horse of western North America.

brontosaurus (bront-ŏ-**sor**-ŭs) *n.* (*pl.* brontosauruses) a large dinosaur that fed on plants.

Bronx cheer (*Amer. informal*) a rude sound made with the mouth, a raspberry.

bronze *n.* **1.** a brown alloy of copper and tin. **2.** a thing made of this, a bronze medal (awarded as third prize). **3.** its colour. —*adj.* made of bronze, bronze-coloured. —*v.* to make or become tanned

by sun. □ **Bronze Age**, the period when weapons and tools were made of bronze.

brooch (*rhymes with* coach) *n.* an ornamental hinged pin fastened with a clasp.

brood *n.* **1.** the young birds or other animals produced at one hatching or birth. **2.** (*humorous*) a family of children. — **brood** *v.* **1.** to sit on eggs to hatch them. **2.** to think long and deeply or resentfully. □ **brood mare**, a mare kept for breeding.

broody *adj.* **1.** (of a hen) wanting to brood. **2.** thoughtful and depressed.

brook[1] *n.* a small stream.

brook[2] *v.* to tolerate, *he would brook no interference.*

broom *n.* **1.** a shrub with yellow or white flowers. **2.** a long-handled brush for sweeping floors. □ **a new broom**, a newly appointed official who gets rid of old methods etc., *a new broom sweeps clean* (proverb).

broomstick *n.* a broom-handle.

Bros. (*pr.* bross) *abbrev.* Brothers.

broth *n.* the water in which meat or fish has been boiled, soup made with this.

brothel (**broth**-ĕl) *n.* a house where women work as prostitutes.

brother *n.* **1.** a son of the same parents as another person. **2.** a man who is a fellow member of a Church or trade union or other association. **3.** a monk who is not a priest; *Brother*, his title. **brotherly** *adj.* □ **brother-in-law** *n.* (*pl.* brothers-in-law) the brother of one's husband or wife, the husband of one's sister.

brotherhood *n.* **1.** the relationship of brothers. **2.** brotherliness, comradeship. **3.** an association of men, its members.

brought *see* bring.

brougham (**broo**-ăm) *n.* **1.** a four-wheeled closed carriage drawn by one horse or electrically driven. **2.** a former type of motor car with the driver's seat open.

brouhaha (**broo**-hah-hah) *n.* a commotion.

brow *n.* **1.** an eyebrow. **2.** the forehead. **3.** a projecting or overhanging part; *the brow of the hill*, the ridge at the top.

browbeat *v.* (browbeat, browbeaten, brow-beating) to intimidate.

brown *adj.* **1.** of a colour between orange and black. **2.** having skin of this colour, sun-tanned. **3.** (of bread) brown in colour, especially through being made with wholemeal flour. —**brown** *n.* **1.** brown colour. **2.** a brown substance or material or thing, brown clothes. **3.** the brown ball in snooker etc. —*v.* to make or become brown. □ **browned off**, (*slang*) bored, fed up. **brown paper**, strong coarse paper for wrapping parcels etc. **brown sugar**, sugar that is only partly refined. **do a person brown**, (*slang*) to cheat him. **in a brown study,** deep in thought.

Brownie *n.* a junior Guide.

browning *n.* a substance for colouring gravy.

brownish *adj.* rather brown.

browse (*rhymes with* cows) *v.* **1.** to feed as animals do, on leaves or grass etc. **2.** to look through a book, or examine items for sale, in a casual leisurely way.

brucellosis (broo-sel-**oh**-sis) *n.* a disease caused by bacteria, affecting cattle and some other farm animals.

bruise (*pr.* brooz) *n.* an injury caused by a knock or by pressure that discolours the skin without breaking it. —*v.* **1.** to cause a bruise or bruises on. **2.** to show the effects of a knock etc.

Brunei (**broon**-I) a country in the island of Borneo.

brunette (broo-**net**) *n.* a woman with darkish skin and/or hair.

brunt *n.* the chief stress or strain, *bore the brunt of the attack.*

brush *n.* **1.** an implement with bristles of hair, wire, or nylon etc. set in a solid base. **2.** a brush like piece of carbon or metal for making a good electrical connection. **3.** a fox's bushy tail. **4.** a short sharp encounter. **5.** brushing, *give it a brush.* — **brush** *v.* **1.** to use a brush on, to remove with a brush or by passing something lightly over the surface of. **2.** to touch lightly in passing. ☐ **brush aside,** to reject casually or curtly. **brush off,** to reject curtly, to snub. **brush-off** *n.* a curt rejection, a snub. **brush up,** to smarten; to study and revive one's former knowledge of. **brush-up** *n.*

brushed *adj.* with raised nap, *brushed nylon.*

brushless *adj.* used without a brush.

brushwood *n.* **1.** undergrowth. **2.** cut or broken twigs.

brushwork *n.* the style of the strokes made with a panter's brush.

brusque (*pr.* bruusk) *adj.* curt and offhand in manner. **brusquely** *adv.*, **brusqueness** *n.*

Brussels the capital of Belgium. **Brussels sprouts,** the edible buds growing thickly on the stem of a kind of cabbage.

brutal *adj.* very cruel, merciless. **brutally** *adv.*, **brutality** *n.*

brutalize *v.* to make brutal.

brute *n.* **1.** an animal other than man. **2.** a brutal person; *brute force,* cruel and unthinking force. **3.** (*informal*) an unpleasant or difficult person or thing. **brutish** *adj.*

bryony (**bry**-ŏni) *n.* a climbing hedge-plant with black or white berries.

B.Sc. *abbrev.* Bachelor of Science.

BST *abbrev.* British Summer Time.

Bt. *abbrev.* Baronet, *Sir John Davis, Bt.*

bubble *n.* **1.** a thin ball of liquid enclosing air or gas. **2.** a small ball of air in a liquid or in a solidified liquid, such as glass. **3.** a transparent domed cover. — **bubble** *v.* **1.** to send up bubbles, to rise in bubbles, to make the sound of these. **2.** to show great liveliness. ☐ **bubble-and-squeak,** cooked cabbage and potato chopped, mixed, and fried. **bubble gum,** chewing-gum that can be blown into large bubbles. **bubble pack,** a package enclosing goods in a transparent domed cover on a backing.

bubbly *adj.* full of bubbles.

buccaneer *n.* a pirate, an unscrupulous adventurer.

Bucharest (bew-kǎ-**rest**) the capital of Romania.

buck¹ *n.* the male of a deer, hare, or rabbit. —*v.* **1.** (of a horse) to jump with the back arched. **2.** (*slang*) to resist or oppose, *bucking the system.* ☐ **buck rarebit** Welsh rarebit served with a poached egg on top. **buck up,** (*slang*) to make haste; to make or become more cheerful.

buck² *n.* an article placed as a reminder before the person whose turn it is to deal at poker. **pass the buck,** (*slang*) to shift responsibility (and possible blame) to someone else. **buck-passing** *n.*

buck³ *n.* (*Amer. & Austral. slang*) a dollar. **a fast buck,** easy money.

buck⁴ *n.* a small vaulting-horse without pommels.

bucked *adj.* cheered and encouraged.

bucket *n.* **1.** a round open container with a handle, used for holding or carrying liquids or substances that are in small pieces. **2.** this with its contents, the amount it contains. —**bucket** *v.* **1.** to move along fast and bumpily. **2.** to pour heavily, *rain was bucketing down.* —**bucketful** *n.* (*pl.* bucketfuls). ☐ **bucket seat,** a seat with a rounded back, for one person.

Buckinghamshire a county of England.

buckle *n.* a device usually with a hinged tongue, through which a belt or strap is threaded to secure it. —*v.* **1.** to fasten with a buckle. **2.** to crumple under pressure, to cause to do this. ☐ **buckle down to,** to set about doing. **buckle to,** to make a vigorous start on work.

buckram (**buk**-rǎm) *n.* stiffened cloth, especially that used for binding books.

Bucks. *abbrev.* Buckinghamshire.

buckshee *adj. & adv.* (*slang*) free of charge.

buckshot *n.* coarse shot.

buckthorn *n.* a kind of thorny shrub.

bucolic (bew-**kol**-ik) *adj.* characteristic of country life.

bud *n.* **1.** a small knob that will develop

into a branch, leaf-cluster, or flower. **2.** a flower or leaf not fully open; *in bud*, putting forth such buds. —**bud** *v.* (budded, budding) **1.** to be in bud. **2.** to graft a bud of (a plant) on to another.

Budapest (bew-dă-**pest**) the capital of Hungary.

Buddha (**buud**-ă) *n.* **1.** the title (often treated as a name) of the Indian philosopher Gautama (5th century BC), and of a series of teachers of Buddhism. **2.** a statue or carving representing Gautama Buddha.

Buddhism (**buud**-izm) *n.* an Asian religion based on the teachings of Buddha. **Buddhist** *adj. & n.*

budding *adj.* beginning to develop, *a budding poet.*

buddleia (**bud**-liă) *n.* a shrub or tree with fragrant lilac or yellow flowers.

buddy *n.* (*informal*) a friend.

budge *v.* **1.** to move slightly. **2.** to cause to alter a position or opinion.

budgerigar (**buj**-er-i-gar) *n.* a kind of Australian parakeet, often kept as a cage-bird.

budget *n.* **1.** an estimate or plan of income and expenditure, that made annually by the Chancellor of the Exchequer. **2.** the amount allotted for a particular purpose. —*v.* (budgeted, budgeting) to plan or allot in a budget.

budgie *n.* (*informal*) a budgerigar.

Buenos Aires (bwayn-ŏs **I**-reez) the capital of Argentina.

buff *n.* **1.** strong velvety dull-yellow leather. **2.** the colour of this. **3.** the bare skin, *stripped to the buff.* **3.** (*Amer. informal*) an enthusiast, *tennis buffs.* —*adj.* dull yellow. —*v.* to polish with soft material.

buffalo *n.* (*pl.* buffaloes *or* buffalo) a kind of ox found in Asia, South Africa, and North America.

buffer *n.* **1.** something that lessens the effect of an impact, a device for this purpose on a railway engine or at the end of a track. **2.** (*slang*) a fellow. —*v.* to act as a buffer to. □ **buffer state**, a small country between two powerful ones, thought to reduce the chance of war between these.

buffet [1] (**buu**-fay) *n.* **1.** a counter where food and drink may be bought and consumed. **2.** provision of food where guests serve themselves, *buffet lunch.* □ **buffet car**, a railway coach serving light meals.

buffet [2] (**buf**-it) *n.* a blow, especially with the hand. —*v.* (buffeted, buffeting) to give a buffet to.

buffoon (buf-**oon**) *n.* a person who plays the fool. **buffoonery** *n.* clowning.

bug *n.* **1.** a flat evil-smelling insect infesting dirty houses and beds. **2.** (*Amer.*) any small insect. **3.** (*slang*) a microbe, especially one causing disease. **4.** (*slang*) a very small hidden microphone installed secretly. **5.** a defect. —**bug** *v.* (bugged, bugging) **1.** (*slang*) to fit with a hidden microphone secretly so that conversations etc. can be overheard from a distance. **2.** (*Amer.*) to annoy. —**bugger** *n.* □ **bug-eyed** *adj.* (*slang*) with bulging eyes.

bugbear *n.* something feared or disliked.

bugger *n.* **1.** a person who practises buggery. **2.** (*vulgar*) an unpleasant or difficult person or thing. —*v.* (*vulgar*) to spoil, to ruin; *bugger off,* go away. —*int.* (*vulgar*) damn. □ **bugger-all** *n.* (*vulgar*) nothing.

buggery *n.* sodomy.

buggy *n.* **1.** (*old use*) a light horse-drawn carriage. **2.** a small sturdy vehicle, *beach buggy.*

bugle [1] *n.* a brass instrument like a small trumpet, used for sounding military signals. **bugler** *n.* one who sounds a bugle.

bugle [2] *n.* a creeping plant with small dark-blue flowers.

bugloss (**bew**-gloss) *n.* a wild plant with bristly leaves and blue flowers.

build *v.* (built, building) to construct by putting parts or material together. —*n.* bodily shape, *of slender build.* □ **build on**, to rely on. **build up**, to accumulate; to establish gradually; to fill in with buildings; to boost with praise or flattering publicity. **build-up** *n.*

builder *n.* one who builds, one whose trade is building houses etc.

building *n.* **1.** the constructing of houses etc. **2.** a permanent built structure that can be entered. □ **building society**, an organization that accepts deposits and lends out money on mortgage to people wishing to buy or build a house etc.

built *see* build. —*adj.* having a specified build, *sturdily built.* **built-in** *adj.* incorporated as part of a structure. **built-up** *adj.* filled in with buildings; *built-up area,* an urban area.

bulb *n.* a thick rounded mass of scale-like leaves from which a stem grows up and roots grow down. **2.** a plant grown from this. **3.** a bulb-shaped object. **4.** an electric lamp, the glass part of this.

bulbous (**bul**-bus) *adj.* **1.** growing from a bulb. **2.** shaped like a bulb.

Bulgaria a country in Europe. **Bulgarian** *adj. & n.*

bulge *n.* a rounded swelling, an outward curve. —*v.* to form a bulge, to cause to swell out.

bulk *n.* **1.** size or magnitude, especially when great. **2.** the greater part, the majority. **3.** a large shape or body or person. —*v.* to increase the size or thickness of, *bulk it out.* □ **bulk buying**, buying a large quantity at one time; the buying of all or most of a producer's output by one purchaser. **bulk large**, to seem important. **in bulk**, in large amounts; in a mass, not packaged.

bulkhead *n.* an upright partition in a ship, aircraft, or vehicle.

bulky *adj.* (bulkier, bulkiest) taking up much space.

bull¹ *n.* **1.** an uncastrated male of any animal of the ox family. **2.** the male of the whale, elephant, and other large animals. **3.** *the Bull,* a sign of the zodiac, Taurus. **4.** (*Stock Exchange*) a person who buys shares etc. in the hope that prices will rise and that he will be able to sell them at a higher price very soon; *a bull market,* a situation where share prices are rising rapidly. **5.** the bull's-eye of a target. □ **bull-nosed** *adj.* with a rounded end.

bull² *n.* an official edict issued by the pope.

bull³ *n.* **1.** an obviously absurd statement, lies, nonsense. **2.** (*slang*) routine tasks regarded as unnecessary.

bulldog *n.* a dog of a powerful courageous breed with a short thick neck. **bulldog clip,** a spring clip that closes very strongly.

bulldoze *v.* **1.** to clear with a bulldozer. **2.** (*informal*) to force or intimidate, *he bulldozed them into accepting it.*

bulldozer *n.* a powerful tractor with a broad steel sheet mounted in front, used for shifting earth or clearing ground.

bullet *n.* a small round or conical missile used in a rifle or revolver. **bullet-proof** *adj.* able to keep out bullets.

bulletin *n.* a short official statement of news.

bullfight *n.* the sport of baiting and killing bulls for public entertainment, as in Spain. **bullfighter** *n.*

bullfinch *n.* a song-bird with a strong beak and a pinkish breast.

bullion *n.* gold or silver in bulk or bars, before coining or manufacture.

bullock *n.* a bull after castration.

bullring *n.* an arena for bullfights.

bull's-eye *n.* **1.** the centre of a target. **2.** a large hard round peppermint sweet.

bull-terrier *n.* a dog of a breed originally produced by crossing a bulldog and a terrier.

bully¹ *n.* a person who uses his strength or power to hurt or frighten others. —*v.* (bullied, bullying) to behave as a bully towards, to intimidate. □ **bully for you,** (*informal*) bravo.

bully² *v.* (bullied, bullying) to start play in hockey, where two opposing players tap the ground and each other's stick alternately three times before hitting the ball, *bully off.* —*n.* this procedure.

bully beef corned beef.

bulrush *n.* a kind of tall rush with a thick velvety head.

bulwark (**buul**-werk) *n.* **1.** a wall of earth built as a defence. **2.** something that acts as a protection or defence. □ **bulwarks** *pl. n.* a ship's side above the level of the deck.

bum¹ *n.* (*slang*) the buttocks.

bum² *n.* (*Amer. slang*) a beggar, a loafer.

bumble *v.* to move or act in a blundering way.

bumble-bee *n.* a large bee with a loud hum.

bumf *n.* (*slang*) **1.** toilet-paper. **2.** (*humorous*) documents, papers.

bummalo (**bum**-ă-loh) *n.* (*pl.* bummalo) a small fish of the coasts of South Asia.

bump *v.* **1.** to knock with a dull-sounding blow, to hurt by this. **2.** to travel with a jolting movement. —**bump** *n.* **1.** a bumping sound or knock or movement. **2.** a raised mark left by a blow. **3.** a swelling or lump on a surface. □ **bump into,** (*informal*) to meet by chance. **bump off,** (*slang*) to kill. **bump up,** (*informal*) to raise, *bumped up the price.*

bumper *n.* **1.** something unusually large or plentiful, *a bumper crop.* **2.** a horizontal bar attached to the front or back of a motor vehicle to lessen the effect of a collision. **3.** a ball in cricket that rises high after pitching.

bumpkin *n.* a country person with awkward manners.

bumptious (**bump**-shŭs) *n.* conceited. **bumptiously** *adv.,* **bumptiousness** *n.*

bumpy *adj.* (bumpier, bumpiest) full of bumps, causing jolts. **bumpiness** *n.*

bun *n.* **1.** a small round sweet cake. **2.** (*Scottish*) rich fruit cake, currant bread. **3.** hair twisted into a bun shape at the back of the head.

bunch *n.* **1.** a cluster, *a bunch of grapes.* **2.** a number of small similar things held or fastened together, *a bunch of keys.* **3.** (*slang*) a mob, a gang. —*v.* to come or bring together into a bunch or in folds.

bunchy *adj.* gathered in clumsy folds.

bundle *n.* **1.** a collection of things loosely fastened or wrapped together, a set of sticks or rods tied together. **2.** (*slang*) a large amount of money. —**bundle** *v.* **1.** to make into a bundle; *bundled up in thick clothes,* cumbersomely dressed in these.

2. to put away hastily and untidily, to push hurriedly, *bundled him into a taxi.* □ **go a bundle on,** (*slang*) to like immensely.

bung *n.* a stopper for closing a hole in a barrel or jar. —*v.* **1.** to close with a bung. **2.** (*slang*) to throw or toss, *bung it over here.* □ **bunged up,** blocked.

bungalow *n.* a one-storeyed house.

bungle *v.* to spoil by lack of skill, to tackle clumsily and without success. —*n.* a bungled attempt. —**bungler** *n.*

bunion *n.* a swelling at the base of the big toe, with thickened skin.

bunk[1] *n.* a built-in shelf-like bed, e.g. on a ship. **bunk beds,** a pair of small single beds mounted one above the other as a unit.

bunk[2] *v.* (*slang*) to run away. **do a bunk,** (*slang*) to run away.

bunk[3] *n.* (*slang*) bunkum.

bunker *n.* **1.** a container for fuel. **2.** a sandy hollow forming a hazard on a golf-course. **3.** a reinforced underground shelter. —*v.* to put fuel into the bunkers of (a ship). □ **bunkered** *adj.* trapped in a bunker at golf.

bunkum *n.* nonsense.

bunny *n.* (*children's use*) a rabbit.

bunt *v.* to push with the head. —*n.* a push given with the head.

bunting[1] *n.* a bird related to the finches.

bunting[2] *n.* **1.** flags and streamers for decorating streets and buildings. **2.** a loosely-woven fabric used for making these.

buoy (*pr.* boi) *n.* an anchored floating object marking a navigable channel or showing the position of submerged rocks etc. —*v.* **1.** to mark with a buoy or buoys. **2.** to keep (a thing) afloat; *buoyed up with new hope,* encouraged.

buoyant (**boy**-ănt) *adj.* **1.** able to float. **2.** light-hearted, cheerful. **buoyantly** *adv.*, **buoyancy** *n.*

bur *n.* a plant's seed-case or flower that clings to hair or clothing, the plant itself.

burble *v.* **1.** to make a gentle murmuring sound. **2.** to speak lengthily.

burden *n.* **1.** something carried, a heavy load. **2.** something difficult to support, *the heavy burden of taxation.* **3.** the chief theme of a speech etc. —*v.* to load, to put a burden on. □ **beast of burden,** an animal that carries packs on its back. **the burden of proof,** the obligation to prove what one says.

burdensome *adj.* troublesome, tiring.

bureau (**bewr**-oh) *n.* (*pl.* bureaus) **1.** a piece of furniture with drawers and a hinged flap for use as a desk. **2.** an office or department, *a travel bureau; the Information Bureau.*

bureaucracy (bewr-**ok**-răsi) *n.* **1.** government by State officials not by elected representatives. **2.** these officials. **3.** excessive official routine, especially because there are too many offices or departments.

bureaucrat (**bewr**-ŏ-krat) *n.* an official who works in a government office, one who applies the rules of his department without exercising much judgement.

bureaucratic (bewr-ŏ-**krat**-ik) *adj.* **1.** of bureaucracy. **2.** of or like bureaucrats.

burette (bewr-**et**) *n.* a graduated glass tube with a tap, used for measuring small quantities of liquid run out of it.

burgeon (**bur**-jŏn) *v.* to begin to grow rapidly.

burger *n.* a hamburger or food resembling this.

burgh (burră) *n.* a borough in Scotland.

burglar *n.* a person who enters a building illegally, especially in order to steal. **burglary** *n.*

burgle *v.* to rob as a burglar.

burgomaster (berg-ŏ-**mah**-ster) *n.* the mayor of a Dutch or Flemish town.

burgundy *n.* **1.** a red or white wine from Burgundy in France, a similar wine from elsewhere. **2.** dark purplish red.

burial *n.* **1.** burying, being buried. **2.** a buried body, *a prehistoric burial was found.*

burlesque (bur-**lesk**) *n.* a mocking imitation.

burly *adj.* (burlier, burliest) *adj.* with a strong heavy body, sturdy. **burliness** *n.*

Burma a country of south-east Asia. **Burmese** *adj.* & *n* (*pl.* Burmese).

burn[1] *v.* (burned *or* burnt (¶ see note at end of entry), burning) **1.** to damage or hurt or destroy by fire or heat or the action of acid. **2.** to be injured or damaged in this way. **3.** to produce (a mark etc.) by heat or fire; *money burns holes in his pocket,* makes him eager to spend it. **4.** to use as fuel. **5.** to produce heat or light, to be alight. **6.** to be able to be set on fire. **7.** to feel or cause to feel hot; *my ears are burning,* they feel hot, jokingly supposed to be a sign that one is being talked about elsewhere. **8.** to make or become brown from heat or light. **9.** to kill or be killed by burning. **10.** (*Amer. slang*) to be electrocuted in the electric chair. —**burn** *n.* **1.** a mark or sore made by burning. **2.** the firing of a spacecraft's rocket(s). □ **burn one's boats** *or* **bridges,** to do something deliberately that makes retreat impossible. **burn the midnight oil,** to study far into the night. **have money to burn,** to have so much that one does not need to take care of it. ¶ The form *burnt* (not *burned*) is always used when an adjective is required, e.g. in *a burnt offering.*

burn² *n.* (*Scottish*) a brook.

burner *n.* the part of a lamp or cooker that shapes the flame.

burnet (**bern**-it) *n.* a plant with brown flowers.

Burnham scale (**ber** năm) a national salary scale for schoolteachers.

burning *see* burn.¹ —*adj.* 1. intense, *a burning desire.* 2. hotly discussed, vital, *a burning question.* □ **burning bush**, a shrub with red fruits or red autumn leaves.

burnish *v.* to polish by rubbing.

burnous (ber-**noos**) *n.* an Arab or Moorish hooded cloak.

burnt *see* burn¹. —*adj.* of a deep shade, *burnt sienna, burnt umber.*

burp *n.* (*slang*) a belch, a belching sound. —*v.* (*slang*) 1. to belch. 2. to cause (a baby) to bring up wind from the stomach.

burr *n.* 1. a whirring sound. 2. the strong pronunciation of 'r', a soft country accent, especially one using this. 3. a small drill. 4. a bur. —*v.* to make a whirring sound.

burrow *n.* a hole or tunnel dug by a fox or rabbit etc. as a dwelling. —*v.* 1. to dig a burrow, to tunnel. 2. to form by tunnelling. 3. to search deeply, to delve.

bursar (**ber**-ser) *n.* 1. a person who manages the finances and other business of a school or college. 2. a student who holds a bursary.

bursary (**ber**-ser-i) *n.* a grant given to a student.

burst *v.* (burst, bursting) 1. to force or be forced open, to fly violently apart because of pressure inside; *buds are bursting,* opening out; *don't burst yourself,* (*slang*) don't injure yourself by making too much effort. 2. to appear or come suddenly and forcefully, *burst into flame.* 3. to let out a violent expression of feeling, *burst into tears, burst out laughing; she burst into song,* suddenly began to sing. —**burst** *n.* 1. a bursting, a split. 2. an explosion or outbreak, a series of shots, *a burst of gunfire, of applause.* 3. a brief violent effort, a spurt.

bursting *adj.* full to breaking-point, *sacks bursting with grain; bursting with energy,* full of it; *we are bursting to tell you,* very eager.

burton *n.* **go for a burton**, (*slang*) to be lost or destroyed or killed.

Burundi (bŭ-**run**-di) a country in East Africa.

bury *v.* (buried, burying) 1. to place (a dead body) in the earth or a tomb or the sea; *she has buried three husbands,* lost them by death. 2. to put underground, to

hide in earth etc., to cover up; *buried himself in the country,* went and lived where he would meet few people; *buried themselves in their books,* gave all their time and attention to reading. □ **bury the hatchet**, to cease quarrelling and become friendly.

bus *n.* (*pl.* buses) 1. a long-bodied passenger vehicle. 2. a busbar. 3. a data highway (*see* highway sense 3). —**bus** *v.* (bused, busing) 1. to travel by bus. 2. to transport by bus, to take (children) to a distant school by bus in order to counteract racial segregation. □ **bus lane**, a strip of road for use by buses only. **bus station**, an area where a number of buses stop, with facilities for passengers etc. as at a railway station. **bus-stop** *n.* the regular stopping-place of a bus.

busbar *n.* an electrical conductor or set of conductors for collecting and distributing electric current.

busby (**buz**-bi) *n.* a tall fur cap worn by the Guards on ceremonial occasions.

bush *n.* 1. a shrub. 2. a thick growth or clump, *a bush of hair.* 3. wild uncultivated land, especially in Africa and Australia. □ **bush telegraph**, a way in which news is passed on unofficially.

bushel *n.* a measure for grain and fruit (8 gallons). **hide one's light under a bushel**, to conceal one's abilities.

bushy *adj.* (bushier, bushiest) 1. covered with bushes. 2. growing thickly. **bushiness** *n.*

business *n.* 1. a task or duty, a thing one is concerned with. 2. one's usual occupation, a profession, a trade. 3. a thing needing to be dealt with, the agenda. 4. a difficult matter, *what a business it is!* 5. an affair or subject or device. 6. buying and selling, trade. 7. a commercial firm, a shop, *they own a grocery business.* □ **business end**, (*informal*) the working end of a tool etc., not the handle. **business-like** *adj.* practical, systematic. **business man**, one who is engaged in trade or commerce. **have no business to**, to have no right to (do something).

busker *n.* an entertainer who performs in the street.

busman *n.* (*pl.* busmen) the driver of a bus. **busman's holiday**, leisure time spent doing something similar to one's usual work.

bust¹ *n.* 1. a sculpture of the head, shoulders, and chest. 2. the bosom. 3. the measurement round a woman's body at the bosom.

bust² *v.* (busted *or* bust, busting) (*slang*) to burst; *the business went bust,* became bankrupt. —*n.* (*slang*) 1. a failure. 2. a spree. —*adj.* (*slang*) **1.** burst, broken. **2.** bankrupt. —**buster** *n.* □ **bust-up** *n.* (*slang*) a quarrel.

bustard *n.* a large swift-running bird.

bustle¹ *v.* **1.** to make a show of hurrying. **2.** to cause to hurry. —*n.* excited activity.

bustle² *n.* padding used to puff out the top of a woman's skirt at the back.

busy *adj.* (busier, busiest) **1.** working, occupied, having much to do; *get busy*, start doing things. **2.** full of activity, *a busy day*; *telephone line is busy*, is engaged. **3.** (of a picture or design) too full of detail. —*v.* (busied, busying) to keep busy, *busy oneself.* —**busily** *adv.*, **busyness** *n.*

busybody *n.* a meddlesome person.

but *adv.* only, no more than, *we can but try.* —*prep.* & *conj.* **1.** however, on the other hand. **2.** except, otherwise than, *there's no one here but me*; *I'd have drowned but for you*, if you had not helped me. —*n.* an objection, *ifs and buts*; *but me no buts*, do not raise objections.

butane (**bew**-tayn) *n.* an inflammable gas produced from petroleum, used in liquid form as a fuel.

butch *n.* (*slang*) **1.** a tough youth or man. **2.** a mannish woman.

butcher *n.* **1.** a person whose trade is to slaughter animals for food, one who cuts up and sells animal flesh. **2.** a person who has people killed needlessly or brutally. —*v.* to kill needlessly or brutally. □ **butcher's** *n.* (*rhyming slang*, short for 'butcher's hook') a look.

butchery *n.* **1.** a butcher's trade. **2.** needless or brutal killing.

butler *n.* the chief manservant of a household, especially one in charge of the wine-cellar.

butt¹ *n.* a large cask or barrel.

butt² *n.* **1.** the thicker end of a tool or weapon. **2.** a short remnant, a stub.

butt³ *n.* **1.** the mound of earth behind the targets on a shooting-range. **2.** a person or thing that is frequently a target for ridicule or teasing. —**butt** *v.* **1.** to push with the head like a ram or goat. **2.** to meet or place edge to edge, *the strips should be butted against each other, not overlapping.* □ **butt in,** to interrupt; to meddle. **butts** *pl. n.* a shooting-range.

butter *n.* **1.** a fatty food substance made from cream by churning. **2.** a similar substance made from other materials, *peanut butter.* —*v.* to spread with butter. □ **butter-cream** *n.* flavoured butter etc. for filling or coating cakes. **buttered** *adj.* cooked or spread with butter. **butter-fingers** *n.* a person likely to drop things. **butter muslin,** a thin loosely-woven

fabric. **butter up,** (*informal*) to flatter.

butter-bean *n.* a large dried haricot bean.

buttercup *n.* a wild plant with bright yellow cup-shaped flowers.

butterfly *n.* **1.** an insect with four often brightly coloured wings and knobbed feelers. **2.** a swimming-stroke in which both arms are lifted at the same time. □ **have butterflies in the stomach,** to feel nervous tremors.

buttermilk *n.* the liquid left after butter has been churned from milk.

butterscotch *n.* a kind of hard toffee.

buttock *n.* either of the two fleshy rounded parts at the lower or rear end of the back of the human or an animal body.

button *n.* **1.** a knob or disc sewn on a garment as a fastener or ornament. **2.** a small rounded object, a knob pressed to operate an electric bell etc. —*v.* (buttoned, buttoning) to fasten with a button or buttons. □ **button chrysanthemum,** one with many small round flower-heads. **button mushroom,** a small unopened mushroom. **button-through** *adj.* fastening by buttons down its whole length.

buttonhole *n.* **1.** a slit through which a button is passed to fasten clothing. **2.** a flower worn in the buttonhole of a coat-lapel. —*v.* to accost and detain with conversation.

buttress *n.* **1.** a support built against a wall. **2.** a thing that supports or reinforces something. —*v.* to prop up.

butty *n.* (*dialect*) a slice of bread and butter, a sandwich.

buxom *adj.* plump and healthy-looking.

buy *v.* (bought, buying) **1.** to obtain in exchange for money or by some sacrifice. **2.** to win over by bribery. **3.** (*slang*) to believe, to accept the truth of, *no one would buy that excuse.* **4.** (*slang*) to receive as a punishment. —*n.* a purchase; *a good buy*, a useful purchase, a bargain. □ **buy it,** (*slang*) to be killed or destroyed. **buy off,** to get rid of by payment. **buy out,** to obtain full ownership by paying (another person) to give up his share. **buy up,** to buy all or as much as possible of.

buyer *n.* **1.** a person who buys something. **2.** an agent choosing and buying stock for a large shop. □ **buyers' market,** a state of affairs when goods are plentiful and prices are low.

buzz *n.* **1.** a vibrating humming sound. **2.** a rumour. **3.** (*slang*) a telephone call, *give me a buzz.* —**buzz** *v.* **1.** to make a buzz. **2.** to be filled with a buzzing noise. **3.** to go about quickly and busily. **4.** to threaten (an aircraft) by flying close to it. □ **buzz off,** (*slang*) to go away.

buzzard *n.* a kind of hawk.

buzzer *n.* a device that produces a buzzing note as a signal.

by *prep.* & *adv.* **1.** near, beside, in reserve; *north by east,* between north and north-north-east. **2.** along, via, past. **3.** during, *came by night.* **4.** through the agency or means of, (of an animal) having as its sire. **5.** (of members or measurements) taking it together with, *multiply six by four; it measures ten feet by eight,* with eight feet as a second dimension. **6.** not later than. **7.** according to, *judging by appearances; sold by the dozen,* a dozen at a time. **8.** after, succeeding, *bit by bit.* **9.** to the extent of, *missed it by inches.* **10.** in respect of, *a tailor, Jones by name; pull it up by the roots.* **11.** in the belief of, *swear by God.* —*adj.* additional, less important, *a by-road.* □ **by and by,** before long. **by and large,** on the whole, considering everything. **by oneself,** alone; without help.

bye *n.* **1.** a run scored in cricket from a ball that passes the batsman without being hit. **2.** a hole or holes remaining unplayed when a golf match is ended. **3.** the state of having no opponent for one round in a tournament and so advancing to the next as if having won.

bye-bye *int.* (*informal*) goodbye.

by-election *n.* election of an MP to fill a single vacancy in the House of Commons, caused by the death or resignation of a member.

bye-line *n.* the goal-line of a football pitch.

bygone *adj.* belonging to the past. **bygones** *pl. n.* things belonging to the past; *let bygones be bygones,* forgive and forget past offences.

by-law *n.* a law or regulation made by a local authority or by a company.

bypass *n.* **1.** a road taking traffic round a congested area. **2.** a secondary channel allowing something to flow when the main route is blocked. —**bypass** *v.* **1.** to avoid by means of a bypass. **2.** to omit or ignore (procedures, regulations, etc.) in order to act quickly.

by-play *n.* action, usually without speech, of minor characters in a play etc.

by-product *n.* a substance produced during the making of something else.

byre *n.* a cow-shed.

by-road *n.* a minor road.

bystander *n.* a person standing near but taking no part when something happens.

byte (*rhymes with* kite) *n.* a fixed number of bits (= binary digits) in a computer, often representing a single character.

byway *n.* a by-road.

byword *n.* **1.** a person or thing spoken of as a notable example, *the firm became a byword for mismanagement.* **2.** a familiar saying.

Byzantine (bĭ-**zan**-tyn) *adj.* **1.** of Byzantium or the eastern Roman Empire. **2.** complicated, devious, underhand.

Cc

C *abbrev.* Celsius, centigrade.

c. *abbrev.* about (short for *circa*).

cab *n.* **1.** a taxi. **2.** a compartment for the driver of a train, lorry, or crane.

cabal (kă-**bal**) *n.* a secret plot, the people engaged in it.

cabaret (**kab**-ă-ray) *n.* an entertainment provided in a restaurant or night-club while the customers are eating.

cabbage *n.* **1.** a vegetable with green or purple leaves usually forming a round head. **2.** (*informal*) a person who lives without interests or ambition.

caber (**kay**-ber) *n.* a roughly-trimmed tree-trunk used in the Scottish sport of tossing the caber.

cabin *n.* **1.** a small dwelling or shelter, especially of wood. **2.** a compartment in a ship or aircraft or spacecraft. **3.** a driver's cab. □ **cabin cruiser,** a large motor boat with a cabin or cabins.

cabinet *n.* **1.** a cupboard or container with drawers or shelves for storing or displaying articles, or containing a radio or TV set. **2.** *the Cabinet,* the group of ministers chosen by the Prime Minister to be responsible for government policy. □ **cabinet-maker** *n.* a skilled joiner.

cable *n.* **1.** a thick rope of fibre or wire. **2.** an anchor-chain. **3.** (as a nautical measure) 200 yards. **4.** a set of insulated wires for carrying electricity or telegraph messages. **5.** a telegram sent abroad. **6.** a knitted pattern (*cable stitch*) looking like twisted rope. —*v.* to send a telegram to (a person) abroad, to transmit (money or information) in this way. □ **cable-car** *n.* one of the cars in a **cable railway,** a railway with cars drawn by an endless cable by means of a stationary engine.

caboodle (kă-**boo**-d'l) *n.* (*slang*) **the whole caboodle,** the whole lot.

cabriole (**kab**-ri-ohl) *n.* a curved leg on furniture, rather like an animal's foreleg.

cacao (kă-**kay**-oh) *n.* **1.** (*pl.* cacaos) a tropical tree producing a seed from which cocoa and chocolate are made. **2.** its seed.

cache (*pr.* kash) *n.* **1.** a hiding-place for treasure or stores. **2.** hidden treasure or stores. —*v.* to place in a cache.

cachou (**kash**-oo) *n.* a small scented lozenge.

cackle *n.* **1.** the loud clucking noise a hen makes after laying. **2.** a loud silly laugh. **3.** noisy chatter. —**cackle** *v.* **1.** to give a cackle. **2.** to chatter noisily.

cacophony (kă-**kof**-ŏni) *n.* a harsh discordant sound. **cacophonous** *adj.*

cactus *n.* (*pl.* cacti, *pr.* **kak**-ty) a plant from a hot dry climate, with a fleshy stem and usually prickles but no leaves. **cactus dahlia,** a dahlia with rolled-back petals that stick out like spikes.

cad *n.* a person who behaves dishonourably. **caddish** *adj.*

cadaverous (kă-**dav**-er-ŭs) *adj.* gaunt and pale.

caddie *n.* **1.** a person who carries a golfer's clubs for him during a game. **2.** (also *caddy*) a small container holding articles ready for use. —*v.* (caddied, caddying) to act as caddie. ◻ **caddie car** *or* **cart,** a light trolley to carry golf-clubs during a game.

caddis-fly *n.* a four-winged insect living near water.

caddy¹ *n.* a small box for holding tea.

caddy² *see* caddie (sense 2).

cadence (**kay**-dĕns) *n.* **1.** rhythm in sound. **2.** the rise and fall of the voice in speaking. **3.** the end of a musical phrase.

cadenza (kă-**den**-ză) *n.* an elaborate passage for a solo instrument or voice, showing off the performer's skill.

cadet (kă-**det**) *n.* a young person receiving elementary training for service in the armed forces or the police force.

cadge *v.* to ask for as a gift, to go about begging. **cadger** *n.*

cadmium (**kad**-miŭm) *n.* a chemical element that looks like tin.

cadre (**kah**-der) *n.* a group forming a nucleus of trained workers that can be increased when necessary.

Caerphilly (kair-**fil**-i) *n.* a mild crumbly white cheese.

Caesar *n.* a title of the Roman emperors.

Caesarean (siz-**air**-iăn) *n.* (*informal*) a **Caesarean section,** a surgical operation by which a child is taken from the womb by cutting through the wall of the abdomen and into the womb (¶ so called from the story that Julius Caesar was born in this way).

café (**kaf**-ay) *n.* a shop that sells refreshments, a small restaurant.

cafeteria (kaf-i-**teer**-iă) *n.* a café where customers serve themselves from a counter.

caffeine (**kaf**-een) *n.* a stimulant found in tea and coffee.

caftan (**kaf**-tăn) *n.* **1.** a long coat-like garment worn by men in the Near East. **2.** a woman's long loose dress.

cage *n.* **1.** a framework with wires or bars in which birds or animals are kept. **2.** any similar structure, the enclosed platform in which people travel in a lift or the shaft of a mine. —*v.* to put or keep in a cage. ◻ **cage-bird** *n.* a bird of a kind usually kept in a cage.

cagey *adj.* (cagier, cagiest) (*informal*) cautious about giving information, secretive. **cagily** *adv.*, **caginess** *n.*

cagoule (kă-**gool**) *n.* a thin waterproof jacket with a hood.

cahoots (kă-**hoots**) *pl. n.* (*Amer. slang*) **in cahoots with,** in league with.

cairn *n.* a pyramid of rough stones set up as a landmark or a monument.

cairngorm *n.* a yellow or wine-coloured semi-precious stone from the Cairngorm mountains in Scotland.

cairn terrier a small shaggy short-legged terrier.

Cairo the capital of Egypt.

caisson (kay-**sŏn**) *n.* a watertight box or chamber inside which work can be carried out on underwater structures.

cajole (kă-**johl**) *v.* to coax. **cajolery** *n.*

cake *n.* **1.** a baked sweet bread-like food. **2.** a mixture cooked in a round flat shape, *fish cakes.* **3.** a shaped or hardened mass, *a cake of soap.* —**cake** *v.* **1.** to harden into a compact mass. **2.** to encrust with a hardened mass.

calabrese (kal-ă-**bray**-say) *n.* a kind of sprouting broccoli.

calamine *n.* a pink powder, chiefly zinc carbonate or oxide, used in skin lotions.

calamity *n.* a disaster. **calamitous** *adj.*

calceolaria (kalsi-ŏ-**lair**-iă) *n.* a garden plant with a slipper-shaped flower.

calcify (**kal**-si-fy) *v.* (calcified, calcifying) to harden by a deposit of calcium salts. **calcification** *n.*

calcium *n.* a greyish-white chemical element present in bones and teeth and forming the basis of lime.

calculable *adj.* able to be calculated.

calculate *v.* **1.** to find out by using mathematics, to count. **2.** to plan deliberately, to intend. **3.** (*Amer. informal*) to suppose, to believe. **calculation** *n.* ◻ **calculated risk,** a risk taken deliberately with full knowledge of the dangers.

calculating *adj.* (of people) shrewd, scheming.

calculator *n.* **1.** a device used in making calculations, especially a small electronic one. **2.** one who calculates.

calculus (**kal**-kew-lŭs) *n.* (*pl.* calculuses) **1.** a stone formed in the body. **2.** a branch of mathematics that deals with problems involving rates of variation.

Caledonian (kali-**doh**-niăn) *adj.* of Scotland.

calendar *n.* **1.** a chart showing the days, weeks, and months of a particular year. **2.** a device displaying the date. **3.** a list of dates or events of a particular kind, *the Racing Calendar.* **4.** the system by which time is divided into fixed periods, *the Gregorian calendar.*

calender *n.* a machine in which cloth or paper is pressed by rollers to glaze or smooth it. —*v.* to press in a calender.

calf¹ *n.* (*pl.* calves) **1.** the young of cattle, also of the seal, whale, and certain other animals. **2.** leather made from calfskin. □ **calf-love** *n.* childish romantic love.

calf² *n.* (*pl.* calves) the fleshy back part of the leg below the knee.

calibrate (**kal**-i-brayt) *v.* **1.** to mark or correct units of measurement on a gauge. **2.** to measure the calibre of. **calibration** *n.*

calibre (**kal**-i-ber) *n.* **1.** the diameter of the inside of a tube or gun-barrel. **2.** the diameter of a bullet or shell. **3.** ability, importance, *we need a man of your calibre.*

calico *n.* a kind of cotton cloth.

Calif. *abbrev.* California.

California a State of the USA. **Californian** *adj.* & *n.* □ **Californian poppy,** a small cultivated poppy.

call *n.* **1.** a shout or cry. **2.** the characteristic cry of a bird. **3.** a signal on a bugle etc. **4.** a short visit. **5.** a summons, an invitation; *the call of the wild,* its attraction. **6.** a demand, a claim, *I have many calls on my time.* **7.** a need, an occasion, *there's no call for you to worry.* **8.** a declaration of trumps etc. in card-games, a player's right or turn to make this. **9.** an act of telephoning, a conversation on the telephone. —**call** *v.* **1.** to shout or speak loudly in order to attract attention etc. **2.** to utter a call. **3.** to pay a short visit. **4.** to name, to describe or address as, *I call that cheating*; *let's call it a fiver,* estimate the amount at £5. **5.** to declare (a trump suit etc.) in card-games. **6.** to rouse deliberately, to summon to get up. **7.** to summon, *call the fire brigade.* **8.** to command or invite, to urge as if by commanding, *call a strike*; *duty calls,* claims my attention. **9.** to communicate with by telephone or radio. — **caller** *n.* □ **call a person's bluff,** to challenge him to carry out his threat. **call-box** *n.* a telephone-box. **call for,** to demand, to require; to come and collect. **call-girl** *n.* a prostitute who accepts appointments by telephone. **call in,** to pay a casual visit; to seek advice or help from; to order the

return of, to take out of circulation. **call it a day,** to decide enough work has been done for one day, and stop working. **call off,** to call away; to cancel, *the strike was called off.* **call of nature,** a need to go to the lavatory. **call on,** to make a short visit to (a person); to appeal to, to request. **call out,** to summon to action; to order to come out on strike. **call-sign, call-signal** *ns.* a signal identifying a radio transmitter, *the call-sign is Alpha Alpha.* **call the tune,** to control the proceedings. **call to mind,** to remember; to cause to remember. **call up,** to telephone to; to bring back to one's mind; to summon for military service. **call-up** *n.* a summons for military service. **on call,** available to be called out on duty. **within call,** near enough to be summoned by calling.

calla lily (**kal**-ă) an arum lily.

calligraphy (kă-**lig**-răfi) *n.* beautiful handwriting, the art of producing this. **calligrapher** *n.*

calling *n.* an occupation, a profession or trade.

calliper (**kal**-i-per) *n.* a metal support for a weak or injured leg. **callipers** *pl. n.* compasses for measuring the diameter of tubes or of round objects.

callosity (kă-**loss**-iti) *n.* **1.** abnormal hardness of the skin. **2.** a callus.

callous (**kal**-ŭs) *adj.* **1.** hardened, having calluses. **2.** unsympathetic. **callously** *adv.,* **callousness** *n.* □ **calloused** *adj.* hardened, having calluses.

callow (*rhymes with* shallow) *adj.* immature and inexperienced. **callowly** *adv.,* **callowness** *n.*

callus (**kal**-ŭs) *n.* (*pl.* calluses) an area of thick hardened skin or tissue.

calm *adj.* **1.** quiet and still, not windy. **2.** not excited or agitated. **3.** casual and confident. —*n.* a calm condition or period, lack of strong winds. —*v.* to make or become calm. —**calmly** *adv.,* **calmness** *n.*

Calor gas (*trade mark*) liquefied butane stored under pressure in containers for domestic use.

calorie *n.* **1.** a unit for measuring a quantity of heat. **2.** a unit for measuring the energy value of food.

calumny (**kal**-ŭm-ni) *n.* **1.** slander. **2.** a slanderous statement.

calve *v.* to give birth to a calf.

Calvinism *n.* the teachings of John Calvin, a French Protestant religious reformer who lived in Switzerland (1509–64), and of his followers. **Calvinist** *n.*

calypso *n.* (*pl.* calypsos) a West Indian

song with a variable rhythm and topical usually improvised lyrics.

calyx (**kay**-liks) *n.* (*pl.* calyxes) a ring of leaves (*sepals*) enclosing an unopened flower-bud.

cam *n.* a projecting part on a wheel or shaft, shaped or mounted so that its circular motion, as it turns, transmits an up-and-down or back-and-forth motion to another part. **camshaft** *n.*

camaraderie (kamă-**rah**-der-i) *n.* comradeship.

camber *n.* a slight arch or upward curve given to a surface especially of a road. **cambered** *adj.*

Cambodia (kam-**boh**-diă) a country (official name *Kampuchea*) in south-east Asia. **Cambodian** *adj.* & *n.*

cambric *n.* thin linen or cotton cloth.

Cambridgeshire a county of England. —*n.* a horse-race run annually at Newmarket in Suffolk.

Cambs. *abbrev.* Cambridgeshire.

came *see* come.

camel *n.* **1.** a long-necked animal with either one or two humps on its back, used in desert countries for riding and for carrying goods. **2.** a fawn colour. □ **camel-hair** *n.* fine soft hair used in artists' brushes, fabric made of this.

camellia (kă-**mee**-liă) **1.** an evergreen flowering shrub from China and Japan. **2.** its flower.

Camembert (**kam**-ĕm-bair) *n.* a soft rich cheese of the kind made in Normandy, France.

cameo (**kam**-i-oh) *n.* (*pl.* cameos) **1.** a small piece of hard stone carved with a raised design, especially with two coloured layers cut so that one serves as a background to the design. **2.** something small but well-executed, e.g. a short description or a part in a play.

camera *n.* an apparatus for taking photographs, moving pictures, or TV pictures.

cameraman *n.* (*pl.* cameramen) a person whose job is to operate a film camera or TV camera.

Cameroon (kam-er-**oon**) a country on the west coast of Africa. **Cameroonian** *adj.* & *n.*

camiknickers *pl. n.* a woman's undergarment combining camisole and knickers.

camisole (**kam**-i-sohl) *n.* a woman's cotton bodice-like garment or undergarment.

camomile (**kam**-ŏ-myl) *n.* a sweet-smelling plant with daisy-like flowers which are dried for use in medicine as a tonic.

camouflage (**kam**-ŏ-flah*zh*) *n.* a method of disguising or concealing objects by colouring or covering them so that they

look like part of their surroundings. —*v.* to conceal in this way.

camp¹ *n.* **1.** a place where people live temporarily in tents, huts, or similar shelters. **2.** the occupants. **3.** a group of people with the same ideals. —**camp** *v.* **1.** to make or live in a camp. **2.** to live temporarily as if in a camp. —**camper** *n.* □ **camp-bed** *n.* a folding portable bed. **camp out**, to sleep in a tent or in the open. **go camping**, to spend a holiday living in tents.

camp² *adj.* **1.** effeminate, homosexual. **2.** exaggerated in style, especially for humorous effect. —*n.* such a style or manner.

campaign *n.* **1.** a series of military operations with a set purpose, usually in one area. **2.** a similar series of planned activities, *an advertising campaign.* —*v.* to take part in a campaign. —**campaigner** *n.*

campanology (kamp-ăn-**ol**-ŏji) *n.* the study of bells (their ringing, founding, etc.). **campanologist** *n.*

campanula (kăm-**pan**-yoo-lă) *n.* a plant with bell-shaped usually blue or white flowers.

camphor *n.* a strong-smelling white substance used in medicine and moth-balls and in making plastics. **camphorated** *adj.* containing camphor.

campion *n.* a wild plant with pink or white flowers.

campus *n.* (*pl.* campuses) the grounds of a university or college.

can¹ *n.* **1.** a metal or plastic container for liquids. **2.** a sealed tin in which food or drink is preserved. **3.** either of these with its contents, the amount it contains. —*v.* (canned, canning) to preserve in a sealed can. —**canner** *n.* □ **carry the can**, (*slang*) to bear the responsibility or blame.

can² *auxiliary verb* expressing ability or knowledge of how to do something (*he can play the violin*) or permission (*you can go*; ¶ *may* is more formal) or desire or liberty to act (*we cannot allow this*).

Canada a country in North America. **Canadian** *adj.* & *n.*

canal *n.* **1.** a channel cut through land for navigation or irrigation. **2.** a tubular passage through which food or air passes in a plant or animal body, *the alimentary canal.*

canalize (kan-ă-lyz) *v.* to channel. **canalization** *n.*

canapé (**kan**-ăpi) *n.* a small piece of bread or pastry spread with savoury food.

canary *n.* a small yellow songbird.

canasta (kă-**nas**-tă) *n.* a card-game played with two packs of 52 cards.

Canberra (kan-ber-ă) the capital of Australia.

cancan *n.* a lively stage dance involving high kicking, performed by women in long skirts and petticoats.

cancel *v.* (cancelled, cancelling) 1. to say that (something already decided upon or arranged) will not be done or take place. 2. to order (a thing) to be discontinued. 3. to neutralize, *forgot to cancel my indicator.* 4. to cross out. 5. to mark (a stamp or ticket) in order to prevent further use. **cancellation** *n.* □ **cancel out,** to counterbalance, to neutralize (each other).

cancer *n.* 1. a tumour, especially a malignant one. 2. a disease in which malignant growths form. 3. something evil that spreads destructively. 4. *Cancer,* a sign of the zodiac, the Crab. **cancerous** *adj.*

candela (kan-dil-ă) *n.* a unit for measuring the brightness of a source of light.

candelabrum (kandi-**lab**-rŭm) *n.* (*pl.* candelabra) a large branched candlestick or holder for lights.

candid *adj.* frank, not hiding one's thoughts. **candidly** *adv.*, **candidness** *n.* □ **candid camera,** a small camera for taking informal pictures, especially without the subject's knowledge.

candidate *n.* 1. a person who seeks or is nominated for appointment to an office or position or membership. 2. a person taking an examination. **candidacy** (**kan**-did-ă-si) *n.*, **candidature** (**kan**-did-ă-cher) *n.*

candied (**kan**-did) *adj.* encrusted with sugar, preserved in sugar. **candied peel,** peel of citrus fruits candied for use in cooking.

candle *n.* a stick of wax with a wick through it, giving light when burning. **candle-light** *n.* the light of a candle or candles. **cannot hold a candle to,** is very inferior to. **game is not worth the candle,** the result does not justify the trouble or cost.

Candlemas *n.* the feast of the Purification of the Virgin Mary, when candles are blessed (2 February).

candlepower *n.* a unit of measurement of light, expressed in candelas.

candlestick *n.* a holder for one or more candles.

candlewick *n.* a fabric with a raised tufted pattern worked in soft cotton yarn.

candour (**kan**-der) *n.* candid speech, frankness.

candy *n.* (*Amer.*) sweets, a sweet. **candy-floss** *n.* a fluffy mass of spun sugar. **candy-stripes** *pl. n.* alternate stripes of white and colour. **candy-striped** *adj.*

candytuft *n.* a plant growing in tufts with white, pink, or purple flowers.

cane *n.* 1. the hollow jointed stem of tall reeds and grasses (e.g. bamboo, sugarcane), the solid stem of slender palms (e.g. Malacca). 2. the material of these used for making furniture etc. 3. a stem or a length of it, or a slender rod, used as a walking-stick or to support a plant etc., or as a stick for use in corporal punishment. 4. a raspberry-plant. —**cane** *v.* 1. to punish by beating with a cane. 2. to weave cane into (a chair etc.). □ **cane-sugar** *n.* sugar obtained from the juice of sugar-cane.

canine[1] (**kay**-nyn) *adj.* of dogs.

canine[2] (**ka**-nyn) *n.* a **canine tooth,** a strong pointed tooth next to the incisors.

canister *n.* 1. a metal box or other container. 2. a cylinder, filled with shot or tear-gas, that bursts and releases its contents when fired from a gun or thrown.

canker *n.* 1. a disease that destroys the wood of plants and trees. 2. a disease that causes ulcerous sores in animals.

cannabis (**kan**-ă-bis) *n.* 1. a hemp plant. 2. a preparation of this for smoking or chewing as an intoxicant drug.

canned *see* can[1]. —*adj.* 1. recorded for reproduction, *canned music.* 2. tinned, *canned fruit.* 3. (*slang*) drunk.

cannelloni (kan-ĕ-**loh**-ni) *pl. n.* rolls of pasta containing meat and seasoning.

cannery *n.* a canning-factory.

cannibal *n.* a person who eats human flesh, an animal that eats its own kind. **cannibalism** *n.*

cannibalize *v.* to dismantle (a machine etc.) in order to provide spare parts for others. **cannibalization** *n.*

cannon *n.* 1. (*pl.* cannon) an old type of large heavy gun firing solid metal balls. 2. an automatic shell-firing gun used in aircraft. 3. a shot in billiards in which the player's ball hits the two other balls in succession. —**cannon** *v.* (cannoned, cannoning) 1. to collide heavily with. 2. to make a cannon at billiards. □ **cannon-fodder** *n.* men regarded merely as material to be expended in war.

cannot = can not.

canny *adj.* (cannier, canniest) shrewd. **cannily** *adv.*, **canniness** *n.*

canoe *n.* a light narrow boat propelled by paddles. —*v.* (canoed, canoeing) to paddle or travel in a canoe. —**canoeist** *n.*

canon *n.* 1. a general principle. 2. a set of writings accepted as genuinely by a particular author, sacred writings included in the Bible. 3. a clergyman who is one of a group with duties in a cathedral. □ **canon law,** church law.

canonical (kă-**non**-ikăl) *adj.* **1**. ordered by canon law. **2**. included in the canon of Scripture. **3**. standard, accepted. **canonically** *adv.* □ **canonicals** *pl. n.* the canonical dress of clergy.

canonize *v.* to declare officially to be a saint. **canonization** *n.*

canopy *n.* **1**. a hanging cover forming a shelter above a throne, bed, or person etc. **2**. any similar covering. **3**. the part of a parachute that spreads in the air. □ **canopied** *adj.* having a canopy.

cant[1] *v.* to slope, to tilt. —*n.* a tilted or sloping position.

cant[2] *n.* **1**. insincere talk. **2**. jargon.

can't = cannot.

cantaloup (**kan**-tă-loop) *n.* a kind of melon.

cantankerous (kan-**tank**-er-ŭs) *adj.* bad-tempered. **cantankerously** *adv.*

cantata (kan-**tah**-tă) *n.* a musical composition for singers, like an oratorio but shorter.

canteen *n.* **1**. a restaurant for the employees of a factory, office, etc. **2**. a case or box containing a set of cutlery. **3**. a soldier's or camper's water-flask.

canter *n.* a slow easy gallop. —*v.* to ride at a canter, to gallop gently.

Canterbury bell a cultivated campanula with large flowers.

canticle (**kan**-ti-kŭl) *n.* a song or chant with words taken from the Bible, e.g. the Magnificat and the Nunc Dimittis.

cantilever (**kan**-ti-lee-ver) *n.* a projecting beam or girder supporting a balcony or similar structure.

canton *n.* a division of a country, especially of Switzerland.

Cantonese *n.* a Chinese language spoken in southern China and in Hong Kong.

canvas *n.* **1**. strong coarse cloth used for making tents and sails etc. and by artists for painting on. **2**. a piece of canvas for painting on, especially in oils, an oil-painting.

canvass *v.* **1**. to visit in order to ask for votes, orders for goods etc., or opinions. **2**. to propose (a plan). —*n.* canvassing. — **canvasser** *n.*

canyon (**kan**-yŏn) *n.* a deep gorge, usually with a river flowing through it.

cap *n.* **1**. a soft head-covering without a brim but often with a peak. **2**. an academic head-dress, a mortar-board. **3**. a cap-like cover or top. **4**. a percussion cap. — **cap** *v.* (capped, capping) **1**. to put a cap on, to cover the top or end of. **2**. to award a sports cap to. **3**. to excel, to outdo; *cap a joke*, to tell another, usually a better one.

capable *adj.* **1**. competent. **2**. having a certain ability or capacity, *quite capable of lying*. **capably** *adv.*, **capability** *n.*

capacious (kă-**pay**-shŭs) *adj.* roomy, able to hold much. **capaciously** *adv.*, **capaciousness** *n.*

capacitor (kă-**pas**-it-er) *n.* a device storing a charge of electricity.

capacity *n.* **1**. the ability to contain or accommodate, the amount that can be contained; *full to capacity*, quite full. **2**. ability, capability; *working at full capacity*, as intensively as possible. **3**. a position or function, *signed it in his capacity as chairman.*

caparison *v.* to deck out.

cape[1] *n.* **1**. a cloak. **2**. a very short similarly shaped part of a coat etc., covering the shoulders.

cape[2] *n.* a coastal promontory. **the Cape**, the Cape of Good Hope.

caper[1] *v.* to jump or run about playfully. —*n.* **1**. capering. **2**. (*slang*) an activity, an occupation, an escapade.

caper[2] *n.* **1**. a bramble-like shrub. **2**. one of its buds which are pickled for use in sauces etc., *caper sauce.*

capercaillie (kap-er-**kayl**-yi) *n.* a kind of bird, the largest European grouse.

Cape Town one of the two capital cities of South Africa.

Cape Verde (kayp **verd**) a group of islands off the west coast of Africa. **Cape Verdean** *adj. & n.*

capillary (kă-**pil**-er-i) *n.* one of the very fine branching blood-vessels that connect veins and arteries. —*adj.* of or like a capillary.

capital *adj.* **1**. principal, most important; *capital city*, the chief town of a country. **2**. (*informal*) excellent. **3**. involving the death penalty, *a capital offence.* **4**. very serious, fatal, *a capital error.* **5**. (of letters) of the form and size used to begin a name or a sentence, *a capital A.* —**capital** *n.* **1**. a capital city. **2**. a capital letter. **3**. the head or top part of a pillar. **4**. wealth or property that is used or invested to produce more wealth, the money with which a business etc. is started. □ **capital gain**, profit from the sale of investments or property. **capital goods**, goods such as ships, railways, machinery, etc., used in producing consumer goods. **capital sum**, a lump sum of money, especially that payable to an insured person. **capital transfer tax**, a tax on capital that is transferred from one person to another, e.g. by inheritance. **make capital out of**, to use (a situation etc.) to one's own advantage.

capitalism (**kap**-it-ăl-izm) *n.* an economic system in which trade and industry are controlled by private owners for profit.

capitalist (**kap**-it-ăl-ist) *n.* one who has much capital invested, a rich person.

capitalize *v.* **1.** to write or print as a capital letter. **2.** to convert into capital, to provide with capital. **capitalization** *n.* ☐ **capitalize on,** to profit by, to use (a thing) to one's advantage.

Capitol the building in Washington DC in which the Congress of the USA meets.

capitulate *v.* to surrender. **capitulation** *n.*

capon (**kay**-pŏn) *n.* a domestic cock castrated and fattened for eating.

cappuccino (kah-poo-**chee**-noh) *n.* espresso coffee made with milk. (¶ Italian.)

caprice (kă-**prees**) *n.* **1.** a whim. **2.** a piece of music in a lively fanciful style.

capricious (kă-**prish**-ŭs) *adj.* **1.** guided by caprice, impulsive. **2.** changeable, *a capricious breeze.* **capriciously** *adv.*, **capriciousness** *n.*

Capricorn *n.* a sign of the zodiac, the Goat.

capsicum (**kap**-si-kŭm) *n.* **1.** a tropical plant with hot-tasting seeds. **2.** its fruit.

capsize *v.* to overturn, *a wave capsized the boat*; *the boat capsized.*

capstan (**kap**-stăn) *n.* **1.** a thick revolving post used to pull in a rope or cable that winds round it as it turns, e.g. for raising a ship's anchor. **2.** a revolving spindle on a tape-recorder. ☐ **capstan lathe,** a lathe with a revolving tool-holder.

capsule *n.* **1.** a seed-case that splits open when ripe. **2.** a small soluble case in which a dose of medicine is enclosed for swallowing. **3.** a detachable compartment of a spacecraft, containing instruments or crew.

captain *n.* **1.** a person given authority over a group or team. **2.** an army officer ranking below a major and above a lieutenant. **3.** a naval officer ranking below a rear-admiral and above a commander. **4.** the person commanding a ship. **5.** the pilot of a civil aircraft. —*v.* to act as captain of. —**captaincy** *n.*

caption (**kap**-shŏn) *n.* **1.** a short title or heading. **2.** a description or explanation printed with an illustration etc. **3.** words shown on a cinema or TV screen.

captious (**kap**-shŭs) *adj.* fond of finding fault or raising objections about trivial matters. **captiously** *adv.*, **captiousness** *n.*

captivate *v.* to capture the fancy of, to charm. **captivation** *n.*

captive *adj.* **1.** taken prisoner. **2.** kept as a prisoner, unable to escape. —*n.* a captive person or animal. ☐ **captive audience,** people who cannot get away easily and therefore cannot avoid being addressed.

captivity *n.* the state of being held captive.

captor *n.* one who captures a person or animal.

capture *v.* **1.** to make a prisoner of. **2.** to take or obtain by force, trickery, attraction, or skill. —**capture** *n.* **1.** capturing. **2.** a thing captured.

Capuchin (**kap**-yoo-chin) *n.* a friar of a branch of the Franciscan order.

car *n.* **1.** a motor car. **2.** a carriage of a specified type, *dining-car*; *jaunting-car.* **3.** the passenger compartment of a cable railway. ☐ **car coat** a short coat designed for car drivers. **car-ferry** *n.* a ferry that can carry cars. **car-park** *n.* an area for parking cars.

Caracas (kă-**rak**-ăs) the capital of Venezuela.

carafe (kă-**raf**) *n.* a glass bottle in which wine or water is served at the table.

caramel *n.* **1.** burnt sugar used for colouring and flavouring food. **2.** a kind of toffee tasting like this.

caramelize *v.* to turn or be turned into caramel. **caramelization** *n.*

carapace (**ka**-ră-payss) *n.* the shell on the back of a tortoise or crustacean.

carat (**ka**-răt) *n.* **1.** a unit of weight for precious stones, 200 milligrams. **2.** a measure of the purity of gold, pure gold being 24 carat.

caravan *n.* **1.** a covered cart or an enclosed carriage used for living in, able to be towed by a horse or car. **2.** a company of people (e.g. merchants) travelling together across desert country. ☐ **caravanning** *n.* travelling by caravan, especially on holiday.

caraway *n.* a plant with spicy seeds that are used for flavouring cakes etc.

carbide (**kar**-byd) *n.* a compound of carbon, the compound used in making acetylene gas.

carbine (**kar**-byn) *n.* a short light automatic rifle.

carbohydrate *n.* an organic compound, such as the sugars and starches, composed of carbon, oxygen, and hydrogen. **carbohydrates** *pl. n.* starchy foods, considered to be fattening.

carbolic *n.* a kind of disinfectant.

carbon *n.* **1.** a chemical element that is present in all living matter and occurs in its pure form as diamond and graphite. **2.** a rod of carbon in an arc lamp. **3.** carbon paper. **4.** a carbon copy. ☐ **carbon copy,** a copy made with carbon paper; an exact copy. **carbon dating,** a method of deciding the age of prehistoric objects by measuring the decay of radiocarbon in them. **carbon dioxide,** a colourless odourless gas formed by the burning of carbon breathed out by animals in respiration. **carbon monoxide,** a very poisonous gas formed when carbon burns incompletely, occurring e.g. in the exhaust of motor engines. **carbon paper,** thin paper coated with carbon, placed between sheets of writing paper for making copies of what is written or typed on the top sheet. **carbon tetrachloride,** a colourless liquid used as a solvent in dry cleaning etc.

carbonade (kar-bŏn-**ayd**) *n.* a rich beef stew containing beer.

carbonate *n.* a compound that releases carbon dioxide when mixed with acid.

carbonated *adj.* charged with carbon dioxide; *carbonated drinks,* made fizzy with this.

carbonize *v.* 1. to convert (a substance that contains carbon) into carbon alone, e.g. by heating or burning it. 2. to coat with carbon. **carbonization** *n.*

carborundum (kar-ber-**un**-dŭm) *n.* a hard compound of carbon and silicon used for polishing and grinding things.

carboy (**kar**-boi) *n.* a large round bottle surrounded by a protecting framework, used for transporting liquids safely.

carbuncle *n.* 1. a severe abscess in the skin. 2. a bright-red gem cut in a knob-like shape.

carburettor *n.* an apparatus for mixing fuel and air in an internal-combustion engine.

carcass *n.* 1. the dead body of an animal, especially one prepared for cutting up as meat. 2. the bony part of the body of a bird before or after cooking. 3. the foundation structure of a tyre.

carcinogen (kar-**sin**-ŏ-jin) *n.* a cancer-producing substance. **carcinogenic** (kar-sin-ŏ-**jen**-ik) *adj.* producing cancer.

carcinoma (kar-sin-**oh**-mǎ) *n.* (*pl.* carcinomata) a cancerous growth.

card¹ *n.* 1. a small piece of stiff paper or thin cardboard, often printed, used e.g. to send messages or greetings, or to record information such as a person's name or the title of a book and used for identification or in a card index. 2. a programme of events at a race-meeting. 3. a playing-card. 4. (*informal*) an odd or amusing person. □ **be on the cards,** to be likely or possible. **card-carrying member,** a registered member of a political party, trade union, etc. **card-game** *n.* a game using playing-cards. **card index,** an index in which each item is entered on a separate card. **cards** *n.* card-playing, a card-game; (*pl. n.*) an employee's official documents

held by his employer; *get one's cards,* be told to leave one's employment. **card-sharp, card-sharper** *ns.* a person who makes a living by cheating others at card-games. **card vote,** a block vote in trade-union meetings. **have a card up one's sleeve,** to have something held in reserve secretly. **play one's cards well,** to behave with good judgement. **put one's cards on the table,** to be frank about one's re-sources and intentions.

card² *n.* a wire brush or toothed instrument for cleaning or combing wool. —*v.* to clean or comb with this.

cardboard *n.* pasteboard, especially for making into boxes.

cardiac (**kar**-di-ak) *adj.* of the heart.

Cardiff the capital of Wales.

cardigan *n.* a knitted jacket.

cardinal *adj.* 1. chief, most important, *the cardinal virtues.* 2. deep scarlet. —*n.* a member of the Sacred College of the RC Church, which elects the pope. □ **cardinal numbers,** the whole numbers, 1, 2, 3, etc. **cardinal points,** the four main points of the compass, North, East, South, and West.

cardiology (kar-di-**ol**-ŏji) *n.* the scientific study of diseases and abnormalities of the heart. **cardiologist** *n.*

care *n.* 1. serious attention and thought, *planned with care.* 2. caution to avoid damage or loss; *handle with care.* 3. protection, ~~charge~~, supervision, *left the child in her sister's care.* 4. worry, anxiety, *freedom from care.* —**care** *v.* 1. to feel concern or interest. 2. to feel affection or liking. 3. to feel willing, *would you care to try one?* □ **care for,** to have in one's care. **care of, c/o,** to the address of (someone who will deliver or forward things), *write to him care of his bank.* **in care,** taken into the care of a local authority. **take care,** to be cautious. **take care of,** to take charge of; to see to the safety or well-being of; to deal with.

careen (kǎ-**reen**) *v.* 1. to tilt or keel over to one side. 2. (*Amer.*) to swerve.

career *n.* 1. an occupation, a way of making a living, especially one with opportunities for advancement or promotion. 2. progress through life, the development and progress of a political party etc. 3. quick or violent forward movement; *stopped him in mid career,* as he was rushing. —*v.* to move swiftly or wildly. □ **career girl** *or* **woman,** a woman who works permanently in a paid occupation.

careerist *n.* a person who is keen to advance in his or her career.

carefree *adj.* lighthearted through being free from anxiety or responsibility.

careful *adj.* **1.** giving serious attention and thought, painstaking, *a careful worker*. **2.** done with care, *careful work*. **3.** cautious, avoiding damage or loss. **carefully** *adv.*, **carefulness** *n.*

careless *adj.* not careful. **carelessly** *adv.*, **carelessness** *n.*

caress (kă-**ress**) *n.* a loving touch, a kiss. —*v.* to touch lovingly, to kiss.

caret (ka-rit) *n.* an omission mark.

caretaker *n.* a person employed to look after a house or building. **caretaker government,** one holding office temporarily until another can be elected.

careworn *adj.* showing signs of prolonged worry.

cargo *n.* (*pl.* cargoes) goods carried on a ship or aircraft.

Caribbean (ka-ri-**bee**-ăn) *adj.* of the Caribbean Sea, a part of the Atlantic off Central America. —*n.* the Caribbean Sea.

caribou (ka-ri-boo) *n.* (*pl.* caribou) a North American reindeer.

caricature (ka-rik-ă-chuur) *n.* a picture or description or imitation of a person or thing that exaggerates certain characteristics, especially for comic effect. —*v.* to make a caricature of.

caries (kair eez) *n.* (*pl.* caries) decay in bones or teeth, *dental caries*.

carillon (kă-**ril**-yŏn) *n.* a set of bells sounded either from a keyboard or mechanically.

Carmelite (kar-měl-lyt) *n.* a member of an order of friars (also called *White Friars*) or of a corresponding order of nuns.

carminative (kar-min-ătiv) *adj.* curing flatulence. —*n.* a carminative drug.

carmine (kar-min) *adj.* & *n.* deep red.

carnage (kar-nij) *n.* the killing of many people.

carnal (kar-năl) *adj.* of the body or flesh, not spiritual, *carnal desires*. **carnally** *adv.*

carnation *n.* a cultivated clove-scented pink.

carnelian *n.* = cornelian.

carnival *n.* festivities and public merrymaking, usually with a procession.

carnivore (kar-niv-or) *n.* a carnivorous animal.

carnivorous (kar-**niv**-er-ŭs) *adj.* feeding on flesh or other animal matter.

carol *n.* a joyful song, especially a Christmas hymn. —*v.* (carolled, carolling) **1.** to sing carols. **2.** to sing joyfully. —**caroller** *n.*

Carolina (ka-rŏ-**ly**-nă) either of two States of the USA, *North* and *South Carolina*.

carotid (kă-**rot**-id) *n.* either of the carotid arteries, the two great arteries (one on

either side of the neck) carrying blood to the head. —*adj.* of these arteries.

carouse (kă-**rowz**, *rhymes with* cows) *v.* to drink and be merry. **carousal** *n.*

carousel (ka-roo-**sel**) *n.* **1.** (*Amer.*) a merry-go-round. **2.** a conveyor or delivery system that rotates like a merry-go-round.

carp[1] *n.* (*pl.* carp) an edible freshwater fish that lives in lakes and ponds.

carp[2] *v.* to keep finding fault, to raise petty objections.

carpal (kar-păl) *adj.* of the wrist joint. —*n.* any of the wrist-bones.

carpel (kar-pěl) *n.* the pistil of a flower, the part in which the seeds develop.

carpenter *n.* a person who makes or repairs wooden objects and structures. **carpentry** *n.*

carpet *n.* **1.** a thick textile covering for floors. **2.** a thick layer underfoot, *a carpet of leaves*. —**carpet** *v.* (carpeted, carpeting) **1.** to cover with a carpet. **2.** (*informal*) to reprimand. □ **carpet slippers,** slippers with cloth uppers. **carpet-sweeper** *n.* a household device with revolving brushes for sweeping carpets. **on the carpet,** (*informal*) being reprimanded.

carpeting *n.* **1.** material for carpets. **2.** (*informal*) a reprimand.

carport *n.* an open-sided shelter for a car, projecting from the side of a house.

carriage *n.* **1.** a wheeled vehicle, usually horse-drawn, for carrying passengers. **2.** a railway vehicle for passengers. **3.** the carrying of goods from place to place, the cost of this. **4.** a gun-carriage. **5.** a moving part carrying or holding something in a machine, the roller of a typewriter. **6.** the posture of the body when walking. □ **carriage clock,** a small portable clock with a rectangular case and a handle on top. **carriage forward,** the cost of sending goods is to be paid by the receiver. **carriage free** *or* **paid,** it is paid by the sender.

carriageway *n.* the part of the road on which vehicles travel.

carrier *n.* **1.** a person or thing that carries something. **2.** a person or company that transports goods or people for payment. **3.** a support for luggage or a seat for a passenger on a bicycle etc. **4.** a person or animal that transmits a disease to others without being affected by it himself. **5.** an aircraft-carrier. **6.** a carrier-bag. □ **carrier-bag** *n.* a paper or plastic bag for holding shopping etc. **carrier pigeon,** a homing pigeon used to carry messages tied to its leg or neck.

carrion (ka-ri-ŏn) *n.* dead and decaying

flesh. □ **carrion crow**, a black crow that lives on carrion and small animals.

carrot *n.* **1.** a plant with a tapering orange-coloured root. **2.** this root, used as a vegetable. **3.** a means of enticing someone to do something; *the carrot and the stick*, bribes and threats. □ **carrots** *n.* (*slang*) red hair, a red-haired person.

carroty *adj.* orange-red.

carry *v.* (carried, carrying) **1.** to take from one place to another. **2.** to have on one's person, *he is carrying a gun*. **3.** to conduct, to take, *wires carry electric current*. **4.** to support the weight of, to bear; *he carries that department*, but for his ability it would collapse. **5.** to involve, to entail, *the crime carries a life sentence*. **6.** to extend; *don't carry modesty too far*, do not be too modest. **7.** to reckon in the next column when adding figures. **8.** to win, to capture; *the motion was carried*, was approved. **9.** (of a newspaper or broadcast) to contain, *they all carried the story*. **10.** to hold and move (the body) in a certain way. **11.** to be transmitted clearly, *sound carries across water*. □ **be carried away**, to be very excited. **carry all before one**, to be very successful. **carry conviction**, to sound convincing. **carry-cot** *n.* a baby's portable cot. **carry forward**, to transfer to a new page of accounts in bookkeeping. **carry off**, to cause the death of; to win (a prize); to deal with (a situation) successfully. **carry on**, to continue; to take part in (a conversation); to manage or conduct (a business etc.); (*informal*) to behave excitedly, to complain lengthily. **carry on with**, (*informal*) to have an affair with, to flirt with. **carry one's bat**, to be 'not out' at the end of one's side's innings in cricket. **carry out**, to put into practice, to accomplish. **carry over**, to carry forward in bookkeeping. **carry weight**, to be influential or important.

carse (*pr.* karss) *n.* (*Scottish*) lowland beside a river.

carsick *adj.* made sick or queasy by the motion of a car. **carsickness** *n.*

cart *n.* **1.** a two-wheeled vehicle used for carrying loads, pulled by a horse etc. **2.** a light vehicle with a shaft, pushed or drawn by hand. —**cart** *v.* **1.** to carry in a cart, to transport. **2.** (*slang*) to carry laboriously, to lug; *carted his family off to Italy*, made them go with him. □ **be in the cart**, (*slang*) to be in a difficult situation. **carthorse** *n.* a strong horse fit for heavy work. **cart-load** *n.* the amount a cart will hold; (*informal*) a large quantity. **cart-track** *n.* a rough track suitable for carts but not for cars. **put the cart before the horse**, to put a thing first when it should logically come second.

cartage (**kar**-tij) *n.* **1.** carting goods. **2.** the cost of this.

carte blanche (kart **blahnsh**) full power to act as one thinks best.

cartel (kar-**tel**) *n.* a combination of business firms to control production, marketing, etc. and avoid competing with one another.

carter *n.* **1.** a person whose job is driving carts. **2.** one whose trade is transporting goods.

Carthusian (kar-**thew**-ziăn) *n.* a member of an order of monks founded at La Grande Chartreuse near Grenoble, France.

cartilage *n.* **1.** tough white flexible tissue attached to the bones of animals. **2.** a structure made of this. **cartilaginous** (karti-**laj**-inŭs) *adj.*

cartography (kar-**tog**-răfi) *n.* map-drawing. **cartographer** *n.*, **cartographic** (kartŏ-**graf**-ik) *adj.*

carton *n.* **1.** a cardboard or plastic container. **2.** the amount it contains.

cartoon *n.* **1.** an amusing drawing in a newspaper etc., especially as a comment on public matters. **2.** a sequence of these telling a comic or serial story. **3.** an animated cartoon. **4.** a drawing made by an artist as a preliminary sketch for a painting etc. —*v.* to draw cartoons, to represent in a cartoon. □ **cartoonist** *n.* a person who draws cartoons.

cartridge *n.* **1.** a tube or case containing explosive for firearms or blasting, with bullet or shot if for a rifle etc. **2.** a sealed case holding film, recording-tape, etc., put into apparatus and removed from it as a unit. **3.** the detachable head of a pick-up on a record-player, holding the stylus. □ **cartridge paper**, thick strong paper.

cartwheel *n.* a handspring in which the body turns with limbs spread like spokes of a wheel, balancing on each hand in turn.

cartwright *n.* a maker of carts.

carve *v.* **1.** to form or produce or inscribe by cutting solid material. **2.** to cut (cooked meat) into slices for eating. **3.** to make by great effort, *carved out a career for himself*. □ **carve up**, to divide into parts or shares.

carvel-built *adj.* (of a boat) made with planks joined smoothly and not overlapping.

carver *n.* **1.** a person who carves. **2.** a knife for carving meat; *carvers,* a carving knife and fork. **3.** an armchair in a set of dining-room chairs.

carving *n.* a carved object or design.

caryatid (ka-ri-**at**-id) *n.* a sculptured female figure used as a supporting pillar in a building.

Casanova (kas-ă-**noh**-vă) *n.* a man with a reputation for having many love affairs. ¶ Named after an Italian adventurer (18th century).

cascade (kas-**kayd**) *n.* **1.** a waterfall. **2.** something falling or hanging like this. —*v.* to fall as or like a cascade.

cascara (kas-**kar**-ă) *n.* the bark of a North American buckthorn, used as a purgative.

case [1] *n.* **1.** an instance or example of the occurrence of something, an actual state of affairs. **2.** a condition of disease or injury, a person suffering from this, *two cases of measles*. **3.** something being investigated by police etc., *a murder case*. **4.** a lawsuit. **5.** a set of facts or arguments supporting something. **6.** the form of a noun or pronoun that shows its relationship to another word, e.g. in *Mary's hat*, *'s* shows the possessive case. □ **case-book** *n.* a record of legal or medical cases. **case history**, a record of the past history of a patient etc. **case-load** *n.* the number of cases being handled by a doctor etc. at one time. **in any case**, whatever the facts are; whatever may happen. **in case**, lest something should happen. **in case of fire** etc., if there should be a fire.

case [2] *n.* **1.** a container or protective covering. **2.** this with its contents, the amount it contains. **3.** a suitcase. —*v.* to enclose in a case.

casein (**kay**-seen) *n.* a protein found in milk, the basis of cheese.

casement *n.* a window that opens on hinges like a door.

casework *n.* social work that involves dealing with people who have problems. **caseworker** *n.*

cash *n.* **1.** money in coin or notes. **2.** immediate payment for goods, as opposed to hire purchase etc. **3.** (*informal*) money, wealth, *they're short of cash*. —*v.* to give or get cash for, *cashed a cheque*. □ **cash and carry**, a method of trading where goods are paid for in cash and taken away by the buyer himself. **cash crop**, a crop grown for selling. **cash desk**, a desk where payment is made in a shop etc. **cash flow**, the movement of money out of and into a business as goods are bought and sold, affecting its ability to make cash payments. **cash register**, a device used in shops, with mechanism for recording the amount of each purchase. **cash in on**, to make a large profit from; to turn to one's advantage. **cash on delivery**, payment to be made when goods are delivered, not at the time of purchase.

cashable *adj.* able to be cashed.

cashew (**kash**-oo) *n.* **1.** the small edible nut of a tropical tree. **2.** this tree.

cashier [1] *n.* a person employed to receive and pay out money in a bank or to receive payments in a shop etc.

cashier [2] *v.* to dismiss from service, especially with disgrace.

cashmere *n.* **1.** a very fine soft wool, especially that from the Kashmir goat. **2.** fabric made from this.

casing *n.* **1.** a protective covering or wrapping. **2.** the material from which this is made.

casino *n.* (*pl.* casinos) a public building or room for gambling and other amusements.

cask *n.* **1.** a barrel, especially for alcoholic drinks. **2.** its contents.

casket *n.* a small usually ornamental box for holding valuables etc.

Cassandra (kă-**san**-dră) *n.* a person who prophesies disaster. ¶ Named after a prophetess in Greek legend who foretold evil events but was doomed never to be believed.

cassata (kă-**sah**-tă) *n.* an ice-cream cake containing fruit and nuts.

cassava (kă-**sah**-vă) *n.* a tropical plant with starchy roots from which tapioca is obtained.

casserole *n.* **1.** a covered dish in which meat etc. is cooked and served. **2.** food cooked in this. —*v.* to cook (meat etc.) in a casserole.

cassette (kă-**set**) *n.* a small sealed case containing a reel of film or magnetic tape.

cassock *n.* a long garment worn by certain clergymen and members of a church choir.

cassowary (kas-ŏ-**wair**-i) *n.* a large bird like an ostrich but smaller.

cast *v.* (cast, casting) **1.** to throw, *cast a net*; *cast a shadow*, cause there to be one. **2.** to shed. **3.** to turn or send in a particular direction; *cast your eye over this*, examine it. **4.** to give (one's vote). **5.** to make (an object) by pouring metal etc. into a mould and letting it harden. **6.** to calculate, *cast a horoscope*. **7.** to select actors for a play etc., to assign a role to. —**cast** *n.* **1.** an act of casting. **2.** something made by putting soft material into a mould to harden, a plaster cast (*see* plaster). **3.** a set of actors cast for parts in a play. **4.** a slight squint. □ **cast about for**, to search or look for. **cast iron**, a hard alloy of iron made by casting in a mould. **cast-iron** *adj.* made of cast iron; very strong. **cast off**, to release a ship from its moorings; (in knitting) to loop stitches off a needle. **cast-offs** *pl. n.* clothes that the owner will not wear again. **cast on**, (in knitting) to loop stitches on to a needle.

castanets (kahst-ă-**nets**) *pl. n.* a pair of shell-shaped pieces of wood or ivory etc., struck together with the fingers especially as an accompaniment to a Spanish dance.

castaway *n.* a shipwrecked person.

caste (*pr.* kahst) *n.* **1.** one of the hereditary Hindu social classes. **2.** any exclusive social class.

castellated (kas-těl-ayt-id) *adj.* having turrets or battlements like a castle.

caster *n.* = castor.

castigate (**kas**-ti-gayt) *v.* to punish with blows or by criticizing severely. **castigation** *n.*, **castigator** *n.*

casting vote a vote that decides the issue when votes on each side are equal.

castle *n.* **1.** a large fortified building or group of buildings. **2.** a chess-piece also called a rook. —*v.* (in chess) to move either rook to next to the king and the king to the other side of that rook. □ **castles in the air,** day-dreams.

castor *n.* **1.** a small container for sugar or salt, with a perforated top for sprinkling from. **2.** one of the small swivelled wheels fixed to the legs of furniture so that it can be moved easily. □ **castor sugar,** finely granulated white sugar.

castor oil oil from the seeds of a tropical plant, used as a purgative and as a lubricant.

castrate (kas-**trayt**) *v.* to remove the testicles of, to geld. **castration** *n.*

casual *adj.* **1.** happening by chance, *a casual encounter*. **2.** made or done without forethought, not serious, *a casual remark.* **3.** not methodical, *a casual inspection.* **4.** informal, for informal occasions, *casual clothes.* **5.** irregular, not permanent, *found some casual work; casual labourers,* doing such work. **casually** *adv.*, **casualness** *n.* □ **casuals** *pl. n.* casual clothes; casual shoes. **casual shoes,** low-heeled slip-on shoes. **casual water,** a temporary puddle or pool on a golf course.

casualty *n.* **1.** a person who is killed or injured in war or in an accident. **2.** a thing lost or destroyed.

cat *n.* **1.** a small furry domesticated animal often kept as a pet. **2.** a wild animal related to this; *the great Cats,* lion, tiger, leopard, etc. **3.** (*informal*) a spiteful or malicious woman. **4.** the cat-o'-nine-tails. □ **cat-and-dog life,** a life with perpetual

quarrels. **cat-and-mouse game,** the practice of taking slight action repeatedly against a weaker party. **cat burglar,** a burglar who enters by climbing a wall or drainpipe etc. **cat-o'-nine-tails** *n.* a whip with nine knotted lashes, formerly used for flogging people. **cat's-cradle** *n.* a game with string forming looped patterns between the fingers. **Catseye** *n.* (*trade mark*), **cat's-eye** *n.* any of a line of reflector studs marking the centre or edge of a road. **cat's-paw** *n.* a person who is used by another to do something risky. (¶ From the fable of the monkey who used the paw of his friend the cat to rake hot chestnuts out of the fire.) **let the cat out of the bag,** to give away a secret. **put the cat among the pigeons,** to put into a group someone who will cause trouble. **see which way the cat jumps,** to refuse to comment or act until it is clear what is likely to happen.

cataclysm (**kat**-ă-klizm) *n.* a violent upheaval or disaster. **cataclysmic** (kată-**kliz**-mik) *adj.*

catacombs (**kat**-ă-koomz) *pl. n.* a series of underground galleries with side recesses for tombs.

catafalque (**kat**-ă-falk) *n.* a decorated platform on which the coffin of a distinguished person stands during the funeral or lying-in-state, or on which it is drawn in procession.

catalepsy (**kat**-ă-lepsi) *n.* a condition in which a person becomes rigid and unconscious. **cataleptic** (kată-**lep**-tik) *adj.*

catalogue *n.* a list of items, usually in systematic order and with a description of each. —*v.* (catalogued, cataloguing) to list in a catalogue. —**cataloguer** *n.*

catalyst (**kat**-ă-list) *n.* **1.** a substance that aids or speeds up a chemical reaction while remaining unchanged itself. **2.** a person or thing that precipitates a change.

catamaran (kat-ă-mă-ran) *n.* a boat with twin hulls.

catapult *n.* **1.** a device with elastic for shooting small stones. **2.** a device for launching a glider, or an aircraft from the deck of a carrier. —**catapult** *v.* **1.** to hurl from a catapult, to fling forcibly. **2.** to rush violently.

cataract *n.* **1.** a large waterfall. **2.** a condition in which the lens of the eye becomes cloudy and obscures sight. **3.** this opaque area.

catarrh (kă-**tar**) *n.* inflammation of mucous membrane, especially of the nose and throat, accompanied by a watery discharge. **catarrhal** *adj.*

catastrophe (kă-**tas**-trŏfi) *n.* a sudden

great disaster. **catastrophic** (kată-**strof**-ik) *adj.*, **catastrophically** *adv.*

catcall *n.* a shrill whistle of disapproval. **catcalling** *n.* making catcalls.

catch *v.* (caught, catching) **1.** to capture in a net or snare or after a chase. **2.** to overtake. **3.** to grasp something moving and hold it; *batsman was caught by Bloggs,* was caught out in cricket etc. **4.** to come unexpectedly upon, to take by surprise, to detect. **5.** to be in time for and get on (a train etc.). **6.** (*informal*) to hear (a broadcast), to watch (a film). **7.** to get briefly, *caught a glimpse of it*; *you have caught the likeness well,* seen and reproduced it in painting etc.; *try and catch his eye,* make him notice you. **8.** to become or cause to become fixed or prevented from moving. **9.** to hit, *the blow caught him on the nose.* **10.** to begin to burn, *the sticks caught* or *caught fire.* **11.** to become infected with, *caught a cold.* —**catch** *n.* **1.** the act of catching. **2.** something caught or worth catching; *he's a good catch,* worth getting as a husband. **3.** a concealed difficulty or disadvantage; *a catch question,* involving a catch. **4.** a device for fastening something. **5.** a round for singing by three or more voices. □ **be caught,** (*slang*) to become pregnant. **catch-as-catch-can,** wrestling in which few or no holds are barred. **catch crop,** a crop that grows quickly and is harvested while the main crop is growing. **catch hold of,** to seize in the hand(s). **catch it,** (*informal*) to be scolded or punished. **catch on,** (*informal*) to become popular; to understand what is meant. **catch out,** to detect in a mistake; to cause (a batsman) to be 'out' in cricket or baseball by catching the ball directly from his bat. **catch-phrase** *n.* a phrase in frequent current use, a catchword or slogan. **catch-22** *n.* (*informal*) a dilemma where the victim is bound to suffer, no matter which course of action etc. he chooses. (¶ the title of a novel by J. Heller, 1961). **catch up,** to come abreast with; to do arrears of work.

catcher *n.* **1.** one who catches. **2.** a baseball fielder who stands behind the batter.

catching *adj.* infectious.

catchment area 1. an area from which rainfall drains into a river or reservoir. **2.** an area from which a hospital draws its patients or a school its pupils.

catchpenny *adj.* intended to sell quickly.

catchweight *adj. & n.* (in sports) accepting a contestant at the weight he happens to be, not at one fixed for that sport.

catchword *n.* a memorable word or phrase that is often used, a slogan.

catchy *adj.* (catchier, catchiest) **1.** pleasant and easy to remember, *a catchy tune.* **2.** tricky, involving a catch.

catechism (**kat**-i-kizm) *n.* **1.** *the Catechism,* a summary of the principles of a religion in the form of questions and answers. **2.** a series of questions.

catechize (**kat**-i-kyz) *v.* to put a series of questions to (a person).

categorical (katig-**o**-ri-kăl) *adj.* absolute, unconditional, *a categorical refusal.* **categorically** *adv.*

categorize (**kat**-ig-eryz) *v.* to place in a particular category.

category (**kat**-ig-eri) *n.* a class of things.

cater (**kay**-ter) *v.* to provide what is needed or wanted, especially food or entertainment, *cater for 50 people*; *cater to people's interest in scandal,* pander to it.

caterer *n.* one whose trade is to supply meals etc.

caterpillar *n.* **1.** the larva of a butterfly or moth. **2.** *Caterpillar,* (*trade mark*) a steel band passing round two wheels of a tractor or tank, enabling it to travel over very rough ground, *Caterpillar track* or *tread.*

caterwaul *v.* to make a cat's howling cry.

catfish *n.* a large usually freshwater fish with whisker-like feelers round the mouth.

catgut *n.* a fine strong cord made from the dried intestines of animals, used for the strings of musical instruments and for sewing up surgical incisions.

catharsis (kă-**thar**-sis) *n.* relief of strong feelings or tension, e.g. by giving vent to them in drama or art etc. **cathartic** *adj.*

cathedral *n.* the principal church of a bishop's see.

Catherine wheel a rotating firework. ¶ Named after St. Catherine, who was martyred on a spiked wheel.

catheter (**kath**-it-er) *n.* a tube that can be inserted into the bladder to extract urine. **catheterize** *v.* to insert a catheter into.

cathode (**kath**-ohd) *n.* the electrode by which current leaves a device. **cathode-ray tube,** a vacuum tube in which beams of electrons are directed against a fluorescent screen where they produce a luminous image, e.g. the picture tube of a TV set.

catholic *adj.* universal, including many or most things, *his tastes are catholic.*

Catholic *adj.* **1.** of all Churches or Christians. **2.** Roman Catholic. —*n.* a Roman Catholic. —**Catholicism** (kă-**thol**-i-sizm) *n.*

cation (**kat**-I-ŏn) *n.* an ion with a positive charge.

catkin *n.* a spike of small soft flowers hanging from trees such as willow and hazel.

catmint *n.* a plant with a strong smell that is attractive to cats.

catnap *n.* a short nap. —*v.* (catnapped, catnapping) to have a catnap.

cattery *n.* a place where cats are bred or boarded.

cattle *pl. n.* large ruminant animals with horns and cloven hoofs, bred for their milk or meat. **cattle-cake** *n.* concentrated food for cattle, in cake form. **cattle-grid** *n.* a grid covering a ditch so that vehicles can pass but not cattle or sheep etc.

catty *adj.* (cattier, cattiest) spiteful, speaking spitefully. **cattily** *adv.*, **cattiness** *n.*

catwalk *n.* a raised narrow pathway.

caucus (kaw-kŭs) *n.* **1.** (*often contemptuous*) the committee of a local branch of a political party, making plans, decisions, etc. **2.** (*Amer.*) a meeting of party leaders to decide policy etc. **3.** (*Austral.*) the parliamentary members of a political party who decide policy etc., a meeting of these.

caudal (kaw-dǎl) *adj.* of or at the tail.

caught see catch.

caul (*pr.* kawl) *n.* **1.** a membrane enclosing a foetus in the womb. **2.** part of this found on a child's head at birth, once thought to be a charm against drowning.

cauldron *n.* a large deep pot for boiling things in.

cauliflower *n.* a cabbage with a large white flower-head. **cauliflower ear,** an ear thickened by repeated blows, e.g. in boxing.

caulk (*pr.* kawk) *v.* to make watertight by filling seams or joints with waterproof material, or by driving edges of plating together. **caulking** *n.* material used to caulk seams etc.

causal *adj.* of or forming a cause.

causality (kaw-zal-iti) *n.* the relationship between cause and effect.

causative (kaw-ză-tiv) *adj.* **1.** acting as a cause. **2.** expressing a cause.

cause *n.* **1.** a person or thing that makes something happen or produces an effect. **2.** a reason, *there is no cause for anxiety.* **3.** a purpose or aim for which efforts are made, a movement or charity; *a good cause,* one deserving support. **4.** a lawsuit; *pleading his cause,* his case. —*v.* to be the cause of, to produce, to make happen. □ **cause célèbre** (kohz say-lebr) a lawsuit or other issue that rouses great interest.

causeway *n.* a raised road across low or wet ground.

caustic *adj.* **1.** able to burn or corrode things by chemical action. **2.** sarcastic. — *n.* a caustic substance. **caustically** *adv.*, **causticity** (kaws-tiss-iti) *n.*

cauterize *v.* to burn the surface of (living tissue) with a caustic substance or a hot

iron in order to destroy infection or stop bleeding. **cauterization** *n.*

caution *n.* **1.** avoidance of rashness, attention to safety. **2.** a warning against danger etc. **3.** a warning and reprimand, *let him off with a caution.* **4.** (*informal*) an amusing person or thing. —**caution** *v.* **1.** to warn. **2.** to warn and reprimand.

cautionary *adj.* conveying a warning.

cautious *adj.* having or showing caution. **cautiously** *adv.*

cavalcade (kav-ăl-kayd) *n.* a procession, especially of people on horseback or in cars etc.

cavalier *n.* **1.** *Cavalier,* a supporter of Charles I in the English Civil War. **2.** (*humorous*) a man escorting a woman. — *adj.* arrogant, offhand, *a cavalier attitude.*

cavalry *n.* troops who fight on horseback.

cave *n.* a natural hollow in the side of a hill or cliff, or underground. —*v.* **cave in,** **1.** to fall inwards, to collapse. **2.** to cause to do this. **3.** to withdraw one's opposition.

caveat (kav-i-at) *n.* a warning.

caveman *n.* **1.** a person of prehistoric times living in caves. **2.** a man with a rough primitive manner towards women.

cavern *n.* a large cave. **cavernous** *adj.*

caviare (kav-i-ar) *n.* the pickled roe of sturgeon or other large fish.

cavil *v.* (cavilled, cavilling) to raise petty objections. —*n.* a petty objection.

caving *n.* the sport of exploring caves.

cavity *n.* a hollow within a solid body. **cavity wall,** a double wall with a cavity between.

cavort (kă-vort) *v.* to caper about excitedly.

caw *n.* the harsh cry of a rook, raven, or crow. —*v.* to make this sound.

cayenne pepper (kay-en) a hot red powdered pepper.

CB *abbrev.* citizens' band (*see* citizen).

CBI *abbrev.* Confederation of British Industry.

cc *abbrev.* **1.** carbon copy. **2.** cubic centimetre(s).

ceanothus (see-ă-noh-thŭss) *n.* a shrub with fluffy blue or pink flowers.

cease *v.* to come or bring to an end, to stop. —*n.* ceasing. □ **cease-fire** *n.* a signal to stop firing guns in war, a truce. **without cease,** not ceasing.

ceaseless *adj.* not ceasing, going on continually. **ceaselessly** *adv.*

cedar (see-der) *n.* **1.** an evergreen tree with hard sweet-smelling wood. **2.** its wood. **cedarwood** *n.*

cede (*pr.* seed) *v.* to give up one's rights to

or possession of, *they were compelled to cede certain territories.*

cedilla (si-**dil**-ă) *n.* a mark written under *c* in certain languages to show that it is pronounced as *s* as in *façade.*

ceilidh (**kay**-li) *n.* (*Scottish* & *Irish*) an informal gathering for music and dancing etc.

ceiling *n.* **1.** the under-surface of the top of a room. **2.** the maximum altitude at which a particular aircraft can fly. **3.** an upper limit or level, *wage ceilings.*

celandine (**sel**-ăn-dyn) *n.* a small wild plant with yellow flowers.

celebrate *v.* **1.** to do something to show that a day or event is important, to honour with festivities, to make merry on such an occasion. **2.** to officiate at (a religious ceremony). **celebration** *n.*

celebrated *adj.* famous.

celebrity (si-**leb**-riti) *n.* **1.** a well-known person. **2.** fame, being famous.

celeriac (si-**le**-ri-ak) *n.* a kind of celery with a turnip-like root.

celerity (si-**le**-riti) *n.* swiftness.

celery *n.* a garden plant with crisp juicy stems used in salads or as a vegetable.

celestial *adj.* **1.** of the sky; *celestial bodies,* stars etc. **2.** of heaven, divine.

celibate (**sel**-ib-ăt) *adj.* remaining unmarried, especially for religious reasons. **celibacy** (**sel**-ib-ăsi) *n.*

cell *n.* **1.** a very small room, e.g. for a monk in a monastery or for confining a prisoner. **2.** a compartment in a honeycomb. **3.** a device for producing electric current by chemical action. **4.** a microscopic unit of living matter, containing a nucleus. **5.** a small group of people forming a centre or nucleus of political activities.

cellar *n.* **1.** an underground room used for storing things. **2.** a room in which wine is stored, a stock of wine.

cellaret (sel-er-**et**) *n.* a case or sideboard for holding bottles of wine.

cellist (**chel**-ist) *n.* a person who plays the cello.

cello (**chel**-oh) *n.* (*pl.* cellos) a violoncello, an instrument like a large violin, played by a seated player who sets it between his knees.

Cellophane (**sel**-ŏ-fayn) *n.* (*trade mark*) thin moisture-proof transparent material used for wrapping things.

cellular (**sel**-yoo-ler) *adj.* **1.** of cells, composed of cells. **2.** woven with an open mesh, *cellular blankets.*

celluloid (**sel**-yoo-loid) *n.* a plastic made from cellulose nitrate and camphor.

cellulose (**sel**-yoo-lohz) *n.* **1.** an organic substance found in all plant tissues, used

in making plastics **2.** paint or lacquer made from this.

Celsius (**sel**-si-ŭs) *adj.* centigrade. ¶ Named after A. Celsius, a Swedish astronomer (1701–44), who devised the centigrade scale.

Celt (*pr.* kelt) *n.* a member of an ancient European people who settled in Britain before the coming of the Romans, or of their descendants especially in Ireland, Wales, Cornwall, and Scotland.

Celtic (**kelt**-ik) *adj.* of the Celts. **Celtic Sea,** the sea between South Ireland and Cornwall.

cement *n.* **1.** a grey powder, made by burning lime and clay, that sets to a stone-like mass when mixed with water and is used for building. **2.** any similar soft substance that sets firm. —**cement** *v.* **1.** to put cement on or in, to join with cement. **2.** to unite firmly.

cemetery *n.* a burial ground other than a churchyard.

cenotaph (**sen**-ŏ-tahf) *n.* a tomb-like monument to persons buried elsewhere.

censer (**sen**-ser) *n.* a container in which incense is burnt, swung on chains in a religious ceremony to disperse its fragrance.

censor (**sen**-ser) *n.* a person authorized to examine letters, books, films, etc. and remove or ban anything regarded as harmful. —*v.* to subject to such examination or removal. —**censorship** *n.*

censorious (sen-**sor**-iŭs) *adj.* severely critical.

censure (**sen**-sher) *n.* strong criticism or condemnation. —*v.* to blame and rebuke. ¶ Do not confuse with censor.

census (**sen**-sŭs) *n.* an official count of the population or of things (e.g. traffic).

cent *n.* **1.** one 100th of a dollar or of certain other metric units of currency, a coin of this value. **2.** (*informal*) a very small amount of money, *I haven't a cent.*

centaur (**sen**-tor) *n.* one of a tribe of wild creatures in Greek mythology, with a man's upper body, head, and arms on a horse's body and legs.

centenarian (sen-tin-**air**-iăn) *n.* a person who is 100 years old or more.

centenary (sen-**teen**-eri) *n.* a 100th anniversary.

centennial (sen-**ten**-iăl) *adj.* of a centenary. —*n.* (*Amer.*) a centenary.

center *n.* & *v.* (*Amer.*) = centre.

centi- (**sent**-i) *prefix* one hundredth.

centigrade (**sent**-i-grayd) *adj.* of or using a temperature scale divided into 100 degrees, 0° being the freezing-point and 100° the boiling-point of water.

centilitre *n.* one 100th of a litre.

centimetre *n.* one 100th of a metre, about 0·4 inch.

centipede *n.* a small crawling creature with a long thin segmented body and many legs, one pair on each segment.

central *adj.* 1. of or at or forming the centre. 2. chief, most important, *the central character in this novel.* □ **Central**, a region of Scotland. **centrally** *adv.*, **centrality** (sen-**tral**-iti) *n.* □ **Central African Republic,** a country in central Africa. **Central America,** *see* America. **central heating,** a system of heating a building from one source by circulating hot water or hot air or steam in pipes or by linked radiators. **Central Intelligence Agency,** a federal agency in the USA responsible for co-ordinating government intelligence activities. **central processor,** the part of a computer that controls and co-ordinates the activities of other units and performs the actions specified in the program.

centralize *v.* to bring under the control of one central authority. **centralization** *n.*

centre *n.* 1. the middle point or part. 2. a point towards which interest is directed or from which administration etc. is organized. 3. a place where certain activities or facilities are concentrated, *a shopping centre.* 4. a political party or group holding moderate opinions, between two extremes. 5. a centre-forward. —**centre** *v.* (centred, centring) 1. to place in or at the centre. 2. to concentrate at one point. 3. to kick or hit from the wing towards the middle of the pitch in football or hockey. □ **centre-board** *n.* a retractable keel in a sailing-boat. **centre-forward** *n.* the player in the middle of the forward line in football or hockey. **centre-half** *n.* the middle player in the half-back line.

centrifugal (sen-**tri**-few-găl) *adj.* 1. moving away from the centre or axis. 2. using **centrifugal force,** a force that appears to cause a body that is travelling round a centre to fly outwards and off its circular path.

centrifuge (**sen**-tri-fewj) *n.* a machine using centrifugal force to separate substances, e.g. milk and cream. —*v.* to separate by centrifuge.

centripetal (sen-**trip**-it'l) *adj.* moving towards the centre or axis.

century *n.* 1. a period of 100 years, one of these periods reckoned from the birth of Christ. 2. 100 runs made by a batsman in one innings at cricket.

ceramic (si-**ram**-ik) *adj.* of pottery or similar substances. —*n.* a ceramic substance. □ **ceramics** *n.* the art of making pottery.

cereal *n.* 1. a grass, such as wheat, rye, oats, or rice, producing an edible grain. 2. its seed. 3. a breakfast food made from such grain.

cerebral (se-ri-brăl) *adj.* 1. of the brain. 2. intellectual. □ **cerebral palsy,** . *see* spastic.

ceremonial *adj.* of a ceremony, used in ceremonies, formal. —*n.* 1. ceremony. 2. a system of rules for ceremonies. — **ceremonially** *adv.*

ceremonious *adj.* full of ceremony, elaborately performed. **ceremoniously** *adv.*

ceremony *n.* 1. a set of formal acts, especially those used on religious or public occasions. 2. formal politeness.

cerise (sĕ-**reez**) *adj. & n.* light clear red.

cert *n.* (*slang*) a certainty, something sure to happen or to be successful.

certain *adj.* 1. feeling sure, convinced. 2. known without doubt. 3. able to be relied on to come or happen or be effective. 4. specific but not named or stated for various reasons. 5. small in amount but definitely there, *I feel a certain reluctance.* 6. existing but not well known, *a certain John Smith.* □ **for certain,** without doubt, as a certainty. **make certain,** to make sure.

certainly *adv.* 1. without doubt. 2. yes.

certainty *n.* 1. being certain. 2. something that is certain; *that horse is a certainty,* is certain to win.

certifiable *adj.* able to be certified. **certifiably** *adv.*

certificate *n.* an official written or printed statement giving certain facts.

certify *v.* (certified, certifying) to declare formally, to show on a certificate or other document.

certitude (**ser**-ti-tewd) *n.* a feeling of certainty.

cervical (ser-vy-kăl *or* ser-vik-ăl) *adj.* 1. of the neck, *cervical vertebrae.* 2. of a cervix, of the cervix of the womb.

cervix (**ser**-viks) *n.* (*pl.* cervices) 1. the neck. 2. a neck-like structure, the neck of the womb.

Cesarewitch (si-**za**-rĕ-wich) *n.* a horse-race run annually at Newmarket, Suffolk.

cessation (sess-ay-shŏn) *n.* ceasing.

cession (sesh-ŏn) *n.* ceding, giving up.

cesspit, cesspool *ns.* a covered pit where liquid waste or sewage is stored temporarily.

Ceylon the former name of Sri Lanka.

cf. *abbrev.* compare (¶ short for the Latin *confer*).

c.f. *abbrev.* carried forward.

Chablis (**shab**-lee) *n.* a white burgundy.

Chad a country in North Africa. **Chadian** *adj. & n.*

chadar *or* **chador** *n.* = chuddar.

chafe (*pr.* chayf) *v.* **1.** to warm by rubbing. **2.** to make or become sore from rubbing. **3.** to become irritated or impatient.

chaff *n.* **1.** corn-husks separated from the seed by threshing or winnowing. **2.** hay or straw cut up as food for cattle. **3.** good-humoured teasing or joking. —*v.* to tease or joke in a good-humoured way.

chaffinch *n.* a common European finch.

chafing-dish (chay-fing-dish) *n.* a pan with a heater under it for cooking food or keeping it warm at the table.

chagrin (shag-rin) *n.* a feeling of annoyance and embarrassment or disappointment. **chagrined** *adj.* affected with chagrin.

chain *n.* **1.** a series of connected metal links, used for hauling or supporting weights or for restraining things or as an ornament. **2.** a connected series or sequence, *chain of mountains, chain of events.* **3.** a number of shops or hotels etc. owned by the same company. **4.** a unit of length for measuring land, 66 ft. —*v.* to make fast with a chain or chains. □ **chain-letter** *n.* a letter of which the recipient is asked to make copies and send these to other people, who will do the same. **chain-plate** *n.* a metal plate to which the lower shrouds of a mast are fastened. **chain reaction,** a chemical or other change forming products that themselves cause more changes; a series of events each of which causes or influences the next. **chain-saw** *n.* a saw with teeth set on an endless chain. **chain-smoke** *v.* to smoke many cigarettes in a continuous succession. **chain-smoker** *n.* a person who chain-smokes. **chain-stitch** *n.* a looped stitch that looks like a chain, in crochet or embroidery. **chain store,** one of a series of similar shops owned by one firm.

chair *n.* **1.** a movable seat, with a back, for one person. **2.** a position of authority at a meeting, the chairmanship; *address your remarks to the chair,* to the chairman. **3.** a professorship. **4.** (*Amer.*) the electric chair. —**chair** *v.* **1.** to seat in a chair of honour. **2.** to carry in triumph on the shoulders of a group. **3.** to act as chairman of. □ **chair-lift** *n.* a series of chairs suspended from an endless cable, for carrying people up a mountain.

chairman *n.* (*pl.* chairmen) **1.** a person who presides over a meeting or a committee. **2.** the president of a board of directors. **chairmanship** *n.* □ **chairwoman** *n.* a female chairman.

¶ The word *chairman* may be used of persons of either sex, a woman being formally addressed as *Madam Chairman.*

chaise longue (shayz lawng) a chair with a very long seat on which the sitter can stretch out his legs.

chalet (shal-ay) *n.* **1.** a Swiss hut or cottage. **2.** a small villa. **3.** a small hut in a holiday camp etc.

chalice (chal-iss) *n.* a large goblet for holding wine, one from which consecrated wine is drunk at the Eucharist.

chalk *n.* **1.** a white soft limestone used for burning into lime. **2.** a piece of this or of similar substance, white or coloured, used in crayons for drawing. —*v.* to write or draw or mark with chalk, to rub with chalk. —**chalky** *adj.* □ **by a long chalk,** by far. **chalk-stripe** *n.* a pattern of thin white stripes on a dark background. **chalk-striped** *adj.* having this pattern. **chalk up,** to make a note of something; to achieve, *chalked up another victory.*

challenge *n.* **1.** a call to demonstrate one's ability or strength. **2.** a call or demand to respond, a sentry's call for a person to identify himself. **3.** a formal objection, e.g. to a juryman. **4.** a difficult or demanding task. —**challenge** *v.* **1.** issue a challenge to. **2.** to raise a formal objection to. **3.** to question the truth or rightness of. — **challenger** *n.*

challenging *adj.* offering problems that test one's ability, stimulating.

challis *n.* a soft light dress-material.

chamber *n.* **1.** (*old use*) a room, a bedroom. **2.** the hall used for meetings of a parliament etc., the members of the group using it. **3.** a chamber-pot. **4.** a cavity or compartment in the body of an animal or plant, or in machinery. □ **chamber-maid** *n.* a woman employed to clean and take care of bedrooms in a hotel. **chamber music,** music written for a small number of players, suitable for performance in a room or small hall. **Chamber of Commerce,** an association of business men etc. to promote local commercial interests. **Chamber of Horrors,** the room of criminals etc. in Madame Tussauds waxworks; a place full of horrifying things. **chamber-pot** *n.* a receptacle for urine etc., used in the bedroom. **chambers** *pl. n.* a set of rooms, a judge's room for hearing cases that do not need to be taken in court.

chamberlain (chaym-ber-lin) *n.* an official who manages the household of the sovereign or a great noble.

chameleon (kă-mee-li-ŏn) *n.* a small lizard that can change colour according to its surroundings.

chamfer (**cham**-fer) *v.* to bevel the edge or corner of.

chamois *n.* (*pl.* chamois) **1.** (*pr.* **sham**-wah) a small wild antelope found in the mountains of Europe and Asia. **2.** (*pr.* **sham**-i) a piece of **chamois-leather**, soft yellowish leather made from the skin of sheep, goats, and deer and used for washing and polishing things.

chamomile (**kam**-ŏ-myl) *n.* = camomile.

champ¹ *v.* **1.** to munch noisily, to make a chewing action or noise. **2.** to show impatience.

champ² *n.* (*slang*) a champion.

champagne *n.* **1.** a sparkling white wine from Champagne in France or elsewhere. **2.** its pale straw colour.

champion *n.* **1.** a person or thing that has defeated all others in a competition. **2.** a person who fights, argues, or speaks in support of another or of a cause. —*adj. & adv.* (*informal* or *dialect*) splendid, splendidly. —*v.* to support as a champion. —**championship** *n.*

chance *n.* **1.** the way things happen through no known cause or agency, luck, fate; *games of chance*, those decided by luck not skill. **2.** a possibility, likelihood. **3.** an opportunity, an occasion when success seems very probable. —**chance** *v.* **1.** to happen without plan or intention. **2.** (*informal*) to risk, *let's chance it.* —*adj.* coming or happening by chance, *a chance meeting.* □ **by chance**, as it happens or happened, without being planned. **chance on**, to come upon or find by chance. **chance one's arm**, (*informal*) to take a chance although failure is probable. **take a chance**, to take a risk, to act in the hope that a particular thing will (or will not) happen. **take chances**, to behave riskily. **take one's chance**, to trust to luck.

chancel (**chahn**-sĕl) *n.* the part of a church near the altar, used by the clergy and choir.

chancellery (**chahn**-sĕl-er-i) *n.* **1.** a chancellor's position, department, or official residence. **2.** an office attached to an embassy or consulate.

chancellor *n.* **1.** a State or law official of various kinds. **2.** the chief minister of State in West Germany and in Austria. **3.** the non-resident head of a university. **chancellorship** *n.* □ **Chancellor of the Exchequer,** the finance minister of the UK, who prepares the budget. **Lord Chancellor,** the highest officer of the Crown, presiding over the House of Lords.

Chancery (**chahn**-ser-i) *n.* the Lord Chancellor's division of the High Court of Justice.

chancy *adj.* (chancier, chanciest) risky, uncertain.

chandelier (shan-dĕ-**leer**) *n.* an ornamental hanging fixture with supports for several lights.

chandler *n.* a dealer in ropes, canvas, and other supplies for ships.

change *v.* **1.** to make or become different. **2.** to pass from one form or phase into another. **3.** to take or use another instead of. **4.** to put fresh clothes or coverings etc. on; *change the baby,* put a fresh napkin on it. **5.** to go from one to another, *change trains.* **6.** to exchange; *can you change £5?*, give small money in change, or give different currency for it. —**change** *n.* **1.** changing, alteration; *a change of the moon,* a fresh phase. **2.** substitution of one thing for another, variety; *pack a change of clothes,* a fresh outfit in reserve. **3.** a fresh occupation or surroundings. **4.** money in small units. **5.** money returned as the balance when the price is less than the amount offered in payment. **6.** *the change,* the change of life, the menopause. □ **change down**, to engage a lower gear. **change hands**, to pass into another person's possession. **change of heart**, a great alteration in one's attitude or feelings. **change of life**, the menopause. **change over**, to change from one system or position to another. **change-over** *n.* a change of this kind. **change-ringing** *n.* ringing a peal of bells in a series of different sequences. **changes** *pl. n.* the different orders in which a peal of bells can be rung. **change up**, to change to a higher gear. **for a change**, for the sake of variety, to vary one's routine. **get no change out of**, (*slang*) to fail to get the better of; to fail to get information from.

changeable *adj.* **1.** able to be changed. **2.** altering frequently, *changeable weather.*

changeling (**chaynj**-ling) *n.* a child or thing believed to have been substituted secretly for another.

channel *n.* **1.** the sunken bed of a stream of water. **2.** the navigable part of a waterway, deeper than the parts on either side. **3.** a stretch of water, wider than a strait, connecting two seas; *the Channel,* the English Channel. **4.** a passage along which a liquid may flow, a sunken course or line along which something may move. **5.** any course by which news or information etc. may travel. **6.** a band of broadcasting frequencies reserved for a particular set of programmes. **7.** a circuit for transmitting electrical signals. **8.** a lengthwise section of recording tape. **9.** (in a computer etc.) =

track *n.* sense 7. **—channel** *v.* (channelled, channelling) **1.** to form a channel or channels in. **2.** to direct through a channel or desired route.

chant *n.* **1.** a tune to which the words of psalms or other works with irregular rhythm are fitted by singing several syllables or words to the same note. **2.** a monotonous song. **3.** a rhythmic call or shout. **—chant** *v.* **1.** to sing, especially a chant. **2.** to call or shout rhythmically. **—chanter** *n.*

chantry *n.* a chapel founded for priests to sing masses for the founder's soul.

chaos (**kay**-oss) *n.* great disorder. **chaotic** (kay-**ot**-ik) *adj.*, **chaotically** *adv.*

chap¹ *v.* (chapped, chapping) (of skin) to split or crack, to become cracked. *n.* a crack in the skin.

chap² *n.* the lower jaw or half of the cheek, especially of a pig, as food.

chap³ *n.* (*informal*) a man.

chapel *n.* **1.** a place used for Christian worship, other than a cathedral or parish church. **2.** a service in this, *go to chapel.* **3.** a place with a separate altar within a church or cathedral. **4.** one section of a trade union in a printing works.

chaperon (**shap**-er-ohn) *n.* an older woman in charge of a girl or young unmarried woman on social occasions. *—v.* to act as chaperon to. **—chaperonage** *n.*

chaplain (**chap**-lin) *n.* a clergyman attached to a chapel in a private house or institution, or to a military unit.

chaplet (**chap**-lit) *n.* **1.** a wreath for the head. **2.** a short rosary.

chappie *n.* (*informal*) a chap, a man.

chaps *pl. n.* long leather leggings worn by cowboys. (¶ Short for *chaparajos.*)

chapter *n.* **1.** a division of a book, usually numbered. **2.** the canons of a cathedral or members of a monastic order, a meeting of these. □ **chapter and verse,** an exact reference to a passage or authority. **chapter-house** *n.* the building used for meetings of a cathedral chapter. **chapter of accidents,** a series of misfortunes.

char¹ *n.* a charwoman. *—v.* (charred, charring) to work as a charwoman.

char² *v.* (charred, charring) to make or become black by burning.

char³ *n.* (*pl.* char) a kind of small trout.

char⁴ *n.* (*slang*) tea.

charabanc (**sha**-ră-bang) *n.* an early form of bus with bench seats from side to side, used for outings.

character *n.* **1.** all those qualities that make a person, group, or thing what he or it is and different from others. **2.** a

person's moral nature. **3.** moral strength. **4.** a person, especially a noticeable or eccentric one. **5.** a person in a novel or play etc. **6.** a description of a person's qualities, a testimonial. **7.** a letter, sign, or mark used in a system of writing or printing etc. **8.** a physical characteristic of a plant or animal. □ **in character,** appropriate to a person's general character. **out of character,** not appropriate.

characteristic *adj.* forming part of the character of a person or thing, showing a distinctive feature. *—n.* a characteristic feature. **—characteristically** *adv.*

characterize *v.* **1.** to describe the character of. **2.** to be a characteristic of. **characterization** *n.*

characterless *adj.* lacking any positive character.

charade (shă-**rahd**) *n.* **1.** a scene acted as a clue to the word to be guessed in the game of *charades.* **2.** an absurd pretence.

charcoal *n.* a black substance made by burning wood slowly in an oven with little air, used as a filtering material or as fuel or for drawing. **charcoal grey,** very dark grey.

chard *n.* a kind of beet with edible leaves and stalks.

charge *n.* **1.** the price asked for goods or services. **2.** the quantity of material that an apparatus holds at one time, the amount of explosive needed for one explosion. **3.** the electricity contained in a substance, energy stored chemically for conversion into electricity. **4.** a task or duty, custody. **5.** a person or thing entrusted. **6.** formal instructions about one's duty or responsibility. **7.** an accusation, especially of having committed a crime. **8.** a rushing attack. **—charge** *v.* **1.** to ask as a price. **2.** to record as a debt, *charge it to my account.* **3.** to load or fill, to put a charge into. **4.** to give an electric charge to, to store energy in. **5.** to give as a task or duty, to entrust. **6.** to accuse formally. **7.** to rush forward in attack; *charge in,* to act impetuously. □ **in charge,** in command. **take charge,** to take control.

chargeable *adj.* able to be charged.

chargé d'affaires (shar-*zhay* da-**fair**) *n.* (*pl.* chargés d'affaires) **1.** an ambassador's deputy. **2.** an envoy to a minor country.

chariot *n.* a two-wheeled horse-drawn carriage used in ancient times in battle and in racing.

charioteer *n.* the driver of a chariot.

charisma (kă-**riz**-mă) *n.* the power to inspire devotion and enthusiasm. **charismatic** (ka-riz-**mat**-ik) *adj.* having this power.

charitable *adj.* **1.** generous in giving to the needy. **2.** of or belonging to charities, *charitable institutions.* **3.** unwilling to think badly of people or acts. **charitably** *adv.*

charity *n.* **1.** loving kindness towards others. **2.** unwillingness to think badly of people or acts. **3.** generosity in giving to the needy. **4.** an institution or fund for helping the needy.

charlady *n.* a charwoman.

charlatan (shar-lă-tăn) *n.* a person who falsely claims to be an expert, especially in medicine.

charlock *n.* wild mustard, a weed with yellow flowers.

charlotte (shar-lŏt) *n.* a pudding made of stewed fruit with a covering or layers of crumbs, biscuits, etc. **charlotte russe** (*pr.* rooss), a mould of custard or cream enclosed in sponge-cake or sponge biscuits.

charm *n.* **1.** attractiveness, the power of arousing love or admiration. **2.** an act or object or words believed to have magic power. **3.** a small ornament worn on a chain or bracelet. —**charm** *v.* **1.** to give pleasure to. **2.** to influence by personal charm. **3.** to influence as if by magic. —**charmer** *n.*

charming *adj.* delightful.

charnel-house (char-nĕl) *n.* a place in which the bodies or bones of the dead are kept.

Charollais (shă-rŏ-lay) *n.* a breed of large white beef-cattle, an animal of this breed.

chart *n.* **1.** a map designed for navigators on water or in the air. **2.** an outline map for showing special information, *a weather chart.* **3.** a diagram, graph, or table giving information in an orderly form, *a temperature chart*; *the charts,* those listing the recordings that are currently most popular. —*v.* to make a chart of, to map.

charter *n.* **1.** a document from a ruler or government granting certain rights or defining the form of an institution. **2.** the chartering of a ship, aircraft, or vehicle. —**charter** *v.* **1.** to grant a charter to, to found by charter. **2.** to let or hire a ship, aircraft, or vehicle. —**charterer** *n.* □ **charter flight,** a flight by chartered aircraft.

chartered *adj.* qualified according to the rules of a professional association which has a royal charter, *chartered accountant.*

chartreuse (shar-trerz) *n.* **1.** a fragrant green or yellow liqueur. **2.** its green colour. **3.** fruit enclosed in jelly.

charwoman *n.* (*pl.* charwomen) a woman employed to clean a house or other building.

chary (chair-i) *adj.* **1.** cautious, wary. **2.** sparing; *chary of giving praise,* seldom praising people.

chase[1] *v.* **1.** to go quickly after in order to capture or overtake or drive away. **2.** to hurry, *chasing round the shops.* **3.** (*informal*) to try to attain. —**chase** *n.* **1.** chasing, pursuit. **2.** hunting, especially as a sport. **3.** a steeplechase. **4.** unenclosed park-land. □ **chase up,** (*informal*) to investigate and find, to try to hasten (suppliers or supplies). **give chase,** to begin to pursue.

chase[2] *v.* to engrave or emboss (metal).

chaser *n.* **1.** a horse for steeplechasing. **2.** (*informal*) a drink taken after a drink of another kind, e.g. spirits after coffee.

chasm (kaz-ŭm) *n.* a deep opening or gap, especially in earth or rock.

chassis (sha-see) *n.* (*pl.* chassis, *pr.* sha-seez) a base-frame, especially of a vehicle, on which other parts are mounted.

chaste (*pr.* chayst) *adj.* **1.** virgin, celibate. **2.** not having sexual intercourse except with the person to whom one is married. **3.** simple in style, not ornate. **chastely** *adv.*

chasten (chay-sĕn) *v.* **1.** to discipline, to punish by inflicting suffering. **2.** to subdue the pride of.

chastise (chas-tyz) *v.* to punish severely, especially by beating. **chastisement** *n.*

chastity *n.* **1.** being chaste, virginity, celibacy. **2.** simplicity of style.

chasuble (chaz-yoo-bŭl) *n.* a loose garment worn over all other vestments by a priest celebrating Mass or Eucharist.

chat *n.* a friendly informal conversation. —*v.* (chatted, chatting) to have a chat. □ **chat a person up,** (*informal*) to chat to a person flirtatiously or with a particular motive. **chat show,** a broadcast programme in which people are interviewed.

château (shat-oh) *n.* (*pl.* châteaux, *pr.* shat-ohz) a castle or large country house in France.

chatelaine (shat-ĕ-layn) *n.* the mistress of a large house.

chattel *n.* a movable possession (as opposed to a house or land).

chatter *v.* **1.** to talk or converse quickly and continuously about unimportant matters. **2.** to make sounds like this, as some birds and animals do. **3.** to make a repeated clicking or rattling sound. — **chatter** *n.* **1.** chattering talk. **2.** a chattering sound. —**chatterer** *n.*

chatterbox *n.* a talkative person.

chatty *adj.* (chattier, chattiest) **1.** fond of chatting. **2.** resembling chat, *a chatty description.* **chattily** *adv.*, **chattiness** *n.*

chauffeur (shoh-fer) *n.* a person employed to drive a car. —*v.* to drive as chauffeur.

chauffeuse (shoh-ferz) *n.* a woman chauffeur.

chauvinism (shoh-vin-izm) *n.* exaggerated patriotism. **male chauvinism**, some men's prejudiced belief in their superiority over women. **chauvinist** *n.*, **chauvinistic** *adj.*

cheap *adj.* **1.** low in price, worth more than it cost; *cheap money*, available at a low rate of interest. **2.** charging low prices, offering good value. **3.** poor in quality, of low value. **4.** showy but worthless, silly. —*adv.* cheaply, *we got it cheap.* —**cheaply** *adv.*, **cheapness** *n.*

cheapen *v.* to make or become cheap.

cheapish *adj.* rather cheap.

cheapjack *n.* a seller of shoddy goods at low prices. —*adj.* of poor quality, shoddy.

cheat *v.* **1.** to act dishonestly or unfairly in order to win some profit or advantage. **2.** to trick, to deceive, to deprive by deceit. —**cheat** *n.* **1.** a person who cheats, an unfair player. **2.** a deception.

check¹ *v.* **1.** to stop or slow the motion of suddenly, to restrain. **2.** to make a sudden stop. **3.** to threaten (an opponent's king) at chess. **4.** to test or examine in order to make sure that something is correct or in good condition; *check the items off*, mark them when you find they are correct. **5.** (*Amer.*) to correspond when compared. —**check** *n.* **1.** a stopping or slowing of motion, a pause. **2.** a loss of the scent in hunting. **3.** exposure of a chess king to possible capture. **4.** a restraint. **5.** a control to secure accuracy. **6.** a test or examination to check that something is correct or in good working order. **7.** a receipt for something handed over. **8.** a bill in a restaurant. **9.** (*Amer.*) a cheque. —**checker** *n.* □ **check in**, to register on arrival, e.g. as a passenger at an airport. **check-list** *n.* a complete list of items, used for reference. **check on** or **up** or **up on**, to examine or investigate the correctness of. **check out**, to register on departure or dispatch; (*Amer.*) to check on. **check-out** *n.* checking out; a place where goods are paid for by customers in a supermarket. **check-point** *n.* a place where documents, vehicles, etc. are checked or inspected. **check-up** *n.* a thorough examination, especially a medical one. **keep in check**, to keep under control.

check² *n.* a pattern of squares like a chess-board, or of crossing lines. **checked** *adj.* having a check pattern.

checkers *n.* (*Amer.*) the game of draughts.

checkmate *n.* **1.** in chess, = **mate**². **2.** a complete defeat. —**checkmate** *v.* **1.** to put into checkmate in chess. **2.** to defeat finally, to foil.

Cheddar *n.* a firm cheese of a kind originally made at Cheddar, Somerset.

cheek *n.* **1.** either side of the face below the eye. **2.** (*slang*) a buttock. **3.** impudent speech, quiet arrogance. —*v.* to address cheekily. □ **cheek by jowl**, close together, in close association.

cheeky *adj.* (**cheekier**, **cheekiest**) **1.** showing bold or cheerful lack of respect. **2.** coquettish. **cheekily** *adv.*, **cheekiness** *n.*

cheep *n.* a weak shrill cry like that made by a young bird. —*v.* to make such a cry.

cheer *n.* **1.** a shout of encouragement or applause; *give three cheers*, three shouts of 'hurray'. **2.** cheerfulness. —**cheer** *v.* **1.** to utter a cheer, to encourage or applaud with cheers. **2.** to comfort, to gladden. □ **cheer up**, to make or become more cheerful.

cheerful *adj.* **1.** happy, contented, in good spirits. **2.** pleasantly bright, *cheerful colours*. **cheerfully** *adv.*, **cheerfulness** *n.*

cheerio *int.* (*informal*) goodbye.

cheerless *adj.* gloomy, dreary.

cheese *n.* **1.** a food made from milk curds. **2.** a shaped mass of this. **3.** thick stiff jam, *damson cheese.* **cheesy** *adj.* □ **cheese-paring** *adj.* & *n.* stingy, stinginess. **cheese straw**, a thin cheese-flavoured strip of pastry.

cheeseburger *n.* a hamburger with cheese in or on it.

cheesecake *n.* **1.** a tart with a filling of sweetened curds. **2.** (*slang*) a picture displaying a woman's shapely body.

cheesecloth *n.* a thin loosely-woven cotton fabric.

cheesed *adj.* (*slang*) bored, exasperated, *cheesed off.*

cheetah (chee-tă) *n.* a very swift kind of leopard that can be trained to hunt deer.

chef (*pr.* shef) *n.* a professional cook, the chief male cook in a restaurant etc.

chef-d'œuvre (shay-dervr) *n.* (*pl.* chefs-d'œuvre, *pr.* shay-dervr) a masterpiece.

Chelsea *n.* **Chelsea bun**, a kind of rolled currant bun. **Chelsea pensioner**, an inmate of the Chelsea Royal Hospital for old or disabled soldiers. ¶ Named after Chelsea in London.

chemical *adj.* **1.** of chemistry. **2.** produced by chemistry. —*n.* a substance obtained by or used in a chemical process. —**chemically** *adv.* □ **chemical engineering**, engineering concerned with processes that involve chemical change and with the equipment needed for these.

chemise (shĕm-eez) *n.* **1.** a loose-fitting

undergarment formerly worn by women, hanging straight from the shoulders. **2.** a dress of similar shape.

chemist *n.* **1.** a scientist skilled in chemistry. **2.** a person or firm dealing in medicinal drugs.

chemistry *n.* **1.** the scientific study of substances and their elements and of how they react when combined or in contact with one another. **2.** chemical structure and properties and reactions.

chemotherapy (kem-ŏ-th'e-ră-pi) *n.* treatment of disease by medicinal drugs and other chemical substances.

chenille (shĕn-**eel**) *n.* a fabric with a long velvety pile, used for furnishings.

cheque *n.* **1.** a written order to a bank to pay out money from an account. **2.** the printed form on which this is written. □ **cheque-book** *n.* a book of printed cheques. **cheque card,** a card guaranteeing payment of a bank customer's cheques.

chequer (**chek**-er) *n.* a pattern of squares, especially of alternate colours. **chequer-board** *n.* a board marked in a pattern of squares, a chess-board. **chequered** *adj.* marked with this pattern or irregularly. **chequered career,** one marked by frequent changes of fortune.

cherish *v.* **1.** to look after lovingly. **2.** to be fond of. **3.** to keep in one's heart, *we cherish hopes of his return.*

cheroot (shĕ-**root**) *n.* a cigar with both ends open.

cherry *n.* **1.** a small soft round fruit with a stone. **2.** a tree producing this or grown for its ornamental flowers. **3.** the wood of this tree. **4.** deep red. —*adj.* deep red. □ **cherry brandy,** a liqueur of brandy in which cherries have been steeped.

chert *n.* a flint-like form of quartz.

cherub *n.* **1.** (*pl.* **cherubim**) one of the angelic beings usually grouped with the seraphim. **2.** a representation (in art) of a chubby infant with wings. **3.** an angelic child.

cherubic (chĕ-**roo**-bik) *adj.* like a cherub, with a plump innocent face.

chervil *n.* a herb used for flavouring.

Ches. *abbrev.* Cheshire.

Cheshire a county of England. —*n.* a kind of cheese originally made in Cheshire. □ **like a Cheshire cat,** with a broad fixed grin.

chess *n.* a game for two players played on a **chess-board,** chequered with 64 squares, and using 32 **chess-men.**

chest *n.* **1.** a large strong box for storing or shipping things in. **2.** the upper front surface of the body, the part containing the heart and lungs. □ **chest of**

drawers, a piece of furniture with drawers for storing clothes etc. **get it off one's chest,** (*informal*) to reveal what one is anxious about. **play it close to one's chest,** to be secretive.

chesterfield *n.* a sofa with a padded back, seat, and ends.

chestnut *n.* **1.** a tree with hard brown nuts, those of the Spanish or sweet chestnut being edible. **2.** the wood of this tree. **3.** its nut. **4.** deep reddish-brown. **5.** a horse of reddish-brown or yellowish-brown colour. **6.** an old joke or story. —*adj.* deep reddish-brown or (of horses) yellowish-brown.

chesty *adj.* (*informal*) **1.** inclined to suffer from bronchial diseases, showing symptoms of these. **2.** having a large chest. **chestiness** *n.*

cheval-glass (shĕv-**al**-glahs) *n.* a tall mirror mounted in a frame so that it can be tilted.

chevalier (shev-ă-**leer**) *n.* a member of certain orders of knighthood or other groups.

chevron (**shev**-rŏn) *n.* a bent line or stripe or bar, especially one worn on the sleeve to show rank.

chew *v.* to work or grind between the teeth, to make this movement. —*n.* **1.** the act of chewing. **2.** something for chewing. □ **chewing-gum** *n.* a sticky substance sweetened and flavoured for prolonged chewing. **chew over,** (*informal*) to think over. **chew the fat** *or* **rag,** (*slang*) to chat; to grouse.

chewy *adj.* **1.** suitable for chewing. **2.** needing to be chewed, not soft.

Chianti (ki-**an**-ti) *n.* a dry Italian wine, usually red.

chiaroscuro (ki-ar-ŏ-**skoor**-oh) *n.* **1.** treatment of the light and dark parts in a painting. **2.** light and shade effects in nature. **3.** use of contrast in literature etc.

chic (*pr.* sheek) *adj.* stylish and elegant. —*n.* stylishness and elegance.

chicane (shi-**kayn**) *n.* **1.** chicanery. **2.** an artificial barrier or obstacle on a motor-racing course. —*v.* to use chicanery, to cheat.

chicanery (shi-**kayn**-er-i) *n.* trickery used to gain an advantage.

chick *n.* **1.** a young bird before or after hatching. **2.** (*slang*) a young woman. □ **chick-pea** *n.* a dwarf pea with yellow seeds.

chicken *n.* **1.** a young bird, especially of the domestic fowl. **2.** the flesh of domestic fowl as food. **3.** (*slang*) a game testing courage in the face of danger, *to play chicken.* —*adj.* (*slang*) afraid to do something cowardly. —*v.* **chicken out,** (*slang*)

to withdraw through cowardice. □ **be no chicken,** (*slang*) to be no longer young.
chicken-feed *n.* food for poultry; (*informal*) something that is small in amount.
chicken-hearted *adj.* cowardly. **chicken wire,** a kind of lightweight wire netting.
chicken-pox *n.* a disease, especially of children, with red spots on the skin.
chickweed *n.* a weed with small white flowers.
chicle (**chik**-ŭl) *n.* the milky juice of a tropical American tree, the main ingredient of chewing-gum.
chicory *n.* a blue-flowered plant cultivated for its salad leaves and for its root, which is roasted, ground, and used with or instead of coffee.
chide *v.* (chided *or* chid, chidden, chiding) (*old use*) to scold.
chief *n.* 1. a leader or ruler. 2. a person with the highest authority; *Chief of Staff*, a senior staff officer. —**chief** *adj.* 1. highest in rank or authority. 2. most important. —**chiefly** *adv.* □ **Chief Constable,** the head of the police force of an area.
chieftain (**cheef**-tŭn) *n.* the chief of a tribe, clan, or other group.
chiff-chaff *n.* a small songbird.
chiffon (**shif**-on) *n.* 1. a thin almost transparent fabric of silk or nylon etc. 2. a very light-textured pudding made with beaten egg-white, *apple chiffon*.
chiffonier (shif-ŏn-**eer**) *n.* 1. a movable low cupboard with a top used as a sideboard. 2. (*Amer.*) a tall chest of drawers.
chignon (**sheen**-yawn) *n.* a knot or roll of long hair, worn at the back of the head by women.
chihuahua (chi-**wah**-wǎ) *n.* a very small smooth-haired dog of a breed that originated in Mexico.
chilblain *n.* a painful swelling on the hand, foot, or ear, caused by exposure to cold and by poor circulation.
child *n.* (*pl.* children) 1. a young human being below the age of puberty, a boy or girl. 2. a son or daughter. □ **child-bearing** *n.* pregnancy and childbirth. **child-minder** *n.* a person who looks after children for payment. **child's play,** something very easy to do.
childbirth *n.* the process of giving birth to a child.
childhood *n.* the condition or period of being a child.
childish *adj.* like a child, unsuitable for a grown person. **childishly** *adv.*, **childishness** *n.*
childless *adj.* having no children.
childlike *adj.* having the good qualities of a child, simple and innocent.

children *see* child.
Chile (**chil**-i) a country in South America. **Chilean** *adj.* & *n.*
chill *n.* 1. unpleasant coldness. 2. an illness with feverish shivering. 3. a feeling of discouragement. —*adj.* chilly. —**chill** *v.* 1. to make or become unpleasantly cold. 2. to preserve at a low temperature without freezing, *chilled beef*.
chilli *n.* (*pl.* chillies) a dried pod of red pepper used as a relish or made into seasoning. **chilli con carne** (*pr.* **kar**-ni), a stew of minced beef flavoured with chillies.
chilly *adj.* (chillier, chilliest) 1. rather cold, unpleasantly cold. 2. cold and unfriendly in manner. **chilliness** *n.*
Chilterns *pl. n.* the Chiltern Hills, in southern England. **Chiltern** *adj.* □ **apply for the Chiltern Hundreds,** (of an MP) to apply for stewardship of a district (formerly called a *hundred*) which includes part of the Chiltern Hills and is Crown property, and hence to be allowed to resign his seat, since the holding of an office of profit under the Crown disqualifies him from being an MP.
chime *n.* a tuned set of bells, a series of notes sounded by these. —*v.* 1. (of bells) to ring. 2. (of a clock) to show the hour by chiming. □ **chime in,** to insert a remark when others are talking. **chime with** *or* **chime in with,** to agree or correspond with.
chimney *n.* (*pl.* chimneys) a structure carrying off smoke or gases from a fire.
chimney-pot *n.* a pipe fitted to the top of a chimney. **chimney-stack** *n.* a number of chimneys standing together. **chimney-sweep** *n.* a man whose trade is to remove soot from inside chimneys.
chimp *n.* (*informal*) a chimpanzee.
chimpanzee *n.* an African ape, smaller than a gorilla.
chin *n.* the front of the lower jaw. **chin-wag** *n.* (*informal*) a chat. **keep one's chin up,** to remain cheerful.
china *n.* 1. fine earthenware, porcelain. 2. articles made of this, *household china*.
China a country in Asia. **China orange,** the common orange (originally from China).
chinagraph *n.* a kind of pencil that can write on china and glass.
Chinaman *n.* (*pl.* Chinamen) a Chinese man. ¶ This word is often considered offensive.
Chinatown a section of a town in which the Chinese live as a group.
chincherinchee (chin-cher-in-**chee**) *n.* a South African plant with white flowers, growing from a bulb.

chinchilla (chin-**chil**-ă) *n.* **1.** a small squirrel-like South American animal. **2.** its soft grey fur. **3.** a breed of domestic cat and rabbit.

chine[1] *n.* an animal's backbone, a joint of meat containing part of this. —*v.* to cut along and separate the backbone in (a joint of meat).

chine[2] *n.* a deep narrow ravine in Dorset and the Isle of Wight.

chine[3] *n.* the join of side and bottom of a flat-bottomed boat.

Chinese *adj.* of China or its people or language. —*n.* **1.** (*pl.* Chinese) a native of China, a person of Chinese descent. **2.** the language of China. □ **Chinese lantern,** a collapsible paper lantern; a plant with an orange-coloured calyx resembling this.

chink[1] *n.* a narrow opening or slit.

chink[2] *n.* a sound like glasses or coins being struck together. —*v.* to make or cause to make this sound.

Chink *n.* (*slang, contemptuous*) a Chinese.

chintz *n.* a cotton cloth with a printed pattern, usually glazed, used for furnishings.

chionodoxa (ky-on-ŏ-**dok**-să) *n.* a blue-flowered plant blooming in early spring, glory-of-the-snow.

chip *n.* **1.** a thin piece cut or broken off something hard. **2.** a fried oblong strip of potato. **3.** (*Amer.*) a potato crisp. **4.** wood split into strips for making baskets, a basket made of such strips. **5.** a place from which a chip has been broken. **6.** a counter used to represent money, especially in gambling. **7.** a microchip. —**chip** *v.* (chipped, chipping) **1.** to cut or break at the surface or edge, to shape or carve by doing this. **2.** to make (potatoes) into chips. **3.** (*informal*) to tease. □ **a chip off the old block,** a child who is very like its father. **a chip on one's shoulder,** something about which one feels bitter or resentful. **chip in,** (*informal*) to interrupt with a remark when someone is speaking; to contribute money. **have had one's chips,** (*slang*) to be defeated, to die. **when the chips are down,** when it comes to the point.

chipboard *n.* thin material made of compressed wood chips and resin.

chipmunk *n.* a small striped squirrel-like animal of North America.

chipolata (chipŏ-**lah**-tă) *n.* a small spicy sausage.

Chippendale *n.* an 18th-century style of English furniture, named after its designer.

chippings *pl. n.* chips of stone etc., used for making a road-surface.

chiropody (ki-**rop**-ŏdi) *n.* the treatment of ailments of the feet. **chiropodist** *n.*

chiropractic (**ky**-rŏ-prak-tik) *n.* treatment of certain disorders by manipulation of the joints, especially those of the spine, not by medicinal drugs or surgery. **chiropractor** *n.* a practitioner of this.

chirp *n.* the short sharp note made by a small bird or a grasshopper. —*v.* to make this sound.

chirpy *adj.* lively and cheerful.

chirrup *n.* a series of chirps. —*v.* to make this sound.

chisel *n.* a tool with a bevelled edge for shaping wood, stone, or metal. —*v.* (chiselled, chiselling) **1.** to cut or shape with a chisel. **2.** (*slang*) to treat unfairly, to swindle. —**chiseller** *n.*

chit[1] *n.* a young child, a small young woman, *only a chit of a girl*.

chit[2] *n.* **1.** a short written note. **2.** a note containing an order or statement of money owed.

chit-chat *n.* chat, gossip.

chitterlings *pl. n.* the small intestines of a pig, cooked as food.

chiv *n.* (*slang*) a knife.

chivalry (**shiv**-ăl-ri) *n.* courtesy and considerate behaviour, especially towards weaker persons. **chivalrous** *adj.*

chive (*rhymes with* hive) *n.* a small herb with onion-flavoured leaves.

chivvy *v.* (chivvied, chivvying) (*informal*) to keep urging (a person) to hurry, to harass.

chloride (**klor**-ryd) *n.* a compound of chlorine and one other element.

chlorinate (**klor**-in-ayt) *v.* to treat or sterilize with chlorine. **chlorination** *n.*

chlorine (**klor**-een) *n.* a chemical element, a poisonous gas used in sterilizing water and in industry.

chloroform (**klo**-rŏ-form) *n.* a liquid that gives off vapour which causes unconsciousness when breathed. —*v.* to make unconscious by this.

chlorophyll (**klo**-rŏ-fil) *n.* the green colouring-matter in plants.

choc *n.* (*informal*) chocolate, a chocolate.

choc-ice *n.* a small bar of ice-cream coated with chocolate.

chock *n.* a block or wedge used to prevent something from moving. —*v.* to wedge with a chock or chocks. □ **chock-a-block** *adv. & adj.* crammed or crowded together. **chock-full** *adj.* crammed full.

chocolate *n.* **1.** a powdered or solid food made from roasted cacao seeds. **2.** a drink made with this. **3.** a sweet made of or covered with this. **4.** dark-brown colour. —**chocolate** *adj.* **1.** flavoured or coated with chocolate. **2.** dark-brown.

choice *n.* **1.** choosing, the right of choosing; *I have no choice,* no alternative. **2.** a variety from which to choose, *a wide choice of holidays.* **3.** a person or thing chosen, *this is my choice.* —*adj.* of the best quality, *choice bananas.* □ **for choice,** preferably.

choir *n.* **1.** an organized band of singers, especially leading the singing in church. **2.** the part of the church where these sit.

choirboy *n.* a boy who sings in a church choir.

choke *v.* **1.** to cause to stop breathing by squeezing or blocking the windpipe or (of smoke etc.) by being unfit to breathe. **2.** to be unable to breathe from such causes. **3.** to make or become speechless from emotion. **4.** to clog, to smother, *the garden is choked with weeds.* —**choke** *n.* **1.** choking, a choking sound. **2.** a valve controlling the flow of air into a petrol engine. □ **choke off,** (*informal*) to silence or discourage, usually by snubbing.

choker *n.* **1.** a high stiff collar, a clerical collar. **2.** a close-fitting necklace.

cholera (kol-er-ǎ) *n.* an infectious and often fatal disease causing severe diarrhoea.

choleric (kol-er-ik) *adj.* easily angered, often angry.

cholesterol (kŏl-est-er-ŏl) *n.* a fatty substance found in animal tissues, thought to cause hardening of the arteries.

choose *v.* (chose, chosen, choosing) **1.** to select out of a greater number of things. **2.** to decide, to prefer, to desire; *there is nothing to choose between them,* they are about equal. —**chooser** *n.*

choosy *adj.* (*informal*) careful and cautious in choosing, hard to please.

chop [1] *v.* (chopped, chopping) **1.** to cut by a blow with an axe or knife. **2.** to hit with a short downward stroke or blow. —**chop** *n.* **1.** a cutting stroke especially with an axe. **2.** a chopping blow. **3.** a thick slice of meat, usually including a rib. □ **chop up,** to chop into small pieces. **get the chop,** (*slang*) to be axed, to be dismissed; to be murdered.

chop [2] *v.* (chopped, chopping) **chop and change,** to keep changing.

chopper *n.* **1.** a chopping tool, a short axe. **2.** (*slang*) a helicopter.

choppy *adj.* **1.** full of short broken waves. **2.** jerky, not smooth. **choppiness** *n.*

chops *pl. n.* the jaws of an animal.

chopstick *n.* one of a pair of sticks used in China etc. to lift food to the mouth.

chop-suey (chop-**soo**-i) *n.* a Chinese dish made with small pieces of meat fried with rice and vegetables.

choral (kor-ǎl) *adj.* written for a choir or

chorus, sung or spoken by these. **chorally** *adv.* □ **choral society,** a society for singing choral music.

chorale (kor-**ahl**) *n.* a choral composition, using the words of a hymn.

chord [1] (*pr.* kord) *n.* a combination of notes sounded together in harmony.

chord [2] (*pr.* kord) *n.* a straight line joining two points on a curve.

chore (*pr.* chor) *n.* a routine task, a tedious task.

choreography (ko-ri-og-rǎfi) *n.* the composition of ballets or stage dances. **choreographer** *n.*

chorister (**ko**-ris-ter) *n.* a member of a choir.

chortle *n.* a loud gleeful chuckle. —*v.* to utter a chortle.

chorus *n.* **1.** a group of singers. **2.** a piece of music for these. **3.** something spoken or sung by many people together, *a chorus of approval.* **4.** the refrain or main part of a song. **5.** a group of singing dancers in a musical comedy. —*v.* (chorused, chorusing) to sing or speak or say in chorus. □ **in chorus,** speaking or singing all together.

chose, chosen see choose.

chough (*pr.* chuf) *n.* a red-legged crow.

choux pastry (*pr.* shoo) very light pastry used for making small cakes.

chow (*rhymes with* cow) *n.* **1.** a long-haired dog of a Chinese breed. **2.** (*slang*) food.

chow mein (*pr.* mayn) a Chinese dish of fried noodles with shredded meat and vegetables.

Christ the title of Jesus (= 'the anointed one'), now treated as a name.

Christadelphian (kristǎ-**del**-fiǎn) *n.* a member of a religious sect rejecting the doctrine of the Trinity and expecting the second coming of Christ.

christen *v.* **1.** to admit to the Christian Church by baptism. **2.** to give a name or nickname to. □ **christening** *n.* the ceremony of baptizing or naming.

Christendom (**kris**-ĕn-dŏm) *n.* all Christians, Christian countries.

Christian *adj.* **1.** of the doctrines of Christianity, believing in or based on these. **2.** of Christians. **3.** showing the qualities of a Christian, kindly, humane. —*n.* one who believes in Christianity. □ **Christian name,** a name given at a christening, a person's given name. **Christian Science,** a religious system claiming that health and healing can be achieved through the mental effect of true Christian faith, without medical treatment. **Christian Scientist,** one who believes in this system.

Christianity *n.* **1.** the religion based on the belief that Christ was the incarnate

Son of God, and on his teachings. **2.** being a Christian.

Christmas *n.* (*pl.* Christmases) the Christian festival (celebrated on 25 December) commemorating Christ's birth, the period about this time. □ **Christmas-box**, a small present or gratuity given at Christmas, especially to employees. **Christmas Day**, 25 December. **Christmas Eve**, 24 December. **Christmas pudding**, rich dark plum pudding eaten at Christmas. **Christmas rose**, white-flowered hellebore, blooming in winter. **Christmas tree**, an evergreen (or artificial) tree decorated at Christmas.

Christmassy *adj.* looking festive, typical of Christmas.

chromatic (krŏ-**mat**-ik) *adj.* of colour, in colours. **chromatic scale**, (in music) a scale that ascends or descends by semitones.

chrome (*pr.* krohm) *n.* **1.** chromium. **2.** yellow colouring matter obtained from a compound of chromium.

chromium (**kroh**-mi-ŭm) *n.* a chemical element, a hard metal used in making stainless steel and for coating other metals, *chromium-plated*.

chromosome (**kroh**-mŏ-sohm) *n.* one of the tiny thread-like structures in animal and plant cells, carrying genes.

chronic *adj.* **1.** (of a disease etc.) affecting a person for a long time, constantly recurring. **2.** having had an illness or a habit for a long time, *a chronic invalid.* **3.** (*slang*) very unpleasant, *this weather is chronic.* **chronically** *adv.*

chronicle (**kron**-ikŭl) *n.* a record of events in the order of their happening. —*v.* to record in a chronicle. —**chronicler** *n.*

chronological (kron-ŏ-**loj**-ikăl) *adj.* arranged in the order in which things occurred. **chronologically** *adv.*

chronology (krŏn-**ol**-ŏji) *n.* the arrangement of events in the order in which they occurred, e.g. in history or geology.

chronometer (krŏn-**om**-it-er) *n.* a time-measuring instrument with special mechanism for keeping exact time.

chrysalis (**kris**-ă-lis) *n.* the stage in an insect's life when it forms a sheath inside which it changes from a grub to an adult insect, especially a butterfly or moth.

chrysanth *n.* (*informal*) a chrysanthemum.

chrysanthemum *n.* a garden plant with bright flowers, blooming in autumn.

chub *n.* (*pl.* chub) a thick-bodied river fish.

chubby *adj.* (chubbier, chubbiest) round and plump. **chubbiness** *n.*

chuck [1] *v.* **1.** (*informal*) to throw carelessly or casually. **2.** (*informal*) to give up, to resign.

3. to touch playfully under the chin. — **chuck** *n.* **1.** a playful touch. **2.** *the chuck*, (*slang*) dismissal. □ **chuck out**, to throw away; to expel (a troublesome person).

chucker-out *n.* (*informal*) a person employed to expel troublesome people from a gathering.

chuck [2] *n.* **1.** the part of a lathe which grips the drill, the part of a drill that holds the bit. **2.** a cut of beef from the neck to the ribs, *chuck steak.*

chuckle *n.* a quiet or half-suppressed laugh. —*v.* to give a chuckle.

chuddar *n.* a large piece of cloth worn as a cloak, leaving only the face exposed, by Muslim women in certain countries.

chuffed *adj.* (*slang*) **1.** pleased. **2.** displeased.

chug *v.* (chugged, chugging) to make a dull short repeated sound, like an engine running slowly. —*n.* this sound.

chukker *n.* a period of play in polo.

chum *n.* (*informal*) a close friend. —*v.* (chummed, chumming) **chum up**, (*informal*) to form a close friendship.

chummy *adj.* very friendly. —*n.* (*police slang*) a nickname for the person who has committed the crime being investigated.

chump *n.* (*slang*) **1.** the head. **2.** a foolish person. □ **chump chop**, a chop from the thick end of a loin of mutton.

chunk *n.* **1.** a thick piece of something. **2.** a substantial amount.

chunky *adj.* **1.** short and thick. **2.** in chunks, containing chunks.

chupatty (chŭ-**pat**-i) *n.* a small flat cake of coarse unleavened bread.

church *n.* **1.** a building for public Christian worship. **2.** a religious service in this, *will see you after church.* **3.** *the Church*, the whole body of Christian believers, a particular group of these, *the Anglican Church.* **4.** *the Church*, the clergy, the clerical profession; *he went into the Church*, became a clergyman. —*v.* to perform the church service of thanksgiving for (a woman) after childbirth. □ **Church of England**, the English branch of the Western Church, rejecting the pope's supremacy.

churchman *n.* (*pl.* churchmen) **1.** a clergyman. **2.** a member of a Church.

churchwarden *n.* a representative of a parish who helps with the business of the church.

churchyard *n.* the enclosed land round a church, often used for burials.

churlish *adj.* ill-mannered, surly. **churlishly** *adv.*, **churlishness** *n.*

churn *n.* **1.** a machine in which milk is beaten to make butter. **2.** a large can in which milk is carried from a farm.

churn v. **1.** to beat (milk) or make (butter) in a churn. **2.** to stir or swirl violently; *the tank churned up the field*, broke up its surface. **3.** to produce in quantity and without quality, *churning out novels at a great rate.*

chute (*pr.* shoot) n. **1.** a sloping or vertical channel down which things can slide or be dropped. **2.** (*informal*) a parachute.

chutney n. a highly seasoned mixture of fruit, vinegar, spices, etc., eaten with meat or cheese.

CIA *abbrev.* Central Intelligence Agency.

ciao (*pr.* chow) *int.* (*informal*) **1.** goodbye. **2.** hullo.

cicada (sik-**ah**-dă) n. a grasshopper-like insect that makes a shrill chirping sound.

cicatrice (**sik** ă triss) n. the scar left by a healed wound.

CID *abbrev.* Criminal Investigation Department.

cider n. a fermented drink made from apples.

c.i.f. *abbrev.* cost, insurance, freight.

cigar n. a roll of tobacco leaves for smoking.

cigarette n. a roll of shredded tobacco enclosed in thin paper for smoking.

cinch (*pr.* sinch) n. (*Amer. slang*) a certainty, an easy task.

cinder n. a small piece of partly burnt coal or wood. **cinders** *pl. n.* ashes. **cinder-track** n. a running-track made with fire cinders.

Cinderella n. a person or thing that is persistently neglected in favour of others.

cine (**sin**-i) *adj.* cinematographic, *cine-camera, cine-film, cine-projector.*

cinema n. **1.** a theatre where motion pictures are shown. **2.** films as an art-form or an industry.

cinematographic (sini-matŏ-**graf**-ik) *adj.* for taking or projecting moving pictures.

cineraria (sin-er-**air**-iă) n. a plant with brightly coloured daisy-like flowers.

cinerary urn (**sin**-er-er-i) an urn for holding a person's ashes after cremation.

cinnamon (**sin**-a-mŏn) n. **1.** spice made from the inner bark of a south-east Asian tree. **2.** its colour, yellowish-brown.

cipher (**sy**-fer) n. **1.** the symbol 0, representing nought or zero. **2.** any Arabic numeral. **3.** a person or thing of no importance. **4.** a set of letters or symbols representing others, used to conceal the meaning of a message etc. —v. to write in cipher.

circa *prep.* about, *china from circa 1850.*

circle n. **1.** a perfectly round plane figure. **2.** the line enclosing it, every point on which is the same distance from the centre. **3.** something shaped like this, a ring. **4.** curved rows of seats rising in tiers at a theatre etc., above the lowest level. **5.** a number of people bound together by similar interests, *in business circles.* —v. to move in a circle, to form a circle round. □ **come full circle**, to pass through a series of events etc. and return to the starting-point. **go round in circles**, to be fussily busy but making no progress.

circlet (**ser**-klit) n. a circular band worn as an ornament, especially round the head.

circs (*pr.* serks) *pl. n.* (*informal*) circumstances.

circuit (**ser**-kit) n. **1.** a line or route or distance round a place. **2.** the journey of a judge round a particular district to hold courts, the district itself. **3.** a group of Methodist churches in a district. **4.** a sequence of sporting events, *the American golf circuit.* **5.** a motor-racing track. **6.** a chain of theatres or cinemas. **7.** a closed path for an electric current. **8.** an apparatus with conductors, valves, etc. through which electric current passes. □ **circuit-breaker** n. a device for interrupting an electric current.

circuitous (ser-**kew**-it-ŭs) *adj.* roundabout, indirect. **circuitously** *adv.*

circuitry (**ser**-kit-ri) n. circuits, the equipment forming these.

circular *adj.* **1.** shaped like a circle. **2.** moving round a circle; *a circular tour,* one by a route that brings travellers back to the starting-point. **3.** (of reasoning) using as evidence for its conclusion the very thing that it is trying to prove. **4.** addressed to a circle of people, *a circular letter.* —n. a circular letter or advertising leaflet. **circularity** (ser-kew-**la**-riti) n.

circularize v. to send a circular to.

circulate v. **1.** to go round continuously. **2.** to pass from place to place. **3.** to cause to move round, to send round, *we will circulate this letter.* **3.** to circularize, *we will circulate these people.*

circulation n. **1.** circulating, being circulated. **2.** the movement of blood round the body, pumped by the heart. **3.** the number of copies sold or distributed, especially of a newspaper.

circulatory (ser-kew-**layt**-er-i) *adj.* of the circulation of blood.

circumcise v. to cut off the foreskin of (a male person) as a religious rite or surgically. **circumcision** n.

circumference (ser-**kum**-fer-ĕns) n. the boundary of a circle, the distance round this.

circumflex accent (**ser**-kum-fleks) a mark over a vowel, as over *e* in *fête.*

circumlocution (ser-kŭm-lŏ-**kew**-shŏn) n.

1. use of many words where a few would do. 2. evasive talk.

circumnavigate *v.* to sail completely round. **circumnavigation** *n.*

circumscribe *v.* 1. to draw a line round. 2. to mark the limits of, to restrict. **circumscription** *n.*

circumspect (ser-kŭm-spekt) *adj.* cautious and watchful, wary. **circumspection** *n.*

circumstance *n.* 1. one of the conditions or facts connected with an event or person or action; *he was a victim of circumstances,* the conditions affecting him were beyond his control; *what are his circumstances?* what is his financial position?; *they live in reduced circumstances,* in poverty that contrasts with their former prosperity. 2. ceremony, *pomp and circumstance.* □ **in** *or* **under the circumstances,** owing to or making allowances for them. **under no circumstances,** not whatever happens.

circumstantial (ser-kŭm-**stan**-shăl) *adj.* 1. giving full details. 2. consisting of facts that strongly suggest something but do not provide direct proof, *circumstantial evidence.* **circumstantially** *adv.*

circumvent (ser-kŭm-**vent**) *v.* to evade, to find a way round, *managed to circumvent the rules.* **circumvention** *n.*

circumvolution (ser-kŭm-vŏ-**loo**-shŏn) *n.* rotation, a twisting movement.

circus *n.* 1. a travelling show with performing animals, acrobats, and clowns. 2. (*informal*) a scene of lively action. 3. (*informal*) a group of people performing in sports or a series of lectures etc. either together or in succession. 4. (*in placenames*) an open space in a town, where streets converge, *Piccadilly Circus.*

cirrhosis (si-**roh**-sis) *n.* a chronic disease, especially of alcoholics, in which the liver hardens into many small projections (*hobnailed liver*).

cirrus (**si**-rŭs) *n.* light wispy clouds.

cissy *n.* an effeminate or timid boy or man.

Cistercian (sis-**ter**-shăn) *n.* a member of a religious order that was founded as a branch of the Benedictines.

cistern (**sis**-tern) *n.* a tank or other vessel for storing water, the tank above a water-closet.

citadel (**sit**-ă-děl) *n.* 1. a fortress overlooking a city. 2. a meeting-hall of the Salvation Army.

cite (*pr. as* sight) *v.* to quote or mention as an example or to support an argument. **citation** *n.*

citizen *n.* 1. an inhabitant of a city. 2. a

person who has full rights in a country or Commonwealth by birth or by naturalization. **citizenship** *n.* □ **citizens' band,** radio frequencies to be used by private persons for local communication.

citric acid (**sit**-rik) the acid in the juice of lemons, limes, etc.

citrus (**sit**-rŭs) *n.* any of a group of related trees including lemon, orange, and grapefruit; *citrus fruit,* fruit from such a tree.

city *n.* 1. a large and important town, a town with special rights given by charter and containing a cathedral. 2. *the City,* the oldest part of London, governed by the Lord Mayor and Corporation, now a centre of commerce and finance.

civet (**siv**-it) *n.* 1. a civet-cat, a cat-like animal of central Africa. 2. a musky-smelling substance obtained from its glands, used in making perfumes.

civic (**siv**-ik) *adj.* of or proper to a city or town, of citizens or citizenship. **civic centre,** an area containing municipal offices and other public buildings. **civics** *n.* the study of municipal government and of the rights and duties of citizens.

civil *adj.* 1. belonging to citizens; *civil liberty,* liberty restricted only by those laws established for the good of the community. 2. of the general public, not the armed forces or the Church; *civil aviation,* non-military; *civil marriage,* with a civil ceremony not a religious one. 3. involving civil law not criminal law, *a civil dispute.* 4. polite and obliging. **civilly** *adv.* □ **civil engineering,** the designing and construction of roads, bridges, canals, etc. **civil law,** law dealing with the private rights of citizens, not with crime. **civil list,** the allowance of money made by Parliament for the sovereign's household expenses. **civil rights,** the rights of a citizen; *civil rights movement,* an organized movement to secure full constitutional rights for Blacks in the USA. **Civil Servant,** an employee of the **Civil Service,** all government departments other than the armed forces. **civil war,** war between groups of citizens of the same country.

civilian *n.* a person not serving in the armed forces.

civility *n.* politeness, an act of politeness.

civilization *n.* 1. making or becoming civilized. 2. a stage in the evolution of organized society, a particular type of this, *ancient civilizations.* 3. civilized conditions or society, *far from civilization.*

civilize *v.* 1. to cause to improve from a savage or primitive stage of human society to a more developed one. 2. to improve the behaviour of.

civvies (siv-iz) *pl. n.* (*slang*) civilian clothes.

cl *abbrev.* centilitre(s).

clack *n.* **1.** a short sharp sound like that made by plates struck together. **2.** the noise of chatter. —*v.* to make such a sound or noise.

clad *adj.* clothed, *warmly clad*; *iron-clad*, protected with iron.

cladding *n.* a metal or other material applied to the surface of another as a protective covering.

clade *n.* a group of organisms that have evolved from a common ancestor.

cladistics (klă-dist-iks) *n.* a method of studying the relationship of groups of living things by tracing the course of their development from a common ancestor, by analysis of shared features.

claim *v.* **1.** to request as one's right or due; *the floods claimed many lives*, people died as a result. **2.** to declare that something is true or has been achieved, to state without being able to prove. —**claim** *n.* **1.** a request for something as one's right; *lay claim to* (see lay³). **2.** the right to something, *a widow has a claim on her deceased husband's estate.* **3.** a statement claiming that something is true, an assertion.

claimant *n.* a person who makes a claim, especially in law.

clairvoyance (klair-voy-ăns) *n.* the supposed power of seeing in the mind either future events or things that are happening or existing out of sight. **clairvoyant** *n.* a person said to have this power.

clam *n.* a large shellfish with a hinged shell. —*v.* (clammed, clamming) **clam up,** (*Amer. slang*) to refuse to talk.

clamber *v.* to climb with some difficulty.

clammy *adj.* unpleasantly moist and sticky. **clamminess** *n.*

clamour *n.* **1.** a loud confused noise especially of shouting. **2.** a loud protest or demand. —*v.* to make a loud protest or demand. **clamorous** *adj.*

clamp¹ *n.* a device for holding things tightly, often with a screw. —*v.* to grip with a clamp, to fix firmly. □ **clamp down on,** to become stricter about, to put a stop to.

clamp² *n.* **1.** a pile of bricks for burning. **2.** a mound of potatoes etc. stored under straw and earth.

clan *n.* **1.** a group with a common ancestor, *the Scottish clans.* **2.** a large family forming a close group.

clandestine (klan-dest-in) *adj.* kept secret, done secretly. **clandestinely** *adv.*

clang *n.* a loud ringing sound. —*v.* to make a clang.

clanger *n.* (*slang*) a blunder; *drop a clanger*, to make a blunder.

clangour (klang-er) *n.* a clanging noise.

clank *n.* a metallic sound like that of metal striking metal. —*v.* to make a clank.

clannish *adj.* showing clan feeling, clinging together and excluding others.

clap¹ *n.* **1.** the sharp noise of thunder. **2.** the sound of the palms of the hands being struck together, especially in applause. **3.** a friendly slap, *gave him a clap on the shoulder.* —**clap** *v.* (clapped, clapping) **1.** to strike the palms loudly together, especially in applause. **2.** to flap (wings) audibly. **3.** to put or place quickly, *clapped him into gaol.* □ **clap eyes on,** (*informal*) to catch sight of. **clapped out,** (*slang*) worn out; exhausted.

clap² *n.* (*vulgar*) venereal disease, gonorrhoea.

clapper *n.* the tongue or striker of a bell. **going like the clappers,** (*slang*) going very fast.

claptrap *n.* talk or ideas used only to win applause.

claque (*pr.* klahk) *n.* a body of people hired to applaud something.

claret (kla-rĕt) *n.* a dry red wine.

clarify *v.* (clarified, clarifying) **1.** to make or become clear or easier to understand. **2.** to remove impurities from (fats), e.g. by heating. **clarification** *n.*

clarinet (kla-rin-et) *n.* a wood-wind instrument with finger-holes and keys. **clarinettist** *n.* a person who plays the clarinet.

clarion (kla-ri-ŏn) *adj.* loud, clear and rousing, *a clarion call.*

clarity *n.* clearness.

clary (klair-i) *n.* a herb with purplish bracts, used for flavouring.

clash *v.* **1.** to strike making a loud harsh sound like that of cymbals. **2.** to conflict, to disagree. **3.** to take place inconveniently at the same time as something else. **4.** (of colours) to produce an unpleasant visual effect by not being harmonious. —**clash** *n.* **1.** a sound of clashing. **2.** a conflict, a disagreement. **3.** a clashing of colours.

clasp *n.* **1.** a device for fastening things, with interlocking parts. **2.** a grasp, a handshake. —**clasp** *v.* **1.** to fasten, to join with a clasp. **2.** to grasp, to hold or embrace closely. □ **clasp-knife** *n.* a folding knife with a catch for fixing it open.

class *n.* **1.** people or animals or things with some characteristics in common. **2.** people of the same social or economic level, *the working class.* **3.** a set of students taught together, a session when these are taught. **4.** a division according to quality, *first class*; *tourist class.* **5.** distinction, high quality, *a tennis player with class.* —*v.* to place in a class, to classify. □ **in a class of its own,** much superior to everything else of its kind.

classic *adj.* **1.** having a high quality that is recognized and unquestioned, *Hardy's classic novel.* **2.** very typical, *a classic case of malnutrition.* **3.** having qualities like those of classical art, simple and harmonious; *classic clothes,* plain and conventional in style. **4.** famous through being long established; *the classic races,* the Two and One Thousand Guineas, Derby, Oaks, and St. Leger. —**classic** *n.* **1.** a classic author or work etc., *'David Copperfield' is a classic.* **2.** a garment in classic style. **3.** a classic race. □ **classics** *n.* the study of ancient Greek and Roman literature, culture, etc.

classical *adj.* **1.** model or first-class, especially in literature. **2.** of ancient Greek and Roman art, literature, and culture; *a classical scholar,* an expert in these. **3.** simple and harmonious in style. **4.** traditional and standard in style, *classical music.* **classically** *adv.*

classifiable *adj.* able to be classified.

classified *adj.* **1.** (of advertisements) arranged according to subject-matter. **2.** (of information) designated as officially secret and available only to specified people.

classify *v.* (classified, classifying) to arrange systematically in classes or groups, to put into a particular class. **classification** *n.*

classless *adj.* without distinctions of social class.

classroom *n.* a room where a class of students is taught.

classy *adj.* (*slang*) stylish, superior.

clatter *n.* **1.** a sound like that of plates rattled together. **2.** noisy talk. —*v.* to make or cause to make a clatter.

clause *n.* **1.** a single part in a treaty, law, or contract. **2.** a part of a complex sentence, with its own verb.

claustrophobia (klaw-strŏ-**foh**-biă) *n.* abnormal fear of being in an enclosed space. **claustrophobic** *adj.* suffering from or causing claustrophobia.

clave *see* cleave².

clavicle (**klav**-ikŭl) *n.* the collar-bone.

claw *n.* **1.** the pointed nail on an animal's or bird's foot, a foot with such nails. **2.** the pincers of a shellfish, *a lobster's claw.* **3.** a device like a claw, used for grappling and holding. —*v.* to grasp or scratch or pull with a claw or with the hands. □ **claw back,** to recoup what has just been given away, *money handed out as family*

allowances was clawed back in taxation.

claw-back *n.* an instance of this.

claw-hammer *n.* a hammer with a head divided at one end for pulling out nails.

clay *n.* stiff sticky earth that becomes hard when baked, used for making bricks and pottery. **clayey** *adj.* □ **clay pigeon,** a breakable disc thrown up as a target for shooting.

claymore *n.* **1.** a Scottish two-edged broadsword. **2.** a broadsword with a basket-like structure protecting the hilt.

clean *adj.* **1.** free from dirt or impurities, not soiled. **2.** not yet used, *a clean page.* **3.** (of a nuclear bomb) producing relatively little fall-out. **4.** with nothing dishonourable in it, (of a licence) with no endorsements. **5.** attentive to cleanliness, with clean habits. **6.** without projections or roughness, smooth and even. **7.** keeping to the rules, not unfair, *a clean fighter.* **8.** free from indecency; *keep it clean,* do not tell improper jokes. —*adv.* completely, entirely, *I clean forgot; clean bowled,* bowled out directly, without the ball touching the bat. —**clean** *v.* **1.** to make clean. **2.** to dry-clean. **3.** to remove the innards of before cooking, to gut, *clean the fish.* —*n.* cleaning, *give it a clean.* —**cleanly** *adv.,* **cleanness** *n.* □ **clean-cut** *adj.* sharply outlined, *clean-cut features.* **clean out,** to clean the inside of; (*slang*) to use up all the supplies or money of. **clean-shaven** *adj.* with beard, moustache, and whiskers shaved off. **clean up,** to make clean, to tidy things up or oneself; to rid of crime and corruption; (*informal*) to make a gain or profit. **make a clean breast of it,** to confess fully. **make a clean sweep,** *see* sweep.

cleaner *n.* **1.** a device or substance used for cleaning things. **2.** a person employed to clean rooms. □ **cleaners** *pl. n.* a dry-cleaning establishment. **take a person to the cleaners,** (*slang*) to rob or defraud him; to criticize him strongly.

cleanly (**klen**-li) *adj.* attentive to cleanness, with clean habits. **cleanliness** *n.*

cleanse (*pr.* klenz) *v.* to make thoroughly clean. **cleanser** *n.* a cleansing substance. **cleansing cream,** for cleansing the skin. **cleansing department,** a local authority department responsible for cleaning the streets and removing refuse.

clear *adj.* **1.** transparent, *clear glass; clear water,* not muddy or cloudy; *clear soup,* not thickened. **2.** free from blemishes. **3.** free from guilt, *a clear conscience.* **4.** easily seen or heard or understood, distinct. **5.** evident, *a clear case of cheating.* **6.** free from doubt, not confused. **7.** free from obstruction or from something undesirable. **8.** net, without deductions, complete, *a clear £1000; give 3 clear days' notice.* —**clear** *adv.* **1.** clearly. **2.** completely. **3.** apart, not in contact, *stand clear!* —**clear** *v.* **1.** to make or become clear. **2.** to free (one's throat) of phlegm or huskiness by a slight cough. **3.** to get past or over, especially without touching. **4.** to get approval or authorization for; *clear goods through customs,* satisfy official requirements there. **5.** to pass (a cheque) through a clearing-house. **6.** to make as net gain or profit; *we cleared our expenses,* made enough money to cover these. —**clearly** *adv.*, **clearness** *n.* ☐ **clear away**, to remove; to remove used crockery etc. after a meal. **clear-cut** *adj.* very distinct; not open to doubt. **clear off**, to get rid of; *(slang)* to go away. **clear the decks**, to clear away hindrances and prepare for action. **clear up**, to tidy up; to become better or brighter; *clear up the mystery,* solve it. **in the clear**, free of suspicion or difficulty.

clearance *n.* **1.** clearing. **2.** authorization, permission. **3.** the space left clear when one object moves within or past another. ☐ **clearance order**, an order for the demolition of buildings.

clearing *n.* an open space from which trees have been cleared in a forest.

clearing-house *n.* **1.** an office at which banks exchange cheques and settle the balances. **2.** an agency that collects and distributes information etc.

clearway *n.* a road on which vehicles must not stop on the carriageway.

cleat *n.* **1.** a short piece of wood or metal with projecting ends round which a rope may be fastened. **2.** a strip or other projecting piece fixed to a gangway etc. or to footwear, to prevent slipping. **3.** a wedge. —*v.* to fasten to a cleat.

cleavage *n.* **1.** a split, a division made by cleaving. **2.** the hollow between full breasts, exposed by a low-cut garment.

cleave[1] *v.* (*see* ¶ *below*) **1.** to divide by chopping, to split or become split. **2.** to make a way through. ¶ The past tense may be either *he cleaved* or *he clove* or *he cleft*, or *he has cloven* or *he has cleft*. The adjectives *cloven* and *cleft* are used of different objects (*see* cleft and cloven).

cleave[2] *v.* (cleaved *or* clave, cleaved, cleaving) (*old use*) to adhere, to cling.

cleaver *n.* a butcher's chopper.

clef *n.* a symbol on a stave in a musical score, showing the pitch of the notes (e.g. treble, bass, etc.).

cleft *see* cleave[1]. —*adj.* split, partly divided; *a cleft chin,* with a V-shaped

hollow. —*n.* a split, a cleavage. ☐ **cleft palate**, a defect in the roof of the mouth where two sides of the palate failed to join before birth. **in a cleft stick**, without room to manœuvre.

clematis (klem-ă-tiss *or* klim-ay-tiss) *n.* a climbing plant with white or purplish flowers.

clemency (klem-ĕn-si) *n.* **1.** mildness, especially of weather. **2.** mercy. **clement** *adj.*

clementine (klem-ĕn-tyn) *n.* a kind of small orange.

clench *v.* **1.** to close (the teeth or fingers) tightly. **2.** to grasp tightly. **3.** to fasten (a nail or rivet) by hammering the point sideways after it is driven through. —*n.* a clenching action, a clenched state.

clerestory (kleer-ster-i) *n.* an upper row of windows in a large church, above the level of the roofs of the aisles.

clergy *n.* the men who have been ordained as priests or ministers of the Christian Church.

clergyman *n.* (*pl.* clergymen) a member of the clergy, especially of the Church of England.

cleric (kle-rik) *n.* a clergyman.

clerical *adj.* **1.** of clerks; *a clerical error,* one made in copying or writing something out. **2.** of the clergy; *clerical collar,* an upright white collar fastening at the back, worn by clergy.

clerihew (kle-ri-hew) *n.* a short witty verse in 4 lines of unequal length, rhyming in couplets.

clerk (*pr.* klark) *n.* **1.** a person employed to keep records or accounts etc. in an office. **2.** an official who keeps the records of a court or council etc. ☐ **clerk of the works**, the overseer of building works.

clerkess *n.* (*Scottish*) a female clerk.

Cleveland a county of England.

clever *adj.* **1.** quick at learning and understanding things, skilful; *he was too clever for us,* he outwitted us. **2.** showing skill, *a clever plan.* **cleverly** *adv.*, **cleverness** *n.* ☐ **clever Dick**, (*slang*) a person who shows off his cleverness.

clew *n.* the lower or after corner of a sail.

cliché (klee-shay) *n.* a hackneyed phrase or idea.

click *n.* a short sharp sound like that of billiard-balls colliding. —*v.* **1.** to make or cause to make a click, to fasten with a click. **2.** (*slang*) to be a success, to become understood.

client *n.* **1.** a person using the services of a lawyer or architect or a professional person other than a doctor, or of a business. **2.** a customer.

clientele (klee-on-**tel**) *n.* clients, customers.

cliff *n.* a steep rock-face, especially on a coast. **cliff-hanger** *n.* a story or contest full of suspense. **cliff-hanging** *adj.*

climacteric (kly-**mak**-ter-ik) *n.* the period of life when physical powers begin to decline.

climate *n.* 1. the regular weather conditions of an area. 2. an area with certain weather conditions, *living in a hot climate.* 3. a general attitude or feeling, an atmosphere, *a climate of hostility.* **climatic** (kly-**mat**-ik) *adj.*

climax *n.* 1. the event or point of greatest interest or intensity. 2. sexual orgasm. —*v.* to reach or bring to a climax.

climb *v.* 1. to go up or over by effort. 2. to move upwards, to go higher, *the plane climbed rapidly.* 3. to grow up a support, *a climbing rose.* —*n.* an ascent made by climbing. □ **climb down**, to go downwards by effort; to retreat from a position taken up in argument. **climb-down** *n.* a retreat of this kind. **climbing-frame** *n.* a structure of joined pipes and bars for children to climb on.

climber *n.* 1. one who climbs, a mountaineer. 2. a climbing plant.

clinch *v.* 1. to fasten securely, to clench (a nail or rivet). 2. (in boxing) to be too close together for a full-arm blow. 3. to settle conclusively, *clinched the deal.* —**clinch** *n.* 1. a clinching position in boxing. 2. (*informal*) an embrace.

cling *v.* (clung, clinging) 1. to hold on tightly. 2. to become attached, to stick. 3. to remain close or in contact, to be emotionally attached or dependent, *the family still cling together.* 4. to refuse to abandon, *clinging to hopes of rescue.* □ **cling peach** *or* **clingstone** *n.* a kind of peach or nectarine in which the stone is difficult to separate from the flesh.

clinic *n.* 1. a private or specialized hospital, *the London Clinic.* 2. a place or session at which specialized treatment or advice is given to visiting persons, *ante-natal clinic.*

clinical *adj.* 1. of a clinic. 2. of or used in the treatment of patients, *clinical thermometer.* 3. of or based on observed signs and symptoms, *clinical medicine.* 4. looking bare and hygienic. 5. unemotional, cool and detached. **clinically** *adv.*

clink¹ *n.* a thin sharp sound like glasses striking together. —*v.* to make or cause to make this sound.

clink² *n.* (*slang*) prison, *in clink.*

clinker *n.* rough stony material left after coal has burnt, a piece of this.

clinker-built *adj.* (of a boat) made with the outside planks or plates overlapping downwards.

clip¹ *n.* 1. a device for holding things tightly or together, a paper-clip. 2. a magazine for a firearm. 3. an ornament fastened by a clip. —**clip** *v.* (clipped, clipping) to fix or fasten with a clip. □ **clip-board** *n.* a portable board with a clip at the top for holding papers. **clip-on** *adj.* attached by a clip.

clip² *v.* (clipped, clipping) 1. to cut or trim with shears or scissors. 2. to punch a small piece from (a ticket) to show that it has been used. 3. (*informal*) to hit sharply, *clipped his ear.* —**clip** *n.* 1. the act or process of clipping, a piece clipped off or out. clipping. 2. the wool cut from a sheep or flock at one shearing. 3. an extract from a film. 4. (*informal*) a sharp blow. 5. a rapid pace, *going at quite a clip.* □ **clip-joint** *n.* (*slang*) a club charging outrageously high prices.

clipper *n.* a fast horse or ship.

clippers *pl. n.* an instrument for clipping hair.

clipping *n.* a piece clipped off or out.

clique (*pr.* kleek) *n.* a small exclusive group. **cliquey** *adj.*, **cliquish** *adj.*

clitoris (**klit**-er-iss) *n.* a small erectile part of the female genitals, at the upper end of the vulva. **clitoral** *adj.*

cloak *n.* 1. a loose sleeveless outdoor garment. 2. something that conceals, *under the cloak of darkness.* —*v.* to cover or conceal. □ **cloak-and-dagger** *adj.* involving dramatic adventures in spying.

cloakroom *n.* a room where outdoor clothes and packages etc. may be left temporarily, often with a lavatory.

clobber¹ *n.* (*slang*) clothing and equipment.

clobber² *v.* (*slang*) to hit repeatedly, to give a beating to, to defeat; *clobbering the taxpayers,* hurting them by heavy taxation.

cloche (*pr.* klosh *or* klohsh) *n.* 1. a portable glass or plastic cover for outdoor plants. 2. a woman's close-fitting bell-shaped hat.

clock¹ *n.* 1. an instrument (other than a watch) for measuring and showing the time. 2. any measuring device with a dial or displayed figures, e.g. a taximeter, an odometer. 3. the seed-head of a dandelion. —**clock** *v.* 1. to time (a race or competitor). 2. (*informal*) to achieve as a speed, *he clocked* or *clocked up 10 seconds for the 100 metres.* 3. (*slang*) to hit. □ **clock golf** a game in which a golf-ball is putted into a hole from points marked round this. **clock in** *or* **on**, to register one's arrival for work. **clock out** *or* **off**, to register one's departure from work. **clock-watcher** *n*. one who is constantly alert for the time when he may legitimately stop working.

clock² *n*. an ornamental pattern on the side of a stocking or sock.

clockwise *adv. & adj*. moving in a curve from left to right, as seen from the centre of the circle.

clockwork *n*. a mechanism with wheels and springs, like that of a clock; *clockwork toys*, toys driven by such mechanism. **like clockwork**, with perfect regularity and precision.

clod *n*. a lump of earth or clay.

clodhoppers *pl. n*. (*informal*) large heavy shoes.

clog *n*. a wooden-soled shoe. —*v*. (clogged, clogging) to cause an obstruction in, to become blocked.

cloister *n*. **1.** a covered walk along the side of a church or other building, looking on a courtyard. **2.** a monastery or convent, life in this.

cloistered *adj*. sheltered, secluded.

clone *n*. a group of plants or organisms produced asexually from one ancestor, a member of this group. —*v*. to propagate or become propagated as a clone.

close¹ (*pr*. klohs) *adj*. **1.** near in space or time. **2.** near in relationship, *a close relative*. **3.** dear to each other, *close friends*. **4.** nearly alike, *a close resemblance*. **5.** in which the competitors are nearly equal, *a close contest*. **6.** dense, compact, with only slight intervals, *a close texture*. **7.** detailed, leaving no gaps or weaknesses, concentrated. **8.** secretive. **9.** stingy. **10.** stuffy, humid, without fresh air. —*adv*. closely, in a near position, *they live close by*. —**close** *n*. **1.** a cul-de-sac. **2.** the grounds round a cathedral or abbey etc., usually with its buildings (houses etc.). — **closely** *adv*., **closeness** *n*. □ **at close quarters**, very close together. **close season**, the season when killing of game etc. is forbidden by law. **a close shave**, *see* shave. **close-up** *n*. a photograph giving a detailed view of something; a detailed description.

close² (*pr*. klohz) *v*. **1.** to shut. **2.** to be or declare to be not open to the public. **3.** to bring or come to an end; *the closing days of the year*, the last ones. **4.** to bring or come closer or into contact, *close the ranks*. **5.** to come within striking distance, to grapple. —*n*. a conclusion, an end. □ **closed book**, a subject one has never studied. **closed-circuit television**, that transmitted by wires, not waves, to a restricted number of screens. **close down**, to shut completely, to cease working.

closedown *n*. an instance of this. **closed shop**, the system whereby membership of a trade union (or of a specified one) is a condition of employment in a certain establishment. **close in**, to approach from all sides so as to shut in or entrap. **close with**, to accept (an offer), to accept the offer made by (a person).

closet *n*. (*Amer*.) **1.** a cupboard. **2.** a storeroom. —*v*. (closeted, closeting) to shut away in private conference or study.

closure (**kloh-***zh*er) *n*. **1.** closing, a closed condition. **2.** a decision in Parliament to take a vote without further debate.

clot *n*. **1.** a small thickened mass formed from blood or other liquid. **2.** (*slang*) a stupid person. —*v*. (clotted, clotting) to form clots. □ **clotted cream**, cream thickened by being scalded.

cloth *n*. **1.** woven or felted material. **2.** a piece of this for a special purpose, a dishcloth, tablecloth, etc. **3.** clerical clothes, the clergy, *respect for his cloth*.

clothe *v*. (clothed *or* clad, clothing) to put clothes upon, to provide with clothes.

clothes *pl. n*. **1.** things worn to cover the body and limbs. **2.** bedclothes. □ **clothes-horse** *n*. a frame with bars over which clothes etc. are hung to air. **clothes-line** *n*. a rope or wire on which washed clothes are hung to dry. **clothes-peg** *n*. a clip or forked device for securing clothes to a clothes-line.

clothier (**kloh-***th*i-er) *n*. a seller of men's clothes.

clothing *n*. clothes, garments.

cloud *n*. **1.** a visible mass of condensed watery vapour, floating in the sky. **2.** a mass of smoke or mist etc. **3.** a mass of things moving in the air, *a cloud of insects*. **4.** a state of gloom or trouble, *casting a cloud over the festivities*. —**cloud** *n*. **1.** to cover or darken with clouds or gloom or trouble. **2.** to become overcast or indistinct or gloomy. □ **under a cloud**, out of favour, under suspicion, in disgrace. **with one's head in the clouds**, daydreaming.

cloudburst *n*. a sudden violent rainstorm.

cloudless *adj*. free from clouds.

cloudy *adj*. (cloudier, cloudiest) **1.** covered with clouds. **2.** not transparent, *a cloudy liquid*. **cloudiness** *n*.

clout *n*. (*informal*) **1.** a blow. **2.** power of effective action, *trade unions with clout*. **3.** (*old use*) an article of clothing, *cast ne'er a clout till May be out*. —*v*. (*informal*) to hit.

clove¹ *see* cleave.

clove[2] *n.* one of the small bulbs making up a compound bulb, *a clove of garlic.*

clove[3] *n.* the dried unopened flower-bud of tropical myrtle, used as a spice.

clove hitch a knot used to secure a rope round a spar or pole.

cloven *see* cleave[1]. □ **cloven hoof**, one that is divided, like those of oxen or sheep.

clover *n.* a plant with three-lobed leaves, used for fodder. **clover-leaf** *n.* an intersection of roads in a pattern resembling a four-leaved clover. **in clover**, in ease and luxury.

clown *n.* 1. a performer, especially in a circus, who does comical tricks and actions. 2. a person who is always behaving comically. —*v.* to perform as a clown, to behave comically.

cloy *v.* to sicken by glutting with sweetness or pleasure, *cloy the appetite.* **cloying** *adj.* sickeningly sweet.

club *n.* 1. a heavy stick with one end thicker than the other, used as a weapon. 2. the headed stick used to hit the ball in golf. 3. a playing-card of the suit (*clubs*) marked with black clover-leaves. 4. a society of people who subscribe to provide themselves with sport or entertainment etc., their buildings or premises, *the tennis club.* 5. an organization offering subscribers certain benefits, *a Christmas club*; *a book club.* —**club** *v.* (clubbed, clubbing) 1. to strike with a club. 2. to join in subscribing, *we clubbed together to buy a boat.* □ **club-foot** *n.* a deformed foot. **club-root** *n.* a disease causing distortion of the root of cabbage and similar plants. **club sandwich**, a three-decker sandwich.

clubbable *adj.* sociable, likely to be a good member of a social club.

cluck *n.* the throaty cry of a hen. —*v.* to utter a cluck.

clue *n.* 1. a fact or idea that gives a guide to the solution of a problem; *she hasn't a clue,* (*informal*) she is stupid or incompetent. 2. a word or words indicating what is to be inserted in a crossword puzzle. —*v.* to provide with a clue. □ **clue up**, (*slang*) to inform.

clueless *adj.* 1. without a clue. 2. (*informal*) stupid or incompetent.

clump *n.* 1. a cluster or mass. 2. a clumping sound. —**clump** *v.* 1. to form a clump, to arrange in a clump. 2. to walk with a heavy tread. 3. (*informal*) to hit.

clumsy *adj.* (clumsier, clumsiest) 1. heavy and ungraceful in movement or shape. 2. large and difficult to handle or use, *a clumsy sideboard.* 3. done without tact or skill, *a clumsy apology.* **clumsily** *adv.*, **clumsiness** *n.*

clung *see* cling.

clunk *n.* a dull sound like thick metal objects striking together. —*v.* to make this sound.

cluster *n.* a small close group. —*v.* to bring or come together in a cluster. □ **cluster bomb**, a bomb that sprays metal pellets when it explodes.

clutch[1] *v.* to grasp tightly; *clutch at,* to try to grasp. —*n.* 1. a tight grasp, a clutching movement. 2. a device for connecting and disconnecting certain working parts in machinery, the pedal or other device operating this. □ **get into a person's clutches**, to come into his possession or under his relentless control.

clutch[2] *n.* 1. a set of eggs for hatching. 2. the chickens hatched from these.

clutter *n.* 1. things lying about untidily. 2. a crowded untidy state. —*v.* to fill with clutter, to crowd untidily.

Clwyd (**kloo**-id) a county of Wales.

Clydesdale *n.* a horse of a heavily-built breed used for pulling things.

cm *abbrev.* centimetre.

Co. *abbrev.* 1. Company, *Briggs & Co.* 2. County, *Co. Durham*; *Co. Derry,* = Co. Londonderry.

CO *abbrev.* Commanding Officer.

c/o *abbrev.* care of (*see* care).

co- *prefix* together with, jointly, *co-author*; *coexistence.*

coach *n.* 1. a large four-wheeled horse-drawn carriage. 2. a railway carriage. 3. a chartered or long-distance single-decker bus. 4. an instructor in sports. 5. a teacher giving private specialized tuition. —*v.* to train or teach.

coachwork *n.* the bodywork of a road or railway vehicle.

coagulate (koh-**ag**-yoo-layt) *v.* to change from liquid to semi-solid, to clot. **coagulation** *n.*

coal *n.* 1. a hard black mineral used for burning to supply heat. 2. a piece of this, one that is burning, *a live coal.* —*v.* to load a supply of coal into (a ship). □ **carry coals to Newcastle**, to take a thing to a place where it is already plentiful. **coal-face** *n.* the exposed surface of coal in a mine. **coalfield** *n.* an area where coal occurs naturally. **coal gas** mixed gases extracted from coal and used for lighting and heating. **coal-mine** *n.* a mine where coal is dug. **coal tar**, tar produced when gas is made from coal. **heap coals of fire**, to cause remorse by returning good for evil.

coalesce (koh-ă-**less**) *v.* to combine and form one whole. **coalescence** *n.*

coalition (koh-ă-**lish**-ŏn) *n.* 1. union. 2. a

temporary union between political parties.

coarse *adj.* **1.** composed of large particles, rough or loose in texture. **2.** rough or crude in manner or behaviour, not refined; *coarse language,* improper, vulgar. **3.** inferior, common; *coarse fish,* freshwater fish other than salmon and trout. **coarsely** *adv.,* **coarseness** *n.*

coarsen *v.* to make or become coarse.

coast *n.* the sea-shore and the land near it, its outline. —*v.* **1.** to sail along a coast. **2.** to ride down a hill or slope without using power. □ **the coast is clear,** there is no chance of being seen or hindered.

coastal *adj.* of or near the coast.

coaster *n.* **1.** a ship that trades between ports on the same coast. **2.** a tray for a decanter, a small mat for a drinking-glass.

coastguard *n.* **1.** a public organization that keeps watch on the coast to report passing ships, prevent or detect smuggling, etc. **2.** one of its members.

coastline *n.* the shape or outline of a coast, *a rugged coastline.*

coat *n.* **1.** an outdoor garment with sleeves. **2.** an animal's hair or fur covering its body. **3.** a covering layer, *a coat of paint.* —*v.* to cover with a layer. □ **coat of arms,** a design on a shield, used as an emblem by a family or a city or an institution.

coatee *n.* a woman's or baby's short coat.

coating *n.* **1.** a covering layer. **2.** material for coats.

coax *v.* **1.** to persuade gently or gradually. **2.** to obtain in this way, *coaxed a smile from her.*

coaxial (koh-**aks**-iăl) *adj.* having an axis in common. **coaxial cable,** an electric cable in which there are two conductors arranged so that one is inside the other with a layer of insulating material between.

cob *n.* **1.** a male swan. **2.** a sturdy short-legged horse for riding. **3.** a large kind of hazel-nut. **4.** a round-headed loaf. **5.** the central part of an ear of maize, on which the corn grows.

cobalt (**koh**-bollt) *n.* **1.** a chemical element, a hard white metal used in many alloys, and with radioactive forms used in medicine and industry. **2.** colouring-matter made from this, its deep-blue colour.

cobber *n.* (*Austral. & N.Z. informal*) a friend, a mate.

cobble[1] *n.* a cobble-stone, a rounded stone used for paving. —*v.* to pave with cobble-stones.

cobble[2] *v.* to put together or mend roughly.

cobbler *n.* **1.** a shoe-repairer. **2.** an iced drink of wine, sugar, and lemon. **3.** fruit pie topped with scones. □ **cobblers** *n.* (*slang*) nonsense.

COBOL (**koh**-bol) *n.* a high-level computer language designed for use in business. (¶ From the initials of Common Business Oriented Language.)

cobra (**koh**-bră *or* **kob**-ră) *n.* a poisonous snake of India and Africa that can rear up.

cobweb *n.* the fine network spun by a spider, a strand of this.

cocaine (kŏ-**kayn**) *n.* a drug used as a local anaesthetic or as a stimulant.

cochineal (koch-in-**eel**) *n.* bright red colouring-matter made from the dried bodies of certain insects.

cock[1] *n.* **1.** a male bird, especially of the domestic fowl; *old cock,* a vulgar way of addressing a man. **2.** a tap or spout for controlling the flow of a liquid. **3.** (*vulgar*) the penis. **4.** a lever in a gun, raised ready to be released by the trigger; *at half cock,* only half-ready for something —**cock** *v.* **1.** to tilt or turn upwards; *the dog cocked his ears,* raised them attentively; *cock an eye,* to glance knowingly. **2.** to raise the cock of (a gun) ready for firing, to set (the shutter of a camera) ready for release. □ **cock-a-doodle doo** *int.* the sound of a cock crowing. **cock-a-hoop** *adj. & adv.* exultant, pleased and triumphant. **cock-a-leekie** *n.* Scottish soup of cock boiled with leeks. **cock-and-bull story,** a foolish story that one should not believe. **cock a snook,** *see* snook. **cock-crow** *n.* dawn, when cocks begin to crow. **cock-fighting** *n.* setting cocks to fight as a sport. **cock of the walk,** the most influential person.

cock[2] *n.* a cone-shaped pile of straw or hay. —*v.* to pile in cocks.

cockade (kok-**ayd**) *n.* a rosette of ribbon worn on a hat as a badge.

cockatoo *n.* (*pl.* cockatoos) a crested parrot.

cockchafer (**kok**-chay-fer) *n.* a large flying beetle.

cocked hat a triangular hat worn with some uniforms. **knock into a cocked hat,** to defeat utterly, to be much superior to.

cockerel *n.* a young domestic cock.

cock-eyed *adj.* (*slang*) **1.** slanting, not straight. **2.** absurd, impractical, *a cock-eyed scheme.*

cockle *n.* **1.** an edible shellfish. **2.** a small shallow boat. **3.** a pucker or bulge. —*v.* to pucker (a stiff substance), to become puckered. □ **warm the cockles of one's heart,** to make one rejoice.

cockney *n.* (*pl.* cockneys) **1.** a native of the East End of London. **2.** the dialect or accent of this area. —*adj.* of cockneys or cockney.

cockpit *n.* **1.** a place made for cock-fighting. **2.** the compartment for the pilot and crew of an aircraft. **3.** the well where the wheel is situated in certain small yachts etc. **4.** the driver's seat in a racing car.

cockroach *n.* a beetle-like insect that infests kitchens.

cocksure *adj.* **1.** quite convinced, very positive. **2.** over-confident of oneself.

cocktail *n.* **1.** a mixed alcoholic drink. **2.** an appetizer containing shellfish or fruit, *prawn* or *grapefruit cocktail.* □ **fruit cocktail,** finely-chopped fruit salad.

cocky *adj.* (cockier, cockiest) conceited and arrogant. **cockily** *adv.,* **cockiness** *n.*

cocoa *n.* **1.** powder made from crushed cacao seeds. **2.** a drink made from this.

coconut *n.* **1.** the hard-shelled nut of a tropical palm-tree containing a milky juice. **2.** its edible white lining. □ **coconut matting,** matting made from the tough fibre of the coconut's outer husk.

cocoon (kŏ-**koon**) *n.* **1.** the silky sheath round a chrysalis. **2.** a protective wrapping. —*v.* to protect by wrapping completely.

cod[1] *n.* (*pl.* cod) a large sea-fish used as food. **cod-liver oil,** oil obtained from cod livers, rich in vitamins A and D.

cod[2] *n.* (*slang*) = codswallop.

COD *abbrev.* cash on delivery.

coda (**koh**-dă) *n.* the concluding passage of a piece of music, after the main part.

coddle *v.* **1.** to cherish and protect carefully. **2.** to cook (eggs) in water just below boiling-point.

code *n.* **1.** a set of laws or rules, *a code of practice for advertisers.* **2.** a pre-arranged word or phrase representing a message, for secrecy. **3.** a system of words, letters, or symbols used to represent others, especially in order to send messages by machine (e.g. the Morse code). **4.** a set of program instructions for use in a computer. —*v.* to put into code.

codeine (**koh**-deen) *n.* a white substance made from opium, used to relieve pain or induce sleep.

codfish *n.* a cod.

codger *n.* (*informal*) a fellow.

codicil (**koh**-di-sil) *n.* an appendix to a will.

codify (**koh**-di-fy) *v.* (codified, codifying) to arrange (laws or rules) systematically into a code. **codification** *n.*

codling[1] *n.* **1.** a kind of cooking-apple. **2.** a moth whose larva feeds on apples.

codling[2] *n.* a small codfish.

codpiece *n.* a bag or flap at the front of men's breeches in 15th and 16th century dress.

co-driver *n.* a person who takes turns in driving a vehicle in a rally.

codswallop *n.* (*slang*) nonsense, humbug.

co-ed *adj.* (*informal*) coeducational. —*n.* (*informal*) a girl at a coeducational school or college.

coeducation *n.* education of boys and girls in the same classes. **coeducational** *adj.*

coefficient (koh-i-**fish**-ěnt) *n.* a multiplier, a mathematical factor.

coelacanth (**seel**-ă-kanth) *n.* a kind of fish that is extinct except for one species.

coeliac disease (**seel**-i-ak) a disease causing inability to digest fats.

coerce (koh-**erss**) *v.* to compel by threats or force. **coercion** (koh-**er**-shŏn) *n.*

coercive (koh-**er**-siv) *adj.* using coercion.

coexist *v.* to exist together.

coexistence *n.* coexisting; *peaceful coexistence,* tolerance of each other by countries with different political and social systems. **coexistent** *adj.*

coextensive *adj.* extending over the same space or time.

C. of E. *abbrev.* Church of England.

coffee *n.* **1.** the bean-like seeds of a tropical shrub, roasted and ground for making a drink. **2.** this drink. **3.** light-brown colour. □ **coffee bar,** a place serving coffee and light refreshments from a counter. **coffee-cup** *n.* a very small cup from which coffee is drunk. **coffee morning,** a morning social gathering at which coffee is served, usually in aid of a good cause. **coffee-pot** *n.* a pot in which coffee is made or served. **coffee shop,** an informal restaurant, especially at a hotel. **coffee-table** *n.* a small low table.

coffer *n.* a large strong box for holding money and valuables. **coffer-dam** *n.* a temporary watertight structure built or placed round an area of water which can then be pumped dry to allow building work etc. to be done within. **coffers** *pl. n.* funds, financial resources.

coffin *n.* a box in which a dead body is placed for burial or cremation.

cog *n.* one of a series of teeth on the edge of a wheel, fitting into and pushing those on another wheel. **cog-wheel** *n.* a wheel with cogs.

cogent (**koh**-jěnt) *adj.* convincing, compelling belief; *a cogent argument.* **cogently** *adv.,* **cogency** *n.*

cogitate (**koj**-i-tayt) *v.* to think deeply. **cogitation** *n.*

cognac (**kon**-yak) *n.* French brandy, that made in Cognac in western France.

cognate (**kog**-nayt) *adj.* having the same source or origin, (of things) related.

cognition (kog-**ni**-shŏn) *n.* the faculty of knowing or perceiving things. **cognitive** (**kog**-ni-tiv) *adj.* of this faculty.

cognizant (**kog**-ni-zănt) *adj.* aware, having knowledge. **cognizance** *n.*

cohabit *v.* to live together as man and wife, especially when not married to each other. **cohabitation** *n.*

cohere (koh-**heer**) *v.* to stick together, to remain united in a mass, *the particles cohere.*

coherent (koh-**heer**-ĕnt) *adj.* **1.** cohering. **2.** connected logically, not rambling in speech or in reasoning. **coherently** *adv.*, **coherence** *n.*

cohesion (koh-**hee**-zhŏn) *n.* cohering, a tendency to stick together. **cohesive** *adj.*

cohort *n.* a division of the ancient Roman army, one tenth of a legion.

coiffure (kwahf-**yoor**) *n.* a hair-style.

coil *v.* to wind into rings or a spiral. —*n.* **1.** something coiled. **2.** one ring or turn in this. **3.** a length of wire wound in a spiral to conduct electric current. **4.** a contraceptive device for insertion into the womb.

coin *n.* metal money, a piece of this. *v.* **1.** to make (coins) by stamping metal. **2.** (*informal*) to make (money) in large quantities as profit. **3.** to invent (a word or phrase).

coinage *n.* **1.** coining. **2.** coins, the system of coins in use. **3.** a coined word or phrase.

coincide (koh-in-**syd**) *v.* **1.** to occur at the same time, *his holidays don't coincide with hers.* **2.** to occupy the same portion of space. **3.** to agree; *our tastes coincide,* are the same.

coincidence (koh-**in**-si-dĕnss) *n.* **1.** coinciding. **2.** a remarkable occurrence of similar or corresponding events at the same time or by chance.

coincident (koh-**in**-si-dĕnt) *adj.* coinciding.

coincidental (koh-in-si-**den**-t'l) *adj.* happening by coincidence. **coincidentally** *adv.*

coir (**koi**-er) *n.* fibre from the outer husk of the coconut, used for ropes, matting, etc.

coition (koh-**ish**-ŏn) *n.* sexual intercourse.

coitus (**koh**-it-ŭs) *n.* coition.

coke[1] *n.* the solid substance left after coal gas and coal tar have been extracted from coal, used as fuel. **coking coal,** coal suitable for being converted into coke.

coke[2] *n.* (*slang*) cocaine.

col *n.* **1.** a depression in a range of mountains. **2.** a region of low pressure between two anticyclones.

colander (**kul**-ăn-der) *n.* a bowl-shaped container with holes for straining water from foods after cooking.

colcannon (kol-**kan**-ŏn) *n.* an Irish and Scottish dish of cabbage and potatoes boiled and pounded.

cold *adj.* **1.** at or having a low temperature, especially when compared with the human body. **2.** not heated, having cooled after being heated or cooked, *cold meat.* **3.** (*slang*) unconscious, *knocked him cold.* **4.** without friendliness or affection or enthusiasm, *got a cold reception.* **5.** (of colours) suggesting coldness. **6.** (of the scent in hunting) faint because no longer fresh. **7.** (in children's games) far from finding or guessing what is sought. —*adv.* in a cold state. —**cold** *n.* **1.** lack of heat or warmth, low temperature. **2.** an infectious illness causing catarrh and sneezing. —**coldly** *adv.*, **coldness** *n.* □ **cold-blooded** *adj.* having a body temperature that varies with the temperature of surroundings, as fish do; unfeeling, deliberately ruthless, *a cold-blooded killer.* **cold chisel,** a chisel for cutting cold metal. **cold comfort,** poor consolation. **cold cream,** ointment for cleansing and softening the skin. **cold frame,** an unheated frame for growing small plants. **cold shoulder,** deliberate unfriendliness. **cold-shoulder** *v.* to treat with deliberate unfriendliness. **cold storage,** storage in a refrigerated place; *in cold storage,* (of plans etc.) postponed but available when required. **cold turkey,** (*Amer. slang*) sudden withdrawal of narcotic drugs from an addict. **cold war,** intense hostility between nations without actual fighting. **get cold feet,** to feel afraid or reluctant. **have a person cold,** (*informal*) to have him at one's mercy. **in cold blood,** without passion, deliberately and ruthlessly. **leave cold,** to fail to affect or impress, *their promises leave me cold.* **leave out in the cold,** to ignore or neglect. **throw** *or* **pour cold water on,** to make discouraging remarks about.

coldish *adj.* rather cold.

coleslaw *n.* finely shredded raw cabbage coated in dressing, as a salad.

coleus (**koh**-li-ŭs) *n.* a plant grown for its variegated leaves.

colic *n.* severe abdominal pain. **colicky** *adj.*

colitis (kŏ-**ly**-tiss) *n.* inflammation of the lining of the colon.

collaborate *v.* to work in partnership. **collaborator** *n.*, **collaboration** *n.*

collage (kol-**ah**zh) *n.* an artistic composition made by fixing bits of paper, cloth, string, etc. to a surface.

collagen (kol-ă-jin) *n.* a protein substance found in bone and tissue.

collapse *v.* **1.** to fall down or in suddenly. **2.** to lose strength or force or value suddenly, *enemy resistance collapsed.* **3.** to fold or be foldable. **4.** to cause to collapse. —*n.* collapsing, a breakdown.

collapsible *adj.* made so as to fold together compactly, *a collapsible canoe.*

collar *n.* **1.** an upright or turned-over band round the neck of a garment. **2.** a band of leather etc. put round the neck of an animal. **3.** a band, ring, or pipe holding part of a machine. **4.** a cut of bacon from near the head. —*v.* (*informal*) to seize, to take for oneself. □ **collar-bone** *n.* the bone joining the breast-bone and shoulder-blade, the clavicle.

collarless *adj.* without a collar.

collate (kŏ-**layt**) *v.* **1.** to compare in detail. **2.** to collect and arrange systematically, *collate information.* **collation** *n.,* **collator** *n.*

collateral (kŏ-**lat**-er-ăl) *adj.* **1.** parallel. **2.** additional but subordinate, *collateral evidence.* **3.** descended from the same ancestor but by a different line, *a collateral branch of the family.* —*n.* a collateral security. —**collaterally** *adv.* □ **collateral security,** an additional security pledged; security lodged by a third party, or consisting of stocks, shares, property, etc. as opposed to a personal guarantee.

colleague *n.* a fellow official or worker, especially in a business or profession.

collect[1] (**kol**-ekt) *n.* a short prayer of the Church of England or the Roman Catholic Church, usually to be read on an appointed day.

collect[2] (kŏ-**lekt**) *v.* **1.** to bring or come together. **2.** to get from a number of people, to ask for (payment or contributions) from people. **3.** to seek and obtain specimens of, especially as a hobby or for study. **4.** to fetch, *collect the children from school.* **5.** to gather (one's thoughts) into systematic order or control; *collect oneself,* to regain control of oneself.

collectable *adj.* suitable for being collected as a hobby etc. —*n.* an object of this kind.

collected *adj.* calm and self-controlled. **collectedly** *adv.*

collection *n.* **1.** collecting. **2.** money collected for a charity etc., e.g. at a church service. **3.** objects collected systematically. **4.** a heap of things that have come together.

collective *adj.* of a group taken as a whole, *our collective impression of the new plan.* —*n.* a collective farm. —**collectively** *adv.* □ **collective bargain-**

ing, bargaining by an organized group of employees. **collective farm,** a farm or group of small-holdings organized and run by its workers, usually under State control. **collective noun,** a noun that is singular in form but denotes many individuals, e.g. *army, cattle, committee, herd.* **collective ownership,** ownership of land etc. by all and for the benefit of all.

collectivize *v.* to bring from private into collective ownership. **collectivization** *n.*

collector *n.* a person who collects things; *a collector's piece,* a thing worth placing in a collection because of its beauty or variety.

colleen (kŏ-**leen**) *n.* (*Irish*) a girl.

college *n.* **1.** an educational establishment for higher or professional education, a small university. **2.** an independent part of a university with its own teachers and students, *the Oxford colleges.* **3.** (in names) a school, *Eton College.* **4.** the buildings of any of these. **5.** an organized body of professional people with common purposes and privileges, *the Royal College of Surgeons.*

collegiate (kŏ-**lee**-ji-ăt) *adj.* of or belonging to a college or college student.

collide *v.* **1.** (of a moving object) to strike violently against something, to meet and strike. **2.** to have a conflict of interests or opinions.

collie *n.* a dog with a long pointed muzzle and shaggy hair.

collier *n.* **1.** a coal-miner. **2.** a ship that carries coal as its cargo.

colliery *n.* a coal-mine and its buildings.

collision *n.* colliding, the striking of one body against another. **collision course,** a set course that is bound to end in a collision.

collocation (kolŏ-**kay**-shŏn) *n.* placing together or side by side.

colloid *n.* a gluey substance.

collop *n.* a slice of meat, an escalope.

colloquial (kŏ-**loh**-kwee-ăl) *adj.* suitable for ordinary conversation but not for formal speech or writing. **colloquially** *adv.*

colloquialism *n.* a colloquial word or phrase.

colloquy (**kol**-ŏ-kwi) *n.* (*formal*) a conversation.

collusion (kŏ-**loo**-zhŏn) *n.* an agreement between two or more people for a deceitful or fraudulent purpose. **collusive** *adj.*

collywobbles *pl. n.* (*informal*) **1.** stomach-ache. **2.** nervousness.

Colo. *abbrev.* Colorado.

cologne (kŏ-**lohn**) *n.* eau-de-Cologne or

other lightly-scented liquid, used to cool and scent the skin.

Colombia a country in South America. **Colombian** *adj.* & *n.*

Colombo the capital of Sri Lanka.

colon¹ (**koh-lŏn**) *n.* the lower and greater part of the large intestine.

colon² (**koh-lŏn**) *n.* the punctuation mark : used (1) to show that what follows is an example or list or summary of what precedes it, or a contrasting idea, (2) between numbers that are in proportion, e.g. $1 : 2 = 2 : 4$.

colonel (**ker-nĕl**) *n.* **1.** an army officer commanding a regiment, ranking next below a brigadier. **2.** a lieutenant-colonel.

colonial *adj.* of a colony or colonies. —*n.* an inhabitant of a colony.

colonialism *n.* the policy of acquiring or maintaining colonies.

colonic (**koh-lon-ik**) *adj.* of the intestinal colon.

colonist *n.* a pioneer settler in a colony.

colonize *v.* to establish a colony in. **colonization** *n.*

colonnade (**kol-ŏn-ayd**) *n.* a row of columns.

colony *n.* **1.** an area of land settled or conquered by a distant State and controlled by it. **2.** its inhabitants. **3.** a group of colonists. **4.** people of one nationality or occupation etc. living in a particular area, the area itself, *the artists' colony.*

Colorado (**kolŏ-rah-doh**) a State of the USA. **Colorado beetle**, a black and yellow beetle that is very destructive to the potato plant.

coloration *n.* colouring.

colossal *adj.* **1.** immense. **2.** (*informal*) remarkable, splendid. **colossally** *adv.*

colossus (**kŏ-los-ŭs**) *n.* (*pl.* colossi, *pr.* kŏ-los-I) **1.** an immense statue, *the Colossus of Rhodes.* **2.** a person of immense importance and influence.

colostomy (**kŏ-lost-ŏmi**) *n.* an artificial opening through which the bowel can empty, made surgically by bringing part of the colon to the surface of the abdomen.

colour *n.* **1.** the sensation produced by rays of light of different wavelengths, a particular variety of this. **2.** the use of all colours, not only black and white; *in colour*, using all colours; *a colour film*, producing photographs that are in colour. **3.** ruddiness of complexion; *she has no colour*, looks pale. **4.** the pigmentation of the skin, especially if dark. **5.** pigment, paint, or dye. **6.** the flag of a ship or regiment. —**colour** *v.* **1.** to put colour on, to paint or stain or dye. **2.** to change colour, to blush. **3.** to give a special character or

bias to; *his political opinions colour his writings.* □ **colour bar**, legal or social discrimination between white and non-white people. **colour-blind** *adj.* unable to see the difference between certain colours. **colours** *pl. n.* an award given to regular or leading members of a sports team. **colour scheme**, a systematic combination of colours. **give** *or* **lend colour to**, to give an appearance of truth to. **in its true colours**, with its real characteristics revealed.

colourant *n.* colouring-matter.

coloured *adj.* **1.** having colour. **2.** wholly or partly of non-white descent. **3.** *Coloured*, (in South Africa) of mixed white and non-white descent. —**coloured** *n.* **1.** a coloured person. **2.** *Coloured*, (in South Africa) a person of mixed white and non-white descent.

colourful *adj.* **1.** full of colour. **2.** with vivid details, *a colourful account of his journey.* **colourfully** *adv.*

colouring *n.* **1.** the way in which something is coloured. **2.** a substance used to colour things.

colourless *adj.* without colour.

colt (*rhymes with* bolt) *n.* a young male horse.

coltsfoot *n.* a weed with yellow flowers.

Columbia, District of a district of the USA coextensive with the city of Washington.

columbine *n.* a garden flower with slender pointed projections on its petals.

column *n.* **1.** a round pillar. **2.** something shaped like this, *a column of smoke*; *the spinal column*, the backbone. **3.** a vertical section of a page, *there are two columns on this page.* **4.** a regular feature in a newspaper, devoted to a special subject. **5.** a long narrow formation of troops or vehicles etc. **columnar** (**kŏ-lum-ner**) *adj.*

columnist (**kol-ŭm-ist**) *n.* a journalist who regularly writes a column of comments.

coma (**koh-mă**) *n.* a state of deep unconsciousness.

comatose (**koh-mă-tohs**) *adj.* **1.** in a coma. **2.** drowsy.

comb *n.* **1.** a strip of bone or plastic etc. with teeth, used for tidying the hair or holding it in place. **2.** something shaped or used like this, e.g. for separating strands of wool or cotton. **3.** the fleshy crest of a fowl. **4.** a honeycomb. —**comb** *v.* **1.** to tidy or untangle with a comb. **2.** to search thoroughly. □ **comb out**, (*informal*) to get rid of (unwanted people or things) from a group.

combat *n.* a fight or contest. —*v.* (combated, combating) to counter, *to combat the effects of alcohol.*

combatant (**kom**-bă-tănt) *adj.* engaged in fighting. —*n.* one who is engaged in fighting.

combe (*pr.* koom) *n.* = coomb.

combination *n.* **1.** combining, being combined. **2.** a number of people or things that are combined. **3.** a sequence of numbers or letters used in opening a combination lock. □ **combination lock,** a lock that can be opened only by turning one or more dials into a particular series of positions, indicated by numbers or letters. **combinations** *pl. n.* a one-piece undergarment covering the body and legs.

combine ¹ (kŏm-**byn**) *v.* to join or be joined into a group or set or mixture.

combine ² (**kom**-byn) *n.* **1.** a combination of people or firms acting together in business. **2.** a **combine harvester,** a combined reaping and threshing machine.

combs (*pr.* komz) *pl. n.* combinations (an undergarment).

combustible (kŏm-**bust**-ibŭl) *adj.* capable of catching fire and burning, used for burning. —*n.* a combustible substance. —**combustibility** *n.*

combustion (kŏm-**bus**-chŏn) *n.* the process of burning, a chemical process (accompanied by heat) in which substances combine with oxygen in air.

come *v.* (came, come, coming) **1.** to move towards the speaker or a place or point. **2.** (of an illness) to begin to develop. **3.** to arrive, to reach a point or condition or result, *when winter comes; we came to a decision,* made one; *for several years to come,* in the future. **4.** to take or occupy a specified position, *what comes next?* **5.** to be available, *the dress comes in 3 sizes; he's as tough as they come,* no one is tougher. **6.** to happen, *how did you come to lose it?* **7.** to occur as a result, *that's what comes of being too confident.* **8.** to be descended; *she comes from a rich family.* **9.** (*slang*) to behave as, *don't come the bully over me!; that's coming it too strong,* exaggerating or overdoing it. —*int.* think again, don't be hasty, *oh come, it's not that bad!* □ **come about,** to happen. **come across,** (*informal*) to find or meet unexpectedly. **come along,** to make progress, to thrive, *coming along nicely; come along!,* hurry up. **come-back** *n.* a return to one's former successful position; a reply or retort. **come between,** to disrupt the relationship between (two people); to prevent (a person) from having something, *nothing must come between him and his career.* **come by,** to obtain (a thing). **come clean,** (*informal*) to confess fully. **come down,** to collapse; to fall, to become lower; *come*

down in the world, to lose one's former high social position; *come down in favour of,* to decide in favour of. **come-down** *n.* a fall in status; an anticlimax. **come down on,** to rebuke. **come forward,** to offer oneself for a task etc. **come from,** to have as one's birthplace or as a place of origin. **come-hither** *adj.* enticing, flirtatious. **come in,** to take a specified position in a race or competition, *he came in third;* to become seasonable or fashionable; to be received as income; to begin one's radio transmission; to have a part to play, to serve a purpose, *it will come in useful; where do I come in?,* what is my role?, where is my advantage? **come in for,** to receive a share of. **come into,** to inherit. **come of age,** to reach adult status. **come off,** to become detached or separated, to be detachable; to fall from, *she came off her bicycle;* (of a series of performances) to end; to fare, to acquit oneself, *they came off well;* to be successful. **come off it!,** (*informal*) stop talking or behaving like that. **come on,** to make progress, to thrive; to come on to the stage, to appear in a filmed scene etc.; to begin, *it's coming on to rain;* to find or meet unexpectedly; (*informal*) to make a demand on (a person or authority); *come on!,* hurry up. **come out,** to go on strike; to emerge from an examination etc. with a specified result; to emerge from behind clouds, *the sun came out;* to become visible in a photograph, *the house has come out well;* to become known, *the truth came out;* to be published; to be solved; to erupt, to become covered (in a rash); to declare one's opinions publicly, *came out in favour of the plan;* (of stains etc.) to be removed. **come out with,** to utter. **come over,** (*informal*) to be affected with a feeling, *she came over faint;* to affect, *what has come over you?* **come round,** to make a casual or informal visit; to recover from faintness or bad temper; to be converted to another person's opinion; to recur. **come to,** to amount to, to be equivalent to; to regain consciousness. **come to pass,** to happen. **come true,** to happen in the way that was prophesied or hoped. **come up,** to arise for discussion etc., to occur, *a problem has come up.* **come-uppance** *n.* (*informal*) a punishment or rebuke that one deserves. **come up to,** to equal, *it doesn't come up to our expectations.* **come up with,** to contribute (a suggestion etc.). **come upon,** to find or meet unexpectedly. **come what may,** whatever may happen.

Comecon (**kom**-i-kon) an economic organization of eastern European countries. (¶The name is formed from the initial

. letters of Council for Mutual Economic Assistance.)

comedian *n.* **1.** an actor who plays comic parts. **2.** a humorous entertainer. **3.** a person who behaves humorously.

comedienne (kŏ-mee-di-en) *n.* a female comedian.

comedy *n.* **1.** a light amusing play or film. **2.** the branch of drama that consists of such plays. **3.** an amusing incident. **4.** humour.

comely (**kum**-li) *adj.* (*old use*) good-looking.

comer (**kum**-er) *n.* one who comes, *the first comers*; *all comers*, anyone who comes or challenges or applies.

comestibles (kŏm-**est**-i-bŭlz) *pl. n.* things to eat.

comet (**kom**-it) *n.* a hazy object that moves round the sun, usually with a star-like centre and a tail pointing away from the sun.

comfort *n.* **1.** a state of ease and contentment. **2.** relief of suffering or grief. **3.** a person or thing that gives this. —*v.* to give comfort to. **comforter** *n.* □ **comfort station**, (*Amer.*) a public lavatory.

comfortable *adj.* **1.** giving ease and contentment. **2.** not close or restricted, *won by a comfortable margin.* **3.** feeling at ease, in a state of comfort. **comfortably** *adv.*

comfrey (**kum**-fri) *n.* a tall plant with rough leaves and purple or white flowers, growing in ditches.

comfy *adj.* (*informal*) comfortable.

comic *adj.* **1.** causing amusement or laughter. **2.** of comedy. —**comic** *n.* **1.** a comedian. **2.** a paper for children, with series of strip cartoons. —**comical** *adj.*, **comically** *adv.*

coming *see* **come**. —*adj.* **1.** approaching, next, *the coming week.* **2.** likely to be important in the near future, *a coming man.* —*n.* arriving, *comings and goings.*

comma *n.* the punctuation mark , indicating a slight pause or break between parts of a sentence, or separating words or figures in a list.

command *n.* **1.** a statement, given with authority, that some action must be performed. **2.** an instruction to a computer. **3.** the right to control others, authority; *he is in command*, has this authority. **4.** ability to use something, mastery, *has a great command of languages.* **5.** a body of troops, *Bomber Command.* —**command** *v.* **1.** to give a command or order to. **2.** to have authority over. **3.** to have at one's disposal, *the firm commands great resources.* **4.** to deserve and get, *they command our respect.* **5.** to look down over or dominate from a strategic position, *the tower commands the harbour; in a commanding position.*

commandant (kom-ăn-**dant**) *n.* the officer in command of a fortress or other military establishment.

commandeer *v.* **1.** to seize for military purposes. **2.** to seize for one's own purposes.

commander *n.* **1.** the person in command. **2.** a naval officer ranking next below a captain. **3.** a police officer at Scotland Yard, ranking below a commissioner. □ **commander-in-chief** *n.* the supreme commander.

commandment *n.* a divine command, any of the ten laws given by God to Moses.

commando *n.* (*pl.* **commandos**) a member of a military unit specially trained for making raids and assaults.

commemorate *v.* **1.** to keep in the memory by means of a celebration or ceremony. **2.** to be a memorial to, *a plaque commemorates the victory.* **commemoration** *n.*, **commemorative** *adj.*

commence *v.* to begin. **commencement** *n.*

commend *v.* **1.** to praise. **2.** to recommend. **3.** to entrust, to commit, *commending his soul to God.* **commendation** *n.*

commendable *adj.* worthy of praise. **commendably** *adv.*

commensurable (kŏ-men-sher-ăbŭl) *adj.* able to be measured by the same standard.

commensurate (kŏ-men-sher-ăt) *adj.* **1.** of the same size or extent. **2.** proportionate, *the salary is commensurate with the responsibilities.*

comment *n.* an opinion given briefly about an event or in explanation or criticism. —*v.* to utter or write comments.

commentary *n.* **1.** a series of descriptive comments on an event or performance. **2.** a collection of explanatory comments, *a new commentary on the Bible.*

commentate *v.* to act as commentator.

commentator *n.* **1.** a person who broadcasts a commentary. **2.** a person who writes a commentary.

commerce (**kom**-erss) *n.* all forms of trade and the services that assist trading, e.g. banking and insurance.

commercial *adj.* **1.** of or engaged in commerce; *commercial vehicles*, those carrying goods or fare-paying passengers; *commercial art*, art used in advertising etc.; *produced on a commercial scale*, in amounts suitable for marketing widely. **2.** financed by firms etc. whose advertisements are included, *commercial radio.* **3.** intended to produce profits rather than to be of artistic or scholarly merit. —*n.* a broadcast advertisement. —**commercially** *adv.* □

commercial traveller, a business firm's representative who visits shops etc. to show samples and get orders.

commercialism *n.* commercial practices and attitudes.

commercialize *v.* to make commercial, to alter in order to make profitable, *a very commercialized resort.* **commercialization** *n.*

Commie *n.* (*slang*) a Communist.

commiserate (kŏ-**miz**-er-ayt) *v.* to express pity for, to sympathize. **commiseration** *n.*

commissariat (kom-i-**sair**-iăt) *n.* a stock of food.

commissary (**kom**-iss-er-i) *n.* a deputy, a delegate.

commission *n.* **1.** the giving of authority to someone to perform a certain task or duty. **2.** the task etc. given, *a commission to paint a portrait.* **3.** the body of people to whom such authority is given. **4.** a warrant conferring authority especially on officers above a certain rank in the armed forces. **5.** performance, committing, *the commission of a crime.* **6.** payment to an agent for selling goods or services etc., often calculated in proportion to the amount sold; *selling goods on commission,* receiving such payment. **commission** *v.* **1.** to give a commission to. **2.** to place an order for, *commissioned a portrait.* □ **commission-agent** *n.* an agent receiving commission; a bookmaker. **commissioned officer,** an officer in the armed forces who holds a commission. **in commission,** (of a warship etc.) manned and ready for service. **out of commission,** not in commission; not in working order.

commissionaire (kŏ-mish-ŏn-**air**) *n.* a uniformed attendant at the entrance to a theatre, large shop, or offices etc.

commissioner *n.* **1.** a member of a commission. **2.** a person who has been given a commission; *a Commissioner for Oaths,* a solicitor before whom oaths may be sworn by persons making affidavits. **3.** the head of Scotland Yard. **4.** a government official in charge of a district abroad.

commit *v.* (committed, committing) **1.** to do, to perform, *commit a crime.* **2.** to entrust for safe keeping or treatment; *commit a prisoner for trial,* send him to prison pending trial; *commit a body to the earth,* bury it with a formal ceremony. **3.** to pledge, to bind with an obligation; *she did not commit herself,* gave no definite statement or opinion. □ **committed** *adj.* dedicated or pledged, especially to support a doctrine or cause. **commit to memory,** to memorize.

commitment *n.* **1.** committing. **2.** the state of being involved in an obligation. **3.** an obligation or pledge.

committal *n.* **1.** committing to prison or other place of confinement. **2.** committing a body at burial or cremation.

committee *n.* a group of people appointed to attend to special business or to manage the business of a club etc.

commode (kŏ-**mohd**) *n.* **1.** a chest of drawers. **2.** a chamber-pot mounted in a chair or box with a cover.

commodious (kŏ-**moh**-di-ŭs) *adj.* roomy.

commodity *n.* a useful thing, an article of trade, a product.

commodore (**kom**-ŏ-dor) *n.* **1.** a naval officer ranking above a captain and below a rear-admiral. **2.** the commander of a squadron or other division of a fleet. **3.** the president of a yacht-club.

common *adj.* **1.** of or affecting the whole community; *it was common knowledge,* was known to most people. **2.** belonging to or shared by two or more people or things; *common ground,* something on which two or more people agree or in which they share an interest. **3.** occurring frequently, familiar, *a common weed.* **4.** without special distinction, ordinary, *the common house-spider.* **5.** ill-bred, not refined in behaviour or style. **6.** *the Commons,* the House of Commons (*see* house¹). —*n.* an area of unfenced grassland for all to use. —**commonly** *adv.,* **commonness** *n.* □ **common law,** unwritten law based on custom and usage and on former court decisions. **common-law husband** *or* **wife,** one recognized by common law without an official ceremony, usually after a period of cohabitation. **Common Market,** the European Economic Community, an association of certain European countries with internal free trade, and common tariffs on their imports from countries outside the community. **common or garden,** (*informal*) ordinary. **common-room** *n.* a room shared for social purposes by pupils or students or teachers of a school or college. **common sense,** normal good sense in practical matters, gained by experience of life not by special study. **common-sense** *adj.* showing common sense. **common time,** (in music) two or four beats (especially four crotchets) in the bar. **in common,** in joint use between two or more people or things, shared as a possession or characteristic or interest.

commoner *n.* one of the common people, not a member of the nobility.

commonplace *adj.* ordinary, usual; *a few commonplace remarks,* lacking originality.

—*n.* something commonplace, *air travel is now a commonplace.*

commonwealth *n.* **1.** an independent State or community. **2.** a republic. **3.** a federation of States, *the Commonwealth of Australia.* □ **the Commonwealth,** an association of the UK and various independent States (formerly subject to Britain) and dependencies. **New Commonwealth,** those countries which have achieved self-government within the Commonwealth since 1945.

commotion *n.* uproar, fuss and disturbance.

communal (**kom**-yoo-năl) *adj.* shared between members of a group or community, *a communal kitchen.* **communally** *adv.*

commune[1] (**kom**-yoon) *n.* **1.** a group of people, not all of one family, sharing accommodation and goods. **2.** a small district of local government in France and certain other European countries.

commune[2] (kŏ-**mewn**) *v.* to communicate mentally or spiritually; *communing with nature,* absorbed in feeling oneself in harmony with it.

communicable *adj.* able to be communicated.

communicant *n.* **1.** a person who receives Holy Communion, one who does this regularly. **2.** a person who communicates information.

communicate *v.* **1.** to make known, *communicate the news to your friends.* **2.** to transfer, to transmit, *communicated the disease to others.* **3.** to pass news and information to and fro, to have social dealings. **4.** to succeed in conveying information, *young people cannot always communicate with older ones.* **5.** to be connected, *the passage communicates with the hall and stairs.*

communication *n.* **1.** communicating. **2.** something that communicates information from one person to another, a letter or message. **3.** a means of communicating, e.g. a road, railway, telegraph line, radio, or other link between places. □ **communication cord,** a cord or chain inside the coaches of a train, to be pulled by passengers who wish to stop the train in an emergency.

communicative (kŏ-**mew**-nik-ătiv) *adj.* ready and willing to talk and give information.

communion *n.* **1.** fellowship, having ideas or beliefs in common; *Churches in communion with each other,* those who accept each other's doctrines and sacraments. **2.** social dealings between people. **3.** a body of Christians belonging to the same denomination, *the Anglican communion.* **4.** *Communion* or *Holy Communion,* the Christian sacrament in which bread and wine are consecrated and consumed, the Eucharist.

communiqué (kŏ-**mew**-ni-kay) *n.* an official communication giving a report of a meeting or a battle etc.

communism *n.* **1.** a social system in which property is owned by the community and each member works for the common benefit. **2.** *Communism,* a political doctrine or movement seeking to overthrow capitalism and establish a form of communism, such a system established in the USSR and elsewhere.

communist *n.* **1.** a supporter of communism. **2.** *Communist,* a member of the **Communist Party,** a political party supporting Communism.

communistic *adj.* of or like communism.

community *n.* **1.** a body of people living in one place or district or country and considered as a whole. **2.** a group with common interests or origins, *the immigrant community.* **3.** fellowship, being alike in some way, *community of interests.* □ **community centre,** a place providing social, recreational, and educational facilities for a neighbourhood. **community home,** a centre for housing young offenders, replacing the former 'approved school' and 'remand home'. **community singing,** organized singing in chorus by a large gathering of people.

commutable *adj.* exchangeable, able to be exchanged for money.

commute *v.* **1.** to exchange for something else; *commuted part of his pension for a lump sum,* chose to take a lump sum in exchange. **2.** to change (a punishment) into something less severe. **3.** to travel regularly by bus or train or car to and from one's daily work in a city.

commuter *n.* a person who commutes to and from his work.

Comoros (kŏm-**or**-ohz) a group of islands off the east coast of Africa. **Comoran** *adj.* & *n.*

compact[1] (**kom**-pakt) *n.* **1.** an agreement, a contract. **2.** a small flat container for face-powder.

compact[2] (kŏm-**pakt**) *adj.* **1.** closely or neatly packed together. **2.** concise. **compactly** *adv.,* **compactness** *n.*

compacted (kŏm-**pak**-tid) *adj.* joined or pressed firmly together, packed into a small space.

companion *n.* **1.** a person who accompanies another or who shares in his work, pleasures, or misfortunes etc. **2.** the title of a member of certain orders, *Companion of Honour*. **3.** a woman employed to live with and accompany another. **4.** one of two things that match or go together, *the companion volume will be published later*. □ **companion-way** *n.* a staircase from a ship's deck to the saloon or cabins.

companionable *adj.* friendly, sociable. **companionably** *adv.*

companionship *n.* the state of being companions, the friendly feeling of being with another or others.

company *n.* **1.** companionship, *travel with us for company*. **2.** a number of people assembled, guests, *we're expecting company*. **3.** the people with whom one spends one's time, *got into bad company*. **4.** people working together or united for business purposes, a firm; *the ship's company*, the officers and crew. **5.** a subdivision of an infantry battalion. □ **keep a person company**, to accompany him, especially for the sake of companionship.

comparable (**kom**-per-ăbŭl) *adj.* able or suitable to be compared, similar. **comparably** *adv.*, **comparability** *n.*

comparative *adj.* **1.** involving comparison, *a comparative study of the output of two firms*. **2.** estimated by comparison; *their comparative merits*, measured in relation to each other; *living in comparative comfort*, comfortably when compared against a previous standard or that of others. **3.** of a grammatical form used in comparing, expressing 'more', e.g. *bigger*, *greater*, *worse*. —*n.* a comparative form of a word. —**comparatively** *adv.*

compare *v.* **1.** to judge the similarity between (one thing and another). **2.** to form the comparative and superlative of (an adjective or adverb). —*n.* comparison, *beautiful beyond compare*. □ **compare notes**, to exchange ideas or conclusions. **compare to**, to liken, to declare to be similar, *he compared the human body to a machine*. **compare with**, to consider (things or people) together so as to judge their similarities and differences; to be worthy of comparison, *he cannot compare with Dickens as a novelist*.

comparison *n.* comparing. **beyond comparison**, not comparable because one is so much better than the other(s).

compartment *n.* **1.** one of the spaces into which a structure or other object is divided, separated by partitions. **2.** such a division of a railway carriage.

compartmentalize (kom-part-**ment**-ă-lyz) *v.* to divide into compartments or categories.

compass *n.* **1.** a device for determining direction, with a needle that points to the magnetic north; *a radio compass*, a similar device using radio. **2.** range, scope. —*v.* to encompass. □ **compass rose**, a circle showing the 32 principal points of the compass. **compasses** *pl. n.* an instrument used for drawing circles, usually with two legs joined at one end.

compassion *n.* a feeling of pity that makes one want to help or show mercy. **compassionate** *adj.*, **compassionately** *adv.*

compatible (kŏm-**pat**-ibŭl) *adj.* **1.** capable of living together harmoniously. **2.** able to exist or be used together, *at a speed compatible with safety*. **compatibly** *adv.*, **compatibility** *n.*

compatriot (kŏm-**pat**-ri-ŏt) *n.* a person from the same country as another.

compel *v.* (compelled, compelling) **1.** to use force or influence to cause (a person) to do something, to allow no choice of action. **2.** to arouse irresistibly, *his courage compels admiration*.

compendious (kŏm-**pen**-di-ŭs) *adj.* giving much information concisely.

compendium (kŏm-**pen**-di-ŭm) *n.* **1.** a concise and comprehensive summary. **2.** a collection of table-games.

compensate *v.* **1.** to make a suitable payment in return for (a loss or damage etc.). **2.** to serve as a counterbalance, *our present success compensates for earlier failures*. **compensation** *n.*

compensatory (kom-pĕn-say-ter-i) *adj.* compensating.

compère (**kom**-pair) *n.* a person who introduces the performers in a variety show etc. —*v.* to act as compère to.

compete *v.* to take part in a competition or other contest.

competent (**kom**-pit-ĕnt) *adj.* **1.** having the ability or authority to do what is required. **2.** adequate, satisfactory, *a competent knowledge of French*. **competently** *adv.*, **competence** *n.*

competition *n.* **1.** a friendly contest in which people try to do better than their rivals. **2.** competing, *competition for export markets*. **3.** those competing with oneself, *we have strong foreign competition*.

competitive *adj.* of or involving competition, *competitive sports*; *the competitive spirit*, enjoying competition; *a competitive examination*, one in which people compete for a prize; *at competitive prices*, at prices which compare favourably with those of rivals. **competitively** *adv.*, **competitiveness** *n.*

competitor *n.* one who competes.

compile *v.* **1.** to collect and arrange (information) into a list or book. **2.** to make up (a book etc.) in this way. **compilation** (kom-pil-**ay**-shŏn) *n.*

compiler *n.* **1.** a person who compiles information or a book etc. **2.** a computer program that translates instructions from a high-level language into a form which can be understood by the computer with little or no further translation.

complacent (kŏm-**play**-sĕnt) *adj.* self-satisfied. **complacently** *adv.*, **complacency** *n.*
¶Do not confuse with complaisant.

complain *v.* **1.** to say that one is dissatisfied, to protest that something is wrong. **2.** to state that one is suffering from a pain etc.

complaint *n.* **1.** a statement saying that one is dissatisfied, a protest. **2.** a cause of dissatisfaction, *a list of complaints.* **3.** an illness.

complaisant (kŏm-**play**-zĕnt) *adj.* willing to do what pleases others. **complaisance** *n.* ¶ Do not confuse with complacent.

complement (**kom**-pli-mĕnt) *n.* **1.** that which makes a thing complete. **2.** the number or quantity needed to fill something, *the bus had its full complement of passengers.* —*v.* to make complete, to form a complement to, *the hat complements the outfit.*
¶ Do not confuse with compliment.

complementary *adj.* completing, forming a complement. **complementary colours**, two colours of light which when mixed have the appearance of white light (e.g. blue and yellow).
¶ Do not confuse with complimentary.

complete *adj.* **1.** having all its parts, not lacking anything. **2.** finished, *the work is now complete.* **3.** thorough, in every way, *a complete stranger.* —**complete** *v.* **1.** to add what is lacking to (a thing) and make it complete. **2.** to finish (a piece of work etc.). **3.** to add what is required to (a thing), *complete the questionnaire.* —**completely** *adv.*, **completeness** *n.*

completion (kŏm-**plee**-shŏn) *n.* completing, being completed.

complex (**kom**-pleks) *adj.* **1.** made up of parts. **2.** complicated. —**complex** *n.* **1.** a complex whole. **2.** a connected group of feelings or ideas that influence a person's behaviour or mental attitude, *a persecution complex.* **3.** a set of buildings. — **complexity** (kŏm-**pleks**-iti) *n.*

complexion *n.* **1.** the colour, texture, and appearance of the skin of the face. **2.** the general character or nature of things; *that puts a different complexion on the matter,* makes it seem different.

compliant (kŏm-**ply**-ănt) *adj.* complying, obedient. **compliance** *n.*

complicate *v.* to make complex or complicated.

complicated *adj.* made up of many parts, difficult to understand or use because of this.

complication *n.* **1.** complicating, being made complicated. **2.** a complex combination of things. **3.** something that complicates or adds difficulties. **4.** an illness or condition that arises during the course of another and makes it worse.

complicity (kŏm-**plis**-iti) *n.* partnership or involvement in wrongdoing.

compliment *n.* an expression of praise or admiration either in words or by action. —*v.* to pay a compliment to, to congratulate. ☐ **compliments** *pl. n.* formal greetings conveyed in a message.
¶ Do not confuse with complement.

complimentary *adj.* **1.** expressing a compliment. **2.** given free of charge.
¶ Do not confuse with complementary.

compline (**kom**-plin) *n.* the last service of the day in the Roman Catholic and High Anglican Church.

comply (kŏm-**ply**) *v.* (**complied, complying**) to do as one is asked or ordered; *comply with the rules,* obey them.

component (kŏm-**poh**-nĕnt) *n.* one of the parts of which a thing is composed. *adj.* being a component.

compose *v.* **1.** to form, to make up, *the group was composed of 20 students.* **2.** to create in music or literature. **3.** to arrange into good order. **4.** to make calm, *to compose oneself.*

composed *adj.* calm, with one's feelings under control. **composedly** (kŏm-**pohz**-id-li) *adv.*

composer *n.* a person who composes music etc.

composite (**kom**-pŏ-zit) *adj.* made up of parts.

composition *n.* **1.** putting together into a whole, composing. **2.** something composed, a piece of music or writing, a short essay written as a school exercise. **3.** the parts of which something is made up, *the composition of the soil.* **4.** the arrangement of parts of a picture. **5.** a compound artificial substance.

compositor *n.* a person who sets up type for printing.

compos mentis in one's right mind, sane. (¶Latin.)

compost *n.* **1.** a mixture of decaying substances used as a fertilizer. **2.** a mixture usually of soil and other ingredients for growing seedlings, cuttings, etc. —*v.* to treat with compost, to make into compost.

composure *n.* calmness of mind or manner.

compote (**kom**-poht) *n.* fruit stewed with sugar.

compound[1] (**kom**-pownd) *adj.* made up of several parts of ingredients. —*n.* a compound thing or substance. ☐ **compound fracture,** one where the fractured bone has pierced the skin. **compound interest,** interest paid on the original capital and on the interest that has been added to it.

compound[2] (kŏm-**pownd**) *v.* **1.** to put together to form a whole, to combine. **2.** to add to or increase. **3.** to come to an agreement, to settle, *he compounded with his creditors.* **4.** to agree to refrain from revealing (a crime), *compounding a felony.*

compound[3] (**kom**-pownd) *n.* a fenced-in enclosure, (in India, China, etc.) an enclosure in which a house or factory stands.

comprehend *v.* **1.** to grasp mentally, to understand. **2.** to include. **comprehension** *n.*

comprehensible *adj.* able to be understood. **comprehensibly** *adv.*, **comprehensibility** *n.*

comprehensive *adj.* inclusive, including much or all. —*n.* a comprehensive school. —**comprehensively** *adv.*, **comprehensiveness** *n.* ☐ **comprehensive school,** a large secondary school providing courses for children of all abilities.

compress[1] (kŏm-**press**) *v.* to squeeze together, to force into less space. **compression** *n.*, **compressor** *n.*

compress[2] (**kom**-press) *n.* a pad or cloth pressed on the body to stop bleeding or to cool inflammation etc.

compressible *adj.* able to be compressed.

comprise (kŏm-**pryz**) *v.* **1.** to include. **2.** to consist of. **3.** to form, to make up, *these three rooms comprise the apartment.* ¶ In sense 3 it is better to use *compose* or *constitute.* Note that it is incorrect to use *comprise* with *of*, as in *the group was comprised of twenty students*; correct usage here is *was composed of.*

compromise (**kom**-prŏ-myz) *n.* **1.** making a settlement by each side giving up part of its demands. **2.** a settlement made in this way. **3.** something that is half-way between opposite opinions or courses of action etc. —**compromise** *v.* **1.** to settle a dispute by a compromise. **2.** to expose to danger or suspicion or scandal etc. by unwise action.

compulsion *n.* **1.** compelling, being compelled. **2.** an irresistible urge.

compulsive *adj.* **1.** compelling. **2.** acting as if from compulsion, *a compulsive gambler.* **compulsively** *adv.*

compulsory *adj.* that must be done, required by the rules etc. **compulsorily** *adv.*

compunction *n.* the pricking of conscience, a slight regret or scruple.

compute *v.* to reckon mathematically, to calculate. **computation** *n.*

computer *n.* an electronic machine for making calculations, storing and analysing information fed into it, and controlling machinery automatically.

computerize *v.* **1.** to process or store (information) by means of a computer. **2.** to convert (a process or machinery etc.) so that it can make use of or be controlled by a computer. **computerization** *n.*

comrade *n.* **1.** a companion who shares one's activities. **2.** a fellow socialist or Communist. **comradely** *adv.*, **comradeship** *n.*

con[1] *v.* (conned, conning) (*informal*) to persuade or swindle after winning a person's confidence. —*n.* (*slang*) a confidence trick. **con man,** (*slang*) a confidence man.

con[2] *see* pro and con.

con[3] *v.* (conned, conning) to direct the steering of (a ship or helicopter).

Conakry (**kon**-ă-kri) the capital of Guinea.

concatenation (kon-kat-in-**ay**-shŏn) *n.* a sequence or combination.

concave *adj.* curving like the surface of a ball as seen from the inside. **concavity** (kon-**kav**-iti) *n.*

conceal *v.* to keep secret or hidden. **concealment** *n.*

concede (kŏn-**seed**) *v.* **1.** to admit that something is true. **2.** to grant, to allow, to yield, *they conceded us the right to cross their land.* **3.** to admit defeat in, especially before the official end of the contest.

conceit *n.* too much pride in oneself.

conceited *adj.* being too proud of oneself. **conceitedly** *adv.*

conceivable *adj.* able to be imagined or believed. **conceivably** *adv.*

conceive *v.* **1.** to become pregnant. **2.** to form (an idea or plan etc.) in the mind, to think.

concentrate *v.* **1.** to employ all one's thought or attention or effort on something. **2.** to bring or come together to one place. **3.** to make less dilute. —*n.* a concentrated substance or solution. —**concentration** *n.* ☐ **concentrated** *adj.* (of a solution etc.) having a large proportion of effective elements, not dilute; intense, *concentrated hatred.* **concentration camp,** a place where civilian political prisoners are brought together and confined.

concentric (kŏn-**sen**-trik) *adj.* having the same centre, *concentric circles*.

concept (**kon**-sept) *n.* an idea, a general notion, *the concept of freedom*.

conception *n.* **1.** conceiving, being conceived. **2.** an idea.

concern *v.* **1.** to be about, to have as its subject, *the story concerns a group of rabbits*. **2.** to be of importance to, to affect. **3.** to take up the time or attention of; *she concerned herself about it*, gave it her care and attention. —**concern** *n.* **1.** something of interest or importance, a responsibility; *it's no concern of mine*, I have nothing to do with it. **2.** a connection, a share, *he has a concern in industry*. **3.** worry, anxiety. **4.** a business, a firm, *a going concern*. **5.** (*informal*) a thing, *smashed the whole concern*.

concerned *adj.* worried, anxious.

concerning *prep.* about, in regard to.

concert *n.* a musical entertainment by more than one performer. **at concert pitch**, in a state of unusually great efficiency or intensity. (¶ A piano intended for use in concerts, especially with an orchestra, needs to be tuned to a pitch which is higher than that needed on an ordinary domestic instrument.) **in concert**, in combination, together.

concerted (kŏn-**sert**-id) *adj.* arranged by mutual agreement, done in co-operation.

concertina *n.* a portable musical instrument with hexagonal ends and bellows, played by squeezing while pressing studs at each end. —*v.* (concertinaed, concertinaing) to fold or collapse like the bellows of a concertina.

concerto (kŏn-**cher**-toh) *n.* (*pl.* concertos) a musical composition for one or more solo instruments and an orchestra.

concession *n.* **1.** conceding. **2.** something conceded **3.** a right given by the owners of land to extract minerals, etc. from it or to sell goods there, *an oil concession*.

conch *n.* the spiral shell of a kind of shellfish, sometimes used as a horn.

conciliate *v.* **1.** to overcome the anger or hostility of, to win the goodwill of. **2.** to reconcile (people who disagree). **conciliation** *n.*, **conciliator** *n.*, **conciliatory** (kŏn-**sil**-i-ătri) *adj.*

concise (kŏn-**syss**) *adj.* brief, giving much information in few words. **concisely** *adv.*, **conciseness** *n.*

conclave (**kon**-klayv) *n.* a private meeting for discussing something, *in conclave*.

conclude *v.* **1.** to bring or come to an end. **2.** to arrange, to settle finally, *they con-*

cluded a treaty. **3.** to arrive at a belief or opinion by reasoning.

conclusion *n.* **1.** ending, an end, *at the conclusion of his speech*. **2.** arrangement, settling, *conclusion of the treaty*. **3.** a belief or opinion based on reasoning. □ **In conclusion**, lastly, to conclude.

conclusive *adj.* ending doubt, completely convincing, *conclusive evidence of his guilt*. **conclusively** *adv.*

concoct (kŏn-**kokt**) *v.* **1.** to prepare by putting ingredients together. **2.** to invent, *concocted an excuse*. **concoction** *n.*

concomitant (kŏn-**kom**-i-tănt) *adj.* accompanying. —*n.* an accompanying thing.

concord *n.* agreement or harmony between people or things. **concordant** (kŏn-**kor**-dănt) *adj.*

concordance (kŏn-**kor**-dănss) *n.* an index of the words used in a book or an author's writings, *a concordance to the Bible*.

concordat (kon-**kor**-dat) *n.* an agreement made, especially between Church and State.

concourse (**kon**-korss) *n.* **1.** a crowd, a gathering. **2.** an open area through which people pass e.g. at a railway terminus.

concrete [1] (**kon**-kreet) *n.* a mixture of cement with sand and gravel, used for building and paving. —*adj.* **1.** existing in material form, able to be touched and felt. **2.** definite, positive, *concrete evidence*. □ **concrete jungle**, a city considered as a place where people have to struggle for survival.

concrete [2] (**kon**-kreet) *v.* **1.** to cover with or embed in concrete. **2.** to form into a solid mass, to solidify.

concretion (kŏn-**kree**-shŏn) *n.* a hard solid mass.

concubine (**konk**-yoo-byn) *n.* a secondary wife in countries where polygamy is customary.

concur (kŏn-**ker**) *v.* (concurred, concurring) **1.** to agree in opinion. **2.** to happen together, to coincide.

concurrence (kŏn-**ku**-rĕns) *n.* **1.** agreement, *concurrence of opinion*. **2.** simultaneous occurrence of events.

concurrent (kŏn-**ku**-rĕnt) *adj.* existing or occurring at the same time. **concurrently** *adv.*

concussed (kŏn-**kust**) *adj.* affected with concussion.

concussion (kŏn-**kush**-ŏn) *n.* injury to the brain caused by a hard blow.

condemn *v.* **1.** to express strong disapproval of. **2.** to pronounce guilty, to convict. **3.** to sentence, *was condemned to death*. **4.** to destine to an unhappy fate. **5.** to declare unfit for use or uninhabitable, *condemned houses*. **condemnation** (kon-dem-

129

nay-shŏn) *n.* □ **condemned cell,** a cell for a prisoner condemned to death.

condemnatory (kŏn-**dem**-nă-ter-i) *adj.* expressing condemnation.

condense *v.* **1.** to make denser or more concentrated. **2.** to change or be changed from gas or vapour into liquid. **3.** to express in fewer words, *a condensed report on the meeting.* **condenser** *n.,* **condensation** (kon-den-**say**-shŏn) *n.* □ **condensed milk,** milk made thick by evaporation and sweetened.

condescend *v.* to behave in a way that shows (pleasantly or unpleasantly) one's feeling of dignity or superiority. **condescension** *n.*

condiment (**kon**-di-mĕnt) *n.* a seasoning (such as salt or pepper) for food.

condition *n.* **1.** the state in which a person or thing is with regard to characteristics and circumstances. **2.** a state of physical fitness or (of things) fitness for use, *get into condition*; *out of condition*, not fully fit. **3.** an abnormality, *she has a heart condition.* **4.** something required as part of an agreement. —**condition** *v.* **1.** to bring into a desired condition, to make physically fit, to put into a proper state for work or use. **2.** to have a strong effect on. **3.** to train, to accustom. —**conditioner** *n.* □ **conditioned reflex** *or* **response,** a reaction produced by training, not a natural one. **conditions** *pl. n.* the facts or situations or surroundings that affect something, *working conditions are good.* **on condition that,** on the understanding that (a thing will be done).

conditional *adj.* not absolute, containing a condition or stipulation, *a conditional agreement.* **conditionally** *adv.*

condole (kŏn-**dohl**) *v.* to express sympathy. **condolence** *n.*

condom (**kon**-dŏm) *n.* a contraceptive sheath (*see* sheath, sense 2).

condone (kŏn-**dohn**) *v.* to forgive or overlook (wrongdoing) without punishment. **condonation** (kon-dŏn-**ay**-shŏn) *n.*

conduce (kŏn-**dewss**) *v.* to help to cause or produce.

conducive (kŏn-**dew**-siv) *adj.* helping to cause or produce, *an atmosphere that is conducive to work.*

conduct[1] (kŏn-**dukt**) *v.* **1.** to lead or guide; *conducted tour,* escorted by a guide. **2.** to be the conductor of (a choir or orchestra or music). **3.** to manage or direct (business or negotiations etc., or an experiment). **4.** to have the property of allowing heat, light, sound, or electricity to pass along or through. □ **conduct oneself,** to behave.

conduct[2] (**kon**-dukt) *n.* **1.** a person's behaviour. **2.** managing or directing affairs; *the conduct of the war,* the way it is being conducted.

conduction *n.* the transmission or conducting of heat or electricity etc.

conductor *n.* **1.** a person who conducts a group or business etc. **2.** one who directs the performance of an orchestra or choir etc. by gestures. **3.** one who collects the fares in a bus. **4.** a substance that conducts heat or electricity etc.

conductress *n.* a woman bus conductor.

conduit (**kon**-dit) *n.* **1.** a pipe or channel for conveying liquids. **2.** a tube or trough protecting insulated electric wires.

cone *n.* **1.** a solid body that narrows to a point from a round flat base. **2.** something shaped like this. **3.** the dry fruit of certain evergreen trees, consisting of woody scales arranged in a shape suggesting a cone.

coney *n.* rabbit-skin or rabbit-fur used in making clothes.

confab (**kon**-fab) *n.* (*informal*) a chat.

confection *n.* something made of various things, especially sweet ones, put together.

confectioner *n.* a maker or retailer of confectionery.

confectionery *n.* sweets, cakes, and pastries.

confederacy *n.* a union of States, a confederation.

confederate *adj.* allied, joined by agreement or treaty. —*n.* **1.** a member of a confederacy. **2.** an ally, an accomplice.

confederated *adj.* united by agreement or treaty.

confederation *n.* **1.** joining in an alliance. **2.** a confederated group of people or organizations or States.

confer *v.* (**conferred, conferring**) **1.** to grant, to bestow. **2.** to hold a conference or discussion.

conference *n.* a meeting for discussion.

conferment (kŏn-**fer**-mĕnt) *n.* granting, bestowing.

conferrable (kŏn-**fer**-ăbŭl) *adj.* able to be conferred.

confess *v.* **1.** to state formally that one has done wrong or has a weakness, *he confessed* or *confessed his crime* or *confessed to the crime.* **2.** to state one's attitude or reaction reluctantly, *I must confess that I am puzzled.* **3.** to declare one's sins formally, especially to a priest. **4.** (of a priest) to hear the confession of. □ **confessedly** (kŏn-**fess**-idli) *adv.* according to a person's own confession.

confession *n.* **1.** confessing. **2.** a thing confessed, a statement of one's wrongdoing.

3. a declaration of one's religious beliefs or one's principles, *a confession of faith.*

confessional *n.* an enclosed stall in a church, where a priest sits to hear confessions.

confessor *n.* **1.** a priest who hears confessions and gives spiritual counsel. **2.** a person who keeps to the Christian faith in the face of danger, *King Edward the Confessor.*

confetti *n.* bits of coloured paper thrown by wedding guests at the bride and bridegroom.

confidant (kon-fid-**ant**) *n.* a person in whom one confides. **confidante** *n.* a female confidant.

confide *v.* **1.** to tell confidentially; *confided in his friend,* told him things confidentially. **2.** to entrust.

confidence *n.* **1.** firm trust. **2.** a feeling of certainty, self-reliance, boldness, *he lacks confidence.* **3.** something told confidentially, *has listened to many confidences.* □ **confidence man,** one who defrauds people by means of a **confidence trick,** in which a victim is persuaded to entrust his valuables to someone who gives a false impression of honesty. **in confidence, as** a secret. **in a person's confidence,** trusted with his secrets.

confident *adj.* feeling confidence, bold. **confidently** *adv.*

confidential *adj.* **1.** spoken or written in confidence, to be kept secret. **2.** entrusted with secrets, *a confidential secretary.* **3.** confiding, *spoke in a confidential tone.* **confidentially** *adv.,* **confidentiality** *n.*

configuration *n.* a method of arrangement (e.g. of apparatus), a shape or outline.

configure *v.* to set up (a system of apparatus etc.) for a particular purpose.

confine *v.* **1.** to keep or restrict within certain limits. **2.** to keep shut up, *the prisoner is confined to his cell; confined to bed,* in bed because of illness.

confined *adj.* narrow, restricted, *a confined space.*

confinement *n.* **1.** confining, being confined. **2.** the time during which a woman is giving birth to a baby.

confines (kon-fynz) *pl. n.* the limits or boundaries of an area.

confirm *v.* **1.** to provide supporting evidence for the truth or correctness of, to prove. **2.** to establish more firmly, *it confirmed him in his dislike of animals.* **3.** to make definite or valid formally, *bookings made by telephone must be confirmed in writing.* **4.** to administer the rite of confirmation to. □ **confirmed** *adj.* firmly settled

in some habit or condition, *a confirmed bachelor.*

confirmation *n.* **1.** confirming. **2.** something that confirms. **3.** a religious rite confirming a baptized person as a member of the Christian Church. **4.** a ceremony confirming a person in the Jewish faith.

confirmatory (kon-**ferm**-ă-ter-i) *adj.* confirming, *we found confirmatory evidence.*

confiscate (kon-fis-kayt) *v.* to take or seize by authority. **confiscation** *n.*

conflagration (kon-flă-**gray**-shŏn) *n.* a great and destructive fire.

conflict[1] (**kon**-flikt) *n.* **1.** a fight, a struggle. **2.** disagreement between people with different ideas or beliefs.

conflict[2] (kŏn-**flikt**) *v.* to be in opposition or disagreement.

confluence (**kon**-floo-ĕns) *n.* the place where two rivers unite.

conform *v.* to keep to rules or general custom, *she refuses to conform.* **conform to,** to act or be in accordance with.

conformation *n.* **1.** the way a thing is formed, its structure. **2.** conforming.

conformist (kŏn-**form**-ist) *n.* a person who readily conforms to established rules or standards etc.

conformity *n.* conforming to established rules or standards etc. **in conformity with,** in accordance with.

confound *v.* **1.** to astonish and perplex, to bewilder. **2.** to confuse. **3.** (*old use*) to defeat, to overthrow. —*int.* an exclamation of annoyance, *confound it!*

confounded *adj.* (*informal*) damned, *a confounded nuisance.*

confront (kŏn-**frunt**) *v.* **1.** to be or come face to face with, *the problems confronting us.* **2.** to face boldly as an enemy or in defiance. **3.** to bring face to face, *we confronted him with his accusers.* **confrontation** (kon-frun-**tay**-shŏn) *n.*

Confucianism (kŏn-**few**-shăn-izm) *n.* the moral and religious system founded by the Chinese philosopher Confucius (550–478 BC). **Confucian** *adj. & n.*

confuse *v.* **1.** to throw into disorder, to mix up. **2.** to throw the mind or feelings of (a person) into disorder, to destroy the composure of. **3.** to mix up in the mind, to fail to distinguish between. **4.** to make unclear, *confuse the issue.* **confusion** *n.*

confused *adj.* (of a person) not mentally sound.

confute (kŏn-**fewt**) *v.* to prove (a person or argument) to be wrong. **confutation** (kon-few-**tay**-shŏn) *n.*

conga *n.* a dance in which people form a long winding line.

congeal (kŏn-**jeel**) *v.* to become semi-solid

instead of liquid. **congelation** (kon-jil-ay-shŏn) *n.*

congenial (kŏn-**jeen**-iăl) *adj.* **1.** pleasant because similar to oneself in character or tastes, *a congenial companion.* **2.** suited or agreeable to oneself, *a congenial climate.*

congenital (kŏn-**jen**-it'l) *adj.* **1.** existing since a person's birth, *a congenital deformity.* **2.** born in a certain condition, *a congenital idiot.* **congenitally** *adv.*

conger (**kong**-er) *n.* a large sea eel.

congested *adj.* **1.** too full, overcrowded. **2.** (of an organ or tissue of the body) abnormally full of blood.

congestion (kŏn-**jes**-chŏn) *n.* a congested condition.

conglomerate (kŏn-**glom**-er-ăt) *adj.* gathered into a mass. —*n.* **1.** a conglomerate mass. **2.** a group formed by merging several different firms.

conglomeration *n.* a mass of different things put together.

Congo a country in West Africa. **Congolese** *adj* & *n.*

congratulate *v.* to praise and tell (a person) that one is pleased about his achievement or good fortune; *congratulating ourselves on our escape,* thinking ourselves fortunate, taking pleasure in it. **congratulation** *n.*

congratulatory (kŏn-**grat**-yoo-lă-ter-i) *adj.* expressing congratulations.

congregate *v.* to flock together into a crowd.

congregation *n.* a group of people gathered together to take part in religious worship. **congregational** *adj.*

congress *n.* **1.** a formal meeting of representatives, for discussion. **2.** *Congress,* the law-making body of a country, especially of the USA. □ **congressional** (kŏn-gresh-ŏn-ăl) *adj.* of a congress.

conic (**kon**-ik) *adj.* of a cone.

conical *adj.* cone-shaped. **conically** *adv.*

conifer (**koh**-ni-fer) *n.* a coniferous tree.

coniferous (koh-**nif**-er-ŭs) *adj.* bearing cones.

conjectural *adj.* based on conjecture.

conjecture *v.* to guess. —*n.* a guess.

conjugal (**kon**-jŭg-ăl) *adj.* of marriage, of the relationship between husband and wife.

conjugate (**kon**-jŭg-ayt) *v.* to give the different forms of (a verb), e.g. *get, gets.* **conjugation** *n.*

conjunction *n.* **1.** a word that joins words or phrases or sentences, e.g. *and, but.* **2.** combination, union, *the four countries acted in conjunction.* **3.** the occurrence of events etc. at the same time. **4.** the apparent nearness of two or more heavenly bodies to each other, *these planets are in conjunction.*

conjunctivitis *n.* inflammation of the surface of the eyeball or inner eyelid.

conjure (**kun**-jer) *v.* **1.** to perform tricks which appear to be magical, especially by movements of the hands, *conjuring tricks.* **2.** to summon (a spirit) to appear. **3.** to produce as if from nothing, *managed to conjure up a meal.* **4.** to produce in the mind, *mention of the Arctic conjures up visions of snow and ice.* □ **a name to conjure with,** a name of great importance.

conjuror *n.* a person who performs conjuring tricks.

conk *n.* (*slang*) the nose, the head. —*v.* (*slang*) to hit on the head. □ **conk out,** (*slang,* of a machine) to break down, to fail; (of a person) to become exhausted and give up, to faint, to die.

conker *n.* (*informal*) the fruit of the horse-chestnut tree. **conkers** *n.* a children's game between players each with a conker on a string.

Conn. *abbrev.* Connecticut.

connect *v.* **1.** to join or be joined. **2.** (of a train etc.) to be timed to arrive so that passengers from one train etc. can catch another in which to continue their journey. **3.** to put into communication by telephone. **4.** to think of (things or persons) as being associated with each other.

connecter *n.* a person who connects things.

Connecticut (kŏn-et-i-kŭt) a State of the USA.

connection *n.* **1.** connecting, being connected. **2.** a place where things connect, a connecting part. **3.** a train etc. timed to connect with another, transfer between such trains. **4.** a relationship. **5.** a person connected by family or marriage. **6.** a number of customers or clients, *a business with a good connection.* □ **in connection with this** *or* **in this connection,** on this subject.

connective *adj.* connecting, *connective tissue.*

connector *n.* a thing that connects others.

conning-tower *n.* a raised structure on a submarine, containing the periscope.

connive (kŏ-**nyv**) *v.* **connive at,** to take no notice of (wrongdoing), thus seeming to consent to it. **connivance** *n.*

connoisseur (kon-ă-**ser**) *n.* a person with expert understanding of artistic and similar subjects.

connote (kŏ-**noht**) *v.* to imply in addition to the literal meaning. **connotation** *n.*

connubial (kŏ-**new**-biăl) *adj.* of marriage,

of the relationship between husband and wife.

conoid (**koh**-noid) *adj.* of or shaped like a cone. —*n.* a conoid object.

conquer *v.* **1.** to overcome in war, to win. **2.** to overcome by effort; *we have conquered Everest,* climbed it successfully. **conqueror** *n.*

conquest *n.* **1.** conquering; *the Conquest* or *Norman Conquest,* conquest of England by the Normans in 1066. **2.** something got by conquering.

consanguinity (kon-sang-**win**-iti) *n.* relationship by descent from the same ancestor.

conscience *n.* **1.** a person's sense of what is right and wrong, especially in his own actions or motives. **2.** a feeling of remorse, *I have no conscience about leaving them.* □ **conscience clause,** a clause (in a rule etc.) exempting a person from complying with this rule if he feels it is morally wrong to do so. **conscience money,** money paid by a person who feels conscience-stricken, especially about having evaded payment previously. **conscience-stricken** *adj.* filled with remorse. **on one's conscience,** causing one to feel guilty or remorseful.

conscientious (kon-shi-en-shŭs) *adj.* showing or done with careful attention. **conscientiously** *adv.,* **conscientiousness** *n.* □ **conscientious objector,** one who refuses to do something (especially to serve in the armed forces in a war) because he believes it is morally wrong.

conscious *adj.* **1.** with one's mental faculties awake, aware of one's surroundings. **2.** aware, *he was conscious of his guilt.* **3.** realized by oneself, intentional, *spoke with conscious superiority; a conscious insult.* **consciously** *adv.,* **consciousness** *n.*

conscript[1] (kŏn-**skript**) *v.* to summon for compulsory military service. **conscription** *n.*

conscript[2] (kon-skript) *n.* a conscripted recruit.

consecrate *v.* to make or declare sacred, to dedicate formally to the service or worship of God. **consecration** *n.*

consecutive (kŏn-**sek**-yoo-tiv) *adj.* following continuously, in unbroken order. **consecutively** *adv.*

consensus (kŏn-**sen**-sŭs) *n.* general agreement in opinion.

consent *v.* to say that one is willing to do or allow what someone wishes. —*n.* agreement to what someone wishes, permission. □ **age of consent,** the age at which a girl's consent to sexual intercourse becomes valid in law.

consequence *n.* **1.** a result produced by some action or condition. **2.** importance,

a person of consequence; the matter is of no consequence, it is not important. □ **consequences** *n.* a round game in which a story is constructed. **in consequence,** as a result. **take the consequences,** to accept whatever results from one's choice or action.

consequent *adj.* following as a result.

consequential (kon-si-**kwen**-shǎl) *adj.* following as a result. **consequentially** *adv.*

consequently *adv.* as a result, therefore.

conservancy *n.* **1.** a committee with authority to control a port or river etc., *the Thames Conservancy.* **2.** official conservation (of forests etc.).

conservation *n.* **1.** conserving, being conserved. **2.** preservation, especially of the natural environment. **conservationist** *n.* a person who supports conservation.

conservatism *n.* a conservative attitude, conservative principles (general or political).

conservative *adj.* **1.** disliking or opposed to great or sudden change. **2.** moderate, avoiding extremes; *a conservative estimate,* a low one. **3.** *Conservative,* of the Conservative Party. —*n.* a conservative person. —**conservatively** *adv.* □ **Conservative** *n.* a member of the **Conservative Party,** a political party favouring private enterprise and freedom from State control.

conservatory *n.* a greenhouse, especially one built against an outside wall of a house which has an opening into it.

conserve[1] (kŏn-**serv**) *v.* to keep from harm, decay, or loss, for future use.

conserve[2] (kon-serv) *n.* jam, especially that made from fresh fruit and sugar.

consider *v.* **1.** to think about, especially in order to make a decision, to weigh the merits of. **2.** to make allowances for, *consider people's feelings.* **3.** to think to be, suppose, *consider yourself lucky.* □ **all things considered,** taking all the events or possibilities into account.

considerable *adj.* fairly great in amount or extent etc., *of considerable importance.* **considerably** *adv.*

considerate *adj.* taking care not to inconvenience or hurt others. **considerately** *adv.*

consideration *n.* **1.** careful thought. **2.** being considerate, kindness. **3.** a fact that must be kept in mind, *time is now an important consideration.* **4.** payment given as a reward, *he will do it for a consideration.* □ **in consideration of,** in return for, on account of. **on no consideration,** no matter what the circumstances may be. **take into consideration,** to allow for. **under consideration,** being considered.

considering *prep.* taking into consideration, *she is very active, considering her age*; *you've done very well, considering,* if we take the circumstances into consideration.

consign *v.* **1.** to hand over or deliver formally. **2.** to give into someone's care.

consignee (kon-sy-**nee**) *n.* one to whom goods etc. are consigned.

consignment *n.* **1.** consigning. **2.** a batch of goods etc. consigned.

consignor (kŏn-**sy**-nor) *n.* one who consigns goods etc. to another.

consist *v.* **1. consist of,** to be made up of, *the flat consists of 3 rooms.* **2. consist in,** to have as its basis or essential feature, *their happiness consists in hoping.*

consistency *n.* **1.** the degree of thickness, firmness, or solidity especially of a liquid or soft mixture, *mix it to the consistency of thick cream.* **2.** being consistent.

consistent *adj.* **1.** conforming to a regular pattern or style, unchanging, *they have no consistent policy.* **2.** not contradictory, *their reforms are consistent with their general policies.* **consistently** *adv.*

consolable *adj.* able to be consoled.

consolation *n.* consoling, being consoled. **consolation prize,** a prize given to a competitor who has just missed winning one of the main prizes.

console[1] (kŏn-**sohl**) *v.* to comfort in time of sorrow or disappointment.

console[2] (**kon**-sohl) *n.* **1.** a bracket to support a shelf. **2.** a frame containing the keyboards and stops etc. of an organ. **3.** a panel holding the controls of electrical or other equipment. **4.** a cabinet containing a radio or TV set, designed to stand on the floor.

consolidate *v.* **1.** to make or become secure and strong, *consolidating his position as leader.* **2.** to combine or become combined, to merge. **consolidation** *n.*

consommé (kŏn-**som**-ay) *n.* clear meat soup.

consonant *n.* **1.** a letter of the alphabet other than a vowel. **2.** the speech-sound it represents. —*adj.* consistent, harmonious, *actions that are consonant with his beliefs.*

consort[1] (**kon**-sort) *n.* a husband or wife, especially of a monarch.

consort[2] (kŏn-**sort**) *v.* to associate, to keep company, *consorting with criminals.*

consortium (kŏn-**sort**-iŭm) *n.* a combination of countries or companies or other groups acting together.

conspectus *n.* a general survey of a subject etc.

conspicuous *adj.* easily seen, attracting attention. **conspicuously** *adv.,* **conspicuousness** *n.*

conspiracy *n.* **1.** conspiring. **2.** a plan made by conspiring. ▢ **conspiracy of silence,** an agreement to say nothing about a certain matter.

conspirator *n.* a person who conspires. **conspiratorial** *adj.,* **conspiratorially** *adv.*

conspire *v.* **1.** to plan secretly with others, especially for some unlawful purpose. **2.** (of events) to seem to combine, *events conspired to bring about his downfall.*

constable *n.* a policeman or policewoman of the lowest rank.

constabulary (kŏn-**stab**-yoo-ler-i) *n.* a police force.

constancy *n.* **1.** the quality of being constant and unchanging. **2.** faithfulness.

constant *adj.* **1.** happening or continuing all the time, happening repeatedly. **2.** unchanging, faithful, *remained constant to his principles.* —*n.* something that is constant and does not vary. —**constantly** *adv.*

constellation *n.* a group of fixed stars.

consternation *n.* great surprise and anxiety or dismay.

constipation *n.* difficulty in emptying the bowels. **constipated** *adj.* suffering from constipation. **constipating** *adj.* causing constipation.

constituency *n.* **1.** a body of voters who elect a representative, especially to parliament. **2.** the district and its residents represented thus.

constituent *adj.* forming part of a whole, *its constituent parts.* —*n.* **1.** a constituent part. **2.** a member of a constituency.

constitute *v.* **1.** to make up, to form, *12 months constitute a year.* **2.** to appoint, *they constituted him chief adviser.* **3.** to establish or be, *this does not constitute a precedent.*

constitution *n.* **1.** constituting. **2.** composition. **3.** the principles according to which a country is organized. **4.** general condition and character, especially of a person's body, *she has a strong constitution.*

constitutional *adj.* **1.** of a country's constitution, established or permitted or limited by this, *a constitutional crisis; constitutional government.* **2.** of or produced by a person's physical or mental constitution, *a constitutional weakness.* —*n.* a walk taken for the sake of one's health.

constrain *v.* to compel, to oblige.

constraint *n.* **1.** constraining or being constrained, compulsion. **2.** a strained manner caused by holding back one's natural feelings.

constrict *v.* to tighten by making narrower, to squeeze. **constriction** *n.,* **constrictor** *n.*

construct v. to make by placing parts together.

construction n. **1.** constructing, being constructed. **2.** something constructed. **3.** two or more words put together to form a phrase or clause or sentence. **4.** an interpretation, *put a bad construction on their refusal.* **constructional** adj.

constructive adj. offering helpful suggestions, *they made constructive criticisms.* **constructively** adv.

construe (kŏn-**stroo**) v. to interpret, to explain, *her words were construed as a refusal.*

consul n. **1.** either of the two chief magistrates in ancient Rome. **2.** an official appointed to live in a foreign city in order to assist and protect his countrymen who live or visit there and to help commercial relations between the two countries. **consular** (**kons**-yoo-ler) adj.

consulate n. **1.** the official premises of a consul. **2.** a consul's position.

consult v. **1.** to seek information or advice from; *a consulting engineer,* one who acts as a consultant. **2.** to confer, *they consulted with their fellow-workers.* **consultation** n. □ **consulting room,** a room in which a doctor interviews patients.

consultant n. a person qualified to give expert professional advice, especially a specialist in a branch of medicine or surgery. **consultancy** n. the position or business of a consultant.

consultative (kŏn-**sult** ă-tiv) adj. for consultation, *a consultative committee.*

consume v. **1.** to use up, *much time was consumed in waiting.* **2.** to eat or drink up, especially in large quantities. **3.** to destroy completely, *fire consumed the building.*

consumer n. a person who buys or uses goods or services. **consumer goods,** those bought and used by individual consumers (not 'capital goods').

consumerism n. (*Amer.*) the protection of consumers' interests.

consuming adj. overwhelming, dominating, *a consuming ambition.*

consummate¹ (**kon**-sŭm-ayt) v. to accomplish, to make complete; *consummate a marriage,* complete it by sexual intercourse between the partners. **consummation** n.

consummate² (kŏn-**sum**-ăt) adj. supremely skilled, *a consummate artist.*

consumption n. **1.** consuming, using up, destruction. **2.** the amount consumed. **3.** (*old use*) tuberculosis of the lungs.

consumptive adj. suffering from tuberculosis of the lungs.

contact (**kon**-takt) n. **1.** touching, coming together. **2.** being in touch, communication.

3. a connection for the passage of electric current. **4.** a person who has recently been near someone with a contagious disease and may carry infection. **5.** an acquaintance who may be contacted when one needs information or help. —v. to get into touch with (a person). □ **contact lens,** a very small lens worn in contact with the eyeball.

contagion (kŏn-**tay**-jŏn) n. **1.** the spreading of disease by contact or close association. **2.** a disease spread in this way.

contagious (kŏn-**tay**-jŭs) adj. **1.** able to be spread by contact or close association, *a contagious disease.* **2.** capable of spreading disease in this way, *all these children are now contagious.*

contain v. **1.** to have within itself, *the atlas contains 40 maps; whisky contains alcohol.* **2.** to consist of, to be equal to, *a gallon contains 8 pints.* **3.** to restrain, *try to contain your laughter.* **4.** to keep within limits, *enemy troops were contained in the valley.*

container n. **1.** a box or bottle etc. designed to contain a substance or goods. **2.** a large box-like receptacle of standard design for transporting goods.

containerize v. to transport by container, to convert to this method of transporting goods. **containerization** n.

containment n. the policy of preventing the expansion of a hostile country or influence.

contaminate v. to pollute. **contamination** n.

contemplate (**kon**-těm-playt) v. **1.** to gaze at thoughtfully. **2.** to consider. **3.** to intend, to have in view as a possibility, *she is contemplating a visit to London.* **4.** to meditate. **contemplation** n.

contemplative (kŏn-**tem**-plă-tiv) adj. thoughtful, fond of contemplation.

contemporary (kŏn-**tem**-per-er-i) adj. **1.** belonging to the same period; *Dickens was contemporary with Thackeray,* lived at the same time. **2.** up-to-date, *contemporary designs.* —**contemporary** n. **1.** a person contemporary with another, *Dickens and his contemporaries.* **2.** one who is approximately the same age as another, *she is my contemporary.*

contempt n. **1.** the process or feeling of despising something. **2.** the condition of being despised; *fell into contempt,* became despised. **3.** disrespect. □ **contempt of court,** disobedience or disrespect towards a court of law or its processes.

contemptible adj. deserving contempt. **contemptibly** adv., **contemptibility** n.

contemptuous adj. feeling or showing

contempt. **contemptuously** *adv.*, **contemptuousness** *n.*

contend *v.* **1.** to strive or fight or struggle, especially in competition or against difficulties. **2.** to assert, to argue, *the defendant contends that he is innocent.* **contender** *n.*

content[1] (kŏn-**tent**) *adj.* contented, satisfied with what one has. —*n.* being contented, satisfaction. —*v.* to make content, to satisfy. —**contentment** *n.* □ **to one's heart's content**, as much as one desires.

content[2] (**kon**-tent) *n.* what is contained in something, *the contents of the barrel*; *butter has a high fat content*, contains much fat; *the table of contents*, the list of chapter-headings etc. showing the subject-matter of a book.

contented *adj.* happy with what one has, satisfied. **contentedly** *adv.*

contention *n.* **1.** contending, quarrelling or arguing. **2.** an assertion made in arguing.

contentious (kŏn-**ten**-shŭs) *adj.* **1.** quarrelsome. **2.** likely to cause contention. **contentiously** *adv.*

contest[1] (**kon**-test) *n.* **1.** a struggle for superiority or victory. **2.** a competition, a test of skill or ability etc. between rivals.

contest[2] (kŏn-**test**) *v.* **1.** to compete for or in, *contest a seat at an election; contest an election.* **2.** to dispute, to challenge; *contest a statement*, try to show that it is wrong; *contest a will*, try to prove that it is not valid.

contestant *n.* one who takes part in a contest, a competitor.

context *n.* **1.** the words that come before and after a particular word or phrase and help to fix its meaning. **2.** the circumstances in which an event occurs, *shortages were tolerated in the context of war.* □ **out of context**, without the surrounding words and therefore giving a false impression of the meaning.

contiguous (kŏn-**tig**-yoo-ŭs) *adj.* adjoining, *Kent is contiguous to Surrey.* **contiguously** *adv.*, **contiguity** (kon-tig-**yoo**-iti) *n.*

continent[1] *n.* one of the main land masses of the earth (Europe, Asia, Africa, North and South America, Australia, Antarctica); *the Continent*, the mainland of Europe as distinct from the British Isles.

continent[2] *adj.* able to control the excretion of one's urine and faeces. **continence** *n.*

continental *adj.* **1.** of a continent. **2.** *Continental*, of the Continent. □ **Continental breakfast**, a light breakfast of coffee and rolls etc. **continental quilt**, a duvet.

contingency (kŏn-**tin**-jĕn-si) *n.* **1.** something unforeseen. **2.** a possibility, something that may occur at a future date; *contingency plans*, plans made in case something happens.

contingent (kŏn-**tin**-jĕnt) *adj.* **1.** happening by chance. **2.** possible, liable to occur but not certain. **3.** depending on something that may or may not happen, *an advantage that is contingent on the success of the expedition.* —**contingent** *n.* **1.** a body of troops or ships etc. contributed to form part of a force. **2.** a group of people forming part of a gathering. —**contingently** *adv.*

continual *adj.* continuing lengthily without stopping or with only short breaks. **continually** *adv.*

continuance *n.* continuing.

continuation *n.* **1.** continuing, starting again after ceasing. **2.** a part etc. by which something is continued, *the book is a continuation of her previous novel.*

continue *v.* **1.** to keep up (an action etc.), to do something without ceasing, *continue to eat; continue the struggle.* **2.** to remain in a certain place or condition, *he will continue as manager.* **3.** to go further, *the road continues beyond the bridge.* **4.** to begin again after stopping, *to be continued next week.*

continuity (kon-tin-**yoo**-iti) *n.* **1.** being continuous. **2.** the uninterrupted succession of things.

continuous *adj.* continuing, without a break. **continuously** *adv.*

continuum (kŏn-**tin**-yoo-ŭm) *n.* something that extends continuously.

contort (kŏn-**tort**) *v.* to force or twist out of its usual shape. **contortion** (kŏn-**tor**-shŏn) *n.*

contortionist (kon-**tor**-shŏn-ist) *n.* a performer who can twist his body into unusual postures.

contour (**kon**-toor) *n.* **1.** an outline. **2.** a line (on a map) joining the points that are the same height above sea level.

contra- *prefix* against.

contraband *n.* **1.** smuggled goods. **2.** smuggling.

contraception (kon-tră-**sep**-shŏn) *n.* the prevention of pregnancy.

contraceptive (kon-tră-**sep**-tiv) *adj.* preventing conception. —*n.* a contraceptive drug or device.

contract[1] (**kon**-trakt) *n.* **1.** a formal agreement between people or groups or countries. **2.** a document setting out the terms of such an agreement. □ **contract bridge**, a form of bridge in which only tricks bid and won count towards the game.

contract[2] (kŏn-**trakt**) v. **1.** to make or become smaller or shorter. **2.** to arrange or undertake by contract, *they contracted to supply oil to the factory*. **3.** to catch (an illness), to form or acquire (a habit, a debt, etc.). **contraction** n., **contractor** n. □ **contract out**, to arrange for oneself or another to be exempt from something, to refuse to take part in something.

contractual (kŏn-**trakt**-yoo-ăl) adj. of a contract.

contradict v. **1.** to state that (what is said) is untrue or that (a person) is wrong. **2.** to state the opposite of, to be contrary to, *these rumours contradict previous ones*. **contradiction** n., **contradictory** adj. □ **a contradiction in terms**, a statement that contradicts itself.

contradistinction n. in **contradistinction to**, as distinct from, *crossing the Atlantic by air takes a few hours, in contradistinction to the longer journey by sea*.

contraflow n. sending vehicles that are travelling one way into part of a carriageway of which the remainder is used by those travelling in the opposite direction.

contralto (kŏn-**tral** toh) n. (pl. **contraltos**) **1.** the lowest female singing-voice. **2.** a singer with such a voice, a part written for it.

contraption n. (*informal*) an odd-looking gadget or machine.

contrariwise (kŏn-**trair**-i-wyz) adv. on the other hand, in the opposite way.

contrary[1] (**kon**-tră-ri) adj. **1.** opposite in nature, opposed, *the result was contrary to expectation*. **2.** opposite in direction; *delayed by contrary winds*, by unfavourable ones. —n. the opposite. —adv. in opposition, against, *acting contrary to instructions*. □ **on the contrary**, in denial of what is just said and stating that the opposite is true. **to the contrary**, proving or indicating the opposite, *there is no evidence to the contrary*.

contrary[2] (kŏn-**trair**-i) adj. doing the opposite of what is expected or advised, wilful. **contrariness** n.

contrast[1] (**kon**-trahst) n. **1.** the act of contrasting. **2.** a difference clearly seen when things are put together. **3.** something showing such a difference. **4.** the degree of difference between tones or colours.

contrast[2] (kŏn-**trahst**) v. **1.** to compare or oppose two things so as to show their differences. **2.** to show a striking difference when compared.

contra-suggestible adj. tending to believe or do the opposite of what is suggested.

contravene (kon-tră-**veen**) v. to act in opposition to, to conflict with, *contravening the law*. **contravention** (kontră-**ven**-shŏn) n.

contretemps (kawn-trĕ-tahn) n. an unfortunate happening.

contribute v. **1.** to give jointly with others, especially to a common fund. **2.** to supply for publication in a newspaper or magazine or book. **3.** to help to bring about, *drink contributed to his ruin*. **contribution** n., **contributor** n.

contributory (kŏn-**trib**-yoo-ter-i) adj. **1.** contributing to a result; *contributory negligence*, failure to have taken proper precautions against an accident etc. in which one becomes involved. **2.** involving contributions to a fund, *a contributory pension scheme*.

contrite (kon-**tryt**) adj. penitent, feeling guilty. **contritely** adv., **contrition** (kŏn-**trish**-ŏn) n.

contrivance (kŏn-**try**-vănss) n. **1.** contriving. **2.** something contrived, a plan. **3.** a mechanical device.

contrive v. to plan cleverly, to achieve in a clever or resourceful way, to manage. **contriver** n.

control n. **1.** the power to give orders or to restrain something. **2.** a means of restraining or regulating; *the controls of a vehicle*, the devices by which it is operated. **3.** restraint, self-restraint. **4.** a standard of comparison for checking the results of an experiment. **5.** a place where cars taking part in a race must stop for inspection etc. **6.** a personality said to direct the actions of a spiritualist medium. —**control** v. (**controlled**, **controlling**) **1.** to have control of, to regulate. **2.** to restrain. — **controller** n. □ **controlling interest**, ownership of so many shares etc. in a business that the holder can control its policies. **in control**, controlling. **out of control**, no longer able to be controlled. **under control**, controlled, in proper order.

controllable adj. able to be controlled.

controversial (kontrŏ-**ver**-shăl) adj. causing controversy.

controversy (**kon**-trŏ-ver-si or kŏn-**trov**-er-si) n. a prolonged argument or dispute. (¶ The traditional pronunciation **kon**-trŏ-ver-si is strongly preferred.)

controvert (kon-trŏ-vert) v. to deny the truth of, to contradict.

controvertible adj. able to be denied or disproved.

contumely (**kon**-tewm-li) n. **1.** an insult. **2.** a disgrace.

contusion (kŏn-**tew**-zhŏn) n. a bruise.

conundrum (kŏ-**nun**-drŭm) *n.* a hard question, a riddle.

conurbation (kon-er-**bay**-shŏn) *n.* a large urban area formed where towns have spread and merged.

convalesce *v.* to regain health after illness. **convalescence** *n.*, **convalescent** *adj. & n.*

convection *n.* the transmission of heat within a liquid or gas by movement of the heated parts.

convector *n.* a heating appliance that circulates warmed air.

convene *v.* to assemble, to cause to assemble. **convener** *n.*

convenience *n.* 1. the quality of being convenient. 2. something that is convenient. 3. a lavatory, *public conveniences.* □ **at your convenience**, whenever or however you find convenient; *at your earliest convenience*, as soon as you can. **convenience foods**, those that are convenient to use because they need little preparation. **make a convenience of someone**, use his services to an unreasonable extent.

convenient *adj.* 1. easy to use or deal with, not troublesome. 2. with easy access, *convenient for station and shops.* **conveniently** *adv.*

convent *n.* 1. a religious community of nuns. 2. a building in which they live. 3. a **convent school**, a school run by members of a convent.

convention *n.* 1. a formal assembly. 2. a formal agreement, especially between countries, *the Geneva Convention.* 3. an accepted custom.

conventional *adj.* done according to conventions, traditional; *conventional weapons*, non-nuclear. **conventionally** *adv.*

converge *v.* to come to or towards the same point. **convergence** *n.*, **convergent** *adj.*

conversant (kŏn-**ver**-sănt) *adj.* **conversant with**, having a knowledge of.

conversation *n.* informal talk between people. **conversational** *adj.*, **conversationally** *adv.* □ **conversationalist** *n.* a person who is good at conversation.

converse[1] (kŏn-**verss**) *v.* to hold a conversation.

converse[2] (**kon**-verss) *adj.* opposite, contrary. —*n.* an idea or statement that is the opposite of another. —**conversely** *adv.*

convert[1] (kŏn-**vert**) *v.* 1. to change from one form or use or character to another. 2. to be able to be changed, *the sofa converts into a bed.* 3. to cause (a person) to change his attitude or beliefs, *he was converted to Christianity.* 4. to score a goal from a try in Rugby football. **converter** *n.*, **conversion** *n.*

convert[2] (**kon**-vert) *n.* a person who is converted, especially to a religious faith.

convertible *adj.* able to be converted. —*n.* a car with a roof that can be folded down or removed. —**convertibility** *n.*

convex (**kon**-veks) *adj.* curving like the surface of a ball as seen from the outside. **convexly** *adv.*, **convexity** (kŏn-**veks**-iti) *n.*

convey *v.* 1. to carry or transport or transmit. 2. to communicate as an idea or meaning. **conveyable** *adj.*

conveyance *n.* 1. conveying. 2. a means of transporting people, a vehicle.

conveyancing *n.* the business of transferring the legal ownership of land etc.

conveyor *n.* a person or thing that conveys, a continuous moving belt for conveying objects in a factory etc.

convict[1] (kŏn-**vikt**) *v.* to prove or declare (a person) to be guilty of a crime.

convict[2] (**kon**-vikt) *n.* a convicted person who is in prison for his crime.

conviction *n.* 1. convicting. 2. being convicted. 3. a firm opinion or belief. □ **carry conviction**, to be convincing.

convince *v.* to make (a person) feel certain that something is true, *I am convinced of his honesty* or *that he is honest.*

convivial (kŏn-**viv**-iăl) *adj.* sociable and lively. **convivially** *adv.*, **conviviality** (kŏn-vivi-**al**-iti) *n.*

convocation *n.* 1. convoking. 2. an assembly convoked.

convoke *v.* to summon (people) to assemble.

convolution (kon-vŏ-**loo**-shŏn) *n.* a coil, a twist.

convolvulus *n.* a twining plant with trumpet-shaped flowers.

convoy (**kon**-voi) *v.* to escort and protect, especially with an armed force or warships. —*n.* a group of ships or vehicles travelling under escort or together.

convulse *v.* 1. to cause violent movement in. 2. to cause to double up with laughter.

convulsion *n.* 1. a violent movement of the body, especially one caused by muscles contracting involuntarily. 2. a violent upheaval.

convulsive *adj.* like a convulsion, producing upheaval. **convulsively** *adv.*

coo *v.* to make a soft murmuring sound. —*n.* a cooing sound. —*int.* (*slang*) an exclamation of surprise.

cooee *int.* a cry to attract someone's attention.

cook *v.* 1. to prepare (food) for eating, by using heat. 2. to undergo this preparation, *lunch is cooking.* 3. (*informal*) to alter or falsify in order to produce a desired result, *cooked the books.* —*n.* a person who cooks, especially as a job. □ **cook a person's goose**, to ruin his chances. **cooking apple**, an apple suitable for cooking. **cook up**, (*informal*) to concoct; to invent, *cook up an excuse*. **what's cooking?**, (*informal*) what is happening or being planned?

cooker *n*. **1.** a container or stove for cooking food. **2.** a cooking apple.

cookery *n*. the art and practice of cooking; *a cookery book*, one containing recipes.

cookie *n*. **1.** (*Scottish*) a plain bun. **2.** (*Amer.*) a sweet biscuit.

cool *adj*. **1.** moderately cold, not hot or warm. **2.** (of colours) suggesting coolness. **3.** calm and unexcited. **4.** not enthusiastic, *got a cool reception*. **5.** casual and confident, *a cool request for a loan*. **6.** full in amount, *cost me a cool thousand*. —**cool** *n*. **1.** coolness, something cool, *the cool of the evening*. **2.** (*slang*) calmness, composure, *keep your cool*. —*v*. to make or become cool. **coolly** *adv*., **coolness** *n*. □ **cooling tower**, a tower for cooling hot water in an industrial process so that it can be re-used. **cool it**, (*slang*) to calm down. **cool one's heels**, to be kept waiting.

coolant *n*. a fluid used for cooling machinery etc.

coolie *n*. an unskilled native labourer in Eastern countries.

coop *n*. a cage for poultry. —*v*. to confine or shut in, *he is cooped up in his room*.

Co-op *n*. (*informal*) **1.** a Co-operative Society. **2.** a shop belonging to such a society.

cooper *n*. a person whose job is making and repairing barrels and tubs.

co-operate *v*. to work with another or others. **co-operation** *n*., **co-operator** *n*.

co-operative *adj*. **1.** of co-operation. **2.** willing to co-operate. **3.** owned and run jointly by its members with profits shared between them. —*n*. a farm or society organized on a co-operative basis. —**co-operatively** *adv*.

co-opt *v*. to appoint to become a member of a group by the invitation of its existing members. **co-option** *n*.

co-ordinate¹ (koh-**ord**-inăt) *adj*. equal in importance. —*n*. **1.** a co-ordinate thing. **2.** (usually *coordinate*) any of the magnitudes used to give the position of a point etc., e.g. latitude and longitude. — **co-ordinately** *adv*. □ **co-ordinates** *pl. n*. items of women's outer clothing that can be worn together harmoniously.

co-ordinate² (koh-**ord**-in-ayt) *v*. to bring (parts etc.) into a proper relationship, to

work or cause to work together efficiently. **co-ordination** *n*., **co-ordinator** *n*.

coot *n*. a kind of water-bird, especially one with a horny white plate on the forehead.

cop¹ *v*. (**copped**, **copping**) (*slang*) to catch, *you'll cop it!* —*n*. (*slang*) **1.** capture, *it's a fair cop*. **2.** a policeman. □ **cop out**, (*Amer. slang*) to escape; to fail to do what one promised. **cop-out** *n*. (*Amer. slang*) *a failure of this kind*. **not much cop**, (*slang*) not worth valuing highly.

cop² *n*. a spool (of yarn).

cope¹ *v*. to manage successfully. **cope with**, to deal successfully with.

cope² *n*. a long loose cloak worn by clergy in certain ceremonies and processions.

copeck (**koh**-pek) *n*. a Russian coin, one hundredth of a rouble.

Copenhagen (koh-pĕn-**hay**-gĕn) the capital of Denmark.

copier *n*. a copying machine.

co-pilot *n*. a second pilot in an aircraft.

coping (**koh**-ping) *n*. the top row of masonry (usually sloping) in a wall; *a coping-stone*, one used in this.

copious *adj*. existing in large amounts, plentiful. **copiously** *adv*.

copper¹ *n*. **1.** a reddish brown metal. **2.** a coin made of copper or a copper alloy. **3.** a reddish-brown colour. —**copper** *adj*. **1.** made of copper. **2.** reddish-brown. □ **copper beech**, a beech-tree with copper-coloured leaves.

copper² *n*. (*slang*) a policeman.

copperplate *n*. neat clear handwriting.

coppice *n*. a wood of small trees and undergrowth, grown for periodic cutting.

copse *n*. a coppice.

copulate (**kop**-yoo-layt) *v*. to come together sexually as in the act of mating. **copulation** *n*.

copy *n*. **1.** a thing made to look like another. **2.** one specimen of a book or document or newspaper. **3.** material for printing; *the trial made good copy*, interesting material for newspaper reporting. —**copy** *v*. (**copied**, **copying**) **1.** to make a copy of. **2.** to try to do the same as, to imitate. □ **copy-cat** *n*. (*slang*) a person who copies another's actions. **copy-typing** *n*. making typewritten copies of documents. **copy-typist** *n*.

copyist *n*. a person who makes copies of documents etc.

copyright *n*. the sole legal right to print, publish, perform, film, or record a literary or artistic or musical work. —*adj*. (of material) protected by copyright.

coquette (kŏ-**ket**) *n*. a woman who flirts. **coquettish** *adj*.

coracle (ko-ră-kŭl) *n.* a small wickerwork boat covered with watertight material.

coral *n.* 1. a hard red, pink, or white substance built by tiny sea creatures; *coral reef,* one formed by coral. 2. reddish-pink colour. —*adj.* reddish-pink.

corbel (kor-bĕl) *n.* a stone or timber projection from a wall, to support something. **corbelled** *adj.*

cord *n.* 1. long thin flexible material made from twisted strands, a piece of this. 2. a similar structure in the body, *the spinal cord.* 3. corduroy material. —*v.* to fasten or bind with cord.

corded *adj.* (of fabric) with raised ridges.

cordial *n.* an essence flavoured with fruit etc., diluted to make a drink. —*adj.* warm and friendly, *cordial greetings.* —**cordially** *adv.,* **cordiality** (kor-di-al-iti) *n.*

cordite (kor-dyt) *n.* a smokeless explosive used as a propellant in bullets and shells.

cordon *n.* 1. a ring of people or military posts etc. enclosing or guarding something. 2. an ornamental cord or braid worn as a badge of honour. 3. a fruit tree with its branches pruned so that it grows as a single stem, usually against a wall or along wires. —*v.* to enclose with a cordon.

cordon bleu (kor-dawn bler) of the highest degree of excellence in cookery.

corduroy *n.* cotton cloth with velvety ridges. **corduroys** *pl. n.* trousers made of corduroy fabric.

core *n.* 1. the horny central part of certain fruits, containing the seeds. 2. the central or most important part of something. 3. a unit in the structure of a computer memory that can represent one bit of data. 4. the part of a nuclear reactor that contains the fissile material. —*v.* to remove the core from. —**corer** *n.* □ **to the core,** thoroughly, entirely.

co-respondent (koh-ri-spon-dĕnt) *n.* the person with whom the person proceeded against in a divorce suit (the *respondent*) is said to have committed adultery.

corgi *n.* (*pl.* corgis) a dog of a small Welsh breed with a fox-like head.

coriander (ko-ri-and-er) *n.* a plant with seeds used for flavouring.

Corinthian (kŏ-rinth-iăn) *adj.* 1. of Corinth, a city of ancient Greece. 2. of the *Corinthian order,* the most ornate of the five classical orders of architecture.

cork *n.* 1. a light tough substance, the thick outer bark of a kind of South European oak. 2. a piece of this used as a float. 3. a bottle-stopper made of this or other material.—*v.* to close or stop up with a cork. □ **corked** *adj.* (of wine) contaminated by a decayed cork.

corker *n.* (*slang*) an excellent person or thing.

corkscrew *n.* 1. a tool for extracting corks from bottles. 2. a spiral thing.

corm *n.* a rounded underground base of a stem, from the top of which buds sprout.

cormorant *n.* a large black sea-bird.

corn[1] *n.* 1. grain or seed, especially of cereal. 2. plants that produce grain. 3. (*Amer.*) maize. 4. a single grain of wheat or pepper etc. 5. (*slang*) something corny.

corn[2] *n.* a small tender area of horny hardened skin on the foot.

corncrake *n.* a bird with a harsh cry.

cornea (korn-iă) *n.* the tough transparent outer covering of the eyeball. **corneal** *adj.*

corned *adj.* preserved in salt, *corned beef.*

cornelian *n.* a reddish or white semi-precious stone.

corner *n.* 1. the angle or area where two lines or sides meet or where two streets join. 2. a hidden or remote place. 3. a free hit or kick from the corner of the field in hockey or Association football. 4. a virtual monopoly of a certain type of goods or services, enabling the holder to control the price. —**corner** *v.* 1. to drive into a corner, to force into a position from which there is no escape. 2. to obtain (all or most of something) for oneself, to establish a monopoly of. 3. to move round a corner, *the car had cornered too fast.* □ **cornerstone** *n.* a basis, a vital foundation, *hard work is the corner-stone of success.*

cornet *n.* 1. a brass musical instrument like a small trumpet. 2. a cone-shaped wafer holding ice-cream.

cornflakes *pl. n.* a breakfast cereal of toasted maize flakes.

cornflour *n.* flour made from maize or rice, used to thicken sauces.

cornflower *n.* a plant that grows wild in cornfields (especially a blue-flowered kind), or cultivated as a garden plant.

cornice (korn-iss) *n.* a band of ornamental moulding round the wall of a room just below the ceiling or crowning a building.

Cornish *adj.* of Cornwall. —*n.* the ancient language of Cornwall. □ **Cornish pasty,** a mixture of meat and vegetables baked in pastry.

cornucopia (kor-new-koh-piă) *n.* a horn of plenty, a horn-shaped container overflowing with fruit and flowers.

Cornwall a county of England.

corny *adj.* (cornier, corniest) hackneyed, repeated so often that people are tired of it, over-sentimental.

corollary (kŏ-rol-er-i) *n.* a natural consequence or result, something that follows logically after something else is proved.

corona (kŏ-**roh**-nă) *n.* a small circle or glow of light round something.

coronary (ko-**rŏn**-er-i) *adj.* of the arteries supplying blood to the heart. —*n.* **1.** a coronary artery. **2.** a **coronary thrombosis**, blockage of a coronary artery by a clot of blood.

coronation *n.* the ceremony of crowning a king or queen or consort.

coroner (ko-**rŏn**-er) *n.* an officer who holds an enquiry into the cause of a death thought to be from violence or unnatural causes, or in cases of treasure trove.

coronet *n.* **1.** a small crown. **2.** a band of gold or jewels etc. for the head.

corporal[1] *adj.* of the body. **corporal punishment,** punishment by whipping or beating.

corporal[2] *n.* a non-commissioned officer ranking just below sergeant.

corporate (**kor**-per-ăt) *adj.* **1.** shared by members of a group, *corporate responsibility.* **2.** united in one group, *a corporate body.*

corporation *n.* **1.** a group of people authorized to act as an individual, especially in business. **2.** a group of people elected to govern a town. **3.** (*informal*) a protruding abdomen.

corps (*pr.* kor) *n.* (*pl.* corps, *pr.* korz) **1.** a military force, an army unit, *the Royal Army Medical Corps.* **2.** a body of people engaged in a special activity, *the diplomatic corps.*

corpse *n.* a dead body.

corpulent (**kor**-pew-lĕnt) *adj.* having a bulky body, fat. **corpulence** *n.*

corpus *n.* a large collection of writings etc.

Corpus Christi a Christian festival in honour of the Eucharist, celebrated on the Thursday after Trinity Sunday.

corpuscle (**kor**-pŭs-ŭl) *n.* one of the red or white cells in the blood.

corral (kŏ-**rahl**) *n.* (*Amer.*) an enclosure for horses, cattle, etc. —*v.* (**corralled, corralling**) (*Amer.*) to put into a corral.

correct *adj.* **1.** true, accurate. **2.** proper, in accordance with an approved way of behaving or working. —**correct** *v.* **1.** to make correct, to set right by altering or adjusting. **2.** to mark the errors in. **3.** to point out faults in (a person), to punish (a person or a fault). —**correctly** *adv.,* **correctness** *n.,* **corrector** *n.*

correction *n.* **1.** correcting, being corrected. **2.** an alteration made to something that was incorrect.

corrective *adj.* correcting what is bad or harmful. —*n.* something that corrects.

correlate (**ko**-rĕl-ayt) *v.* **1.** to compare or connect systematically. **2.** to have a systematic connection. **correlation** *n.,* **correlative** (kŏ-**rel**-ătiv) *adj.*

correspond *v.* **1.** to be in harmony or agreement, *this corresponds with what I've heard.* **2.** to be similar or equivalent, *an assembly that corresponds to our parliament.* **3.** to write letters to each other.

correspondence *n.* **1.** corresponding, harmony. **2.** communicating by writing letters, the letters themselves. □ **correspondence course,** instruction by means of materials sent by post.

correspondent *n.* **1.** a person who writes letters. **2.** a person who is employed to gather news and contribute reports to a newspaper or radio station etc.

corridor *n.* a long narrow passage, especially one from which doors open into rooms or compartments.

corrigendum (ko-rig-**en**-dŭm) *n.* (*pl.* corrigenda) an error, especially in a printed book, for which a correction is printed.

corroborate (kŏ-**rob**-er-ayt) *v.* to get or give supporting evidence. **corroboration** *n.,* **corroborative** (kŏ-**rob**-er-ătiv) *adj.,* **corroboratory** (kŏ-**rob**-er-ă-ter-i) *adj.*

corrode *v.* to destroy gradually by chemical action, *rust corrodes metal.* **corrosion** *n.,* **corrosive** *adj.*

corrugated *adj.* shaped into alternate ridges and grooves, *corrugated iron.*

corrupt *adj.* **1.** dishonest, accepting bribes. **2.** immoral, wicked. **3.** decaying. —**corrupt** *v.* **1.** to cause to become dishonest or immoral, to persuade to accept bribes. **2.** to spoil, to taint. —**corruption** *n.*

corruptible *adj.* able to be corrupted. **corruptibility** *n.*

corsair (**kor**-sair) *n.* (*old use*) **1.** a pirate ship. **2.** a pirate.

corset *n.* a close-fitting undergarment worn to shape or support the body.

corsetière (kor-sit-**yair**) *n.* a woman whose job is to make or fit corsets.

cortège (kor-**tayzh**) *n.* a funeral procession.

cortex *n.* **1.** an outer layer of tissue (e.g. of a kidney or a plant stem), the bark of a tree. **2.** the outer grey matter of the brain. **cortical** *adj.*

cortisone (**kor**-tiz-ohn) *n.* a hormone produced by the adrenal glands or made synthetically.

corvette (kor-**vet**) *n.* a small fast gunboat designed for escorting merchant ships.

cos (*pr.* koss) *n.* a kind of lettuce with long leaves.

'cos (*pr.* koz) *adv.* & *conj.* (*informal*) because.

cosh *n.* a weighted weapon for hitting people. —*v.* to hit with a cosh.

cosine *n.* (in a right-angled triangle) the ratio of the length of a side adjacent to one of the acute angles to the length of the hypotenuse.

cosmetic *n.* a substance for beautifying the body, especially the face. —*adj.* for beautifying or improving the appearance, *cosmetic surgery.*

cosmic (**koz**-mik) *adj.* of the universe. **cosmic rays,** high-energy radiation that reaches the earth from outer space.

cosmonaut *n.* a Russian astronaut.

cosmopolitan *adj.* **1.** of or from many parts of the world, containing people from many countries, *a cosmopolitan crowd* or *city.* **2.** free from national prejudices and at home in all parts of the world, *a cosmopolitan outlook.* —*n.* a cosmopolitan person.

cosmos[1] (**koz**-moss) *n.* the universe.

cosmos[2] (**koz**-moss) *n.* a garden plant with pink, white, or purple flowers.

Cossack (**koss**-ak) *n.* a member of a people of south Russia, famous as horsemen. **Cossack hat,** a brimless fur hat widening towards the top.

cosset (**koss**-it) *v.* (cosseted, cosseting) to pamper.

cost *n.* **1.** an amount given or required as payment. **2.** an expenditure of time or labour, a loss suffered in achieving something, *succeeded at the cost of his life.* —**cost** *v.* (cost in sense 3 costed), costing) **1.** to be obtainable at a certain price. **2.** to require a certain effort or loss etc. **3.** to estimate the cost involved; *a costing clerk,* one who does this for a firm. □ **at all costs,** no matter what the risk or loss involved may be. **at cost,** at cost price. **cost accountant,** one employed to supervise a firm's expenditure. **cost-effective** *adj.* producing useful results in relation to its cost. **cost of living,** the general level of prices. **cost price,** the price at which a thing is bought by someone who intends to re-sell it or process it. **costs** *pl. n.,* the expenses involved in having something settled in a lawcourt. **to one's cost,** involving bitter experience.

co-star *n.* a stage or cinema star performing with another or others of equal importance. —*v.* (co-starred, co-starring) to perform or include as a co-star.

Costa Rica (kostă **ree**-kǎ) a country in Central America. **Costa Rican** *adj.* & *n.*

costermonger (**kost**-er-mung-er) *n.* a person who sells fruit etc. from a barrow in the street.

costly *adj.* (costlier, costliest) costing much, expensive. **costliness** *n.*

costume *n.* **1.** a style of clothes belonging to a particular place or period or group or suitable for a particular activity, *peasant costume*; *a skating costume.* **2.** special garments worn by an actor; *costume plays,* in which the actors wear historical costume. □ **costume jewellery,** jewellery made of inexpensive materials.

cosy *adj.* (cosier, cosiest) warm and comfortable. —*n.* a cover placed over a teapot or boiled egg to keep it hot. —**cosily** *adv.,* **cosiness** *n.*

cot *n.* a child's bed with high sides. **cot-death,** an unexplained death of a sleeping baby.

coterie (**koh**-ter-i) *n.* an exclusive group of people.

cotoneaster (kŏ-toh-ni-**ast**-er) *n.* a shrub or tree with red berries.

Cotswolds *pl. n.* the Cotswold Hills, in Gloucestershire. **Cotswold** *adj.*

cottage *n.* a small simple house in the country. **cottage cheese,** soft white cheese made from curds without pressing. **cottage industry,** one that can be carried on at home, e.g. knitting and some kinds of weaving. **cottage loaf,** a round loaf with a small mass on top of a larger one. **cottage piano,** a small upright piano. **cottage pie,** a dish of minced meat topped with mashed potato. **cottage suite,** a small three-piece suite of furniture.

cottager *n.* a person who lives in a cottage.

cotton *n.* **1.** a soft white substance round the seeds of a tropical plant. **2.** the plant itself. **3.** thread made from this. **4.** fabric made from this thread. —*v.* **cotton on,** (*slang*) to understand. □ **cotton wool,** raw cotton as prepared for wadding.

cottony *adj.* like cotton.

cotyledon (kot-i-lee-dŏn) *n.* the first leaf growing from a seed.

couch *n.* **1.** a piece of furniture like a sofa but with the back extending along half its length and only one raised end. **2.** a sofa or settee. **3.** a bed-like structure on which a doctor's patient can lie for examination. —*v.* to express in words of a certain kind, *the request was couched in polite terms.*

couchette (koo-**shet**) *n.* a sleeping-berth in a railway compartment that can be converted to form an ordinary compartment with seats during the day.

couch-grass *n.* a kind of grass with long creeping roots.

cougar (**koog**-er) *n.* (*Amer.*) a puma.

cough *v.* **1.** to send out air or other matter from the lungs with a sudden sharp sound. **2.** (*slang*) to reveal information. —**cough** *n.* **1.** an act or sound of coughing. **2.** an illness causing frequent coughing. □ **cough up**, (*slang*) to reveal (information); to give (money etc.) with some reluctance.

could *auxiliary verb* **1**. used as the past tense of can². **2**. to feel inclined to, *I could laugh for joy*. □ **could be**, might be; *he could have been delayed*, this is possible.

couldn't = could not.

council *n*. **1**. an assembly of people to advise on or discuss or organize something. **2**. an elected body organizing municipal affairs. □ **council house** *or* **flat**, one owned and let by a municipal council. **council estate**, an estate of council houses.
¶ Do not confuse with counsel.

councillor *n*. a member of a council. ¶ Do not confuse with counsellor.

counsel *n*. **1**. advice, suggestions, *give counsel*. **2**. (*pl*. counsel) a barrister or group of barristers giving advice in a legal case. —*v*. (counselled, counselling) to advise, to give advice to people professionally on social problems. □ **a counsel of perfection**, advice that is ideal in theory but impossible to follow in practice. **keep one's own counsel**, to keep one's views or plans secret. **take counsel with**, to consult. ¶ Do not confuse with council.

counsellor *n*. an adviser. ¶ Do not confuse with councillor.

count¹ *v*. **1**. to find the total of. **2**. to say or name the numbers in order. **3**. to include or be included in a reckoning, *six of us, counting the dog*; *this will count against him*, will be a disadvantage to his reputation. **4**. to be important, to be worth reckoning; *fine words count for nothing*, are of no value. **5**. to regard or consider, *I should count it an honour*. —**count** *n*. **1**. counting, a calculation. **2**. a number reached by counting, a total. **3**. one of the points being considered, one of the charges against an accused person, *he was found guilty on all counts*. □ **count down**, to count numerals backwards to zero, as in the procedure before launching a rocket. **count-down** *n*. this procedure. **count in**, to include in a reckoning. **count on**, to rely on; to expect confidently. **count one's chickens before they are hatched**, to assume that something will be successful before this is certain. **count out**, to count one by one from a stock; to exclude from a reckoning; (of a referee) to count up to ten seconds over (a boxer or wrestler who has been knocked or fallen to the floor). **count up**, to find the sum of. **out for the count**, defeated in a boxing match by failing to rise within ten seconds after being knocked to the floor;

(*informal*) out of action. **take the count**, to be out for the count in boxing.

count² *n*. a foreign nobleman corresponding to an earl.

countable *adj*. able to be counted.

countenance *n*. **1**. the expression of the face. **2**. an appearance of approval, *lending countenance to their plan*. —*v*. to give approval to.

counter¹ *n*. **1**. a flat-topped fitment over which goods are sold or served or business is transacted with customers. **2**. a small disc used for keeping account in table-games. **3**. an apparatus for counting things. □ **under the counter**, sold or transacted in an underhand way.

counter² *adv*. in the opposite direction. —*adj*. opposed. —*v*. to hinder or defeat by an opposing action.

counteract *v*. to reduce or prevent the effects of. **counteraction** *n*.

counter-attack *n*. an attack directed against an enemy who has already attacked or invaded. *v*. to make a counter-attack.

counterbalance *n*. a weight or influence that balances another. —*v*. to act as a counterbalance to.

counterblast *n*. a powerful retort.

countercheck *n*. an obstruction checking movement or operating against another.

counter-claim *n*. a claim made in opposition to another claim.

counter-espionage (es-pi-ón-ah*zh*) *n*. action taken to uncover and counteract enemy spying.

counterfeit (**cownt**-er-feet) *adj*. fake. —*n*. a fake. —*v*. to fake.

counterfoil *n*. a detachable section of a cheque or receipt etc. kept by the sender as a record.

counter-intelligence *n*. counter-espionage.

countermand *v*. to cancel (a command or order).

countermarch *v*. to march in the opposite direction from before.

countermeasure *n*. action taken to counteract a threat or danger etc.

counter-offensive *n*. a large-scale counter-attack.

counterpane *n*. a bedspread.

counterpart *n*. a person or thing corresponding to another in position or use.

counterpoint *n*. **1**. a melody added as an accompaniment to another. **2**. a method of combining melodies according to fixed rules.

counterpoise *n*. a counterbalance. —*v*. to counterbalance.

counter-productive *adj.* having the opposite of the desired effect.

Counter-Reformation *n.* the reformation in the Church of Rome following on the Protestant Reformation.

countersign *n.* a password. —*v.* to add another signature to (a document) to give it authority.

countersink *v.* (countersunk, countersinking) to enlarge the top of (a hole) so that the head of a screw or bolt will lie level with or below the surface, to sink (a screw etc.) in such a hole.

countervail *v.* **1.** to counterbalance. **2.** to avail against.

counterweight *n.* a counterbalancing weight or influence. —*v.* **1.** to counterbalance. **2.** to fit with a counterweight.

countess *n.* **1.** the wife or widow of a count or earl. **2.** a woman holding the rank of a count or earl.

countless *adj.* too many to be counted.

countrified *adj.* having the characteristics of the country or country life.

country *n.* **1.** a nation or State, the land it occupies. **2.** land consisting of fields and woods with few houses or other buildings. **3.** an area of land with certain features, *hill country.* **4.** country-and-western. □ **across country,** across fields, not keeping to main roads or to a direct road. **country-and-western** *n.* rural or cowboy songs sung to a guitar etc. **country dance,** a traditional English dance, often with couples face to face in lines. **go to the country,** to test public opinion by holding a general election.

countryman *n.* (*pl.* countrymen) **1.** a man living in the country, not in a town. **2.** a man of one's own country, a compatriot. **countrywoman** *n.*

countryside *n.* country districts.

county *n.* **1.** one of the main areas into which a country is divided for purposes of local government. **2.** the people of such an area. **3.** the families of high social level long-established in a county. □ **county court,** a local court where civil cases are tried.

coup (*pr.* koo) *n.* (*pl.* coups, *pr.* kooz) a sudden action taken to obtain power or achieve a desired result.

coup de grâce (koo dĕ grahs) a stroke or blow that puts an end to something.

coup d'état (koo day-tah) the sudden overthrowing of a government by force or by unconstitutional means.

coupé (koo-pay) *n.* a closed two-door car with a sloping back.

couple *n.* **1.** two people or things considered together. **2.** a man and woman who are engaged or married. **3.** partners in a dance. —**couple** *v.* **1.** to fasten or link together, to join by a coupling. **2.** to copulate.

couplet (**kup**-lit) *n.* two successive lines of verse that rhyme and have the same metre.

coupling *n.* a device for connecting two railway carriages or parts of machinery.

coupon *n.* **1.** a detachable ticket or part of a document etc. that entitles the holder to receive something or that can be used as an application form. **2.** an entry-form for a football pool or similar competition.

courage *n.* the ability to control fear when facing danger or pain, bravery. **have the courage of one's convictions,** to be brave enough to do what one feels to be right.

courageous (kŏ-**ray**-jŭs) *adj.* having or showing courage. **courageously** *adv.*

courgette (koor-*zh*et) *n.* a variety of small vegetable marrow.

courier (**koor**-i-er) *n.* **1.** a messenger carrying news or important papers. **2.** a person employed to guide and assist a group of tourists.

course *n.* **1.** an onward movement in space or time, *in the ordinary course of events.* **2.** the direction taken or intended, *the course of the river; the ship was off course.* **3.** a series of things one can do to achieve something, *your best course is to start again.* **4.** a series of talks or lessons or treatment etc., *a course of lectures* or *injections.* **5.** an area of land on which golf is played, a stretch of land or water over which a race takes place. **6.** a continuous layer of brick or stone etc. in a wall. **7.** one of the parts of a meal, *the first course was soup.* —**course** *v.* **1.** to hunt (especially hares) with hounds that follow game by sight not by scent. **2.** to follow a course. **3.** to move or flow freely, *blood coursed through his veins.* □ **in course of,** in the process of, *the bridge is in course of construction.* **in the course of,** during; *in the course of nature,* as part of the normal sequence of events; *in the course of time,* after some time has passed. **of course,** without a doubt, as was to be expected; admittedly.

court *n.* **1.** a courtyard. **2.** a yard surrounded by houses, opening off a street. **3.** an enclosed area for certain games, e.g. squash, tennis. **4.** a sovereign's establishment with attendants, councillors, etc.; *the Court of St. James's,* the British sovereign's court. **5.** a lawcourt. —**court** *v.* **1.** to try to win the favour or support of. **2.** to try to win the affection of, especially in order to marry. **3.** (of animals) to try to attract sexually. **4.** to behave as though trying to provoke something harmful, *courting danger*. □ **court-card** *n*. the king, queen, or jack in playing-cards. **Court of Session,** the supreme civil court in Scotland. **pay court to,** to pay special attention to a person in order to win their favour or interest.

courteous (ker-ti-ŭs) *adj*. polite. **courteously** *adv*.

courtesan (kor-ti-**zan**) *n*. (*old use*) a prostitute with wealthy or upper-class clients.

courtesy (**kur**-ti-si) *n*. courteous behaviour. **by courtesy of,** by the permission or favour of. **courtesy light,** a light (in a motor vehicle) that is switched on by opening the door.

courtier (**kor**-ti-er) *n*. (*old use*) one of a sovereign's companions at court.

courtly (**kort**-li) *adj*. dignified and polite. **courtliness** *n*.

court martial (*pl*. courts martial) **1.** a court for trying offences against military law. **2.** trial by such a court. **court martial** *v*. (court-martialled, court-martialling) to try by a court martial.

courtship *n*. courting, the period during which this takes place.

courtyard *n*. a space enclosed by walls or buildings.

cousin *n*. a child of one's uncle or aunt (also called *first cousin*); *second cousin*, a child of one's parent's first cousin. **cousinly** *adv*.

couture (koo-**tewr**) *n*. the design and making of high-class fashionable clothes.

couturier (koo-**tewr**-i-ay) *n*. a designer of high-class fashionable clothes.

cove¹ *n*. a small bay.

cove² *n*. (*slang*) a man.

coven (**kuv**-ĕn) *n*. an assembly, especially of witches.

covenant (**kuv**-ĕn-ănt) *n*. a formal agreement, a contract. —*v*. to undertake by covenant.

Coventry (**kov**-ĕn-tri) *n*. **send a person to Coventry,** to refuse to speak to him or associate with him.

cover *v*. **1.** to place a thing over or in front of, to conceal or protect in this way. **2.** to spread (a thing) over; *covered with shame,* obviously ashamed. **3.** to lie or extend over, to occupy the surface of, *the factory covers a large area*; *a covering letter,* an explanatory letter sent with a document or goods. **4.** to travel over (a distance), *we covered ten miles a day*. **5.** to protect by dominating the approach to, to have within range of one's gun(s), to keep a gun aimed at. **6.** to protect by providing insurance or a guarantee, *covering you*

against fire or theft. **7.** to be enough money to pay for, *£10 will cover the fare*. **8.** to include, to deal with (a subject). **9.** to investigate or report for a newspaper etc., *who is covering the conference?* —**cover** *n*. **1.** a thing that covers. **2.** the binding of a book etc., either half of this. **3.** a wrapper or envelope. **4.** a place or area giving shelter or protection, *there was no cover*. **5.** a supporting force etc. protecting another from attack, *fighter cover*. **6.** a screen or pretence, *under cover of friendship*. **7.** insurance against loss or damage etc. **8.** a place laid at table for a meal. □ **cover charge,** an extra charge per person in a restaurant. **cover for,** to deputize temporarily for. **cover much ground,** to travel far; to deal with a variety of topics. **cover up,** to conceal (a thing or fact). **cover-up** *n*. concealment, especially of facts. **under separate cover,** in a separate envelope or package.

coverage *n*. **1.** the act or fact of covering. **2.** the area or amount covered.

covert (**kuv**-ert) *n*. **1.** an area of thick undergrowth in which animals hide. **2.** a bird's feather covering the base of another. —*adj*. concealed, done secretly, *covert glances*. —**covertly** *adv*.

covet (**kuv**-it) *v*. (coveted, coveting) to desire eagerly, especially something belonging to another person.

covetous (**kuv**-it-ŭs) *adj*. coveting. **covetously** *adv*., **covetousness** *n*.

covey (**kuv**-i) *n*. (*pl*. coveys) a brood or small flock of partridges.

cow¹ *n*. **1.** the fully-grown female of cattle or of certain other large animals (e.g. elephant, whale, seal). **2.** (*slang*) a woman one dislikes. **3.** (*Austral. slang*) something bad or difficult, *it's a fair cow*.

cow² *v*. to subdue by frightening with threats or force.

coward *n*. a person who lacks courage. **cowardly** *adj*., **cowardliness** *n*.

cowardice *n*. lack of courage.

cowboy *n*. **1.** a man in charge of grazing cattle in the western USA. **2.** (*informal*) a person who uses reckless or unscrupulous methods in business etc.

cower *v*. to crouch or shrink back in fear.

cowl *n*. **1.** a monk's hood or hooded robe. **2.** a hood-shaped covering e.g. on a chimney.

cowling *n*. a removable metal cover over an engine.

cowman *n*. (*pl*. cowmen) a man employed to look after cattle.

cowrie *n*. a mollusc found in tropical seas, with a glossy often brightly-coloured shell.

cowshed *n.* a shed where cattle are kept when not at pasture.

cowslip *n.* a wild plant with small fragrant yellow flowers.

cox *n.* a coxswain —*v.* to act as cox of a racing-boat.

coxswain (**kok**-swayn, *naval pr.* **kok**-sŭn) *n.* 1. a person who steers a rowing-boat. 2. a sailor in charge of a ship's boat. 3. a senior petty officer on certain naval vessels.

coy *n.* pretending to be shy or embarrassed, bashful. **coyly** *adv.*, **coyness** *n.*

coypu (**koi**-poo) *n.* a beaver-like water animal, originally from South America.

crab *n.* 1. a ten-footed shellfish. 2. its flesh as food. 3. *the Crab,* a sign of the zodiac, Cancer. —*v.* (crabbed, crabbing) (*informal*) to find fault with, to grumble. □ **crab-apple** *n.* a kind of small sour apple.

crabbed (**krab**-id) *adj.* 1. bad-tempered. 2. (of writing) difficult to read or decipher.

crabby *adj.* bad-tempered.

crack *n.* 1. a sudden sharp explosive noise. 2. a sharp blow. 3. (*informal*) a wisecrack, a joke. 4. a chink. 5. a line of division where something is broken but has not come completely apart. —*adj.* (*informal*) first-rate. —**crack** *v.* 1. to make or cause to make a sudden sharp explosive sound; *cracked his head against the wall,* gave his head a sharp blow. 2. to tell (a joke). 3. to break with a sharp sound. 4. to break into (a safe etc.). 5. to find the solution to (a code or problem). 6. to break without coming completely apart. 7. (of a voice) to become suddenly harsh, especially with emotion. 8. to collapse under strain, to cease to resist. 9. to break down (heavy oils) in order to produce lighter ones. □ **crack-brained** *adj.* (*informal*) crazy. **crack down on,** (*informal*) to take severe measures against (something illegal or against rules). **crack of dawn,** daybreak. **crack of doom,** a thunder-peal announcing Judgement Day. **crack up,** (*informal*) to praise highly; to have a physical or mental breakdown. **get cracking,** (*informal*) to get busy on work that is waiting to be done. **have a crack at,** (*informal*) to attempt.

cracked *adj.* (*slang*) crazy.

cracker *n.* 1. a firework that explodes with a sharp crack. 2. a small paper toy made so as to explode harmlessly when the ends are pulled. 3. a thin dry biscuit. □ **crackers** *adj.* (*slang*) crazy.

cracking *adj.* (*slang*) very good.

crackle *v.* to make or cause to make a series of slight cracking sounds. —*n.* these sounds.

crackling *n.* crisp skin on roast pork.

crackpot *n.* (*slang*) a person with crazy or impractical ideas.

cradle *n.* 1. a small bed or cot for a baby, usually on rockers. 2. a place where something originates, *the cradle of civilization.* 3. a supporting framework or structure. —*v.* to hold or support as if in a cradle.

craft *n.* 1. an occupation in which skill is needed. 2. such a skill or technique. 3. cunning, deceit. 4. (*pl.* craft) a ship or boat or raft, an aircraft or spacecraft.

craftsman *n.* (*pl.* craftsmen) a workman who is skilled in a craft. **craftsmanship** *n.*

crafty *adj.* (craftier, craftiest) cunning, using underhand methods. **craftily** *adv.*, **craftiness** *n.*

crag *n.* a steep or rugged rock. **craggy** *adj.*, **cragginess** *n.*

cram *v.* (crammed, cramming) 1. to force into too small a space so that the container is overfull. 2. to overfill in this way. 3. to study intensively for an examination.

cramp *n.* 1. sudden painful involuntary tightening of a muscle. 2. a metal bar with bent ends for holding masonry etc. together. —*v.* to keep within too narrow limits. □ **cramp a person's style,** to prevent him from acting freely or showing his best abilities.

cramped *adj.* 1. put or kept in too narrow a space, without room to move. 2. (of writing) small and with letters close together.

crampon (**kram**-pŏn) *n.* an iron plate with spikes, worn on boots for walking or climbing on ice.

cranberry *n.* 1. the small acid red berry of a kind of shrub, used for making jelly and sauce. 2. the shrub itself.

crane *n.* 1. a large wading bird with long legs, neck, and bill. 2. an apparatus for moving heavy objects, usually by suspending them from a jib by ropes or chains. —*v.* to stretch (one's neck) in order to see something.

crane-fly *n.* a flying insect with very long legs.

cranium (**kray**-ni-ŭm) *n.* the bones enclosing the brain, the skull. **cranial** *adj.*

crank¹ *n.* an L-shaped part for converting to-and-fro motion into circular motion. —*v.* to cause to move by means of a crank. □ **crankshaft** *n.* a shaft turned by a crank.

crank² *n.* a person with very strange ideas. **cranky** *adj.*, **crankiness** *n.*

cranny *n.* a crevice.

crap *n.* (*vulgar*) 1. faeces. 2. nonsense, rubbish. **crappy** *adj.*

crape *n.* black crêpe formerly used for mourning.

craps *n.* (*Amer.*) a gambling game played with a pair of dice; *shooting craps*, playing this game.

crash[1] *n.* **1.** a sudden violent noise like that of something breaking by impact. **2.** a violent collision or fall. **3.** financial collapse. —**crash** *v.* **1.** to make a crash, to move or go with a crash. **2.** to cause (a vehicle or aircraft) to have a collision, to be involved in a crash. **3.** (*informal*) to enter without permission, to gatecrash; *crash the lights*, to drive past a red light without stopping. **4.** to collapse financially. —*adj.* involving intense effort to achieve something rapidly, *a crash programme.* □ **crash barrier**, a protective fence erected where there is danger of vehicles leaving a road. **crash-dive** *n.* a sudden dive by an aircraft or submarine, especially in an emergency, (*v.*) to dive in this way. **crash-helmet** *n.* a padded helmet worn to protect the head in case of a crash. **crash-land** *v.* to land (an aircraft) in an emergency, especially with damage to it; to be landed in this way. **crash-landing** *n.*

crash[2] *n.* a kind of coarse linen or cotton fabric.

crashing *adj.* (*informal*) overwhelming, *a crashing bore.*

crass *adj.* **1.** gross, *crass stupidity.* **2.** very stupid. **crassly** *adv.*, **crassness** *n.*

crate *n.* **1.** a packing-case made of wooden slats. **2.** (*slang*) an old aircraft or car. **3.** a divided container for holding milk-bottles. —*v.* to pack into a crate.

crater *n.* a bowl-shaped cavity or hollow.

cravat (krǎ-**vat**) *n.* **1.** a short scarf. **2.** a necktie.

crave *v.* **1.** to long for, to have a strong desire. **2.** to ask earnestly for, *crave mercy* or *for mercy.*

craven *adj.* cowardly.

craving *n.* a strong desire, a longing.

crawfish *n.* (*pl.* crawfish) a large spiny lobster that lives in the sea.

crawl *v.* **1.** to move as snakes or ants do, with the body close to the ground or other surface. **2.** to move on hands and knees. **3.** to move slowly or with difficulty. **4.** (*informal*) to seek favour by behaving in a servile way, *he crawls to the boss.* **5.** to be covered with crawling things, *it was crawling with ants.* **6.** to feel as if covered with crawling things. —**crawl** *n.* **1.** a crawling movement. **2.** a very slow pace, *at a crawl.* **3.** a swimming stroke with an overarm movement of each arm alternately. —**crawler** *n.*

crayfish *n.* (*pl.* crayfish) a freshwater shellfish like a very small lobster.

crayon *n.* a stick of coloured chalk or other material for drawing. —*v.* to draw or colour with crayons.

craze *n.* **1.** great but often short-lived enthusiasm for something. **2.** the object of this.

crazed *adj.* driven insane, *crazed with grief.*

crazy *adj.* (crazier, craziest) **1.** insane. **2.** very foolish, not sensible, *this crazy plan.* **crazily** *adv.*, **craziness** *n.* □ **crazy paving**, paving made up of oddly-shaped pieces fitted together. **like crazy**, (*informal*) like mad, very much.

creak *n.* a harsh squeak like that of an unoiled hinge. —*v.* to make such a sound.

cream *n.* **1.** the fatty part of milk. **2.** its colour, yellowish-white. **3.** a food containing or like cream, *chocolate cream.* **4.** a soft cream-like substance, especially a cosmetic. **5.** the best part of something, *the cream of society.* —*adj.* cream-coloured. —**cream** *v.* **1.** to remove the cream from; *creaming off the best students*, removing them for some special purpose. **2.** to make creamy; *cream the butter and sugar*, beat it to a creamy consistency. **3.** to apply a cream to. □ **cream cheese**, soft cheese made from curds of cream or unskimmed milk without pressing. **cream of tartar**, a compound of potassium used in cookery.

creamery *n.* a place where milk and milk products are processed or sold.

creamy *adj.* (creamier, creamiest) **1.** rich in cream. **2.** like cream. **creaminess** *n.*

crease *n.* **1.** a line caused by crushing or folding or pressing. **2.** a line marking the limit of the bowler's and batsman's positions in cricket. —**crease** *v.* **1.** to make a crease or creases in. **2.** to develop creases.

create *v.* **1.** to bring into existence, to originate. **2.** to give rise to, to produce by what one does, *create a good impression.* **3.** to give a new rank or position to, *he was created Duke of Edinburgh.* **4.** (*slang*) to make a fuss, to grumble. **creation** *n.*

creative *adj.* **1.** having the power or ability to create things. **2.** showing imagination and originality as well as routine skill, *creative work.* **creatively** *adv.*

creator *n.* one who creates something; *the Creator*, God.

creature *n.* **1.** a living being, especially an animal. **2.** a person; *a poor creature*, someone who is pitied or despised. □ **creature comforts**, things that make one's life comfortable, e.g. good food. **creature of habit**, a person who does things from force of habit.

crèche (*pr.* kresh) *n.* a day nursery for babies.

credence (kree-děnss) *n.* belief. ¶ Do not confuse with credibility.

credentials (kri-**den**-shälz) *pl. n.* letters or papers showing that a person is who or what he claims to be.

credibility *n.* the quality of being credible.

credibility gap, people's disinclination to trust official statements or the person(s) making these.

credible *adj.* able to be believed, convincing. **credibly** *adv.* ¶ Do not confuse with creditable.

credit *n.* **1.** belief that something is true. **2.** honour given for some achievement or good quality. **3.** a source of honour, *a credit to the firm.* **4.** a system of doing business by trusting that a person will pay at a later date for goods or services supplied to him; *buy on credit,* with an arrangement to pay later. **5.** the power to buy in this way. **6.** the amount of money in a person's bank account or entered in an account-book as paid to the holder. — **credit** *v.* (credited, crediting) **1.** to believe. **2.** to attribute; *credit Strauss with this waltz,* say that he wrote it. **3.** to enter as credit in an account-book. □ **credit card,** a card authorizing a person to buy on credit. **credit note,** a document crediting a sum of money to a customer, e.g. for goods returned. **credits** *pl. n.* credit titles. **credit sale,** the selling of something that will be paid for, by agreement, at a later date. **credit titles,** a list of acknowledgements shown at the end of a film or TV programme. **credit transfer,** a system of transferring credit from one person's bank account to another's. **do credit to,** to bring credit upon.

creditable *adj.* deserving praise. **creditably** *adv.* ¶ Do not confuse with credible.

creditor *n.* a person to whom money is owed.

credulous (**kred**-yoo-lŭs) *adj.* too ready to believe things. **credulity** (krid-**yoo**-liti) *n.*

creed *n.* **1.** a formal summary of Christian beliefs. **2.** a set of beliefs or principles.

creek *n.* **1.** a narrow inlet of water especially on the coast. **2.** (*Amer.*) a small stream, a tributary to a river. **3.** (*Austral.* & *N.Z.*) a stream, a brook. □ **up the creek,** (*slang*) in difficulties.

creel *n.* a fisherman's wicker basket for carrying fish.

creep *v.* (crept, creeping) **1.** to move with the body close to the ground. **2.** to move timidly or slowly or stealthily, to come on gradually. **3.** (of plants) to grow along the ground or other surface. **4.** to feel as if covered with crawling things; *it will make your flesh creep,* have this effect by causing fear or dislike. —**creep** *n.* **1.** creeping. **2.** (*slang*) a person one dislikes, one who seeks favour by behaving in a servile way. □ **give a person the creeps,** (*informal*) to make his flesh creep.

creeper *n.* **1.** a person or thing that creeps. **2.** a creeping plant.

creepy *adj.* (creepier, creepiest) making one's flesh creep, feeling this sensation. **creepiness** *n.* □ **creepy-crawly** *n.* (*informal*) a crawling insect.

cremate *v.* to burn (a corpse) to ashes. **cremation** *n.*

crematorium (krem-ă-**tor**-iŭm) *n.* (*pl.* crematoria) a place where corpses are cremated.

crème de menthe (krem dĕ **mahnth**) a green liqueur flavoured with peppermint.

crenellated (**kren**-ĕl-ay-tid) *adj.* having battlements. **crenellation** (kren-ĕl-**ay**-shŏn) *n.*

Creole (**kree**-ohl) *n.* **1.** a descendant of European settlers in the West Indies or Central or South America. **2.** the dialect spoken by these.

creosote (**kree**-ŏ-soht) *n.* **1.** a thick brown oily liquid obtained from coal tar, used as a preservative for wood. **2.** a colourless liquid obtained from wood tar, used as an antiseptic. —*v.* to treat with creosote.

crêpe (*pr.* krayp) *n.* **1.** fabric with a wrinkled surface. **2.** rubber with a wrinkled texture, used for shoe-soles. □ **crêpe paper,** thin crêpe-like paper. **crêpe Suzette,** a small sweet pancake served flambé.

crept *see* creep.

crepuscular (kri-**pus**-kew-ler) *adj.* appearing or active at dusk or dawn, not at light or in full daylight.

crescendo (kri-**shen**-doh) *adj. & adv.* gradually becoming louder. —*n.* (*pl.* crescendos) a gradual increase in loudness.

crescent *n.* **1.** a narrow curved shape tapering to a point at each end. **2.** something shaped like this. **3.** a curved street.

cress *n.* any of various plants with hot-tasting leaves used in salads.

crest *n.* **1.** a tuft or fleshy outgrowth on a bird's or animal's head. **2.** a plume on a helmet. **3.** the top of a slope or hill, the white top of a large wave. **4.** a design above the shield on a coat of arms, or used separately on a seal or notepaper etc. **crested** *adj.*

crestfallen *adj.* downcast, disappointed at failure.

Cretan *adj.* of Crete, an island in the East Mediterranean.

cretin (**kret**-in) *n.* **1.** a person who is deformed and mentally undeveloped through lack of thyroid hormone. **2.** (*informal*) a very stupid person. **cretinous** *adj.*

cretonne (kret-**on**) *n.* heavy cotton cloth with a printed pattern, used in furnishings.

crevasse (kri-**vass**) *n.* a deep open crack, especially in the ice of a glacier.

crevice (**krev**-iss) *n.* a narrow opening or crack, especially in a rock or wall.

crew[1] *see* **crow**[2].

crew[2] *n.* **1.** the people working a ship or aircraft. **2.** all these except the officers. **3.** a group of people working together, *the camera crew.* **4.** a gang. —*v.* to act as crew. □ **crew-cut** *n.* a closely-cropped style of haircut for men.

crewel (**kroo**-ĕl) *n.* fine worsted yarn used for tapestry and embroidery.

crib *n.* **1.** a wooden framework from which animals can pull out fodder. **2.** a baby's cot. **3.** a model of the manger-scene at Bethlehem. **4.** cards given by other players to the dealer at cribbage. **5.** (*informal*) cribbage. **6.** something copied from another person's work. **7.** a literal translation (for use by students) for something written in a foreign language. —*v.* (cribbed, cribbing) to copy unfairly or without acknowledgement.

cribbage *n.* a card-game in which the dealer scores also from cards in the crib (*see* crib sense 4).

crick *n.* a painful stiffness in the neck or back. —*v.* to cause a crick in.

cricket[1] *n.* an outdoor summer game played with a ball, bats, and wickets, between two sides of 11 players. □ **not cricket**, (*informal*) not fair play.

cricket[2] *n.* a brown grasshopper-like insect that makes a shrill chirping sound. **cricketer** *n.* a cricket player.

cri de coeur (kri dĕ **ker**) a passionate appeal, complaint, or protest. (¶ French, = cry from the heart.)

crime *n.* **1.** a serious offence, one for which there is punishment by law. **2.** such offences, serious law-breaking, *the detection of crime.* **3.** (*informal*) a shame, a senseless act, *it would be a crime to miss such a chance.*

Crimean (kry-**mee**-ăn) *adj.* of the Crimea, a peninsula in the south of the USSR.

crime passionel (kreem pas-yŏn-**el**) a crime (especially murder) caused by sexual jealousy. (¶ French, = crime of passion.)

criminal *n.* a person who is guilty of

crime. —*adj.* **1.** of or involving crime, *a criminal offence.* **2.** concerned with crime and its punishment, *criminal law.*

criminology *n.* the scientific study of crime. **criminologist** *n.* an expert in criminology.

crimp *v.* to press into small folds or ridges.

crimson *adj.* & *n.* deep-red.

cringe *v.* to shrink back in fear, to cower.

crinkle *v.* to make or become wrinkled. —*n.* a wrinkle, a crease. —**crinkly** *adj.*

crinoline (**krin**-ŏ-lin) *n.* a light framework formerly worn to make a long skirt stand out, a skirt shaped by this.

cripple *n.* a person who is permanently lame. —*v.* **1.** to make a cripple of. **2.** to disable, to weaken or damage seriously, *the business was crippled by lack of money.*

crisis *n.* (*pl.* crises, *pr.* **kry**-seez) **1.** a decisive time. **2.** a time of acute difficulty or danger.

crisp *adj.* **1.** brittle, breaking with a snap, *crisp pastry.* **2.** slightly stiff, *a crisp £5 note*; *crisp curls.* **3.** cold and bracing, *a crisp winter morning.* **4.** brisk and decisive, *a crisp manner.* —*n.* a thin fried slice of potato (usually sold in packets). —*v.* to make or become crisp. **crisply** *adv.* **crispness** *n.* □ **burnt to a crisp**, burnt until it is crisp, badly burnt.

crispy *adj.* (crispier, crispiest) crisp.

criss-cross *n.* a pattern of crossing lines. —*adj.* with crossing lines. —*v.* to mark or form or move in this pattern.

criterion (kry-**teer**-iŏn) *n.* (*pl.* criteria) a standard of judgement. ¶ Note that *criteria* is a plural; it is incorrect to speak of *a criteria* or *this criteria*, or of *criterias*.

critic *n.* **1.** a person who finds fault with something. **2.** a person who forms and expresses judgements about books or art or musical works etc.

critical *adj.* **1.** looking for faults. **2.** expressing criticism, *critical remarks.* **3.** of or at a crisis; *the critical moment,* one when there will be a decisive change; *the patient's condition is critical,* he is dangerously ill. **critically** *adv.* □ **critical path analysis,** the study of a complex set of operations (e.g. in building a ship) to decide in what order these should be carried out in order to complete the work as quickly and efficiently as possible.

criticism *n.* **1.** finding fault, a remark pointing out a fault. **2.** the work of a critic, judgements about books or art or music etc., *expert criticism.*

criticize *v.* **1.** to find fault with. **2.** to examine critically, to express judgements about.

critique (kri-**teek**) *n.* a critical essay or review.

croak *n.* a deep hoarse cry or sound, like that of a frog. —*v.* **1.** to utter or speak with a croak. **2.** (*slang*) to die.

crochet (**kroh**-shay) *n.* a kind of handiwork in which thread is looped into a pattern of connected stitches by means of a hooked needle. —*v.* (crocheted, crocheting) to do this needlework, to make (an article) by this.

crock¹ *n.* **1.** an earthenware pot or jar. **2.** a broken piece of this.

crock² *n.* (*informal*) **1.** a person who suffers from bad health or lameness etc. **2.** a very old or worn-out vehicle or ship. —*v.* (*informal*) **crock up**, to make or become a crock.

crockery *n.* household china.

crocodile *n.* **1.** a large tropical reptile with a thick skin, long tail, and huge jaws. **2.** its skin, used to make bags, shoes, etc. **3.** a long line of schoolchildren, walking in pairs. □ **crocodile tears**, insincere sorrow (¶ so called from the belief that the crocodile wept while devouring its victim).

crocus *n.* (*pl.* crocuses) a small plant growing from a corm, with yellow, purple, or white flowers.

croft *n.* (in Scotland) a small enclosed field, a small rented farm. **crofter** *n.* the tenant of a croft.

croissant (krwass-ahn) *n.* a rich crescent-shaped bread roll.

cromlech (**krom**-lek) *n.* a dolmen.

crony *n.* a close friend or companion.

crook *n.* **1.** a hooked stick or staff, that used by a shepherd. **2.** something bent or curved, *carried it in the crook of her arm.* **3.** (*informal*) a person who makes a living dishonestly. —*v.* to bend into the shape of a crook.

crooked *adj.* **1.** not straight or level, having curves or bends or twists. **2.** dishonest, not straightforward. **crookedly** *adv.*, **crookedness** *n.*

croon *v.* to sing softly and gently.

crop *n.* **1.** a batch of plants grown for their produce. **2.** the harvest from this. **3.** a group or quantity appearing or produced at one time, *this year's crop of students.* **4.** the bag-like part of a bird's throat where food is broken up for digestion before passing into the stomach. **5.** the handle of a whip, one with a loop instead of a lash. **6.** a very short haircut. —**crop** *v.* (cropped, cropping) **1.** to cut or bite off, *sheep crop the grass closely.* **2.** to cut (hair) very short. **3.** to bear a crop. □ **crop up**, to occur unexpectedly.

cropper *n.* a plant producing a crop; *a good cropper,* one producing a good crop. □ **come a cropper,** (*slang*) to have a heavy fall or a bad failure.

croquet (**kroh**-kay) *n.* a game played on a lawn with wooden balls that are driven through hoops with mallets.

croquette (kroh-**ket**) *n.* a fried ball or roll of potato, meat, or fish.

crore *n.* (in India) ten millions, 100 lakhs.

crosier (**kroh**-zi-er) *n.* a hooked staff carried by a bishop as a symbol of office.

cross *n.* **1.** a mark made by drawing one line across another, × or +. **2.** an upright post with another piece of wood across it, used in ancient times for crucifixion; *the Cross,* that on which Christ died. **3.** a model of this as a Christian emblem, a monument in this form. **4.** an affliction, an annoying thing one has to bear. **5.** a cross-shaped emblem or medal, *the Victoria Cross.* **6.** an animal or plant produced by cross-breeding. **7.** a mixture of two different things. —**cross** *v.* **1.** to place crosswise; *a crossed telephone line,* an accidental connection. **2.** draw a line across, *cross the t's*; *cross a cheque,* mark it with two parallel lines so that it must be paid into a bank. **3.** to make the sign of the Cross on or over; *cross oneself,* as a sign of religious awe or to call upon God for protection. **4.** to go or extend across. **5.** to frustrate, to oppose the wishes or plans of. **6.** to cross-breed (animals), to cross-fertilize (plants). —**cross** *adj.* **1.** passing from side to side; *cross winds,* blowing across one's direction of travel. **2.** annoyed, showing bad temper. —**crossly** *adv.,* **crossness** *n.* □ **at cross purposes,** misunderstanding or conflicting with each other. **cross a person's path,** to come across him. **cross in the post,** (of letters between two people) to be in the post at the same time. **cross off,** to cross out. **cross one's mind,** to come briefly into one's mind. **cross out,** to draw a line through (an item on a list) to show that it is no longer valid. **cross swords,** to have a controversy. **keep one's fingers crossed,** to hope that nothing unfortunate will happen, crooking one finger over another to bring good luck. **on the cross,** crosswise, on the bias.

crossbar *n.* a horizontal bar.

crossbow *n.* a powerful bow with mechanism for drawing and releasing the string.

cross-breed *v.* (cross-bred, cross-breeding) to produce by mating an animal with one of a different kind. —*n.* an animal produced in this way.

cross-check *v.* to check by a different method.

cross-country *adj. & adv.* across fields, not keeping to main roads or to a direct road.

cross-dressing *n.* transvestism.

crosse *n.* a netted crook used in lacrosse.

cross-examine *v.* to cross-question, especially in a lawcourt. **cross-examination** *n.*

cross-eyed *adj.* having one or both eyes turned towards the nose.

cross-fertilize *v.* to fertilize (a plant) from one of a different kind. **cross-fertilization** *n.*

crossfire *n.* the firing of guns from two or more points so that the lines of fire cross.

cross-grained *adj.* 1. (of wood) with the grain in crossing directions. 2. bad-tempered.

crossing *n.* 1. a journey across water, *we had a smooth crossing.* 2. a place where things cross. 3. a specially marked place for pedestrians to cross a road.

cross-legged *adj. & adv.* with the ankles crossed and knees apart.

cross-patch *n.* a bad-tempered person.

cross-ply *adj.* (of tyres) having fabric layers with cords lying crosswise.

cross-pollinate *v.* to pollinate (a plant) from another. **cross-pollination** *n.*

cross-question *v.* to question closely in order to test answers given to previous questions.

cross-reference *n.* a note directing people to another part of a book or index for further information.

crossroads *n.* a place where two or more roads intersect.

cross-section *n.* 1. a diagram showing the internal structure of something as though it has been cut through. 2. a representative sample.

cross-talk *n.* 1. conversation heard on a crossed telephone line. 2. dialogue, especially between two comedians in an entertainment.

cross-trees *pl.n.* a pair of horizontal timbers for supporting the mast of a ship.

crossways *or* **crosswise** *adv. & adj.* in the form of a cross, with one crossing another.

crossword *n.* a puzzle in which intersecting words, indicated by clues, have to be inserted into blank squares in a diagram.

crotch *n.* 1. a place where things fork. 2. the part of the body or of a garment where the legs fork.

crotchet (kroch-it) *n.* a note in music, equal to half a minim.

crotchety *adj.* peevish.

crouch *v.* to lower the body with the limbs bent and close to it, to be in this position.

croup (*pr.* kroop) *n.* a children's disease in which inflammation of the windpipe causes a hard cough and difficulty in breathing.

croupier (kroop-i-er) *n.* a person who rakes in the money at a gambling table and pays out winnings.

croûton (kroo-tawn) *n.* a small piece of fried or toasted bread served with soup etc.

crow [1] *n.* a large black bird. **as the crow flies,** in a straight line. **crow's-feet** *pl. n.* wrinkles in the skin at the side of the eyes. **crow's nest,** a protected look-out platform high on the mast of a ship.

crow [2] *v.* (crowed *or* crew, crowing) 1. (of a cock) to make a loud shrill cry. 2. (of a baby) to make sounds of pleasure. 3. to express gleeful triumph. —*n.* a crowing cry or sound.

crowbar *n.* a bar of iron with a beak-like end, used as a lever.

crowd *n.* a large group of people gathered together. —*v.* 1. to come together in a crowd. 2. to fill or occupy fully or cram with people or things. —**crowded** *adj.* □ **crowd out,** to keep out by crowding.

crowfoot *n.* a small wild plant of the buttercup family.

crown *n.* 1. an ornamental headdress worn by a king or queen. 2. the sovereign, his or her authority, *loyalty to the crown.* 3. *the Crown,* the supreme governing power in Britain; *Crown property,* owned by the Crown; *a Crown Colony,* one governed completely by Britain. 4. a wreath worn on the head, especially as a symbol of victory. 5. a crown-shaped object or ornament. 6. the top part of something (e.g. of the head or a hat or a tooth), the highest part of something arched, *the crown of the road.* —**crown** *v.* 1. to place a crown on, as a symbol of royal power or victory; *the crowned heads of Europe,* kings and queens. 2. to form or cover or ornament the top part of. 3. to make a successful conclusion to, *our efforts were crowned with success; to crown it all,* completing one's good or bad fortune. 4. to put an artificial top on (a tooth). 5. (*slang*) to hit on the head. □ **Crown Court,** a court where criminal cases are tried in England and Wales. **Crown Derby,** a kind of china made at Derby and often marked with a crown. **Crown jewels,** the sovereign's crown, sceptre, orb, etc. used at coronations. **Crown prince** *or* **princess,** the heir to the throne.

crucial (kroo-shăl) *adj.* very important,

deciding an important issue. **crucially** *adv.*

crucible (**kroo**-si-bŭl) *n.* a pot in which metals are melted.

crucifix *n.* a model of the Cross or of Christ on the Cross.

crucifixion *n.* crucifying, being crucified; *the Crucifixion*, that of Christ.

crucify *v.* (crucified, crucifying) 1. to put to death by nailing or binding to a cross. 2. to cause extreme mental pain to.

crude *adj.* 1. in a natural state, not refined, *crude oil.* 2. not well finished or worked out, rough, *a crude attempt.* 3. without good manners, vulgar. —**crude** *n.* crude oil. —**crudely** *adv.*, **crudity** *n.*

cruel *adj.* (crueller, cruellest) 1. feeling pleasure in another's suffering. 2. causing pain or suffering, *this cruel war.* **cruelly** *adv.*, **cruelty** *n.*

cruet *n.* 1. a small stoppered glass bottle for holding oil or vinegar for use at the table. 2. a stand holding this and salt, pepper, etc.

cruise *v.* 1. to sail about for pleasure or on patrol. 2. (of a vehicle or aircraft) to travel at a moderate speed that is economical of fuel. 3. to drive at moderate speed, or at random when looking for passengers etc. —*n.* a cruising voyage.

cruiser *n.* 1. a fast warship. 2. a yacht for cruising, a cabin cruiser (*see* cabin).

crumb *n.* a small fragment, especially of bread or other food.

crumble *v.* to break or fall into small fragments. —*n.* fruit cooked with a crumbly topping, *apple crumble.*

crumbly *adj.* easily crumbled.

crummy *adj.* (crummier, crummiest) (*slang*) 1. dirty, squalid. 2. inferior, worthless.

crumpet *n.* 1. a soft cake of yeast mixture, baked on a griddle and eaten toasted. 2. (*slang*) the head. 3. (*slang*) a sexually attractive woman or women.

crumple *v.* 1. to crush or become crushed into creases. 2. to collapse loosely.

crunch *v.* 1. to crush noisily with the teeth. 2. to walk or move with a sound of crushing, to make such a sound. □ **when it comes to the crunch**, (*informal*) when there is a show-down.

crusade (kroo-**sayd**) *n.* 1. any of the military expeditions made by Europeans in the Middle Ages to recover the Holy Land from the Muslims. 2. a campaign against something believed to be bad. —*v.* to take part in a crusade. —**crusader** *n.*

crush *v.* 1. to press so as to break or injure or wrinkle, to squeeze tightly. 2. to pound into small fragments. 3. to become crushed.

4. to defeat or subdue completely. —**crush** *n.* 1. a crowd of people pressed together. 2. a drink made from crushed fruit. 3. (*slang*) an infatuation.

crushable *adj.* able to be crushed easily.

crust *n.* 1. the hard outer layer of something, especially bread. 2. the rocky outer portion of the earth.

crustacean (krus-**tay**-shŏn) *n.* an animal that has a hard shell (e.g. crab, lobster, shrimp, etc.).

crusty *adj.* (crustier, crustiest) 1. having a crisp crust. 2. having a harsh manner. **crustiness** *n.*

crutch *n.* 1. a support for a lame person, usually fitting under the armpit. 2. the crotch of the body or of a garment.

crux *n.* (*pl.* cruxes) the vital part of a problem.

cry *n.* 1. a loud wordless sound expressing pain, grief, joy, etc. 2. a shout. 3. the call of a bird or animal. 4. an appeal, a demand. 5. a battle-cry. 6. a spell of weeping, *have a good cry.* —**cry** *v.* (cried, crying) 1. to shed tears; *cry one's heart* or *eyes out*, to weep bitterly. 2. to call out loudly in words. 3. to appeal, to demand; *a crying shame*, one demanding attention. 4. (of an animal) to utter its cry. 5. to announce for sale, *crying their wares.* □ **cry-baby** *n.* a person who weeps easily without good cause. **cry off**, to withdraw from a promise or arrangement. **in full cry**, giving tongue in hot pursuit.

cryosurgery *n.* surgical application of intense cold, e.g. to destroy diseased or damaged tissue.

crypt (*pr.* kript) *n.* a room below the floor of a church.

cryptic (**krip**-tik) *adj.* concealing its meaning in a puzzling way. **cryptically** *adv.*

crypto-Communist *n.* a person who secretly sympathizes with Communism.

cryptogam (**krip**-tŏ-gam) *n.* a flowerless plant such as a fern, moss, or fungus.

cryptogram (**krip**-tŏ-gram) *n.* something written in cipher.

crystal *n.* 1. a clear transparent colourless mineral. 2. a piece of this. 3. very clear glass of high quality. 4. one of the pieces into which certain substances solidify, *crystals of ice.* □ **crystal ball**, a globe of glass used in crystal-gazing. **crystal-gazing** *n.* looking into a crystal ball in an attempt to see future events pictured there.

crystalline (**krist**-ă-lyn) *adj.* 1. like or containing crystals. 2. transparent, very clear.

crystallize *v.* 1. to form crystals. 2. (of ideas or plans) to become clear and definite in form. **crystallization** *n.* □

crystallized fruit, fruit preserved in and coated with sugar.

CSE *abbrev.* Certificate of Secondary Education.

cub *n.* **1.** the young of certain animals, e.g. fox, bear, lion; *a cub reporter*, an inexperienced reporter. **2.** *Cub*, or *Cub Scout*, a member of the junior branch of the Scout Association.

Cuba an island in the West Indies. **Cuban** *adj. & n.*

cubbing *n.* the sport of hunting fox-cubs.

cubby-hole *n.* a small compartment.

cube *n.* **1.** a solid body with six equal square sides. **2.** a block shaped like this. **3.** the product of a number multiplied by itself twice, *the cube of 3 is 27* $(3 \times 3 \times 3 = 27)$. —**cube** *v.* **1.** to cut (food) into small cubes. **2.** to find the cube of (a number). □ **cube root**, *see* root[1] (sense 7).

cubic *adj.* of three dimensions; *one cubic centimetre*, the volume of a cube with sides one centimetre long (used as a unit of measurement for volume).

cubical *adj.* cube-shaped.

cubicle *n.* a small division of a large room, an enclosed space screened for privacy.

cubist (**kew**-bist) *n.* an artist who paints in a style in which objects are represented as geometrical shapes. **cubism** *n.* this style.

cuckold (**kuk**-ōld) *n.* a man whose wife has committed adultery during their marriage. —*v.* to make a cuckold of (a married man).

cuckoo *n.* a bird with a call that is like its name, belonging to a family of which some members lay their eggs in the nests of other birds. **cuckoo-clock** *n.* a clock that strikes the hours with a sound like a cuckoo's call. **cuckoo-pint** *n.* wild arum.

cucumber *n.* **1.** a long green-skinned fleshy fruit eaten as salad or pickled. **2.** the plant producing this.

cud *n.* the food that cattle etc. bring back from the stomach into the mouth and chew again, *chewing the cud*.

cuddle *v.* **1.** to hold closely and lovingly in one's arms. **2.** to nestle. —*n.* an affectionate hug. □ **cuddlesome, cuddly** *adjs.* pleasant to cuddle.

cudgel (**kuj**-ĕl) *n.* a short thick stick used as a weapon. —*v.* (cudgelled, cudgelling) to beat with a cudgel. □ **cudgel one's brains**, to think hard about a problem. **take up the cudgels for**, to defend vigorously.

cue[1] *n.* something said or done which serves as a signal for something else to be done, e.g. for an actor to speak in a play. —*v.* (cued, cueing) to give a cue to.

cue[2] *n.* a long rod for striking the ball in billiards and similar games.

cuff[1] *n.* **1.** a doubled strip of cloth forming a band round the end part of a sleeve, or a separate band worn similarly. **2.** the part of a glove covering the wrist. □ **cuff-link** *n.* one of a pair of fasteners for shirt-cuffs, used instead of buttons. **off the cuff**, without rehearsal or preparation. **off-the-cuff** *adj.*

cuff[2] *v.* to strike with the open hand. —*n.* a cuffing blow.

cui bono? (kwee **boh**-noh) who gains by this? ¶ This is sometimes incorrectly used as if it meant 'what is the use?'.

cuirass (kwi-**rass**) *n.* **1.** a piece of armour consisting of a breastplate and a similar plate protecting the back. **2.** something shaped like this, especially a device for artificial respiration.

cuisine (kwi-**zeen**) *n.* a style of cooking.

cul-de-sac (kul-dĕ-sak) *n.* (*pl.* culs-de-sac) a street with an opening at one end only.

culinary (**kul**-in-er-ı) *adj.* **1.** of a kitchen or cooking. **2.** used in cooking, *culinary herbs*.

cull *v.* **1.** to pick (flowers). **2.** to select. **3.** to pick out and kill (surplus animals from a flock). —*n.* culling, thing(s) culled.

cullet *n.* broken glass added to new material in glass-making.

culminate *v.* to reach its highest point or degree, *the argument culminated in a fight*. **culmination** *n.*

culottes (kew-**lot**) *pl. n.* women's trousers styled to look like a skirt.

culpable (**kul**-pă-bŭl) *adj.* deserving blame. **culpably** *adv.*, **culpability** *n.*

culprit *n.* a person who has committed a slight offence.

cult *n.* **1.** a system of religious worship. **2.** devotion to or admiration of a person or thing.

cultivate *v.* **1.** to prepare and use (land) for crops. **2.** to produce (crops) by tending them. **3.** to spend time and care in developing (a thing); *cultivate a person*, try to win his good will. **cultivation** *n.*, **cultivator** *n.*

cultural *adj.* of culture. **culturally** *adv.*

culture *n.* **1.** the appreciation and understanding of literature, arts, music, etc. **2.** the customs and civilization of a particular people or group, *West Indian culture*. **3.** improvement by care and training, *physical culture*. **4.** the cultivating of plants, the rearing of bees, silkworms, etc. **5.** a quantity of bacteria grown for study. —*v.* to grow (bacteria) for study.

cultured *adj.* educated to appreciate literature, arts, music, etc. **cultured pearls**,

pearls formed by an oyster when a foreign body is inserted artificially into its shell.

culvert (**kul**-vert) *n.* a drain that crosses under a road or railway etc.

cum *prep.* with. **cum dividend**, including a dividend that is about to be paid.

cumbersome (**kum**-ber-sŏm) *adj.* clumsy to carry or wear or manage.

Cumbria a county of England.

cum div. *abbrev.* cum dividend.

cumin (**kum**-in) *n.* a plant with fragrant seeds that are used for flavouring.

cummerbund *n.* a sash worn round the waist.

cumulative (**kew**-mew-lă-tiv) *adj.* increasing in amount by one addition after another. **cumulatively** *adv.*

cuneiform (**kew**-ni-form) *adj.* of or written in the wedge-shaped strokes used in the inscriptions of ancient Assyria, Persia, etc. —*n.* cuneiform writing.

cunning *adj.* **1.** skilled at deceiving people, crafty. **2.** ingenious, *a cunning device*. **3.** (*Amer.*) attractive, quaint. —*n.* craftiness.

cunt *n.* (*vulgar*) **1.** the female genitals, the vagina. **2.** (*contemptuous*) a person, especially a woman.

cup *n.* **1.** a small open container for drinking from, usually bowl-shaped and with a handle, used with a saucer. **2.** its contents, the amount it contains (used as a measure in cookery). **3.** something shaped like a cup. **4.** an ornamental goblet-shaped vessel awarded as a prize. **5.** flavoured wine or cider etc., *claret cup*. —**cup** *v.* (**cupped**, **cupping**) **1.** to form into a cup-like shape, *cupped his hands*. **2.** hold as if in a cup, *with her chin cupped in her hands*. — **cupful** *n.* (*pl.* cupfuls). □ **Cup Final**, the final match in a **cup-tie**, a competition for a cup. **not my cup of tea**, (*informal*) not what I like, not what interests me.

cupboard *n.* a recess or piece of furniture with a door, in which things may be stored. **cupboard love**, a display of affection put on in the hope of obtaining a reward.

Cupid the Roman god of love. —*n.* a picture or statue of a beautiful boy with wings and a bow and arrows.

cupidity (kew-**pid**-iti) *n.* greed for gain.

cupola (**kew**-pŏ-lă) *n.* a small dome on a roof.

cuppa *n.* (*slang*) a cup of tea.

cur *n.* a bad-tempered or worthless dog.

curable *adj.* able to be cured.

curaçao (**kewr**-ă-soh) *n.* a liqueur flavoured with peel of bitter oranges.

curacy *n.* the position of a curate.

curare (kewr-**ar**-i) *n.* a bitter substance obtained from certain South American plants, used by some Indian tribes there to poison their arrows.

curate *n.* a clergyman who assists a parish priest.

curative (**kewr**-ă-tiv) *adj.* helping to cure illness.

curator (kewr-**ay**-ter) *n.* a person in charge of a museum or other collection.

curb *n.* **1.** something that restrains, *put a curb on spending*. **2.** a chain or strap passing under a horse's lower jaw, used to restrain it. —*v.* to restrain.

curd *n.* **1.** (often *curds*) the thick soft substance formed when milk turns sour. **2.** the edible head of a cauliflower.

curdle *v.* to form or cause to form curds. **curdle one's blood**, to fill one with horror.

cure *v.* **1.** to restore to health. **2.** to get rid of (a disease or troublesome condition). **3.** to preserve (meat, fruit, tobacco, or skins) by salting, drying, etc. **4.** to vulcanize (rubber). —**cure** *n.* **1.** curing, being cured, *cannot guarantee a cure*. **2.** a substance or treatment that cures a disease, a remedy.

curettage (kewr-i-**tij**) *n.* scraping surgically to remove tissue or growths.

curfew *n.* a signal or time after which people must remain indoors until the next day.

Curia *n.* the papal court, the government department of the Vatican.

curio *n.* (*pl.* curios) an object that is interesting because it is rare or unusual.

curiosity *n.* **1.** a desire to find out and know things. **2.** something that is of interest because it is rare or unusual.

curious *adj.* **1.** eager to learn or know something. **2.** strange, unusual. **curiously** *adv.*

curl *v.* **1.** to bend, to coil into a spiral. **2.** to move in a spiral form, *smoke curled upwards*. —**curl** *n.* **1.** something curved inwards or coiled. **2.** a coiled lock of hair. **3.** a curling movement. □ **curl up**, (*informal*) to lie or sit with the knees drawn up comfortably.

curler *n.* a device for curling the hair.

curlew (**kerl**-yoo) *n.* a wading bird with a long slender curved bill.

curlicue (**kerl**-i-kew) *n.* a curly ornamental line.

curling *n.* a game played with large flat round stones which are sent along ice towards a mark.

curly *adj.* (curlier, curliest) curling, full of curls.

curmudgeon (ker-**muj**-ŏn) *n.* a bad-tempered person.

currant *n.* 1. the dried fruit of a small seedless grape, used in cookery. 2. a small round red, white, or black berry, the shrub that produces it.

currency *n.* 1. money in actual use in a country. 2. the state of being in common or general use; *the rumour gained currency*, became generally known and believed.

current *adj.* 1. belonging to the present time, happening now, *current events.* 2. in general circulation or use, *some words are no longer current.* —**current** *n.* 1. water or air etc. moving in a certain direction, a running stream. 2. the flow of electricity through something or along a wire or cable. —**currently** *adv.* □ **current account**, a bank account from which money may be drawn without previous notice being given.

curricle *n.* an old type of light open two-wheeled carriage drawn by two horses abreast.

curriculum (kŭ-**rik**-yoo-lŭm) *n.* (*pl.* curricula) a course of study. **curriculum vitae** (*pr.* **vee**-ty), a brief account of one's previous career. (¶ Latin, = course of life.)

curry¹ *n.* 1. seasoning made with hot-tasting spices. 2. a dish flavoured with this. —*v.* (curried, currying) to flavour with curry.

curry² *v.* (curried, currying) to groom (a horse) with a **curry-comb**, a pad with rubber or plastic projections. □ **curry favour**, to win favour by flattery.

curse *n.* 1. a call for evil to come upon a person or thing. 2. the evil produced by this. 3. a violent exclamation of anger. 4. something that causes evil or harm. 5. *the curse*, (*informal*) menstruation. —**curse** *v.* 1. to utter a curse against. 2. to exclaim violently in anger. □ **be cursed with**, to have as a burden or source of harm.

cursed (ker-sid) *adj.* damnable.

cursor *n.* 1. the transparent slide, bearing the reference line, on a slide rule. 2. an indicator (usually a flashing light) on a VDU screen, showing a specific position in the matter displayed.

cursory (**ker**-ser-i) *adj.* hasty and not thorough, *a cursory inspection.* **cursorily** *adv.*

curt *adj.* noticeably or rudely brief. **curtly** *adv.*, **curtness** *n.*

curtail *v.* to cut short, to reduce. **curtailment** *n.*

curtain *n.* 1. a piece of cloth or other material hung up as a screen, especially at a window or between the stage and auditorium of a theatre. 2. the fall of a stage-curtain at the end of an act or scene. 3. a curtain-call. —*v.* to provide or shut off with a curtain or curtains. □ **curtain-call** *n.* applause calling for an actor etc. to take a bow after the curtain has been lowered.

curtains *n.* (*slang*) the end.

curtsy *n.* a movement of respect made by women and girls, bending the knees and lowering the body with one foot forward. —*v.* (curtsied, curtsying) to make a curtsy.

curvaceous (ker-**vay**-shŭs) *adj.* (*informal*) having a shapely figure.

curvature (**ker**-vă-cher) *n.* curving, a curved form, *the curvature of the earth.*

curve *n.* 1. a line of which no part is straight. 2. a smooth continuous surface of which no part is flat. 3. a curved form or thing. —*v.* to bend or shape so as to form a curve. —**curvy** *adj.*

curvet (ker-vet) *n.* a horse's frisky leap. —*v.* (curvetted, curvetting) to make a curvet.

cushion *n.* 1. a bag of cloth or other fabric filled with soft or firm or springy material, used to make a seat etc. more comfortable. 2. a soft pad or other means of support or of protection against jarring. 3. the elastic border round a billiard table, from which the balls rebound. —**cushion** *v.* 1. to furnish with a cushion or cushions. 2. to lessen the impact of (a blow, or shock). 3. to protect from the effects of something harmful.

cushy *adj.* (cushier, cushiest) (*informal*) pleasant and easy, *a cushy job.*

cusp *n.* a pointed end where two curves meet, e.g. the horn of a crescent moon.

cuss *v.* (*informal*) to curse. —*n.* 1. (*informal*) a curse. 2. (*slang*) a difficult person, *an awkward cuss.*

cussed (**kus**-id) *adj.* (*informal*) 1. cursed. 2. awkward and stubborn. **cussedness** *n.*

custard *n.* 1. a dish or sauce made with beaten eggs and milk. 2. a sweet sauce made with milk and flavoured cornflour.

custodian (kus-**toh**-diăn) *n.* a guardian or keeper, especially of a public building.

custody *n.* 1. the right or duty of taking care of something, guardianship; *in safe custody*, safely guarded. 2. imprisonment. □ **take into custody**, to arrest.

custom *n.* 1. a usual way of behaving or of doing something. 2. the regular support given to a tradesman or a business by customers □ **custom-built** *adj.* made according to a customer's order. **custom**

car, one built or modified to the owner's design.

customary *adj.* in accordance with custom, usual. **customarily** *adv.*

customer *n.* **1.** a person who buys goods or services from a shop or business. **2.** a person one has to deal with.

customs *n.* **1.** duty charged on goods imported from other countries. **2.** *Customs,* the government department dealing with these. **3.** the area at a port or airport where Customs officials examine goods and baggage brought into a country. □ **customs union,** a group of countries that have arranged to charge the same amount of duty on imported goods.

cut *v.* (cut, cutting) **1.** to divide or wound or detach with an edged instrument; *the knife won't cut,* is blunt. **2.** to shape or make or shorten in this way. **3.** to be able to be cut, *cotton fabric cuts easily.* **4.** to have (a tooth) appear through the gum. **5.** to cross, to intersect; *you can cut across the field,* go across it as a shorter way. **6.** to reduce by removing part, *cut taxes*; *two scenes were cut by the censor.* **7.** to switch off (electric power, an engine, etc.). **8.** to lift and turn up part of a pack of cards, e.g. in deciding who is to deal. **9.** to hit a ball with a chopping movement in cricket etc. **10.** to stay away deliberately from, *cut the lecture.* **11.** to ignore (a person) deliberately. **12.** (*Amer.*) to dilute (spirits for drinking). —**cut** *n.* **1.** the act of cutting, a division or wound made by this. **2.** a stroke with a sword or whip or cane. **3.** a stroke made by cutting a ball in cricket etc. **4.** a piece of meat cut from the carcass of an animal. **5.** the way a thing is cut, the style in which clothes are made by cutting. **6.** a cutting remark. **7.** a reduction, *tax cuts*; *power cut,* a temporary reduction or stoppage of electric current. **8.** the cutting out of part of a play or film etc. **9.** (*slang*) a share of profits, commission. □ **a cut above,** noticeably superior to. **cut and dried,** planned or prepared in advance. **cut back,** to reduce; to prune. **cut-back** *n.* a reduction. **cut both ways,** to have two appropriate and opposite ways of being applied. **cut a corner,** to pass round it as closely as possible; to scamp one's work. **cut a dash,** to make a brilliant show in appearance and behaviour. **cut in,** to interrupt; to return too soon to one's own side of the road, obstructing the path of an overtaken vehicle; to give a share of the profits to. **cut no ice,** (*slang*) to have no influence or effect. **cut off,** to prevent from continuing; to keep from union or contact;

cut off with a shilling, to leave (a person) a very small amount in a will instead of a large inheritance. **cut one's losses,** to abandon a scheme that causes loss, before one loses too much. **cut out,** to shape by cutting; to outdo (a rival); to cease or cause to cease functioning, *the engine cut out: cut it out,* (*slang*) stop doing that. **cut-out** *n.* a shape cut out of paper etc.; a device that disconnects something automatically. **cut out for,** having the qualities and abilities needed for. **cut the ground from under someone's feet,** to anticipate his arguments or plans and leave him with no foundation for these. **cut up,** to cut into pieces; to cut in on (a vehicle) in driving; *be very cut up,* to be greatly distressed. **cut up rough,** (*informal*) to show anger or resentment.

cute *adj.* (*informal*) **1.** sharp-witted. **2.** ingenious, cleverly made. **3.** (*Amer.*) attractive, quaint. **cutely** *adv.,* **cuteness** *n.*

cuticle (**kew**-ti-kŭl) *n.* skin at the base of a finger-nail or toe-nail.

cutlass *n.* a short sword with a slightly curved blade.

cutlery *n.* knives, forks, and spoons used in eating or serving food.

cutlet *n.* **1.** a neck-chop of mutton or lamb. **2.** a piece of veal etc. for frying. **3.** minced meat cooked in the shape of a cutlet.

cutter *n.* **1.** a person or thing that cuts. **2.** a kind of small boat with one mast.

cut-throat *n.* a person who cuts throats, a murderer. —*adj.* **1.** intense and merciless, *cut-throat competition.* **2.** (of card-games) three-handed. **3.** (of a razor) having a long blade set in a handle.

cutting see **cut.** —*adj.* (of words) hurtful, *cutting remarks.* —*n.* **1.** a piece cut from something, a section cut from a newspaper etc. and kept for reference. **2.** an excavation through high ground for a road or railway. **3.** a piece cut from a plant for replanting to form a new plant.

cuttlefish *n.* a sea creature that sends out a black liquid when attacked.

c.v. *abbrev.* curriculum vitae.

cwm (*pr.* koom) *n.* a bowl-shaped hollow on a mountain.

cyan (sy-ăn) *adj.* & *n.* greenish-blue.

cyanide (sy-ă-nyd) *n.* a very poisonous chemical substance.

cyanosis (sy-ă-**noh**-sis) *n.* a condition in which the skin appears blue, caused by lack of oxygen in the blood.

cybernetics (sy-ber-**net**-iks) *n.* the science of communication and control in animals (e.g. by the nervous system) and in machines (e.g. computers).

cyclamen (sik-lă-měn) *n.* a plant with pink, purple, or white flowers with petals that turn back.

cycle *n.* **1.** a series of events or operations that are regularly repeated in the same order, *the cycle of the seasons.* **2.** the time needed for one such series. **3.** one complete occurrence of a continually recurring process such as electrical oscillation or alternation of electric current. **4.** a complete set or series e.g. of songs or poems. **5.** a bicycle or motor cycle. —*v.* to ride a bicycle.

cyclic (sy-klik) *adj.* **1.** recurring in cycles or series. **2.** forming a cycle. **cyclical** *adj.*, **cyclically** *adv.*

cyclist *n.* a person who rides a cycle.

cyclo-cross *n.* cross-country racing on bicycles.

cyclone (sy-klohn) *n.* **1.** a wind rotating round a calm central area. **2.** a violent destructive form of this. **cyclonic** (sy-**klon**-ik) *adj.*

cyclopaedia (sy-klŏ-**pee**-diă) *n.* an encyclopaedia.

cyclostyle (sy-klŏ-styl) *n.* an apparatus for printing copies from a stencil. —*v.* to print or reproduce with this.

cyclotron (sy-klŏ-tron) *n.* an apparatus for accelerating charged particles by making them move spirally in a magnetic field.

cygnet (sig-nit) *n.* a young swan.

cylinder *n.* **1.** a solid or hollow object with straight sides and circular ends. **2.** a machine-part shaped like this, the chamber in which a piston moves in an engine. **cylindrical** *adj.*

cymbal *n.* a percussion instrument consisting of a brass plate struck with another or with a stick. **cymbalist** *n.* a person who plays the cymbals.

cynic (sin-ik) *n.* a person who believes people's motives are bad or selfish and shows this by sneering at them. **cynical** *adj.*, **cynically** *adv.* □ **cynicism** (sin-i-sizm) *n.* the attitude of a cynic.

cynosure (sy-nŏz-yoor) *n.* a centre of attraction or admiration.

cypress *n.* a coniferous evergreen tree with dark feathery leaves.

Cyprus an island in the East Mediterranean. **Cypriot** (sip-ri-ŏt) *adj.* & *n.*

Cyrillic (si-ril-ik) *adj.* of the alphabet used by Slavonic peoples of the Eastern Church.

cyst (*pr.* sist) *n.* an abnormal sac formed in the body, containing fluid or semi-solid matter.

cystic (sis-tik) *adj.* **1.** of the bladder. **2.** like a cyst.

cystitis (sis-ty-tiss) *n.* inflammation of the bladder.

cytology (sy-tol-ŏji) *n.* the scientific study of cells.

czar (*pr.* zar) *n.* = tsar.

Czech (*pr.* chek) *n.* **1.** a native or the language of western Czechoslovakia. **2.** a Czechoslovak.

Czechoslovakia a country in central Europe. **Czechoslovak** (chek-ŏ-**sloh**-vak) *or* **Czechoslovakian** *adjs.* & *ns.*

Dd

d. *abbrev.* (until 1971) penny or pence (¶ short for the Latin *denarius*).

dab[1]. *n.* **1.** a light or feeble blow, a tap. **2.** quick gentle pressure on a surface with something soft, *a dab with a sponge.* **3.** a small amount of a soft substance applied to a surface. **4.** *dabs*, (*slang*) fingerprints. —**dab** *v.* (dabbed, dabbing) **1.** to strike lightly or feebly. **2.** to press quickly and lightly.

dab[2] *n.* a kind of flat-fish.

dab[3] *n.* (*informal*) an adept, *a dab* or *dab hand at tennis.*

dabble *v.* **1.** to wet by splashing or by putting in and out of water. **2.** to move the feet, hands, or bill lightly in water or mud. □ **dabble in**, to study or work at something casually not seriously. **dabbler** *n.*

dabchick *n.* the little grebe.

dabster *n.* (*informal*) = dab[3].

Dacca (dak-ă) the capital of Bangladesh.

dace (*pr.* dayss) *n.* (*pl.* dace) a small freshwater fish related to the carp.

dachshund (daks-huund) *n.* a small dog of a breed with a long body and very short legs.

dad *n.* (*informal*) father.

daddy *n.* (*children's informal*) father.

daddy-long-legs *n.* a crane-fly.

dado (day-doh) *n.* (*pl.* dados) the lower part of the wall of a room or corridor when it is coloured or faced differently from the upper part.

daffodil *n.* a yellow flower with a trumpet-shaped central part, growing from a bulb.

daft *adj.* (*informal*) silly, foolish, crazy.

dagger *n.* a short pointed two-edged weapon used for stabbing. **at daggers drawn**, hostile and on the point of quarrelling. **look daggers**, to stare angrily.

dago (day-goh) *n.* (*pl.* dagoes) (*slang, contemptuous*) a foreigner, especially one from southern Europe.

dahlia (**day**-liă) *n.* a garden plant with large brightly-coloured flowers and tuberous roots.

Dáil (*pr.* doil) *n.* the **Dáil Éireann** (*pr.* doil air-ăn), the lower house of Parliament in the Republic of Ireland.

daily *adj.* happening or appearing on every day (or every weekday). —*adv.* once a day. —*n.* **1.** a daily newspaper. **2.** (*informal*) a charwoman. □ **daily bread,** one's livelihood.

dainty *adj.* (daintier, daintiest) **1.** small and pretty, delicate. **2.** fastidious, especially about food. **daintily** *adv.,* **daintiness** *n.* □ **dainties** *pl. n.* choice foods, delicacies.

daiquiri (**dy**-kwi-ri) *n.* (*pl.* daiquiris) a cocktail of rum, lime juice, etc.

dairy *n.* **1.** a room or building where milk and milk products are processed. **2.** a shop where these are sold. □ **dairy cream,** real cream (not synthetic). **dairy farm,** a farm producing chiefly milk and butter etc.

dairyman *n.* (*pl.* dairymen) a dealer in milk etc.

dais (**day**-iss) *n.* a low platform, especially at one end of a hall.

daisy *n.* a flower with many petal-like rays surrounding a centre. **daisy wheel,** a type of printer used on a word processor etc., with characters arranged round the circumference of a segmented disc. **pushing up the daisies,** (*slang*) dead and buried.

Dakar (**dak**-ar) the capital of Senegal.

Dakota (dă-**koh**-tă) either of two States of the USA, *North* and *South Dakota.*

Dalai Lama (dal-I **lah**-mă) the chief Lama of Tibet.

dale *n.* a valley, especially in north England.

dally *v.* (dallied, dallying) **1.** to idle, to dawdle. **2.** to flirt. **dalliance** *n.*

Dalmatian (dal-**may**-shăn) *adj.* of Dalmatia, the central region of the coast of Yugoslavia. —*n.* a large white dog with dark spots.

dam[1] *n.* a barrier built across a river etc. to hold back water and control its flow or form a reservoir. —*v.* (dammed, damming) **1.** to hold back with a dam. **2.** to obstruct (a flow).

dam[2] *n.* the mother of a four-footed animal.

damage *n.* **1.** something done or suffered that reduces the value or usefulness of the thing affected or spoils its appearance. **2.** (*slang*) cost or charge, *what's the damage?* —*v.* to cause damage to. □ **damages** *pl. n.* money claimed or paid as compensation for an injury.

Damascus the capital of Syria.

damask (**dam**-ăsk) *n.* silk or linen material woven with a pattern that is visible on either side. **damask rose,** an old sweet-scented variety of rose.

dame *n.* **1.** (*old use* or *Amer. slang*) a woman. **2.** a comic female character in pantomime, usually played by a man. **3.** *Dame,* the title of a woman who has been awarded an order of knighthood (corresponding to the title of *Sir* for a Knight).

damn *v.* **1.** to condemn to eternal punishment in hell; *I'll be damned,* (*informal*) I am astonished; *I'm damned if I know,* (*informal*) I certainly do not know. **2.** to condemn as a failure. **3.** to swear at, to curse. —*int.* an exclamation of anger or annoyance; *let's go, and damn the expense,* never mind the expense. —*n.* 'damn' said as a curse; *we don't give or care a damn,* we do not care at all. —*adj. & adv.* damned. □ **damn all,** (*slang*) nothing at all.

damnable *adj.* hateful, annoying. **damnably** *adv.*

damnation *n.* being damned or condemned to hell. —*int.* an exclamation of anger or annoyance.

damned *adj.* (*informal*) damnable. —*adv.* damnably, extremely, *it's damned hot.* □ **do one's damnedest,** to do one's very best.

Damocles (**dam**-ŏ-kleez) *n.* **sword of Damocles,** imminent danger. ¶From the story of *Damocles,* a Greek of the 4th century BC above whose head a sword was once hung by a hair while he ate.

damp *n.* **1.** moisture in the air or on a surface or throughout something. **2.** foul or explosive gas in a mine. —*adj.* slightly or moderately wet. —**damp** *v.* **1.** to make damp. **2.** to make sad or dull, to discourage, *damped their enthusiasm.* **3.** to stop the vibration of (a string in music). — **damply** *adv.,* **dampness** *n.* □ **damp course,** a layer of damp-proof material built into a wall near the ground to prevent damp from rising. **damp down,** to heap ashes on (a fire) to make it burn more slowly.

damper *n.* **1.** a movable metal plate that regulates the flow of air into the fire in a stove or furnace. **2.** a person or thing that damps or discourages enthusiasm, *cast a damper over the proceedings.* **3.** a small pad that presses against a piano-string to stop it vibrating.

damsel (**dam**-zĕl) *n.* (*old use*) a young woman.

damselfly *n.* an insect like a dragon-fly but with wings that fold while it rests.

damson *n.* **1.** a small dark-purple plum. **2.** the tree that bears it. **3.** dark-purple.

dan *n.* **1.** a degree of proficiency in judo. **2.** one who reaches this.

dance *v.* **1.** to move with rhythmical steps or movements, usually to music, to perform in this way. **2.** to move in a quick or lively way, to bob up and down. ― **dance** *n.* **1.** a piece of dancing. **2.** a piece of music for dancing to. **3.** a social gathering for the purpose of dancing. ―**dancer** *n.* □ **dance attendance on,** to follow about and help dutifully.

d. and c. *abbrev.* dilatation (of the cervix) and curettage (of the womb).

dandelion *n.* a wild plant with bright-yellow flowers.

dander *n.* (*informal*) fighting spirit; *his dander is up,* he is angry and aggressive.

dandified *adj.* like a dandy.

dandle *v.* to dance or nurse (a child) in one's arms.

dandruff *n.* flakes of scurf on the scalp and amongst the hair.

dandy *n.* a man who pays excessive attention to the smartness of his appearance and clothes. ―*adj.* (*informal*) very good of its kind.

dandy-brush *n.* a stiff brush for cleaning horses.

Dane *n.* a native of Denmark.

danger *n.* **1.** liability or exposure to harm or death. **2.** a thing that causes this. □ **danger money,** payment above basic wages for people doing dangerous work.

dangerous *adj.* causing danger. **dangerously** *adv.*

dangle *v.* **1.** to hang loosely. **2.** to hold or carry (a thing) so that it swings loosely. **3.** to hold out (hopes) to a person temptingly.

Danish *adj.* of Denmark or its people or language. ―*n.* the language of Denmark. □ **Danish blue,** soft white cheese with veins of blue mould. **Danish pastry,** a yeast cake topped with icing, nuts, etc.

dank *adj.* unpleasantly damp and cold.

daphne (daf-ni) *n.* a kind of flowering shrub.

dapper *n.* neat and smart in dress and appearance, *a dapper little man.*

dapple *v.* to mark with spots or patches of shade or a different colour. **dapple-grey** *adj.* grey with darker markings.

Darby and Joan a devoted old married couple. **Darby and Joan Club,** a social club for elderly people.

dare *v.* **1.** to have the courage or impudence to do something, to be bold enough, *he didn't dare go* or *dare to go.* **2.** to take the risk of, to face as a danger. **3.** to challenge (a person) to do something risky. ―*n.* a challenge to do something risky. □ **I dare say,** I am prepared to believe, it is very likely, I do not deny it.

daredevil *n.* a recklessly daring person.

Dar es Salaam the capital of Tanzania.

daring *n.* boldness. ―*adj.* **1.** bold, taking risks boldly. **2.** boldly dramatic or unconventional. ―**daringly** *adv.*

dariole (da-ri-ohl) *n.* **1.** a savoury or sweet dish cooked in a small mould. **2.** the mould itself.

dark *adj.* **1.** with little or no light. **2.** (of colour) of a deep shade closer to black than to white, *dark-grey; a dark suit.* **3.** (of people) having a brown or black skin, having dark hair. **4.** gloomy, cheerless, dismal, *the long dark years of the war.* **5.** secret, *keep it dark.* **6.** mysterious, remote and unexplored, *in darkest Africa.* ―**dark** *n.* **1.** absence of light. **2.** a time of darkness, night or nightfall, *out after dark.* **3.** a dark colour. ―**darkly** *adv.,* **darkness** *n.* □ **Dark Ages,** the early part of the Middle Ages in Europe, when learning and culture were in decline. **Dark Blues,** Oxford men, an Oxford team etc. **dark horse,** a successful competitor of whose abilities little was known before the contest. **dark-room** *n.* a room where light is excluded so that photographs can be processed. **in the dark,** having no information about something.

darken *v.* to make or become dark or darker. **darken a person's door,** to come to visit him.

darkish *adj.* rather dark.

darling *n.* **1.** a dearly loved or lovable person or thing, a favourite. **2.** (*informal*) something charming. ―*adj.* dearly loved, (*informal*) charming.

darn[1] *v.* to mend by weaving yarn across a hole. ―*n.* a place mended by darning.

darn[2] *int. & adj.* = damn, damned.

darned *adj.* = damned.

darnel *n.* a grass that grows as a weed among corn.

dart *n.* **1.** a small pointed missile. **2.** a small metal-tipped object used in the game of darts. **3.** a darting movement. **4.** a tapering stitched tuck in a garment. ―**dart** *v.* **1.** to spring or move suddenly and rapidly in some direction. **2.** to send out rapidly, *darted an angry look at him.* □ **darts** *n.* an indoor game in which darts are thrown at a target.

dartboard *n.* a circular board used as a target in the game of darts.

dash *v.* **1.** to run rapidly, to rush. **2.** to

knock or drive or throw (a thing) with force against something, to shatter (a thing) in this way; *our hopes were dashed,* were destroyed. **3.** to write hastily, *dashed off a letter.* **4.** (*slang*) to give as a bribe. — *int.* (*informal*) damn. —**dash** *n.* **1.** a short rapid run, a rush. **2.** a small amount of liquid or flavouring added. **3.** a dashboard. **4.** energy, vigour. **5.** lively spirit or appearance. **6.** the punctuation mark — used to show a break in sense. **7.** the longer of the two signals used in the Morse code.

dashboard *n.* a board below the windscreen of a motor vehicle, carrying various instruments and controls.

dashing *adj.* spirited, showy.

dastardly *adj.* contemptible and cowardly.

data (**day**-tă) *pl. n.* facts or information to be used as a basis for discussing or deciding something, or prepared for being processed by a computer etc. ¶ This word is now often used with a singular verb (like 'information') e.g. *the data is here,* but it is by origin a Latin plural (the singular is *datum*) and should be used (like 'facts') with a plural verb, *the data are here.* **data bank,** a large store of computerized data. **data base,** a store of computerized data, especially lists of articles, reports, etc. **data bus** *or* **data highway** = highway (sense 3). **data processing,** the performance of operations on data, especially using a computer, to obtain information, solutions to problems, etc.

datable *adj.* able to be dated.

date [1] *n.* **1.** the day on which something happened or was written or is to happen etc., a statement of this in terms of day, month, and year (or any of these). **2.** the period to which something belongs, *objects of prehistoric date.* **3.** (*informal*) an appointment to meet socially. **4.** (*Amer. informal*) a person of the opposite sex with whom one has a social appointment. — **date** *v.* **1.** to mark with a date. **2.** to assign a date to. **3.** to originate from a particular date, *the custom dates from Victorian times.* **4.** to show up the age of, to show signs of becoming out of date, *dated fashions*; *some fashions date quickly.* **5.** (*Amer. informal*) to make a social appointment with. □ **date-line** *n.* a line from north to south roughly along the meridian 180° from Greenwich, east and west of which the date differs (east being one day earlier). **out of date,** *see* out. **to date,** so far, until now, *here are our sales figures to date.* **up to date,** *see* up.

date [2] *n.* the small brown sweet edible

fruit of the **date-palm,** a palm tree of North Africa and south-west Asia.

dateless *adj.* **1.** having no date. **2.** not becoming out of date.

datum (**day**-tŭm) *n.* **1.** (*pl.* data; see the entry for data) an item of information, a unit of data. **2.** (*pl.* datums) the starting-point from which something is measured or calculated.

daub *v.* to cover or smear roughly with a soft substance, to paint clumsily. —*n.* **1.** a clumsily-painted picture. **2.** a covering or smear of something soft.

daughter *n.* **1.** a female child in relation to her parents. **2.** a female descendant, *daughters of Eve.* □ **daughter-in-law** *n.* (*pl.* daughters-in-law) a son's wife.

daunt *v.* to make afraid or discouraged; *nothing daunted,* not discouraged.

dauntless *adj.* brave, not daunted. **dauntlessly** *adv.*

dauphin (**daw**-fin) *n.* the eldest son of the king of France in the days when France was ruled by a king.

davit (**dav**-it) *n.* a kind of small crane on board ship.

Davy Jones (*slang*) the evil spirit of the sea. **Davy Jones's locker,** the bottom of the sea as the graveyard of those who are drowned or buried at sea.

dawdle *v.* to walk slowly and idly, to take one's time. **dawdler** *n.*

dawn *n.* **1.** the first light of day. **2.** the beginning, *the dawn of civilization.* —**dawn** *v.* **1.** to begin to grow light. **2.** to begin to appear; *the truth dawned on him,* became evident to him.

day *n.* **1.** the time during which the sun is above the horizon. **2.** the time for one rotation of the earth, a period of 24 hours, especially from one midnight to the next. **3.** the hours given to work, *an eight-hour day.* **4.** a specified or appointed day, *Coronation day.* **5.** a period, time, or era, *in Queen Victoria's day*; *in my young days,* when I was young. **6.** a period of success; *colonialism has had its day,* its successful period is over. **7.** victory in a contest, *win the day.* □ **day-boy, day-girl** *ns.* a pupil attending a boarding-school but living at home. **day-break** *n.* the first light of day, dawn. **day by day,** daily. **day centre,** a place where social and other facilities are provided for elderly or handicapped people during the day. **day in day out,** every day, unceasingly. **day nursery,** a place where young children are looked after while their parents are at work. **day release,** a system of allowing employees to have days off work for education. **day-return** *n.* a ticket sold at a reduced rate for a journey both ways in one day.

daybook *n.* a book in which sales are noted as they take place, being transferred later to a ledger.

day-dream *n.* idle and pleasant thoughts. —*v.* to have day-dreams.

daylight *n.* **1.** the light of day. **2.** dawn. □ **daylight robbery**, unashamed swindling.

daylights *pl.* *n.* (*slang*) the internal organs; *beat* or *scare the daylights out of him,* beat him severely, scare him greatly. **see daylight**, to begin to understand what was previously puzzling.

daytime *n.* the time of daylight.

daze *v.* to make (a person) feel stunned or bewildered. —*n.* a dazed state.

dazzle *v.* **1.** to make (a person) unable to see clearly because of too much bright light. **2.** to amaze and impress or confuse (a person) by a splendid display. —*n.* bright confusing light.

DC *abbrev.* **1.** (also **d.c.**) direct current. **2.** District of Columbia.

D-Day *n.* the date on which an important operation is planned to begin.

deacon *n.* **1.** a clergyman ranking below a priest in Episcopal churches. **2.** a layman attending to church business in Nonconformist churches. □ **deaconess** *n.* a woman with similar duties.

dead *adj.* **1.** no longer alive. **2.** numb, without feeling. **3.** no longer used, *a dead language.* **4.** lifeless and without lustre or resonance or warmth; *a dead match,* already struck and burnt out. **5.** no longer active or functioning, *the microphone went dead.* **6.** dull, without interest or movement or activity, *it's a dead place on Sundays.* **7.** (of a ball in games) out of play. **8.** complete, abrupt, exact, *dead silence*; *a dead stop*; *dead centre*; *he is a dead shot,* shoots very accurately. —**dead** *adv.* completely, exactly, *dead drunk*; *dead level.* —**dead** *n.* an inactive or silent time, *the dead of night.* □ **dead-alive** *adj.* (of a place) very dreary. **dead beat**, tired out. **dead-beat** *n.* a down-and-out. **dead duck**, (*slang*) something useless or unsuccessful. **dead end**, the closed end of a road or passage, a blind alley. **dead-end job**, a job with no prospects of advancement. **dead heat**, the result of a race in which two or more competitors finish exactly even. **dead-heat** *v.* to finish in a dead heat. **dead letter**, a rule or law that is no longer observed. **dead man's handle**, a controlling device (on a train etc.) that disconnects the driving power if it is released. **dead march**, a funeral march. **dead nettle**, a plant with nettle-like leaves that does not sting. **dead-pan** *adj.* (*informal*) with an ex-

pressionless face. **dead reckoning**, calculating a ship's position by log and compass etc. when observations are impossible. (¶ Note that this does not mean 'a reckoning that is exactly right'.) **Dead Sea**, an inland salt lake between Israel and Jordan.

dead set, a determined attack; *make a dead set at a person,* try to attract him or her. **dead weight**, a heavy inert weight.

deaden *v.* to deprive of or lose vitality, loudness, feeling, etc.

deadline *n.* a time-limit. ¶ Originally this meant the line round a military prison beyond which a prisoner was liable to be shot.

deadlock *n.* a complete standstill or lack of progress. —*v.* to reach a deadlock, to cause to do this.

deadly *adj.* (**deadlier**, **deadliest**) **1.** causing or capable of causing fatal injury or death. **2.** death-like, *a deadly silence.* **3.** (*informal*) very dreary. —**deadly** *adv.* **1.** as if dead, *deadly pale.* **2.** extremely, *deadly serious.* —**deadliness** *n.* □ **deadly nightshade**, a plant with poisonous black berries. **the seven deadly sins**, those that result in damnation for a person's soul.

deaf *adj.* **1.** wholly or partly without the sense of hearing, unable to hear. **2.** refusing to listen, *deaf to all advice; turned a deaf ear to our requests.* **deafness** *n.* □ **deaf-aid** *n.* a hearing-aid. **deaf mute**, a person who is both deaf and dumb.

deafen *v.* to make deaf or unable to hear by a very loud noise.

deal^1 *n.* fir or pine timber.

deal^2 *v.* (dealt, dealing) **1.** to distribute among several people, to hand out (cards) to players in a card-game. **2.** to give, to inflict, *dealt him a severe blow.* **3.** to do business, to trade, *we deal at Smith's; they deal in fancy goods.* —**deal** *n.* **1.** dealing, a player's turn to deal, a round of play after dealing. **2.** a business transaction, *the deal fell through; it's a deal,* I agree to this. **3.** treatment, *didn't get a fair deal.* **4.** (*informal*) a large amount. —**dealer** *n.* □ **a good deal, a great deal**, a large amount. **deal with**, to do business with; to take action about or be what is needed by (a problem etc.); *deal with a subject,* discuss it in a book or speech etc.

dean *n.* **1.** a clergyman who is head of a cathedral chapter. **2.** an official in certain universities, responsible for the organization of studies or for discipline. □ **rural dean**, a clergyman with authority over a group of parishes.

deanery *n.* **1.** the position of dean. **2.** a dean's official residence. **3.** a rural dean's area of office.

dear *adj.* **1.** much loved, cherished. **2.** esteemed; *Dear Sir*, a polite phrase beginning a letter. **3.** costing more than it is worth, not cheap. —*n.* a dear person. —*adv.* dearly, at a high price. —*int.* an exclamation of surprise or distress. —**dearly** *adv.*, **dearness** *n.*

dearth (*pr.* derth) *n.* a scarcity.

death *n.* **1.** the process of dying, the end of life. **2.** the state of being dead. **3.** a cause of death, *drink was the death of him.* **4.** the ending or destruction of something, *the death of our hopes.* □ **at death's door**, close to death. **death-bed** *n.* the bed on which a person is dying or dies. **death certificate**, an official statement of the date, place, and cause of a person's death. **death duty**, tax levied on property after the owner's death. **death penalty**, punishment for a crime by being put to death. **death-rate** *n.* the number of deaths in one year for every 1000 persons. **death-roll** *n.* a list of those killed in a battle or an accident etc. **death's head**, a picture of a skull as a symbol of death. **death-trap** *n.* a dangerous place. **death-watch beetle**, a beetle whose larva bores holes in old wood and makes a ticking sound. **put to death**, to kill, to execute. **to death**, extremely, to the utmost limit, *bored to death.* **to the death**, until one or other is killed, *a fight to the death.*

deathless *adj.* immortal.

deathly *adj.* & *adv.* like death, *a deathly hush; deathly pale.*

débâcle (day-**bahkl**) *n.* a sudden disastrous collapse.

debar *v.* (debarred, debarring) to exclude, to prohibit.

debase *v.* to lower in quality or value. **debasement** *n.*

debatable *adj.* questionable, open to dispute. **debatably** *adv.*

debate *n.* a formal discussion. —*v.* **1.** to hold a debate about. **2.** to discuss, to consider.

debauch (di-**bawch**) *v.* to make dissolute, to lead into debauchery.

debauchery (di-**bawch**-er-i) *n.* over-indulgence in harmful or immoral pleasures.

debenture (di-**ben**-cher) *n.* a certificate or bond acknowledging a debt on which fixed interest is being paid.

debilitate *v.* to cause debility in.

debility *n.* feebleness, weakness.

debit *n.* an entry in an account-book of a sum owed by the holder. —*v.* (debited, debiting) to enter as a debit in an account.

debonair (deb-ŏn-**air**) *adj.* having a carefree self-confident manner.

debrief *v.* (*informal*) to question (a person) in order to obtain information from him about a mission he has just completed.

debris (**deb**-ree) *n.* scattered broken pieces.

debt *n.* something owed by one person to another. **in debt**, owing something.

debtor *n.* a person who owes money to another.

debug *v.* (debugged, debugging) to free from bugs (= insects, faults and errors, or secret microphones).

debunk *v.* (*informal*) to show up (a claim or theory) as exaggerated or false.

début (**day**-bew) *n.* a first public appearance.

débutante (**deb**-yoo-tahnt) *n.* (*old use*) a young woman making her first appearance in society.

decade (**dek**-ayd) *n.* a period of ten years.

decadent (**dek**-ă-dĕnt) *adj.* becoming less worthy, deteriorating in standard. **decadence** *n.*

decaffeinated (di-**kaf**-in-ayt-id) *adj.* with the caffeine removed or reduced.

Decalogue (**dek**-ă-log) *n.* the Ten Commandments.

decamp *v.* to go away suddenly or secretly.

decant (di-**kant**) *v.* **1.** to pour (liquid) gently from one container into another without disturbing the sediment. **2.** (*informal*) to transfer from one place to another.

decanter (di-**kant**-er) *n.* a stoppered glass bottle into which wine etc. may be decanted before serving.

decapitate (di-**kap**-it-ayt) *v.* to behead. **decapitation** *n.*

decathlon (dik-**ath**-lŏn) *n.* an athletic contest in which each competitor takes part in the ten events it includes.

decay *v.* **1.** to become rotten, to cause to rot. **2.** to lose quality or strength. —*n.* decaying, rot.

decease (di-**seess**) *n.* (*formal*) death.

deceased *adj.* dead; *the deceased*, the person(s) who died recently.

deceit *n.* deceiving, a deception.

deceitful *adj.* deceiving people. **deceitfully** *adv.*

deceive *v.* **1.** to cause (a person) to believe something that is not true. **2.** to be sexually unfaithful to. **deceiver** *n.*

decelerate (dee-**sel**-er-ayt) *v.* to cause to slow down, to decrease one's speed. **deceleration** *n.*

December *n.* the twelfth month of the year.

decency *n.* being decent; *the decencies,* the requirements of respectable behaviour in society.

decent *adj.* 1. conforming to the accepted standards of what is proper, not immodest or obscene. 2. respectable, *ordinary decent people.* 3. (*informal*) quite good, *earns a decent salary.* 4. (*informal*) kind, generous, obliging. **decently** *adv.*

decentralize *v.* to divide and distribute (powers etc.) from a central authority to places or branches away from the centre. **decentralization** *n.*

deception *n.* 1. deceiving, being deceived. 2. something that deceives people.

deceptive *adj.* deceiving, easily mistaken for something else. **deceptively** *adv.*

decibel (**dess**-i-bel) *n.* a unit for measuring the relative loudness of sound.

decide *v.* 1. to think about and make a choice or judgement, to come to a decision. 2. to settle by giving victory to one side, *this goal decided the match.* 3. to cause to reach a decision, *that decided me.* **decider** *n.*

decided *adj.* 1. having clear opinions, determined. 2. clear, definite, *a decided difference.* **decidedly** *adv.*

deciduous (di-**sid**-yoo-ŭs) *adj.* 1. (of a tree) shedding its leaves annually. 2. falling off or shed after a time, *a deer has deciduous antlers.*

decimal (**dess**-im-ăl) *adj.* reckoned in tens or tenths. —*n.* a decimal fraction. □ **decimal currency,** currency in which each unit is ten or one hundred times the value of the one next below it. **decimal fraction,** a fraction whose denominator is a power of 10, expressed in figures after a dot (the **decimal point**), e.g. $0.5 = 5/10$, $0.52 = 52/100$. **decimal system,** a system of weights and measures with each unit ten times that immediately below it. **go decimal,** to adopt a decimal currency or system.

decimalize *v.* 1. to express as a decimal. 2. to convert to a decimal system. **decimalization** *n.*

decimate (**dess**-im-ayt) *v.* to destroy one tenth of, to destroy a large proportion of. **decimation** *n.*

decipher (di-**sy**-fer) *v.* to make out the meaning of (a coded message, bad handwriting, or something difficult to interpret). **decipherment** *n.*

decision *n.* 1. deciding, making a reasoned judgement about something. 2. the judgement itself. 3. the ability to form clear opinions and act on them.

decisive (di-**sy**-siv) *adj.* 1. settling something conclusively, *a decisive battle.* 2. showing decision and firmness. **decisively** *adv.*

deck [1] *n.* 1. any of the horizontal floors in a ship. 2. a similar floor or platform especially one of two or more, *the top deck of a bus.* 3. the turntable of a record-player. 4. a device for holding and carrying magnetic tape, and for playing it or transferring information to or from it. □ **deckchair** *n.* a portable folding chair of canvas on a wood or metal frame. **hit the deck,** (*slang*) to fall to the ground or floor.

deck [2] *v.* to decorate, to dress up, *decked with flags; decked out in her finest clothes.*

deckle edge a ragged edge like that on hand-made paper. **deckle-edged** *adj.*

declaim (di-**klaym**) *v.* to speak or say impressively or dramatically. **declamation** (deklă-**may**-shŏn) *n.*

declare *v.* 1. to make known, to announce openly or formally or explicitly. 2. to state firmly, *he declares that he is innocent.* 3. to inform customs officials that one has (goods) on which duty may be payable. 4. to choose to close one's side's innings at cricket before ten wickets have fallen. **declaration** *n.* □ **declare war,** to announce that a state of war exists.

decline *v.* 1. to refuse; *decline the invitation,* say politely that one cannot accept it. 2. to slope downwards. 3. to decrease, to lose strength or vigour; *one's declining years,* old age. —*n.* a gradual decrease or loss of strength. □ **in decline,** decreasing.

declivity (di-**kliv**-iti) *n.* a downward slope.

declutch *v.* to disengage the clutch of a motor vehicle.

decoction *n.* boiling down to extract an essence, the extract itself.

decode *v.* to put (a coded message) into plain language, to translate (coded characters in a computer).

decoder *n.* 1. a person or machine that decodes messages etc. 2. a device for analysing stereophonic signals and passing them to separate amplifier-channels.

decoke *v.* (*informal*) to remove a carbon deposit from (an engine). —*n.* (*informal*) the process of decoking.

décolletage (day-**kol**-tahzh) *n.* a low neckline. **décolleté** (day-**kol**-tay) *adj.* having a low neckline.

decompose *v.* 1. to separate (a substance etc.) into its parts. 2. to decay, to cause to decay. **decomposition** *n.*

decompress *v.* to subject to decompression.

decompression *n.* 1. release from compression. 2. the gradual and safe reduction of air pressure on a person who has been in compressed air; *decompression chamber,* an enclosed space where this can be done.

decongestant (dee-kŏn-**jest**-ănt) *n.* a medicinal substance that relieves congestion.

decontaminate *v.* to rid of radioactive or other contamination. **decontamination** *n.*

decontrol *v.* (decontrolled, decontrolling) to release from government control. —*n.* decontrolling.

décor (**day**-kor) *n.* the style of furnishings and decoration used in a room etc.

decorate *v.* 1. to make (a thing) look attractive or striking or festive with objects or details added for this purpose. 2. to put fresh paint or paper on the walls etc. of. 3. to confer a medal or other award upon.

decoration *n.* 1. decorating. 2. something that decorates; *decorations,* flags etc. put up on festive occasions. 3. a medal etc. awarded and worn as an honour.

decorative (**dek**-er-ătiv) *adj.* ornamental, pleasing to look at.

decorator *n.* a person who decorates, especially one whose job is to paint and paper houses.

decorous (**dek**-er-ŭs) *adj.* polite and well-behaved, decent. **decorously** *adv.*

decorum (di-**kor**-ŭm) *n.* correctness and dignity of behaviour.

decoy (di-**koi**) *n.* something used to lure an animal or person into a trap or situation of danger. —*v.* to lure by means of a decoy.

decrease *v.* to make or become shorter or smaller or less. —*n.* 1. decreasing. 2. the amount by which something decreases.

decree *n.* 1. an order given by a government or other authority and having the force of a law. 2. a judgement or decision of certain lawcourts. —*v.* (decreed, decreeing) to order by decree. □ **decree nisi** (*pr.* **ny**-sy), a provisional order for divorce, made absolute unless cause to the contrary is shown within a fixed period.

decrepit (di-**krep**-it) *adj.* made weak by old age or hard use, dilapidated. **decrepitude** *n.* the state of being decrepit.

decriminalize *v.* to pass a law causing (an action, etc.) to cease to be treated as a crime. **decriminalization** *n.*

decry (di-**kry**) *v.* (decried, decrying) to disparage.

dedicate *v.* 1. to devote to a sacred person or use, *the church is dedicated to St. Peter.* 2. to devote one's time and energy to a

special purpose, *a dedicated scientist.* 3. (of an author etc.) to address (a book or piece of music etc.) to a person as a compliment, putting his name at the beginning. **dedication** *n.,* **dedicator** *n.*

dedicatory (**ded**-i-kayt-er-i) *adj.* making a dedication, *a dedicatory inscription.*

deduce (di-**dewss**) *v.* to arrive at (knowledge or a conclusion) by reasoning from observed facts. **deducible** *adj.* able to be deduced.

deduct *v.* to take away (an amount or quantity), to subtract.

deductible *adj.* able to be deducted.

deduction *n.* 1. deducting, something that is deducted. 2. deducing, a conclusion reached by reasoning. 3. logical reasoning that something must be true because it is a particular case of a general law that is known to be true.

deductive *adj.* based on reasoning.

deed *n.* 1. something done, an act. 2. a written or printed legal agreement, especially one giving ownership or rights, bearing the giver's signature and seal. □ **deed-box** *n.* a strong box for holding deeds and other documents. **deed of covenant,** an undertaking to make an annual subscription for a period of years to a society etc. which is allowed to reclaim, in addition, the tax paid on this amount by the contributor. **deed poll,** a deed made by one party only making a formal declaration, *change one's name by deed poll.*

deem *n.* (*formal*) to believe, to consider, to judge.

deep *adj.* 1. going or situated far down or back or in, *a deep cut; deep cupboards; a deep sigh,* coming from far down. 2. (in cricket) distant from the batsman. 3. intense, extreme, *a deep sleep; deep colours,* strong in tone. 4. low-pitched and resonant, not shrill, *a deep voice.* 5. absorbed, *deep in thought.* 6. heartfelt, *deep sympathy.* 7. difficult to understand, obscure, *that's too deep for me; he's a deep one,* (*slang*) he is secretive and not easy to know. —*adv.* deeply, far down or in. —*n.* a deep place; *the deep,* the sea. —**deeply** *adv.,* **deepness** *n* □ **deep-fry** *v.* to fry (food) in fat that covers it. **deep-seated** *adj.* firmly established, not superficial, *a deep-seated distrust.* **deep space,** the far distant regions beyond the earth's atmosphere or those beyond the solar system. **go off the deep end,** (*informal*) to give way to emotion or anger.

deepen *v.* to make or become deep or deeper.

deep-freeze *n.* a freezer. —*v.* (deep-froze, deep-frozen, deep-freezing) to freeze (food) quickly for storage.

deer *n.* (*pl.* deer) a ruminant swift-footed animal, the male of which usually has antlers.

deerstalker *n.* a soft cloth cap with one peak in front and another at the back.

deface *v.* to spoil or damage the surface of. **defacement** *n.*

de facto (dee **fak**-toh) existing in fact (whether by right or not). (¶ Latin.)

defalcation (dee-fal-**kay**-shŏn) *n.* misappropriation of funds, a breach of trust concerning money.

defamatory (di-**fam**-ă-ter-i) *adj.* defaming.

defame (di-**faym**) *v.* to attack the good reputation of, to speak ill of. **defamation** (def-ă-**may**-shŏn) *n.*

default *v.* to fail to fulfil one's obligations. —*n.* failure to fulfil an obligation or to appear; *they won by default,* because the other side did not appear; *in default of this,* if this does not take place, since it is not here. —**defaulter** *n.*

defeat *v.* **1.** to win a victory over. **2.** to cause to fail, to frustrate, *this defeats our hopes for reform.* **3.** to baffle, *the problem defeats me.* —**defeat** *n.* **1.** defeating others. **2.** being defeated, a lost battle or contest.

defeatist *n.* a person who expects to be defeated or accepts defeat too easily. **defeatism** *n.*

defecate (**dee**-fik-ayt) *v.* to empty the bowels. **defecation** *n.*

defect [1] (di-**fekt** *or* **dee**-fekt) *n.* a deficiency, an imperfection.

defect [2] (di-**fekt**) *v.* to desert one's country, to abandon one's allegiance to a cause. **defection** *n.*, **defector** *n.*

defective *adj.* **1.** having defects, imperfect, incomplete. **2.** mentally deficient. **defectively** *adv.*, **defectiveness** *n.*

defence *n.* **1.** defending from or resistance against attack. **2.** something that defends or protects against attack. **3.** a justification put forward in response to an accusation. **4.** the defendant's case in a lawsuit, the lawyer(s) representing an accused person.

defenceless *adj.* having no defence, unable to defend oneself.

defend *v.* **1.** to protect by warding off an attack. **2.** to try to preserve; *the champion is defending his title,* trying to defeat one who challenges him. **3.** to uphold by argument, to put forward a justification of. **4.** to represent the defendant in a lawsuit. **defender** *n.*

defendant *n.* a person accused or sued in a lawsuit.

defensible *adj.* able to be defended. **defensibly** *adv.*, **defensibility** *n.*

defensive *adj.* used or done for defence, protective. **defensively** *adv.* □ **on the defensive,** in an attitude of defence, ready to defend oneself against criticism.

defer [1] *v.* (deferred, deferring) to put off to a later time, to postpone. **deferment** *n.*, **deferral** *n.* □ **deferred shares,** shares on which dividends are paid only after they have been paid on all other shares.

defer [2] *v.* (deferred, deferring) to give way to a person's wishes or judgement or authority, to yield.

deference (**def**-er-ĕns) *n.* polite respect. **in deference to,** out of respect for.

deferential (def-er-en-**shăl**) *adj.* showing deference. **deferentially** *adv.*

defiance *n.* defying, open disobedience, bold resistance.

defiant *adj.* showing defiance. **defiantly** *adv.*

deficiency (di-**fish**-ĕn-si) *n.* **1.** being deficient. **2.** a lack or shortage, the amount by which something falls short of what is required. □ **deficiency disease,** a disease caused by lack of vitamins or other essential elements in food.

deficient (di-**fish**-ĕnt) *adj.* **1.** not having enough, *deficient in vitamins;* mentally deficient, see mental. **2.** insufficient or not present at all.

deficit (**def**-i-sit) *n.* **1.** the amount by which a total falls short of what is required. **2.** the excess of expenditure over income, or of liabilities over assets.

defile [1] *v.* to make dirty, to pollute. **defilement** *n.*

defile [2] *n.* a narrow pass through which troops etc. can pass only in file.

definable (di-**fyn**-ăbŭl) *adj.* able to be defined.

define *v.* **1.** to give a definition of (a word etc.). **2.** to state or explain precisely, *customers' rights are defined by the law.* **3.** to outline clearly, to mark out the boundary of.

definite *adj.* **1.** having exact limits. **2.** clear and unmistakable, not vague, *I want a definite answer.* **3.** certain, settled, *is it definite that we are to move?* **definitely** *adv.* □ **definite article,** the word 'the'. ¶ See the note under definitive.

definition *n.* **1.** a statement of the precise meaning of a word or phrase, or of the nature of a thing. **2.** making or being distinct, clearness of outline.

definitive (di-**fin**-itiv) *adj.* finally fixing or settling something, conclusive. ¶ This word is sometimes confused with definite. A *definite* offer is one that is clearly stated. A *definitive* offer is one that must be accepted or refused without trying to alter its terms. A *definitive edition* is one with authoritative status.

deflate *v.* **1.** to let out air or gas from (an inflated tyre etc.). **2.** to cause (a person) to lose his confidence or self-esteem. **3.** to counteract inflation in (a country's economy), e.g. by reducing the amount of money in circulation. **4.** to become deflated. **deflation** *n.*, **deflationary** *adj.*

deflect *v.* to turn or cause to turn aside. **deflexion** *n.*, **deflector** *n.*

defoliant (dee-**foh**-li-ănt) *n.* a chemical substance that destroys foliage.

defoliate (dee-**foh**-li-ayt) *v.* to strip of leaves, to destroy the foliage of by chemical means. **defoliation** *n.*

deform *v.* to spoil the form or appearance of, to put out of shape. **deformation** (dee-for-**may**-shŏn) *n.* □ **deformed** *adj.* badly or abnormally shaped.

deformity *n.* **1.** being deformed. **2.** a deformed part of the body.

defraud *v.* to deprive by fraud.

defray *v.* to provide money to pay (costs or expenses). **defrayal** *n.*

defrost *v.* **1.** to remove frost or ice from. **2.** to unfreeze, *defrost the chicken*; *let the chicken defrost*.

deft *adj.* skilful, handling things neatly. **deftly** *adv.*, **deftness** *n.*

defunct (di-**funkt**) *adj.* **1.** dead. **2.** no longer existing or used or functioning.

defuse *v.* **1.** to remove the fuse of, to make (an explosive) unable to explode. **2.** to reduce the dangerous tension in (a situation).

defy *v.* (defied, defying) **1.** to resist openly, to refuse to obey. **2.** to challenge (a person) to try and do something that one believes he cannot or will not do, *I defy you to prove this*. **3.** to offer difficulties that cannot be overcome by, *the door defied all attempts to open it*.

degenerate[1] (di-**jen**-er-ayt) *v.* to become worse or lower in standard, to lose good qualities. **degeneration** *n.*

degenerate[2] (di-**jen**-er-ăt) *adj.* having degenerated.

degrade *v.* **1.** to reduce to a lower rank or status. **2.** to bring disgrace or contempt on. **degradation** (deg-ră-**day**-shŏn) *n.*

degrading *adj.* shaming, humiliating.

degree *n.* **1.** a step or stage in an ascending or descending series. **2.** a stage in intensity or amount, *a high degree of skill*. **3.** an academic rank awarded to a person who has successfully completed a course of study or as an honour. **4.** a unit of measurement for angles or arcs, indicated by the symbol °, e.g. 45°. **5.** a unit of measurement in a scale e.g. of temperatures. □ **by degrees**, step by step, gradually.

dehorn *v.* to remove the horns from (an animal).

dehumanize *v.* to take away human qualities, to make impersonal or machine-like.

dehydrate *v.* **1.** to remove the moisture content from. **2.** to lose moisture. **dehydration** *n.*

de-ice *v.* to remove or prevent the formation of ice on (a windscreen or other surface). **de-icer** *n.*

deify (**dee**-i-fy) *v.* (deified, deifying) to make a god of, to treat as a god. **deification** *n.*

deign (*pr.* dayn) *v.* to condescend, to be kind or gracious enough to do something, *she did not deign to reply*.

deity (**dee**-iti) *n.* **1.** a god or goddess, *Roman deities; the Deity*, God. **2.** divinity.

déjà vu (day-*zh*a vew) a feeling of having experienced the present situation before.

dejected *adj.* in low spirits, depressed. **dejectedly** *adv.*

dejection *n.* lowness of spirits, depression.

Del. *abbrev.* Delaware.

Delaware a State of the USA.

delay *v.* **1.** to make or be late, to hinder. **2.** to put off until later, to postpone. — **delay** *n.* **1.** delaying, being delayed. **2.** the amount of time for which something is delayed, *a two-hour delay*. □ **delayed-action** *adj.* operating after an interval of time.

delectable *adj.* delightful, enjoyable.

delectation (dee-lek-**tay**-shŏn) *n.* enjoyment, delight, *for your delectation*.

delegacy (**del**-ig-ăsi) *n.* a body of delegates.

delegate[1] (**del**-i-găt) *n.* a person who represents others and acts according to their instructions.

delegate[2] (**del**-i-gayt) *v.* to entrust (a task, power, or responsibility) to an agent.

delegation (del-i-**gay**-shŏn) *n.* **1.** delegating. **2.** a body of delegates.

delete (di-**leet**) *v.* to strike out (something written or printed), **deletion** *n.*

deleterious (del-i-**teer**-iŭs) *adj.* harmful to the body or mind.

delft *n.* (also *delftware*) a kind of glazed earthenware, usually decorated in blue.

Delhi (**del**-i) the capital of India.

deliberate[1] (di-**lib**-er-ăt) *adj.* **1.** done or said on purpose, intentional, *a deliberate insult*. **2.** slow and careful, unhurried, *entered with deliberate steps*. **deliberately** *adv.*

deliberate[2] (di-**lib**-er-ayt) *v.* to think over or discuss carefully before reaching a decision.

deliberation *n.* 1. careful consideration or discussion. 2. careful slowness.

deliberative (di-**lib**-er-ătiv) *adj.* for the purpose of deliberating or discussing things, *a deliberative assembly.*

delicacy *n.* 1. delicateness. 2. avoidance of what is immodest or offensive or hurtful to others. 3. a choice food.

delicate *adj.* 1. fine in texture, soft, slender. 2. of exquisite quality or workmanship. 3. (of colour or flavour) pleasant and not strong or intense. 4. easily injured, liable to illness, (of plants) unable to withstand cold. 5. requiring careful handling, *a delicate operation; the situation is delicate.* 6. skilful and sensitive, *has a delicate touch.* 7. taking great care to avoid what is immodest or offensive or hurtful to others. **delicately** *adv.*, **delicateness** *n.*

delicatessen (del-i-kă-**tess**-ĕn) *n.* a shop selling prepared delicacies and relishes.

delicious *adj.* delightful, especially to the senses of taste or smell. **deliciously** *adv.*

delight *v.* 1. to please greatly. 2. to be greatly pleased, to feel great pleasure, *she delights in giving surprises.* —**delight** *n.* 1. great pleasure. 2. something that causes this.

delightful *adj.* giving delight. **delightfully** *adv.*

Delilah (di-**ly**-lă) *n.* a seductive and treacherous woman. ¶ Named after a woman in the Bible, who betrayed Samson to the Philistines.

delimit (dee-**lim**-it) *v.* to fix the limits or boundaries of. **delimitation** *n.*

delineate (di-**lin**-i-ayt) *v.* to show by drawing or by describing. **delineation** *n.*

delinquent (di-**link**-wĕnt) *adj.* committing an offence or failing to perform a duty. — *n.* a delinquent person, especially a young offender against the law. —**delinquency** *n.*

delirious (di-**li**-ri-ŭs) *adj.* 1. affected with delirium, raving. 2. wildly excited. **deliriously** *adv.*

delirium (di-**li**-ri-ŭm) *n.* 1. a disordered state of mind, especially during feverish illness. 2. wild excitement or emotion. □ **delirium tremens** (**tree**-menz), a form of delirium with tremors and terrifying delusions, caused by heavy drinking.

deliver *v.* 1. to take (letters or goods etc.) to the addressee or purchaser. 2. to transfer, to hand over, to present. 3. to utter (a speech). 4. to aim or launch (a blow, an attack), to bowl (a ball) in cricket etc. 5. to rescue, to save or set free. 6. to assist (a female) in giving birth; *she was delivered of a child,* gave birth to it. **deliverer** *n.*

deliverance *n.* rescue, setting free.

delivery *n.* 1. delivery, being delivered. 2. a periodical distribution of letters or goods etc. 3. the manner of delivering a speech. 4. the manner of bowling or sending a ball in cricket etc. □ **delivery note,** a note accompanying goods sent by a seller, listing the items sent so that the recipient can check them.

dell *n.* a small wooded hollow or valley.

delphinium *n.* a garden plant with tall spikes of flowers, usually blue.

delta *n.* 1. the fourth letter of the Greek alphabet, $=$ d (written Δ). 2. a triangular patch of land accumulated at the mouth of a river between two or more of its branches, *the Nile Delta.* □ **delta wing aircraft,** an aircraft with swept-back wings that give it a triangular appearance.

delude (di-**lood**) *v.* to deceive.

deluge (**del**-yooj) *n.* 1. a great flood, a heavy fall of rain; *the Deluge,* the flood in Noah's time. 2. anything coming in a heavy rush, *a deluge of questions.* —*v.* to flood, to come down on like a deluge.

delusion *n.* 1. a false belief or opinion. 2. a persistent false belief that is a symptom or form of madness.

delusive *adj.* deceptive, raising vain hopes.

de luxe of very high quality, luxurious.

delve *v.* 1. (*old use*) to dig. 2. to search deeply for information.

demagogue (**dem**-ă-gog) *n.* a leader or agitator who wins support by appealing to people's feelings and prejudices rather than by reasoning.

demand *n.* 1. a request made imperiously or as if one had a right. 2. a desire for goods or services by people who wish to buy or use these, *there's a great demand for typists.* 3. an urgent claim, *there are many demands on my time.* —**demand** *v.* 1. to make a demand for. 2. to need, *the work demands great skill.* □ **demand note,** a request for payment. **in demand,** sought after. **on demand,** as soon as the demand is made, *payable on demand.*

demanding *adj.* 1. making many demands. 2. requiring skill or effort, *a demanding job.*

demarcation (dee-mar-**kay**-shŏn) *n.* marking of the boundary or limits of something; *demarcation dispute,* a dispute between trade unions about work they consider to belong to different trades.

demean *v.* to lower the dignity of, *I wouldn't demean myself to ask for it.*

demeanour *n.* the way a person behaves.

demented *adj.* driven mad, crazy.

demerara (dem-er-**air**-ă) *n.* brown raw cane sugar.

demerit *n.* a fault, a defect.

demesne (di-**meen**) *n.* **1.** a domain. **2.** a landed estate.

demilitarized *adj.* (of an area) required (by treaty or agreement) to have no military forces or installations in it.

demise (di-**myz**) *n.* (*formal*) death.

demisemiquaver *n.* a note in music, equal to half a semiquaver.

demist *v.* to clear mist from (a windscreen etc.). **demister** *n.*

demo *n.* (*pl.* demos) (*informal*) a demonstration.

demob *v.* (demobbed, demobbing) (*informal*) to demobilize. —*n.* (*informal*) demobilization.

demobilize *v.* to release from military service. **demobilization** *n.*

democracy *n.* **1.** government by the whole people of a country, especially through representatives whom they elect. **2.** a country governed in this way.

democrat *n.* **1.** a person who favours democracy. **2.** *Democrat*, a member of the Democratic party in the USA.

democratic *adj.* **1.** of or like or supporting democracy. **2.** in accordance with the principle of equal rights for all, *a democratic decision*. **3.** *Democratic*, of the Democratic Party, one of the two main political parties in the USA. **democratically** *adv.*

democratize (di-**mok**-ră-tyz) *v.* to make democratic. **democratization** *n.*

demolish *v.* **1.** to pull or knock down (a building). **2.** to destroy (a person's argument or theory etc.). **3.** (*informal*) to eat up. **demolition** (dem-ŏ-**lish**-ŏn) *n.*

demon *n.* **1.** a devil or evil spirit. **2.** a cruel or forceful person; *a demon bowler,* a very fast bowler; *a demon for work,* a very energetic worker.

demoniac (di-**moh**-ni-ak) *adj.* **1.** of or like a demon. **2.** possessed by an evil spirit. **3.** fiercely energetic, frenzied.

demoniacal (dee-mŏn-**I**-ăkăl) *adj.* of or like a demon.

demonic (dee-**mon**-ik) *adj.* of or like a demon.

demonstrable (**dem**-ŏn-stră-bŭl) *adj.* able to be shown or proved. **demonstrably** *adv.*

demonstrate *v.* **1.** to show evidence of, to prove. **2.** to describe and explain by the help of specimens or examples; *demonstrate the machine to customers,* show them how it works. **3.** to take part in a demonstration. **demonstrator** *n.*

demonstration *n.* **1.** demonstrating. **2.** a

show of feeling. **3.** an organized gathering or procession to express the opinion of a group publicly. **4.** a display of military force.

demonstrative (di-**mon**-stră-tiv) *adj.* **1.** showing or proving. **2.** expressing one's feelings openly; *she is not a demonstrative child,* does not readily show affection openly. **demonstratively** *adv.,* **demonstrativeness** *n.* ☐ **demonstrative pronoun,** *see* pronoun.

demoralize *v.* to weaken the morale of, to dishearten. **demoralization** *n.*

demote (dee-**moht**) *v.* to reduce to a lower rank or category. **demotion** *n.*

demur (di-**mer**) *v.* (demurred, demurring) to raise objections, *they demurred at working on Sundays.* —*n.* an objection raised, *they went without demur.*

demure (di-**mewr**) *adj.* quiet and serious or pretending to be so. **demurely** *adv.,* **demureness** *n.*

den *n.* **1.** a wild animal's lair. **2.** a place where people gather for some illegal activity, *an opium den*; *a den of vice.* **3.** a small room in which a person shuts himself away to work or relax.

denationalize *v.* to transfer (an industry) from national to private ownership. **denationalization** *n.*

denatured (dee-**nay**-cherd) *adj.* having had its natural qualities changed; *denatured alcohol,* alcohol made unfit for drinking but remaining usable for other purposes.

deniable *adj.* able to be denied.

denial *n.* **1.** denying. **2.** a statement that a thing is not true. **3.** refusal of a request or wish.

denier (**den**-yer) *n.* a unit of weight by which the fineness of silk, rayon, or nylon yarn is measured.

denigrate (**den**-i-grayt) *v.* to blacken the reputation of, to sneer at. **denigration** *n.*

denim *n.* a strong twilled cotton fabric used for making clothes. **denims** *pl. n.* trousers made of denim.

denizen (**den**-i-zĕn) *n.* a person or plant living or often present in a particular place, *denizens of the Arctic.*

Denmark a country in northern Europe.

denomination *n.* **1.** a name or title. **2.** a distinctively named Church or religious sect, *Baptists and other Protestant denominations.* **3.** a unit of measurement a unit of money, *coins of small denomination.*

denominational *adj.* of a particular religious denomination.

denominator *n.* the number written below the line in a fraction, e.g. 4 in ¾, showing how many parts the whole is divided into; *the common denominator of a group,* the feature that its members have in common.

denote (di-**noht**) *v.* to be the sign or symbol or name of, to indicate, *in road signs,* P *denotes a parking place.* **denotation** (dee-noh-**tay**-shŏn) *n.*

dénouement (day-**noo**-mahn) *n.* the clearing up, at the end of a play or story, of the complications of the plot.

denounce *v.* 1. to speak publicly against. 2. to give information against, *denounced him as a spy.* 3. to announce that one is ending (a treaty or agreement).

dense *adj.* 1. thick, not easy to see through, *dense fog.* 2. massed closely together, *dense crowds.* 3. stupid. **densely** *adv.*, **denseness** *n.*

density *n.* 1. a dense or concentrated condition, *the density of the fog.* 2. stupidity. 3. the relation of weight to volume, *the density of water is 62½ pounds per cubic foot.*

dent *n.* a depression left by a blow or by pressure. —*v.* 1. to make a dent in. 2. to become dented.

dental *adj.* 1. of or for the teeth. 2. of dentistry, *a dental practice.* □ **dental floss,** strong thread used for cleaning between the teeth.

dentifrice (**dent**-i-friss) *n.* toothpaste or tooth-powder.

dentist *n.* a person who is qualified to fill or extract teeth, fit artificial ones, etc.

dentistry *n.* the work or profession of a dentist.

denture *n.* a set of artificial teeth.

denude *v.* 1. to make naked or bare, to strip the cover from, *the trees were denuded of their leaves.* 2. to take away from (a person), *creditors denuded him of every penny.* **denudation** (dee-new-**day**-shŏn) *n.*

denunciation (di-nun-si-**ay**-shŏn) *n.* denouncing.

deny *v.* (denied, denying) 1. to say that (a thing) is not true or does not exist. 2. to disown, to refuse to acknowledge, *Peter denied Christ.* 3. to refuse to give what is asked for or needed, to prevent from having, *no one can deny you your rights.* □ **deny oneself,** to restrict one's food or drink or pleasure.

deodorant (dee-**oh**-der-ănt) *n.* a substance that removes or conceals unwanted odours. —*adj.* deodorizing.

deodorize *v.* to destroy the odour of. **deodorization** *n.*

depart *v.* 1. to go away, to leave. 2. (of trains or buses) to start, to begin a journey.

3. to cease following a particular course, *departing from our normal procedure.*

departed *adj.* 1. bygone, *departed glories.* 2. *the departed,* the dead.

department *n.* one of the units, each with a specialized function, into which a business, shop, or organization is divided. **department store,** a large shop in which there are various departments each dealing in a separate type of goods.

departmental (dee-part-**men**-tăl) *adj.* of a department.

departure *n.* 1. departing, going away. 2. setting out on a new course of action or thought.

depend *v.* **depend on, 1.** to be controlled or determined by, *whether we can picnic depends on the weather.* 2. to be unable to do without, *she depends on my help.* 3. to trust confidently, to feel certain about, *you can depend on John to be there when he's needed.*

dependable *adj.* able to be relied on. **dependably** *adv.*, **dependability** *n.*

dependant *n.* one who depends on another for support, *he has four dependants.* ¶ In standard English usage the spelling is *-ant* for the noun and *-ent* for the adjective; in the USA *-ent* is used for both.

dependence *n.* depending, being dependent.

dependency *n.* a country that is controlled by another.

dependent *adj.* 1. depending, conditioned, *promotion is dependent on ability.* 2. needing the help of, unable to do without, *he is dependent on drugs.* 3. controlled by another, not independent, *our dependent territories.* ¶ See the note under dependant.

depict *v.* 1. to show in the form of a picture. 2. to describe in words. **depiction** *n.*

depilatory (di-**pil**-ă-ter-i) *n.* a substance that removes superfluous hair. —*adj.* removing hair.

deplete (di-**pleet**) *v.* to use up large quantities of, to reduce in number or quantity. **depletion** *n.*

deplorable *adj.* 1. regrettable. 2. exceedingly bad, shocking. **deplorably** *adv.*

deplore *v.* 1. to regret deeply, *we deplore his death.* 2. to find deplorable, *we deplore their incompetence.*

deploy *v.* to spread out, to bring or come into action systematically, *deploying his troops* or *resources; the ships deployed into line.* **deployment** *n.*

depopulate *v.* to reduce the population of. **depopulation** *n.*

deport *v.* to remove (an unwanted person) from a country. **deportation** *n.*

deportment *n.* behaviour, a person's way of holding himself in standing and walking.

depose *v.* **1.** to remove from power, *the king was deposed.* **2.** to testify or bear witness, especially on oath in court.

deposit *n.* **1.** a thing deposited for safe keeping. **2.** a sum of money paid into a bank. **3.** a sum paid as a guarantee or a first instalment. **4.** a layer of matter deposited or accumulated naturally, *new deposits of copper were found.* —**deposit** *v.* (deposited, depositing) **1.** to lay or put down, *she deposited the books on the desk.* **2.** to store or entrust for safe keeping, to pay (money) into a bank. **3.** to pay as a guarantee or first instalment. **4.** to leave as a layer or covering of matter, *floods deposited mud on the land.* □ **deposit account,** a sum placed in a bank, not to be withdrawn without notice, and on which interest is payable. **on deposit,** in a deposit account; as a deposit of money.

deposition *n.* **1.** deposing or being deposed from power. **2.** a statement made on oath. **3.** depositing.

depositor *n.* a person who deposits money or property.

depository *n.* a storehouse.

depot (**dep**-oh) *n.* **1.** a storehouse, especially for military supplies. **2.** the headquarters of a regiment. **3.** a place where goods are deposited or from which goods, vehicles, etc. are dispatched. **4.** (*Amer.*) a bus station or railway station.

deprave (di-**prayv**) *v.* to make morally bad, to corrupt. **depravation** (dep-ră-**vay**-shŏn) *n.*

depraved *adj.* **1.** immoral, wicked, *a depraved character.* **2.** made bad, perverted, *depraved tastes.*

depravity (di-**prav**-iti) *n.* moral corruption, wickedness.

deprecate (**dep**-ri-kayt) *v.* **1.** to feel and express disapproval of. **2.** to try to turn aside (praise or blame etc.) politely. **deprecation** *n.,* **deprecatory** (**dep**-ri-kay-ter-i) *adj.*
¶ Do not confuse with depreciate.

depreciate (di-**pree**-shi-ayt) *v.* **1.** to make or become lower in value. **2.** to belittle, to disparage. **depreciation** *n.* □ **depreciatory** (di-**pree**-shă-ter-i) *adj.* disparaging.
¶ Do not confuse with deprecate.

depredation (dep-ri-**day**-shŏn) *n.* plundering, destruction.

depress *v.* **1.** to make sad, to lower the spirits of. **2.** to make less active; *the stock market is depressed,* values are low. **3.** to press down, *depress the lever.*

depressant *n.* a substance that reduces the activity of the nervous system, a sedative.

depression *n.* **1.** a state of excessive sadness or hopelessness, often with physical symptoms. **2.** a long period of inactivity in business and trade, with widespread unemployment. **3.** a lowering of atmospheric pressure, an area of low pressure which may bring rain. **4.** a sunken place or hollow on a surface. **5.** pressing down.

depressive *adj.* **1.** depressing. **2.** involving mental depression. —*n.* a person suffering from mental depression.

deprival (di-**pry**-văl) *n.* depriving, being deprived.

deprivation (dep-ri-**vay**-shŏn) *n.* **1.** deprival. **2.** a keenly felt loss.

deprive *v.* to take a thing away from, to prevent from using or enjoying, *the prisoner had been deprived of food.* **deprived child,** one who has been prevented from having a normal home life.

depth *n.* **1.** being deep. **2.** the distance from the top down, or from the surface inwards, or from front to back. **3.** deep learning or thought or feeling. **4.** intensity of colour or darkness. **5.** lowness of pitch in a voice or sound. **6.** the deepest or most central part, *living in the depths of the country.* □ **depth-charge** *n.* a bomb that will explode under water, for use against submarines etc. **in depth,** with thorough and intensive investigations, *studied it in depth; defence in depth,* a system of successive areas of resistance. **out of one's depth,** in water that is too deep to stand in; attempting something that is beyond one's ability.

deputation *n.* a body of people appointed to go on a mission on behalf of others.

depute [1] (di-**pewt**) *v.* **1.** to delegate (a task) to a person. **2.** to appoint (a person) to act as one's representative.

depute [2] (**dep**-ewt) *n.* (*Scottish*) a deputy.

deputize *v.* to act as deputy.

deputy *n.* **1.** a person appointed to act as substitute for another. **2.** a member of a parliament in certain countries, *the Chamber of Deputies.*

derail *v.* (derailed, derailing) to cause (a train) to leave the rails. **derailment** *n.*

derange *v.* **1.** to throw into confusion, to disrupt. **2.** to make insane. **derangement** *n.*

derate *v.* to abolish or lower the rates on.

Derby (**dar**-bi) *n.* **1.** an annual horse-race at Epsom. **2.** a similar race elsewhere. **3.** an important sporting contest; *a local Derby,* one between two teams from the same district. **4.** *derby* (*Amer. pr.* **der**-bi), (*Amer.*) a bowler hat.

Derbyshire a county of England.

derelict *adj.* abandoned, deserted and left to fall into ruin. —*n.* a person who is abandoned by society or who does not fit into a normal social background.

dereliction (derri-**lik**-shŏn) *n.* **1.** neglect of duty. **2.** abandoning, being abandoned.

derestrict *v.* to remove restrictions from; *a derestricted road,* one where a special speed limit has been removed or has not been imposed. **derestriction** *n.*

deride (di-**ryd**) *v.* to laugh at scornfully, to treat with scorn.

de rigueur (dĕ rig-**er**) required by custom or etiquette, *evening dress is de rigueur.*

derision (di-**rizh**-ŏn) *n.* scorn, ridicule.

derisive (di-**ry**-siv) *adj.* scornful, showing derision, *derisive cheers.* **derisively** *adv.*

derisory (di-**ry**-ser-i) *adj.* **1.** showing derision. **2.** deserving derision, too insignificant for serious consideration, *a derisory offer.*

derivation (derri-**vay**-shŏn) *n.* **1.** deriving. **2.** origin.

derivative (di-**riv**-ătiv) *adj.* derived from a source. —*n.* a thing that is derived from another.

derive *v.* **1.** to obtain from a source, *he derived great pleasure from music*; *some English words are derived from Latin,* originate from Latin words. **2.** to show or assert that something is derived from (a source).

dermatitis (der-mă-**ty**-tiss) *n.* inflammation of the skin.

dermatology (der-ma-**tol**-ŏji) *n.* the scientific study of the skin and its diseases. **dermatologist** *n.* a specialist in dermatology.

derogatory (di-**rog**-ă-ter-i) *adj.* disparaging, contemptuous.

derrick *n.* **1.** a kind of crane with an arm pivoted to the base of a central post or to a floor. **2.** a framework over an oil-well or bore-hole, holding the drilling machinery etc.

derris *n.* **1.** a tropical climbing plant. **2.** an insecticide made from its powdered root.

derv *n.* fuel oil for heavy road-vehicles. ¶ From the initials of *d*iesel-engined *r*oad *v*ehicle.

dervish *n.* a member of a Muslim religious order, vowed to poverty.

descale *v.* to remove scale from (a kettle or boiler etc.).

descant *n.* a melody sung or played in accompaniment to the main melody.

descend *v.* **1.** to come or go down. **2.** to slope downwards. **3.** to make a sudden attack or visit, *the whole family descended on us for Easter.* **4.** to sink or stoop to unworthy behaviour, to lower oneself, *they would never descend to cheating.* **5.** to be passed down by inheritance, *the title descended to his son.* □ **be descended from,** to come by descent from (a specified person or family or people).

descendant *n.* a person who is descended from another, *the descendants of Queen Victoria.*

descent *n.* **1.** descending. **2.** a way by which one may descend. **3.** a downward slope. **4.** a sudden attack or invasion, *the Danes made descents upon the English coast.* **5.** lineage, family origin, *they are of French descent.*

describe *v.* **1.** to set forth in words, to say what something is like. **2.** to mark out or draw the outline of, to move in a certain pattern, *described a complete circle.*

description *n.* **1.** describing. **2.** an account or picture in words. **3.** a kind or class of thing, *there's no food of any description.*

descriptive *adj.* giving a description.

desecrate (**dess**-i-krayt) *v.* to treat (a sacred thing) with irreverence or disrespect. **desecration** *n.,* **desecrator** *n.*

desert[1] (**dez** ert) *n.* a dry barren often sand-covered area of land. —*adj.* **1.** barren and uncultivated. **2.** uninhabited, *a desert island.*

desert[2] (di-**zert**) *v.* **1.** to abandon, to leave without intending to return, to forsake. **2.** to leave service in the armed forces without permission. **deserter** *n.,* **desertion** *n.*

deserts (di-**zerts**) *pl. n.* what one deserves.

deserve *v.* to be worthy of or entitled to (a thing) because of actions or qualities. **deservedly** (di-**zerv**-idli) *adv.* according to what is deserved, justly.

deserving *adj.* worthy, worth rewarding or supporting, *a deserving charity; those who are deserving of our sympathy.*

desiccate *v.* (**dess**-i-kayt) to dry out the moisture from, to dry (solid food) in order to preserve it, *desiccated coconut.* **desiccation** *n.*

desideratum (di-sid-er-**ay**-tŭm) *n.* (*pl.* desiderata) something that is lacking but needed or desired.

design *n.* **1.** a drawing that shows how something is to be made. **2.** the art of making such drawings, *she studied design.* **3.** the general form or arrangement of something, *the design of the building is good.* **4.** a combination of lines or shapes to form a decoration. **5.** a mental plan, a purpose. —**design** *v.* **1.** to prepare a drawing or design for (a thing). **2.** to plan, to intend for a specific purpose, *the book is*

designed for students. —**designer** *n.* □
designedly (di-**zyn**-id-li) *adv.* intentionally.
have designs on, to plan to get possession of.
designate¹ (**dez**-ig-năt) *adj.* appointed
but not yet installed in office, *the bishop
designate.*
designate² (**dez**-ig-nayt) *v.* **1.** to mark or
point out clearly, to specify, *the river was
designated as the western boundary.* **2.** to
describe as, to give a name or title to. **3.**
to appoint to a position, *designated Smith
as his successor.*
designation (dez-ig-**nay**-shŏn) *n.* **1.** de-
signating. **2.** a name or title.
designing *adj.* crafty, scheming.
desirable *adj.* **1.** arousing desire, worth
desiring, *a desirable riverside house.* **2.**
advisable, worth doing, *it is desirable
that you should be present.* **desirably** *adv.,*
desirability *n.*
desire *n.* **1.** a feeling that one would get
pleasure or satisfaction by obtaining or
possessing something. **2.** an expressed wish,
a request, *at the desire of Her Majesty.* **3.**
an object of desire, *all your heart's desires.*
4. sexual urge. —**desire** *v.* **1.** to have a
desire for. **2.** to ask for. □ **leave much to
be desired,** to be very imperfect.
desirous *adj.* having a desire, desiring.
desist (di-**zist**) *v.* to cease from an action
etc.
desk *n.* **1.** a piece of furniture with a flat
top and often drawers, used when reading
or writing etc. **2.** a counter behind which a
cashier or receptionist etc. sits, *ask at the
information desk.* **3.** a section of a newspaper office dealing with specified topics.
desolate (**dess**-ŏ-lăt) *adj.* **1.** solitary, lonely.
2. deserted, uninhabited, barren, dismal,
a desolate landscape. **3.** forlorn and unhappy.
desolated (**dess**-ŏ-lay-tid) *adj.* feeling
lonely and wretched.
desolation *n.* **1.** a desolate or barren condition. **2.** loneliness. **3.** grief, wretchedness.
despair *n.* **1.** complete loss or lack of hope.
2. a thing that causes this. —*v.* to lose all
hope.
desperado (dess-per-**ah**-doh) *n.* (*pl.* desper-
adoes) a reckless criminal.
desperate *adj.* **1.** leaving little or no hope,
extremely serious, *the situation is desperate.*
2. made reckless by despair or urgency, *a
desperate criminal; they are desperate for
food.* **3.** done or used in a nearly hopeless
situation, *a desperate remedy.* **desperately**
adv.
desperation *n.* **1.** hopelessness. **2.** being
desperate, recklessness caused by despair.
despicable (**dess**-pik-ăbŭl *or* di-**spik**-ăbŭl)

adj. deserving to be despised, contemptible.
despicably *adv.*
despise *v.* to regard as inferior or worthless, to feel disrespect for.
despite *prep.* in spite of.
despondent *adj.* in low spirits, dejected.
despondently *adv.,* **despondency** *n.*
despot (**dess**-pot) *n.* a tyrant, a ruler who
has unrestricted power.
despotic (dis-**pot**-ik) *adj.* having unrestricted power. **despotically** *adv.*
despotism (**dess**-pŏt-izm) *n.* **1.** tyranny,
government by a despot. **2.** a country ruled
by a despot.
dessert (di-**zert**) *n.* **1.** the sweet course of a
meal. **2.** a course of fruit, nuts, etc. at the
end of dinner. □ **dessert-spoon** *n.* a
medium-sized spoon used in eating
puddings etc. **dessertspoonful** *n.* (*pl.*
dessertspoonfuls)
destination *n.* the place to which a
person or thing is going.
destine *v.* to settle or determine the future
of, to set apart for a purpose; *he was destined to become President,* this was his
destiny.
destiny *n.* **1.** fate considered as a power.
2. that which happens to a person or
thing, thought of as determined in advance by fate.
destitute *adj.* **1.** penniless, without the
necessaries of life. **2.** lacking in something,
a landscape destitute of trees.
destitution *n.* being destitute, extreme
poverty.
destroy *v.* **1.** to pull or break down, to
reduce to a useless form, to spoil completely. **2.** to kill (a sick or unwanted
animal) deliberately, *the dog had to be
destroyed.* **3.** to put out of existence, *it
destroyed our chances.*
destroyer *n.* **1.** a person or thing that
destroys. **2.** a fast warship designed to
protect other ships.
destructible *adj.* able to be destroyed.
destructibility *n.*
destruction *n.* **1.** destroying, being destroyed, **2.** a cause of destruction or
ruin, *gambling was his destruction.*
destructive *adj.* **1.** destroying, causing destruction. **2.** frequently destroying things,
some children are very destructive.
desuetude (dis-**yoo**-i-tewd *or* **dess**-wi-tewd)
n. a state of disuse, *the custom fell into
desuetude.*
desultory (**dess**-ŭl-ter-i) *adj.* going constantly from one subject to another, not systematic. **desultorily** *adv.,* **desultoriness**
n.
detach *v.* to release or remove from
something else or from a group.

detachable *adj.* able to be detached.

detached *adj.* **1.** (of a house) not joined to another. **2.** (of the mind or opinions) free from bias or emotion.

detachment *n.* **1.** detaching, being detached. **2.** freedom from bias or emotion, aloofness, lack of concern. **3.** a group of people or ships etc. detached from a larger group for a special duty.

detail *n.* **1.** an individual item, a small or subordinate particular. **2.** a number of such particulars, *the description is full of detail.* **3.** the minor decoration in a building or picture etc., *look at the detail in the carvings.* **4.** a small military detachment assigned to special duty. —**detail** *v.* **1.** to give particulars of, to describe fully. **2.** to assign to special duty. □ **go into details**, to explain things in detail. **in detail**, describing the individual parts or events etc. fully.

detailed *adj.* giving or showing many details.

detain *v.* **1.** to keep in confinement or under restraint. **2.** to keep waiting, to cause delay to, to keep from proceeding.

detainee (di-tayn-ee) *n.* a person who is detained by the authorities.

detect *v.* **1.** to discover the existence or presence of. **2.** to find (a person) doing something bad or secret, *like a boy detected in robbing an orchard.*

detection *n.* **1.** detecting, being detected. **2.** the work of a detective.

detective *n.* a person, especially a member of the police force, whose job is to investigate crimes. **detective story**, a story that tells of crime and the detection of criminals.

detector *n.* a device for detecting the presence of something, *a smoke-detector.*

detent (di-tent) *n.* a catch that has to be released in order to allow machinery to operate.

détente (day-tahnt) *n.* the easing of strained relations between countries.

detention *n.* **1.** detaining, being detained. **2.** being kept in custody. **3.** being kept in school after hours as a punishment. □ **detention centre**, an institution where young offenders are kept in detention for a short time.

deter *v.* (deterred, deterring) to discourage or prevent from doing something through fear or dislike of the consequences. **determent** *n.*

detergent *n.* a cleansing substance, especially a synthetic substance other than soap. —*adj.* having a cleansing effect.

deteriorate *v.* to become worse. **deterioration** *n.*

determinable *adj.* able to be settled or

calculated, *its age is not determinable.*

determinant *n.* a decisive factor.

determinate (di-ter-min-ăt) *adj.* limited, of fixed and definite scope or nature.

determination *n.* **1.** firmness of purpose. **2.** the process of deciding, determining, or calculating.

determine *v.* **1.** to find out or calculate precisely, *we must determine the height of the mountain.* **2.** to settle, to decide, *determine what is to be done.* **3.** to be the decisive factor or influence on, *income determines one's standard of living.* **4.** to decide firmly, *he determined to become a doctor.*

determined *adj.* showing determination, firm and resolute. **determinedly** *adv.*

deterrent (di-te-rĕnt) *n.* a thing that deters, a nuclear weapon that deters countries from attacking the one who has it.

detest *v.* to dislike intensely, to loathe. **detestation** *n.*

detestable *adj.* intensely disliked, hateful. **detestably** *adv.*

dethrone *v.* to remove from a throne, to depose. **dethronement** *n.*

detonate (det-ŏn-ayt) *v.* to explode or cause to explode loudly. **detonation** *n.*

detonator *n.* a device that detonates an explosive.

detour (dee-toor) *n.* a deviation from one's direct or intended course, a roundabout route, *make a detour.*

detract (di-trakt) *v.* to take away a part, to lessen (a quantity, value, etc.), *it will not detract from our pleasure.* **detraction** *n.*

detractor (di-trakt-er) *n.* a person who criticizes something unfavourably, *the plan has its detractors.*

detriment (det-ri-mĕnt) *n.* harm, damage, *worked long hours to the detriment of his health.*

detrimental (det-ri-men-tăl) *adj.* causing harm, *smoking is detrimental to health.* **detrimentally** *adv.*

detritus di-try-tŭs) *n.* debris.

de trop (dĕ troh) not wanted, in the way.

deuce [1] *n.* **1.** (in tennis) the score of 40 all. **2.** the two on dice.

deuce [2] *n.* (in exclamations of surprise or annoyance) the Devil, *where the deuce is it?*

deuterium (dew-teer-iŭm) *n.* a heavy form of hydrogen.

Deutschmark (doich-mark) *n.* the unit of money in West Germany.

deutzia (doit-siă) *n.* an ornamental shrub, usually with white flowers.

devalue *v.* to reduce the value of (currency) in relation to other currencies or to gold. **devaluation** *n.*

devastate *v.* to lay waste, to cause great destruction to. **devastation** *n.*

devastating *adj.* **1.** causing destruction. **2.** overwhelming, *a devastating handicap.*

develop *v.* (developed, developing) **1.** to make or become larger or fuller or more mature or organized. **2.** to bring or come gradually into existence, *a storm developed.* **3.** to begin to exhibit or suffer from, to acquire gradually, *develop measles; develop bad habits.* **4.** to convert (land) to a new purpose so as to use its resources, to use (an area) for the building of houses or shops or factories etc. **5.** to treat (a photographic film or plate etc.) so as to make the picture visible. □ **developing country,** a poor or primitive country that is developing better economic and social conditions.

developer *n.* **1.** one who develops. **2.** a person or firm that develops land. **3.** a substance used for developing photographic film etc.

development *n.* **1.** developing, being developed. **2.** something that has developed or been developed, *the latest developments in foreign affairs.* □ **development area,** an area where new industries are encouraged by government action, in order to counteract severe unemployment there.

deviant (**dee**-vi-ănt) *adj.* deviating from what is accepted as normal or usual. —*n.* a person who deviates from accepted standards in his beliefs or behaviour.

deviate (**dee**-vi-ayt) *v.* to turn aside or diverge from a course of action, a rule, truth, etc. **deviation** *n.*

deviationist *n.* a Communist who deviates from accepted party doctrines or practices.

device *n.* **1.** a thing that is made or used for a particular purpose, *a device for opening tins.* **2.** a plan or scheme for achieving something. **3.** a design used as a decoration or emblem. □ **leave a person to his own devices,** to leave him to do as he wishes without help or advice.

devil *n.* **1.** *the Devil,* (in Jewish and Christian teaching) the supreme spirit of evil and enemy of God. **2.** an evil spirit. **3.** a wicked or cruel or annoying person. **4.** a person of great energy or cleverness. **5.** (*informal*) something difficult or hard to manage. **6.** (*informal*) a person, *poor devil; lucky devil.* **7.** (*informal*) used in exclamations of surprise or annoyance, *where the devil is it?* —**devil** *v.* (devilled, devilling) **1.** to cook (food) with hot seasoning,

devilled kidneys. **2.** to do research or other work for an author or barrister. — **devilish** *adj.* □ **devil-may-care** *adj.* cheerful and reckless. **devil's advocate,** one who tests a theory by putting forward possible objections to it. **like the devil,** with great energy, intensely. **play the devil with,** to cause severe damage to. **the devil to pay,** trouble to be expected.

devilment *n.* mischief.

devilry *n.* **1.** wickedness. **2.** devilment.

devious (**dee**-vi-ŭs) *adj.* **1.** winding, roundabout. **2.** not straightforward, underhand. **deviously** *adv.,* **deviousness** *n.*

devise (di-**vyz**) *v.* to think out, to plan, to invent.

devoid (di-**void**) *adj.* lacking or free from something, *devoid of merit.*

devolution (dee-vŏ-**loo**-shŏn) *n.* **1.** the handing down of property etc. to an heir. **2.** the delegation or transference of work or power from a central administration to a local or regional one.

devolve *v.* to pass or be passed on to a deputy or successor, *this work will devolve on the new manager.*

Devon, Devonshire a county of southwest England. ¶ *Devon* is the official name.

devote *v.* to give or use for a particular activity or purpose, *devoted himself* or *his time to sport.* **devoted** *adj.* showing devotion, very loyal or loving. **devotedly** *adv.*

devotee (dev-ŏ-**tee**) *n.* a person who is devoted to something, an enthusiast, *devotees of sport.*

devotion *n.* **1.** great love or loyalty, enthusiastic zeal. **2.** religious worship. □ **devotions** *pl. n.* prayers.

devotional *adj.* used in religious worship.

devour *v.* **1.** to eat hungrily or greedily. **2.** to destroy completely, to consume, *fire devoured the forest.* **3.** to take in greedily with the eyes or ears, *they devoured the story.* **4.** to absorb the attention of, *she was devoured by curiosity.*

devout *adj.* **1.** earnestly religious. **2.** earnest, sincere, *a devout supporter.* **devoutly** *adv.,* **devoutness** *n.*

dew *n.* **1.** small drops of moisture that condense on cool surfaces during the night from water vapour in the air. **2.** moisture in small drops on a surface.

dew-claw *n.* a small claw on the inner side of a dog's leg, not reaching the ground in walking.

dewdrop *n.* a drop of dew.

Dewey system a decimal system for classifying books in libraries.

dewlap *n.* a fold of loose skin that hangs

from the throat of cattle and other animals.

dewy *adj.* wet with dew. **dewy-eyed** *adj.* innocently trusting or sentimental.

dexter *n.* one of a small hardy breed of Irish cattle.

dexterity (deks-te-riti) *n.* skill in handling things.

dextrous (**deks**-trŭs) *adj.* showing dexterity. **dextrously** *adv.*

dhoti (**doh**-ti) *n.* (*pl.* dhotis) a loincloth worn by male Hindus.

diabetes (dy-ă-**bee**-teez) *n.* a disease in which sugar and starch are not properly absorbed by the body.

diabetic (dy-ă-**bet**-ik) *adj.* of diabetes. —*n.* a person suffering from diabetes.

diabolic (dy-ă-**bol**-ik) *adj.* of the Devil.

diabolical (dy-ă-**bol**-ikăl) *adj.* **1.** like a devil, very cruel or wicked. **2.** fiendishly clever or cunning or annoying. **diabolically** *adv.*

diabolism (dy-**ab**-ŏl-izm) *n.* worship of the Devil.

diadem (**dy**-ă-dem) *n.* a crown or headband worn as a sign of sovereignty.

diaeresis (dy-**eer**-i-sis) *n.* (*pl.* diaereses) a mark placed over a vowel to show that it is sounded separately, as in *naïve.*

diagnose (**dy**-ăg-nohz) *v.* to make a diagnosis of, *typhoid fever was diagnosed in six patients.*

diagnosis (dy-ăg-**noh**-sis) *n.* (*pl.* diagnoses) a statement of the nature of a disease or other condition made after observing its signs and symptoms.

diagnostic (dy-ăg-**noss**-tik) *adj.* of or used in diagnosis, *diagnostic procedures.*

diagonal (dy-**ag**-ŏn-ăl) *adj.* slanting, crossing from corner to corner. —*n.* a straight line joining two opposite corners. —**diagonally** *adv.*

diagram *n.* a drawing that shows the parts of something or how it works.

diagrammatic (dy-ă-gră-**mat**-ik) *adj.* in the form of a diagram. **diagrammatically** *adv.*

dial *n.* **1.** the face of a clock or watch. **2.** a similar flat plate marked with a scale for the measurement of something and having a movable pointer that indicates the amount registered. **3.** a plate or disc etc. on a radio or TV set showing the wavelength or channel selected. **4.** a movable disc with finger-holes over a circle of numbers or letters, manipulated in order to connect one telephone with another. **5.** (*slang*) a person's face. —**dial** *v.* (**dialled, dialling**) **1.** to select or regulate by means of a dial. **2.** to make a telephone connection by using a dial.

dialect (**dy**-ă-lekt) *n.* the words and pronunciation that are used in a particular area and differ from what is regarded as standard in the language as a whole.

dialectic (dy-ă-**lek**-tik) *n.* investigation of truths in philosophy etc. by systematic reasoning.

dialogue (**dy**-ă-log) *n.* **1.** a conversation or discussion. **2.** the words spoken by characters in a play or story.

dialysis (dy-**al**-i-sis) *n.* purification of the blood by causing it to flow through a suitable membrane.

diamanté (dee-ă-**mahn**-tay) *adj.* decorated with fragments of crystal or other sparkling substance.

diameter (dy-**am**-it-er) *n.* **1.** a straight line passing from side to side through the centre of a circle or sphere. **2.** the length of this.

diametrical (dy-ă-**met**-rik-ăl) *adj.* of or along a diameter; *the diametrical opposite,* the exact opposite. **diametrically** *adv.*

diamond *n.* **1.** a very hard brilliant precious stone of pure crystallized carbon. **2.** a figure with four equal sides and with angles that are not right angles. **3.** something shaped like this. **4.** a playing-card of the suit (*diamonds*) marked with red figures of this shape. —*adj.* made of or set with diamonds. ☐ **diamond wedding,** the 60th (or 75th) anniversary of a wedding.

diaper (**dy**-ă-per) *n.* a baby's napkin.

diaphanous (dy-**af**-ăn-ŭs) *adj.* (of fabric) light, delicate, and almost transparent.

diaphragm (**dy**-ă-fram) *n.* **1.** the midriff, the internal muscular partition that separates the chest from the abdomen and is used in breathing. **2.** a vibrating disc in a microphone or telephone receiver etc. **3.** a device for varying the aperture of a camera lens. **4.** a thin contraceptive cap fitting over the neck of the womb.

diarist (**dy**-er-ist) *n.* one who keeps a diary.

diarrhoea (dy-ă-**ree**-ă) *n.* a condition in which bowel movements are very frequent and fluid.

diary *n.* **1.** a daily record of events or thoughts. **2.** a book for this or for noting engagements.

diathermy (**dy**-ă-therm-i) *n.* a kind of medical heat-treatment by means of high-frequency electric currents.

diatonic (dy-ă-**tonn**-ik) *adj.* (in music) using the notes of the major or minor scale only, not of the chromatic scale.

diatribe (**dy**-ă-tryb) *n.* a violent attack in words, abusive criticism.

dibber *n.* a hand tool used to make holes in the ground for seeds or young plants.

dice *n.* **1.** (*pl.* dice) a small cube marked on each side with a number of spots (1–6), used in games of chance. **2.** a game played with these. —**dice** *v.* **1.** to gamble using dice. **2.** to take great risks, *dicing with death.* **3.** to cut into small cubes, *diced carrots.* □ **no dice**, (*Amer. slang*) no success.

dicey *adj.* (*slang*) risky, unreliable.

dichotomy (dy-kot-ŏmi) *n.* division into two parts or kinds.

dick *n.* (*slang*) a detective.

dickens *n.* (in exclamations of surprise or annoyance) the deuce, the Devil, *where the dickens is it?*

dicker *v.* (*informal*) to bargain, to haggle.

dicky¹ *n.* (*informal*) a false shirt-front.

dicky² *adj.* (*slang*) unsound, likely to collapse or fail, *a dicky heart.*

Dictaphone *n.* (*trade mark*) a machine that records and plays back dictation.

dictate *v.* **1.** to say or read aloud (words) to be written down by a person or recorded by a machine. **2.** to state or order with the force of authority, *dictate terms to a defeated enemy.* **3.** to give orders officiously, *I will not be dictated to.* **dictation** *n.*

dictates (dik-tayts) *pl. n.* authoritative commands, *the dictates of conscience.*

dictator *n.* **1.** a ruler who has unrestricted authority, especially one who has taken control by force. **2.** a person with supreme authority in any sphere, one who dictates what is to be done. **3.** a domineering person. **dictatorship** *n.*

dictatorial (dik-tă-tor-iăl) *adj.* **1.** of or like a dictator. **2.** domineering. **dictatorially** *adv.*

diction (dik-shŏn) *n.* a person's manner of uttering or pronouncing words.

dictionary *n.* a book that lists and explains the words of a language or the words and topics of a particular subject, usually in alphabetical order.

dictum *n.* (*pl.* dicta) **1.** a formal expression of opinion. **2.** a saying.

did *see* do.

didactic (dy-dak-tik) *adj.* **1.** giving instruction. **2.** having the manner of one who is lecturing pupils. **didactically** *adv.*

diddle *v.* (*slang*) to cheat, to swindle.

didn't = did not.

die¹ *v.* (died, dying) **1.** to cease to be alive. **2.** to cease to exist; *the laugh died on his lips*, ceased abruptly. **3.** to cease to function, to stop, *the engine sputtered and died.* **4.** (of a fire or flame) to go out. **5.** to become exhausted, *we were dying with laughter.* **6.** to feel an intense longing, *we are dying to go; dying for a drink.* □ **die away**, to become fainter or weaker and then cease, *the noise died away.* **die back,**

(of plants) to decay from the tip towards the root. **die down**, to become less loud or less violent, *the excitement died down.*

die-hard *n.* a person who obstinately refuses to abandon old theories or policies, one who resists change. **die off**, to die one by one. **die out**, to pass out of existence, *the custom has died out*; *the family has died out*, no members of it are still alive. **never say die**, keep up courage, do not give in.

die² *n.* a dice. **the die is cast**, a step has been taken and its consequences must follow. **straight as a die**, quite straight; very honest.

die³ *n.* an engraved device that stamps a design on coins or medals etc., a device that stamps or cuts or moulds material into a particular shape. **die-cast** *adj.* made by casting metal in a mould. **die-stamping** *n.* stamping with a die that leaves an embossed design.

diesel (dee-zĕl) *n.* **1.** a diesel engine, a vehicle driven by this. **2.** fuel for a diesel engine. □ **diesel-electric** *adj.* driven by electric current from a generator driven by a diesel engine. **diesel engine**, an oil-burning engine in which ignition is produced by the heat of highly compressed air.

diet¹ *n.* **1.** the sort of foods usually eaten by a person or animal or community. **2.** a selection of food to which a person is restricted. —**diet** *v.* (dieted, dieting) **1.** to restrict oneself to a special diet, especially in order to control one's weight. **2.** to restrict (a person) to a special diet. —**dieter** *n.*

diet² *n.* a congress, a parliamentary assembly in certain countries, e.g. Japan.

dietary (dy-it-er-i) *adj.* of or involving diet, *the dietary rules of Hindus.*

dietetic (dy-i-tet-ik) *adj.* of diet and nutrition. **dietetics** (dy-i-tet-iks) *pl. n.* the scientific study of diet and nutrition.

dietitian (dy-i-tish-ăn) *n.* an expert in dietetics.

differ *v.* **1.** to be unlike, to be distinguishable from something else. **2.** to disagree in opinion.

difference *n.* **1.** the state of being different or unlike. **2.** the point in which things differ, the amount or degree of unlikeness. **3.** the quantity by which amounts differ, the remainder left after subtraction, *the difference between 8 and 5 is 3.* **4.** a disagreement in opinion, a quarrel. □ **make all the difference**, to make a very important or vital difference.

different *adj.* **1.** unlike, of other nature or form or quality, *different from* or *to others.* (¶ *Different from* is the preferred phrase; *different to* is acceptable when it feels natural in a particular context, e.g. when *similar to* occurs near by; *different than* is common in American use, but should be avoided in standard English although it was used in the 18th-19th centuries.) **2.** separate, distinct, *several different people.* **3.** unusual, *try Finland for a holiday that's different.* **differently** *adv.*

differential (dif-er-**en**-shăl) *adj.* of or showing or depending on a difference. —*n.* **1.** an agreed difference in wages between industries or between different classes of workers in the same industry. **2.** a differential gear. □ **differential gear**, an arrangement of gears that allows a motor vehicle's rear wheels to revolve at different speeds in rounding corners.

differentiate (dif-er-en-shi-ayt) *v.* **1.** to be a difference between, to make different, *the features that differentiate one breed from another.* **2.** to recognize as different, to distinguish, to discriminate; *the pension scheme does not differentiate between male and female employees,* does not treat them differently. **3.** to develop differences, to become different. **differentiation** *n.*

difficult *adj.* **1.** needing much effort or skill, not easy to do or practise. **2.** troublesome, perplexing, *these are difficult times.* **3.** not easy to please or satisfy, *a difficult employer.*

difficulty *n.* **1.** being difficult. **2.** a difficult problem or thing, a hindrance to action. **3.** a difficult state of affairs, trouble; *in financial difficulties,* short of money. □ **make difficulties,** to raise objections, to put obstacles in the way of progress. **with difficulty,** not easily.

diffident (dif-i-dĕnt) *adj.* lacking self-confidence, hesitating to put oneself or one's ideas forward. **diffidently** *adv.,* **diffidence** *n.*

diffraction *n.* the process of breaking up a beam of light into a series of dark and light bands or the coloured bands of the spectrum.

diffuse[1] (di-**fewss**) *adj.* **1.** spread out, diffused, not concentrated, *diffuse light.* **2.** wordy, not concise, *a diffuse style.* **diffusely** *adv.,* **diffuseness** *n.*

diffuse[2] (dif-**fewz**) *v.* **1.** to spread widely or thinly throughout something, *to diffuse knowledge* or *light* or *heat.* **2.** to mix (liquids or gases) slowly, to become intermingled. **diffusion** *n.,* **diffuser** *n.* □ **diffused lighting,** lighting that is spread or filtered so that there is no glare.

dig *v.* (dug, digging) **1.** to break up and move ground with a tool or machine or claws etc., to make (a way or a hole) by doing this, *dig the ground; dig through the hill; dig a tunnel.* **2.** to obtain or remove by digging, *dig potatoes.* **3.** to excavate archaeologically. **4.** to seek or discover by investigation, *dug up some useful information.* **5.** to thrust, to plunge, *dig a knife into it.* **6.** to prod, to nudge, *dug him in the ribs.* **7.** (*slang*) to appreciate, to enjoy, to understand, *they don't dig pop music; do you dig?* —**dig** *n.* **1.** a piece of digging. **2.** an archaeological excavation. **3.** a thrust, a poke, *a dig in the ribs.* **4.** a cutting remark; *that was a dig at me,* a remark directed against me. □ **dig in** or **into,** to mix (a substance) with the soil by digging; (*informal*) to begin eating or working energetically. **dig oneself in,** to dig a defensive trench or pit; to establish oneself securely. **dig one's heels** or **toes in,** to become obstinate, to refuse to give way.

digest[1] (dy-**jest**) *v.* **1.** to dissolve (food) in the stomach etc. so that it can be absorbed by the body; *this food digests easily,* is easily digested. **2.** to think over, to absorb into the mind, *digesting the information.*

digest[2] (**dy**-jest) *n.* **1.** a methodical summary. **2.** a periodical publication giving excerpts and summaries of news, writings, etc.

digestible *adj.* able to be digested. **digestibility** *n.*

digestion *n.* **1.** the process of digesting. **2.** the power of digesting food, *has a good digestion.*

digestive *adj.* **1.** of or aiding digestion. **2.** having the function of digesting food, *the digestive system.* —*n.* a digestive biscuit. □ **digestive biscuit,** a kind of wholemeal biscuit.

digger *n.* **1.** one who digs. **2.** a mechanical excavator.

digit (**dij**-it) *n.* **1.** any numeral from 0 to 9, especially when forming part of a number. **2.** a finger or toe.

digital (**dij**-it-ăl) *adj.* of digits. **digital clock,** a clock that shows the time by displaying a row of figures. **digital computer,** a device that makes calculations etc. with data represented as a series of digits. **digital recording,** conversion of sound into electrical pulses (representing binary digits) for recording.

digitalin (dij-i-**tay**-lin) *n.* a poisonous substance extracted from foxglove leaves.

digitalis (dij-i-**tay**-lis) *n.* a drug prepared from dried foxglove leaves, used as a heart-stimulant.

dignified *adj.* having or showing dignity.

dignify *v.* (dignified, dignifying) **1.** to give dignity to. **2.** to make (a thing) sound more important than it is, *they dignified the school with the name of 'college'*.

dignitary (**dig**-ni-ter-i) *n.* a person holding a high rank or position, especially in the Church.

dignity *n.* **1.** a calm and serious manner or style, showing suitable formality or indicating that one deserves respect. **2.** worthiness, *the dignity of labour.* **3.** a high rank or position. □ **beneath one's dignity**, not worthy enough for one to do. **stand on one's dignity**, to insist on being treated respectfully.

digress (dy-**gress**) *v.* to depart from the main subject temporarily in speaking or writing. **digression** *n.*

digs *pl. n.* (*informal*) lodgings.

dike *n.* **1.** a long wall or embankment to keep back water and prevent flooding. **2.** a ditch for draining water from land.

dilapidated *adj.* falling to pieces, in a state of disrepair.

dilapidation *n.* a state of disrepair, bringing or being brought into this state.

dilatation (dy-lă-**tay**-shŏn) *n.* **1.** dilation. **2.** widening of the neck of the womb, e.g. for surgical curettage.

dilate (dy-**layt**) *v.* **1.** to make or become wider or larger. **2.** to speak or write at length, *dilating upon this subject.* **dilation** *n.*, **dilator** *n.*

dilatory (**dil**-ă-ter-i) *adj.* **1.** slow in doing something, not prompt. **2.** designed to cause delay. **dilatorily** *adv.*, **dilatoriness** *n.*

dildo (**dil**-doh) *n.* (*pl.* dildos) an artificial penis used by women for sexual pleasure.

dilemma (dil-**em**-ă) *n.* **1.** a perplexing situation, in which a choice has to be made between alternatives that are equally undesirable. **2.** a problem or difficult choice, *what to do with one's spare time is a modern dilemma.* (¶ Many people regard the use in sense 2 as unacceptable.)

dilettante (dili-**tan**-ti) *n.* a person who dabbles in a subject for his own enjoyment.

diligent (**dil**-i-jĕnt) *adj.* **1.** hard-working, putting care and effort into what one does. **2.** done with care and effort, *a diligent search.* **diligently** *adv.*, **diligence** *n.*

dill *n.* a yellow-flowered herb with spicy seeds used for flavouring pickles.

dilly-dally *v.* (*informal*) to dawdle, to waste time by not making up one's mind.

dilute (dy-**lewt**) *v.* **1.** to thin down, to make a liquid less concentrated by adding water or other liquid. **2.** to weaken or reduce the forcefulness of, to water down. —*adj.* diluted, *a dilute acid.* —**dilution** *n.*

dim *adj.* (dimmer, dimmest) **1.** faintly lit,

luminous but not bright. **2.** indistinct, not clearly seen or heard or remembered. **3.** not seeing clearly, *eyes dim with tears.* **4.** (*informal*) stupid. —*v.* (dimmed, dimming) to make or become dim. —**dimly** *adv.*, **dimness** *n.* □ **dim-wit** *n.* (*informal*) a stupid person. **dim-witted** *adj.* stupid. **take a dim view of,** (*informal*) to disapprove of; to feel gloomy about.

dime *n.* a ten-cent coin of the USA.

dimension (dy-**men**-shŏn) *n.* **1.** a measurement such as length, breadth, thickness, area, or volume. **2.** size; *of great dimensions,* very large. **3.** extent, scope, *gave the problem a new dimension.* **dimensional** *adj.*

diminish *v.* to make or become smaller or less.

diminuendo (dim-in-yoo-**en**-doh) *adj.* & *adv.* (in music) gradually becoming quieter.

diminution (dim-in-**yoo**-shŏn) *n.* **1.** diminishing, being diminished. **2.** a decrease.

diminutive (dim-**in**-yoo-tiv) *adj.* remarkably small. —*n.* a word for a small specimen of something (e.g. *booklet, duckling*), or an affectionate form of a name etc. (e.g. *dearie, Johnnie*).

dimmer *n.* a device for reducing the brightness of lights.

dimple *n.* a small hollow or dent, especially a natural one on the skin of the cheek or chin. —*v.* **1.** to produce dimples in. **2.** to show dimples.

din *n.* a loud resonant and annoying noise. —*v.* (dinned, dinning) **1.** to make a din. **2.** to force (information) into a person by continually repeating it, *din it into him.*

dinar (**dee**-nar) *n.* a unit of currency in Yugoslavia and various countries of the Middle East and North Africa.

dine *v.* **1.** to eat dinner. **2.** to entertain to dinner, *we were wined and dined.* □ **dining-car** *n.* a railway carriage in which meals are served. **dining-room** *n.* a room in which meals are eaten.

diner *n.* **1.** a person who dines. **2.** a dining-car on a train. **3.** a dining-room.

dinette (dy-**net**) *n.* **1.** a small room or part of a room used for meals. **2.** a compact set of furniture for dining.

ding-dong *n.* the sound of a clapper bell or alternate strokes of two bells. —*adj.* with vigorous and alternating action, *a ding-dong argument*; *a ding-dong struggle,* in which each contestant has the better of it alternately.

dinghy (**ding**-i) *n.* (*pl.* dinghies) **1.** a small open boat driven by oars or sails. **2.** a small inflatable rubber boat.

dingo *n.* (*pl.* dingoes) an Australian wild dog.

dingy (**din**-ji) *adj.* (dingier, dingiest) dirty-looking, not fresh or cheerful. **dingily** *adv.*, **dinginess** *n.*

dinkum *adj.* (*Austral.* & *N.Z. informal*) true, real.

dinky *adj.* (*informal*) attractively small and neat.

dinner *n.* **1.** the chief meal of the day, whether at midday or in the evening. **2.** a formal evening meal in honour of a person or event. ☐ **dinner-jacket** *n.* a man's short (usually black) jacket for evening wear.

dinosaur (**dy**-nŏ-sor) *n.* an extinct lizard-like creature, often of enormous size.

dint *n.* a dent. **by dint of**, by means of.

diocese (**dy**-ŏ-sis) *n.* a district under the care of a bishop. **diocesan** (dy-**oss**-i-săn) *adj.*

diode (**dy**-ohd) *n.* **1.** a simple thermionic valve with only two electrodes. **2.** a rectifier made of semiconducting materials and having two terminals.

dioxide (dy-**ok**-syd) *n.* an oxide with two atoms of oxygen to one of a metal or other element.

dip *v.* (dipped, dipping) **1.** to put or lower into liquid; *dip sheep,* wash them in a vermin-killing liquid; *dip fabrics,* dye them in liquid. **2.** to go under water and emerge quickly. **3.** to go down, *the sun dipped below the horizon.* **4.** to put a hand or ladle etc. into something in order to take something out; *dip into one's pocket* or *reserves,* take out money etc. and use it. **5.** to lower for a moment, *dip the flag; dip headlights,* lower their beam to avoid dazzling other drivers. **6.** to slope or extend downwards, *the path dips down to the river.* **7.** to read short passages here and there in a book, *I've dipped into 'War and Peace'.* —**dip** *n.* **1.** the act of dipping. **2.** a quick plunge, a short bathe. **3.** a downward slope. **4.** a liquid into which something is dipped, *sheep-dip.* **5.** a creamy mixture into which biscuits etc. are dipped before eating. ☐ **dip-stick** *n.* a rod for measuring the depth of liquid. **dip-switch** *n.* a switch for dipping a vehicle's headlights.

diphtheria (dif-**theer**-iă) *n.* an acute infectious disease causing severe inflammation of a mucous membrane especially in the throat.

diphthong (**dif**-thong) *n.* a compound vowel-sound produced by combining two simple ones, e.g. *oi* in *point, ou* in *loud.*

diploma *n.* a certificate awarded by a college etc. to a person who has successfully completed a course of study.

diplomacy (dip-**loh**-mă-si) *n.* **1.** the handling of international relations, skill in this. **2.** tact.

diplomat (**dip**-lŏ-mat) *n.* **1.** a member of the diplomatic service. **2.** a tactful person.

diplomatic (diplŏ-**mat**-ik) *adj.* **1.** of or engaged in diplomacy; *the diplomatic service,* the officials engaged in diplomacy on behalf of their country. **2.** tactful, *a diplomatic person* or *reply.* **diplomatically** *adv.*

dipper *n.* **1.** a diving bird, especially the water ouzel. **2.** a ladle.

dipso (**dip**-soh) *n.* (*pl.* dipsos) (*slang*) a dipsomaniac.

dipsomania (dip-sŏ-**may**-niă) *n.* an uncontrollable craving for alcohol. **dipsomaniac** *n.* a person suffering from this.

dire *adj.* **1.** dreadful, terrible, *in dire peril.* **2.** ominous, predicting trouble, *dire warnings.* **3.** extreme and urgent, *in dire need.*

direct *adj.* **1.** going in a straight line, not curved or crooked or roundabout, *the direct route.* **2.** with nothing or no one in between, in an unbroken line, *in direct contact; direct taxes,* those charged on income, as distinct from those on goods or services. **3.** straightforward, frank, going straight to the point, *a direct way of speaking.* **4.** exact, complete, *the direct opposite.* —**direct** *adv.* by a direct route, *travelled to Rome direct.* (¶ Note that *directly* is not used with this meaning.) —**direct** *v.* **1.** to tell or show how to do something or get somewhere, *can you direct me to the station?* **2.** to address (a letter or parcel etc.). **3.** to cause to have a specified direction or target, to utter (remarks) to a particular hearer, *direct our energies towards higher productivity; the remark was directed at me.* **4.** to control, to manage, *there was no one to direct the workmen; direct a film,* supervise the acting and filming of it. **5.** to command, to order, *directed his men to advance.* —**directness** *n.* ☐ **direct access,** *see* access. **direct current,** electric current flowing in one direction only. **direct debit,** a system of debiting a person's bank account at the request of his creditor.

direction *n.* **1.** directing, aiming, guiding, managing. **2.** the line along which something moves or faces, *in the direction of London.* ☐ **directions** *pl. n.* instructions. **sense of direction,** a person's ability to get his bearings without guidance.

directional *adj.* **1.** of or indicating direction. **2.** operating or sending radio signals in one direction only.

directive *n.* a general instruction issued by authority.

directly *adv.* **1.** in a direct line, in a direct manner. (¶ See also direct *adv.*) **2.** without delay. **3.** very soon. —*conj.* (*informal*) as soon as, *I went directly I knew.*

director *n.* **1.** a person who supervises or manages things, especially a member of the board managing a business company on behalf of shareholders. **2.** a person who directs a film or play. **directorship** *n.*

directorate *n.* a board of directors.

directory *n.* a book containing a list of telephone subscribers, inhabitants of a district, members of a profession, business firms, etc.

dirge (*pr.* derj) *n.* a slow mournful song, a lament for the dead.

dirigible (di-**rij**-ibŭl) *adj.* capable of being guided. —*n.* a dirigible balloon or airship.

dirk *n.* a kind of dagger.

dirndl (**dern**-d'l) *n.* a full skirt gathered into a tight waistband.

dirt *n.* **1.** unclean matter that soils something. **2.** earth, soil. **3.** anything worthless or not deserving respect. **4.** foul words or talk, scandal. □ **dirt cheap**, (*slang*) very cheap. **dirt-track** *n.* a racing track made of earth or rolled cinders etc.

dirty *adj.* (dirtier, dirtiest) **1.** soiled, unclean; *a dirty job,* causing the doer to become dirty. **2.** (of a nuclear bomb) producing much fall-out. **3.** not having clean habits. **4.** dishonourable, mean, unfair, *a dirty trick; a dirty fighter.* **5.** (of weather) rough and stormy. **6.** lewd, obscene, *dirty jokes.* —**dirty** *v.* (dirtied, dirtying) to make or become dirty. □ **dirty look**, a disapproving look. **dirty money**, extra money paid to those who have to handle dirty materials. **dirty word**, an obscene word; a word denoting something that is regarded as discreditable, *charity became a dirty word.* **dirty work**, dishonourable dealings. **do the dirty on**, to play a mean trick on.

disability *n.* something that disables or disqualifies a person, a physical incapacity caused by injury or disease etc.

disable *v.* to deprive of some ability, to make unfit or useless. **disablement** *n.* □ **disabled** *adj.* having a physical disability.

disabuse (dis-ă-**bewz**) *v.* to disillusion, to free from a false idea, *he was soon disabused of this notion.*

disadvantage *n.* **1.** an unfavourable condition or circumstance; *at a disadvantage,* in an unfavourable position. **2.** damage to one's interest or reputation; *to our disadvantage,* causing us loss or inconvenience etc. —*v.* to put at a disadvantage.

disadvantaged *adj.* suffering from unfavourable conditions of life.

disadvantageous (dis-ad-văn-**tay**-jŭs) *adj.* causing disadvantage.

disaffected *adj.* discontented, having lost one's feelings of loyalty. **disaffection** *n.*

disagree *v.* (disagreed, disagreeing) **1.** to have a different opinion. **2.** to be unlike, to fail to correspond, *your statement disagrees with your brother's.* **3.** to quarrel. **4.** (of food or climate etc.) to have bad effects, *hot weather disagrees with him.* **disagreement** *n.*

disagreeable *adj.* **1.** unpleasant. **2.** bad-tempered. **disagreeably** *adv.*

disallow *v.* to refuse to allow or accept as valid, *the judge disallowed the claim.*

disappear *v.* to cease to be visible, to pass from sight or from existence, *the problem may disappear.* **disappearance** *n.*

disappoint *v.* to fail to do or be equal to what was hoped or desired or expected by. **disappointment** *n.* □ **disappointed** *adj.* feeling disappointment, *we were disappointed at the failure* or *in* or *with a thing* or *of one's expectations.*

disapprobation (dis-ap-rŏ-**bay**-shŏn) *n.* disapproval.

disapprove *v.* to have or express an unfavourable opinion. **disapproval** *n.*

disarm *v.* **1.** to deprive of weapons or of the means of defence. **2.** to disband or reduce armed forces. **3.** to defuse (a bomb). **4.** to make it difficult for a person to feel anger or suspicion or doubt, *his friendliness dispelled their hostility.*

disarmament *n.* reduction of a country's armed forces or weapons of war.

disarrange *v.* to put into disorder, to disorganize. **disarrangement** *n.*

disarray *n.* disorder. —*v.* to disarrange.

disassociate *v.* = dissociate.

disaster *n.* **1.** a sudden great misfortune. **2.** a complete failure, *the performance was a disaster.* **disastrous** (diz-**ah**-strŭs) *adj.,* **disastrously** *adv.* □ **disaster area**, an area in which a major disaster (e.g. an earthquake) has recently occurred.

disavow *v.* to disclaim. **disavowal** *n.*

disband *v.* to break up, to separate, *disbanded the choir; the troops disbanded.* **disbandment** *n.*

disbelieve *v.* to refuse or be unable to believe. **disbeliever** *n.,* **disbelief** *n.*

disbud *v.* (disbudded, disbudding) to remove unwanted buds from (a plant).

disburse *v.* to pay out (money), *disbursing large amounts.* **disbursement** *n.*

disc *n.* **1.** a thin circular plate of any material. **2.** something shaped or looking like this, *the sun's disc.* **3.** a layer of cartilage between vertebrae; *a slipped disc,* one that has become displaced, causing pain from pressure on nerves. **4.** a gramophone record. **5.** a circular plate resembling a gramophone record, coated with magnetic material on which data can be recorded for use in a computer etc. □ **disc brake,** one in which a flat plate presses against a plate at the centre of a wheel. **disc drive,** an apparatus that turns the disc on a computer etc. while data are recorded or retrieved. **disc jockey,** (*informal*) the compère of a broadcast programme of records of light and popular music. **disc parking,** a system in which vehicles may park for a limited time by displaying a disc indicating their time of arrival. **disc wheel,** a solid wheel without spokes.

discard [1] (dis-**kard**) *v.* to throw away, to put aside as useless or unwanted.

discard [2] (**dis**-kard) *n.* something discarded.

discern (dis-**sern**) *v.* to perceive clearly with the mind or senses. **discernment** *n.*

discernible (dis-**sern**-ibŭl) *adj.* able to be discerned.

discerning (dis-**sern**-ing) *adj.* perceptive, showing good judgement.

discharge *v.* **1.** to give or send out, *the pipes discharge their contents into the river*; *the river discharges into the sea,* flows into it; *the wound is still discharging,* matter is coming out. **2.** to give out an electric charge, to cause to do this. **3.** to fire (a missile or gun). **4.** to dismiss from employment, *a discharged servant.* **5.** to allow to leave, *the patient was discharged from hospital*; *a discharged bankrupt,* a bankrupt who has done what the court required and is now freed from its control. **6.** to pay (a debt), to perform or fulfil (a duty or contract). —**discharge** *n.* **1.** discharging, being discharged. **2.** something that is discharged, *the discharge from the wound.*

disciple (di-**sy**-pŭl) *n.* **1.** one of the original followers of Christ. **2.** a person who follows the teachings of another whom he accepts as a leader.

disciplinarian (dis-i-plin-**air**-iăn) *n.* one who enforces or believes in strict discipline.

disciplinary (**dis**-i-plin-er-i) *adj.* of or for discipline.

discipline (**dis**-i-plin) *n.* **1.** training that produces obedience, self-control, or a particular skill. **2.** controlled behaviour produced by such training. **3.** punishment given to correct a person or enforce obedience. **4.** a branch of instruction or learning. —**discipline** *v.* **1.** to train to be obedient and orderly. **2.** to punish.

disclaim *v.* to disown; *they disclaim responsibility for the accident,* say that they are not responsible. **disclaimer** *n.* a statement disclaiming something.

disclose *v.* to expose to view, to reveal, to make known. **disclosure** *n.*

disco *n.* (*pl.* discos) (*informal*). a discothèque.

discography (dis-**kog**-răfi) *n.* a descriptive catalogue or study of gramophone records.

discolour *v.* **1.** to spoil the colour of, to stain. **2.** to become changed in colour or stained. **discoloration** *n.*

discomfit (dis-**kum**-fit) *v.* (discomfited, discomfiting) to disconcert. **discomfiture** (dis-**kum**-fi-cher) *n.*

discomfort *n.* **1.** being uncomfortable in body or mind. **2.** something that causes this.

discompose *v.* to disturb the composure of, to agitate. **discomposure** *n.*

disconcert (dis-kŏn-**sert**) *v.* to upset the self-possession of, to fluster.

disconnect *v.* to break the connection of, to put out of action by disconnecting certain parts. **disconnection** *n.*

disconnected *adj.* lacking orderly connection between its parts, *a disconnected speech.*

disconsolate (dis-**kon**-sŏ-lăt) *adj.* unhappy at the loss of something, disappointed. **disconsolately** *adv.*

discontent *n.* dissatisfaction, lack of contentment.

discontented *adj.* not contented, feeling discontent.

discontinue *v.* to put an end to, to come to an end. **discontinuance** *n.*

discontinuous *adj.* not continuous. **discontinuity** (dis-kon-tin-**yoo**-iti) *n.*

discord (**dis**-kord) *n.* **1.** disagreement, quarrelling. **2.** a combination of notes producing a harsh or unpleasant sound. **discordant** (dis-**kor**-dănt) *adj.,* **discordantly** *adv.*

discothèque (**dis**-kŏ-tek) *n.* **1.** a club or party etc. where amplified recorded music is played for dancing. **2.** the equipment for playing such records.

discount [1] (**dis**-kownt) *n.* an amount of money taken off the full price or total. **at a discount,** below the nominal or usual price; not valued as it used to be, *is honesty at a discount nowadays?* **discount shop,** one selling goods regularly at less than the standard price.

discount [2] (dis-**kownt**) *v.* **1.** to disregard partly or wholly, *we cannot discount this possibility.* **2.** to purchase a bill of exchange for less than its value will be when matured.

discourage v. 1. to dishearten. 2. to dissuade. 3. to deter. **discouragement** n.

discourse[1] (dis-korss) n. a speech or lecture, a written treatise on a subject.

discourse[2] (dis-**korss**) v. to utter or write a discourse.

discourteous (dis-**ker**-ti-ŭs) adj. lacking courtesy. **discourteously** adv., **discourtesy** n.

discover v. 1. to obtain sight or knowledge of, especially by searching or other effort. 2. to be the first to do this, *Herschel discovered a new planet.* **discoverer** n.

discovery n. 1. discovering, being discovered. 2. something that is discovered.

discredit v. (discredited, discrediting) 1. to damage the good reputation of. 2. to refuse to believe. 3. to cause to be disbelieved. —**discredit** n. 1. damage to reputation. 2. something that causes this. 3. doubt, lack of credibility.

discreditable adj. bringing discredit, shameful. **discreditably** adv.

discreet adj. 1. showing caution and good judgement in what one does, not giving away secrets. 2. not showy or obtrusive. **discreetly** adv.
¶ Do not confuse with discrete.

discrepancy (dis-**krep**-ănsi) n. difference, failure to tally, *there were several discrepancies between the two accounts.* **discrepant** adj.

discrete (dis-**kreet**) adj. discontinuous, individually distinct. **discretely** adv.
¶ Do not confuse with discreet.

discretion (dis-**kresh**-ŏn) n. 1. being discreet in one's speech, keeping secrets. 2. good judgement, *he acted with discretion.* 3. freedom to act according to one's judgement, *the treasurer has full discretion.* □ **at a person's discretion**, in accordance with his decision. **years** or **age of discretion**, the age at which a person is considered capable of managing his own affairs.

discretionary (dis-**kresh**-ŏn-er-i) adj. done or used at a person's discretion, *discretionary powers.*

discriminate v. 1. to have good taste or judgement. 2. to make a distinction, to give unfair treatment, especially because of prejudice, *they had discriminated against him.* **discrimination** n.

discursive adj. rambling from one subject to another.

discus n. a heavy thick-centred disc, thrown in contests of strength.

discuss v. to examine by means of argument, to talk or write about. **discussion** n.

disdain n. scorn, contempt. —v. 1. to regard with disdain, to treat as unworthy of notice. 2. to refrain because of disdain, *she disdained to reply.* —**disdainful** adj., **disdainfully** adv.

disease n. an unhealthy condition caused by infection or diet or by faulty functioning of a bodily process.

diseased adj. affected with disease.

disembark v. to put or go ashore. **disembarkation** n.

disembodied adj. (of the soul or spirit) freed from the body.

disembowel v. (disembowelled, disembowelling) to take out the bowels of.

disenchant v. to free from enchantment, to disillusion, *they are disenchanted with the government.* **disenchantment** n.

disengage v. to free from engagement, to detach. **disengagement** n.

disengaged adj. not engaged in attending to another person or to business, free.

disentangle v. to free from tangles or confusion, to extricate. **disentanglement** n.

disestablish v. to end the established state of, to deprive (the Church) of its official connection with the State. **disestablishment** n.

disfavour n. dislike, disapproval.

disfigure v. to spoil the appearance of. **disfigurement** n.

disfranchise (dis-**fran**-chyz) v. to deprive of the right to vote for a parliamentary representative. **disfranchisement** n.

disgorge v. 1. to throw out from the gorge or throat, *the whale swallowed Jonah and then disgorged him.* 2. to pour forth, *the river disgorges itself into the sea.* 3. (*informal*) to hand over, *made him disgorge the stolen property.*

disgrace n. 1. loss of favour or respect. 2. something that causes this. —v. to bring disgrace upon, to humiliate. —**disgraceful** adj., **disgracefully** adv.

disgruntled adj. discontented, resentful.

disguise v. 1. to conceal the identity of. 2. to conceal; *there's no disguising the fact,* it cannot be concealed. —**disguise** n. 1. something worn or used for disguising. 2. disguising, a disguised condition.

disgust n. a strong feeling of dislike, finding a thing very unpleasant or against one's principles. —v. to cause disgust in.

disgusted adj. feeling disgust.

dish n. 1. a shallow flat-bottomed container for holding or serving food; *wash the dishes,* wash all the utensils after use at a meal. 2. the amount a dish contains. 3. the food itself, a particular kind of food. 4. a shallow concave object. 5. (*slang*) an attractive person. —v. (*informal*) to ruin, to spoil hopes or expectations, *it has dished* *our chances.* ☐ **dish out.** (*informal*) to distribute. **dish up,** to put food into dishes ready for serving; (*slang*) to serve up as facts etc., *dished up the usual excuses.*

dish-water *n.* water in which used dishes have been washed.

disharmony *n.* lack of harmony.

dishcloth *n.* a cloth for washing dishes.

dishearten *v.* to cause to lose hope or confidence. **disheartenment** *n.*

dished *adj.* concave.

dishevelled (dish-ev-ĕld) *adj.* ruffled and untidy. **dishevelment** *n.*

dishonest *adj.* not honest. **dishonestly** *adv.*, **dishonesty** *n.*

dishonour *n.* 1. loss of honour or respect, disgrace. 2. something that causes this. —*v.* to bring dishonour upon, to disgrace.

dishonourable *adj.* not honourable, shameful. **dishonourably** *adv.*

dishwasher *n.* a machine for washing dishes etc. automatically.

dishy *adj.* (dishier, dishiest) (*slang*) very attractive.

disillusion *v.* to set free from pleasant but mistaken beliefs. —*n.* the state of being disillusioned. —**disillusionment** *n.*

disincentive *n.* something that discourages an action or effort.

disinclination *n.* unwillingness, a slight dislike.

disincline *v.* to make (a person) feel reluctant or unwilling to do something.

disinfect *v.* to cleanse by destroying bacteria that may cause disease. **disinfection** *n.*

disinfectant *n.* a substance used for disinfecting things.

disinflation *n.* the process of counteracting inflation without producing the disadvantages of deflation. **disinflationary** *adj.*

disinformation *n.* deliberately false information.

disingenuous (dis-in-jen-yoo-ŭs) *adj.* insincere, not frank.

disinherit *v.* to deprive (a person) of an inheritance by making a will naming another or others as one's heir(s).

disintegrate *v.* to break or cause to break into small parts or pieces. **disintegration** *n.*

disinter (dis-in-ter) *v.* (disinterred, disinterring) to dig up (something buried), to unearth.

disinterested *adj.* 1. unbiased, not influenced by self-interest. 2. uninterested, uncaring. (¶ This use is regarded as unacceptable because it obscures a useful distinction between *disinterested* and *uninterested*.) **disinterestedly** *adv.*

disjoin *v.* to separate.

disjointed *adj.* (of talk) disconnected.

disk *n.* = disc.

diskette *n.* = disc (sense 5).

dislike *n.* a feeling of not liking something. —*v.* to feel dislike for.

dislocate *v.* 1. to put (a thing) out of place in relation to connecting parts, to displace (a bone) from its proper position in a joint. 2. to put out of order, to disrupt, *fog dislocated traffic.* **dislocation** *n.*

dislodge *v.* to move or force from an established position.

disloyal *adj.* not loyal. **disloyally** *adv.*, **disloyalty** *n.*

dismal *adj.* 1. causing or showing gloom, dreary. 2. feeble, *a dismal attempt at humour.* **dismally** *adv.*

dismantle *v.* to take away fittings or furnishings from, to take to pieces.

dismay *n.* a feeling of surprise and discouragement. —*v.* to fill with dismay.

dismember *v.* 1. to remove the limbs of. 2. to divide into parts, to partition (a country etc.). **dismemberment** *n.*

dismiss *v.* 1. to send away from one's presence or employment. 2. to put out of one's thoughts, to mention or discuss only briefly. 3. to reject without further hearing, *the case was dismissed for lack of evidence.* 4. to put (a batsman or side) out in cricket, *dismissed him for 6 runs.* **dismissal** *n.*

dismount *v.* 1. to get off or down from something on which one is riding. 2. to cause to fall off, to unseat.

disobedient *adj.* not obedient. **disobediently** *adv.*, **disobedience** *n.*

disobey *v.* (disobeyed, disobeying) to disregard orders, to fail to obey.

disorder *n.* 1. lack of order, untidiness. 2. a disturbance of public order, a riot. 3. disturbance of the normal working of body or mind, *a nervous disorder.* —*v.* to throw into disorder, to upset. —**disorderly** *adj.*

disorganize *v.* to throw into confusion, to upset the orderly system or arrangement of. **disorganized** *adj.* lacking organization or an orderly system.

disorientate (dis-or-i-ĕn-tayt) *v.* to confuse (a person) and make him lose his bearings.

disown *v.* to refuse to acknowledge as one's own, to reject all connection with.

disparage (dis-pa-rij) *v.* to speak of in a slighting way, to belittle. **disparagingly** *adv.*, **disparagement** *n.*

disparate (dis-per-ăt) *adj.* different in kind.

disparity (dis-pa-riti) *n.* inequality, difference.

dispassionate *adj.* free from emotion, calm, impartial. **dispassionately** *adv.*

dispatch *v.* **1.** to send off to a destination or for a purpose. **2.** to give the death-blow to, to kill. **3.** to complete or dispose of quickly. —**dispatch** *n.* **1.** dispatching, being dispatched. **2.** promptness, speed, *he acted with dispatch.* **3.** an official message or report sent with speed. **4.** a news report sent to a newspaper or news agency etc. □ **dispatch-box** *n.* a container for carrying official documents. **dispatch-rider** *n.* a messenger who travels by motor cycle.

dispel *v.* (dispelled, dispelling) to drive away, to scatter, *wind dispelled the fog; how can we dispel their fears?*

dispensable *adj.* not essential.

dispensary *n.* a place where medicines are dispensed, *the hospital dispensary.*

dispensation *n.* **1.** dispensing, distributing. **2.** ordering or management, especially of the world by Providence. **3.** exemption from a penalty or duty.

dispense *v.* **1.** to distribute, to deal out; *dispense justice,* to administer it. **2.** to prepare and give out (medicines etc.) according to prescriptions. □ **dispense with,** to do without; to make unnecessary. **dispensing chemist,** one who is qualified to dispense medicines.

dispenser *n.* **1.** a person who dispenses medicines. **2.** a device that deals out a quantity of something, *a soap dispenser.*

dispersant *n.* a substance that disperses something.

disperse *v.* to scatter, to go or drive or send in different directions. **dispersal** *n.,* **dispersion** *n.*

dispirited *adj.* depressed, disheartened.

displace *v.* **1.** to shift from its place. **2.** to take the place of, to oust, *weeds tend to displace other plants.* **displacement** *n.*

display *v.* **1.** to show, to arrange (a thing) so that it can be seen. **2.** (of birds and animals) to make a display (see sense 3 below). —**display** *n.* **1.** displaying, being displayed. **2.** something displayed conspicuously. **3.** a special pattern of behaviour used by birds and animals as a means of communication. □ **display terminal,** a computer terminal that displays information on a screen.

displease *v.* to offend, to arouse the disapproval or anger of.

displeasure *n.* a displeased feeling, dissatisfaction.

disport *v.* (*formal*) to play, to amuse oneself, *disporting themselves on the beach.*

disposable *adj.* **1.** able to be disposed of. **2.** at one's disposal; *disposable income,* the amount left after taxes have been deducted.

3. designed to be thrown away after being used once.

disposal *n.* disposing of something. **at one's disposal,** available for one's use.

dispose *v.* **1.** to place suitably or in order, *disposed the troops in two lines.* **2.** to determine the course of events, *man proposes, God disposes.* **3.** to make willing or ready to do something, to incline, *their friendliness disposed us to accept the invitation; we felt disposed to accept.* □ **be well disposed towards,** to be friendly towards, to favour. **dispose of,** to get rid of, to deal with.

disposition *n.* **1.** setting in order, arrangement, *the disposition of troops.* **2.** a person's natural qualities of mind and character, *has a cheerful disposition.* **3.** a natural tendency or inclination, *they show a disposition to move house frequently.*

dispossess *v.* to deprive (a person) of the possession of something. **dispossession** *n.*

disproportion *n.* lack of proper proportion, being out of proportion.

disproportionate *adj.* out of proportion, relatively too large or too small. **disproportionately** *adv.*

disprove *v.* to show to be false or wrong.

disputable (dis-**pewt**-ăbŭl) *adj.* able to be disputed, questionable.

disputant (dis-**pew**-tănt) *n.* a person engaged in a dispute.

disputation *n.* argument, debate.

dispute[1] (dis-**pewt**) *v.* **1.** to argue, to debate. **2.** to quarrel. **3.** to question the truth or validity of, *dispute a claim; the disputed territory,* that which is the subject of a dispute.

dispute[2] (dis-**pewt** *or* **dis**-pewt) *n.* **1.** an argument or debate. **2.** a quarrel. □ **in dispute,** being argued about.

disqualify *v.* (disqualified, disqualifying) **1.** to debar from a competition because of an infringement of the rules. **2.** to make unsuitable or ineligible, *weak eyesight disqualifies him for military service.* **disqualification** *n.*

disquiet *n.* uneasiness, anxiety. —*v.* to make uneasy or anxious. —**disquieting** *adj.* causing disquiet.

disquisition (dis-kwi-**zish**-ŏn) *n.* a long elaborate spoken or written account of something.

disregard *v.* to pay no attention to, to treat as of no importance. —*n.* lack of attention to something, treating it as of no importance, *complete disregard for his own safety.*

disrepair *n.* a bad condition caused by lack of repairs, *in a state of disrepair.*

disreputable (dis-**rep**-yoo-tăbŭl) *adj.*

having a bad reputation, not respectable in character or appearance. **disreputably** *adv.*

disrepute (dis-ri-**pewt**) *n.* lack of good repute, discredit, *fell into disrepute*.

disrespect *n.* lack of respect, rudeness. **disrespectful** *adj.*

disrobe *v.* to take off official or ceremonial robes, to undress.

disrupt *v.* to cause to break up, to throw into disorder, to interrupt the flow or continuity of, *party quarrels disrupted the coalition*; *floods disrupted traffic*. **disruption** *n.*

disruptive *adj.* causing disruption.

dissatisfaction *n.* lack of satisfaction or of contentment.

dissatisfied *adj.* not satisfied, feeling dissatisfaction.

dissect (dis-**sekt**) *v.* 1. to cut apart, especially in order to examine internal structure. 2. to examine (a theory etc.) part by part. **dissection** *n.*, **dissector** *n.*

dissemble *v.* to conceal (one's feelings).

disseminate (dis-**sem**-in-ayt) *v.* to spread (ideas etc.) widely. **dissemination** *n.* □ **disseminated sclerosis**, multiple sclerosis.

dissension *n.* disagreement that gives rise to strife.

dissent *v.* to have or express a different opinion. —*n.* a difference in opinion. — **dissenter** *n.*

dissentient (dis-**sen**-shĕnt) *adj.* dissenting. —*n.* one who dissents.

dissertation *n.* a spoken or written discourse.

disservice *n.* a harmful action done by a person who intended to help.

dissident (**dis**-i-dĕnt) *adj.* disagreeing. —*n.* one who disagrees, one who opposes the authorities. —**dissidence** *n.*

dissimilar *adj.* unlike. **dissimilarity** *n.*

dissimulation *n.* dissembling.

dissipate (**dis**-i-payt) *v.* 1. to dispel, to disperse. 2. to squander or fritter away.

dissipation *n.* 1. dissipating, being dissipated. 2. dissipated living.

dissipated *adj.* indulging one's vices, living a dissolute life.

dissociate (dis-**soh**-si-ayt) *v.* to separate in one's thoughts, *it is difficult to dissociate the man from his work*; *dissociate oneself from a thing*, to declare that one has no connection with it. **dissociation** *n.*

dissolute (**dis**-ŏ-loot) *adj.* lacking moral restraint or self-discipline.

dissolution *n.* the dissolving of an assembly or partnership, the ending of the existence of monasteries in the reign of Henry VIII.

dissolve *v.* 1. to make or become liquid, to disperse or cause to be dispersed in a liquid. 2. to cause to disappear, to disappear gradually. 3. to dismiss or disperse (an assembly, e.g. parliament), to annul or put an end to (a partnership, e.g. a marriage). 4. to give way to emotion, *she dissolved into tears*.

dissonant (**dis**-ŏn-ănt) *adj.* discordant. **dissonance** *n.*

dissuade *v.* to discourage or persuade against a course of action, *dissuaded her from going*. **dissuasion** *n.*

dissuasive *adj.* dissuading.

distaff (**dis**-tahf) *n.* a cleft stick holding wool etc. for spinning. **on the distaff side**, on the mother's side of a family.

distance *n.* 1. the length of space between one point and another. 2. a distant part, *in the distance*. 3. being distant, remoteness. —*v.* to outdistance in a race. □ **at a distance**, far off, not very near; *keep someone at a distance*, to avoid becoming too friendly. **keep one's distance**, to remain at a safe distance; to behave aloofly, to be not very friendly. **within walking distance**, near enough to be reached easily by walking.

distant *adj.* 1. at a specified or considerable distance away, *three miles distant*. 2. remote, much apart in space or time or relationship etc., *the distant past*; *a distant cousin*. 3. not friendly, aloof. —**distantly** *adv.*

distaste *n.* dislike.

distasteful *adj.* unpleasant, arousing distaste. **distastefully** *adv.*

distemper *n.* 1. a disease of dogs and certain other animals, with coughing and weakness. 2. a kind of paint made from powdered colouring matter mixed with glue or size. —*v.* to paint with this.

distend *v.* to swell or become swollen by pressure from within. **distension** *n.*

distil *v.* (distilled, distilling) 1. to treat by distillation, to make or produce or purify in this way. 2. to undergo distillation.

distillation *n.* 1. the process of turning a substance to vapour by heat then cooling the vapour so that it condenses and collecting the resulting liquid, in order to purify it or separate its constituents or extract an essence. 2. something distilled.

distiller *n.* a person who distils, one who makes alcoholic liquors by distillation. **distillery** *n.* a place where this is done.

distinct *adj.* 1. able to be perceived clearly by the senses or the mind, definite and unmistakable, *a distinct improvement*. 2. different in kind, separate, *his hobbies are* *quite distinct from his work.* **distinctly** *adv.,* **distinctness** *n.*

distinction *n.* **1.** seeing or making a difference between things. **2.** a difference seen or made. **3.** a thing that differentiates one thing from another. **4.** a mark of honour. **5.** excellence, *a person of distinction.*

distinctive *adj.* serving to distinguish a thing by making it different from others. ¶ Do not confuse with distinct. A *distinct* sign is one that can be seen clearly; a *distinctive* sign is one not commonly found elsewhere.

distinguish *v.* **1.** to see or point out a difference between, to draw distinctions, *we must distinguish facts from rumours.* **2.** to make different, to be a characteristic mark or property of, *speech distinguishes man from animals.* **3.** to make out by listening or looking, *unable to distinguish distant objects.* **4.** to make notable, to bring honour to, *he distinguished himself by his bravery.*

distinguished *adj.* **1.** showing excellence. **2.** famous for great achievements. **3.** having an air of distinction and dignity.

distort *v.* **1.** to pull or twist out of its usual shape. **2.** to misrepresent, to twist out of the truth. **distortion** *n.*

distract *v.* to draw away the attention of, *distracted him from his work.*

distracted *adj.* distraught.

distraction *n.* **1.** something that distracts the attention and prevents concentration. **2.** an amusement or entertainment. **3.** mental upset or distress. □ **to distraction,** almost to a state of madness.

distrain *v.* to levy a distraint (upon a person or his goods).

distraint *n.* seizure of a person's possessions in order to make him pay what he owes, or in order to sell them to meet his debts.

distraught (dis-**trawt**) *adj.* greatly upset, nearly crazy with grief or worry.

distress *n.* **1.** suffering caused by pain, worry, illness, or exhaustion. **2.** the condition of being damaged or in danger and requiring help, *a ship in distress.* —*v.* to cause distress to.

distribute *v.* **1.** to divide and give a share to each of a number, to deal out. **2.** to spread or scatter, to place at different points, *distributed his forces.* **distribution** *n.*

distributive *adj.* of or concerned with distribution.

distributor *n.* **1.** one who distributes things, an agent who markets goods. **2.** a device for passing current to the sparking-plugs in an engine.

district *n.* part of a country, city, or county, having a particular feature or regarded as a unit for a special purpose, *the Lake District; a postal district.*

distrust *n.* lack of trust, suspicion. —*v.* to feel distrust in. —**distrustful** *adj.*

disturb *v.* **1.** to break the rest or quiet or calm of. **2.** to cause to move from a settled position. □ **disturbed** *adj.* emotionally or mentally unstable or abnormal.

disturbance *n.* **1.** disturbing, being disturbed. **2.** a commotion, an outbreak of social or political disorder.

disunity *n.* lack of unity.

disuse *n.* the state of not being used, *rusty from disuse.* **disused** *adj.* no longer used.

ditch *n.* a long narrow trench to hold or carry off water or to serve as a boundary. —*v.* **1.** to make or repair ditches, *hedging and ditching.* **2.** to drive (a vehicle) into a ditch. **3.** (*informal*) to make a forced landing on the sea. **4.** (*slang*) to abandon, to discard, to leave in the lurch. □ **dull as ditch-water,** very dull.

dither *v.* **1.** to tremble, to quiver. **2.** to hesitate indecisively. —*n.* a state of dithering, nervous excitement or fear, *all of a dither.*

ditto *n.* (used in lists to avoid repeating something) the same again. **say ditto to,** (*informal*) to endorse what is said, to agree with it.

ditty *n.* a short simple song.

diuretic (dy-yoor-et-ik) *n.* a substance that causes more urine to be secreted.

diurnal (dy-**ern**-ăl) *adj.* **1.** of the day, not nocturnal. **2.** occupying one day.

divan (div-**an**) *n.* a low couch without a raised back or ends, a bed resembling this.

dive *v.* **1.** to plunge head first into water. **2.** (of an aircraft) to plunge steeply downwards. **3.** (of a submarine or diver) to go under water. **4.** to go down or out of sight suddenly, to rush headlong, *dived into a shop.* **5.** to move a thing (e.g. one's hand) quickly downwards into something. — **dive** *n.* **1.** an act of diving. **2.** a sharp downward movement or fall. **3.** (*slang*) a disreputable place. □ **dive-bomb** *v.* to drop bombs from a diving aircraft. **diving bird,** one that dives for its food. **diving-board** *n.* a board for diving from. **diving-suit** *n.* a watertight suit, usually with a helmet and air supply, for work under water.

diver *n.* **1.** one who dives. **2.** a person who works underwater in a diving-suit.

diverge (dy-**verj**) *v.* **1.** to go in different directions from a common point or from each other, to become further apart. **2.** to go aside from a path; *diverge from the* *truth,* depart from it. **divergent** *adj.,* **divergence** *n.*

divers (**dy**-verz) *adj.* (*old use*) several, various.

diverse (dy-**vers**) *adj.* of differing kinds.

diversify *v.* (diversified, diversifying) to introduce variety into, to vary. **diversification** *n.*

diversion *n.* **1.** diverting something from its course. **2.** diverting of attention; *create a diversion,* do something to divert attention. **3.** a recreation, an entertainment. **4.** an alternative route when a road is temporarily closed to traffic. **diversionary** *adj.*

diversity (dy-**vers**-iti) *n.* variety.

divert *v.* **1.** to turn (a thing) from its course, *divert the stream*; *divert attention,* distract it; *divert traffic,* cause it to go by a different route. **2.** to entertain or amuse with recreations.

diverticulitis (dy-ver-tik-yoo-**ly**-tiss) *n.* inflammation of a side-branch of a cavity or passage in the body.

diverting *adj.* entertaining, amusing.

divest (dy-**vest**) *v.* **1.** to strip of clothes, *divested himself of his robes.* **2.** to take away, to deprive, *divested him of his power.*

divide *v.* **1.** to separate into parts, to split or break up, *divide the money between you*; *the river divides into two channels.* **2.** to separate from something else, *the Pyrenees divide France from Spain.* **3.** to arrange in separate groups, to classify. **4.** to cause to disagree, *this controversy divided the party.* **5.** (in parliament) to part or cause to part in order to vote, *the House divided*; *they decided not to divide the House,* not to ask for a vote to be taken. **6.** to find how many times one number contains another, *divide 12 by 3.* **7.** to be able to be divided. — **divide** *n.* a dividing line, a watershed.

dividend *n.* **1.** a number that is to be divided. **2.** a share of profits paid to shareholders or winners in a football pool. **3.** a benefit from an action; *his long training paid dividends,* produced benefits.

divider *n.* something that divides; *a room divider,* a screen or piece of furniture to divide a room into two parts. **dividers** *pl. n.* measuring-compasses.

divination (div-in-**ay**-shŏn) *n.* divining, foretelling future events or discovering hidden knowledge.

divine *adj.* **1.** of, from, or like God or a god. **2.** (*informal*) excellent, very beautiful, *this divine weather.* —**divine** *v.* to discover or learn about future events by what are alleged to be magical means, or by inspiration or guessing. —**divinely** *adv.,* **diviner** *n.* □ **divining-rod** *n.* a forked stick or rod used in dowsing.

divinity *n.* **1.** being divine. **2.** a god. **3.** the study of Christianity.

divisible (di-**viz**-ibŭl) *adj.* able to be divided. **divisibility** *n.*

division *n.* **1.** dividing, being divided. **2.** (in parliament) separation of members into two sections for counting votes. **3.** a dividing line, a partition. **4.** one of the parts into which a thing is divided. **5.** a major unit of an organization, *our export division.* □ **division sign,** the sign ÷ (as in 12 ÷ 4) indicating that one quantity is to be divided by another. **divisional** *adj.*

divisive (di-**vy**-siv) *adj.* tending to cause disagreement among members of a group.

divisor (di-**vy**-zer) *n.* a number by which another is to be divided.

divorce *n.* **1.** the legal termination of a marriage. **2.** the separation of things that were together. —**divorce** *v.* **1.** to end a marriage with (one's husband or wife) by divorce. **2.** to separate, especially in thought or organization.

divorcee (div-or-**see**) *n.* a divorced person.

divot (**div**-ŏt) *n.* a piece of turf cut out by a club-head in making a stroke in golf.

divulge (dy-**vulj**) *v.* to reveal (information). **divulgation** (dy-vul-**gay**-shŏn) *n.*

divvy *n.* (*informal*) a dividend. —*v.* (divvied, divvying) **divvy up,** (*informal*) to share out.

Diwali (di-**wah**-li) *n.* a Hindu religious festival at which lamps are lit, held in October or November.

dixie *n.* a large iron pot in which stew or tea is made by campers etc.

Dixie *n.* the southern States of the USA.

Dixieland *n.* **1.** Dixie. **2.** a kind of jazz with strong two-beat rhythm.

DIY *abbrev.* do-it-yourself.

dizzy *adj.* (dizzier, dizziest) **1.** giddy, feeling confused. **2.** causing giddiness, *dizzy heights,* **dizzily** *adv.,* **dizziness** *n.*

DJ *abbrev.* disc jockey.

Djakarta = Jakarta.

DNA *abbrev.* deoxyribonucleic acid, a substance in chromosomes that stores genetic information.

do *v.* (did, done, doing) **1.** to perform, to carry out, to fulfil or complete (a work, duty, etc.). **2.** to produce, to make, *do five copies*; *we do meals,* provide them. **3.** to deal with, to set in order, to solve, *do a crossword*; *do the room,* clean or decorate it; *do the flowers,* arrange them; *do it in the oven,* cook it there; *they did us for £50,* (*slang*) cheated us out of it; *did the supermarket,* (*slang*) robbed or burgled it. **4.** to cover (a distance) in travelling. **5.** to visit, to see the sights, *we did Rome last year.*

187

6. to undergo; *did time for robbery*, was in prison. **7.** to provide food etc. for, *they do you well here.* **8.** to act or proceed, *do as you like.* **9.** to fare, to get on, to achieve something; *they did well out of it*, profited by it. **10.** to be suitable or acceptable, to serve a purpose, *it doesn't do to worry*; *that will do!*, stop it. **11.** to be in progress; *what is to do?*, what is happening? —**do** *auxiliary verb,* **1.** used to indicate present or past tense, *what does he think, what did he think?* **2.** used for emphasis, *I do like nuts.* **3.** used to avoid repetition of a verb just used, *we work as hard as they do.* —**do** *n. (pl.* **dos** *or* **do's**) **1.** a statement of what should be done, *do's and dont's.* **2.** (*informal*) an entertainment, a party. **3.** (*slang*) a swindle, a hoax. □ **do away with,** to abolish, to get rid of. **do down,** (*informal*) to get the better of, to swindle. **do for,** (*informal*) to ruin, to destroy, to kill; to do housework for. **do-gooder** *n.* a person who is well-meaning but unrealistic or officious in trying to promote social work or reform. **do in,** (*slang*) to ruin, to kill; (*informal*) to tire out. **do-it-yourself** *adj.* for use or making etc. by an amateur handyman. **do or die,** to make a supreme effort, disregarding danger. **do out,** to clean or redecorate (a room). **do up,** to fasten, to wrap up; to repair or redecorate; to tire out. **do with,** to get on with; to tolerate; to need or want. **do without,** to manage without.

doc *n.* (*informal*) doctor.

docile (**doh**-syl) *adj.* willing to obey. **docilely** *adv.,* **docility** (dŏ-**sil**-iti) *n.*

dock [1] *n.* a weed with broad leaves.

dock [2] *v.* **1.** to cut short (an animal's tail). **2.** to reduce or take away part of (wages, supplies, etc.).

dock [3] *n.* an artificially enclosed body of water where ships are admitted for loading, unloading, or repair. —*v.* **1.** to bring or come into dock. **2.** to join (two or more spacecraft) together in space, to become joined thus. □ **docks** *pl. n.* a dockyard.

dock [4] *n.* an enclosure in a criminal court for a prisoner. **dock brief,** a brief handed in court to a barrister chosen by a prisoner in the dock.

docker *n.* a labourer who loads and unloads ships in a dockyard.

docket *n.* a document or label listing goods delivered or the contents of a package, or recording payment of customs dues etc. —*v.* (**docketed, docketing**) to enter on a docket, to label with a docket.

dockland *n.* the district near a dockyard.

dockyard *n.* an area with docks and equipment for building and repairing ships.

doctor *n.* **1.** a person who is qualified to be a practitioner of medicine, a physician. **2.** a person who holds a doctorate, *Doctor of Civil Law.* —**doctor** *v.* **1.** to treat medically. **2.** to castrate or spay. **3.** to patch up (machinery etc.). **4.** to tamper with or falsify, *doctored the evidence.*

doctorate (**dok**-ter-ăt) *n.* the highest degree at a university, entitling the holder to the title of 'doctor'.

doctrinaire (dok-trin-**air**) *adj.* applying theories or principles without regard for practical considerations, *doctrinaire socialism.* —*n.* a person who does this.

doctrine (**dok**-trin) *n.* a principle or set of principles and beliefs held by a religious or political or other group. **doctrinal** (dok-**try**-năl) *adj.*

document *n.* a paper giving information or evidence about something. —*v.* to prove or provide with documents; *a heavily documented report,* supporting its statements by many references to evidence. —**documentation** *n.*

documentary (dok-yoo-**ment**-er-i) *adj.* **1.** consisting of documents, *documentary evidence.* **2.** giving a factual filmed report of a subject or activity. —*n.* a documentary film.

dodder *v.* to tremble or totter because of age or frailty. **dodderer** *n.,* **doddery** *adj.*

doddle *n.* (*slang*) an easy task.

dodecaphonic (doh-deka-**fon**-ik) *adj.* (of music) using the twelve chromatic notes of the octave arranged in a chosen order, without a conventional key.

dodge *v.* **1.** to move quickly to one side, to change position or direction in order to avoid something. **2.** to evade by cunning or trickery, *dodged military service.* —**dodge** *n.* **1.** a quick movement to avoid something. **2.** (*informal*) a clever trick, an ingenious way of doing something. —**dodger** *n.*

dodgem (**doj**-ĕm) *n.* one of the small electrically-driven cars in an enclosure at a fun-fair, in which each driver tries to bump other cars and dodge those trying to bump his car.

dodgy *adj.* (**dodgier, dodgiest**) (*informal*) **1.** cunning, artful. **2.** awkward, difficult.

dodo (**doh**-doh) *n.* (*pl.* **dodos**) a large non-flying bird that formerly lived in Mauritius but has long been extinct.

doe *n.* the female of the fallow deer, reindeer, hare, or rabbit.

doer *n.* a person who does something, one who takes action rather than thinking or talking about things.

doesn't = does not.

doff *v.* to take off (one's hat etc.).

dog *n.* **1.** a four-legged carnivorous animal, commonly kept as a pet or trained for use in hunting etc. **2.** the male of this or of the wolf or fox. **3.** (*informal*) a person, *lucky dog*; *dirty dog*, a despicable person. **4.** a mechanical device for gripping things. **5.** *the dogs*, (*informal*) greyhound racing. —**dog** *v.* (dogged, dogging) to follow closely or persistently, *dogged his footsteps*. —**doglike** *adj.* □ **dog-collar** *n.* (*informal*) a clerical collar. **dog-eared** *adj.* (of a book) having the corners of the pages turned down through use. **dog-eat-dog** *n.* ruthless competition. **dog in the manger**, one who keeps for himself something he cannot use, in order to prevent others from having it. **dog-paddle** *n.* a simple swimming stroke with short quick movements of the arms and legs. **dog's life**, a life of misery. **dog-star** *n.* the star Sirius. **dog-tired** *adj.* tired out. **dog-violet** *n.* an unscented wild violet. **dog-watch** *n.* one of the two-hour watches on a ship (4–6 or 6–8 p.m.). **go to the dogs**, (*slang*) to become worthless, to be ruined. **not a dog's chance**, not the slightest chance. **put on dog**, (*informal*) to show off.

doge (*pr.* dohj) *n.* the former ruler of Venice.

dogfight *n.* **1.** a fight between dogs. **2.** (*informal*) a battle between (usually two) fighter aircraft.

dogged (**dog**-id) *adj.* determined, not giving up easily. **doggedly** *adv.*

doggerel (**dog**-er-ĕl) *n.* bad verse.

doggie *n.* (*children's informal*) a dog.

doggo *adv.* lie doggo, (*slang*) to lie motionless or making no sign.

doggy *adj.* **1.** of dogs. **2.** (*informal*) fond of dogs.

doghouse *n.* (*Amer.*) a dog's kennel, in the doghouse, (*slang*) in disgrace.

dogma *n.* a doctrine or doctrines put forward by some authority, especially the Church, to be accepted as true without question.

dogmatic (dog-**mat**-ik) *adj.* **1.** of or like dogmas. **2.** putting forward statements in a very firm authoritative way. **dogmatically** *adv.*

dogmatism (**dog**-mă-tizm) *n.* being dogmatic.

dogmatize (**dog**-mă-tyz) *v.* to make dogmatic statements.

dogrose *n.* a wild hedge-rose.

dogsbody *n.* (*informal*) a drudge.

dogwood *n.* a shrub with dark red bran-ches, greenish-white flowers, and purple berries, found in woods and hedgerows.

doh *n.* a name for the keynote of a scale in music, or the note C.

doily *n.* a small ornamental mat placed under a dish or under cake etc. on a dish.

doings *pl. n.* **1.** things done or being done. **2.** (*slang*) things needed.

dojo (**doh**-joh) *n.* (*pl.* dojos) a room or hall, or a mat, for practising judo.

doldrums *pl. n.* **1.** the ocean regions near the equator where there is little or no wind. **2.** a period of inactivity. □ **in the doldrums**, in low spirits.

dole *v.* to distribute, *dole it out.* —*n.* (*informal*) a State payment to insured persons who are unable to find employment; *on the dole*, receiving this.

doleful *adj.* mournful, sad. **dolefully** *adv.*

doll *n.* **1.** a small model of a human figure, especially as a child's toy. **2.** a pretty but empty-headed young woman. **3.** (*slang*) a young woman. —*v.* (*informal*) to dress smartly, *dolled herself up.*

dollar *n.* the unit of money in the USA. and certain other countries.

dollop *n.* (*informal*) a mass or quantity, a shapeless lump of something soft.

dolly *n.* **1.** (*children's informal*) a doll. **2.** a movable platform for a cine camera. □ **dolly-bird** *n.* (*informal*) an attractive young woman.

dolman sleeve a loose sleeve cut in one piece with the body of a garment.

dolmen (**dol**-men) *n.* a prehistoric structure with a large flat stone laid on upright ones.

Dolomites (**dol**-ŏ-myts) *pl. n.* a rocky mountain range in north Italy.

dolorous (**dol**-er-ŭs) *adj.* mournful.

dolphin *n.* a sea animal like a porpoise but larger and with a beak-like snout.

dolt (*pr.* dohlt) *n.* a stupid person.

Dom *n.* **1.** a title put before the names of some Roman Catholic dignitaries and of Benedictine and Carthusian monks. **2.** a Portuguese title put before a man's Christian name.

domain (dŏm-**ayn**) *n.* **1.** a district or area under someone's control. **2.** a field of thought or activity, *the domain of science.*

dome *n.* **1.** a rounded roof with a circular base. **2.** something shaped like this. □ **domed** *adj.* having a dome, shaped like a dome.

Domesday Book (**doomz**-day) a record of the ownership of lands in England made in 1086 by order of William the Conqueror.

domestic *adj.* **1.** of the home or household or family affairs. **2.** of one's own country, not foreign or international, *domestic air services*. **3**. (of animals) kept by man, not wild. —**domestic** *n*. a servant in a household. —**domestically** *adv*. □ **domestic science**, the study of household management.

domesticated *adj*. **1**. (of animals) trained to live with and be kept by man. **2**. (of people) enjoying household work and home life.

domesticity (dom-es-**tiss**-iti) *n*. being domestic, domestic or home life.

domicile (**dom**-i-syl) *n*. a person's place of residence. **domiciled** *adj*. dwelling in a place.

domiciliary (dom-i-**sil**-yer-i) *adj*. **1**. of a dwelling-place. **2**. visiting a patient in his home, *domiciliary physiotherapist*.

dominant *adj*. dominating. **dominance** *n*.

dominate *v*. **1**. to have a commanding influence over. **2**. to be the most influential or conspicuous person or thing. **3**. (of a high place) to tower over, *the mountain dominates the whole valley*. **domination** *n*.

domineer *v*. to behave in a forceful way, making others obey.

Dominica (dom-in-**eek**-ă) an island in the West Indies. **Dominican** (dom-in-**eek**-ăn) *adj*. & *n*.

Dominican[1] (dŏm-**in**-ikăn) *n*. a member of an order of friars (also called *Black Friars*) founded by St. Dominic, or of a corresponding order of nuns.

Dominican[2] (dŏm-**in**-ikăn) *adj*. of the *Dominican Republic*, a country in the West Indies. —*n*. a native or inhabitant of this country.

dominion *n*. **1**. authority to rule, control. **2**. territory controlled by a ruler or government, a domain.

domino *n*. (*pl*. dominoes) one of the small oblong pieces marked with up to 6 pips on each half, used in the game of **dominoes**. □ **domino effect**, an effect compared to a row of dominoes falling, when a political or other event in one place seems to cause similar events elsewhere.

don[1] *v*. (donned, donning) to put on.

don[2] *n*. a head or fellow or tutor of a college, especially at Oxford or Cambridge.

Don *n*. a Spanish title put before a man's Christian name. **Don Juan** (*pr*. joo-ăn), a man who has many love affairs.

donate *v*. to give as a donation.

donation *n*. a gift of money etc. to a fund or institution.

done *see* do. —*adj*. **1**. cooked sufficiently; *done to a turn*, cooked perfectly. **2**. (*informal*) tired out. **3**. (*informal*) socially acceptable, *the done thing*; *it isn't done*. —*int*. (in reply to an offer) I accept. □ **done**

with, finished with; *it's over and done with*, ended.

donkey *n*. (*pl*. donkeys) an animal of the horse family, with long ears. **donkey engine**, a small auxiliary engine. **donkey jacket**, a workman's thick weatherproof jacket. **donkey's years**, (*informal*) a very long time. **donkey-work** *n*. drudgery, the laborious part of a job.

Donna *n*. the title of an Italian or Spanish or Portuguese lady.

donnish *adj*. like a don (don[2]).

donor *n*. **1**. one who gives or donates something. **2**. one who provides blood for transfusion or semen for insemination or tissue for transplantation.

don't = do not. —*n*. a prohibition, *do's and don'ts*.

doodle *v*. to scribble while thinking about something else. —*n*. a drawing or marks made by doodling.

doom *n*. a grim fate, death or ruin. —*v*. to destine to a grim fate.

doomsday *n*. the day of the Last Judgement, the end of the world.

door *n*. **1**. a hinged, sliding, or revolving barrier that closes an entrance or exit; *they live three doors away*, three houses away. **2**. a doorway. **3**. a means of obtaining or approaching something, *closed the door to any agreement*, made it impossible. □ **doorbell** *n*. a bell inside a house, rung from outside by visitors as a signal. **door-keeper** *n*. a doorman. **doorknob** *n*. a knob for turning to release the latch of a door. **doorman** *n*. a person on duty at the entrance to a hotel or large building. **doormat** *n*. a mat placed at a door, for wiping dirt from shoes; a person who meekly allows himself to be bullied. **doorstep** *n*. a step or area just outside a door; (*slang*) a thick slice of bread; *on one's doorstep*, very near. **doorstop** *n*. a device for keeping a door open or preventing it from striking a wall when it opens. **door-to-door** *adj*. (of selling etc.) done at each house in turn. **doorway** *n*. an opening filled by a door.

dope *n*. **1**. a thick liquid used as a lubricant etc. **2**. (*informal*) a medicine or drug, a narcotic; a drug given to an athlete or horse or greyhound to affect his or its performance. **3**. (*slang*) information. **4**. (*slang*) a stupid person. —**dope** *v*. **1**. to treat with dope. **2**. to give a narcotic or stimulant to. **3**. to take drugs that cause addiction.

dopey *adj*. (*slang*). **1**. half asleep, stupefied by a drug. **2**. stupid. **dopiness** *n*.

Doric (*rhymes with* historic) *adj*. of the *Doric order*, the simplest of the five classical orders of architecture.

dormant *adj.* **1.** sleeping, lying inactive as if in sleep. **2.** (of plants) alive but not actively growing. **3.** temporarily inactive, *a dormant volcano.*

dormer window an upright window under a small gable built out from a sloping roof.

dormitory *n.* a room with a number of beds, especially in a school or institution. **dormitory town,** one from which people travel to work elsewhere because there are few or no industries locally.

dormouse *n.* (*pl.* dormice) a mouse-like animal that hibernates in winter.

dormy *adj.* as many holes ahead in a score at golf as there are holes left to play, *dormy five.*

dorsal *adj.* of or on the back of an animal or plant, *a dorsal fin.*

Dorset a county of England.

dory *n.* an edible sea-fish.

dosage *n.* **1.** the giving of medicine in doses. **2.** the size of a dose.

dose *n.* **1.** an amount of medicine to be taken at one time. **2.** an amount of radiation received by a person or thing. **3.** (*informal*) an amount of flattery or punishment etc. **4.** (*slang*) a venereal infection. —*v.* to give a dose or doses of medicine to.

doss *v.* (*slang*) to sleep, especially in a doss-house. **dosser** *n.* ☐ **doss down,** (*slang*) to sleep on a makeshift bed. **doss-house** *n.* (*slang*) a cheap lodging-house.

dossier (dos-i-er) *n.* a set of documents containing information about a person or event.

dot *n.* **1.** a small round mark, a point. **2.** the shorter of the two signals used in the Morse code. —**dot** *v.* (dotted, dotting) **1.** to mark with a dot or dots, to place a dot over a letter. **2.** to scatter here and there, *dot them about; the sea was dotted with ships.* **3.** (*slang*) to hit, *dotted him one.* ☐ **dotted line,** a line of dots showing where a signature etc. is to be entered on a document. **dot the i's and cross the t's,** to be minutely accurate and explicit about details. **on the dot,** exactly on time. **the year dot,** (*informal*) a very long time ago.

dotage (doh-tij) *n.* a state of weakness of mind caused by old age, *in his dotage.*

dotard (doh-terd) *n.* a person who is in his dotage.

dote *v.* to show great fondness, *a doting husband; she dotes on her grandchildren.*

doth (*old use*) the present tense of do, used with *he, she, it,* and *they.*

dottle *n.* unburnt tobacco left in a pipe.

dotty *adj.* (dottier, dottiest) (*informal*) feeble-minded, eccentric, silly. **dottiness** *n.*

double *adj.* **1.** consisting of two things or parts that form a pair. **2.** twice as much or as many; *a double whisky,* twice the standard portion. **3.** designed for two persons or things, *a double bed.* **4.** combining two things or qualities, *it has a double meaning.* **5.** (of flowers) having more than one circle of petals. —**double** *adv.* **1.** twice the amount or quantity, *it costs double what it cost last year.* **2.** in twos; *see double,* to see two things where there is only one. — **double** *n.* **1.** a double quantity or thing. **2.** a person or thing that looks very like another. **3.** a hit between the two outer circles of the board in darts, scoring double. **4.** a bet where winnings and stake from one race are re-staked on another. — **double** *v.* **1.** to make or become twice as much or as many. **2.** to bend or fold in two. **3.** to turn sharply back from a course, *the fox doubled back on its tracks.* **4.** to sail round, *the ship doubled the Cape.* **5.** to act two parts in the same play. — **doubly** *adv.* ☐ **at the double,** running, hurrying. **double agent,** one who spies for two rival countries. **double-barrelled** *adj.* (of a gun) having two barrels; (of a surname) having two parts. **double-bass** *n.* the lowest-pitched instrument of the violin family. **double-breasted** *adj.* (of a coat) having fronts that overlap to fasten across the breast. **double-check** *v.* to verify twice or in two ways. **double chin,** a chin with a fold of loose flesh below it. **double cream,** thick cream with a high fat content. **double-cross** *v.* to deceive or cheat a person with whom one pretends to be collaborating. **double-dealing** *n.* deceit, especially in business. **double-decker** *n.* a bus with two decks. **double Dutch,** unintelligible talk. **double entry,** a system of book-keeping in which each transaction is entered as a debit in one account and a credit in another. **double figures,** any number from 10 to 99 inclusive. **double glazing,** two layers of glass in a window, with an air space between. **double-jointed** *adj.* having very flexible joints that allow the fingers, arms, or legs to bend in unusual ways. **double or quits,** a throw (with dice etc.) deciding whether a person shall pay twice what he owes or nothing at all. **double-park** *v.* to park a car alongside one already parked at the side of a street. **double-quick** *adj. & adv.* very quick, very quickly. **doubles** *pl. n.* a game between two pairs of players. **double take,** a delayed reaction to a situation etc., coming immediately after one's first reaction. **double-talk** *n.* a kind of talk that means something very different from its apparent meaning. **double time,** payment of an employee at twice the normal rate.

double entendre (doobl ahn-**tahndr**) *n.* a phrase with two meanings, one of which is usually indecent. (¶ French.)

doublet (**dub**-lit) *n.* **1.** a man's close-fitting jacket, with or without sleeves, worn in the 15th–17th centuries. **2.** either of a pair of similar things. **3.** a combination of two simple lenses.

doubt *n.* **1.** a feeling of uncertainty about something, an undecided state of mind. **2.** a feeling of disbelief. **3.** an uncertain state of affairs. —**doubt** *v.* **1.** to feel uncertain or undecided about. **2.** to hesitate to believe. —**doubter** *n.* □ **doubting Thomas,** a person who (like St. Thomas) refuses to believe something until it has been fully proved. **no doubt,** certainly. **without doubt** *or* **without a doubt,** certainly.

doubtful *adj.* **1.** feeling doubt. **2.** causing doubt; *a doubtful ally,* unreliable; *a doubtful reputation,* not a good one. **doubtfully** *adv.*

doubtless *adv.* no doubt.

douche (*pr.* doosh) *n.* **1.** a jet of liquid applied to a part of the body to cleanse it or for medical purposes. **2.** a device for applying this. —*v.* to treat with a douche, to use a douche.

dough (*rhymes with* go) *n.* **1.** a thick mixture of flour etc. and liquid, to be baked as bread, cake, or pastry. **2.** (*slang*) money. **doughy** *adj.*

doughnut *n.* a small sweetened fried cake of dough.

dour (*rhymes with* poor) *adj.* stern, severe, gloomy-looking. **dourly** *adv.,* **dourness** *n.*

douse (*rhymes with* mouse) *v.* **1.** to put into water, to throw water over. **2.** to extinguish, *douse the light.* ¶ Do not confuse with **dowse.**

dove *n.* **1.** a kind of bird with short legs, a small head, and a thick body, that makes a cooing sound. **2.** a person who favours a policy of peace and negotiation rather than violence.

dovecote *n.* a shelter for domesticated pigeons. **flutter the dovecotes,** to cause alarm or surprise to quiet people.

dovetail *n.* a wedge-shaped joint interlocking two pieces of wood. —*v.* **1.** to join by such a joint. **2.** to fit closely together, to combine neatly, *my plans dovetailed with hers.*

dowager (**dow**-ă-jer) *n.* **1.** a woman who holds a title or property from her dead husband, *the dowager duchess.* **2.** (*informal*) a dignified elderly woman.

dowdy *adj.* (dowdier, dowdiest) **1.** (of clothes) unattractively dull, not stylish. **2.** dressed in dowdy clothes. **dowdily** *adv.,* **dowdiness** *n.*

dowel (*rhymes with* fowl) *n.* a headless wooden or metal pin for holding two pieces of wood or stone together by fitting into a corresponding hole in each. —*v.* (dowelled, dowelling) to fasten with a dowel. □ **dowelling** *n.* round rods for cutting into dowels.

dower *n.* a widow's share of her husband's estate. **dower house,** a smaller house near a large one, forming part of a widow's dower.

down[1] *n.* an area of open rolling land. **the downs,** the chalk uplands of south England.

down[2] *n.* very fine soft furry feathers or short hairs.

down[3] *adv.* **1.** from an upright position to a horizontal one, *fell down.* **2.** to or in or at a lower place or level or value or condition, to a smaller size, further south; *they are two goals down,* are losing by this amount; *we are £5 down on the transaction,* have lost this amount; *I'm down to my last penny,* have only this left. **3.** so as to be less active, *quieten down.* **4.** incapacitated by illness, *is down with flu.* **5.** away from a central place or a university, *he is down from headquarters.* **6.** from an earlier to a later time, *down to the present day.* **7.** in writing, *note it down; he is down to speak,* is listed in the programme. **8.** to the source or the place where something is, *track it down.* **9.** as a payment at the time of purchase, *paid £5 down.* —**down** *prep.* **1.** downwards along or through or into, along, from top to bottom of. **2.** at a lower part of, *Oxford is further down the river.* —**down** *adj.* **1.** directed downwards, *a down draught.* **2.** travelling away from a central place, *a down train; the down platform,* one for such a train. —**down** *v.* (*informal*) **1.** to knock or bring down; *down tools,* to cease work for the day or in a strike. **2.** to swallow. —**down** *n.* **1.** misfortune, *ups and downs.* **2.** a throw in wrestling **3.** (*informal*) a dislike, a grudge against someone, *has a down on him.* □ **down and out,** completely destitute. **down-and-out** *n.* a destitute person. **down at heel,** shabby. **down-hearted** *adj.* in low spirits. **down in the mouth,** looking unhappy. **down on,** disapproving or hostile towards, *she is down on smoking.* **down on one's luck,** suffering misfortune. **down stage,** at or towards the front of a theatre stage. **down-to-earth** *adj.* sensible and practical. **down under,** in Australia or other countries of the antipodes. **down**

with, may (a person or party etc.) be overthrown.

Down a county of Northern Ireland.

downbeat *n.* an unaccented beat in music, when the conductor's baton moves downwards.

downcast *adj.* **1.** looking downwards, *downcast eyes.* **2.** (of a person) dejected.

downfall *n.* a fall from prosperity or power, something that causes this.

downgrade *v.* to reduce to a lower grade or rank.

downhill *adv.* in a downward direction, on a downward slope. —*adj.* going or sloping downwards. □ **go downhill,** to deteriorate.

Downing Street a street in London containing the official residences of the Prime Minister and other members of the government.

downpour *n.* a great fall of rain.

downright *adj.* **1.** frank, straightforward. **2.** thorough, complete, *a downright lie.* —*adv.* thoroughly, *felt downright scared.*

downs *see* down¹.

downstairs *adv.* down the stairs, to or on a lower floor. —*adj.* situated downstairs.

downstream *adj. & adv.* in the direction in which a stream or river flows.

downtrodden *adj.* trampled underfoot, oppressed.

downturn *n.* a decline in activity or prosperity.

downward *adj.* moving or leading or pointing towards what is lower or less important or later, *a downward movement.* —*adv.* downwards. —**downwards** *adv.* towards what is lower etc., *moved downwards.*

downwind *adj. & adv.* in the direction towards which the wind is blowing.

downy *adj.* (downier, downiest) **1.** like or covered with soft down. **2.** (*slang*) clever, knowing.

dowry (*rhymes with* floury) *n.* property or money brought by a bride to her husband.

dowse (*rhymes with* cows) *v.* to search for underground water or minerals by using a Y-shaped stick or rod. **dowser** *n.* ¶ Do not confuse with douse.

doyen (**doy**-ĕn) *n.* the senior member of a staff, profession, etc. **doyenne** *n.* a female doyen.

doze *v.* to sleep lightly; *dozed off,* fell into a doze. —*n.* a short light sleep.

dozen *n.* a set of twelve, *pack them in dozens; dozens of things,* very many. ¶ Correct use is *ten dozen* (not *ten dozens*).

Dr *abbrev.* **1.** Doctor. **2.** debtor.

drab *adj.* **1.** dull, uninteresting. **2.** of dull

greyish-brown colour. —*n.* drab colour. —**drably** *adv.,* **drabness** *n.*

drachm (*pr.* dram) *n.* one eighth of an ounce or of a fluid ounce.

drachma (**drak**-mă) *n.* (*pl.* drachmas *or* drachmae, *pr.* **drak**-mee) the unit of money in Greece.

Draconian (dră-**koh**-niăn) *adj.* very harsh, *Draconian laws.* ¶ Named after *Draco,* who is said to have established severe laws in ancient Athens.

draft *n.* **1.** a rough preliminary written version, *a draft of a speech.* **2.** a written order for the payment of money by a bank, the drawing of money by this. **3.** a group detached from a larger group for special duty, the selection of these. **4.** (*Amer.*) conscription. —**draft** *v.* **1.** to prepare a written draft of. **2.** to select for a special duty, *he was drafted to the Paris branch.* **3.** (*Amer.*) to conscript.
¶ This is also the American spelling of draught.

drag *v.* (dragged, dragging) **1.** to pull along with effort or difficulty. **2.** to trail or allow to trail along the ground, to move slowly and with effort. **3.** to search the bottom of water with grapnels, nets, etc., *drag the river.* **4.** to continue slowly in a dull manner, *the speeches dragged on.* **5.** to draw at a cigarette etc., *dragged at his pipe.* —**drag** *n.* **1.** something that is made for pulling along the ground, e.g. a heavy harrow, a drag-net. **2.** something that slows progress, something boring. **3.** (*slang*) women's clothes worn by men. **4.** (*slang*) a draw at a cigarette etc. □ **drag-hunt** *n.* a hunt in which hounds follow the trail of a strong-smelling object dragged over the ground. **drag in,** to bring in (a subject) unnecessarily or in an artificial way. **drag-net** *n.* a net drawn through a river or across ground to trap fish or game. **drag one's feet** *or* **heels,** to be deliberately slow or reluctant. **drag out,** to prolong unnecessarily. **drag race,** a race between cars to see which can accelerate fastest from a standstill. **drag up,** (*informal*) to rear (a child) roughly and without proper training; to revive a forgotten scandal etc.

dragon *n.* **1.** an imaginary reptile usually with wings, able to breathe out fire. **2.** a fierce person.

dragonfly *n.* a long-bodied insect with wings that spread while it is resting.

dragoon *v.* to force into doing something.

Dragoon Guards any of several cavalry regiments.

drain *v.* **1.** to draw off (liquid) by means of

channels or pipes etc. **2.** to flow or trickle away. **3.** to dry or become dried when liquid flows away. **4.** to deprive gradually of (strength or resources). **5.** to drink, to empty (a glass etc.) by drinking its contents. —**drain** n. **1.** a channel or pipe through which liquid or sewage is carried away. **2.** something that drains one's strength or resources. □ **down the drain**, (*informal*) lost, wasted. **draining-board** n. a sloping surface beside a sink, on which washed dishes are put to drain. **drain-pipe** n. a pipe used in a system of drains.

drainage n. **1.** draining. **2.** a system of drains. **3.** what is drained off.

drake n. a male duck.

dram n. **1.** a drachm. **2.** a small drink of spirits.

drama (drah-mă) n. **1.** a play for acting on the stage or for broadcasting. **2.** plays as a branch of literature, their composition and performance. **3.** a dramatic series of events. **4.** dramatic quality, *the drama of the situation*.

dramatic (dră-**mat**-ik) adj. **1.** of drama. **2.** exciting, impressive, *a dramatic change*. **dramatically** adv. □ **dramatics** pl. n. the performance of plays; exaggerated behaviour.

dramatist (**dram**-ă-tist) n. a writer of dramas.

dramatize (**dram**-ă-tyz) v. **1.** to make (a story etc.) into a play. **2.** to make (a thing) seem dramatic. **dramatization** n.

drank see drink.

drape v. **1.** to cover loosely or decorate with cloth etc. **2.** to arrange loosely or in graceful folds. —n. the way a fabric hangs in folds.

draper n. a retailer of cloth or clothing.

drapery n. **1.** a draper's trade or fabrics. **2.** fabric arranged in loose folds.

drastic adj. having a strong or violent effect. **drastically** adv.

drat int. (*informal*) curse. **dratted** adj. (*informal*) cursed.

draught (*rhymes with* craft) n. **1.** a current of air in an enclosed place. **2.** pulling; a *draught-horse*, one used for pulling heavy loads. **3.** the pulling in of a net of fish, the fish caught in this. **4.** the depth of water needed to float a ship. **5.** the drawing of liquor from a cask etc. **6.** one continuous process of swallowing liquid, the amount swallowed. □ **draught beer**, beer drawn from a cask, not bottled. **draughts** pl. n. a game for two players using 24 round pieces, played on a **draught-board** (the same as a chess-board). **feel the draught**, to feel the effect of financial or other difficulties.

draughtsman (*rhymes with* craftsman) n. (pl. **draughtsmen**) **1.** one who makes drawings or plans or sketches. **2.** a piece used in the game of draughts. **draughtsmanship** n.

draughty (*rhymes with* crafty) adj. (draughtier, draughtiest) letting in sharp currents of air.

draw v. (drew, drawn, drawing) **1.** to pull; *draw a bow*, pull back its string; *draw the curtains*, pull them across the window. **2.** to attract, *draw attention*. **3.** to take in, *draw breath*; *he drew at his pipe*, sucked smoke from it; *chimney draws well*, has a good draught. **4.** to take out, *drew the cork*; *draw water*; *draw £10*, withdraw it from one's account; *draw a salary*, receive it from one's employer; *draw an abscess*, cause blood or pus to concentrate; *draw a fowl*, take out its inside before cooking it; *draw on one's imagination*, use it as a source. **5.** to draw lots, to obtain in a lottery, *drew for partners*; *drew the winner*. **6.** to get information from, *tried to draw him about his plans*. **7.** to finish a contest with neither side winning. **8.** to (require a certain depth of water) in which to float, *ship draws 10 feet*. **9.** to produce a picture or diagram by making marks on a surface. **10.** to formulate, *draw a conclusion*. **11.** to write out (a cheque etc.) for encashment. **12.** to search (a covert) for game. **13.** to make one's way, *draw near*; *train drew in*, entered a station and stopped. **14.** (of tea) to infuse. —**draw** n. **1.** the act of drawing; *quick on the draw*, quick at drawing a gun. **2.** a person or thing that draws custom, an attraction. **3.** the drawing of lots. **4.** a drawn game. □ **draw blank** or **a blank**, to get no response or result. **draw in**, (of the time of daylight) to become shorter. **draw in one's horns**, to become less aggressive or less ambitious. **draw out**, to prolong (a discussion etc.); to encourage (a person) to talk; (of the time of daylight) to become longer. **draw rein**, to check a horse by pulling the reins. **draw-sheet** n. one that can be taken from under a patient without remaking the bed. **draw-string** n. one that can be pulled to tighten an opening. **draw the line at**, to refuse to do or tolerate. **draw the teeth of**, to make harmless. **draw up**, to come to a halt; to compose (a contract etc.); *draw oneself up*, to make oneself stiffly erect.

drawback n. a disadvantage.

drawbridge n. a bridge over a moat, hinged at one end so that it can be drawn up.

drawer n. **1.** a person who draws something, one who draws (= writes out) a cheque. **2.** a box-like compartment without a lid, that can be slid horizontally in and out of a piece of furniture.

drawers *pl. n.* knickers, underpants.

drawing *n.* a picture etc. drawn but not coloured. **drawing-board** *n.* a flat board on which paper is stretched while a drawing is made; *back to the drawing-board*, we must begin planning afresh. **drawing-pin** *n.* a flat-headed pin for fastening paper etc. to a surface.

drawing-room *n.* a room in which guests are received in a private house, a sitting-room.

drawl *v.* to speak lazily or with drawn-out vowel sounds. —*n.* a drawling manner of speaking.

drawn *see* draw. —*adj.* (of a person's features) looking strained from tiredness or worry. □ **drawn-thread-work** *n.* needlework in which threads are drawn from fabric which is then stitched ornamentally.

dray *n.* a strong low flat cart for heavy loads. **drayman** *n.*

dread *n.* great fear. —*v.* to fear greatly. —*adj.* (*old use*) dreaded.

dreadful *adj.* 1. causing dread. 2. (*informal*) troublesome, boring, very bad, *dreadful weather*. **dreadfully** *adv.*

dreadlocks *pl. n.* hair worn in many ringlets or plaits, especially by Rastafarians.

dream *n.* 1. a series of pictures or events in a sleeping person's mind. 2. the state of mind of one dreaming or day-dreaming, *goes round in a dream*. 3. an ambition, an ideal. 4. a beautiful person or thing. — **dream** *v.* (dreamt (*pr.* dremt) or dreamed (*pr.* dremt), dreaming) 1. to have a dream or dreams while sleeping. 2. to have an ambition, *dreamt of being champion*. 3. to think of as a possibility, *never dreamt it would happen*; *wouldn't dream of allowing it*, will certainly not allow it. —**dreamer** *n.*, **dreamless** *adj.* □ **dream up**, to imagine, to invent.

dreamy *adj.* 1. day-dreaming. 2. (*informal*) wonderful. **dreamily** *adv.*, **dreaminess** *n.*

dreary *adj.* (drearier, dreariest) dull, boring, (of places, etc.) gloomy. **drearily** *adv.*, **dreariness** *n.*

dredge[1] *n.* an apparatus for scooping things from the bottom of a river or the sea. —*v.* to bring up or clean out with a dredge. □ **dredger** *n.* a dredge, a boat with a dredge.

dredge[2] *v.* to sprinkle with flour or sugar etc. —**dredger** *n.* a container with a perforated lid, used for sprinkling things.

dregs *pl. n.* 1. bits of worthless matter that sink to the bottom of a liquid. 2. the worst and useless part, *the dregs of society*.

drench *v.* to make wet through.

Dresden china fine china made at Meissen, near Dresden, in Germany.

dress *n.* 1. clothing, especially the visible part of it. 2. a woman's or girl's garment with a bodice and skirt. —**dress** *v.* 1. to put clothes upon, to put on one's clothes, to provide clothes for; *she dresses well*, chooses and wears good clothes. 2. to put on evening dress, *they dress for dinner*. 3. to decorate; *dress a shop window*, arrange goods in it. 4. to put a dressing on (a wound etc.). 5. to groom and arrange (hair). 6. to finish or treat the surface of, *to dress leather*. 7. to prepare (poultry, crab, etc.) for cooking or eating, to coat (salad) with dressing. 8. to arrange (soldiers) into a straight line. □ **dress circle**, the first gallery in theatres, where evening dress was formerly required. **dress rehearsal**, a rehearsal in full costume. **dress shirt**, a shirt suitable for wearing with evening dress. **dress up**, to put on special clothes; to make (a thing) look more interesting.

dressage (**dress**-ah*zh*) *n.* the management of a horse to show its obedience and deportment

dresser[1] *n.* one who dresses a person or thing.

dresser[2] *n.* a kitchen sideboard with shelves for dishes etc.

dressing *n.* 1. a sauce or stuffing for food. 2. manure etc. spread over land. 3. a bandage, ointment, etc for a wound. 4. a substance used to stiffen fabrics during manufacture. □ **dressing-case** *n.* a case for brushes, cosmetics, etc. when travelling. **dressing down**, a scolding. **dressing-gown** *n.* a loose gown worn when one is not fully dressed. **dressing-room** *n.* a room for dressing or changing one's clothes. **dressing-table** *n.* a table with a mirror, for use while dressing.

dressmaker *n.* a woman who makes women's clothes. **dressmaking** *n.* making women's clothes.

dressy *adj.* (dressier, dressiest) 1. wearing stylish clothes. 2. (of clothes) elegant, elaborate.

drew *see* draw.

drey (*pr.* dray) *n.* (*pl.* dreys) a squirrel's nest.

dribble *v.* 1. to allow saliva to flow from the mouth. 2. to flow or allow to flow in drops. 3. to move the ball forward in football or hockey with slight touches of the feet or stick. —*n.* a dribbling flow.

driblet *n.* a small amount; *in driblets*, a little at a time.

dribs and drabs small amounts.

dried see dry. —*adj.* (of foods) preserved by drying, *dried apricots.*

drier *n.* a device for drying hair, laundry, etc.

drift *v.* 1. to be carried by or as if by a current of water or air. 2. to move casually or aimlessly. 3. to be piled into drifts by wind, *the snow had drifted.* 4. to cause to drift. —**drift** *n.* 1. a drifting movement. 2. a mass of snow or sand piled up by wind. 3. deviation from a set course. 4. the general tendency or meaning of a speech etc. □ **drift-net** *n.* a large net for catching herring etc., allowed to drift with the tide.

drifter *n.* 1. a boat used for fishing with a drift-net. 2. an aimless person.

driftwood *n.* wood floating on the sea or washed ashore by it.

drill¹ *n.* 1. a pointed tool or a machine used for boring holes or sinking wells. 2. training in military exercises. 3. thorough training by practical exercises, usually with much repetition. 4. (*informal*) a routine procedure to be followed, *what's the drill?* —**drill** *v.* 1. to use a drill, to make (a hole) with a drill. 2. to train or be trained by means of drill.

drill² *n.* 1. a furrow. 2. a machine for making or sowing seed in furrows. 3. a row of seeds sown in this way. —*v.* to plant in drills.

drill³ *n.* strong twilled linen or cotton cloth.

drily *adv.* in a dry way.

drink *v.* (drank, drunk, drinking) 1. to swallow (liquid). 2. (of plants, the soil, etc.) to take in or absorb liquid. 3. to take alcoholic liquors, especially in excess; *drank himself to death,* caused his death by drinking. 4. to pledge good wishes to by drinking, *drank his health.* —**drink** *n.* 1. liquid for drinking. 2. alcoholic liquors. 3. a portion of liquid for drinking. 4. (*slang*) the sea. —**drinker** *n.* □ **drink in,** to watch or listen to with delight or eagerness.

drip *v.* (dripped, dripping) to fall or let fall in drops. —*n.* 1. liquid falling in drops, one of these drops. 2. the sound of this. 3. (*slang*) a weak or dull person. □ **dripping wet,** very wet.

drip-dry *v.* (drip-dried, drip-drying) to dry easily when hung up wet, without wringing or ironing. —*adj.* made of fabric that will drip-dry.

dripping *n.* fat melted from roast meat.

drive *v.* (drove, driven, driving) 1. to urge or send in some direction by blows, threats, violence, etc. 2. to push, send, or carry along. 3. to strike and propel (a ball etc.) forcibly. 4. to force to penetrate, *drove a stake into the ground*; *drove a*

tunnel through the hill, dug it. 5. to operate (a vehicle or locomotive) and direct its course. 6. to travel or convey in a private vehicle, *we drive to work*; *he drove me to the station.* 7. (of steam or other power) to keep (machinery) going. 8. to cause, to compel, *was driven by hunger to steal*; *he drives himself too hard,* overworks; *drove him mad,* forced him into this state. 9. to rush, to move or be moved rapidly, *driving rain.* — **drive** *n.* 1. a journey in a vehicle. 2. a stroke made by driving in cricket or golf etc. 3. the transmission of power to machinery, *front-wheel drive*; *left-hand drive,* having the steering wheel on the left of the vehicle. 4. energy, persistence, a psychological urge. 5. an organized effort to achieve something, *a sales drive.* 6. a social gathering to play card-games etc., changing partners and tables. 7. a road, especially a scenic one. 8. a private road leading to a house. —**driver** *n.* □ **drive a hard bargain,** to conclude one without making concessions. **drive at,** to intend to convey as a meaning, *what was he driving at?* **drive-in** *adj.* (of a cinema, bank, etc.) able to be used without getting out of one's car. **driving-wheel** *n.* a wheel that communicates motive power in machinery, or to which driving power is applied.

drivel *n.* silly talk, nonsense. —*v.* (drivelled, drivelling) to talk or write drivel.

drizzle *n.* very fine rain. —*v.* to rain in very fine drops. —**drizzly** *adj.*

drogue (*pr.* drohg) *n.* a funnel-shaped piece of fabric used as a wind-sock, brake, target, etc.

droll (*pr.* drohl) *adj.* amusing in an odd way. **drolly** *adv.* □ **drollery** *n.* quaint humour.

dromedary (**drom**-ĕd-er-i) *n.* a light one-humped camel bred for riding.

drone *n.* 1. a male honey-bee. 2. an idler. 3. a deep humming sound. —**drone** *v.* 1. to make a deep humming sound. 2. to speak or utter monotonously.

drool *v.* 1. to water at the mouth, to dribble. 2. to show gushing appreciation.

droop *v.* to bend or hang downwards through tiredness or weakness. —*n.* a drooping attitude. —**droopy** *adj.*

drop *n.* 1. a small rounded or pear-shaped mass of liquid. 2. something shaped like this, e.g. a sweet or a hanging ornament. 3. a very small quantity. 4. the act of dropping. 5. a fall, *a drop in prices.* 6. a steep or vertical descent, the distance of this, *a drop of 10 feet from the window.* 7. the length of a hanging curtain. 8. a thing that drops or is dropped, a platform withdrawn from under the feet of a person executed by hanging. —**drop** v. (dropped, dropping) **1.** to fall by force of gravity from not being held, to allow to fall. **2.** to sink from exhaustion; *feel ready to drop*, very tired. **3.** to form a steep or vertical descent, *the cliff drops sharply to the sea*. **4.** to lower, to become lower or weaker, *drop the hem*; *prices dropped*; *drop one's voice*; *drop a curtsy*, make this movement. **5.** to allow oneself to move to a position further back, *dropped behind the others*. **6.** to utter or send casually, *drop a hint*; *drop me a note*. **7.** to omit, to fail to pronounce or insert, *drop one's h's*. **8.** to set down (a passenger or parcel etc.). **9.** to fell with an axe, blow, or bullet. **10.** to give up, to reject, to cease to associate with, *dropped the habit*; *has dropped his friends*; *drop the subject*, cease talking about it. **11.** to lose money in gambling etc. **12.** to score by a drop-kick. — **dropper** n. □ **drop by** or **drop in**, to pay a casual visit. **drop-kick** n. a kick made by dropping a football and kicking it as it falls to the ground. **drop off**, to fall asleep. **drop on a person**, to reprimand or punish him. **drop out**, to cease to participate. **drop-out** n. one who drops out from a course of study or from conventional society. **drops** pl. n. liquid medicine to be measured by drops. **drop scone**, a scone made by dropping a spoonful of batter on a cooking surface.

droplet n. a small drop.

droppings pl. n. dung of animals or birds.

dropsy n. a disease in which watery fluid collects in the body. **dropsical** adj.

dross n. **1.** scum on molten metal. **2.** impurities, rubbish.

drought (*rhymes with* out) n. continuous dry weather.

drove see drive. —n. **1.** a moving herd or flock. **2.** a moving crowd, *droves of people*.

drover n. a person who herds cattle or sheep to market or pasture.

drown v. **1.** to kill or be killed by suffocating in water or other liquid. **2.** to flood, to drench. **3.** to deaden (grief etc.) with drink, *drown one's sorrows*. **4.** to overpower (a sound) with greater loudness.

drowse (*rhymes with* cows) v. to be half asleep.

drowsy adj. (drowsier, drowsiest) half asleep. **drowsily** adv., **drowsiness** n.

drub v. (drubbed, drubbing) **1.** to thrash. **2.** to defeat thoroughly. □ **drubbing** n. a beating, a severe defeat.

drudge n. a person who does dull or laborious or menial work. —v. to do such work. —**drudgery** n.

drug n. **1.** a substance used in medicine. **2.** a substance that acts on the nervous system, e.g. a narcotic or stimulant, especially one causing addiction. —**drug** v. (drugged, drugging) **1.** to add a drug to (food or drink). **2.** to give drugs to, to stupefy. **3.** to take drugs as an addict. □ **drug on the market**, something that is plentiful but not in demand.

drugget (**drug**-it) n. coarse woven fabric used for floor-coverings.

druggist n. a pharmaceutical chemist.

drugstore n. (*Amer.*) a chemist's shop also selling light refreshments and many kinds of goods.

Druid (**droo**-id) n. a priest of an ancient Celtic religion. **Druidism** n.

drum n. **1.** a percussion instrument consisting of a parchment or skin stretched tightly across a round frame. **2.** the sound of this being struck, a similar sound. **3.** a cylindrical structure or object or container. **4.** the ear-drum. — **drum** v. (drummed, drumming) **1.** to play a drum or drums. **2.** to make a drumming sound, to tap or thump continuously or rhythmically. **3.** to drive (facts etc.) into a person's mind by constant repetition □ **drum brake**, one in which curved pads on a vehicle press against the inner cylindrical part of a wheel. **drum major**, the leader of a marching band. **drum majorette**, a female drum major. **drum up**, to obtain through vigorous effort, *drum up support*.

drummer n. a person who plays a drum or drums.

drumstick n. **1.** a stick for beating a drum. **2.** the lower part of a cooked fowl's leg.

drunk see drink. —adj. excited or stupefied with alcoholic drink; *drunk with success*, made greatly excited by it. —n. **1.** a drunken person. **2.** (*slang*) a bout of drinking.

¶ See the note under drunken.

drunkard n. a person who is often drunk.

drunken adj. **1.** intoxicated, frequently in this condition. **2.** happening during or because of drunkenness, *a drunken brawl*. **drunkenly** adv., **drunkenness** n.

¶ This word is used before a noun (e.g. *a drunken man*), whereas *drunk* is usually used after a verb (e.g. *he is drunk*).

drupe (*pr.* droop) n. a fruit with juicy flesh round a stone with a kernel, e.g. a peach.

dry adj. (drier, driest) **1.** without water or moisture; *a dry country*, with little rainfall; *dry land*, not under water; *dry shampoo*, for use without water; *a dry cough*, without phlegm; *dry wall*, built without mortar or cement; *the cows are dry*, not producing milk. **2.** eaten without butter etc., *dry bread*. **3.** thirsty. **4.** (of wine) not sweet. **5.** uninteresting, *a dry book*. **6.** expressed with pretended seriousness, *dry humour*. **7.** not allowing the sale of alcohol. —**dry** *v.* (dried, drying) **1.** to make or become dry. **2.** to preserve (food) by removing its moisture. —**drily** *adv.*, **dryness** *n.* □ **dry-clean** *v.* to clean (clothes etc.) by a solvent which evaporates very quickly, not by water. **dry dock**, a dock which can be emptied of water, used for repairing ships. **dry-fly** *adj.* (of fishing) using an artificial fly that floats. **dry measure**, a measure of capacity for dry goods (e.g. corn). **dry rot**, decay of wood that is not well ventilated; the fungi that cause this; any moral or social decay. **dry run**, (*informal*) a dummy run. **dry-shod** *adv.* without wetting one's shoes. **dry up**, to dry washed dishes; (*informal*) to cease talking; (of an actor) to forget one's lines.

dryad *n.* a wood-nymph.

drystone *adj.* (of a stone wall) built without mortar.

d.t.'s *abbrev.* delirium tremens.

dual *adj.* composed of two parts, double. **duality** (dew-al-iti) *n.* □ **dual carriageway**, a road with a dividing strip between traffic in opposite directions. **dual control**, two linked sets of controls, enabling either of two persons to operate a car or aircraft. **dual-purpose** *adj.* suitable for two purposes.

dub *v.* (dubbed, dubbing) **1.** to make (a man) a knight by touching him on the shoulder with a sword. **2.** to give a nickname to. **3.** to replace or add to the sound-track of (a film), especially in a different language.

dubbin *n.* thick grease for softening and waterproofing leather.

dubious (dew-bi-ŭs) *adj.* doubtful. **dubiously** *adv.*

Dublin the capital of the Republic of Ireland.

ducal *adj.* of or like a duke.

duchess *n.* **1.** a duke's wife or widow. **2.** a woman whose rank is equal to that of a duke.

duchy *n.* the territory of a duke or duchess.

duck¹ *n.* **1.** a swimming-bird of various kinds. **2.** the female of this. **3.** its flesh as food. **4.** (*informal*) dear. **5.** a batsman's score of 0. **6.** a ducking movement. — **duck** *v.* **1.** to dip the head under water and emerge, to push (a person) under water. **2.** to bob down, especially to avoid being seen or hit. **3.** to dodge, to avoid (a

task etc.). □ **duck-boards** *pl. n.* boards forming a narrow path in a trench or over mud.

duck² *n.* strong linen or cotton cloth. **ducks** *pl. n.* trousers made of this.

duckling *n.* a young duck.

duckweed *n.* a plant that forms on the surface of ponds etc.

duct *n.* **1.** a tube or channel for conveying liquid, gas, air, cable, etc. **2.** a tube in the body through which fluid passes, *tear ducts*. —*v.* to convey through a duct. □ **ductless glands**, glands that pour their secretions directly into the blood, not through a duct.

ductile *adj.* (of metal) able to be drawn out into fine strands.

dud *n.* (*slang*) something that is useless or counterfeit or that fails to work. —*adj.* (*slang*) useless, defective.

dude (*pr.* dewd) *n.* (*Amer.*) a dandy. **dude ranch**, a ranch used as a holiday centre.

dudgeon (duj-ŏn) *n.* resentment, indignation, *in high dudgeon*.

duds *pl. n.* (*slang*) clothes.

due *adj.* **1.** owed as a debt or obligation. **2.** payable immediately, *it has become due*. **3.** that ought to be given to a person, rightful, adequate, *with due respect*. **4.** scheduled to do something or to arrive, *he is due to speak tonight; the train is due at 7.30.* —*adv.* exactly, *sailed due east.* —*n.* a person's right, what is owed to him; *give the Devil his due*, give a disliked person credit for one of his good qualities or actions. □ **in due course**, in the proper order, at the appropriate time. **dues** *pl. n.* a fee, *harbour dues*; what one owes, *pay one's dues*. **due to**, caused by.
¶ The phrase *due to* is often used like *because of*, e.g. *play was stopped, due to rain*. This usage is incorrect and *due to* should be used only with a noun (often after a linking verb), e.g. *the stoppage was due to rain*.

duel *n.* **1.** a fight with weapons between two persons. **2.** a contest between two persons or sides. —*v.* (duelled, duelling) to fight a duel. —**duellist** *n.*

duet *n.* a musical composition for two performers.

duff *adj.* (*slang*) worthless, useless, counterfeit.

duffel *n.* heavy woollen cloth with a thick nap. **duffel bag**, a cylindrical canvas bag closed by a draw-string. **duffel coat**, a hooded overcoat made of duffel, fastened with toggles.

duffer *n.* an inefficient or stupid person.

dug¹ *see* dig.

dug² *n.* an udder, a teat.

dug-out *n.* **1.** an underground shelter. **2.** a canoe made by hollowing a tree-trunk.

duke *n.* **1.** a nobleman of the highest rank. **2.** the male ruler of a duchy or of certain small countries. □ **dukedom** *n.* the position or lands of a duke.

dulcet (**dul**-sit) *adj.* sounding sweet.

dulcimer (**dul**-sim-er) *n.* a musical instrument with strings struck by two hammers.

dull *adj.* **1.** not bright or clear. **2.** slow in understanding, stupid. **3.** not sharp, (of pain) not felt sharply, (of sound) not resonant. **4.** not interesting or exciting, boring. —*v.* to make or become dull. — **dully** *adv.,* **dullness** *n.*

dullard *n.* a mentally dull person.

duly (**dew**-li) *adv.* in a correct or suitable way.

dumb *adj.* **1.** unable to speak. **2.** temporarily silent; *was struck dumb,* speechless from surprise etc. **3.** (*informal*) stupid. — **dumbly** *adv.,* **dumbness** *n.* □ **dumbbell** *n.* a short bar with a weight at each end, lifted to exercise the muscles. **dumb show,** gestures without words. **dumb waiter,** a stand with shelves for holding food ready to be served; a lift for conveying food etc.

dumbfound *v.* to astonish, to strike dumb with surprise.

dumdum bullet a soft-nosed bullet that expands on impact.

Dumfries and Galloway (dum-**freess**, gal-ŏ-way) a region of Scotland.

dummy *n.* **1.** a sham article. **2.** a model of the human figure, used to display clothes. **3.** a rubber teat for a baby to suck. **4.** (in card-games) a player whose cards are placed upwards on the table and played by his partner. —*adj.* sham. □ **dummy run,** a trial run, a practice.

dump *v.* **1.** to deposit as rubbish. **2.** to put down carelessly. **3.** to get rid of (something unwanted). **4.** to market goods abroad at a lower price than is charged in the home market. —**dump** *n.* **1.** a rubbish-heap, a place where rubbish may be deposited. **2.** a temporary store, *an ammunition dump.* **3.** (*informal*) a dull or unattractive place.

dumpling *n.* **1.** a ball of dough cooked in stew etc. or baked with fruit inside it. **2.** a small fat person.

dumps *pl. n.* (*informal*) low spirits, *in the dumps.*

dumpy *adj.* short and fat. **dumpiness** *n.* □ **dumpy level,** a spirit-level with a fixed short telescope, used in surveying.

dun[1] *adj. & n.* greyish brown.

dun[2] *v.* (dunned, dunning) to ask persistently for payment of a debt.

dunce *n.* a person who is slow at learning.

Dundee cake a rich fruit cake decorated with almonds.

dune (*pr.* dewn) *n.* a sand-dune (*see* sand).

dung *n.* animal excrement. **dunghill** *n.* a heap of dung in a farmyard.

dungarees (dung-er-**eez**) *pl. n.* overalls or trousers of coarse cotton cloth.

dungeon (**dun**-jŏn) *n.* a strong underground cell for prisoners.

dunk *v.* to dip into liquid.

Dunkirk *n.* **Dunkirk spirit,** refusal to surrender or despair in a crisis. ¶The name of a seaport in northern France from which British troops were evacuated in 1940.

duo (**dew**-oh) *n.* (*pl.* duos) a pair of performers.

duodecimal (dew-ŏ-**dess**-imăl) *adj.* based on 12, reckoning by twelves.

duodenum (dew-ŏ-**deen**-ŭm) *n.* the first part of the small intestine, immediately below the stomach. **duodenal** *adj.*

duologue (**dew**-ŏ-log) *n.* a dialogue between two persons.

dupe *n.* a person who is deceived or tricked. —*v.* to deceive, to trick.

duplex (**dew**-pleks) *adj.* **1.** having two parts. **2.** (of a flat) on two floors.

duplicate[1] (**dew**-plik-ăt) *n.* **1.** one of two or more things that are exactly alike. **2.** an exact copy. —*adj.* exactly like another thing, being a duplicate. □ **in duplicate,** as two identical copies.

duplicate[2] (**dew**-plik-ayt) *v.* **1.** to make or be an exact copy of something. **2.** to repeat or do something twice. **duplication** *n.*

duplicator *n.* a machine for copying documents.

duplicity (dew-**pliss**-iti) *n.* double-dealing, deceitfulness.

durable *adj.* likely to last, not wearing out or decaying quickly. **durably** *adv.,* **durability** *n.* □ **durables** *pl. n.* durable goods.

duration *n.* the time during which a thing continues.

duress (dewr-**ess**) *n.* the use of force or threats to procure something.

Durham a county of England.

during *prep.* throughout or at a point in the continuance of.

dusk *n.* the darker stage of twilight.

dusky *adj.* (duskier, duskiest) **1.** shadowy, dim. **2.** dark-coloured. **duskiness** *n.*

dust *n.* fine particles of earth or other matter. —*v.* **1.** to sprinkle with dust or powder. **2.** to clear of dust by wiping, to clear furniture etc. of dust. □ **dust-**

cover, **dust-jacket** *ns.* a paper jacket on a book. **dust-sheet** *n.* a sheet put over furniture to protect it from dust. **dust-up** *n.* (*informal*) a noisy argument, a fight. **throw dust in a person's eyes,** to prevent him from seeing the truth.

dustbin *n.* a bin for household rubbish.

dustcart *n.* a vehicle for collecting and removing the contents of dustbins and other rubbish.

duster *n.* a cloth for dusting furniture etc.

dustman *n.* (*pl.* dustmen) a man employed by a local authority to empty dustbins and cart away rubbish.

dustpan *n.* a pan into which dust is brushed from a floor.

dusty *adj.* (dustier, dustiest) **1.** like dust, full of dust, covered with dust. **2.** (of a colour) greyish, *dusty pink.* **dustiness** *n.* □ **dusty answer,** a sharp rejection of a request. **dusty miller,** a kind of primula with white dust on its leaves and flowers; an artificial fishing-fly. **not so dusty,** (*slang*) fairly good.

Dutch *adj.* of the Netherlands or its people or language. —*n.* **1.** the Dutch language. **2.** *the Dutch,* Dutch people. —**Dutchman, Dutchwoman** *ns.* □ **Dutch auction,** one in which the price asked is gradually reduced until a buyer is found. **Dutch barn,** one consisting of a roof supported on poles. **Dutch cap,** a contraceptive diaphragm. **Dutch courage,** that obtained by drinking alcohol. **Dutch elm disease,** a disease of elm trees, caused by a fungus, first found in the Netherlands. **Dutch oven,** a covered dish for cooking meat etc. slowly. **Dutch treat,** an outing where each person pays his own expenses. **go Dutch,** to share expenses on an outing. **talk like a Dutch uncle,** to lecture a person severely but kindly.

dutch *n.* (*costermongers' slang*) a wife.

dutiable (**dew**-ti-ăbŭl) *adj.* on which customs or other duties must be paid.

dutiful *adj.* doing one's duty, showing due obedience. **dutifully** *adv.*

duty *n.* **1.** a moral or legal obligation. **2.** a task that must be done, action required from a particular person, *household duties; the duties of a postman.* **3.** a tax charged on certain goods or on imports. □ **do duty for,** to serve as (something else). **in duty bound,** obliged by duty. **on** *or* **off duty,** actually engaged or not engaged in one's regular work.

duvet (**doo**-vay) *n.* a thick soft quilt used instead of bedclothes.

dwarf *n.* (*pl.* dwarfs) **1.** a person, animal, or plant much below the usual size. **2.** (in fairy-tales) a small being with magic

powers. —*adj.* of a kind that is very small in size. —**dwarf** *v.* **1.** to stunt. **2.** to make seem small by contrast or distance.

dwell *v.* (dwelt, dwelling) to live as an inhabitant. **dwell on,** to think or speak or write lengthily about, *dwell on a subject.* **dweller** *n.*

dwelling *n.* a house etc. to live in. **dwelling-house** *n.* one used as a residence, not as a shop or warehouse etc.

dwindle *v.* to become gradually less or smaller.

dye *v.* (dyed, dyeing) **1.** to colour, especially by dipping in a liquid. **2.** to be able to be dyed, *this fabric dyes well.* —**dye** *n.* **1.** a substance used for dyeing. **2.** a colour given by dyeing. —**dyer** *n.*

Dyfed (**duv**-id) a county of Wales.

dying *see* die [1].

dyke *n.* = dike.

dynamic *adj.* **1.** of force producing motion (as opposed to *static*). **2.** (of a person) energetic, having force of character. —**dynamically** *adv.* □ **dynamics** *n.* a branch of physics that deals with matter in motion.

dynamite *n.* **1.** a powerful explosive made of nitroglycerine. **2.** something likely to cause violent or dangerous reactions, *the frontier question is dynamite.* **3.** a person or thing with great vitality or effectiveness. —*v.* to fit with a charge of dynamite, to blow up with dynamite.

dynamo *n.* (*pl.* dynamos) a small compact generator producing electric current; *a human dynamo,* a dynamic person.

dynasty (**din**-ă-sti) *n.* a line of hereditary rulers. **dynastic** *adj.*

dysentery (**dis**-ĕn-tri) *n.* a disease with inflammation of the intestines, causing severe diarrhoea.

dysfunction (dis-**funk**-shŏn) *n.* failure to function normally.

dyslexia (dis-**leks**-iă) *n.* abnormal difficulty in reading and spelling, caused by a brain condition. **dyslexic** *adj.* & *n.*

dyspepsia (dis-**pep**-siă) *n.* indigestion. **dyspeptic** *adj.* suffering from dyspepsia or the resultant irritability.

dystrophy (**dis**-trŏ-fi) *n.* a hereditary condition causing progressive weakening of the muscles, *muscular dystrophy.*

Ee

E. *abbrev.* east, eastern.

each *adj.* every one of two or more, *each child.* —*pronoun* each person or thing, *each of them*; *give them two each*; *we see each other*, each of us sees the other, we meet. □ **each way**, (of a bet) backing a horse etc. to win and to be placed.

eager *adj.* full of strong desire, enthusiastic. **eagerly** *adv.*, **eagerness** *n.* □ **eager beaver**, (*informal*) an excessively diligent person.

eagle *n.* 1. a large bird of prey. 2. a score of two strokes under par or bogey for a hole at golf. □ **eagle eye**, very sharp eyesight, keen watchfulness. **eagle-eyed** *adj.*

eaglet *n.* a young eagle.

ear[1] *n.* 1. the organ of hearing in man and certain animals, the external part of this. 2. the ability to distinguish sounds accurately; *has an ear for music*, enjoys it. 3. listening, attention; *lend an ear*, listen; *have a person's ear*, to have his favourable attention. 4. an ear-shaped thing. □ **be all ears**, to listen attentively. **ear-drum** *n.* a membrane inside the ear that vibrates when sound-waves strike it. **ear-plug** *n.* a plug inserted in the ear to keep out noise or water. **ear-ring** *n.* an ornament worn on the lobe of the ear. **ear-splitting** *adj.* piercingly loud. **have one's ear to the ground**, to be alert to rumours or trends of opinion. **up to the ears**, (*informal*) deeply involved or occupied in something.

ear[2] *n.* the seed-bearing part of corn.

earache *n.* pain in the ear-drum.

earful *n.* (*informal*) 1. a large amount of talk. 2. a strong reprimand.

earl *n.* a British nobleman ranking between marquis and viscount. **earldom** *n.* the position or lands of an earl. **Earl Marshal**, an officer of state with ceremonial duties.

early *adj. & adv.* (earlier, earliest) 1. before the usual or expected time. 2. not far on in a period of time or a development or a series, *his early years*. **earliness** *n.* □ **early bird**, a person who gets up early or arrives early. **early closing**, the shutting of business premises on a particular afternoon every week. **early on**, at an early stage.

earmark *n.* a distinguishing mark. —*v.* 1. to put a distinguishing mark on. 2. to set aside for a particular purpose.

earn *v.* (earned, earning) 1. to get or deserve as a reward for one's work or merit. 2. (of money lent or invested) to gain as interest. □ **earned income**, income derived from paid employment. **earnings** *pl. n.* money earned.

earnest *adj.* showing serious feeling or intentions. —*n.* 1. money paid as an instalment or to confirm a contract etc. 2. a foretaste or token, *an earnest of what is to come.* —**earnestly** *adv.*, **earnestness** *n.* □ **in earnest**, seriously, not jokingly; with determination, intensively.

earphone *n.* a headphone.

earshot *n.* range of hearing, *within earshot.*

earth *n.* 1. the planet (*Earth*) on which we live, the world in which we live. 2. its surface, dry land, the ground, *it fell to earth.* 3. *the earth*, (*informal*) a huge amount of money, *it cost the earth.* 4. soil. 5. the hole of a fox or badger. 6. an oxide with little taste or smell. 7. connection to the ground as completion of an electrical circuit. — **earth** *v.* 1. to cover roots of plants with heaped-up earth, *earth them up.* 2. to connect an electrical circuit to earth. □ **on earth**, in existence, in this world (as distinct from a future life); *why on earth*, why ever; *look* or *feel like nothing on earth*, very bad. **run a thing to earth**, to find it after a long search.

earthen *adj.* 1. made of earth. 2. made of baked clay.

earthenware *n.* pottery made of coarse baked clay.

earthly *adj.* of this earth, of man's life on it. **no earthly use**, (*informal*) no use at all. **not an earthly**, (*slang*) no chance at all.

earthquake *n.* a violent natural movement of a part of the earth's crust.

earthwork *n.* an artificial bank of earth.

earthworm *n.* a common worm that lives in the soil.

earthy *adj.* 1. like earth or soil. 2. gross, coarse, *earthy humour.*

earwig *n.* a small insect with pincers at the end of its body (formerly thought to enter the head through the ear).

ease *n.* 1. freedom from pain or trouble or anxiety. 2. relief from pain. 3. absence of painful effort, *did it with ease.* —**ease** *v.* 1. to relieve from pain or anxiety. 2. to make less tight or forceful or burdensome. 3. to move gently or gradually, *ease it in.* 4. to slacken, to reduce in severity or pressure etc., *it will ease off* or *up.* □ **at ease**, free from anxiety, in comfort; standing relaxed with feet apart. **at one's ease**, relaxed, not feeling awkward or embarrassed.

easel *n.* a wooden frame to support a painting or a blackboard etc.

easily *adv.* 1. in an easy way, with ease. 2. by far, *easily the best.*

east *n.* 1. the point on the horizon where the sun rises, the direction in which this point lies. 2. the eastern part of something. 3. *the East*, the part of the world lying east of Europe, the Communist countries of eastern Europe. —*adj. & adv.* towards or in the east; *an east wind*, blowing from the east. □ **East Anglia**, an area of England comprising the counties of Norfolk and Suffolk. **East End**, the eastern part of London. **East Germany**, the German Democratic Republic. **East Side**, (*Amer.*) the eastern part of Manhattan. **East Sussex**, a county of England.

Easter *n.* the Christian festival (celebrated on a Sunday in March or April) commemorating Christ's resurrection, the period about this time. □ **Easter egg**, a chocolate artificial egg given as a gift at Easter.

easterly *adj.* in or towards the east; *an easterly wind*, blowing from the east (approximately). —*n.* an easterly wind.

eastern *adj.* of or in the east.

eastward *adj.* towards the east. **eastwards** *adv.*

easy *adj.* (**easier, easiest**) **1.** not difficult, done or obtained without great effort. **2.** free from pain, trouble, or anxiety, *with an easy mind*; *easy manners*, relaxed and pleasant; *in easy circumstances*, with enough money to live comfortably. —*adv.* in an easy way, with ease. — **easiness** *n.* □ **easy chair**, a large comfortable chair. **easy-going** *adj.* not strict, placid and tolerant. **easy on the eye**, (*informal*) pleasant to look at. **Easy Street**, (*informal*) a state of affluence. **go easy with**, to be careful with; *go easy on the butter*, do not use too much. **I'm easy**, (*informal*) I do not mind. **stand easy**, stand at ease. **take it easy**, to proceed comfortably or carefully; to rest or relax.

eat *v.* (**ate, eaten, eating**) **1.** to take food into the mouth and swallow it for nourishment, to chew and swallow. **2.** to have a meal, *when do we eat?* **3.** to destroy gradually, to consume, *acids eat into metals*; *the car ate up the miles*, covered the distance rapidly. □ **eating apple**, an apple suitable for eating raw. **eat one's heart out**, to suffer greatly with vexation or longing. **eat one's words**, to be obliged to withdraw what one has said. **eats** *pl. n.* (*informal*) food. **what's eating you?**, (*slang*) why are you annoyed?

eatable *adj.* fit to be eaten (because of its condition). **eatables** *pl. n.* food.

eater *n.* **1.** one who eats. **2.** an eating apple.

eau-de-Cologne (oh-dĕ-kŏ-**lohn**) *n.* a delicate perfume originally made at Cologne.

eaves *pl. n.* the overhanging edge of a roof.

eavesdrop *v.* (**eavesdropped, eavesdropping**) to listen secretly to a private conversation. **eavesdropper** *n.*

ebb *n.* **1.** the outward movement of the tide, away from land. **2.** a condition of lowness or decline. —**ebb** *v.* **1.** (of tides) to flow away from land. **2.** to become lower, to weaken, *his strength ebbed*.

ebony *n.* the hard black wood of a tropical tree. —*adj.* black as ebony.

ebullient (i-**bul**-iĕnt) *adj.* exuberant, bubbling over with high spirits. **ebullience** *n.*

eccentric *adj.* **1.** unconventional in appearance or behaviour. **2.** (of circles) not concentric, (of orbits) not circular, (of a pivot) not placed centrally. —*n.* an eccentric person. —**eccentrically** *adv.*, **eccentricity** *n.*

Eccles cake (ek-**ūlz**) a round cake of pastry filled with currants.

ecclesiastical (i-kleez-i-**ast**-ikăl) *adj.* of the Church or the clergy.

echelon (**esh**-ĕ-lŏn) *n.* **1.** a formation of troops or aircraft etc. like a series of steps, with each unit to the right (or left) of the one in front. **2.** a level of rank or authority, *the upper echelons of the Civil Service*.

echo *n.* (*pl.* **echoes**) **1.** repetition of sound by the reflection of sound-waves, a secondary sound produced in this way. **2.** a close imitation or imitator. —**echo** *v.* (**echoed, echoing**) **1.** to repeat (sound) by echo, to resound. **2.** to repeat or imitate.

éclair (ay-**klair**) *n.* a finger-shaped cake of choux pastry with cream filling.

eclampsia (i-**klamp**-siă) *n.* a kind of epileptic convulsion affecting women in pregnancy or childbirth. **eclamptic** *adj.*

eclectic (i-**klek**-tik) *adj.* choosing or accepting from various sources.

eclipse *n.* **1.** the blocking of light from one heavenly body by another. **2.** a loss of brilliance or power or reputation. —**eclipse** *v.* **1.** to cause an eclipse of. **2.** to outshine, to throw into obscurity.

ecliptic (i-**klip**-tik) *n.* the sun's apparent path among stars during the year.

ecologist *n.* an expert in ecology.

ecology (ee-**kol**-ŏji) *n.* **1.** the scientific study of living things in relation to each other and to their environment. **2.** this relationship. **ecological** (ee-kŏ-**loj**-ikăl) *adj.*

economic (ee-kŏ-**nom**-ik *or* ek-ŏ-**nom**-ik) *adj.* **1.** of economics, *the government's economic policies*. **2.** sufficient to give a good return for the money or effort outlaid, *an economic rent*. □ **economics** *n.* the science concerned with the production and consumption or use of goods and services; (as *pl. n.*) the financial aspects of something, *the economics of farming*.

economical (ee-kŏ-**nom**-ikăl) *adj.* thrifty, avoiding waste. **economically** *adv.*

economist (i-**kon**-ŏmist) *n.* an expert in economics.

economize *v.* to be economical, to use or spend less than before, *economize on fuel.*

economy *n.* **1.** being economical, *practise economy.* **2.** an instance of this, a saving, *make economies.* **3.** a community's system of using its resources to produce wealth; *an agricultural economy,* one where agriculture is the chief industry. **4.** the state of a country's prosperity.

ecru (**ay**-kroo) *n.* light fawn colour.

ecstasy (**ek**-stă-si) *n.* a feeling of intense delight. **ecstatic** (ik-**stat**-ik) *adj.,* **ecstatically** *adv.*

ECT *abbrev.* electroconvulsive therapy.

ectoplasm (**ek**-tŏ-plazm) *n.* **1.** the outer portion of the protoplasm of an animal or vegetable cell. **2.** a substance supposed to be exuded from a spiritualist medium during a trance.

Ecuador (**ek**-wă-dor) a country in South America. **Ecuadorean** *adj. & n.*

ecumenical (ee-kew-**men**-ikăl) *adj.* **1.** of the whole Christian Church, not only of separate sects. **2.** seeking world-wide Christian unity, *the ecumenical movement.*

eczema *n.* a skin disease causing scaly itching patches.

Edam (**ee**-dam) *n.* a round Dutch cheese, usually with a red rind.

eddy *n.* a swirling patch of water or air or fog etc. —*v.* (eddied, eddying) to swirl in eddies.

edelweiss (**ay**-del-vys) *n.* an alpine plant with white flowers and woolly leaves.

Eden the place where Adam and Eve lived at their creation. —*n.* a delightful place.

edge *n.* **1.** the sharpened side of a blade. **2.** its sharpness, *has lost its edge.* **3.** the line where two surfaces meet at an angle. **4.** a rim, the narrow surface of a thin or flat object, *the pages have gilt edges.* **5.** the outer limit or boundary of an area, *the edge of the forest.* —**edge** *v.* **1.** to supply with a border, to form the border of. **2.** to move gradually, *edging towards the door.* □ **be on edge,** to be tense and irritable. **have the edge on,** (*informal*) to have an advantage over. **set a person's teeth on edge,** to upset his nerves by causing an unpleasant sensation. **take the edge off,** to dull or soften; *take the edge off one's appetite,* to make one's hunger less acute.

edgeways *adv.* with the edge forwards or outwards. **get a word in edgeways,** to manage to break into a lengthy monologue.

edging *n.* something placed round an edge to define or strengthen or decorate it.

edgy *adj.* with nerves on edge, irritable.

edible *adj.* fit to be eaten (because of its nature). **edibility** *n.*

edict (**ee**-dikt) *n.* an order proclaimed by an authority.

edifice (**ed**-i-fis) *n.* a large building.

edify (**ed**-i-fy) *v.* (edified, edifying) to be an uplifting influence on the mind of (a person). **edification** *n.*

Edinburgh the capital of Scotland.

edit *v.* (edited, editing) **1.** to act as editor of (a newspaper etc.). **2.** to prepare (written material) for publication. **3.** to reword for a purpose. **4.** to prepare (data) for processing by computer. **5.** to prepare (a film or recording) by selecting individual sections and arranging them in sequence.

edition *n.* **1.** the form in which something is published, *a pocket edition.* **2.** the copies of a book or newspaper printed from one set of type. **3.** the total number of a product (e.g. a commemorative medal) issued at one time.

editor *n.* **1.** a person who is responsible for the content and writing of a newspaper etc. or a section of this, *our financial editor.* **2.** one who edits written material for publication. **3.** one who edits cinema film or recording tape.

editorial *adj.* of an editor, *editorial work.* —*n.* a newspaper article giving the editor's comments on current affairs.

educate *v.* to train the mind and abilities of, to provide education for. **educator** *n.*

education *n.* systematic training and instruction designed to impart knowledge and develop skill. **educational** *adj.* □ **educationist, educationalist** *ns.* expert in educational methods.

Edwardian (ed-**wor**-diăn) *adj.* of the time of King Edward VII's reign (1901–10). —*n.* a person living at this time.

EEC *abbrev.* European Economic Community.

eel *n.* a snake-like fish.

eelworm *n.* a small worm infesting plants.

eerie *adj.* (eerier, eeriest) causing a feeling of mystery and fear. **eerily** *adv.,* **eeriness** *n.*

eff *v.* (*vulgar*) fuck, *eff off.*

efface *v.* to rub out, to obliterate. **effacement** *n.* □ **efface oneself,** to make oneself inconspicuous.

effect *n.* **1.** a change produced by an action or cause, a result; *have an effect,* to produce such a change. **2.** an impression produced on a spectator or hearer etc., *special lighting gave the effect of moonlight; did it only for effect,* in order to impress people. **3.** a state of being operative, *the law came into effect last week.* — *v.* to bring about, to accomplish, *effect one's purpose*; *effect a cure*; *effect an insurance policy,* obtain one. (¶ See the note under affect.) □ **effects** *pl. n.* property, *personal effects*; sounds and lighting etc. provided to accompany a broadcast or film. **in effect,** in fact, really, *it is, in effect, a refusal.* **take effect,** to produce its effect(s); to become operative. **to that effect,** with that implication, *words to that effect.* **with effect from,** coming into operation at (a stated time).

effective *adj.* 1. producing an effect, powerful in its effect. 2. making a striking impression. 3. actual, existing; *the effective membership,* the real (not nominal) number of members. 4. operative, *the law is effective from 1 April.* **effectively** *adv.*, **effectiveness** *n.*

effectual *adj.* answering its purpose, sufficient to produce an effect. **effectually** *adv.*

effectuate *v.* to cause to happen.

effeminate (i-**fem**-in-ăt) *adj.* unmanly, having qualities associated with women. **effeminacy** *n.*

effervesce (ef-er-**vess**) *v.* to give off small bubbles of gas. **effervescent** *adj.*, **effervescence** *n.*

effete (ef-**eet**) *adj.* having lost its vitality. **effeteness** *n.*

efficacious (ef-i-**kay**-shŭs) *adj.* producing the desired result. **efficacy** (**ef**-ik-ăsi) *n.*

efficient (i-**fish**-ĕnt) *adj.* acting effectively, producing results with little waste of effort. **efficiently** *adv.*, **efficiency** *n.*

effigy (**ef**-iji) *n.* a sculpture or model of a person.

effluent (**ef**-loo-ĕnt) *adj.* flowing out. —*n.* something that flows out, especially sewage.

effort *n.* 1. the use of physical or mental energy to achieve something. 2. the energy exerted, *it was quite an effort to give up smoking.* 3. something produced by this, *this painting is a good effort.*

effortless *adj.* done without effort. **effortlessly** *adv.*

effrontery (i-**frunt**-er-i) *n.* shameless insolence.

effusion (i-**few**-zhŏn) *n.* 1. a pouring forth. 2. an unrestrained outpouring of thought or feeling.

effusive (i-**few**-siv) *adj.* expressing emotions in an unrestrained way. **effusively** *adv.*, **effusiveness** *n.*

e.g. *abbrev.* = for example. (¶ From the Latin *exempli gratia.*)

egalitarian (i-gal-it-**air**-iăn) *adj.* holding the principle of equal rights for all persons. —*n.* one who holds this principle.

egg[1] *n.* 1. a reproductive cell produced by the female of birds, fish, reptiles, etc. 2. the hard-shelled egg of a domestic hen, used as food. □ **bad egg,** (*informal*) a worthless or dishonest person. **egg-cup** *n.* a small cup for holding a boiled egg. **egg custard,** custard made with egg. **egg-plum** *n.* a small yellow plum. **egg-timer** *n.* a device for timing the cooking of a boiled egg.

egg[2] *v.* to urge a person to do something, *egging him on.*

egghead *n.* (*informal*) an intellectual person.

egg-plant *n.* 1. a plant with deep-purple fruit used as a vegetable. 2. its fruit, aubergine.

eggshell *n.* the shell of an egg. —*adj.* 1. (of china) very fragile. 2. (of paint) with a slightly glossy finish.

eglantine (eg-lăn-tyn) *n.* sweet-brier.

ego (eg-oh) *n.* (*pl.* egos) 1. the self. 2. self-esteem, conceit. □ **ego-trip** *n.* (*informal*) an activity undertaken with the sole purpose of indulging in one's own interests or in self-expression.

egocentric (eg-oh-**sen**-trik) *adj.* self-centred.

egoism (eg-oh-izm) *n.* self-centredness.

egotism (eg-oh-tizm) *n.* the practice of talking too much about oneself, conceit. □ **egotist** *n.* a conceited person. **egotistic, egotistical** *adjs.*

egregious (i-**gree**-jŭs) *adj.* outstandingly bad, *egregious folly.*

egress (ee-gress) *n.* an exit.

egret (ee-grit) *n.* a kind of heron with beautiful long tail-feathers.

Egypt a country in north-east Africa. **Egyptian** *adj. & n.*

Egyptology *n.* the study of Egyptian antiquities. **Egyptologist** *n.* an expert in Egyptology.

eh (*pr.* ay) *int.* (*informal*) an exclamation of enquiry or surprise.

eiderdown *n.* a quilt stuffed with soft material.

eight *adj. & n.* 1. one more than seven (8, VIII). 2. an eight-oared rowing-boat or its crew. □ **have had one over the eight,** (*informal*) to be slightly drunk.

eighteen *adj. & n.* one more than seventeen (18, XVIII). **eighteenth** *adj. & n.*

eighth *adj. & n.* 1. next after seventh. 2. one of eight equal parts of a thing. **eighthly** *adv.*

eightsome *adj.* for eight people, *an eightsome reel.*

eighty *adj. & n.* eight times ten (80, LXXX). **eightieth** *adj. & n.* □ **eighties** *pl. n.*

the numbers or years or degrees of temperature from 80 to 89.

Eire (**air**-ĕ) a former name of the Republic of Ireland, still often used in newspapers etc. to distinguish the country from Northern Ireland.

eisteddfod (I-ste*th*-vod) *n.* an annual Welsh gathering of poets and musicians for competitions.

either (**I**-*th*er *or* ee-*th*er) *adj.* & *pron.* 1. one or the other of two, *either of you can go.* 2. each of two, *there are fields on either side of the river.* —**either** *adv.* & *conj.* 1. as one alternative, *he is either mad or drunk.* 2. likewise, any more than the other, *the new lid doesn't fit, either.*

ejaculate (i-jak-yoo-layt) *v.* 1. to say suddenly and briefly. 2. to eject fluid (especially semen) from the body. **ejaculation** *n.*

eject *v.* 1. to thrust or send out forcefully, *the gun ejects spent cartridges.* 2. to expel, to compel to leave. **ejection** *n.,* **ejectment** *n.,* **ejector** *n.* ☐ **ejector seat,** a seat that can eject the occupant out of an aircraft in an emergency so that he can descend by parachute.

eke (*pr.* eek) *v.* 1. to supplement, *eke out coal by re-using cinders.* 2. to make (a living) laboriously, *eke out a living.*

elaborate¹ (i-**lab**-er-ăt) *adj.* with many parts or details, complicated, *an elaborate pattern.* **elaborately** *adv.*

elaborate² (i-**lab**-er-ayt) *v.* to work out or describe in detail. **elaboration** *n.*

elapse *v.* (of time) to pass away.

elastic *adj.* 1. going back to its original length or shape after being stretched or squeezed. 2. adaptable, not rigid, *the rules are somewhat elastic.* —*n.* cord or material made elastic by interweaving strands of rubber etc. —**elasticity** (el-ass-**tiss**-iti) *n.*

elasticated *adj.* made elastic by being interwoven with elastic thread.

elated (i-**lay**-tid) *adj.* feeling very pleased or proud. **elation** *n.*

elbow *n.* 1. the joint between the forearm and upper arm, its outer part. 2. the part of a sleeve covering this. 3. a sharp bend in a pipe etc. —*v.* to thrust with one's elbow. ☐ **elbow-grease** *n.* vigorous polishing; hard work. **elbow-room** *n.* plenty of room to work or move.

elder¹ *adj.* older, *elder sister.* —*n.* 1. an older person, *respect your elders.* 2. an official in certain Churches. ☐ **elder statesman,** an elderly influential person whose advice is valued because of his years of experience.

elder² *n.* a tree or shrub with white flowers and dark berries. **elderberry** *n.* its berry.

elderly *adj.* rather old, past middle age.

eldest *adj.* oldest, first-born, *eldest son.*

eldorado (el-dor-**ah**-doh) *n.* (*pl.* **eldorados**) an imaginary land of riches.

elect *v.* 1. to choose by vote, *elect a chairman.* 2. to choose as a course, to decide, *he elected to become a lawyer.* —*adj.* chosen; *the president elect,* chosen but not yet in office.

election *n.* 1. choosing or being chosen, especially by vote. 2. the process of electing representatives, especially Members of Parliament.

electioneering *n.* busying oneself in an election campaign.

elective *adj.* 1. having the power to elect, *an elective assembly.* 2. chosen or filled by election, *an elective office.*

elector *n.* one who has the right to vote in an election. **electoral** *adj.* of electors.

electorate *n.* the whole body of electors.

electric *adj.* 1. of or producing electricity. 2. worked by electricity. 3. causing sudden excitement, *the news had an electric effect.* ☐ **electric chair,** a chair in which criminals are executed by electrocution. **electric eel,** an eel-like fish able to give an electric shock. **electric guitar,** a guitar with a built-in microphone. **electric hare,** a dummy hare propelled by electricity, used in greyhound racing. **electrics** *pl. n.* electrical fittings. **electric shock,** the effect of a sudden discharge of electricity through the body of a person or animal, stimulating the nerves and contracting the muscles. **electric storm,** a violent disturbance of the electrical condition of the atmosphere.

electrical *adj.* 1. of or concerned with electricity, *electrical engineering.* 2. causing sudden excitement. **electrically** *adv.*

electrician (i-lek-**trish**-ăn) *n.* a person whose job is dealing with electricity and electrical equipment.

electricity *n.* 1. a form of energy occurring in certain particles (electrons and protons) and hence in larger bodies, since they contain these. 2. a supply of electric current for lighting, heating, etc.

electrify *v.* (electrified, electrifying) 1. to charge with electricity. 2. to convert (a railway, farm, etc.) to the use of electric power. 3. to startle or excite suddenly. **electrification** *n.*

electrocardiogram *n.* the pattern traced by an electrocardiograph.

electrocardiograph *n.* an instrument for detecting and recording the electric currents generated by heartbeats.

electroconvulsive therapy treatment of mental illness by means of electric shocks that produce convulsions.

electrocute *v.* to kill by electricity. **electrocution** *n.*

electrode (i-**lek**-trohd) *n.* a solid conductor through which electricity enters or leaves a vacuum tube etc.

electroencephalogram *n.* the pattern traced by an electroencephalograph.

electroencephalograph *n.* an instrument for detecting and recording the electric currents generated by activity of the brain.

electrolysis (i-lek-**trol**-ĭ-sis) *n.* **1.** chemical decomposition by electric current. **2.** the breaking up of tumours, hair-roots, etc. by electric current.

electrolyte (i-**lek**-trŏ-lyt) *n.* a solution that conducts electric current, especially in an electric cell or battery. **electrolytic** (i-lek-trŏ-**lit**-ik) *adj.*

electromagnet *n.* a magnet consisting of a metal core magnetized by a coil, carrying electric current, wound round it.

electromagnetic *adj.* having both electrical and magnetic properties. **electromagnetically** *adv.*

electromotive *adj.* producing electric current.

electron (i-**lek**-tron) *n.* a particle of matter with a negative electric charge. **electron microscope,** a very high-powered microscope that uses beams of electrons instead of rays of light.

electronic (i-lek-**tron**-ik) *adj.* **1.** produced or worked by a flow of electrons in a vacuum, gas, or certain solids. **2.** of or concerned in electronics, *electronic engineering.* **electronically** *adv.* □ **electronics** *n.* the development and application of electronic devices, e.g. in transistors, computers, etc.; (as *pl. n.*) electronic circuits.

electroplate *v.* to coat with a thin layer of silver etc. by electrolysis. —*n.* objects plated in this way.

elegant *adj.* tasteful, refined, and dignified in appearance or style. **elegantly** *adv.,* **elegance** *n.*

elegy (**el**-i-ji) *n.* a sorrowful or serious poem.

element *n.* **1.** one of the parts that make up a whole. **2.** one of about 100 substances that cannot be split up by chemical means into simpler substances. **3.** an environment that is suitable or satisfying; *water is a fish's element,* its natural habitat; *he is in his element when organizing things,* he enjoys and is good at this. **4.** a trace, *there's an element of truth in the story.* **5.** the wire that gives out heat in an electric heater, cooker, etc. **elemental** *adj.* □ **elements** *pl. n.* atmospheric agencies or forces, e.g. wind, rain, etc., *exposed to the elements;* the basic or elementary principles of a subject; the bread and wine used in the Eucharist.

elementary *adj.* dealing with the simplest facts of a subject. **elementary particle,** any of the subatomic particles that are thought not to be able to be divided into smaller particles.

elephant *n.* a very large land animal with a trunk and long curved ivory tusks. **elephant's ear,** a begonia or a kind of arum with very large leaves.

elephantiasis (eli-făn-**ty**-ă-sis) *n.* a tropical disease in which the legs etc. become grossly enlarged and the skin thickens.

elephantine (el-i-**fan**-tyn) *adj.* **1.** of or like elephants. **2.** very large or clumsy.

elevate *v.* **1.** to raise to a higher place or position, to lift up. **2.** to raise to a higher moral or intellectual level.

elevation *n.* **1.** elevating, being elevated. **2.** the altitude of a place. **3.** a piece of rising ground, a hill. **4.** the angle that the direction of something (e.g. a gun) makes with the horizontal. **5.** a plan or drawing showing one side of a structure, *a south elevation of the house.*

elevator *n.* **1.** something that hoists or raises things. **2.** (*Amer.*) a lift (= lift *n.* sense 3).

eleven *adj.* & *n.* **1.** one more than ten (11, XI). **2.** a team of eleven players at cricket, football, etc. □ **eleven-plus** *n.* an examination taken at the age of 11, before entering secondary school. **elevenses** *pl. n.* light refreshments at about 11 a.m.

eleventh *adj.* & *n.* **1.** next after tenth. **2.** one of eleven equal parts of a thing. □ **at the eleventh hour,** at the latest possible time for doing something.

elf *n.* (*pl.* **elves**) an imaginary small being with magic powers. **elfin** *adj.,* **elfish** *adj.*

elicit (i-**lis**-it) *v.* to draw out (information, a response, etc.).

eligible (**el**-i-ji-bŭl) *adj.* **1.** qualified to be chosen for a position or allowed a privilege etc., *he is eligible for a pension.* **2.** regarded as suitable or desirable, especially for marriage, *eligible young men.* **eligibility** *n.*

eliminate (i-**lim**-in-ayt) *v.* **1.** to get rid of (something that is not wanted), *eliminate errors.* **2.** to exclude from a further stage of a competition etc. through defeat, *was eliminated in the fourth round.* **elimination** *n.,* **eliminator** *n.*

elision (i-**lizh**-ŏn) *n.* omission of part of a word in pronouncing it (e.g. *I'm* = I am).

élite (ay-**leet**) *n.* **1.** a group of people regarded as superior in some way and therefore favoured. **2.** a size of letters in typewriting (12 per inch). □ **élitist** *n.* one who advocates selecting and treating certain people as an élite. **élitism** *n.*

elixir (i-**liks**-er) *n.* **1.** a fragrant liquid used as a medicine or flavouring. **2.** a remedy believed to cure all ills.

Elizabethan *adj.* of the time of Queen Elizabeth I's reign (1558–1603). —*n.* a person living at this time.

elk *n.* a large deer of northern Europe and Asia.

ellipse (i-**lips**) *n.* a regular oval that can be divided into four identical quarters.

ellipsis (i-**lip**-sis) *n.* (*pl.* ellipses) the omission of words needed to complete a meaning or a grammatical construction.

elliptical (i-**lip**-ti-kăl) *adj.* **1.** shaped like an ellipse. **2.** containing an ellipsis, having omissions. **elliptically** *adv.*

elm *n.* **1.** a deciduous tree with rough serrated leaves. **2.** its wood.

elocution (el-ŏ-**kew**-shŏn) *n.* a person's style of speaking, the art of speaking expressively.

elongate (**ee**-long-ayt) *v.* to lengthen, to prolong. **elongation** *n.*

elope (i-**lohp**) *v.* to run away secretly with a lover, especially in order to get married. **elopement** *n.*

eloquence (**el**-ŏ-kwĕns) *n.* fluent and powerful speaking. **eloquent** *adj.* speaking fluently and powerfully. **eloquently** *adv.*

El Salvador (el **sal**-vă-dor) a country in Central America.

else *adv.* **1.** besides, other, *someone else.* **2.** otherwise, if not, *run or else you'll be late.*

elsewhere *adv.* somewhere else.

elucidate (i-**loo**-sid-ayt) *v.* to throw light on (a problem), to make clear. **elucidation** *n.*

elude (i-**lood**) *v.* **1.** to escape skilfully from, to avoid, *eluded his pursuers.* **2.** to escape a person's understanding or memory etc., *the answer eludes me.* **elusion** *n.*

elusive (i-**loo**-siv) *adj.* **1.** eluding, escaping. **2.** eluding a person's understanding or memory etc. **elusiveness** *n.*

¶ Do not confuse with illusive.

elver *n.* a young eel.

'em *pronoun* (*informal*) = them.

emaciated (i-**may**-si-ayt-id) *adj.* having become very thin from illness or starvation. **emaciation** *n.*

emanate (**em**-ăn-ayt) *v.* to issue or originate from a source, *pleasant smells emanated from the kitchen.* **emanation** *n.*

emancipate (i-**man**-sip-ayt) *v.* to liberate,

to set free from slavery or some form of restraint. **emancipation** *n.*, **emancipator** *n.*

emasculate (i-**mas**-kew-layt) *v.* to deprive of force; *an emasculated law,* one made weak by alterations to it. **emasculation** *n.*

embalm (im-**bahm**) *v.* to preserve (a corpse) from decay by using spices or chemicals.

embankment *n.* a long mound of earth or a stone structure to keep a river from spreading or to carry a road or railway.

embargo (im-**bar**-goh) *n.* (*pl.* embargoes) an order forbidding commerce or other activity.

embark *v.* **1.** to put or go on board a ship or aircraft at the start of a journey. **2.** to begin an undertaking, *they embarked on a programme of expansion.* **embarkation** *n.*

embarrass *v.* to make (a person) feel awkward or ashamed. **embarrassment** *n.*

embassy *n.* **1.** an ambassador and his staff. **2.** his official headquarters. **3.** a deputation sent to a foreign government.

embattled *adj.* **1.** prepared for battle, *embattled troops.* **2.** fortified against attack.

embed *v.* (embedded, embedding) to fix firmly in a surrounding mass.

embellish (im-**bel**-ish) *v.* **1.** to ornament. **2.** to improve (a story etc.) by adding details that are entertaining but invented. **embellishment** *n.*

Ember days a group of three days in each of the four seasons, observed as days of fasting and prayer in certain Churches.

embers *pl. n.* small pieces of live coal or wood in a dying fire.

embezzle *v.* to take fraudulently for one's own use money or property placed in one's care. **embezzlement** *n.*, **embezzler** *n.*

embitter *v.* to arouse bitter feelings in.

emblazon (im-**blay**-zŏn) *v.* to ornament with heraldic or other devices.

emblem *n.* a symbol, a device that represents something, *the crown is the emblem of kingship.*

emblematic (em-blim-**at**-ik) *adj.* serving as an emblem, symbolic.

embody *v.* (embodied, embodying) **1.** to express principles or ideas in a visible form, *the house embodied her idea of a home.* **2.** to incorporate, to include, *parts of the old treaty are embodied in the new one.* **embodiment** *n.*

embolden *v.* **1.** to make bold, to encourage. **2.** to cause to be printed in boldface type.

embolism (**em**-bŏl izm) *n.* obstruction of an artery or vein by a clot of blood, airbubble, etc.

emboss *v.* to decorate with a raised design.

embrace *v.* **1.** to hold closely and affectionately in one's arms. **2.** to accept eagerly, *embraced the opportunity*. **3.** to adopt (a religion etc.). **4.** to include. —*n.* the act of embracing, a hug.

embrasure (im-**bray**-*zhe*r) *n.* **1.** an opening in a wall for a door or window, with splayed sides. **2.** a similar opening for a gun, widening towards the outside.

embrocation *n.* liquid for rubbing on the body to relieve aches or bruises.

embroider *v.* **1.** to ornament with needlework. **2.** to embellish (a story). **embroidery** *n.* embroidering, embroidered material.

embroil *v.* to involve in an argument or quarrel etc.

embryo (**em**-bri-oh) *n.* (*pl.* embryos) **1.** an animal in the early stage of its development, before birth or emergence from an egg (used of a child in the first eight weeks of its development in the womb). **2.** a rudimentary plant contained in a seed. **3.** something in its very early stages. □ **in embryo,** existing but undeveloped.

embryonic (em-bri-**on**-ik) *adj.* existing in embryo.

emend (i-**mend**) *v.* to alter (something written) in order to remove errors. **emendation** (ee-men-**day**-shŏn) *n.*

emerald *n.* **1.** a bright-green precious stone. **2.** its colour.

emerge (i-**merj**) *v.* **1.** to come up or out into view. **2.** (of facts or ideas) to be revealed by investigation, to become obvious. **emergence** *n.,* **emergent** *adj.*

emergency *n.* a serious happening or situation needing prompt action.

emery (**em**-er-i) *n.* coarse abrasive used for polishing metal or wood etc. **emery-board** *n.* a small stiff strip of wood or cardboard coated with emery, used for filing the nails. **emery-paper** *n.* paper coated with emery.

emetic (i-**met**-ik) *n.* medicine used to cause vomiting.

emigrate *v.* to leave one country and go to settle in another. **emigration** *n.* □ **emigrant** *n.* one who emigrates.

eminence (**em**-in-ĕns) *n.* **1.** the state of being famous or distinguished, *a surgeon of great eminence*. **2.** a piece of rising ground. **3.** a cardinal's title, *His Eminence*.

eminent (**em**-in-ĕnt) *adj.* **1.** famous, distinguished. **2.** conspicuous, outstanding, *a man of eminent goodness*. **eminently** *adv.*

emir (em-**eer**) *n.* the title of various Muslim rulers. **emirate** (**em**-er-ăt) *n.* the territory of an emir.

emissary (**em**-iss-er-i) *n.* a person sent to conduct negotiations.

emit (i-**mit**) *v.* (emitted, emitting) **1.** to send out (light, heat, fumes, lava, etc.). **2.** to utter, *she emitted a shriek.* **emission** *n.,* **emitter** *n.*

emollient (i-**mol**-iĕnt) *adj.* softening or soothing the skin. —*n.* an emollient substance.

emolument (i-**mol**-yoo-mĕnt) *n.* a fee received, a salary.

emotion *n.* an intense mental feeling, e.g. love or hate.

emotional *adj.* **1.** of emotions. **2.** showing emotion excessively. **emotionally** *adv.*

emotive (i-**moh**-tiv) *adj.* rousing emotion.

empanel (im-**pan**-ĕl) *v.* (empanelled, empanelling) to list or select for service on a jury.

empathy (**em**-păthi) *n.* the ability to identify oneself mentally with a person or thing and so understand his feelings or its meaning.

emperor *n.* the male ruler of an empire.

emphasis (**em**-fă-sis) *n.* (*pl.* emphases) **1.** special importance given to something, prominence, *the emphasis is on quality*. **2.** vigour of expression or feeling or action, *nodded his head with emphasis*. **3.** the extra force used in speaking a particular syllable or word, or on a sound in music.

emphasize (**em**-fă-syz) *v.* to lay emphasis on.

emphatic (im-**fat**-ik) *adj.* using or showing emphasis, expressing oneself with emphasis. **emphatically** *adv.*

emphysema (em-fi-**see**-mă) *n.* a condition in which the air cells in the lungs become dilated and lose their elasticity, causing difficulty in breathing.

empire *n.* **1.** a group of countries ruled by a single supreme authority. **2.** supreme political power. **3.** a large commercial organization controlled by one person or group. □ **empire-building** *n.* the process of deliberately acquiring extra territory or authority etc. **Empire style,** a style of furniture or dress fashionable during the first (1804–14) or second (1852–70) French Empire.

empirical (im-**pi**-ri-kăl) *adj.* (of knowledge) based on observation or experiment, not on theory.

emplacement *n.* a place or platform for a gun or battery of guns.

employ *v.* **1.** to give work to, to use the services of. **2.** to make use of, *how do you employ your spare time?* —*n.* **in the employ of,** employed by.

employable *adj.* able to be employed.

employee (im-**ploi**-ee) *n.* a person who works for another in return for wages.

employer *n.* a person or firm that employs people.

employment *n.* **1.** employing. **2.** the state of being employed. **3.** work done as an occupation or to earn a livelihood.

emporium (em-**por**-iŭm) *n.* **1.** a centre of commerce. **2.** a large shop.

empower *v.* to give power or authority to, *police are empowered to arrest people.*

empress *n.* **1.** the female ruler of an empire. **2.** the wife or widow of an emperor.

empty *adj.* **1.** containing nothing, *empty boxes*; *empty trucks*, not loaded. **2.** without an occupant, *an empty chair*; *empty streets*, without people or traffic. **3.** without effectiveness, *empty promises.* **4.** lacking good sense or intelligence, *an empty head.* **5.** (*informal*) hungry, *feel rather empty.* —**empty** *v.* (emptied, emptying) **1.** to make or become empty. **2.** to transfer (the contents of one thing) into another, to discharge itself or its contents. **emptily** *adv.*, **emptiness** *n.* □ **empties** *pl. n.* emptied boxes or bottles or trucks etc. **empty-handed** *adj.* bringing or taking away nothing. **empty-headed** *adj.* lacking good sense or intelligence.

emu (**ee**-mew) *n.* a large Australian bird rather like an ostrich.

emulate (**em**-yoo-layt) *v.* to try to do as well as or better than. **emulation** *n.*, **emulator** *n.*

emulsify (i-**mul**-si-fy) *v.* (emulsified, emulsifying) to convert or be converted into an emulsion.

emulsion (i-**mul**-shŏn) *n.* **1.** a creamy liquid in which particles of oil or fat are evenly distributed. **2.** a medicine or paint in this form. **3.** the light-sensitive coating on photographic film, a mixture of silver compound in gelatine.

enable *v.* to give the means or authority to do something.

enact (in-**akt**) *v.* **1.** to decree, to make into a law. **2.** to perform, to act (a play etc.). □ **enactment** *n.* a law enacted.

enamel *n.* **1.** a glass-like substance used for coating metal or pottery. **2.** paint that dries hard and glossy. **3.** the hard outer covering of teeth. —*v.* (enamelled, enamelling) to coat or decorate with enamel.

enamoured (i-**nam**-erd) *adj.* fond, *he was very enamoured of the sound of his own voice.*

en bloc (ahn **blok**) in a block, all at the same time.

encamp *n.* to settle in a camp.

encampment *n.* a camp.

encase *v.* to enclose in a case.

enchant *v.* **1.** to put under a magic spell. **2.** to fill with intense delight. **enchantment** *n.*, **enchanter**, **enchantress** *ns.*

encircle *v.* to surround. **encirclement** *n.*

enclave (**en**-klayv) *n.* a small territory wholly within the boundaries of another.

enclose *v.* **1.** to put a wall or fence etc. round, to shut in on all sides. **2.** to shut up in a receptacle, to put into an envelope along with a letter or into a parcel along with the contents. □ **enclosed** *adj.* (of a religious community) living in isolation from the outside world.

enclosure *n.* **1.** enclosing. **2.** an enclosed area. **3.** something enclosed with a letter etc.

encode *v.* to put into code, to put (data) into a coded form for processing by computer. **encoder** *n.*

encomium (en-**koh**-miŭm) *n.* high praise given in a speech or writing.

encompass *v.* to surround, to encircle.

encore (**ong**-kor) *int.* a call for repetition of a performance. —*n.* **1.** this call. **2.** the item performed in response to it. —*v.* to call for such a repetition.

encounter *v.* **1.** to meet, especially by chance or unexpectedly. **2.** to find oneself faced with, *encounter difficulties.* **3.** to meet in battle. —**encounter** *n.* **1.** a sudden or unexpected meeting. **2.** a battle.

encourage *v.* **1.** to give hope or confidence to. **2.** to urge, *encouraged him to try.* **3.** to stimulate, to help to develop, *to encourage exports.* **encouragement** *n.*

encroach *v.* **1.** to intrude upon someone's territory or rights or time. **2.** to advance beyond the original or proper limits, *the sea encroached gradually upon the land.* **encroachment** *n.*

encrust *v.* **1.** to cover with a crust of hard material. **2.** to ornament with a layer of jewels etc. **encrustation** *n.*

encumber *v.* to be a burden to, to hamper. **encumbrance** *n.* something that encumbers.

encyclical (en-**sik**-lik-ăl) *n.* a letter written by the pope for wide circulation.

encyclopaedia *n.* a book or set of books giving information on all branches of knowledge or of one subject, usually arranged alphabetically.

encyclopaedic *adj.* giving or possessing information about many subjects or branches of one subject.

end *n.* **1.** the extreme limit of something. **2.** the part or surface forming this; *to the ends of the earth*, to its furthest points; *no problem at my end*, in my share of the work.

3. *the end,* (*informal*) the limit of what one can endure. **4.** half of a sports pitch or court defended or occupied by one side or player. **5.** the finish or conclusion of something, the latter or final part. **6.** destruction, downfall, death. **7.** a purpose or aim, *to gain his own ends.* —**end** *v.* **1.** to bring to an end, to put an end to. **2.** to come to an end, to reach a certain place or state eventually, *ended up laughing.* □ **end it all,** (*informal*) to commit suicide. **end on,** with the end facing one or adjoining the end of the next object. **end-product** *n.* the final product of a manufacturing process. **keep one's end up,** to do one's part in spite of difficulties. **make ends meet,** to keep one's expenditure within one's income. **no end,** (*informal*) to a great extent. **no end of,** (*informal*) much or many of. **put an end to,** to abolish or stop or destroy.

endanger *v.* to cause danger to.

endear *v.* to cause to be loved, *endeared herself to us all.* **endearing** *adj.* inspiring affection.

endearment *n.* a word or words expressing love.

endeavour (in-**dev**-er) *v.* to attempt, to try. —*n.* an attempt.

endemic (en-**dem**-ik) *adj.* commonly found in a particular country or district or group of people, *the disease is endemic in Africa.*

ending *n.* the final part.

endive (**en**-div) *n.* **1.** a curly-leaved plant used as salad. **2.** (*Amer.*) chicory.

endless *adj.* without end, never stopping, *endless patience.* **endless belt,** one with the ends joined so that it forms a continuous strip for use in machinery etc.

endmost *adj.* nearest the end.

endocrine (**end**-ŏ-kryn) *adj.* (of a gland) pouring its secretions straight into the blood, not through a duct.

endorphin (en-**dor**-fin) *n.* any of a group of pain-killing substances produced naturally within the brain and spinal cord.

endorse *v.* **1.** to sign or add a comment on (a document), to sign the back of (a cheque) in order to obtain the money indicated. **2.** to make an official entry on (a licence) about an offence by the holder. **3.** to confirm (a statement), to declare one's approval of. **endorsement** *n.*

endow *v.* **1.** to provide with a permanent income, *endow a school.* **2.** to provide with a power or ability or quality, *was endowed with great talents.*

endowment *n.* **1.** endowing. **2.** an endowed income. **3.** a natural ability. □ **endowment assurance,** a form of life insurance in which a fixed sum is paid to the insured person on a specified date or to his estate if he dies before this date.

endue *v.* to provide with a talent or quality etc., *endue us with gentleness.*

endurable *adj.* able to be endured.

endurance *n.* ability to withstand pain or hardship or prolonged use or strain.

endure *v.* **1.** to experience pain or hardship or difficulties, to bear patiently. **2.** to tolerate. **3.** to remain in existence, to last.

endways *adv.* **1.** with its end foremost. **2.** end to end.

enema (**en**-im-ă) *n.* **1.** the insertion of liquid into the rectum through the anus by means of a syringe, for medical purposes. **2.** this liquid.

enemy *n.* **1.** one who is hostile towards another and seeks to harm the other. **2.** a member of a hostile army or nation etc., an opposing military force, ship, aircraft etc.

energetic *adj.* full of energy, done with energy. **energetically** *adv.*

energize (**en**-er-jyz) *v.* **1.** to give energy to. **2.** to cause electricity to flow to.

energy *n.* **1.** the capacity for vigorous activity. **2.** the ability of matter or radiation to do work either because of its motion (*kinetic energy*), or because of its mass (released in nuclear fission etc.), or because of its electric charge etc. **3.** fuel and other resources used for the operation of machinery etc., *the country's energy requirements.*

enervate (**en**-er-vayt) *v.* to cause to lose vitality, *an enervating climate.*

enfant terrible (ahn-fahn te-**reebl**) a person whose behaviour is embarrassing or indiscreet or irresponsible.

enfeeble *v.* to make feeble.

enfilade (en-fil-**ayd**) *n.* gunfire directed along a line from end to end. —*v.* to rake with gunfire.

enfold *v.* **1.** to wrap up. **2.** to clasp.

enforce *v.* to compel obedience to, to impose by force or compulsion, *the law was firmly enforced.* **enforcement** *n.*

enforceable *adj.* able to be enforced.

enfranchise *v.* to give municipal rights to (a town), to give (a person) the right to vote in elections. **enfranchisement** *n.*

engage *v.* **1.** to take into one's employment, *engage a typist.* **2.** to arrange beforehand to occupy (a seat etc.). **3.** to promise, to pledge. **4.** to occupy the attention of, *engaged her in conversation.* **5.** to occupy oneself, *he engages in politics.* **6.** to begin a battle against, *engaged the enemy troops.* **7.** to interlock (parts of a gear) so that it transmits power, to become interlocked in this way.

engaged *adj.* **1.** having promised to marry, *an engaged couple.* **2.** occupied or reserved by a person, occupied with business etc., *I'm afraid the manager is engaged.* **3.** (of a telephone line) already in use.

engagement *n.* **1.** engaging something, being engaged. **2.** an appointment made with another person. **3.** a battle.

engaging *adj.* attractive, charming.

engender (in-**jen**-der) *v.* to give rise to.

engine *n.* **1.** a mechanical contrivance consisting of several parts working together, especially as a source of power. **2.** the engine of a railway train. **3.** a fire-engine.

engineer *n.* **1.** a person who is skilled in a branch of engineering. **2.** one who is in charge of machines and engines, e.g. on a ship. **3.** one who plans or organizes something. —**engineer** *v.* **1.** to construct or control as an engineer. **2.** to contrive or bring about, *he engineered a meeting between them.*

engineering *n.* the application of scientific knowledge for the control and use of power e.g. in works of public utility such as the building of roads and bridges (*civil engineering*), machines (*mechanical engineering*), electrical apparatus (*electrical engineering*), etc.

England the country forming the southern part of Great Britain.

English *adj.* of England or its people or language. —*n.* **1.** the English language, used in Britain and most Commonwealth countries and the USA. **2.** *the English,* English people. **Englishman, Englishwoman** *ns.*

engrave *v.* **1.** to cut or carve (a design) into a hard surface, to ornament with a design in this way. **2.** to fix deeply in the mind or memory. **engraver** *n.*

engraving *n.* a print made from an engraved metal plate.

engross (in-**grohs**) *v.* **1.** to occupy fully by absorbing the attention. **2.** to express in legal form. **engrossment** *n.*

engulf *v.* to surround or cause to disappear by flowing round or over, to swamp.

enhance (in-**hahns**) *v.* to increase the attractiveness or other qualities of. **enhancement** *n.*

enigma (in-**ig**-mă) *n.* something very difficult to understand.

enigmatic (en-ig-**mat**-ik) *adj.* mysterious and puzzling. **enigmatically** *adv.*

enjoin *v.* to order, to command.

enjoy *v.* **1.** to get pleasure from. **2.** to have as an advantage or benefit, *to enjoy good health.* **enjoyment** *n.* □ **enjoy oneself,** to experience pleasure from what one is doing.

enjoyable *adj.* giving enjoyment, pleasant. **enjoyably** *adv.*

enlarge *v.* **1.** to make or become larger. **2.** to reproduce (a photograph) on a larger scale. **3.** to say more about something, *enlarge upon this matter.* □ **enlarger** *n.* an apparatus for making photographic enlargements.

enlargement *n.* **1.** enlarging, being enlarged. **2.** something enlarged, a photograph printed larger than its negative.

enlighten *v.* to give knowledge to, to inform. **enlightenment** *n.* □ **enlightened** *adj.* freed from ignorance or prejudice, *in these enlightened days.*

enlist *v.* **1.** to take into or join the armed forces, *enlist as a soldier.* **2.** to secure as a means of help or support, *enlisted their sympathy.* **enlistment** *n.*

enliven *v.* to make more lively. **enlivenment** *n.*

en masse (ahn **mass**) all together.

enmesh *v.* to entangle as if in a net.

enmity *n.* hostility between enemies.

ennoble *v.* **1.** to make (a person) a noble. **2.** to make (a thing) noble or more dignified. **ennoblement** *n.*

enormity (in-**orm**-iti) *n.* **1.** great wickedness, *the enormity of this crime.* **2.** a serious crime, *these enormities.* **3.** enormous size, hugeness, *the enormity of their task.* (¶ Many people regard this use as unacceptable.)

enormous *adj.* very large, huge. **enormously** *adv.*, **enormousness** *n.*

enough *adj., n., & adv.* as much or as many as necessary.

enquire *v.* to ask. **enquiry** *n.* ¶ Although these words are often used in exactly the same way as *inquire* and *inquiry,* there is a tendency to use *en-* as a formal word for 'ask' and *in-* for an investigation.

enrage *v.* to make furious.

enrapture *v.* to fill with intense delight.

enrich *v.* **1.** to make richer. **2.** to improve the quality of by adding things, *this food is enriched with vitamins.* **enrichment** *n.*

enrobe *v.* to put a robe on.

enrol *v.* (enrolled, enrolling) **1.** to become a member of a society, institution, etc. **2.** to admit as a member. **enrolment** *n.*

en route (ahn **root**) on the way, *met him en route from Rome to London.*

ensconce (in-**skons**) *v.* to establish securely or comfortably.

ensemble (ahn-**sahmbl**) *n.* **1.** a thing viewed as a whole. **2.** a group of musicians who perform together. **3.** a woman's outfit of harmonizing items.

enshrine *v.* **1.** to enclose in a shrine. **2.** to serve as a shrine for.

enshroud *v.* to cover completely.

ensign (**en**-syn) *n.* a military or naval flag, a special form of the national flag flown by ships.

enslave *v.* to make a slave of. **enslavement** *n.*

ensue (ens-**yoo**) *v.* to happen afterwards or as a result, *a quarrel ensued.*

ensure *v.* to make safe or certain, to secure, *good food will ensure good health.* ¶ This word is never used to mean 'to provide with financial insurance'.

entablature (en-**tab**-la-cher) *n.* the section including the architrave, frieze, and cornice of a building or structure, above the supporting columns.

entail (in-**tayl**) *v.* **1.** to make necessary, to involve, *these plans entail great expense.* **2.** to leave (land) to a line of heirs so that none of them can give it away or sell it. — *n.* the entailing of landed property, the property itself.

entangle *v.* **1.** to tangle. **2.** to entwine in something that it is difficult to escape from. **3.** to involve in something complicated. **entanglement** *n.*

entente (ahn-**tahnt**) *n.* a friendly understanding between countries.

enter *v.* **1.** to go or come in or into. **2.** to come on stage. **3.** to penetrate, *the bullet entered his leg.* **4.** to become a member of, *he entered the Navy.* **5.** to put (a name, details, etc.) on a list or in a book. **6.** to register as a competitor. **7.** to record formally, to present for consideration, *entered a plea of not guilty; entered a protest.* □ **enter into,** to take part in (a conversation, an agreement, etc.); to form part of (calculations, plans, etc.). **enter on,** to begin (a process, stage of work, etc.); to take possession of (an inheritance, an appointment, etc.). **enter up,** to record (names or details) in a book.

enteritis (en-ter-**I**-tiss) *n.* inflammation of the intestines.

enterprise *n.* **1.** an undertaking, especially a bold or difficult one. **2.** initiative. **3.** business activity, *private enterprise.*

enterprising *adj.* full of initiative.

entertain *v.* **1.** to amuse, to occupy agreeably. **2.** to receive (a person) with hospitality, *they entertained me to lunch.* **3.** to have in the mind, *entertain doubts.* **4.** to consider favourably, *refused to entertain the idea.* □ **entertainer** *n.* one who performs in entertainments, especially as an occupation.

entertainment *n.* **1.** entertaining, being entertained. **2.** amusement. **3.** something performed before an audience to amuse or interest them.

enthral (in-**thrawl**) *v.* (enthralled, enthralling) to hold spellbound.

enthrone *v.* to place on a throne, especially with ceremony. **enthronement** *n.*

enthuse (in-**thewz**) *v.* **1.** to show enthusiasm. **2.** to fill with enthusiasm.

enthusiasm *n.* **1.** a feeling of eager liking for or interest in something. **2.** the object of this, *one of my enthusiasms.*

enthusiast *n.* one who is full of enthusiasm for something, *a sports enthusiast.*

enthusiastic *adj.* full of enthusiasm. **enthusiastically** *adv.*

entice *v.* to attract or persuade by offering something pleasant. **enticement** *n.*

entire *adj.* whole, complete. **entirely** *adv.*

entirety (in-**tyr**-ĕti) *n.* completeness, the total; *in its entirety,* in its complete form.

entitle *v.* **1.** to give a title to (a book etc.). **2.** to give a right, *the ticket entitles you to a seat.* **entitlement** *n.*

entity (**en**-titi) *n.* something that exists as a separate thing.

entomb (in-**toom**) *v.* to place in a tomb, to bury.

entomology (en-tŏ-**mol**-ŏji) *n.* the scientific study of insects. **entomological** (en-tŏm-ŏ-**loj**-ikăl) *adj.* □ **entomologist** *n.* an expert in entomology.

entourage (on-toor-**ah**zh) *n.* the people accompanying an important person.

entrails (**en**-traylz) *pl. n.* the intestines.

entrance[1] (**en**-trăns) *n.* **1.** entering. **2.** a door or passage by which one enters. **3.** the right of admission, the fee charged for this.

entrance[2] (in-**trahns**) *v.* to fill with intense delight.

entrant *n.* one who enters, especially as a competitor.

entreat *v.* to request earnestly or emotionally. **entreaty** *n.*

entrecôte (**on**-trĕ-koht) *n.* boned steak cut off the sirloin.

entrée (**on**-tray) *n.* **1.** the right or privilege of admission. **2.** a dish served between the fish and meat courses of a meal.

entrench (in-**trench**) *v.* to establish firmly in a well-defended position; *entrenched ideas,* ideas firmly fixed in the mind.

entrenchment *n.* **1.** entrenching, being entrenched. **2.** a trench made for defence.

entrepreneur (on-trĕ-prĕn-**er**) *n.* **1.** a person who organizes and manages a commercial undertaking, especially one involving commercial risk. **2.** a contractor acting as intermediary. **entrepreneurial** *adj.*

entropy (en-trŏp-i) *n.* a measure of the disorder of the molecules in substances etc. that are mixed or in contact with each other, indicating the amount of energy that (although it still exists) is not available for use because it has become more evenly distributed instead of being concentrated.

entrust *v.* to give as a responsibility, to place (a person or thing) in a person's care.

entry *n.* 1. entering. 2. a place of entrance. 3. an alley between buildings. 4. an item entered in a list, diary, etc. 5. a person or thing entered in a race or competition, the number of entrants.

entryism *n.* infiltration, especially of the Labour Party by left-wing extremists seeking to use the party's political organization to further their revolutionary aims. **entryist** *n.*

Entryphone *n.* (*trade mark*) a telephone at the entrance to a building, for visitors to use in order to identify themselves before they are allowed to enter.

entwine *v.* to twine round, to interweave.

enumerate (in-**new**-mer-ayt) *v.* to count, to mention (items) one by one. **enumeration** *n.*

enunciate (i-**nun**-si-ayt) *v.* 1. to pronounce (words). 2. to state clearly. **enunciation** *n.*

envelop (in-**vel**-ŏp) *v.* (enveloped, enveloping) to wrap up, to cover on all sides, *the hill was enveloped in mist.* **envelopment** *n.*

envelope (en-vĕ-lohp) *n.* a wrapper or covering, especially a folded and gummed cover for a letter.

enviable (**en**-vi-ăbŭl) *adj.* desirable enough to arouse envy. **enviably** *adv.*

envious *adj.* full of envy. **enviously** *adv.*

environment *n.* surroundings, especially those affecting people's lives. **environmental** (in-vyr-ŏn-**men**-tăl) *adj.* □ **environmentalist** *n.* one who seeks to protect or improve the environment.

environs (in-**vyr**-ŏnz) *pl. n.* the surrounding districts, especially round a town.

envisage (in-**viz**-ăj) *v.* 1. to visualize, to imagine. 2. to foresee, *changes are envisaged.*

envoy (**en**-voi) *n.* 1. a messenger or representative. 2. a diplomatic minister ranking below an ambassador.

envy *n.* 1. a feeling of discontent aroused by someone else's possession of things one would like to have oneself. 2. the object of this, *his car is the envy of the neighbourhood.* —*v.* (envied, envying) to feel envy of.

enzyme (**en**-zym) *n.* 1. a protein formed in living cells and assisting chemical processes (e.g. in digestion). 2. a similar substance produced synthetically for use in chemical processes, household detergents, etc.

epaulette (ep-ă-let) *n.* an ornamental shoulder-piece worn on uniforms.

epergne (i-**pern**) *n.* an ornament for a dinner-table, with small bowls or vases on branched supports.

ephedrine (**ef**-i-drin) *n.* a stimulant drug used to relieve asthma, hay fever, etc.

ephemeral (if-**em**-er-ăl) *adj.* lasting only a very short time.

epic *n.* 1. a long poem or other literary work telling of heroic deeds or history. 2. a book or film resembling this. 3. a subject fit to be told in an epic. —*adj.* of or like an epic, on a grand scale.

epicentre *n.* the point at which an earthquake reaches the earth's surface.

epicure (**ep**-i-kewr) *n.* a person with refined tastes in food, literature, etc.

epicurean (ep-i-kewr-ee-ăn) *adj.* devoted to sensuous pleasure and luxury. —*n.* an epicurean person.

epidemic *n.* an outbreak of a disease etc. spreading rapidly through a community.

epidermis (epi-**der**-mis) *n.* the outer layer of the skin.

epidural (epi-**dewr**-ăl) *adj.* (of an anaesthetic) injected round the nerves in the spine and having the effect of anaesthetizing the lower part of the body. —*n.* an epidural anaesthetic.

epigram *n.* a short witty saying.

epilepsy *n.* a disorder of the nervous system causing mild or severe convulsions, sometimes with loss of consciousness. **epileptic** *adj. & n.*

epilogue (**ep**-i-log) *n.* a short concluding section in a literary work.

Epiphany (i-**pif**-ăni) *n.* the Christian festival commemorating the showing of Christ to the Magi, celebrated on 6 January.

episcopal (ip-**iss**-kŏ-păl) *adj.* of a bishop or bishops, governed by bishops.

Episcopalian (ip-iss-kŏ-**pay**-li-ăn) *adj.* of an episcopal church. —*n.* a member of an episcopal church.

episiotomy (ep-isi-**ot**-omi) *n.* a cut made at the opening of the vagina during childbirth, to facilitate delivery of the baby.

episode *n.* 1. an incident or event forming one part of a sequence. 2. an incident in a story, one part of a serial.

epistle (ip-**iss**-ŭl) *n.* 1. (*humorous*) a letter. 2. *Epistle,* any of the letters in the New Testament, written by the Apostles.

epitaph (ep-i-tahf) *n.* words inscribed on a tomb or describing a dead person.

epithet (ep-i-thet) *n.* a descriptive word or phrase, e.g. 'the Great' in *Alfred the Great*.

epitome (ip-**it**-ŏmi) *n.* something that shows on a small scale the qualities of something much larger, a person who embodies a quality, *she is the epitome of kindness*.

EPNS *abbrev.* electroplated nickel silver.

epoch (ee-pok) *n.* a particular period of history. **epoch-making** *adj.* very important or remarkable, marking the beginning of a new epoch.

Epsom salts magnesium sulphate, used as a purgative.

equable (**ek**-wă-bŭl) *adj.* **1.** even, unvarying; *an equable climate,* free from extremes of heat and cold. **2.** even-tempered. **equably** *adv.*

equal *adj.* **1.** the same in size, amount, value, etc. **2.** having the same rights or status. **3.** having enough strength or courage or ability etc., *he was equal to the task.* —*n.* a person or thing that is equal to another. —**equal** *v.* (equalled, equalling) **1.** to be equal to. **2.** to produce or achieve something to match, *no one has equalled this score.* —**equally** *adv.*

equalitarian (ee-kwol-i-**tair**-iăn) *adj.* = egalitarian.

equality *n.* being equal.

equalize *v.* **1.** to make or become equal. **2.** (in games) to equal an opponent's score. **equalization** *n.* □ **equalizer** *n.* an equalizing goal etc.

equanimity (ek-wă-**nim**-iti) *n.* calmness of mind or temper.

equate (i-**kwayt**) *v.* to consider to be equal or equivalent.

equation (i-kway-zhŏn) *n.* **1.** a mathematical statement that two expressions (connected by the sign =) are equal. **2.** making equal.

equator (i-**kway**-ter) *n.* an imaginary line round the earth at an equal distance from the North and South Poles.

equatorial (ee-wă-**tor**-iăl) *adj.* of or near the equator. **Equatorial Guinea,** a country on the west coast of Africa.

equerry (**ek**-wer-i) *n.* an officer of the British royal household, attending members of the royal family.

equestrian (i-**kwest**-riăn) *adj.* of horse-riding; *an equestrian statue,* a statue of a person on a horse. —*n.* a person who is skilled at horse-riding.

equidistant (ee-kwi-**dis**-tănt) *adj.* at an equal distance.

equilateral (ee-kwi-**lat**-er-ăl) *adj.* having all sides equal.

equilibrium (ee-kwi-**lib**-riŭm) *n.* a state of balance.

equine (**ek**-wyn) *adj.* of or like a horse.

equinox (**ek**-win-oks) *n.* the time of year when day and night are of equal length. **equinoctial** (ek-wi-**nok**-shăl) *adj.*

equip *v.* (equipped, equipping) to supply with what is needed.

equipment *n.* **1.** equipping. **2.** the outfit, tools, and other things needed for a particular job or expedition etc.

equipoise (**ek**-wi-poiz) *n.* **1.** equilibrium. **2.** a counterbalance.

equitable (**ek**-wit-ăbŭl) *adj.* fair and just. **equitably** *adv.*

equity (**ek**-wi-ti) *n.* **1.** fairness, impartiality. **2.** *Equity,* the actors' trade union. □ **equities** *pl. n.* stocks and shares not bearing fixed interest.

equivalent *adj.* equal in value, importance, meaning, etc. —*n.* an equivalent thing or amount or word. —**equivalence** *n.*

equivocal (i-**kwiv**-ŏkăl) *adj.* **1.** able to be interpreted in two ways, ambiguous. **2.** questionable, suspicious, *an equivocal character.* **equivocally** *adv.*

equivocate (i-**kwiv**-ŏkayt) *v.* to use ambiguous words in order to conceal the truth, to avoid committing oneself. **equivocation** *n.*

ER *abbrev.* Elizabetha Regina. (¶ Latin, = Queen Elizabeth.)

era (**eer**-ă) *n.* a period of history; *the Christian era,* the period reckoned from the birth of Christ.

eradicate (i-**rad**-ik-ayt) *v.* to get rid of, to remove all traces of. **eradication** *n.*

erase (i-**rayz**) *v.* to rub or scrape out (marks, writing, etc.), to wipe out a recorded signal from (magnetic tape).

eraser *n.* a thing that erases marks etc., a piece of rubber or other substance for rubbing out marks or writing.

erasure (i-**ray**-zher) *n.* **1.** erasing. **2.** a word etc. that has been erased.

erect *adj.* **1.** standing on end, upright, vertical. **2.** (of a part of the body) enlarged and rigid from sexual excitement. —*v.* to set up, to build. —**erector** *n.*

erectile (i-**rek**-tyl) *adj.* (of parts of the body) able to become enlarged and rigid from sexual excitement.

erection *n.* **1.** erecting, being erected. **2.** something erected, a building. **3.** swelling and hardening (especially of the penis) in sexual excitement.

ergonomics (ergŏ-**nom**-iks) *n.* study of work and its environment and conditions in order to achieve maximum efficiency.

ergot (**er**-got) *n.* a fungus affecting rye and other cereals, dried for use in medicine.

erigeron (e-**rij**-er-ŏn) *n.* a hardy plant with daisy-like flowers.

ermine *n.* **1.** an animal of the weasel family, with brown fur that turns white in winter. **2.** this white fur.

Ernie *n.* a device for drawing the prize-winning numbers of Premium Bonds, named from the initial letters of *e*lectronic *r*andom *n*umber *i*ndicator *e*quipment.

erode (i-**rohd**) *v.* to wear away gradually, especially by rubbing or corroding. **erosion** (i-**roh**-zhŏn) *n.*

erogenous (i-**roj**-in-ŭs) *adj.* arousing sexual desire, particularly sensitive to sexual stimulation.

erotic (i-**rot**-ik) *adj.* of sexual love, arousing sexual desire. **erotically** *adv.*

err (*rhymes with* fur) *v.* (erred, erring) **1.** to make a mistake, to be incorrect. **2.** to sin.

errand *n.* **1.** a short journey on which a person goes or is sent to carry a message or deliver goods etc. **2.** the purpose of a journey. □ **errand of mercy,** a journey to bring help or relieve distress etc.

errant (**e**-rănt) *adj.* **1.** misbehaving. **2.** travelling in search of adventure, *a knight errant.*

erratic (i-**rat**-ik) *adj.* irregular or uneven in movement, quality, habit, etc. **erratically** *adv.*

erratum (e-**rah** tŭm) *n.* (*pl.* **errata**) an error in printing or writing, = corrigendum.

erroneous (i-**roh**-niŭs) *adj.* mistaken, incorrect. **erroneously** *adv.*

error *n.* **1.** a mistake. **2.** the condition of being wrong in opinion or conduct. **3.** the amount of inaccuracy in a calculation or a measuring-device, *an error of 2 per cent.* □ **in error,** mistakenly, by mistake.

Erse *n.* Irish Gaelic or Highland Gaelic language. —*adj.* of or in Erse.

erstwhile *adj.* & *adv.* former, formerly.

erudite (**e**-rew-dyt) *adj.* having or showing great learning. **erudition** (e rew **dish** ŏn) *n.*

erupt *v.* **1.** to break out suddenly and violently. **2.** (of a volcano) to shoot forth lava etc., (of a geyser) to spurt water. **3.** to form spots or patches on the skin. **eruption** *n.*

eruptive *adj.* **1.** erupting, liable to erupt. **2.** formed or characterized by eruptions.

erysipelas (e-ri-**sip**-ilăs) *n.* inflammation of the skin, caused by a type of bacterium.

escalate (**esk**-ă-layt) *v.* to increase or cause to increase in intensity or extent. **escalation** *n.*

escalator *n.* a staircase with an endless line of steps moving up or down.

escallonia (esk-ă-**loh**-niă) *n.* a kind of flowering shrub.

escalope (esk-ă-lohp) *n.* a slice of boneless meat, especially veal.

escapade (esk-ă-**payd**) *n.* a piece of reckless or mischievous conduct.

escape *v.* **1.** to get oneself free from confinement or control. **2.** (of liquid or gas etc.) to get out of a container, to leak. **3.** to succeed in avoiding (capture, punishment, etc.). **4.** to be forgotten or unnoticed by; *his name escapes me,* I have forgotten it. **5.** (of words, a sigh, etc.) to be uttered unintentionally. —**escape** *n.* **1.** the act of escaping, the fact of having escaped. **2.** a means of escaping. **3.** a temporary distraction or relief from reality or worry. — **escaper** *n.* □ **escape clause,** a clause releasing a person etc. from a contract under certain conditions. **escape-hatch** *n.* a means of emergency exit from a ship etc. **escape velocity,** the minimum velocity needed for one body to escape from the gravitational pull of another.

escapee (ess-kay-**pee**) *n.* an escaper.

escapement *n.* mechanism regulating the movement of a watch or clock etc., a movable catch engaging the projections of a toothed wheel.

escapist *n.* one who likes to escape from the realities of life by absorbing the mind in entertainment or fantasy. **escapism** *n.*

escargot (ess-**kar**-goh) *n.* an edible snail.

escarpment *n.* a steep slope at the edge of a plateau.

eschew (ess-**choo**) *v.* to avoid or abstain from (certain kinds of action or food etc.).

eschscholtzia (iss-**kol**-shă) *n.* the Californian poppy.

escort[1] (**ess**-kort) *n.* **1.** one or more persons or ships etc. accompanying a person or thing to give protection or as an honour. **2.** a person accompanying a member of the opposite sex socially.

escort[2] (i-**skort**) *v.* to act as escort to.

escritoire (ess-krit-**wahr**) *n.* a writing-desk with drawers.

escudo (ess-**kew**-doh) *n.* (*pl.* **escudos**) the unit of money in Portugal.

escutcheon (i-**skuch**-ŏn) *n.* a shield or emblem bearing a coat of arms. **a blot on one's escutcheon,** a stain on one's reputation.

Eskimo *n.* (*pl.* **Eskimos** *or* **Eskimo**) **1.** a member of a people living near the Arctic coast of America and eastern Siberia. **2.** their language.

esoteric (ess-oh-te-**rik**) *adj.* intended only for people with special knowledge or interest.

ESP *abbrev.* extra-sensory perception.

espadrille (**ess**-pă-dril) *n.* a canvas shoe with a sole of plaited fibre.

espalier (iss-**pal**-i-er) *n.* a trellis or framework on which fruit-trees or ornamental shrubs are trained, a tree etc. trained on this.

esparto (ess-**par**-toh) *n.* a kind of grass of Spain and North Africa, used in paper-making.

especial *adj.* **1.** special, outstanding, *of especial interest.* **2.** belonging chiefly to one person or thing, *for your especial benefit.*

especially *adv.* chiefly, more than in other cases.

Esperanto (ess-per-**an**-toh) *n.* an artificial language designed in 1887 for use by people of all nations.

espionage (**ess**-pi-ŏn-ah*zh*) *n.* spying or using spies to obtain secret information.

esplanade (ess-plăn-**ayd**) *n.* a level area of ground where people may walk or ride for pleasure.

espouse (i-**spowz**, *rhymes with* cows) *v.* **1.** to give support to (a cause). **2.** to marry, to give (a woman) in marriage. **espousal** *n.*

espresso *n.* (*pl.* espressos) **1.** an apparatus for making coffee by forcing steam through powdered coffee-beans. **2.** coffee made in this way. **3.** a place where such coffee is sold.

esprit de corps (ess-pree dĕ **kor**) loyalty and devotion uniting the members of a group.

espy *v.* (espied, espying) to catch sight of.

Esq. *abbrev.* = **Esquire**, a courtesy title (in formal use) placed after a man's surname where no title is used before his name.

essay¹ (**ess**-ay) *n.* **1.** a short literary composition in prose. **2.** an attempt. □ **essayist** *n.* a writer of essays.

essay² (ess-**ay**) *v.* (essayed, essaying) to attempt.

essence *n.* **1.** all that makes a thing what it is, its nature. **2.** an indispensable quality or element. **3.** an extract of something, containing all its important qualities in concentrated form. **4.** a liquid perfume.

essential *adj.* **1.** indispensable. **2.** of or constituting a thing's essence; *its essential qualities,* those that make it what it is. **essentially** *adv.* □ **essential oil,** an oil that is like an essence, with the characteristic smell of the plant from which it is extracted. **essentials** *pl. n.* indispensable elements or things.

Essex a county of England.

establish *v.* **1.** to set up (a business or government etc.) on a permanent basis. **2.** to settle (a person or oneself) in a place or position. **3.** to cause people to accept (a custom or belief etc.). **4.** to show to be

true, to prove, *established his innocence.* □ **established** *adj.* (of a Church or religion) that is made officially a country's national Church or religion.

establishment *n.* **1.** establishing, being established. **2.** an organized body of people maintained for a purpose, a household or staff of servants etc. **3.** a business firm or public institution, its members or employees or premises. **4.** a Church system established by law. □ **the Establishment,** people who are established in positions of power and authority, exercising influence in the background of public life or other activity and generally resisting changes.

estate *n.* **1.** landed property. **2.** a residential or industrial district planned as a unit. **3.** all that a person owns, especially that left at his death. **4.** (*old use*) condition, *the holy estate of matrimony.* □ **estate agent,** one whose business is the selling or letting of houses and land. **estate car,** a saloon car that can carry both passengers and goods in one compartment.

esteem *v.* **1.** to think highly of. **2.** to consider or regard, *I should esteem it an honour.* —*n.* favourable opinion, respect.

ester (**ess**-ter) *n.* a chemical compound formed when an acid and an alcohol interact in a certain way.

estimable (**ess**-tim-ăbŭl) *adj.* worthy of esteem.

estimate¹ (**ess**-tim-ăt) *n.* **1.** a judgement of a thing's approximate value or amount etc. **2.** a contractor's statement of the sum which he estimates he will charge for performing specified work. **3.** a judgement of character or qualities.

estimate² (**ess**-tim-ayt) *v.* to form an estimate of. **estimator** *n.*

estimation *n.* **1.** estimating. **2.** judgement of a person's or thing's worth.

estrange (is-**straynj**) *v.* to cause (people formerly friendly or loving) to become unfriendly or indifferent. **estrangement** *n.*

estuary (**ess**-tew-er-i) *n.* the mouth of a large river where its flow is affected by ebb and flow of tides.

etc. *abbrev.* = **et cetera**, and other similar things, and the rest. **etceteras** *pl. n.* the usual extras, sundries.

etch *v.* **1.** to make (a pattern or picture) by engraving a metal plate with acids or corrosive substances, especially so that copies can be printed from this. **2.** to impress deeply, *the scene is etched on my mind.* **etcher** *n.*

etching *n.* a copy printed from an etched plate.

eternal *adj.* **1.** existing always without beginning or end. **2.** unchanging, not affected by time. **3.** (*informal*) ceaseless, too frequent, *these eternal arguments.* **eternally** *adv.* □ **the Eternal City,** Rome. **eternal triangle,** two men and a woman or two women and a man, with problems resulting from conflict of sexual attractions.

eternity *n.* **1.** infinite time, past or future. **2.** the endless period of life after death. **3.** (*informal*) a very long time. □ **eternity ring,** a finger ring with gems set all round it, symbolizing eternity.

ethanoic acid (eth-ă-**noh**-ik) acetic acid.

ether (ee-ther) *n.* **1.** the clear sky, the upper regions beyond the clouds. **2.** a kind of substance formerly thought to fill all space and act as a medium for transmission of radio waves etc. **3.** a colourless liquid produced by the action of acids on alcohol, used as an anaesthetic and as a solvent.

ethereal (i-**theer**-iăl) *adj.* **1.** light and delicate especially in appearance. **2.** of heaven, heavenly. **ethereally** *adv.*

ethic (eth-ik) *adj.* of or involving morals. —*n.* a moral principle or set of principles. **ethical** (eth-ikăl) *adj.* **1.** of ethics. **2.** morally correct, honourable. **3.** (of medicines) not advertised to the general public and usually available only on a doctor's prescription. **ethically** *adv.*

ethics *n.* moral philosophy (*see* moral). —*pl. n.* moral principles; *medical ethics,* those observed by the medical profession.

Ethiopia a country of north-east Africa. **Ethiopian** *adj. & n.*

ethnic *adj.* **1.** of a racial group. **2.** (of clothes etc.) resembling the peasant clothes of primitive peoples. **ethnically** *adv.*

ethnologist *n.* an expert in ethnology.

ethnology (eth-**nol**-ŏji) *n.* the scientific study of human races and their characteristics. **ethnological** (eth-nŏ-**loj**-ikăl) *adj.*

ethos (ee-thoss) *n.* the characteristic spirit and beliefs of a community, person, or literary work.

etiolate (ee-tiŏ-layt) *v.* to make (a plant) pale through lack of light. **etiolation** *n.*

etiquette (et-i-ket) *n.* the rules of correct behaviour in society or among the members of a profession.

Etonian (ee-**toh**-niăn) *adj.* of Eton College, a public school near Windsor, Berks. —*n.* a member of Eton College.

étude (ay-tewd) *n.* a short musical composition.

etymologist *n.* an expert in etymology.

etymology (et-im-ol-ŏji) *n.* **1.** an account of the origin and development of a word and its meaning. **2.** the study of words and

their origins. **etymological** (et-im-ŏ-**loj**-ikăl) *adj.,* **etymologically** *adv.*

eucalyptus (yoo-kă-**lip**-tŭs) *n.* (*pl.* eucalyptuses) **1.** a kind of evergreen tree. **2.** a strong-smelling oil obtained from its leaves.

Eucharist (yoo-kă-rist) *n.* **1.** the Christian sacrament in which bread and wine are consecrated and consumed. **2.** the consecrated elements, especially the bread. **Eucharistic** *adj.*

eulogistic (yoo-lŏ-**jist**-ik) *adj.* eulogizing.

eulogize (yoo-lŏ-jyz) *v.* to write or utter a eulogy of.

eulogy (yoo-lŏ-ji) *n.* a speech or piece of writing in praise of a person or thing.

eunuch (yoo-nŭk) *n.* a castrated man.

euphemism (yoo-fim-izm) *n.* a mild or roundabout expression substituted for one considered improper or too harsh or blunt, *pass away' is a euphemism for die'.* **euphemistic** (yoo-fim-**ist**-ik) *adj.,* **euphemistically** *adv.*

euphonium (yoo-**foh**-niŭm) *n.* a large brass wind instrument, a tenor tuba.

euphony (yoo-fŏni) *n.* pleasantness of sounds, especially in words. **euphonious** (yoo-**foh**-niŭs) *adj.*

euphoria (yoo-**for**-iă) *n.* a feeling of general happiness. **euphoric** (yoo-fo-rik) *adj.*

Eurasian (yoor-ay-**zh**ăn) *adj.* **1.** of Europe and Asia. **2.** of mixed European and Asian parentage. —*n.* a Eurasian person.

eureka (yoor-**eek**-ă) *int.* I have found it, an exclamation of triumph at a discovery. ¶ Said to have been uttered by the Greek mathematician Archimedes (3rd century BC) on realizing that the volume of an object can be calculated by the amount of water it displaces.

Eurocommunism *n.* a form of Communism in European countries, seeking independence of the Soviet Communist Party. **Eurocommunist** *n.*

Europe (yoor-ŏp) a continent extending from Asia to the Atlantic Ocean. **European** *adj. & n.* □ **European Economic Community,** *see* Common Market.

euthanasia (yooth-ăn-**ay**-ziă) *n.* the bringing about of a gentle and easy death for a person suffering from a painful incurable disease.

evacuate *v.* **1.** to send (people) away from a place considered dangerous, to remove the occupants of (a place). **2.** to empty (a vessel) of air etc. **3.** to empty the contents of (the bowel or other organ). **evacuation** *n.*

evacuee *n.* an evacuated person.

evade (i-vayd) *v.* to avoid (a person or thing) by cleverness or trickery; *evade the* *question*, to avoid giving a direct answer.

evaluate *v.* to find out or state the value of, to assess. **evaluation** *n.*

evanescent (ev-ăn-**ess**-ĕnt) *adj.* (of an impression etc.) fading quickly.

evangelical (ee-van-**jel**-ikăl) *adj.* 1. according to the teaching of the gospel or the Christian religion. 2. of a Protestant group believing that salvation is achieved by faith in the Atonement through Christ. —*n.* a member of this group.

evangelism (i-**van**-jĕl-izm) *n.* preaching or spreading of the gospel.

evangelist (i-**van**-jĕl-ist) *n.* 1. any of the authors of the four Gospels (Matthew, Mark, Luke, John). 2. a person who preaches the gospel.

evangelize *v.* to preach or spread the gospel to, to win over to Christianity. **evangelization** *n.*

evaporate *v.* 1. to turn or be turned into vapour. 2. to lose or cause to lose moisture in this way. 3. to cease to exist, *their enthusiasm evaporated*. **evaporation** *n.* □ **evaporated milk**, unsweetened milk thickened by partial evaporation and tinned.

evasion (i-**vay**-zhon) *n.* 1. evading. 2. an evasive answer or excuse.

evasive (i-**vay**-siv) *adj.* evading, not frank or straightforward. **evasively** *adv.*, **evasiveness** *n.*

eve *n.* 1. the evening or day before a festival, *Christmas Eve*. 2. the time just before an event, *on the eve of an election*. 3. (*old use*) evening.

Eve (in Hebrew tradition) the first woman. **daughter of Eve**, a woman.

even¹ *adj.* 1. level, free from irregularities, smooth. 2. uniform in quality. 3. (of temper) calm, not easily upset. 4. equally balanced or matched, equal. 5. equal in number or amount. 6. (of a number) exactly divisible by two. 7. (of money or time or quantity) exact, not involving fractions, *an even dozen*. —*v.* to make or become even. — **evenly** *adv.*, **evenness** *n.* □ **be** *or* **get even with**, to have one's revenge on. **even chance**, when success is as likely as failure. **even-handed** *adj.* impartial. **even money** *or* **evens** *pl. n.* with equal stakes on both sides in a bet. **even up**, to make or become equal.

even² *adv.* 1. (used to emphasize a comparison) to a greater degree, *ran even faster*. 2. (used to suggest that something mentioned is unlikely or is an extreme case or should be compared with what might have happened etc.) *does he even suspect the danger?*; *even a child could understand that*; *didn't even try to avoid it* (let alone succeed). □ **even now**, in addition to previously; at this very moment. **even so**, although that is the case.

evening *n.* the part of the day between afternoon and bedtime. **evening dress**, the kind of clothing usually worn for formal occasions in the evening; a woman's long formal dress. **evening paper**, one published at about or later than midday. **evening primrose**, a plant with pale yellow flowers that open in the evening. **evening star**, a planet (especially Venus) when conspicuous in the west after sunset.

evensong *n.* the service of evening prayer in the Church of England.

event *n.* 1. something that happens, especially something important. 2. the fact of a thing happening; *in the event of his death*, if he dies. 3. an item in a sports programme. □ **at all events**, **in any event**, in any case. **in the event**, as things turned out.

eventful *adj.* full of incidents.

eventide *n.* (*old use*) evening.

eventual *adj.* coming at last, ultimate, *his eventual success*. **eventually** *adv.*

eventuality (i-ven-tew-**al**-iti) *n.* a possible event.

eventuate *v.* to result, to be the outcome.

ever *adv.* 1. at all times, always, *ever hopeful*. 2. at any time, *the best thing I ever did*. 3. (used for emphasis) in any possible way, *why ever didn't you say so?* □ **did you ever?**, (*informal*) an exclamation of surprise, = did you ever see or hear the like? **ever so**, (*informal*) very; very much, *it's ever so easy, thanks ever so*. **yours ever**, see yours.

evergreen *adj.* (of a tree or shrub) having green leaves throughout the year. —*n.* an evergreen tree or shrub.

everlasting *adj.* 1. lasting for ever. 2. lasting a very long time. 3. lasting too long, repeated too often, *his everlasting complaints*. 4. (of flowers) keeping shape and colour when dried. **everlastingly** *adv.*

evermore *adv.* for ever, always.

every *adj.* 1. each single one without exception, *enjoyed every minute*. 2. each in a series, *came every fourth day*. 3. all possible, *she shall be given every care*. □ **every one**, each one. (¶ This should be followed by a singular verb, *every one of them is* (not *are*) *guilty*.) **every other day** *or* **week** etc., with one between each two selected.

everybody *pronoun* every person.

everyday *adj.* 1. worn or used on ordinary days. 2. usual, commonplace.

Everyman *n.* the ordinary or typical person, the 'man in the street'.

everyone *pronoun* everybody. ¶ Do not confuse with *every one* = each one (*see* every).

everything *pronoun* 1. all things, all. 2. the most important thing, *speed is everything*. □ **have everything**, (*informal*) to possess every advantage or attraction.

everywhere *adv.* in every place.

evict (i-**vikt**) *v.* to expel (a tenant) by legal process. **eviction** *n.*

evidence *n.* 1. anything that establishes a fact or gives reason for believing something. 2. statements made or objects produced in a lawcourt as proof or to support a case. —*v.* to indicate, to be evidence of. □ **be in evidence**, to be conspicuous.

evident *adj.* obvious to the eye or mind. **evidently** *adv.*

evidential (ev-i-**den**-shăl) *adj.* of or based on or providing evidence.

evil *adj.* 1. morally bad, wicked. 2. harmful, intending to do harm. 3. very unpleasant or troublesome, *an evil temper*. —*n.* an evil thing, sin, harm. —**evilly** *adv.* □ **the evil eye**, a gaze or stare superstitiously believed to cause harm.

evince (i-**vins**) *v.* to indicate, to show that one has (a quality).

eviscerate (i-**vis**-er-ayt) *v.* 1. to take out the intestines of. 2. to empty (a thing) of its vital contents. **evisceration** *n.*

evocative (i-**vok**-ătiv) *adj.* tending to evoke.

evoke (i-**vohk**) *v.* to call up or produce or inspire (memories, feelings, a response, etc.). **evocation** (ev-ŏ-**kay**-shŏn) *n.*

evolution (ee-vŏ-**loo**-shŏn) *n.* 1. the process by which something develops gradually into a different form. 2. the origination of living things by development from earlier forms, not by special creation. **evolutionary** *adv.*

evolve (i-**volv**) *v.* 1. to develop or work out gradually, *evolve a plan*. 2. to develop or modify by evolution. **evolvement** *n.*

ewe *n.* a female sheep. **ewe lamb**, one's most cherished possession.

ewer (**yoo**-er) *n.* a wide-mouthed pitcher for holding water.

ex[1] *prep.* 1. (of goods) as sold from (a ship, factory, etc.); *ex-works price*, the amount payable for goods at a factory etc., excluding the cost of delivery to the buyer. 2. without, excluding. □ **ex dividend**, not including a dividend that is about to be paid.

ex[2] *n.* (*informal*) a former husband or wife.

ex- *prefix* former, *ex-convict*, *Ex-President*.

exacerbate (eks-**ass**-er-bayt) *v.* 1. to make (pain, disease, anger etc.) worse. 2. to irritate (a person). **exacerbation** *n.*

exact[1] *adj.* 1. correct in every detail, free from error. 2. giving all details, *gave me exact instructions*. 3. capable of being precise, *the exact sciences*. **exactness** *n.*

exact[2] *v.* to insist on and obtain, *exacted payment* or *obedience*. **exaction** *n.*

exacting *adj.* making great demands, requiring or insisting on great effort, *an exacting task* or *teacher*.

exactitude *n.* exactness.

exactly *adv.* 1. in an exact manner. 2. (said in agreement) quite so, as you say. □ **not exactly**, (*informal*) by no means, *didn't exactly enjoy it*.

exaggerate *v.* to make (a thing) seem larger or better or smaller or worse than it really is; *with exaggerated courtesy*, with excessive courtesy. **exaggeration** *n.*

exalt (ig-**zawlt**) *v.* 1. to raise (a person) in rank or power or dignity. 2. to praise highly.

exaltation *n.* 1. exalting, being exalted. 2. elation, spiritual delight.

exam *n.* (*informal*) an examination.

examination *n.* 1. examining, being examined or looked at. 2. the testing of knowledge or ability by oral or written questions or by exercises. 3. a formal questioning of a witness or an accused person in a lawcourt.

examine *v.* 1. to look at in order to learn about or from, to look at closely. 2. to put questions or exercises etc. in order to test knowledge or ability. 3. to question formally in order to get information. **examiner** *n.*

examinee *n.* a person being tested in an examination.

example *n.* 1. a fact that illustrates a general rule, a thing that shows the quality or characteristics of others in the same group or of the same kind. 2. something (especially conduct) that is worthy of imitation, *his courage is an example to us all*. □ **for example**, by way of illustrating a general rule. **make an example of**, to punish as a warning to others. **set an example**, to behave in a way that is worthy of imitation.

exasperate *v.* to annoy greatly. **exasperation** *n.*

ex cathedra (eks kăth-ee-dră) given by the pope as an infallible judgement.

excavate *v.* 1. to make (a hole or channel) by digging, to dig out (soil). 2. to reveal or extract by digging. **excavation** *n.*, **excavator** *n.*

exceed *v.* 1. to be greater or more numerous than. 2. to go beyond the limit of, to do more than is warranted by, *exceeded his authority*.

exceedingly *adv*. very, extremely.

excel *v*. (excelled, excelling) 1. to be better than. 2. to be very good at something. □ **excel oneself**, to do better than one has ever done before.

excellence *n*. very great merit or quality.

Excellency *n*. the title of high officials such as ambassadors and governors.

excellent *adj*. extremely good. **excellently** *adv*.

excelsior (ik-**sel**-si-or) *int*. (as a motto etc.) higher.

except *prep*. not including, *they all left except me*. —*v*. to exclude from a statement or calculation etc.

excepting *prep*. except.

exception *n*. 1. excepting, being excepted. 2. a thing that does not follow the general rule. □ **take exception to**, to object to. **the exception proves the rule**, the excepting of some cases proves that the rule exists, or that it applies to all other cases. **with the exception of**, except.

exceptionable *adj*. open to objection.

exceptional *adj*. 1. forming an exception, very unusual. 2. outstandingly good. **exceptionally** *adv*.

excerpt¹ (**ek**-serpt) *n*. an extract from a book or film or piece of music etc.

excerpt² (ek-**serpt**) *v*. to select excerpts from.

excess *n*. 1. the exceeding of due limits. 2. an amount by which one number or quantity etc. exceeds another. 3. an agreed amount subtracted by an insurer from the total payment to be made to an insured person who makes a claim. □ **excess baggage**, the amount that is over the weight for free carriage. **excesses** *pl. n*. immoderation in eating or drinking. **in excess of**, more than.

excessive *adj*. greater than what is normal or necessary, too much. **excessively** *adv*.

exchange *v*. 1. to give or receive (one thing) in place of another. 2. to give to and receive from another person; *they exchanged glances*, looked at each other. — **exchange** *n*. 1. exchanging (goods, prisoners, words, blows, etc.). 2. the exchanging of money for its equivalent in another currency, the relation in value between the money of two or more countries. 3. a place where merchants or stockbrokers etc. assemble to do business, *a stock exchange*. 4. the central telephone office of a district, where connections are made between lines concerned in calls.

exchangeable *adj*. able to be exchanged.

exchequer *n*. 1. the government department in charge of national revenue. 2. a national treasury. 3. a person's supply of money.

excise¹ (**ek**-syz) *n*. duty or tax levied on certain goods and licences etc.

excise² (ek-**syz**) *v*. to remove by cutting out or away, *excise tissue from the body*; *excise a passage from a book*. **excision** (ek-**si**-zhŏn) *n*.

excitable *adj*. (of a person) easily excited. **excitability** *n*.

excite *v*. 1. to rouse the feelings of, to cause (a person) to feel strongly, to make eager. 2. to cause (a feeling or reaction), *it excited curiosity*. 3. to produce activity in (a nerve or organ of the body etc.).

excited *adj*. feeling or showing excitement. **excitedly** *adv*.

excitement *n*. 1. a state of great emotion, especially that caused by something pleasant. 2. something causing this.

exciting *adj*. causing great interest or eagerness. **excitingly** *adv*.

exclaim *v*. to cry out or utter suddenly from pain, pleasure, surprise, etc.

exclamation *n*. 1. exclaiming. 2. a word or words etc. exclaimed. □ **exclamation mark**, the punctuation mark ! placed after an exclamation.

exclamatory (iks-**klam**-ă-ter-i) *adj*. of or containing or being an exclamation.

exclude *v*. 1. to keep out (a person or thing) from a place or group or privilege etc. 2. to omit, to ignore as irrelevant, *do not exclude this possibility*. 3. to make impossible, to prevent. **exclusion** *n*.

exclusive *adj*. 1. not admitting something else; *the schemes are mutually exclusive*, if you accept one you must reject the other. 2. (of groups or societies) admitting only certain carefully selected people to membership. 3. (of shops or their goods) high-class, catering only for the wealthy, expensive. 4. (of terms etc.) excluding all but what is specified. 5. (of an article in a newspaper or goods in a shop) not published or obtainable elsewhere. 6. done or held etc. so as to exclude everything else, *his exclusive occupation*; *we have the exclusive rights*, not shared with others. —*adv*. not counting, *20 men exclusive of our own*. — **exclusively** *adv.*, **exclusiveness** *n*.

excommunicate *v*. to cut off (a person) from participation in a Church, especially in its sacraments. **excommunication** *n*.

excoriate (eks-**kor**-i-ayt) *v*. 1. to remove some skin from (a person etc.), e.g. by grazing. 2. to criticize severely. **excoriation** *n*.

excrement (**eks**-kri-měnt) *n*. faeces.

excrescence (iks-**kress**-ĕns) *n.* **1.** an outgrowth, especially an abnormal one, on an animal body or a plant. **2.** an ugly or disfiguring addition, e.g. to a building.

excreta (iks-**kree**-tă) *pl. n.* waste matter expelled from the body, especially faeces.

excrete (iks-**kreet**) *v.* to separate and expel (waste matter) from the body or tissues. **excretion** *n.*

excretory (iks-**kree**-ter-i) *adj.* of or used in excretion.

excruciating (iks-**kroo**-shi-ayting) *adj.* intensely painful.

exculpate (eks-**kŭl**-payt) *v.* to free (a person) from blame, to clear of a charge of wrongdoing. **exculpation** *n.*

excursion *n.* **1.** a short journey or ramble (returning afterwards to the starting-point). **2.** a pleasure-trip made by a number of people.

excursus (iks-**ker**-sŭs) *n.* (*pl.* excursuses) a digression.

excusable *adj.* able to be excused. **excusably** *adv.*

excuse [1] (iks-**kewz**) *v.* **1.** to overlook or pardon (a slight offence or a person committing it) because of circumstances or some other reason. **2.** (of a thing or circumstance) to justify a fault or error, *nothing can excuse such rudeness.* **3.** to release from an obligation or duty, to grant exemption to. □ **excuse me,** a polite apology for interrupting or disagreeing etc. **excuse oneself,** to ask permission or apologize for leaving.

excuse [2] (iks-**kewss**) *n.* a reason put forward as a ground for excusing a fault etc.

ex-directory *adj.* (of a telephone number or subscriber) deliberately not listed in a telephone directory.

ex div. *abbrev.* ex dividend (*see* ex[1]).

execrable (eks-i-kră-bŭl) *adj.* abominable. **execrably** *adv.*

execrate (eks-i-krayt) *v.* to detest greatly, to utter curses upon. **execration** *n.*

execute *v.* **1.** to carry out (an order), to put (a plan etc.) into effect. **2.** to perform (an action or manœuvre). **3.** to produce (a work of art). **4.** to make legally valid e.g. by signing, *execute a will.* **5.** to inflict capital punishment on.

execution *n.* **1.** the carrying out or performance of something. **2.** skill in playing music. **3.** executing a condemned person.

executioner *n.* one who executes a condemned person.

executive (ig-**zek**-yoo-tiv) *n.* a person or group that has administrative or managerial powers in a business or commercial organization, or with authority to put the laws or agreements etc. of a government into effect. —*adj.* having the powers to execute plans or to put laws or agreements etc. into effect.

executor (ig-**zek**-yoo-ter) *n.* a person appointed by a testator to carry out the terms of his or her will. **executrix** *n.* a woman executor.

exemplary (ig-**zem**-pler-i) *adj.* serving as an example; *exemplary conduct,* very good, an example to others; *exemplary damages,* very high damages, serving as a warning.

exemplify (ig-**zem**-pli-fy) *v.* (exemplified, exemplifying) to serve as an example of. **exemplification** *n.*

exempt *adj.* not liable, free from an obligation or payment etc. that is required of others or in other cases. —*v.* to make exempt. —**exemption** *n.*

exercise *n.* **1.** the using or application of mental powers or of one's rights. **2.** activity requiring physical exertion, done for the sake of health. **3.** an activity or task designed for bodily or mental training; *military exercises,* a series of movements or operations designed for the training of troops. **4.** an act of worship, *religious exercises.* —**exercise** *v.* **1.** to use or employ (mental powers, rights, etc.). **2.** to take or cause to take exercise, to train by means of exercises. **3.** to perplex, to worry. □ **exercise book,** a book for writing in, with a limp cover and ruled pages.

exert *v.* to bring (a quality or influence etc.) into use, *exert all one's strength.* **exert oneself,** to make an effort.

exertion *n.* **1.** exerting, being exerted. **2.** a great effort.

exeunt (eks-i-ŭnt) *v.* (*stage direction*) they leave the stage.

ex gratia (eks **gray**-shă) done or given as a concession, without legal compulsion, *an ex gratia payment.* (¶ Latin, = from favour.)

exhale *v.* to breathe out. **exhalation** *n.*

exhaust *v.* **1.** to use up completely. **2.** to make empty, to draw out the contents of, *exhaust a well.* **3.** to tire out, *exhaust oneself.* **4.** to find out or say all there is to say about (a subject); *exhaust the possibilities,* to try them all in turn. —**exhaust** *n.* **1.** waste gases or steam expelled from an engine etc. **2.** the device through which they are sent out.

exhaustion (ig-**zaws**-chŏn) *n.* **1.** exhausting something, being exhausted. **2.** total loss of strength.

exhaustive *adj.* thorough, trying all possibilities, *we made an exhaustive search.* **exhaustively** *adv.*

exhibit (ig-**zib**-it) *v.* to display, to present for the public to see. —*n.* a thing or collection of things exhibited. —**exhibitor** *n.*

exhibition *n.* **1.** exhibiting, being exhibited. **2.** a display or show, *an exhibition of temper*. **3.** a public display of works of art or industrial products etc. or of a skilled performance. □ **make an exhibition of oneself**, to behave so that one appears ridiculous.

exhibitionist *n.* a person who behaves in a way designed to attract attention to himself. **exhibitionism** *n.* a tendency towards this kind of behaviour.

exhilarate (ig-**zil**-er-ayt) *v.* to make very happy or lively. **exhilaration** *n.*

exhort (ig-**zort**) *v.* to urge or advise earnestly. **exhortation** (eg-zor-**tay**-shŏn) *n.*

exhume (ig-**zewm**) *v.* to dig up (something buried), e.g. for examination. **exhumation** (eks-yoo-**may**-shŏn) *n.*

exigency (**eks**-i-jĕn-si) *n.* **1.** an urgent need, *the exigencies of the situation*. **2.** an emergency.

exigent (**eks**-i-jĕnt) *adj.* **1.** urgent. **2.** exacting, requiring much. **exigently** *adv.*

exiguous (eg-**zig**-yoo-ŭs) *adj.* very small, scanty.

exile *n.* **1.** being sent away from one's country as a punishment. **2.** long absence from one's country or home. **3.** an exiled person. —*v.* to send (a person) into exile.

exist *v.* **1.** to have place as part of what is real, *do fairies exist?* **2.** to have being under specified conditions, to occur or be found. **3.** to continue living, *we cannot exist without food.*

existence *n.* **1.** the state of existing, occurrence, presence. **2.** continuance in life or being, *the struggle for existence.*

existent *adj.* existing, actual, current.

existentialism (eg-zis-**ten**-shăl-izm) *n.* a philosophical theory emphasizing that man is responsible for his own actions and free to choose his development and destiny. **existentialist** *n.*

exit *v.* (*stage direction*) he or she leaves the stage. —*n.* **1.** an actor's or performer's departure from the stage. **2.** the act of going away or out, departure from a place or position etc. **3.** a passage or door to go out by. □ **exit permit**, permission to leave a country.

exodus *n.* **1.** a departure of many people. **2.** *Exodus*, the second book of the Old Testament, telling of the exodus of the Jews from Egypt.

ex officio (eks ŏ-**fish**-i-oh) because of his or her official position, *the director is a member of this committee ex officio.* — **ex-officio** *adj.* holding a position etc. ex officio, *an ex-officio member.*

exonerate (ig-**zon**-er-ayt) *v.* to free from

blame, to declare (a person) to be blameless. **exoneration** *n.*

exorbitant (ig-**zorb**-i-tănt) *adj.* (of a price or demand) much too great.

exorcize (**eks**-or-syz) *v.* **1.** to drive out (an evil spirit) by prayer. **2.** to free (a person or place) of evil spirits. **exorcism** *n.*, **exorcist** *n.*

exoskeleton *n.* an external bony or leathery covering on an animal, e.g. the shell of a lobster.

exotic (ig-**zot**-ik) *adj.* **1.** (of plants, words, or fashions) introduced from abroad, not native. **2.** striking and attractive through being colourful or unusual. **exotically** *adv.*

expand *v.* **1.** to make or become larger, to increase in bulk or importance. **2.** to unfold or spread out. **3.** to give a fuller account of, to write out in full (what is condensed or abbreviated). **4.** to become genial, to throw off one's reserve.

expandable *adj.* able to be expanded.

expanse *n.* a wide area or extent of open land or space, etc.

expansible *adj.* able to be expanded.

expansion *n.* expanding, increase, extension.

expansionist *n.* a person who wishes a country or business to expand.

expansive *adj.* **1.** able or tending to expand. **2.** (of a person or his manner) genial, communicating thoughts and feelings readily. **expansively** *adv.*, **expansiveness** *n.*

expatiate (iks-**pay**-shi-ayt) *v.* to speak or write about (a subject) at great length or in detail. **expatiation** *n.*

expatriate [1] (eks-**pat**-ri-ayt) *v.* to banish, to withdraw (oneself) from one's native country and live abroad.

expatriate [2] (eks-**pat**-ri-ăt) *adj.* expatriated, living abroad. —*n.* an expatriate person.

expect *v.* **1.** to think or believe that (a person or thing) will come or that (a thing) will happen. **2.** to wish for and be confident that one will receive, to consider necessary, *he expects obedience.* **3.** to think, to suppose. □ **be expecting**, (*informal*) to be pregnant. **expecting a baby**, pregnant.

expectant *adj.* filled with expectation. **expectantly** *adv.*, **expectancy** *n.* □ **expectant mother**, a woman who is pregnant.

expectation *n.* **1.** expecting, looking forward with hope or pleasure. **2.** a thing that is expected to happen. **3.** the probability that a thing will happen. □ **expectation of life**, the average period that persons of a certain age are expected to live.

expectations *pl. n.* prospects of inheritance.

expectorant *n.* a medicine that causes a person to expectorate.

expectorate *v.* to cough and spit out phlegm from the throat or lungs, to spit. **expectoration** *n.*

expedient (iks-**pee**-diĕnt) *adj.* 1. suitable for a particular purpose. 2. advantageous rather than right or just. —*n.* a means of achieving something. —**expediently** *adv.*, **expediency** *n.*

expedite (**eks**-pi-dyt) *v.* to help or hurry the progress of (business etc.), to perform (business) quickly.

expedition *n.* 1. a journey or voyage for a particular purpose. 2. the people or ships etc. making this. 3. promptness, speed, *solved it with expedition.*

expeditionary *adj.* of or used in an expedition, *an expeditionary force.*

expeditious (eks-pi-**dish**-ŭs) *adj.* acting or done speedily and efficiently. **expeditiously** *adv.*

expel *v.* (expelled, expelling) 1. to force or send or drive out. 2. to compel (a person) to leave a school or country etc.

expend *v.* to spend (money, time, care, etc.), to use up.

expendable *adj.* 1. able to be expended. 2. not worth preserving, suitable for sacrificing in order to gain an objective.

expenditure *n.* 1. spending of money etc. 2. the amount expended.

expense *n.* 1. the cost or price of an activity. 2. a cause of spending money, *the car was a great expense.* □ **at the expense of,** so as to cause loss or damage to, *succeeded but at the expense of his health*; *had a good laugh at my expense,* by making fun of me. **expense account,** a record of an employee's expenses to be paid by his employer. **expenses** *pl. n.* the amount spent in doing something, reimbursement for this.

expensive *adj.* involving great expenditure, costing or charging more than the average. **expensively** *adv.*, **expensiveness** *n.*

experience *n.* 1. actual observation of facts or events, activity or practice in doing something. 2. skill or knowledge gained in this way. 3. an event or activity that gives one experience. —*v.* to observe or share in (an event etc.) personally, to be affected by (a feeling). □ **experienced** *adj.* having knowledge or skill gained from much experience.

experiment *n.* a test or trial carried out to see how something works or to find out what happens or to demonstrate a known fact. —*v.* to conduct an experiment. — **experimentation** *n.*

experimental *adj.* 1. of or used in or based on experiments. 2. still being tested. **experimentally** *adv.*

expert *n.* a person with great knowledge or skill in a particular thing. —*adj.* having great knowledge or skill. —**expertly** *adv.*

expertise (eks-per-**teez**) *n.* expert knowledge or skill.

expiate (**eks**-pi-ayt) *v.* to make amends for (wrongdoing). **expiation** *n.*

expire *v.* 1. to breathe out (air). 2. to breathe one's last, to die. 3. to come to the end of its period of validity, *this licence has expired.* **expiration** (eks-per-**ay**-shŏn) *n.*

expiry *n.* the end of a period of validity, e.g. of a licence or contract.

explain *v.* 1. to make plain or clear, to show the meaning of. 2. to account for, *that explains his absence.* □ **explain away,** to show why a fault etc. should not be blamed. **explain oneself,** to make one's meaning clear; to give an account of one's motives or conduct.

explanation *n.* 1. explaining. 2. a statement or fact that explains something.

explanatory (iks-**plan**-ă-ter-i) *adj.* serving or intended to explain something.

expletive (iks-**plee**-tiv) *n.* a violent or meaningless exclamation, an oath.

explicable (**eks**-plik-ăbŭl) *adj.* able to be explained.

explicate (**eks**-plik-ayt) *v.* to bring out the implicit meaning of (an idea or statement) more fully or clearly.

explicit (iks-**pliss**-it) *adj.* stating something in exact terms, not merely implying things. **explicitly** *adv.*, **explicitness** *n.*

explode *v.* 1. to expand suddenly with a loud noise because of the release of internal energy, to cause (a bomb etc.) to do this. 2. (of feelings) to burst out, (of a person) to show sudden violent emotion, *exploded with laughter.* 3. (of a population or a supply of goods etc.) to increase suddenly or rapidly. 4. to destroy (a theory) by showing it to be false. □ **exploded diagram,** one showing the parts of a structure in their relative positions but slightly separated from each other.

exploit[1] (**eks**-ploit) *n.* a bold or notable deed.

exploit[2] (iks-**ploit**) *v.* 1. to work or develop (mines and other natural resources). 2. to take full advantage of, to use (workers, colonial possessions, etc.) for one's own advantage and their disadvantage. **exploitation** *n.*

exploratory (iks-**plo**-ră-ter-i) *adj.* for the purpose of exploring.

explore *v.* 1. to travel into or through (a

223

country etc.) in order to learn about it. **2.** to examine by touch. **3.** to examine or investigate (a problem, possibilities, etc.). **exploration** *n.*

explorer *n.* a person who explores unknown regions.

explosion *n.* **1.** exploding, being exploded, a loud noise caused by this. **2.** a sudden outburst of anger, laughter, etc. **3.** a sudden great increase, *the population explosion.*

explosive *adj.* **1.** able to explode, tending to explode. **2.** likely to cause violent and dangerous reactions, dangerously tense, *an explosive situation.* —*n.* an explosive substance.

exponent (iks-**poh**-něnt) *n.* **1.** a person who sets out the facts or interprets something. **2.** one who favours a particular theory or policy.

export[1] (eks-**port** *or* eks-port) *v.* to send (goods etc.) to another country for sale. **exportation** *n.*, **exporter** *n.*

export[2] (eks-port) *n.* **1.** exporting. **2.** a thing exported.

exportable *adj.* able to be exported.

expose *v.* **1.** to leave (a person or thing) uncovered or unprotected, especially from the weather. **2.** to subject to a risk etc. **3.** to allow light to reach (photographic film or plate). **4.** to make visible, to reveal. **5.** to make known or reveal (a crime, fraud, impostor, etc.), to reveal the wrongdoings of (a person). □ **exposed** *adj.* (of a place) not sheltered. **expose oneself**, to expose one's body indecently.

exposition *n.* **1.** expounding, an explanatory account of a plan or theory etc. **2.** a large public exhibition.

expostulate (iks-**poss**-tew-layt) *v.* to make a friendly protest, to reason or argue with a person. **expostulation** *n.*

exposure *n.* **1.** exposing or being exposed to air or cold or danger etc.; *died of exposure,* from the effects of being exposed to cold. **2.** the exposing of photographic film or plate to the light, the length of time for which this is done. **3.** a section of film exposed as a unit. **4.** publicity. □ **exposure meter**, a device measuring light and indicating the length of time needed for a photographic exposure.

expound *v.* to set forth or explain in detail.

express[1] *adj.* **1.** definitely stated, not merely implied. **2.** going or sent quickly, designed for high speed, (of a train or lift etc.) travelling rapidly to its destination with few or no intermediate stops. **3.** (of a letter or parcel) delivered quickly by a special messenger or service. —*adv.* at high speed, by express service. —*n.* an

express train. —*v.* to send by express service.

express[2] *v.* **1.** to make known (feelings or qualities). **2.** to put (thought etc.) into words. **3.** to represent by means of symbols, e.g. in mathematics. **4.** to press or squeeze out. □ **express oneself**, to communicate one's thoughts or feelings.

expressible *adj.* able to be expressed.

expression *n.* **1.** expressing, being expressed. **2.** a word or phrase. **3.** a look that expresses one's feelings. **4.** a manner of speaking or playing music in a way that shows feeling for the meaning. **5.** a collection of mathematical symbols expressing a quantity.

expressionism *n.* a style of painting, drama, or music seeking to express the artist's or writer's emotional experience rather than to represent the physical world realistically. **expressionist** *n.*

expressionless *adj.* without positive expression, not revealing one's thoughts or feelings, *an expressionless face.*

expressive *adj.* **1.** serving to express, *a tone expressive of contempt.* **2.** full of expression, *an expressive voice.* **expressively** *adv.*, **expressiveness** *n.*

expressly *adv.* **1.** explicitly. **2.** for a particular purpose.

expressway *n.* (*Amer.*) an urban motorway.

expulsion *n.* expelling, being expelled.

expulsive *adj.* expelling.

expunge (iks-**punj**) *v.* to wipe or rub out, to delete.

expurgate (eks-per-gayt) *v.* to remove objectionable matter from (a book etc.), to remove (such matter). **expurgation** *n.*, **expurgator** *n.*

exquisite (eks-kwiz-it) *adj.* **1.** having special beauty. **2.** having excellent discrimination, *exquisite taste in dress.* **3.** acute, keenly felt, *exquisite pain.* **exquisitely** *adv.*

ex-service *adj.* formerly belonging to the armed services.

ex-serviceman *n.* (*pl.* ex-servicemen) a former member of the armed services.

extant (eks-**tant**) *adj.* still existing.

extempore (eks-**tem**-per-i) *adv. & adj.* spoken or done without preparation, impromptu.

extemporize (eks-**tem**-peryz) *v.* to speak or produce extempore. **extemporization** *n.*

extend *v.* **1.** to make longer in space or time. **2.** to stretch out (a hand or foot or limb etc.). **3.** to reach, to be continuous over an area or from one point to another, *our land extends to the river.* **4.** to enlarge, to increase the scope of. **5.** to offer or grant, *extend a welcome.* **6.** (of a task) to stretch the ability of (a person) fully.

extender n. □ **extended family,** a family including all relatives living near.

extendible, extensible adjs. able to be extended.

extension n. **1.** extending, being extended. **2.** extent, range. **3.** an addition or continuance, a section extended from the main part. **4.** an additional period. **5.** a subsidiary telephone distant from the main one, its number. **6.** extramural instruction by a university or college, *extension lectures.*

extensive adj. **1.** large in area, *extensive gardens.* **2.** wide-ranging, large in scope, *extensive knowledge.* **extensively** adv., **extensiveness** n.

extent n. **1.** the space over which a thing extends. **2.** the range or scope of something, *the full extent of his power.* **3.** a large area, *an extent of marsh.*

extenuate (eks-**ten**-yoo-ayt) v. to make (a person's guilt or offence) seem less great by providing a partial excuse, *there were extenuating circumstances.* **extenuation** n.

exterior adj. on or coming from the outside. —n. an exterior surface or part or appearance.

exterminate v. to get rid of by destroying all members or examples of (a race, disease, etc.). **extermination** n., **exterminator** n.

external adj. **1.** of or on the outside or visible part of something. **2.** of or on the outside of the body, *for external use only.* **3.** coming or obtained from an independent source, *external influences.* **4.** belonging to the world outside a person or people, not in the mind. **externally** adv. □ **externals** pl. n. outward appearances.

extinct adj. **1.** no longer burning, (of a volcano) no longer active. **2.** no longer existing in living form, *extinct animals.*

extinction n. **1.** extinguishing, being extinguished. **2.** making or becoming extinct.

extinguish v. **1.** to put out (a light or fire or flame). **2.** to end the existence of (hope, passion, etc.).

extinguisher n. a device for discharging liquid chemicals or foam to extinguish a fire.

extirpate (**eks**-ter-payt) v. to root out and destroy completely. **extirpation** n.

extol (eks-**tohl**) v. (extolled, extolling) to praise enthusiastically.

extort v. to obtain by force or threats or intimidation etc. **extortion** n. extorting (especially money). —**extortioner** n.

extortionate (iks-**tor**-shŏn-ăt) adj. excessively high in price, (of demands) excessive. **extortionately** adv.

extra adj. additional, more than is usual or expected. —adv. **1.** more than usually, *extra strong.* **2.** in addition, *postage extra.* — **extra** n. **1.** an extra thing, something additional. **2.** a thing for which an additional charge is made. **3.** a run in cricket scored otherwise than from a hit by the bat. **4.** a special issue of a newspaper etc. **5.** a person engaged temporarily for a minor part or to form one of a crowd in a cinema film.

extra- prefix outside or beyond (a boundary), not coming within the scope of.

extract[1] (iks-**trakt**) v. **1.** to take out by force or effort (something firmly fixed). **2.** to obtain (money, information etc.) from someone unwilling to give it. **3.** to obtain (juice) by suction or pressure, to obtain (a substance) as an extract. **4.** to obtain (information from a book etc., to take or copy passages from (a book). **5.** to derive (pleasure etc.) from. **extractor** n.

extract[2] (**eks**-trakt) n. **1.** a substance separated from another by dissolving it or by other treatment. **2.** a concentrated substance prepared from another. **3.** a passage from a book, play, film, or music.

extraction n. **1.** extracting. **2.** descent, lineage, *he is of Indian extraction.*

extraditable (eks-trǎ-**dy**-tǎbŭl) adj. liable to extradition, (of a crime) warranting extradition.

extradite (**eks**-trǎ-dyt) v. **1.** to hand over (a person accused or convicted of a crime) to the country where the crime was committed. **2.** to obtain (such a person) for trial or punishment. **extradition** (eks-trǎ-**dish**-ŏn) n.

extramarital (eks-trǎ-**ma**-ri-t'l) adj. of sexual relationships outside marriage.

extramural (eks-trǎ-**mewr**-ǎl) adj. (of university teaching or studies) for students who are non-resident or who are not members of the university.

extraneous (iks-**tray**-niŭs) adj. **1.** of external origin. **2.** not belonging to the matter or subject in hand.

extraordinary adj. **1.** very unusual or remarkable. **2.** beyond what is usual or ordinary, *an extraordinary general meeting.* **extraordinarily** adv.

extrapolate (iks-**trap**-ŏ-layt) v. to make an estimate of (something unknown and outside the range of one's data) on the basis of available data. **extrapolation** n.

extra-sensory adj. (of perception) achieved by some means other than the known senses.

extraterrestrial adj. of or from outside the earth or its atmosphere.

extravagant adj. **1.** spending much more

than is necessary. **2.** (of prices) excessively high. **3.** (of ideas or praise or behaviour etc.) going beyond what is reasonable, not properly controlled. **extravagantly** *adv.*, **extravagance** *n.*

extravaganza (iks-trav-ă-**gan**-ză) *n.* **1.** a fanciful composition in music. **2.** a lavish spectacular film or theatrical production.

extreme *adj.* **1.** very great or intense, *extreme cold.* **2.** at the end(s), furthest, outermost, *the extreme edge.* **3.** going to great lengths in actions or views, not moderate. —**extreme** *n.* **1.** either end of anything. **2.** an extreme degree or act or condition. —**extremely** *adv.* □ **go to extremes,** to take an extreme course of action. **in the extreme,** to an extreme degree.

extremist *n.* a person who holds extreme views, especially in politics.

extremity (iks-**trem**-iti) *n.* **1.** an extreme point, the end of something. **2.** an extreme degree of feeling or need or danger etc. □ **extremities** *pl. n.* the hands and feet.

extricable (**eks**-trik-ăbŭl) *adj.* able to be extricated.

extricate (**eks**-trik-ayt) *v.* to disentangle or release from an entanglement or difficulty etc. **extrication** *n.*

extrovert (**eks**-trŏ-vert) *n.* a person more interested in the people and things around him than in his own thoughts and feelings, a lively sociable person. **extroverted** *adj.* having these characteristics.

extrude *v.* **1.** to thrust or squeeze out. **2.** to shape (metal or plastic etc.) by forcing through a die. **extrusion** *n.*

exuberant (ig-**zew**-ber-ănt) *adj.* **1.** full of high spirits, very lively. **2.** growing profusely, *plants with exuberant foliage.* **exuberantly** *adv.*, **exuberance** *n.*

exude (ig-**zewd**) *v.* **1.** to give off like sweat or a smell, (of liquid etc.) to ooze out in this way. **2.** to show pleasure, confidence etc.) freely. **exudation** (eks-yoo-**day**-shŏn) *n.*

exult (ig-**zult**) *v.* to rejoice greatly. **exultation** *n.* □ **exultant** *adj.* exulting.

eye *n.* **1.** the organ of sight in man and animals. **2.** the iris of this, *blue eyes.* **3.** the region round it, *gave him a black eye.* **4.** the power of seeing, observation, *sharp eyes.* **5.** a thing like an eye, the spot on a peacock's tail, the leaf-bud of a potato. **6.** the hole in a needle, through which thread is passed. —**eye** *v.* (eyed, eyeing) to look at, to watch. □ **all my eye,** (*slang*) nonsense. **an eye for an eye,** retaliation in the same form as the injury done. **cast** *or* **run an eye over,** to examine quickly. **do a**

person in the eye, (*slang*) to cheat or thwart him. **eye of a storm,** a relatively calm spot at the centre of a storm. **eye of the wind,** the point from which the wind is blowing. **eyes down,** the start of a bingo game. **get one's eye in,** to become accustomed to the conditions in batting or playing tennis etc. so as to be able to judge speed and distance accurately. **in the eyes of,** in the opinion or judgement of. **keep an eye on,** to watch carefully, to take care of. **keep one's eyes open** *or* **skinned,** to watch carefully, to be observant. **make eyes at,** to gaze at flirtatiously. **see eye to eye,** to be in full agreement with a person. **up to the eyes,** deeply involved or occupied in something. **wind's eye,** = eye of the wind (see above); *in the wind's eye,* directly against the wind. **with an eye to,** with the aim or intention of; with prudent attention to benefiting. **with one's eyes open,** with full awareness.

eyeball *n.* the ball of the eye, within the lids. **eyeball to eyeball,** (*informal*) confronting a person closely.

eyebath *n.* a small cup shaped to fit round the eye, used for applying liquid to the eyeball.

eyebrow *n.* the fringe of hair growing on the ridge above the eye-socket.

eyeful *n.* (*pl.* eyefuls) **1.** something thrown or blown into one's eye, *got an eyeful of sand.* **2.** (*informal*) a thorough look, *having an eyeful.* **3.** (*informal*) a remarkable or attractive sight.

eyelash *n.* one of the fringe of hairs on the edge of each eyelid.

eyeless *adj.* having no eyes.

eyelet *n.* **1.** a small hole through which a rope or cord etc. is passed. **2.** a metal ring strengthening this.

eyelid *n.* either of the two folds of skin that can be moved together to cover the eyeball.

eye-liner *n.* a cosmetic applied as a line round the eye.

eye-opener *n.* a fact or circumstance that brings enlightenment or great surprise.

eyepiece *n.* the lens or lenses to which the eye is applied at the end of a telescope or microscope etc.

eye-shade *n.* a device to protect eyes from strong light.

eye-shadow *n.* a cosmetic applied to the skin round the eyes.

eyesight *n.* **1.** the ability to see. **2.** range of vision, *within eyesight.*

eyesore *n.* a thing that is ugly to look at.

eye-tooth *n.* (*pl.* eye-teeth) a canine tooth in the upper jaw, under the eye.

eyewash *n.* **1.** a lotion for the eye. **2.**

(*slang*) talk or behaviour intended to create a misleadingly good impression.

eyewitness *n.* a person who actually saw an accident or crime etc. take place.

eyrie (I-ri) *n.* **1.** the nest of an eagle or other bird of prey. **2.** a house etc. perched high up.

Ff

F *abbrev.* Fahrenheit.

fable *n.* **1.** a short (usually supernatural) story not based on fact, often with animals as characters and conveying a moral. **2.** these stories or legends collectively. **3.** untrue statements, *sort out fact from fable.*

fabled *adj.* told of in fables, legendary.

fabric *n.* **1.** cloth, woven or knitted or felted material. **2.** a plastic resembling this. **3.** the frame or structure of something, the walls and floors and roof of a building.

fabricate *v.* **1.** to construct, to manufacture. **2.** to invent (a story), to forge (a document). **fabrication** *n.*, **fabricator** *n.*

fabulous *adj.* **1.** told of in fables. **2.** incredibly great, *fabulous wealth.* **3.** (*informal*) wonderful, marvellous. **fabulously** *adv.*

façade (fă-sahd) *n.* **1.** the principal face or the front of a building. **2.** an outward appearance, especially a deceptive one.

face *n.* **1.** the front part of the head from forehead to chin. **2.** the expression shown by its features, *a cheerful face; make* or *pull a face,* make a grimace. **3.** the outward show or aspect of something. **4.** the front or façade or right side of something, the dial-plate of a clock, the distinctive side of a playing-card. **5.** the coal-face. **6.** the striking-surface of a bat etc., the working-surface of a tool. —**face** *v.* **1.** to have or turn the face towards (a certain direction). **2.** to be opposite to. **3.** to meet confidently or defiantly, to accept and be prepared to deal with (unpleasant facts or problems). **4.** to meet (an opponent) in a contest. **5.** to present itself to, *the problem that faces us.* **6.** to turn (a card) face upwards. **7.** to cover (a surface) with a layer of different material, to put a facing on (a garment etc.). □ **face the music,** to face unpleasant consequences bravely. **face to face,** facing; confronting a person or danger etc. **face up to,** to face (a difficulty etc.) resolutely. **face value,** the value printed or stamped on money; *take a thing at its face value,* assume that it is genuinely what it seems to be. **have the face,** to be impudent enough. **in the face of,** despite. **lose face,**

to suffer loss of prestige through a humiliation. **on the face of it,** judging by appearances. **put a good face on it,** to make an outward show of cheerful acceptance of something. **save a person's face,** to prevent him from losing prestige. **to a person's face,** openly in his presence.

face-cloth *n.* **1.** a face-flannel. **2.** a smooth-surfaced woollen cloth.

face-flannel *n.* a cloth for washing one's face.

faceless *adj.* **1.** without a face. **2.** without identity. **3.** purposely not identifiable.

face-lift *n.* **1.** the operation of having one's face lifted (*see* lift). **2.** an alteration etc. that improves the appearance e.g. of a building. **face-lifting** *n.*

facer *n.* a sudden great difficulty.

facet (fas-it) *n.* **1.** one of the many sides of a cut stone or jewel. **2.** one aspect of a situation or problem.

facetious (fă-see-shŭs) *adj.* intended or intending to be amusing. **facetiously** *adv.*, **facetiousness** *n.*

facia (fay-shă) *n.* **1.** the instrument panel of a motor vehicle, the dashboard. **2.** the plate over a shop-front with the occupier's name etc.

facial (fay-shăl) *adj.* of the face. —*n.* a beauty treatment for the face.

facile (fa-syl) *adj.* **1.** easily done. **2.** (of a person) able to do something easily, *a facile speaker.* **3.** achieved easily but without attention to quality, superficial, *a facile solution.*

facilitate (fă-sil-i-tayt) *v.* to make easy, to lessen the difficulty of. **facilitation** *n.*

facility (fă-sil-iti) *n.* **1.** the quality of being easy, absence of difficulty. **2.** ease in doing something, *reads music with great facility.* **3.** an aid or equipment etc. that makes it easy to do something, *you shall have every facility*; *sports facilities.*

facing *n.* **1.** an outer layer covering a surface. **2.** a layer of material covering part of a garment etc. for contrast or to strengthen it.

facsimile (fak-sim-ili) *n.* a reproduction of a document or book or painting etc.

fact *n.* **1.** something known to have happened or to be true or to exist. **2.** a thing asserted to be true as a basis for reasoning, *his facts are disputed.* □ **facts of life,** (*informal*) knowledge of human sexual functions. **in fact,** in reality; (in summarizing) in short.

faction (fak-shŏn) *n.* a small united group within a larger one, especially in politics.

factor *n.* **1.** a circumstance or influence that contributes towards a result; *safety factor,* the margin of security against risks.

2. one of the numbers or mathematical expressions by which a larger number etc. can be divided exactly, *2, 3, 4, and 6 are factors of 12*. **3.** (in Scotland) a land-agent, a steward.

factory *n.* a building or buildings in which goods are manufactured. **factory farm,** one organized on industrial lines. **factory ship,** one that quick-freezes its catch while still at sea.

factotum (fak-**toh**-tŭm) *n.* a servant or assistant doing all kinds of work.

factual *adj.* based on or containing facts. **factually** *adv.*

faculty (**fak**-ŭl-ti) *n.* **1.** any of the powers of the body or mind, *the faculty of sight*. **2.** a particular kind of ability, *a faculty for learning languages*. **3.** a department teaching a particular subject in a university or college, *the faculty of Law*. **4.** authorization given by Church authorities, e.g. to move the gravestones in a churchyard.

fad *n.* a person's particular like or dislike, a craze.

faddy *adj.* having petty likes and dislikes, e.g. about food. **faddiness** *n.*

fade *v.* **1.** to lose or cause to lose colour, freshness, or vigour. **2.** to disappear gradually, to become indistinct. **3.** to cause (the sound or picture in broadcasting or cinema) to decrease or increase gradually. □ **fade-out** *n.* the fading out of something, especially a broadcast or cinema sound or picture.

faeces (**fee**-seez) *pl. n.* waste matter discharged from the bowels. **faecal** (**fee**-kăl) *adj.* of faeces.

fag *v.* (fagged, fagging) **1.** to toil. **2.** (of work) to make tired. **3.** (at schools) to perform services for a senior pupil. —**fag** *n.* **1.** tiring work, drudgery, *what a fag!* **2.** exhaustion, *brain-fag*. **3.** (at schools) a pupil who has to fag for a senior. **4.** (*slang*) a cigarette. □ **fag-end** *n.* an inferior or worthless remnant; (*slang*) a cigarette-end. **fagged** *or* **fagged out,** tired out.

faggot *n.* **1.** a bundle of sticks or twigs bound together. **2.** a ball of chopped seasoned liver, served baked. **3.** (*slang*) an unpleasant woman. **4.** (*slang*) a male homosexual.

faggoting *n.* embroidery in which threads are fastened together like faggots.

Fahrenheit (**fa**-rĕn-hyt) *adj.* of or using a temperature scale with the freezing-point of water at 32° and the boiling-point at 212°.

faience (fy-ahns) *n.* pottery decorated with an opaque glaze.

fail *v.* **1.** to be unsuccessful in what is attempted. **2.** to be or become insufficient, (of crops) to produce a very poor harvest. **3.** to become weak or ineffective, to cease functioning, *the engine failed*. **4.** to neglect or forget or be unable to do something, *he failed to appear*. **5.** to disappoint the hopes of. **6.** to become bankrupt. **7.** to grade (a candidate) as not having passed an examination. —*n.* failure in an examination. □ **failed** *adj.* unsuccessful, *a failed author*. **fail safe,** (of equipment) to revert to a danger-free condition in the event of a breakdown or other failure. **without fail,** for certain, whatever happens.

failing *n.* a weakness or fault. —*prep.* if (a thing) does not happen, if (a person) is not available.

failure *n.* **1.** failing, non-performance of something, lack of success. **2.** the ceasing of mechanism or power or a part of the body etc. to function, *heart failure*. **3.** becoming bankrupt. **4.** an unsuccessful person or thing or attempt.

fain *adj. & adv.* (*old use*) willing or willingly under the circumstances.

faint *adj.* **1.** not clearly perceived by the senses, indistinct, not intense in colour or sound or smell. **2.** weak, vague, *a faint hope*. **3.** timid, feeble. **4.** about to lose consciousness. —*v.* to lose consciousness temporarily through failure in the supply of blood to the brain. —*n.* an act or state of fainting. —**faintly** *adv.*, **faintness** *n.* □ **faint-hearted** *adj.* timid.

fair [1] *n.* **1.** a periodical gathering for the sale of goods, often with shows and entertainments. **2.** an exhibition of commercial or industrial goods. **3.** a fun-fair. □ **fair-ground** *n.* an open space where a fair is held.

fair [2] *adj.* **1.** (of the hair or skin) light in colour, (of a person) having fair hair. **2.** (*old use*) beautiful. **3.** (of weather) fine, (of winds) favourable. **4.** just, unbiased, in accordance with the rules. **5.** of moderate quality or amount. —*adv.* in a fair manner. □ **fair and square,** straightforwardly, above-board; exactly. **fair copy,** a neat copy of a corrected document. **a fair crack of the whip,** (*informal*) a fair chance to share in something. **fair enough!,** (*informal*) that is a reasonable or satisfactory proposition. **fair play,** equal opportunities and treatment for all. **the fair sex,** women. **in a fair way to,** at the stage where something is likely, *he's in a fair way to succeed*.

fairing *n.* a structure added to the exterior of a ship or aircraft etc. to streamline it.

Fair Isle one of the Shetland Islands, noted for its knitting designs in coloured wools.

fairlead *n.* (on a ship) a device through which a rope is passed to lead it in the right direction or to prevent chafing.

fairly *adv.* 1. in a fair manner. 2. moderately, *fairly difficult.* 3. actually, *fairly jumped for joy.* **fairly and squarely,** = fair and square.

fairway *n.* 1. a navigable channel. 2. part of a golf-course between tee and green, kept free from rough grass.

fairy *n* 1. an imaginary small being supposed to have magical powers. 2. (*slang*) a male homosexual. □ **fairy godmother,** a benefactress who provides a sudden unexpected gift. **fairy lights,** strings of small coloured lights used for decoration. **fairy ring,** a ring of darker grass caused by fungi, but superstitiously said to be caused by fairies dancing. **fairy story, fairy-tale** *n.* a tale about fairies or magic; an incredible story; a falsehood.

fairyland *n.* 1. the world of fairies. 2. a very beautiful place.

fait accompli (fayt ah-**kom**-pli) a thing that is already done and not reversible.

faith *n.* 1. reliance or trust in a person or thing. 2. belief in religious doctrine. 3. a system of religious belief, *the Christian faith.* 4. a promise, loyalty, sincerity. □ **break faith,** to break one's promise or loyalty. **faith-cure** *n.* something that heals a person because he believes that it will do so. **faith-healer** *n.* a person who practises **faith-healing,** healing by prayer and religious faith, not by medical skill. **in good faith,** with honest intention.

faithful *adj.* 1. loyal, trustworthy, conscientious. 2. true to the facts, accurate. 3. *the faithful,* true believers (especially Muslims), loyal supporters. **faithfully** *adv.,* **faithfulness** *n.* □ **Yours faithfully,** *see* yours.

faithless *adj.* 1. lacking religious faith. 2. false to promises, disloyal.

fake *n.* 1. something that looks genuine but is not, a forgery. 2. a person who tries to deceive others by pretending falsely to be something that he is not. —*adj.* faked, not genuine. —**fake** *v.* 1. to make (a thing) that looks genuine, in order to deceive people. 2. to pretend, *he faked illness.* —**faker** *n.*

fakir (**fay**-keer) *n.* a Muslim or Hindu religious beggar regarded as a holy man.

falcon (**fawl**-kŏn) *n.* a small long-winged hawk. **falconry** *n.* the breeding and training of hawks.

fall *v.* (fell, fallen, falling) 1. to come or go down freely, e.g. by force of weight or loss of balance or becoming detached. 2. to come as if by falling, *silence fell.* 3. to lose one's position or office, *fell from power.* 4. to hang down. 5. to decrease in amount or number or intensity, *prices fell; her spirits fell,* she became depressed; *the barometer is falling,* is showing that atmospheric pressure is becoming lower. 6. to slope downwards. 7. (of the face) to show dismay. 8. to cease to stand; *six wickets fell,* six batsmen were out. 9. to die in battle. 10. (of a fortress or city) to be captured. 11. (of a woman) to become pregnant. 12. to take a specified direction or place, *his glance fell on me.* 13. to come by chance or be assigned as what one must have or do, *the honour falls to you.* 14. to happen to come, *fell into bad company.* 15. to pass into a specified state, to become, *fall in love; fell asleep.* 16. to occur, to have as a date, *Easter fell early.* —**fall** *n.* 1. the act of falling. 2. giving way to temptation; *the Fall (of man),* Adam's sin and its results. 3. the amount by which something falls. 4. (*Amer.*) autumn. 5. a wrestling-bout, a throw that causes the opponent to remain on the ground for a specified time. □ **fall back on,** to retreat to; to turn to for help when something else has failed. **fall down on,** to fail in. **fall flat,** to fail to produce a result. **fall for,** (*informal*) to fall in love with; to be taken in by (a deception). **fall foul of,** to collide with; to get into trouble with. **fall guy,** (*Amer. slang*) an easy victim; a scapegoat. **fall in,** to take one's place in a military formation, to cause (troops) to do this; (of a building) to collapse inwards; (of a lease) to run out. **falling star,** a meteor. **fall in with,** to meet by chance; to agree to. **fall off,** to decrease in size or number or quality. **fall on one's feet,** to get out of a difficulty successfully. **fall out,** to quarrel; to happen; to leave one's place in a military formation, to cause (troops) to do this. **fall-out** *n.* airborne radioactive debris from a nuclear explosion. **fall over oneself,** to be very awkward; to be very hasty or eager. **fall pipe** *n.* a vertical drainage-pipe. **fall short,** to be insufficient or inadequate. **fall short of,** to fail to obtain or reach. **fall through,** (of a plan) to fail, to come to nothing. **fall to,** to begin working or fighting or eating.

fallacious (fă-**lay**-shŭs) *adj.* containing a fallacy.

fallacy (**fal**-ăsi) *n.* 1. a false or mistaken belief. 2. false reasoning.

fallible (**fal**-ibŭl) *adj.* liable to make mistakes. **fallibility** (fal-i-**bil**-iti) *n.*

Fallopian tubes (fă-**loh**-piăn) the two tubes carrying egg-cells from the ovaries to the womb.

fallow (**fal**-oh) *adj.* (of land) ploughed but left unplanted in order to restore its fertility.
fallow deer a kind of small deer, white-spotted in summer.
falls *pl. n.* a waterfall.
false *adj.* **1.** wrong, incorrect. **2.** deceitful, lying, unfaithful. **3.** not genuine, sham, artificial, *false teeth*; *false economy*, one that does not result in a genuine saving. **4.** improperly so called; *the false acacia*, not really an acacia tree. **falsely** *adv.*, **falseness** *n.* □ **false alarm**, an alarm raised without genuine cause. **false pretences**, acts intended to deceive.
falsehood *n.* **1.** an untrue statement, a lie. **2.** telling lies.
falsetto (fol-**set**-oh) *n.* (*pl.* falsettos) a high-pitched voice above one's natural range, especially when used by male singers. —*adv.* in a falsetto voice.
falsify *v.* (falsified, falsifying) **1.** to alter (a document) fraudulently. **2.** to misrepresent (facts). **falsification** *n.*
falsity *n.* **1.** falseness. **2.** a falsehood, an error.
falter *v.* **1.** to go or function unsteadily. **2.** to become weaker, to begin to give way, *his courage faltered*. **3.** to speak or utter hesitatingly, to stammer.
fame *n.* **1.** the condition of being known to many people. **2.** a good reputation.
famed *adj.* famous.
familiar *adj.* **1.** well known, often seen or experienced, *a familiar sight*. **2.** lacking formality, friendly and informal, *addressed him in familiar terms*. **3.** too informal, assuming a greater degree of informality or friendship than is proper. **familiarly** *adv.*, **familiarity** *n.* □ **familiar with**, having a good knowledge of (a thing); well acquainted with (a person).
familiarize *v.* **1.** to make well acquainted (with a person or thing). **2.** to make well known. **familiarization** *n.*
family *n.* **1.** parents and their children. **2.** a person's children, *they have a large family*. **3.** a set of relatives. **4.** all the descendants of a common ancestor, their line of descent. **5.** a group of things that are alike in some way. **6.** a group of related plants or animals, *lions belong to the cat family*. □ **family circle**, a group of close relatives. **family man**, one who is fond of home life with his family. **family planning**, birth-control. **family tree**, a diagram showing how people in a family are related. **in the family way**, (*informal*) pregnant.
famine *n.* extreme scarcity (especially of food) in a region.
famished, famishing *adjs.* suffering from extreme hunger.

famous *adj.* known to very many people.
famously *adv.* extremely well, *getting on famously*.
fan [1] *n.* a device waved in the hand or operated mechanically to create a current of air. —*v.* (fanned, fanning) **1.** to drive a current of air upon, with or as if with a fan. **2.** to stimulate (flames etc.) in this way. **3.** to spread from a central point, *troops fanned out*. □ **fan belt**, a belt driving the fan that cools the radiator of a motor vehicle.
fan [2] *n.* an enthusiastic admirer or supporter. (¶ Originally short for *fanatic*.) **fan club**, an organized group of a person's admirers. **fan mail**, letters from fans to the person they admire.
fanatic (fă-**nat**-ik) *n.* a person filled with excessive enthusiasm for something. **fanatical** *adj.*, **fanatically** *adv.*
fanaticism (fă-**nat**-i-sizm) *n.* excessive enthusiasm.
fancier *n.* **1.** a person with special knowledge of and love for something, *a dog-fancier*. **2.** one whose hobby is breeding animals or growing plants.
fanciful *adj.* **1.** (of people) using the imagination freely, imagining things. **2.** existing only in the imagination. **3.** (of things) designed in a quaint or imaginative style. **fancifully** *adv.*
fancy *n.* **1.** the power of imagining things, especially of an unreal or fantastic sort. **2.** something imagined, an unfounded idea or belief. **3.** an unreasoning desire for something. **4.** a liking. —**fancy** *adj.* **1.** ornamental, not plain, elaborate. **2.** based on imagination not fact. —**fancy** *v.* (fancied, fancying) **1.** to imagine. **2.** to be inclined to believe or suppose. **3.** (*informal*) to take a fancy to, to like, to find (a person) attractive. □ **fancy-free** *adj.* not in love. **fancy dress**, a costume worn for a party etc. where the guests dress to represent animals, characters of history or fiction, etc. **fancy goods**, (in a shop) ornamental novelties. **fancy man**, (*slang*) a woman's lover; a ponce. **fancy oneself**, (*informal*) to be rather conceited, to admire oneself. **fancy prices**, excessively high prices. **fancy woman**, (*slang*) a man's mistress. **take a fancy to**, to develop a liking for. **take a person's fancy**, to become liked by him.
fandango *n.* (*pl.* fandangoes) **1.** a lively Spanish dance for two people, music for this. **2.** nonsense, tomfoolery.
fanfare *n.* a short showy or ceremonious sounding of trumpets.
fang *n.* **1.** a long sharp tooth, especially of dogs and wolves. **2.** a snake's tooth with which it injects venom.

fanlight *n.* a semicircular window above a door, a small window above another window or a door.

fanny *n.* 1. (*Amer. slang*) the buttocks. 2. (*vulgar*) the female genitals.

fantail *n.* a kind of pigeon with a semicircular tail.

fantasia (fan-**tay**-ziă) *n.* an imaginative musical or other composition.

fantasize (**fan**-tă-syz) *v.* to imagine in fantasy, to day-dream.

fantastic *adj.* 1. absurdly fanciful. 2. designed in a very imaginative style. 3. (*informal*) very remarkable, excellent. **fantastically** *adv.*

fantasy *n.* 1. imagination, especially when producing very fanciful ideas. 2. a wild or fantastic product of the imagination, a day-dream. 3. a fanciful design, a fantasia.

far *adv.* (farther *or* further, farthest *or* furthest) at or to or by a great distance. —*adj.* distant, remote. □ **a far cry from**, greatly different from. **by far**, by a great amount. **far and away**, by far. **far and wide**, over a large area. **far-away** *adj.* remote; (of a look) dreamy; (of the voice) sounding as if from a distance. **far be it from me**, I would certainly not. **Far East**, China, Japan, and other countries of east and south-east Asia. **far fetched** *adj.* (of an explanation etc.) strained, traced from something very remote and therefore unlikely. **far-reaching** *adj.* having a wide range or influence or effect. **far-seeing** *adj.* showing great foresight.

farce *n.* 1. a light comedy. 2. this kind of drama. 3. absurd and useless proceedings, a pretence. **farcical** (**far**-sik-ăl) *adj.*

fare *n.* 1. the price charged for a passenger to travel. 2. a passenger who pays a fare, especially for a hired vehicle. 3. food provided. —*v.* to have good or bad treatment, to progress, *how did they fare?* □ **fare-stage** *n.* a stopping place marking one of the sections of a bus route that are regarded as a unit in calculating fares.

farewell *int.* goodbye. —*n.* leave-taking.

farm *n.* 1. an area of land and its buildings, owned or rented by one management, used for raising crops or livestock. 2. a farmhouse. 3. a stretch of water used for raising fish etc. —**farm** *v.* 1. to grow crops or raise livestock. 2. to use (land) for this purpose. □ **farm out**, to send out or delegate (work) to be done by others.

farmer *n.* a person who owns or manages a farm.

farmhouse *n.* the farmer's house on a farm; *farmhouse butter* or *cheese,* that made on a farm not in a factory.

farmstead (**farm**-sted) *n.* a farm and its buildings.

farmyard *n.* the enclosed area round farm buildings.

Faroes (**fair**-ohz) *pl. n.* the Faroe Islands in the North Atlantic, belonging to Denmark. **Faroese** *adj. & n.*

farrago (fă-**rah**-goh) *n.* a hotch-potch.

farrier (**fa**-ri-er) *n.* a smith who shoes horses.

farrow (**fa**-roh) *v.* (of a sow) to give birth to young pigs. —*n.* 1. farrowing. 2. a litter of young pigs.

Farsi *n.* the Persian language.

fart *v.* (*vulgar*) to send out wind through the anus. —*n.* (*vulgar*) the sending out of wind in this way.

farther *adv. & adj.* at or to a greater distance, more remote. **farthest** *adv. & adj.* at or to the greatest distance, most remote. ¶ These words are not commonly used except where the sense of 'distance' is involved, and even then many people prefer to use *further* and *furthest*.

farthing *n.* a former British coin worth one quarter of a penny.

fascia (**fay**-shă) *n.* 1. a long flat vertical surface of wood or stone, e.g. under eaves or a cornice. 2. = facia.

farthingale *n.* a hooped petticoat or padded roll of material formerly worn under a skirt (especially in the reign of Queen Elizabeth I) to make it stand out.

fascicle (**fas**-ikŭl) *n.* one section of a book that is published in instalments.

fascinate *v.* 1. to attract and hold the interest of, to charm greatly. 2. to deprive (a victim) of the power of escape by a fixed look, as a snake does. **fascination** *n.,* **fascinator** *n.* □ **fascinating** *adj.* having great attraction or charm.

fascism (**fash**-izm) *n.* a system of extreme right-wing dictatorial government. **fascist** *n.*

fash *v.* (*Scottish*) to bother or trouble, *don't fash yourself.*

fashion *n.* 1. a manner or way of doing something, *continue in this fashion.* 2. the popular style of dress, customs, etc. at a given time; *fashion shoes,* shoes made with fashion (not function) in mind. —*v.* to make into a particular form or shape. □ **after** *or* **in a fashion**, to some extent but not very satisfactorily. **in fashion**, fashionable. **out of fashion**, not fashionable.

fashionable *adj.* 1. in or adopting a style that is currently popular. 2. frequented or used by stylish people, *a fashionable hotel.* **fashionably** *adv.*

fast[1] *adj.* 1. moving or done quickly.

2. producing or allowing quick movement, *a fast road.* **3.** (of a clock etc.) showing a time ahead of the correct one. **4.** (of a person) spending too much time and energy on pleasure, immoral. **5.** (of photographic film) very sensitive to light, (of a lens) having a large aperture, allowing a short exposure to be used. **6.** firmly fixed or attached. **7.** (of colours or dyes) unlikely to fade or run. —**fast** *adv.* **1.** quickly. **2.** firmly, tightly, securely, *stuck fast; fast asleep.* □ **fast food,** quickly-prepared food, especially that served or cooked in a restaurant. **fast-talk** *v.* (*Amer. informal*) to persuade by eloquent or deceitful talk. **fast worker,** one who makes rapid progress especially in furthering his own interests. **play fast and loose,** to change one's attitude repeatedly, to ignore one's obligations.

fast² *v.* to go without food or without certain kinds of food, especially as a religious duty. —*n.* fasting, a day or season appointed for this.

fastback *n.* a car with a long sloping back, the back itself.

fasten *v.* **1.** to fix firmly, to tie or join together. **2.** to fix (one's glance or attention) intently. **3.** to become fastened, *the door fastens with a latch.* □ **fastener, fastening** *ns.* a device for fastening something. **fasten off,** to tie or secure the end of a thread etc. **fasten on,** to lay hold of; to single out for attack; to seize as a pretext.

fastidious (fas-**tid**-iŭs) *adj.* selecting carefully, choosing only what is good, easily disgusted. **fastidiously** *adv.,* **fastidiousness** *n.*

fastness *n.* **1.** the state of being fast or firm, *colour fastness.* **2.** a stronghold, a fortress.

fat *n.* **1.** a whitish or yellowish substance, insoluble in water, found in animal bodies and certain seeds. **2.** this substance prepared for use in cooking. —**fat** *adj.* (fatter, fattest) **1.** containing much fat, covered with fat. **2.** excessively plump. **3.** (of an animal) made plump for slaughter. **4.** thick, *a fat book.* **5.** fertile, *fat lands.* **6.** richly rewarding, *a nice fat job.* —**fatness** *n.* □ **fat cat,** (*Amer. slang*) a wealthy person. **a fat lot** *or* **chance,** (*informal*) none, no chance at all. **the fat will be in the fire,** there will be an explosion of anger. **live off the fat of the land,** to have the best of everything to eat.

fatal *adj.* **1.** causing or ending in death. **2.** causing disaster, *a fatal mistake.* **3.** fateful, *the fatal day.* **fatally** *adv.*

fatalist *n.* a person who accepts and submits to what happens, regarding it as inevitable. **fatalism** *n.,* **fatalistic** *adj.*

fatality (fă-**tal**-iti) *n.* death caused by accident or in war etc.

fate *n.* **1.** a power thought to control all events and impossible to resist. **2.** a person's destiny.

fated *adj.* destined by fate, doomed.

fateful *adj.* bringing or producing great and usually unpleasant events.

fat-head *n.* (*informal*) a stupid person.

father *n.* **1.** a male parent. **2.** a male ancestor, *land of our fathers.* **3.** the founder or originator of something. **4.** *Father,* God, the first person of the Trinity. **5.** the title of certain priests, especially those belonging to religious orders. —**father** *v.* **1.** to beget, to be the father of. **2.** to found or originate (an idea or plan etc). **3.** to fix the paternity of (a child) on a certain person. —**fatherly** *adj.,* **fatherhood** *n.* □ **Father Christmas,** an old man dressed in a red robe, symbolic of Christmas festivities and identified with Santa Claus. **father-figure** *n.* an older man who is respected and trusted by others like a father. **father-in-law** *n.* (*pl.* fathers-in-law) the father of one's wife or husband. **Father of the House of Commons,** the MP with the longest continuous service. **Father's Day,** a day (usually the third Sunday in June) on which special tribute is paid to fathers. **Father Time,** the personification of time, shown as an old man with a scythe and an hourglass.

fatherland *n.* one's native country.

fatherless *adj.* without a living father, without a known father.

fathom *n.* a measure of 6 ft., used in stating the depth of water. —*v.* **1.** to measure the depth of. **2.** to get to the bottom of, to understand. □ **fathomless** *adj.* too deep to fathom.

fatigue *n.* **1.** tiredness resulting from hard work or exercise. **2.** weakness in metals etc. caused by repeated stress. **3.** any of the non-military duties of soldiers such as cooking, cleaning, etc. —*v.* to cause fatigue to.

fatstock *n.* livestock fattened for slaughter as food.

fatted *adj.* (of animals) fattened as food, *the fatted calf.*

fatten *v.* (fattened, fattening) to make or become fat.

fattish *adj.* rather fat.

fatty *adj.* like fat, containing fat. —*n.* (*informal*) a fat person.

fatuous (**fat**-yoo-ŭs) *adj.* foolish, silly. **fatuously** *adv.,* **fatuousness** *n.,* **fatuity** (fă-**tew**-iti) *n.*

faucet (**faw**-sit) *n.* **1.** a tap for a barrel. **2.** (*Amer.*) any kind of tap.

fault *n.* **1.** a defect or imperfection. **2.** an offence, something wrongly done. **3.** the responsibility for something wrong. **4.** a break in the continuity of layers of rock, caused by movement of the earth's crust. **5.** an incorrect serve in tennis etc. —**fault** *v.* **1.** to find fault with, to declare to be faulty. **2.** to make imperfect. □ **at fault**, responsible for a mistake or shortcoming. **fault-finding** *adj.* & *n.* finding fault. **find fault with**, to seek and find mistakes in, to complain about. **to a fault**, excessively, *generous to a fault.*

faultless *adj.* without fault. **faultlessly** *adv.*

faulty *adj.* (faultier, faultiest) having a fault or faults, imperfect. **faultily** *adv.*, **faultiness** *n.*

faun (*pr.* fawn) *n.* one of a class of gods of the woods and fields in ancient mythology, with the legs and horns of a goat.

fauna *n.* the animals of an area or period of time.

faux pas (foh **pah**) (*pl.* faux pas, *pr.* foh **pahz**) an embarrassing blunder. (¶ French, = false step.)

favour *n.* **1.** liking, goodwill, approval. **2.** an act that is kindly or helpful beyond what is due or usual. **3.** support or preference given to one person or group at the expense of another. **4.** an ornament or badge etc. worn to show that one supports a certain political or other party. —**favour** *v.* **1.** to regard or treat with favour. **2.** to be in favour of. **3.** to oblige, *favour us with a song.* **4.** (of events or circumstances) to make possible or easy, to be advantageous to. **5.** to resemble (one parent etc.), *the boy favours his father.* □ **be in** *or* **out of favour**, to have or not have a person's goodwill. **in favour of**, in support of, in sympathy with; to the advantage of, *the exchange rate is in our favour;* (of cheques) made out to (a person or his account).

favourable *adj.* **1.** giving or showing approval. **2.** pleasing, satisfactory, *made a favourable impression.* **3.** helpful, advantageous, *favourable winds.* **favourably** *adv.*

favourite *adj.* liked or preferred above others. —*n.* **1.** a favoured person or thing. **2.** a competitor generally expected to win.

favouritism *n.* unfair favouring of one person or group at the expense of another.

fawn[1] *n.* **1.** a fallow deer in its first year. **2.** light yellowish brown. —*adj.* fawn-coloured.

fawn[2] *v.* **1.** (of a dog etc.) to try to win affection or attention by crouching close to a person and licking him. **2.** to try to win favour by obsequious behaviour.

FBI *abbrev.* Federal Bureau of Investigation.

fealty (**feel**-ti) *n.* loyalty, *oath of fealty.*

fear *n.* **1.** an unpleasant emotion caused by the nearness of danger or expectation of pain etc. **2.** the reverence or awe felt for God. —**fear** *v.* **1.** to feel fear of, to be afraid. **2.** to reverence (God). **3.** to have an uneasy feeling, to be politely regretful, *I fear there's none left.* □ **for fear of**, because of the risk of. **put the fear of God into**, to terrify. **without fear or favour**, impartially.

fearful *adj.* **1.** causing horror. **2.** feeling fear. **3.** (*informal*) very great, extremely bad. **fearfully** *adv.*

fearless *adj.* feeling no fear. **fearlessly** *adv.*, **fearlessness** *n.*

fearsome *adj.* frightening or alarming in appearance, very great, *a fearsome task.*

feasible (**fee**-zi-bŭl) *adj.* **1.** able to be done, possible. **2.** likely, plausible, *a feasible explanation.* **feasibly** *adv.*, **feasibility** (fee-zi-**bil**-iti) *n.*

feast *n.* **1.** a large elaborate meal. **2.** a religious festival of rejoicing. —**feast** *v.* **1.** to eat heartily. **2.** to give a feast to. □ **feast one's eyes on**, to gaze admiringly at.

feat *n.* a remarkable action or achievement.

feather *n.* **1.** one of the structures that grow from a bird's skin and cover its body, consisting of a central shaft with a fringe of fine strands on each side. **2.** long silky hair on a dog's or horse's legs. —**feather** *v.* **1.** to cover or fit with feathers. **2.** to turn (an oar) so that the blade passes through the air edgeways. **3.** to make (propeller blades) rotate in such a way as to lessen the resistance of the air or water. □ **a feather in one's cap**, an achievement one can be proud of. **feather bed**, a mattress stuffed with feathers. **feather-bed** *v.* (feather-bedded, feather-bedding) to make things financially easy for, to pamper. (**feather-brained**) *adj.* empty-headed. **feather one's nest**, to enrich oneself when an opportunity occurs. **feather-stitch** *n.* an ornamental stitch producing a feather-like pattern.

featherweight *n.* **1.** a boxing-weight (57kg) between lightweight and bantamweight. **2.** a very lightweight thing or person. **3.** a person of little or no influence.

feathery *adj.* **1.** light and soft like feathers. **2.** covered with feathers.

feature *n.* **1.** one of the named parts of the face (e.g. mouth, nose, eyes) which together make up its appearance. **2.** a distinctive or noticeable quality of a thing. **3.** a prominent article in a newspaper etc. **4.** a long film forming the main item in a cinema programme. **5.** a broadcast based on one specific theme. —**feature** v. **1.** to give special prominence to. **2.** to be a feature of or in.

featureless adj. without distinctive features.

febrile (fee-bryl) adj. of or involving fever, feverish.

February the second month of the year.

feckless adj. feeble and incompetent, irresponsible. **fecklessness** n.

fecund (fek-ūnd) adj. fertile. **fecundity** (fi-**kund**-iti) n.

fed see feed. □ **fed up,** (informal) discontented, displeased.

federal adj. **1.** of a system of government in which several States unite under a central authority but remain independent in internal affairs. **2.** belonging to this group as a whole (not to its separate parts), federal laws. **3.** of an association of units that are largely independent. **federally** adv. □ **Federal Bureau of Investigation,** a section of the Department of Justice in the USA, responsible for investigating violations of federal law and safeguarding national security.

federate v. **1.** to unite on a federal basis. **2.** to band together for a common object.

federation n. **1.** federating. **2.** a federated society or group of States.

fee n. **1.** a sum payable to an official or a professional person for advice or services. **2.** a sum payable for membership of a society, entrance for an examination, transfer of a footballer, etc. □ **fees** pl. n. charges for instruction at a school or university.

feeble adj. weak, without strength or force or effectiveness. **feebly** adv., **feebleness** n. □ **feeble-minded** adj. mentally deficient, especially with a mental age of 8 or 9.

feed v. (fed, feeding) **1.** to give food to, to put food into the mouth of. **2.** to give as food to animals, feed oats to horses. **3.** (of animals) to take food. **4.** serve as food for, to nourish. **5.** to supply, to pass a supply of material to. **6.** to send passes to (a player) in football etc. —**feed** n. **1.** a meal (chiefly for animals or babies). **2.** food for animals. **3.** a pipe or channel etc. by which material is carried to a machine, the material itself. □ **feeding-bottle** n. a bottle with a teat, for feeding babies. **feed on,** to consume as food, to be nourished or sustained by.

feedback n. **1.** return of part of the output of a system to its source, especially so as to modify the output. **2.** the return of

information about a product etc. to its supplier.

feeder n. **1.** (of plants and animals) one that takes in food in a certain way, a dainty feeder. **2.** a baby's feeding-bottle. **3.** a baby's bib. **4.** a hopper or feeding apparatus in a machine. **5.** a branch railway line, airline, canal, etc. linking outlying areas with a central line or service etc.

feel v. (felt, feeling) **1.** to explore or perceive by touch. **2.** to be conscious of, to be aware of being, feel a pain; feel happy. **3.** to be affected by, feels the cold badly. **4.** to give a certain sensation or impression, the water feels warm. **5.** to have a vague conviction or impression of something. **6.** to have as an opinion, to consider, we felt it was necessary to do this. —**feel** n. **1.** the sense of touch. **2.** the act of feeling. **3.** the sensation produced by something touched, silk has a soft feel. □ **feel for a person,** to sympathize with him. **feel free,** (informal) an expression of permission. **feel like,** to be in the mood for. **feel one's way,** to find one's way by feeling about; to proceed cautiously.

feeler n. **1.** a long slender part or organ in certain animals, used for testing things by touch. **2.** a cautious proposal or suggestion put forward to test people's reactions. □ **feeler gauge,** a gauge with blades that can be inserted to measure gaps.

feeling n. **1.** the power and capacity to feel, had lost all feeling in his legs. **2.** mental or physical awareness, emotion. **3.** an idea or belief not wholly based on reason, had a feeling of safety. **4.** readiness to feel, sympathy, showed no feeling for the sufferings of others. **5.** opinion, attitude, the feeling of the meeting was against it. □ **feelings** pl. n. the emotional side of a person's nature (contrasted with the intellect); sympathies, opinions, we have strong feelings on this matter. **good feeling,** friendliness.

feet see foot.

feign (pr. fayn) v. to pretend.

feint (pr. faynt) n. a slight attack or movement made in one place to divert attention from the main attack coming elsewhere. —v. to make a feint. —adj. (of ruled lines) faint.

felicitate (fi-**liss**-i-tayt) v. to congratulate. **felicitation** n.

felicitous (fil-**iss**-i-tŭs) adj. (of words or remarks) well chosen, apt. **felicitously** adv.

felicity n. **1.** being happy, great happiness. **2.** a pleasing manner or style, expressed himself with great felicity.

feline (fee-lyn) *adj.* of cats, cat-like. —*n.* an animal of the cat family.

fell[1] *n.* a stretch of moorland or hilly land in north England.

fell[2] *adj.* (*poetical*) ruthless, cruel, destructive. **at one fell swoop**, in a single deadly action.

fell[3] *v.* **1.** to strike down by a blow. **2.** to cut (a tree) down. **3.** to stitch down (the edge of a seam) so that it lies flat.

fell[4] *see* fall.

fellow *n.* **1.** one who is associated with another, a comrade. **2.** a thing of the same class or kind, the other of a pair. **3.** a member of a learned society. **4.** a member of the governing body of certain colleges. **5.** (*informal*) a man or boy. □ **fellow-feeling** *n.* sympathy with a person. **fellow-traveller** *n.* one who sympathizes with the aims of the Communist Party but is not a member of it.

fellowship *n.* **1.** friendly association with others, companionship. **2.** a number of people associated together, a society, membership of this. **3.** the position of a college fellow.

felon (fel-ŏn) *n.* a person who has committed a felony.

felony (fel-ŏni) *n.* (in former use) a crime regarded by the law as serious, usually involving violence.

felt[1] *n.* a kind of cloth made by matting and pressing fibres. —*v.* **1.** to make or become matted together like felt. **2.** to cover with felt.

felt[2] *see* feel.

female *adj.* **1.** of the sex that can bear offspring or produce eggs. **2.** (of plants) fruit-bearing, having a pistil and no stamens. **3.** of a woman or women. —*n.* a female animal or plant.

feminine *adj.* **1.** of or like or suitable for women, having the qualities or appearance considered characteristic of a woman. **2.** having the grammatical form suitable for the names of females or for words corresponding to these, *'lioness' is the feminine noun corresponding to 'lion'.* —*n.* a feminine word or gender. —**femininity** *n.*

feminist *n.* a supporter of women's claims to be given rights equal to those of men. **feminism** *n.*

femur (fee-mer) *n.* the thigh-bone.

fen *n.* a low-lying marshy or flooded tract of land. **the Fens**, those in Cambridgeshire and nearby regions.

fence *n.* **1.** a structure of rails, stakes, wire, etc. put round a field or garden to mark a boundary or keep animals from straying. **2.** a raised structure for a horse to jump. **3.** a person who knowingly buys and re-sells stolen goods. —**fence** *v.* **1.** to surround with a fence. **2.** to act as a fence for (stolen goods). **3.** to engage in fencing. —**fencer** *n.* □ **sit on the fence,** *see* sit.

fencing *n.* **1.** fences, a length of fence. **2.** the sport of fighting with foils or other kinds of sword.

fend *v.* **fend for,** to provide a livelihood for, to look after. **fend off,** to ward off.

fender *n.* **1.** a low frame bordering a fireplace, to keep falling coals etc. from rolling into the room. **2.** a pad or a bundle of rope hung over a vessel's side to prevent damage when it is alongside a wharf or another vessel.

fennel *n.* a fragrant yellow-flowered herb used for flavouring.

Fermanagh (fer-man-ă) a county of Northern Ireland.

ferment[1] (fer-ment) *v.* **1.** to undergo fermentation, to cause fermentation in. **2.** to seethe with excitement or agitation.

ferment[2] (fer-ment) *n.* **1.** fermentation. **2.** something that causes this. **3.** a state of seething excitement or agitation.

fermentation *n.* a chemical change caused by the action of an organic substance such as yeast, involving effervescence and the production of heat, e.g. when sugar is converted into alcohol.

fern *n.* a kind of flowerless plant with feathery green leaves.

ferocious *adj.* fierce, savage. **ferociously** *adv.*, **ferocity** (fi-ross-iti) *n.*

ferret *n.* a small animal of the weasel family kept for driving rabbits from burrows, killing rats, etc. —*v.* (ferreted, ferreting) to search, to rummage. □ **ferreting** *n.* hunting with ferrets, *go ferreting.* **ferret out,** to discover by searching or rummaging. **ferrety** *adj.* (of the face) narrow and pointed like a ferret's.

ferroconcrete *n.* reinforced concrete.

ferrous (fe-rŭs) *adj.* containing iron, *ferrous and non-ferrous metals.*

ferrule (fe-rool) *n.* a metal ring or cap strengthening the end of a stick or tube.

ferry *v.* (ferried, ferrying) **1.** to convey (people or things) in a boat etc. across a stretch of water. **2.** to transport from one place to another, especially as a regular service. —**ferry** *n.* **1.** a boat etc. used for ferrying. **2.** the place where it operates. **3.** the service it provides. —**ferryman** *n.*

fertile *adj.* **1.** (of soil) rich in the materials needed to support vegetation. **2.** (of plants) able to produce fruit, (of animals) able or likely to conceive or beget young. **3.** (of seeds or eggs) capable of developing into a new plant or animal, fertilized. **4.** (of the mind) able to produce ideas, inventive. **fertility** *n.*

fertilize *v.* **1.** to make (soil etc.) fertile or productive. **2.** to introduce pollen or sperm into (a plant or egg or female animal) so that it develops seed or young. **fertilization** *n.*

fertilizer *n.* material (natural or artificial) added to soil to make it more fertile.

fervent (fer-vĕnt) *adj.* showing warmth of feeling. **fervently** *adv.*

fervid *adj.* fervent. **fervidly** *adv.*

fervour *n.* warmth and intensity of feeling, zeal.

fescue (fess-kew) *n.* a kind of grass used as pasture and fodder.

festal *adj.* of a festival.

fester *v.* **1.** to make or become septic and filled with pus. **2.** to cause continuing resentment.

festival *n.* **1.** a day or time of religious or other celebration. **2.** a series of performances of music, drama, films, etc. given periodically, *the Edinburgh Festival.*

festive *adj.* of or suitable for a festival.

festivity *n.* a festive occasion or celebration.

festoon *n.* a chain of flowers, leaves, ribbons, etc. hung in a curve or loop as a decoration. —*v.* to decorate with hanging ornaments.

fetch *v.* **1.** to go for and bring back, *fetch a doctor.* **2.** to cause to come out, *fetched a sigh*; *fetch tears to the eyes.* **3.** (of goods) to sell for (a price), *your books won't fetch much.* **4.** (*informal*) to give (a blow) to, *fetched him a slap.* —*n.* a distance of water between two points. □ **fetch up**, (*informal*) to arrive or end up at a place or in a certain position.

fetching *adj.* attractive.

fête (*pr.* fayt) *n.* **1.** a festival. **2.** an outdoor entertainment or sale, usually to raise funds for a cause or charity. —*v.* (**fêted**, **fêting**) to entertain (a person) in celebration of some achievement etc.

fetid (fet-id) *adj.* stinking.

fetish (fet-ish) *n.* **1.** an object worshipped by primitive peoples who believe it to have magical powers or to be inhabited by a spirit. **2.** anything to which foolishly excessive respect or attention is given.

fetlock *n.* the part of a horse's leg above and behind the hoof.

fetter *n.* a chain or shackle for a prisoner's ankles. —*v.* **1.** to put into fetters. **2.** to impede or restrict.

fettle *n.* condition, trim, *in fine fettle.*

feu (*pr.* few) *n.* (*Scottish*) **1.** a perpetual lease at a fixed rent. **2.** land held in this way. —*v.* to lease by feu.

feud (*pr.* fewd) *n.* lasting hostility between people or groups. —*v.* to carry on a feud.

feudal (few-d'l) *adj.* of or according to the **feudal system**, a method of holding land (during the Middle Ages in Europe) by giving one's services to the owner. **feudalism** *n.*, **feudalistic** *adj.*

fever *n.* **1.** an abnormally high body temperature. **2.** a disease characterized by this. **3.** a state of nervous excitement or agitation. □ **fever pitch**, a high level of excitement.

fevered *adj.* affected with fever.

feverish *adj.* **1.** having a fever, caused or accompanied by a fever. **2.** restless with excitement or agitation. **feverishly** *adv.*, **feverishness** *n.*

few *adj.* & *n.* not many. (¶ See the note under **less**.) **fewness** *n.* □ **a few**, some, not none. **a good few** *or* **quite a few**, (*informal*) a fairly large number.

fey (*pr.* fay) *adj.* **1.** (*Scottish*) clairvoyant. **2.** having a strange other-worldly charm. **feyness** *n.*

fez *n.* (*pl.* fezzes) a man's high flat-topped red cap with a tassel, worn by Muslims in certain countries.

fiancé, fiancée (fee-ahn-say) *ns.* a man (*fiancé*) or woman (*fiancée*) to whom one is engaged to be married.

fiasco (fi-ass-koh) *n.* (*pl.* fiascos) a complete and ludicrous failure in something attempted.

fiat (fy-at) *n.* an order or decree.

fib *n.* an unimportant lie. —*v.* (fibbed, fibbing) to tell a fib. —**fibber** *n.*

fibre *n.* **1.** one of the thin strands of which animal and vegetable tissue or textile substance is made, a thread-like piece of glass. **2.** a substance consisting of fibres. **3.** strength of character, *moral fibre.*

fibreboard *n.* board made of compressed fibres.

fibreglass *n.* **1.** textile fabric made from glass fibres. **2.** plastic containing glass fibres.

fibroid (fy-broid) *adj.* consisting of fibrous tissue. —*n.* a benign fibroid tumour in the womb.

fibrosis (fy-broh-sis) *n.* development of excessive fibrous tissue.

fibrositis (fy-brŏ-sy-tiss) *n.* rheumatic pain in any tissue other than bones and joints.

fibrous (fy-brŭs) *adj.* like fibres, made of fibres.

fibula (fib-yoo-lă) *n.* the bone on the outer side of the lower part of the leg.

fiche (*pr.* feesh) *n.* (*pl.* fiche) a microfiche.

fickle *adj.* often changing, not constant or loyal. **fickleness** *n.*

fiction *n.* **1.** a product of the imagination. **2.** an invented story. **3.** a class of literature consisting of books containing such stories. **fictional** *adj.*

fictionalize *v.* to make into a fictional narrative.

fictitious (fik-**tish**-ŭs) *adj.* imagined, not real, not genuine, *gave a fictitious account of his movements.*

fiddle *n.* **1.** (*informal*) a violin. **2.** (*slang*) a piece of cheating, a swindle. —**fiddle** *v.* **1.** (*informal*) to play the fiddle. **2.** to fidget with something, to handle a thing aimlessly. **3.** (*slang*) to cheat or swindle, to falsify (accounts etc.), to get by cheating. — **fiddler** *n.*

fiddlesticks *int.* nonsense.

fiddling *adj.* petty, trivial.

fiddly *adj.* (*informal*) small and awkward to use or do.

fidelity (fid-**el**-iti) *n.* **1.** faithfulness, loyalty. **2.** accuracy, truthfulness. **3.** the quality or precision of the reproduction of sound.

fidget *v.* (fidgeted, fidgeting) **1.** to make small restless movements. **2.** to be uneasy, to make (a person) uneasy, to worry. —*n.* a person who fidgets. ◻ **fidgets** *pl. n.* fidgeting movements.

fidgety *adj.* inclined to fidget.

fie *int.* (*old use*) for shame!

field *n.* **1.** a piece of open ground, especially one used for pasture or cultivation. **2.** an area of land rich in some natural product, a coalfield or gasfield or oilfield. **3.** a battlefield. **4.** a sports ground, the playing area marked out on this. **5.** the space within which an electric or magnetic or gravitational influence etc. can be felt, the force of that influence. **6.** the area that can be seen or observed, *one's field of vision.* **7.** the range of a subject or activity or interest, *an expert in the field of music.* **8.** (in computers) one section of a record, representing a unit of information, *the firm's payroll record has one field for gross pay, one for deductions, and one for net pay.* **9.** the scene or area of fieldwork, *field archaeology.* **10.** all the competitors in an outdoor contest or sport, all except the one(s) specified, the fielding side in cricket. **field** *v.* **1.** to act as a fieldsman in cricket etc. **2.** to stop and return (the ball) in cricket etc. **3.** to put (a football or other team) into the field. **4.** to deal successfully with (a series of questions). ◻ **field-day** *n.* a day of much activity, especially of brilliant and exciting events. **field events,** athletic sports other than races, e.g. jumping, weight-putting, etc. **field-glasses** *pl. n.* binoculars for outdoor use. **Field Marshal,** an army officer of the highest

rank. **field-mouse** *n.* the type of mouse found in open country. **field sports,** outdoor sports such as hunting, shooting, and fishing.

fielder *n.* a fieldsman.

fieldfare *n.* a kind of thrush that spends the winter (but not summer) in Britain.

fieldsman *n.* (*pl.* fieldsmen) a member of the side not batting in cricket etc.

fieldwork *n.* practical work done outside libraries and laboratories e.g. by surveyors, scientists, and social workers who visit people in their homes. **fieldworker** *n.*

fiend (*pr.* feend) *n.* **1.** an evil spirit. **2.** a very wicked or cruel person, one who causes mischief or annoyance. **3.** a devotee or addict, *a fresh-air fiend.* **fiendish** *adj.*, **fiendishly** *adv.*

fierce *adj.* **1.** violent in temper or manner or action, not gentle. **2.** eager, intense, *fierce loyalty.* **3.** unpleasantly strong or extreme, *fierce heat.* **fiercely** *adv.*, **fierceness** *n.*

fiery *adj.* **1.** consisting of fire, flaming. **2.** looking like fire, bright red. **3.** intensely hot, producing a burning sensation. **4.** intense, passionate, *a fiery speech.* **5.** easily roused to anger.

fiesta (fee-**est**-ă) *n.* a religious festival in Spanish-speaking countries.

fife *n.* a kind of small shrill flute used with a drum in military music.

Fife a region of Scotland.

fifteen *adj. & n.* **1.** one more than fourteen (15, XV). **2.** a Rugby Union football team of fifteen players. **fifteenth** *adj. & n.*

fifth *adj. & n.* **1.** next after fourth. **2.** one of five equal parts of a thing. **fifthly** *adv.* ◻ **fifth column,** an organized body working for the enemy within a country at war. (¶ General Mola, leading four columns of troops towards Madrid in the Spanish Civil War, declared that he had a fifth column inside the city.) **fifth columnist,** a member of such a group.

fifty *adj. & n.* five times ten (50, L). **fiftieth** *adj. & n.* ◻ **fifties** *pl. n.* the numbers or years or degrees of temperature from 50 to 59. **fifty-fifty** *adj. & adv.* (*informal*) shared or sharing equally between two; *a fifty-fifty chance,* an equal chance of winning or losing, or of surviving, etc.

fig *n.* **1.** a broad-leaved tree bearing a soft pear-shaped fruit. **2.** this fruit. **fig-leaf** *n.*

fight *v.* (fought, fighting) **1.** to struggle against (a person or country) in physical combat or in war. **2.** to carry on (a battle). **3.** to struggle or contend in any way, to strive to obtain or accomplish something.

4. to strive to overcome or destroy, *they fought the fire.* **5.** to make one's way by fighting or effort. —**fight** *n.* **1.** fighting, a battle. **2.** a struggle or contest or conflict of any kind. **3.** a boxing-match. □ **fight back**, to show resistance. **fighting chance**, a chance of succeeding provided that one makes a great effort. **fighting fit**, very fit. **fight it out**, to settle something by fighting or arguing until one side wins. **fight off**, to drive away by fighting. **fight shy of**, to be unwilling to undertake or approach (a task etc.). **show fight**, to show readiness to fight.

fighter *n.* **1.** a person who fights. **2.** one who does not yield without a struggle. **3.** a fast military aircraft designed for attacking other aircraft.

figment *n.* a thing that does not exist except in the imagination.

figurative (fig-yoor-ătiv) *adj.* using or containing a figure of speech, metaphorical, not literal. **figuratively** *adv.*

figure *n.* **1.** the written symbol of a number. **2.** a diagram. **3.** a decorative pattern, a pattern traced in dancing or skating. **4.** a representation of a person or animal in drawing, painting, sculpture, etc. **5.** a person as seen or studied, *saw a figure leaning against the door; the most terrible figure in our history.* **6.** external form or shape, bodily shape, *has a good figure.* **7.** a geometrical shape enclosed by lines or surfaces. —**figure** *v.* **1.** to represent in a diagram or picture. **2.** to picture mentally, to imagine. **3.** to form part of a plan etc., to appear or be mentioned, *he figures in all books on the subject.* □ **figure-head** *n.* a carved image at the prow of a ship; a person at the head of an organization etc. but without real power. **figure of fun**, a person who looks ridiculous. **figure of speech**, a word or phrase used for vivid or dramatic effect and not literally. **figure on**, (*Amer.*) to count on, to expect. **figure out**, to work out by arithmetic; (*Amer.*) to interpret, to understand. **figures** *pl. n.* arithmetic, calculating, *she is no good at figures.*

figured *adj.* ornamented, decorated; *figured silk*, with designs woven into it.

figurine (fig-yoor-een) *n.* a statuette.

Fiji (fee-jee) an island in the South Pacific. **Fijian** (fee-jee-ăn) *adj.* & *n.*

filament *n.* **1.** a thread-like strand. **2.** a fine wire in an electric lamp, giving off light when heated by the current.

filbert *n.* the nut of a cultivated hazel.

filch *v.* to pilfer, to steal (something of small value).

file¹ *n.* a steel tool with a roughened surface for shaping or smoothing things. —*v.* to shape or smooth with a file.

file² *n.* **1.** a holder or cover or box etc. for keeping papers together and in order for reference purposes. **2.** its contents. **3.** an organized collection of related data in a computer. **4.** a line of people or things one behind the other; *in single file*, one at a time. —**file** *v.* **1.** to place in a file. **2.** to place on record, *file an application.* **3.** to march in file, *they filed out.*

filial (fil-iăl) *adj.* of or due from a son or daughter, *filial duty.*

filibuster *n.* (*Amer.*) **1.** a person who tries to delay or prevent the passage of a bill by making long speeches. **2.** this action. —*v.* to delay things in this way.

filigree (fil-i-gree) *n.* ornamental lace-like work in metal.

filing-cabinet *n.* a metal or wooden container with drawers for filing documents.

filings *pl. n.* particles rubbed off by a file.

Filipino (fili-pee-noh) *n.* (*pl.* Filipinos) a native of the Philippine Islands.

fill *v.* **1.** to make or become full, to occupy the whole of. **2.** to block up (a hole or cavity). **3.** to spread over or through, *smoke began to fill the room.* **4.** to hold (a position), to appoint a person to (a vacant post). **5.** to occupy (vacant time). —**fill** *n.* **1.** enough to fill something. **2.** enough to satisfy a person's appetite or desire. □ **fill in**, to complete by writing or drawing inside an outline; to complete (an unfinished document etc.); (*informal*) to inform (a person) more fully; to act as a substitute. **fill out**, to enlarge, to become enlarged or plumper. **fill the bill**, to be suitable for what is required. **fill up**, to fill completely; to fill in (a document); to fill the petrol tank of a car.

filler *n.* an object or material used to fill a cavity or to increase the bulk of something.

fillet *n.* **1.** a piece of boneless meat from near the loins or ribs, a thick boneless piece of fish. **2.** a strip of ribbon etc. worn round the head. —*v.* (filleted, filleting) to remove the bones from (fish etc.).

filling *n.* **1.** material used to fill a tooth-cavity, the process of inserting this. **2.** material put into a container, between layers of bread to form a sandwich, etc. □ **filling station**, a place where petrol is supplied to motorists from pumps.

fillip *n.* **1.** a quick smart blow or stroke given with a finger. **2.** something that boosts or stimulates (trade etc.). —*v.* (filliped, filliping) to propel with a fillip.

filly *n.* a young female horse.

film *n*. **1**. a thin coating or covering layer. **2**. a rolled strip or sheet coated with light-sensitive material used for taking photographs or making a motion picture, a single roll of this. **3**. a motion picture. —**film** *v*. **1**. to cover or become covered with a thin coating or covering layer. **2**. to make a film of (a story etc.) □ **films** *pl. n*. the cinema industry. **film star**, a star actor or actress in films. **film-strip** *n*. a series of transparencies for projection, especially as a teaching aid.

filmy *adj*. (filmier, filmiest) thin and almost transparent.

filter *n*. **1**. a device or substance for holding back the impurities in a liquid or gas passed through it. **2**. a screen for preventing light of certain wavelengths from passing through. **3**. a device for suppressing electrical or sound waves of frequencies other than the ones required. **4**. an arrangement for the filtering of traffic. —**filter** *v*. **1**. to pass or cause to pass through a filter, to remove impurities in this way. **2**. to come or make a way in or out gradually, *news filtered out*; *people filtered into the hall*. **3**. to allow (traffic) or be allowed to pass in a certain direction while other traffic is held up. □ **filter-bed** *n*. a tank or reservoir containing a layer of sand etc. for filtering large quantities of liquid. **filter-tip** *n*. a cigarette with a filter at the mouth end to purify the smoke.

filth *n*. **1**. disgusting dirt. **2**. obscenity.

filthy *adj*. (filthier, filthiest) **1**. disgustingly dirty. **2**. obscene. **filthily** *adv*., **filthiness** *n*.

filtrate *n*. filtered liquid. —*v*. to filter. **filtration** *n*.

fin *n*. **1**. a thin flat projection from the body of a fish etc., used by the animal for propelling and steering itself in the water. **2**. an underwater swimmer's rubber flipper. **3**. a small projection shaped like a fish's fin, e.g. to improve the stability of an aircraft or rocket.

finagle (fin-**ay**-gul) *v*. (*Amer. informal*) to behave or obtain dishonestly.

final *adj*. **1**. at the end, coming last. **2**. putting an end to doubt or discussion or argument. —**final** *n*. **1**. the last of a series of contests in sports or a competition. **2**. the edition of a newspaper published latest in the day. **finally** *adv*. □ **finals** *pl. n*. the last set of examination in a series.

finale (fin-**ah**-li) *n*. the final section of a musical composition or a drama.

finalist *n*. one who competes in the final.

finality (fy-**nal**-iti) *n*. the quality of being final.

finalize *v*. **1**. to bring to an end. **2**. to put into its final form. **finalization** *n*.

finance (fy-**nanss**) *n*. **1**. the management of money. **2**. money as support for an undertaking. —*v*. to provide the money for. □ **finance company** *or* **house**, a company that is mainly concerned with lending money for hire-purchase transactions. **finances** *pl. n*. the money resources of a country or company or person.

financial (fy-**nan**-shǎl) *adj*. of finance. **financially** *adv*.

financier (fy-**nan**-si-er) *n*. a person who is engaged in financing businesses etc. on a large scale.

finch *n*. any of a number of related birds most of which have short stubby bills.

find *v*. (found, finding) **1**. to discover by search or effort or inquiry or by chance. **2**. to become aware of, to discover (a fact). **3**. to arrive at naturally, *water finds its own level*. **4**. to succeed in obtaining, *can't find time to do it*. **5**. to supply, to provide, *who will find the money for the expedition?* **6**. (of a jury etc.) to decide and declare, *found him innocent*; *found for the plaintiff*. —**find** *n*. **1**. the finding of something. **2**. a thing found, especially something useful or pleasing. □ **find favour**, to be acceptable. **find one's feet**, to become able to stand or walk; to develop one's powers and become able to act independently. **find oneself**, to discover one's natural powers or one's vocation. **find out**, to get information about; to detect (a person) who has done wrong, to discover (a deception or fraud).

finder *n*. **1**. one who finds something. **2**. the viewfinder of a camera. **3**. a small telescope attached to a larger one to locate an object for observation.

findings *pl. n*. the conclusions reached by means of an inquiry.

fine¹ *n*. a sum of money fixed as a penalty for an offence. —*v*. to punish by a fine.

fine² *adj*. **1**. of high quality. **2**. excellent, of great merit. **3**. (of weather) bright and clear, free from rain and fog etc. **4**. of slender thread or thickness, small-sized, consisting of small particles. **5**. requiring very skilful workmanship. **6**. difficult to perceive, *making fine distinctions*. **7**. complimentary especially in an insincere way, *said fine things about them*. **8**. in good health, comfortable, *I'm fine, thank you*. —**fine** *adv*. **1**. finely. **2**. (*informal*) very well, *that will suit me fine*. —*v*. to make or become finer or thinner or less coarse. —**finely** *adv*., **fineness** *n*. □ **fine arts**, those appealing to the sense of beauty, especially painting, sculpture, and architecture. **fine-drawn** *adj*. subtle; extremely thin. **fine-tooth**

comb, a comb with narrow close-set teeth; *go through something with a fine-tooth comb*, to examine it closely and thoroughly. **not to put too fine a point on it**, to express it bluntly.

finery *n.* fine clothes or decorations.

fines herbes (feenz **airb**) mixed herbs used to flavour cooking. (¶ French.)

finesse (fin-ess) *n.* **1.** delicate manipulation. **2.** tact and cleverness in dealing with a situation.

finger *n.* **1.** one of the five parts extending from each hand, or one of these other than the thumb. **2.** the part of a glove that fits over a finger. **3.** a finger-like object. **4.** (*slang*) the breadth of a finger (about ¾ inch) as a measure of alcohol in a glass. — **finger** *v.* **1.** to touch or feel with the fingers. **2.** to play (a musical instrument) with the fingers. □ **finger-bowl** *n.* a small bowl for rinsing one's fingers at the table. **finger-mark** *n.* a mark left on a surface by a finger. **finger-nail** *n.* a nail at the tip of the finger. **finger-plate** *n.* a plate fastened on a door to prevent finger-marks. **finger-post** *n.* a signpost pointing down a road. **finger-stall** *n.* a sheath to cover an injured finger. **have a finger in the pie**, to be actively involved in a project.

fingering *n.* **1.** a method of using the fingers in playing a musical instrument or in typing. **2.** an indication of this in a musical score, usually by numbers.

fingerprint *n.* an impression of the ridges of the skin on the pad of a finger, especially as a means of identification.

fingertip *n.* the tip of a finger. **have at one's fingertips**, to be thoroughly familiar with (a thing).

finicking *adj. & n.* **1.** being fastidious. **2.** giving or requiring extreme care about details. **finical, finicky** *adjs.* finicking.

finish *v.* **1.** to bring or come to an end, to complete. **2.** to reach the end of a task or race etc. **3.** to consume or get through all of, *finish the pie*. **4.** to put the final touches to, to complete the manufacture of (woodwork, cloth, etc.) by surface treatment. — **finish** *n.* **1.** the last stage of something. **2.** the point at which a race etc. ends. **3.** the state of being finished or perfect. **4.** the method or texture or material used for finishing woodwork etc. □ **finishing school**, a private school preparing girls for life in fashionable society. **finish with**, to complete one's use of; to end one's association with.

finite (fy-nyt) *adj.* limited, not infinite.

Finland a country of north-east Europe.

Finn *n.* a native of Finland.

finnan haddock (fin-ăn) haddock cured with smoke of green wood or of turf or peat.

Finnish *adj.* of the Finns or their language. —*n.* the language of the Finns.

fiord (fi-ord) *n.* a long narrow inlet of the sea between high cliffs as in Norway.

fir *n.* **1.** a kind of evergreen cone-bearing tree with needle-like leaves on its shoots. **2.** its wood.

fire *n.* **1.** combustion producing light and heat. **2.** destructive burning, *insured against fire*. **3.** burning fuel in a grate or furnace etc., an electric or gas fire. **4.** angry or excited feeling, enthusiasm. **5.** the firing of guns, *hold your fire*. —**fire** *v.* **1.** to set fire to. **2.** to catch fire. **3.** to supply (a furnace etc.) with fuel. **4.** to bake (pottery or bricks), to cure (tea or tobacco) by artificial heat. **5.** to excite, to stimulate, *fired them with enthusiasm*. **6.** to send a bullet or shell from a gun, to detonate. **7.** (of a firearm) to discharge its missile. **8.** to dismiss (an employee) from a job. — **firer** *n.* □ **fire-alarm** *n.* a bell or other device giving warning of fire. **fire away**, (*informal*) to begin, to go ahead. **fire-brick** *n.* a fireproof brick used in grates. **fire brigade**, an organized body of men trained and employed to extinguish fires. **fire-drill** *n.* rehearsal of the procedure to be used in case of fire. **fire-eater** *n.* a conjurer who appears to eat fire; a person who is fond of fighting or quarrelling. **fire-engine** *n.* a vehicle fitted with equipment used for fighting large fires. **fire-escape** *n.* a special staircase or apparatus by which people may escape from a burning building etc. in case of fire. **fire in the belly**, intense ambition or enthusiasm. **fire-irons** *pl. n.* a poker, tongs, and shovel for tending a domestic fire. **fire-lighter** *n.* a piece of inflammable material to help start a fire in a grate. **fire station**, the headquarters of the fire brigade. **fire-storm** *n.* a high wind or storm following fire caused by bombs. **fire-trap** *n.* a building without sufficient exits in case of fire.

firearm *n.* a rifle, gun, pistol, or revolver.

firebrand *n.* a person who stirs up trouble.

firedamp *n.* the miners' name for methane, which is explosive when mixed in certain proportions with air.

firefly *n.* a kind of beetle that gives off a phosphorescent light.

firelight *n.* the light from a fire in a fireplace.

fireman *n.* (*pl.* firemen) **1.** a member of a fire brigade. **2.** one whose job is to tend a furnace etc.

firemaster *n.* the head of a fire brigade.

fireplace *n.* **1.** an open recess for a domestic fire, at the base of a chimney. **2.** the surrounding structure.

fireproof *adj.* **1.** that does not catch fire. **2.** that does not break when heated, *fireproof dishes.*

fireside *n.* the part of a room near a fireplace, this as the centre of one's home.

firewood *n.* wood for use as fuel.

firework *n.* a device containing chemicals that burn or explode with spectacular effect, used at celebrations. **fireworks** *pl. n.* a display of fireworks; an outburst of anger.

firing-line *n.* **1.** the front line of a battle, from which troops fire at the enemy. **2.** a position at the forefront of an activity.

firing-squad *n.* a group ordered to fire a salute during a military funeral, or to shoot a condemned man.

firm¹ *n.* a partnership for carrying on a business, a commercial establishment.

firm² *adj.* **1.** not yielding when pressed, hard, solid. **2.** steady, not shaking. **3.** securely fixed. **4.** established, not easily changed or influenced, *a firm belief; a firm offer,* one that is not liable to be cancelled. *—adv.* firmly, *stand firm. —v.* to make or become firm or compact, to fix firmly.

firmament *n.* the sky with its clouds and stars.

first *adj.* coming before all others in time or order or importance. *—n.* **1.** something that is first, the first day of a month, the first occurrence or achievement of something. **2.** first-class honours in a university degree. **3.** first gear. *—first adv.* **1.** before all others. **2.** before another event or time; *must finish this work first,* before doing something else. **3.** for the first time, *when did you first see him?* **4.** in preference, *will see him damned first.* **5.** first class, *I usually travel first.* □ **at first,** at the beginning. **at first hand,** obtained directly, from the original source. **first aid,** treatment given to an injured person before a doctor comes. **first base,** the first of the bases that must be reached to score a run in baseball; *get to first base,* to achieve the first step towards an objective. **first blood,** the first success in a contest. **first-born** *adj. & n.* eldest, the eldest child. **first class,** a set of persons or things grouped together as better than others; the best accommodation in a boat or train or aircraft etc.; a category of mail that is to be delivered quickly; (used adverbially) in or by first class accommodation etc., *we travelled first class.* **first-class** *adj.* of the best quality; very good; of or using first-class accommodation etc. **first cousin,** *see* cousin. **first-**

footing *n.* (*Scottish*) the custom or practice of being the first to cross the threshold in the New Year. **first-fruits** *pl. n.* the first of a season's agricultural products, offered to God; the first results of work etc. **first gear,** the slowest and most powerful gear of a motor vehicle, used when starting. **First Lady,** (*Amer.*) the wife of the President of the USA. **first name,** a personal or Christian name. **first night,** the first public performance of a play etc. **first offender,** a person with no previous conviction for an offence. **first officer,** the mate on a merchant ship. **first past the post,** (of an election-candidate) winning because receiving the most votes though perhaps not having an absolute majority. **first person,** *see* person. **first-rate** *adj. & adv.* of the best class, excellent; (*informal*) very well. **first thing,** (*informal*) before anything else, *shall do it first thing.* **first violin,** one of the group playing the leading part of two or more parts.

firsthand *adj. & adv.* obtained directly from the original source.

firstly *adv.* first, as a first consideration.

firth *n.* an estuary or a narrow inlet of the sea in Scotland.

fiscal *adj.* of public revenue.

fish *n.* (*pl.* usually fish) **1.** a cold-blooded animal living wholly in water. **2.** its flesh as food. **3.** (*informal*) a person, *an odd fish.* **4.** *the Fish* or *Fishes,* a sign of the zodiac, Pisces. *—fish v.* **1.** to try to catch fish; *fish the river,* try to catch fish from it. **2.** to search for something in or under water or by reaching into something. **3.** (*informal*) to bring out or up in this way, *fished out his keys.* **4.** to try to obtain by hinting or indirect questioning, *fishing for information.* □ **fish cake,** a small cake of shredded fish and mashed potato. **fish-eye lens,** a very wide-angled lens producing a distorting effect. **fish finger,** a small oblong piece of fish in batter or breadcrumbs. **fish-hook** *n.* a barbed hook for catching fish. **fish-kettle** *n.* an oval pan for boiling fish. **fish-meal** *n.* ground dried fish used as a fertilizer. **fish-net** *adj.* (of fabric) made in a kind of open mesh. **fish out of water,** a person who is out of his element. **have other fish to fry,** to have more important business to attend to.

fisherman *n.* (*pl.* fishermen) **1.** a man who earns a living by fishing. **2.** one who goes fishing as a sport. □ **fisherman knit,** a kind of ribbed knitting.

fishery *n.* **1.** part of the sea where fishing is carried on. **2.** the business of fishing.

fishing *n.* trying to catch fish. **fishing-ground** *n.* an area used for fishing.

fishing-rod *n.* a long rod to which a line is attached, used for fishing. **fishing-tackle** *n.* equipment used in fishing.

fishmonger *n.* a shopkeeper who sells fish.

fish-plate *n.* one of two iron plates holding rails together.

fishy *adj.* (fishier, fishiest) **1.** like fish, smelling or tasting of fish. **2.** (*informal*) causing disbelief or suspicion, *a fishy story.* **fishiness** *n.*

fissile (fi-syl) *adj.* **1.** tending to split. **2.** capable of undergoing nuclear fission.

fission *n.* **1.** splitting of the nucleus of certain atoms, with release of energy. **2.** splitting or division of biological cells as a method of reproduction.

fissionable *adj.* capable of undergoing nuclear fission.

fissure (fish-er) *n.* a cleft made by splitting or separation of parts.

fist *n.* **1.** the hand when tightly closed, with the fingers bent into the palm. **2.** (*slang*) handwriting.

fisticuffs *n.* fighting with the fists.

fistula (fiss-tew-lă) *n.* **1.** a long pipe-like ulcer. **2.** an abnormal or surgically made passage in the body. **3.** a natural pipe or spout in whales, insects, etc.

fit¹ *n.* **1.** a brief spell of an illness or its symptoms, *a fit of coughing.* **2.** a sudden violent seizure of epilepsy, apoplexy, etc., with convulsions or loss of consciousness. **3.** an attack of strong feeling, *a fit of rage.* **4.** a short period of a certain feeling or activity, an impulse, *a fit of energy.* □ **in fits and starts**, in short bursts of activity, not steadily or regularly.

fit² *adj.* (fitter, fittest) **1.** suitable or well adapted for something, good enough. **2.** right and proper, fitting. **3.** feeling in a suitable condition to do something; *worked till they were fit to drop*, ready to drop from exhaustion. **4.** in good athletic condition or health, *fit as a fiddle.* —**fit** *v.* (fitted, fitting) **1.** to be the right shape and size for something. **2.** to put clothing on (a person) and adjust it to the right shape and size. **3.** to put into place, *fit a lock on the door.* **4.** to make or be suitable or competent, *his training fitted him for the position.* —*n.* the way a thing fits, *coat is a good fit.* —**fitly** *adv.*, **fitness** *n.* □ **fit in**, to make room or time etc. for; to be or cause to be harmonious or in a suitable relationship. **fit out** *or* **up**, to supply or equip. **fitted carpet**, one cut to fit the floor exactly. **see** *or* **think fit**, to decide or choose to do something, especially when this is unwise or without good reason.

fitful *adj.* occurring in short periods, not regularly or steadily. **fitfully** *adv.*

fitment *n.* a piece of fixed furniture.

fitter *n.* **1.** a person who supervises the fitting of clothes etc. **2.** a mechanic who fits together and adjusts the parts of machinery.

fitting *adj.* proper, suitable. —*n.* the process of having a garment etc. fitted. □ **fittings** *pl. n.* the fixtures and fitments of a building.

five *adj. & n.* one more than four (5, V). **five-star** *adj.* of the highest class.

fivefold *adj. & adv.* **1.** five times as much or as many. **2.** consisting of five parts.

fiver *n.* (*informal*) £5, a five-pound note.

fives *n.* a game in which a ball is struck with gloved hands or a bat against the walls of a court.

fix *v.* **1.** to fasten firmly. **2.** to implant (facts or ideas) firmly in the mind or memory. **3.** to direct (the eyes or attention) steadily. **4.** to establish, to specify, *fixed a time for the meeting; how are you fixed for cash,* what is your situation as regards money? **5.** to treat (a photographic image or a colour etc.) with a substance that prevents it from fading or changing colour. **6.** to repair. **7.** (*slang*) to deal with, to get even with. **8.** (*slang*) to use bribery or deception or improper influence on, to arrange (the result of a race etc.) fraudulently. **9.** (*slang*) to inject oneself with a narcotic. —**fix** *n.* **1.** (*informal*) an awkward situation, a dilemma, *be in a fix.* **2.** the finding of the position of a ship or aircraft etc. by taking bearings, the position found. **3.** (*slang*) an addict's dose of a narcotic drug. □ **fixed star**, an ordinary star, one that (unlike the sun and planets) is so far from the earth that it seems to have no motion of its own. **fix up**, to arrange; to organize; to provide for, *fixed him up for the night.*

fixation (fiks-ay-shŏn) *n.* **1.** fixing, being fixed. **2.** an abnormal emotional attachment to a person or thing. **3.** concentration on one idea, an obsession. □ **fixated** *adj.* having a fixation.

fixative *n.* **1.** a substance for keeping things in position. **2.** a substance for fixing colours etc., or for preventing perfumes from evaporating too quickly

fixedly (fiks-id-li) *adv.* in a fixed way.

fixer *n.* **1.** a person or thing that fixes something. **2.** a substance for fixing photographic images.

fixity *n.* a fixed state, stability, permanence.

fixture *n.* **1.** a thing that is fixed in position. **2.** a person or thing that is firmly established and unlikely to leave. **3.** a date appointed for a match or race etc., the match or race itself.

fizz *v.* to make a hissing or spluttering sound as when gas escapes in bubbles from a liquid. —*n.* **1.** this sound. **2.** a fizzy drink, *gin fizz*. —**fizzy** *adj.*, **fizziness** *n.*

fizzle *v.* to make a feeble fizzing sound. **fizzle out**, to end feebly or unsuccessfully.

fjord *n.* = fiord.

Fla. *abbrev.* Florida.

flab *n.* (*informal*) fat, flabbiness.

flabbergast *v.* to overwhelm with astonishment.

flabby *adj.* (flabbier, flabbiest) fat and limp, not firm. **flabbily** *adv.*, **flabbiness** *n.*

flaccid (**flak**-sid) *adj.* hanging loose or wrinkled, not firm. **flaccidly** *adv.*, **flaccidity** (flak-**sid**-iti) *n.*

flag¹ *n.* **1.** a piece of cloth attached by one edge to a staff or rope and used as the distinctive symbol of a country or as a signal. **2.** an oblong device used as a signal that a taxi is for hire. **3.** a small paper device resembling a flag. —**flag** *v.* (flagged, flagging) **1.** to mark out with flags. **2.** to signal with or as if with a flag; *flagged the vehicle down*, signalled to it to stop. □ **flag-day** *n.* a day on which money is raised for a cause by the sale of small paper flags to passers-by. **flag of convenience**, a foreign flag of the nationality under which a ship is registered to evade taxation or certain regulations.

flag² *v.* (flagged, flagging) **1.** to hang down limply, to droop. **2.** to lose vigour, to become weak, *interest flagged*.

flag³ *n.* a plant with blade-like leaves, especially an iris.

flag⁴ *n.* a flagstone. **flagged** *adj.* paved with flagstones.

flagellate (**flaj**-ěl-ayt) *v.* to whip. **flagellation** *n.*

flageolet (flaj-ŏ-**let**) *n.* **1.** a small pipe like a recorder. **2.** an organ stop producing a similar quality of sound.

flagon *n.* **1.** a large rounded bottle in which wine or cider etc. is sold, usually holding twice as much as an ordinary bottle. **2.** a vessel with a handle, lip, and lid for serving wine at the table.

flagrant (**flay**-gránt) *adj.* (of an offence or error or an offender) very bad and obvious. **flagrantly** *adv.*, **flagrancy** *n.*

flagship *n.* **1.** a ship that carries an admiral and flies his flag. **2.** the principal vessel of a shipping-line. **3.** a firm's best or most important product.

flagstone *n.* a flat slab of rock used for paving.

flail *n.* an old-fashioned tool for threshing grain, consisting of a strong stick hinged on a long handle. —*v.* **1.** to beat with or as

if with a flail. **2.** to wave or swing about wildly.

flair *n.* a natural ability to do something well or to select and recognize what is good or useful etc.

flak *n.* shells fired by anti-aircraft guns. **flak jacket**, a heavy protective jacket, reinforced with metal.

flake *n.* **1.** a small light flat piece of snow. **2.** a small thin leaf-like piece of something. **3.** dogfish or other shark sold as food. — **flake** *v.* **1.** to come off in flakes. **2.** to separate into flakes. —**flaky** *adj.* □ **flake out**, (*informal*) to faint or fall asleep from exhaustion.

flambé (**flahm**-bay) *adj.* (of food) covered with spirit and served alight.

flamboyant *adj.* **1.** coloured or decorated in a very showy way. **2.** (of people) having a very showy appearance or manner. **flamboyantly** *adv.*, **flamboyance** *n.*

flame *n.* **1.** a bright tongue-shaped portion of ignited gases burning visibly. **2.** bright red. **3.** passion, especially of love. — **flame** *v.* **1.** to burn with flames, to send out flames. **2.** to become bright red, *his face flamed with anger*. □ **flame gun**, a device that projects a flame for destroying weeds etc. **flame-tree** *n.* any of several trees with brilliant red or yellow flowers. **old flame**, (*informal*) a former sweetheart.

flamenco (flǎ-**menk**-oh) *n.* (*pl.* flamencos) a Spanish gypsy style of song or dance.

flaming *adj.* **1.** very hot or bright. **2.** (*informal*) damned, *that flaming cat*.

flamingo (flǎ-**ming**-oh) *n.* (*pl.* flamingoes) a long-legged wading bird with a long neck and pinkish feathers.

flammable *adj.* able to be set on fire. **flammability** *n.*

¶ See the note under inflammable.

flan *n.* an open pastry or sponge case filled with fruit or a savoury filling.

flange (*pr.* flanj) *n.* a projecting rim or edge.

flank *n.* **1.** the fleshy part of the side of the body between the last rib and the hip. **2.** the side of a building or mountain. **3.** the right or left side of a body of troops etc. —*v.* to place or be situated at the side of.

flannel *n.* **1.** a kind of loosely-woven woollen fabric. **2.** a cloth used for washing the face etc. **3.** (*slang*) nonsense, flattery, bragging. □ **flannels** *pl. n.* trousers made of flannel or similar fabric.

flannelette *n.* cotton fabric made to look and feel like flannel.

flap *v.* (flapped, flapping) **1.** to sway or be swayed up and down or from side to side, to wave about. **2.** to give a light blow with something flat, *flapped at a fly*. **3.** (*slang*) to get into a flap or panic. —**flap** *n*. **1**. the action or sound of flapping. **2**. a light blow with something flat. **3**. a broad piece hinged or attached at one side, a hinged or sliding section on an aircraft wing etc. used to control lift. **4**. (*slang*) a state of agitation or fuss, *he is in a flap*. □ **with ears flapping**, (*informal*) listening eagerly.

flapjack *n*. **1**. a kind of pancake. **2**. a sweet oatcake.

flare *v*. **1**. to blaze with a sudden irregular flame. **2**. to burst into sudden activity or anger, *tempers flared*. **3**. to widen gradually outwards. —**flare** *n*. **1**. a sudden outburst of flame. **2**. a device producing a flaring light as a signal or for illumination. **3**. a flared shape, a gradual widening. □ **flare up**, to become suddenly angry.

flash *v*. **1**. to give out a brief or intermittent bright light. **2**. to come suddenly into view or into the mind, *the idea flashed upon me*. **3**. to move rapidly, *the train flashed past*. **4**. (of water) to rush along, to rise and flow. **5**. to cause to shine briefly. **6**. to signal with a light or lights. **7**. to send (news etc.) by radio or telegraph. **8**. (*slang*) to expose one's genitals briefly in an indecent way. — **flash** *n*. **1**. a sudden burst of flame or light. **2**. a sudden showing of wit or feeling. **3**. a very brief time, *in a flash*. **4**. a rush of water. **5**. a brief news item sent out by radio etc. **6**. a device producing a brief bright light in photography. **7**. a coloured patch of cloth as an emblem on a military uniform etc. **8**. (*slang*) a brief act of indecent exposure. —*adj*. (*informal*) flashy. —**flasher** *n*. □ **flash bulb**, a bulb used in producing a flash of light for photography. **flash flood**, a sudden destructive flood. **flash in the pan**, something that makes a promising start and then fails. (¶ Originally an explosion of gunpowder in the 'pan' of an old gun without actually firing the charge.)

flashback *n*. the changing of the scene in a story or film to a scene at an earlier time.

flashing *n*. a strip of metal to prevent water entering at a joint in roofing etc.

flashlight *n*. an electric torch.

flashpoint *n*. **1**. the temperature at which vapour from oil etc. will ignite. **2**. the point at which anger is ready to break out.

flashy *adj*. showy, gaudy. **flashily** *adv.*, **flashiness** *n*.

flask *n*. **1**. a narrow-necked bottle. **2**. a vacuum flask.

flat *adj*. (flatter, flattest) **1**. horizontal, level. **2**. spread out, lying at full length. **3**. smooth and even, with a broad level surface and little depth, *a flat cap*. **4**. (of a tyre) deflated because of a puncture etc. **5**.

absolute, unqualified, *a flat refusal*. **6**. dull, monotonous. **7**. (of drink) having lost its effervescence. **8**. (of a battery etc.) unable to generate any more electric current. **9**. (in music) below the correct pitch; *D flat* etc., a semitone lower than the corresponding note or key of natural pitch. —**flat** *adv*. **1**. in a flat manner. **2**. (*informal*) completely, *am flat broke*. **3**. (*informal*) exactly, *in ten seconds flat*. **4**. below the correct pitch in music, *was singing flat*. —**flat** *n*. **1**. a flat thing or part, level ground. **2**. a set of rooms on one floor, used as a residence. **3**. *the flat*, the season of flat races for horses. **4**. (in music) a note that is a semitone lower than the corresponding one of natural pitch, the sign indicating this. — **flatly** *adv.*, **flatness** *n*. □ **fall flat**, to fail to win applause or appreciation.

flat-fish *n*. a type of fish with a flattened body, swimming on its side. **flat feet**, feet with less than the normal arch beneath. **flat-footed** *adj*. having flat feet; resolute; unprepared, *was caught flat-footed*. **flat-iron** *n*. a heavy iron heated by external means. **flat out**, at top speed; using all one's strength or resources. **flat race**, a race over level ground, as distinct from a hurdle-race or steeplechase. **flat rate**, a rate that is the same in all cases, not proportional.

flatlet *n*. a small flat (*see* flat *n.*, sense 2).

flatten *v*. to make or become flat.

flatter *v*. **1**. to compliment (a person) excessively or insincerely, especially in order to win favour. **2**. to gratify by honouring, *we were flattered to receive an invitation*. **3**. to represent (a person or thing) favourably in a portrait etc. so that good looks are exaggerated. **flatterer** *n*. □ **flatter oneself**, to please or delude oneself with a belief.

flattery *n*. **1**. flattering. **2**. excessive or insincere compliments.

flattish *adj*. rather flat.

flatulent (flat-yoo-lĕnt) *adj*. causing or suffering from the formation of gas in the digestive tract. **flatulence** *n*.

flatworm *n*. a type of worm with a flattened body.

flaunt *v*. **1**. to display proudly or ostentatiously. **2**. (of a flag etc.) to wave proudly. ¶ This word is sometimes used incorrectly in place of flout.

flautist (flaw-tist) *n*. a flute-player.

flavour *n*. **1**. a distinctive taste. **2**. a special quality or characteristic, *the story has a romantic flavour*. —*v*. to give a flavour to, to season.

flavouring *n*. a substance used to give flavour to food.

flaw *n.* an imperfection, a blemish. —*v.* to spoil with a flaw.

flawless *adj.* without a flaw. **flawlessly** *adv.*, **flawlessness** *n.*

flax *n.* **1.** a blue-flowered plant cultivated for the textile fibre obtained from its stem and for its seeds (linseed). **2.** its fibre.

flaxen *adj.* **1.** made of flax. **2.** pale yellow in colour like dressed flax, *flaxen hair.*

flay *v.* **1.** to strip off the skin or hide of. **2.** to criticize severely.

flea *n.* a small wingless jumping insect that feeds on human and animal blood. **fleabag** *n.* (*slang*) a sleeping-bag. **flea-bite** *n.* the bite of a flea; a trivial inconvenience or expense. **flea market**, (*humorous*) a street market. **with a flea in his ear**, (*informal*) with a stinging rebuke.

fleck *n.* **1.** a very small patch of colour. **2.** a small particle, a speck. □ **flecked** *adj.* marked with flecks.

fled *see* flee.

fledged *adj.* **1.** (of young birds) with fully grown wing feathers, able to fly. **2.** mature, trained and experienced, *a fully-fledged engineer.*

fledgeling *n.* a young bird that is just fledged.

flee *v.* (fled, fleeing) **1.** to run or hurry away. **2.** to run away from, *fled the country.* **3.** to pass away swiftly, to vanish, *all hope had fled.*

fleece *n.* **1.** the woolly hair of a sheep or similar animal. **2.** a soft fabric used for linings etc. —*v.* to defraud, to rob by trickery. —**fleecy** *adj.*

fleet[1] *n.* **1.** the naval force of a country, a number of warships under one commander. **2.** a number of ships or aircraft or buses etc. moving or working under one command or ownership.

fleet[2] *adj.* moving swiftly, nimble. **fleetly** *adv.*, **fleetness** *n.*

fleeting *adj.* passing quickly, brief, *a fleeting glimpse.*

Fleet Street London newspapers, the English national papers (most of which have headquarters in Fleet Street, London).

Flemish *adj.* of Flanders or its people or language. —*n.* the Flemish language.

flesh *n.* **1.** the soft substance of an animal body, consisting of muscle and fat. **2.** this tissue of animal bodies (excluding fish and sometimes fowl) as food. **3.** the body as opposed to mind or soul. **4.** the pulpy part of fruits and vegetables. □ **flesh and blood**, human nature, people with their emotions and weaknesses; *one's own flesh and blood*, relatives, descendants. **flesh-coloured** *adj.* yellowish pink. **flesh-**

wound *n.* a wound that does not reach a bone or vital organ. **in the flesh**, in bodily form, in person.

fleshy *adj.* **1.** of or like flesh. **2.** having much flesh, plump, (of plants or fruits etc.) pulpy. **fleshiness** *n.*

fleur-de-lis (fler-dĕ-lee) *n.* (*pl.* fleurs-de-lis) a design of three petal-like parts used in heraldry.

flew *see* fly[2].

flex[1] *v.* to bend (a joint or limb), to move (a muscle) so that it bends a joint.

flex[2] *n.* flexible insulated wire used for carrying electric current to a lamp, iron, etc.

flexible *adj.* **1.** able to bend easily without breaking. **2.** adaptable, able to be changed to suit circumstances. **flexibly** *adv.*, **flexibility** *n.*

flexion *n.* bending, a bent state, especially of a joint or limb.

flexitime, *n.* a system of flexible working hours.

flick *n.* a quick light blow or stroke e.g. with a whip. —*v.* to strike or remove with a quick light blow, to make a flicking movement. □ **flick knife** *n.* a weapon with a blade that springs out when a button is pressed. **flick through**, to turn over cards or pages etc. quickly.

flicker *v.* **1.** to burn or shine unsteadily. **2.** (of hope etc.) to occur briefly. **3.** to quiver, to move quickly to and fro. *n.* a flickering movement or light, a brief occurrence of hope etc.

flicks *pl. n.* (*informal*) a performance of films at a cinema.

flier *n.* = flyer.

flies *pl. n.* (*informal*) the fly fastening down the front of a pair of trousers (*see* fly[2] *n.*, sense 2).

flight[1] *n.* **1.** the process of flying, the movement or path of a thing through the air. **2.** a journey made by air, transport in an aircraft making a particular journey, *there are three flights a day to Rome.* **3.** a flock of birds or insects. **4.** a number of aircraft regarded as a unit, *an aircraft of the Queen's flight.* **5.** a series of stairs in a straight line or between two landings. **6.** swift passage (of time). **7.** an effort that is above the ordinary, *a flight of the imagination.* **8.** the feathers etc. on a dart or arrow. —**flight** *v.* **1.** to shoot (a bird etc.) while it is flying. **2.** to give (a ball etc.) a certain path through the air. □ **flight-deck** *n.* the cockpit of a large aircraft. **in the first** *or* **top flight**, taking a leading place, excellent of its kind.

flight[2] *n.* fleeing, running or going away. **put to flight**, to cause to flee. **take flight** *or* **take to flight**, to flee.

flightless *adj.* (of birds, e.g. penguins) non-flying.

flighty *adj.* (flightier, flightiest) (of a girl or woman) without a serious purpose or interest, frivolous. **flightiness** *n.*

flimsy *adj.* (flimsier, flimsiest) 1. light and thin, of loose structure, fragile. 2. unconvincing, *a flimsy excuse.* **flimsily** *adv.*, **flimsiness** *n.*

flinch *v.* 1. to draw back in fear, to wince. 2. to shrink from one's duty etc.

fling *v.* (flung, flinging) 1. to throw violently or angrily or hurriedly; *fling caution to the winds,* act rashly. 2. to put or send suddenly or forcefully, *flung him into prison.* 3. to rush, to go angrily or violently, *she flung out of the room.* —**fling** *n.* 1. the act or movement of flinging. 2. a kind of vigorous dance, *the Highland fling.* 3. a spell of indulgence in pleasure, *have one's fling.*

flint *n.* 1. a very hard kind of stone that can produce sparks when struck against steel. 2. a piece of this. 3. a piece of hard alloy used to produce a spark.

flintlock *n.* an old type of gun fired by a spark from a flint.

flinty *adj.* (flintier, flintiest) like flint, very hard.

flip *v.* (flipped, flipping) 1. to flick. 2. to toss (a thing) with a sharp movement so that it turns over in the air. 3. (*slang*) to show great anger. —**flip** *n.* 1. the action of flipping something. 2. (*informal*) a short flight in an aircraft. 3. a quick tour. □ **flip one's lid,** (*slang*) to show great anger. **flip side,** the reverse side of a gramophone record.

flippant *adj.* not showing proper seriousness. **flippantly** *adv.*, **flippancy** *n.*

flipper *n.* 1. a limb of certain sea animals (e.g. seals, turtles, penguins), used in swimming. 2. one of a pair of large flat rubber attachments worn on the feet for underwater swimming.

flipping *adj.* (*slang*) damned.

flirt *v.* 1. to pretend lightheartedly to court a person. 2. to toy, *flirted with the idea*; *flirting with death,* taking great risks. 3. to move (a thing) to and fro in short rapid jerks. —*n.* a person who flirts. —**flirtation** *n.*

flirtatious *adj.* flirting, fond of flirting. **flirtatiously** *adv.*

flit *v.* (flitted, flitting) 1. to fly or move lightly and quickly. 2. to decamp in a stealthy way. —*n.* a stealthy move of this kind.

flitch *n.* a side of bacon.

float *v.* 1. to rest or drift on the surface of a liquid without sinking, to be held up

freely in air or gas. 2. to cause to do this. 3. to move lightly or casually. 4. to have or allow (currency) to have a variable rate of exchange. 5. to launch (a business company or a scheme), especially by getting financial support from the sale of shares. —**float** *n.* 1. a thing designed to float on liquid, a cork or quill used on a fishingline to show when the bait has been taken, one of the corks supporting the edge of a fishing net. 2. a floating device to control the flow of water, petrol, etc. 3. a structure to enable an aircraft to float on water. 4. a low-bodied cart, a milk-float, a platform on wheels carrying a display in a procession. 5. a sum of money made available for minor expenditures or for giving change. □ **floating rib,** one of the ribs not joined to the breastbone. **floating voter,** a voter who is not attached to any political party.

floater *n.* 1. a thing that floats. 2. (*slang*) a blunder.

flock[1] *n.* 1. a number of sheep, goats, or birds kept together or feeding or travelling together. 2. a large number of people together. 3. a number of people in someone's charge, a Christian congregation. —*v.* to gather or go in a flock.

flock[2] *n.* 1. a tuft of wool or cotton etc. 2. wool or cotton waste used for stuffing mattresses etc., powdered wool or cloth. **flocked** *adj.* decorated with flock.

floe *n.* a sheet of floating ice.

flog *v.* (flogged, flogging) 1. to beat severely with a rod or whip, as a punishment. 2. (*slang*) to sell. **flogging** *n.*

flood *n.* 1. the coming of a great quantity of water over a place that is usually dry, the water itself; *the Flood,* that described in Genesis. 2. a great outpouring or outburst, *a flood of abuse.* 3. the inflow of the tide. —**flood** *v.* 1. to cover or fill with a flood, to overflow. 2. (of a river etc.) to become flooded. 3. to come in great quantities, *letters flooded in.* 4. to have a haemorrhage of the womb. □ **be flooded out,** to be forced to leave because of a flood. **flood-tide** *n.* the advancing tide.

floodgate *n.* a gate that can be opened or closed to control the flow of water, especially the lower gate of a lock.

floodlight *n.* a lamp used for producing a broad bright beam of light to light up a stage or building etc. —*v.* (floodlit, floodlighting) to illuminate with this.

floor *n.* 1. the lower surface of a room, the part on which one stands. 2. the bottom of the sea or of a cave etc. 3. (in legislative assemblies) the part of the assembly hall where members sit. 4. a minimum level for wages or prices. **5.** a storey of a building, all the rooms having a continuous floor. —**floor** v. **1.** to put a floor into (a building). **2.** to knock down (a person) in a fight. **3.** to baffle, to overwhelm (a person) with a problem or argument. □ **floor manager**, the stage manager of a TV production. **floor show**, an entertainment presented on the floor of a nightclub etc. **have the floor**, to have the right to speak next in a debate.

floorboard n. one of the boards forming the floor of a room.

floorcloth n. a cloth for washing floors.

flop v. (flopped, flopping) **1.** to hang or sway heavily and loosely. **2.** to fall or move or sit down clumsily. **3.** (slang) to be a failure. —**flop** n. **1.** a flopping movement or sound. **2.** (slang) a failure. —adv. with a flop.

floppy adj. (floppier, floppiest) hanging heavily and loosely, not firm or rigid. **floppiness** n. □ **floppy disc**, a flexible disc bearing machine-readable data.

flora n. the plants of an area or period of time.

floral adj. of flowers.

Florentine (flo-rĕn-tyn) adj. of Florence, a city of north Italy.

floribunda (flor-i-**bun**-dă) n. a rose or other plant bearing dense clusters of flowers.

florid (flo-rid) adj. **1.** elaborate and ornate. **2.** (of the complexion) ruddy.

Florida (flo-rid-ă) a State of the USA.

florin (flo-rin) n. **1.** a Dutch guilder. **2.** a former British coin worth two shillings.

florist (flo-rist) n. a person whose business is the selling or growing of flowers.

floss n. **1.** a mass of silky fibres. **2.** silk thread with little or no twist, used in embroidery. **flossy** adj.

flotation n. floating, especially the launching of a commercial venture.

flotilla (flŏ-**til**-ă) n. **1.** a small fleet. **2.** a fleet of boats or small ships.

flotsam n. wreckage found floating. **flotsam and jetsam**, odds and ends; vagrants, tramps, etc.

flounce[1] v. to go in an impatient annoyed manner, flounced out of the room. —n. a flouncing movement.

flounce[2] n. a deep frill of material sewn by its upper edge to a skirt etc. **flounced** adj. trimmed with a flounce.

flounder[1] n. a small edible flat-fish.

flounder[2] v. **1.** to move clumsily and with difficulty as in mud. **2.** to make mistakes or become confused when trying to do something.

flour n. fine meal or powder made from grain after the bran has been sifted out, used in cooking. —v. to cover or sprinkle with flour. —**floury** adj.

flourish v. **1.** to thrive in growth or development. **2.** to prosper, to be successful. **3.** (of famous people) to be alive and active at a certain time, Beethoven flourished in the early 19th century. **4.** to wave (a thing) dramatically. —**flourish** n. **1.** a dramatic sweeping gesture. **2.** a flowing ornamental curve in writing etc. **3.** a fanfare.

flout v. to disobey openly and scornfully. ¶ See the note under flaunt.

flow v. **1.** to glide along as a stream, to move freely like a liquid or gas. **2.** to proceed steadily and continuously, keep the traffic flowing. **3.** (of talk or literary style) to proceed smoothly and evenly. **4.** to hang loosely, (of a line or curve) to be smoothly continuous. **5.** to gush forth, (of the tide) to come in, to rise. **6.** to come (from a source), to be the result. —**flow** n. **1.** a flowing movement or mass. **2.** the amount that flows. **3.** an outpouring, a copious supply. **4.** the inward movement of the tide, towards the land, ebb and flow. □ **flow chart**, a diagram showing the movement of things through a series of processes, e.g. in manufacturing.

flower n. **1.** the part of a plant from which seed or fruit develops. **2.** a blossom and its stem for use as a decoration etc., usually in groups. **3.** a plant that is noticeable or cultivated for its fine flowers. **4.** the best part of something. —**flower** v. **1.** (of a plant) to produce flowers. **2.** to cause or allow (a plant) to produce flowers. □ **flowered** adj. ornamented with flowers. **flowers of sulphur**, a fine powder produced when sulphur evaporates and condenses. **in flower**, with the flowers out.

flowerless adj. (of plants) non-flowering.

flowerpot n. a pot in which a plant may be grown.

flowery adj. **1.** full of flowers. **2.** (of language) full of ornamental phrases.

flown see fly[2].

flu n. influenza.

fluctuate v. (of levels, prices, etc.) to vary irregularly, to rise and fall. **fluctuation** n.

flue n. **1.** a smoke-duct in a chimney. **2.** a channel for conveying heat.

fluent (floo-ĕnt) adj. **1.** (of a person) able to speak smoothly and readily. **2.** (of speech) coming smoothly and readily. **fluently** adv., **fluency** n.

fluff n. **1.** a light soft downy substance. **2.** (slang) a bungled attempt, a mistake in speaking. —**fluff** v. **1.** to shake into a soft mass. **2.** (slang) to bungle.

fluffy *adj.* (fluffier, fluffiest) having or covered with a soft mass of fur or fibres. **fluffiness** *n.*

fluid *n.* a substance that is able to flow freely as liquids and gases do. —*adj.* **1.** able to flow freely, not solid or rigid. **2.** (of a situation) not stable. —**fluidity** (floo-**id**-iti) *n.* ☐ **fluid ounce,** one twentieth of a pint; (*Amer.*) one sixteenth of an American pint.

fluke[1] *n.* an accidental stroke of good luck.

fluke[2] *n.* **1.** the broad triangular flat end of each arm of an anchor. **2.** the barbed head of a harpoon etc. **3.** one of the lobes of a whale's tail.

fluke[3] *n.* **1.** a kind of flat-fish, especially the flounder. **2.** a flatworm found as a parasite in sheep's liver.

flummox *v.* (*informal*) to baffle.

flung *see* fling.

flunk *v.* (*Amer. informal*) to fail, especially in an examination.

flunkey *n.* (*pl.* flunkeys) (*informal*) a liveried servant.

fluorescent (floo-er-**ess**-ĕnt) *adj.* (of substances) taking in radiations and sending them out in the form of light, (of lamps) containing such a substance, (of a screen) coated with this. **fluorescence** *n.*

fluoridation (floo-er-id-**ay**-shŏn) *n.* the addition of traces of fluoride to drinking-water to prevent or reduce tooth-decay.

fluoride *n.* a compound of fluorine and one other element.

fluorine (**floo**-er-een) *n.* a chemical element, a pale-yellow corrosive gas.

flurry *n.* **1.** a short sudden rush of wind or rain or snow. **2.** a commotion. **3.** a state of nervous agitation. —*v.* (flurried, flurrying) to fluster.

flush[1] *v.* **1.** to become red in the face because of a rush of blood to the skin. **2.** to cause (the face) to redden in this way. **3.** to fill with pride, *flushed with success.* **4.** to cleanse (a drain or lavatory etc.) with a flow of water, to dispose of in this way. **5.** (of water) to rush out in a flood. — **flush** *n.* **1.** flushing of the face, a blush. **2.** excitement caused by emotion, *the first flush of victory.* **3.** a rush of water. **4.** fresh growth of vegetation. —**flush** *adj.* **1.** level, in the same plane, without projections, *doors that are flush with the walls.* **2.** (*informal*) well supplied with money.

flush[2] *n.* (in poker) a hand of cards all of one suit. **straight flush,** a flush that is a straight sequence. **royal flush,** a straight flush headed by an ace.

flush[3] *v.* to cause (a bird) to fly up and away, to drive out.

fluster *v.* to make nervous and confused. —*n.* a flustered state.

flute *n.* **1.** a wind instrument consisting of a long pipe with holes stopped by fingers or keys and a mouth-hole at the side. **2.** an ornamental groove. —**flute** *v.* **1.** to play on the flute. **2.** to speak or utter in flute-like tones. **3.** to make ornamental grooves in.

fluting *n.* ornamental grooves.

flutter *v.* **1.** to move the wings hurriedly in flying or trying to fly. **2.** to wave or flap quickly and irregularly, (of the heart) to beat feebly and irregularly. —**flutter** *n.* **1.** a fluttering movement or beat. **2.** a state of nervous excitement. **3.** a stir, a sensation. **4.** (*informal*) a slight gamble, *have a flutter.* **5.** rapid variation in the pitch or loudness of reproduced sound.

flux *n.* **1.** a continuous succession of changes, *in a state of flux.* **2.** flowing, flowing out.

fly[1] *n.* **1.** a two-winged insect. **2.** a disease caused by one of various flies. **3.** a natural or artificial fly used as bait in fishing. ☐ **fly-blown** *adj.* (of meat etc.) tainted by flies' eggs. **fly-fishing** *n.* fishing with flies as bait. **fly in the ointment,** one small thing that spoils enjoyment. **fly-paper** *n.* a paper for trapping or poisoning flies. **fly-spray** *n.* a liquid to be sprayed from a canister etc. to kill flies. **like flies,** in large numbers, *dying like flies.* **there are no flies on him,** (*slang*) he is very astute.

fly[2] *v.* (flew, flown, flying) **1.** to move through the air by means of wings as a bird does. **2.** to travel through the air or through space. **3.** to travel in an aircraft. **4.** to direct or control the flight of (an aircraft etc.), to transport in an aircraft. **5.** to raise (a flag) so that it waves, (of a flag) to wave in the air. **6.** to make (a kite) rise and stay aloft. **7.** to go or move quickly, to rush along, (of time) to pass quickly. **8.** to be scattered violently, *sparks flew in all directions.* **9.** to become angry etc. quickly, *flew into a rage.* **10.** to flee from, *must fly the country.* —**fly** *n.* **1.** flying. **2.** a flap of material on a garment to contain or cover a fastening, a flap at the entrance of a tent. **3.** a speed-regulating device in clockwork or machinery. ☐ **fly a kite,** (*informal*) to do something in order to test public opinion. **fly at,** to attack violently, either physically or with words. **fly-by-night** *n.* one who makes night excursions or decamps by night. **fly-half** *n.* a stand-off half in Rugby football. **fly high,** to behave very ambitiously. **fly in the face of,** to disregard or disobey openly. **fly off the handle,** (*informal*) to become uncontrollably angry. **fly-past** *n.* a ceremonial flight of aircraft past a person or place. **send flying,** to knock (a person or thing) violently aside.

fly[3] *adj. (slang)* astute, knowing.

flycatcher *n.* a bird that catches insects in the air.

flyer *n.* **1.** a bird etc. that flies. **2.** an animal or vehicle that moves very fast. **3.** an airman. **4.** a high-flyer.

flying *adj.* able to fly. **flying buttress,** a buttress that springs from a separate structure, usually forming an arch with the wall it supports. **flying colours,** great credit gained in a test etc., *passed with flying colours.* **flying fish,** a tropical fish with wing-like fins, able to rise into the air. **flying fox,** a fruit-eating bat. **flying leap,** a forward leap made while moving swiftly. **flying picket,** a picket organized for moving from place to place. **flying saucer,** an unidentified saucer-shaped object reported as seen in the sky. **flying squad,** a detachment of police etc. organized for rapid movement. **flying start,** a vigorous start giving one an initial advantage. **flying tackle,** a tackle in football etc. made while running or jumping. **flying visit,** a brief or hasty visit.

flyleaf *n.* a blank leaf at the beginning or end of a book etc.

flyover *n.* a bridge that carries one road or railway over another.

flysheet *n.* a circular etc. with two or four pages.

flyweight *n.* a boxing-weight (51 kg) below bantamweight.

flywheel *n.* a heavy wheel revolving on a shaft to regulate machinery.

foal *n.* the young of a horse or of a related animal. —*v.* to give birth to a foal. □ **in foal,** (of a mare) pregnant.

foam *n.* **1.** a collection of small bubbles formed in or on a liquid. **2.** the froth of saliva or perspiration. **3.** rubber or plastic in a light spongy form. —*v.* to form or send out foam. —**foamy** *adj.*

fob[1] *n.* an ornament worn hanging from a watch-chain etc., a tab on a key-ring.

fob[2] *v.* (fobbed, fobbing) **fob off,** to palm (a thing) off, to get (a person) to accept something of little or no value instead of what he is seeking.

focal *adj.* of or at a focus.

fo'c's'le (fohk-sŭl) *n.* = forecastle.

focus (foh-kŭs) *n.* (*pl.* focuses *or* foci, *pr.* foh-sy) **1.** the point at which rays meet or from which they appear to proceed. **2.** the point or distance at which an object is most clearly seen by the eye or through a lens. **3.** an adjustment on a lens to produce a clear image at varying distances. **4.** a centre of activity or interest etc. —**focus**

v. (focused, focusing) **1.** to adjust the focus of (a lens or the eye). **2.** to bring into focus. **3.** to concentrate or be concentrated or directed (on a centre etc.). □ **in** *or* **out of focus,** seen or not seen sharply by the eye or a lens.

fodder *n.* dried food, hay, etc. for horses and farm animals.

foe *n.* an enemy.

foetal (fee-t'l) *adj.* of a foetus.

foetus (fee-tŭs) *n.* (*pl.* foetuses) a developed embryo in the womb or egg, a human embryo more than 8 weeks after conception.

fog *n.* **1.** thick mist that is difficult to see through. **2.** cloudiness on a photographic negative etc., obscuring the image. —**fog** *v.* (fogged, fogging) **1.** to cover or become covered with fog or condensed vapour. **2.** to cause cloudiness on (a negative etc.). **3.** to bewilder, to perplex. □ **fog-horn** *n.* a sounding instrument for warning ships in fog. **fog-lamp** *n.* a lamp for use on a car etc. in fog.

fogey *n.* (*pl.* fogies) a person with old-fashioned ideas, *an old fogey.*

foggy *adj.* (foggier, foggiest) **1.** full of fog. **2.** made opaque by condensed vapour etc., clouded. **3.** obscure, vague, *only a foggy idea.* **fogginess** *n.* □ **not the foggiest,** (*informal*) no idea at all.

foible (foi-bŭl) *n.* a harmless peculiarity in a person's character.

foil[1] *n.* **1.** metal hammered or rolled into a thin sheet, *tin foil.* **2.** a person or thing that contrasts strongly with another and therefore makes the other's qualities more obvious.

foil[2] *v.* to thwart, to frustrate.

foil[3] *n.* a long thin sword with a button on the point, used in fencing.

foist *v.* to cause a person to accept (something inferior or unwelcome or undeserved), *the job was foisted on us.*

fold[1] *v.* **1.** to bend or turn (a flexible thing) so that one part lies on another, to close or flatten by pressing parts together. **2.** to become folded, to be able to be folded. **3.** to clasp (the arms etc.) about, to hold (a person or thing) close to one's breast. **4.** to envelop. **5.** to blend (an ingredient) in cooking by spooning one part over another. **6.** to collapse, to cease to function, *the business had folded* or *folded up.* —**fold** *n.* **1.** a folded part, a hollow between two thicknesses. **2.** a line made by folding. **3.** a hollow among hills or mountains. □ **fold one's arms,** to place them together or entwined across one's chest. **fold one's hands,** to clasp or place them together.

fold[2] *n.* **1.** an enclosure for sheep. **2.** an

established body of people with the same beliefs or aims, the members of a Church. □ **return to the fold**, to rejoin such a group.

folder *n.* **1.** a folding cover for loose papers. **2.** a folded leaflet.

foliage (foh-li-ij) *n.* the leaves of a tree or plant.

folic acid (foh-lik) a vitamin of the B-group, deficiency of which causes anaemia.

folio (foh-li-oh) *n.* (*pl.* folios) **1.** a large sheet of paper folded once, making two leaves of a book. **2.** a book made of such sheets, the largest-sized volume. **3.** the page-number of a printed book.

folk *n.* **1.** people in general. **2.** the people of a certain group or nation etc., *country folk.* **3.** one's relatives. □ **folk-dance, folk song** etc., a dance, song, etc., in the traditional style of a country.

folklore *n.* the traditional beliefs and tales etc. of a community.

folksy *adj.* **1.** simple in manner. **2.** friendly, sociable.

folkweave *n.* a kind of loosely-woven fabric used chiefly for furnishings.

follicle (fol-i-kŭl) *n.* a very small sac or cavity in the body, especially one containing a hair-root.

follow *v.* **1.** to go or come after. **2.** to go along (a path or road etc.). **3.** to provide with a sequel or successor. **4.** to take as a guide or leader or example; *follow the fashion*, conform to it. **5.** to grasp the meaning of, to understand. **6.** to take an interest in the progress of (events, a team, etc.). **7.** to happen as a result, to result from. **8.** to be necessarily true in consequence of something else. □ **follow on**, (of a side in cricket) to be compelled by the lowness of the score to bat again immediately after the first innings. **follow-on** *n.* an example of this. **follow one's nose**, to be guided by instinct. **follow suit**, to play a card of the suit led; to follow a person's example. **follow up**, to add a further action or blow etc. to a previous one; to perform further work or investigation etc. upon. **follow-up** *n.*

follower *n.* **1.** one who follows. **2.** a person who believes in or supports a religion or teacher or cause etc.

following *n.* a body of believers or supporters. —*adj.* now to be mentioned, *answer the following questions.* —*prep.* as a sequel to, after, *following the fall of sterling, prices rose sharply.* ¶ Many people regard this use as unacceptable. It should always be avoided when it obscures the meaning, as in *police arrested a man following the hunt.*

folly *n.* **1.** foolishness, a foolish act. **2.** a costly ornamental building serving no practical purpose.

foment (fŏ-ment) *v.* to arouse or stimulate (trouble, discontent, etc.).

fomentation (foh-men-tay-shŏn) *n.* **1.** fomenting. **2.** hot lotion applied to part of the body to relieve pain or inflammation.

fond *adj.* **1.** affectionate, loving. **2.** over-affectionate, doting. **3.** (of hopes) cherished but unlikely to be fulfilled. **fondly** *adv.*, **fondness** *n.* □ **fond of**, having a liking for; much inclined to.

fondant *n.* a soft sweet made of flavoured sugar.

fondle *v.* to touch or stroke lovingly.

fondue (fon-dew) *n.* a dish of flavoured melted cheese.

font *n.* a basin or vessel (often of carved stone) in a church, to hold water for baptism.

fontanelle (fon-tăn-el) *n.* a space under the skin on the top of an infant's head where the bones of the skull have not yet grown together.

food *n.* **1.** any substance that can be taken into the body of an animal or plant to maintain its life and growth. **2.** a solid substance of this kind, *food and drink.* □ **food for thought**, something that needs thinking about. **food poisoning**, illness caused by bacteria or toxins in food. **food processor**, an electrically driven device with blades for mixing or slicing food. **food value**, the nourishing power of a food.

foodstuff *n.* a substance used as food.

fool *n.* **1.** a person who acts unwisely, one who lacks good sense or judgement. **2.** a jester or clown in a household during the Middle Ages. **3.** a creamy pudding of fruit purée mixed with cream or custard. —**fool** *v.* **1.** to behave in a joking or teasing way. **2.** to play about idly. **3.** to trick or deceive (a person). □ **fool's errand**, a useless errand. **fool's paradise**, happiness that is based on an illusion. **make a fool of**, to make (a person) look foolish, to trick or deceive.

foolery *n.* foolish acts or behaviour.

foolhardy *adj.* bold but rash, delighting in taking unnecessary risks. **foolhardiness** *n.*

foolish *adj.* **1.** lacking good sense or judgement. **2.** (of actions) unwise. **3.** ridiculous, *felt foolish.* **foolishly** *adv.*, **foolishness** *n.*

foolproof *adj.* **1.** (of rules or instructions) plain and simple and unable to be misinterpreted. **2.** (of machinery) very simple to operate.

foolscap *n.* a large size of writing-paper. ¶ So called from the use of a *fool's cap* (a jester's cap with bells) as a watermark.

foot *n.* (*pl.* feet) **1.** the end part of the leg below the ankle. **2.** a similar part in animals, used in moving or for attaching the animal to things. **3.** the lower end of a table or bed etc., the end opposite the head. **4.** the part of a stocking covering the foot. **5.** a person's step or tread or pace of movement, *fleet of foot.* **6.** a lower usually projecting part of something (e.g. of a table-leg), the part of a sewing-machine that is lowered on to the material to hold it steady. **7.** the lowest part of something that has height or length, the bottom of a hill, ladder, page, list, etc. **8.** a measure of length, = 12 inches (30·48 cm). (¶ Correct usage is *a ten-foot pole; it is ten feet long.*) **9.** a unit of rhythm in a line of poetry, containing a stressed syllable, e.g. each of the four divisions in *Jack/and Jill/went up/the hill.* —**foot** *v.* to walk not ride, *shall have to foot it.* □ **feet of clay,** a great weakness, in a person or thing that is honoured. **foot-and-mouth disease,** a contagious disease of cattle etc., causing ulceration of the mouth and feet. **Foot Guards,** the infantry regiments of the Household troops. **foot the bill,** to be the one responsible for paying the bill. **have a foot in both camps,** to be a member of each of two opposing factions. **have one foot in the grave,** to be nearing death or very old. **my foot!,** an exclamation of scornful contradiction. **on foot,** walking not riding. **to one's feet,** to a standing position. **under foot,** on the ground, in a position to be trodden on. **under one's feet,** in danger of being trodden on, in the way.

footage *n.* a length measured in feet, especially of exposed cinema or TV film.

football *n.* **1.** a large round or elliptical inflated leather ball. **2.** a game played with this on a field, between two teams of players. □ **footballer** *n.* one who plays football. **footballing** *n.* playing football. **football pool,** a form of gambling on the results of a number of football matches.

foot-bridge *n.* a bridge for pedestrians, not for traffic.

footfall *n.* the sound of a footstep.

foothill *n.* one of the low hills near the bottom of a mountain or range.

foothold *n.* **1.** a place just wide enough for a foot to be placed on when climbing etc. **2.** a small but secure position gained in a business etc.

footing *n.* **1.** a placing of the feet, a foothold; *lost his footing,* slipped. **2.** a status, conditions, *they were on a friendly footing; put the army on a war footing.*

footlights *pl. n.* a row of lights along the front of a stage floor.

footling (foo-tling) *adj.* (*slang*) trivial, petty.

footloose *adj.* independent, without responsibilities.

footman *n.* (*pl.* footmen) a manservant (usually in livery) who admits visitors, waits at table, etc.

footmark *n.* a footprint.

foot-muff *n.* a bag lined with fur etc. into which both feet are thrust to keep them warm.

footnote *n.* a note printed at the bottom of a page.

footpath *n.* a path for pedestrians, a pavement.

footplate *n.* a platform for the driver and fireman in a locomotive.

footprint *n.* an impression left by a foot or shoe.

foot-slog *v.* (foot-slogged, foot-slogging) (*informal*) to walk, to march.

footsore *adj.* having feet that are sore from walking.

footstep *n.* a step taken in walking, the sound of this. □ **follow in someone's footsteps,** to do as an earlier person did.

footstool *n.* a stool for resting the feet on when sitting.

footwear *n.* shoes and stockings.

footwork *n.* the manner of moving or using the feet in dancing, boxing, football, etc.

foozle *v.* (*slang*) to bungle.

fop *n.* a dandy.

for *prep.* **1.** in place of. **2.** as the price or penalty of, *was fined for speeding.* **3.** in defence or support or favour of. **4.** with a view to, in order to find or obtain, *went for a walk; looking for a job.* **5.** with regard to, in respect of, *ready for dinner.* **6.** in the direction of, *set out for home.* **7.** intended to be received by or belong to, *bought shoes for the children.* **8.** so as to happen at a stated time, *an appointment for two o'clock* **9.** because of, on account of, *famous for its cider.* **10.** to the extent or duration of, *walked for two miles; it will last for years.* —**for** *conj.* because, *they hesitated, for they were afraid.* □ **be for it,** (*slang*) to be about to meet with punishment or trouble. **for ever,** for all time; continually, repeatedly, *he is for ever complaining.*

forage (*rhymes with* porridge) *n.* **1.** food for horses and cattle. **2.** foraging. —*v.* to go searching, to rummage.

foray (fo-ray) *n.* a sudden attack or raid, especially to obtain something.

forbade *see* forbid.

forbear *v.* (forbore, forborne, forbearing) to refrain, to refrain from, *could not for-*

bear criticizing or *from criticizing*; *forbore to mention it.*

forbearance *n.* patience, tolerance.

forbearing *adj.* & *n.* being patient or tolerant.

forbid *v.* (forbade (*pr.* for-**bad**), forbidden, forbidding) **1.** to order (a person) not to do something or not to enter, *forbid him to go*; *forbid him the court.* **2.** to refuse to allow, *forbid the marriage*; *he is forbidden wine*, not allowed to drink it.

forbidding *adj.* looking unfriendly or un-inviting, stern.

force *n.* **1.** strength, power, intense effort. **2.** (in scientific use) a measurable influence tending to cause movement of a body, its intensity. **3.** a body of troops or police. **4.** a body of people organized or available for a purpose, *a labour force.* **5.** compulsion. **6.** effectiveness, legal validity, *the new rules come into force next week.* —**force** *v.* **1.** to use force in order to get or do something, to compel, to oblige. **2.** to exert force on, to break open by force, *forced the lock.* **3.** to strain to the utmost, to overstrain. **4.** to impose, to inflict; *force a card on someone*, make him select a particular one by trickery. **5.** to cause or produce by effort, *forced a smile.* **6.** to cause (plants etc.) to reach maturity earlier than is normal. □ **force a person's hand**, to compel him to take action. **forced march**, a lengthy march requiring special effort by troops etc. **force-land** *v.* to make a **forced landing**, an emergency landing of an aircraft. **force the issue**, to make an immediate decision necessary. **force the pace**, to adopt a high speed in a race etc. and so tire out others who are taking part.

force-feed *v.* (force-fed, force-feeding) to feed (a prisoner etc.) against his will.

forceful *adj.* powerful and vigorous, effective. **forcefully** *adv.*, **forcefulness** *n.*

forcemeat *n.* finely-chopped meat seasoned and used as stuffing.

forceps (for-seps) *n.* (*pl.* forceps) pincers or tongs used by dentists, surgeons, etc. for gripping things.

forcible *adj.* done by force, forceful. **forcibly** *adv.*

ford *n.* a shallow place where a river may be crossed by wading or riding or driving through. —*v.* to cross in this way.

fordable *adj.* able to be forded.

fore *adj.* situated in front. —*adv.* in or at or towards the front. —*n.* the fore part. —*int.* a cry to warn a person who may be hit by a golf ball that is about to be played. □ **fore-and-aft** *adj.* (of sails) set lengthwise

on a ship or boat (as opposed to *square-rigged*). **to the fore,** in front; conspicuous.

forearm [1] *n.* the arm from elbow to wrist or fingertips.

forearm [2] *v.* to arm or prepare in advance against possible danger etc.

forebears *pl. n.* ancestors.

forebode *v.* to be an advance sign or token of (trouble). **foreboding** *n.* a feeling that trouble is coming.

forecast *v.* (forecast, forecasting) to tell in advance (what is likely to happen). —*n.* a statement that forecasts something.

forecastle (**fohk**-sŭl) *n.* the forward part of certain ships, where formerly the crew had their accommodation.

foreclose *v.* **1.** (of a firm etc. that has lent money on mortgage) to take possession of property when the loan is not duly repaid, *the Bank decided to foreclose* or *to foreclose the mortgage.* **2.** to bar from a privilege. **foreclosure** *n.*

forecourt *n.* **1.** an enclosed space in front of a building, an outer court. **2.** the outer part of a filling station where petrol is sold.

forefathers *pl. n.* ancestors.

forefinger *n.* the finger next to the thumb.

forefoot *n.* (*pl.* forefeet) an animal's front foot.

forefront *n.* the very front.

foregoing *adj.* preceding, previously mentioned.

foregone conclusion a result that can be foreseen easily and with certainty.

foreground *n.* **1.** the part of a scene or picture that is nearest to an observer. **2.** the most conspicuous position.

forehand *adj.* **1.** (of a stroke in tennis etc.) played with the palm of the hand turned forwards. **2.** on the side on which this is made. —*n.* a forehand stroke.

forehead (fo-rid *or* for-hed) *n.* the part of the face above the eyes.

foreign *adj.* **1.** of or in or from another country, not of one's own country. **2.** dealing with or involving other countries, *foreign affairs.* **3.** not belonging naturally, *jealousy is foreign to her nature.* **4.** coming from outside, *a foreign body in the eye.* □ **Foreign Legion,** *see* legion. **Foreign Secretary,** the head of the British government department dealing with foreign affairs.

foreigner *n.* a person who was born in or comes from another country.

foreknowledge *n.* knowledge of something before it occurs.

foreland *n.* a cape or promontory.

foreleg *n.* an animal's front leg.

forelock *n.* a lock of hair just above the forehead.

foreman *n.* (*pl.* foremen) **1.** a workman whose job is to superintend other workmen. **2.** a man acting as president and spokesman of a jury.

foremast *n.* the mast nearest to the bow in a sailing-ship.

foremost *adj.* **1.** most advanced in position or rank. **2.** most important. —*adv.* in the foremost position etc.

forename *n.* a person's first name, a Christian name.

forensic (fer-en-sik) *adj.* **1.** of or used in lawcourts. **2.** of or involving **forensic medicine**, the medical knowledge needed in legal matters or police investigations (e.g. in a poisoning case).

foreordain *v.* to destine beforehand, *it was foreordained by God.*

forerunner *n.* a person or thing that comes in advance of another which it foreshadows.

foresee *v.* (foresaw, foreseen, foreseeing) to be aware of or realize (a thing) before-hand.

foreseeable *adj.* able to be foreseen; *the foreseeable future*, the period during which the course of events can be predicted.

foreshadow *v.* to be a sign of (something that is to come).

fore-sheets *n.* the forward part of a sailing-boat.

foreshore *n.* the shore between high-water mark and low-water mark, or between water and land that is cultivated or built on.

foreshorten *v.* to represent (an object, when drawing it) with shortening of certain lines to give an effect of distance, to cause such an effect in.

foresight *n.* the ability to foresee and prepare for future needs.

foreskin *n.* the loose skin at the end of the penis.

forest *n.* trees and undergrowth covering a large area. **forested** *adj.* covered in forest.

forestall *v.* to prevent or foil (a person or his plans) by taking action first.

forestay *n.* a stay from the head of the mast or foremast to a ship's deck.

forester *n.* an officer in charge of a forest or of growing timber.

forestry *n.* the science or practice of planting and caring for forests.

foretaste *n.* an experience of something in advance of what is to come.

foretell *v.* (foretold, foretelling) to forecast, to prophesy.

forethought *n.* careful thought and planning for the future.

forever *adv.* (*Amer.*) for ever.

forewarn *v.* to warn beforehand.

forewoman *n.* (*pl.* forewomen) **1.** a woman whose job is to superintend other workers. **2.** a woman acting as president and spokesman of a jury.

foreword *n.* introductory remarks at the beginning of a book, usually written by someone other than the author.

forfeit (for-fit) *n.* something that has to be paid or given up as a penalty. —*adj.* paid or given up in this way. —*v.* to pay or give up as a forfeit.

forfeiture (for-fi-cher) *n.* forfeiting.

forgather *v.* to assemble.

forge[1] *v.* to make one's way forward by effort, *forged ahead.*

forge[2] *n.* **1.** a workshop with a fire and an anvil where metals are heated and shaped, especially one used by a smith for shoeing horses and working iron. **2.** a furnace or hearth for melting or refining metal, the workshop containing it. —**forge** *v.* **1.** to shape by heating in fire and hammering. **2.** to make an imitation or copy of (a thing) in order to pass it off fraudulently as real. —**forger** *n.*

forgery *n.* **1.** forging, imitating fraudulently. **2.** something forged.

forget *v.* (forgot, forgotten, forgetting) **1.** to lose remembrance of (a thing or duty etc.). **2.** to put out of one's mind, to stop thinking about, *decided to forget our quarrels.* □ **forget oneself**, to behave without suitable dignity.

forgetful *adj.* tending to forget things. **forgetfulness** *n.*

forget-me-not *n.* a plant with small blue flowers.

forgive *v.* (forgave, forgiven, forgiving) to cease to feel angry or bitter towards (a person) or about (an offence). **forgiveness** *n.*

forgo *v.* (forwent, forgone, forgoing) to give up, to go without.

fork *n.* **1.** a pronged instrument used in eating or cooking. **2.** a pronged agricultural implement used for digging or lifting things. **3.** a thing shaped like this. **4.** a place where something separates into two or more parts, one of these parts. —**fork** *v.* **1.** to lift or dig with a fork. **2.** (of an object or road etc.) to form a fork by separating into two branches. **3.** (of a person) to follow one of these branches, *fork left.* □ **fork out**, (*slang*) to hand over, to pay out money.

fork-lift truck a truck with a fork-like mechanical device for lifting and moving heavy objects.

forlorn *adj.* left alone and unhappy.

forlornly *adv.* □ **forlorn hope,** the only faint hope left.

form *n.* **1.** the shape of something, its outward or visible appearance. **2.** its structure. **3.** a person or animal as it can be seen or touched. **4.** the way in which a thing exists, *ice is a form of water.* **5.** a class in a school. **6.** a fixed or usual method of doing something, a formality, a set order of words in a ritual etc. **7.** a document with blank spaces that are to be filled in with information. **8.** (of a horse or athlete) condition of health and training; *is in good form,* performing well, (of a person) in good spirits. **9.** details of previous performances, *study form before betting.* **10.** (*slang*) a criminal record, *has he got form?* **11.** a bench. **12.** a hare's lair. —**form** *v.* **1.** to shape, to mould, to produce or construct. **2.** to bring into existence, to constitute, *form a committee.* **3.** to take shape, to become solid, *icicles formed.* **4.** to develop in the mind, *formed a plan; formed a habit,* developed it. **5.** to arrange in a certain formation.

formal *adj.* **1.** conforming to accepted rules or customs, showing or requiring formality, *a formal greeting* or *party.* **2.** outward, *only a formal resemblance.* **3.** regular or geometrical in design, *formal gardens.* **formally** *adv.*

formaldehyde (for-**mal**-di-hyd) *n.* a colourless gas used in solution as a preservative and disinfectant.

formality (for-**mal**-iti) *n.* **1.** strict observance of rules and conventions. **2.** a formal act, something required by law or custom, *legal formalities; it's just a formality,* is done only to comply with a rule.

formalize *v.* to make formal or official. **formalization** *n.*

format (for-mat) *n.* **1.** the shape and size of a book etc. **2.** style of arrangement or procedure. **3.** an arrangement of data etc. for processing or storage by computer. — *v.* (formatted, formatting) to arrange in a format, especially for a computer. **formatter** *n.*

formation *n.* **1.** forming, being formed. **2.** a thing formed. **3.** a particular arrangement or order.

formative (form-ātiv) *adj.* forming something; *a child's formative years,* while its character is being formed.

former *adj.* **1.** of an earlier period, *in former times.* **2.** mentioned before another; *the former,* the one mentioned first of two. (¶When referring to the first of three or more, *the first,* not *the former,* should be used.).

formerly *adv.* in former times.

Formica (for-**my**-kǎ) *n.* (*trade mark*) a hard heat-resistant plastic used on surfaces.

formic acid a colourless acid contained in fluid emitted by ants.

formidable (for-mid-ǎbǔl) *adj.* **1.** inspiring fear or awe. **2.** difficult to do or overcome, *a formidable task.* **formidably** *adv.*

formless *adj.* without distinct or regular form.

formula (form-yoo-lǎ) *n.* (*pl.* formulas *or* in scientific usage formulae, *pr.* **form**-yoolee) **1.** a fixed series of words, especially one used on social or ceremonial occasions. **2.** a list of ingredients for making something; *diplomats seeking a formula,* a set of statements that can be agreed on, e.g. in order to produce a peace treaty. **3.** a set of chemical symbols showing the constituents of a substance. **4.** a mathematical rule or statement expressed in algebraic symbols. **5.** the classification of a racing car, especially by its engine capacity.

formulate *v.* to express clearly and exactly. **formulation** *n.*

fornicate (**for**-ni-kayt) *v.* (of unmarried people) to have sexual intercourse voluntarily. **fornication** *n.,* **fornicator** *n.*

forsake *v.* (forsook, forsaken, forsaking) **1.** to give up, to renounce, *forsaking their former way of life.* **2.** to withdraw one's help or friendship or companionship from, *forsook his wife and children.*

forswear *v.* (forswore, forsworn, forswearing) to give up doing or using something, to renounce.

forsythia (for-**syth**-iǎ) *n.* a shrub with yellow flowers, blooming in spring.

fort *n.* a fortified building or position.

forte[1] (**for**-ti) *n.* a person's strong point.

forte[2] (**for**-ti) *adv.* (in music) loudly.

forth *adv.* **1.** out. **2.** onwards, forwards, *from this day forth.* □ **and so forth,** and so on. **back and forth,** to and fro.

forthcoming *adj.* **1.** about to come forth or appear; *forthcoming events,* things about to take place. **2.** made available when needed, *money was not forthcoming.* **3.** (*informal*) willing to give information, *the girl was not very forthcoming.*

forthright *adj.* frank, outspoken.

forthwith *adv.* immediately.

fortieth *see* forty.

fortification *n.* **1.** fortifying. **2.** a wall or building constructed to defend a place.

fortify *v.* (fortified, fortifying) **1.** to strengthen (a place) against attack, especially by constructing fortifications. **2.** to strengthen (a person) mentally or morally, to increase the vigour of. **3.** to increase the food value of (bread etc.) by adding vitamins, to strengthen (wine, e.g. sherry) with alcohol.

fortissimo *adv.* (in music) very loudly.

fortitude *n.* courage in bearing pain or trouble.

fortnight *n.* a period of two weeks. **fortnightly** *adv.* & *adj.* happening or appearing once a fortnight.

FORTRAN *n.* a high-level computer language used in scientific work. (¶ From the first letters of *For*mula *Tra*nslation.)

fortress *n.* a fortified building or town.

fortuitous (for-tew-it-ŭs) *adj.* happening by chance. **fortuitously** *adv.*

fortunate *adj.* having or bringing or brought by good fortune. **fortunately** *adv.*

fortune *n.* **1.** the events that chance brings to a person or undertaking. **2.** chance as a power in the affairs of mankind. **3.** a person's destiny. **4.** prosperity, success, *seek one's fortune.* **5.** a great amount of wealth, *left him a fortune.* □ **fortuneteller** *n.* a person who claims to foretell future events in people's lives. **tell fortunes**, to be a fortune-teller.

forty *adj.* & *n.* four times ten (40, XL). **fortieth** *adj.* & *n.* □ **forties** *pl. n.* the numbers or years or degrees of temperature from 40 to 49. **forty winks**, a nap.

forum *n.* a place or meeting where a public discussion is held.

forward *adj.* **1.** directed or moving towards the front, situated in the front. **2.** of or relating to the future, *forward buying.* **3.** having made more than the normal progress. **4.** too bold in one's manner, presumptuous. —*n.* an attacking player near the front in football or hockey (= striker), his position. —*adv.* forwards, in advance, ahead, towards the future. —**forward** *v.* **1.** to send on (a letter etc.) to a new address. **2.** to send or dispatch (goods) to a customer. **3.** to help to advance (a person's interests). — **forwardness** *n.*

forwards *adv.* **1.** towards the front, onward so as to make progress. **2.** with the front foremost.

forwent *see* forgo.

fosse *n.* a long ditch or trench, especially in fortification.

fossick *v.* (*Austral.* & *N.Z. slang*) to rummage, to search.

fossil *n.* **1.** the remains or traces of a prehistoric animal or plant once buried in earth and now hardened like rock. **2.** a person who is out of date and unable to accept new ideas. □ **fossil fuel**, coal etc. formed in the geological past, especially as distinguished from nuclear fuel.

fossilize *v.* to turn or be turned into a fossil. **fossilization** *n.*

foster *v.* **1.** to promote the growth or development of. **2.** to take care of and bring up (a child that is not one's own). □ **foster-brother, foster-child**, etc. *ns.* a child fostered in this way. **foster home**, a family home in which a foster-child is brought up. **foster-mother** *n.* a woman who fosters a child.

fought *see* fight.

foul *adj.* **1.** causing disgust, having an offensive smell or taste. **2.** morally offensive, evil. **3.** (of language) disgusting, obscene. **4.** (of weather) rough, stormy. **5.** clogged, choked, overgrown with barnacles etc. **6.** in collision or entangled. **7.** unfair, against the rules of a game, *a foul stroke.* —*n.* a foul stroke or blow etc., breaking the rules of a game. —**foul** *v.* **1.** to make or become foul. **2.** to entangle or collide with, to obstruct. **3.** to commit a foul in a game. —**foully** *adv.* □ **foul-mouthed** *adj.* using foul language. **foul play**, a foul in sport; a violent crime, especially murder.

foulard (foo-lar) *n.* a kind of silky material used for ties etc.

found[1] *see* find.

found[2] *v.* **1.** to establish, to originate, to provide money for starting (an institution etc.). **2.** to base or construct, *a novel that is founded on fact.* **founder** *n.*, **foundress** *n.*

found[3] *v.* **1.** to melt and mould (metal), to fuse (materials for glass). **2.** to make (an object) in this way. **founder** *n.*

foundation *n.* **1.** the founding of an institution etc. **2.** the institution itself, a fund of money established for a charitable purpose. **3.** the strong base from which a building is built up. **4.** a cosmetic applied to the skin as the first layer of make-up. **5.** the underlying principle or idea etc. on which something is based. □ **foundation garment**, a woman's supporting undergarment, e.g. a corset. **foundation-stone** *n.* a stone laid ceremonially to celebrate the founding of a building.

founder[1,2] *ns. see* found[2], found[3].

founder[3] *v.* **1.** to stumble or fall. **2.** (of a ship) to fill with water and sink. **3.** to fail completely, *the plan foundered.*

foundling *n.* a deserted child of unknown parents.

foundry *n.* a factory or workshop where metal or glass is founded (*see* found[3]).

fount *n.* **1.** a fountain, a source. **2.** a set of printing-type of one style and size.

fountain *n.* **1.** a spring of water, especially a jet of water made to spout artificially as an ornament. **2.** a structure providing a supply of drinking-water in a public place,

□ **fountain-pen** *n.* a pen that can be filled with a supply of ink.

four *adj. & n.* **1.** one more than three (4, IV). **2.** a four-oared boat or its crew. □ **four figures,** a figure with four digits, e.g. 1000. **four-letter word,** a short word referring to sexual or excretory functions and regarded as obscene. **four-poster** *n.* a bed with four posts to support a canopy. **four-square** *adj.* solidly based, steady, (*adv.*) squarely. **four-wheel** *adj.* applied to all four wheels of a vehicle, *four-wheel drive.*

fourfold *adj. & adv.* **1.** four times as much or as many. **2.** consisting of four parts.

foursome *n.* **1.** a company of four people. **2.** a golf match between two pairs, with partners playing the same ball. —*adj.* for four people, *a foursome reel.*

fourteen *adj. & n.* one more than thirteen (14, XIV). **fourteenth** *adj. & n.*

fourth *adj.* next after third. —*n.* **1.** something that is fourth. **2.** fourth-class honours in a university degree. **3.** one of four equal parts of a thing. —**fourthly** *adv.*

fowl *n.* **1.** kind of bird often kept at houses and farms to supply eggs and flesh for food. **2.** the flesh of birds as food, *fish, flesh, and fowl.*

fowler *n.* a person who goes fowling.

fowling *n.* catching or shooting or snaring wildfowl.

fox *n.* **1.** a wild animal of the dog family with a pointed snout and reddish fur and a bushy tail. **2.** its fur. **3.** a crafty person. —*v.* to deceive or puzzle by acting craftily.

foxed *adj.* (of things) discoloured by brown spots caused by damp. **foxing** *n.*

foxglove *n.* a tall plant with purple or white flowers like glove-fingers.

foxhound *n.* a kind of hound bred and trained to hunt foxes.

fox-terrier *n.* a kind of short-haired terrier.

foxtrot *n.* a ballroom dance with slow and quick steps, music for this. —*v.* to dance a foxtrot.

foxy *adj.* (foxier, foxiest) **1.** reddish brown. **2.** crafty. **3.** looking like a fox.

foyer (**foi**-ay) *n.* the entrance hall of a theatre or cinema or of a hotel.

fracas (**frak**-ah) *n.* (*pl.* fracas, *pr.* **frak**-ahz) a noisy quarrel or disturbance.

fraction *n.* **1.** a number that is not a whole number, e.g. ⅓, 0·5. **2.** a very small part or piece or amount.

fractional *adj.* **1.** of a fraction. **2.** very small, *a fractional difference.* **fractionally** *adv.*

fractious (**frak**-shŭs) *adj.* irritable, peevish.

fractiously *adv.*, **fractiousness** *n.*

fracture *n.* breaking or breakage, especially of a bone. —*v.* to cause a fracture in, to suffer a fracture.

fragile *adj.* **1.** easily damaged or broken. **2.** of delicate constitution, not strong. **fragilely** *adv.*, **fragility** (frǎ-**jil**-iti) *n.*

fragment¹ (**frag**-mĕnt) *n.* **1.** a piece broken off something. **2.** an isolated part, *a fragment of the conversation.*

fragment² (frag-**ment**) *v.* to break or be broken into fragments. —**fragmentation** *n.*

fragmentary (**frag**-mĕnt-er-i) *adj.* consisting of fragments.

fragrance *n.* **1.** being fragrant. **2.** something fragrant, perfume.

fragrant *adj.* having a pleasant smell. **fragrantly** *adv.*

frail *adj.* not strong, physically weak.

frailty *n.* **1.** being frail, weakness. **2.** moral weakness, liability to yield to temptation.

frame *n.* **1.** a rigid structure forming a support for other parts of a building, vehicle, piece of furniture, etc.; *spectacle frames,* a framework to hold the lenses of a pair of spectacles. **2.** an open case or a border in which a picture, door, pane of glass, etc. may be set. **3.** the human or an animal body with reference to its size, *a small frame.* **4.** a single exposure on a strip of cinema film. **5.** a box-like structure used for protecting plants from the cold. **6.** a triangular structure for setting up balls in snooker etc., a round of play using this. —**frame** *v.* **1.** to put or form a frame round. **2.** to construct. **3.** to compose, to express in words, *frame a treaty* or *a question.* **4.** (*slang*) to arrange false evidence against, so that an innocent person appears to be guilty. □ **frame of mind,** a temporary state of mind. **frame of reference,** a set of principles or standards by which ideas and behaviour etc. are evaluated. **frame-up** *n.* (*slang*) the arrangement of false evidence against an innocent person.

framework *n.* the supporting frame of a building or other construction.

franc *n.* the unit of money in France, Belgium, Switzerland, and certain other countries.

France a country in western Europe.

franchise (**fran**-chyz) *n.* **1.** the right to vote at public elections. **2.** authorization to sell a company's goods or services in a particular area.

Franciscan (fran-**sis**-kǎn) *n.* a member of an order of friars (also called *Grey Friars*) founded by St. Francis of Assisi, or of a corresponding order of nuns.

Franco- *prefix* French; *a Franco-German treaty,* between France and Germany.

frank[1] *adj.* showing one's thoughts and feelings unmistakably. **frankly** *adv.*, **frankness** *n.*

frank[2] *v.* to mark in a **franking-machine,** a device that marks letters etc. passed through it and automatically counts up the total charge for these.

frankfurter *n.* a smoked sausage (¶ originally made at Frankfurt in Germany).

frankincense *n.* a kind of sweet-smelling gum burnt as incense.

frantic *adj.* wildly excited or agitated by anxiety etc., frenzied. **frantically** *adv.*

fraternal (frǎ-**ter**-nǎl) *adj.* of a brother or brothers. **fraternally** *adv.*

fraternity (frǎ-**tern**-iti) *n.* **1.** being fraternal, brotherly feeling. **2.** a religious brotherhood. **3.** a guild or company of people with common interests.

fraternize (**frat**-er-nyz) *v.* to associate with others in a friendly way. **fraternization** *n.*

Frau (*rhymes with* brow) *n.* (*pl.* Frauen) the title of a German married woman, = Mrs.

fraud *n.* **1.** criminal deception, a dishonest trick. **2.** a person or thing that is not what it seems or pretends to be, an impostor.

fraudulent (**fraw**-dew-lěnt) *adj.* acting with fraud, obtained by fraud. **fraudulently** *adv.*, **fraudulence** *n.*

fraught (*pr.* frawt) *adj.* filled, involving, *fraught with danger.*

Fräulein (**froi**-lyn) *n.* the title of a German unmarried woman, = Miss.

fray[1] *n.* a fight, a conflict, *ready for the fray.*

fray[2] *v.* (frayed, fraying) **1.** to make worn so that there are loose threads, especially at the edge. **2.** to strain or upset (nerves or temper). **3.** to become frayed.

frazzle *n.* a completely exhausted state, *worn to a frazzle.*

freak *n.* **1.** a person or thing that is abnormal in form. **2.** something very unusual or irregular, *a freak storm.* **3.** a person who dresses absurdly. **4.** one who freaks out, a drug addict. —*v.* **freak out,** to have hallucinations from narcotic drugs, to have a strong emotional experience; to adopt an unconventional life-style. **freak-out** *n.*

freakish *adj.* like a freak.

freckle *n.* a light brown spot on the skin. —*v.* to become or cause to become spotted with freckles.

free *adj.* (freer, freest) **1.** (of a person) not a slave, not in the power of another or others, having social and political liberty. **2.** (of a country or its citizens or institutions) not controlled by a foreign or despotic government, having representative government, having private rights which are respected. **3.** not fixed or held down, able to move without hindrance. **4.** unrestricted, not controlled by rules. **5.** without, not subject to or affected by (an influence etc.), *free from blame; harbour is free of ice.* **6.** without payment, costing nothing to the recipient. **7.** (of a place or time) not occupied, not being used, (of a person) without engagements or things to do. **8.** coming or given or giving readily, *he is very free with his advice.* —**free** *v.* (freed, freeing) **1.** to make free, to set at liberty. **2.** to relieve, to rid or ease, *freed him from suspicion.* **3.** to clear, to disengage or disentangle. —**freely** *adv.* □ **for free,** (*Amer.*) provided without payment. **free and easy,** informal. **Free Church,** a nonconformist Church. **free enterprise,** freedom of private business to operate without government control. **free fall,** the unrestricted fall of a body towards earth under the force of gravity; the movement of a spacecraft in space without thrust from the engines. **free fight,** a general fight in which anyone present may join. **free-for-all** *n.* a free fight; a discussion in which anyone present may join. **free hand,** the right of taking what action one chooses. **free-hand** *adj.* (of a drawing) done without ruler or compasses etc. **free house,** an inn or public house that is not controlled by a brewery and is therefore able to stock more than one brand of beer etc. **free kick,** a kick allowed to be taken in football without interference from opponents, as a minor penalty against them. **free lance,** a person who sells his services to various employers, not employed by one only. **free-lance** *v.* to work as a free lance. **free-loader** *n.* (*slang*) a sponger. **free love,** sexual intercourse irrespective of marriage. **free on board** *or* **rail,** without charge for delivery (of goods) to a ship or railway wagon. **free port,** one open to all traders alike. **free-range** *adj.* (of hens) allowed to range freely in search of food, not kept in a battery; (of eggs) from such hens. **free speech,** the right to express opinions of any kind. **free-standing** *adj.* not supported by a framework. **free-style** *adj.* (of swimming races and other sports) in which any style may be used; (of wrestling) with few restrictions on the holds permitted. **free vote,** a parliamentary vote in which members are not subject to party discipline. **free-wheel** *v.* to ride a bicycle without pedalling; to act without effort. **free will,** the power

of choosing one's own course of action.
free world, the non-Communist countries' name for themselves.
freedom *n.* **1.** the condition of being free, independence. **2.** frankness, outspokenness. **3.** exemption from a defect or duty etc. **4.** unrestricted use, *has the freedom of the library.* □ **freedom of the city,** the full rights of citizenship, given to a person as an honour.
freehold *n.* the holding of land or a house etc. in absolute ownership. **freeholder** *n.*
freeman *n.* (*pl.* freemen) a holder of the freedom of a city.
freemartin *n.* a calf that is incapable of propagation.
Freemason *n.* a member of an international fraternity (called the *Free and Accepted Masons*) for mutual help and fellowship, with elaborate secret rituals. **Freemasonry** *n.* their system and institutions. **freemasonry** *n.* sympathy and mutual help between people of similar interests.
freesia *n.* a fragrant flowering plant growing from a bulb.
Freetown the capital of Sierra Leone.
freeway *n.* (*Amer.*) a motorway on which there are no tolls.
freewill *adj.* voluntary.
freeze *v.* (froze, frozen, freezing) **1.** to be so cold that water turns to ice, *it was freezing last night.* **2.** to change or be changed from a liquid to a solid by extreme cold, to become full of ice or covered in ice. **3.** to become very cold or rigid from cold or fear etc, to chill by cold or fear etc. **4.** to preserve (food) by refrigeration to below freezing-point. **5.** to make (credits or assets) unable to be realized. **6.** to hold (prices, wages, etc.) at a fixed level. — **freeze** *n.* **1.** a period of freezing weather. **2.** the freezing of prices, wages, etc. □ **freeze-dry** *v.* to freeze and dry by evaporation of ice in a vacuum. **freezing-point** *n.* the temperature at which a liquid freezes. **freeze on to,** (*slang*) to take or keep tight hold of. **freeze out,** (*slang*) to exclude from business or social dealings. **freeze up,** to obstruct by the formation of ice. **freeze-up** *n.*
freezer *n.* a refrigerated container or compartment for preserving and storing perishable goods by freezing them and keeping them at a very low temperature.
freight (*pr.* frayt) *n.* **1.** the transport of goods in containers or by water or by air (in the USA also by land). **2.** the goods transported, cargo. **3.** the charge for this. —*v.* to load (a ship) with cargo, to send or carry as cargo.

freighter (**frayt**-er) *n.* a ship or aircraft carrying mainly freight.
French *adj.* of France or its people or language. —*n.* **1.** the French language. **2.** *the French,* French people. **3.** (*informal*) bad language, *excuse my French.* —**Frenchman, Frenchwoman** *ns.* □ **French bean,** a kidney bean or haricot bean used as a vegetable both as unripe pods and as ripe seeds. **french chalk,** finely powdered talc used as a lubricant etc. **French dressing,** salad dressing of seasoned oil and vinegar. **French horn,** a brass wind instrument with a long tube coiled in a circle. **French knickers,** knickers with wide legs. **French letter,** (*informal*) a condom. **french-polish** *v.* to polish (wood) with shellac polish. **French seam,** a seam with the raw edges enclosed. **french window,** a door with long glass panes on an outside wall, serving as both door and window. **take French leave,** to absent oneself without permission.
frenzied *adj.* in a state of frenzy, wildly excited or agitated. **frenziedly** *adv.*
frenzy *n.* violent excitement or agitation.
frequency *n.* **1.** the state of being frequent, frequent occurrence. **2.** the rate of the occurrence or repetition of something. **3.** the number of cycles per second of a carrier wave, a band or group of similar frequencies.
frequent[1] (**free**-kwĕnt) *adj.* happening or appearing often. **frequently** *adv.*
frequent[2] (fri-**kwent**) *v.* to go frequently to, to be often in (a place).
fresco (**fress**-koh) *n.* (*pl.* frescoes) a picture painted on a wall or ceiling before the plaster is dry.
fresh *adj.* **1.** newly made or produced or gathered etc., not stale. **2.** newly arrived. **3.** new or different, not previously known or used. **4.** (of food) not preserved by salting or pickling or tinning or freezing etc. **5.** not salty, not bitter. **6.** (of air or weather) cool, refreshing, (of wind) moderately strong. **7.** bright and pure in colour, not dull or faded. **8.** not weary, feeling vigorous. **9.** (*Amer.*) presumptuous, forward. —**freshly** *adv.*, **freshness** *n.*
freshen *v.* to make or become fresh.
freshwater *adj.* of fresh (not salty) water, not of the sea, *freshwater fish.*
fret[1] *v.* (fretted, fretting) **1.** to make or become unhappy, to worry, to vex. **2.** to wear away by gnawing or rubbing. —*n.* a state of unhappiness or worry, vexation.
fret[2] *n.* a bar or ridge on the finger-board of a guitar, banjo, etc., as a guide for the fingers to press the strings at the correct place.

fretful *adj.* constantly worrying or crying. **fretfully** *adv.*, **fretfulness** *n.*

fretsaw *n.* a very narrow saw fixed in a frame, used for cutting thin wood in ornamental patterns.

fretted *adj.* (of a ceiling etc.) decorated with carved or embossed work.

fretwork *n.* carved work in decorative patterns, especially in wood cut with a fretsaw.

Freudian (**froi**-di-ăn) *adj.* of Sigmund Freud, an Austrian physician (1856–1939), the founder of psychoanalysis, or his theories.

friable (**fry**-ă-bŭl) *adj.* easily crumbled.

friar *n.* a man who is a member of certain Roman Catholic religious orders (especially the Franciscans, Augustinians, Dominicans, and Carmelites), working among people in the outside world and not as enclosed orders. **friar's balsam**, a kind of oil used as an inhalant.

friary *n.* a monastery of friars.

fricassee (**frik**-ă-see) *n.* a dish of stewed or fried pieces of meat served in a thick sauce.

friction *n.* **1.** the rubbing of one thing against another. **2.** the resistance of one surface to another that moves over it. **3.** conflict between people with different ideas or personalities. **frictional** *adj.*

Friday the day of the week following Thursday.

fridge *n.* (*informal*) a refrigerator.

fried *see* fry¹.

friend *n.* **1.** a person with whom one is on terms of mutual affection independently of sexual or family love. **2.** a helpful thing or quality, *darkness was our friend*. **3.** a helper or sympathizer; *Friends of the cathedral*, people who regularly contribute money towards its upkeep. **4.** *Friend*, a member of the Society of Friends, a Quaker. **friendship** *n.*

friendless *adj.* without a friend.

friendly *adj.* (friendlier, friendliest) **1.** like a friend, kindly. **2.** (of things) favourable, helpful. **friendliness** *n.* ◻ **friendly match**, a match played for enjoyment and not in competition for a cup etc. **Friendly Society**, a society for the mutual benefit of its members e.g. during illness or old age.

Friesian (**free**-zhăn) *n.* one of a breed of large black-and-white dairy cattle originally from Friesland, a province of the Netherlands.

frieze *n.* a band of sculpture or decoration round the top of a wall or building.

frigate (**frig**-ăt) *n.* a small fast naval escort vessel or a small destroyer.

fright *n.* **1.** sudden great fear. **2.** a ridiculous-looking person or thing.

frighten *v.* **1.** to cause fright to. **2.** to feel fright, *he doesn't frighten easily*. **3.** to drive or compel by fright, *frightened them into concealing it.* ◻ **be frightened of**, to be afraid of.

frightful *adj.* **1.** causing horror. **2.** ugly. **3.** (*informal*) very great, extreme, extremely bad, *a frightful expense*; *frightful weather.* **frightfully** *adv.*

frigid (**frij**-id) *adj.* **1.** intensely cold. **2.** very cold and formal in manner. **3.** (of a woman) unresponsive sexually. **frigidly** *adv.*, **frigidity** (fri-**jid**-iti) *n.*

frill *n.* **1.** a gathered or pleated strip of trimming attached at one edge. **2.** an unnecessary extra, *simple accommodation with no frills.* **frilled** *adj.*, **frilly** *adj.*

fringe *n.* **1.** an ornamental edging of hanging threads or cords etc. **2.** something resembling this. **3.** front hair cut short to hang over the forehead. **4.** the edge of an area or a group etc. —**fringe** *v.* **1.** to decorate with a fringe. **2.** to form a fringe to. ◻ **fringe benefits**, benefits that are provided for an employee in addition to wages or salary.

frippery *n.* showy unnecessary finery or ornaments.

frisk *v.* **1.** to leap or skip playfully. **2.** to pass one's hands over (a person) in order to search for concealed weapons etc.

frisky *adj.* (friskier, friskiest) lively, playful. **friskiness** *n.*

fritillary (fri-**til**-er-i) *n.* **1.** a plant with speckled bell-shaped flowers. **2.** a kind of spotted butterfly.

fritter¹ *n.* a small flat fried cake of batter containing sliced fruit or meat etc.

fritter² *v.* to waste little by little, especially on trivial things, *fritter away one's time* or *money*.

frivol *v.* (frivolled, frivolling) to spend one's time frivolously.

frivolous *adj.* lacking a serious purpose, pleasure-loving. **frivolously** *adv.*, **frivolity** *n.*

frizz *v.* to curl into a wiry mass. —*n.* a frizzed condition, frizzed hair. —**frizzy** *adj.*, **frizziness** *n.*

frizzle *v.* to fry crisp.

fro *adv.* **to and fro,** *see* to.

frock *n.* a woman's or girl's dress.

frog *n.* **1.** a small cold-blooded jumping animal living both in water and on land. **2.** a horny substance in the sole of a horse's foot. **3.** a fastener consisting of a button and an ornamentally looped cord. ◻ **have a frog in one's throat,** to be unable to speak except hoarsely.

frogman *n.* (*pl.* frogmen) a swimmer equipped with a rubber suit, flippers etc., and an oxygen supply for swimming and working under water.

frog-march *v.* to hustle (a person) forward forcibly with his arms held fast.

frolic *v.* (frolicked, frolicking) to play about in a lively cheerful way. —*n.* lively cheerful playing or entertainment.

from *prep.* expressing separation or origin, **1.** indicating the place or time or limit that is the starting-point, *travelled from London*; *from ten o'clock*. **2.** indicating source or origin, *took water from the well*. **3.** indicating separation, prevention, escape, etc. *was released from prison*; *cannot refrain from laughing*. **4.** indicating difference or discrimination, *can't tell red from green*. **5.** indicating cause or agent or means, *died from starvation*. **6.** indicating material used in a process, *wine is made from grapes*. □ **from day to day**, daily. **from time to time**, at intervals of time.

frond *n.* a leaf-like part of a fern or other flowerless plant or of a palm tree.

front *n.* **1.** the foremost or most important side or surface. **2.** the part normally nearer or towards the spectator or line of motion, *the front of a bus*. **3.** the area where fighting is taking place in a war, the foremost line of an army etc. **4.** outward appearance or show, something serving as a cover for secret activities. **5.** the forward edge of an advancing mass of cold or warm air. **6.** the promenade of a seaside resort. **7.** the part of a garment covering the front of the body. **8.** the part of a theatre where the audience sits, in front of the stage. **9.** (in names) an organized political group, *the Patriotic Front*. —*adj.* of the front, situated in front. —**front** *v.* **1.** to face, to have the front towards, *fronting the sea* or *on the sea*. **2.** (*slang*) to serve as a front or cover for secret activities. □ **front-bencher** *n.* an MP entitled to sit on the front benches in Parliament, which are reserved for government ministers and members of the shadow cabinet. **front runner**, the contestant who seems most likely to succeed. **in front**, at the front of something; *in front of the children*, in their presence.

frontage *n.* **1.** the front of a building. **2.** the land bordering its front.

frontal *adj.* of or on the front; *full frontal nudity*, of a completely naked person seen from the front. **frontally** *adv.*

frontier *n.* **1.** the land-border of a country. **2.** the limit of attainment or knowledge achieved in a subject.

frontispiece (**frunt**-iss-peess) *n.* an illus-

tration placed opposite the title-page of a book.

frost *n.* **1.** a weather condition with temperature below the freezing-point of water. **2.** a white powder-like coating of frozen vapour produced by this. **3.** (*slang*) a failure, a disappointing thing. —**frost** *v.* **1.** to injure (a plant etc.) with frost. **2.** to cover with frost or frosting. **3.** to make (glass) opaque by roughening the surface. □ **frost-bite** *n.* injury to tissue of the body from freezing. **frost-bitten** *adj.* affected with frost-bite.

frosting *n.* sugar icing for cakes.

frosty *adj.* (frostier, frostiest) **1.** cold with frost. **2.** very cold and unfriendly in manner. **frostily** *adv.*, **frostiness** *n.*

froth *n.* foam. —*v.* to cause froth in, to foam. —**frothy** *adj.*

frown *v.* **1.** to wrinkle one's brow in thought or disapproval. **2.** to be disapproving, *they frown on gambling*. —*n.* a frowning movement or look.

frowsty *adj.* fusty, stuffy.

frozen *see* freeze. □ **the frozen limit**, (*slang*) something extremely objectionable.

frugal (**froo**-găl) *adj.* **1.** careful and economical. **2.** scanty, costing little, *a frugal meal*. **frugally** *adv.*, **frugality** (froo-**gal**-iti) *n.*

fruit *n.* **1.** the seed-containing part of a plant. **2.** this used as food. **3.** any plant product used as food, *the fruits of the earth*. **4.** the product or rewarding outcome of labour. **5.** currants etc. used in food. — **fruit** *v.* **1.** (of a plant) to produce fruit. **2.** to cause or allow (a plant) to produce fruit. □ **fruit machine**, a kind of coin-operated gambling machine, often using symbols representing fruit. **fruit salad**, various fruits cut up and mixed.

fruiterer *n.* a shopkeeper who deals in fruit.

fruitful *adj.* **1.** producing much fruit. **2.** producing good results. **fruitfully** *adv.*, **fruitfulness** *n.*

fruition (froo-**ish**-ŏn) *n.* the fulfilment of hopes, results attained by work. ¶ This word does not mean 'fruiting' or 'becoming fruitful'.

fruitless *adj.* producing little or no result. **fruitlessly** *adv.*, **fruitlessness** *n.*

fruity *adj.* (fruitier, fruitiest) **1.** like fruit in smell or taste. **2.** (*informal*) of full rich quality, *a fruity voice*. **3.** (*informal*) full of rough humour or scandal, *fruity stories*.

frump *n.* a dowdily-dressed woman. **frumpish** *adj.*

frustrate *v.* to prevent (a person) from achieving what he intends, to make (efforts) useless. **frustration** *n.*

fry [1] *v.* (fried, frying) to cook or be cooked in boiling fat. —*n.* various internal parts of animals usually fried, *lamb's fry*. ☐ **frying-pan** *n.* a shallow pan used in frying; *out of the frying-pan into the fire*, from a bad situation to a worse one. **fry-pan** *n.* a frying-pan. **fry up**, to heat or reheat (food) by frying. **fry-up** *n.*

fry [2] *pl. n.* young or newly hatched fishes. **small fry**, children; people of little importance.

ft. *abbrev.* foot or feet (as a measure).

fuchsia (few-shǎ) *n.* an ornamental shrub with red or purple or white drooping flowers.

fuck *v.* (*vulgar*) **1.** to have sexual intercourse with. **2.** (used in exclamations etc.) *fuck off*, go away. —*n.* (*vulgar*) **1.** sexual intercourse. **2.** a damn, *doesn't care a fuck*. —**fucking** *adj. & adv.* (*vulgar*) damned.

fuddle *v.* to stupefy, especially with alcoholic drink.

fuddy-duddy *adj.* (*slang*) out of date, unable to accept new ideas. —*n.* (*slang*) a person of this kind.

fudge [1] *n.* a soft sweet made of milk, sugar, and butter.

fudge [2] *v.* to put together in a makeshift or dishonest way, to fake.

fuel *n.* **1.** material burnt or lit as a source of warmth or light or energy, or used as a source of nuclear energy. **2.** something that increases anger or other strong feelings. —*v.* (fuelled, fuelling) to supply with fuel.

fug *n.* (*informal*) fustiness of air in a room. **fuggy** *adj.*, **fugginess** *n.*

fugitive (few-ji-tiv) *n.* a person who is fleeing or escaping from something. —*adj.* **1.** fleeing, escaping. **2.** transient.

fugue (*pr.* fewg) *n.* a musical composition in which one or more themes are introduced and then repeated in a complex pattern.

fulcrum (ful-krŭm) *n.* (*pl.* fulcra) the point on which a lever turns.

fulfil *v.* (fulfilled, fulfilling) **1.** to accomplish, to carry out (a task). **2.** to do what is required by (a treaty etc.), to satisfy the requirements of. **3.** to make (a prophecy) come true. **fulfilment** *n.* ☐ **fulfil oneself** *or* **be fulfilled**, (of persons) to develop and use one's abilities etc. fully.

full *adj.* **1.** holding or having as much as the limits will allow. **2.** having much or many, crowded, showing, *full of vitality*. **3.** completely occupied with thinking of, *full of himself*; *full of the news*, unable to keep from talking about it. **4.** fed to satisfaction, *ate till he was full*. **5.** copious, *give full details*. **6.** complete, reaching the usual or specified extent or limit etc., *in full*

bloom; *waited a full hour*. **7.** plump, rounded, *a full figure*. **8.** (of clothes) fitting loosely, made with much material hanging in folds. **9.** (of a tone) deep and mellow. — **full** *adv.* **1.** completely. **2.** exactly, *hit him full on the nose*. —**fully** *adv.*, **fullness** *n.* ☐ **full age**, the age at which a person has an adult's legal rights and responsibilities. **full back**, one of the defensive players near the goal in football, hockey, etc. **full-blown** *adj.* fully developed. **full-blooded** *adj.* vigorous, hearty; sensual. **full board**, provision of bed and all meals at a hotel etc. **full brothers**, those who have the same parents, not half-brothers. **full face**, with all the face towards the spectator. **full marks**, the maximum marks possible in an examination etc. **full moon**, the moon with its whole disc illuminated; the time when this occurs. **full-scale** *adj.* of the actual size, complete, not reduced. **full speed ahead!**, an order to move or work with maximum speed. **full stop**, the punctuation mark . used at the end of a sentence or abbreviation; *come to a full stop*, cease completely, be unable to proceed. **full time**, the whole of a working day or week; the end of a football match etc. **full-time** *adj.* for or during the whole of the working day or week. **full-timer** *n.* one employed to work a full working week. **in full**, with nothing omitted; for the whole amount, *paid in full*. **in the fullness of time**, at the proper or destined time. **to the full**, thoroughly, completely.

fuller *n.* a person who cleans and thickens freshly woven cloth. **fuller's earth**, a type of clay used for this process.

fulmar *n.* an Arctic sea-bird related to the petrels.

fulminate (ful-min-ayt) *v.* to protest loudly and bitterly. **fulmination** *n.*

fulsome (fuul-sŏm) *adj.* praising something excessively and sickeningly. ¶ It is regarded as unacceptable to use this word in current English to mean 'full' or 'copious' or 'plentiful'.

fumble *v.* **1.** to touch or handle something awkwardly. **2.** to grope about.

fume *n.* (usually *fumes*) strong-smelling smoke or gas or vapour. —*v.* **1.** to treat with chemical fumes, especially to darken wood, *fumed oak*. **2.** to emit fumes. **3.** to seethe with anger.

fumigate (few-mig-ayt) *v.* to disinfect by means of fumes. **fumigation** *n.*

fun *n.* **1.** light-hearted amusement. **2.** a source of this. ☐ **like fun**, (*informal*) very much, intensively. **make fun of**, to cause people to laugh at (a person or thing) by making it appear ridiculous.

function *n*. **1**. the special activity or purpose of a person or thing. **2**. an important social or official ceremony. **3**. any of the basic operations of a computer etc.

functional *adj*. **1**. of a function or functions. **2**. designed to perform a particular function without being decorative or luxurious. **functionally** *adv*.

functionary *n*. an official.

fund *n*. **1**. a stock of money, especially that available for a particular purpose. **2**. an available stock or supply, *a fund of jokes*. —*v*. to provide with money.

fundamental *adv*. **1**. of the basis or foundation of a subject etc., serving as a starting-point. **2**. very important, essential. **fundamentally** *adv*. □ **fundamentals** *pl*. *n*. fundamental facts or principles.

fundamentalism *n*. strict maintenance of traditional orthodox religious beliefs, belief that the Bible contains accurate historical records, e.g. of the creation of the world, and should be accepted strictly and literally as the basis of Protestant Christianity. **fundamentalist** *n*.

funeral *n*. **1**. the ceremony of burying or cremating the dead. **2**. a procession to this. **3**. (*slang*) a person's unpleasant responsibility or concern, *that's your funeral*.

funerary (**few**-ner-er-i) *adj*. of or used for burial or a funeral.

funereal (few-**neer**-iăl) *adj*. suitable for a funeral, dismal, dark.

fun-fair *n*. a fair consisting of amusements and side-shows.

fungicide (**fun**-ji-syd) *n*. a fungus-destroying substance. **fungicidal** *adj*.

fungoid (**fung**-oid) *adj*. like a fungus.

fungous (**fung**-ŭs) *adj*. like a fungus.

fungus *n*. (*pl*. fungi, *pr*. **fung**-I) any of those plants without leaves, flowers, or green colouring-matter, growing on other plants or on decaying matter and including mushrooms, toadstools, and moulds.

funicular (few-**nik**-yoo-ler) *n*. a cable railway with ascending and descending cars counterbalancing each other.

funk *n*. (*slang*) **1**. fear. **2**. a coward. —*v*. (*slang*) to show fear, to fear and shirk.

funky *adj*. (*slang*) **1**. (of jazz etc.) uncomplicated, emotional. **2**. fashionable. **3**. having a strong smell.

funnel *n*. **1**. a tube or pipe wide at the top and narrow at the bottom, for pouring liquids or powders etc. into small openings. **2**. a metal chimney on a steam engine or ship. —**funnel** *v*. (funnelled, funnelling) to move through a funnel or a narrowing space.

funny *adj*. (funnier, funniest) **1**. causing amusement. **2**. puzzling, hard to account for. **3**. (*informal*) slightly unwell or insane. **funnily** *adv*. □ **funny-bone** *n*. part of the elbow over which a very sensitive nerve passes. **funny business**, trickery.

fur *n*. **1**. the short fine soft hair covering the bodies of certain animals. **2**. animal skin with the fur on it, especially when used for making or trimming clothes etc. **3**. fabric imitating this. **4**. a coat or cape etc. of real or imitation fur. **5**. a coating formed on a sick or unhealthy person's tongue. **6**. the coating formed by hard water on the inside of a kettle or pipes etc. —*v*. (furred, furring) to cover or become covered with fur.

furbelows *pl*. *n*. showy trimmings, *frills and furbelows*.

furbish *v*. to polish, to clean or renovate.

furious *adj*. **1**. full of anger. **2**. violent, intense, *a furious pace*. **furiously** *adv*.

furl *v*. (furled, furling) to roll up and fasten (a sail, flag, or umbrella).

furlong *n*. one eighth of a mile, 220 yards.

furlough (**fer**-loh) *n*. leave of absence, especially that granted to servicemen.

furnace *n*. **1**. a closed fireplace for heating water to warm a building etc. by hot pipes. **2**. an enclosed space for heating minerals or metals etc. or for making glass.

furnish *v*. **1**. to equip (a room or house etc.) with furniture. **2**. to provide or supply.

furnishings *pl*. *n*. furniture and fitments, curtains, etc., in a room or house.

furniture *n*. the movable articles (such as tables, chairs, beds, etc.) needed in a room or house etc.

furore (fewr-**or**-i) *n*. an uproar of enthusiastic admiration or fury.

furrier (**fu**-ri-er) *n*. a person who deals in furs or fur clothes.

furrow *n*. **1**. a long cut in the ground made by a plough or other implement. **2**. a groove resembling this, a deep wrinkle in the skin. —*v*. to make furrows in.

furry *adj*. (furrier, furriest) **1**. like fur. **2**. covered with fur.

further *adv*. & *adj*. **1**. more distant in space or time. **2**. to a greater extent, more, additional, *shall enquire further*; *made further enquiries*. (¶ See the note under farther.) —*v*. to help the progress of, *further someone's interests*. □ **further education**, formal education provided for people above school age.

furtherance *n*. the furthering of someone's interests etc.

furthermore *n*. in addition, moreover.

furthermost *adj*. most distant.

furthest *adj*. most distant. —*adv*. to or at the greatest distance.
¶ See the note under farther.

furtive *adj.* sly, stealthy. **furtively** *adv.*, **furtiveness** *n.*

fury *n.* **1.** wild anger, rage. **2.** violence of weather etc., *the storm's fury.* **3.** a violently angry person, especially a woman. **4.** *the Furies*, snake-haired goddesses in Greek mythology, sent from the underworld to punish crime. □ **like fury**, (*informal*) intensely, furiously.

furze *n.* gorse.

fuse¹ *v.* to blend or amalgamate (metals, living bones, institutions, etc.) into a whole.

fuse² *n.* (in an electric circuit) a short piece of wire designed to melt and break the circuit if the current exceeds a safe level. —*v.* **1.** to fit (a circuit or appliance) with a fuse. **2.** to cease or cause to cease functioning through melting of a fuse. □ **fuse-box** *n.* a small cupboard or box containing the fuses of an electrical system.

fuse³ *n.* a length of easily burnt material for igniting a bomb or an explosive charge. —*v.* to fit a fuse to.

fuselage (**few**-zĕl-ah*zh*) *n.* the body of an aeroplane.

fusible *adj.* able to be fused.

Fusiliers (few-zi-**leerz**) *pl. n.* any of several infantry regiments formerly armed with light muskets.

fusillade (few-zi-**layd**) *n.* **1.** a simultaneous or continuous firing of guns. **2.** a great outburst of questions, criticism, etc.

fusion (**few**-*zh*ŏn) *n.* **1.** fusing, the blending or uniting of different things into a whole. **2.** the union of atomic nuclei to form a heavier nucleus, usually with release of energy.

fuss *n.* **1.** unnecessary excitement or activity. **2.** a display of worry about something unimportant. **3.** a vigorous protest or dispute. —*v.* to make a fuss, to bother (a person) with unimportant matters or by fussing. □ **fuss-pot** *n.* (*informal*) a person who continually makes a fuss. **make a fuss**, to complain vigorously. **make a fuss of** *or* **over**, to treat (a person) with a great display of attention or affection.

fussy *adj.* (fussier, fussiest) **1.** often fussing. **2.** fastidious. **3.** full of unnecessary detail or decoration. **fussily** *adv.*, **fussiness** *n.*

fusty *adj.* (fustier, fustiest) **1.** (of a room) stale-smelling, stuffy. **2.** smelling of damp and mould. **3.** old-fashioned in ideas etc. **fustiness** *n.*

futile (**few**-tyl) *adj.* producing no result, useless. **futility** (few-**til**-iti) *n.*

future *adj.* belonging to the time coming after the present. —*n.* future time or events or condition; *there's no future in it,* no prospects of success or advancement. □

future life, existence after death. **in future**, from this time onwards.

futuristic (few-tewr-**ist**-ik) *adj.* looking suitable for the distant future, not traditional.

futurity (few-**tewr**-iti) *n.* future time.

fuzz *n.* **1.** fluff, something fluffy or frizzy. **2.** (*slang*) the police.

fuzzy *adj.* (fuzzier, fuzziest) **1.** like fuzz, covered with fuzz. **2.** frizzy. **3.** blurred, indistinct. **fuzzily** *adv.*, **fuzziness** *n.*

Gg

g *abbrev.* **1.** gram(s). **2.** gravity, the acceleration due to this.

Ga. *abbrev.* Georgia.

gab *n.* (*informal*) chatter. **have the gift of the gab**, to be good at talking.

gabardine (gab-er-**deen**) *n.* a strong fabric woven in a twill pattern.

gabble *v.* to talk quickly and indistinctly. —*n.* gabbled talk. **gabbler** *n.*

gable *n.* the triangular upper part of an outside wall, between sloping roofs. **gabled** *adj.* having a gable or gables.

Gabon (gă-**bon**) a country on the west coast of Africa. **Gabonese** (gab-ŏn-**eez**) *adj. & n.* (*pl.* Gabonese)

Gaborone (kab-oo-**roo**-ni) the capital of Botswana.

gad *v.* (gadded, gadding) **1.** to be a gadabout. **2.** (of cattle etc.) to leap about when pestered by flies that bite.

gadabout *n.* a person who goes about constantly in search of pleasure.

gadfly *n.* a fly that bites horses and cattle.

gadget *n.* a small mechanical device or tool. **gadgetry** *n.* gadgets.

Gael (*pr.* gayl) *n.* a Scottish or Irish Celt.

Gaelic *n.* **1.** (*pr.* **gal**-ik) the Celtic language of the Scots. **2.** (*pr.* **gay**-lik) the Irish language. —*adj.* of or in Gaelic. □ **Gaelic coffee** (*pr.* **gay**-lik) coffee made with cream and Irish whiskey.

gaff *n.* a stick with an iron hook for landing large fish caught with rod and line. —*v.* to seize with a gaff, *gaffing a salmon.*

gaffe *n.* a blunder.

gaffer *n.* (*informal*) **1.** an elderly man. **2.** a boss or foreman.

gag *n.* **1.** something put into a person's mouth or tied across it to prevent him from speaking or crying out. **2.** a device used by a dentist or surgeon for holding a patient's jaws open. **3.** anything that prevents freedom of speech or of writing. **4.** a joke or funny story, especially as part of a comedian's act. —**gag** v. (gagged, gagging) **1.** to put a gag into or over the mouth of. **2.** to prevent from having freedom of speech or of writing, *we cannot gag the press.* **3.** to tell jokes or gags. **4.** to retch or choke.

gaga (gah-gah) *adj.* (*slang*) **1.** senile. **2.** crazy.

gage *n.* a greengage.

gaggle *n.* **1.** a flock of geese. **2.** a group of talkative people. —v. to cackle like geese.

gaiety *n.* **1.** cheerfulness, a happy and light-hearted manner. **2.** merrymaking.

gaily *adv.* **1.** in a cheerful light-hearted manner. **2.** in bright colours.

gain v. **1.** to obtain, especially something desirable. **2.** to make a profit. **3.** to acquire gradually, to build up for oneself, *gained strength after illness.* **4.** (of a clock etc.) to become ahead of the correct time. **5.** to get nearer in racing or pursuit, *our horse was gaining on the favourite.* **6.** to reach (a desired place), *gained the shore.* —**gain** *n.* **1.** an increase in wealth or possessions. **2.** an improvement, an increase in amount or power. —**gainer** *n.* □ **gain ground,** to make progress. **gain time,** to improve one's chances by arranging or accepting a delay.

gainful *adj.* profitable. **gainfully** *adv.*

gainsay v. (gainsaid, gainsaying) (*formal*) to deny or contradict, *there is no gainsaying it.*

gait *n.* **1.** a manner of walking or running. **2.** any of the forward movements of a horse, such as trotting or cantering.

gaiter *n.* a covering of cloth or leather for the leg from knee to ankle, or for the ankle, or for part of a machine.

gala (gah-lă) *n.* a festive occasion, a fête.

galactic (gă-lak-tik) *adj.* **1.** of a galaxy or galaxies. **2.** of the Galaxy or Milky Way.

galantine (gal-ăn-teen) *n.* white meat boned and spiced and cooked in the form of a roll, served cold.

galaxy (gal-ăk-si) *n.* **1.** any of the large independent systems of stars existing in space; *the Galaxy,* that containing the earth. **2.** the Milky Way. **3.** a brilliant company of beautiful or famous people.

gale *n.* **1.** a very strong wind; *gale-force winds,* winds with a speed of 35–50 m.p.h. **2.** a noisy outburst, *gales of laughter.*

gall ¹ (*pr.* gawl) *n.* **1.** bile. **2.** bitterness of feeling. **3.** (*slang*) impudence. □ **gall-bladder** *n.* a pear-shaped organ attached to the liver, storing and releasing bile.

gallstone *n.* a small hard mass that sometimes forms in the gall-bladder.

gall ² (*pr.* gawl) *n.* a sore spot on the skin of an animal, especially a horse, caused by rubbing. —v. to rub and make sore.

gall ³ (*pr.* gawl) *n.* an abnormal growth produced by an insect, fungus, or bacterium on a plant, especially on an oak-tree.

gallant (gal-ănt) *adj.* **1.** brave, chivalrous. **2.** fine, stately, *our gallant ship.* **gallantly** *adv.,* **gallantry** *n.*

galleon (gal-i-ŏn) *n.* a large Spanish sailing ship used in the 15th–17th centuries.

gallery *n.* **1.** a platform projecting from the inner wall of a church or hall. **2.** the highest balcony in a theatre, the people occupying this. **3.** the spectators at a golf-match. **4.** a raised covered platform or passage along the wall of a building. **5.** a long room or passage, especially one used for a special purpose, *a shooting gallery.* **6.** a room or building for showing works of art. □ **play to the gallery,** to try to win favour by appealing to the taste of the general public.

galley *n.* (*pl.* galleys) **1.** a long low medieval ship propelled by sails and oars. **2.** an ancient Greek or Roman warship propelled by oars. **3.** the kitchen in a ship or aircraft. **4.** an oblong tray for holding type for printing. □ **galley-proof** *n.* a printed proof made from type set in a galley.

Gallic (gal-ik) *adj.* **1.** of ancient Gaul. **2.** of France, typically French, *Gallic wit.*

galling (gawl-ing) *adj.* vexing, humiliating.

gallipot (gal-i-pot) *n.* a small earthenware or metal pot for holding ointments etc.

gallivant v. (*informal*) to gad about.

gallon *n.* a measure for liquids, = 4 quarts (4·546 litres).

gallop *n.* **1.** a horse's fastest pace, with all four feet off the ground simultaneously in each stride. **2.** a ride at this pace. —**gallop** v. (galloped, galloping) **1.** to go at a gallop, to cause a horse to do this. **2.** to go very fast, to rush; *galloping inflation,* getting worse rapidly.

Galloway (gal-ŏ-way) *see* Dumfries and Galloway. —**galloway** *n.* **1.** a horse of a small strong breed from Galloway. **2.** a small horse. **3.** one of a breed of cattle from Galloway.

gallows *n.* **1.** a framework with a suspended noose for the hanging of criminals. **2.** *the gallows,* execution by hanging.

gallstone *n.* (*see* gall ¹).

Gallup poll an estimate of public opinion, made by questioning a representative sample of people and used especially to forecast how people will vote in an election. ¶ Named after G. H. Gallup (1901–), an American statistician.

galore adv. in plenty, *whisky galore.*

galosh n. one of a pair of overshoes, usually rubber.

galumph (gă-**lumf**) v. (*informal*) **1.** to prance in triumph. **2.** to move noisily or clumsily.

galvanic (gal-**van**-ik) adj. **1.** producing an electric current by chemical action, *a galvanic cell.* **2.** stimulating people into sudden activity. **galvanically** adv.

galvanize v. **1.** to stimulate into sudden activity. **2.** to coat (iron) with zinc in order to protect it from rust, *galvanized iron.* **galvanization** n.

Gambia a country in West Africa, also called *the Gambia.* **Gambian** adj. & n.

gambit n. **1.** an opening move in chess in which a player deliberately sacrifices a pawn or piece in order to gain a favourable position. **2.** an action or statement intended to secure some advantage.

gamble v. **1.** to play games of chance for money. **2.** to stake or risk money etc. in the hope of great gain; *gambled his fortune away,* lost it by gambling. **3.** to stake one's hopes; *gambled on its being a fine day,* made plans in the hope of this. —**gamble** n. **1.** gambling. **2.** a risky attempt or undertaking. —**gambler** n.

gambol v. (gambolled, gambolling) to jump or skip about in play. —n. a gambolling movement.

game¹ n. **1.** a form of play or sport, especially one with rules. **2.** a single section forming a scoring unit in some games (e.g. in tennis or bridge). **3.** a scheme or plan, a trick, *so that's his little game!* **4.** wild animals or birds hunted for sport or food. **5.** their flesh as food, *game pie.* —v. to gamble for money stakes; *gaming-rooms,* licensed for gambling. **game** adj. **1.** brave. **2.** having spirit or energy, *are you game for a lark?* —**gamely** adv., **gameness** n. □ **game chips,** thin round potato chips served with game. **game laws,** laws regulating the killing and preservation of game. **game point,** the stage in a game when one side will win if it gains the next point; this point. **games** pl. n. athletics or sports, a sporting contest, *the Olympic Games.* **give the game away,** to reveal a secret or scheme. **make game of,** to make fun of, to ridicule. **on the game,** (*slang*) involved in prostitution or thieving. **the game is up,** the secret or deception is revealed.

game² adj. lame, *a game leg.*

gamekeeper n. a person employed to protect and breed game.

gamesmanship n. the art of winning contests by upsetting the confidence of one's opponent.

gamete (gam-eet) n. a sexual cell capable of fusing with another in reproduction.

gamin (gam-an) n. a street urchin, a child who looks or behaves like this.

gamine (gam-een) n. **1.** a girl gamin. **2.** a small mischievous-looking young woman.

gamma n. the third letter of the Greek alphabet, = g.

gammon n. **1.** the bottom piece of a flitch of bacon, including a hind leg. **2.** cured or smoked ham.

gammy adj. (*informal*) = game², *a gammy leg.*

gamut (gam-ŭt) n. **1.** the whole range of musical notes used in medieval or modern music. **2.** the whole series or range or scope of anything; *the whole gamut of emotion,* from greatest joy to deepest despair.

gander n. a male goose.

gang¹ n. **1.** a number of workmen working together, *a road gang.* **2.** a band of people going about together or working together, especially for some criminal purpose. —v. to combine in a gang; *they ganged up on him,* combined against him. □ **gang rape,** rape of a woman by a gang of men on the same occasion.

gang² v. (*Scottish*) to go.

ganger n. the foreman of a gang of workmen.

gangling adj. tall, thin, and awkward-looking.

ganglion n. (*pl.* ganglia) **1.** a group of nerve-cells from which nerve-fibres radiate. **2.** a cyst on a tendon-sheath. **3.** a centre of activity.

gangplank n. a movable plank used as a bridge for walking into or out of a boat.

gangrene n. death and decay of body tissue, usually caused by blockage of the blood supply to that part. **gangrenous** (gang-rin-ŭs) adj.

gangster n. a member of a gang of violent criminals.

gangway n. **1.** a gap left for people to pass between rows of seats or through a crowd. **2.** a passageway, especially on a ship. **3.** a movable bridge from a ship to the land, the opening in a ship's side into which this fits. —int. make way!

ganja n. marijuana.

gannet (gan-it) n. a large sea-bird.

gantry n. a light bridge-like overhead framework for supporting a travelling crane, railway signals over several tracks, etc.

gaol (*pr.* jayl) n. **1.** a public prison. **2.**

confinement in this; *he was sentenced to three years' gaol.* —*v.* (gaoled, gaoling) to put into gaol.

¶ The spellings *gaol* and *jail* are both in general use, but *gaol* is preferred in official documents and *jail* in the USA.

gaolbird *n.* a person who is or has been in prison, a habitual criminal.

gaolbreak *n.* an escape from gaol.

gaoler *n.* a person in charge of a gaol or its prisoners.

gap *n.* 1. a break or opening in something continuous such as a hedge or fence or wall, or between hills. 2. an unfilled space or interval, *a gap between programmes.* 3. something lacking, *a gap in one's education.* 4. a wide difference in ideas.

gape *v.* 1. to open the mouth wide. 2. to stare with open mouth, in surprise or wonder. 3. to open or be open wide, *a gaping chasm.* —*n.* an open-mouthed stare.

garage (ga-rah*zh* or ga-rij) *n.* 1. a building in which to keep a motor vehicle or vehicles. 2. a commercial establishment where motor vehicles are repaired and serviced. 3. a roadside establishment selling petrol and oil etc. —*v.* to put or keep in a garage.

garb *n.* clothing, especially of a distinctive kind; *a man in clerical garb.* —*v.* to clothe.

garbage *n.* rubbish or refuse of all kinds, domestic waste.

garble *v.* to give a confused account of something, so that a message or story is distorted or misunderstood.

garden *n.* a piece of cultivated ground, especially attached to a house. —*v.* to tend a garden. □ **garden centre,** an establishment where plants and gardening tools etc. are sold. **garden city,** a town laid out with many open spaces and planted with numerous trees. **garden of England,** a very fertile area such as Kent or the Vale of Evesham. **garden party,** a party held on a lawn or in a garden or park. **gardens** *pl. n.* ornamental public grounds. **Gardens** *pl. n.* the name of a group or street of houses, *Burlington Gardens.* **lead up the garden path,** to entice, to mislead deliberately.

gardener *n.* a person who tends a garden, either as a job or as a hobby.

gardenia (gar-**deen**-iă) *n.* 1. a tree or shrub with large fragrant white or yellow flowers. 2. its flower.

gargantuan (gar-**gan**-tew-ăn) *adj.* gigantic.

gargle *v.* to wash or rinse the inside of the throat with liquid held there by air

breathed out from the lungs. —*n.* a liquid used for this.

gargoyle *n.* a grotesque carved face or figure, especially as a gutter-spout carrying water clear of a wall.

garish (**gair**-ish) *adj.* excessively bright, gaudy, over-decorated. **garishly** *adv.*

garland *n.* a wreath of flowers etc. worn or hung as a decoration. —*v.* to deck with a garland or garlands.

garlic *n.* 1. an onion-like plant. 2. its bulbous root that has a strong taste and smell, used for flavouring. **garlicky** *adj.*

garment *n.* an article of clothing.

garner *v.* to store up, to collect.

garnet *n.* a semi-precious stone of deep transparent red.

garnish *v.* to decorate (especially food for the table). —*n.* something used for garnishing.

garret *n.* an attic, especially a poor one.

garrison *n.* 1. troops stationed in a town or fort to defend it; *a garrison town,* one that has a permanent garrison. 2. the building or fort they occupy. —**garrison** *v.* 1. to place a garrison in. 2. to occupy and defend, *troops garrisoned the town.*

garrotte (gă-**rot**) *n.* 1. a Spanish method of capital punishment by strangulation with a metal collar. 2. the apparatus used for this. 3. a cord or wire used to strangle a victim. —*v.* to execute or strangle with a garrotte.

garrulous (ga-**roo**-lŭs) *adj.* talkative. **garrulously** *adv.,* **garrulousness** *n.,* **garrulity** (gă-**roo**-liti) *n.*

garter *n.* 1. a band especially of elastic worn round the leg to keep a stocking up. 2. *the Garter,* the highest order in English knighthood, its badge.

gas *n.* (*pl.* gases) 1. a substance with particles that can move freely, especially one that does not become liquid or solid at ordinary temperatures (other gases are usually called 'vapours'). 2. one of the gases or mixtures of gases used for lighting, heating, or cooking; *gas cooker, gas fire, etc.,* domestic appliances using gas as fuel. 3. poisonous gas used to disable an enemy in war, dangerous gas occurring naturally in a coal-mine. 4. nitrous oxide or other gas used as an anaesthetic. 5. (*slang*) empty talk. 6. (*Amer. informal,* short for *gasoline*) petrol; *step on the gas,* press the accelerator pedal, hurry. —**gas** *v.* (gassed, gassing) 1. to expose to gas, to poison or overcome by gas. 2. (*informal*) to talk idly for a long time. □ **gas chamber,** a room that can be filled with poisonous gas to kill animals or prisoners. **gas-fired** *adj.* heated by burning gas. **gas fitter,** a workman who fits pipes etc. for gas heating or lighting. **gas mask,** a protective device worn over the face to protect the wearer against poisonous gas. **gas oven,** the oven of a gas cooker; a gas chamber. **gas poker,** a hollow poker through which gas flows, used to light fires. **gas ring,** a hollow perforated ring through which gas flows for cooking on.

gasbag *n.* (*informal*) a person who talks too much.

gaseous (gas-iŭs) *adj.* of or like a gas.

gash *n.* a long deep slash or cut or wound. —*v.* to make a gash in.

gasholder *n.* a gasometer.

gasify *v.* (gasified, gasifying) to change or become changed into gas.

gasket *n.* a flat sheet or ring of rubber or other soft material used for sealing a joint between metal surfaces to prevent gas or steam or liquid from entering or escaping.

gaslight *n.* light given by a jet of burning gas.

gasoline *n.* **1.** a liquid distilled from petroleum, used for heating and lighting. **2.** (*Amer.*) petrol.

gasometer (gas-**om**-it-er) *n.* a large round tank in which gas is stored and from which it is distributed through pipes.

gasp *v.* **1.** to struggle for breath with the mouth open. **2.** to draw in the breath sharply in astonishment etc. **3.** to speak in a breathless way. —*n.* a breath drawn in sharply; *was at his last gasp,* was exhausted or at the point of death.

gassy *adj.* of or like a gas.

gastric *adj.* of the stomach. **gastric flu,** sickness and diarrhoea of unknown origin.

gastritis (gas-**try**-tiss) *n.* inflammation of the stomach.

gastro-enteritis (gas-troh-en-ter-**I**-tiss) *n.* inflammation of the stomach and intestines.

gastronomy (gas-**tron**-ŏmi) *n,* the science of good eating and drinking. **gastronomic** (gas-trŏ-**nom**-ik) *adj.*

gasworks *n.* a place where gas for lighting and heating is manufactured.

gate *n.* **1.** a movable barrier, usually on hinges, serving as door in a wall or fence, or regulating the passage of water etc. **2.** the opening it covers. **3.** a means of entrance or exit. **4.** an arrangement of slots controlling the movement of a gear lever in a motor vehicle. **5.** an electrical device that controls the passage of electrical signals, (in computers) a circuit with one output that is activated only by a combination of input signals. **6.** the number of spectators entering by payment to see a football match etc., the amount of money taken. —*v.* to confine to college or

school entirely or after certain hours, as a punishment. ☐ **gate-legged** *adj.* (of a table) having legs that can be moved out or in to support or lower drop leaves.

gateau (gat-oh) *n.* (*pl.* gateaux, *pr.* gat-ohz) a large rich cream cake.

gatecrash *v.* to go to a private party etc. without being invited. **gatecrasher** *n.*

gatehouse *n.* a house built at the side of or over a large gate.

gatekeeper *n.* a person on duty at a gate.

gateway *n.* **1.** an opening or structure framing a gate. **2.** any means of entrance or exit, *the gateway to success.*

gather *v.* **1.** to bring or come together. **2.** to collect, to obtain gradually. **3.** to collect as harvest, to pluck. **4.** to increase gradually, *gather speed.* **5.** to understand or conclude, *I gather your proposal was accepted.* **6.** to draw (parts) together; *his brow was gathered in thought,* was wrinkled. **7.** to pull fabric into gathers; *a gathered skirt,* made with gathers at the waist. **8.** (of a sore) to swell up and form pus. ☐ **gathers** *pl. n.* a series of folds formed by drawing up fabric on a thread run through it like a draw-string.

gathering *n.* **1.** an assembly of people. **2.** an inflamed swelling with pus in it.

gauche (*pr.* gohsh) *adj.* lacking in ease and grace of manner, awkward and tactless.

gaucherie (goh-sher-i) *n.* gauche manners, a gauche action.

gaudy *adj.* (gaudier, gaudiest) showy or bright in a tasteless way. **gaudily** *adv.,* **gaudiness** *n.*

gauge (*pr.* gayj) *n.* **1.** a standard measure of contents, fineness of textile, thickness of sheet metal, or diameter of bullets. **2.** the distance between pairs of rails or between opposite wheels. **3.** an instrument used for measuring, marked with regular divisions or units of measurement.. —**gauge** *v.* **1.** to measure exactly. **2.** to estimate, to form a judgement of.

Gaullist (**goh**-list) *n.* a supporter of the principles of Charles de Gaulle (1890 1970), French general and statesman.

gaunt *adj.* **1.** lean and haggard. **2.** grim or desolate-looking. **gauntness** *n.*

gauntlet[1] *n.* **1.** a glove with a wide cuff covering the wrist. **2.** the cuff itself. **3.** a glove with metal plates worn by soldiers in the Middle Ages. ☐ **throw down the gauntlet,** to make a challenge to a fight.

gauntlet[2] *n.* **run the gauntlet,** to be exposed to continuous severe criticism or risk. ¶ The phrase is derived from a former military and naval punishment in which the victim was made to pass between two rows of men who struck him as he passed.

gauss (*rhymes with* house) *n.* (*pl.* gauss) an electromagnetic unit of magnetic induction.

gauze *n.* **1.** thin transparent woven material of silk or cotton etc. **2.** fine wire mesh. **gauzy** *adj.*

gave *see* give.

gavel (**gav**-ĕl) *n.* a hammer used by an auctioneer or a chairman to call for attention or order.

gavotte (gă-**vot**) *n.* a lively old French dance, the music for it.

Gawd *n.* (*vulgar*) God.

gawky *adj.* awkward and ungainly. **gawkiness** *n.*

gawp *v.* (*informal*) to stare stupidly.

gay *adj.* **1.** light-hearted and cheerful, happy and full of fun. **2.** bright-coloured, dressed or decorated in bright colours. **3.** (*informal*) homosexual, of homosexuals. **gayness** *n.*

gaze *v.* to look long and steadily. —*n.* a long steady look.

gazebo (gă-**zee**-boh) *n.* (*pl.* gazebos) a structure, such as a raised turret or summer-house, with a wide view.

gazelle *n.* a small graceful Asian or African antelope.

gazette *n.* the title of certain newspapers, or of official journals that contain public notices and lists of government appointments.

gazetteer (gaz-it-**eer**) *n.* an index of place-names, names of rivers and mountains, etc.

gazpacho (gahs-**pah**-choh) *n.* Spanish cold vegetable soup.

gazump *v.* (*slang*) to disappoint (an intended purchaser) by raising the price after accepting his offer, especially for a house.

GB *abbrev.* Great Britain.

GC *abbrev.* George Cross.

GCE *abbrev.* General Certificate of Education.

GDR *abbrev.* German Democratic Republic.

gear *n.* **1.** equipment, *hunting-gear.* **2.** (*informal*) clothes, *teenage gear.* **3.** apparatus, appliances, *aircraft's landing gear.* **4.** a set of toothed wheels working together in a machine, those connecting the engine of a motor vehicle to the road wheels. —**gear** *v.* **1.** to put machinery in gear. **2.** to provide with or connect by gears. **3.** to adjust or adapt; *a factory geared to the export trade,* organized for this specifically. □ **in gear,** with gear mechanism engaged. **out of gear,** with it disengaged. **out of gear with,** not

proceeding or produced uniformly with (other parts etc.).

gearbox, gearcase *ns.* a case enclosing gear mechanism.

gecko (**gek**-oh) *n.* a house-lizard of warm climates, able to climb walls by the adhesive pads on its toes.

gee, gee whiz *int.* (*Amer.*) a mild exclamation.

gee-up *int.* a command to a horse to move on or go faster.

geezer *n.* (*slang*) a person, an old man.

Geiger counter (**gy**-ger) a cylindrical device for detecting and measuring radioactivity.

geisha (**gay**-shă) *n.* a Japanese hostess trained to entertain men by dancing and singing.

gel (*pr.* jel) *n.* a jelly-like substance. —*v.* (gelled, gelling) to set as a gel.

gelatine *n.* a clear tasteless substance made by boiling the bones, skins, and connective tissue of animals, used in foods, medicine, and photographic film.

gelatinous (jil-**at**-in-ŭs) *adj.* of or like gelatine, jelly-like.

geld *v.* to castrate, to spay.

gelding *n.* a gelded animal, especially a horse.

gelignite (**jel**-ig-nyt) *n.* an explosive containing nitro-glycerine.

gem *n.* **1.** a precious stone, especially when cut and polished. **2.** something valued because of its excellence or beauty; *the gem of the collection,* the most prized item.

Gemini (**jem**-in-I) a sign of the zodiac, the Twins. **Geminean** *adj.* & *n.*

gen (*pr.* jen) *n.* (*slang*) information.

gender *n.* **1.** the class in which a noun or pronoun is placed in grammatical grouping (in English, these are masculine, feminine, neuter, and common). **2.** (*informal*) a person's sex.

gene (*pr.* jeen) *n.* one of the factors controlling heredity, carried by a chromosome.

genealogy (jeeni-**al**-ŏji) *n.* **1.** an account of descent from an ancestor given by listing the intermediate persons, pedigree. **2.** the science or study of family pedigrees. **genealogical** (jeeni-ă-**loj**-ikăl) *adj.* □ **genealogist** *n.* an expert in genealogy.

genera *see* genus.

general *adj.* **1.** of or affecting all or nearly all, not partial or local or particular. **2.** involving various kinds, not specialized, *a general education.* **3.** involving only main features, not detailed or specific, *spoke only in general terms.* **4.** chief, head, *the general secretary; the Attorney-General.* —**general** *n.* **1.** an army officer ranking below a

Field Marshal. **2.** a lieutenant-general or major-general. **3.** *the General,* (*informal*) the General Post Office. □ **general election,** an election for representatives in Parliament from the whole country. **general knowledge,** knowledge of a wide variety of subjects. **general meeting,** one open to all members. **general practitioner,** a doctor who treats cases of all kinds in a section of the community. **general staff,** officers assisting a military commander at headquarters. **in general,** as a general rule, usually; for the most part.

generalissimo *n.* a commander of combined military, naval, and air forces, or of several armies.

generalist *n.* a person who is competent in several different fields (as opposed to a *specialist*).

generality (jen-er-**al**-iti) *n.* **1.** being general. **2.** a general statement lacking precise details.

generalize *v.* **1.** to draw a general conclusion from particular instances. **2.** to speak in general terms, to use generalities. **3.** to bring into general use. **generalization** *n.*

generally *adv* **1** usually, as a general rule. **2.** widely, for the most part, *the plan was generally welcomed.* **3.** in a general sense, without regard to details, *speaking generally.*

generate *v.* to bring into existence, to produce.

generation *n.* **1.** generating, being generated. **2.** a single stage in descent or pedigree; *three generations,* children, parents, and grandparents. **3.** all persons born about the same time and therefore of the same age, *my generation; first generation Americans,* Americans whose parents were of some other nationality. **4.** the average period (regarded as about 30 years) in which children grow up and take the former place of their parents. **5.** (of machinery etc.) a set of models at one stage of development, *a new generation of computers.* □ **generation gap,** lack of understanding between people of different generations.

generator *n.* **1.** an apparatus for producing gases, steam, etc. **2.** a machine for converting mechanical energy into electricity.

generic (jin-e-rik) *adj.* of a whole genus or group. **generically** *adv.*

generous *adj.* **1.** giving or ready to give freely, free from meanness or prejudice. **2.** given freely, plentiful, *a generous gift; a generous portion.* **generously** *adv.*, **generosity** *n.*

genesis *n.* **1.** a beginning or origin. **2.**

Genesis, the first book of the Old Testament, telling of the creation of the world.

genetic (ji-**net**-ik) *adj.* **1.** of genes. **2.** of genetics. **genetically** *adv.* □ **genetic code,** the system of storage of genetic information in chromosomes. **genetic engineering,** deliberate modification of hereditary features by treatment to transfer certain genes. **genetics** *pl. n.* the scientific study of heredity.

genial (jee-niăl) *adj.* **1.** kindly, pleasant, and cheerful. **2.** mild, pleasantly warm, *a genial climate.* **genially** *adv.,* **geniality** (jee-ni-**al**-iti) *n.*

genie (jee-ni) *n.* (in Arabian tales) a spirit or goblin with strange powers.

genital (jen-i-t'l) *adj.* of animal reproduction or reproductive organs. **genitals** *pl. n.* the external sex organs of people and animals.

genitive (jen-i-tiv) *n* the grammatical case showing source or possession in certain languages, corresponding to the use of *of* or *from* in English.

genius *n.* (*pl.* geniuses) **1.** exceptionally great mental ability, any great natural ability. **2.** a person possessing this. **3.** a guardian spirit, *one's good* or *evil genius.*

genocide (jen-ŏ-syd) *n.* deliberate extermination of a race of people.

genre (*pr.* zhahnr) *n.* a particular kind or style of art or literature.

gent *n.* **1.** (*slang*) a man, a gentleman. **2.** *the Gents,* (*informal*) a men's public lavatory.

genteel (jen-**teel**) *adj.* affectedly polite and refined. **genteelly** *adv.*

gentian (jen-shăn) *n.* an alpine plant usually with deep blue bell-like flowers. **gentian violet,** a dye used as an antiseptic.

Gentile (jen-tyl) *n.* anyone who is not Jewish.

gentility (jen-**til**-iti) *n.* good manners and elegance.

gentle *adj.* **1.** mild, moderate, not rough or severe, *a gentle breeze.* **2.** of good family, *is of gentle birth.* —*n.* a maggot used as bait. —*v.* to coax. —**gently** *adv.,* **gentleness** *n.* □ **the gentle sex,** women.

gentlefolk *n.* people of good family.

gentleman *n.* (*pl.* gentlemen) **1.** a man of honourable and kindly behaviour. **2.** a man of good social position. **3.** (in polite use) a man. **4.** *the Gentlemen's,* a men's public lavatory. **gentlemanly** *adj.* □ **gentleman-at-arms** *n.* one of the sovereign's bodyguard. **gentleman's agreement,** one that is regarded as binding in honour but not enforceable at law. **gentleman's gentleman,** a valet.

gentlewoman *n.* (*pl.* gentlewomen) (*old use*) a lady.

gentry *pl. n.* **1.** people next below the nobility in position and birth. **2.** (*contemptuous*) people, *these gentry*.

genuflect (jen-yoo-flekt) *v.* to bend the knee and lower the body, especially in worship. **genuflexion** *n.*

genuine *adj.* really what it is said to be, *genuine pearls*; *with genuine pleasure*. **genuinely** *adv.*, **genuineness** *n.*

genus (jee-nŭs) *n.* (*pl.* genera, *pr.* jen-er-ă) **1.** a group of animals or plants with common characteristics, usually containing several species. **2.** (*informal*) a kind or sort.

geodesy (ji-od-i-si) *n.* the scientific study of the earth's shape and size. **geodesic** (ji-ŏ-dee-sik) *adj.*, **geodetic** (ji-ŏ-det-ik) *adj.* □ **geodesic** (*or* **geodetic**) **dome**, a dome built of short struts holding flat or triangular polygonal pieces, fitted together to form a rough hemisphere.

geographer *n.* an expert in geography.

geography *n.* **1.** the scientific study of the earth's surface and its physical features, climate, products, and population. **2.** the physical features and arrangement of a place. **geographical** *adj.*, **geographically** *adv.*

geologist *n.* an expert in geology.

geology (ji-ol-ŏji) *n.* **1.** the scientific study of the earth's crust and its strata. **2.** the features and strata of the earth's crust. **geological** *adj.*, **geologically** *adv.*

geometry (ji-om-itri) *n.* the branch of mathematics dealing with the properties and relations of lines, angles, surfaces, and solids. **geometric** (ji-ŏ-met-rik), **geometrical** *adjs.*, **geometrically** *adv.*

Geordie (jor-di) *n.* a person from Tyneside.

Georgetown the capital of Guyana.

georgette (jor-jet) *n.* a thin silky dress-material.

Georgia **1.** a State of the USA. **2.** a region of the USSR.

Georgian (jor-jăn) *adj.* of the time of the Georges, kings of England, especially 1714–1830.

geranium *n.* a garden plant with red, pink, or white flowers.

gerbil (jer-bil) *n.* a desert rodent with long hind legs.

geriatrics (je-ri-at-riks) *n.* the branch of medicine dealing with the diseases and care of old people. **geriatric** *adj.* □ **geriatrician** (je-ri-ă-trish-ăn) *n.* a specialist in geriatrics.

germ *n.* **1.** a portion of a living organism capable of becoming a new organism, the embryo of a seed, *wheat germ*. **2.** a beginning or basis from which something may develop, *the germ of an idea*. **3.** a micro-organism, especially one causing disease.

German *adj.* of Germany or its people or language. —*n.* **1.** a native of Germany. **2.** the language of Germany. □ **German measles**, a contagious disease like mild measles.

germane (jer-mayn) *adj.* relevant.

Germanic (jer-man-ik) *adj.* having German characteristics.

Germany a country in Europe, divided between the Federal Republic of Germany (= West Germany) and the German Democratic Republic (= East Germany).

germicide (jerm-i-syd) *n.* a substance that kills germs or micro-organisms. **germicidal** *adj.*

germinate *v.* **1.** to begin to develop and grow, to put forth shoots. **2.** to cause to do this. **germination** *n.*

gerontology (je-ron-tol-ŏji) *n.* the scientific study of the process of ageing and of old people's special problems.

gerrymander (je-ri-man-der) *v.* to arrange the boundaries of constituencies so as to give unfair advantages to one party or class in an election. ¶ Named after Governor Gerry of Massachusetts, who rearranged boundaries for this purpose in 1812.

Gestapo (ges-tah-poh) *n.* the German secret police of the Nazi regime.

gestation (jes-tay-shŏn) *n.* **1.** the process of carrying or being carried in the womb. **2.** the time of this, from conception until birth. **3.** private development of a plan etc.

gesticulate (jes-tik-yoo-layt) *v.* to make expressive movements of the hands and arms. **gesticulation** *n.*

gesture (jes-cher) *n.* **1.** an expressive movement of any part of the body. **2.** something done to convey one's intentions or attitude, *a gesture of friendship*. —*v.* to make a gesture.

get *v.* (got, getting) **1.** to come into possession of, to obtain or receive. **2.** to obtain radio transmissions from, to reach by telephone. **3.** to fetch, *get your coat*. **4.** to suffer (a punishment etc.), to contract (an illness); *Bill got his,* (*slang*) was killed; *she has got religion,* has become very religious suddenly. **5.** to capture, to catch; *I'll get him for that,* catch and kill or injure him; *the bullet got him in the leg,* struck him. **6.** (*informal*) to understand, *I don't get your meaning*. **7.** to prepare (a meal). **8.** to bring or come into a certain condition, *get your hair cut*; *got wet*. **9.** to move in a par-

glandular (glan-dew-ler) adj. of or like a gland. glandular fever, a feverish illness in which certain glands are swollen.

glare v. 1. to shine with an unpleasant dazzling light. 2. to stare angrily or fiercely. —glare n. 1. a strong unpleasant light; the glare of publicity, intense publicity. 2. an angry or fierce stare.

glaring adj. 1. bright and dazzling. 2. very obvious, a glaring error. glaringly adv.

glass n. 1. a hard brittle substance (as used in windows), usually transparent. 2. an object made of this, e.g. a mirror; 50 acres of glass, of greenhouses. 3. a glass container for drinking from, its contents. 4. objects made of glass. 5. a barometer. —v. to fit or enclose with glass. □ glass-blowing n. shaping semi-molten glass by blowing air into it through a tube. glass-cloth n. a cloth for drying objects made of glass. glasses pl. n. spectacles, binoculars. glass fibre, fabric woven from glass filaments; plastic reinforced with glass filaments. glass-paper n. paper coated with glass particles, used for smoothing things.

glassful n. (pl. glassfuls) the amount contained by a drinking-glass.

glasshouse n. 1. a greenhouse. 2. (slang) a military prison.

glassy adj. 1. like glass in appearance. 2. with a dull expressionless stare, glassy-eyed. glassily adv., glassiness n.

Glaswegian (glaz-wee-jǎn) adj. of Glasgow. —n. a native or inhabitant of Glasgow.

glaucoma (glaw-koh-mǎ) n. a condition caused by increased pressure of the fluid within the eyeball, causing weakening or loss of sight.

glaze v. 1. to fit or cover with glass. 2. to coat with a glossy surface. 3. to become glassy. —n. a shiny surface or coating especially on pottery, the substance forming this.

glazier (glay-zi-er) n. a person whose trade is to fit glass in windows etc.

GLC abbrev. Greater London Council.

gleam n. 1. a beam or ray of soft light, especially one that comes and goes. 2. a brief show of some quality, a gleam of hope. —v. to send out gleams.

glean v. 1. to pick up grain left by harvesters. 2. to gather scraps of information. gleaner n. □ gleanings pl. n. things gleaned.

glee n. 1. lively or triumphant joy. 2. a part-song, especially for male voices. □ glee club, a type of choral society.

gleeful adj. full of glee. gleefully adv.

glen n. a narrow valley.

glengarry (glen-ga-ri) n. a Scotch cap with a pointed front and usually a pair of ribbons hanging from the back.

glib adj. ready with words but insincere or superficial, a glib tongue; a glib excuse. glibly adv., glibness n.

glide v. 1. to move along smoothly. 2. to fly in a glider or in an aeroplane without engine power. — n. a gliding movement.

glider n. an aircraft without an engine.

gliding n. the sport of flying in gliders.

glimmer n. a faint gleam. —v. to gleam faintly.

glimpse n. a brief view. —v. to catch a glimpse of.

glint n. a very brief flash of light. —v. to send out a glint.

glissade (glis-ayd) v. 1. to glide or slide skilfully down a steep slope, especially in mountaineering. 2. to make a gliding step in dancing. —n. a glissading movement or step.

glisten v. to shine like something wet or polished.

glitter v. to sparkle. —n. a sparkle.

gloaming n. the evening twilight.

gloat v. to be full of greedy or malicious delight.

global adj. 1. of the whole world, world wide. 2. of or in the whole of a computer program or set of data. globally adv.

globe n. 1. an object shaped like a ball, especially one with a map of the earth on it. 2. the world, travelled all over the globe. 3. a hollow round glass object, such as an electric light bulb. □ globe artichoke, the edible flower of an artichoke. globe-trotting n. & adj. travelling all over the world as a tourist.

globular (glob-yoo-ler) adj. shaped like a globe.

globule (glob-yool) n. a small rounded drop.

globulin (glob-yoo-lin) n. a kind of protein found in animal and plant tissue.

glockenspiel (glok-en-speel) n. a musical instrument consisting of tuned steel bars fixed in a frame and struck by two hammers, or with steel tubes or plates played from a keyboard.

gloom n. 1. semi-darkness. 2. a feeling of sadness and depression. —v. to look sullen, to feel sad and depressed.

gloomy adj. (gloomier, gloomiest) 1. almost dark, unlighted. 2. depressed, sullen. 3. dismal, depressing. gloomily adv., gloominess n.

glorify v. (glorified, glorifying) 1. to praise highly. 2. to worship. 3. to make something seem more splendid than it is, their patio is only a glorified back yard. glorification n.

ticular direction, to succeed in coming or going or bringing, get off the grass; we got from here to London in an hour. 10. to succeed in bringing or persuading, got a message to her; got her to agree. □ get across, (slang) to become on bad terms with. get along, to get on. get at, to reach; (informal) to mean, to imply; (slang) to imply a criticism of, he keeps getting at the trade unions; (slang) to tamper with, to bribe. get-at-able adj. (informal) able to be reached. get away, to escape; get away with something, do it and yet escape blame or punishment or misfortune. getaway n. an escape after committing a crime; the getaway car, the car used in this. get by, (informal) to pass, to be accepted; to manage to survive. get down, to swallow (a thing); to record in writing; (informal) to cause depression in (a person). get down to, to begin working on. get going, (informal) to begin moving or operating, to begin to be in progress. get in, to arrive. get off, to begin a journey; to be acquitted; to escape with little or no punishment; to obtain an acquittal for, a clever lawyer got him off. get off with, to become friendly with (a person), especially after attracting him or her deliberately. get on, to manage; to make progress; to be on friendly or harmonious terms; to advance in age; he is getting on, is elderly; getting on for, approaching an age or time. get on!, (informal) don't expect me to believe that. get one's own back, (informal) to have one's revenge. get out of, to avoid or get round. get-out n. a means of evading something; like all get-out, (slang) with great vigour. get over, to overcome (a difficulty); to recover from (an illness or shock etc.). get round, to influence in one's favour, to coax; to evade a law or rule without actually breaking it. get round to, to find time to deal with. get there, to reach one's goal; (informal) to succeed in understanding. get through, to finish or use up; to pass an examination; to make contact by telephone. get through to, (informal) to make (a person) understand. get-together n. (informal) a social gathering. get up, to stand after sitting or kneeling etc., to get out of bed or from one's chair etc.; to prepare or organize; to acquire a knowledge of; to produce in a specified style; to dress in an outfit or costume. get-up n. (informal) an outfit or costume. get up to, to become involved in (mischief etc.).

geum (jee-ŭm) n. a perennial garden plant with yellow, red, or white flowers.

gewgaw (g- as in get) n. a showy but valueless ornament or fancy article.

geyser n. 1. (pr. gy-zer) a natural spring sending up a column of hot water or steam at intervals. 2. (pr. gee-zer) a kind of water-heater.

Ghana (gah-nǎ) a country in West Africa. Ghanaian (gah-nay-ǎn) adj. & n.

ghastly adj. 1. causing horror or fear, a ghastly accident. 2. (informal) very unpleasant, very bad, a ghastly mistake. 3. pale and ill-looking. ghastliness n.

ghat (pr. gawt) n. (in India) 1. a flight of steps down to a river, a landing-place. 2. a mountain pass; Eastern and Western Ghats, mountains along the east and west coasts of south India.

gherkin (ger-kin) n. a small cucumber used for pickling.

ghetto (get-oh) n. (pl. ghettos) a slum area occupied by a particular group, especially as a result of social or economic conditions.

ghost n. 1. a person's spirit appearing after his death. 2. something very slight; he hasn't the ghost of a chance, he has no chance at all. 3. a duplicated image in a defective telescope or a television picture. v. to write as a ghost-writer. —ghostly adj., ghostliness n. □ ghost town, a town abandoned by all or most of its former inhabitants. ghost-writer n. a person who writes a book, article, or speech for another to pass off as his own. give up the ghost, to die.

ghoul (pr. gool) n. 1. (in Muslim stories) a spirit that robs graves and devours the corpses in them. 2. a person who enjoys gruesome things. ghoulish adj., ghoulishly adv.

giant n. 1. (in fairy-tales) a man of very great height and size. 2. a man, animal, or plant that is much larger than the usual size. 3. a person of outstanding ability or influence. —adj. of a kind that is very large in size. □ giantess n. a female giant.

Gib (pr. jib) abbrev. (informal) Gibraltar.

gibber (jib-er) v. to make unintelligible or meaningless sounds, especially when shocked or terrified.

gibberish (jib-er-ish) n. unintelligible talk or sounds, nonsense.

gibbet (jib-it) n. 1. a gallows. 2. an upright post with an arm from which an executed criminal was hung.

gibbon n. a long-armed ape of south-east Asia.

gibbous (jib-ŭs) adj. 1. convex, protuberant, humped. 2. (of a moon or planet) having more than half (but less than the whole) of its disc illuminated.

gibe (*pr.* jyb) *v.* to jeer. —*n.* a jeering remark.

giblets (**jib**-lits) *pl. n.* the edible parts of the inside of a bird, taken out before it is cooked.

giddy *adj.* (giddier, giddiest) **1.** having the feeling that everything is spinning round. **2.** causing this feeling, *giddy heights.* **3.** frivolous, flighty. **giddily** *adv.*, **giddiness** *n.*

gift *n.* **1.** a thing given or received without payment. **2.** a natural ability, *has a gift for languages.* **3.** an easy task. □ **gift token,** a voucher (given as a gift) for money to buy something. **look a gift-horse in the mouth,** to accept something ungratefully, examining it for faults.

gifted *adj.* having great natural ability.

gift-wrap *v.* (gift-wrapped, gift-wrapping) to wrap attractively as a gift.

gig[1] (g- *as in* get) *n.* a light two-wheeled horse-drawn carriage.

gig[2] (g- *as in* get) *n.* (*informal*) an engagement to play jazz etc., especially for a single performance.

gigantic *adj.* very large. **gigantically** *adv.*

giggle *v.* to laugh in a silly or nervous way. —*n.* **1.** this kind of laugh. **2.** (*informal*) something amusing, a joke, *did it for a giggle.*

gigolo (**jig**-ŏ-loh) *n.* (*pl.* gigolos) a man who is paid by an older woman to be her escort or lover.

gild[1] *v.* (gilded *or* gilt, gilding) to cover with a thin layer of gold or gold paint. **gild the lily,** to spoil something already beautiful by trying to improve it.

gild[2] *n. see* guild.

gill (*pr.* jil) *n.* one quarter of a pint.

gillie (**gil**-i) *n.* a man or boy attending someone shooting or fishing in Scotland.

gills (g- *as in* get) *pl. n.* **1.** the organ with which a fish breathes in water. **2.** the vertical plates on the under-side of a mushroom cap. □ **green about the gills,** looking sickly.

gilt[1] *adj.* gilded, gold-coloured. —*n.* a substance used for gilding. □ **gilt-edged** *adj.* (of investments) considered to be very safe. **gilts** *pl. n.* gilt-edged securities. **take the gilt off the gingerbread,** to make a situation lose its attractiveness.

gilt[2] *n.* a young sow.

gimbals (**jim**-bălz) *pl. n.* a contrivance of rings and pivots for keeping instruments horizontal in a moving ship etc.

gimcrack (**jim**-krak) *adj.* showy, worthless, and flimsy, *gimcrack ornaments.*

gimlet (**gim**-lit) *n.* a small tool with a screw-like tip for boring holes.

gimmick (**gim**-ik) *n.* a trick, device, or mannerism used for attracting notice or publicity, or for making an entertainer etc. easily recognized and remembered. **gimmicky** *adj.*

gin[1] (*pr.* jin) *n.* **1.** a trap or snare for catching animals. **2.** a machine for separating raw cotton from its seeds. —*v.* (ginned, ginning) to treat (cotton) in a gin.

gin[2] (*pr.* jin) *n.* a colourless alcoholic spirit flavoured with juniper berries. **gin rummy,** a form of rummy for two players. **gin sling,** a sweetened drink of gin and fruit-juice etc.

ginger *n.* **1.** the hot-tasting root of a tropical plant. **2.** this plant. **3.** liveliness. **4.** light reddish yellow. —*v.* to make more lively, *ginger things up.* —*adj.* ginger-coloured. □ **ginger ale, ginger beer,** ginger-flavoured fizzy drinks. **ginger group,** a group within a larger group, urging a more active or livelier policy. **ginger-nut** *n.* a ginger-flavoured biscuit.

gingerbread *n.* a ginger-flavoured cake or biscuit.

gingerly *adv.* cautiously. —*adj.* cautious, *in a gingerly way.*

gingham (**ging**-ăm) *n.* a cotton fabric often with a striped or checked pattern.

gingivitis (jin-ji-vy-tiss) *n.* inflammation of the gums.

gippy tummy (**jip**-i) (*informal*) diarrhoea affecting visitors to hot countries.

gipsy *n.* = gypsy.

giraffe *n.* a long-necked African animal.

gird *v.* to encircle or attach with a belt or band, *he girded on his sword.* **gird up one's loins,** to prepare for an effort.

girder *n.* a metal beam supporting part of a building or a bridge.

girdle[1] *n.* **1.** a belt or cord worn round the waist. **2.** an elastic corset. **3.** a connected ring of bones in the body, *the pelvic girdle.* —*v.* to surround.

girdle[2] *n.* a round iron plate for cooking things over heat (also called a *griddle*).

girl *n.* **1.** a female child. **2.** a young woman. **3.** (*informal*) a woman of any age, a woman assistant or employee. **4.** a man's girl-friend. —**girlhood** *n.* □ **Girl Friday,** a young woman doing general duties in an office etc. (¶ named after Man Friday in Defoe's book 'Robinson Crusoe'). **girl-friend** *n.* a female friend, especially a man's usual companion.

girlie *n.* (*informal*) a girl. **girlie magazines,** magazines containing erotic pictures of young women.

girlish *adj.* like a girl. **girlishly** *adv.*, **girlishness** *n.*

giro (**jy**-roh) *n.* (*pl.* giros) a system, used in banking or operated by the Post Office, by which one customer can make a payment to another by transferring credit from his own account to the other person's, instead of paying him directly.

girt *adj.* (*poetical*) girded.

girth *n.* **1.** the distance round a thing. **2.** a band passing under a horse's belly, holding the saddle in place.

gist (*pr.* jist) *n.* the essential points or general sense of anything.

give *v.* (gave, given, giving) **1.** to cause another person to receive or have (especially something in one's possession or at one's disposal), to supply; *give me Spain for holidays,* I prefer it. **2.** to deliver (a message). **3.** (*informal*) to tell what one knows. **4.** to utter, *gave a laugh.* **5.** to pledge, *give one's word.* **6.** to make over in exchange or payment; *I don't give a damn,* don't care at all. **7.** to make or perform (an action or effort), to affect another person or thing with this, *gave him a scolding; gave the door a kick; I was given to understand,* was told. **8.** to provide (a meal or party) as host. **9.** to perform or present (a play etc.) in public. **10.** to yield as a product or result. **11.** to be the source of. **12.** to permit a view of or access to, *the window gives on the street.* **13.** to declare (judgement) authoritatively, *the umpire gave the batsman out.* **14.** to be flexible, to yield when pressed or pulled; *woollen fabric gives,* it stretches slightly. **15.** (*informal*) to be happening, *what gives?* —**give** *n.* springiness, elasticity. □ **give-and-take** *n.* an exchange of talk and ideas; willingness on both sides to make concessions. **give away,** to give as a present; to hand over (the bride) to the groom at a wedding; to reveal (a secret etc.) unintentionally. **give-away** *n.* (*informal*) a thing given without charge; something that reveals a secret. **give in,** to hand in (a document etc.); to acknowledge that one is defeated. **give it to a person,** (*informal*) to reprimand or punish him; to award praise to him. **give off,** to produce and emit, *petrol gives off fumes.* **give or take,** (*informal*) add or subtract (an amount) in estimating. **give out,** to distribute; to announce; to emit, *chimney was giving out smoke;* to become exhausted or used up. **give over,** to devote, *afternoons are given over to sport;* (*informal*) to cease doing something. **give tongue,** to speak one's thoughts; (of hounds) to bark, especially on finding the scent. **give up,** to cease (doing something); to part with; to surrender; to abandon hope; to declare a person to be incurable or a problem to be too difficult for oneself to solve; *he was*

given up for dead, was assumed to be dead. **give way,** to yield, to allow other traffic to go first; to collapse.

given *see* give. —*adj.* **1.** specified or stated, *all the people in a given area.* **2.** having a certain tendency, *he is given to swearing.* □ **given name,** a Christian name, a first name (given in addition to a family name).

giver *n.* a person who gives.

gizzard *n.* a bird's second stomach, in which food is ground.

glacé (**gla**-say) *adj.* iced with sugar, preserved in sugar, *glacé fruits; glacé icing,* made from icing sugar and water.

glacial (**glay**-shăl) *adj.* **1.** icy. **2.** of or from glaciers or other ice, *glacial deposits.* **glacially** *adv.*

glaciated (**glas**-i-ayt-id) *adj.* covered with glaciers, affected by their action. **glaciation** *n.*

glacier (**glas**-i-er) *n.* a river of ice moving very slowly.

glad *adj.* (gladder, gladdest) **1.** pleased, expressing joy. **2.** giving joy, *the glad news.* □ **glad of,** to be glad of. **gladly** *adv.*, **gladness** *n.* □ **be glad of,** to be grateful for. **glad eye,** (*slang*) an inviting look towards a member of the opposite sex. **glad hand,** (*informal*) a hearty welcome. **glad rags,** (*informal*) dressy clothes.

gladden *v.* to make glad.

glade *n.* an open space in a forest.

gladiator (**glad**-i-ay-ter) *n.* a man trained to fight at public shows in ancient Rome. **gladiatorial** (gladi-ă-**tor**-iăl) *adj.*

gladiolus *n.* (*pl.* gladioli, *pr.* glad-i-**oh**-ly) a garden plant with spikes of brightly-coloured flowers.

Gladstone bag a small case shaped like a portmanteau. ¶ Named after W. E. Gladstone, 19th-century English statesman.

Glam. *abbrev.* Glamorgan.

Glamorgan a former county of Wales, now *Mid, South,* and *West Glamorgan.*

glamorize *v.* to make glamorous or romantic.

glamour *n.* **1.** alluring beauty. **2.** attractive and exciting qualities that arouse envy. **glamorous** *adj.*

glance *v.* **1.** to look briefly. **2.** to strike at an angle and glide off an object, *a glancing blow; the ball glanced off his bat.* —*n.* **1.** a brief look. **2.** a stroke in cricket with the bat's face turned slantwise to the ball.

gland *n.* an organ that separates from the blood substances that are to be used in the body or expelled from it.

glanders *n.* a contagious disease of horses.

glorious *adj.* **1.** possessing or bringing glory. **2.** splendid, *a glorious view*; *a glorious muddle*, very great. **gloriously** *adv.*

glory *n.* **1.** fame and honour won by great deeds. **2.** adoration and praise in worship, *glory to God*. **3.** beauty, magnificence, *the glory of a sunset*. **4.** a thing deserving praise and honour. —*v.* (gloried, glorying) to rejoice or pride oneself, *glorying in their success*. □ **glory hole** *n.* (*slang*) an untidy room or cupboard etc. **go to glory**, (*slang*) to be destroyed; to die.

Glos. *abbrev.* Gloucestershire.

gloss *n.* **1.** the shine on a smooth surface. **2.** an explanatory comment. —*v.* to make glossy. □ **gloss over**, to cover up (a mistake or fault). **gloss paint**, a paint with a glossy finish.

glossary (**glos**-er-i) *n.* a list of technical or special words with their definitions.

glossy *adj.* (glossier, glossiest) shiny; *glossy magazine*, one printed on glossy paper, with many illustrations. **glossily** *adv.*, **glossiness** *n.*

Gloucester (**glos**-ter) *n.* a kind of cheese from Gloucestershire. **double Gloucester**, the kind made from very rich milk.

Gloucestershire a county of England.

glove *n.* a covering for the hand, usually with separate divisions for each finger and the thumb. **fit like a glove**, to fit exactly. **glove puppet**, one fitting over the hand so that the fingers can move it. **with the gloves off**, arguing in earnest, striving mercilessly.

gloved *adj.* wearing a glove or gloves.

glover *n.* a person whose trade is the making of gloves.

glow *v.* **1.** to send out light and heat without flame. **2.** to have a warm or flushed look, colour, or feeling; *a glowing account*, very enthusiastic or favourable. —*n.* a glowing state, look, or feeling. □ **glow-worm** *n.* a kind of beetle which can give out a greenish light at its tail.

glower (*rhymes with* flower) *v.* to scowl, to stare angrily.

gloxinia (glok-**sin**-iă) *n.* a tropical plant with bell-shaped flowers.

glucose (**gloo**-kohz) *n.* a form of sugar found in fruit-juice.

glue *n.* a sticky substance used for joining things. —*v.* (glued, gluing) **1.** to fasten with glue. **2.** to attach or hold closely, *his ear was glued to the keyhole*. —**gluey** *adj.*

glum *adj.* (glummer, glummest) sad and gloomy. **glumly** *adv.*, **glumness** *n.*

glut *v.* (glutted, glutting) **1.** to supply with much more than is needed, *glut the market*. **2.** to satisfy fully with food, *glut oneself* or *one's appetite*. —*n.* an excessive supply, *a glut of apples*.

glutamate (**gloo**-tă-mayt) *n.* a substance used to bring out the flavour in food.

gluten (**gloo**-tĕn) *n.* a sticky protein substance that remains when starch is washed out of flour. **gluten bread**, bread that contains much gluten and little starch.

glutinous (**gloo** tin ŭs) *adj.* glue-like, sticky.

glutton *n.* **1.** a person who eats far too much. **2.** a person with a great desire or capacity for something; *a glutton for punishment*, one who enjoys arduous tasks. **3.** an animal of the weasel family. **gluttonous** *adj.*, **gluttony** *n.*

glycerine (**glis**-er-een) *n.* a thick sweet colourless liquid used in ointments and medicines and in the manufacture of explosives.

G-man *n.* (*pl.* G-men) (*Amer. slang*) an agent of the Federal Bureau of Investigation.

GMT *abbrev.* Greenwich Mean Time.

gnarled (*pr.* narld) *adj.* (of a tree or hands) covered with knobbly lumps, twisted and misshapen.

gnash *v.* **1.** to grind (one's teeth). **2.** (of teeth) to strike together.

gnat *n.* a small biting fly.

gnaw *v.* to bite persistently at something hard; *a gnawing pain*, hurting continuously.

gnome *n.* **1.** a kind of dwarf in fairy-tales, living underground and guarding the treasures of the earth. **2.** a model of such a dwarf as a garden ornament. **3.** *Gnomes of Zurich*, important international financiers with secret influence.

gnu (*pr.* noo) *n.* an ox-like antelope.

go[1] *v.* (went, gone, going) **1.** to begin to move, to be moving, to pass from one point to another; *we must go at one o'clock*, must leave; *go shopping*, go out for this purpose. **2.** to extend or lead from one place to another, *the road goes to York*. **3.** to be in a specified state, *they went hungry*. **4.** to be functioning, *that clock doesn't go*. **5.** to make a specified movement or sound, *the gun went bang*; *the whistle has gone*, has sounded as a signal. **6.** (of time) to pass, (of a distance) to be traversed or accomplished, *ten miles to go*. **7.** to be allowable or acceptable, *anything goes*; *what he says, goes*, has final authority; *that goes without saying*, is too obvious to need to be mentioned. **8.** to belong in some place or position, *plates go on the shelf*. **9.** to be on the average, *it is cheap as things go nowadays*. **10.** (of a story or tune etc.) to have a certain wording or content, *I forget how the* *chorus goes.* **11.** to pass into a certain condition, *the fruit went bad.* **12.** to make progress, to fare, *all went well; make the party go,* to make it lively and successful. **13.** to be sold, *it's going cheap.* **14.** (of money or supplies) to be spent or used up. **15.** to be given up, dismissed, abolished, or lost, *some luxuries must go; my sight is going,* is becoming weaker. **16.** to fail, to give way, to die. **17.** to carry an action to a certain point; *that's going too far,* beyond the limits of what is reasonable or polite; *will go to £50 for it,* will pay as much as that. **18.** to be able to be put, *your clothes won't go into that suitcase; 3 into 12 goes 4,* 3 is contained in 12 four times. **19.** to be given or allotted, *his estate went to his nephew.* **20.** to contribute, to serve, *it all goes to prove what I said.* —**go** *n.* (*pl.* goes) **1.** energy, *full of go.* **2.** a turn or try, *have a go.* **3.** a success; *make a go of it,* make it succeed. **4.** an attack of illness, *a bad go of flu.* —*adj.* (*informal*) functioning properly; *all systems are go,* everything is ready. □ **go about,** to go to social functions; *he goes about grumbling,* grumbles to everyone he meets; *go about work efficiently,* tackle it efficiently. **go ahead,** to proceed immediately. **go-ahead** *n.* a signal to proceed immediately, (*adj.*) energetic, willing to try new methods. **go a long way,** to go far; to last long or buy much; to have a great effect towards achieving something. **go along with,** to agree with. **go back on one's word,** to fail to keep a promise. **go-between** *n.* one who acts as a messenger or negotiator. **go by,** to be guided or directed by. **go-by** (*n.*) *give a person the go-by,* to ignore him. **go down,** (of a ship) to sink, (of the sun) to appear to descend towards the horizon, to set; to be written down; to be swallowed; to be received or accepted, *the suggestion went down very well;* (*slang*) to go to prison. **go down with,** to become ill with (a disease). **go far,** to achieve much; to contribute greatly towards something. *it doesn't go far,* does not last long or buy much. **go for,** to like, to prefer, to choose; (*slang*) to attack. **go-getter** *n.* (*informal*) one who is successful through being pushful and energetic. **go-go** *adj.* (*informal*) very active or energetic; *go-go dancers,* (*Amer.*) performers of lively erotic dancing at night-clubs etc. **go in for,** to compete in; to engage in (an activity). **go into,** to become a member or occupant or patient in (an institution); to investigate (a problem). **go it!,** (*slang*) an encouragement to act vigorously. **go it alone,** to take action by oneself without assistance. **go off,** to explode; to lose

quality, to become stale; to fall asleep; to proceed, *the party went off well;* to dislike what one liked formerly, *I've gone off tea lately.* **go on,** to continue; to talk lengthily; *to go on at someone,* (*informal*) to nag him; *enough to be going on with,* enough for the moment. **go on!,** (*informal*) do not expect me to believe that. **go out,** to go to social functions; to be broadcast, *the programme goes out live;* to be extinguished; to cease to be fashionable; (*Amer. informal*) to lose consciousness; *my heart went out to him,* I sympathized with him. **go out with,** to have as a social companion of the opposite sex. **go round,** to be enough for everyone. **go slow,** to work at a deliberately slow pace as a form of industrial protest. **go-slow** *n.* a deliberately slow pace of this kind. **go to a person's head,** (of alcohol) to make him slightly drunk; (of success etc.) to make him conceited. **go up,** to rise in price; to explode; to burn rapidly. **go with,** to match, to harmonize with. **go without,** to put up with the lack of something. **on the go,** in constant motion, active. **to go,** (*Amer.,* of foods) to be taken away for consumption, *two ham sandwiches to go.*

go[2] *n.* a Japanese board game.

goad *n.* **1.** a pointed stick for prodding cattle to move onwards. **2.** something stimulating a person to activity. —*v.* to act as a stimulus to, *goaded her into answering back.*

goal *n.* **1.** a structure or area into which players try to send a ball in certain games. **2.** a point scored in this way. **3.** an objective. □ **goal difference,** (in league football) the difference between the total of goals scored by a team and those against it in a series of matches. **goal-line** *n.* the end line of a football or hockey pitch. **goal-post** *n.* either of the pair of posts marking the limits of the goal.

goalie *n.* (*informal*) a goalkeeper.

goalkeeper *n.* a player whose chief task is to keep the ball out of the goal.

goat *n.* **1.** a small horned animal kept for its milk. **2.** a related wild animal, *mountain goat.* **3.** *the Goat,* a sign of the zodiac, Capricorn. □ **act the goat,** to behave comically. **get someone's goat,** (*slang*) to annoy him.

goatee (goh-**tee**) *n.* a short pointed beard.

goatherd *n.* a person who looks after a herd of goats.

gob[1] *n.* (*vulgar*) a clot of a slimy substance.

gob[2] *n.* (*slang*) the mouth. **gob-stopper** *n.* a large sweet for sucking.

gobbet *n.* an extract from a text, e.g. one set for comment in an examination.

gobble *v.* 1. to eat quickly and greedily. 2. to make a throaty sound like a turkey-cock.

gobbledegook *n.* (*slang*) pompous language used by officials.

goblet *n.* 1. a drinking-glass with a stem and a foot. 2. the container of liquid in a liquidizer.

goblin *n.* a mischievous ugly elf.

go-cart *n.* a simple four-wheeled structure for a child to play on.

god *n.* 1. *God*, the creator and ruler of the universe in Christian, Jewish, and Muslim teaching. 2. a superhuman being regarded and worshipped as having power over nature and human affairs, *Mars was the Roman god of war*. 3. an image of a god, an idol. 4. a person or thing that is greatly admired or adored, *money is his god.* □ **God-fearing** *adj.* sincerely religious. **God forbid**, I wish that this may not happen. **God-forsaken** *adj.* wretched, dismal. **God knows**, this is something we cannot hope to know; I call God to witness. **God will-ing**, if circumstances allow it. **good God! my God!, ye gods!**, exclamations of surprise or pain. **the gods**, (*informal*) the gallery in a theatre.

godchild *n.* (*pl.* **godchildren**) a child in relation to its godparent(s).

god-daughter *n.* a female godchild.

goddess *n.* a female god.

godetia (gŏ-dee-shǎ) *n.* a garden plant with brightly-coloured flowers.

godfather *n.* 1. a male godparent. 2. (*Amer.*) the mastermind behind an illegal organization.

godhead *n.* divine nature; *the Godhead*, God.

godless *adj.* not having belief in God, wicked. **godlessly** *adv.*, **godlessness** *n.*

godlike *adj.* like God or a god.

godly *adj.* (**godlier**, **godliest**) sincerely religious. **godliness** *n.*

godmother *n.* a female godparent.

godparent *n.* a person who undertakes, when a child is baptized, to see that it is brought up as a Christian.

godsend *n.* a piece of unexpected good fortune.

godson *n.* a male godchild.

Godspeed *n.* an expression of good wishes to a person starting a journey.

goer *n.* a person or thing that goes; *car is a nice goer*, runs well; *church-goer*, a person who goes to church regularly.

goffer (goh-fer) *v.* to crimp frills etc. with hot irons.

goggle *v.* to stare with wide-open eyes.

goggle-box *n.* (*slang*) a television set.

goggle-eyed *adj.* with wide-open eyes.

goggles *pl. n.* spectacles for protecting the eyes from wind, dust, or water etc.

go-go *see* go¹.

going *see* go¹. —*n.* 1. moving away, departing, *comings and goings*. 2. the state of the ground for walking or riding on, *rough going*. 3. rate of progress, *it was good going to get there by noon*. —**going** *adj.* 1. moving away, departing; *he has everything going for him*, all is operating in his favour. 2. existing, available, *there is cold beef going*. 3. current; *the going rate*, the current price. 4. active and prosperous, *a going concern*. □ **be going to do some-thing**, to be about to do it, to be likely to do it. **going-over** *n.* (*informal*) an inspection or overhaul; (*slang*) a thrashing. **goings-on** *pl. n.* surprising behaviour or events. **while the going is good**, while conditions are favourable.

goitre (goi-ter) *n.* an enlarged thyroid gland, often showing as a swelling in the neck.

go kart *n.* a kind of miniature racing-car. **go-karting** *n.* the sport of racing in this.

gold *n.* 1. a yellow metal of very high value. 2. coins or other articles made of gold. 3. its colour. 4. the bull's-eye of an archery target, a shot that strikes this. 5. a gold medal (awarded as first prize). 6. something very good or precious. —*adj.* made of gold, coloured like gold. □ **gold brick**, something that looks valuable on the surface but is sham beneath. **gold-digger** *n.* a woman who uses her attractions to obtain money from men. **gold-dust** *n.* gold found naturally in fine particles. **gold-field** *n.* an area where gold is found as a mineral. **gold-mine** *n.* a place where gold is mined; a source of great wealth, *the shop was a little gold-mine*. **gold-plated** *adj.* coated with gold. **gold reserve**, gold held by a central bank to guarantee the value of a country's currency. **gold-rush** *n.* a rush to a newly discovered gold-field. **gold standard**, a system by which the value of money is based on that of gold. **Gold Stick**, the bearer of a gilt rod carried on State occasions.

goldcrest *n.* a very small bird with a golden crest.

golden *adj.* 1. made of gold. 2. coloured like gold. 3. precious, excellent, *a golden opportunity*. □ **golden age**, a time of great prosperity. **golden boy** *or* **girl**, a popular or successful person. **golden handshake**, a generous cash payment given by a firm to one of its executives as compensation for being dismissed or forced to retire.

277

Golden Gate, a channel of water in California between San Francisco Bay and the Pacific, spanned by a suspension bridge. **Golden Horn**, the harbour at Istanbul. **golden jubilee**, the 50th anniversary of a sovereign's accession or other event. **golden mean**, neither too much nor too little. **golden retriever**, a retriever dog with a thick golden coat. **golden rod**, a plant with spikes of yellow flowers, blooming in late summer. **golden rule**, a basic principle of action. **Golden Syrup**, (*trade mark*) a kind of pale treacle. **golden wedding**, the 50th anniversary of a wedding.

goldfinch *n.* a songbird with a band of yellow across each wing.

goldfish *n.* (*pl.* goldfish) a small reddish Chinese carp kept in a bowl or pond.

goldsmith *n.* a person whose trade is making articles in gold.

golf *n.* a game in which a small hard ball is struck with clubs towards and into a series of holes. —*v.* to play golf. □ **golf ball**, a ball used in golf. **golf-club** *n.* a club used in golf. **golf club**, an association for playing golf, its premises. **golf-course**, **golf-links** *ns.* an area of land on which golf is played.

golfer *n.* **1.** a golf-player. **2.** a woman's cardigan that buttons to the neck, a man's cardigan.

golliwog *n.* a male Negro doll made in soft material with fuzzy hair and brightly coloured clothes.

golly *int.* (*informal*) an exclamation of surprise.

golosh *n.* = galosh.

gondola (gon-dŏl-ă) *n.* **1.** a boat with high pointed ends, used on the canals in Venice. **2.** a basket-like structure suspended beneath a balloon, for carrying passengers etc.

gondolier (gond-ŏ-**leer**) *n.* a man who propels a gondola by means of a pole.

gone *see* go¹. —*adj.* **1.** departed, past; *it's gone six o'clock*, later than this. **2.** dead. **3.** (*informal*) pregnant for a specified time, *she is six months gone*. □ **gone on**. (*slang*) infatuated with.

goner *n.* (*slang*) a person or thing that is dead, ruined, or doomed.

gong *n.* **1.** a round metal plate that resounds when struck, especially one used as a signal for meals. **2.** a similar device operated electrically. **3.** (*slang*) a medal.

gonorrhoea (gon-ŏ-**ree**-ă) *n.* a venereal disease causing a thick discharge from the sexual organs.

goo *n.* (*slang*) **1.** sticky wet material. **2.** sickly sentiment.

good *adj.* (better, best) **1.** having the right or desirable properties, satisfactory, *good food*. **2.** right, proper, expedient. **3.** morally correct, virtuous, kindly. **4.** (of a child) well-behaved. **5.** gratifying, enjoyable, beneficial, *have a good time*; *good morning*, *good evening*, forms of greeting or farewell. **6.** efficient, suitable, competent, *a good driver*; *good at chess*. **7.** thorough, considerable, *a good beating*. **8.** not less than, full, *walked a good ten miles*. **9.** used in exclamations, *good God!* —**good** *adv.* (*Amer. informal*) **1.** well, *doing pretty good*. **2.** entirely; *good and angry*, very angry. —**good** *n.* **1.** that which is morally right; *up to no good*, doing something mischievous or criminal. **2.** profit, benefit, *it will do him good*; *£5 to the good*, having made this profit. **3.** *the good*, virtuous people. □ **as good as**, practically, almost, *the war is as good as over*. **for good and all**, permanently, finally. **good for**, beneficial to; able to pay or undertake; *he is good for £100, for a 10-mile walk*; *good for you!*, well done! **good-for-nothing** *adj.* worthless, (*n.*) a worthless person. **Good Friday**, the Friday before Easter, commemorating the Crucifixion. **good-looking** *adj.* having a pleasing appearance. **good-tempered** *adj.* having or showing good temper. **goodwill** *n.* a friendly feeling; the established custom or popularity of a business, considered as an asset that can be sold. **good will**, an intention that good shall result; *good-will token*, a token of this. **in good time**, with no risk of being late; *all in good time*, in due course but without haste.

goodbye *int.* & *n.* farewell, an expression used when parting or at the end of a telephone call. □ **goodbye to**, there will be no more of.

goodish *adj.* **1.** fairly good. **2.** rather large or great, *it's a goodish way from the station*.

goodness *n.* **1.** the quality of being good. **2.** the good element of something; *the goodness is in the gravy*, this is the most nourishing part. **3.** used instead of 'God' in exclamations, *goodness knows*; *for goodness' sake*; *thank goodness*. □ **have the goodness to**, to be kind enough to (do something).

goods *pl. n.* **1.** movable property. **2.** articles of trade, *leather goods*. **3.** things to be carried by road or rail; *goods train*, a train carrying goods not passengers. □ **the goods**, (*informal*) the genuine article, the real thing; *deliver the goods*, to produce what one has promised; *have the goods on a person*, to have evidence of his guilt.

goodwill *see* good.

goody *n.* (*informal*) **1.** something good or attractive, especially to eat. **2.** a person of

grant *v.* **1.** to give or allow as a privilege; *grant a request*, permit what is requested. **2.** to admit or agree that something is true, *I grant that your offer is generous.* — *n.* something granted, especially a sum of money; *students' grants*, their allowances from public funds. ☐ **take for granted**, to assume that something is true or sure to happen; to be so used to having something that one no longer appreciates it.

granular (gran-yoo-ler) *adj.* like grains or granules.

granulate (gran-yoo-layt) *v.* **1.** to form into grains or granules, *granulated sugar.* **2.** to make rough and grainy on the surface. **granulation** *n.*

granule (gran-yool) *n.* a small grain.

grape *n.* a green or purple berry growing in clusters on vines, used for making wine. ☐ **grape hyacinth**, a small hyacinth-like plant with clusters of rounded usually blue flowers. **grape-vine** *n.* the kind of vine on which grapes grow; a way by which news is passed on unofficially, *heard it on the grape-vine.*

grapefruit *n.* (*pl.* **grapefruit**) a large round yellow citrus fruit with an acid juicy pulp.

graph *n.* a diagram consisting of a line or lines showing the relationship between corresponding values of two quantities. — *v.* to draw a graph of. ☐ **graph paper**, paper ruled into small squares, used for plotting graphs.

graphic (graf-ik) *adj.* **1.** of drawing or painting or lettering or engraving, *the graphic arts*; *a graphic artist.* **2.** giving a vivid description, *a graphic account of the fight.* ☐ **graphics** *n.* the use of diagrams in calculation or in design; lettering and drawings, *the graphics are by John James.*

graphical (graf-ik-ăl) *adj.* **1.** using diagrams or graphs. **2.** = graphic (sense 1).

graphically *adv.* in a graphic or graphical way.

graphite *n.* a soft black form of carbon used in lubrication, as a moderator in nuclear reactors, and in lead pencils.

graphology (gră-fol-ŏji) *n.* the scientific study of handwriting, especially as a guide to the writer's character. **graphological** *adj.* **graphologist** *n.*

grapnel *n.* **1.** a small anchor with three or more flukes, used for boats and balloons. **2.** a hooked grappling instrument used in dragging the bed of a lake or river.

grapple *v.* **1.** to seize or hold firmly. **2.** to struggle at close quarters; *grapple with a problem*, try to deal with it. ☐ **grappling-iron** *n.* a grapnel.

grasp *v.* **1.** to seize and hold firmly, especially with one's hands or arms. **2.** to understand, *he couldn't grasp what we meant.* — **grasp** *n.* **1.** a firm hold or grip; *within his grasp*, close enough for him to grasp or obtain it. **2.** a mental hold, understanding, *a thorough grasp of his subject.* ☐ **grasp at**, to snatch at. **grasp the nettle**, to tackle a difficulty or danger boldly.

grasping *adj.* greedy for money or possessions.

grass *n.* **1.** any of a group of common wild low-growing plants with green blades and stalks that are eaten by animals. **2.** any species of this plant (in botanical use including cereal plants, reeds, and bamboos). **3.** ground covered with grass, lawn, or pasture; *put animals out to grass*, put them to graze. **4.** (*slang*) marijuana. **5.** (*slang*) a person who grasses, an act of grassing or betraying. — **grass** *v.* **1.** to cover with grass. **2.** (*slang*) to betray a conspiracy, to turn informer. ☐ **grass roots**, the fundamental level or source; ordinary people, the rank-and-file of a political party or other group. **grass snake**, a small harmless snake. **grass widow**, a wife whose husband is absent for some time.

grasshopper *n.* a jumping insect that makes a shrill chirping noise.

grassland *n.* a wide area covered in grass and with few trees.

grassy *adj.* like grass, covered with grass.

grate¹ *n.* **1.** a metal framework that keeps fuel in a fireplace. **2.** the recess where the fire burns, the surrounding structure.

grate² *v.* **1.** to shred into small pieces by rubbing against a jagged surface. **2.** to make a harsh noise by rubbing, to sound harshly, *a grating laugh.* **3.** to have an unpleasant irritating effect.

grateful *adj.* feeling or showing that one values a kindness or benefit received. **gratefully** *adv.*

grater *n.* a device with a jagged surface for grating food.

gratify *v.* (gratified, gratifying) to give pleasure to, to satisfy (wishes etc.). **gratification** *n.*

grating *n.* a screen of spaced metal or wooden bars placed across an opening.

gratis (gray-tiss) *adv. & adj.* free of charge, *you can have the leaflet gratis.*

gratitude *n.* being grateful.

gratuitous (gră-tew-it-ŭs) *adj.* **1.** given or done without payment. **2.** given or done without good reason, *a gratuitous insult.* **gratuitously** *adv.*

gratuity (gră-tew-iti) *n.* money given in

good character, *the goodies and the baddies.* — *adj.* smugly virtuous. — *int.* (children's use) an exclamation of delight.

goody-goody *adj.* smugly virtuous. — *n.* a goody-goody person.

gooey *adj.* (*slang*) **1.** wet and sticky. **2.** sickly and sentimental.

goof *n.* (*slang*) **1.** a stupid person. **2.** a mistake.

goofy *adj.* (*slang*) stupid.

googly *n.* a ball bowled in cricket so that it breaks in the opposite direction from what the batsman expected.

goose *n.* (*pl.* **geese**) **1.** a web-footed bird larger than a duck. **2.** its flesh as food. **3.** (*informal*) a stupid person. ☐ **all his geese are swans**, he refuses to believe that there are any faults in the people or ideas he supports. **goose-flesh** *or* **goose-pimples** *ns.* rough bristling skin caused by cold or fear. **goose-neck** *n.* a thing shaped like the neck of a goose. **goose step**, a way of marching without bending the knees.

gooseberry *n.* **1.** a thorny shrub. **2.** its edible berry. **3.** a chaperon or an unwelcome companion to a pair of lovers, *to play gooseberry.*

Gordian *adj.* **cut the Gordian knot**, to solve a problem forcefully or by some unexpected means. ¶ An intricate knot was tied by Gordius, king of ancient Phrygia; it was eventually cut, rather than untied, by Alexander the Great.

gore¹ *n.* thickened blood from a cut or wound.

gore² *n.* a triangular or tapering section of a skirt or a sail etc. **gored** *adj.* made with gores.

gore³ *v.* to pierce with a horn or tusk. — *n.*

gorge *n.* a narrow steep-sided valley. — *v.* **1.** to eat greedily; *gorge oneself*, stuff oneself with food. **2.** to fill full, to choke up. ☐ **make a person's gorge rise**, to sicken or disgust him.

gorgeous *adj.* **1.** richly coloured, magnificent. **2.** (*informal*) very pleasant, beautiful. **gorgeously** *adv.*, **gorgeousness** *n.*

gorgon (gor-gŏn) *n.* a terrifying woman. ¶ Named after the *Gorgons* in Greek mythology, three snake-haired sisters whose looks turned to stone anyone who saw them.

Gorgonzola (gor-gŏn-zoh-lă) *n.* a rich strong blue-veined cheese from Gorgonzola in north Italy or elsewhere.

gorilla *n.* a large powerful African ape.

gormandize (gor-măn-dyz) *v.* to eat greedily. **gormandizer** *n.*

gormless *adj.* (*slang*) stupid.

gorse *n.* a wild evergreen shrub with yellow flowers and sharp thorns.

gory *adj.* **1.** covered with blood. **2.** involving bloodshed, *a gory battle.*

gosh *int.* (*slang*) an exclamation of surprise.

gosling (goz-ling) *n.* a young goose.

gospel *n.* **1.** the teachings of Christ recorded in the first four books of the New Testament. **2.** *Gospel*, any of these books. **3.** a thing one may safely believe, *you can take it as gospel.* **4.** a set of principles that one believes in.

gossamer *n.* **1.** a fine filmy piece of cobweb made by small spiders. **2.** any flimsy delicate material.

gossip *n.* **1.** casual talk especially about other people's affairs. **2.** a person who is fond of gossiping. — *v.* to engage in or spread gossip. — **gossipy** *adj.* ☐ **gossip column**, a section of a newspaper containing titbits of information about people or social incidents.

got *see* **get**. ☐ **have got**, to possess, *she has got a car.* **have got to do it**, must do it.

Gothic (goth-ik) *adj.* of the style of architecture common in western Europe in the 12th–16th centuries, with pointed arches and rich stone carving. — *n.* this style. ☐ **Gothic novel**, a kind of novel with sensational or horrifying events, popular in the 18th–19th centuries.

gotten an alternative form of **got**, used in the USA (*he has gotten him a job*) but not now used in standard English except in certain expressions such as *ill-gotten gains.*

Gouda (gow-dă) *n.* a flat round Dutch cheese.

gouge (*pr.* gowj) *n.* a chisel with a concave blade, used for cutting grooves. — *v.* **1.** to cut out with a gouge. **2.** to scoop or force out; *gouge out his eye*, force it out with one's thumb.

goulash (goo-lash) *n.* a stew of meat and vegetables, seasoned with paprika.

gourd (*pr.* goord) *n.* **1.** the hard-skinned fleshy fruit of a climbing plant. **2.** this plant. **3.** a bowl or container made from the dried hollowed-out rind of this fruit.

gourmand (goor-mănd) *n.* a lover of food, a glutton. ¶ This word is often applied to a person contemptuously, whereas *gourmet* is not.

gourmet (goor-may) *n.* a connoisseur of good food and drink. ¶ See the note under gourmand.

gout *n.* a disease causing inflammation of the joints, especially the toes, knees, and fingers. **gouty** *adj.*

govern *v.* **1.** to rule with authority, to conduct the affairs of a country or an organization. **2.** to keep under control, *to govern one's temper.* **3.** to influence or direct, *be governed by the experts' advice.*

governance *n.* governing, control.

governess *n.* a woman employed to teach children in a private household.

government *n.* **1.** governing, the system or method of governing. **2.** the group or organization governing a country. **3.** the State as an agent; *a government grant,* given from State funds. **governmental** *adj.* □ **government securities,** securities issued by the government. **government surplus,** unused equipment sold to the public by the government.

governor *n.* **1.** a person who governs a province or colony. **2.** the head of each State in the USA. **3.** the head or one of the governing body of an institution; *the governor of the prison,* the official in charge of it. **4.** (*slang*) one's employer, one's father. **5.** (*slang*) a form of address to a man regarded as being of superior status. **6.** a mechanism that automatically controls speed or the intake of gas or water etc. in a machine. □ **Governor-General** *n.* the representative of the Crown in a Commonwealth country that recognizes the Queen as head of the State.

gown *n.* **1.** a loose flowing garment, especially a woman's long dress. **2.** a loose outer garment that is the official robe of members of a university, judges, etc. **3.** a kind of overall, *a surgeon's gown.* **gowned** *adj.* wearing a gown.

GP *abbrev.* general practitioner.

grab *v.* (grabbed, grabbing) **1.** to grasp suddenly. **2.** to take something greedily. **3.** to operate harshly or jerkily, *the brakes are grabbing.* **4.** (*slang*) to make an impression on someone; *how does that music grab you?,* do you like it? —**grab** *n.* **1.** a sudden clutch or an attempt to seize. **2.** a mechanical device for gripping things and lifting them. □ **grab handle** *or* **rail,** a handle or bar for a person to hold in order to steady himself. **up for grabs,** (*Amer. slang*) available for anyone to take.

grace *n.* **1.** the quality of being attractive, especially in movement, manner, or design. **2.** elegance of manner; *he had the grace to apologize,* realized that this was right and proper, and did it. **3.** favour, goodwill. **4.** a delay or postponement granted as a favour, not as a right, *give him a week's grace.* **5.** God's loving mercy towards mankind. **6.** a short prayer of thanks before or after a meal. **7.** the title used in speaking of or to a duke, duchess, or archbishop, *his Grace, her Grace, their Graces.* —*v.* to confer honour or dignity on, to be an

ornament to. □ **be in a person's good graces,** to have his favour and approval. **days of grace,** the time allowed by law or custom after the day on which a payment is officially due. **grace and favour house,** a house occupied by permission of the British sovereign. **grace-note** *n.* a music note that is not essential to the harmony but is added as an embellishment. **with a good grace,** as if willingly.

graceful *adj.* having or showing grace. **gracefully** *adv.,* **gracefulness** *n.*

graceless *adj.* **1.** inelegant. **2.** ungracious.

gracious *adj.* **1.** kind and pleasant in manner to inferiors. **2.** of royal persons or their acts, *Her gracious Majesty the Queen; by gracious permission of His Royal Highness.* **3.** showing divine grace, merciful. **4.** showing qualities associated with good taste and breeding, *gracious living.* —*int.* an exclamation of surprise, *good gracious!* **graciously** *adv.,* **graciousness** *n.*

gradation (gră-**day**-shŏn) *n.* a process of gradual change, a stage in such a process, *the gradations of colour between blue and green.*

grade *n.* **1.** a step or stage or degree in some rank, quality, or value, *Grade A milk.* **2.** a class of people or things of the same rank or quality etc. **3.** the mark given to a student for his standard of work. **4.** gradient, slope. —**grade** *v.* **1.** to arrange in grades. **2.** to give a grade to a student. **3.** to adjust the gradient of a road. □ **grade school,** (*Amer.*) an elementary school. **make the grade,** to reach the desired standard. **on the up grade,** going up, rising in standard; *on the down grade,* falling in standard.

gradient (**gray**-di-ĕnt) *n.* **1.** the amount of slope in a road or railway: *the road has a gradient of 1 in 10,* it rises 1 foot in every 10 feet of its length. **2.** a sloping road or railway.

gradual *adj.* taking place by degrees, not sudden or steep. **gradually** *adv.*

graduate¹ (**grad**-yoo-ăt) *n.* a person who holds a university degree.

graduate² (**grad**-yoo-ayt) *v.* **1.** to take a university degree. **2.** to divide into graded sections. **3.** to mark into regular divisions or units of measurement. **graduation** *n.*

graffito (gră-**fee**-toh) *n.* (*pl.* **graffiti,** *pr.* gră-**fee**-tee) words or a drawing roughly scratched or scribbled on a wall. ¶ Note that *graffiti* is plural; it is incorrect to speak of *a graffiti* or of *graffitis.*

graft¹ *n.* **1.** a shoot from one tree fixed into a cut in another to form a new growth. **2.** a piece of living tissue transplanted surgically to replace diseased or damaged tissue. **3.** (*slang*) hard work. —**graft** *v.* **1.** to

put a graft in or on. **2.** to join (a thing) inseparably to another. **3.** (*slang*) to work hard.

graft² *n.* **1.** obtaining some advantage in business or politics by bribery or unfair influence or other shady means. **2.** a bribe or bribery used in this way. **3.** the advantage gained by it.

Grail *n.* the **Holy Grail,** the cup or the platter used (according to legend) by Christ at the Last Supper and in which Joseph of Arimathea received drops of Christ's blood at the Crucifixion, sought in prolonged quests by knights in the Middle Ages.

grain *n.* **1.** a small hard seed of a food plant such as wheat or rice. **2.** the gathered seeds of such plants. **3.** the plants themselves. **4.** a small hard particle, *a grain of sand.* **5.** a unit of weight, about 65 milligrams. **6.** the smallest possible amount, *he hasn't a grain of sense.* **7.** the texture produced by the particles in flesh, stone, etc., or in photographic prints. **8.** the pattern of lines made by fibres in wood or by layers in rock or coal etc. □ **against the grain,** cutting or lying across a natural layer; contrary to one's natural inclinations.

grainy *adj.* like grains in form or appearance or texture. **graininess** *n.*

gram *n.* a unit of mass in the metric system, one thousandth part of a kilogram.

grammar *n.* **1.** the study of words and of the rules for their formation and their relationships to each other in sentences. **2.** the rules themselves. **3.** a book about these. **4.** speech or writing judged as good or bad according to these rules, *his grammar is appalling.* □ **grammar school,** a kind of secondary school for pupils with academic ability.

grammatical *adj.* in accordance with the rules of grammar. **grammatically** *adv.*

gramophone *n.* a record-player, especially the kind that is not operated electrically.

Grampian a region of Scotland.

grampus *n.* **1.** a large dolphin-like sea animal. **2.** a person breathing loudly and heavily.

gran *n.* (*informal*) grandmother.

granary *n.* a storehouse for grain.

grand *adj.* **1.** splendid, magnificent. **2.** of the highest rank, *the Grand Duke Alexis.* **3.** dignified, imposing, *she puts on a grand manner.* **4.** (*informal*) very enjoyable or satisfactory, *we had a grand time.* **5.** including everything, final, *the grand total.* —**grand** *n.* **1.** a grand piano. **2.** (*slang*)

a thousand pounds or dollars, *five grand.* —**grandly** *adv.,* **grandness** *n.* □ **Grand Canyon,** a gorge one mile deep through which the Colorado River flows in Arizona. **Grand National,** a steeplechase held annually at Aintree, Liverpool. **grand opera,** opera in which everything is sung and there are no spoken parts. **grand piano,** a large full-toned piano with horizontal strings. **Grand Prix** (*pr.* grahn **pree**) any of several important international motor-racing events. **grand slam,** *see* slam.

grandad *n.* (*informal*) **1.** grandfather. **2.** an elderly man.

grandchild *n.* (*pl.* grandchildren) the child of a person's son or daughter.

granddaughter *n.* the daughter of a person's son or daughter.

grandee (gran-**dee**) *n.* a person of high rank.

grandeur (**grand**-yer) *n.* splendour, magnificence, grandness.

grandfather *n.* the father of a person's father or mother. **grandfather clock,** a clock in a tall wooden case, worked by weights.

grandiloquent (gran-**dil**-ŏ-kwĕnt) *adj.* using pompous language. **grandiloquently** *adv.,* **grandiloquence** *n.*

grandiose (**gran**-di-ohss) *adj.* **1.** imposing, planned on a large scale. **2.** trying to be grand, pompous. **grandiosity** (grandi-**oss**-iti) *n.*

grandma *n.* (*informal*) grandmother.

grandmother *n.* the mother of a pers[on's] father or mother. **grandmother cloc[k,]** clock like a grandfather clock but [a] smaller case.

grandpa *n.* (*informal*) grandfather.

grandparent *n.* a grandfather or g[rand]mother.

grandsire *n.* (*old use*) grandfather.

grandson *n.* the son of a person's [son or] daughter.

grandstand *n.* the principal roofe[d build]ing with rows of seats for specta[tors at] races and sports-meetings. **gra[ndstand] finish,** a close and exciting en[d to a] race.

grange *n.* a country house wi[th farm] buildings that belong to it.

granite *n.* a hard grey stone used [for build]ing; *the granite city,* Aberdeen.

granny *n.* (*informal*) grandm[other.] **granny flat,** a flat in someo[ne's house] where his elderly relative can liv[e indepen]dently but close to the fami[ly.] **granny knot,** a reef-knot with the thre[ads crossed] the wrong way and therefo[re liable to] slip.

recognition of services rendered, a tip.

grave[1] *n*. **1**. a hole dug in the ground to bury a corpse. **2**. the place where a corpse is buried; *someone is walking on my grave*, said when one shivers without reason. **3**. *the grave*, death, being dead.

grave[2] *adj*. **1**. serious, causing great anxiety, *grave news*. **2**. solemn, not smiling. **gravely** *adv*. □ **grave accent** (*pr*. grahv), a backward-sloping mark over a vowel, as in *à la carte*.

gravel *n*. coarse sand with small stones, as used for roads and paths. —*v*. (gravelled, gravelling) **1**. to cover with gravel. **2**. to perplex or puzzle.

gravelly *adj*. **1**. like gravel. **2**. rough-sounding, *a gravelly voice*.

graven *adj*. carved, *a graven image*; *graven on my memory*, firmly fixed in it.

Graves (*pr*. grahv) *n*. a light white or red French wine.

gravestone *n*. a stone monument over a grave.

graveyard *n*. a burial ground.

gravitate *v*. to move or be attracted towards.

gravitation *n*. **1**. gravitating **2**. the force of gravity. **gravitational** *adj*.

gravity *n*. **1**. seriousness, *the gravity of the situation*. **2**. solemnity. **3**. the force that attracts bodies towards the centre of the earth. □ **centre of gravity**, the central point in an object about which its mass is evenly balanced. **gravity feed**, a supply system in which a substance falls from a higher level to a lower one by force of gravity rather than by mechanical means. **specific gravity**, *see* specific.

gravy *n*. **1**. juice that comes out of meat while it is cooking. **2**. sauce made from this. **3**. (*slang*) money or profit easily or unexpectedly acquired. □ **gravy train**, (*slang*) a source of easy money.

grayling *n*. a silver-grey freshwater fish.

graze[1] *v*. **1**. to eat growing grass, *cattle grazing in the fields*. **2**. to put (animals) into a field to eat the grass.

graze[2] *v*. **1**. to touch or scrape lightly in passing. **2**. to scrape the skin from. —*n*. a raw place where the skin has been scraped.

grazier (gray-zi-er) *n*. **1**. a person who farms grazing animals. **2**. (*Austral*.) a sheep-farmer.

grazing *n*. grass growing in a field etc. and suitable for animals to eat.

grease *n*. **1**. animal fat melted soft. **2**. any thick semi-solid oily substance —*v*. to put grease on or in. □ **grease a person's palm**, (*slang*) to bribe him. **grease-gun** *n*. a device for forcing grease into the parts

of a machine. **grease-paint** *n*. make-up used by actors and other performers. **like greased lightning**, (*slang*) very fast.

greaser *n*. **1**. a man who greases machinery. **2**. a ship's engineer.

greasy *adj*. (greasier, greasiest) **1**. covered with grease. **2**. containing much grease. **3**. slippery, *the road was greasy after the storm*. **4**. oily in manner. **greasily** *adv*., **greasiness** *n*.

great *adj*. **1**. much above average in size or amount or intensity. **2**. larger than others of similar kind, *the great auk*, *Great Malvern*. **3**. of remarkable ability or character, important, *one of the great painters*; *Peter the Great*; *the great*, great people; *the greatest*, (*slang*) a very remarkable person or thing. **4**. elaborate, intense, *told in great detail*. **5**. doing something frequently or intensively or very well, *a great reader*. **6**. (*informal*) very enjoyable or satisfactory, *we had a great time*. **7**. of a family relationship that is one generation removed in ancestry or descent, as *great-grandfather*, *great-niece*; *great-great-grandfather*, *great-grandfather's* father. —**greatly** *adv*., **greatness** *n*. □ **Great Britain**, England, Wales, and Scotland. **Great Dane**, a dog of a very large powerful smooth-haired breed. **Greater London**, London together with the nearby urban areas. **Greater Manchester**, a metropolitan county of England. **Great Lakes**, a series of five large lakes along the boundary between Canada and the USA. **Great Powers**, important countries with international influence. **Great Scott!**, an exclamation of surprise. **Great Seal**, the official seal affixed to important State papers in Britain. **great toe**, the big toe. **Great War**, the war of 1914–18.

greatcoat *n*. a heavy overcoat.

greave *n*. a piece of armour worn on the leg to protect the shin.

grebo (*pr*. greeb) *n*. a diving bird.

Grecian (gree-shăn) *adj*. Greek. **Grecian nose**, a straight nose that continues the line of the forehead without a dip. **Grecian slippers**, soft slippers with low sides.

Greece a country in south-east Europe.

greed *n*. an excessive desire for food or wealth.

greedy *adj*. (greedier, greediest) **1**. showing greed. **2**. very eager or keen for something. **greedily** *adv*., **greediness** *n*.

Greek *adj*. of Greece or its people or language. —*n*. **1**. a member of the people living in ancient or modern Greece. **2**. their language. □ **Greek Church**, the Greek Orthodox Church (*see* orthodox). **it's**

Greek to me, I cannot understand its meaning.

green *adj.* **1.** of the colour between blue and yellow, the colour of growing grass. **2.** covered with grass or with growing leaves; *a green Christmas,* mild and without snow. **3.** unripe, not seasoned; *wood is green,* not yet dry enough to burn well; *green bacon,* not smoked. **4.** immature, inexperienced, easily deceived. **5.** pale and sickly-looking; *green with envy,* very jealous. —**green** *n.* **1.** green colour. **2.** a green substance or material, green clothes. **3.** a green light. **4.** a piece of grassy public land, *the village green.* **5.** a grassy area, *a putting-green.* —**greenly** *adv.,* **greenness** *n.* ☐ **green belt,** an area of open land round a town, where the amount of building is restricted. **green card,** an international insurance document for motorists. **green-eyed monster,** jealousy. **green fingers,** skill in making plants grow. **green light,** a signal to proceed on a road; (*informal*) permission to go ahead with a project. **Green Paper,** a government report of proposals which are being considered but not yet accepted. **green pound,** the agreed value of the £ according to which payments to agricultural producers are reckoned in the EEC. **green revolution,** greatly increased crop production in developing countries. **green-room** *n.* a room in a theatre, for the use of actors when they are not on the stage. **greens** *pl. n.* (*informal*) green vegetables. **green salad,** salad consisting of leafy vegetables. **greenstick fracture,** a kind of fracture, usually in children, in which the bone is partly broken and partly bent. **green tea,** tea made from leaves that are steam-dried, not fermented. **green thumb,** = green fingers.

greenery *n.* green foliage or growing plants.

greenfinch *n.* a finch with green and yellow feathers.

greenfly *n.* **1.** one of the small green insects that suck juices from plants. **2.** these insects collectively.

greengage *n.* a round plum with a greenish skin.

greengrocer *n.* a shopkeeper selling vegetables and fruit. **greengrocery** *n.* a greengrocer's shop or goods.

greenhorn *n.* an inexperienced person.

greenhouse *n.* a building with glass sides and roof, for rearing plants.

greenish *adj.* rather green.

greenstone *n.* **1.** a kind of green rock. **2.** a variety of jade found in New Zealand.

greenstuff *n.* green vegetables.

Greenwich (**gren**-ich) *n.* a suburb of London, the former site of the Royal Observatory. **Greenwich mean time,** time on the line of longitude which passes through Greenwich, used as a basis for calculating time throughout the world.

greeny *adj.* rather green, *greeny-yellow.*

greet *v.* **1.** to address (a person) on meeting or arrival. **2.** to receive with a certain reaction, *the news was greeted with dismay.* **3.** to present itself to one's sight or hearing, *the sight that greeted our eyes.*

greeting *n.* **1.** words or gestures used to greet a person. **2.** expressions of goodwill, *birthday greetings.*

gregarious (gri-**gair**-iŭs) *adj.* **1.** living in flocks or communities. **2.** fond of company. **gregariously** *adv.* **gregariousness** *n.*

Gregorian calendar (gri-**gor**-iăn) the calendar introduced by Pope Gregory XIII in 1582, replacing the Julian calendar and still in general use.

gremlin *n.* (*slang*) a mischievous spirit said to cause mishaps to machinery.

Grenada (gren-**ay**-dă) an island country in the West Indies.

grenade *n.* a small bomb thrown by hand or fired from a rifle.

Grenadier Guards (gren-ă-**deer**) the first regiment of the Household infantry.

grew *see* grow.

grey *adj.* **1.** of the colour between black and white, coloured like ashes or lead; *he is going grey,* his hair is losing its colour; *a grey day,* without sun. **2.** intermediate in character —**grey** *n.* **1.** grey colour. **2.** a grey substance or material, grey clothes. **3.** a grey horse. **4.** *the Greys* or *Scots Greys,* 2nd Dragoons. —*v.* to make or become grey. —**greyness** *n.* ☐ **grey area,** that part of a matter where there are no exact rules about right and wrong etc. **grey cells,** (*humorous*) brain or intelligence. **Grey Friars,** Franciscan friars. **grey-headed** *adj.* with grey hair. **grey matter,** the material of the brain and spinal cord; (*informal*) brain or intelligence.

greyhound *n.* a slender smooth-haired dog noted for its swiftness, used in coursing hares and in racing.

greyish *adj.* rather grey.

greylag *n.* the **greylag goose,** a grey wild European goose.

grid *n.* **1.** a grating. **2.** a framework of spaced parallel spirals or networks of wires in a valve. **3.** a network of squares on maps, numbered for reference. **4.** any network of lines, an arrangement of electric-power cables or gas-supply lines for distributing current or supplies over a large area. **5.** a pattern of lines marking the starting-places on a car-racing track. **6.** a gridiron. ☐ **gridded** *adj.* marked with a grid.

griddle *n.* = girdle².

gridiron (grid-I-ern) *n.* **1.** a framework of metal bars for cooking on. **2.** a field on which American football is played, with parallel lines marking the area of play.

grief *n.* **1.** deep sorrow. **2.** something causing this. ☐ **come to grief**, to meet with disaster, to fail, to fall.

grievance *n.* a real or imagined cause of complaint.

grieve *v.* **1.** to cause grief to. **2.** to feel grief.

grievous (gree-vŭs) *adj.* **1.** causing grief. **2.** serious; *grievous bodily harm*, serious injury. **grievously** *adv.*

griffin *n.* a creature in Greek mythology, with an eagle's head and wings on a lion's body.

griffon *n.* **1.** one of a breed of terrier-like dogs with coarse hair. **2.** a kind of vulture.

grill *n.* **1.** a metal grid, a grating. **2.** a grid-iron for cooking on. **3.** a device on a cooker for radiating heat downwards. **4.** meat, fish, or vegetables cooked under this or on a gridiron. **5.** a grill-room. —**grill** *v.* **1.** to cook under a grill or on a gridiron. **2.** to be exposed to great heat. **3.** to question closely and severely. ☐ **grill-room** *n.* a restaurant or room where grills and other foods are served.

grille *n.* a grating, especially in a door or window.

grilse *n.* a young salmon returning from the sea to fresh water to spawn for the first time.

grim *adj.* (grimmer, grimmest) **1.** stern or severe in appearance. **2.** severe, unrelenting, merciless, *held on like grim death.* **3.** without cheerfulness, unattractive, *a grim prospect.* **grimly** *adv.*, **grimness** *n.*

grimace (grim-ayss) *n.* a contortion of the face expressing pain or disgust, or intended to cause amusement. —*v.* to make a grimace.

grime *n.* dirt or soot ingrained in a surface or in the skin. —*v.* to blacken with grime. —**grimy** *adj.*, **griminess** *n.*

grin *v.* (grinned, grinning) **1.** to smile broadly, showing the teeth; *grin and bear it*, endure something without complaining. **2.** to express by a grin, *he grinned his approval.* —*n.* a broad smile.

grind *v.* (ground, grinding) **1.** to crush or be crushed into grains or powder. **2.** to produce in this way. **3.** to oppress or crush by cruelty. **4.** to sharpen or smooth by fric-

tion. **5.** to rub harshly together, *grind one's teeth*; *the bus ground to a halt*, stopped laboriously with a sound of grating. **6.** to work something by turning a handle; *grind out a tune on the barrel-organ*, produce it in this way. **7.** to study hard, *grinding away at his algebra.* —**grind** *n.* **1.** the act of grinding. **2.** the size of ground particles, *a coarse grind.* **3.** hard monotonous work.

grinder *n.* **1.** a person or thing that grinds. **2.** a molar tooth.

grindstone *n.* a thick revolving disc used for sharpening or grinding things; *keep a person's nose to the grindstone*, make him work hard without rest.

grip (gripped, gripping) *v.* **1.** to take a firm hold of. **2.** to hold a person's attention, *a gripping story.* —**grip** *n.* **1.** a firm grasp or hold. **2.** the power of gripping, a way of grasping or holding. **3.** understanding, mental hold or control, *has a good grip of his subject.* **4.** the part of a tool or machine etc. that grips things. **5.** the part (of a weapon or device) designed to be held. **6.** a hair-grip. **7.** (*Amer.*) a suitcase or travelling-bag. ☐ **come to grips with**, to begin to cope with, to deal with (a problem) firmly. **get a grip on oneself**, to regain one's self-control. **to stop being slack. lose one's grip**, to become less competent than one was formerly.

gripe *v.* **1.** to cause colic. **2.** (*slang*) to grumble. —*n.* (*slang*) a grumble. ☐ **gripe-water** *n.* a medicine to relieve colic in babies.

grisly *adj.* causing fear or horror or disgust, *all the grisly details.*

grist *n.* **1.** grain to be ground or already ground; *all is grist that comes to his mill*, he makes use of everything. **2.** malt crushed for brewing.

gristle *n.* tough flexible tissue of animal bodies, especially in meat. **gristly** *adj.*

grit *n.* **1.** particles of stone or sand. **2.** courage and endurance. —**grit** (gritted, gritting) *v.* **1.** to make a slightly grating sound. **2.** to clench; *grit one's teeth*, to keep the jaws tightly to-gether especially when enduring pain or trouble. **3.** to spread grit on. —**gritty** *adj.*, **grittiness** *n.*

grizzle *v.* (*informal*) to whimper or whine, to complain. —*n.* a bout of grizzling. —**grizzler** *n.*

grizzled *adj.* streaked with grey hairs.

grizzly *adj.* grey, grey-haired. —*n.* a **grizzly bear**, a large fierce grey bear of North America.

groan *v.* **1.** to make a long deep sound expressing pain or grief or disapproval. **2.** to make a creaking noise resembling this. —*n.* the sound made in groaning.

groats *pl. n.* crushed grain, especially oats.

grocer *n.* a shopkeeper who sells foods and household stores. **groceries** *pl. n.* goods sold by a grocer. **grocery** *n.* a grocer's shop or goods.

grog *n.* **1.** a drink of spirits mixed with water. **2.** (*Austral.*) any alcoholic drink.

groggy *adj.* weak and unsteady, especially after illness. **groggily** *adv.,* **grogginess** *n.*

groin *n.* **1.** the groove where each thigh joins the trunk. **2.** this area of the body, where the genitals are situated. **3.** the curved edge where two vaults meet in a roof, an arch supporting a vault. □ **groined** *adj.* built with groins.

grommet *n.* = grummet.

groom *n.* **1.** a person employed to look after horses. **2.** the title of certain officers of the Royal Household, chiefly in the Lord Chamberlain's department. **3.** a bridegroom. —**groom** *v.* **1.** to clean and brush (an animal). **2.** to make neat and trim. **3.** to prepare (a person) for a career or position.

groove *n.* **1.** a long narrow channel in the surface of hard material. **2.** a spiral cut on a gramophone disc for the needle or stylus. **3.** a way of living that has become a habit, a rut. —*v.* to make a groove or grooves in.

groovy *adj.* (*slang*) excellent, admired.

grope *v.* **1.** to feel about as one does in the dark, to seek by feeling. **2.** to search mentally with some uncertainty, *groping for an answer.*

grosgrain (**groh**-grayn) *n.* corded fabric of silky thread, used for ribbons etc.

gross (*pr.* grohss) *adj.* **1.** thick, large-bodied; *a gross fellow*, repulsively fat; *gross vegetation*, growing thickly. **2.** not refined, vulgar, *gross manners.* **3.** glaringly obvious, outrageous, *gross negligence.* **4.** total, whole, without deductions; *gross income*, income before tax etc. is deducted. —**gross** *n.* (*pl.* gross) twelve dozen (144) items; *ten gross*, 1440. —*v.* to produce or earn as total profit. □ **gross national product**, the total value of goods produced and services provided in a country in one year. **gross up**, to work out (a gross amount) by taking the net amount and adding to it the total of tax etc. already paid or payable on this.

grotesque (groh-**tesk**) *adj.* very odd or unnatural, fantastically ugly or absurd. —*n.* a comically distorted figure, a design using fantastic human, animal, and plant forms. —**grotesquely** *adv.,* **grotesqueness** *n.*

grotto (**grot**-oh) *n.* (*pl.* grottoes) a picturesque cave.

grotty *adj.* (*slang*) unpleasant, dirty, or useless.

grouch *v.* (*informal*) to grumble. —*n.* (*informal*) **1.** a grumble. **2.** a grumbler. —**groucher** *n.,* **grouchy** *adj.*

ground[1] *n.* **1.** the solid surface of the earth, especially contrasted with the air surrounding it. **2.** an area or position or distance on the earth's surface, *gain* or *lose ground.* **3.** a foundation or reason for a theory or action, *there are no grounds for suspicion.* **4.** soil, earth, *marshy ground.* **5.** an area used for a particular purpose, *a football ground.* **6.** the underlying part, a surface worked upon in embroidery or painting. —**ground** *v.* **1.** to run aground. **2.** to prevent (an aircraft or airman) from flying, *all aircraft were grounded because of the fog.* **3.** to teach thoroughly, to give good basic training to. **4.** to base it, *is grounded on fact.* □ **above ground**, alive; not yet buried. **below ground**, dead and buried. **down to the ground**, completely, *the job suits me down to the ground.* **get off the ground**, to rise in the air; to make a successful start. **ground floor**, the floor at ground level in a building; *get in on the ground floor*, to be one of the first to have the advantage of sharing in a promising business. **ground frost**, frost on the surface of the ground or in the top layer of soil. **ground ivy**, a creeping plant with bluish-purple flowers. **ground-nut** *n.* a peanut. **ground-plan** *n.* a plan of a building at ground level; an outline or general design of a scheme. **ground-rent** *n.* the rent paid for land that is leased for building. **ground swell**, heavy slow-moving waves caused by a distant or recent storm.

ground[2] *see* grind. —*adj.* **ground glass**, glass made non-transparent by grinding. **ground rice**, rice reduced to fine powder.

grounding *n.* thorough teaching, basic training, *a good grounding in arithmetic.*

groundless *adj.* without basis, without good reason, *your fears are groundless.* **groundlessly** *adv.*

grounds *pl. n.* **1.** an area of enclosed land belonging to a large house or an institution. **2.** solid particles that sink to the bottom of a liquid, *coffee grounds.*

groundsel *n.* a weed with small starry flowers.

groundsheet *n.* a waterproof sheet for spreading on the ground.

groundsman *n.* (*pl.* groundsmen) a man employed to look after a sports ground.

groundwork n. preliminary or basic work.

group n. **1.** a number of persons or things gathered, placed, or classed together, or working together for some purpose. **2.** a number of commercial companies under one owner. **3.** a pop group. —v. to form or gather into a group or groups. ☐ **group captain,** an officer in the RAF. **group practice,** a medical practice in which several doctors are associated. **group sex,** sexual activity in which more than two persons take part simultaneously. **group therapy,** therapy in which patients with a similar condition are brought together to assist one another psychologically.

grouper (groop-er) n. a sea-fish used as food.

groupie n. (slang) a girl who follows touring pop groups.

grouse[1] (pl. grouse) **1.** a game-bird with feathered feet. **2.** its flesh as food.

grouse[2] v. (informal) to grumble. —n. (informal) a grumble. —**grouser** n.

grout n. thin fluid mortar used to fill narrow cavities such as joints between stone or wall-tiles. —v. to fill with grout.

grove n. a group of trees, a small wood.

grovel v. (grovelled, grovelling) **1.** to lie or crawl with the face downwards in a show of humility or fear. **2.** to humble oneself.

grow v. (grew, grown, growing) **1.** to increase in size or quantity, to become greater. **2.** to develop; the seeds are growing, putting out shoots. **3.** to be capable of developing as a plant, to flourish, rice grows in warm climates. **4.** to become gradually, he grew rich. **5.** to cause or allow to grow, to produce by cultivation, grow a beard; grow roses. **6.** to become firmly established or more acceptable, it's a habit that grows on you. ☐ **growing pains,** neuralgic pain in children's legs, usually caused by tiredness; problems arising because a project or development is in its early stages. **grow out of,** (of a growing child) to become too large to wear (certain clothes); to become too mature for, grew out of his childish habits; to have as a source, to arise or develop from. **grow up,** to develop, to become adult or mature.

growable adj. able to be grown.

grower n. **1.** a person who grows plants, fruit, or vegetables commercially. **2.** a plant that grows in a certain way a rapid grower.

growl v. **1.** to make a low threatening sound. **2.** to speak or say in a growling manner, to grumble. —**growl** n. **1.** a growling sound. **2.** a grumble. —**growler** n.

grown see grow. —adj. **1.** fully developed, adult, a grown man. **2.** covered with a growth, a wall grown over with ivy. ☐ **grown-up** adj. adult, (n.) an adult person.

growth n. **1.** the process of growing, development. **2.** cultivation of produce. **3.** something that grows or has grown, a thick growth of weeds. **4.** an abnormal formation of tissue in the body, a tumour. ☐ **growth industry,** one developing faster than most others. **growth shares** or **stocks,** investments thought likely to increase in capital value rather than yield high income.

groyne n. a structure of wood, stone, or concrete projecting towards the sea, preventing sand and pebbles from being washed away by the current. —v. to protect with groynes.

grub n. **1.** the thick-bodied worm-like larva of certain insects. **2.** (slang) food. — **grub** v. (grubbed, grubbing) **1.** to dig the surface of the soil. **2.** to clear away roots by digging, to dig up by the roots. **3.** to search laboriously, to rummage. ☐ **grub-screw** n. a headless screw.

grubby adj. (grubbier, grubbiest) **1.** infested with grubs. **2.** dirty, unwashed. **grubbily** adv., **grubbiness** n.

grudge v. to resent having to give or allow something; I don't grudge him his success, I admit that he deserves it. —n. a feeling of resentment or ill will. —**grudging** adj., **grudgingly** adv.

gruel (groo-ĕl) n. a thin porridge made by boiling oatmeal in milk or water, especially for invalids.

gruelling (groo-ĕl-ing) adj. very tiring, exhausting.

gruesome (groo-sŭm) adj. filling one with horror or disgust, revolting, the gruesome details of the murder.

gruff adj. **1.** (of the voice) low and harsh, hoarse. **2.** having a gruff voice. **3.** surly in manner. **gruffly** adv., **gruffness** n.

grumble v. **1.** to complain in a bad-tempered way. **2.** to rumble, thunder was grumbling in the distance. —**grumble** n. **1.** a complaint, especially a bad-tempered one. **2.** a rumble. ☐ **grumbler** n. a person who grumbles constantly. **grumbling appendix,** (informal) one that causes pain from time to time without developing into appendicitis.

grummet n. **1.** an insulating washer placed round an electrical conductor where it passes through a hole in metal etc. **2.** a ring of twisted rope used as a fastening, rowlock, etc.

grumpy adj. bad-tempered and gloomy. **grumpily** adv., **grumpiness** n.

grunt v. **1.** to make the gruff snorting

sound characteristic of a pig. **2.** to speak or utter with such a sound, *he grunted a reply*. **3.** to grumble. —*n.* a grunting sound.

gruyère (groo-yair) *n.* a kind of cheese with many holes.

gryphon (grif-ŏn) *n.* a griffin.

G-string *n.* **1.** a string on a musical instrument, tuned to the note G. **2.** a very brief covering for the genitals, attached to a string round the hips.

G-suit *n.* a close-fitting inflatable suit worn by airmen flying at high speed to prevent blood from draining away from the head and causing blackouts (G = gravity).

GT *abbrev.* gran turismo. (¶ Italian, = grand touring.)

guano (gwah-noh) *n.* **1.** dung of sea-birds, used as manure. **2.** an artificial manure, especially that made from fish.

guarantee *n.* **1.** a formal promise to do what has been agreed, or that a thing is of specified quality and durability, with penalties for failure. **2.** a formal promise given by one person to another that he will be responsible for something to be done, or for a debt to be paid, by a third person. **3.** something offered or accepted as security. **4.** a guarantor. —**guarantee** *v.* (guaranteed, guaranteeing) **1.** to give or be a guarantee for; *guarantee his debts*, undertake to pay them if he does not. **2.** to promise, to state with certainty.

guarantor (ga-răn-tor) *n.* a person who gives a guarantee.

guard *v.* **1.** to watch over and protect, to keep safe. **2.** to watch over and supervise or prevent escape. **3.** to keep in check, to restrain; *guard your tongue*, do not be outspoken or indiscreet. **4.** to take precautions, *guard against errors*. —**guard** *n.* **1.** a state of watchfulness or alertness for possible danger. **2.** a defensive attitude in boxing, fencing, cricket etc. **3.** a protector, a sentry. **4.** a railway official in charge of a train. **5.** a body of soldiers or others guarding a place or a person, serving as escort, or forming a separate part of an army. **6.** *the Guards*, the Household troops. **7.** a protecting part or device. □ **off one's guard**, unprepared against attack or surprise. **on one's guard**, alert for possible danger etc. **stand guard**, to guard, to act as a protector or sentry.

guarded *adj.* cautious, discreet, *a guarded statement*.

guardian *n.* **1.** one who guards or protects. **2.** a person who undertakes legal responsibility for someone who is incapable of managing his own affairs, such as an orphaned child. **guardianship** *n.* □ **guardian angel**, an angel thought of as watching over a person or place.

guardsman *n.* **1.** a soldier acting as guard. **2.** a member of the Guards.

Guatemala (gwati-**mah**-lă) **1.** a country in Central America. **2.** its capital city. **Guatemalan** *adj.* & *n.*

guava (gwah-vă) *n.* **1.** a tropical American tree. **2.** its edible orange-coloured acid fruit.

gudgeon[1] (guj-ŏn) *n.* a small freshwater fish used as bait.

gudgeon[2] (guj-ŏn) *n.* **1.** a kind of pivot. **2.** a socket for a rudder. **3.** a metal pin or red, *the gudgeon-pin holds the piston and connecting-rod together.*

guelder rose (geld-er) a shrub with bunches of round white flowers, the snowball tree.

Guernsey (gern-zi) *n.* (*pl.* Guernseys) one of a breed of dairy cattle originally from the island of Guernsey. □ **Guernsey lily**, a kind of amaryllis with large red flowers, originally from South Africa.

guernsey *n.* (*pl.* guernseys) **1.** a thick knitted woollen sweater. **2.** (*Austral.*) a football jersey.

guerrilla (gĕ-**ril**-ă) *n.* a person who takes part in **guerrilla warfare**, fighting or harassment by small groups acting independently.

guess *v.* **1.** to form an opinion or make a statement or give an answer without calculating or measuring and without definite knowledge. **2.** to think something likely. **3.** (*Amer.*) to suppose, *I guess we ought to be going.* —*n.* an opinion formed by guessing.—**guesser** *n.* □ **keep a person guessing**, (*informal*) to keep him uncertain of one's feelings or future actions etc.

guesstimate (gess-tim-ăt) *n.* (*informal*) an estimate based on guesswork and reasoning.

guesswork *n.* the process of guessing, an example of this.

guest *n.* **1.** a person staying at another's house or visiting him by invitation or being entertained to a meal. **2.** a person lodging at a hotel. **3.** a visiting performer taking part in an entertainment, *a guest artist.* □ **guest-house** *n.* a superior boarding-house. **guest-night** *n.* an evening on which members of a club or other society may invite guests. **guest-room** *n.* a room kept for the use of guests.

guff *n.* (*slang*) empty talk, nonsense.

guffaw *n.* a coarse noisy laugh. —*v.* to give a guffaw.

guidance *n.* **1.** guiding, being guided. **2.** advising or advice on problems.

guide *n.* **1.** a person who shows others the way. **2.** one employed to point out interesting sights on a journey or visit. **3.** an adviser, a person or thing that directs or influences one's behaviour. **4.** a book of information about a place or a subject, *A Guide to Italy*. **5.** a thing that marks a position, guides the eye, or steers moving parts. **6.** *Guide*, a member of the Girl Guides Association, an organization for girls, similar to the Scout Association —*v.* to act as guide to. □ **guide-dog** *n.* a dog trained to guide a blind person. **guided missile**, a missile that is under remote control or directed by equipment within itself. **guide-lines** *pl. n.* statements of principles giving practical guidance.

guidebook *n.* a book of information about a place, for travellers or visitors.

Guider *n.* an adult leader in the Girl Guides Association.

guild *n.* (¶the older spelling is **gild**) a society of people with similar interests and aims, one of the associations of craftsmen or merchants in the Middle Ages.

guilder (**gild**-er) *n.* a unit of money in the Netherlands, a florin.

Guild-hall *n.* a hall built or used as a meeting-place by a guild or corporation, a town hall. **Guildhall**, that of the Corporation of the City of London, used for official banquets and receptions.

guile (*rhymes with* mile) *n.* treacherous cunning, craftiness. **guileful** *adj.* full of guile. **guileless** *adj.* without guile. **guilelessness** *n.*

guillemot (**gil**-i-mot) *n.* a kind of auk.

guillotine (**gil**-ŏ-teen) *n.* **1.** a machine with a heavy blade sliding down in grooves, used for beheading criminals in France. **2.** a machine with a long blade for cutting paper or metal. **3.** the fixing of times for taking votes on a bill in Parliament, in order to prevent it from being obstructed by an excessively long debate. — **guillotine** *v.* **1.** to execute with a guillotine. **2.** to cut short by parliamentary guillotine.

guilt *n.* **1.** the fact of having committed some offence. **2.** a feeling that one is to blame for something.

guiltless *adj.* without guilt, innocent.

guilty *adj.* (guiltier, guiltiest) **1.** having done wrong. **2.** feeling or showing guilt. **guiltily** *adv.*, **guiltiness** *n.*

guinea *n.* **1.** a former British gold coin worth 21 shillings (£1.05). **2.** this sum of money used in stating professional fees etc.; *the 2000 Guineas*, a horse-race with this prize.

Guinea a country in West Africa. **Guinean** *adj. & n.*

Guinea-Bissau (**bis**-ow) a country between Guinea and Senegal.

guinea-fowl *n.* a domestic fowl of the pheasant family, with grey feathers spotted with white.

guinea-pig *n.* **1.** a short-eared animal like a large rat, kept as a pet or for biological experiments. **2.** a person or thing used as a subject for experiment.

guise (*pr. as* guys) *n.* an outward manner or appearance put on in order to conceal the truth, a pretence, *they exploited him under the guise of friendship*.

guitar (gi-**tar**) *n.* a stringed musical instrument, played by plucking with the fingers or a plectrum; *electric guitar*, one with a built-in microphone. **guitarist** *n.* a person who plays the guitar.

gulf *n.* **1.** an area of sea (larger than a bay) that is partly surrounded by land. **2.** a deep hollow. **3.** a wide difference in opinions or outlook. □ **Gulf Stream**, a warm ocean current flowing from the Gulf of Mexico to Europe.

gull *n.* a large sea-bird with long wings.

gullet *n.* the passage by which food goes from the mouth to the stomach, the throat.

gullible (**gul**-i-bŭl) *adj.* easily deceived. **gullibility** (gul-i-**bil**-iti) *n.*

gully *n.* **1.** a narrow channel cut by water or made for carrying rainwater away from a building. **2.** (in cricket) a fieldsman between point and slips, his position.

gulp *v.* **1.** to swallow (food or drink) hastily or greedily. **2.** to suppress something by swallowing hard, *he gulped back his rage*. **3.** to make a gulping movement, to choke or gasp, *gulping for breath*. —**gulp** *n.* **1.** the act of gulping. **2.** a large mouthful of liquid.

gum [1] *n.* the firm flesh in which the teeth are rooted.

gum [2] *n.* **1.** a sticky substance exuded by some trees and shrubs, used for sticking things together. **2.** chewing-gum. **3.** a gum-drop. **4.** a gum-tree. —*v.* (gummed, gumming) to smear or cover with gum, to stick together with gum. □ **gum arabic**, gum exuded by some kinds of acacia. **gum-drop** *n.* a hard transparent sweet made of gelatine or gum arabic. **gum-tree** *n.* a tree that exudes gum, a eucalyptus; *up a gum-tree*, (slang) in great difficulties. **gum up**, (*informal*) to cause confusion or delay in, to spoil; *gum up the works*, to interfere with the smooth running of something.

gum [3] *n.* (*slang*, in oaths) God, *by gum!*

gumboil *n.* a small abscess on the gum.

gumboot *n.* a rubber boot, a wellington.

gummy *adj.* **1.** sticky with gum. **2.** showing the gums, toothless. **gumminess** *n.*

gumption (**gump**-shŏn) *n.* (*informal*) common sense and initiative.

gumshoe *n.* (*Amer.*) a galosh.

gun *n.* **1.** any kind of firearm that sends shells or bullets from a metal tube. **2.** a starting-pistol. **3.** a device that forces out a substance through a tube, *a grease-gun.* **4.** a person using a sporting gun as a member of a shooting-party. **5.** (*Amer.*) a gunman, *a professional gun.* —**gun** *v.* (gunned, gunning) **1.** to shoot with a gun, *gunned him down.* **2.** to accelerate (an engine) briskly. □ **at gunpoint,** under threat of being shot by a gun held ready. **be gunning for,** to have as one's target for attack, to seek to destroy. **great guns,** vigorously, intensively, *blowing* or *going great guns.* **gun-carriage** *n.* a wheeled structure on which a gun is mounted for transport. **gun-cotton** *n.* an explosive made of acid-soaked cotton. **gun dog,** a dog trained to retrieve game for sportsmen who use guns. **gun-metal** *adj.* & *n.* dull bluish-grey, like the colour of metal formerly used for guns. **gun-runner** *n.* a person engaged in **gun-running,** extensive smuggling of guns and ammunition into a country.

gunboat *n.* a small armed vessel with heavy guns. **gunboat diplomacy,** diplomacy backed by threat of force.

gunfire *n.* the firing of guns.

gunja *n.* = ganja.

gunman *n.* (*pl.* gunmen) a man armed with a gun.

gunner *n.* **1.** a soldier in an artillery unit, the official term for a private. **2.** a warrant officer in the navy, in charge of a battery of guns. **3.** a member of an aircraft crew who operates a gun, *rear-gunner.*

gunnery *n.* the construction and operating of large guns.

gunny *n.* **1.** a coarse material used for making sacks and bales. **2.** a sack made from this.

gunpowder *n.* an explosive of saltpetre, sulphur, and charcoal. **Gunpowder Plot,** a plot to blow up Parliament (5 November 1605).

gunroom *n.* **1.** a room where sporting guns are kept in a house. **2.** a room for junior officers in a warship.

gunship *n.* **helicopter gunship,** an armed helicopter.

gunshot *n.* **1.** a shot fired from a gun. **2.** the range of a gun, *within gunshot.*

gunsmith *n.* a person whose trade is making and repairing small firearms.

gunwale (**gun**-ăl) *n.* the upper edge of a small ship's or boat's side.

gurdwara (gerd-**wah**-ră) *n.* a Sikh temple.

gurgle *n.* a low bubbling sound. —*v.* to make this sound.

Gurkha (ger-kă) *n.* a member of a Hindu people in Nepal, forming regiments in the British army.

guru (**goor**-oo) *n.* (*pl.* gurus) **1.** a Hindu spiritual teacher or head of a religious sect. **2.** an influential or revered teacher.

gush *v.* **1.** to flow or pour out suddenly or in great quantities. **2.** to talk with extravagant enthusiasm or emotion, especially in an affected manner. —**gush** *n.* **1.** a sudden or great outflow. **2.** an outpouring of feeling, effusiveness.

gusher *n.* **1.** an effusive person. **2.** an oil-well from which oil flows strongly without needing to be pumped.

gusset *n.* a triangular or diamond-shaped piece of cloth inserted in a garment to strengthen or enlarge it. **gusseted** *adj.* fitted with a gusset.

gust *n.* **1.** a sudden rush of wind. **2.** a burst of rain or smoke or sound. —*v.* to blow in gusts. —**gusty** *adj.,* **gustily** *adv.*

gusto *n.* zest, great enjoyment in doing something.

gut *n.* **1.** the lower part of the alimentary canal, the intestine. **2.** a thread made from the intestines of animals, used surgically and for violin and racket strings. —**gut** *adj.* **1.** fundamental, basic, *a gut issue.* **2.** instinctive, *a gut reaction.* —**gut** *v.* (gutted, gutting) **1.** to remove the guts from (a fish). **2.** to remove or destroy the internal fittings or parts of (a building); *the factory was gutted by fire.* □ **guts** *pl. n.* **1.** the internal organs of the abdomen. **2.** the strength or vitality of something. **3.** (*informal*) courage and determination. □ **hate a person's guts,** (*informal*) to hate him intensely. **sweat one's guts out,** (*informal*) to work extremely hard.

gutless *adj.* (*informal*) lacking courage and determination.

gutsy *adj.* (*slang*) **1.** greedy. **2.** courageous.

gutta-percha *n.* a tough rubber-like substance made from the juice of various Malayan trees.

gutter *n.* **1.** a shallow trough under the eaves of a building, or a channel at the side of a street, for carrying off rain-water. **2.** a slum environment. —*v.* (of a candle) to burn unsteadily so that melted wax flows freely down the sides.

guttering *n.* gutters, a length of gutter.

guttersnipe *n.* a dirty badly-dressed child who plays in slum streets.

guttural (gut-er-ăl) *adj.* throaty, harsh-sounding, *a guttural voice.* **gutturally** *adv.*

guv *n.* (*slang*) governor.

guy[1] *n.* a rope or chain used to keep something steady or secured, *guy ropes.*

guy[2] *n.* **1.** a figure in the form of a man dressed in old clothes, representing Guy Fawkes and burnt on 5 November in memory of the Gunpowder Plot. **2.** an oddly-dressed person. **3.** (*slang*) a man. —*v.* to ridicule, especially by comic imitation.

Guyana (gy-**an**-ă) a country in South America. **Guyanese** (gy-an-**eez**) *adj.* & *n.* (*pl.* Guyanese)

guzzle *v.* to eat or drink greedily. **guzzler** *n.*

Gwent a county of Wales.

Gwynedd (gwin-*eth*) a county of Wales.

gybe (*pr.* j-) *v.* **1.** (of a sail or boom) to swing across in wearing or running before the wind. **2.** to make (a sail) do this. **3.** to change course, to change the course of (a ship) so that this happens.

gym (*pr.* jim) *n.* (*informal*) **1.** a gymnasium. **2.** gymnastics. □ **gym-slip, gym-tunic** *ns* a sleeveless tunic worn by girls as part of school uniform.

gymkhana (jim-**kah**-nă) *n.* a public display of athletics and sports competitions, especially horse-riding.

gymnasium *n.* a room fitted up for physical training and gymnastics.

gymnast (**jim**-nast) *n.* an expert performer of gymnastics.

gymnastics *pl. n.* exercises performed to develop the muscles or demonstrate agility; *mental gymnastics,* mental agility, elaborate reasoning. —*n.* gymnastics as a subject of study or practice. □ **gymnastic** *adj.* of gymnastics.

gynaecologist (gy-ni-kol-ŏ-jist) *n.* a specialist in gynaecology.

gynaecology (gy-ni-**kol**-ŏji) *n.* the scientific study of the female reproductive system and its diseases. **gynaecological** *adj.*

gyp (*pr.* jip) *n.* **give a person gyp,** (*informal*) to scold or punish or defeat him severely, to cause him pain.

gypsophila (jip-**sof**-ilă) *n.* a garden plant with many small white flowers.

gypsum (**jip**-sum) *n.* a chalk-like substance from which plaster of Paris is made, also used as a fertilizer.

gypsy *n.* a member of a wandering race in Europe. **gypsy's warning,** a cryptic or sinister warning.

gyrate (jy-**rayt**) *v.* to move round in circles or spirals, to revolve. **gyration** (jy-**ray**-shŏn) *n.*

gyratory (jy-ră-ter-i) *adj.* gyrating, following a circular or spiral path.

gyro (jy-roh) *n.* (*pl.* gyros) (*informal*) a gyroscope.

gyrocompass (jy-rŏ-kum-păs) *n.* a navigation compass using a gyroscope and so independent of the earth's rotation.

gyroscope (jy-rŏ-skohp) *n.* a device consisting of a heavy wheel which, when spinning fast, keeps the direction of its axis unchanged, used in navigation instruments in ships and in spacecraft etc. **gyroscopic** (jy-rŏ-**skop**-ik) *adj.*

Hh

ha *int.* an exclamation of triumph or surprise.

habeas corpus (haybi-ăs **kor**-pŭs) an order requiring a person to be brought before a judge or into court, especially in order to investigate the right of the authorities to keep him imprisoned. (¶ Latin, = you must have the body.)

haberdasher *n.* a shopkeeper dealing in accessories for dress and in sewing-goods. **haberdashery** *n.* these goods.

habit *n.* **1.** a settled way of behaving, something done frequently and almost without thinking, something that is hard to give up. **2.** the long dress worn by a monk or nun. **3.** a woman's riding-dress. □ **habit-forming** *adj.* causing addiction.

habitable *adj.* suitable for living in.

habitat (**hab**-i-tat) *n.* the natural environment of an animal or plant.

habitation *n.* **1.** a place to live in. **2.** inhabiting, being inhabited.

habitual *adj.* **1.** done constantly, like or resulting from a habit. **2.** regular, usual, *in his habitual place.* **3.** doing something as a habit, *a habitual smoker.* **habitually** *adv.*

habituate *v.* to accustom. **habituation** *n.*

habitué (hă-**bit**-yoo-ay) *n.* one who visits a place frequently or lives there.

hacienda (ha-si-**en**-dă) *n.* (in Spanish-speaking countries) a large estate with a dwelling house.

hack[1] *v.* **1.** to cut or chop roughly. **2.** to deal a rough blow or kick, *hacked at his shins.* **3.** to cough harshly.

hack[2] *n.* **1.** a horse for ordinary riding, one that may be hired. **2.** a person paid to do hard and uninteresting work, especially as a writer. —*v.* to ride on horseback at an ordinary pace, especially along roads.

hacking *adj.* (of a cough) short, dry, and frequent.

hackles *pl. n.* the long feathers on the neck of a domestic cock and other birds. **with his hackles up,** (of a person) angry and ready to fight.

hackney carriage a vehicle that plies for hire, especially a taxi.

hackneyed (**hak**-nid) *adj.* (of a saying) having lost its original impact through long over-use.

hack-saw *n.* a saw for cutting metal, with a short blade in a frame.

had *see* have.

haddock *n.* (*pl.* haddock) a sea-fish like cod but smaller, used for food.

Hades (**hay**-deez) *n.* **1.** (in Greek mythology) the underworld, the place where the spirits of the dead go. **2.** hell.

hadn't = had not.

haematology (hee-mă-**tol**-ŏji) *n.* the scientific study of blood and its diseases. **haematologist** *n.*

haemoglobin (heem-ŏ-**gloh**-bin) *n.* the red oxygen-carrying substance in the blood.

haemophilia (heem-ŏ-**fil**-iă) *n.* a tendency (usually inherited) to bleed severely from even a slight injury, through failure of the blood to clot quickly. **haemophiliac** *n.* a person suffering from this.

haemorrhage (**hem**-er-ij) *n.* bleeding, especially when this is heavy. —*v.* to bleed heavily.

haemorrhoids (**hem**-er-oidz) *pl. n.* varicose veins at or near the anus.

haft *n.* the handle of a knife or dagger or cutting-tool.

hag *n.* an ugly old woman.

haggard *adj.* looking ugly from prolonged worry or illness or exhaustion.

haggis *n.* a Scottish dish made from sheep's heart, lungs, and liver.

haggle *v.* to argue about price or terms when settling a bargain.

Hague (*pr.* hayg), **The.** the seat of government of the Netherlands.

ha-ha¹ *int.* an outburst of laughter.

ha-ha² *n.* a sunk fence (*see* sunk).

haiku (**hy**-koo) *n.* a Japanese three-line poem of 17 syllables, an English imitation of this.

hail¹ *v.* **1.** to greet, to call to (a person or ship) in order to attract his attention, to signal to and summon (a taxi, etc.); *within hailing distance,* close enough to do this. **2.** to originate, to have come, *where does he hail from?* □ **be hail-fellow-well-met,** to be very friendly towards strangers. **Hail Mary,** a prayer to the Virgin Mary

beginning with these words.

hail² *n.* **1.** pellets of frozen rain falling in a shower. **2.** something coming in great numbers, *a hail of blows.* —**hail** *v.* **1.** to fall as hail in a shower, *it is hailing.* **2.** to come or send down like hail. □ **hailstone** *n.* a pellet of hail. **hailstorm** *n.* a storm of hail.

hair *n.* **1.** one of the fine thread-like strands that grow from the skin of people and animals or on certain plants. **2.** a mass of these, especially on the human head. □ **get in a person's hair,** to encumber or annoy him. **hair-do** *n.* (*pl.* hair-dos) a hairstyle; the process of arranging a woman's hair. **hair-grip** *n.* a strong springy clip for holding the hair in place. **hair-line** *n.* the edge of a person's hair round the face; a very thin line. **hair-piece** *n.* false hair worn to increase the amount of a person's natural hair. **hair-raising** *adj.* terrifying, causing one's hair to stand on end in fear. **hair's breadth escape,** a very narrow escape. **hair-splitting** *n.* splitting hairs (*see below*). **hair-style** *n.* the style in which hair is arranged. **hair-trigger** *n.* a trigger that causes a gun to fire at the very slightest pressure. **split hairs,** to make distinctions of meaning that are too small to be of any real importance.

hairbrush *n.* a brush for grooming the hair.

haircut *n.* **1.** shortening the hair by cutting it. **2.** the style in which it is cut.

hairdresser *n.* a person whose trade is to arrange and cut hair.

hairless *adj.* without hair, bald.

hairpin *n.* a U-shaped pin for keeping the hair in place. **hairpin bend,** a V-shaped bend in a road.

hairspring *n.* a fine spring regulating the balance-wheel in a watch.

hairy *adj.* (hairier, hairiest) **1.** having much hair. **2.** (*slang*) hair-raising, difficult. **hairiness** *n.*

Haiti (**hy**-ti) a country in the West Indies. **Haitian** *adj.* & *n.*

hake *n.* (*pl.* hake) a fish of the cod family, used as food.

halcyon (**hal**-si-ŏn) *adj.* (of a period) happy and prosperous, *halcyon days.* ¶ Named after a bird formerly believed to have the power of calming wind and waves while it nested on the sea.

hale *adj.* strong and healthy, *hale and hearty.*

half *n.* (*pl.* halves) **1.** one of two equal or corresponding parts into which a thing is divided. **2.** a half-price ticket for a child on a bus or train. **3.** (*informal*) half-past, *half seven.* —*adj.* amounting to a half. —*adv.* to the extent of a half, partly, *half-cooked; I'm half inclined to agree.* □ **by half,** excessively, *too clever by half.* **by halves,** lacking thoroughness, *they never do things by halves.* **go halves,** to share a thing equally. **half a dozen,** six. **half-and-half,** *adj.* being half of one thing and half of another. **half-back** *n.* a player between the forwards and the full backs in football and hockey; his position. **half-baked** *adj.* (*informal*) not competently planned; foolish. **half board,** provision of bed, breakfast, and one main meal at a hotel etc. **half-breed** *n.* a person of mixed race. **half-brother** *n.* a brother with only one parent in common with another. **half-caste** *n.* a person of mixed race. **half-cock** *n.* the state of being only half-ready, *at half-cock.* **half-hardy** *adj.* (of plants) able to withstand cold weather but not severe frost. **half-hearted** *adj.* lacking enthusiasm. **half holiday,** a day of which the afternoon is taken as a holiday. **half-hour** *n.* thirty minutes; a point of time 30 minutes after any hour o'clock. **half-landing** *n.* a landing half-way up a flight of stairs. **half-life** *n.* the time it takes the radioactivity of a substance to fall to half its original value. **half-mast** *n.* a point about half-way up a mast, to which a flag is lowered as a mark of respect for a dead person. **half measures,** a policy lacking thoroughness. **half nelson,** a hold in wrestling, with an arm under the opponent's arm and behind his back. **half-plate** *n.* a size of photograph $16 \cdot 5 \times 10 \cdot 8$ cm. **half-past** *n.* half an hour after (any hour o'clock). **half-price** *n.* a price reduced to half the standard price. **half-seas-over** *adj.* (*slang*) intoxicated. **half-term** *n.* a short holiday half-way through a school term. **half-timbered** *adj.* (of a building) having a timber frame with the spaces filled in by brick or plaster. **half-time** *n.* the interval between the two halves of a game of football or hockey etc. **half-tone** *n.* a black-and-white illustration in which light and dark shades are reproduced by means of small and large dots. **half-truth** *n.* a statement conveying only part of the truth. **half-way** *adj.* & *adv.* at a point between and equally distant from two others; *a half-way house,* a compromise. **half-wit** *n.* a half-witted person. **half-witted** *adj.* mentally retarded; stupid.

halfpenny (**hayp**-ni) *n.* (*pl.* halfpennies for separate coins, halfpence for a sum of money) a coin worth half a penny. **halfpennyworth** *n.* the amount this will buy.

halibut *n.* (*pl.* halibut) a large flat-fish used for food.

halitosis (hal-i-**toh**-sis) *n.* breath that smells unpleasant.

hall *n.* **1.** a large room or a building for meetings, meals, concerts, etc. **2.** a large country house, especially one with a landed estate. **3.** a space or passage into which the front entrance of a house etc. opens. □ **hall of residence,** a building for university students to live in.

hallelujah *int.* & *n.* = alleluia.

halliard *n.* = halyard.

hallmark *n.* **1.** a mark used at Goldsmiths' Hall (and by assay offices) for marking the standard of gold, silver, and platinum on articles made of these. **2.** a distinguishing characteristic, *the bombing bears the hallmark of recent guerrilla attacks.* **hallmarked** *adj.* marked with a hallmark.

hallo *int.* & *n.* an exclamation used in greeting or to call attention or express surprise, or to answer a call on the telephone.

halloo *int.* & *n.* a cry to urge on hounds or attract a person's attention. —*v.* to shout 'halloo'.

hallow *v.* to make holy, to honour as holy.

Hallowe'en *n.* 31 October, the eve of All Saints' Day.

hallucination (hă-loo-sin-**ay**-shŏn) *n.* **1.** the illusion of seeing or hearing something when no such thing is present. **2.** the thing seen or heard in this way.

hallucinatory (hă-loo-sin-ă-ter-i) *adj.* of or causing hallucinations.

hallucinogenic (hă-loo-sin-ŏ-**jen**-ik) *adj.* causing hallucinations.

halo *n.* (*pl.* haloes) **1.** a disc or ring of light shown round the head of a sacred figure in paintings etc. **2.** a disc of diffused light round a luminous body such as the sun or moon. **haloed** *adj.*

halt *n.* **1.** a temporary stop, an interruption of progress, *work came to a halt.* **2.** a stopping-place on a railway-line, used for local services only and without station buildings. —*v.* to come or bring to a halt.

halter *n.* **1.** a length of rope or a leather strap put round a horse's head so that it may be led or fastened by this. **2.** a style of dress-top held up by a strap passing round the back of the neck, leaving back and shoulders bare.

halting *adj.* **1.** walking slowly as if unsure of oneself. **2.** spoken hesitantly, *a halting explanation.*

halve *v.* **1.** to divide or share equally between two. **2.** to reduce by half.

halves *see* half.

halyard (**hal**-yerd) *n.* a rope or tackle for raising or lowering a sail or yard or flag etc.

ham *n.* **1.** the upper part of a pig's leg,

dried and salted or smoked. **2.** meat from this. **3.** the back of the thigh, the thigh and buttock. **4.** (*slang*) a poor actor or performer. **5.** (*informal*) the operator of an amateur radio station, *a radio ham.* —*v.* (hammed, hamming) (*slang*) to overact, to exaggerate one's actions deliberately, *hamming it up.* ☐ **ham-fisted, ham-handed** *adjs.* (*slang*) clumsy.

hamburger *n.* a flat round cake of minced beef served fried, often eaten in a bread roll. ¶ Named after *Hamburg* in Germany.

hamlet *n.* a small village, usually without a church.

hammer *n.* **1.** a tool with a heavy metal head used for breaking things, driving nails in, etc. **2.** something shaped or used like this, e.g. an auctioneer's mallet, part of the firing device in a gun, a lever striking the string in a piano. **3.** a metal ball of about 7 kg, attached to a wire for throwing as an athletic contest. —**hammer** *v.* to hit or beat with a hammer, to strike loudly; *hammer an idea into someone,* din it into him. ☐ **come under the hammer,** to be sold by auction. **hammer and sickle,** the symbols of manual worker and peasant used as the emblem of the USSR. **hammer and tongs,** fighting or arguing with great energy and noise.

hammer-beam *n.* a beam that projects a short way into a hall etc. from the foot of one of the roof's principal rafters. **hammer-beam roof,** a timber roof in which the rafters are supported by a series of brackets each resting on the one below. **hammer-lock** *n.* a hold in which a wrestler's arm is bent behind his back. **hammer out,** to devise (a plan) with great effort. **hammer-toe** *n.* a toe that is permanently bent downwards.

hammock *n.* a hanging bed of canvas or rope network.

hamper[1] *n.* **1.** a basketwork packing-case. **2.** a hamper or box of food as a present.

hamper[2] *v.* to prevent the free movement or activity of, to hinder.

Hampshire a county of England.

hamster *n.* a small rat-like rodent with cheek-pouches for carrying grain.

hamstring *n.* **1.** any of the five tendons at the back of the human knee. **2.** the great tendon at the back of an animal's hock. — **hamstring** *v.* (hamstrung, hamstringing) **1.** to cripple by cutting the hamstrings. **2.** to cripple the activity or efficiency of.

hand *n.* **1.** the end part of the arm below the wrist; *a hand of pork,* a part of the foreleg. **2.** possession, control, care, *the child is in good hands.* **3.** influence, activity, *many people had a hand in it.* **4.** active help, *give him a hand.* **5.** a pledge of marriage, *asked for her hand.* **6.** a manual worker in a factory or farm etc., a member of a ship's crew. **7.** skill or style of workmanship, a person with reference to skill, *has a light hand with pastry; an old hand at this,* an experienced person. **8.** style of handwriting. **9.** a pointer on a dial etc. **10.** side or direction, the right or left side, one of two contrasted sides in an argument etc., *on every hand; on the other hand.* **11.** a unit of 4 inches used in measuring a horse's height. **12.** the cards dealt to a player in a card-game, one round of a card-game. **13.** (*informal*) applause, *got a big hand.* **14.** done or operated or carried etc. by hand, *hand-sewn; hand-brake; hand-luggage.* —**hand** *v.* **1.** to give or pass with one's hand(s) or otherwise. **2.** to help (a person) into a vehicle etc. ☐ **at hand,** close by; about to happen. **by hand,** by a person (not a machine); delivered by a messenger, not through the post. **hand in glove with,** working in close association with. **hand in hand,** holding each other's hand; closely associated, linked together. **hand it to a person,** (*informal*) to award praise to him. **hand-out** *n.* something distributed free of charge; a prepared statement issued to the press etc. **hand over,** to put (a person or thing) into the custody or control of another person; to present. **hand over fist,** (*informal*) with rapid progress, *making money hand over fist.* **hand-picked** *adj.* carefully chosen. **hands down,** (of a victory won) easily, completely. **hands off!,** do not touch or interfere. **a hand's turn,** the slightest amount of work. **hands up!,** an order to raise one hand (e.g. in agreement) or both hands in surrender. **in hand,** in one's possession; in control; (of business) being dealt with. **live from hand to mouth,** to supply only one's immediate needs without provision for the future. **on hand,** available. **on one's hands,** resting on one as a responsibility. **out of hand,** out of control; without delay or preparation, *rejected it out of hand.* **to hand,** within reach.

handbag *n.* **1.** a woman's bag to hold a purse and small personal articles. **2.** a travelling-bag.

handbook *n.* a small book giving useful facts.

h. & c. *abbrev.* hot and cold water.

handcraft *v.* to make by handicraft.

handcuff *n.* one of a pair of linked metal rings for securing a prisoner's wrists. —*v.* to put handcuffs on (a prisoner).

handful *n.* (*pl.* handfuls) **1.** a quantity that fills the hand. **2.** a small number of people or things. **3.** (*informal*) a person who is difficult to control, a troublesome task.

handicap *n.* **1.** a disadvantage imposed on a superior competitor in order to equalize chances. **2.** a race or contest in which this is imposed. **3.** the number of strokes by which a golfer normally exceeds par for the course. **4.** anything that lessens one's chance of success or makes progress difficult. **5.** a physical or mental disability. —*v.* (handicapped, handicapping) to impose or be a handicap on. —**handicapper** *n.* ☐ **handicapped** *adj.* suffering from a physical or mental disability.

handicraft *n.* work that needs both skill with the hands and artistic design, e.g. woodwork, needlework, pottery, etc.

handily *adv.* in a handy way.

handiwork *n.* **1.** something done or made by the hands. **2.** something done or made by a named person.

handkerchief *n.* (*pl.* handkerchiefs) a small square of cloth for wiping the nose etc.

handle *n.* **1.** the part of a thing by which it is to be held or carried or controlled. **2.** a fact that may be taken advantage of, *gave a handle to his critics.* —**handle** *v.* **1.** to touch or feel or move with the hands. **2.** to be able to be operated, *the car handles well.* **3.** to manage, to deal with, *knows how to handle people.* **4.** to deal in (goods). **5.** to discuss or write about (a subject). ☐ **have a handle to one's name**, to have a title of nobility.

handlebar *n.* **1.** the steering-bar of a bicycle etc., with a handle at each end. **2.** a thick curving moustache shaped like this.

handler *n.* a person who handles things, one in charge of a trained police dog.

handrail *n.* a narrow rail for people to hold as a support.

handshake *n.* grasping and shaking a person's hand with one's own as a greeting.

handsome *adj.* **1.** good-looking. **2.** generous, *a handsome present.* **2.** (of a price or fortune etc.) very large. **handsomely** *adv.*, **handsomeness** *n.*

handspring *n.* a somersault in which a person lands first on his hands then on his feet.

handstand *n.* balancing on one's hands with the feet in the air.

handwriting *n.* **1.** writing done by hand with a pen or pencil. **2.** a person's style of this.

handwritten *adj.* written by hand.

handy *adj.* (handier, handiest) **1.** convenient to handle or use. **2.** conveniently placed for being reached or used. **3.** clever with one's hands. **handily** *adv.*, **handiness** *n.*

handyman *n.* (*pl.* handymen) a person who is clever at doing household repairs etc. or who is employed to do odd jobs.

hang *v.* (hung in senses 5 and 6 hanged), hanging) **1.** to support or be supported from above so that the lower end is free. **2.** to cause (a door or gate) to rest on hinges so that it swings freely to and fro, to be placed in this way. **3.** to stick (wallpaper) to a wall. **4.** to decorate with drapery or hanging ornaments. **5.** to execute or kill by suspending from a rope that tightens round the neck, to be executed in this way. **6.** (*informal*) to damn, *I'm hanged if I know.* **7.** to droop; *people hung over the gate,* leant over it. **8.** to remain in the air, *smoke hung over the area; the threat is hanging over him,* remains as something unpleasant. —*int.* (*informal*) damn. —**hang** *n.* **1.** the way something hangs. **2.** (*informal*) a very small amount, *doesn't care a hang.* ☐ **get the hang of,** (*informal*) to get the knack of. **hang about** or **around,** to loiter, not to disperse. **hang back,** to show reluctance to take action or to advance. **hang fire,** (of a gun) to be slow in going off; (of events) to be slow in developing. **hang on,** to hold tightly; to depend on, *much hangs on this decision;* to attend closely to, *they hung on his words;* to remain in office, to stick to one's duty etc.; (*slang*) to wait for a short time, *hung on a minute;* (*informal*, in telephoning) to hold the line and not ring off. **hang out,** (*slang*) to have one's home, to reside; *let it all hang out,* (*slang*) be uninhibited. **hang-out** (*slang*) a place of residence. **hang together,** (of people) to help or support one another; (of statements) to fit well together, to be consistent. **hang up,** to end a telephone conversation by replacing the receiver; to cause delay or difficulty to. **hang-up** *n.* (*slang*) a difficulty; an inhibition.

hangar *n.* a shed for housing aircraft.

hangdog *adj.* shamefaced.

hanger *n.* **1.** a person who hangs things. **2.** a loop or hook by which something is hung. **3.** a shaped piece of wood or plastic for hanging a garment on. **4.** a wood on the side of a hill, *the beech hanger.* ☐ **hanger-on** *n.* (*pl.* hangers-on) a person who attaches himself to another in the hope of personal gain.

hang-gliding *n.* the sport of being suspended in an airborne frame controlled by one's own movements. **hang-glider** *n.* this frame.

hangings *pl. n.* draperies hung on walls.

hangman *n.* a man whose job is to hang persons condemned to death.

hangnail *n.* torn skin at the root of a finger-nail.

hangover *n.* **1.** a severe headache or other unpleasant after-effects from drinking much alcohol. **2.** something left from an earlier time.

hank *n.* **1.** a coil or length of wool or thread etc. **2.** a ring or hoop of metal for securing a jib or staysail to a stay.

hanker *v.* to crave, to feel a longing.

hanky *n.* (*informal*) a handkerchief.

hanky-panky *n.* (*slang*) **1.** trickery, dishonest dealing. **2.** naughtiness.

Hanoi the capital of Vietnam.

Hansard *n.* the official report of proceedings in parliament. ¶ Named after the English printer whose firm originally compiled it.

Hants *abbrev.* Hampshire.

haphazard (hap-**haz**-erd) *adj.* done or chosen at random, without planning. **haphazardly** *adv.*

hapless *adj.* unlucky.

ha'p'orth (**hay**-perth) *n.* **1.** = halfpennyworth. **2.** a very small amount, *not a ha'p'orth of difference.*

happen *v.* **1.** to occur (by chance or otherwise). **2.** to have the (good or bad) fortune to do something, *we happened to see him.* **3.** to find by chance, *I happened on this book.* **4.** to be the fate or experience of, *what happened to you?* □ **happening** *n.* something that happens, an event.

happy *adj.* (happier, happiest) **1.** feeling or showing pleasure or contentment. **2.** fortunate. **3.** (of words or behaviour) very suitable, pleasing. **happily** *adv.*, **happiness** *n.* □ **happy-go-lucky** *adj.* taking events cheerfully as they happen. **happy hunting-ground**, a good place for finding things. **happy medium**, something that achieves satisfactory avoidance of extremes.

hara-kiri (ha-rä-**ki**-ri) *n.* suicide involving disembowelment, formerly practised by Japanese army officers when in disgrace or under sentence of death.

harangue (hǎ-**rang**) *n.* a lengthy earnest speech. —*v.* to make a harangue to.

Harare (hǎ-**rah**-ri) the capital of Zimbabwe.

harass (**ha**-rǎs) *v.* **1.** to trouble and annoy continually. **2.** to make repeated attacks on (an enemy). **harassment** (**ha**-rǎs-měnt) *n.* ¶ The pronunciations hǎ-**ras** and hǎ-**ras**-měnt are American but not standard English.

harassed (**ha**-rǎst) *adj.* tired and irritated by continual worry.

harbinger (**har**-bin-jer) *n.* a person or thing whose presence announces the approach of another.

harbour *n.* a place of shelter for ships. —*v.* **1.** to give shelter to, to conceal (a criminal etc.). **2.** to keep in one's mind, *harbour a grudge.*

hard *adj.* **1.** firm, not yielding to pressure, not easily cut; *hard facts,* not disputable. **2.** difficult to do or understand or answer. **3.** causing unhappiness, difficult to bear. **4.** severe, harsh, unsympathetic. **5.** energetic, *a hard worker.* **6.** (of weather) severe, frosty. **7.** (of currency) not likely to drop suddenly in value. **8.** (of drinks) strongly alcoholic. **9.** (of water) containing mineral salts that prevent soap from lathering freely and cause a hard coating to form inside kettles, water-tanks, etc. **10.** (of colours or sounds) harsh to the eye or ear. **11.** (of consonants) sounding sharp not soft, *the letter 'g' is hard in 'gun' and soft in 'gin'.* —**hard** *adv.* **1.** with great effort, intensively, *worked hard; it's raining hard.* **2.** with difficulty, *hard-earned money.* **3.** so as to be hard, *hard-baked.* —**hardness** *n.* □ **hard and fast rules,** rules that cannot be altered to fit special cases. **hard bargaining,** making few concessions. **hard-boiled** *adj.* (of eggs) boiled until white and yolk have become solid; (of people) callous. **hard by,** close by. **hard cash,** coins and banknotes, not a cheque or a promise to pay later. **hard copy,** material produced in printed form by a computer or from a microfilm etc. and able to be read without a special device. **hard core,** the stubborn unyielding nucleus of a group. **hard court,** a tennis court with a hard (not grass) surface. **hard disc,** (in computers) a rigid disc, capable of holding more data than a floppy disc. **hard drugs,** drugs that are strong and likely to cause addiction. **hard-headed** *adj.* practical, not sentimental. **hard-hearted** *adj.* unsympathetic. **hard line,** unyielding adherence to a firm policy. **hard lines,** worse luck than is deserved. **hard of hearing,** slightly deaf. **hard pornography,** highly obscene. **hard sell,** aggressive salesmanship. **hard shoulder,** a strip of hardened land beside a motorway for vehicles leaving the road in an emergency. **hard up,** (*informal*) short of money; *hard up for ideas,* short of these. **hard-wearing** *adj.* able to stand much wear.

hardboard *n.* stiff board made of compressed wood-pulp.

harden *v.* **1.** to make or become hard or hardy. **2.** to make or become unyielding, *attitudes have hardened in the dispute.* **hardener** *n.*

hardly *adv.* **1.** in a hard manner. **2.** only

with difficulty. **3.** scarcely; *one can hardly expect it*, cannot reasonably expect it.

hardship *n.* severe discomfort or lack of the necessaries of life, a circumstance causing this.

hardstanding *n.* an area with a hard surface for a vehicle to stand on.

hardware *n.* **1.** tools and household implements etc. sold by a shop. **2.** weapons, machinery. **3.** the mechanical and electronic parts of a computer.

hardwood *n.* the hard heavy wood obtained from deciduous trees, e.g. oak and teak.

hardy *adj.* (hardier, hardiest) **1.** capable of enduring cold or difficult conditions. **2.** (of plants) able to grow in the open air all the year round. **hardiness** *n.* □ **hardy annual**, an annual plant hardy enough to be sown in the open; a subject that comes up at regular intervals.

hare *n.* a field animal like a rabbit but larger. —*v.* to run rapidly. □ **hare-brained** *adj.* wild and foolish, rash.

harebell *n.* a wild plant with blue bell-shaped flowers on a slender stalk.

harelip *n.* a deformed lip (usually the upper lip) with a vertical slit in it like that of a hare.

harem (hair-ĕm) *n.* **1.** the women of a Muslim household, living in a separate part of the house. **2.** their apartments.

haricot bean (ha-rik-oh) the white dried seed of a kind of bean.

hark *v.* listen. **hark back**, to return to an earlier subject.

harl *v.* (*Scottish*) to roughcast with lime and small gravel. **harling** *n.* this material.

harlequin *adj.* in varied colours. ¶ Named after *Harlequin*, a former pantomime character usually dressed in a diamond-patterned costume.

Harley Street a London street associated with eminent medical specialists.

harlot *n.* (*old use*) a prostitute.

harm *n.* damage, injury. —*v.* to cause harm to.

harmful *adj.* causing harm. **harmfully** *adv.*

harmless *adj.* **1.** unlikely to cause harm. **2.** inoffensive. **harmlessly** *adv.*, **harmlessness** *n.*

harmonic *adj.* full of harmony.

harmonica *n.* a mouth-organ.

harmonious *adj.* **1.** forming a pleasing or consistent whole. **2.** free from disagreement or ill-feeling. **3.** sweet-sounding, tuneful. **harmoniously** *adv.*

harmonium *n.* a musical instrument with a keyboard, in which notes are produced by air pumped through reeds.

harmonize *v.* **1.** to make or be harmonious. **2.** to produce an agreeable artistic effect. **3.** to add notes to (a melody) to form chords. **harmonization** *n.*

harmony *n.* **1.** the state of being harmonious. **2.** the combination of musical notes to produce chords. **3.** a sweet or melodious sound.

harness *n.* **1.** the straps and fittings by which a horse is controlled and fastened to the cart etc. that it pulls. **2.** fastenings resembling this (e.g. for attaching a parachute to its wearer). —**harness** *v.* **1.** to put harness on (a horse), to attach by a harness. **2.** to control and use (a river or other natural force) to produce electrical power etc.

harp *n.* a musical instrument consisting of strings stretched on a roughly triangular frame, played by plucking with the fingers. —*v.* **harp on**, to talk repeatedly and tiresomely about (a subject).

harpist *n.* a person who plays the harp.

harpoon *n.* a spear-like missile with a rope attached, for catching whales etc. —*v.* to spear with a harpoon.

harpsichord (harp-si-kord) *n.* an instrument rather like a piano but with the strings sounded by a mechanism that plucks them, used especially in the 16th–18th centuries.

harpy *n.* a grasping unscrupulous person. ¶ Named after the *Harpies*, creatures in Greek mythology with a woman's head and body and a bird's wings and claws.

harridan (ha-rid-ăn) *n.* a bad-tempered old woman.

harrier *n.* **1.** a hound used for hunting hares. **2.** a kind of falcon.

harrow *n.* a heavy frame with metal spikes or discs for breaking up clods, covering seed, etc. —*v.* **1.** to draw a harrow over (land). **2.** to distress greatly, *harrowed their feelings*.

harry *v.* (harried, harrying) to harass.

harsh *adj.* **1.** rough and disagreeable, especially to the senses, *a harsh texture* or *voice*. **2.** severe, cruel, *harsh treatment*. **harshly** *adv.*, **harshness** *n.*

hart *n.* an adult male deer. **hart's-tongue** *n.* a fern with long undivided fronds.

harum-scarum *adj.* (*informal*) wild and reckless. — *n.* (*informal*) a wild and reckless person.

harvest *v.* **1.** the gathering of a crop or crops, the season when this is done. **2.** the season's yield of any natural product. **3.** the product of any action. —*v.* to gather a crop, to reap. □ **harvest moon**, the full moon nearest to the autumnal equinox (22 or 23 September).

harvester *n.* **1.** a reaper. **2.** a reaping-machine.

has *see* have. □ **has-been** *n.* (*pl.* has-beens) (*informal*) a person or thing that is no longer as famous or successful as formerly.

hash¹ *n.* **1.** a dish of cooked or preserved meat cut into small pieces and recooked. **2.** a jumble, a mixture. —*v.* to make (meat) into a hash. □ **make a hash of,** (*slang*) to make a mess of, to bungle. **settle a person's hash,** (*slang*) to deal with and subdue him.

hash² *n.* (*informal*) hashish.

hashish *n.* the top leaves and tender parts of hemp, dried for chewing or smoking as a narcotic.

haslet (**hayz**-lit) *n.* a meat loaf made from pig's offal, eaten cold.

hasn't = has not.

hasp *n.* a hinged metal strip with a slit in it that fits over a U-shaped staple through which a pin or padlock is then passed.

hassle *n.* (*informal*) a quarrel or struggle. —*v.* (*informal*) **1.** to quarrel. **2.** to jostle, to harass.

hassock *n.* a thick firm cushion for kneeling on in church.

hast (*old use*) the past tense of have, used with *thou.*

haste *n.* urgency of movement or action, hurry. **in haste,** quickly, hurriedly. **make haste,** to act quickly.

hasten *v.* **1.** to hurry. **2.** to cause (a thing) to be done earlier or to happen earlier.

hasty *adj.* (hastier, hastiest) **1.** hurried, acting too quickly. **2.** said or made or done too quickly. **hastily** *adv.*, **hastiness** *n.*

hat *n.* **1.** a covering for the head, worn out of doors. **2.** this thought of as symbolizing a person's official position; *wear two hats,* to have two official positions. □ **hat trick,** the taking of 3 wickets in cricket by 3 successive balls from the same bowler; the scoring of 3 goals or winning of 3 victories by one person. **keep it under your hat,** keep it secret. **pass the hat round,** to collect contributions of money.

hatband *n.* a band of ribbon etc. round a hat just above the brim.

hatch¹ *n.* **1.** an opening in a door or floor or ceiling, an opening in a ship's deck. **2.** a movable cover over any of these. **3.** an opening in a wall between two rooms.

hatch² *v.* **1.** (of a young bird or fish etc.) to emerge from an egg, (of an egg) to produce a young animal. **2.** to cause (eggs) to produce young by incubating them. **3.** to devise (a plot). —*n.* hatching, a brood hatched.

hatch³ *v.* to mark with close parallel lines. **hatching** *n.* these marks.

hatchback *n.* a car with a sloping back hinged at the top so that it can be opened, the back itself.

hatchery *n.* a place for hatching eggs, especially of fish, *a trout hatchery.*

hatchet *n.* a light short-handled axe. **hatchet-faced** *adj.* having a long sharp-featured face. **hatchet-man** *n.* a person employed to attack and destroy people's reputations.

hatchway *n.* a cover on a hatch in a ship's deck.

hate *n.* **1.** hatred. **2.** (*informal*) a hated person or thing. —**hate** *v.* **1.** to feel hatred towards. **2.** to dislike greatly. **3.** (*informal*) to be reluctant, *I hate to interrupt you, but it's time to go.* —**hater** *n.*

hateful *adj.* arousing hatred.

hath (*old use*) has.

hatful *n.* the amount a hat will hold.

hatless *adj.* not wearing a hat.

hatred *n.* violent dislike or enmity.

hatter *n.* a person whose trade is making or selling hats.

haughty (**haw**-ti) *adj.* (haughtier, haughtiest) proud of oneself and looking down on other people. **haughtily** *adv.*, **haughtiness** *n.*

haul *v.* **1.** to pull or drag forcibly. **2.** to transport by a truck etc., to cart. **3.** to turn a ship's course. —**haul** *n.* **1.** hauling. **2.** the amount gained as a result of effort, booty, *made a good haul.* **3.** a distance to be traversed, *it's only a short haul from here.*

haulage *n.* transport of goods, the charge for this.

haulier (**hawl**-i-er) *n.* a person or firm whose trade is transporting goods by road.

haunch *n.* **1.** the fleshy part of the buttock and thigh. **2.** the leg and loin of deer etc. as food.

haunt *v.* **1.** (of ghosts) to be frequently in (a place) with manifestations of their presence and influence. **2.** to be persistently in (a place). **3.** to linger in the mind of, *the memory haunts me.* —*n.* a place often visited by the person(s) named, *the inn is a favourite haunt of fishermen.* □ **haunted** *adj.* frequented by a ghost or ghosts.

Havana (hă-**van**-ă) the capital of Cuba.

have *v.* (had, having) **1.** to be in possession of (a thing or quality), to possess in a certain relationship, *he has many enemies.* **2.** to contain, *the house has six rooms.* **3.** to experience, to undergo, *had a shock.* **4.** to give birth to. **5.** to put into a certain condition, *you had me worried; you have me there,* have me defeated or at a disadvantage.

6. (*slang*) to cheat or deceive, *we've been had.* **7.** to have sexual intercourse with. **8.** to engage in, to carry on, *had a talk with him; had breakfast,* ate it. **9.** to allow, to tolerate, *won't have him bullied.* **10.** to be under the obligation of, *we have to go now.* **11.** to let (a feeling etc.) be present in the mind, *have no doubt.* **12.** to show a quality, *have mercy on us.* **13.** to receive, to accept, *we had news of her; will you have a cigarette?* **14.** to cause a thing to be done, *have one's hair cut; have three copies made.* —**have** *auxiliary verb,* used to form past tenses of verbs, *he has gone; we had expected it.* □ **had better,** would find it wiser. **have had it,** (*informal*) to have missed one's chance; to be near death, no longer usable, etc. **have it,** to have a sudden inspiration about a problem etc., *I have it!*; to win a decision in a vote, *the ayes have it; let him have it,* give him the punishment etc. **have it coming,** (*informal*) to deserve one's punishment or bad luck. **have it in for,** (*informal*) to show ill will towards (a person). **have it off,** (*slang*) to have sexual intercourse. **have it out,** to settle a problem by frank discussion. **have on,** (*informal*) to hoax. **have over,** (*informal*) to discuss, to talk over. **haves and have-nots,** people with and without wealth or privilege. **have up,** to bring (a person) before a court of justice or an interviewer.

haven *n.* a refuge.

haven't = have not.

haver (hay-ver) *v.* **1.** to hesitate. **2.** (*Scottish*) to talk foolishly.

haversack *n.* a strong bag carried on the back or over the shoulder.

havoc (hav-ŏk) *n.* widespread destruction, great disorder. **play havoc with,** to create havoc in.

haw[1] *n.* a hawthorn berry, *hips and haws.*

haw[2] *v. see* hum[2].

Hawaii (hă-wy-i) a State of the USA consisting of a group of islands in the Pacific. **Hawaiian** (hă-wy-ăn) *adj. & n.*

hawk[1] *n.* **1.** a bird of prey with rounded wings shorter than a falcon's. **2.** a person who favours an aggressive policy. □ **hawk-eyed** *adj.* keen-sighted.

hawk[2] *v.* to clear the throat of phlegm noisily.

hawk[3] *v.* to carry (goods) about for sale. **hawker** *n.* one who does this for a living.

hawser (haw-zer) *n.* a heavy rope or cable for mooring or towing a ship.

hawthorn *n.* a thorny tree or shrub with small red berries.

hay *n.* grass mown and dried for fodder. **hay fever,** catarrh caused by pollen or dust.

haymaking *n.* tossing grass and spreading it to dry after mowing. **make hay while the sun shines,** to seize opportunities for profit. **make hay of,** to throw into confusion.

haystack *n.* a regularly shaped pile of hay firmly packed for storing, with a pointed or ridged top.

haywire *adj.* (*informal*) badly disorganized, out of control.

hazard (haz-erd) *n.* **1.** risk, danger, a source of this. **2.** an obstacle (e.g. a pond or bunker etc.) on a golf-course. —*v.* to risk; *hazard a guess,* venture to make one.

hazardous *adj.* risky. **hazardously** *adv.*

haze *n.* **1.** thin mist. **2.** mental confusion or obscurity.

hazel *n.* **1.** a bush with small edible nuts. **2.** a light brownish colour. **hazel-nut** *n.*

hazy *adj.* (hazier, haziest) **1.** misty. **2.** vague, indistinct. **3.** feeling confused or uncertain. **hazily** *adv.,* **haziness** *n.*

H-bomb *n.* a hydrogen bomb.

he *pronoun* **1.** the male person or animal mentioned. **2.** a person (male or female), *he who hesitates is lost.* *n.* a male, animal; *a he-goat,* a male goat. □ **he-man** *n.* a masterful or robust-looking man.

head *n.* **1.** the part of the body containing the eyes, nose, mouth, and brain. **2.** this as a measure of length, *the horse won by a head.* **3.** the intellect, the imagination, the mind, *use your head.* **4.** a mental ability or faculty, *has a good head for figures* or *heights.* **5.** an image or picture of a person's head *ruler's head appears.* **6.** (*informal*) a headache. **7.** a person, an individual person or animal, *crowned heads; it costs £1 per head.* **8.** a number of animals, *20 head of cattle.* **9.** a thing like a head in form or position, e.g. the rounded end of a pin, the cutting or striking part of a tool etc., a rounded mass of leaves or petals etc. at the top of a stem, the flat surface of a drum or cask **10.** foam on top of beer etc. **11.** the top of something long (e.g. a stair or mast) or of a list. **12.** the top part of a boil where it tends to break. **13.** the upper end or part of a table (where the host sits) or lake (where a river enters) or bed etc. (where a person's head rests). **14.** a body of water kept at a height (e.g. to work a water-mill), a confined body of steam for exerting pressure. **15.** the leading part in a procession or army; *at the head,* in a position of command. **16.** (in place-names) a promontory, *Beachy Head.* **17.** the chief person of a group or organization etc., a headmaster or headmistress. —**head** *v.* **1.** to be at the head or top of. **2.** to strike (a ball) with one's head in football. **3.** to move in a certain direction, *we headed south*; *heading for disaster*. **4.** to force to turn back or aside by getting in front of, *head him off*. □ **come to a head**, (of matters) to reach a crisis. **give him his head**, let him move or act freely. **go to a person's head**, (of alcohol) to make him dizzy or slightly drunk; (of success) to make him conceited. **head-on** *adj. & adv.* with the head pointed directly towards something; colliding head to head. **head over heels**, turning one's body upside down in a circular movement; very much, *he is head over heels in love with her*. **heads will roll**, some people will be punished or dismissed. **head wind**, a wind blowing from directly in front. **in one's head**, in one's mind, not written down. **keep one's head**, to remain calm in a crisis. **lose one's head**, to act foolishly. **make head or tail of**, to be able to understand. **off one's head**, crazy. **over one's head**, (of another's promotion etc.) when one has a prior or stronger claim. **put heads together**, to pool ideas. **turn a person's head**, to make him vain.

headache *n.* **1.** a continuous pain in the head. **2.** a problem causing worry.

headboard *n.* an upright panel along the head of a bed.

head-dress *n.* an ornamental covering or band worn on the head.

header *n.* **1.** a dive or plunge with head first. **2.** heading of the ball in football.

headgear *n.* a hat or head-dress.

heading *n.* **1.** a word or words put at the top of a section of printed or written matter as a title etc. **2.** a horizontal passage in a mine.

headlamp *n.* a headlight.

headland *n.* a promontory.

headless *n.* having no head.

headlight *n.* **1.** a powerful light mounted on the front of a motor vehicle or railway engine. **2.** the beam from this.

headline *n.* a heading in a newspaper, especially the largest one at the top of the front page; *the news headlines*, a brief broadcast summary of news.

headlong *adv. & adj.* **1.** falling or plunging with the head first. **2.** in a hasty and rash way.

headmaster, headmistress *ns.* the principal master or mistress in a school, responsible for organizing it.

headphone *n.* a radio or telephone receiver held over the ear(s) by a band fitting over the head.

headquarters *pl. n.* the place from which a military or other organization is controlled.

headroom *n.* clearance above the head of

a person or the top of a vehicle etc.

headscarf *n.* a scarf worn tied round the head.

head-shrinker *n.* (*slang*) a psychiatrist.

headstone *n.* a stone set up at the head of a grave.

headstrong *n.* self-willed and obstinate.

headwater *n.*, **headwaters** *pl. n.* the stream(s) forming the sources of a river.

headway *n.* progress.

heady *adj.* (headier, headiest) **1.** (of drinks) likely to intoxicate people. **2.** (of success etc.) likely to cause conceit.

heal *v.* **1.** (of sore or wounded parts) to form healthy flesh again, to unite after being cut or broken. **2.** to cause to do this. **3.** to cure, *healing the sick*. **healer** *n.*

health *n.* **1.** the state of being well and free from illness, *was restored to health*. **2.** the condition of the body, *ill health*. □ **health centre**, the headquarters of a group of local medical services. **health farm**, an establishment where improved health is sought by dieting etc. **health foods**, foods thought to have health-giving qualities; natural unprocessed foods. **health service**, a public service providing medical care. **health visitor**, a trained person visiting babies or sick or elderly people at their homes.

healthful *adj.* producing good health, beneficial.

healthy *adj.* (healthier, healthiest) **1.** having or showing or producing good health. **2.** beneficial. **3.** (of things) functioning well. **healthily** *adv.*, **healthiness** *n.*

heap *n.* a number of things lying on one another, a mass of material so shaped. —*v.* **1.** to pile or become piled in a heap. **2.** to load with large quantities, to give large quantities of, *heaped the plate with food*; *they heaped insults on him*. □ **heaps** *pl. n.* (*informal*) a great amount, plenty, *there's heaps of time*.

hear *v.* (heard, hearing) **1.** to perceive (sounds) with the ear. **2.** to listen or pay attention to. **3.** to listen to and try (a case) in a lawcourt. **4.** to receive information or a message or letter etc. **hearer** *n.* □ **have heard of**, to have knowledge or information about, *we have never heard of this firm*. **hear a person out**, to listen to the whole of what he has to say. **hear!, hear!**, I agree. **not hear of**, to refuse to allow, *won't hear of my paying for it*.

heard *see* hear.

hearing *n.* **1.** the ability to hear; *within hearing distance*, near enough to be heard; *in my hearing*, in my presence, where I can hear. **2.** an opportunity of being heard, trial of a case in a lawcourt (especially before a judge without a jury), *got a fair hearing.* □ **hearing-aid** *n.* a small sound amplifier worn by a deaf person to improve the hearing.

hearsay *n.* things heard in rumours or gossip.

hearse (*pr.* herss) *n.* a vehicle for carrying the coffin at a funeral.

heart *n.* **1.** the hollow muscular organ that keeps blood circulating in the body by contracting rhythmically. **2.** the part of the body where this is, the bosom. **3.** the centre of a person's emotions or affections or inmost thoughts, *knew it in her heart.* **4.** the ability to feel emotion, *a tender heart.* **5.** courage, *take heart.* **6.** enthusiasm, *his heart isn't in it.* **7.** a beloved person, *dear heart.* **8.** the innermost part of a thing, the close compact head of a cabbage etc.; *the heart of the matter,* the vital part of it. **9.** a symmetrical figure conventionally representing a heart. **10.** a red figure shaped like this on playing-cards, a playing-card of the suit (*hearts*) marked with these. —*v.* (of cabbage etc.) to form a heart. □ **after one's own heart,** exactly to one's liking. **at heart,** basically. **by heart,** memorized thoroughly. **change of heart,** a change of feeling towards something. **have a heart!,** (*informal*) be considerate or sympathetic. **have the heart to,** to be hard-hearted enough to (do something). **heart attack** *or* **heart failure,** sudden failure of the heart to function normally. **heart-break** *n.* overwhelming unhappiness. **heart-breaking** *adj.* causing this. **heart-broken** *adj.* suffering from this. **heart-lung machine,** a pumping machine that enables these organs to be bypassed during a surgical operation by taking over their functions in blood-circulation. **heart-rending** *adj.* very distressing. **heart-searching** *n.* examination by oneself of one's own feelings and motives. **heart-strings** *pl. n.* one's deepest feelings of love or pity. **heart-throb** *n.* (*slang*) the person with whom someone is infatuated. **heart-to-heart** *adj.* frank and personal, *a heart-to-heart talk.* **heart-warming** *adj.* causing people to rejoice. **heart-whole** *adj.* not in love. **his heart is in the right place,** he has kindly intentions. **his heart was in his mouth,** he was violently alarmed. **set one's heart on,** to desire eagerly. **take to heart,** to be deeply troubled by. **to one's heart's content,** as much as one wishes. **with all one's heart,** sincerely, with the greatest goodwill.

heartache *n.* mental pain, deep sorrow.

heartburn *n.* a burning sensation in the lower part of the chest.

heartburning *n.* jealousy.

hearten *v.* to make (a person) feel encouraged.

heartfelt *adj.* felt deeply or earnestly.

hearth (*pr.* harth) *n.* **1.** the floor of a fireplace, the area in front of this. **2.** the fireside as the symbol of domestic comfort, *hearth and home.*

hearthrug *n.* a rug laid in front of a fireplace.

heartily *adv.* **1.** in a hearty way. **2.** very, *heartily sick of it.*

heartland *n.* the central or most important part of an area.

heartless *adj.* not feeling pity or sympathy. **heartlessly** *adv.*, **heartlessness** *n.*

heartwood *n.* the dense inner part of a tree-trunk, yielding the hardest timber.

hearty *adj.* (heartier, heartiest) **1.** showing warmth of feeling, enthusiastic. **2.** vigorous, strong, *hale and hearty.* **3.** (of meals or appetites) large. —*n.* a hearty person. — **heartiness** *n.*

heat *n.* **1.** a form of energy produced by the movement of molecules. **2.** the sensation produced by this, hotness. **3.** hot weather. **4.** a condition of sexual excitement and readiness for mating in female animals, *be in* or *on* or *at heat.* **5.** an intense feeling (especially of anger), tension, the most vigorous stage of a discussion; *take the heat out of a situation,* to reduce the anger or tension. **6.** one of the preliminary contests of which winners take part in further contests or the final. —*v.* to make or become hot or warm. □ **heat-stroke** *n.* illness caused by too much exposure to heat or sun. **heat wave,** a period of very hot weather.

heated *adj.* (of a person or discussion) angry. **heatedly** *adv.*

heater *n.* a stove or other device supplying heat.

heath *n.* **1.** an area of flat uncultivated land with low shrubs. **2.** a small shrubby plant of the heather kind.

heathen (hee-*thĕn*) *n.* a person who is not a believer in any of the world's chief religions, especially one who is neither Christian, Jew, nor Muslim.

heather *n.* an evergreen plant or shrub with small purple or pinkish or white bell-shaped flowers, growing on uplands. **heather mixture,** a speckled mixture of the soft shades of the heather plant.

Heath Robinson (of equipment) elaborate and clumsily contrived. ¶ Named after a cartoonist who drew machines of this kind.

heave *v.* (heaved (in sense 6 hove), heaving) **1.** to lift or haul (something heavy) with great effort. **2.** to utter with effort, *heaved* a sigh. **3.** (*informal*) to throw, *heave a brick at him.* **4.** to rise and fall regularly like waves at sea. **5.** to pant, retch. **6.** (in nautical use) to come; *heave in sight,* come into view. —*n.* the act of heaving. □ **heave to,** to bring (a ship) or come to a standstill without anchoring or mooring.

heaven *n.* **1.** the abode of God and of the righteous after death. **2.** *Heaven,* God, Providence; *heavens,* an exclamation of surprise. **3.** a place or state of supreme bliss, something delightful. **4.** *the heavens,* the sky as seen from the earth, in which the sun, moon, and stars appear. □ **heaven-sent** *adj.* providential, fortunate.

heavenly *adj.* **1.** of heaven, divine. **2.** of the heavens or sky; *heavenly bodies,* the sun and stars etc. **3.** (*informal*) very pleasing.

heavy *adj.* (heavier, heaviest) **1.** having great weight, difficult to lift or carry or move. **2.** of more than average weight or amount or force, *heavy artillery*; *heavy rain.* **3.** (of work) needing much physical effort. **4.** severe, intense; *a heavy sleeper,* not easily woken. **5.** dense, *a heavy mist*; *heavy bread,* doughy from not having risen. **6.** (of ground) clinging, difficult to travel over. **7.** (of food) stodgy and difficult to digest. **8.** (of the sky) gloomy and full of clouds. **9.** clumsy or ungraceful in appearance or effect or movement. **10.** unhappy, *with a heavy heart.* **11.** dull and tedious, serious in tone. **12.** stern, *the heavy father.* —**heavily** *adv.,* **heaviness** *n.* □ **heavy-duty** *adj.* intended to withstand hard use. **heavy going,** progress made only with difficulty; a person who is difficult to talk to sociably. **heavy-handed** *adj.* clumsy. **heavy industry,** industry producing metal, machines, etc. **heavy metal,** a type of loud rock music with a heavy beat. **heavy mob,** (*informal*) a group using brutal techniques. **heavy water,** deuterium oxide, a substance with the same chemical properties as water but greater density. **make heavy weather of,** to find (a thing) more difficult than it really is.

heavyweight *n.* **1.** a person of more than average weight. **2.** the heaviest boxing-weight; *light heavyweight,* 81 kg. **3.** a person of great influence. —*adj.* having great weight or influence.

hebe (hee-bee) *n.* a small shrub with blue or violet or white flowers in spikes.

Hebrew *n.* **1.** a member of a Semitic people in ancient Palestine. **2.** their language, a modern form of this used in Israel.

Hebrides (heb-ri-deez) two groups of islands off the north-west coast of Scotland. **Hebridean** (heb-ri-dee-ăn) *adj.* & *n.*

heck *n.* (*informal,* in oaths) hell.

heckle *v.* to interrupt and harass (a public speaker) with aggressive questions and abuse. **heckler** *n.*

hectare (hek-tair *or* hek-tar) *n.* a unit of area, 10,000 sq. metres (2·471 acres).

hectic *adj.* with feverish activity, *a hectic day.* **hectically** *adv.*

hectogram *n.* one hundred grams.

hector *v.* to intimidate by bullying.

he'd = he had, he would.

hedge *n.* **1.** a fence of closely-planted bushes or shrubs. **2.** a means of protecting oneself against possible loss, *bought diamonds as a hedge against inflation.* —**hedge** *v.* **1.** to surround or bound with a hedge. **2.** to make or trim hedges, *hedging and ditching.* **3.** to reduce the possible loss on (a bet etc.) by another speculation. **4.** to avoid giving a direct answer or commitment. —**hedger** *n.* □ **hedge-sparrow** *n.* a common British bird resembling a thrush.

hedgehog *n.* a small insect-eating animal with a pig-like snout and a back covered in stiff spines, able to roll itself up into a ball when attacked.

hedgerow *n.* a row of bushes etc. forming a hedge.

hedonist (hee-dŏn-ist) *n.* one who believes that pleasure is the chief good in life.

heebie-jeebies *pl. n.* (*slang*) nervous anxiety or depression.

heed *v.* to pay attention to. —*n.* careful attention, *take heed.*

heedless *adj.* not taking heed. **heedlessly** *adv.*

hee-haw *n.* a donkey's bray.

heel¹ *n.* **1.** the rounded back part of the human foot. **2.** the part of a stocking etc. covering this. **3.** a built-up part of a boot or shoe that supports a person's heel. **4.** something like a heel in shape or position; *the heel of the hand,* the front part next to the wrist. **5.** (*slang*) a dishonourable man. —**heel** *v.* **1.** to repair the heels of (shoes etc.). **2.** to pass the ball with the heel in Rugby football. □ **at** *or* **on the heels of,** following closely after. **down at heel,** (of a shoe) with the heel worn down by wear; (of a person) shabby. **take to one's heels,** to run away. **well-heeled** *adj.* rich.

heel² *v.* to tilt (a ship) or become tilted to one side, *heeled over.*

heel³ *v.* = hele.

heelless *adj.* (of shoes) with no built-up part under the heel.

hefty *adj.* (heftier, heftiest) **1.** (of a person) big and strong. **2.** (of a thing) large and heavy, powerful.

hegemony (hig-em-on-i) *n.* leadership,

especially by one country.

Hejira (hej-i-ră) *n.* the flight of Muhammad from Mecca (AD 622), from which the Muslim era is reckoned.

heifer (hef-er) *n.* a young cow, especially one that has not given birth to a calf.

heigh-ho *int.* an exclamation of boredom or disappointment.

height *n.* **1**. measurement from base to top, the measurement of a person etc. from head to foot as he stands. **2**. the distance (of an object or position) above ground or sea level. **3**. a high place or area, *is afraid of heights*. **4**. the highest degree of something, *dressed in the height of fashion*; *the height of the tourist season*, its most active time.

heighten *v.* to make or become higher or more intense.

heinous (hay-nŭs) *adj.* very wicked.

heir (*pr.* air) *n.* a person who inherits property or rank etc. from its former owner. **heir apparent**, the legal heir whose claim cannot be set aside by the birth of a person with a stronger claim to inherit. **heir presumptive**, one whose claim may be set aside in this way.

heiress (air-ĕss) *n.* a female heir, especially to great wealth.

heirloom (air-loom) *n.* a possession that has been handed down in a family for several generations.

heist (*rhymes with* sliced) *n.* (*Amer. slang*) a robbery. —*v.* (*Amer. slang*) to rob.

held *see* hold¹.

hele *v.* to set (a plant) in the ground and cover its roots, *hele it in*.

helical (hel-i-kăl) *adj.* like a helix.

helicopter (hel-i-kop-ter) *n.* a kind of aircraft with horizontal revolving blades or rotors.

heliotrope (hee-li-ŏ-trohp) *n.* **1**. a plant with small sweet-smelling purple flowers. **2**. a light purple colour.

heliport (hel-i-port) *n.* a place equipped for helicopters to take off and land.

helium (hee-li-ŭm) *n.* a light colourless gas that does not burn, used in airships.

helix (hee-liks) *n.* (*pl.* helices, *pr.* hee-li-seez) a spiral, especially a three-dimensional one, either like a corkscrew or flat like a watch-spring.

hell *n.* **1**. the place of punishment for the wicked after death, the abode of devils. **2**. a place or state of supreme misery, something extremely unpleasant. **3**. (*informal*) used in oaths, exclamations, and comparisons etc. to express anger or intensify a meaning or indicate something extreme, *what the hell does he want?*; *ran like hell*; *for the hell of it*, for amusement despite the discomfort or trouble involved. □ **beat** *or* **knock hell out of**, to pound heavily. **come hell or high water**, no matter what the obstacles. **hell-bent** *adj.* recklessly determined. **hell-fire** *n.* the fire(s) of hell. **hell for leather**, at full speed. **hell's angels**, violent lawless young motor-cyclists.

he'll = he will.

hellebore (hel-i-bor) *n.* a poisonous plant with white or greenish flowers, the Christmas rose.

Hellene (hel-een) *n.* a Greek.

Hellenistic *adj.* of the Greek language and culture of the 4th–1st centuries BC.

hellish *adj.* very unpleasant.

hello *int.* & *n.* = hallo.

helm *n.* the tiller or wheel by which a ship's rudder is controlled. **at the helm**, at the head of an organization etc., in control.

helmet *n.* a protective head-covering worn by a policeman, fireman, diver, motor-cyclist, etc.

helmsman *n.* (*pl.* helmsmen) a person who steers a ship by means of its helm.

help *v.* **1**. to do part of another person's work for him. **2**. to make it easier for (a person) to do something or for (a thing) to happen. **3**. to do something for the benefit of (someone in need). **4**. to prevent, to remedy, *it can't be helped*; *I couldn't help myself*, I was unable to avoid taking a certain action. —**help** *n.* **1**. the action of helping or being helped. **2**. a person or thing that helps. **3**. a person employed to help with housework. —**helper** *n.* □ **help a person to food**, to serve him with it at a meal. **help oneself to**, to serve oneself with (food) at a meal; to take without seeking assistance or permission. **help out**, to give help (especially in a crisis).

helpful *adj.* giving help, useful. **helpfully** *adv.*, **helpfulness** *n.*

helping *n.* a portion of food given to one person at a meal.

helpless *adj.* **1**. unable to manage without help, dependent on others. **2**. incapable of action, indicating this, *helpless with laughter*; *gave him a helpless glance*. **helplessly** *adv.*, **helplessness** *n.*

helpmate *n.* a helper, a companion or partner who helps.

Helsinki (hel-sink-i) the capital of Finland.

helter-skelter *adv.* in disorderly haste. — *n.* a tower-shaped structure in a fun-fair etc., with a spiral track outside it down which people may slide on a mat.

helve *n.* the handle of a tool or weapon.

hem *n.* the border of cloth where the edge is turned under and sewn or fixed down. —*v.* (hemmed, hemming) **1**. to turn and sew a hem on. **2.** to surround and restrict the movement of, *hemmed in by enemy forces.* —**hemmer** *n.* ☐ **hem-line** *n.* the lower edge of a skirt or dress.

hemisphere *n.* **1.** half a sphere. **2.** either of the halves into which the earth is divided either by the equator (the *Northern* and *Southern hemisphere*) or by a line passing through the poles (*the Eastern hemisphere,* including Europe, Asia, and Africa; *the Western hemisphere,* the Americas).

hemispherical (hem-iss-**fe**-ri-kăl) *adj.* shaped like a hemisphere.

hemlock *n.* a poisonous plant with small white flowers.

hemp *n.* **1.** a plant from which coarse fibres are obtained for the manufacture of rope and cloth. **2.** a narcotic drug made from this plant. **hempen** *adj.*

hem-stitch *v.* to decorate with a kind of drawn-thread-work.

hen *n.* a female bird, especially of the common domestic fowl. **hen-party** *n.* (*informal*) a party of women only.

henbane *n.* a kind of poisonous plant.

hence *adv.* **1.** (*old use*) from here. **2.** from this time, *five years hence.* **3.** for this reason. **henceforth, henceforward** *advs.* from this time on, in future.

henchman *n.* (*pl.* henchmen) a trusty supporter.

henna *n.* **1.** a reddish-brown dye used especially on the hair. **2.** the tropical plant from which this is obtained. ☐ **hennaed** (**hen**-ăd) *adj.* treated with henna.

henpecked *adj.* (of a husband) nagged by a domineering wife.

hepatic (hip-**at**-ik) *adj.* of the liver.

hepatitis (hep-ă-**ty**-tiss) *n.* inflammation of the liver.

Hepplewhite *n.* a light and graceful style of furniture named after George Hepplewhite, an 18th-century cabinet-maker.

heptagon (**hep**-tă-gŏn) *n.* a geometric figure with seven sides.

her *pronoun* **1.** the objective case of she, *we saw her.* **2.** (*informal*) = she, *it's her all right.* —**her** *adj.* **1.** of or belonging to her. **2.** used in women's titles, *Her Majesty.* ¶ It is incorrect to write *her's* (see the note under its).

herald *n.* **1.** an official in former times who made announcements and carried messages from a ruler. **2.** a person or thing indicating the approach of something, *heralds of spring.* **3.** an official of the *Heralds' College,* a corporation that records people's pedigrees and grants coats of arms. —*v.* to proclaim the approach of.

heraldic (hi-**ral**-dik) *adj.* of heralds or heraldry.

heraldry *n.* the study of the coats of arms of old families.

herb *n.* a soft-stemmed plant that dies down to the ground after flowering, one with leaves or seeds etc. that are used as food or in medicine or for flavouring. **herby** *adj.*

herbaceous (her-**bay**-shŭs) *adj.* of or like herbs. **herbaceous border,** a garden border containing perennial flowering plants.

herbage *n.* grass and other field plants.

herbal *adj.* of herbs used in medicine or for flavouring. —*n.* a book with descriptions of these.

herbalist *n.* a dealer in medicinal herbs.

herbicide *n.* a substance that is poisonous to plants, used to destroy unwanted vegetation.

herbivore (**her**-biv-or) *n.* a herbivorous animal.

herbivorous (her-**biv**-er-ŭs) *adj.* feeding on plants.

herculean (her-kew-lee-ăn) *adj.* **1.** as strong as Hercules, a hero in Greek mythology. **2.** needing great strength or effort, *a herculean task.*

herd *n.* **1.** a number of cattle or other animals feeding or staying together. **2.** a mob. —**herd** *v.* **1.** to gather or stay or drive as a group. **2.** to tend (a herd of animals). ☐ **herd instinct,** the instinct to think and behave like the majority of people.

herdsman *n.* (*pl.* herdsmen) a person who tends a herd of animals.

here *adv.* **1.** in or at or to this place. **2.** at this point in a process or a series of events. —*int.* an exclamation calling attention to something or making a protest, or used as a reply (=I am here) in answer to a roll-call. ☐ **here and there,** in or to various places. **here goes,** I am about to begin. **here's to,** I drink to the health of.

hereabouts *adv.* somewhere near here.

hereafter *adv.* in future, from now on; *the hereafter,* the future, life after death.

hereby *adv.* by this means, by this act or decree etc.

hereditary (hi-**red**-it-er-i) *adj.* **1.** inherited, able to be passed or received from one generation to another, *hereditary characteristics.* **2.** holding a position by inheritance, *hereditary ruler.*

heredity (hi-**red**-iti) *n.* inheritance of physical or mental characteristics from parents or ancestors.

Hereford *n.* one of a breed of red and white beef cattle.

Hereford and Worcester a county of England.

heresy (**herri**-si) *n.* **1.** an opinion that is contrary to the accepted beliefs of the Christian Church or to those on any subject. **2.** the holding of such an opinion.

heretic (**herri**-tik) *n.* a person who holds a heresy or is guilty of heresy. **heretical** (hi-**ret**-ikăl) *adj.*

herewith *adv.* with this, *enclosed herewith.*

heritable *adj.* able to be inherited.

heritage *n.* that which has been or may be inherited, inherited circumstances or benefits.

hermaphrodite (her-**maf**-rŏ-dyt) *n.* a creature that has both male and female sexual organs in one individual.

hermetic *adj.* with an airtight closure, *hermetic sealing.* **hermetically** *adv.*

hermit *n.* a person (especially a man in early Christian times) who has withdrawn from human society and lives in solitude. □ **hermit-crab** *n.* a crab that uses a cast-off shell to protect its soft hinder parts.

hermitage *n.* a hermit's dwelling-place.

hernia *n.* an abnormal condition in which a part or organ of the body protrudes through a wall of the cavity (especially the abdomen) that normally contains it, a rupture.

hero *n.* (*pl.* **heroes**) **1.** a man who is admired for his brave or noble deeds. **2.** the chief male character in a story, play, or poem. □ **hero-worship** *n.* excessive devotion to an admired person. **hero-worshipper** *n.*

heroic *adj.* having the characteristics of a hero, very brave. **heroically** *adv.* □ **heroics** *pl. n.* over-dramatic talk or behaviour.

heroin *n.* a powerful sedative drug prepared from morphine, used medically and by addicts.

heroine *n.* a female hero.

heroism *n.* heroic conduct.

heron *n.* a long-legged long-necked wading-bird living in marshy places.

heronry *n.* a place where herons breed

herpes (**her**-peez) *n.* a virus disease causing blisters on the skin. **herpes simplex,** a painless form of this. **herpes zoster** (*pr.* **zoh**-ster), shingles.

Herr (*pr.* hair) *n.* (*pl.* **Herren**) the title of a German man, = Mr.

herring *n.* a North Atlantic fish much used for food. **herring-bone** *n.* a zigzag pattern or arrangement; *herring-bone tweed,* woven in this pattern.

hers *possessive pronoun,* of or belonging to her, the thing(s) belonging to her, *it is hers; hers are best.* ¶ It is incorrect to write *her's* (see the note under *its*).

herself *pronoun* corresponding to *she* and *her,* used in the same ways as himself.

Hertfordshire (**har**-ferd-sher) a county of England.

Herts. *abbrev.* Hertfordshire.

hertz *n.* (*pl.* **hertz**) a unit of frequency of electromagnetic waves, = one cycle per second.

he's = he is, he has.

hesitant *adj.* hesitating. **hesitantly** *adv.,* **hesitancy** *n.*

hesitate *v.* **1.** to be slow to speak or act or move because one feels uncertain or reluctant, to pause in doubt. **2.** to be reluctant, to scruple, *wouldn't hesitate to break the rules if it suited him.* **hesitation** *n.*

hessian *n.* strong coarse cloth of hemp or jute, sack-cloth.

het *adj.* **het up,** (*slang*) excited, over-wrought.

heterodox (**het**-er-ŏ-doks) *adj.* not orthodox.

heterogeneous (het-er-ŏ-**jee**-niŭs) *adj.* made up of people or things that are unlike each other.

heterosexual *adj.* feeling sexually attracted to people of the opposite sex, not homosexual. —*n.* a heterosexual person.

hew *v.* (**hewed, hewn, hewing**) to chop or cut with an axe or sword etc., to cut into shape. **hewer** *n.* □ **hewn** *adj.* made or shaped by hewing.

hex *n.* (*Amer.*) a magic spell, a curse. —*v.* (*Amer.*) to put a hex on, to bewitch.

hexagon (**heks**-ă-gŏn) *n.* a geometric figure with six sides. **hexagonal** (heks-**ag**-ŏn-ăl) *adj.* six-sided.

hey *int.* an exclamation calling attention or expressing surprise or inquiry.

heyday *n.* the time of greatest success or prosperity, *it was in its heyday.*

HF *abbrev.* high frequency.

hg *abbrev.* hectogram(s).

HGV *abbrev.* heavy goods vehicle.

hi *int.* an exclamation calling attention or (*Amer.*) expressing greeting.

hiatus (hy-**ay**-tŭs) *n.* (*pl.* **hiatuses**) a break or gap in a sequence or series.

hibernate (**hy**-ber-nayt) *v.* (of certain animals) to spend the winter in a state like deep sleep. **hibernation** *n.*

hibiscus (hib-**isk**-ŭs) *n.* a cultivated shrub or tree with trumpet-shaped flowers.

hiccup *n.* **1.** a sudden stopping of the breath with a gulp-like sound; *hiccups,* an attack of hiccuping. **2.** a brief hitch. —*v.* to make a hiccup.

hick *n.* (*Amer. informal*) a country bumpkin.

hickory *n.* **1.** a North American tree related to the walnut. **2.** its hard wood.

hid, hidden *see* hide².

hide¹ *n.* **1.** an animal's skin (raw or dressed) as an article of commerce and manufacture. 2. (*informal*) the human skin; *save one's hide*, save oneself from a beating or other punishment.

hide² *v.* (hid, hidden, hiding) **1**. to put or keep out of sight, to prevent from being seen. **2**. to keep secret. **3**. to conceal oneself. —*n.* a place of concealment used when observing or hunting wild animals, *built a hide.* ☐ **hide-and-seek** *n.* a children's game in which some players conceal themselves and others try to find them. **hide-out** *n.* (*informal*) a hiding-place.

hidebound *adj.* narrow-minded, refusing to abandon old customs and prejudices.

hideous *adj.* very ugly, revolting to the senses or the mind. **hideously** *adv.*, **hideousness** *n.*

hidey-hole *n.* (*informal*) a hiding-place.

hiding¹ *n.* (*informal*) a thrashing. **on a hiding to nothing**, (*slang*) bound to lose or fail.

hiding² *n.* the state of being or remaining hidden, *went into hiding*. **hiding-place** *n.* a place where a person or thing is or could be hidden.

hierarchy (**hyr**-ark-i) *n.* a system with grades of status or authority ranking one above another in a series. **hierarchical** (hyr-**ark**-ikăl) *adj.* of or arranged in a hierarchy.

hieroglyph (**hyr**-ŏ-glif) *n.* **1**. one of the pictures or symbols used in ancient Egypt and elsewhere to represent sounds or words or ideas. **2**. a written symbol with a secret or cryptic meaning.

hieroglyphic (hyr-ŏ-**glif**-ik) *adj.* of or written in hieroglyphs. **hieroglyphics** *pl. n.* hieroglyphs.

hi-fi *adj.* (*informal*) high-fidelity. —*n.* (*informal*) hi-fi equipment.

higgledy-piggledy *adj. & adv.* completely mixed up, in utter disorder.

high *adj.* **1**. extending far upwards, extending above the normal or average level. **2**. situated far above the ground or above sea level. **3**. measuring a specified distance from base to top. **4**. ranking above others in importance or quality, *High Admiral*; *the higher animals* or *plants,* those of complex structure, highly developed. **5**. extreme, intense, greater than what is normal or average, *high temperatures*; *high prices*; *a high opinion*, very favourable. **6**. (of time) fully reached, *high noon*; *it's high time we left.* **7**. noble, virtuous, *high ideals.* **8**. (of a sound or voice) having rapid vibrations, not deep or low. **9**. (of meat) beginning to go bad, (of game) hung until slightly decomposed and ready to cook. **10**. (*slang*) intoxicated, under the influence of drugs. —**high** *n.* **1**. a high level or figure, *exports reached a new high.* **2**. an area of high bar-

ometric pressure. —**high** *adv.* **1**. in or at or to a high level or position. **2**. in or to a high degree; *play high*, play for high stakes; *feelings ran high*, were strong. ☐ **high altar**, the chief altar of a church. **high and dry**, aground; stranded, isolated. **high and low**, everywhere, *hunted high and low*. **high and mighty**, arrogant. **high chair**, an infant's chair with long legs and usually a tray, for use at meals. **High Church**, that section of the Church of England that gives an important place to ritual and to the authority of bishops and priests. **high-class** *adj.* of high quality or social class. **high colour**, a flushed complexion. **High Commission**, an embassy from one Commonwealth country to another. **High Commissioner**, the head of this. **High Court of Justice**, the supreme court for civil cases. **high explosive**, explosive with a violently shattering effect. **high-falutin** *adj.* (*informal*) pompous. **high fidelity**, reproduction of sound with little or no distortion. **high finance**, dealing with large sums of money. **high-flyer** *n.* a person or thing with capacity for great achievements. **high frequency**, (in radio) 3 to 30 megahertz. **high-handed** *adj.* using authority arrogantly. **high jump**, an athletic competition of jumping over a high horizontal bar; *be for the high jump*, liable to receive drastic punishment. **high-level** *adj.* (of negotiations) conducted by people of high rank; (of a computer language) designed for convenience in programming and requiring translation by an intermediate program before it can be understood by the computer. **high life** *or* **living**, a luxurious way of living. **high-minded** *adj.* having high moral principles. **a high old time**, (*informal*) a most enjoyable time. **high-pitched**, (of a voice or sound) high. **high-powered** *adj.* using great power or energy, forceful. **high priest**, the chief priest. **high-rise** *adj.* (of a building) with many storeys. **high road**, the main road. **high school**, a secondary school (especially a grammar school). **high sea** *or* **seas**, the open seas not under any country's jurisdiction. **high season**, the period when a resort etc. regularly has most visitors. **high-speed** *adj.* operating at great speed. **high-spirited** *adj.* in high spirits, happy and lively. **high spot**, (*slang*) an important place or feature. **high street**, the principal street of a town, with shops etc. **high tea**, an evening meal with tea and meat or similar cooked food. **high tide**, the tide at its highest level; the time when this occurs. **high treason**, treason against one's country or ruler. **high-up** *n.* (*in-*

formal) a person of high rank. **high water**, high tide. **high-water mark**, the level reached at high water; the highest point or value etc. recorded. **high wire**, a high tightrope.

highball *n*. (*Amer.*) a drink with spirits and soda etc. served in a tall glass.

highbrow *adj.* very intellectual, cultured. —*n*. a highbrow person.

higher *adj. & adv.* more high; *higher animals* or *plants*, those which are highly developed and of complex structure. — *adv.* in or to a higher position etc. □ **higher education**, education above the level given in schools. **higher-ups** *pl. n.* (*informal*) people of higher rank.

highland *adj.* of or in highlands; *Highland*, of the Scottish Highlands. **Highland**, a region of Scotland. **highlander** *n.* a native or inhabitant of highlands. **highlands** *pl. n.* mountainous country; *the Highlands*, that of northern Scotland.

highlight *n*. **1.** a light or bright area in a painting etc. **2.** the brightest or most outstanding feature of something, *the highlight of the tour* —*v.* to draw special attention to, to emphasize.

highly *adv.* **1.** in a high degree, extremely, *highly amusing*; *highly commended.* **2.** very favourably, *thinks highly of her.* □ **highly-strung** *adj.* (of a person) easily upset.

Highness *n.* the title used in speaking of or to a prince or princess, *His* or *Her* or *Your Highness*.

highway *n.* **1.** a public road **2.** a main route by land of sea or air. **3.** (also *data highway*) a route along which signals travel to and from several destinations and sources in a computer. □ **Highway Code**, a set of rules issued officially for the guidance of road-users.

highwayman *n.* (*pl.* highwaymen) a man (usually on horseback) who robbed passing travellers in former times.

hijack *v.* to seize control of (a vehicle or aircraft in transit) in order to steal its goods or take its passengers hostage or force it to a new destination. —*n.* a hijacking. —**hijacker** *n.*

hike *n.* a long walk, especially a cross-country walk taken for pleasure. —*v.* **1.** to go for a hike. **2.** to walk laboriously. — **hiker** *n.*

hilarious *adj.* **1.** noisily merry. **2.** extremely funny. **hilarity** (hi-**la**-riti) *n.*

Hilary term the university and law term beginning in January.

hill *n.* **1.** a natural elevation of the earth's surface, not as high as a mountain. **2.** a slope in a road etc. **3.** a heap or mound, *an ant-hill*.

hill-billy *n.* folk music like that of southern USA.

hillock *n.* a small hill, a mound.

hillside *n.* the sloping side of a hill.

hilly *adj.* full of hills.

hilt *n.* the handle of a sword or dagger etc. **to the hilt**, completely, *his guilt was proved up to the hilt*.

him *pronoun* **1.** the objective case of he, *we saw him.* **2.** (*informal*) = he, *it's him all right.*

Himalayas (him-ă-**lay**-ăz) *pl. n.* the Himalaya Mountains in Nepal and adjacent countries. **Himalayan** *adj.*

himself *pronoun* the form of him used in reflexive constructions (e.g. *he cut himself*) and for emphasis (e.g. *he himself had said it; told me himself*). **be himself**, to behave in a normal manner without constraint; *he is not himself today*, is not in his normal good health or spirits. **by himself**, without companions; without help.

hind[1] *n.* a female deer.

hind[2] *adj.* situated at the back, *hind legs*.

hinder[1] (**hin**-der) *v.* to keep (a person or thing) back by delaying progress.

hinder[2] (**hynd**-er) *adj.* hind, *the hinder part*.

Hindi (**hin**-di) *n.* **1.** one of the official languages of India, a form of Hindustani. **2.** a group of spoken languages of northern India.

hindmost *adj.* furthest behind.

hindquarters *pl. n.* the hind legs and parts adjoining these of a quadruped.

hindrance *n.* **1.** something that hinders. **2.** hindering, being hindered, *went forward without hindrance*.

hindsight *n.* wisdom about an event after it has occurred.

Hindu *n.* a person whose religion is Hinduism. —*adj.* of the Hindus.

Hinduism (**hin**-doo-izm) *n.* a religion and philosophy of India, with a caste system and belief in reincarnation.

Hindustani (hin-du-**stah**-ni) *n.* the language of much of northern India and Pakistan.

hinge *n.* **1.** a joint on which a lid, door, or gate etc. turns or swings. **2.** a natural joint working similarly. **3.** a small piece of gummed paper for fixing stamps in an album. —**hinge** *v.* **1.** to attach or be attached by a hinge or hinges. **2.** to depend on, *everything hinges on this meeting*.

hint *n.* **1.** a slight indication, a suggestion made indirectly. **2.** a small piece of practical information, *household hints.* —*v.* to make a hint. □ **hint at**, to refer indirectly to.

hinterland *n.* a district lying behind a

coast etc. or served by a port or other centre.

hip¹ *n.* the projection formed by the pelvis and upper part of the thigh-bone on each side of the body; *hips,* the measurement round the body here. **hipped** *adj.* □ **hip-bath** *n.* a small portable bath in which a person can sit immersed to the hips. **hip-bone** *n.* the bone forming the hip. **hip-flask** *n.* a small flask for spirits etc., carried in the **hip-pocket** just behind the hip.

hip² *n.* the fruit (red when ripe) of the wild rose.

hip³ *int.* used in cheering, *hip, hip, hurray.*

hip⁴ *adj.* (*slang*) well-informed, stylish.

hippeastrum (hip-i-ass-trŭm) *n.* a South American plant with large showy red or white flowers, growing from a bulb.

hippie *n.* (*slang*) a young person who joins with others in adopting an unconventional style of dress etc., rejecting conventional ideas and organized society and often using (or thought to be using) hallucinogenic drugs.

hippo *n.* (*pl.* hippos) (*informal*) a hippopotamus.

Hippocratic (hip-ŏ-krat-ik) *adj.* of Hippocrates, a Greek physician of the 5th century BC. **Hippocratic oath,** an oath taken by those beginning medical practice, to observe the code of professional behaviour.

hippopotamus *n.* (*pl.* hippopotamuses *or* hippopotami) a large African river animal with tusks, short legs, and thick dark skin.

hipster *adj.* (of a garment) hanging from the hips rather than from the waist.

hire *v.* to engage or grant the services of (a person) or the use of (a thing) temporarily, for payment. —*n.* hiring, payment for this. —**hirer** *n.* □ **hire-purchase** *n.* a system by which a thing becomes the hirer's after a certain number of payments.

hireable *adj.* able to be hired.

hirsute (herss-yoot) *adj.* hairy, shaggy.

his *adj. & possessive pronoun.* 1. of or belonging to him, the thing(s) belonging to him. 2. used in men's titles, *His Majesty.*

Hispanic (hiss-pan-ik) *adj.* 1. of Spain, of Spain and Portugal. 2. of Spain and other Spanish-speaking countries.

hiss *n.* a sound like that of *s.* —*v.* 1. to make this sound. 2. to express disapproval in this way.

histamine (hist-ă-min) *n.* a chemical compound present in all body tissues, causing some allergic reactions.

historian (hiss-tor-iăn) *n.* an expert in history, a writer of history.

historic *adj.* famous or important in history.

historical *adj.* 1. belonging to or dealing with history or past events (as opposed to legend or prehistory), *historical novels.* 2. concerned with history, *a historical society.* **historically** *adv.*

historicity (hiss-ter-iss-iti) *n.* the historical genuineness of an alleged event etc.

history *n.* 1. a continuous methodical record of important or public events. 2. past events, those connected with a person or thing. 3. an interesting or eventful past, *the house has a history.* 4. the study of past events, especially of human affairs. □ **make history,** to do something memorable, to be the first to do something.

histrionic (histri-on-ik) *adj.* 1. of acting. 2. dramatic or theatrical in manner. **histrionics** *pl. n.* theatricals; dramatic behaviour intended to impress people.

hit *v.* (hit, hitting) 1. to strike with a blow or missile, to aim a blow etc., to come against (a thing) with force; *it hits you in the eye,* is very obvious. 2. to propel (a ball etc.) with a bat or club, to score runs or points in this way. 3. to have an effect on (a person), to cause to suffer. 4. to get at, to come to (a thing aimed at), to find (what is sought). 5. to reach, *can't hit the high notes; hit a snag,* encountered a difficulty. —**hit** *n.* 1. a blow, a stroke. 2. a shot etc. that hits its target. 3. a success; *make a hit,* to win popularity. □ **hit-and-run** *adj.* causing harm or damage and making off immediately. **hit back,** to retaliate. **hit it off,** to get on well (with a person). **hit man,** (*Amer.*) a hired assassin. **hit off,** to represent exactly. **hit on,** to discover suddenly or by chance. **hit-or-miss** *adj.* aimed or done carelessly. **hit parade,** a list or programme of the most popular tunes. **hit the bottle,** (*slang*) to drink alcohol heavily. **hit the nail on the head,** to guess right, to express the truth exactly. **hit the road** *or* **trail,** (*Amer. slang*) to depart.

hitch *v.* 1. to move (a thing) with a slight jerk. 2. to fasten or be fastened with a loop or hook etc.; *hitch one's wagon to a star,* to be very ambitious. 3. to hitch-hike, to obtain (a lift) in this way. —**hitch** *n.* 1. a slight jerk. 2. a noose or knot of various kinds. 3. a temporary stoppage, a snag. □ **get hitched,** (*slang*) to get married.

hitch-hike *v.* to travel by begging free rides in passing vehicles. **hitch-hiker** *n.*

hither *adv.* to or towards this place. **hither and thither,** to and fro.

hitherto *adv.* until this time.

hive *n.* 1. a box or other container for bees to live in. 2. the bees living in this. —*v.* to gather or live in a hive. □ **hive off,** to swarm off separately like a group of bees; to assign (work) to a subsidiary department or company. **hive of industry,** a place full of people working busily.

hiya *int.* (*Amer. informal*) an exclamation of greeting.

h'm *int.* = hum.

HM *abbrev.* His (or Her) Majesty's. **HMS,** His (or Her) Majesty's Ship. **HMSO,** His (or Her) Majesty's Stationery Office.

ho *int.* an exclamation of triumph or scorn, or calling attention.

hoard *n.* a carefully saved and guarded store of money or food or treasured objects. —*v.* to save and store away. **hoarder** *n.*

hoarding *n.* a fence of light boarding, often used for displaying advertisements.

hoar-frost *n.* a white frost.

hoarse *adj.* 1. (of the voice) sounding rough, as if from a dry throat. 2. (of a person) having a hoarse voice, **hoarsely** *adv.*, **hoarseness** *n.*

hoary *adj.* (hoarier, hoariest) 1. white or grey, *hoary hair.* 2. with hoary hair, aged. 3. (of a joke etc.) old.

hoax *v.* to deceive jokingly.   *n.* a joking deception. —**hoaxer** *n.*

hob *n.* a flat metal shelf at the side of a fireplace, where a kettle or pan etc. can be heated.

hobbit *n.* one of an imaginary race of half-sized persons in stories by J. R. R. Tolkien.

hobble *v.* 1. to walk lamely. 2. to fasten the legs of (a horse etc.) so as to limit but not entirely prevent movement. —*n.* a hobbling walk.

hobby *n.* an occupation that a person does for pleasure, not as his main business.

hobby-horse *n.* 1. a figure of a horse used in a morris dance etc. 2. a rocking-horse. 3. a stick with a horse's head, used as a toy. 4. a topic that a person is fond of discussing.

hobgoblin *n.* a mischievous or evil spirit.

hobnail *n.* a heavy-headed nail for boot-soles. **hobnailed** *adj.* studded with these. **hobnailed liver,** *see* cirrhosis.

hob-nob *v.* (hob-nobbed, hob-nobbing) to spend time together in a friendly way.

Hobson's choice a situation in which there is no alternative to the thing offered. ¶ Thomas Hobson (17th century) hired out horses and made people take the one nearest to the stable door.

hock[1] *n.* the middle joint of an animal's hind leg.

hock[2] *n.* a German white wine, that of Hochheim on the river Main.

hock[3] *v.* (*Amer. slang*) to pawn. **in hock,** in pawn; in prison; in debt.

hockey *n.* 1. a game played on a field between two teams of players with curved sticks and a small hard ball. 2. ice hockey.

hocus-pocus *n.* trickery.

hod *n.* 1. a trough on a staff used by bricklayers for carrying mortar or bricks. 2. a cylindrical container for shovelling and holding coal.

hoe *n.* a tool with a blade on a long handle, used for loosening soil or scraping up weeds etc. —*v.* (hoed, hoeing) to dig or scrape with a hoe.

hog *n.* 1. a castrated male pig reared for meat. 2. (*informal*) a greedy person. —*v.* (hogged, hogging) (*informal*) to take more than one's fair share of, to hoard selfishly. □ **go the whole hog,** (*slang*) to do something thoroughly. **hog's-back** *n.* a steep-sided hill ridge.

hogmanay (hog-mă-nay) *n.* (*Scottish*) the last day of the year, 31 December.

hogshead *n.* 1. a large cask. 2. a liquid or dry measure for various commodities, usually about 50 gallons.

hogweed *n.* any of several weeds liable to be eaten by animals.

hoick *v.* (*slang*) to lift or bring out, especially with a jerk.

hoi polloi (hoi pŏ-loi) the common people, the masses.

hoist *v.* to raise or haul up, to lift with ropes and pulleys etc. —*n.* 1. an apparatus for hoisting things. 2. a pull or haul up, *give it a hoist.*

hoity-toity *adj.* haughty.

hokey-pokey *n.* (*slang*) deception, trickery.

hokum (hoh-kŭm) *n.* (*slang*) hunkum

hold[1] *v.* (held, holding) 1. to take and keep in one's arms, hand(s), teeth, etc. 2. to keep in a particular position or condition, to grasp or keep so as to control, to detain in custody; *hold him to his promise,* insist that he keeps it. 3. to be able to contain, *jug holds two pints.* 4. to have in one's possession or as something one has gained, *he holds the record for the high jump.* 5. to support, to bear the weight of. 6. to remain unbroken under strain, to continue, *the rope failed to hold; will the fine weather hold?; the law still holds,* remains valid. 7. to keep possession of (a place or position etc.) against attack. 8. to keep (a person's attention) by being interesting. **9.** to have the position of, to occupy (a job etc.), *held the chairmanship.* **10.** to cause to take place, to conduct, *hold a meeting* or *investiture* or *conversation.* **11.** to restrain; *hold your tongue,* stop talking; *hold it, hold everything,* cease action or movement. **12.** to believe, to consider, to assert. —**hold** *n.* **1.** the act or manner of holding something. **2.** an opportunity or means of holding. **3.** a means of exerting influence on a person. —**holder** *n.* □ **get hold of,** to acquire; to make contact with (a person). **hold down,** to be competent enough to keep (one's job). **hold forth,** to speak lengthily. **hold good,** to remain valid. **hold off,** to wait, not to begin, *the rain held off.* **hold on,** to keep one's grasp of something; to refrain from ringing off (on the telephone); (*informal*) wait. **hold one's ground,** to stand firm, to refuse to yield. **hold one's peace** to keep silent. **hold out,** to offer (an inducement or hope); to last, *if supplies hold out.* **hold out for,** to refuse to accept anything other than. **hold out on,** (*informal*) to refuse the requests etc. of. **hold over,** to postpone; *holds the threat over him,* exerts influence on him by this threat. **hold the fort,** to act as a temporary substitute, to cope in an emergency. **hold the line,** to refrain from ringing off (on the telephone). **hold up,** to hinder; to stop by the use of threats or force for the purpose of robbery. **hold-up** *n.* a stoppage or delay; robbery by armed robbers. **hold water,** (of reasoning) to be sound. **hold with,** (*slang*) to approve of, *we don't hold with bribery.* **no holds barred,** all methods are permitted. **take hold,** to grasp; to become established.

hold² *n.* a cavity below a ship's deck, where cargo is stored.

holdall *n.* a portable case for carrying miscellaneous articles.

holding *n.* something held or owned, land held by an owner or tenant. **holding company,** one formed to hold the shares of other companies which it then controls. **holding operation,** a temporary expedient to prevent change.

hole *n.* **1.** an empty place in a solid body or mass, a sunken place on a surface. **2.** an animal's burrow. **3.** a small or dark or wretched place. **4.** (*slang*) an awkward situation. **5.** a hollow or cavity into which a ball etc. must be sent in various games. **6.** a section of a golf-course between tee and hole, a point scored by a player who reaches the hole with the fewest strokes. **7.** an opening through something. —**hole** *v.* **1.** to make a hole or holes in; *the ship was holed,* its side was pierced. **2.** to put

into a hole. □ **hole-and-corner** *adj.* underhand. **hole in the wall,** a small dingy establishment.**hole up,** (*Amer. slang*) to hide oneself. **hole out,** to get the ball into the hole in golf. **in holes,** worn so much that holes have formed. **make a hole in,** to use a large amount of (one's supply).

holey *adj.* full of holes.

holiday *n.* **1.** a day of festivity or recreation, when no work is done. **2.** (also *holidays*) a period of this. —*v.* (holidayed, holidaying) to spend a holiday. □ **holiday-maker** *n.* a person who is on holiday.

holiness *n.* being holy or sacred. **His Holiness,** the title of the pope.

holland *n.* a smooth hard-wearing linen fabric.

Holland the Netherlands.

hollandaise sauce (hol-ăn-dayz) a creamy sauce containing butter, egg-yolks, and vinegar.

hollow *adj.* **1.** having a hole inside, not solid. **2.** sunken, *hollow cheeks.* **3.** (of sound) echoing, as if from something hollow. **4.** empty, worthless, *a hollow triumph*; *a hollow laugh,* cynical. —*n.* a hollow or sunken place, a hole, a valley. —*adv.* completely, *beat them hollow.* —*v.* to make or become hollow, *hollow it out.* —**hollowly** *adv.*

holly *n.* an evergreen shrub with prickly leaves and red berries.

hollyhock *n.* a plant with large showy flowers on a tall stem.

holm-oak (hohm-ohk) *n.* an evergreen oak.

holocaust (hol-ŏ-kawst) *n.* large-scale destruction, especially by fire; *the Holocaust,* mass murder of Jews by Nazis in 1939–45.

holograph (hol-ŏ-grahf) *n.* a document that is handwritten by its author.

holster (hohl-ster) *n.* a leather case for a pistol or revolver, fixed to a belt or saddle or under the arm.

holy *adj.* (holier, holiest) **1.** of God and therefore regarded with reverence, associated with God or religion, *the Holy Bible.* **2.** consecrated, sacred, *holy water.* **3.** devoted to the service of God, *a holy man.* □ **holier-than-thou** *adj.* self-righteous. **Holy Communion,** *see* Communion. **Holy Father,** a title of the pope. **Holy Ghost,** the Holy Spirit. **Holy Land,** the country west of the river Jordan, revered by Christians; a region revered in non-Christian religions. **holy of holies,** a place or thing regarded as most sacred; the sacred inner chamber of a Jewish temple. **holy orders,** *see* order. **Holy See,** the position or diocese of the pope, the papal court. **Holy Spirit,**

the Third Person of the Trinity, God acting spiritually. **holy terror**, (*informal*) a troublesome child; a formidable person. **Holy Week**, the week before Easter Sunday. **Holy Writ**, the Bible.

homage *n.* **1.** things said as a mark of respect, *paid homage to his achievements*. **2.** a formal expression of loyalty to a ruler etc.

Homburg *n.* a man's soft felt hat with a narrow curled brim and a lengthwise dent in the crown.

home *n.* **1.** the place where one lives, especially with one's family. **2.** one's native land, the district where one was born or where one has lived for a long time or to which one feels attached. **3.** a dwelling-house, *Homes For Sale*. **4.** an institution where those needing care may live, *an old people's home*. **5.** the natural environment of an animal or plant. **6.** the place to be reached by a runner in a race or in certain games. **7.** a home match, (in football pools) a home win. —**home** *adj.* **1.** of or connected with one's own home or country, *done, or produced there, home industries; home produce*. **2.** played on one's own ground, *a home match* —**home** *adv.* **1.** to or at one's home, *go home; stay home*, (*Amer.*) to stay at home. **2.** to the point aimed at, *the thrust went home; the criticism went home*, made itself felt as true; *drive a nail home*, right in. —**home** *v.* **1.** (of a trained pigeon) to fly home. **2.** to be guided to a target, to make for a particular destination. ☐ **at home**, *see* at. **bring home to**, to cause to realize fully. **come home to**, to become fully realized by. **home-bird** *n.* a person who enjoys home life and staying at home. **homecoming** *n.* arrival at home. **Home Counties**, the counties nearest to London. **home farm**, a farm worked by the owner of an estate on which there are other farms. **home from home**, a place (other than home) where one feels comfortable and at home. **home-grown** *adj.* grown at home. **home help**, a person who helps with housework etc., especially in a service organized by local authorities. **homemade** *adj.* made at home. **Home Office**, the British government department dealing with law and order in England and Wales. **home rule**, government of a country by its own citizens. **home run**, a hit in baseball that allows the batter to make a complete circuit of the bases. **Home Secretary**, the government minister in charge of the Home Office. **home straight** *or* **stretch**, the stretch of a racecourse between the last turn and the finish-ing-line. **home truth**, an unpleasant truth affecting himself that a person is made to realize.

homeland *n.* **1.** one's native land. **2.** one of the areas reserved for Bantus in the Republic of South Africa.

homeless *adj.* lacking a dwelling-place.

homely *adj.* **1.** simple and informal, not pretentious. **2.** (*Amer.*, of a person's appearance) plain, not beautiful. **homeliness** *n.*

Homeric (hoh-**merr**ik) *adj.* of the writings or heroes of Homer, traditional author of the Greek epic poems called the *Iliad* and the *Odyssey*.

homesick *adj.* feeling depressed through longing for one's home when one is away from it. **homesickness** *n.*

homespun *adj.* made of yarn spun at home. —*n.* homespun fabric.

homestead (**hohm**-sted) *n.* a farmhouse or similar building with the land and buildings round it.

homeward *adj.* & *adv.* going towards home. **homewards** *adv.* towards home.

homework *n.* **1.** work that a pupil is required to do away from school. **2.** (*informal*) preparatory work to be done before a discussion etc. takes place.

homey *adj.* home-like, homely.

homicide (**hom**-i-syd) *n.* the killing of one person by another. **homicidal** *adj.*

homily *n.* a sermon, a moralizing lecture.

homing *adj.* (of a pigeon) trained to fly home, bred for long-distance racing.

homo (**hoh**-moh) *n.* (*pl.* homos) (*informal*) a male homosexual.

homoeopathic (hohm-i-ŏ-**path**-ik) *adj.* treating a disease by very small doses of drugs etc. that in a healthy person would produce symptoms like those of the disease itself, *homoeopathic remedies*.

homoeopathy (hohm-i-**op**-ă-thi) *n.* homoeopathic treatment.

homogeneous (hom-ŏ-**jee**-niŭs) *adj.* of the same kind as the others, formed of parts that are all of the same kind. **homogeneity** (hom-ŏ-jin-**ee**-iti) *n.*

homogenize (hŏ-**moj**-i-nyz) *v.* to treat (milk) so that the particles of fat are broken down and cream does not separate.

homograph (**hom**-ŏ-grahf) *n.* a word that is spelt like another but has a different meaning or origin, e.g. *bat* (a flying animal) and *bat* (for striking a ball).

homonym (**hom**-ŏ-n'm) *n.* a word of the same spelling or sound as another but with a different meaning, e.g. *grate* (= fireplace), *grate* (= to rub), *great* (= large).

homophone (**hom**-ŏ-fohn) *n.* a word with the same sound as another, e.g. *son, sun*.

Homo Sapiens (hoh-moh **sap**-i-enz) mankind regarded as a species.

homosexual (hoh-mŏ-**seks**-yoo-ăl) *adj.* feeling sexually attracted only to people of the same sex as himself or herself. —*n.* a homosexual person. —**homosexuality** *n.*

Hon. *abbrev.* **1.** Honorary. **2.** Honourable.

Honduras (hon-**dewr**-ăs) a country in Central America. **Honduran** *adj.* & *n.*

hone (*rhymes with* stone) *n.* a fine-grained stone used for sharpening razors and tools. —*v.* to sharpen on this.

honest *adj.* **1.** truthful, trustworthy. **2.** (of an act or feeling) showing such qualities, *an honest opinion*; *an honest piece of work*, done conscientiously. **3.** (of gain etc.) got by fair means, *earn an honest penny*, earn money fairly. □ **honest-to-goodness** *adj.* (*informal*) real, straightforward. **make an honest woman of her**, marry a woman with whom one has already had a sexual relationship.

honestly *adv.* **1.** in an honest way. **2.** really, *that's all I know, honestly*.

honesty *n.* **1.** being honest. **2.** a plant with seeds that form in round translucent pods.

honey *n.* (*pl.* honeys) **1.** a sweet sticky yellowish substance made by bees from nectar. **2.** its colour. **3.** sweetness, pleasantness, a sweet thing. **4.** (*informal*) darling. □ **honey-bee** *n.* the common bee that lives in a hive.

honeycomb *n.* **1.** a bees' wax structure of six-sided cells for holding their honey and eggs. **2.** a pattern or arrangement of six-sided sections. —**honeycomb** *v.* **1.** to fill with holes or tunnels, *the rock was honeycombed with passages.* **2.** to mark or sew in a honeycomb pattern.

honeydew melon a cultivated variety of melon with pale skin and sweet green flesh.

honeymoon *n.* a holiday spent together by a newly-married couple. —*v.* to spend a honeymoon.

honeysuckle *n.* a climbing shrub with fragrant yellow and pink flowers.

honk *n.* a loud harsh sound, the cry of the wild goose, the sound made by an old-style motor horn. —*v.* to make a honk, to sound (a horn).

honky-tonk *n.* a kind of ragtime music played on a piano, often with strings that give a tinny sound.

Honolulu the capital of Hawaii.

honorarium (on-er-**air**-iŭm) *n.* (*pl.* honorariums) a voluntary payment made for services where no fee is legally required.

honorary *adj.* **1.** given as an honour, *an*

honorary degree. **2.** unpaid, *the honorary treasurer.*

honour *n.* **1.** great respect, high public regard. **2.** a mark of this, a privilege given or received; *passed with honours*, gained special distinction in an examination. **3.** a source of this, a person or thing that brings honour. **4.** good personal character, a reputation for honesty and loyalty etc. **5.** a title of respect given to certain judges or people of importance, *your Honour.* **6.** the right of driving off first in golf, held by the player who won the previous hole. **7.** (in certain card-games) any of the cards of the highest value. —**honour** *v.* **1.** to feel honour for. **2.** to confer honour on. **3.** to acknowledge and pay (a cheque etc.). □ **do the honours**, to perform the usual civilities to guests or visitors etc. **honours degree**, a university degree requiring a higher level of attainment than a pass degree. **honours list**, a list of people awarded honours by the sovereign. **in honour bound** *or* **on one's honour**, under a moral obligation to do something. **on my honour**, I swear it.

honourable *adj.* **1.** deserving honour. **2.** possessing or showing honour. **3.** *Honourable*, the courtesy title of certain high officials and judges, also of the children of viscounts and barons, the younger sons of earls, and used during debates by MPs to one another. **honourably** *adv.*

hood[1] *n.* **1.** a covering for the head and neck, either forming part of a garment or separate. **2.** a loose hood-like garment forming part of academic dress. **3.** something resembling a hood in shape or use, e.g. a folding roof over a car, a canopy over a machine etc. **4.** (*Amer.*) the bonnet of a car. □ **hooded** *adj.* having a hood, (of animals) with a hood-like part.

hood[2] *n.* (*Amer. slang*) a gangster or gunman.

hoodlum *n.* a hooligan, a young thug.

hoodoo *n.* (*Amer.*) a thing or person thought to cause bad luck.

hoodwink *v.* to deceive.

hoof *n.* (*pl.* hoofs *or* hooves) the horny part of the foot of a horse and other animals. —*v.* **hoof it**, (*slang*) to go on foot. **hoof out**, (*slang*) to kick (a person) out. **on the hoof**, (of cattle) live, not yet slaughtered.

hoo-ha *n.* (*slang*) a commotion.

hook *n.* **1.** a bent or curved piece of metal etc. for catching hold or for hanging things on. **2.** something shaped like this; *the Hook of Holland*, a projecting point of land on the coast of Holland. **3.** a curved cutting-tool, *reaping-hook.* **4.** a hooked stroke in cricket or golf, (in boxing) a short swinging blow with the elbow bent. —**hook** v. **1.** to grasp or catch with a hook, to fasten with a hook or hooks. **2.** (*slang*) to obtain, to steal. **3.** to propel (a ball) in a curving path, to pass (the ball) backward with the foot in Rugby football. **4.** to make (a rug) by looping yarn through canvas with a hook. □ **be hooked on**, (*slang*) to be addicted to or captivated by. **by hook or by crook**, by some means no matter what happens. **hook and eye**, a small metal hook and loop for fastening a dress etc. **hooked** *adj.* hook-shaped, *a hooked nose.* **hook it**, (*slang*) to run away. **hook, line, and sinker**, entirely. **hook-up** n. (*informal*) interconnection of broadcasting transmissions. **off the hook**, freed from a difficulty.

hookah (**huuk**-ă) n. an oriental tobacco-pipe with a long tube passing through a glass container of water that cools the smoke as it is drawn through.

hooker n. **1.** a player in the front row of the scrummage in Rugby football, who tries to get the ball by hooking it. **2.** (*Amer. slang*) a prostitute.

hookey n. (*Amer. slang*) truant, *play hookey.*

hookworm n. a worm (the male of which has hook-like spines) that can infest the intestines of men and animals.

hooligan n. a young ruffian. **hooliganism** n.

hoop n. **1.** a band of metal or wood etc. forming part of a framework. **2.** this used as a child's toy for bowling along the ground, or for circus riders and animals to jump through. **3.** a small iron arch used in croquet. —v. to bind or encircle with hoops. □ **be put** or **go through the hoops**, to undergo a test or ordeal.

hoop-la n. a game in which rings are thrown to encircle a prize.

hoopoe (**hoo**-poo) n. a bird with a fan-like crest and striped plumage.

hooray *int. & n.* = hurray.

hoot n. **1.** the cry of an owl. **2.** the sound made by a vehicle's horn or a steam whistle. **3.** a cry expressing scorn or disapproval. **4.** (*informal*) laughter, a cause of this. — **hoot** v. **1.** to make a hoot or hoots. **2.** to receive or drive away with scornful hoots. **3.** to sound (a horn). □ **doesn't care a hoot** or **two hoots**, (*slang*) doesn't care at all.

hooter n. **1.** a siren or steam-whistle used as a signal. **2.** a car horn.

Hoover n. (*trade mark*) a vacuum cleaner. —**hoover** v. to clean (a carpet etc.) with a vacuum cleaner.

hop[1] v. **1.** (of an animal) to spring from

all feet at once, (of a person) to jump on one foot. **2.** to cross by hopping. **3.** (*informal*) to make a short quick trip. —**hop** n. **1.** a hopping movement. **2.** an informal dance. **3.** a short flight or one stage in a long-distance flight. □ **hop in** or **out**, (*informal*) to get into or out of a car. **hopping mad**, (*informal*) very angry. **hop it**, (*slang*) go away. **on the hop**, (*informal*) bustling about; unprepared, *we were caught on the hop.*

hop[2] n. a plant cultivated for its cones (*hops*) which are used for giving a bitter flavour to beer.

hope n. **1.** a feeling of expectation and desire combined, a desire for certain events to happen. **2.** a person or thing or circumstance that gives cause for this. **3.** what one hopes for. —v. to feel hope, to expect and desire, to feel fairly confident. □ **hoping against hope**, hoping for something that is barely possible.

hopeful *adj.* **1.** feeling hope. **2.** causing hope, seeming likely to be favourable or successful. —n. a person who hopes or seems likely to succeed, *young hopefuls.*

hopefully *adv.* **1.** in a hopeful way. **2.** it is to be hoped, *hopefully, we shall be there by one o'clock.* (¶ Many people regard the second use as unacceptable.)

hopeless *adj.* **1.** feeling no hope. **2.** admitting no hope, *a hopeless case.* **3.** inadequate, incompetent, *is hopeless at tennis.* **hopelessly** *adv.*, **hopelessness** n.

hopper n. **1.** one who hops, a hopping insect. **2.** a V-shaped container with an opening at the base through which its contents can be discharged into a machine etc.

hopsack n. a kind of coarsely-woven fabric.

hopscotch n. a children's game of hopping and jumping over marked squares to retrieve a stone tossed into these.

horde n. a large group or crowd.

horehound n. a herb with woolly leaves and white flowers, producing a bitter juice.

horizon n. **1.** the line at which earth and sky appear to meet. **2.** the limit of a person's experience or knowledge or interests. □ **on the horizon**, (of an event) about to happen, just becoming apparent.

horizontal *adj.* parallel to the horizon, going across from left to right or right to left. **horizontally** *adv.*

hormone (**hor**-mohn) n. a substance produced within the body of an animal or plant (or made synthetically) and carried by the blood or sap to an organ which it

stimulates. **hormonal** (hor-moh-nal) *adj.*
□ **hormone cream,** a cosmetic cream containing hormones.

horn *n.* **1.** a hard pointed outgrowth on the heads of certain animals. **2.** the hard smooth substance of which this consists. **3.** a projection resembling a horn. **4.** any of various wind instruments (originally made of horn) with a trumpet-shaped end. **5.** a device for sounding a warning signal. —**horn** *v.* **1.** to shorten or cut off the horns of (cattle). **2.** to gore with the horns. □ **horned** *adj.* having horns. **horn in,** (*slang*) to intrude, to interfere. **horn of plenty,** *see* cornucopia. **horn-rimmed** *adj.* (of spectacles) with frames made of a material like horn or tortoiseshell.

hornbeam *n.* a tree with hard tough wood, often used in hedges.

hornbill *n.* a tropical bird with a horn-like projection on its beak.

hornblende *n.* a black or green or dark brown mineral.

hornet *n.* a large kind of wasp inflicting a serious sting. **stir up a hornets' nest,** to cause an outburst of angry feeling.

hornpipe *n.* a lively dance usually for one person, traditionally associated with sailors.

horny *adj.* (hornier, horniest) **1.** of or like horn. **2.** hardened and calloused, *horny hands.*

horoscope *n.* **1.** an astrologer's diagram showing the relative positions of the planets and stars at a particular time. **2.** a forecast of future events, based on this.

horrendous *adj.* (*informal*) horrifying.

horrible *adj.* **1.** causing horror. **2.** (*informal*) unpleasant. **horribly** *adv.*

horrid *adj.* horrible. **horridly** *adv.*

horrific *adj.* horrifying. **horrifically** *adv.*

horrify *v.* (horrified, horrifying) to arouse horror in, to shock.

horror *n.* **1.** a feeling of loathing and fear. **2.** intense dislike or dismay. **3.** a person or thing causing horror. □ **horror comic** *or* **film,** one full of violence presented sensationally for entertainment. **horror-struck** *or* **horror-stricken** *adjs.* horrified, shocked. **the horrors,** a fit of horror or depression.

hors-d'œuvre (*pr.* or-dervr) *n.* food served as an appetizer at the start of a meal.

horse *n.* **1.** a four-legged animal with a flowing mane and tail, used for riding on or to carry loads or pull carts etc. **2.** an adult male horse. **3.** cavalry. **4.** a frame on which something is supported, a clothes-horse. **5.** a vaulting-horse (*see* vault²). —*v.* (*informal*) to indulge in horseplay. □ **horse-box** *n.* a closed vehicle for trans-

porting a horse. **horse-brass** *n.* a brass ornament worn by a horse. **horse-drawn** *adj.* (of a vehicle) pulled by a horse. **Horse Guards,** a cavalry brigade of the Household troops; its headquarters in Whitehall. **horse-laugh** *n.* a loud coarse laugh. **horse-racing** *n.* the sport of conducting horse-races, races between horses with riders. **horse sense,** (*informal*) plain rough common sense. **horse-trading** *n.* (*Amer.*) dealing in horses; shrewd bargaining. **on horseback,** mounted on a horse. **straight from the horse's mouth,** (of information) from a first-hand source.

horse-chestnut *n.* **1.** a large tree with conical clusters of white or pink or red flowers. **2.** its dark brown fruit.

horseflesh *n.* **1.** the flesh of horses, as food. **2.** horses, *a good judge of horseflesh.*

horsehair *n.* hair from a horse's mane or tail, used for padding furniture etc.

horseman *n.* (*pl.* horsemen) a rider on horseback, especially a skilled one. **horsemanship** *n.*

horseplay *n.* boisterous play.

horsepower *n.* a unit for measuring the power of an engine (550 foot-pounds per second, about 750 watts).

horse-radish *n.* a plant with a hot-tasting root used to make a sauce.

horseshoe *n.* **1.** a U-shaped strip of metal nailed to a horse's hoof. **2.** anything shaped like this.

horsewhip *n.* a whip for horses. —*v.* (horsewhipped, horsewhipping) to beat with a horsewhip.

horsewoman *n.* (*pl.* horsewomen) a woman rider on horseback, especially a skilled one.

horsy *adj.* **1.** of or like a horse. **2.** interested in horses and horse-racing, showing this in one's dress and conversation etc.

horticulture *n.* the art of garden cultivation. **horticultural** *adj.* □ **horticulturist** *n.* an expert in horticulture.

Hosanna *int.* & *n.* a cry of adoration to God and the Messiah.

hose *n.* **1.** (in shops) stockings and socks. **2.** a hose-pipe. **3.** (*old use*) breeches, *doublet and hose.* —*v.* to water or spray with a hose, *hose the car down.*

hose-pipe *n.* a flexible tube for conveying water.

hosier *n.* a dealer in stockings and socks.

hosiery *n.* (in shops) stockings and socks (in trade use also knitted or woven underclothing).

hospice (hos-pis) *n.* **1.** a lodging for travellers, especially one kept by a religious order. **2.** a home for destitute or sick people.

hospitable (hos-pit-ăbŭl *or* hos-**pit**-ăbŭl) *adj.* giving and liking to give hospitality. **hospitably** *adv.*

hospital *n.* an institution providing medical and surgical treatment for persons who are ill or injured.

hospitality *n.* friendly and generous reception and entertainment of guests.

hospitalize (hos-pit-ă-lyz) *v.* to send or admit (a patient) to a hospital. **hospitalization** *n.*

host¹ *n.* a large number of people or things.

host² *n.* **1.** a person who receives and entertains another as his guest. **2.** an organism on which another organism lives as a parasite. —*v.* to act as host to (a person) or at (an event).

host³ *n.* the bread consecrated in the Eucharist.

hostage *n.* a person held as security that the holder's demands will be satisfied.

hostel *n.* a lodging-house for young travellers, students, or other special groups.

hostess *n.* **1.** a woman who receives and entertains a person as her guest. **2.** a woman employed to welcome and entertain people at a night-club etc.

hostile *adj.* **1.** of an enemy, *hostile aircraft.* **2.** unfriendly, *a hostile glance*; *they are hostile towards reform*, are opposed to it. **hostilely** *adv.* □ **hostile witness**, one who gives evidence unfairly and appears hostile to the party calling him.

hostility *n.* being hostile, enmity. **hostilities** *pl. n.* acts of warfare.

hot *adj.* (hotter, hottest) **1.** having great heat or high temperature, giving off heat, feeling heat. **2.** producing a burning sensation to the taste. **3.** eager, angry, excited, or excitable, *in hot pursuit*; *a hot temper*; *he's hot on punctuality*, keen on it. **4.** (of the scent in hunting) fresh and strong, (of news) fresh. **5.** (*informal*, of a player) very skilful, **6.** (of jazz etc.) strongly rhythmical and emotional. **7.** (*slang*) radioactive. **8.** (*slang*, of goods etc.) recently stolen, determinedly sought by the police and hence risky to handle. —*hot adv.* hotly, eagerly, angrily. —*v.* (hotted, hotting) (*informal*) to heat, to make or become hot; *things are hotting up*, becoming active or exciting. —*hotly adv.*, **hotness** *n.* □ **hot air**, (*slang*) excited or boastful talk. **hot cross bun**, a bun marked with a cross, to be eaten hot on Good Friday. **hot dog**, a hot sausage sandwiched in a roll of bread. **hot favourite**, a competitor strongly fancied to win. **hot gospeller**, (*informal*) an eager and enthusiastic preacher of the gospel. **hot-headed** *adj.* impetuous, excitable. **hot**

line, a direct line of communication, especially that between heads of governments in Washington and Moscow. **hot-pot** *n.* a stew containing meat with potatoes and other vegetables. **hot potato**, (*informal*) a situation etc. likely to cause trouble to the person handling it. **hot rod**, a motor vehicle modified to have extra power and speed. **hot seat**, (*slang*) the position of someone who has difficult responsibilities. **hot stuff**, (*slang*) a person of high spirit or skill or passions; something high-powered. **hot-tempered** *adj.* easily becoming very angry. **hot under the collar**, angry, resentful, or embarrassed. **hot-water bottle**, a small container to be filled with hot water for warmth in bed. **in hot water**, (*informal*) in trouble or disgrace. **make things hot for a person**, to make it uncomfortable for him by persecution. **sell like hot cakes**, to sell very readily.

hotbed *n.* **1.** a bed of earth heated by fermenting manure. **2.** a place favourable to the growth of something evil.

hotchpotch *n.* a jumble.

hotel *n.* a building where meals and rooms are provided for travellers.

hotelier (hoh-tel-i er) *n.* a hotel-keeper.

hotfoot *adv.* in eager haste. **hotfooting it**, hurrying eagerly.

hothead *n.* an impetuous person.

hothouse *n.* a heated building made of glass, for growing plants in a warm temperature.

hotplate *n.* a heated surface for cooking food or keeping it hot.

Hottentot *n.* a member of a Black people of South Africa.

hottish *adj.* rather hot.

hound *n.* **1.** a dog used in hunting, a fox-hound. **2.** a contemptible man. —**hound** *v.* **1.** to harass or pursue, *hounded him out of society*. **2.** to urge, to incite, *hound them on*.

hour *n.* **1.** a twenty-fourth part of a day and night, 60 minutes. **2.** a time of day, a point of time, *always comes at the same hour*; *17.00 hours*, this time on the 24-hour clock; *bus leaves on the hour*, when the clock indicates a whole number of hours from midnight. **3.** a short period of time, the time for action, the present time, *the hour has come*; *question of the hour*. **4.** (in the RC Church) prayers to be said at one of the seven times of day appointed for prayer, *a book of hours*. **5.** a period for a specified activity, *the lunch hour*. □ **hours** *pl. n.* a fixed period for daily work, *office hours are 9 to 5*; *after hours*.

hourglass *n.* a wasp-waisted glass container holding a quantity of fine sand that takes one hour to trickle from the upper to the lower section.

houri (**hoor**-i) *n.* a young and beautiful woman of the Muslim paradise.

hourly *adj.* **1.** done or occurring once an hour, *an hourly bus service.* **2.** continual, frequent, *lives in hourly dread of discovery.* —*adv.* every hour.

house[1] (*pr.* howss) *n.* **1.** a building made for people (usually one family) to live in. **2.** the people living in this, a household. **3.** a building used for a particular purpose, *the opera house.* **4.** a boarding-school residence, the pupils in this, one of the divisions of a day-school for sports competitions etc. **5.** a building used by an assembly, the assembly itself, *the Houses of Parliament*; *the House,* the House of Commons or Lords. **6.** a business firm, *a banking house.* **7.** the audience of a theatre, the theatre itself, a performance in this, *a full house*; *second house starts at 9 o'clock.* **8.** a family or dynasty, *the House of Windsor.* **9.** one of the twelve parts into which the heavens are divided in astrology. □ **house-agent** *n.* an estate agent. **house-bound** *adj.* unable to leave one's house. **house-dog** *n.* a dog kept to guard a house. **house-fly** *n.* a common fly found in houses. **house-martin** *n.* a bird that builds a mud nest on house walls. **house of cards,** an insecure scheme. **House of Commons,** the assembly of elected representatives in parliament; the building where it meets. **House of Keys,** a similar assembly in the Isle of Man. **House of Lords,** the assembly of members of the nobility and bishops in parliament; the building where it meets. **house party,** a number of guests staying at a house. **house-physician, house-surgeon** *ns.* one living in a hospital as a member of its staff. **house-plant** *n.* a plant for growing indoors. **house-proud** *adj.* giving great attention to the care and appearance of the home. **house-room** *n.* space to accommodate a thing in one's house, *wouldn't give it house-room.* **house-to-house** *adj.* calling at each house in turn. **house-trained** *adj.* (of animals) trained to be clean in the house. **house-warming** *n.* a party to celebrate the occupation of a new home. **like a house on fire,** vigorously, excellently. **on the house,** (of drinks) at the innkeeper's expense. **put one's house in order,** to make the necessary reforms. **under house arrest,** under detention in one's own house, not in prison.

house[2] (*pr.* howz) *v.* **1.** to provide accommodation for. **2.** to store (goods etc.). **3.** to encase (a part or fixture).

houseboat *n.* a barge-like boat fitted up as a dwelling.

housebreaker *n.* **1.** a burglar. **2.** a person employed in demolishing old buildings. **housebreaking** *n.*

housecoat *n.* a woman's long dress-like garment for informal wear in the house.

housecraft *n.* skill in household management.

houseful *n.* all that a house can hold.

household *n.* all the occupants of a house living as a family. **Household troops,** the troops nominally employed to guard the sovereign. **household word,** a familiar saying or name.

householder *n.* a person owning or renting a house.

housekeeper *n.* a woman employed to look after a household.

housekeeping *n.* **1.** management of household affairs. **2.** (*informal*) money to be used for this.

houseleek *n.*, a plant with pink flowers growing on walls and roofs.

housemaid *n.* a woman servant in a house, especially one who cleans rooms. **housemaid's knee,** inflammation of the kneecap, caused by kneeling.

housemaster, housemistress *ns.* a teacher in charge of a school boarding-house.

housewife *n.* a woman managing a household. **housewifely** *adj.* ¶ From the old meaning of *wife* = 'woman' (as in *fishwife*), not 'married woman'.

housewifery (**howss**-wif-ri) *n.* household management.

housework *n.* the cleaning and cooking etc. done in housekeeping.

housing *n.* **1.** accommodation. **2.** a rigid casing enclosing machinery. **3.** a shallow trench or groove cut in a piece of wood. □ **housing estate,** a number of houses in an area planned as a unit.

hove *see* heave.

hovel (**hov**-ĕl) *n.* a miserable dwelling.

hover *v.* **1.** (of a bird etc.) to remain in one place in the air. **2.** to wait about, to linger, to wait close at hand. □ **hover-fly** *n.* a fly like a slim wasp that hovers with rapidly beating wings.

hovercraft *n.* a vehicle supported by air thrust downwards from its engines.

hoverport *n.* a port used by hovercraft.

hovertrain *n.* a train supported like a hovercraft.

how *adv.* **1.** by what means, in what way. **2.** to what extent or amount etc. **3.** in what condition. □ **and how!**, (*slang*) very much so. **how about,** what is your feeling about (this thing)?; would you like (this)?

how come, (*informal*) why, how did it happen? **how do you do?,** a formal greeting.

how-d'ye-do *n.* (*informal*) an awkward state of affairs. **how many,** what total. **how much,** what amount, what price.

howdah (how-dă) *n.* a seat, usually with a canopy, on an elephant's back.

however *adv.* 1. in whatever way, to whatever extent, *will not succeed, however hard he tries.* 2. all the same, nevertheless, *later, however, he decided to go.*

howl *n.* 1. the long loud wailing cry of a dog etc. 2. a loud cry of amusement or pain or scorn. 3. a similar noise made by a strong wind or in an electrical amplifier. —**howl** *v.* 1. to make a howl. 2. to weep loudly. 3. to utter with a howl. □ **howl down,** to prevent (a speaker) from being heard by howling scorn at him.

howler *n.* (*informal*) a foolish mistake.

hoyden *n.* a girl who behaves boisterously. **hoydenish** *adj.*

HP *abbrev.* 1. hire-purchase. 2. (also h.p.) horse-power.

HRH *abbrev.* His or Her Royal Highness.

hub *n.* 1. the central part of a wheel, from which spokes radiate. 2. a central point of activity, *the hub of the universe.* □ **hub-cap** *n.* a round metal cover over the hub of a car wheel.

hubble-bubble *n.* a simple form of hookah.

hubbub *n.* a loud confused noise of voices.

huckaback *n.* a strong linen or cotton fabric used for towels.

huckleberry *n.* 1. a low shrub of North America. 2. its blue or black fruit.

huckster *n.* a hawker. —*v.* to haggle.

huddle *v.* 1. to heap or crowd together into a small space. 2. to curl one's body closely, to nestle. —*n.* a confused mass; *go into a huddle,* to hold a close or secret conference.

hue [1] *n.* a colour, a tint.

hue [2] *n.* **hue and cry,** a general outcry of alarm or demand or protest.

huff *n.* a fit of annoyance; *in a huff,* annoyed and offended. —*v.* to blow; *huffing and puffing,* blowing or blustering.

huffy, huffish *adjs.* in a huff.

hug *v.* (hugged, hugging) 1. to squeeze tightly in one's arms. 2. to keep close to, *the ship hugged the shore.* —*n.* a strong clasp with the arms. □ **hug oneself,** to be very pleased with oneself.

huge *adj.* extremely large, enormous. **hugely** *adv.*, **hugeness** *n.*

hugger-mugger *adj.* & *adv.* 1. secretly, full of secrecy. 2. in disorder.

hulk *n.* 1. the body of an old ship. 2. a large clumsy-looking person or thing.

hulking *adj.* (*informal*) bulky, clumsy.

hull *n.* 1. the framework of a ship or airship. 2. the cluster of leaves on a strawberry. 3. the pod of peas and beans. —*v.* to remove the hulls of (strawberries etc.).

hullabaloo *n.* an uproar.

hullo *int.* & *n.* = hallo.

hum *v.* (hummed, humming) 1. to make a low steady continuous sound like that of a spinning object. 2. to utter a slight sound in hesitating. 3. to sing with closed lips. 4. (*informal*) to be in a state of activity, *things started humming; make things hum.* 5. (*slang*) to give off a bad smell. —*int.* an exclamation of hesitation. —**hum** *n.* 1. a humming sound. 2. an exclamation of hesitation, *hums and haws.* 3. (*slang*) a bad smell. □ **hum and haw,** to hesitate.

human *adj.* 1. of or consisting of human beings (*see* man sense 1), *the human race.* 2. having the qualities that distinguish mankind, not divine or animal or mechanical. —*n.* a human being. □ **human interest,** something that appeals to personal emotions (in a newspaper story etc.). **human rights,** those held to be claimable by any living person.

humane (hew-**mayn**) *adj.* kind-hearted, compassionate, merciful. **humanely** *adv.* □ **humane killer,** an instrument for the painless killing of animals.

humanist (hew-măn-ist) *n.* a person who is concerned with the study of mankind and human affairs (as opposed to theological subjects), or who seeks to promote human welfare. **humanism** *n.* this study. **humanistic** *adj.*

humanitarian (hew-man-i-**tair**-iăn) *adj.* concerned with human welfare and the reduction of suffering. —*n.* a humanitarian person.

humanity *n.* 1. the human race, people, *crimes against humanity.* 2. being human. 3. being humane, kind-heartedness. □ **humanities** *pl. n.* arts subjects (especially study of the Greek and Latin classics) as opposed to the sciences.

humanize *v.* 1. to make human, to give a human character to. 2. to make humane. **humanization** *n.*

humanly *adv.* 1. in a human way. 2. by human means, with human limitations, *as accurate as is humanly possible.*

humanoid *adj.* having a human form or human characteristics. —*n.* a humanoid thing.

Humberside a county of England.

humble *adj.* 1. having or showing a modest estimate of one's own importance, not proud. 2. offered with such feelings, *humble apologies*. **3**. of low social or political rank. **4**. (of a thing) not large or showy or elaborate, *a humble cottage*. —*v*. to make humble, to lower the rank or self-importance of. —**humbly** *adv*., **humbleness** *n*. ☐ **eat humble pie**, to make a humble apology. (¶ From *umble pie*, that made with 'umbles', the edible offal of deer.)

humble-bee *n*. a bumble-bee.

humbug *n*. **1**. misleading behaviour or talk that is intended to win support or sympathy. **2**. a person who behaves or talks in this way. **3**. a kind of hard boiled sweet usually flavoured with peppermint.

humdinger *n*. (*slang*) a remarkable person or thing.

humdrum *adj*. dull, commonplace, monotonous.

humerus (**hew**-mer-ŭs) *n*. the bone in the upper arm, from shoulder to elbow.

humid (**hew**-mid) *adj*. (of the air or climate) damp. **humidity** (hew-**mid**-iti) *n*. dampness of the air.

humidifier (hew-**midi**-fy-er) *n*. a device for keeping the air moist in a room or enclosed space.

humiliate *v*. to cause (a person) to feel disgraced. **humiliation** *n*.

humility *n*. a humble condition or attitude of mind.

humming-bird *n*. a small tropical bird that vibrates its wings rapidly, producing a humming sound.

hummock *n*. a hump in the ground.

humoresque (hew-mer-**esk**) *n*. a light and lively musical composition.

humorist *n*. a writer or speaker who is noted for his humour.

humorous *adj*. full of humour. **humorously** *adv*.

humour *n*. **1**. the quality of being amusing. **2**. the ability to perceive and enjoy amusement, *sense of humour*. **3**. a state of mind, *in a good humour*. —*v*. to keep (a person) contented by giving way to his wishes.

hump *n*. **1**. a rounded projecting part. **2**. a deformity on a person's back, where there is abnormal curvature of the spine. **3**. *the hump*, (*slang*) a fit of depression or annoyance. —**hump** *v*. **1**. to form into a hump. **2**. to hoist or shoulder (one's pack etc.). —**humped** *adj*.

humpback *n*. a hunchback. **humpback bridge**, a small steeply-arched bridge.

humus (**hew**-mus) *n*. a rich dark organic material, formed by the decay of dead leaves and plants etc. and essential to the fertility of soil.

hunch *v*. to bend into a hump. —*n*. **1**. a

hump, a hunk. **2**. a feeling based on intuition.

hunchback *n*. a person with a hump on his back.

hundred *adj*. & *n*. ten times ten (100, C), *a few hundred* (¶ not *a few hundreds*) **Chiltern Hundreds**, *see* Chilterns. **hundredth** *adj*. & *n*. ☐ **hundred per cent**, entirely, completely. **hundreds and thousands**, tiny coloured sweets used for decorating cakes etc.

hundredfold *adj*. & *adv*. one hundred times as much or as many.

hundredweight *n*. a measure of weight, 112 lb or (*metric hundredweight*) 50 kg.

hung *see* hang. ☐ **hung-over** *adj*. (*slang*) having a hangover. **a hung parliament**, one that cannot reach decisions because there is no clear majority in voting.

Hungary a country of central Europe. **Hungarian** (hung-**air**-iăn) *adj*. & *n*.

hunger *n*. **1**. need for food, the uneasy sensation felt when one has not eaten for some time. **2**. a strong desire for something. —*v*. to feel hunger. ☐ **hunger-strike** *n*. refusal of food, as a form of protest. **hunger-striker** *n*.

hungry *adj*. (hungrier, hungriest) feeling hunger. **hungrily** *adv*.

hunk *n*. a large or clumsy piece.

hunt *v*. **1**. to pursue (wild animals) for food or sport. **2**. to pursue with hostility, to drive, *was hunted away*. **3**. to make a search, *hunted for it everywhere*; *hunt it out*, seek and find it. **4**. to search (a district) for game. **5**. to use (a horse or hounds) in hunting. **6**. (of an engine) to run too fast and too slow alternately. —**hunt** *n*. **1**. hunting. **2**. an association of people hunting with a pack of hounds, the district where they hunt. ☐ **hunt ball**, a ball given by members of a hunt. **hunt down**, to hunt (an animal etc.) until it is caught or killed; to hunt for and find. **hunt up**, to search for and find.

hunter *n*. **1**. one who hunts. **2**. a horse used for hunting. **3**. a watch with a hinged metal cover over the dial. ☐ **hunter-killer submarine**, a submarine designed to track down and destroy enemy ships. **hunter's moon**, the first full moon after the harvest moon.

huntsman *n*. (*pl*. huntsmen) **1**. a man who hunts. **2**. a man in charge of a pack of hounds.

hurdle *n*. **1**. a portable rectangular frame with bars, used for a temporary fence. **2**. an upright frame to be jumped over in a *hurdle-race*. **3**. an obstacle or difficulty. ☐ **hurdler** *n*. one who runs in hurdle-races. **hurdles** *pl*. *n*. a hurdle-race.

hurdy-gurdy *n.* **1.** a musical instrument with a droning sound, played by turning a handle. **2.** (*informal*) a barrel-organ.

hurl *v.* **1.** to throw violently. **2.** to utter vehemently, *hurl insults.* —*n.* a violent throw.

hurly-burly *n.* a rough bustle of activity.

hurrah *int. & n.* = hurray.

hurray *int. & n.* an exclamation of joy or approval.

hurricane (**hurri-kăn**) *n.* **1.** a storm with violent wind, especially a West Indian cyclone. **2.** a wind of 73 m.p.h. or more.

hurried *adj.* done with great haste. **hurriedly** *adv.*

hurry *n.* great haste, the need or desire for this. —*v.* (hurried, hurrying) to move or do something with eager haste or too quickly, to cause to move etc. in this way. □ **hurry-scurry** *n.* disorderly haste. **hurry up,** (*informal*) make haste. **in a hurry,** hurrying; easily or willingly, *you won't beat that in a hurry; shan't ask again in a hurry.*

hurt *v.* (hurt, hurting) **1.** to cause pain or damage or injury to. **2.** to cause mental pain to, to distress. **3.** to cause or feel pain, *my leg hurts.* —*n.* an injury, harm.

hurtful *adj.* causing hurt.

hurtle *v.* to move or hurl rapidly.

husband *n.* a married man in relation to his wife. —*v.* to use economically, to try to save, *husband one's resources.*

husbandry *n.* **1.** farming. **2.** management of resources.

hush *v.* to make or become silent or quiet; *hush a thing up,* to prevent it from becoming generally known. —*n.* silence. □ **hush-hush** *adj.* (*informal*) kept very secret. **hush-money** *n.* money paid to prevent something discreditable from being revealed.

husk *n.* the dry outer covering of certain seeds and fruits. —*v.* to remove the husk(s) from.

husky[1] *adj.* (huskier, huskiest) **1.** dry, like husks. **2.** (of a person or his voice) dry in the throat, hoarse. **3.** big and strong, burly. **huskily** *adv.*, **huskiness** *n.*

husky[2] *n.* an Eskimo dog, used for pulling sledges.

Hussars (**hŭ-zarz**) *n.* any of several cavalry regiments.

hussy *n.* a cheeky young woman.

hustings *n.* parliamentary election proceedings. ¶ Originally a temporary platform from which candidates for parliament could address the electors.

hustle *v.* **1.** to jostle, to push roughly. **2.** to hurry. **3.** to bustle (a person), to make (a person) act quickly and without time to consider things, *was hustled into a decision.*

—*n.* hustling. —**hustler** *n.*

hut *n.* a small roughly-made house or shelter.

hutch *n.* a box-like pen for rabbits.

hyacinth *n.* **1.** a plant with fragrant bell-shaped flowers, growing from a bulb. **2.** purplish-blue.

hybrid *n.* **1.** an animal or plant that is the offspring of two different species or varieties. **2.** something made by combining two different elements. —*adj.* produced in this way.

hydra *n.* a thing that is hard to get rid of. ¶ Named after the *Hydra* in Greek mythology, a water-snake with many heads that grew again if cut off.

hydrangea (**hy-drayn-jă**) *n.* a shrub with white, pink, or blue flowers growing in clusters.

hydrant *n.* a pipe from a water-main (especially in a street) with a nozzle to which a hose can be attached for fire-fighting or street-cleaning etc.

hydrate *n.* a chemical compound of water with another compound or element.

hydraulic (**hy-draw-lik**) *adj.* **1.** of water conveyed through pipes or channels. **2.** operated by the movement of water, *a hydraulic lift.* **3.** concerned with the use of water in this way, *hydraulic engineer.* **4.** hardening under water, *hydraulic cement.* **hydraulically** *adv.*

hydro *n.* (*pl.* hydros) (*informal*) **1.** a hotel etc. providing hydrotherapy. **2.** a hydro-electric power plant.

hydrocarbon *n.* any of a class of compounds of hydrogen and carbon which are found in petrol, coal, and natural gas.

hydrocephalus (**hy-droh-sef-ă-lus**) *n.* a condition (especially of children) in which fluid accumulates on the brain.

hydrochloric acid (**hy-drŏ-klor-ik**) a colourless corrosive acid containing hydrogen and chlorine.

hydrocyanic acid prussic acid.

hydrodynamic *adj.* of the force exerted by a moving liquid, especially water. **hydrodynamics** *n.* the scientific study of this force.

hydroelectric *adj.* using water-power to produce electricity.

hydrofoil *n.* **1.** a boat equipped with a structure designed to raise the hull out of the water when the boat is in motion, enabling it to travel fast and economically. **2.** this structure.

hydrogen *n.* a colourless odourless tasteless gas, the lightest substance known, combining with oxygen to form water. **hydrogen bomb,** an immensely power-

-ful bomb releasing energy by fusion of hydrogen nuclei.

hydrolysis (hy-**drol**-i-sis) *n.* decomposition of a substance by the chemical action of water.

hydrometer (hy-**drom**-it-er) *n.* an instrument that measures the density of liquids.

hydrophobia (hy-drŏ-**foh**-biǎ) *n.* **1.** abnormal fear of water, especially as a symptom of rabies in man. **2.** rabies.

hydroplane *n.* a light fast motor boat designed to skim over the surface of water.

hydroponics (hy-drŏ-**pon**-iks) *n.* the art of growing plants without soil, in sand etc. containing water to which nutrients have been added.

hydrostatic *adj.* of the pressure and other characteristics of water or other liquid at rest. **hydrostatics** *n.* the scientific study of these characteristics.

hydrotherapy *n.* the use of water (internally and externally) in the treatment of disease and abnormal physical conditions.

hydrous (**hy**-drŭs) *adj.* (of substances) containing water.

hyena *n.* a flesh-eating animal like a wolf, with a howl that sounds like wild laughter.

hygiene (**hy**-jeen) *n.* the practice of cleanliness in order to maintain health and prevent disease.

hygienic (hy-**jeen**-ik) *adj.* **1.** according to the principles of hygiene. **2.** clean and free from disease-germs. **hygienically** *adv.*

hygrometer (hy-**grom**-it-er) *n.* an instrument that measures humidity.

hymen *n.* a membrane partly closing the external opening of the vagina of a virgin girl or woman.

hymn *n.* a song of praise to God or a sacred being. **hymn-book** *n.* a book of hymns.

hymnal *n.* a hymn-book.

hyoscine (**hy**-ŏ-seen) *n.* a poisonous substance from which a sedative is made, found in plants of the nightshade family.

hype[1] *n.* (*slang*) **1.** a hypodermic needle or injection. **2.** a drug addict. ☐ **hyped up,** (*slang*) stimulated by or as if by an injection of drugs.

hype[2] *n.* (*slang*) trickery, misleading publicity. —*v.* (*slang*) to deceive by this.

hyperactive *adj.* (of children) abnormally and excessively active. **hyperactivity** *n.*

hyperbola (hy-**per**-bŏlǎ) *n.* the curve produced when a cone is cut by a plane that makes a larger angle with the base than the side of the cone does. **hyperbolic** (hy-per-**bol**-ik) *adj.*

hyperbole (hy-**per**-bŏli) *n.* an exaggerated statement that is not meant to be taken literally, e.g. *a stack of work a mile high.* **hyperbolical** (hy-per-**bol**-ikǎl) *adj.*

hypercritical *adj.* excessively critical.

hypermarket *n.* a very large self-service store with a sales area of at least 5000 sq. metres, selling a wide range of goods and a number of services (e.g. hairdressing), usually situated outside a town.

hypersensitive *adj.* excessively sensitive.

hypertension *n.* **1.** abnormally high blood pressure. **2.** great emotional tension.

hyphen *n.* the sign - used to join two words together (e.g. *fruit-tree*) or to divide a word into parts. —*v.* to hyphenate.

hyphenate *v.* to join or divide with a hyphen. **hyphenation** *n.*

hypnosis (hip-**noh**-sis) *n.* **1.** the sleep-like condition produced by hypnotism. **2.** hypnotism.

hypnotic (hip-**not**-ik) *adj.* **1.** of or producing hypnosis or a similar condition. **2.** (of a drug) producing sleep. —*n.* a hypnotic drug. —**hypnotically** *adv.*

hypnotism (**hip**-nŏ-tizm) *n.* the production of a sleep-like condition in a person who is then very susceptible to suggestion and who acts only if told to do so.

hypnotist (**hip**-nŏ-tist) *n.* a person who produces hypnosis in another.

hypnotize (**hip**-nŏ-tyz) *v.* **1.** to produce hypnosis in (a person). **2.** to fascinate, to dominate the mind or will of.

hypocaust (**hy**-pŏ-kawst) *n.* a system of under-floor heating by hot air, used in ancient Roman houses.

hypochondria (hy-pŏ-**kon**-driǎ) *n.* a mental condition in which a person constantly imagines that he is ill. **hypochondriac** *n.* one who suffers from this.

hypocrisy (hip-**ok**-risi) *n.* falsely pretending to be virtuous, insincerity.

hypocrite (**hip**-ŏ-krit) *n.* a person who is guilty of hypocrisy. **hypocritical** (hip-ŏ-**krit**-ikǎl) *adj.,* **hypocritically** *adv.*

hypodermic *adj.* injected beneath the skin, used for such injections. —*n.* a **hypodermic syringe,** a syringe fitted with a hollow needle through which a liquid can be injected beneath the skin. —**hypodermically** *adv.*

hypotension *n.* abnormally low blood pressure.

hypotenuse (hy-**pot**-i-newz) *n.* the side opposite the right angle in a right-angled triangle.

hypothesis (hy-**poth**-i-sis) *n.* (*pl.* hypotheses, *pr.* -seez) a supposition or conjecture put forward to account for certain facts and used as a basis for further investigation by which it may be proved or disproved.

hypothermia (hy-pŏ-**therm**-iă) *n.* the condition of having an abnormally low body-temperature.

hypothetical (hy-pŏ-**thet**-ikăl) *adj.* of or based on a hypothesis, supposed but not necessarily true. **hypothetically** *adv.*

hysterectomy (hiss-ter-**ek**-tŏmi) *n.* surgical removal of the womb.

hysteria (hiss-**teer**-iă) *n.* wild uncontrollable emotion or excitement.

hysterical (hiss-**terri**-kăl) *adj.* caused by hysteria, suffering from this. **hysterically** *adv.* □ **hysterics** *pl. n.* a hysterical outburst.

Hz *abbrev.* hertz.

Ii

I *pronoun* the person who is speaking or writing and referring to himself.

iambic (I-**am**-bik) *adj.* of or using a metrical foot with one short or unstressed syllable followed by one long or stressed syllable. **iambics** *pl. n.* lines of verse in iambic metre.

iatrogenic (I at roh **jen** ik) *adj.* (of disease) caused unintentionally by a doctor through his method of diagnosis, manner, or treatment.

IBA *abbrev.* Independent Broadcasting Authority.

Iberian (I-**beer**-iăn) *adj.* of the peninsula in south-west Europe comprising Spain and Portugal.

ibex (I-beks) *n.* (*pl.* **ibexes** or **ibex**) a mountain goat with long curving horns.

ibid. *abbrev.* ibidem, = in the same book or passage etc.

ibis (I-bis) *n.* a wading-bird with a long curved bill, found in warm climates.

ice *n.* 1. frozen water, a brittle transparent solid. 2. a sheet of this. 3. a portion of ice cream or water-ice. —**ice** *v.* 1. to become covered with ice, *the pond iced over.* 2. to make very cold, *iced beer.* 3. to decorate with icing. □ **Ice Age**, a period when much of the nothern hemisphere was covered with glaciers. **ice-blue** *adj. & n.* very pale blue. **ice-cap** *n.* the permanent covering of ice in polar regions. **ice-cold** *adj.* as cold as ice. **ice-cream**, a sweet creamy frozen food. **ice hockey**, a game resembling hockey, played on ice between teams of skaters with a flat disc (a *puck*) instead of a ball. **ice lolly**, a water-ice on a small stick. **ice-plant** *n.* a plant with

leaves that glisten as if with ice. **ice-show** *n.* an entertainment by skaters on ice.

iceberg *n.* a huge mass of ice floating in the sea with the greater part under water. **tip of the iceberg**, a small evident part of something much larger that lies concealed.

Iceland an island country in the North Atlantic. **Icelander** *n.*

Icelandic *adj.* of Iceland or its people or language. —*n.* the language of Iceland.

ichneumon (ik-**new**-mŏn) *n.* a small insect that lays its eggs on or inside the larva of another insect.

ICI *abbrev.* Imperial Chemical Industries.

icicle *n.* a pointed piece of ice hanging down, formed when dropping water freezes.

icing *n.* a mixture of sugar etc. used to decorate cakes and biscuits. **icing sugar**, powdered sugar used for making this.

icon (I-kon) *n.* (in the Orthodox Church) a painting or mosaic of a sacred person, itself regarded as sacred.

iconoclast (I-**kon**-ŏ-klast) *n.* a person who attacks cherished beliefs.

icy *adj.* (**icier**, **iciest**) 1. very cold, as cold as ice, *icy winds.* 2. covered with ice, *icy roads.* 3. very cold and unfriendly in manner, *an icy voice.* **icily** *adv.,* **iciness** *n.*

I'd = I had, I would.

Idaho (I-dă-hoh) a State of the USA.

idea *n.* 1. a plan etc. formed in the mind by thinking. 2. a mental impression, *give him an idea of what is needed.* 3. an opinion, *tries to force his ideas on us.* 4. a vague belief or fancy, a feeling that something is likely, *I have an idea that we shall be late.* □ **have no idea**, (*informal*) not to know; to be utterly incompetent. **the very idea!**, that is outrageous.

ideal *adj.* satisfying one's idea of what is perfect, *ideal weather for sailing.* —*n.* a person or thing or idea that is regarded as perfect or as a standard for attainment or imitation, *the high ideals of the Christian religion.* —**ideally** *adv.*

idealist (I-dee-ăl-ist) *n.* a person who has high ideals and tries in an unrealistic way to achieve these. **idealistic** *adj.,* **idealism** *n.*

idealize *v.* to regard or represent as perfect.

identical *adj.* 1. the same, *this is the identical place we stayed in last year.* 2. similar in every detail, exactly alike, *no two people have identical fingerprints.* **identically** *adv.* □ **identical twins**, twins developed from a single fertilized ovum and therefore of the same sex and very similar in appearance.

identifiable *adj.* able to be identified.

identify *v.* (identified, identifying) **1.** to establish the identity of, to recognize as being a specified person or thing. **2.** to consider to be identical, to equate, *one cannot identify riches and happiness.* **3.** to associate very closely in feeling or interest, *he has identified himself with the progress of the firm.* **4.** to regard oneself as sharing the characteristics or fortunes of another person, *people like to identify with the characters in a film.* **identification** *n.*

Identikit *n.* (*trade mark*) a set of pictures of features that can be put together to form a likeness (especially of a person who is sought by the police) constructed from descriptions.

identity *n.* **1.** the state of being identical, absolute sameness. **2.** the condition of being a specified person or thing; *established his identity,* established who he was. □ **identity card** *or* **disc** etc., one that is worn or carried and bears a person's name or an assigned number etc.

ideogram (**id**-i-ŏ-gram) *n.* a symbol indicating the idea (not the sounds forming the name) of a thing, e.g. numerals, Chinese characters, and symbols used in road signs.

ideology (I-dee-**ol**-ŏji) *n.* the ideas that form the basis of an economic or political theory etc., *in Marxist ideology.* **ideological** *adj.* of or based on an ideology.

idiocy *n.* **1.** the state of being an idiot. **2.** extreme stupidity. **3.** stupid behaviour, a stupid action.

idiom (**id**-i-ŏm) *n.* **1.** a phrase that must be taken as a whole, usually having a meaning that is not clear from the meanings of the individual words, e.g. *foot the bill* and *a change of heart.* **2.** the use of particular words or of words in an order that is regarded as standard, *the English idiom is 'wash up the dishes' but not 'wash up the baby'.* **3.** the language used by a people or group, *in the scientific idiom.* **4.** a characteristic style of expression in art or music etc.

idiomatic (idi-ŏ-**mat**-ik) *adj.* **1.** in accordance with idioms. **2.** full of idioms. **idiomatically** *adv.*

idiosyncrasy (idi-ŏ-**sink**-răsi) *n.* a person's own attitude of mind or way of behaving etc. that is unlike that of others. **idiosyncratic** (idi-ŏ-sin-**krat**-ik) *adj.*

idiot *n.* **1.** a mentally deficient person who is permanently incapable of rational conduct. **2.** (*informal*) a very stupid person.

idiotic *adj.* very stupid. **idiotically** *adv.*

idle *adj.* **1.** doing no work, not employed, not active or in use. **2.** (of time) not spent in doing something. **3.** avoiding work, lazy, *an idle fellow.* **4.** worthless, having no special purpose, *idle gossip; idle curiosity.* — **idle** *v.* **1.** to pass (time) without working, to be idle. **2.** (of an engine) to run slowly in a neutral gear. —**idly** *adv.,* **idleness** *n.,* **idler** *n.*

idol *n.* **1.** an image of a god, used as an object of worship. **2.** a person or thing that is the object of intense admiration or devotion.

idolater (I-**dol**-ă-ter) *n.* a person who worships an idol or idols.

idolatry (I-**dol**-ă-tri) *n.* **1.** worship of idols. **2.** excessive admiration or devotion. **idolatrous** *adj.*

idolize *v.* to feel excessive admiration or devotion to (a person or thing).

idyll (**id**-il) *n.* **1.** a short description (usually in verse) of a peaceful or romantic scene or incident, especially in country life. **2.** a scene or incident of this kind.

idyllic (id-**il**-ik) *adj.* like an idyll, peaceful and happy. **idyllically** *adv.*

i.e. *abbrev.* = that is. (¶ From the Latin *id est.*)

if *conj.* **1.** on condition that, *he'll do it only if you pay him.* **2.** in the event that, *if you are tired we will rest.* **3.** supposing or granting that, *even if she said it she didn't mean it.* **4.** even though, *I'll finish it, if it takes me all day.* **5.** whenever, *if they asked for food, it was brought.* **6.** whether, *see if you can turn the handle.* **7.** (in exclamations of wish or surprise), *if only he would come!; well, if it isn't Simon!* —*n.* a condition or supposition, *too many ifs about it.*

igloo *n.* a dome-shaped Eskimo hut built of blocks of hard snow.

igneous (**ig**-ni-ŭs) *adj.* (of rocks) formed when molten matter has solidified, either underground or after being expelled by a volcano.

ignite (ig-**nyt**) *v.* **1.** to set fire to. **2.** to catch fire.

ignition (ig-**nish**-ŏn) *n.* **1.** igniting, being ignited. **2.** the mechanism providing the spark that ignites the fuel in an internal-combustion engine.

ignoble *adj.* not noble in character or aims or purpose. **ignobly** *adv.*

ignominious (ignŏ-**min**-iŭs) *adj.* bringing contempt or disgrace, humiliating. **ignominiously** *adv.*

ignominy (**ig**-nŏm-ini) *n.* disgrace, humiliation.

ignoramus (ig-ner-**ay**-mŭs) *n.* (*pl.* ignoramuses) an ignorant person.

ignorant *adj.* **1.** lacking knowledge. **2.** behaving rudely through lack of know-

ledge of good manners. **ignorantly** *adv.*, **ignorance** *n.*

ignore *v.* **1.** to take no notice of, to disregard. **2.** to refrain deliberately from acknowledging or greeting (a person).

iguana (ig-**wah**-nă) *n.* a large tree-climbing lizard of the West Indies and tropical America.

ileostomy (ili-**ost**-ŏmi) *n.* an artificial opening through which the bowel can empty, made surgically by bringing part of the ileum to the surface of the abdomen.

ileum (**il**-iŭm) *n.* the lowest part of the small intestine.

iliac (**il**-i-ak) *adj.* of the flank or hip-bone.

ilium (**il**-iŭm) *n.* the bone forming the upper part of the pelvis.

ilk *n.* (*informal*) kind, *others of that ilk.*

I'll = I shall, I will.

ill *adj.* **1.** physically or mentally unwell. **2.** (of health) unsound, not good. **3.** harmful, *no ill effects.* **4.** not favourable, *ill luck.* **5.** hostile, unkind, *no ill feelings, ill humour,* bad temper. —**ill** *adv.* **1.** badly, wrongly. **2.** unfavourably. **3.** imperfectly, scarcely, *ill provided for*; *can ill afford to do this.* —*n.* evil, harm, or injury. □ **ill-advised** *adj.* unwise. **ill at ease,** uncomfortable, embarrassed. **ill-bred** *adj.* having bad manners. **ill-fated** *adj.* unlucky. **ill-favoured** *adj.* unattractive. **ill-gotten** *adj.* gained by evil or unlawful means. **ill-mannered** *adj.* having bad manners. **ill-natured** *adj.* unkind. **ill-starred** *adj.* unlucky. **ill-timed** *adj.* done or occurring at an unfortunate time. **ill-treat** *v.* to treat badly or cruelly. **ill-use** *v.* to ill-treat. **ill will,** hostility, unkind feeling.

Ill. *abbrev.* Illinois.

illegal *adj.* against the law. **illegally** *adv.*, **illegality** (ili-**gal**-iti) *n.*

illegible (i-**lej**-ibŭl) *adj.* not legible. **illegibly** *adv.*, **illegibility** *n.*

illegitimate (ili-**jit**-im-ăt) *adj.* **1.** born of parents not married to each other. **2.** contrary to law or to rules. **3.** (of a conclusion in an argument etc.) not logical, wrongly inferred. **illegitimately** *adv.*, **illegitimacy** *n.*

illicit (i-**lis**-it) *adj.* unlawful, not allowed. **illicitly** *adj.*

Illinois (il-in-oi) a State of the USA.

illiterate (i-**lit**-er-ăt) *adj.* unable to read and write, showing lack of education. —*n.* an illiterate person. **illiteracy** *n.*

illness *n.* **1.** the state of being ill in body or mind. **2.** a particular form of ill health.

illogical *adj.* not logical, contrary to logic. **illogically** *adv.*, **illogicality** (i-loj-i-**kal**-iti) *n.*

illuminate *v.* **1.** to light up, to make bright.

2. to throw light on (a subject), to make understandable. **3.** to decorate (a street or building etc.) with lights. **4.** to decorate (a manuscript) with coloured designs. **illumination** *n.*

illusion (i-loo-*zh*ŏn) *n.* **1.** something that a person wrongly supposes to exist. **2.** a false belief about the nature of something. **illusionist** *n.* a conjuror.

illusive (i-**loo**-siv) *adj.* illusory.

illusory (i-**loo**-ser-i) *adj.* based on illusion, not real.

illustrate *v.* **1.** to supply (a book or newspaper etc.) with drawings or pictures. **2.** to make clear or explain by examples or pictures etc. **3.** to serve as an example of. **illustrator** *n.*

illustration *n.* **1.** illustrating. **2.** a drawing or picture in a book etc. **3.** an example used to explain something.

illustrative (il-**ŭs**-tră-tiv) *adj.* serving as an illustration or example.

illustrious (i-**lus**-triŭs) *adj.* famous and distinguished.

I'm = I am.

image *n.* **1.** a representation of the outward form of a person or thing, a statue. **2.** the optical appearance of something, produced in a mirror or through a lens etc. **3.** something very like another in appearance, *he's the very image of his father.* **4.** a mental picture. **5.** the general impression of a person or firm or product etc. as perceived by the public.

imagery *n.* **1.** images. **2.** the use of metaphorical language to produce pictures in the minds of readers or hearers.

imaginable *adj.* able to be imagined.

imaginary *adj.* existing only in the imagination, not real.

imagination *n.* imagining, the ability to imagine creatively or to use this ability in a practical way (e.g. in dealing with difficulties).

imaginative *adj.* having or showing imagination. **imaginatively** *adv.*

imagine *v.* **1.** to form a mental image of, to picture in one's mind. **2.** to think or believe, to suppose, *don't imagine you'll get away with it.* **3.** to guess, *can't imagine where it has gone.*

imam (im-**ahm**) *n.* **1.** the leader of prayers in a mosque. **2.** *Imam,* the title of various Muslim religious leaders.

imbalance *n.* lack of balance, disproportion.

imbecile (**im**-bi-seel) *n.* **1.** a mentally deficient person, an adult whose intelligence is equal to that of an average five-year-old child. **2.** a stupid person. —*adj.* idiotic. — **imbecility** (imbi-**sil**-iti) *n.*

imbibe (im-**byb**) *v.* **1.** to drink. **2.** to absorb (ideas etc.) into the mind.

imbroglio (im-**brohl**-yoh) *n.* (*pl.* imbroglios) a confused situation, usually involving a disagreement.

imbue (im-**bew**) *v.* to fill (a person) with certain feelings or qualities or opinions.

IMF *abbrev.* International Monetary Fund.

imitable *adj.* able to be imitated.

imitate *v.* **1.** to copy the behaviour of, to take as an example that should be followed. **2.** to mimic playfully or for entertainment. **3.** to make a copy of, to be like (something else). **imitator** *n.*

imitation *n.* **1.** imitating. **2.** something produced by this, a copy; *imitation leather*, a material made to look like leather. **3.** the act of mimicking a person or thing for entertainment, *he does imitations*.

imitative (**im**-it-ātiv) *adj.* imitating.

immaculate *adj.* **1.** spotlessly clean. **2.** free from moral blemish. **3.** free from fault, right in every detail. **immaculately** *adv.*, **immaculacy** *n.* □ **Immaculate Conception**, the Roman Catholic doctrine that the Virgin Mary, from the moment of her conception by her mother, was and remained free from the taint of original sin.

immanent (**im**-ă-něnt) *adj.* **1.** (of qualities) inherent. **2.** (of God) permanently pervading the universe. **immanence** *n.*

immaterial *adj.* **1.** having no physical substance, *as immaterial as a ghost*. **2.** of no importance or relevance, *it is now immaterial whether he goes or stays*; *some immaterial objections*.

immature *adj.* not mature. **immaturity** *n.*

immeasurable *adj.* not measurable, immense. **immeasurably** *adv.*

immediate *adj.* **1.** occurring or done at once, without delay. **2.** nearest, next, with nothing between, *the immediate neighbourhood*; *my immediate family*. **immediately** *adv.* & *conj.*, **immediacy** *n.*

immemorial *adj.* existing from before what can be remembered or found recorded, *from time immemorial*.

immense *adj.* exceedingly great. **immensity** *n.* □ **immensely** *adv.* extremely.

immerse *v.* **1.** to put completely into water or other liquid. **2.** to absorb or involve deeply in thought or business etc.

immersion *n.* **1.** immersing, being immersed. **2.** baptism by putting the whole body into water. □ **immersion heater,** an electric heating element designed to be placed in the liquid that is to be heated, especially as a fixture in a hot-water tank.

immigrant *adj.* **1.** immigrating. **2.** of immigrants. —*n.* a person who has immigrated.

immigrate *v.* to come into a foreign country as a permanent resident. **immigration** *n.*

imminent *adj.* (of events) about to occur, likely to occur at any moment. **imminence** *n.*

immobile *adj.* **1.** immovable. **2.** not moving. **immobility** *n.*

immobilize *v.* to make or keep immobile. **immobilization** *n.*

immoderate *adj.* excessive, lacking moderation. **immoderately** *adv.*

immodest *adj.* **1.** lacking in modesty, indecent. **2.** conceited. **immodestly** *adv.*, **immodesty** *n.*

immolate (**im**-ŏ-layt) *v.* to sacrifice. **immolation** *n.*

immoral *adj.* not conforming to the accepted rules of morality, morally wrong (especially in sexual matters). **immorally** *adv.*, **immorality** (im-er-**al**-iti) *n.*

immortal *adj.* **1.** living for ever, not mortal. **2.** famous for all time. —*n.* an immortal being or person. **immortality** *n.*

immortalize *v.* to make immortal.

immortelle (im-or-**tel**) *n.* a flower with a papery texture that retains its shape and colour when dried.

immovable *adj.* **1.** unable to be moved. **2.** unyielding, not changing in one's purpose. **immovably** *adv.*

immune *adj.* having immunity, *immune from* or *against* or *to infection* etc.

immunity *n.* **1.** the ability of an animal or plant to resist infection. **2.** special exemption from a tax or duty or penalty.

immunize *v.* to make immune, especially against infection. **immunization** *n.*

immunology (im-yoo-**nol**-ŏji) *n.* the scientific study of resistance to infection.

immure (im-**yoor**) *v.* to imprison, to shut in.

immutable (i-**mewt**-ăbŭl) *adj.* unchangeable. **immutably** *adv.*, **immutability** *n.*

imp *n.* **1.** a small devil. **2.** a mischievous child.

impact[1] (**im**-pakt) *n.* **1.** a collision. **2.** the force exerted when one body collides with another. **3.** the force exerted by the influence of new ideas.

impact[2] (**im**-pakt) *v.* to pack or drive or wedge firmly into something or together. **impaction** *n.* □ **impacted** *adj.* (of a tooth) wedged in the jaw so that it cannot grow through the gum normally.

impair *v.* to damage, to cause weakening of, *impair one's health*. **impairment** *n.*

impala (im-**pah**-lă) *n.* (*pl.* impala) a small antelope of southern Africa.

impale *v.* to fix or pierce by passing a sharp-pointed object into or through. **impalement** *n.*

impalpable (im-**palp**-ăbŭl) *adj.* unable to be touched or felt.

impart *v.* 1. to give. 2. to reveal or make (information etc.) known.

impartial (im-**par**-shăl) *adj.* not favouring one more than another. **impartially** *adv.*, **impartiality** (im-par-shi-**al**-iti) *n.*

impassable *adj.* (of roads or barriers) impossible to travel on or over.

impasse (**am**-pahs) *n.* a deadlock.

impassioned (im-**pash**-ŏnd) *adj.* full of deep feeling, *an impassioned appeal.*

impassive *adj.* not feeling or showing emotion. **impassively** *adv.*, **impassiveness** *n.*, **impassivity** *n.*

impatient *adj.* 1. unable to wait patiently. 2. showing lack of patience, irritated, *got an impatient reply.* 3. intolerant, *impatient of delay.* **impatiently** *adv.*, **impatience** *n.*

impeach *v.* 1. to accuse of treason or other serious crime against the State, and bring for trial (in the UK, accusation would be by the House of Commons and trial by the House of Lords). 2. to call in question. **impeachment** *n.*

impeccable *adj.* faultless. **impeccably** *adv.*

impecunious (impi-**kew**-niŭs) *adj.* having little or no money. **impecuniosity** *n.*

impedance (im-**pee**-dăns) *n.* 1. the total resistance of an electric circuit to the flow of alternating current. 2. a similar mechanical property.
¶ Do not confuse with impediment.

impede *v.* to hinder.

impediment *n.* 1. a hindrance, an obstruction. 2. a defect that prevents something functioning properly; *has an impediment in his speech,* has a lisp or stammer.
¶ Do not confuse with impedance.

impedimenta (im-ped-i-**ment**-ă) *pl. n.* encumbrances, baggage.

impel *v.* (impelled, impelling) 1. to urge or drive to do something, *curiosity impelled her to investigate.* 2. to send or drive forward, to propel.

impending *adj.* imminent.

impenetrable *adj.* unable to be penetrated. **impenetrability** *n.*

impenitent *adj.* not penitent, not repentant. **impenitently** *adv.*, **impenitence** *n.*

imperative (im-pe-**ră**-tiv) *adj.* 1. expressing a command. 2. essential, obligatory, *further economies are imperative.* — **imperative** *n.* 1. a command, a form of a verb used in making commands (e.g. *come* in *come here!*). 2. something essential or obligatory, *survival is the first imperative.*

imperceptible *adj.* not perceptible, very slight or gradual and therefore difficult to see. **imperceptibly** *adv.*

imperfect *adj.* not perfect. **imperfectly** *adv.*

imperfection *n.* 1. being imperfect. 2. a mark or fault or characteristic that prevents a thing from being perfect.

imperial *adj.* 1. of an empire or emperor or empress. 2. majestic. 3. (of weights and measures) used by statute in the UK, formerly for all goods and still for certain goods, *an imperial gallon.* —**imperially** *adv.*

imperialism *n.* belief in the desirability of acquiring colonies and dependencies. **imperialist** *n.*, **imperialistic** *adj.*

imperil *v.* (imperilled, imperilling) to endanger.

imperious (im-**peer**-iŭs) *adj.* commanding, bossy. **imperiously** *adv.*

impermanent *adj.* not permanent. **impermanence** *n.*, **impermanently** *adv.*

impermeable (im-**per**-mi-ăbŭl) *adj.* not able to be penetrated, especially by liquid. **impermeability** *n.*

impersonal *adj.* 1. not influenced by personal feeling, showing no emotion. 2. not referring to any particular person. 3. having no existence as a person, *nature's impersonal forces.* 4. (of verbs) used with 'it' to make general statements such as 'it is raining' or 'it is hard to find one'. **impersonally** *adv.*, **impersonality** *n.*

impersonate *v.* 1. to play the part of. 2. to pretend to be (another person) for entertainment or in fraud. **impersonation** *n.*, **impersonator** *n.*

impertinent *adj.* insolent, not showing proper respect. **impertinently** *adv.*, **impertinence** *n.*

imperturbable (im-per-**terb**-ăbŭl) *adj.* not excitable, calm. **imperturbably** *adv.*, **imperturbability** *n.*

impervious (im-**per**-viŭs) *adj.* 1. not able to be penetrated, *impervious to water.* 2. not influenced by, *impervious to fear* or *argument.*

impetigo (imp-i-**ty**-goh) *n.* a contagious skin disease causing spots that form yellowish crusts.

impetuous (im-**pet**-yoo-ŭs) *adj.* 1. moving quickly or violently, *an impetuous dash.* 2. acting or done on impulse. **impetuously** *adv.*, **impetuosity** *n.*

impetus (**im**-pit-ŭs) *n.* (*pl.* impetuses) 1. the force or energy with which a body moves. 2. a driving force, *the treaty gave an impetus to trade.*

impiety (im-**py**-iti) *n.* lack of reverence.

impinge *v.* **1.** to make an impact. **2.** to encroach.

impious (**imp**-iŭs) *adj.* not reverent, wicked. **impiously** *adv.*

impish *adj.* of or like an imp. **impishly** *adv.*, **impishness** *n.*

implacable (im-**plak**-ăbŭl) *adj.* not able to be placated, relentless. **implacably** *adv.*, **implacability** *adv.*

implant[1] (im-**plahnt**) *v.* to plant, to insert or fix (ideas etc.) in the mind, to insert (tissue or other substance) in a living thing. **implantation** *n.*

implant[2] (**im**-plahnt) *n.* implanted tissue etc.

implausible *adj.* not plausible.

implement[1] (**im**-pli-měnt) *n.* a tool or instrument for working with.

implement[2] (**im**-pli-ment) *v.* to put into effect, *we implemented the scheme.* —**implementation** *n.*

implicate *v.* to involve or show (a person) to be involved in a crime etc.

implication *n.* **1.** implicating, being implicated. **2.** implying, being implied. **3.** something that is implied.

implicit (im-**pliss**-it) *adj.* **1.** implied though not made explicit. **2.** absolute, unquestioning, *expects implicit obedience.* **implicitly** *adv.*

implore *v.* to request earnestly, to entreat. **imploringly** *adv.*

imply *v.* (implied, implying) **1.** to suggest without stating directly, to hint. **2.** to mean. **3.** to involve the truth or existence of, *the beauty of the carving implies that they had skilled craftsmen.*

impolite *adj.* not polite. **impolitely** *adv.*

impolitic (im-**pol**-i-tik) *adj.* unwise, inexpedient.

imponderable (im-**pon**-der-ăbŭl) *adj.* not able to be estimated. **imponderables** *pl. n.* things such as emotions, qualities, etc., the effect of which is imponderable.

import[1] (im-**port**) *v.* **1.** to bring in from abroad or from an outside source. **2.** to imply, to indicate. **importation** *n.*, **importer** *n.*

import[2] (**im**-port) *n.* **1.** the importing of goods etc., something imported. **2.** meaning. **3.** importance.

important *adj.* **1.** having or able to have a great effect. **2.** (of a person) having great authority or influence. **3.** pompous, *he has an important manner.* **importantly** *adv.*, **importance** *n.*

importunate (im-**por**-tew-năt) *adj.* making persistent requests. **importunity** (im-per-**tewn**-iti) *n.*

importune (im-per-**tewn**) *v.* to make persistent requests.

impose *v.* **1.** to put (a tax or obligation etc.), *imposed heavy duties on tobacco.* **2.** to inflict, *imposed a great strain on our resources.* **3.** to force to be accepted, *imposed his ideas on the group.* **4.** to take unfair advantage, *we don't want to impose on your hospitality.*

imposing *adj.* impressive.

imposition *n.* **1.** the act of imposing something. **2.** something imposed, e.g. a tax or duty. **3.** a burden imposed unfairly.

impossible *adj.* **1.** not possible, unable to be done or to exist. **2.** unendurable, *an impossible person.* **impossibly** *adv.*, **impossibility** *n.*

impostor *n.* a person who fraudulently pretends to be someone else.

imposture *n.* a fraudulent deception.

impotent (**im**-pŏ-těnt) *adj.* **1.** powerless, unable to take action. **2.** (of a man) unable to copulate or reach orgasm, unable to procreate. **impotently** *adv.*, **impotence** *n.*

impound *v.* to take (another person's property) into a pound or into legal custody, to confiscate.

impoverish *v.* **1.** to cause to become poor. **2.** to exhaust the natural strength or fertility of, *impoverished soil.* **impoverishment** *n.*

impracticable *adj.* incapable of being put into practice. **impracticability** *n.*

impractical *adj.* not practical, unwise.

imprecation (impri-**kay**-shŏn) *n.* a spoken curse.

imprecise *adj.* not precise. **imprecisely** *adj.*, **imprecision** *n.*

impregnable (im-**preg**-năbŭl) *adj.* safe against attack, *an impregnable fortress.*

impregnate (im-**preg**-nayt) *v.* **1.** to introduce sperm or pollen into and fertilize (a female animal or plant). **2.** to penetrate all parts of (a substance), to fill or saturate, *the water was impregnated with salts.* **impregnation** *n.*

impresario (impri-**sar**-i-oh) *n.* (*pl.* impresarios) the manager of an operatic or concert company.

impress[1] (im-**press**) *v.* **1.** to make (a person) form a strong (usually favourable) opinion of something. **2.** to fix firmly in the mind, *impressed on them the need for haste.* **3.** to press a mark into, to stamp with a mark.

impress[2] (**im**-press) *n.* an impressed mark.

impression *n.* **1.** an effect produced on the mind. **2.** an uncertain idea or belief or remembrance. **3.** an imitation of a person or sound, done for entertainment. **4.** the impressing of a mark, an impressed mark.

5. a reprint of a book etc. made with few or no alterations to its contents. □ **be under the impression,** to think (that something is a fact).

impressionable *adj.* easily influenced.

Impressionist *n.* one of the painters of the late 19th century who adopted a style giving the general impression of a subject, especially by using the effects of light, without elaborate detail. **Impressionism** *n.*

impressive *adj.* making a strong impression, arousing admiration and approval. **impressively** *adv.*

imprint¹ (**im**-print) *n.* a mark made by pressing or stamping a surface; *the imprint of a foot,* a footprint.

imprint² (im-**print**) *v.* **1.** to impress or stamp a mark etc. on. **2.** to establish firmly in the mind.

imprison *v.* **1.** to put into prison. **2.** to keep in confinement. **imprisonment** *n.*

improbable *adj.* not likely to be true or to happen. **improbably** *adv.*, **improbability** *n.*

impromptu (im-**promp**-tew) *adv. & adj.* without preparation or rehearsal —*n* a musical composition that gives the impression of being composed impromptu.

improper *adj.* **1.** wrong, incorrect, *made improper use of the blade.* **2.** not conforming to the rules of social or lawful conduct. **3.** indecent. **improperly** *adv.* □ **improper fraction,** one that is greater than unity, with the numerator greater than the denominator, e.g. ⅗.

impropriety (im-prŏ-**pry**-iti) *n.* being improper, an improper act or remark etc.

improvable *adj.* able to be improved.

improve *v.* **1.** to make or become better. **2.** to make good or better use of, *improved the occasion.* □ **improve on,** to produce something better than.

improvement *n.* **1.** improving, being improved. **2.** an addition or alteration that improves something or adds to its value.

improver *n.* a person who works at a trade for little or no payment in order to improve his skill.

improvident (im-**prov**-idĕnt) *adj.* not providing for future needs, wasting one's resources. **improvidently** *adv.*, **improvidence** *n.*

improvise (**im**-prŏ-vyz) *v.* **1.** to compose (a thing) impromptu. **2.** to provide, in time of need, using whatever materials are at hand, *improvised a bed from cushions and rugs.* **improvisation** *n.*, **improviser** *n.*

imprudent (im-**proo**-dĕnt) *adj.* unwise, rash. **imprudently** *adv.*, **imprudence** *n.*

impudent *adj.* impertinent, cheeky. **impudently** *adv.*, **impudence** *n.*

impugn (im-**pewn**) *v.* to express doubts about the truth or honesty of, to try to discredit, *we do not impugn their motives.*

impulse *n.* **1.** a push or thrust, impetus. **2.** a stimulating force in a nerve, causing a muscle to react. **3.** a sudden inclination to act, without thought for the consequences, *did it on impulse.* □ **impulse buying,** buying of goods on impulse and not because of previous planning.

impulsive *adj.* **1.** (of a person) habitually acting on impulse. **2.** (of an action) done on impulse. **impulsively** *adv.*, **impulsiveness** *n.*

impunity (im-**pewn**-iti) *n.* freedom from punishment or injury.

impure *adj.* not pure.

impurity *n.* **1.** being impure. **2.** a substance that makes another substance impure by being present in it.

impute (im-**pewt**) *v.* to attribute, to ascribe. **imputation** *n.* imputing; an accusation of wrongdoing.

in *prep.* expressing position or state. **1.** of inclusion within the limits of space or time or circumstance or surroundings etc. **2.** of quantity or proportion, *they are packed in tens.* **3.** of form or arrangement, *hanging in folds.* **4.** of activity or occupation or membership, *he is in the army.* **5.** wearing as dress or colour etc., *in gumboots.* **6.** of method or means of expression, *spoke in French.* **7.** with the instrument or means of, *written in ink.* **8.** of identity, *found a friend in Mary.* **9.** under the influence of, *spoke in anger.* **10.** with respect to, *lacking in courage.* **11.** as the content of; *there's not much in it,* no great difference between the advantages or merits of various schemes or competitors etc. **12.** after the time of, *back in ten minutes.* **13.** (of a female animal) pregnant with, *in calf.* **14.** into. **15.** towards, *ran in all directions.* —*adv.* **1.** expressing position bounded by certain limits, or to a point enclosed by these. **2.** at home, *will you be in?* **3.** on or towards the inside, *with the fur side in.* **4.** in fashion or season or office, elected, in effective or favourable action, *my luck was in; the tide was in,* was high. **5.** (in cricket and baseball) batting, *which side is in?* **6.** (of a domestic fire) burning. **7.** having arrived or been gathered or received, *train is in; harvest is in.* —**in** *adj.* **1.** internal, living etc. inside. **2.** fashionable, *it's the in thing to do.* □ **be in for,** to be about to experience, *she is in for a surprise;* to be competing in. **be in on,** (*informal*) to be aware of or sharing in (a secret or activity). **in all,** in total number. **in-built** *adj.* built-in. **in camera,** (of the hearing of evidence or lawsuits) in the judge's private room; in private or in secret. **in-depth** *adj*. thorough, very detailed, *an in-depth survey*. **in memoriam**, in memory of a person who has died. **in-patient** *n*. a person who remains resident in a hospital while undergoing treatment. **ins and outs**, the passages in a building etc.; the details of an activity or procedure. **in shore**, on the water near or nearer to the shore. **in situ** (*pr*. **sit**-yoo), in its present or original place. **in so far as**, to the extent that, *he carried out orders only in so far as he did not openly disobey them*. **in toto**, totally. **in-tray** *n*. a tray to hold documents awaiting the owner's attention.

in. *abbrev*. inch(es).

inability *n*. being unable.

inaccessible *adj*. not accessible, unapproachable. **inaccessibility** *n*.

inaccurate *adj*. not accurate. **inaccurately** *adv*., **inaccuracy** *n*.

inaction *n*. lack of action, doing nothing.

inactive *adj*. not active, showing no activity. **inactivity** *n*.

inadequate *adj*. **1.** not adequate, insufficient. **2.** not sufficiently able or competent, *felt inadequate*. **inadequately** *adv*., **inadequacy** *n*.

inadmissible *adj*. not allowable.

inadvertent (in-ăd-**ver**-těnt) *adj*. unintentional. **inadvertently** *adv*., **inadvertency** *n*.

inadvisable *adj*. not advisable.

inalienable (in-**ay**-li-ěn-ăbŭl) *adj*. not able to be given away or taken away, *an inalienable right*.

inamorata (in-am-er-**ah**-tă) *n*. a woman with whom a man is in love.

inane *adj*. silly, lacking sense. **inanely** *adv*., **inanity** (in-**an**-iti) *n*.

inanimate (in-**an**-im-ăt) *adj*. **1.** (of rocks and other objects) lifeless, (of plants) lacking animal life. **2.** showing no sign of life.

inapplicable (in-**ap**-lik-ăbŭl) *adj*. not applicable.

inapprehensible (in-ap-ri-**hen**-si-bŭl) *adj*. that cannot be grasped by the mind or perceived by the senses.

inappropriate (in-ă-**proh**-pri-ăt) *adj*. unsuitable.

inarticulate (in-ar-**tik**-yoo-lăt) *adj*. **1.** not expressed in words, *an inarticulate cry*. **2.** unable to speak distinctly, *was inarticulate with rage*. **3.** unable to express one's ideas clearly.

inartistic *adj*. not artistic. **inartistically** *adv*.

inattention *n*. lack of attention, neglect.

inattentive *adj*. not attentive, not paying attention.

inaudible (in-**aw**-dibŭl) *adj*. not audible, unable to be heard. **inaudibly** *adv*., **inaudibility** *n*.

inaugural (in-**awg**-yoor-ăl) *adj*. of or for an inauguration, *the inaugural ceremony*.

inaugurate (in-**awg**-yoor-ayt) *v*. **1.** to admit (a person) to office with a ceremony. **2.** to enter ceremonially upon (an undertaking), to open (a building or exhibition etc.) formally. **3.** to be the beginning of, to introduce, *Concorde inaugurated a new era in jet travel*. **inauguration** *n*., **inaugurator** *n*.

inauspicious (in-aw-**spish**-ŭs) *adj*. not auspicious.

inboard *adj*. & *adv*. within the sides of or towards the centre of a ship, aircraft, or vehicle.

inborn *adj*. existing in a person or animal from birth, natural, *an inborn ability*.

inbred *adj*. **1.** produced by inbreeding. **2.** inborn.

inbreeding *n*. breeding from closely related individuals.

Inc. *abbrev*. (*Amer*.) Incorporated.

Inca *n*. a member of an American Indian people in Peru etc. before the Spanish conquest.

incalculable *adj*. unable to be calculated.

incandescent (in-kan-**dess**-ěnt) *adj*. glowing with heat, shining. **incandescent lamp**, an electric or other lamp in which a white-hot filament gives off light. **incandescence** *n*.

incantation (in-kan-**tay**-shŏn) *n*. words or sounds to be uttered as a magic spell, the uttering of these.

incapable *adj*. not capable; *drunk and incapable*, so drunk as to be helpless. **incapability** *n*.

incapacitate (in-kă-**pas**-i-tayt) *v*. **1.** to disable. **2.** to make ineligible. **incapacitation** *n*.

incapacity *n*. inability, lack of sufficient strength or power.

incarcerate (in-**kar**-ser-ayt) *v*. to imprison. **incarceration** *n*.

incarnate (in-**kar**-năt) *adj*. embodied, in human form, *a devil incarnate*.

incarnation (in-kar-**nay**-shŏn) *n*. embodiment, especially in human form. **the Incarnation**, the embodiment of God in human form as Christ.

incautious (in-**kaw**-shŭs) *adj*. not cautious, rash. **incautiously** *adv*.

incendiary (in-**sen**-di-er-i) *adj*. **1.** (of a bomb etc.) designed to cause a fire, containing chemicals that ignite. **2.** of arson, guilty of arson. **3.** tending to stir up strife, inflammatory. —**incendiary** *n*. **1.** an incendiary bomb etc. **2.** an arsonist. **3.** a person who stirs up strife.

incense[1] (**in**-sens) *n.* **1.** a substance that produces a sweet smell when burning. **2.** its smoke, used especially in religious ceremonies.

incense[2] (in-**sens**) *v.* to make angry.

incentive (in-**sen**-tiv) *n.* something that rouses or encourages a person to some action or effort.

inception (in sep shŏn) *n.* the beginning of the existence of something.

incertitude *n.* uncertainty.

incessant (in-**sess**-ănt) *adj.* unceasing, continually repeated.

incest (**in**-sest) *n.* sexual intercourse between people regarded as too closely related to marry each other. **incestuous** (in-**sess**-tew-ŭs) *adj.* involving incest, guilty of incest.

inch *n.* **1.** a measure of length, one twelfth part of a foot (= 2·54 cm). **2.** an amount of rainfall that would cover a surface to a depth of 1 inch. **3.** a very small amount, *would not yield an inch.* —*v.* to move slowly and gradually, *they inched forward.* □ **every inch**, entirely, *looked every inch a soldier.* **within an inch of his life**, almost to death.

inchoate (in-**koh**-ăt) *adj.* just begun, not yet fully developed.

incidence (**in**-si-dĕns) *n.* **1.** the rate at which something occurs or affects people or things, *studied the incidence of the disease.* **2.** the falling of something (e.g. a ray of light) on a surface.

incident *n.* **1.** an event, especially a minor one. **2.** a piece of hostile activity, *frontier incidents.* **3.** a public disturbance or accident, *the protest march took place without incident.* **4.** an event that attracts general attention. —**incident** *adj.* **1.** liable to happen, accompanying something, *the risks incident to a pilot's career.* **2.** (of rays of light etc.) falling on a surface, *incident light.*

incidental *adj.* **1.** occurring as a minor accompaniment, *incidental expenses.* **2.** liable to occur in consequence of or in connection with something, *the incidental hazards of exploration.* **3.** casual, occurring by chance. □ **incidental music**, music played as a background to the action of a play.

incidentally *adv.* **1.** in an incidental way. **2.** as an unconnected comment, by the way.

incinerate (in-**sin**-er-ayt) *v.* to reduce to ashes, to destroy by fire. **incineration** *n.*

incinerator (in-**sin**-er-ayt-er) *n.* a furnace or enclosed device for burning rubbish.

incipient (in-**sip**-iĕnt) *adj.* in its early stages, beginning, *incipient decay.*

incise (in-**syz**) *v.* to make a cut in (a surface), to engrave by cutting.

incision (in-**si**-zhŏn) *n.* **1.** incising. **2.** a cut, especially one made surgically into the body.

incisive (in-**sy**-siv) *adj.* clear and decisive, *made incisive comments.* **incisively** *adv.,* **incisiveness** *n.*

incisor (in-**sy**-zer) *n.* any of the sharp-edged front teeth in the upper and lower jaws.

incite (in-**syt**) *v.* to urge on to action, to stir up. **incitement** *n.*

incivility *n.* lack of civility, an impolite act or remark.

inclement (in-**klem**-ĕnt) *adj.* (of weather) cold or wet or stormy.

inclination *n.* **1.** a slope or slant, a leaning or bending movement. **2.** a tendency. **3.** a liking or preference; *against my inclination, against my wish.*

incline[1] (in-**klyn**) *v.* **1.** to lean, to slope. **2.** to bend (the head or body) forward. **3.** to have or cause a certain tendency, to influence, *his manner inclines me to believe him.* □ **be inclined**, to have a certain tendency or willingness, *the door is inclined to bang; I'm inclined to agree.*

incline[2] (**in**-klyn) *n.* a slope.

include *v.* **1.** to have or regard or treat as part of a whole. **2.** to put into a certain category or list. **inclusion** *n.*

inclusive *adj.* **1.** including all that is mentioned, *pages 7 to 26 inclusive.* **2.** including much or everything; *inclusive terms,* (at a hotel etc.) including all charges. —**inclusively** *adv.*

incognito (in-**kog**-nit-oh) *adj. & adv.* with one's identity kept secret, *she was travelling incognito.* —*n.* the identity assumed by one who is incognito.

incognizant (in-**kog**-ni-zănt) *adj.* unaware.

incoherent (in-koh-**heer**-ĕnt) *adj.* rambling in speech or in reasoning. **incoherently** *adv.,* **incoherence** *n.*

incombustible *adj.* not able to be burnt by fire.

income *n.* money received during a certain period (especially a year) as wages or salary, interest on investments, etc. **income tax,** tax that must be paid on annual income.

incoming *adj.* **1.** coming in, *the incoming tide.* **2.** succeeding another person, *the incoming president.*

incommode (in-kŏ-**mohd**) *v.* to inconvenience.

incommunicado (in-kŏ-mew-ni-**kah**-doh)

adj. not allowed to communicate with others, *the prisoner was held incommunicado.*

incomparable (in-**komp**-er-ăbŭl) *adj.* without an equal, beyond comparison. **incomparably** *adv.*

incompatible (in-kŏm-**pat**-ibŭl) *adj.* 1. not compatible. 2. inconsistent; *the two statements are incompatible,* cannot both be true. **incompatibility** *n.*

incompetent (in-**kom**-pi-tĕnt) *adj.* not competent. **incompetently** *adv.,* **incompetence** *n.*

incomplete *adj.* not complete. **incompletely** *adv.,* **incompleteness** *n.*

incomprehensible (in-kom-pri-**hen**-sibŭl) *adj.* not able to be understood. **incomprehensibly** *adv.*

incomprehension (in-kom-pri-**hen**-shŏn) *n.* failure to understand.

inconceivable *adj.* 1. unable to be imagined. 2. (*informal*) impossible to believe. **inconceivably** *adv.*

inconclusive *adj.* (of evidence or an argument etc.) not fully convincing, not decisive. **inconclusively** *adv.,* **inconclusiveness** *n.*

incongruous (in-**kong**-roo-ŭs) *adj.* unsuitable, not harmonious. **incongruously** *adv.* **incongruity** (in-kong-**roo**-iti) *n.*

inconsequent (in-**kon**-si-kwĕnt) *adj.* not following logically, irrelevant. **inconsequently** *adv.*

inconsequential (in-kon-si-**kwen**-shăl) *adj.* not following logically, irrelevant. **inconsequentially** *adv.*

inconsiderable *adj.* not worth considering, of small size or amount or value.

inconsiderate *adj.* not considerate towards other people. **inconsiderately** *adv.,* **inconsiderateness** *n.*

inconsistent *adj.* not consistent. **inconsistently** *adv.,* **inconsistency** *n.*

inconsolable (in-kŏn-**soh**-lă-bŭl) *adj.* not able to be consoled. **inconsolably** *adv.*

inconspicuous *adj.* not conspicuous. **inconspicuously** *adv.*

incontestable (in-kŏn-**test**-ăbŭl) *adj.* indisputable. **incontestably** *adv.*

incontinent *adj.* 1. unable to control the excretion of one's urine and faeces. 2. lacking self-restraint in sexual desire. **incontinence** *n.*

incontrovertible (in-kon-trŏ-**vert**-ibŭl) *adj.* indisputable, undeniable. **incontrovertibly** *adv.*

inconvenience *n.* 1. being inconvenient. 2. a circumstance that is inconvenient. — *v.* to cause inconvenience or slight difficulty to.

inconvenient *adj.* not convenient, not suiting one's needs or requirements, slightly troublesome. **inconveniently** *adv.*

incorporate *v.* 1. to include as a part, *your suggestions will be incorporated in the plan.* 2. to form into a legal corporation. **incorporation** *n.*

incorrect *adj.* not correct. **incorrectly** *adv.,* **incorrectness** *n.*

incorrigible (in-**ko**-ri-jibŭl) *adj.* (of a person or his faults etc.) not able to be reformed or improved, *an incorrigible liar.* **incorrigibly** *adv.,* **incorrigibility** *n.*

incorruptible (in-kŏ-**rupt**-ibŭl) *adj.* 1. not liable to decay. 2. not able to be corrupted morally, e.g. by bribes. **incorruptibility** *n.*

increase[1] (in-**kreess**) *v.* to make or become greater in size or amount or intensity. **increasingly** *adv.* more and more.

increase[2] (**in**-kreess) *n.* 1. the process of increasing. 2. the amount by which something increases.

incredible *adj.* 1. unbelievable. 2. (*informal*) hard to believe, very surprising. **incredibly** *adv.*

incredulous (in-**kred**-yoo-lŭs) *adj.* unbelieving, showing disbelief. **incredulously** *adv.,* **incredulity** (in-kri-**dew**-liti) *n.*

increment (**in**-kri-mĕnt) *n.* an increase, an added amount, *a salary with annual increments of £100.*

incriminate *v.* to indicate as involved in wrongdoing, *his statement incriminated the guard.* **incrimination** *n.*

incriminatory (in-**krim**-in-ayt-er-i) *adj.* causing incrimination.

incrustation *n.* 1. encrusting, being encrusted. 2. a crust or deposit formed on a surface.

incubate *v.* 1. to hatch (eggs) by warmth of a bird's body as it sits on them or by artificial heat. 2. to cause (bacteria etc.) to develop in suitable conditions. **incubation** *n.* incubating; *the incubation period,* the time it takes for symptoms of a disease to become apparent in an infected person.

incubator *n.* 1. an apparatus for hatching eggs by artificial warmth. 2. an apparatus in which babies born prematurely can be kept in a constant controlled heat and supplied with oxygen etc.

incubus (**ink**-yoo-bŭs) *n.* (*pl.* incubuses) a burdensome person or thing.

inculcate (**in**-kul-kayt) *v.* to implant (ideas or habits) by persistent urging, *desiring to inculcate obedience in the young.* **inculcation** *n.*

inculpate (**in**-kul-payt) *v.* to involve in a charge of wrongdoing, to incriminate.

incumbent (in-**kum**-bĕnt) *adj.* forming an obligation or duty, *it is incumbent on you to warn people of the danger.* —*n.* 1. a person who holds a particular office. **2.** the holder of a church benefice, a rector or vicar.

incur *v.* (incurred, incurring) to bring upon oneself, *incurred great expense.*

incurable *adj.* unable to be cured. —*n.* a person with an incurable disease. —**incurably** *adv.*

incurious *adj.* feeling or showing no curiosity about something.

incursion (in-ker-shŏn) *n.* a raid or brief invasion into someone else's territory etc.

incurved *adj.* curved inwards.

Ind. *abbrev.* Indiana.

indebted *adj.* owing money or gratitude. **indebtedness** *n.*

indecent *adj.* **1.** offending against recognized standards of decency. **2.** unseemly, *with indecent haste.* **indecently** *adv.*, **indecency** *n.* □ **indecent assault**, sexual assault not involving rape. **indecent exposure**, exposing one's genitals publicly with the intention of causing offence.

indecipherable *adj.* unable to be deciphered.

indecision *n.* inability to make up one's mind, hesitation.

indecisive *adj.* not decisive.

indecorous (in-dek-er-ŭs) *adj.* improper, not in good taste. **indecorously** *adv.*

indeed *adv.* **1.** truly, really, *it was indeed remarkable*; *indeed?*, is that so? **2.** used to intensify a meaning, *very nice indeed.* **3.** admittedly, *it is, indeed, his first attempt.* **4.** used to express surprise or contempt, *does she indeed!*

indefatigable (indi-fat-ig-ăbŭl) *adj.* not becoming tired. **indefatigably** *adv.*

indefensible *adj.* unable to be defended, unable to be justified.

indefinable (indi-fy-năbŭl) *adj.* unable to be defined or described clearly.

indefinite *adj.* not clearly defined or stated or decided, vague. **indefinite article**, the word 'a' or 'an'.

indefinitely *adv.* **1.** in an indefinite way. **2.** for an unlimited period.

indelible *adj.* **1.** (of a mark or stain or feeling) unable to be removed or washed away. **2.** (of a pencil etc.) making an indelible mark. **indelibly** *adv.*

indelicate *adj.* **1.** slightly indecent. **2.** tactless. **indelicately** *adv.*

indemnify (in-dem-ni-fy) *v.* (indemnified, indemnifying) **1.** to protect or insure (a person) against penalties incurred by his actions etc. **2.** to compensate (a person) for injury suffered.

indemnity *n.* **1.** protection or insurance against penalties incurred by one's actions.

2. compensation for damage done.

indent[1] (in-dent) *v.* **1.** to make recesses or tooth-like notches in; *an indented coastline*, one with deep recesses. **2.** to start (a line of print or writing) further from the margin than the others, *indent the first line of each paragraph.* **3.** to place an indent for goods or stores. **indentation** *n.*

indent[2] (in-dent) *n.* an official order for goods or stores.

indenture (in-den-cher) *n.* a written contract or agreement. **indentures** *pl. n.* an agreement binding an apprentice to work for a master. **indentured** *adj.* bound by indentures.

independence *n.* being independent. **Independence Day**, 4 July, celebrated in the USA as the anniversary of the date in 1776 when the American colonies formally declared themselves free and independent of Britain; a similar festival elsewhere.

independent *adj.* **1.** not dependent on or controlled by another person or thing, *he is now independent of his parents.* **2.** (of broadcasting) not financed by licence-fees. **3.** not depending for its validity or operation on the thing(s) involved; *independent proof*, from another source. **4.** self-governing. **5.** having or providing a sufficient income to make it unnecessary for the possessor to earn his living, *he has independent means.* **6.** not influenced by others in one's ideas or conduct. **7.** unwilling to be under an obligation to others. —**independently** *adv.* □ **Independent** *n.* a politician who is not committed to any political party. **independent school**, one that is not controlled by a local authority and does not receive a government grant.

indescribable *adj.* unable to be described, too great or beautiful or bad etc. to be described. **indescribably** *adv.*

indestructible *adj.* unable to be destroyed.

indeterminable *adj.* impossible to discover or decide. **indeterminably** *adv.* ¶ Do not confuse with indeterminate.

indeterminate *adj.* not fixed in extent or character etc., vague, left doubtful. ¶ Do not confuse with indeterminable.

index *n.* (*pl.* indexes) **1.** a list of names, titles, subjects, etc., especially an alphabetical list indicating where in a book etc. each can be found. **2.** a figure indicating the relative level of prices or wages compared with that at a previous date. **index** *v.* **1.** to make an index to (a book or collection of books etc.). **2.** to enter in an index. **3.** to make (wages, pensions, etc.) index-linked. —**indexer** *n.* □ **index finger**, the forefinger. **index-linked** *adj.*

(of wages, pensions etc.) increased according to increases in the cost-of-living index.

indexation *n.* the practice of making wages, pensions, etc. index-linked.

India 1. a large peninsula of Asia south of the Himalayas, forming a subcontinent. **2.** a country consisting of the greater part of this.

Indian *adj.* of India or Indians. —*n.* **1.** a native of India. **2.** an **American Indian**, one of the original inhabitants of the continent of America (other than Eskimos) or their descendants. □ **Indian clubs**, a pair of wooden or metal bottle-shaped clubs for swinging to exercise the arms. **indian corn**, maize. **Indian file**, single file. **indian ink**, ink made with a black pigment (made originally in China and Japan). **Indian Ocean**, the ocean between India and Australia. **Indian summer**, a period of dry sunny weather in late autumn; a period of tranquil enjoyment late in life.

Indiana (indi-**an**-ă) a State of the USA.

indiarubber *n.* a rubber for rubbing out pencil or ink marks.

indicate *v.* **1.** to point out, to make known. **2.** to be a sign of, to show the presence of. **3.** to show the need of, to require. **4.** to state briefly. **indication** *n.*

indicative (in-**dik**-ătiv) *adj.* **1.** giving an indication, *the style is indicative of the author's origin.* **2.** (of a form of a verb) used in making a statement, not in a command or wish etc., e.g. *he said* or *he is coming.* —*n.* this form of a verb.

indicator *n.* **1.** a thing that indicates or points to something. **2.** a meter or other device giving information about the functioning of a machine etc. **3.** a board giving information about something that is constantly changing, e.g. the arrival or departure of trains or aircraft. **4.** a device on a vehicle showing when the direction of travel is about to be altered.

indict (in-**dyt**) *v.* to make an indictment against (a person).

indictable (in-**dyt**-ăbŭl) *adj.* (of an action) making the doer liable to be charged with a crime.

indictment (in-**dyt**-měnt) *n.* **1.** a written statement of charges against an accused person. **2.** an accusation, especially of serious wrongdoing.

indifferent *adj.* **1.** feeling or showing no interest or sympathy, unconcerned. **2.** neither good nor bad. **3.** not of good quality or ability, *he is an indifferent footballer.* **indifferently** *adv.,* **indifference** *n.*

indigenous (in-**dij**-in-ŭs) *adj.* (of plants or animals or inhabitants) native.

indigent (**in**-dij-ěnt) *adj.* needy, poverty-stricken. **indigence** *n.*

indigestible (indi-**jest**-ibŭl) *adj.* difficult or impossible to digest. **indigestibility** *n.*

indigestion (indi-**jes**-chŏn) *n.* pain caused by difficulty in digesting food.

indignant *adj.* feeling or showing indignation. **indignantly** *adv.*

indignation *n.* anger aroused by something thought to be unjust or wicked etc.

indignity *n.* **1.** the quality of being humiliating. **2.** treatment that makes a person feel undignified or humiliated.

indigo *n.* a deep-blue dye or colour.

indirect *adj.* not direct. **indirectly** *adv.* □ **indirect taxes**, those paid in the form of increased prices for goods etc., not on income or capital.

indiscernible (indi-**sern**-ibŭl) *adj.* not discernible. **indiscernibly** *adv.*

indiscreet *adj.* **1.** not discreet, revealing secrets. **2.** not cautious, unwise. **indiscreetly** *adv.*

indiscretion (in-dis-**kresh**-ŏn) *n.* an indiscreet action or statement.

indiscriminate *adj.* showing no discrimination, doing or giving things without making a careful choice. **indiscriminately** *adv.*

indispensable *adj.* not able to be dispensed with, essential. **indispensability** *n.*

indisposed *adj.* **1.** slightly ill. **2.** unwilling, *they seem indisposed to help us.*

indisposition *n.* **1.** slight illness. **2.** unwillingness.

indisputable (in-dis-**pewt**-ăbŭl) *adj.* not able to be disputed, undeniable. **indisputably** *adv.*

indissoluble (indi-**sol**-yoo-bŭl) *adj.* firm and lasting, not able to be dissolved or destroyed, *indissoluble bonds of friendship.*

indistinct *adj.* not distinct. **indistinctly** *adv.,* **indistinctness** *n.*

indistinguishable *adj.* not distinguishable. **indistinguishably** *adv.*

indite (in-**dyt**) *v.* to put into words, to compose and write (a letter etc.).

individual *adj.* **1.** single, separate, *each individual strand.* **2.** of or for one person, *baked in individual portions.* **3.** characteristic of one particular person or thing, *has a very individual style.* —**individual** *n.* **1.** one person or plant or animal considered separately. **2.** (*informal*) a person, *a most unpleasant individual.* —**individually** *adv.,* **individuality** (indi-vid-yoo-**al**-iti) *n.*

individualist *n.* a person who is very independent in thought or action.

indivisible (indi-**viz**-ibŭl) *adj.* not divisible. **indivisibility** *adv.*

indoctrinate (in-**dok**-trin-ayt) *v.* to fill (a person's mind) with particular ideas or doctrines. **indoctrination** *n.*

Indo-European *adj.* of the family of languages spoken over most of Europe and Asia as far as north India. —*n.* a speaker of one of these languages.

indolent (in-dŏl-ĕnt) *adj.* lazy. **indolently** *adv.*, **indolence** *n.*

indomitable (in-**dom**-it-ăbŭl) *adj.* having an unyielding spirit, stubbornly persistent when faced with difficulty or opposition. **indomitably** *adv.*

Indonesia (indŏ-**nee**-*zh*ă) a country in south-east Asia. **Indonesian** *adj.* & *n.*

indoor *adj.* situated or used or done inside a building, *indoor games*; *an indoor aerial.* **indoors** *adv.* inside a building.

indubitable (in-**dew**-bit-ăbŭl) *adj.* that cannot reasonably be doubted. **indubitably** *adv.*

induce (in-**dewss**) *v.* **1.** to persuade. **2.** to produce or cause. **3.** to bring on (labour in childbirth) by artificial means.

inducement *n.* **1.** inducing, being induced. **2.** an attraction or incentive.

induct *v.* to install (a clergyman) ceremonially into a benefice.

inductance *n.* the property of producing an electric current by induction, the measure of this.

induction *n.* **1.** inducting. **2.** inducing. **3.** logical reasoning that a general law exists because particular cases that seem to be examples of it exist. **4.** production of an electric or magnetic state in an object by bringing an electrified or magnetic object close to but not touching it. **5.** drawing of a fuel mixture into the cylinder(s) of an internal combustion engine. **6.** production of an electric current in a circuit by varying the magnetic field.

inductive *adj.* **1.** of or using induction, *inductive reasoning.* **2.** of inductance.

indulge *v.* **1.** to allow (a person) to have what he wishes. **2.** to gratify (a wish). **3.** to allow oneself something that gives pleasure, *he indulges in a cigar after lunch.*

indulgence *n.* **1.** indulging. **2.** being indulgent. **3.** something allowed as a pleasure or privilege.

indulgent *adj.* indulging a person's wishes too freely; kind and lenient. **indulgently** *adv.*

industrial *adj.* **1.** of or engaged in industries, *industrial workers.* **2.** for use in industries. **3.** having many highly developed industries, *an industrial country.* **industrially** *adv.* □ **industrial action**, a strike or other disruptive activity.

Industrial Revolution, the rapid development of British industry by use of machines in the early 19th century.

industrialized *adj.* (of a country or area) made industrial. **industrialization** *n.*

industrialist *n.* a person who owns or is engaged in managing an industrial business.

industrious *adj.* hard-working. **industriously** *adv.*, **industriousness** *n.*

industry *n.* **1.** the manufacture or production of goods. **2.** a particular branch of this, any business activity, *the tourist industry.* **3.** the quality of being industrious.

inebriate (in-ee-bri-ăt) *adj.* drunken. — *n.* a drunken person, a drunkard.

inebriated (in-ee-bri-ayt-id) *adj.* drunken.

inedible (in-ed-ibŭl) *adj.* not edible (because of its nature).

ineducable (in-ed-yoo-kăbŭl) *adj.* incapable of being educated.

ineffable (in-ef-ăbŭl) *adj.* too great to be described, *ineffable joy.*

ineffective *adj.* **1.** not effective. **2.** (of a person) inefficient. **ineffectively** *adv.*

ineffectual *adj.* not effectual. **ineffectually** *adv.*

inefficient *adj.* not efficient. **inefficiently** *adv.*, **inefficiency** *n.*

inelegant *adj.* not elegant. **inelegantly** *adv.*, **inelegance** *n.*

ineligible (in-el-i-ji-bŭl) *adj.* not eligible. **ineligibility** *n.*

inept *adj.* unsuitable, absurd. **ineptly** *adv.*, **ineptitude** *n.*

inequality *n.* lack of equality in size or standard or rank etc.

inequitable (in-ek-wit-ăbŭl) *adj.* unfair, unjust.

ineradicable (in-i-**rad**-ik-ăbŭl) *adj.* unable to be eradicated.

inert *adj.* **1.** (of matter) without power to move or act. **2.** without active chemical or other properties, incapable of reacting, *an inert gas.* **3.** not moving, slow to move or take action. **inertly** *adv.*, **inertness** *n.*

inertia (in-er-shă) *n.* **1.** inertness, slowness to take action. **2.** the property of matter by which it remains in a state of rest or, if it is in motion, continues moving in a straight line, unless acted upon by an external force. □ **inertia reel**, a type of reel round which one end of a safety-belt is wound so that the belt will tighten automatically over the wearer if it is pulled suddenly. **inertia selling**, the sending of goods to a person who has not ordered them, in the hope that he will not take action to refuse them and must later make payment.

inescapable *adj.* unavoidable. **inescapably** *adv.*

inessential *adj.* not essential. —*n.* an inessential thing.

inestimable (in-**est**-im-ăbŭl) *adj.* too great or intense or precious etc. to be estimated. **inestimably** *adv.*

inevitable (in-**ev**-it-ăbŭl) *adj.* 1. not able to be prevented, sure to happen or appear. 2. (*informal*) tiresomely familiar, *the tourist with his inevitable camera.* **inevitably** *adv.*, **inevitability** *n.*

inexact *adj.* not exact. **inexactly** *adv.*, **inexactitude** *n.*

inexcusable *adj.* unable to be excused or justified. **inexcusably** *adv.*

inexhaustible *adj.* not able to be totally used up, available in unlimited quantity.

inexorable (in-**eks**-er-ăbŭl) *adj.* relentless, unable to be persuaded by request or entreaty. **inexorably** *adv.*

inexpedient *adj.* not expedient. **inexpediency** *n.*

inexpensive *adj.* not expensive, offering good value for the price. **inexpensively** *adv.*

inexperience *n.* lack of experience. **inexperienced** *adj.*

inexpert *adj.* not expert, unskilful. **inexpertly** *adv.*

inexplicable (in-**eks**-plik-ăbŭl *or* in-eks-**plik**-ăbŭl) *adj.* unable to be explained or accounted for. **inexplicably** *adv.*

in extremis (in eks-**tree**-mees) 1. at the point of death. 2. in very great difficulties. (¶ Latin.)

inextricable (in-**eks**-trik-ăbŭl) *adj.* 1. unable to be extricated. 2. unable to be disentangled or sorted out. **inextricably** *adv.*

infallible (in-**fal**-ibŭl) *adj.* 1. incapable of making a mistake or being wrong. 2. never failing, *an infallible remedy.* **infallibly** *adv.*, **infallibility** (in-fali-**bil**-iti) *n.*

infamous (**in**-fă-mŭs) *adj.* having or deserving a very bad reputation, detestable. **infamy** (**in**-fă-mi) *n.*

infancy *n.* 1. early childhood, babyhood. 2. an early stage of development.

infant *n.* a child during the earliest period of its life.

infanticide (in-**fant**-i-syd) *n.* murder of an infant soon after its birth.

infantile (**in**-făn-tyl) *adj.* 1. of infants or infancy. 2. very childish. □ **infantile paralysis**, polio.

infantry *n.* troops who fight on foot.

infatuated *adj.* temporarily filled with an intense unreasoning love for a person or thing. **infatuation** *n.*

infect *v.* 1. to affect or contaminate with a disease or with bacteria etc. that produce

a diseased condition. 2. to inspire with one's feeling.

infection *n.* 1. infecting, being infected. 2. the spreading of disease, especially by air or water etc. 3. a disease that is spread in this way, a diseased condition.

infectious *adj.* 1. (of a disease) able to spread by air or water etc. 2. infecting with disease. 3. quickly spreading to others, *his fear was infectious.*

infer *v.* (inferred, inferring) 1. to reach (an opinion) from facts or reasoning. 2. to imply. (¶ This use should be avoided because it conceals a useful distinction between *infer* and *imply*.) **inference** *n.*

inferable (in-**fer**-ăbŭl) *adj.* able to be inferred.

inferior *adj.* low or lower in rank or importance or quality or ability. —*n.* a person who is inferior to another, especially in rank. **inferiority** *n.* □ **inferiority complex**, a feeling of general inferiority, sometimes with aggressive behaviour in compensation; (*informal*) great lack of self-confidence.

infernal *adj.* 1. of hell, *the infernal regions.* 2. (*informal*) detestable, tiresome, *an infernal nuisance.* **infernally** *adv.*

inferno (in-**fer**-noh) *n.* (*pl.* infernos) a place resembling hell, somewhere intensely hot, a raging fire.

infertile *adj.* not fertile. **infertility** *n.*

infest *v.* (of pests or vermin etc.) to be numerous and troublesome in (a place). **infestation** *n.*

infidelity *n.* unfaithfulness.

infighting *n.* 1. boxing with an opponent nearer than arm's length. 2. hidden conflict within an organization.

infilling *n.* placing of buildings to occupy gaps between earlier ones.

infiltrate (**in**-fil-trayt) *v.* 1. to enter gradually and without being noticed, e.g. as settlers or spies. 2. to cause to do this. **infiltration** *n.*, **infiltrator** *n.*

infinite (**in**-fin-it) *adj.* 1. having no limit, endless. 2. too great or too many to be measured or counted. **infinitely** *adv.*

infinitesimal (in-fini-**tess**-imăl) *adj.* extremely small. **infinitesimally** *adv.*

infinitive (in-**fin**-itiv) *n.* a form of a verb that does not indicate a particular tense or number or person, in English used with or without *to*, e.g. *go* in 'let him go' or 'allow him to go'.

infinitude *n.* 1. being infinite. 2. infinity.

infinity (in-**fin**-iti) *n.* an infinite number or extent or time.

infirm *adj.* physically weak, especially from old age or illness; *infirm of purpose,* not resolute, hesitant.

infirmary *n.* **1.** a hospital. **2.** a room or rooms for sick people in a school or monastery etc.

infirmity *n.* **1.** being infirm. **2.** a particular physical weakness.

inflame *v.* **1.** to provoke to strong feeling or emotion, to arouse anger in. **2.** to cause inflammation in.

inflammable *adj.* able to be set on fire. ¶ This word means the same as *flammable*; its opposite is *non-inflammable*.

inflammation *n.* redness and heat and pain produced in the body, especially as a reaction to injury or infection.

inflammatory (in-**flam**-ă-ter-i) *adj.* likely to arouse strong feeling or anger, *inflammatory speeches*.

inflatable (in-**flayt**-ăbŭl) *adj.* able to be inflated.

inflate *v.* **1.** to fill or become filled with air or gas and swell up, to increase artificially; *at an inflated price*, an excessively high price.

inflation *n.* **1.** inflating, being inflated. **2.** a general increase of prices and fall in the purchasing value of money.

inflationary *adj.* causing inflation.

inflect *v.* **1.** to change the pitch of (the voice) in speaking. **2.** to change the ending or form of (a word) to show its grammatical relation or number etc., e.g. *sing* changes to *sang* or *sung*; *child* changes to *children*. **inflexion** *n.*

inflexible *adj.* **1.** not flexible, unable to be bent. **2.** not able to be altered, *an inflexible rule*. **3.** refusing to alter one's demands etc., unyielding. **inflexibly** *adv.*, **inflexibility** *n.*

inflict *v.* to cause (a blow or penalty etc.) to be suffered. **infliction** *n.*

inflorescence (in-flor-**ess**-ĕns) *n.* the head of a flower.

inflow *n.* an inward flow, the amount that flows in, *a large inflow of cash*.

influence *n.* **1.** the power to produce an effect, *the influence of the moon on the tides*. **2.** the ability to affect someone's character or beliefs or actions. **3.** a person or thing with this ability. —*v.* to exert influence on.

influential (in-floo-**en**-shăl) *adj.* having great influence.

influenza *n.* a virus disease causing fever, muscular pain, and catarrh.

influx *n.* an inflow, especially of people or things into a place.

inform *v.* **1.** to give information to. **2.** to reveal information to the police etc. about secret or criminal activities. □ **informed** *adj.* having good or sufficient knowledge of something, *informed opinion*.

informal *adj.* not formal, without formal-ity or ceremony. **informally** *adv.*, **informality** (in-for-**mal**-iti) *n.*

¶ In this dictionary, words marked *informal* are used in everyday speech but should not be used when speaking or writing formally.

informant *n.* a person who gives information.

information *n.* **1.** facts told or heard or discovered. **2.** facts fed into a computer etc. **3.** the process of informing. □ **information science** *or* **technology,** the study or use of processes (especially computers, microelectronics, and telecommunications) for storing, retrieving, and sending information of all kinds (e.g. words, numbers, pictures).

informative *adj.* giving information.

informer *n.* a person who reveals information to the police etc. about secret or criminal activities.

infra dig. (*informal*) beneath one's dignity. (¶ From the Latin *infra dignitatem*.)

infrangible (in-**fran**-ji-bŭl) *adj.* unbreakable, inviolable.

infra-red *adj.* **1.** (of radiation) having a wavelength that is slightly longer than that of visible light-rays at the red end of the spectrum. **2.** of or using this radiation.

infrastructure *n.* the subordinate parts and installations etc. that form the basis of an enterprise.

infrequent *adj.* not frequent. **infrequently** *adv.*, **infrequency** *n.*

infringe *v.* **1.** to break or act against (a rule or agreement etc.), to violate. **2.** to encroach, *do not infringe upon his rights.* **infringement** *n.*

infuriate *v.* to enrage.

infuse *v.* **1.** to imbue, to instil, *infused them with courage; infused courage into them.* **2.** to steep (tea or herbs etc.) in a liquid in order to make flavour or soluble constituents pass into the liquid, to allow (tea etc.) to undergo this process.

infusion *n.* **1.** infusing, being infused. **2.** a liquid made by infusing. **3.** something added or introduced into a stock, *an infusion of new blood to improve the breed.*

ingenious *adj.* **1.** clever at inventing new things or methods. **2.** cleverly contrived, *an ingenious machine.* **ingeniously** *adv.*, **ingenuity** (in-jin-**yoo**-iti) *n.*

ingenuous (in-**jen**-yoo-ŭs) *adj.* without artfulness, unsophisticated, *an ingenuous manner.* **ingenuously** *adv.*, **ingenuousness** *n.*

¶ Do not confuse with ingenious.

ingest (in-**jest**) *v.* to take in as food. **ingestion** *n.*

ingle-nook *n.* a nook forming a place for

sitting beside a deeply recessed fireplace.

inglorious *adj.* **1.** ignominious. **2.** not bringing glory, obscure.

ingot (**ing**-ŏt) *n.* a brick-shaped lump of cast metal.

ingrained *adj.* **1.** (of habits or feelings or tendencies) firmly fixed. **2.** (of dirt) marking a surface deeply.

ingratiate (in-**gray**-shi-ayt) *v.* **ingratiate oneself,** to bring oneself into a person's favour, especially in order to gain an advantage.

ingratitude *n.* lack of due gratitude.

ingredient *n.* one of the parts or elements in a mixture or combination.

ingrowing *adj.* growing abnormally into the flesh, *an ingrowing toe-nail.*

inhabit *v.* to live in (a place) as one's home or dwelling-place.

inhabitable *adj.* able to be inhabited.

inhabitant *n.* one who inhabits a place.

inhalant (in-**hay**-lănt) *n.* a medicinal substance to be inhaled.

inhale *v.* **1.** to breathe in, to draw into the lungs by breathing. **2.** to take tobacco-smoke into the lungs. **inhalation** (in-hă-**lay**-shŏn) *n.*

inhaler *n.* a device that produces or sends out a medicinal vapour to be inhaled.

inherent (in-**heer**-ĕnt) *adj.* existing in something as a natural or permanent characteristic or quality. **inherently** *adv.*

inherit *v.* **1.** to receive (property or a title etc.) by legal right of succession or by a will etc. when its previous owner or holder has died. **2.** to receive from a predecessor, *this government inherited many problems from the last one.* **3.** to receive (a characteristic) from one's parents or ancestors. **inheritor** *n.*

inheritance *n.* **1.** inheriting. **2.** a thing that is inherited.

inhibit *v.* **1.** to restrain, to prevent, *this substance inhibits the growth of moss.* **2.** to hinder the impulses of (a person), to cause inhibitions.

inhibition (in-hib-**ish**-ŏn) *n.* **1.** inhibiting, being inhibited. **2.** repression of or resistance to an instinct or impulse or feeling.

inhospitable (in-**hoss**-pit-ăbŭl *or* in-hoss-pit-**ă**bŭl) *adj.* **1.** not hospitable. **2.** (of a place or climate) giving no shelter or no favourable conditions.

inhuman *adj.* brutal, lacking normal human qualities of kindness, pity, etc. **inhumanity** (in-hew-**man**-iti) *n.*

inhumane (in-hew-**mayn**) *n.* not humane.

inimitable (in-**im**-it-ăbŭl) *adj.* impossible to imitate.

iniquitous (in-**ik**-wit-ŭs) *adj.* very unjust.

iniquity *n.* great injustice; wickedness.

initial *adj.* of or belonging to the beginning, *the initial stages of the work.* —*n.* the first letter of a word or name; *a person's initials,* those of his names, often used as a signature etc. —*v.* (initialled, initialling) to sign or mark with initials. —**initially** *adv.*

initiate (in-ish-i-ayt) *v.* **1.** to cause to begin, to start (a scheme) working, *he initiated certain reforms.* **2.** to admit (a person) into membership of a society etc., often with special ceremonies. **3.** to give (a person) basic instruction or information about something that is new to him. —*n.* an initiated person. **initiation** *n.,* **initiator** *n.*

initiative (in-ish-ă-tiv) *n.* **1.** the first step in a process. **2.** the power or right to begin something. **3.** the ability to initiate things, enterprise, *he lacks initiative.* □ **have the initiative,** to be in a position to control the course of events, e.g. in a war. **on one's own initiative,** without being prompted by others. **take the initiative,** to be the first to take action.

inject *v.* **1.** to force or drive (a liquid etc.) into something, especially by means of a syringe. **2.** to introduce (a new element), *inject some new ideas into the committee.*

injection *n.* **1.** injecting, an instance of this. **2.** a liquid etc. that is injected. □ **fuel injection,** the spraying of liquid fuel into the cylinder(s) of an internal-combustion engine.

injudicious (in-joo-**dish**-ŭs) *adj.* showing lack of good judgement, unwise. **injudiciously** *adv.*

injunction *n.* an order or command, especially an order from a lawcourt stating that something must or must not be done.

injure *v.* to cause injury to, to hurt.

injured *adj.* **1.** damaged, harmed, hurt. **2.** showing that one feels offended, *in an injured voice.* **3.** wronged, *the injured party in a divorce.*

injurious (in-**joor**-iŭs) *adj.* causing or likely to cause injury.

injury *n.* **1.** damage, harm. **2.** a particular form of this, *a leg injury.* **3.** a wrong or unjust act.

injustice *n.* **1.** lack of justice. **2.** an unjust action or treatment. □ **do a person an injustice,** to make an unfair judgement about him.

ink *n.* a coloured liquid used in writing with a pen, a coloured paste used in printing etc. and in ball-point pens. —*v.* to mark or cover with ink, to apply ink to; *ink these words out,* obliterate them with ink.

inkling *n.* a hint, a slight knowledge or suspicion.

inky *adj.* (inkier, inkiest) **1.** covered or stained with ink. **2.** black like ink, *inky darkness*.

inlaid *see* inlay¹.

inland *adj. & adv.* in or towards the interior of a country. **Inland Revenue,** the government department responsible for assessing and collecting taxes and inland duties.

in-laws *pl. n.* (*informal*) a person's relatives by marriage.

inlay¹ (in-**lay**) *v.* (inlaid, inlaying) to set (pieces of wood or metal etc.) into a surface so that they lie flush with it and form a design.

inlay² (in-**lay**) *n.* **1.** inlaid material. **2.** a design formed by this. **3.** a dental filling shaped to fit a tooth-cavity.

inlet *n.* **1.** a strip of water extending into the land from a sea or lake, or between islands. **2.** a piece of material inserted in a garment etc. **3.** a way in, e.g. for water into a tank, *the inlet pipe*.

inmate *n.* one of a number of inhabitants of a house or other building, especially a hospital or prison or other institution.

inmost *adj.* furthest inward.

inn *n.* **1.** a hotel, especially in the country. **2.** a public house. □ **Inn of Court,** any of the four law societies in London with the exclusive right of admitting people to practise as barristers in England; a similar society in Ireland.

innards *pl. n.* (*informal*) **1.** the stomach and bowels, entrails. **2.** any inner parts.

innate (in-**ayt**) *adj.* inborn.

inner *adj.* nearer to the centre or inside, interior, internal. —*n.* the division of a target next to the bull's eye, a shot that strikes this. □ **inner city,** the central area of a city, usually with overcrowding and poverty. **inner tube,** a separate inflatable tube inside the cover of a pneumatic tyre.

innermost *adj.* furthest inward.

innings *n.* (*pl.* innings) **1.** a batsman's or side's turn at batting in cricket. **2.** a period of power or of opportunity to show one's ability. **inning** *n.* a turn at batting in baseball.

innkeeper *n.* a person who keeps an inn.

innocent *adj.* **1.** not guilty of a particular crime etc. **2.** free of all evil or wrongdoing, *as innocent as a new-born babe*. **3.** harmless, not intended to be harmful, *innocent amusements; an innocent remark*. **4.** foolishly trustful. —*n.* a person (especially a child) who is free of all evil or who is foolishly trustful. —**innocently** *adv.*, **innocence** *n.*

innocuous (in-**ok**-yoo-ŭs) *adj.* harmless.

innovate *v.* to introduce a new process or way of doing things. **innovation** *n.*, **innovator** *n.*

innuendo (in-yoo-**en**-doh) *n.* (*pl.* innuendoes) an unpleasant insinuation.

innumerable *adj.* too many to be counted.

innumerate *adj.* not numerate. **innumeracy** *n.*

inoculate *v.* to treat (a person or animal) with vaccines or serums etc., especially in order to protect him or it against a disease. **inoculation** *n.*

inoffensive *adj.* not offensive, harmless.

inoperable (in-**op**-er-ăbŭl) *adj.* unable to be cured by surgical operation.

inoperative *adj.* not functioning.

inopportune (in-**op**-er-tewn) *adj.* coming or happening at an unsuitable time.

inordinate (in-**or**-din-ăt) *adj.* excessive.

inorganic (in-or-**gan**-ik) *adj.* of mineral origin, not organic. **inorganic chemistry,** a branch of chemistry dealing with inorganic substances.

input *n.* **1.** what is put in. **2.** the place where energy or information etc. enters a system. **3.** the data, programs, etc., supplied to a computer. —*v.* (input *or* inputted, inputting) to supply (data, programs, etc.) to a computer.

inquest *n.* **1.** a judicial investigation to establish facts, especially about a death which may not be the result of natural causes. **2.** (*informal*) a detailed discussion of something that is over, e.g. the playing of a card-game.

inquire *v.* to make an inquiry. **inquirer** *n.* □ **inquiry** *n.* an investigation, especially an official one. ¶ See the note under enquire.

inquisition (inkwi-**zish**-ŏn) *n.* a detailed questioning or investigation. **the Inquisition,** a tribunal of the Roman Catholic Church in the Middle Ages, especially the very severe one in Spain, to discover and punish heretics.

inquisitive *adj.* **1.** eagerly seeking knowledge. **2.** prying. **inquisitively** *adv.*

inquisitor (in-**kwiz**-it-er) *n.* a person who questions another searchingly.

inquisitorial (in-kwiz-i-**tor**-iăl) *adj.* of or like an inquisitor, prying.

inroad *n.* a sudden attack made into a country. **make inroads on** *or* **into,** to use up large quantities of (resources etc.).

inrush *n.* a rush in, a violent influx.

insalubrious (in-să-**loo**-briŭs) *adj.* (of a place or climate) unhealthy.

insane *adj.* **1.** not sane, mad. **2.** extremely foolish. **insanely** *adv.*, **insanity** *n.*

insanitary *adj.* unclean and likely to be harmful to health.

insatiable (in-say-shă-bŭl) *adj.* unable to be satisfied, *an insatiable appetite.* **insatiably** *adv.*

insatiate (in-saysh-yăt) *adj.* never satisfied.

inscribe *v.* 1. to write or cut words etc. on (a surface), *inscribed their names on the stone; inscribed it with their names.* 2. to draw (one geometrical figure) within another so that certain points of their boundaries coincide.

inscription *n.* words or names inscribed on a monument or coin or stone etc.

inscrutable (in-skroot-ăbŭl) *adj.* baffling, impossible to understand or interpret.

insect *n.* a small animal with six legs, no backbone, and a body divided into three parts (head, thorax, abdomen).

insecticide *n.* a substance for killing insects.

insectivorous (in-sek-tiv-er-ŭs) *adj.* feeding on insects.

insecure *adj.* not secure or safe. **insecurely** *adv.*, **insecurity** *n.*

inseminate (in-sem-in-ayt) *v.* to insert semen into. **insemination** *n.*

insensible *adj.* 1. unconscious. 2. without feeling, unaware, *seemed insensible of his danger.* 3. callous. 4. (of changes) imperceptible.

insensitive *adj.* not sensitive. **insensitivity** *n.*

insentient (in-sen-shĕnt) *adj.* not sentient.

inseparable *adj.* 1. unable to be separated. 2. liking to be constantly together, *inseparable companions.*

insert¹ (in-sert) *v.* to put (a thing) in or between or among. **insertion** *n.*

insert² (in-sert) *n.* a thing inserted.

inset¹ (in-set) *v.* (inset, insetting) to set or place in, to decorate with an inset, *the crown was inset with jewels.*

inset² (in-set) *n.* something set into a larger thing.

inshore *adv. & adj.* near or nearer to the shore.

inside *n.* 1. the inner side, surface, or part. 2. (*informal*) the organs in the abdomen, the stomach and bowels. —*adj.* on or coming from the inside; *inside information,* information that is not available to outsiders; *an inside job,* a crime committed by someone living or working on the premises where it occurred. —**inside** *adv.* 1. on or in or to the inside. 2. (*slang*) in prison. —*prep.* on the inner side of, within; *inside an hour,* in less than an hour. □ **inside left** *or* **right,** (in football etc.) a player on

the forward line near to the centre on the left or right side; his position. **inside out,** with the inner surface turned to face the outside; *turn a place inside out,* to search it thoroughly; *know a subject inside out,* to know it thoroughly.

insider *n.* an accepted member of a certain group.

insidious (in-sid-iŭs) *adj.* spreading or developing or acting inconspicuously but with harmful effect. **insidiously** *adv.*, **insidiousness** *n.*

insight *n.* 1. the ability to perceive and understand the true nature of something. 2. knowledge obtained by this.

insignia (in-sig-niă) *pl. n.* 1. the symbols of authority or office (e.g. the crown and sceptre of a king). 2. the identifying badge of a regiment etc.

insignificant *adj.* having little or no importance or value or influence. **insignificantly** *adv.*, **insignificance** *n.*

insincere *adj.* not sincere. **insincerely** *adv.*, **insincerity** *n.*

insinuate (in-sin-yoo-ayt) *v.* 1. to insert gradually or craftily, *insinuate oneself into a person's good graces.* 2. to hint artfully or unpleasantly. **insinuation** *n.*

insipid (in-sip-id) *adj.* 1. lacking in flavour. 2. lacking in interest or liveliness. **insipidity** (in-si-pid-iti) *n.*

insist *v.* 1. to declare emphatically. 2. to demand emphatically, *I insist on your being there.*

insistent *adj.* 1. insisting, declaring or demanding emphatically. 2. forcing itself on one's attention, *the insistent throb of the engines.* **insistently** *adv.*, **insistence** *n.*

insobriety (in-sŏ-bry-iti) *n.* lack of sobriety, drunkenness.

insole *n.* 1. the inner sole of a boot or shoe. 2. a loose piece of material laid in the bottom of a shoe for warmth or comfort.

insolent *adj.* behaving insultingly, arrogant, contemptuous. **insolently** *adv.*, **insolence** *n.*

insoluble *adj.* 1. unable to be dissolved. 2. unable to be solved, *an insoluble problem.* **insolubility** *n.*

insolvent *adj.* unable to pay one's debts. **insolvency** *n.*

insomnia *n.* inability to sleep sufficiently.

insomniac *n.* a person who suffers from insomnia.

insouciant (in-soo-si-ănt *or* an-soo-si-ahn) *adj.* carefree, unconcerned. **insouciance** *n.*

inspect *v.* 1. to examine (a thing) carefully and critically, especially looking for flaws. 2. to examine officially, to visit in order to make sure that rules and standards are being observed. **inspection** *n.*

inspector *n.* **1.** a person whose job is to inspect things or supervise services etc. **2.** a police officer above sergeant and below superintendent. □ **inspector of taxes,** an official assessing the amount of income tax to be paid.

inspiration *n.* **1.** inspiring. **2.** an inspiring influence. **3.** a sudden brilliant idea.

inspire *v.* **1.** to stimulate (a person) to creative or other activity or to express certain ideas. **2.** to fill with or instil a certain feeling, *he inspires confidence in us.* **3.** to communicate ideas etc. by a divine agency, *the prophets were inspired by God.*

inspiriting *adj.* encouraging.

inst. *abbrev.* instant, = of the current month, *on the 6th inst.* ¶ This use is regarded as artificial and undesirable.

instability *n.* lack of stability.

install *v.* **1.** to place (a person) in office, especially with ceremonies. **2.** to set (apparatus) in position and ready for use. **3.** to settle in a place, *he was comfortably installed in an armchair.*

installation (in-stă-**lay**-shŏn) *n.* **1.** installing, being installed. **2.** apparatus etc. installed.

instalment *n.* any of the parts in which something is presented or supplied, or a debt is paid, over a period of time.

instance *n.* a case or example of something. —*v.* to mention as an instance. □ **in the first instance,** firstly.

instant *adj.* **1.** occurring immediately, *there was instant relief.* **2.** (of food) designed to be prepared quickly and easily. —**instant** *n.* **1.** an exact point of time, the present moment, *come here this instant!* **2.** a very short space of time, a moment, *not an instant too soon.*

instantaneous (in-stăn-**tay**-niŭs) *adj.* occurring or done instantly, *death was instantaneous.* **instantaneously** *adv.*

instantly *adv.* immediately.

instead *adv.* as an alternative or substitute.

instep *n.* **1.** the upper surface of the foot between toes and ankle. **2.** the part of a shoe etc. covering this.

instigate *v.* to urge or incite, to bring about by persuasion, *instigated them to strike*; *instigated an inquiry.* **instigation** *n.*, **instigator** *n.*

instil *v.* (instilled, instilling) to implant (ideas etc.) into a person's mind gradually.

instinct *n.* **1.** an inborn impulse or tendency to perform certain acts or behave in certain ways. **2.** a natural ability, *has an instinct for finding a good place.*

instinctive *adj.* prompted by instinct. **instinctively** *adv.*

institute *n.* **1.** a society or organization for promotion of a scientific or educational or social etc. activity. **2.** the building used by this. —**institute** *v.* **1.** to establish, to found. **2.** to cause (an inquiry or a custom) to be started.

institution *n.* **1.** instituting, being instituted. **2.** an institute, especially for a charitable or social activity. **3.** an established law or custom or practice, (*informal*) a person who has become a familiar figure in some activity.

institutional *adj.* of or like an institution.

institutionalize *v.* **1.** to make (a thing) institutional. **2.** to place or keep (a person) in an institution that will provide the care he needs; *become institutionalized,* to be so used to living in an institution that one cannot live independently.

instruct *v.* **1.** to give (a person) instruction in a subject or skill. **2.** to inform, *we are instructed by our agents that you owe us £50.* **3.** to give instructions to. **4.** to authorize (a solicitor or counsel) to act on one's behalf. **instructor** *n.*, **instructress** *n.*

instruction *n.* **1.** the process of teaching. **2.** knowledge or teaching imparted. **3.** an expression in a computer program defining and effecting an operation. □ **instructions** *pl. n.* statements making known to a person what he is required to do; an order.

instructional *adj.* imparting knowledge.

instructive *adj.* giving or containing instruction, enlightening.

instrument *n.* **1.** a tool or implement used for delicate or scientific work. **2.** a measuring-device giving information about the operation of an engine etc. or used in navigation. **3.** a device designed for producing musical sounds, *musical instruments.* **4.** a person used and controlled by another to perform an action, *was made the instrument of another's crime.* **5.** a formal or legal document, *signed the instrument of abdication.*

instrumental *adj.* **1.** serving as an instrument or means of doing something, *was instrumental in finding her a job.* **2.** performed on musical instruments, *instrumental music.*

instrumentalist *n.* a musician who plays a musical instrument (as distinct from one who is a singer).

instrumentation *n.* **1.** the arrangement or composition of music for instruments.

2. the provision or use of mechanical or scientific instruments.

insubordinate *adj.* disobedient, rebellious. **insubordination** *n.*

insubstantial *adj.* **1.** not existing in reality, imaginary. **2.** not made of a strong or solid substance; *insubstantial evidence,* weak, not well founded.

insufferable *adj.* **1.** unbearable. **2.** unbearably conceited or arrogant.

insufficient *adj.* not sufficient. **insufficiently** *adv.*, **insufficiency** *n.*

insular (**ins**-yoo-ler) *adj.* **1.** of or on an island. **2.** of or like people who live on an island and are isolated from outside influences, narrow-minded, *insular prejudices.* **insularity** (ins-yoo-**la**-riti) *n.*

insulate (**ins**-yoo-layt) *v.* **1.** to cover or protect (a thing) with a substance or device that prevents the passage of electricity or sound or the loss of heat; *insulating tape,* tape that prevents the passage of electricity. **2.** to isolate (a person or place) from influences that might affect it. **insulation** *n.*, **insulator** *n.*

insulin (**ins**-yoo-lin) *n.* a hormone produced in the pancreas, controlling the absorption of sugar by the body.

insult¹ (in-**sult**) *v.* to speak or act in a way that hurts the feelings or pride of (a person) and rouses his anger.

insult² (**in**-sult) *n.* an insulting remark or action.

insuperable (in-**soop**-er-ăbŭl) *adj.* unable to be overcome, *an insuperable difficulty.*

insupportable *adj.* unbearable.

insurable *adj.* able to be insured.

insurance *n.* **1.** a contract undertaking to provide compensation for loss or damage or injury etc., in return for a payment made in advance once or regularly. **2.** the business of providing such contracts. **3.** the amount payable to the company etc. providing the contract, a premium. **4.** the amount payable by the company etc. in compensation. **5.** anything done as a safeguard against loss or failure etc. ¶ See the note under assurance.

insure *v.* **1.** to protect by a contract of insurance; *the insured,* the person protected by this. **2.** (*Amer.*) to ensure. **insurer** *n.*

insurgent (in-**ser**-jĕnt) *adj.* rebellious, rising in revolt. —*n.* a rebel.

insurmountable (in-ser-**mownt**-ăbŭl) *adj.* unable to be surmounted, insuperable.

insurrection (in-ser-**ek**-shŏn) *n.* rising in open resistance to established authority, rebellion.

insusceptible (in-sus-**ep**-tibŭl) *adj.* not susceptible.

intact *adj.* undamaged, complete.

intaglio (in-**tal**-yoh) *n.* (*pl.* intaglios) a kind of carving in which the design is sunk below the surface.

intake *n.* **1.** the process of taking something in, the place where liquid or air etc. is channelled into something. **2.** the number or quantity of people or things etc. accepted or received, *a school's annual intake of pupils.*

intangible (in-**tan**-jibŭl) *adj.* not tangible, not material.

integer (**in**-ti-jer) *n.* a whole number such as 0, 3, 19, etc., not a fraction.

integral (**in**-ti-grăl) *adj.* **1.** (of a part) constituent, necessary to the completeness of a whole, *Cornwall is an integral part of England.* **2.** complete, forming a whole, *an integral design.*

integrate (**in**-ti-grayt) *v.* **1.** to combine or form (a part or parts) into a whole. **2.** to bring or come into equal membership of a community. **integration** *n.* □ **integrated circuit,** a microchip, designed to replace a conventional circuit of many components.

integrity (in-**teg**-riti) *n.* honesty, incorruptibility.

integument (in-**teg**-yoo-mĕnt) *n.* skin.

intellect (**in**-ti-lekt) *n.* **1.** the mind's power of reasoning and acquiring knowledge (contrasted with feeling and instinct). **2.** ability to use this power, *people of intellect.*

intellectual (inti-**lek**-tew-ăl) *adj.* **1.** of the intellect. **2.** needing use of the intellect, *an intellectual occupation.* **3.** having a well-developed intellect and a taste for advanced knowledge. —*n.* an intellectual person. —**intellectually** *adv.*

intelligence *n.* **1.** mental ability, the power of learning and understanding. **2.** information, news, especially that of military value. **3.** the people engaged in collecting this. □ **intelligence quotient,** a number that shows how a person's intelligence compares with that of an average normal person.

intelligent *adj.* **1.** having great mental ability. **2.** (of a device in a computer system) containing in itself a capacity to process information. **intelligently** *adv.*

intelligentsia (in-tel-i-**jent**-siă) *n.* intellectual people regarded as a class.

intelligible (in-**tel**-i-jibŭl) *adj.* able to be understood. **intelligibly** *adv.*, **intelligibility** *n.*

intemperate *adj.* drinking alcohol excessively. **intemperance** *n.*

intend *v.* **1.** to have in mind as what one wishes to do or achieve. **2.** to plan that (a thing) shall be used or interpreted in a particular way, *we intended this room for you*; *the remark was intended as an insult.*

intense *adj.* **1.** strong in quality or degree, *intense heat.* **2.** (of a person) emotional. **intensely** *adv.*, **intensity** *n.*

intensify *v.* (intensified, intensifying) to make or become more intense. **intensification** *n.*

intensive *adj.* employing much effort, concentrated. **intensively** *adv.*

intent *n.* intention, *with intent to kill.* —*adj.* **1.** intending, having one's mind fixed on some purpose, *intent on killing.* **2.** with one's attention concentrated, *an intent gaze.* —**intently** *adv.*, **intentness** *n.* □ **to all intents and purposes**, practically, virtually.

intention *n.* what one intends to do or achieve, one's purpose.

intentional *adj.* done on purpose, intended, not accidental. **intentionally** *adv.*

inter (in-ter) *v.* (interred, interring) to bury (a dead body) in the earth or in a tomb.

inter- *prefix* between, among.

interact *v.* to have an effect upon each other. **interaction** *n.*

interactive *adj.* **1.** interacting. **2.** (in computers) allowing information to be transferred immediately both to and from a computer system and its user.

inter alia (ay-liă) among other things. (¶ Latin.)

interbreed *v.* (interbred, interbreeding) to breed with each other, to crossbreed.

intercede (inter-seed) *v.* to intervene on behalf of another person or as a peacemaker.

intercept[1] (inter-sept) *v.* to stop or catch (a person or thing) between his or its starting-point and destination. **interception** *n.*, **interceptor** *n.*

intercept[2] (in-ter-sept) *n.* **1.** a message or conversation that is picked up by intercepting a letter or a telephone or radio conversation. **2.** a device for performing such interception.

intercession (inter-sesh-ŏn) *n.* interceding.

interchange[1] (inter-chaynj) *v.* **1.** to put (each of two things) into the other's place. **2.** to make an exchange of, to give and receive (one thing for another). **3.** to alternate.

interchange[2] (in-ter-chaynj) *n.* **1.** interchanging. **2.** a road junction designed so that streams of traffic do not intersect on the same level.

interchangeable *adj.* able to be interchanged. **interchangeability** *n.*

intercom (in-ter-kom) *n.* (*informal*) a

system of communication operating like a telephone.

interconnected *adj.* connected.

intercontinental *adj.* connecting or carried on between two continents, (of missiles) able to be fired from one continent to another.

intercourse *n.* **1.** any dealings or communication between people or countries. **2.** sexual intercourse (*see* sexual), copulation.

interdependent *adj.* dependent on each other. **interdependence** *n.*

interdict[1] (inter-dikt) *v.* to prohibit or forbid authoritatively. **interdiction** *n.*

interdict[2] (in-ter-dikt) *n.* an authoritative prohibition.

interest *n.* **1.** a feeling of curiosity or concern about something. **2.** the quality of arousing such feeling, *the subject has no interest for me.* **3.** a thing towards which one feels it, *music is one of his interests.* **4.** advantage, benefit, *she looks after her own interests.* **5.** a legal right to a share in something, a financial stake in a business etc. **6.** money paid for the use of money lent; *return someone's kindness with interest,* give back more than one received. —**interest** *v.* **1.** to arouse the interest of. **2.** to cause to take an interest in, *interested herself in welfare work.*

interested *adj.* **1.** feeling or showing interest or curiosity. **2.** having a private interest in something, *interested parties.*

interesting *adj.* arousing interest.

interface *n.* **1.** a surface forming a common boundary between two regions. **2.** a place or piece of equipment where interaction occurs between two processes etc., (in computers etc.) a device designed to accept data in one format and transmit them in another. —*v.* to connect by means of an interface.

interfacing *n.* stiffish material placed between two layers of fabric in a garment etc.

interfere *v.* **1.** to take part in dealing with other people's affairs without right or invitation. **2.** to obstruct wholly or partially.

interference *n.* **1.** interfering. **2.** the fading of received radio signals because of atmospherics or unwanted signals.

interferon (inter-feer-on) *n.* a protein substance that prevents the development of a virus in living cells.

interim (in-ter-im) *n.* an intervening period of time, *in the interim.* —*adj.* of or in such a period; *an interim report,* one made before the main report, showing what has happened so far.

interior *adj.* nearer to the centre, inner. —*n.* **1.** an interior part or region, the central or inland part of a country. **2.** the inside of a building or room; *interior design* or *decoration*, decoration of this.

interject *v.* to put in (a remark) when someone is speaking.

interjection *n.* **1.** interjecting. **2.** an interjected remark. **3.** an exclamation such as *oh!* or *good heavens!*

interlace *v.* to weave or lace together.

interlard *v.* to insert contrasting remarks here and there in (a speech etc.), *interlarded his speech with quotations.*

interline *v.* to put an extra layer of material between the fabric of (a garment) and its lining in order to give firmness or extra warmth. **interlining** *n.* this material.

interlock *v.* to fit into each other, especially so that parts engage. —*n.* machine-knitted fabric with fine stitches.

interloper *n.* an intruder, one who interferes in the affairs of others.

interlude *n.* **1.** an interval between parts of a play etc. **2.** something performed during this. **3.** an intervening time or event etc. of a different kind from the main one.

intermarry *v.* (intermarried, intermarrying) **1.** (of tribes or nations or families etc.) to become connected by marriage. **2.** to marry within one's own family. **intermarriage** *n.*

intermediary (inter-**meed**-i-er-i) *n.* a mediator, a go-between. —*adj.* **1.** acting as an intermediary. **2.** intermediate in position or form.

intermediate *adj.* coming between two things in time or place or order.

interment (in-ter-**měnt**) *n.* burial.
¶ Do not confuse with internment.

intermezzo (inter-**mets**-oh) *n.* (*pl.* intermezzos) a short musical composition to be played between acts of a play etc. or between sections of a larger work or independently.

interminable (in-ter-min-ăbŭl) *adj.* endless, long and boring. **interminably** *adv.*

intermingle *v.* to mingle.

intermission *n.* an interval, a pause in work or action.

intermittent *adj.* occurring at intervals, not continuous, *intermittent rain.* **intermittently** *adv.*

intermix *v.* to mix.

intern (in-**tern**) *v.* to compel (an enemy alien or prisoner of war etc.) to live in a special area or camp.

internal *adj.* **1.** of or in the inside of a thing. **2.** of or in the interior of the body, *internal organs.* **3.** of the domestic affairs of a country. **internally** *adv.* □ **internal-combustion engine,** an engine that produces

power by burning fuel inside the engine itself rather than externally. **internal evidence,** evidence contained in the thing being discussed.

international *adj.* of or existing or agreed between two or more countries. —*n.* **1.** a sports contest between players representing different countries. **2.** one of these players. —**internationally** *adv.*

internecine (inter-**nee**-syn) *adj.* destructive to each of the parties involved, *internecine war.*

internee (in-ter-**nee**) *n.* a person who is interned.

internment *n.* interning, being interned.
¶ Do not confuse with interment.

interplanetary *adj.* between planets.

interplay *n.* interaction.

Interpol International Criminal Police Commission, an organization that coordinates investigations made by the police forces of member countries into crimes with an international basis.

interpolate (in-ter-pŏl-ayt) *v.* **1.** to interject. **2.** to insert (new material) misleadingly into a book etc. **interpolation** *n.*

interpose *v.* **1.** to insert between, to interject. **2.** to intervene.

interpret *v.* **1.** to explain the meaning of. **2.** to understand in a specified way. **3.** to act as interpreter. **interpretation** *n.*

interpretative (in-ter-prit-ătiv) *adj.* interpreting.

interpreter *n.* a person whose job is to translate a speech etc. into another language orally, in the presence of the speaker.

interregnum (inter-**reg**-nŭm) *n.* a period between the rule of two successive rulers.

interrelated *adj.* related to each other.

interrogate (in-te-rŏ-gayt) *v.* to question closely or formally. **interrogation** *n.*, **interrogator** *n.*

interrogative (inter-**rog**-ătiv) *adj.* questioning, having the form of a question, *an interrogative tone.* **interrogatively** *adv.* □ **interrogative pronoun,** *see* pronoun.

interrogatory (inter-**rog**-ă-ter-i) *adj.* questioning.

interrupt *v.* **1.** to break the continuity of. **2.** to break the flow of a speech etc. by inserting a remark. **3.** to obstruct (a view etc.). **interruption** *n.*, **interrupter** *n.*

intersect *v.* **1.** to divide (a thing) by passing or lying across it. **2.** (of lines or roads etc.) to cross each other.

intersection *n.* **1.** intersecting. **2.** a place where lines or roads etc. intersect.

intersperse *v.* to insert contrasting material here and there in (a thing).

interstellar *adj.* between stars.

interstice (in-ter-stiss) *n.* a small intervening space, a crevice.

intertwine *v.* to twine together, to entwine.

interval *n.* **1.** a time between two events or parts of an action. **2.** a pause between two parts of a performance. **3.** a space between two objects or points. **4.** the difference in musical pitch between two notes. ☐ **at intervals**, with some time or distance between, not continuous

intervene (inter-veen) *v.* **1.** to occur in the time between events, *in the intervening years*. **2.** to cause hindrance by occurring, *we should have finished harvesting but a storm intervened*. **3.** to enter a discussion or dispute etc. in order to change its course or resolve it. **intervention** (inter-ven-shŏn) *n.*

interview *n.* a formal meeting or conversation with a person, held in order to assess his merits as a candidate etc. or to obtain comments and information from him. *v.* to hold an interview with. — **interviewer** *n.*

interweave *v.* (interwove, interwoven, interweaving) to weave (strands etc.) into one another, to become woven together.

intestate (in-test-ăt) *adj.* not having made a valid will before death occurs, *he died intestate*. **intestacy** (in-test-asi) *n.*

intestine (in-test-in) *n.* the long tubular section of the alimentary canal, extending from the outlet of the stomach to the anus. **intestinal** *adj.* ☐ **large intestine**, the broader and shorter part of this, including the colon and rectum. **small intestine**, the narrower and longer part.

intimate¹ (in-tim-ăt) *adj.* **1.** having a close acquaintance or friendship with a person. **2.** having a sexual relationship with a person, especially outside marriage. **3.** private and personal. **4.** (of knowledge) detailed and obtained by much study or experience. —*n.* an intimate friend. —**intimately** *adv.*, **intimacy** *n.*

intimate² (in-tim-ayt) *v.* to make known, especially by hinting. **intimation** *n.*

intimidate (in-tim-i-dayt) *v.* to subdue or influence by frightening with threats or force. **intimidation** *n.*

into *prep.* **1.** to the inside of, to a point within, *went into the house*; *fell into the river*; *far into the night*. **2.** to a particular state or condition or occupation, *got into trouble*; *grew into an adult*; *went into banking*. **3.** actively interested and participating in, *he is into rock music*. **4.** (in mathematics) *4 into 20*, 20 divided by 4.

intolerable *adj.* unbearable. **intolerably** *adv.*

intolerant *adj.* not tolerant, unwilling to tolerate ideas or beliefs etc. that differ from one's own, *intolerant of opposition*. **intolerantly** *adv.*, **intolerance** *n.*

intonation (in-tŏn-ay-shŏn) *n.* **1.** intoning. **2.** the tone or pitch of the voice in speaking. **3.** a slight accent, *a Welsh intonation*.

intone *v.* to recite in a chanting voice, especially on one note.

intoxicant *adj.* causing intoxication. —*n.* intoxicant drink.

intoxicated *adj.* (of a person) drunk; *intoxicated by success*, made greatly excited or reckless by it. **intoxication** *n.*

intra- *prefix* within.

intractable (in-trakt-ăbŭl) *adj.* unmanageable, hard to deal with or control, *an intractable difficulty*; *intractable children*. **intractability** *n.*

intramuscular *adj.* into a muscle, *intramuscular injections*.

intransigent (in-transs-i-jĕnt) *adj.* unwilling to compromise, stubborn. **intransigence** *n.*

intransitive (in-transs-itiv) *adj.* (of a verb) used without being followed by a direct object, e.g. *hear* in *we can hear* (but not in *we can hear you*). **intransitively** *adv.*

intravenous (intră-vee-nŭs) *adj.* into a vein. **intravenously** *adv.*

intrepid (in-trep-id) *adj.* fearless, brave. **intrepidly** *adv.*, **intrepidity** (in-trip-id-iti) *n.*

intricate *adj.* very complicated. **intricately** *adv.*, **intricacy** (in-trik-ăsi) *n.*

intrigue (in-treeg) *v.* **1.** to plot with someone in an underhand way, to use secret influence. **2.** to rouse the interest or curiosity of, *the subject intrigues me*. — **intrigue** *n.* **1.** underhand plotting, an underhand plot. **2.** a secret love affair.

intrinsic (in-trin-sik) *adj.* belonging to the basic nature of a person or thing; *the intrinsic value of a coin*, the value of the metal in it as opposed to its face value. **intrinsically** *adv.*

introduce *v.* **1.** to make (a person) known by name to others. **2.** to announce (a speaker or broadcast programme etc.) to listeners or viewers. **3.** to bring (a bill) before Parliament. **4.** to cause (a person) to become acquainted with a subject. **5.** to bring (a custom or idea etc.) into use or into a system. **6.** to bring or put in, *introduce the needle into a vein*.

introduction *n.* **1.** introducing, being introduced. **2.** the formal presentation of one person to another. **3.** a short explanatory section at the beginning of a book or speech etc. **4.** an introductory treatise. **5.** a short preliminary section leading up to the main part of a musical composition.

introductory *adj.* introducing a person or subject.

introspection *n.* examination of one's own thoughts and feelings. **introspective** *adj.* characterized by introspection.

introvert (**in**-trŏ-vert) *n.* a person who is concerned more with his own thoughts and feelings than with the people and things round him, a shy person. **introverted** *adj.* having these characteristics.

intrude *v.* to come or join in without being invited or wanted. **intrusion** *n.*

intruder *n.* **1.** a person who intrudes. **2.** a burglar. **3.** an enemy aircraft over one's territory.

intrusive *adj.* intruding.

intuition (in-tew-**ish**-ŏn) *n.* the power of knowing or understanding something immediately without reasoning or being taught.

intuitive (in-**tew**-itiv) *adj.* of or possessing or based on intuition. **intuitively** *adv.*

inundate (**in**-ŭn-dayt) *v.* **1.** to flood, to cover with water. **2.** to overwhelm as if with a flood. **inundation** *n.*

inure (in-**yoor**) *v.* to accustom, especially to something unpleasant.

invade *v.* **1.** to enter (territory) with armed forces in order to attack or damage or occupy it. **2.** to crowd into, *tourists invaded the city.* **3.** to penetrate harmfully, *the disease had invaded all parts of the body.* **invader** *n.*

invalid[1] (**in**-vă-leed) *n.* a person who is weakened by illness or injury, one who suffers from ill health for a long time. —*v.* to remove from active service because of ill health or injury, *he was invalided out of the army.*

invalid[2] (in-**val**-id) *adj.* not valid. **invalidity** (in-vă-**lid**-iti) *n.* □ **invalidate** (in-**val**-i-dayt) *v.* to make invalid. **invalidation** *n.*

invaluable *adj.* having a value that is too great to be measured.

invariable (in-**vair**-i-ăbŭl) *adj.* not variable, always the same. **invariably** *adv.*

invasion *n.* invading, being invaded.

invasive (in-**vay**-siv) *adj.* invading; *an invasive plant,* one that spreads freely into areas where it is not wanted.

invective (in-**vek**-tiv) *n.* a violent attack in words, abusive language.

inveigh (in-**vay**) *v.* to attack violently or bitterly in words.

inveigle (in-**vay**-gŭl) *v.* to entice.

invent *v.* **1.** to create by thought, to make or design (something that did not exist before). **2.** to construct (a false or fictional story), *invented an excuse.* **inventor** *n.*

invention *n.* **1.** inventing, being invented. **2.** something invented.

inventive *adj.* able to invent things.

inventory (**in**-věn-ter-i) *n.* a detailed list of goods or furniture etc. —*v.* (inventoried, inventorying) to make an inventory of, to enter in an inventory.

inverse *adj.* reversed in position or order or relation; *in inverse proportion,* with the first quantity increasing in proportion as the other decreases, or vice versa. —*n.* **1.** an inverse state. **2.** a thing that is the exact opposite of another. —**inversely** *adv.*

invert *v.* to turn (a thing) upside-down, to reverse the position or order or relationship etc. of. **inversion** *n.* □ **inverted commas,** quotation-marks ' ' or " ".

invertebrate (in-**vert**-ibrăt) *adj.* not having a backbone. —*n.* an invertebrate animal.

invest *v.* **1.** to use (money) to buy stocks or shares or property etc. in order to earn interest or bring profit for the buyer. **2.** to spend money or time or effort on something that will be useful, *invest in a freezer.* **3.** to confer a rank or office or power upon (a person). **4.** to endow with a quality.

investigate *v.* **1.** to make a careful study of (a thing) in order to discover the facts about it. **2.** to make a search or systematic inquiry, to examine. **investigation** *n.*, **investigator** *n.*

investigatory (in-**vest**-i-gayt-er-i) *adj.* investigating.

investiture (in-**vest**-i-cher) *n.* the process of investing a person with rank or office etc., a ceremony at which the sovereign confers honours.

investment *n.* **1.** investing. **2.** a sum of money invested. **3.** something in which money or time or effort is invested.

investor *n.* one who invests money.

inveterate (in-**vet**-er-ăt) *adj.* **1.** habitual, *an inveterate smoker.* **2.** firmly established, *inveterate prejudices.*

invidious (in-**vid**-iŭs) *adj.* likely to cause resentment because of real or imagined injustice. **invidiously** *adv.*

invigilate (in-**vij**-i-layt) *v.* to supervise candidates at an examination. **invigilation** *n.*, **invigilator** *n.*

invigorate (in-**vig**-er-ayt) *v.* to fill with vigour, to give strength or courage to.

invincible (in-**vin**-si-bŭl) *adj.* unconquerable. **invincibly** *adv.*, **invincibility** *n.*

inviolable (in-vy-**ŏl**-ăbŭl) *adj.* not to be violated. **inviolability** *n.*

inviolate (in-vy-**ŏ**-lăt) *adj.* not violated.

invisible *adj.* not visible, unable to be seen.

invisibly adv., **invisibility** n. □ **invisible exports** or **imports**, payment for services (such as insurance or shipping) made to or by another country. **invisible ink**, colourless ink for writing words etc. that cannot be seen until the paper is heated or treated in some way.

invite v. **1.** to ask (a person) in a friendly way to come to one's house or to a gathering etc. **2.** to ask (a person) formally to do something. **3.** to ask for (comments, suggestions, etc.). **4.** to act so as to be likely to cause (a thing) unintentionally, *you are inviting disaster*. **5.** to attract, to tempt. —n. (*slang*) an invitation. **invitation** n.

inviting adj. attracting one to do something, pleasant and tempting.

invocation (invŏ-**kay**-shŏn) n. invoking, calling upon God in prayer.

invoice n. a list of goods sent or services performed, with prices and charges. —v. **1.** to make an invoice of (goods). **2.** to send an invoice to (a person).

invoke (in-**vohk**) v. **1.** to call upon (God) in prayer. **2.** to call for the help or protection of, *invoked the law*. **3.** to summon up (a spirit) with words.

involuntary adj. done without intention or without conscious effort of the will; *an involuntary movement* (e.g. jumping when startled). **involuntarily** adv.

involve v. **1.** to contain within itself, to make necessary as a condition or result, *the plan involves much expense*. **2.** to include or affect in its operation, *the safety of the nation is involved*. **3.** to bring (a person or thing) into difficulties, *it will involve us in much expense*. **4.** to show (a person) to be concerned in a crime etc. **involvement** n.

involved adj. **1.** complicated. **2.** concerned in something.

invulnerable (in-**vul**-ner-ăbŭl) adj. not vulnerable. **invulnerability** n.

inward adj. **1.** situated on the inside. **2.** going towards the inside. **3.** in the mind or spirit, *inward happiness*. —adv. inwards. □

inwardly adv. on the inside; in the mind or spirit. **inwards** adv. towards the inside; in the mind or spirit.

iodine (**I**-ŏ-deen) n. a chemical substance found in seawater and certain seaweeds, used in solution as an antiseptic.

iodize (**I**-ŏ-dyz) v. to impregnate with iodine or a compound of it.

IOM abbrev. Isle of Man.

ion (**I**-ŏn) n. one of the electrically charged particles in certain substances.

Ionic (I-**on**-ik) adj. of the *Ionic order*, one of the five classical orders of architecture, characterized by columns with a scroll-like ornamentation at the top.

ionize (I-ŏ-nyz) v. to convert or be converted into ions. **ionization** n.

ionosphere (I-**on**-ŏ-sfeer) n. an ionized region of the upper atmosphere, able to reflect radio waves for transmission to another part of the earth.

iota (I-**oh**-tă) n. **1.** the Greek letter i. **2.** the smallest possible amount, a jot, *it doesn't make an iota of difference*.

IOU n. a signed paper acknowledging that one owes a sum of money to the holder (= *I owe you*).

IOW abbrev. Isle of Wight.

Iowa (I-ŏ-wă) a State of the USA.

ipecacuanha (ipi-kak-yoo-**an**-ă) n. the dried root of a South American plant, used as an emetic or purgative.

ipso facto (ip-soh **fak**-toh) by that very fact or act. (¶ Latin.)

IQ abbrev. intelligence quotient.

IRA abbrev. Irish Republican Army, an organization seeking to achieve by force a united Ireland independent of Britain.

Iran (i-**rahn**) a country in south-west Asia, Persia. **Iranian** (I-**ray**-niăn) adj. & n.

Iraq (i-**rahk**) a country lying between Iran and Saudi Arabia. **Iraqi** (i-**rah**-ki) adj. & n. (*pl.* Iraqis)

irascible (i-**ras**-ibŭl) adj. irritable, hot-tempered. **irascibly** adv., **irascibility** n.

irate (I-**rayt**) adj. angry, enraged. **irately** adv.

ire n. anger.

Ireland an island west of Great Britain, divided into Northern Ireland (which forms part of the UK) and the Republic of Ireland.

iridescent (i-ri-**dess**-ĕnt) adj. showing rainbow-like colours, showing a change of colour when its position is altered. **iridescence** n.

iris n. **1.** the flat circular coloured membrane in the eye, with a circular opening (the *pupil*) in the centre. **2.** a plant with sword-shaped leaves and showy (often purple) flowers with large petals.

Irish adj. of Ireland or its people or language. —n. **1.** the Celtic language of Ireland. **2.** *the Irish*, people of Irish birth or descent. **3.** (*informal*) bad temper; *with his Irish up*, angry. —**Irishman, Irishwoman** ns. □ **Irish stew**, a stew of mutton, potatoes, and onions.

irk v. to annoy, to be tiresome to.

irksome adj. tiresome.

iron n. **1.** a very common hard grey metal, capable of being magnetized. **2.** a tool made of this, *branding iron*. **3.** a golf-club with an iron or steel head. **4.** an implement with a flat base that is heated for smoothing cloth or clothes etc. **5.** a metal splint or support worn on the leg. **6.** a preparation of iron as a tonic. **7.** something thought to be as unyielding as iron, *a will of iron.* — **iron** *adj.* **1.** made of iron. **2.** as strong or unyielding as iron, *an iron constitution*; *an iron will.* —*v.* to smooth (clothes etc.) with an iron; *iron out the difficulties,* deal with and remove them. □ **Iron Age,** the period when weapons and tools were made of iron. **Iron Curtain,** an invisible barrier of secrecy and restriction, preventing the free passage of people and information between the USSR (and countries under its influence) and the Western world. **iron-grey** *adj.* & *n.* grey like the colour of freshly-broken iron. **ironing-board** *n.* a narrow flat strip on which clothes etc. are ironed. **iron lung,** a rigid case fitting over a patient's body, used for administering artificial respiration for a prolonged period by means of mechanical pumps. **iron-mould** *n.* a brown spot caused by iron rust. **iron rations,** a small supply of tinned food etc. to be used only in an emergency. **irons** *pl. n.* fetters, *in irons.* **many irons in the fire,** many undertakings or resources.

ironic (I-**ron**-ik), **ironical** (I-**ron**-ikăl) *adjs.* using or expressing irony. **ironically** *adv.*

ironmonger (I-ern-mung-er) *n.* a shopkeeper who sells tools and household implements etc. **ironmongery** *n.* an ironmonger's shop or goods.

ironstone *n.* **1.** hard iron ore. **2.** a kind of hard white pottery.

ironwork *n.* articles such as gratings, rails, railings, etc. made of iron.

ironworks *n.* a place where iron is smelted or where heavy iron goods are made.

irony (I-rŏn-i) *n.* **1.** the expression of one's meaning by using words of the opposite meaning in order to make one's remarks forceful, e.g. *that will please him* (used of something that will not please him at all). **2.** (of an occurrence) the quality of being so unexpected or ill-timed that it appears to be deliberately perverse.

irradiate (i-ray-di-ayt) *v.* to shine upon, to subject to radiation. **irradiation** *n.*

irrational (i-**rash**-ŏn-ăl) *adj.* **1.** not rational, not guided by reasoning, illogical, *irrational fears* or *behaviour.* **2.** not capable of reasoning. **irrationally** *adv.*, **irrationality** *n.*

irreconcilable *adj.* unable to be reconciled. **irreconcilably** *adv.*

irrecoverable *adj.* unable to be recovered. **irrecoverably** *adv.*

irredeemable *adj.* unable to be re-

deemed. **irredeemably** *adv.*

irreducible (i-ri-**dew**-sibŭl) *adj.* unable to be reduced, *an irreducible minimum.*

irrefutable (i-**ref**-yoo-tăbŭl) *adj.* unable to be refuted. **irrefutably** *adv.*

irregular *adj.* **1.** not regular, uneven, varying. **2.** contrary to rules or to established custom. **3.** (of troops) not belonging to the regular armed forces. **irregularly** *adv.*, **irregularity** *n.*

irrelevant (i-**rel**-i-vănt) *adj.* not relevant. **irrelevantly** *adv.*, **irrelevance** *n.*

irreligious (i-ri-**lij**-ŭs) *adj.* not religious, irreverent.

irremovable (i-ri-**moo**-văbŭl) *adj.* unable to be removed.

irreparable (i-**rep**-er-ăbŭl) *adj.* unable to be repaired or made good, *irreparable damage* or *loss.*

irreplaceable *adj.* unable to be replaced, being a loss that cannot be made good.

irrepressible (i-ri-**press**-ibŭl) *adj.* unable to be repressed or restrained.

irreproachable *adj.* blameless, faultless.

irresistible *adj.* too strong or convincing or delightful to be resisted. **irresistibly** *adv.*

irresolute (i-**rez**-ŏ-loot) *adj.* feeling or showing uncertainty, hesitating.

irrespective *adj.* not taking something into account, *prizes are awarded to winners irrespective of nationality.*

irresponsible *adj.* not showing a proper sense of responsibility. **irresponsibly** *adv.*

irretrievable *adj.* not retrievable. **irretrievably** *adv.*

irreverent *adj.* not reverent, not respectful. **irreverently** *adv.*, **irreverence** *n.*

irreversible *adj.* not reversible, unable to be altered or revoked.

irrevocable (i-**rev**-ŏk-ăbŭl) *adj.* unable to be revoked, final and unalterable. **irrevocably** *adv.*

irrigate *v.* **1.** to supply (land or crops) with water by means of streams, channels, pipes, etc. **2.** to wash (a wound) with a constant flow of liquid. **irrigation** *n.*

irritable *adj.* easily annoyed, bad-tempered. **irritably** *adv.*, **irritability** *n.*

irritant *adj.* causing irritation. —*n.* something that causes irritation.

irritate *v.* **1.** to annoy, to rouse impatience or slight anger in (a person). **2.** to cause itching. **irritation** *n.*

is *see* be.

ISBN *abbrev.* international standard book number.

ischium (isk-iŭm) *n.* the curved bone forming the base of each half of the pelvis.

Islam (iz-lahm) *n.* **1.** the Muslim religion, based on the teaching of Muhammad.

2. the Muslim world. **Islamic** (iz-**lam**-ik) *adj.*

Islamabad (iz-**lahm**-ă-bad) the capital of Pakistan.

island (**I**-lănd) *n.* **1.** a piece of land surrounded by water. **2.** something resembling this because it is detached or isolated; *a traffic island*, a paved or raised area in the middle of a road, where people crossing may be safe from traffic. □ **islander** *n.* an inhabitant of an island.

isle (*rhymes with* mile) *n.* an island. **Isle of Wight**, an island off the south coast of England, a county of England.

isn't = is not.

isobar (**I**-sŏ-bar) *n.* a line, drawn on a map, connecting places that have the same atmospheric pressure.

isolate *v.* **1.** to place apart or alone. **2.** to separate (an infectious person) from others. **3.** to separate (one substance etc.) from a compound. **isolation** *n.*

isolationism *n.* the policy of holding aloof from other countries or groups.

isometric (I-sŏ-**met**-rik) *adj.* **1.** (of muscle action) developing tension while the muscle is prevented from contracting. **2.** (of a drawing or projection) drawing a three-dimensional object, without perspective, so that equal lengths along the three axes are drawn equal.

isosceles (I-**sos**-i-leez) *adj.* (of a triangle) having two sides equal.

isotherm (**I**-sŏ-therm) *n.* a line, drawn on a map, connecting places that have the same temperature.

isotope (**I**-sŏ-tohp) *n.* one of two or more forms of a chemical element with different atomic weight and different nuclear properties but the same chemical properties.

Israel[1] *n.* the Hebrew nation or people (also called *children of Israel*) traditionally descended from Jacob. **Israelite** *adj. & n.*

Israel[2] a country in the Middle East, at the eastern end of the Mediterranean Sea. **Israeli** (iz-**ray**-li) *adj. & n.* (*pl.* **Israelis**)

issue *n.* **1.** an outgoing or outflow. **2.** the issuing of things for use or for sale, the number or quantity issued. **3.** one set of publications in a series issued regularly, *the May issue*. **4.** a result, an outcome. **5.** the point in question, an important topic for discussion, *what are the real issues?* **6.** offspring, *died without male issue.* —**issue** *v.* **1.** to come or go or flow out. **2.** to supply or distribute for use, *campers were issued with blankets*. **3.** to put out for sale, to publish. **4.** to send out, *issue orders*. **5.** to result, to originate. □ **at issue**, being discussed or disputed or risked. **join** *or* **take issue**, to proceed to argue.

isthmus (**iss**-mŭs) *n.* (*pl.* isthmuses) a narrow strip of land connecting two masses of land that would otherwise be separated by water.

it *pronoun* **1.** the thing mentioned or being discussed. **2.** the person in question, *who is it?; it's me.* **3.** used as the subject of a verb making a general statement about the weather (e.g. *it is raining*) or about circumstances etc. (e.g. *it is 6 miles to Oxford*), or as an indefinite object (*run for it!*). **4.** used as the subject or object of a verb, with reference to a following clause or phrase, e.g. *it is seldom that he fails*; *I take it that you agree.* **5.** exactly what is needed. **6.** (in children's games) the player who has to catch others. ¶ See the note under its.

Italian *adj.* of Italy or its people or language. —*n.* **1.** a native of Italy. **2.** the Italian language.

italic (i-**tal**-ik) *adj.* **1.** (of printed letters) sloping *like this.* **2.** (of handwriting) compact and pointed like an early form of Italian handwriting. □ **italics** *pl. n.* sloping printed letters *like these.*

italicize (i-**tal**-i-syz) *v.* to put into italics. **italicization** *n.*

Italy a country in southern Europe.

itch *n.* **1.** an itching feeling in the skin. **2.** a restless desire or longing. —**itch** *v.* **1.** to have or feel a tickling sensation in the skin, causing a desire to scratch the affected part. **2.** to feel a restless desire or longing. —**itchy** *adj.* □ **have an itching palm**, to be greedy for money.

item *n.* **1.** a single thing in a list or number of things. **2.** a single piece of news in a newspaper or bulletin.

itemize *v.* to list, to state the individual items involved.

itinerant (i-**tin**-er-ănt) *adj.* travelling from place to place, *an itinerant preacher.*

itinerary (I-**tin**-er-er-i) *n.* a route, a list of places to be visited on a journey.

it'll = it will.

its *possessive pronoun*, of or belonging to it. ¶ Do not confuse with *it's*, which has a different meaning (see the next entry). The word *its* is the possessive form of *it*, and (like *hers*, *ours*, *theirs*, *yours*) has no apostrophe; correct usage is *wagged its tail* (not *it's*), *the dog is hers* (not *her's*), *these are ours* (not *our's*).

it's = it is, it has, *it's very hot*; *it's broken all records.* ¶ Do not confuse with its.

itself *pronoun* corresponding to *it*, used in the same ways as himself.

ITV *abbrev.* Independent Television.

IUD *abbrev.* intra-uterine device, a coil

placed inside the womb as a contraceptive.

ivory *n.* **1.** the hard creamy-white substance forming the tusks of elephants etc.
2. an object made of this. **3.** creamy-white
colour. —*adj.* creamy-white. □ **ivory
tower**, a place or situation where people
live secluded from the harsh realities of
everyday life.

Ivory Coast a country in West Africa.

ivy *n.* a climbing evergreen shrub with
shiny often five-pointed leaves.

ixia (**iks**-iă) *n.* a plant of the iris family.

Jj

jab *v.* (jabbed, jabbing) to poke roughly,
to thrust (a thing) into. —*n.* **1.** a rough
blow or thrust, especially with something
pointed. **2.** (*informal*) an injection.

jabber *v.* **1.** to talk rapidly and
unintelligibly. **2.** to chatter like monkeys. —
n. jabbering talk or sound.

jabot (*zh*ab-oh) *n.* ornamental frilling down
the front of a shirt or blouse or dress.

jacaranda *n.* **1.** a tropical American tree
with hard scented wood. **2.** a tropical tree
with blue flowers.

jack *n.* **1.** a portable device for raising
heavy weights off the ground, especially
one for raising the axle of a motor vehicle
so that a wheel may be changed. **2.** a ship's
flag (smaller than an ensign) flown at the
bow of a ship to show its nationality. **3.** a
playing-card ranking below a queen in
card-games. **4.** a small white ball aimed at
in the game of bowls. **5.** a male donkey.
6. (*slang*) a detective. —*v.* to raise with a
jack. □ **before you can say Jack Robinson**, very quickly or suddenly. **every
man Jack**, every individual man. **Jack
Frost**, frost personified. **jack-in-office** *n.*
a fussy conceited official. **jack-in-the-box**
n. a toy figure that springs out of a box when
the lid is lifted. **jack of all trades**, one who
can do many different kinds of work.

jackal (**jak**-awl) *n.* a wild flesh-eating
animal of Africa and Asia, related to the
dog, formerly supposed to hunt up the
lion's prey for him.

jackass *n.* **1.** a male donkey. **2.** a stupid or
foolish person.

jackdaw *n.* a thievish small crow.

jacket *n.* **1.** a short coat, usually reaching
to the hips. **2.** an outer covering round a
boiler or water-tank etc. to lessen loss of
heat. **3.** a coloured paper wrapper in which
a bound book is issued. **4.** the skin of a

potato baked without being peeled, *baked
in their jackets.*

jack-knife *n.* **1.** a large clasp-knife. **2.** a
dive in which the body is first bent double
and then straightened. —*v.* (of an articulated vehicle) to fold one part against another accidentally.

jackpot *n.* the accumulated stakes in various games, increasing in value until won.
hit the jackpot, to have sudden great
success or good fortune.

Jacobean (jak-ŏ-**bee**-ăn) *adj.* of the reign
of James I of England (1603–25).

Jacobite (**jak**-ŏ-byt) *n.* a supporter of
James II of England after his abdication
(1688), or of the exiled Stuarts.

jacquard (**jak**-ard) *n.* a fabric woven with
an intricate figured pattern.

Jacuzzi (ja-**koo**-zi) *n.* (*trade mark*) a bath
in which underwater jets of water are projected against the body.

jade *n.* **1.** a hard green, blue, or white
stone from which ornaments are carved.
2. its green colour.

jaded *adj.* **1.** feeling or looking tired and
bored. **2.** (of the appetite) dulled, lacking
zest for food.

Jaffa *n.* a large oval thick-skinned variety
of orange, originally grown near the port
of Jaffa in Israel.

jag *n.* (*slang*) a drinking-bout, a spree.

Jag *n.* (*informal*) a Jaguar car.

jagged (**jag**-id) *adj.* having an uneven
edge or outline with sharp projections.

jaguar *n.* a large flesh-eating animal of the
cat family, found in tropical America.

jail *n.* = gaol.

Jain (*rhymes with* mine) *n.* a member of an
Indian sect with doctrines like those of
Buddhism. —*adj.* of this sect.

Jakarta (jă-**kar**-tă) the capital of Indonesia.

jalopy (jă-**lop**-i) *n.* a battered old car.

jam¹ *v.* (jammed, jamming) **1.** to squeeze
or wedge into a space, to become wedged.
2. to make (part of a machine) immovable
so that the machine will not work, to
become unworkable in this way. **3.** to
crowd or block (an area) with people or
things. **4.** to thrust or apply forcibly,
jammed the brakes on. **5.** to cause interference to (a radio transmission), making it
unintelligible. —**jam** *n.* **1.** a squeeze or
crush or stoppage caused by jamming. **2.** a
crowded mass making movement difficult,
traffic jams. **3.** (*informal*) a difficult situation, *I'm in a jam.* □ **jam-packed** *adj.*
(*informal*) packed full and tightly. **jam
session**, improvised playing by a group
of jazz musicians.

jam² *n.* **1.** a sweet substance made by boiling fruit with sugar to a thick consistency. **2.** (*informal*) something easy or pleasant. —**jam** *v.* (jammed, jamming) **1.** to spread with jam. **2.** to make into jam.

Jamaica an island in the Caribbean Sea. **Jamaican** *adj.* & *n.*

jamb (*pr.* jam) *n.* the vertical side post of a doorway or window frame.

jamboree (jam-ber-**ee**) *n.* **1.** a large party, a celebration. **2.** a large rally of Scouts.

jammy *adj.* smeared with jam.

jangle *n.* a harsh metallic sound. —*v.* **1.** to make or cause to make this sound. **2.** to cause irritation to (nerves etc.) by discord.

janitor (jan-it-er) *n.* the caretaker of a building. **janitorial** (jan-i-**tor**-iǎl) *adj.*

January the first month of the year.

Jap *n.* & *adj.* (*informal*) = Japanese.

Japan a country in eastern Asia. **Japanese** *adj.* & *n.* (*pl.* Japanese)

japanned (jǎ-**pand**) *adj.* made black and glossy with a kind of hard varnish.

japonica (jǎ-**pon**-ikǎ) *n.* an ornamental variety of quince, with red flowers.

jar¹ *n.* **1.** a cylindrical container made of glass or earthenware. **2.** this with its contents, the amount it contains. **3.** (*informal*) a glass of beer etc.

jar² *v.* (jarred, jarring) **1.** to make a sound that has a discordant or painful effect. **2.** (of an action etc.) to be out of harmony, to have a harsh or disagreeable effect. **3.** to cause an unpleasant jolt or a sudden shock. —*n.* a jarring movement or effect.

jardinière (*z*har-din-**yair**) *n.* a large ornamental pot for holding indoor plants.

jargon *n.* words or expressions developed for use within a particular group, hard for outsiders to understand and sounding ugly, *scientists' jargon.*

jasmine *n.* a shrub with yellow or white flowers.

jasper *n.* an opaque variety of quartz, usually red, yellow, or brown.

jaundice (**jawn**-dis) *n.* a condition in which the skin becomes abnormally yellow as a result of excessive bile in the bloodstream. **jaundiced** *adj.* discoloured by jaundice; filled with resentment or jealousy.

jaunt *n.* a short trip, especially one taken for pleasure. **jaunting** *n.* making a jaunt. □ **jaunting-car** *n.* a light two-wheeled horse-drawn vehicle used in Ireland.

jaunty *adj.* (jauntier, jauntiest) **1.** cheerful and self-confident in manner. **2.** (of clothes) stylish and cheerful. **jauntily** *adv.*, **jauntiness** *n.*

Java (jah-vǎ) an island of Indonesia. **Javanese** *adj.* & *n.* (*pl.* Javanese)

javelin (jav-ĕlin) *n.* a light spear.

jaw *n.* **1.** either of the two bones that form the framework of the mouth and in which the teeth are set. **2.** the lower of these, the part of the face covering it. **3.** (*informal*) talkativeness, a lecture, a gossiping talk. —*v.* (*slang*) to talk long and boringly, to gossip. □ **jaw-bone** *n.* either of the bones of the jaw. **jaw-breaker** *n.* a word that is very long or difficult to pronounce. **jaw-line** *n.* the outline of the lower jaw. **jaws** *pl. n.* something resembling a pair of jaws, e.g. the gripping-part of a tool.

jay *n.* a noisy chattering bird with bright blue, black, and white feathers.

jay-walking *n.* walking carelessly in a road, without regard for traffic. **jaywalker** *n.*

jazz *n.* **1.** a type of music with strong rhythm and much syncopation, often improvised. **2.** (*slang*) a matter, especially something regarded as pretentious or as nonsense, *talked of the honour of the firm and all that jazz.* —**jazz** *v.* **1.** to play or arrange as jazz. **2.** to brighten, *jazz it up.*

jazzy *adj.* **1.** of or like jazz. **2.** (*slang*) flashy, showy, *a jazzy sports car.*

jealous (jel-ŭs) *adj.* **1.** feeling or showing resentment towards a person whom one thinks of as a rival. **2.** taking watchful care, *is very jealous of his own rights.* **jealously** *adv.*, **jealousy** *n.*

jeans *pl. n.* trousers of strong twilled cotton for informal wear.

Jeep *n.* (*trade mark*) a small sturdy motor vehicle with four-wheel drive.

jeer *v.* to laugh or shout at rudely and scornfully. *n.* a jeering remark or shout.

Jehovah (ji-hoh-vǎ) the name of God in the Old Testament. **Jehovah's Witnesses,** an organization believing that the end of the world is near for all except their own adherents, and rejecting allegiance to any country.

jejune (ji-**joon**) *adj.* **1.** scanty, poor, (of land) barren. **2.** unsatisfying to the mind.

Jekyll-and-Hyde *adj.* having a dual personality, one good and the other evil. ¶ Named after the hero of a story (by R. L. Stevenson) who could transform himself from the respectable Dr Jekyll into the evil Mr Hyde by means of a potion which he drank.

jell *v.* (*informal*) **1.** to set as jelly. **2.** to take definite form, *our ideas began to jell.*

jellaba (jel-ǎ-bǎ) *n.* a loose hooded cloak worn by Arab men in some countries.

jellied *adj.* set in jelly, *jellied eels.*

jelly n. **1.** a soft solid food made of liquid set with gelatine, especially one prepared in a mould as a sweet dish. **2.** a kind of jam made of strained fruit juice and sugar. **3.** a substance of similar consistency, *petroleum jelly*. **4.** (*slang*) gelignite.

jellyfish n. (*pl.* jellyfish) a sea animal with a jelly-like body and stinging tentacles.

jemmy n. a short crowbar used by burglars to force doors and windows and drawers.

jenny n. a female donkey.

jeopardize (jep-er-dyz) v. to endanger.

jeopardy (jep-er-di) n. danger.

jerboa (jer-boh-ă) n. a small rat-like animal of the North African desert, with long hind legs used for leaping.

jeremiad (je-ri-my-ăd) n. a long mournful lament about one's troubles. ¶ Named after *Jeremiah*, a Hebrew prophet (7th–6th centuries BC) and the book of the Old Testament containing his account of the troubles of the Jews at that time.

Jeremiah (je-ri-my-ah) n. a pessimistic person. (¶ See the note on *Jeremiad*.)

jerk n. **1.** a sudden sharp movement, an abrupt pull or push or throw. **2.** (*slang*) a stupid or insignificant person. —v. to pull or throw or stop with a jerk, to move with a jerk or in short uneven movements.

jerkin n. a sleeveless jacket.

jerky adj. making abrupt starts and stops, not moving or acting smoothly. **jerkily** adv., **jerkiness** n.

jerry-built adj. built badly and with poor materials.

jerrycan n. a kind of 5-gallon can for petrol or water.

jersey n. **1.** plain machine-knitted fabric used for making clothes. **2.** (*pl.* jerseys) a close-fitting woollen pullover with sleeves.

Jersey n. (*pl.* Jerseys) one of a breed of light-brown dairy cattle originally from the island of Jersey.

Jerusalem 1. the ancient capital of Judaea; the holy city of the Jews, sacred also to Christians and Muslims. **2.** the capital of modern Israel.

jest n. a joke. —v. to make jokes. □ **in jest**, in fun, not seriously.

jester n. **1.** a person who makes jokes. **2.** a professional entertainer employed at a king's court in the Middle Ages.

Jesuit (jez-yoo-it) n. a member of the Society of Jesus, a Roman Catholic religious order.

jet[1] n. **1.** a hard black mineral that can be polished, used as a gem. **2.** its colour, deep glossy black. **jet-black** adj.

jet[2] n. **1.** a stream of water, gas, or flame etc. shot out from a small opening. **2.** a spout or opening from which this comes, a burner on a gas cooker. **3.** a jet engine, a jet-propelled aircraft. —**jet** v. (jetted, jetting) **1.** to spurt in jets. **2.** (*informal*) to travel or convey by jet-propelled aircraft. □ **jet engine**, an engine using jet propulsion to give forward thrust. **jet-foil** n. a vessel that travels above the surface of the water on struts attached to underwater hydrofoils. **jet lag**, delayed physical effects of tiredness etc. felt after a long flight by jet-propelled aircraft. **jet-propelled** adj. propelled by jet engines. **jet propulsion**, propulsion by engines that give forward thrust by sending out a high-speed jet of gases etc. at the back. **jet set**, wealthy people making frequent air journeys between social or business events. **jet stream**, a jet from a jet engine; a strong wind blowing in a narrow range of altitudes in the upper atmosphere.

jetsam n. goods thrown overboard from a ship in distress to lighten it, especially those that are washed ashore.

jettison v. **1.** to throw (goods) overboard or (goods or fuel) from an aircraft, especially to lighten a ship or aircraft in distress. **2.** to discard (what is unwanted).

jetty n. a breakwater or landing-stage.

Jew n. **1.** a person of Hebrew descent, or one whose religion is Judaism. **2.** (*informal, contemptuous*) a person who drives hard bargains in buying and selling. —**Jewess** n. □ **jew's harp,** a musical instrument consisting of a small U-shaped metal frame held in the teeth while a projecting metal strip is twanged with a finger.

jewel n. **1.** a precious stone. **2.** an ornament for wearing, containing one or more precious stones. **3.** a person or thing that is highly valued. □ **jewelled** adj. ornamented or set with jewels.

jeweller n. a person who makes or deals in jewels or jewellery.

jewellery (joo-ĕl-ri) n. jewels or similar ornaments to be worn. (¶ It is incorrect to pronounce this word as **jool**-er-i.)

Jewish adj. of Jews.

Jewry n. the Jewish people.

jib n. **1.** a triangular sail stretching forward from the mast. **2.** the projecting arm of a crane. —**jib** v. (jibbed, jibbing) **1.** (of a horse) to stop suddenly and refuse to go forwards. **2.** to refuse to proceed in some action; *jibbed at it*, showed unwillingness or dislike. □ **the cut of his jib,** his general appearance.

jibbah n. a long cloth coat worn by Muslim men in some countries.

Jibuti (ji-boo-ti) **1.** a country on the north-east coast of Africa. **2.** its capital city.

jiffy n. (*informal*) a moment, *in a jiffy*.

jig *n.* **1.** a lively jumping dance, the music for this. **2.** a device that holds a piece of work and guides the tools working on it. **3.** a template. **4.** (*slang*) a piece of trickery; *the jig is up*, the game is up. —**jig** *v.* (jigged, jigging) **1.** to dance a jig. **2.** to move up and down rapidly and jerkily.

jigger *n.* a measure of spirits etc., a glass holding this amount.

jiggered *adj.* I'll be jiggered, (*informal*) an exclamation of astonishment.

jiggery-pokery *n.* (*informal*) trickery, underhand dealing.

jiggle *v.* to rock or jerk lightly.

jigsaw *n.* **1.** a mechanically operated fretsaw. **2.** a jigsaw puzzle, a picture pasted on board and cut with a jigsaw into irregular pieces which are then shuffled and reassembled for amusement.

jilt *v.* to drop or abandon (a person) after having courted or promised to marry him or her.

jingle *v.* to make or cause to make a metallic ringing or clinking sound like that of small bells or of keys struck together. —*n.* **1.** a jingling sound. **2.** verse or words with simple catchy rhymes or repetitive sounds.

jingoism (jing-oh-izm) *n.* an aggressive attitude combining excessive patriotism and contempt for other countries.

jink *v.* to dodge by turning suddenly and sharply. —**high jinks**, noisy merry-making, boisterous fun.

jinn, jinnee *ns.* (*pl.* jinn) **1.** (in Muslim mythology) one of an order of spirits able to exercise supernatural influence over people. **2.** = genie.

jinx *n.* (*informal*) a person or thing that is thought to bring bad luck.

jitter *v.* (*informal*) to feel nervous, to behave nervously. **jitters** *pl. n.* (*informal*) nervousness. **jittery** *adj.* (*informal*) nervy.

jive *n.* fast lively jazz music, dancing to this. *v.* to dance to such music.

jizz *n.* the characteristic impression given by an animal or bird or plant, *he identifies a bird by its jizz*.

job *n.* **1.** a piece of work to be done. **2.** (*slang*) a crime, especially a robbery. **3.** something completed, a product of work, *a neat little job*. **4.** a paid position of employment, *got a job at the factory*. **5.** something one has to do, a responsibility, *it's your job to lock the gates*. **6.** (*informal*) a difficult task, *you'll have a job to move it*. □ **a bad job**, a difficult state of affairs, *make the best of a bad job*; *gave it up as a bad job*, a thing on which time or effort would be wasted. **a good job**, a satisfactory or fortunate state of affairs. **job lot**, a

collection of miscellaneous articles bought together. **jobs for the boys**, (*informal*) the assurance of gain or profitable positions for one's friends. **job-sheet** *n.* a document recording the details of jobs done. **just the job**, (*slang*) exactly what is wanted. **make a job** *or* **a good job of**, to do thoroughly or successfully.

Job (*pr.* johb) *n.* **Job's comforter**, a person who aggravates the distress of the person he is supposed to be comforting. **the patience of Job**, great patience like that of Job, a Hebrew patriarch who endured his troubles patiently.

jobber *n.* a stockjobber.

jobbing *adj.* doing single specific pieces of work for payment, *a jobbing gardener*.

jobcentre *n.* a government office in a town centre where information about jobs available is displayed.

jobless *adj.* unemployed, out of work.

jockey *n.* (*pl.* jockeys) a person who rides horses in horse-races, especially a professional rider. —*v.* (jockeyed, jockeying) to manœuvre in order to gain an advantage, *jockeying for position*; *jockeyed him into doing it*, forced him by skilful or unfair methods.

jock-strap *n.* a support or protective covering for the male genitals, worn while taking part in sport etc.

jocose (jŏk-ohss) *adj.* joking.

jocular (jok-yoo-ler) *adj.* joking, avoiding seriousness. **jocularly** *adv.*, **jocularity** (jok-yoo-la-riti) *n.*

jocund (jok-ŭnd) *adj.* merry, cheerful.

jodhpurs (jod-perz) *pl. n.* riding-breeches reaching to the ankle, fitting closely below the knee and loosely above it.

joey *n.* (*Austral.*) **1.** a young kangaroo. **2.** a young animal.

jog *v.* (jogged, jogging) **1.** to give a slight knock or push to, to shake with a push or jerk. **2.** to rouse or stimulate, *jogged his memory*. **3.** to move up and down with an unsteady movement. **4.** (of a horse) to move at a jogtrot. **5.** to run at a leisurely pace with short strides, as a form of exercise. —**jog** *n.* **1.** a slight shake or push, a nudge. **2.** a slow walk or trot. □ **jog on** *or* **along**, to proceed slowly or laboriously.

joggle *v.* to shake slightly, to move by slight jerks. —*n.* a joggling movement, a slight shake.

jogtrot *n.* a slow regular trot.

John Bull a typical Englishman, the English people.

johnny *n.* (*informal*) a fellow. **johnny-come-lately** *n.* a recently arrived person, an upstart.

joie de vivre (zhwah dĕ **veevr**) a feeling of

great enjoyment of life. (¶ French, = joy of living.)

join *v.* **1.** to put together, to fasten or unite or connect. **2.** to come together, to become united; *the Cherwell joins the Thames at Oxford*, meets and flows into it. **3.** to take part with others in doing something, *joined in the chorus*. **4.** to come into the company of, *join us for lunch*. **5.** to become a member of, *joined the Navy*. **6.** to take or resume one's place in, *joined his ship*. —*n.* a point or line or surface where things join. □ **join battle**, to begin fighting. **join forces**, to combine efforts. **join hands**, to clasp each other's hands. **join up**, to enlist in the armed forces.

joiner *n.* **1.** a person who makes furniture, house fittings, and other woodwork that is lighter than a carpenter's products. **2.** (*informal*) a person who readily joins clubs etc. □ **joinery** *n.* the work of a joiner.

joint *adj.* **1.** shared or held or done by two or more people together, *a joint account*. **2.** sharing in an activity etc., *joint authors*. —*joint* *n.* **1.** a place where two things are joined. **2.** a structure in an animal body by which bones are fitted together. **3.** a place or device at which two parts of a structure are joined. **4.** one of the parts into which a butcher divides a carcass, this cooked and served. **5.** (*slang*) a place where people meet for gambling or drinking etc. **6.** (*slang*) a marijuana cigarette. —*joint* *v.* **1.** to connect by a joint or joints. **2.** to fill up masonry joints with mortar etc., to point. **3.** to divide (a carcass) into joints; *joint a chicken*, divide it into pieces by cutting through each joint. □ **joint-stock company**, a business company with capital contributed and held jointly by a number of people. **out of joint**, dislocated; in disorder.

jointly *adv.* so as to be shared or done by two or more people together.

joist *n.* one of the parallel beams, extending from wall to wall, on which floor boards or ceiling laths are fixed.

joke *n.* **1.** something said or done to cause laughter. **2.** a ridiculous person or thing or circumstance. —*v.* to make jokes. — **jokingly** *adv.* □ **it's no joke**, it is a serious matter.

joker *n.* **1.** a person who jokes. **2.** (*slang*) a fellow. **3.** an extra playing-card used in certain card-games as the highest trump.

jokey *adj.* joking, not serious.

jollification *n.* merry-making, festivity.

jollity *n.* being jolly, merriment, merry-making.

jolly *adj.* (jollier, jolliest) **1.** full of high spirits, cheerful, merry. **2.** cheerful be-

cause slightly drunk. **3.** very pleasant, delightful. —*adv.* (*informal*) very, *jolly good*. —*v.* (jollied, jollying) (*informal*) to keep (a person) in a good humour, especially in order to win his co-operation, *jolly him along*. □ **Jolly Roger**, the pirates' black flag with a white skull and crossbones.

jolt *v.* **1.** to shake or dislodge with a jerk. **2.** to move along jerkily, as on a rough road. —**jolt** *n.* **1.** a jolting movement or effect. **2.** a surprise or shock.

jonquil (jon-kwil) *n.* a kind of narcissus with clusters of fragrant flowers.

Jordan the **Hashemite Kingdom of Jordan**, a country in the Middle East, bordering on the east of Israel. **Jordanian** (jor-**day**-niăn) *adj. & n.*

josh *v.* (*Amer.*) to joke or tease.

josser *n.* (*slang*) a fellow.

joss-stick *n.* a thin stick which burns to give off a smell of incense.

jostle *v.* to push roughly, especially when in a crowd.

jot *n.* a very small amount, *not one jot or tittle*. —*v.* (jotted, jotting) to write down briefly or hastily, *jot it down*. —**jottings** *pl. n.* jotted notes.

jotter *n.* a note-pad or notebook.

joule (*pr.* jool) *n.* a unit of energy.

journal (jer-năl) *n.* **1.** a daily record of news or events or business transactions. **2.** a newspaper or periodical.

journalese (jer-năl-**eez**) *n.* a style of language used in inferior newspaper writing, full of hackneyed or artificially elaborate phrases.

journalist (jer-nal-ist) *n.* a person employed in writing for a newspaper or magazine. **journalism** *n.*, **journalistic** *adj.*

journey *n.* (*pl.* journeys) **1.** a continued course of going or travelling. **2.** the distance travelled or the time required for this, *a day's* or *4 days' journey*. —*v.* (journeyed, journeying) to make a journey.

journeyman *n.* (*pl.* journeymen) **1.** a workman who has completed his apprenticeship and works for an employer. **2.** a reliable but not outstanding workman.

joust (*pr.* jowst) *v.* to fight on horseback with lances.

Jove Jupiter, the king of the gods in Roman mythology. **by Jove**, an exclamation of surprise.

jovial (joh-viăl) *adj.* full of cheerful good humour. **jovially** *adv.*, **joviality** (joh-vi-**al**-iti) *n.*

jowl (*rhymes with* howl) *n.* **1.** the jaw or cheek. **2.** an animal's dewlap, similar loose skin on a person's throat.

joy *n.* **1.** a deep emotion of pleasure, gladness. **2.** a thing that causes delight. □ **no joy**, (*informal*) no satisfaction or success.

joyful *adj.* full of joy. **joyfully** *adv.*, **joyfulness** *n.*

joyless *adj.* without joy.

joyous *adj.* joyful. **joyously** *adv.*

joy-ride *n.* a car ride taken for pleasure, usually without the owner's permission. **joy-rider** *n.*, **joy-riding** *n.*

JP *abbrev.* Justice of the Peace.

jubilant *adj.* showing joy, rejoicing.

jubilation *n.* rejoicing.

jubilee *n.* **1.** a special anniversary, *silver* (25th), *golden* (50th), or *diamond* (60th) *jubilee.* **2.** a time of rejoicing.

Judaism (**joo**-day-izm) *n.* the religion of the Jewish people, with belief in one God and based on the teachings of the Old Testament and the Talmud.

Judas *n.* a betrayer or traitor. ¶ Named after Judas Iscariot who betrayed Christ.

judder *v.* to shake noisily or violently. —*n.* a juddering movement or effect.

judge *n.* **1.** a public officer appointed to hear and try cases in a lawcourt. **2.** a person appointed to decide who has won a contest. **3.** a person who is able to give an authoritative opinion on the merits of something. —**judge** *v.* **1.** to try (a case) in a lawcourt. **2.** to act as judge of (a contest). **3.** to form and given an opinion about. **4.** to estimate, *judged the distance accurately.* □ **Judges' Rules**, a set of rules about an accused person's statements and answers to police questioning.

judgement *n.* (in Law contexts the spelling **judgment** is used) **1.** judging, being judged. **2.** the decision of a judge etc. in a lawcourt, *the judgement was in his favour.* **3.** ability to judge wisely, good sense, *he lacks judgement.* **4.** misfortune considered or jokingly said to be a punishment sent by God, *it's a judgement on you!* **5.** an opinion, *in the judgement of most people* □ **Judgement Day** *or* **Day of Judgement**, the day of the Last Judgement, when God will judge all mankind.

judicature (joo-dik-ă-choor) *n.* **1.** the administration of justice. **2.** a body of judges.

judicial (joo-**dish**-ăl) *adj.* **1.** of lawcourts or the administration of justice. **2.** of a judge or judgement. **3.** able to judge things wisely, *a judicial mind.* □ **judicial murder**, sentence of death that is legal but unjust.

judiciary (joo-**dish**-er-i) *n.* the whole body of judges in a country.

judicious (joo-**dish**-ŭs) *adj.* judging wisely, showing good sense. **judiciously** *adv.*

judo *n.* a Japanese system of unarmed combat. **judoka** (*pr.* **joo**-doh-kă) *n.* (*pl.* judoka), **judoist** *n.* a student of or expert in judo.

jug *n.* **1.** a vessel for holding and pouring liquids, with a handle and a shaped lip. **2.** (*slang*) prison, *in jug.* —**jug** *v.* (jugged, jugging) **1.** to cook (hare) by stewing it (formerly in a jug or jar). **2.** (*slang*) to put into prison. — **jugful** *n.*

juggernaut *n.* **1.** a large overwhelmingly powerful object or institution etc. **2.** a very large long-distance transport vehicle. ¶ *Juggernaut* was a title of a Hindu god whose image was drawn in procession on a huge wheeled vehicle; devotees are said to have thrown themselves under its wheels.

juggle *v.* **1.** to toss and catch a number of objects skilfully for entertainment, keeping one or more in the air at one time. **2.** to manipulate skilfully when handling several objects. **3.** to rearrange (facts or figures) in order to achieve something or to deceive people. □ **juggler** *n.* one who juggles, an entertainer who performs juggling tricks.

jugular (**jug**-yoo-ler) *n.* a **jugular vein**, one of the great veins of the neck, carrying blood from the head.

juice *n.* **1.** the fluid content of fruits or vegetables or meat. **2.** fluid secreted by an organ of the body, *the digestive juices.* **3.** (*slang*) electricity. **4.** (*slang*) petrol used in an engine etc.

juicy *adj.* (juicier, juiciest) **1.** full of juice. **2.** (*informal*) interesting, especially because of its scandalous nature, *juicy stories.* **juicily** *adv.*, **juiciness** *n.*

jujube *n.* a jelly-like sweet.

juke-box *n.* a machine that automatically plays a selected record when a coin is inserted.

Julian calendar the calendar introduced by Julius Caesar, replaced by the Gregorian calendar.

julienne (joo-li-**en**) *n.* clear meat soup containing vegetables cut in thin strips.

July *n.* the seventh month of the year.

jumble *v.* to mix in a confused way. —*n.* **1.** articles jumbled together, a muddle. **2.** articles for a **jumble sale**, a sale of miscellaneous second-hand goods to raise money for a charity.

jumbo *n.* (*pl.* jumbos) **1.** something very large of its kind. **2.** a **jumbo jet**, a very large jet aircraft able to carry several hundred passengers.

jump *v.* **1.** to move up off the ground etc. by bending and then extending the legs or (of fish) by a movement of the tail. **2.** to move suddenly with a jump or bound, to rise suddenly from a seat etc.; **jump in**, to get quickly into a car etc. **3.** to pass over by jumping, to use (a horse) for jumping. **4.** to pass over (a thing) to a point beyond, to skip (part of a book etc.) in reading or studying. **5.** to give a sudden movement from shock or excitement. **6.** to rise suddenly in amount or price or value. **7.** to leave (rails or a track) accidentally. **8.** to pounce on, to attack suddenly. — **jump** *n.* **1.** a jumping movement. **2.** a sudden movement caused by shock etc. **3.** a sudden rise in amount or price or value. **4.** a sudden change to a different condition or set of circumstances, a gap in a series etc. **5.** an obstacle to be jumped over. □ **have the jump on**, (*slang*) to have an advantage over. **jump at**, to accept eagerly. **jump bail**, to fail to come for trial when summoned after being released on bail. **jump down a person's throat**, to reprimand him severely. **jumped-up** *adj.* having risen suddenly from a low position or status. **jumping-off place**, a starting-point. **jump-jet** *n.* a jet aircraft that can take off directly upwards. **jump-lead** *n.* a cable for conveying current from one battery through another. **jump-off** *n.* a deciding round between competitors with equal scores in a horse-riding contest. **jump ship**, (of a seaman) to desert one's ship. **jump suit**, a one-piece garment for the whole body, like that worn by paratroops. **jump the gun**, to start or act before the permitted time. **jump the queue**, to obtain something without waiting for one's proper turn. **jump to conclusions**, to reach them too hastily. **jump to it**, to make an energetic start. **one jump ahead**, one stage ahead of one's rival. **the jumps**, (*slang*) extreme nervousness.

jumper [1] *n.* a person or animal that jumps, *is a good jumper.*

jumper [2] *n.* **1.** a woman's knitted garment for the upper part of the body. **2.** the upper part of a sailor's uniform. **3.** (*Amer.*) a pinafore dress.

jumpy *adj.* nervous.

junction *n.* **1.** a place where things join. **2.** a place where roads or railway lines etc. meet and unite.

juncture (**junk**-cher) *n.* a point of time, a critical convergence of events.

June *n.* the sixth month of the year.

jungle *n.* **1.** land overgrown with tangled vegetation, especially in the tropics. **2.** a wild tangled mass. **3.** a scene of struggle, *the blackboard jungle* (in schools), *concrete jungle* (in cities).

junior *adj.* **1.** younger in age; *Tom Brown junior,* the younger person of that name. **2.** lower in rank or authority. **3.** for younger children, *junior school.* —**junior** *n.*

1. a junior person. **2.** a person employed to work in a junior capacity, *the office junior.* **3.** a member of a junior school; *he is my junior,* is younger than I am. **4.** (*Amer. informal*) the son in a family.

juniper (joo-nip-er) *n.* an evergreen shrub with prickly leaves and dark purplish berries.

junk [1] *n.* **1.** discarded material, rubbish. **2.** (*informal*) anything regarded as useless or of little value, *all that junk in the boot of the car.* **3.** (*slang*) a narcotic drug, heroin. □ **junk-shop** *n.* a shop selling miscellaneous cheap second-hand goods.

junk [2] *n.* a kind of flat-bottomed ship with sails, used in the China seas.

junket *n.* a sweet custard-like food made of milk curdled with rennet and flavoured.

junketing *n.* feasting and merry-making.

junkie *n.* (*slang*) a drug addict.

junta *n.* a group of people who combine to rule a country, especially having seized power after a revolution.

jurisdiction (joor-iss-**dik**-shŏn) *n.* **1.** authority to interpret and apply the law. **2.** official power exercised within a particular sphere of activity. **3.** the extent or territory over which legal or other power extends.

jurisprudence (joor-iss-**proo**-dĕns) *n.* the study of law or of a particular part of law, *medical jurisprudence.*

juror (**joor**-er) *n.* a member of a jury.

jury *n.* **1.** a body of people sworn to give a verdict on a case presented to them in a court of law. **2.** a body of people appointed to select the winner(s) in a competition. □ **jury-box** *n.* an enclosure for the jury in a lawcourt. **juryman, jurywoman** *ns.* a juror.

jury-rigged *adj.* set up as a makeshift.

just *adj.* **1.** giving proper consideration to the claims of everyone concerned. **2.** deserved, right in amount etc., *a just reward.* — **just** *adv.* **1.** exactly, *just at that spot.* **2.** barely, no more than, by only a short distance, *I just managed it; just below the knee.* **3.** at this moment or only a little time ago, *he has just gone.* **4.** (*informal*) merely, *we are just good friends.* **5.** really, certainly, *it's just splendid.* **justly** *adv.*, **justness** *n.* □ **just about**, (*informal*) almost exactly or completely. **just in case**, as a precaution. **just now**, at this moment; a little time ago. **just so**, exactly arranged, *she likes everything just so*; it is exactly as you say.

justice *n.* **1.** just treatment, fairness. **2.** legal proceedings, *a court of justice.* **3.** a magistrate. **4.** a judge, the title of a judge, *Mr Justice Humphreys.* □ **do justice to**, to show (a thing) to advantage; to show appreciation of. **Justice of the Peace,** a non-professional magistrate.

justiciary (jus-**tish**-er-i) *n.* one who administers justice. **Court of Justiciary,** the supreme criminal court in Scotland.

justifiable *adj.* able to be justified. **justifiably** *adv.*

justify *v.* (justified, justifying) **1.** to show (a person or statement or act etc.) to be right or just or reasonable. **2.** to be a good or sufficient reason for, *increased production justifies an increase in wages.* **3.** to adjust (a line of type in printing) so that it fills a space neatly. **justification** *n.*

jut *v.* (jutted, jutting) to project, *it juts out.*

jute *n.* fibre from the bark of certain tropical plants, used for making sacks etc.

juvenile (joo-vĕ-nyl) *adj.* **1.** youthful, childish. **2.** for young people. —*n.* a young person. ☐ **juvenile delinquent,** a young offender against the law, below the age when he may be held legally responsible for his actions. **juvenile delinquency.**

juxtapose (juks-tă-**pohz**) *v.* to put (things) side by side. **juxtaposition** *n.*

Kk

K *abbrev.* **1.** kelvin(s) **2.** one thousand, *32 K.*

Kaaba (**kah**-ă-bă) *n.* a shrine at Mecca containing a sacred black stone.

- **Kabul** (**kah**-bŭl) the capital of Afghanistan.

Kaiser (**ky**-zer) *n.* the title of the German and Austrian emperors until 1918.

kale *n.* a kind of cabbage with curly leaves that do not form a compact head.

kaleidoscope (kăl-**I**-dŏ-skohp) *n.* a toy consisting of a tube containing small brightly-coloured fragments of glass etc. and mirrors which reflect these to form changing patterns. **kaleidoscopic** (kăl-I-dŏ-**skop**-ik) *adj.*

kameez (kă-**meez**) *n.* a tunic worn by both sexes in some countries of southern Asia.

Kampala (kam-**pah**-lă) the capital of Uganda.

kampong *n.* a Malayan enclosure or village.

Kampuchea (kam-puu-**chee**-ă) = Cambodia.

kangaroo *n.* an Australian animal that jumps along on its strong hind legs, the female having a pouch on the front of the body in which young are carried. **kangaroo court,** a court formed illegally by a group

of people (e.g. prisoners or strikers) to settle disputes among themselves.

Kans. *abbrev.* Kansas.

Kansas a State of the USA.

kaolin (**kay**-ŏ-lin) *n.* a fine white clay used in making porcelain and in medicine.

kapok (**kay**-pok) *n.* a substance resembling cotton wool, used for padding things.

kaput (kă-**puut**) *adj.* (*slang*) done for, ruined, out of order.

karate (kă-**rah**-ti) *n.* a Japanese system of unarmed combat in which the hands and feet are used as weapons.

karma *n.* (in Buddhism and Hinduism) the sum of a person's actions in one of his successive existences, thought to decide his fate for the next.

Katmandu (kat-man-**doo**) the capital of Nepal.

kauri (**kowr**-i) *n.* a coniferous tree of New Zealand, yielding **kauri-gum.**

kayak (**ky**-ak) *n.* **1.** an Eskimo canoe with a sealskin covering closed round the waist of the occupant. **2.** a small covered canoe resembling this.

kc/s *abbrev.* kilocycle(s) per second.

kebabs (kib-**abz**) *pl. n.* small pieces of meat cooked on a skewer.

kedge *v.* to move (a boat) or be moved by means of a hawser attached to a small anchor. —*n.* this anchor.

kedgeree (kej-er-**ee**) *n.* a cooked dish of rice and fish or eggs.

keel *n.* the timber or steel structure along the base of a ship, on which the ship's framework is built up. —*v.* to become tilted, to overturn, to collapse, *keeled over.* ☐ **on an even keel,** steady.

keen¹ *adj.* **1.** sharp, having a sharp edge or point. **2.** (of sound or light) acute, penetrating. **3.** piercingly cold, *keen wind.* **4.** (of prices) low because of competition. **5.** intense, *keen interest.* **6.** showing or feeling intense interest or desire, *a keen swimmer; is keen to go.* **7.** perceiving things very distinctly, *keen sight.* **keenly** *adv.*, **keenness** *n.* ☐ **keen on,** (*informal*) much attracted to.

keen² *n.* an Irish funeral song accompanied by wailing. —*v.* to utter the keen, to utter in a wailing tone.

keep *v.* (kept, keeping) **1.** to remain or cause to remain in a specified state or position or condition. **2.** to prevent or hold back from doing something, to detain, *what kept you?* **3.** to put aside for a future time. **4.** to pay proper respect to; *keep the law,* or *a promise,* not break it. **5.** to celebrate (a feast or ceremony). **6.** to guard or protect, to keep safe; *keep goal* or *wicket,* be goalkeeper or wicket-keeper. **7.** to continue to have, to have and not give away, *keep the change*. **8.** to provide with the necessities of life; *it keeps him in cigarettes*, provides him with money for these. **9.** to own and look after (animals) for one's use or enjoyment, *keep hens*. **10.** to manage, *keep a shop*. **11.** to have (a commodity) regularly in stock or for sale. **12.** to make entries in (a diary or accounts etc.), to record in this way. **13.** to continue doing something, to do frequently or repeatedly, *the strap keeps breaking*. **14.** to continue in a specified direction, *keep straight on*. **15.** (of food) to remain in good condition; *the work* or *news will keep*, can be put aside until later. —**keep** *n.* **1.** provision of the necessities of life, the food required for this, *she earns her keep*. **2.** the central tower or other strongly fortified structure in a castle. □ **for keeps**, (*informal*) permanently. **keep a secret**, not tell it to others. **keep down**, to keep low in amount or number, *it keeps the weeds down*; to eat and not vomit (food). **keep early hours**, to go to bed early. **keep fit**, to be and remain healthy. **keep house**, to look after a house or a household. **keep in with**, to remain on good terms with. **keep on**, to continue doing something; to nag, *she keeps on at me*. **keep one's feet**, not fall. **keep one's hair on**, (*slang*) to remain calm. **keep one's head above water**, to keep out of debt. **keep the peace**, to obey the laws and refrain from causing trouble. **keep to oneself**, to keep (a thing) secret; to avoid meeting people, *keeps himself to himself*. **keep under**, to repress. **keep up**, to progress at the same pace as others; to prevent from sinking or getting low; to continue to observe, *keep up old customs*; to continue, *kept up the attack all day*; to maintain in proper condition, *the cost of keeping up a large house*. **keep up with the Joneses**, to strive to remain on terms of obvious social equality with one's neighbours.

keeper *n.* **1.** a person who keeps or looks after something, the custodian of a museum or forest etc. **2.** a fruit that keeps well.

keeping *n.* **1.** custody, charge, *in safe keeping*. **2.** harmony, conformity, *a style that is in keeping with his dignity*.

keepsake *n.* a thing that is kept in memory of the giver.

keffiyeh (kef-ee-ay) *n.* a kerchief worn as a head-dress by Arab men in some countries.

keg *n.* a small barrel. **keg beer**, beer supplied from metal containers.

kelp *n.* a large brown seaweed.

kelvin *n.* a degree (equivalent to the Celsius degree) of the **Kelvin scale** of temperature (with zero at absolute zero, $-273 \cdot 15°C$).

ken *n.* the range of sight or knowledge, *beyond my ken*. —*v.* (*Scottish*) to know.

kendo *n.* the Japanese art of fencing with two-handed bamboo swords.

kennel *n.* **1.** a shelter for a dog kept as a pet, or for hounds. **2.** a pack of dogs. —*v.* (kennelled, kennelling) to put into a kennel. □ **kennels** *pl. n.* a boarding or breeding establishment for dogs.

Kent a county of England. **Kentish** *adj.*

Kentucky a State of the USA.

Kenya (keen-yǎ) a country in east Africa. **Kenyan** *adj.* & *n.*

kept *see* keep.

keratin (ke-rǎ-tin) *n.* a strong protein substance forming the basis of horns, claws, nails, feathers, hair, etc.

kerb *n.* a stone edging to a pavement or raised path. **kerbstone** *n.*

kerchief *n.* a square scarf worn on the head.

kerfuffle *n.* (*informal*) fuss, commotion.

kernel *n.* **1.** the softer (usually edible) part inside the shell of a nut or stone-fruit. **2.** the part of a grain or seed within the husk. **3.** the central or important part of a subject or plan or problem etc.

kerosene (kerrŏ-seen) *n.* a fuel oil distilled from petroleum etc., paraffin oil.

kestrel *n.* a kind of small falcon.

ketch *n.* a small sailing-boat with two masts.

ketchup *n.* a thick sauce made from tomatoes and vinegar etc., used as a seasoning.

kettle *n.* a metal container with a spout and handle, for boiling water in. **a pretty kettle of fish**, an awkward state of affairs.

kettledrum *n.* a percussion instrument consisting of a hollow shaped body over which parchment is stretched.

key *n.* **1.** a small piece of metal shaped so that it will move the bolt of a lock and so lock or unlock something. **2.** a similar instrument for grasping and turning something, e.g. for winding a clock or tightening a spring etc. **3.** something that provides access or control or insight, *the key to the mystery; a key industry*, one that is important to other industries and to a country's economy. **4.** a set of answers to problems, a word or set of symbols for interpreting a code etc., or for extracting items of data from a computer. **5.** a system of related notes in music, based on a particular note, *the key of C major*. **6.** the general tone or degree of intensity of something; *all in the same key,* monotonous in character. **7.** roughness of surface helping plaster or paint to adhere to it. **8.** a piece of wood or metal etc. inserted between others to hold them secure. **9.** one of a set of levers to be pressed by the fingers in playing a musical instrument or operating a typewriter etc. **10.** a device for making or breaking an electric circuit, e.g. in telegraphy or to operate the ignition in a motor vehicle. **11.** the winged fruit of certain trees, e.g. sycamore. —**key** v. (keyed, keying) **1.** to roughen (a surface) so that plaster or paint will adhere well. **2.** to link closely with something else, *the factory is keyed to the export trade.* □ **keyed up,** stimulated, nervously tense. **key money,** payment demanded from an incoming tenant, nominally for the provision of the key to the premises. **key-pad** n. a small keyboard of numbered buttons for use instead of a dial on a telephone or for selecting a channel etc. on a TV set. **key-ring** n. a ring on which keys are threaded.

keyboard n. the set of keys on a piano or typewriter etc.

keyhole n. the hole by which a key is put into a lock.

keynote n. **1.** the note on which a key in music is based. **2.** the prevailing tone or idea of a speech etc.

keystone n. the central wedge-shaped stone at the summit of an arch, locking the others in position.

keyword n. the key to a cipher etc.

kg *abbrev.* kilogram(s).

KGB *abbrev.* the secret police of the USSR since 1954.

khaki (**kah**-ki) *adj.* & *n.* dull brownish-yellow, the colour used for military uniforms.

Khartoum (kar-**toom**) the capital of Sudan.

kHz *abbrev.* kilohertz.

kibbutz (kib-**uuts**) n. (pl. kibbutzim, pr. kib-uuts-eem) a communal settlement in Israel.

kibbutznik (kib-**uuts**-nik) n. a member of a kibbutz.

kick v. **1.** to strike or thrust or propel with the foot. **2.** to score by kicking the ball into goal. **3.** to treat contemptuously, *gets kicked around.* **4.** (of a gun) to recoil when fired. —**kick** n. **1.** an act of kicking, a blow from being kicked. **2.** (*informal*) a thrill, a pleasurable effect, *get a kick out of it*; *did it for kicks*. **3.** (*informal*) an interest or activity, *the health food kick*. **4.** the recoil of a gun when it is fired. —**kicker** n. □ **alive and kicking,** (*informal*) fully active. **kick-down** n. a device for gear-

changing in a motor vehicle by full depression of the accelerator. **kick off,** to start a football game by kicking the ball; (*informal*) to begin proceedings. **kick-off** n. kicking off in football. **kick one's heels,** to be kept waiting. **kick out,** (*informal*) to drive out forcibly; to dismiss. **kick over the traces,** *see* trace². **kick the bucket,** (*slang*) to die. **kick the habit,** (*slang*) to give it up. **kick up,** (*informal*) to create a fuss or noise). **kick upstairs,** to promote (a person) to a higher position, which is in fact less influential, in order to get rid of him.

kickback n. **1.** a recoil. **2.** (*informal*) payment for help in making a profit etc.

kick-start v. to start (a motor cycle etc.) by pushing down a lever with one's foot. **kick-starter** n.

kid n. **1.** a young goat. **2.** leather made from its skin. **3.** (*slang*) a child. —**kid** v. (kidded, kidding) **1.** to give birth to a young goat. **2.** (*slang*) to deceive (especially for fun), to tease. □ **kid-glove treatment,** tactfulness.

kiddy n. (*slang*) a child.

kidnap v. (kidnapped, kidnapping) to carry off (a person) by force or fraud in order to obtain a ransom, **kidnapper** n.

kidney n. (pl. kidneys) **1.** either of a pair of glandular organs that remove waste products from the blood and secrete urine. **2.** this as food. □ **kidney bean,** a French bean; a climbing bean with purple pods; a runner bean. **kidney dish,** a kidney-shaped dish, oval and indented at one side. **kidney machine,** an apparatus that performs the functions of a kidney.

kie-kie (**kee**-kee) n. a New Zealand climbing plant with leaves that are used for making baskets etc.

kill v. **1.** to cause the death of (a person), to destroy the vitality of (a plant etc.). **2.** to put an end to (a feeling etc.); *kill a light or an engine,* switch it off. **3.** to make (a colour) seem insipid by contrast. **4.** to spend (time) unprofitably while waiting for something. **5.** (*informal*) to cause severe pain to, *my feet are killing me.* —**kill** n. **1.** the act of killing. **2.** the animal(s) killed by a hunter. —**killer** n. □ **in at the kill,** present at the time of victory. **kill off,** to get rid of by killing. **kill two birds with one stone,** to achieve two purposes with one action. **kill with kindness,** to harm with excessive kindness. **make a killing,** to have a great financial success.

killing *adj.* (*informal*) very amusing. **killingly** *adv.*

killjoy *n.* a person who spoils the enjoyment of others.

kiln *n.* an oven for hardening or drying things such as pottery or bricks or hops, or for burning lime.

kilo (kee-loh) *n.* (*pl.* kilos) a kilogram.

kilo- (kil-ŏ) *prefix* one thousand.

kilocycle *n.* **1.** 1000 cycles as a unit of wave-frequency. **2.** (*informal*) kilohertz.

kilogram *n.* the basic unit of mass in the International System of Units (2·205 lb).

kilohertz *n.* a unit of frequency of electromagnetic waves, = 1000 cycles per second.

kilometre (kil-ŏ-meet-er *or* kil-**om**-it-er) *n.* a distance of 1000 metres (0·62 mile).

kilovolt *n.* 1000 volts.

kilowatt *n.* the power of 1000 watts. **kilowatt-hour** *n.* an amount of energy equal to one kilowatt operating for one hour.

kilt *n.* a knee-length pleated skirt-like garment of tartan wool, worn as part of a Highland man's dress or by women and children. **kilted** *adj.* wearing a kilt.

kimono (kim-**oh**-noh) *n.* (*pl.* kimonos) **1.** a long loose Japanese robe with wide sleeves, worn with a sash. **2.** a dressing-gown resembling this.

kin *n.* a person's relative(s).

kind¹ *n.* a class of similar things or animals, a type. **a kind of,** something that belongs approximately to the class named, *he's a kind of stockbroker.* **in kind,** (of payment) in goods or natural produce, not in money; *repaid his insolence in kind,* by being insulting in return. **of a kind,** similar. **kind of,** (*informal*) slightly, *I felt kind of sorry for him.* ¶ Correct usage is *this kind of thing* or *these kinds of things,* not *these kind of things.*

kind² *adj.* gentle and considerate in one's manner or conduct towards others. **kind-hearted** *adj.,* **kindness** *n.*

kindergarten *n.* a school for very young children.

kindle¹ **1.** to set on fire, to cause (a fire) to begin burning. **2.** to arouse or stimulate, *kindled our hopes.* **3.** to become kindled. □ **kindling** *n.* small pieces of wood for lighting fires.

kindle² *v.* (of rabbits) to produce offspring. —*n.* **in kindle,** (of a female rabbit) pregnant.

kindly *adj.* (kindlier, kindliest) kind in character or manner or appearance. —*adv.* **1.** in a kind way. **2.** please, *kindly shut the door.* —**kindliness** *n.* □ **not take kindly to,** to be displeased by.

kindred (**kin**-drid) *n.* a person's relative(s). —*adj.* **1.** related. **2.** of similar kind, *chemistry and kindred subjects.* □ **a kindred spirit,** a person whose tastes are similar to one's own.

kinetic (kin-et-ik) *adj.* of or produced by movement, characterized by movement. **kinetic art,** art that depends for its effect on the movement of some of its parts, e.g. in air currents. **kinetic energy,** *see* energy.

king *n.* **1.** a man who is the supreme ruler of an independent country by right of succession to the throne. **2.** a person or thing regarded as supreme in some way; *king of beasts,* the lion. **3.** a large species of animal, *king penguin.* **4.** the piece in chess that has to be protected from checkmate. **5.** a piece in draughts that has been crowned on reaching the opponent's end of the board. **6.** a playing-card bearing a picture of a king and ranking next above queen. □ **King Charles spaniel,** a small black-and-tan spaniel. **King of Arms,** the title of the chief heralds at the College of Arms and in Scotland. **king-size** *or* **king-sized** *adjs.* extra large.

kingcup *n.* a marsh marigold.

kingdom *n.* **1.** a country ruled by a king or queen. **2.** the spiritual reign of God; *thy Kingdom come,* may the rule of God be established. **3.** a division of the natural world, *the animal* or *vegetable kingdom.* □ **kingdom-come** *n.* (*slang*) the next world; *till kingdom-come,* for an unending period.

kingfisher *n.* a small bird with bright bluish plumage that dives to catch fish.

kingly *adj.* of or like or suitable for a king.

kingpin *n.* **1.** a vertical bolt used as a pivot. **2.** an indispensable person or thing.

kingship *n.* being a king, a king's position or reign.

Kingston the capital of Jamaica.

kink *n.* **1.** a short twist in a wire or rope or hair etc. **2.** a mental or moral peculiarity. —*v.* to form or cause to form kinks.

kinky *adj.* (kinkier, kinkiest) **1.** full of kinks. **2.** (*informal*) bizarre, eccentric, especially in sexual behaviour.

kinsfolk *pl. n.* a person's relatives. **kinsman** *n.,* **kinswoman** *n.*

Kinshasa (kin-**shah**-să) the capital of Zaire.

kiosk (kee-osk) *n.* **1.** a small light open structure where newspapers or refreshments are sold. **2.** a public telephone booth.

kip *n.* (*slang*) **1.** a place to sleep. **2.** a sleep. —*v.* (kipped, kipping) (*slang*) to lie down for sleep, to sleep.

kipper *n.* a kippered herring. —*v.* to cure

(fish) by splitting, cleaning, and drying it in the open air or in smoke.

Kiribati (ki-ri-**bas**) a group of islands in the Pacific north-west of Australia. —*adj.* of Kiribati or its inhabitants. **i-Kiribati** *n.* a native or inhabitant of Kiribati.

kirk *n.* (*Scottish*) a church. **kirk-session** *n.* the lowest court in the Church of Scotland, composed of ministers and elders.

kirsch (*pr.* keersh) *n.* a colourless brandy made from the juice of wild cherries.

kirtle *n.* (*old use*) **1.** a woman's gown or outer petticoat. **2.** a man's tunic or coat.

kismet (**kiz**-met) *n.* destiny, fate.

kiss *n.* a touch or caress given with the lips. —*v.* to touch with the lips in affection or as a greeting or in reverence. □ **kiss hands,** to greet the sovereign ceremonially on being appointed to high office. **kiss of death,** an apparently friendly act causing ruin. **kiss of life,** mouth-to-mouth resuscitation.

kisser *n.* (*slang*) the mouth or face.

kit *n.* **1.** the clothing and personal equipment of a soldier etc. or a traveller. **2.** the equipment needed for a particular activity or situation, *riding-kit; a first-aid kit; a workman's kit,* his outfit of tools etc. **3.** a set of parts sold together to be assembled, *in kit form.* —*v.* (kitted, kitting) to equip with kit, *kit a person out* or *up.*

kitbag *n.* a bag for holding a soldier's or traveller's kit.

kitchen *n.* a room in which meals are prepared. **kitchen garden,** a garden for growing one's own fruit and vegetables.

kitchenette *n.* a small room or an alcove used as a kitchen.

kite *n.* **1.** a large bird of prey of the hawk family. **2.** a toy consisting of a light framework to be flown in a strong wind on the end of a long string. **3.** (*slang*) an aeroplane. □ **fly a kite,** to make an experiment in order to gauge people's opinion.

Kitemark *n.* an official kite-shaped mark affixed to goods approved by the British Standards Institution.

kith *n.* **kith and kin,** kinsfolk, one's relatives.

kitsch (*pr.* kich) *n.* pretentiousness and lack of good taste in art, art of this type.

kitten *n.* the young of a cat or of a hare or rabbit or ferret. —*v.* to give birth to kittens. —**kittenish** *adj.* □ **have kittens,** (*slang*) to be very agitated or nervous.

kitty *n.* **1.** the pool of stakes to be played for in some card games. **2.** a fund of money for communal use.

kiwi (**kee**-wee) *n.* a New Zealand bird that does not fly, with a long bill, rudimentary wings, and no tail. **Kiwi** *n.* (*pl.* Kiwis) (*informal*) a New Zealander.

kleptomania (kleptō-**may**-niă) *n.* an uncontrollable tendency to steal things, with no desire to use or profit by them. **kleptomaniac** *n.* a person with this tendency.

km *abbrev.* kilometre(s).

knack *n.* **1.** the ability to do something skilfully. **2.** the habit of doing, *it has a knack of going wrong.*

knacker *n.* a person who buys and slaughters useless horses, selling the meat and hides.

knackered *adj.* (*slang*) exhausted, worn out.

knapsack *n.* a bag worn strapped on the back for carrying necessaries, used by soldiers on a march or by hikers.

knapweed *n.* a common weed like a thistle but without prickles.

knave *n.* **1.** (*old use*) a rogue. **2.** the jack in playing-cards. **knavish** *adj.*, **knavery** *n.*

knead *v.* **1.** to work (moist flour or clay) into dough by pressing and stretching it with the hands. **2.** to make (bread etc.) in this way. **3.** to massage with kneading movements.

knee *n.* **1.** the joint between the thigh and the lower part of the human leg, the corresponding joint in animals; *fall on* or *to one's knees,* to kneel. **2.** the part of a garment covering this. **3.** the upper surface of the thigh of a sitting person, *sit on my knee.* **4.** something shaped like a bent knee. —*v.* to touch or strike with the knee. □ **knee-breeches** *pl. n.* breeches reaching to or just below the knee. **knee-deep** *adj.* of or in sufficient depth to cover a person up to the knees; *knee-deep in work,* deeply occupied. **knee-hole** *adj.* (of a desk) with space for the knees between pedestals fitted with drawers. **knee-jerk** *n.* an involuntary jerk of the leg when a tendon below the knee is struck. **knee length** *adj.* reaching to the knees. **knees-up** *n.* (*informal*) a lively party with dancing.

kneecap *n.* **1.** the small bone covering the front of the knee joint. **2.** a protective covering for the knee. **kneecapping** *n.* shooting in the legs to lame a person as a punishment.

kneel *v.* (knelt, kneeling) to take or be in a position where the body is supported on the knees with the lower leg bent back, especially in prayer or reverence.

kneeler *n.* a hassock for kneeling on.

knell *n.* the sound of a bell tolled solemnly after a death or at a funeral.

knelt *see* kneel.

knew *see* know.

knickerbockers *pl. n.* loose-fitting breeches gathered in at the knee.

knickers *pl. n.* a woman's or girl's undergarment covering the lower part of the body and having separate legs or leg-holes.

knick-knack *n.* a small ornamental article.

knife *n.* (*pl.* knives) **1.** a cutting instrument or weapon consisting of a sharp blade with a handle. **2.** the cutting-blade of a machine. —*v.* to cut or stab with a knife. □ **have got one's knife into a person,** to be persistently malicious or vindictive towards him. **knife-pleats** *pl. n.* narrow flat pleats. **on a knife-edge,** in a situation involving extreme tension or anxiety about the outcome. **war to the knife,** relentless enmity.

knight *n.* **1.** a man on whom a rank is conferred as an honour, lower than that of baronet, having the title 'Sir'. **2.** a chess piece, usually with the form of a horse's head. —*v.* to confer a knighthood on. — **knightly** *adv.*

knighthood *n.* the rank of knight.

knit *v.* (knitted *or* knit, knitting) **1.** to make (a garment or fabric etc.) from yarn formed into interlocking loops either by long needles held in the hands or on a machine. **2.** to form (yarn) into fabric etc. in this way. **3.** to make a plain (not purl) stitch in knitting. **4.** to unite or grow together, *the broken bones had knit well*; *a well-knit frame,* compact bodily structure. —*n.* a garment or fabric made by knitting. —**knitter** *n.* □ **knit one's brow,** to frown. **knitting** *n.* work in the process of being knitted. **knitting-needle** *n.* one of the long needles used for knitting by hand.

knitwear *n.* knitted garments.

knob *n.* **1.** a rounded projecting part, especially one forming the handle of a door or drawer or for turning to adjust a dial-setting etc. **2.** a small lump of butter, coal, etc. **knobby** *adj.* □ **with knobs on,** (*slang*) that and more.

knobbly *adj.* with many small projecting lumps.

knock *v.* **1.** to strike with an audible sharp blow. **2.** to make a noise by striking something, e.g. at a door to summon a person or gain admittance. **3.** (of an engine) to make a thumping or rattling noise while running, to pink. **4.** to drive or make by knocking, *knock a nail in*; *knocked a hole in it.* **5.** (*slang*) to say critical or insulting things about, *stop knocking Britain.* — **knock** *n.* **1.** an act or sound of knocking. **2.** a sharp blow. **3.** (in an engine) knocking, pinking. □ **knock about,** to treat

roughly; to wander casually. **knock back,** (*slang*) to swallow (a drink). **knock down,** to dispose of (an article) at auction. **knockdown** *adj.* (of prices) very low; (of furniture) easy to dismantle and re-assemble. **knock-for-knock agreement,** an agreement between insurers that each will pay his own policy-holder's claims arising from a collision between two vehicles, regardless of the degree of liability of each driver. **knock-kneed** *adj.* having **knock knees,** an abnormal inward curving of the legs at the knees. **knock off,** (*informal*) to cease work; to complete (work) quickly; to deduct (an amount) from a price; (*slang*) to steal. **knock-on effect,** an alteration that causes similar alterations elsewhere. **knock out,** to make unconscious by hitting on the head, to disable (a boxer) in this way so that he is unable to rise or continue in a specified time; to defeat in a knock-out competition; to exhaust or disable. **knock spots off,** to be easily superior to. **knock up,** to rouse by knocking at the door; to make or arrange hastily; to score (runs) at cricket; to make exhausted or ill. **knock-up** *n.* a practice or casual game at tennis etc.

knocker *n.* **1.** a person who knocks. **2.** a hinged metal flap for rapping against a door to summon a person.

knock-out *adj.* knocking a person out, (of a competition) in which the loser of each successive round is eliminated; *knock-out drops,* liquid added to a drink to cause unconsciousness when swallowed. —*n.* **1.** a blow that knocks a boxer out. **2.** a knock-out competition. **3.** (*slang*) an outstanding or irresistible person or thing.

knoll (*pr.* nohl) *n.* a hillock, a mound.

knot *n.* **1.** an intertwining of one or more pieces of thread or rope etc. to fasten them together; *a knot of ribbon,* a piece tied and used as an ornament. **2.** a tangle. **3.** a hard mass in something, especially on a tree-trunk where a branch joins it. **4.** a round cross-grained spot in timber where a branch joined; *knot-hole,* a hole formed where this has fallen out. **5.** a cluster of people or things. **6.** a unit of speed used by ships at sea and by aircraft, = one nautical mile per hour. —**knot** *v.* (knotted, knotting) **1.** to tie or fasten with a knot. **2.** to entangle. □ **at a rate of knots,** (*informal*) very rapidly. **get knotted!,** (*slang*) stop annoying me. **tie in knots,** (*informal*) to make (a person) baffled or confused.

knot-grass *n.* a common weed with nodes in its stems and small pale pink flowers.

knotty *adj.* (knottier, knottiest) **1.** full of knots. **2.** puzzling, full of problems or difficulties.

know *v.* (knew, known, knowing) **1.** to have in one's mind or memory as a result of experience or learning or information. **2.** to feel certain, *I know I left it here!* **3.** to recognize (a person), to have had social contact with, to be familiar with (a place). **4.** to recognize with certainty, *knows a bargain when she sees one.* **5.** to understand and be able to use (a subject or language or skill), *she knows how to please people*; *knows better than to do that,* is too wise or well-mannered to do it. □ **in the know,** (*informal*) having inside information. **know-all** *n.* a person who behaves as if he knows everything. **know-how** *n.* practical knowledge or skill in a particular activity. **know one's own mind,** to know firmly what one wants or intends.

knowable *adj.* able to be known.

knowing *adj.* showing knowledge or awareness, showing that one has inside information. **knowingly** *adv.*

knowledge *n.* **1.** knowing. **2.** all that a person knows. **3.** all that is known, an organized body of information.

knowledgeable *adj.* well-informed.

knuckle *n.* **1.** a finger-joint. **2.** the knee joint of an animal, or the part joining the leg to the foot, especially as a joint of meat. —*v.* to strike or press or rub with the knuckles. □ **knuckle down,** to begin to work earnestly. **knuckle under,** to yield, to submit.

knuckleduster *n.* a metal device worn over the knuckles to protect them and increase the injury done by a blow.

KO *abbrev.* knock-out. **KO'd,** knocked out.

koala (koh-**ah**-lă) *n.* a **koala bear,** an Australian tree-climbing animal with thick grey fur and large ears, feeding on the leaves of the gum-tree.

kohlrabi (kohl-**rah**-bi) *n.* a cabbage with an edible turnip-shaped stem.

kookaburra *n.* a giant kingfisher of Australia, the *laughing jackass.*

kopje (kop-i) *n.* = koppie.

koppie *n.* (in South Africa) a small hill.

Koran (kor-**ahn**) *n.* the sacred book of the Muslims containing the revelations of Muhammad, written in Arabic.

Korea (kŏ-**ree**-ă) a country in Asia, divided between the Republic of Korea (= South Korea) and the Democratic People's Republic of Korea (= North Korea). **Korean** *adj. & n.*

kosher (koh-sher) *adj.* (of food etc.) conforming to the requirements of Jewish dietary laws.

kowhai (koh-I) *n.* a New Zealand tree or shrub with golden flowers.

kowtow *v.* to behave with exaggerated respect towards a person. ¶ The *kowtow* was a former Chinese custom of touching the ground with one's forehead as a sign of worship or submission.

k.p.h. *abbrev.* kilometres per hour.

kraal (*pr.* krahl) *n.* (in South Africa) **1.** a village of huts enclosed by a fence. **2.** an enclosure for cattle or sheep.

kremlin *n.* a citadel within a Russian town, especially that of Moscow. **the Kremlin,** the government of the USSR.

krill *n.* the mass of tiny crustaceans that forms the principal food of certain whales.

kromesky (krŏ-**mess**-ki) *n.* a small roll of minced meat or fish wrapped in bacon and fried.

krona (kroh-nă) *n.* the unit of money in Sweden (*pl.* kronor) and Iceland (*pl.* krónur).

krone (kroh-nĕ) *n.* (*pl.* kroner) the unit of money in Denmark and Norway.

krugerrand (**kroog**-er-ahnt) *n.* a South African gold coin bearing a portrait of President Kruger (1825–1904).

Kuala Lumpur (kwah-lă **lum**-poor) the capital of Malaysia.

kudos (**kew**-doss) *n.* (*informal*) honour and glory.

Ku-Klux-Klan *n.* an American secret society hostile to Blacks, originally formed in the southern States after the Civil War.

kulak (koo-lak) *n.* (in the USSR) a peasant proprietor working for his own profit.

kümmel (kuu-mĕl) *n.* a sweet liqueur flavoured with caraway seeds.

kumquat (**kum**-kwot) *n.* a plum-sized orange-like fruit used in preserves.

kung fu (kuung **foo**) a Chinese form of unarmed combat, similar to karate.

Kurd *n.* a member of a pastoral people of Kurdistan, a mountainous region of east Turkey, north Iraq, and north-west Iran. **Kurdish** *adj. & n.*

Kuwait (koo-**wayt**) **1.** a country bordering on the Persian Gulf. **2.** its capital city. **Kuwaiti** *adj. & n.*

kV *abbrev.* kilovolt(s).

kW *abbrev.* kilowatt(s).

kWh *abbrev.* kilowatt-hour(s).

Ky. *abbrev.* Kentucky.

kyloe (ky-loh) *n.* one of a breed of small long-horned Scottish cattle.

Ll

L *abbrev.* learner, *L-driver*.

l *abbrev.* litre(s).

La. *abbrev.* Louisiana.

LA *abbrev.* Los Angeles.

lab *n.* (*informal*) a laboratory.

label *n.* **1.** a slip of paper or cloth or metal etc. fixed on or beside an object and showing its nature, owner, name, destination, or other information about it. **2.** a descriptive word or phrase classifying people etc. —**label** *v.* (labelled, labelling) **1.** to attach a label to. **2.** to describe or classify, *he was labelled as a troublemaker.*

labia (lay-bi-ă) *pl. n.* the lips of the female genitals; *labia majora,* the fleshy outer folds; *labia minora,* the inner folds.

labial (lay-bi-ăl) *adj.* of the lips.

laboratory (lă-**bo**-ră-ter-i) *n.* a room or building equipped for scientific experiments or research etc.

laborious *adj.* **1.** needing much effort or perseverance. **2.** showing signs of great effort, not spontaneous, forced. **3.** hardworking. **laboriously** *adv.*

labour *n.* **1.** physical or mental work, exertion. **2.** a task; *a labour of Hercules,* a herculean task. **3.** the pains or contractions of the womb at childbirth. **4.** workers, working people distinguished from management or considered as a political force. **5.** *Labour,* the Labour Party. —**labour** *v.* **1.** to exert oneself, to work hard. **2.** to have to make a great effort, to operate or progress only with difficulty, *the engine was labouring.* **3.** to treat at great length or in excessive detail, *I will not labour the point.* □ **labour camp,** a penal settlement with forced labour by prisoners. **Labour Day,** 1 May, celebrated in honour of workers; (in the USA) a public holiday on the first Monday in September. **Labour Exchange,** (*informal*) an employment exchange. **labour-intensive** *adj.* (of an industry) needing to employ many people. **Labour Party,** a political party in Britain, representing the interests of workers. **labour-saving** *adj.* designed to reduce the amount of work or effort needed.

laboured *adj.* showing signs of great effort, not spontaneous.

labourer *n.* a person employed to do unskilled manual work or to assist a skilled worker, *a bricklayer's labourer.*

Labourite *n.* a supporter of the Labour Party.

Labrador (lab-ră-dor) a region of Canada. —*n.* a retriever dog of a breed with a smooth black or golden coat.

laburnum *n.* an ornamental tree with hanging clusters of yellow flowers.

labyrinth (lab-er-inth) *n.* a complicated network of paths through which it is difficult to find one's way.

LAC *abbrev.* Leading Aircraftman.

lace *n.* **1.** fabric or trimming made in an ornamental openwork design. **2.** a cord or narrow leather strip threaded through holes or hooks for pulling opposite edges together and securing them. —**lace** *v.* **1.** to fasten with a lace or laces. **2.** to pass (a cord) through, to intertwine. **3.** to flavour or fortify (a drink) with a dash of spirits.

lacerate (**las**-er-ayt) *v.* **1.** to injure (flesh) by tearing. **2.** to wound (feelings). **laceration** *n.*

lachrymal (lak-rim-ăl) *adj.* of tears, secreting tears, *lachrymal ducts.*

lachrymose (lak-rim-ohs) *adj.* tearful.

lack *n.* the state or fact of not having something. —*v.* to be without or not have (a thing) when it is needed; *they lack for nothing,* have plenty of everything. □ **lacking** *adj.* undesirably absent, *money was lacking*; deficient, *he is lacking in courage.* **lack-lustre** *adj.* (of the eye etc.) not bright, dull.

lackadaisical (lak-ă-**day**-zikăl) *adj.* lacking vigour or determination, unenthusiastic.

lackey *n.* (*pl.* lackeys) **1.** a footman, a servant. **2.** a person's servile follower.

laconic (lă-**kon**-ik) *adj.* terse. **laconically** *adv.*

lacquer (lak-er) *n.* a hard glossy varnish. —*v.* to coat with lacquer.

lacrosse (lă-**kross**) *n.* a game resembling hockey but with players using a netted crook (a *crosse*) to catch or carry or throw the ball.

lactation (lak-tay-shŏn) *n.* the secreting of milk in breasts or udder, the period during which this occurs.

lacuna (lă-**kew**-nă) *n.* (*pl.* lacunae, *pr.* lă-kew-nee) a gap, a section missing from a book or argument etc.

lacy *adj.* like lace.

lad *n.* **1.** a boy, a young fellow. **2.** (*informal*) a fellow. **3.** a stable-lad (*see* stable².).

ladder *n.* **1.** a set of cross-bars (*rungs*) between two uprights of wood etc., used as a means of climbing up or down something. **2.** a vertical ladder-like flaw in a stocking etc. caused by a stitch or stitches becoming undone through several rows. **3.** a means or series of stages by which a person may advance in his career etc., *the political ladder.* —*v.* to cause a ladder in (a stocking etc.), to develop a ladder.

laddie *n.* a lad.

laden *adj.* loaded with a cargo or burden.

la-di-da *adj.* (*informal*) having an affected manner or pronunciation.

lading (**lay**-ding) *n.* cargo; *bill of lading* (*see* bill¹).

ladle *n.* a utentsil with a deep bowl and a long handle, for transferring liquids. —*v.* to transfer with a ladle.

lady *n.* **1.** a woman of good social position, a woman of polite and kindly behaviour. **2.** (in polite use) a woman. **3.** (*old use*) a wife, *the colonel's lady.* **4.** *Lady,* a title used with the surname of the wives or widows of certain noblemen, or with the Christian name of daughters of a duke or marquis or earl. **5.** a woman with authority over a household etc., *the lady of the house.* **6.** a woman to whom a man is chivalrously devoted. **7.** *the Ladies* or *ladies' room,* a women's public lavatory. □ **ladies' man,** a man who is fond of female society. **Lady chapel,** a chapel within a large church, dedicated to the Virgin Mary. **lady-in-waiting** *n.* a lady attending a queen or princess. **Lady Day,** the Feast of the Annunciation, 25 March. **lady's maid,** a lady's personal maidservant. **lady's slipper,** a wild or garden flower of the orchid family, with a bloom shaped like a slipper or pouch.

ladybird *n.* a small flying beetle, usually reddish-brown with black spots.

ladylike *adj.* polite and suitable for a lady, *ladylike manners.*

ladyship *n.* a title used in speaking to or about a woman of the rank of Lady, *your ladyship.*

lady-smock *n.* a wild flower with pale pinkish petals, growing in damp ground.

lag¹ *v.* (**lagged, lagging**) to go too slow, to fail to keep up with others. —*n.* lagging, a delay.

lag² *v.* (**lagged, lagging**) to encase (pipes or a boiler etc.) in a layer of insulating material to prevent loss of heat.

lag³ *n.* (*slang*) a convict, *old lags.*

lager (**lahg**-er) *n.* a kind of light beer.

laggard *n.* a person who lags behind.

lagoon *n.* **1.** a salt-water lake separated from the sea by a sandbank or coral reef etc. **2.** a small freshwater lake near a larger lake or river.

Lagos (**lay**-goss) the capital of Nigeria.

laid *see* lay³. □ **laid-back** *adj.* (*slang*) relaxed. **laid paper,** paper with the surface marked in fine ribs; *cream laid,* cream laid paper.

lain *see* lie².

lair *n.* **1.** a sheltered place where a wild animal regularly sleeps or rests. **2.** a person's hiding-place.

laird *n.* (*Scottish*) a landowner.

laissez-faire (lay-say-**fair**) *n.* the policy of non-interference. (¶ French, = let act.)

laity (**lay**-iti) *n.* laymen, *the laity.*

lake *n.* a large body of water entirely surrounded by land. **Lake District,** the district round the lakes in Cumbria.

lakh (*pr.* lak) *n.* (in India) a hundred thousand, *a lakh of rupees.*

lam *v.* (**lammed, lamming**) (*slang*) to hit hard, to thrash; *lammed into him,* attacked him physically or verbally.

lama (**lah**-mă) *n.* a priest of the form of Buddhism found in Tibet and Mongolia.

lamasery (lă-**mah**-ser-i) *n.* a monastery of lamas.

lamb *n.* **1.** a young sheep. **2.** its flesh as food. **3.** (*informal*) a gentle or endearing person. —*lamb v.* **1.** to give birth to a lamb. **2.** to tend lambing ewes. □ **Lamb of God,** Christ (compared to the lamb sacrificed by Jews at the Passover).

lambaste (lam-**bayst**) *v.* (*informal*) to thrash or beat or reprimand severely.

lambskin *n.* the skin of a lamb, either with its wool on (used in making clothing etc.) or as leather.

lambswool *n.* soft fine wool used in making machine-knitted garments.

lame *adj.* **1.** unable to walk normally because of an injury or defect, especially in a foot or leg. **2.** (of an excuse or argument) weak, unconvincing. —*v.* to make lame. —**lamely** *adv.,* **lameness** *n.* □ **lame duck,** a person or firm etc. that is in difficulties and unable to manage without help.

lamé (**lah**-may) *n.* a fabric in which gold or silver thread is interwoven.

lament *n.* **1.** a passionate expression of grief. **2.** a song or poem expressing grief. —*v.* to feel or express great sorrow or regret. □ **lamented** *adj.* mourned for.

lamentable (**lam**-ĕn-tă-bŭl) *adj.* regrettable, deplorable. **lamentably** *adv.*

lamentation (lam-ĕn-**tay**-shŏn) *n.* **1.** lamenting. **2.** a lament, an expression of grief.

laminate (**lam**-in-ăt) *n.* a laminated material.

laminated *adj.* made of layers joined one upon the other, *laminated plastic.*

Lammas *n.* the first day of August, formerly observed as a harvest festival.

lamp *n.* **1.** a device for giving light, either by the use of electricity or gas or by burning oil or spirit. **2.** a glass container enclosing a filament that is made to glow by electricity. **3.** an electrical device producing radiation, *an infra-red lamp.* □ **lamp standard** *n.* a lamppost.

lampoon (lam-**poon**) *n.* a piece of writing

that attacks a person by ridiculing him. —*v.* to ridicule in a lampoon.

lamppost *n.* a tall post supporting a street lamp.

lamprey *n.* (*pl.* lampreys) a small eel-like water animal with a round mouth used as a sucker for attaching itself to things.

lampshade *n.* a shade placed over a lamp to soften or screen its light.

Lancashire a county of England.

lance *n.* a weapon used for spearing fish etc., consisting of a long wooden shaft with a pointed steel head, resembling that used by mounted knights or cavalry in the Middle Ages. —*v.* to prick or cut open with a lancet. □ **lance-corporal** *n.* an NCO ranking below a corporal.

lancer *n.* a soldier of a certain cavalry regiment formerly armed with lances.

lancet (**lahn**-sit) *n.* 1. a pointed two-edged knife used by surgeons. 2. a tall narrow pointed arch or window.

Lancs. *abbrev.* Lancashire.

land *n.* 1. the solid part of the earth's surface, the part not covered by water or sea. 2. the ground or soil as used for farming etc. 3. an expanse of country, *forest land.* 4. a country or State or nation, *Land of Hope and Glory*; *in the land of the living,* alive. 5. property consisting of land. —**land** *v.* 1. to arrive or put on land from a ship. 2. to bring (an aircraft or its passengers etc.) down to the ground or other surface, to come down in this way. 3. to alight after a jump or fall. 4. to bring (a fish) to land, to win (a prize) or obtain (an appointment etc.), *landed an excellent job.* 5. to arrive or cause to arrive at a certain place or stage or position, *landed up in gaol; landed us all in a mess.* 6. to strike with a blow, *landed him one in the eye.* 7. to present with a problem etc., *landed us with the job of sorting it out.* □ **land-locked** *adj.* almost or entirely surrounded by land. **land-mine** *n.* an explosive mine laid in or on the ground.

Land's End, the westernmost point of the mainland of Britain, in Cornwall.

landed *adj.* 1. owning land, *landed gentry.* 2. consisting of land, *landed estates.*

landfall *n.* approach to land after a journey by sea or air.

landing *n.* 1. the process of coming or bringing something to land or of alighting after a jump etc. 2. a place where people and goods may be landed from a boat etc. 3. a level area between or at the top of flights or a flight of stairs. □ **landing-craft** *n.* naval craft designed for putting ashore troops and equipment. **landing-gear** *n.* the undercarriage of an aircraft. **landing-stage** *n.* a platform on which

people and goods are landed from a boat. **landing-strip** *n.* an airstrip.

landlady *n.* 1. a woman who lets rooms etc. to tenants. 2. a woman who keeps an inn or boarding-house.

landlord *n.* 1. a person who lets land or a house or a room etc. to a tenant. 2. one who keeps an inn or boarding-house.

landlubber *n.* (*sailors' informal*) a person who is not accustomed to the sea and seamanship.

landmark *n.* 1. a conspicuous and easily recognized feature of a landscape. 2. an event that marks a stage or change in the history of something.

landowner *n.* a person who owns a large area of land.

landrail *n.* a corncrake.

landscape *n.* 1. the scenery of a land area. 2. a picture of this. —*v.* to lay out (an area) attractively, with natural features. □ **landscape gardening,** laying out a garden in imitation of natural scenery.

landslide *n.* 1. a landslip. 2. an overwhelming majority of votes for one side in an election.

landslip *n.* the sliding down of a mass of land on a slope or mountain.

landsman *n.* (*pl.* landsmen) a person who is not a sailor.

landward *adj.* & *adv.* towards the land. **landwards** *adv.*

lane *n.* 1. a narrow road or track, often between hedges. 2. a narrow road or alley between buildings. 3. a passage made or left between rows of people. 4. a strip of road for a single line of traffic, a strip of track or water for a runner or rower or swimmer in a race. 5. a route prescribed for or regularly followed by ships or aircraft, *shipping lanes.*

language *n.* 1. words and their use. 2. a system of words used in one or more countries. 3. a system of signs or symbols used for conveying information. 4. a system of words, phrases, and symbols by means of which a computer can be programmed. 5. a particular style of wording. 6. the vocabulary of a particular group of people, *medical language.* □ **language laboratory,** a room equipped with tape recorders etc. for learning a language by repeated practice.

languid (**lang**-wid) *adj.* lacking vigour or vitality. **languidly** *adv.*

languish (**lang**-wish) *v.* 1. to lose or lack vitality. 2. to live under miserable conditions, to be neglected. □ **languishing** *adj.* putting on a languid look in an attempt to win sympathy or affection.

languor (lang-er) *n*. **1**. tiredness, listlessness, lack of vitality. **2**. a languishing expression. **3**. oppressive stillness of the air. **languorous** *adj*.

langur (lăng-**oor**) *n*. a long-tailed monkey of Asia.

lank *adj*. **1**. tall and lean. **2**. (of grass) long and limp, (of hair) straight and limp.

lanky *adj*. (lankier, lankiest) ungracefully lean and long or tall. **lankiness** *n*.

lanolin (**lan**-ŏ-lin) *n*. fat extracted from sheep's wool and used as a basis for ointments.

lantern *n*. a transparent case for holding a light and shielding it against wind etc. outdoors. **lantern-jawed** *adj*. having long thin jaws so that the face has a hollow look.

lanyard *n*. **1**. a short rope or line used on a ship to fasten something or secure it. **2**. a cord worn round the neck or on the shoulder, to which a knife or whistle etc. may be attached.

Laos (*rhymes with* mouse) a country in south-east Asia. **Laotian** (lah-**oh**-shăn) *adj. & n.*

lap[1] *n*. **1**. the flat area formed by the upper part of the thighs of a seated person. **2**. the part of a dress etc. covering this. □ **in a person's lap**, as his responsibility; *in the lap of the gods*, for fate to decide. **in the lap of luxury**, in great luxury. **lap-dog** *n*. a small pampered dog.

lap[2] *n*. **1**. an overlapping part, the amount of overlap. **2**. a single circuit of something, e.g. of a racecourse. **3**. one section of a journey, *the last lap*. —**lap** *v*. (lapped, lapping) **1**. to fold or wrap round. **2**. to overlap. **3**. to be one or more laps ahead of (another competitor) in a race. □ **lap of honour**, a ceremonial circuit of a racetrack or sports field etc. by the winner(s).

lap[3] *v*. (lapped, lapping) **1**. to take up (liquid) by movements of the tongue, as a cat does. **2**. to flow with ripples making a gentle splashing sound, *waves lapped the shore* or *against the shore*.

La Paz the capital of Bolivia.

lapel (lă-**pel**) *n*. a flap at the edge of each front of a coat etc., folded back to lie against its outer surface. **lapelled** *adj*. having lapels.

lapidary (**lap**-id-er-i) *adj*. of stones, engraved on stone.

lapis lazuli (lap-iss laz-yoo-li) a bright-blue semi-precious stone.

Lapland a region at the north of Scandinavia. **Laplander** *n*. a native or inhabitant of Lapland.

Lapp *n*. **1**. a Laplander. **2**. the language of Lapland.

lapse *n*. **1**. a slight error, especially one caused by forgetfulness or weakness or inattention. **2**. backsliding, a decline into an inferior state. **3**. the passage of a period of time, *after a lapse of six months*. **4**. the termination of a privilege or legal right through disuse. —**lapse** *v*. **1**. to fail to maintain one's position or standard. **2**. (of rights and privileges) to be lost or no longer valid because not used or claimed or renewed.

lapwing *n*. a peewit.

larceny (**lar**-sin-i) *n*. theft of personal goods.

larch *n*. a tall cone-bearing deciduous tree of the pine family.

lard *n*. a white greasy substance prepared from pig-fat and used in cooking. —*v*. **1**. to place strips of fat bacon in or on (meat) before cooking, in order to prevent it from becoming dry while roasting. **2**. to interlard.

larder *n*. a room or cupboard for storing food.

lardy *adj*. like lard. **lardy-cake** *n*. cake made with lard and containing currants.

large *adj*. **1**. of considerable size or extent. **2**. of the larger kind, *the large intestine*. — *adv*. in a large way, on a large scale, *bulk or loom large*. —**largeness** *n*. □ **at large**, free to roam about, not in confinement; in a general way, at random; as a whole, in general, *is popular with the country at large*.

large-scale *adj*. drawn to a large scale so that many details can be shown, *a large-scale map*; extensive, involving large quantities etc., *large-scale operations*.

largely *adv*. to a great extent, *his success was largely due to luck*.

largesse (lar-**jess**) *n*. money or gifts generously given.

largish *adj*. fairly large.

lariat (la-ri-ăt) *n*. a lasso, a rope used to catch or tether a horse etc.

lark[1] *n*. any of several small sandy-brown birds, especially the skylark. **rise with the lark**, to get up early.

lark[2] *n*. **1**. a playful adventurous action. **2**. an amusing incident. —*v*. to play about lightheartedly.

larkspur *n*. a plant with spur-shaped blue or pink flowers.

larn *v*. (*humorous*) = learn (sense 3); *that'll larn him*, will train him by punishment or unpleasant experience.

larrikin *n*. (*Austral*.) a lout, a hooligan.

larva *n*. (*pl*. larvae, *pr*. **lar**-vee) an insect in the first stage of its life after coming out of the egg. **larval** *adj*.

laryngitis (la-rin-**jy**-tiss) *n*. inflammation of the larynx.

larynx (la-rinks) *n.* the part of the throat containing the vocal cords.

lasagne (lă-san-yeh) *pl. n.* pasta formed into ribbon-like strips, served with a sauce containing minced meat.

Lascar (lask-er) *n.* a seaman from the countries south-east of India.

lascivious (lă-siv-i-ŭs) *adj.* lustful. **lasciviously** *adv.,* **lasciviousness** *n.*

laser (lay-zer) *n.* a device that generates an intense and highly concentrated beam of light, *laser beams.*

lash *v.* 1. to move in a whip-like movement, *lashed its tail.* 2. to strike with a whip, to beat or strike violently, *rain lashed against the panes.* 3. to attack violently in words. 4. to fasten or secure with cord etc., *lashed them together.* —**lash** *n.* 1. a stroke with a whip etc. 2. the flexible part of a whip. 3. an eyelash. □ **lash out**, to attack with blows or words; to spend lavishly. **lash-up** *n.* an improvised structure.

lashings *pl. n.* (*slang*) a lot, *lashings of cream.*

lass *or* **lassie** *ns.* (*Scottish & N. England*) a girl, a young woman.

Lassa fever a serious disease of tropical Africa, caused by a virus. ¶ Named after Lassa in Nigeria.

lassitude *n.* tiredness, listlessness.

lasso (la-soo) *n.* (*pl.* lassoes) a rope with a running noose, used (especially in America) for catching cattle. —*v.* (lassoed, lassoing) to catch with a lasso.

last¹ *n.* a block of wood or metal shaped like a foot, used in making and repairing shoes.

last² *adj. & adv.* 1. after all others in position or time, coming at the end. 2. latest, most recent, most recently; *last night*, in the night that has just passed. 3. remaining as the only one(s) left, *our last hope.* 4. least likely or suitable, *she is the last person I'd have chosen.* —**last** *n.* 1. a person or thing that is last. 2. the last performance of certain actions, *breathe or look one's last.* 3. the last mention or sight of something, *shall never hear the last of it.* □ **at last** *or* **at long last**, in the end, after much delay. **last ditch**, a place of final desperate defence. **last-minute** *adj.* at the latest possible time when an event etc. can be altered or influenced. **last post**, a military bugle-call sounded at sunset, also at military funerals etc. **last straw**, a slight addition to one's difficulties that makes them unbearable. **Last Supper**, the meal eaten by Christ and his disciples on the eve of the Crucifixion. **last trump**, a trumpet-call to

wake the dead on Judgement Day. **last word**, the final statement in a dispute; a definitive statement; the latest fashion. **on one's** *or* **its last legs**, near death or the end of usefulness.

last³ *v.* 1. to continue for a period of time, to endure. *the rain lasted all day.* 2. to be sufficient for one's needs, *enough food to last us for three days.* □ **last out**, to be strong enough or sufficient to last.

lasting *adj.* able to last for a long time.

lastly *adv.* in the last place, finally.

latch *n.* 1. a small bar fastening a door or gate, lifted from its catch by a lever. 2. a spring-lock that catches when the door is closed. —*v.* to fasten or be fastened with a latch. □ **latch on to**, (*informal*) to cling to; to get possession of; to take in as an idea. **on the latch**, fastened by a latch but not locked.

latchkey *n.* the key of an outer door; *latchkey children*, those left to look after themselves because neither parent is at home when they return from school etc.

late *adj. & adv.* 1. after the proper or usual time. 2. flowering or ripening late in the season. 3. far on in the day or night or a period of time or a series etc., *in the late 1920s.* 4. of recent date or time, *the latest news.* 5. no longer alive, no longer holding a certain position, *the late president.* —**lateness** *n.* □ **late in the day**, at a late stage in the proceedings. **of late**, lately.

lateen (lă-teen) *n.* 1. (of a sail) triangular and hung on a long spar at an angle of 45° to the mast. 2. (of a ship) rigged with such a sail.

lately *adv.* in recent times, not long ago.

latent (lay-těnt) *adj.* existing but not yet active or developed or visible.

lateral (lat-er-ăl) *adj.* of or at or towards the side(s). **laterally** *adv.* □ **lateral thinking**, seeking to solve problems by unusual methods.

latex (lay-teks) *n.* 1. a milky fluid exuded from the cut surfaces of certain plants, e.g. the rubber plant. 2. a synthetic product resembling this, used in paints and adhesives.

lath (*pr.* lath) *n.* (*pl.* laths) a narrow thin strip of wood, used in trellises or as a support for plaster etc.

lathe (*pr.* layth) *n.* a machine for holding and turning pieces of wood or metal etc. against a tool that will shape them.

lather *n.* 1. a froth produced by soap or detergent mixed with water. 2. frothy sweat, especially on horses. —**lather** *v.* 1. to cover with lather. 2. to form a lather.

Latin *n.* the language of the ancient Romans. —*adj.* 1. of or in Latin. 2. of the countries or peoples (e.g. France, Spain, Portugal, Italy) using languages developed from Latin. □ **Latin America**, the parts of Central and South America where Spanish or Portuguese is the main language. **Latin-American** *adj.* of these parts, (*n.*) a native of these parts. **Latin Church**, the Roman Catholic Church.

latitude *n.* **1.** the distance of a place from the equator, measured in degrees. **2.** a region, especially with reference to temperature; *high latitudes*, regions near the North or South Pole; *low latitudes*, near the equator. **3.** freedom from restrictions or actions or opinions.

latrine (lă-**treen**) *n.* a lavatory in a camp or barracks etc., a trench or pit for human excreta where there are no sewers.

latter *adj.* **1.** mentioned after another; *the latter*, the one mentioned second of two things. (¶ When referring to the last of three or more, *the last*, not *the latter*, should be used.) **2.** nearer to the end, *the latter half of the year*. □ **latter-day** *adj.* modern, recent. **Latter-day Saints**, Mormons' name for themselves.

latterly *adv.* of late, nowadays.

lattice (**lat**-iss) *n.* **1.** a framework of crossed laths or bars with spaces between, used as a screen or fence etc. **2.** a structure resembling this. □ **lattice window**, one made with a lattice or with small panes set in strips of lead.

laud *v.* (*formal*) to praise.

laudable (**law**-dă-bŭl) *adj.* praiseworthy. **laudably** *adv.*

laudanum (**lawd**-nŭm) *n.* opium prepared for use as a sedative.

laudatory (**law**-dă-ter-i) *adj.* praising. ¶ Do not confuse with laudable.

laugh *v.* **1.** to make the sounds and movements of the face and body that express lively amusement or amused scorn. **2.** to have these emotions. **3.** to utter or treat with a laugh; *laughed him out of it*, ridiculed him until he stopped a habit etc. — **laugh** *n.* **1.** an act or sound or manner of laughing. **2.** (*informal*) an amusing incident. □ **laugh in a person's face**, to show one's amused scorn for him openly. **laughing-gas** *n.* nitrous oxide, which can cause involuntary laughter in a person who inhales it. **laughing jackass**, the kookaburra. **laughing-stock** *n.* a person or thing that is ridiculed. **laugh it off**, to get rid of embarrassment by making a joke about it. **laugh on the other side of one's face**, to change from amusement to dismay. **laugh out of court**, to make fun of (a thing) so that no one gives it serious consideration. **no laughing matter**,

not fit subject for laughter.

laughable *adj.* causing people to laugh, ridiculous.

laughter *n.* the act or sound or manner of laughing.

launch[1] *v.* **1.** to send forth by hurling or thrusting, to send on its course, *launch a rocket*. **2.** to cause (a ship) to move or slide from land into the water. **3.** to put into action, *launch an attack* or *a business*. **4.** to enter boldly or freely into a course of action. —*n.* the process of launching a ship or spacecraft. □ **launching pad** *or* **launch pad**, a concrete platform from which spacecraft are launched. **launch out**, to spend money freely; to start on an ambitious enterprise.

launch[2] *n.* a large motor boat.

launder *v.* **1.** to wash and iron (clothes etc.). **2.** to be washable. **3.** to transfer (funds etc.) so as to make their source seem legitimate.

launderette (lawn-der-et) *n.* an establishment fitted with washing-machines to be used by customers for a fee.

laundry *n.* **1.** a place where clothes etc. are laundered, a business establishment that launders things for customers. **2.** a batch of clothes etc. sent to or from a laundry.

laureate (**lorri**-ăt) *adj.* **Poet Laureate**, the poet appointed to write poems for State occasions.

laurel (*rhymes with* quarrel) *n.* an evergreen shrub with smooth glossy leaves. **look to one's laurels**, to beware of losing one's position of superiority. **rest on one's laurels**, to cease to strive for further successes. (¶ From the ancient use of a branch or wreath of laurel as a token of victory.)

lav *n.* (*informal*) a lavatory.

lava (**lah**-vă) *n.* flowing molten rock discharged from a volcano, the solid substance formed when this cools.

lavatory *n.* **1.** a pan (usually a fixture) into which urine and faeces may be discharged for hygienic disposal. **2.** a room or building or compartment equipped with this.

lavender *n.* **1.** a shrub with fragrant purple flowers that are dried and used to scent linen etc. **2.** light purple. □ **lavender-water** *n.* a delicate perfume made from lavender.

laver (**lay**-ver) *n.* an edible seaweed of various kinds.

lavish (**lav**-ish) *adj.* **1.** giving or producing something in large quantities. **2.** plentiful, *a lavish display*. —*v.* to bestow lavishly. — **lavishly** *adv.*, **lavishness** *n.*

law *n.* **1.** a rule established among a community by authority or custom. **2.** a body of such rules. **3.** their controlling influence, their operation as providing a remedy against wrongs, *law and order*. **4.** the subject or study of such rules. **5.** (*informal*) the police. **6.** something that must be obeyed, *his word was law*. **7.** a factual statement of what always happens in certain circumstances, e.g. of regular natural occurrences, *the laws of nature; the law of gravity*. □ **go to law**, to ask a lawcourt to decide about a problem or claim. **law-abiding** *adj.* obeying the law. **law-breaker** *n.* one who breaks the law. **Law Lord**, a member of the House of Lords who is qualified to perform its legal work. **a law unto one-self** *or* **itself**, a person or thing that does not behave in the customary fashion. **take the law into one's own hands**, to right a wrong oneself without legal sanction.

lawcourt *n.* a room or building in which legal cases are heard and judged.

lawful *adj.* permitted or recognized by law, *lawful business; his lawful wife*. **lawfully** *adv.*

lawless *adj.* **1.** (of a country) where laws do not exist or are not applied. **2.** disregarding the law, uncontrolled, *lawless brigands*. **lawlessly** *adv.*, **lawlessness** *n.*

lawn¹ *n.* fine woven cotton or synthetic material.

lawn² *n.* an area of closely-cut grass in a garden or park, or used for a game, *croquet lawn*. **lawn-mower** *n.* a machine with revolving blade(s) for cutting the grass of lawns. **lawn tennis**, *see* tennis.

lawsuit *n.* the process of bringing a problem or claim etc. before a court of law for settlement.

lawyer (**loi**-er) *n.* a person who is trained and qualified in legal matters.

lax *adj.* slack, not strict or severe, *discipline was lax*. **laxly** *adv.*, **laxity** *n.*

laxative (**laks**-ă-tiv) *n.* a medicine that stimulates the bowels to empty. —*adj.* having this effect.

lay¹ *n.* (*old use*) a poem meant to be sung, a ballad.

lay² *adj.* **1.** not ordained into the clergy. **2.** not professionally qualified, especially in law or medicine; *lay opinion*, the opinion of non-professional people.

lay³ *v.* (laid, laying) **1.** to place or put on a surface or in a certain position. **2.** to place or arrange in a horizontal position, to put in place, *lay a carpet; lay the table* or *breakfast* etc., arrange things on a table for a meal; *lay the fire*, put fuel etc. ready for lighting; *lay the paint evenly*, apply it evenly. **3.** (*slang*, of a man) to have sexual intercourse with (a woman). **4.** to place or assign, *lay emphasis on neatness; laid the blame on her*. **5.** to formulate, to establish,

we laid our plans. **6.** to cause to be in a certain condition, *laid himself open to suspicion*. **7.** to cause to subside, *laid the dust; laid the ghost*, made it cease being troublesome. **8.** to present or put forward for consideration, *laid claim to it*. **9.** (of a hen bird) to produce (an egg or eggs) from the body. **10.** to stake as a wager, to bet. **11.** (*incorrect use*) = lie². —**lay** *n.* **1.** the way in which something lies. **2.** (*slang*) sexual intercourse, a female partner in this. □ **in lay**, (of hens) laying eggs regularly. **lay about one**, to hit out on all sides. **lay claim to**, to claim as one's right. **lay down**, to put on the ground etc.; to give up (office); to establish as a rule or instruction; to store (wine) in a cellar for future use. **lay down the law**, to talk authoritatively or as if sure of being right. **lay hold of**, to grasp. **lay in**, to provide oneself with a stock of. **lay into**, (*slang*) to thrash; to reprimand harshly. **lay it on the line**, (*slang*) to offer without reserve; to speak frankly. **lay it on thick** *or* **with a trowel**, (*slang*) to exaggerate greatly; to flatter a person excessively. **lay low**, to overthrow; to humble; to incapacitate by illness. **lay off**, to discharge (workers) temporarily owing to shortage of work; (*informal*) to cease, especially from causing trouble or annoyance. **lay-off** *n.* a temporary discharge. **lay on**, to inflict blows forcefully; to provide; *gas is laid on*, a supply is available. **lay open**, to break the skin of (part of the body); to expose to criticism. **lay out**, to arrange according to a plan; to prepare (a body) for burial; to spend (money) for a purpose; to knock unconscious; *laid himself out to help us*, made every effort. **layout** *n.* an arrangement of parts etc. according to a plan. **lay to rest**, to bury in a grave. **lay up**, to store or save; to cause to be confined to bed or unfit for work etc. **lay waste**, to destroy the crops and buildings etc. of (a district). ¶ Do not confuse *lay* (= put down; past tense is *laid*) with *lie* (= recline; past tense is *lay*). Correct uses are as follows: *go and lie down; she went and lay down; please lay it on the floor; they laid it on the floor*. Incorrect use is *go and lay down*.

layabout *n.* a loafer, a person who lazily avoids working for a living.

lay-by *n.* (*pl.* lay-bys) **1.** an extra strip of road beside a carriageway, where vehicles may stop without obstructing the flow of traffic. **2.** a similar arrangement on a canal or railway.

layer *n.* **1.** a person etc. that lays; *hen is a poor layer*, lays few eggs. **2.** a thickness of material (often one of several) laid over a surface. **3.** a shoot fastened down for propagation by layering. —**layer** v. **1.** to arrange in layers. **2.** to propagate by fastening down a shoot to take root while still attached to the parent plant. □ **layer cake,** cake consisting of layers with filling between.

layette n. the clothes and bedding etc. prepared for a new-born baby.

lay figure a jointed wooden figure of the human body, used by artists for arranging drapery on etc. ¶ From an old Dutch word *led* = joint.

layman n. (laymen) a lay person (= non-professional; see **lay**², sense 2).

layshaft n. a secondary or intermediate shaft for transmitting power in a machine.

laze v. to spend time idly or in idle relaxation. —n. an act or period of lazing.

lazy adj. (lazier, laziest) **1.** unwilling to work, doing little work. **2.** showing or characterized by lack of energy, *a lazy yawn.* **lazily** adv., **laziness** n. □ **lazy-bones** n. a lazy person. **lazy-tongs** n. an arrangement of zigzag levers for picking up distant objects.

lb abbrev. = pound(s) weight. (¶ From the Latin *libra*.)

lbw abbrev. leg before wicket.

leach v. to make (liquid) percolate through soil or ore etc., to remove (soluble matter) in this way, *leach it out.*

lead¹ (*pr.* leed) v. (led, leading) **1.** to cause to go with oneself, to guide, especially by going in front or by holding the hand or an attached rein etc. **2.** to influence the actions or opinions of, *what led you to believe this?* **3.** to be a route or means of access, *the door leads into a passage.* **4.** to have as its result, *this led to confusion.* **5.** to live or pass (one's life), *was leading a double life.* **6.** to be in first place or position in, to be ahead, *lead the world in electronics.* **7.** to be the leader or head of, to control. **8.** to make one's start, *Ali led with his left.* **9.** (in card-games) to play as one's first card, to be the first player. — **lead** n. **1.** guidance given by going in front, an example. **2.** a clue, *it gave us a lead.* **3.** a leading place, leadership, the amount by which one competitor is in front, *take the lead; a lead of 5 points.* **4.** an electrical conductor (usually a wire) conveying current from a source to a place of use. **5.** a strap or cord etc. for leading an animal, one fixed to a dog's collar and held to keep the dog under restraint. **6.** the act or right of playing one's card first in a card-game, the card played. **7.** the chief part in a play or other performance, one who takes this part, *play the lead; the lead singer.* □ **lead**

astray, to lead into error or wrongdoing. **lead by the nose,** to control the actions of (a person) completely. **lead someone a dance,** to cause him much trouble, especially by making him search. **lead someone on,** to entice him. **lead up the garden path,** to mislead. **lead up to,** to serve as an introduction to or preparation for; to direct the conversation towards (a subject).

lead² (*pr.* led) n. **1.** a heavy metal of dull greyish colour. **2.** a thin stick of graphite forming the writing substance in a pencil. **3.** a lump of lead used in taking soundings in water. □ **leaded** adj. covered or framed or mixed with lead. **leads** pl. n. strips of lead used to cover a roof, a piece of roof covered with these; a framework of lead strips holding the glass of a window. **swing the lead,** (*slang*) to pretend to be ill in order to avoid work.

leaden (led'n) adj. **1.** made of lead. **2.** heavy, slow as if weighted with lead. **3.** lead-coloured, dark grey, *leaden skies.*

leader n. **1.** a person or thing that leads. **2.** one who has the principal part in something, the head of a group etc., (in an orchestra) the principal first-violin player. **3.** one whose example is followed, *a leader of fashion.* **4.** a leading article in a newspaper. □ **Leader of the House,** a member of the government in the House of Commons or of Lords who arranges and announces the business of the House.

leadership n. **1.** being a leader. **2.** ability to be a leader. **3.** the leaders of a group.

leading¹ (leed-ing) see **lead**¹. □ **leading aircraftman** or **seaman,** one ranking just below an NCO. **leading article,** a long article in a newspaper, giving the editor's opinions. **leading lady** or **man,** one taking the chief part in a play etc. **leading light,** a prominent member of a group. **leading question,** one that is worded so that it prompts a person to give the desired answer (¶ not the same as a *searching question*).

leading² (led-ing) n. a covering or framework of lead (metal).

leaf n. (pl. leaves) **1.** a flat organ (usually green) growing from the stem or branch of a plant or directly from the root. **2.** the state of having leaves out, *tree is in leaf.* **3.** a single thickness of the paper forming the pages of a book. **4.** a very thin sheet of metal, *gold leaf.* **5.** a hinged flap of a table, an extra section inserted to extend a table. —v. to turn over the leaves or pages of a book, *leafed through it.* □ **leaf-mould** n. soil or compost consisting chiefly of decayed leaves. **take a leaf out of someone's book,** to follow his example.

leafless *adj.* having no leaves.

leaflet *n.* **1.** a small leaf or leaf-like part of a plant. **2.** a printed sheet of paper (sometimes folded but not stitched) giving information, especially for distribution free of charge.

leafy *adj.* **1.** covered in leaves. **2.** consisting of leaves, *leafy vegetables.*

league *n.* **1.** a group of people or countries who combine formally for a particular purpose. **2.** a group of sports clubs which compete against each other for a championship. **3.** a class of contestants, *he is out of his league.* **4.** a measure of length, about 3 miles. —*v.* to form a league. □ **in league** with, allied with; conspiring with. **league table,** a table of contestants etc. in order of merit.

leak *n.* **1.** the process of leaking. **2.** a hole or crack etc. through which liquid or gas may wrongly get in or out. **3.** the liquid or gas that passes through this. **4.** a similar escape of an electric charge, the charge itself. **5.** a disclosure of secret information.— **leak** *v.* **1.** (of liquid or gas etc.) to escape wrongly through an opening. **2.** (of a container) to allow such an escape, to let out (liquid or gas). **3.** to disclose, *leaked the news to a reporter.* □ **leak out,** (of a secret) to become known despite efforts to keep it secret.

leakage *n.* **1.** leaking. **2.** a thing or amount that has leaked out.

leaky *adj.* liable to leak.

lean ¹ *adj.* **1.** (of a person or animal) without much flesh. **2.** (of meat) containing little or no fat. **3.** scanty, *a lean harvest.* —*n.* the lean part of meat. —**leanness** *n.* □ **lean years,** years of scarcity.

lean ² *v.* (leaned, leant, leaning) **1.** to put or be in a sloping position. **2.** to rest against or on something for support. **3.** to rely or depend on for help. □ **lean on,** (*informal*) to seek to influence by intimidation. **lean-to** *n.* a building with its roof resting against the side of a larger building.

¶ The past tense is 'he *leaned* or he *had leant* against the wall.'

leaning *n.* a tendency or partiality, *has leanings towards socialism.*

leap *v.* (leaped, leapt, leaping) to jump vigorously. —*n.* a vigorous jump. □ **by leaps and bounds,** with very rapid progress. **leap year,** a year with an extra day (29 February).

¶ The past tense is 'he *leaped* or he *had leapt* over the wall.'

leap-frog *n.* a game in which each player in turn vaults with parted legs over an-

other who is bending down. —*v.* (leap-frogged, leap-frogging) **1.** to perform this vault. **2.** to overtake alternately.

learn *v.* (learned (*pr.* lernt *or* lernd), learnt, learning) **1.** to gain knowledge of or skill in a subject etc. by study or experience or by being taught; *learn it by heart,* memorize it thoroughly so that one can repeat it. **2.** to become aware by information or from observation. **3.** (*incorrect* or *humorous use*) to teach, *he is learning her to drive; that'll learn you!*

¶ The past tense is 'he *learned* French' or 'he *has learnt* French' or 'French *was learnt* at school'.

learned (**lern**-id) *adj.* **1.** having much knowledge acquired by study, *learned men.* **2.** of or for learned people, *a learned society.* **learnedly** *adv.*

learner *n.* a person who is learning a subject or skill. **learner-driver** *n.* one who is learning to drive a motor vehicle but has not yet passed the driving test.

learning *n.* knowledge obtained by study.

lease *n.* a contract by which the owner of land or a building etc. allows another person to use it for a specified time, usually in return for payment. —*v.* **1.** to grant the use of (a property) by lease. **2.** to obtain or hold (a property) by lease. □ **a new lease of life,** a chance to continue living or to live more happily because of recovery from illness or anxiety, or (of things) to continue in use after repair.

leasehold *n.* the holding of land or a house or flat etc. by means of a lease. **leaseholder** *n.*

leash *n.* a thong by which hounds etc. are held under restraint, a dog's lead. —*v.* to hold on a leash.

least *adj.* **1.** smallest in amount or degree. **2.** lowest in rank or importance. —*n.* the least amount or degree. —*adv.* in the least degree. □ **at least,** not less than what is stated; anyway. **in the least,** at all, in the smallest degree. **to say the least of it,** putting the case moderately.

leather *n.* **1.** material made from animal skins by tanning or a similar process. **2.** the leather part(s) of something. **3.** a piece of leather for polishing with. —*v.* to wipe or polish with a leather. □ **leather-jacket** *n.* a crane-fly grub (which has a tough skin).

leathery *adj.* as tough as leather.

leave *v.* (left, leaving) **1.** to go away from, to go away finally or permanently. **2.** to cease to belong to (a group) or live at (a place), to cease working for an employer. **3.** to cause or allow to remain, to depart without taking, *left the door open; left my* *gloves in the bus; he leaves a wife and two children*, is survived by these. **4.** to give as a legacy. **5.** to allow to stay or proceed without interference, *left him to get on with it; leave the dog alone.* **6.** to refrain from consuming or dealing with, *left all the fat; let's leave the washing-up.* **7.** to entrust or commit to another person; *was left with the problem*, had this as a burden; *leave it to me*, I will deal with it. **8.** to deposit for collection or transmission, *leave your coat in the hall; leave a message.* **9.** to abandon, to desert, *was left in the lurch.* —**leave** *n.* **1.** permission. **2.** official permission to be absent from duty, the period for which this lasts; *on leave*, absent in this way. □ **leave off**, to cease; to cease to wear. **leave out**, to omit, not to include. **leave-taking** *n.* taking one's leave. **take leave of one's senses**, to go mad. **take one's leave**, to say farewell and go away.

leaven (lev-ĕn) *n.* **1.** a substance (e.g. yeast) that produces fermentation in dough. **2.** a quality or influence that lightens or enlivens something. —**leaven** *v.* **1.** to add leaven to. **2.** to enliven.

leavings *pl. n.* what is left.

Lebanon (leb-ă-nŏn) a country at the eastern end of the Mediterranean Sea. **Lebanese** *adj.* & *n.* (*pl.* Lebanese).

lecher *n.* a lecherous man. **lecherous** *adj.* of or characterized by lechery. **lechery** *n.* unrestrained indulgence of sexual lust.

lectern *n.* a stand with a sloping top to hold a Bible (from which the lesson is read) in church, or a lecturer's notes etc.

lectionary (lek-shŏn-ri) *n.* a list or book containing portions of Scripture appointed to be read at church services.

lecture *n.* **1.** a speech giving information about a subject to an audience or class. **2.** a long serious speech, especially one giving reproof or warning. —**lecture** *v.* **1.** to give a lecture or series of lectures. **2.** to talk to (a person) seriously or reprovingly. —**lecturer** *n.*

led *see* lead [1].

ledge *n.* a narrow horizontal projection, a narrow shelf.

ledger *n.* a tall narrow book used by a business firm as an account-book or to record trading transactions.

lee *n.* shelter, the sheltered side or part of something, *under the lee of the hedge.*

leech[1] *n.* **1.** a small blood-sucking worm usually living in water. **2.** a person who drains the resources of another.

leech[2] *n.* a vertical side of a square sail, the side of a fore-and-aft sail away from the mast or stay.

leek *n.* a plant related to the onion but with broader leaves and a cylindrical white bulb.

leer *v.* to look slyly or maliciously or lustfully. —*n.* a leering look.

leery *adj.* (*slang*) wary, suspicious.

lees *pl. n.* sediment that settles at the bottom of a quantity of wine etc.

leeward (lee-werd; *in nautical use* loo-erd) *adj.* situated on the side turned away from the wind. —*n.* the leeward side or region.

leeway *n.* **1.** a ship's sideways drift from its course. **2.** a degree of freedom of action, *these instructions give us plenty of leeway.* □ **make up leeway**, to make up lost time, to get back into position.

left[1] *see* leave. □ **left luggage**, luggage deposited temporarily at a railway office etc. **left-overs** *pl. n.* things remaining when the rest is finished, especially food not finished at a meal.

left[2] *adj.* & *adv.* on or towards the left-hand side. —*n.* **1.** the left-hand side or region. **2.** the left hand, a blow with this. **3.** (in marching) the left foot. **4.** *the Left*, the left wing of a political party or other group. □ **left hand**, the hand that in most people is less used, on the same side of the body as the heart. **left-hand** *adj.* of or towards this side of a person or the corresponding side of a thing. **left-handed** *adj.* using the left hand usually, by preference; (of a blow or tool) made with or operated by the left hand; (of a screw) to be tightened by turning towards the left; (of a compliment) ambiguous in meaning, back-handed. **left-hander** *n.* a left-handed person or blow. **left wing**, *see* wing sense 8; those who support a more extreme form of socialism than others in their group. **left-winger** *n.*

leftist *n.* a supporter of socialism, one who belongs to the left of a socialist group. —*adj.* of the left wing in politics etc.

lefty *n.* (*informal*) a left-handed person.

leg *n.* **1.** one of the projecting parts of an animal's body, on which it stands or moves. **2.** this as food. **3.** either of the two lower limbs of the human body, an artificial replacement of this. **4.** the part of a garment covering this. **5.** one of the projecting supports beneath a chair or other piece of furniture. **6.** one branch of a forked object. **7.** one section of a journey. **8.** one of a pair of matches between the same opponents. **9.** the side of a cricket field opposite the off side and behind the batsman; *long leg, short leg, square leg*, fieldsmen at various positions there. □ **give him a leg up**, help him to mount or to get over an obstacle or difficulty. **has not a leg to**

stand on, has no facts to support his argument. **leg before wicket**, (of a batsman) out because of illegally obstructing the ball with any part of the body other than the hand. **leg it**, (*informal*) to walk or run rapidly, to go on foot. **leg-pull** *n*. (*informal*) a hoax. **leg-rest** *n*. a support for a seated person's leg. **leg-room** *n*. space for a seated person to extend his legs.

legacy (leg-ăsi) *n*. **1**. money or an article left to someone in a will. **2**. something handed down by a predecessor, *a legacy of distrust*.

legal *adj*. **1**. of or based on law; *my legal adviser*, a solicitor etc. **2**. in accordance with the law, authorized or required by law. **legally** *adv.*, **legality** (lig-al-iti) *n*. □ **legal aid**, payment from public funds towards the cost of legal advice or proceedings.

legalize *v*. to make legal.

legate (leg-ăt) *n*. an envoy, especially one representing the pope.

legatee (leg-ă-tee) *n*. a person who receives a legacy.

legation (lig-ay-shŏn) *n*. **1**. a diplomatic minister and his staff. **2**. his official residence.

legato (lig-ah-toh) *adv*. (in music) in a smooth even manner.

legend (lej-ĕnd) *n*. **1**. a story (which may or may not be true) handed down from the past. **2**. such stories collectively. **3**. an inscription on a coin or medal.

legendary (lej-ĕn-der-i) *adj*. **1**. of or based on legends, described in a legend. **2**. (*informal*) famous, often talked about.

legerdemain (lej-er-dĕ-mayn) *n*. sleight of hand, conjuring tricks.

leger line (lej-er) a short line added in a musical score for notes above or below the range of the staff.

leggings *pl. n*. protective outer coverings for each leg from knee to ankle.

leggy *adj*. having noticeably long legs.

leghorn *n*. one of a small hardy breed of domestic fowl.

legible (lej-i-bŭl) *adj*. (of print or handwriting) clear enough to be deciphered, readable. **legibly** *adv.*, **legibility** *n*.

legion (lee-jŏn) *n*. **1**. a division of the ancient Roman army. **2**. a vast group, a multitude, *they are legion* or *their name is Legion*. □ **Foreign Legion**, a body of foreign volunteers in an army, especially the French army. **Royal British Legion**, an organization of ex-service men and women.

legionnaire (lee-jŏn-**air**) *n*. a member of the foreign legion or of the American or Royal British Legion. **legionnaires' disease**, a form of bacterial pneumonia

first identified in an outbreak at a meeting of the American Legion in 1976.

legislate (lej-iss-layt) *v*. to make laws. **legislation** *n*. legislating, the laws themselves.

legislative (lej-iss-lă-tiv) *adj*. making laws, *a legislative assembly*.

legislator (lej-iss-layt-er) *n*. a member of a legislative assembly.

legislature (lej-iss-lă-cher) *n*. a country's legislative assembly.

legitimate (li-jit-i-măt) *adj*. **1**. in accordance with the law or rules. **2**. logical, justifiable, *a legitimate reason for absence*. **3**. (of a child) born of parents who are married to each other. **legitimately** *adv.*, **legitimacy** *n*.

legitimize (li-jit-i-myz) *v*. to make legitimate.

legless *adj*. without legs.

legman *n*. (*pl*. legmen) a person employed to go round gathering news etc.

legume (leg-yoom) *n*. **1**. a leguminous plant. **2**. a pod of this, especially when edible.

leguminous (lig-yoo-min-ŭs) *adj*. of the family of plants that bear their seeds in pods, e.g. peas and beans.

lei (*pr*. lay) *n*. (in Polynesian countries) a garland of flowers worn round the neck.

Leicestershire a county of England.

Leics. *abbrev*. Leicestershire.

leisure (lezh-er) *n*. time that is free from work, time in which one can do as one chooses. **at leisure**, not occupied; in an unhurried way. **at one's leisure**, when one has time.

leisured *adj*. having plenty of leisure.

leisurely (lezh-er-li) *adj*. & *adv*. without hurry.

lemming *n*. a small mouse-like rodent of arctic regions, one species of which migrates in large numbers and is said to continue running into the sea and drown.

lemon *n*. **1**. an oval fruit with acid juice. **2**. the tree that bears it. **3**. its pale yellow colour. **4**. (*slang*) something disappointing or unsuccessful. **lemony** *adj*. □ **lemon cheese** *or* **curd**, a thick creamy-textured jam made with lemons.

lemonade *n*. a lemon-flavoured soft drink.

lemon sole a kind of plaice.

lemur (lee-mer) *n*. a monkey-like animal of Madagascar.

lend *v*. (lent, lending) **1**. to give or allow the use of (a thing) temporarily on the understanding that it or its equivalent will be returned. **2**. to provide (money) temporarily in return for payment of interest. **3**. to contribute as a temporary help or effect etc., *lend dignity to the occasion; lend a hand,* help; *lend an ear,* listen. **4.** to be of use, to be suitable, *this garden lends itself to relaxation.* **lender** *n.*

length *n.* **1.** measurement or extent from end to end, especially along a thing's greatest dimension. **2.** the amount of time occupied by something, *the length of our holiday.* **3.** the distance a thing extends used as a unit of measurement, the length of a horse or boat etc. as a measure of the lead in a race. **4.** the degree of thoroughness in an action, *went to great lengths.* **5.** a piece of cloth or other material from a larger piece, *a length of wire; a dress length,* one long enough to make a dress. □ **at length,** after a long time; taking a long time, in detail.

lengthen *v.* to make or become longer.

lengthways *adv.* in the direction of the length of something. **lengthwise** *adv. & adj.*

lengthy *adj.* (lengthier, lengthiest) very long, long and boring. **lengthily** *adv.*

lenient (lee-ni-ěnt) *adj.* merciful, not severe (especially in awarding punishment), mild. **leniently** *adv.,* **lenience** *n.*

lens *n.* (*pl.* **lenses**) **1.** a piece of glass or glass-like substance with one or both sides curved, for use in optical instruments. **2.** a combination of lenses used in photography etc. **3.** the transparent part of the eye, behind the pupil.

lent *see* **lend.**

Lent *n.* the period from Ash Wednesday to Easter Eve, of which the 40 weekdays are observed as a time of fasting and penitence. **Lenten** *adj.*

lentil *n.* **1.** a kind of bean plant. **2.** its edible seed, *lentil soup.*

Leo (lee-oh) *n.* a sign of the zodiac, the Lion.

leonine (lee-ŏ-nyn) *adj.* of or like a lion.

leopard (lep-erd) *n.* a large African and South Asian flesh eating animal of the cat family (also called a *panther*), having a yellowish coat with dark spots or a black coat. **leopardess** *n.*

leotard (lee-ŏ-tard) *n.* a close-fitting one-piece garment worn by acrobats etc.

leper *n.* a person with leprosy.

leprechaun (lep-rĕ-kawn) *n.* (in Irish folklore) an elf resembling a little old man.

leprosy *n.* an infectious disease affecting skin and nerves, resulting in mutilations and deformities. **leprous** *adj.*

lesbian *n.* a homosexual woman. **lesbianism** *n.*

lèse-majesté (layz-ma-zhess-tay) *n.* **1.** an insult to a sovereign or ruler. **2.** (*humorous*) presumptuous behaviour.

lesion (lee-zhŏn) *n.* a harmful change in the tissue of an organ of the body, caused by injury or disease.

Lesotho (lě-soo-too) a country surrounded by the Republic of South Africa.

less *adj.* **1.** not so much of, a smaller quantity of, *eat less meat.* **2.** smaller in amount or degree etc., *of less importance.* —*adv.* to a smaller extent. —*n.* a smaller amount or quantity etc., *will not take less.* —*prep.* minus, deducting, *a year less three days; was paid £100, less tax.*

¶ The word *less* is used of things that are measured by amount (e.g. in *eat less butter; use less fuel*). Its use of things measured by number is regarded as incorrect (e.g. in *we need less workers;* correct usage is *fewer workers*).

lessee (less-ee) *n.* a person who holds a property by lease.

lessen *v.* to make or become less.

lesser *adj.* not so great as the other, *the lesser evil.*

lesson *n.* **1.** a thing to be learnt by a pupil. **2.** an amount of teaching given at one time; *give lessons in a subject,* give systematic instruction in it. **3.** an example or experience by which one can learn, *let this be a lesson to you!* **4.** a passage from the Bible read aloud during a church service.

lessor (less-or) *n.* a person who lets a property on lease.

lest *conj.* **1.** in order that not, to avoid the risk that, *lest we forget.* **2.** that, *were afraid lest we should be late.*

let¹ *n.* **1.** stoppage, *without let or hindrance.* **2.** (in tennis etc.) an obstruction of the ball in certain ways, requiring the ball to be served again.

let² *v.* (let, letting) **1.** to allow to, not prevent or forbid, *let me see it.* **2.** to cause to, *let us know what happens.* **3.** to allow or cause to come or go or pass, *let the dog in; let the rope down; a piece was let into it, was inserted, especially into the surface.* **4.** to allow the use of (rooms or land) for payment; *house to let,* available in this way. **5.** used as an auxiliary verb in requests or commands (*let's try; let there be light*), assumptions (*let AB equal CD*), and challenges (*let him do his worst*). —*n.* the letting of property etc., *a long let.* □ **let alone,** to refrain from interfering with or doing; apart from, far less or more than, *too tired to walk, let alone run.* **let be,** to refrain from interfering with or doing. **let down,** to let out air from (a balloon or tyre etc.); to fail to support or satisfy, to disappoint; to lengthen (a garment) by adjusting the hem; *let one's hair down,* to abandon conventional restraint in one's behaviour; *let him down gently*, do not treat him too severely. **let-down** *n.* a disappointment. **let fly**, to shoot or send out violently; to hurl strong abuse. **let go**, to set at liberty; to loose one's hold of; to cease discussion of, to ignore; *let oneself go*, to behave in an unrestrained way, to cease to take trouble. **let in for**, to involve in (loss or difficulty). **let loose**, to release. **let off**, to fire (a gun); to cause (a bomb) to explode; to ignite (a firework); to excuse from doing (duties etc.); to give little or no punishment to. **let off steam**, to allow it to escape; to do something that relieves one's pent-up energy or feelings. **let on**, (*slang*) to reveal a secret. **let out**, to release from restraint or obligation; to make (a garment) looser by adjusting the seams; to let (rooms etc.) to tenants. **let-out** *n.* a way of escaping an obligation. **let slip**, to reveal (a secret); to miss (an opportunity). **let up**, (*informal*) to become less intense, to relax one's efforts. **let-up** *n.* a reduction in intensity, relaxation of effort.

lethal (lee-thǎl) *adj.* causing or able to cause death. **lethally** *adv.*, **lethality** (lith-al-iti) *n.*

lethargy (leth-er-ji) *n.* extreme lack of energy or vitality. **lethargic** (lith-ar-jik) *adj.*, **lethargically** *adv.*

let's = let us.

letter *n.* 1. a symbol representing a sound used in speech. 2. a written message addressed to one or more persons, usually sent by post. —*v.* to inscribe letters on, to draw or inscribe letters. □ **letter-bomb** *n.* a terrorist explosive device disguised as a letter sent by post. **letter-box** *n.* a slit in a door, with a movable flap, through which letters are delivered; a post-box. **letter-card** *n.* a folded card with a gummed edge that can be posted without using an envelope. **letter of the law**, its exact requirements (as opposed to its spirit or true purpose). **to the letter**, paying strict attention to every detail.

letterhead *n.* a printed heading on stationery, stationery with this.

lettuce *n.* a garden plant with broad crisp leaves much used as salad.

leucocyte (lew-kŏ-syt) *n.* a white blood-cell.

leucorrhoea (lew-kŏ-ree-ǎ) *n.* an abnormal white discharge from the vagina.

leucotomy (lew-kot-ŏmi) *n.* an incision into the white tissue at the front of the brain to relieve some types of mental disorder.

leukaemia (lew-kee-miǎ) *n.* a disease in which the white corpuscles multiply un-

controllably in the body tissues and usually in the blood.

Levant (li-vant) *n.* the countries and islands in the eastern part of the Mediterranean Sea. **Levantine** (lev-ǎn-tyn) *adj.* & *n.*

levee (lev-i) *n.* (*old use*) an assembly of visitors, especially at a formal reception.

level *n.* 1. an imaginary line or plane joining points of equal height. 2. a measured height or value etc., position on a scale, *the level of alcohol in the blood.* 3. relative position in rank or class or authority, *decisions at Cabinet level.* 4. a more or less flat surface or layer or area. 5. an instrument for testing a horizontal line. —**level** *adj.* 1. horizontal. 2. (of ground) flat, without hills or hollows. 3. on a level with, at the same height or rank or position on a scale. 4. steady, uniform, (of a voice) not changing in tone. —**level** *v.* (levelled, levelling) 1. to make or become level or even or uniform; *level up* or *down*, to bring up or down to a standard; *level out*, to become level. 2. to knock down (buildings) to the ground. 3. to aim (a gun or missile). 4. to direct (an accusation or criticism) at a person. —**levelly** *adv.*, **leveller** *n.* □ **do one's level best**, (*informal*) to make all possible efforts. **find one's level**, to reach one's right place in relation to others. **level crossing**, a place where a road and a railway (or two railways) cross each other at the same level. **level-headed** *adj.* mentally well-balanced, sensible. **level pegging**, equal scores or achievements. **on the level**, (*informal*) with no dishonesty or deception.

lever (lee-ver) *n.* 1. a bar or other device pivoted on a fixed point (the *fulcrum*) in order to lift something or force something open. 2. a projecting handle used in the same way to operate or control machinery etc. —*v.* to use a lever, to lift or move by this.

leverage *n.* 1. the action or power of a lever. 2. power, influence.

leveret (lev-er-it) *n.* a young hare.

leviathan (li-vy-ǎth-ǎn) *n.* something of enormous size and power. ¶ Named after a sea-monster in the Bible.

levitate *v.* to rise or cause to rise and float in the air in defiance of gravity. **levitation** *n.*

levity (lev-iti) *n.* a humorous attitude, especially towards matters that should be treated with respect.

levy *v.* (levied, levying) to impose or collect (a payment etc.) by authority or by force. —*n.* 1. levying. 2. the payment levied.

lewd *adj.* 1. indecent, treating sexual matters in a vulgar way. **2.** lascivious. **lewdly** *adv.*, **lewdness** *n.*

lexicography (leksi-**kog**-răfi) *n.* the process of compiling a dictionary. **lexicographer** *n.*

lexicon *n.* a dictionary of certain languages, especially Greek and Hebrew.

ley[1] (*pr.* lay) *n.* (*pl.* **leys**) land that is temporarily sown with grass.

ley[2] (*pr.* lee *or* lay) *n.* (*pl.* **leys**) the supposed straight line of a prehistoric track, usually between hilltops.

LF *abbrev.* low frequency.

liability *n.* **1.** being liable. **2.** (*informal*) a handicap, a disadvantage. □ **liabilities** *pl. n.* debts, obligations.

liable (**ly**-ăbŭl) *adj.* **1.** held responsible by law, legally obliged to pay a tax or penalty etc. **2.** able or likely to do or suffer something, *cliff is liable to crumble; she is liable to colds.*

liaise (lee-**ayz**) *v.* (*informal*) to act as a liaison or go-between.

liaison (lee-**ay**-zŏn) *n.* **1.** communication and co-operation between units of an organization. **2.** a person who acts as a link or go-between.

liar *n.* a person who tells lies.

Lib *n.* (*informal*) liberation, *Women's Lib.*

libel (**ly**-běl) *n.* **1.** a published false statement that damages a person's reputation. **2.** the act of publishing it, *was charged with libel.* **3.** (*informal*) a statement or anything that brings discredit on a person or thing, *the portrait is a libel on him.* —*v.* (**libelled, libelling**) to utter or publish a libel against. —**libellous** *adj.*

liberal *adj.* **1.** giving generously. **2.** ample, given in large amounts. **3.** not strict or literal, *a liberal interpretation of the rules.* **4.** (of education) broadening the mind in a general way, not only training it in technical subjects. **5.** tolerant, open-minded, especially in religion and politics. **6.** *Liberal,* of the Liberal Party. **liberally** *adv.*, **liberality** (lib-er-**al**-iti) *n.* □ **Liberal** *n.* a member of the Liberal Party, a political party more socialist than the Conservative Party but less so than the Labour Party. **Liberalism** *n.*

liberalize *v.* to make less strict. **liberalization** *n.*

liberate *v.* to set free, especially from control by an authority that is considered to be oppressive. **liberation** *n.*, **liberator** *n.*

Liberia (ly-**beer**-iă) a country on the coast of West Africa. **Liberian** *adj.* & *n.*

libertine (**lib**-er-teen) *n.* a man who lives an irresponsible and immoral life.

liberty *n.* **1.** freedom from captivity, slav-

ery, imprisonment, or despotic control by others. **2.** the right or power to do as one chooses. **3.** a right or privilege granted by authority. **4.** the setting aside of convention, improper familiarity; *take the liberty of doing* or *to do something,* venture to do it. □ **at liberty,** (of a person) not imprisoned, free; allowed, *you are at liberty to leave;* not occupied or engaged. **Liberty Hall,** a place where one may do as one likes. **take liberties,** to behave too familiarly towards a person; to interpret facts etc. too freely.

libido (lib-**ee**-doh) *n.* (*pl.* **libidos**) emotional energy or urge, especially that associated with sexual desire.

Lib-Lab *adj.* of a combination of the Liberal and Labour Parties.

Libra (**lib**-ră) *n.* a sign of the zodiac, the Scales. **Libran** *adj.* & *n.*

librarian *n.* a person in charge of or assisting in a library. **librarianship** *n.*

library (**ly**-bră-ri) *n.* **1.** a collection of books for reading or borrowing. **2.** a room or building where these are kept. **3.** a similar collection of records, films, etc.

libretto (lib-**ret**-oh) *n.* (*pl.* **librettos**) the words of an opera or other long musical work.

Libreville (leeh-ră-vil) the capital of Gabon.

Libya a country in North Africa. **Libyan** *adj.* & *n.*

lice *see* louse.

licence *n.* **1.** a permit from the government or other authority to own or do something or to carry on a certain trade. **2.** permission. **3.** disregard of rules or customs etc., lack of due restraint in behaviour. **4.** a writer's or artist's exaggeration, or disregard of rules etc., for the sake of effect, *poetic licence.*

license *v.* to grant a licence to or for, to authorize, *licensed to sell tobacco; licensed premises,* licensed to sell alcoholic drinks.

licensee *n.* a person who holds a licence, especially to sell alcoholic drinks.

licentiate (ly-**sen**-shi-ăt) *n.* one who holds a certificate showing that he is competent to practise a certain profession, *Licentiate in Dental Surgery.*

licentious (ly-**sen**-shŭs) *adj.* disregarding the rules of conduct, especially in sexual matters. **licentiousness** *n.*

lichee (lee-chee) *n.* = litchi.

lichen (**ly**-kěn) *n.* a dry-looking plant that grows on rocks, walls, tree-trunks, etc., usually green or yellow or grey.

lich-gate *n.* a roofed gateway to a churchyard.

lick *v.* **1.** to pass the tongue over, to take up or make clean by doing this. **2.** (of waves or flame) to move like a tongue, to touch lightly. **3.** (*slang*) to defeat. —**lick** *n.* **1.** an act of licking with the tongue. **2.** a blow with a stick etc. **3.** a slight application (of paint etc.). **4.** (*slang*) a fast pace, *going at quite a lick.* ☐ **lick a person's boots,** to be servile towards him. **lick into shape,** to make presentable or efficient. **lick one's lips,** to show pleasure and eagerness or satisfaction. **lick one's wounds,** to remain in retirement trying to recover after a defeat.

licking *n.* (*slang*) **1.** a defeat. **2.** a thrashing.

lid *n.* **1.** a hinged or removable cover for a box or pot etc. **2.** an eyelid. ☐ **that puts the lid on it,** (*slang*) that forms a climax to it; that puts a stop to it. **with the lid off,** with all the horrors etc. exposed to view.

lido (**lee**-doh) *n.* (*pl.* **lidos**) a public open-air swimming-pool or pleasure-beach.

lie[1] *n.* **1.** a statement that the speaker knows to be untrue, *tell a lie.* **2.** a thing that deceives, an imposture. —**lie** *v.* (**lied, lying**) **1.** to tell a lie or lies; *lied himself out of the trouble,* got himself out of it by lying. **2.** to be deceptive. ☐ **give the lie to,** to show that something is untrue. **lie-detector** *n.* an instrument that can detect changes in the pulse-rate or respiration etc. brought on by the tension caused by telling lies.

lie[2] *v.* (**lay, lain, lying**) (¶ See the note on lay[3].) **1.** to have or put one's body in a flat or resting position on a more or less horizontal surface. **2.** (of a thing) to be at rest on a surface. **3.** to be or be kept or remain in a specified state, *the road lies open; machinery lay idle; lie in ambush.* **4.** to be situated, *the island lies near the coast.* **5.** to exist or be found, *the remedy lies in education.* **6.** (in Law) to be admissible or able to be upheld, *an action or appeal will not lie.* —*n.* the way or position in which something lies. ☐ **how the land lies,** what the situation is. **it lies with you,** it is your business or right. **lie-abed** *n.* a person who lies idly in bed late in the morning. **lie down,** to have a brief rest in or on a bed etc. **lie-down** *n.* such a rest. **lie down under,** to accept (an insult etc.) without protest. **lie in,** (*informal*) to lie idly in bed late in the morning. **lie-in** *n.* such lying. **lie in state,** (of a dead eminent person) to be laid in a public place of honour before burial or cremation. **lie low,** to conceal oneself or one's intentions. **take it lying**

down, to accept an insult etc. without protest.

Liechtenstein (**lik**-těn-styn) a country between Austria and Switzerland.

lien (*pr.* **leen**) *n.* the right to keep another person's property until a debt owed in respect of it (e.g. for repairing it) is paid.

lieu (*pr.* **lew**) *n.* **in lieu,** instead, in place, *accepted a cheque in lieu of cash.*

lieutenant (lef-**ten**-ănt) *n.* **1.** an army officer next below a captain. **2.** a navy officer next below a lieutenant-commander. **3.** an officer ranking just below one specified, *lieutenant-colonel, lieutenant-commander.* **4.** a deputy, a chief assistant.

life *n.* (*pl.* **lives**) **1.** being alive, the ability to function and grow that distinguishes animals and plants (before their death) from rocks and synthetic substances. **2.** living things, *plant life; is there life on Mars?* **3.** a living form or model, *portrait is drawn from life.* **4.** liveliness, interest, *full of life.* **5.** the period for which a person or organism is or has been or will be alive; *life imprisonment* or *a life sentence,* a sentence of imprisonment for the rest of one's life. **6.** (*informal*) a life sentence. **7.** (in insurance) a person with regard to the number of years that he is likely to live; *a good life,* one who is likely to live for a long time. **8.** a person's or people's activities or fortunes or manner of existence, *in private life; village life.* **9.** the business and pleasures and social activities of the world, *we do see life!* **10.** a biography. **11.** a period during which something exists or continues to function, *the battery has a life of two years.* ☐ **a matter of life and death,** an event or decision etc. that could cause a person to die; something of vital importance. **for life,** for the rest of one's life. **for one's life** *or* **for dear life,** in order to escape death or as if to do this. **life-blood** *n.* a person's or animal's blood, necessary to his or its life; an influence that gives vitality to something. **life cycle,** the series of forms into which a living thing changes until the first form appears again. **life-guard** *n.* an expert swimmer employed to rescue bathers who are in danger of drowning. **Life Guards,** a regiment of the Household cavalry. **life-jacket** *n.* a jacket of buoyant or inflatable material to support a person's body in the water. **life peer,** a peer whose title is granted only to himself, not to be passed to his heirs. **life-preserver** *n.* a short stick with a loaded end, used as a weapon of defence; a lifebelt or life-jacket. **life sciences,** biology and related subjects. **life-size, life-sized** *adjs.* of the same size as the person or thing represented. **life-style** *n.* a person's way of life. **life-support** *adj.* (of equipment) providing an environment in which the crew of a spacecraft etc. can live, or (in medical use) making possible the continued functioning of the body, e.g. when vital natural functions have failed. **not on your life,** (*informal*) most certainly not. **this life,** life on earth (as opposed to an existence after death). **to the life,** exactly like the original.

lifebelt *n.* a belt of buoyant or inflatable material to support a person's body in the water.

lifeboat *n.* **1.** a small boat carried on a ship for use if the ship has to be abandoned at sea. **2.** a boat specially constructed for going to the help of people in danger at sea along a coast.

lifebuoy *n.* a device to keep a person afloat.

lifeless *adj.* **1.** without life, dead or never having had life. **2.** unconscious. **3.** lacking vitality. **lifelessness** *n.*

lifelike *adj.* exactly like a real person or thing.

lifeline *n.* **1.** a rope etc. used in rescuing people, e.g. one attached to a lifebelt. **2.** a diver's signalling line. **3.** a sole means of communication or transport.

lifelong *adj.* continued all one's life.

lifer *n.* (*slang*) a life sentence, a person sentenced to life imprisonment.

lifetime *n.* the duration of a person's life or of a thing's existence; *the chance of a lifetime,* the best chance one will ever get.

lift *v.* **1.** to raise to a higher level or position; *lift one's eyes,* look up. **2.** to take up from the ground or from its resting-place. **3.** to dig up, (e.g. potatoes etc. at harvest or plants for storing). **4.** (*informal*) to steal, to copy from another source. **5.** to go up, to rise, (of fog etc.) to disperse. **6.** to remove or abolish (restrictions). —**lift** *n.* **1.** lifting, being lifted. **2.** a ride as a passenger without payment. **3.** an apparatus for transporting people or goods from one floor of a building to another. **4.** a ski-lift or chair-lift. **5.** the upward pressure that air exerts on an aircraft in flight. **6.** a feeling of elation, *the praise gave me a lift.* □ **have one's face lifted,** to have an operation for removing wrinkles on the face by tightening the skin. **lift-off** *n.* the vertical take-off of a rocket or spacecraft.

ligament *n.* the tough flexible tissue that holds bones together or keeps organs in place in the body.

ligature (**lig-ă-cher**) *n.* **1.** a thing used in tying, especially in surgical operations. **2.** a tie in music. **3.** joined printed letters such as œ. —*v.* to tie with a ligature.

light[1] *n.* **1.** the agent that stimulates the sense of sight, a kind of radiation. **2.** the presence or amount or effect of this. **3.** a source of light, especially an electric lamp, *leave the light on.* **4.** a flame or spark, something used to produce this. **5.** brightness, the bright parts of a picture etc. **6.** enlightenment; *light dawned on him,* he began to understand. **7.** the aspect of something, the way it appears to the mind, *sees the matter in a different light.* **8.** a window or opening to admit light. —**light** *adj.* **1.** full of light, not in darkness. **2.** pale, *light blue.* —**light** *v.* (lit, lighted (¶ see note at end of entry), lighting) **1.** to set burning, to begin to burn. **2.** to cause to give out light. **3.** to provide with light, to guide with a light. **4.** to brighten. □ **bring** *or* **come to light,** to reveal or be revealed, to make or become known. **in the light of this,** with the help given by these facts. **light meter,** an exposure meter. **light pen,** a pen-like photoelectric device for communicating with a computer by movement, either applied to the screen of a terminal (e.g. to cause the computer to draw lines or select an item from a list), or (also called *wand*) passed over a bar code (*see* bar[1]). **lights** *pl. n.* traffic lights (*see* traffic); a person's mental attitude, *did his best according to his lights.* **light up,** to put lights on at dusk; to make or become bright with light or colour or animation, to begin to smoke a pipe or cigarette. **light-year** *n.* the distance light travels in one year (about 6 million million miles). ¶ Preferred use is *he lit the lamps, the lamps were lit* (rather than *lighted* in either phrase), but *holding a lighted torch* (not *a lit torch*).

light[2] *adj.* **1.** having little weight, not heavy, easy to lift or carry or move. **2.** of less than average weight or amount or force, *light traffic; light artillery,* armed with lighter weapons than heavy artillery. **3.** (of work) needing little physical effort. **4.** not intense; *a light sleeper,* one easily woken. **5.** not dense, *light mist.* **6.** (of food) easy to digest. **7.** moving easily and quickly. **8.** cheerful, free from worry, *with a light heart.* **9.** not profound or serious, intended as entertainment, *light music.* —*adv.* lightly, with little load, *we travel light.* —**lightly** *adv.,* **lightness** *n.* □ **light-fingered** *adj.* apt to steal. **light-headed** *adj.* feeling slightly faint, dizzy; delirious. **light-hearted** *adj.* cheerful, without cares; too casual, not treating a thing seriously. **light industry,** industry producing small or light articles. **make light of,** to treat as unimportant; *made light of his injuries,* said they were not serious.

light³ *v.* (lit *or* lighted, (¶ preferred use is lit), lighting) to find accidentally, *we lit on this book.* **light into,** (*slang*) to attack. **light out,** (*slang*) to depart, *lit out for home.*

lighten¹ *v.* **1.** to shed light on. **2.** to make or become brighter. **3.** to produce lightning.

lighten² *v.* **1.** to make or become lighter in weight. **2.** to relieve or be relieved of care or worry.

lighter¹ *n.* a device for lighting cigarettes and cigars.

lighter² *n.* a flat-bottomed boat used for loading and unloading ships that are not brought to a wharf or into a harbour, and for transporting goods in a harbour. **lighterman** *n.* (*pl.* lightermen) one who works on a lighter.

lighthouse *n.* a tower or other structure containing a beacon light to warn or guide ships.

lighting *n.* equipment for providing light to a room or building or street etc., the light itself. **lighting-up time,** the time after which vehicles on a road must show prescribed lights.

lightish *adj.* fairly light.

lightning *n.* a flash of bright light produced by natural electricity, between clouds or cloud and ground. —*adj.* very quick, *with lightning speed; a lightning strike,* a labour strike begun without warning. □ **lightning-conductor** *n.* a metal rod or wire fixed to an exposed part of a building etc., to divert lightning into the earth. **like lightning,** with very great speed.

lights *pl. n.* the lungs of sheep, pigs, etc., used as food for animals.

lightship *n.* a moored or anchored ship with a beacon light, serving the same purpose as a lighthouse.

lightweight *n.* **1.** a person of less than average weight. **2.** a boxing-weight (60 kg) between welterweight and featherweight. **3.** a person of little influence. —*adj.* not having great weight or influence

like¹ *adj.* **1.** having some or all of the qualities or appearance etc. of, similar; *what is he like?,* what sort of person is he? **2.** characteristic of, *it was like him to do that.* **3.** in a suitable state or the right mood for something, *it looks like rain; we felt like a walk.* **4.** such as, for example, *in subjects like music.* —**like** *prep.* in the manner of, to the same degree as, *he swims like a fish.* —**like** *conj.* **1.** in the same manner as, to the same degree as, *do it like I do.* **2.** (*Amer.*) as if, *she doesn't act like she belongs here.* —*adv.* (*informal*) likely, *as like*

as not they'll refuse. —*n.* one that is like another, a similar thing, *shall not see his like again; the likes of you,* people like you. □ **and the like,** and similar things. **like-minded** *adj.* having similar tastes or opinions.

like² *v.* **1.** to find pleasant or satisfactory. **2.** to wish for, *should like to think it over.* □ **likes** *pl. n.* the things one likes or prefers.

likeable *adj.* pleasant, easy for a person to like.

likelihood *n.* being likely, probability.

likely *adj.* (likelier, likeliest) **1.** such as may reasonably be expected to occur or be true etc., *he is likely to be late; rain is likely.* **2.** seeming to be suitable, *the likeliest place.* **3.** showing promise of being successful, *a likely lad.* —*adv.* probably. —**likeliness** *n.* □ **not likely!,** (*informal*) this will certainly not be possible.
¶ The use of *likely* as an adverb without *very, quite, most,* or *more* (e.g. in *the rain will likely die out*) is common in the USA but is not used in standard English.

liken *v.* to point out the resemblance of (one thing to another), *likened the heart to a pump.*

likeness *n.* **1.** being like, a resemblance. **2.** a copy, portrait, or picture.

likewise *adv.* **1.** moreover, also. **2.** similarly, *do likewise.*

liking *n.* **1.** what one likes, one's taste, *is it to your liking?* **2.** one's feeling that one likes something, *a liking for it.*

lilac *n.* **1.** a shrub with fragrant purplish or white flowers. **2.** pale purple. —*adj.* of lilac colour.

liliaceous (lil-i-**ay**-shŭs) *adj.* lily-like, of the lily family.

lilliputian (lili-**pew**-shăn) *adj.* very small. —*n.* a very small person. ¶ Named after the inhabitants of Lilliput, a country in Swift's *Gulliver's Travels,* who were only six inches tall.

lilt *n.* a light pleasant rhythm, a song or tune having this. **lilting** *adj.* having a light pleasant rhythm.

lily *n.* **1.** a plant growing from a bulb, with large white or reddish flowers. **2.** a plant of this family. □ **lily of the valley,** a spring flower with small fragrant white bell-shaped flowers. **lily-white** *adj.* as white as a lily.

Lima (**lee**-mă) the capital of Peru.

limb *n.* **1.** a projecting part of an animal body, used in movement or in grasping things. **2.** a main branch of a tree. **3.** a mischievous child. □ **out on a limb,** isolated, stranded; at a disadvantage because separated from others.

limber *adj.* flexible, supple, lithe. —*v.* to make limber. ☐ **limber up**, to exercise in preparation for athletic activity.

limbo¹ *n.* (*pl.* limbos) **1.** *Limbo*, in certain Christian teachings, the supposed abode of souls not admitted to heaven (e.g. because not baptized) but not condemned to punishment. **2.** an intermediate state or condition (e.g. of a plan not yet accepted but not rejected), a condition of being neglected and forgotten.

limbo² *n.* (*pl.* limbos) a West Indian dance in which the dancer bends back and passes repeatedly under a gradually lowered horizontal bar.

lime¹ *n.* a white substance (calcium oxide) used in making cement and mortar and as a fertilizer. —*v.* to treat with lime.

lime² *n.* **1.** a round fruit like a lemon but smaller and more acid. **2.** (also *lime-green*) its yellowish-green colour. **lime-juice** *n.*

lime³ *n.* a tree with smooth heart-shaped leaves and fragrant yellow flowers, a linden. **lime-tree** *n.*

limelight *n.* great publicity. ¶ Named after the brilliant light, obtained by heating lime, formerly used to illuminate the stages of theatres.

limerick *n.* a type of humorous poem with five lines. ¶ Named after *Limerick*, a town in Ireland.

limestone *n.* a kind of rock from which lime is obtained by heating.

limey *n.* (*pl.* limeys) (*Amer. slang*) a British person. ¶ Named after *lime-juice* which was formerly issued to British sailors as a drink to prevent scurvy.

limit *n.* **1.** the point or line or level beyond which something does not continue. **2.** the greatest amount allowed, *the speed limit*. **3.** (*slang*) something that is as much as or more than one can tolerate, *she really is the limit!* —*v.* to set or serve as a limit, to keep within limits. ☐ **limited** *adj.* confined within limits; few, scanty. **limited liability company**, a business company whose members are liable for its debts only to the extent of the capital sum they have provided.

limitation *n.* **1.** limiting, being limited. **2.** a lack of ability; *knows his limitations*, knows what he cannot achieve.

limousine (lim-oo-**zeen**) *n.* a luxurious car.

limp¹ *v.* to walk or proceed lamely. —*n.* a limping walk.

limp² *adj.* **1.** not stiff or firm. **2.** lacking strength or energy, wilting. **limply** *adv.*, **limpness** *n.*

limpet *n.* a small shellfish that sticks tightly to rocks.

limpid *adj.* (of liquids etc.) clear, transparent.

linchpin *n.* **1.** a pin passed through the end of an axle to keep the wheel in position. **2.** a person or thing that is vital to an organization or plan etc.

Lincolnshire a county of England.

Lincs. *abbrev.* Lincolnshire.

linctus *n.* a soothing syrupy cough-mixture.

linden *n.* a lime-tree.

line¹ *n.* **1.** a straight or curved continuous extent of length without breadth. **2.** a long narrow mark on a surface. **3.** something resembling this, a band of colour, a wrinkle or crease in the skin; *the Line*, the equator. **4.** an outline, the shape to which something is designed; *a proposal along these lines*, with these general features. **5.** a limit, a boundary. **6.** one of a set of military fieldworks or boundaries of an encampment. **7.** a row of people or things, a row of words on a page or in a poem; *an actor's lines*, the words of his part in a play. **8.** a brief letter, *drop me a line*. **9.** a series of ships or buses or aircraft etc. regularly travelling between certain places, the company running these, *Cunard Line*. **10.** a connected series, several generations of a family, *a line of kings*. **11.** a direction or course or track, *line of march*. **12.** a single pair of rails in a railway, one branch of a system, *the main line north*. **13.** a course of procedure or thought or conduct, *in the line of duty; don't take that line with me*. **14.** a department of activity, a type of business; *not my line*, not among my interests or skills. **15.** a class of goods, *a nice line in handbags*. **16.** a piece of cord used for a particular purpose, *fishing with rod and line*. **17.** a wire or cable used to connect electricity or telephones, connection by this, *the line is bad*. —**line** *v.* **1.** to mark with lines. **2.** to arrange in a line, *line them up*. ☐ **come** *or* **bring into line**, to become or cause to become a straight line or row; to conform or cause to conform with others. **get a line on**, (*informal*) to discover information about. **in line**, so as to form a straight line. **in line for**, likely to get (e.g. promotion). **in line with**, in accordance with. **line-drawing** *n.* a drawing done with pen or pencil or a pointed instrument, chiefly in lines and solid masses. **line-out** *n.* parallel lines of opposing forwards formed in Rugby football when the ball is thrown in. **line printer**, a high-speed printing device (for use with a computer etc.) that prints a complete line of a page at a time. **line-up** *n.* a line of people formed for inspection etc. **out of line**, not in line.

line² *v*. **1.** to cover the inside surface of (a thing) with a layer of different material. **2.** to be the lining of. □ **line one's pockets** *or* **purse**, to make a lot of money, especially by underhand or dishonest methods.

lineage (**lin**-i-ăj) *n*. ancestry, the line of descendants of an ancestor.

lineal (**lin**-i-ăl) *adj*. of or in a line, especially as a descendant.

lineaments (**lin**-iă-mĕnts) *pl. n.* the features of the face.

linear (**lin**-i-er) *adj*. **1.** of a line, of length. **2.** arranged in a line.

linen *n*. **1.** cloth made of flax. **2.** shirts and household articles (such as sheets, tablecloths, etc.) which were formerly made of this.

liner¹ *n*. **1.** a large passenger or cargo ship travelling on a regular route. **2.** a freight train travelling regularly.

liner² *n*. a removable lining, *nappy-liners*.

linesman *n*. (*pl*. linesmen) **1.** an official assisting the referee in certain games, especially in deciding whether or where a ball crosses a line. **2.** a man employed to test the safety of railway lines, or to keep electrical or telephone wires in repair.

ling¹ *n*. a kind of heather.

ling² *n*. a sea-fish of northern Europe, used (usually salted) as food.

linger *v*. **1.** to stay a long time, especially as if reluctant to leave. **2.** to dawdle. **3.** to remain alive although becoming weaker.

lingerie (**lan**-*zh*er-ee) *n*. women's underwear.

lingo *n*. (*pl*. lingoes) (*humorous* or *contemptuous*) a foreign language, jargon.

lingua franca (ling-wă **frank**-ă) a language used between the people of an area where several languages are spoken.

linguist (**ling**-wist) *n*. a person who knows foreign languages well.

linguistic (ling-**wist**-ik) *adj*. of language or linguistics. □ **linguistics** *n*. the scientific study of languages and their structure.

liniment *n*. embrocation, especially one made with oil.

lining *n*. **1.** a layer of material used to line something, the material itself. **2.** the tissue covering the inner surface of an organ of the body.

link *n*. **1.** one ring or loop of a chain. **2.** a cuff-link. **3.** a connecting part, a person who is a connection between others. —*v*. to make or be a connection between; *link hands*, to clasp each other's hand.

linkage *n*. linking, a link.

linkman *n*. (*pl*. linkmen) **1.** a player be-

tween the forwards and half-backs of the strikers and backs in football etc. **2.** a person providing continuity in a broadcast programme or between programmes.

links *n*. or *pl. n.* a golf-course.

linnet (**lin**-it) *n*. a kind of finch.

lino (**ly**-noh) *n*. linoleum.

linocut *n*. a design cut in relief on a layer of thick linoleum, a print made from this.

linoleum (lin-**oh**-liŭm) *n*. a kind of floor-covering made by pressing a thick coating of powdered cork and linseed oil etc. on to a canvas backing.

Linotype *n*. (*trade mark*) a machine that sets a line of type as a single strip of metal.

linseed *n*. the seed of flax, pressed to form **linseed oil**, an oil used in paint and varnish. **linseed cake**, linseed from which the oil has been pressed out, used as cattle-food.

lint *n*. **1.** a soft material for dressing wounds, consisting of linen with one side scraped so that it is fluffy. **2.** fluff.

lintel *n*. a horizontal piece of timber or stone etc. over a door or other opening.

lion *n*. **1.** a large powerful flesh-eating animal of the cat family. **2.** *the Lion*, a sign of the zodiac, Leo. **lioness** *n*. □ **lion-hearted** *adj*. very brave. **the lion's share**, the largest or best part of something that is divided. (¶ In the fable the lion demanded most (or, in one version, all) of the prey in return for his help in the kill.)

lionize *v*. to treat (a person) as a celebrity.

lip *n*. **1.** either of the fleshy edges of the mouth-opening. **2.** (*slang*) impudence. **3.** the edge of a cup or other hollow container or of an opening. **4.** a projecting part of such an edge shaped for pouring. **lipped** *adj*. □ **lip-read** *v*. to understand what a person is saying by watching the movements of his lips, not by hearing. **pay lip-service to,** to state that one approves of something but fail to support it by actions.

lipsalve *n*. ointment for sore lips.

lipstick *n*. **1.** a stick of cosmetic for colouring the lips. **2.** this cosmetic.

liquefy *v*. (liquefied, liquefying) to make or become liquid. **liquefaction** *n*.

liqueur (lik-**yoor**) *n*. a strong sweet alcoholic spirit with fragrant flavouring. **liqueur brandy**, brandy of special quality for drinking as a liqueur.

liquid *n*. a substance like water or oil that flows freely but is not a gas. —*adj*. **1.** in the form of a liquid. **2.** having the clearness of water. **3.** (of sounds) flowing clearly and pleasantly, *blackbird's liquid notes*. **3.**

(of assets) easily converted into cash. — **liquidity** (li-**kwid**-iti) *n.*

liquidate *v.* **1.** to pay or settle (a debt). **2.** to close down (a business) and divide its assets between its creditors. **3.** to get rid of, especially by killing. **liquidation** *n.,* **liquidator** *n.* ☐ **go into liquidation,** (of a business) to be closed down and its assets divided, especially in bankruptcy.

liquidize *v.* to cause to become liquid, to crush into a liquid pulp.

liquidizer *n.* a device for liquidizing fruit and vegetables.

liquor (**lik**-er) *n.* **1.** alcoholic drink. **2.** juice produced in cooking, liquid in which food has been boiled.

liquorice (**lik**-er-iss) *n.* **1.** a black substance used in medicine and as a sweet. **2.** the plant from whose root it is obtained.

lira (**leer**-ă) *n.* (*pl.* **lire**) the unit of money in Italy and Turkey.

Lisbon the capital of Portugal.

lisle (*rhymes with* mile) *n.* a fine smooth cotton thread used especially for stockings.

lisp *n.* a speech defect in which s is pronounced like th (as in *thin*) and z like *th* (as in *they*). —*v.* to speak or utter with a lisp.

lissom (**liss**-ŏm) *adj.* lithe, agile.

list[1] *n.* a series of names, items, figures, etc. written or printed. —*v.* to make a list of, to enter (a name etc.) in a list. ☐ **enter the lists,** to make or accept a challenge, especially in a controversy. **listed building,** a building entered in an official list as being of architectural or historical importance and therefore protected from demolition etc. **list price,** the published or advertised price of goods.

list[2] *v.* (of a ship) to lean over to one side. —*n.* a listing position, a tilt.

listen *v.* **1.** to make an effort to hear something, to wait alertly in order to hear a sound. **2.** to hear by doing this, to pay attention. **3.** to allow oneself to be persuaded by a suggestion or request. ☐ **listen in,** to overhear a conversation, especially by telephone; to listen to a radio broadcast.

listener *n.* **1.** a person who listens; *a good listener,* one who can be relied on to listen attentively or sympathetically. **2.** a person listening to a radio broadcast.

listless *adj.* without energy or vitality, showing no enthusiasm. **listlessly** *adv.,* **listlessness** *n.*

lit *see* light[1], light[3].

litany *n.* **1.** a form of prayer consisting of a series of supplications to God, recited by a priest and with set responses by the congregation; *the Litany,* that in the Book of Common Prayer. **2.** a long monotonous recital, *a litany of complaints.*

litchi (**lee**-chee) *n.* (*pl.* **litchis**) **1.** a fruit consisting of a sweetish white pulp in a thin brown shell. **2.** the tree (originally from China) that bears this.

literacy (**lit**-er-ăsi) *n.* the ability to read and write.

literal *adj.* **1.** in accordance with the primary meaning of a word or the actual words of a phrase, as contrasted with a metaphorical or exaggerated meaning (¶ see the note under **metaphorical**); *a literal translation,* keeping strictly to the words of the original. **2.** (of a person) tending to interpret things in a literal way, unimaginative. **literally** *adv.,* **literalness** *n.*

¶ The word *literally* is sometimes used thoughtlessly in statements that are clearly not to be taken literally, e.g. *he was literally glued to the TV set every night.*

literary (**lit**-er-er-i) *adj.* of or concerned with literature.

literate (**lit**-er-ăt) *adj.* able to read and write. —*n.* a literate person.

literature *n.* **1.** writings that are valued for their beauty of form, especially novels and poetry and plays etc. as contrasted with technical works and journalism. **2.** the writings of a country or a period or a particular subject. **3.** (*informal*) printed pamphlets or leaflets etc., *some literature about coach tours.*

lithe (*rhymes with* scythe) *adj.* flexible, supple, agile.

litho (**lyth**-oh) *n.* the lithographic process.

lithograph *n.* a picture etc. printed by lithography.

lithography (lith-**og**-răfi) *n.* a process of printing from a smooth surface (e.g. a metal plate) treated so that ink will adhere to the design to be printed and not to the rest of the surface. **lithographic** *adj.*

litigant (**lit**-i-gănt) *n.* a person who is involved in a lawsuit, one who goes to law.

litigation (lit-i-**gay**-shŏn) *n.* a lawsuit, the process of going to law.

litigious (lit-**ij**-ŭs) *adj.* **1.** of lawsuits. **2.** giving matter for a lawsuit. **3.** fond of going to law. **litigiousness** *n.*

litmus *n.* a blue colouring-matter that is turned red by acids and can be restored to blue by alkalis. **litmus-paper** *n.* paper stained with this, used to tell whether a solution is acid or alkaline.

litre (**lee**-ter) *n.* a unit of capacity in the metric system, (about 1 pints) used for measuring liquids.

litter *n.* **1.** odds and ends of rubbish left lying about. **2.** straw etc. put down as bedding for animals. **3.** the young animals brought forth at a birth. —**litter** *v.* **1.** to make untidy by scattering odds and ends, to scatter as litter. **2.** to give birth to (a litter of young).

little *adj.* **1.** small in size or amount or intensity etc., not great or big or much. **2.** smaller than others of the same kind, *little finger*; *Little Malvern*; *Little Venice*, a small area resembling Venice. **3.** working on only a small scale, *a little ironmonger*. **4.** young, younger, *our little boy*; *his little sister*. **5.** unimportant, *bothers me with every little detail*. —*n.* only a small amount, some but not much, a short time or distance. —**little** *adv.* **1.** to a small extent only, *little-known authors*. **2.** not at all, *he little knows*. □ **little by little**, gradually, by a small amount at a time. **the little people**, the fairies. **the little woman**, (*informal*) a person's wife.

liturgy (**lit**-er-ji) *n.* a fixed form of public worship used in churches. **liturgical** (lit-er-ji-kăl) *adj.*, **liturgically** *adv.*

live[1] (*rhymes with* hive) *adj.* **1.** alive. **2.** actual, not pretended, *a real live burglar*. **3.** glowing, burning, *a live coal*. **4.** (of a shell or match) not yet exploded or used. **5.** (of a wire or cable etc.) charged with or carrying electricity. **6.** of interest or importance at the present time, *pollution is a live issue*. **7.** (of a broadcast) transmitted while actually happening or being performed, not recorded or edited. □ **a live wire**, a highly energetic forceful person.

live[2] (*rhymes with* give) *v.* **1.** to have life, to be or remain alive, (of things without life) to remain in existence. **2.** to be kept alive, *living on fruit*. **3.** to get a livelihood, *they lived on* or *off her earnings*; *live by one's wits*, to get money or food etc. by ingenious or dishonest methods. **4.** to have one's dwelling-place, *they lived in tents*. **5.** to conduct one's life in a certain way, *lived like a hermit*; *lived a peaceful life*; *live a lie*, express it by one's life. **6.** to enjoy life to the full, *I don't call that living*. □ **lived-in** *adj.* inhabited, (of a room) used frequently. **live down**, to live in such a way that (a past guilt or scandal etc.) becomes forgotten. **live in** *or* **out**, (of an employee) to live on *or* off the premises. **live it up**, to live in a lively extravagant way. **live together**, to live in the same house etc.; (of a man and woman not his wife) to live as if married. **live up to**, to live or behave in accordance with, *did not live up to his principles*. **live with**, to live together; to tolerate, *you will have to learn to live with it*.

liveable (**liv**-ăbŭl) *adj.* suitable for living;

felt that life wasn't liveable, was unbearable; *liveable-in*, (of a house etc.) suitable for living in; *liveable-with*, easy to live with.

livelihood (**lyv**-li-huud) *n.* a means of living, a way in which a person earns a living.

livelong (**liv**-long) *adj.* **the livelong day**, the whole length of the day.

lively *adj.* (livelier, liveliest) full of life or energy, vigorous and cheerful, full of action. **liveliness** *n.* □ **look lively**, to move more quickly or energetically.

liven *v.* to make or become lively, *liven it up*; *things livened up*.

liver *n.* **1.** a large organ in the abdomen, secreting bile. **2.** the liver of certain animals, used as food. **3.** dark reddish brown.

liveried *adj.* wearing a livery.

liverish *adj.* **1.** suffering from a disorder of the liver. **2.** irritable, glum.

Liverpudlian *adj.* of Liverpool. —*n.* a native or inhabitant of Liverpool.

liverwort (**liv**-er-wert) *n.* any of a group of small creeping plants growing in damp places, of which some kinds have liver-shaped leaves and some resemble mosses.

livery *n.* a distinctive uniform worn by male servants in a great household or by members of the London trade guilds (*Livery Companies*). **livery stables**, stables where horses are kept for their owner in return for a fee, or where horses may be hired.

livestock *n.* animals kept for use or profit, e.g. cattle or sheep etc. on a farm.

livid *adj.* **1.** of the colour of lead, bluish-grey. **2.** (*informal*) furiously angry.

living *adj.* **1.** alive; *the living*, people who are now alive. **2.** (of a likeness) exact, true to life, *she is the living image of her mother*. **3.** (of rock) not detached from the earth, (of water) always flowing. —**living** *n.* **1.** being alive. **2.** a means of earning or providing enough food etc. to sustain life. **3.** a manner of life, *their standard of living*. **4.** a position held by a clergyman and providing him with an income and/or property. □ **living-room** *n.* a room for general use during the day. **living wage**, a wage on which it is possible to live. **within living memory**, within the memory of people who are still alive.

lizard *n.* a reptile with a rough or scaly hide, four legs, and a long tail.

llama (**lah**-mă) *n.* a South American animal related to the camel but with no hump, kept as a beast of burden and for its soft woolly hair.

Lloyd's a corporation of underwriters in

London. **Lloyd's Register,** an annual list of all the ships in various classes.

lo *int.* (*old use*) see.

loach *n.* a small edible freshwater fish.

load *n.* **1.** something carried. **2.** the quantity that can be carried, e.g. on a cart. **3.** a unit of weight or measure for certain substances. **4.** the amount of electric current supplied by a dynamo or generating station. **5.** a burden of responsibility or worry or grief.
　　load *v.* **1.** to put a load in or on, to fill with goods or cargo etc., to receive a load. **2.** to fill heavily. **3.** to weight with something heavy, *a loaded stick; loaded dice,* dice weighted so as to fall in a known way; *the dice were loaded against him,* he did not have a fair chance. **4.** to put ammunition into (a gun) or film into (a camera) ready for use, to place (ammunition or film) thus. **5.** to put (a program or data etc.) into a computer, to instruct (a computer) thus. **6.** to add an extra charge to (an insurance premium) for special reasons. □ **get a load of this,** (*slang*) take notice. **loaded** *adj.* (*slang*) very rich. **loaded question,** one that is worded so as to trap a person into saying something damaging. **load line,** a ship's Plimsoll line. **loads** *pl. n.* (*informal*) plenty, *loads of time.*

load-shedding *n.* cutting off of the supply of electric current on certain lines when the demand is greater than the supply available.

loader *n.* **1.** a person who loads things, an attendant loading a sportman's guns. **2.** a device for loading something. **3.** something, loaded in a certain way, *breech-loader; front-loader.*

loadstone *n.* **1.** a magnetic oxide of iron. **2.** a piece of this used as a magnet.

loaf[1] *n.* (*pl.* loaves) **1.** a mass of bread shaped in one piece. **2.** minced or chopped meat moulded into an oblong shape. **3.** (*slang*) the head, *use your loaf!* □ **loaf sugar,** lump sugar.

loaf[2] *v.* to spend time idly, to stand or saunter about. **loafer** *n.*

loam *n.* rich soil containing clay and sand and decayed vegetable matter. **loamy** *adj.*

loan *n.* **1.** something lent, especially a sum of money. **2.** lending, being lent; *on loan,* lent; *have the loan of,* borrow. —*v.* to lend. (¶ Many people regard the use of this verb as unacceptable.)

loath (*rhymes with* both) *adj.* unwilling, *was loath to depart.* **nothing loath,** quite willing.

loathe (*rhymes with* clothe) *v.* to feel great hatred and disgust for. **loathing** *n.* this feeling. **loathsome** *adj.* arousing loathing, repulsive.

loaves *see* loaf.[1]

lob *v.* (lobbed, lobbing) to send or strike (a ball) slowly or in a high arc in cricket or tennis etc. —*n.* a lobbed ball in tennis etc., a slow underarm delivery in cricket.

lobar (loh-ber) *adj.* of a lobe, especially of the lung, *lobar pneumonia.*

lobby *n.* **1.** a porch or entrance-hall or ante-room. **2.** (in the House of Commons) a large hall open to the public and used for interviews with MPs etc. **3.** one of two corridors to which MPs retire when a vote is taken in the House, *division lobby.* **4.** a body of people lobbying an MP etc. or seeking to influence legislation, *the anti-abortion lobby.* —*v.* (lobbied, lobbying) to seek to persuade (an MP or other person) to support one's cause, by interviewing him in the lobby or by writing letters etc.

lobe *n.* a rounded flattish part or projection (especially of an organ of the body), the lower soft part of the ear. **lobed** *adj.* having lobes.

lobelia (lŏ-bee-liă) *n.* a low-growing garden plant with blue, red, white, or purple flowers, used especially for edging.

lobster *n.* **1.** a large shellfish with eight legs and two long claws that turns scarlet after being boiled. **2.** its flesh as food. □ **lobster-pot** *n.* a basket for trapping lobsters.

lobworm *n.* a large earthworm used as fishing-bait.

local *adj.* **1.** belonging to a particular place or a small area, *letters for local delivery; the local bus,* of the neighbourhood and not long-distance. **2.** affecting a particular place, not general, *a local anaesthetic.* —*local n.* **1.** an inhabitant of a particular district. **2.** (*informal*) the public house of a neighbourhood. —**locally** *adv.* □ **local authority,** the body of people given responsibility for administration in local government. **local call,** a telephone call to a nearby place. **local colour,** details characteristic of the scene in which a novel etc. is set, added to make it seem more real. **local government,** the system of administration of a district or county etc. by the elected representatives of people who live there.

locale (lŏ-kahl) *n.* the scene or locality of operations or events.

locality (lŏ-kal-iti) *n.* a thing's position, the site or neighbourhood of something.

localize *v.* to make local not general, to confine within a particular area, *a localized infection.*

locate *v.* **1.** to discover the place where something is, *locate the electrical fault.* **2.** to assign to or establish in a particular location; *the town hall is located in the city centre,* is situated there.

location *n.* **1.** the place where something is situated. **2.** finding the location of, being found. **3.** the basic unit in a computer memory, able to hold a single item of data. □ **on location,** (of making a cinema film) being filmed in a suitable environment instead of in a film studio.

loch (*pr.* lok) *n.* (*Scottish*) a lake or an arm of the sea.

lock¹ *n.* a portion of hair that hangs together. **locks** *pl. n.* the hair of the head.

lock² *n.* **1.** a device for fastening a door or lid etc. into position when it is closed, with a bolt that needs a key or other device to work it; *under lock and key,* locked up. **2.** a wrestling hold that keeps an opponent's arm or leg etc. from moving. **3.** a player in the second row of the scrum in Rugby football. **4.** mechanism for exploding the charge in a gun. **5.** a section of a canal or river where the water level changes, fitted with gates and sluices so that water can be let in or out to raise or lower boats from one level to another. **6.** a decompression chamber. **7.** the interlocking of parts. **8.** the turning of a vehicle's front wheels by use of the steering wheel, the maximum extent of this. —**lock** *v.* **1.** to fasten or be able to be fastened with a lock. **2.** to shut into a place that is fastened by a lock. **3.** to store away securely or inaccessibly, *his capital is locked up in land.* **4.** to bring or come into a rigidly fixed position, to jam. **5.** to go or convey (a boat) through a lock. □ **lock-keeper** *n.* a person in charge of a lock on a canal or river. **lock out,** to shut out by locking a door. **lock-out** *n.* an employer's procedure of refusing to allow workmen to enter their place of work until certain conditions are agreed to. **lock-stitch** *n.* a sewing-machine stitch that locks threads firmly together. **lock, stock, and barrel,** completely, including everything. **lock-up** *adj.* able to be locked up; (*n.*) premises that can be locked up, a room or building where prisoners can be detained temporarily.

locker *n.* a small cupboard or compartment where things can be stowed safely, especially for an individual's use in a public place.

locket *n.* a small ornamental case holding a portrait or lock of hair etc., worn on a chain round the neck.

lockjaw *n.* a form of tetanus in which the jaws become rigidly closed.

locksmith *n.* a maker and mender of locks.

locomotion *n.* moving or the ability to move from place to place.

locomotive *n.* an engine for drawing a train along rails. —*adj.* of locomotion, *locomotive power.*

locomotor (loh-kŏ-moh-ter) *adj.* of or affecting locomotion; *locomotor ataxy,* a disease affecting the co-ordination of bodily movements.

locum (loh-kŭm) *n.* a deputy acting for a doctor or clergyman in his absence.

locus (loh-kŭs) *n.* (*pl.* loci, *pr.* loh-sy) **1.** the exact place of something. **2.** the line or curve etc. formed by all the points satisfying certain conditions or by movement of a point or line etc. □ **locus classicus,** the best-known or most authoritative passage on a subject.

locust (loh-kŭst) *n.* a kind of grasshopper that migrates in swarms and eats all the vegetation of a district. **locust tree,** *see* acacia.

locution (lŏ-kew-shŏn) *n.* a word or phrase.

lode *n.* a vein of metal ore.

lodestar *n.* a star used as a guide in navigation, especially the pole-star.

lodestone *n.* = loadstone.

lodge *n.* **1.** a small house at the gates of a park or in the grounds of a large house, occupied by a gate-keeper or other employee. **2.** a country house for use in certain seasons, *a hunting lodge.* **3.** a porter's room in the chief entrance to a block of flats or college or factory etc. **4.** the members or meeting-place of a branch of a society such as the Freemasons. **5.** a beaver's or otter's lair. —**lodge** *v.* **1.** to provide with sleeping-quarters or temporary accommodation. **2.** to live as a lodger. **3.** to deposit, to be or become embedded, *bullet lodged in his brain.* **4.** to present formally for attention, *lodged a complaint.*

lodger *n.* a person living in another's house and paying for his accommodation.

lodging *n.* a place where one lodges. **lodging-house** *n.* a house in which lodgings are let. **lodgings** *pl. n.* a room or rooms (not in a hotel) rented for living in.

loess (loh-iss) *n,* a layer of fine light-coloured dust, found in large areas of Asia, Europe, and America and very fertile when irrigated, thought to have been deposited by winds during the Ice Age.

loft *n.* **1.** a space under the roof of a house. **2.** a space under the roof of a stable or barn, used for storing hay etc. **3.** a gallery or upper level in a church or hall, *the organ-loft.* **4.** a backward slope in the face of a golf-club. **5.** a lofted stroke. —*v.* to send (a ball) in a high arc.

lofty *adj.* (loftier, loftiest) **1.** (of things) very tall, towering. **2.** (of thoughts or aims etc.) noble. **3.** haughty, *a lofty manner.* **loftily** *adv.*, **loftiness** *n.*

log[1] *n.* **1.** a length of tree-trunk that has fallen or been cut down. **2.** a short piece of this, especially as firewood. **3.** a device for gauging a ship's speed. **4.** a detailed record of a ship's voyage or an aircraft's flight, any similar record. —**log** *v.* (logged, logging) **1.** to enter (facts) in a log-book. **2.** to achieve (a certain speed or distance or number of hours worked etc.) as recorded in a log-book or similar record, *the pilot had logged 200 hours on jets.* —**logger** *n.,* □ **log-book** *n.* a book in which details of a voyage etc. or of the registration details of a motor vehicle are recorded. **log cabin,** a hut built of logs. **log in** *or* **out,** to connect or disconnect a terminal correctly to or from a multi-access computer system. **log-rolling** *n.* unprincipled assistance to help each other's projects (¶ from the phrase *you roll my log and I'll roll yours*).

log[2] *n.* a logarithm, *log tables.*

loganberry *n.* a large dark-red fruit resembling a blackberry.

logarithm (log-er-i*th*'m) *n.* one of a series of numbers set out in tables which make it possible to work out problems by adding and subtracting numbers instead of multiplying and dividing. **logarithmic** *adj.*

loggerheads *pl. n.* **at loggerheads,** disagreeing, arguing, or quarrelling.

loggia (loj-ă) *n.* an open-sided gallery or arcade, especially one looking on an open court or forming part of a house and facing a garden.

logging *see* log[1]. —*n.* (*Amer.*) the work of cutting down forest trees for timber.

logic (loj-ik) *n.* **1.** the science of reasoning. **2.** a particular system or method of reasoning. **3.** a chain of reasoning regarded as good or bad. **4.** the ability to reason correctly. **5.** the principles used in designing a computer or any of its units, the circuit(s) involved in this.

logical (loj-ikăl) *adj.* **1.** of or according to logic, correctly reasoned. **2.** (of an action etc.) in accordance with what seems reasonable or natural. **3.** capable of reasoning correctly. **logically** *adv.*, **logicality** (loj-i-kal-iti) *n.*

logistics (lŏj-ist-iks) *pl. n.* the organization of supplies and services etc. **logistic** *adj.*

logo (**log-**oh) *n.* (*pl.* logos) a printed symbol (not a heraldic device) used by a corporation or business company etc. as its emblem.

loin *n.* **1.** the side and back of the body between the ribs and the hip-bone. **2.** a joint of meat that includes the vertebrae of this part.

loincloth *n.* a piece of cloth worn round the body at the hips, especially as the only garment.

loiter *v.* to linger or stand about idly, to proceed slowly with frequent stops. **loiterer** *n.*

loll *v.* **1.** to lean lazily against something, to stand or sit or rest lazily. **2.** to hang loosely, *tongue lolling out.*

lollipop *n.* a large round usually flat boiled sweet on a small stick. **lollipop man** *or* **lady,** (*informal*) an official using a circular sign on a stick to signal traffic to stop so that children may cross a road.

lollop *v.* (lolloped, lolloping) (*informal*) to flop about, to move in clumsy bounds.

lolly *n.* (*informal*) **1.** a lollipop. **2.** (*Austral.*) a sweet. **3.** (*slang*) money. □ **ice lolly** *or* **iced lolly,** an ice cream on a small stick.

London the capital of England and of the United Kingdom. **London pride,** a saxifrage with pink flowers.

Londonderry a county of Northern Ireland.

Londoner *n.* a native or inhabitant of London.

lone *adj.* solitary, without companions, *a lone horseman.* **play a lone hand,** to take action without the support of others. **lone wolf,** a person who prefers to do this or to be by himself.

lonely *adj.* (lonelier, loneliest) **1.** solitary, without companions. **2.** sad because one lacks friends or companions. **3.** (of places) far from inhabited places, remote, not often frequented, *a lonely road.* **loneliness** *n.* □ **lonely heart,** a person who feels permanently lonely.

loner *n.* one who prefers not to associate with others.

lonesome *adj.* lonely, causing loneliness.

long[1] *adj.* **1.** having great length in space or time. **2.** having a certain length or duration, *two miles* or *two hours long.* **3.** seeming to be longer than it really is, *ten long years.* **4.** lasting, going far into the past or future, *a long memory; take the long view,* consider the later effects. **5.** (*informal*) having much of a certain quality, *he's not long on tact.* **6.** of elongated shape. **7.** (of vowel sounds) having a pronunciation that is considered to last longer than that of a corresponding 'short' vowel (the *a* in *cane* is long, in *can* it is short). — **long** *adv.* **1.** for a long time, by a long time; *I shan't be long*, shall not take a long time. **2.** throughout a specified time, *all day long*; *I am no longer a child*, am not one now or henceforth. □ **as** *or* **so long as**, provided that, on condition that. **in the long run**, in the end, over a long period. **the long and the short of it**, all that need be said; the general effect or result. **long-distance** *adj.* travelling or operating between distant places. **long division**, the process of dividing one number by another with all calculations written down. **long drink**, one that is large in quantity or filling a tall glass. **long face**, a dismal expression. **long hop**, a short-pitched ball in cricket, easily hit. **long in the tooth**, rather old. **long johns**, *(informal)* underpants or knickers with long legs. **long jump**, an athletic competition of jumping as far as possible along the ground in one leap. **long-legged** *adj.* having long legs. **long-life** *adj.* remaining usable or serviceable for a long time. **long-lived** *adj.* having a long life; lasting for a long time. **long odds**, very uneven odds in betting. **long-playing** *adj.* (of a record) playing for about 10 to 30 minutes on each side. **long-range** *adj.* having a long range; relating to a period far into the future. **long shot**, a wild guess or venture. **long-sighted** *adj.* able to see clearly only what is at a distance. **long-standing** *adj.* having existed for a long time, *a long-standing grievance*. **long-suffering** *adj.* bearing provocation patiently. **long suit**, many playing-cards of one suit in a hand; a thing at which one excels, *modesty is not his long suit*. **long-term** *adj.* of or for a long period. **long ton**, see ton. **long wave**, a radio wave of more than 1000 metres wavelength. **long-winded** *adj.* talking or writing at tedious length.

long² *v.* to feel a longing.
longevity (lon-**jev**-iti) *n.* long life.
longhand *n.* ordinary writing, contrasted with shorthand or typing or printing.
longhorn *n.* one of a breed of cattle with long horns.
longing *n.* an intense persistent wish.
longish *adj.* rather long.
longitude (**lonj**-i-tewd) *n.* the distance east or west (measured in degrees) from the meridian of Greenwich.
longitudinal (lonji-**tew**-din-ăl) *adj.* **1.** of longitude. **2.** of or in length, measured lengthwise. **longitudinally** *adv.*
long-shore *adj.* found on the shore, employed along the shore, especially near a port. **long-shoreman** *n.* one who is employed in loading and unloading ships or in fishing from the shore.

longways, longwise *advs.* lengthways.
loo *n.* *(informal)* a lavatory.
loofah (**loo**-fă) *n.* the dried pod of a kind of gourd, used as a rough sponge.
look *v.* **1.** to use or direct one's eyes in order to see or search or examine. **2.** to direct one's eyes or one's attention, to consider; *they look to her for help*, rely on her to provide it. **3.** (of things) to face in a certain direction. **4.** to have a certain appearance, to seem to be, *the fruit looks ripe*; *made him look a fool*. —**look** *n.* **1.** the act of looking, a gaze or glance. **2.** an inspection or search, *have a look for it*. **3.** appearance, *is blessed with good looks*; *wet-look paint*; *I don't like the look of this*, find it alarming. □ **look after**, to take care of; to attend to. **look-alike** *n.* (*Amer.*) a person or thing closely resembling another. **look down on** *or* **look down one's nose at**, to regard with contempt. **look forward to**, to be waiting eagerly (or sometimes with anxiety etc.) for an expected thing or event. **look here!**, an exclamation of protest. **look in**, to make a short visit; *(informal)* to watch television. **look-in** *n.* a chance of participation or success. **look into**, to investigate. **look on**, to be a spectator. **look out**, to be vigilant; to select or find by inspection, *I'll look out some books for you*. **look-out** *n.* looking out, a watch; one who keeps watch; a place from which observation is kept; a prospect of luck, *it's a poor look-out for us*; a person's own concern, *that's his look-out*. **look sharp**, be alert. **look up**, to search for information about, *look up words in a dictionary*; to improve in prospects, *things are looking up*; to go to visit, *look us up*. **look up to**, to admire and respect as superior.
looker-on *n.* (*pl.* **lookers-on**) a mere spectator.
looking-glass *n.* a glass mirror.
loom¹ *n.* an apparatus for weaving cloth.
loom² *v.* to come into view suddenly, to appear close at hand or with threatening aspect.
loon *n.* a diving-bird with a loud wild cry.
loony *n.* *(slang)* a lunatic. —*adj.* *(slang)* crazy. □ **loony-bin** *n.* *(slang)* a mental home or mental hospital.
loop *n.* **1.** the shape produced by a curve that crosses itself. **2.** any path or pattern shaped roughly like this. **3.** a length of cord or wire etc. that crosses itself and is fastened at the crossing. **4.** a complete circuit for electrical current. **5.** a set of computer instructions that is carried out repeatedly until some specified condition

is satisfied. **6.** a curved piece of metal serving as a handle. **7.** a contraceptive coil. **8.** a strip of fabric etc. attached to a garment or object so that it can be hung on a peg. —**loop** v. **1.** to form into a loop or loops. **2.** to fasten or join with a loop or loops. **3.** to enclose in a loop. □ **loop-line** n. a railway or telegraph line that leaves the main line and joins it again. **loop the loop**, (of an aircraft) to fly in a vertical circle, turning upside down between climb and dive.

loophole n. **1.** a narrow opening in the wall of a fort etc., for shooting or looking through or to admit light or air. **2.** a way of evading a rule or contract etc., especially through an omission or inexact wording in its provisions.

loose adj. **1.** freed from bonds or restraint, (of an animal) not tethered or shut in; a loose ball, (in football etc.) not in any player's possession. **2.** detached or detachable from its place, not rigidly fixed. **3.** not fastened together, not held or packed or contained in something. **4.** not organized strictly, a loose confederation. **5.** slack, relaxed, not tense or tight, loose skin; loose bowels, with a tendency to diarrhoea; a loose tongue, indiscreet. **6.** not compact, not dense in texture, arranged at wide intervals, a loose weave. **7.** inexact, vague; a loose translation, approximate, not close to the original; loose fielding, careless. **8.** slack in moral principles or conduct, promiscuous, loose women. —adv. loosely, loose-fitting. —**loose** v. **1.** to release. **2.** to untie or loosen. **3.** to fire a gun or missile, loosed off a round of ammunition. —**loosely** adv., **looseness** n. □ **at a loose end**, without definite occupation. **loose box**, a stall in which a horse can move about. **loose covers**, removable covers for chairs etc. **loose-leaf** adj. (of a notebook etc.) with each leaf separate and removable.

loosen v. to make or become loose or looser. **loosen a person's tongue**, to make him talk freely. **loosen up**, to relax, to limber up.

loosestrife n. a kind of marsh plant.

loot n. goods taken from an enemy or by theft. —v. to plunder, to take as loot, to steal from or rob shops or houses left unprotected after a violent event. —**looter** n.

lop v. (lopped, lopping) to cut away branches or twigs of, to cut off.

lope v. to run with a long bounding stride. —n. a long bounding stride.

lop-eared adj. having drooping ears.

lop-sided adj. with one side lower or smaller or heavier than the other.

loquacious (lŏ-**kway**-shŭs) adj. talkative. **loquaciously** adv., **loquacity** (lŏ-**kwass**-iti) n.

lord n. **1.** a master or ruler or sovereign; the Lord, God; Our Lord, Christ. **2.** a nobleman; live like a lord, live sumptuously. **3.** the title or form of address to certain peers or high officials, the Lord Bishop of Oxford; the Lord Chief Justice. **4.** the Lords, the House of Lords (see house [1]). —v. to domineer, lording it over the whole club. □ **Lord Chancellor**, see chancellor. **Lord Mayor**, the mayor of certain large cities. **lord of the manor**, (in the Middle Ages) the master from whom men held land and to whom they owed service. **lords and ladies**, wild arum. **the Lord's Prayer**, the prayer taught by Christ to his disciples, beginning 'Our Father'. **lords spiritual**, the bishops and archbishops in the House of Lords. **lords temporal**, peers other than these. **Lord's Supper**, the Eucharist.

lordly adj. (lordlier, lordliest) **1.** haughty, imperious. **2.** suitable for a lord, a lordly mansion.

lordship n. a title used in speaking to or about a man of the rank of 'Lord', your lordship.

lore n. a body of traditions and knowledge on a subject or possessed by a class of people, bird lore; gypsy lore.

lorgnette (lorn-yet) n. a pair of eyeglasses or opera-glasses held to the eyes on a long handle.

lorry n. a large strong motor vehicle for transporting heavy goods or troops.

lose v. (lost, losing) **1.** to be deprived of, (e.g. by death or accident). **2.** to cease to have or maintain, lose confidence; lose one's balance; car lost speed. **3.** to become unable to find, to miss from amongst one's possessions. **4.** to fail to keep (a thing etc.) in sight or to follow (a piece of reasoning) mentally; lose one's way, to fail to find the right path etc. **5.** to fail to obtain or catch, lost the contract. **6.** to get rid of, lose weight; managed to lose our pursuers. **7.** to be defeated in a contest or lawsuit or argument etc. **8.** to have to forfeit, the Liberal candidate lost his deposit. **9.** to waste time or an opportunity, lost twenty minutes through bursting a tyre. **10.** to suffer loss, to be worse off, we lost on the deal. **11.** to cause (a person) the loss of, delay lost them the contract. **12.** (of a clock) to become slow; it loses two minutes a day, becomes this amount behind the correct time. —**loser** n. □ **lose ground**, to be forced to retreat or give way. **lose one's heart**, to fall in love. **lose one's**

life, to be killed. **lose out,** (*informal*) to be unsuccessful; to suffer loss. **losing battle,** one in which defeat seems certain.

loss *n.* **1.** losing, being lost. **2.** a person or thing lost. **3.** money lost in a business transaction, the excess of outlay over returns. **4.** a disadvantage or suffering caused by losing something; *it's no loss,* the loss does not matter. □ **be at a loss,** to be puzzled, to be unable to know what to do or say. **loss-leader** *n.* a popular article sold at a loss to attract customers who will then buy other articles.

lost *see* lose. —*adj.* **1.** strayed or separated from its owner, *a lost dog.* **2.** engrossed, *lost in thought.* □ **be lost on,** to fail to influence or draw the attention of, *our hints were lost on him.* **get lost!,** (*slang*) cease being annoying. **lost cause,** an undertaking that can no longer be successful. **lost to,** no longer affected by, *she seems lost to a sense of duty.*

lot¹ *n.* **1.** one of a set of objects used in making a selection by methods depending on chance, *cast* or *draw lots for it.* **2.** this method of selecting, the choice resulting from it, *was chosen by lot*; *the lot fell on me.* **3.** a person's share, what falls to him by lot or chance, his fate or appointed task etc. **4.** a piece of land, (*Amer.*) an area for a particular purpose, *a parking lot.* **5.** an article or set of articles put up for sale at an auction etc. □ **bad lot,** a person of bad character. **cast** *or* **throw in one's lot with,** to decide to join and share the fortunes of.

lot² *n.* **1.** a number of people or things of the same kind; *the lot,* the total quantity. **2.** (*informal*) a large number or amount, *has a lot of friends*; *there's lots of time,* plenty. **3.** much, *feeling a lot better.*

Lothian (**loh**-*th*i-ăn) a region of Scotland.

lotion *n.* a medicinal or cosmetic liquid applied to the skin.

lottery *n.* **1.** a system of raising money by selling numbered tickets and distributing prizes to the holders of numbers drawn at random. **2.** something where the outcome is governed by luck.

lotto *n.* a game resembling bingo but with numbers drawn instead of called.

lotus (**loh**-tŭs) *n.* (*pl.* lotuses) **1.** a kind of tropical water-lily. **2.** a mythical fruit represented as inducing a state of lazy and luxurious dreaminess. □ **lotus position,** a cross-legged position adopted for meditating.

loud *adj.* **1.** easily heard, producing much noise. **2.** (of colours etc.) unpleasantly bright, gaudy. —*adv.* loudly. —**loudly** *adv.,*

loudness *n.* □ **loud hailer,** an electronic device that amplifies the sound of a voice which can then be heard at a distance. **out loud,** aloud.

loudspeaker *n.* an apparatus (especially part of a radio) that converts electrical impulses into audible sound.

lough (*pr.* lok) *n.* (*Irish*) a lake or an arm of the sea.

Louisiana (loo-eez-i-**an**-ă) a State of the USA.

lounge *v.* to loll, to sit or stand about idly. —*n.* **1.** a waiting-room at an airport etc., with seats for waiting passengers. **2.** a public room (in a hotel) for sitting in. **3.** a sitting-room in a house. —**lounger** *n.* □ **lounge suit,** a man's ordinary suit for day wear.

lour (*rhymes with* sour) *v.* **1.** to frown or scowl. **2.** (of clouds or the sky etc.) to look dark and threatening.

louse *n.* **1.** (*pl.* lice) a small insect that lives as a parasite on animals or plants. **2.** (*pl.* louses) (*slang*) a contemptible person. —*v.* **louse up,** (*slang*) to make a mess of.

lousy *adj.* (lousier, lousiest) **1.** infested with lice. **2.** (*slang*) disgusting, very bad or ill. **3.** (*slang*) well provided, swarming, *he's lousy with money*; *lousy with tourists.*

lout *n.* a clumsy ill-mannered young man. **loutish** *adj.* like a lout.

louver *or* **louvre** (loo-ver) *ns.* one of a set of overlapping slats arranged to admit air but exclude light or rain. **louvered** *or* **louvred** *adjs.* fitted with these.

lovable *adj.* easy to love.

lovage (**luv**-ij) *n.* a herb with leaves that are used for flavouring soups and in salads.

love *n.* **1.** warm liking or affection for a person, affectionate devotion; *there's no love lost between them,* they dislike each other. **2.** sexual affection or passion, the relation between sweethearts. **3.** God's benevolence towards mankind. **4.** strong liking for a thing, *love of music.* **5.** affectionate greetings, *send one's love.* **6.** a loved person, a sweetheart, (*informal*) a form of address to a woman or child. **7.** (*informal*) a delightful person or thing. **8.** (in games) no score, nil; *love all,* neither side has yet scored; *a love game,* in which the loser has not scored at all. —**love** *v.* **1.** to feel love for. **2.** to like greatly, to take pleasure in having or doing something. □ **for love,** because of affection; without receiving payment; *cannot get it for love or money,* by any means. **in love,** feeling love (especially sexual love) for another person. **love-affair** *n.* a romantic or sexual relationship between two people who are in love. **love-bird** *n.* a kind of parakeet that seems to show great affection for its mate. **love-child** *n.* an illegitimate child. **love-hate relationship,** an intense emotional response involving both love and hate. **love-letter** *n.* a letter between sweethearts and concerning their love. **love-lies-bleeding** *n.* a garden plant with a long drooping spike of dark-red bloom. **love-match** *n.* a marriage made because the two people are in love with each other. **love-song** *n.* a song expressing love. **love-story** *n.* a novel etc. of which the main theme is romantic love.

loveless *adj.* without love, *a loveless marriage.*

lovelorn *adj.* pining with love, forsaken by one's lover.

lovely *adj.* (lovelier, loveliest) **1.** beautiful, attractive. **2.** (*informal*) delightful, *having a lovely time.* —*n.* (*informal*) a pretty woman. **loveliness** *n.*

lover *n.* **1.** someone (especially a man) who is in love with another person, a suitor. **2.** a person (especially a man) having an illicit love affair. **3.** one who likes or enjoys something, *lovers of music*; *music-lovers.*

lovesick *adj.* languishing because of love.

loving *adj.* feeling or showing love. **lovingly** *adv.*

low[1] *n.* the deep sound made by cattle, a moo. —*v.* to make this sound.

low[2] *adj.* **1.** not high or tall, not extending far upwards. **2.** (of ground) not far above sea level, low in relation to surrounding land. **3.** ranking below others in importance or quality. **4.** ignoble, vulgar, *low cunning*; *keeps low company.* **5.** less than what is normal in amount or intensity etc., *low prices*; *a low opinion*, unfavourable. **6.** (of a sound or voice) deep not shrill, having slow vibrations. **7.** not loud, *spoke in a low voice.* **8.** lacking in vigour, depressed. —**low** *n.* **1.** a low level or figure, *share prices reached a new low.* **2.** an area of low barometric pressure. —**low** *adv.* **1.** in or at or to a low level or position. **2.** in or to a low degree. **3.** in a low tone, (of sound) at a low pitch. □ **Low Church,** that section of the Church of England that gives only a low place to ritual and the authority of bishops and priests. **low-class** *adj.* of low quality or social class. **Low Countries,** the Netherlands, Belgium, and Luxemburg. **low-down** *adj.* dishonourable, (*n.*) (*slang*) the true facts, inside information. **low frequency,** (in radio) 30 to 300 kilohertz. **low-key** *adj.* restrained, not intense or emotional. **low-level** *adj.* (of a computer language) using instructions which corres-

pond closely to the individual operations that the computer will perform. **Low Mass,** with no music and the minimum of ceremony. **low-pitched** *adj.* (of a voice or sound) low. **low season,** the period when a resort etc. has relatively few visitors. **Low Sunday,** the next Sunday after Easter. **low tide,** the tide at its lowest level; the time when this occurs. **low water,** low tide; *in low water,* short of money.

lowbrow *adj.* not intellectual or cultured. —*n.* a lowbrow person.

lower[1] *adj.* **1.** less high in place or position. **2.** situated on less high land or to the south; *Lower Egypt,* the part nearest to the Nile delta. **3.** ranking below others; *the lower animals* or *plants,* those of relatively simple structure, not highly developed; *lower classes,* people of the lowest social rank. —*adv.* in or to a lower position etc. —*v.* **1.** to let or haul down. **2.** to make or become lower, to reduce in amount or quantity etc.; *lower one's eyes,* to direct one's gaze downwards. □ **lower case,** letters (for printing-type) that are not capitals. **Lower Chamber** *or* **House,** the House of Commons as an assembly. **lower deck,** the petty officers and lower ranks of a ship or of the Navy.

lower[2] *v.* —lour.

lowland *n.* low-lying land. —*adj.* of or in lowland. □ **lowlander** *n.* a native or inhabitant of lowlands.

lowly *adj.* (lowlier, lowliest) of humble rank or condition. **lowliness** *n.*

loyal *adj.* steadfast in one's allegiance to a person or cause or to one's country or sovereign. **loyally** *adv.,* **loyalty** *n.*

loyalist *n.* a person who is loyal, especially to the established government during a revolt.

lozenge *n.* **1.** a four-sided diamond-shaped figure. **2.** a small tablet of flavoured sugar or medicine or meat essence etc., to be dissolved in the mouth.

LP *abbrev.* a long-playing record.

L-plate *n.* a sign bearing the letter 'L', fixed to a motor vehicle that is being driven by a learner-driver.

LSD *n.* a powerful drug that produces hallucinations (= lysergic acid diethylamide).

Ltd. *abbrev.* Limited (= 'limited liability company', now used only by private companies; public companies use PLC).

Luanda (loo-an-dă) the capital of Angola.

lubricant (loo-brik-ănt) *n.* a lubricating substance.

lubricate (loo-brik-ayt) *v.* to oil or grease (machinery etc.) so that it moves easily. **lubrication** *n.*

lucerne (loo-**sern**) *n.* a clover-like plant used for fodder.

lucid (**loo**-sid) *adj.* **1.** clearly expressed, easy to understand. **2.** sane; *lucid intervals,* periods of sanity between periods of insanity. **lucidly** *adv.,* **lucidity** (loo-**sid**-iti) *n.*

luck *n.* **1.** chance thought of as a force that brings either good or bad fortune. **2.** the events etc. (either favourable or unfavourable to one's interests) that it brings. **3.** good fortune, *it will bring you luck.* ☐ **in luck,** having good fortune. **out of luck,** not in luck.

luckless *adj.* unlucky.

lucky *adj.* (luckier, luckiest) having or bringing or resulting from good luck. **luckily** *adv.* ☐ **lucky dip,** a receptacle at bazaars etc. containing small articles of various values which people may take out at random, taking the chance of getting something of good value.

lucrative (**loo**-krǎ-tiv) *adj.* profitable, producing much profit. **lucrativeness** *n.*

lucre (**loo**-ker) *n.* (*contemptuous*) money, money-making as a motive for action. **filthy lucre,** (*humorous*) money.

Luddite (**lud**-dyt) *n.* a member of the bands of English workers (1811–16) who destroyed newly introduced machinery which they thought would cause unemployment. ¶ Probably named after Ned *Lud,* an insane person who destroyed some machinery in about 1779.

ludicrous (**loo**-dik-rǔs) *adj.* absurd, ridiculous, laughable. **ludicrously** *adv.*

ludo *n.* a simple game played with dice and counters on a special board.

luff *v.* to bring a ship's head nearer to the direction from which the wind is blowing.

lug[1] *v.* (lugged, lugging) to drag or carry with great effort.

lug[2] *n.* an ear-like part or projection on an object, by which it may be carried or fixed in place etc.

luggage *n.* suitcases and bags etc. containing a person's belongings taken on a journey.

lugubrious (lŭ-**goo**-briŭs) *adj.* dismal, mournful. **lugubriously** *adv.*

lugworm *n.* a large marine worm used as bait.

lukewarm *adj.* **1.** only slightly warm. **2.** not enthusiastic, *got a lukewarm reception.*

lull *v.* **1.** to soothe or send to sleep. **2.** to calm (suspicions etc.). **3.** (of a storm or noise) to lessen, to become quiet. —*n.* a temporary period of quiet or inactivity.

lullaby *n.* a soothing song sung to put a child to sleep.

lumbago (lum-**bay**-goh) *n.* rheumatic pain in the muscles of the loins.

lumbar *adj.* of or in the loins.

lumber *n.* **1.** unwanted articles of furniture etc. that are stored away or take up room, useless material of any kind. **2.** (*Amer.*) timber sawn into planks. —**lumber** *v.* **1.** to encumber, to fill up (space) inconveniently. **2.** to move in a heavy clumsy way. ☐ **lumber-room** *n.* a room in which lumber (= unwanted articles) is kept.

lumberjack *n.* (*Amer.*) one whose trade is the cutting or conveying or preparing of lumber (= timber).

lumber-jacket *n.* a hip-length jacket fastening up to the neck.

luminary (**loo**-min-er-i) *n.* **1.** a natural light-giving body, especially the sun or moon. **2.** an eminent or influential person.

luminescent (loo-min-ess-ĕnt) *adj.* emitting light without being hot. **luminescence** *n.*

luminous (**loo**-min-ŭs) *adj.* emitting light, glowing in the dark. **luminosity** (loo-min-**oss**-iti) *n.*

lump[1] *n.* **1.** a hard or compact mass, usually one without a regular shape. **2.** a protuberance or swelling. **3.** a heavy dull or stupid person. **4.** (*slang*) a great quantity, a lot. **5.** *the lump,* the body of casual workers in the building trade etc. —*v.* to put or consider together, to treat as alike, *lump them together.* ☐ **lump in the throat,** a feeling of pressure there caused by emotion. **lump sugar,** sugar in small lumps or cubes. **lump sum,** a single payment covering a number of items or paid all at once not in instalments.

lump[2] *v.* **lump it,** (*informal*) to put up with something one dislikes.

lumpish *adj.* heavy and dull or stupid.

lumpy *adj.* (lumpier, lumpiest) full of lumps, covered in lumps. **lumpiness** *n.*

lunacy *n.* **1.** insanity. **2.** great folly.

lunar *adj.* of the moon. **lunar month,** the interval between new moons (about 29½ days); four weeks.

lunatic *n.* an insane person, one who is extremely foolish or reckless. —*adj.* insane, extremely foolish or reckless. ☐ **lunatic asylum,** (*old use*) a mental home or mental hospital. **lunatic fringe,** a few eccentric or fanatical members of a political or other group.

lunch *n.* **1.** a meal taken in the middle of the day. **2.** light refreshment at mid morning. —**lunch** *v.* **1.** to eat lunch. **2.** to entertain to lunch.

luncheon *n.* (*formal*) lunch. **luncheon meat,** tinned meat loaf ready for serving, made from pork or ham. **luncheon voucher,** a voucher given to an employee, exchangeable for food at certain restaurants.

lung *n.* either of the two breathing-organs, in the chest of man and most vertebrates, that draw in air and bring it into contact with the blood. **lung-power** *n.* power of voice.

lunge *n.* **1.** a sudden forward movement of the body towards something, a thrust. **2.** a long rope on which a horse is held by its trainer while it is made to canter in a circle. —**lunge** *v.* (lunged, lunging) **1.** to make a lunge. **2.** to exercise (a horse) on a lunge.

lupin *n.* a garden plant with tall tapering spikes of flowers, bearing seeds in pods.

lurch[1] *n.* **leave in the lurch**, to abandon (a person etc.) so that he is left in an awkward situation.

lurch[2] *n.* an unsteady swaying movement to one side. —*v.* to make such a movement, to stagger.

lurcher *n.* a dog that is a cross between a collie and a greyhound, often used by poachers for retrieving game.

lure (*rhymes with* pure) *n.* **1.** something that attracts or entices or allures. **2.** its power of attracting. **3.** a bait or decoy for wild animals, a device used to attract and recall a trained hawk. —*v.* to entice, to attract by the promise of pleasure or gain.

lurid (**lewr**-id) *adj.* **1.** in glaring colours or combinations of colour. **2.** sensationally and shockingly vivid, *the lurid details.* **luridly** *adv.*, **luridness** *n.*

lurk *v.* **1.** to lie hidden while waiting to attack. **2.** to wait near a place furtively or unobtrusively. **3.** to be latent or lingering, *a lurking sympathy for the rebels.*

Lusaka (loo-**sah**-kă) the capital of Zambia.

luscious (**lush**-ŭs) *adj.* **1.** richly sweet in taste or smell. **2.** voluptuously attractive, *a luscious blonde.* **lusciously** *adv.*, **lusciousness** *n.*

lush[1] *adj.* **1.** (of grass etc.) growing thickly and strongly. **2.** luxurious, *lush furnishings.* **lushly** *adv.*, **lushness** *n.*

lush[2] *v.* (*slang*) to ply with drink or good food etc., *lush him up.* —*n.* (*Amer. slang*) a drunkard.

lust *n.* **1.** intense sexual desire. **2.** any intense desire for something, *lust for power.* —*v.* to feel lust. —**lustful** *adj.*

lustre (**lus**-ter) *n.* **1.** the soft brightness of a smooth or shining surface. **2.** glory, distinction, *add lustre to the assembly.* **3.** a kind of metallic glaze on pottery and porcelain. **lustrous** (**lus**-trŭs) *adj.*

lusty *adj.* (lustier, lustiest) strong and vigorous, full of vitality. **lustily** *adv.*, **lustiness** *n.*

lute (*pr.* loot) *n.* a guitar-like instrument with a pear-shaped body, popular in the 14th–17th centuries.

Lutheran (loo-ther-ăn) *adj.* of Martin Luther (1483–1546), leader of the Protestant Reformation in Germany, or his teachings.

Luxemburg 1. a country between France and Germany. **2.** its capital city. **Luxemburger** *n.*

luxuriant *adj.* growing profusely. **luxuriance** *n.* ¶ Do not confuse with luxurious.

luxuriate *v.* to feel great enjoyment, to enjoy as luxury, *luxuriating in the warm sun.*

luxurious *adj.* supplied with luxuries, very comfortable. **luxuriously** *adv.*, **luxuriousness** *n.* ¶ Do not confuse with luxuriant.

luxury *n.* **1.** surroundings and food, dress, etc. that are choice and costly. **2.** luxuriousness, self-indulgence. **3.** something costly that is enjoyable but not essential.

LV *abbrev.* luncheon voucher.

lych (*pr.* lich) *n.* = lich.

lying *see* lie[1], lie[2].

lymph (*pr.* limf) *n.* **1.** a colourless fluid from tissues or organs of the body, containing white blood-cells. **2.** the fluid used in vaccination against smallpox. **lymphatic** (lim-**fat**-ik) *adj.*

lynch (*pr.* linch) *v.* (of a mob) to execute or punish violently, without a lawful trial.

lynx (*pr.* links) *n.* (*pl.* lynxes) a wild animal of the cat family with spotted fur, noted for its keen sight. **lynx-eyed** *adj.* keen-sighted.

lyre *n.* an ancient musical instrument with strings fixed in a U-shaped frame. **lyre-bird** *n.* an Australian bird, the male of which can spread its tail in the shape of a lyre.

lyric (**li**-rik) *adj.* of poetry that expresses the poet's thoughts and feelings. —*n.* **1.** a lyric poem. **2.** the words of a song.

lyrical (**li**-ri-kăl) *adj.* **1.** = lyric, using language suitable for this. **2.** (*informal*) expressing oneself enthusiastically. **lyrically** *adv.*

lysin (**ly**-sin) *n.* a substance that is able to cause disintegration of living cells or bacteria.

Mm

m *abbrev.* **1.** metre(s). **2.** mile(s). **3.** million(s).

ma *n.* (*vulgar*) mother.

MA *abbrev.* Master of Arts.

ma'am (*pr.* mam) *n.* madam (used in addressing the Queen or a royal princess).

mac *n.* (*informal*) a mackintosh.

macabre (mă-**kahbr**) *adj.* gruesome, suggesting death.

macadam (mă-**kad**-ăm) *n.* layers of broken stone used in road-making, each layer being rolled hard before the next is put down. **macadamized** *adj.* made with layers in this way.

macaroni *n.* pasta formed into long tubes.

macaroon *n.* a small flat sweet cake or biscuit made with sugar, white of egg, and ground almonds or coconut.

macaw (mă-**kaw**) *n.* a brightly coloured American parrot with a long tail.

mace[1] *n.* a ceremonial staff carried or placed before an official, especially that symbolizing the Speaker's authority in the House of Commons.

mace[2] *n.* a spice made from the dried outer covering of nutmeg.

macedoine (**mas**-id-wahn) *n.* a mixture of chopped fruits or vegetables, often served set in jelly.

macerate (**mas**-er-ayt) *v.* to make or become soft by steeping in a liquid. **maceration** *n.*

mach (*pr.* mahk) *n.* **mach number**, the ratio of the speed of a body to the speed of sound in the same medium; a body travelling at *mach one* is travelling at the speed of sound, *mach two* is twice this.

machete (mă-**chay**-ti) *n.* a broad heavy knife used in Central America and the West Indies as a tool and weapon.

machiavellian (maki-ă-**vel**-iăn) *adj.* elaborately cunning or deceitful. ¶ Named after Niccolo dei Machiavelli (1469–1527), an Italian statesman who advised the use of any means, however unscrupulous, that would strengthen the State.

machinations (mash-in-ay-**shŏn**z) *pl. n.* clever scheming, things done by this.

machine *n.* **1.** an apparatus for applying mechanical power, having several parts each with a definite function. **2.** something operated by such apparatus, e.g. a bicycle or aircraft. **3.** a complex controlling system of an organization, *the publicity machine.* —*v.* to make or produce or work on (a thing) with a machine, to stitch with a sewing-machine. ☐ **machine language**, a language (see language sense 4) to which a particular computer can respond directly without further translation. **machine-readable** *adj.* in a form that a computer can respond to. **machine tool**, a mechanically operated tool.

machine-gun *n.* a mounted gun operated automatically, that can deliver a rapid and continuous fire of bullets. —*v.* to shoot at with a machine-gun.

machinery *n.* **1.** machines. **2.** mechanism. **3.** an organized system for doing something.

machinist *n.* a person who makes or works machinery, one who operates machine tools.

machismo (mă-**chis**-moh) *n.* virility or manly courage, a show of this.

macho (**mach**-oh) *adj.* exhibiting machismo.

mackerel *n.* (*pl.* mackerel) an edible sea-fish. **mackerel sky**, rows of small white fleecy clouds.

mackintosh *n.* **1.** waterproof material of rubber and cloth. **2.** a raincoat.

macramé (mă-**krah**-mi) *n.* **1.** a fringe or trimming of knotted thread or cord. **2.** the art of making this.

macroscopic (makrŏ-**skop**-ik) *adj.* **1.** visible to the naked eye. **2.** regarded in terms of large units. **macroscopically** *adv.*

mad *adj.* (madder, maddest) **1.** having a disordered mind, not sane. **2.** extremely foolish, *a mad scheme.* **3.** wildly enthusiastic, *is mad about sport.* **4.** (*informal*) very annoyed. **5.** frenzied, *a mad scramble.* **6.** (of an animal) suffering from rabies, *a mad dog.* **madly** *adv.*, **madness** *n.* ☐ **like mad**, with great haste or energy or enthusiasm.

Madagascar an island off the south-east coast of Africa.

madam *n.* **1.** a word used in speaking politely to a woman, or prefixed to the name of her office in formal address, *Madam Chairman.* **2.** a conceited or presumptuous young woman. **3.** (*informal*) a woman in charge of a brothel.

Madame (mă-**dahm**) *n.* (*pl.* Mesdames, *pr.* may-**dahm**) the title of a French-speaking woman, = Mrs or madam.

madcap *n.* a wildly impulsive person. — *adj.* wildly impulsive.

madden *v.* to make mad or angry, to irritate.

madder *n.* **1.** a plant with yellowish flowers. **2.** a red dye got from its root or made synthetically.

made *see* make.

Madeira *n.* a fortified white wine produced in the island of Madeira. ☐ **Madeira cake**, a rich cake containing no fruit.

madeleine (**mad**-ĕ-layn) *n.* a small rich plain cake baked in a round narrow tapering tin.

Mademoiselle (mad-mwă-**zel**) *n.* (*pl.* Mesdemoiselles, *pr.* mayd-mwă-**zel**) the title of a French-speench-speaking girl or unmarried woman, = Miss or madam.

madhouse *n.* (*informal*) **1.** a mental home

or mental hospital. **2.** a scene of confused uproar.

madman *n.* (*pl.* madmen) a man who is mad.

madonna *n.* a picture or statue of the Virgin Mary. **madonna lily,** a tall lily with white flowers.

madras (mă-**dras**) *n.* a light cotton fabric often with coloured stripes.

Madrid the capital of Spain.

madrigal (**mad**-ri-găl) *n.* a part-song for voices, usually without instrumental accompaniment.

madwoman *n.* (*pl.* madwomen) a woman who is mad.

maelstrom (**mayl**-strŏm) *n.* a great whirlpool.

maestro (**my**-stroh) *n.* (*pl.* maestros) **1.** a great musical composer or teacher or conductor. **2.** a master of any art.

Mae West (*slang*) an inflatable life-jacket. ¶ Named after an American film actress (1892–1980) noted for her large bust.

Mafia (**mah**-fiă) *n.* **1.** a secret organization in Sicily, opposed to legal authority and engaged in crime. **2.** a similar organization in the USA and elsewhere, thought to be involved in smuggling, racketeering, etc. **3.** *mafia,* a network of persons regarded as exerting hidden influence.

mafioso (mah-fi-**oh**-soh) *n.* (*pl.* mafiosi, *pr.* mah-fi-**oh**-see) a member of the Mafia.

magazine *n.* **1.** a paper-covered illustrated periodical publication containing articles or stories etc. by a number of writers. **2.** a store for arms and ammunition, or for explosives. **3.** a chamber for holding cartridges to be fed into the breech of a gun. **4.** a similar device in a camera or slide-projector.

magenta (mă-**jen**-tă) *n.* & *adj.* bright purplish red.

maggot *n.* a larva, especially of the blue-bottle. **maggoty** *adj.*

Magi (**mayj**-I) *pl. n.* the 'wise men' from the East who brought offerings to the infant Christ at Bethlehem.

magic *n.* **1.** the supposed art of controlling events or effects etc. by supernatural power. **2.** superstitious practices based on belief in this. **3.** a mysterious and enchanting quality, *the magic of a spring day.* — *adj.* of magic, used in producing magic, *magic words.* —**magical** *adj.,* **magically** *adv.* □ **magic carpet,** a mythical carpet able to transport a person on it to any place.

magician (mă-**jish**-ăn) *n.* **1.** one who is s skilled in magic. **2.** a conjuror.

magisterial (ma-jis-**teer**-iăl) *adj.* **1.** of a magistrate. **2.** having or showing authority, imperious. **magisterially** *adv.*

magistrate *n.* an official with authority to administer the law, hear and judge minor cases, and hold preliminary hearings. **magistrates' court,** a court where such cases and hearings are held.

Magna Charta (**kar**-tă) the charter establishing people's rights concerning personal and political liberty, obtained by the English from King John in 1215.

magnanimous (mag-**nan**-imŭs) *adj.* noble and generous in one's conduct, not petty. **magnanimously** *adv.,* **magnanimity** (mag-nă-**nim**-iti) *n.*

magnate (**mag**-nayt) *n.* a wealthy and influential person, especially in business.

magnesia (mag-**nee**-shă) *n.* a white powder that is a compound of magnesium, used as an antacid and mild laxative.

magnesium (mag-**nee**-ziŭm) *n.* a silvery-white metal that burns with an intensely bright flame.

magnet *n..***1.** a piece of iron or steel etc. that can attract iron and that points north and south when suspended. **2.** a person or thing that exerts a powerful attraction.

magnetic *adj.* **1.** having the properties of a magnet. **2.** produced or acting by magnetism. **3.** having the power to attract people, *a magnetic personality.* **magnetically** *adv.* □ **magnetic compass,** one using a **magnetic needle** that points north and south. **magnetic north pole,** the point indicated by a magnetic needle, close to the geographical North Pole but not identical with it. **magnetic tape,** a strip of plastic coated or impregnated with magnetic particles for use in the recording and reproduction of sound or other signals.

magnetism *n.* **1.** the properties and effects of magnetic substances. **2.** the scientific study of these. **3.** great charm and attraction, *personal magnetism.*

magnetize *v.* **1.** to give magnetic properties to. **2.** to attract as a magnet does. **3.** to exert attraction on (a person or people). **magnetization** *n.*

magneto (mag-**nee**-toh) *n.* (*pl.* magnetos) a small electric generator using permanent magnets, especially one used to produce electricity for the spark in the ignition system of an engine.

Magnificat *n.* a canticle beginning 'My soul doth magnify the Lord', the words of the Virgin Mary at the Annunciation.

magnification *n.* **1.** magnifying. **2.** the amount by which a lens etc. magnifies things.

magnificent *adj.* **1.** splendid in appearance etc. **2.** excellent in quality. **magnificently** *adv.,* **magnificence** *n.*

magnify v. (magnified, magnifying) **1.** to make (an object) appear larger than it really is, as a lens or microscope does. **2.** to exaggerate. **3.** (old use) to praise, My soul doth magnify the Lord. **magnifier** n. □ **magnifying glass**, a lens (often mounted in a frame) that magnifies things.

magnitude n. **1.** largeness, size. **2.** importance. **3.** the degree of brightness of a star. □ **of the first magnitude**, very important.

magnolia (mag-**noh**-liă) n. a tree cultivated for its large wax-like usually white or pale pink flowers.

magnum n. a bottle containing two quarts of wine or spirits.

magpie n. **1.** a noisy bird with black-and-white plumage. **2.** a chatterer. **3.** a person who collects objects at random.

Magyar (**mag**-yar) n. **1.** a member of a people originally from Finland and western Siberia, now predominant in Hungary. **2.** their language. —adj. of the Magyars. □ **magyar sleeve**, a plain sleeve cut in one piece with the body of a garment.

maharaja (mah-hă-**rah**-jă) n. the former title of certain Indian princes.

maharishi (mah-hă-**rish**-i) n. a Hindu man of great wisdom.

mahatma (mă-**hat**-mă) n. (in India etc.) a title of respect for a person regarded with reverence.

mah-jong n. a Chinese game for four people, played with pieces called tiles.

mahogany (mă-**hog**-ăni) n. **1.** a very hard reddish-brown wood much used for furniture. **2.** the tropical tree that produces this. **3.** its colour.

maid n. **1.** (old use) a maiden, a girl. **2.** a woman servant doing indoor work. □ **maid of honour**, an unmarried lady attending a queen or princess; a kind of small custard tart.

maiden n. (old use) a girl or young unmarried woman, a virgin. —adj. **1.** unmarried, maiden aunt. **2.** (of a horse) not yet having won a prize. **3.** first, a maiden speech; maiden voyage. —**maidenly** adj., **maidenhood** n. □ **maiden name**, a woman's family name before she marries. **maiden over**, an over in cricket in which no runs are scored.

maidenhair n. a fern with fine hair-like stalks and delicate foliage.

mail[1] n. = post[3]. —v. to send by post. □ **mail-bag** n. a large bag for carrying mail. **mailing list**, a list of people to whom advertising matter etc. is to be posted. **mail order**, an order for goods to be sent by post; mail-order firm, a firm

doing business mainly by this system. **mail train**, a train carrying mail.

mail[2] n. body-armour made of metal rings or chains.

maim v. to wound or injure so that some part of the body is useless.

main adj. principal, most important, greatest in size or extent. —n. **1.** the main pipe or channel or cable in a public system for conveying water, gas, or (usually mains) electricity; we have main drainage, our drains are connected to a public system. —**mainly** adv. □ **have an eye to the main chance**, to be considering one's own interests. **in the main**, for the most part, on the whole. **main frame**, a very large computer system.

Maine a State of the USA.

mainland n. a country or continent without its adjacent islands.

mainmast n. the principal mast of a sailing-ship.

mainspring n. **1.** the principal spring of a watch or clock etc. **2.** the chief force motivating the actions of a person or group.

mainstay n. **1.** the strong cable that secures the mainmast. **2.** the chief support.

mainstream n. the dominant trend of opinion or style etc.

maintain v. **1.** to cause to continue, to keep in existence. **2.** to keep in repair, the house is well maintained. **3.** to support, to provide for, to bear the expenses of, maintaining his son at college. **4.** to assert as true.

maintenance n. **1.** maintaining, being maintained. **2.** keeping equipment etc. in repair; maintenance man, one employed to do this. **3.** provision of the means to support life, an allowance of money for this.

maisonette (may-zŏn-et) n. **1.** a small house. **2.** part of a house (usually not all on one floor) let or used separately as a self-contained dwelling.

maize n. **1.** a tall cereal plant bearing grain on large cobs. **2.** its grain. **3.** the yellow colour of maize cobs.

majestic adj. stately and dignified, imposing. **majestically** adv.

majesty n. **1.** impressive stateliness. **2.** sovereign power. **3.** the title used in speaking of or to a sovereign or a sovereign's wife or widow, His or Her or Your Majesty.

majolica (mă-**yol**-ika) n. **1.** Italian earthenware of the Renaissance period with coloured ornamentation on white enamel. **2.** a modern imitation of this.

major[1] adj. **1.** greater, very important, major roads. **2.** (of a surgical operation) involving danger to the patient's life.

3. (in music) of or based on a scale which has a semitone next above the third and seventh notes and a whole tone elsewhere. —*n.* an officer in charge of a section of band instruments, *drum major.* —*v.* (*Amer.*) to specialize (in a certain subject) at college or university

major [2] *n.* an army officer below lieutenant-colonel and above captain. **major-general** *n.* an army officer next below a lieutenant-general.

major-domo (may-jer-**doh**-moh) *n.* (*pl.* major-domos) the head steward of a great household.

majorette *n.* a drum majorette (*see* drum).

majority *n.* 1. the greatest part of a group or class. 2. the number by which votes for one party etc. exceed those for the next or for all combined. 3. (in law) full age, *attained his majority.* □ **majority verdict,** a verdict supported by more than half of a jury but not unanimous.

make *v.* (made, making) 1. to construct or create or prepare from parts or from other substances. 2. to draw up as a legal document or contract, *make a will.* 3. to establish (laws or rules or distinctions). 4. to arrange ready for use, *make the beds.* 5. to cause to exist, to produce, *make difficulties; make peace.* 6. to result in, to amount to, *two and two make four.* 7. to cause to be or become, *it made me happy; don't make a habit of it; make a day of it,* to carry on an activity etc. so that it fills a day. 8. to frame in the mind, *made a decision.* 9. to succeed in arriving at or achieving a position, *we made London by midnight; she finally made the team.* 10. (*slang*) to catch (a train etc.), to achieve sexual intercourse with (a woman). 11. to form, to serve for, to turn out to be, *this makes pleasant reading; she made him a good wife.* 12. to gain or acquire, *make a profit; make friends,* to become friends. 13. to consider to be, *what do you make the time?; see what you can make of her letter,* how to interpret it. 14. to cause or compel, *make him repeat it.* 15. to perform (an action etc.), *make an attempt; make war.* 16. to ensure the success of, *wine can make the meal; this made my day.* 17. to act as if intending to do something, *he made to go.* —**make** *n.* 1. making, the way a thing is made. 2. the origin of manufacture, *British make; our own make of shoes.* □ **be made for,** to be ideally suited to. **be the making of,** to be the main factor in the success of. **have it made,** (*slang*) to be sure of success. **have the makings of,** to have the essential qua-

lities for becoming, *he had the makings of a good manager.* **a made man,** one who has attained success in his life or career. **make believe,** to pretend. **make-believe** *adj.* pretended, (*n.*) pretence. **make conversation,** to converse only as a social duty. **make do,** to manage with something that is not really adequate or satisfactory. **make for,** to proceed towards, to try to reach; to tend to bring about, *it makes for domestic harmony.* **make good,** to become successful or prosperous; *make good the loss,* pay compensation; *make good the damage,* repair it; *made good his escape,* succeeded in escaping. **make it,** to achieve what one wanted, to be successful. **make it up,** to become reconciled after a quarrel. **make it up to someone,** to compensate him. **make love,** to embrace and kiss in courtship; to have sexual intercourse. **make money,** to make a large profit. **make much** *or* **little of,** to treat as important or unimportant; *make much of a person,* to give him much flattering attention. **make off,** to go away hastily. **make off with,** to carry away, to steal. **make out,** to write out (a list etc.); to manage to see or read something, *made out a shadowy figure;* to understand the nature of, *I can't make him out;* to assert or claim or pretend to be, *made him out to be a fool;* (*informal*) to fare, *how did you make out?* **make over,** to transfer the ownership of; to convert for a new purpose. **make room,** to clear a space for something by moving another person or thing. **make shift,** = make do. **make time,** to contrive to find time to do something. **make up,** to form or constitute; to put together, to prepare (medicine etc.); to invent (a story etc.); to compensate (for a loss or mistake); to complete (an amount) by supplying what is lacking; to apply cosmetics to; *make up one's mind,* to decide. *make up to a person,* to curry favour with him. **make-up** *n.* cosmetics applied to the skin, especially of the face; the way something is made up, its composition or constituent parts; a person's character and temperament. **on the make,** (*slang*) intent on gain.

maker *n.* one who makes something. **our Maker,** God.

makeshift *n.* a temporary or improvised substitute. —*adj.* serving as this.

makeweight *n.* 1. a small quantity added to make up the full weight. 2. anything added to make up for a deficiency.

Malacca (mă-**lak**-ă) *n.* a brown cane made from the stem of a kind of palm-tree.

malachite (**mal**-ă-kyt) *n.* a green mineral that can be polished.

maladjusted *adj.* (of a person) not well-adjusted to his own circumstances. **maladjustment** *n.*

maladministration *n.* bad or improper management of business or public affairs.

maladroit (**mal**-ă-droit) *adj.* bungling.

malady (**mal**-ă-di) *n.* an illness, a disease.

Malagasy (mală-**gas**-i) *adj.* of Madagascar. —*n.* a native or inhabitant of Madagascar.

malaise (mal-**ayz**) *n.* a feeling of illness or mental uneasiness.

malapropism (**mal**-ă-prop-izm) *n.* a comical confusion of words, e.g. *it will percussion the blow* (for *cushion the blow*). ¶ Named after Mrs. Malaprop in Sheridan's play *The Rivals*, who made mistakes of this kind.

malaria (mă-**lair**-iă) *n.* a disease causing fever which recurs at intervals, transmitted by mosquitoes. **malarial** *adj.*

malathion (mal-ath-I-ŏn) *n.* an insecticide containing phosphorus.

Malawi (mă-**lah**-wi) a country in central Africa. **Malawian** *adj. & n.*

Malay (mă-**lay**) *adj.* of a people living in Malaysia and Indonesia. —*n.* **1.** a member of this people. **2.** their language.

Malaya a group of States forming part of Malaysia. **Malayan** *adj. & n.*

Malaysia (mă-**lay**-*zh*ă) a country in southeast Asia. **Malaysian** *adj & n.*

malcontent (**mal**-kŏn-tent) *n.* a person who is discontented and inclined to rebel.

Maldive Islands (**mawl**-div) a group of islands south-west of India. **Maldivian** (mawl-**div**-iăn) *adj. & n.*

male *adj.* **1.** of the sex that can beget offspring by fertilizing egg-cells produced by the female. **2.** (of plants) having flowers that contain pollen-bearing organs and not seeds. **3.** of a man or men, *male voice choir.* —*n.* a male person or animal or plant.

malediction (mali-**dik**-shŏn) *n.* a curse.

malefactor (**mal**-i-fak-ter) *n.* a wrongdoer.

malevolent (mă-**lev**-ŏ-lĕnt) *adj.* wishing harm to others. **malevolence** *n.*

malformation *n.* faulty formation. **malformed** *adj.* faultily formed.

malfunction *n.* faulty functioning. —*v.* to function faultily.

Mali (**mah**-li) a country in West Africa. **Malian** *adj. & n.*

malice *n.* a desire to harm others or to tease.

malicious (mă-**lish**-ŭs) *adj.* feeling or showing or caused by malice. **maliciously** *adv.*

malign (mă-**lyn**) *adj.* **1.** harmful, *a malign influence.* **2.** showing malice. —*v.* to say unpleasant and untrue things about, *maligning an innocent person.* —**malignity** (mă-**lig**-niti) *n.*

malignant (mă-**lig**-nănt) *adj.* **1.** (of a tumour) growing uncontrollably. **2.** feeling or showing great ill will. **malignantly** *adv.,* **malignancy** *n.*

malinger (mă-**ling**-er) *v.* to pretend to be ill in order to avoid work. **malingerer** *n.*

mall (*pr.* mal *or* mawl) *n.* **shopping mall,** *see* shopping.

mallard (**mal**-erd) *n.* (*pl.* mallard) a kind of wild duck, the male of which has a glossy green head.

malleable (**mal**-i-ăbŭl) *adj.* **1.** able to be hammered or pressed into shape. **2.** easy to influence, adaptable. **malleability** *n.*

mallee (**mal**-i) *n.* (*Austral.*) any of the kinds of eucalyptus tree that flourish in dry areas, scrub formed by these.

mallet *n.* **1.** a hammer, usually of wood. **2.** a similarly shaped instrument with a long handle, for striking the ball in croquet or polo.

mallow *n.* a plant with hairy stems and leaves, bearing purple or pink or white flowers.

malmsey (**mahm**-zi) *n.* a kind of strong sweet wine.

malnutrition *n.* insufficient nutrition.

malodorous (mal-**oh**-der-ŭs) *adj.* stinking.

malpractice *n.* wrongdoing.

malt *n.* **1.** grain (usually barley) that has been allowed to sprout and then dried, used for brewing or distilling or vinegar-making. **2.** (*informal*) malt liquors. —*v.* to make or be made into malt. □ **malted milk,** a drink made from dried milk and malt.

Malta an island in the Mediterranean Sea. **Maltese** *adj. & n.* (*pl.* Maltese) □ **Maltese cross,** a cross with four equal arms broadening outwards, often indented at the ends.

maltreat *v.* to ill-treat. **maltreatment** *n.*

mama (mă-**mah**) *n.* (*old use*) mother.

mamba *n.* a poisonous black or green South African tree-snake.

mamma (mă-**mah**) *n.* (*old use*) mother.

mammal *n.* a member of the class of animals that suckle their young. **mammalian** (mă-**may**-liăn) *adj.*

mammary (**mam**-er-i) *adj.* of the breasts. **mammary gland,** a milk-secreting gland.

Mammon *n.* wealth personified, regarded as an evil influence.

mammoth *n.* a large extinct elephant with a hairy coat and curved tusks. —*adj.* huge.

mammy *n.* (*children's informal*) mother.

man *n.* (pl. men) **1.** a human being, a creature distinguished from other animals by superior mental development, power of articulate speech, and upright posture. **2.** mankind. **3.** an adult male person. **4.** an individual male person considered as an expert or one's assistant or opponent etc., *if you want a good teacher, he's your man.* **5.** a person of either sex, an individual person, *every man for himself.* **6.** a manly person; *is he man enough to do it?,* is he brave enough? **7.** a male servant or employee or workman, *masters and men.* **8.** an ordinary soldier etc., not an officer. **9.** one of the set of small objects moved on a board in playing board-games such as chess and draughts. —*v.* (manned, manning) to supply with men for service or to operate something, *man the pumps.* □ **as one man,** in unison. **be one's own man,** to be independent. **man about town,** a man who spends much of his time in sophisticated social amusements. **man-hour** *n.* the amount of work that one person can do in an hour, considered as a unit. **man-hunt** *n.* an organized search for a person, especially a criminal. **man in the street,** an ordinary person, not an expert. **man-made** *adj.* made by man not by nature, synthetic. **man of the house,** the male head of a household. **man of the world,** *see* world. **man-sized** *adj.* of the size of a man; adequate for a man. **man to man,** with frankness. **to a man,** all without exception.

Man. *abbrev.* Manitoba.

manacle (man-ă-kŭl) *n.* one of a pair of fetters for the hands. —*v.* to fetter with manacles.

manage *v.* **1.** to have under effective control. **2.** to be the manager of (a business etc.). **3.** to operate (a tool or machinery) effectively. **4.** to succeed in doing or producing something (often with inadequate means), to be able to cope, *managed without help.* **5.** to contrive to persuade (a person) to do what one wants, by use of tact or flattery or other means.

manageable *adj.* able to be managed.

management *n.* **1.** managing, being managed. **2.** the process of managing a business, people engaged in his.

manager *n.* **1.** a person who is in charge of the affairs of a business etc. **2.** one who deals with the business affairs of a sports team or entertainer etc. **3.** one who manages household affairs in a certain way, *she is a good manager.* **managerial** (mană-**jeer**-iăl) *adj.* □ **manageress** *n.* a woman manager of a business etc.

managing *adj.* **1.** having executive control or authority, *managing director.* **2.** fond of

being in control, bossy.

Manama (man-ah-mă) the capital of Bahrain.

Managua (mă-**nag**-wă) the capital of Nicaragua.

Mancunian (man-**kew**-niăn) *adj.* of Manchester. —*n.* a native or inhabitant of Manchester.

mandarin (**man**-der-in) *n.* **1.** a high-ranking influential official. **2.** a kind of small flattened orange grown in China and North Africa. **3.** the former standard spoken language of China. □ **mandarin collar,** a high upright collar not quite meeting in front.

mandatary (**man**-dă-ter-i) *n.* the holder of a mandate.

mandate *n.* authority given to someone to perform a certain task or apply certain policies.

mandatory (**man**-dă-ter-i) *adj.* obligatory, compulsory.

mandible (**man**-dib-ŭl) *adj.* **1.** a jaw. **2.** either of the parts of a bird's beak. **3.** the corresponding part in insects etc.

mandolin (man-dŏl-in) *n.* a musical instrument rather like a guitar, played with a plectrum.

mandrake *n.* a poisonous plant with white or purple flowers and large yellow fruit.

mane *n.* **1.** the long hair on a horse's or lion's neck. **2.** a person's long hair.

manful *adj.* brave, resolute. **manfully** *adv.*

manganese (mang-ă-neez) *n.* a hard brittle grey metal or its black oxide.

mange (*pr.* maynj) *n.* a skin-disease affecting hairy animals, caused by a parasite.

mangel-wurzel *n.* a large beet used as cattle food.

manger *n.* a long open trough or box in a stable etc. for horses or cattle to eat from.

mangle[1] *n.* a wringer. —*v.* to press (clothes etc.) in a mangle.

mangle[2] *v.* to damage by cutting or crushing roughly, to mutilate.

mango *n.* (*pl.* mangoes) **1.** a tropical fruit with yellowish flesh. **2.** the tree that bears it.

mangrove *n.* a tropical tree or shrub growing in shore-mud and swamps, with many tangled roots above ground.

mangy (**mayn**-ji) *adj.* (mangier, mangiest) **1.** having mange. **2.** squalid, shabby.

manhandle *v.* **1.** to move (a thing) by human effort alone. **2.** to treat roughly.

manhole *n.* an opening (usually with a cover) through which a person can enter a sewer or pipe or boiler etc. to inspect or repair it.

manhood *n.* **1.** the state of being a man; *reach manhood,* become an adult male person. **2.** manly qualities, courage. **3.** the men of a country.

mania (**may**-niă) *n.* **1.** violent madness. **2.** extreme enthusiasm for something, *a mania for sport.*

maniac (**may**-ni-ak) *n.* a person affected with mania.

maniacal (mă-**ny**-ă-kăl) *adj.* of or like a mania or a maniac. **maniacally** *adv.*

manic-depressive (**man**-ik) *adj.* of a mental disorder with alternating bouts of excitement and depression —*n.* a person suffering from this disorder.

manicure *n.* cosmetic care and treatment of the hands and finger-nails. —*v.* to apply such treatment to. ☐ **manicurist** *n.* a person whose job is to manicure people's hands.

manifest *adj.* clear and unmistakable. —*v.* to show (a thing) clearly, to give signs of, *the crowd manifested its approval by cheering.* —*n.* a list of cargo or passengers carried by a ship or aircraft etc. —**manifestation** *n.*

manifesto *n.* (*pl.* manifestos) a public declaration of principles and policy.

manifold *adj.* of many kinds, very varied. —*n.* a pipe or chamber (in a piece of mechanism) with several openings that connect with other parts.

manikin *n.* a little man, a dwarf.

Manila (mă-**nil**-ă) the capital of the Philippines.

manilla (mă-**nil**-ă) *n.* a kind of brown paper used for wrapping and for envelopes.

manioc (**man**-i-ok) *n.* **1.** cassava. **2.** flour made from this.

manipulate *v.* **1.** to handle or manage or use (a thing) skilfully. **2.** to arrange or influence cleverly or craftily; *manipulate figures,* alter or adjust them to suit one's purposes. **manipulation** *n.,* **manipulator** *n.*

Manitoba (man-i-**toh**-bă) a province of Canada.

mankind *n.* human beings in general, the human race.

manly *adj.* having the qualities expected of a man (e.g. strength and courage), suitable for a man. **manliness** *n.*

manna *n.* **1.** (in the Bible) a substance miraculously supplied as food to the Israelites in the wilderness after the exodus from Egypt. **2.** something unexpected and delightful.

manned *see* man. —*adj.* (of a spacecraft etc.) containing a human crew, *manned flights.*

mannequin (**man**-i-kin) *n.* a woman who models clothes.

manner *n.* **1.** the way a thing is done or

happens. **2.** a person's bearing or way of behaving towards others. **3.** kind, sort; *all manner of things,* every kind of thing. ☐ **in a manner of speaking,** as one might say (used to qualify or weaken what one says).

manners *pl. n.* social behaviour, *good manners;* polite social behaviour, *has no manners.*

mannered *adj.* **1.** having manners of a certain kind, *well-mannered.* **2.** full of mannerisms, *a mannered style.*

mannerism *n.* a distinctive personal habit or way of doing something.

mannerly *adj.* polite.

mannish *adj.* having masculine characteristics, suitable for a man.

manœuvre (mă-**noo**-ver) *n.* **1.** a planned and controlled movement of a vehicle or a body of troops etc. **2.** a skilful or crafty proceeding, a trick, *the manœuvres of politicians to achieve their purposes.* —**manœuvre** *v.* **1.** to move a thing's position or course etc. carefully, *manœuvred the car into the garage.* **2.** to perform manœuvres. **3.** to guide skilfully or craftily, *manœuvred the conversation towards money.* ☐ **manœuvres** *pl. n.* large-scale exercises of troops or ships, *on manœuvres.*

man-of-war *n.* (*pl.* men-of-war) an armed ship of a country's navy.

manor *n.* **1.** a large country house or the landed estate belonging to it; *manor-house,* this house. **2.** (*slang*) an area under the administration of a unit of police. **manorial** (man-**or**-iăl) *adj.*

manpower *n.* **1.** power supplied by human physical effort. **2.** the number of people working on a particular task or available for work or service.

mansard (**man**-sard) *n.* a type of roof that has a steep lower part and a less steep upper part on all four sides of a building.

manse *n.* a church minister's house, especially in Scotland.

manservant *n.* (*pl.* menservants) a male servant.

mansion (**man**-shŏn) *n.* **1.** a large stately house. **2.** *Mansions,* a name given to a block of flats, *Victoria Mansions.* ☐ **the Mansion House,** the official residence of the Lord Mayor of London.

manslaughter *n.* the act of killing a person unlawfully but not intentionally, or by negligence.

mantel *n.* a structure of wood or marble etc. above and around a fireplace.

mantelpiece *n.* a shelf above a fireplace.

mantilla (man-**til**-ă) *n.* a lace veil worn by Spanish women over the hair and shoulders.

mantis *n.* an insect resembling a grass-hopper.

mantle *n.* **1.** a loose sleeveless cloak. **2.** something likened to this, a covering, *a mantle of secrecy.* **3.** a fragile gauzy cover fixed round the flame of a gas lamp, producing a strong light when heated. —*v.* to envelop or cover as if with a mantle.

mantra *n.* a word or words to be said or sung as an incantation in Buddhism, also used similarly in yoga or forms of meditation.

mantrap *n.* a trap for catching trespassers or poachers etc.

manual *adj.* **1.** of the hands. **2.** done or operated by the hand(s), *manual labour*; *manual gear-change,* operated by the driver, not automatically. —**manual** *n.* **1.** a handbook. **2.** an organ keyboard that is played with the hands, not with the feet. —**manually** *adv.*

manufacture *v.* **1.** to make or produce (goods) on a large scale by machinery. **2.** to invent, *manufactured an excuse.* —*n.* the process of manufacturing. —**manufacturer** *n.*

manure *n.* any substance (e.g. dung or compost or artificial material) used as a fertilizer.—*v.* to apply manure to.

manuscript (**man**-yoo-skript) *n.* **1.** something written by hand, not typed or printed. **2.** an author's work as written or typed, not a printed book.

Manx *adj.* of the Isle of Man.—*n.* the Celtic language of the Manx people. — **Manxman** *n.* (*pl.* Manxmen), **Manxwoman** *n.* (*pl.* Manxwomen) □ **Manx cat,** a tailless variety of domestic cat.

many *adj.* (more, most) great in number, numerous, *many a time,* many times. —*n.* many people or things, *many were found.*

Maoism (**mow**-izm; *first part rhymes with* cow) *n.* the doctrines of Mao Zedong (= Mao Tse-tung), a Chinese Communist statesman (1893–1976). **Maoist** *n.*

Maori (**mow**-ri; *first part rhymes with* cow) *n.* (*pl.* Maoris) a member of the brown aboriginal race in New Zealand.

map *n.* a representation (usually on a plane surface) of the earth's surface or a part of it, or of the sky showing the positions of the stars etc. —*v.* (mapped, mapping) **1.** to make a map of. **2.** to plan in detail, *map out one's time.* □ **put a thing on the map,** (*informal*) to make it become famous or important.

maple *n.* a kind of tree with broad leaves, grown for ornament or for its wood.

Maputo (mă-**poo**-toh) the capital of Mozambique.

mar *v.* (marred, marring) to damage, to spoil.

marabou (ma-ră-boo) *n.* **1** African stork. **2.** its down used ming.

maraschino (ma-ră-**skee**-noh) *n.* a sweet liqueur made from small black matian cherries.

marathon *n.* **1.** a long-distance foot-race, especially that of 26 miles in the modern Olympic Games. (¶ Named after *Marathon* in Greece, where an invading Persian army was defeated in 490 BC; a man who fought at the battle ran to Athens, announced the victory, and died.) **2.** any very long race or other test of endurance.

marauding (mă-**raw**-ding) *adj.* going about in search of plunder or prey. **marauder** *n.* one who does this.

marble *n.* **1.** a kind of limestone that can be polished, used in sculpture and building. **2.** a piece of sculpture in marble, *the Elgin Marbles.* **3.** a small ball made of glass or clay etc. used in games played by children. —*adj.* like marble, hard and smooth and white or mottled, □ **marbled** *adj.* having a veined or mottled appearance, (of meat) with alternating layers of lean and fat.

marcasite (**mark**-ă-syt) *n.* crystallized iron pyrites, a piece of this used as an ornament.

March *n.* the third month of the year.

march *v.* **1.** to walk in a military manner with regular paces, to walk in an organized column **2.** to walk purposefully, *marched up to the manager.* **3.** to cause to march or walk, *marched them up the hill*; *he was marched off.* **4.** to progress steadily, *time marches on.* —**march** *n.* **1.** marching, the distance covered by marching troops etc.; *a protest march,* a demonstration taking the form of a parade. **2.** progress, *the march of events.* **3.** music suitable for marching to. —**marcher** *n.* □ **get one's marching orders,** to be told to go. **march-past** *n.* a ceremonial march past a saluting-point. **on the march,** marching, advancing.

marches *pl. n.* border regions.

marchioness (mar-shŏn-ess) *n.* **1.** the wife or widow of a marquis. **2.** a woman holding the rank of marquis in her own right.

mare *n.* the female of a horse or related animal. **mare's nest,** a discovery that is thought to be interesting but turns out to be false or worthless.

margarine (mar-jer-**een** *or* marg-er-**een**) *n.* a substance used like butter, made from animal or vegetable fats.

marge *n.* (*informal*) margarine.

margin *n.* **1.** an edge or border of a surface. **2.** a blank space round printed or written matter on a page. **3.** an amount over and above the essential minimum, *was defeated by a narrow margin*; *margin of safety*. **4.** (in commerce) the difference between cost price and selling price, *profit margins*.

marginal *adj*. **1.** written in a margin, *marginal notes*. **2.** of or at an edge. **3.** very slight in amount, *its usefulness is marginal*; *marginal seat* or *constituency*, one where an MP has only a small majority and may easily be defeated at the next election. **marginally** *adv*.

marguerite (marg-er-eet) *n*. a large daisy-like flower with a yellow centre and white petals.

marigold *n*. a garden plant with golden or bright yellow flowers.

marijuana (ma-ri-hwah-nă) *n*. the dried leaves, stems, and flowering tops of the hemp plant, used to make a hallucinogenic drug, especially in the form of cigarettes.

marina (mă-ree-nă) *n*. a harbour for yachts and pleasure-boats.

marinade (ma-rin-ayd) *n*. a seasoned flavoured liquid in which meat or fish is steeped before being cooked. —*v*. to steep in a marinade.

marine (mă-reen) *adj*. **1.** of or living in the sea, *marine animals*. **2.** of shipping, nautical, *marine insurance*. **3.** for use at sea. — **marine** *n*. **1.** a country's shipping, *the mercantile marine*. **2.** a member of a body of troops trained to serve on land or sea. □ **tell that to the marines**, (*informal*) I do not believe you.

mariner (ma-rin-er) *n*. a sailor, a seaman.

marionette (ma-ri-ŏn-et) *n*. a puppet worked by strings.

marital (ma-rit'l) *adj*. of marriage, of or between husband and wife.

maritime (ma-ri-tym) *adj*. **1.** living or situated or found near the sea, *maritime provinces*. **2.** of seafaring or shipping, *maritime law*.

marjoram (mar-jer-ăm) *n*. a herb with fragrant leaves, used in cooking.

mark[1] *n*. the unit of money in Germany.

mark[2] *n*. **1.** a line or area that differs in appearance from the rest of a surface, especially one that spoils it. **2.** a distinguishing feature or characteristic. **3.** something that indicates the presence of a quality or feeling, *as a mark of respect*. **4.** a symbol placed on a thing to indicate its origin or ownership or quality; *Mark One* or *Two*, the first (or second) design of a machine or piece of equipment etc. **5.** a written or printed symbol, *punctuation marks*. **6.** a lasting impression, *poverty had left its mark*. **7.** a unit awarded for the merit or quality of a piece of work or a perform-

ance, *got high marks*; *deserves a good mark for effort*, deserves credit. **8.** a target, a standard to be aimed at; *not feeling up to the mark*, not feeling well. **9.** a line or object serving to indicate position. —**mark** *v*. **1.** to make a mark on. **2.** to distinguish with a mark, to characterize. **3.** to assign marks of merit to. **4.** to notice, to watch carefully, *mark my words!* **5.** to keep close to (an opposing player) in football etc. so as to hamper him if he receives the ball. □ **make one's mark**, to make a significant achievement, to become famous. **mark down**, to notice and remember the place etc. of; to reduce the price of. **mark off**, to separate by a boundary. **mark out**, to mark the boundaries of; to destine, to single out, *is marked out for promotion*. **mark time**, to move the feet rhythmically as if in marching but without advancing; to occupy time in routine work without making progress. **mark up**, to increase the price of. **mark-up** *n*. the amount a seller adds to the cost price of an article to determine his selling-price. **off the mark**, off the point, irrelevant; having made a start.

marked *adj*. clearly noticeable, *a marked improvement*. **markedly** (mark-id-li) *adv*. □ **a marked man**, one who is singled out, e.g. as an object of vengeance.

marker *n*. **1.** a person or tool that marks, one who records the score in games etc. **2.** something that serves to mark a position.

market *n*. **1.** a gathering for the sale of goods or livestock. **2.** a space or building used for this. **3.** the conditions or opportunity for buying or selling, *found a ready market*. **4.** a place where goods may be sold, a particular class of buyers, *foreign markets*; *the teenage market*. **5.** the stock market. **6.** *the Market*, the Common Market. —*v*. to offer for sale; *go marketing*, to go buying food etc. for domestic use. □ **be in the market for**, to wish to buy. **market-day** *n*. the day on which a market is regularly held. **market garden**, one in which vegetables are grown for market. **market-place** *n*. an open space where a market is held in a town. **market research**, study of consumers' needs and preferences. **market town**, one where a market is held regularly. **market value**, the amount for which something can be sold, its current value. **on the market**, offered for sale.

marketable *adj*. able or fit to be sold.

marking *n*. **1.** a mark or marks. **2.** the colouring of an animal's skin or feathers or fur.

marksman *n.* (*pl.* marksmen) a person who is a skilled shot. **marksmanship** *n.*

marl[1] *n.* a soil consisting of clay and lime, a valuable fertilizer. **marly** *adj.*

marl[2] *n.* a fabric with a mottled effect.

marmalade *n.* a kind of jam made from citrus fruit, especially oranges.

marmoset (mar-mŏ-zet) *n.* a small bushy-tailed monkey of tropical America.

marmot (mar-mŏt) *n.* a small burrowing animal of the squirrel family.

marocain (ma-rŏ-kayn) *n.* a kind of crêpe dress-fabric.

maroon[1] *n.* 1. a brownish-red colour. 2. a kind of firework that explodes with a sound like a cannon, used as a warning signal. —*adj.* brownish-red.

maroon[2] *v.* to abandon or isolate (a person), e.g. on an island or in a deserted place.

marquee (mar-kee) *n.* a large tent used for a party or an exhibition etc.

marquetry (mar-kit-ri) *n.* inlaid work in wood or ivory etc.

marquis (mar-kwis) *n.* a nobleman rank ing between duke and earl or count.

marquisette (mar-ki-zet) *n* fine light net fabric used for curtains etc.

marriage *n.* 1. the state in which a man and a woman are formally united for the purpose of living together (usually in order to procreate children) and with certain legal rights and obligations towards each other. 2. the act or ceremony of being married. □ **marriage bureau,** an agency that arranges meetings between people of opposite sexes who wish to marry. **marriage guidance,** advice given by authorized counsellors about marital problems.

marriageable *adj.* old enough or fit for marriage.

marrow *n.* 1. the soft fatty substance in the cavities of bones; *felt chilled to the marrow,* right through. 2. the large white-fleshed fruit of a plant of the gourd family, used as a vegetable.

marrowbone *n.* a bone containing edible marrow.

marrowfat *n.* a kind of large pea.

marry *v.* (married, marrying) 1. to unite or give or take in marriage. 2. to take a husband or wife in marriage, *she never married.* 3. to unite, to put (things) together as a pair.

Marsala (mar-sah-lă) *n.* a dark sweet fortified wine of a kind originally made in Sicily.

Marseillaise (mar-sĕ-layz) *n.* the national anthem of France.

marsh *n.* low-lying watery ground. **marshy**

adj. □ **marsh-gas** *n.* methane. **marsh marigold,** a kind of large buttercup.

marshal *n.* 1. an officer of high or the highest rank, *Air Marshal; Field Marshal.* 2. an official with responsibility for arranging certain public events or ceremonies. 3. an official accompanying a judge on circuit, with secretarial duties. 4. an official at a race. —*marshal* *v.* (marshalled, marshalling) 1. to arrange in proper order. 2. to cause to assemble. 3. to usher, *marshalled him into the governor's office.* □ **marshalling yard,** a railway yard in which goods trains etc. are assembled for dispatch.

marshland *n.* marshy land.

marshmallow *n.* a soft sweet made from sugar, egg-white, and gelatine.

marsupial (mar-soo-piăl) *n.* an animal such as the kangaroo, the female of which has a pouch in which its young are carried until they are fully developed.

mart *n.* a market.

marten *n.* a weasel-like animal with thick soft fur.

martial (mar-shăl) *adj.* of war, warlike, *martial music.* **martial law,** military rule imposed on a country temporarily in an emergency, suspending ordinary law.

Martian (mar-shăn) *adj.* of the planet Mars. —*n.* (in science fiction etc.) an inhabitant of Mars.

martin *n.* a bird of the swallow family.

martinet (mar-tin-et) *n.* a person who demands strict obedience.

Martini (mar-tee-ni) *n.* (*trade mark*) a cocktail of gin and vermouth.

Martinmas *n.* St. Martin's day, 11 November.

martyr *n.* 1. a person who suffers death rather than give up the Christian faith. 2. one who undergoes death or great suffering in support of a belief or cause or principle. 3. one who suffers greatly; *is a martyr to rheumatism,* suffers constantly from this. —*v.* to put to death or torment as a martyr. —**martyrdom** *n.*

marvel *n.* a wonderful thing. —*v.* (marvelled, marvelling) to be filled with wonder.

marvellous *adj.* astonishing, excellent. **marvellously** *adv.*

Marxism *n.* the political and economic theory of Karl Marx, a German socialist writer (1818–83), on which Communism is based. **Marxist** *adj.* & *n.*

Maryland a State of the USA.

marzipan (mar-zi-pan) *n.* a paste of ground almonds and sugar, made into small cakes or sweets or used to coat large cakes.

mascara *n.* a cosmetic for darkening the eyelashes.

mascot *n.* **1.** a person or thing believed to bring good luck to its owner. **2.** a figurine mounted on the bonnet of a car etc.

masculine *adj.* **1.** of or like or suitable for men, having the qualities or appearance considered characteristic of a man. **2.** having the grammatical form suitable for the names of males or for words corresponding to these, *'hero' is a masculine noun, heroine' is the corresponding feminine noun.* —*n.* a masculine word or gender. —**masculinity** *n.*

mash *n.* **1.** grain or bran etc. cooked in water to form a soft mixture, used as animal food. **2.** (*informal*) mashed potatoes. **3.** a mixture of malt and hot water used in brewing. —*v.* to beat or crush into a soft mixture.

mask *n.* **1.** a covering worn over the face (or part of it) as a disguise or for protection. **2.** a carved or moulded replica of a face. **3.** a respirator worn over the face to filter air for breathing or to supply gas for inhaling. **4.** the face or head of a fox. **5.** a screen used in photography to exclude part of the image. —**mask** *v.* **1.** to cover with a mask. **2.** to disguise or screen or conceal.

masochist (**mas**-ŏ-kist) *n.* **1.** a person who derives sexual excitement and satisfaction from his own pain or humiliation. **2.** one who enjoys what seems to be painful or tiresome. **masochism** *n.,* **masochistic** *adj.*

mason *n.* **1.** a person who builds or works with stone. **2.** *Mason,* a Freemason.

Masonic (mă-**sonn**-ik) *adj.* of Freemasons.

masonry *n.* **1.** mason's work, stonework. **2.** *Masonry,* Freemasonry.

masquerade (mas-ker-**ayd**) *n.* a false show or pretence. —*v.* to pretend to be what one is not, *masqueraded as a policeman.*

mass¹ *n.* (especially in the RC Church) **1.** a celebration of the Eucharist. **2.** the form of service used in this, a musical setting for the words of it.

mass² *n.* **1.** a coherent unit of matter with no specific shape. **2.** a large quantity or heap, an unbroken extent; *the garden was a mass of flowers,* was full of flowers. **3.** (in technical usage) the quantity of matter a body contains (called *weight* in non-technical usage). —*v.* to gather or assemble into a mass. □ **mass media,** *see* media. **mass meeting,** one attended by a large number of people. **mass-produce** *v.* to manufacture in large numbers of identical articles by standardized processes. **mass-production** *n.* manufacturing in this way. **the masses,** the common people.

Mass. *abbrev.* Massachusetts.

Massachusetts a State of the USA.

massacre *n.* slaughter of a large number of people or animals.—*v.* to slaughter in large numbers.

massage (mas-ah*z*h) *n.* rubbing and kneading the body to lessen pain or stiffness. —*v.* to treat in this way.

masseur (ma-**ser**) *n.* a man who practises massage professionally. **masseuse** (ma-**serz**) *n.* a woman who does this.

massive *adj.* **1.** large and heavy or solid. **2.** unusually large. **3.** substantial, *a massive improvement.* **massiveness** *n.*

mast¹ *n.* **1.** a long upright pole that supports a ship's sails. **2.** a tall pole from which a flag is flown. **3.** a tall steel structure for the aerials of a radio or TV transmitter. **masted** *adj.* □ **before the mast,** serving as an ordinary seaman (quartered in the forecastle).

mast² *n.* the fruit of beech, oak, chestnut, and other forest trees, used as food for pigs.

mastectomy (mas-**tek**-tŏmi) *n.* surgical removal of a breast.

master *n.* **1.** a man who has control of people or things. **2.** the captain of a merchant ship. **3.** the male head of a household. **4.** the male owner of a dog etc. **5.** an employer, *masters and men.* **6.** a male teacher, a schoolmaster. **7.** *Master,* the holder of a university degree as *Master of Arts* etc. **8.** a respected teacher. **9.** a person with very great skill, a great artist. **10.** a chess player of proved ability at international level. **11.** a document or film or record etc. from which a series of copies is made. **12.** *Master,* a title prefixed to the name of a boy who is not old enough to be called *Mr.* —**master** *v.* **1.** to overcome, to bring under control. **2.** to acquire knowledge or skill in. □ **master-key** *n.* a key that opens a number of locks, each also opened by a separate key. **master mariner,** the captain of a merchant ship. **Master of Ceremonies,** a person in charge of a social or other occasion, who introduces the events or performers. **master-stroke** *n.* an outstandingly skilful act of policy etc.

masterful *adj.* **1.** domineering. **2.** very skilful. **masterfully** *adv.*

masterly *adj.* worthy of a master, very skilful.

master-mind *n.* **1.** a person with outstanding mental ability. **2.** the person directing an enterprise. —*v.* to plan and direct, *master-minded the whole scheme.*

masterpiece *n.* **1.** an outstanding piece of workmanship. **2.** a person's best piece of work.

mastery *n.* **1.** complete control, supremacy. **2.** thorough knowledge or skill, *his mastery of Arabic.*

masticate *v.* to chew (food). **mastication** *n.*

mastiff *n.* a large strong dog with drooping ears.

mastoid *n.* **1.** part of a bone behind the ear. **2.** (*informal*) mastoiditis. □ **mastoiditis** *n.* inflammation of the mastoid.

masturbate *v.* to excite oneself or (another person) sexually by stimulating the genitals with the hand, not by sexual intercourse. **masturbation** *n.*

mat *n.* **1.** a piece of material used as a floor covering, a door-mat. **2.** a small pad or piece of material placed under an ornament or vase etc. or under a hot dish, to protect the surface on which it stands. **3.** a thick pad for landing on in gymnastics etc. —*v.* (matted, matting) to make or become entangled to form a thick mass, *matted hair.* □ **on the mat,** (*slang*) being reprimanded.

Matabele (mat-ă-**bee**-li) *n.* (*pl.* Matabele) a member of a Bantu-speaking people of Zimbabwe.

matador (**mat**-ă-dor) *n.* a performer whose task is to fight and kill the bull in a bullfight.

match[1] *n.* a short piece of wood (a *matchstick*) or pasteboard with a head made of material that bursts into flame when rubbed on a rough or specially prepared surface. **matchbox** *n.* a box for holding matches.

match[2] *n.* **1.** a contest in a game or sport. **2.** a person or animal with abilities equalling those of another whom he meets in contest, *meet one's match*; *you are no match for him,* not strong enough or skilled enough to defeat him. **3.** a person or thing exactly like or corresponding to another. **4.** a marriage; *they made a match of it,* married. **5.** a person considered as a partner for marriage, especially with regard to rank or fortune. —**match** *v.* **1.** to place in competition, *the teams were matched with* or *against each other.* **2.** to equal in ability or skill etc. **3.** to be alike or correspond in colour, quality, quantity, etc. **4.** to find something similar to, *I want to match this wool.* **5.** to put or bring together as corresponding, *matching unemployed workers with vacant posts.* □ **match point,** the stage in a match when one side will win if it gains the next point; this point.

matchboard *n.* board with a tongue cut along one edge and a groove along another, so as to fit with similar boards.

matchless *adj.* unequalled.

matchmaker *n.* a person who is fond of scheming to bring about marriages. **matchmaking** *adj.* & *n.*

matchwood *n.* **1.** wood that splinters easily. **2.** wood reduced to splinters.

mate[1] *n.* **1.** a companion, a fellow worker (also used informally as a form of address to an equal, especially among labourers). **2.** one of a mated pair of birds or animals. **3.** (*informal*) a partner in marriage. **4.** a fellow member or sharer, *team-mate*; *room-mate.* **5.** an officer on a merchant ship ranking next below the master. **6.** a worker's assistant, *plumber's mate.* — **mate** *v.* **1.** to put or come together as a pair or as corresponding. **2.** to put (two birds or animals) together so that they can breed, to come together in order to breed.

mate[2] *n.* a situation in chess in which the capture of a king cannot be prevented.

mater (**may**-ter) *n.* (*slang*) mother.

material *n.* **1.** the substance or things from which something is or can be made or with which something is done, *clay is used as material for bricks*; *writing materials*; *select those regarded as officer material,* those with qualities that make them suitable to become officers. **2.** cloth, fabric. **3.** facts or information or events etc. to be used in composing something, *gathering material for a book on poverty.* —**material** *adj.* **1.** of matter, consisting of matter, of the physical (as opposed to spiritual) world, *material things*; *had no thought of material gain.* **2.** of bodily comfort, *our material well-being.* **3.** important, significant, *at the material time*; *is this material to the issue?* —**materially** *adv.*

materialism *n.* **1.** belief that only the material world exists. **2.** excessive concern with material possessions rather than spiritual or intellectual values. **materialist** *n.,* **materialistic** *adj.*

materialize *v.* **1.** to appear or become visible, *the ghost didn't materialize*; *the boy failed to materialize,* (*informal*) did not come. **2.** to become a fact, to happen, *if the threatened strike materializes.* **materialization** *n.*

maternal (mă-**ter**-năl) *adj.* **1.** of a mother, of motherhood. **2.** motherly. **3.** related through one's mother; *maternal uncle,* one's mother's brother. **maternally** *adv.*

maternity (mă-**ter**-niti) *n.* **1.** motherhood. **2.** of or suitable or caring for women in pregnancy or childbirth, *maternity dress*; *maternity ward.*

matey *adj.* (matier, matiest) sociable, friendly. —*n.* (*informal,* as a form of address) mate. —**matily** *adv.*, **matiness** *n.*

mathematics *n.* the science of number, quantity, and space. —*pl. n.* the use of mathematics in calculation, *his mathematics are weak*. —**mathematical** *adj.*, **mathematically** *adv.* □ **mathematician** *n.* a person who is skilled in mathematics.

maths *n.* (*informal*) mathematics.

matinée (**mat**-in-ay) *n.* an afternoon performance at a theatre or cinema. **matinée coat** *or* **jacket**, a baby's short coat.

matins *n.* (in the Church of England) morning prayer.

matriarch (**may**-tri-ark) *n.* a woman who is head of a family or tribe. **matriarchal** (may-tri-**ark**-ăl) *adj.* □ **matriarchy** *n.* a social organization in which the mother is head of the family and descent is through the female line; a society in which women have most of the authority.

matricide (**may**-tri-syd) *n.* the act of killing one's mother. **matricidal** *adj.*

matriculate (mă-**trik**-yoo-layt) *v.* to admit or be admitted to membership of a university. **matriculation** *n.*

matrimony (**mat**-tri-mŏni) *n.* marriage. **matrimonial** (mat-ri-**moh**-niăl) *adj.*

matrix (**may**-triks) *n.* (*pl.* matrixes *or* matrices) **1.** a mould in which something is cast or shaped. **2.** a place in which a thing is developed. **3.** an array of mathematical quantities etc. in rows and columns. **4.** (in computers) an interconnected array of circuit elements that resembles a lattice or grid.

matron *n.* **1.** a married woman, especially one who is middle-aged or elderly and dignified. **2.** a woman managing the domestic affairs of a school etc. **3.** (*formerly*) the senior nursing officer in a hospital or other institution. □ **matron of honour,** a married woman as the chief attendant of the bride at a wedding.

matronly *adj.* like or suitable for a dignified married woman.

matt *adj.* (of a colour or surface etc.) having a dull finish, not shiny.

matter *n.* **1.** that which occupies space in the visible world, as opposed to spirit or mind or qualities etc. **2.** a particular substance or material, *colouring matter*. **3.** a discharge from the body, pus. **4.** material for thought or expression, the content of a book or speech as distinct from its form, *subject-matter*. **5.** things of a specified kind, *reading matter*. **6.** a situation or business being considered, *it's a serious matter*; *a matter for complaint*. **7.** a quantity, *for a matter of 40 years*. —*v.* to be of importance, *it doesn't matter*. □ **for that matter,** as far as that is concerned. **a**

matter of course, an event etc. that follows naturally or is to be expected. **a matter of fact,** something that is a fact not an opinion etc. **matter-of-fact** *adj.* strictly factual and not imaginative or emotional, down-to-earth. **no matter,** it is of no importance. **the matter,** the thing that is amiss, the trouble or difficulty, *what's the matter?*

matting *n.* mats, material for making these.

mattock *n.* an agricultural tool with the blade set at right angles to the handle, used for loosening soil and digging out roots.

mattress *n.* a fabric case filled with soft or firm or springy material, used on or as a bed.

maturation (mat-yoor-**ay**-shŏn) *n.* the process of maturing, ripening.

mature *adj.* **1.** having reached full growth or development. **2.** having or showing fully developed mental powers, capable of reasoning and acting sensibly. **3.** (of wine) having reached a good stage of development. **4.** (of a bill of exchange etc.) due for payment. —*v.* to make or become mature. —**maturely** *adv.*, **maturity** *n.*

matutinal (mă-**tew**-tin-ăl) *adj.* of or occurring in the morning.

maudlin *adj.* sentimental in a silly or tearful way, especially from drunkenness.

maul *v.* to treat roughly, to injure by rough handling or clawing.

maunder *v.* to talk in a rambling way.

Maundy *n.* **1.** the distribution of Maundy money. **2.** the money itself. **3.** (in the RC Church) the ceremony of washing people's feet on Maundy Thursday. □ **Maundy money,** specially minted silver coins distributed by the sovereign to the poor on **Maundy Thursday,** the Thursday before Easter, celebrated in commemoration of the Last Supper.

Mauritania a country in north-west Africa. **Mauritanian** *adj. & n.*

Mauritius (mă-**rish**-ŭs) an island in the Indian Ocean. **Mauritian** *adj. & n.*

mausoleum (maw-sŏ-**lee**-ŭm) *n.* a magnificent tomb. ¶ Named after that erected at Halicarnassus in Asia Minor for King Mausolus in the 4th century BC.

mauve (*rhymes with* cove) *adj. & n.* pale purple.

maverick (**mav**-er-ik) *n.* **1.** (*Amer.*) an unbranded calf or other young animal. **2.** a person of unorthodox independence, one who dissents from the ideas and beliefs of an organized political or other group to which he belongs.

maw *n.* the jaws or mouth or stomach of a voracious animal.

mawkish *adj.* sentimental in a sickly way. **mawkishly** *adv.*, **mawkishness** *n.*

maxim *n.* a general truth or rule of conduct, e.g. 'waste not, want not'.

maximal *adj.* greatest possible.

maximize *v.* to increase to a maximum. **maximization** *n.*

maximum *n.* (*pl.* maxima) the greatest or greatest possible number or amount or intensity etc. —*adj.* greatest, greatest possible.

may[1] *auxiliary verb*, (also might) expressing possibility (*it may be true*) or permission (*you may go*) or wish (*long may she reign*), or uncertainty (*whoever it may be*).

may[2] *n.* hawthorn blossom.

May *n.* the fifth month of the year. **May Day**, 1 May, kept as a festival with dancing or as an international holiday in honour of workers. **May Queen**, a girl crowned with flowers as queen of the festivities on May Day.

Maya (**mah**-yă) *n.* a member of an American Indian people living in Mexico until the 15th century AD. **Mayan** *adj.*

maybe *adv.* perhaps, possibly.

mayday *n.* an international radio signal of distress. ¶ Representing the pronunciation of French *m'aider* = help me.

mayfly *n.* an insect with two or three long hair-like tails, living briefly in spring.

mayhem *n.* violent or damaging action.

mayn't = may not.

mayonnaise (may-ŏn-**ayz**) *n.* **1.** a creamy sauce made with egg-yolks, oil, and vinegar. **2.** a dish with a dressing of this, *salmon mayonnaise*.

mayor *n.* the head of the municipal corporation of a city or borough, or of a district council with borough status. **mayoral** (**mair**-ăl) *adj.* □ **mayoress** *n.* a mayor's wife, or other lady performing her ceremonial duties; a woman mayor.

maypole *n.* a tall pole for dancing round on May Day, with ribbons attached to its top.

maze *n.* **1.** a complicated network of paths, a labyrinth. **2.** a network of paths and hedges designed as a puzzle in which to try and find one's way. **3.** a state of bewilderment.

mazurka (mă-**zerk**-ă) *n.* a lively Polish dance in triple time, music for this.

MC *abbrev.* Master of Ceremonies.

MCC (— Marylebone Cricket Club) the governing body that makes the rules of cricket.

Mc/s *abbrev.* megacycle(s) per second (=megahertz).

Md. *abbrev.* Maryland.

me *pronoun* **1.** the objective case of I. (¶ See the note under between sense 6.) **2.** (*informal*) = I, *it's me*.

Me. *abbrev.* Maine.

mead *n.* an alcoholic drink of fermented honey and water.

meadow *n.* a field of grass.

meadowsweet *n.* a meadow plant with fragrant creamy-white flowers.

meagre (**meeg**-er) *adj.* scanty in amount.

meal[1] *n.* **1.** an occasion when food is eaten. **2.** the food itself. □ **make a meal of**, to make (a task) seem unnecessarily laborious. **meal-ticket** *n.* a person or thing that provides one with food. **mealtime** *n.* the usual time for a meal.

meal[2] *n.* coarsely-ground grain or pulse.

mealy *adj.* **1.** like or containing meal, dry and powdery. **2.** mealy-mouthed. □ **mealy-mouthed** *adj.* trying excessively to avoid offending people.

mean[1] *adj.* (of a point or quantity) equally far from two extremes, average. —*n.* a middle point or condition or course etc. □ **in the mean time**, in the intervening period of time.

mean[2] *v.* (meant, meaning) **1.** to have as one's purpose or intention. **2.** to design or destine for a purpose; *it was meant for you*, you were intended to receive or hear it; *are we meant to go this way?*, are we supposed to? **3.** to intend to convey (a sense) or to indicate or refer to (a thing). **4.** (of words) to have an equivalent in the same or another language, *'maybe' means 'perhaps'*. **5.** to entail, to involve, *it means catching the early train*. **6.** to be likely or certain to result in, *this means war*. **7.** to be of a specified importance, *the honour means a lot to me*. □ **mean business**, (*informal*) to be ready to take action, not merely talk. **mean it**, not be joking or exaggerating; really intend to do what is said. **mean well**, to have good intentions. **what do you mean by it?**, how can you justify such behaviour?

mean[3] *adj.* **1.** poor in quality or appearance, low in rank; *he is no mean cricketer*, he is a very good one. **2.** unkind, spiteful, *a mean trick*. **3.** not generous, miserly. **4.** (*Amer.*) vicious. **meanly** *adv.*, **meanness** *n.*

meander (mee-**an**-der) *v.* **1.** (of a stream) to follow a winding course, flowing slowly and gently. **2.** to wander in a leisurely way. —*n.* a winding course.

meaning *n.* what is meant. —*adj.* full of meaning, expressive, *gave him a meaning* *look*. □ **with meaning**, full of meaning, significantly.

meaningful *adj*. full of meaning, significant. **meaningfully** *adv*.

meaningless *adj*. with no meaning. **meaninglessly** *adv*.

means *n*. that by which a result is brought about; *transported their goods by means of lorries*, by using lorries. —*pl. n*. resources, money or other wealth considered as a means of supporting oneself, *has private means*. □ **by all means**, certainly. **by no means** not nearly, *it is by no means certain*. **means test**, an official inquiry to establish a person's neediness before financial help is given from public funds.

meant *see* mean².

meantime *adv*. meanwhile. **mean time**, *see* mean¹.

meanwhile *adv*. 1. in the intervening period of time. 2. at the same time, while something else takes place.

measles *n*. an infectious disease producing small red spots on the whole body.

measly *adj*. 1. affected with measles. 2. (*slang*) meagre.

measurable *adj*. able to be measured.

measure *n*. 1. the size or quantity of something, found by measuring. 2. extent or amount, *he is in some measure responsible*; *had a measure of success*. 3. a unit or standard or system used in measuring, *the metre is a measure of length*. 4. a device used in measuring, e.g. a container of standard size (*pint measure*) or a marked rod or tape. 5. the rhythm or metre of poetry, the time of a piece of music, a bar of music. 6. suitable action taken for a particular purpose, a law or proposed law, *measures to stop tax evasion*. 7. a layer of rock or mineral. —**measure** *v*. 1. to find the size or quantity or extent of something by comparing it with a fixed unit or with an object of known size. 2. to be of a certain size, *it measures two metres by four*. 3. to mark or deal out a measured quantity, *measured out their rations*. 4. to estimate (a quality etc.) by comparing it with some standard. □ **beyond measure**, very great, very much, *kind* or *kindness beyond measure*. **for good measure**, in addition to what was needed; as a finishing touch. **made to measure**, made in accordance with measurements taken. **measure one's length**, to fall flat on the ground. **measure up to**, to reach the standard required by.

measured *adj*. 1. rhythmical, regular in movement, *measured tread*. 2. carefully considered, *in measured language*.

measurement *n*. 1. measuring. 2. size etc.

found by measuring and expressed in units.

meat *n*. 1. animal flesh as food (usually excluding fish and poultry). 2. informative matter, *the book has a lot of meat in it*. **meatless** *adj*.

meaty *adj*. (meatier, meatiest) 1. like meat. 2. full of meat, fleshy. 3. full of informative matter, *a meaty book*.

Mecca *n*. a place that a person or people with certain interests are anxious to visit. ¶ The name of a city in Saudi Arabia, the birthplace of Muhammad and chief place of Muslim pilgrimage.

mechanic *n*. a skilled workman who uses or repairs machines or tools.

mechanical *adj*. 1. of machines or mechanism. 2. worked or produced by machinery. 3. (of a person or action) like a machine, as if acting or done without conscious thought. 4. (of work) needing little or no thought. 5. of or belonging to the science of mechanics. **mechanically** *adv*.

mechanics *n*. 1. the scientific study of motion and force. 2. the science of machinery. —*pl. n*. the processes by which something is done or functions.

mechanism *n*. 1. the way a machine works. 2. the structure or parts of a machine. 3. the process by which something is done, *the mechanism of government*.

mechanize (mek-ă-nyz) *v*. to equip with machines, to use machines in or for; *a mechanized army unit*, one that is equipped with tanks and armoured cars etc. **mechanization** *n*.

Med *n*. (*informal*) the Mediterranean Sea.

medal *n*. a small flat piece of metal, usually shaped like a coin, bearing a design and commemorating an event or given as an award for an achievement.

medallion (mid-al-yŏn) *n*. 1. a large medal. 2. a large circular ornamental design, e.g. on a carpet.

medallist *n*. one who wins a medal as a prize, *gold medallist*.

meddle *v*. 1. to interfere in people's affairs. 2. to tinker. **meddler** *n*.

meddlesome *adj*. often meddling.

Mede *n*. one of the inhabitants of ancient Persia. **the law of the Medes and Persians**, an unchanging law.

media (meed-iă) *pl. n*. see medium. □ **the media**, newspapers and broadcasting, by which information is conveyed to the general public. ¶ This word is the plural of *medium* and should have a plural verb, e.g. *the media are* (not *is*) *influential*. It is incorrect to refer to one of these services (e.g. television) as *a media* or *the media*, or to several of them as *medias*.

mediaeval *adj*. = medieval.

medial (**mee**-di-ăl) *adj.* situated in the middle, intermediate between two extremes. **medially** *adv.*

median (**mee**-di-ăn) *adj.* situated in or passing through the middle. —*n.* a median point or line etc.

mediate (**mee**-di-ayt) *v.* **1.** to act as negotiator or peacemaker between the opposing sides in a dispute. **2.** to bring about (a settlement) in this way. **mediation** *n.*, **mediator** *n.*

medic *n.* (*informal*) a doctor or medical student.

medical *adj.* of or involving the science of medicine, of this as distinct from surgery; *medical examination,* physical examination by a doctor to determine a person's state of health. —*n.* (*informal*) a medical examination. —**medically** *adv.* ☐ **medical practitioner,** a physician or surgeon.

medicament (mid-ik-ă-měnt) *n.* any medicine or ointment etc.

medicate *v.* to treat or impregnate with a medicinal substance, *medicated gauze.* **medication** *n.*

medicinal (mid-**iss**-in-ăl) *adj.* of a medicine, having healing properties. **medicinally** *adv.*

medicine (**med**-s'n) *n.* **1.** the scientific study of the prevention and cure of diseases and disorders of the body. **2.** this as distinct from surgery. **3.** a substance used to treat a disease etc., especially one taken by mouth. ☐ **medicine-man** *n.* a witch-doctor. **take one's medicine,** to submit to punishment for one's wrongdoing.

medico *n.* (*pl.* medicos) (*informal*) a doctor or medical student.

medieval (med-i-ee-văl) *adj.* of the Middle Ages.

mediocre (meed-i-**oh**-ker) *adj.* **1.** of medium quality, neither good nor bad. **2.** second-rate. **mediocrity** (meed-i-**ok**-riti) *n.*

meditate *v.* **1.** to think deeply and quietly. **2.** to plan in one's mind. **meditation** *n.*

meditative (**med**-it-ătiv) *adj.* meditating, accompanied by meditation. **meditatively** *adv.*

Mediterranean *adj.* of or characteristic of the Mediterranean Sea or the regions bordering on it. —*n.* the **Mediterranean Sea,** a sea lying between Europe and North Africa.

medium *n.* (*pl.* media, in sense 7 mediums) **1.** a middle quality or degree of intensiveness etc.; *the happy medium,* avoidance of extremes which are unpleasant. **2.** a substance or surroundings in which something exists or moves or is transmitted, *air is the medium through which sound travels.* **3.** an environment. **4.** a liquid (e.g. oil or water) in which pigments are mixed for use in painting. **5.** an agency or means by which something is done, *the use of television as a medium for advertising.* (¶ See the entry for media.) **6.** the material or form used by an artist or composer, *sculpture is his medium.* **7.** (*pl.* mediums) a person who claims to be able to communicate with the spirits of the dead. *adj.* intermediate between two extremes or amounts, average, moderate. ☐ **medium wave,** a radio wave having a wavelength between 100 and 1000 metres.

mediumistic *adj.* of spiritualist mediums.

medlar *n.* **1.** a fruit like a small brown apple that is not edible until it begins to decay. **2.** the tree that bears it.

medley *n.* (*pl.* medleys) **1.** an assortment of things. **2.** music combining passages from different sources.

meek *adj.* quiet and obedient, making no protest. **meekly** *adv.,* **meekness** *n.*

meerschaum (**meer**-shăm) *n.* a tobacco-pipe with a bowl made from a white clay-like substance.

meet [1] *adj.* (*old use*) suitable, proper.

meet [2] *v.* (met, meeting) **1.** to come face to face with, to come together (e.g. socially or for discussion). **2.** to come into contact, to touch. **3.** to go to a place to be present at the arrival of, *I will meet your train.* **4.** to make the acquaintance of, to be introduced. **5.** to come together as opponents in a contest or battle. **6.** to find oneself faced (with a thing), to experience or receive, *met with difficulties; met his death.* **7.** to deal with (a problem), to satisfy (a demand etc.), to pay (the cost or what is owing). —*n.* a meeting of people and hounds for a hunt, or of athletes etc. for a competition. ☐ **meet a person half-way,** to respond readily to his advances; to make a compromise with him. **meet the case,** to be adequate or satisfactory. **meet the eye** or **ear,** to be visible or audible; *there's more in it than meets the eye,* there are hidden qualities or complications; *meet a person's eye,* to look directly at the eyes of a person who is looking at one's own. **meet up with,** (*informal*) to meet (a person).

meeting *n.* **1.** coming together. **2.** an assembly of people for discussion etc. or (of Quakers) for worship. **3.** a race-meeting. ☐ **meeting-place** *n.* a place appointed for a meeting.

mega- (**meg**-ă) *prefix* **1.** large. **2.** one million, *megavolts, megawatts.*

megacycle *n.* **1.** one million cycles as a

unit of wave frequency. **2.** (*informal*) megahertz.

megadeath *n.* the death of one million people (regarded as a unit in estimating the possible casualties in nuclear war).

megahertz *n.* a unit of frequency of electromagnetic waves, = one million cycles per second.

megalith (**meg-ă-lith**) *n.* a huge stone used in the building of prehistoric monuments, **megalithic** (megă-**lith**-ik) *adj.* using such stones.

megalomania (meg-ăl-ŏ-**may**-niă) *n.* **1.** a form of madness in which a person has exaggerated ideas of his own importance etc. **2.** an obsessive desire to do things on a grand scale.

megaphone *n.* a funnel-shaped device used for directing and amplifying a speaker's voice so that it can be heard at a distance.

megaton (**meg-ă-tun**) *n.* a unit of explosive power equal to that of one million tons of TNT.

melamine (**mel-ă-meen**) *n.* a resilient kind of plastic.

melancholia (mel-ăn-**koh**-liă) *n.* mental depression. **melancholic** (mel-ăn-**kol**-ik) *adj.*

melancholy (**mel**-ăn-kŏli) *n.* **1.** mental depression, thoughtful sadness. **2.** an atmosphere of gloom. —*adj.* sad, gloomy, depressing.

mélange (may-**lahn**zh) *n.* a mixture.

melanin (**mel-ăn-in**) *n.* a dark pigment found in skin and hair.

Melba toast thin crisp toast.

mêlée (**mel**-ay) *n.* **1.** a confused fight. **2.** a muddle.

mellifluous (mel-**if**-loo-ŭs) *adj.* sweet-sounding.

mellow *adj.* **1.** sweet and rich in flavour. **2.** (of sound or colour) soft and rich, free from harshness or sharp contrast. **3.** made kindly and sympathetic by age or experience. **4.** genial, jovial. —*v.* to make or become mellow. —**mellowly** *adv.*, **mellowness** *n.*

melodic (mil-**od**-ik) *adj.* of melody.

melodious (mil-**oh**-diŭs) *adj.* full of melody. **melodiously** *adv.*

melodrama (**mel**-ŏ-drah-mă) *n.* **1.** a play full of suspense in a sensational and emotional style. **2.** plays of this kind. **3.** a situation in real life resembling this. **melodramatic** (mel-ŏ-dră-**mat**-ik) *adj.*, **melodramatically** *adv.*

melody *n.* **1.** sweet music, tunefulness. **2.** a song or tune, *old Irish melodies*. **3.** the main part in a piece of harmonized music.

melon *n.* the large sweet fruit of various gourds.

melt *v.* **1.** to make into or become liquid by heat. **2.** (of food) to be softened or dissolved easily, *it melts in the mouth*. **3.** to make or become gentler through pity or love. **4.** to dwindle or fade away, to pass slowly into something else, *one shade of colour melted into another*. **5.** (*informal*, of a person) to depart unobtrusively. □ **melt down**, to melt completely; to melt (metal articles) in order to use the metal as raw material. **melting-point** *n.* the temperature at which a solid melts. **melting-pot** *n.* a place or situation where things are being mixed or reconstructed, *all our ideas must go back into the melting-pot*.

melton *n.* heavy woollen cloth with close-cut nap, used for overcoats.

member *n.* **1.** a person or thing that belongs to a particular group or society. **2.** *Member*, a **Member of Parliament**, one who is elected as representative of a constituency to take part in the proceedings of the House of Commons. — **membership** *n.* being a member; the total number of members.

membrane (**mem**-brayn) *n.* thin flexible skin-like tissue, especially that covering or lining organs or other structures in animals and plants. **membranous** (mem-**brăn**-ŭs) *adj.*

memento (mim-**ent**-oh) *n.* (*pl.* mementoes) a souvenir.

memo (**mem**-oh) *n.* (*pl.* memos) (*informal*) a memorandum.

memoir (**mem**-wahr) *n.* a written account of events that one has lived through or of the life or character of a person whom one knew, *write one's memoirs*.

memorable (**mem**-er-ăbŭl) *adj.* worth remembering, easy to remember. **memorably** *adv.*, **memorability** *n.*

memorandum (mem-er-**an**-dŭm) *n.* (*pl.* memoranda) **1.** a note or record of events written as a reminder, for future use. **2.** an informal written communication from one person to another in an office or organization.

memorial *n.* an object or institution or custom established in memory of an event or person. —*adj.* serving as a memorial.

memorize *v.* to learn (a thing) so as to know it from memory.

memory *n.* **1.** the ability to keep things in one's mind or to recall them at will. **2.** remembering, a thing remembered, *memories of childhood; of happy memory*, remembered with pleasure. **3.** the length of time over which people's memory extends, *within living memory*. **4.** (in a computer etc.) = store *n.* sense 4. □ **from memory**, recalled into one's mind without the aid of notes etc. **in memory of,** in honour of a person or thing that is remembered with respect.

men *see* man.

menace *n.* **1.** something that seems likely to bring harm or danger, a threatening quality. **2.** an annoying or troublesome person or thing. —*v.* to threaten with harm or danger. —**menacingly** *adv.*

ménage (may-**nah***zh*) *n.* a household. **ménage à trois** (*pr.* ah trwah), a household consisting of husband, wife, and the lover of one of these.

menagerie (min-**aj**-er-i) *n.* a collection of wild or strange animals in captivity, for exhibition.

mend *v.* **1.** to make whole (something that is damaged), to repair. **2.** to make or become better; *mend one's manners,* improve them; *mend matters,* to set right or improve the state of affairs. —*n.* a repaired place. □ **on the mend,** improving in health or condition.

mendacious (men-**day**-shŭs) *adj.* untruthful, telling lies. **mendaciously** *adv.,* **mendacity** (men-**dass**-iti) *n.*

mender *n.* one who mends things.

mendicant (**men**-dik-ănt) *adj.* begging; *mendicant friars,* friars who depend on alms for a living. —*n.* a beggar, a mendicant friar.

mending *n.* clothes etc. to be mended.

menfolk *pl. n.* men in general, the men of one's family.

menhir (**men**-heer) *n.* a tall upright stone set up in prehistoric times.

menial (**meen**-iăl) *adj.* lowly, degrading, *menial tasks.* —*n.* (*contemptuous*) a servant, a person who does humble tasks.

meninges (min-**in**-jeez) *pl. n.* the membranes that enclose the brain and spinal cord. **meningitis** (men-in-**jy**-tiss) *n.* inflammation of these.

menopause (**men**-ŏ-pawz) *n.* the time of life during which a woman finally ceases to menstruate. **menopausal** *adj.*

menses *pl. n.* the blood etc. discharged in menstruation.

menstrual (**men**-stroo-ăl) *adj.* of or in menstruation.

menstruate (**men**-stroo-ayt) *v.* to experience the discharge of blood from the womb that normally occurs in women between puberty and middle age at approximately monthly intervals. **menstruation** *n.*

mensuration (men-sewr-**ay**-shŏn) *n.* measuring, the mathematical rules for finding lengths, areas, and volumes.

menswear *n.* (in shops) clothes for men.

mental *adj.* **1.** of the mind, existing in or performed by the mind; *mental arithmetic,*

calculations done without the aid of written figures. **2.** (*informal*) suffering from a disorder of the mind, mad. **mentally** *adv.* □ **mental age,** the level of a person's mental development expressed as the age at which this level is reached by an average person. **mental deficiency,** lack of normal intelligence through imperfect mental development. **mentally deficient,** suffering from this. **mental home** *or* **hospital,** an establishment for the care of patients suffering from mental illness.

mentality (men-**tal**-iti) *n.* a person's mental ability or characteristic attitude of mind.

menthol (**men**-thol) *n.* a solid white substance obtained from peppermint oil or made synthetically, used as a flavouring and to relieve pain. **mentholated** *adj.* impregnated with menthol.

mention *v.* to speak or write about briefly, to refer to by name; *was mentioned in dispatches,* mentioned by name for bravery. —*n.* mentioning, being mentioned. □ **don't mention it,** a polite reply to thanks or to an apology. not to mention, and as another important thing.

mentor (**men**-tor) *n.* a trusted adviser.

menu (**men**-yoo) *n.* **1.** a list of dishes to be served or available in a restaurant etc. **2.** a list of options, displayed on a screen, from which a user selects what he requires a computer to do.

MEP *abbrev.* Member of the European Parliament.

mercantile (**mer**-kăn-tyl) *adj.* trading, of trade or merchants. **mercantile marine,** the merchant navy.

mercenary (**mer**-sin-er-i) *adj.* **1.** working merely for money or other reward, grasping. **2.** (of professional soldiers) hired to serve a foreign country. —*n.* a professional soldier serving a foreign country.

mercerized *adj.* (of cotton fabric or thread) treated with a substance that gives greater strength and a slight gloss.

merchandise *n.* goods or commodities bought and sold, goods for sale. —*v.* **1.** to buy and sell, to trade. **2.** to promote sales of (goods etc.).

merchant *n.* **1.** a wholesale trader. **2.** (*Amer. & Scottish*) a retail trader. **3.** (*slang*) a person who is fond of a certain activity, *speed merchants.* □ **merchant bank,** a bank dealing in commercial loans and the financing of businesses. **merchant navy,** shipping employed in commerce. **merchant ship,** a ship carrying merchandise.

merchantable *adj.* saleable, marketable.

merciful *adj.* **1.** showing mercy. **2.** giving relief from pain or suffering, *a merciful* *death.* **mercifully** *adv.* in a merciful way; (*informal*) thank goodness.

merciless *adj.* showing no mercy. **mercilessly** *adv.*

mercurial (mer-**kewr**-iăl) *adj.* **1.** of or caused by mercury, *mercurial poisoning.* **2.** having a lively temperament. **3.** liable to sudden changes of mood.

mercury *n.* a heavy silvery normally liquid metal, used in thermometers and barometers etc. **mercuric** (mer-**kewr**-ik) *adj.*

mercy *n.* **1.** refraining from inflicting punishment or pain on an offender or enemy etc. who is in one's power. **2.** a disposition to behave in this way, *a tyrant without mercy.* **3.** a merciful act, a thing to be thankful for, *it's a mercy no one was killed.* —*int.* an exclamation of surprise or fear, *mercy on us!* □ **at the mercy of,** wholly in the power of, liable to danger or harm from. **mercy killing,** euthanasia.

mere [1] *adj.* nothing more or better than what is specified, *she is a mere child*; *mere words,* words alone, without deeds; *it's no mere theory,* is not only a theory. **merely** *adv.* □ **merest** *adj.* very small or insignificant, *the merest trace of colour.*

mere [2] *n.* a lake.

meretricious (merri-**trish**-ŭs) *adj.* showily attractive but cheap or insincere.

merganser (mer-**gan**-ser) *n.* a diving duck that feeds on fish.

merge *v.* **1.** to unite or combine into a whole, *the two companies merged* or *were merged.* **2.** to pass slowly into something else, to blend or become blended.

merger *n.* the combining of two commercial companies etc. into one.

meridian (mer-**rid**-iăn) *n.* any of the great semicircles on the globe, passing through a given place and the North and South Poles; *the meridian of Greenwich,* the meridian shown on maps as 0° longitude.

meringue (mer-**rang**) *n.* **1.** a mixture of sugar and white of egg baked crisp. **2.** a small cake of this.

merino (mer-**ree**-noh) *n.* (*pl.* merinos) **1.** a kind of sheep with fine soft wool. **2.** a kind of fine soft woollen yarn or fabric.

merit *n.* **1.** the quality of deserving to be praised, excellence. **2.** a feature or quality that deserves praise; *judge it on its merits,* according to its own qualities. —*v.* (merited, meriting) to deserve.

meritocracy (merri-**tok**-răsi) *n.* **1.** government or control by people of high ability, selected by some form of competition. **2.** these people.

meritorious (merri-**tor**-iŭs) *adj.* having merit, deserving praise.

mermaid *n.* an imaginary sea-creature, a woman with a fish's tail in place of legs.

merman *n.* (*pl.* mermen) a similar male creature.

merry *adj.* (merrier, merriest) **1.** cheerful and lively, joyous. **2.** (*informal*) cheerful because slightly drunk. **merrily** *adv.,* **merriment** *n.* □ **make merry,** to hold lively festivities. **merry-making** *n.* lively festivities. **merry men,** (*humorous*) a person's companions or henchmen.

merry-go-round *n.* **1.** a machine at funfairs with a circular revolving platform with models of horses or cars etc. for riding on while it revolves. **2.** a busy repeated series of occupations or events in social or business life.

Merseyside a metropolitan county of England.

mescaline (**mesk**-ă-leen) *n.* a drug that produces hallucinations, made from the button-like tops of a Mexican cactus.

Mesdames *see* Madame.

Mesdemoiselles *see* Mademoiselle.

mesembryanthemum (miz-em-bri-**anth**-imŭm) *n.* a low-growing plant with pink, orange, or white daisy-like flowers opening at about noon.

mesh *n.* **1.** one of the spaces between threads in a net or sieve or wire screen etc. **2.** network fabric. —*v.* (of a toothed wheel etc.) to engage with another or others.

mesmerize *v.* to hypnotize, to dominate the attention or will of.

mesolithic (mess-ŏ-**lith**-ik) *adj.* of the Stone Age between palaeolithic and neolithic.

mess *n.* **1.** a dirty or untidy condition, an untidy collection of things, something spilt. **2.** a difficult or confused situation, trouble. **3.** any disagreeable substance or concoction, a domestic animal's excreta. **4.** (*informal*) a person who looks untidy or dirty or slovenly. **5.** (in the armed forces) a group who take meals together, the place where such meals are eaten. —**mess** *v.* **1.** to make untidy or dirty. **2.** to muddle or bungle (business etc.), *messed it up.* **3.** to potter, *mess about* or *around.* **4.** to meddle or tinker, *don't mess with the transistor.* **5.** to take one's meals with a military or other group, *they mess together.* □ **make a mess of,** to bungle.

message *n.* **1.** a spoken or written communication. **2.** the inspired moral or social teaching of a prophet or writer etc., *a film with a message.* □ **get the message,** (*informal*) to understand what is meant or implied.

messenger *n.* the bearer of a message.

Messiah (mi-**sy**-ă) *n.* **1.** the expected deliverer and ruler of the Jewish people, whose coming was prophesied in the Old Testament. **2.** Christ, regarded by Christians as this.

Messianic (mess-i-**an**-ik) *adj.* of the Messiah.

Messieurs *see* Monsieur.

Messrs (**mess**-erz) *abbrev.* plural of Mr.

messy *adj.* (messier, messiest) **1.** untidy or dirty, slovenly. **2.** causing a mess, *a messy task*. **3.** complicated and difficult to deal with. **messily** *adv.*, **messiness** *n.*

met[1] *see* meet[2].

met[2] *adj.* (*informal*) meteorological. **the Met**, the Meteorological Office.

metabolism (mi-**tab**-ŏl-izm) *n.* the process by which food is built up into living material or used to supply energy in a living organism. **metabolic** (met-ă-**bol**-ik) *adj.*

metabolize (mi-**tab**-ŏ-lyz) *v.* to process (food) in metabolism.

metal *n.* any of a class of mineral substances such as gold, silver, copper, iron, uranium, etc., or an alloy of any of these. —*adj.* made of metal.

metalled *adj.* (of a road) made or mended with road-metal.

metallic (mi-**tal**-ik) *adj.* **1.** of or like metal. **2.** (of sound) like metals struck together, sharp and ringing.

metallurgist (mi-**tal** er-jist) *n.* an expert in metallurgy.

metallurgy (mi-tal-er-ji) *n.* the scientific study of the properties of metals and alloys, the art of working metals or of extracting them from their ores. **metallurgical** (met-ăl-**er**-jikăl) *adj.*

metamorphose (met-ă-**mor**-fohs) *v.* to change or be changed in form or character.

metamorphosis (met-ă-**mor**-fŏ-sis) *n.* (*pl.* metamorphoses) a change of form or character. **metamorphic** *adj.*

metaphor (**met**-ă-fer) *n.* the application of a word or phrase to something that it does not apply to literally, in order to indicate a comparison with the literal usage, e.g. the *evening* of one's life, *food* for thought, *cut off one's nose to spite one's face*. **mixed metaphor**, an unsuitable combination of metaphors, e.g. *the only thing this government will listen to is muscle.*

metaphorical (met-ă-**fo**-rikăl) *adj.* in a metaphor, not literal. **metaphorically** *adv.*

metaphysics (met-ă-**fiz**-iks) *n.* a branch of philosophy that deals with the nature of existence and of truth and knowledge. **metaphysical** (metă-**fiz**-ikăl) *adj.*

mete (*pr.* meet) *v.* **mete out**, to give as what is due, *mete out punishment to wrongdoers.*

meteor (**meet**-i-er) *n.* a bright moving body seen in the sky, formed by a small mass of matter from outer space that becomes luminous from compression of air as it enters the earth's atmosphere.

meteoric (meet-i-o-rik) *adj.* **1.** of meteors. **2.** like a meteor in brilliance or sudden appearance, *a meteoric career.*

meteorite (**meet**-i-er-ryt) *n.* a fallen meteor, a fragment of rock or metal reaching the earth's surface from outer space.

meteoroid (**meet**-i-er-oid) *n.* a body moving through space, of the same nature as those which become visible as meteors when they enter the earth's atmosphere.

meteorologist (meet-i-er-**ol**-ŏ-jist) *n.* an expert in meteorology.

meteorology (meet-i-er-**ol**-ŏji) *n.* the scientific study of atmospheric conditions, especially in order to forecast weather. **meteorological** *adj.* □ **Meteorological Office**, a government department providing information and forecasts about the weather.

meter[1] *n.* a device designed to measure and indicate the quantity of a substance supplied, or the distance travelled and fare payable, or the time that has elapsed, etc. —*v.* (metered, metering) to measure by meter.

meter[2] *n.* (*Amer.*) = metre.

methane (**mee**-thayn) *n.* a colourless inflammable gas that occurs in coal-mines and marshy areas.

method *n.* **1.** a procedure or way of doing something. **2.** orderliness, *he's a man of method.*

methodical (mi-**thod**-ikăl) *adj.* orderly, systematic. **methodically** *adv.*

Methodist *n.* a member of a Protestant religious denomination originating in the 18th century and based on the teachings of John and Charles Wesley and their followers. **Methodism** *n.*

meths *n.* (*informal*) methylated spirit.

methyl (**meth**-il) *n.* a chemical unit present in methane and in many organic compounds. **methylated spirit**, a form of alcohol (made unpleasant for drinking) used as a solvent and for heating.

meticulous (mi-**tik**-yoo-lŭs) *adj.* giving or showing great attention to detail, very careful and exact. **meticulously** *adv.*, **meticulousness** *n.*

metre *n.* **1.** a unit of length in the metric system (about 39·4 inches). **2.** rhythm in poetry, a particular form of this.

metric *adj.* **1.** of or using the metric system. **2.** of poetic metre. **metrically** *adv.* □ **go metric**, (*informal*) to adopt the metric system. **metric system**, a decimal system of weights and measures, using the metre, litre, and gram as units. **metric ton,** a tonne (1000 kilograms).

metrical *adj.* of or composed in rhythmic metre, not prose, *metrical psalms.*

metricate *v.* to change or adapt to the metric system of measurement. **metrication** *n.*

Metro *n.* (*informal*) the underground railway in Paris. —*adj.* (*informal*) metropolitan.

metronome (**met**-rŏ-nohm) *n.* a device, often with an inverted pendulum, that sounds a click at a regular interval, used to indicate tempo for a person practising music.

metropolis (mi-**trop**-ŏlis) *n.* the chief city of a country or region.

metropolitan (metrŏ-**pol**-ităn) *adj.* of a metropolis. **metropolitan county,** any of the six new English counties formed in 1974, treated as a unit for some purposes (e.g. transport and planning) and divided into districts for others. **metropolitan magistrate,** a paid professional magistrate in London. **Metropolitan Police,** the police force of London.

mettle *n.* courage or strength of character. **on one's mettle,** determined to show one's courage or ability.

mettlesome *adj.* spirited, courageous.

mew *n.* the characteristic cry of a cat. —*v.* to make this sound.

mews *n.* a set of what were formerly stables in a small street or square, now rebuilt or converted into dwellings or garages.

Mexico a country in Central America. **Mexican** *adj.* & *n.* □ **Mexico City,** its capital city.

mezzanine (**mets**-ă-neen) *n.* an extra storey between ground floor and first floor, often in the form of a wide balcony.

mezzo (**met**-soh) *adv.* (in music) moderately; *mezzo forte,* moderately loudly.

mezzo-soprano *n.* a voice between soprano and contralto; a singer with this voice; a part written for it.

mezzotint (**met**-soh-tint) *n.* **1.** a method of engraving in which the plate is roughened to give areas of shadow and smoothed to give areas of light. **2.** a print produced by this.

mg *abbrev.* milligram(s).

M. Glam. *abbrev.* Mid Glamorgan.

MHz *abbrev.* megahertz.

miaow *n.* & *v.* = mew.

miasma (mi-**az**-mă) *n.* unpleasant or unwholesome air.

mica (**my**-kă) *n.* a mineral substance used as an electrical insulator.

mice *see* mouse.

Mich. *abbrev.* Michigan.

Michaelmas (**mik**-ĕl-măs) *n.* a Christian festival in honour of St. Michael (29 September). **Michaelmas daisy,** a kind of perennial aster flowering in autumn, with purple, dark red, pink, or white blooms. **Michaelmas term,** the university and law term beginning at Michaelmas.

Michigan (**mish**-i-găn) a State of the USA.

mickey *n.* **take the mickey out of,** (*slang*) to tease or ridicule.

micro- *prefix* **1.** very small. **2.** one millionth of a unit, *microgram.*

microbe *n.* a micro-organism, especially one that causes disease or fermentation.

microchip *n.* a very small piece of silicon or similar material made so as to work like a complex wired electric circuit.

microcomputer *n.* a very small computer in which the central processor is a microprocessor.

microcosm (**my**-krŏ-kozm) *n.* a world in miniature, something regarded as resembling something else on a very small scale.

microdot *n.* a photograph of a document etc. reduced to the size of a dot.

microfiche (**my**-krŏ-feesh) *n.* (*pl.* microfiche) a sheet of microfilm in a form suitable for filing like an index-card.

microfilm *n.* a length of film on which written or printed material is photographed in greatly reduced size. —*v.* to photograph on this.

micrographic *adj.* of or using minute photographic reproductions, e.g. of printed matter.

micro-organism *n.* an organism that cannot be seen by the naked eye, e.g. a bacterium or virus.

microphone *n.* an instrument for picking up sound waves for recording, amplifying, or broadcasting.

microprocessor *n.* a miniature computer (or a unit of this) consisting of one or more microchips.

microscope *n.* an instrument with lenses that magnify objects or details too small to be seen by the naked eye.

microscopic *adj.* **1.** of the microscope. **2.** too small to be visible without the aid of a microscope. **3.** extremely small.

microsecond *n.* one millionth of a second.

microwave *n.* an electromagnetic wave of length between about 50 cm and ¼ mm. **microwave oven,** an oven using such waves to heat food very quickly.

mid *adj.* in the middle of, middle, *in mid-air; to mid-August.* **mid-off, mid-on** *ns.* a fieldsman in cricket near the bowler on the off (or on) side, his position.

Midas (**my**-das) *n*. **the Midas touch**, ability to make money in all one's activities. ¶ Named after a legendary king in Asia Minor, whose touch turned all things to gold.

midday *n*. the middle of the day, noon.

midden *n*. a heap of dung, a rubbish-heap.

middle *adj*. **1**. at an equal distance from extremes or outer limits. **2**. occurring half-way between beginning and end. **3**. intermediate in rank or quality, moderate in size etc., *a man of middle height*. —**middle** *n*. **1**. a middle point, position, time, area, or quality etc. **2**. the waist. □ **in the middle of**, during or half-way through (an activity etc.). **in the middle of nowhere**, (*informal*) in a very remote place. **middle age**, the period between youth and old age. **middle-aged** *adj*. of middle age. **Middle Ages**, about AD 1000–1400. **middle-brow** *adj*. moderately intellectual, (*n*.) a middle brow person. **middle C**, the note C that occurs near the middle of the piano keyboard. **middle class**, the class of society between the upper and working classes, including business and professional people. **Middle East**, the area covered by countries from Egypt to Iran inclusive. **middle-of-the-road** *adj*. favouring a moderate policy, avoiding extremes. **middle school**, the middle forms of an independent school; a school for children aged about 9–13 years. **middle-sized** *adj*. of medium size. **Middle West**, the region of the USA near the northern Mississippi.

middleman *n*. (*pl*. middlemen) any of the traders handling a commodity between producer and consumer.

Middlesex a former county of England.

middleweight *n*. a boxing-weight (75 kg) between light heavyweight and welterweight.

middling *adj*. & *adv*. moderately good, moderately well.

Middx. *abbrev*. Middlesex.

middy *n*. (*informal*) a midshipman.

midge *n*. a small biting gnat-like insect.

midget *n*. an extremely small person or thing. —*adj*. extremely small.

midland *adj*. of the Midlands or the middle part of a country. **the Midlands**, the inland counties of central England.

midnight *n*. twelve o'clock at night, the time near this.

midriff *n*. the front part of the body or of a garment just above the waist.

midshipman *n*. (*pl*. midshipmen) a naval rank between cadet and sub-lieutenant.

midst *n*. the middle part. **in the midst of**, among, surrounded by.

midsummer *n*. the middle of the summer, about 21 June. **Midsummer's Day**, 24 June.

midway *adv*. half-way between places.

Midwest *n*. (*Amer*.) = Middle West.

midwife *n*. (*pl*. midwives) a person trained to assist women in childbirth. **midwifery** (**mid**-wif-ri) *n*. the work of a midwife.

midwinter *n*. the middle of the winter, about 22 December.

mien (*pr*. meen) *n*. a person's manner or bearing.

might[1] *n*. great strength or power, *with all one's might*. **with might and main**, with all one's power and energy.

might[2] *auxiliary verb* used as the past tense of may[1]; *you might call at the baker's*, I should like you to do so; *you might have offered*, ought to have offered. □ **might-have-been** *n*. an event that might have happened but did not.

mightn't = might not.

mighty *adj*. (mightier, mightiest) **1**. having or showing great strength or power. **2**. very great in size. —*adv*. (*informal*) very, *mighty fine*. —**mightily** *adv*., **mightiness** *n*.

mignonette (min-yon-et) *n*. an annual plant with fragrant greyish-green leaves.

migraine (**mee**-grayn) *n*. a severe form of headache that tends to recur.

migrant (**my**-grant) *adj*. migrating. —*n*. a migrant person or animal.

migrate (my-**grayt**) *v*. **1**. to leave one place and settle in another. **2**. (of animals) to go periodically from one place to another, living in each place for part of a year. **migration** *n*.

migratory (**my**-gra-ter-i) *adj*. of or involving migration, migrating.

Mikado (mi-**kah**-doh) *n*. (*pl*. mikados) the emperor of Japan.

mike *n*. (*informal*) a microphone.

milch *adj*. giving milk. **milch cow**, a cow kept for its milk rather than for beef; a person or organization from whom money is easily obtained.

mild *adj*. **1**. moderate in intensity or character or effect, not severe or harsh or drastic. **2**. (of a person) gentle in manner. **3**. not strongly flavoured, not sharp or strong in taste. **mildly** *adv*., **mildness** *n*. □ **mild steel**, steel that is strong and tough but not readily tempered.

mildew *n*. a minute fungus that forms a white coating on things exposed to damp.

mildewed *adj*. coated with mildew.

mile *n*. **1**. a measure of length, 1760 yards

(about 1·609 kilometres); *nautical mile,* a unit used in navigation, 2025 yards (1·852 kilometres). **2.** (*informal*) a great distance or amount, *miles too big.* **3.** a race extending over a mile. ☐ **mile-post** *n.* a post marking the point one mile from the finish of a race.

mileage *n.* **1.** distance measured in miles. **2.** the number of miles a vehicle travels on one gallon of fuel. **3.** travelling expenses at a fixed rate per mile. **4.** (*informal*) benefit, *he gets a lot of mileage out of his family name.*

miler *n.* a person who specializes in races that are one mile in length.

milestone *n.* **1.** a stone set up beside a road to show the distance in miles to a given point. **2.** a significant event or stage in life or history.

milfoil *n.* yarrow.

milieu (**meel**-yer) *n.* (*pl.* milieus) environment, surroundings.

militant *adj.* prepared to take aggressive action in support of a cause. —*n.* a militant person. —**militancy** *n.*

militarism (**mil**-it-er-izm) *n.* reliance on military strength and methods. **militarist** *n.* ☐ **militaristic** *adj.* warlike.

military *adj.* of soldiers or the army or all armed forces, *military service*; *the military,* armed forces as distinct from police or civilians. **military band,** a combination of woodwind, brass, and percussion instruments.

militate (**mil**-i-tayt) *v.* to serve as a strong influence, *several factors militated against the success of our plan.*

militia (mil-ish-ă) *n.* a military force, especially one consisting of civilians trained as soldiers and available to supplement the regular army in an emergency.

milk *n.* **1.** a white fluid secreted by female mammals as food for their young. **2.** the milk of cows, used as food by human beings. **3.** a milk-like liquid, e.g. that in a coconut. —**milk** *v.* **1.** to draw milk from (a cow or goat etc.). **2.** to extract juice from (a tree etc.). **3.** to exploit or get money undeservedly from, *milking the Welfare State.* ☐ **in milk,** (of cows) secreting milk. **milk bar** *n.* a bar for the sale of non-alcoholic drinks, especially those made from milk, and light refreshments. **milk chocolate,** chocolate (for eating) made with milk. **milk-float** *n.* a light low vehicle used in delivering milk. **milk loaf,** a loaf of white bread made with milk. **milk-powder** *n.* dehydrated milk. **milk shake,** a drink made of milk and flavouring mixed or shaken until frothy. **milk-tooth** *n.* any of the first (temporary) teeth in young mammals. **milk-white** *adj.* white like milk.

milker *n.* **1.** a person who milks an animal. **2.** an animal that gives milk, *that cow is a good milker.*

milkmaid *n.* a woman who milks cows.

milkman *n.* (*pl.* milkmen) a man who delivers milk to customers' houses.

milksop *n.* a boy or man who is weak or timid, a weakling.

milkweed *n.* any of several wild plants with milky juice.

milky *adj.* (milkier, milkiest) **1.** of or like milk. **2.** made with milk, containing much milk. **3.** (of a gem or liquid) cloudy, not clear. **milkiness** *n.* ☐ **Milky Way,** the broad faintly luminous band of stars encircling the sky, the Galaxy.

mill *n.* **1.** machinery for grinding corn, a building fitted with this. **2.** any machine for grinding or crushing a solid substance into powder or pulp, *coffee-mill.* **3.** a machine or a building fitted with machinery for processing material of certain kinds, *cotton-mill*; *paper-mill*; *saw-mill.* —**mill** *v.* **1.** to grind or crush in a mill. **2.** to produce in a mill. **3.** to produce regular markings on the edge of (a coin), *silver coins with a milled edge.* **4.** to cut or shape (metal) with a rotating tool. **5.** (of people or animals) to move round and round in a confused mass. ☐ **go** *or* **put through the mill,** to undergo or subject to training or experience or suffering. **mill-pond** *n.* water dammed in a stream for use in a water-mill; *sea was like a mill-pond,* very calm. **mill-wheel** *n.* the wheel that drives a water-mill.

millennium (mil-en-iŭm) *n.* (*pl.* millenniums) **1.** a period of 1000 years. **2.** the thousand-year reign of Christ on earth prophesied in the Bible. **3.** a period of great happiness and prosperity for everyone.

millepede (**mil**-i-peed) *n.* **1.** a small crawling creature like a centipede but usually with two pairs of legs on each segment of its body. **2.** a woodlouse or similar animal.

miller *n.* a person who owns or runs a corn-grinding mill.

millet *n.* **1.** a kind of cereal plant growing 3–4 ft. high and producing a large crop of small seeds. **2.** its seeds, used as food.

milli- *prefix* one thousandth.

millibar *n.* one thousandth of a bar as a unit of pressure in meteorology.

milligram *n.* one thousandth of a gram.

millilitre *n.* one thousandth of a litre.

millimetre *n.* one thousandth of a metre (0·04 inch).

milliner *n.* a person who makes or sells women's hats. **millinery** *n.* a milliner's work; women's hats sold in a shop.

million *adj. & n.* **1.** one thousand thousand (1,000,000), *a few million* (¶ not *a few millions*). **2.** a million pounds or dollars. **3.** an enormous number. **millionth** *adj. & n.*

millionaire *n.* a person who possesses a million pounds, one who is extremely wealthy.

millstone *n.* **1.** one of a pair of circular stones between which corn is ground. **2.** a great burden that impedes progress, *a millstone round one's neck*.

milometer (my-**lom**-it-er) *n.* an instrument for measuring the number of miles travelled by a vehicle.

milt *n.* the roe of a male fish, fish-sperm discharged into the water over the eggs laid by the female.

mime *n.* acting with gestures and without words, a performance using this. —*v.* to act with mime.

mimic *v.* (mimicked, mimicking) **1.** to copy the appearance or ways of (a person etc.) playfully or for entertainment. **2.** to pretend to be, (of things) to resemble closely. — *n.* a person who is clever at mimicking others, especially for entertainment. —**mimicry** *n.*

mimosa (mim-**oh**-ză) *n.* any of several usually tropical trees or shrubs, especially the kind with clusters of small ball-shaped fragrant flowers.

mina (**my**-nă) *n.* an Asian bird of the starling family.

minaret (min er-et) *n.* a tall slender tower on or beside a mosque, with a balcony from which a muezzin calls Muslims to prayer.

minatory (**min**-ă-ter-i) *adj.* threatening.

mince *v.* **1.** to cut into small pieces in a machine with revolving blades. **2.** to walk or speak in an affected way, trying to appear refined. —*n.* minced meat. □ **mince pie,** a pie containing mincemeat. **not to mince matters** or **one's words,** to speak bluntly.

mincemeat *n.* a mixture of currants, raisins, sugar, apples, candied peel, etc., used in pies. **make mincemeat of,** to destroy utterly in argument.

mincer *n.* a machine with revolving blades for mincing food.

mind *n.* **1.** the ability to be aware of things and to think and reason, originating in the brain. **2.** a person's thoughts and attention, *keep your mind on the job.* **3.** remembrance, *keep it in mind.* **4.** opinion, *change one's mind; to my mind he's a genius.* **5.** a way of thinking and feeling, *state of mind.* **6.** sanity, normal mental faculties; *in one's right mind,* sane; *out of one's mind,* insane

or extremely agitated. —**mind** *v.* **1.** to take care of, to attend to, *minding the baby* or *the shop.* **2.** to feel annoyance or discomfort at, to object to, *she doesn't mind the cold; I shouldn't mind a cup of tea,* should like one. **3.** to bear in mind, to give heed to or concern oneself about, *never mind the expense; mind you,* please take note. **4.** to remember and take care, *mind you lock the door.* **5.** to be careful about, *mind the step; mind how you carry that tray.* □ **have a good** or **half a mind to,** to feel tempted or inclined to. **have a mind of one's own,** to be capable of forming opinions independently of others. **mind-bending** *adj.* strongly influencing the mind. **mind-boggling** *adj.* causing the mind to boggle or be overwhelmed with amazement. **mind one's P's and Q's,** to be careful in one's speech or behaviour. **mind-reader** *n.* a thought-reader. **mind's eye,** the faculty of imagination. **on one's mind,** constantly in one's thoughts, causing worry. **put a person in mind of,** to remind him of. **a triumph of mind over matter,** a triumph of determination overcoming physical or other obstacles.

minded *adj.* **1.** having a mind of a certain kind, *independent-minded.* **2.** having certain interests, *politically minded; car-minded.* **3.** inclined or disposed to do something, *if she's minded to help; could do it if he were so minded.*

minder *n.* a person whose job is to attend to or take care of something, *machine-minder.*

mindful *adj.* taking thought or care of something, *mindful of his public image.*

mindless *adj.* without a mind, without intelligence. **mindlessly** *adv.*

mine [1] *adj. & possessive pronoun,* of or belonging to me, the thing(s) belonging to me.

mine [2] *n.* **1.** an excavation in the earth for extracting metal or coal etc. **2.** an abundant source of something, *a mine of information.* **3.** a receptacle filled with explosive, placed in or on the ground or in water ready to explode when something strikes it or passes near it. —**mine** *v.* **1.** to dig for minerals, to extract (metal or coal etc.) in this way. **2.** to lay explosive mines in (an area). □ **mine-detector** *n.* an instrument for detecting the presence of explosive mines.

minefield *n.* an area where explosive mines have been laid.

miner *n.* a man who works in a mine.

mineral *n.* **1.** an inorganic sub~~~~~ occurs naturally in the earth~~~~ other substance obtained by~~~~ non-alcoholic usually fizzy ~~~~

of or containing minerals. □ **mineral water**, water that is found naturally containing dissolved mineral salts or gases; a non-alcoholic usually fizzy drink.

mineralogy (min-er-**al**-ŏji) *n*. the scientific study of minerals. **mineralogical** *adj*., **mineralogist** *n*.

minestrone (mini-**stroh**-ni) *n*. an Italian soup containing chopped mixed vegetables and pasta.

minesweeper *n*. a ship for clearing away explosive mines laid in the sea.

mineworker *n*. a miner.

Ming *n*. porcelain belonging to the time of the Ming dynasty in China (1368–1644).

mingle *v*. **1**. to mix, to blend. **2**. to go about among people, *mingled with the crowd*.

mingy *adj*. (*informal*) mean, stingy.

Mini *n*. (*pl*. Minis) (*trade mark*) a type of small car.

mini- *prefix* miniature.

miniature (**min**-i-cher) *adj*. very small, made or represented on a small scale. —*n*. **1**. a very small and detailed portrait. **2**. a small-scale copy or model of something. □ **in miniature**, on a very small scale. **miniature camera**, one that produces small negatives.

miniaturist *n*. a person who paints miniatures.

miniaturize *v*. to make miniature, to produce in a very small version. **miniaturization** *n*.

minibus *n*. a small vehicle like a bus with seats for only a few people.

minicab *n*. a car like a taxi that can be booked but does not ply for hire.

minicomputer *n*. a computer that is small in size and in its storage capacity.

minim *n*. **1**. a note in music, lasting half as long as a semibreve. **2**. one sixtieth of a fluid drachm, about one drop.

minimal *adj*. very small, the least possible. **minimally** *adv*.

minimize *v*. **1**. to reduce to a minimum. **2**. to estimate at the smallest possible amount, to represent at less than the true value or importance.

minimum *n*. (*pl*. minima) the lowest or lowest possible number or amount or intensity etc.

mining *n*. **1**. the process of extracting minerals etc. from the earth. **2**. the process of laying explosive mines.

minion (**min**-yŏn) *n*. (*contemptuous*) a subordinate assistant.

miniskirt *n*. a very short skirt ending at about the middle of the thighs.

minister *n*. **1**. a person at the head of a ʳovernment department or a main branch

of this. **2**. a diplomatic representative usually ranking below ambassador. **3**. a clergyman, especially in Presbyterian and Nonconformist Churches. —*v*. to attend to people's needs, *nurses ministered to the wounded*. **ministerial** (min-iss-**teer**-iăl) *adj*.

ministry *n*. **1**. a government department headed by a minister, *Ministry of Defence*. **2**. a period of government under one premier, his body of ministers. **3**. the profession or functions of a clergyman or religious leader.

mink *n*. **1**. a small stoat-like animal of the weasel family. **2**. its highly valued fur. **3**. a coat made of this.

Minn. *abbrev*. Minnesota.

Minnesota (mini-**soh**-tă) a State of the USA.

minnow (**min**-oh) *n*. a small freshwater fish of the carp family.

Minoan (min-**oh**-ăn) *adj*. of the Bronze Age civilization of Crete (about 3000–1000 BC). —*n*. a person of this civilization. ¶ Named after *Minos*, a legendary king of Crete.

minor *adj*. **1**. lesser, less important, *minor roads*; *a minor operation*, a surgical operation that does not involve danger to the patient's life. **2**. (in music) of or based on a scale which has a semitone next above the second note. —*n*. a person under full age.

minority *n*. **1**. the smallest part of a group or class. **2**. a small group differing from others. **3**. (in law) the state of being under full age, *during his minority*.

minster *n*. a name given to certain large or important churches, *York Minster*.

minstrel *n*. a travelling singer and musician in the Middle Ages.

mint[1] *n*. **1**. a place authorized to make a country's coins. **2**. a vast amount, *left him a mint of money*. —**mint** *v*. **1**. to make (coins) by stamping metal. **2**. to invent or coin (a word etc.). □ **in mint condition**, fresh and unsoiled as if newly from the mint.

mint[2] *n*. **1**. a plant with fragrant leaves that are used for flavouring sauces and drinks etc. **2**. peppermint, a sweet flavoured with this. **minty** *adj*.

minuet (min-yoo-**et**) *n*. a slow stately dance in triple time, music suitable for this.

minus (**my**-nŭs) *prep*. **1**. reduced by the subtraction of, *seven minus three equals four* $(7 - 3 = 4)$. **2**. below zero, *temperatures of minus ten degrees Centigrade* $(- 10°C)$. **3**. (*informal*) without, *returned minus his shoes*. —*adj*. less than zero $(= negative)$, less than the amount or number indicated, *a minus quantity*; *alpha minus,* a grade slightly below alpha (written as A −). —**minus** *n.* **1**. the sign −. **2**. a disadvantage.

minuscule (**min**-ŭs-kewl) *adj.* extremely small.

minute[1] (**min**-it) *n.* **1**. one sixtieth of an hour. **2**. a very short time, a moment. **3**. an exact point of time. **4**. one sixtieth of a degree used in measuring angles. **5**. a memorandum. —*v.* to make a note of, to record in the minutes of an assembly's proceedings. □ **minutes** *pl. n.* an official record of the proceedings of an assembly or committee etc. made during a meeting. **minute steak,** a thin slice of steak that can be cooked quickly.

minute[2] (my-**newt**) *adj.* **1**. extremely small. **2**. very detailed and precise, *a minute examination.* **minutely** *adv.*

minutiae (min-**yoo**-shi-ee) *pl. n.* very small details.

minx *n.* a cheeky or mischievous girl.

miracle *n.* **1**. a remarkable and welcome event that seems impossible to explain by means of the known laws of nature and which is therefore attributed to a supernatural agency. **2**. a remarkable example or specimen, *it's a miracle of ingenuity.*

miraculous *adj.* of or like a miracle, wonderful. **miraculously** *adv.*

mirage (**mi**-rah*zh*) *n.* an optical illusion caused by atmospheric conditions, especially making sheets of water seem to appear in a desert or on a hot road.

mire *n.* **1**. swampy ground, bog. **2**. mud or sticky dirt.

mirror *n.* a piece of glass backed with amalgam so that reflections can be seen in it. —*v.* to reflect in or as if in a mirror. □ **mirror image,** a reflection or copy in which the right and left sides of the original are reversed.

mirth *n.* merriment, laughter. **mirthful** *adj.*, **mirthless** *adj.*

mis- *prefix* badly, wrongly.

misadventure *n.* a piece of bad luck; *death by misadventure,* (in law) death caused unintentionally by a deliberate act but with no crime involved.

misanthropist (mis-**an**-thrŏp-ist), **misanthrope** (**mis**-ăn-throhp) *ns.* a person who is full of misanthropy.

misanthropy (mis-**an**-thrŏpi) *n.* dislike of people in general. **misanthropic** (misăn-**throp**-ik) *adj.*

misapprehend (mis-apri-**hend**) *v.* to misunderstand. **misapprehension** *n.*

misappropriate (mis-ă-**proh**-pri-ayt) *v.* to take dishonestly, especially for one's own use. **misappropriation** *n.*

misbegotten *adj.* contemptible.

misbehave *v.* to behave badly. **misbehaviour** *n.*

miscalculate *v.* to calculate incorrectly. **miscalculation** *n.*

miscall *v.* to give a wrong or inappropriate name to.

miscarriage (mis-**ka**-rij) *n.* **1**. abortion occurring without being induced. **2**. a mistake or failure to achieve the correct result, *a miscarriage of justice.* **3**. the miscarrying of a letter or goods or of a scheme etc.

miscarry *v.* (miscarried, miscarrying) **1**. (of a pregnant woman) to have a miscarriage. **2**. (of a scheme etc.) to go wrong, to fail. **3**. (of a letter etc.) to fail to reach its destination.

miscast *v.* (miscast, miscasting) to cast (an actor) in an unsuitable role.

miscellaneous (mis-ĕl-**ay**-niŭs) *adj.* **1**. of various kinds, *miscellaneous items.* **2**. of mixed composition or character, *a miscellaneous collection.*

miscellany (mi-**sel**-ăni) *n.* a collection of various items.

mischance *n.* misfortune.

mischief *n.* **1**. conduct (especially of children) that is annoying or does slight damage but is not malicious. **2**. a tendency to tease or cause annoyance playfully, *full of mischief.* **3**. harm or damage, *did a lot of mischief.* □ **do someone a mischief,** to injure him. **make mischief,** to cause discord or ill-feeling. **mischief-maker** *n.* a person who does this.

mischievous (**mis**-chiv-ŭs) *adj.* (of a person) full of mischief, (of an action) brought about by mischief. **mischievously** *adv.*

miscible (**mis**-ibŭl) *adj.* able to be mixed.

misconceive (mis-kŏn-**seev**) *v.* to misunderstand, to interpret incorrectly.

misconception (mis-kŏn-**sep**-shŏn) *n.* a wrong interpretation.

misconduct (mis-**kon**-dukt) *n.* **1**. bad behaviour. **2**. adultery. **3**. mismanagement.

misconstrue (mis-kŏn-**stroo**) *v.* to misinterpret. **misconstruction** *n.* misinterpretation.

miscopy *v.* (miscopied, miscopying) to copy incorrectly.

miscount *v.* to count incorrectly. —*n.* an incorrect count.

miscreant (**mis**-kri-ănt) *n.* a wrongdoer, a villain.

misdeal *v.* (misdealt, misdealing) to make a mistake in dealing playing-cards. —*n.* an incorrect dealing.

misdeed *n.* a wrong or improper act, a crime.

misdemeanour (mis-dim-**een**-er) *n.* a misdeed, wrongdoing.

misdirect *v.* to direct incorrectly. **misdirection** *n.*

miser *n.* a person who hoards money and spends as little as possible. **miserly** *adj.*, **miserliness** *n.*

miserable *adj.* 1. full of misery, feeling very unhappy or uneasy or uncomfortable. 2. surly and discontented, disagreeable. 3. unpleasant, *miserable weather*. 4. wretchedly poor in quality or surroundings etc., *a miserable attempt*; *miserable slums*. **miserably** *adv.*

miserere (miz-er-**air**-i) *n.* = misericord, *miserere seats*.

misericord (miz-e-ri-kord) *n.* a small projection on the under-side of a hinged seat in the choir stall of a church, giving support (when the seat was turned up) to a person standing.

misery *n.* 1. a feeling of great unhappiness or discomfort. 2. something causing this. 3. *(informal)* a discontented or disagreeable person.

misfire *v.* 1. (of a gun) to fail to go off correctly. 2. (of an engine etc.) to fail to start, to function correctly. 3. to fail to have the intended effect, *the joke misfired*.

misfit *n.* 1. a garment etc. that does not fit the person it was meant for. 2. a person who is not well suited to his work or his environment.

misfortune *n.* bad luck, an unfortunate event.

misgiving *n.* a feeling of doubt or slight fear or mistrust.

misguided *adj.* mistaken in one's opinions or actions, ill-judged. **misguidedly** *adv.*

mishandle *v.* to deal with (a thing) badly or inefficiently.

mishap (**mis**-hap) *n.* an unlucky accident.

mishear *v.* (misheard, mishearing) to hear incorrectly.

mishmash *n.* a confused mixture.

misinform *v.* to give wrong information to.

misinterpret *v.* to interpret incorrectly. **misinterpretation** *n.*

misjudge *v.* to form a wrong opinion of, to estimate incorrectly. **misjudgement** *n.*

mislay *v.* (mislaid, mislaying) to put (a thing) in a place and be unable to remember where it is, to lose temporarily.

mislead *v.* (misled, misleading) to cause (a person) to gain a wrong impression of something.

mismanage *v.* to manage (affairs) badly or wrongly. **mismanagement** *n.*

misname *v.* to miscall.

misnomer (mis-**noh**-mer) *n.* a name or description that is wrongly applied to something.

misogynist (mis-**oj**-in-ist) *n.* a person who hates women.

misplace *v.* 1. to put (a thing) in the wrong place. 2. to place (one's confidence etc.) unwisely. 3. to use (words or action) in an unsuitable situation, *misplaced humour*.

misprint *n.* an error in printing.

misquote *v.* to quote incorrectly. **misquotation** *n.*

misread *v.* (misread (*pr.* mis-**red**), misreading) to read or interpret incorrectly.

misrepresent *v.* to represent in a false or misleading way. **misrepresentation** *n.*

misrule *n.* bad government.

miss[1] *v.* 1. to fail to hit or reach or catch (an object). 2. to fail to see or hear or understand etc., *we missed the signpost*; *missed that remark*. 3. to fail to catch (a train etc.) or keep (an appointment) or meet (a person), to fail to seize (an opportunity). 4. to omit, to lack. 5. to notice the absence or loss of. 6. to feel regret at the absence or loss of; *old Smith won't be missed*, no one will feel regret at his absence or death. 7. to avoid, *go this way and you'll miss the traffic*. 8. (of an engine etc.) to misfire. —*n.* failure to hit or attain what is aimed at. □ **give a thing a miss**, to avoid it, to leave it alone. **miss out**, to omit. **miss out on**, (*Amer.*) to fail to get benefit or enjoyment from. **miss the boat** *or* **the bus**, (*informal*) to lose an opportunity.

miss[2] *n.* 1. a girl or unmarried woman. 2. *Miss*, a title used of or to a girl or unmarried woman, *Miss Smith* (pl. *the Miss Smiths*); *Miss France, Miss Brighton*, the title of the winner of a beauty contest in the specified region etc. 3. (in shops) one of a range of sizes of garments suitable for women of average build, *Miss size 14*; *misses' dresses*.

Miss. *abbrev.* Mississippi.

missal *n.* a book containing the prayers used in the Mass in the Roman Catholic Church.

misshapen *adj.* badly shaped, distorted.

missile *n.* an object or weapon suitable for throwing or projecting or directing at a target.

missing *adj.* 1. lost, not in its place, *two pages are missing*. 2. not present, *he's always missing when there's work to be done*. 3. absent from home and with one's whereabouts unknown, *she's listed as a missing person*. 4. (of a soldier etc.) neither present after a battle nor known to have been killed. □ **missing link**, a thing lacking to complete a series; a type of animal supposed to have existed between the anthropoid apes and the development of man.

mission *n*. **1**. a body of envoys sent to a foreign country or to an international organization. **2**. an establishment of missionaries. **3**. an organization for spreading the Christian faith, a series of religious services etc. for this purpose. **4**. the work or premises of a religious or other mission. **5**. a person's vocation, *his mission in life*.

missionary *n*. a person who is sent to spread the Christian faith amongst a community.

missis *n*. **1**. (*vulgar*, used by employees) = mistress, a woman in relation to servants etc. **2**. (*humorous*) wife, *how's the missis?* **3**. (*vulgar*) a form of address to a woman, used without her name.

Mississippi a State of the USA.

missive *n*. a written message, a letter.

Missouri a State of the USA.

misspell *v*. (misspelt, misspelling) to spell incorrectly.

misspend *v*. (misspent, misspending) to spend badly or unwisely.

mist *n*. **1**. water vapour near the ground in drops smaller than raindrops, clouding the atmosphere less thickly than fog does. **2**. condensed vapour clouding a window etc. **3**. something resembling mist in its form or effect. —*v*. to cover or become covered with mist, *the windscreen misted up*.

mistakable *adj*. able to be mistaken for another person or thing.

mistake *n*. an incorrect idea or opinion, something done incorrectly; *by mistake*, as the result of carelessness or forgetfulness etc. —*v*. (mistook, mistaken, mistaking) **1**. to misunderstand the meaning or intention of. **2**. to choose or identify wrongly, *mistake one's vocation; she is often mistaken for her sister*. □ **mistaken** *adj*. wrong in one's opinion, *you are mistaken*; applied unwisely, *mistaken kindness*. **mistakenly** *adv*.

mister *n*. (*vulgar*) a form of address to a man, used without his name.

mistime *v*. to say or do (a thing) at a wrong time.

mistletoe *n*. a plant with white berries that grows as a parasite on trees.

mistress *n*. **1**. a woman who is in a position of authority or control. **2**. the female head of a household. **3**. the female owner of a dog or other animal. **4**. a female teacher. **5**. a man's female lover with whom he has a continuing illicit sexual relationship.

mistrust *v*. to feel no trust in. —*n*. lack of trust. —**mistrustful** *adj*.

misty *adj*. (mistier, mistiest) **1**. full of mist. **2**. indistinct in form or idea etc. **mistily** *adv*., **mistiness** *n*.

misunderstand *v*. (misunderstood, misunderstanding) to form an incorrect interpretation or opinion of.

misuse[1] (mis-**yooz**) *v*. **1**. to use wrongly or incorrectly. **2**. to treat badly.

misuse[2] (mis-**yooss**) *n*. wrong or incorrect use.

mite *n*. **1**. a very small spider-like animal found in food, *cheese-mites*. **2**. a very small contribution, *offered a mite of comfort*. **3**. a very small creature, a small child.

mitigate (**mit**-i-gayt) *v*. to make less intense or serious or severe; *mitigating circumstances*, facts that partially excuse wrongdoing. **mitigation** *n*. ¶ Do not confuse with *militate*.

mitre (**my**-ter) *n*. **1**. the tall head-dress worn by bishops and abbots as a symbol of office. **2**. a joint or join of two pieces of wood or cloth etc. with their ends evenly tapered so that together they form a right angle. —*v*. (mitred, mitring) to join in this way, *mitred corners*.

mitt *n*. a mitten.

mitten *n*. a kind of glove that leaves the fingers and thumb-tip bare or that has no partition between the fingers.

mix *v*. **1**. to put different things together so that the substances etc. are no longer distinct, to make or prepare (a thing) by doing this. **2**. to be capable of being blended, *oil will not mix with water*. **3**. to combine, to be able to be combined, *mix business with pleasure; drinking and driving don't mix*. **4**. (of a person) to be sociable or harmonious. —**mix** *n*. **1**. a mixture. **2**. a mixture prepared commercially from suitable ingredients for making something, *cake mix; concrete mix*. □ **mix it**, (*informal*) to start fighting. **mix up**, to mix thoroughly; to confuse (things) in one's mind; to make (a person) feel confused; *be mixed up in a crime* etc., to be involved in it. **mix-up** *n*.

mixed *adj*. **1**. composed of various qualities or elements. **2**. containing people from various races or social classes. **3**. for people of both sexes, *a mixed school*. □ **mixed bag**, an assortment of different things or people. **mixed blessing**, a thing that has advantages and also disadvantages. **mixed doubles**, a doubles game in tennis with a man and woman as partners on each side. **mixed farming**, with both crops and livestock. **mixed feelings**, a mixture of pleasure and dismay at the same event. **mixed**

grill, a dish of various grilled meats and vegetables. **mixed marriage**, a marriage between people of different race or religion. **mixed-up** *adj.* (*informal*) having problems of the emotions and behaviour through not being well-adjusted socially.

mixer *n.* **1.** a device that mixes or blends things, *food-mixers*. **2.** a person who gets on in a certain way with others, *a good mixer*.

mixture *n.* **1.** mixing, being mixed. **2.** something made by mixing, a combination of things or ingredients or qualities etc.

mizen *n.* **1.** a mizen-sail. **2.** a mizen-mast. □ **mizen-mast** *n.* the mast that is next aft of the mainmast. **mizen-sail** *n.* the lowest sail, set lengthways, on a mizen-mast.

ml *abbrev.* millilitre(s).

mm *abbrev.* millimetre(s).

mnemonic (nim-**on**-ik) *adj.* aiding the memory. —*n.* a verse or other aid to help one remember facts.

mo *n.* (*slang*) a moment, *half a mo*.

Mo. *abbrev.* Missouri.

moan *n.* **1.** a low mournful inarticulate sound, usually indicating pain or suffering. **2.** a grumble. —**moan** *v.* **1.** to utter a moan, to say with a moan. **2.** (of wind etc.) to make a sound like a moan. **3.** to grumble.

moat *n.* a deep wide ditch surrounding a castle or house etc., usually filled with water.

moated *adj.* surrounded by a moat.

mob *n.* **1.** a large disorderly crowd of people. **2.** *the mob*, the common people, the rabble. **3.** (*slang*) a gang. —*v.* (mobbed, mobbing) to crowd round in great numbers either to attack or to admire. □ **mob-cap** *n.* a large round cap worn indoors by women in the 18th and early 19th centuries. **mob rule**, rule imposed and enforced by the mob.

mobile (**moh**-byl) *adj.* **1.** movable, not fixed, able to move or be moved easily and quickly. **2.** (of the features of the face) readily changing expression. —*n.* a structure of metal or plastic or cardboard etc. that may be hung so that its parts move freely in currents of air. —**mobility** (moh-**bil**-iti) *n.* □ **mobile home**, a large caravan permanently parked and used as a residence.

mobilize (**moh**-bi-lyz) *v.* **1.** to assemble (troops) for service, to prepare for war or other emergency. **2.** to assemble for a particular purpose, *they mobilized support from all parties*. **mobilization** *n.*

moccasin (**mok**-ă-sin) *n.* a kind of soft leather shoe, stitched round the vamp.

mocha (**moh**-kă) *n.* a kind of coffee, flavouring made with this.

mock *v.* **1.** to make fun of by imitating, to mimic. **2.** to scoff or jeer, to defy contemptuously. —*adj.* sham, imitation, *a mock battle*. □ **mocking-bird** *n.* a bird that mimics the notes of other birds. **mock orange**, a shrub with strongly scented white flowers. **mock turtle soup**, soup made from calf's head or other meat, to resemble turtle soup. **mock-up** *n.* a model of something, to be used for testing or study.

mockery *n.* **1.** ridicule, contempt. **2.** a ridiculous or unsatisfactory imitation, a travesty.

modacrylic (mod-ă-**kril**-ik) *adj.* of a type of acrylic fibre that is more fire-resistant than ordinary acrylic. —*n.* this fibre.

mode *n.* **1.** the way in which a thing is done. **2.** the current fashion.

model *n.* **1.** a three-dimensional reproduction of something, usually on a smaller scale. **2.** a design or style of structure, e.g. of a car, *this year's model*. **3.** a garment by a well-known designer, a copy of this. **4.** a person or thing regarded as excellent of its kind and worthy of imitation. **5.** a person employed to pose for an artist. **6.** a person employed to display clothes in a shop etc. by wearing them. —*adj.* excellent of its kind, exemplary. —*v.* (modelled, modelling) **1.** to make a model of (a thing) in clay or wax etc., to shape (clay etc.) into a model. **2.** to design or plan (a thing) in accordance with a model, *the new method is modelled on the old one*. **3.** to work as an artist's model or as a fashion model, to display (clothes) in this way.

modem (**moh**-děm) *n.* a device linking a computer system and a telephone line so that data can be transmitted at high speeds.

moderate[1] (**mod**-er-ăt) *adj.* **1.** medium in amount or intensity or quality etc. **2.** keeping or kept within reasonable limits, not extreme or excessive; *a moderate climate*, mild, not intensely hot or intensely cold. **3.** not holding extremist views. **moderately** *adv.*

moderate[2] (**mod**-er-ayt) *v.* to make or become moderate or less intense etc. **moderation** *n.* □ **in moderation**, in moderate amounts.

moderator *n.* a Presbyterian minister presiding over a church court or assembly.

modern *adj.* **1.** of the present or recent times, *modern history*. **2.** in current fashion, not antiquated. **3.** (of artistic or literary forms) new and experimental, not following traditional styles. —*n.* a person of modern times or with modern tastes or style. —**modernity** (mŏ-**dern**-iti) *n.*

modernism *n.* modern views or methods. **modernist** *n.* one who favours modernism. **modernistic** *adj.*

modernize *v.* to make modern, to adapt to modern ideas or tastes etc. **modernization** *n.*

modest *adj.* 1. not vain, not boasting about one's merits or achievements. 2. rather shy, not putting oneself forward. 3. moderate in size or amount etc., not showy or splendid in appearance. 4. (of a woman) showing regard for conventional decencies in dress or behaviour. **modestly** *adv.*, **modesty** *n.*

modicum (mod-i-kŭm) *n.* a small amount.

modify *v.* (modified, modifying) 1. to make less severe or harsh or violent. 2. to make partial changes in, *some clauses in the agreement have been modified.* 3. (in grammar) to qualify by describing, *adjectives modify nouns.* **modification** *n.*

modish (**moh**-dish) *adj.* fashionable.

modulate *v.* 1. to adjust or regulate, to moderate. 2. to vary the tone or pitch of (one's voice). 3. to pass from one key to another in music. 4. to alter the amplitude or frequency or phase of (a carrier wave) so as to convey a particular signal. **modulation** *n.*

module (**mod**-yool) *n.* 1. a unit or standard used in measuring. 2. a standardized part or an independent unit in furniture or buildings or a spacecraft etc. □ **modular** *adj.* consisting of independent units.

modus operandi (moh-dŭs op-er-**an**-di) 1. a person's method of working. 2. the way a thing operates.

modus vivendi (moh dŭs viv-**en**-di) an arrangement that enables parties who are in dispute to carry on instead of having their activities paralysed until the dispute has been settled. (¶ Latin, = way of living.)

Mogadishu (mog-ă-**dish**-oo) the capital of Somalia.

mogul (**moh**-gŭl) *n.* (*informal*) an important or influential person.

mohair *n.* 1. the fine silky hair of the angora goat, or a mixture of it with wool or cotton. 2. yarn or fabric made from this.

Mohammedan *adj.* Muslim. —*n.* a Muslim.

Mohican (moh-**hee**-kăn) *n.* a member of a warlike tribe of North American Indians, formerly living in western Connecticut and Massachusetts.

moiré (**mwah**-ray) *n.* fabric that looks like watered silk.

moist *adj.* slightly wet, damp. **moistness** *n.*

moisten (**moi**-sĕn) *v.* to make or become moist.

moisture *n.* water or other liquid diffused through a substance or present in the air as vapour or condensed on a surface.

moisturize *v.* to make (the skin) less dry by use of certain cosmetics. **moisturizer** *n.*

molar (**moh**-ler) *n.* any of the teeth at the back of the jaw that have broad tops and are used for grinding food in chewing. —*adj.* of these teeth.

molasses (mŏ-**las**-iz) *n.* 1. uncrystallized syrup drained from raw sugar. 2. (*Amer.*) treacle.

mole[1] *n.* a small permanent dark spot on the human skin.

mole[2] *n.* a structure built out into the sea as a breakwater or causeway.

mole[3] *n.* 1. a small burrowing animal with dark velvety fur and very small eyes. 2. a person working within an organization who secretly passes confidential information to another organization or country.

molecule (**mol**-i-kewl) *n.* 1. the smallest unit (usually consisting of a group of atoms) into which a substance can be divided while still retaining the substance's chemical qualities. 2. a small particle. **molecular** (mŏ-**lek**-yoo-ler) *adj.*

molehill *n.* a small mound of earth thrown up by a burrowing mole; *make a mountain out of a molehill,* to behave as if a small difficulty were a very great one.

molest (mŏ-**lest**) *v.* to annoy or pester a person in a hostile way or in a way that causes injury. **molestation** *n.*

moll *n.* (*informal*) a gangster's female companion.

mollify *v.* (mollified, mollifying) to soothe the anger of. **mollification** *n.*

mollusc (**mol**-ŭsk) *n.* any of a group of animals which have soft bodies and hard shells (e.g. snails, oysters, mussels) or no shell (e.g. slugs, octopuses).

mollycoddle *v.* to coddle excessively, to pamper. —*n.* a mollycoddled person.

Molotov cocktail a kind of incendiary bomb thrown by hand. ¶ Named after a Russian statesman.

molten (**mohl**-tĕn) *adj.* melted, made liquid by very great heat.

Molucca Islands (mŏ-**luk**-ă) a group of islands in Indonesia. **Moluccan** *adj.* & *n.*

moment *n.* 1. a very brief portion of time. 2. an exact point of time; *he'll be here any moment,* at any time now, very soon. 3. importance, *these are matters of great moment.* □ **at the moment,** now. **for the moment,** for now, temporarily. **in a**

moment, instantly; very soon. **the man of the moment**, the one who is important or the centre of attention now. **moment of truth**, a time of test or crisis (¶ from a Spanish phrase referring to the final sword-thrust in a bull-fight).

momentary (moh-měn-ter-i) *adj*. lasting only a moment. **momentarily** *adv*.

momentous (moh-**ment**-ŭs) *adj*. of great importance.

momentum (moh-**ment**-ŭm) *n*. impetus gained by movement, *the sledge gathered momentum as it ran downhill*.

Monaco (mon-ă-koh) 1. a country on the French Riviera. 2. its capital city. **Monacan** (mon-ă-kăn) *adj*. & *n*., **Monegasque** (mon-i-gask) *adj*. & *n*.

monarch (mon-erk) *n*. 1. a ruler with the title of king, queen, emperor, or empress. 2. a large orange-and-black butterfly. **monarchic** (mon-**ark**-ik), **monarchical** *adjs*.

monarchist (mon-er-kist) *n*. a person who favours government by a monarch or who supports a monarch against opponents of this system. **monarchism** *n*.

monarchy (mon-er-ki) *n*. 1. a form of government in which a monarch is the supreme ruler. 2. a country with this form of government.

monastery (mon-ă-ster-i) *n*. a building in which monks live as a secluded community under religious vows.

monastic (mon-ast-ik) *adj*. of monks or monasteries. **monasticism** (mŏn-ast-i-sizm) *n*. the way of life practised by monks.

monaural (mon-or-ăl) *adj*. monophonic.

Monday *n*. the day of the week following Sunday.

monetarism (mun-it-er-izm) *n*. the theory that governments create inflation by putting more money into the economy. **monetarist** *n*. one who supports this theory.

monetary (mun-it-er-i) *adj*. 1. of a country's currency, *our monetary system*. 2. of or involving money, *its monetary value*.

money *n*. 1. coin, portable pieces of stamped metal in use as a medium of exchange. 2. coins and banknotes. 3. (*pl*. moneys *or* monies) any form of currency. 4. an amount of money, wealth; *there's money in it*, much profit can be made from it. □ **get one's money's worth**, to get good value for one's money. **in the money**, (*informal*) winning money prizes; having plenty of money. **make money**, to make a profit, to become rich by doing this. **marry money**, to marry a rich person.

money-back *adj*. (of a guarantee) promising to return a customer's money if he is not satisfied. **money-bags** *n*. (*slang*) a rich person. **money-box** *n*. a closed box into which savings or contributions are dropped through a slit. **money for jam** *or* **for old rope**, (*slang*) profit for little or no trouble. **money-grubber** *n*. one who is greedily intent on making money. **money-lender** *n*. one whose business it is to lend money in return for payment of interest. **money of account**, a unit of money used in reckoning but not currently issued as coin (e.g. guineas). **money order**, a printed order for the payment of money, issued by the Post Office for payment at any of its branches. **money-spinner** *n*. something that brings in much profit.

moneyed (mun-id) *adj*. wealthy.

Mongol (mong-ŏl) *adj*. Mongolian. —*n*. a Mongolian person.

mongol (mong-ŏl) *n*. a person suffering from mongolism.

Mongolia (mong-oh-liă) a country north of China, formerly extending to East Europe. **Mongolian** *adj*. & *n*.

mongolism (mong-ŏl-izm) *n*. an abnormal congenital condition in which a person has a broad flattened skull, slanting eyes, and mental deficiency.

Mongoloid (mong-ŏ-loid) *adj*. resembling the Mongols in racial characteristics, having yellowish skin, a broad flat face, and straight black hair. —*n*. a Mongoloid person.

mongoose (mon-gooss) *n*. (*pl*. mongooses) a stoat-like tropical animal that can attack and kill venomous snakes.

mongrel (mung-rĕl) *n*. 1. a dog of no definable type or breed. 2. an animal of mixed breed. —*adj*. of mixed origin or character.

monitor *n*. 1. a device used for observing or testing the operation of something. 2. a person who monitors broadcasts etc. 3. a monitor screen. 4. a pupil who is given special duties in a school. —*v*. to keep watch over, to record or test or control the working of. □ **monitor screen**, a TV screen used in a studio to check or select transmissions.

monitress *n*. a girl pupil who is a monitor.

monk *n*. a member of a community of men living apart from the world under the rules of a religious order.

monkey *n*. (*pl*. monkeys) 1. an animal of a group closely related to man, especially one of the small long-tailed species. 2. a mischievous person. —*v*. (monkeyed, monkeying) to play about mischievously;

don't monkey with the switch, do not tamper with it. □ **monkey business,** (*slang*) mischief; underhand dealings. **monkey engine,** a machine hammer of the kind used in pile-driving. **monkey-nut** *n.* a peanut. **monkey puzzle,** an evergreen tree with narrow stiff sharp leaves and interlaced branches. **monkey tricks,** (*slang*) mischief. **monkey-wrench** *n.* a wrench with an adjustable jaw.

monkish *adj.* of or like a monk.

monkshood *n.* a poisonous plant with blue hood-shaped flowers.

mono *adj.* monophonic. —*n.* (*pl.* monos) 1. monophonic sound or recording. 2. a monophonic record.

monochrome (**mon**-ŏ-krohm) *adj.* done in only one colour, black-and-white.

monocle (**mon**-ŏ-kŭl) *n.* an eye-glass for one eye only.

monocular (mŏn-**ok**-yoo-ler) *adj.* with one eye, using or intended for use with one eye. —*n.* a monocular telescope or other optical device.

monogamy (mŏn-**og**-ămi) *n.* the system of being married to only one person at a time.

monogram (**mon**-ŏ-gram) *n.* two or more letters (especially a person's initials) combined in one design. **monogrammed** *adj.* marked with a monogram.

monograph (**mon**-ŏ-grahf) *n.* a scholarly treatise on a single subject or on some aspect of a subject.

monolith (**mon**-ŏ-lith) *n.* a large single upright block of stone.

monolithic (monŏ-**lith**-ik) *adj.* 1. consisting of one or more monoliths. 2. like a monolith in being single and massive, *a monolithic organization.*

monologue (**mon**-ŏ-log) *n.* a long speech by one performer or by one person in a group.

monomania (monŏ-**may**-niă) *n.* an obsession with one idea or interest.

monophonic (mon-ŏ-**fon**-ik) *adj.* (of sound reproduction) using only one transmission channel.

monoplane *n.* a type of aeroplane with only one set of wings.

monopolist (mŏn-**op**-ŏlist) *n.* one who has a monopoly. **monopolistic** *adj.*

monopolize *v.* to take exclusive control or use of; *monopolize the conversation,* give others no chance to join in. **monopolization** *n.*

monopoly (mŏn-**op**-ŏli) *n.* 1. exclusive possession of the sale of some commodity or service. 2. sole possession or control of anything. 3. *Monopoly,* (*trade mark*) a board game in which squares represent properties which players 'buy' with imitation money.

monorail *n.* a railway in which the track consists of a single rail.

monosyllable (**mon**-ŏ-sil-ăbŭl) *n.* a word of one syllable. **monosyllabic** (monŏ-sil-**ab**-ik) *adj.*

monotheism (**mon**-ŏth-ee-ism) *n.* the doctrine that there is only one God. **monotheist** *n.,* **monotheistic** *adj.*

monotone (**mon**-ŏ-tohn) *n.* a level unchanging tone of voice in speaking or singing.

monotonous (mŏn-**ot**-ŏn-ŭs) *adj.* lacking in variety or variation, tiring or boring because of this. **monotonously** *adv.*

monotony (mŏn-**ot**-ŏn-i) *n* a monotonous condition.

monoxide (mŏn-**ok**-syd) *n.* an oxide with one atom of oxygen.

Monrovia (mŏn-**roh**-viă) the capital of Liberia.

Monseigneur (mawn-sen-**yer**) *n.* the title of an eminent Frenchman.

Monsieur (mŏs-**yer**) *n.* (*pl.* Messieurs, *pr.* mes-**yer**) the title of a Frenchman, = Mr or sir.

Monsignor (mon-**seen**-yor) *n.* the title of certain Roman Catholic priests and officials.

monsoon *n.* 1. a seasonal wind blowing in South Asia. 2. the rainy season accompanying the south-west monsoon.

monster *n.* 1. a large ugly or frightening creature. 2. an animal or plant that is very abnormal in form. 3. anything of huge size. 4. an extremely cruel or wicked person.

monstrance (**mon**-stráns) *n.* (in the RC Church) a framed open or transparent holder in which the consecrated bread of the Eucharist is exposed for veneration.

monstrosity (mon-**stros**-iti) *n.* a monstrous thing.

monstrous (**mon**-strŭs) *adj.* 1. like a monster, huge. 2. outrageous, very wrong or absurd.

Mont. *abbrev.* Montana.

montage (mon-**tah**zh) *n.* 1. the joining of a number of short disconnected shots (in a cinema film) to indicate passage of time, change of place, etc. 2. the process of making a composite picture by putting together pieces from other pictures or designs. 3. a picture produced in this way.

Montana (mon-**tan**-ă) a State of the USA.

montbretia (mon-**bree**-shă) *n.* a plant of the iris family with small bright orange-coloured flowers on long stems.

Montevideo (monti-vi-**day**-oh) the capital of Uruguay.

month *n.* **1.** any of the twelve portions into which a year is divided. **2.** the period between the same dates in successive months. □ **month of Sundays**, a very long time.

monthly *adj.* happening or published or payable etc. once a month. —*adv.* once a month. —*n.* a monthly magazine etc.

monument *n.* **1.** anything (especially a structure) designed or serving to celebrate or commemorate a person or event etc. **2.** a structure that is preserved because of its historical importance.

monumental *adj.* **1.** of or serving as a monument, *monumental brasses in the church*. **2.** (of a literary work) massive and of permanent importance. **3.** extremely great, *a monumental achievement* or *blunder*. □ **monumental mason**, a maker of tombstones etc.

moo *n.* the low deep sound made by a cow. —*v.* to make this sound.

mooch *v.* (*slang*) to walk slowly and aimlessly.

mood *n.* **1.** a temporary state of mind or spirits. **2.** the feeling or tone conveyed by a literary or artistic work, *the visual mood of a film*. **3.** a fit of bad temper or depression, *he's in one of his moods*. **4.** a grammatical form of a verb that shows whether it is a statement (e.g. *he stopped*) or a command (e.g. *stop!*) etc.

moody *adj.* (moodier, moodiest) gloomy, sullen, liable to become like this. **moodily** *adv.*, **moodiness** *n.*

moon *n.* **1.** the natural satellite of the earth, made visible by light that it reflects from the sun. **2.** this when it is visible, *there's no moon tonight*. **3.** a natural satellite of any planet. **4.** something regarded as unlikely to be attained, *cry for the moon*; *promised us the moon*, made very extravagant promises. —*v.* to move or look or pass time dreamily or listlessly. □ **moon-daisy** *n.* an ox-eye daisy.

moonbeam *n.* a ray of moonlight.

moonless *adj.* without a moon, *moonless nights*.

moonlight *n.* light from the moon; *a moonlight flit*, see flit. **moonlighting** *n.* (*informal*) having two paid jobs, one during the day and the other in the evening.

moonlit *adj.* lit by the moon.

moonrise *n.* the rising of the moon, the time of this.

moonshine *n.* foolish ideas.

moonstone *n.* a semi-precious stone, a form of felspar with a pearly appearance.

moony *adj.* listless, dreamy.

moor¹ *n.* **1.** a stretch of open uncultivated land with low shrubs (e.g. heather). **2.** this used for preserving game for shooting, *a grouse moor*.

moor² *v.* to secure (a boat or other floating thing) to a fixed object by means of cable(s). **moorings** *pl. n.* cables etc. by which something is moored; a place where a boat is moored.

Moor *n.* a member of a Muslim people living in north-west Africa. **Moorish** *adj.*

moorhen *n.* a small water-bird.

moose *n.* (*pl.* moose) a large animal of North America closely related to or the same as the European elk.

moot *adj.* debatable, undecided, *that's a moot point*. —*v.* to raise (a question) for discussion.

mop *n.* **1.** a bundle of yarn or soft material fastened at the end of a stick, used for cleaning floors. **2.** a small device of similar shape for various purposes, *dish-mop*. **3.** a thick mass of hair. —*v.* (mopped, mopping) to clean or wipe with a mop etc., to wipe away. □ **mop up**, to wipe up with a mop etc.; to finish off a task; to clear (an area) of the remnants of enemy troops etc. after a victory. **Mrs Mopp**, (*informal*) a charwoman.

mope *v.* to be in low spirits and listless.

moped (**moh**-ped) *n.* a motorized bicycle.

moquette (mŏ-**ket**) *n.* a material with raised loops or cut pile used for carpets and upholstery.

moraine (mŏ-**rayn**) *n.* a mass of debris carried down and deposited by a glacier.

moral *adj.* **1.** of or concerned with the goodness and badness of human character or with the principles of what is right and wrong in conduct, *moral philosophy*. **2.** virtuous. **3.** capable of understanding and living by the rules of morality. **4.** based on people's sense of what is right or just, not on legal rights and obligations, *we had a moral obligation to help*. **5.** psychological, mental not physical or concrete, *moral courage*; *moral support*, encouragement and approval. —*n.* a moral lesson or principle. —**morally** *adv.* □ **moral certainty**, a probability so great that no reasonable doubt is possible. **morals** *pl. n.* a person's moral habits, especially sexual conduct. **moral victory**, a triumph, although nothing concrete is obtained by it.

morale (mŏ-**rahl**) *n.* the state of a person's or group's spirits and confidence.

moralist *n.* a person who expresses or teaches moral principles.

morality (mŏ-**ral**-iti) *n.* **1.** moral principles or rules. **2.** a particular system of morals, *commercial morality*. **3.** being moral, conforming to moral principles, goodness or rightness.

moralize v. to talk or write about the principles of right and wrong and conduct etc.

morass (mo-**rass**) n. **1.** a marsh, a bog. **2.** an entanglement, something that confuses or impedes people.

moratorium (mo-ră-**tor**-iŭm) n. (pl. moratoriums) **1.** legal authorization to debtors to postpone payment. **2.** a temporary ban or suspension on some activity, asked for a moratorium on strikes.

morbid adj. **1.** (of the mind or ideas) unwholesome, preoccupied with gloomy or unpleasant things. **2.** caused by or indicating disease, unhealthy, a morbid growth. **morbidly** adv., **morbidness** n., **morbidity** (mor-**bid**-iti) n.

mordant (mor-dănt) adj. characterized by a biting sarcasm, his mordant wit.

more adj. greater in quantity or intensity etc. —n. a greater quantity or number. — adv. **1.** in a greater degree, was more frightened than hurt. **2.** again, once more. ◻ **more or less**, in a greater or less degree; approximately.

morello (mŏ-**rel**-oh) n. (pl. morellos) a bitter kind of dark cherry.

moreover adv. besides, in addition to what has already been said.

morganatic (mor-găn-**at**-ik) adj. (of a marriage) between a man of high rank and a woman of low rank who retains her former status, their children having no claim to the father's possessions or title.

morgue (pr. morg) n. a mortuary.

moribund (morri-bund) adj. in a dying state.

Mormon (mor-mŏn) n. a member of a religious organization (the Church of Jesus Christ of Latter-day Saints) founded in the USA in 1830.

morning n. **1.** the early part of the day, ending at noon or at the midday meal. **2.** sunrise, dawn, when morning broke. **3.** (informal, used as a greeting) = good morning. ◻ **morning after**, (informal) a hangover. **morning dress**, formal dress for a man consisting of a tail-coat, striped trousers, and top hat. **morning glory**, a climbing plant with trumpet-shaped flowers that often close in the afternoons. **morning star**, a bright star or planet (especially Venus) seen in the east before sunrise.

Morocco a country in North Africa. **Moroccan** adj. & n.

morocco n. a fine flexible leather made (originally in Morocco) from goatskins, or an imitation of this.

moron (mor-on) n. **1.** an adult with intelligence equal to that of an average child of 8–12 years. **2.** (informal) a very stupid person. **moronic** (mŏ-**ron**-ik) adj.

morose (mŏ-**rohss**) adj. sullen, gloomy, and unsociable. **morosely** adv., **moroseness** n.

morphia (mor-fiă) n. = morphine.

morphine (mor-feen) n. a drug made from opium, used for relieving pain.

morris dance a traditional English folkdance performed by men in costume with ribbons and bells, **morris dancers**.

morrow n. (old use) the following day.

Morse n. the **Morse code** (used in signalling) in which letters of the alphabet are represented by various combinations of short and long sounds or flashes of light (dots and dashes).

morsel n. a small quantity, a small amount or piece of food.

mortal adj. **1.** subject to death. **2.** causing death, fatal, a mortal wound. **3.** deadly, lasting until death, mortal enemies; in mortal combat. **4.** (slang) intense, in mortal fear. **5.** (slang) without exception, sold every mortal thing. —n. a person who is subject to death, a human being. —**mortally** adv. ◻ **mortal sin**, (in RC teaching) sin that causes death of the soul or that is fatal to salvation.

mortality (mor-**tal**-iti) n. **1.** being mortal, subject to death. **2.** loss of life on a large scale. ◻ **mortality rate**, the death rate. **mortality tables**, tables showing the expectation of life of people according to their age.

mortar n. **1.** a mixture of lime or cement with sand and water, for joining bricks or stones. **2.** a vessel of hard material in which substances are pounded with a pestle. **3.** a short cannon for firing shells at a high angle. —v. to plaster or join (bricks etc.) with mortar. ◻ **mortar-board** n. a cap with a stiff square top worn as part of academic dress.

mortgage (mor-gij) v. to give someone a claim on (property) as security for payment of a debt or loan. —n. **1.** mortgaging. **2.** an agreement giving a claim of this kind. **3.** the amount of money borrowed or lent against the security of a property in this way. ◻ **mortgagee** (mor-gij-ee) n. a person or firm (e.g. a building society) to whom property is mortgaged. **mortgager** or **mortgagor** (mor-gij-or) ns. one who mortgages his property.

mortician (mor-**tish**-ăn) n. (Amer.) an undertaker.

mortify v. (mortified, mortifying) **1.** to humiliate greatly. **2.** to subdue by discipline or self-denial. **3.** (of flesh) to become gangrenous. **mortification** *n.*

mortise (mor-tiss) *n.* a hole in one part of a wooden structure into which the end of another part is inserted so that the two are held together. —*v.* to cut a mortise in, to join with a mortise. □ **mortise lock**, a lock that is set into (not on) the framework of a door.

mortuary (mor-tew-er-i) *n.* a place where dead bodies may be kept temporarily.

mosaic (mŏ-zay-ik) *n.* a pattern or picture made by placing together small pieces of glass or stone etc. of different colours.

Mosaic (mŏ-zay-ik) *adj.* of Moses or his teaching, *Mosaic Law.*

Moscow the capital of the USSR.

moselle (moh-zel) *n.* a dry white wine from the Moselle valley in Germany.

Moslem (moz-lĕm) *adj. & n.* = Muslim.

mosque (*pr.* mosk) *n.* a Muslim place of worship.

mosquito (mos-kee-toh) *n.* (*pl.* mosquitoes) a kind of gnat, the female of which bites and sucks blood from men and animals.

moss *n.* a small flowerless plant that forms a dense growth on moist surfaces or in bogs. **moss-rose** *n.* a cultivated variety of rose with a moss-like growth on the stem and calyx. **moss-stitch** *n.* a pattern formed of alternating plain and purl stitches in knitting.

mossy *adj.* (mossier, mossiest) like moss, covered in moss.

most *adj.* greatest in quantity or intensity etc. —*n.* the greatest quantity or number. —*adv.* **1.** in the greatest degree. **2.** very, *a most amusing book.* □ **at most** *or* **at the most,** not more than. **for the most part,** in most cases, in most of its extent. **make the most of,** to use to the best advantage; to represent at its best or at its worst.

mostly *adv.* for the most part.

MOT *abbrev.* (*formerly*) Ministry of Transport. **MOT test,** (*informal*) a compulsory annual test of cars of more than a specified age.

motel (moh-tel) *n.* a roadside hotel or group of furnished cabins providing accommodation for motorists and their vehicles.

moth *n.* **1.** an insect resembling a butterfly but usually flying at night. **2.** a small similar insect that lays its eggs in cloth or fur fabrics on which its larvae feed. □ **mothball** *n.* a small ball of pungent substance for keeping moths away from clothes; *in moth-balls,* stored out of use for a considerable time. **moth-eaten** *adj.* damaged by moth-larvae; antiquated, decrepit.

mother *n.* **1.** a female parent. **2.** a quality

or condition that gives rise to another, *necessity is the mother of invention.* **3.** a woman who is head of a female religious community, *Mother Superior.* **4.** (*informal*) a title used in addressing an old woman. **5.** an apparatus generating warmth, used for rearing chickens without a hen. —*v.* to look after in a motherly way. — **motherhood** *n.* □ **mother country,** a country in relation to its colonies. **Mothering Sunday,** the fourth Sunday in Lent, with a custom of giving a gift to one's mother. **mother-in-law** *n.* (*pl.* mothers-in-law) the mother of one's wife or husband. **mother-in-law's tongue,** a plant with very long pointed leaves blotched with yellow. **mother-of-pearl** *n.* a pearly substance lining the shells of oysters and mussels etc. **Mother's Day,** Mothering Sunday. **mother tongue,** one's native language.

mothercraft *n.* skill in looking after one's children as a mother.

motherland *n.* one's native country.

motherless *adj.* without a living mother.

motherly *adj.* like a mother, showing a mother's kindliness and tenderness. **motherliness** *n.*

motif (moh-teef) *n.* **1.** a recurring design or feature in a literary or artistic work. **2.** a short melody or theme that recurs and is developed in a piece of music. **3.** an ornament sewn on a dress etc.

motion *n.* **1.** moving, change of position. **2.** manner of movement. **3.** change of posture, a particular movement, a gesture. **4.** a formal proposal that is to be discussed and voted on at a meeting. **5.** emptying of the bowels, faeces. —*v.* to make a gesture directing a person to do something, *motioned him to sit beside her.* □ **go through the motions,** to do something in a perfunctory or insincere manner. **in motion,** moving, not at rest. **motion picture,** a story or record of events recorded on cine film for showing to an audience in a cinema or elsewhere.

motionless *adj.* not moving.

motivate (moh-tiv-ayt) *v.* **1.** to give a motive or incentive to, to be the motive of, *she was motivated by kindness.* **2.** to stimulate the interest of, to inspire. **motivation** *n.* □ **motivated** *adj.* having a definite and positive desire to do things.

motive *n.* that which induces a person to act in a certain way. —*adj.* producing movement or action; *motive power,* that which drives machinery etc.

motley *adj.* **1.** multi-coloured. **2.** made up of various sorts, *a motley collection.*

motor *n.* **1.** a machine that supplies motive power for a vehicle or boat etc. or for another device with moving parts, an internal combustion engine. **2.** a motor car. —**motor** *adj.* **1.** giving or producing motion; *motor nerves,* those that carry impulses from the brain etc. to the muscles. **2.** driven by a motor, *motor boat; motor mower.* **3.** of or for motor vehicles, *the motor show.* —*v.* to go or convey in a motor car. □ **motor bike,** (*informal*) a motor cycle. **motor car,** a short-bodied motor vehicle that can carry a driver and usually passengers. **motor cycle,** a two-wheeled motor-driven road vehicle that cannot be driven by pedals. **motor-cyclist** *n.* one who rides a motor cycle. **motor vehicle,** a vehicle with a motor engine, for use on ordinary roads.

motorcade *n.* (*Amer.*) a procession or parade of motor vehicles.

motorist *n.* the driver of a motor car.

motorize *v.* **1.** to equip with a motor or motors. **2.** to equip (troops) with motor vehicles.

motorway *n.* a road specially constructed and controlled for fast motor traffic.

mottled *adj.* marked or patterned with irregular patches of colour.

motto *n.* (*pl.* mottoes) **1.** a short sentence or phrase adopted as a rule of conduct or as expressing the aims and ideals of a family or country or institution etc. **2.** a maxim or verse or riddle etc. inside a paper cracker.

mould[1] *n.* **1.** a hollow container into which a soft or liquid substance is poured to set or cool into a desired shape. **2.** a pudding etc. made in a mould. —**mould** *v.* **1.** to cause to have a certain shape, to produce by shaping. **2.** to guide or control the development of, *mould a person's character.*

mould[2] *n.* a fine furry growth of very small fungi, forming on things that lie in moist warm air.

mould[3] *n.* soft fine loose earth that is rich in organic matter, *leaf-mould.*

moulder[1] *n.* **1.** a person who moulds or shapes things. **2.** a workman who makes moulds for casting metal.

moulder[2] *v.* to decay into dust, to rot away.

moulding *n.* a moulded object, especially an ornamental strip of plaster or wood etc. decorating or outlining something.

mouldy *adj.* (mouldier, mouldiest) **1.** covered with mould. **2.** stale, smelling of mould. **3.** (*slang*) dull, worthless. **mouldiness** *n.*

moult (*pr.* mohlt) *v.* (of a bird or animal or insect) to shed feathers or hair or skin etc. before a new growth. —*n.* the process of moulting.

mound *n.* a mass of piled-up earth or stones, a small hill.

mount[1] *n.* a mountain or hill, *Mount Everest.*

mount[2] *v.* **1.** to ascend, to go upwards, to rise to a higher level. **2.** to get or put on to a horse etc. for riding, to provide with a horse for riding. **3.** to increase in amount or total or intensity, *the death toll mounted.* **4.** to put into place on a support, to fix in position for use or display or study. **5.** to take action to effect (something); *mount an offensive,* to arrange and begin it. **6.** to place on guard, *mount sentries round the palace; mount guard over it,* keep watch to protect it. —**mount** *n.* **1.** a horse for riding. **2.** something on which a thing is mounted for support or display etc. □ **mounted** *adj.* serving on horseback, *mounted police.*

mountain *n.* **1.** a mass of land that rises to a great height, especially of over 1000 ft. **2.** a large heap or pile, a huge quantity. **3.** a large surplus stock, *the butter mountain.* □ **mountain ash,** the rowan tree.

mountaineer *n.* a person who is skilled in mountain climbing. **mountaineering** *n.* the sport of climbing mountains.

mountainous *adj.* **1.** full of mountains, *mountainous country.* **2.** huge.

mountebank (**mownt**-i-bank) *n.* a swindler or charlatan.

Mountie *n.* (*informal*) a member of the Royal Canadian Mounted Police.

mourn *v.* to feel or express sorrow for a person who has died or regret for a thing that is lost or past. **mourner** *n.* one who mourns, one who attends a funeral.

mournful *adj.* sorrowful, showing grief. **mournfully** *adv.,* **mournfulness** *n.*

mourning *n.* black or dark clothes worn as a conventional sign of bereavement.

mousaka (moo-**sah**-kă) *n.* a Greek dish consisting of layers of minced meat and aubergine, usually topped with cheese sauce.

mouse *n.* (*pl.* mice) **1.** a small rodent with a long thin tail. **2.** a shy or timid person. □ **mouse-coloured** *adj.* dull greyish-brown.

mouser *n.* a cat as a hunter of mice.

mousetrap *n.* **1.** a trap for catching mice. **2.** (*informal*) cheese of poor quality.

mousing *n.* hunting mice.

mousse (*pr.* mooss) *n.* **1.** a dish of cream or a similar substance flavoured with fruit or chocolate. **2.** meat or fish purée mixed with cream etc. and shaped in a mould.

mousseline (**mooss**-lin) *n.* a kind of thin soft dress material.

moustache (mŭs-**tahsh**) *n.* hair allowed to grow on a man's upper lip.

mousy *adj.* **1.** mouse-coloured. **2.** quiet and shy or timid.

mouth[1] (*pr.* mow*th*) *n.* **1.** the opening through which food is taken into an animal's body. **2.** (*slang*) talkativeness, impudence. **3.** the opening of a bag, cave, cannon, trumpet, etc. **4.** the place where a river enters the sea. □ **keep one's mouth shut,** (*slang*) to refrain from revealing a secret. **mouth-watering** *adj.* making one's mouth water, appetizing. **out of a person's own mouth,** by using his own words. **put words into a person's mouth,** to tell him what to say; to represent him as having said this. **take words out of a person's mouth,** to say what he was about to say.

mouth[2] (*pr.* mow*th*) *v.* **1.** to form (words) with the lips without speaking them aloud. **2.** to declaim words pompously or with exaggerated distinctness.

mouthful *n.* **1.** an amount that fills the mouth. **2.** a small quantity of food etc. **3.** a lengthy word or phrase, one that is difficult to utter. **4.** (*Amer. slang*) an important statement, *you've said a mouthful.*

mouth-organ *n.* a small rectangular wind-instrument played by passing it along the lips while blowing or sucking air.

mouthpiece *n.* **1.** the part of a device or musical instrument etc. that is placed between or near the lips. **2.** a person who speaks on behalf of another or others.

mouthwash *n.* a liquid for cleansing the mouth.

movable *adj.* able to be moved; *a movable feast,* one that changes its date each year (e.g. Easter). **movables** *pl. n.* furniture and other possessions that can be moved, not fixtures.

move *v.* **1.** to change or cause to change in position or place or posture. **2.** to be or cause to be in motion. **3.** to change one's place of residence. **4.** to cause (bowels) to empty, to be emptied thus. **5.** to make progress, *the work moves slowly.* **6.** to make a move at chess etc. **7.** to provoke a reaction or emotion in, *moved her to laughter; felt very moved,* very affected with emotion. **8.** to prompt or incline, to motivate, *what moved them to invite us?; he works as the spirit moves him,* only when he chooses. **9.** to put forward formally for discussion and decision at a meeting. **10.** to initiate some action, *unless the employers move quickly, there will be a strike.* **11.** to live or be active in a particular group, *she moves in the best circles.* —**move** *n.* **1.** the act or process of moving. **2.** the moving of a piece in chess etc., a player's turn to do this. **3.** a

calculated action done to achieve some purpose, *a move towards settling the dispute.* —**mover** *n.* □ **get a move on,** (*informal*) to hurry. **move in,** to take possession of a new dwelling-place etc. **move over** *or* **up,** to alter position in order to make room for another. **on the move,** moving from one place to another; progressing.

movement *n.* **1.** moving, being moved. **2.** action, activity, *watch every movement.* **3.** the moving parts in mechanism especially of a clock or watch. **4.** a series of combined actions by a group to achieve some purpose, the group itself, *the Women's Lib movement.* **5.** a trend, *the movement towards more casual styles in fashion.* **6.** market activity in some commodity; *the movement in stocks and shares,* their rise and fall in price. **7.** one of the principal divisions in a long musical work.

movie *n.* (*Amer. informal*) a cinema film.

moving *adj.* affecting the emotions, *a very moving story.* **moving pavement,** a structure like a conveyer belt for carrying pedestrians. **moving picture,** a motion picture. **moving staircase,** an escalator.

mow (*rhymes with* go) *v.* (mowed, mown, mowing) to cut down (grass or grain etc.), to cut the grass etc. from, *mow the lawn.* **mow down,** to kill or destroy at random or in great numbers. **mower** *n.* a person or machine that mows.

Mozambique (moh-zam-**beek**) a country in East Africa. **Mozambican** *n.*

MP *abbrev.* Member of Parliament. ¶ Note the placing or absence of an apostrophe in *MPs* (= Members of Parliament), *an MP's salary, MPs' salaries.*

m.p.h. *abbrev.* miles per hour.

Mr *n.* (*pl.* Messrs) the title prefixed to a man's name or to the name of his office, *Mr Jones; Mr Speaker.*

Mrs *n.* (*pl.* Mrs) the title prefixed to a married woman's name.

Ms (*pr.* miz) *n.* the title prefixed to a woman's name without distinction of married or unmarried status.

MS *abbrev.* (*pl.* MSS) manuscript.

Mt. *abbrev.* Mount.

much *adj.* existing in great quantity. —*n.* a great quantity. —*adv.* **1.** in a great degree, *much to my surprise.* **2.** approximately, *much the same.* □ **much as,** even though, however much, *I can't go, much as I should like to.* **I thought as much,** I thought so. **much of a muchness,** very alike, very nearly the same. **not much,** (*slang*) certainly not; *not much of a poet,* (*informal*) not a good one.

muck *n.* **1.** farmyard manure. **2.** (*informal*) dirt, filth. **3.** (*informal*) untidy things, a mess. —*v.* to make dirty, to mess. □ **make a muck of**, (*slang*) to bungle. **muck about** *or* **around**, (*slang*) to mess about. **muck in**, (*slang*) to share tasks or expenses equally. **muck out**, to remove muck from, *mucking out the stables*. **muck-raking** *n.* seeking for and exposing scandal. **muck sweat**, (*slang*) a profuse sweat. **muck up**, (*slang*) to spoil.

mucky *adj.* (muckier, muckiest) covered with muck, dirty.

mucous (mew-kŭs) *adj.* of or like mucus, covered with mucus; *mucous membrane*, the moist skin lining the nose, mouth, throat, etc.

mucus (mew-kŭs) *n.* the moist sticky substance that lubricates and forms a protective covering on the inner surface of hollow organs of the body.

mud *n.* **1.** wet soft earth. **2.** a chemical fluid used as a coolant and lubricant and to prevent leakage when drilling for oil or gas. □ *his name is mud*, (*informal*) he is in disgrace. **mud-flap** *n.* a flap behind the wheel of a vehicle to prevent mud etc. from being thrown up as it travels. **mud-flats** *pl. n.* stretches of muddy land left uncovered at low tide. **mud-slinging** *n.* (*slang*) speaking evil of someone, trying to damage someone's reputation.

muddle *v.* **1.** to bring into a state of confusion and disorder. **2.** to confuse (a person) mentally. **3.** to confuse or mistake (one thing for another). —*n.* a muddled condition, disorder. —**muddler** *n.* □ **muddle-headed** *adj.* liable to muddle things, mentally confused. **muddle on** *or* **along**, to work in a haphazard way. **muddle through**, to succeed in the end in spite of one's inefficiency.

muddy *adj.* (muddier, muddiest) **1.** like mud, full of mud. **2.** (of colour) not clear or pure. —*v.* (muddied, muddying) to make muddy. —**muddiness** *n.*

mudguard *n.* a curved cover above the wheel of a cycle etc. to protect the rider from the mud it throws up.

mudlark *n.* **1.** a child who plays in mud. **2.** a person who scavenges articles from the mud, e.g. beside a tidal river.

muesli (mooz-li) *n.* a food of mixed crushed cereals, dried fruit, nuts, etc.

muezzin (moo-ez-in) *n.* a man who proclaims the hours of prayer for Muslims, usually from a minaret.

muff [1] *n.* a short tube-like covering of fur etc. into which both hands are thrust from opposite ends to keep them warm.

muff [2] *v.* (*informal*) to bungle or blunder.

muffin *n.* a light flat round spongy cake, eaten toasted and buttered.

muffle *v.* **1.** to wrap or cover for warmth or protection. **2.** to wrap up or pad in order to deaden the sound of. **3.** to deaden, to make less loud or less distinct.

muffler *n.* **1.** a scarf worn round the neck for warmth. **2.** something used to muffle sound.

mufti *n.* plain clothes worn by one who has the right to wear uniform, *in mufti*.

mug [1] *n.* **1.** a large drinking-vessel (usually with a handle) for use without a saucer. **2.** its contents. **3.** (*slang*) the face or mouth. **4.** (*slang*) a person who is easily deceived. —*v.* (mugged, mugging) to rob (a person) with violence, especially in a public place. —**mugger** *n.* □ **a mug's game**, (*slang*) an activity that is unlikely to bring profit or reward.

mug [2] *v.* (*slang*) to learn (a subject) by studying hard, *mugged it up*.

muggins *n.* (*informal*) a person who is easily deceived or victimized.

muggy *adj.* (muggier, muggiest) oppressively damp and warm, *a muggy day*; *muggy weather*. **mugginess** *n.*

mulatto (mew-lat-oh) *n.* (*pl.* mulattos) a person who has one white and one Black parent.

mulberry *n.* **1.** a purple or white fruit rather like a blackberry. **2.** the tree that bears it. **3.** dull purplish-red.

mulch *n.* a mixture of wet straw, grass, leaves, etc., spread on the ground to protect plants or retain moisture. —*v.* to cover with a mulch.

mulct *v.* to take away money from (a person), e.g. by a fine or taxation, or by dubious means.

mule [1] *n.* an animal that is the offspring of a horse and a donkey, known for its stubbornness.

mule [2] *n.* a backless slipper.

mulish (mewl-ish) *adj.* stubborn. **mulishly** *adv.*, **mulishness** *n.*

mull [1] *v.* to heat (wine or beer etc.) with sugar and spices, as a drink.

mull [2] *v.* **mull over**, to think over, to ponder, *mulled it over*.

mull [3] *n.* (*Scottish*) a promontory, *Mull of Kintyre*.

mullah (mul-ă) *n.* a Muslim who is learned in Islamic theology and sacred law.

mullein (mul-in) *n.* a biennial herb with downy leaves and tall spikes of yellow flowers.

mullet (mul-it) *n.* a kind of fish used for food, *red mullet*; *grey mullet*.

mulligatawny (mul-ig-ă-taw-ni) *n.* a highly seasoned soup flavoured like curry.

mullion (**mul**-iŏn) *n.* an upright strip between the panes of a tall window.

multi- *prefix* many, *multi-coloured.* **multi-access** *adj.* (of a computer) able to serve several terminals at the same time.

multifarious (multi-**fair**-iŭs) *adj.* very varied, of many kinds, *his multifarious duties.*

multilateral (multi-**lat**-er-ăl) *adj.* (of an agreement etc.) involving three or more parties.

multimillionaire *n.* a person with a fortune of several million pounds or dollars etc.

multinational *adj.* (of a business company) operating in several countries. —*n.* a multinational company.

multiple *adj.* having several or many parts or elements or components. —*n.* a quantity that contains another (a *factor*) a number of times without remainder, *30 is a multiple of 10.* □ **multiple sclerosis,** a chronic progressive disease in which patches of tissue harden in the brain or spinal cord, causing partial or complete paralysis. **multiple shop** *or* **store,** a chain store.

multiplex *adj.* having many parts or forms, consisting of many elements.

multiplication *n.* multiplying, being multiplied. **multiplication sign,** the sign × (as in 2 × 3) indicating that one quantity is to be multiplied by another. **multiplication tables,** a series of lists showing the results when a number is multiplied by each number (especially 1 to 12) in turn.

multiplicity (multi-**plis**-iti) *n.* a great variety.

multiplier *n.* the number by which a quantity is multiplied.

multiply *v.* (multiplied, multiplying) **1.** (in mathematics) to take a specified quantity a specified number of times and find the quantity produced, *multiply 6 by 4 and get 24.* **2.** to make or become many; *multiply examples,* to produce large numbers of examples; *rabbits multiply rapidly,* they increase in number by breeding.

multiracial (multi-**ray**-shăl) *adj.* composed of people of many races, *a multiracial society.*

multi-storey *adj.* having several storeys, *a multi-storey block of flats.*

multitude *n.* a great number of things or people; *the multitude,* the common people.

multitudinous (multi-**tewd**-in-ŭs) *adj.* very numerous.

mum¹ *adj.* (*informal*) silent, *keep mum; mum's the word,* say nothing about this.

mum² *n.* (*informal*) mother.

mumble *v.* to speak or utter indistinctly. —*n.* indistinct speech. **mumbler** *n.*

mumbo-jumbo *n.* **1.** meaningless ritual. **2.** words or actions that are deliberately obscure in order to mystify or confuse people.

mummer *n.* an actor in a traditional mime.

mummify *v.* (mummified, mummifying) to preserve (a corpse) by embalming it as in ancient Egypt.

mummy¹ *n.* **1.** the body of a person or animal embalmed for burial so as to preserve it, especially in ancient Egypt. **2.** a dried-up body preserved from decay by an accident of nature.

mummy² *n.* (*informal*) mother.

mumps *n.* a virus disease that causes painful swellings in the neck.

munch *v.* to chew steadily and vigorously.

mundane (mun-**dayn**) *adj.* **1.** dull, routine. **2.** worldly, not spiritual.

municipal (mew-**nis**-i-păl) *adj.* of a town or city or its self-government.

municipality (mew-nis-i-**pal**-iti) *n.* a self-governing town or district.

munificent (mew-**nif**-i-sĕnt) *adj.* splendidly generous. **munificently** *adv.,* **munificence** *n.*

muniments (**mew**-ni-mĕnts) *pl. n.* title-deeds and similar records.

munitions (mew-**nish**-ŏnz) *pl. n.* military weapons and ammunition and equipment etc.

mural (**mewr**-ăl) *adj.* of or on a wall. —*n.* a wall-painting, a fresco.

murder *n.* **1.** the intentional and unlawful killing of one person by another. **2.** (*informal*) something very difficult or unpleasant or painful. —**murder** *v.* **1.** to kill (a person) unlawfully and intentionally. **2.** (*informal*) to ruin by bad performance or pronunciation etc. —**murderer** *n.,* **murderess** *n.*

murderous *adj.* **1.** involving murder, capable of or intent on murder. **2.** very angry, suggesting murder, *a murderous look.*

murky *adj.* (murkier, murkiest) **1.** dark, gloomy. **2.** (of liquid) muddy, full of sediment. **3.** secretly scandalous, *his murky past.* **murkiness** *n.*

murmur *n.* **1.** a low continuous sound. **2.** a low abnormal sound made by the heart. **3.** softly spoken words. **4.** a subdued expression of feeling, *murmurs of discontent.* —*v.* to make a murmur, to speak or utter in a low voice.

muscat (**musk**-ăt) *n.* a musk-flavoured grape.

Muscat (**musk**-at) the capital of Oman.

muscatel (musk-ă-**tel**) *n.* a muscat or a raisin made from this.

muscle *n.* **1.** a band or bundle of fibrous tissue able to contract and relax and so produce movement in an animal body. **2.** a part of the body made chiefly of such tissue. **3.** muscular power. **4.** strength, *trade unions with plenty of muscle.* —*v.* **muscle in,** (*Amer. slang*) to force one's way.

Muscovite (**musk**-ŏ-vyt) *adj.* of Moscow. —*n.* a native or inhabitant of Moscow.

muscular *adj.* **1.** of or affecting the muscles. **2.** having well-developed muscles. **muscularity** (mus-kew-**la**-riti) *n.*

muse *v.* to ponder.

Muse *n.* one of the nine sister goddesses in Greek and Roman mythology, presiding over branches of learning and the arts.

museum *n.* a building or room in which antiques or other objects of historical or scientific interest are collected and exhibited. **museum piece** *n.* a fine specimen suitable for a museum; (*contemptuous*) an antiquated person or thing.

mush *n.* soft pulp.

mushroom *n.* **1.** an edible fungus with a stem and domed cap, noted for its rapid growth. **2.** pale yellowish-brown. — **mushroom** *v.* **1.** to spring up rapidly in large numbers, *launderettes mushroomed in all towns.* **2.** to rise and spread in the shape of a mushroom.

mushy *adj.* (mushier, mushiest) **1.** as or like mush. **2.** feebly sentimental. **mushiness** *n.*

music *n.* **1.** the art of arranging the sounds of voice(s) or instrument(s) or both in a pleasing sequence or combination. **2.** the sound(s) or composition(s) produced, a written or printed score for this. **3.** any pleasant sound or series of sounds, e.g. bird-song. □ **music centre,** equipment combining a radio, record-player, and tape recorder. **music-hall** *n.* a hall or theatre used for variety entertainment, the entertainment itself.

musical *adj.* **1.** of music; *musical instruments,* devices producing music by means of tuned strings or membranes or air in pipes, or electronically. **2.** fond of or skilled in music. **3.** accompanied by music, set to music. —*n.* a musical comedy, a cinema film resembling this. —**musically** *adv.* □ **musical box,** a box with a mechanical device that produces music by means of a toothed cylinder which strikes a comb-like metal plate. **musical chairs,** a game in which players walk round chairs (one fewer than the number of players) till the music stops, when the one who finds no chair is eliminated and a chair is removed before the next round. **musical comedy,** a light play in which songs and dancing alternate with the dialogue.

musician *n.* a person who is skilled at music, one whose profession is music.

musk *n.* **1.** a substance secreted by the male musk-deer or certain other animals, or produced artificially, used as the basis of perfumes. **2.** a plant with a musky smell. □ **musk-deer** *n.* a small hornless deer of Central Asia. **musk-rat** *n.* a large rat-like water animal of North America, valued for its fur (*musquash*). **musk-rose** *n.* a rambling rose with large white flowers that have a musky fragrance.

musket *n.* a long-barrelled gun formerly used by infantry, now replaced by the rifle. **musketeer** *n.* a soldier armed with this.

musky *adj.* smelling like musk.

Muslim *n.* one who believes in the Islamic faith. —*adj.* of Muslims or their faith.

muslin *n.* a kind of thin cotton cloth.

musquash (**mus**-kwosh) *n.* **1.** the musk-rat. **2.** its fur.

muss *v.* **muss up,** (*Amer. informal*) to make untidy.

mussel *n.* a kind of bivalve mollusc, the marine variety of which is edible.

must [1] *auxiliary verb,* used to express necessity or obligation (*you must go*), certainty (*night must fall*), insistence (*I must repeat, all precautions were taken*). —*n.* (*informal*) a thing that should not be overlooked or missed, *the exhibition is a must.*

must [2] *n.* grape-juice etc. undergoing fermentation, new wine.

mustang (**mus**-tang) *n.* a wild horse of Mexico and California.

mustard *n.* **1.** a plant with yellow flowers and with black or white sharp-tasting seeds in long pods. **2.** these seeds ground and made into paste as a condiment. **3.** darkish yellow colour. —*adj.* darkish yellow. □ **mustard gas,** a kind of poison gas that burns the skin.

muster *v.* **1.** to assemble or cause to assemble. **2.** to summon, *muster* or *muster up one's strength.* —*n.* an assembly or gathering of people or things. □ **pass muster,** to be accepted as adequate.

mustn't = must not.

musty *adj.* (mustier, mustiest) **1.** stale, smelling or tasting mouldy. **2.** antiquated. **mustiness** *n.*

mutable (**mew**-tă-bŭl) *adj.* liable to change, fickle. **mutability** *n.*

mutant (**mew**-tănt) *n.* a living thing that differs basically from its parents as a result of genetic change. —*adj.* differing in this way.

mutate (mew-**tayt**) v. to undergo or cause to undergo mutation. **mutation** n. change or alteration in form; a mutant.

mutatis mutandis (moo-tah-teess moo-tan-deess) when the necessary alteration of details has been made (in comparing things). (¶ Latin.)

mute adj. 1. silent, refraining from speaking. 2. not having the power of speech, dumb. 3. not expressed in words, *in mute adoration.* 4. (of a letter) not pronounced, *the e in 'house' is mute.* 5. (of colour) subdued. —**mute** n. 1. a dumb person. 2. a device fitted to a musical instrument to deaden its sound. —v. to deaden or muffle the sound of. —**mutely** adv., **muteness** n.

mutilate v. to injure or disfigure by cutting off an important part. **mutilation** n., **mutilator** n.

mutineer (mew-tin-**eer**) n. one who mutinies.

mutinous (mew-tin-ŭs) adj. rebellious, ready to mutiny. **mutinously** adv.

mutiny (mew-tin-i) n. open rebellion against authority, especially by members of the armed forces against their officers. —v. (mutinied, mutinying) to engage in mutiny.

mutt n. (*slang*) a stupid person.

mutter v. 1. to speak or utter in a low unclear tone. 2. to utter subdued grumbles. —n. muttering, muttered words.

mutton n. the flesh of sheep as food. **mutton dressed as lamb,** (*informal*) a middle-aged or elderly woman dressed in too youthful a style.

mutual (mew-tew-ăl) adj. 1. (of a feeling or action) felt or done by each towards or to the other, *mutual affection*; *mutual aid.* 2. having the same specified relationship to each other, *mutual enemies.* 3. (*informal*) common to two or more people, *our mutual friend.* (¶ Many people object to the use in sense 3 although it was used by Dickens, George Eliot, and others; the alternative word 'common' could be taken to mean 'ill-bred'.) **mutually** adv.

Muzak (mew-zak) n. (*trade mark*) piped music, recorded light music as a background.

muzzle n. 1. the projecting nose and jaws of certain animals (e.g. dogs). 2. the open end of a firearm. 3. a strap or wire etc. put over an animal's head to prevent it from biting or feeding. —**muzzle** v. 1. to put a muzzle on (an animal). 2. to silence, to prevent (a person or newspaper etc.) from expressing opinions freely.

muzzy adj. dazed, feeling stupefied. **muzziness** n.

MW *abbrev.* megawatt(s).

mW *abbrev.* milliwatt(s).

my adj. 1. of or belonging to me. 2. used in forms of address (*my lord, my dear*), or exclamations of surprise etc. (*my God!*).

myalgia (my-**al**-jiă) n. pain in the muscles.

Mycenaean (my-sin-ee-ăn) adj. of a Bronze Age civilization of Greece, remains of which were found at Mycenae in the Peloponnese and elsewhere. —n. 1. a member of this civilization. 2. its language.

mynah (my-nă) n. = mina.

myopia (my-oh-piă) n. short-sightedness.

myopic (my-op-ik) adj. short-sighted.

myosotis (my-ŏ-soh-tiss) n. the forget-me-not and flowers related to this.

myriad (mirri-ăd) n. a vast number.

myrmidon (mer-mid-ŏn) n. a henchman.

myrrh¹ (*rhymes with* fur) n. a kind of gum resin used in perfumes and medicine and incense.

myrrh² (*rhymes with* fur) n. a white-flowered herb, = sweet cicely.

myrtle (mer-t'l) n. an evergreen shrub with dark leaves and scented white flowers.

myself *pronoun* corresponding to *I* and *me*, used in the same ways as himself.

mysterious adj. full of mystery, puzzling or obscure. **mysteriously** adv.

mystery n. 1. a matter that remains unexplained or secret. 2. the quality of being unexplained or obscure, *its origins are wrapped in mystery.* 3. the practice of making a secret of things. 4. a religious truth that is beyond human powers to understand. 5. a story or play that deals with a puzzling crime. □ **mystery tour** *or* **trip,** a pleasure excursion to an unspecified destination.

mystic (mis-tik) adj. 1. of hidden or symbolic meaning, especially in religion, *mystic ceremonies.* 2. inspiring a sense of mystery and awe. —n. a person who seeks to obtain union with God by spiritual contemplation and self-surrender.

mystical (mis-tik-ăl) adj. 1. of mystics or mysticism. 2. having spiritual meaning or value or symbolism. **mystically** adv.

mysticism (mis-ti-sizm) n. 1. mystical quality. 2. being a mystic.

mystify v. (mystified, mystifying) to cause (a person) to feel puzzled. **mystification** n.

mystique (mis-teek) n. an aura of mystery or mystical power.

myth (*pr.* mith) n. 1. a traditional story containing ideas or beliefs about ancient times or about natural events (such as the four seasons). 2. such stories collectively, *in* *myth and legend.* **3.** an imaginary person or thing. **4.** an idea that forms part of the beliefs of a group or class but is not founded on fact.

mythical (**mith**-i-kăl) *adj.* **1.** of myths, existing in myths. **2.** imaginary, fancied.

mythology (mith-**ol**-ŏji) *n.* **1.** a body of myths, *Greek mythology.* **2.** study of myths. **mythological** *adj.,* **mythologist** *n.*

myxomatosis (miksŏ-mă-**toh**-sis) *n.* a fatal virus disease of rabbits.

Nn

N. *abbrev.* North.

Naafi (**naf**-i) *n.* a canteen for servicemen, organized by the Navy, Army, and Air Force Institutes.

nab *v.* (nabbed, nabbing) (*slang*) **1.** to catch (a wrongdoer) in the act, to arrest. **2.** to seize, to grab

nadir (**nay**-deer) *n.* the lowest point, the time of deepest depression.

naevus (**nee**-vŭs) *n.* (*pl.* naevi, *pr.* **nee**-vy) a birthmark consisting of a red patch on the skin or a mole.

nag¹ *n.* (*informal*) a horse.

nag² *v.* (nagged, nagging) **1.** to make scolding remarks to, to find fault continually. **2.** (of pain or worry) to be felt persistently.

naiad (**ny**-ad) *n.* a water-nymph.

nail *n.* **1.** the layer of horny substance over the outer tip of a finger or toe. **2.** a claw or talon. **3.** a small metal spike driven in with a hammer to hold things together or as a peg or protection or ornament. —**nail** *v.* **1.** to fasten with a nail or nails. **2.** to catch or arrest, *nailed the intruder.* □ **hit the nail on the head,** *see* hit. **nail-brush** *n.* a brush for scrubbing one's nails. **nail down,** to pin down (*see* pin). **nail-file, nail-scissors** *ns.* those designed for shaping and trimming the nails. **nail polish** *or* **varnish,** a substance for giving a shiny tint to the nails. **on the nail,** (especially of payment) without delay.

nainsook (**nayn**-suuk) *n.* a kind of fine soft cotton fabric, shiny on one side.

Nairobi (ny-**roh**-bi) the capital of Kenya.

naïve (nah-**eev**) *adj.* showing a lack of experience or of informed judgement. **naïvely** *adv.,* **naïvety** *or* **naïveté** (nah-**eev**-tay) *n.*

naked *adj.* **1.** without clothes on, nude. **2.** without the usual coverings or ornamentation etc.; *a naked sword,* without its sheath. **3.** undisguised, *the naked truth.* **nakedly** *adv.,* **nakedness** *n.* □ **naked**

eye, the eye unassisted by a telescope or microscope etc.

NALGO *or* **Nalgo** (**nal**-goh) *abbrev.* National and Local Government Officers' Association.

namby-pamby *adj.* lacking positive character, feeble, not manly. —*n.* a person of this kind.

name *n.* **1.** a word or words by which a person or animal or place or thing is known or indicated. **2.** a reputation, *has got a bad name; made a name for himself,* became famous. **3.** a famous person, *the film has some big names in it.* —**name** *v.* **1.** to give a name to. **2.** to state the name(s) of. **3.** to nominate or appoint to an office etc. **4.** to mention or specify; *name the day,* to arrange a date, especially of a woman fixing the date for her wedding. □ **call a person names,** to speak abusively to him or about him. **have to one's name,** to possess. **in name only,** so called but not so in reality. **in the name of,** invoking or calling to witness, *in the name of God, what are you doing?;* by authority of, *open in the name of the law!;* under the designation or pretence of, *did it all in the name of friendship.* **name-dropping** *n.* mention of famous people's names in order to impress others by implying that one is familiar with such people. **the name of the game,** (*informal*) the purpose or essence of an activity. **name-tape** *n.* a tape (fixed to a garment etc.) bearing the name of the owner.

nameable *adj.* able to be named.

nameless *adj.* **1.** having no name or no known name. **2.** not mentioned by name, anonymous, *others who shall be nameless.* **3.** too bad to be named, *nameless horrors.*

namely *adv.* that is to say, specifically.

namesake *n.* a person or thing with the same name as another.

Namibia (nă-**mib**-iă) a country in south-west Africa.

nan *n.* (*children's informal*) nanny.

nancy *n.* (*slang*) an effeminate or homosexual man or boy.

nankeen (nan-**keen**) *n.* a kind of cotton cloth, originally made in Nanking in China from naturally yellow cotton.

nanny *n.* **1.** a child's nurse. **2.** (*children's informal*) grandmother. **3.** a nanny-goat. □ **nanny-goat** *n.* a female goat.

nap¹ *n.* a short sleep or doze, especially during the day. —*v.* (napped, napping) to have a nap. □ **catch a person napping,** to catch a person off his guard.

nap² *n.* short raised fibres on the surface of cloth or leather.

nap³ *n.* **1.** a card-game in which players have five cards and declare how many tricks they expect to take. **2.** a call of five in this game. **3.** betting all of one's money on one chance, a tipster's choice for this. —*v.* (napped, napping) to name as a choice for this kind of bet. □ **go nap**, to make a call of five in nap; to risk all on one chance.

napalm (**nay**-pahm) *n.* a jelly-like petrol substance used in incendiary bombs.

nape *n.* the back part of the neck.

naphtha (**naf**-thă) *n.* an inflammable oil obtained from coal or petroleum.

naphthalene (**naf**-thă-leen) *n.* a strong-smelling white substance obtained from coal-tar, used in dyes and as a moth-repellent.

napkin *n.* **1.** a square piece of cloth or paper used at meals to protect one's clothes or for wiping one's lips or fingers. **2.** a piece of towelling or similar fabric worn by a baby to absorb or retain its excreta. □ **napkin-ring** *n.* a ring in which a table-napkin is placed when not in use.

Napoleonic *adj.* of Napoleon (1769–1821), a French general, emperor of France 1804–15.

nappa (**nap**-ă) *n.* leather made by a special process from the skin of sheep or goats.

nappy *n.* a baby's napkin.

narcissus (nar-**sis**-ŭs) *n.* (*pl.* narcissi, *pr.* nar-**sis**-I) any of a group of flowers including jonquils and daffodils, especially the kind with heavily-scented single white flowers.

narcosis (nar-**koh**-sis) *n.* a state of sleep or drowsiness produced by drugs or by electricity.

narcotic (nar-**kot**-ik) *adj.* causing sleep or drowsiness. —*n.* a narcotic drug.

nark *n.* (*slang*) **1.** a police spy or informer. **2.** (*Austral.*) an annoying person or thing. —*v.* (*slang*) to annoy. □ **nark it,** (*slang*) stop it, be quiet.

narrate (nă-**rayt**) *v.* to tell (a story), to give an account of, to utter or write a narrative. **narration** *n.*, **narrator** *n.*

narrative (**na**-ră-tiv) *n.* a spoken or written account of something. —*adj.* in the form of a narrative.

narrow *adj.* **1.** of small width in proportion to length. **2.** having or allowing little space, *within narrow bounds.* **3.** with little scope or variety, small, *a narrow circle of friends.* **4.** with little margin, *a narrow escape; a narrow majority.* **5.** narrow-minded. —*v.* to make or become narrower. —**narrowly** *adv.*, **narrowness** *n.* □ **narrow boat,** a long narrow boat used on canals. **narrow-minded** *adj.* rigid in one's views and sympathies, not tolerant.

narwhal (**nar**-wăl) *n.* an Arctic animal re-lated to the whale, the male of which has a long tusk with a spiral groove.

nasal (**nay**-zăl) *adj.* **1.** of the nose. **2.** (of a voice or speech) sounding as if the breath came out through the nose. **nasally** *adv.*

Nassau (**nass**-aw) the capital of the Bahamas.

nasturtium (nă-**ster**-shŭm) *n.* a trailing garden plant with bright orange or yellow or red flowers and round flat leaves.

nasty *adj.* (nastier, nastiest) **1.** unpleasant. **2.** unkind, spiteful. **3.** difficult to deal with, *a nasty problem.* **nastily** *adv.*, **nastiness** *n.* □ **nasty piece of work,** (*informal*) an unpleasant person.

natal (**nay**-t'l) *adj.* of or from one's birth.

nation *n.* a large community of people of mainly common descent, language, history, etc., usually inhabiting a particular territory and under one government. **nation-wide** *adj.* extending over the whole of a nation.

national *adj.* of a nation, common to a whole nation. —*n.* **1.** a citizen or subject of a particular country. **2.** *the National,* the Grand National (*see* grand). —**nationally** *adv.* □ **national anthem,** a song of loyalty or patriotism adopted by a country. **National Debt,** the total amount owed by a country to those who have lent money to it. **National Front,** a political group in Britain holding extreme nationalistic views and opposing immigration. **National Health Service,** the public service in Britain that provides medical care. **National Insurance,** a system of compulsory contributions from adults and employers to provide State assistance to people who are ill or unemployed or retired etc. **national park,** an area of countryside declared to be public property for the use and enjoyment of the people. **national service,** a period of compulsory service in a country's armed forces.

nationalism *n.* **1.** patriotic feeling or principles or efforts. **2.** a movement favouring independence for a country that is controlled by or forms part of another. □ **nationalist** *n.* a supporter of nationalism. **nationalistic** *adj.*

nationality *n.* the condition of belonging to a particular nation.

nationalize *v.* to convert (industries etc.) from private to government ownership. **nationalization** *n.*

native *adj.* **1.** belonging to a person or thing by nature, inborn, natural. **2.** (of a person) belonging to a particular place by birth, (of a thing) belonging to a person because of his place of birth, *one's native* *land* or *language*. **3**. grown or produced or originating in a specified place. **4**. of the natives of a place. —**native** *n*. **1**. a person who was born in a specified place, *a native of Canada*. **2**. a local inhabitant of a place. **3**. (*Austral.*) a white person born in Australia. **4**. a member of a non-European or less civilized native people, (in South Africa) a Black. **5**. an animal or plant grown or originating in a specified place. □ **native bear**, (*Austral.*) the koala.

nativity *n*. **1**. a person's birth with regard to its place or circumstances, especially *the Nativity*, that of Christ. **2**. *Nativity*, a picture of a scene with Christ as a new-born infant. □ **Nativity play**, a play dealing with the birth of Christ.

NATO or **Nato** (**nay**-toh) *abbrev*. North Atlantic Treaty Organization.

natter *v*. (*informal*) to chat. —*n*. (*informal*) a chat.

natterjack *n*. a kind of small toad with a yellow stripe down its back, that runs instead of hopping.

natty *adj*. (nattier, nattiest) neat and trim, dapper. **nattily** *adv*.

natural *adj*. **1**. of or existing in or produced by nature; *a country's natural resources*, its mineral deposits, forests, etc. **2**. in accordance with the course of nature, normal, *a natural death*. **3**. (of a person) having certain inborn qualities or abilities, *a natural leader*. **4**. not looking artificial, not affected in manner etc. **5**. not surprising, to be expected. **6**. (in music, of a note) neither sharp nor flat, *B natural*. **natural** *n*. **1**. a person or thing that seems to be naturally suited for something. **2**. (in music) a natural note, the sign for this (♮). **3**. pale fawn colour. —**naturally** *adv*., **naturalness** *n*. □ **natural childbirth**, a system of childbirth in which the mother has been taught to relax and so needs little or no anaesthetic. **natural gas**, gas found in the earth's crust, not manufactured. **natural history**, the study of animal and vegetable life. **natural selection**, survival of the organisms that are best adapted to their environment while the less well adapted ones die out.

naturalism *n*. realism in art and literature, drawing or painting or representing things as they are in nature. **naturalistic** *adj*.

naturalist *n*. an expert in natural history.

naturalize *v*. **1**. to admit (a person of foreign birth) to full citizenship of a country. **2**. to adopt (a foreign word or custom) into the language or customs of a country. **3**. to introduce and acclimatize (an animal or plant) into a country where

it is not native. **4**. to cause to appear natural; *daffodil bulbs suitable for naturalizing*, suitable for planting so that they appear to be growing wild. **naturalization** *n*.

nature *n*. **1**. the world with all its features and living things, the physical power that produces these; *Nature*, this power personified. **2**. a kind or sort or class, *things of this nature*; *the request was in the nature of a command*. **3**. the complex of qualities and characteristics innate in a person or animal. **4**. a thing's essential qualities, its characteristics. □ **back to nature**, returning to what are regarded as the natural conditions of living before the spread of civilization. **in a state of nature**, in an uncultivated or undomesticated state; totally naked. **nature study**, (in schools) the practical study of plant and animal life. **nature trail**, a path through woods or countryside where interesting natural objects can be seen.

naturist *n*. a nudist. **naturism** *n*.

naught *n*. (*old use*) nothing, = nought.

naughty *adj*. (naughtier, naughtiest) **1**. behaving badly, disobedient. **2**. improper, shocking or amusing people by mild indecency. **naughtily** *adv*., **naughtiness** *n*.

Nauru (now-**roo**) an island country in the Pacific. **Nauruan** *adj*. & *n*.

nausea (**naw**-ziă) *n*. a feeling of sickness or disgust.

nauseate (**naw**-zi-ayt) *v*. to affect with nausea.

nauseous (**naw**-zi-ŭs) *adj*. causing nausea.

nautical *adj*. of sailors or seamanship. **nautical mile**, *see* mile.

naval *adj*. of a navy, of warships; *a naval power*, a country with a strong navy.

navarin (**nav**-er-an) *n*. casserole of lamb or mutton with vegetables.

nave *n*. the body of a church apart from the chancel, aisles, and transepts.

navel (**nay**-věl) *n*. **1**. the small hollow in the centre of the abdomen where the umbilical cord was attached. **2**. the central point of something. □ **navel orange**, a large orange with a navel-like formation at the top.

navigable (**nav**-ig-ăbŭl) *adj*. **1**. (of rivers or seas) suitable for ships to sail in. **2**. (of a ship etc.) able to be steered and sailed. **navigability** *n*.

navigate *v*. **1**. to sail in or through (a sea or river etc.). **2**. to direct the course of (a ship or aircraft or vehicle etc.). **navigation** *n*., **navigator** *n*.

navvy *n*. a labourer employed in making

roads, railways, canals, etc. where digging is necessary.

navy *n*. **1**. a country's warships. **2**. the officers and men of these. **3**. navy blue. —*adj*. navy blue. □ **navy blue**, very dark blue like that used in naval uniform.

nay *adv*. (*old use*) no.

Nazi (**nah**-tsi) *n*. (*pl*. Nazis) a member of the National Socialist party in Germany, brought to power by Hitler. —*adj*. of the Nazis. —**Nazism** *n*.

NB *abbrev*. **1**. New Brunswick. **2**. note well (¶ from the Latin *nota bene*).

NBG *abbrev*. (*informal*) no bloody good.

NC *abbrev*. North Carolina.

NCO *abbrev*. non-commissioned officer.

N. Dak. *abbrev*. North Dakota.

NE *abbrev*. north-east, north-eastern.

Neanderthal (ni-**an**-der-tǎl) *adj*. of **Neanderthal man**, an extinct type of mankind living in the Old Stone Age in Europe.

neap *n*. **neap tide**, the tide when there is the least rise and fall of water, half-way between spring tides.

Neapolitan (nee-ǎ-**pol**-itǎn) *adj*. of Naples. —*n*. a native or inhabitant of Naples. □ **Neapolitan ice**, ice cream made in layers of different colours and flavours.

near *adv*. **1**. at or to or within a short distance or interval. **2**. nearly, *as near as I can guess*. —*prep*. near to. —**near** *adj*. **1**. with only a short distance or interval between, *in the near future*. **2**. closely related. **3**. (of a part of a vehicle or horse or road) on the left side, *the near side front wheel; near hind leg*. **4**. with little margin, *a near escape*. **5**. stingy. —*v*. to draw near. —**nearness** *n*. □ **near by**, not far off, *they live near by*. (¶ Written as two words except when used as an adjective; *see* nearby.) **Near East**, the Middle East. **near miss**, something that missed its objective only narrowly; not a direct hit but near enough to do damage. **near-sighted** *adj*. short-sighted. **near thing**, something achieved or missed by only a narrow margin; a narrow escape.

nearby *adj*. near in position, *a nearby house*. (¶ See the note on *near by* in entry for near.)

nearly *adv*. **1**. closely; *we are nearly related*, are closely related. **2**. almost. □ **not nearly**, nothing like, far from, *not nearly enough*.

neat *adj*. **1**. simple and clean and orderly in appearance. **2**. done or doing things in a precise and skilful way. **3**. undiluted, *neat whisky*. **neatly** *adv*., **neatness** *n*.

neaten *v*. to make or become neat.

Neb. *abbrev*. Nebraska.

Nebraska (nib-**ras**-kǎ) a State of the USA.

nebula (**neb**-yoo-lǎ) *n*. (*pl*. nebulae, *pr*. **neb**-yoo-lee) a bright or dark patch in the sky caused by distant stars or a cloud of dust or gas.

nebulous (**neb**-yoo-lǔs) *adj*. indistinct, having no definite form, *nebulous ideas*.

necessarily *adv*. as a necessary result, inevitably.

necessary *adj*. **1**. essential in order to achieve something. **2**. unavoidable, happening or existing by necessity, *the necessary consequence*. □ **necessaries** *pl*. *n*. things without which life cannot be maintained or is exceedingly harsh. **the necessary**, (*slang*) money or action needed for a purpose, *do* or *provide the necessary*.

necessitate (ni-**sess**-i-tayt) *v*. to make necessary, to involve as a condition or accompaniment or result.

necessitous (ni-**sess**-i-tǔs) *adj*. needy.

necessity (ni-**sess**-iti) *n*. **1**. the state or fact of being necessary, *the necessity of adequate food*. **2**. a necessary thing. **3**. the compelling power of circumstances. **4**. a state of need or great poverty or hardship.

neck *n*. **1**. the narrow part of the body connecting the head to the shoulders. **2**. the part of a garment round this. **3**. the length of a horse's head and neck as a measure of its lead in a race. **4**. the flesh of an animal's neck as food. **5**. a narrow part of anything (especially of a bottle or cavity), a narrow connecting part or channel. —*v*. (*slang*, of couples) to kiss and caress each other lovingly. □ **get it in the neck**, (*slang*) to suffer a reprimand or a severe blow. **neck and crop**, headlong, bodily. **neck and neck**, running level in a race. **neck or nothing**, in a desperate attempt, staking all on success. **risk** *or* **save one's neck**, to risk or save one's own life. **up to one's neck in**, (*informal*) very deeply involved in.

neckband *n*. a strip of material round the neck of a garment.

necklace *n*. an ornament of precious stones or metal or beads etc. worn round the neck.

necklet *n*. **1**. a necklace. **2**. a fur worn round the neck.

neckline *n*. the outline formed by the edge of a garment at or below the neck.

necromancy (**nek**-rŏ-man-si) *n*. **1**. the art of predicting events by allegedly communicating with the dead. **2**. witchcraft. **necromancer** *n*.

necropolis (nek-**rop**-ŏ-lis) *n*. a cemetery, especially an ancient one.

necktie *n*. a strip of material worn round the neck, passing under the collar and knotted in front.

nectar

Negroid

nectar *n.* **1.** (in Greek mythology) the drink of the gods. **2.** any delicious drink. **3.** sweet fluid produced by plants and collected by bees for making honey.

nectarine (**nek**-ter-in) *n.* a kind of peach that has a thin skin with no down and firm flesh.

nectary (**nek**-ter-i) *n.* the nectar-secreting part of a plant or flower.

Neddy *n.* (*informal*) the National Economic Development Council.

née (*pr.* nay) *adj.* born (used in giving a married woman's maiden name, *Mrs Jane Smith, née Jones*).

need *n.* **1.** circumstances in which a thing or course of action is required, *there is no need to worry*. **2.** a situation of great difficulty or misfortune, *a friend in need*. **3.** lack of necessaries, poverty. **4.** a requirement, a thing necessary for life, *my needs are few.* —**need** *v.* **1.** to be in need of, to require. **2.** to be under a necessity or obligation, *need you ask?* □ **if need be,** if necessary. **needs** *adv.* of necessity; *must needs do it,* foolishly insists on doing it, cannot help doing it; *needs must do it,* must do it.

needful *adj.* necessary. **the needful,** (*slang*) what is necessary; money or action needed for a purpose.

needle *n.* **1.** a small thin piece of polished steel with a point at one end and a hole for thread at the other, used in sewing. **2.** something resembling this in shape or use, e.g. one of the long thin leaves of pine trees, a sharp pointed rock, an obelisk (*Cleopatra's Needle*), the sharp hollow end of a hypodermic syringe. **3.** a long thin piece of smooth metal or plastic etc. with one or both ends pointed, used in knitting by hand. **4.** the pointer of a compass or gauge. —*v.* to annoy or provoke. □ **needle in a haystack,** a thing so buried amongst others that search for it is hopeless.

needlecord *n.* very fine corduroy fabric.

needlecraft *n.* skill in needlework.

needleloom *n.* a machine with vertical needles that fasten loose fibres into a backing to make carpet fabric.

needlepoint *n.* a kind of fine embroidery on canvas.

needless *adj.* not needed, unnecessary. **needlessly** *adv.*

needlewoman *n.* a woman with a certain skill in needlework, *a good needlewoman.*

needlework *n.* sewing or embroidery.

needn't = need not.

needy *adj.* (needier, neediest) lacking the necessaries of life, extremely poor.

ne'er-do-well *n.* a good-for-nothing person.

nefarious (ni-**fair**-iŭs) *adj.* wicked. **nefariously** *adv.*

negate (ni-**gayt**) *v.* to nullify, to disprove. **negation** *n.*

negative *adj.* **1.** expressing or implying denial or refusal or prohibition; *a negative reply,* saying 'no'. **2.** not positive, lacking positive qualities or characteristics; *the result of the test was negative,* indicated that a specific substance etc. was not present. **3.** (of a quantity) less than zero, minus. **4.** containing or producing the kind of electric charge carried by electrons; *negative terminal of a battery,* the one through which current enters from an external circuit. **5.** (of a photograph) having the lights and shades of the actual object or scene reversed, or its colours represented by complementary ones. —**negative** *n.* **1.** a negative statement or reply or word; *the answer is in the negative,* is 'no'. **2.** a negative quality or quantity. **3.** a negative photograph, from which positive pictures can be obtained. —**negative** *v.* **1.** to veto. **2.** to contradict (a statement). **3.** to neutralize (an effect). **negatively** *adv.* □ **negative pole,** the south-seeking pole of a magnet. **negative sign,** the sign .

neglect *v.* **1.** to pay no attention or not enough attention to. **2.** to fail to take proper care of. **3.** to omit to do something, e.g. through carelessness or forgetfulness. —*n.* neglecting, being neglected. —**neglectful** *adj.*

négligé (**neg**-li-zhay) *n.* a woman's light flimsy ornamental dressing-gown.

negligence (**neg**-li-jĕns) *n.* lack of proper care or attention, carelessness. **negligent** *adj.*, **negligently** *adv.*

negligible (**neg**-lij-ibŭl) *adj.* very small in amount etc. and not worth taking into account.

negotiable (nig-oh-**shă**-bŭl) *adj.* **1.** able to be modified after discussion, *the salary is negotiable.* **2.** (of a cheque etc.) able to be converted into cash or transferred to another person.

negotiate (nig-**oh**-shi-ayt) *v.* **1.** to try to reach an agreement or arrangement by discussion, to arrange in this way, *negotiated a treaty.* **2.** to get or give money in exchange for (a cheque or bonds etc.). **3.** to get over or through (an obstacle or difficulty) successfully. **negotiation** *n.,* **negotiator** *n.*

Negro *n.* (*pl.* Negroes) a member of the black-skinned race of mankind that originated in Africa. **Negress** *n.*

Negroid *adj.* having the physical characteristics that are typical of Negroes, with

437

black skin, woolly hair, and flat nose.—*n.* a Negroid person.

neigh (*pr.* nay) *n.* the long high-pitched cry of a horse. —*v.* to make this cry.

neighbour *n.* **1.** a person who lives near or next to another. **2.** a person to whom one should be friendly or kind. **3.** a person or thing situated near or next to another, *Britain's nearest neighbour is France.*

neighbourhood *n.* **1.** a district. **2.** the people living in it. □ **in the neighbourhood of**, somewhere near, approximately, *in the neighbourhood of £500.*

neighbouring *adj.* living or situated near by.

neighbourly *adj.* kind and friendly, as one neighbour should be to another. **neighbourliness** *n.*

neither (**ny**-*th*er *or* **nee**-*th*er) *adj. & pron.* not either, *neither of them likes it.* (¶ Note the use of the singular verb; *neither of them like it* would be incorrect.) —*adv. & conj.* **1.** not either, *she neither knew nor cared.* **2.** also not, *you don't know and neither do I.* **3.** (*incorrect use*) either, *I don't know that neither.* □ **be neither here nor there**, to be of no importance or relevance.

nelson *n.* a kind of hold in wrestling in which the arm is passed under the opponent's arm from behind and the hand applied to his neck.

nem. con. *abbrev.* unanimously. (¶ From the Latin *nemine contradicente* = with nobody disagreeing.)

nemesia (ni-**mee**-*zh*ă) *n.* a plant with variously coloured flowers with irregular petals.

nemesis (**nem**-i-sis) *n.* the infliction of deserved and unavoidable punishment.

neo- *prefix* new, recent, a new form of.

neo-classical *adj.* of or in a style of art, literature or music that is based on or influenced by classical style.

Neo-Impressionist *n.* any of a group of painters whose style was similar to that of the impressionists but with greater detail. **Neo-Impressionism** *n.*

neolithic (nee-ŏ-**lith**-ik) *adj.* of the later part of the Stone Age.

neologism (ni-**ol**-ŏ-jizm) *n.* a newly-coined word.

neon (**nee**-on) *n.* a kind of gas much used in illuminated signs because it glows orange-red when electricity is passed through it.

neoprene (**nee**-ŏ-preen) *n.* a tough synthetic rubber-like substance.

Nepal (nĕ-**pawl**) a country north-east of India. **Nepalese** (nep-ă-**leez**) *adj. & n.* (*pl.* Nepalese)

nephew (**nef**-yoo) *n.* one's brother's or sister's son.

nephritis (ni-**fry**-tiss) *n.* inflammation of the kidneys.

ne plus ultra (*pr.* nay) the furthest point attainable, the highest form of something. (¶ Latin, = do not go beyond this point.)

nepotism (**nep**-ŏ-tizm) *n.* favouritism shown to relatives in appointing them to jobs.

nerine (ni-**ry**-ni) *n.* the Guernsey lily or a similar garden flower.

nerve *n.* **1.** any of the fibres or bundles of fibres carrying impulses of sensation or of movement between the brain or spinal cord and all parts of the body. **2.** courage, coolness in danger, *lose one's nerve.* **3.** (*informal*) impudent boldness, *had the nerve to ask for more.* —*v.* to give strength or vigour or courage to; *nerve oneself,* to brace oneself to face danger or suffering. □ **get on a person's nerves**, to be irritating to him. **nerve-centre** *n.* a centre of control from which instructions are sent out. **nerve-racking** *adj.* inflicting great strain on the nerves. **nerves** *pl. n.* nervousness, *he doesn't know what nerves are*; a condition in which a person suffers from mental stress and easily becomes anxious or upset.

nerveless *adj.* incapable of effort or movement, *the knife fell from his nerveless fingers.*

nervous *adj.* **1.** of the nerves or nervous system, *a nervous disorder.* **2.** excitable, easily agitated, timid. **3.** uneasy, *a nervous laugh.* **nervously** *adv.*, **nervousness** *n.* □ **nervous breakdown**, loss of mental and emotional stability. **nervous system**, the system of nerves throughout the body.

nervy *adj.* (nervier, nerviest) nervous, easily agitated, uneasy.

nest *n.* **1.** a structure or place in which a bird lays its eggs and shelters its young. **2.** a place where certain creatures (e.g. mice, wasps) live, or produce and keep their young. **3.** a snug place. **4.** a secluded shelter or hiding-place. **5.** a set of similar articles designed to fit inside each other in a series, *a nest of tables.* —*v.* to make or have a nest. □ **nest-egg** *n.* a sum of money saved for future use.

nesting *n.* collecting wild birds' nests or eggs.

nestle *v.* **1.** to curl up or press oneself comfortably into a soft place. **2.** to lie half-hidden or sheltered.

nestling *n.* a bird too young to leave the nest.

net[1] *n.* **1.** open-work material of thread or cord or wire etc. woven or joined at intervals. **2.** a piece of this used for a particular purpose, e.g. covering or protecting something, catching fish, dividing a tennis court, surrounding a goal-space, etc. —**net** v. (netted, netting) **1.** to make by forming threads into a net, to make netting. **2.** to place nets in, to cover or confine with or as if with a net. **3.** to catch in or as if in a net.

net² adj. **1.** remaining when nothing more is to be taken away; *net profit*, profit after tax etc. has been deducted from the gross profit; *net weight*, weight of contents only, excluding wrappings. **2.** (of an effect etc.) positive, excluding unimportant effects or those that cancel each other out, *the net result.* —v. (netted, netting) to obtain or yield as net profit.

netball n. a team game in which a ball has to be thrown so that it falls into a net hanging from a ring on a high post.

nether (neth-er) adj. lower, *the nether regions.* **nethermost** adj.

Netherlands, The. a country in Europe, also called *Holland.* **Netherlander** n.

netting n. fabric of netted thread or cord or wire etc.

nettle n. **1.** a common wild plant with hairs on its leaves that sting and redden the skin when they are touched. **2.** a plant resembling this. —v. to irritate, to provoke. □ **nettle-rash** n. an eruption on the skin with red patches like those made by nettle stings.

network n. **1.** an arrangement or pattern with intersecting lines, *a network of railways.* **2.** a chain of interconnected people or operations, or broadcasting stations, *a spy network.*

neural (newr-ăl) adj. of nerves.

neuralgia (newr-al-jă) n. sharp intermittent pain along the course of a nerve, especially in the head or face. **neuralgic** adj.

neuritis (newr-I-tiss) n. inflammation of a nerve or nerves.

neurology (newr-ol-ŏji) n. the scientific study of nerve systems and their diseases. **neurological** adj., **neurologist** n.

neurosis (newr-oh-sis) n. (pl. neuroses) a mental disorder producing depression or abnormal behaviour, sometimes with physical symptoms but with no evidence of disease.

neuro-surgery n. surgery performed on the nervous system.

neurotic (newr-ot-ik) adj. **1.** of or caused by a neurosis. **2.** (of a person) subject to abnormal anxieties or obsessive behaviour. —n. a neurotic person. —**neurotically** adv.

neuter (new-ter) adj. **1.** (of a noun) neither masculine nor feminine. **2.** (of plants) without male or female parts. **3.** (of insects) sexually undeveloped, sterile. —n. a neuter word or plant or insect, a castrated animal. —v. to castrate.

neutral adj. **1.** not supporting or assisting either side in a dispute or conflict. **2.** belonging to a country or person etc. that is neutral, *neutral ships.* **3.** having no positive or distinctive characteristics, not definitely one thing or the other. **4.** (of colours) not strong or positive, grey or fawn. —**neutral** n. **1.** a neutral person or country, one who is a subject of a neutral country. **2.** grey or fawn colour. **3.** neutral gear. —**neutrally** adv., **neutrality** (new-tral-iti) n. □ **neutral gear**, a position of a gear mechanism in which the engine is disconnected from driven parts.

neutralize v. to make ineffective by means of an opposite force or effect. **neutralization** n.

neutron (new-tron) n. a particle with no electric charge, present in the nuclei of all atoms except those of certain isotopes of hydrogen. **neutron bomb**, a nuclear bomb that kills people by intense radiation but does little damage to buildings etc.

Nev. abbrev. Nevada.

Nevada (ně-vah-dă) a State of the USA.

never adv. **1.** at no time, on no occasion; *never-ending, never-failing,* not ending or failing ever. **2.** not at all, *never fear.* **3.** (informal) surely not, *you never left the key in the lock!* **4.** not, *never a care in the world.* —int. (informal) surely not. □ **never mind**, do not be troubled; do not trouble about, you may ignore, *never mind the bread*; I refuse to answer your question. **the never-never** n. (informal) hire-purchase. **well I never!**, an exclamation of surprise.

nevermore adv. at no future time.

nevertheless adv. & conj. in spite of this.

new adj. **1.** not existing before, recently made or invented or discovered or experienced. **2.** unfamiliar, unaccustomed, *it was new to me, I am new to the job.* **3.** recently changed or renewed, different, *the new chairman.* —adv. newly, recently, just, *new-born; new-laid.* —**newness** n. □ **New Brunswick**, a province of Canada. **New Commonwealth**, see commonwealth. **New England**, a group of 6 States in the north-east of the USA. **New Englander**, a native or inhabitant of New England. **New Hampshire, New Jersey**, States of the USA. **new look**, a fresh and up-to-date appearance. **New Mexico**, a State of the USA. **new moon**, the moon when it is seen in the evening as a crescent; (on calendars) the precise moment when the moon is in conjunction with the sun and is invisible. **New South Wales,** a State of Australia. **New Testament,** *see* testament. **new town,** a town established as a completely new settlement, with government sponsorship. **New World,** the Americas. **new year,** the first few days of January. **New Year's Day,** 1 January. **New Year's Eve,** 31 December. **New York,** a State and city of the USA. **New Yorker,** a native or inhabitant of New York. **New Zealand,** a country south-east of Australia. **New Zealander,** a native or inhabitant of New Zealand.

newcomer *n.* a person who has arrived recently.

newel (**new**-ĕl) *n.* **1.** a post that supports the handrail of a stair at the top or bottom of a staircase. **2.** the centre pillar of a winding stair.

newfangled *adj.* (*contemptuous*) objectionably new in method or style.

Newfoundland (**new**-fŭnd-lănd) a province of Canada. —*n.* a dog of a large breed with a thick dark coat. — **Newfoundlander** *n.*

newish *adj.* fairly new.

newly *adv.* recently, freshly. **newly-wed** *adj.* recently married, (*n.*) a recently-married person.

news *n.* **1.** information about recent events. **2.** a broadcast report of this. **3.** newsworthy information, *when a man bites a dog, that's news.* □ **news-stand** *n.* a stall where newspapers are sold.

newsagent *n.* a shopkeeper who sells newspapers.

newscast *n.* a broadcast news report. **newscaster** *n.* a person who reads this.

newsletter *n.* an informal printed report giving information that is of interest to members of a club etc.

newspaper *n.* **1.** a printed publication, usually issued daily or weekly, containing news reports, advertisements, articles on various subjects, etc. **2.** the sheets of paper forming this, *wrapped in newspaper.*

newsprint *n.* the type of paper on which a newspaper is printed.

newsreel *n.* a cinema film showing current items of news.

newsvendor *n.* a newspaper-seller.

newsworthy *adj.* important or interesting enough to be mentioned as news.

newsy *adj.* (*informal*) full of news.

newt *n.* a small lizard-like creature that can live in water or on land.

Newtonian (new-**toh**-niăn) *adj.* of the theories etc. devised by the English scientist Sir Isaac Newton (1642–1727).

next *adj.* **1.** lying or living or being nearest to something. **2.** coming nearest in order or time or sequence, soonest come to. —*adv.* in the next place or degree, on the next occasion. —*n.* the next person or thing. □ **next best,** second best. **next door,** in the next house or room, *they live next door.* **next-door** *adj.* living or situated next door, *my next-door neighbour.* **next door to,** not far from, almost, *it's next door to impossible.* **next of kin,** one's closest relative. **next world,** life after death.

nexus *n.* (*pl.* nexuses; it is incorrect to use *nexi*) a connected group or series.

Nfld. *abbrev.* Newfoundland.

NH *abbrev.* New Hampshire.

NHS *abbrev.* National Health Service.

nib *n.* the metal point of a pen.

nibble *v.* **1.** to take small quick or gentle bites. **2.** to eat in small amounts, *no nibbling between meals.* **3.** to show interest in (an offer etc.) but without being definite. — **nibble** *n.* **1.** a small quick bite. **2.** a small amount of food. —**nibbler** *n.*

Nicaragua (nik-er-**ag**-yoo-ă) a country in Central America. **Nicaraguan** *adj. & n.*

nice *adj.* **1.** pleasant, satisfactory. **2.** (*ironically*) difficult, bad, *this is a nice mess.* **3.** needing precision and care, involving fine distinctions, *it's a nice point.* **4.** fastidious. **nicely** *adv.*, **niceness** *n.*

nicety (**ny**-sit-i) *n.* **1.** precision. **2.** a subtle distinction or detail. □ **to a nicety,** exactly.

niche (*rhymes with* pitch) *n.* **1.** a shallow recess, especially in a wall. **2.** a position in life or employment to which the holder is well suited, *has found his niche.*

nick *n.* **1.** a small cut or notch. **2.** (*slang*) a police station, prison. —**nick** *v.* **1.** to make a nick in. **2.** (*slang*) to steal. **3.** (*slang*) to catch or arrest (a criminal). □ **in good nick,** (*slang*) in good condition. **in the nick of time,** only just in time.

nickel *n.* **1.** a hard silvery-white metal much used in alloys. **2.** (*Amer.*) a 5-cent piece. □ **nickel silver,** an alloy of nickel, zinc, and copper.

nickname *n.* a name given humorously to a person instead of or as well as his real name. —*v.* to give a nickname to.

Nicosia (nik-ŏ-**see**-ă) the capital of Cyprus.

nicotine (**nik**-ŏ-teen) *n.* a poisonous substance found in tobacco. **nicotinic acid,** a vitamin of the B group obtained from nicotine.

niece *n.* one's brother's or sister's daughter.

Niger (nee-*zh*air) a country in central Africa.

Nigeria a country in West Africa. **Nigerian** *adj. & n.*

niggardly (**nig**-erd-li) *adj.* stingy.

nigger *n.* (*contemptuous*) a Black. □ **a nigger in the woodpile**, a concealed fact or influence capable of having a bad effect.

niggle *v.* to fuss over details, to find fault in a petty way.

nigh (*rhymes with* by) *adv. & prep.* near.

night *n.* **1.** the dark hours between sunset and sunrise. **2.** nightfall. **3.** a specified or appointed night, an evening on which a performance or other activity occurs, *the first night of the play.* □ **make a night of it**, to spend a night in festivity etc. **night and day**, at all times, without ceasing. **night-cap** *n.* a soft cap for wearing in bed; a drink taken just before going to bed. **night-clothes** *pl. n.* garments for wearing in bed. **night-club** *n.* a club that is open at night, providing meals and entertainment. **night-life** *n.* entertainments available in towns at night. **night-light** *n.* a faint light kept burning in a bedroom (e.g. of a child or invalid) at night. **night-long** *adj. & adv.* throughout the night. **night-night**, (*informal*) good night. **night safe**, a receptacle provided at a bank so that money etc. can be deposited when the bank is closed. **night-school** *n.* instruction provided in the evening for people who are at work during the day. **night-shift** *n.* a shift of workers employed during the night. **night-time** *n.* night. **night-watchman** *n.* a man employed to keep watch at night in a building that is closed.

nightdress *n.* a woman's or child's loose garment for wearing in bed.

nightfall *n.* the coming of darkness at the end of the day.

nightgown *n.* a nightdress.

nightie *n.* (*informal*) a nightdress.

nightingale *n.* a small reddish-brown thrush, the male of which sings melodiously both by night and in the day.

nightjar *n.* a night-flying bird with a harsh cry.

nightly *adj.* **1.** happening or done or existing etc. in the night. **2.** happening every night. —*adv.* every night.

nightmare *n.* **1.** a bad dream. **2.** (*informal*) a terrifying or very unpleasant experience. **nightmarish** *adj.*

nightshade *n.* any of several wild plants with poisonous berries.

nightshirt *n.* a boy's or man's long shirt for wearing in bed.

nil *n.* nothing.

nimble *adj.* **1.** able to move quickly, agile. **2.** (of the mind or wits) able to think quickly. **nimbly** *adv.*

nincompoop *n.* a foolish person.

nine *adj. & n.* one more than eight (9, IX). **dressed up to the nines**, dressed very elaborately. **nine days' wonder**, something that attracts much attention at first but is soon forgotten.

ninepins *n.* the game of skittles played with nine objects to be knocked down by rolling a ball. **ninepin** *n.* one of these objects.

nineteen *adj. & n.* one more than eighteen (19, XIX). **nineteenth** *adj. & n.* □ **talk nineteen to the dozen**, to talk continually.

ninety *adj. & n.* nine times ten (90, XC). **ninetieth** *adj. & n.* □ **nineties** *pl. n.* the numbers or years or degrees of temperature from 90 to 99.

ninny *n.* a foolish person.

ninth *adj. & n.* **1.** next after eighth. **2.** one of nine equal parts of a thing. **ninthly** *adv.*

nip¹ *v.* (nipped, nipping) **1.** to pinch or squeeze sharply, to bite quickly with the front teeth. **2.** to break off by doing this, *nip off the side-shoots.* **3.** to pain or harm with biting cold, *a nipping wind.* **4.** (*slang*) to go quickly, *nip out.* —**nip** *n.* **1.** a sharp pinch or squeeze or bite. **2.** biting coldness, *a nip in the air.* □ **nip in the bud**, to destroy at an early stage of development.

nip² *n.* a small drink of spirits. —*v.* (nipped, nipping) to take frequent nips.

nipper *n.* **1.** (*slang*) a young boy or girl. **2.** the great claw of a lobster or similar animal. □ **nippers** *pl. n.* pincers or forceps for gripping things or breaking things off.

nipple *n.* **1.** a small projection in the centre of a male or female mammal's breasts, containing (in females) the outlets of the milk-secreting organs. **2.** the teat of a feeding-bottle. **3.** a nipple-like projection.

nippy *adj.* (*informal*) **1.** nimble, quick. **2.** bitingly cold. **nippiness** *n.*

nirvana (ner-**vah**-nă) *n.* (in Buddhist and Hindu teaching) the state of perfect bliss attained when the soul is freed from all suffering and absorbed into the supreme spirit.

nisi *adj. see* decree nisi.

Nissen hut a tunnel-shaped hut of corrugated iron with a cement floor.

nit *n.* **1.** the egg of a louse or other parasite, the insect laying this. **2.** (*slang*) a stupid or foolish person. □ **nit-picking** *n.* fault-finding in a petty way.

nitrate (**ny**-trayt) *n.* **1.** a salt or ester of nitric acid. **2.** potassium or sodium nitrate used as a fertilizer.

nitric (**ny**-trik) *adj.* of or containing nitrogen. **nitric acid,** a colourless caustic highly corrosive acid.

nitrobenzene (ny-trŏ-**ben**-zeen) *n.* a poisonous yellow oil used as a solvent and in making certain dyes.

nitrogen (**ny**-trŏ-jĕn) *n.* a colourless odourless gas forming about four-fifths of the atmosphere. **nitrogenous** (ny-**troj**-in-ŭs) *adj.*

nitro-glycerine (ny-trŏ-**gliss**-er-een) *n.* a powerful explosive made by adding glycerine to a mixture of nitric and sulphuric acids.

nitrous (**ny**-trŭs) *adj.* of or containing nitrogen. **nitrous oxide,** a colourless gas used as an anaesthetic, laughing-gas.

nitty-gritty *n.* (*slang*) the basic facts or realities of a matter.

nitwit *n.* (*informal*) a stupid or foolish person.

nix *n.* (*slang*) nothing.

NJ *abbrev.* New Jersey.

N. Mex. *abbrev.* New Mexico.

no *adj.* **1.** not any. **2.** not a, quite other than, *she is no fool.* —*no adv.* **1.** used as a denial or refusal of something. **2.** not at all, *no better than before.* —*n.* (*pl.* noes) a negative reply or vote, a person voting against something. □ **no-ball** *n.* an unlawfully delivered ball in cricket etc., (*v.*) to declare (a bowler) to have bowled this. **no-claim bonus,** a reduction of an insurance premium for a person who has not claimed payment under the insurance since the previous renewal. **no fear,** (*informal*) it is not likely; certainly not. **no go,** the task is impossible, the situation is hopeless. **no-go area,** an area to which entry is forbidden to certain people or groups. **no man's land,** an area not firmly assigned to any one owner; a space between the fronts of two opposing armies in war. **no one,** no person, nobody. **no way,** (*informal*) that is impossible.

No. *or* **no.** *abbrev.* number.

nob[1] *n.* (*slang*) the head.

nob[2] *n.* (*slang*) a person of high rank.

nobble *v.* (*slang*) **1.** to tamper with (a racehorse) to prevent its winning. **2.** to get hold of or influence by underhand means. **3.** (*slang*) to catch (a criminal).

Nobel prize (noh-**bel**) any of the prizes awarded annually for outstanding achievements in the sciences, literature, economics, and the promotion of world peace, from the bequest of Alfred Nobel (1833–96), the Swedish inventor of dynamite.

nobility (noh-**bil**-iti) *n.* nobleness of mind or character or rank; *the nobility,* people

of aristocratic birth or rank, titled people.

noble *adj.* **1.** belonging to the aristocracy by birth or rank. **2.** possessing excellent qualities, especially in one's character, free from pettiness or meanness. **3.** imposing in appearance, *a noble edifice.* —*n.* a nobleman or noblewoman. —**nobly** *adv.,* **nobleness** *n.* □ **nobleman, noblewoman** *ns.* a member of the nobility.

noblesse oblige (noh-bless ŏ-**bleezh**) noble people must behave nobly, privilege entails responsibility.

nobody *pronoun* no person. —*n.* a person of no importance or authority, *he's nobody* or *a nobody.* □ **like nobody's business,** (*informal*) very much, intensively.

nocturnal (nok-**ter**-năl) *adj.* **1.** of or in the night. **2.** active in the night, *nocturnal animals.*

nocturne (**nok**-tern) *n.* a dreamy piece of music.

nod *v.* (nodded, nodding) **1.** to move the head down and up again quickly as a sign of agreement or casual greeting, to indicate (agreement etc.) in this way. **2.** to let the head fall forward in drowsiness, to be drowsy. **3.** (of plumes or flowers etc.) to bend downwards and sway. —*n.* a nodding movement in agreement or greeting; *give* or *get the nod,* to give or get agreement or a signal to proceed. □ **a nodding acquaintance,** a slight acquaintance with a person or subject. **land of Nod,** sleep. **nod through,** to authorize without discussion. **on the nod,** (*informal*) on credit; on request, without discussion.

node (*rhymes with* load) *n.* **1.** a knob-like swelling. **2.** the point on the stem of a plant where a leaf or bud grows out.

nodule (**nod**-yool) *n.* a small rounded lump, a small node. **nodular** *adj.*

Noel (noh-el) *n.* (in carols) Christmas.

noggin *n.* a small measure of alcohol, usually $\frac{1}{4}$ pint.

nohow *adv.* in no way.

noise *n.* a sound, especially one that is loud or harsh or confused or undesired. —*v.* to make public; *noised it abroad,* made it generally known.—**noiseless** *adj.*

noisome (**noi**-sŏm) *adj.* (*literary*) harmful, evil-smelling, objectionable.

noisy *adj.* (noisier, noisiest) making much noise. **noisily** *adv.,* **noisiness** *n.*

nomad (**noh**-mad) *n.* **1.** a member of a tribe that roams from place to place seeking pasture for its animals. **2.** a wanderer. **nomadic** (nŏ-**mad**-ik) *adj.*

nom de plume (nom dĕ **ploom**) a writer's pseudonym.

nomenclature (nŏ-**men**-klă-cher) *n.* a

system of names, e.g. those used in a particular science.

nominal (**nom**-in-ăl) *adj.* **1.** in name only, *nominal ruler of that country.* **2.** (of an amount or sum of money) very small but charged or paid as a token that payment is required, *a nominal fee.* **nominally** *adv.* □ **nominal value,** the face value of a coin etc.

nominate (**nom**-in-ayt) *v.* **1.** to name as candidate for or future holder of an office. **2.** to appoint as a place or date for a meeting etc., **nomination** *n.,* **nominator** *n.*

nominative (**nom**-in-ă-tiv) *n.* the form of a noun used when it is the subject of a verb.

nominee (nom-in-ee) *n.* a person who is nominated by another.

non- *prefix* not.

nonagenarian (noh-nă-jin-**air**-iăn) *n.* a person who is in his or her nineties.

non-alcoholic *adj.* containing no alcohol.

non-aligned (non-ă-**lynd**) *adj.* not in alliance with any bloc. **non-alignment** *n.*

nonchalant (**non**-shă-lănt) *adj.* not feeling or showing anxiety or excitement, calm and casual. **nonchalantly** *adv.,* **nonchalance** *n.*

non-combatant (non-**com**-bă-tănt) *n.* **1.** a member of an army etc. whose duties do not involve fighting, e.g. a doctor or chaplain. **2.** a civilian during a war.

non-commissioned *adj.* not holding a commission, *non-commissioned officers.*

non-committal (non-kŏ-**mi**-t'l) *adj.* not committing oneself, not showing what one thinks or which side one supports.

non compos mentis insane.

non-conductor *n.* a substance that does not conduct heat or electricity.

non-conformist *n.* **1.** a person who does not conform to established principles. **2.** *Nonconformist,* a member of certain Protestant sects that do not conform to the teaching or practices of the Church of England or other established Churches.

non-contributory *adj.* not involving payment of contributions, *a non-contributory pension scheme.*

nondescript (**non**-dis-kript) *adj.* lacking in distinctive characteristics and therefore not easy to classify. —*n.* a nondescript person or thing.

none *pronoun* **1.** not any. ¶ This word may be followed by either a singular or a plural verb. The singular construction is preferred (*none of the candidates has failed*), but the plural is very common (*none of them are required*). **2.** no person(s), no one, *none can tell.* —*adv.* by no amount, not at all, *is none the worse for it.* □ **none other,**

no other person. **none the less,** nevertheless. **none too,** not very, not at all, *he's none too pleased.*

nonentity (non-**en**-titi) *n.* a person or thing of no importance.

non-event *n.* an event that was expected or intended to be important but proves to be disappointing.

non-existent *adj.* not existing.

non-fiction *n.* a class of literature that includes books in all subjects other than fiction.

non-flammable *adj.* unable to be set on fire. ¶ See the note under inflammable.

non-inflammable *adj.* unable to be set on fire.

non-intervention *n.* the policy of not interfering in other people's disputes.

non-iron *adj.* (of fabric) not needing to be ironed.

non-pareil (**non**-per-el) *adj.* unrivalled. —*n.* an unrivalled person or thing.

non-party *adj.* not belonging to or supported by a political party.

nonplussed (non-**plust**) *adj.* completely perplexed.

non-resident *adj.* **1.** not living on the premises, *a non-resident caretaker.* **2.** (of a job) not requiring the holder to live in. —*n.* a person not staying at a hotel etc., *open to non residents.*

nonsense *n.* **1.** words put together in a way that does not make sense. **2.** absurd or foolish talk or ideas or behaviour.

nonsensical (non-**sens**-ikăl) *adj.* not making sense, absurd, foolish. **nonsensically** *adv.*

non sequitur (non **sek**-wit-er) a conclusion that does not follow from the evidence given. (¶ Latin, = it does not follow.)

non-skid *adj.* (of tyres) designed to prevent or reduce skidding.

non-smoker *n.* **1.** a person who does not smoke. **2.** a train-compartment where smoking is forbidden.

non-starter *n.* **1.** a horse which is entered for a race but does not run in it. **2.** a person or an idea etc. that is not worth considering for a particular purpose.

non-stick *adj.* coated with a substance that food will not stick to during cooking.

non-stop *adj.* **1.** (of a train or plane etc.) not stopping at intermediate places. **2.** not ceasing, *non-stop chatter.* —*adv.* without stopping or pausing.

non-U (non-**yoo**) *adj.* (*informal*) not characteristic of upper-class speech or behaviour.

non-union *adj.* not belonging to a trade union.

non-white *adj.* not belonging to the white

race of mankind. —*n.* a non-white person.

noodle *n.* a foolish person.

noodles *pl. n.* pasta in narrow strips, used in soups etc.

nook *n.* a secluded place or corner, a recess.

noon *n.* twelve o'clock in the day, midday. **noonday** *n.*, **noontide** *n.*

noose *n.* a loop of rope etc. with a knot that tightens when pulled.

nor *conj.* & *adv.* and not.

Nordic *adj.* of the racial type found especially in Scandinavia, tall and blond with blue eyes.

Norfolk (**nor**-fŏk) a county of England.

norm *n.* **1.** a standard or pattern or type considered to be representative of a group. **2.** a standard amount of work etc. to be done or produced.

normal *adj.* **1.** conforming to what is standard or usual. **2.** free from mental or emotional disorders. **normally** *adv.*, **normality** *n.*

normalize *v.* to make or become normal. **normalization** *n.*

Norman *adj.* of the Normans. —*n.* a member of the people of Normandy in northern France. □ **Norman Conquest,** *see* conquest.

Norse *adj.* of ancient Norway or Scandinavia. —*n.* the Norwegian language or the Scandinavian group of languages.

north *n.* **1.** the point or direction to the left of a person facing east. **2.** the northern part of something. —*adj.* & *adv.* towards or in the north; *a north wind,* blowing from the north. □ **north country,** the part of England north of the Humber. **north-countryman** *n.* a person from this area. **North Pole,** the northernmost point of the earth. **north pole,** (of a magnet) the pole that is attracted to the north. **North Star,** the pole-star.

Northamptonshire a county of England.

Northants *abbrev.* Northamptonshire.

Northd. *abbrev.* Northumberland.

north-east *n.* the point or direction midway between north and east. **north-easterly** *adj.* & *n.*, **north-eastern** *adj.*

northerly *adj.* in or towards the north; *a northerly wind,* blowing from the north (approximately). —*n.* a northerly wind.

northern *adj.* of or in the north. **Northern Ireland,** *see* Ireland. **northern lights,** the aurora borealis. **Northern Territory,** a territory in north Australia.

northerner *n.* a native or inhabitant of the north.

northernmost *adj.* furthest north.

Northumberland a county of England.

Northumbrian *adj.* of ancient Northumbria (= England north of the Humber) or modern Northumberland.

northward *adj.* & *adv.* towards the north. **northwards** *adv.*

north-west *n.* the point or direction midway between north and west. **north-westerly** *adj.* & *n.*, **north-western** *adj.* □ **Northwest Territories,** part of Canada lying north of the 60th parallel.

Norway a country in northern Europe.

Norwegian *adj.* of Norway or its people or language. —*n.* **1.** a native or inhabitant of Norway. **2.** the language of Norway.

Nos. *or* **nos.** *abbrev.* numbers.

nose *n.* **1.** the organ at the front of the head in man and animals, containing the nostrils and used for breathing and smelling. **2.** a sense of smell. **3.** the ability to detect things of a particular kind, *has a nose for scandal.* **4.** the open end of a tube or piping etc. **5.** the front end or projecting front part of something. —**nose** *v.* **1.** to detect or search by using one's sense of smell. **2.** to smell at, to rub with the nose, to push the nose against or into. **3.** to push one's way cautiously ahead, *the car nosed past the obstruction.* □ **by a nose,** by a very narrow margin. **keep one's nose clean,** to stay out of trouble. **pay through the nose,** to pay an unfairly high price. **put someone's nose out of joint,** to make him envious because of another's success or promotion etc. **rub his nose in it,** to remind him humiliatingly of his error. **turn up one's nose at,** to reject or ignore contemptuously. **under a person's nose,** where he can or should see it clearly. **with one's nose in the air,** haughtily.

nosebag *n.* a bag containing fodder, for hanging on a horse's head.

nosebleed *n.* bleeding from the nose.

nosedive *n.* **1.** an aeroplane's steep downward plunge with the nose first. **2.** any sudden drop or plunge. —*v.* to make this.

nosegay *n.* a small bunch of flowers.

nosey *adj.* (**nosier, nosiest**) (*slang*) inquisitive. **nosily** *adv.*, **nosiness** *n.* □ **Nosey Parker,** an inquisitive person, a busybody.

nosh *n.* (*slang*) food. —*v.* (*slang*) to eat. □ **nosh-up** *n.* (*slang*) a meal.

nostalgia (noss-**tal**-jă) *n.* sentimental memory of or longing for things of the past. **nostalgic** *adj.* feeling or producing nostalgia. **nostalgically** *adv.*

nostril *n.* either of the two openings in the nose through which air is admitted.

nostrum (**noss**-trŭm) *n.* a quack remedy.

not *adv.* expressing a negative or denial or

refusal. **not at all,** a polite reply to thanks.
not half, not nearly, *not half enough*; (*informal*) not at all, *it's not half bad*; (*slang*) very much, *he didn't half swear.*

notability *n.* **1.** being notable. **2.** a notable person.

notable *adj.* worthy of notice, remarkable, eminent. —*n.* an eminent person.

notably *adv.* remarkably; especially.

Notary Public (**noh**-ter-i) (*pl.* Notaries Public) a person officially authorized to witness the signing of documents and to perform other formal transactions.

notation *n.* a system of signs or symbols representing numbers, quantities, musical notes, etc.

notch *n.* **1.** a V-shaped cut or indentation. **2.** one of the levels in a graded system, *everyone moved up a notch.* —**notch** *v.* **1.** to make a notch or notches in. **2.** to score, *notched up another win.*

note *n.* **1.** a brief record of something, written down to aid the memory. **2.** a short or informal letter, a memorandum, a formal diplomatic communication. **3.** a short comment on or explanation of a word or passage in a book etc. **4.** a written or printed promise to pay money, a banknote, *£5 notes.* **5.** a tone of definite pitch made by a voice or instrument or engine etc. **6.** a written sign representing the pitch and duration of a musical sound. **7.** one of the keys on a piano etc. **8.** a significant sound or indication of feelings etc., *a note of optimism.* **9.** eminence, distinction, *a family of note.* **10.** notice, attention; *take note of what he says,* pay attention to it. —**note** *v.* **1.** to notice, to pay attention to. **2.** to write down, *noted it down.*

notebook *n.* a book with blank pages on which to write memoranda.

notecase *n.* a wallet for holding banknotes.

noted *adj.* famous, well-known.

notelets *pl. n.* a set of pieces of small folded ornamental notepaper.

notepaper *n.* paper for writing letters on.

noteworthy *adj.* worthy of notice, remarkable.

nothing *n.* **1.** no thing, not anything. **2.** no amount, nought. **3.** non-existence, what does not exist. **4.** a person or thing of no importance. —*adv.* not at all, in no way, *it's nothing like as good.* □ **for nothing,** without payment, free; without a reward or result. **nothing doing,** (*slang*) a statement of refusal or failure. **nothingness** *n.* non-existence, *faded into nothingness.*

notice *n.* **1.** news or information of what has happened or is about to happen; *at short notice,* with little time for preparation. **2.** a formal announcement that one is to end an agreement or leave a job at a specified time, *gave him a month's notice.* **3.** written or printed information or instructions displayed publicly. **4.** attention, observation, *it escaped my notice.* **5.** an account or review in a newspaper. —**notice** *v.* **1.** to perceive, to become aware of, to take notice of. **2.** to remark upon, to speak of. □ **notice-board** *n.* a board on which notices may be displayed. **take notice,** to show signs of interest; *take no notice of it,* ignore it, take no action about it.

noticeable *adj.* easily seen or noticed. **noticeably** *adv.*

notifiable *adj.* that must be notified; *notifiable diseases,* those that must be reported to the public health authorities.

notify *v.* (**notified, notifying**) **1.** to inform. **2.** to report, to make (a thing) known. **notification** *n.*

notion *n.* **1.** an idea or opinion, especially one that is vague or probably incorrect. **2.** an understanding or intention, *has no notion of discipline.* □ **notions** *pl. n.* (*Amer.*) small items used in sewing (e.g. reels of cotton, buttons), haberdashery.

notional (**noh**-shŏn-ăl) *adj.* hypothetical, assumed to be correct or valid for a particular purpose, *an estimate based on notional figures.* **notionally** *adv.*

notorious (noh-**tor**-iŭs) *adj.* well known, especially in an unfavourable way. **notoriously** *adv.,* **notoriety** (noh-ter-I-iti) *n.*

Nottinghamshire a county of England.

Notts. *abbrev.* Nottinghamshire.

notwithstanding *prep.* in spite of. —*adv.* nevertheless.

nougat (**noo**-gah) *n.* a chewy sweet made of nuts, sugar or honey, and egg-white.

nought (*pr.* nawt) *n.* **1.** the figure 0. **2.** nothing.

noun *n.* a word or phrase used as the name of a person or place or thing. **common nouns,** words such as *man, dog, table,* and *sport,* which are used of whole classes of people or things. **proper nouns,** words such as *John* and *Smith* and *London* which name a particular person or thing.

nourish (**nu**-rish) *v.* **1.** to keep (a person or animal or plant) alive and well by means of food. **2.** to foster or cherish (a feeling etc.). **nourishment** *n.*

nous (*rhymes with* house) *n.* (*informal*) common sense.

nova (**noh**-vă) *n.* (*pl.* novas) a star that suddenly becomes much brighter for a short time.

Nova Scotia (noh-vă **skoh**-shă) a province of Canada.

novel *n.* a book-length story. —*adj.* of a new kind, *a novel experience.*

novelette *n.* a short novel.

novelist *n.* a writer of novels.

novelty *n.* 1. the quality of being novel. 2. a novel thing or occurrence. 3. a small unusual object, especially one suitable for giving as a present, *a stall selling novelties.*

November *n.* the eleventh month of the year.

novice (**nov**-iss) *n.* 1. a person who is inexperienced in the work etc. that he is doing, a beginner. 2. one who has been accepted into a religious order but has not yet taken the final vows.

noviciate (nŏ-**vish**-i-ăt) *n.* the period of being a novice in a religious order.

now *adv.* 1. at the time when or of which one is writing or speaking. 2. by this time. 3. immediately, *must go now.* 4. (with no reference to time, giving an explanation or comfort etc.) I beg or wonder or warn you or am telling you, *now why didn't I think of that?* —*conj.* as a consequence of the fact, simultaneously with it, *now that you have come, we'll start; I do remember, now you mention it.* —*n.* the present time, *they ought to be here by now.* □ **for now,** until a later time, *goodbye for now.* **now and again** *or* **now and then,** occasionally.

nowadays *adv.* at the present time (contrasted with years ago).

nowhere *adv.* not anywhere. **be nowhere** *or* **come in nowhere,** to fail to be placed in a race or competition. **come from nowhere,** to be suddenly present. **get nowhere,** to make no progress.

nowise *adv.* in no way, not at all.

nowt *n.* (*informal*) nothing.

noxious (**nok**-shŭs) *adj.* unpleasant and harmful.

nozzle *n.* the vent or spout of a hosepipe etc. through which a stream of liquid or air is directed.

NS *abbrev.* Nova Scotia.

NSW *abbrev.* New South Wales.

NT *abbrev.* 1. New Testament. 2. (*Austral.*) Northern Territory.

nth *adj.* **to the nth degree,** to the utmost.

nuance (**new**-ahns) *n.* a subtle difference in meaning, a shade of meaning.

nub *n.* 1. a small knob or lump. 2. the central point or core of a matter or problem.

nubbly *adj.* full of small lumps, *nubbly tweeds.*

nubile (**new**-byl) *adj.* marriageable, physically attractive, *nubile young women.*

nuclear *adj.* 1. of a nucleus. 2. of or using nuclear energy, *nuclear weapons; nuclear power.* □ **nuclear energy,** energy that is released or absorbed during reactions taking place in the nuclei of atoms. **nuclear physics,** the branch of physics dealing with atomic nuclei and their reactions.

nucleonics (new-kli-**on**-iks) *n.* the branch of science and engineering that deals with the practical uses of nuclear energy.

nucleus (**new**-kli-ŭs) *n.* (*pl.* nuclei, *pr.* **new**-kli-I) 1. the central part or thing round which others are collected. 2. something established that will receive additions, *this collection of books will form the nucleus of a new library.* 3. the central positively charged portion of an atom.

nude *adj.* not clothed, naked. —*n.* a nude human figure in a painting etc. **nudity** *n.* □ **in the nude,** not clothed, naked.

nudge *v.* 1. to poke (a person) gently with the elbow in order to draw his attention quietly. 2. to push slightly or gradually. —*n.* this movement.

nudist (**newd**-ist) *n.* a person who believes that going unclothed is good for the health. **nudism** *n.* □ **nudist camp,** a settlement where people live unclothed.

nugget (**nug**-it) *n.* 1. a rough lump of gold or platinum as found in the earth. 2. something small and valuable, *nuggets of information.*

nuisance *n.* a source of annoyance, an annoying person or thing.

null *adj.* having no legal force, *declared the agreement null and void.* **nullity** *n.*

nullify *v.* (nullified, nullifying) 1. to make (a thing) null. 2. to cancel or neutralize the effect of. **nullification** *n.*

numb *adj.* deprived of the power to feel or move, *numb with cold* or *shock.* —*v.* to make numb. **numbly** *adv.,* **numbness** *n.*

number *n.* 1. a symbol or word indicating how many, a numeral. 2. a numeral identifying a person or thing (e.g. a telephone or a house in a street) by its position in a series. 3. a single issue of a magazine. 4. a song or piece of music. etc., especially as an item in a theatrical performance. 5. (*informal*) an object (such as garment or car) considered as an item. 6. a total of people or things; *a number of,* some; *numbers of,* very many. 7. the category 'singular' or 'plural' in grammar. —**number** *v.* 1. to count, to find out how many. 2. to amount to. 3. to assign a number to (each in a series), to distinguish in this way. 4. to include or regard as, *I number him among my friends.* □ **by numbers,** following simple instructions identified by numbers. **have a person's number,** (*slang*) to understand him or his motives. **his days are numbered,** he has not long to live or to remain in his present position. **number one,** (*slang*) oneself, *always takes care of number one.* **number-plate** *n.* a plate on a motor vehicle, bearing its registration number.

numeral (**new**-mer-ăl) *n.* a symbol that represents a certain number, a figure.

numerate (**new**-mer-ăt) *adj.* having a good basic knowledge and understanding of mathematics and science. **numeracy** *n.*

numeration (new-mer-ay-shŏn) *n.* numbering.

numerator (**new**-mer-ayter) *n.* the number written above the line in a vulgar fraction, showing how many of the parts indicated by the denominator are to be taken (e.g. 2 in $\frac{2}{3}$).

numerical (new-**merri**-kăl) *adj.* of a number or series of numbers, *placed in numerical order.*

numerous (**new**-mer-ŭs) *adj.* many, consisting of many items.

numismatics (new-miz-**mat**-iks) *n.* the scientific study of coins and similar objects (e.g. medals).

numismatist (new-**miz**-mă-tist) *n.* an expert in numismatics.

nun *n.* a member of a community of women living apart from the world under the rules of a religious order.

nuncio (**nun**-shi-oh) *n.* (*pl.* nuncios) a diplomatic representative of the pope, accredited to a civil government.

nunnery *n.* a convent for nuns.

nuptial (**nup**-shăl) *adj.* of marriage, of a wedding ceremony. **nuptials** *pl. n.* a wedding.

nurse *n.* **1.** a person trained to assist a doctor in caring for sick or injured or infirm people. **2.** a woman employed to take charge of young children. —**nurse** *v.* **1.** to work as a nurse, to look after in this way. **2.** to feed or be fed at the breast or udder. **3.** to hold carefully. **4.** to give special care to; *nurse a constituency,* try to keep its favour by continued attentions. □ **nursing home,** a privately run hospital or home for invalids. **nursing mother,** one who is suckling an infant.

nursemaid *n.* a young woman employed to take charge of young children.

nursery *n.* **1.** a room set apart for young children. **2.** a day nursery (*see* day). **3.** a place where young plants are reared for transplantation and usually for sale. □ **nursery rhyme,** a simple traditional song or story in rhyme for children. **nursery school,** a school for children below normal school age. **nursery slopes,** easy slopes

suitable for beginners at a skiing resort. **nursery stakes,** a race for two-year-old horses.

nurseryman *n.* (*pl.* nurserymen) one who owns or works in a plant nursery.

nursling *n.* a baby or young animal that is being suckled.

nurture (**ner**-cher) *v.* **1.** to nourish and rear. **2.** to bring up, *a delicately nurtured girl.* —*n.* nurturing.

nut *n.* **1.** fruit consisting of a hard shell round an edible kernel. **2.** this kernel. **3.** (*slang*) the head. **4.** (*slang*) an insane or eccentric person. **5.** a small piece of metal with a hole in its centre, designed for use with a bolt; *the nuts and bolts of something,* practical details. **6.** a small lump of a solid substance, e.g. coal or butter. □ **nut-brown** *adj.* brown like a ripe hazelnut. **nut-case** *n.* (*slang*) a crazy person. **nut-house** *n.* (*slang*) a mental home or hospital. **nuts** *adj.* (*slang*) crazy; *be nuts about,* to be very enthusiastic about.

nutcrackers *pl. n.* a pair of pincers for cracking nuts.

nuthatch *n.* a small climbing bird that feeds on nuts and insects.

nutmeg *n.* the hard fragrant seed of a tropical tree, ground or grated as spice.

nutria (**new**-tri-ă) *n.* the skin or fur of a beaver-like water animal of South America.

nutrient (**new**-tri-ĕnt) *adj.* nourishing. —*n.* a nourishing substance.

nutriment (**new**-trim-ĕnt) *n.* nourishing food.

nutrition (new-**trish**-ŏn) *n.* nourishment. **nutritional** *adj.*

nutritious (new-**trish**-ŭs) *adj.* nourishing, efficient as food.

nutritive (**new**-tri-tiv) *adj.* nourishing. —*n.* a nourishing substance.

nutshell *n.* the hard outer shell of a nut. *in a nutshell,* expressed in the briefest possible way.

nutter *n.* (*slang*) a crazy person.

nutting *n.* gathering nuts, *go nutting.*

nutty *adj.* **1.** full of nuts. **2.** tasting like nuts. **3.** (*slang*) crazy.

nuzzle *v.* to press or rub gently with the nose.

NW *abbrev.* north-west, north-western.

NWT *abbrev.* Northwest Territories.

NY *abbrev.* New York.

nylon *n.* **1.** a synthetic fibre of great lightness and strength. **2.** fabric made from this.

nymph (*pr.* nimf) *n.* **1.** (in mythology) a semi-divine maiden living in the sea or woods etc. **2.** a young insect that resembles its parents in form.

nympho (**nim**-foh) *n.* (*pl.* nymphos) (*informal*) a nymphomaniac.

nymphomania (nim-fŏ-**may**-niă) *n.* excessive and uncontrollable sexual desire in women. **nymphomaniac** *n.* a woman suffering from this.

nystagmus (nis-**tag**-mŭs) *n.* abnormal continual rapid involuntary movement of the eyeballs.

NZ *abbrev.* New Zealand.

Oo

oaf *n.* (*pl.* oafs) an awkward lout. **oafish** *adj.* like an oaf.

oak *n.* **1.** a deciduous forest tree with irregularly-shaped leaves, bearing acorns. **2.** its wood. □ **oak-apple** *n.* = gall³. **the Oaks**, an annual race at Epsom for three-year-old fillies.

oaken *adj.* made of oak.

OAP *abbrev.* old-age pensioner.

oar *n.* **1.** a pole with a flat blade at one end, used to propel a boat by its leverage against water. **2.** an oarsman, *he's a good oar.* □ **put one's oar in**, to interfere.

oarsman *n.* (*pl.* oarsmen) a rower.

oarsmanship *n.* skill in rowing.

oasis (oh-**ay**-sis) *n.* (*pl.* oases, *pr.* oh-**ay**-seez) a fertile spot in a desert, with a spring or well or water.

oast *n.* a kiln for drying hops. **oast-house** *n.* a building containing this.

oatcake *n.* a thin cake made of oatmeal.

oath *n.* **1.** a solemn undertaking to do something or that something is true, appealing to God or a revered object as witness. **2.** casual use of the name of God etc. in anger or to give emphasis. □ **on** *or* **under oath**, having made a solemn oath.

oatmeal *n.* **1.** meal prepared from oats, used to make porridge etc. **2.** greyish-fawn colour.

oats *pl. n.* **1.** a hardy cereal plant grown in cool climates for food (*oats* for horses, *oatmeal* for people). **2.** its grain. □ **sow one's wild oats**, to lead a wild life while young, before becoming steady.

obbligato (obli-**gah**-toh) *n.* (*pl.* obbligatos) an important accompanying part in a musical composition.

obdurate (**ob**-dewr-ăt) *adj.* stubborn and unyielding. **obduracy** *n.*

obedient *adj.* doing what one is told to do, willing to obey. **obediently** *adv.*, **obedience** *n.*

obeisance (ŏ-**bay**-săns) *n.* a deep bow or curtsy.

obelisk (**ob**-ĕl-isk) *n.* a tall pillar set up as a monument.

obese (ŏ-**beess**) *adj.* very fat. **obesity** (ŏ-**beess**-iti) *n.*

obey *v.* (obeyed, obeying) to do what is commanded by (a person or law or instinct etc.), to be obedient.

obituary (ŏ-**bit**-yoo-eri) *n.* a notice of a person's death, especially in a newspaper, often with a short account of his life and achievements.

object¹ (**ob**-jikt) *n.* **1.** something solid that can be seen or touched. **2.** a person or thing to which some action or feeling is directed, *an object of pity.* **3.** a purpose, an intention. **4.** (in grammar) a noun or its equivalent acted upon by a transitive verb or by a preposition ('him' is the object in *the dog bit him* and *against him*). □ **no object**, not forming an important or limiting factor; *expense no object*, the cost will not be grudged. **object lesson**, a striking practical illustration of some principle.

object² (ŏb-**jekt**) *v.* to say that one is not in favour of something, to protest. **objector** *n.*

objection *n.* **1.** a feeling of disapproval or opposition, a statement of this. **2.** a reason for objecting, a drawback in a plan etc.

objectionable *adj.* causing objections or disapproval, unpleasant. **objectionably** *adv.*

objective (ŏb-**jek**-tiv) *adj.* **1.** having real existence outside a person's mind, not subjective. **2.** not influenced by personal feelings or opinions, *an objective account of the problem.* **3.** (in grammar) of the objective case. —*n.* something one is trying to achieve or reach or capture. —**objectively** *adv.* □ **objective case**, the form of a word used when it is the object of a verb or preposition.

objet d'art (ob-*zhay* **dar**) (*pl.* objets d'art, *pr.* ob-*zhay* **dar**) a small artistic object.

obligation *n.* **1.** being obliged to do something. **2.** what one must do in order to comply with an agreement or law etc., one's duty. □ **under an obligation**, owing gratitude to another person for some service or benefit.

obligatory (ŏ-**blig**-ă-ter-i) *adj.* required by law or rule or custom, compulsory not optional.

oblige *v.* **1.** to compel by law or agreement or custom or necessity. **2.** to help or gratify by performing a small service, *oblige me with a loan.* □ **be obliged to a person**, indebted to him for some service. **much obliged**, thank you.

obliging *adj.* courteous and helpful. **obligingly** *adv.*

oblique (ŏ-**bleek**) *adj.* **1.** slanting. **2.** expressed indirectly, not going straight to the point, *an oblique reply.* **obliquely** *adv.* □ **oblique angle,** an acute or obtuse angle.

obliterate (ŏ-**blit**-er-ayt) *v.* to blot out, to destroy and leave no clear traces of. **obliteration** *n.*

oblivion (ŏ-**bliv**-iŏn) *n.* **1.** the state of being forgotten. **2.** the state of being oblivious.

oblivious (ŏ-**bliv**-iŭs) *adj.* unaware or unconscious of something, *oblivious of* or *to her surroundings.*

oblong *n.* a rectangular shape that is longer than it is broad. —*adj.* having this shape.

obnoxious (ŏb-**nok**-shŭs) *adj.* very unpleasant, objectionable. **obnoxiously** *adv.*

oboe (**oh**-boh) *n.* a woodwind instrument of treble pitch. **oboist** (**oh**-boh-ist) *n.* a person who plays the oboe.

obscene (ŏb-**seen**) *adj.* indecent in a repulsive or very offensive way. **obscenely** *adv.*

obscenity (ŏb-**sen**-iti) *n.* **1.** being obscene. **2.** an obscene action or word etc.

obscuration *n.* making or being made obscure.

obscure *adj.* **1.** dark, indistinct. **2.** remote from people's observation. **3.** not famous, *an obscure poet.* **4.** not easily understood, not clearly expressed. —*v.* to make obscure, to conceal from view. —**obscurely** *adv.*, **obscurity** *n.*

obsequies (**ob**-si-kwiz) *pl. n.* funeral rites.

obsequious (ŏb-**see**-kwi-ŭs) *adj.* excessively or sickeningly respectful. **obsequiously** *adv.*

observable *adj.* able to be observed.

observance *n.* the keeping of a law or rule or custom etc., the keeping or celebrating of a religious festival or or of a holiday.

observant *adj.* quick at noticing things. **observantly** *adv.*

observation *n.* **1.** observing, being observed. **2.** a comment or remark.

observatory (ŏb-**zerv**-ă-ter-i) *n.* a building designed and equipped for scientific observation of the stars or weather.

observe *v.* **1.** to see and notice, to watch carefully. **2.** to pay attention to (rules etc.). **3.** to keep or celebrate, *not all countries observe New Year's Day.* **4.** to remark. **observer** *n.*

obsess (ŏb-**sess**) *v.* to occupy the thoughts of (a person) continually.

obsession (ŏb-**sesh**-ŏn) *n.* **1.** obsessing, being obsessed. **2.** a persistent idea that dominates a person's thoughts.

obsessive *adj.* of or causing or showing obsession. **obsessively** *adv.*

obsolescent (obsŏ-**less**-ĕnt) *adj.* becoming obsolete, going out of use or out of fashion. **obsolescence** *n.*

obsolete (**ob**-sŏ-leet) *adj.* no longer used, antiquated.

obstacle *n.* a thing that obstructs progress. **obstacle-race** *n.* a race in which artificial or natural obstacles have to be passed.

obstetrician (ob-stit-**rish**-ăn) *n.* a specialist in obstetrics.

obstetrics (ŏb-**stet**-riks) *n.* the branch of medicine and surgery that deals with childbirth. **obstetric, obstetrical** *adjs.*

obstinate *adj.* **1.** keeping firmly to one's opinion or to one's chosen course of action, not easily persuaded. **2.** not easily overcome, *an obstinate cold.* **obstinately** *adv.*, **obstinacy** *n.*

obstreperous (ŏb-**strep**-er-ŭs) *adj.* noisy, unruly, *obstreperous children.*

obstruct *v.* **1.** to prevent or hinder movement along (a path etc.) by means of an object or objects placed in it, *obstructing the highway.* **2.** to prevent or hinder the movement or progress or activities of, *obstructing the police.*

obstruction *n.* **1.** obstructing, being obstructive. **2.** a thing that obstructs.

obstructionist *n.* a person who seeks to obstruct plans or legislation etc.

obstructive *adj.* causing or intended to cause obstruction.

obtain *v.* **1.** to get, to come into possession of (a thing) by effort or as a gift. **2.** to be established or in use as a rule or custom, *this custom still obtains in some districts.*

obtainable *adj.* able to be obtained.

obtrude (ŏb-**trood**) *v.* to force (oneself or one's ideas) on others. **obtrusion** (ŏb-**troo**-zhŏn) *n.*

obtrusive (ŏb-**troo**-siv) *adj.* obtruding oneself, unpleasantly noticeable. **obtrusively** *adv.*

obtuse (ŏb-**tewss**) *adj.* **1.** of blunt shape, not sharp or pointed. **2.** stupid, slow at understanding. **obtusely** *adv.*, **obtuseness** *n.* □ **obtuse angle,** an angle of more than 90° but less than 180°.

obverse (**ob**-verss) *n.* the side of a coin or medal etc. that bears the head or the principal design.

obviate (**ob**-vi-ayt) *v.* to make unnecessary, *the bypass obviates the need to drive through the town.*

obvious *adj.* easy to see or recognize or understand. **obviously** *adv.*

occasion *n.* **1.** the time at which a particular event takes place. **2.** a special event, *this is quite an occasion.* **3.** a suitable time for doing something, an opportunity. **4.** a need or reason or cause, *had no occasion to speak French.* —*v.* to cause. □ **on occasion**, when need arises, occasionally.

occasional *adj.* **1.** happening from time to time but not regularly or frequently, *occasional showers.* **2.** used or meant for a special event, *occasional verses.* **occasionally** *adv.* □ **occasional table**, a small table for use as required.

Occident (oks-i-děnt) *n.* the West as opposed to the Orient.

occidental (oksi-**den**-t'l) *adj.* western. **Occidental** *n.* a native of the western world.

occlude *v.* to stop up, to obstruct. **occlusion** *n.* □ **occluded front** *or* **occlusion**, the atmospheric condition that occurs when a cold front overtakes a mass of warm air, and warm air is driven upwards.

occult (ŏ-**kult**) *adj.* **1.** secret, hidden except from those with more than ordinary knowledge. **2.** involving the supernatural, *occult powers.*

occupant *n.* a person occupying a place or dwelling or position. **occupancy** *n.*

occupation *n.* **1.** occupying, being occupied. **2.** taking or holding possession by force, especially of a defeated country or district. **3.** an activity that keeps a person busy, one's employment.

occupational *adj.* of or caused by one's occupation. **occupational hazard**, a risk of accident or illness associated with a certain job. **occupational therapy**, creative activities designed to aid recovery from certain illnesses.

occupy *v.* (occupied, occupying) **1.** to dwell in, to inhabit. **2.** to take possession of and establish one's troops in (a country or strategic position etc.) in war. **3.** to place oneself in (a building etc.) as a political or other demonstration. **4.** to take up or fill (space or a position). **5.** to hold as one's official position, *he occupies the post of manager.* **6.** to keep (a person or his time) filled with activity. **occupier** *n.*

occur *v.* (occurred, occurring) **1.** to come into being as an event or process. **2.** to be found to exist in some place or conditions, *these plants occur in marshy areas.* **3.** to come into a person's mind, *it did not occur to me to mention it.*

occurrence (ŏ-**ku**-rěns) *n.* **1.** occurring. **2.** an incident or event.

ocean *n.* the sea surrounding the continents of the earth, especially one of the five large named areas of this, *the Atlantic, Pacific, Indian, Arctic, and Antarctic Oceans.* □ **ocean-going** *adj.* (of ships) made for

crossing the sea, not for coastal or river journeys.

oceanic (oh-shi-**an**-ik) *adj.* of the ocean.

oceanography (oh-shăn-**og**-răfi) *n.* the scientific study of the ocean.

ocelot (**oh**-sil-ot) *n.* **1.** a leopard-like animal of Central and South America. **2.** its fur.

ochre (**oh**-ker) *n.* **1.** a yellow, red, or brownish mineral consisting of clay and iron oxide, used as a pigment. **2.** pale brownish yellow.

o'clock *adv.* **1.** = of the clock (used in specifying the hour), *six o'clock.* **2.** according to a method for indicating relative position by imagining a clock-dial with the observer at the centre, 'twelve o'clock' being directly ahead of or above him, *enemy aircraft approaching at two o'clock.*

octagon (**ok**-tă-gŏn) *n.* a geometric figure with eight sides. **octagonal** (ok-**tag**-ŏn-ăl) *adj.* having eight sides.

octahedron (oktă-**hee**-drŏn) *n.* a solid geometric shape with eight faces.

octane (**ok**-tayn) *n.* a hydrocarbon compound occurring in petrol. **high-octane** *adj.* (of fuel) having a high percentage of a certain form of octane and therefore good anti-knock properties. **octane number**, a measure of the anti-knock properties of a petrol in comparison with those of a fuel taken as standard.

octave (**ok**-tiv) *n.* **1.** a note that is six whole tones above or below a given note. **2.** the interval between these notes. **3.** the series of notes filling this.

octavo (ok-**tay**-voh) *n.* the size of a book or page given by folding a sheet of standard size three times to form eight leaves.

octet (ok-**tet**) *n.* a group of eight instruments or voices, a musical composition for these.

October *n.* the tenth month of the year.

octogenarian (ok-toh-jin-**air**-iăn) *n.* a person who is in his or her eighties.

octopus *n.* (*pl.* octopuses) a sea animal with a soft body and eight long tentacles.

ocular (**ok**-yoo-ler) *adj.* of or for or by the eyes, visual.

oculist (**ok**-yoo-list) *n.* a specialist in the treatment of diseases and defects of the eyes.

odd *adj.* **1.** (of a number) not even, not exactly divisible by 2. **2.** designated by such a number. **3.** being the remaining one of a set or series of which the other member(s) are lacking, *found an odd glove*; *several odd volumes*; *you're wearing odd socks,* two that do not form a pair. **4.** exceeding a round number or amount, *keep the odd money*; *forty odd,* between 40 and

50. **5.** not regular or habitual or fixed, *does odd jobs*; *at odd moments*. **6.** unusual, strange, eccentric, *an odd sort of person*. **oddly** *adv.*, **oddness** *n.* □ **odd man out**, a person or thing differing in some way from others of a group.

oddball *n.* (*slang*) an eccentric person.

oddity *n.* **1.** strangeness. **2.** an unusual person or thing or event.

oddment *n.* something left over, an isolated article.

odds *pl. n.* **1.** the probability that a certain thing will happen, this expressed as a ratio, *the odds are 5 to 1 against throwing a six.* **2.** the ratio between amounts staked by parties to a bet, *gave odds of 3 to 1.* □ **at odds with**, in disagreement or conflict with. **it makes no odds**, it makes no difference; *it's no odds to him,* does not concern him. **odds and ends**, oddments. **odds-on** *adj.* with success more likely than failure; with betting-odds in favour of its success, *the odds-on favourite.*

ode *n.* a poem expressing noble feelings, often addressed to a person or celebrating an event.

odious (oh-di-ŭs) *adj.* hateful, detestable. **odiously** *adv.*, **odiousness** *n.*

odium (oh-di-ŭm) *n.* widespread hatred or disgust felt towards a person or his actions.

odometer (od-om-it-er) *n.* an instrument for measuring the distance travelled by a wheeled vehicle.

odour (oh-der) *n.* a smell. **odourless** *adj.*, **odorous** *adj.*

odyssey (od-iss-i) *n.* (*pl.* odysseys) a long adventurous journey. ¶ Named after *the Odyssey,* a Greek epic poem telling of the wanderings of the hero Odysseus.

oedema (ee-dee-ma) *n.* excess of fluid in the tissues, causing swelling.

Oedipus complex (ee-dip-ŭs) sexual feeling towards one's parents, involving attraction to the parent of the opposite sex (especially the mother) and jealousy of the other parent. ¶ Named after *Oedipus* in Greek legend, who in ignorance killed his father and married his mother.

oesophagus (ee-sof-ă-gŭs) *n.* the canal from the mouth to the stomach, the gullet.

oestrogen (ees-trŏ-jin) *n.* a hormone capable of developing and maintaining female bodily characteristics.

of *prep.* indicating relationships, **1.** belonging to or originating from. **2.** concerning, *told us of his travels.* **3.** composed or made from, *built of brick*; *a farm of 100 acres.* **4.** with reference or regard to, *never heard of it.* **5.** for or involving or directed towards, *love of one's country.* **6.** so as to bring separation or relief from, *cured him of smoking.* **7.** during, *he comes of an evening.* □ **of itself**, by itself or in itself.

off *adv.* **1.** away, at or to a distance, *rode off*; *is 3 miles* or *3 years off.* **2.** out of position, not touching or attached, separate, *take the lid off.* **3.** disconnected, not functioning, no longer obtainable, cancelled, *turn the gas off*; *the wedding is off*; *take the day off,* away from work. **4.** to the end, completely, so as to be clear, *finish it off*; *sell them off.* **5.** situated as regards money or supplies, *how are you off for cash?* **6.** (in a theatre) behind or at the side(s) of the stage, *noises off.* **7.** (of food) beginning to decay. —**off** *prep.* **1.** from, away from, not on, *fell off a ladder*; *off duty.* **2.** abstaining from, not attracted by for the time being, *is off his food* or *off smoking*; *off form* or *off his game,* not performing as well as usual. **3.** leading from, not far from, *in a street off the Strand.* **4.** at sea a short distance from, *sank off Cape Horn.* —**off** *adj.* **1.** (of a part of a vehicle or horse or road) on the right-hand side, *the off side front wheel.* **2.** in or from or towards the side of a cricket field to the right-hand side of the wicket-keeper. —**off** *n.* **1.** the off side in cricket. **2.** the start of a race etc., *ready for the off.* □ **off-beat** *adj.* unconventional, unusual. **off chance**, a slight possibility. **off colour**, not in the best of health. **off-cut** *n.* a remnant of timber etc. **off-day** *n.* a day when a person is not at his best. **off-key** *adj.* out of tune. **off-licence** *n.* a licence to sell alcoholic drinks for consumption away from the premises; a place holding such a licence. **off-line** *adj.* (of processing by a computer) carried out on equipment that is not under the control of the central processor; (of equipment) suitable for use in such processing. **off-load** *v.* to unload. **off-peak** *adj.* in or used at a time that is less popular or less busy, *off-peak electricity.* **off-putting** *adj.* (*informal*) repellent, disconcerting. **off-season** *n.* the time when business etc. is fairly slack. **off-stage** *adj. & adv.* not on the stage, not visible to the audience. **off white**, white with a grey or yellowish tinge. **off-white** *adj.*

offal *n.* the edible parts (e.g. heart, kidneys, liver, head) which are considered less valuable than the flesh when an animal carcass is cut up for food.

offence *n.* **1.** breaking of the law, an illegal act. **2.** a feeling of annoyance or resentment, *give* or *take offence.*

offend *v.* **1.** to cause offence or displeasure to. **2.** to do wrong, *offend against the law*. **offender** *n*.

offensive *adj*. **1.** causing offence, insulting, *offensive remarks*. **2.** disgusting, repulsive, *an offensive smell*. **3.** used in attacking, aggressive, *offensive weapons*. —*n*. an aggressive action or campaign; *take the offensive*, to begin hostilities. — **offensively** *adv*., **offensiveness** *n*.

offer *v*. (offered, offering) **1.** to present (a thing) so that it may be accepted or rejected, or considered. **2.** to state what one is willing to do or pay or give. **3.** to show for sale. **4.** to provide, to give opportunity, *the job offers prospects of promotion*. **5.** to show an intention, *the dog didn't offer to bark*. — **offer** *n*. **1.** an expression of willingness to give or do or pay something. **2.** an amount offered, *offers above £500*. □ **on offer**, for sale at a certain price or at a reduced price.

offering *n*. a gift or contribution etc. that is offered.

offertory *n*. **1.** the act of offering bread and wine for consecration at the Eucharist. **2.** money collected in a religious service. □ **offertory box**, a box placed in a church so that visitors may insert contributions of money.

offhand *adj*. **1.** without previous thought or preparation. **2.** (of behaviour etc.) casual or curt and unceremonious. —*adv*. in an offhand way. —**offhanded** *adj*., **offhandedly** *adv*.

office *n*. **1.** a room or building used as a place of business, especially for clerical and similar work or for a special department, *the enquiry office*. **2.** the staff working there. **3.** the premises or staff or authority of certain government departments, *the Foreign and Commonwealth Office*. **4.** a position of authority or trust, the holding of an official position, *seek office*; *be in office*, hold such a position. **5.** an authorized form of Christian worship, *the Office for the Dead*. **6.** a piece of kindness or a service, *through the good offices of his friends; the last offices*, ceremonial rites for the dead. □ **office-block** *n*. a large building designed to contain business offices. **office-boy** *n*. a youth employed to do minor jobs in a business office. **office hours**, the hours during which business is regularly conducted. **offices** *pl. n*. (in a house) rooms devoted to household work etc. (e.g. kitchen, pantry, laundry), *the usual offices*. **office-worker** *n*. an employee in a business office.

officer *n*. **1.** a person holding a position of authority or trust, an official, *customs officers*. **2.** a person who holds authority in any of the armed services (especially with

a commission), mercantile marine, or on a passenger ship. **3.** a policeman.

official *adj*. **1.** of an office or position of authority, *in his official capacity*. **2.** suitable for or characteristic of officials and bureaucracy, *official red tape*. **3.** properly authorized, *the news is official*. —*n*. a person holding office. —**officially** *adv*.

officiate (ŏ-**fish**-i-ayt) *v*. to act in an official capacity, to be in charge.

officious (ŏ-**fish**-ŭs) *adj*. asserting one's authority, bossy. **officiously** *adv*.

offing *n*. **in the offing**, in view, not far away in distance or future time.

offset *v*. (offset, offsetting) to counterbalance or compensate for. —*n*. **1.** an offshoot. **2.** a method of printing in which the ink is transferred to a rubber surface and from this to paper.

offshoot *n*. **1.** a side shoot. **2.** a subsidiary product.

offshore *adj*. **1.** (of wind) blowing from the land towards the sea. **2.** at sea some distance from the shore.

offside *adj. & adv*. (of a player in football etc.) in a position where he may not legally play the ball.

offspring *n*. (*pl*. offspring) **1.** the child or children of a particular person or persons. **2.** the young of an animal.

oft *adv*. (*old use*) often.

often *adv*. **1.** frequently, many times, at short intervals. **2.** in many instances.

ogive (**oh**-jyv) *n*. **1.** a diagonal groin or rib of a vault. **2.** a pointed arch.

ogle (**oh**-gŭl) *v*. to eye flirtatiously.

ogre *n*. **1.** a cruel or man-eating giant in fairy-tales and legends. **2.** a terrifying person. **ogress** *n*.

oh *int*. **1.** an exclamation of surprise or delight or pain. **2.** used for emphasis, *oh yes I will*.

Ohio (oh-**hy**-oh) a State of the USA.

ohm (*rhymes with* Rome) *n*. a unit of electrical resistance.

OHMS *abbrev*. On His or Her Majesty's Service.

oil *n*. **1.** a thick slippery liquid that will not dissolve in water. **2.** petroleum. **3.** a form of petroleum used as fuel; *oil-heater, oil-lamp, oil-stove*, domestic appliances using oil as fuel. **4.** oil-colour. **5.** (*informal*) an oil-painting. **6.** (*slang*) flattery. —*v*. to apply oil to, to lubricate or treat with oil; *oiled silk*, silk made waterproof by being treated with oil. □ **oil-colour** *n*. paint made by mixing powdered pigment in oil. **oil-fired** *adj*. using oil as fuel. **oil-paint** *n*. = oil-colour. **oil-painting** *n*. a picture painted in oil-colours; *she is no oil-painting*, is ugly. **oil-tanker** *n*. a ship with tanks for transporting fuel oil in bulk. **oil the wheels,** to make things go smoothly by tactful behaviour or flattery etc. **oil-well** *n.* a well yielding mineral oil.

oilcake *n.* cattle food made from linseed or similar seeds after the oil has been pressed out.

oilcan *n.* a can with a long nozzle through which oil flows, used for oiling machinery.

oilcloth *n.* strong fabric treated with oil and used to cover tables etc.

oilfield *n.* an area where oil is found in the ground or beneath the sea.

oilskin *n.* cloth waterproofed by treatment with oil. **oilskins** *pl. n.* waterproof clothing made of this.

oily *adj.* (oilier, oiliest) **1.** of or like oil, covered in oil, containing much oil. **2.** unpleasantly smooth in manner, trying to win favour by flattery. **oiliness** *n.*

ointment *n.* a thick slippery paste rubbed on the skin to heal roughness or injuries or inflammation etc.

OK *adv. & adj. (informal)* all right, satisfactory. —*n. (informal)* approval, agreement to a plan etc. —*v. (informal)* to give one's approval or agreement to.

okapi (ō-**kah**-pi) *n. (pl.* okapis) an animal of Central Africa, like a giraffe but with a shorter neck and a striped body.

okay *adv., adj., n., & v. (informal)* = OK.

okey-doke *adv. (slang)* OK.

Okla *abbrev.* Oklahoma.

Oklahoma a State of the USA.

okra (**oh**-krǎ) *n.* a tropical plant with seed-pods that are used as a vegetable.

old *adj.* **1.** having lived or existed for a long time; *the old,* old people. **2.** made long ago, used or established or known for a long time. **3.** shabby from age or wear. **4.** of a particular age, *ten years old, a ten-year-old.* **5.** not recent or modern, *in the old days.* **6.** former, original, *in its old place.* **7.** skilled through long experience, *an old hand at negotiating.* **8.** (*informal*) used for emphasis in friendly or casual mention, *good old Winnie; any old time.* **oldness** *n.* □ **of old,** of or in former times; *we know him of old,* since long ago. **old age,** the period of a person's life from about 65 to 70 onwards. **old-age pension,** a State pension paid to people above a certain age. **old-age pensioner,** a person receiving this. **Old Bailey,** the Central Criminal Court in London. **old boy,** a former member of a school; (*informal*) an elderly man, a man or male animal regarded affectionately. **old country,** a mother country. **old-fashioned** *adj.* in a fashion that is no longer in style; having the ways or tastes

current in former times; *an old-fashioned look,* a dignified and reproving glance. **old girl,** (used in ways corresponding to *old boy*). **Old Glory,** (*Amer.*) the Stars and Stripes. **old gold,** dull gold colour. **old guard,** the original or past or conservative members of a group. **old maid,** an elderly spinster. **old-maidish** *adj.* fussy and prim. **old man,** (*informal*) one's employer or manager or husband or father. **old man's beard,** a kind of clematis with masses of grey fluffy hairs round the seeds. **old master,** a great painter of former times (especially 13th–17th centuries in Europe); a painting by such a painter. **Old Nick,** the Devil. **Old Testament,** *see* testament. **old-time** *adj.* belonging to former times. **old-timer** *n.* a person with long experience or standing. **old wives' tale,** an old but foolish belief. **old woman,** a fussy or timid man; (*informal*) a wife. **Old World,** Europe, Asia, and Africa, as distinct from the Americas. **old year,** the year just ended or about to end.

olden *adj.* (*old use*) old-time.

oldie *n.* (*informal*) an old person or thing.

oldish *adj.* fairly old.

oleander (oh-li-**an**-der) *n.* a poisonous evergreen shrub of Mediterranean regions, with red or white or pink flowers.

O level Ordinary level in GCE.

olfactory (ol-**fak**-ter-i) *adj.* concerned with smelling, *olfactory organs.*

oligarchy (**ol**-i-gar-ki) *n.* **1.** a form of government in which power is in the hands of a few people. **2.** these people. **3.** a country governed in this way.

olive *n.* **1.** a small oval fruit with a hard stone and bitter pulp from which an oil (*olive oil*) is obtained. **2.** the evergreen tree that bears it. **3.** a greenish colour —*adj.* greenish like an unripe olive or (of the complexion) yellowish-brown. □ **olive-branch** *n.* something done or offered to show one's desire to make peace.

Olympian (ō-**limp**-iǎn) *adj.* (of manners etc.) majestic and imposing.

Olympic (ō-**limp**-ik) *adj.* of the **Olympic Games,** athletic and other contests held every 4th year at Olympia in Greece in ancient times and revived since 1896 as international competitions, held each time in a different part of the world. **Olympics** *pl. n.* the Olympic Games.

Oman (ō-**mahn**) a country in Arabia. **Omani** (ō-**mah**-ni) *adj. & n.*

ombudsman (**om**-buudz-mǎn) *n.* (*pl.* ombudsmen) an official appointed to investigate individuals' complaints about maladministration by public authorities.

omega (**oh**-mig-ă) *n.* the last letter of the Greek alphabet, = o.

omelette (**om**-lit) *n.* a dish made of beaten eggs cooked in a frying-pan, often served folded round a savoury or sweet filling.

omen (**oh**-men) *n.* an event regarded as a prophetic sign.

ominous (**om**-in-ŭs) *adj.* looking or seeming as if trouble is at hand, *an ominous silence.*

omission *n.* **1.** omitting, being omitted. **2.** something that has been omitted or not done.

omit *v.* (omitted, omitting) **1.** to leave out, not insert or include. **2.** to leave not done, to neglect or fail to do.

omnibus *n.* **1.** a bus. **2.** an **omnibus book**, one volume containing a number of books or stories.

omnipotent (om-**nip**-ŏ-těnt) *adj.* having unlimited power or very great power. **omnipotence** *n.*

omniscient (om-**nish**-ěnt) *adj.* knowing everything, having very extensive knowledge. **omniscience** (om-**nish**-ěns) *n.*

omnivorous (om-**niv**-er-ŭs) *adj.* **1.** feeding on both plants and animal flesh. **2.** (*humorous*) reading whatever comes one's way.

on *prep.* **1.** supported by or attached to or covering, *sat on the floor*; *lives on her pension*; *got any money on you?*, are you carrying any with you? **2.** using as a basis or ground or reason etc., *was arrested on suspicion*; *profits on sales*. **3.** close to, in the direction of, *they live on the coast*; *the army advanced on Paris*; *on form* or *on his game*, performing at his usual high standard. **4.** (of time) exactly at, during, *on the next day*. **5.** in a certain manner or state, *on the cheap*; *on one's best behaviour*. **6.** concerning, engaged with, so as to affect, *a book on grammar*; *on holiday*; *is on the Pill*, taking it; *the drinks are on me*, at my expense. **7.** added to, *5p on the price of petrol*. —**on** *adv.* **1.** so as to be supported by or attached to or covering something, *put the lid on.* **2.** further forward, towards something, *move on*; *from that day on*; *broadside on*, with that part forward. **3.** with continued movement or action, *slept on.* **4.** in operation or activity, (of a play etc.) being performed or broadcast, (of an actor etc.) performing on the stage, (of gas or water or electric current) running or available or activated, (of an event) due to take place, not cancelled, (of an employee) on duty. —**on** *adj.* in or from or towards the part of a cricket field opposite the off side and in front of the batsman. —*n.* the on side in cricket. □ **be on**, (*informal*) to be willing to participate in something;

to be practicable or acceptable, *this plan just isn't on*; *you're on!*, (*informal*) I accept your proposition or wager. **be** *or* **keep on at**, (*informal*) to nag. **be on to a thing**, to notice it or realize its importance. **on and off**, from time to time, not continually. **on and on**, continuing, continually. **on high**, in or to heaven or a high place. **on-licence** *n.* a licence to sell alcoholic drinks for consumption on the premises; a place holding such a licence. **on-line** *adj.* (of processing by a computer) carried out on equipment that is directly under the control of the central processor; (of equipment) suitable for use in such processing. **on to**, to a position on (*see* onto).

once *adv., conj., & n.* **1.** on one occasion only, one time or occurrence, *once is enough*. **2.** at all, ever, as soon as, *once I can get this job done*. **3.** formerly, *people who once lived here*. □ **once and for all**, in a final manner, conclusively. **once in a while**, from time to time, not often. **once more**, an additional time. **once-over** *n.* (*informal*) a rapid inspection, *give it the once-over*. **once upon a time**, at some vague time in the past.

oncoming *adj.* approaching.

one *adj.* single, individual, forming a unity. —*n.* **1.** the smallest whole number (1, I). **2.** a single thing or person. **3.** (*informal*) a joke, *do you know the one about the dog that could play poker?* **4.** (*informal*) a drink, *one for the road*. **5.** (*informal*) a blow, *dotted him one*. —**one** *pronoun* **1.** a person, *loved ones*. **2.** any person, the speaker or writer as representing people in general, *one doesn't want to seem mean*. □ **one another**, each other. **one-armed bandit**, (*slang*) a fruit-machine or similar device, operated by pulling down an arm-like handle. **one day**, at some unspecified date. **one in the eye for**, (*informal*) something that will be an unwelcome surprise to (a person) and put him at a disadvantage. **one-man** *adj.* done or managed by one person, *one-man bus*. **one-off** *adj.* made as a single article only, not repeated, *a one-off job*. **one-sided** *adj.* (of opinions or judgements) unfair, prejudiced. **one-time** *adj.* former. **one too many for**, such as to outwit or baffle (a person). **one-track mind**, a mind that can think of only one topic. **one-upmanship** *n.* the art of maintaining a psychological advantage over others. **one-way street**, a street in which traffic may move in one direction only. **one-way ticket**, a single ticket, not a return.

onerous (**on**-er-ŭs) *adj.* burdensome.

oneself *pronoun* corresponding to one (*pronoun*, sense 2), used in the same ways as himself.

ongoing *adj.* continuing to exist or progress. ¶The cliché phrase *an ongoing situation* should be avoided at all times.

onion *n.* a vegetable with an edible rounded bulb that has a strong smell and strong flavour. **oniony** *adj.* □ **know one's onions**, (*slang*) to know one's subject or one's job thoroughly.

onlooker *n.* a spectator.

only *adj.* **1.** being the one specimen or all the specimens of a class, sole. **2.** most or best worth considering, *gliding is the only sport.* —**only** *adv.* **1.** without anything or anyone else, and that is all. **2.** no longer ago than, *saw her only yesterday.* —*conj.* but then, *he makes good resolutions, only he never keeps them.* □ **only too**, extremely, *we'll be only too pleased.*

onomatopoeia (on-ŏ-mat-ŏ-**pee**-ă) *n.* formation of words that imitate or suggest what they stand for, e.g. *cuckoo, plop, sizzle.* **onomatopoeic** *adj.*

onrush *n.* an onward rush.

onset *n.* **1.** a beginning, *the onset of winter.* **2.** an attack or assault.

onshore *adj.* (of wind) blowing from the sea towards the land.

onslaught (**on**-slawt) *n.* a fierce attack.

Ont. *abbrev.* Ontario.

Ontario (on-**tair**-i-oh) **1.** a province of Canada. **2.** one of the Great Lakes between Canada and the USA.

onto *prep.* to a position on. Note that *onto* cannot be used where *on* is an adverb, e.g. *we walked on to the river* (= continued walking until we reached it). ¶ Many people prefer not to use *onto*, and write *on* to *to* in all cases.

ontology (on-**tol**-ŏji) *n.* a branch of philosophy dealing with the nature of being. **ontological** *adj.*

onus (**oh**-nŭs) *n.* the duty or responsibility of doing something; *the onus of proof rests with you,* you must prove what you say.

onward *adv.* & *adj.* with an advancing motion, further on. **onwards** *adv.*

onyx (**on**-iks) *n.* a stone like marble with different colours in layers.

oodles *n.* (*informal*) a great quantity.

ooh *int.* an exclamation of surprise or pleasure or pain.

ooze *v.* **1.** (of liquid) to trickle or flow out slowly. **2.** (of a substance or wound etc.) to exude a liquid, to allow to trickle out slowly. **3.** to show (a feeling) freely, *ooze confidence.* —*n.* mud at the bottom of a river or sea.

op *n.* (*informal*) an operation.

opacity (ŏ-**pas**-iti) *n.* being opaque.

opal *n.* an iridescent quartz-like stone often used as a gem.

opalescent (oh-pă-**less**-ĕnt) *adj.* iridescent like an opal. **opalescence** *n.*

opaque (ŏ-**payk**) *adj.* **1.** not transparent, not allowing light to pass through. **2.** (of a statement etc.) not clear.

op art art in a style that gives an illusion of movement. (¶ The word *op* is short for *optical.*)

OPEC (**oh**-pek) *abbrev.* Organization of Petroleum Exporting Countries.

open *adj.* **1.** not closed or blocked up or sealed or locked. **2.** not covered or concealed or restricted; *an open championship,* for which anyone may enter. **3.** admitting visitors or customers, *the shops are open.* **4.** spread out, unfolded. **5.** with wide spaces between solid parts, *open texture.* **6.** frank, communicative, *was quite open about her reasons.* **7.** not yet settled or decided. **8.** available, *three courses are open to us.* **9.** willing to receive, *we are open to offers.* **10.** (of a cheque) not crossed. — **open** *n.* **1.** *the open,* open space or country or air. **2.** an open championship or competition. —**open** *v.* **1.** to make or become open or more open. **2.** to begin or establish, to make a start, *open a business* or *a debate*; *to open fire, to begin firing.* **3.** to declare ceremonially to be open to the public. —**openness** *n.* □ **in the open air,** not inside a house or building. **open-air** *adj.* taking place in the open air. **open-and-shut** *adj.* (*informal*) perfectly straightforward. **open a person's eyes,** to make him realize something that surprises him. **open day,** a day when the public may visit a place that is not normally open to them. **open-ended** *adj.* with no fixed limit, *an open-ended contract.* **open-handed** *adj.* generous in giving. **open-heart surgery,** surgery with the heart exposed and with blood circulating temporarily through a bypass. **open house,** hospitality to all comers. **open letter,** a letter of comment or protest addressed to a person by name but printed in a newspaper. **open mind,** a mind that is unprejudiced or undecided. **open-plan** *adj.* without partition walls or fences. **open prison,** a prison with few physical restraints on the prisoners. **open question,** a matter on which no final verdict has yet been made or on which none is possible. **open sandwich,** a slice of bread covered with a layer of meat or cheese etc. **open secret,** one known to so many people that it is no longer a secret. **open sesame,** *see* sesame. **Open University,** an organization giving university teaching mainly by broadcasts and correspondence, open to all, including those without scholastic qualifications. **open verdict**, a verdict that does not specify whether a crime is involved in the case of a person's death. **open-work** *n.* a pattern with spaces between threads or strips of metal etc. **with open arms**, with an enthusiastic welcome.

opencast *adj.* (of a mine or mining) with layers of earth removed from the surface and worked from above, not from shafts.

opener *n.* **1.** a person or thing that opens something. **2.** a device for opening tins or bottles.

opening *n.* **1.** a space or gap, a place where something opens. **2.** the beginning of something. **3.** an opportunity.

openly *adv.* without concealment, publicly, frankly.

opera *n.* **1.** a play in which the words are sung to a musical accompaniment. **2.** dramatic works of this kind. —*pl. n.* see **opus**. □ **opera-glasses** *pl. n.* small binoculars for use at the opera or theatre.

operable *adj.* **1.** able to be operated. **2.** able to be treated by surgical operation.

operate *v.* **1.** to be in action, to produce an effect, *the new tax operates to our advantage.* **2.** to control the functioning of, *he operates the lift.* **3.** to perform a surgical or other operation. □ **operating system**, a controlling computer program that organizes the running of a number of other programs at the same time. **operating-theatre** *n.* a room for surgical operations.

operatic *adj.* of or like opera.

operation *n.* **1.** operating, being operated. **2.** the way a thing works. **3.** a piece of work, something to be done, *begin operations.* **4.** strategic military activities in war or during manœuvres. **5.** an act performed by a surgeon, on any part of the body, to take away or deal with a diseased or injured or deformed part.

operational *adj.* **1.** of or engaged in or used in operations. **2.** able to function, *is the system operational yet?*

operative *adj.* **1.** having an effect, working or functioning. **2.** of surgical operations. —*n.* a worker, especially in a factory.

operator *n.* **1.** a person who operates a machine or engages in business or runs a business etc. **2.** one who makes connections of lines at a telephone exchange.

operetta *n.* a short or light opera.

ophthalmic (off-**thal**-mik) *adj.* of or for the eyes.

opthalmologist (off-thal-**mol**-ŏ-jist) *n.* a specialist in opthalmology.

ophthalmology (off-thal-**mol**-ŏji) *n.* the

scientific study of the eye and its diseases.

ophthalmoscope (off-**thal**-mŏ-skohp) *n.* an instrument for examining the retina and other parts of the eye.

opiate (**oh**-piăt) *n.* **1.** a sedative drug containing opium. **2.** a thing that soothes the feelings or dulls activity.

opine (ŏ-**pyn**) *v.* to express or hold as one's opinion.

opinion *n.* **1.** a belief or judgement that is held firmly but without actual proof of its truth, a view held as probable. **2.** what one thinks on a particular point, *public opinion.* **3.** a judgement or comment(s) given by an expert who is consulted. **4.** an estimate, *have a low opinion of him.* □ **opinion poll**, an estimate of public opinion as in a Gallup poll.

opinionated *adj.* having strong opinions and holding them obstinately.

opium *n.* a drug made from the juice of certain poppies, smoked or chewed as a stimulant or narcotic, and used in medicine as a sedative.

opossum (ŏ-**poss**-ŭm) *n.* a small furry American or Australian marsupial that lives in trees.

opponent *n.* a person or group opposing another in a contest or war.

opportune (**op**-er-tewn) *adj.* **1.** (of time) suitable or favourable for a purpose. **2.** done or occurring at a favourable time. **opportunely** *adv.*

opportunist (**op**-er-tewn-ist) *n.* one who grasps opportunities, often in an unprincipled way. **opportunism** *n.*

opportunity *n.* a time or set of circumstances that are suitable for a particular purpose.

oppose *v.* **1.** to show resistance to, to argue or fight against. **2.** to place opposite, to place or be in opposition to. **3.** to represent (things) as contrasting. □ **as opposed to**, in contrast with.

opposite *adj.* **1.** having a position on the other or further side, facing. **2.** of a contrary kind, as different as possible from; *the opposite sex*, men in relation to women or vice versa; *they travelled in opposite directions*, moving away from or towards each other. —*n.* an opposite thing or person. —*adv. & prep.* in an opposite place or position or direction to (a person or thing). □ **one's opposite number**, a person holding a similar position to oneself in another group or organization.

opposition *n.* **1.** resistance, being hostile or in conflict or disagreement. **2.** the people who oppose a proposal etc., one's competitors or rivals; *the Opposition*, the chief parliamentary party opposed to the one that is in office. **3.** placing or being placed opposite, contrast.

oppress *v.* **1.** to govern harshly, to treat with continual cruelty or injustice. **2.** to weigh down with cares or unhappiness. **oppression** *n.*, **oppressor** *n.*

oppressive *adj.* **1.** oppressing. **2.** difficult to endure. **3.** (of weather) sultry and tiring. **oppressively** *adv.*, **oppressiveness** *n.*

opprobrious (ŏ-**proh**-briŭs) *adj.* (of words etc.) showing scorn or reproach, abusive.

opprobrium (ŏ-**proh**-briŭm) *n.* great disgrace brought by shameful conduct.

opt *v.* to make a choice. **opt out,** to choose not to participate.

optic *adj.* of the eye or the sense of sight. □ **optics** *n.* the scientific study of sight and of light as its medium.

optical *adj.* **1.** of the sense of sight. **2.** aiding sight; *optical instruments*, telescopes etc. **optically** *adv.* □ **optical illusion,** a mental misinterpretation of something seen, caused by its deceptive appearance.

optician (op-**tish**-ăn) *n.* a maker or seller of spectacles and other optical equipment. **ophthalmic optician,** one qualified to prescribe spectacles etc. as well as to dispense them.

optimal *adj.* optimum.

optimism *n.* a tendency to take a hopeful view of things, or to expect that results will be good. **optimist** *n.*

optimistic *adj.* showing optimism, hopeful. **optimistically** *adv.*

optimum *adj.* best, most favourable. —*n.* the best or most favourable conditions or amount etc.

option *n.* **1.** freedom to choose, *had no option but to go.* **2.** a thing that is or may be chosen, *none of the options is satisfactory.* **3.** the right to buy or sell something at a certain price within a limited time, *we have 10 days' option on the house.* □ **keep one's options open,** to avoid committing oneself, so that one still has a choice.

optional *adj.* not compulsory. **optionally** *adv.*

opulent (**op**-yoo-lĕnt) *adj.* **1.** wealthy, rich. **2.** abundant, luxuriant. **opulently** *adv.*, **opulence** *n.*

opus (**oh**-pŭs) *n.* (*pl.* opera, *pr.* **op**-er-ă) a musical composition numbered as one of a composer's works (usually in order of publication), *Beethoven opus 15.*

or *conj.* **1.** as an alternative, *are you coming or going?* **2.** also known as, *hydrophobia or rabies.*

oracle *n.* **1.** a place where the ancient Greeks consulted one of their gods for advice or prophecy. **2.** the reply given. **3.** a person or thing regarded as able to give wise

guidance. **oracular** (or-**ak**-yoo-ler) *adj.*

oral (**or**-ăl) *adj.* **1.** spoken not written, *oral evidence.* **2.** of the mouth, done or taken by mouth, *oral contraceptives*; *oral sex,* sucking or licking a partner's genitals as a method of giving sexual satisfaction to him or her. —*n.* (*informal*) a spoken (not written) examination. —**orally** *adv.*

orange *n.* **1.** a round juicy citrus fruit with reddish-yellow peel. **2.** reddish-yellow. —*adj.* orange-coloured, reddish-yellow. □ **orange-blossom** *n.* white sweet-scented flowers of the orange tree, traditionally worn by brides. **orange-stick** *n.* a small thin stick (originally of wood from an orange-tree) designed for manicuring the nails.

orangeade *n.* an orange-flavoured soft drink.

Orangeman *n.* (*pl.* Orangemen) a member of a political society formed to support Protestantism in Ireland. ¶ Named after William of Orange (William III).

orang-utan (or-ang-oo-**tan**) *n.* a large long-armed ape of Borneo and Sumatra.

oration (or-**ay**-shŏn) *n.* a long speech, especially of a ceremonial kind.

orator *n.* a person who makes public speeches, one who is good at public speaking.

oratorio (o-ră-**tor**-i-oh) *n.* (*pl.* oratorios) a musical composition for solo voices, chorus, and orchestra, usually with a biblical theme.

oratory[1] (**o**-ră-ter-i) *n.* **1.** the art of public speaking. **2.** eloquent speech. **oratorical** (o-răt-**o**-ri-kăl) *adj.*

oratory[2] (**o**-ră-ter-i) *n.* a small chapel or place for private worship.

orb *n.* **1.** a sphere or globe. **2.** an ornamental globe surmounted by a cross, forming part of the royal regalia.

orbit *n.* **1.** the curved path of a planet or satellite or spacecraft etc. round another body; *in orbit,* moving in an orbit. **2.** a sphere of influence. —*v.* to move in an orbit, to travel in an orbit round (a body).

orbital (**or**-bit'l) *adj.* **1.** (of a road) passing round the outside of a city. **2.** of an orbit, *orbitual velocity.*

Orcadian (or-**kay**-diăn) *adj.* of Orkney. —*n.* a native or inhabitant of Orkney.

orchard *n.* **1.** a piece of land planted with fruit-trees. **2.** these trees.

orchestra *n.* **1.** a large body of people playing various musical instruments, including stringed and wind instruments. **2.** the part of a theatre where these sit, in front of the stalls and lower than the stage.

orchestral (or-**kess**-trăl) *adj.*

orchestrate (**or**-kis-trayt) *v.* **1.** to compose or arrange (music) for performance by an orchestra. **2.** to co-ordinate (things) deliberately, *an orchestrated series of protests.* **orchestration** *n.*

orchid (**or**-kid) *n.* **1.** a kind of plant with showy often irregularly-shaped flowers. **2.** its flower.

orchis (**or**-kis) *n.* an orchid, especially a wild one.

ordain *v.* **1.** to appoint ceremonially to the Christian ministry, *was ordained priest.* **2.** (of God or fate) to destine, *providence ordained that they should meet.* **3.** to appoint or decree authoritatively.

ordeal (or-**deel**) *n.* a difficult experience that tests a person's character or power of endurance.

order *n.* **1.** the way in which things are placed in relation to one another. **2.** a proper or customary sequence. **3.** a condition in which every part or unit is in its right place or in a normal or efficient state, *in good working order*; *out of order.* **4.** the condition brought about by good and firm government and obedience to the laws, *law and order.* **5.** a system of rules or procedure. **6.** a command, an instruction given with authority. **7.** a request to supply goods, the goods themselves. **8.** a written direction (especially to a bank or post office) to pay money, or giving authority to do something, *a postal order*; *an estate agent's order to view property.* **9.** a rank or class in society, *the lower orders.* **10.** a kind or sort or quality, *showed courage of the highest order.* **11.** a monastic organization or institution, *the Franciscan Order.* **12.** *orders* = holy orders (see below). **13.** a company of people to which distinguished people are admitted as an honour or reward, the insignia worn by its members, *the Order of the Garter.* **14.** a style of ancient Greek or Roman architecture distinguished by the type of column used, *there are five classical orders.* **15.** a group of plants or animals classified as similar in many ways. —**order** *v.* **1.** to put in order, to arrange methodically. **2.** to issue a command, to command that something shall be done. **3.** to give an order for (goods etc.), to tell a waiter to serve (certain food). □ **holy orders,** the status of an ordained clergyman, *in holy orders*; *take holy orders,* to be ordained. **in order to** or **that,** with the intention that, with the purpose of. **made to order,** made according to the buyer's instructions. **on order,** (of goods) ordered but not yet received.

order about, to keep on giving commands to. **order-book** *n.* a book in which a tradesman enters orders. **order-form** *n.* a form to be filled in by a customer ordering goods. **order-paper** *n.* a written or printed programme of business for a committee or parliament etc. on a particular day.

orderly *adj.* **1.** well arranged, in good order, tidy. **2.** methodical, *an orderly mind.* **3.** obedient to discipline, well behaved, *an orderly crowd.* —**orderly** *n.* **1.** a soldier in attendance on an officer to assist him or take messages etc. **2.** an attendant in a hospital. —**orderliness** *n.* □ **orderly officer,** the officer on duty on a particular day. **orderly room,** a room where business is conducted in a military barracks.

ordinal *n.* any of the **ordinal numbers,** the numbers defining a thing's position in a series (e.g. *first, fifth, twentieth*).

ordinance *n.* a rule made by authority, a decree.

ordinand (**or**-din-and) *n.* a candidate for ordination.

ordinary *adj.* usual, customary, not exceptional. **ordinarily** *adv.* □ **in the ordinary way,** if the circumstances were not exceptional. **Ordinary level,** the GCE examination of basic standard. **ordinary seaman,** one ranking lower than an able seaman.

ordination *n.* ordaining or being ordained as a clergyman.

ordnance *n.* military supplies and materials, the government service dealing with these. **Ordnance Survey,** an official survey of Great Britain preparing accurate and detailed maps of the whole country.

ore *n.* solid rock or mineral, found in the earth's crust, from which metal or other useful or valuable substances can be extracted, *iron ore.*

Oreg. *abbrev.* Oregon.

Oregon (**o**-ri-gŏn) a State of the USA.

organ *n.* **1.** a musical instrument consisting of pipes that sound notes when air is forced through them, played by keys pressed with the fingers and pedals pressed with the feet. **2.** a distinct part of an animal or plant body, adapted for a particular function, *digestive organs*; *organs of speech.* **3.** a medium of communication (e.g. a newspaper) giving the views of a particular group. □ **organ-grinder** *n.* a person who plays a barrel-organ.

organdie (or-**gan**-di) *n.* a kind of fine translucent usually stiffened cotton fabric.

organic (or-**gan**-ic) *adj.* **1.** of or affecting an organ or organs of the body, *organic* *diseases.* **2.** of or formed from living things, *organic matter.* **3.** (of food etc.) produced without the use of artificial fertilizers or pesticides. **4.** organized or arranged as a system of related parts, *the business forms an organic whole.* **organically** *adv.* □ **organic chemistry,** chemistry of carbon compounds, which are present in all living matter and in substances derived from it.

organism *n.* a living being, an individual animal or plant.

organist *n.* one who plays the organ.

organization *n.* **1.** organizing, being organized. **2.** an organized body of people, an organized system. **organizational** *adj.*

organize *v.* **1.** to arrange in an orderly or systematic way. **2.** to make arrangements for, *organize a picnic.* **3.** to form (people) into an association for a common purpose. **organizer** *n.*

organza (or-**gan**-ză) *n.* thin stiff transparent dress-fabric of silk or synthetic fibre.

orgasm (or-gazm) *n.* the climax of sexual excitement.

orgy *n.* **1.** a wild drunken party or revelry. **2.** great indulgence in one or more activities, *an orgy of spending.*

oriel window (or-i-ĕl) a kind of projecting window in an upper storey.

Orient (or-i-ĕnt) *n.* the East, countries east of the Mediterranean, especially East Asia.

orient (or-i-ĕnt) *v.* to orientate.

oriental (or i en t'l) *adj.* of the Orient, of the eastern or Asian world or its civilization. **Oriental** *n.* a native of the Orient.

orientate (or-i-ĕn-tayt) *v.* **1.** to place or determine the position of (a thing) with regard to the points of the compass; *orientate a map,* place it so that its bearings correspond to one's own. **2.** to face or direct (towards a certain direction). **orientation** *n.* □ **orientate oneself,** to get one's bearings; to become accustomed to a new situation.

orienteering (or-i-ĕn-**teer**-ing) *n.* the sport of finding one's way on foot across rough country by map and compass.

orifice (o-ri-fiss) *n.* the opening of a cavity.

origami (o-ri-**gah**-mi) *n.* the Japanese art of folding paper into attractive shapes.

origin *n.* **1.** the point or source or cause from which a thing begins its existence. **2.** a person's ancestry or parentage, *a man of humble origin.*

original *adj.* **1.** existing from the first, earliest. **2.** being a thing from which a copy or translation has been made. **3.** first-hand, not imitative, new in character or design. **4.** thinking or acting for oneself, inventive, creative, *an original mind.* —*n.* the first

form of something, the thing from which another is copied. —**originally** *adv.,* **originality** *n.* □ **original sin,** the condition of wickedness thought to be common to all mankind since Adam's sin.

originate *v.* **1.** to give origin to, to cause to begin. **2.** to have origin, to begin, *the quarrel originated in rivalry*; *from what country did the custom originate?* **origination** *n.,* **originator** *n.*

oriole (or-i-ohl) *n.* a kind of bird of which the male has black and yellow plumage.

Orkney an island area of Scotland consisting of the *Orkney Islands* (or *Orkneys*), situated off the north coast.

ormolu (or-mŏ-loo) *n.* **1.** gilded bronze or a gold-coloured alloy of copper, used in decorating furniture. **2.** articles made of or decorated with this.

ornament *n.* **1.** a decorative object or detail. **2.** decoration, adornment, *this is for use, not only for ornament.* **3.** a person or thing that adds distinction, *he is an ornament to his profession.* —*v.* to decorate, to be an ornament to. —**ornamentation** *n.*

ornamental *adj.* serving as an ornament.

ornate (or-**nayt**) *adj.* elaborately ornamented.

ornithology (orni-**thol**-ŏji) *n.* the scientific study of birds. **ornithological** *adj.* □ **ornithologist** *n.* an expert in ornithology.

orphan *n.* a child whose parents are dead. —*v.* to make (a child) an orphan.

orphanage *n.* an institution where orphans are housed and cared for.

orris (o-riss) *n.* a kind of iris that has a fragrant root (*orris-root*) which is dried for use in perfumery and medicine.

orthodontics (orthŏ-**don**-tiks) *n.* correction of irregularities in the teeth and jaws. **orthodontic** *adj.* □ **orthodontist** *n.* a specialist in orthodontics.

orthodox *adj.* of or holding correct or conventional or currently accepted beliefs, especially in religion; *orthodox Jews,* those who follow traditional observances strictly. **orthodoxy** *n.* □ **Orthodox Church,** the Eastern or Greek Church (recognizing the Patriarch of Constantinople as its head), and the national Churches of Russia, Romania, etc. in communion with it.

orthographic (orthŏ-**graf**-ik) *or* **orthographical** *adjs.* of orthography. □ **orthographic projection,** a way of drawing a three-dimensional object without showing perspective.

orthography (or-**thog**-ră-fi) *n.* correct spelling.

orthopaedics (orthŏ-**pee**-diks) *n.* the branch of surgery dealing with the correction of deformities in bones or muscles. **orthopaedic** *adj.* ☐ **orthopaedist** *n.* a specialist in orthopaedics.

orthoptics (or-**thop**-tiks) *n.* remedial treatment of the eye-muscles. **orthoptic** *adj.* ☐ **orthoptist** *n.* a specialist in orthoptics.

ortolan (**or**-tŏ-lăn) *n.* a kind of bunting with a pink bill and pink legs.

oryx (**o**-riks) *n.* a large African antelope with straight horns.

OS *abbrev.* outsize.

Oscar *n.* one of the statuettes awarded by the Academy of Motion Picture Arts and Sciences for excellence in the acting or directing of films.

oscillate (**oss**-i-layt) *v.* **1.** to move to and fro like a pendulum. **2.** to vary between extremes of opinion or condition etc. **oscillation** *n.*

oscilloscope (ŏ-**sil**-ŏ-skohp) *n.* a device for showing oscillations as a display on the screen of a cathode-ray tube.

osier (**oh**-zi-er) *n.* **1.** a kind of willow with flexible twigs used in basketwork. **2.** a twig from this.

Oslo (**oz**-loh) the capital of Norway.

osmosis (oz-**moh**-sis) *n.* diffusion of fluid through a porous partition into another fluid.

osprey (**oss**-pri) *n.* (*pl.* ospreys) a large bird preying on fish in inland waters.

ossify *v.* (ossified, ossifying) **1.** to change into bone, to make or become hard like bone. **2.** to make or become rigid and unprogressive, *their ideas had ossified.* **ossification** *n.*

ostensible (oss-**ten**-sibŭl) *adj.* pretended, put forward as a reason etc. to conceal the real one, *their ostensible motive was trade.* **ostensibly** *adv.*

ostentation *n.* a showy display intended to impress people. **ostentatious** (oss-ten-tay-shŭs) *adj.*, **ostentatiously** *adv.*

osteo-arthritis *n.* a form of arthritis in which the joints degenerate.

osteopath (**oss**-tiŏp-ath) *n.* a practitioner who treats certain diseases and abnormalities by manipulating bones and muscles. **osteopathy** (osti-**op**-ăthi) *n.* this treatment. **osteopathic** (osti-ŏp-**ath**-ik) *adj.*

ostracize (**oss**-tră-syz) *v.* to refuse to associate with, to cast out from a group or from society. **ostracism** *n.*

ostrich *n.* **1.** a swift-running African bird that cannot fly, said to bury its head in the sand when pursued, in the belief that it then cannot be seen. **2.** a person who refuses to face facts.

OT *abbrev.* Old Testament.

other *adj.* **1.** alternative, additional, being the remaining one or set of two or more, *has no other income*; *try the other shoe*; *my other friends.* **2.** not the same, *wouldn't want her to be other than she is.* —*n. & pronoun* the other person or thing, *where are the others?* —*adv.* otherwise. ☐ **other ranks,** soldiers other than commissioned officers. **the other day** *or* **week** etc., a few days or weeks etc. ago. **the other world,** life after death.

otherwise *adv.* **1.** in a different way, *could not have done otherwise.* **2.** in other respects, *is otherwise correct.* **3.** if circumstances were different, or else, *write it down, otherwise you'll forget.* —*adj.* in a different state, not as supposed, *the truth is quite otherwise.*

Ottawa the capital of Canada.

otter *n.* a fish-eating water animal with webbed feet, a flat tail, and thick brown fur.

ottoman *n.* **1.** a long cushioned seat without back or arms. **2.** a storage box with a padded top.

ouch *int.* an exclamation of sudden pain or annoyance.

ought *auxiliary verb* expressing duty or rightness or advisability or strong probability. **oughtn't,** = ought not.

ounce *n.* a unit of weight equal to one sixteenth of a pound (about 28 grams). **fluid ounce,** *see* fluid.

our *adj.* of or belonging to us. **ours** *possessive pronoun,* belonging to us, the thing(s) belonging to us. ¶ It is incorrect to write *our's* (see the note under its).

ourselves *pronoun* corresponding to *we* and *us,* used in the same ways as himself.

oust (*pr.* ow- *as in* cow) *v.* to drive out, to eject from office or a position or employment etc.

out *adv.* **1.** away from or not in a place, not in its normal or usual state, not at home; *the tide is out,* is low. **2.** not in effective or favourable action, no longer in fashion or in office, (in cricket etc.) having had one's innings ended, (of workers) on strike, (of a light or fire etc.) no longer burning. **3.** in error, *the estimate was 10% out.* **4.** no longer visible, *paint it out.* **5.** not possible, *skating is out until the ice thickens.* **6.** unconscious. **7.** into the open, into existence or hearing or view etc., visible, revealed, *the sun is out; the secret is out; the flowers are out,* opened, no longer in bud; *the best game out,* the best one known to exist. **8.** to or at an end, completely, *tired out; sold out.* **9.** in finished form, *type it out.* **10.** (in radio conversations) transmission ends. —**out** *prep.* out of. —*n.* a way of escape. —*int.* get out. ☐ **be out to**, to be acting with the intention of, *is out to cause trouble.* **out-and-out** *adj.* thorough, extreme. **out of**, from within or among; beyond the range of; so as to be without a supply of; (of an animal) having as its dam. **out of date**, no longer fashionable or current or valid, *this passport is out of date.* **out-of-date** *adj.* out of date, *an out-of-date passport.* **out of doors**, in the open air. **out of the way**, no longer an obstacle; remote; unusual. **out of this world**, incredibly good, indescribable. **out of work**, having no work, unable to find paid employment. **out-patient** *n.* a person who visits a hospital for treatment but does not remain resident there. **out-tray** *n.* a tray to hold documents that have been dealt with and are ready for dispatch. **out with it**, say what you are thinking.

out- *prefix* more than, so as to exceed, *outbid, outgrow, out-talk.*

outback *n.* (*Austral.*) remote inland districts.

outbid *v.* (outbid, outbidding) to bid higher than (another person).

outboard *adj. & adv.* on or towards the outside of a ship, aircraft, or vehicle; (of a motor) attached to the outside of the stern of a boat.

outbreak *n.* a breaking out of anger or war or a disease etc.

outbuilding *n.* an outhouse.

outburst *n.* a bursting out of steam or anger or laughter etc.

outcast *n.* a person who has been driven out of a group or rejected by society.

outclass *v.* to surpass greatly.

outcome *n.* the result or effect of an event etc.

outcrop *n.* 1. part of an underlying layer of rock that projects on the surface of the ground. 2. a breaking out.

outcry *n.* 1. a loud cry. 2. a strong protest.

outdated *adj.* out of date.

outdistance *v.* to get far ahead of (a person) in a race etc.

outdo *v.* (outdid, outdone, outdoing) to do better than (another person).

outdoor *adj.* 1. of or for use in the open air. 2. enjoying open-air activities, *she's not an outdoor type.* ☐ **outdoors** *adv.* in or to the open air.

outer *adj.* further from the centre or from the inside, exterior, external. —*n.* the division of a target furthest from the bull's-eye, a shot that strikes this. ☐ **outer space**, the universe beyond the earth's atmosphere.

outermost *adj.* furthest outward, most remote.

outface *v.* to disconcert (a person) by one's defiant or confident manner.

outfall *n.* an outlet where water falls or flows out.

outfield *n.* the outer part of a cricket or baseball field.

outfit *n.* 1. complete equipment or a set of things for a purpose. 2. a set of clothes to be worn together. 3. (*informal*) an organization, a group of people regarded as a unit.

outfitter *n.* a supplier of equipment or of men's clothing.

outflank *v.* to get round the flank of (an enemy).

outflow *n.* an outward flow, the amount that flows out.

outgoing *adj.* 1. going out. 2. sociable and friendly. ☐ **outgoings** *pl. n.* expenditure.

outgrow *v.* (outgrew, outgrown, outgrowing) 1. to grow faster than. 2. to grow out of (clothes or habits); *outgrow one's strength*, to grow too quickly during childhood so that health suffers.

outgrowth *n.* 1. something that grows out of another thing. 2. a natural development, an effect.

outhaul *n.* a rope etc. by which a sail is hauled outboard along a spar.

out-herod *v.* **out-herod Herod**, to exceed Herod in evil or extravagance.

outhouse *n.* a building (e.g. a shed or barn etc.) belonging to but separate from a house.

outing *n.* a pleasure-trip.

outlandish *adj.* looking or sounding strange or foreign. **outlandishness** *n.*

outlast *v.* to last longer than.

outlaw *n.* (in the Middle Ages) a person who was punished by being placed outside the protection of the law. —*v.* 1. to make (a person) an outlaw. 2. to declare to be illegal.

outlay *n.* what is spent on something.

outlet *n.* 1. a way out for water or steam etc. 2. a means or occasion for giving vent to one's feelings or energies. 3. a market for goods.

outline *n.* 1. a line or lines showing the shape or boundary of something. 2. a statement or summary of the chief facts about something. 3. a symbol in shorthand. —*v.* to draw or describe in outline, to mark the outline of. ☐ **in outline**, giving only an outline.

outlive *v.* to live longer than.

outlook *n.* 1. a view on which one looks out, *a pleasant outlook over the lake.* 2. a person's mental attitude or way of looking at something. **3.** future prospects.

outlying *adj.* situated far from a centre, remote.

outmanœuvre *v.* to outdo in manœuvring.

outmoded (owt-**moh**-did) *adj.* no longer fashionable.

outmost *adj.* **1.** outermost. **2.** uttermost.

outnumber *v.* to exceed in number.

outpace *v.* to go faster than.

outpost *n.* **1.** a detachment of troops stationed at a distance from the main army. **2.** any distant branch or settlement.

output *n.* the amount produced. *—v.* (output *or* outputted, outputting) (of a computer) to supply (results).

outrage *n.* **1.** an act that shocks public opinion. **2.** violation of rights, *safe from outrage.* *—v.* to commit an outrage against, to shock and anger greatly.

outrageous *adj.* greatly exceeding what is moderate or reasonable, shocking. **outrageously** *adv.*

outrank *v.* to be of higher rank than.

outrider *n.* a mounted attendant or a motor-cyclist riding as guard with a carriage or procession.

outrigger *n.* **1.** a beam or spar or structure projecting from the side of a ship for various purposes. **2.** a strip of wood fixed parallel to a canoe by struts projecting from it, to give stability. **3.** a boat with either of these.

outright *adv.* **1.** completely, entirely, not gradually; *bought the house outright*, by a single payment. **2.** openly, frankly, *told him outright.* *—adj.* thorough, complete, *an outright fraud.*

outrun *v.* (outran, outrun, outrunning) **1.** to run faster or further than. **2.** to go beyond (a specified point or limit).

outsell *v.* (outsold, outselling) to sell or be sold in greater quantities than.

outset *n.* the beginning, *from the outset of his career.*

outshine *v.* (outshone, outshining) to surpass in splendour or excellence.

outside *n.* the outer side, surface, or part. *—adj.* **1.** of or coming from the outside; *her outside interests*, interests other than work or household. **2.** (of a player in football etc.) positioned nearest to the edge of the field, *outside left.* **3.** greatest possible, *the outside price.* *—adv.* on or at or to the outside. *— prep.* on the outer side of, at or to the outside of, other than, *has no interests outside his work.* □ **at the outside**, (of amounts) at most. **outside broadcast**, one that is not made from a studio.

outsider *n.* **1.** a non-member of a certain group or profession. **2.** a horse or person

thought to have no chance in a race or competition for which he has entered.

outsize *adj.* much larger than average.

outskirts *pl. n.* the outer districts or outlying parts, especially of a town.

outsmart *v.* (*informal*) to outwit.

outspoken *adj.* speaking or spoken without reserve, very frank.

outspread *adj.* spread out.

outstanding *adj.* **1.** conspicuous. **2.** exceptionally good. **3.** not yet paid or settled, *some of his debts are still outstanding.* **outstandingly** *adv.*

outstay *v.* to stay longer than.

outstretched *adj.* stretched out.

outstrip *v.* (outstripped, outstripping) **1.** to outrun. **2.** to surpass.

outvote *v.* to defeat by a majority of votes.

outward *adj.* **1.** situated on the outside. **2.** going towards the outside. **3.** in one's expression or actions etc. as distinct from in one's mind or spirit. *—adv.* outwards. □ **Outward Bound Trust**, an organization running schools for character-building through adventure.

outwardly *adv.* on the outside.

outwards *adv.* towards the outside.

outweigh *v.* to be greater in weight or importance or significance than.

outwit *v.* (outwitted, outwitting) to get the better of (a person) by one's cleverness or craftiness.

outwith *prep.* (*Scottish*) outside.

outwork *n.* an advanced or detached part of a fortification.

outworn *adj.* worn out, damaged by wear.

ouzel (oo-zĕl) *n.* **1.** a small bird of the thrush family, *ring ouzel.* **2.** a kind of diving bird, *water ouzel.*

ova *see* ovum.

oval *n.* a rounded symmetrical shape longer than it is broad. *—adj.* having this shape.

ovary (**oh**-ver-i) *n.* **1.** either of the two organs in which egg-cells are produced in female animals. **2.** part of the pistil in a plant, from which fruit is formed. **ovarian** (ŏ-**vair**-iăn) *adj.*

ovation (ŏ-**vay**-shŏn) *n.* enthusiastic applause.

oven *n.* an enclosed chamber in which things are cooked or heated. **ovenware** *n.* dishes for cooking and serving food.

over *adv.* **1.** with movement outwards and downwards from the brink or from an upright position. **2.** with movement from one side to the other or so that a different side is showing. **3.** across a street or other space or distance, *is over here from America.* **4.** so as to cover or touch a whole surface, *the lake froze over*; *brush it over*. **5.** with transference or change from one hand or one side or one owner etc. to another, *went over to the enemy*; *hand it over*; *over to you*, I await your action. **6.** (in radio conversation) it is your turn to transmit. **7.** besides, in addition or excess. **8.** with repetition, *ten times over*. **9.** thoroughly, with detailed consideration, *think it over*. **10.** at an end, *the battle is over*. —*n.* a series of 6 (or 8) balls bowled in cricket. — **over** *prep.* **1.** in or to a position higher than. **2.** above and across, so as to clear. **3.** throughout the length or extent of, during, *over the years*; *stayed over the weekend*. **4.** so as to visit or examine all parts, *saw over the house*; *went over the plan again*. **5.** transmitted by, *heard it over the radio*. **6.** while engaged with, *we can talk over dinner*. **7.** concerning, *quarrelled over money*. **8.** more than, *it's over a mile away*. **9.** in superiority or preference to, *their victory over United*. □ **over and above**, besides. **over and over**, so that the same point comes uppermost repeatedly; repeated many times. **over the moon**, (*Informal*) highly excited, in raptures.

over- *prefix* **1.** above, *overlay*. **2.** too much, excessively, *over-anxiety*, *over-anxious*.

overact *v.* to act one's part in an exaggerated manner.

overall *n.* a garment worn to protect other clothing, which it covers. —*adj.* **1.** including everything, total. **2.** taking all aspects into account. —*adv.* in all parts, taken as a whole. □ **overalls** *pl. n.* a one-piece garment covering body and legs, worn as protective clothing.

overarm *adj. & adv.* **1.** (in cricket etc.) bowling or bowled with the hand brought forward and down from above shoulder level. **2.** (in swimming) with the arm lifted out of the water and stretched forward beyond the head.

overawe *v.* to overcome with awe.

overbalance *v.* to lose balance and fall over, to cause to do this.

overbearing *adj.* domineering.

overblown *adj.* (of a flower etc.) too fully open, past its prime.

overboard *adv.* from within a ship into the water. **go overboard**, (*informal*) to be very enthusiastic. **throw overboard**, to abandon, to discard.

overbook *v.* to book too many passengers or visitors for (an aircraft flight or a hotel etc.).

overburden *v.* to burden excessively.

overcall *v.* to make a higher bid than a previous one, or higher than is justified, e.g. in the game of bridge.

overcast *adj.* (of the sky) covered with cloud. —*v.* (overcast, overcasting) to stitch over (an edge) to prevent it from fraying.

overcharge *v.* **1.** to charge too high a price. **2.** to fill too full.

overcoat *n.* a warm outdoor coat.

overcome *v.* (overcame, overcome, overcoming) **1.** to win a victory over, to succeed in subduing. **2.** to be victorious. **3.** to make helpless, to deprive of proper control of oneself, *they were overcome by gas fumes or by grief*. **4.** to find a way of dealing with (a problem etc.).

overcrowd *v.* to crowd too many people into (a place or vehicle etc.).

overdo *v.* (overdid, overdone, overdoing) **1.** to do (a thing) excessively. **2.** to cook (food) too long. □ **overdo it** or **things**, to work too hard; to exaggerate.

overdose *n.* too large a dose of a drug etc.

overdraft *n.* overdrawing of a bank account, the amount by which an account is overdrawn.

overdraw *v.* (overdrew, overdrawn, overdrawing) to draw more from (a bank account) than the amount credited; *be overdrawn*, to have done this.

overdrive *n.* mechanism providing an extra gear above the normal top gear in a vehicle.

overdue *adj.* not paid or arrived etc. by the due or expected time.

overeat *v.* (overate, overeaten, overeating) to eat too much.

overestimate *v.* to form too high an estimate of.

over-expose *v.* to expose for too long. **over-exposure** *n.*

overfeed *v.* (overfed, overfeeding) to feed too much.

overfill *v.* to fill too full or to overflowing.

overfish *v.* to catch so many fish from (a certain area) that next season's supply is reduced.

overflow *v.* **1.** to flow over (the edge or limits or banks etc.). **2.** (of a crowd) to spread beyond the limits of (a room etc.). —**overflow** *n.* **1.** what overflows. **2.** an outlet for excess liquid.

overfly *v.* (overflew, overflown, overflying) to fly over (a place or territory).

overfull *adj.* overfilled, too full.

overgrown *adj.* **1.** having grown too large. **2.** covered with weeds etc.

overhand *adj. & adv.* = overarm.

overhang *v.* (overhung, overhanging) to jut out over. —*n.* an overhanging part.

overhaul *v.* **1.** to examine and make any necessary repairs or changes. **2.** to overtake. —*n.* an examination and repair etc.

overhead *adv.* & *adj.* above the level of one's head, in the sky. **overheads** *pl. n.* the expenses involved in running a business.

overhear *v.* (overheard, overhearing) to hear accidentally or without the speaker's knowledge or intention.

overheat *v.* to make or become too hot.

overjoyed *adj.* filled with very great joy.

overkill *n.* a surplus of capacity for destruction above what is needed to defeat or destroy an enemy.

overland *adv.* & *adj.* by land, not by sea.

overlap *v.* (overlapped, overlapping) 1. to extend beyond the edge of (a thing) and partly cover it. 2. to coincide partially, *our holidays overlap.* —*n.* overlapping, an overlapping part or amount.

overlay¹ (oh-ver-**lay**) *v.* (overlaid, overlaying) 1. to cover with a surface layer. 2. to lie on top of.

overlay² (**oh**-ver-lay) *n.* a thing laid over another, a coverlet.

overleaf *adv.* on the other side of a leaf of a book etc.

overload *v.* to put too great a load on or into. —*n.* a load that is too great.

overlook *v.* 1. to have a view of or over (a place) from above. 2. to oversee. 3. to fail to observe or consider. 4. to take no notice of, to allow (an offence) to go unpunished.

overlord *n.* a supreme lord.

overly *adv.* (*Scottish* & *Amer.*) excessively.

overman *v.* (overmanned, overmanning) to provide with too many people as workmen or crew etc.

overmantel *n.* ornamental shelves etc. over a mantelpiece.

overmuch *adv.* too much.

overnight *adv.* 1. during the length of a night. 2. on the night before, *put it ready overnight.* —*adj.* of or for or during a night, *an overnight stop in Rome.*

overpass *n.* a road that crosses another by means of a bridge.

overpay *v.* (overpaid, overpaying) to pay too highly.

overplay *v.* **overplay one's hand,** to take unjustified risks by overestimating one's strength.

overpower *v.* to overcome by greater strength or numbers.

overpowering *adj.* (of heat or feelings) extremely intense.

overprint *v.* 1. to print (a photograph) darker than was intended. 2. to print further matter on (an already printed surface, e.g. a postage stamp), to print (further matter) thus.

overrate *v.* 1. to have too high an opinion of. 2. to assess the rates of (a place) too highly.

overreach *v.* **overreach oneself,** to fail through being too ambitious.

over-react *v.* to respond more strongly than is justified.

override *v.* (overrode, overridden, overriding) 1. to set aside (an order) by having, or behaving as if one had, superior authority. 2. to prevail over, *considerations of safety override all others.* 3. to intervene and cancel the operation of (automatic mechanism).

overrider *n.* a vertical attachment on the bumper of a car to prevent another bumper from becoming locked behind it.

overripe *adj.* too ripe.

overrule *v.* to set aside (a decision etc.) by using one's authority.

overrun *v.* (overran, overrun, overrunning) 1. to spread over and occupy or injure, *the place is overrun with mice.* 2. to exceed (a limit or time allowed etc.), *the broadcast overran its allotted time.*

overseas *adv.* & *adj.* across or beyond the sea, abroad.

oversee *v.* (oversaw, overseen, overseeing) to superintend. **overseer** *n.*

oversew *v.* (oversewed, oversewn, oversewing) to sew together (two edges) so that each stitch lies over the edges.

over-sexed *adj.* having unusually great sexual desires.

overshadow *v.* 1. to cast a shadow over. 2. to make (a person or thing) seem unimportant in comparison.

overshoe *n.* a shoe worn over an ordinary one as a protection against wet etc.

overshoot *v.* (overshot, overshooting) to pass beyond (a target or limit etc.), *the plane overshot the runway when landing.*

overshot *adj.* (of a water-wheel) turned by water falling on it from above.

oversight *n.* 1. supervision. 2. an unintentional omission or mistake.

over-simplify *v.* (over-simplified, over-simplifying) to misrepresent (a problem etc.) by stating it in terms that are too simple.

oversized *adj.* of more than the usual size.

oversleep *v.* (overslept, oversleeping) to sleep longer than one intended.

overspend *v.* (overspent, overspending) to spend too much.

overspill *n.* 1. what spills over or overflows. 2. the surplus population of a town etc.

who seek accommodation in other districts.

overstaffed *adj.* having more than the necessary number of staff.

overstate *v.* to exaggerate.

overstay *v.* to stay longer than; *overstay one's welcome*, to stay so long that one is no longer welcome.

oversteer *v.* (of a car etc.) to have a tendency to turn more sharply than was intended. —*n.* this tendency.

overstep *v.* (overstepped, overstepping) to go beyond (a limit).

overstrung *adj.* (of a piano) with strings in sets crossing each other obliquely.

overstuffed *adj.* (of cushions etc.) filled with much or too much stuffing.

over-subscribed *adj.* with applications for (an issue of shares etc.) in excess of the number offered.

overt (ŏ-vert) *adj.* done or shown openly, *overt hostility*. **overtly** *adv.*

overtake *v.* (overtook, overtaken, overtaking) 1. to come abreast with or level with. 2. to pass (a moving person or vehicle) by faster movement. 3. to exceed (a compared value or amount).

overtax *v.* 1. to levy excessive taxes on. 2. to put too heavy a burden or strain on.

overthrow *v.* (overthrew, overthrown, overthrowing) to cause the downfall of, *overthrew the government*. —*n.* 1. downfall, defeat. 2. a fielder's throwing of a ball beyond an intended point.

overtime *adv.* in addition to regular working hours. —*n.* 1. time worked in this way. 2. payment for this.

overtone *n.* an additional quality or implication, *overtones of malice in his comments*.

overtook *see* overtake.

overtrick *n.* a trick taken in excess of one's contract in the game of bridge.

overture *n.* 1. an orchestral composition forming a prelude to an opera or ballet etc. 2. a composition resembling this. **overtures** *pl. n.* a friendly approach showing willingness to begin negotiations, a formal proposal or offer.

overturn *v.* to turn over, to cause to turn over.

over-use[1] (oh-ver-**yooz**) *v.* to use excessively.

over-use[2] (oh-ver-**yoos**) *n.* excessive use.

overweight *adj.* weighing more than is normal or required or permissible.

overwhelm *v.* 1. to bury or drown beneath a huge mass. 2. to overcome completely, especially by force of numbers. 3. to make helpless with emotion.

overwhelming *adj.* irresistible through

force of numbers or amount or influence etc.

overwind *v.* (overwound, overwinding) to wind (a watch etc.) beyond the proper stopping-point.

overwork *v.* 1. to work or cause to work so hard that one becomes exhausted. 2. to make excessive use of, *an overworked phrase*. *n.* excessive work causing exhaustion.

overwrought (oh-ver-**rawt**) *adj.* in a state of nervous agitation through over-excitement.

ovoid (**oh**-void) *adj.* egg-shaped, oval. —*n.* an ovoid shape or mass.

ovulate (ov-yoo-layt) *v.* to produce or discharge an ovum from an ovary. **ovulation** *n.*

ovule (**oh**-vewl) *n.* 1. a small part in a plant's ovary that develops into a seed when fertilized. 2. an unfertilized ovum.

ovum (**oh**-vŭm) *n.* (*pl.* ova) a female egg-cell capable of developing into a new individual when fertilized by male sperm.

owe *v.* 1. to be under an obligation to pay or repay (money etc.) in return for what one has received, to be in debt. 2. to have a duty to render, *owe allegiance to the Queen*. 3. to feel (gratitude etc.) towards another in return for a service. 4. to have (a thing) as a result of the work or action of another person or cause, *we owe this discovery to Newton; he owes his success to luck*

owing *adj.* owed and not yet paid. **owing to**, caused by; because of.

owl *n.* a bird of prey with a large head, large eyes, and a hooked beak, usually flying at night.

owlet *n.* a small or young owl.

owlish *adj.* like an owl. **owlishly** *adv.*

own[1] *adj.* belonging to oneself or itself. **get one's own back**, (*informal*) to have one's revenge. **hold one's own**, to succeed in holding one's position; not lose strength of one's own, belonging to oneself exclusively. **on one's own**, alone; independently. **own brand**, a class of goods marked with the trade mark of the retailer instead of that of the manufacturer. **own goal**, a goal scored by a member of a team against his own side.

own[2] *v.* 1. to have as one's property, to possess. 2. to acknowledge that one is the author or possessor or father etc. of. 3. to confess, *she owns to having said it*. □ **own up**, (*informal*) to confess, to admit that one is guilty.

owner *n.* one who owns something as his property. **ownership** *n.*, □ **owner-driver, owner-occupier** *ns.* a person who both owns and drives a vehicle, or occupies a house.

ownerless *adj.* having no owner or no known owner.

ox *n.* (*pl.* oxen) **1.** an animal of the kind kept as domestic cattle or related to these. **2.** a fully-grown bullock, used as a draught animal or as food.

Oxbridge *n.* the universities of Oxford and Cambridge as distinct from newer (*redbrick*) foundations.

ox-eye *n.* any of several daisy-like flowers with a large centre from which petals radiate, *ox-eye daisy.*

Oxfam *abbrev.* Oxford Committee for Famine Relief.

Oxfordshire a county of England.

oxidation *n.* the process of combining or causing to combine with oxygen.

oxide *n.* a compound of oxygen and one other element.

oxidize *v.* **1.** to combine or cause to combine with oxygen. **2.** to coat with an oxide. **3.** to make or become rusty.

Oxon. *abbrev.* **1.** Oxfordshire. **2.** of Oxford University.

Oxonian (oks-**oh**-niăn) *adj.* of Oxford University. —*n.* a member of Oxford University.

oxtail *n.* the tail of an ox, used to make soup or stew.

oxy-acetylene (oksi-ă-**set**-i-leen) *adj.* using a mixture of oxygen and acetylene, especially in the cutting and welding of metals.

oxygen *n.* a colourless odourless tasteless gas existing in air and combining with hydrogen to form water.

oxygenate *v.* to supply or treat or mix with oxygen. **oxygenation** *n.*

oxymoron (oksi-**mor**-ŏn) *n.* putting together words which seem to contradict one another, e.g. *bitter-sweet.*

oxytocin (oksi-**toh**-sin) *n.* a hormone controlling contractions of the womb, used in synthetic form to induce labour in childbirth.

oyster *n.* a kind of shellfish used as food, some types of which produce pearls inside their shells.

oz. *abbrev.* ounce(s).

ozone (**oh**-zohn) *n.* **1.** a form of oxygen with a sharp smell. **2.** (*humorous*) invigorating air at the seaside.

Pp

p *abbrev.* penny or pence (in decimal coinage).

p. *abbrev.* page.

pa *n.* (*slang*) father.

Pa. *abbrev.* Pennsylvania.

PA *abbrev.* **1.** personal assistant. **2.** Press Association (a news-reporting agency).

pace[1] *n.* **1.** a single step made in walking or running. **2.** the distance passed in this. **3.** a style of walking or running (especially of horses). **4.** speed in walking or running. **5.** the rate of progress in some activity. —**pace** *v.* **1.** to walk with a slow or regular pace. **2.** to walk to and fro across (a room etc.). **3.** to measure by pacing, *pace it out.* **4.** to set the pace for (a runner etc.). — **pacer** *n.* ◻ **keep pace**, to advance at an equal rate. **put a person through his paces**, to test his ability.

pace[2] (**pay**-si *or* **pah**-chay) *prep.* although (a named person) may not agree. (¶ Latin, = with the permission of.)

pacemaker *n.* **1.** a runner etc. who sets the pace for another. **2.** an electrical device placed on the heart to stimulate contractions.

pachyderm (**pak**-i-derm) *n.* a thick-skinned animal, especially an elephant or rhinoceros.

pacific (pă-**sif**-ik) *adj.* peaceful, making or loving peace. **pacifically** *adv.*

Pacific *adj.* of the Pacific Ocean. —*n.* the **Pacific Ocean**, the ocean lying between the Americas and Asia/Australia.

pacifist (**pas**-i-fist) *n.* a person who totally opposes war, believing that disputes should be settled by peaceful means. **pacifism** *n.*

pacify (**pas**-i-fy) *v.* (pacified, pacifying) **1.** to calm and quieten. **2.** to establish peace in. **pacification** *n.*

pack[1] *n.* **1.** a collection of things wrapped or tied together for carrying. **2.** a set of things packed for selling. **3.** a complete set of playing-cards (usually 52). **4.** a group of hounds or wolves etc. **5.** a gang of people, an organized group of Cub Scouts or Brownies, a Rugby football team's forwards. **6.** a large amount or collection, *a pack of lies.* **7.** a face-pack. — **pack** *v.* **1.** to put (things) into a container for transport or storing or for marketing, to fill with things in this way. **2.** to be able to be packed, *this dress packs easily.* **3.** to cram or press or crowd together into, to fill (a space) in this way; *the hall was packed out,* was very crowded. **4.** to cover or protect (a thing) with something pressed tightly on or in or round it. —**packer** *n.* ◻ **pack a gun**, (*slang*) to carry a gun. **pack a punch**, (*slang*) to be capable of delivering a powerful blow. **pack-drill** *n.* a military punishment of being made to walk up and down in full marching equipment; *no names no pack-drill*, discretion will prevent punishment. **pack-horse** *n.* a horse for carrying packs. **pack-ice** *n.* large crowded floating pieces of ice in the sea. **packing-case** *n.* a wooden case or framework for packing goods in. **pack it in**, (*slang*) to cease doing something. **pack off**, to send (a person) away. **pack up**, to put one's things together in readiness for departing or ceasing work; (*slang*, of machinery etc.) to break down. **send packing**, to dismiss abruptly.

pack [2] *v.* to select (a jury etc.) fraudulently so that their decisions will be in one's favour.

package *n.* 1. a parcel. 2. a box etc. in which goods are packed. 3. a set of items that go together, a package deal. —*v.* to put together in a package. □ **package deal**, a number of proposals offered or accepted as a whole. **package holiday** *or* **tour**, one with set arrangements at an inclusive price.

packet *n.* 1. a small package. 2. (*informal*) a considerable sum of money, *won a packet*. 3. a mail-boat. □ **catch** *or* **stop a packet**, (*slang*) to be severely injured or wounded.

pact *n.* an agreement, a treaty.

pad [1] *n.* 1. a flat cushion, a piece of soft material used to protect against jarring or to add bulk or to hold or absorb fluid etc., or used for rubbing. 2. a padded protection for the leg and ankle in certain games. 3. a set of sheets of writing paper or drawing paper fastened together at one edge. 4. the soft fleshy underpart at the end of a finger, or of the foot of certain animals. 5. a flat surface from which spacecraft are launched or helicopters take off. 6. (*slang*) a lodging. —**pad** *v.* (padded, padding) 1. to put a pad or pads on or into. 2. to stuff. 3. to fill (a book or speech etc.) with unnecessary material in order to lengthen it. □ **padded cell**, a room with padded walls in a mental hospital etc. **padding** *n.* material used to pad things.

pad [2] *v.* (padded, padding) to walk, especially with a soft dull steady sound of steps.

paddle [1] *n.* 1. a short oar with a broad blade, used without a rowlock. 2. an instrument shaped like this. 3. one of the boards on a paddle-wheel. —**paddle** *v.* 1. to propel by using a paddle or paddles. 2. to row gently. □ **paddle one's own canoe**, to be independent. **paddle-wheel** *n.* a wheel with boards round its rim that drive a boat by pressing against the water as the wheel revolves.

paddle [2] *v.* to walk with bare feet in shallow water for pleasure, to dabble (the feet or hands) gently in water. —*n.* a spell of paddling. □ **paddling pool**, a shallow pool in which children may paddle.

paddock *n.* 1. a small field where horses are kept. 2. an enclosure at a racecourse where horses or racing-cars are brought together before a race.

paddy [1] *n.* (*informal*) rage, temper.

paddy [2] *n.* 1. a field where rice is grown. 2. rice that is still growing or in the husk.

padlock *n.* a detachable lock with a U-shaped bar or a chain etc. that fastens through the loop of a staple or ring. —*v.* to fasten with a padlock.

padre (pah-dray) *n.* the title used in speaking to or of a chaplain in the armed forces.

paean (pee-ăn) *n.* a song of praise or triumph.

paederast (peed-er-ast) *n.* = pederast.

paediatrician (peed-i-ă-**trish**-ăn) *n.* a specialist in paediatrics.

paediatrics (peed-i-**at**-riks) *n.* the branch of medicine dealing with children and their diseases. **paediatric** *adj*

paedophilia (peed-ŏ-**fil**-iă) *n.* sexual love by an adult for a child.

paella (pah-**el**-ă) *n.* a Spanish dish of rice, chicken, seafood, etc., cooked and served in a large shallow pan.

pagan (pay-găn) *adj.* heathen. —*n.* a heathen. —**paganism** *n.*

page [1] *n.* 1. a leaf in a book or newspaper etc. 2. one side of this.

page [2] *n.* 1. a liveried boy employed to go on errands or act as door attendant etc. 2. a boy attendant of a person of rank or a bride. —*v.* to summon (a person) by means of a page or by calling his name until he is found.

pageant (paj-ĕnt) *n.* a public show consisting of a procession of people in costume, or an outdoor performance of a historical play. **pageantry** *n.*

pagination (paj-in-ay-shŏn) *n.* the numbering of the pages of a book.

pagoda (pă-**goh**-dă) *n.* a Hindu temple shaped like a pyramid, or a Buddhist tower with several storeys, in India and countries of the Far East.

paid *see* pay. —*adj.* receiving money in exchange for goods or services, *a paid assistant*; *paid holidays*, during which normal wages continue to be paid. □ **paid-up** *adj.* for which all the necessary payments have been made. **put paid to**, (*informal*) to put an end to the hopes or prospects or activities of.

pail *n.* a bucket.

pain *n.* 1. an unpleasant feeling caused by

injury or disease of the body. **2.** mental suffering. **3.** (*old use*) punishment, *pains and penalties*; *on* or *under pain of death*, with the threat of this punishment. —*v.* to cause pain to. □ **a pain in the neck**, (*informal*) an annoying or tiresome person or thing. **pain-killer** *n.* a medicine that lessens pain. **pains** *pl. n.* careful effort, trouble taken, *take pains with the work*.

pained *adj.* distressed and annoyed, *a pained look*.

painful *adj.* **1.** causing pain. **2.** (of a part of the body) suffering pain. **3.** causing trouble or difficulty, laborious. **painfully** *adv.*, **painfulness** *n.*

painless *adj.* not causing pain. **painlessly** *adv.*, **painlessness** *n.*

painstaking *adj.* careful, using or done with great care and effort.

paint *n.* colouring-matter for applying in liquid form to a surface. —*v.* **1.** to coat or decorate with paint. **2.** to make a picture or portray by using paint(s). **3.** to describe vividly; *he's not so black as he is painted*, not as bad as he is said to be. **4.** to apply (liquid or cosmetic) to the skin; *paint one's face*, to use or apply make-up. □ **painted lady**, an orange butterfly with black and white spots. **paints** *pl. n.* a collection of tubes or cakes of paint. **paint the town red**, (*slang*) to hold a riotous spree.

paintbox *n.* a box holding dry paints for use by an artist.

paintbrush *n.* a brush for applying paint.

painter [1] *n.* a person who paints as an artist or as a decorator.

painter [2] *n.* a rope attached to the bow of a boat for tying it up.

painting *n.* a painted picture.

paintwork *n.* **1.** a painted surface. **2.** the work of painting.

pair *n.* **1.** a set of two things or people, a couple. **2.** an article consisting of two joined corresponding parts, *a pair of scissors*. **3.** an engaged or married couple. **4.** two mated animals. **5.** the other member of a pair, *can't find a pair to this sock*. **6.** either or both of two MPs of opposite parties who are absent from a division by mutual arrangement. —*pair v.* **1.** to arrange or be arranged in couples. **2.** (of animals) to mate. **3.** to partner (a person) with a member of the opposite sex. **4.** to make a pair in Parliament. □ **pair off**, to form into pairs.

Paisley *adj.* having a pattern of tapering petal-shaped figures with much detail.

Paki (**pak**-i) *n.* (*slang*) a Pakistani.

Pakistan (pah-kis-**tahn**) a country in southern Asia. **Pakistani** *adj.* & *n.* (*pl.* Pakistanis).

pal *n.* (*informal*) a friend. —*v.* (palled, palling) **pal up**, (*informal*) to become friends.

palace *n.* **1.** the official residence of a sovereign or of an archbishop or bishop. **2.** a splendid mansion. □ **palace revolution**, overthrow of a ruler without civil war.

palaeolithic (pay-li-ŏ-**lith**-ik) *adj.* of the early part of the Stone Age.

palatable (**pal**-ă-tă-bŭl) *adj.* pleasant to the taste or to the mind.

palate (**pal**-ăt) *n.* **1.** the roof of the mouth. **2.** the sense of taste.

¶ Do not confuse with palette and pallet.

palatial (pă-**lay**-shăl) *adj.* like a palace, spacious and splendid.

palaver (pă-**lah**-ver) *n.* **1.** (*old use*) a parley, especially with primitive peoples of Africa. **2.** (*informal*) fuss.

pale [1] *adj.* **1.** (of a person's face) having little colour, lighter than normal. **2.** (of colour or light) faint, not bright or vivid. —*v.* to turn pale. —**palely** *adv.*, **paleness** *n.*

pale [2] *n.* **1.** a stake forming part of a fence. **2.** a boundary. □ **beyond the pale**, outside the bounds of acceptable behaviour.

Palestine the former name of a country at the eastern end of the Mediterranean Sea, now divided between Israel and Jordan. **Palestinian** *adj.* & *n.*

palette (**pal**-it) *n.* a thin board, with a hole for the thumb by which it is held, on which an artist mixes colours when painting. **palette-knife** *n.* an artist's knife for mixing or spreading paint; a knife with a long blunt round-ended flexible blade for spreading or smoothing soft substances in cookery etc.

¶ Do not confuse with palate and pallet.

palindrome (**pal**-in-drohm) *n.* a word or phrase that reads the same backwards as forwards, e.g. *rotator, nurses run*.

paling (**pay**-ling) *n.* **1.** fencing made of wooden posts or railings. **2.** one of its uprights.

palisade (pal-i-**sayd**) *n.* a fence of pointed stakes.

palish *adj.* rather pale.

pall (*pr.* pawl) *n.* **1.** a cloth spread over a coffin. **2.** something forming a dark heavy covering, *a pall of smoke*. —*v.* to become uninteresting or boring, *the subject began to pall on us*. □ **pallbearer** *n.* one of the people carrying or walking beside the coffin at a funeral.

pallet [1] (**pal**-it) *n.* **1.** a mattress stuffed with straw. **2.** a hard narrow bed, a makeshift bed.

¶ Do not confuse with palate and palette.

pallet[2] (**pal**-it) *n.* a large tray or platform for carrying goods that are being lifted or in storage, especially one that can be raised by a fork-lift truck.

¶ Do not confuse with palate and palette.

palliasse (**pal**-yas) *n.* a straw mattress.

palliate (**pal**-i-ayt) *v.* to make less intense or less severe. **palliation** *n.*

palliative (**pal**-i-ătiv) *adj.* reducing the bad effects of something. —*n.* something that does this.

pallid (**pal**-id) *adj.* pale, especially from illness.

pallor (**pal**-er) *n.* paleness.

pally *adj.* (*informal*) friendly.

palm *n.* **1.** the inner surface of the hand between the wrist and the fingers. **2.** the part of a glove that covers this. **3.** a palmtree. **4.** an imaginary award for success, *carried off the palm.* —*v.* to conceal in one's hand. □ **palm off**, to get (a thing) accepted fraudulently; *palmed it off on them,* induced them to accept something false or inferior, or something one did not want. **Palm Sunday,** the Sunday before Easter, commemorating Christ's triumphal entry into Jerusalem when the people strewed leaves in his path. **palm-tree** *n.* a kind of tree growing in warm or tropical climates, with no branches and with large leaves growing in a mass at the top.

palmate (**pal**-mayt) *adj.* shaped like a hand with the fingers spread out.

palmetto (**pal**-**met**-oh) *n.* (*pl.* **palmettos**) a kind of small palm tree with fan-shaped leaves.

palmistry (**pahm**-ist-ri) *n.* the supposed art of telling a person's future or interpreting his character by examining the lines or creases etc. in the palm of his hand. **palmist** *n.* a person who does this.

palmy (**pahm**-i) *adj.* (palmier, palmiest) **1.** full of palms. **2.** flourishing, *in their former palmy days.*

palpable (**pal**-pă-bŭl) *adj.* **1.** able to be touched or felt. **2.** easily perceived, obvious. **palpably** *adv.,* **palpability** *n.*

palpate (**pal**-payt) *v.* to examine by feeling with the hands, especially as part of a medical examination. **palpation** *n.*

palpitate (**pal**-pit-ayt) *v.* **1.** to pulsate, to throb rapidly. **2.** (of a person) to quiver with fear or excitement. **palpitation** *n.*

palsy (**pawl**-zi) *n.* paralysis, especially with involuntary tremors. **palsied** (**pawl**-zid) *adj.* affected with palsy.

paltry (**pol**-tri) *adj.* (paltrier, paltriest) worthless, trivial, contemptible.

pampas (**pam**-păs) *n.* vast grassy plains in South America. **pampas-grass** *n.* a kind of tall ornamental grass with feathery plumes.

pamper *v.* to treat very indulgently.

pamphlet (**pamf**-lit) *n.* a leaflet or papercovered booklet containing information or a treatise.

pan[1] *n.* **1.** a metal or earthenware vessel with a flat base and often without a lid, used for cooking and other domestic purposes. **2.** its contents. **3.** any similar vessel. **4.** the bowl of a pair of scales. **5.** the bowl of a water-closet. —**pan** *v.* (panned, panning) **1.** to wash (gravel) in a pan in search of gold. **2.** (*informal*) to criticize severely. — **panful** *n.* □ **pan out,** (of circumstances or events) to turn out, to be successful in outcome.

pan[2] *v.* (panned, panning) **1.** to turn (a camera) horizontally to give a panoramic effect or follow a moving object. **2.** (of a camera) to turn in this way.

pan[3] *adj.* panchromatic.

pan- *prefix* all-, of the whole of a continent or racial group etc., *pan-African, pan-American.*

panacea (pan-ă-**see**-ă) *n.* a remedy for all kinds of diseases or troubles.

panache (păn-**ash**) *n.* a confident stylish manner.

Panama (pan-ă-**mah**) a country in Central America. **Panamanian** (pană-**may**-niăn) *adj. & n.*

panama (pan-ă-**mah**) *n.* **1.** a hat of fine pliant straw-like material. **2.** a woven fabric used for jackets and skirts etc.

panatella (pan-ă-**tel**-ă) *n.* a thin cigar.

pancake *n.* **1.** a thin round cake of batter fried on both sides, sometimes rolled up with filling. **2.** make-up in the form of a flat cake. □ **Pancake Day,** Shrove Tuesday, on which pancakes are traditionally eaten. **pancake landing,** a landing in which an aircraft descends vertically in a level position.

panchromatic (pan-krŏ-**mat**-ik) *adj.* sensitive to all colours of the visible spectrum, *panchromatic film.*

pancreas (**pank**-ri-ăs) *n.* a gland near the stomach discharging a digestive secretion into the duodenum and insulin into the blood. **pancreatic** (pank-ri-**at**-ik) *adj.*

panda *n.* **1.** a large rare bear-like blackand-white animal living in the mountains of south-west China, also called the *giant panda.* **2.** a racoon-like animal of India. **3.** a panda car. □ **panda car,** a police patrol car, often with doors coloured differently from the rest of the body.

pandemic (pan-**dem**-ik) *adj.* (of a disease) occurring over a whole country or the whole world.

pandemonium (pandi-**moh**-niŭm) *n.* uproar.

pander *v.* **pander to**, to gratify (weakness or vulgar tastes), *pandering to the public interest in scandal.* —*n.* a pimp.

Pandora's box (in Greek mythology) a box which, when opened, let loose all kinds of misfortunes upon mankind.

p. & p. *abbrev.* postage and packing.

pane *n.* a single sheet of glass in a window or door.

panegyric (pan-i-**ji**-rik) *n.* a speech or piece of writing praising a person or thing.

panel *n.* 1. a distinct usually rectangular section of a surface. 2. a strip of board or other material forming a separate section of a wall or door or cabinet etc., a section of the metal bodywork of a vehicle. 3. a strip of material set lengthwise in or on a garment. 4. a group of people assembled to discuss or decide something. 5. a list of jurors, a jury. —*v.* (panelled, panelling) to cover or decorate with panels. □ **panel game**, a quiz or similar form of entertainment in which a panel of people take part.

panelling *n.* 1. a series of panels in a wall. 2. wood used for making panels.

panellist *n.* a member of a panel.

pang *n.* a sudden sharp feeling of pain or a painful emotion, *pangs of jealousy.*

panic *n.* sudden terror, wild infectious fear. —*v.* (panicked, panicking) to affect or be affected with panic. —**panicky** *adj.* □ **panic button**, a button to be pressed as a signal etc. in an emergency. **panic stations**, positions taken up in an emergency. **panic-stricken**, **panic-struck** *adjs.* affected with panic.

panicle *n.* a loose branching cluster of flowers.

pannier *n.* 1. a large basket, especially one of a pair carried on either side of a pack animal. 2. a bag carried similarly on a motor cycle etc.

panoply (**pan**-ŏ-pli) *n.* a splendid array.

panorama *n.* 1. a view of a wide area, a picture or photograph of this. 2. a view of a constantly changing scene or series of events. **panoramic** (pan-er-**am**-ik) *adj.*

pan-pipes *n.* a musical instrument made of a series of pipes fixed together and with the mouthpieces in line.

pansy *n.* 1. a garden plant of the violet family, with broad flat rounded richly-coloured petals. 2. (*informal*) an effeminate man, a male homosexual.

pant[1] *v.* 1. to breathe with short quick breaths. 2. to utter breathlessly. 3. to be extremely eager. —*n.* a panting breath.

pant[2] *see* pants.

pantaloons *pl. n.* (*humorous* & *Amer.*) trousers.

pantechnicon (pan-**tek**-nik-ŏn) *n.* a large van for transporting furniture.

panther *n.* a leopard.

panties *pl. n.* (*informal*) short knickers for women or children.

pantihose *n.* tights (sense 1).

pantile (**pan**-tyl) *n.* a curved roof-tile.

pantomime *n.* 1. a type of drama based on a fairy-tale, usually produced at Christmas. 2. expressive movements of the face and body used to convey a story or meaning. —*v.* to express a story or meaning by such movements.

pantry *n.* 1. a room in which china, glasses, cutlery, table-linen, etc. are kept. 2. a larder.

pants *pl. n.* (*informal*) 1. trousers. 2. a man's underpants. 3. knickers. □ **pant suit** *or* **pants suit**, a trouser suit.

panzer (**pants**-er) *adj.* (of German troops) armoured, *panzer divisions.*

pap *n.* 1. soft or semi-liquid food suitable for infants or invalids. 2. mash, pulp.

papa *n.* (*old use,* children's word) father.

papacy (**pay**-pă-si) *n.* the position or authority of the pope, the system of Church government by popes.

papal (**pay**-păl) *adj.* of the pope or the papacy.

papaw (pă-**paw**) *n.* 1. an oblong orange-coloured edible fruit. 2. the palm-like tropical American tree bearing this.

paper *n.* 1. a substance manufactured in thin sheets from wood fibre, rags, etc., used for writing or printing or drawing on or for wrapping things. 2. a newspaper. 3. wallpaper. 4. a set of examination questions, *the biology paper.* 5. a document; *a ship's papers,* documents establishing its identity etc. 6. an essay or dissertation, especially one read to a learned society. —*v.* to cover (walls etc.) with wallpaper. □ **on paper**, in writing; in theory, when judged from written or printed evidence, *the scheme looks good on paper.* **paper-boy**, **paper-girl** *ns.* one who delivers newspapers. **paper-clip** *n.* a piece of bent wire or plastic for holding a few sheets of paper together. **paper-knife** *n.* a blunt knife for slitting open uncut pages or sealed envelopes etc. **paper money**, banknotes and money orders etc. as distinct from coin. **paper over the cracks**, to seek to conceal flaws or disagreement. **paper tiger**, a person or thing that has a threatening appearance but can do no harm.

paperback *adj.* bound in a flexible paper binding, not in a stiff cover. —*n.* a book bound in this way.

paperweight *n.* a small heavy object placed on top of loose papers to keep them in place.

paperwork *n.* routine clerical work and record-keeping.

papery *adj.* like paper in texture.

papier mâché (pap-yay ma-shay) moulded paper pulp used for making boxes or trays or ornaments etc.

papillon (pă-**pil**-yŏn) *n.* a dog of a very small breed with ears shaped like a butterfly's wings.

papist (**pay**-pist) *n.* (*contemptuous*) a Roman Catholic.

papoose (pă-**pooss**) *n.* a North American Indian baby.

paprika (**pap**-rik-ă) *n.* red pepper.

Papua New Guinea (**pap**-oo-ă) a country consisting of a group of islands between Asia and Australia.

papyrus (pă-**py**-rŭs) *n.* 1. a reed-like water-plant with thick fibrous stems from which a kind of paper was made by the ancient Egyptians. 2. this paper. 3. (*pl.* papyri) a manuscript written on this.

par *n.* 1. an average or normal amount or condition or degree etc., *was feeling below par.* 2. the face value of stocks and shares etc.; *at par,* at face value. 3. (in golf) the number of strokes that a first-class player should normally require for a hole or course. □ **on a par with,** on an equal footing with.

para *n.* (*informal*) 1. a parachutist or paratrooper. 2. a paragraph.

parable *n.* a story told to illustrate a moral or spiritual truth.

parabola (pă-**rab**-ŏ-lă) *n.* a curve like the path of an object thrown into the air and falling back to earth.

parabolic (pa-ră-**bol**-ik) *adj.* 1. of or expressed in a parable. 2. of or like a parabola.

parachute *n.* an umbrella-shaped device used to slow the descent of a person or heavy object falling from a great height, especially from a moving aircraft; *parachute troops,* troops trained to descend by parachute. —*v.* to descend by parachute, to drop (supplies etc.) by parachute. — **parachutist** *n.*

parade *n.* 1. a formal assembly of troops for inspection or roll-call etc. 2. a place where this is regularly held. 3. a procession of people or things, especially in a display or exhibition. 4. an ostentatious display, *makes a parade of his virtues.* 5. a public square or promenade. —**parade** *v.* 1. to assemble for parade. 2. to march or walk with display. 3. to make a display of. □ **on parade,** taking part in a parade.

paradigm (pa-ră-dym) *n.* something serving as an example or model of how things should be done.

paradise *n.* 1. heaven. 2. Eden.

paradox (pa-ră-doks) *n.* a statement etc. that seems to contradict itself or to conflict with common sense but which contains a truth (e.g. 'more haste, less speed'). **paradoxical** (pa-ră-**doks**-ikăl) *adj.,* **paradoxically** *adv.*

paraffin *n.* an oil obtained from petroleum or shale, used as a fuel. **liquid paraffin,** a tasteless form of this used as a mild laxative. **paraffin wax,** paraffin in solid form.

paragon (pa-ră-gŏn) *n.* a model of excellence, an apparently perfect person or thing.

paragraph *n.* one or more sentences on a single theme, forming a distinct section of a piece of writing and beginning on a new (usually indented) line. —*v.* to arrange in paragraphs.

Paraguay (pa-ră-gwy) a country in South America. **Paraguayan** (pa-ră-**gwy**-ăn) *adj.* & *n.*

parakeet (pa-ră-keet) *n.* a kind of small parrot, often with a long tail.

paraldehyde (pă-**ral**-di-hyd) *n.* a substance used as a sedative.

parallax (pa-ră-laks) *n.* an apparent difference in the position or direction of an object when it is viewed from different points.

parallel *adj.* 1. (of lines or planes) continuously at the same distance from each other. 2. having this relationship, *the road runs parallel to* (or *with*) *the railway.* 3. similar, having features that correspond, *parallel situations.* —**parallel** *n.* 1. an imaginary line on the earth's surface or a corresponding line on a map parallel to and passing through all points equidistant from the equator. 2. a person or situation etc. that is parallel to another. 3. a comparison, *drew a parallel between the two situations.* — **parallel** *v.* (paralleled, paralleling) 1. to be parallel to. 2. to find or mention something parallel or corresponding, to compare. —**parallelism** *n.*

parallelogram (pa-ră-**lel**-ŏ-gram) *n.* a plane four-sided figure with its opposite sides parallel to each other.

paralyse *v.* 1. to affect with paralysis, to make unable to act or move normally. 2. to bring to a standstill.

paralysis *n.* 1. loss of the power of movement, caused by disease or injury to nerves. 2. inability to move normally.

paralytic (pa-ră-**lit**-ik) *adj.* 1. affected with paralysis. 2. (*slang*) very drunk.

—*n.* a person affected with paralysis.

paramedical *adj.* (of services etc.) supplementing and supporting medical work.

parameter (pă-**ram**-it-er) *n.* **1.** (in mathematics) a quantity that is constant in the case considered but varies in different cases. **2.** a variable quantity or quality that restricts or gives a particular form to the thing it characterizes. **3.** a specification that is used in a computer program or routine and that can be given a different value whenever this is repeated. **4.** (*incorrect use*) a limit.

¶ Do not confuse with perimeter.

paramilitary *adj.* organized like a military force but not part of the armed services. —*n.* a member of a paramilitary organization.

paramount *adj.* chief in importance, supreme.

paramour (**pa**-ră-moor) *n.* a married person's illicit lover.

parang (**par**-ang) *n.* a heavy Malayan sheath-knife.

paranoia (pa-ră-**noi**-ă) **1.** a mental disorder in which a person has delusions, e.g. of grandeur or persecution. **2.** an abnormal tendency to suspect and mistrust others.

paranoiac (pa-ră-**noi**-ak) *adj.* of or like or suffering from paranoia. —*n.* a person suffering from paranoia.

paranoid (**pa**-ră-noid) *adj.* & *n.* = paranoiac.

parapet (**pa**-ră-pit) *n.* a low protective wall along the edge of a balcony or roof or bridge etc.

paraphernalia (pa-ră-fer-**nay**-liă) *n.* numerous small pieces of equipment etc.

paraphrase (**pa**-ră-frayz) *v.* to express the meaning of (a passage) in other words. —*n.* re-wording in this way, a re-worded passage.

paraplegia (pa-ră-**plee**-jiă) *n.* paralysis of the legs and part or all of the trunk. **paraplegic** *adj.* & *n.*

parapsychology (pa-ră-sy-**kol**-ŏji) *n.* the scientific study of mental perceptions (e.g. those occuring in clairvoyance and telepathy) that seem to be outside normal mental abilities.

paraquat (**pa**-ră-kwot) *n.* an extremely poisonous weed-killer.

parasite *n.* **1.** an animal or plant that lives on or in another from which it draws its nourishment. **2.** a person who lives off another or others and gives no useful return. **parasitic** (pa-ră-**sit**-ik) *adj.*

parasol *n.* a light umbrella used to give shade from the sun.

parathion (pa-răth-**I**-ŏn) *n.* an extremely poisonous insecticide.

paratroops *pl. n.* parachute troops. **paratrooper** *n.* a member of these. ¶ It is incorrect to use 'a paratroop' to mean 'a paratrooper'.

paratyphoid (pa-ră-**ty**-foid) *n.* a kind of fever resembling typhoid but milder.

parboil *v.* to boil (food) until it is partly cooked.

parcel *n.* **1.** a thing or things wrapped up for carrying or for sending by post. **2.** a piece of land. —*v.* (parcelled, parcelling) **1.** to wrap up as a parcel. **2.** to divide into portions, *parcelled it out.*

parch *v.* to make hot and dry or thirsty.

parchment *n.* **1.** a heavy paper-like material made from animal skins. **2.** a kind of paper resembling this.

pardon *n.* **1.** forgiveness. **2.** cancellation of the punishment incurred through a crime or conviction, *a free pardon.* **3.** kind indulgence, e.g. for a slight discourtesy or for failing to hear or understand, *I beg your pardon.* —*v.* (pardoned, pardoning) to forgive, to overlook (a slight discourtesy etc.) kindly.

pardonable *adj.* able to be pardoned. **pardonably** *adv.*

pare (*pr.* pair) *v.* **1.** to trim by cutting away the edges of, to peel. **2.** to reduce little by little, *pared down their expenses.* □ **parings** *pl. n.* pieces pared off, *nail parings.*

parent *n.* **1.** one who has procreated offspring, a father or mother. **2.** an ancestor. **3.** a person who has adopted a child. **4.** an animal or plant from which others are derived. **5.** a source from which other things are derived, *the parent company.* **parenthood** *n.*

parentage (**pair**-ĕn-tij) *n.* descent from parents, ancestry.

parental (pă-**ren**-t'l) *adj.* of parents.

parenthesis (pă-**ren**-thi-sis) *n.* (*pl.* parentheses) **1.** an additional word or phrase or sentence inserted in a passage which is grammatically complete without it, and usually marked off by brackets or dashes or commas. **2.** either of the pair of round brackets (like these) used for this. □ **in parenthesis**, between brackets as a parenthesis; as an aside or digression in a speech etc.

parenthetic (pa-rĕn-**thet**-ik) *adj.* **1.** of or as a parenthesis. **2.** interposed as an aside or digression. **parenthetical** *adj.*, **parenthetically** *adv.*

par excellence (par **eks**-el-ahnss) more than all others, in the highest degree. (¶ French)

parfait (**par**-fay) *n.* **1.** a rich iced pudding made of eggs and cream or ice cream.

2. layers of ice cream and fruit etc. served in a tall glass.

pariah (pă-ry-ă) *n.* an outcast.

parietal (pă-ry-ĕt'l) *n.* either of the **parietal bones**, those forming part of the sides and top of the skull.

Paris the capital of France. **Parisian** (pă-**riz**-iăn) *adj.* & *n.*

parish *n.* **1.** an area within a diocese, having its own church and clergyman. **2.** a distinct area within a county, constituted for purposes of local government. **3.** the people of a parish. □ **parish clerk**, an official having various duties in connection with the parish church. **parish council**, an administrative body in a civil parish. **parish register**, a book recording the christenings, marriages, and burials that have taken place at the parish church.

parishioner (pă-**rish**-ŏn-er) *n.* an inhabitant of a parish.

parity (**pa**-riti) *n.* **1.** equality, equal status or pay etc. **2.** being valued at par.

park *n.* **1.** a public garden or recreation ground in a town. **2.** an enclosed area of grassland (usually with trees) attached to a country house or a mansion. **3.** a parking area for vehicles. —**park** *v.* **1.** to place and leave (a vehicle) temporarily. **2.** (*informal*) to deposit temporarily; *park oneself*, to sit down. □ **parking-lot** *n.* (*Amer.*) an outdoor area for parking vehicles. **parking-meter** *n.* a coin-operated meter in which fees are inserted for parking a vehicle beside it in the street. **parking-ticket** *n.* a notice of a fine imposed for parking a vehicle illegally.

parka *n.* **1.** a skin jacket with hood attached, worn by Eskimos. **2.** a jacket or coat shaped like this.

parkin *n.* gingerbread made with oatmeal and treacle.

Parkinson's disease a disease of the nervous system causing tremor and weakness of the muscles.

Parkinson's law any of several facts humorously formulated by C. Northcote Parkinson, especially 'work expands so as to fill the time available for its completion'.

parky *adj.* (*slang*, of weather) chilly.

parlance (**par**-lăns) *n.* phraseology.

parley *n.* (*pl.* parleys) a discussion, especially between enemies or opponents to settle points in dispute. —*v.* (parleyed, parleying) to hold a parley.

parliament (**par**-lă-mĕnt) *n.* an assembly that makes the laws of a country; *Parliament*, that of the UK, consisting of the House of Commons and the House of Lords.

parliamentarian (parlă-men-**tair**-iăn) *n.* a person who is skilled at debating in parliament.

parliamentary (parlă-**ment**-eri) *adj.* of parliament; *parliamentary language*, polite, as required in parliamentary debates.

parlour *n.* **1.** (*old use*) the sitting-room of a family in a private house. **2.** a room in a mansion or convent etc. where people may receive visitors and converse privately. **3.** a place for milking cows. □ **parlour game**, an indoor game. **parlour tricks**, (*contemptuous*) social accomplishments.

parlourmaid *n.* a maid who waits on a household at meals.

Parmesan (par-mi-**zan**) *n.* a kind of hard cheese made at Parma and elsewhere, usually grated before use.

parochial (pă-**roh**-kiăl) *adj.* **1.** of a church parish. **2.** merely local, showing interest in a limited area only. **parochialism** *n.*

parody (**pa**-rŏ-di) *n.* **1.** a comic imitation of a well-known person or literary work or style etc. **2.** a grotesque imitation, a travesty. —*v.* (parodied, parodying) to mimic humorously, to compose a parody of.

parole (pă-**rohl**) *n.* **1.** a person's word of honour. **2.** a prisoner's promise that he will not try to escape if given a limited freedom. **3.** release of a convicted person from a prison before his sentence has expired, on condition of good behaviour. —*v.* to release on parole.

paroxysm (**pa**-rŏk-sizm) *n.* a spasm, a sudden attack or outburst of pain or rage or laughter etc.

parquet (**par**-kay) *n.* flooring of wooden blocks arranged in a pattern.

parrot *n.* **1.** a tropical bird with a short hooked bill and often with brightly-coloured plumage. **2.** a person who repeats another's words or imitates his actions unintelligently.

parry *v.* (parried, parrying) **1.** to ward off (an opponent's weapon or blow) by using one's own weapon etc. to block the thrust. **2.** to evade (an awkward question) skilfully. —*n.* parrying.

parse (*pr.* parz) *v.* to explain the grammatical form and function of (a word or words in a sentence).

parsec (**par**-sek) *n.* a unit of distance used in astronomy, about 3½ light-years.

Parsee (par-**see**) *n.* a person who believes in Zoroastrianism.

parsimonious (par-si-**moh**-niŭs) *adj.* stingy, very sparing in the use of resources. **parsimoniously** *adv.*, **parsimony** (**par**-sim-ŏni) *n.*

parsley *n.* a garden plant with crinkled green leaves used for seasoning and decorating food and in sauces.

parsnip *n.* **1.** a plant with a large yellowish tapering root that is used as a vegetable. **2.** this root.

parson *n.* **1.** a rector or vicar. **2.** (*informal*) a clergyman. □ **parson's nose**, the rump of a cooked fowl.

parsonage *n.* a rectory or vicarage.

part *n.* **1.** some but not all of a thing or number of things. **2.** a division of a book or broadcast serial etc., especially as much as is issued at one time. **3.** a region. **4.** an integral element, *she is part of the family*. **5.** a distinct portion of a human or animal body or of a plant. **6.** a component of a machine or structure. **7.** each of several equal portions of a whole; *a fourth part*, a quarter; *three parts*, three-quarters. **8.** a portion allotted, a share of work etc. **9.** the character assigned to an actor in a play etc., the words spoken by this character, a copy of these. **10.** the melody or other line of music assigned to a particular voice or instrument. **11.** a side in an agreement or in a dispute; *for* or *on my part*, as far as I am concerned. —*adv.* in part, partly. — **part** *v.* **1.** to separate or divide, to cause to do this; *part one's hair*, to make a parting. **2.** (*informal*) to pay out money. □ **in good part**, good-humouredly, without taking offence. **in part**, partly. **a man of parts**, one with many abilities. **part and parcel of**, an essential part of. **part company**, to go different ways after being together; to cease to associate. **part-exchange** *n.* a transaction in which an article is given as part of the payment for a more expensive one. **part of speech**, one of the classes into which words are divided in grammar (noun, adjective, pronoun, verb, adverb, preposition, conjunction, interjection). **part-owner** *n.* one who shares the ownership of something with other people. **part-song** *n.* a song with three or more voice-parts, often without accompaniment. **part time**, less than full time. **part-time** *adj.* for or during only part of the working day or week. **part-timer** *n.* one employed in part-time work. **part with**, to give up possession of, to hand over.

partake *v.* (partook, partaken, partaking) **1.** to participate. **2.** to take a part or portion, especially of food. **partaker** *n.*

Parthian (par-thi-ăn) *adj.* **Parthian shot**, a sharp remark made by a person as he departs. ¶ The horsemen of ancient Parthia were renowned for turning to shoot their arrows at the enemy while retreating.

partial (par-shăl) *adj.* **1.** in part but not complete or total, *a partial eclipse*. **2.** biased, unfair. **partially** *adv.* □ **be partial to**, to have a strong liking for.

partiality (par-shi-al-iti) *n.* **1.** bias, favouritism. **2.** a strong liking.

participate (par-tiss-i-payt) *v.* to have a share, to take part in something. **participant** *n.*, **participation** *n.*

participle (par-tiss-ipŭl) *n.* a word formed from a verb (e.g. *going, gone; burning, burnt*) and used in compound verb-forms (*she is going* or *has gone*) or as an adjective (*a going concern*). **participial** (par-ti-sip-iăl) *adj.* □ **past participle**, e.g. *burnt, frightened, wasted*. **present participle,** e.g. *burning, frightening, wasting*.

particle *n.* **1.** a very small portion of matter. **2.** the smallest possible amount, *he hasn't a particle of sense*. **3.** a minor part of speech or a common prefix or suffix, e.g. *non-, un-, -ness*.

particoloured *adj.* coloured partly in one colour and partly in another or others.

particular *adj.* **1.** relating to one person or thing as distinct from others, individual, *this particular tax is no worse than others*. **2.** special, exceptional, *took particular trouble*. **3.** selecting carefully, insisting on certain standards, *is very particular about what he eats*. —*n.* a detail, a piece of information, *gave particulars of the stolen property*. —**particularly** *adv.*, **particularity** (per-tik-yoo-la-riti) *n.* □ **in particular**, particularly, especially, *we liked this one in particular*; specifically, *did nothing in particular*.

particularize *v.* to specify, to name specially or one by one.

parting *n.* **1.** leave-taking. **2.** a line where hair is combed away in different directions. □ **parting shot**, = Parthian shot.

partisan (parti-zan) *n.* **1.** a strong and often uncritical supporter of a person or group or cause. **2.** a guerrilla. **partisanship** *n.*

partition (par-tish-ŏn) *n.* **1.** division into parts. **2.** a part formed in this way. **3.** a structure that divides a room or space, a thin wall. —**partition** *v.* **1.** to divide into parts, to share out in this way. **2.** to divide (a room etc.) by means of a partition.

partly *adv.* to some extent but not completely or wholly.

partner *n.* **1.** one who shares with another or others in some activity, especially in a business firm where he shares risks and profits. **2.** either of two people dancing together or playing tennis or cards etc. on the same side. **3.** a husband or wife. —*v.* to be the partner of, to put together as partners. —**partnership** *n*.

partridge *n*. **1.** a game-bird with brown feathers and a plump body. **2.** its flesh as food.

parturition (par-tewr-**ish**-ŏn) *n*. the process of giving birth to young, childbirth.

party *n*. **1.** a social gathering, usually of invited guests. **2.** a number of people travelling or working together as a unit, *a search party*. **3.** a group of people united in support of a cause or policy etc., especially a political group organized on a national basis to put forward its policies and candidates for office. **4.** the person(s) forming one side in an agreement or dispute. **5.** a person who participates in or knows of or supports an action or plan etc., *refused to be a party to the conspiracy*. **6.** (*humorous*) a person. □ **party line**, a shared telephone line; the set policy of a political party.

party-wall *n*. a wall that is common to two rooms or buildings which it divides.

paschal (**pas**-kăl) *adj*. **1.** of the Jewish Passover; *the paschal lamb*, one sacrificed at Passover. **2.** of Easter.

pasha *n*. a former Turkish title (placed after a name) for an official of high rank, *Glubb Pasha*.

Pashto (**pu**'sh-toh) *n*. the Iranian language of the Pathans.

pass *v*. (passed, passing) **1.** to go or proceed or move onward or past something. **2.** to cause to move across or over or past. **3.** to go from one person to another, to be transferred, *his title passed to his eldest son*. **4.** to hand or transfer, (in football etc.) to send the ball to another player of one's own side. **5.** to discharge from the body as or with excreta. **6.** to change from one state or condition into another. **7.** to come to an end. **8.** to happen, to be done or said, *we heard what passed between them*. **9.** to occupy (time). **10.** to circulate, to be accepted or currently known in a certain way. **11.** to be tolerated or allowed. **12.** to examine and declare satisfactory, to approve (a law etc.), especially by vote. **13.** to achieve the required standard in performing (a test), to be accepted as satisfactory. **14.** to go beyond. **15.** to utter, to pronounce as a decision, *passed some remarks*; *pass judgement*. **16.** (in cards) to refuse one's turn (e.g. in bidding). —**pass** *n*. **1.** passing, especially of an examination or at cards. **2.** a movement made with the hand(s) or something held. **3.** a permit to go into or out of a place or to be absent from one's quarters. **4.** transference of the ball to another player of one's own side in football etc. **5.** a gap in a mountain range, allowing access to the other side. **6.** a critical state of affairs, *things have come to a pretty pass*. □ **make a pass at**, (*informal*) to try to attract sexually. **pass away**, to cease; to die. **pass off**, to cease gradually; (of an event) to take place and be completed, *the meeting passed off smoothly*; to offer or dispose of (a thing) under false pretences, *passed it off as his own*; to evade or dismiss (an awkward remark etc.) lightly. **pass out**, to complete one's military training; (*informal*) to faint. **pass over**, to disregard; to ignore the claims of (a person) to promotion etc. **pass the buck**, *see* buck². **pass up**, (*informal*) to refuse to accept (an opportunity etc.). **pass water**, to urinate.

passable *adj*. **1.** able to be passed. **2.** satisfactory, fairly good but not outstanding. **passably** *adv*.

passage *n*. **1.** the process of passing. **2.** the right to pass through, right of conveyance as a passenger by sea or air, *book your passage*. **3.** a journey by sea or air. **4.** a way through, especially with walls on either side. **5.** a tube-like structure through which air or secretions etc. pass in the body; (*informal*), *back passage*, the rectum, *front passage*, the vagina. **6.** a conversation or dispute, *angry passages during the debate*. **7.** a particular section of a literary or musical work □ **passage of arms**, a fight; a dispute.

passageway *n*. a passage giving a way through.

passbook *n*. a book recording a customer's deposits and withdrawals from a bank or building society account.

passé (**pas**-ay) *adj*. past its or his prime, no longer fashionable.

passenger *n*. **1.** a person (other than the driver or pilot or member of crew etc.) travelling in a vehicle or ship or aircraft. **2.** a member of a team or crew who does no effective work. □ **passenger seat**, the seat beside the driver's seat in a motor vehicle. **passenger train**, a train for carrying passengers not goods.

passer-by *n*. (*pl.* passers-by) a person who happens to be going past a thing.

passing *adj*. not lasting long, casual, *a passing glance*. —*n*. the end of something, a death.

passion *n*. **1.** strong emotion. **2.** an outburst of anger. **3.** sexual love. **4.** great enthusiasm for something, the object of this, *chess is his passion*. **5.** *Passion*, the sufferings of Christ on the cross, the account of this in the Gospels, a musical setting for this account. □ **passionflower** *n*. a climbing plant with flowers thought to resemble the crown of thorns and other things associated with the Passion of Christ. **passion-fruit** *n.* the edible fruit of some kinds of passion-flower. **Passion Sunday,** the fifth Sunday in Lent.

passionate *adj.* **1.** full of passion, showing or moved by strong emotion. **2.** (of emotion) intense. **passionately** *adv.*

passive *adj.* **1.** acted upon and not active. **2.** not resisting, submissive. **3.** lacking initiative or forceful qualities. **4.** (of substances) inert, not active. —*n.* the form of a verb used when the subject of the sentence receives the action, e.g. *was seen* in *he was seen there.* —**passively** *adv.,* **passiveness** *n.,* **passivity** (pa-**siv**-iti) *n.* ☐ **passive resistance,** resistance by refusal to co-operate.

passkey *n.* **1.** a key to a door or gate. **2.** a master-key.

Passover *n.* **1.** a Jewish festival commemorating the liberation of the Jews from slavery in Egypt. **2.** the paschal lamb.

passport *n.* **1.** an official document issued by a government identifying the holder as one of its citizens and entitling him to travel abroad under its protection. **2.** a thing that enables one to obtain something, *such ability is a passport to success.*

password *n.* a selected word or phrase known only to one's own side, enabling sentries to distinguish friend from enemy.

past *adj.* belonging to the time before the present, (of time) gone by. —*n.* **1.** time that is gone by, *in the past.* **2.** past events. **3.** a person's past life or career, especially one that is discreditable, *a man with a past.* —**past** *prep.* **1.** beyond in time or place, *hurried past me.* **2.** beyond the limits or power or range or stage of, *past belief; she's past caring what happens.* —*adv.* beyond in time or place, up to and further, *drove past.* ☐ **past it,** (*slang*) too old to be able to do it, too decrepit to be usable. **past master,** a thorough master in or of a subject, an expert. **would not put it past him,** (*informal*) regard him as morally capable of (doing it).

pasta (**pas**-tă) *n.* **1.** dried paste made with flour and produced in various shapes (e.g. macaroni, spaghetti). **2.** a cooked dish made with this.

paste *n.* **1.** a moist fairly stiff mixture, especially of a powdery substance and a liquid. **2.** an adhesive. **3.** an edible doughy substance, *almond paste.* **4.** an easily spread preparation of ground meat or fish etc., *anchovy paste.* **5.** a hard glass-like substance used in making imitation gems. —**paste** *v.* **1.** to fasten with paste.

2. to coat with paste. **3.** (*slang*) to beat or thrash.

pasteboard *n.* a kind of thin board made of layers of paper or wood fibres pasted together.

pastel (**pas**-t'l) *n.* **1.** a chalk-like crayon. **2.** a drawing made with this. **3.** a light delicate shade of colour.

pastern (**pas**-tern) *n.* the part of a horse's foot between fetlock and hoof.

pasteurize (**pahs**-chĕryz) *v.* to sterilize (milk etc.) partially by heating and then chilling it. **pasteurization** *n.* ¶ The method was devised by Louis Pasteur (1822–95), a French chemist.

pastiche (pas-**teesh**) *n.* a musical or other composition made up of selections from various sources.

pastille (**pas**-t'l) *n.* a small flavoured sweet for sucking, a lozenge.

pastime *n.* something done to pass time pleasantly, a recreation.

pastor (**pah**-ster) *n.* a clergyman in charge of a church or congregation.

pastoral (**pah**-ster-ăl) *adj.* **1.** of shepherds or country life, *a pastoral scene.* **2.** of a pastor, concerned with spiritual guidance of Christians.

pastry *n.* **1.** dough made of flour, fat, and water, used for covering pies or holding filling. **2.** food made with this. **3.** a cake in which pastry is used.

pasturage (**pahs**-cher-ij) *n.* **1.** pasture-land. **2.** the right to graze animals on this.

pasture *n.* **1.** land covered with grass and similar plants suitable for grazing cattle. **2.** grass etc. on such land. —**pasture** *v.* **1.** to put (animals) to graze in a pasture. **2.** (of animals) to graze.

pasty [1] (**pas**-ti) *n.* pastry with a filling of meat or fruit or jam etc., baked without a dish.

pasty [2] (**pay**-sti) *adj.* **1.** of or like paste. **2.** unhealthily pale, *pasty-faced.*

pat *v.* (patted, patting) **1.** to tap gently with the open hand or with something flat. **2.** to flatten or shape by doing this. —**pat** *n.* **1.** a patting movement. **2.** the sound of this. **3.** a small mass of butter or other soft substance. —*adv. & adj.* known and ready for any occasion, *had his answer pat.* ☐ **a pat on the back,** praise, congratulations. **stand pat,** to stick firmly to what one has said.

patch *n.* **1.** a piece of material or metal etc. put over a hole to mend it. **2.** a piece of plaster or a pad placed over a wound etc., or a shield over the eye, to protect it. **3.** a large or irregular area on a surface, differing in colour or texture etc. from the rest. **4.** a piece of ground, especially for growing vegetables, *cabbage patch.* **5.** a small area of anything, *patches of fog.* **6.** a short period, *went through a bad patch last summer.* —**patch** *v.* **1.** to put a patch or patches on. **2.** to serve as a patch for. **3.** to piece (things) together. □ **not a patch on,** (*informal*) not nearly as good as. **patchpocket** *n.* a pocket made by sewing a piece of cloth on the surface of a garment. **patch up,** to repair with patches; to put together hastily or as a makeshift; to settle (a quarrel etc.).

patchouli (pa-choo-li) *n.* **1.** a fragrant plant grown in the Far East. **2.** perfume made from this.

patchwork *n.* **1.** a kind of needlework in which assorted small pieces of cloth are joined edge to edge, often in a pattern. **2.** anything made of assorted pieces.

patchy *adj.* (patchier, patchiest) **1.** having patches, existing in patches, *patchy fog.* **2.** uneven in quality. **patchily** *adv.*, **patchiness** *n.*

pate (*pr.* payt) *n.* (*old use*) the head.

pâté (**pa** tay) *n.* paste of meat etc.

patella (pă-tel-ă) *n.* the kneecap.

paten (pa-t'n) *n.* a metal plate on which bread is placed at the Eucharist.

patent¹ (pay-t'nt) *adj.* **1.** obvious, unconcealed, *his patent dislike of the plan.* **2.** protected by a patent, *patent medicines.* *v.* to obtain or hold a patent for. —**patently** *adv.* □ **letters patent,** an official document conferring a right or title, especially one giving the holder the sole right to make or use or sell an invention. **patent leather,** leather with a glossy varnished surface.

patent² (pa-t'nt *or* pay-t'nt) *n.* **1.** letters patent, the right granted by these. **2.** an invention or process protected in this way. □ **Patent Office,** the government office from which patents are issued.

patentee (pay-t'n-tee) *n.* one who holds a patent.

paternal (pă-ter-năl) *adj.* **1.** of a father, of fatherhood. **2.** fatherly. **3.** related through one's father; *paternal grandmother,* one's father's mother. **paternally** *adv.*

paternalism (pă-ter-năl-izm) *n.* the policy of governing or controlling people in a paternal way, providing for their needs but giving them no responsibility. **paternalistic** *adj.*

paternity (pă-tern-iti) *n.* **1.** fatherhood, being a father. **2.** descent from a father. □ **paternity test,** a test to determine from blood samples whether a man may be the father of a particular child.

paternoster (pat-er-nost-er) *n.* the Lord's Prayer, especially in Latin.

path *n.* **1.** a way by which people pass on

foot, a track. **2.** a line along which a person or thing moves. **3.** a course of action.

Pathan (pă-tahn) *n.* a member of a people living in parts of Afghanistan, Pakistan, and the Indian peninsula.

pathetic (pă-thet-ik) *adj.* **1.** arousing pity or sadness. **2.** miserably inadequate. **pathetically** *adv.*

pathological (pa-thŏ-loj-ikăl) *adj.* **1.** of pathology. **2.** of or caused by a physical or mental disorder, *a pathological liar.* **pathologically** *adv.*

pathologist (pă-thol-ŏ-jist) *n.* an expert in pathology.

pathology (pă-thol-ŏji) *n.* **1.** the scientific study of diseases of the body. **2.** abnormal changes in body tissue, caused by disease.

pathos (pay-thoss) *n.* a quality that arouses pity or sadness.

patience *n.* **1.** calm endurance of hardship or annoyance or inconvenience or delay etc. **2.** perseverance. **3.** a card-game (usually for one player) in which cards have to be brought into a particular arrangement. □ **have no patience with,** to feel irritated by.

patient *adj.* having or showing patience. —*n.* a person receiving treatment (or registered to receive any necessary treatment) by a doctor or dentist etc. **patiently** *adv.*

patina (pat-in-ă) *n.* **1.** an attractive green incrustation on the surface of old bronze. **2.** a gloss on the surface of woodwork, produced by age.

patio (pat-i-oh) *n.* (*pl.* patios) **1.** an inner courtyard, open to the sky, in a Spanish or Spanish-American house. **2.** a paved area beside a house, used for outdoor meals or relaxation.

Patna rice rice with long firm grains like that grown at Patna in India.

patois (pat-wah) *n.* a dialect.

patriarch (pay-tri-ark) *n.* **1.** the male head of a family or tribe; *the Patriarchs,* the men named in the book of Genesis as the ancestors of mankind or of the tribes of Israel. **2.** a bishop of high rank in certain Churches. **3.** a venerable old man. **patriarchal** (pay-tri-ar-kăl) *adj.*

patrician (pă-trish-ăn) *n.* a member of the aristocracy, especially in ancient Rome. —*adj.* aristocratic.

patricide (pat-ri-syd) *n.* the crime of murdering one's own father.

patrimony (pat-rim-ŏni) *n.* **1.** property inherited from one's father or ancestors, a heritage. **2.** a church's endowed income or property.

patriot (**pay**-tri-ŏt *or* **pat**-ri-ŏt) *n.* a patriotic person.

patriotic (pat-ri-**ot**-ik) *adj.* loyally supporting one's country. **patriotically** *adv.*, **patriotism** (**pat**-riŏ-tizm) *n.*

patrol *v.* (patrolled, patrolling) to walk or travel regularly through (an area or building) in order to see that all is secure and orderly. —*n.* **1.** patrolling, *on patrol.* **2.** the person(s) or ship(s) or aircraft whose job is to patrol an area. **3.** a unit of usually 6 members of a Scout troop or Guide company. —**patrolman** *n.*

patron (**pay**-trŏn) *n.* **1.** a person who gives encouragement or financial or other support to an activity or cause etc. **2.** a regular customer of a shop or restaurant etc. **3.** a patron saint. **patroness** *n.* □ **patron saint**, a saint regarded as giving special protection to a person or place or activity.

patronage (**pat**-rŏn-ij) *n.* **1.** support given by a patron. **2.** the right of appointing a person to a benefice or other position. **3.** patronizing behaviour.

patronize (**pat**-rŏ-nyz) *v.* **1.** to act as a patron towards, to support or encourage. **2.** to be a regular customer at (a shop etc.). **3.** to treat in a condescending way.

patronizing *adj.* condescending. **patronizingly** *adv.*

patronymic (pat-rŏ-**nim**-ik) *n.* a person's name that is taken from the name of his father or a male ancestor.

patter¹ *v.* **1.** to make a series of light quick taps. **2.** to run with short quick steps. —*n.* a series of light quick tapping sounds.

patter² *n.* rapid and often glib or deceptive speech, e.g. that used by a conjuror or salesman etc.

pattern *n.* **1.** an arrangement of lines or shapes or colours, a decorative design. **2.** a model or design or instructions according to which something is to be made. **3.** a sample of cloth or other material. **4.** an excellent example, a model. **5.** the regular form or order in which a series of actions or qualities etc. occur, *behaviour patterns.* —**pattern** *v.* **1.** to model according to a pattern. **2.** to decorate with a pattern.

patty *n.* a small pie or pasty.

paucity (**paw**-siti) *n.* smallness of supply or quantity.

paunch *n.* **1.** the belly. **2.** a protruding abdomen. —*v.* to disembowel (an animal).

pauper *n.* a very poor person. —*v.* to make a pauper of.

pause *n.* a temporary stop in action or speech. —*v.* to make a pause. □ **give pause to**, to cause (a person) to hesitate.

pave *v.* to cover (a road or path etc.) with

stones or concrete etc. to make a hard surface. **pave the way**, to prepare the way for changes etc. **paving-stone** *n.* a slab of stone for paving.

pavement *n.* a paved surface, a paved path for pedestrians at the side of a road.

pavilion *n.* **1.** a light building or other structure used as a shelter, e.g. in a park. **2.** an ornamental building used for dances and concerts etc. **3.** a building on a sports ground for use by players and spectators.

pavlova (pav-**loh**-vă) *n.* an open meringue case filled with cream and fruit. ¶ Named after Anna Pavlova, a Russian ballerina (1885–1931).

paw *n.* **1.** the foot of an animal that has claws. **2.** (*informal*) a person's hand. —**paw** *v.* **1.** to strike with a paw. **2.** to scrape (the ground) with a hoof. **3.** (*informal*) to touch awkwardly or rudely with the hands.

pawky *adj.* (pawkier, pawkiest) drily humorous. **pawkily** *adv.*, **pawkiness** *n.*

pawl *n.* a lever with a catch that engages with the notches of a ratchet.

pawn¹ *n.* **1.** a chess-man of the smallest size and value. **2.** a person whose actions are controlled by others.

pawn² *v.* to deposit (a thing) with a pawnbroker as security for money borrowed. —*n.* something deposited as a pledge. □ **in pawn**, deposited as a pawn. **pawnbroker** *n.* a person licensed to lend money on the security of personal property deposited with him. **pawnbroking** *n.* the occupation of a pawnbroker. **pawnshop** *n.* his place of business. **pawn-ticket** *n.* a receipt for a thing deposited with a pawnbroker.

pawpaw *n.* = papaw.

pay *v.* (paid, paying) **1.** to give (money) in return for goods or services. **2.** to give what is owed, to hand over the amount of (wages, a debt, ransom, etc.), to undergo (a penalty). **3.** to bear the cost of something. **4.** to be profitable or worth while. **5.** to bestow or render or express, *pay attention*; *paid them a visit*; *paid them a compliment.* **6.** to let out (a rope) by slackening it. —**pay** *n.* **1.** payment. **2.** wages. **3.** paid employment, *he is in the pay of the enemy.* —**payer** *n.* □ **pay-as-you-earn** *n.* a method of collecting income tax by deducting it at source from wages or interest etc. **pay-bed** *n.* a bed in an NHS hospital for which the user is charged a fee. **pay-claim** *n.* a demand for an increase of wages. **pay for**, to suffer or be punished because of (a mistake etc.). **paying guest**, one who pays for his board and lodging. **pay its way**, to make enough profit to cover expenses. **pay off**, to pay in full and be free from (a debt) or discharge (an employee); (*informal*) to yield good results, *the risk paid off*; *pay off old scores*, to get even with a person for past wrongdoing. **pay-off** *n.* (*slang*) payment; reward or retribution; a climax, especially of a joke or story. **pay one's way**, not get into debt. **pay out**, to punish or be revenged on (a person). **pay-packet** *n.* a packet containing an employee's wages. **pay up**, to pay in full; to pay what is demanded.

payable *adj.* which must or may be paid.

PAYE *abbrev.* pay-as-you-earn.

payee (pay-**ee**) *n.* a person to whom money is paid or is to be paid.

payload *n.* **1.** the part of an aircraft's load from which revenue is derived (e.g. passengers or cargo). **2.** the total weight of bombs or instruments carried by an aircraft or rocket etc.

paymaster *n.* an official who pays troops or workmen etc. **Paymaster-General** *n.* the minister at the head of the department of the Treasury through which payments are made.

payment *n.* **1.** paying. **2.** money given in return for goods or services. **3.** reward, compensation.

payola (pay-**oh**-lă) *n.* **1.** a bribe offered to one who promotes a commercial product by dishonestly making use of his position or influence etc. **2.** bribery of this kind.

payroll *n.* a list of a firm's employees receiving regular pay.

PC *abbrev.* police constable.

p.d.q. *abbrev.* (*slang*) pretty damn quick.

pea *n.* **1.** a climbing plant bearing seeds in pods. **2.** the seed of certain varieties of this, used as a vegetable. □ **pea-green** *adj.* & *n.* bright green like vegetable peas. **pea-shooter** *n.* a toy tube from which peas or pellets are shot by blowing. **pea-souper** *n.* (*informal*) a thick yellowish fog.

peace *n.* **1.** a state of freedom from war, cessation of war. **2.** a treaty ending a war, *signed the peace*. **3.** freedom from civil disorder, *a breach of the peace*. **4.** quiet, calm; *peace of mind*, freedom from anxiety. **5.** a state of harmony between people, absence of strife. □ **peace-offering** *n.* something offered to show that one is willing to make peace.

peaceable *adj.* **1.** not quarrelsome, desiring to be at peace with others. **2.** peaceful, without strife, *a peaceable settlement*. **peaceably** *adv.*

peaceful *adj.* **1.** characterized by peace. **2.** belonging to a state of peace not of war, *peaceful uses of atomic energy*. **peacefully** *adv.*, **peacefulness** *n.*

peacemaker *n.* a person who brings about peace.

peach *n.* **1.** a round juicy fruit with downy yellowish or reddish skin and a rough stone. **2.** the tree that bears this. **3.** (*slang*) a person or thing that is greatly admired, an attractive young woman. **4.** yellowish-pink colour. —*adj.* yellowish-pink. —**peachy** *adj.* □ **peach Melba**, a dish of ice cream and peaches with raspberry syrup.

peacock *n.* a male bird with long tail-feathers that can be spread upright like a fan. —*v.* to show one's pride ostentatiously. □ **peacock blue**, brilliant blue like the feathers on a peacock's neck.

peahen *n.* the female of a peacock.

peak[1] *n.* **1.** a pointed top, especially of a mountain. **2.** the mountain itself. **3.** any shape or edge or part that tapers to form a point. **4.** a projecting part of the edge of a cap. **5.** the point of highest value or achievement or intensity etc., *at the peak of his career*; *peak hours*, the hours when traffic is heaviest or consumption of electric current etc. is at its highest. —*v.* to reach its peak in value or intensity etc. □ **Peak District**, an area in Derbyshire where there are many peaks.

peak[2] *v.* to waste away, *peak and pine*.

peaked[1] *adj.* having a peak.

peaked[2], **peaky** *adjs.* having a drawn and sickly appearance.

peal *n.* **1.** the loud ringing of a bell or set of bells. **2.** a set of bells with different notes. **3.** a loud burst of thunder or laughter. —*v.* to sound or cause to sound in a peal.

peanut *n.* **1.** a plant bearing pods that ripen underground, containing two edible seeds. **2.** this seed. □ **peanut butter**, a paste of ground roasted peanuts. **peanuts** *pl. n.* (*slang*) a trivial or contemptibly small amount, especially of money.

pear *n.* **1.** a rounded fleshy fruit that tapers towards the stalk. **2.** the tree that bears this.

pearl *n.* **1.** a round usually white mass of a lustrous substance formed inside the shells of certain oysters, valued as a gem. **2.** an imitation of this. **3.** something resembling it in shape. **4.** something valued because of its excellence or beauty. —*adj.* (of an electric-light bulb) made of opaque glass. □ **cast pearls before swine**, to offer a good thing to someone who is incapable of appreciating it. **pearl barley**, barley grains ground small. **pearl button**, a button made of real or imitation mother-of-pearl. **pearl-diver**, **pearl-fisher** *ns.* one who dives or fishes for oysters containing pearls. **pearl onion**, a very small onion used in pickles.

pearled *adj.* formed into or covered with pearl-like drops.

pearling *n.* fishing or diving for pearls.

pearly *adj.* **1.** like pearls. **2.** with pearls. □ **pearlies** *pl. n.* pearly kings and queens; their clothes. **Pearly Gates,** (*humorous*) the gates of heaven. **pearly king and queen,** a London costermonger and his wife wearing clothes decorated with many pearl buttons.

pearmain (per-**mayn**) *n.* a variety of apple with firm white flesh.

peasant (**pez**-ănt) *n.* (in some countries) a member of the class of farm labourers and small farmers. **peasantry** *n.* peasants.

pease-pudding *n.* a pudding of peas and eggs etc., boiled in a cloth.

peat *n.* vegetable matter decomposed by the action of water in bogs etc. and partly carbonized, used in horticulture or cut in pieces as fuel. **peaty** *adj.*

pebble *n.* **1.** a small stone worn round and smooth by the action of water. **2.** a kind of rock-crystal used for spectacle lenses, a lens of this; *pebble glasses*, spectacles with thick lenses. **pebbly** *adj.* □ **pebble-dash** *n.* mortar with pebbles in it, used as a coating for an outside wall.

peccadillo (pek-ă-**dil**-oh) *n.* (*pl.* peccadilloes) a trivial offence.

peccary (**pek**-er-i) *n.* a wild pig of tropical America.

peck¹ *n.* a measure of capacity for dry goods, = 2 gallons or 8 quarts.

peck² *v.* **1.** to strike or nip or pick up with the beak. **2.** to make (a hole) with the beak. **3.** to kiss lightly and hastily. —**peck** *n.* **1.** a stroke or nip made with the beak. **2.** a light hasty kiss. □ **pecking order,** a series of ranks of status or authority in which people dominate those below themselves and are dominated by those above (as observed among domestic fowls).

pecker *n.* a bird that pecks. **keep your pecker up,** (*slang*) stay cheerful.

peckish *adj.* (*informal*) hungry.

pectin *n.* a gelatinous substance found in ripe fruits etc., causing jams to set.

pectoral (**pek**-ter-ăl) *adj.* **1.** of or in or on ·the chest or breast, *pectoral muscles.* **2.** worn on the breast, *a pectoral cross.*

peculation (pek-yoo-**lay**-shŏn) *n.* embezzlement.

peculiar *adj.* **1.** strange, eccentric. **2.** belonging exclusively to a particular person or place or thing, *customs peculiar to the 18th century.* **3.** particular, special, *a point of peculiar interest.*

peculiarity *n.* **1.** being peculiar. **2.** a characteristic. **3.** something unusual, an eccentricity.

peculiarly *adv.* **1.** in a peculiar way. **2.** especially, *peculiarly annoying.*

pecuniary (pi-**kew**-ni-er-i) *adj.* of or in money, *pecuniary aid.*

pedagogue (**ped**-ă-gog) *n.* (*contemptuous*) a person who teaches in a pedantic way.

pedal *n.* a lever operated by the foot in a motor vehicle or cycle or other machine, or in certain musical instruments. —*v.* (pedalled, pedalling) **1.** to work the pedal(s) of. **2.** to move or operate by means of pedals, to ride a bicycle.

pedalo (**ped**-ă-loh) *n.* (*pl.* pedalos) a pleasure-boat operated by pedals.

pedant (**ped**-ănt) *n.* a person who parades his learning or who insists unimaginatively on strict observance of formal rules and details in the presentation of knowledge. **pedantry** (**ped**-ăn-tri) *n.*, **pedantic** (pid-**an**-tik) *adj.,* **pedantically** *adv.*

peddle *v.* to sell (goods) as a pedlar.

pederast (**peed**-er-ast) *n.* one who commits sodomy with a boy. **pederasty** *n.*

pedestal *n.* **1.** a base supporting a column or pillar or statue etc. **2.** each of the two supports of a knee-hole table or desk. □ **pedestal table,** one with a single central support. **put a person on a pedestal,** to admire or respect him greatly.

pedestrian *n.* a person who is walking, especially in a street. —*adj.* **1.** of walking, of or for pedestrians. **2.** unimaginative, dull. □ **pedestrian crossing,** a street crossing where pedestrians have priority over traffic.

pedicure (**ped**-i-kewr) *n.* care or treatment of the feet and toe-nails.

pedigree *n.* a line or list of ancestors, especially of a distinguished kind. —*adj.* (of animals) having a recorded line of descent that shows pure breeding, *pedigree cattle.*

pediment (**ped**-i-měnt) *n.* a triangular part crowning the front of a building.

pedlar *n.* a person who goes from house to house selling small articles usually carried in a pack.

pedometer (pid-**om**-it-er) *n.* a device that calculates the distance a person walks by counting the number of steps taken.

pee *v.* (*informal*) to urinate. —*n.* (*informal*) **1.** urination. **2.** urine.

peek *v.* to peep or glance. —*n.* a peep or glance.

peel¹ *n.* the skin of certain fruits and vegetables, the outer coating of prawns etc. —*v.* **1.** to remove the peel of. **2.** to strip away, to pull off (a skin or covering). **3.** to be able to be peeled. **4** to come off in strips or layers, to lose skin or bark etc. in this way. □ **peelings** *pl. n.* strips of skin peeled from potatoes etc. **peel off,** to veer away from a formation of which one formed part.

peel² *n.* a small square tower built as a fortification in the 16th century near the border between England and Scotland.

peep¹ *v.* **1.** to look through a narrow opening. **2.** to look quickly or surreptitiously or from a concealed place. **3.** to come briefly or partially into view, to show slightly. —*n.* a brief or surreptitious look. □ **peep-hole** *n.* a small hole to peep through. **peeping Tom,** a man who furtively watches someone undressing or engaging in sexual activities. (¶ Named after the Coventry tailor in the story of Lady Godiva.) **peep of day,** dawn. **peep-toe** *or* **peep-toed** *adjs.* (of shoes) with a small opening at the tip of the toe.

peep² *n.* a weak high chirping sound like that made by young birds. —*v.* to make this sound.

peer¹ *v.* **1.** to look searchingly or with difficulty. **2.** to peep out.

peer² *n.* **1.** a member of the peerage in Britain, a duke, marquis, earl, viscount, or baron, also called *peers of the realm,* with the right to sit in the House of Lords. **2.** one who is the equal of another in rank or merit or quality etc. □ **peer group,** a group of people who are associated and of equal status.

peerage *n.* **1.** peers, the nobility. **2.** the rank of peer or peeress. **3.** a book containing a list of peers.

peeress *n.* a female peer, a peer's wife.

peerless *adj.* without equal, superb.

peeved *adj.* (*slang*) annoyed.

peevish *adj.* irritable. **peevishly** *adv.,* **peevishness** *n.*

peewit *n.* a kind of plover named from its cry.

peg *n.* **1.** a wooden or metal pin or bolt for fastening things together, hanging things on, holding a tent-rope taut, or marking a position; *a peg on which to hang a sermon* etc., a suitable theme or pretext for it. **2.** a clothes-peg. **3.** a wooden screw for tightening or loosening the strings of a violin etc. **4.** a drink or measure of spirits. — **peg** *v.* (**pegged, pegging**) **1.** to fix or mark by means of a peg or pegs. **2.** to keep (wages or prices) at a fixed amount; *peg a person down,* make him keep to certain rules etc. □ **off the peg,** (of clothes) ready-made. **peg away,** to work diligently, to be persistent in doing something. **peg-board** *n.* a board with holes and pegs. **peg out,** (*slang*) to die. **take a**

person down a peg, to reduce his pride, to humble him.

PEI *abbrev.* Prince Edward Island.

pein (*pr.* payn) *n.* the pointed or wedge-shaped or ball-shaped end of the head of a hammer.

pejorative (pij-o-ră-tiv) *adj.* disparaging, derogatory. **pejoratively** *adv.*

peke *n.* (*informal*) a Pekingese dog.

Peking (pee-**king**) = Beijing.

Pekingese *n.* (*pl.* Pekingese) a dog of a breed with short legs, flat face, and long silky hair.

pekoe (pee-koh) *n.* a kind of black tea made from young leaves.

pelargonium (pel-er-goh-niŭm) *n.* a plant with showy flowers and fragrant leaves (the cultivated variety is usually called *geranium*).

pelican *n.* a large water-bird of warm regions, with a pouch in its long bill for storing fish. □ **pelican crossing,** a pedestrian crossing with traffic lights operated by pedestrians.

pellagra (pil-**ag**-ră) *n.* a deficiency disease causing cracking of the skin, often ending in insanity.

pellet *n.* **1.** a small rounded closely-packed mass of a soft substance. **2.** a slug of small shot. □ **pelleted** *adj.* formed into pellets; *pelleted seeds,* seeds coated individually with fertilizer etc.

pell-mell *adv. & adj.* in a hurrying disorderly manner, headlong.

pellucid (pil-**oo**-sid) *adj.* very clear.

pelmet (**pel**-mit) *n.* a valance or ornamental strip above a window etc., especially to conceal a curtain rod.

pelt¹ *n.* an animal skin, especially with the fur or hair still on it.

pelt² *v.* **1.** to throw missiles at. **2.** (of rain etc.) to come down fast. **3.** to run fast. □ **at full pelt,** as fast as possible.

pelvis *n.* the basin-shaped framework of bones at the lower end of the body. **pelvic** *adj.*

pemmican *n.* a food like that made by North American Indians from a paste of dried pounded meat.

pen¹ *n.* a small fenced enclosure especially for cattle, sheep, poultry, etc. —*v.* (**penned, penning**) to shut in or as if in a pen.

pen² *n.* a device with a metal point for writing with ink. —*v.* (**penned, penning**) to write (a letter etc). □ **pen-friend** *n.* a friend with whom a person corresponds without meeting. **pen-light** *n.* a small electric torch shaped like a fountain-pen. **pen-name** *n.* an author's pseudonym. **pen-pushing** *n.* (*informal*) clerical work.

pen[3] *n.* a female swan.

pen[4] *n.* (*Amer.*) a penitentiary.

penal (**pee**-năl) *adj.* of or involving punishment, especially according to law; *a penal offence*, one for which the law imposes a punishment; *penal taxation*, heavy taxation inflicted as if intended to be a punishment.

penalize *v.* **1.** to inflict a penalty on. **2.** to place at a serious disadvantage. **penalization** *n.*

penalty *n.* **1.** a punishment for breaking a law or rule or contract. **2.** a disadvantage or hardship brought on by some action or quality, *the penalties of fame.* **3.** a disadvantage to which a sports player or team must submit for breaking a rule. **4.** a handicap imposed on a player or team that has won a previous contest. □ **penalty area**, an area in front of the goal on a football field in which a foul by the defenders involves the award of a penalty kick. **penalty box**, a place for penalized players and some officials in ice hockey. **penalty kick**, a free kick at goal awarded as a penalty in football.

penance (**pen**-ănss) *n.* **1.** an act performed as an expression of penitence. **2.** (in the RC and Orthodox Church), a sacrament including confession, absolution, and an act of penitence imposed by the priest. □ **do penance**, to perform an act of this kind.

pence *see* penny.

penchant (**pahn**-shahn) *n.* a liking or inclination, *has a penchant for Indian music.*

pencil *n.* **1.** an instrument for drawing or writing, consisting of a thin stick of graphite or coloured chalk etc. enclosed in a cylinder of wood or fixed in a metal case. **2.** something used or shaped like this. —*v.* (pencilled, pencilling) to write or draw or mark with a pencil. □ **pencil in**, to enter (a suggested date or estimate etc.) provisionally.

pendant *n.* a hanging ornament, especially one attached to a chain worn round the neck.

pendent *adj.* hanging.

pending *adj.* **1.** waiting to be decided or settled. **2.** about to come into existence, *patent pending.* —**pending** *prep.* **1.** during, *pending these negotiations.* **2.** until, *pending his return.* □ **pending-tray** *n.* a tray for documents that are awaiting decision.

pendulous (**pen**-dew-lŭs) *adj.* hanging downwards, hanging so as to swing freely.

pendulum (**pen**-dew-lŭm) *n.* **1.** a weight hung from a cord so that it can swing freely. **2.** a rod with a weighted end that regulates the movement of a clock etc. □ **swing of the pendulum**, the tendency for public opinion to favour an opposite policy or political party etc. after a time.

penetrable (**pen**-i-tră-bŭl) *adj.* able to be penetrated. **penetrability** *n.*

penetrate *v.* **1.** to make a way into or through, to pierce. **2.** to enter and permeate. **3.** to see into or through, *our eyes could not penetrate the darkness.* **4.** to discover or understand, *penetrated their secrets.* **5.** to be absorbed by the mind, *my hint didn't penetrate.* **penetration** *n.*, **penetrator** *n.*

penetrating *adj.* **1.** having or showing great insight. **2.** (of a voice or sound) loud and carrying, piercing.

penetrative (**pen**-i-tră-tiv) *adj.* able to penetrate, penetrating.

penguin *n.* a sea-bird of the Antarctic and nearby regions, with wings developed into scaly flippers used for swimming.

penicillin (pen-i-**sil**-in) *n.* an antibiotic of the kind obtained from mould fungi.

peninsula (pĕn-**ins**-yoo-lă) *n.* a piece of land that is almost surrounded by water or projecting far into the sea. **peninsular** *adj.*

penis (**pee**-nis) *n.* the organ by which a male animal copulates and (in mammals) urinates.

penitent *adj.* feeling or showing regret that one has done wrong. —*n.* a penitent person. —**penitently** *adv.*, **penitence** *n.*

penitential (pen-i-**ten**-shăl) *adj.* of penitence or penance.

penitentiary (pen-i-**ten**-sher-i) *n.* (*Amer.*) a federal or State prison.

penknife *n.* a small folding knife, usually carried in a person's pocket.

Penn. *abbrev.* Pennsylvania.

pennant (**pen**-ănt) *n.* a long tapering flag flown on a ship.

penniless *adj.* having no money, very poor, destitute.

Pennines *pl. n.* the Pennine Chain, a system of hills in northern England.

pennon *n.* **1.** a long narrow triangular or swallow-tailed flag. **2.** a long pointed streamer on a ship. **3.** a flag.

penn'orth *n.* (*informal*) = pennyworth.

Pennsylvania a State of the USA. **Pennsylvanian** *adj.* & *n.*

penny *n.* (*pl.* pennies for separate coins, pence for a sum of money) **1.** a British bronze coin worth $\frac{1}{100}$ of £1, or a former coin worth $\frac{1}{12}$ of a shilling. **2.** (*Amer.*

informal) a cent. **3.** a very small sum of money, *won't cost you a penny.* □ **in penny numbers**, in small quantities at a time. **penny black**, the first adhesive postage stamp (1840), printed in black. **penny farthing**, an old type of bicycle with a very large front wheel and a small rear one. **penny-pinching** *adj.* niggardly, (*n.*) niggardliness. **penny wise and pound foolish**, careful in small matters but wasteful in large ones.

pennywort (pen-i-wert) *n.* a plant with rounded leaves, either *wall pennywort* (growing in crevices) or *marsh pennywort* (in marshy places).

pennyworth *n.* the amount a penny will buy.

penology (pee-**nol**-ŏji) *n.* the scientific study of crime, its punishment, and prison management. **penological** *adj.*

pension [1] (**pen**-shŏn) *n.* an income consisting of a periodic payment made by the State to people who are above a certain age or widowed or to certain disabled people, or by an employer to a retired employee. —*v.* **1.** to pay a pension to. **2.** to dismiss or allow to retire with a pension, *pensioned him off.*

pension [2] (**pahn**-si-awn *or* pen-shŏn) a boarding-house on the Continent.

pensionable *adj.* **1.** entitled to receive a pension. **2.** (of a job) entitling a person to receive a pension.

pensioner *n.* a person who receives a pension.

pensive *adj.* deep in thought, thoughtful and gloomy. **pensively** *adv.*, **pensiveness** *n.*

pent *adj.* shut in a confined space, *pent in* or *up.* **pent-up** *adj.* shut in; kept from being expressed openly, *pent up anger.*

pentacle (**pen**-tă-kŭl) *n.* a pentagram or other figure used as a symbol, especially in magic.

pentagon (**pen**-tă-gŏn) *n.* **1.** a geometric figure with five sides. **2.** *the Pentagon,* a five-sided building near Washington, headquarters of the USA Department of Defence and of the leaders of the armed forces; the department itself.

pentagonal (pen-**tag**-ŏn-ăl) *adj.* five-sided.

pentagram (**pen**-tă-gram) *n.* a five-pointed star.

pentameter (pen-**tam**-it-er) *n.* a line of verse with five metrical feet.

Pentateuch (**pen**-tă-tewk) *n.* the first five books of the Old Testament.

pentathlon (pen-**tath**-lŏn) *n.* an athletic contest in which each competitor takes part in the five events it includes.

Pentecost (**pen**-ti-kost) *n.* **1.** the Jewish harvest festival, fifty days after the second day of the Passover. **2.** Whit Sunday.

penthouse *n.* **1.** a sloping roof (especially for a shelter or shed) attached to the wall of a main building. **2.** a flat or dwelling (usually with a terrace) on the roof of a tall building.

penultimate (pĕn-**ul**-tim-ăt) *adj.* last but one.

penumbra (pin-**um**-bră) *n.* (*pl.* penumbrae) a region of partial shadow surrounding the umbra, where some light, but not the full amount, reaches a surface.

penurious (pin-**yoor**-iŭs) *adj.* **1.** poverty-stricken. **2.** stingy

penury (**pen**-yoor-i) *n.* extreme poverty.

peony (**pee**-ŏni) *n.* a garden plant with large round red or pink or white flowers.

people *pl. n.* **1.** human beings in general. **2.** the persons belonging to a place or forming a group or social class, the subjects or citizens of a State. **3.** ordinary persons, those who are not nobles or not in high office etc. **4.** a person's parents or other relatives. —*n.* the persons composing a community or tribe or race or nation, *the English-speaking peoples; a warlike people.* —*v.* to fill (a place) with people, to populate.

pep *n.* vigour, energy. —*v.* (pepped, pepping) to fill with vigour, to enliven, *pep it up.* □ **pep pill**, a pill containing a stimulant drug. **pep talk**, a talk urging the hearer(s) to great effort or courage.

peplum *n.* a short flounce from the waist of a garment.

pepper *n.* **1.** a hot-tasting powder made from the dried berries of certain plants, used to season food. **2.** a kind of capsicum grown as a vegetable, its fruit used unripe (*green pepper*) or ripe (*red* or *yellow pepper*); *sweet pepper,* one with a relatively mild taste. —**pepper** *v.* **1.** to sprinkle with pepper. **2.** to pelt with small missiles. **3.** to sprinkle here and there, *a speech peppered with jokes.* □ **pepper-and-salt** *adj.* woven with light and dark threads producing an effect of small dots. **pepper-pot** *n.* a small container with a perforated lid for sprinkling pepper.

peppercorn *n.* the dried black berry from which pepper is made. **peppercorn rent**, a very low rent, virtually nothing.

peppermint *n.* **1.** a kind of mint grown for its strong fragrant oil, used in medicine and in sweets etc. **2.** the oil itself. **3.** a sweet flavoured with this.

peppery *adj.* **1.** like pepper, containing much pepper. **2.** hot-tempered.

pepsin *n.* an enzyme contained in gastric juice, helping to digest food.

peptic *adj.* of digestion; *peptic ulcer*, an ulcer in the stomach or duodenum.

per *prep.* **1.** for each, *£1 per gallon*. **2.** in accordance with, *as per instructions*; *as per usual*, (*informal*) as usual. **3.** by means of, *per post*. □ **per annum**, for each year. **per capita**, (*incorrect use*) = per caput. **per caput**, for each person. **per cent**, in or for every hundred, *three per cent* (3).

perambulate (per-**am**-bew-layt) *v.* **1.** to walk through or over or round (an area), to travel through and inspect. **2.** to walk about. **perambulation** *n.*

perambulator *n.* a child's pram.

perceive *v.* to become aware of, to see or notice.

percentage (per-**sen**-tij) *n.* **1.** the rate or proportion per cent (*see* per). **2.** a proportion or part.

perceptible (per-**sep**-tibŭl) *adj.* able to be perceived. **perceptibly** *adv.*, **perceptibility** *n.*

perception *n.* perceiving, ability to perceive.

perceptive (per-**sep**-tiv) *adj.* having or showing insight and sensitive understanding. **perceptively** *adv.*, **perceptiveness** *n.*, **perceptivity** (per-sep-**tiv**-iti) *n.*

perch[1] *n.* **1.** a bird's resting-place (e.g. a branch), a bar or rod provided for this purpose. **2.** a high place or narrow ledge etc. on which a person sits or positions himself. —*v.* to rest or place on or as if on a perch.

perch[2] *n.* (*pl.* perch) an edible freshwater fish with spiny fins.

perchance *adv.* (*old use*) perhaps.

percipient (per-**sip**-i-ĕnt) *adj.* perceiving, perceptive. **percipience** *n.*

percolate (per-**kŏl**-ayt) *v.* **1.** to filter or cause to filter, especially through small holes. **2.** to prepare (coffee) in a percolator. **percolation** *n.*

percolator *n.* a pot in which coffee is made and served, in which boiling water is made to circulate repeatedly up a central tube and downwards through ground coffee held in a perforated drum near the top.

percussion (per-**kush**-ŏn) *n.* **1.** the striking of one object against another. **2.** percussion instruments in an orchestra. □ **percussion cap**, a small metal or paper device containing explosive powder that explodes when this is struck, used as a detonator or in a toy pistol. **percussion instrument**, a musical instrument (e.g. drum, cymbals) played by striking.

perdition (per-**dish**-ŏn) *n.* eternal damnation.

peregrination (pe-ri-grin-**ay**-shŏn) *n.* travelling, a journey.

peregrine (pe-ri-grin) *n.* a kind of falcon that can be trained to hunt and catch small animals and birds.

peremptory (per-**emp**-ter-i) *adj.* imperious, insisting on obedience. **peremptorily** *adv.*

perennial (per-en-yăl) *adj.* **1.** lasting a long time or for ever, constantly recurring, *a perennial problem*. **2.** (of a plant) living for several years. —*n.* a perennial plant. — **perennially** *adv.*

perfect[1] (**per**-fikt) *adj.* **1.** complete, having all its essential qualities. **2.** faultless, excellent. **3.** exact, precise, *a perfect circle*. **4.** entire, total, *a perfect stranger*.

perfect[2] (per-**fekt**) *v.* to make perfect.

perfection *n.* **1.** making or being perfect. **2.** a person or thing considered perfect. □ **to perfection**, perfectly.

perfectionist *n.* a person who is satisfied with nothing less than what he thinks is perfect. **perfectionism** *n.*

perfectly *adv.* **1.** in a perfect way. **2.** completely, quite, *perfectly satisfied*.

perfidious (per-**fid**-iŭs) *adj.* treacherous, disloyal. **perfidy** (**per**-fid-i) *n.*

perforate *v.* **1.** to make a hole or holes through, to pierce with a row or rows of tiny holes so that part(s) can be torn off easily. **2.** to penetrate. **perforation** *n.*

perforce *adv.* by force of circumstances, necessarily.

perform *v.* **1.** to carry into effect, to accomplish, to do. **2.** to go through (a particular proceeding), to execute, *performed the ceremony*. **3.** to function, *the car performed well when tested*. **4.** to act in a play etc., to play an instrument or sing or do tricks before an audience. **performer** *n.*

performance *n.* **1.** the process or manner of performing. **2.** a notable action or achievement. **3.** the performing of a play or other entertainment, *two performances a day*.

perfume *n.* **1.** a sweet smell. **2.** a fragrant liquid for giving a pleasant smell, especially to the body. —*v.* to give a sweet smell to, to apply perfume to.

perfumery (per-**fewm**-er-i) *n.* perfumes, the preparation of these.

perfunctory (per-**funk**-ter-i) *adj.* **1.** done as a duty or routine but without much care or interest. **2.** (of a person) acting in this way. **perfunctorily** *adv.*, **perfunctoriness** *n.*

pergola (**per**-gŏl-ă) *n.* an arbour or covered walk formed of climbing plants trained over trellis-work.

perhaps *adv.* it may be, possibly.

pericardium *n.* the membranous sac enclosing the heart.

perigee (pe-ri-jee) *n.* the point in the orbit of the moon or any planet when it is nearest to earth.

peril *n.* serious danger.

perilous *adj.* full of risk, dangerous. **perilously** *adv.*

perimeter (per-**im**-it-er) *n.* **1.** the outer edge or boundary of a closed geometric figure or of an area. **2.** the length of this.

perineum (pe-ri-**nee**-ŭm) *n.* the region of the body between the anus and the scrotum or vulva. **perineal** *adj.*

period *n.* **1.** a length or portion of time. **2.** a time with particular characteristics, *the colonial period.* **3.** the time allocated for a lesson in school. **4.** an occurrence of menstruation. **5.** a complete sentence. **6.** a full stop in punctuation. —*adj.* (of furniture or dress or architecture) belonging to a past age.

periodic *adj.* occurring or appearing at intervals.

periodical *adj.* periodic. —*n.* a magazine etc. published at regular intervals. — **periodically** *adv.*

periodontal (pe-ri-o-**don**-t'l) *adj.* of the tissues surrounding the teeth, *periodontal diseases.*

peripatetic (pe-ri-pă-**tet**-ik) *adj.* going from place to place.

peripheral (per-**if**-er-ăl) *adj.* **1.** of or on the periphery. **2.** of minor but not central importance to something. —*n.* any input, output, or storage device that can be controlled by the central processing unit of a computer (e.g. a magnetic tape, floppy disc, line printer).

periphery (per-**if**-er-i) *n.* **1.** the boundary of a surface or area, the region immediately inside or beyond this. **2.** the fringes of a subject etc.

periphrasis (per-**if**-ră-sis) *n.* (*pl.* periphrases) a roundabout phrase or way of speaking, a circumlocution.

periscope *n.* an apparatus with a tube and mirror(s) by which a person in a trench or submerged submarine or at the rear of a crowd etc. can see things that are otherwise out of sight.

perish *v.* **1.** to suffer destruction, to become extinct, to die a violent or untimely death. **2.** to rot, to lose or cause (rubber or other fabric) to lose its normal qualities. **3.** to distress or wither by cold or exposure.

perishable *adj.* liable to decay or go bad in a short time. **perishables** *pl. n.* perishable foods.

perisher *n.* (*slang*) an annoying person.

perishing *adj.* (*slang*) **1.** damned. **2.** very cold.

peritoneum (pe-ri-tŏn-ee-ŭm) *n.* the membrane lining the abdomen.

peritonitis (pe-ri-tŏn-I-tiss) *n.* inflammation of the peritoneum.

periwinkle [1] *n.* an evergreen trailing plant with blue or white flowers.

periwinkle [2] *n.* a winkle.

perjure (**per**-jer) *v.* **perjure oneself**, to make a perjured statement.

perjured *adj.* **1.** involving perjury, *perjured evidence.* **2.** guilty of perjury.

perjury (**per**-jer-i) *n.* the deliberate giving of false evidence while on oath, the evidence itself.

perk [1] *v.* to raise (the head etc.) briskly or jauntily. **perk up**, to regain or cause to regain courage or confidence or vitality; to smarten up.

perk [2] *n.* (*informal*) a perquisite.

perk [3] *v.* (*informal*) to percolate (coffee), to bubble up in a percolator.

perky *adj.* (perkier, perkiest). lively and cheerful. **perkily** *adv.*, **perkiness** *n.*

perm [1] *n.* a permanent wave. —*v.* to give a perm to.

perm [2] *n.* (in football pools) a permutation. —*v.* to make a perm of.

permafrost *n.* the permanently frozen subsoil in polar regions.

permanency *n.* **1.** permanence. **2.** a permanent thing or arrangement.

permanent *adj.* lasting or meant to last indefinitely. **permanently** *adv.*, **permanence** *n.* □ **permanent wave**, a long-lasting artificial wave in the hair. **permanent way**, the foundation and track of a railway.

permanganate (per-**mang**-ăn-ayt) *n.* a salt of an acid containing manganese.

permeable (**per**-mi-ăbŭl) *adj.* able to be permeated by fluids etc. **permeability** *n.*

permeate (**per**-mi-ayt) *v.* to pass or flow or spread into every part of. **permeation** *n.*

permissible *adj.* such as may be permitted, allowable. **permissibly** *adv.*

permission *n.* consent or authorization to do something.

permissive *adj.* **1.** giving permission. **2.** tolerant, allowing much freedom in social conduct and sexual matters. **permissiveness** *n.*

permit [1] (per-**mit**) *v.* (permitted, permitting) **1.** to give permission or consent, to authorize. **2.** to give opportunity, to make possible, *weather permitting.*

permit [2] (**per**-mit) *n.* a written order giving permission, especially for entry into a place.

permutation (per-mew-**tay**-shŏn) *n.* **1.** variation of the order of a set of things.

2. any one of these arrangements. **3.** a selection of specified items from a larger group, to be arranged in a number of combinations (e.g. in a football pool).

permute (per-**mewt**) *v.* to vary the order or arrangement of.

pernicious (per-**nish**-ŭs) *adj.* having a very harmful effect.

pernickety *adj.* (*informal*) fastidious, scrupulous.

peroration (pe-rer-**ay**-shŏn) *n.* a lengthy speech, the last part of this.

peroxide *n.* a compound containing the maximum proportion of oxygen, especially **hydrogen peroxide** which is used as an antiseptic or to bleach hair. —*v.* to bleach with hydrogen peroxide.

perpendicular *adj.* **1.** at a right angle (90°) to another line or surface. **2.** upright, at right angles to the horizontal. **3.** (of a cliff etc.) having a vertical face. **4.** *Perpendicular*, of the style of English Gothic architecture in the 14th–15th centuries, with vertical tracery in large windows. — *n.* a perpendicular line or direction. — **perpendicularly** *adv.*, **perpendicularity** *n.*

perpetrate (**per**-pit-rayt) *v.* to commit (a crime or error), to be guilty of (a blunder etc.). **perpetration** *n.*, **perpetrator** *n.*

perpetual *adj.* **1.** lasting for a long time, not ceasing. **2.** (*informal*) frequent, often repeated, *this perpetual quarrelling*. **perpetually** *adv.* □ **perpetual calendar**, one that can be used for any year or over a long period.

perpetuate *v.* to preserve from being forgotten or from going out of use, *his invention will perpetuate his memory*. **perpetuation** *n.*

perpetuity (per-pi-**tew**-iti) *n.* the state or quality of being perpetual. **in perpetuity**, for ever.

perplex *v.* **1.** to bewilder, to puzzle. **2.** to make more complicated. □ **perplexedly** (per-**pleks**-idli) *adv.* in a perplexed way.

perplexity *n.* bewilderment.

perquisite (**per**-kwiz-it) *n.* a profit or allowance or privilege etc. given or looked upon as one's right in addition to wages or salary.

perry *n.* a drink like cider, made from the fermented juice of pears.

persecute *v.* **1.** to subject to constant hostility or cruel treatment, especially because of religious or political beliefs. **2.** to harass. **persecution** *n.*, **persecutor** *n.* □ **persecution complex**, an insane delusion that one is being persecuted.

persevere *v.* to continue steadfastly, especially in something that is difficult or tedious. **perseverance** *n.*

Persia the ancient and now the alternative name of Iran.

Persian *adj.* of Persia or its people or language. —*n.* **1.** a native or inhabitant of Persia. **2.** the language of Persia. **3.** a Persian cat. □ **Persian cat**, a cat of a breed that has long silky fur. **Persian lamb**, the silky tightly-curled fur of lambs of a kind of Asian sheep.

persiflage (**per**-si-flah*zh*) *n.* banter.

persist *v.* **1.** to continue firmly or obstinately, *she persists in breaking the rules*. **2.** to continue to exist, *the custom persists in some areas*. **persistent** *adj.*, **persistently** *adv.*, **persistence** *n.*, **persistency** *n.*

person *n.* **1.** an individual human being. **2.** the living body of a human being; *offences against the person*, bodily attacks etc. **3.** the genitals, *exposing his person*. **4.** one of the three modes of being of the Godhead; *the three Persons of the Trinity*, the Father (*First Person*), the Son (*Second Person*), the Holy Spirit (*Third Person*). **5.** (in grammar) any of the three classes of personal pronouns and verb-forms, referring to the person speaking (*first person*, = I, me, we, us), or spoken to (*second person*, = thou, thee, you) or spoken of (*third person*, he, him, she, her, it, they, them). □ **in person**, physically present.

persona (per-**soh**-nă) *n.* = personality (sense 1).

personable (per-**sŏn**-ăbŭl) *adj.* good-looking.

personage (**per**-sŏn-ij) *n.* a person, especially one of importance or distinction.

persona grata (per-soh-nă **grah**-tă) a person who is acceptable, especially a diplomat acceptable to a foreign government. **persona non grata**, one who is not acceptable.

personal *adj.* **1.** one's own or a particular person's own, *will give it my personal attention*. **2.** of one's own or another's private life, *a personal matter*. **3.** making remarks about a person's appearance or his private affairs, especially in a critical or hostile way, *don't let us become personal*. **4.** done or made etc. in person, *several personal appearances*. **5.** of the body and clothing, *personal hygiene*. **6.** existing as a person, *a personal God*. □ **personal assistant**, a confidential assistant helping an official or business man etc. **personal column**, a column of private messages or advertisements in a newspaper. **personal pronoun**, *see* pronoun.

personality *n.* **1.** a person's own distinctive character. **2.** a person with distinctive qualities, especially pleasing ones. **3.** a celebrity. □ **personality cult**, veneration of a famous or successful person, hero-worship. **personalities** *pl. n.* personal remarks (*see* personal, sense 3).

personalize *v.* **1.** to make personal, especially by marking as one's own property. **2.** to personify.

personally *adv.* **1.** in person, not through an agent, *showed us round personally*. **2.** as a person, in a personal capacity, *we don't know him personally*. **3.** in a personal manner, *don't take it personally*. **4.** as regards oneself, *personally, I like it*.

personify (per-**sonn**-i-fy) *v.* (personified, personifying) **1.** to represent (an idea) in human form or (a thing) as having human characteristics, *Justice is personified as a blindfolded woman holding a pair of scales*. **2.** to embody in one's life or behaviour, *he was meanness personified*. **personification** *n.*

personnel (per-sŏn-**el**) *n.* **1.** the body of people employed in any work, staff. **2.** the department (in a business firm etc.) dealing with employees and their problems and welfare.

perspective *n.* **1.** the art of drawing solid objects on a flat surface so as to give the right impression of their relative position, size, solidity, etc. **2.** the apparent relationship between visible objects as to position, distance, etc. **3.** a view of a visible scene or of facts and events. **4.** a mental picture of the relative importance of things. □ **in perspective**, drawn according to the rules of perspective; with its relative importance understood.

Perspex *n.* (*trade mark*) a tough unsplinterable transparent plastic material.

perspicacious (per-spi-**kay**-shŭs) *adj.* having or showing great insight. **perspicaciously** *adv.*, **perspicacity** (per-spi-**kas**-iti) *n.*

perspicuity (per-spi-**kew**-iti) *n.* **1.** clearness of statement or explanation. **2.** (*incorrect use*) perspicacity.

perspicuous (per-**spik**-yoo-ŭs) *adj.* **1.** expressed or expressing things clearly. **2.** (*incorrect use*) perspicacious. **perspicuously** *adv.*, **perspicuousness** *n.*

perspire *v.* to sweat. **perspiration** *n.*

persuadable *adj.* able to be persuaded.

persuade *v.* to cause (a person) to believe or do something by reasoning with him.

persuasion *n.* **1.** persuading, being persuaded. **2.** persuasiveness. **3.** belief, especially religious belief, *people of the same persuasion*.

persuasive *adj.* able or trying to persuade people. **persuasively** *adv.*, **persuasiveness** *n.*

pert *adj.* **1.** cheeky. **2.** (*Amer.*) lively. **pertly** *adv.*, **pertness** *n.*

pertain (per-**tayn**) *v.* **1.** to be relevant, *evidence pertaining to the case*. **2.** to belong as part, *the mansion and lands pertaining to it*.

pertinacious (per-tin-ay-shŭs) *adj.* holding firmly to an opinion or course of action, persistent and determined. **pertinaciously** *adv.*, **pertinacity** (per-tin-**ass**-iti) *n.*

pertinent *adj.* pertaining, relevant. **pertinently** *adv.*, **pertinence** *n.*

perturb *v.* to disturb greatly, to make anxious or uneasy. **perturbation** *n.*

Peru a country in South America. **Peruvian** (per-**oo**-viăn) *adj. & n.*

peruse (per-**ooz**) *v.* to read (a document etc.) carefully. **perusal** (per-**oo**-zăl) *n.*

pervade *v.* to spread or be present throughout, to permeate, *a pervading atmosphere of optimism*. **pervasion** *n.*

pervasive (per-**vay**-siv) *adj.* pervading, able to pervade. **pervasiveness** *n.*

perverse (per-**verss**) *adj.* **1.** obstinately doing something different from what is reasonable or required, intractable. **2.** indicating or characterized by a tendency of this kind, *a perverse satisfaction*. **perversely** *adv.*, **perverseness** *n.*, **perversity** *n.*

perversion *n.* **1.** perverting, being perverted. **2.** a perverted form of something. **3.** preference for a form of sexual activity that is considered abnormal or unacceptable.

pervert[1] (per-**vert**) *v.* **1.** to turn (a thing) from its proper course or use, *pervert the course of justice*. **2.** to lead astray from right behaviour or beliefs, to corrupt.

pervert[2] (**per**-vert) *n.* a perverted person, one showing perversion of sexual instincts.

peseta (pĕ-**say**-tă) *n.* the unit of money in Spain.

peso (**pay**-soh) *n.* (*pl.* pesos) the unit of money in Chile and several Latin-American countries, and in the Philippines.

pessary (**pess**-er-i) *n.* **1.** a device placed in the vagina to prevent displacement of the womb or as a contraceptive. **2.** a vaginal suppository.

pessimism *n.* a tendency to take a gloomy view of things or to expect that results will be bad. **pessimist** *n.*

pessimistic *adj.* showing pessimism. **pessimistically** *adv.*

pest *n.* **1.** a troublesome or annoying

person or thing. 2. an insect or animal that is destructive to cultivated plants or to stored food etc.

pester v. to make persistent requests, to annoy with frequent requests or questions.

pesticide n. a substance for destroying harmful insects etc.

pestiferous (pest-**if**-erŭs) adj. troublesome.

pestilence n. a deadly epidemic disease.

pestilential (pest-i-**len**-shăl) adj. troublesome, pernicious.

pestle n. a club-shaped instrument for pounding substances in a mortar.

pet n. 1. an animal that is tamed and treated with affection, kept for companionship or amusement. 2. a darling or favourite. —**pet** adj. 1. kept or treated as a pet, pet lamb. 2. favourite; pet aversion, something one particularly dislikes. —**pet** v. (petted, petting) 1. to treat with affection. 2. to fondle erotically. □ **pet name**, a name (other than the real name) used affectionately.

petal n. one of the bright or delicately-coloured outer parts of a flower-head.

petard (pit-**ard**) n. (old use) a kind of small bombshell; hoist with his own petard, injured by his own devices against others.

peter v. **peter out**, to diminish gradually and cease to exist.

petersham n. strong corded ribbon used to strengthen waistbands etc.

pethidine (**peth**-i-deen) n. a soluble synthetic drug used for relieving pain.

petit (pĕ-**tee**) adj. **petit bourgeois** (pr. **boor**-zhwah), a member of the lower middle classes. **petit mal**, a mild form of epilepsy without loss of consciousness. **petit point** (pr. pwan), embroidery on canvas using small stitches.

petite (pĕ-**teet**) adj. (of a woman) of small dainty build.

petition n. 1. an earnest request. 2. a formal document appealing to an authority for a right or benefit etc., especially one signed by a large number of people. 3. a formal application made to a court of law for a writ or order etc. —v. to make or address a petition to. —**petitioner** n.

petrel n. a kind of sea-bird that flies far from land.

petrify v. (petrified, petrifying) 1. to change or cause to change into a stony mass. 2. to paralyse or stun with astonishment or fear etc. **petrification** n.

petrochemical n. a chemical substance obtained from petroleum or natural gas.

petrodollar n. a dollar earned by a

country that exports petroleum (= oil).

petrol n. an inflammable liquid made from petroleum, used as fuel in internal-combustion engines. **petrol pump**, a machine for transferring petrol from a storage tank into the tank of a motor vehicle.

petroleum (pi-**troh**-liŭm) n. a mineral oil found underground, refined for use as fuel (e.g. petrol, paraffin) or for use in dry-cleaning etc. **petroleum jelly**, a greasy translucent substance obtained from petroleum, used as a lubricant etc.

petticoat n. a woman's or girl's dress-length undergarment worn hanging from the shoulders or waist beneath a dress or skirt.

pettifogging adj. trivial, paying too much attention to unimportant details.

petting n. 1. affectionate treatment. 2. erotic fondling.

pettish adj. peevish, irritable or unreasonably impatient. **pettishly** adv., **pettishness** n.

petty adj. (pettier, pettiest) 1. unimportant, trivial, petty details. 2. minor, on a small scale. 3. small-minded, petty spite. **pettily** adv., **pettiness** n. □ **petty cash**, a small amount of money kept by an office etc. for or from small payments. **petty officer**, an NCO in the navy. **petty sessions**, a meeting of magistrates for summary trial of minor offences.

petulant (**pet**-yoo-lănt) adj. peevish, unreasonably impatient. **petulantly** adv., **petulance** n.

petunia n. a garden plant with funnel-shaped flowers in bright colours.

pew n. 1. one of the long bench-like seats with a back and sides, usually fixed in rows, for the congregation in a church. 2. (informal) a seat, take a pew.

pewter n. 1. a grey alloy of tin with lead or other metal, used for making mugs and dishes etc. 2. articles made of this.

pH (pee-**aych**) n. a measure of the acidity or alkalinity of a solution.

phaeton (**fay**-tŏn) n. an old type of open horse-drawn carriage with four wheels.

phalanx n. a number of people forming a compact mass or banded together for a common purpose.

phallic (**fal**-ik) adj. of or resembling a model of the penis in erection, symbolizing generative power in nature, phallic emblems.

phantasm (**fan**-tazm) n. a phantom.

phantasmagoria (fan-taz-mă-**gor**-iă) n. a shifting scene of real or imagined figures.

phantom n. 1. a ghost, an apparition. 2. something without reality, as seen in a dream or vision, phantom ships.

Pharaoh (**fair**-oh) *n*. the title of the king of ancient Egypt.

Pharisee *n*. **1.** a member of an ancient Jewish sect represented in the New Testament as making a show of sanctity and piety. **2.** *pharisee*, a hypocritical self-righteous person. **pharisaical** (fa-ri-**say**-ikăl) *adj*.

pharmaceutical (farm-ă-**sewt**-ikăl) *adj*. of or engaged in pharmacy, of medicinal drugs, *a pharmaceutical chemist*.

pharmacist (**farm**-ă-sist) *n*. a person who is skilled in pharmacy, a pharmaceutical chemist.

pharmacology (farm-ă-**kol**-ŏji) *n*. the scientific study of medicinal drugs and their effects on the body.

pharmacopoeia (farm-ă-kŏ-**pee**-ă) *n*. **1.** a book containing a list of medicinal drugs with directions for their use. **2.** a stock of medicinal drugs.

pharmacy (**farm**-ăsi) *n*. **1.** the preparation and dispensing of medicinal drugs. **2.** a shop where these are sold, a dispensary.

pharyngitis (fa-rin-**jy**-tiss) *n*. inflammation of the pharynx.

pharynx (**fa**-rinks) *n*. the cavity at the back of the nose and throat.

phase *n*. **1.** a stage of change or development or of a recurring sequence of changes. **2.** any of the forms in which the moon or a planet appears as part or all of its disc is seen illuminated (new moon, first quarter, full moon, last quarter). —*v*. to carry out (a programme etc.) in stages. □ **phase in** *or* **out**, to bring gradually into or out of use.

Ph.D. *abbrev*. Doctor of Philosophy.

pheasant (**fez**-ănt) *n*. **1.** a long-tailed game-bird with bright feathers. **2.** its flesh as food.

phenacetin (fin-**ass**-it-in) *n*. a medicinal drug used to reduce fever.

phenobarbitone (feen-ŏ-**bar**-bit-ohn) *n*. a medicinal drug used to calm the nerves and induce sleep.

phenomenal *adj*. extraordinary, remarkable. **phenomenally** *adv*.

phenomenon (fin-**om**-inŏn) *n* (*pl*. phenomena) **1.** a fact or occurrence or change perceived by any of the senses or by the mind, *snow is a common phenomenon in winter*. **2.** a remarkable person or thing, a wonder. ¶ Note that *phenomena* is a plural; it is incorrect to speak of *this phenomena*.

pheromone (**ferrŏ**-mohn) *n*. a substance, secreted by an animal, that is detected by others of the same species and produces a response in them.

phew *int*. an exclamation of wonder

or surprise or impatience or discomfort etc.

phial (**fy**-ăl) *n*. a small glass bottle, especially for perfume or liquid medicine.

philander (fil-**and**-er) *v*. (of a man) to flirt. **philanderer** *n*.

philanthropic (fil-ăn-**throp**-ik) *adj*. **1.** benevolent. **2.** concerned with human welfare and the reduction of suffering. **philanthropically** *adv*.

philanthropist (fil-**an**-thrŏp-ist) *n*. a philanthropic person.

philanthropy (fil-**an**-thrŏp-i) *n*. love of mankind, benevolence, philanthropic acts and principles.

philately (fil-**at**-ĕl-i) *n*. stamp-collecting. **philatelist** *n*., **philatelic** (fil-ă-**tel**-ik) *adj*.

philharmonic (fil-ar-**mon**-ik) *adj*. (in names of symphony orchestras and music societies) devoted to music.

Philippine (**fil**-i-peen) *adj*. of the Philippines, Filipino. **Philippines** *pl. n*. the Philippine Islands, a group of islands in the western Pacific.

Philistine (**fil**-i-styn) *n*. **1.** a member of a people in ancient Palestine who were enemies of the Israelites. **2.** *philistine*, an uncultured person, one whose interests are material and commonplace. —**philistine** *adj*. having or showing uncultured tastes.

philology (fil-**ol**-ŏji) *n*. the scientific study of languages and their development. **philological** *adj*., **philologist** *n*.

philosopher *n*. **1.** an expert in philosophy or in one of its branches. **2.** one who expounds a particular philosophical system. **3.** one who speaks or behaves philosophically.

philosophical *adj*. **1.** of philosophy. **2.** calmly reasonable, bearing unavoidable misfortune unemotionally. **philosophically** *adv*.

philosophize *v*. to reason like a philosopher, to moralize.

philosophy *n*. **1.** the search, by logical reasoning, for understanding of the basic truths and principles of the universe, life, and morals, and of human perception and understanding of these. **2.** a system of ideas concerning this or a particular subject, a system of principles for the conduct of life. **3.** advanced learning in general, *Doctor of Philosophy*. **4.** calm endurance of misfortune etc.

philtre (**fil**-ter) *n*. a supposedly magic potion.

phlebitis (fli-**by**-tiss) *n*. inflammation of the walls of a vein.

phlegm (*pr*. flem) *n*. thick mucus in the throat and bronchial passages, ejected by coughing.

phlegmatic (fleg-**mat**-ik) *adj.* **1**. not easily excited or agitated. **2**. sluggish, apathetic. **phlegmatically** *adv.*

phlox (*pr.* floks) *n.* a plant with a cluster of reddish or purple or white flowers at the end of each stem.

Phnom-Penh (fnom-**pen**) the capital of Cambodia.

phobia (**foh**-biǎ) *n.* a lasting abnormal fear or great dislike of something.

Phoenician (fin-**ish**-ǎn) *n.* **1**. a member of an ancient Semitic people of the eastern Mediterranean. **2**. their language. —*adj.* of the Phoenicians or their language.

phoenix (**fee**-niks) *n.* a mythical bird of the Arabian desert, said to live for hundreds of years and then burn itself on a funeral pile, rising from its ashes young again to live for another cycle.

phone *n.* a telephone. —*v.* to telephone. □ **on the phone,** using the telephone; having an instrument connected to a telephone system. **over the phone,** by use of the telephone. **phone-in** *n.* a broadcast programme in which listeners telephone the studio and participate.

phonetic (fŏ-**net**-ik) *adj.* **1**. representing each speech-sound by a particular symbol which is always used for that sound; *the phonetic alphabet,* a set of symbols used in this way. **2**. (of spelling) corresponding to pronunciation. **phonetically** *adv.*

phoney *adj.* (phonier, phoniest) (*slang*) sham, not genuine, insincere. —*n.* (*slang*) a phoney person or thing.

phonograph (**fohn**-ŏ-grahf) *n.* (*Amer.*) a record-player.

phosphate (**foss**-fayt) *n.* a salt or ester of phosphoric acid, an artificial fertilizer composed of or containing this.

phosphoresce (foss-fer-**ess**) *v.* to be phosphorescent.

phosphorescent (foss-fer-**ess**-ěnt) *adj.* luminous, glowing with a faint light without burning or perceptible heat. **phosphorescence** *n.*

phosphoric (foss-**fo**-rik) *adj.* of or containing phosphorus.

phosphorus (**foss**-fer-ŭs) *n.* a chemical element existing in several forms, a yellowish wax-like form of it that appears luminous in the dark.

photo *n.* (*pl.* photos) (*informal*) a photograph. **photo finish,** a very close finish of a race, photographed to enable the judge to decide the winner.

photocopy *n.* a copy (of a document etc.) made by photographing the original. —*v.* (photocopied, photocopying) to make a photocopy of. □ **photocopier** *n.* a machine for photocopying documents.

photoelectric *adj.* of or using the electrical effects of light. **photoelectric cell,** an electronic device which emits an electric current when light falls on it, used e.g. to measure light for photography, to count objects passing it, or to cause a door to open when someone approaches it.

photofit *n.* a likeness of a person (especially one who is sought by the police) that is put together by assembling photographs of separate features.

photogenic (foh-tŏ-**jen**-ik) *adj.* being a good subject for photography, coming out well in photographs.

photograph *n.* a picture formed by means of the chemical action of light or other radiation on a sensitive surface. —*v.* **1**. to take a photograph of. **2**. to come out in a certain way when photographed, *it photographs badly.*

photographer *n.* a person who takes photographs.

photographic *adj.* **1**. of or used on or produced by photography. **2**. (of the memory) recalling accurately what was seen, as if by a process of photography. **photographically** *adv.*

photography *n.* the taking of photographs.

photolithography (foh-toh-lith-**og**-rǎfi) *n.* lithography with plates made photographically.

photon (**foh**-tonn) *n.* an indivisible unit of electromagnetic radiation.

photosynthesis (foh-toh-**sin**-thi-sis) *n.* the process by which green plants use sunlight to convert carbon dioxide (taken from the air) and water into complex substances.

phototropic (foh-tŏ-**trop**-ik) *adj.* (of the movement or growth of a plant) responding to the direction from which light falls upon it.

phrase *n.* **1**. a group of words forming a unit, especially as an idiom or a striking or clever way of saying something. **2**. a group of words (usually without a finite verb) forming a unit within a sentence or clause, e.g. *in the garden.* **3**. the way something is worded, *we didn't like his choice of phrase.* **4**. a short distinct passage forming a unit in a melody. —**phrase** *v.* **1**. to express in words. **2**. to divide (music) into phrases. □ **phrase-book** *n.* a book listing common phrases and their equivalents in a foreign language, for use by travellers.

phraseology (fray-zi-**ol**-ŏji) *n.* wording, the way something is worded.

phrenology (frin-**ol**-ŏji) *n.* study of the external shape of a person's skull as a supposed indication of his character and abilities. **phrenological** *adj.*

phut *n.* a sound like air etc. escaping in a short burst. **go phut,** to burst or explode with this sound; (*informal*) to come to nothing.

phylum (fy-lŭm) *n.* (*pl.* phyla) any of the larger groups into which plants and animals are divided, containing species with the same general form.

physic (fiz-ik) *n.* (*informal*) medicine.

physical *adj.* **1.** of the body, *physical fitness; a physical examination.* **2.** of matter or the laws of nature (as opposed to moral or spiritual or imaginary things), *the physical world; a physical map,* one showing mountains and rivers and other natural features. **3.** of physics. —*n.* (*informal*) a physical examination. —**physically** *adv.* □ **physical chemistry,** a branch of chemistry in which physics is used to study substances and their reactions. **physical geography,** a branch of geography dealing with the natural features of the earth's surface (e.g. mountains, lakes, rivers).

physician (fiz-**ish**-ăn) *n.* a doctor, especially one who practises medicine (as distinct from surgery) or is a specialist in this (as distinct from a general practitioner).

physicist (**fiz**-i-sist) *n.* an expert in physics.

physics (**fiz**-iks) *n.* **1.** the scientific study of the properties and interactions of matter and energy. **2.** these properties etc.

physiognomy (fiz-i-**on**-ŏmi) *n.* the features of a person's face.

physiology (fiz-i-**ol**-ŏji) *n.* **1.** the scientific study of the bodily functions of living organisms and their parts. **2.** these functions. **physiological** (fizi-ŏ-**loj**-ikăl) *adj.* **physiologist** *n.*

physiotherapist (fiz-i-oh-th'e-ră-pist) *n.* an expert in physiotherapy.

physiotherapy (fiz-i-oh-th'e-ră-pi) *n.* treatment of a disease or injury or deformity or weakness by massage, exercises, heat, etc.

physique (fiz-**eek**) *n.* a person's physical build and muscular development, *a man of powerful physique.*

pi (*rhymes with* my) *n.* a letter of the Greek alphabet (π, = p) used as a symbol for the ratio of the circumference of a circle to its diameter (approximately 3·14159).

pianissimo *adv.* (in music) very softly.

pianist *n.* a person who plays the piano.

piano[1] (pee-**an**-oh) *n.* (*pl.* pianos) a musical instrument in which metal strings are struck by hammers operated by pressing the keys of a keyboard. **piano-accordion** *n.* an accordion in which the melody is played on a small piano-like keyboard.

piano[2] (pee-**ah**-noh) *adv.* (in music) softly.

pianoforte (pi-ah-noh-**for**-ti) *n.* a piano.

Pianola (pee-ă-**noh**-lă) *n.* **1.** (*trade mark*) a device for playing a piano automatically. **2.** *pianola,* a player-piano.

piastre (pee-**ast**-er) *n.* a small coin of various Middle Eastern countries.

piazza (pee-**ats**-ă) *n.* a public square in an Italian town.

pibroch (**pee**-brok) *n.* a series of variations on a theme, for bagpipes. ¶ Note that this does not mean the bagpipes themselves.

pica *n.* **1.** (*pr.* **pee**-kă) a size of letters in typewriting (10 per inch). **2.** (*pr.* **py**-kă) a unit of length for measuring printing type, about one sixth of an inch.

picador (**pik**-ă-dor) *n.* a mounted man with a lance in bullfighting.

piccalilli *n.* pickle of chopped vegetables, mustard, and hot spices.

piccaninny *n.* **1.** a small Negro. **2.** an Australian Aboriginal child.

piccolo *n.* (*pl.* piccolos) a small flute sounding an octave higher than the ordinary one.

pick[1] *n.* **1.** a pickaxe. **2.** plectrum.

pick[2] *v.* **1.** to use a pointed instrument or the fingers or beak etc. in order to make a hole in or remove bits from (a thing); *pick at one's food,* to eat it in small bits or without appetite. **2.** to detach (a flower or fruit) from the plant bearing it. **3.** to select carefully; *pick a winner,* choose a person or thing that will later prove to be successful. —**pick** *n.* **1.** picking. **2.** selection; *have first pick,* have the right to choose first. **3.** the best part; *pick of the bunch,* the best of the lot. —**picker** *n.* □ **pick a lock,** to use a piece of wire or a pointed tool to open it without a key. **pick and choose,** to select with excessive care. **pick a person's brains,** to extract ideas or information from him for one's own use. **pick a person's pocket,** to steal its contents while he is wearing the garment. **pick a quarrel,** to provoke one deliberately. **pick holes in,** to find fault with. **pick-me-up** *n.* a tonic to restore health or relieve depression. **pick off,** to pluck off; to select and shoot or destroy one by one as opportunity arises. **pick on,** to single out, especially as a target for nagging or harassment. **pick out,** to take from among a number of things; to recognize; to distinguish from surrounding objects or areas; to play (a tune) by searching for the right notes. **pick over,** to select the best of. **pick up**, to lift or take up; to call for and take with one, to take aboard (passengers or freight etc.); (of police etc.) to catch, to find and take into custody; to get or acquire by chance or casually; to meet casually and become acquainted with; to succeed in seeing or hearing by means of apparatus; to recover health, to show an improvement; to recover speed; *pick up speed*, accelerate; *pick up the bill*, be the one who pays it. **pick-up** *n.* picking up; an acquaintance met informally; a small open motor truck; the part carrying the stylus in a record-player.

pick-a-back *adv.* = piggy-back.

pickable *adj.* suitable for being picked.

pickaxe *n.* a tool consisting of a curved iron bar with one or both ends pointed, mounted at right angles to its handle, used for breaking hard ground or stones etc.

picket *n.* **1.** a pointed stake set into the ground, e.g. as part of a fence. **2.** an outpost of troops, a party of sentries. **3.** one or more persons stationed by strikers outside their place of work to dissuade others from entering. —**picket** *v.* (picketed, picketing) **1.** to secure or enclose with a stake or stakes. **2.** to station or act as a picket during a strike.

pickings *pl. n.* **1.** scraps of good food etc. remaining, gleanings. **2.** odd gains or perquisites, profits from pilfering.

pickle *n.* **1.** food (especially a vegetable) preserved in vinegar or brine. **2.** vinegar or brine used for this. **3.** (*informal*) a plight, a mess. **4.** (*informal*) a mischievous child. — *v.* to preserve in pickle.

pickled *adj.* (*slang*) drunk.

picklock *n.* a device used for picking locks.

pickpocket *n.* a thief who picks people's pockets.

picnic *n.* **1.** an informal meal taken in the open air for pleasure, an excursion for this. **2.** (*informal*) something very agreeable or easily done. —*v.* (picnicked, picnicking) to take part in a picnic. —**picnicker** *n.*

picot (**pee**-koh) *n.* one of a series of small loops of twisted thread forming an ornamental edging.

picric acid a yellow substance used in dyeing and in explosives.

Pict *n.* a member of an ancient people of northern Britain. **Pictish** *adj.*

pictogram *or* **pictograph** *n.* **1.** a pictorial symbol used as a form of writing. **2.** a chart using pictures to represent statistical information. **pictographic** *adj.*

pictorial *adj.* **1.** of or expressed in a picture or pictures. **2.** illustrated by pictures. **3.** picturesque. —*n.* a newspaper or magazine in which pictures are the main feature. —**pictorially** *adv.*

picture *n.* **1.** a representation of a person or people or object(s) etc. made by painting, drawing, or photography, especially as a work of art. **2.** a portrait. **3.** something that looks beautiful, *the garden is a picture.* **4.** a scene, the total impression produced on one's sight or mind. **5.** a perfect example, *she is a picture of health.* **6.** a cinema film; *go to the pictures*, go to a cinema performance. **7.** the image on a TV screen. —**picture** *v.* **1.** to represent in a picture. **2.** to describe vividly. **3.** to form a mental picture of, *picture to yourself a deserted beach.* □ **in the picture**, fully informed, *let me put you in the picture.*

picture-gallery *n.* a hall etc. containing a collection of pictures. **picture hat,** a woman's wide-brimmed highly decorated hat. **picture postcard,** a postcard with a picture on one side. **picture window,** a large window facing an attractive view.

picturesque (pik-cher-**esk**) *adj.* **1.** forming a striking and pleasant scene, *picturesque villages.* **2.** (of words or a description) very expressive, vivid. **picturesquely** *adv.*, **picturesqueness** *n.*

piddle *v.* (*children's informal*) to urinate.

piddling *adj.* (*informal*) trivial, unimportant.

pidgin (**pij**-in) *n.* a simplified form of English or another language, containing elements of the local language(s) and used for communication (e.g. in parts of the Far East) between people speaking different languages, *pidgin English.*

pie *n.* a baked dish of meat or fish or fruit etc. enclosed in or covered with pastry or other crust. □ **pie in the sky**, a prospect (considered unrealistic) of future happiness.

piebald *adj.* (of a horse etc.) with irregular patches of white and black or other dark colour.

piece *n.* **1.** one of the distinct portions of which a thing is composed or into which it is divided or broken. **2.** one of a set of things, *three-piece suite.* **3.** something regarded as a unit, *a fine piece of work.* **4.** a musical or literary or artistic composition. **5.** (*contemptuous*) a person, especially a woman or child, *a spoilt little piece.* **6.** a coin, *ten-cent piece.* **7.** one of the set of small objects moved on a board in playing board-games, a chess-man other than a pawn. **8.** a slice of bread. **9.** a fixed unit of work, *payment by the piece, piece-rates,* payment according to this (not by the hour). —*v.* to make by joining or adding pieces together; *piece it together*, put parts together to form a whole. □ **go to pieces,** (of a person) to lose one's strength or ability etc., to collapse. **in one piece,** not broken. **of a piece,** of the same kind, consistent. **a piece of cake,** (*informal*) something very easy or pleasant. **a piece of one's mind,** a reproach or scolding giving one's frank criticisms. **piece-work** *n.* work paid according to the quantity done, not by the time spent on it. **say one's piece,** to make a prepared statement; to give one's opinion.

pièce de résistance (pee-ess dĕ ray-**zee**-stahns) **1.** the principal dish at a meal. **2.** the most important or remarkable item.

piecemeal *adj. & adv.* done piece by piece, part at a time.

pied (*rhymes with* tide) *adj.* particoloured, piebald, *pied wagtail*; *Pied Piper* (dressed in particoloured clothing).

pied-à-terre (pee-ayd-ah-**tair**) *n.* (*pl.* pieds-à-terre, *pr.* pee-ayd-) a small place for use as temporary quarters when needed.

pier (*pr.* peer) *n.* **1.** a structure built out into the sea to serve as a breakwater or landing-stage or promenade. **2.** one of the pillars or similar structures supporting an arch or bridge. **3.** solid masonry between windows etc.

pierce *v.* **1.** to go into or through like a sharp-pointed instrument, to make a hole in (a thing) in this way. **2.** to force one's way into or through.

piercing *adj.* (of cold or wind etc.) penetrating sharply; (of a voice or sound) shrilly audible.

piety (**py**-iti) *n.* piousness.

piffle *n.* (*slang*) nonsense, worthless talk. —*v.* (*slang*) to talk nonsense.

piffling *adj.* (*slang*) trivial, worthless.

pig *n.* **1.** a domestic or wild animal with short legs, cloven hooves, and a broad blunt snout. **2.** (*informal*) a greedy, dirty, or unpleasant person, a difficult or unpleasant thing. **3.** (*slang, contemptuous*) a policeman. **4.** an oblong mass of metal from a smelting-furnace, pig-iron. —*v.* (pigged, pigging) *pig it,* to live in dirty conditions or in a disorderly way. □ **buy a pig in a poke,** to buy a thing without seeing it or knowing whether it will be satisfactory. **pig-headed** *adj.* obstinate, stubborn. **pig-iron** *n.* crude iron from a smelting-furnace.

pigeon *n.* **1.** a bird of the dove family. **2.** (*informal*) a person's business or responsibility, *that's your pigeon* (¶ from a Chinese pronunciation of the word *business*). □ **pigeon-chested** *adj.* (of a person) having a deformed chest in which

the breastbone forms a protruding curve.
pigeon-toed *adj.* having the toes turned inwards.

pigeon-hole *n.* **1.** a small recess for a pigeon to nest in. **2.** one of a set of small compartments in a desk or cabinet, used for holding papers or letters etc. — **pigeon-hole** *v.* **1.** to put away for future consideration or indefinitely. **2.** to classify mentally as belonging to a particular group or kind.

piggery *n.* **1.** a pig-breeding establishment. **2.** a pigsty.

piggish *adj.* like a pig, dirty or greedy.

piggy *adj.* like a pig; *piggy eyes*, small eyes like those of a pig. **piggy-back** *adv.* so as to be carried on the shoulders and back or on the top of a larger object. **piggy bank,** a money-box made in the shape of a pig.

piglet *n.* a young pig.

pigment *n.* colouring-matter. —*v.* to colour (skin or other tissue) with natural pigment. —**pigmentation** *n.*

pigskin *n.* leather made from the skin of pigs.

pigsty *n.* **1.** a partly covered pen for pigs. **2.** a very dirty or untidy place.

pigtail *n.* long hair worn hanging in a plait at the back of the head.

pike *n.* **1.** a long wooden shaft with a pointed metal head. **2.** a pointed or peaked summit of a hill, especially in the Lake District, *Langdale Pikes*. **3.** (*pl.* pike) a large voracious freshwater fish with a long narrow snout.

piked *adj.* (of a position in acrobatics etc.) with the legs straight and forming an angle with the body at the hips, *piked somersault*.

pikelet *n.* a crumpet.

pikestaff *n.* **plain as a pikestaff,** quite plain or obvious. ¶ From *packstaff*, a pedlar's smooth staff.

pilaff (pil **af**) *n.* a dish of rice with meat or fish, spices, etc.

pilaster (pil-**ast**-er) *n.* a rectangular column, especially an ornamental one that projects from a wall into which it is set.

pilchard *n.* a small sea-fish related to the herring.

pile[1] *n.* a heavy beam of metal or concrete or timber driven vertically into the ground as a foundation or support for a building or bridge. **pile-driver** *n.* a machine for driving piles into the ground.

pile[2] *n.* **1.** a number of things lying one upon another. **2.** a funeral pyre. **3.** (*informal*) a large quantity, *a pile of work.* **4.** (*informal*) a large quantity of money, *made* *a pile.* **5.** a lofty building or complex of buildings. —**pile** *v.* **1.** to heap or stack or load. **2.** to crowd, *they all piled into one car.* □ **pile it on,** (*informal*) to exaggerate. **pile up,** to accumulate; to run (a ship) on the rocks or aground; to cause (a vehicle) to crash. **pile-up** *n.* a collision of several motor vehicles.

pile³ *n.* cut or uncut loops on the surface of a fabric.

piles *pl. n.* haemorrhoids.

pilfer *v.* to steal small items or in small quantities. **pilferer** *n.*

pilferage *n.* loss caused by theft of goods during transit or storage.

pilgrim *n.* a person who travels to a sacred or revered place as an act of religious devotion. **Pilgrim Fathers,** the English Puritans who founded the colony of Plymouth, Massachusetts, in 1620.

pilgrimage *n.* a pilgrim's journey, a journey made to a place as a mark of respect (e.g. to a person's birth-place).

pill¹ *n.* a small ball or flat round piece of medicinal substance for swallowing whole. **bitter pill,** a humiliation. **the pill,** (*informal*) a contraceptive pill; *on the pill,* taking this regularly.

pill² *v.* (of fabric) to form tiny balls of fibre on the surface.

pillage *v.* to plunder. —*n.* plunder. — **pillager** *n.*

pillar *n.* **1.** a vertical structure used as a support or ornament. **2.** something resembling this in shape, *a pillar of rock.* **3.** a person regarded as one of the chief supporters of something, *a pillar of the community.* □ **from pillar to post,** from one place or situation to another. **pillar-box** *n.* a hollow red-painted pillar about 5ft. high into which letters may be posted through a slit.

pillbox *n.* **1.** a small round box for holding pills. **2.** a hat shaped like this. **3.** a small concrete shelter for a gun emplacement.

pillion *n.* a saddle for a passenger seated behind the driver of a motor cycle. **ride pillion,** to ride on this as a passenger.

pillory *n.* a wooden framework with holes for the head and hands, into which offenders were formerly locked for exposure to public ridicule. —*v.* (pilloried, pillorying) **1.** to put into the pillory as a punishment. **2.** to hold up to public ridicule or scorn.

pillow *n.* a cushion used (especially in bed) for supporting the head. —*v.* to rest or prop up on or as if on a pillow. □ **pillowcase, pillowslip** *ns.* a cloth cover into which a pillow is placed for use. **pillow sham,** a decorative cover for a pillow that is not in use.

pilot *n.* **1.** a person who operates the flying

controls of an aircraft. **2.** a person qualified to take charge of ships entering or leaving a harbour or travelling through certain waters. **3.** a guide. —**pilot** *v.* (piloted, piloting) **1.** to act as pilot of. **2.** to guide. —*adj.* experimental, testing (on a small scale) how a scheme etc. will work, *a pilot project.* □ **pilot-light** *n.* a small jet of gas kept alight and lighting a larger burner when this is turned on; an electric indicator light. **pilot officer,** an officer of the lowest commissioned rank in the RAF.

pilotage *n.* piloting, the charge for this.

pilotless *adj.* having no pilot.

pimento (pim-**ent**-oh) *n.* (*pl.* pimentos) **1.** allspice, the West Indian tree yielding this. **2.** a sweet pepper.

pimp *n.* **1.** a man who solicits clients for a prostitute or brothel. **2.** a ponce. —*v.* to be a pimp.

pimpernel (**pimp**-er-nel) *n.* a wild plant with small scarlet or blue or white flowers that close in cloudy or wet weather.

pimple *n.* a small hard inflamed spot on the skin. **pimply** *adj.* covered with pimples, especially on the face.

pin *n.* **1.** a short thin stiff piece of metal with a sharp point and a round broadened head, used for fastening fabrics or papers etc. together or (with an ornamental head) as a decoration. **2.** a peg of wood or metal used for various purposes. **3.** a stick with a flag on it, placed in a hole on a golf-course to mark its position. **4.** a drawing-pin, hair-pin, ninepin, rolling-pin, or safety-pin. —**pin** *v.* (pinned, pinning) **1.** to fasten with a pin or pins. **2.** to transfix with a weapon or arrow etc. and hold fast, to restrict and make unable to move, *he was pinned under the wreckage.* **3.** to attach or fix; *we pinned our hopes on you,* counted on you to succeed; *pinned the blame on her,* made her the scapegoat. □ **pin down,** to establish clearly; to make (a person) agree to keep to a promise or arrangement etc. or declare his intentions definitely. **pin-money** *n.* money allowed to a woman or earned by her for private expenses. **pin-point** *n.* the point of a pin, something very small or sharp, (*adj.*) showing or needing care and precision, (*v.*) to locate or identify precisely. **pins** *pl. n.* (*informal*) legs, *quick on his pins.* **pins and needles,** a tingling sensation; *on pins and needles,* in a state of anxiety or suspense. **pin-stripe** *n.* a very narrow stripe on cloth; cloth with parallel stripes of this kind. **pin-striped** *adj.* having pin-stripes. **pin-table** *n.* a board on which pinball is played. **pin-tuck** *n.* a very narrow ornamental tuck.

pin-tucked *adj.* ornamented with pin-tucks.

pin-up *n.* (*informal*) a picture of an attractive or famous person, for pinning on a wall; the subject of this.

pinafore *n.* an apron. **pinafore dress,** a dress without collar or sleeves, worn over a blouse or jumper.

pinball *n.* a game played on a sloping board on which a ball is projected so that it strikes pins or targets or falls into a pocket.

pince-nez (**panss**-nay) *n.* (*pl.* pince-nez) a pair of glasses with a spring that clips on the nose and no side-pieces.

pincers *pl. n.* **1.** a tool for gripping and pulling things, consisting of a pair of pivoted jaws with handles that are pressed together to close them. **2.** a claw-like part of a lobster etc. □ **pincer movement,** an attack in which forces converge from each side on an enemy position.

pinch *v.* **1.** to squeeze tightly or painfully between two surfaces, especially between finger and thumb; *look pinched with cold,* have a drawn appearance from feeling unpleasantly cold. **2.** to shorten or remove by squeezing, *pinch out the tops of the plants.* **3.** to stint, to be niggardly, *pinching and scrimping.* **4.** (*slang*) to steal. **5.** (*slang*) to arrest. —**pinch** *n.* **1.** pinching, squeezing. **2.** stress or pressure of circumstances, *began to feel the pinch.* **3.** as much as can be held between the tips of the thumb and forefinger. □ **at a pinch,** in time of difficulty or necessity.

pincushion *n.* a small pad into which pins are stuck to keep them ready for use.

pine[1] *n.* **1.** an evergreen tree with needle-shaped leaves growing in clusters. **2.** its wood.

pine[2] *v.* **1.** to waste away through grief or yearning. **2.** to feel an intense longing.

pineapple *n.* **1.** a large juicy tropical fruit with a tough prickly segmented skin. **2.** the plant that bears it.

ping *n.* a short sharp ringing sound. —*v.* to make or cause to make this sound. — **pinger** *n.*

ping-pong *n.* table tennis.

pinion[1] (**pin**-yŏn) *n.* a bird's wing, especially the outer segment. —*v.* **1.** to clip the wings of (a bird) to prevent it from flying. **2.** to restrain (a person) by holding or binding his arms or legs.

pinion[2] (**pin**-yŏn) *n.* a small cog-wheel that engages with a larger one or with a rack.

pink[1] *n.* **1.** pale red colour. **2.** a garden plant with fragrant white or pink or variegated flowers. **3.** the best or most perfect condition, *the pink of perfection.* —**pink** *adj.*

1. of pale red colour. **2.** (*slang*) mildly Communist. —**pinkness** *n.* □ **in the pink,** (*slang*) in very good health. **pink gin,** a drink of gin and angostura.

pink[2] *v.* **1.** to pierce slightly. **2.** to cut a zigzag edge on. □ **pinking shears,** dressmaker's scissors with serrated blades for cutting a zigzag edge.

pink[3] *v.* (of an engine) to make slight explosive sounds when running imperfectly.

pinkish *adj.* rather pink.

pinnacle *n.* **1.** a pointed ornament on a roof. **2.** a peak. **3.** the highest point, *the pinnacle of his fame.*

pinprick *n.* a small annoyance.

pint *n.* **1.** a measure for liquids, ⅛ of a gallon (in Britain 4546 cc, in the USA 3785 cc). **2.** this quantity of liquid, especially milk or beer.

pinta *n.* (*informal*) a pint of milk.

pintle (**pin**-t'l) *n.* a pin or bolt, especially one on which another part turns.

piny *adj.* like pine-trees, *a piny smell.*

pioneer (py-ŏn-**eer**) *n.* a person who is one of the first to enter or settle a new region or to investigate a new subject or method etc. —*v.* to be a pioneer, to take part in (a course of action etc.) that leads the way for others to follow.

pious *adj.* **1.** devout in religion. **2.** ostentatiously virtuous. **piously** *adv.,* **piousness** *n.*

pip[1] *n.* one of the small seeds of an apple, pear, orange, etc.

pip[2] *n.* **1.** a spot on a domino or dice or playing-card. **2.** a star (indicating rank) on the shoulder of an army officer's uniform.

pip[3] *v.* (pipped, pipping) (*informal*) **1.** to hit with a shot. **2.** to defeat. □ **pip at the post,** to defeat at the last moment.

pip[4] *n.* a disease of poultry and other birds. **the pip,** (*slang*) a feeling of disgust or depression or bad temper.

pip[5] *n.* a short high-pitched sound, usually one produced mechanically, *the six pips of the time-signal.*

pipe *n.* **1.** a tube through which something can flow. **2.** a wind instrument consisting of a single tube, each of the tubes by which sound is produced in an organ; *the pipes,* bagpipes. **3.** a boatswain's whistle, its sounding. **4.** a narrow tube with a bowl at one end in which tobacco burns for smoking, the quantity of tobacco held by this. — **pipe** *v.* **1.** to convey (water etc.) through pipes. **2.** to transmit (music or a broadcast programme etc.) by wire or cable. **3.** to play (music) on a pipe, to lead or bring or summon by sounding a pipe etc. **4.** to utter in a shrill voice. **5.** to ornament (a dress etc.) with piping. **6.** to force (icing or cream etc.) through an aperture to make ornamental shapes. □ **pipe down,** (*informal*) to cease talking, to become less noisy or less insistent. **pipe-dream** *n.* an impractical hope or scheme. **pipe up,** to begin to play a pipe or to sing or speak.

pipeline *n.* **1.** a pipe for conveying petroleum etc. to a distance. **2.** a channel of supply or information. □ **in the pipeline,** on the way, in the process of being prepared.

piper *n.* a person who plays on a pipe or bagpipes.

pipette (pip-et) *n.* a slender tube, usually filled by suction, used in a laboratory for transferring or measuring small quantities of liquids.

piping *n.* **1.** pipes, a length of pipe. **2.** a pipe-like fold (often enclosing a cord) ornamenting edges or seams of clothing or upholstery. **3.** a cord-like ornamental line of icing etc. piped on food. **4.** a cutting from a pink or similar plant, taken off at a joint. □ **piping hot,** (of water or food) very hot.

pipit *n.* a kind of small bird resembling a lark.

pippin *n.* a kind of apple.

pipsqueak *n.* (*slang*) a small or unimportant but self-assertive fellow.

piquant (pee-kănt) *adj.* **1.** pleasantly sharp in its taste or smell. **2.** pleasantly stimulating or exciting to the mind. **piquantly** *adv.*, **piquancy** *n.*

pique (*pr.* peek) *v.* **1.** to hurt the pride or self-respect of. **2.** to stimulate, *their curiosity was piqued.* —*n.* a feeling of hurt pride.

piqué (pee-kay) *n.* a firm fabric especially of cotton, with a lengthwise corded effect or (*waffle piqué*) a woven honeycomb pattern.

piranha (pi-rahn-yă) *n.* a fierce tropical American freshwater fish.

pirate *n.* **1.** a person on a ship who unlawfully attacks and robs another ship at sea, or who makes a plundering raid on the shore. **2.** the ship used for this. **3.** one who infringes another's copyright or business rights, or who broadcasts without authorization, *a pirate radio station.* —*v.* to reproduce (a book etc.) or trade (goods) without due authorization. —**piratical** *adj.*, **piracy** (pyr-ăsi) *n.*

pirouette (pi-roo-et) *n.* a spinning movement of the body while balanced on the point of the toe or the ball of the foot. —*v.* to perform a pirouette.

Pisces (py-seez) *n.* a sign of the zodiac, the Fishes. **Piscean** *adj.* & *n.*

piss *v.* (*vulgar*) to urinate; *piss off,* go

away. —*n.* (*vulgar*) **1.** urination. **2.** urine.

pistachio (pis-tash-i-oh) *n.* (*pl.* pistachios) a kind of nut with an edible green kernel.

piste (*pr.* peest) *n.* a ski-track of compacted snow.

pistil *n.* the seed-producing part of a flower, comprising ovary, style, and stigma.

pistol *n.* a small gun. **pistol-grip** *n.* a handle shaped and held like the butt of a pistol.

piston *n.* **1.** a sliding disc or cylinder fitting closely inside a tube in which it moves up and down as part of an engine or pump. **2.** the sliding valve in a trumpet or other brass wind-instrument.

pit *n.* **1.** a hole in the ground, especially one from which material is dug out, *chalk-pit.* **2.** a coal-mine. **3.** a depression in the skin or in any surface; *pit of the stomach,* the depression between the ribs below the breastbone. **4.** seats on the ground floor of a theatre behind the stalls. **5.** a sunken area in a workshop floor, giving access to the underside of motor vehicles. **6.** a place (at a race-course) at which racing cars are refuelled etc. during a race. —**pit** *v.* (pitted, pitting) **1.** to make pits or depressions in, to become marked with hollows, *pitted with craters.* **2.** to match or set in competition, *was pitted against a strong fighter.* □ **pit-head** *n.* the top of a coal-mine shaft, the area surrounding this. **pit pony,** a pony kept underground for hauling wagons in coal-mines.

pit-a-pat *n.* a quick tapping sound. —*adv.* with this sound.

pitch[1] *n.* a dark resinous tarry substance that sets hard, used for caulking seams of ships etc. —*v.* to coat with pitch. □ **pitch-black, pitch-dark** *adjs.* quite black, with no light at all. **pitch-pine** *n.* a kind of pine-tree that yields much resin.

pitch[2] *v.* **1.** to throw or fling. **2.** to erect and fix (a tent or camp). **3.** to set at a particular degree or slope or level, *pitched their hopes high.* **4.** to fall heavily. **5.** (in cricket) to cause the ball to strike the ground near the wicket in bowling, (of a bowled ball) to strike the ground. **6.** (in baseball) to throw (the ball) to the batter. **7.** (of a ship or vehicle) to plunge forward and backward alternately. **8.** (*slang*) to tell (a yarn or excuse etc.). —**pitch** *n.* **1.** the act or process of pitching. **2.** the steepness of a slope. **3.** the intensity of a quality etc. **4.** the degree of highness or lowness of a musical note or a voice. **5.** a place at which a street performer or trader etc. is stationed. **6.** a playing-field for football etc., the area between and near the wickets in cricket.

7. a salesman's persuasive talk. □ **pitched battle,** a battle fought by troops in prepared positions, not a skirmish. **pitch in,** (*informal*) to begin to work vigorously. **pitch into,** (*informal*) to attack or reprimand vigorously. **pitch on,** to happen to select.

pitchblende *n.* a mineral ore (uranium oxide) that yields radium.

pitcher[1] *n.* the baseball player who delivers the ball to the batter.

pitcher[2] *n.* a large (usually earthenware) jug or two-handled vessel for holding and pouring liquids; *little pitchers have long ears,* children are apt to overhear things. **pitcher-plant** *n.* a plant with pitcher-shaped leaves holding a secretion in which insects become trapped.

pitchfork *n.* a long-handled fork with two prongs, used for pitching hay. —*v.* **1.** to lift or move (a thing) with a pitchfork. **2.** to thrust (a person) forcibly into a position or office etc.

piteous *adj.* deserving or arousing pity. **piteously** *adv.*

pitfall *n.* an unsuspected danger or difficulty.

pith *n.* **1.** the spongy tissue in the stems of certain plants or lining the rind of oranges etc. **2.** the essential part, *the pith of the argument.*

pithy *adj.* (pithier, pithiest) **1.** like pith, containing much pith. **2.** brief and full of meaning, *pithy comments.*

pitiable *adj.* deserving or arousing pity or contempt. **pitiably** *adv.*

pitiful *adj.* pitiable. **pitifully** *adv.*

pitiless *adj.* showing no pity. **pitilessly** *adv.*

piton (**pee**-tonn) *n.* a spike or peg with a hole through which a rope can be passed, driven into a rock or crack as a support in rock-climbing.

pitot tube (**pee**-toh) an open-ended tube bent at right angles, used in instruments that measure wind speed, the rate of flow of liquids, etc.

pittance *n.* a very small allowance of money.

pitted *see* pit.

pitter-patter *n.* a light tapping sound.

pituitary (pit-**yoo**-it-eri) *n.* the **pituitary gland,** a small ductless gland at the base of the brain, with important influence on growth and bodily functions.

pity *n.* **1.** a feeling of sorrow for another person's suffering. **2.** a cause for regret, *what a pity.* —*v.* (pitied, pitying) to feel pity for. □ **take pity on,** to feel concern for and therefore help (a person who is in difficulty).

pivot *n.* **1.** a central point or shaft etc. on which something turns or swings. **2.** a pivoting movement. —*v.* (pivoted, pivoting) to turn or place to turn on a pivot.

pivotal *adj.* **1.** of a pivot. **2.** vitally important.

pixie *n.* a small supernatural being in fairytales. **pixie hood,** a woman's or child's hood with a pointed crown.

pizza (**peets**-ă) *n.* an Italian dish consisting of a layer of dough baked with a savoury topping.

pizzicato (pits-i-**kah**-toh) *adv.* plucking the string of a musical instrument (instead of using the bow).

placard *n.* a poster or other notice for displaying. —*v.* to post up placards on (a wall etc.).

placate (plă-**kayt**) *v.* to pacify, to conciliate. **placatory** *adj.*

place *n.* **1.** a particular part of space or of an area on a surface. **2.** a particular town or district or building etc., *one of the places we visited.* **3.** (in names) a short street, a square or the buildings round it, a country mansion. **4.** a passage or part in a book etc., the part one has reached in reading, *lose one's place.* **5.** a proper position for a thing, a position in a series, one's rank or position in a community a duty appropriate to this. **6.** a position of employment. **7.** a space or seat or accommodation for a person, *keep me a place on the train.* **8.** one's home or dwelling. **9.** (in racing) a position among placed competitors, especially second or third. **10.** a step in the progression of an argument or statement, *in the first place, the dates are wrong.* **11.** the position of a figure after a decimal point etc., *correct to 3 decimal places.* —**place** *v.* **1.** to put into a particular place or rank or position or order etc., to find a place for. **2.** to locate, to identify in relation to circumstances etc., *I know his face but can't place him.* **3.** to put or give, *placed an order with the firm.* □ **be placed,** (in a race) to be among the first three. **go places,** (*informal*) to become successful. **in place,** in the right position; suitable. **in place of,** instead of. **out of place,** in the wrong position or environment; unsuitable. **place-kick** *n.* a kick made in football when the ball is placed on the ground for that purpose. **place-setting** *n.* a set of dishes or cutlery for one person at table.

placebo (plă-**see**-boh) *n.* (*pl.* placebos) a harmless substance given as if it were medicine, to humour a patient or as a dummy pill etc. in a controlled experiment.

placement *n.* placing.

placenta (plă-**sent**-ă) *n.* an organ that develops in the womb during pregnancy and supplies the developing foetus with nourishment.

placid *adj.* calm and peaceful, not easily made anxious or upset. **placidly** *adv.*, **placidity** (plă-**sid**-iti) *n.*

placket *n.* an opening in a woman's skirt to make it easy to put on and take off.

plagiarize (**play**-ji-ă-ryz) *v.* to take and use (another person's ideas or writings or inventions) as one's own. **plagiarism** *n.*

plague (*pr.* playg) *n.* **1.** a deadly contagious disease, especially the bubonic plague in London in 1665. **2.** an infestation of a pest, *a plague of caterpillars.* **3.** (*informal*) a nuisance. —*v.* to annoy, to pester.

plaice *n.* (*pl.* plaice) a kind of flat-fish used as food.

plaid (*pr.* plad, *Scottish pr.* playd) *n.* **1.** a long piece of woollen cloth, usually with a tartan or similar pattern, worn over the shoulder as part of Highland dress. **2.** this pattern.

Plaid Cymru (plyd **kum**-ri) the Welsh nationalist party.

plain *adj.* **1.** unmistakable, easy to see or hear or understand. **2.** not elaborate or intricate or luxurious, *plain cooking*; *plain water*, without flavouring etc.; *plain cake*, not containing fruit; *plain chocolate*, manufactured without milk. **3.** straightforward, candid, *some plain speaking.* **4.** ordinary, homely in manner, without affectation. **5.** lacking beauty. —*adv.* plainly, simply, *it's plain stupid.* —**plain** *n.* **1.** a large area of level country. **2.** the ordinary stitch in knitting, producing a smooth surface towards the knitter. —**plainly** *adv.*, **plainness** *n.* □ **plain clothes**, civilian clothes as distinct from uniform or official dress. **plain flour,** flour that does not contain a raising agent. **plain sailing,** a course of action that is free from difficulties. **plain-spoken** *adj.* frank.

plainsong *n.* a medieval type of church music for voices singing in unison, without regular rhythm.

plaintiff *n.* the party that brings an action in a court of law (opposed to the *defendant*).

plaintive *adj.* sounding sad. **plaintively** *adv.*, **plaintiveness** *n.*

plait (*pr.* plat) *v.* to weave or twist (three or more strands) into one rope-like length. —*n.* something plaited.

plan *n.* **1.** a drawing showing the relative position and size of parts of a building etc. **2.** a map of a town or district. **3.** a method

or way of proceeding thought out in advance; *it all went according to plan*, happened as planned. —**plan** *v.* (planned, planning) **1.** to make a plan or design of. **2.** to arrange a method etc. for, to make plans. —**planner** *n.* □ **planning** *n.* making plans, especially with reference to the controlled design of buildings and development of land.

planchette (plahn-**shet**) *n.* a small board on castors with a vertical pencil said to trace marks on paper at spiritualist seances without conscious direction by hand.

plane¹ *n.* a tall spreading tree with broad leaves.

plane² *n.* **1.** a flat or level surface. **2.** an imaginary surface of this kind. **3.** a level of thought or existence or development, *on the same plane as a savage.* **4.** an aeroplane. —*adj.* lying in a plane, level, *a plane figure* or *surface.*

plane³ *n.* **1.** a tool with a blade projecting from the base, used for smoothing the surface of wood by paring shavings from it. **2.** a similar tool for smoothing metal. —*v.* to smooth or pare with a plane.

planet *n.* one of the heavenly bodies moving round the sun. **planetary** *adj.*

planetarium (plan-i-**tair**-iŭm) *n.* a room with a domed ceiling on which lights are projected to show the appearance of the stars and planets in the sky at any chosen place or time.

plangent (**plan**-jĕnt) *adj.* (of sounds) **1.** resonant, reverberating. **2.** loud and mournful. **plangency** *n.*

plank *n.* **1.** a long flat piece of timber several inches thick. **2.** one of the basic principles of a political platform. —*v.* to lay with planks. □ **plank-bed** *n.* a bed of boards without a mattress.

planking *n.* a structure or floor of planks.

plankton *n.* the forms of organic life (chiefly microscopic) that drift or float in the sea or in fresh water.

planned *see* plan.

plant *n.* **1.** a living organism that makes its own food from inorganic substances and has neither the power of movement nor special organs of sensation and digestion. **2.** a small plant (distinguished from a tree or shrub). **3.** a factory or its machinery and equipment. **4.** (*slang*) something deliberately placed for discovery by others, a hoax or trap. —**plant** *v.* **1.** to place in the ground or in soil for growing, to put plants or seeds into (ground or soil) for growing. **2.** to fix or set or place in position, *planted his foot on the ladder.* **3.** to station (a person) as a look-out or spy. **4.** to conceal (stolen or incriminating articles) in a place where they will be discovered and mislead the discoverer. ☐ **plant out**, to transfer (a plant) from a pot or frame to open ground; to set out (seedlings) at intervals.

Plantagenet (plan-**taj**-in-it) *n.* any of the kings of England from Henry II to Richard II (1154–1399).

plantain¹ (**plan**-tin) *n.* a common wild plant with broad flat leaves, bearing seeds that are used as food for cage-birds.

plantain² (**plan**-tin) *n.* a tropical tree and fruit resembling the banana.

plantation *n.* **1.** a number of cultivated plants or trees, the area of land on which they grow. **2.** an estate on which cotton or tobacco or tea etc. is cultivated.

planter *n.* **1.** a person who owns or manages a plantation, especially in a tropical or sub-tropical country. **2.** a machine for planting things, *potato-planter*. **3.** a container for decorative plants.

plaque (*pr.* plak) *n.* **1.** a flat metal or porcelain plate fixed on a wall as an ornament or memorial. **2.** a soft substance that forms on teeth, where bacteria can live.

plash *v.* to splash. —*n.* a splashing sound.

plasma (**plaz**-mă) *n.* **1.** the colourless fluid part of blood, in which the corpuscles are suspended. **2.** a kind of gas containing positively and negatively charged particles in approximately equal numbers.

plaster *n.* **1.** a soft mixture of lime, sand, and water etc. used for coating walls and ceilings. **2.** plaster of Paris, a cast made of this fitted round a broken limb etc. **3.** sticking-plaster, a piece of this. —**plaster** *v.* **1.** to cover (a wall etc.) with plaster or a similar substance. **2.** to coat or daub, to cover thickly. **3.** to make smooth with a fixative etc., *his hair was plastered down*. — **plasterer** *n.* ☐ **plaster cast**, a cast of a statue etc. made in plaster; plaster moulded round a part of the body to keep it rigid. **plaster of Paris**, white paste made from gypsum, used for making moulds or casts. **plaster saint**, a person wrongly regarded as being without moral faults and human frailty.

plasterboard *n.* board with a core of plaster, used for making partitions etc.

plastered *adj.* (*slang*) drunk.

plastic (**plass**-tik) *n.* a synthetic resinous substance that can be given any permanent shape, e.g. by moulding it under pressure while heated. —*adj.* **1.** made of plastic, *plastic bag.* **2.** able to be shaped or moulded, *clay is a plastic substance.* **3.** giving form to clay or wax etc.; *the plastic arts,* those concerned with sculpture or ceram-

ics etc. —**plasticity** (plas-**tiss**-iti) *n.* ☐ **plastic surgeon**, a specialist in plastic surgery, the repairing or replacing of injured or defective external tissue.

Plasticine *n.* (*trade mark*) a plastic substance used for modelling things.

plasticize (**plast**-i-syz) *v.* to make or become plastic. **plasticizer** *n.*

plate *n.* **1.** an almost flat usually circular utensil from which food is eaten or served, its contents. **2.** a similar shallow vessel for the collection of money in church. **3.** dishes and other domestic utensils made of gold or silver or other metal. **4.** plated metal, objects made of this. **5.** a silver or gold cup as a prize for a horse-race etc., the race itself. **6.** a flat thin sheet of metal or glass or other rigid material. **7.** this coated with material sensitive to light or other radiation, for use in photography etc. **8.** a flat piece of metal on which something is engraved or bearing a name or registration-number etc. **9.** an illustration on special paper in a book. **10.** a thin flat structure or formation in a plant or animal body. **11.** a piece of plastic material moulded to the shape of the gums or roof of the mouth for holding artificial teeth, (*informal*) a denture. **12.** a flat piece of whitened rubber marking the station of the batter (*home plate*) or pitcher in baseball. —**plate** *v.* **1.** to cover with plates of metal. **2.** to coat (metal) with a thin layer of silver or gold or tin. ☐ **on a plate**, (*informal*) available without the recipient having to make an effort. **on one's plate**, (*informal*) for one to deal with or consider. **plate glass**, glass of fine quality for shop windows etc. **plate-rack** *n.* a rack in which plates are kept or placed to drain.

plateau (**plat**-oh) *n.* (*pl.* plateaux, *pr.* **plat**-oh) **1.** an area of fairly level high ground. **2.** a state in which there is little variation following an increase, *the firm's export trade reached a plateau.*

plateful *n.* (*pl.* platefuls) **1.** as much as a plate will hold. **2.** (*informal*) a large amount of work etc. to deal with.

platelayer *n.* a person employed to fix and repair railway rails.

platen (**pla**-t'n) *n.* the roller of a typewriter, against which the paper is held.

platform *n.* **1.** a level surface raised above the surrounding ground or floor, especially one from which a speaker addresses an audience. **2.** a raised area along the side of the line at a railway station, where passengers wait for or board or alight from trains. **3.** a floor area at the entrance to a bus or tram. **4.** the declared policy or programme of a political party.

platinum *n.* a silver-white metal that does not tarnish. **platinum blonde,** a woman with very light blonde hair.

platitude (**plat**-i-tewd) *n.* a commonplace remark, especially one uttered solemnly as if it were new. **platitudinous** (plat-i-**tewd**-in-ŭs) *adj.*

Platonic (plă-**ton**-ik) *adj.* of the ancient Greek philosopher Plato (4th century BC) or his doctrines; *platonic love* or *friendship,* affection (not involving sexual love) between a man and a woman.

platoon *n.* a subdivision of a military company.

platter *n.* **1.** (*old use*) a flat dish or plate, often of wood. **2.** (*Amer.*) a large shallow dish or plate for serving food.

platypus (**plat**-i-pŭs) *n.* (*pl.* platypuses) an Australian animal with a duck-like beak and a flat tail, that lays eggs but suckles its young.

plaudits (**plaw**-dits) *pl. n.* a round of applause, an emphatic expression of approval.

plausible (**plaw**-zib-ŭl) *adj.* **1.** (of a statement) seeming to be reasonable or probable but not proved. **2.** (of a person) persuasive but deceptive. **plausibly** *adv.,* **plausibility** *n.*

play *v.* **1.** to occupy oneself in a game or other recreational activity. **2.** to take part in (a game), *play football.* **3.** to compete against (a player or team) in a game. **4.** to occupy (a specified position) in a game. **5.** to move (a piece) or put (a card) on the table or strike (a ball etc.) in a game. **6.** to act in a drama etc., to act the part of; *play the politician,* to behave like one. **7.** to perform (a part in a process). **8.** to perform on (a musical instrument), to perform (a piece of music). **9.** to cause (a record or tape, or a record-player or tape-recorder etc.) to produce sound. **10.** to move lightly or irregularly, to allow (light or water) to fall on something, (of a fountain or hosepipe) to discharge water. **11.** to allow (a hooked fish) to exhaust itself by its pulling against the line. —**play** *n.* **1.** playing; *a play on words,* a pun. **2.** activity, operation, *other influences came into play.* **3.** a literary work written for performance on the stage, a similar work for broadcasting. **4.** free movement, *bolts should have half an inch of play.* □ **in** *or* **out of play,** (of a ball) being used, or temporarily out of use according to the rules, in a game. **play about** *or* **around,** to behave irresponsibly. **play-acting** *n.* playing a part in a play; pretending. **play along,** to pretend to co-operate. **play at,** to perform in a trivial or half-hearted way. **play back,** to play (what has recently

been recorded) on a tape-recorder etc. **play-back** *n.* playing back sound, a device for doing this. **play ball,** (*informal*) to co-operate. **play by ear,** to perform (music) without having seen a written score; to proceed in (a matter) step by step going by one's instinct or by results. **play down,** to minimize the importance of. **played out,** exhausted of energy. **play for safety,** to avoid taking risks. **play for time,** to seek to gain time by delaying. **play-group** *n.* a group of young children who play together regularly under supervision. **play into someone's hands,** to do something, that unwittingly gives him an advantage. **play off,** to play an extra match to decide a drawn position; *play off one person against another,* to oppose one person to another in order to serve one's own interests. **play-off** *n.* a match played to decide a draw or tie. **play on,** to affect and make use of (a person's sympathy etc.). **play one's cards well,** to make good use of one's opportunities. **play-pen** *n.* a portable enclosure for a young child to play in. **play safe,** to avoid taking risks. **play the game,** to keep the rules; to behave honourably. **play the market,** to speculate in stocks etc. **play up,** to put all one's energy into a game; (*informal*) to be mischievous and unruly, to annoy by doing this. **play up to,** to try to win the favour of or encourage (a person) by flattery etc. **play with,** to toy with; *play with fire,* to treat frivolously something that could prove dangerous.

playboy *n.* a pleasure-loving usually rich man.

player *n.* **1.** a person who takes part in a game. **2.** a performer on a musical instrument. **3.** an actor. **4.** a record-player. □ **player-piano** *n.* a piano fitted with apparatus that enables it to play automatically.

playfellow *n.* a playmate.

playful *adj.* **1.** full of fun. **2.** in a mood for play, not serious. **playfully** *adv.,* **playfulness** *n.*

playground *n.* **1.** a piece of ground for children to play on. **2.** a favourite place for recreation.

playing-card *n.* one of a pack or set of 52 oblong pieces of pasteboard used to play a variety of games, marked on one side to show one of 13 ranks in one of 4 suits.

playing-field *n.* a field used for outdoor games.

playleader *n.* an adult who leads or helps with children's play, especially at a play-group.

playmate *n.* a child's companion in play.

plaything *n.* **1.** a toy. **2.** something treated as a thing to play with.

playtime *n.* time assigned for children to play.

playwright *n.* a person who writes plays, a dramatist.

plaza (**plah**-ză) *n.* a public square in a Spanish town.

PLC *abbrev.* public limited company.

plea *n.* **1.** a formal statement (especially of 'guilty' or 'not guilty') made by or on behalf of a person charged in a lawcourt. **2.** an appeal or entreaty, *a plea for mercy.* **3.** an excuse, *on the plea of ill health.* □ **plea bargaining,** the procedure whereby a defendant agrees to plead guilty in return for a light sentence or other leniency.

plead *v.* (pleaded (*Scottish & Amer.* pled), pleading) **1.** to put forward as a plea in a lawcourt. **2.** to address a lawcourt as an advocate, to put forward (a case) in court. **3.** to make an appeal or entreaty; *plead with a person,* to entreat him. **4.** to put forward as an excuse, *pleaded a previous engagement.*

pleasant *adj.* **1.** pleasing, giving pleasure to the mind or feelings or senses. **2.** having an agreeable manner. **pleasantly** *adv.,* **pleasantness** *n.*

pleasantry *n.* being humorous, a humorous remark.

please *v.* **1.** to give pleasure to, to make (a person etc.) feel satisfied or glad. **2.** to be so kind as to, *please ring the bell.* **3.** to think fit, to have the desire, *take what you please.* —*adv.* a polite phrase of request. □ **if you please,** (*formal*) please; an ironical phrase, pointing out unreasonableness, *and so, if you please, we're to get nothing!* **please oneself,** to do as one chooses.

pleased *adj.* feeling or showing pleasure or satisfaction.

pleasurable *adj.* causing pleasure. **pleasurably** *adv.*

pleasure *n.* **1.** a feeling of satisfaction or joy, enjoyment. **2.** a source of pleasure, *it's a pleasure to talk to him.* **3.** choice, desire, *at your pleasure.* —*adj.* done or used for pleasure, *a pleasure trip.* □ **with pleasure,** willingly, gladly.

pleat *n.* a flat fold made by doubling cloth on itself. —*v.* to make a pleat or pleats in.

plebeian (pli-**bee**-ăn) *adj.* **1.** of the lower social classes. **2.** uncultured, vulgar, *plebeian tastes.* —*n.* a member of the lower classes.

plebiscite (**pleb**-i-sit) *n.* a referendum, a vote by all the people of a country on an important public matter.

plebs *pl. n.* (*slang*) plebeians.

plectrum *n.* a small piece of metal or bone or ivory for plucking the strings of a musical instrument.

pledge *n.* **1.** a thing deposited as security for payment of a debt or fulfilment of a contract etc., and liable to be forfeited in case of failure. **2.** a token of something, *as a pledge of his devotion.* **3.** a toast drunk to someone's health. **4.** a solemn promise, *under pledge of secrecy.* —**pledge** *v.* **1.** to deposit (an article) as a pledge. **2.** to promise solemnly. **3.** to drink to the health of.

plenary (**pleen**-er-i) *adj.* attended by all members, *a plenary session of the assembly.*

plenipotentiary (plen-i-pŏ-**ten**-sher-i) *n.* an envoy with full powers to take action or make decisions etc. on behalf of the government he represents. —*adj.* having these powers.

plentiful *adj.* in large quantities or numbers, abundant. **plentifully** *adv.*

plenty *n.* quite enough, as much as one could need or desire. —*adv.* (*informal*) quite, fully, *it's plenty big enough.*

plesiosaurus (plee-si-ŏ-**sor**-ŭs) *n.* (*pl.* plesiosauri *or* plesiosauruses) an extinct reptile that lived in the sea, with a long neck, short tail, and four large paddle-like flippers.

pleonasm (**plee**-ŏn-azm) *n.* an expression in which a word is redundant, as in 'a sure certainty'.

plethora (**pleth**-er-ă) *n.* an over abundance.

pleurisy (**ploor**-i-si) *n.* inflammation of the membrane lining the chest and surrounding the lungs.

pliable *adj.* **1.** bending easily, flexible. **2.** easily influenced. **pliably** *adv.,* **pliability** *n.*

pliant (**ply**-ănt) *adj.* pliable. **pliantly** *adv.,* **pliancy** *n.*

pliers *pl. n.* pincers having jaws with flat surfaces that can be brought together for gripping small objects or wire etc.

plight[1] *n.* a serious and difficult situation.

plight[2] *v.* (*old use*) to pledge.

plimsoll *n.* a rubber-soled canvas sports shoe.

Plimsoll line *or* **mark** a mark on a ship's side showing how far it may legally go down in the water when loaded.

plinth *n.* a block or slab forming the base of a column or a support for a vase etc.

plissé (**plee**-say) *n.* fabric that has been treated to give it a crinkled appearance, *cotton plissé.*

PLO *abbrev.* Palestine Liberation Organization.

plod *v.* (plodded, plodding) **1.** to walk doggedly or laboriously, to trudge. **2.** to work at a slow but steady rate. —*n.* plodding. —**plodder** *n.*

plonk[1] *v.* to throw or place or drop down heavily.

plonk[2] *n.* (*slang*) cheap or inferior wine.

plop *n.* a sound like that of something dropping into water without a splash.

plot *n.* 1. a small measured piece of land, *building plots.* 2. the story in a play or novel or film. 3. a conspiracy, a secret plan, *Gunpowder Plot.* —**plot** *v.* (plotted, plotting) 1. to make a plan or map of. 2. to mark on a chart or diagram. 3. to plan secretly, to contrive a secret plan. — **plotter** *n.*

plough (*rhymes with* cow) *n.* 1. an implement for cutting furrows in soil and turning it up, drawn by a tractor or horse(s). 2. an implement resembling a plough, *snow-plough.* 3. *the Plough,* a constellation also called the Great Bear. —**plough** *v.* 1. to turn up (earth) or cast out (roots etc.) with a plough, to cut (a furrow). 2. to make one's way or advance laboriously, *ploughed through the snow* or *through a book.* 3. to advance violently, *the lorry ploughed into the barrier as it crashed.* 4. (*slang*) to fail (an examination), to declare that (a candidate) has failed. □ **plough back,** to turn (growing grass etc.) into the soil to enrich it; to reinvest (profits) in the business that produced them.

ploughman *n.* (*pl.* ploughmen) a man who guides a plough. **ploughman's lunch,** a meal of bread and cheese and beer.

ploughshare *n.* the cutting-blade of a plough.

plover (**pluv**-er) *n.* a kind of wading bird.

ploy *n.* (*informal*) 1. an undertaking or occupation, *they were out on various ploys.* 2. a cunning manœuvre to gain an advantage.

PLR *abbrev.* public lending right (a proposed system of remunerating authors whose books are borrowed from public libraries).

pluck *v.* 1. to pick (a flower or fruit), to pull out (a hair or feather etc.). 2. to strip (a bird) of its feathers. 3. to pull at or twitch. 4. to sound (the string of a musical instrument) by pulling and then releasing it with the finger(s) or a plectrum. —**pluck** *n.* 1. plucking, a pull. 2. courage, spirit. 3. an animal's heart, liver, and lungs as food. □ **pluck up courage,** to summon up one's courage.

plucky *adj.* (pluckier, pluckiest) showing pluck, brave. **pluckily** *adv.*

plug *n.* 1. something fitting into and stopping or filling a hole or cavity. 2. a device with metal pins that fit into a socket to make an electrical connection, (*informal*)

the socket. 3. (*informal*) the release-mechanism of the apparatus flushing a water-closet, *pull the plug.* 4. a sparking-plug. 5. a cake of tobacco, a piece of this cut off for chewing. 6. (*informal*) a piece of favourable publicity for a commercial product. —**plug** *v.* (plugged, plugging) 1. to put a plug into, to stop with a plug. 2. (*slang*) to shoot or strike (a person etc.). 3. (*informal*) to mention favourably, to seek to popularize (a song or product or policy etc.) by constant commendation. □ **plug away,** to work diligently or persistently. **plug in,** to connect electrically by inserting a plug into a socket. **plug-in** *adj.* able to be connected in this way.

plum *n.* 1. a fleshy fruit with sweet pulp and a flattish pointed stone. 2. the tree that bears it. 3. (*old use*) a dried grape or raisin used in cooking; *plum cake* or *pudding,* containing such fruit. 4. reddish-purple colour. 5. a good thing, the best of a collection, something considered good and desirable, *a plum job.*

plumage (**ploo**-mij) *n.* a bird's feathers.

plumb[1] (*pr.* plum) *n.* a piece of lead tied to the end of a cord, used for finding the depth of water or testing whether a wall etc. is vertical. —*adv.* 1. exactly, *plumb in the middle.* 2. (*Amer. informal*) completely, *plumb crazy.* —**plumb** *v.* 1. to measure or test with a plumb-line. 2. to reach, *plumbed the depths of misery.* 3. to get to the bottom of (a matter). □ **plumb-line** *n.* a cord with a plumb attached.

plumb[2] (*pr.* plum) *v.* 1. to work as a plumber. 2. to provide with a plumbing system, to fit (a thing) as part of this.

plumber (**plum**-er) *n.* a person whose job is to fit and repair plumbing.

plumbing (**plum**-ing) *n.* a system of water-pipes, cisterns, and drainage-pipes etc. in a building.

plume (*pr.* ploom) *n.* 1. a feather, especially a large one used for ornament. 2. an ornament of feathers or similar material. 3. something resembling this, *a plume of smoke.* —*v.* to preen, *the bird plumed itself* or *its feathers.* □ **plume oneself,** to pride oneself.

plumed (*pr.* ploomd) *adj.* ornamented with plumes.

plummet *n.* a plumb or plumb-line. —*v.* (plummeted, plummeting) to fall or plunge steeply.

plummy *adj.* 1. full of plums. 2. (of the voice) sounding affectedly full and rich in tone.

plump[1] *adj.* having a full rounded shape. —*v.* to make or become plump. — **plumpness** *n.*

plump[2] *v.* to drop or plunge abruptly, *plumped down.* —*adv.* with a sudden or heavy fall. □ **plump for,** to choose or vote for whole-heartedly, to decide on.

plunder *v.* to rob (a place or person) forcibly or systematically, to steal or embezzle. —*n.* **1.** the taking of goods or money etc. in this way. **2.** the goods etc. acquired. —**plunderer** *n.*

plunge *v.* **1.** to thrust or go forcefully into something. **2.** to descend suddenly. **3.** to jump or dive into water. **4.** to enter or cause to enter a condition or set of circumstances, *plunged the world into war.* **5.** (of a horse) to start forward violently, (of a ship) to thrust its bows down into the water, to pitch. **6.** to gamble heavily or run deeply into debt. —*n.* plunging, a dive. □ **take the plunge,** to take a bold decisive step.

plunger *n.* **1.** the part of a mechanism that works with a plunging or thrusting movement. **2.** a rubber cup on a handle for removing blockages by alternate thrusting and suction.

plunk *v.* – plonk[1].

plural (**ploor**-ăl) *n.* the form of a noun or verb used with reference to more than one person or thing, *the plural of 'child' is 'children'.* —*adj.* **1.** of this form. **2.** of more than one; *plural vote* or *voting,* a vote by one person in more than one constituency.

plus *prep.* **1.** with the addition of. **2.** above zero, *temperature between minus ten and plus ten degrees.* **3.** (*informal*) with, having gained, possessing, *arrived plus dog.* —*adj.* more than the amount or number indicated; *beta plus,* a grade slightly above beta (written as B+). —**plus** *n.* **1.** the sign +. **2.** an advantage. □ **plus-fours,** *pl. n.* knickerbockers worn especially by golfers (¶ so named because the length is increased by 4 inches to produce the overhang). **plus sign,** the sign +.

plush *n.* a kind of cloth with long soft nap, used in furnishings. —*adj.* **1.** made of plush. **2.** plushy.

plushy *adj.* luxurious. **plushiness** *n.*

plutocrat (**ploo**-tŏ-krat) *n.* a person who is powerful because of his wealth. **plutocratic** *adj.*

plutonium (ploo-**toh**-niŭm) *n.* a radioactive substance used in nuclear weapons and reactors.

ply[1] *n.* **1.** a thickness or layer of wood or cloth etc. **2.** a strand in yarn, *3-ply wool.* **3.** plywood.

ply[2] *v.* (plied, plying) **1.** to use or wield (a tool or weapon). **2.** to work at, *ply one's trade.* **3.** to work steadily. **4.** to keep offering or supplying, *plied her with food* or

with questions. **5.** to go to and fro regularly, *the boat plies between the two harbours.* **6.** (of a taxi-driver or boatman etc.) to drive or row or wait about looking for custom, *ply for hire.*

Plymouth Brethren (**plim**-ŭth) a Calvinistic religious body formed about 1830 at Plymouth in Devon.

plywood *n.* strong thin board made by glueing layers with the grain crosswise.

p.m. *abbrev.* after noon. (¶ From the Latin *post meridiem.*)

PM *abbrev.* Prime Minister.

pneumatic (new-**mat**-ik) *adj.* filled with or operated by compressed air, *pneumatic drills.* **pneumatically** *adv.*

pneumonia (new-**moh**-niă) *n.* inflammation of one or both lungs.

PO *abbrev.* **1.** postal order. **2.** Post Office.

poach[1] *v.* **1.** to cook (an egg removed from its shell) in boiling water or in a poacher. **2.** to cook (fish or fruit etc.) by simmering it in a small amount of liquid. □ **poacher** *n.* a pan with one or more cup-shaped containers in which eggs are placed for cooking over boiling water.

poach[2] *v.* **1.** to take (game or fish) illegally from private land or water. **2.** to trespass or encroach on something that properly belongs to another person. **poacher** *n.*

pochette (posh-et) *n.* a woman's envelope-shaped handbag.

pock *n.* **1.** one of the spots that erupt on the skin in smallpox. **2.** a scar left by this. □ **pock-marked** *adj.* marked by scars or pits.

pocket *n.* **1.** a small bag-like part sewn into or on a garment, for holding money or small articles. **2.** one's resources of money; *beyond my pocket,* more than I can afford. **3.** a pouch-like compartment in a suitcase or on a car door etc. **4.** one of the pouches at the corners or sides of a billiard-table, into which balls are driven. **5.** an isolated group or area, *small pockets of resistance.* —*adj.* of a size or shape suitable for carrying in a pocket, *pocket calculators.* —**pocket** *v.* **1.** to put into one's pocket. **2.** to take for oneself (dishonestly or otherwise). **3.** to send (a ball) into a pocket on a billiard-table. **4.** to suppress or hide (one's feelings), *pocketing his pride.* □ **in a person's pocket,** intimate with him; completely under his influence. **in pocket,** having gained in a transaction. **out of pocket,** having lost in a transaction. **out-of-pocket expenses,** cash expenses incurred while doing something. **pocket-book** *n.* a notebook; a small book-like case for holding money or papers. **pocket-knife**

n. a knife with folding blade(s), for carrying in the pocket. **pocket-money** *n.* money for small expenses; money allowed regularly to children.

pocketful *n.* (*pl.* pocketfuls) the amount that a pocket will hold.

pod *n.* a long seed-vessel like that of a pea or bean. —*v.* (podded, podding) to bear or form pods.

podgy *adj.* (podgier, podgiest) short and fat.

podium (**poh**-di-ŭm) *n.* (*pl.* podia) a pedestal or platform.

poem *n.* a literary composition in verse, especially one expressing deep feeling or noble thought in an imaginative way.

poet *n.* a writer of poems. **poetess** *n.* □ **Poet Laureate**, *see* Laureate.

poetic *adj.* of or like poetry, of poets. **poetic justice**, well-deserved punishment or reward.

poetical *adj.* poetic, written in verse, *poetical works.* **poetically** *adv.*

poetry *n.* **1.** poems, a poet's art or work. **2.** a quality that pleases the mind as poetry does, *the poetry of motion.*

po-faced *adj.* solemn-faced, not showing amusement.

pogrom (**pog**-rŏm) *n.* an organized massacre.

poignant (**poin**-yănt) *adj.* arousing sympathy, deeply moving to the feelings, keenly felt, *poignant grief.* **poignantly** *adv.*, **poignancy** *n.*

poinsettia (poin-**set**-iă) *n.* a plant with large scarlet petal-like leaves.

point *n.* **1.** the tapered or sharp end of something, the tip. **2.** a projection, a promontory of land. **3.** (in geometry) that which has position but not magnitude, e.g. the intersection of two lines. **4.** a dot used as a punctuation mark, a decimal point. **5.** a particular place or spot, an exact moment, a stage or degree of progress or increase or temperature etc. **6.** one of the directions marked on the compass, a corresponding direction towards the horizon. **7.** a unit of measurement or value or scoring. **8.** a separate item or detail, *we differ on several points.* **9.** a distinctive feature or characteristic; *it has its points,* has certain useful features. **10.** the essential thing, the thing under discussion, *come to the point.* **11.** the important feature of a story or joke or remark. **12.** effectiveness, purpose, value, *there's no point in wasting time.* **13.** a fieldsman in cricket near the batsman on the off side, his position. **14.** an electrical socket, *power points.* **15.** one of the tapering movable rails by which a train is directed from one line to another. —

point *v.* **1.** to direct or aim, *pointed a gun at her.* **2.** to be directed or aimed. **3.** to direct attention, to indicate; *it all points to a conspiracy,* is evidence of one. **4.** to sharpen. **5.** to fill in the joints of (brickwork etc.) with mortar or cement. □ **a case in point**, one that is relevant to what has just been said. **make a point of**, to treat as important, to do something with ostentatious care. **on the point of**, on the very verge of (an action). **point-duty** *n.* (of a policeman etc.) being stationed at a particular point to regulate traffic. **point of no return**, the point in a long-distance journey at which one must continue onward because supplies are insufficient to enable one to return to the starting-point; the point after which one cannot withdraw from an action. **point of view**, a way of looking at a matter. **point out**, to indicate, to draw attention to. **point-to-point** *n.* a horse-race over a course defined only by certain landmarks. **point up**, to emphasize. **to the point**, relevant, relevantly.

point-blank *adj.* **1.** (of a shot) aimed or fired at very close range. **2.** (of a remark) direct, straightforward, *a point-blank refusal.* —*adv.* in a point-blank manner, *refused point-blank.*

pointed *adj.* **1.** tapering or sharpened to a point. **2.** (of a remark or manner) clearly aimed at a particular person or thing, emphasized. **pointedly** *adv.*

pointer *n.* **1.** a thing that points to something, a mark or rod that points to figures etc. on a dial or scale. **2.** a rod used to point to things on a blackboard etc. **3.** (*informal*) a hint or indication. **4.** a dog of a breed that on scenting game stands rigidly with muzzle pointing towards it.

pointless *adj.* **1.** without a point. **2.** having no purpose or meaning. **pointlessly** *adv.*

poise *v.* **1.** to balance or be balanced. **2.** to hold suspended or supported. —**poise** *n.* **1.** balance, the way something is poised. **2.** a dignified and self-assured manner.

poised *adj.* (of a person) having poise, dignified and self-assured.

poison *n.* **1.** a substance that can destroy the life or harm the health of a living animal or plant. **2.** a harmful influence. —**poison** *v.* **1.** to give poison to, to kill with poison. **2.** to put poison on or in. **3.** to corrupt, to fill with prejudice, *poisoned their minds.* —**poisoner** *n.* □ **poison pen**, a person who writes malicious or slanderous anonymous letters.

poisonous *adj.* **1.** containing or having the effect of poison. **2.** likely to corrupt people, *a poisonous influence.*

poke *v.* **1.** to thrust with the end of a finger

or a stick etc.; *poke the fire*, lever or thrust the coals etc. with a poker. **2.** to thrust or be thrust forward, to protrude. **3.** to produce by poking, *poked a hole in it.* **4.** to search, to pry, *poking about in the attic.* — *n.* poking, a thrust or nudge. □ **poke fun at**, to ridicule. **poke one's nose into something**, to pry or intrude.

poker¹ *n.* a stiff metal rod for poking a fire.

poker² *n.* a card-game in which players bet on whose hand of cards has the highest value. **poker-face** *n.* a face that does not reveal thoughts or feelings; a person with such a face.

poky *adj.* (pokier, pokiest) small and cramped, *poky little rooms.*

Poland a country in eastern Europe.

polar *adj.* **1.** of or near the North Pole or South Pole. **2.** of one of the poles of a magnet. **3.** directly opposite in character or tendency. □ **polar bear**, a white bear living in Arctic regions.

polarity (poh-la-riti) *n.* the possessing of negative and positive poles.

polarize *v.* **1.** to confine similar vibrations of (light-waves etc.) to a single direction or plane. **2.** to give polarity to. **3.** to set or become set at opposite extremes of opinion, *public opinion had polarized.* **polarization** *n.*

Polaroid *n.* (*trade mark*) **1.** a material that polarizes the light passing through it, used in spectacle lenses etc. to protect the eyes from glare. **2.** a kind of camera that develops and prints a photograph instantly when an exposure is made.

pole¹ *n.* **1.** a long slender rounded piece of wood or metal, especially one used as part of a supporting structure or in propelling a barge etc. **2.** a measure of land, $5\frac{1}{2}$ yds. or $30\frac{1}{4}$ sq. yds. —*v.* to push along by using a pole. □ **pole-jump**, **pole-vault** *ns.* a vault over a high crossbar with the help of a pole held in the hands. **up the pole**, (*slang*) in a difficulty; crazy; drunk.

pole² *n.* **1.** either extremity of the earth's or other body's axis, either of two points in the sky about which the stars appear to rotate, the North Pole or South Pole. **2.** each of the two points in a magnet which attract or repel magnetic bodies. **3.** the positive or negative terminal of an electric cell or battery. **4.** each of two opposed principles. □ **be poles apart**, to differ greatly. **pole-star** *n.* a star in the Little Bear, near the North Pole in the sky.

Pole *n.* a Polish person.

pole-axe *n.* **1.** a battleaxe with a long handle. **2.** a butcher's implement for

slaughtering cattle. —*v.* to strike down with or as if with a pole-axe.

polecat *n.* **1.** a small dark-brown animal of the weasel family with an unpleasant smell. **2.** (*Amer.*) a skunk.

polemic (pol-em-ik) *n.* a verbal attack on a belief or opinion. —*adj.* **1.** controversial. **2.** argumentative. — **polemical** *adj.*

police *n.* **1.** a civil force responsible for the keeping of public order, its members. **2.** a force responsible for enforcing the regulations of an organization etc., *military police*; *railway police.* —*v.* to keep order in (a place) by means of police, to provide with police. □ **police-officer** *n.* a policeman or policewoman. **police state**, a country (usually a totalitarian State) in which political police supervise and control citizens' activities. **police station**, the office of a local police force.

policeman *n.* (*pl.* policemen) a man who is a member of a police force.

policewoman *n.* (*pl.* policewomen) a woman member of a police force.

policy¹ *n.* the course or general plan of action adopted by a government or party or person.

policy² *n.* a contract of insurance, the document containing this.

polio (poh-li-oh) *n.* poliomyelitis.

poliomyelitis (poh-li-oh-my-il-I-tiss) *n.* an infectious disease caused by a virus, producing temporary or permanent paralysis.

polish *v.* **1.** to make or become smooth and glossy by rubbing. **2.** to make better by correcting or putting finishing touches. — **polish** *n.* **1.** smoothness and glossiness. **2.** the process of polishing. **3.** a substance for polishing a surface. **4.** a high degree of elegance. —**polisher** *n.* □ **polish off**, to finish off.

Polish *adj.* of Poland or its people or language. —*n.* **1.** a native or inhabitant of Poland. **2.** the language of Poland.

polished *adj.* elegant, refined, perfected, *polished manners*; *a polished performance.*

Politburo (pol-it-bewr-oh) *n.* (*pl.* Politburos) the principal committee of a Communist party.

polite *adj.* **1.** having good manners, socially correct. **2.** refined, *polite society.* **politely** *adv.*, **politeness** *n.*

politic *adj.* showing good judgement, prudent. **the body politic**, the State or a similar organized system.

political *adj.* **1.** of or engaged in politics. **2.** of the way a country is governed, *its political system.* **politically** *adv.* □ **political asylum**, refuge in foreign territory for refugees from political persecution.

political prisoner, a person imprisoned for a political offence.

politician *n.* a person who is engaged in politics, an MP.

politics *n.* **1.** the science and art of governing a country. **2.** political affairs or life. **3.** manœuvring for power etc. within a group, *office politics.* —*pl. n.* political principles or affairs or tactics. ☐ **not practical politics,** unlikely to occur; liable to meet practical difficulties.

polka *n.* a lively dance for couples, of Bohemian origin. **polka dots,** round dots evenly spaced to form a pattern on fabric.

poll (*rhymes with* hole) *n.* **1.** voting at an election, the counting of votes, the number of votes recorded, *a heavy poll.* **2.** the place where voting is held. **3.** an estimate of public opinion made by questioning a representative sample of people. **4.** (*old use*) the head. —**poll** *v.* **1.** to vote at an election. **2.** (of a candidate) to receive as votes. **3.** to cut off the horns of (cattle) or the top of (a tree etc.). ☐ **polling-booth, polling-station** *ns.* a place where votes are recorded.

pollack (**pol**-ăk) *n.* a sea-fish related to the cod, used as food.

pollard (**pol**-erd) *n.* **1.** a tree that is polled so as to produce a close head of young branches. **2.** an animal that has cast or lost its horns, an ox or sheep or goat of a hornless breed. —*v.* to make (a tree) into a pollard, *pollarded willows.*

pollen *n.* a fine powdery substance produced by the anthers of flowers, containing the fertilizing element. **pollen count,** an index of the amount of pollen in the air, published as a warning to those who are allergic to it.

pollinate *v.* to shed pollen on, to fertilize with pollen. **pollination** *n.*

pollster *n.* a person conducting a public-opinion poll.

pollutant *n.* a substance causing pollution.

pollute *v.* **1.** to make dirty or impure, especially by adding harmful or offensive substances. **2.** to corrupt, *polluting the mind.* **pollution** *n.*

polo *n.* a game like hockey, played by teams on horseback with long-handled mallets. **polo neck,** a high round turned-over collar.

polonaise (pol-ŏ-**nayz**) *n.* a stately dance of Polish origin, music for this or in this style.

polony (pŏ-**loh**-ni) *n.* a sausage made of partly-cooked pork.

poltergeist (**pol**-ter-gyst) *n.* a ghost or spirit that throws things about noisily.

poly (**pol**-i) *n.* (*pl.* polys) (*informal*) a polytechnic.

poly- *prefix* **1.** many (as in *polyhedron*). **2.** (in names of plastics) polymerized.

polyandry (**pol**-i-an-dri) *n.* the system of having more than one husband at a time.

polyanthus *n.* a kind of cultivated primrose produced from hybridized primulas.

polychrome (**pol**-i-krohm) *adj.* painted or printed or decorated in many colours.

polyester *n.* a polymerized substance, especially as a synthetic resin or fibre.

polygamy (pŏ-**lig**-ămi) *n.* the system of having more than one wife at a time. **polygamous** *adj.,* **polygamist** *n.*

polyglot (**pol**-i-glot) *adj.* knowing or using or written in several languages. —*n.* a person who knows several languages.

polygon (**pol**-i-gŏn) *n.* a geometric figure with many (usually five or more) sides. **polygonal** (pŏ-**lig**-ŏnăl) *adj.*

polyhedron (poli-**hee**-drŏn) *n.* a solid figure with many (usually seven or more) faces.

polymath (**pol**-i-math) *n.* a person with knowledge of many subjects.

polymer (**pol**-im-er) *n.* a compound whose molecule is formed from a large number of simple molecules combined.

polymerize (**pol**-im-er-ryz) *v.* to combine or become combined into a polymer. **polymerization** *n.*

Polynesia (poli-**nee**-zhă) a group of islands in the Pacific Ocean, including New Zealand, Hawaii, and Samoa. **Polynesian** *adj. & n.*

polyp (**pol**-ip) *n.* **1.** a simple organism with a tube-shaped body, e.g. one of the organisms of which coral is composed. **2.** an abnormal growth projecting from a mucous membrane, e.g. in the nose.

polystyrene (poli-**styr**-een) *n.* a kind of plastic, a polymer of styrene.

polysyllabic (poli-sil-**ab**-ik) *adj.* having many syllables, *polysyllabic words.*

polytechnic (poli-**tek**-nik) *n.* an institution giving instruction in many subjects at an advanced level.

polytheism (**pol**-ith-ee-ism) *n.* belief in or worship of more than one god.

polythene *n.* a kind of tough light plastic material.

polyunsaturated *adj.* of a kind of fat or oil that (unlike animal and dairy fats) is not associated with the formation of cholesterol in the blood.

polyurethane (poli-**yoor**-i-thayn) *n.* a kind of synthetic resin or plastic.

polyvinyl (poli-**vy**-nil) *adj.* made from polymerized vinyl. **polyvinyl chloride,** a plastic used for insulation and as fabric for furnishings etc.

pom *n.* **1.** a Pomeranian. **2.** (*Austral. & N.Z. slang*) a pommy.

pomander (pŏm-**an**-der) *n.* a ball of mixed sweet-smelling substances or a round container for this, used to perfume cupboards etc.

pomegranate (**pom**-i-gran-it) *n.* **1.** a tropical fruit with tough rind and reddish pulp enclosing many seeds. **2.** the tree that produces it.

Pomeranian (pom-er-**ayn**-iän) *n.* a dog of a small silky-haired breed.

pommel (**pum**-ĕl) *n.* **1.** a knob on the handle of a sword. **2.** an upward projection at the front of a saddle. —*v.* (pommelled, pommelling) to pummel.

pommy *n.* (*Austral.* & *N.Z. slang*) a British person, especially a recent immigrant.

pomp *n.* a stately and splendid ceremonial.

pom-pom *n.* = pompon.

pompon *n.* **1.** a decorative tuft or ball. **2.** a type of dahlia or other flower with small tightly-clustered petals.

pompous *adj.* full of ostentatious dignity and self-importance. **pompously** *adv.*, **pomposity** (pom-**poss**-iti) *n.*

ponce *n.* a man who lives off a prostitute's earnings. —*v.* **1.** to act as a ponce. **2.** to walk or move in an effeminate way.

poncho *n.* (*pl.* ponchos) **1.** a blanket-like piece of cloth with a slit in the centre for the head, worn as a cloak. **2.** a garment shaped like this.

pond *n.* a small area of still water.

ponder *v.* **1.** to be deep in thought. **2.** to think something over thoroughly.

ponderous *adj.* **1.** heavy, unwieldy. **2.** laborious in style. **ponderously** *adv.*

pong *n.* (*slang*) a stink. —*v.* (*slang*) to stink.

Pontefract-cake (**pont**-i-frakt) *n.* a small round flat liquorice sweet made at Pontefract in West Yorkshire.

pontifical (pon-**tif**-ikăl) *adj.* pompously dogmatic. **pontifically** *adv.*

pontificate (pon-**tif**-i-kayt) *v.* to speak in a pontifical way.

pontoon[1] *n.* **1.** a kind of flat-bottomed boat. **2.** one of a number of boats or hollow metal cylinders etc. used to support a temporary bridge.

pontoon[2] *n.* **1.** a card-game in which players try to acquire cards with face-value totalling 21. **2.** a score of 21 from two cards in this game.

pony *n.* a horse of any small breed. **ponytail** *n.* a woman's or girl's long hair drawn back and tied at the back of the head so that it hangs down. **pony-trekking** *n.* travelling across country on ponies for pleasure.

poodle *n.* a dog with thick curly hair often clipped or shaved in a pattern.

poof *n.* (*informal*) an effeminate man, a male homosexual.

pooh *int.* an exclamation of impatience or contempt. **pooh-pooh** *v.* to dismiss (an idea etc.) scornfully.

pool[1] *n.* **1.** a small area of still water, especially one that is naturally formed. **2.** a shallow patch of water or other liquid lying on a surface, a puddle. **3.** a swimming-pool. **4.** a deep place in a river.

pool[2] *n.* **1.** a common fund, e.g. that containing the total stakes in a gambling venture. **2.** a common supply of vehicles or commodities or services etc. for sharing between a number of people or firms. **3.** a game resembling snooker. —*v.* to put into a common fund or supply, for sharing. □ **the pools**, football pools.

poop *n.* the stern of a ship, a raised deck at the stern.

poor *adj.* **1.** having little money or means; *the poor*, poor people. **2.** deficient in something, *poor in minerals*. **3.** scanty, inadequate, less good than is usual or expected, *a poor crop*; *he is a poor driver*; *poor soil*, not fertile. **4.** lacking in spirit, despicable. **5.** deserving pity or sympathy, unfortunate, *poor fellow!* **poorness** *n.* □ **poor-spirited** *adj.* lacking courage, timid.

poorly *adv.* in a poor way, badly. —*adj.* unwell, *feeling poorly*.

pop[1] *n.* **1.** a small sharp explosive sound. **2.** a fizzy drink. —**pop** *v.* (popped, popping) **1.** to make or cause to make a pop. **2.** to put quickly or suddenly, *pop it in the oven*. **3.** to come or go quickly or suddenly or unexpectedly, *popped out for coffee*. **4.** (*slang*) to pawn. □ **pop-eyed** *adj.* with bulging eyes. **pop off**, (*slang*) to die. **pop-shop** *n.* (*slang*) a pawnbroker's shop. **pop the question**, (*informal*) to propose marriage. **pop-up** *adj.* (of a machine etc.) operating so that something comes upwards automatically.

pop[2] *n.* (*slang*) father.

pop[3] *adj.* in a popular modern style. —*n.* pop music, a record of this, *top of the pops*; *pop group,* performing pop music; *pop festival,* at which pop music is performed.

popadam *n.* = poppadam.

popcorn *n.* maize heated so that it bursts to form fluffy balls.

pope *n.* the bishop of Rome, head of the Roman Catholic Church.

popery *n.* (*contemptuous*) the papal system, the Roman Catholic religion.

popgun *n.* a child's toy gun that shoots a cork etc. with a popping sound.

popish *adj.* (*contemptuous*) of Roman Catholicism or the papal system.

poplar *n.* a kind of tall slender tree often with leaves that quiver easily.

poplin *n.* a plain woven fabric usually of cotton.

poppadam (**pop**-ă-dăm) *n.* a thin crisp biscuit made of lentil-flour.

poppet *n.* (*informal*) a small or dainty person, a darling.

popping-crease *n.* a line marking the limit of the batsman's position in cricket.

poppy *n.* a plant with showy flowers and milky juice.

poppycock *n.* (*slang*) nonsense.

populace (**pop**-yoo-lăs) *n.* the general public.

popular *adj.* **1.** liked or enjoyed by many people. **2.** of or for the general public. **3.** (of a belief etc.) held by many people, *popular superstitions.* **popularly** *adv.*, **popularity** *n.* □ **popular front**, a political party representing left-wing groups.

popularize *v.* **1.** to make generally liked. **2.** to make generally known, to present (a subject etc.) so that it can be understood by ordinary people. **popularization** *n.*, **popularizer** *n.*

populate *v.* to supply with a population, to form the population of.

population *n.* the inhabitants of a place or district or country, the total number of these.

populous *adj.* thickly populated.

porcelain (**por**-sĕl-in) *n.* **1.** the finest kind of china. **2.** objects made of this.

porch *n.* a roofed shelter forming the approach to the entrance of a building.

porcupine *n.* an animal related to the squirrel, with a body and tail covered with protective spines.

pore¹ *n.* one of the tiny openings on an animal's skin or on a leaf, through which moisture may be emitted (e.g. as sweat) or taken in.

pore² *v.* **pore over**, to study (a thing) with close attention.

pork *n.* unsalted pig-flesh as food.

porker *n.* a pig raised for food, a young fattened pig.

porn *n.* (*slang*) pornography.

pornography *n.* writings or pictures or films etc. that are intended to stimulate erotic feelings by description or portrayal of sexual activity. **pornographic** *adj.*, **pornographer** *n.*

porous (**por**-ŭs) *adj.* **1.** containing pores. **2.** able to be permeated by fluid or air. **porosity** (por-**oss**-iti) *n.*

porphyry (**por**-fi-ri) *n.* a kind of rock containing crystals of minerals.

porpoise (**por**-pŭs) *n.* a sea animal resembling a dolphin or small whale, with a blunt rounded snout.

porridge *n.* **1.** a food made by boiling oatmeal or other meal or cereal to a thick paste in water or milk. **2.** (*slang*) imprisonment.

porringer *n.* a small basin-shaped dish from which porridge is eaten, especially by children.

port¹ *n.* **1.** a harbour, a town with a harbour, especially one where goods are imported or exported by ship. **2.** any place (e.g. Heathrow Airport) where goods pass in and out of a country by ship or aircraft and where customs officers are stationed to supervise this.

port² *n.* **1.** an opening in a ship's side for entrance, loading, etc. **2.** a porthole. **3.** a place where signals enter or leave a data-transmission system or device.

port³ *n.* the left-hand side (when facing forward) of a ship or aircraft. —*v.* to turn this way, *port your helm.*

port⁴ *n.* a strong sweet usually dark-red wine of Portugal.

portable *adj.* able to be carried, *portable typewriters.* —*n.* a portable kind of typewriter, television set, etc. —**portability** *n.*

portal *n.* a doorway or gateway, especially an imposing one.

portcullis *n.* a strong heavy vertical grating that can be lowered in grooves to block the gateway to a castle etc.

portend (por-**tend**) *v.* to foreshadow.

portent (**por**-tent) *n.* an omen, a significant sign of something to come.

portentous (por-**tent**-ŭs) *adj.* ominous, being a sign of some extraordinary (usually calamitous) event. ¶ Do not confuse with pretentious.

porter¹ *n.* a gatekeeper or door-keeper of a large building.

porter² *n.* a person employed to carry luggage or other goods.

porterage *n.* the services of a porter.

porterhouse steak a choice cut of beef-steak.

portfolio *n.* (*pl.* portfolios) **1.** a case for holding loose sheets of paper or drawings etc. **2.** a set of investments held by one investor. **3.** the position of a minister of State. **Minister without portfolio**, a Cabinet Minister who is not in charge of any department of State.

porthole *n.* a window-like structure in the side of a ship or aircraft.

portico (**port**-i-koh) *n.* (*pl.* porticoes) a structure consisting of a roof supported on columns, usually forming a porch to a building.

portion *n.* **1.** a part or share of something. **2.** the amount of food allotted to one person. **3.** one's destiny or lot. —*v.* to divide into portions, to distribute in portions, *portion it out.*

Portland cement a kind of cement coloured like limestone (*Portland stone*) from the Isle of Portland in Dorset.

portly *adj.* (portlier, portliest) stout and dignified. **portliness** *n.*

portmanteau (port-**man**-toh) *n.* a trunk for clothes etc. that opens into two equal parts. **portmanteau word,** an invented word combining the sounds and meanings of two others, e.g. *motel, Oxbridge.*

portrait *n.* **1.** a picture or drawing or photograph of a person or animal. **2.** a description in words.

portray (por-**tray**) *v.* **1.** to make a picture of. **2.** to describe in words or represent in a play etc., *she is portrayed as a pathetic character.* **portrayal** *n.*

Port Salut (por sal-**yoo**) a pale mild type of French cheese.

Portugal a country in south-west Europe.

Portuguese *adj.* of Portugal or its people or language. —*n.* **1.** (*pl.* Portuguese) a native of Portugal. **2.** the language of Portugal. □ **Portuguese man-of-war,** a sea animal with tentacles that have a poisonous sting.

pose *v.* **1.** to put into or take a desired position for a portrait or photograph etc. **2.** to take a particular attitude for effect. **3.** to pretend to be, *posed as an expert.* **4.** to put forward, to present, *pose a question* or *a problem.* —**pose** *n.* **1.** an attitude in which a person etc. is posed. **2.** an affectation, a pretence.

poser *n.* a puzzling question or problem.

poseur (poh-**zer**) *n.* a person who poses for effect or behaves affectedly.

posh *adj.* (*slang*) very smart, luxurious. ¶ The suggestion that this word is derived from the initials of 'port out, starboard home', referring to the more expensive side for accommodation on ships formerly travelling between England and India, is often put forward but lacks foundation.

position *n.* **1.** the place occupied by a person or thing. **2.** the proper place for something, *in* or *out of position.* **3.** an advantageous location, *manœuvring for position.* **4.** the way in which a thing or its parts are placed or arranged. **5.** a situation in relation to other people or things, *this puts me in a difficult position.* **6.** a point of view, *what is their position about tax reform?* **7.** rank or status, high social standing,

people of position. **8.** paid employment, a job. —*v.* to place in a certain position.

positive *adj.* **1.** stated formally or explicitly, *positive rules.* **2.** definite, leaving no room for doubt, *we have positive proof.* **3.** holding an opinion confidently. **4.** (*informal*) clear, out-and-out, *it's a positive miracle.* **5.** constructive and helpful, *made some positive suggestions.* **6.** having specific or definite qualities or characteristics; *the result of the test was positive,* indicated that a specific substance etc. was present. **7.** (of a quantity) greater than zero. **8.** containing or producing the kind of electrical charge produced by rubbing glass with silk; *positive terminal of a battery,* the one through which electric current leaves the battery. **9.** (of a photograph) having the lights and shades or colours as in the actual object or scene photographed, not as in a negative. —*n.* a positive quality or quantity or photograph etc. —**positively** *adv.,* **positiveness** *n.* □ **positive discrimination,** the policy of deliberately favouring members of a group that is felt to be underprivileged, especially when resources or opportunities are being allocated. **positive pole** the north-seeking pole of a magnet. **positive sign,** the sign +.

posse (**poss**-i) *n.* a body of constables, a strong force or company.

possess *v.* **1.** to hold belonging to oneself, to have or own. **2.** to occupy or dominate the mind of, *be possessed by a devil* or *with an idea; fought like one possessed,* as if strengthened by an evil spirit or a powerful emotion. **possessor** *n.* □ **possess oneself of,** to take.

possession *n.* **1.** possessing, being possessed. **2.** a thing possessed. □ **take possession of,** to become the owner or possessor of.

possessive *adj.* **1.** of or indicating possession; *the possessive form of a word,* e.g. *John's, the baker's.* **2.** showing a desire to possess or to retain what one possesses. **possessively** *adv.,* **possessiveness** *n.* □ **possessive pronoun,** *see* pronoun.

possibility *n.* **1.** the fact or condition of being possible. **2.** something that may exist or happen, *thunder is a possibility today.* **3.** capability of being used or of producing good results, *the plan has distinct possibilities.*

possible *adj.* capable of existing or happening or being done or used etc. —*n.* a candidate who may be successful, one who may become a member of a team.

possibly *adv.* **1.** in accordance with possibility, *can't possibly do it.* **2.** perhaps, for all one knows to the contrary.

possum *n.* an opossum, especially in Australia. **play possum,** to pretend to be unaware of something (¶ from the possum's habit of feigning death when in danger).

post[1] *n.* **1.** a piece of timber or metal set upright in the ground etc. to support something or to mark a position. **2.** the starting-post or winning-post in a race; *left at the post,* outdistanced from the start; *beaten at the post,* defeated at the last moment. —*v.* to announce by putting up a notice or placard etc.; *post no bills,* a warning that notices must not be pasted up; *the ship was posted as missing,* was announced to be missing.

post[2] *n.* **1.** the place where a soldier is on watch, a place of duty, *the sentries are at their posts.* **2.** a place occupied by soldiers, especially a frontier fort, the soldiers there. **3.** a place occupied for purposes of trade, especially in a region that is not yet fully settled, *trading-posts.* **4.** a position of paid employment, *got a post with a textile firm.* —**post** *v.* **1.** to place or station, *we posted sentries.* **2.** to appoint to a post or command. □ last post, *see* last[2].

post[3] *n.* **1.** the official conveyance of letters etc. **2.** the letters etc. conveyed. **3.** a single collection or delivery of these. — **post** *v.* **1.** to put (a letter etc.) into a post office or post-box for transmission. **2.** to enter in an official ledger. □ **keep a person posted,** to keep him informed.

post-box *n.* a box into which letters are inserted for transmission. **post-code** *n.* a group of letters and figures included in a postal address to assist sorting. **Post Office,** a public department or corporation responsible for postal services. **post office,** a building or room where postal business is carried on. **post-office box,** a numbered place in a post office where letters are kept until called for. **post town,** a town that acts as a clearing-point for post sent to a particular district.

post- *prefix* after, *post-war.*

postage *n.* the charge for sending something by post. **postage stamp,** a small adhesive stamp for sticking on things to be posted, showing the amount paid.

postal *adj.* **1.** of the post. **2.** by post, *postal vote.* □ **postal order,** a kind of money order.

postcard *n.* a card for sending messages by post without an envelope.

post-date *v.* to put a date on (a document or cheque etc.) that is later than the actual one.

poster *n.* a large sheet of paper announcing or advertising something, for display in a public place.

poste restante (pohst ress-**tahnt**) a department in a post office where letters are kept until called for.

posterior *adj.* situated behind or at the back. —*n.* the buttocks.

posterity (poss-**te**-riti) *n.* **1.** future generations. **2.** a person's descendants.

postern (**poss**-tern) *n.* a small entrance at the back or side of a fortress etc.

post-graduate *adj.* (of studies) carried on after taking a first degree. —*n.* a student engaged on such studies.

post-haste *adv.* with great speed or haste.

posthumous (**poss**-tew-mŭs) *adj.* **1.** (of a child) born after its father's death. **2.** coming or happening after a person's death, *a posthumous award; a posthumous novel,* published after the author's death. **posthumously** *adv.*

postilion (pos-**til**-yŏn) *n.* a rider on a near-side horse drawing a coach etc. when there is no coach-driver.

Post-Impressionist *n.* a painter using a style that was a reaction against Impressionism. **Post-Impressionism** *n.*

postman *n.* (*pl.* postmen) one who delivers or collects letters etc.

postmark *n.* an official mark stamped on something sent by post, giving the place and date of marking. —*v.* to mark with a postmark.

postmaster *n.* a man in charge of a post office.

postmistress *n.* a woman in charge of a post office.

post-mortem *adv. & adj.* after death. —*n.* **1.** an examination made after death to determine its cause. **2.** (*informal*) a detailed discussion of something that is over.

post-natal (pohst-**nay**-t'l) *adj.* existing or occurring immediately after birth or childbirth.

postpone *v.* to keep (an event) from occurring until a later time, *postpone the meeting.* **postponement** *n.*

postprandial *adj.* taking place after lunch or after dinner.

postscript *n.* a paragraph added at the end of something (especially in a letter, after the signature).

postulant (**poss**-tew-lănt) *n.* a candidate for admission to a religious order.

postulate[1] (**poss**-tew-layt) *v.* to assume (a thing) to be true, especially as a basis for reasoning. **postulation** *n.*

postulate[2] (**poss**-tew-lăt) *n.* something postulated.

posture (**poss**-cher) *n.* an attitude of the body, the way a person etc. stands or sits or walks. —v. to assume a posture, especially for effect. —**postural** adj., **posturer** n.

post-war adj. existing or occurring after a war.

posy n. a small bunch of flowers.

pot[1] n. **1.** a rounded vessel of earthenware or metal or glass etc. used for holding liquids or solids, or for cooking in. **2.** the contents of a pot. **3.** (slang) a prize in an athletic contest, especially a silver cup. **4.** (slang) a large amount, pots of money. **5.** (slang) a pot-belly. —**pot** v. (potted, potting) **1.** to plant in a pot. **2.** to pocket (a ball) in billiards etc. **3.** (informal) to abridge, a potted edition. **4.** to shoot, to kill by a pot-shot. **5.** (informal) to put (a child) to sit on a chamber-pot. □ **go to pot**, (slang) to deteriorate, to become ruined. **pot-belly** n. a protuberant belly, a person with this. **pot-boiler** n. a literary or artistic work done merely to make a living. **pot-bound** adj. (of a plant) with roots filling a flowerpot tightly and lacking room to spread. **pot-boy** n. a publican's assistant. **pot-herb** n. a herb used in cooking. **pot luck**, whatever is available for a meal etc., take pot luck with us. **pot plant**, a plant grown in a flowerpot. **pot-roast** n. a piece of meat cooked slowly in a covered dish, (v.) to cook in this way. **pot shot** n. a shot aimed casually.

pot[2] n. (slang) marijuana. ¶ From the Mexican Spanish phrase potación de guaya (= drink of grief) for a drink made by soaking cannabis seed-pods in wine or brandy.

potable (poh-tăbŭl) adj. drinkable.

potash n. any of various salts of potassium, especially potassium carbonate.

potassium (pŏ-tas-iŭm) n. a soft silvery-white metallic element.

potato n. (pl. potatoes) **1.** a plant with starchy tubers that are used as food. **2.** one of these tubers.

potent (poh-tĕnt) adj. having great natural power or influence, able to have a strong effect, potent drugs. **potency** n.

potentate (poh-tĕn-tayt) n. a monarch or ruler.

potential (pŏ-ten-shăl) adj. capable of coming into being or of being developed or used etc., a potential source of energy. —n. **1.** an ability or capacity or resources etc. available for development or use. **2.** the voltage between two points. — **potentially** adv., **potentiality** n.

pot-hole n. **1.** a deep cylindrical hole formed in rock (e.g. in limestone) by the action of water, an underground cave. **2.** a hole in the surface of a road. —v. to explore underground pot-holes. —**pot-holer** n.

potion (poh-shŭn) n. liquid for drinking as a medicine or drug etc.

potman n. (pl. potmen) a publican's assistant.

pot-pourri (poh-poor-ee) n. **1.** a scented mixture of dried petals and spices. **2.** a literary or musical medley.

potsherd (pot-sherd) n. a broken piece of earthenware, especially in archaeology.

potted see pot[1]. —adj. (of food) preserved in a pot; potted meat, meat paste.

potter[1] n. a person who makes earthenware dishes or ornaments etc.

potter[2] v. to work on trivial tasks in a leisurely relaxed way. **potterer** n.

pottery n. **1.** vessels and other objects made of baked clay. **2.** a potter's work or workshop. □ **the Potteries**, a district in north Staffordshire where the pottery industry is carried on.

potting-shed n. a shed where delicate plants are grown in pots for planting out.

potty[1] adj. (pottier, pottiest) (slang) **1.** trivial, insignificant. **2.** crazy.

potty[2] n. (informal) a chamber-pot for a child.

pouch n. a small bag or bag-like formation. —v. **1.** to put into a pouch, to pocket. **2.** to make (part of a dress) hang like a pouch.

pouf (pr. poof) n. = poof.

pouffe (pr. poof) n. a padded stool.

poulterer n. a dealer in poultry and game.

poultice (pohl-tiss) n. a soft heated mass of bread or kaolin etc. applied to an inflamed or sore area of skin. —v. to apply a poultice to.

poultry (pohl-tri) n. domestic fowls, ducks, geese, turkeys, etc., especially as a source of food.

pounce v. to spring or swoop down on and grasp, e.g. as prey; pounce on a mistake, to spot it quickly. —n. a pouncing movement.

pound[1] n. **1.** a measure of weight, 16 oz. avoirdupois (0·4536 kg) or 12 oz. troy (0·3732 kg). **2.** the unit of money of Britain and certain other countries. □ **pound note**, a banknote for £1. ¶ Correct usage is a five-pound note (or weight); it costs (or weighs) five pounds.

pound[2] n. a place where stray animals, or motor vehicles left in unauthorized places, are taken and kept until claimed.

pound[3] v. **1.** to crush or beat with heavy repeated strokes. **2.** to deliver heavy blows or repeated gunfire etc. **3.** to make one's way heavily, pounding along. **4.** (of the heart) to beat heavily, to thump.

poundage n. **1.** a charge of so much for

each £. **2.** a charge for a postal order. **3.** an allowance of so much in the £. **4.** payment per pound weight.

pour *v.* **1.** to flow or cause to flow in a stream or shower. **2.** to pour tea etc. into cups, to serve by pouring. **3.** to rain heavily. **4.** to come or go or send out in large amounts or numbers, *refugees poured out of the country*; *letters poured in.* **5.** to send (words or music etc.) out freely, *he poured out his story.* —**pourer** *n.* □ **pour cold water on,** *see* cold.

pout¹ *v.* to push out one's lips, (of lips) to be pushed out, especially as a sign of annoyance or sulking. —*n.* a pouting expression.

pout² *n.* **1.** an edible sea-fish related to the cod. **2.** an eel-like freshwater fish.

poverty *n.* **1.** being poor, great lack of money or resources; *monks who were vowed to poverty,* who renounced the right to individual ownership of property. **2.** scarcity, lack. **3.** inferiority, poorness. □ **poverty line,** the minimum income level needed to obtain the necessities of life. **poverty-stricken** *adj.* affected by poverty. **poverty trap,** the condition of being so dependent on State benefits that an increase in one's income means that one loses some of these and is no better off.

POW *abbrev.* prisoner of war.

powder *n.* **1.** a mass of fine dry particles. **2.** a medicine or cosmetic in this form. **3.** gunpowder. —*v.* to apply powder to, to cover with powder. □ **powder blue,** pale blue. **powder-puff** *n.* a soft or fluffy pad for applying powder to the skin. **powder-room** *n.* a ladies' cloakroom. **powder snow,** loose dry snow.

powdered *adj.* made into powder.

powdery *adj.* like powder.

power *n.* **1.** the ability to do something. **2.** vigour, energy, strength. **3.** a property, *great heating power.* **4.** control, influence, *the party in power.* **5.** authority, *their powers are defined by law.* **6.** an influential person or country or organization etc. **7.** (*informal*) a large amount, *did me a power of good.* **8.** (in mathematics) the product of a number multiplied by itself a given number of times, *the third power of* $2 = 2 \times 2 \times 2 = 8$. **9.** mechanical or electrical energy as opposed to hand-labour; *power tools,* using such energy. **10.** the electricity supply, *a power failure.* **11.** capacity for exerting mechanical force, horsepower. **12.** the magnifying capacity of a lens. □ **power-dive** *n.* an aircraft's dive made without shutting off engine power. **power point,** a socket on a wall etc. where electrical appliances can be connected to the

mains. **power politics,** political action based on threats to use force. **power-station** *n.* a building where electrical power is generated for distribution. **the powers that be,** the people in authority.

powered *adj.* equipped with mechanical or electrical power.

powerful *adj.* having great power or strength or influence. **powerfully** *adv.*

powerhouse *n.* a power-station.

powerless *adj.* without power to take action, wholly unable.

powwow *n.* a meeting for discussion.

Powys (**poh**-iss) a county of Wales.

pp. *abbrev.* pages.

p.p. *abbrev.* by proxy, through an agent (Latin *per procurationem*). ¶ Although the logical sequence would be 'signed by AB (principal) p.p. CD (agent)', it is customary to treat the phrase as meaning 'on behalf of' and to use 'signed by CD (agent) p.p. AB (principal)'.

PPS *abbrev.* post-postscript, = an additional postscript.

PQ *abbrev.* Province of Quebec.

practicable *adj.* able to be done. **practicability** *n.*

practical *adj.* **1.** involving activity as distinct from study or theory, *has had practical experience.* **2.** suitable for use, *an ingenious but not very practical invention.* **3.** (of people) clever at doing and making things, *a practical handyman.* **4.** virtual, *he has practical control of the firm.* —*n.* a practical examination, practical study. **practicality** (prakti-**kal**-iti) *n.* □ **practical joke,** a humorous trick played on a person by a **practical joker.**

practically *adv.* **1.** in a practical way. **2.** virtually, almost.

practice *n.* **1.** action as opposed to theory, *it works well in practice.* **2.** a habitual action, custom, *it is our practice to supply good material.* **3.** repeated exercise to improve one's skill, a spell of this, *target practice.* **4.** professional work, the business carried on by a doctor or lawyer, the patients or clients regularly consulting these, *has a large practice.* □ **out of practice,** no longer possessing a former skill.

practise *v.* **1.** to do something repeatedly in order to become skilful. **2.** to carry out in action, to do something habitually, *practise what you preach.* **3.** to do something actively, *a practising Catholic.* **4.** (of a doctor or lawyer etc.) to be actively engaged in professional work.

practised *adj.* experienced, expert.

practitioner (prak-**tish**-ŏn-er) *n.* a professional or practical worker, especially in medicine.

pragmatic (prag-**mat**-ik) *adj.* treating things from a practical point of view, *a pragmatic approach to the problem.* **pragmatically** *adv.*, **pragmatism** (prag-mă-tizm) *n.*

Prague (*pr.* prahg) the capital of Czechoslovakia.

prairie *n.* a large treeless tract of grassland, especially in North America.

praise *v.* **1.** to express approval or admiration of. **2.** to honour (God) in words. —*n.* praising, approval expressed in words.

praiseworthy *adj.* deserving praise.

praline (**prah**-leen) *n.* a sweet made by browning nuts in boiling sugar.

pram *n.* a four-wheeled carriage for a baby, pushed by a person walking.

prance *v.* to move springily in eagerness, *prancing horses.*

prang *v.* (*slang*) to crash an aircraft or vehicle, to damage by impact. —*n.* (*slang*) a crash, damage by impact.

prank *n.* mischief, a practical joke.

prattle *v.* to chatter in a childish way. —*n.* childish chatter.

prawn *n.* an edible shellfish like a large shrimp.

pray *v.* **1.** to say prayers. **2.** to entreat. **3.** = please, *pray be seated.*

prayer *n.* **1.** a solemn request or thanksgiving to God or to an object of worship. **2.** a set form of words used in this, *the Lord's Prayer.* **3.** a religious service, *morning prayer.* **4.** the act of praying. **5.** entreaty to a person. □ **prayer-book** *n.* a book of set prayers. **prayer-mat** *n.* a small carpet on which Muslims kneel to pray.

pre- *prefix* before, beforehand.

preach *v.* **1.** to deliver (a sermon or religious address), to speak in public in support of a religion; *preach the gospel,* make it known by preaching. **2.** to advocate, to urge people to a certain quality or practice or action, *they preached economy.* **3.** to give moral advice in an obtrusive way. **preacher** *n.*

preamble (pree-**am**-bŭl) *n.* a preliminary statement, the introductory part of a document or law etc.

pre-arrange *v.* to arrange beforehand. **pre-arrangement** *n.*

prebendary (**preb**-ĕn-der-i) *n.* **1.** a clergyman receiving a stipend from a cathedral revenue. **2.** an honorary canon (not receiving such a stipend).

precarious (pri-**kair**-iŭs) *adj.* unsafe, not secure. **precariously** *adv.*

precast *adj.* (of concrete) cast in blocks before use.

precaution *n.* something done in advance to avoid a risk; *take precautions,* do things as a precaution. **precautionary** *adj.*

precede (pri-**seed**) *v.* to come or go or place before in time or order etc.

precedence (**press**-i-dĕnss) *n.* priority in time or order. **take precedence,** to have priority.

precedent (**press**-i-dĕnt) *n.* a previous case that is taken as an example to be followed.

precentor (pri-**sent**-er) *n.* a member of the clergy of a cathedral who is in general charge of music there.

precept (**pree**-sept) *n.* a command, a rule of conduct.

preceptor (pri-**sept**-er) *n.* a teacher, an instructor. **preceptress** *n.*

pre-Christian *adj.* of the time before Christianity.

precinct (**pree**-sinkt) *n.* **1.** an enclosed area, especially around a place of worship. **2.** a district where traffic is prohibited in a town, *pedestrian precinct.* **3.** (*Amer.*) a subdivision of a county or city or ward for election and police purposes. □ **precincts** *pl. n.* the area surrounding a place, *in the precincts of the forest.*

precious *adj.* **1.** of great value or worth. **2.** beloved. **3.** affectedly refined. **4.** (*informal,* used ironically) considerable, *did him a precious lot of good.* —*adv.* (*informal*) very, *there's precious little money left.* —**preciously** *adv.*, **preciousness** *n.* □ **precious metals,** gold, silver, and platinum. **precious stone,** a piece of mineral having great value, especially as used in jewellery.

precipice (**press**-i-piss) *n.* a very steep or vertical face of a cliff or rock etc.

precipitate[1] (pri-**sip**-i-tayt) *v.* **1.** to throw down headlong. **2.** to send rapidly into a certain state or condition, *precipitated the country into war.* **3.** to cause to happen suddenly or soon, *this action precipitated a crisis.* **4.** to cause (a substance) to be deposited in solid form from a solution in which it is present. **5.** to condense (vapour) into drops which fall as rain or dew etc. **precipitation** *n.*

precipitate[2] (pri-**sip**-i-tăt) *n.* a substance precipitated from a solution, moisture condensed from vapour and deposited (e.g. rain, dew). —*adj.* **1.** headlong, violently hurried, *a precipitate departure.* **2.** (of a person or action) hasty, rash. — **precipitately** *adv.*

precipitous (pri-**sip**-itŭs) *adj.* like a precipice, steep. **precipitously** *adv.* ¶ Do not confuse with precipitate[2] *adj.*

précis (**pray**-see) *n.* (*pl.* précis, *pr.* **pray**-seez) a summary. —*v.* (précised, précising) to make a précis of.

precise *adj.* **1.** exact, correctly and clearly stated. **2.** taking care to be exact, *she is very precise.*

precisely *adv.* **1.** in a precise manner, exactly. **2.** (said in agreement) quite so, as you say.

precision (pri-si*z*h-ŏn) *n.* accuracy; *precision tools,* tools designed for very accurate work.

preclude (pri-klood) *v.* to exclude the possibility of, to prevent.

precocious (pri-koh-shŭs) *adj.* **1.** (of a child) having developed certain abilities earlier than is usual. **2.** (of abilities or knowledge) showing such development. **precociously** *adv.,* **precocity** (pri-koss-iti) *n.*

preconceived (pree-kŏn-seevd) *adj.* (of an idea or opinion) formed beforehand, formed before full knowledge or evidence is available. **preconception** *n.* a preconceived idea.

pre-condition *n.* a condition that must be fulfilled before something else can happen.

precursor (pri-ker-ser) *n.* **1.** a person or thing that precedes another, a forerunner. **2.** a thing that precedes a later and more developed form, *rocket bombs were the precursors of space-probes.*

predator (pred-ă-ter) *n.* a predatory animal.

predatory (pred-ă-ter-i) *adj.* **1.** (of animals) preying upon others. **2.** plundering or exploiting others.

predecease (pree-di-seess) *v.* to die earlier than (another person).

predecessor (pree-di-sess-er) *n.* **1.** the former holder of an office or position. **2.** an ancestor. **3.** a thing to which another has succeeded, *it will share the fate of its predecessor.*

predestination *n.* **1.** the doctrine that God has foreordained all that happens, or that certain souls are destined for salvation and eternal life and others are not. **2.** destiny, fate.

predestine *v.* to destine beforehand, to appoint as if by fate.

predetermine *v.* to decide in advance, to predestine.

predicament (pri-dik-ă-měnt) *n.* a difficult or unpleasant situation.

predicate (pred-i-kăt) *n.* the part of a sentence that says something about the subject, e.g. 'is short' in *life is short.*

predicative (pri-dik-ătiv) *adj.* forming part or the whole of the predicate, e.g. 'old' in *the dog is old* (but not in *the old dog*). **predicatively** *adv.*

predict *v.* to forecast, to prophesy. **prediction** *n.,* **predictor** *n.*

predictable *adj.* able to be predicted. **predictably** *adv.,* **predictability** *n.*

predilection (pree-di-lek-shŏn) *n.* a special liking, a preference.

predispose *v.* **1.** to influence in advance, *circumstances predispose us to be lenient*; *we are predisposed in his favour,* inclined to favour him. **2.** to render liable, e.g. to a disease.

predisposition *n.* a state of mind or body that renders a person liable to act or behave in a certain way or to be subject to certain diseases, *a predisposition to bronchitis.*

predominant *adj.* predominating. **predominantly** *adv.,* **predominance** *n.*

predominate *v.* **1.** to be greater than others in number or intensity etc., to be the main element. **2.** to have or exert control.

pre-eminent *adj.* excelling others, outstanding. **pre-eminently** *adv.,* **pre-eminence** *n.*

pre-empt *v.* to take possession of (a thing) before anyone else can do so. **pre-emption** *n.*

pre-emptive *adj.* pre-empting; *a pre-emptive attack,* one intended to disable an enemy and prevent him from attacking.

preen *v.* (of a bird) to smooth (its feathers) with its beak. **preen oneself,** to groom oneself; to congratulate oneself, to show self-satisfaction.

prefab *n.* (*informal*) a prefabricated building.

prefabricate *v.* to manufacture in sections that are ready for assembly on a site. **prefabrication** *n.*

preface (pref-ăs) *n.* an introductory statement at the beginning of a book or speech. —*v.* **1.** to provide or introduce with a preface. **2.** to lead up to (an event), *the music that prefaced the ceremony.*

prefatory (pref-ă-ter-i) *adj.* serving as a preface, preliminary, *prefatory remarks.*

prefect *n.* **1.** a senior pupil in a school, authorized to maintain discipline. **2.** the chief administrative official in certain departments in France, Japan, and other countries.

prefer *v.* (preferred, preferring) **1.** to choose as more desirable, to like better. **2.** to put forward (an accusation etc.) for consideration by an authority, *they preferred charges of forgery against him.* **3.** to promote (a person).

preferable (pref-er-ăbŭl) *adj.* more desirable. **preferably** *adv.*

preference (pref-er-ěns) *n.* **1.** preferring,

being preferred, *do this in preference to that.* **2.** a thing preferred. **3.** a prior right to something. **4.** the favouring of one person or country etc. rather than another. □ **preference shares** or **stock,** that on which dividend is paid before profits are distributed to holders of ordinary shares etc.

preferential (pref-er-**en**-shăl) *adj.* giving or receiving preference, *preferential treatment.*

preferment *n.* promotion.

prefix *n.* (*pl.* prefixes) **1.** a word or syllable (e.g. *co-, ex-, non-, out-, pre-*) placed in front of a word to add to or change its meaning. **2.** a title (e.g. *Mr*) placed before a name. —**prefix** *v.* **1.** to put as a prefix. **2.** to put as an introduction.

pregnant *adj.* **1.** (of a woman or female animal) having a child or young developing in the womb. **2.** full of meaning, significant, *there was a pregnant pause.* **3.** full, *the situation was pregnant with danger.* **pregnancy** *n.*

prehensile (pri-**hen**-syl) *adj.* (of an animal's foot or tail etc.) able to grasp things.

prehistoric *adj.* **1.** of the ancient period before written records of events were made. **2.** (*informal*) completely out of date.

prehistory *n.* prehistoric events or times, the study of these.

prejudge *v.* to form a judgement on (a person or action etc.) before a proper inquiry is held or before full information is available.

prejudice *n.* **1.** an unreasoning opinion or like or dislike of something, *racial prejudice,* prejudice against people of other races. **2.** harm to someone's rights etc. **prejudice** *v.* **1.** to cause (a person) to have a prejudice. **2.** to cause harm to, *it may prejudice our rights.* □ **without prejudice,** (of an offer made for the purpose of settling a dispute) which must not be interpreted as an admission of liability, or used in evidence.

prejudiced *adj.* having a prejudice.

prejudicial (prej-oo-**dish**-ăl) *adj.* harmful to someone's rights or claims etc.

prelate (**prel**-ăt) *n.* a clergyman of high rank.

preliminary *adj.* coming before a main action or event etc. and preparing for it, *some preliminary negotiations.* —*n.* a preliminary action or event or examination etc.

prelude (**prel**-yood) *n.* **1.** an action or event that precedes another and leads up to it. **2.** the introductory part of a poem etc. **3.** (in music) an introductory move-

ment preceding a fugue or forming the first piece of a suite, a short piece of music of similar type.

pre-marital (pree-ma-rit'l) *adj.* of the time before marriage.

premature (**prem**-ă-tewr) *adj.* occurring or done before the usual or proper time, too early; *premature baby,* one born between 3 and 12 weeks before the expected time. **prematurely** *adv.*

premeditated (pree-**med**-i-tayt-id) *adj.* planned beforehand, *a premeditated crime.* **premeditation** *n.*

pre-menstrual (pree-**men**-stroo-ăl) *adj.* of the time immediately before each menstruation.

premier (**prem**-i-er) *adj.* first in importance or order or time. —*n.* a prime minister. —**premiership** *n.*

première (**prem**-yair) *n.* the first public performance or showing of a play or film.

premise (**prem**-iss) *n.* = premiss.

premises (**prem**-i-siz) *pl. n.* a house or other building with its grounds and outbuildings etc.; *on the premises,* in the buildings or grounds concerned.

premiss (**prem**-iss) *n.* a statement on which reasoning is based.

premium (**pree**-mi-ŭm) *n.* **1.** an amount or instalment to be paid for an insurance policy. **2.** an addition to ordinary wages or charges etc., a bonus. **3.** a fee for instruction, especially that paid by an apprentice. □ **at a premium,** above the nominal or usual price; highly valued or esteemed. **Premium Bond,** a government security that pays no interest but offers a chance of a cash prize at intervals. **put a premium on,** to attach especial value to; to provide an incentive for (a certain action etc.).

premonition (pree-mŏn-**ish**-ŏn) *n.* a presentiment. **premonitory** (pri-**mon**-it-er-i) *adj.*

preoccupation *n.* **1.** the state of being preoccupied. **2.** a thing that fills one's thoughts.

preoccupied *adj.* having one's thoughts deeply engaged in something, inattentive in manner because of this.

prep *n.* **1.** school work that a child is required to do outside lessons. **2.** a school period during which this is done. □ **prep school,** a preparatory school.

pre-pack *v.* to pack (goods) ready for sale before distributing them.

pre-package *v.* to pre-pack.

preparation *n.* **1.** preparing, being prepared. **2.** a thing done to make ready for something; *make preparations for,* prepare for. **3.** = prep. **4.** a substance or mixture prepared for use, e.g. as food or medicine, *a preparation of bismuth.*

preparatory (pri-**pa**-rä-ter-i) *adj.* preparing for something, *preparatory training.* — *adv.* in a preparatory way. □ **preparatory school**, a school where pupils are prepared for a higher school or (in America) for college or university.

prepare *v.* **1.** to make or get ready. **2.** to make (food or other substances) ready for use. □ **be prepared to**, to be ready and willing to (do something). **preparedness** (pri-**pair**-id-ness) *n.* readiness.

prepay *v.* (prepaid, prepaying) to pay (a charge) beforehand, to pay the postage of (a letter etc.) beforehand, e.g. by buying and affixing a stamp. **prepayment** *n.*

preponderant (pri-**pond**-er-ănt) *adj.* preponderating. **preponderantly** *adv.*, **preponderance** *n.*

preponderate (pri-**pond**-er-ayt) *v.* to be greater than others in number or intensity etc.

preposition *n.* a word used with a noun or pronoun to show place or position or time or means, e.g. *at* home, *in* the hall, *on* Sunday, *by* train. **prepositional** *adj.*

prepossessing *adj.* attractive, making a good impression, *not very prepossessing.*

preposterous (pri-**poss**-ter-ŭs) *adj.* utterly absurd, outrageous.

prepuce (**pree**-pewss) *n.* **1.** the foreskin. **2.** a similar structure at the tip of the clitoris.

Pre-Raphaelite (pree-**raf**-ĕ-lyt) *n.* one of a group of 19th-century artists who aimed at producing work in the style of the Italian artists of before the time of Raphael.

prerequisite (pree-**rek**-wiz-it) *adj.* required as a condition or in preparation for something else. —*n.* a prerequisite thing.

prerogative (pri-**rog**-ătiv) *n.* a right or privilege belonging to a particular person or group.

presage[1] (**pres**-ij) *n.* **1.** an omen. **2.** a presentiment.

presage[2] (pre-**sayj**) *v.* **1.** to foreshadow, to be an advance sign of. **2.** to predict.

Presbyterian (prezbi-**teer**-iăn) *adj.* of a **Presbyterian Church**, one governed by elders who are all of equal rank, especially the national Church of Scotland. —*n.* a member of the Presbyterian Church. — **Presbyterianism** *n.*

pre-school *adj.* of the time before a child is old enough to attend school.

prescribe *v.* **1.** to advise the use of (a medicine etc.). **2.** to lay down as a course or rule to be followed.

prescript (**pree**-skript) *n.* a law or rule or command.

prescription *n.* **1.** a doctor's written instruction for the composition and use of a medicine. **2.** the medicine prescribed in this way. **3.** prescribing.

presence *n.* **1.** being present in a place, *your presence is required.* **2.** a person's bearing, impressiveness of bearing, *has a fine presence.* **3.** a person or thing that is or seems to be present in a place, *felt a presence in the room.* □ **presence of mind**, ability to act quickly and in a practical way in an emergency.

present[1] (**prez**-ĕnt) *adj.* **1.** being in the place in question, *no one else was present.* **2.** being dealt with or discussed, *in the present case.* **3.** existing or occurring now, *the present Duke.* —*n.* present time, the time now passing. □ **at present**, now. **for the present**, for now, temporarily. **present-day** *adj.* of present times, modern.

present[2] (**prez**-ĕnt) *n.* something given or received as a gift.

present[3] (pri-**zent**) *v.* **1.** to give as a gift or award, to offer for acceptance; *the cheque has not been presented,* has not been handed in for payment. **2.** to introduce (a person) to another or others. **3.** to bring (a play or new product etc.) to the public. **4.** to show, to reveal, *presented a brave front to the world.* **5.** to level or aim (a weapon). **presenter** *n.* □ **present arms**, to hold a rifle etc. vertically in front of the body as a salute. **present oneself**, to appear or attend, e.g. for an examination.

presentable *adj.* fit to be presented to someone, of good appearance.

presentation *n.* **1.** presenting, being presented. **2.** something that is presented.

presentiment (pri-**zent**-i-měnt) *n.* a feeling of something that is about to happen, a foreboding.

presently *adv.* **1.** soon, after a short time. **2.** (*Scottish & Amer.*) now.

preservation *n.* preserving, being preserved.

preservative *adj.* preserving things. —*n.* a substance that preserves perishable foods.

preserve *v.* **1.** to keep safe, to keep in an unchanged condition. **2.** to keep from decay, to treat (food, e.g. fruit or meat) so that it can be kept for future use. **3.** to keep (game, or a river etc.) undisturbed, for private use. —**preserve** *n.* **1.** (also *preserves*) preserved fruit, jam. **2.** an area where game or fish are preserved. **3.** activities or interests etc. regarded as belonging to a particular person. — **preserver** *n.*

pre-set v. (pre-set, pre-setting) to set beforehand.

pre-shrunk adj. (of fabric) subjected to a shrinking process before being used or sold, so that it will not shrink further when laundered.

preside v. to be president or chairman, to have the position of authority or control.

president n. 1. a person who is the head of a club or society or council etc. 2. the head of a republic. **presidency** n., **presidential** (prez-i-**den**-shăl) adj.

press¹ v. 1. to apply weight or force steadily to (a thing). 2. to squeeze juice etc. from. 3. to make by pressing. 4. to flatten or smooth, to iron (clothes etc.). 5. to exert pressure on (an enemy etc.), to oppress. 6. to urge or entreat, to demand insistently, *press for a 35-hour week.* 7. to force the acceptance of, *they pressed sweets upon us.* 8. to insist upon, *don't press that point.* 9. to throng closely. 10. to push one's way. 11. (in golf) to strike the ball imperfectly by trying too hard for a long hit. —**press** n. 1. pressing, *give it a slight press.* 2. crowding, a throng of people. 3. hurry, pressure of affairs, *the press of modern life.* 4. an instrument or machinery for compressing or flattening or shaping something. 5. a printing-press, a printing or publishing firm. 6. newspapers and periodicals, the people involved in writing or producing these, *a press photographer.* 7. a large cupboard with shelves for linen or books. □ **be pressed for**, to have barely enough of, *we are pressed for time.* **press conference**, an interview given to journalists by a person who wishes to make an announcement or answer questions. **press cutting**, a cutting from a newspaper. **press-stud** n. a small fastener for clothes etc., with two parts that engage when pressed together. **press-ups** pl. n. an exercise in which a person lies face downwards and presses down on his hands so that the shoulders and trunk are raised.

press² v. (old use) to force to serve in the army or navy. **press-gang** n. a group who coerce people into doing something, (v.) to force into doing or joining something. **press into service**, to bring into use as a makeshift.

pressing adj. 1. urgent, *a pressing need.* 2. urging something strongly, *a pressing invitation.* —n. a thing made by pressing, a gramophone record or series of these made at one time.

pressure n. 1. the exertion of continuous force upon something. 2. the force exerted, that of the atmosphere, *pressure is high in*

eastern areas. 3. a compelling or oppressive influence, *is under pressure to vote against it; the pressures of business life.* —v. to pressurize (a person etc.). □ **pressure-cooker** n. a pan in which things can be cooked quickly by steam under high pressure. **pressure group**, an organized group seeking to influence policy by concerted action and intensive propaganda.

pressurize v. 1. to try to compel (a person) into some action. 2. to keep (a closed compartment, e.g. an aircraft cabin) at a constant atmospheric pressure. **pressurization** n.

prestige (press-**teezh**) n. respect for a person resulting from his good reputation, past achievements, etc.

prestigious (press-**tij**-ŭs) adj. having or bringing prestige.

presto adv. (especially in music) quickly. **hey presto!**, a conjuror's words used at a moment of sudden change.

pre-stressed adj. (of concrete) strengthened by means of stretched wires within it.

presumable adj. able to be presumed. **presumably** adv.

presume v. 1. to take for granted, to suppose to be true. 2. to take the liberty of doing something, to venture, *may we presume to advise you?* 3. to be presumptuous. □ **presume on**, to take unwarranted liberties because of, *they are presuming on her good nature.*

presumption n. 1. presuming a thing to be true, something presumed. 2. presumptuous behaviour.

presumptive adj. giving grounds for presumption. **heir presumptive**, see **heir**.

presumptuous (pri-**zump**-tew-ŭs) adj. behaving with impudent boldness, acting without authority. **presumptuously** adv., **presumptuousness** n.

presuppose v. 1. to take for granted. 2. to require as a prior condition, *effects presuppose causes.* **presupposition** n.

pre-tax adj. before tax has been deducted.

pretence n. 1. pretending, make-believe. 2. claim, e.g. to merit or knowledge. 3. pretentiousness.

pretend v. 1. to create a false appearance of something, either in play or so as to deceive others. 2. to claim falsely that one has or is something. 3. to lay claim, *he pretended to the title; pretended to exact knowledge,* claimed to have this. **pretendedly** adv.

pretender n. 1. a person who pretends. 2. a person who claims a throne or title etc.; *the Old Pretender and Young Preten-*

der, the son and grandson of James II, claimants to the British throne.

pretension *n.* **1.** the assertion of a claim to something. **2.** pretentiousness.

pretentious (pri-**ten**-shŭs) *adj.* showy, pompous. **pretentiously** *adv.*, **pretentiousness** *n.* ¶ Do not confuse with portentous.

preternatural (pree-ter-**nach**-er-ăl) *adj.* outside the ordinary course of nature, unusual. **preternaturally** *adv.*

pretext (**pree**-tekst) *n.* a reason put forward to conceal one's true reason.

Pretoria (pri-**tor**-iă) the administrative capital of South Africa.

prettify *v.* (prettified, prettifying) to make (a thing) look superficially pretty or pleasing.

pretty *adj.* (prettier, prettiest) **1.** attractive in a delicate way. **2.** considerable; *cost me a pretty penny*, a lot of money. —*adv.* fairly, moderately, *pretty good*. —**prettily** *adv.*, **prettiness** *n.* □ **pretty much** *or* **nearly** *or* **well**, almost. **pretty-pretty** *adj.* with the prettiness overdone.

pretzel (**pret**-zĕl) *n.* a crisp knot-shaped biscuit flavoured with salt.

prevail *v.* **1.** to be victorious, to gain the mastery. **2.** to be more usual or frequent than others, to exist or occur generally, *the prevailing wind*. □ **prevail on**, to persuade.

prevalent (**prev**-ă-lĕnt) *adj.* existing or occurring generally, widespread. **prevalently** *adv.*, **prevalence** *n.*

prevaricate (pri-**va**-ri-kayt) *v.* to speak evasively or misleadingly. **prevarication** *n.*, **prevaricator** *n.*

prevent *v.* **1.** to keep (a thing) from happening, to make impossible. **2.** to keep (a person) from doing something. **prevention** *n.*

preventable *adj.* able to be prevented.

preventative *adj.* preventive. —*n.* a preventive.

preventive *adj.* preventing something. —*n.* a thing that prevents something. □ **preventive detention**, imprisonment of a person who is thought likely to commit a crime. **preventive medicine**, the branch of medicine concerned with the prevention of disease.

preview *n.* an advance showing or viewing of a film or play etc. before it is shown to the general public.

previous *adj.* **1.** coming before in time or order. **2.** done or acting prematurely, *you have been a little too previous*. **previously** *adv.*

pre-war *adj.* existing or occurring before a certain war, especially before that of 1914–18 or 1939–45.

prey (*pr.* pray) *n.* **1.** an animal that is hunted or killed by another for food. **2.** a person or thing that falls victim to an enemy or fear or disease etc. —*v.* (preyed, preying) **prey on**, to seek or take as prey; to have a harmful influence on, *the problem preyed on his mind*. □ **bird** *or* **beast of prey**, one that kills and eats four-footed animals or other birds.

price *n.* **1.** the amount of money for which a thing is bought or sold. **2.** the odds in betting. **3.** what must be given or done etc. in order to achieve something, *peace at any price*. —*v.* to fix or find or estimate the price of. □ **a price on someone's head** *or* **life**, a reward offered for his capture or killing. **at a price**, at a high cost. **price oneself out of the market**, to charge such a high price for one's goods or services that no one will buy them.

priceless *adj.* **1.** invaluable. **2.** (*slang*) very amusing or absurd.

pricey *adj.* (pricier, priciest) (*informal*) expensive.

prick *v.* **1.** to pierce slightly, to make a tiny hole in. **2.** to goad by causing mental awareness, *my conscience is pricking me*. **3.** to feel a pricking sensation. **4.** to mark (a pattern etc.) with pricks or dots. —**prick** *n.* **1.** pricking, a mark or puncture made by this. **2.** (*vulgar*) the penis, (*contemptuous*) a man. —**pricker** *n.* □ **prick out**, to plant out (seedlings) in small holes pricked in soil. **prick up one's ears**, (of a dog) to raise the ears erect when on the alert; (of a person) to become suddenly attentive.

prickle *n.* **1.** a small thorn. **2.** one of the hard-pointed spines on a hedgehog etc. **3.** a pricking sensation. —*v.* to feel or cause a sensation of pricking.

prickly *adj.* (pricklier, prickliest) **1.** having prickles. **2.** (of a person) irritable, touchy. **prickliness** *n.* □ **prickly pear**, a kind of cactus with pear-shaped edible fruit; its fruit.

pride *n.* **1.** a feeling of pleasure or satisfaction in one's actions or qualities or possessions etc. **2.** a person or thing that is a source of pride. **3.** a proper sense of what is fitting for one's position or character, self-respect. **4.** unduly high opinion of one's own qualities or merits. **5.** a company (of lions). —*v.* **pride oneself on**, to be proud of. □ **pride of place**, the most prominent position.

priest *n.* **1.** a clergyman. **2.** a person who is appointed to perform religious rites in non-Christian religions. **priestess** *n.*, **priesthood** *n.*

priestly *adj.* of or like or suitable for a priest.

prig *n.* a self-righteous person, one who displays or demands exaggerated correctness, especially in behaviour. **priggish** *adj.*

prim *adj.* (primmer, primmest) stiffly formal and precise in manner or appearance or behaviour, disliking what is rough or improper. **primly** *adv.*, **primness** *n.*

prima (pree-mă) *adj.* **prima ballerina**, the chief female dancer in a ballet. **prima donna**, the chief female singer in an opera.

primacy (pry-mă-si) *n.* **1.** pre-eminence. **2.** the office of a primate of the Church.

prima facie (pry-mă fay-shee) at first sight, based on a first impression; *made out a prima facie case against him*, one that seemed, at first sight, to be valid.

primal (pry-măl) *adj.* **1.** primitive, primeval. **2.** chief, fundamental.

primary *adj.* **1.** earliest in time or order, first in a series, *the primary meaning of a word.* **2.** of the first importance, chief. **primarily** (pry-mer-ili) *adv.* □ **primary colours**, those colours from which all others can be made by mixing, (of paint) red and yellow and blue, (of light) red and green and violet. **primary education** *or* **school**, that in which the rudiments of knowledge are taught, elementary.

primate (pry-măt) *n.* **1.** an archbishop; *Primate of England,* Archbishop of York; *Primate of all England,* Archbishop of Canterbury. **2.** a member of the highly-developed order of animals that includes man, apes, and monkeys.

prime¹ *adj.* **1.** chief, most important, *the prime cause.* **2.** first-rate, excellent, *prime beef.* **3.** basic, fundamental. —*n.* the state of greatest perfection, the best part, *in the prime of life.* □ **prime minister**, the chief minister in a government. **prime number**, a number (e.g. 2, 3, 5, 7, 11) that can be divided exactly only by itself and unity.

prime² *v.* **1.** to prepare (a thing) for use or action; *prime a pump,* cause liquid to flow into it to start it working. **2.** to prepare (a surface) for painting by coating it with a substance that prevents the first coat of paint from being absorbed. **3.** to equip (a person) with information. **4.** to give (a person) plenty of food or drink in preparation for something.

primer¹ (pry-mer) *n.* a substance used to prime a surface for painting.

primer² (pry-mer) *n.* an elementary textbook.

primeval (pry-mee-văl) *adj.* of the earliest times of the world, ancient.

primitive *adj.* **1.** of or at an early stage of civilization, *primitive tribes.* **2.** simple or crude, using unsophisticated techniques, *primitive tools.* **primitively** *adv.*

primogeniture (pry-mŏ-jen-i-cher) *n.* **1.** the fact of being a first-born child. **2.** the system by which an eldest son inherits all his parents' property.

primordial (pry-mor-di-ăl) *adj.* primeval.

primrose *n.* **1.** a plant bearing pale yellow flowers in spring. **2.** its flower. **3.** pale yellow. □ **primrose path**, a way of life devoted to ease and pleasure.

primula *n.* a perennial plant (of a kind including the primrose and polyanthus) with clusters of flowers in various colours.

Primus (pry-mŭs) *n.* (*trade mark*) a portable cooking stove burning vaporized oil as fuel.

prince *n.* **1.** a male member of a royal family, (in Britain) a son or grandson of the sovereign. **2.** a ruler, especially of a small State, *Prince Rainier of Monaco.* **3.** a nobleman of various countries. □ **prince consort**, a title conferred on the husband (who is himself a prince) of a reigning queen. **Prince Edward Island**, a province of Canada. **Prince of Wales**, a title usually conferred on the heir apparent to the British throne.

princely *adj.* **1.** of a prince, worthy of a prince. **2.** splendid, generous.

princess *n.* **1.** the wife of a prince. **2.** a female member of a royal family, (in Britain) a daughter or granddaughter of the sovereign. —*adj.* (of a woman's garment) made in panels extending from shoulder to hem and with a flared skirt, *princess style.* □ **princess royal**, a title that may be conferred on the eldest daughter of the British sovereign.

principal *adj.* first in rank or importance, chief. —*n.* **1.** the person with highest authority in an organization etc., the head of certain schools or colleges. **2.** a person who takes a leading part in an activity or in a play etc. **3.** a person for whom another acts as agent, *I must consult my principal.* **4.** a capital sum as distinguished from the interest or income on it. □ **principal boy**, the leading male part in a pantomime, traditionally played by a woman.

¶ Do not confuse with *principle*, which is never used of a person.

principality (prin-si-pal-iti) *n.* a country ruled by a prince; *the Principality,* Wales.

principally *adv.* for the most part, chiefly.

principle *n.* **1.** a basic truth or a general law or doctrine that is used as a basis of reasoning or a guide to action or behaviour.

2. a personal code of right conduct, *a man of principle*; *has no principles*. **3.** a general or scientific law shown in the way something works or used as the basis for the construction of a machine etc. □ **in principle**, as regards the main elements but not necessarily the details. **on principle**, because of the principles of conduct one accepts, *we refused on principle*. ¶ See the note under principal.

print *v.* **1.** to press (a mark or design etc.) on a surface, to impress or stamp (a surface or fabric etc.) in this way. **2.** to produce (lettering on a book or newspaper etc.) by applying inked type to paper, to publish in this way. **3.** to write with letters like those used in printing books etc. **4.** to produce a positive picture from (a photographic negative or transparency) by transmission of light. —**print** *n.* **1.** a mark or indentation left where something has pressed on a surface. **2.** printed lettering or writing, words in printed form. **3.** a printed picture or design. **4.** printed cotton fabric. □ **in print**, available from a publisher, not out of print. **out of print**, = all copies have been sold. **printed circuit**, an electric circuit with thin strips of conducting material on a flat insulating sheet (instead of wires). **print-out** *n.* material produced in printed form from a computer or teleprinter.

printer *n.* **1.** a person whose job or business is the printing of books, newspapers, etc. **2.** a printing instrument.

prior[1] *adj.* earlier, coming before another or others in time or order or importance. —*adv.* **prior to**, before, *prior to that date*.

prior[2] *n.* the monk who is head of a religious house or order or (in an abbey) ranking next below an abbot. **prioress** *n.*

priority *n.* **1.** being earlier or more important, precedence in rank etc, the right to be first. **2.** something that is more important than other items or considerations, *has got his priorities wrong*.

priory *n.* a monastery governed by a prior, a nunnery governed by a prioress.

prise *v.* to force out or open by leverage.

prism *n.* **1.** a solid geometric shape with ends that are similar, equal, and parallel. **2.** a transparent body of this form, usually triangular and made of glass, that breaks up light into the colours of the rainbow.

prismatic (priz-**mat**-ik) *adj.* **1.** of or like a prism. **2.** (of colours) formed or distributed as if by a prism, rainbow-like. **prismatically** *adv.*

prison *n.* **1.** a building used to confine people who are convicted or (in certain cases) accused of crimes. **2.** any place of custody or confinement. **3.** imprisonment as a punishment. □ **prison-camp** *n.* a camp serving as a prison for prisoners of war etc.

prisoner *n.* **1.** a person kept in prison. **2.** a person who is in custody and on trial for a criminal offence, *prisoner at the bar*. **3.** a captive. **4.** a person or thing kept in confinement or held in another's grasp etc. □ **prisoner of war**, an enemy captured in a war.

prissy *adj.* prim.

pristine (**pris**-teen) *adj.* **1.** ancient and unspoilt, *of some pristine era*. **2.** fresh as if new, *a pristine layer of snow*. (¶ Many people object to the use in sense 2.)

privacy (**priv**-ăsi) *n.* being private, seclusion.

private *adj.* **1.** of or belonging to a particular person or persons, not public, *private property*. **2.** not holding public office, *speaking as a private citizen*; *in private life*, as a private person, not as an official or public performer etc. **3.** not to be made known publicly, confidential. **4.** (of a place) secluded. **5.** of or belonging to a profession practised on one's own financial account and not as an employee of a government, *private medicine*; *private patients*, those treated by a doctor etc. for payment and not under a public health service; *private ward*, a hospital ward for private patients. —*n.* a soldier of the lowest rank. —**privately** *adv.* □ **in private**, in the presence only of the person(s) directly concerned, not in public. **private detective**, one who undertakes investigations etc. for a fee, not as a member of a police force. **private enterprise**, management of business by private individuals or companies (contrasted with State ownership or control); an individual's initiative. **private eye**, (*informal*) a private detective. **private hotel**, a hotel that is not obliged to accept all comers. **private means**, an income available from investments etc., not as an earned wage or salary. **private member**, an MP not holding a government appointment. **private parts**, the genitals. **private school**, a school supported wholly by pupils' fees or endowments. **private soldier**, an ordinary soldier, other than officers.

privation (pry-**vay**-shŏn) *n.* loss or lack of something, especially of the necessaries of life.

privet (**priv**-it) *n.* a bushy evergreen shrub with small leaves, much used for hedges.

privilege *n.* a special right or advantage granted to one person or group.

privileged *adj.* having privileges.

privy *adj.* (*old use*) hidden, secret. —*n.* (*old use & Amer.*) a lavatory. —**privily** *adv.* □ **be privy to,** to be sharing in the secret of (a person's plans etc.). **Privy Council,** a body of distinguished people advising the sovereign on matters of State. **Privy Counsellor,** a member of the Privy Council. **privy purse,** an allowance from public revenue for the sovereign's private expenses. **privy seal,** a State seal formerly affixed to documents of minor importance; *Lord Privy Seal,* a senior Cabinet Minister without official duties (formerly keeper of the privy seal).

prize[1] *n.* **1.** an award given as a symbol of victory or superiority. **2.** something striven for or worth striving for. **3.** something that can be won in a lottery etc. —*adj.* winning or likely to win a prize, excellent of its kind. —*v.* to value highly. □ **prize-fighter** *n.* a professional boxer. **prize-winner** *n.* the winner of a prize.

prize[2] *n.* a ship or property captured at sea during a war.

prize[0] *v.* = prise.

pro *n.* (*pl.* pros) (*informal*) a professional.

pro and con for and against. **pros and cons,** arguments for and against something.

probability *n.* **1.** being probable. **2.** something that is probable, the most probable event. **3.** a ratio expressing the chances that a certain event will occur. □ **in all probability,** most probably.

probable *adj.* likely to happen or be true. —*n.* a candidate likely to be successful, one who will probably become a member of a team. —**probably** *adv.*

probate (proh-bayt) *n.* **1.** the official process of proving that a will is valid. **2.** a copy of a will with a certificate that it is valid, handed to executors.

probation *n.* **1.** the testing of a person's behaviour or abilities etc. **2.** a system whereby certain offenders are supervised by an official (*probation officer*) as an alternative to imprisonment. **probationary** *adj.*

probationer *n.* a person who is undergoing a probationary period of testing, e.g. a hospital nurse at an early stage of training.

probe *n.* **1.** a device for exploring an otherwise inaccessible place or object etc., a blunt-ended surgical instrument for exploring a wound; *space probe,* an unmanned exploratory spacecraft transmitting information about its environment etc. **2.** a penetrating investigation, *ordered a probe into their expense accounts.* —**probe** *v.*

1. to explore with a probe. **2.** to penetrate with something sharp. **3.** to make a penetrating investigation of.

probity (proh-biti) *n.* honesty, integrity.

problem *n.* **1.** something difficult to deal with or understand. **2.** something difficult that has to be accomplished or answered or dealt with.

problematic *or* **problematical** *adj.* difficult to deal with or understand. **problematically** *adv.*

proboscis (prŏ-boss-iss) *n.* **1.** a long flexible snout, an elephant's trunk. **2.** an elongated mouth-part in certain insects, used for sucking things.

procedure *n.* a series of actions done or appointed to be done in order to accomplish something, a way of conducting business. **procedural** *adj.*

proceed (prŏ-seed) *v.* **1.** to go forward or onward, to make one's way. **2.** to continue, to carry on an activity, *please proceed with your work.* **3.** to start a lawsuit, *he proceeded against the newspaper for libel.* **4.** to come forth, to originate, *the evils that proceed from war.*

proceedings *pl. n.* **1.** a lawsuit, *start proceedings for divorce.* **2.** what takes place at a formal meeting of a society etc. **3.** a published report of a discussion or conference etc., *Proceedings of the Royal Society.*

proceeds (proh-seedz) *pl. n.* the amount of money produced by a sale or performance etc.

process[1] (proh-sess) *n.* **1.** a series of actions or operations used in making or manufacturing or achieving something. **2.** a series of changes, a natural operation, *the digestive process.* **3.** a course of events or time. **4.** a lawsuit, a summons or writ. **5.** a natural projection on the body or on a plant. —**process** *v.* **1.** to put through a manufacturing or other process or course of treatment; *your application is being processed,* is being dealt with. **2.** to perform operations on (data). □ **processed cheese,** cheese treated to avoid further ripening or deterioration during storage. **processer** *n.* a person who processes things. **processor** *n.* a machine that processes things.

process[2] (prŏ-sess) *v.* to go in procession.

procession *n.* a number of people or vehicles or boats etc. going along in an orderly line. **processional** *adj.*

proclaim *v.* **1.** to announce officially or publicly, to declare. **2.** to make known unmistakably as being, *his accent proclaimed him a Scot.* **proclamation** *n.*

proclivity (prŏ-kliv-iti) *n.* a tendency.

procrastinate (prŏ-**kras**-tin-ayt) *v.* to postpone action, to be dilatory. **procrastination** *n.*, **procrastinator** *n.*

procreate (proh-kri-**ayt**) *v.* to bring (a living thing) into existence by the natural process of reproduction, to generate. **procreation** *n.*

procrustean (prŏ-**krust**-iăn) *adj.* seeking to enforce conformity with a theory etc. by violent methods (e.g. by omitting all that contradicts it). ¶ Named after Procrustes, a robber in Greek legend, who fitted victims to his bed by stretching them or lopping bits off.

proctor *n.* either of two officials at Oxford and Cambridge universities, with disciplinary functions. **Queen's** *or* **King's Proctor,** an official with the right to intervene in certain legal cases (e.g. probate and divorce) where suppression of facts is alleged.

procurable *adj.* able to be procured.

procuration (prok-yoor-**ay**-shŏn) *n.* procuring.

procurator (**prok**-yoor-ayt-er) *n.* an agent or proxy. **procurator fiscal,** (in Scotland) the public prosecutor and coroner of a district.

procure *v.* to obtain by care or effort, to acquire. **procurement** *n.* □ **procurer** *n.* one who procures something; a pimp. **procuress** (prŏ-**kewr**-ess) *n.* a female pimp.

prod *v.* (prodded, prodding) **1.** to poke. **2.** to urge or stimulate into action. —**prod** *n.* **1.** a poke. **2.** a stimulus to action. **3.** a pointed instrument for prodding things.

prodigal *adj.* **1.** recklessly wasteful or extravagant. **2.** lavish. —*n.* a recklessly extravagant person. **prodigally** *adv.*, **prodigality** (prod-i-**gal**-iti) *n.*

prodigious (prŏ-**dij**-us) *adj.* **1.** marvellous, amazing, *a prodigious achievement.* **2.** enormous, *spent a prodigious amount.* **prodigiously** *adv.*

prodigy (**prod**-iji) *n.* **1.** a person with exceptional qualities or abilities, a child with abilities very much beyond those appropriate to his age. **2.** a marvellous thing, a wonderful example of something.

produce¹ (prŏ-**dewss**) *v.* **1.** to bring forward for inspection or consideration or use, *will produce evidence.* **2.** to bring (a play or performance etc.) before the public. **3.** to bring into existence, to cause (a reaction or sensation etc.), to bear or yield (offspring or products). **4.** to manufacture. **5.** to extend (a line).

produce² (**prod**-yewss) *n.* **1.** an amount or thing produced. **2.** agricultural and natural products, *dairy produce.*

producer *n.* **1.** a person producing articles or agricultural products etc. (contrasted with a *consumer*). **2.** one who directs the acting of a play. **3.** one who is responsible for control of expenditure, schedule, and quality in the production of a film or a broadcast programme.

product *n.* **1.** something produced by a natural process or by agriculture or manufacture or as a result. **2.** (in mathematics) the result obtained by multiplying two quantities together.

production *n.* **1.** producing, being produced; *go into production,* begin being manufactured. **2.** a thing produced, especially a play or film. **3.** the amount produced. □ **production line,** a sequence of machines and workers through which things move to undergo successive stages of production.

productive *adj.* tending or able to produce things, especially in large quantities. **productively** *adv.*, **productiveness** *n.*

productivity *n.* productiveness, efficiency in industrial production.

profane (prŏ-**fayn**) *adj.* **1.** secular, not sacred, *sacred and profane music.* **2.** irreverent, blasphemous. —*v.* to treat (a thing) with irreverence or lack of due respect. —**profanely** *adv.*, **profanity** (prŏ-**fan**-iti) *n.*

profess *v.* **1.** to state that one has (a quality or feeling etc.), to pretend, *she professed ignorance* or *to be ignorant of this law.* **2.** to affirm one's faith in (a religion).

professed *adj.* **1.** avowed, openly acknowledged by oneself, *a professed Christian.* **2.** falsely claiming to be something, *a professed friend.* **3.** having taken the vows of a religious order, *a professed nun.* **professedly** (prŏ-**fess**-idli) *adv.*

profession *n.* **1.** an occupation, especially one that involves knowledge and training in a branch of advanced learning, *the dental profession.* **2.** the people engaged in an occupation of this kind. **3.** a declaration or avowal, *made professions of loyalty.*

professional *adj.* **1.** of or belonging to a profession or its members. **2.** having or showing the skill of a professional. **3.** doing a certain kind of work as a full-time occupation or to make a living or (of sportsmen, contrasted with *amateur*) for payment. —**professional** *n.* **1.** a person working or performing for payment. **2.** someone highly skilled. —**professionally** *adv.* □ **professional foul,** a deliberate foul committed in order to halt the game when a member of the opposing team seems virtually certain to score.

professionalism *n.* the qualities or skills of a profession or professionals.

professor *n.* a university teacher of the highest rank. **professorship** *n.*, **professorial** (prof-i-**sor**-iăl) *adj.*

proffer (**prof**-er) *v.* to offer. —*n.* an offer.

proficient (prŏ-**fish**-ĕnt) *adj.* doing something correctly and competently through training or practice, skilled. **proficiently** *adv.*, **proficiency** *n.*

profile (**proh**-fyl) *n.* 1. a side view, especially of the human face. 2. a drawing or other representation of this. 3. a short account of a person's character or career.

profit *n.* 1. an advantage or benefit obtained from doing something. 2. money gained in a business transaction, the excess of returns over outlay. —**profit** *v.* (profited, profiting) 1. to bring advantage to. 2. to obtain an advantage or benefit.

profitable *adj.* bringing profit or benefits. **profitably** *adv.*, **profitability** *n.*

profiteer *n.* a person who makes excessive profits, especially by taking advantage of times of difficulty or scarcity (e.g. in war). **profiteering** *n.* being a profiteer.

profiterole (prŏ-**fit**-er-ohl) *n.* a small hollow cake of choux pastry with sweet or savoury filling.

profligate (**prof**-lig-ăt) *adj.* 1. recklessly wasteful or extravagant. 2. dissolute. —*n.* a profligate person. —**profligacy** *n.*

pro forma as a matter of form. (¶ Latin.)

profound *adj.* 1. deep, intense, *takes a profound interest in it.* 2. having or showing great knowledge of or insight into a subject. **profoundly** *adv.*, **profundity** *n.*

profuse (prŏ-**fewss**) *adj.* 1. lavish, extravagant, *profuse gratitude.* 2. plentiful, *a profuse variety.* **profusely** *adv.*, **profuseness** *n.*

profusion (prŏ-**few**-zhŏn) *n.* abundance, a plentiful supply, *a profusion of roses.*

progenitor (proh-**jen**-it er) *n.* an ancestor.

progeny (**proj**-ini) *n.* offspring, descendants.

progesterone (prŏ-**jest**-er-ohn) *n.* a hormone that prevents ovulation.

prognosis (prog-**noh**-sis) *n.* an advance indication, a forecast of the course of a disease.

prognostication (prŏg-nos-ti-**kay**-shŏn) *n.* a forecast.

program *n.* 1. (*Amer.*) = programme. 2. a series of coded instructions for a computer or electronic calculator. —*v.* (programmed, programming) to instruct (a computer etc.) by means of a program. — **programmer** *n.*

programmable *adj.* able to be programmed.

programme *n.* 1. a plan of intended procedure. 2. a descriptive notice or list of an organized series of events (e.g. of a concert or a course of study). 3. these events. 4. a broadcast performance.

progress [1] (**proh**-gress) *n.* 1. forward or onward movement. 2. an advance or development, especially to a better state. □ **in progress**, taking place, in the course of occurring.

progress [2] (prŏ-**gress**) *v.* 1. to move forward or onward. 2. to advance or develop, especially to a better state. 3. to deal with at successive stages, *allow them to progress their own work to completion.* **progression** *n.*

progressive *adj.* 1. making continuous forward movement. 2. proceeding steadily or in regular degrees, *a progressive improvement.* 3. (of a card-game or dance etc.) with a periodic change of partners. 4. (of a disease) gradually increasing in its effect. 5. advancing in social conditions or efficiency etc., *a progressive nation* or *firm.* 6. favouring rapid progress or reform, *a progressive party* or *policy.* —*n.* one who favours a progressive policy. —**progressively** *adv.*, **progressiveness** *n.*

prohibit *v.* (prohibited, prohibiting) to forbid. **prohibition** *n.*

prohibitive *adj.* preventing or intended to prevent the use or abuse or purchase of something, *prohibitive taxes.*

project [1] (prŏ-**jekt**) *v.* 1. to extend outward from a surface, *a projecting balcony.* 2. to cast or throw outward. 3. to cause (a picture or shadow) to fall on a surface. 4. to imagine (a thing or oneself) in another situation or another person's feelings or a future time. 5. to plan (a scheme or course of action). 6. to represent (a solid thing) systematically on a plane surface, as maps of the earth are made.

project [2] (**proj**-ekt) *n.* 1. a plan or scheme or undertaking. 2. a task set as an educational exercise, requiring students to do their own research and present the results.

projectile (prŏ-**jek**-tyl) *n.* a missile (e.g. a bullet or arrow or rocket) that can be projected forcefully.

projection *n.* 1. projecting, being projected. 2. something that projects from a surface. 3. a thing that is projected. 4. a representation of the surface of the earth on a plane surface. 5. an estimate of future situations or trends etc. based on a study of present ones.

projectionist *n.* a person whose job is to operate a projector.

projector *n.* an apparatus for projecting photographs or a cinema film etc. on to a screen.

prolapse[1] (prŏ-**laps**) v. (of an organ of the body) to slip forward or down out of its place.

prolapse[2] (**proh**-laps) n. the prolapsing of an organ of the body.

prole n. (*informal*) a member of the proletariat.

proletarian (proh-li-**tair**-iăn) adj. of the proletariat. —n. a member of the proletariat.

proletariat (proh-li-**tair**-iăt) n. the working class (contrasted with the bourgeoisie).

proliferate (prŏ-**lif**-er-ayt) v. to produce new growth or offspring rapidly, to multiply. **proliferation** n.

prolific (prŏ-**lif**-ik) adj. producing much fruit or many flowers or offspring; *a prolific writer*, one who writes many works. **prolifically** adv.

prologue (**proh**-log) n. 1. an introduction to a poem or play etc. 2. an act or event serving as an introduction to something.

prolong (prŏ-**long**) v. to lengthen (a thing) in extent or duration. **prolongation** (proh-long-**ay**-shŏn) n. □ **prolonged** adj. continuing for a long time.

prom n. (*informal*) 1. a promenade along a sea front. 2. a promenade concert.

promenade (prom-ĕn-**ahd**) n. 1. a leisurely walk in a public place. 2. a paved public walk (especially along a sea front), an esplanade. —v. to go or take for a promenade, to parade. □ **promenade concert**, one at which part of the audience is not seated and can move about. **promenade deck**, an upper deck on a passenger ship, where passengers may promenade.

prominent adj. 1. jutting out, projecting. 2. conspicuous. 3. important, well-known, *prominent citizens*. **prominently** adv., **prominence** n.

promiscuous (prŏ-**miss**-kew-ŭs) adj. 1. indiscriminate. 2. having sexual relations with many people. **promiscuously** adv., **promiscuity** (prom-iss-**kew**-iti) n.

promise n. 1. a declaration that one will give or do or not do a certain thing. 2. an indication of something that may be expected to come or occur. 3. an indication of future success or good results, *his work shows promise*. —**promise** v. 1. to make a promise to, to declare that one will give or do or not do something. 2. to make (a thing) seem likely; *it promises well*, seems likely to give good results. □ **Promised Land**, Canaan, which was promised by God to Abraham and his descendants; any place of expected happiness.

promising adj. likely to turn out well or produce good results.

promissory (**prom**-iss-er-i) adj. conveying a promise. **promissory note**, a signed promise to pay a sum of money.

promontory (**prom**-ŏn-ter-i) n. high land jutting out into the sea or a lake.

promote v. 1. to raise (a person) to a higher rank or office. 2. to initiate or help the progress of, *promote friendship between nations*. 3. to publicize (a product) in order to sell it. **promoter** n.

promotion n. promoting, being promoted. **promotional** adj.

prompt adj. 1. made or done or doing something without delay. 2. punctual. —adv. punctually. —**prompt** v. 1. to incite or stimulate (a person) to action. 2. to cause (a feeling or thought or action). 3. to assist by supplying (an actor or speaker) with words that should or could come next. —**promptly** adv., **promptness** n., **promptitude** n. □ **prompt side**, the side of a stage (usually to the actors' left) where the prompter is placed.

prompter n. a person (placed out of sight of the audience) who prompts actors on the stage.

promulgate (**prom**-ul-gayt) v. to make known to the public, to proclaim. **promulgation** n.

prone adj. 1. lying face downwards (contrasted with *supine*). 2. likely to do or suffer something, *prone to jealousy*; *strike-prone industries*. **proneness** n.

prong n. one of the projecting pointed parts of a fork. **pronged** adj. having a certain number or kind of prongs, *a three-pronged attack*, in three areas.

pronoun (**proh**-nown) n. a word used as a substitute for a noun; *demonstrative pronouns*, this, that, these, those; *interrogative pronouns*, who? what? which? etc.; *personal pronouns*, I, me, we, us, thou, thee, you, ye, he, him, she, her, it, they, them; *possessive pronouns*, my, your, etc.; *reflexive pronouns*, myself, oneself, etc.; *relative pronouns*, who, what, which, that.

pronounce v. 1. to utter (a speech-sound) distinctly or correctly or in a certain way, *can't pronounce the letter r*. 2. to declare formally, *I now pronounce you man and wife*. 3. to declare as one's opinion, *the wine was pronounced excellent*.

pronounced adj. definite, noticeable, *walks with a pronounced limp*.

pronouncement n. a declaration.

pronto adv. (*slang*) immediately.

pronunciation n. 1. the way a word is pronounced. 2. the way a person pronounces words. ¶ Note that the word should not be written or spoken as 'pronounciation'.

proof *n.* **1.** a fact or thing that shows or helps to show that something is true or exists. **2.** a demonstration of the truth of something, *in proof of my statement.* **3.** the process of testing whether something is true or good or valid, *put it to the proof.* **4.** a standard of strength for distilled alcoholic liquors, *80% proof.* **5.** a trial impression of printed matter, produced so that corrections can be made. **6.** a trial print of a photograph. —*adj.* able to resist or withstand penetration or damage, *bullet-proof; proof against the severest weather.* —**proof** *v.* **1.** to make a proof of (printed matter etc.). **2.** to make (a fabric) proof against something, especially water or bullets. □ **proofreader** *n.* a person employed to read and correct proofs. **proof-reading** *n.*

prop¹ *n.* **1.** a support used to keep something from falling or sagging. **2.** a person or thing depended on for support or help. —*v.* (propped, propping) to support with or as if with a prop, to keep from falling or failing, *prop it up.*

prop² *n.* (*informal*) a stage property.

propaganda *n.* publicity intended to spread ideas or information that will persuade or convince people.

propagate *v.* **1.** to breed or reproduce from parent stock, *propagate these plants from seeds or cuttings.* **2.** to spread (news or ideas etc.). **3.** to transmit, *the vibrations are propagated through the rock.* **propagation** *n.*, **propagator** *n.*

propel *v.* (propelled, propelling) to drive or push forward, to give an onward movement to. **propelling pencil**, one with a lead that can be moved forwards by turning the outer case.

propellant *n.* a propelling agent, e.g. an explosive that propels a bullet from a firearm, fuel that provides thrust for a rocket, compressed gas that forces out the contents of an aerosol container.

propeller *n.* a revolving device with blades for propelling a ship or aircraft to which it is fitted.

propensity (prŏ-**pen**-siti) *n.* a tendency or inclination, *a propensity to laziness.*

proper *adj.* **1.** suitable, appropriate, *not a proper time for singing.* **2.** correct, according to rules, *the proper way to hold the bat.* **3.** according to social conventions, respectable. **4.** strictly so called, *we drove from the suburbs to the city proper.* **5.** (*informal*) thorough, complete, *there was a proper row about it.* —**properly** *adv.* □ **proper fraction**, one that is less than unity, with the numerator less than the denominator, e.g.¾. **proper name** *or* **noun**, the name

of an individual person or thing, e.g. *Jane, London.*

property *n.* **1.** a thing or things owned. **2.** real estate, someone's land, *their property borders on ours.* **3.** a movable object (other than furniture or scenery) used on stage during a performance of a play etc. **4.** a quality or characteristic, *it has the property of dissolving grease.*

prophecy (**prof**-i-si) *n.* **1.** the power of prophesying, *the gift of prophecy.* **2.** a statement that tells what will happen.

prophesy (**prof**-i-sy) *v.* (prophesied, prophesying) to declare beforehand (what will happen), to foretell things as if by divine inspiration.

prophet *n.* **1.** a person who foretells the future. **2.** a religious teacher inspired by God. **prophetess** *n.* □ **the Prophet,** Muhammad.

prophetic (prŏ-**fet**-ik) *adj.* prophesying the future.

prophetical (prŏ-**fet**-ikăl) *adj.* **1.** of a prophet or prophets. **2.** prophetic. **prophetically** *adv.*

prophylactic (proh-fil-**ak**-tik) *adj.* tending to prevent a disease or misfortune. —*n.* a prophylactic substance or procedure. —**prophylactically** *adv.*

prophylaxis (proh-fil-**aks**-iss) *n.* preventive treatment against a disease etc.

propinquity (prŏ-**pink**-witi) *n.* nearness.

propitiate (prŏ-**pish**-i-ayt) *v.* to win the favour or forgiveness of, to placate. **propitiation** *n.*, **propitiatory** (prŏ-**pish**-ă-ter-i) *adj.*

propitious (prŏ-**pish**-ŭs) *adj.* favourable, giving a good omen or a suitable opportunity. **propitiously** *adv.*

proportion *n.* **1.** a fraction or share of a whole. **2.** a ratio, *the proportion of skilled workers to unskilled.* **3.** the correct relation in size or amount or degree between one thing and another or between parts of a thing. □ **proportioned** *adj.* having certain proportions, *a well-proportioned room.* **proportions** *pl. n.* size, dimensions, *a ship of majestic proportions.*

proportional *adj.* in correct proportion, corresponding in size or amount or degree. **proportionally** *adv.* □ **proportional representation,** an electoral system in which each party has a number of seats in proportion to the number of votes for its candidates.

proportionate *adj.* in proportion, corresponding, *the cost is proportionate to the quality.* **proportionately** *adv.*

proposal *n.* **1.** the proposing of something. **2.** the thing proposed. **3.** a request that a person should agree to be married to the person asking.

propose *v.* **1.** to put forward for consideration; *propose a toast,* ask people formally to drink a toast. **2.** to have and declare as one's plan or intention, *we propose to wait.* **3.** to nominate as a candidate. **4.** to make a proposal of marriage. **proposer** *n.*

proposition *n.* **1.** a statement, an assertion. **2.** a proposal, a scheme. **3.** (*informal*) a problem or undertaking, something to be dealt with, *not a paying proposition.* —*v.* (*informal*) to put a proposal to (a person), to suggest immoral sexual intercourse to (a woman).

propound *v.* to put forward for consideration. **propounder** *n.*

proprietary (prŏ-**pry**-ĕt-er-i) *adj.* **1.** manufactured and sold by one particular firm, usually under a patent, *proprietary medicines.* **2.** of an owner or ownership.

proprietor (prŏ-**pry**-ĕt-er) *n.* the owner of a business. **proprietress** *n.*

proprietorial (prŏ-pry-ĕ-**tor**-iăl) *adj.* of or indicating ownership.

propriety (prŏ-**pry**-ĕti) *n.* **1.** being proper or suitable. **2.** correctness of behaviour or morals; *the proprieties,* the requirements of correct behaviour in society.

propulsion *n.* the process of propelling or being propelled.

pro rata (proh **ray**-tă) proportional, proportionally, *if costs increase, there will be a pro rata increase in prices* or *prices will increase pro rata.* (¶ Latin, = according to the rate.)

prosaic (prŏ-**zay**-ik) *adj.* lacking poetic beauty or fantasy, unimaginative, plain and ordinary. **prosaically** *adv.*

proscenium (prŏ-**seen**-iŭm) *n.* the part of a theatre stage in front of the curtain, with its enclosing arch.

proscribe *v.* to forbid by law.

prose *n.* written or spoken language not in verse form.

prosecute *v.* **1.** to take legal proceedings against (a person etc.) for a crime. **2.** to carry on or conduct, *prosecuting their trade.* **prosecutor** *n.*

prosecution *n.* **1.** prosecuting, being prosecuted. **2.** the party prosecuting another for a crime.

proselyte (**pross**-i-lyt) *n.* a convert to a religion or opinion etc., especially to the Jewish faith.

proselytize (**pross**-il-i-tyz) *v.* to try to convert people to one's beliefs or opinions.

prosody (**pross**-ŏ-di) *n.* the study of verse-forms and poetic metres.

prospect[1] (**pross**-pekt) *n.* **1.** an extensive view of a landscape etc., a mental view

of matters. **2.** an expectation, a possibility, *prospects of success.* **3.** a chance of success or advancement, *a job with prospects.* **4.** a possible customer or client etc., a competitor likely to be successful.

prospect[2] (prŏ-**spekt**) *v.* to explore in search of something, *prospecting for gold.* **prospector** *n.*

prospective (prŏ-**spek**-tiv) *adj.* expected to be or to occur, future, possible, *prospective customers.*

prospectus (prŏ-**spek**-tŭs) *n.* a printed document describing and advertising the chief features of a school or business enterprise.

prosper *v.* to be successful, to thrive.

prosperous *adj.* financially successful. **prosperously** *adv.,* **prosperity** *n.*

prostate (**pross**-tayt) *n.* the **prostate gland,** a gland round the neck of the bladder in males. **prostatic** (prŏ-**stat**-ik) *adj.*

prosthesis (**pros**-thē-sis) *n.* (*pl.* prostheses) an artificial limb or similar appliance.

prostitute *n.* a woman who engages in promiscuous sexual intercourse for payment, a man who engages in homosexual acts for payment. —*v.* **1.** to make a prostitute of, *prostitute oneself.* **2.** to put to an unworthy use, *prostituting their artistic abilities.* —**prostitution** *n.*

prostrate[1] (**pross**-trayt) *adj.* **1.** face downwards. **2.** lying horizontally. **3.** overcome, exhausted, *prostrate with grief.*

prostrate[2] (pross-**trayt**) *v.* to cause to be prostrate; *prostrate oneself,* to cast oneself face downward on the ground in humility or adoration. **prostration** *n.*

prosy (**proh**-zi) *adj.* prosaic, dull.

protagonist (proh-**tag**-ŏn-ist) *n.* **1.** the chief person in a drama. **2.** one of the chief contenders in a contest. **3.** (*incorrect use,* as if the opposite of 'antagonist') an advocate or champion of a cause etc.

protect *v.* to keep from harm or injury. **protection** *n.*

protectionism *n.* the policy of protecting home industries from foreign competition, e.g. by controlling imports. **protectionist** *n.*

protective *adj.* protecting, giving protection. **protectively** *adv.*

protector *n.* a person or thing that protects something.

protectorate *n.* a weak or under-developed country that is under the official protection and partial control of a stronger one.

protégé (**prot**-ezhay) *n.* someone who is being helped by a person taking an interest in his welfare or career. **protégée**

(**prot**-ezhay) *n.* a female protégé.

protein (**proh**-teen) *n.* an organic compound containing nitrogen, occurring in plant and animal tissue and forming an essential part of the food of animals.

pro tem (*informal*) for the time being, temporarily. (¶ From the Latin *pro tempore*.)

protest[1] (**proh**-test) *n.* a statement or action showing one's disapproval of something. □ **under protest**, unwillingly and after making protests.

protest[2] (prŏ-**test**) *v.* 1. to express one's disapproval of something. 2. to declare firmly or solemnly, *protesting their innocence*. **protester** *n.*

Protestant (**prot**-i-stănt) *n.* a member of any of the Christian bodies that separated from the Church of Rome in the Reformation, or of their later branches. **Protestantism** *n.*

protestation (prot-i-**stay**-shŏn) *n.* a firm declaration, *protestations of loyalty*.

protocol (**proh**-tŏ-kol) *n.* 1. etiquette with regard to people's rank or status. 2. the first or original draft of an agreement (especially between States), signed by those making it, in preparation for a treaty.

proton (**proh** ton) *n.* a particle of matter with a positive electric charge.

protoplasm (**proh**-tŏ-plazm) *n.* a colourless jelly-like substance that is the main constituent of all animal and vegetable cells and tissues.

prototype (**proh**-tŏ-typ) *n.* a first or original example of something from which others have been or will be developed, a trial model (e.g. of an aircraft).

protract (prŏ-**trakt**) *v.* to prolong in duration. **protraction** *n.*

protractor *n.* an instrument for measuring angles, usually a semicircle marked off in degrees.

protrude *v.* to project from a surface. **protrusion** *n.*

protuberant (prŏ-**tew**-ber-ănt) *adj.* bulging outwards from a surface. **protuberance** *n.* a bulging part.

proud *adj.* 1. feeling or showing justifiable pride. 2. marked by such feeling, *a proud day for us.* 3. full of self-respect and independence, *too proud to ask for help.* 4. having an unduly high opinion of one's own qualities or merits. —*adv.* (*informal*) proudly; *they did us proud*, treated us lavishly or with great honour. —**proudly** *adv.*

provable *adj.* able to be proved.

prove *v.* 1. to give or be proof of. 2. to establish the validity of (a will). 3. to be

found to be, *it proved to be a good thing.* 4. (of dough) to rise because of the action of yeast, before being baked. □ **prove oneself**, to show that one has the required character or abilities.

proven (**proh**-věn) *adj.* proved, *a person of proven ability.* **not proven**, (in Scottish law) the evidence is insufficient to establish either guilt or innocence.

provenance (**prov**-in-ăns) *n.* a place of origin.

Provençal (prov-ahn-**sahl**) *adj.* of Provence, a region of southern France.

provender (**prov**-in-der) *n.* 1. fodder. 2. (*humorous*) food.

proverb *n.* a short well-known saying stating a general truth, e.g. *many hands make light work*. **Proverbs**, a book of the Old Testament, containing proverbs ascribed to Solomon.

proverbial (prŏ-**verb**-iăl) *adj.* 1. of or like a proverb, mentioned in a proverb. 2. well-known, notorious, *his meanness is proverbial*. **proverbially** *adv.*

provide *v.* 1. to cause (a person) to have possession or use of something, to supply. 2. to give or supply the necessities of life, *has to provide for his family.* 3. to make suitable preparation for something, *try to provide against emergencies*. **provider** *n.*

provided *conj.* on the condition, *we will come provided that our expenses are paid.*

providence *n.* 1. being provident. 2. God's or nature's care and protection. 3. *Providence*, God.

provident *adj.* showing wise forethought for future needs or events, thrifty.

providential (prov-i-**den**-shăl) *adj.* happening very luckily. **providentially** *adv.*

providing *conj.* = provided.

province *n.* 1. one of the principal administrative divisions in certain countries. 2. a district consisting of a group of adjacent dioceses, under the charge of an archbishop. 3. a range of learning or knowledge or responsibility or concern, *estimates of expenditure are the treasurer's province.* □ **the provinces**, the whole of a country outside its capital city.

provincial (prŏ-**vin**-shăl) *adj.* 1. of a province or provinces, *provincial government.* 2. having only limited interests and narrow-minded views, *provincial attitudes.* —*n.* a native or inhabitant of a province or of the provinces. —**provincialism** *n.*

provision *n.* 1. providing, preparation of resources etc. for future needs, *made provision for their old age.* 2. a statement or clause in a treaty or contract etc. stipulating something, *under the provisions of his will.* —*v.* to supply with provisions of food etc. □ **provisions** *pl. n.* a supply of food and drink.

provisional *adj.* arranged or agreed upon temporarily but possibly to be altered later. **provisionally** *adv.* □ **Provisional** *n.* a member of the Provisional wing of the IRA (¶ taking its name from the 'Provisional Government of the Republic of Ireland' which was declared in 1916).

proviso (prŏ-vy-zoh) *n.* (*pl.* provisos) something that is insisted upon as a condition of an agreement.

Provo (**proh**-voh) *n.* (*pl.* Provos) (*informal*) a member of the Provisionals.

provocation *n.* **1**. provoking, being provoked. **2**. something that provokes anger or retaliation.

provocative (prŏ-**vok**-ătiv) *adj.* **1**. arousing or likely to arouse anger or interest or sexual desire. **2**. deliberately annoying. **provocatively** *adv.*

provoke *v.* **1**. to make angry. **2**. to rouse or incite (a person) to action. **3**. to produce as a reaction or effect, *the joke provoked laughter.*

provoking *adj.* annoying.

provost (**prov**-ŏst) *n.* **1**. the head of certain colleges. **2**. the head of the chapter in certain cathedrals. **3**. the head of a municipal corporation or burgh in Scotland.

prow (*rhymes with* cow) *n.* the projecting front part of a ship or boat.

prowess (-ow- *as in* cow) *n.* great ability or daring.

prowl *v.* **1**. to go about stealthily in search of prey or plunder. **2**. to pace or wander restlessly. —*n.* prowling, *on the prowl.* — **prowler** ·*n.*

proximate (**proks**-im-ăt) *adj.* nearest, next before or after.

proximity (proks-**im**-iti) *n.* **1**. nearness. **2**. neighbourhood, *in the proximity of the station.*

proxy *n.* a person authorized to represent or act for another, the use of such a person, *voted by proxy.*

prude (*pr.* prood) *n.* a person of extreme or exaggerated propriety concerning behaviour or speech, one who is easily shocked by sexual matters. **prudery** *n.*

prudent *adj.* showing carefulness and foresight, avoiding rashness. **prudently** *adv.,* **prudence** *n.*

prudential (proo-**den**-shăl) *adj.* showing or involving prudence.

prudish (**proo**-dish) *adj.* like a prude, showing prudery. **prudishly** *adv.* **prudishness** *n.*

prune[1] *n.* a dried plum.

prune[2] *v.* **1**. to trim by cutting away dead

or overgrown branches or shoots. **2**. to shorten and improve (a speech or book etc.) by removing unnecessary parts. **3**. to reduce, *costs must be pruned.*

prurient (**proor**-i-ĕnt) *adj.* having or arising from lewd thoughts. **prurience** *n.*

pruritus (proor-I-tŭs) *n.* itching.

Prussian *adj.* of Prussia, a former country of north Europe. **Prussian blue**, a deep blue colour.

prussic acid a highly poisonous acid.

pry[1] *v.* (pried, prying) to inquire or investigate or peer impertinently (and often furtively).

pry[2] *v.* (pried, prying) (*Amer.*) = prise.

PS *abbrev.* postscript.

psalm (*pr.* sahm) *n.* a sacred song, especially one of those in the Book of Psalms in the Old Testament. **psalmist** *n.* a writer of psalms.

psalter (**sol**-ter) *n.* a copy of the Book of Psalms.

psephology (see-**fol**-ŏji) *n.* the study of trends in elections and voting. **psephologist** *n.*

pseudo (s'**yoo**-doh) *adj.* false, insincere.

pseudo- (s'yoo-doh) *prefix* false.

pseudonym (s'**yoo**-dŏn-im) *n.* a false name used by an author.

psoriasis (sor-**I**-ă-sis) *n.* a skin disease causing red scaly patches.

psst *int.* an exclamation to attract someone's attention furtively.

psych (*pr.* syk) *v.* (*Amer. slang*) **1**. to psychoanalyse. **2**. to work out the intentions of (a person) or the solution of (a problem) by use of psychology. **3**. to intimidate (a person) by making him feel uneasy. □ **psych up**, *v.* (*Amer. slang*) to make (oneself or another person) ready emotionally.

psyche (**sy**-ki) *n.* **1**. the human soul or spirit. **2**. the human mind.

psychedelic (sy-ki-**del**-ik) *adj.* of or producing hallucinations and similar experiences, full of vivid or luminous colours.

psychiatrist (sy-**ky**-ă-trist) *n.* a specialist in psychiatry.

psychiatry (sy-**ky**-ă-tri) *n.* the study and treatment of mental disease. **psychiatric** (sy-ki-**at**-rik) *adj.*

psychic (**sy**-kik) *adj.* **1**. of the soul or mind. **2**. concerned with processes that seem to be outside physical or natural laws, having or involving extra-sensory perception or occult powers.

psychical (**sy**-kik-ăl) *adj.* psychic, *psychical research.* **psychically** *adv.*

psycho (**sy**-koh) *adj.* (*informal*) psychotic. —*n.* (*pl.* psychos) (*informal*) a psychotic person.

psychoanalyse *v.* to treat (a person) by psychoanalysis.

psychoanalysis *n.* a method of examining or treating mental conditions that involves bringing to light certain things in a person's conscious mind that may be influencing behaviour and mental state. **psychoanalytical** *adj.*

psychoanalyst *n.* a specialist in psychoanalysis.

psychological *adj.* 1. of or affecting the mind and its workings. 2. of psychology. **psychologically** *adv.* □ **at the psychological moment**, (*informal*) at the most appropriate moment. **psychological warfare**, actions or propaganda etc. designed to weaken an enemy's morale.

psychologist *n.* a specialist or expert in psychology.

psychology *n.* 1. the study of the mind and how it works. 2. mental characteristics.

psychopath (**sy**-kŏ-path) *n.* a person suffering from a severe mental disorder, especially with aggressive antisocial behaviour. **psychopathic** (sy-kŏ-**pa**-thik) *adj.*

psychosis (sy-**koh**-sis) *n.* (*pl.* **psychoses**) a severe mental disorder involving a person's whole personality.

psychosomatic (sy-kŏ-sŏ-**mat**-ik) *adj.* of or involving both the mind and the body; *psychosomatic illness,* one that is caused or aggravated by mental stress. **psychosomatically** *adv.*

psychotherapy (sy-kŏ-th'e-răpi) *n.* treatment of mental disorders by the use of psychological methods.

PT *abbrev.* physical training.

pt. *abbrev.* pint.

ptarmigan (**tar**-mig-ăn) *n.* a bird of the grouse family with plumage that turns white in winter.

pterodactyl (te-rŏ-**dak**-til) *n.* an extinct reptile with wings.

PTO *abbrev.* please turn over.

pub *n.* (*informal*) a public house. **pub-crawl** *n.* a journey to several pubs, with one or more drinks at each.

puberty (**pew**-ber-ti) *n.* the stage at which a person's reproductive organs are in the process of becoming mature and he or she becomes capable of producing offspring.

pubic (**pew**-bik) *adj.* of the lower part of the abdomen, at the front of the pelvis, *pubic hair.*

public *adj.* of or for or known to people in general, not private. —*n.* members of the community in general or a particular section of this, *the British public.* □ **in public**, openly, not in private. **public-address system**, a system of loudspeakers to make

something audible over a wide area. **public health**, protection of the public from infection and disease, by means of hygienic living-conditions and environment. **public house**, a building (not a hotel) licensed to sell beer and other alcoholic drinks to the general public for consumption on the premises (and not only with meals). **public prosecutor**, a law officer conducting prosecutions on behalf of the State or in the public interest. **Public Record Office**, an institution where official documents are kept for public inspection. **public relations**, the promotion of good will between an organization etc. and the general public. **public school**, an endowed secondary school (usually a boarding-school) for fee-paying pupils; (in Scotland, USA, etc.) a school managed by public authorities. **public spirit**, readiness to do things for the benefit of people in general. **public-spirited** *adj.* showing public spirit.

publican *n.* 1. the keeper of a public house. 2. (in the Bible) a tax-collector.

publication *n.* 1. publishing, being published. 2. something published, e.g. a book or newspaper.

publicity *n.* 1. public attention directed upon a person or thing. 2. the process of drawing public attention to a person or thing, the spoken or written or other material by which this is done.

publicize *v.* to bring to the attention of the public, to advertise.

publicly *adv.* in public, openly.

publish *v.* 1. to issue copies of (a book etc.) to the public. 2. to make generally known. 3. to announce formally, *publish the banns of marriage.*

publisher *n.* a person or firm that issues copies of a book or newspaper etc. to the public (distinguished from a *printer* who prints books etc. but does not issue them).

puce (*pr.* pewss) *adj.* & *n.* brownish-purple.

puck *n.* the hard rubber disc used in ice hockey.

pucker *v.* to come together in small wrinkles or bulges, to cause to do this. —*n.* a wrinkle or bulge made in this way.

puckish *adj.* impish.

pud *n.* (*informal*) pudding.

pudding *n.* 1. any of a number of foods containing or enclosed in a mixture of flour (or a similar substance) and other ingredients, cooked by baking or boiling or steaming. 2. the sweet course of a meal. 3. a kind of sausage, *black pudding* (see black). 4. a fat and rather stupid person.

puddle *n.* a small pool of rainwater on a

road or of other liquid on a surface. —*v.*
1. to stir (molten iron) so as to expel
carbon and produce wrought iron. **2.** to
work into a wet mixture. **3.** to saturate the
soil round (a plant) when planting, *puddle
it in*.

pudenda (pew-**den**-dă) *pl. n.* the genitals,
especially of a woman. **pudendal** *adj.*

pudgy *adj.* (pudgier, pudgiest) podgy.

pueblo (**pweb**-loh) *n.* (*pl.* pueblos) a communal village dwelling built by American
Indians in Mexico and the south-west
USA. **Pueblo** *n.* a member of a tribe
living in these.

puerile (**pew**-er-ryl) *adj.* showing immaturity, suitable only for children, *asking
puerile questions*. **puerility** (pew-er-**il**-iti) *n.*

puerperal (pew-er-per-ăl) *adj.* of or associated with childbirth, *puerperal fever*.

Puerto Rico (pwer-toh-**ree**-koh) an island
in the West Indies. **Puerto Rican** *adj.* &
n.

puff *n.* **1.** a short light blowing of breath
or wind etc., smoke or vapour sent out by
this. **2.** a powder-puff. **3.** a cake of puff
pastry or choux pastry filled with cream
etc., *cream puffs*. **4.** a piece of extravagant
praise in a review or advertisement for a
book or play etc. —**puff** *v.* **1.** to send out
a puff or puffs, to blow (smoke etc.) in
puffs, to smoke (a pipe etc.) in puffs. **2.** to
breathe hard, to pant. **3.** to make or
become inflated, to swell. □ **puff-adder**
n. a large poisonous African viper that
inflates the upper part of its body when
excited. **puff-ball** *n.* a fungus with a ball-
shaped spore-case that bursts open when
ripe. **puff pastry**, very light flaky pastry.
puff *or* **puffed sleeve**, a sleeve that is
very full at the shoulder.

puffin *n.* a sea-bird with a short striped
bill.

puffy *adj.* (puffier, puffiest) puffed out,
swollen. **puffiness** *n.*

pug *n.* a dog of a dwarf breed resembling
the bulldog. **pug-nosed** *adj.* having a
short flattish nose.

pugilist (**pew**-jil-ist) *n.* a professional boxer.
pugilism *n.*, **pugilistic** *adj.*

pugnacious (pug-**nay**-shŭs) *adj.* eager to
fight, aggressive. **pugnaciously** *adv.*,
pugnacity (pug-**nas**-iti) *n.*

puissance (**pwee**-săns) *n.* (in show-jumping) a test of a horse's ability to jump high
obstacles.

puke *v.* (*vulgar*) to vomit.

pukka (**puk**-ă) *adj.* (*informal*) real,
genuine.

pull *v.* **1.** to exert force upon (a thing) so as
to move it towards oneself or towards the
source of the force; *pull a muscle*, damage

it by abnormal strain; *pull a gun*, draw it
and prepare to use it; *pull a horse*, to check
it so as to lose a race. **2.** to remove by pulling, *pull the cork*. **3.** to propel (a boat) by
pulling on its oars. **4.** (in cricket) to strike
the ball to the leg side, (in golf) to hit the
ball widely to the left. **5.** to exert a pulling
or driving force, *the engine is pulling well*.
6. to attract, *attractions that pull the crowds*.
—**pull** *n.* **1.** the act of pulling, the force
exerted by this. **2.** a means of exerting influence. **3.** a deep draught of a drink, a
draw at a pipe etc. **4.** a prolonged effort in
walking etc., *the long pull up the hill*. □
pull a fast one, (*slang*) to act unfairly in
order to gain an advantage. **pull a person's
leg**, to tease him. **pull back**, to retreat or
withdraw, to cause to do this. **pull down**,
to demolish a building; to cause general
weakness or ill health in, *his illness pulled
him down*. **pull in**, to obtain as wages or
profit; (of a train) to enter and stop at a
station; (of a vehicle) to move to the side
of the road or off the road; (*informal*) to
take into custody. **pull-in** *n.* a place where
vehicles may pull in, a roadside café. **pull
off**, to succeed in achieving or winning
something, *pulled it off*. **pull oneself together**, to regain one's self-control. **pull
one's punches**, to avoid using one's full
force. **pull one's weight**, to do one's fair
share of work. **pull out**, to withdraw or
cause to withdraw; (of a train) to move
out of a station; (of a vehicle) to move
away from the side of a road, or from
behind another vehicle to overtake it. **pull-
out** *n.* a middle section of a magazine etc.,
detachable by pulling. **pull rank**, to make
unfair use of one's senior rank in demanding obedience. **pull round**, to recover or
cause to recover from illness. **pull strings**,
to use one's influence, often secretly.
pull through, to come or bring successfully through an illness or difficulty. **pull
together**, to co-operate. **pull up**, to stop or
cause (a person or vehicle etc.) to stop; to
reprimand. **pull-up** *n.* a pull-in. **pull wires**,
= pull strings. **pull your finger out**,
(*slang*) hurry up, begin work in earnest.

pullet *n.* a young domestic hen from the
time of beginning to lay until the first
moult.

pulley *n.* (*pl.* pulleys) a wheel over which
a rope or chain or belt passes, used in lifting things or to drive or be driven by an
endless belt.

Pullman *n.* a type of railway carriage with
luxurious furnishings and without compartments.

pullover *n.* a knitted garment (with no
fastenings) for the upper part of the body.

pulmonary (**pul**-mŏn-er-i) *adj.* of or affecting the lungs.

pulp *n.* **1.** the soft moist part of fruit. **2.** the soft tissue inside a tooth. **3.** any soft moist mass of material, especially of wood fibre as used for making paper. —*v.* to reduce to pulp, to become pulpy. □ **pulp magazines**, cheap popular magazines (originally printed on rough paper made from woodpulp).

pulpit *n.* a raised enclosed platform in a church, used for preaching from.

pulpy *adj.* like pulp, containing much pulp.

pulsar *n.* a source (in space) of radio signals that pulsate in a rapid regular rhythm.

pulsate (pul-**sayt**) *v.* to expand and contract rhythmically, to vibrate, to quiver. **pulsation** *n.*

pulse[1] *n.* **1.** the rhythmical throbbing of the arteries as blood is propelled along them, this as felt in the wrists or temples etc. **2.** any steady throb. **3.** a single beat or throb. —*v.* to pulsate.

pulse[2] *n.* the edible seed of peas, beans, lentils, etc.

pulverize *v.* **1.** to crush into powder. **2.** to become powder. **3.** to defeat thoroughly. **pulverization** *n.*

puma (**pew**-ma) *n.* a large brown American animal of the cat family.

pumice (**pum**-iss) *n.* a light porous kind of lava used for rubbing stains from the skin or as powder for polishing things. **pumicestone** *n.* pumice; a piece of this.

pummel *v.* (pummelled, pummelling) to strike repeatedly, especially with the fist(s).

pump[1] *n.* **1.** a machine or device for forcing liquid, air, or gas into or out of something. **2.** a fire-engine with pumping apparatus. **3.** a machine for raising water for domestic use. —**pump** *v.* **1.** to raise or move or inflate by means of a pump. **2.** to use a pump. **3.** to empty by using a pump, *pump the ship dry*. **4.** to move vigorously up and down like a pump-handle. **5.** to pour or cause to pour forth as if by pumping. **6.** to question (a person) persistently to obtain information.

pump[2] *n.* **1.** a light shoe worn for dancing etc. **2.** a plimsoll.

pumpernickel *n.* German wholemeal rye bread.

pumpkin *n.* the large round orange-coloured fruit of a trailing vine, used as a vegetable and (in the USA) as a filling for pies.

pun *n.* a humorous use of a word to suggest another that sounds the same, e.g. 'the sole has no feet and therefore no sole, poor soul'. **punning** *adj.* & *n.* making a pun or puns.

punch[1] *v.* **1.** to strike with the fist. **2.** (*Amer.*) to herd, *cattle-punching*. — **punch** *n.* **1.** a blow with the fist. **2.** (*slang*) vigour, effective force, *a speech with plenty of punch in it*. □ **punch-drunk** *adj.* stupefied through being severely punched. **punch line**, words that give the climax of a joke or story. **punch-up** *n.* (*informal*) a fight with fists, a brawl.

punch[2] *n.* a device for making holes in metal or leather, or for stamping a design on material. —*v.* to perforate with a punch, to make (a hole etc.) with a punch. □ **punched card**, a card perforated with holes according to a code, for giving instructions or data to a computer etc.

punch[3] *n.* a drink made of wine or spirits mixed with fruit juices etc. **punch-bowl** *n.* a bowl in which this is mixed.

punctilious (punk-**til**-iŭs) *adj.* very careful to carry out duties or details of ceremony etc. correctly, conscientious. **punctiliously** *adv.*, **punctiliousness** *n.*

punctual *adj.* arriving or doing things at the appointed time, neither early nor late. **punctually** *adv.*, **punctuality** *n.*

punctuate *v.* **1.** to insert punctuation marks in. **2.** to interrupt at intervals, *his speech was punctuated with cheers.*

punctuation *n.* punctuating, the marks used for this. **punctuation mark,** any of the marks (e.g. full stop, comma, question mark) used in written or printed material to separate sentences etc. and to make the meaning clear.

puncture *n.* a small hole made by something sharp, especially one made accidentally in a pneumatic tyre. *v.* **1.** to make a puncture in, to suffer a puncture. **2.** to reduce the pride or confidence of, *punctured his conceit.*

pundit *n.* a person who is an authority on a subject.

pungent (**pun**-jĕnt) *adj.* **1.** having a strong sharp taste or smell. **2.** (of remarks) penetrating, biting. **pungently** *adv.*, **pungency** *n.*

punish *v.* **1.** to cause (an offender) to suffer for his offence. **2.** to inflict a punishment for, *vandalism should be severely punished.* **3.** to treat roughly, to test severely. *the race was run at a punishing pace.*

punishable *adj.* liable to be punished, especially by law, *punishable offences.*

punishment *n.* **1.** punishing, being punished. **2.** that which an offender is made to suffer because of his wrongdoing.

punitive (**pew**-nit-iv) *adj.* inflicting or

intended to inflict punishment.

punk *n.* **1.** (*slang*) worthless stuff, nonsense. **2.** (*slang*) a worthless person, a young ruffian. **3.** a devotee of punk rock. —**punk** *adj.* **1.** (*slang*) worthless. **2.** of punk rock or its devotees. □ **punk rock**, a type of rock music involving outrage and shock effects in music, behaviour, and dress.

punnet (**pun**-it) *n.* a small chip or similar plastic container for fruit etc.

punster *n.* a person who makes puns.

punt¹ *n.* a flat-bottomed boat propelled by thrusting a long pole against the bottom of a river. —*v.* **1.** to propel (a punt) with a pole in this way. **2.** to carry or travel in a punt. —**punter** *n.*

punt² *v.* to kick (a football) after it has dropped from the hands and before it touches the ground. —*n.* a kick of this kind. —**punter** *n.*

punt³ *v.* **1.** to lay a stake against the bank in certain card-games. **2.** (*informal*) to bet on a horse etc., to speculate in shares. **punter** *n.*

puny (**pew**-ni) *adj.* (punier, puniest) undersized, feeble.

pup *n.* **1.** a young dog; *in pup*, (of a bitch) pregnant. **2.** a young wolf, rat, or seal. —*v.* (pupped, pupping) to give birth to a pup or pups. □ **pup tent**, a small tent of simple design. **sell someone a pup**, to swindle him by pretending that the thing sold is more valuable than it really is.

pupa (**pew**-pă) *n.* (*pl.* pupae, *pr.* pew-pee) a chrysalis. **pupal** *adj.*

pupil *n.* **1.** a person who is taught by another. **2.** an opening in the centre of the iris of the eye, through which light passes to the retina.

puppet *n.* **1.** a kind of doll that can be made to move by various means as an entertainment. **2.** a person or group whose actions are entirely controlled by another. □ **puppet show**, an entertainment using puppets.

puppetry *n.* manipulation of puppets.

puppy *n.* a young dog. **puppy fat**, temporary fatness of a child or adolescent.

purchase *v.* to buy. —*n.* **1.** buying. **2.** something bought. **3.** a firm hold to pull or raise something or prevent it from slipping, leverage. —**purchaser** *n.*

purdah (**per**-dă) *n.* the system in Muslim or Hindu communities of keeping women from the sight of men or strangers.

pure *adj.* **1.** not mixed with any other substance, free from impurities. **2.** mere, nothing but, *pure nonsense.* **3.** free from evil or sin. **4.** chaste. **5.** dealing with theory only, not with practical applications, *pure mathematics.* **pureness** *n.*

purée (**pewr**-ay) *n.* pulped fruit or vegetables etc. —*v.* to make into purée.

purely *adv.* **1.** in a pure way. **2.** entirely, only, *came purely out of interest.*

purgative (**per**-gă-tiv) *n.* a strong laxative.

purgatory (**per**-gă-ter-i) *n.* **1.** (in RC belief) a place or condition in which souls undergo purification by temporary punishment. **2.** a place or condition of suffering. **purgatorial** (per-gă-**tor**-iăl) *adj.*

purge (*pr.* perj) *v.* **1.** to cause emptying of the bowels of (a person) by means of a purgative. **2.** to rid of people or things considered undesirable or harmful. **3.** to atone for (an offence, especially contempt of court). —*n.* purging, ridding of undesirable things etc.

purify *v.* (purified, purifying) to make pure, to cleanse from impurities. **purifier** *n.*, **purification** *n.*

purist (**pewr**-ist) *n.* a stickler for correctness, especially in language.

Puritan *n.* **1.** a member of the party of English Protestants in the 16th and 17th centuries who wanted simpler forms of church ceremony and strictness and gravity in behaviour. **2.** *puritan*, a person who is extremely strict in morals and who looks upon some kinds of fun and pleasure as sinful. **puritanical** (pewr-i-**tan**-ikăl) *adj.*

purity *n.* pureness.

purl *n.* a knitting-stitch that produces a ridge towards the knitter. —*v.* to make this stitch.

purler *n.* (*informal*) a headlong fall.

purlieus (**per**-lewz) *pl. n.* the outskirts of a place.

purloin (per-**loin**) *v.* (*formal* or *humorous use*) to steal.

purple *n.* a colour obtained by mixing red and blue. —*adj.* of this colour. —*v.* to become purple. □ **born in the purple**, (*old use*) born in a reigning family; born into an aristocratic or influential family. **purple emperor**, a large butterfly with purple wings. **purple passage**, a very ornate passage in a literary work.

purplish *adj.* rather purple.

purport¹ (**per**-port) *n.* the meaning or intention of something said or written.

purport² (per-**port**) *v.* to pretend, to be intended to seem, *the letter purports to come from you.* **purportedly** *adv.*

purpose *n.* **1.** an intended result, something for which effort is being made, *this will serve our purpose.* **2.** intention to act, determination. —*v.* to intend. □ **on purpose**, by intention in order to do something, not by chance. **purpose-built**

adj. built for a particular purpose. **to no purpose,** with no result.

purposeful *adj.* having or showing a particular purpose, with determination. **purposefully** *adv.*, **purposefulness** *n.*

purposeless *adj.* without a purpose.

purposely *adv.* on purpose.

purr *v.* 1. (of a cat etc.) to make the low vibrant sound that a cat makes when pleased. 2. (of machinery etc.) to make a similar sound. —*v.* a purring sound.

purse *n.* 1. a small pouch of leather etc. for carrying money. 2. (*Amer.*) a handbag. 3. money, funds. 4. a sum of money as a present or prize. —*v.* to pucker, *pursing her lips.* □ **hold the purse-strings,** to have control of expenditure. **purse-proud** *adj.* arrogant because of one's wealth.

purser *n.* a ship's officer in charge of accounts, especially on a passenger ship.

pursuance *n.* performance or carrying out of something, *in pursuance of my duties.*

pursuant *adv.* **pursuant to,** in accordance with.

pursue *v.* 1. to chase in order to catch or kill. 2. to afflict continually, *was pursued by misfortunes.* 3. to continue, to proceed along, *we pursued our course.* 4. to engage in, *pursuing her hobby.* **pursuer** *n.*

pursuit *n.* 1. pursuing, *in pursuit of the fox.* 2. an activity, something at which one works or gives one's time.

purvey (per-**vay**) *v.* (purveyed, purveying) to supply (articles of food) as a trader. **purveyor** *n.*

purview (per-view) *n.* 1. the scope or range of a document, scheme, occupation, etc. 2. the range of physical or mental vision.

pus *n.* thick yellowish matter produced from inflamed or infected tissue.

push *v.* 1. to exert force upon (a thing) so as to move it away from oneself or from the source of the force; *push one's way,* go forward by pushing. 2. to thrust or cause to thrust outwards. 3. to extend by effort, *the frontier was pushed further north.* 4. to make a vigorous effort in order to succeed or to surpass others. 5. to press (a person) to do something, to put a strain on the abilities or tolerance of, *don't push him for payment.* 6. to urge the use or adoption of (goods or ideas etc.), e.g. by advertisement; *push drugs,* sell them illegally. — **push** *n.* 1. the act of pushing, the force exerted by this. 2. a vigorous effort, a military attack made in order to advance. 3. enterprise, self-assertion, determination to get on. —**pusher** *n.* □ **at a push,** in time of difficulty or necessity. **be pushed for,** (*informal*) to have barely enough of, *I'm pushed for time.* **give** *or* **get the push,** (*slang*) to dismiss or be dismissed (from one's job etc.). **push around,** to treat contemptuously and unfairly; to bully. **push-bike** *n.* a bicycle worked by pedalling, as distinct from a motor cycle. **push-button** *adj.* operated automatically by pressing a button. **push-chair** *n.* a folding chair on wheels, in which a child can be pushed along. **push off,** (*slang*) to go away. **push one's luck,** (*informal*) to take undue risks. **push-over** *n.* (*informal*) something that is easily done; a person who is easily convinced or charmed etc. **push-start** *v.* to start (a motor vehicle) by pushing it along to turn the engine, (*n.*) a start made in this way. **push the boat out,** (*informal*) to celebrate. **push-up** *n.* a press-up.

pushful *adj.* self-assertive, determined to get on. **pushfulness** *n.*

pushing *adj.* (of a person) 1. pushful. 2. (*informal*) having nearly reached (a certain age), *pushing forty.*

Pushtu (pu'sh-too) *n.* = Pashto.

pusillanimous (pew-zı-**lan**-ımŭs) *adj.* timid, cowardly.

puss *n.* a cat.

pussy *n.* 1. (*children's use*) a cat. 2. (*vulgar*) the vulva. □ **pussy willow,** a willow with furry catkins.

pussyfoot *v.* (*Amer.*) 1. to move stealthily. 2. to act cautiously, to avoid committing oneself.

pustule (**pus**-tewl) *n.* a pimple or blister, especially one containing pus.

put *v.* (put, putting) 1. to move (a thing) to a specified place, to cause to occupy a certain place or position, to send. 2. to cause to be in a certain state or relationship, *put the machine out of action*; *put her at her ease.* 3. to subject, *put it to the test.* 4. to estimate, *I put the cost at £400.* 5. to express or state, *put it tactfully.* 6. to impose as a tax etc. 7. to stake (money) in a bet. 8. to place as an investment, *put his money into land.* 9. to lay (blame) on. 10. (of ships) to proceed, *put into harbour.* —*n.* a throw of the shot or weight. □ **be hard put,** to have difficulty in doing or providing something. **not put a foot wrong,** to make no mistakes. **put across,** to succeed in communicating (an idea etc.), to make seem acceptable. **put away,** (*informal*) to put into prison or into a mental home; to consume as food or drink. **put by,** to save for future use. **put down,** to suppress by force or authority; to snub; to have (an animal) destroyed; to enter (a person's name) as one who will subscribe; to reckon or consider, *put him down as a fool;*

to attribute, *put it down to nervousness.* **put in**, to make (an appearance); to enter (a claim); to spend (time) working. **put in for**, to apply for. **put it across a person**, (*slang*) to make him believe something false. **put it on**, (*informal*) to pretend an emotion. **put off**, to postpone; to postpone an engagement with (a person); to make excuses and try to avoid; to dissuade, to repel, *the smell puts me off.* **put on**, to stage (a play etc.); to increase, *putting on weight*; to cause to operate. **put one's feet up**, to take a rest. **put one's foot down**, to insist on something firmly; to accelerate a motor vehicle. **put one's foot in it**, to make a blunder. **put out**, to disconcert or annoy or inconvenience (a person); to extinguish (a light or fire); to dislocate (a joint). **put over**, = put across. **put pen to paper**, to start writing. **put the clock back**, to go back to a past age or an out-of-date practice. **put the shot** *or* **weight**, to hurl it as an athletic exercise. **put through**, to complete (a business transaction) successfully; to connect by telephone; to cause to undergo, *put it through severe tests.* **put two and two together**, to draw a conclusion from the facts one knows. **put up**, to construct or build; to raise the price of; to provide or contribute, *the firm will put up the money*; to make (a prayer); to offer for sale; to display (a notice); to present as an idea or proposal; to give or receive accommodation; to pack up into a parcel or receptacle; to attempt or offer, *they put up no resistance.* **put-up** *adj.* concocted fraudulently, *a put-up job.* **put up to**, to instigate (a person) in, *who put him up to it?* **put up with**, to endure, to tolerate.

putative (**pew**-tă-tiv) *adj.* reputed, supposed, *his putative father.*

putonghua (poo-tuung-**hwah**) *n.* the standard language of China.

putrefy (**pew**-tri-fy) *v.* (putrefied, putrefying) to rot, to decay or cause to decay. **putrefaction** (pew-tri-**fak**-shŏn) *n.*

putrescent (pew-**tress**-ĕnt) *adj.* decaying, rotting. **putrescence** *n.*

putrid (**pew**-trid) *adj.* **1.** decomposed, rotting. **2.** foul-smelling. **3.** (*slang*) very distasteful or unpleasant.

putt (*rhymes with* cut) *v.* to strike (a golf ball) lightly to make it roll along the ground —*n.* a stroke of this kind. □ **putter** *n.* a golf-club used in putting. **putting-green** *n.* (in golf) a smooth area of grass round a hole.

puttee *n.* a strip of cloth wound spirally round the leg from ankle to knee for support or protection.

putty *n.* a soft paste that sets hard, used for fixing glass in window frames, filling up holes, etc.

puzzle *n.* **1.** a question that is difficult to answer, a problem. **2.** a problem or toy designed to test one's knowledge or ingenuity or patience. —**puzzle** *v.* **1.** to make hard thought necessary, *a puzzling problem.* **2.** to use hard thought, *she puzzled over it*; *puzzle it out*, solve or understand it by patient thought or ingenuity. **puzzlement** *n.*

puzzler *n.* a puzzling problem.

PVC *abbrev.* polyvinyl chloride.

pygmy (**pig**-mi) *n.* **1.** a person or thing of unusually small size. **2.** *Pygmy*, a member of a dwarf Black people of equatorial Africa. —*adj.* very small.

pyjamas *pl. n.* a suit of loose-fitting jacket and trousers for sleeping in; *pyjama top*, the jacket of this.

pylon *n.* **1.** a tall lattice-work structure used for carrying overhead electricity cables or as a boundary. **2.** a structure marking a path for aircraft.

Pyongyang the capital of North Korea.

pyorrhoea (py-ŏ-**ree**-ă) *n.* a disease of the tooth-sockets causing discharge of pus and loosening of the teeth.

pyramid *n.* a structure with a flat (usually square) base and with sloping sides that meet at the top, especially one built by the ancient Egyptians as a tomb or by the Aztecs and Mayas as a platform for a temple. **pyramidal** (pi-**ram**-id'l) *adj.* □ **pyramid selling**, a method of selling goods whereby distributors pay a premium for the right to sell a company's goods and then sell part of that right to a number of others.

pyre (*rhymes with* fire) *n.* a pile of wood etc. for burning a corpse as part of a funeral rite.

Pyrenees *pl. n.* a range of mountains between France and Spain. **Pyrenean** (pi-ri-**nee**-ăn) *adj.*

pyrethrum (py-**ree**-thrŭm) *n.* **1.** a kind of chrysanthemum with finely-divided leaves. **2.** an insecticide made from its dried flowers.

pyrites (py-**ry**-teez) *n.* a mineral that is a sulphide of iron (*iron pyrites*) or copper and iron (*copper pyrites*).

pyromaniac (pyr-ŏ-**may**-ni-ak) *n.* a person with an uncontrollable impulse to set things on fire.

pyrotechnic (py-rŏ-**tek**-nik) *adj.* of or like fireworks. **pyrotechnics** *pl. n.* a firework display.

Pyrrhic victory (**pi**-rik) a victory gained at too great a cost, like that of Pyrrhus (king of Epirus) over the Romans in 279 BC.

python (py-thŏn) *n.* a large snake that crushes its prey.

pyx (*pr.* piks) *n.* **1.** a vessel in which bread consecrated for Holy Communion is kept. **2.** a box in which specimen coins are deposited at the Royal Mint.

Qq

Qatar (**kat**-ar) a country on the Persian Gulf. **Qatari** *adj.* & *n.* (*pl.* Qataris)

QC *abbrev.* Queen's Counsel.

QED *abbrev.* quod erat demonstrandum. (Latin, = which was the thing that had to be proved.)

Qld. *abbrev.* Queensland.

qt. *abbrev.* quart(s).

q.t. *n.* **on the q.t.**, (*slang*) on the quiet.

qua (*pr.* kway) *conj.* in the capacity or character of, *putting his duty qua citizen above other loyalties.* (¶ Latin.)

quack[1] *n.* the harsh cry of a duck. —*v.* to utter this sound.

quack[2] *n.* a person who falsely claims to have medical skill or to have remedies which will cure diseases etc.

quad[1] (*pr.* kwod) *n.* **1.** a quadrangle. **2.** one of a set of quadruplets.

quad[2] *adj.* & *n.* quadraphonic.

Quadragesima (kwod-ră-**jess**-imă) *n.* the first Sunday in Lent.

quadrangle (**kwod**-rang-ŭl) *n.* a four-sided court bordered by large buildings.

quadrant (**kwod**-rănt) *n.* **1.** a quarter of a circle or of its circumference. **2.** an instrument with an arc of 90° marked off in degrees, for measuring angles.

quadraphonic (kwod-ră-**fon**-ik) *adj.* (of sound-reproduction) using four transmission channels. —*n.* quadraphonic transmission.

quadratic (kwod-**rat**-ik) *adj.* **quadratic equations**, equations involving the square (and no higher power) of one or more of the unknown quantities or variables. **quadratics** *pl. n.* such equations.

quadrennial (kwod-**ren**-iăl) *adj.* **1.** lasting for four years. **2.** happening every fourth year.

quadrilateral (kwod-ri-**lat**-er-ăl) *n.* a geometric figure with four sides. —*adj.* having four sides.

quadrille (kwod-**ril**) *n.* a square dance for four couples, the music for this.

quadriplegia (kwodri-**plee**-jiă) *n.* paralysis of both arms and both legs. **quadriplegic** *adj.* & *n.*

quadruped (**kwod**-ruu-ped) *n.* a four-footed animal.

quadruple *adj.* **1.** consisting of four parts, involving four people or groups, *a quadruple alliance.* **2.** four times as much as, *shall need quadruple that number of lights.* —*v.* to multiply or become multiplied by four; *costs had quadrupled,* had increased to four times the original amount.

quadruplet (**kwod**-ruu-plit) *n.* one of four children born at one birth.

quadruplicate (kwod-**roo**-plik-ăt) *n.* in **quadruplicate,** in four exactly similar examples or copies.

quaff (*pr.* kwof) *v.* to drink (a thing) in long draughts.

quagmire (**kwag**-myr) *n.* a bog or marsh.

quail[1] *n.* (*pl.* quail *or* quails) a bird related to the partridge, used as food.

quail[2] *v.* to flinch, to show fear.

quaint *adj.* odd in a pleasing way, attractive through being unusual or old-fashioned. **quaintly** *adv.*, **quaintness** *n.*

quake *v.* to shake or tremble from unsteadiness, to shake with fear. —*n.* **1.** a quaking movement. **2.** (*informal*) an earthquake.

Quaker *n.* a member of the Society of Friends, a Christian sect with no written creed or ordained ministers, formerly noted for simplicity of dress and of lifestyle.

qualification *n.* **1.** qualifying, being qualified. **2.** a thing that qualifies a person to do something or to have a certain right etc. **3.** something that limits or restricts a meaning, *this statement needs certain qualifications.*

qualificatory *adj.* of or giving or involving qualifications.

qualify *v.* (qualified, qualifying) **1.** to make or become competent or eligible or legally entitled to do something. **2.** to make (a statement etc.) less general or extreme, to limit its meaning, *'in all cases' needs to be qualified as 'in all known cases';* *gave it only qualified approval,* not complete approval. **3.** to describe, to attribute some quality to, *they qualified him as ambitious; adjectives qualify nouns.* —**qualifier** *n.*

qualitative (**kwol**-i-tă-tiv) *adj.* of or concerned with quality, *qualitative analysis.*

quality *n.* **1.** a degree or level of excellence, *goods of high quality.* **2.** general excellence, *it has quality.* **3.** a characteristic, something that is special in a person or thing, *has the quality of inspiring confidence.*

qualm (*pr.* kwahm) *n.* **1.** a misgiving, a pang of conscience. **2.** a sudden feeling of sickness or faintness.

quandary (kwon-der-i) *n.* a state of perplexity, a difficult situation.

quango *n.* (*pl.* quangos) an administrative body with financial support from and senior appointments made by the government but not controlled by it. ¶ From the initials of quasi-autonomous non-governmental organization.

quantifiable (kwon-ti-fy-ăbŭl) *adj.* able to be quantified.

quantify (kwon-ti-fy) *v.* (quantified, quantifying) to express as a quantity.

quantitative (kwon-ti-tă-tiv) *adj.* of or concerned with quantity, *quantitative analysis.*

quantity *n.* **1.** an amount or number of things, a specified or considerable amount or number; *it is found in quantity* or *in quantities,* in large amounts. **2.** ability to be measured through having size or weight or amount or number. **3.** a thing that has this ability, a figure or symbol representing it. □ **quantity surveyor,** a person who measures and prices building-work.

quantum (kwon-tŭm) *n.* (*pl.* quanta) the amount required or desired. **quantum theory,** a theory of physics based on the assumption that energy exists in indivisible units.

quarantine (kwo-răn-teen) *n.* **1.** isolation imposed on people or animals who may have been exposed to an infectious or contagious disease which they could spread to others. **2.** the period of this isolation. —*v.* to put into quarantine.

quarrel *n.* **1.** a violent disagreement, breaking of friendly relations. **2.** a cause for complaint against a person or his actions, *we have no quarrel with him.* —**quarrel** *v.* (quarrelled, quarrelling) **1.** to engage in a quarrel, to break off friendly relations. **2.** to disagree with or complain about, *we are not quarrelling with this decision.*

quarrelsome *adj.* liable to quarrel with people.

quarry[1] *n.* **1.** an intended prey or victim being hunted. **2.** something that is sought or pursued.

quarry[2] *n.* an open excavation from which stone or slate etc. is obtained. —*v.* (quarried, quarrying) **1.** to obtain (stone etc.) from a quarry. **2.** to search laboriously in order to extract information etc.

quart *n.* a measure of capacity for liquids, 2 pints or a quarter of a gallon.

quarter *n.* **1.** one of the four equal parts into which a thing is divided. **2.** (*Amer.* & *Canada*) a quarter of a dollar, 25 cents. **3.** a grain-measure of 8 bushels, one quarter of a hundredweight. **4.** a fourth part of a year, for which payments become due on quarter-day. **5.** a fourth part of a lunar month. **6.** a point of time 15 minutes before or after every hour. **7.** a direction or point of the compass, a district, a division of a town. **8.** a person or group, especially regarded as a possible source of help or information etc., *got no sympathy from that quarter.* **9.** mercy towards an enemy or opponent, *gave no quarter.* —**quarter** *v.* **1.** to divide into quarters. **2.** to place (a symbol) in one of the divisions of a shield or coat of arms. **3.** to put (soldiers etc.) into lodgings. **4.** (of a dog etc.) to search (ground) in every direction. □ **quarterday** *n.* one of the four days regarded as beginning the quarters of a year for financial purposes or tenancies etc., (in England) 25 March, 24 June, 29 September, 25 December, (in Scotland) 2 February, 15 May, 1 August, 11 November. **quarterfinal** *n.* one of the matches or rounds preceding a semi-final. **quarter-light** *n.* a small triangular window in a car. **quarterplate** *n.* a size of photograph 8·3 × 10·8 cm.

quarters *pl. n.* lodgings, accommodation; *married quarters,* accommodation for married people.

quarterdeck *n.* part of the upper deck of a ship nearest the stern, usually reserved for the ship's officers.

quarterly *adj.* & *adv.* produced or occurring once in every quarter of a year. —*n.* a quarterly periodical.

quartermaster *n.* **1.** (in the army) a regimental officer in charge of stores and assigning quarters etc. **2.** a naval petty officer in charge of steering and signals etc.

quartet *n.***1.** a group of four instruments or voices, a musical composition for these. **2.** a set of four.

quarto *n.* the size of a book or page or sheet of paper given by folding a sheet of standard size twice to form four leaves.

quartz (*pr.* kwortz) *n.* a kind of hard mineral occurring in various forms.

quasar (kway-zar) *n.* a star-like object that is the source of intense electromagnetic radiation.

quash *v.* **1.** to annul, to reject (by legal authority) as not valid, *quashed the conviction.* **2.** to suppress or crush (a rebellion etc.).

quasi- (kwayz-I) *prefix* seeming to be something but not really so, *a quasiscientific explanation.*

quatercentenary (kwat-er-sen-teen-er-i) *n.* a 400th anniversary.

quatrain (kwot-rayn) *n.* a stanza of four lines.

quaver *v.* **1.** to tremble, to vibrate. **2.** to speak in a trembling voice. —**quaver** *n.*

1. a quavering sound. **2.** a note in music, lasting half as long as a crotchet.

quay (*pr.* kee) *n.* a landing-place, usually built of stone or iron, alongside which ships can be tied up for loading and unloading. **quayside** *n.* land forming or beside a quay.

queasy *adj.* (queasier, queasiest) **1.** feeling slightly sick. **2.** having a digestion that is easily upset. **3.** (of food) causing a feeling of sickness. **4.** squeamish. **queasiness** *n.*

Quebec a province of Canada.

queen *n.* **1.** a woman who is the supreme ruler of an independent country by right of succession to the throne. **2.** a king's wife. **3.** a woman or place or thing regarded as supreme in some way, *Venice, the queen of the Adriatic.* **4.** a playing-card bearing a picture of a queen. **5.** (*slang*) a male homosexual, especially an elderly one. **6.** a piece in chess. **7.** a perfect fertile female of a bee or ant or similar insect. —*v.* to convert (a pawn in chess) to a queen when it reaches the opponent's end of the board, to be converted in this way. □ **queen it,** to behave as if supreme. **queen mother,** a dowager queen who is the mother of a reigning king or queen. **Queen's Counsel,** counsel to the Crown, taking precedence over other barristers. **Queen's Messenger,** a courier in the diplomatic service.

queenly *adj.* like a queen in appearance or manner. **queenliness** *n.*

Queensberry Rules the standard rules of boxing.

Queensland a State of Australia.

queer *adj.* **1.** strange, odd, eccentric. **2.** causing one to feel suspicious, of questionable character. **3.** slightly ill or faint, *felt queer.* **4.** (*slang*) homosexual. —*n.* (*slang*) a homosexual. —*v.* to spoil. — **queerly** *adv.,* **queerness** *n.* □ **in Queer Street,** (*slang*) in difficulties, in debt or trouble. **queer a person's pitch,** to spoil his chances beforehand.

quell *v.* to suppress, to reduce to submission, *quelled the rebellion.*

quench *v.* **1.** to extinguish (a fire or flame). **2.** to satisfy (one's thirst) by drinking. **3.** to cool (a heated thing) by water.

quern *n.* a hand-mill for grinding corn or pepper.

querulous (**kwe**-rew-lŭs) *adj.* complaining peevishly. **querulously** *adv.,* **querulousness** *n.*

query *n.* **1.** a question. **2.** a question mark. —*v.* (queried, querying) to ask a question or express doubt about.

quest *n.* the act of seeking something, a search.

question *n.* **1.** a sentence requesting information or an answer. **2.** something being discussed or for discussion, a problem requiring solution. **3.** the raising of doubt, *whether we shall win is open to question.* —**question** *v.* **1.** to ask questions of (a person). **2.** to express doubt about. —**questioner** *n.* □ **in question,** being referred to or discussed; being disputed, *his honesty is not in question.* **it is a question of,** this is what is required or involved; *it is only a question of time,* it will happen sooner or later. **no question of,** no possibility of. **out of the question,** completely impracticable. **question mark,** the punctuation mark ? placed after a question. **question-master** *n.* the person who puts the questions to people taking part in a quiz game or similar entertainment.

questionable *adj.* open to doubt or suspicion, not certainly true or advisable or honest. **questionably** *adv.*

questionnaire (kwes-chŏn-**air**) *n.* a list of questions seeking information about people's opinions or customs etc., especially for use in a survey.

queue *n.* a line or series of people awaiting their turn for something. —*v.* (queued, queuing) to wait in a queue, *queueing up.*

quibble *n.* a petty objection. —*v.* to make petty objections.

quiche (*pr.* keesh) *n.* an open tart, usually with a savoury filling.

quick *adj.* **1.** taking only a short time to do something or to be done. **2.** able to notice or learn or think quickly. **3.** (of temper) easily roused. **4.** (*old use*) alive, *the quick and the dead.* —*n.* the sensitive flesh below the nails; *be cut to the quick,* to have one's feelings deeply hurt. —*adv.* quickly, *quick-drying.* —**quickly** *adv.,* **quickness** *n.* □ **quick-freeze** *v.* to freeze (food) rapidly for storing, so that it keeps its natural qualities. **quick-witted** *adj.* quick at understanding a situation or making jokes.

quicken *v.* **1.** to make or become quicker. **2.** to stimulate, to make or become livelier, *our interest quickened.* **3.** to reach a stage in pregnancy (*the quickening*) when the foetus makes movements that can be felt by the mother.

quickie *n.* (*informal*) something done or made quickly or hastily.

quicklime *n.* = lime [1].

quicksand *n.* an area of loose wet deep sand into which heavy objects will sink.

quickset *adj.* (of a hedge) formed of plants set in the ground to grow.

quicksilver *n.* mercury.

quickstep *n.* a ballroom dance with quick steps, music for this.

quid[1] *n.* (*pl.* quid) (*slang*) £1. **quids in,** (*slang*) in a position of profit.

quid[2] *n.* a lump of tobacco for chewing.

quid pro quo a thing given in return for something. (¶ Latin, = something for something.)

quiescent (kwi-**ess**-ĕnt) *adj.* inactive, quiet. **quiescence** *n.*

quiet *adj.* 1. with little or no sound, not loud or noisy. 2. with little or no movement. 3. free from disturbance or vigorous activity, peaceful. 4. silent, *be quiet!* 5. unobtrusive, done in a restrained manner, *had a quiet laugh about it.* 6. (of colours or dress etc.) subdued, not showy. —*n.* quietness. —*v.* to make or become quiet, to calm. — **quietly** *adv.,* **quietness** *n.* □ **on the quiet,** unobtrusively, secretly.

quieten *v.* to make or become quiet.

quietude (**kwy**-i-tewd) *n.* quietness.

quiff *n.* an upright tuft of hair above a man's forehead.

quill *n.* 1. one of the large feathers on a bird's wing or tail. 2. an old type of pen made from this, *a quill-pen.* 3. one of a porcupine's spines. 4. the hollow stem of a feather, a plectrum or other device made of this.

quilt *n.* a padded bed-cover. —*v.* to line with padding and fix with cross-lines of stitching.

quin *n.* one of a set of quintuplets.

quince *n.* 1. a hard yellowish pear-shaped fruit used for making jam. 2. the tree bearing it.

quincentenary (kwin-sen-**teen**-er-i) *n.* a 500th anniversary.

quinine (kwin-**een**) *n.* a bitter-tasting medicinal drug used to treat malaria and in tonics.

Quinquagesima (kwinkwă-**jess**-imă) *n.* the Sunday before Lent (50 days before Easter).

quinquennial (kwin-**kwen**-iăl) *adj.* 1. lasting for five years. 2. happening every fifth year.

quinsy (**kwin**-zi) *n.* severe inflammation of the throat, often with an abscess on one of the tonsils.

quintessence (kwin-**tess**-ĕns) *n.* 1. an essence of a substance. 2. the essence or essential part of a theory or speech or condition etc. 3. a perfect example of a quality.

quintet *n.* 1. a group of five instruments or voices, a musical composition for these. 2. a set of five.

quintuple (**kwin**-tew-pŭl) *adj.* 1. consisting of five parts, involving five people or groups. 2. five times as much —*v.* to mul-

tiply or become multiplied by five.

quintuplet (kwin-**tew**-plit) *n.* one of five children born at one birth.

quip *n.* a witty or sarcastic remark. —*v.* (quipped, quipping) to utter as a quip.

quirk *n.* 1. a peculiarity of a person's behaviour. 2. a trick of fate.

quisling (**kwiz**-ling) *n.* a traitor, especially one who collaborates with an enemy occupying his country. ¶ Named after V. Quisling, a pro-Nazi Norwegian leader in the war of 1939–45.

quit *v.* (quitted, quitting) 1. to go away from, to leave; *gave him notice to quit,* gave him (a tenant) notice to leave the premises he occupies. 2. to give up or abandon (a task etc.). 3. (*informal*) to cease, *quit grumbling.* —*adj.* rid, *glad to be quit of the trouble.* □ **quitter** *n.* (*informal*) a person who gives up too easily.

quitch *n.* = couch-grass.

quite *adv.* 1. completely, entirely, *quite finished.* 2. to some extent, somewhat, *quite a long time.* 3. really, actually, *it's quite a change.* 4. (as an answer) I agree, *quite* or *quite so.* □ **quite a few,** a considerable number. **quite something,** a remarkable thing.

quits *adj.* even with, on even terms as a result of retaliation or repayment. **call it quits,** to acknowledge that things are now even, to agree to cease quarrelling.

Quito (**kee**-toh) the capital of Ecuador.

quiver[1] *n.* a case for holding arrows.

quiver[2] *v.* to shake or vibrate with a slight rapid motion. —*n.* a quivering movement or sound.

qui vive (kee **veev**) **on the qui vive,** on the alert, watchful.

quixotic (kwik-**sot**-ik) *adj.* chivalrous and unselfish to an extravagant or impractical extent. **quixotically** *adv.* ¶ Named after Don Quixote, hero of a Spanish story.

quiz *n.* (*pl.* quizzes) a series of questions testing people's general knowledge, especially as a form of entertainment. —*v.* (quizzed, quizzing) 1. to examine by questioning. 2. (*old use*) to stare at curiously.

quizzical (**kwiz**-ikăl) *adj.* 1. done in a questioning way. 2. gently amused. **quizzically** *adv.*

quod *n.* (*slang*) prison, *in quod.*

quoit (*pr.* koit) *n.* a ring of metal or rubber or rope thrown to encircle a peg in the game of **quoits.**

quorum (**kwor**-ŭm) *n.* the minimum number of people that must be present at a meeting before its proceedings are to be regarded as valid.

quota *n.* 1. a fixed share that must be done or contributed or received. 2. the maximum number or amount of people or things that may be admitted e.g. to a country or institution or as imports.

quotable *adj.* worth quoting.

quotation *n.* **1.** quoting, being quoted. **2.** a passage quoted. **3.** an amount stated as the current price of stocks or commodities. **4.** a contractor's statement of the sum for which he is willing to perform specified work. □ **quotation-marks** *pl. n.* punctuation marks (either single ' ' or double " ") enclosing words quoted or put by way of apology round a slang or similar word.

quote *v.* **1.** to repeat or write out words from a book or speech, *quote the Bible* or *from the Bible*. **2.** to mention in support of a statement, *can you quote a recent example?* **3.** to state the price of (goods or services), to give a quotation or estimate. **4.** (in dictation etc.) begin the quotation, open the inverted commas (*see* unquote).

quoth (*rhymes with* both) *v.* (*old use*) said.

quotient (**kwoh**-shĕnt) *n.* the result obtained when one amount is divided by another (e.g. 3 in '12 ÷ 4 = 3').

q.v. *abbrev.* which see (used as an indication that the reader should look at the reference given). From the Latin *quod vide.*

Rr

R. *abbrev.* **1.** Regina, *Elizabeth R.* **2.** Rex, *George R.*

Rabat one of the two capitals of Morocco.

rabbet *n.* a step-shaped channel cut along the edge of a piece of wood etc. to receive another piece or the glass of a window etc. —*v.* (rabbeted, rabbeting) **1.** to join or fix with a rabbet. **2.** to cut a rabbet in.

rabbi (**rab**-I) *n.* (*pl.* rabbis) the religious leader of a Jewish congregation.

rabbinical (ră-**bin**-ikăl) *adj.* of rabbis or Jewish doctrines or law.

rabbit[1] *n.* **1.** a burrowing animal with long ears and a short furry tail. **2.** (*informal*) a person who is a poor performer at a game, especially tennis. **rabby** *adj.* □ **rabbiting** *n.* hunting rabbits. **rabbit-punch** *n.* a short chop with the edge of one's hand on the back of a person's neck. **Welsh rabbit,** *see* Welsh.

rabbit[2] *v.* (rabbited, rabbiting) (*informal*) to talk lengthily or in a rambling way.

rabble *n.* **1.** a disorderly crowd, a mob. **2.** *the rabble,* the common people, the lowest social classes.

rabid (**rab**-id) *adj.* **1.** furious, fanatical, *rabid hate; a rabid Socialist.* **2.** affected with rabies. **rabidly** *adv.,* **rabidity** (ră-**bid**-iti) *n.*

rabies (**ray**-beez) *n.* a contagious fatal virus disease affecting dogs and similar animals, transmitted to man usually by the bite of an infected animal.

race[1] *n.* **1.** a contest of speed in reaching a certain point or in doing or achieving something; *a race against time,* an effort to get something done before a certain time. **2.** a strong fast current of water. **3.** a channel for the balls in a ball-bearing. —**race** *v.* **1.** to compete in a race, to have a race with. **2.** to engage in horse-racing, *a racing man.* **3.** to move or cause to move or operate at full speed, *raced his engine.* —**racer** *n.* □ **race-meeting** *n.* a horse-racing fixture. **race-track** *n.* a track for horse or vehicle races. **the races,** a race-meeting, a series of races for horses or dogs at fixed times on a regular course.

race[2] *n.* **1.** one of the great divisions of mankind with certain inherited physical characteristics in common (e.g. colour of skin and hair, shape of eyes and nose). **2.** a number of people related by common descent. **3.** a genus or species or breed or variety of animals or plants; *the race* or *the human race,* mankind. □ **race relations,** relations between members of different races in the same country.

racecourse *n.* a ground where horse-races are run.

racehorse *n.* a horse bred or kept for racing.

raceme (ră-**seem**) *n.* flowers evenly spaced along a central stem, with the ones at the base opening first (as in lupins, hyacinths, etc.).

rachel (ră-**shel**) *n.* a pale fawn colour used in cosmetics. —*adj.* of this colour.

racial (**ray**-shăl) *adj.* of or based on race. **racially** *adv.*

racialism (**ray**-shăl-izm) *n.* **1.** belief in the superiority of a particular race. **2.** antagonism between people of different races. **racialist** *n.*

racism (**ray**-sizm) *n.* **1.** = racialism. **2.** the theory that human abilities are determined by race. **racist** *n.*

rack[1] *n.* **1.** a framework, usually with bars or pegs, for holding things or for hanging things on. **2.** a shelf or framework of bars for holding light luggage in a train or bus etc. **3.** a bar or rail with teeth or cogs into which those of a wheel or gear etc. fit. **4.** an instrument of torture on which people were tied and stretched —*v.* to inflict great torment on, *was racked with pain.* □ **rack one's brains,** to think hard about a problem. **rack-railway** *n.* a railway having a cogged rail with which a cogged wheel on the train engages for driving the train up a steep slope.

rack[2] *n.* destruction, *go to rack and ruin.*

rack[3] *v.* to draw (wine or beer) off the lees.

racket[1] *n.* a stringed bat used in tennis and similar games. **rackets** *pl. n.* a ball-game for two or four people played with rackets in a four-walled court.

racket[2] *n.* **1.** a din, a noisy fuss. **2.** a business or other activity in which dishonest methods are used. **3.** (*slang*) a line of business, a dodge. —*v.* to move about noisily, to engage in wild social activities, *racketing about.* ☐ **stand the racket,** (*informal*) to bear the costs or consequences.

racketeer *n.* a person who runs or works in a racket or dishonest business. **racketeering** *n.*

rackety *adj.* noisy.

raconteur (rak-on-**ter**) *n.* a person who tells anecdotes, *a good raconteur.*

racy *adj.* (racier, raciest) spirited and vigorous in style, *a racy description of his adventures.* **racily** *adv.,* **raciness** *n.*

radar *n.* **1.** a system for detecting the presence or position or movement etc. of objects by sending out short radio waves which they reflect. **2.** apparatus used for this. ☐ **radar trap,** an arrangement using radar to detect vehicles travelling faster than the speed limit.

radial (**ray**-di-ăl) *adj.* of rays or radii, having spokes or lines etc. that radiate from a central point. —*n.* a radial-ply tyre. —**radially** *adv.* ☐ **radial-ply** *adj.* (of a tyre) having fabric layers with cords lying radial to the hub of the wheel (not crossing each other).

radiant *adj.* **1.** giving out rays of light. **2.** looking very bright and happy. **3.** transmitting heat by radiation, (of heat) transmitted in this way. **radiantly** *adv.,* **radiance** *n.*

radiate *v.* **1.** to spread outwards (especially in lines or rays) from a central point, to cause to do this. **2.** to send out (light or heat etc.) in rays, to be sent out as radiation. **3.** to give forth a feeling of, *she radiated confidence.*

radiation *n.* **1.** radiating, being radiated. **2.** the sending out of the rays and atomic particles characteristic of radioactive substances, these rays and particles.

radiator *n.* **1.** an apparatus that radiates heat, especially a metal case through which steam or hot water circulates. **2.** an engine-cooling apparatus in a motor vehicle or an aircraft.

radical *adj.* **1.** going to the root or foundation of something, fundamental. **2.** drastic, thorough, *radical changes* or *reforms.* **3.** desiring radical reforms, holding extremist views. —*n.* a person desiring radical

reforms or holding extremist views. —**radically** *adv.*

radicle *n.* an embryo root (e.g. of a pea or bean).

radio *n.* (*pl.* radios) **1.** the process of sending and receiving messages etc. by invisible electromagnetic radiation. **2.** an apparatus for sending or receiving messages etc. in this way, a transmitter or receiver. **3.** sound-broadcasting, a sound-broadcasting station, *Radio Oxford.* —**radio** *adj.* **1.** of or using radio. **2.** of or involving stars etc. from which radio waves are received or reflected, *radio astronomy.* —*v.* (radioed, radioing) to send or signal or communicate with by radio. ☐ **radio cab,** a cab equipped with radio for communicating with its headquarters. **radio star,** a small celestial object emitting strong radio waves.

radioactive *adj.* of or showing radioactivity.

radioactivity *n.* the property of having atoms that break up spontaneously and send out radiation capable of penetrating opaque bodies and producing electrical and chemical effects.

radio-carbon *n.* a radioactive form of carbon that is present in organic materials and is used in carbon dating (*see* carbon).

radio-frequency *n.* a range of electromagnetic wave frequencies used in radio and TV transmission.

radiogram *n.* a piece of furniture incorporating a radio and a record-player.

radiographer *n.* a person who is skilled in radiography.

radiography (ray-di-**og**-răfi) *n.* the production of X-ray photographs.

radiologist *n.* a specialist in radiology.

radiology (ray-di-**ol**-ŏji) *n.* the scientific study of X-rays and similar radiation.

radiotherapy *n.* treatment of disease etc. by X-rays or similar forms of radiation.

radish *n.* **1.** a plant with a crisp hot-tasting root that is eaten raw. **2.** its root.

radium *n.* a radioactive metal obtained from pitchblende.

radius *n.* (*pl.* radii, *pr.* **ray**-di-I) **1.** a straight line extending from the centre of a circle or sphere to its circumference. **2.** the length of this line, the distance from a centre, *all schools within a radius of 20 miles.* **3.** the thicker of the two long bones in the forearm, the corresponding bone in animals.

RAF *abbrev.* Royal Air Force.

raffia *n.* soft fibre from the leaves of a kind of palm-tree, used for tying up plants and for making mats etc.

raffish *adj.* looking vulgarly flashy or disreputable or rakish. **raffishness** *n.*

raffle *n.* a lottery with an object as the prize, especially as a method of raising money for a charity. —*v.* to offer (a thing) as the prize in a raffle.

raft *n.* a flat floating structure made of timber or other materials, used especially as a substitute for a boat.

rafter *n.* one of the sloping beams forming the framework of a roof.

rag¹ *n.* **1.** a torn or frayed or worn piece of woven material. **2.** rags used as material for stuffing things or making paper etc. **3.** (*contemptuous*) a newspaper. □ **rag-and-bone man,** an itinerant dealer in old clothes and discarded articles. **rag-bag** *n.* a bag in which scraps of fabric etc. are kept for future use. **rags** *pl. n.* old and torn clothes.

rag² *v.* (ragged, ragging) (*slang*) to tease, to play practical jokes on (a person). —*n.* **1.** (*slang*) a practical joke, a piece of fun. **2.** a carnival held by students to collect money for charity

raga (**rah-gă**) *n.* (in Indian music) **1.** notes used as a basis for improvisation. **2.** a piece of music using a particular raga.

ragamuffin *n.* a person in ragged dirty clothes.

rage *n.* **1.** violent anger, a fit of this. **2.** a craze; *be all the rage,* to be temporarily very popular or fashionable. —**rage** *v.* **1.** to show violent anger. **2.** (of a storm or battle etc.) to be violent, to continue furiously.

ragged (**rag**-id) *adj.* **1.** torn, frayed. **2.** wearing torn clothes. **3.** jagged. **4.** faulty, lacking finish or smoothness or uniformity, *that crew's rowing is a bit ragged.* **raggedly** *adv.,* **raggedness** *n.* □ **ragged robin,** crimson-flowered campion with ragged petals.

raglan *n.* a type of sleeve that continues to the neck and is joined to the body of the garment by sloping seams.

ragout (**rag**-oo) *n.* a stew of meat and vegetables.

ragtime *n.* a form of jazz music with much syncopation.

ragwort *n.* a wild plant with yellow flowers and ragged leaves.

raid *n.* **1.** a sudden attack and withdrawal made by a military party or by ships or aircraft. **2.** an attack made in order to steal. **3.** a surprise visit by police etc. to arrest suspected people or seize illicit goods. —*v.* to make a raid on (a place etc.); *raid the larder,* to take food from it. —**raider** *n.*

rail¹ *n.* **1.** a horizontal or sloping bar forming part of a fence or the top of

banisters or a protection against contact or falling over etc., or for hanging things on. **2.** one of the lines of metal bars on which trains or trams run. **3.** railways as a means of transport, *send it by rail.* —*v.* to fit or protect with a rail, *rail it off.* □ **go off the rails,** (*informal*) to become disorganized or out of control or crazy.

rail² *n.* a kind of small wading-bird.

rail³ *v.* to complain or protest or reproach strongly, *railing at him.*

railing *n.* a fence of rails supported on upright metal bars.

raillery *n.* good-humoured joking or teasing.

railman *n.* (*pl.* railmen) = railwayman.

railroad *n.* (*Amer.*) a railway. —*v.* to rush, to force into hasty action, *railroaded him into accepting.*

railway *n.* **1.** a set of rails on which trains run. **2.** a system of transport using these, the organization and people required for its working. **3.** a track on which equipment with wheels is run.

railwayman *n.* (*pl.* railwaymen) a railway employee.

raiment *n.* (*old use*) clothing.

rain *n.* **1.** condensed moisture of the atmosphere falling in separate drops. **2.** a fall or spell of this; *the rains,* the rainy season in tropical countries. **3.** a shower of things. —*v.* to send down or fall as or like rain; *it rains* or *is raining,* rain falls; *it rains in,* rain penetrates the house etc. □ **be rained off,** (of an event) to be prevented by rain from taking place. **rain forest,** thick forest in tropical areas where there is heavy rainfall. **rain-water** *n.* water that has fallen as rain, not obtained from wells etc.

rainbow *n.* an arch of colours formed in rain or spray by the sun's rays.

raincoat *n.* a waterproof or water-resistant coat.

raindrop *n.* a single drop of rain.

rainfall *n.* the total amount of rain falling within a given area in a given time.

rainy *adj.* (rainier, rainiest) in or on which much rain falls. **save for a rainy day,** to save money etc. for a time when one may need it.

raise *v.* **1.** to bring to or towards a higher or upright position. **2.** to increase the amount or heighten the level of, *raise prices.* **3.** to cause, to rouse, *raise doubts; raise a laugh,* cause people to laugh. **4.** to breed or grow, *raise sheep* or *corn.* **5.** to bring up, to rear, *raise a family.* **6.** to collect, to manage to obtain, *raise an army; raise a loan.* **7.** to put forward, *raise objections.* **8.** to cause to come or appear, *raise* *the ghost.* —*n.* (*Amer.*) an increase in wages or salary. □ **raise Cain** *or* **hell** etc., (*informal*) to make an uproar; to show great anger. **raise from the dead,** to restore to life. **raise one's eyebrows,** to show disdain or suspicion. **raise one's glass to,** to drink a toast to. **raise one's voice,** to speak; to speak more loudly. **raise the alarm,** to give a warning of imminent danger. **raise the siege,** to end it by withdrawing the besieging forces or compelling them to withdraw. **raise the wind,** to obtain money for some purpose. **raising agent,** a substance (e.g. yeast or baking-powder) that makes bread or cake etc. swell and become light in texture.

raisin *n.* a partially dried grape.

raison d'être (ray-zawn **detr**) the reason for or purpose of a thing's existence. (¶ French.)

raj (*pr.* rahj) *n.* the period of British rule in India.

rajah (**rah**-jă) *n.* (in former times) an Indian king or prince.

rake¹ *n.* **1.** a tool with prongs used for drawing together hay or fallen leaves etc. or for smoothing loose soil or gravel. **2.** an implement resembling this, used e.g. by a croupier for drawing in money at a gaming-table. —**rake** *v.* **1.** to gather or smooth with a rake. **2.** to search, *have been raking among old records.* **3.** to direct gunfire along (a line) from end to end, to direct one's eyes or a camera in this way. □ **rake-off** *n.* (*informal*) a commission or share of profits. **rake up,** to revive the memory of (a quarrel or other unpleasant incident).

rake² *n.* a backward slope (e.g. of a ship's mast or funnel, or of a driver's seat). —*v.* to set at a sloping angle.

rake³ *n.* a man who lives an irresponsible and immoral life. **rakish** *adj.* like a rake; jaunty.

rally *v.* (rallied, rallying) **1.** to bring or come together for a united effort. **2.** to reassemble for effort after defeat. **3.** to rouse or revive, *rally one's courage.* **4.** to recover one's strength after illness. **5.** (of share-prices etc.) to increase after falling. —**rally** *n.* **1.** an act of rallying, a recovery of energy or spirits etc. **2.** (in tennis etc.) a series of strokes before a point is scored. **3.** a mass meeting of people with a common interest. **4.** a driving competition for cars or motor cycles over public roads.

ram *n.* **1.** an uncastrated male sheep. **2.** *the Ram,* a sign of the zodiac, Aries. **3.** a battering-ram or similar device. **4.** a striking or plunging device in various machines. — **ram** *v.* (rammed, ramming) **1.** to force or drive into place by pressure. **2.** to strike

and push heavily, to crash against. — **rammer** *n.* □ **ram-jet** *n.* a type of jet engine in which air is drawn in and compressed by motion through the air.

Ramadan (ram-ă-**dahn**) *n.* the ninth month of the Muslim year, when Muslims fast between sunrise and sunset.

ramble *v.* **1.** to take a ramble. **2.** to talk or write disconnectedly, to wander from the subject. —*n.* a walk taken for pleasure, with or without a definite route.

rambler *n.* **1.** a person who rambles, one who goes for a ramble. **2.** a climbing rose.

rambling *adj.* **1.** wandering. **2.** speaking or spoken or written disconnectedly, wandering from one subject to another. **3.** (of a plant) straggling, climbing. **4.** (of a house or street or village etc.) extending in various directions irregularly.

ramekin (**ram**-i-kin) *n.* **1.** a small mould for baking and serving an individual portion of food. **2.** something baked and served in this, *cheese ramekins.*

ramification *n.* **1.** an arrangement of branching parts. **2.** a part of a complex structure, something arising from it, *the ramifications of the plot.*

ramp¹ *n.* **1.** a slope joining two levels of floor or road etc. **2.** a movable set of stairs put beside an aircraft so that people may enter or leave.

ramp² *n.* (*slang*) a swindle or racket, especially one that involves charging excessively high prices.

rampage¹ (ram-**payj**) *v.* to behave violently, to race about wildly or destructively.

rampage² (**ram**-payj) *n.* violent behaviour. **on the rampage,** rampaging.

rampant *adj.* **1.** (in heraldry, of a lion etc.) standing on one hind leg with the opposite foreleg raised, *a lion rampant.* **2.** unrestrained, flourishing excessively, *disease was rampant in the poorer districts.*

rampart *n.* a broad bank of earth built as a fortification, usually topped with a parapet and wide enough for troops etc. to walk on.

ramrod *n.* an iron rod formerly used for ramming a charge into muzzle-loading guns; *like a ramrod,* stiff and straight.

ramshackle *adj.* tumbledown, rickety.

ran *see* run.

ranch *n.* **1.** a cattle-breeding establishment in North America. **2.** a farm where certain other animals are bred, *a mink ranch.* —*v.* to farm on a ranch. —**rancher** *n.*

rancid (**ran**-sid) *adj.* smelling or tasting unpleasant like stale fat. **rancidity** (ran-**sid**-iti) *n.*

rancour (**rank**-er) *n.* bitter feeling or ill will. **rancorous** *adj.*, **rancorously** *adv.*

rand (*pr.* rahnt) *n.* **1.** (in South Africa) a ridge of high ground on either side of a river. **2.** the unit of money in South African countries.

random *adj.* done or made or taken etc. at random, *a random choice.* □ **at random**, without a particular aim or purpose or principle. **random access**, *see* access.

randy *adj.* (**randier**, **randiest**) **1.** lustful, eager for sexual gratification. **2.** (*Scottish*) loud-voiced, boisterous. **randiness** *n.*

rang *see* ring².

range *n.* **1.** a line or tier or series of things, *a range of mountains.* **2.** an extent, the limits between which something operates or varies. **3.** the distance over which one can see or hear, or to which a sound or signal or missile can travel, the distance that a ship or aircraft etc. can travel without refuelling. **4.** the distance to a thing being aimed at or looked at, *at close range.* **5.** a large open stretch of grazing or hunting ground. **6.** a place with targets for shooting-practice. **7.** a fireplace with ovens etc. for cooking in. —**range** *v.* **1.** to arrange in a row or ranks or in a specified way. **2.** to extend, to reach. **3.** to vary between limits. **4.** to wander or go about a place. □ **range-finder** *n.* a device for calculating the distance of an object to be shot at or photographed.

ranger *n.* **1.** a keeper of a royal park or forest. **2.** a member of a body of mounted troops policing a thinly-populated area. **3.** *Ranger,* a senior Guide.

ranging-rod *n.* a rod used in surveying for setting a straight line.

Rangoon (rang-**oon**) the capital of Burma.

rangy (**rayn**-ji) *adj.* (**rangier**, **rangiest**) tall and thin.

rank¹ *n.* **1.** a line of people or things; *the ranks,* ordinary soldiers (not officers). **2.** a place where taxis stand to await hire. **3.** a place in a scale of quality or value etc., a position or grade, *ministers of Cabinet rank.* **4.** high social position, *people of rank.* — **rank** *v.* **1.** to arrange in a rank. **2.** to assign a rank to. **3.** to have a certain rank or place, *he ranks among the great statesmen.* □ **close the ranks**, to maintain solidarity. **the rank and file**, the ordinary undistinguished people of an organization.

rank² *adj.* **1.** growing too thickly and coarsely. **2.** (of land) full of weeds. **3.** foul-smelling. **4.** unmistakably bad, out-and-out, *rank poison; rank injustice.* **rankly** *adv.*, **rankness** *n.*

rankle *v.* to cause lasting and bitter annoyance or resentment.

ransack *v.* **1.** to search thoroughly or roughly. **2.** to rob or pillage (a place).

ransom *n.* the release of a captive in return for money or other payment demanded by his captors, the payment itself. —*v.* **1.** to obtain the release of (a captive) in return for payment. **2.** to hold (a captive) to ransom. □ **hold to ransom**, to hold (a captive) and demand ransom for his release; to demand concessions from (a person etc.) by threatening some damaging action.

rant *v.* to make a speech loudly and violently and theatrically.

ranunculus (ră-**nunk**-yoo-lŭs) *n.* (*pl.* ranunculi, *pr.* ră-**nunk**-yool-I) a plant of the buttercup family.

rap¹ *n.* **1.** a quick sharp blow. **2.** a knock, a tapping sound. **3.** (*slang*) blame, punishment. —**rap** *v.* (**rapped**, **rapping**) **1.** to strike quickly and sharply. **2.** to make a knocking or tapping sound. **3.** to reprimand. □ **rap out**, to say suddenly or sharply. **take the rap**, (*slang*) to take the blame, to suffer the punishment.

rap² *n.* not care or give a rap, not care at all.

rapacious (ră-**pay**-shŭs) *adj.* greedy and grasping (especially for money), plundering and robbing others. **rapaciously** *adv.*, **rapacity** (ră-**pas**-iti) *n.*

rape¹ *n.* the act or crime of having sexual intercourse with a person without her consent or his, either by using force or by fraudulent means. —*v.* to commit rape on (a person). —**rapist** *n.*

rape² *n.* a plant grown as food for sheep and for its seed from which oil is obtained.

rapid *adj.* **1.** quick, swift. **2.** (of a slope) descending steeply. **rapidly** *adv.*, **rapidity** (ră-**pid**-iti) *n.* □ **rapids** *pl. n.* a swift current in a river, caused by a steep downward slope in the river-bed.

rapier (**rayp**-i-er) *n.* a thin light double-edged sword, used for thrusting.

rapport (rap-**or**) *n.* a harmonious and understanding relationship between people.

rapscallion *n.* a rascal.

rapt *adj.* very intent and absorbed, enraptured. **raptly** *adv.*

rapture *n.* intense delight. **rapturous** *adj.*, **rapturously** *adv.* □ **in raptures**, feeling or expressing rapture.

rare¹ *adj.* **1.** seldom found or occurring, very uncommon. **2.** (*informal*) exceptionally good, *had a rare time.* **3.** of low density, thin, *the rare atmosphere in the Himalayas.* **rarely** *adv.*, **rareness** *n.* □ **rare earth**, any of a group of metallic elements with similar chemical properties.

rare[2] *adj.* (of meat) cooked so that the inside is still red.

rarebit *n.* **Welsh rarebit,** *see* Welsh.

rarefied (**rair**-i-fyd) *adj.* (of air etc.) less dense than is normal, thin, like that on high mountains.

raring (**rair**-ing) *adj.* (*informal*) enthusiastic, *raring to go.*

rarity (**rair**-iti) *n.* **1.** rareness. **2.** something uncommon, a thing valued because it is rare.

rascal *n.* **1.** a dishonest person. **2.** a mischievous person. **rascally** *adj.*

raschel (ră-**shel**) *n.* loosely-knitted textile fabric.

rash[1] *n.* an eruption of spots or patches on the skin.

rash[2] *adj.* acting or done without due consideration of the possible consequences or risks. **rashly** *adv.*, **rashness** *n.*

rasher *n.* a slice of bacon or ham.

rasp *n.* **1.** a coarse file with raised sharp points on its surface. **2.** a rough grating sound. —**rasp** *v.* **1.** to scrape with a rasp. **2.** to make a rough grating sound, *a rasping voice.* **3.** to utter gratingly, *he rasped out orders.* **4.** to have a grating effect upon (a person's feelings).

raspberry *n.* **1.** an edible sweet red conical berry. **2.** the bramble that bears it. **3.** (*slang*) a vulgar sound or expression of disapproval or rejection.

Rastafarian (ras-tă-**fair**-iăn) *n.* a member of a Jamaican sect regarding Blacks as a people chosen by God for salvation and having their true homeland in Africa. — *adj.* of Rastafarians.

rat *n.* **1.** a rodent resembling a mouse but larger. **2.** a scoundrel, a treacherous person. —*v.* (**ratted, ratting**) *v.* to withdraw treacherously from an undertaking, to break a promise, *he ratted on us.* □ **rat race,** a fiercely competitive struggle to maintain one's position in work or life.

ratafia (rat-ă-**fee**-ă) *n.* a liqueur or biscuit flavoured with fruit kernels.

ratchet (**rach**-it) *n.* **1.** a series of notches on a bar or wheel in which a pawl engages to prevent backward movement. **2.** the bar or wheel bearing these.

rate[1] *n.* **1.** a standard of reckoning, obtained by expressing the quantity or amount of one thing with respect to another, *walked at a rate of four miles per hour.* **2.** a measure of value or charge or cost, *postal rates.* **3.** speed, *drove at a great rate.* **4.** a local taxation assessed on the value of land and buildings; *the rates,* the amount payable. —**rate** *v.* **1.** to estimate the worth or value of. **2.** to assign a value to. **3.** to consider, to regard as, *we rate him*

among our benefactors. **4.** to rank or be regarded in a certain way, *he rates as a benefactor.* **5.** (*Amer.*) to deserve, *that joke didn't rate a laugh.* **6.** to levy rates on (property), to value (property) for the purpose of assessing rates. □ **at any rate,** in any possible case, no matter what happens; at least. **at this** *or* **that rate,** (*informal*) if this is true or a typical specimen.

rate[2] *v.* to scold angrily.

rateable *adj.* liable to rates (*see* rate[1] *n.* sense 4). **rateable value,** the value at which a house etc. is assessed for rates.

ratepayer *n.* a person liable to pay rates (*see* rate[1] *n.* sense 4).

rather *adv.* **1.** slightly, more so than not, *rather dark.* **2.** more exactly, *he is lazy rather than incompetent.* **3.** more willingly, by preference, *would rather not go.* **4.** (*informal*) emphatically yes, *do you like it? Rather!*

ratify *v.* (**ratified, ratifying**) to confirm or assent formally and make (an agreement etc.) officially valid. **ratification** *n.*

rating *n.* **1.** the classification assigned to a person or thing in respect of quality, popularity, etc. **2.** the amount payable as a local rate. **3.** a non-commissioned sailor.

ratio (**ray**-shi-oh) *n.* (*pl.* ratios) the relationship between two amounts reckoned as the number of times one contains the other.

ration *n.* a fixed quantity (especially of food) allowed to one person. —*v.* to limit (food etc.) to a fixed ration, to allow (a person) only a certain amount.

rational *adj.* **1.** able to reason. **2.** sane. **3.** based on reasoning, not unreasonable. **rationally** *adv.*, **rationality** (rash-ŏn-**al**-iti) *n.*

rationale (rash-ŏn-**ahl**) *n.* a fundamental reason, the logical basis of something.

rationalize *v.* **1.** to make logical and consistent, *tried to rationalize English spelling.* **2.** to invent a rational explanation of, *tried to rationalize their fears.* **3.** to make (a process or an industry) more efficient by reorganizing so as to eliminate waste of labour or time or materials. **rationalization** *n.*

ratline (**rat**-lin) *n.* any of the small lines fastened across a ship's shrouds like rungs of a ladder.

rattan (rat-**an**) *n.* **1.** a climbing palm with long thin jointed pliable stems. **2.** a piece of this stem used as a cane etc.

ratter *n.* a dog as a hunter of rats.

ratting *n.* hunting rats.

rattle *v.* **1.** to make or cause to make a rapid series of short sharp hard sounds, to cause such sounds by shaking something. **2.** to move or travel with a rattling noise.

3. to utter rapidly, *rattled off the oath.* **4.** (*slang*) to agitate or fluster, to make nervous. —**rattle** *n.* **1.** a rattling sound. **2.** a device or toy for making a rattling sound. **3.** noise, an uproar.

rattlesnake *n.* a poisonous American snake with a rattling structure in its tail.

rattling *adj.* **1.** that rattles. **2.** vigorous, brisk, *a rattling pace.* —*adv.* (*informal*) very, *a rattling good story.*

ratty *adj.* (rattier, rattiest) (*slang*) angry, irritable.

raucous (raw-kŭs) *adj.* loud and harshsounding. **raucously** *adv.*, **raucousness** *n.*

raunchy *adj.* (raunchier, raunchiest) (*Amer.*) **1.** slovenly, disreputable. **2.** coarsely outspoken. **3.** boisterous.

ravage *v.* to do great damage to, to devastate. **ravages** *pl. n.* damage, devastation.

rave *v.* **1.** to talk wildly or furiously, to talk nonsensically in delirium; *raving mad,* completely mad. **2.** (of the wind or sea) to howl, to roar. **3.** to speak with rapturous admiration. —**rave** *n.* **1.** (*informal*) a very enthusiastic review of a book or play etc. **2.** (*slang*) an infatuation. □ **rave-up** *n.* (*slang*) a lively party.

ravel *v.* (ravelled, ravelling) to tangle, to become tangled —*n.* a tangle.

raven *n.* a large bird with glossy black feathers and a hoarse cry. —*adj.* (especially of hair) glossy black.

ravening (rav-ĕn-ing) *adj.* hungrily seeking prey.

ravenous (rav-ĕn-ŭs) *adj.* very hungry. **ravenously** *adv.*

ravine (ră-veen) *n.* a deep narrow gorge or cleft between mountains.

ravioli (rav-i-oh-li) *n.* an Italian dish consisting of small pasta cases containing meat.

ravish *v.* **1.** to rape (a woman or girl). **2.** to fill with delight, to enrapture.

ravishing *adj.* very beautiful, filling people with delight.

raw *adj.* **1.** not cooked. **2.** in its natural state, not yet or not fully processed or manufactured, *raw hides.* **3.** (of alcohol) undiluted. **4.** crude in artistic quality, lacking finish. **5.** inexperienced, untrained, fresh to something, *raw recruits.* **6.** stripped of skin and with the underlying flesh exposed, sensitive because of this. **7.** (of an edge of cloth) not a selvage and not hemmed. **8.** (of weather) damp and chilly. —*n.* a raw and sensitive patch on the skin; *touched him on the raw,* wounded his feelings on something about which he was sensitive. —**rawness** *n.* □ **in the raw,** in a raw state; crude, without a softening or refining influence, *life in the raw.*

raw-boned *adj.* gaunt. **raw deal,** unfair treatment. **raw material,** any material or product that is processed to make another; that from which something is made; people who are to be trained.

rawhide *n.* untanned leather.

ray[1] *n.* **1.** a single line or narrow beam of light or other radiation. **2.** a trace of something good, *a ray of hope.* **3.** one of a set of radiating lines or parts or things.

ray[2] *n.* any of several large sea-fish related to the shark and used as food, especially the skate.

rayon *n.* a synthetic fibre or fabric made from cellulose.

raze *v.* to destroy completely, to tear down to the ground.

razor *n.* an instrument with a sharp blade or cutters, used in cutting hair especially from the skin.

razzle *n.* **on the razzle,** (*slang*) on the spree.

razzmatazz *n.* (*informal*) showy publicity or display.

RC *abbrev.* Roman Catholic.

RD *abbrev.* refer to drawer (written on a cheque by a bank when the account has insufficient money to pay it).

re (*pr.* ree) *prep.* in the matter of, about, concerning.

re- *prefix* **1.** again. **2.** back again.

reach *v.* **1.** to stretch out or extend. **2.** to go as far as, to arrive at. **3.** to stretch out one's hand in order to touch or grasp or take something, *reached for his gun.* **4.** to establish communication with, *you can reach me by phone.* **5.** to achieve, to attain, *reached a speed of 100 m.p.h.; reached a conclusion.* **4.** to sail with the wind blowing at right angles to the ship's course. — **reach** *n.* **1.** an act of reaching. **2.** the distance over which a person or thing can reach, the extent covered by one's mental powers or abilities. **3.** a continuous extent of a river between two bends or of a canal between two locks.

reachable *adj.* able to be reached.

react *v.* to cause or undergo a reaction.

reaction *n.* **1.** a response to a stimulus or act or situation etc. **2.** a chemical change produced by two or more substances acting upon each other. **3.** the occurrence of one condition after a period of the opposite, e.g. of depression after excitement.

reactionary *adj.* opposed to progress or reform. —*n.* a person who favours reactionary policies.

reactor *n.* an apparatus for the controlled production of nuclear energy.

read (*pr.* reed) *v.* (read (*pr.* red), reading) **1.** to be able to understand the meaning of (written or printed words or symbols). **2.** to speak (written or printed words etc.) aloud, *read to the children*; *read them a story.* **3.** to study or discover by reading, *we read about the accident.* **4.** to carry out a course of study; *he is reading for the bar,* is studying to become a barrister. **5.** to interpret mentally, to find implications, *don't read too much into it.* **6.** to have a certain wording, *the sign reads 'Keep Left'.* **7.** to copy, extract, or transfer (computerized data), to do this in or on (any storage device or medium). **8.** (of a measuring instrument) to indicate or register, *the thermometer reads 20°.* —**read** *n.* (*informal*) **1.** a session of reading, *had a nice quiet read.* **2.** a thing in regard to its readability, *an interesting read.* □ **read a person's hand,** to interpret the markings on it as a fortune-teller does. **read between the lines,** to discover a hidden or implicit meaning in something. **read-only** *adj.* (of a computer memory) with contents that can be copied, extracted, or transferred but not changed by program instructions. **read proofs,** to read and mark corrections on a printer's proofs. **read up,** to make a special study of (a subject) by reading. **well read,** (of a person) having knowledge of a subject or good general acquaintance with literature through reading.

readable *adj.* **1.** pleasant and interesting to read. **2.** legible. **readability** *n.*

readdress *v.* to alter the address on (a letter etc.).

reader *n.* **1.** a person who reads. **2.** a higher grade of lecturer in some universities, *Reader in Chemistry.* **3.** a book containing passages for practice in reading by students of a language.

readership *n.* **1.** the readers of a newspaper etc., the number of these. **2.** the position of reader at a university.

readily *adv.* **1.** without reluctance, willingly. **2.** without difficulty.

readiness *n.* being ready.

reading *n.* **1.** the act of one who reads. **2.** being read, the way something is read, an occasion when something is read. **3.** books etc. intended to be read. **4.** the amount that is indicated or registered by a measuring instrument. □ **reading age,** the age of an average child with the same reading ability as the one in question. **reading-desk** *n.* a desk for supporting a book etc. while it is being read. **reading-lamp** *n.* a lamp for giving light by which a person can read. **reading-room** *n.* a room (in a club or lending-library etc.) set aside for people who wish to read.

readjust *v.* **1.** to adjust (a thing) again.

2. to adapt oneself again. **readjustment** *n.*

ready *adj.* (readier, readiest) **1.** in a fit state for immediate action or use. **2.** willing, *always ready to help a friend.* **3.** about or inclined to do something, *looked ready to collapse.* **4.** quick, *a ready wit.* **5.** easily available, *found a ready market.* —*adv.* beforehand, *ready cooked.* □ **at the ready,** ready for action. **ready-made** *adj.* (of clothes) made for selling in standard shapes and sizes, not to individual customers' orders; (of opinions or excuses etc.) of a standard type, not original. **ready money,** actual coin or notes; payment on the spot, not credit. **ready reckoner,** a collection of answers to the kind of calculations commonly needed in business etc.

reagent (ree-ay-jěnt) *n.* a substance used to produce a chemical reaction.

real *adj.* **1.** existing as a thing or occurring as a fact, not imaginary. **2.** genuine, natural, not imitation, *real pearls.* **3.** true, complete, worthy of the name, *there's no real cure*; *now you're in real trouble,* in great trouble. **4.** (of income or value etc.) with regard to its purchasing power. **5.** consisting of immovable property such as land or houses, *real property, real estate.* —*adv.* (*Scottish & Amer. informal*) really, very. □ **real time,** (of a computer system) able to receive continually changing data from outside sources, process these data rapidly, and supply results that influence their sources.

realism *n.* **1.** (in art and literature) being true to nature, representing things as they are in reality. **2.** the attitude of a realist.

realist *n.* a person who faces facts, one whose ideas and practices are based on facts not on ideals or illusions.

realistic *adj.* **1.** true to nature, closely resembling what is imitated or portrayed. **2.** facing facts, based on facts not on ideals or illusions. **3.** (of wages or prices) high enough to pay the worker or seller adequately. **realistically** *adv.*

reality *n.* **1.** the quality of being real, resemblance to an original. **2.** all that is real, the real world as distinct from imagination or fantasy, *lost his grip on reality.* **3.** something that exists or that is real, *the realities of the situation.*

realize *v.* **1.** to be fully aware of, to accept as a fact, *realized his mistake.* **2.** to convert (a hope or plan) into a fact, *our hopes were realized.* **3.** to convert (securities or property) into money by selling. **4.** to obtain or bring in as profit, (of goods) to fetch as a price. **realization** *n.*

really *adv.* **1.** in fact. **2.** positively, indeed, *a really nice girl.* **3.** an expression of interest or surprise or mild protest. □

realm (*pr.* relm) *n.* **1.** a kingdom, *peers of the realm.* **2.** a field of activity or interest, *the realms of science.*

ream *n.* a quantity of paper (about 500 sheets) of the same size. **reams** *pl. n.* a great quantity of written matter.

reap *v.* **1.** to cut (grain or a similar crop) as harvest. **2.** to receive as the consequence of actions, *reaped great benefit from their training.* **reaper** *n.*

reappear *v.* to appear again. **reappearance** *n.*

reappraisal (ree-ă-**pray**-zăl) *n.* a new appraisal.

rear[1] *n.* the back part of something. — *adj.* situated at or in the rear. □ **bring up the rear,** *see* bring. **rear-admiral,** *see* admiral. **rear-lamp, rear-light** *ns.* a light on the back of a vehicle. **rear-view mirror,** a mirror placed so that the driver of a vehicle can see traffic etc. behind reflected in it.

rear[2] *v.* **1.** to bring up and educate (children), to breed and look after (animals), to cultivate (crops). **2.** to build or set up (a monument etc.). **3.** (of a horse etc.) to raise itself on its hind legs. **4.** (of a building) to extend to a great height.

rearguard *n.* a body of troops whose job is to protect the rear of the main force.

rearm *v.* to arm again. **rearmament** *n.*

rearmost *adj.* furthest back.

rearrange *v.* to arrange in a different way or order. **rearrangement** *n.*

rearward *adj. & adv.* towards the rear. **rearwards** *adv.*

reason *n.* **1.** a motive or cause or justification of something, a fact put forward as this. **2.** the ability to think and understand and draw conclusions. **3.** sanity, *lost his reason.* **4.** good sense or judgement, what is right or practical or possible, *will do anything within reason,* anything that seems reasonable. —**reason** *v.* **1.** to use one's ability to think and draw conclusions, to state as a step in this, *reasoning that the burglar was familiar with the house.* **2.** to try to persuade someone by giving reasons, *reasoned with the rebels.*

reasonable *adj.* **1.** ready to use or listen to reason, sensible, *a reasonable person.* **2.** in accordance with reason, not absurd, logical. **3.** moderate, not expensive or extortionate, *reasonable prices.* **reasonably** *adv.,* **reasonableness** *n.*

reassemble *v.* to assemble again.

reassure (ree-ă-**shoor**) *v.* to restore confidence to, to remove the fears or doubts of. **reassurance** *n.*

rebarbative (ri-**barb**-ă-tiv) *adj.* repellent, unattractive.

rebate (**ree**-bayt) *n.* a reduction in the amount to be paid, a partial refund.

rebel[1] (**reb**-ĕl) *n.* a person who rebels.

rebel[2] (ri-**bel**) *v.* (rebelled, rebelling) **1.** to refuse to continue allegiance to an established government, to take up arms against it. **2.** to resist authority or control, to refuse to obey, to protest strongly.

rebellion *n.* open resistance to authority, especially organized armed resistance to an established government.

rebellious *adj.* rebelling, insubordinate. **rebelliously** *adv.*

rebirth *n.* a return to life or activity, a revival.

rebound[1] (ri-**bownd**) *v.* **1.** to spring back after an impact with something. **2.** to have an adverse effect upon the originator.

rebound[2] (**ree**-bownd) *n.* an act or instance of rebounding. **on the rebound,** (of a hit or catch) made to a ball that is rebounding; (of an action etc.) done while still reacting to depression or disappointment.

rebuff *n.* an unkind or contemptuous refusal, a snub. —*v.* to give a rebuff to.

rebuild *v.* (rebuilt, rebuilding) to build again after destruction or demolition.

rebuke *v.* to reprove sharply or severely. —*n.* a sharp or severe reproof.

rebus (**ree**-bŭs) *n.* (*pl.* rebuses) a representation of a name or word by means of a picture or pictures suggesting its syllables.

rebut (ri-**but**) *v.* (rebutted, rebutting) to refute or disprove (evidence or an accusation). **rebuttal** *n.*

recalcitrant (ri-**kal**-si-trănt) *adj.* disobedient, resisting authority or discipline. **recalcitrance** *n.*

recall *v.* **1.** to summon (a person) to return from a place. **2.** to bring back into the mind, to remember or cause to remember. —*n.* recalling, being recalled.

recant (ri-**kant**) *v.* to withdraw one's former statement or belief etc. formally, rejecting it as wrong or heretical. **recantation** *n.*

recap (**ree**-kap) *v.* (recapped, recapping) (*informal*) to recapitulate. —*n.* (*informal*) a recapitulation.

recapitulate (ree-kă-**pit**-yoo-layt) *v.* to state again the main points of what has been said or discussed. **recapitulation** *n.*

recapture *v.* **1.** to capture (a person or thing that has escaped or been lost to an enemy). **2.** to succeed in experiencing (a former state or emotion) again. —*n.* recapturing.

recast *v.* (recast, recasting) to cast again, to put into a different form, *recast the question in different words.*

recce (**rek**-i) n. (*informal*) a reconnaissance.

recede v. **1.** to go or shrink back from a certain point, to seem to go away from the observer, *the floods receded*; *the shore receded as we sailed away*. **2.** to slope backwards, *a receding forehead*.

receipt (ri-**seet**) n. **1.** receiving, being received, *on receipt of your letter*. **2.** a written acknowledgement that something has been received or that money has been paid. **3.** (*old use*) a recipe. —v. to mark (a bill) as having been paid.

receive v. **1.** to acquire or accept or take in (something offered or sent or given). **2.** to experience, to be treated with, *it received close attention*. **3.** to take the force or weight or impact of. **4.** to serve as a receptacle for. **5.** to allow to enter as a member or guest. **6.** to greet on arrival. □ **be on the receiving end**, to be the one who has to submit to something unpleasant.

receiving n. the crime of accepting stolen goods while knowing them to be stolen.

receiving-order n. a lawcourt's order to an official (the *receiver*) to take charge of the property of a bankrupt or insane person or of property that is the subject of litigation.

receiver n. **1.** a person or thing that receives something. **2.** one who accepts stolen goods while knowing them to be stolen. **3.** an official who administers property under a receiving-order. **4.** a radio or television apparatus that receives broadcast signals and converts them into sound or a picture. **5.** the part of a telephone that receives the incoming sound and is held to the ear.

recent adj. not long past, happening or begun in a time shortly before the present. **recently** adv.

receptacle n. something for holding or containing what is put into it.

reception n. **1.** receiving, being received. **2.** the way something is received, *the speech got a cool reception*. **3.** an assembly held to receive guests, *wedding reception*. **4.** a place where hotel guests or a firm's clients are received on arrival. **5.** the receiving of broadcast signals, the efficiency of this, *reception was poor*. □ **reception-room** n. a room where visitors are received, (in house-agents' use) a living-room as distinct from a bedroom or kitchen etc.

receptionist n. a person employed to receive and direct callers or clients or patients.

receptive adj. able or quick or willing to receive knowledge or ideas or suggestions etc. **receptiveness** n., **receptivity** n.

receptor n. an organ of the body that is able to respond to a stimulus (such as light or pressure) and transmit a signal through a sensory nerve.

recess (ri-**sess**) n. **1.** a part or space set back from the line of a wall etc., a small hollow place inside something. **2.** temporary cessation from business, a time of this, *while parliament is in recess*. —v. to make a recess in or of (a wall etc.), to set back.

recession n. **1.** receding from a point or level. **2.** a temporary decline in economic activity or prosperity.

recessional n. a hymn sung while clergy and choir withdraw after a church service.

recessive adj. **1.** tending to recede. **2.** (of inherited characteristics) remaining latent when a dominant characteristic is present.

recharge v. to charge (a battery or gun etc.) again. **recharge one's batteries**, to have a period of rest and recovery.

rechargeable adj. able to be recharged.

réchauffé (ri-**shoh**-fay) n. warmed-up or re-cooked food.

recherché (rĕ-**shair**-shay) adj. **1.** devised or selected with care. **2.** far-fetched.

recidivist (ri-**sid**-i-vist) n. a person who constantly commits crimes and seems unable to be cured of criminal tendencies, a persistent offender. **recidivism** n.

recipe n. **1.** directions for preparing a dish etc. in cookery. **2.** a way of achieving something, *a recipe for success*.

recipient (ri-**sip**-iĕnt) n. a person who receives something.

reciprocal (ri-**sip**-rŏ-kăl) adj. **1.** given or received in return, *reciprocal help*. **2.** given or felt by each towards the other, mutual, *reciprocal affection*. **3.** corresponding but the other way round, *I thought he was a waiter, while he made the reciprocal mistake and thought that I was*. —n. a mathematical expression related to another in the way that $\frac{2}{3}$ is related to $\frac{3}{2}$. —**reciprocally** adv.

reciprocate (ri-**sip**-rŏ-kayt) v. **1.** to give and receive, to make a return for something done or given or felt. **2.** (of a machine part) to move backward and forward alternately. **reciprocation** n.

reciprocity (ress-i-**pross**-iti) n. a reciprocal condition or action, the giving of privileges in return for similar privileges.

recital n. **1.** reciting. **2.** a long account of a series of events. **3.** a musical entertainment given by one performer or group, a similar entertainment (e.g. by a dancer).

recitation n. **1.** reciting. **2.** a thing recited.

recitative (ress-i-tă-**teev**) n. a narrative or conversational part of an opera or oratorio, sung in a rhythm imitating that of ordinary speech.

recite *v.* **1.** to repeat (a passage) aloud from memory, especially before an audience. **2.** to state (facts) in order.

reckless *adj.* wildly impulsive, rash. **recklessly** *adv.*, **recklessness** *n.*

reckon *v.* **1.** to count up. **2.** to include in a total or as a member of a particular class. **3.** to have as one's opinion, to feel confident, *I reckon we shall win.* **4.** to rely or base one's plans, *we reckoned on your support.* □ **day of reckoning**, the time when one must atone for one's actions or be punished. **reckon with**, to take into account; *a person* or *thing to be reckoned with,* one that must be considered as important.

reckoner *n.* an aid to reckoning, a ready reckoner (*see* ready).

reclaim *v.* **1.** to take action so as to recover possession of. **2.** to make (flooded or waste land) usable, e.g. by draining or irrigating it. **reclamation** (rek-lă-**may**-shŏn) *n.*

recline *v.* to have or put one's body in a more or less horizontal or leaning position.

recluse (ri-**klooss**) *n.* a person who lives alone and avoids mixing with people.

recognition *n.* recognizing, being recognized; *a presentation in recognition of his services,* as a token of appreciation.

recognizable *adj.* able to be recognized. **recognizably** *adv.*

recognizance (ri-**kog**-ni-zǎns) *n.* a pledge made to a lawcourt or magistrate that a person will observe some condition (e.g. keep the peace) or appear when summoned, a sum of money pledged as surety for this.

recognize *v.* **1.** to know again, to identify from one's previous knowledge or experience. **2.** to realize or admit the nature of, *recognized the hopelessness of the situation.* **3.** to acknowledge or accept formally as genuine or valid, *France has recognized the island's new government.* **4.** to show appreciation of (ability or service etc.) by giving an honour or reward. **5.** (of a chairman in a formal debate) to allow (a particular person) the right to speak next.

recoil *v.* **1.** to move or spring back suddenly, to rebound. **2.** to draw oneself back in fear or disgust. **3.** to have an adverse effect upon the originator. —*n.* the act or sensation of recoiling.

recollect *v.* to remember. **recollection** *n.*

recommence (ree-kŏ-**menss**) *v.* to begin again. **recommencement** *n.*

recommend *v.* **1.** to advise (a course of action or a treatment etc.). **2.** to praise as worthy of employment or favour or trial

etc. **3.** (of qualities or conduct) to make acceptable or desirable, *this plan has much to recommend it.* **recommendation** *n.*

recompense (rek-ŏm-penss) *v.* to repay or reward, to compensate. —*n.* payment or reward etc. in return for something.

reconcile (**rek**-ŏn-syl) *v.* **1.** to restore friendship between (people) after an estrangement or quarrel. **2.** to induce (a person or oneself) to accept an unwelcome fact or situation, *this reconciled him to living far from home.* **3.** to bring (facts or statements etc.) into harmony or compatibility when they appear to conflict. **reconciliation** *n.*

recondite (rek-ŏn-dyt) *adj.* (of a subject) obscure, (of an author) writing about an obscure subject.

recondition *v.* to overhaul and make any necessary repairs to.

reconnaissance (ri-kon-i-săns) *n.* an exploration or examination of an area in order to obtain information about it (especially for military purposes), a preliminary survey.

reconnoitre (rek-ŏn-**oi**-ter) *v.* to make a reconnaissance of (an area), to make a preliminary survey.

reconsider *v.* to consider again, especially with the possibility of changing one's former decision. **reconsideration** *n.*

reconstitute *v.* to reconstruct, to reorganize. **reconstitution** *n.* □ **reconstituted** *adj.* (of food) dried and later restored to its original form, usually by adding water.

reconstruct *v.* **1.** to construct or build again. **2.** to create or enact (past events) again, e.g. in investigating the circumstances of a crime. **reconstruction** *n.*

record [1] (**rek**-ord) *n.* **1.** information preserved in a permanent form, especially in writing. **2.** a document etc. bearing this. **3.** a disc bearing recorded sound. **4.** facts known about a person's past, *has a good record of service; have a record* or *a police record,* to have past convictions which are on record. **5.** the best performance or most remarkable event etc. of its kind that is known; *hold the record,* to be the one who achieved this. —*adj.* best or highest or most extreme hitherto recorded, *a record crop.* □ **for the record**, so that facts may be recorded. **off the record**, stated unofficially or not for publication. **on record**, preserved in written records. **record-breaking** *adj.* surpassing all previous records. **record-player** *n.* an apparatus for reproducing sound from discs on which it is recorded.

record [2] (ri-**kord**) *v.* **1.** to set down in writing or other permanent form. **2.** to preserve (sound) on a disc or magnetic tape for later reproduction. **3.** (of a measuring instrument) to register. □ **recorded delivery,** a postal delivery in which a receipt is obtained from the recipient as proof of delivery. **recording angel,** an angel popularly supposed to register people's good and bad actions.

recorder *n.* **1.** a person or thing that records something. **2.** a judge in certain law-courts. **3.** a kind of flute held forward and downwards from the mouth as it is played.

recount (ri-**kownt**) *v.* to narrate, to tell in detail, *recounted his adventures.*

re-count (**ree**-kownt) *v.* to count again. — *n.* a second counting, especially of election votes to check the totals.

recoup (ri-**koop**) *v.* **1.** to recover what one has lost or its equivalent, *recoup oneself* or *recoup one's losses.* **2.** to reimburse or compensate, *recoup a person for his losses.*

recourse (ri-**korss**) *n.* a source of help. **have recourse to,** to turn to (a person or thing) for help.

recover *v.* **1.** to regain possession or use or control of. **2.** to obtain as compensation, *sought to recover damages from the company.* **3.** to return to a normal condition after illness or unconsciousness. **recovery** *n.* □ **recover oneself,** to regain consciousness or calmness, or one's balance.

re-create *v.* to create again.

recreation (rek-ri-**ay**-shŏn) *n.* the process or means of refreshing or entertaining oneself after work by some pleasurable activity. **recreational** *adj.* □ **recreation ground,** a public playground for children.

recrimination *n.* an angry retort or accusation made in retaliation.

recrudesce (ree-roo-**dess**) *v.* (of a disease or sore or discontent) to break out again. **recrudescent** *adj.,* **recrudescence** *n.*

recruit *n.* **1.** a person who has just joined the armed forces and is not yet trained. **2.** a new member of a society or other group. —**recruit** *v.* **1.** to form (an army or other group) by enlisting recruits. **2.** to enlist (a person) as a recruit. **3.** to refresh, *recruit one's strength.* —**recruitment** *n.*

rectal *adj.* of the rectum.

rectangle *n.* a four-sided geometric figure with four right angles, especially one with adjacent sides unequal in length.

rectangular *adj.* shaped like a rectangle.

rectifiable *adj.* able to be rectified.

rectifier *n.* a device that converts alternating current to direct current.

rectify *v.* (rectified, rectifying) **1.** to put right, to correct, *rectify the error.* **2.** to purify or refine, especially by distillation. **3.** to convert (alternating current) to direct current. **rectification** *n.*

rectilinear (rek-ti-**lin**-i-er) *adj.* bounded by straight lines, *a rectilinear figure.*

rectitude *n.* moral goodness, correctness of behaviour or procedure.

rector *n.* **1.** a clergyman in charge of a parish (in the Church of England, one formerly entitled to receive all the tithes of his parish). **2.** the head of certain universities, colleges, schools, and religious institutions. **3.** the students' elected representative on the governing body of a Scottish university.

rectory *n.* the house of a rector.

rectum *n.* the last section of the large intestine, between colon and anus.

recumbent *adj.* lying down, reclining.

recuperate (ri-**kew**-per-ayt) *v.* **1.** to recover, to regain (one's health or strength) after illness or exhaustion. **2.** to recover (losses). **recuperation** *n.*

recuperative (ri-**kew**-per-ătiv) *adj.* of recuperation, *great recuperative powers.*

recur *v.* (recurred, recurring) to happen again, to keep occurring. **recurring decimal,** a decimal fraction in which the same figures are repeated indefinitely, e.g. $3·999 . . . .$ or $4·014014 . . . .$

recurrent (ri-**ku**-rĕnt) *adj.* recurring, *a recurrent problem.* **recurrence** *n.*

recurve (ri-**kerv**) *v.* to bend or be bent backwards, *a flower with recurved petals.*

recycle *v.* to convert (waste material) into a form in which it can be re-used.

red *adj.* (redder, reddest) **1.** of the colour of blood or a colour approaching this. **2.** (of the face) flushed with anger or shame, (of the eyes) bloodshot or reddened with weeping. **3.** Communist, favouring Communism. **4.** anarchist. —**red** *n.* **1.** red colour. **2.** a red substance or material, red clothes. **3.** a red light. **4.** the debit side of an account; *in the red,* having a debit balance, in debt. **5.** a Communist. **6.** an anarchist. —**redly** *adv.,* **redness** *n.* □ **red admiral,** *see* admiral. **Red Army,** the army of the USSR. **red-blooded** *adj.* full of vigour. **red carpet,** privileged treatment given to an important visitor. **Red Cross,** an international organization for the treatment of the sick and wounded in war and the help of those afflicted by large-scale natural disasters. **red ensign,** the flag of the merchant navy. **red flag,** a flag used as a warning of danger; the symbol of a left-wing revolutionary group; *The Red Flag,* a revolutionary song with this title. **red-handed** *adj.* in the act of crime, *was caught red-handed.* **red herring,** a smoked herring; a misleading clue; something that draws attention away from the matter under consideration. **red-hot** *adj.* so hot that it glows red; highly excited or angry; (of news) fresh, completely new. **red-hot poker**, a garden plant with spikes of red or yellow flowers. **Red Indian**, a North American Indian, with reddish skin. **red lead**, red oxide of lead, used as a pigment. **red-letter day**, a day that is memorable because of some joyful occurrence. **red light**, a signal to stop on a road or railway; a danger-signal. **red-light district**, a district containing many brothels. **red tape**, excessive formalities in official transactions.

redbreast *n.* a robin.

redbrick *adj.* of English universities founded in the 19th century or later, as distinct from Oxford and Cambridge (*Oxbridge*).

redcap *n.* a member of the military police.

redden *v.* to make or become red.

reddish *adj.* rather red.

redecorate *v.* to decorate freshly. **redecoration** *n.*

redeem *v.* **1.** to buy back, to recover (a thing) by payment or by doing something. **2.** to clear (a debt etc.) by paying it off, *redeem the mortgage.* **3.** to convert (tokens etc.) into goods or cash. **4.** to obtain the freedom of (a person) by payment. **5.** to save from damnation or from the consequences of sin. **6.** to make up for faults or deficiencies, *it has one redeeming feature.* □ **redeem oneself**, to make up for one's former fault.

redeemable *adj.* able to be redeemed.

redeemer *n.* one who redeems something. **the Redeemer**, Christ as the redeemer of mankind.

redemption *n.* redeeming, being redeemed.

redeploy *v.* to send (troops or workers etc.) to a new place or task. **redeployment** *n.*

redevelop *v.* (redeveloped, redeveloping) to develop (especially land) afresh. **redevelopment** *n.*

redhead *n.* a person with reddish hair.

rediffusion *n.* relaying of broadcast programmes from a central receiver.

redirect *v.* to direct or send to another place, to readdress. **redirection** *n.*

redo (ree-doo) *v.* (redid, redone, redoing) **1.** to do again. **2.** to redecorate.

redolent (red-ŏ-lĕnt) *adj.* **1.** smelling strongly, *redolent of onions* (¶ not *redolent of the smell of onions*). **2.** full of memories, *a town redolent of age*

and romance. **redolence** *n.*

redouble *v.* **1.** to double again. **2.** to make or become more intense, *redoubled their efforts.*

redoubtable *adj.* formidable, especially as an opponent.

redound *v.* to come back as an advantage or disadvantage, to accrue, *this will redound to our credit.*

redress (ri-dress) *v.* to set right, to rectify, *redress the balance.* —*n.* reparation, amends for a wrong done, *has no chance of redress for this damage.*

redstart *n.* a kind of songbird with a red tail.

reduce *v.* **1.** to make or become less. **2.** to make lower in rank or status. **3.** to slim. **4.** to subdue, to bring by force or necessity into a specified state or condition, *was reduced to despair* or *to borrowing.* **5.** to convert into a simpler or more general form, *reduce the fraction to its lowest terms; the problem may be reduced to two main elements.* **6.** to restore (a fractured or dislocated bone) to its proper position. — **reducer** *n.* □ **reduced circumstances**, poverty after a period of prosperity.

reducible *adj.* able to be reduced.

reduction *n.* **1.** reducing, being reduced. **2.** the amount by which something is reduced, especially in price.

redundant *adj.* **1.** superfluous. **2.** (of workers) no longer needed for any available job and therefore liable to dismissal. **3.** (of apparatus etc.) being a duplicate in case of failure of the corresponding part or unit. **redundancy** *n.*

reduplicate *v.* to double (a letter or syllable), *e.g. bye-bye, goody-goody, superduper.* **reduplication** *n.*

redwood *n.* **1.** a very tall evergreen coniferous tree of California. **2.** its reddish wood.

re-echo *v.* (re-echoed, re-echoing) to echo, to echo repeatedly, to resound.

reed *n.* **1.** a water or marsh plant with tall straight hollow stems. **2.** its stem. **3.** a vibrating part that produces the sound in certain wind instruments.

reedy *adj.* (reedier, reediest) **1.** full of reeds. **2.** like a reed in slenderness or (of grass) thickness. **3.** (of the voice) having the thin high tone of a reed instrument. **reediness** *n.*

reef[1] *n.* a ridge of rock or shingle or sand that reaches to or close to the surface of water.

reef[2] *n.* one of several strips at the top or bottom of a sail that can be drawn in so as to reduce the area of sail exposed to the wind. —*v.* to shorten (a sail) by drawing in a reef or reefs.

reefer *n.* **1.** a thick double-breasted jacket. **2.** (*slang*) a marijuana cigarette.

reef-knot *n.* a symmetrical double knot that is very secure.

reek *n.* a foul or stale smell. —*v.* to smell strongly or unpleasantly.

reel *n.* **1.** a cylinder or similar device on which something is wound. **2.** this and what is wound on it, the amount held by a reel. **3.** a lively folk dance or Scottish dance, music for this. —**reel** *v.* **1.** to wind on or off a reel. **2.** to pull (a thing) in by using a reel. **3.** to stagger, to have a violent swinging or spinning motion. □ **reel off**, to rattle off (a story etc.).

re-elect *v.* to elect again. **re-election** *n.*

re-enter *v.* to enter again. **re-entry** *n.*

re-establish *v.* to establish again. **re-establishment** *n.*

re-examine *v.* to examine again. **re-examination** *n.*

ref *n.* (*informal*) a referee (= umpire).

refectory (ri-**fek**-teri) *n.* the dining-room of a monastery or college or similar establishment. **refectory table,** a long narrow table with a broad supporting upright at each end, or with turned or carved legs, joined by a bar.

refer *v.* (referred, referring) **1.** to make an allusion, to direct people's attention by words, *I wasn't referring to you.* **2.** to send on or direct (a person) to some authority or specialist or source of information. **3.** to turn to (a thing) for information, *referred to the list of rules.* **4.** to ascribe. □ **referred pain,** one felt in a part of the body other than its true source.

referable (ri-**fer**-ăbŭl) *adj.* able to be referred.

referee *n.* **1.** an umpire, especially in football and boxing. **2.** a person to whom disputes are referred for decision, an arbitrator. **3.** a person willing to testify to the character or ability of someone applying for a job. —*v.* (refereed, refereeing) to act as referee in (a football match etc.).

reference *n.* **1.** the act of referring. **2.** something that can be referred to as an authority or standard. **3.** a statement referring to or mentioning something, *made no reference to recent events.* **4.** a direction to a book or page or file etc. where information can be found, the book or passage etc. cited in this way. **5.** a testimonial. **6.** a person willing to testify to a person's character or ability or financial circumstances. □ **in** *or* **with reference to,** in connection with, about. **reference book,** a book providing information for reference but not designed to be read straight through. **reference library** *or* **room,** one

containing books that can be consulted but not taken away.

referendum *n.* (*pl.* referendums (not *referenda*). (¶ This word is now fully established as an English noun and the plural is formed by adding -*s*.) the referring of a question to the people of a country etc. for direct decision by a general vote, a vote taken in this way.

referral (ri-**fer**-ăl) *n.* referring, being referred.

refill[1] (ree-**fil**) *v.* to fill again.

refill[2] (ree-fil) *n.* **1.** a second or later filling. **2.** the material used for this, a thing that replaces something used up.

refine *v.* **1.** to remove impurities or defects from. **2.** to make elegant or cultured.

refinement *n.* **1.** refining, being refined. **2.** elegance of behaviour or manners etc. **3.** an improvement added to something, *the oven has automatic cleaning and other refinements.* **4.** a piece of subtle reasoning, a fine distinction.

refiner *n.* one whose business is to refine crude oil or metal or sugar etc.

refinery *n.* a factory where crude substances are refined.

refit[1] (ree-**fit**) *v.* (refitted, refitting) to renew or repair the fittings of. **refitment** *n.*

refit[2] (ree-fit) *n.* refitting.

reflate *v.* to cause reflation of (a financial system). **reflation** *n.* the process of restoring a financial system to its previous condition when deflation has been carried out too fast or too far. **reflationary** *adj.*

reflect *v.* **1.** to throw back (light or heat or sound). **2.** to be thrown back in this way. **3.** (of a mirror etc.) to show an image of. **4.** to correspond to (a thing) because of its influence, *improved methods of agriculture were soon reflected in larger crops.* **5.** to bring (credit or discredit). **6.** to bring discredit, *this failure reflects upon the whole industry.* **7.** to think deeply, to consider, to remind oneself of past events.

reflection *n.* **1.** reflecting, being reflected. **2.** reflected light or heat etc., a reflected image. **3.** discredit, a thing that brings this. **4.** deep thought, an idea or statement produced by this.

reflective *adj.* **1.** reflecting. **2.** thoughtful, *in a reflective mood.*

reflector *n.* **1.** a thing that reflects light or heat or images. **2.** a red disc or fitment on the back of a vehicle, making it visible in the dark by reflecting the lights of vehicles behind it.

reflex (ree-fleks) *n.* **1.** a reflex action. **2.** a reflex camera. □ **reflex action,** an involuntary or instinctive movement in response to a stimulus. **reflex angle,** an angle of more than 180°. **reflex camera,** one in which the image given by the lens is reflected through the lens to the view-finder.

reflexive *adj.* (of a word or form) refer-ring back to the subject of the verb, in which the action of the verb is performed on its subject, e.g. *he washed himself.* —*n.* a reflexive word or form. □ **reflexive pronoun,** any of the pronouns *myself, himself, itself, themselves,* etc.

refloat *v.* to set (a stranded ship) afloat again.

reform *v.* to make or become better by removal or abandonment of imperfections or faults. —*n.* reforming, being reformed. —**reformer** *n.* □ **Reformed Church,** one that accepted the principles of the Reformation, especially the Calvinist Church.

reformation (ref-er-**may**-shŏn) *n.* reform-ing, being reformed, a great change for the better in public affairs. **the Reformation,** the 16th-century movement for reform of certain doctrines and practices of the Church of Rome, resulting in the estab-lishment of Reformed or Protestant Churches.

reformatory (ri-**form**-ă-ter-i) *n.* an insti-tution where young offenders against the law are sent to be reformed.

refract (ri-**frakt**) *v.* to bend (a ray of light) at the point where it enters water or glass etc. obliquely. **refraction** *n.,* **refractor** *n.*

refractory (ri-**frakt**-er-i) *adj.* **1.** resisting control or discipline, stubborn, *a refrac-tory child.* **2.** (of a disease etc.) not yielding to treatment. **3.** (of a substance) resistant to heat, hard to fuse or work.

refrain[1] *n.* **1.** the lines of a song that are repeated at the end of each verse. **2.** the main part of a song, after the verse. **3.** the music for either of these.

refrain[2] *v.* to keep oneself from doing something, *please refrain from talking.*

refresh *v.* to restore the strength and vigour of (a person etc.) by food or drink or rest. **refresh a person's memory,** to stimulate his memory by reminding him.

refresher *n.* **1.** an extra fee paid to coun-sel while a case is proceeding in a law-court. **2.** (*informal*) a drink. □ **refresher course,** a course of instruction enabling a qualified person to keep abreast of recent developments in his subject.

refreshing *adj.* **1.** restoring strength and vigour. **2.** welcome and interesting because of its novelty.

refreshment *n.* **1.** refreshing, being re-freshed. **2.** something that refreshes, espe-

cially food and drink. □ **refreshments** *pl. n.* food and drink that does not consti-tute a meal.

refrigerant *n.* a substance used for cool-ing things or for keeping things cold.

refrigerate *v.* to make extremely cold, especially in order to preserve and store food. **refrigeration** *n.*

refrigerator *n.* a cabinet or room in which food is stored at a very low tempera-ture.

refuel *v.* (refuelled, refuelling) to re-plenish the fuel supply of (a ship or air-craft).

refuge *n.* shelter from pursuit or danger or trouble, a place giving this; *took refuge in silence,* became silent in order to avoid difficulty.

refugee *n.* a person who has left his home and seeks refuge elsewhere e.g. from war or persecution or some natural disaster.

refund[1] (ri-**fund**) *v.* to pay back (money received, or expenses that a person has incurred).

refund[2] (**ree**-fund) *n.* money refunded, repayment.

refurbish *v.* to make clean or bright again, to redecorate.

refusal *n.* refusing, being refused. **first refusal,** the right to accept or refuse some-thing before the choice is offered to others.

refuse[1] (ri-**fewz**) *v.* **1.** to say or show that one is unwilling to accept or give or do something, *refused to go; refused him permission to go; refused my request; car refused to start,* would not start. **2.** (of a horse) to be unwilling to jump (a fence).

refuse[2] (**ref**-yooss) *n.* what is rejected as worthless, waste material.

refutable (ri-**fewt**-ăbŭl) *adj.* able to be re-futed.

refute *v.* to prove that (a statement or opinion or person) is wrong. (¶ This word is sometimes incorrectly used to mean 'to deny' or 'to repudiate'.) **refutation** (ref-yoo-**tay**-shŏn) *n.*

regain *v.* **1.** to obtain possession or use or control of (a thing) again after losing it. **2.** to reach again, *regained the shore.*

regal (**ree**-găl) *adj.* like or fit for a king. **regally** *adv.,* **regality** (ri-**gal**-iti) *n.*

regale (ri-**gayl**) *v.* to feed or entertain well, *regaled themselves on caviare; regaled them with stories of the campaign.*

regalia (ri-**gay**-li-ă) *pl. n.* **1.** the emblems of royalty used at coronations, *the regalia include crown, sceptre, and orb.* **2.** the emblems or costumes of an order (e.g. the Order of the Garter) or of a certain rank or office; *the mayoral regalia,* the mayor's chain of office etc.

regard *v.* **1.** to look steadily at. **2.** to consider to be, *we regard the matter as serious.* **3.** to concern or have a connection with, *he is innocent as regards the first charge.* — **regard** *n.* **1.** a steady gaze. **2.** heed, consideration, *acted without regard to the safety of others.* **3.** respect, *we have a great regard for him as our chairman.* □ **regards** *pl. n.* kindly greetings conveyed in a message, *give him my regards.*

regarding *prep.* concerning, with reference to, *laws regarding picketing.*

regardless *adv.* heedlessly, paying no attention to something, *regardless of expense.*

regatta *n.* a number of boat or yacht races organized as a sporting event.

regency *n.* **1.** being a regent, a regent's period of office. **2.** a group of people acting as regent. **3.** *the Regency,* the period 1810–20 in England, when George, Prince of Wales, acted as regent.

regenerate (ri-**jen**-er-ayt) *v.* **1.** to give new life or vigour to. **2.** to reform spiritually or morally. **regeneration** *n.*

regent *n.* a person appointed to rule a country while the monarch is too young or unable to rule, or is absent. —*adj.* acting as regent, *Prince Regent.*

reggae (**reg**-ay) *n.* a West Indian style of music with a strongly accented subsidiary beat.

regime (ray-*zh*eem) *n.* a method or system of government or administration.

regiment *n.* **1.** a permanent unit of an army, usually divided into companies or troops or battalions. **2.** an operational unit of artillery, tanks, armoured cars, etc. **3.** a large array or number of things. —*v.* to organize (people or work or data etc.) rigidly into groups or into a pattern. — **regimentation** *n.*

regimental *adj.* of an army regiment. **regimentals** *pl. n.* the uniform of an army regiment.

Regina (ri-**jy**-nä) *n.* reigning queen; *Regina v. Jones,* (as the title of a lawsuit) the Crown versus Jones.

region *n.* **1.** a continuous part of a surface or space or body, with or without definite boundaries or with certain characteristics. **2.** an administrative division of a country. **regional** *adj.* □ **in the region of,** approximately.

register *n.* **1.** an official list of names or items or attendances etc. **2.** the book or other document(s) in which this is kept. **3.** a mechanical device for indicating or recording speed, force, numbers, etc. automatically, *cash register.* **4.** an adjustable plate for widening or narrowing an open-

ing, e.g. for regulating the draught in a fire-grate. **5.** exact correspondence of position; *out of register,* not corresponding exactly. **6.** the range of a human voice or of a musical instrument. —**register** *v.* **1.** to enter or cause to be entered in a register. **2.** to set down formally in writing, to present for consideration. **3.** to notice and remember. **4.** (of an instrument) to indicate or record something automatically. **5.** to make an impression on a person's mind, *his name did not register with me.* **6.** to express (an emotion) on one's face or by gesture. □ **registered letter,** a letter sent by post with special precautions for its safety. **register office,** a place where civil marriages are performed in the presence of a registrar, and where records of births, marriages, and deaths are made.

registrar (rej-i-**strar**) *n.* **1.** an official with responsibility for keeping written records or registers. **2.** a judicial and administrative officer of the High Court. **3.** a doctor undergoing hospital training to be a specialist.

registration *n.* registering, being registered. **registration number,** a combination of letters and figures identifying a motor vehicle.

registry *n.* **1.** registration. **2.** a place where written records or registers are kept. □ **registry office,** a register office.

regress[1] (ri-**gress**) *v.* to go back to an earlier or more primitive form or state. **regression** *n.*

regress[2] (**ree**-gress) *n.* regressing.

regressive *adj.* tending to regress.

regret *n.* a feeling of sorrow for the loss of a person or thing, or of annoyance or disappointment or repentance; *send one's regrets,* to send polite expressions of regret or apology. —*v.* (regretted, regretting) to feel regret about.

regretful *adj.* feeling regret. **regretfully** *adv.*

regrettable *adj.* that is to be regretted, *a regrettable incident.* **regrettably** *adv.*

regroup *v.* to form into new groups.

regular *adj.* **1.** acting or recurring or done in a uniform manner, or constantly at a fixed time or interval, *regular customers; his pulse is regular; keep regular hours,* to get up and go to bed at about the same times always. **2.** conforming to a principle or to a standard of procedure. **3.** even, symmetrical; *a regular pentagon,* with sides of equal length. **4.** usual, normal, habitual, *has no regular occupation.* **5.** belonging to the permanent armed forces of a country, *regular soldiers; the regular navy.* **6.** (of a verb or noun etc.) having inflexions that

are of a normal type. **7.** (*informal*) complete, out-and-out, *it's a regular mess.* —
regular *n.* **1.** a member of the permanent armed forces of a country. **2.** (*informal*) a regular customer or client etc. —
regularly *adv.*, **regularity** *n.*

regularize *v.* **1.** to make regular. **2.** to make lawful or correct, *regularize the position* or *situation.* **regularization** *n.*

regulate *v.* **1.** to control or direct by means of rules and restrictions. **2.** to adjust or control (a thing) so that it works correctly or according to one's requirements. **regulator** *n.*

regulation *n.* **1.** regulating, being regulated. **2.** a rule or restriction; *the Queen's Regulations,* those applying to the armed forces; *regulation dress* or *size* or *speed* etc., that required by regulations.

regurgitate (ri-**gerj**-it-ayt) *v.* **1.** to bring (swallowed food) up again to the mouth. **2.** to cast or pour out again. **regurgitation** *n.*

rehabilitate *v.* **1.** to restore (a person) to a normal life by training, after a period of illness or imprisonment. **2.** to reinstate. **3.** to restore (a building etc.) to a good condition or for a new purpose. **rehabilitation** *n.*

rehash [1] (ree-**hash**) *v.* to put (old material) into a new form with no great change or improvement.

rehash [2] (ree-hash) *n.* **1.** rehashing. **2.** something made of rehashed material, *the programme was a rehash of old newsreels.*

rehearsal *n.* **1.** rehearsing. **2.** a practice or trial performance.

rehearse *v.* **1.** to practise before performing in public. **2.** to train (a person) by doing this. **3.** to say over, to give an account of, *rehearsing his grievances.*

re-heat *v.* to heat again.

rehouse (ree-**howz**) *v.* to provide with new accommodation.

Reich (*rhymes with* like) *n.* the former German State; *the Third Reich,* Germany under the Nazi regime (1933–45).

reign (*pr.* rayn) *n.* **1.** a sovereign's rule, the period of this. **2.** the controlling or dominating effect of a person or thing, *the reign of terror.* —**reign** *v.* **1.** to rule as king or queen. **2.** to be supreme, to dominate; *silence reigned,* there was silence; *the reigning champion,* the one who is champion at present.

reimburse *v.* to repay, to refund. **reimbursement** *n.*

rein *n.* (also *reins*) **1.** a long narrow strap fastened to the bit of a bridle and used to guide or check a horse being ridden or driven. **2.** a means of control, *hold the reins of government.* —*v.* to check or control

with reins; *rein in,* to pull in or restrain with reins. □ **give free rein to,** to allow freedom to, *give one's imagination free rein.*
keep a tight rein on, to allow little freedom to.

reincarnate [1] (ree-in-**kar**-nayt) *v.* to bring back (a soul after death) into another body. **reincarnation** *n.*

reincarnate [2] (ree-in-**kar**-năt) *adj.* reincarnated.

reindeer *n.* (*pl.* reindeer) a kind of deer with large antlers, living in arctic regions.

reinforce *v.* to strengthen or support by additional men or material or quantity. **reinforcement** *n.* □ **reinforced concrete,** concrete with metal bars or wire embedded in it to increase its strength. **reinforcements** *pl. n.* additional men or ships etc. sent to reinforce armed forces.

reinstate *v.* to restore to a previous position. **reinstatement** *n.*

reissue *v.* to issue (a thing) again. —*n.* something reissued.

reiterate (ree-**it**-er-ayt) *v.* to say or do again or repeatedly. **reiteration** *n.*

reject [1] (ri-**jekt**) *v.* **1.** to refuse to accept, to put aside or send back as not to be chosen or used or done etc. **2.** to react against, *the body may reject the transplanted tissue.* **3.** to fail to give due affection to, *the child was rejected by both his parents.* **rejection** *n.*

reject [2] (**ree**-jekt) *n.* a person or thing that is rejected, especially as being below standard.

rejig *v.* (rejigged, rejigging) to re-equip (a factory etc.) for a new type of work.

rejoice *v.* **1.** to feel or show great joy. **2.** to make glad, *this will rejoice your heart.*

rejoin [1] (ree-**join**) *v.* to join again.

rejoin [2] (ri-**join**) *v.* to say in answer, to retort. **rejoinder** *n.* something said in answer or retort.

rejuvenate (ri-**joo**-věn-ayt) *v.* to restore youthful appearance or vigour to. **rejuvenation** *n.*

relapse *v.* to fall back into a previous condition, or into a worse state after improvement. —*n.* relapsing, especially after partial recovery from illness.

relate *v.* **1.** to narrate, to tell in detail. **2.** to bring into relation. □ **relate to,** to establish a relation between, *trying to relate these effects to a possible cause;* to have reference to or a connection with, *he notices nothing but what relates to himself;* to establish a sympathetic or successful relationship with (a person or thing), *learning to relate to children.*

related *adj.* having a common descent or origin.

relation *n.* **1.** the way in which one thing is related to another, a similarity or correspondence or contrast between people or things or events. **2.** being related. **3.** a person who is a relative. **4.** narrating, being narrated. **relationship** *n.* □ **relations** *pl. n.* dealings with others, *the country's foreign relations*; sexual intercourse, *had relations with him.*

relative *adj.* **1.** considered in relation or proportion to something else, *the relative merits of the two plans*; *lived in relative comfort.* **2.** having a connection with, *facts relative to the matter in hand.* **3.** (in grammar) referring or attached to an earlier noun or clause or sentence; *relative pronoun,* e.g. 'who' in 'the man who came to dinner'. — **relative** *n.* **1.** a person who is related to another by parentage or descent or marriage. **2.** (in grammar) a relative pronoun or adverb. — **relatively** *adv.*, **relativeness** *n.*

relativity *n.* **1.** relativeness. **2.** Einstein's theory of the universe, showing that all motion is relative and treating time as a fourth dimension related to space.

relax *v.* **1.** to become or cause to become less tight or tense. **2.** to make or become less strict, *relax the rules.* **3.** to make or become less anxious or formal, to cease work or effort and indulge in recreation. **relaxation** *n.*

relay [1] (ree-lay) *n.* **1.** a fresh set of people or animals taking the place of others who have completed a spell of work, *operating in relays.* **2.** a fresh supply of material to be used or worked on. **3.** a relay race. **4.** a relayed message or transmission. **5.** an electronic device that receives and passes on a signal, often strengthening it. □ **relay race**, a race between teams in which each person in turn covers a part of the total distance.

relay [2] (ree-lay) *v.* (relayed, relaying) to receive and pass on or re-transmit (a message or broadcast etc.).

release *v.* **1.** to set free. **2.** to remove from a fixed position, to allow to fall or fly etc.; *released an arrow.* **3.** to issue (a film) for general exhibition, to make (information or a recording etc.) available to the public. —**release** *n.* **1.** releasing, being released; *a happy release,* death as a merciful release from suffering. **2.** a handle or catch etc. that unfastens a device or machine-part. **3.** information or a film or recording etc. that is released to the public, *a press release.*

relegate (rel-i-gayt) *v.* **1.** to send or consign to a less important place or condition. **2.** to transfer (a sports team) to a lower

division of a league etc. **relegation** *n.*

relent *v.* to become less stern, to abandon one's harsh intentions and be more lenient.

relentless *adj.* **1.** not relenting. **2.** unceasing in its severity, *the relentless pressure of business life.* **relentlessly** *adv.*

relevant (rel-i-vănt) *adj.* related to the matter in hand. **relevance** *n.*

reliable *adj.* **1.** able to be relied on. **2.** consistently good in quality or performance. **reliably** *adv.*, **reliability** *n.*

reliance *n.* **1.** relying. **2.** trust or confidence felt about something. **reliant** *adj.*

relic (rel-ik) *n.* **1.** something that survives from an earlier age. **2.** a surviving trace of a custom or practice. **3.** part of a holy person's body or belongings kept after his death as an object of reverence. □ **relics** *pl. n.* remnants, residue.

relief [1] *n.* **1.** ease given by reduction or removal of pain or anxiety or a burden etc. **2.** something that relaxes tension or breaks up monotony, *a humorous scene serving as comic relief.* **3.** assistance given to people in special need, *a relief fund for the earthquake victims.* **4.** a person taking over another's turn of duty. **5.** a bus etc. supplementing an ordinary service. **6.** the raising of the siege of a besieged town, *the relief of Mafeking.* □ **relief road**, a bypass or other road by which traffic can avoid a congested area.

relief [2] *n.* **1.** a method of carving or moulding in which the design projects from the surface. **2.** a piece of carving etc. done in this way. **3.** a similar effect achieved by the use of colour or shading. □ **relief map**, a map showing hills and valleys either by shading or by their being moulded in relief.

relieve *v.* **1.** to give relief to, to bring or be a relief to. **2.** to introduce variation into, to make less monotonous. **3.** to take a thing from (a person), *the thief had relieved him of his watch.* **4.** to raise the siege of (a town). **5.** to release (a person) from a duty or task by taking his place or providing a substitute. □ **relieve one's feelings**, to use strong language or vigorous behaviour when annoyed. **relieve oneself**, to urinate or defecate.

religion *n.* **1.** belief in the existence of a superhuman controlling power, especially of God or gods, usually expressed in worship. **2.** a particular system of faith and worship, *the Christian religion.* **3.** something compared to religious faith as a controlling influence on a person's life, *football is his religion.*

religious *adj.* **1.** of religion, *a religious ser-*

vice. **2.** believing firmly in a religion and paying great attention to its practices. **3.** of a monastic order; *a religious house,* a monastery or convent. **4.** very conscientious, *with religious attention to detail.* **religiously** *adv.*

relinquish *v.* **1.** to give up or cease from (a plan or habit or belief etc.). **2.** to surrender possession of. **3.** to cease to hold, *relinquished the reins.* **relinquishment** *n.*

reliquary (**rel**-i-kwer-i) *n.* a receptacle for a relic or relics of a holy person.

relish *n.* **1.** great enjoyment of food or other things. **2.** an appetizing flavour or attractive quality. **3.** a strong-tasting substance or food eaten with plainer food to add flavour. —*v.* to enjoy greatly.

reload *v.* to load again.

relocate (ree-lŏ-**kayt**) *v.* to move (a person or thing) to a different place. **relocation** *n.*

reluctant *adj.* unwilling, grudging one's consent. **reluctantly** *adv.,* **reluctance** *n.*

rely *v.* (relied, relying) **rely on,** to trust confidently, to depend on for help etc.

remain *v.* **1.** to be there after other parts have been removed or used or dealt with. **2.** to be in the same place or condition during further time, to continue to be, *remained in London; remained faithful.*

remainder *n.* **1.** the remaining people or things or part. **2.** the quantity left after subtraction or division. —*v.* to dispose of unsold copies of (a book) at a reduced price.

remains *pl. n.* **1.** what remains after other parts or things have been removed or used. **2.** ancient buildings or objects that have survived when others are destroyed, relics. **3.** a dead body, *his mortal remains.*

remake *v.* (remade, remaking) to make again. —*n.* something remade.

remand *v.* to send back (a prisoner) into custody while further evidence is sought. —*n.* remanding, being remanded. □ **on remand,** held in custody after being remanded. **remand centre,** a place where young offenders are sent temporarily.

remark *n.* a written or spoken comment, anything that is said. —*v.* **1.** to make a remark, to say. **2.** to notice.

remarkable *adj.* worth noticing, exceptional, unusual. **remarkably** *adv.*

remarry *v.* (remarried, remarrying) to marry again.

remedial (ri-**meed**-iăl) *adj.* providing a remedy for a disease or deficiency, *remedial exercises.*

remedy *n.* something that cures or relieves a disease or that puts right a matter. —*v.* (remedied, remedying) to be a remedy for, to put right.

remember *v.* **1.** to keep in one's mind. **2.** to recall knowledge or experience to one's mind, to be able to do this. **3.** to make a present to, *remembered me in his will.* **4.** to mention as sending greetings, *remember me to your mother.* □ **remember oneself,** to remember one's intentions or to behave with suitable dignity after a lapse.

remembrance *n.* **1.** remembering, being remembered, memory. **2.** something that reminds people, a memento or memorial. □ **Remembrance Sunday,** the Sunday nearest to 11 November, when those killed in the wars of 1914–18 and 1939–45 are commemorated.

remind *v.* to cause to remember or think of something.

reminder *n.* a thing that reminds someone, a letter sent to remind someone.

reminisce (rem-in-**iss**) *v.* to think or talk about past events and experiences.

reminiscence (rem-in-**iss**-ĕns) *n.* **1.** thinking or talking about past events. **2.** a spoken or written account of what one remembers, *wrote his reminiscences.* **3.** a thing that is reminiscent of something else.

reminiscent (rem-in-**iss**-ĕnt) *adj.* **1.** inclined to reminisce, *she was in a reminiscent mood.* **2.** having characteristics that recall something to one's mind, *his style is reminiscent of Picasso's.* **reminiscently** *adv.*

remiss (ri-**miss**) *adj.* negligent, *you have been remiss in your duties* or *very remiss.*

remission *n.* **1.** God's pardon or forgiveness of sins. **2.** the remitting of a debt or penalty, shortening of a convict's prison sentence on account of his good behaviour. **3.** reduction of the force or intensity of something, *slight remission of the pain.*

remit *v.* (remitted, remitting) **1.** (of God) to forgive (sins). **2.** to cancel (a debt), to refrain from inflicting (a punishment). **3.** to make or become less intense, *we must not remit our efforts.* **4.** to send (money etc.) to a person or place, *please remit the interest to my home address.* **5.** to send (a matter for decision) to some authority. **6.** to postpone.

remittance *n.* the sending of money to a person, the money sent.

remnant *n.* **1.** a small remaining quantity or part or number of people or things. **2.** a surviving trace of something. **3.** a small piece of cloth left when the rest of the roll has been used or sold.

remodel *v.* (remodelled, remodelling) to model again or differently, to reconstruct or reorganize.

remonstrance (ri-**mon**-străns) *n.* remonstrating, a protest.

remonstrate (**rem**-ŏn-strayt) *v.* to make a

protest, *remonstrated with him about his behaviour.*

remorse *n.* deep regret for one's wrongdoing. **remorseful** *adj.,* **remorsefully** *adv.*

remorseless *adv.* relentless. **remorselessly** *adv.*

remote *adj.* **1.** far apart, far away in place or time, *the remote past.* **2.** far from civilization, *a remote village.* **3.** not close in relationship or connection, *a remote ancestor; remote causes.* **4.** slight, *I haven't the remotest idea.* **remotely** *adv.,* **remoteness** *n.* □ **remote control,** control of apparatus etc. from a distance, usually by means of electricity or radio.

remount *v.* to mount again.

removable *adj.* able to be removed.

removal *n.* **1.** removing, being removed. **2.** transfer of furniture etc. to a different house.

remove *v.* **1.** to take off or away from the place occupied. **2.** to take off (clothing). **3.** to dismiss from office. **4.** to get rid of, *this removes the last of my doubts.* — **remove** *n.* **1.** a form or division in some schools. **2.** a stage or degree, a degree of difference, *this is several removes from the truth.* —**remover** *n.* □ **removed** *adj.* distant, remote, *a dialect not far removed from Cockney; a cousin once removed,* a cousin's child or parent, *twice removed,* a cousin's grandchild or grandparent.

remunerate (ri-**mewn**-er-ayt) *v.* to pay or reward (a person) for services rendered. **remuneration** *n.*

remunerative (ri-**mewn**-er-ătiv) *adj.* giving good remuneration, profitable.

Renaissance (rĕ-**nay**-săns) *n.* **1.** the revival of art and literature in Europe (influenced by classical forms) in the 14th–16th centuries, the period of this. **2.** *renaissance,* any similar revival.

renal (**ree**-năl) *adj.* of the kidneys.

rename *v.* to give a fresh name to.

rend *v.* (rent, rending) to tear.

render *v.* **1.** to give, especially in return or exchange or as something due, *a reward for services rendered.* **2.** to present or send in; *account rendered,* a bill previously sent in and not yet paid. **3.** to cause to become, *rendered him helpless.* **4.** to give a performance of (a play or character). **5.** to translate, *rendered into English.* **6.** to melt down (fat).

rendezvous (**ron**-day-voo) *n.* (*pl.* rendezvous, *pr.* **ron**-day-vooz) **1.** a pre-arranged meeting. **2.** a pre-arranged or regular meeting-place. —*v.* (rendezvoused, rendezvousing) to meet at a rendezvous.

rendition (ren-**dish**-ŏn) *n.* the way a dramatic role or musical piece etc.

is rendered or performed.

renegade (**ren**-i-gayd) *n.* someone who deserts from a group or cause or faith etc.

renege (ri-**neeg**) *v.* to fail to keep a promise etc., *reneged on their agreement.*

renew *v.* **1.** to restore to its original state. **2.** to replace with a fresh supply, *the tyres need renewing.* **3.** to get or make or give again, *renewed their acquaintance* or *requests.* **4.** to arrange for a continuation or continued validity of, *renew one's subscription* or *lease* or *licence.* **renewal** *n.*

renewable *adj.* able to be renewed.

rennet (**ren**-it) *n.* a substance used to curdle milk in making cheese or junket.

renounce *v.* **1.** to give up (a claim or right etc.) formally, *renounced his title.* **2.** to reject, to refuse to abide by (an agreement etc.). **renouncement** *n.*

renovate (**ren**-ŏ-vayt) *v.* to repair, to renew. **renovation** *n.,* **renovator** *n.*

renown (*rhymes with* down) *n.* fame. **renowned** *adj.* famous, celebrated.

rent[1] *see* rend. —*n.* a torn place in a garment etc., a split.

rent[2] *n.* payment made periodically for the use of land or accommodation or machinery, or for the availability of a telephone instrument etc. —*v.* **1.** to pay rent for temporary use of. **2.** to allow to be used in return for payment of rent. □ **rent-free** *adj. & adv.* with exemption from payment of rent.

rentable *adj.* able to be rented.

rental *n.* **1.** the amount paid or received as rent. **2.** renting.

renumber *v.* to change the numbering of.

renunciation (ri-nun-si-**ay**-shŏn) *n.* renouncing, giving something up.

reopen *v.* to open again.

reorder *v.* **1.** to order again, to order further supplies of. **2.** to put into a different order.

reorganize *v.* to organize in a new way. **reorganization** *n.*

rep[1] *n.* textile fabric with a corded effect, used for curtains and upholstery.

rep[2] *n.* (*informal*) a business firm's travelling representative.

rep[3] *n.* (*informal*) repertory, *a rep company.*

repaint *v.* to paint again or differently.

repair[1] *v.* **1.** to put into good or sound condition after damage or the effects of wear and tear. **2.** to put right, to make amends for; *repaired the omission,* did what had been omitted. —**repair** *n.* **1.** the act or process of repairing something. **2.** condition as regards being repaired, *keep it in good repair.* —**repairer** *n.*

repair[2] *v.* to go, *repaired to the coffee room.*

repairable *adj.* able to be repaired.

reparation (rep-er-**ay**-shŏn) *n.* making amends. **reparations** *pl. n.* compensation for war damage, demanded by the victor from a defeated enemy.

repartee (rep-ar-**tee**) *n.* a witty reply, ability to make witty replies.

repast (ri-**pahst**) *n.* (*formal*) a meal.

repatriate (ree-**pat**-ri-ayt) *v.* to send or bring back (a person) to his own country. **repatriation** *n.*

repay *v.* (repaid, repaying) 1. to pay back (money). 2. to do or make or give in return, *repaid kindness with kindness.* **repayment** *n.*

repayable *adj.* able or needing to be repaid.

repeal *v.* to withdraw (a law) officially. — *n.* the repealing of a law.

repeat *v.* 1. to say or do or occur again. 2. to say aloud (something heard or learnt by heart), *repeat the oath after me.* 3. to tell to another person (something told to oneself). 4. (of food) to produce a taste in one's mouth intermittently for some time after being eaten. 5. to supply a further consignment of, *we cannot repeat this article.* —**repeat** *n.* 1. repeating. 2. something that is repeated; *a repeat order,* an order for a further consignment of similar goods. □ **repeat itself,** to recur in the same form. **repeat oneself,** to say or do the same thing again.

repeatable *adj.* able to be repeated, suitable for being repeated.

repeatedly *adv.* again and again.

repeater *n.* a device that repeats a signal.

repel *v.* (repelled, repelling) 1. to drive away, *repelled the attackers.* 2. to refuse to accept, *repelled all offers of help.* 3. to be impossible for (a substance) to penetrate, *the surface repels moisture.* 4. to push away from itself by an unseen force (the opposite of *attract*), *one north magnetic pole repels another.* 5. to be repulsive or distasteful to.

repellent *adj.* 1. repelling, arousing distaste. 2. not penetrable by a specified substance, *the fabric is water-repellent.* — *n.* a substance that repels something, *insect repellents.*

repent *v.* to feel regret about (what one has done or failed to do). **repentance** *n.,* **repentant** *adj.*

repercussion (ree-per-**kush**-ŏn) *n.* 1. the recoil of something after impact. 2. an echo. 3. an indirect effect or reaction.

repertoire (**rep**-er-twar) *n.* a stock of songs or plays or acts etc. that a person or company knows and is prepared to perform.

repertory (**rep**-er-ter-i) *n.* 1. a repertoire. 2. theatrical performances of various plays for short periods (not for long runs as in London theatres); *repertory company* or *theatre,* one giving these.

repetition *n.* repeating, being repeated, an instance of this.

repetitious (rep-i-**tish**-ŭs) *adj.* repetitive.

repetitive (ri-**pet**-it-iv) *adj.* characterized by repetition. **repetitively** *adv.*

replace *v.* 1. to put back in place. 2. to take the place of. 3. to find or provide a substitute for. **replacement** *n.*

replaceable *adj.* able to be replaced.

replay[1] (ree-**play**) *v.* to play (a match or recording etc.) again.

replay[2] (ree-**play**) *n.* replaying of a match or of a recorded incident in a game etc.

replenish *v.* to fill (a thing) again, to renew (a supply etc.). **replenishment** *n.*

replete (ri-**pleet**) *adj.* 1. well stocked or supplied. 2. full, gorged. **repletion** *n.*

replica (**rep**-lik-ă) *n.* an exact copy or reproduction of something.

replicate (**rep**-lik-ayt) *v.* to make a replica of. **replication** *n.*

reply *v.* (replied, replying) to make an answer, to say in answer. — *n.* 1. replying. 2. what is replied, an answer.

report *v.* 1. to give an account of (something seen or done or studied), to tell as news; *report progress,* to state what has been done so far. 2. to write or give a description of (an event etc.) for publication or broadcasting. 3. to make a formal accusation about (an offence or offender). 4. to present oneself as arrived or returned, *report to me on Monday.* 5. to be responsible to a certain person as one's superior or supervisor. —**report** *n.* 1. a spoken or written account of something seen or done or studied. 2. a description for publication or broadcasting. 3. a periodical statement about a pupil's or employee's work and conduct. 4. rumour, a piece of gossip. 5. an explosive sound like that made by a gun.

reportage (rep-or-**tah**zh) *n.* the reporting of news for the press etc., a typical style of doing this.

reportedly *adv.* according to reports.

reporter *n.* a person employed to report news etc. for publication or broadcasting.

repose[1] *n.* 1. rest, sleep. 2. a peaceful state or effect, tranquillity. —*v.* to rest, to lie.

repose[2] *v.* to place (trust etc.) in.

repository *n.* a place where things are stored.

repossess *v.* to regain possession of

559

(goods on which hire-purchase payments have not been kept up). **repossession** *n.*

repp *n.* = rep¹.

reprehend (rep-ri-**hend**) *v.* to rebuke.

reprehensible (rep-ri-hen-sibŭl) *adj.* deserving rebuke. **reprehensibly** *adv.*

represent *v.* 1. to show (a person or thing or scene) in a picture or play etc. 2. to describe or declare to be, *representing himself as an expert.* 3. to state in polite protest or remonstrance, *we must represent to them the risks involved.* 4. to symbolize, *in Roman numerals C represents 100.* 5. to be an example or embodiment of, *the election results represent the views of the electorate.* 6. to act as a deputy or agent or spokesman for, *the Queen was represented by the Duke.* **representation** *n.*

representative *adj.* 1. typical of a group or class. 2. containing examples of a number of types, *a representative selection.* 3. consisting of elected representatives, based on representation by these, *representative government.* —**representative** *n.* 1. a sample or specimen of something. 2. a person's or firm's agent. 3. a person chosen to represent another or others, or to take part in a legislative assembly on their behalf. □ **House of Representatives,** the lower house of Congress in the USA and of other national parliaments.

repress *v.* to keep down, to suppress, to keep (emotions etc.) from finding an outlet. **repression** *n.* □ **repressed** *adj.* suffering from repression of the emotions.

repressive *adj.* serving or intended to repress a person or thing. **repressively** *adv.*

reprieve (ri-**preev**) *n.* 1. postponement or cancellation of a punishment, especially of the death sentence. 2. temporary relief from danger, postponement of trouble. —*v.* to give a reprieve to.

reprimand (**rep**-ri-mahnd) *n.* a rebuke, especially a formal or official one. —*v.* to give a reprimand to.

reprint¹ (ree-**print**) *v.* to print again in the same or a new form.

reprint² (**ree**-print) *n.* reprinting of a book, a book reprinted.

reprisal (ri-**pry**-zăl) *n.* an act of retaliation; *take reprisals,* retaliate.

reproach *v.* to express disapproval to (a person) for a fault or offence. —*n.* 1. reproaching, an instance of this. 2. a thing that brings disgrace or discredit. □ **above** *or* **beyond reproach,** deserving no blame, perfect.

reproachful *adj.* expressing reproach. **reproachfully** *adv.*

reprobate (**rep**-rŏ-bayt) *n.* an immoral or unprincipled person.

reprobation (rep-rŏ-**bay**-shŏn) *n.* strong condemnation.

reproduce *v.* 1. to produce a copy of (a picture etc.). 2. to cause to be seen or heard again or to occur again. 3. to have a specified quality when reproduced, *some colours don't reproduce well.* 4. to produce further members of the same species by natural means, to produce (offspring).

reproducible *adj.* able to be reproduced.

reproduction *n.* 1. reproducing, being reproduced. 2. a copy of a painting etc.; *reproduction furniture,* made in imitation of an earlier style.

reproductive *adj.* of or belonging to reproduction, *the reproductive system.*

reproof *n.* an expression of condemnation for a fault or offence.

reprove *v.* to give a reproof to.

reptile *n.* a member of the class of cold-blooded animals with a backbone and relatively short legs or no legs at all, e.g. snakes, lizards, crocodiles, tortoises. **reptilian** (rep-**til**-iăn) *adj.*

republic *n.* a country in which the supreme power is held by the people or their elected representatives, or by an elected or nominated president.

republican *adj.* of or like or advocating a republic. —*n.* 1. a person advocating republican government. 2. *Republican,* a member of the *Republican Party,* one of the two main political parties in the USA.

repudiate (ri-**pew**-di-ayt) *v.* to reject or disown utterly, to deny, *repudiate the accusation; repudiate the agreement,* to refuse to abide by it. **repudiation** *n.*

repugnant (ri-**pug**-nănt) *adj.* distasteful, objectionable. **repugnance** *n.*

repulse *v.* 1. to drive back (an attacking force). 2. to reject (an offer or help etc.) firmly, to rebuff.

repulsion *n.* 1. repelling, being repelled. 2. a feeling of strong distaste, revulsion.

repulsive *adj.* 1. arousing disgust. 2. repelling things, *a repulsive force.* **repulsively** *adv.,* **repulsiveness** *n.*

reputable (**rep**-yoo-tăbŭl) *adj.* having a good reputation, respected.

reputation *n.* 1. what is generally said or believed about a person or thing, *a reputation for honesty.* 2. public recognition for one's abilities or achievements, *built up a reputation.*

repute (ri-**pewt**) *n.* reputation, *I know him by repute.*

reputed (ri-**pewt**-id) *adj.* said or thought to be; *his reputed father,* the man thought to be his father. **reputedly** *adv.*

request *n.* asking or being asked for a

thing or to do something, a thing asked for; *a request programme*, one consisting of items asked for by the public. —*v.* to make a request for. □ **by** *or* **on request**, in response to a request. **request stop**, a place where a bus etc. stops only on a passenger's request.

requiem (rek-wi-em) *n.* a special Mass for the repose of the soul(s) of the dead, a musical setting for this.

require *v.* **1.** to need, to depend on for success or fulfilment etc., *cars require regular servicing.* **2.** to order or oblige, *Civil Servants are required to sign the Official Secrets Act.* **3.** to wish to have, *will you require tea?*

requirement *n.* a need.

requisite (rek-wiz-it) *adj.* required by circumstances, necessary to success. —*n.* a thing needed for some purpose.

requisition *n.* a formal written demand for something that is needed, an official order laying claim to the use of property or materials. —*v.* to demand or order by a requisition.

reredos (reer-doss) *n.* an ornamental screen covering the wall above the back of an altar.

re-route (ree-root) *v.* to send or carry by a different route.

resale *n.* sale to another person of something one has bought.

rescind (ri-sind) *v.* to repeal or cancel (a law or rule etc.).

rescue *v.* to save or bring away from attack or capture or danger etc. —*n.* rescuing, being rescued. —**rescuer** *n.*

research (ri-serch) *n.* careful study and investigation, especially in order to discover new facts or information. —*v.* to do research into, *the subject has been fully researched.* —**researcher** *n.*

resect *v.* to cut out part of (a lung etc.) or pare down (a bone etc.) surgically. **resection** *n.*

resell *v.* (resold, reselling) to sell (what one has bought) to another person.

resemble *v.* to be like (another person or thing). **resemblance** *n.*

resent (ri-zent) *v.* to feel displeased and indignant about, to feel insulted by (something said or done). **resentment** *n.*

resentful *adj.* feeling resentment. **resentfully** *adv.*

reservation *n.* **1.** reserving, being reserved. **2.** a reserved seat or accommodation etc., a record of this, *our hotel reservations.* **3.** a limitation on one's agreement or acceptance of an idea etc., *we accept the plan in principle but have certain reservations; without reservation,* completely, whole-

heartedly. **4.** a strip of land between the carriageways of a road. **5.** (*Amer.*) an area of land reserved for occupation by an Indian tribe.

reserve *v.* **1.** to put aside for a later occasion or for special use. **2.** to retain, *the company reserves the right to offer a substitute.* **3.** to order or set aside (seats or accommodation etc.) for a particular person to use at a future date. **4.** to postpone, *reserve judgement.* —**reserve** *n.* **1.** something reserved for future use, an extra amount or stock kept available for use when needed. **2.** (also **reserves**) forces outside the regular armed services and liable to be called out in an emergency, a member of these. **3.** an extra player chosen in case a substitute should be needed in a team. **4.** an area of land reserved for some special purpose, *a nature reserve.* **5.** the reservation between carriageways of a road. **6.** a limitation on one's agreement or acceptance of an idea etc. **7.** a reserve price. **8.** a tendency to avoid showing one's feelings and to lack cordiality towards other people. □ **in reserve,** in a state of being unused but available. **reserve price,** the lowest price that will be accepted for something sold by public auction or from an exhibition.

reserved *adj.* (of a person) showing reserve of manner.

reservist *n.* a member of a country's reserve forces.

reservoir (rez-er-vwar) *n.* **1.** a natural or artificial lake that is a source or store of water for a town etc. **2.** a container for a supply of fuel or other liquid. **3.** a supply or collection of information etc.

reshuffle *v.* **1.** to shuffle (cards) again. **2.** to interchange the posts or responsibilities of (a group of people). —*n.* reshuffling; *a Cabinet reshuffle,* redistribution of Cabinet posts among the same people.

reside *v.* **1.** to have one's home (in a certain place), to dwell permanently. **2.** to be present or vested in a person, *supreme authority resides in the President.*

residence *n.* **1.** a place where one resides. **2.** a dwelling-house, *desirable residence for sale.* **3.** residing; *take up one's residence,* to begin to dwell. □ **in residence,** living in a specified place for the performance of one's work or duties.

resident *adj.* residing, in residence. —*n.* **1.** a permanent inhabitant of a place, not a visitor. **2.** (at a hotel) a person staying overnight.

residential (rez-i-den-shăl) *adj.* **1.** containing or suitable for private houses, *a residential area.* **2.** connected with or based on residence, *residential qualifications for voters.*

residual (ri-**zid**-yoo-ăl) *adj.* left over as a residue.

residuary (ri-**zid**-yoo-er-i) *adj.* 1. residual. 2. of the residue of an estate; *residuary legatee,* the one who inherits the remainder of an estate after specific items have been allotted to others.

residue (**rez**-i-dew) *n.* the remainder, what is left over.

residuum (ri-**zid**-yoo-ŭm) *n.* (*pl.* residua) a residue, especially after combustion or evaporation.

resign *v.* to give up or surrender (one's job or property or claim etc.). **resign oneself to,** to be ready to accept and endure, to accept as inevitable.

resigned *adj.* having or showing patient acceptance of an unwelcome task or situation. **resignedly** (ri-**zyn**-idli) *adv.* □ **be resigned to,** to resign oneself to.

resignation *n.* 1. resigning. 2. a document or statement conveying that one wishes to resign. 3. a resigned attitude or expression.

resilient (ri-**zil**-iĕnt) *adj.* 1. springing back to its original form after being bent or stretched, springy. 2. (of a person) readily recovering from shock or depression etc. **resiliently** *adv.,* **resilience** *n.*

resin (**rez**-in) *n.* 1. a sticky substance that oozes from fir and pine trees and from many other plants, used in making varnish etc. 2. a similar substance made synthetically, used as a plastic or in making plastics. **resinous** *adj.*

resist *v.* 1. to oppose, to use force in order to prevent something from happening or being successful. 2. to regard (a plan or idea) unfavourably. 3. to be undamaged or unaffected by, to prevent from penetrating, *pans that resist heat.* 4. to refrain from accepting or yielding to, *can't resist chocolates* or *temptation.*

resistance *n.* 1. resisting, the power to resist something. 2. an influence that hinders or stops something. 3. the property of not conducting heat or electricity, the measure of this. 4. a secret organization resisting the authorities, especially in a conquered or enemy-occupied country. □ **the line of least resistance,** the easiest method or course.

resistant *adj.* offering resistance, capable of resisting, *heat-resistant plastics.*

resistive *adj.* 1. resistant. 2. having electrical resistance.

resistivity (rez-iss-**tiv**-iti) *n.* the power of a specified material to resist the passage of electric current.

resistor *n.* a device having resistance to the passage of electric current.

resit *v.* (resat, resitting) to sit (an examination) again after a previous failure.

resole *v.* to put a new sole on (a shoe).

resolute (**rez**-ŏ-loot) *adj.* showing great determination. **resolutely** *adv.,* **resoluteness** *n.*

resolution *n.* 1. the quality of being resolute, great determination. 2. a mental pledge, something one intends to do, *New Year resolutions.* 3. a formal statement of opinion agreed on by a committee or assembly. 4. the solving of a problem or question. 5. the process of separating something or being separated into constituent parts.

resolve *v.* 1. to decide firmly. 2. (of a committee or assembly) to pass a resolution. 3. to solve or settle (a problem or doubts etc.). 4. to separate into constituent parts; *the resolving power of a lens,* its ability to magnify things distinctly. —**resolve** *n.* 1. something one has decided to do, a resolution, *and she kept her resolve.* 2. great determination.

resolved *adj.* (of a person) resolute.

resonant (**rez**-ŏn-ănt) *adj.* resounding, echoing. **resonance** *n.*

resort (ri-**zort**) *v.* 1. to turn for help, to adopt as an expedient, *resorted to violence.* 2. to go, especially as a frequent or customary practice, *police watched the bars to which he was known to resort.* —**resort** *n.* 1. an expedient, resorting to this, *compulsion is our only resort; without resort to violence.* 2. a place resorted to, a popular holiday place. □ **in the last resort,** when everything else has failed.

resound (ri-**zownd**) *v.* 1. (of a voice or sound etc.) to fill a place with sound, to produce echoes. 2. (of a place) to be filled with sound, to echo.

resounding *adj.* (of an event etc.) notable, *a resounding victory.*

resource *n.* 1. something to which one can turn for help or support or to achieve one's purpose. 2. a means of relaxation or amusement. 3. ingenuity, quick wit □ **resources** *pl. n.* available assets, *we pooled our resources;* a source of wealth to a country, *natural resources such as minerals.*

resourceful *adj.* clever at finding ways of doing things. **resourcefully** *adv.,* **resourcefulness** *n.*

respect *n.* 1. admiration felt towards a person or thing that has good qualities or achievements, politeness arising from this. 2. attention, consideration, *showing respect for people's feelings.* 3. relation, reference, *this is true with respect to English* *but not to French.* **4.** a particular detail or aspect, *in this one respect.* —*v.* to feel or show respect for. —**respecter** *n.* □ **be no respecter of persons,** to treat everyone in the same way without being influenced by their importance. **respects** *pl. n.* polite greetings; *pay one's respects,* make a polite visit, *pay one's last respects,* by attending a person's funeral or a lying-in-state.

respectable *adj.* **1.** of moderately good social standing, honest and decent, proper in appearance or behaviour. **2.** of a moderately good standard or size etc., not bringing disgrace or embarrassment, *a respectable score.* **respectably** *adv.*, **respectability** *n.*

respectful *adj.* showing respect. **respectfully** *adv.*

respecting *prep.* concerning, with respect to.

respective *adj.* belonging to each as an individual, *were given places according to their respective ranks.* **respectively** *adv.* for each separately, in the order mentioned.

respiration *n.* **1.** breathing. **2.** a plant's absorption of oxygen and emission of carbon dioxide.

respirator *n.* **1.** a device worn over the nose and mouth to filter or purify the air before it is inhaled. **2.** an apparatus for giving artificial respiration.

respiratory (ress-per-ayt-er-i *or* ri-**spyr**-ă-ter-i) *adj.* of or involving respiration.

respire *v.* to breathe, (of plants) to perform the process of respiration.

respite (ress pyt) *n.* **1.** an interval of rest or relief. **2.** delay permitted before an obligation must be fulfilled or a penalty suffered.

resplendent *adj.* brilliant with colour or decorations. **resplendently** *adv.*

respond *v.* to make an answer. **respond to,** to act or behave in answer to or because of, *the horse responds to the bridle, the vehicle responds to its controls; the disease did not respond to treatment,* was not cured or relieved by it; *she responds to kindness,* behaves better if treated kindly.

respondent *n.* the defendant in a lawsuit, especially in a divorce case.

response *n.* **1.** an answer. **2.** any part of the liturgy said or sung in answer to the priest. **3.** an act or feeling or movement produced by a stimulus or by another's action.

responsibility *n.* **1.** being responsible. **2.** something for which one is responsible.

responsible *adj.* **1.** legally or morally

obliged to take care of something or to carry out a duty, liable to be blamed for loss or failure etc. **2.** having to account for one's actions, *you will be responsible to the president himself.* **3.** capable of rational conduct. **4.** trustworthy, *a responsible person.* **5.** involving important duties, *a responsible position.* **6.** being the cause of something, *the plague was responsible for many deaths.* **responsibly** *adv.*

responsive *adj.* responding warmly and favourably to an influence. **responsiveness** *n.*

rest [1] *v.* **1.** to be still, to cease from movement or action or working, especially in order to regain one's vigour; *be resting,* (of an actor) to be out of work. **2.** to cause or allow to do this, *sit down and rest your feet.* **3.** (of a matter under discussion) to be left without further investigation. **4.** to place or be placed for support, *rested the parcel on the table.* **5.** to rely, *the case rests on evidence of identification.* **6.** (of a look) to alight, to be directed, *his gaze rested on his son.* —**rest** *n.* **1.** inactivity or sleep as a way of regaining one's vigour, a period of this. **2.** a prop or support for an object. **3.** an interval of silence between notes in music, a sign indicating this. □ **at rest,** not moving; free from trouble or anxiety. **come to rest,** to cease movement. **restcure** *n.* a prolonged period of rest, usually in bed, as medical treatment. **rested** *adj.* refreshed by resting.

rest [2] *v.* **1.** to be left in the hands or charge of, *it rests with you to suggest terms.* **2.** to remain in a specified state, *rest assured, it will be a success.* —*n.* **the rest,** the remaining part, the others.

restaurant (rest-er-ahn) *n.* a place where meals can be bought and eaten.

restful *adj.* giving rest or a feeling of rest. **restfully** *adv.*, **restfulness** *n.*

restitution *n.* **1.** restoration of a thing to its proper owner or its original state. **2.** reparation for injury or damage.

restive *adj.* restless, resisting control because made impatient by delay or restraint. **restively** *adv.*, **restiveness** *n.*

restless *adj.* **1.** unable to rest or to be still. **2.** without rest or sleep, *a restless night.* **restlessly** *adv.*, **restlessness** *n.*

restoration *n.* restoring, being restored. **the Restoration,** the re-establishment of the monarchy in Britain in 1660 when Charles II became king.

restorative (ri-sto-ră-tiv) *adj.* tending to restore health or strength. —*n.* a restorative food or medicine or treatment.

restore *v.* **1.** to bring back to its original state, e.g. by repairing or rebuilding. **2.** to bring back to good health or vigour. **3.** to put back in its former position, to reinstate. **restorer** *n.*

restrain *v.* to hold back (a person or thing) from movement or action, to keep under control.

restrained *adj.* showing restraint.

restraint *n.* **1.** restraining, being restrained. **2.** something that restrains, a limiting influence. **3.** avoidance of exaggeration in literary or artistic work.

restrict *v.* to put a limit on, to subject to limitations. **restriction** *n.* □ **restricted area**, an area where there is a special speed limit for motor vehicles, lower than that applied elsewhere.

restrictive *adj.* restricting. **restrictive practices**, practices that prevent labour or materials from being used in the most efficient way.

result *n.* **1.** that which is produced by an activity or operation, an effect. **2.** a statement of the score or marks or the name of the winner in a sporting event or competition or examination. **3.** an answer or formula etc. obtained by calculation. — **result** *v.* **1.** to occur as a result, *the troubles that resulted from the merger.* **2.** to have a specified result, *the match resulted in a draw.* □ **get results**, to achieve a significant and satisfactory result.

resultant *adj.* occurring as a result, *the resultant profit.*

resume *v.* **1.** to get or take or occupy again; *resume one's seat*, to sit down again. **2.** to begin again, to begin to speak or work or use again. **resumption** *n.*

résumé (rez-yoom-ay) *n.* a summary.

resurgence (ri-ser-jĕns) *n.* a rise or revival after defeat or destruction or disappearance etc. **resurgent** *adj.*

resurrect *v.* to bring back into use, *resurrect an old custom.*

resurrection *n.* **1.** rising from the dead; *the Resurrection,* that of Christ. **2.** revival after disuse.

resuscitate (ri-sus-i-tayt) *v.* **1.** to bring or come back from unconsciousness. **2.** to revive (a custom or institution etc.). **resuscitation** *n.*

retail *n.* the selling of goods to the general public (not for resale). —*adj. & adv.* in the retail trade. —*v.* **1.** to sell or be sold in the retail trade. **2.** to recount, to relate details of. —**retailer** *n.*

retain *v.* **1.** to keep in one's possession or use. **2.** to continue to have, not lose, *the fire had retained its heat.* **3.** to keep in one's memory, *she retained a clear impression of the building.* **4.** to hold in place; *a retaining wall,* one supporting and confin-

ing a mass of earth or water. **5.** to book the services of (a barrister).

retainer *n.* **1.** a fee paid to retain certain services. **2.** (*old use*) an attendant of a person of rank. □ **old retainer,** (*humorous use*) a faithful old servant.

retake *v.* (retook, retaken, retaking) to take again.

retaliate (ri-tal-i-ayt) *v.* to repay an injury or insult etc. with a similar one, to make a counter-attack. **retaliation** *n.*, **retaliatory** (ri-tal-yă-ter-i) *adj.*

retard (ri-tard) *v.* to cause delay to, to slow the progress of. **retardation** *n.*

retarded *adj.* backward in mental or physical development.

retch (*rhymes with* fetch) *v.* to strain one's throat as if vomiting.

retell *v.* (retold, retelling) to tell (a story etc.) again.

retention *n.* retaining.

retentive *adj.* able to retain things, *a retentive memory.*

rethink *v.* (rethought, rethinking) to think about again, to plan again and differently.

reticent (ret-i-sĕnt) *adj.* not revealing one's thoughts and feelings readily, discreet. **reticently** *adv.*, **reticence** *n.*

reticulated (ri-tik-yoo-layt-id) *adj.* divided into a network or into small squares with intersecting lines. **reticulation** *n.*

retina (ret-in-ă) *n.* (*pl.* retinas) a layer of membrane at the back of the eyeball, sensitive to light.

retinue (ret-in-yoo) *n.* a number of attendants accompanying an important person.

retire *v.* **1.** to give up one's regular work because of advancing age, to cause (an employee) to do this. **2.** to withdraw, to retreat. **3.** to go to bed or to one's private room. **retirement** *n.*

retiring *adj.* shy, avoiding society.

retort[1] *v.* to make a quick or witty or angry reply. —*n.* retorting, a reply of this kind.

retort[2] *n.* **1.** a vessel (usually of glass) with a long downward-bent neck, used in distilling liquids. **2.** a receptacle used in making gas or steel.

retouch *v.* to improve or alter (a picture or photograph) by making minor alterations or removing flaws etc.

retrace *v.* to trace back to the source or beginning; *retrace one's steps,* go back the way one came.

retract *v.* **1.** to pull (a thing) back or in, *snail retracts its horns.* **2.** to withdraw (a statement), to refuse to keep to (an agreement). **retraction** *n.*, **retractor** *n.*

retractable *adj.* able to be retracted.

retrain *v.* to train again or for something different.

retread (ree-tred) *n.* a tyre made by moulding rubber to a used foundation.

retreat *v.* to withdraw after being defeated or when faced with danger or difficulty, to go away to a place of shelter. —*n.* 1. retreating, the military signal for this. 2. a military bugle-call at sunset. 3. withdrawal into privacy or seclusion, a place for this. 4. a period of withdrawal from worldly activities for prayer and meditation.

retrench *v.* 1. to reduce the amount of, *retrench one's operations.* 2. to reduce one's expenditure or operations, *we shall have to retrench.* **retrenchment** *n.*

retrial *n.* the trying of a lawsuit again.

retribution (ret-ri-**bew**-shŏn) *n.* a deserved punishment.

retributive (ri-**trib**-yoo-tiv) *adj.* happening or inflicted as retribution.

retrievable *adj.* able to be retrieved.

retrieval *n.* retrieving, being retrieved.

retrieve *v.* 1. to regain possession of. 2. to find again or extract (stored information etc.) 3. (of a dog) to find and bring in (killed or wounded game). 4. to rescue, to restore to a flourishing state, *retrieve one's fortunes.* 5. to set right (a loss or error or bad situation). —*n.* possibility of recovery, *beyond retrieve.*

retriever *n.* a dog of a breed that is often trained to retrieve game.

retroactive *adj.* effective as from a past date.

retrograde *adj.* 1. going backwards, *retrograde motion.* 2. reverting to a less good condition.

retrogress (ret-rŏ-**gress**) *v.* to move backwards, to deteriorate. **retrogression** *n.*

retro-rocket *n.* an auxiliary rocket discharging its exhaust in the opposite direction to the main rockets, used for slowing a spacecraft.

retrospect *n.* a survey of past time or events. **in retrospect**, when one looks back on a past event or situation.

retrospective *adj.* 1. looking back on the past. 2. applying to the past as well as the future, *the law could not be made retrospective.* **retrospectively** *adv.*

retroussé (rĕ-**troo**-say) *adj.* (of the nose) turned up at the tip.

retroverted (ret-roh-ver-tid) *adj.* turned backwards. **retroversion** *n.*

retry *v.* (retried, retrying) to try (a lawsuit or a defendant) again.

retsina (ret-**seen**-ă) *n.* resin-flavoured Greek wine.

return *v.* 1. to come or go back. 2. to bring or give or put or send back. 3. to say in reply. 4. to state or describe officially, especially in answer to a formal demand for information. 5. to elect as an MP, *she was returned as MP for Finchley.* —**return** *n.* 1. coming or going back. 2. bringing or giving or putting or sending back. 3. the proceeds or profits of a transaction, *brings a good return on one's investment.* 4. a return ticket. 5. a return match or game. 6. a formal report, e.g. of a set of transactions, *income-tax return.* □ **returning officer**, the official conducting an election in a constituency and announcing the result. **return match** *or* **game**, a second match or game between the same opponents. **return ticket**, a ticket for a journey to a place and back to one's starting-point.

returnable *adj.* that can be or must be returned.

retype *v.* to type again.

reunion *n.* 1. reuniting, being reunited. 2. a social gathering of people who were formerly associated.

reunite *v.* to unite again after separation.

reusable *adj.* able to be reused.

reuse¹ (ree-**yooz**) *v.* to use again.

reuse² (ree-**yooss**) *n.* using or being used again.

Reuters (**roi**-terz) an international news agency owned and directed by various newspaper associations of Britain and the Commonwealth.

rev *n.* a revolution of an engine. —*v.* (revved, revving) 1. (of an engine) to revolve. 2. to cause (an engine) to run quickly, especially when starting.

Rev. *abbrev.* Reverend, *the Rev. John Smith* or *the Rev. J. Smith* or *the Rev. Mr. Smith* (¶ not *the Rev. Smith*).

revalue *v.* to re-assess the value of. **revaluation** *n.*

revamp *v.* to renovate, to give a new appearance to.

Revd. *abbrev.* Reverend. ¶ See the note under Rev.

reveal *v.* to make known, to uncover and allow to be seen.

reveille (ri-**val**-i) *n.* a military waking-signal sounded on a bugle or drums.

revel *v.* (revelled, revelling) 1. to take great delight, *some people revel in gossip.* 2. to hold revels. —**reveller** *n.* □ **revels** *pl. n.* lively festivities or merrymaking.

revelation *n.* 1. revealing, making known something that was secret or hidden. 2. something revealed, especially something surprising. 3. *Revelation,* the last book of the New Testament (*see* Apocalypse). ¶ This book is often referred to incorrectly as *Revelations.*

revelry *n.* revelling, revels.

revenge *n.* **1.** punishment or injury inflicted in return for what one has suffered. **2.** a desire to inflict this. **3.** opportunity to defeat in a return game an opponent who won the first game. —*v.* to avenge; *be revenged* or *revenge oneself,* to get satisfaction by inflicting vengeance. —**revengeful** *adj.*

revenue (rev-ĕn-yoo) *n.* a country's annual income from taxes, duties, etc., used for paying public expenses.

reverberate (ri-verb-er-ayt) *v.* to echo, to resound. **reverberation** *n.*

revere (ri-veer) *v.* to feel deep respect or religious veneration for.

reverence *n.* **1.** a feeling of awe and respect or veneration. **2.** (*old use* or *humorous*) a title used in speaking to or about a clergyman, *your* or *his reverence.* —*v.* to feel or show reverence towards.

reverend *adj.* **1.** deserving to be treated with respect. **2.** *the Reverend,* the title of a clergyman (*Very Reverend,* of a dean, *Right Reverend,* of a bishop, *Most Reverend,* of an archbishop or Irish Roman Catholic bishop; ¶ see the note under Rev.). —*n.* (*informal*) a clergyman. ☐ **Reverend Mother,** the Mother Superior of a convent.

reverent *adj.* feeling or showing reverence. **reverently** *adv.*

¶ Do not confuse with reverend.

reverie (rev-er-i) *n.* a day-dream, a state of day-dreaming.

revers (ri-veer) *n.* (*pl.* revers, *pr.* ri-veerz) a turned-back front edge at the neck of a jacket or bodice.

reversal *n.* reversing, being reversed.

reverse *adj.* facing or moving in the opposite direction, opposite in character or order, upside down. —*v.* **1.** to turn the other way round or up or inside out. **2.** to convert to the opposite kind or effect, *reversed the tendency; reverse the charges,* make the recipient (not the caller) pay for a telephone call. **3.** to annul (a decree or decision etc.). **4.** to move in the opposite direction, (of a vehicle) to travel backwards. **5.** to make (an engine or machine) work in the opposite direction, to cause (a vehicle) to travel backwards. —**reverse** *n.* **1.** the reverse side or effect. **2.** the opposite of the usual manner, *the name was printed in reverse.* **3.** a piece of misfortune, *suffered several reverses.* **4.** reverse gear. — **reversely** *adv.* ☐ **reverse gear,** a gear used to make a vehicle etc. travel backwards.

reversible *adj.* able to be reversed, (of a garment) able to be worn with either side turned outwards.

reversion *n.* **1.** reverting. **2.** the legal right to possess something when its present holder relinquishes it, the returning of a right or property in this way. **reversionary** *adj.*

¶ Note that *reversion* does not mean *reversal.*

revert *v.* **1.** to return to a former condition or habit. **2.** to return to a subject in talk or thought. **3.** (of property etc.) to return or pass to another owner by reversion.

revetment (ri-vet-mĕnt) *n.* a facing of masonry on a rampart etc., a retaining wall.

review *n.* **1.** a general survey of past events or of a subject. **2.** a re-examination or reconsideration; *the salary scale is under review,* is being reconsidered. **3.** a ceremonial inspection of troops or a fleet etc. **4.** a published report assessing the merits of a book or play etc. —**review** *v.* **1.** to survey. **2.** to re-examine or reconsider. **3.** to inspect (troops or a fleet etc.) ceremonially. **4.** to write a review of (a book or play etc.). —**reviewer** *n.*

¶ Do not confuse with revue.

revile *v.* to criticize angrily in abusive language. **revilement** *n.*

revise *v.* **1.** to re-examine and alter or correct. **2.** to go over (work already learnt) in preparation for an examination. **revision** *n.* ☐ **Revised Version,** the revision (1870–84) of the Authorized Version of the Bible.

revisionist (ri-vizh-ŏn-ist) *n.* a Communist who insists on modifying the Marxist theories or practices that are considered authoritative.

revival *n.* **1.** reviving, being revived. **2.** something brought back into use or fashion. **3.** a reawakening of interest in religion, a special effort with meetings etc. to promote this.

revivalist *n.* a person who organizes or conducts meetings to promote a religious revival.

revive *v.* **1.** to come or bring back to life or consciousness or strength. **2.** to come or bring back into use or activity or fashion etc. **reviver** *n.*

revoke (ri-vohk) *v.* **1.** to withdraw or cancel (a decree or licence etc.). **2.** to fail to follow suit in a card-game when able to do so. —*n.* revoking in a card-game.

revolt *v.* **1.** to take part in a rebellion. **2.** to be in a mood of protest or defiance. **3.** to feel strong disgust. **4.** to cause a feeling of strong disgust in (a person). —**revolt** *n.*

1. an act or state of rebelling or defying authority. **2.** a sense of disgust.

revolting *adj.* causing disgust.

revolution *n.* **1.** substitution of a new system of government, especially by force. **2.** any complete change of method or conditions etc., *a revolution in the treatment of burns.* **3.** revolving, rotation, a single complete orbit or movement of this kind.

revolutionary *adj.* **1.** of political revolution. **2.** involving a great change, *revolutionary new ideas.* —*n.* a person who begins or supports a political revolution.

revolutionize *v.* to alter (a thing) completely, *the discovery will revolutionize our lives.*

revolve *v.* **1.** to turn or cause to turn round, to rotate. **2.** to move in a circular orbit. **3.** to turn over (a problem etc.) in one's mind.

revolver *n.* a pistol with a revolving mechanism that makes it possible to fire it a number of times without reloading.

revue *n.* an entertainment consisting of a series of items. ¶ Do not confuse with review.

revulsion *n.* **1.** a feeling of strong disgust. **2.** a sudden violent change of feeling, *a revulsion of public feeling in favour of the accused woman.*

reward *n.* **1.** something given or received in return for what is done or for a service or merit. **2.** a sum of money offered for the detection of a criminal, return of lost property, etc. —*v.* to give a reward to.

rewarding *adj.* (of an occupation) well worth doing.

rewire *v.* to renew the electrical wiring of.

reword *v.* to change the wording of.

rewrite *v.* (rewrote, rewritten, rewriting) to write (a thing) again in a different form or style.

Rex *n.* reigning king (¶ used in the same ways as Regina).

Reykjavik (**rayk**-yǎ-vik) the capital of Iceland.

Rh *abbrev.* Rhesus.

rhapsodize *v.* to talk or write about something in an ecstatic way.

rhapsody *n.* **1.** an ecstatic written or spoken statement. **2.** a romantic musical composition in an irregular form.

rheostat (**ree**-ŏ-stat) *n.* an instrument used to control the current in an electrical circuit by varying the amount of resistance in it.

rhesus (**ree**-sŭs) *n.* a small monkey common in northern India, used in biological experiments. **Rhesus factor**, a substance present in the blood of most people and some animals, causing a blood disorder in a new-born baby whose blood is *Rhesus-positive* (= containing this substance) while its mother's blood is *Rhesus-negative* (= not containing it).

rhetoric (**ret**-er-ik) *n.* **1.** the art of using words impressively, especially in public speaking. **2.** language used for its impressive sound, affected or exaggerated expressions.

rhetorical (rit-o-ri-kǎl) *adj.* expressed in a way that is designed to be impressive. **rhetorically** *adv.* □ **rhetorical question**, something phrased as a question only for dramatic effect and not to seek an answer, e.g. *who cares?* (= nobody cares).

rheumatic (roo-**mat**-ik) *adj.* of or affected with rheumatism. **rheumaticky** *adj.*, **rheumatically** *adv.* □ **rheumatic fever**, a serious form of rheumatism with fever, chiefly in children. **rheumatics** *pl. n.* (*informal*) rheumatism.

rheumatism (**room**-ă-tizm) *n.* any of several diseases causing pain in the joints or muscles or fibrous tissue, especially rheumatoid arthritis.

rheumatoid (**room**-ŭ-toid) *adj.* of rheumatism: *rheumatoid arthritis,* a disease causing inflammation and stiffening of the joints.

rheumatology (roo-mă-**tol**-ŏji) *n.* the scientific study of rheumatic diseases.

Rhineland the region of Germany lying west of the river Rhine.

rhinestone *n.* an imitation diamond.

rhino *n.* (*pl.* rhino *or* rhinos) (*slang*) a rhinoceros.

rhinoceros *n.* (*pl.* rhinoceroses) a large thick-skinned animal of Africa and south Asia, with a horn or two horns on its nose.

rhizome (**ry**-zohm) *n.* a root-like stem growing along or under the ground and sending out both roots and shoots.

Rhode Island a State of the USA.

Rhodesia (roh-**dee**-shǎ) the former name of Zimbabwe. **Rhodesian** *adj. & n.*

rhododendron (roh-dŏ-**den**-drŏn) *n.* an evergreen shrub with large clusters of trumpet-shaped flowers.

rhomboid (**rom**-boid) *adj.* like a rhombus.

rhombus (**rom**-bŭs) *n.* a geometric figure shaped like the diamond on playing-cards.

rhubarb *n.* a garden plant with fleshy reddish leaf-stalks that are used like fruit.

rhyme *n.* **1.** identity of sound between words or syllables or the endings of lines of verse (e.g. *line/mine/pine, visit/is it*). **2.** a poem with rhymes. **3.** a word providing a rhyme to another. —*v.* to form a rhyme, to have rhymes. □ **rhyming slang**, slang in which words are replaced by words that rhyme with them, e.g. *apples and pears* = stairs. **without rhyme or reason**, with no sensible or logical reason.

rhythm (ri*th*-ĕm) *n.* **1.** the pattern produced by emphasis and duration of notes in music or by long and short syllables in words. **2.** a movement with a regular succession of strong and weak elements, *the rhythm of the heart beating*. **3.** a constantly recurring sequence of events. **rhythmic** *adj.*, **rhythmical** *adj.*, **rhythmically** *adv.* □ **rhythm method**, contraception by avoiding sexual intercourse near the time of ovulation (which recurs regularly).

RI *abbrev.* Rhode Island.

rib *n.* **1.** one of the curved bones round the chest. **2.** a cut of meat from this part of an animal. **3.** a curved structural part resembling a rib, e.g. a raised moulding on a ceiling. **4.** one of the hinged rods forming the framework of an umbrella. **5.** a raised pattern of lines in knitting. —**rib** *v.* (**ribbed**, **ribbing**) **1.** to support (a structure) with ribs. **2.** to knit as rib, *the cuffs are ribbed*. **3.** (*informal*) to tease. □ **rib-cage** *n.* the framework of ribs round the chest.

ribald (rib-ăld) *adj.* humorous in a cheerful but vulgar or disrespectful way. **ribaldry** *n.*

riband (rib-ănd) *n.* a ribbon.

ribbed *adj.* **1.** with raised ridges. **2.** knitted in rib.

ribbon *n.* **1.** a narrow band of fine ornamental material used for decoration or for tying something. **2.** a ribbon of special colour or pattern worn to indicate the award of a medal or order etc. **3.** a long narrow strip of material, e.g. an inked strip used in a typewriter; *in ribbons* or *torn to ribbons*, torn into ragged strips. □ **ribbon development**, the building of houses along a main road, extending outwards from a town or village.

rice *n.* **1.** a kind of grass grown in marshes in hot countries, producing seeds that are used as food. **2.** these seeds.

rich *adj.* **1.** having much wealth. **2.** having a large supply of something, *the country is rich in natural resources*. **3.** splendid, made of costly materials, elaborate, *rich furniture*. **4.** producing or produced abundantly, *rich soil; a rich harvest*. **5.** (of food) containing a large proportion of fat, butter, eggs, or spices etc. **6.** (of a mixture in an internal combustion engine) containing more than the normal proportion of fuel. **7.** (of a colour or sound or smell) pleasantly deep or strong. **8.** highly amusing. **richness** *n.* □ **riches** *pl. n.* a great quantity of money or property or valuable possessions.

richly *adv.* **1.** in a rich way. **2.** thoroughly, *the book richly deserves its success*.

Richter scale (rik-ter) a scale for measuring the magnitude of earthquakes.

rick¹ *n.* a built stack of hay etc.

rick² *n.* a slight sprain or strain. —*v.* to sprain or strain slightly.

rickets *n.* a children's disease caused by deficiency of vitamin D, resulting in softening and deformity of the bones.

rickety *adj.* shaky, insecure.

rickrack *n.* = ricrac.

rickshaw *n.* a light two-wheeled hooded vehicle used in countries of the Far East, drawn by one or more people.

ricochet (rik-ŏ-shay) *v.* (**ricocheted** (*pr.* **rik**-ŏ-shayd), **ricocheting**, *pr.* **rik**-ŏ-shaying) to rebound from a surface as a missile does when it strikes with a glancing blow. —*n.* a rebound of this kind, a hit made by it.

ricrac *n.* a zigzag braid trimming.

rid *v.* (**rid**, **ridding**) to free from something unpleasant or unwanted, *rid the house of mice*; *was glad to be rid of him*. **get rid of**, to cause to go away; (*informal*) to succeed in selling.

riddance *n.* ridding. **good riddance**, a welcome freedom from a person or thing one is rid of.

ridden *adj.* full of or dominated by, *rat-ridden cellars*; *guilt-ridden*.

riddle¹ *n.* **1.** a question or statement designed to test ingenuity or give amusement in finding its answer or meaning. **2.** something puzzling or mysterious.

riddle² *n.* a coarse sieve for gravel or cinders etc. —*v.* **1.** to pass (gravel etc.) through a riddle, *riddle the ashes*. **2.** to pierce with many holes, *riddled the car with bullets*. **3.** to permeate thoroughly, *riddled with disease*.

ride *v.* (**rode**, **ridden**, **riding**) **1.** to sit on and be carried by (a horse etc.). **2.** to go on horseback or bicycle or train or other conveyance. **3.** to sit on and manage a horse. **4.** to be supported on, to float or seem to float, *the ship rode the waves* or *at anchor*; *the moon was riding high*. **5.** to yield to (a blow) so as to reduce its impact. —**ride** *n.* **1.** a spell of riding. **2.** a journey in a vehicle, *only a short ride into town*. **3.** a track for riding on, especially through woods. **4.** the feel of a ride, *the car gives a smooth ride*. □ **let it ride**, to take no further action. **ride down**, to overtake or trample deliberately while riding on horseback. **ride for a fall**, to act riskily. **ride high**, to be successful. **ride out the storm**, to survive a storm or difficulty successfully. **ride up**, (of a garment) to work upwards when worn. **take for a ride**, (*slang*) to take away by car and murder (a person); to deceive or swindle.

rider *n.* **1.** a person who rides a horse or bicycle etc. **2.** an additional clause supplementing a statement etc., an expression of opinion added to a verdict.

riderless *adj.* without a rider.

ridge *n.* **1.** a narrow raised strip, a line where two upward-sloping surfaces meet. **2.** an elongated region of high barometric pressure.

ridged *adj.* formed into ridges.

ridgeway *n.* a road along the ridge of a hill-top.

ridicule *n.* the process of making a person or thing appear ridiculous. —*v.* to subject to ridicule, to make fun of.

ridiculous *adj.* **1.** deserving to be laughed at, especially in a malicious or scornful way. **2.** not worth serious consideration, preposterous. **ridiculously** *adv.*

Riding *n.* one of the former divisions of Yorkshire, *East, North,* and *West Riding*.

riding-light *n.* a light shown by a ship riding at anchor.

Riesling (rees-ling) *n.* a kind of dry white wine.

rife *adj.* **1.** occurring frequently, widespread, *crime was rife in the city*. **2.** well provided, full, *the country was rife with rumours of war*.

riffle *v.* **1.** to turn (pages) in quick succession, to leaf through quickly, *riffled through the book*. **2.** to shuffle (playing-cards) rapidly by flexing and combining two halves of the pack.

riff-raff *n.* the rabble, disreputable people.

rifle *n.* a gun with a long barrel cut with spiral grooves to make the bullet spin and so travel more accurately when fired; *the Rifles*, a unit of troops armed with rifles. —*v.* **1.** to search and rob, *rifled the safe*. **2.** to cut spiral grooves in (a gun-barrel).

rift *n.* **1.** a cleft in earth or rock. **2.** a crack or split in an object, a break in cloud. **3.** a breach in friendly relations between people or in the unity of a group. □ **rift-valley** *n.* a steep-sided valley formed by subsidence of the earth's crust.

rig¹ *v.* (rigged, rigging) **1.** to provide with clothes or equipment, *rigged them out*. **2.** to fit (a ship) with spars, ropes, sails, etc. **3.** to set up (a structure) quickly or with makeshift materials. — **rig** *n.* **1.** the way a ship's masts and sails etc. are arranged. **2.** equipment for a special purpose, e.g. for drilling an oil-well, *a test rig; an oil rig*. **3.** (*informal*) an outfit of clothes. □

rig-out *n.* (*informal*) an outfit of clothes.

rig² *v.* (rigged, rigging) to manage or control fraudulently, *the election was rigged; rig the market*, to cause an artificial rise or fall in share-prices.

rigging *n.* the ropes etc. used to support masts and set or work the sails on a ship.

right *adj.* **1.** (of conduct or actions etc.) morally good, in accordance with justice. **2.** proper, correct, true, *the right answer; right side*, (of fabric) the side meant to show. **3.** in a good or normal condition, *all's right with the world; in his right mind*, sane. **4.** (*informal*) real, properly so called, *made a right old mess of it*. **5.** of the right-hand side. —**right** *n.* **1.** what is just, a fair claim or treatment, something one is entitled to. **2.** the right-hand part or region. **3.** the right hand, a blow with this. **4.** (in marching) the right foot. **5.** *the Right*, the right wing of a political party or other group. —**right** *v.* **1.** to restore to a proper or correct or upright position, *managed to right the boat*. **2.** to set right, to make amends or take vengeance for, *to right the wrong*. **3.** to correct, *the fault will right itself*. —**right** *adv.* **1.** on or towards the right-hand side, *turn right*. **2.** straight, *go right on*. **3.** (*informal*) immediately, *I'll be right back*. **4.** all the way, completely, *went right round it*. **5.** exactly, *right in the middle*. **6.** very, fully, *dined right royally*. **7.** rightly, *you did right to come*. **8.** all right, that is correct, I agree. □ **by right** *or* **rights**, if right were done. **in the right**, having justice or truth on one's side. **on the right side of**, in the favour of or liked by (a person); *on the right side of forty*, not yet 40 years old. **right angle**, an angle of 90°; *at right angles*, placed at or turning through a right angle. **right-angled** *adj.* having a right angle. **right away**, immediately. **right-down** *adj. & adv.* thorough, thoroughly, *it's right-down dishonest*. **right hand**, the hand that in most people is used more than the left, on the side opposite the left hand. **right-hand** *adj.* of or towards this side of a person or the corresponding side of a thing; *a person's right-hand man*, his indispensable or chief assistant. **right-handed** *adj.* using the right hand usually, by preference; (of a blow or tool) made with or operated by the right hand; (of a screw) to be tightened by turning towards the right. **right-hander** *n.* a right-handed person or blow. **Right Honourable**, the title of earls, viscounts, barons, privy councillors, and certain others. **right-minded** *adj.* having proper or honest principles. **right of way**, the right to pass over another's land, a path that is subject to such a right; the right to proceed, while another vehicle must wait. **right oh!**, (*informal*) an exclamation of agreement to what is suggested. **Right Reverend**, *see* reverend. **right wing**, *see* wing (sense 8); those who support more conservative or traditional policies than others in their group. **rightwinger** *n.*

righteous *adj.* **1.** doing what is morally right, making a show of this. **2.** morally justifiable, *full of righteous indignation.* **righteously** *adv.*, **righteousness** *n.*

rightful *adj.* in accordance with what is just or proper or legal. **rightfully** *adv.*

rightist *n.* a member of the right wing of a political party. —*adj.* of the right wing in politics etc.

rightly *adv.* justly, correctly, properly, justifiably.

rightness *n.* being just or correct or proper or justifiable.

rigid *adj.* **1.** stiff, not bending or yielding. **2.** strict, inflexible, *rigid rules.* **rigidly** *adv.*, **rigidity** (ri-**jid**-iti) *n.*

rigmarole (**rig**-mă-rohl) *n.* **1.** a long rambling statement. **2.** a complicated formal procedure.

rigor mortis (**ry**-ger **mor**-tiss) stiffening of the body after death.

rigorous (**rig**-er-ŭs) *adj.* **1.** strict, severe, *rigorous discipline.* **2.** strictly accurate or detailed, *a rigorous search.* **3.** harsh, unpleasant, *a rigorous climate.* **rigorously** *adv.*

rigour (**rig**-er) *n.* **1.** severity, strictness. **2.** harshness of weather or conditions, *the rigours of famine.*

rile (*rhymes with* mile) *v.* (*informal*) to annoy, to irritate.

rill *n.* a small stream.

rim *n.* **1.** the edge or border of something more or less circular. **2.** the outer edge of a wheel, on which a tyre is fitted.

rime *n.* frost. **rimed** *adj.* coated with frost.

rimless *adj.* (of spectacles) made without frames.

rimmed *adj.* edged, bordered, *red-rimmed eyes.*

rind (*rhymes with* mind) *n.* a tough outer layer or skin on fruit, cheese, bacon, etc.

ring¹ *n.* **1.** the outline of a circle. **2.** something shaped like this, a circular band. **3.** a small circular band of precious metal worn on the finger. **4.** a circular or other enclosure for a circus or sports event or cattle-show etc., a square area in which a boxing-match or wrestling-match is held. **5.** *the ring,* bookmakers. **6.** a combination

of people acting together for control of operations or policy etc. —**ring** *v.* **1.** to enclose with a ring, to encircle. **2.** to put a ring on (a bird etc.) to identify it. **3.** to cut a ring in the bark of (a tree), especially to retard its growth and improve fruit-production. □ **make** *or* **run rings round**, to do things much better than (another person). **ring-dove** *n.* a large species of pigeon. **ring-finger** *n.* the third finger, especially of the left hand, on which a wedding-ring is worn. person in charge of a circus performance. **ring road**, a bypass encircling a town.

ring² *v.* (rang, rung, ringing) **1.** to give out a loud clear resonant sound, like that of a bell when struck. **2.** to cause (a bell) to do this. **3.** to sound a bell as a summons, to signal by ringing, *bells rang out the old year.* **4.** to be filled with sound, *the stadium rang with cheers.* **5.** (of ears) to be filled with a ringing or humming sound. **6.** to telephone. **7.** (*informal*) to alter and sell (a stolen vehicle). —**ring** *n.* **1.** the act of ringing a bell. **2.** a ringing sound or tone. **3.** a tone or feeling of a particular kind; *it has the ring of truth,* sounds true. **4.** (*informal*) a telephone call. □ **ring a bell,** (*informal*) to arouse a vague memory, to sound faintly familiar. **ring off,** to end a telephone call by replacing the receiver. **ring the changes,** to vary things. **ring the curtain up** *or* **down,** to signal that the curtain on a theatre stage should be raised or lowered; to mark the beginning or end of an enterprise etc. **ring up,** to make a telephone call to (a person etc.); to record (an amount) on a cash register.

ringer *n.* **1.** a person who rings bells. **2.** (*Amer.*) a racehorse etc. fraudulently substituted for another. **3.** a person's double.

ringleader *n.* a person who leads others in mischief or wrongdoing or opposition to authority.

ringlet *n.* a long tubular curl.

ringmaster *n.* the person in charge of a circus performance.

ringside *n.* the area immediately beside a boxing ring. **ringside seat,** a position from which one has a clear view of the scene of action.

ringworm *n.* a skin disease producing round scaly patches on the skin, caused by a fungus.

rink *n.* a skating-rink (*see* skate²).

rinse *v.* **1.** to wash lightly with water. **2.** to wash out soap or impurities from. — **rinse** *n.* **1.** rinsing. **2.** a solution washed through hair to tint or condition it.

riot *n.* **1.** a wild disturbance by a crowd of

people. **2.** a profuse display of something, *a riot of colour*. **3.** (*informal*) a very amusing thing or person. —*v.* to take part in a riot or in disorderly revelry. —**rioter** *n.* □ **Riot Act**, an Act of Parliament dealing with the prevention of riots; *read the Riot Act*, to insist that noise or disobedience etc. must cease. **riot shield**, a shield for use by police or soldiers dealing with riots. **run riot**, to behave in an unruly way; (of plants) to grow or spread in an uncontrolled way.

riotous *adj.* **1.** disorderly, unruly. **2.** boisterous, unrestrained, *riotous laughter*. **riotously** *adv.*

rip *v.* (ripped, ripping) **1.** to tear apart, to remove by pulling roughly. **2.** to become torn. **3.** to rush along. —*n.* ripping, a torn place. —**ripper** *n.* □ **let rip**, (*informal*) to refrain from checking the speed of (a thing) or from interfering; to speak or utter violently. **rip-cord** *n.* a cord for pulling to release a parachute from its pack. **rip into**, to criticize or scold severely. **rip off**, (*slang*) to defraud; to steal. **rip-off** *n.* (*slang*) something fraudulent, theft. **rip-roaring** *adj.* wildly noisy.

RIP *abbrev.* rest in peace. (¶ From the Latin, *requiescat* (or *requiescant*) *in pace*.)

ripe *adj.* **1.** (of fruit or grain etc.) ready to be gathered and used. **2.** matured and ready to be eaten or drunk, *ripe cheese*. **3.** (of a person's age) advanced, *lived to a ripe old age*. **4.** ready, prepared or able to undergo something, *the time is ripe for revolution; the land is ripe for development*. **ripely** *adv.*, **ripeness** *n.*

ripen *v.* to make or become ripe.

riposte (ri-**posst**) *n.* a quick counterstroke, a quick retort. —*v.* to deliver a riposte.

ripple *n.* **1.** a small wave or series of waves. **2.** something resembling this in appearance or movement. **3.** a gentle sound that rises and falls, *a ripple of laughter*. —*v.* to form or cause ripples.

rise *v.* (rose, risen, rising) **1.** to come or go or grow or extend upwards. **2.** to get up from lying or sitting or kneeling, to get out of bed. **3.** (of a meeting) to cease to sit for business. **4.** to become upright or erect. **5.** to come to life again after death, *Christ is risen*. **6.** to rebel, *rise in revolt*. **7.** (of the wind) to begin to blow or to blow more strongly. **8.** (of the sun etc.) to become visible above the horizon. **9.** to increase in amount or number or intensity, *prices are rising; her spirits rose*, she began to feel more cheerful. **10.** to achieve a higher position or status, *rose to the rank of colonel; rise to the occasion*, to prove oneself able

to deal with an unexpected situation. **11.** (of bread or cake etc.) to swell by the action of yeast or other raising agent. **12.** to have its origin, to begin or begin to flow, *the Thames rises in the Cotswolds*. —**rise** *n.* **1.** rising, an upward movement. **2.** an upward slope, a small hill. **3.** increase in amount or number or intensity, an increase in wages. **4.** an upward movement in rank or status. □ **get** *or* **take a rise out of**, to draw (a person) into a display of annoyance or into making a retort. **give rise to**, to cause. **rising five** etc., (of a child) nearing the age of five. **rising generation**, young people, those who are growing up.

riser *n.* **1.** a person or thing that rises, *an early riser*. **2.** a vertical piece between treads of a staircase.

rising *n.* a revolt.

risk *n.* **1.** the possibility of meeting danger or suffering harm or loss, exposure to this. **2.** a person or thing insured or similarly representing a source of risk, *not a good risk*. —*v.* to expose to the chance of injury or loss, to accept the risk of.

risky *adj.* (riskier, riskiest) full of risk. **riskily** *adv.*, **riskiness** *n.*

risotto (ri-**zot**-oh) *n.* (*pl.* risottos) an Italian dish of rice containing chopped meat or cheese and vegetables.

risqué (**risk**-ay) *adj.* (of a story) slightly indecent.

rissole *n.* a small ball or cake of minced meat or fish mixed with potato or breadcrumbs etc. and usually fried.

rite *n.* a religious or other solemn ritual.

ritual *n.* **1.** the series of actions used in a religious or other ceremony, a particular form of this. **2.** a procedure regularly followed. *adj.* of or done as a ritual. — **ritually** *adv.*, **ritualistic** *adj.*

rival *n.* **1.** a person or thing competing with another. **2.** a person or thing that can equal another in quality. —*adj.* being a rival or rivals. —*v.* (rivalled, rivalling) to be comparable to, to seem or be as good as. —**rivalry** *n.*

riven (**riv**-ĕn) *adj.* split, torn violently.

river *n.* **1.** a large natural stream of water flowing in a channel. **2.** a great flow, *rivers of blood*.

rivet (**riv**-it) *n.* a nail or bolt for holding two pieces of metal together, its headless end being beaten or pressed down to form a head when it is in place. —*v.* (riveted, riveting) **1.** to fasten with a rivet. **2.** to flatten (the end of a bolt) when it is in place. **3.** to fix, to make immovable, *she stood riveted to the spot*. **4.** to attract and hold the attention of. —**riveter** *n.*

Riviera (rivi-**air**-ă) *n.* **1.** *the Riviera,* the region along the Mediterranean coast of south-east France, Monaco, and north-west Italy, famous for its natural beauty and containing many holiday resorts. **2.** a region thought to resemble this.

rivulet (**riv**-yoo-lit) *n.* a small stream.

Riyadh (ree-**ad**) the capital of Saudi Arabia.

roach[1] *n.* (*pl.* roach) a small freshwater fish related to the carp.

roach[2] *n.* the curve in the side or foot of a sail.

road *n.* **1.** a way by which people or animals or vehicles may pass between places, especially one with a prepared surface. **2.** a way of reaching or achieving something, *the road to success; you're in the road,* in the way, as an obstruction. □ **on the road,** travelling, especially as a salesman or performer or beggar. **road-block** *n.* a barricade set up by the police or army to stop traffic for inspection or search etc. **road-hog** *n.* a reckless or inconsiderate driver. **road-house** *n.* an inn or club or restaurant on a main road in a country district. **road-metal** *n.* broken stone for making the foundation of a road or railway. **road sense,** ability to behave safely on roads, especially in traffic. **road test,** a test of a vehicle by using it on a road. **road-test** *v.* to test in this way. **road-works** *pl. n.* construction or repair of roads.

roadside *n.* the border of a road.

roadway *n.* a road, this as distinct from a footpath beside it.

roadworthy *adj.* (of a vehicle) fit to be used on a road. **roadworthiness** *n.*

roam *v.* to wander. —*n.* a wander.

roan *adj.* (of an animal) having a coat that is thickly sprinkled with white or grey hairs; *strawberry roan,* red mixed with white or grey. —*n.* a roan horse or other animal.

roar *n.* **1.** a long deep loud sound, like that made by a lion. **2.** loud laughter. —**roar** *v.* **1.** to give a roar. **2.** to express in this way, *the crowd roared its approval.* **3.** to be full of din. —**roarer** *n.*

roaring *adj.* **1.** noisy. **2.** briskly active, *did a roaring trade.* —*adv.* noisily, *roaring drunk.*

roast *v.* **1.** to cook (meat etc.) in an oven or by exposure to heat. **2.** to expose to great heat. **3.** to undergo roasting. —*adj.* roasted, *roast beef.* —*n.* roast meat, a joint of meat for roasting.

roasting *adj.* very hot.

rob *v.* (robbed, robbing) **1.** to steal from, to take unlawfully. **2.** to deprive of what is due or normal, *robbing us of our sleep.*

robber *n.,* **robbery** *n.* □ **rob Peter to pay Paul,** to pay one debt by borrowing what one needs and so incurring another.

robe *n.* a long loose garment, especially a ceremonial one or one worn as an indication of rank etc. —*v.* to dress in a robe.

robin *n.* a small brown red-breasted bird.

robot (**roh**-bot) *n.* **1.** (in science fiction) a machine that resembles and can act like a person. **2.** a piece of apparatus operated by remote control. **3.** a person who seems to act like a machine. **4.** (in Southern Africa) traffic lights. **robotic** (rŏ-**bot**-ik) *adj.* □ **robotics** *pl. n.* use of robots in manufacturing.

robust (rŏ-**bust**) *adj.* strong, vigorous. **robustly** *adv.,* **robustness** *n.*

rock[1] *n.* **1.** the hard part of the earth's crust, underlying the soil. **2.** a mass of this, a large stone or boulder. **3.** a hard sugar sweet made in cylindrical sticks, usually flavoured with peppermint. **4.** *the Rock,* Gibraltar. □ **on the rocks,** (*informal*) short of money; (of a drink) served neat with ice cubes. **rock-bottom** *adj.* (*informal,* of prices etc.) very low. **rock-cake** *n.* a small fruit cake with a flat base and a rugged surface. **rock-garden** *n.* an artificial mound or bank containing large stones and planted with rock-plants. **rock-plant** *n.* a plant growing on or among rocks. **rock salmon,** dogfish sold as food.

rock[2] *v.* **1.** to move or be moved gently to and fro while supported on something. **2.** to shake violently. **3.** to disturb greatly by shock, *the scandal rocked the country.* —**rock** *n.* **1.** rocking, a rocking movement. **2.** a kind of popular modern music usually with a strong beat, rock 'n' roll. □ **rock 'n' roll,** a kind of popular music with a strong beat, containing elements of blues. **rock the boat,** (*informal*) to do something that upsets the plans or progress of one's group.

rocker *n.* **1.** a thing that rocks something or is rocked. **2.** one of the curved bars on which a rocking-chair etc. is mounted. **3.** a rocking-chair. **4.** a switch that pivots between the 'on' and 'off' positions.

rockery *n.* a rock-garden.

rocket *n.* **1.** a firework or similar device that rises into the air when ignited and then explodes. **2.** a structure that flies by expelling gases that are the products of combustion, used to propel a warhead or spacecraft, a bomb or shell propelled by this. **3.** (*slang*) a reprimand. —*v.* (rocketed, rocketing) to move rapidly upwards or away.

rocketry *n.* the science or practice of using

rockets for propelling missiles or space-craft.

Rockies *pl. n.* the Rocky Mountains, a range of mountains in North America.

rocking-chair *n.* a chair mounted on rockers or with springs so that it can be rocked by the sitter.

rocking-horse *n.* a wooden horse mounted on rockers or springs so that it can be rocked by a child sitting on it.

rocky¹ *adj.* (rockier, rockiest) **1.** of or like rock. **2.** full of rocks.

rocky² *adj.* (rockier, rockiest) unsteady.

rococo (rŏ-koh-koh) *n.* an ornate style of decoration common in Europe in the 18th century. —*adj.* of this style.

rod *n.* **1.** a slender straight round stick or metal bar. **2.** a cane or birch used for flogging people. **3.** a fishing-rod, an angler with the right to use this on a specified stretch of water.

rode *see* ride.

rodent *n.* an animal (e.g. rat, mouse, squirrel) with strong front teeth used for gnawing things.

rodeo (roh-day-oh) *n.* (*pl.* rodeos) **1.** a round-up of cattle on a ranch, for branding etc. **2.** an exhibition of cowboys' skill in handling animals. **3.** an exhibition of motor-cycle riding.

roe¹ *n.* a mass of eggs in a female fish's ovary (*hard roe*), a male fish's milt (*soft roe*).

roe² *n.* (*pl.* roe *or* roes) a kind of small deer. **roebuck** *n.* a male roe.

rogations *pl. n.* a special litany for use on **Rogation Days**, the three days before Ascension Day. **Rogation Sunday**, the Sunday before this.

roger *int.* (in signalling) your message has been received and understood.

rogue *n.* **1.** a dishonest or unprincipled person. **2.** a mischievous person. **3.** a wild animal driven away from the herd or living apart from it, *rogue elephant*. **roguery** *n.* □ **rogues' gallery**, a collection of photographs of criminals.

roguish *adj.* mischievous, affectedly playful. **roguishly** *adv.*, **roguishness** *n.*

roistering *adj. & n.* merrymaking noisily. **roisterer** *n.*

role *n.* **1.** an actor's part. **2.** a person's or thing's function.

roll *v.* **1.** to move or cause to move along in contact with a surface, either on wheels or by turning over and over. **2.** to turn on an axis or over and over, to cause to revolve. **3.** to form into a cylindrical or spherical shape; *rolled into one*, combined in one person or thing. **4.** to wind in or as a covering. **5.** to flatten by means of a roller, *roll out the pastry*. **6.** to rock from side to

side, e.g. in walking. **7.** to move or pass steadily, *the years rolled on*. **8.** to undulate, *rolling hills*. **9.** to make a long continuous vibrating sound, *the thunder rolled*. **10.** (*Amer. slang*) to attack and rob (a person). —**roll** *n.* **1.** a cylinder formed by turning flexible material over and over upon itself without creasing it. **2.** something having this shape, an undulation, *rolls of fat*. **3.** a small individual portion of bread baked in a rounded shape, this split and containing filling. **4.** an official list or register; *strike off the rolls*, to debar (a person) from practising his profession, e.g. after dishonesty. **5.** a rolling movement. **6.** a long steady vibrating sound. □ **roll-call** *n.* the calling of a list of names, to check that all are present. **rolled gold**, a thin coating of gold applied to another metal. **roll in**, to arrive in great numbers or quantities; (*informal*) to arrive casually. **rolled oats**, husked and crushed oats. **rolling-mill** *n.* a machine or factory for rolling metal into various shapes. **rolling-pin** *n.* a cylindrical device rolled over dough to flatten this. **rolling-stock** *n.* railway engines and carriages and wagons etc. **rolling stone**, a person who does not settle and live or work in one place. **roll of honour**, a list of names whose achievements are honoured. **roll-on** *adj.* (of a cosmetic) applied by means of a ball that rotates in the neck of a container. **roll-on, roll-off**, (of a ferry) that vehicles can be driven on to and off. **roll-top desk**, a desk with a flexible cover that slides in curved grooves. **roll up**, (*informal*) to arrive in a vehicle, to arrive casually.

roller *n.* **1.** a cylinder used for flattening or spreading things, or on which something is wound. **2.** a long swelling wave. □ **roller-coaster** *n.* a switchback at a fair etc. **roller-skate** *n.* see skate². **roller-skating** *n.* skating on roller-skates. **roller towel**, a towel with its ends joined so that it is continuous, hung over a roller.

rollicking *adj.* full of boisterous high spirits.

rolling *adj.* (*informal*) wealthy.

rollmop *n.* a rolled pickled herring fillet.

roly-poly *n.* a pudding consisting of suet pastry spread with jam, rolled up, and boiled. —*adj.* plump, podgy.

Rolls *n.* a Rolls-Royce car.

Roman *adj.* **1.** of ancient or modern Rome. **2.** of the ancient Roman republic or empire. **3.** of the Christian Church of Rome, Roman Catholic. —**Roman** *n.* **1.** a member of the ancient Roman republic or empire. **2.** a native or inhabitant of Rome. **3.** a Roman Catholic. **4.** *roman*, plain upright type (not italic), like that used for the definitions in this dictionary. □ **Roman candle**, a tubular firework that sends out coloured sparks. **Roman Catholic**, of the Church that acknowledges the Pope as its head; a member of this Church. **Roman Catholicism**, the faith of the Roman Catholic Church. **Roman holiday**, enjoyment provided by the discomfort of others. **Roman nose**, a nose with a high bridge. **Roman numerals**, letters representing numbers (I = 1, V = 5, X = 10, L = 50, C = 100, D = 500, M = 1000).

romance (rŏ-**manss**) *n*. **1**. an imaginative story, literature of this kind, *medieval romances*. **2**. a romantic situation or event or atmosphere. **3**. a love story, a love affair resembling this. **4**. a picturesque exaggeration or falsehood. —*v*. to exaggerate or distort the truth in an imaginative way. □ **Romance languages**, those descended from Latin (French, Italian, Spanish, etc.).

Romanesque (roh-măn-**esk**) *n*. a style of art and architecture in Europe in about 1050–1200, with massive vaulting and round arches.

Romania a country in eastern Europe. **Romanian** *adj*. & *n*.

romantic *adj*. **1**. appealing to the emotions by its imaginative or heroic or picturesque quality. **2**. involving a love affair. **3**. enjoying romantic situations. **4**. (of music or literature) richly imaginative, not conforming to classical conventions. —*n*. a person who enjoys romantic situations etc. —**romantically** *adv*.

Romany (**rom**-ă-ni) *n*. **1**. a gypsy. **2**. the language of gypsies. —*adj*. of Romanies or their language.

Rome 1. the capital of Italy. **2**. the ancient Roman republic or empire. **3**. Roman Catholicism.

romp *v*. **1**. to play about together in a lively way, as children do. **2**. (*informal*) to get along easily; *romped home*, came in as an easy winner. —*n*. a spell of romping.

rompers *pl. n*. a young child's one-piece garment, usually covering the trunk only.

rondo *n*. (*pl*. rondos) a piece of music with a theme that recurs several times.

rood *n*. **1**. a crucifix, especially one raised on the middle of the rood-screen. **2**. a quarter of an acre. □ **Holy Rood**, (*old use*) the Cross of Christ. **rood-screen** *n*. a carved wooden or stone screen separating the nave from the chancel.

roof *n*. **1**. a structure covering the top of a house or building. **2**. the top of a car or tent etc.; *roof of the mouth*, a structure forming the upper part of the mouth cavity. —*v*. to cover with a roof, to be the roof

of. □ **have a roof over one's head**, to have somewhere to live. **hit** *or* **raise the roof**, (*informal*) to become very angry. **roof-garden** *n*. a garden on the flat roof of a building. **roof-rack** *n*. a framework to carry luggage etc. on the roof of a car.

rook[1] *n*. a black crow that nests in colonies. —*v*. to swindle, to charge (a person) an extortionate price.

rook[2] *n*. a chess piece with a top shaped like battlements.

rookery *n*. **1**. a colony of rooks, a place where these nest. **2**. a colony or breeding-place of penguins or seals.

room *n*. **1**. space that is or could be occupied by something; *make room for*, to clear a space or position etc. for a person or thing. **2**. part of a building enclosed by walls or partitions, the people present in this. **3**. opportunity or scope or ability to allow something, *no room for dispute*. □ **room-divider** *n*. a piece of furniture used to divide a room into sections. **room-mate** *n*. a person sharing a room with another. **rooms** *pl. n*. a set of rooms occupied by a person or family. **room service**, service of food etc. to a hotel guest in his room.

roomful *n*. the amount that a room will hold.

roomy *adj*. (roomier, roomiest) having plenty of room to contain things.

roost *n*. a place where birds perch or where they settle for sleep. —*v*. (of birds) to perch, to settle for sleep. □ **come home to roost**, (of an action) to react unfavourably on the doer.

rooster *n*. (*Amer*.) a male domestic fowl.

root[1] *n*. **1**. the part of a plant that attaches it to the earth and absorbs water and nourishment from the soil; *a person's roots*, what attaches him emotionally to a place where he or his ancestors lived for a long time. **2**. a similar part attaching ivy etc. to its support, a rhizome. **3**. a small plant with root attached, for transplanting. **4**. an edible root, a plant with this (e.g. carrot, turnip), *root crops*. **5**. the part of a bodily organ or structure that is embedded in tissue, *the root of a tooth*. **6**. a source or basis, *the root of all evil*; *get to the root of the matter*, discover its source and tackle it there. **7**. a number in relation to a given number which it produces when multiplied by itself once (= *square root*) or a specified number of times, *2 is the cube root of 8* (2 × 2 × 2 = 8). —**root** *v*. **1**. to take root, to cause to do this. **2**. to cause to stand fixed and unmoving, *was rooted to the spot by fear*. **3**. to establish deeply and firmly, *the feeling is deeply rooted*. □ **root out** *or* **up**, to drag or dig up by the roots; to get rid of. **root-stock** *n.* a rhizome. **take root**, to send down roots; (of an idea etc.) to become established.

root² *v.* **1.** (of an animal) to turn up ground with its snout or beak in search of food. **2.** to rummage, to find or extract by doing this, *root out some facts and figures*. **3.** (*Amer. slang*) to support actively by applause etc., *rooting for their team*.

rootless *adj.* **1.** having no root or roots. **2.** (of a person) having no roots in a community.

rope *n.* **1.** strong thick cord, a length of this. **2.** a quantity of similar things strung together, *a rope of pearls*. —**rope** *v.* **1.** to fasten or secure or catch with rope. **2.** to fence off with rope(s). □ **give a person enough rope**, to allow him freedom of action in the hope that he will bring about his own downfall. **rope a person in**, to persuade him to take part in an activity. **rope-ladder** *n.* a ladder made of two long ropes connected by short cross-pieces. **the ropes**, the procedure for doing something, *know* or *learn the ropes*.

ropy *adj.* (**ropier, ropiest**) **1.** (of a substance) forming long sticky threads. **2.** (*informal*) poor in quality. **ropiness** *n.*

Roquefort (**rok**-for) *n.* (*trade mark*) a kind of blue cheese, made from ewes' milk.

rosaceous (roh-**zay**-shŭs) *adj.* rose-like, of the large family of plants comprising roses and similar flowers.

rosary *n.* **1.** a set series of prayers used in the Roman Catholic Church, a book containing this. **2.** a string of 55 or 165 beads for keeping count of this. **3.** a similar bead-string used in other religions.

rose¹ *n.* **1.** a bush or shrub bearing ornamental usually fragrant flowers. **2.** its flower. **3.** deep pink colour; *see things through rose-coloured spectacles*, to take an unduly cheerful view of things; *roses in her cheeks*, a rosy complexion. **4.** the perforated sprinkling-nozzle of a watering-can or hose-pipe. —*adj.* deep pink. □ **rose-water** *n.* a fragrant liquid perfumed with roses. **rose window** *n.* a circular window in a church, with a pattern of tracery.

rose² *see* **rise**.

rosé (**roh**-zay) *n.* a light pink wine.

roseate (**roh**-zi-ăt) *adj.* deep pink, rosy.

rosebud *n.* the bud of a rose.

rosemary (**rohz**-mer-i) *n.* an evergreen shrub with fragrant leaves that are used for flavouring food.

rosette *n.* **1.** a rose-shaped badge or ornament made of ribbon etc. **2.** a rose-shaped carving.

rosewood *n.* any of several fragrant close-grained woods used for making furniture.

rosin (**roz**-in) *n.* a kind of resin.

roster (**ros**-ter) *n.* a list showing people's turns of duty etc. —*v.* to place on a roster.

rostrum (**ros**-trŭm) *n.* (*pl.* **rostra**) a platform for one person, especially for public speaking.

rosy *adj.* (**rosier, rosiest**) **1.** rose-coloured, deep pink. **2.** promising, hopeful, *a rosy future*. **rosily** *adv.*, **rosiness** *n.*

rot *v.* (**rotted, rotting**) **1.** (of animal or vegetable matter) to lose its original form by chemical action caused by bacteria or fungi etc. **2.** to perish or become weak through lack of use or activity. —**rot** *n.* **1.** rotting, rottenness. **2.** (*slang*) nonsense, an absurd statement or argument. **3.** a series of failures, *a rot set in*.

rota (**roh**-tă) *n.* a list of duties to be done or people to do them in rotation.

Rotarian (roh-**tair**-iăn) *n.* a member of a Rotary Club.

rotary *adj.* rotating, acting by rotating, *a rotary drill*. **Rotary Club**, a local branch of an international association formed by business men for the purpose of rendering service to the community.

rotate *v.* **1.** to revolve or cause to revolve. **2.** to arrange or deal with in a recurrent series. **rotation** *n.*, **rotator** *n.*

rotatory (roh-tă-ter-i) *adj.* rotating.

rote *n.* **by rote**, by memory without thought of the meaning, *knew it only by rote*; by a fixed procedure, *working by rote*.

rotisserie (rŏ-**tiss**-er-i) *n.* a cooking-device for roasting food on a revolving spit.

rotor *n.* a rotating part of a machine, a helicopter vane.

rotten *adj.* **1.** rotting, rotted, breaking easily or falling to pieces from age or use. **2.** morally corrupt. **3.** (*informal*) contemptible, worthless. **4.** (*informal*) unpleasant, *rotten weather*. **rottenness** *n.*

rotter *n.* (*slang*) a contemptible person.

rotund (rŏ-**tund**) *adj.* rounded, plump. **rotundity** *n.*

rotunda (rŏ-**tun**-dă) *n.* a circular domed building or hall.

rouble (**roo**-bŭl) *n.* the unit of money in Russia.

roué (**roo**-ay) *n.* a dissolute elderly man.

rouge (*pr.* roozh) *n.* **1.** a reddish cosmetic for colouring the cheeks. **2.** a fine red powder used for polishing metal. —*v.* to colour with rouge.

rough *adj.* **1.** having an uneven or irregular surface, coarse in texture, not level or smooth. **2.** not gentle or restrained or careful, violent; *rough weather*, stormy; *rough luck*, hard luck. **3.** lacking finish or delicacy, not perfected or detailed; *a rough estimate,* approximate. —*adv.* roughly, in rough conditions; *sleeping rough,* not in a proper bed etc., especially out of doors. — **rough** *n.* **1.** something rough, rough ground. **2.** hardship, *take the rough with the smooth.* **3.** an unfinished state. **4.** a rough drawing or design etc. **5.** a ruffian or hooligan. —**rough** *v.* **1.** to make rough. **2.** to shape or plan or sketch roughly, *roughed out a scheme.* —**roughly** *adv.,* **roughness** *n.* ☐ **rough-and-ready** *adj.* full of rough vigour and not refined; rough or crude but effective. **rough-and-tumble** *n.* a haphazard fight or struggle. **rough diamond,** a diamond not yet cut; a person of good nature but lacking polished manners. **rough grazing,** pasture in a natural state. **rough house,** (*slang*) a disturbance with violent behaviour or fighting. **rough it,** to do without ordinary comforts. **rough justice,** treatment that is approximately fair. **rough shooting,** shooting (as a sport) without the help of beaters etc. **rough stuff,** (*slang*) violent behaviour. **rough up,** (*slang*) to treat (a person) violently.

roughage *n.* indigestible material in plants which are used as food (e.g. bran, green vegetables, and certain fruits), that stimulates the action of the intestines.

roughcast *n.* plaster of lime and gravel, used for covering the outsides of buildings. —*v.* (roughcast, roughcasting) to coat with this.

roughen *v.* to make or become rough.

roughneck *n.* a worker in an oil-drilling crew.

roughshod *adj.* (of a horse) having shoes with the nail-heads left projecting to prevent slipping. **ride roughshod over,** to treat inconsiderately or arrogantly.

rouleau (roo-loh) *n.* (*pl.* rouleaux, *pr.* roo-loh) a narrow tubular piece of trimming etc., *a rouleau belt.*

roulette (roo-let) *n.* a gambling game in which a small ball falls at random into one of the compartments on a revolving disc.

round *adj.* **1.** having a curved shape or outline, shaped like a circle or sphere or cylinder. **2.** full, complete, *a round dozen.* —**round** *n.* **1.** a round object, a slice of bread cut across the loaf. **2.** a circular or recurring course or series; *the daily round,* ordinary occupations of the day; *a round of drinks,* one for each person in a group. **3.** a route on which things are to be inspected or delivered, *make* or *go one's rounds; a round of golf,* playing all holes on a course once. **4.** a musical composition for two or more voices in which each sings

the same melody but starts at a different time. **5.** a single shot or volley of shots from one or more firearms, ammunition for this. **6.** one stage in a competition or struggle, one section of a boxing-match. —**round** *prep.* **1.** so as to circle or enclose. **2.** at points on or near the circumference of, *sat round the table; talked round the subject,* did not tackle it directly. **3.** having as its axis or central point, *the earth moves round the sun.* **4.** visiting in a series or all over, to all points of interest in, *went round the cafés; were shown round the museum.* **5.** on or to the further side of, *the shop round the corner.* —**round** *adv.* **1.** in a circle or curve, by a circuitous route. **2.** so as to face in a different direction, *turn the chair round.* **3.** round a place or group, in every direction. **4.** to a person's house etc., *I'll be round in an hour.* **5.** into consciousness after unconsciousness, *he isn't round yet.* —**round** *v.* **1.** to make or become round. **2.** to make into a round figure or number; *round it up,* increase it in order to do this (e.g. make £1.90 into £2.00); *round it down,* decrease it similarly. **3.** to travel round, *the car rounded the corner.* ☐ **in the round,** (of sculpture) with all sides shown, not attached to a background; (of a theatre) with seats on all sides of the stage. **round about,** near by; approximately. **round and round,** turning or going round several times. **round dance,** one in which dancers form a ring. **round figure** *or* **number,** one without odd units. **round game,** a game for any number of players, with no teams or partners. **round off,** to bring (a thing) into a complete state. **round on,** to make an attack or retort in retaliation, especially unexpectedly. **round robin,** a statement signed by a number of people (often with signatures in a circle to conceal who signed first); a letter sent in turn to members of a group, each of whom adds something before sending it on. **round-table conference,** a conference where people meet round a table to discuss something. **round the clock,** continuously throughout day and night. **round trip,** a trip to one or more places and back again. **round up,** to gather (animals or people or things) into one place. **round-up** *n.*

roundabout *n.* **1.** a merry-go-round at a funfair; *lose on the swings what you gain on the roundabouts,* break even. **2.** a road junction with a circular structure round which traffic has to pass in the same direction. —*adj.* indirect, not using the shortest or most direct route or phrasing etc., *heard the news in a roundabout way.*

roundel *n.* a circular identifying mark on an aircraft etc.

rounders *n.* a team game played with bat and ball, in which players have to run round a circuit. **rounder** *n.* the unit of scoring in rounders.

Roundhead *n.* a supporter of the Parliament party in the English Civil War (¶ so called because they wore their hair cut short at a time when long hair was in fashion for men).

roundish *adj.* approximately round in shape.

roundly *adv.* **1.** thoroughly, severely, *was roundly scolded.* **2.** in a rounded shape.

roundsman *n.* (*pl.* roundsmen) a tradesman's employee delivering goods on a regular round.

roundworm *n.* a worm with a rounded body.

rouse *v.* **1.** to cause (a person) to wake. **2.** to cause to become active or excited. **3.** (of a person etc.) to wake.

rousing *adj.* vigorous, stirring.

roustabout *n.* a labourer on an oil rig.

rout[1] *n.* utter defeat, a disorderly retreat of defeated troops. —*v.* to defeat completely, to put to flight.

rout[2] *v.* **1.** to fetch or force out, *routed him out of bed.* **2.** to rummage.

route (*pr.* root) *n.* the course or way taken to get from starting-point to destination. —*v.* (routed, routeing) to send by a certain route. □ **route march**, a training-march for troops.

router (*rhymes with* outer) *n.* a type of two-handled plane for cutting grooves etc.

routine (roo-**teen**) *n.* **1.** a standard course of procedure, a series of acts performed regularly in the same way. **2.** a set sequence of movements in a dance or other performance. —*adj.* in accordance with routine. —**routinely** *adv.*

roux (*pr.* roo) *n.* a mixture of heated fat and flour used as a basis for a sauce.

rove *v.* to roam. **rover** *n.* □ **roving commission**, authority to travel as may be necessary in connection with one's enquiries or other work. **roving eye**, a tendency to flirt.

row[1] (*rhymes with* go) *n.* **1.** a number of people or things in a line. **2.** a line of seats across a theatre etc.

row[2] (*rhymes with* go) *v.* **1.** to propel (a boat) by using oars. **2.** to carry in a boat that one rows. **3.** to row a race with. **4.** to be a member of a rowing-boat's crew. —*n.* a spell of rowing, an excursion in a rowing-boat. □ **row-boat** *n.* a rowing-boat. **rowing-boat** *n.* a boat for rowing. **rowing-machine** *n.* a machine for exercising the muscles that are used in rowing.

row[3] (*rhymes with* cow) *n.* (*informal*) **1.** a loud noise. **2.** a quarrel, a heated argument. **3.** the process or condition of being reprimanded, *got into a row for being late.* —**row** *v.* (*informal*) **1.** to quarrel or argue heatedly. **2.** to reprimand.

rowan (roh-ăn) *n.* a tree that bears hanging clusters of scarlet berries, the mountain ash.

rowdy (*rhymes with* cloudy) *adj.* (rowdier, rowdiest) noisy and disorderly. —*n.* a rowdy person. —**rowdily** *adv.*, **rowdiness** *n.*, **rowdyism** *n.*

rowlock (rol-ŏk) *n.* a device on the side of a boat serving as a fulcrum for an oar and keeping it in place.

royal *adj.* **1.** of or suitable for or worthy of a king or queen. **2.** belonging to the family of a king or queen, in the service or under the patronage of royalty; *Royal Air Force, Royal Marines, Royal Navy,* the British air force etc. **3.** splendid, first-rate, of exceptional size etc. —*n.* (*informal*) a member of a royal family. —**royally** *adv.* □ **royal blue**, deep vivid blue. **Royal Commission**, a body of people appointed by the Crown to investigate and report on something. **royal flush**, see flush[2]. **royal icing**, hard icing for cakes, made with icing sugar and egg-white.

royalist *n.* **1.** a person who favours monarchy. **2.** *Royalist,* a supporter of the monarchy in the English Civil War.

royalty *n.* **1.** being royal. **2.** a royal person or persons, *in the presence of royalty.* **3.** payment by a mining or oil company to the owner of the land, *oil royalties.* **4.** payment to an author etc. for each copy of his book sold or for each public performance of his work, payment to a patentee for the use of his patent.

RSVP *abbrev.* (in an invitation) please reply. (¶ From the French, *répondez s'il vous plaît.*)

Rt. Hon. *abbrev.* Right Honourable.

Rt. Rev., Rt. Revd. *abbrevs.* Right Reverend.

rub *v.* (rubbed, rubbing) **1.** to press something against (a surface) and slide it to and fro, to apply in this way. **2.** to polish or clean by rubbing, to make or become dry or smooth or sore etc. in this way; *rub brasses,* to take an impression of brass memorial tablets by rubbing coloured wax or chalk etc. over paper laid upon them. —**rub** *n.* **1.** the act or process of rubbing. **2.** a difficulty or impediment, *there's the rub.* □ **rub along**, (*informal*) to manage to get on without undue difficulty. **rub**

down, to dry or smooth or reduce the level of (a thing) by rubbing. **rub it in**, to emphasize or remind a person constantly of an unpleasant fact. **rub off**, to be removed or transferred by or as if by rubbing. **rub out**, to remove (marks etc.) by using a rubber; (*slang*) to murder. **rub a person's nose in it**, (*slang*) = rub it in. **rub shoulders with**, to associate with (certain people). **rub up**, to polish; to brush up (a subject etc.). **rub up the wrong way**, to irritate or repel (a person) by one's actions.

rubber [1] *n.* **1.** a tough elastic substance made from the coagulated juice of certain tropical plants or synthetically. **2.** a piece of this or other substance for rubbing out pencil or ink marks. **3.** a person who rubs something, a device for rubbing things. □ **rubber goods**, contraceptive devices and sexual aids. **rubber stamp**, a device for imprinting a mark on to a surface; one who mechanically gives approval to the actions of another person or group. **rubber-stamp** *v.* to approve automatically without due consideration.

rubber [2] *n.* a match of three successive games at bridge or whist etc.

rubberize *v.* to treat or coat with rubber.

rubberneck *n.* (*Amer. slang*) a gaping sightseer, an inquisitive person. —*v.* (*Amer. slang*) to behave as a rubberneck.

rubbery *adj.* like rubber.

rubbish *n.* **1.** waste or worthless material. **2.** nonsense. **rubbishy** *adj.*

rubble *n.* waste or rough fragments of stone or brick etc.

Rubicon (roo-bi-kŏn) *n.* **cross the Rubicon**, to take a decisive step that commits one to an enterprise. ¶ The river Rubicon was the ancient boundary between Gaul and Italy; by crossing it into Italy Julius Caesar committed himself to war with Pompey.

rubicund (roo-bik-ŭnd) *adj.* (of the complexion) red, ruddy.

Rubik cube *or* **Rubik's cube** (roo-bik) (*trade mark*) a puzzle consisting of a cube formed of 27 smaller cubes with their faces painted in different colours, each layer of three cubes being capable of being rotated independently with the aim of restoring a single colour to appear on each face of the large cube. (¶ Named after E. Rubik, its Hungarian inventor.)

rubric (roo-brik) *n.* words put as a heading or a note of explanation or a direction of how something must be done.

ruby *n.* **1.** a red gem. **2.** deep red colour. —*adj.* deep red. □ **ruby wedding**, the 40th anniversary of a wedding.

ruche (*pr.* roosh) *n.* a gathered trimming. —*v.* to gather (fabric) ornamentally.

ruck [1] *v.* to crease, to wrinkle. —*n.* a crease or wrinkle.

ruck [2] *n.* **1.** an undistinguished crowd of people or things. **2.** (in Rugby football) a loose scrum with the ball on the ground.

rucksack *n.* a bag worn slung by straps from both shoulders and resting on the back, used by walkers and climbers for carrying their possessions.

ructions *pl. n.* (*informal*) protests and noisy argument, a row.

rudder *n.* a vertical piece of metal or wood hinged to the stern of a boat or rear of an aeroplane and used for steering.

ruddy *adj.* (ruddier, ruddiest) **1.** reddish, (of a person's face) having a fresh healthy reddish colour. **2.** (*slang*) bloody. **ruddily** *adv.*, **ruddiness** *n.*

rude *adj.* **1.** impolite, showing no respect or consideration. **2.** primitive, roughly made, *rude stone implements*. **3.** vigorous, hearty, *rude health*. **4.** violent, startling, *a rude awakening*. **rudely** *adv.*, **rudeness** *n.*

rudery *n.* (*informal*) rudeness.

rudiment (roo-dim-ĕnt) *n.* a part or organ that is incompletely developed. **rudiments** *pl. n.* basic or elementary principles, *learning the rudiments of chemistry*. **rudimentary** (roodi-**ment**-er-i) *adj.*

rue [1] *n.* a shrub with bitter leaves formerly used in medicine.

rue [2] *v.* to repent or regret; *he'll live to rue it*, will some day regret it.

rueful *adj.* showing or feeling good-humoured regret. **ruefully** *adv.*

ruff [1] *n.* **1.** a deep starched pleated frill worn round the neck in the 16th century. **2.** a projecting or coloured ring of feathers or fur round the neck of a bird or animal. **3.** a bird of the sandpiper family.

ruff [2] *v.* to trump in a card-game. —*n.* trumping.

ruffian *n.* a violent lawless person.

ruffle *v.* **1.** to disturb the smoothness or evenness of. **2.** to upset the calmness or even temper of (a person). **3.** to become ruffled. —*n.* a gathered ornamental frill.

rug *n.* **1.** a thick floor-mat. **2.** a piece of thick warm fabric used as a blanket or coverlet. □ **pull the rug from under**, to remove the support of (a theory etc.).

Rugby *n.* the game of **Rugby football**, a kind of football played with an oval ball which may be kicked or carried. ¶ Named after Rugby School in Warwickshire, where it was first played.

rugged *adj.* **1.** having an uneven surface or an irregular outline, craggy. **2.** rough but

kindly and honest, *a rugged individualist*.
ruggedly *adv.*, **ruggedness** *n.*
rugger *n.* (*informal*) Rugby football.
ruin *n.* **1.** severe damage or destruction.
2. complete loss of one's fortune or resources or prospects. **3.** the remains of
something decayed or destroyed, *the house
was a ruin*; *the ruins of Pompeii.* **4.** a
cause of ruin. —*v.* to damage (a thing) so
severely that it is useless, to bring into a
ruined condition. —**ruination** *n.*
ruinous *adj.* **1.** bringing or likely to bring
ruin. **2.** in ruins, ruined, *the house is in a
ruinous condition.* **ruinously** *adv.*
rule *n.* **1.** a statement of what can or must
or should be done in a certain set of circumstances or in playing a game. **2.** the
customary or normal state of things or
course of action, *seaside holidays became
the rule.* **3.** exercise of authority, control,
governing, *countries that were under
French rule.* **4.** a straight often jointed
measuring device used by carpenters etc.
  rule *v.* **1.** to have authoritative control
over people or a country, to govern. **2.** to
keep (a person or feeling etc.) under control, to dominate. **3.** to give a decision as
judge or other authority, *the chairman
ruled that the question was out of order.*
4. to draw (a line) using a ruler or other
straight edge, to mark parallel lines on
(writing-paper etc.). □ **as a rule**, usually,
more often than not. **rule of the road**, the
rules regulating the movements of vehicles
or riders or ships with respect to each other.
rule of thumb, a rough practical method
of procedure. **rule out**, to exclude as irrelevant or ineligible. **rule the roost**, to be the
dominant person. **run the rule over**, to
examine briefly for correctness or fitness.
ruler *n.* **1.** a person who rules by authority. **2.**
a straight strip of wood or metal etc. used for
measuring or for drawing straight lines.
rum[1] *n.* alcoholic spirit distilled from
sugar-cane residues or molasses.
rum[2] *adj.* (*informal*) strange, odd.
Rumania = Romania.
rumba *n.* a ballroom dance of Cuban
origin, music for this.
rumble[1] *v.* **1.** to make a deep heavy
continuous sound, like thunder. **2.** to utter
in a deep voice. —*n.* a rumbling sound.
rumble[2] *v.* (*slang*) to detect the true character of, to see through (a deception).
rumbustious *adj.* (*informal*) boisterous,
uproarious.
ruminant (roo-min-ănt) *n.* an animal that
chews the cud. —*adj.* ruminating.
ruminate (roo-min-ayt) *v.* **1.** to chew the
cud. **2.** to meditate, to ponder.
rumination *n.*

ruminative (roo-min-ătiv) *adj.* meditative,
pondering.
rummage *v.* to make a search by turning
things over or disarranging them. —*n.* a
search of this kind. □ **rummage sale**, a
jumble sale.
rummy *n.* a card-game in which players
try to form sets or sequences of cards.
rumour *n.* information spread by word of
mouth but not certainly true. —*v.* **be
rumoured**, to be spread as a rumour.
rump *n.* **1.** the buttocks, the corresponding
part of a bird. **2.** a cut of meat from an
animal's hindquarters.
rumple *v.* to make or become crumpled,
to make (something smooth) untidy.
rumpus *n.* (*slang*) an uproar, an angry dispute.
run *v.* (ran, run, running) **1.** to move with
quick steps, never having both or all feet
on the ground at once. **2.** to go or travel
smoothly or swiftly, (of salmon) to go up
river in large numbers from the sea; *run
free,* (of a sailing-ship) travelling with the
wind blowing from astern. **3.** to compete in a
race or contest, to seek election, *run for
president.* **4.** to spread rapidly or beyond the
intended limit, *the dye has run.* **5.** to flow
or cause to flow, to exude liquid, *run some
water into it*; *smoke makes my eyes run*;
run dry, to become dry; *feeling ran high,*
became intense. **6.** to function, to be in
action, *left the engine running.* **7.** (of a film
or magnetic tape etc.) to pass between
spools so as to show or play or perform its
contents. **8.** to travel or convey from point
to point, *the bus runs every hour*; *we'll run
you home*; *run the blockade,* to continue to
pass through it; *run contraband goods,*
smuggle them in. **9.** to extend, *a fence runs
round the estate*; *the money won't run to it,*
will not be enough. **10.** to be current or
operative or valid, *the lease runs for 20
years*; *musical ability runs in the family.*
11. to pass or cause to pass (into a specified condition), *supplies are running low*;
run a temperature, to be feverish. **12.** to
cause to run or go or extend or function.
13. to manage, to organize, *who runs the
country?* **14.** to own and use (a vehicle etc.).
15. (of a newspaper) to print as an item.
16. to sew (fabric) loosely or quickly. —
run *n.* **1.** an act or spell or course of running. **2.** a point scored in cricket or baseball.
3. a ladder in a stocking or knitted fabric.
4. a continuous stretch or sequence or spell.
5. a general demand for goods etc., *there
has been a run on tinned meat*; *a run on the
bank,* a sudden withdrawal of deposits by
many customers. **6.** a large number of
salmon going up river from the sea. **7.** a

general type or class of things. **8.** an enclosure where domestic aniimals can range. **9.** a track for some purpose, *ski-run*. **10.** permission to make unrestricted use of something, *he has the run of the house*. □ **on the run**, fleeing from pursuit or capture. **run across**, to happen to meet or find. **run after**, to seek the company or attentions of. **run away**, to leave quickly or secretly. **run away with**, to elope with (a person); to win (a prize etc.) easily; to accept (an idea) too hastily; to require (much money) in expense. **run down**, to stop because not rewound; to reduce the numbers of; to knock down with a moving vehicle or ship; to discover after searching; to speak of in a slighting way; *be run down*, to be weak or exhausted. **run-down** *n.* a detailed analysis. **run for it**, to try to escape by running. **run in**, (*informal*) to arrest and take into custody; to run (a new engine) carefully into good working order. **run into**, to collide with; to happen to meet. **run off**, to run away; to produce (copies) on a machine. **run-of-the-mill** *adj.* ordinary, not special. **run on**, to talk continually. **run out**, (of time or a stock of something) to become used up, (of a person) to have used up one's stock; to escape from a container; to jut out; to complete a required score; to put down the wicket of (a batsman while he is running). **run over**, to knock down or crush with a vehicle; to study or repeat quickly. **run risks**, to take risks. **run through**, to study or repeat quickly. **run up**, to raise (a flag) on a mast; to allow (a bill) to mount; to add up (a column of figures); to make quickly by sewing, *run up some curtains*. **run-up** *n.* the period leading to an event.

runaway *n.* a person who has run away. —*adj.* **1.** having run away or become out of control. **2.** won easily, *a runaway victory*.

rune (*pr.* roon) *n.* any of the letters in an alphabet used by early Germanic peoples. **runic** *adj.*

rung[1] *n.* one of the cross-pieces of a ladder etc.

rung[2] *see* ring[2].

runner *n.* **1.** a person or animal that runs, one taking part in a race. **2.** a messenger. **3.** a creeping stem that issues from the main stem and takes root. **4.** a groove or rod or roller for a thing to move on, one of the long strips on which a sledge etc. slides. **5.** a long narrow strip of carpet, or of ornamental cloth for a table etc. □ **runner bean**, a kind of climbing bean. **runner-up** *n.* a person or team finishing second in a competition.

running *see* run. —*adj.* **1.** performed while running, *a running jump* or *kick*. **2.** following each other without interval, *for four days running*. **3.** continuous, *a running battle*; *running commentary*, one on an event as it happens. □ **in** *or* **out of the running**, with a good chance *or* with no chance of winning. **make the running**, to set the pace. **running-stitch** *n.* a line of evenly-spaced stitches made by a straight thread passing in and out of the material.

runny *adj.* **1.** semi-liquid. **2.** tending to flow or exude fluid.

runt *n.* an undersized person or animal; *the runt of a litter*, the smallest animal in a litter.

runway *n.* a prepared surface on an airfield, on which aircraft take off and land.

rupee (roo-**pee**) *n.* the unit of money in India, Pakistan, and certain other countries.

rupture *n.* **1.** breaking, breach. **2.** an abdominal hernia. —**rupture** *v.* **1.** to burst or break (tissue etc.), to become burst or broken. **2.** to affect with hernia.

rural *adj.* of or in or like the countryside. **rural dean**, *see* dean.

ruse (*pr.* rooz) *n.* a deception or trick.

rush[1] *n.* a marsh plant with a slender pithy stem used for making mats, chair-seats, baskets, etc.

rush[2] *v.* **1.** to go or come or convey with great speed. **2.** to act hastily, to force into hasty action; *rush one's fences*, to act with undue haste. **3.** to attack or capture with a sudden assault. —**rush** *n.* **1.** rushing, an instance of this. **2.** a period of great activity. **3.** a sudden great demand for goods etc. **4.** (*informal*) the first print of a cinema film before it is cut and edited. —*adj.* done with haste or with minimum delay, *a rush job*. □ **rush-hour** *n.* the time each day when traffic is busiest.

rusk *n.* a kind of biscuit, especially one used for feeding babies.

russet *adj.* soft reddish-brown. —*n.* **1.** russet colour. **2.** an apple with a rough skin of this colour.

Russia a country extending from eastern Europe to the Pacific, the USSR.

Russian *adj.* of Russia or its people or language. —*n.* **1.** a native or inhabitant of Russia. **2.** the language of Russia. □ **Russian roulette**, an act of bravado in which a person holds to his head a revolver of which one (unknown) chamber contains a bullet, and pulls the trigger. **Russian salad**, salad of mixed diced vegetables in mayonnaise.

rust *n.* **1.** a reddish-brown or yellowish-brown coating formed on iron or other metal by the effect of moisture, and gradually corroding it. **2.** reddish-brown. **3.** a plant disease with rust-coloured spots, the fungus causing this. —**rust** *v.* **1.** to affect or be affected with rust. **2.** to lose quality or efficiency by lack of use. —**rustless** *adj.*, **rust-proof** *adj.*

rustic *adj.* **1.** having the qualities ascribed to country people or peasants, simple and unsophisticated, rough and unrefined. **2.** made of rough timber or untrimmed branches, *rustic seat* or *bridge.* —*n.* a countryman, a peasant.

rusticate *v.* to settle in the country and live a rural life. **rustication** *n.*

rustle *v.* **1.** to make a sound like that of paper being crumpled, to cause to do this. **2.** (*Amer.*) to steal (horses or cattle), *cattle rustling.* —*n.* a rustling sound. —**rustler** *n.* ☐ **rustle up**, (*informal*) to prepare or produce, *try and rustle up a meal.*

rusty *adj.* (rustier, rustiest) **1.** affected with rust. **2.** rust-coloured. **3.** having lost quality or efficiency by lack of use. **rustiness** *n.*

rut[1] *n.* **1.** a deep track made by wheels in soft ground. **2.** a habitual usually dull course of life, *getting into a rut.* **rutted** *adj.*

rut[2] *n.* the periodic sexual excitement of a male deer or goat or ram etc. —*v.* (rutted, rutting) to be affected with this.

ruthless *adj.* having no pity or compassion. **ruthlessly** *adv.*, **ruthlessness** *n.*

Rwanda (roo-an-dǎ) a country in East Africa. **Rwandan** *adj. & n.*

rye *n.* **1.** a kind of cereal used for making flour or as food for cattle. **2.** a kind of whisky made from rye.

Ss

S. *abbrev.* south.

s. *abbrev.* shilling (¶ originally short for the Latin *solidus*).

SA *abbrev.* **1.** South Africa. **2.** South Australia.

sabbath *n.* **1.** a religious rest-day appointed for Jews on the last day of the week (Saturday). **2.** Sunday as a Christian day of abstinence from work and play.

sabbatical (sǎ-bat-ikǎl) *adj.* of or like the sabbath. **sabbatical leave**, leave granted at intervals to a university professor etc. for study and travel.

sable *n.* **1.** a small weasel-like animal of arctic and adjacent regions, valued for its dark-brown fur. **2.** its fur. —*adj.* black, gloomy.

sabot (sab-oh) *n.* a shoe hollowed out

from one piece of wood, or with a wooden sole.

sabotage (sab-ŏ-tahzh) *n.* wilful damaging of machinery or materials, or disruption of work, by dissatisfied workmen or hostile agents. —*v.* **1.** to commit sabotage on. **2.** to destroy or render useless, *sabotaged my plans.*

saboteur (sab-ŏ-ter) *n.* one who commits sabotage.

sabre (say-ber) *n.* a cavalry sword with a curved blade.

sac *n.* a bag-like part in an animal or plant.

saccharin (sak-er-in) *n.* a very sweet substance used as a substitute for sugar.

saccharine (sak-er-een) *adj.* intensely and unpleasantly sweet.

sachet (sash-ay) *n.* **1.** a small bag filled with a sweet-smelling substance for laying among clothes etc. to scent them. **2.** a sealed plastic or paper pack containing a single portion of a substance.

sack[1] *n.* **1.** a large bag of strong coarse fabric for storing and carrying goods. **2.** this with its contents, the amount it contains. **3.** *the sack*, (*informal*) dismissal from one's employment or position, *got the sack.* —**sack** *v.* **1.** to put into a sack or sacks. **2.** (*informal*) to dismiss from a job. — **sackful** *n.* (*pl.* sackfuls) ☐ **sack-race** *n.* a race in which each competitor is tied in a sack up to his waist or neck and moves by jumping.

sack[2] *v.* to plunder (a captured town etc.) in a violent destructive way. —*n.* the act or process of sacking a place.

sackcloth *n.* coarse fabric for making sacks; *sackcloth and ashes,* a symbol of regret and repentance. (¶ From the ancient custom of wearing sackcloth and sprinkling ashes on one's head in penitence or mourning.)

sacking *n.* material for making sacks.

sacrament *n.* **1.** any of the symbolic Christian religious ceremonies, especially baptism and the Eucharist. **2.** the consecrated elements in the Eucharist, especially the bread. **sacramental** *adj.*

sacred *adj.* **1.** associated with or dedicated to God or a god, or regarded with reverence because of this. **2.** dedicated to some person or purpose, *sacred to the memory of those who fell in battle.* **3.** connected with religion, not secular, *sacred music.* **4.** sacrosanct. ☐ **sacred cow**, an idea or institution which its supporters will not allow to be criticized. (¶ The phrase refers to the Hindus' respect for the cow as a sacred animal.)

sacrifice *n.* **1.** the slaughter of a victim or

the presenting of a gift or doing of an act in order to win the favour of a god. **2.** the giving up of a valued thing for the sake of another that is more important or more worthy. **3.** the thing offered or given up. **4.** the sale of something at much less than its real value. —**sacrifice** v. **1.** to offer or give up as a sacrifice. **2.** to give up (a thing) in order to achieve something else, *her description of events sacrificed accuracy to vividness.* **3.** to sell at much less than its real value. **sacrificial** (sak-ri-**fish**-ăl) *adj.*

sacrilege (**sak**-ri-lij) *n.* disrespect or damage to something regarded as sacred. **sacrilegious** (sak-ri-**lij**-us) *adj.*

sacristan (**sak**-ri-stăn) *n.* the person in charge of the contents of a church, especially the sacred vessels etc. used in worship.

sacristy (**sak**-rist-i) *n.* the place in a church where sacred vessels etc. are kept.

sacrosanct (**sak**-roh-sankt) *adj.* reverenced or respected and therefore secure from violation or damage.

sacrum (**say**-krŭm) *n.* the triangular bone that forms the back of the pelvis.

sad *adj.* (**sadder, saddest**) **1.** showing or causing sorrow, unhappy. **2.** regrettable. **3.** (of cake or pastry etc.) dense from not having risen. **sadly** *adv.*, **sadness** *n.*

sadden v. to make sad.

saddle *n.* **1.** a seat for a rider, placed on a horse or other animal or forming part of a bicycle etc. **2.** a saddle-shaped thing. **3.** a ridge of high land between two peaks. **3.** a joint of meat consisting of the two loins. — **saddle** v. **1.** to put a saddle on (an animal). **2.** to burden (a person) with a task. □ **in the saddle**, in a controlling position. **saddle-bag** *n.* a strong bag fixed behind a saddle or as one of a pair slung over a horse etc. **saddle stitching**, a long running-stitch made with thick thread, used decoratively.

saddleback *n.* a black pig with a white stripe round its body.

saddler *n.* one who makes or deals in saddles and harness. **saddlery** *n.* a saddler's goods or business.

sadism (**say**-dizm) *n.* enjoyment of inflicting or watching cruelty, this as a form of sexual perversion. **sadist** *n.*, **sadistic** (să-**dis**-tik) *adj.*, **sadistically** *adv.*

s.a.e. *abbrev.* stamped addressed envelope.

safari (să-**far**-i) *n.* **1.** a hunting or exploratory expedition, especially in East Africa. **2.** a similar expedition organized as a holiday tour. □ **safari jacket**, a belted jacket in linen or similar fabric. **safari park**, a park where exotic wild animals are kept in the open for visitors to see.

safe *adj.* **1.** free from risk or danger, not dangerous. **2.** providing security or protection. —*adv.* safely; *play safe*, not take risks. —**safe** *n.* **1.** a strong locked cupboard or cabinet for valuables. **2.** a ventilated cabinet for storing food. —**safely** *adv.*, **safeness** *n.* □ **on the safe side**, allowing a margin of security against risks. **safe conduct**, the right to pass through a district on a particular occasion without risk of arrest or harm (e.g. in time of war). **safe deposit**, a building containing safes and strong-rooms for hire separately. **safe period**, (in birth control) the time in a woman's menstrual cycle when sexual intercourse is least likely to result in conception.

safeguard *n.* a means of protection. —*v.* to protect.

safety *n.* being safe, freedom from risk or danger. **safety-catch** *n.* a device that prevents a mechanism from being operated accidentally or dangerously; a locking device on a gun-trigger. **safety curtain**, a fireproof curtain that can be lowered to cut off a theatre stage from the auditorium. **safety lamp**, a miner's lamp with the flame protected so that it will not ignite firedamp. **safety net**, a net placed to catch an acrobat etc. in case he falls from a height. **safety-pin** *n.* a brooch-like pin with a guard protecting the point to prevent it from pricking the user or coming out. **safety razor**, a razor with a guard to prevent the blade from cutting the skin deeply. **safety-valve** *n.* a valve that opens automatically to relieve excessive pressure in a steam boiler; an outlet for releasing feelings of anger or excitement etc. harmlessly.

saffron *n.* **1.** the orange-coloured stigmas of a kind of crocus, used for colouring and flavouring food. **2.** the colour of these.

sag v. (**sagged, sagging**) **1.** to sink or curve down in the middle under weight or pressure. **2.** to hang loosely and unevenly, to droop. —*n.* sagging.

saga (**sah**-gă) *n.* a long story with many episodes.

sagacious (să-**gay**-shŭs) *adj.* showing wisdom in one's understanding and judgement of things. **sagaciously** *adv.*, **sagacity** (să-**gas**-iti) *n.*

sage[1] *n.* a herb with fragrant greyish-green leaves used to flavour food.

sage[2] *adj.* profoundly wise, having wisdom gained from experience. —*n.* a profoundly wise man. —**sagely** *adv.*

Sagittarius (saj-i-**tair**-iŭs) a sign of the zodiac, the Archer. **Sagittarian** *adj. & n.*

sago *n.* a starchy food in the form of hard white grains, used in puddings, obtained from the pith of a kind of palm-tree (the *sago palm*).

sahib (sah-ib) *n.* a former title of address to European men in India.

said *see* say.

sail *n.* 1. a piece of canvas or other fabric spread on rigging to catch the wind and drive a ship or boat along. 2. these sails collectively. 3. a journey by ship or boat, *Haifa is three days' sail from Naples.* 4. something resembling a sail in function, *the sails of a windmill.* —sail *v.* 1. to travel on water by use of sails or engine-power. 2. to start on a voyage, *we sail next week.* 3. to travel on or over (water) in a ship or boat, *sailed the seas.* 4. to control the navigation of (a ship), to set (a toy boat) afloat. 5. to move swiftly and smoothly, to walk in a stately manner.

sailboard *n.* a kind of surfboard to which a sail is fixed. **sailboarding** *n.* the sport of riding on this (also called *windsurfing*). **sailboarder** *n.*

sailcloth *n.* 1. canvas for sails. 2. a strong canvas-like dress-material.

sailing-ship *n.* a ship driven by sails.

sailor *n.* 1. a man who works as a member of a ship's crew, a member of a country's navy, especially one below the rank of officer. 2. a traveller considered as liable or not liable to sea-sickness, *a bad* or *good sailor.* □ **sailor hat**, a straw hat with a flat top and straight brim.

saint *n.* 1. a holy person, one declared (in the RC or Orthodox Church) to have won a high place in heaven and to be worthy of veneration. 2. *Saint*, the title of such a person or of one receiving veneration, or used in the name of a church not called after a saint (e.g. *St. Saviour's, St. Cross*). 3. one of the souls of the dead in paradise. 4. a member of the Christian Church or (in certain religious bodies) of one's own branch of it. 5. a very good or patient or unselfish person. **sainthood** *n.* □ **St. Kitts-Nevis** (nee-vis), **St. Lucia** (loo-shă), **St. Vincent**, islands in the West Indies. **St. Vitus's dance**, a children's disease in which the limbs twitch uncontrollably.

saintly *adj.* (saintlier, saintliest) like a saint. **saintliness** *n.*

saithe (*rhymes with* faith) *n.* a fish related to the cod, with a skin which soils the fingers like wet coal.

sake *n.* **for the sake of**, in order to please or honour (a person) or get or keep (a thing).

salaam (să-lahm) *n.* an Oriental salutation, a low bow. —*v.* to make a salaam to.

salacious (să-lay-shŭs) *adj.* lewd, erotic. **salaciously** *adv.*, **salaciousness** *n.*, **salacity** (să-lass-iti) *n.*

salad *n.* a cold dish consisting of one or more vegetables (usually raw), often chopped or sliced and seasoned. **salad days**, the time when one was youthful and inexperienced.

salamander (sal-ă-mand-er) *n.* 1. a lizard-like animal related to the newts. 2. (in mythology) a lizard-like animal living in fire.

salami (să-lah-mi) *n.* a strongly flavoured Italian sausage.

salaried *adj.* receiving a salary.

salary *n.* a fixed payment made by an employer at regular intervals to a person doing other than manual or mechanical work, usually calculated on an annual or quarterly or monthly basis.

sale *n.* 1. selling, being sold. 2. an instance of this, the amount sold, *made a sale; our sales were enormous.* 3. an event at which goods are sold, especially by public auction or for charity. 4. disposal of a shop's stock at reduced prices, e.g. at the end of a season. □ **for** *or* **on sale**, offered for purchase. **sales department**, the department concerned with selling its firm's products. **sales talk**, persuasive talk designed to make people buy goods or accept an idea.

saleable *adj.* fit for sale, likely to find a purchaser.

saleroom *n.* a room where goods are displayed for sale or in which auctions are held.

Salesian (să-lee-zhăn) *n.* a member of a Roman Catholic religious order engaged in teaching.

salesman *n.* (*pl.* salesmen) a man employed to sell goods.

salesmanship *n.* skill in selling.

salesperson *n.* a salesman or saleswoman.

saleswoman *n.* (*pl.* saleswomen) a woman employed to sell goods.

salient (say-li-ĕnt) *adj.* projecting, prominent, most noticeable, *the salient features of the plan.* —*n.* a projecting part, especially of a battle-line.

saline (say-lyn) *adj.* salty, containing salt or salts. **salinity** (să-lin-iti) *n.*

saliva (să-ly-vă) *n.* the colourless liquid discharged into the mouth by various glands, assisting in chewing and digestion.

salivary (să-ly-ver-i) *adj.* of or producing saliva, *salivary glands.*

salivate (sal-i-vayt) *v.* to produce saliva. **salivation** *n.*

sallee (sal-ee) *n.* (*Austral.*) any of several species of acacia.

sallow[1] *adj.* (of a person's skin or complexion) yellowish. **sallowness** *n.*

sallow[2] *n.* a willow-tree, especially of a low-growing or shrubby kind.

sally *n.* 1. a sudden rush forward in attack, a sortie. 2. an excursion. 3. a lively or witty remark. —*v.* (sallied, sallying). **sally out** *or* **forth**, to make a sally (in attack) or an excursion.

salmi (sal-mi) *n.* a ragout or casserole, especially of game-birds.

salmon *n.* 1. (*pl.* salmon) a large fish with pinkish flesh, much valued for food and sport. 2. salmon-pink. □ **salmon-pink** *adj.* & *n.* orange-pink like the flesh of salmon. **salmon trout**, a trout resembling salmon.

salon (sal-awn) *n.* 1. an elegant room in a continental great house, used for receiving guests. 2. a room or establishment where a hairdresser, beauty specialist, or couturier etc. receives clients.

saloon *n.* 1. a public room for a specified purpose, *billiard saloon.* 2. a public room on a ship. 3. (*Amer.*) a place where alcoholic drinks may be bought and drunk. 4. a saloon car. □ **saloon bar**, a first-class bar in a public house. **saloon car**, a car for a driver and passengers, with a closed body.

salsify (sal-si-fi) *n.* a plant with a long fleshy root cooked as a vegetable.

salt *n.* 1. sodium chloride, a substance obtained from mines or by evaporation of sea-water (in which it is present), used to flavour and preserve food. 2. a chemical compound of a metal and an acid. 3. a salt-cellar. —*adj.* tasting of salt, impregnated with or preserved in salt. —**salt** *v.* 1. to season with salt. 2. to preserve in salt. 3. to put aside for the future, *salt it away.* 4. to make (a mine) appear rich by fraudulently inserting precious metal into it before it is viewed. □ **old salt**, an experienced sailor. **salt-cellar** *n.* a dish or perforated pot holding salt for use at meals. **salt-lick** *n.* a place where animals go to lick rock or earth impregnated with salt. **salt-marsh** *n.* a marsh that is flooded by the sea at high tide. **salt of the earth**, people with a wholesome influence upon society. **salt-pan** *n.* a natural or artificial hollow by the sea where salt is obtained from sea-water by evaporation. **salts** *pl. n.* a substance resembling salt in form, especially a laxative. **take it with a grain** *or* **pinch of salt**, not believe it wholly. **worth one's salt**, competent, deserving one's position.

SALT *abbrev.* Strategic Arms Limitation Talks.

saltire (sal-tyr) *n.* a St. Andrew's cross X, dividing a shield into four compartments.

saltpetre (solt-peet-er) *n.* a salty white powder (potassium nitrate) used in making gunpowder and preserving meat, and medicinally.

salty *adj.* (saltier, saltiest) containing or tasting of salt. **saltiness** *n.*

salubrious (să-loo-bri-ŭs) *adj.* health-giving. **salubrity** *n.*

saluki (să-loo-ki) *n.* (*pl.* salukis) a tall swift slender silky-coated dog.

salutary (sal-yoo-ter-i) *adj.* producing a beneficial or wholesome effect.

salutation (sal-yoo-tay-shŏn) *n.* a word or words or gesture of greeting, an expression of respect.

salute *n.* 1. a gesture of respect or greeting or polite recognition. 2. a formal military movement or position of the body, or a discharge of guns or use of flags, as a sign of respect. —**salute** *v.* 1. to greet with a polite gesture. 2. to perform a formal military salute, to greet with this. 3. to express respect or admiration for.

Salvadorean (sal-vă-dor-iăn) *adj.* of El Salvador. —*n.* a native or inhabitant of El Salvador.

salvage *n.* 1. rescue of a wrecked or damaged ship or its cargo, rescue of property from fire or other disaster. 2. the goods or property saved. 3. the saving and use of waste paper, scrap metal, etc. 4. the items saved. —*v.* to save from loss or for use as salvage.

salvation *n.* 1. saving of the soul from sin and its consequences, the state of being saved. 2. preservation from loss or calamity, a thing that preserves from these, *the loan was our salvation.* □ **Salvation Army**, an international Christian organization founded on military lines to do charitable work and spread Christianity.

salve *n.* 1. a soothing ointment. 2. something that soothes conscience or wounded feelings. —*v.* to soothe (conscience etc.).

salver *n.* a tray (usually of metal) on which letters or cards or refreshments are placed for handing to people.

salvia (sal-viă) *n.* a plant with spikes of red or blue flowers.

salvo *n.* (*pl.* salvoes) 1. the firing of a number of guns simultaneously, especially as a salute. 2. a volley of applause.

sal volatile (sal vŏ-lat-ili) *n.* a flavoured solution of ammonium carbonate, used for drinking as a remedy for faintness.

Samaritan *n.* 1. *good Samaritan*, someone who readily gives help to a person in distress who has no claim on him. (¶ Named after the parable of the Good Samaritan in the Bible.) **2.** a member of an organization (*the Samaritans*) offering help and friendship to those in despair.

same *adj.* **1.** being of one kind, not changed or changing or different. **2.** previously mentioned. **3.** *the same,* the same person or thing, *would do the same again.* **4.** *the same,* in the same manner, *we still feel the same about it.* —*pron.* & *adv.* (*informal*) = the same (senses 3 and 4 above), *same for me, please*; *we feel same as you do.* □ **sameness** *n.* being the same, lack of variety. **same here,** (*informal*) the same applies to me, I agree.

samizdat (**sam**-iz-dat) *n.* a system of secret publication of banned literature in the USSR.

Samoa (să-**moh**-ă) a group of islands in the Pacific Ocean, of which the eastern part (*American Samoa*) is a territory of the USA, and the western part (*Western Samoa*) is an independent country. **Samoan** *adj.* & *n.*

samovar (**sam**-ŏ-var) *n.* a metal urn with an interior heating-tube to keep water at boiling-point for making tea, used in Russia and elsewhere.

sampan *n.* a small flat-bottomed boat used along coasts and rivers of China.

samphire (**sam**-fyr) *n.* a plant with fragrant fleshy leaves, growing on cliffs.

sample *n.* a small separated part showing the quality of the whole, a specimen. —*v.* to test by taking a sample or getting an experience of.

sampler *n.* **1.** a thing that takes samples. **2.** a piece of embroidery worked in various stitches to display skill in needlework.

samurai (**sam** oor-I) *n.* (*pl.* samurai) **1.** a Japanese army officer. **2.** a member of the former military caste in Japan.

Sana'a (**sah**-nă) the capital of the Yemen Arab Republic.

sanatorium *n.* (*pl.* sanatoriums) an establishment for treating chronic diseases (e.g. tuberculosis) or convalescents.

sanctify *v.* (sanctified, sanctifying) to make holy or sacred. **sanctification** *n.*

sanctimonious (sank-ti-**moh**-niŭs) *adj.* making a show of righteousness or piety. **sanctimoniously** *adv.*, **sanctimoniousness** *n.*

sanction *n.* **1.** permission or approval for an action or behaviour etc. **2.** action taken by a country to penalize and coerce a country or organization that is considered to have violated a law or code of practice or basic human rights. —*v.* to give sanction or approval to, to authorize.

sanctity *n.* sacredness, holiness.

sanctuary *n.* **1.** a sacred place. **2.** the holiest part of a temple, the part of a chancel containing the altar. **3.** an area where birds or wild animals are protected and encouraged to breed. **4.** refuge, a place of refuge, *seek sanctuary.*

sanctum *n.* **1.** a holy place. **2.** a person's private room.

sand *n.* **1.** very fine loose fragments resulting from the wearing down of rock, found in deserts, sea-shores, river-beds, etc.; *the sands are running out,* the time allowed is nearly at an end (¶ from the use of sand in an hour-glass). **2.** an expanse of sand, a sandbank, *Goodwin Sands.* **3.** light brown colour like that of sand. —**sand** *v.* **1.** to sprinkle or cover with sand. **2.** to smooth or polish with sand or sandpaper. —**sander** *n.* □

sand-blast *v.* to clean with a jet of sand driven by compressed air or steam. **sand-castle** *n.* a structure of sand made by a child on the sea-shore. **sand-dune** *or* **sand-hill** *ns.* loose sand formed into a mound by wind. **sand-pit** *n.* a hollow partly filled with sand for children to play in. **sand-shoe** *n.* a light shoe, especially with a rubber or rope sole, for use on sand. **sand-yacht** *n.* a sailing dinghy or canoe-shaped structure on 3 or 4 wheels, with one or more sails, driven over sands by wind.

sandal *n.* a light shoe consisting of a sole with straps or thongs over the foot. **sandalled** *adj.* wearing sandals.

sandalwood *n.* a kind of scented wood from a tropical tree.

sandbag *n.* a bag filled with sand, used to protect a wall or building (e.g. in war, or as a defence against rising flood-water), or as a ruffian's weapon. —*v.* (sandbagged, sandbagging) **1.** to protect with sandbags. **2.** to hit with a sandbag.

sandbank *n.* a deposit of sand under water, causing a river etc. to be shallow at that point.

sandpaper *n.* paper with a coating of sand or other abrasive substance, used for smoothing or polishing surfaces. —*v.* to smooth or polish with sandpaper.

sandpiper *n.* any of several birds with long pointed bills, living in open wet sandy places.

sandstone *n.* rock formed of compressed sand.

sandstorm *n.* a desert storm of wind with clouds of sand.

sandwich *n.* **1.** two or more slices of bread with a layer of filling between. **2.** something resembling this in arrangement. —*v.* to insert (a thing) between two others. □ **sandwich course,** a course of training with alternating periods of instruction and practical work. **sandwich-man** *n.* a man walking in the street with advertisement boards hung one before and one behind him.

sandy *adj.* (sandier, sandiest) **1.** like sand, covered with sand. **2.** (of hair) yellowish-red, (of a person) having hair of this colour. **sandiness** *n.*

sane *adj.* **1.** having a sound mind, not mad. **2.** showing good judgement, sensible and practical. **sanely** *adv.*

sang *see* sing.

sang-froid (sahn-**frwah**) *n.* calmness in danger or difficulty.

sanguinary (**sang**-win-er-i) *adj.* **1.** full of bloodshed. **2.** bloodthirsty.

sanguine (**sang**-win) *adj.* hopeful, optimistic, *they are not very sanguine about their chances of winning.*

sanitary (**san**-it-er-i) *n.* **1.** of hygiene, hygienic. **2.** of sanitation. □ **sanitary towel**, an absorbent pad worn during menstruation.

sanitation *n.* arrangements to protect public health, especially by drainage and the efficient disposal of sewage.

sanitize *v.* to make hygienic.

sanity *n.* the state or condition of being sane.

San José (san **hoh**-say) the capital of Costa Rica.

sank *see* sink.

San Marino (mǎ-**ree**-noh) a small independent republic in north-east Italy.

Sanskrit *n.* the ancient language of the Hindus in India, one of the oldest known Indo-European languages.

Santa Claus Father Christmas. ¶ From the Dutch name *Sante Klaas* = St. Nicholas.

Santiago (san-ti-**ah**-goh) the capital of Chile.

São Tomé (sah-oo tŏm-**ay**) the capital of **São Tomé and Príncipe** (*pr.* **prin**-sipi), a country consisting of two islands off the west coast of Africa.

sap¹ *n.* **1.** the vital liquid that circulates in plants, carrying food to all parts. **2.** (*slang*) a foolish person. —*v.* (sapped, sapping) to exhaust (strength etc.) gradually.

sap² *n.* a trench or tunnel made in order to get closer to an enemy.

sapele (sǎ-**pee**-li) *n.* **1.** the hard mahogany-like wood of a West African tree. **2.** the tree itself.

sapling *n.* a young tree.

sapper *n.* a soldier (especially a private) of the Royal Engineers.

sapphire *n.* **1.** a transparent blue precious stone. **2.** its colour. —*adj.* bright blue.

saprophyte (**sap**-rŏ-fyt) *n.* a fungus or similar plant living on dead organic matter. **saprophytic** (sap-rŏ-**fit**-ik) *adj.*

Saracen (**sa**-rǎ-sĕn) *n.* an Arab or Muslim of the time of the Crusades.

sarcasm (**sar**-kazm) *n.* **1.** an ironical remark or taunt. **2.** the use of such taunts.

sarcastic (sar-**kas**-tic) *adj.*, using or showing sarcasm. **sarcastically** *adv.*

sarcoma (sar-**koh**-mǎ) *n.* a malignant tumour on connective tissue.

sarcophagus (sar-**kof**-ǎ-gǔs) *n.* (*pl.* sarcophagi) a stone coffin, often decorated with carvings.

sardine *n.* a young pilchard or similar small fish, often tinned as food tightly packed in oil.

sardonic (sar-**don**-ik) *adj.* humorous in a grim or sarcastic way. **sardonically** *adv.*

sarge *n.* (*slang*) sergeant.

sari (**sar**-i) *n.* (*pl.* saris) a length of cotton or silk cloth draped round the body, worn as the main garment by Hindu women.

sarong (sǎ-**rong**) *n.* a Malay and Javanese garment worn by both sexes, consisting of a strip of cloth worn tucked round the waist or under the armpits.

sarsen (**sar**-sĕn) *n.* one of the large sandstone boulders found especially in Wiltshire.

sarsenet (**sar**-snit) *n.* a soft silk fabric used mainly for linings.

sartorial (sar-**tor**-iǎl) *adj.* of tailoring, of men's clothing, *sartorial elegance.*

sash¹ *n.* a long strip of cloth worn round the waist or over one shoulder and across the body for ornament or as part of a uniform.

sash² *n.* either of a pair of frames holding the glass panes of a window and sliding up and down in grooves. **sash-cord** *n.* strong cord used for attaching a weight to each end of a sash so that it can be balanced at any height.

Sask. *abbrev.* Saskatchewan.

Saskatchewan (sǎ-**skach**-i-wǎn) a province of Canada.

Sassenach (**sas**-ĕn-ak) *n.* (*Scottish & Irish,* usually *contemptuous*) an Englishman.

sat *see* sit.

Satan the Devil.

Satanic (sǎ-**tan**-ik) *adj.* **1.** of Satan. **2.** *satanic,* devilish, hellish.

Satanism *n.* worship of Satan, using distorted forms of Christian worship.

satchel *n.* a small bag for carrying light articles (especially school books), hung over the shoulder or carried on the back.

sate (*pr.* sayt) *v.* to satiate.

sateen (sǎ-**teen**) *n.* a closely-woven cotton fabric resembling satin.

satellite *n.* **1.** a heavenly body revolving round a planet, an artificial body placed in orbit to revolve similarly. **2.** a person's follower or hanger-on. **3.** a country that is subservient to another and follows its lead. □ **satellite town**, a smaller town dependent on a larger one near it.

satiate (say-shi-ayt) *v.* to satisfy fully, to glut or cloy with an excess of something. **satiation** *n.*

satiety (să-ty-ĕti) *n.* the condition or feeling of being satiated.

satin *n.* a silky material woven in such a way that it is glossy on one side only. — *adj.* smooth as satin. —**satiny** *adj.*

satinette (sat-in-et) *n.* fabric resembling satin.

satinwood *n.* **1.** the smooth hard wood of various tropical trees, used for making furniture. **2.** a tree yielding this.

satire *n.* **1.** the use of ridicule or irony or sarcasm in speech or writing. **2.** a novel or play or film etc. that ridicules people's hypocrisy or foolishness in this way, often by parody.

satirical (să ti ri kăl) *adj.* using satire, criticizing in a humorous or sarcastic way. **satirically** *adv.*

satirist (sat-i-rist) *n.* a person who writes satires or uses satire.

satirize (sat-i-ryz) *v.* to attack with satire, to describe satirically.

satisfaction *n.* **1.** satisfying, being satisfied. **2.** something that satisfies a desire or gratifies a feeling. **3.** compensation for injury or loss, *demand satisfaction.*

satisfactory *adj.* satisfying expectations or needs, adequate. **satisfactorily** *adv.*

satisfy *v.* (satisfied, satisfying) **1.** to give (a person) what he wants or demands or needs, to make pleased or contented; *he satisfied with something* or *to do something,* to demand no more than this, to consider that this is enough. **2.** to put an end to (a demand or craving) by giving what is required, *satisfy one's hunger.* **3.** to provide with sufficient proof, to convince; *the police are satisfied that his death was accidental,* they feel certain of this. **4.** to pay (a creditor).

satsuma (sat-soo-mă) *n.* a kind of mandarin orange originally grown in Japan.

saturate *v.* **1.** to make thoroughly wet, to soak. **2.** to cause to absorb or accept as much as possible; *the market for used cars is saturated,* can take no more. **saturation** *n.*

Saturday *n.* the day of the week following Friday.

saturnalia (sat-er-**nay**-liă) *n.* wild revelry.

saturnine (sat-er-nyn) *adj.* (of a person or his looks) having a gloomy forbidding appearance.

satyr (sat-er) *n.* **1.** one of a class of woodland gods in ancient Greek and Roman mythology, in human form but having a goat's ears, tail, and legs. **2.** a grossly lustful man.

sauce *n.* **1.** a liquid or semi-liquid preparation served with food to add flavour or richness. **2.** (*informal*) impudence.

saucepan *n.* a metal cooking-pot with a long handle at the side, used for boiling things over heat.

saucer *n.* **1.** a small shallow curved dish on which a cup stands. **2.** something shaped like this.

saucy *adj.* (saucier, sauciest) **1.** impudent. **2.** jaunty. **saucily** *adv.*, **sauciness** *n.*

Saudi (*rhymes with* dowdy) *n.* (*pl.* Saudis) a native or inhabitant of **Saudi Arabia** a country in the Middle East.

sauerkraut (sowr-krowt, *rhymes with* our, out) a German dish of chopped pickled cabbage.

sauna (saw-na) *n.* a Finnish-style steam bath, a building or room for this.

saunter *v.* to walk in a leisurely way. —*n.* a leisurely walk or walking-pace.

saurian (sor-iăn) *adj.* of or like a lizard. — *n.* an animal of the lizard family.

sausage *n.* minced seasoned meat enclosed in a cylindrical case made from animal entrails or synthetic material. **sausage-meat** *n.* meat prepared for this or as a stuffing etc. **sausage roll**, a sausage or sausage-meat enclosed in a cylindrical roll of pastry.

sauté (soh-tay) *adj.* fried quickly in a small amount of fat, *sauté potatoes.* —*v.* (sautéd, sautéing) to cook in this way.

Sauternes (soh-tern) *n.* a light sweet white French wine.

savage *adj.* **1.** in a primitive or uncivilized state, *savage tribes.* **2.** wild and fierce, *savage animals.* **3.** cruel and hostile, *savage criticism.* **4.** (*informal*) very angry. —*n.* a member of a savage tribe. —*v.* to attack savagely, to maul. —**savagely** *adv.*, **savageness** *n.*, **savagery** *n.*

savannah (să-van-ă) *n.* a grassy plain in hot regions, with few or no trees.

savarin (sav-er-in) *n.* a sponge-like cake made with yeast, often baked in a ring mould and filled with fruit.

save *v.* **1.** to rescue, to keep from danger or harm or capture. **2.** to free from the power of sin or its spiritual consequences. **3.** to avoid wasting, *save fuel.* **4.** to keep for future use or enjoyment, to put aside (money) for future use. **5.** to make unnecessary, *did it to save a journey* or *to save you a journey.* **6.** (in sports) to prevent an opponent from scoring. —*n.* the act of saving in football etc. —*prep.* except, *in all cases save one.* —**saver** *n.* □ **save-as-you-earn** *n.* a method of putting aside money as savings by having an amount deducted regularly from one's income. **save one's breath,** to keep silent because it would be useless to speak. **saving grace,** a good quality that redeems a person whose other qualities are not good.

saveloy (sav-ĕl-oi) *n.* a kind of highly seasoned sausage.

saving *prep.* except.

savings *pl. n.* money put aside for future use. **savings bank,** a bank that pays interest on money deposited but does not offer other banking facilities to its customers.

saviour *n.* a person who rescues or delivers people from harm or danger; *the* or *our Saviour,* Christ as the saviour of mankind.

savoir-faire (sav-wahr-**fair**) *n.* knowledge of how to behave in any situation that may arise, social tact.

savory *n.* a low-growing herb with a spicy smell and flavour, used in cooking.

savour *n.* **1.** the taste or smell of something. **2.** the power to arouse enjoyment, *felt that life had lost its savour.* —**savour** *v.* **1.** to have a certain taste or smell. **2.** to taste or smell (a thing) with enjoyment. **3.** to give a certain impression, *the reply savours of impertinence.*

savoury *adj.* **1.** having an appetizing taste or smell. **2.** having a salt or piquant and not sweet flavour. —*n.* a savoury dish, especially one served at the end of a meal. —**savouriness** *n.*

savoy *n.* a hardy cabbage with wrinkled leaves.

savvy *n.* (*slang*) common sense, understanding. —*v.* (*slang*) to understand.

saw ¹ *see* see ¹.

saw ² *n.* a tool with a zigzag edge for cutting wood etc. —*v.* (sawed, sawn, sawing) **1.** to cut with a saw. **2.** to make a to-and-fro movement like that of sawing.

sawdust *n.* powdery fragments of wood produced when timber is sawn.

sawfish *n.* a large sea-fish having a blade-like snout with jagged edges that it uses as a weapon.

sawfly *n.* an insect that is destructive to plants which it pierces with a jagged organ in order to lay its eggs.

sawmill *n.* a mill with power-operated saws where timber is cut into planks etc.

sawyer *n.* a workman who saws timber.

sawn *see* saw². □ **sawn-off** *adj.* (of a gun) with part of the barrel removed by

sawing, so that it can be handled more easily.

sax *n.* (*informal*) a saxophone.

saxe *n.* (also *saxe-blue*) light blue with a greyish tinge.

saxifrage (saks-i-frij) *n.* a rock plant with clusters of small white, yellow, or red flowers.

Saxon *n.* **1.** a member of a Germanic people who occupied parts of England in the 5th–6th centuries. **2.** their language. —*adj.* of the Saxons or their language.

saxophone *n.* a brass wind instrument with a reed in the mouthpiece, and with keys operated by the player's fingers.

saxophonist (saks-off-ŏn-ist) *n.* a person who plays the saxophone.

say *v.* (said, saying) **1.** to utter or recite in a speaking voice. **2.** to state, to express in words, to have a specified wording, *the notice says 'keep out'.* **3.** to give as an argument or excuse, *there's much to be said on both sides.* **4.** to give as one's opinion or decision, *it's hard to say which of them is taller.* **5.** to suppose as a possibility, to take (a specified amount) as being near enough, *let's allow, say, an hour for the meeting.* —*n.* the power to decide, *has no say in the matter.* —*int.* (*Amer. informal*) = I say. □ **have one's say,** to say all one wishes to say. **I'll say,** (*informal*) yes indeed. **I say,** an expression of surprise or admiration, or calling attention or opening a conversation. **say-so** *n.* the power to decide something; a command; a mere assertion without proof.

SAYE *abbrev.* save-as-you-earn.

saying *n.* a well-known phrase or proverb or other statement.

SC *abbrev.* South Carolina.

scab *n.* **1.** a crust forming over a sore as it heals. **2.** a skin-disease or plant-disease that causes scab-like roughness. **3.** (*informal, contemptuous*) a blackleg. **scabby** *adj.*

scabbard *n.* the sheath of a sword or dagger or bayonet.

scabies (skay-beez) *n.* a contagious skin-disease causing itching.

scabious (skay-bi-ŭs) *n.* a wild or cultivated annual herbaceous plant with thickly-clustered blue, pink, or white flowers.

scabrous (skab-rŭs) *adj.* **1.** (of the surface of a plant or animal) rough, scurfy. **2.** (of a subject or situation) hard to handle with decency. **3.** indecent, salacious.

scaffold *n.* **1.** a wooden platform for the execution of criminals; *the scaffold,* death by execution. **2.** scaffolding. —*v.* to fit scaffolding to (a building). —**scaffolder** *n.*

scaffolding *n.* **1.** a temporary structure of poles or tubes and planks providing workmen with platforms to stand on while building or repairing a house etc. 2. the poles etc. from which this is made.

scalable *adj.* able to be scaled.

scald *v.* 1. to injure or pain with hot liquid or steam. 2. to heat (milk) to near boiling-point. 3. to cleanse (pans etc.) with boiling water. —*n.* an injury to the skin by scald-ing.

scale¹ *n.* 1. one of the thin overlapping plates of horny membrane or hard sub-stance that protect the skin of many fishes and reptiles. 2. something resembling this (e.g. on a plant), a flake of skin. 3. an in-crustation inside a boiler or kettle etc. in which hard water is regularly used, a sim-ilar incrustation on teeth. —**scale** *v.* 1. to remove scales or scale from. 2. to come off in scales or flakes. □ **the scales fell from his eyes**, he was no longer deceived.

scale² *n.* the pan of a balance. **scales** *pl. n.* an instrument for weighing things; *the Scales,* a sign of the zodiac, Libra. **tip** *or* **turn the scale(s),** to be the decisive factor in a situation. **turn the scales at,** to weigh, *turned the scales at 12 stone.*

scale³ *n.* 1. an ordered series of units or degrees or qualities etc. for purposes of measurement or classification. 2. an arrange-ment of notes in a system of music, ascen-ding or descending by fixed intervals. 3. the ratio of the actual measurements of something and those of a drawing or map or model of it, a line with marks showing this, *the scale is 1 inch to the mile*; *a scale model,* one with measurements in uniform proportion to those of the original. 4. the relative size or extent of something, *war on a grand scale.* —**scale** *v.* 1. to climb, *scaled the cliff.* 2. to represent in measurements or extent in proportion to the size of the original; *scale it up or down,* make it larger *or* smaller in proportion.

scallop (skol-ŏp) *n.* 1. a shellfish with two hinged fan-shaped shells. 2. one shell of this, used as a container in which food is cooked and served. 3. one of a series of semicircular curves used as an orna-mental edging. **scallop** *v.* (scalloped, scalloping) 1. to cook in a scallop-shell. 2. to ornament with scallops. —**scallop-ing** *n.*

scallywag *n.* (*slang*) a rascal.

scalp *n.* 1. the skin of the head excluding the face. 2. this with the hair, formerly cut as a trophy from an enemy's head by American Indians. —*v.* to take the scalp of. □ **out for scalps,** in an aggressive mood.

scalpel (skal-pĕl) *n.* a surgeon's small light straight knife.

scaly *adj.* (scalier, scaliest) covered in scales or scale (*see* scale ¹).

scamp *n.* a rascal. —*v.* to do (work) hastily and inadequately.

scamper *v.* to run hastily, to run about playfully as a child does. —*n.* a scamper-ing run.

scampi (skamp-i) *pl. n.* large prawns, these as food.

scan *v.* (scanned, scanning) 1. to look at all parts of (a thing) intently. 2. to glance at quickly and not thoroughly. 3. to sweep a radar or electronic beam over (an area) in search of something. 4. to resolve (a pic-ture) into elements of light and shade for TV transmission. 5. to analyse the rhythm of (a line of verse). 6. (of verse) to be cor-rect in rhythm. —*n.* scanning.

scandal *n.* 1. something shameful or dis-graceful. 2. gossip, about other people's fault and wrongdoing.

scandalize *v.* to shock by something shameful or disgraceful.

scandalmonger *n.* a person who invents or spreads scandal.

scandalous *adj.* 1. shameful, disgraceful. 2. containing scandal, *scandalous reports.* **scandalously** *adv.*

Scandinavia Norway, Sweden, Denmark, and Iceland considered as a unit. **Scandinavian** *adj. & n.*

scanner *n.* a device for scanning or sys-tematically examining all parts of some-thing (*see* scan *v.* sense 3).

scansion (skan-shŏn) *n.* the scanning of lines of verse, the way verse scans.

scant *adj.* scanty, insufficient, *was treated with scant courtesy.*

scanty *adj.* (scantier, scantiest) 1. of small amount or extent, *scanty vegetation.* 2. barely enough. **scantily** *adv.*, **scantiness** *n.*

scapegoat *n.* a person who is made to bear blame or punishment that should rightly fall on others. ¶ Named after the goat which, in ancient Jewish religious custom, was allowed to escape into the wilderness after the high priest had sym-bolically laid the sins of the people upon it.

scapula (skap-yoo-lă) *n.* (*pl.* scapulae, *pr.* skap-yoo-lee) the shoulder-blade.

scar *n.* 1. a mark left where a wound or injury or sore has healed, or on a plant from which a leaf has fallen. 2. a mark left by damage. 3. a lasting effect produced by grief etc. —*v.* (scarred, scarring) to mark with a scar, to form a scar or scars.

scarab (ska-răb) *n.* a carving of a beetle, engraved with symbols on the flat side and used in ancient Egypt as a charm.

scarce *adj.* not enough to supply a

scarcely

schedule

demand or need, rare. **make oneself scarce**, (*informal*) to go away, to depart quietly.

scarcely *adv.* **1**. only just, almost not, *she is scarcely 17 years old; I scarcely know him.* **2**. not, surely not, *you can scarcely expect me to believe that.*

scarcity *n.* being scarce, a shortage.

scare *v.* to frighten or become frightened suddenly. —*n.* a sudden fright, alarm caused by a rumour, *a bomb scare.*

scarecrow *n.* **1**. a figure of a man dressed in old clothes, set up in a field to scare birds away from crops. **2**. a badly-dressed or grotesque person.

scaremonger *n.* a person who raises unnecessary or excessive alarm. **scaremongering** *n.*

scarf *n.* (*pl.* scarves) **1**. a long narrow strip of material worn for warmth or ornament round the neck. **2**. a square of material worn round the neck or tied over a woman's hair.

scarify¹ (**skair**-i-fy *or* **ska**-ri-fy) *v.* (scarified, scarifying) **1**. to loosen the surface of (soil etc.). **2**. to make slight cuts in (skin or tissue) surgically.

scarify² (**skair**-i-fy) *v.* (scarified, scarifying) (*slang*) to scare.

scarlet *adj.* of brilliant red colour. —*n.* **1**. scarlet colour. **2**. a scarlet substance or material, scarlet clothes. □ **scarlet fever**, an infectious fever caused by bacteria, producing a scarlet rash. **scarlet runner**, a climbing bean with scarlet flowers. **scarlet woman**, (*old use*) a notorious prostitute.

scarp *n.* a steep slope on a hillside.

scarper *v.* (*slang*) to run away.

scary *adj.* (scarier, scariest) **1**. frightening. **2**. easily frightened.

scathing (**skay**-*th*'ing) *adj.* **1**. (of criticism) very severe. **2**. making very severe criticisms.

scatter *v.* **1**. to throw or put here and there, to cover in this way, *scatter gravel on the road* or *scatter the road with gravel; there were some scattered villages,* situated far apart. **2**. to go or send in different directions. —*n.* scattering, the extent over which something is scattered. □ **scatter-brain** *n.* a scatter-brained person. **scatter-brained** *adj.* unable to concentrate or do things in a systematic way, frivolous. **scatter cushions,** cushions for placing here and there decoratively.

scatty *adj.* (scattier, scattiest) (*slang*) scatter-brained, crazy.

scaup (*pr.* skawp) *n.* a kind of diving duck of northern coasts.

scavenge *v.* **1**. (of an animal) to search for decaying flesh as food. **2**. to search for

usable objects or material among rubbish or discarded things. **scavenger** *n.*

scenario (sin-**ar**-i-oh) *n.* (*pl.* scenarios) **1**. the outline or script of a film, with details of the scenes. **2**. a detailed summary of the action of a play, with notes on scenery and special effects. **3**. an imagined sequence of future events.

scene *n.* **1**. the place of an actual or fictional event; *the scene of the crime,* where it happened. **2**. a piece of continuous action in a play or film, a subdivision of an act. **3**. an incident thought of as resembling this. **4**. a dramatic outburst of temper or emotion, a stormy interview, *made a scene.* **5**. stage scenery. **6**. a landscape or view as seen by a spectator, *the rural scene before us.* **7**. (*slang*) an area of action, a way of life, *the drug scene; not my scene,* not what I like or want to take part in. □ **be on the scene**, to be present. **scene-shifter** *n.* a person who moves the scenery on a theatre stage.

scenery *n.* **1**. the general appearance of a landscape. **2**. picturesque features of a landscape. **3**. structures used on a theatre stage to represent features in the scene of the action.

scenic (**seen**-ik) *adj.* having fine natural scenery, *the scenic road along the coast.* **scenic railway,** a miniature railway running through artificial picturesque scenery as an amusement at a fair.

scent *n.* **1**. the characteristic pleasant smell of something. **2**. a sweet-smelling liquid made from essence of flowers or aromatic chemicals. **3**. the trail left by an animal and perceptible to hounds' sense of smell, indications that can be followed similarly, *followed* or *lost the scent; on the scent of talent.* **4**. an animal's sense of smell, *dogs hunt by scent.* —*scent* *v.* **1**. to discover by sense of smell, *the dog scented a rat.* **2**. to begin to suspect the presence or existence of, *she scented trouble.* **3**. to put scent on (a thing), to make fragrant. —**scented** *adj.*

sceptic (**skep**-tik) *n.* a sceptical person, one who doubts the truth of religious doctrines.

sceptical (**skep**-tik-ăl) *adj.* inclined to disbelieve things, doubting or questioning the truth of claims or statements etc. **sceptically** *adv.*

scepticism (**skep**-ti-sizm) *n.* a sceptical attitude of mind.

sceptre (**sep**-ter) *n.* a staff carried by a king or queen as a symbol of sovereignty.

schedule (**shed**-yool) *n.* a programme or timetable of planned events or of work. —*v.* to include in a schedule, to appoint for a certain time, *the train is scheduled to stop* *at Bletchley.* □ **on schedule,** punctual according to the timetable.

schematic (skee-**mat**-ik) *adj.* in the form of a diagram or chart. **schematically** *adv.*

scheme (*pr.* skeem) *n.* **1.** a plan of work or action. **2.** a secret or underhand plan, *a scheme to defraud people.* **3.** an orderly planned arrangement, *a colour scheme.* — *v.* to make plans, to plan in a secret or underhand way. —**schemer** *n.*

scherzo (**skairts**-oh) *n.* (*pl.* scherzos) a lively vigorous musical composition or independent passage in a longer work.

schism (*pr.* sizm) *n.* division into opposing groups because of a difference in belief or opinion, especially in a religious body.

schismatic (siz-**mat**-ik) *adj.* of schism. — *n.* a person who takes part in a schism.

schizo (**skidz**-oh) *adj.* & *n.* (*pl.* schizos) (*informal*) = schizophrenic.

schizoid (**skidz**-oid) *adj.* resembling or suffering from schizophrenia. —*n.* a schizoid person.

schizophrenia (skidz-ŏ-**freen**-iă) *n.* a mental disorder in which a person becomes unable to act or reason in a rational way, often with delusions and withdrawal from social relationships.

schizophrenic (skidz-ŏ-**fren**-ik) *adj.* of or suffering from schizophrenia. —*n.* a schizophrenic person.

schmaltz (*pr.* shmawlts) *n.* sugary sentimentality, especially in music or literature.

schnapps (*pr.* shnaps) *n.* a kind of strong gin.

schnitzel (**shnits**-ĕl) *n.* a fried veal cutlet.

scholar *n.* **1.** a person with great learning in a particular subject. **2.** a person who is skilled in academic work. **3.** a person who holds a scholarship. **scholarly** *adj.*

scholarship *n.* **1.** a grant of money towards education, usually gained by means of a competitive examination. **2.** great learning in a particular subject. **3.** the methods and achievements characteristic of scholars and academic work.

scholastic (skŏl-**ast**-ik) *adj.* of schools or education, academic.

school[1] *n.* a shoal, e.g. of fish or whales.

school[2] *n.* **1.** an institution for educating children or for giving instruction. **2.** its buildings. **3.** its pupils. **4.** the time during which teaching is done there, *school ends at 4.30 p.m.* **5.** the process of being educated in a school, *always hated school.* **6.** the department of one branch of study in a university, *the history school.* **7.** experience that gives discipline or instruction, *learned his tactics in a hard school.* **8.** a group or suc-

cession of philosophers, artists, etc. following the same teachings or principles. —*v.* to train or discipline. □ **of the old school,** according to old standards, *a gentleman of the old school.* **schooling** *n.* education in a school. **school-leaver** *n.* a person who has just left school for good. **school of thought,** a particular way of looking at a problem; those who hold this. **schoolboy** *n.* a boy at school.

schoolchild *n.* (*pl.* schoolchildren) a child at school.

schoolgirl *n.* a girl at school.

schoolmaster *n.* a male schoolteacher.

schoolmistress *n.* a female schoolteacher.

schoolroom *n.* a room used for lessons in a school or private house.

schoolteacher *n.* a teacher in a school.

schooner (**skoo**-ner) *n.* **1.** a kind of sailing-ship with two or more masts. **2.** a measure for beer or sherry etc.

sciatic (sy-**at**-ik) *adj.* of the hip or the **sciatic nerve,** the largest nerve in the human body, running from pelvis to thigh.

sciatica (sy-**at**-ik-ă) *n.* neuralgia of the hip and thigh, pain in the sciatic nerve.

science *n.* **1.** a branch of knowledge requiring systematic study and method, especially one of those dealing with substances, animal and vegetable life, and natural laws, *natural sciences,* e.g. biology, geology, and the physical sciences; *physical sciences,* e.g. physics, chemistry. **2.** an expert's skilful technique, *with skill and science.* □ **science fiction,** stories based on imaginary future scientific discoveries or changes of the environment or space travel and life on other planets.

scientific *adj.* **1.** of or used in a science, *scientific apparatus.* **2.** of scientists. **3.** using careful and systematic study, observations, and tests of conclusions etc. **scientifically** *adv.*

scientist *n.* an expert in one or more of the natural or physical sciences.

scilla (**sil**-ă) *n.* a plant with small blue hanging flowers, growing from a bulb.

Scillies *pl. n.* the Scilly Islands, off the west of Cornwall. **Scillonian** (sil-**oh**-niăn) *adj.*

scimitar (**sim**-it-er) *n.* a short curved Oriental sword.

scintilla (sin-**til**-ă) *n.* a trace, *not a scintilla of evidence.*

scintillate (**sin**-til-ayt) *v.* **1.** to sparkle, to give off sparks. **2.** to be brilliant, *a scintillating discussion.* **scintillation** *n.*

scion (**sy**-ŏn) *n.* a descendant of a family, especially a noble one.

scissors *pl. n.* a cutting instrument made

of two blades with handles for the thumb and finger(s) of one hand, pivoted so that the cutting edges can be closed on what is to be cut.

sclerosis (skleer-**oh**-sis) *n.* a diseased condition in which soft tissue (e.g. of arteries) hardens.

scoff [1] *v.* to jeer, to speak contemptuously. **scoffer** *n.*

scoff [2] *v.* (*slang*) to eat (food) quickly or greedily.

scold *v.* to rebuke (a child or servant). —*n.* (*old use*) a nagging woman. □ **scolding** *n.* a lengthy rebuke to a child or servant.

sconce *n.* an ornamental bracket fixed to a wall for holding a candle or electric light.

scone (*pr.* skon *or* skohn) *n.* a soft flat cake of barley-meal or oatmeal or flour, baked quickly and eaten buttered.

scoop *n.* **1.** a deep shovel-like tool for taking up and moving grain, sugar, coal, etc. **2.** a ladle, a device with a small round bowl and a handle used for serving ice-cream etc. **3.** a scooping movement. **4.** a piece of news discovered and published by one newspaper in advance of its rivals. — **scoop** *v.* **1.** to lift or hollow with or as if with a scoop. **2.** to forestall (a rival newspaper) with a news scoop.

scoot *v.* to run or dart, to go away hastily.

scooter *n.* **1.** a child's toy vehicle with a footboard on wheels and a long steering-handle. **2.** a kind of lightweight motor cycle with a protective shield extending from below the handles to where the rider's feet rest. □ **scooterist** *n.* a person who rides a scooter.

scope *n.* **1.** the range of something, *the subject is outside the scope of this inquiry.* **2.** opportunity, outlet, *a kind of work that gives scope for her abilities.*

scorch *v.* **1.** to burn or become burnt on the surface, to make or become discoloured in this way. **2.** (*slang*) to drive or ride at a very high speed. —*n.* a mark made by scorching.

scorcher *n.* (*informal*) a very hot day.

scorching *adj.* (*informal*) extremely hot.

score *n.* **1.** the number of points made by each player or side in a game, or gained in a competition etc. **2.** a record of this, a reckoning. **3.** a reason or motive, *was rejected on the score of being old-fashioned*; *on that score,* so far as that matter is concerned. **4.** a set of twenty; *scores of things,* very many. **5.** a line or mark cut into something. **6.** a copy of a musical composition showing the notes on sets of staves. **7.** the music for an opera or musical comedy etc.

—**score** *v.* **1.** to gain (a point or points) in a game etc., to make a score. **2.** to keep a record of the score. **3.** to be worth as points in a game, *a goal scores 6 points.* **4.** to achieve, *scored a great success.* **5.** to have an advantage, *he scores by knowing the language well.* **6.** to make a clever retort that puts an opponent at a disadvantage; *score off a person,* to humiliate him in this way. **7.** to cut a line or mark(s) into (a thing); *score it out,* cancel it by drawing a line through the words etc. **8.** to write out as a musical score, to arrange (a piece of music) for instruments. —**scorer** *n.* □ **know the score,** (*informal*) to be aware of the essential facts. **score-board** *n.* a board where the score is displayed.

scorn *n.* strong contempt; *laughed it to scorn,* ridiculed it. —*v.* **1.** to feel or show strong contempt for. **2.** to reject or refuse scornfully, *would scorn to ask for favours.*

scornful *adj.* feeling or showing scorn. **scornfully** *adv.,* **scornfulness** *n.*

Scorpio *n.* a sign of the zodiac, the Scorpion. **Scorpian** *adj.* & *n.*

scorpion *n.* **1.** a small animal of the spider group with lobster-like claws and a sting in its long jointed tail. **2.** *the Scorpion,* a sign of the zodiac, Scorpio.

Scot *n.* a native of Scotland.

scotch *v.* to put an end to, *scotched the rumour.*

Scotch *adj.* of Scotland or Scottish people or their form of English. (¶ Modern Scots prefer to use the words *Scots* and *Scottish,* not *Scotch,* except when the word is applied to whisky and in the compounds listed below.) —*n.* **1.** the Scottish dialect. **2.** Scotch whisky, the kind distilled in Scotland especially from malted barley. □ **Scotch broth,** soup or stew containing pearl barley and vegetables. **Scotch cap,** a man's wide beret, like that worn as part of Highland dress. **Scotch egg,** a hard-boiled egg enclosed in sausage-meat. **Scotch terrier,** a small terrier with rough hair and short legs. **Scotch woodcock,** scrambled eggs on toast, garnished with anchovies.

scot-free *adj.* **1.** unharmed, not punished. **2.** free of charge.

Scotland the country forming the northern part of Great Britain.

Scotland Yard 1. the headquarters of the London Metropolitan Police. **2.** its Criminal Investigation Department.

Scots *adj.* Scottish. —*n.* the Scottish dialect. —**Scotsman** *n.,* **Scotswoman** *n.*

Scotticism (skot-i-sizm) *n.* a Scottish word or phrase.

Scottish *adj.* of Scotland or its people or

their form of the English language.

scoundrel *n.* a dishonest or unprincipled person.

scour¹ *v.* **1.** to cleanse or brighten by rubbing. **2.** to clear out (a channel or pipe etc.) by the force of water flowing through or over it. **3.** to purge drastically. —*n.* scouring, the action of water on a channel etc., *the scour of the tide.* —**scourer** *n.*

scour² *v.* to travel over (an area) in search of something, to search thoroughly.

scourge (*pr.* skerj) *n.* **1.** a whip for flogging people. **2.** a person or thing regarded as a great affliction, *the scourge of war.* — **scourge** *v.* **1.** to flog with a whip. **2.** to afflict greatly.

scouse (*rhymes with* house) *n.* **1.** a native of Liverpool. **2.** Liverpool dialect. —*adj.* of Liverpool people or dialect.

scout¹ *n.* **1.** a person sent out to gather information, e.g. about an enemy's movements or strength. **2.** a ship or aircraft designed for reconnoitring. **3.** *Scout,* a member of the Scout Association, a boys' organization intended to develop character by outdoor activities. —*v.* to act as scout, to make a search. □ **Scouting** *n.* the activities of the Scout Association.

scout² *v.* to reject (an idea) scornfully.

Scouter *n.* an adult leader in the Scout Association.

scowl *n.* a sullen or angry frown. —*v* to make a scowl.

scrabble *v.* **1.** to make a scratching movement or sound with the hands or feet. **2.** to grope busily or struggle to find or obtain something.

Scrabble *n.* (*trade mark*) a game played on a board in which words are built up from letters printed on small square counters.

scrag *n.* the bony part of an animal's carcass as food, neck of mutton or the less meaty end (*scrag-end*) of this. —*v.* (scragged, scragging) (*slang*) to seize roughly by the neck, to handle roughly.

scraggy *adj.* (scraggier, scraggiest) lean and bony.

scram *v.* (*slang*) to go away.

scramble *v.* **1.** to move as best one can over rough ground, to move hastily and awkwardly. **2.** to struggle eagerly to do or obtain something. **3.** (of aircraft or their crew) to hurry and take off quickly, e.g. in order to attack an invading enemy. **4.** to mix together indiscriminately. **5.** to cook (egg) by mixing its contents and heating the mixture in a pan until it thickens. **6.** to make (a telephone conversation etc.) unintelligible except to a person with a special receiver, by altering the frequencies on which it is transmitted. —**scramble** *n.* **1.** a

climb or walk over rough ground. **2.** an eager struggle to do or obtain something. **3.** a motor-cycle race over rough ground.

scrambler *n.* an electronic device for scrambling a transmitted telephone conversation or unscrambling it at the receiving end.

scrap¹ *n.* **1.** a small detached piece of something, a fragment, a remnant. **2.** rubbish, waste material, discarded metal suitable for being reprocessed. —*v.* (scrapped, scrapping) to discard as useless. □ **scrap-book** *n.* a book in which newspaper cuttings and similar souvenirs are mounted. **scrap-heap** *n.* a heap of waste material.

scrap² *n.* (*informal*) a fight or quarrel. — *v.* (scrapped, scrapping) (*informal*) to fight, to quarrel.

scrape *v.* **1.** to make (a thing) clean or smooth or level by passing the hard edge of something across it. **2.** to pass (an edge) across in this way. **3.** to remove by doing this, *scrape mud off shoes.* **4.** to excavate by scraping, *scrape a hole.* **5.** to damage by scraping. **6.** to make the sound of scraping. **7.** to pass along or through something with difficulty, with or without touching it. **8.** to obtain or amass with difficulty or by careful saving, *scrape a living*; *scrape something together* or *up.* **9.** to be very economical. **scrape** *n.* **1.** a scraping movement or sound. **2.** a scraped mark or injury. **3.** a thinly applied layer of butter etc. on bread. **4.** an awkward situation resulting from an escapade. □ **scrape acquaintance,** to contrive to become acquainted (with a person). **scrape through,** to get through a testing situation or pass (an examination etc.) by only a small margin. **scrapings** *pl. n.* fragments produced by scraping. **scraping the barrel,** driven to using one's last and inferior resources because the better ones are finished.

scraper *n.* a device used for scraping things.

scrappy *adj.* (scrappier, scrappiest) made up of scraps or odds and ends or disconnected elements.

scratch *v.* **1.** to make a shallow mark or wound on (a surface) with something sharp. **2.** to form by scratching. **3.** to scrape with the fingernails in order to relieve itching; *scratch my back and I'll scratch yours,* promote my interests and I will promote yours. **4.** to make a thin scraping sound. **5.** to obtain with difficulty, *scratch a living.* **6.** to cancel by drawing a line through, *scratch it out.* **7.** to withdraw from a race or competition, *was obliged to scratch*; *scratched* *his horse.* —**scratch** *n.* **1.** a mark or wound made by scratching. **2.** a spell of scratching. **3.** a line from which competitors start in a race when they receive no handicap; *a scratch player,* one who receives no handicap in a game. —*adj.* collected from whatever is available, *a scratch team.* □ **start from scratch,** to begin at the very beginning; to begin with no advantage or preparation. **up to scratch,** up to the required standard.

scratchy *adj.* (scratchier, scratchiest) **1.** (of a pen) tending to make a scratching sound or catch in paper. **2.** (of a drawing) looking like a series of scratches. **3.** tending to cause itching. **scratchily** *adv.,* **scratchiness** *n.*

scrawl *n.* bad handwriting, something written in this. —*v.* to write in a scrawl.

scrawny *adj.* (scrawnier, scrawniest) scraggy.

scream *v.* **1.** to make a long piercing cry of pain or terror or annoyance or excitement. **2.** to utter in a screaming tone. **3.** (of the wind or a machine etc.) to make a loud piercing sound. **4.** to laugh uncontrollably. —**scream** *n.* **1.** a screaming cry or sound. **2.** (*slang*) an extremely amusing person or thing. □ **screamingly** *adv.* so as to cause screams of laughter, *screamingly funny.*

scree *n.* a mass of loose stones on a mountain side, sliding when trodden on.

screech *n.* a harsh high-pitched scream or sound. —*v.* to make a screech, to utter with a screech. □ **screech-owl** *n.* an owl that makes a screeching cry (not a hoot).

screed *n.* **1.** a tiresomely long list or letter or other document. **2.** a strip of plaster or wood or other material fixed to a wall or floor etc. as a guide to the correct thickness of a coat of plaster or concrete to be laid. **3.** a finishing layer of mortar, cement, etc., spread over a floor.

screen *n.* **1.** an upright structure used to conceal or protect or divide something. **2.** anything serving a similar purpose, *under the screen of night.* **3.** a windscreen. **4.** a blank surface on which pictures or cinema films or TV transmissions etc. are projected. **5.** a large sieve or riddle, especially one used for sorting grain or coal etc. into sizes. —**screen** *v.* **1.** to shelter or conceal or protect. **2.** to protect (a person) from discovery or deserved blame by diverting suspicion from him. **3.** to show (images or a cinema film etc.) on a screen. **4.** to pass (grain or coal etc.) through a screen. **5.** to examine systematically in order to discover something, e.g. a person's suitability for a post where national

security is involved, or the presence or absence of a substance or disease. □ **screenprinting** *n.* a process like stencilling with ink or dye forced through a prepared sheet of fine fabric. **screen test,** a test of a person's suitability for taking part in a film.

screenplay *n.* the script of a film.

screw *n.* **1.** a metal pin with a spiral ridge (the *thread*) round its length, used for holding things together by being twisted in under pressure, or secured by a nut. **2.** a thing turned like a screw and used for tightening something or exerting pressure. **3.** a propeller, especially of a ship or motor boat. **4.** the act of screwing. **5.** (*slang*) the amount of a person's wages or salary, *earning a good screw.* **6.** (*slang*) a prison warder. —**screw** *v.* **1.** to fasten or tighten with a screw or screws, to fasten by twisting like a screw; *her head is screwed on the right way,* she has sound common sense; *screw up one's courage,* muster it. **2.** to turn (a screw), to twist or become twisted; *screw up one's face,* to twist it out of the natural expression, e.g. in disgust. **3.** to oppress, to extort; *screwed a promise out of her.* **4.** (*slang*) to extort money from, *how much did they screw you for?* **5.** (*vulgar*) to have sexual intercourse with. □ **have a screw loose,** (*informal*) to be slightly mad. **put the screw** *or* **screws on,** (*informal*) to put pressure on, e.g. to intimidate or extort money. **screwcap, screw-top** *ns.* a cap that screws on to the opening of a container. **screwtopped** *adj.*

screwball *adj. & n.* (*Amer. slang*) crazy, a crazy person.

screwdriver *n.* a tool with a narrow end for turning screws that have a slotted head into which this fits.

screwed *adj.* (*slang*) drunk.

screwy *adj.* (screwier, screwiest) (*slang*) **1.** crazy, eccentric. **2.** drunk.

scribble *v.* **1.** to write hurriedly or carelessly. **2.** to make meaningless marks; *scribble it out,* obliterate it by scribbling on it. —*n.* something scribbled, hurried or careless writing, scribbled meaningless marks. —**scribbler** *n.* □ **scribbling-pad** *n.* a pad of paper for casual jottings.

scribe *n.* **1.** a person who (before the invention of printing) made copies of writings. **2.** (in New Testament times) a professional religious scholar.

scrim *n.* a loosely-woven cotton fabric.

scrimmage *n.* a confused struggle, a skirmish.

scrimp *v.* to skimp.

scrimshank *v.* (*slang*) to shirk work, to malinger. **scrimshanker** *n.*

scrip *n.* an extra share or shares (in a business company) issued instead of a dividend, *a scrip issue.*

script *n.* **1.** handwriting. **2.** a style of printed or typewritten characters resembling this. **3.** the text of a play or film or broadcast talk etc. **4.** a candidate's written answer-paper in an examination. —*v.* to write a script for (a film etc.).

scripture *n.* **1.** any sacred writings. **2.** *Scripture* or *the Scriptures,* the sacred writings of the Christians (the Old and New Testaments) or the Jews (the Old Testament). **scriptural** *adj.*

scrofula (**skrof**-yoo-lă) *n.* a disease causing glandular swellings.

scroll *n.* **1.** a roll of paper or parchment. **2.** an ornamental design resembling a scroll or in spiral form.

Scrooge *n.* a miser. ¶ Named after a character in Dickens's novel 'A Christmas Carol'.

scrotum (**skroh**-tŭm) *n.* the pouch of skin that encloses the testicles in most mammals, behind the penis.

scrounge *v.* (*slang*) **1.** to cadge. **2.** to collect by foraging. **scrounger** *n.*

scrub¹ *n.* vegetation consisting of stunted trees or shrubs, land covered with this.

scrub² *v.* (scrubbed, scrubbing) **1.** to rub hard with something coarse or bristly, to clean thus with a wet brush. **2.** (*slang*) to cancel, to scrap, *we'll have to scrub our plans.* —*n.* scrubbing, being scrubbed, *give it a scrub.* □ **scrub up,** (of a surgeon etc.) to clean the hands and arms by scrubbing, before an operation.

scrubber *n.* **1.** (*Austral.*) an animal that lives in scrub country, an inferior animal, especially one of the stray livestock that has run wild, breeding indiscriminately with other strays. **2.** (*slang*) a promiscuous woman.

scrubby *adj.* (scrubbier, scrubbiest) small and mean or shabby.

scruff *n.* the back of the neck as used to grasp or lift or drag a person or animal.

scruffy *adj.* (scruffier, scruffiest) shabby and untidy. **scruffily** *adv.,* **scruffiness** *n.*

scrum *n.* **1.** a scrummage. **2.** a milling crowd, a confused struggle. □ **scrum-half** *n.* a half-back who puts the ball into the scrum.

scrummage *n.* (in Rugby football) the grouping of the forwards of each side to push against each other and seek possession of the ball thrown on the ground between them.

scrumping *n.* (*informal*) stealing apples from trees.

scrumptious *adj.* (*informal*) delicious, delightful.

scrunch *v.* to crunch.

scruple *n.* a feeling of doubt or hesitation about doing or allowing an action, produced by one's conscience or principles. —*v.* to hesitate because of scruples.

scrupulosity (skroo-pew-**loss**-iti) *n.* scrupulousness.

scrupulous (**skroo**-pew-lŭs) *adj.* **1.** very conscientious even in small matters, painstakingly careful and thorough. **2.** strictly honest or honourable, *they are not very scrupulous in their business dealings.* **scrupulously** *adv.,* **scrupulousness** *n.*

scrutinize *v.* to look at or examine carefully.

scrutiny *n.* a careful look or examination of something.

scuba *n.* self-contained underwater breathing apparatus. ¶ Named from the initials of these words.

scud *v.* (scudded, scudding) to move along straight and fast and smoothly, *clouds were scudding across the sky.* —*n.* clouds or spray driven by the wind, a short shower of driving rain.

scuff *v.* **1.** to scrape or drag (one's feet) in walking. **2.** to mark or wear away by doing this. **3.** to scrape (a thing) with one's foot or feet.

scuffle *n.* a confused struggle or fight at close quarters. —*v.* to take part in a scuffle.

scull *n.* **1.** one of a pair of small oars used by a single rower. **2.** an oar that rests on the stern of a boat, worked with a screwlike movement. —*v.* to row with sculls.

scullery *n.* a room where dishes etc. are washed up.

sculpt *v.* (*informal*) to sculpture.

sculptor *n.* a person who makes sculptures.

sculptural *adj.* of sculpture.

sculpture *n.* **1.** the art of carving in wood or stone or producing shapes in cast metal. **2.** a work made in this way. —*v.* to represent in sculpture, to decorate with sculptures, to be a sculptor.

scum *n.* **1.** impurities that rise to the surface of a liquid, a film of material floating on the surface of a stretch of water. **2.** people regarded as the most worthless part of the population. **scummy** *adj.*

scupper *n.* an opening in a ship's side to carry off water from the deck. —*v.* **1.** to sink (a ship) deliberately. **2.** (*informal*) to wreck.

scurf *n.* **1.** flakes of dry skin, especially from the scalp. **2.** any dry scaly matter on a surface.

scurrilous (**sku**-ril-us) *adj.* **1.** abusive and

insulting, *a scurrilous attack on his charac-ter*. **2.** coarsely humorous. **scurrilously** *adv.*, **scurrility** (sku-**ril**-iti) *n*.

scurry *v.* (scurried, scurrying) to run or move hurriedly, especially with quick short steps, to hurry. —*n*. **1.** scurrying, a rush. **2.** a flurry of rain or snow.

scurvy *n*. a disease caused by lack of vita-min C in the diet.

scut *n*. a short tail, especially that of a hare or rabbit or deer.

scutter *v.* (*informal*) to scurry. —*n*. a scurrying movement or sound.

scuttle¹ *n*. **1.** a bucket or portable box-like container for holding a supply of coal in a room. **2.** the part of a car body im-mediately behind the bonnet.

scuttle² *n*. a small opening with a lid, on a ship's deck or side or in a roof or wall. —*v*. to let water into (a ship) in order to sink her.

scuttle³ *v*. to scurry, to hurry away. —*n*. scurrying.

scythe *n*. an implement with a slightly curved blade on a long wooden pole with two handles, used for cutting long grass or grain. —*v*. to cut with a scythe.

S. Dak. *abbrev*. South Dakota.

SDP *abbrev*. Social Democratic Party.

SE *abbrev*. south-east, south-eastern.

sea *n*. **1.** the expanse of salt water that covers most of the earth's surface and sur-rounds the continents. **2.** any part of this as opposed to dry land or fresh water, a named section of it partly enclosed by land, *the Mediterranean Sea*. **3.** a large inland lake of either salt or fresh water, *the Sea of Galilee*. **4.** the waves of the sea, the movement or state of these; *a heavy sea*, with great waves. **5.** a vast expanse of something, *a sea of faces*. □ **at sea**, in a ship on the sea; perplexed, not knowing how to proceed. **by sea**, carried or con-veyed in a ship. **on the sea**, in a ship on the sea; situated on a coast. **sea anemone**, a tube-shaped sea animal with petal-like tentacles round its mouth. **sea-bird** *n*. a bird that frequents the sea or land near the sea. **sea-fish** *n*. a fish living in the sea, not a freshwater fish. **sea front**, the part of a town facing the sea. **sea-green** *adj*. & *n*. bluish-green. **sea holly**, an evergreen plant with spiny leaves and blue flowers. **sea-horse** *n*. a small fish with a horse-like head at right angles to its body, and a tail that can be wrapped round a support. **sea-kale** *n*. a perennial plant of which the young shoots are used as a vegetable. **sea lane**, a lane for ships (*see* lane, sense 5). **sea-legs** *pl. n*. ability to walk steadily on the deck of a moving ship, *hasn't got his sea-legs yet*.

sea-level *n*. the level corresponding to that of the surface of the sea half-way be-tween high and low water. **sea-lion** *n*. a kind of large seal of the Pacific Ocean. **Sea Lord**, a naval member of the Admiralty Board. **sea-mew** *n*. a gull. **sea-pink** *n*. a seashore or alpine plant with bright pink flowers. **sea-salt** *n*. salt obtained from sea-water by evaporation. **sea serpent**, a huge serpentine monster reported as seen in the sea. **sea shell**, the shell of any mollusc living in salt water. **sea-shore** *n*. land close to the sea. **sea-urchin** *n*. a sea animal with a round shell covered in sharp spikes.

seaboard *n*. the coast or its outline.

seafarer *n*. a seafaring person.

seafaring *adj*. & *n*. working or travelling on the sea, especially as one's regular occupation.

seafood *n*. fish or shellfish from the sea eaten as food.

seagoing *adj*. **1.** (of ships) ocean-going. **2.** (of people) seafaring.

seagull *n*. a gull.

seal¹ *n*. an amphibious sea animal with short limbs that serve chiefly for swim-ming, and thick fur or bristles. **sealing** *n*. hunting seals.

seal² *n*. **1.** a gem or piece of metal etc. with an engraved design that is pressed on with wax or other soft material to leave an impression; *seals of office*, those held by a person while he holds a certain position, e.g. as Lord Chancellor or Secretary of State. **2.** this impression or a piece of wax bearing it, attached to a document as a guarantee of authenticity, or to an enve-lope or box or room etc. to show that (while the seal is unbroken) the contents have not been tampered with since it was affixed. **3.** a mark or event or action etc. serving to confirm or guarantee some-thing, *gave it their seal of approval*. **4.** a small decorative paper sticker resembling a postage stamp. **5.** a substance or fitting used to close an opening etc. and prevent air or liquid etc. from passing through it. — **seal** *v*. **1.** to affix a seal to. **2.** to stamp or certify as authentic in this way. **3.** to close securely so as to prevent penetration, to coat or surface with a protective substance or sealant, to stick down (an envelope etc.); *it's a sealed book to me*, it is a subject of which I have no understanding. **4.** to settle or decide, *his fate was sealed*. □ **sealing-wax** *n*. a substance that is soft when heated but hardens when cooled, used for sealing letters or for impressing with an engraved design. **seal off**, to pre-vent access to (an area). **seal-ring** *n*. a signet-ring.

sealant *n.* a substance used for coating a surface to make it watertight.

sealskin *n.* the skin or prepared fur of a seal used as a clothing material.

Sealyham (**see**-li-ăm) *n.* a breed of terrier with short legs and wiry hair.

seam *n.* **1.** the line or groove where two edges join, especially of cloth or leather etc. or wood. **2.** a surface line such as a wrinkle or scar. **3.** a layer of coal etc. in the ground. —**seam** *v.* **1.** to join by means of a seam. **2.** to mark with a wrinkle or scar etc. ☐ **seam bowler**, a bowler in cricket who makes the ball bounce off its seam.

seaman *n.* (*pl.* **seamen**) **1.** a sailor, especially one below the rank of officer. **2.** a person who is skilled in seafaring.

seamanship *n.* skill in seafaring.

seamstress (**sem**-stris) *n.* a woman whose job is sewing things.

seamy *adj.* (**seamier**, **seamiest**) showing seams. **seamy side**, the less presentable or less attractive aspect of life.

seance (**say**-ahns) *n.* a spiritualist meeting.

seaplane *n.* an aeroplane, especially one with floats, designed to alight on and take off from a stretch of water.

seaport *n.* a port on the coast.

sear *v.* to scorch or burn the surface of; *a searing pain*, a burning pain.

search *v.* **1.** to look or go over (a place etc.) in order to find something. **2.** to examine the clothes and body of (a person) to see if something is concealed there. **3.** to examine thoroughly, *search your conscience*. —*n.* the act or process of searching. —**searcher** *n.* ☐ **search-party** *n.* a group of people organized to look for a lost person or thing. **search-warrant** *n.* a warrant allowing officials to enter the premises of a person thought to be concealing stolen property etc.

searching *adj.* (of a scrutiny or examination) thorough.

searchlight *n.* **1.** an outdoor electric lamp with a reflector producing a powerful beam that can be turned in any direction, used e.g. for discovering hostile aircraft. **2.** its beam.

seascape *n.* a picture or view of the sea.

seasick *adj.* made sick or queasy by the motion of a ship. **seasickness** *n.*

seaside *n.* the sea-coast, especially as a place for holidays.

season *n.* **1.** a section of the year with distinct characteristics of temperature and rainfall. **2.** the time of year when something is common or plentiful, or when an

activity takes place, *the hunting season*. **3.** (*informal*) a season ticket. —**season** *v.* **1.** to give extra flavour to (food) by adding salt or pepper or other sharp-tasting substances. **2.** to bring into a fit condition for use by drying or treating or allowing to mature, to become seasoned in this way. **3.** to make (people) experienced by training and practice, *seasoned soldiers*. ☐ **season**, (of food) available plentifully and in good condition for eating; (of an animal) on heat; (of advice) given when likely to be heeded. **out of season**, (of food) not in season. **season-ticket** *n.* a ticket that allows a person to travel between certain destinations, or to attend performances etc. for a specified period.

seasonable *adj.* **1.** suitable for the season, *hot weather is seasonable in summer*. **2.** timely, opportune. **seasonably** *adv.* ¶ Do not confuse with **seasonal**.

seasonal *adj.* of a season or seasons, varying according to these, *the seasonal migration of geese; fruit-picking is seasonal work*. ¶ Do not confuse with **seasonable**.

seasoning *n.* a substance used to season food.

seat *n.* **1.** a thing made or used for sitting on. **2.** a place where one sits, a place for one person to sit in a theatre or vehicle etc. **3.** the right to sit as a member of a council or committee or parliament etc. **4.** the horizontal part of a chair etc. on which a sitter's body rests. **5.** the part supporting another part in a machine. **6.** the buttocks, the part of a skirt or trousers covering these. **7.** the place where something is based or located, *seats of learning, such as Oxford and Cambridge*. **8.** a country mansion, *the family seat in Norfolk*. **9.** the manner in which a person sits on a horse etc.

seat *v.* **1.** to cause to sit; *seat oneself* or *be seated*, to sit down. **2.** to provide sitting accommodation for, *the hall seats 500*. **3.** to put a seat on (a chair). **4.** to put (machinery) on its support. ☐ **seat-belt** *n.* a strap securing a person to his seat in a vehicle or aircraft, for safety.

seated *adj.* **1.** sitting. **2.** (of garments) having the seat worn out or misshapen from sitting.

seaward *adj.* & *adv.* towards the sea. **seawards** *adv.*

seaweed *n.* any plant that grows in the sea or on rocks washed by the sea.

seaworthy *adj.* (of a ship) in a fit state for a sea voyage.

sebaceous (si-**bay**-shŭs) *adj.* secreting an oily or greasy substance, *sebaceous glands*.

secateurs (sek-ă-**terz** or **sek**-ă-terz) *pl. n.*

clippers used with one hand for pruning plants.

secede (si-**seed**) *v.* to withdraw oneself from membership of an organization.

secession (si-**sesh**-ŏn) *n.* seceding.

seclude *v.* to keep (a person) apart from others. **secluded** *adj.* (of a place) screened or sheltered from view.

seclusion (si-**kloo**-*zh*ŏn) *n.* secluding, being secluded, privacy.

second [1] (**sek**-ŏnd) *adj.* **1.** next after first. **2.** another after the first, *a second chance.* **3.** of a secondary kind, subordinate, inferior, *second quality*; *the second eleven.* — **second** *n.* **1.** something that is second, the second day of a month. **2.** second-class honours in a university degree. **3.** second gear. **4.** an attendant of a person taking part in a duel or boxing-match. **5.** a sixtieth part of a minute of time or angular measurement. **6.** (*informal*) a short time, *wait a second.* —**second** *adv.* **1.** in second place or rank or position. **2.** second class, *travelling second.* —**second** *v.* **1.** to assist. **2.** to state formally that one supports a motion that has been put forward by another person, in order to show that the proposer is not isolated or as a means of bringing it to be voted on. —**seconder** *n.* □ **second-best** *adj.* of second or inferior quality; *come off second best*, to be the loser in a contest or dispute. **second childhood**, childishness caused by mental weakness in old age. **second class**, a group of persons or things, or a standard of accommodation etc., less good than first class (but better than third); a category of mail that is to be given lower priority than first-class mail; (used adverbially) in or by second-class accommodation etc., *we travelled second class.* **second-class** *adj.* of second or inferior quality; or of using less good accommodation etc. than first-class. **second cousin**, *see* cousin. **second fiddle**, a subsidiary or secondary role, *had to play second fiddle to his brother.* **second gear**, the second lowest gear in a vehicle. **second-guess** *v.* (*Amer. informal*) to criticize (a person) or explain (a situation) from hindsight. **at second hand**, obtained indirectly, not from the original source. **second-hand** *adj. & adv.* bought after use by a previous owner; dealing in used goods, *a second-hand shop*; at second hand, obtained or experienced in this way. **second in command**, the person next in rank to the commanding or chief officer or official. **second lieutenant**, an army officer immediately below lieutenant. **second name**, a surname. **second nature**, a habit or characteristic that has become auto-

matic, *secrecy is second nature to him.* **second officer**, the assistant mate on a merchant ship. **second person**, *see* person. **second-rate** *adj.* not of the best quality, rated second-class. **seconds** *pl. n.* goods rated second-class in quality, having some flaw(s); a second helping of food; a second course at a meal. **second sight**, the supposed power to foresee future events. **second teeth**, adults' permanent teeth, appearing after the milk teeth have fallen out. **second thoughts**, a change of mind after reconsideration. **second wind**, recovery of one's ease of breathing during exercise, after having become out of breath.

second [2] (si-**kond**) *v.* to transfer (an officer or official) temporarily to another appointment or department. **secondment** *n.*

secondary *adj.* **1.** coming after what is primary. **2.** of lesser importance or rank etc. than the first. **3.** derived from what is primary or original, *secondary sources.* **secondarily** *adv.* □ **secondary colours**, colours obtained by mixing two primary colours. **secondary education** *or* **school**, that for people who have received primary education but have not yet proceeded to a university or occupation. **secondary picketing**, (during an industrial dispute) picketing of firms that are not directly involved in order to increase the effect of a strike etc.

secondly *adv.* second, as a second consideration.

secrecy *n.* **1.** being kept secret. **2.** keeping things secret, *was pledged to secrecy.*

secret *adj.* **1.** kept or intended to be kept from the knowledge or view of others, to be known only by specified people. **2.** working or operating secretly. —**secret** *n.* **1.** something kept or intended to be kept secret. **2.** a mystery, a thing no one properly understands, *the secrets of nature.* **3.** a method (not known to everyone) for attaining something, *the secret of good health.* — **secretly** *adv.* □ **in secret**, secretly. **in the secret**, among those who know something kept secret from most people. **secret agent**, a spy acting for a country. **secret ballot**, one in which individual voters' choices are not made public. **secret police**, a police force operating in secret for political purposes. **Secret Service**, a government department responsible for conducting espionage. **secret society**, a society whose members are sworn to secrecy about it.

secretaire (sek-ri-**tair**) *n.* a piece of furniture with a hinged front over a part that is fitted for use when writing.

secretarial (sek-ri-**tair**-iăl) *adj.* of the work of a secretary.

secretariat (sek-ri-**tair**-i-at) *n.* **1.** a staff of secretaries of a large organization. **2.** an administrative office or department headed by a government Secretary or by a Secretary-General, its premises.

secretary (sek-rĕ-tri) *n.* **1.** a person employed to help deal with correspondence, typing, filing, and similar routine work. **2.** an official in charge of the correspondence and records of an organization. **3.** the principal assistant of a government minister or ambassador. □ **secretary-bird** *n.* a long-legged African bird with a crest likened to quill-pens placed behind a writer's ear. **Secretary-General** *n.* the principal administrator of a large organization. **Secretary of State,** the head of a major government department.

secrete (si-**kreet**) *v.* **1.** to put (an object) into a place of concealment. **2.** to form and send out (a substance) into the body, either for excretion (*kidneys secrete urine*) or for use within the body (*the liver secretes bile*). **secretor** *n.*

secretion (si-**kree**-shŏn) *n.* **1.** secreting, being secreted. **2.** a substance secreted by an organ or cell of the body.

secretive (**seek**-rĭt-ĭv *or* si-**kreet**-iv) *adj.* making a secret of things unnecessarily, uncommunicative. **secretively** *adv.,* **secretiveness** *n.*

sect *n.* a group of people with religious or other beliefs that differ from those more generally accepted.

sectarian (sek-**tair**-iăn) *adj.* **1.** of or belonging to a sect or sects. **2.** narrow-mindedly putting the beliefs or interests of one's sect before more general interests.

section *n.* **1.** a distinct part or portion of something. **2.** a cross-section. **3.** the process of cutting or separating something surgically. —*v.* to divide into sections.

sectional *adj.* **1.** of a section or sections. **2.** of one section of a group or community as distinct from others or from the whole. **3.** made in sections, *sectional fishing-rod.*

sector *n.* **1.** one of the parts into which a battle area is divided for the purpose of controlling operations. **2.** a similar division of an activity, *the private sector of industry.* **3.** a section of a circular area between two lines drawn from its centre to its circumference.

secular (**sek**-yoo-ler) *adj.* **1.** concerned with worldly affairs rather than spiritual ones. **2.** not involving or belonging to religion, *secular music; secular clergy,* clergy who are not members of a monastic community.

secure *adj.* safe (especially against attack),

certain not to slip or fail, reliable. —*v.* **1.** to make secure. **2.** to fasten securely. **3.** to obtain. **4.** to guarantee by pledging something as security. *the loan is secured on landed property.* —**securely** *adv.*

security *n.* **1.** a state or feeling of being secure, something that gives this. **2.** the safety of a country or organization against espionage or theft or other danger. **3.** a thing that serves as a guarantee or pledge, *offered the deeds of his house as security for the loan.* **4.** a certificate showing ownership of financial stocks or bonds or shares.

sedan (si-**dan**) *n.* **1.** a sedan-chair. **2.** (*Amer.*) a saloon car. □ **sedan-chair** *n.* an enclosed chair for one person (used in the 17th–18th centuries), mounted on two poles and carried by two bearers.

sedate[1] (si-**dayt**) *adj.* calm and dignified, not lively. **sedately** *adv.,* **sedateness** *n.*

sedate[2] (si-**dayt**) *v.* to treat (a person) with sedatives. **sedation** *n.*

sedative (**sed**-ă-tiv) *adj.* having a calming or soothing effect. —*n.* a sedative medicine or influence.

sedentary (**sed**-ĕn-ter-i) *adj.* **1.** spending much time seated, *sedentary workers.* **2.** requiring much sitting, *sedentary work.*

sedge *n.* a grass-like plant growing in marshes or near water, a bed of this.

sediment *n.* **1.** very fine particles of solid matter suspended in a liquid or settling to the bottom of it. **2.** solid matter (e.g. sand, gravel) that is carried by water or wind and settles on the surface of land.

sedimentary (sed-i-**ment**-er-i) *adj.* of or like sediment; *sedimentary rocks,* those formed from sediment carried by water or wind.

sedition (si-**dish**-ŏn) *n.* words or actions that make people rebel against the authority of the State. **seditious** (si-**dish**-ŭs) *adj.*

seduce (si-**dewss**) *v.* **1.** to persuade (especially into wrongdoing) by offering temptations, *was seduced into betraying his country.* **2.** to tempt (a person) immorally into sexual intercourse. **seducer** *n.*

seduction *n.* **1.** seducing, being seduced. **2.** a tempting and attractive feature, *the seductions of country life.*

seductive *adj.* tending to seduce, alluring. **seductively** *adv.,* **seductiveness** *n.*

sedulous (**sed**-yoo-lŭs) *adj.* diligent and persevering. **sedulously** *adv.*

sedum (**see**-dŭm) *n.* a kind of plant with fleshy leaves, often with pink or white or yellow flowers.

see[1] *v.* (saw, seen, seeing) **1.** to perceive with the eyes, to have or use the power of doing this. **2.** to perceive with the mind, to understand, *I can't see why not*; *see? do you understand?* **3.** to have a certain opinion about; *as I see it,* in my opinion. **4.** to consider, to take time to do this, *must see what can be done*; *let me see, how can we fix it?* **5.** to watch, to be a spectator of, *went to see a film.* **6.** to look at for information, *see page 310.* **7.** to meet, to be near and recognize, *saw her in church.* **8.** to discover, *see who is at the door.* **9.** to experience, to undergo, *saw service during the war*; *won't see 50 again,* is over this age. **10.** to grant or obtain an interview with, to consult, *the manager will see you now*; *must see the doctor about my wrist.* **11.** to escort, to conduct, *see her to the door.* **12.** to make sure, *see that this letter goes today.* □ **see about,** to attend to. **see off,** to accompany (a person) to his point of departure for a journey and take leave of him when he sets out; (of a dog) to chase away (an intruder). **see red,** to be suddenly filled with fury. **see stars,** to see dancing lights before one's eyes as the result of a blow on the head. **see the back of,** to be rid of. **see the light,** to understand after failing to do so, to realize one's mistakes. **see things,** to have hallucinations. **see through,** to understand the true nature of, not be deceived by; *see a thing through,* not abandon it before it is completed. **see-through** *adj.* transparent. **see to,** to attend to.

see [2] *n.* the position or district of a bishop or archbishop, *the see of Canterbury.*

seed *n.* (*pl.* seeds *or* seed) **1.** a fertilized ovule of a plant, capable of developing into a plant like its parent. **2.** seeds as collected for sowing, *to be kept for seed.* **3.** semen, milt. **4.** (*old use*) offspring, descendants, *Abraham and his seed.* **5.** something from which a tendency or feeling etc. can develop, *sowing the seeds of doubt in their minds.* **6.** (*informal*) a seeded player. —**seed** *v.* **1.** to plant seeds in, to sprinkle with seeds. **2.** to place particles in (a cloud) to cause condensation and produce rain. **3.** to remove seeds from (fruit). **4.** to name (a strong player) as not to be matched against another named in this way in the early rounds of a knock-out tournament, so as to increase the interest of later rounds. □ **go** *or* **run to seed,** to cease flowering as seed develops; to become shabby and careless of appearance; to deteriorate in ability or efficiency. **seed-bed** *n.* a bed of fine soil in which seeds are sown. **seed-cake** *n.* cake containing caraway seeds as flavouring. **seed-pearl** *n.* a very small pearl. **seed-potato**

n. a potato kept for seed.

seedless *adj.* not containing seeds.

seedling *n.* a very young plant growing from a seed.

seedsman *n.* (*pl.* seedsmen) a tradesman who deals in seeds.

seedy *adj.* (seedier, seediest) **1.** full of seeds. **2.** (*informal*) looking shabby and disreputable. **3.** (*informal*) feeling slightly ill.

seeing *see* see [1]. □ **seeing that,** in view of the fact that, because.

seek *v.* (sought, seeking) to make a search or inquiry for, to try to find or obtain or do. **seek out,** to seek specially, to make a special effort to meet and address (a person).

seem *v.* to appear to be or to exist or to be true. **seeming** *adj.* having an appearance of being something but not necessarily being this in fact.

seemly *adj.* proper, suitable, in accordance with accepted standards of good taste.

seen *see* see [1].

seep *v.* to ooze slowly out or through.

seepage (**seep**-ij) *n.* seeping, the amount that seeps out.

seer *n.* a prophet, a person who sees visions.

seersucker *n.* fabric woven with a puckered surface.

see-saw *n.* **1.** a children's amusement consisting of a long board balanced on a central support so that when a person sits on each end they can make each end go up and the other down alternately. **2.** an up-and-down change that is constantly repeated. —*v.* to ride on a see-saw, to make this movement.

seethe *v.* **1.** to bubble or surge as in boiling. **2.** to be very agitated or excited.

segment (**seg**-měnt) *n.* a part cut off or separable or marked off as though separable from the other parts of a thing.

segmented (seg-**ment**-id) *adj.* divided into segments.

segregate (**seg**-ri-gayt) *v.* **1.** to put apart from the rest, to isolate. **2.** to separate (people) according to their race. **segregation** *n.* □ **segregationist** *n.* a person who is in favour of racial segregation.

seine (*pr.* sayn) *n.* a large fishing-net that hangs vertically with floats at the top and weights at the bottom, the ends being drawn together to enclose fish as it is hauled ashore.

seismic (**sy**-zmik) *adj.* **1.** of an earthquake or earthquakes. **2.** of or using vibrations of the earth that are produced artificially by explosions. □ **seismic survey,** the collection of data about earthquakes or other earth vibrations in an area.

seismograph (sy-zmŏ-grahf) *n.* an instrument for detecting, recording, and measuring earthquakes.

seize *v.* **1.** to take hold of (a thing) forcibly or suddenly or eagerly. **2.** to take possession of (a thing) forcibly or by legal right, *seize smuggled goods.* **3.** to have a sudden overwhelming effect on, *panic seized us.* **4.** to seize up. □ **seize on**, to make use of (an excuse etc.) eagerly. **seize up**, (of a moving part or the machine containing it) to become stuck or jam because of friction or undue heat.

seizure (see-zher) *n.* **1.** seizing, being seized. **2.** a sudden attack of epilepsy or apoplexy etc., a stroke.

seldom *adv.* rarely, not often.

select *v.* to pick out as best or most suitable. —*adj.* **1.** chosen for excellence. **2.** (of a society) exclusive, admitting only certain people as members. □ **select committee**, a small committee appointed to make a special investigation.

selection *n.* **1.** selecting, being selected. **2.** the people or things selected **3.** a collection of things from which a choice can be made, *they stock a large selection of goods.*

selective *adj.* chosen or choosing carefully. **selectively** *adv.*, **selectivity** *n.*

selector *n.* **1.** a person who selects, a member of a committee selecting a national sports team. **2.** a device that selects the appropriate gear or circuit etc. in machinery.

self *n.* (*pl.* selves) **1.** a person as an individual, *one's own self.* **2.** a person's special nature; *she is her old self again*, has regained her former personality. **3.** one's own interests or advantage or pleasure, *always puts self first.* **4.** (*humorous* or in commerce) myself, herself, himself, etc., *have got tickets for self and friend; the cheque is payable to self.* —*adj.* of the same colour or material as that used for the whole, *a dress with self belt.*

self- *prefix* of or to or done by oneself or itself.

self-addressed *adj.* (of an envelope for containing a reply) addressed to oneself.

self-assertive *adj.* asserting oneself confidently.

self-assured *adj.* self-confident. **self-assurance** *n.*

self-catering *adj.* catering for oneself (instead of having meals provided in rented accommodation), especially while on holiday.

self-centred *adj.* thinking chiefly of oneself or one's own affairs, selfish.

self-command *n.* self-control.

self-confident *adj.* having confidence in one's own abilities. **self-confidence** *n.*

self-conscious *adj.* embarrassed or unnatural in manner from knowing that one is being observed by others. **self-consciousness** *n.*

self-contained *adj.* **1.** complete in itself, (of accommodation) having all the necessary facilities and not sharing these. **2.** (of a person) able to do without the company of others, reserved.

self-control *n.* ability to control one's behaviour and not act emotionally. **self-controlled** *adj.*

self-defeating *adj.* (of a course of action etc.) frustrating the purpose for which it was intended.

self-defence *n.* defence of oneself, or of one's rights or good reputation etc., against attack.

self-denial *n.* deliberately going without the things one would like to have.

self-employed *adj.* working independently and not for an employer.

self-evident *adj.* clear without proof or explanation or further evidence.

self-explanatory *adj.* so easy to understand that it needs no further explanation.

self-governing *adj.* (of a country) governing itself. **self-government** *n.*

self-help *n.* use of one's own powers to achieve things, without dependence on aid from others.

self-important *adj.* having a high opinion of one's own importance, pompous. **self-importance.** *n.*

self-indulgent *adj.* greatly indulging one's own desires for comfort and pleasure. **self-indulgence** *n.*

self-interest *n.* one's own personal advantage.

selfish *adj.* acting or done according to one's own interests and needs without regard for those of others, keeping good things for oneself and not sharing. **selfishly** *adv.*, **selfishness** *n.*

selfless *adj.* unselfish. **selflessly** *adv.*, **selflessness** *n.*

self-made *adj.* having risen from poverty or obscurity and achieved success by one's own efforts, *a self-made man.*

self-pity *n.* pity for oneself.

self-portrait *n.* a portrait of himself by an artist, an account of himself by a writer.

self-possessed *adj.* calm and dignified. **self-possession** *n.*

self-preservation *n.* protection of oneself from harm or injury, the instinct to ensure one's own survival.

self-raising *adj.* (of flour) containing a raising agent and for use without additional baking-powder.

self-reliant *adj.* independent, relying on one's own abilities and resources. **self-reliance** *n.*

self-respect *n.* proper regard for oneself and one's own dignity and principles etc.

self-righteous *adj.* smugly sure of one's own righteousness.

self-sacrifice *n.* sacrifice of one's own interests and desires so that others may benefit. **self-sacrificing** *adj.*

selfsame *adj.* the very same, *died in the selfsame house where he was born.*

self-satisfied *adj.* pleased with oneself and one's own achievements, conceited. **self-satisfaction** *n.*

self-seeking *adj. & n.* seeking to promote one's own interests rather than those of others.

self-service *adj.* (of a restaurant or shop or filling station) at which customers help themselves and pay a cashier for what they have taken.

self-styled *adj.* using a name or description one has adopted without right, *one of these self-styled fast safe drivers.*

self-sufficient *adj.* able to provide what one needs without outside help.

self-supporting *adj.* able to support oneself or itself without help.

self-taught *adj.* having taught oneself without formal teaching from another person.

self-willed *adj.* obstinately doing what one wishes, stubborn.

self-winding *adj.* (of a watch or clock) having a mechanism that winds it automatically.

sell *v.* (sold, selling) **1.** to transfer the ownership of (goods etc.) in exchange for money. **2.** to keep a stock of (goods) for sale, to be a dealer in, *do you sell tobacco?* **3.** to promote sales of, *the author's name alone will sell many copies.* **4.** (of goods) to find buyers, *the book is selling well.* **5.** to be on sale at a certain price, *it sells for £1.50.* **6.** to persuade a person into accepting (a thing) by convincing him of its merits, *tried to sell him the idea of merging the two departments.* —**sell** *n.* **1.** the manner of selling something; *hard sell (see* hard*).* **2.** (*informal*) a deception, a disappointment. □ **sell down the river,** to betray or defraud. **selling-race** *n.* a race in which the winning horse must then be auctioned. **sell off,** to dispose of by selling, especially at a reduced price. **sell out,** to dispose of (all one's stock etc.) by selling; to betray. **sell-out** *n.* the selling of all tickets for a

show etc., a great commercial success; a betrayal. **sell up,** to sell one's house or business etc.; to sell the goods of (a debtor) so as to repay his creditors.

sellable *adj.* able to be sold.

seller *n.* **1.** a person who sells something. **2.** a thing that sells well or badly, *those sandals were good sellers.* □ **seller's market,** a state of affairs when goods are scarce and prices are high.

Sellotape *n.* (*trade mark*) an adhesive usually transparent cellulose or plastic tape. —**sellotape** *v.* to fix or seal with tape of this kind.

selvage *n.* **1.** an edge of cloth so woven that it does not unravel. **2.** a tape-like border along the edge of cloth, intended to be removed or hidden.

selvedge *n.* = selvage.

semantic (sim-**an**-tik) *adj.* of meaning in language, of semantics. **semantically** *adv.* □ **semantics** *pl. n.* the branch of philology concerned with meanings; meaning, connotation; interpretation of symbols other than words (e.g. road signs).

semaphore (sem-ă-for) *n.* **1.** a system of signalling by holding the arms in certain positions to indicate letters of the alphabet. **2.** a device with mechanically moved arms, used for signalling on railways. —*v.* to signal by semaphore.

semblance (sem-blăns) *n.* **1.** an outward appearance (either real or pretended), a show, *spoke with a semblance of friendship.* **2.** a resemblance or likeness to something.

semen (see-men) *n.* the whitish sperm-bearing fluid produced by male animals.

semester (sim-est-er) *n.* a half-year course or term in an American university.

semi *n.* (*pl.* semis) (*informal*) a semi-detached house.

semi- *prefix* half, partly.

semi-basement *n.* a storey (in a house etc.) that is partly below ground level.

semibreve (sem-i-breev) *n.* the longest note in common use in music, equal to two minims in length.

semicircle *n.* half of a circle, something arranged in this shape. **semicircular** *adj.*

semicolon (sem-i-koh-lŏn) *n.* the punctuation-mark ; used to separate parts of a sentence where there is a more distinct break than that represented by a comma.

semiconductor *n.* a substance that (in certain conditions) conducts electricity but not as well as most metals do.

semi-detached *adj.* (of a house) being one of a pair of houses that have one wall in common with each other but are detached from other houses.

semifinal *n.* the match or round preceding the final. **semifinalist** *n.* one who takes part in this.

semi-fitted *adj.* (of a garment) shaped to the body but not closely fitted.

seminal (sem-in-ăl) *adj.* 1. of seed or semen. 2. giving rise to new developments, *seminal ideas.*

seminar (sem-in-ar) *n.* a small class for advanced discussion and research.

seminary (sem-in-er-i) *n.* a training college for priests or rabbis.

semi-precious *adj.* (of a gem-stone) less valuable than those called precious.

semiquaver *n.* a note in music equal to half a quaver.

semi-skilled *adj.* having or requiring some training but less than that needed for skilled work.

semi-sweet *adj.* (of biscuits) slightly sweetened.

Semite (see-myt) *n.* a member of the group of races that includes the Jews and Arabs and formerly the Phoenicians and Assyrians.

Semitic (sim-it-ik) *adj.* of the Semites or their languages.

semitone *n.* the smallest interval used in European music, half of a tone.

semolina *n.* hard round grains left when wheat has been ground and sifted, used to make puddings and pasta.

SEN *abbrev.* State Enrolled Nurse.

senate (sen-ăt) *n.* 1. the governing council in ancient Rome. 2. *Senate,* the upper house of the parliamentary assemblies of the USA, France, and certain other countries. 3. the governing body of certain universities.

senator (sen-ă-ter) *n.* a member of a senate.

send *v.* (sent, sending) 1. to order or cause or enable to go to a certain destination, to have (a thing) conveyed. 2. to send a message or letter, *she sent to say she was coming.* 3. to cause to move or go; *sent him flying,* knocked him headlong; *sent his temperature up; the sermon sent us to sleep.* 4. to cause to become, *sent him mad.* **sender** *n.* □ **send away for,** to order (goods etc.) by post. **send down,** to expel from a university. **send for,** to order (a person) to come to one's presence; to order (a thing) to be brought or delivered from elsewhere. **send-off** *n.* a friendly demonstration at a person's departure. **send up,** (*informal*) to make fun of (a thing) by imitating it. **send-up** *n.* (*informal*) a humorous imitation. **send word,** to send information.

Senegal (sen-i-gawl) a country in West Africa. **Senegalese** (sen-i-gawl-eez) *adj.* & *n.* (*pl.* Senegalese)

senile (see-nyl) *adj.* suffering from bodily or mental weakness because of old age, (of illness etc.) characteristic of elderly people. **senility** (sin-il-iti) *n.*

senior *adj.* 1. older in age; *Tom Brown senior,* the older person of that name. 2. higher in rank or authority. 3. for older children, *senior school.* —**senior** *n.* a senior person, a member of a senior school; *he is my senior,* is older than I am. **seniority** *n.* □ **senior citizen,** an elderly person, one who has retired. **senior service,** the Royal Navy.

senna *n.* the dried pods or leaves of a tropical tree, used as a laxative.

señor (sen-yor) *n.* (*pl.* señores) the title of a Spanish-speaking man, = Mr or sir.

señora (sen-yor-ă) *n.* the title of a Spanish-speaking woman, = Mrs or madam.

señorita (sen-yor-eet-ă) *n.* the title of a Spanish-speaking girl or unmarried woman, = Miss or madam.

sensation *n.* 1. an awareness or feeling produced by stimulation of a sense-organ or of the mind. 2. ability to feel such stimulation, *loss of sensation in the fingers.* 3. a condition of eager interest or excitement or admiration aroused in a number of people, a person or thing arousing this.

sensational *adj.* 1. producing eager interest or excitement or admiration in many people. 2. (*informal*) extraordinary. **sensationally** *adv.*

sensationalism *n.* use of subject-matter or words or style etc. in order to produce excessive emotional excitement in people. **sensationalist** *n.*

sense *n.* 1. any of the special powers by which a living thing becomes aware of things; *the five senses,* the faculties of sight, hearing, smell, taste, and touch, by which the external world is perceived; *sixth sense (see* sixth). 2. ability to perceive or feel or be conscious of a thing, awareness or recognition of something, *has no sense of shame; sense of humour,* ability to appreciate humour. 3. the power of making a good judgement about something, practical wisdom, *had the sense to get out of the way.* 4. the way in which a word or phrase or passage etc. is to be understood, its meaning or one of its meanings. 5. possession of a meaning or of reasonableness. —**sense** *v.* 1. to perceive by one of the senses. 2. to become aware of (a thing) by getting a mental impression, *sensed that he was unwelcome.* 3. (of a machine) to detect. □ **come to one's senses,** to regain consciousness; to become sensible after behaving stupidly. **in a sense** *or* **in one sense**, if the statement is understood in a particular way, *what you say is true in a sense*. **make sense**, to have a meaning; to be a sensible and practicable idea. **make sense of**, to find a meaning in. **sense-organ** *n.* any of the organs (e.g. the eye or ear) by which the body becomes aware of stimuli from the external world. **senses** *pl. n.* sanity; *in one's senses*, sane; *has taken leave of his senses*, has gone mad.

senseless *adj.* **1.** not showing good sense, foolish. **2.** unconscious. **senselessness** *n.*

sensibility *n.* the ability to feel things mentally, sensitiveness, delicacy of feeling. ¶ This word does not mean 'possession of good sense'.

sensible *adj.* **1.** having or showing good sense. **2.** aware, *we are sensible of the honour you have done us*. **3.** (of clothing) practical rather than fashionable, *sensible shoes*. **sensibly** *adv.*

sensitive *adj.* **1.** affected by something, responsive to stimuli, *plants are sensitive to light*. **2.** receiving impressions quickly and easily, *sensitive fingers*. **3.** alert and considerate about other people's feelings. **4.** easily hurt or offended. **5.** (of an instrument etc.) readily responding to or recording slight changes of condition. **6.** (of a subject) requiring tactful treatment. **sensitively** *adv.*, **sensitivity** *n.* □ **sensitive plant**, mimosa or another plant with leaves that fold or droop when touched.

sensitize *v.* to make sensitive or abnormally sensitive. **sensitization** *n.*

sensor *n.* a device (e.g. a photoelectric cell) that reacts to a certain stimulus.

sensory (sen-ser-i) *adj.* of the senses, receiving or transmitting sensations, *sensory nerves*.

sensual (sens-yoo-ăl) *adj.* **1.** physical, gratifying to the body, *sensual pleasures*. **2.** indulging oneself with physical pleasures, showing that one does this, *a sensual face*. **sensually** *adv.*, **sensuality** (sens-yoo-al-iti) *n.* ¶ See the note under sensuous.

sensuous (sens-yoo-ŭs) *adj.* affecting or appealing to the senses, especially by beauty or delicacy. **sensuously** *adv.* ¶ This word does not have the implication of undesirable behaviour that *sensual* can have.

sent *see* send.

sentence *n.* **1.** a set of words containing a verb (either expressed or understood), that is complete in itself as an expression of thought. **2.** the punishment awarded by a lawcourt to a person convicted in a crim-

inal trial, declaration of this. —*v.* to pass sentence upon (a person), to condemn (to punishment).

sententious (sen-ten-shŭs) *adj.* putting on an air of wisdom, dull and moralizing. **sententiously** *adv.*, **sententiousness** *n.*

sentient (sen-shĕnt) *adj.* capable of perceiving and feeling things, *sentient beings*.

sentiment *n.* **1.** a mental attitude produced by one's feeling about something, an opinion. **2.** emotion as opposed to reason, sentimentality.

sentimental *adj.* **1.** showing or influenced by romantic or nostalgic feeling. **2.** characterized by emotions as opposed to reason. **sentimentally** *adv.*, **sentimentality** (senti-men-tal-iti) *n.*

sentinel *n.* a sentry.

sentry *n.* a soldier posted to keep watch and guard something. **sentry-box** *n.* a wooden structure large enough to shelter a standing sentry. **sentry-go** *n.* the duty of pacing up and down as a sentry.

Seoul (*pr. as* sole) the capital of South Korea.

sepal (sep-ăl) *n.* one of the leaf-like parts forming the calyx of a flower.

separable (sep-er-ăbŭl) *adj.* able to be separated.

separate[1] (sep-er-ăt) *adj.* forming a unit by itself, not joined or united with others. **separately** *adv.* □ **separates** *pl. n.* individual items of outer clothing for wearing together in various combinations.

separate[2] (sep-er-ayt) *v.* **1.** to divide, to make separate, to keep apart; *separate the cream*, extract it from the milk. **2.** to be between, *the Channel separates England from France*. **3.** to become separate, to go different ways, to withdraw oneself from a union, to cease to live together as a married couple.

separation *n.* **1.** separating, being separated. **2.** a legal arrangement by which a married couple live apart but without ending the marriage.

separatist (sep-er-ă-tist) *n.* a person who favours separation from a larger unit, e.g. so as to achieve political independence. **separatism** *n.*

separator *n.* a machine that separates things (e.g. cream from milk).

sepia (seep-iă) *n.* **1.** brown colouring-matter originally made from the black fluid of the cuttlefish, used in inks and water-colours. **2.** rich reddish-brown colour. —*adj.* of sepia colour.

sepsis *n.* a septic condition.

September *n.* the ninth month of the year.

septet *n.* a group of seven instruments or voices, a musical composition for these.

septic *adj.* infected with harmful microorganisms that cause pus to form. **septic tank,** a tank into which sewage is conveyed and in which it remains until the activity of bacteria makes it liquid enough to drain away.

septicaemia (septi-**seem**-iă) *n.* blood-poisoning.

septuagenarian (sep-tew-ă-jin-**air**-iăn) *n.* a person in his or her seventies.

Septuagesima (sep-tew-ă-**jess**-imă) *n.* the Sunday before Sexagesima.

Septuagint (**sep**-tew-ă-jint) *n.* the Greek version of the Old Testament.

septum *n.* a partition between two cavities, e.g. that in the nose between the nostrils.

sepulchral (sip-**ul**-krăl) *adj.* **1.** of a tomb, *sepulchral monument.* **2.** looking or sounding dismal, funereal; *a sepulchral voice,* deep and hollow-sounding.

sepulchre (**sep**-ŭl-ker) *n.* a tomb.

sequel *n.* **1.** what follows or arises out of an earlier event. **2.** a novel or film etc. that continues the story of an earlier one.

sequence *n.* **1.** the following of one thing after another in an orderly or continuous way. **2.** a series without gaps, a set of things that belong next to each other in a particular order; *in sequence,* in this order; *out of sequence,* not in it. **3.** a section dealing with one scene or topic in a cinema film.

sequential (si-**kwen**-shăl) *adj.* **1.** forming a sequence, following in succession. **2.** occurring as a result. **sequentially** *adv.*

sequester (si-**kwest**-er) *v.* **1.** to seclude. **2.** to confiscate.

sequestrate (si-**kwes**-trayt) *v.* to confiscate. **sequestration** *n.*

sequin (**see**-kwin) *n.* a circular spangle ornamenting clothing or other material. **sequinned** *adj.*

sequoia (si-**kwoi**-ă) *n.* a coniferous tree of California, growing to a great height.

seraglio (si-**rahl**-yoh) *n.* (*pl.* seraglios) the harem of a Muslim palace.

seraph *n.* (*pl.* seraphim) a member of the highest order of angels in ancient Christian belief. **seraphic** (ser-**af**-ik) *adj.* like a seraph, angelic. **seraphically** *adv.*

serenade *n.* a song or tune played by a lover to his lady, or suitable for this. —*v.* to sing or play a serenade to.

serendipity (se-rĕn-**dip**-iti) *n.* the making of pleasant discoveries by accident, the knack of doing this.

serene *adj.* **1.** calm and cheerful. **2.** the title used in speaking of or to members of certain European royal families, *His* or *Her* or *Your Serene Highness.* **serenely** *adv.,* **serenity** (ser-**en**-iti) *n.*

serf *n.* **1.** a farm labourer who was forced to work for his landowner in the Middle Ages. **2.** an oppressed labourer. **serfdom** *n.*

serge *n.* a strong twilled worsted fabric used for making clothes.

sergeant *n.* **1.** a non-commissioned army officer ranking above corporal. **2.** a police officer ranking just below inspector. □ **sergeant-major** *n.* a warrant officer assisting the adjutant of a regiment or battalion.

serial *n.* a story presented in a series of instalments. —*adj.* of or forming a series. □ **serial number,** a number that identifies one item in a series of things.

serialize *v.* to produce as a serial. **serialization** *n.*

seriatim (se-ri-**ay**-tim) *adv.* point by point, taking one subject etc. after another in an orderly sequence.

series *n.* (*pl.* series) **1.** a number of things of the same kind, or related to each other in a similar way, occurring or arranged or produced in order. **2.** a set of stamps or coins etc. issued at one time or in one reign.

serio-comic *adj.* partly serious and partly comic.

serious *adj.* **1.** solemn and thoughtful, not smiling. **2.** sincere, in earnest, not casual or light-hearted, *made a serious attempt.* **3.** important, *this is a serious decision.* **4.** causing great concern, not slight, *serious illness.* **seriously** *adv.,* **seriousness** *n.*

serjeant-at-arms *n.* an official of parliament, or of a court or city, with ceremonial duties.

sermon *n.* **1.** a talk on a religious or moral subject, especially one delivered by a clergyman during a religious service. **2.** a long moralizing talk.

sermonize *v.* to give a long moralizing talk.

serpent *n.* a snake, especially a large one.

serpentine *adj.* twisting and curving like a snake, *a serpentine road.*

serrated (ser-**ay**-tid) *adj.* having a series of small projections like the teeth of a saw. **serration** *n.*

serried (*rhymes with* buried) *adj.* (of rows of people or things) arranged in a close series.

serum (**seer**-ŭm) *n.* (*pl.* sera *or* serums) **1.** the thin yellowish fluid that remains from blood when the rest has clotted. **2.** this taken from an immunized animal and used for inoculations. **3.** any watery fluid from animal tissue (e.g. in a blister).

servant *n.* **1.** a person employed to do domestic work in a household or as a personal attendant on a master or mistress. **2.** a person engaged in service, an employee considered as performing services for his employer, *a faithful servant of the company*.

serve *v.* **1.** to perform services for (a person or community etc.), to work for, *served his country; served the national interest*, helped it. **2.** to be employed or performing a spell of duty, to be a member of the armed forces, *served in the Navy*. **3.** to be suitable for, to do what is required, *it will serve our purpose; it will serve*. **4.** to provide a facility for, *the area is served by a number of buses*. **5.** to spend time in, to undergo, *served his apprenticeship; served a prison sentence*. **6.** (of a male animal) to copulate with. **7.** to set out or present (food etc.) for others to consume, to attend to (customers in a shop). **8.** (of a quantity of food) to be enough for, *this recipe serves six persons*. **9.** to set the ball in play at tennis etc. **10.** to assist the priest officiating in a religious service. **11.** to deliver (a legal writ etc.) to the person named, *served him with the writ* or *served the writ on him*. **12.** to treat in a certain way, *she was most unjustly served*. —*n.* a service in tennis etc., a person's turn for this, the ball served. —**server** *n.* □ **it serves him right**, an expression of satisfaction at seeing a person get something unpleasant that he deserved. **serve up**, to offer for acceptance, *served up the same old entertainments again*.

service *n.* **1.** being a servant, a servant's status, *be in service; go into service*. **2.** the occupation or process of working for an employer or of assisting another person or persons. **3.** a department of people employed by the Crown or by a public organization; *the Civil Service* (*see* civil). **4.** a system or arrangement that performs work for customers or supplies public needs, *laundry services are available; the bus service; essential services*, public supply of water, electricity, etc. **5.** a branch of the armed forces; *the services*, the navy, army, and air force. **6.** use, assistance, a helpful or beneficial act, *did me a service; be of service*, to be useful, to help. **7.** a meeting of a congregation for worship of God, a religious ceremony. **8.** the serving of a legal writ. **9.** the serving of food or goods, provision of help for customers or clients, *quick service*. **10.** a service charge. **11.** a set of dishes, plates, etc. for serving a meal, *a dinner service*. **12.** the act or manner or turn

of serving in tennis etc., the game in which one serves, *lost his service*. **13.** maintenance and repair of a car or of machinery or appliances at intervals. **14.** the serving of a mare etc. by a male animal. —**service** *v.* **1.** to maintain or repair (a piece of machinery etc.). **2.** to supply with service(s). **3.** to pay the interest on, *the amount needed to service this loan*. □ **service area**, an area beside a motorway where petrol and refreshments etc. are available. **service charge**, an additional charge for service. **service flat**, a flat in which domestic service and sometimes meals are provided by the management. **service industry**, an industry providing services (e.g. gas, electricity) not goods. **service road**, a road giving access to houses etc. but not intended for through traffic. **service station**, a place where petrol etc. is available, beside a road.

serviceable *adj.* **1.** usable. **2.** suitable for ordinary use or wear, hard-wearing. **serviceably** *adv.*

serviceman *n.* (*pl.* servicemen) a man who is a member of the armed services.

servicewoman *n.* (*pl.* servicewomen) a woman who is a member of the armed services.

serviette *n.* a table-napkin.

servile (ser-vyl) *adj.* **1.** suitable for a servant, menial, *servile tasks*. **2.** excessively submissive, lacking independence, *servile flattery* or *imitation*. **servility** (ser-**vil**-iti) *n.*

serving *n.* a helping.

servitude *n.* the condition of being forced to work for others and having no freedom.

servo- *prefix* power-assisted, *servo-mechanism*.

sesame (sess-ǎ-mi) *n.* **1.** a plant of tropical Asia with seeds that are used as food or as a source of oil. **2.** its seeds. □ **Open Sesame**, a special way of obtaining access to something that is usually inaccessible. (¶ These words were used, in one of the *Arabian Nights* stories, to cause a door to open.)

session *n.* **1.** a meeting or series of meetings for discussing or deciding something. **2.** a period spent continuously in an activity, *a session of Scottish dancing*. **3.** the academic year in certain universities, (*Amer.*) a university term. **4.** the governing body of a Presbyterian church. □ **Court of Session**, *see* court.

set *v.* (set, setting) **1.** to put or place, to cause to stand in position. **2.** to put in contact with; *set fire to*, to cause to burn. **3.** to fix in position, to adjust the hands of (a clock) or the mechanism of (a trap etc.);

set the table, lay it for a meal. **4.** to represent as happening in a certain place, or at a certain time, *the story is set in Egypt in 2000 BC.* **5.** to provide a tune for, *set it to music.* **6.** to make or become hard or firm or established; *they are set against change,* have this as a permanent attitude; *the blossom fell before it* (or *the fruit*) *had set,* before fruit had developed from it. **7.** (of fabric etc.) to fall or hang in a certain way, *the collar sets well.* **8.** to fix or decide or appoint, *set a date for the wedding.* **9.** to arrange and protect (a broken bone) so that it will heal. **10.** to fix (hair) while it is damp so that it will dry in the desired style. **11.** to place (a jewel) in a surrounding framework, to decorate with jewels, *the bracelet is set with emeralds.* **12.** to establish, *set a new record for the high jump.* **13.** to offer or assign as something to be done, *set them a task.* **14.** to put into a specified state, *set them free; set it swinging.* **15.** to have a certain movement, *the current sets strongly eastwards.* **16.** to be brought towards or below the horizon by the earth's movement, *the sun sets.* **17.** (in certain dances) to face another dancer and make certain steps, *set to your partners.* **18.** (*dialect* or *incorrect use*) to sit. —**set** *n.* **1.** a number of people or things that are grouped together as similar or forming a unit. **2.** a group of games forming a unit or part of a match in tennis etc. **3.** (in mathematics) a collection of things having a common property. **4.** a radio or television receiver. **5.** the way something sets or is set or placed or arranged, *the set of his shoulders.* **6.** the process or style of setting hair. **7.** the scenery in use for a play or film, the stage etc. where this is being performed, *be on the set by 7 a.m.* **8.** a badger's burrow. **9.** a paving-block. **10.** a slip or shoot for planting, *onion sets.* ☐ **be set on,** to be determined about. **set about,** to begin (a task); to attack with blows or words. **set back,** to halt or slow the progress of, to cause a change for the worse; (*slang*) to cost, *it set me back £50.* **set-back** *n.* something that sets back progress. **set by the ears,** to cause to quarrel or argue. **set eyes on,** to catch sight of. **set forth,** to set out. **set in,** to become established, *depression had set in.* **set off,** to begin a journey; to cause to begin, *set off a chain reaction;* ignite or cause to explode; to improve the appearance of (a thing) by providing a contrast. **set one's hand to,** to begin (a task); to sign (a document). **set one's teeth,** to clench them. **set out,** to declare or make known, *set out the terms of the agreement;* to begin a journey; *set out to*

do something, to make a start with the intention of doing it. **set piece,** an arrangement of fireworks on scaffolding etc.; any formal or elaborate arrangement, especially in art or literature. **set sail,** to hoist sail(s); to begin a voyage. **set square,** a draughtsman's right-angled triangular plate for drawing lines in a certain relation to each other. **set theory,** the study of sets in mathematics, without regard to the nature of their individual constituents. **set to,** to begin doing something vigorously; to begin fighting or arguing. **set-to** *n.* a fight or argument. **set up,** to place in view; to arrange; to begin or create (a business etc.); to establish in some capacity; to begin making (a loud sound); to cause; to supply adequately, *I'm set up with reading matter for the journey; set up house,* to establish a household. **set-up** *n.* (*informal*) the structure of an organization.

sett *n.* = set *n.* (senses 8 and 9).

settee *n.* a long seat with a back and usually with arms, for two or more people.

setter *n.* **1.** a person or thing that sets something, *type-setter.* **2.** a dog of a long-haired breed that is trained to stand rigid when it scents game.

setting *n.* **1.** the way or place in which something is set. **2.** music for the words of a song etc. **3.** a set of cutlery or crockery for one person.

settle[1] *n.* a wooden seat for two or more people, with a high back and arms and often a box-like compartment from seat to floor.

settle[2] *v.* **1.** to place (a thing etc.) so that it stays in position. **2.** to establish or become established more or less permanently. **3.** to make one's home, to occupy as settlers, *settled in Canada; colonists settled the coast.* **4.** to sink or come to rest, to cause to do this, to become compact in this way, *dust settled on the shelves; let the earth settle after digging.* **5.** to arrange as desired, to end or arrange conclusively, to deal with, *settled the dispute.* **6.** to make or become calm or orderly, to stop being restless; *she can't settle to work,* she is too restless to concentrate steadily. **7.** to pay (a debt or bill or claim etc.). **8.** to bestow legally, *settled all his property on his wife.* ☐ **settle down,** to become settled after wandering or movement or restlessness or disturbance etc. **settle a person's hash,** *see* hash[1]. **settle up,** to pay what is owing.

settlement *n.* **1.** settling, being settled. **2.** a business or financial arrangement. **3.** an amount or property settled legally on a person. **4.** a place occupied by settlers or colonists etc.

settler *n.* a person who goes to live permanently in a previously unoccupied land, a colonist.

seven *adj. & n.* one more than six (7, VII).

sevenfold *adj. & adv.* seven times as much or as many.

seventeen *adj. & n.* one more than sixteen (17, XVII). **seventeenth** *adj. & n.*

seventh *adj. & n.* **1.** next after sixth. **2.** one of seven equal parts of a thing. **seventhly** *adv.* □ **seventh heaven,** a state of intense delight.

seventy *adj. & n.* seven times ten (70, LXX). **seventieth** *adj. & n.* □ **seventies** *pl. n.* the numbers or years or degrees of temperature from 70 to 79.

sever (sev-er) *v.* (severed, severing) to cut or break off from a whole, to separate; *sever a contract,* to end it.

several *adj.* **1.** a few, more than two but not many. **2.** separate, individual, *we all went our several ways.* —*pronoun* several people or things.

severally *adv.* separately.

severance (sev-er-ănss) *n.* severing, being severed. **severance pay,** an amount of money paid to an employee on termination of his contract.

severe (si-veer) *adj.* **1.** strict, without sympathy, imposing harsh rules on others. **2.** intense, forceful, *severe gales.* **3.** making great demands on endurance or energy or ability etc., *the pace was severe.* **4.** plain and without decoration, *a severe style of dress.* **severely** *adv.*, **severity** (si-ve-riti) *n.* □ **let it severely alone,** avoid meddling or dealing with it.

Seville (sev-il) *n.* a **Seville orange,** a bitter orange used for making marmalade. ¶ Named after Seville in Spain.

Sèvres (*pr.* sayvr) *n.* fine porcelain made at Sèvres in France.

sew *v.* (sewed, sewn *or* sewed, sewing) **1.** to fasten by passing thread again and again through material, using a threaded needle or an awl etc. or a sewing-machine. **2.** to make or attach or fasten by sewing. **3.** to work with needle and thread or with a sewing-machine.

sewage *n.* liquid waste matter drained away from houses, towns, factories, etc. for disposal. □ **sewage-farm** *n.* a farm on which a town's sewage is treated and used as manure. **sewage-works** *n.* a place where sewage is purified so that it can safely be discharged into a river etc.

sewer [1] (soh-er) *n.* a person or thing that sews.

sewer [2] (*rhymes with* fewer) *n.* a pipe connecting drains for carrying away sewage. —*v.* to provide or drain with sewers. □ **sewerage** *n.* a system of sewers, drainage by this; sewage.

sewing-machine *n.* a machine for sewing or stitching things.

sewn *see* sew. □ **have a thing sewn up,** (*informal*) to have it all arranged.

sex *n.* **1.** either of the two main groups (*male* and *female*) into which living things are placed according to their reproductive functions, the fact of belonging to one of these. **2.** sexual feelings or impulses, mutual attraction between members of the two sexes. **3.** sexual intercourse, *have sex with someone.* —*v.* to judge the sex of, *to sex chickens.* —**sexer** *n.* □ **sex act,** sexual intercourse. **sex appeal,** sexual attractiveness. **sexed** *adj.* having sexual characteristics or impulses, *highly sexed.* **sex life,** a person's sexual activities. **sex-starved** *adj.* lacking sexual gratification.

sexagenarian (seks-ă-jin-**air**-iăn) *n.* a person in his or her sixties.

Sexagesima (seks-ă-**jes**-imă) *n.* the Sunday before Quinquagesima.

sexist *adj.* **1.** discriminating in favour of members of one sex. **2.** assuming that a person's abilities and social functions are predetermined by his or her sex. —*n.* a person who does this. —**sexism** *n.*

sexless *adj.* **1.** lacking sex, neuter. **2.** not involving sexual feelings. **sexlessly** *adv.*

sexology *n.* study of human sexual relationships. **sexological** *adj.,* **sexologist** *n.*

sexpot *n.* (*slang*) a sexy person.

sextant *n.* an instrument used in navigating and surveying, for finding one's position by measuring the altitude of the sun etc.

sextet *n.* a group of six instruments or voices, a musical composition for these.

sextile (**seks**-til) *adj.* (of stars) in the position of being 60° distant from each other.

sexton *n.* an official whose job is to take care of a church and churchyard.

sextuple (**seks**-tew-pŭl) *adj.* sixfold.

sextuplet (**seks**-tew-plit) *n.* one of six children born at one birth.

sexual *adj.* **1.** of sex or the sexes or the relationship or feelings etc. between them. **2.** (of reproduction) occurring by fusion of male and female cells. **sexually** *adv.* □ **sexual intercourse,** copulation (especially of man and woman), insertion of the penis into the vagina.

sexuality (seks-yoo-**al**-iti) *n.* **1.** the fact of belonging to one of the sexes. **2.** sexual characteristics or impulses.

sexy *adj.* (sexier, sexiest) sexually attractive or stimulating.

Seychelles (say-**shelz**) a group of islands in the Indian Ocean.

sez = says. **sez you**, (*slang*) that is your opinion but I disagree.

SF *abbrev.* science fiction.

sh *int.* hush.

shabby *adj.* (shabbier, shabbiest) **1.** worn and threadbare, not kept in good condition, (of a person) poorly dressed. **2.** unfair, dishonourable, *a shabby trick*. **shabbily** *adv.*, **shabbiness** *n.* □ **shabby-genteel** *adj.* shabby but trying to keep up a dignified appearance.

shack *n.* a roughly-built hut or shed. —*v.* **shack up**, (*slang*) to cohabit with a person.

shackle *n.* one of a pair of iron rings joined by a chain, for fastening a prisoner's wrists or ankles. —*v.* **1.** to put shackles on. **2.** to impede or restrict, *shackled by tradition*.

shade *n.* **1.** comparative darkness or coolness found where something blocks rays of light or heat. **2.** shelter from the sun's light and heat, a place sheltered from these. **3.** the darker part of a picture. **4.** a colour, a degree or depth of colour, *in shades of blue*. **5.** a differing variety, *all shades of opinion*. **6.** a small amount, *she's a shade better today*. **7.** a ghost. **8.** a screen used to block or moderate light or heat, a translucent cover for making a lamp less glaringly bright or for directing its beam, an eye-shield. **9.** (*Amer.*) a window-blind. — **shade** *v.* **1.** to block the rays of. **2.** to give shade to, to make dark. **3.** to darken (parts of a drawing etc.) so as to give effects of light and shade or gradations of colour. **4.** to pass gradually into another colour or variety, *the blue here shades into green*, *where socialism shaded into communism*. □ **put in the shade**, to cause to appear inferior by contrast, to outshine. **shades** *pl. n.* the darkness of night or evening; (*Amer.*) sun-glasses; reminders of some person or thing, *shades of the 1930s*.

shadow *n.* **1.** shade. **2.** a patch of this with the shape of the body that is blocking the rays. **3.** a person's inseparable attendant or companion. **4.** a slight trace, *no shadow of doubt*. **5.** a shaded part of a picture. **6.** gloom, *the news cast a shadow over the proceedings*. **7.** something weak or unsubstantial, a ghost, *worn to a shadow*. —**shadow** *v.* **1.** to cast shadow over. **2.** to follow and watch secretly. —**shadower** *n.* □ **shadow-boxing** *n.* boxing against an imaginary opponent as a form of training. **Shadow Cabinet**, members of the Opposition party who act as spokesmen on matters for which Cabinet ministers hold responsibility; *Shadow Chancellor, Shadow Foreign Secretary*, members with these functions.

shadowy *adj.* **1.** like a shadow. **2.** full of shadows.

shady *adj.* (shadier, shadiest) **1.** giving shade. **2.** situated in the shade, *a shady corner*. **3.** disreputable, not completely honest, *shady dealings*. **shadiness** *n.*

shaft *n.* **1.** a spear or arrow or similar device, its long slender stem. **2.** a remark aimed or striking like an arrow, *shafts of wit*. **3.** a ray (of light), a bolt (of lightning). **4.** any long narrow straight part of something, e.g. of a supporting column or a golf-club. **5.** a large axle. **6.** one of a pair of long bars between which a horse is harnessed to draw a vehicle. **7.** a vertical or sloping passage or opening giving access to a mine or giving an outlet for air or smoke etc.

shag *n.* **1.** a rough mass of hair or fibre. **2.** a strong coarse kind of tobacco. **3.** a cormorant.

shaggy *adj.* (shaggier, shaggiest) **1.** having long rough hair or fibre. **2.** rough and thick and untidy, *shaggy hair*. **shagginess** *n.* □ **shaggy-dog story**, a lengthy anecdote with a peculiar twist of humour at the end.

shah *n.* the king of Iran.

shake *v.* (shook, shaken, shaking) **1.** to move quickly and often jerkily up and down or to and fro. **2.** to dislodge by doing this, *shook snow off his hat*. **3.** to make uneasy, to shock or disturb, to upset the calmness of. **4.** to make less firm. **5.** (of a voice) to tremble, to become weak or faltering. **6.** to shake hands, *let's shake on it*. —**shake** *n.* **1.** shaking, being shaken. **2.** a shaking movement. **3.** a jolt or shock. **4.** a milk shake. **5.** a moment, *shall be there in two shakes* or *a brace of shakes*. □ **no great shakes**, (*slang*) not very good. **shake down**, to become harmoniously adjusted to new conditions etc.; to sleep in an improvised bed. **shakedown** *n.* this process; an improvised bed. **shake hands**, to clasp right hands in greeting or parting or agreement. **shake in one's shoes**, to tremble with fear. **shake one's fist**, to make this threatening gesture at a person. **shake one's head**, to turn it from side to side in refusal or denial or disapproval. **shake up**, to mix by shaking; to restore to shape by shaking; to rouse from sluggishness or a set habit. **shake-up** *n.* an upheaval, a re-organization.

shaker *n.* **1.** a person or thing that shakes something. **2.** a container in which ingredients for cocktails etc. are mixed by being shaken.

Shakespearian *adj.* of Shakespeare.

shaky *adj.* (shakier, shakiest) **1.** shaking, unsteady, trembling. **2.** unreliable, wavering. **shakily** *adv.*, **shakiness** *n.*

shale *n.* stone that splits easily into fine pieces, rather like slate.

shall *auxiliary verb* (shalt is used with *thou*) **1.** used with *I* and *we* to express the future tense in statements and questions (but *will* is used with other words), *I shall arrive tomorrow* (but *they will arrive*); *shall I open the window?* **2.** used with words other than *I* and *we* in promises or statements of intention or obligation, *you shall have it* (but *I will have it* = I intend to have it); *thou shalt not kill.* **3.** sometimes *shall* is used in questions with words other than *I* and *we* because *will* would look like a request, e.g. *shall you take the children?*

shallot (shă-**lot**) *n.* an onion-like plant that forms clusters of bulbs as it grows.

shallow *adj.* **1.** not deep, *a shallow stream.* **2.** not thinking or thought out deeply, not capable of deep feelings. —*n.* a shallow place. —*v.* to make or become shallow. — **shallowly** *adv.*, **shallowness** *n.*

shalwar (**shul**-var) *n.* loose trousers worn by both sexes in some countries of southern Asia.

shalt *see* shall.

sham *n.* **1.** a pretence, a thing or feeling that is not genuine. **2.** a person who shams. —*adj.* pretended, not genuine. —*v.* (shammed, shamming) to pretend or pretend to be, *to sham illness, sham dead.* — **shammer** *n.*

shamble *v.* to walk or run in an awkward or lazy way. —*n.* a shambling movement.

shambles *n.* a scene or condition of great bloodshed or disorder.

shame *n.* **1.** a painful mental feeling aroused by a sense of having done something wrong or dishonourable or improper or ridiculous. **2.** ability to feel this, *he has no shame.* **3.** a person or thing that causes shame. **4.** something regrettable, a pity, *it's a shame you can't come.* —*v.* to bring shame on, to make ashamed, to compel by arousing feelings of shame, *was shamed into contributing more.*

shamefaced *adj.* looking ashamed.

shameful *adj.* causing shame, disgraceful. **shamefully** *adv.*

shameless *adj.* having or showing no feeling of shame, impudent. **shamelessly** *adv.*

shammy *n.* chamois-leather.

shampoo *n.* **1.** a liquid used to lather and wash the hair; *dry shampoo*, a powder brushed into hair to clean without wetting

it. **2.** a liquid or chemical for cleaning the surface of a carpet or upholstery, or for washing a car. **3.** shampooing, *booked a shampoo and set.* —*v.* to wash or clean with a shampoo.

shamrock *n.* a clover-like plant with three leaves on each stem, the national emblem of Ireland.

shandy *n.* a mixed drink of beer and ginger-beer or lemonade.

shanghai (shang-**hy**) *v.* (shanghaied, shanghaiing) to take (a person) by force or trickery and compel him to do something.

shank *n.* **1.** the leg, *long shanks.* **2.** the leg from knee to ankle, the corresponding part of an animal's leg (especially as a cut of meat). **3.** a long narrow part of something, a shaft.

shan't = shall not.

shantung *n.* a kind of soft Chinese silk, fabric resembling this.

shanty[1] *n.* a shack. **shanty town**, a town consisting of shanties.

shanty[2] *n.* a sailors' traditional song.

shape *n.* **1.** an area or form with a definite outline, the appearance produced by this. **2.** the form or condition in which something appears, *a monster in human shape.* **3.** the proper form or condition of something, *get it into shape.* **4.** a pattern or mould. **5.** a jelly etc. shaped in a mould. — **shape** *v.* **1.** to give a certain shape to. **2.** to develop into a certain shape or condition; *it is shaping well or shaping up well*, looks promising. **3.** to adapt or modify (one's plans or ideas etc.). —**shaper** *n.*

shapeless *adj.* **1.** having no definite shape. **2.** not shapely. **shapelessly** *adv.*

shapely *adj.* (shapelier, shapeliest) having a pleasing shape, well formed or proportioned. **shapeliness** *n.*

share[1] *n.* **1.** a part given to an individual out of a larger amount which is being divided or of a burden or achievement, the part one is entitled to have or do. **2.** one of the equal parts forming a business company's capital and entitling the holder to a proportion of the profits. —**share** *v.* **1.** to give portions of (a thing) to two or more people, *share it out.* **2.** to give away part of, *would share his last crust.* **3.** to have a share of, to use, possess, endure, or benefit from (a thing) jointly with others, *share a room*; *we share the credit.* —**sharer** *n.* □ **go shares** to share things equally. **sharecropper** *n.* a tenant farmer who pays part of his crop as rent to the owner. **sharecropping** *n.* doing this. **share-out** *n.* a distribution of profits or proceeds etc. in shares.

share² *n.* a ploughshare.

shareholder *n.* a person who owns a share or shares in a business company.

shark *n.* **1.** a sea-fish with a triangular fin on its back, some kinds of which are large and dangerous to bathers. **2.** a person who ruthlessly extorts money from another or others, a swindler.

sharp *adj.* **1.** having a fine edge or point that is capable of cutting or piercing, not blunt. **2.** narrowing to a point or edge, *a sharp ridge.* **3.** steep, angular, not gradual, *a sharp slope*; *a sharp turn.* **4.** well-defined, distinct, *in sharp focus.* **5.** intense, forceful, loud and shrill, (of temper) irritable; *she has a sharp tongue,* often speaks harshly and angrily. **6.** (of tastes and smells) producing a smarting sensation. **7.** quick to see or hear or notice things, intelligent. **8.** quick to seize an advantage; *be too sharp for someone,* to outwit him. **9.** unscrupulous. **10.** vigorous, brisk, *a sharp walk.* **11.** (in music) above the correct pitch; *C sharp, F sharp,* etc., a semitone higher than the corresponding note or key of natural pitch. —*sharp adv.* **1.** punctually, *at six o'clock sharp.* **2.** suddenly, *stopped sharp.* **3.** at a sharp angle, *turn sharp right at the junction.* **4.** above the correct pitch in music, *was singing sharp.* —*sharp n.* **1.** (in music) a note that is a semitone higher than the corresponding one of natural pitch, the sign ♯ indicating this. **2.** (*informal*) a swindler. —**sharply** *adv.*, **sharpness** *n.* □ **sharp-eyed** *adj.* quick at noticing things. **sharp practice,** business dealings that are dishonest or barely honest.

sharpen *v.* to make or become sharp. **sharpener** *n.*

sharper *n.* a swindler, especially at cards.

sharpish *adj.* rather sharp. *adv.* (*informal*) quickly, briskly.

sharpshooter *n.* a skilled marksman.

shatter *v.* **1.** to break or become broken violently into small pieces. **2.** to destroy utterly, *shattered our hopes.* **3.** to disturb or upset the calmness of, *we were shattered by the news.*

shave *v.* **1.** to scrape (growing hair) off the skin with a razor, to remove hair from the chin etc. **2.** to cut or scrape thin slices from the surface of (wood etc.). **3.** to graze gently in passing. **4.** to reduce or remove, *shave production costs*; *shave ten per cent off our estimates.* —*n.* the shaving of hair from the face, *needs a shave.* □ **close shave,** (*informal*) a narrow escape from injury or risk or failure. **shaving-brush** *n.* a brush for lathering the chin etc. before shaving. **shaving-cream** *n.* cream for applying to the chin etc. to assist shaving.

shaving-stick *n.* a cylindrical piece of soap for making lather to assist shaving.

shaven *adj.* shaved.

shaver *n.* **1.** a person or thing that shaves. **2.** an electric razor. **3.** (*informal*) a youngster.

shavings *pl. n.* thin strips of wood etc. shaved off the surface of a piece.

shawl *n.* a large piece of fabric worn round the shoulders or head, or wrapped round a baby, as a covering. **shawled** *adj.* covered in a shawl.

she *pronoun* the female person or animal mentioned, a thing (e.g. a vehicle or ship or aircraft) personified as female. —*n.* a female animal; *she-bear,* a female bear.

sheaf *n.* (*pl.* sheaves) **1.** a bundle of stalks of corn etc. tied together after reaping. **2.** a bundle of arrows or papers or other things laid lengthwise together.

shear *v.* (sheared, shorn *or* sheared, shearing) **1.** to cut or trim with shears or other sharp device, to remove (a sheep's wool) in this way. **2.** to strip bare, to deprive, *shorn of his glory.* **3.** to break or distort, or become broken or distorted, by shear. —*n.* a type of fracture or distortion produced by pressure, in which each successive layer (e.g. of a mass of rock) slides over the next. —**shearer** *n.*

shears *pl. n.* a clipping or cutting instrument working like scissors but much larger and usually operated with both hands.

shearwater *n.* a sea-bird with long wings, skimming close to the water as it flies.

sheath *n.* (*pl.* sheaths, *pr.* sheeths *or* sheethz) **1.** a close-fitting covering, a cover for a blade or tool. **2.** a covering for wearing on the penis during sexual intercourse as a contraceptive. **3.** a woman's close-fitting dress. □ **sheath-knife** *n.* a dagger-like knife carried in a sheath.

sheathe (*pr.* sheeth) *v.* **1.** to put into a sheath. **2.** to encase in a covering.

shed¹ *n.* a one-storeyed building for storing things or sheltering livestock etc. or for use as a workshop.

shed² *v.* (shed, shedding) **1.** to lose (a thing) by a natural falling off, *trees shed their leaves.* **2.** to take off, *shed one's clothes.* **3.** allow to pour forth, *shed tears*; *shed one's blood,* to be wounded or killed for one's country etc. **4.** to send forth, *shed light.*

she'd = she had, she would.

sheen *n.* gloss, lustre. **sheeny** *adj.*

sheep *n.* (*pl.* sheep) a grass-eating animal with a thick fleecy coat, kept in flocks for its fleece and for its flesh as meat; *as well be hanged for a sheep as a lamb,* commit a big crime rather than a small one if the punishment is the same. **like sheep,** (of people) easily led or influenced. **make sheep's eyes at,** *see* eye. **separate the sheep from the goats,** to separate the good from the wicked. **sheep-dip** *n.* a liquid for cleansing sheep of vermin or preserving their wool. **sheep-dog** *n.* a dog trained to guard and herd sheep; *Old English sheep-dog,* a dog of a large shaggy-coated breed. **sheep-farmer** *n.* one who breeds sheep. **sheep-fold** *n.* an enclosure into which sheep can be penned.

sheepish *adj.* bashful, embarrassed through shame. **sheepishly** *adv.,* **sheepishness** *n.*

sheepshank *n.* a knot used to shorten a rope without cutting it.

sheepskin *n.* 1. a garment or rug made of sheep's skin with the fleece on. 2. leather made from sheep's skin.

sheer[1] *adj.* 1. pure, not mixed or qualified, *sheer luck.* 2. (of a rock or fall etc.) having a vertical or almost vertical surface, with no slope. 3. (of fabric) very thin, transparent. —*adv.* directly, straight up or down, *the cliff rises sheer from the sea.*

sheer[2] *v.* to swerve from a course. **sheer off,** to go away, to leave (a person or topic that one dislikes or wishes to avoid).

sheet[1] *n.* 1. a large rectangular piece of cotton or similar fabric, used in pairs as inner bedclothes between which a person sleeps. 2. a large thin piece of any material (e.g. paper, glass, metal). 3. a piece of paper for writing or printing on, a complete and uncut piece (of the size in which it is made). 4. a wide expanse of water or snow or flame etc. □ **sheeted** *adj.* covered with a sheet or sheets. **sheeting** *n.* material for making sheets. **sheet lightning,** lightning that looks like a sheet of light across the sky. **sheet music,** music published on loose sheets of paper and not bound into a book.

sheet[2] *n.* a rope or chain attached to the lower corner of a sail, to secure or adjust it. □ **sheet-anchor** *n.* a thing on which one depends for security or stability.

sheikh (*pr.* shayk) *n.* the leader of an Arab tribe or village. **sheikhdom** *n.* the territory of a sheikh.

sheila *n.* (*Austral. slang*) a young woman, a girl.

shekel (shek-ĕl) *n.* the unit of money in Israel. **shekels** *pl. n.* (*informal*) money, riches.

sheldrake *n.* (*pl.* shelduck) a wild duck with bright plumage, living on coasts. **shelduck** *n.* a female sheldrake.

shelf *n.* (*pl.* shelves) 1. a flat rectangular piece of wood or metal or glass etc. fas-

tened horizontally to a wall or in a cupboard or bookcase for things to be placed on. 2. something resembling this, a ledge or step-like projection. □ **on the shelf,** (of a person) made to be inactive as no longer of use; (of an unmarried woman) past the age when she is regarded as likely to be sought in marriage. **shelf-life** *n.* the time for which a stored thing remains usable. **shelf-mark** *n.* a number marked on a book to show its place in a library.

shell *n.* 1. the hard outer covering of eggs, nut-kernels, and of animals such as snails and crabs and tortoises. 2. the walls of an unfinished or burnt-out building or ship. 3. any structure that forms a firm framework or covering. 4. the metal framework of the body of a vehicle. 5. a light boat for rowing races. 6. a metal case filled with explosive, to be fired from a large gun. —**shell** *v.* 1. to remove the shell of, *shell peas.* 2. to fire explosive shells at. □ **come out of one's shell,** to become more sociable and less shy. **shell out,** (*slang*) to pay out (money, or a required amount). **shell-pink** *adj. & n.* delicate pale pink. **shell-shock** *n.* nervous breakdown resulting from exposure to battle conditions.

she'll = she will.

shellac (shĕl-**ak**) *n.* thin flakes of a resinous substance used in making varnish. —*v.* (shellacked, shellacking) to varnish with shellac.

shellfish *n.* a water animal that has a shell, especially one of edible kinds such as oysters, crabs, and shrimps.

shelter *n.* 1. something that serves as a shield or barrier against attack, danger, heat, wind, etc. 2. a structure built to keep rain etc. off people, *a bus shelter.* 3. refuge, a shielded condition, *sought shelter from the rain.* —**shelter** *v.* 1. to provide with shelter. 2. to protect from blame or trouble or competition. 3. to find or take shelter.

shelve *v.* 1. to arrange on a shelf or shelves. 2. to fit (a wall or cupboard etc.) with shelves. 3. to put aside for later consideration, to reject (a plan etc.) temporarily or permanently. 4. to slope, *the river-bottom shelves here.*

shelving *n.* shelves, material for making these.

shemozzle *n.* (*slang*) a rumpus, a brawl.

shenanigans (shin-**an**-i-gănz) *pl. n.* (*Amer. slang*) 1. high-spirited behaviour. 2. trickery.

shepherd *n.* a man who tends a flock of sheep while they are at pasture. —*v.* to guide or direct (people). —**shepherdess** *n.*

□ **shepherd's pie**, a pie of minced meat topped with mashed potato.

Sheraton (sh'e-ră-tŏn) *n.* a late 18th-century style of English furniture, named after its designer.

sherbet *n.* **1.** a cooling Oriental drink of weak sweet fruit-juice. **2.** a fizzy sweet drink or the powder from which this is made. **3.** a flavoured water-ice.

sheriff *n.* **1.** the chief executive officer of the Crown in a county, with certain legal and ceremonial duties. **2.** the chief judge of a district in Scotland. **3.** (*Amer.*) the chief law-enforcing officer of a county.

Sherpa *n.* a member of a Himalayan people living on the borders of Nepal and Tibet.

sherry *n.* a strong white wine (either sweet or dry), originally from southern Spain.

she's = she is, she has.

Shetland an islands area of Scotland. — *adj.* of Shetland or the Shetland Islands. □ **Shetland pony**, a pony of a very small rough-coated breed. **Shetland wool**, fine loosely-twisted wool from Shetland sheep.

Shetlander *n.* a native or inhabitant of Shetland or the Shetland Islands.

shibboleth (**shib**-ŏ-leth) *n.* an old slogan or principle that is still considered essential by some members of a party, *outworn shibboleths*. ¶ From the story in the Bible, in which shibboleth' was a kind of password.

shield *n.* **1.** a piece of armour carried on the arm to protect the body against missiles or thrusts. **2.** a drawing or model of a triangular shield used for displaying a coat of arms, a trophy in the form of this. **3.** an object or structure or layer of material that protects something. —*v.* to protect or screen, to protect from discovery.

shift *v.* **1.** to change or move from one position to another. **2.** to change form or character. **3.** to transfer (blame or responsibility etc.). **4.** (*slang*) to move quickly. **5.** to manage to do something. —**shift** *n.* **1.** a change of place or form or character etc. **2.** a set of workers who start work as another set finishes, the time for which they work, *the night-shift*. **3.** a piece of evasion. **4.** a scheme for achieving something. **5.** a woman's straight-cut dress. —**shifter** *n.* □ **make shift**, *see* make. **shift for oneself**, to manage without help. **shift one's ground**, to change the basis of one's argument.

shiftless *adj.* lazy and inefficient, lacking resourcefulness. **shiftlessly** *adv.*, **shiftlessness** *n.*

shifty *adj.* (shiftier, shiftiest) evasive, not straightforward in manner or character, untrustworthy. **shiftily** *adv.*, **shiftiness** *n.*

shilling *n.* a former British coin, = 5p.

shilly-shally *v.* (shilly-shallied, shilly-shallying) to be unable to make up one's mind firmly.

shim *n.* a thin wedge or slip of material used in machinery to make parts fit together.

shimmer *v.* to shine with a soft light that appears to quiver. —*n.* a shimmering effect.

shin *n.* **1.** the front of the leg below the knee. **2.** the lower part of the foreleg in cattle, especially as a cut of beef. —*v.* (shinned, shinning) to climb by using arms and legs (not on a ladder).

shindy *n.* (*informal*) a din, a brawl.

shine *v.* (shone (in sense 5 shined), shining) **1.** to give out or reflect light, to be bright, to glow. **2.** (of the sun etc.) to be visible and not obscured by clouds. **3.** to excel in some way, *does not shine in maths*; *shining example*, an excellent one. **4.** to direct the light of, *shine the torch on it.* **5.** (*informal*) to polish. —**shine** *n.* **1.** brightness. **2.** a high polish. □ **take a shine to**, (*Amer.*) to take a liking to.

shiner *n.* (*slang*) a black eye.

shingle[1] *n.* a rectangular slip of wood used as a roof-tile. —*v.* **1.** to roof with shingles. **2.** to cut (a woman's hair) in a short tapering style at the back, with all ends exposed.

shingle[2] *n.* small rounded pebbles, a stretch of these on a shore.

shingles *n.* a painful disease caused by the chickenpox virus, with blisters forming along the path of a nerve or nerves.

shinty *n.* a game resembling hockey.

shiny *adj.* (shinier, shiniest) shining, rubbed until glossy.

ship *n.* a large seagoing vessel. —*v.* (shipped, shipping) **1.** to put or take on board a ship for conveyance to a destination. **2.** to transport. □ **ship a sea**, (of a boat) to be overwhelmed by a wave. **ship canal**, a canal deep and wide enough to admit large ships. **ship one's oars**, to take them from the rowlocks and lay them in the boat. **take ship**, to go on board a ship for a journey.

shipboard *adj.* used or ocurring on board a ship.—*n.* **on shipboard**, on board a ship.

shipbuilding *n.* the business of constructing ships. **shipbuilder** *n.* a person engaged in this.

shipload *n.* as much as a ship will hold.

shipmate *n.* a person travelling or working on the same ship as another.

shipment *n.* **1.** the putting of goods on a

ship. 2. the amount shipped, a consignment.

shipowner *n.* a person who owns a ship or holds shares in a shipping company.

shipper *n.* a person or firm whose business is transporting goods by ship.

shipping *n.* **1.** ships, especially those of a country or port. **2.** transporting goods by ship.

shipshape *adv. & adj.* in good order, tidy.

shipwreck *n.* destruction of a ship by storm or striking rock etc. **shipwrecked** *adj.* having suffered a shipwreck.

shipwright *n.* a shipbuilder.

shipyard *n.* a shipbuilding establishment.

shire *n.* **1.** a county. **2.** (*Austral.*) a rural area with its own elected council. □ **shirehorse** *n.* a heavy powerful breed of horse used for pulling loads.

shirk *v.* to avoid (a duty or work etc.) selfishly or unfairly. **shirker** *n.*

shirr *v.* to gather (cloth) with parallel threads run through it. **shirring** *n.*

shirt *n.* **1.** a man's loose-fitting garment of cotton or silk etc. for the upper part of the body. **2.** a shirt blouse. □ **in one's shirtsleeves,** with no jacket over one's shirt. **put one's shirt on,** (*slang*) to bet all one has on (a horse etc.); to be sure of. **shirt blouse,** a woman's blouse in a plain style like a man's shirt. **shirt dress,** a shirtwaister. **shirt-front** *n.* the breast of a shirt, especially when stiffened or starched.

shirting *n.* material for making shirts.

shirtwaister *n.* a woman's dress with the bodice shaped like a shirt.

shirty *adj.* (shirtier, shirtiest) (*slang*) annoyed, angry. **shirtily** *adv.,* **shirtiness** *n.*

shit *n.* (*vulgar*) **1.** faeces. **2.** a contemptible person or thing. —*v.* (*vulgar*) to empty the bowels, to defecate.

shiver[1] *v.* to tremble slightly especially with cold or fear. —*n.* a shivering movement; *it gives me the shivers,* makes me shiver with fear or horror. —**shivery** *adj.*

shiver[2] *v.* to shatter. **shivers** *pl. n.* shattered fragments.

shoal[1] *n.* a great number of fish swimming together. —*v.* to form shoals.

shoal[2] *n.* a shallow place, an underwater sandbank. —*v.* to become shallower. □ **shoals** *pl. n.* hidden dangers or difficulties.

shock[1] *n.* a bushy untidy mass of hair.

shock[2] *n.* **1.** the effect of a violent impact or shake. **2.** a violent shake of the earth's crust in an earthquake. **3.** a sudden violent effect upon a person's mind or emotions (e.g. by news of a disaster). **4.** an acute state of weakness caused by physical injury or pain or by mental shock. **5.** an

electric shock (*see* electric). —**shock** *v.* **1.** to affect with great indignation or horror or disgust, to seem highly improper or scandalous or outrageous to (a person). **2.** to give an electric shock to. **3.** to cause an acute state of weakness in (a person or animal). □ **shock absorber,** a device for absorbing vibration in a vehicle. **shock tactics,** sudden violent action taken to achieve one's purpose. **shock therapy** *or* **treatment,** treatment of psychiatric patients by means of an electric shock or a drug causing a similar effect. **shock troops,** troops specially trained for violent assaults. **shock wave,** a sharp wave of increased atmospheric pressure, caused by an explosion or by a body moving faster than sound.

shocker *n.* (*informal*) a shocking person or thing, a very bad specimen of something.

shocking *adj.* **1.** causing great astonishment or indignation or disgust, scandalous. **2.** (*informal*) very bad, *shocking weather.* **shockingly** *adv.*

shod *see* shoe. —*adj.* having shoes of a certain kind, *sensibly shod.*

shoddy *n.* **1.** fibre made from old cloth shredded. **2.** cloth made partly from this. —*adj.* (shoddier, shoddiest) of poor quality or workmanship. —**shoddily** *adv.,* **shoddiness** *n.*

shoe *n.* **1.** an outer covering for a person's foot, with a fairly stiff sole. **2.** a horseshoe. **3.** an object like a shoe in appearance or use. **4.** the part of a brake that presses against the wheel or its drum in a vehicle. —*v.* (shod, shoeing) to fit with a shoe or shoes. □ **be in a person's shoes,** to be in his situation or plight. **on a shoestring,** with only a small amount of capital and resources, e.g. in running a business. **shoe-tree** *n.* a shaped block for keeping a shoe in shape.

shoehorn *n.* a curved piece of metal or other stiff material for easing one's heel into the back of a shoe.

shoelace *n.* a cord for fastening the edges of a shoe's uppers.

shoemaker *n.* a person whose trade is making or mending boots and shoes.

shoeshine *n.* (*Amer.*) the polishing of shoes.

shone *see* shine.

shoo *int.* a sound uttered to frighten animals away. —*v.* (shooed, shooing) to drive away by this.

shook *see* shake.

shoot *v.* (shot, shooting) **1.** to fire (a gun or other weapon, or a missile), to use a gun etc., *can't shoot straight.* **2.** to kill or wound with a missile from a gun etc. **3.** to hunt with a gun for sport, to go over (an area) in shooting game. **4.** to send out swiftly or violently, *shot the rubbish into the bin.* **5.** to move swiftly, *the car shot past me.* **6.** (of a plant) to put forth buds or shoots. **7.** to slide (the bolt of a door) into or out of its fastening. **8.** to have one's boat move swiftly under (a bridge) or over (rapids etc.). **9.** to take a shot at goal. **10.** to photograph or film. **11.** *shoot!,* (*Amer. slang*) say what you have to say. — **shoot** *n.* **1.** a young branch or new growth of a plant. **2.** an expedition for shooting game, land where this is held. — **shooter** *n.* □ **have shot one's bolt,** to have made one's last possible effort. **shoot a line,** (*informal*) to try to impress or convince someone by boastful talk. **shoot dice,** (*Amer.*) to play at dice. **shoot down,** to cause (a flying aircraft) to fall to the ground by shooting. **shooting-box** *n.* a small house for use in the shooting season. **shooting-brake** *n.* an estate car. **shooting-gallery** *n.* a place for shooting at targets with rifles etc. **shooting star,** a small meteor appearing like a star, moving rapidly and then disappearing. **shooting-stick** *n.* a walking-stick with a small folding seat at the handle end. **shoot it out,** (*slang*) to engage in a decisive gun-battle. **shoot one's mouth off,** (*slang*) to talk too freely. **shoot up,** to rise suddenly; (of a person) to grow rapidly. **the whole shoot,** (*slang*) everything.

shop *n.* **1.** a building or room where goods or services are on sale to the public. **2.** a workshop. **3.** one's own work or profession as a subject of conversation, *is always talking shop.* —**shop** *v.* (shopped, shopping) **1.** to go to a shop or shops to buy things. **2.** (*slang*) to inform against (a person), especially to the police. □ **all over the shop,** (*slang*) in great disorder, scattered everywhere. **shop around,** to look for the best bargain. **shop-floor** *n.* workers as distinct from management or senior officials of a trade union. **shop-soiled** *adj.* soiled or faded from being on display in a shop. **shop steward,** a trade union official elected by fellow workers as their spokesman. **shop-worn** *adj.* shop-soiled.

shopkeeper *n.* a person who owns or manages a shop.

shop-lifter *n.* a person who steals goods that are on display in a shop, after entering as a customer. **shop-lifting** *n.*

shopper *n.* **1.** a person who shops. **2.** a shopping-bag.

shopping *n.* **1.** buying goods in shops. **2.** the goods bought. □ **shopping-bag** *n.*

a bag for holding goods bought. **shopping centre,** an area where shops are concentrated. **shopping mall** (*pr.* mal *or* mawl), (*Amer.*) a shopping precinct. **shopping-trolley** *n.* a trolley with a large shopping-bag mounted on it.

shore [1] *n.* the land along the edge of the sea or of a large body of water.

shore [2] *v.* to prop or support with a length of timber set at a slant. —*n.* a support of this kind. □ **shoring** *n.* a number of shores supporting something.

shoreward *adj. & adv.* towards the shore. **shorewards** *adv.*

shorn *see* shear.

short *adj.* **1.** measuring little from end to end in space or time. **2.** seeming to be shorter than it really is, *for one short hour.* **3.** not lasting, not going far into the past or future, *a short memory.* **4.** insufficient, having an insufficient supply, *water is short; we are short of water; short-staffed.* **5.** (*informal*) having little of a certain quality, *he's short on tact.* **6.** concise, brief. **7.** curt. **8.** (of vowel sounds) relatively brief or light (*see* long, sense 6). **9.** (of an alcoholic drink) small and concentrated, made with spirits. **10.** (of temper) easily lost. **11.** (of pastry) rich and crumbly through containing much fat. —*adv.* suddenly, abruptly, *stopped short.* —**short** *n.* (*informal*) **1.** a short drink. **2.** a short circuit. —*v.* (*informal*) to short-circuit. □ **for short,** as an abbreviation, *Raymond is called Ray for short.* **get** *or* **have by the short hairs,** to have at one's mercy or forced to obey. **in short supply,** scarce. **make short work of,** to deal with (a thing) rapidly. **short-change** *v.* to rob by giving insufficient change; to cheat (a person). **short circuit,** a connection (usually a fault) in an electrical circuit in which current flows by a shorter route than the normal one. **short-circuit** *v.* to cause a short circuit in; to bypass. **short cut,** a route or method that is quicker than the usual one. **short division,** the process of dividing one number by another without writing down one's calculations. **short for,** an abbreviation of, *'Ray' is short for 'Raymond'.* **short-handed** *adj.* having an insufficient number of workmen or helpers. **short list,** a list of selected candidates from whom the final choice will be made. **short-list** *v.* to put on a short list. **short-lived** *adj.* having a short life, not lasting long. **short odds,** nearly even odds in betting. **short of,** without going the length of, *will do anything for her short of having her to stay.* **short rations,** very small rations. **shorts** *pl. n.* trousers that do not reach to the knee. **short shrift,** curt treatment. **short-sighted** *adj.* able to see clearly only what is close; lacking foresight. **short-sleeved** *adj.* with sleeves not reaching below the elbow. **short-tempered** *adj.* easily becoming angry. **short-term** *adj.* of or for a short period. **short time,** a reduced working day or week. **short ton,** *see* ton. **short wave,** a radio wave of about 10 to 100 metres wavelength.

shortage *n.* a lack of something that is needed, insufficiency.

shortbread *n.* a rich sweet biscuit.

shortcake *n.* shortbread.

shortcoming *n.* failure to reach a required standard, a fault.

shorten *v.* to make or become shorter.

shortening *n.* fat used to make pastry etc. rich and crumbly.

shortfall *n.* a deficit.

shorthand *n.* a method of writing very rapidly, using quickly-made symbols.

shorthorn *n.* one of a breed of cattle with short horns.

shortish *adj.* rather short.

shortly *adv.* **1.** in a short time, not long, soon, *coming shortly; shortly afterwards.* **2.** in a few words. **3.** curtly.

shorty *n.* (*informal*) a person or garment that is shorter than average.

shot *see* shoot. —*adj.* (of fabric) woven or dyed so that different colours show at different angles. —*n.* **1.** the firing of a gun etc., the sound of this. **2.** a person with regard to his skill in shooting, *he's a good shot.* **3.** (*pl.* shot) a single missile for a cannon or gun, a non-explosive projectile. **4.** lead pellets for firing from small guns. **5.** a heavy ball thrown as a sport. **6.** the launching of a rocket or spacecraft. **7.** a stroke in tennis or cricket or billiards etc. **8.** an attempt to hit something or reach a target. **9.** an attempt to do something, *have a shot at this crossword.* **10.** an injection. **11.** (*informal*) a dram of spirits. **12.** a photograph, the scene photographed, a single continuous photographed scene in a cinema film. □ **like a shot,** without hesitation, willingly. **shot-gun** *n.* a gun for firing small shot at close range; *shot-gun wedding,* one that is enforced, especially because the bride is pregnant. **shot in the arm,** a stimulus or encouragement. **shot in the dark,** a mere guess.

should *auxiliary verb,* used to express **1.** duty or obligation, *you should have told me.* **2.** an expected future event, *they should be here by ten.* **3.** a possible event, *if you should happen to see him.* **4.** with *I* and *we* to form a polite statement or a conditional clause, *I should like to come; if their fore-*

cast had been right, they would have won and we should (¶ not would) have lost; I should say it's about right.

shoulder *n.* **1.** the part of the body at which the arm or foreleg or wing is attached, the part of the human body between this and the neck. **2.** the part of a garment covering the shoulder. **3.** the upper foreleg and adjacent parts of an animal as a cut of meat. **4.** a projection compared to the human shoulder, *the shoulder of a bottle.* —**shoulder** *v.* **1.** to push with one's shoulder. **2.** to take (a burden) upon one's shoulders. **3.** to take (blame or responsibility) upon oneself. □ **put one's shoulder to the wheel,** to make an effort. **shoulder arms,** to hold a rifle with the barrel against one's shoulder. **shoulder-bag** *n.* a handbag hung on a strap over the shoulder. **shoulder-blade** *n.* either of the two large flat bones at the top of the back. **shoulder-high** *n.* up to or as high as the shoulders. **shoulder-strap** *n.* a strap that passes over the shoulder, especially to support something. **shoulder to shoulder,** side by side and close together.

shouldn't = should not.

shout *n.* **1.** a loud cry or utterance of words calling attention or expressing joy or excitement or disapproval. **2.** (*Austral. informal*) a person's turn to buy a round of drinks. —**shout** *v.* **1.** to utter a shout, to utter or call loudly. **2.** (*Austral. informal*) to buy a round of drinks. □ **shout down,** to silence (a person) by shouting.

shove (*pr.* shuv) *n.* a rough push. —*v.* **1.** to push roughly. **2.** (*informal*) to put, *shove it in the drawer.* □ **shove off,** to push a boat so that it moves from the shore; (*informal*) to go away.

shovel *n.* **1.** a tool for scooping up earth or snow etc. usually shaped like a spade with the edges turned up. **2.** a large mechanically-operated device used for the same purpose. —**shovel** *v.* (shovelled, shovelling) **1.** to shift or clear with or as if with a shovel. **2.** to scoop or thrust roughly, *shovelling food into his mouth.*

shovelboard *n.* a game in which discs are driven over a marked surface, especially on a ship's deck.

shoveller *n.* a duck with a broad shovel-like beak.

show *v.* (showed, shown, showing) **1.** to allow or cause to be seen, to offer for inspection or viewing. **2.** to demonstrate, to point out, to prove, to cause (a person) to understand, *show us how it works; showed them the door,* dismissed them. **3.** to conduct, *show them in* or *out.* **4.** to present an image of, *this picture shows the hotel.* **5.** to exhibit in a show. **6.** to treat in a certain way, *showed us much kindness.* **7.** to be able to be seen, *the lining is showing.* **8.** (*informal*) to prove one's ability or worth to, *we'll show them!* —**show** *n.* **1.** showing, being shown. **2.** a display, a public exhibition for competition or entertainment or advertisement etc., a pageant, *a dog show*; *a puppet show*; *the motor show*; *the Lord Mayor's Show.* **3.** (*informal*) any public entertainment or performance. **4.** (*slang*) any business or undertaking, *he runs the whole show.* **5.** an outward appearance, an insincere display, *under a show of friendship.* **6.** a pompous display. **7.** a discharge of blood from the vagina at the start of childbirth or menstruation. □ **bad show!**, (*informal*) that was badly done or unfortunate. **give the show away**, to reveal things that were intended to be secret. **good show!**, (*informal*) well done. **nothing to show for it**, no visible result of one's efforts. **show a leg**, (*informal*) get out of bed. **showbiz** *n.* (*slang*) = **show business**, the entertainment or theatrical profession. **show-case** *n.* a glass-covered case in which things are exhibited. **show-down** *n.* a final test, disclosure of intentions or conditions etc. **show house** *or* **flat**, one prepared as a sample of those available on the rest of an estate etc. **show-jumping** *n.* the sport of riding horses to jump over obstacles, in competition. **show off**, to display well or proudly or ostentatiously; to try to impress people; to have a tantrum. **show-off** *n.* a person who tries to impress others. **show of hands**, raising of hands to vote for or against something. **show oneself**, to be seen in public. **show one's face**, to let oneself be seen. **show-piece** *n.* an excellent specimen used for exhibition. **show-place** *n.* a place that tourists etc. go to see. **show-room** *n.* a room in which goods are displayed for inspection. **show up**, to make or be clearly visible; to reveal (a fault or inferiority etc.); (*informal*) to appear, to be present.

shower *n.* **1.** a brief fall of rain or snow etc., or of bullets, dust, or stones etc. **2.** a sudden influx of letters or gifts etc. **3.** a device or cabinet in which water is sprayed on a person's body to wash him, a wash in this. **4.** (*Amer.*) a party for giving presents to a person, especially to a bride-to-be. **5.** (*slang*) a contemptible or unpleasant person. —**shower** *v.* **1.** to pour down or come in a shower. **2.** to send or give (many letters or gifts etc.) to. **3.** to wash oneself in sprayed water.

showerproof *adj.* (of fabric) able to keep

out slight rain. —*v.* to make showerproof.

showery *adj.* (of weather) with many showers.

showing *n.* the evidence or quality that a person shows, *on today's showing, he will fail.*

showman *n.* (*pl.* showmen) **1.** an organizer of circuses or similar entertainments. **2.** a person who is good at showmanship.

showmanship *n.* skill in presenting an entertainment or goods or one's abilities to the best advantage.

shown *see* show.

showy *adj.* (showier, showiest) **1.** making a good display. **2.** brilliant, gaudy. **showily** *adv.*

shrank *see* shrink.

shrapnel *n.* **1.** an artillery shell containing bullets or pieces of metal which it scatters as it explodes. **2.** the pieces it scatters.

shred *n.* **1.** a small piece torn or cut from something. **2.** a small amount, *not a shred of evidence.* —*v.* (shredded, shredding) to tear or cut into shreds. —**shredder** *n.*

shrew *n.* **1.** a small mouse-like animal. **2.** a sharp-tempered scolding woman.

shrewd *adj.* having or showing sound judgement and common sense, clever. **shrewdly** *adv.*, **shrewdness** *n.*

shrewish *adj.* sharp-tempered and scolding.

shriek *n.* a shrill cry or scream. —*v.* to make a shriek, to utter with a shriek.

shrift *n.* **short shrift**, *see* short.

shrike *n.* a bird with a strong hooked beak that impales its prey (small birds and insects) on thorns.

shrill *adj.* piercing and high-pitched in sound. —*v.* to sound or utter shrilly. **shrilly** *adv.*, **shrillness** *n.*

shrimp *n.* **1.** a small shellfish often used as food, pink when boiled. **2.** (*informal*) a very small person.

shrimping *n.* fishing for shrimps.

shrine *n.* an altar or chapel or other place that is hallowed because of its special associations.

shrink *v.* (shrank, shrunk, shrinking) **1.** to make or become smaller, especially by the action of moisture or heat or cold, *it shrank*; *it has shrunk.* **2.** to draw back so as to avoid something, to withdraw, to be unwilling to do something (e.g. because of shame or dislike). —*n.* (*slang*, short for *head shrinker*) a psychiatrist. □ **shrink fit**, an extremely tight fit formed by shrinking one metal part round another. **shrink-wrap** *v.* to wrap (an article) in material that shrinks tightly round it.

shrinkage *n.* the process of shrinking, the

amount by which something has shrunk.

shrive v. (shrove, shriven) (old use) to hear the confession of and give absolution to (a penitent).

shrivel v. (shrivelled, shrivelling) 1. to shrink and wrinkle from great heat or cold or lack of moisture. 2. to cause to shrivel.

shriven see shrive.

Shropshire a county of England.

shroud n. 1. a sheet in which a dead body is wrapped for burial, a garment for the dead. 2. something that conceals, *wrapped in a shroud of secrecy*. 3. one of a set of ropes supporting the mast of a ship. — **shroud** v. 1. to wrap in a shroud. 2. to protect or conceal in wrappings. 3. to conceal, *his past life is shrouded in mystery*.

shrove see shrive. **Shrove Tuesday**, the day before Ash Wednesday, on which and the two preceding days **(Shrovetide)** it was formerly customary to be shriven.

shrub n. a woody plant smaller than a tree and usually divided into separate stems from near the ground. **shrubby** adj.

shrubbery n. an area planted with shrubs.

shrug v. (shrugged, shrugging) to raise (the shoulders) as a gesture of indifference or doubt or helplessness. —n. this movement. □ **shrug off**, to dismiss (a thing) as unimportant.

shrunk see shrink.

shrunken adj. having shrunk.

shudder v. 1. to shiver violently with horror or fear or cold. 2. to make a strong shaking movement.—n. a shuddering movement.

shuffle v. 1. to walk without lifting the feet clear of the ground, to move (one's feet) in this way. 2. to slide (cards) over one another so as to change their order. 3. to rearrange, to jumble. 4. to keep shifting one's position. 5. to get rid of (a burden etc.) shiftily, *shuffled off the responsibility on to others; shuffled out of it.* —**shuffle** n. 1. a shuffling movement or walk. 2. shuffling of cards etc. 3. a rearrangement, *the latest Cabinet shuffle.* **shuffler** n.

shuffleboard = shovelboard.

shun v. (shunned, shunning) to avoid, to keep away from.

'shun int. stand to attention.

shunt v. 1. to move (a train) on to a side track. 2. to divert into an alternative course. —**shunt** n. 1. shunting, being shunted. 2. (slang) a collision in which a vehicle knocks the back of the one in front of it, *a rear-end shunt.* —**shunter** n.

shush int. & v. (informal) = hush.

shut v. (shut, shutting) 1. to move (a door or lid or window etc.) into position so that

it blocks an opening. 2. to move or be moved into such a position, *the lid shuts automatically*. 3. to prevent access to (a place or receptacle etc.) by shutting a door etc.; *shut one's eyes* or *ears* or *mind to a thing*, to refuse to take notice of it or hear it. 4. to bring or fold the parts of (a thing) together, *shut the book*. 5. to keep in or out by shutting a door etc., *shut out the noise*. 6. to trap (a finger or dress etc.) by shutting something on it. —adj. (slang) rid, *glad to be shut of it.* □ **shut a person's mouth**, (slang) to prevent him from revealing something. **shut down**, to cease working or business, either for the day or permanently; to cause to do this. **shut-down** n. this process. **shut-eye** n. (slang) sleep. **shut off**, to stop the flow of (water or gas etc.) by shutting a valve. **shut up**, to shut securely; to shut all the doors and windows of (a house); to put away in a box etc.; (informal) to stop talking or making a noise, to cause to do this, to silence; *shut up shop*, = shut down. **shut your mouth**, (slang) be silent.

shutter n. 1. a panel or screen that can be closed over a window. 2. a device that opens and closes the aperture of a camera lens to allow light to fall on the film. **shuttered** adj. fitted with shutters; with the shutters closed.

shuttle n. 1. a holder carrying the weft-thread to and fro across the loom in weaving. 2. a holder carrying the lower thread in a sewing-machine. 3. a vehicle used in a shuttle service. 4. a shuttlecock. —v. to move or travel or send to and fro. □ **shuttle diplomacy**, diplomacy that involves travelling between the countries involved in a dispute. **shuttle service**, a transport service in which a vehicle goes to and fro over a relatively short distance.

shuttlecock n. 1. a small rounded piece of cork with a ring of feathers, or of other material made in this shape, struck to and fro in badminton. 2. something that is passed repeatedly to and fro.

shy[1] adj. (shyer, shyest) 1. (of a person) timid and lacking self-confidence in the presence of others, avoiding company, reserved. 2. (of behaviour) showing shyness, *a shy smile*. 3. (of an animal) timid and avoiding observation. —v. (shied, shying) to jump or move suddenly in alarm, *the horse shied at the noise*. —**shyly** adv., **shyness** n.

shy[2] v. (shied, shying) to fling or throw (a stone etc.). —n. a throw.

SI abbrev. Système International. (¶ French, = International System of Units.)

Siamese adj. of Siam (now called Thailand) or its people or language. —*n.* (*pl.* Siamese) **1.** a native of Siam. **2.** the language of Siam. **3.** a Siamese cat. □ **Siamese cat**, a cat of a breed that has short pale fur with darker face, ears, tail, and feet. **Siamese twins**, twins whose bodies are joined in some way at birth.

Siberian *adj.* of Siberia, a northern region of the USSR.

sibilant *adj.* having a hissing sound. —*n.* one of the speech-sounds that sound like hissing, e.g. *s, sh.* —**sibilance** *n.*

sibling *n.* a child in relation to another or others of the same parent, a brother or sister.

sic (*pr.* seek) *adv.* used or spelt in that way. (Latin, = thus). ¶ This word is placed in brackets after a word that seems odd or is wrongly spelt, to show that one is quoting it exactly as it was given.

Sicilian *adj.* of Sicily. —*n.* a native or inhabitant of Sicily.

sick *adj.* **1.** physically or mentally unwell. **2.** likely to vomit, *feel sick.* **3.** distressed or disgusted, *sick at heart; their ignorance makes me sick.* **4.** bored with something through having already had or done too much of it, *I'm sick of cricket.* **5.** finding amusement in misfortune or in morbid subjects, *sick jokes.* —*v.* (*slang*) to vomit, *sicked it up.* —*n.* (*informal*) vomit. □ **be sick**, to vomit. **sick-bay** *n.* a room or rooms for sick people in a ship or boarding-school etc. **sick-bed** *n.* the bed of a sick person. **sick-leave** *n.* leave of absence because of illness. **sick-list** *n.* a list of people who are ill, especially in a regiment; *on the sick-list*, ill. **sick-pay** *n.* pay given to an employee who is absent through illness. **sick-room** *n.* a room occupied by a sick person, or kept ready for this.

sicken *v.* **1.** to begin to be ill; *be sickening for a disease*, showing the first signs of it. **2.** to make or become distressed or disgusted.

sickening *adj.* annoying, disgusting.

sickle *n.* **1.** a tool with a curved blade and a short handle, used for cutting corn etc. **2.** something shaped like this, e.g. the crescent moon.

sickly *adj.* (sicklier, sickliest) **1.** often ill, *a sickly child.* **2.** unhealthy-looking. **3.** causing ill health, *a sickly climate.* **4.** causing sickness or distaste, *sickly smell; sickly sentimentality.* **5.** weak, *sickly smile.*

sickness *n.* **1.** illness. **2.** a disease. **3.** vomiting.

side *n.* **1.** one of the more or less flat inner or outer surfaces of an object, especially as distinct from the top and bottom, front and back, or ends. **2.** either surface of a flat object (e.g. a piece of paper). **3.** any of

the bounding lines of a plane figure such as a triangle or square. **4.** either of the two halves into which an object or body can be divided by a line down its centre. **5.** the part near the edge and away from the centre of something; *take* or *put on one side,* aside. **6.** a slope of a hill or ridge. **7.** the region next to a person or thing, *stood at my side.* **8.** one aspect or view of something, *study all sides of the problem; she is on the fat side,* rather fat. **9.** one of two opposing groups or teams etc. **10.** the line of descent through father or mother, *his mother's side of the family.* **11.** (*slang*) swank, *puts on side.* —*adj.* at or on the side, *side door.* —*v.* to take the side of a person in a dispute, *sided with his son.* □ **on the side**, as a sideline; as a surreptitious or illicit activity. **side by side**, standing close together. **side-car** *n.* a small vehicle attached to the side of a motor cycle, to seat a passenger. **side-drum** *n.* a small double-headed drum. **side-effect** *n.* a secondary (usually less desirable) effect. **side-issue** *n.* an issue that is not the main one. **side-road** *n.* a road leading off a main road; a minor road. **side-saddle** *n.* a saddle for a woman rider to sit on with both legs on the same side of the horse, not astride, (*adv.*) sitting in this way. **side-show** *n.* a small show forming part of a large one (e.g. at a fair). **side-step** *v.* to avoid by stepping sideways; to evade (a question or responsibility etc.). **side-street** *n.* a street lying aside from main ones. **side-stroke** *n.* a stroke towards or from a side; a swimming stroke in which the swimmer lies on his side. **side-table** *n.* a table at the side of a room or apart from the main table. **side-track** *v.* to divert from the main course or issue. **side-view** *n.* a view of something sideways. **side-whiskers** *pl. n.* whiskers on the cheek. **side wind**, a wind from one side (not front or back).

sideboard *n.* a table or flat-topped piece of dining-room furniture with drawers and cupboards for china etc. **sideboards** *pl. n.* (*slang*) side-whiskers.

sideburns *pl. n.* short side-whiskers.

sidekick *n.* (*Amer. informal*) a close associate.

sidelight *n.* **1.** light from one side (not front or back). **2.** minor or casual light shed on a subject etc. **3.** one of a pair of small lights at the front of a vehicle. **4.** a light at either side of a ship under way.

sideline *n.* something done in addition to one's main work or activity. **sidelines** *pl. n.* the lines bounding a football pitch etc. at its sides; the space just outside these; a place for spectators as distinct from participants.

sidelong *adv. & adj.* to one side, sideways, *a sidelong glance.*

sidereal (sy-**deer**-iăl) *adj.* of or measured by the stars.

sidesman *n.* (*pl.* sidesmen) an assistant churchwarden.

sidewalk *n.* (*Amer.*) a pavement at the side of a road.

sideways *adv. & adj.* **1.** to or from one side (not forwards or back). **2.** with one side facing forwards, *sat sideways.*

siding *n.* a short track by the side of a railway, used for shunting.

sidle (*rhymes with* bridle) *v.* to advance in a timid or furtive or cringing manner, to edge.

siege *n.* the surrounding and blockading of a town or fortified place, in order to capture it, or of a house etc. that is occupied by persons using force or threats. **lay siege to**, to begin besieging. **raise the siege**, *see* raise.

sienna (si-en-ă) *n.* a kind of clay used as colouring-matter. **burnt sienna**, reddish-brown. **raw sienna**, brownish-yellow.

sierra (si-e-ră) *n.* a long chain of mountains with sharp slopes and an irregular outline, in Spain or Spanish America.

Sierra Leone (si-e-ră li-**ohn**) a country in West Africa. **Sierra Leonean** *adj. & n.*

siesta (si-est-ă) *n.* an afternoon nap or rest, especially in hot countries.

sieve (*pr.* siv) *n.* a utensil consisting of a frame with wire mesh or gauze, used for sorting solid or coarse matter (which is retained in it) from liquid or fine matter (which passes through), or for reducing a soft mixture squeezed through it to a uniform pulp. —*v.* to put through a sieve.

sift *v.* **1.** to sieve. **2.** to sprinkle lightly from a perforated container. **3.** to examine carefully and select or analyse. **4.** (of snow or light) to fall as if from a sieve. —**sifter** *n.*

sigh *n.* a long deep breath given out audibly, expressing sadness, tiredness, relief, etc. —*v.* **1.** to give a sigh, to express with a sigh. **2.** (of wind etc.) to make a similar sound. **3.** to yearn.

sight *n.* **1.** the faculty of seeing, ability to see. **2.** seeing or being seen, *lost sight of it.* **3.** the range over which a person can see or an object can be seen, *within sight of the castle.* **4.** a thing seen or visible or worth seeing, a display, *our tulips are a wonderful sight this year.* **5.** something regarded as unsightly or looking ridiculous, *she looks a sight in those clothes.* **6.** (*informal*) a great quantity, *it cost a sight of money*; *a darned sight better.* **7.** a device looked

through to help aim or observe with a gun or telescope etc., aim or observation using this; *set one's sights on*, aim at. —**sight** *v.* **1.** to get a sight of, to observe the presence of, *we sighted land.* **2.** to aim or observe by using the sight in a gun or telescope etc. □ **at** *or* **on sight**, as soon as a person or thing has been seen; *she plays music at sight*, without preliminary practice or study of the score. **in sight**, visible; clearly near at hand, *victory was in sight.* **lower one's sights**, to adopt a less ambitious policy. **sight-reading** *n.* playing or singing music at sight. **sight-screen** *n.* a large movable white structure placed in line with the wicket to help the batsman see the ball in cricket. **sight unseen**, without previous inspection.

sightless *adj.* blind.

sightseeing *n.* visiting places of interest in a town etc. **sightseer** *n.* one who does this.

sign *n.* **1.** something perceived that suggests the existence of a fact or quality or condition, either past or present or future, *it shows signs of decay* or *of being a success.* **2.** a mark or device with a special meaning, a symbol. **3.** a signboard or other visible object used similarly, the device on this, a notice. **4.** an action or gesture conveying information or a command etc. **5.** any of the twelve divisions of the zodiac (*see* zodiac), a symbol representing one of these. —**sign** *v.* **1.** to make a sign, *signed to me to come.* **2.** to write (one's name) on a document etc. to guarantee that it is genuine or has one's authority or consent, or to acknowledge receipt of something, *signed his name*; *signed the letter*; *sign here.* **3.** to convey by signing a document, *signed away her right to the house.* **4.** to engage or be engaged as an employee by signing a contract of employment. □ **sign off**, (in broadcasting) to announce the end of one's programme or transmission. **sign on** *or* **up**, to sign a contract of employment; to register oneself (e.g. at an employment exchange).

signal *n.* **1.** a sign or gesture giving information or a command, a message made up of such signs. **2.** an act or event that immediately produces a general reaction, *his arrival was the signal for an outburst of cheering.* **3.** an object placed to give notice or warning, *traffic signals*; *railway signals.* **4.** a sequence of electrical impulses or radio waves transmitted or received. —*v.* (signalled, signalling) to make a signal or signals, to direct or communicate with or announce in this way. (¶ This word is sometimes used in mistake for *single* in the phrase *to single out.*) —*adj.* remarkably good or bad, *a signal success.* —**signaller**

n., **signally** *adv.* □ **signal-box**, a small railway building with signalling apparatus.

signalize *v.* to make noteworthy.

signalman *n.* (*pl.* signalmen) one who is responsible for displaying naval signals or operating railway signals.

signatory (sig-nă-ter-i) *n.* any of the parties who sign a treaty or other agreement.

signature *n.* 1. a person's name or initials written by himself in signing something. 2. a key signature or time signature in music. 3. a section of a book made from one sheet folded and cut, often marked with a letter or figure as a guide to the binder. □ **key signature**, the sharps or flats after the clef in a musical score, showing its key. **signature tune**, a special tune used to announce a particular programme or performer. **time signature**, a fraction (e.g. $\frac{3}{4}$) printed at the beginning of a piece of music, showing the number of beats in the bar and their rhythm.

signboard *n.* a board bearing the name or device of a shop or inn etc. and displayed in front of it.

signet (sig-nit) *n.* a person's seal used with or instead of a signature. **signet-ring** *n.* a finger-ring with an engraved design, formerly used as a seal.

significance *n.* 1. what is meant by something, *what is the significance of this symbol?* 2. being significant, importance, *the event is of no significance.*

significant *adj.* 1. having a meaning. 2. full of meaning, *a significant glance.* 3. important, noteworthy, *significant developments.* **significantly** *adv.*

signification *n.* meaning.

signify *v.* (signified, signifying) 1. to be a sign or symbol of. 2. to have as a meaning. 3. to make known, *signified her approval.* 4. to be of importance, to matter, *it doesn't signify.*

signor (seen-yor) *n.* the title of an Italian man, = Mr or sir.

signora (seen-yor-ä) *n.* the title of an Italian woman, = Mrs or madam.

signorina (seen-yor-een-ä) *n.* the title of an Italian unmarried woman or girl, = Miss or madam.

signpost *n.* a post at a road junction etc. with arms showing the names of places along each of the roads to which these point. —*v.* to provide with a post or posts of this kind.

Sikh (*pr.* seek) *n.* a member of a certain Indian religious sect. **Sikhism** *n.*

silage (sy-lij) *n.* green fodder stored and fermented in a silo.

silence *n.* 1. absence of sound. 2. avoidance or absence of speaking or of making a sound. 3. the fact of not mentioning something or of refusing to betray a secret. —*v.* to make silent. □ **in silence**, without speaking or making a sound.

silencer *n.* a device for reducing the sound made by a gun or a vehicle's exhaust etc.

silent *adj.* 1. not speaking, not making or accompanied by a sound. 2. saying little. **silently** *adv.* □ **silent majority**, people of moderate opinions who rarely make themselves heard.

silhouette (sil-oo-et) *n.* 1. a dark shadow or outline seen against a light background. 2. a profile portrait in solid black. —*v.* to show as a silhouette, *she was silhouetted against the screen.*

silica (sil-i-kă) *n.* a compound of silicon occurring as quartz or flint and in sandstone and other rocks.

silicate (sil-i-kayt) *n.* any of the insoluble compounds of silica.

silicon (sil-i-kŏn) *n.* a chemical substance found widely in the earth's crust in its compound forms. **silicon chip**, a microchip made of silicon.

silicone (sil-i-kohn) *n.* any of the organic compounds of silicon, widely used in paints, varnish, and lubricants.

silicosis (sil-i-koh-sis) *n.* an abnormal condition of the lungs caused by inhaling dust that contains silica.

silk *n.* 1. the fine strong soft fibre produced by a silkworm in making its cocoon, or by certain other insects or spiders. 2. thread or cloth made from it, fabric resembling this. 3. clothing made from silk. 4. (*informal*) a Queen's Counsel, entitled to wear a silk gown; *take silk*, to become a Queen's Counsel. 5. fine soft strands like threads of silk. **silken** *adj.* like silk.

silkworm *n.* a caterpillar (of a kind of moth) which feeds on mulberry leaves and spins its cocoon of silk.

silky *adj.* (silkier, silkiest) as soft or fine or smooth as silk. **silkily** *adv.*, **silkiness** *n.*

sill *n.* a strip of stone or wood or metal at the base of a window or door.

silly *adj.* (sillier, silliest) 1. lacking good sense, foolish, unwise. 2. feeble-minded. 3. (of a fieldsman's position in cricket) close to the batsman, *silly mid-on.* —*n.* (*informal*) a foolish person. —**silliness** *n.* □ **silly-billy** *n.* (*informal*) a foolish person.

silo (sy-loh) *n.* (*pl.* silos) 1. a pit or airtight structure in which green crops are pressed and undergo fermentation for use as fodder. 2. a pit or tower for storing grain or cement or radioactive waste. 3. an underground place where a missile is kept ready for firing.

silt *n.* sediment deposited by water in a channel or harbour etc. —*v.* to block or clog or become blocked with silt, *the harbour is* or *has silted up.*

silver *n.* **1.** a shiny white precious metal. **2.** coins made of this or of an alloy resembling it. **3.** silver dishes or ornaments, household cutlery of any metal. **4.** a silver medal (awarded as second prize). **5.** the colour of silver. —*adj.* made of silver, coloured like silver. —**silver** *v.* **1.** to coat or plate with silver. **2.** to give a silvery appearance to, to become silvery, (of hair) to turn grey or white. □ **born with a silver spoon in one's mouth**, destined to be wealthy. **silver birch**, a birch tree with silver-coloured bark. **silver-fish** *n.* a silver-coloured fish; a small insect with a fish-like body found in books and damp places. **silver fox**, a fox with black fur tipped with white; its fur. **silver gilt**, gilded silver; imitation gilding of yellow lacquer over silver leaf. **silver-grey** *adj.* & *n.* very pale grey. **silver jubilee**, the 25th anniversary of a sovereign's accession or other event. **silver lining**, a consolation or hopeful prospect in the midst of misfortune. **silver paper**, tin foil. **silver-plated** *adj.* coated with silver. **silver sand**, very fine sand used in gardening. **silver wedding**, the 25th anniversary of a wedding.

silverside *n.* a joint of beef cut from the haunch, below topside.

silversmith *n.* a person whose trade is making articles in silver.

silverware *n.* articles made of silver.

silvery *adj.* **1.** like silver in colour or appearance. **2.** having a clear gentle ringing sound.

simian (sim-iăn) *adj.* monkey-like.

similar *adj.* **1.** like, alike, resembling something but not the same. **2.** of the same kind or nature or amount. **similarly** *adv.*, **similarity** (sim-i-**la**-riti) *n.*

simile (sim-i-li) *n.* a figure of speech in which one thing is compared to another, e.g. *he's as fit as a fiddle; went through it like a hot knife through butter.*

similitude (sim-**il**-i-tewd) *n.* similarity.

simmer *v.* **1.** to keep (a pan or its contents) almost at boiling point, to be kept like this, to boil very gently. **2.** to be in a state of excitement or anger or laughter which is only just kept under control. □ **simmer down**, to become less excited or agitated.

simnel cake a rich cake (especially for Mothering Sunday or Easter), covered with marzipan and decorated.

simper *v.* to smile in an affected way. —*n.* an affected smile.

simple *adj.* **1.** of one element or kind, not compound or complex. **2.** not complicated or elaborate, not showy or luxurious. **3.** foolish, inexperienced. **4.** feeble-minded. **5.** of humble rank, *simple ordinary people.* —**simply** *adv.* □ **simple interest**, interest paid only on the original capital, not on the interest added to it. **simple-minded** *adj.* unsophisticated; without cunning; feeble-minded.

simpleton *n.* a foolish or easily-deceived person, a half-wit.

simplicity *n.* being simple. **be simplicity itself**, to be very easy.

simplify *v.* (simplified, simplifying) to make simple, to make easy to do or understand. **simplification** *n.*

simulate (**sim**-yoo-layt) *v.* **1.** to reproduce the conditions of (a situation), e.g. by means of a model, for study or testing or training etc. **2.** to pretend to have or feel, *they simulated indignation.* **3.** to imitate the form or condition of. —**simulation** *n.*, **simulator** *n.* □ **simulated** *adj.* (of furs or pearls etc.) manufactured to look like natural products.

simultaneous (sim-ŭl-**tayn**-iŭs) *adj.* occurring or operating at the same time. **simultaneously** *adv.*, **simultaneity** (simul-tăn-ee-iti) *n.*

sin *n.* **1.** the breaking of a religious or moral law, an act which does this. **2.** a serious fault or offence. **3.** something contrary to common sense, *it's a sin to stay indoors on this fine day.* —*v.* (sinned, sinning) to commit a sin. □ **for my sins**, (*humorous*) as a penalty for something or other that I have done. **live in sin**, (*informal*) to cohabit without marrying.

since *adv.*, *prep.*, & *conj.* **1.** after (a certain event or past time), between then and now. **2.** ago, before now, *it happened long since.* **3.** for the reason that, because, *since we have no money, we can't buy it.*

sincere *adj.* free from pretence or deceit in feeling or manner or actions. **sincerely** *adv.*, **sincerity** (sin-se-ri-ti) *n.* □ **Yours sincerely**, *see* yours.

sine (*rhymes with* mine) *n.* (in a right-angled triangle) the ratio of the length of a side opposite one of the acute angles to the length of the hypotenuse.

sinecure (**sy**-ni-kewr) *n.* an official position that gives the holder profit or honour with no work attached.

sine die (sy-ni **dy**-i) indefinitely, with no appointed date, *the business was adjourned sine die.* (¶ Latin, = without a day.)

sine qua non (sy-ni kway **non** *or* sin-i kwah **nohn**) an indispensable condition or qualification. (¶ Latin, = without which not.)

sinew (**sin**-yoo) *n.* **1.** tough fibrous tissue uniting muscle to bone. **2.** a tendon. ☐ **sinews** *pl. n.* muscles, strength. **sinewy** *adj.* like sinew; muscular.

sinful *adj.* full of sin, wicked. **sinfully** *adv.*, **sinfulness** *n.*

sing *v.* (sang, sung, singing) **1.** to make musical sounds with the voice, especially in a set tune. **2.** to perform (a song). **3.** to make a humming or buzzing or whistling sound, *the kettle sings.* **4.** (*slang*) to turn informer. ☐ **sing a person's praises**, to praise him greatly. **sing out**, to call out loudly. **sing small**, to adopt a humbler tone.

Singapore an island forming (with others) a country south of the Malay peninsula.

singe (*pr.* sinj) *v.* (singed, singeing) to burn slightly, to burn the ends or edges of. —*n.* a slight burn.

singer *n.* a person who sings, especially as a professional.

single *adj.* **1.** one only, not double or multiple. **2.** designed for one person or thing, *single beds.* **3.** taken separately, *every single thing.* **4.** unmarried. **5.** (of a ticket) valid for an outward journey only, not to return. **6.** (of a flower) having only one circle of petals. —**single** *n.* **1.** one person or thing, a single one. **2.** a room etc. for one person. **3.** a single ticket. **4.** a pop record with one piece of music on each side. **5.** a hit for one run in cricket. —*v.* to choose or distinguish from others, *singled him out.* —**singly** *adv.* ☐ **single-breasted** *adj.* (of a coat) fastening but not overlapping widely across the breast. **single combat**, a duel. **single-decker** *n.* a bus with only one deck. **single figures**, any number from 1 to 9 inclusive. **single file**, *see* file². **single-handed** *adj.* without help from others. **single-minded** *adj.* with one's mind set on a single purpose. **single parent**, a person bringing up children without a marital partner. **singles** *pl. n.* a game with one player on each side.

singlet *n.* a man's garment worn under or instead of a shirt, a vest.

singleton (**sing**-ĕl-tŏn) *n.* something occurring singly, not as one of a group.

singsong *adj.* with a monotonous rise and fall of the voice in speaking. —*n.* **1.** a singsong manner of speaking. **2.** an informal singing of well-known songs by a group of people.

singular *n.* the form of a noun or verb used with reference to one person or thing, *the singular is 'man', the plural is 'men'.* —

adj. **1.** of this form. **2.** uncommon, extraordinary, *spoke with singular shrewdness.* —**singularly** *adv.*, **singularity** (sing-yoo-la-riti) *n.*

singularize *v.* to make different from others.

Sinhalese (sing-hă-**leez**) *adj.* of Sri Lanka or its people or language. —*n.* (*pl.* Sinhalese) **1.** a Sinhalese person. **2.** the Sinhalese language.

sinister *adj.* **1.** suggestive of evil. **2.** involving wickedness, criminal, *sinister motives.*

sink *v.* (sank, sunk, sinking) **1.** to fall slowly downwards, to come gradually to a lower level or pitch. **2.** to become wholly or partly submerged in water etc., (of a ship) to go to the bottom of the sea. **3.** to pass into a less active condition, *she sank into sleep.* **4.** to lose value or strength etc. gradually. **5.** to cause or allow to sink; *must sink our differences,* disregard them. **6.** to dig (a well) or bore (a shaft). **7.** to engrave (a die). **8.** to send (a ball) into a pocket or hole in billiards, golf, etc. **9.** to invest (money). —**sink** *n.* **1.** a fixed basin with a drainage pipe and usually with a water supply, in a kitchen etc. **2.** a cesspool; *a sink of iniquity,* a place where evil people or practices tend to collect. ☐ **sink in**, to penetrate; to become understood. **sinking feeling**, a feeling caused by hunger or fear. **sinking-fund** *n.* a fund set aside for the purpose of wiping out a country's or business company's debt gradually.

sinker *n.* a weight used to sink a fishing-line or a line used in taking soundings.

sinless *adj.* free from sin.

sinner *n.* a person who sins.

Sinn Fein (shin-**fayn**) a nationalist political party in Ireland.

sinuous (**sin**-yoo-ŭs) *adj.* with many curves, undulating. **sinuously** *adv.*

sinus (**sy**-nŭs) *n.* (*pl.* sinuses) a cavity in bone or tissue, especially that in the skull connecting with the nostrils. **sinusitis** (sy-nŭs-I-tiss) *n.* inflammation of this.

sip *v.* (sipped, sipping) to take a sip, to drink in small mouthfuls. —*n.* **1.** the act of sipping. **2.** a small mouthful of liquid.

siphon (**sy**-fŏn) *n.* **1.** a pipe or tube in the form of an upside-down U, used for forcing liquid to flow from one container to another by utilizing atmospheric pressure. **2.** a bottle from which aerated water is forced out through a tube by pressure of gas. **3.** the sucking-tube of some insects or small animals. —**siphon** *v.* **1.** to flow or draw out through a siphon. **2.** to take from a source, *funds were siphoned off for this purpose.*

sir *n*. **1**. a polite form of address to a man. **2**. *Sir*, a title prefixed to the name of a knight or baronet, *Sir John Moore, Sir J. Moore, Sir John.* —*v*. to address as sir, *don't sir me.*

sire *n*. **1**. (*old use*) a father or male ancestor. **2**. (*old use*) a title of respect, used to a king. **3**. the male parent of an animal. —*v*. (of an animal) to be the sire of, to beget.

siren *n*. **1**. a device that makes a loud prolonged sound as a signal. **2**. a dangerously fascinating woman. ¶ Named after the *Sirens* in Greek legend, women who lived on an island and by their singing lured seafarers to destruction on the rocks surrounding it.

sirloin *n*. the upper (best) part of loin of beef.

sirocco (si-**rok**-oh) *n*. (*pl*. siroccos) a hot wind that reaches Italy from Africa.

sisal (**sy**-săl) *n*. **1**. rope-fibre made from the leaves of a tropical plant. **2**. the plant itself.

siskin *n*. a greenish song-bird related to the goldfinch.

sissy *n*. an effeminate boy or man, a cowardly person.

sister *n*. **1**. a daughter of the same parents as another person. **2**. a fellow woman, one who is a fellow member of a group or sect. **3**. a nun; *Sister*, the title of a nun. **4**. a female hospital nurse in authority over others. **sisterly** *adj*. □ **sister-in-law** *n*. (*pl*. sisters-in-law) the sister of one's husband or wife, the wife of one's brother. **sister ship**, a ship built in the same design as another.

sisterhood *n*. **1**. the relationship of sisters. **2**. an order of nuns, a society of women doing religious or charitable work.

sit *v*. (sat, sitting) **1**. to take or be in a position in which the body rests more or less upright on the buttocks, *we were sitting* (¶ not *we were sat*) *gossiping*; *sit one's horse*, to sit or keep one's seat on it. **2**. to cause to sit, to place in a sitting position, *sat him down*. **3**. to pose for a portrait. **4**. (of birds) to perch, (of certain animals) to rest with legs bent and body along the ground. **5**. (of birds) to remain on the nest to hatch eggs. **6**. to be situated, to lie. **7**. to be a candidate for, *sit an examination*; *sit for a scholarship*. **8**. to occupy a seat as a member of a committee etc. **9**. (of Parliament or a lawcourt or committee) to be in session. **10**. (of clothes) to fit in a certain way, *the coat sits badly on the shoulders*. □ **be sitting pretty**, to be in an advantageous situation. **sit at a person's feet**, to be his pupil or disciple. **sit back**, to relax one's efforts. **sit down**, to take a seat after

standing. **sit-down** *adj*. (of a meal) taken seated; *sit-down strike*, in which strikers refuse to leave their place of work. **sit down under**, to submit tamely to (an insult etc.). **sit-in** *n*. occupation of a building etc. as a form of protest. **sit in judgement**, to make judgements about other people. **sit in on**, to be present as an observer at (a meeting etc.). **sit on**, (*informal*) to delay action concerning, *the Government has been sitting on the report*; (*slang*) to repress or snub, *he wants sitting on*. **sit on on the fence**, to avoid taking sides in a dispute. **sit out**, to take no part in (a dance etc.); to stay till the end of, *had to sit the concert out*. **sit tight**, (*informal*) to remain firmly where one is, to take no action and not yield. **sit up**, to rise to a sitting posture from lying down; to sit upright and not slouch; to remain out of bed, *sat up late*; *make a person sit up*, to cause him surprise or alarm, to arouse his interest.

sitar (**sit**-ar *or* si-**tar**) *n*. an Indian musical instrument resembling a guitar.

sitcom *n*. (*informal*) a situation comedy.

site *n*. **1**. the ground on which a town or building stood or stands or is to stand. **2**. the place where some activity or event takes place or took place, *camping site*; *the site of the battle*. —*v*. to locate, to provide with a site.

sitter *n*. **1**. a person who is seated. **2**. one who is sitting for a portrait. **3**. a sitting hen. **4**. (also *sitter-in*) a baby-sitter. **5**. (*slang*) an easy catch or shot, something easy to do.

sitting *see* sit. —*adj*. (of an animal) not running, (of a game-bird) not flying, *shot a sitting pheasant*. —*n*. **1**. the time during which a person or assembly etc. sits continuously, *an all-night sitting of Parliament*; *lunch is served in two sittings*. **2**. a clutch of eggs. □ **sitting duck** *or* **target**, a person or thing that is a helpless victim of attack. **sitting-room** *n*. a room used for sitting in, not a bedroom. **sitting tenant**, one already in occupation of rented accommodation etc.

situate *v*. to place or put in a certain position. **be situated**, to be in a certain position.

situation *n*. **1**. a place (with its surroundings) that is occupied by something. **2**. a set of circumstances. (¶ It is bad style to use this word in phrases such as 'when there is a strike situation' instead of 'when there is a strike'.) **3**. a position of employment. □ **save the situation**, to prevent a disaster. **situation comedy**, a comedy in which humour derives from characters' misunderstandings and embarrassments.

six *adj*. & *n*. one more than five (6, VI).

□ **at sixes and sevens,** in disorder. **hit** *or* **knock a person for six,** to surprise or defeat him utterly. **six-footer** *n.* a person or thing 6 ft. tall.

sixer *n.* the leader of a group of six Brownies or Cub Scouts.

sixpence *n.* **1.** the sum of 6p. **2.** (*old use*) the sum of 6d, a coin worth this. □ **sixpenny** *adj.* costing sixpence.

sixteen *adj. & n.* one more than fifteen (16, XVI). **sixteenth** *adj. & n.*

sixth *adj. & n.* **1.** next after fifth. **2.** one of six equal parts of a thing. **sixthly** *adv.* □ **sixth form,** a form for pupils aged 16–18 in a secondary school. **sixth sense,** a supposed extra power of perception other than the five physical ones, intuition.

sixty *adj. & n.* six times ten (60, LX). **sixtieth** *adj. & n.* □ **sixties** *pl. n.* the numbers or years or degrees of temperature from 60 to 69.

size[1] *n.* **1.** the measurements or extent of something. **2.** any of the series of standard measurements in which things of the same kind are made and sold. —*v.* to group or sort according to size. □ **size up,** to estimate the size of; (*informal*) to form a judgement of (a person or situation etc.). **the size of it,** (*informal*) the way it is, the facts about it.

size[2] *n.* a gluey solution used to glaze paper or stiffen textiles etc. —*v.* to treat with size.

sizeable *adj.* of large or fairly large size.

sizzle *v.* **1.** to make a hissing sound like that of frying. **2.** (*informal*) to be very hot, to be angry or resentful.

SJ *abbrev.* Society of Jesus.

skate[1] *n.* (*pl.* skate) a large flat-fish used as food.

skate[2] *n.* one of a pair of blades or sets of four wheels (*roller-skates*) attached to the soles of boots or shoes so that the wearer can glide over ice or a hard surface. —*v.* to move on skates, to perform (a specified figure) in this way. —**skater** *n.* □ **get one's skates on,** (*slang*) to make haste. **skate over a subject,** to make only a passing reference to it. **skating-rink** *n.* a stretch of natural or artificial ice used for skating; a smooth floor used for roller-skating.

skateboard *n.* a small board with wheels like those of roller-skates, for riding on (as a sport) while standing. **skateboarding** *n.,* **skateboarder** *n.*

skedaddle *v.* (*slang*) to go away quickly.

skein (*pr.* skayn) *n.* **1.** a loosely-coiled bundle of yarn or thread. **2.** a number of wild geese etc. in flight.

skeletal (skel-i-t'l) *adj.* of or like a skeleton.

skeleton *n.* **1.** the supporting structure of an animal body, consisting of bones. **2.** the shell or other hard structure covering or supporting an invertebrate animal. **3.** a very lean person or animal. **4.** any supporting structure or framework, e.g. of a building. **5.** an outline of a literary work etc. □ **skeleton crew,** a permanent nucleus ready for supplementing. **skeleton in the cupboard,** a discreditable secret. **skeleton key,** a key made so as to fit many locks. **skeleton staff,** the minimum needed to do the essential things in work which normally requires more staff.

skep *n.* **1.** a wooden or wicker basket of various forms. **2.** the amount it contains. **3.** a straw or wicker beehive.

skerry *n.* (*Scottish*) a small island.

sketch *n.* **1.** a rough drawing or painting. **2.** a brief account of something. **3.** a short usually comic play. —*v.* to make a sketch or sketches, to make a sketch of. — **sketcher** *n.* □ **sketch-book** *n.* a pad of drawing-paper for sketching on. **sketch-map** *n.* a roughly-drawn map.

sketchy *adj.* (sketchier, sketchiest) rough and not detailed or careful or substantial. **sketchily** *adv.,* **sketchiness** *n.*

skew *adj.* slanting, askew. —*v.* to make skew, to turn or twist round. □ **on the skew,** askew.

skewbald *adj.* (of an animal) with irregular patches of white and another colour (strictly, not including black; *see* piebald).

skewer *n.* a pin thrust through meat to hold it compactly together while it is cooked. —*v.* to pierce or hold in place with a skewer or other pointed object.

ski (*pr.* skee) *n.* (*pl.* skis) one of a pair of long narrow strips of wood etc. fixed under the feet for travelling over snow. — *v.* (ski'd, skiing) to travel on skis. —**skier** *n.* □ **ski-lift** *n.* a device for carrying skiers up a slope, usually on seats slung from an overhead cable. **ski-run** *n.* a slope suitable for skiing down as a sport.

skid *v.* (skidded, skidding) (of a vehicle or its wheels) to slide uncontrollably on slippery ground. —*n.* **1.** a skidding movement. **2.** a log or plank etc. used to make a track over which heavy objects may be dragged or rolled. **3.** a runner on a helicopter, for use when landing. **4.** a wedge or a wooden or metal shoe that acts as a braking device on the wheel of a cart. □ **put the skids under,** (*slang*) to cause to hurry; to hasten the downfall of. **skid-pan** *n.* a surface specially prepared to cause skids, used for practice in controlling skidding vehicles. **skid row,** (*Amer.*) a slum area where vagrants live.

skiff *n.* a small light boat for rowing or sculling.

skilful *adj.* having or showing great skill. **skilfully** *adv.*

skill *n.* ability to do something well.

skilled *adj.* **1.** skilful. **2.** (of work) needing great skill, (of a worker) highly trained or experienced in such work.

skillet *n.* **1.** a metal cooking-pot with a long handle and usually legs. **2.** (*Amer.*) a frying-pan.

skim *v.* (skimmed, skimming) **1.** to take (floating matter) from the surface of a liquid, to clear (a liquid) in this way. **2.** to move lightly and quickly over a surface, to glide through air. **3.** to read quickly, noting only the chief points, *skim through a newspaper* or *skim it.* —**skimmer** *n.* □ **skim milk**, milk from which cream has been removed. **skim the cream**, to take the best part.

skimp *v.* to supply or use rather less than what is needed, to scrimp.

skimpy *adj.* (skimpier, skimpiest) scanty, especially through being skimped. **skimpily** *adv.*, **skimpiness** *n.*

skin *n.* **1.** the flexible continuous covering of the human or other animal body. **2.** an animal's skin removed from its body, with or without the hair still attached. **3.** material made from this. **4.** a vessel for water or wine, made from an animal's whole skin. **5.** a person's complexion. **6.** an outer layer or covering. **7.** the skin-like film that forms on the surface of certain liquids. —**skin** *v.* (skinned, skinning) **1.** to strip or scrape the skin from. **2.** to cover or become covered with new skin, *the wound had skinned over.* □ **be nothing but skin and bone**, to be very thin. **by the skin of one's teeth**, only just, barely. **get under a person's skin**, (*informal*) to interest or annoy him greatly. **save one's skin**, to avoid injury or loss. **skin-deep** *adj.* superficial. **skin-diver** *n.* one who engages in **skin-diving**, the sport of swimming deep under water with flippers and breathing apparatus. **skin-food** *n.* a cosmetic to nourish the skin. **skin game**, (*Amer. slang*) a swindling game. **skin-tight** *adj.* (of clothing) very close-fitting.

skinflint *n.* a miserly person.

skinful *n.* (*informal*) enough alcohol to make a person very drunk.

skinhead *n.* a youth with close-cropped hair.

skinny *adj.* (skinnier, skinniest) **1.** (of a person or animal) very thin. **2.** miserly.

skint *adj.* (*slang*) having no money left.

skip[1] *v.* (skipped, skipping) **1.** to move along lightly, especially by taking two steps with each foot in turn. **2.** to jump with a skipping-rope. **3.** to pass quickly from one subject or point to another. **4.** to omit in reading or dealing with a thing. **5.** (*slang*) to go away hastily or secretly. —*n.* a skipping movement. □ **skip bail**, to jump bail (*see* jump). **skip it!**, (*slang*) leave that subject. **skipping-rope** *n.* a length of rope, usually with a handle at each end, turned over the head and under the feet as a person jumps in play or exercise.

skip[2] *n.* **1.** a cage or bucket in which men or materials are raised and lowered in mines and quarries. **2.** a large metal container for holding and carrying away builders' rubbish etc.

skip[3] *n.* a skep.

skipper[1] *n.* **1.** one who skips. **2.** a small dark thick-bodied butterfly.

skipper[2] *n.* a captain. —*v.* to captain.

skirl *n.* the shrill sound characteristic of bagpipes. —*v.* to make this sound.

skirmish *n.* a minor fight or conflict. —*v.* to take part in a skirmish.

skirt *n.* **1.** a woman's garment hanging from the waist, this part of a garment. **2.** (*vulgar*) a woman. **3.** the flap of a saddle. **4.** the hanging part round the base of a hovercraft. **5.** a cut of beef from the lower flank. —**skirt** *v.* **1.** to go or be situated along the edge of. **2.** to avoid dealing directly with (a question or controversial topic etc).

skirting *n.* (also *skirting-board*) a narrow board round the wall of a room, close to the floor.

skit *n.* a short play or piece of writing that is a humorous imitation of a serious one, a piece of humorous mimicry.

skittish *adj.* frisky. **skittishly** *adv.*, **skittishness** *n.*

skittle *n.* one of the wooden pins set up to be bowled down with a ball or disc in the game of *skittles.* —*v.* **skittle out**, to get (batsmen) out rapidly in cricket.

skive *v.* (*slang*) to dodge a duty. **skiver** *n.* □ **skive off**, (*slang*) to go away in order to dodge a duty.

skivvy *n.* (*informal*) a lowly female servant.

skua (skew-ă) *n.* a kind of large seagull.

skulduggery *n.* (*informal*) trickery.

skulk *v.* to loiter or move or conceal oneself stealthily.

skull *n.* **1.** the bony framework of the head, the part of this protecting the brain. **2.** a representation of this; *skull and crossbones*, this with two thigh-bones crossed below it as an emblem of death or piracy. □ **skull-cap** *n.* a small close-fitting cap with no peak, worn on top of the head.

skunk *n.* **1.** a black bushy-tailed American animal about the size of a cat, able to spray an evil-smelling liquid from glands near its tail. **2.** (*slang*) a contemptible person.

sky *n.* **1.** the region of the clouds or upper air. **2.** climate or weather shown by this, *the sunny skies of Italy.* —*v.* (skied, skying) to hit (a ball) to a great height. □ **sky-blue** *adj.* & *n.* bright clear blue. **sky-diver** *n.* one who engages in the sport of **sky-diving**, jumping from an aircraft and not opening the parachute until the last safe moment. **sky-high** *adj.* & *adv.* very high. **sky-rocket** *n.* a rocket that rises high into the air before exploding, (*v.*) to rise sharply.

Skye terrier a variety of Scotch terrier with long hair and a long body.

skylark *n.* a lark that soars while singing. —*v.* to play about lightheartedly.

skylight *n.* a window set in the line of a roof or ceiling.

skyscape *n.* a picture or view of the sky.

skyscraper *n.* a very tall building with many storeys.

slab *n.* a flat broad fairly thick piece of something solid.

slack¹ *adj.* **1.** loose, not tight or tense. **2.** slow, sluggish, negligent. **3.** (of trade or business) with little happening, not busy. —*n.* the slack part of a rope etc., *haul in the slack.* —**slack** *v.* **1.** to slacken. **2.** to be idle or lazy about work. **slacker** *n.*, **slackly** *adv.*, **slackness** *n.*

slack² *n.* coal-dust or very small pieces of coal left when coal is screened.

slacken *v.* to make or become slack.

slacks *pl. n.* trousers for informal or sports wear.

slag *n.* solid non-metallic waste matter left when metal has been separated from ore by smelting. **slag-heap** *n.* a mound of waste matter from a mine etc.

slain *see* slay.

slake *v.* **1.** to satisfy or make less strong, *slake one's thirst.* **2.** to combine (lime) chemically with water.

slalom (slah-lŏm) *n.* **1.** a ski-race down a zigzag course. **2.** an obstacle race in canoes.

slam *v.* (slammed, slamming) **1.** to shut forcefully with a loud noise. **2.** to put or knock or hit forcefully. **3.** (*slang*) to criticize severely. —**slam** *n.* **1.** a slamming noise. **2.** the winning of 12 or 13 tricks in the game of bridge. □ **grand slam**, the winning of all 13 tricks in the game of bridge; the winning of all of a group of championships in tennis or golf etc.

slander *n.* **1.** a false statement uttered maliciously that damages a person's reputa-tion. **2.** the crime of uttering this. —*v.* to utter a slander about. —**slanderous** *adj.*, **slanderously** *adv.*

slang *n.* words, phrases, or particular meaning of these, that are used very informally for vividness or novelty or to avoid being conventional. —*v.* to use abusive language to. —**slangy** *adj.* □ **slanging-match** *n.* a prolonged exchange of insults.

slant *v.* **1.** to slope. **2.** to present (news etc.) from a particular point of view. —**slant** *n.* **1.** a slope. **2.** the way something is presented, an attitude or bias. □ **slantwise** *adv.* in a slanting position.

slap *v.* (slapped, slapping) **1.** to strike with the open hand or with something flat. **2.** to lay forcefully, *slapped the money on the counter.* **3.** to place hastily or carelessly, *slapped paint on the walls.* —*n.* a blow with the open hand or with something flat. —*adv.* with a slap, directly, *ran slap into him.* □ **slap a person down**, to snub or reprimand him. **slap-happy** *adj.* (*informal*) cheerfully casual or irresponsible. **slap-up** *adj.* (*slang*) first-class, *a slap-up meal.*

slapdash *adj.* hasty and careless —*adv.* in a slapdash way.

slapstick *n.* comedy with boisterous activities.

slash *v.* **1.** to make a sweeping stroke or strokes with a sword or knife or whip etc., to strike in this way. **2.** to make an ornamental slit in (a garment), especially to show underlying fabric. **3.** to reduce drastically, *prices were slashed.* **4.** to criticize vigorously. —*n.* a slashing cut, a wound made by this.

slat *n.* one of the thin narrow strips of wood or metal or plastic arranged so as to overlap and form a screen, e.g. in a Venetian blind.

slate *n.* **1.** a kind of rock that is easily split into flat smooth plates. **2.** a piece of this used as roofing-material or (formerly) for writing on. —**slate** *v.* **1.** to cover or roof with slates. **2.** (*informal*) to criticize severely, to scold. —**slaty** *adj.* □ **a clean slate**, a record of good conduct with nothing discreditable; *wipe the slate clean,* to forgive and forget past offences. **on the slate**, (*informal*) recorded as a debt, on credit. **slate-blue** *adj.* & *n.* greyish-blue. **slate-grey** *adj.* & *n.* bluish-grey.

slattern *n.* a slovenly woman. **slatternly** *adj.*

slaughter *n.* **1.** the killing of animals for food. **2.** the ruthless killing of a great number of people or animals, a massacre. —**slaughter** *v.* **1.** to kill (animals) for food. **2.** to kill ruthlessly or in great num-

bers. **3.** (*informal*) to defeat utterly. —
slaughterer *n.*

slaughterhouse *n.* a place where animals
are killed for food.

Slav *n.* a member of any of the peoples of
East and Central Europe who speak a Slavonic language.

slave *n.* **1.** a person who is the property of
another and obliged to work for him.
2. one who is dominated by another
person or by an influence, *a slave to duty*.
3. a person compelled to work very hard
for someone else, a drudge. **4.** mechanism
controlled by other mechanism and repeating its actions. —*v.* to work very hard.
□ **slave-driver** *n.* a person who makes
others work very hard. **slave-driving** *n.*

slaver (**slav**-er *or* **slay**-ver) *v.* to have saliva
flowing from the mouth.

slavery *n.* **1.** the condition of a slave. **2.** the
existence of slaves, *to abolish slavery*. **3.**
very hard work, drudgery.

slavish *adj.* **1.** like a slave, excessively submissive. **2.** showing no independence or originality. **slavishly** *adv.*, **slavishness** *n.*

Slavonic (slă-**von**-ik) *adj.* of the group of
languages including Russian and Polish.

slay *v.* (slew, slain, slaying) to kill.

sleazy *adj.* (sleazier, sleaziest) (*informal*)
dirty and slovenly.

sled *n.* (*Amer.*) a sports sledge.

sledge *n.* a narrow cart with runners instead of wheels, used for travelling on snow
or bare ground or in sport for travelling
downhill at speed. **sledging** *n.* this sport.

sledge-hammer *n.* a large heavy hammer
used with both hands.

sleek *adj.* **1.** smooth and glossy, *sleek hair*.
2. looking well-fed and thriving. —*v.* to
make sleek by smoothing. —**sleekly** *adv.*,
sleekness *n.*

sleep *n.* **1.** the natural recurring condition
of rest in animals, in which there is unconsciousness with the nervous system
inactive and muscles relaxed. **2.** a spell of
this, *a long sleep*. **3.** the inert condition of
hibernating animals. —**sleep** *v.* (slept, sleeping) **1.** to be in a state of sleep **2.** to spend
(time) in sleeping; *sleep it off*, get rid of a
hangover etc. by sleeping. **3.** to stay for a
night's sleep. **4.** to provide with sleeping
accommodation, *the cottage sleeps four*. □
sleep around, (*informal*) to be sexually
promiscuous. **sleep in**, to sleep late.
sleeping-bag *n.* a padded bag for sleeping
in, especially while camping. **sleeping-car**
n. a railway coach fitted with berths or
beds for passengers. **sleeping partner**, a
partner in a business firm who does not
take part in its actual work. **sleeping-pill**
n. a pill to help a person to sleep. **sleeping**

sickness, a disease with symptoms that
include extreme sleepiness, spread by the
bite of the tsetse-fly. **sleeping-suit** *n.* a
child's one-piece garment for sleeping in.
sleep on it, to delay deciding about
something until the next day. **sleep-**
walker *n.* a person who walks about while
asleep. **sleep-walking** *n.* this condition.
sleep with, to have sexual intercourse
with.

sleeper *n.* **1.** one who sleeps. **2.** one of the
beams on which the rails of a railway etc.
rest. **3.** a sleeping-car, a berth in this. **4.** a
ring worn in a pierced ear to keep the hole
from closing.

sleepless *adj.* unable to sleep, without
sleep. **sleeplessly** *adv.*, **sleeplessness** *n.*

sleepy *adj.* (sleepier, sleepiest) **1.** feeling or
showing a desire to sleep. **2.** inactive, without stir or bustle, *a sleepy little town*. **3.** (of
fruit) tasteless and dry from being overripe and about to decay. **sleepily** *adv.*,
sleepiness *n.*

sleepyhead *n.* a sleepy person.

sleet *n.* snow and rain falling at the same
time, hail or snow that melts while falling.
—*v.* (of sleet) to fall in a shower, *it is sleet-*
ing. —**sleety** *adj.*

sleeve *n.* **1.** the part of a garment covering
the arm or part of it. **2.** a tube enclosing a
rod or another tube. **3.** a wind-sock, a
drogue towed by an aircraft. **4.** the cover of
a gramophone record. —**sleeved** *adj.* □
sleeve-board *n.* a small ironing-board on
which a sleeve fits for being ironed. **up**
one's sleeve, concealed but available for
use, in reserve; *laugh up one's sleeve*, to
laugh secretly or be secretly pleased with
oneself.

sleeveless *adj.* without sleeves.

sleigh (*pr.* slay) *n.* a sledge, especially one
used as a passenger vehicle drawn
by horses. **sleighing** *n.* travelling in a
sleigh.

sleight (*rhymes with* bite) *n.* **sleight of**
hand, great skill in using the hands to
perform conjuring tricks etc.

slender *adj.* **1.** slim and graceful. **2.** small in
amount, scanty, *slender means*. **slender-**
ness *n.*

slenderize *v.* to make or become slender.

slept *see* sleep.

sleuth (*pr.* slooth) *n.* a detective. **sleuth-**
ing *n.* searching for information as a
detective does.

slew¹ *v.* to turn or swing round.

slew² *see* slay.

slice *n.* **1.** a thin broad piece (or a wedge)
cut from something. **2.** a portion or share.
3. an implement with a thin broad blade
for lifting or serving fish etc. **4.** a slicing

stroke in golf. —**slice** v. **1.** to cut into slices. **2.** to cut from a larger piece. **3.** to cut cleanly or easily. **4.** to strike (a ball, in golf) badly so that it spins away from the direction intended, going to the right of a right-handed player. —**slicer** n. □ **sliced bread**, bread that is sliced and wrapped before being sold.

slick adj. **1.** done or doing things smoothly and cleverly but perhaps with some trickery. **2.** smooth in manner or speech. **3.** smooth and slippery, *the roads were slick with mud*. —n. a slippery place, a thick patch of oil floating on the sea. —v. to make sleek.

slicker n. (*Amer. informal*) a stylish townsman with a smooth but deceptive manner.

slide v. (slid, sliding) **1.** to move or cause to move along a smooth surface with the same area in continuous contact with this. **2.** to glide more or less erect over ice or other smooth surface without skates. **3.** to move or cause to move quietly or unobtrusively, *slid a coin into his hand*. **4.** to pass gradually into a condition or habit. —**slide** n. **1.** the act of sliding. **2.** a smooth surface for sliding on. **3.** a chute for goods etc. or for children to play on. **4.** a sliding part of a machine or instrument. **5.** a small glass plate on which things are placed for examination under a microscope. **6.** a mounted picture or transparency for showing on a blank surface by means of a projector. **7.** a hair-slide. □ **let things slide**, to fail to give them proper attention, to make no effort to control them. **slide-rule** n. a ruler with a sliding central strip, marked with logarithmic scales and used for making calculations rapidly. **sliding door**, a door that slides across an opening, not turning on hinges. **sliding scale**, a scale of fees or taxes or wages etc. that varies in accordance with the variation of some standard.

slight adj. **1.** not much or great or thorough; *paid me not the slightest attention*, paid none at all. **2.** slender, not heavily built. —v. to treat or speak of (a person etc.) as not worth one's attention, to insult by lack of respect or courtesy. —n. an insult given in this way. —**slightly** adv., **slightness** n.

slim adj. (slimmer, slimmest) **1.** of small girth or thickness, not heavily built. **2.** small, insufficient, *only a slim chance of success*. —**slim** v. (slimmed, slimming) **1.** to make oneself slimmer by dieting, exercise, etc. **2.** to reduce in numbers or scale, *slim down the work-force*. —**slimly** adv., **slimness** n., **slimmer** n.

slime n. an unpleasant slippery thick liquid substance.

slimline adj. of slender design.

slimy adj. (slimier, slimiest) **1.** like slime, covered or smeared with slime. **2.** disgustingly dishonest or meek or flattering. **slimily** adv., **sliminess** n.

sling n. **1.** a belt or strap or chain etc. looped round an object to support or lift it. **2.** a bandage looped round the neck to form a support for an injured arm. **3.** a looped strap used to throw a stone or other missile. —**sling** v. (slung, slinging) **1.** to suspend or lift with a sling. **2.** to hurl (a stone) with a sling. **3.** (*informal*) to throw. □ **sling-back** adj. (of a shoe) with a strap round the back of the foot. **sling mud at**, see mud. **sling one's hook**, (*slang*) to run away.

slink v. (slunk, slinking) to move in a stealthy or guilty or shamefaced way.

slinky adj. **1.** moving in a slinking way. **2.** smooth and sinuous. **3.** (of clothes) close-fitting and flowing.

slip v. (slipped, slipping) **1.** to slide accidentally, to lose one's balance in this way. **2.** to go or put or be put with a smooth movement. **3.** to escape hold or capture by being slippery or not grasped firmly. **4.** to make one's way quietly or unobserved. **5.** to detach or release; *slip a stitch*, (in knitting) to transfer it to the other needle without looping the yarn through it. **6.** to escape, to become detached from, *the ship slipped her moorings*; *it slipped my memory*. —**slip** n. **1.** the act of slipping. **2.** an accidental or casual mistake. **3.** a loose covering or garment, a petticoat, a pillow-case. **4.** a slipway. **5.** a long narrow strip of thin wood or paper etc. **6.** a cutting taken from a plant for grafting or planting; *a slip of a girl*, a small slim girl. **7.** a fieldsman in cricket stationed on the off side just behind the wicket, his position; *the slips*, this part of the field. **8.** a thin liquid containing fine clay, for coating pottery. □ **give a person the slip**, to escape from him or avoid him skilfully. **let slip**, to release accidentally or deliberately; to miss (an opportunity); to reveal news etc. unintentionally or thoughtlessly. **slip it across** or **over someone**, to trick him. **slip-knot** n. a knot that can slide easily along the rope etc. on which it is tied, or one that can be undone by pulling. **slip of the pen** or **tongue**, a small mistake in which one thing is written or said accidentally instead of another. **slip-on** adj. (of clothes) easily slipped on, usually without fastenings. **slipped disc**, see disc sense 3. **slip-road** n. a road for entering or leaving a motorway or other main road. **slip-stitch** *n.* a loose hemming-stitch in sewing, a slipped stitch in knitting, (*v.*) to sew with a slip-stitch. **slip-stream** *n.* a current of air driven backward as something is propelled forward. **slip up**, (*informal*) to make an accidental or casual mistake. **slip-up** *n.*

slipper *n.* a light loose comfortable shoe for indoor wear.

slippery *adj.* 1. smooth and difficult to hold, causing slipping by its wetness or smoothness. 2. (of a person) not to be trusted to keep an agreement etc., *a slippery customer.*

slippy *adj.* (*informal*) slippery. **look slippy**, (*informal*) to make haste.

slipshod *adj.* not doing things carefully, not done or arranged carefully.

slipway *n.* a sloping structure used as a landing-stage or on which ships are built or repaired.

slit *n.* a narrow straight cut or opening. — *v.* (slit, slitting) 1. to cut a slit in. 2. to cut into strips.

slither *v.* (*informal*) to slide unsteadily, to move with an irregular slipping movement.

slithery *adj.* (*informal*) causing slithering, liable to slither.

sliver (**sliv**-er) *n.* a thin strip cut or split from wood or glass etc.

slob *n.* (*slang, contemptuous*) a stupid or clumsy person.

slobber *v.* to slaver or dribble; *slobber over a person,* to behave with repulsively excessive affection to him.

sloe (*rhymes with* go) *n.* blackthorn, its small bluish-black plum-like fruit. **sloe-eyed** *adj.* with eyes of this colour. **sloe gin**, a liqueur of gin in which sloes have been steeped.

slog *v.* (slogged, slogging) 1. to hit hard. 2. to work or walk hard and steadily. — **slog** *n.* 1. a hard hit. 2. a spell of hard steady work or walking. —**slogger** *n.*

slogan *n.* a word or phrase adopted as a motto, a short catchy phrase used in advertising.

sloop *n.* a kind of ship with one mast.

slop¹ *v.* (slopped, slopping) 1. to spill over or cause to spill, to splash liquid on. 2. to plod clumsily, especially through mud or puddles etc. —**slop** *n.* 1. weak unappetizing drink or liquid food. 2. a quantity of slopped liquid. 3. swill fed to pigs. □ **slop-basin** *n.* a basin into which dregs from teacups are poured at the table. **slop out**, (in prison) to carry slops out from cells. **slop-pail** *n.* a pail for collecting or carrying slops. **slops** *pl. n.* household

liquid refuse; contents of chamber-pots; dregs from teacups.

slop² *n.* (also *slops*) a loose outer garment worn by a workman.

slope *v.* 1. to lie or turn at an angle from the horizontal or vertical. 2. to place in this position. —**slope** *n.* 1. a sloping surface or direction, a stretch of rising or falling ground. 2. the amount by which something slopes. □ **slope off**, (*slang*) to go away.

sloppy *adj.* (sloppier, sloppiest) 1. having a liquid consistency that splashes easily, excessively liquid, *sloppy porridge.* 2. slipshod. 3. weakly sentimental. **sloppily** *adv.*, **sloppiness** *n.*

slosh *v.* (*slang*) 1. to hit, *sloshed him on the chin.* 2. to pour (liquid) clumsily. 3. to splash, to move with a splashing sound. — **slosh** *n.* (*slang*) 1. a blow. 2. a splashing sound. —**sloshed** *adj.* (*slang*) drunk.

slot *n.* 1. a narrow opening through which something is to be put. 2. a groove or channel or slit into which something fits. 3. a position in a series or scheme; *the programme has its regular slot,* its regular time for transmission. —**slot** *v.* (slotted, slotting) 1. to make a slot or slots in. 2. to put into a slot. □ **slot-machine** *n.* a machine operated by a coin put in a slot, e.g. to dispense small articles.

sloth (*rhymes with* both) *n.* 1. laziness. 2. an animal of tropical America that lives in trees and is capable of only very slow movement.

slothful *adj.* lazy. **slothfully** *adv.*

slouch *v.* to stand or sit or move in a lazy awkward way, not with an upright posture. —*n.* a slouching movement or posture. —**sloucher** *n.* □ **slouch hat**, a hat with a wide flexible brim.

slough¹ (*rhymes with* cow) *n.* a swamp or marshy place.

slough² (*pr.* sluf) *v.* to shed, *a snake sloughs its skin periodically.* —*n.* a snake's cast skin, dead tissue that drops away.

slovenly (**sluv**-ĕn-li) *adj.* careless and untidy in appearance, not methodical in work. **slovenliness** *n.*

slow *adj.* 1. not quick or fast, acting or moving or done without haste or rapidity. 2. (of a clock) showing a time earlier than the correct one. 3. mentally dull, stupid. 4. lacking liveliness, sluggish, *business is slow today.* 5. (of photographic film) not very sensitive to light, (of a lens) having only a small aperture, needing a long exposure. 6. tending to cause slowness. — *adv.* slowly, *go slow.* —*v.* to reduce the speed of, to go more slowly, *slow down* or *up.* —**slowly** *adv.*, **slowness** *n.* □ **slow motion**, (of a cinema film) making movements appear to be performed much more slowly than in real life.

slowcoach *n.* a person who is slow in his actions or work.

slowish *adj.* rather slow.

slow-worm *n.* a small European lizard with no legs.

slub *n.* a thick lump in yarn or thread.

sludge *n.* thick greasy mud, something resembling.

slug¹ *n.* **1.** a small slimy animal like a snail without a shell. **2.** a roundish lump of metal, a bullet of irregular shape, a pellet for firing from an airgun.

slug² *v.* (slugged, slugging) to strike with a hard heavy blow. —*n.* a blow of this kind.

sluggard *n.* a slow or lazy person.

sluggish *adj.* slow-moving, not alert or lively. **sluggishly** *adv.*, **sluggishness** *n.*

sluice (*pr.* slooss) *n.* **1.** a sliding gate for controlling the volume or flow of water in a stream etc. **2.** the water controlled by this. **3.** a channel carrying off water. **4.** a place where objects are rinsed. **5.** the act of rinsing. —**sluice** *v.* **1.** to let out (water) by means of a sluice. **2.** to flood or scour or rinse with a flow of water.

slum *n.* a dirty overcrowded district inhabited by very poor people. **slumming** *n.* visiting a slum for curiosity or for charitable purposes.

slumber *n.* sleep. —*v.* to sleep. — **slumberer** *n*

slump *n.* a sudden or great fall in prices or values or in the demand for goods etc. —*v.* **1.** to undergo a slump. **2.** to sit or flop down heavily and slackly.

slung *see* sling.

slunk *see* slink.

slur *v.* (slurred, slurring) **1.** to write or pronounce indistinctly with each letter or sound running into the next. **2.** to mark (notes) with a slur in music, to perform in the way indicated by this. **3.** to pass lightly over (a fact etc.), *slurred it over.* **4.** (*Amer.*) to speak ill of. —**slur** *n.* **1.** a slurred letter or sound. **2.** a curved line placed over notes in music to show that they are to be sung to one syllable or played smoothly without a break. **3.** discredit, *there is no slur on his reputation.*

slurp *v.* to make a noisy sucking sound in eating or drinking. —*n.* this sound.

slurry (*rhymes with* hurry) *n.* thin mud, thin liquid cement.

slush *n.* **1.** partly melted snow on the ground. **2.** silly sentimental talk or writing. **slushy** *adj.* □ **slush fund**, (*Amer.*) a fund of money for illegal purposes such as bribing officials.

slut *n.* a slovenly woman. **sluttish** *adj.*

sly *adj.* (slyer, slyest) **1.** done or doing things in an unpleasantly cunning and secret way. **2.** mischievous and knowing, *with a sly smile.* **slyly** *adv.*, **slyness** *n.* □ **on the sly**, slyly, secretly.

smack¹ *n.* **1.** a slap. **2.** a hard hit. **3.** a loud kiss. —*v.* to slap, to hit hard; *smack one's lips,* to close and then part them noisily in enjoyment. —*adv.* (*informal*) with a smack, directly, *went smack through the window.* □ **have a smack at**, (*informal*) to attempt, to attack.

smack² *n.* a slight flavour or trace of something. —*v.* to have a slight flavour or trace of something, *his manner smacks of conceit.*

smack³ *n.* a boat with a single mast used for coasting or fishing.

smacker *n.* (*slang*) **1.** a loud kiss, a sounding blow. **2.** £1, (*Amer.*) a dollar.

small *adj.* **1.** not large or big. **2.** not great in size or importance or number etc. **3.** of the smaller kind, *the small intestine.* **4.** doing things on a small scale, *a small farmer.* **5.** petty. —*n.* the most slender part of something; *small of the back,* the part at the back at the waist. —*adv.* in a small size or way, into small pieces, *chop it small.* — **smallness** *n.* □ **look** or **feel small**, to be humiliated. **no small thing**, something considerable. **small beer**, something trivial. **small change**, coins as opposed to notes. **small fry**, *see* fry². **small hours**, the hours soon after midnight. **small-minded** *adj.* narrow or selfish in outlook. **small print**, matter printed in small type, limitations (in contract etc.) stated inconspicuously in this way. **smalls** *pl. n.* (*informal*) small articles of laundry, especially underwear. **small-scale** *adj.* drawn to a small scale so that few details are shown; not extensive, involving only small quantities etc. **small talk**, social conversation on unimportant subjects. **small-time** *adj.* of an unimportant level, *small-time crooks.*

smallholder *n.* the owner or tenant of a smallholding.

smallholding *n.* a piece of land of more than one acre in area but usually less than 50 acres, sold or let for cultivation.

smallpox *n.* a contagious disease caused by a virus, with pustules that often leave disfiguring scars.

smarmy *adj.* (*informal*) trying to win favour by flattery or excessive politeness, fulsome.

smart *adj.* **1.** forceful, brisk, *a smart pace.* **2.** clever, ingenious. **3.** neat and elegant. — *v.* to feel a stinging pain (bodily or mental). —*n.* a stinging pain. —**smartly**

adv., **smartness** *n.* □ **smart aleck,** (*informal*) a know-all.

smarten *v.* to make or become smarter.

smash *v.* **1.** to break or become broken suddenly and noisily into pieces. **2.** to strike or move with great force. **3.** to strike (a ball) forcefully downwards in tennis etc. **4.** to crash (a vehicle), to have a crash. **5.** to overthrow or destroy, *police smashed the drug ring.* **6.** to ruin or become ruined financially. —**smash** *n.* **1.** the act or sound of smashing. **2.** a collision. **3.** a disaster, financial ruin. □ **smash-and-grab raid,** a robbery done by smashing a shop window and grabbing goods. **smash hit,** (*slang*) an extremely successful thing.

smasher *n.* (*informal*) an excellent person or thing.

smashing *adj.* (*informal*) excellent.

smattering *n.* a slight superficial knowledge of a language or subject.

smear *v.* **1.** to spread with a greasy or sticky or dirty substance. **2.** to try to damage the reputation of. —**smear** *n.* **1.** something smeared on a surface, a mark made by this. **2.** a specimen of material smeared on a microscope slide for examination. **3.** an attempt to damage a reputation, *a smear campaign.*

smeary *adj.* **1.** smeared. **2.** tending to smear things.

smell *n.* **1.** the faculty of perceiving things by their action on the sense-organs of the nose. **2.** the quality that is perceived in this way. **3.** an unpleasant quality of this kind. **4.** an act of smelling something. —**smell** *v.* (smelt, smelling) **1.** to perceive the smell of, to detect or test by one's sense of smell. **2.** to give off a smell. **3.** to give off an unpleasant smell. □ **smelling-salts** *pl. n.* a solid preparation of ammonia used for smelling as a stimulant to relieve faintness etc.

smelly *adj.* (smellier, smelliest) having a strong or unpleasant smell.

smelt[1] *see* smell.

smelt[2] *v.* to heat and melt (ore) so as to obtain the metal it contains, to obtain (metal) in this way.

smelt[3] *n.* a small fish related to salmon.

smilax (**smy**-laks) *n.* **1.** a kind of climbing shrub. **2.** a kind of climbing asparagus cultivated for its decorative leaves.

smile *n.* a facial expression indicating pleasure or amusement, with the lips stretched and turning upwards at their ends. —*v.* **1.** to give a smile, to express by smiling, *smiled her thanks.* **2.** to look bright or favourable; *fortune smiled on us,* favoured us. —**smiler** *n.*

smirch *v.* **1.** to smear or soil. **2.** to bring

discredit upon (a reputation). —*n.* a smear, discredit.

smirk *n.* a self-satisfied smile. —*v.* to give a smirk.

smite *v.* (smote, smitten, smiting) **1.** to hit hard. **2.** to have a sudden effect on, *his conscience smote him.*

smith *n.* **1.** a person who makes things in metal. **2.** a blacksmith.

smithereens *pl. n.* small fragments.

smithy *n.* **1.** a blacksmith. **2.** his workshop.

smitten *see* smite. □ **smitten with,** affected by (a disease or desire or fascination etc.).

smock *n.* an overall shaped like a long loose shirt. —*v.* to ornament with smocking.

smocking *n.* a decoration of close gathers stitched into a honeycomb pattern.

smog *n.* fog polluted by smoke.

smoke *n.* **1.** the visible vapour given off by a burning substance. **2.** an act or spell of smoking tobacco, *wanted a smoke.* **3.** (*informal*) a cigarette or cigar. **4.** *the Smoke,* (*informal*) London. —**smoke** *v.* **1.** to give out smoke or steam or other visible vapour. **2.** (of a fireplace) to send smoke into a room instead of up the chimney. **3.** to darken with smoke, *smoked glass.* **4.** to preserve by treating with smoke, *smoked salmon.* **5.** to draw into the mouth the smoke from a cigarette or cigar or tobacco-pipe, to use (a cigarette etc.) in this way, to do this as a habit. □ **smoke-bomb** *n.* a bomb that gives out dense smoke when it explodes. **smoke out,** to drive out by means of smoke. **smoke-screen** *n.* a mass of smoke used to conceal the movements of troops; something intended to conceal or disguise one's activities.

smokeless *adj.* **1.** free from smoke. **2.** producing little or no smoke, *smokeless fuel.*

smoker *n.* **1.** a person who smokes tobacco as a habit. **2.** a compartment where smoking is permitted on a train.

smoko *n.* (*Austral. informal*) a brief stoppage of work for rest and a smoke.

smoky *adj.* (smokier, smokiest) **1.** giving off much smoke. **2.** covered or filled with smoke. **3.** greyish, *smoky blue.*

smooth *adj.* **1.** having an even surface with no projections, free from roughness. **2.** not harsh in sound or taste. **3.** moving evenly without jolts or bumping. **4.** pleasantly polite but perhaps insincere. —*adv.* smoothly, *the course of true love never did run smooth.* —**smooth** *v.* **1.** to make or become smooth. **2.** to remove problems or dangers from, *smooth a person's path.* —*n.*

a smoothing touch or stroke. —**smoothly**
adv., **smoothness** *n.* □ **smooth-tongued**
adj. pleasantly polite or convincing but
insincere.

smorgasbord (smor-găs-bord) *n.* Swedish
hors d'œuvres, a buffet meal with a variety of dishes.

smote *see* smite.

smother *v.* 1. to suffocate or stifle, to be
suffocated. 2. to put out or keep down
(a fire) by heaping ash on it. 3. to
cover thickly. 4. to restrain or suppress,
smothered a smile. —*n.* a dense cloud of
dust or smoke etc.

smoulder *v.* 1. to burn slowly with smoke
but no flame. 2. to burn inwardly with
concealed anger or jealousy etc. 3. (of feelings) to exist in a suppressed state, *discontent smouldered.*

smudge *n.* a dirty or blurred mark. —*v.*
1. to make a smudge on or with. 2. to
become smudged or blurred. —**smudgy** *adj.*

smug *adj.* (smugger, smuggest) self-satisfied. **smugly** *adv.*, **smugness** *n.*

smuggle *v.* 1. to convey secretly. 2. to
bring (goods) into or out of a country illegally, especially without paying customs
duties. **smuggler** *n.*

smut *n.* 1. a small flake of soot, a small
black mark made by this or otherwise.
2. indecent talk or pictures or stories.

smutty *adj.* (smuttier, smuttiest) 1. marked
with smuts. 2. (of talk or pictures or
stories) indecent.

snack *n.* a small or casual or hurried meal.
snack-bar *n.* a place where snacks are
sold.

snaffle *n.* a horse's bit without a curb. —
v. (*slang*) to take for oneself.

snag *n.* 1. a jagged projection. 2. a tear in
fabric that has caught on a snag. 3. an
unexpected difficulty. —*v.* (snagged,
snagging) to catch or tear or be caught
on a snag.

snail *n.* a soft-bodied animal with a shell
that can enclose its whole body. **snail's
pace**, a very slow pace.

snake *n.* 1. a reptile with a long narrow
body and no legs. 2. a treacherous person.
3. *the snake*, a set of European currencies
which retain their exchange-rates with
regard to each other while able to fluctuate against others. —**snaky** *adj.* □
snake-charmer *n.* an entertainer who
seems to make snakes move to music.

snakeskin *n.* leather made from snakes'
skins.

snap *v.* (snapped, snapping) 1. to make or
cause to make a sharp cracking sound.
2. to break suddenly or with a cracking
sound, *the rope snapped.* 3. to bite or try to

bite with a snatching movement, *the dog
snapped at her ankles.* 4. to take or accept
eagerly, *snapping up bargains.* 5. to speak
with sudden irritation. 6. to move smartly,
snapped to attention. 7. to take a snapshot
of. —**snap** *n.* 1. the act or sound of snapping. 2. a fastener that closes with a snap.
3. a small crisp brittle biscuit, *ginger snaps.*
4. a sudden brief spell of cold weather. 5. a
snapshot. 6. *Snap*, a card-game in which
players call 'Snap' when two similar cards
are exposed. —*adv.* with a snapping
sound. —*adj.* sudden, done or arranged at
short notice, *a snap election.* □ **snap one's
fingers**, to make a cracking noise by flipping the thumb against a finger, usually in
order to draw attention; *snap one's fingers
at*, to defy. **snap out of it,** (*slang*) to make
oneself recover quickly from an illness or
mood etc.

snapdragon *n.* a garden plant with flowers that have a mouth-like opening.

snapper *n.* 1. a person or thing that snaps.
2. any of several sea-fish used as food.

snappish *adj.* bad-tempered and inclined
to snap at people. **snappishly** *adv.*

snappy *adj.* (snappier, snappiest)
(*informal*) 1. brisk, vigorous. 2. neat and
elegant. **snappily** *adv.* □ **make it
snappy,** (*informal*) be quick about it.

snapshot *n.* a photograph taken informally or casually.

snare *n.* 1. a trap for catching birds or animals, usually with a noose. 2. something
liable to entangle a person or expose him
to danger or failure etc. 3. one of the
strings of gut or hide stretched across a
side-drum to produce a rattling effect. 4. a
snare drum. —*v.* to trap in a snare. □ **snare
drum**, a drum with snares.

snarl[1] *v.* 1. to growl angrily with the
teeth bared. 2. to speak or utter in a bad-
tempered way. —*n.* the act or sound of
snarling.

snarl[2] *v.* to tangle, to become entangled.
—*n.* a tangle. □ **snarl up**, to make or
become jammed or tangled, *traffic was
snarled up.* **snarl-up** *n.*

snatch *v.* 1. to seize quickly or eagerly.
2. to take quickly or when a chance
occurs, *snatched a few hours' sleep.* —
snatch *n.* 1. the act of snatching. 2. a
short or brief part, *snatches of song; works
in snatches,* in short spells.

snazzy *adj.* (*slang*) smart, stylish.

sneak *v.* 1. to go or convey furtively.
2. (*slang*) to steal furtively. 3. (*school slang*)
to tell tales. —*n.* (*school slang*) a telltale.
—*adj.* acting or done without warning,
sneak raider. —**sneaky** *adj.* □ **sneak-
thief** *n.* a burglar who enters by sneaking

or reaching through an open door or window.

sneakers *pl. n.* (*Amer.*) soft-soled shoes.

sneaking *adj.* persistent but not openly acknowledged, *had a sneaking affection for him.*

sneer *n.* a scornful expression or remark. —*v.* to show contempt by a sneer.

sneeze *n.* a sudden audible involuntary expulsion of air through the nose and mouth, to expel an irritant substance from the nostrils. —*v.* to give a sneeze. □ **not to be sneezed at**, (*slang*) not to be despised, worth having.

snick *n.* **1.** a small cut or notch. **2.** a batsman's light glancing stroke. —**snick** *v.* **1.** to cut a snick in. **2.** to hit with a light glancing stroke.

snicker *v.* to snigger. —*n.* a snigger.

snide *adj.* (*informal*) **1.** (of coins etc.) counterfeit. **2.** sneering in a sly way.

sniff *v.* **1.** to draw up air audibly through the nose. **2.** to draw in through the nose as one breathes, to try the smell of. —*n.* the act or sound of sniffing. —**sniffer** *n.* □ **sniff at**, (*informal*) to show contempt for. **sniffer dog**, a dog trained to scent the presence of drugs or explosives.

sniffle *v.* to sniff slightly or repeatedly. —*n.* the act or sound of sniffling.

sniffy *adj.* (*informal*) contemptuous. **sniffily** *adv.*

snigger *n.* a sly giggle. —*v.* to give a snigger.

snip *v.* (snipped, snipping) to cut with scissors or shears in small quick strokes. —*n.* **1.** the act or sound of snipping. **2.** a piece snipped off. **3.** (*slang*) a bargain, a certainty, something very easy to do.

snipe *n.* (*pl.* snipe) a wading-bird with a long straight bill, frequenting marshes. —*v.* **1.** to fire shots from a hiding-place. **2.** to make sly critical remarks attacking a person or thing. —**sniper** *n.*

snippet *n.* **1.** a small piece cut off. **2.** a fragment of information or news, a brief extract.

snitch *v.* (*slang*) to steal.

snivel *v.* (snivelled, snivelling) to cry or complain in a miserable whining way.

snob *n.* a person who has an exaggerated respect for social position or wealth or for certain attainments or tastes, and who despises people whom he considers inferior; *snob appeal* or *value*, qualities that appeal to people's snobbish feelings. **snobbery** *n.*

snobbish *adj.* of or like a snob. **snobbishly** *adv.*, **snobbishness** *n.*

snogging *n.* (*slang*) kissing and caressing.

snood *n.* a loose bag-like ornamental net

in which a woman's hair is held at the back.

snook *n.* (*slang*) a contemptuous gesture with thumb to nose and fingers spread out. **cock a snook**, to make this gesture; to show cheeky contempt.

snooker *n.* a game played on a billiard-table with 15 red and 6 other coloured balls. **snookered** *adj.* in a position in snooker where a direct shot would lose points; (*slang*) thwarted or defeated.

snoop *v.* (*informal*) to pry inquisitively. **snooper** *n.*

snooty *adj.* (snootier, snootiest) (*informal*) haughty and contemptuous. **snootily** *adv.*

snooze *n.* a nap. —*v.* to take a snooze.

snore *n.* a snorting or grunting sound made during sleep. —*v.* to make such sounds. —**snorer** *n.*

snorkel *n.* **1.** a breathing-tube to enable a person to swim under water. **2.** a device by which a submerged submarine can take in and expel air. □ **snorkelling** *n.* swimming with the aid of a snorkel.

snort *n.* a rough sound made by forcing breath suddenly through the nose, usually expressing annoyance or disgust. —*v.* to utter a snort.

snorter *n.* (*slang*) something remarkable for its vigour or violence, a difficult task.

snot *n.* (*vulgar*) **1.** mucous discharge from the nose. **2.** a contemptible person. **snotty** *adj.*

snout *n.* **1.** an animal's long projecting nose or nose and jaws. **2.** the projecting front part of something.

snow *n.* **1.** crystals of ice that form from atmospheric vapour and fall to earth in light white flakes. **2.** a fall or layer of snow. **3.** something resembling snow, a dessert made with fruit and egg-white, *apple snow.* **4.** (*slang*) cocaine. —**snow** *v.* **1.** (of snow) to fall, *it is snowing.* **2.** to scatter or fall like snow. □ **snow-bound** *adj.* prevented by snow from going out or travelling; blocked by snow. **snow-drift** *n.* snow heaped up by wind. **snowed under**, covered with snow; overwhelmed with a mass of letters or work etc. **snowed up**, snow-bound, blocked with snow. **snow-field** *n.* a permanent wide expanse of snow. **snow-goose** *n.* a white goose of arctic areas. **snow-line** *n.* the level above which an area is covered permanently with snow. **snow-plough** *n.* a device for clearing a road or railway track by pushing snow aside. **snow-shoe** *n.* a device shaped like a racket-head, attached to the bottom of a shoe and enabling the wearer to walk

over snow without sinking in. **snow-white**
adj. pure white.

snowball *n.* snow pressed into a small
compact mass for throwing in play. —*v.*
1. to throw snowballs at, to play in this
way. **2.** to grow quickly in size or intensity,
as a snowball does when rolled in more
snow, *opposition to the war snowballed.* □
snowball-tree *n.* the guelder rose.

snowdrop *n.* a small flower growing from
a bulb, with hanging white flowers blooming in early spring.

snowfall *n.* a fall of snow, the amount
that falls.

snowflake *n.* a flake of snow.

snowman *n.* (*pl.* snowmen) a figure made
in snow roughly in the shape of a man.

snowstorm *n.* a storm in which snow falls.

snowy *adj.* (snowier, snowiest) **1.** with
snow falling, *snowy weather.* **2.** covered
with snow. **3.** as white as snow.

SNP *abbrev.* Scottish National Party.

snub [1] *v.* (snubbed, snubbing) to reject
or humiliate (a person) by treating him
scornfully or in an unfriendly way —*n*
treatment of this kind.

snub [2] *adj.* (of the nose) short and stumpy.
snub-nosed *adj.*

snuff [1] *n.* powdered tobacco for sniffing
into the nostrils. **snuff-coloured** *adj.* dark
yellowish-brown.

snuff [2] *v.* to put out (a candle) by covering
or pinching the flame. **snuffer** *n.* □
snuff it, (*slang*) to die.

snuffle *v.* to sniff in a noisy way, to
breathe noisily through a partly blocked
nose. —*n.* a snuffling sound.

snug *adj.* (snugger, snuggest) cosy, (of a
garment) close-fitting. **snugly** *adv.*

snuggle *v.* to nestle, to cuddle.

so *adv.* & *conj.* **1.** to the extent or in the
manner or with the result indicated, *it was
so dark that we could not see.* **2.** very, *we
are so pleased to see you.* **3.** for that
reason, *and so they ran away.* **4.** also, *if you
go, so shall I.* —*pronoun* that, the same
thing, *do you think so?; and so say all of us.*
□ **and so on,** and others of the same
kind. **or so,** or about that number or
amount, *two hundred or so.* **so-and-so** *n.* a
person or thing that need not be named;
(*informal,* to avoid using a vulgar word) a
disliked person, *he is a so-and-so!* **so as to,**
in order to. **so-called** *adj.* called by that
name or description but perhaps not deserving it. **so far, so good,** progress has
been satisfactory up to this point. **so
long!,** (*informal*) goodbye till we meet
again. **so many,** nothing but, *went down
like so many skittles.* **so much,** nothing
but, *melted like so much snow; so much for*

that idea, no more need be said of it. **so-
so** *adj.* & *adv.* (*informal*) only moderately
good or well. **so that,** in order that. **so
what?,** that fact has no importance.

soak *v.* **1.** to place or lie in a liquid so as to
become thoroughly wet. **2.** (of liquid) to
penetrate gradually, (of rain etc.) to drench.
3. to absorb, *soak it up with a sponge; soak
up knowledge.* **4.** (*slang*) to extract much
money from (a person) by charging or
taxing him very heavily. — **soak** *n.* **1.** the act
or process of soaking. **2.** (*slang*) a heavy
drinker.

soap *n.* a substance used for washing and
cleaning things, made of fat or oil combined with an alkali. —*v.* to apply soap to.
□ **soap-flakes** *pl. n.* soap prepared in
small flakes for washing clothes etc. **soap
opera,** (*Amer. informal*) a sentimental
broadcast serial with a domestic setting.
soap powder, powder of soap with addi-
tives.

soapstone *n.* steatite.

soapsuds *pl. n.* froth of soapy water.

soapy *adj.* **1.** like soap. **2.** covered or impregnated with soap. **3.** (*informal*) trying
to win favour by flattery or excessive
politeness. **soapiness** *n.*

soar *v.* **1.** to rise high in flight. **2.** to rise
very high, *prices soared.*

sob *n.* uneven drawing of breath in weeping or when out of breath. —*v.* (sobbed,
sobbing) to weep or breathe or utter with
sobs. □ **sob-stuff** *n.* (*Amer.*) sentimental
writing or statements intended to arouse
sympathy or sadness.

sober *adj.* **1.** not intoxicated. **2.** serious and
self-controlled, not frivolous. **3.** (of colour)
not bright or conspicuous. —*v.* to make or
become sober, *sober up* or *down.* —
soberly *adv.* □ **sober-sides** *n.* a sedate
person.

sobriety (sŏ-bry-ĕti) *n.* being sober.

sobriquet (soh-brik-ay) *n.* a nickname.

soccer *n.* (*informal*) Association football.

sociable (soh-shă-bŭl) *adj.* fond of company, characterized by friendly companionship. **sociably** *adv.*, **sociability** *n.*

social *adj.* **1.** living in an organized community, not solitary. **2.** of society or its
organization, of the mutual relationships
of people or classes living in an organized
community, *social problems.* **3.** of or designed for companionship and sociability,
a social club. **4.** sociable. —*n.* a social gathering. —**socially** *adv.* □ **social climber,** a
person seeking to gain a higher rank in
society. **Social Democrat,** a member of the
Social Democratic Party, a political party
with moderate socialist aims. **social engineering,** the process of reorganizing society.

social science, the scientific study of human society and social relationships. **social security,** State assistance for those who lack economic security through being unemployed or ill or disabled etc. **social services,** welfare services provided by the State, including the education, health, housing, and pensions services. **social worker,** a person trained to help people with social problems.

socialism n. a political and economic theory advocating that land, transport, natural resources, and the chief industries should be owned and managed by the State. **socialist** n., **socialistic** adj.

socialite (soh-shǎ-lyt) n. a person who is prominent in fashionable society.

socialize v. 1. to organize in a socialistic manner. 2. to behave sociably, to take part in social activities. **socialization** n.

society n. 1. an organized community, the system of living in this. 2. people of the higher social classes. 3. company, companionship, *always enjoy his society; he is at his best in society.* 4. a group of people organized for some common purpose. □ **Society of Friends,** Quakers. **Society of Jesus,** Jesuits.

sociologist (soh-si-ol-ŏ-jist) n. an expert in sociology.

sociology (soh-si-ol-ŏji) n. the scientific study of human society and its development and institutions, or of social problems. **sociological** adj.

sock¹ n. 1. a short stocking not reaching the knee. 2. a loose insole. □ **pull one's socks up,** (*informal*) to make an effort to do better. **put a sock in it,** (*slang*) be quiet.

sock² v. (*slang*) to hit forcefully. —n. (*slang*) a forceful blow. □ **sock it to a person,** (*slang*) to attack him forcefully.

socket n. 1. a hollow into which something fits, *a tooth socket.* 2. a device for receiving an electric plug or bulb in order to make a connection.

socketed adj. fitted with a socket.

sockeye n. a kind of salmon.

sod¹ n. turf, a piece of this.

sod² n. (*vulgar*) a person, a man. —v. (*vulgar*) damn; *sod off,* go away.

soda n. 1. a compound of sodium in common use, especially sodium carbonate (*washing-soda*), bicarbonate (*baking-soda*), or hydroxide (*caustic soda*). 2. soda-water, *whisky and soda.* □ **soda-bread** n. bread made with baking-soda (not yeast). **soda-fountain** n. an apparatus in which soda-water is stored under pressure, ready to be drawn out; a shop equipped with this. **soda-water** n. water made fizzy by being charged with carbon dioxide under pressure.

sodden adj. made very wet.

sodium (soh-di-ǔm) n. a soft silver-white metal. **sodium lamp,** a lamp using an electrical discharge in sodium vapour and giving a yellow light, often used in street lighting.

sodomy (sod-ŏ-mi) n. a copulation-like act between male persons or between a person and an animal.

sofa n. a long upholstered seat with a back and raised ends or arms.

soffit n. the under-surface of an arch or architrave.

Sofia (soh-fee-ǎ) the capital of Bulgaria.

soft adj. 1. not hard or firm. 2. smooth, not rough or stiff. 3. not loud. 4. gentle, soothing; *a soft answer,* a good-tempered one. 5. not physically robust, feeble. 6. easily influenced, tender-hearted. 7. (*slang*) easy, comfortable, *a soft job; soft living.* 8. (of currency) likely to drop suddenly in value. 9. (of drinks) non-alcoholic. 10. (of water) free from mineral salts that prevent soap from lathering. 11. (of colour or light) not bright or dazzling, (of an outline) not sharp. 12. (of consonants) not hard (*see* hard, sense 11). —adv. softly; *fall soft,* on a soft surface. —**softly** adv., **softness** n. □ **soft-boiled** adj. (of eggs) boiled but without allowing yolk and white to become set. **soft drugs,** drugs that are not likely to cause addiction. **soft fruit,** small stoneless fruits such as strawberries and currants. **soft furnishings,** curtains and rugs etc. **soft-hearted** adj. compassionate. **soft option,** the easier alternative. **soft-pedal** v. (*informal*) to refrain from emphasizing. **soft pornography,** not highly obscene. **soft soap,** semi-liquid soap; (*informal*) persuasive talk, flattery. **soft spot,** a feeling of affection towards a person or thing.

soften v. to make or become soft or softer. **softener** n. □ **soften up,** to make weaker by attacking repeatedly; to make less able to resist (salesmanship etc.) by making preliminary approaches.

softie n. (*informal*) a person who is physically weak or not hardy, or who is soft-hearted.

software n. computer programs or the tapes containing these (as distinct from *hardware*).

softwood n. wood from coniferous trees, which is relatively soft.

soggy adj. 1. sodden. 2. moist and heavy in texture, *soggy bread.* **sogginess** n.

soigné (swahn-yay) adj. (of a woman, soignée) well-groomed and sophisticated.

soil¹ n 1. the loose upper layer of earth

in which plants grow. **2.** ground as territory, *on British soil.*

soil [2] *v.* to make or become dirty.

soirée (swah-ray) *n.* a social gathering in the evening, e.g. for music.

sojourn (soj-ern) *n.* a temporary stay. —*v.* to stay at a place temporarily.

solace (sol-ăs) *n.* comfort in distress, something that gives this. —*v.* to give solace to.

solar (soh-ler) *adj.* **1.** of or derived from the sun, *solar energy.* **2.** reckoned by the sun, *solar time.* □ **solar heating,** heating derived from solar energy. **solar plexus,** the network of nerves at the pit of the stomach; this area. **solar system,** the sun with the heavenly bodies that revolve round it.

solarium (sŏl-air-iŭm) *n.* a room or balcony, often enclosed with glass, where sunlight can be enjoyed for medical purposes or for pleasure.

sold *see* sell. □ **sold again!,** *(slang)* deceived or disappointed again. **sold on,** *(slang)* enthusiastic about.

solder (sohl-der) *n.* a soft alloy used to cement metal parts together. —*v.* to join with solder. □ **soldering-iron** *n.* a tool used hot for applying solder.

soldier *n.* a member of an army, especially a private or NCO. —*v.* to serve as a soldier. □ **soldier of fortune,** an adventurous person ready to serve any country or person that will hire him. **soldier on,** *(informal)* to persevere doggedly.

soldierly *adj.* like a soldier.

soldiery *n.* soldiers collectively or as a class.

sole [1] *n.* **1.** the under-surface of a foot. **2.** the part of a shoe or stocking etc. that covers this (often excluding the heel). —*v.* to put a sole on (a shoe).

sole [2] *n.* a kind of flat-fish used as food.

sole [3] *adj.* **1.** one and only, *our sole objection is this.* **2.** belonging exclusively to one person or group, *we have the sole right to sell these cars.* **solely** *adv.*

solecism (sol-i-sizm) *n.* a mistake in the use of language, an offence against good manners or etiquette.

solemn *adj.* **1.** not smiling or cheerful. **2.** dignified and impressive, *a solemn occasion.* **3.** formal, accompanied by a religious or other ceremony. **solemnly** *adv.,* **solemnity** (sŏl-em-niti) *n.*

solemnize (sol-ĕm-nyz) *v.* **1.** to celebrate (a festival etc.). **2.** to perform (a marriage ceremony) with formal rites. **solemnization** *n.*

solenoid (soh-lin-oid) *n.* a coil of wire that becomes magnetic when an electrical

current is passed through it.

sol-fa (sol-fah) *n.* the system of syllables *doh, ray, me, fah, soh, la, te,* used to represent notes of a musical scale.

solicit (sŏl-iss-it) *v.* **1.** to seek to obtain, to ask for earnestly, *solicit votes* or *for votes.* **2.** (of a prostitute) to make an immoral sexual offer, especially in a public place. **solicitation** *n.*

solicitor *n.* a lawyer who advises clients on legal matters and prepares legal documents for them but who does not represent them as an advocate except in certain lower courts.

solicitous (sŏl-iss-it-ŭs) *adj.* anxious and concerned about a person's welfare or comfort. **solicitously** *adv.,* □ **solicitude** *n.* solicitous concern.

solid *adj.* **1.** keeping its shape, firm, not liquid or gas. **2.** not hollow. **3.** of the same substance throughout, *solid silver.* **4.** continuous, without a break, *for two solid hours.* **5.** strongly constructed, not flimsy. **6.** having three dimensions, concerned with solids, *solid geometry.* **7.** sound and reliable, *there are solid arguments against it.* **8.** unanimous, *the miners are solid on this issue.* —**solid** *n.* **1.** a solid substance or body or food. **2.** a body or shape with three dimensions. —**solidly** *adv.,* **solidity** (sŏl-id-iti) *n.* □ **solid-state** *adj.* using transistors (which make use of the electronic properties of solids) instead of valves.

solidarity *n.* unity resulting from common interests or feelings or sympathies.

solidify (sŏl-id-i-fy) *v.* (solidified, solidifying) to make or become solid.

soliloquize (sŏl-il-ŏ-kwyz) *v.* to utter a soliloquy.

soliloquy (sŏl-il-ŏ-kwi) *n.* a speech in which a person expresses his thoughts aloud without addressing any person.

solitaire (sol-i-tair) *n.* **1.** a diamond or other gem set by itself. **2.** a game for one person, in which marbles are removed from their places on a special board after jumping others over them. **3.** (*Amer.*) the card-game of patience.

solitary *adj.* **1.** alone, without companions. **2.** single, *a solitary example.* **3.** not frequented, lonely, *a solitary valley.* —**solitary** *n.* **1.** a recluse. **2.** (*slang*) solitary confinement. —**solitarily** *adv.* □ **solitary confinement,** isolation in a separate cell as a punishment.

solitude *n.* being solitary.

solo *n.* (*pl.* solos) **1.** a musical composition or passage for a single voice or instrument. **2.** solo whist. **3.** a pilot's flight in an aircraft without an instructor or companion. —*adj. & adv.* unaccompanied, alone, *for* *solo flute*; *flying solo.* □ **solo whist,** a card-game like whist in which one player may oppose the others.

soloist *n.* a person who performs a solo.

solstice (**sol**-stis) *n.* either of the times in the year when the sun is furthest from the equator, the point reached by the sun at these times; *summer solstice,* about 21 June; *winter solstice,* about 22 December.

soluble (**sol**-yoo-bŭl) *adj.* **1.** able to be dissolved in liquid. **2.** able to be solved. **solubility** (sol-yoo-**bil**-iti) *n.*

solution *n.* **1.** a liquid in which something is dissolved. **2.** dissolving or being dissolved into liquid form. **3.** the process of solving a problem etc., the answer found.

solvable *adj.* able to be solved.

solve *v.* to find the answer to (a problem or puzzle) or the way out of (a difficulty). **solver** *n.*

solvent *adj.* **1.** having enough money to pay one's debts and liabilities. **2.** able to dissolve another substance. —*n.* a liquid used for dissolving something. —**solvency** *n.*

Somalia (sŏm-**ah**-liă) a country in East Africa. **Somali** *adj. & n.* (*pl.* **Somalis**).

somatic (sŏ-**mat**-ik) *adj.* of the body, physical as distinct from mental or spiritual.

sombre (**som**-ber) *adj.* dark, gloomy, dismal. **sombrely** *adv.*

sombrero (som-**brair**-oh) *n.* (*pl.* **sombreros**) a felt or straw hat with a very wide brim, worn especially in Latin-American countries.

some *adj. & pronoun* **1.** an unspecified quantity, *buy some apples*; *some few,* some but not many. **2.** an amount that is less than the whole, *some of them were late.* **3.** an unspecified person or thing, *some fool locked the door.* **4.** a considerable quantity, *that was some years ago.* **5.** approximately, *waited some 20 minutes.* **6.** (*slang*) remarkable, *that was some storm!* □ **some time,** at some point in time. (¶ To be written as two words; do not confuse with *sometime* and *sometimes.*)

somebody *n. & pronoun* **1.** an unspecified person. **2.** a person of importance.

somehow *adv.* **1.** in some unspecified or unexplained manner, *I never liked her, somehow.* **2.** by one means or another, *must get it finished somehow.*

someone *n. & pronoun* somebody.

somersault (**sum**-er-solt) *n.* an acrobatic movement in which a person rolls his body head over heels on the ground or in the air. —*v.* to turn a somersault.

Somerset (**sum**-er-set) a county of England.

something *n. & pronoun* **1.** an unspecified thing; *see something of a person,* meet him occasionally or for a short time; *he is something of an expert,* to some extent. **2.** an important or praiseworthy thing. □ **something like,** approximately, *it cost something like £10*; rather like, *it's something like a rabbit*; (*informal*) impressive, *that's something like!*

sometime *adj.* former, *her sometime friend.* —*adv.* formerly. ¶ See the note on *some time* (see entry for some).

sometimes *adv,.* at some times but not all the time. ¶ See the note on *some time* (see entry for some).

somewhat *adv.* to some extent, *it's somewhat difficult.* **more than somewhat,** (*informal*) very.

somewhere *adv.* at or in or to an unspecified place or position. **get somewhere,** (*informal*) to achieve some success.

somnambulist (som-**nam**-bew-list) *n.* a sleep-walker.

somnolent (**som**-nŏl-ĕnt) *adj.* sleepy, asleep. **somnolence** *n.*

son *n.* **1.** a male child in relation to his parents. **2.** a male descendant. **3.** a form of address to a boy or young man. □ **son-in-law** *n.* (*pl.* **sons-in-law**) a daughter's husband. **son of a bitch,** (*vulgar*) an unpleasant person. **son of a gun,** (*humorous*) a person.

sonar (**soh**-ner) *n.* a device for detecting objects under water by reflection of sound-waves.

sonata (sŏn-**ah**-tă) *n.* a musical composition for one instrument or two, usually with three or four movements.

sonatina (sonn-ă-**teen**-ă) *n.* a simple or short sonata.

son et lumière (sonn ay **loom**-yair) an entertainment given at night, a dramatic account of the history of a building or place, with lighting effects and recorded sound. (¶ French = sound and light.)

song *n.* **1.** singing. **2.** a musical composition for singing. □ **going for a song,** being sold very cheaply. **make a song and dance,** (*informal*) to make a great fuss.

songbird *n.* a bird with a musical cry.

songster *n.* **1.** a singer. **2.** a song-bird.

sonic *adj.* of or involving sound-waves. **sonic boom,** a loud noise heard when the shock wave caused by an aircraft travelling at supersonic speed reaches the hearer.

sonnet *n.* a poem of 14 lines with lengths and rhymes in accordance with one of several patterns.

sonny *n.* (*informal*) a form of address to a boy or young man.

sonorous (**sonn**-er-ŭs) *adj.* resonant, giving a deep powerful sound.

soon *adv.* **1.** in a short time, not long after the present or a specified time. **2.** early, quickly, *spoke too soon.* □ **as soon,** as readily, as willingly. **as soon as,** at the moment that, as early as; as readily or willingly as. **sooner or later,** at some time, eventually.

soot *n.* the black powdery substance that rises in the smoke of coal or wood etc. — *v.* to cover with soot.

soothe *v.* to calm, to ease (pain etc.). **soothing** *adj.*

sooty *adj.* (sootier, sootiest) **1.** full of soot, covered with soot. **2.** like soot, black.

sop *n.* **1.** a piece of bread dipped in liquid before being eaten or cooked. **2.** a concession that is made in order to pacify or bribe a troublesome person. —**sop** *v.* (sopped, sopping) **1.** to dip (a thing) in liquid. **2.** to soak up (liquid) with something absorbent.

sophisticated (sŏf-**ist**-i-kaytid) *adj.* **1.** characteristic of fashionable life and its ways, experienced in this and lacking natural simplicity. **2.** complicated, elaborate, *sophisticated electronic devices.* **sophistication** *n.*

sophistry (**sof**-ist-ri) *n.* clever and subtle but perhaps misleading reasoning.

soporific (sop-er-**if**-ik) *adj.* tending to cause sleep. —*n.* a medicinal substance that causes sleep.

sopping *adj.* very wet, drenched.

soppy *adj.* (soppier, soppiest) **1.** very wet. **2.** (*informal*) sentimental in a sickly way. **soppiness** *n.*

soprano (sŏ-**prah**-noh) *n.* (*pl.* sopranos) **1.** the highest female or boy's singing-voice. **2.** a singer with such a voice, a part written for it.

sorbet *n.* a flavoured water-ice.

sorcerer *n.* a magician, especially one supposedly aided by evil spirits. **sorceress** *n.*

sorcery *n.* a sorcerer's art or practices.

sordid *adj.* **1.** dirty, squalid. **2.** (of motives or actions) lacking dignity, not honourable, mercenary. **sordidly** *adv.*, **sordidness** *n.*

sore *adj.* **1.** causing pain from injury or disease. **2.** suffering pain, *felt sore all over.* **3.** causing mental pain or annoyance, *a sore subject.* **4.** (*old use*) serious, *in sore need.* **5.** distressed, vexed. —**sore** *n.* **1.** a sore place, especially where the skin is raw. **2.** a source of distress or annoyance. **soreness** *n.*

sorely *adv.* seriously, very, *I was sorely tempted.*

Soroptimist (ser-**op**-tim-ist) *n.* a member of an international association (*Soroptim-ist Club*) of clubs for business and professional women, similar to the Rotary Club.

sorrel [1] (*rhymes with* coral) *n.* a herb with sharp-tasting leaves used in salads.

sorrel [2] (*rhymes with* coral) *adj.* & *n.* light reddish-brown, a horse of this colour.

sorrow *n.* **1.** mental suffering caused by loss or disappointment etc. **2.** something that causes this. —*v.* to feel sorrow, to grieve.

sorrowful *adj.* feeling or showing sorrow. **sorrowfully** *adv.*

sorry *adj.* (sorrier, sorriest) **1.** feeling pity or regret or sympathy; *sorry!,* I am sorry, I beg your pardon. **2.** wretched, *in a sorry plight.*

sort *n.* **1.** a particular kind or variety. **2.** (*informal*) a person with regard to his character, *quite a good sort.* —*v.* to arrange according to sort or size or destination etc. —**sorter** *n.* □ **of a sort** *or* **of sorts,** not fully deserving the name given. **out of sorts,** slightly unwell or depressed. **sort of,** (*informal*) somewhat, rather, *I sort of expected it.* **sort out,** to disentangle; to select from others; (*slang*) to deal with or punish; *sort out the men from the boys,* show which people are truly competent.

¶ Correct usage is *this sort of thing* or *these sorts of things,* not *these sort of thing.*

sortie (**sor**-tee) *n.* **1.** an attack by troops coming out from a besieged place. **2.** a flight of an aircraft on a military operation.

SOS the international code-signal of extreme distress. —*n.* an urgent appeal for help or response.

sot *n.* a drunkard.

sotto voce (sot-oh **voh**-chi) in an undertone. (¶ Italian.)

soufflé (soo-flay) *n.* a light spongy dish made with beaten egg-white.

sought *see* seek. □ **sought-after** *adj.* much sought for purchase or use etc.

souk (*pr.* sook) *n.* a market-place in Muslim countries.

soul *n.* **1.** the spiritual or immortal element in a person. **2.** a person's mental or moral or emotional nature, *his whole soul revolted from it; cannot call his soul his own,* is completely under the control of another person. **3.** a personification or pattern; *she is the soul of honour,* incapable of dishonourable conduct. **4.** a person, *there's not a soul about.* **5.** Black American culture and racial identity. □ **soul-destroying** *adj.* deadeningly monotonous or depressing. **soul mates,** people ideally suited to each other. **soul music,** an emotional style of jazz-playing. **soul-searching** *n.* examination of one's conscience.

soulful *adj.* **1.** having or showing deep feeling. **2.** emotional. **soulfully** *adv.*

soulless *adj.* **1.** lacking sensitivity or noble qualities. **2.** dull, uninteresting.

sound[1] *n.* **1.** vibrations that travel through the air and are detectable (at certain frequencies) by the ear. **2.** the sensation produced by these vibrations, a particular kind of it, *the sound of music.* **3.** a sound made in speech. **4.** sound reproduced in a film etc. **5.** the mental impression produced by a statement or description etc., *we don't like the sound of the new scheme.* —**sound** *v.* **1.** to produce or cause to produce sound, *sound the trumpet.* **2.** to utter, to pronounce, *the 'h' in 'hour' is not sounded.* **3.** to give an impression when heard, *it sounds like an owl; the news sounds good,* seems to be good. **4.** to give an audible signal for, *sound the retreat.* **5.** to test by noting the sound produced, *the doctor sounds a patient's lungs with a stethoscope.* —**sounder** *n.* □ **sound barrier,** the high resistance of air to objects moving at speeds near that of sound. **sound broadcasting,** radio as opposed to TV. **sound effects,** sounds (other than speech or music) made artificially for use in a play or film etc. **sounding-board** *n.* a board to reflect sound or increase resonance. **sound off,** (*Amer. informal*) to express one's opinions loudly and freely. **sound out,** to question cautiously. **sound-proof** *adj.* not able to be penetrated by sound, (*v.*) to make sound-proof. **sound-track** *n.* a narrow strip at the side of a cinema film for carrying recorded sound, the sound itself.

sound[2] *adj.* **1.** healthy, not diseased or damaged. **2.** correct, logical, well-founded, *sound reasoning.* **3.** financially secure, *a sound investment.* **4.** thorough, *a sound thrashing; sound sleep,* deep and unbroken. —*adv.* soundly, *is sound asleep.* —**soundly** *adv.,* **soundness** *n.*

sound[3] *v.* **1.** to test the depth or quality of the bottom of (the sea or a river etc.) especially by a weighted line (*sounding-line*), to measure depth etc. in this way. **2.** to examine with a probe. —*n.* a surgeon's probe. —**sounder** *n.*

sound[4] *n.* a strait.

sounding[1] *n.* measurement of the depth of water (*see* sound[3]).

sounding[2] *adj.* resounding.

soup *n.* liquid food made of stock from stewed meat or fish or vegetables etc. —*v.* **soup up,** (*informal*) to increase the power of (an engine); to enliven. —**soupy** *adj.* □

in the soup, (*slang*) in difficulties. **soup-kitchen** *n.* a place where soup and other food is supplied free to the needy in times of distress.

soupçon (**soop-sawn**) *n.* a very small quantity, a trace, *add a soupçon of garlic.*

sour *adj.* **1.** tasting sharp like unripe fruit. **2.** not fresh, tasting or smelling sharp or unpleasant from fermentation or staleness. **3.** (of soil) excessively acid, deficient in lime. **4.** bad-tempered, disagreeable in manner, *gave me a sour look.* —*n.* an acid drink; *a whisky sour,* whisky with lemon-juice or lime-juice. —*v.* to make or become sour, *was soured by misfortune.* —**sourly** *adv.,* **sourness** *n.* □ **sour cream,** cream deliberately fermented by the action of bacteria. **sour grapes,** said when a person pretends to despise something he cannot have. (¶ From the fable of the fox who wanted some grapes but found that they were out of reach and so pretended that they were sour and undesirable anyway.)

source *n.* **1.** the place from which something comes or is obtained. **2.** the starting-point of a river. **3.** a person or book etc. supplying information. □ **at source,** at the point of origin.

sourpuss *n.* (*slang*) a sour-tempered person.

souse (*rhymes with* house) *v.* **1.** to steep in pickle, *soused herrings.* **2.** to plunge or soak in liquid, to drench, to throw (liquid) over a thing. □ **soused** *adj.* (*slang*) drunk.

south *n.* **1.** the point or direction opposite north. **2.** the southern part of something. —*adj. & adv.* towards or in the south; *a south wind,* blowing from the south. □ **South Africa,** a republic in the south of Africa. **South African,** of southern Africa or of the republic of South Africa; a native or inhabitant of the republic of South Africa. **South Australia,** a State of Australia. **South Pole,** the southernmost pole of the earth. **south pole,** (of a magnet) the pole that is attracted to the south. **South Sea,** the southern Pacific Ocean.

south-east *n.* the point or direction midway between south and east. **south-easterly** *adj. & n.,* **south-eastern** *adj.*

southerly *adj.* in or towards the south; *a southerly wind,* blowing from the south (approximately). —*n.* a southerly wind.

southern *adj.* of or in the south. **southern lights,** the aurora australis.

southerner *n.* a native or inhabitant of the south.

southernmost *adj.* furthest south.

southpaw *n.* a left-handed person, especially in sports.

southward *adj.* towards the south. **southwards** *adv.*

south-west *n.* the point or direction midway between south and west. **south-westerly** *adj.* & *n.*, **south-western** *adj.*

souvenir (soo-věn-eer) *n.* something bought or given or kept as a reminder of an incident or a place visited.

sou'wester *n.* a waterproof hat, usually of oilskin, with a broad flap at the back.

sovereign (sov-rin) *n.* 1. a king or queen who is the supreme ruler of a country. 2. a British gold coin, nominally worth £1. — **sovereign** *adj.* 1. supreme, *sovereign power*. 2. possessing sovereign power, independent, *sovereign states*. 3. very effective, *a sovereign remedy*. —**sovereignty** *n.*

soviet (soh-vi-ĕt *or* sov-i-ĕt) *n.* an elected council in the USSR. —**Soviet** *adj.* of the Soviet Union. □ **Soviet Union,** the USSR. **Supreme Soviet,** the governing council of the USSR or of one of its constituent republics.

sow¹ (*rhymes with* go) *v.* (sowed, sown *or* sowed, sowing) 1. to plant or scatter (seed) for growth, to plant seed in (a field etc.). 2. to implant or spread (feelings or ideas), *they sowed hatred amongst the people*. —**sower** *n.*

sow² (*rhymes with* cow) *n.* a fully-grown female pig. **sowthistle** *n.* a weed with thistle-like leaves and milky juice.

soy *n.* the soya bean. **soy sauce,** a sauce made by fermenting soya beans in brine.

soya bean a kind of bean (originally from south-east Asia) from which an edible oil and flour are obtained.

sozzled *adj.* (*slang*) very drunk.

spa (*pr.* spah) *n.* a curative mineral spring, a place with such a spring.

space *n.* 1. the boundless expanse in which all objects exist and move. 2. a portion of this, an area or volume for a particular purpose, *the box takes too much space*; *parking spaces*. 3. an interval between points or objects, an empty area, *separated by a space of 10 ft.*; *there's a space for your signature*. 4. the area of paper used in writing or printing something, *would take too much space to explain in detail*. 5. a large area, *the wide open spaces*. 6. outer space (*see* outer). 7. an interval of time, *within the space of an hour*. —*v.* to arrange with spaces between, *space them out*. □ **space-heater** *n.* a self-contained device for heating the room etc. in which it is placed. **space probe,** an unmanned rocket with instruments to detect conditions in outer space. **space shuttle,** a spacecraft for repeated use e.g. between earth and a space station. **space station,** an artificial satel-

lite used as a base for operations in space. **space suit,** a sealed pressurized suit allowing the wearer to leave a spacecraft and move about independently in outer space. **space-time continuum,** fusion of the concepts of space and time, with time as a fourth dimension. **space travel,** travel in outer space.

spacecraft *n.* (*pl.* spacecraft) a vehicle for travelling in outer space.

spaceman *n.* (*pl.* spacemen) a person who travels in outer space.

spaceship *n.* a spacecraft.

spacious (spay-shŭs) *adj.* providing much space, roomy. **spaciousness** *n.*

spade¹ *n.* 1. a tool for digging ground, with a broad metal blade and a wooden handle. 2. a tool of similar shape for other purposes. **spadeful** *n.* (*pl.* spadefuls). □ **call a spade a spade,** to call a thing by its proper name, to speak plainly or bluntly.

spade² *n.* a playing-card of the suit (*spades*) marked with black figures shaped like an inverted heart with a short stem.

spadework *n.* hard work done in preparation for something.

spaghetti (spă-get-i) *n.* pasta made in solid sticks, between macaroni and vermicelli in thickness.

Spain a country in south-west Europe.

span¹ *n.* 1. the extent from end to end or across. 2. the distance (about 9 inches or 23 cm) between the tips of a person's thumb and little finger when these are stretched apart. 3. the distance or part between the uprights supporting an arch or bridge. 4. length in time from beginning to end, *the span of life*. 5. (in South Africa) a team of two or more pairs of oxen. —**span** *v.* (spanned, spanning) 1. to extend across, to bridge. 2. to stretch one's hand across in one span, *span an octave on the piano*.

span² *see* spick.

spangle *n.* a small thin piece of glittering material, especially one of many ornamenting a dress etc. —*v.* to cover with spangles or sparkling objects.

Spaniard *n.* a native of Spain.

spaniel *n.* a kind of dog with long drooping ears and a silky coat.

Spanish *adj.* of Spain or its people or language. —*n.* the language of Spain.

spank *v.* to slap on the buttocks.

spanking *adj.* (*informal*) brisk, lively, *a spanking pace*.

spanner *n.* a tool for gripping and turning the nut on a screw etc. **throw a spanner into the works,** to sabotage a scheme.

spar¹ *n.* a strong pole used for a mast or yard or boom on a ship.

spar [2] *n.* any of several kinds of non-metallic mineral that split easily.

spar [3] *v.* (sparred, sparring) **1.** to box, especially for practice. **2.** to quarrel or argue. □ **sparring partner**, a boxer employed to give another boxer practice; a person with whom one enjoys frequent arguments.

spare *v.* **1.** to be merciful towards, to refrain from hurting or harming; *spare me this ordeal*, do not inflict it on me; *if I am spared*, if I live so long. **2.** to use with great restraint; *does not spare himself*, works very hard. **3.** to part with, to be able to afford to give, *we can't spare him until next week*; *can you spare me a moment?*; *enough and to spare*, more than is needed. — **spare** *adj.* **1.** additional to what is usually needed or used, in reserve for use when needed, *a spare wheel*; *spare time*, time not needed for work or other purposes. **2.** thin; lean. **3.** small in quantity, *on a spare diet*. —*n.* a spare part or thing kept in reserve for use when needed. —**sparely** *adv.*, **spareness** *n.* □ **go spare**, *(slang)* to become very annoyed. **spare my blushes**, do not embarrass me by praise. **spare-rib** *n.* a cut of pork from the lower ribs. **spare tyre**, *(informal)* a roll of fat round the waist.

sparing (**spair**-ing) *adj.* economical, not generous or wasteful. **sparingly** *adv.*

spark *n.* **1.** a fiery particle, e.g. one thrown off by a burning substance or caused by friction. **2.** a flash of light produced by an electrical discharge. **3.** a particle of a quality or of energy or genius, *hasn't a spark of generosity in him*. **4.** a lively young fellow. —*v.* to give off a spark or sparks. □ **sparking-plug** *or* **spark-plug** *ns.* a device producing an electrical spark to fire the mixture in an internal combustion engine. **spark off**, to trigger off.

sparkle *v.* **1.** to shine brightly with flashes of light. **2.** to show brilliant wit or liveliness. —*n.* a sparkling light or brightness. □ **sparkling wine**, wine that is effervescent.

sparkler *n.* a sparking firework. **sparklers** *pl. n.* (*slang*) diamonds.

sparrow *n.* a small brownish-grey bird. **sparrow-hawk** *n.* a small hawk that preys on small birds.

sparse *adj.* thinly scattered, not dense. **sparsely** *adv.*, **sparsity** *n.*, **sparseness** *n.*

spartan *adj.* (of conditions) simple and sometimes harsh, without comfort or luxuries. ¶ Named after the citizens of Sparta in ancient Greece, who were renowned for hardiness.

spasm *n.* **1.** a strong involuntary contraction of a muscle. **2.** a sudden brief spell of activity or emotion, *a spasm of coughing.* .

spasmodic (spaz-**mod**-ik) *adj.* **1.** occurring at irregular intervals. **2.** of or like a spasm, characterized by spasms. **spasmodically** *adv.*

spastic *adj.* physically disabled because of cerebral palsy, a condition in which there are faulty links between the brain and the motor nerves, causing jerky or involuntary movements through difficulty in controlling the muscles. —*n.* a person suffering from this condition. —**spasticity** (spas-**tiss**-iti) *n.*

spat [1] *see* spit [1].

spat [2] *n.* a short gaiter covering the instep and ankle.

spat [3] *n.* (*Amer. informal*) a slight quarrel.

spate (*pr.* spayt) *n.* a sudden flood or rush, *a spate of orders*. **in spate**, (of a river) flowing strongly at an abnormally high level.

spathe (*pr.* spay*th*) *n.* a large petal-like part of a flower, surrounding a central spike.

spatial (**spay**-shăl) *adj.* of or relating to space, existing in space. **spatially** *adv.*

spatter *v.* **1.** to scatter or fall in small drops. **2.** to splash with drops, *spattered her dress with mud*. —*n.* a splash or splashes, the sound of spattering.

spatula (**spat**-yoo-lă) *n.* **1.** a tool like a knife with a broad blunt flexible blade. **2.** a strip of stiff material used by a doctor for pressing down the tongue etc.

spatulate (**spat**-yoo-lăt) *adj.* shaped like a spatula, with a broad rounded end.

spawn *n.* **1.** the eggs of fish or frogs or shellfish. **2.** (*contemptuous*) offspring. **3.** the thread-like matter from which fungi grow, *mushroom spawn*. —**spawn** *v.* **1.** to deposit spawn, to produce from spawn. **2.** to generate, especially in large numbers, *the reports spawned by that committee*.

spay *v.* to sterilize (a female animal) by removing the ovaries.

speak *v.* (spoke, spoken, speaking) **1.** to utter words in an ordinary voice (not singing), to hold a conversation, to make a speech, *spoke for an hour*. **2.** to utter (words), to express or make known, *spoke the truth*. **3.** to use or be able to use (a certain language) in speaking, *we speak French*. **4.** to make a polite or friendly remark, *she always speaks when we meet*; *they haven't spoken for years*, avoid conversing through not being on friendly terms. **5.** to be evidence of something; *it speaks volumes for his patience*, is good or favourable evidence of it; *the facts speak for themselves*, need no supporting evidence. □ **be on speaking terms**, to be on friendly terms with each other. **not** *or*

nothing to speak of, very little, only very slightly. **so to speak**, if I may express it this way. **speak for oneself**, to give one's own opinion. **speaking-tube** *n*. a tube for conveying a voice from one room etc. to another. **speak one's mind**, to give one's opinion frankly. **speak out**, to speak loudly or freely; to speak one's mind. **speak up**, to speak more loudly, to speak out.

speaker *n*. **1.** a person who speaks, one who makes a speech. **2.** a loudspeaker. **3.** *the Speaker*, the person presiding over the House of Commons or a similar assembly.

spear *n*. **1.** a weapon for hurling, with a long shaft and a pointed tip. **2.** a pointed stem, e.g. of asparagus. —*v*. to pierce with or as if with a spear.

spearhead *n*. the foremost part of an attacking or advancing force. —*v*. to be the spearhead of.

spearmint *n*. a common garden mint used in cookery and to flavour chewing-gum.

spec *n*. **on spec**, (*slang*) as a speculation, without being certain of achieving what one wants.

special *adj*. **1.** of a particular kind, for a particular purpose, not general, *a special key*; *special training*. **2.** exceptional in amount or quality or intensity, *take special care of it*. —*n*. a special thing, a special train or edition etc., a special constable. — **specially** *adv*. □ **Special Branch**, the police department that deals with problems of national security. **special constable**, a person sworn in to assist the police in an emergency. **special licence**, a licence allowing a marriage to take place at very short notice or at a place other than one duly authorized. **special pleading**, (*informal*) persuasive but unfair reasoning.

specialist *n*. a person who is an expert in a special branch of a subject, especially of medicine.

speciality (spesh-i-**al**-iti) *n*. a special quality or characteristic or product, an activity in which a person specializes.

specialize *v*. **1.** to become a specialist. **2.** to have a product etc. to which one devotes special attention, *the shop specializes in sports goods*. **3.** to adapt for a particular purpose, *specialized organs such as the ear*. **specialization** *n*.

species (**spee**-shiz) *n*. (*pl*. species) **1.** a group of animals or plants within a genus, differing only in minor details from the others. **2.** a kind or sort, *a species of sledge*.

specific (spi-**sif**-ik) *adj*. **1.** particular, clearly distinguished from others, *the money was given for a specific purpose*. **2.** expressing oneself in exact terms, not vague, *please be specific about your requirements*. —*n*. a specific aspect or influence, a remedy for a specific disease or condition. —**specifically** *adv*. □ **specific gravity**, the ratio between the weight of a substance and that of the same volume of a standard substance (usually water for liquids and solids, air for gases).

specification *n*. **1.** specifying, being specified. **2.** the details describing something to be done or made.

specify *v*. (**specified**, **specifying**) to mention (details, ingredients, etc.) clearly and definitely, to include in a list of specifications.

specimen *n*. **1.** a part or individual taken as an example of a whole or of a class, especially for investigation or scientific examination. **2.** a quantity of a person's urine etc. taken for testing. **3.** (*informal*) a person of a specified sort, *he seems a peculiar specimen*.

specious (**spee**-shŭs) *adj*. seeming good or sound at first sight but lacking real merit, *specious reasoning*. **speciously** *adv*.

speck *n*. a small spot or particle.

speckle *n*. a small spot, a speck, especially as a natural marking. **speckled** *adj*. marked with speckles.

specs *pl. n.* (*informal*) spectacles.

spectacle *n*. **1.** a striking or impressive sight, *a magnificent spectacle*. **2.** a lavish public show or pageant. **3.** a ridiculous sight, *made a spectacle of himself*. □ **spectacles** *pl. n.* a pair of lenses set in a frame, worn before the eyes to assist sight or for protection from sunlight or dust etc.

spectacular *adj*. striking, impressive, amazing. —*n*. **1.** a spectacular performance. **2.** a lavishly-produced film etc. — **spectacularly** *adv*.

spectator *n*. a person who watches a show or game or incident etc. **spectator sports**, sports that attract many spectators.

spectra *see* spectrum.

spectral *adj*. **1.** of or like a spectre. **2.** of the spectrum.

spectre (**spek**-ter) *n*. **1.** a ghost. **2.** a haunting fear of future trouble, *the spectre of defeat loomed over them*.

spectrometer (spek-**trom**-it-er) *n*. a spectroscope that can be used for measuring spectra.

spectroscope (**spek**-trŏ-skohp) *n*. an instrument for producing and measuring spectra.

spectrum *n*. (*pl*. spectra) **1.** the bands of colour as seen in a rainbow, forming a series according to their wavelengths. **2.** a similar series of bands of sound. **3.** an entire range of related qualities or ideas etc., *the whole spectrum of science.*

speculate *v.* **1.** to form opinions about something without having definite knowledge or evidence. **2.** to buy or sell goods or stocks and shares etc. in the hope of making a profit but with risk of loss, to do this rashly. **speculation** *n.,* **speculator** *n.*

speculative (**spek**-yoo-lă-tiv) *adj.* **1.** of or based on speculation, *speculative reasoning.* **2.** involving financial speculation and risk of loss. **speculatively** *adv.*

speculum (**spek**-yoo-lŭm) *n.* a medical instrument for looking inside cavities of the body.

sped *see* speed.

speech *n.* **1.** the act or power or manner of speaking; *have speech with a person,* talk with him. **2.** words spoken, a spoken communication to an audience. **3.** language or dialect. □ **speech-day** *n.* an annual day of celebration at a school, when speeches are made. **speech-therapy** *n.* treatment to improve a stammer or other defect of speech.

speechifying *n.* (*informal*) making a speech or speeches, talking as if doing this.

speechless *adj.* silent, unable to speak because of great emotion. **speechlessly** *adv.*

speed *n.* **1.** the rate of time at which something moves or operates. **2.** rapidity of movement. **3.** the sensitivity of photographic film to light, the power of a lens to admit light. **4.** (*slang*) an amphetamine drug. —**speed** *v.* (sped (in sense 3 speeded), speeding) **1.** to move or pass quickly, *the years sped by.* **2.** to send quickly, *to speed you on your way.* **3.** to travel at an illegal or dangerous speed. □ **at speed,** rapidly. **speed up,** to move or work or cause to work at greater speed. **speed-up** *n.*

speedboat *n.* a fast motor boat.

speedometer (spee-**dom**-it-er) *n.* a device in a motor vehicle, showing its speed.

speedway *n.* **1.** an arena for motor-cycle racing. **2.** (*Amer.*) a road or track reserved for fast traffic.

speedwell *n.* a wild plant with small blue flowers.

speedy *adj.* (speedier, speediest) **1.** moving quickly. **2.** done or coming without delay. **speedily** *adv.*

speleology (spel-i-**ol**-ŏji) *n.* the exploration and scientific study of caves. **speleological** *adj.,* **speleologist** *n.*

spell[1] *n.* **1.** words supposed to have magic power. **2.** the state of being influenced by this, *laid them under a spell.*

3. fascination, attraction, *the spell of eastern countries.*

spell[2] *v.* (spelt, spelling) **1.** to write or name in their correct sequence the letters that form (a word or words). **2.** (of letters) to form as a word, *c a t spells 'cat'.* **3.** to have as a necessary result, *these changes spell ruin to the farmer.* **speller** *n.* □ **spell out,** to spell aloud; to make out (words) laboriously letter by letter; to state explicitly, to explain in detail.

spell[3] *n.* **1.** a period of time. **2.** a period of a certain type of weather, *during the cold spell.* **3.** a period of a certain activity, *did a spell of driving.* **4.** (*Austral.*) a rest period. —*v.* to relieve (a person) in work etc. by taking one's turn.

spellbound *adj.* with the attention held as if by a spell, entranced.

spelling-bee *n.* a competition in spelling.

spelt[1] *see* spell[2].

spelt[2] *n.* a kind of wheat.

spencer *n.* a woman's undergarment like a thin jumper, worn under a dress etc. for warmth.

spend *v.* (spent, spending) **1.** to pay out (money) in buying something. **2.** to use for a certain purpose, to use up, *don't spend too much time on it.* **3.** to pass, *spent a holiday in Greece.* —**spender** *n.* □ **spend a penny,** (*informal*) to urinate or defecate.

spendthrift *n.* a person who spends money extravagantly and wastefully.

spent *see* spend. —*adj.* used up, having lost its force or strength; *a spent match,* one that has been struck and extinguished and is now useless.

sperm *n.* **1.** (*pl.* sperms or sperm) a male reproductive cell, capable of fertilizing an ovum. **2.** semen. □ **sperm whale,** a large whale from which a waxy oil is obtained.

spermatic *adj.* of sperm; *spermatic cord,* that supporting the testicle within the scrotum.

spermicide (**sperm**-i-syd) *n.* a substance that kills sperm. **spermicidal** *adj.*

spew *v.* **1.** to vomit. **2.** to cast out in a stream.

sphagnum (**sfag**-nŭm) *n.* a kind of moss that grows on bogs.

sphere (*pr.* sfeer) *n.* **1.** a perfectly round solid geometric figure. **2.** something shaped like this. **3.** a field of action or influence or existence, a person's place in society, *took him out of his sphere.*

spherical (**sfe**-ri-kăl) *adj.* shaped like a sphere.

spheroid (**sfeer**-oid) *n.* a sphere-like but not perfectly spherical solid.

sphincter (**sfink**-ter) *n.* a ring of muscle surrounding an opening in the body and able to close it by contracting.

sphinx *n.* **1.** *the Sphinx,* (in Greek mythology) a winged monster at Thebes that killed all who could not answer the riddle it put to them. **2.** any of the ancient stone statues in Egypt with a recumbent lion's body and a human or animal's head, especially the large one near the pyramids at Giza. **3.** a statue resembling these. **4.** a person who does not reveal his thoughts and feelings.

spice *n.* **1.** a substance (obtained from plants) with a strong taste or smell, used for flavouring food. **2.** such substances collectively, *the spice market.* **3.** a thing that adds zest or excitement, *variety is the spice of life.* —*v.* to flavour with spice.

spick *adj.* **spick and span,** neat and clean, new-looking.

spicy *adj.* (spicier, spiciest) **1.** like spice, flavoured with spice. **2.** (of stories) slightly scandalous or improper. **spiciness** *n.*

spider *n.* an animal (not an insect) with a segmented body and eight jointed legs, spinning webs to trap insects which are its prey. □ **spider-man** *n.* a man who works at a great height in constructing buildings. **spider plant,** a grass-like plant with arching stems carrying young plants.

spidery *adj.* **1.** having thin angular lines like a spider's legs. **2.** like a cobweb. **3.** full of spiders.

spied *see* spy.

spiel (*pr.* speel) *n.* (*Amer. slang*) a glib or lengthy speech, usually intended to persuade. —*v.* (spieled, spieling) (*Amer. slang*) to talk glibly or lengthily.

spigot (**spig**-ŏt) *n.* a peg or plug used to stop the vent-hole of a cask or to control the flow of a tap.

spike *n.* **1.** a sharp projecting point, a pointed piece of metal. **2.** an ear of corn. **3.** a long cluster of flowers with short stalks (or no stalks) on a central stem. — **spike** *v.* **1.** to put spikes on, *spiked running-shoes.* **2.** to pierce or fasten with a spike. **3.** (*informal*) to add alcohol to (a drink). —**spiky** *adj.* □ **spike a person's guns,** to spoil his plans.

spill[1] *n.* a thin strip of wood or of twisted paper used to transfer flame, e.g. for lighting a pipe.

spill[2] *v.* (spilt, spilling) **1.** to cause or allow (a liquid etc.) to run over the edge of its container. **2.** (of liquid etc.) to become spilt. **3.** (*slang*) to make known, *spilt the news.* —*n.* spilling, being spilt, a fall. □ **spill blood,** to shed blood in killing or wounding. **spill over,** to overflow from something that is full. **spill the beans,** (*slang*) to let out information indiscreetly.

spillage *n.* spilling, the amount spilt.

spin *v.* (spun, spinning) **1.** to turn or cause to turn rapidly on its axis; *spin a coin,* toss it; *my head is spinning,* I feel dizzy. **2.** to draw out and twist (raw cotton or wool etc.) into threads, to make (yarn) in this way. **3.** (of a spider or silkworm) to make from a fine thread-like material emitted from the body, *spinning its web.* —**spin** *n.* **1.** a spinning movement. **2.** a short drive in a vehicle. □ **spin a yarn,** to tell an invented story, especially in order to deceive someone. **spin bowler,** a bowler who gives the ball a spinning movement. **spin-drier** *n.* a machine with a rapidly rotating drum in which moisture is removed from washed articles by centrifugal force. **spin-dry** *v.* to dry in a spin-drier. **spin-off** *n.* a benefit or product produced incidentally from a larger process or while developing this. **spin out,** to cause to last a long time.

spina bifida (spy-nă **bif**-id-ă) · an abnormal congenital condition in which certain bones of the spine are not properly developed and allow the meninges or spinal cord to protrude.

spinach *n.* a vegetable with dark-green leaves.

spinal *adj.* of the spine. **spinal column,** the spine. **spinal cord,** the rope-like mass of nerve-fibres enclosed within the spinal column.

spindle *n.* **1.** a slender rod on which thread is twisted or wound in spinning. **2.** a pin or axis that revolves or on which something revolves. **3.** a spindle-tree. □ **spindle-berry** *n.* the fruit of the spindle-tree. **spindle-shanks** *n.* (*slang*) a person with long thin legs. **spindle-tree** *n.* a shrub or small tree with pink or red berries and hard wood formerly used for spindles.

spindly *adj.* long or tall and thin.

spindrift *n.* spray blown along the surface of the sea.

spine *n.* **1.** the backbone. **2.** one of the sharp needle-like projections on certain plants (e.g. cacti) and animals (e.g. hedgehogs). **3.** the part of a book where the pages are hinged, this section of the jacket or cover. □ **spine-chiller** *n.* a book or film etc. that causes a thrill of terror. **spine-chilling** *adj.*

spineless *adj.* **1.** having no backbone. **2.** lacking determination or strength of character. **spinelessness** *n.*

spinet (spin-et) *n.* a kind of small harpsichord.

spinnaker (**spin**-ă-ker) *n.* a large triangular extra sail on a racing-yacht.

spinner *n.* a person or thing that spins.

spinney n. (pl. spinneys) a small wood, a thicket.

spinning-wheel n. a household device for spinning fibre into yarn, with a spindle driven by a wheel.

spinster n. a woman who has not married.

spiny adj. full of spines, prickly.

spiraea (spy-**ree**-ă) n. a kind of shrub or plant with small white or pink flowers.

spiral adj. advancing or ascending in a continuous curve (either two-dimensional or three-dimensional) that winds round a central point or axis. —n. **1.** a spiral line, a thing of spiral form. **2.** a continuous increase or decrease in two or more quantities alternately because of their dependence on each other, *the spiral of rising wages and prices.* —v. (spiralled, spiralling) to move in a spiral course. —**spirally** adv.

spire n. a pointed structure in the form of a tall cone or pyramid, especially on a church tower.

spirit n. **1.** a person's mind or feelings or animating principle as distinct from his body, *shall be with you in spirit.* **2.** soul. **3.** a disembodied soul, a ghost. **4.** life and consciousness not associated with a body, *God is pure spirit*; *the Spirit,* the Holy Spirit (*see* holy). **5.** a person's nature. **6.** a person with certain mental or moral qualities, *a few brave spirits went swimming.* **7.** the characteristic quality or mood of something, *the spirit of the times*; *the spirit of the law,* its real purpose as distinct from a strict interpretation of its words. **8.** liveliness, readiness to assert oneself, *answered with spirit.* **9.** a distilled extract. —v. to carry off swiftly and secretly, *spirited him away.* □ **spirit-lamp** n. a lamp that burns methylated spirit or a similar fluid. **spirit-level** n. a glass tube nearly filled with liquid and containing an air-bubble, used to test whether something is horizontal by means of the position of this bubble. **spirits** pl. n. a person's feeling of cheerfulness or depression, *raised their spirits*; strong distilled alcoholic drink, e.g. whisky, gin.

spirited adj. **1.** full of spirit, lively, ready to assert oneself. **2.** having mental spirit or spirits of a certain kind, *a poor-spirited creature.* **spiritedly** adv.

spiritless adj. not spirited.

spiritual adj. **1.** of the human spirit or soul, not physical or worldly. **2.** of the Church or religion; *lords spiritual,* see lord. —n. a religious folk-song of American Blacks or one resembling this. — **spiritually** adv., **spirituality** n.

spiritualism n. the belief that spirits of the dead can and do communicate with the living, practices based on this. **spiritualist** n.

spirituous adj. containing much alcohol; *spirituous liquors,* those that are distilled and not only fermented.

spit[1] v. (spat or spit, spitting) **1.** to eject from the mouth, to eject saliva. **2.** to make a noise like spitting as a cat does when angry or hostile, (of a person) to show anger, *spitting with fury.* **3.** to utter violently, *spat curses at me.* **4.** to fall lightly, *it's spitting with rain.* —spit n. **1.** spittle. **2.** the act of spitting. **3.** an exact likeness, *he's the dead spit of his father.* □ **spit and polish,** cleaning and polishing of equipment etc., especially by soldiers. **spit it out,** (slang) say what you wish without delay. **spitting image,** an exact likeness.

spit[2] n. **1.** a long thin metal spike thrust through meat to hold it while it is roasted. **2.** a long narrow strip of land projecting into the sea. —v. (spitted, spitting) to pierce with or as if with a spit.

spit[3] n. a spade's depth of earth, *dig it two spits deep.*

spite n. malicious desire to hurt or annoy or humiliate another person. —v. to hurt or annoy etc. from spite. □ **in spite of,** not being prevented by, *enjoyed ourselves in spite of the weather.*

spiteful adj. full of spite, showing or caused by spite. **spitefully** adv., **spitefulness** n.

spitfire n. a fiery-tempered person.

spittle n. saliva, especially that ejected from the mouth.

spittoon n. a receptacle for spitting into.

spiv n. (slang) a smartly-dressed person who makes money by shady dealings, not by regular work.

splash v. **1.** to cause (liquid) to fly about in drops, to wet with such drops. **2.** (of liquid) to be splashed. **3.** to move or fall with splashing, *we splashed through the puddles.* **4.** to decorate with irregular patches of colour etc. **5.** to display in large print, *the news was splashed across the Sunday papers.* **6.** to spend (money) freely and ostentatiously. —**splash** n. **1.** splashing, a sound or mark made by this. **2.** a quantity of liquid splashed. **3.** (informal) a small quantity of soda-water or other liquid in a drink. **4.** a patch of colour or light. **5.** a striking or ostentatious display or effect. —**splashy** adj. □ **splash-down** n. the alighting of a spacecraft on the sea.

splashback n. a panel behind a sink etc. to protect a wall from splashes.

splatter v. to splash noisily. —n. a noisy splashing sound.

splay v. to spread apart, to slant (the sides of an opening) so that the inside is wider than the outside or vice versa; *splayed his feet*, placed them with the toes turned outwards not forwards. —adj. splayed.

spleen n. an organ of the body situated at the left of the stomach and involved in maintaining the proper condition of the blood.

splendid adj. 1. magnificent, displaying splendour. 2. excellent, *a splendid achievement*. **splendidly** adv.

splendour n. brilliance, magnificent display or appearance, grandeur.

splice v. 1. to join (two ends of rope) by untwisting and interweaving the strands of each. 2. to join (pieces of film or timber etc.) by overlapping the ends. —n. a join made by splicing. □ **get spliced**, (*slang*) to get married.

splint n. a strip of rigid material bound to an injured part of the body to prevent movement, e.g. while a broken bone heals. —v. to secure with a splint.

splinter n. a thin sharp piece of wood or stone etc. broken off from a larger piece. —v. to break or become broken into splinters. **splintery** adj. □ **splinter group**, a small group that has broken away from a larger one, e.g. in a political party.

split v. (split, splitting) 1. to break or become broken into parts, especially lengthwise or along the grain of wood etc. 2. to divide into parts, to divide and share. 3. to come apart, to tear, *this coat has split at the seams*. 4. to divide or become divided into disagreeing or hostile groups. 5. (*slang*) to reveal a secret; *split on a person*, to inform on him. —split n. 1. splitting, being split. 2. the place where something has split or torn. 3. something split or divided. 4. a sweet dish of split fruit with cream or ice-cream etc., *banana split*. □ **split hairs**, *see* hair. **split infinitive**, an infinitive with a word placed between *to* and the verb, e.g. *to thoroughly understand*. (¶ Many people dislike this construction and it can usually be avoided, e.g. by putting *to understand thoroughly*.) **split-level** adj. (of a building) having adjoining rooms at a level midway between successive storeys in other parts; (of a cooker) having the oven placed separately from the burners or hotplates not below them, so that it can be at a convenient height. **split one's sides**, to laugh very heartily. **split personality**, schizophrenia. **split pin**, a metal pin with split ends that hold it in position when these are splayed.

split ring, a ring with ends not joined but closely overlapping. **splits** n. an acrobatic position in which the legs are stretched along the floor in opposite directions and at right angles to the trunk. **split second**, a very brief moment. **split-second** adj. extremely rapid; accurate to a very small fraction of time, *split-second timing*. **split shift**, a shift in which there are two or more periods of duty. **split the difference**, to take an amount half-way between two proposed amounts. **split up**, to split, to separate; (of a married couple) to cease to live together.

splitting adj. (of a headache) very severe, feeling as if it will split one's head.

splotch n. a splash or blotch on material etc. —v. to mark with splotches.

splurge n. an ostentatious display, especially of wealth. —v. to make a splurge, to spend money freely.

splutter v. 1. to make a rapid series of spitting sounds. 2. to speak or utter rapidly or indistinctly (e.g. in rage) —n. a spluttering sound.

spoil v. (spoilt *or* spoiled, spoiling) 1. to damage, to make useless or unsatisfactory. 2. to become unfit for use. 3. to harm the character of (a person) by lack of discipline or excessive generosity or pampering. —n. = spoils. □ **be spoiling for**, to desire eagerly, *he is spoiling for a fight*. **spoils** pl. n. plunder; benefits gained by a victor, profitable advantages of an official position. **spoil-sport** n. a person who spoils the enjoyment of others.

spoiler n. a device on an aircraft to slow it down by interrupting the air flow, a similar device on a vehicle to prevent it from being lifted off the road when travelling very fast.

spoke[1] n. one of the bars or wire rods that connect the centre or hub of a wheel to its rim. **put a spoke in a person's wheel**, to thwart his intentions.

spoke[2], **spoken** *see* speak.

spokeshave n. a tool for planing something curved.

spokesman n. (*pl.* spokesmen) a person who speaks on behalf of a group.

spoliation (spoh-li-ay-shŏn) n. pillaging.

sponge n. 1. a kind of water animal with a porous structure. 2. the skeleton of this, or a substance of similar texture, used for washing, cleaning, or padding. 3. a thing of light open texture, something absorbent. 4. sponge-cake. 5. sponging, a wash with a sponge. —sponge v. 1. to wipe or wash with a sponge. 2. to live off the generosity of others, to cadge, *to sponge on people*. □

sponge-bag *n.* a waterproof bag for toilet articles. **sponge-cake** *n.* a cake with a light, open texture. **sponge pudding,** a pudding like a sponge-cake. **sponge rubber,** rubber made with many small spaces like a sponge. **throw up the sponge,** *see* throw.

spongeable *adj.* able to be cleaned by sponging.

sponger *n.* a person who sponges on others.

spongy *adj.* (spongier, spongiest) like a sponge in texture, soft and springy.

sponson *n.* a projection on the side of a ship or tank or seaplane, an air-filled structure fitted along the gunwale of a canoe to make it more stable and buoyant.

sponsor *n.* 1. a person who makes himself responsible for another who is undergoing training etc. 2. a godparent. 3. a person who puts forward a proposal, e.g. for a new law. 4. a person or firm that provides funds for a broadcast or for a musical, artistic, or sporting event. 5. a person who subscribes to charity in return for a specified activity by another person. —*v.* to act as sponsor for. —**sponsorship** *n.*

spontaneous (spon-tay-niŭs) *adj.* resulting from natural impulse, not caused or suggested from outside, not forced. **spontaneously** *adv.,* **spontaneity** (spontăn-ee-iti) *n.* □ **spontaneous combustion,** the bursting into flame of a substance (e.g. a mass of oily rags) because of heat produced by its own rapid oxidation and not by flame etc. from an external source.

spoof *n.* (*slang*) a hoax, a humorous imitation.

spook *n.* (*informal*) a ghost.

spooky *adj.* (*informal*) ghostly, eerie.

spool *n.* a reel on which something is wound, e.g. yarn or photographic film.

spoon *n.* 1. a utensil consisting of an oval or round bowl and a handle, used for conveying food to the mouth or for stirring or measuring. 2. the amount it contains. — **spoon** *v.* 1. to take or lift with a spoon. 2. to hit (a ball) feebly upwards.

spoonbill *n.* a wading-bird with a very broad flat tip to its bill.

spoonerism *n.* interchange of the initial sounds of two words, usually as a slip of the tongue, e.g. *he's a boiled sprat* (= spoiled brat). ¶ Named after the Rev. W. A. Spooner (1884–1930), said to have made such errors in speaking.

spoon-feed *v.* (spoon-fed, spoon-feeding) 1. to feed with liquid food from a spoon. 2. to give excessive help to (a person etc.) so that the recipient does not need to make any effort.

spoonful *n.* (*pl.* spoonfuls) as much as a spoon will hold.

spoor *n.* the track or scent left by an animal.

sporadic (sper-**ad**-ik) *adj.* occurring here and there, scattered. **sporadically** *adv.*

spore *n.* one of the tiny reproductive cells of plants such as fungi and ferns.

sporran (spo-răn) *n.* a pouch worn hanging in front of the kilt as part of Highland dress.

sport *n.* 1. an athletic (especially outdoor) activity. 2. any game or pastime, an outdoor pastime such as hunting or fishing. 3. such activities or pastimes collectively, the world of sport. 4. amusement, fun, *said it in sport.* 5. (*slang*) a sportsmanlike person. 6. an animal or plant that is strikingly different from its parent(s). —**sport** *v.* 1. to play, to amuse oneself. 2. to wear or display, *sported a gold tie-pin.* □ **sports** *pl. n.* athletic activities, a meeting for competition in these, *the school sports.* **sports car,** an open low-built fast car. **sports coat,** a man's jacket for informal wear (not part of a suit).

sporting *adj.* 1. interested in sport, concerned with sport, *a sporting man.* 2. sportsmanlike. □ **a sporting chance,** a reasonable chance of success.

sportive *adj.* playful. **sportively** *adv.*

sportsman *n.* (*pl.* sportsmen) 1. a man who takes part in sports. 2. a sportsmanlike person. —**sportswoman** *n.* (*pl.* sportswomen), **sportsmanship** *n.*

sportsmanlike *adj.* behaving fairly and generously.

sporty *adj.* (*informal*) 1. fond of sport. 2. dashing.

spot *n.* 1. a roundish area different in colour from the rest of a surface. 2. a roundish mark or stain. 3. a pimple. 4. a particular place or locality. 5. (*informal*) a small amount of something, *a spot of leave.* 6. a drop, *a few spots of rain.* 7. a spotlight. —**spot** *v.* (spotted, spotting) 1. to mark with a spot or spots. 2. (*informal*) to catch sight of, to detect or recognize, *spotted him at once as an American.* 3. to watch for and take note of, *train-spotting.* —**spotter** *n.* □ **in a spot,** (*slang*) in difficulties. **on the spot,** without delay or change of place; at the scene of action; (of a person) alert, equal to dealing with a situation; *put a person on the spot,* to put him in a difficult position, to compel him to take action or justify himself. **spot cash,** cash down. **spot check,** a check made suddenly on something chosen at random. **spot-on** *adv.* (*informal*) precisely. **spotted Dick,** suet pudding containing currants. **spot**

welding, welding of small areas that are in contact.

spotless *adj.* free from stain or blemish, perfectly clean. **spotlessly** *adv.*

spotlight *n.* a beam of light directed on a small area, a lamp giving this. —*v.* (spotlighted, spotlighting) **1.** to direct a spotlight on. **2.** to draw attention to, to make conspicuous.

spotty *adj.* (spottier, spottiest) marked with spots.

spouse *n.* a person's husband or wife.

spout *n.* **1.** a projecting tube through which liquid is poured or conveyed. **2.** a jet of liquid. —**spout** *v.* **1.** to come or send out forcefully as a jet of liquid, *water spouted from the pump*; *the wound was spouting blood.* **2.** to utter or speak lengthily. □ **up the spout**, (*slang*) broken or ruined, in a hopeless condition.

sprain *v.* to injure (a joint or its muscles or ligaments) by wrenching it violently. —*n.* an injury caused in this way.

sprang *see* spring.

sprat *n.* a small herring-like fish.

sprawl *v.* **1.** to sit or lie or fall with the arms and legs spread out loosely. **2.** to spread out in an irregular or straggling way. —*n.* a sprawling attitude or movement or arrangement.

spray [1] *n.* **1.** a single shoot or branch with its leaves and twigs and flowers. **2.** a bunch of cut flowers etc. arranged decoratively. **3.** an ornament in similar form.

spray [2] *n.* **1.** water or other liquid dispersed in very small drops. **2.** a liquid preparation for spraying. **3.** a device for spraying liquid. —*v.* to send out (liquid) or be sent out in very small drops, to wet with liquid in this way. —**sprayer** *n.* □ **spray-gun** *n.* a gun-like device for spraying liquid.

spread *v.* (spread, spreading) **1.** to open out, to unroll or unfold, *the peacock spreads its tail*; *spread the map out.* **2.** to become longer or wider, *the stain began to spread.* **3.** to cover the surface of, to apply as a layer, *spread the bread with jam*; *spread the paint evenly.* **4.** to be able to be spread, *it spreads like butter.* **5.** to make or become more widely known or felt or suffered, *spread the news*; *panic spread.* **6.** to distribute or become distributed, *settlers spread inland.* **7.** to distribute over a period, *spread the payments over 12 months.* — **spread** *n.* **1.** spreading, being spread. **2.** the extent or expanse or breadth of something. **3.** expansion; *middle-aged spread*, increased bodily girth in middle age. **4.** a bedspread. **5.** (*informal*) a lavish meal. **6.** the range of something. **7.** a sweet

or savoury paste for spreading on bread. □ **spread eagle**, the figure of an eagle with legs and wings extended, as an emblem. **spread-eagle** *v.* to spread out (a person's body) in this way. **spread oneself**, to talk or write lengthily; to spend or provide things lavishly.

spree *n.* (*informal*) a lively outing, some fun; *a shopping* or *spending spree*, an outing or period in which one shops or spends freely.

sprig [1] *n.* **1.** a small branch, a shoot. **2.** an ornament or decoration in this form.

sprig [2] *n.* a small tapering headless tack.

sprightly *adj.* (sprightlier, sprightliest) lively, full of energy. **sprightliness** *n.*

spring *v.* (sprang, sprung, springing) **1.** to jump, to move rapidly or suddenly, especially in a single movement. **2.** to grow or issue, to arise, *weeds sprang up*; *their discontent springs from distrust of their leaders.* **3.** to become warped or split. **4.** to rouse (game) from an earth or covert; *spring a prisoner from gaol*, to contrive his escape. **5.** to cause to operate suddenly, *sprang the trap.* **6.** to produce or develop suddenly or unexpectedly, *sprang a surprise on us.* — **spring** *n.* **1.** the act of springing, a jump. **2.** a device (usually of bent or coiled metal) that reverts to its original position after being compressed or tightened or stretched, used to drive clockwork or (in groups) to make a seat etc. more comfortable. **3.** elasticity. **4.** a place where water or oil comes up naturally from the ground, the flow of this. **5.** the season in which vegetation begins to appear, from March to May in the northern hemisphere. □ **spring a leak**, to develop a leak. **spring balance**, a device that measures weight by tension of a spring. **spring-clean** *v.* to clean one's home thoroughly, especially in spring. **spring-cleaning** *n.* this process. **spring mattress**, one containing springs. **spring onion**, a young onion eaten raw in salad. **spring tide**, the tide when there is the largest rise and fall of water, occurring shortly after the new and full moon.

springboard *n.* a flexible board for giving impetus to a person who jumps on it, used in gymnastics and in diving.

springbok *n.* a South African gazelle that can spring high into the air.

springtime *n.* the season of spring.

springy *adj.* (springier, springiest) able to spring back easily after being squeezed or stretched. **springiness** *n.*

sprinkle *v.* to scatter or fall in small drops or particles, to scatter small drops etc. on (a surface). —*n.* a sprinkling.

sprinkler *n.* a device for sprinkling water.

sprinkling *n.* **1.** something sprinkled. **2.** a few here and there.

sprint *v.* to run at full speed, especially over a short distance. —*n.* a run of this kind, a similar spell of maximum effort in swimming, cycling, etc. —**sprinter** *n.*

sprit *n.* a small spar reaching diagonally from a mast to the upper outer corner of a sail.

sprite *n.* an elf or fairy or goblin.

sprocket *n.* one of a series of teeth on a wheel, engaging with links on a chain.

sprout *v.* **1.** to begin to grow or appear, to put forth shoots. **2.** to cause to spring up as a growth, *has sprouted horns.* —**sprout** *n.* **1.** the shoot of a plant. **2.** a Brussels sprout (*see* Brussels).

spruce ¹ *adj.* neat and trim in appearance, smart. —*v.* to smarten, *spruce oneself up.* —**sprucely** *adv.*, **spruceness** *n.*

spruce ² *n.* a kind of fir with dense foliage, its wood.

sprung *see* spring. —*adj.* fitted with springs, *a sprung seat.*

spry *adj.* (spryer, spryest) active, nimble, lively. **spryly** *adv.*, **spryness** *n.*

spud *n.* **1.** a small narrow spade for digging up weeds or cutting their roots. **2.** (*slang*) a potato.

spume *n.* froth, foam.

spun *see* spin. □ **spun silk,** yarn or fabric made from waste silk. **spun sugar,** a fluffy mass made from boiled sugar drawn into long threads.

spunk *n.* (*slang*) courage.

spur *n.* **1.** a pricking device with a projecting point or toothed wheel, worn on a horseman's heel. **2.** a stimulus or incentive. **3.** something shaped like a spur, a hard projection on a cock's leg, a slender hollow projection on a flower. **4.** a ridge projecting from a mountain. **5.** a branch road or railway. —**spur** *v.* (spurred, spurring) **1.** to urge (one's horse) on by pricking it with spurs. **2.** to urge on, to incite, *spurred the men to greater effort.* **3.** to stimulate, *spurred their interest.* □ **on the spur of the moment,** on an impulse, without previous planning. **win one's spurs,** to prove one's ability, to win distinction.

spurge *n.* a kind of plant or bush with a bitter milky juice. **spurge laurel,** a shrub related to daphne.

spurious (spewr-iŭs) *adj.* not genuine or authentic. **spuriously** *adv.*

spurn *v.* to reject scornfully.

spurred *adj.* having spurs, fitted with spurs.

spurt *v.* **1.** to gush, to send out (a liquid) suddenly. **2.** to increase one's speed suddenly. —**spurt** *n.* **1.** a sudden gush. **2.** a

short burst of activity, a sudden increase in speed.

sputnik (spuut-nik) *n.* a Russian artificial satellite orbiting the earth.

sputter *v.* to splutter, to make a series of quick explosive sounds, *sausages sputtered in the pan.* —*n.* a sputtering sound.

sputum (spew-tŭm) *n.* spittle, matter that is spat out.

spy *n.* a person who secretly watches or gathers information about the activities of others and reports the result, one employed by a government to do this in another country. —*v.* (spied, spying) **1.** to see, to catch sight of. **2.** to be a spy, to keep watch secretly, *he was spying on them*; *spy out the land,* investigate its features etc. secretly.

sq. *abbrev.* square.

squab (*pr.* skwob) *n.* **1.** a young pigeon. **2.** a stuffed seat or cushion, especially as part (usually the back) of a car seat.

squabble *v.* to quarrel in a petty or noisy way, as children do. —*n.* a quarrel of this kind.

squad *n.* a small group of people working or being trained together.

squadron *n.* **1.** a division of a cavalry unit or armoured formation, consisting of two troops. **2.** a detachment of warships. **3.** a unit of the RAF (10 to 18 aircraft). □ **squadron leader,** an officer commanding a squadron in the RAF.

squalid *adj.* **1.** dirty and unpleasant, especially because of neglect or poverty. **2.** morally degrading. **squalidly** *adv.*, **squalor** *n.*

squall *n.* **1.** a harsh cry or scream, especially of a baby. **2.** a sudden storm of wind, especially with rain or snow or sleet. —*v.* to utter a squall. —**squally** *adj.* □ **look out for squalls,** to be on one's guard against trouble.

squander *v.* to spend wastefully.

square *n.* **1.** a geometric figure with four equal sides and four right angles. **2.** an area or object shaped like this. **3.** a four-sided area surrounded by buildings, *Belgrave Square.* **4.** (in astrology) the aspect of two planets 90° apart, regarded as having on unfavourable influence. **5.** an L-shaped or T-shaped instrument for obtaining or testing right angles. **6.** the product obtained when a number is multiplied by itself, *9 is the square of 3* $(9 = 3 \times 3)$. **7.** (*slang*) a person considered old-fashioned or conventional, one who does not know or does not like the current trends. —**square** *adj.* **1.** of square shape. **2.** right-angled, *the desk has square corners.* **3.** of or using units that express the measure of an area; *one square metre*, a unit equal to the area of a square with sides one metre long. **4.** of comparatively broad sturdy shape, *a man of square frame*. **5.** properly arranged, tidy, *get things square*. **6.** equal, with no balance of advantage or debt etc. on either side, *the golfers were all square at the fourth hole*. **7.** straightforward, uncompromising, *got a square refusal*. **8.** fair, honest, *a square deal*. **9.** (*slang*) old-fashioned, conventional. —*adv.* squarely, directly, *hit him square on the jaw*. —**square** *v.* **1.** to make right-angled, *square the corners*. **2.** to mark with squares, *squared paper*. **3.** to place evenly or squarely, *squared his shoulders*. **4.** to multiply (a number) by itself, *3 squared is 9 ($3^2 = 9$), 3 × 3 = 9.* **5.** to settle or pay, *that squares the account*. **6.** (*informal*) to secure the co-operation of (a person) by payment or bribery, *try and square the porter*. **7.** to be or make consistent, *his story doesn't square with yours; try and square the two stories*. —**squarely** *adv.*, **squareness** *n.* □ **back to square one,** back to the starting-point in an enterprise etc., with no progress made. **on the square,** (*informal*) honest, honestly. **square dance,** a dance in which four couples face inwards from four sides. **square leg,** a fieldsman in cricket on the batsman's leg-side and nearly in line with the wicket, his position. **square meal,** a large satisfying meal. **square peg in a round hole,** a person who is not fitted for his job. **square-rigged** *adj.* with the principal sails at right angles to the length of the ship. **square root,** a number of which the given number is the square (*see n.* sense 6), *3 is the square root of 9.* **square up to,** to assume a boxer's fighting attitude; to face and tackle (a difficulty) resolutely.

squarish *adj.* approximately square.

squash¹ *v.* **1.** to crush, to squeeze or become squeezed flat or into pulp. **2.** to pack tightly, to crowd, to squeeze into a small space. **3.** to suppress, *squashed the rebellion*. **4.** to silence with a crushing reply. —**squash** *n.* **1.** a crowd of people squashed together. **2.** the sound of something being squashed. **3.** a crushed mass. **4.** a fruit-flavoured soft drink. **5.** squash rackets. —**squashy** *adj.* □ **squash rackets,** a game played with rackets and a small ball in a closed court.

squash² *n.* a kind of gourd used as a vegetable, the plant that bears it.

squat *v.* (**squatted, squatting**) **1.** to sit on one's heels or crouch with knees drawn up closely. **2.** (of an animal) to crouch close to the ground. **3.** (*informal*) to sit. **4.** to be a squatter, to occupy as a squatter. —**squat**

n. **1.** a squatting posture. **2.** occupying a place as a squatter, the place itself. —*adj.* short and thick, dumpy.

squatter *n.* **1.** one who sits in a squatting posture. **2.** a person who settles on unoccupied land in order to acquire a legal right to it. **3.** a person who takes temporary possession of unoccupied buildings for living in, without authority. **4.** (*Austral.*) a sheep-farmer.

squaw *n.* a North American Indian woman or wife.

squawk *n.* a loud harsh cry. —*v.* **1.** to utter a squawk. **2.** (*slang*) to complain.

squeak *n.* a short high-pitched cry or sound. —*v.* **1.** to utter or make a squeak. **2.** (*slang*) to become an informer. —**squeaker** *n.* □ **a narrow squeak,** (*informal*) a narrow escape from danger or failure.

squeaky *adj.* (**squeakier, squeakiest**) making a squeaking sound.

squeal *n.* a long shrill cry or sound. —*v.* **1.** to utter a squeal, to make this sound. **2.** (*slang*) to protest sharply. **3.** (*slang*) to become an informer.

squeamish *adj.* **1.** easily sickened or disgusted or shocked. **2.** excessively scrupulous about principles. **squeamishness** *n.*

squeegee (skwee-jee) *n.* a tool with a rubber blade or roller on a handle, used for sweeping or squeezing away water or moisture. —*v.* to treat with a squeegee.

squeeze *v.* **1.** to exert pressure on from opposite or all sides. **2.** to treat in this way so as to extract moisture or juice, to extract (moisture etc.) by squeezing. **3.** to force into or through, to force one's way, to crowd, *we squeezed six people into the car; she squeezed through the gap*. **4.** to produce by pressure or effort. **5.** to obtain by compulsion or strong urging, *squeezed a promise from them*. **6.** to extort money etc. from, to harass in this way, *heavy taxation is squeezing small firms.* — **squeeze** *n.* **1.** squeezing, being squeezed. **2.** an affectionate clasp or hug. **3.** a small amount of liquid produced by squeezing, *a squeeze of lemon-juice*. **4.** a crowd or crush, the pressure of this, *we all got in, but it was a tight squeeze*. **5.** hardship or difficulty caused by shortage of money or time etc. **6.** restrictions on borrowing etc. during a financial crisis.

squeezer *n.* a device for squeezing juice from fruit by pressure.

squelch *v.* to make a sound like someone treading in thick mud. —*n.* this sound.

squib *n.* a small firework that makes a hissing sound and then explodes. **damp**

squib, something intended to impress people but failing to do so.

squid *n.* a sea creature related to the cuttlefish, with ten arms round the mouth.

squiggle *n.* a short curly line, especially in handwriting.

squill *n.* 1. a wild variety of scilla. 2. a seashore plant whose bulbs are dried and used in medicines. 3. a kind of crustacean that burrows in the sea-shore.

squint *v.* 1. to have an eye that is turned abnormally from the line of gaze of the other, to be cross-eyed. 2. to look at (a thing) with the eyes turned sideways or half shut, or through a narrow opening. — **squint** *n.* 1. a squinting position of the eyeballs. 2. a stealthy or sideways glance. 3. (*informal*) a look, *have a squint at this.* —*adj.* (*informal*) askew.

squire *n.* 1. a country gentleman, especially the chief landowner in a district. 2. (as an informal form of address) sir.

squirm *v.* 1. to wriggle or writhe. 2. to feel embarrassment or uneasiness. —*n.* a squirming movement.

squirrel *n.* 1. a small tree-climbing animal with a bushy tail and red or grey fur. 2. its fur.

squirt *v.* to send out (liquid) or be sent out from or as if from a syringe, to wet in this way. —*n.* 1. a syringe. 2. a jet of liquid. 3. (*informal*) a small or unimportant but self-assertive fellow.

Sri Lanka a large island (formerly called Ceylon) south of India. **Sri Lankan** *adj.* & *n.*

SRN *abbrev.* State Registered Nurse.

St. *abbrev.* 1. Saint. 2. Street.

stab *v.* (stabbed, stabbing) 1. to pierce or wound with a pointed tool or weapon. 2. to aim a blow with or as if with a pointed weapon. 3. to cause a sensation of being stabbed, *a stabbing pain.* —*n.* 1. the act of stabbing, a blow or thrust or wound made by stabbing. 2. a sensation of being stabbed, *felt a stab of fear.* 3. (*informal*) an attempt; *have a stab at it,* try to do it. □ **a stab in the back,** a treacherous attack.

stability (stă-**bil**-iti) *n.* being stable.

stabilize (stay-bĭ-lyz) *v.* to make or become stable. **stabilization** *n.* □ **stabilizer** *n.* a device to prevent a ship from rolling or to aid in keeping a child's bicycle upright.

stable [1] *adj.* firmly fixed or established, not readily changing or fluctuating, not easily destroyed or decomposed. **stably** *adv.*

stable [2] *n.* 1. a building in which horses are kept. 2. an establishment for training racehorses, the horses from a particular establishment. 3. racing-cars or products or people originating from or working for the same establishment. —*v.* to put or keep in a stable. **stable-boy, stable-lad** *ns.* a person (of either sex) who works in a stable.

stabling *n.* accommodation for horses.

staccato (stă-**kah**-toh) *adj.* & *adv.* (especially in music) in a sharp disconnected manner, not running on smoothly.

stack *n.* 1. a haystack. 2. an orderly pile or heap. 3. (*informal*) a large quantity, *have stacks* or *a whole stack of work to get through.* 4. a number of aircraft stacked for landing. 5. a number of chimneys standing together. 6. an isolated tall factory chimney, a chimney or funnel for smoke on a steamer etc. —**stack** *v.* 1. to pile in a stack or stacks. 2. to arrange (cards) secretly for cheating; *the cards were stacked against him,* circumstances put him at a disadvantage. 3. to instruct (aircraft) to fly round the same point at different altitudes while waiting to land.

staddle-stone *n.* a mushroom-shaped stone like those formerly used for supporting a rick.

stadium *n.* sports ground surrounded by tiers of seats for spectators.

staff *n.* 1. a stick or pole used as a weapon or support or measuring-stick, or as a symbol of authority. 2. a body of officers assisting a commanding officer and concerned with an army or regiment or fleet etc. as a whole. 3. a group of assistants by whom a business is carried on, those responsible to a manager or person of authority. 4. people in authority within an organization (as distinct from pupils etc.), or those doing administrative work as distinct from manual work. 5. (*pl.* staves) one of the sets of five horizontal lines on which music is written. —*v.* to provide with a staff of employees or assistants. □ **staff officer,** a member of a military staff (*see* sense 2).

Staffordshire a county of England.

Staffs. *abbrev.* Staffordshire.

stag *n.* a fully-grown male deer. **stag-beetle** *n.* a beetle with branched projecting mouth-parts that resemble a stag's antlers. **stag-party** *n.* a party of or for men only.

stage *n.* 1. a platform on which plays etc. are performed before an audience. 2. *the stage,* theatrical work, the profession of actors and actresses. 3. a raised floor or platform, e.g. on scaffolding. 4. a point or period in the course or development of something, *the talks have reached a critical* *stage.* **5.** a stopping-place on a route, the distance between two of these; *we travelled by easy stages,* a short distance at a time. **6.** a section of a space-rocket with a separate engine, jettisoned when its fuel is exhausted. —**stage** *v.* **1.** to present (a play etc.) on the stage. **2.** to arrange and carry out, *decided to stage a sit-in.* □ **go on the stage,** to become an actor or actress. **stage fright,** nervousness on facing an audience. **stage-coach** *n.* a horse-drawn coach that formerly ran regularly between two places. **stage-manage** *v.* to organize things as or like a stage-manager. **stage-manager** *n.* the person responsible for the scenery and other practical arrangements in the production of a play. **stage-struck** *adj.* having an obsessive desire to become an actor or actress. **stage whisper,** a whisper that is meant to be overheard.

stager *n.* **old stager,** an old hand, an experienced person.

stagflation *n.* a state of inflation without a corresponding increase in demand and employment.

stagger *v.* **1.** to move or go unsteadily, as if about to fall. **2.** to shock deeply, to cause astonishment or worry or confusion to, *we were staggered by the news.* **3.** to place in a zigzag or alternating arrangement; *a staggered junction,* a crossroads where the side-roads are not exactly opposite each other. **4.** to arrange (people's holidays or hours of work etc.) so that their times do not coincide exactly. —*n.* an unsteady staggering movement.

staging *n.* **1.** scaffolding, a temporary platform or support. **2.** a platform of boards for plants to stand on in a greenhouse. □ **staging post,** a regular stopping-place on a long route.

staggering *adj.* bewildering, astonishing, *the total cost is staggering.*

stagnant *adj.* **1.** (of water) not flowing, still and stale. **2.** showing no activity, *business was stagnant.*

stagnate (stag-**nayt**) *v.* **1.** to be stagnant. **2.** (of a person) to become dull through inactivity and lack of variety or opportunity. **stagnation** *n.*

stagy (stay-ji) *adj.* theatrical in style or manner.

staid (*pr.* stayd) *adj.* steady and serious in manner, tastes, etc., sedate.

stain *v.* **1.** to discolour or become discoloured by a substance. **2.** to blemish, *it stained his good reputation.* **3.** to colour with a pigment that penetrates. —**stain** *n.* **1.** a mark caused by staining. **2.** a blemish, *without a stain on his character.* **3.** a liquid used for staining things. □ **stained**

glass, glass coloured with transparent colouring.

stainless *adj.* free from stains or blemishes. **stainless steel,** steel containing chromium and not liable to rust or tarnish under ordinary conditions.

stair *n.* one of a flight of fixed indoor steps. **stair-rod** *n.* a rod for securing a stair-carpet in the angle between two stairs. **stairs** *pl. n.* a flight of indoor steps.

staircase *n.* a flight of stairs (often with banisters) and its supporting structure.

stairway *n.* a staircase.

stake *n.* **1.** a stick or post sharpened at one end for driving into the ground as a support or marker etc. **2.** the post to which a person was bound for execution by being burnt alive; *the stake,* this method of execution. **3.** money etc. wagered on the result of a race or other event; *stakes,* (in names of horse-races) money offered as a prize, the race itself, *the Queen Anne Stakes.* **4.** something invested in an enterprise and giving a share or interest in it. —**stake** *v.* **1.** to fasten or support with stakes. **2.** to mark (an area) with stakes. **3.** to wager or risk (money etc.) on an event. **4.** (*Amer. informal*) to give financial or other support to. □ **at stake,** being risked, depending on the outcome of an event. **stake a claim,** to claim or obtain a right to something. **stake-boat** *n.* a boat moored or anchored as the starting-point or other mark in a boat-race.

stalactite (stal-ăk-tyt) *n.* a deposit of calcium carbonate hanging like an icicle from the roof of a cave etc.

stalagmite (stal-ăg-myt) *n.* a deposit like a stalactite but standing like a pillar on the floor of a cave etc.

stale *adj.* **1.** lacking freshness, dry or musty or unpleasant because not fresh. **2.** uninteresting because not new or because heard often before, *stale news* or *jokes.* **3.** having one's ability to perform spoilt by too much practice. —*v.* to make or become stale. —**stalely** *adv.,* **staleness** *n.*

stalemate *n.* **1.** a drawn position in chess, in which a player can make no move without putting his king in check. **2.** a deadlock, a drawn contest. —*v.* to bring to a position of stalemate or deadlock.

Stalinism (stah-lin-izm) *n.* the policy of Joseph Stalin (1879–1953) in government of the USSR.

stalk[1] *n.* **1.** the main stem of a plant. **2.** a stem attaching a leaf or flower or fruit to another stem or to a twig. **3.** a similar support of a part or organ in animals or of a device.

stalk[2] *v.* **1.** to walk in a stately or imposing manner. **2.** to track or pursue (game etc.) stealthily. —**stalker** *n.* □ **stalking-horse** *n.* a person or thing used to conceal one's real intentions.

stall *n.* **1.** a stable or cow-house, a compartment for one animal in this. **2.** a compartment for one person. **3.** a seat with its back and sides more or less enclosed, in a church etc. **4.** one of the set of seats (*the stalls*) in the part of a theatre nearest to the stage. **5.** a stand from which things are sold. **6.** stalling of an engine or aircraft. — **stall** *v.* **1.** to place or keep (an animal) in a stall, especially for fattening. **2.** (of an engine) to stop suddenly because of an overload or insufficient fuel. **3.** (of an aircraft) to begin to drop because the speed is too low for the plane to answer to its controls. **4.** to cause (an engine or aircraft) to stall. **5.** to use delaying tactics in order to gain time, to stave off (a person or request) in this way.

stallion (**stal**-yŏn) *n.* an uncastrated male horse, especially one kept for breeding.

stalwart (**stawl**-wert) *adj.* **1.** sturdy. **2.** strong and faithful, *stalwart supporters.* — *n.* a stalwart person.

stamen (**stay**-men) *n.* the male fertilizing-organ of flowering plants, bearing pollen.

stamina (**stam**-in-ă) *n.* staying-power, ability to withstand prolonged physical or mental strain.

stammer *v.* to speak or utter with involuntary pauses or rapid repetitions of the same syllable. —*n.* stammering speech, a tendency to stammer. —**stammerer** *n.*

stamp *v.* **1.** to bring one's foot down heavily on the ground, *stamped hard* or *stamped his foot.* **2.** to walk with loud heavy steps. **3.** to strike or press with a device that leaves a mark or pattern etc., to cut or shape in this way. **4.** to fix a postage or other stamp to. **5.** to give a certain character to, *this achievement stamps him as a genius.* —**stamp** *n.* **1.** the act or sound of stamping. **2.** an instrument for stamping a pattern or mark, the mark itself. **3.** a piece of paper bearing an official design, for affixing to an envelope or document to indicate that postage or duty or other fee has been paid. **4.** a distinguishing mark, a clear indication, *the story bears the stamp of truth.* □ **stamp-collecting** *n.* the collecting of postage stamps as objects of interest or value. **stamping-ground** *n.* (*informal*) a person's or animal's usual haunt or place of action. **stamp on**, to crush by stamping; to quell. **stamp out**, to extinguish by stamping, *stamped out the fire*; to suppress (a rebellion etc.) by force.

stampede *n.* **1.** a sudden rush of a herd of frightened animals. **2.** a rush of people under a sudden common impulse. —*v.* to take part or cause to take part in a stampede, to cause to act hurriedly.

stance (*pr.* stanss) *n.* the position in which a person or animal stands, a player's attitude for making a stroke.

stanch *v.* to restrain the flow of (blood etc.) or from (a wound).

stanchion (**stan**-shŏn) *n.* an upright bar or post forming a support.

stand *v.* (**stood, standing**) **1.** to have or take or keep a stationary upright position, *we were standing* (¶ not *we were stood*) *talking about the weather.* **2.** to be situated. **3.** to place, to set upright, *stand the vase on the table.* **4.** to remain firm or valid or in a specified condition, *the offer still stands*; *the thermometer stood at 90°.* **5.** to remain stationary or unused. **6.** to offer oneself for election, *she stood for Parliament.* **7.** to undergo, *he stood trial for murder.* **8.** to steer a specified course in sailing. **9.** to put up with, to endure, *can't stand that noise.* **10.** to provide at one's own expense, *stood him a drink.* —**stand** *n.* **1.** a stationary condition. **2.** a position taken up, *took his stand near the door.* **3.** resistance to attack, the period of this, *made a stand.* **4.** a halt to give a performance, *the band did a one-night stand.* **5.** a rack or pedestal etc. on which something may be placed, *umbrella stand.* **6.** a raised structure with seats at a sports ground etc. **7.** a table or booth or other (often temporary) structure where things are exhibited or sold. **8.** a standing-place for vehicles, *taxi stand.* **9.** (*Amer.*) a witness-box. □ **as it stands**, in the present state of affairs; in its present condition, unaltered. **it stands to reason**, it is obvious or logical. **stand a chance**, to have a chance of success. **stand alone**, to be unequalled. **stand by**, to look on without interfering; to support or side with (a person) in a difficulty or dispute; to stand ready for action; to keep to (a promise or agreement). **stand-by** *adj.* ready for use or action as a substitute etc., (*n.*) a person or thing available as a substitute or in an emergency. **stand down**, to withdraw (e.g. from a competition). **stand for**, to represent, '*US' stands for 'United States'*; (*informal*) to tolerate. **stand in**, to deputize. **stand-in** *n.* a person who takes the place of an actor while lighting etc. is arranged; (*informal*) a person who deputizes for another. **stand off**, to remain at a distance; to lay off (employees) temporarily. **stand-off** *adj.* (of missile) launched by an aircraft but having a long range and its own guidance system, so that the aircraft can turn away and travel a great distance before the missile explodes. **stand-off half,** a half-back in Rugby football who forms the link between scrum-half and three-quarters. **stand-offish** *adj.* (*informal*) aloof in manner. **stand on,** to insist on formal observance of, *stand on ceremony.* **stand on end,** (of hair) to become erect from fear or horror. **stand on one's own feet,** to be independent. **stand one's ground,** not yield. **stand out,** to be conspicuous; to persist in opposition or in one's demands, *they stood out for a ten per cent rise.* **stand over,** to supervise (a person or thing) closely; to be postponed. **stand to,** to stand ready for action. **stand treat,** (*informal*) to pay for another person's drink or entertainment etc. **stand up,** to come to or place in a standing position; to be valid, *that argument won't stand up*; *stand a person up,* fail to keep an appointment with him. **stand-up** *adj.* (of a collar) upright, not turned down; (of a fight) vigorous, actual; (of a meal) eaten while standing. **stand up for,** to defend or support (a person or opinion). **stand up to,** to resist courageously; to remain durable in (hard use or wear).

standard *n.* **1.** a thing or quality or specification by which something may be tested or measured. **2.** the required level of quality, *was rejected as being below standard.* **3.** the average quality, *the standard of her work is high.* **4.** a specified level of proficiency. **5.** a distinctive flag, *the royal standard.* **6.** an upright support. **7.** a shrub that has been grafted on an upright stem, *standard roses.* —**standard** *adj.* **1.** serving as or conforming to a standard, *standard measures of length.* **2.** of average or usual quality, not of special design etc., *the standard model of this car.* **3.** of recognized merit or authority, *the standard book on spiders.* **4.** widely used and regarded as the usual form, *standard English.* □ **standard lamp,** a household lamp set on a tall pillar on a base. **standard of living,** the level of material comfort enjoyed by a person or group.

standardize *v.* to cause to conform to a standard. **standardization** *n.*

standee *n.* (*informal*) a person who stands in a bus or theatre etc. because all seats are occupied.

standing *adj.* **1.** upright; *standing corn,* not yet harvested. **2.** (of a jump) performed without a run. **3.** permanent, remaining effective or valid, *a standing invitation.* —**standing** *n.* **1.** status, *people of high standing.* **2.** past duration, *a friendship of long standing.* □ **standing ovation,** an ovation by people rising from

their seats to applaud. **standing-room** *n.* space for people to stand in.

stand-pipe *n.* a vertical pipe for fluid to rise in, e.g. to provide a water supply outside or at a distance from buildings.

standpoint *n.* a point of view.

standstill *n.* a stoppage, inability to proceed.

stank *see* stink.

stanza *n.* a verse of poetry.

staphylococcus *n.* (*pl.* staphylococci, *pr.* staf-il-ŏ-**kok**-I) a kind of micro-organism that causes pus to form.

staple[1] *n.* **1.** a U-shaped piece of metal or wire for holding something in place. **2.** a piece of metal or wire driven into papers etc. and clenched to fasten them. —*v.* to secure with a staple or staples. —**stapler** *n.*

staple[2] *adj.* principal, standard, *rice is their staple food.* —*n.* a staple food or product etc.

star *n.* **1.** a celestial body appearing as a point of light in the night sky. **2.** (in astronomy) any large light-emitting gaseous ball, such as the sun. **3.** a celestial body regarded as influencing a person's fortunes, *thank your lucky stars.* **4.** a figure or object or ornament with rays or radiating points, an asterisk, a star-shaped mark indicating a category of excellence. **5.** a brilliant person, a famous actor or actress or other performer. —**star** *v.* (starred, starring) **1.** to put an asterisk or star symbol beside (a name or item in a list etc.). **2.** to present or perform as a star actor. □ **star-gazing** *n.* (*humorous*) studying the stars as an astronomer or astrologer; day-dreaming. **Star of David,** the six-pointed star used as a Jewish and Israeli symbol. **Stars and Stripes,** the national flag of the USA. **Star-Spangled Banner,** the national anthem of the USA. **star turn,** the principal item in an entertainment.

starboard *n.* the right-hand side (when facing forward) of a ship or aircraft. —*v.* to turn this way.

starch *n.* **1.** a white carbohydrate that is an important element in human food. **2.** a preparation of this or other substances for stiffening fabrics. **3.** stiffness of manner. —*v.* to stiffen with starch. □ **starch-reduced** *adj.* containing less than the normal proportion of starch.

starchy *adj.* (starchier, starchiest) **1.** of or like starch. **2.** containing much starch. **3.** stiff and formal in manner. **starchiness** *n.*

stardom *n.* being a star actor or performer.

stare *v.* **1.** to gaze fixedly with the eyes wide open, especially in astonishment. **2.** (of the eyes) to be wide open with fixed gaze.

—*n.* a staring gaze. ☐ **stare a person in the face**, to be glaringly obvious or clearly imminent, *ruin stared him in the face.*

starfish *n.* a star-shaped sea creature.

stark *adj.* **1.** stiff in death. **2.** desolate, cheerless, *stark prison conditions.* **3.** sharply evident, *in stark contrast.* **4.** downright, complete, *stark madness.* **5.** completely naked. —*adv.* completely, wholly, *stark raving mad.* —**starkly** *adv.*, **starkness** *n.*

starlight *n.* light from the stars.

starling *n.* a noisy bird with glossy blackish speckled feathers, that forms large flocks.

starlit *adj.* lit by starlight.

starry *adj.* (starrier, starriest) **1.** set with stars. **2.** shining like stars. ☐ **starry-eyed** *adj.* romantically enthusiastic; enthusiastic but impractical.

start *v.* **1.** to begin or cause to begin a process or course of action, (of an engine) to begin running. **2.** to cause or enable to begin, to establish or found, *the council started a play-group*; *start a baby*, to conceive. **3.** to begin a journey. **4.** to make a sudden movement from pain or surprise etc. **5.** to spring suddenly, *started from his seat.* **6.** (of timber) to spring from its proper position. **7.** to rouse (game etc.) from its lair or covert. —**start** *n.* **1.** the beginning of a journey or activity or race, the place where a race starts. **2.** an opportunity for or assistance in starting. **3.** an advantage gained or allowed in starting, the amount of this, *had 10 seconds* or *10 yards start.* **4.** a sudden movement of surprise or pain etc. ☐ **for a start**, as a thing to start with. **start in**, (*informal*) to begin. **starting-gate** *n.* a removable barrier behind which horses are lined up at the start of a race. **starting-point** *n.* the point from which something begins. **starting price**, the final odds on a horse etc. at the start of a race. **start off**, to begin, to begin to move. **start out**, to begin, to begin a journey; to intend when starting, *started out to write a novel.* **start up**, to start; to set in motion, to start an activity etc.

starter *n.* **1.** a person or thing that starts something. **2.** one who gives the signal for a race to start. **3.** a horse or competitor at the start of a race, *list of probable starters.* **4.** the first course of a meal. ☐ **for starters**, (*slang*) to start with.

startle *v.* to cause to make a sudden movement from surprise or alarm, to take by surprise.

startling *adj.* surprising, astonishing.

starve *v.* **1.** to die or suffer acutely from lack of food, to cause to do this. **2.** to

suffer or cause to suffer for lack of something needed, *was starved of affection.* **3.** (*informal*) to feel very hungry or very cold. **4.** to force by starvation, *starved them into surrender.* **starvation** *n.* ☐ **starvation diet**, not enough food to support life adequately.

starveling (starv-ling) *n.* a starving or ill-fed person or animal.

stash *v.* (*slang*) to stow.

state *n.* **1.** the quality of a person's or thing's characteristics or circumstances. **2.** an excited or agitated condition of mind, *she got into a state.* **3.** a grand imposing style, *arrived in state.* **4.** (often *State*) an organized community under one government (*the State of Israel*) or forming part of a federal republic (*States of the USA*). **5.** civil government, *matters of state.* —**state** *adj.* **1.** of or for or concerned with the State; *state schools*, those run by public authorities. **2.** involving ceremony, used or done on ceremonial occasions, *the state apartments.* —**state** *v.* **1.** to express in spoken or written words. **2.** to fix or specify, *must be inspected at stated intervals.* ☐ **lie in state**, see lie². **State Department**, the department of foreign affairs in the government of the USA. **the States**, the USA.

stateless *adj.* (of a person) not a citizen or subject of any country.

stately *adj.* (statelier, stateliest) dignified, imposing, grand. **stateliness** *n.*

statement *n.* **1.** stating. **2.** something stated. **3.** a formal account of facts, a written report of a financial account.

stateroom *n.* **1.** a state apartment. **2.** a passenger's private compartment on a ship.

statesman *n.* (*pl.* statesmen) a person who is skilled or prominent in the management of State affairs. **statesmanship** *n.*, **stateswoman** *n.*

static *adj.* **1.** of force acting by weight without motion (as opposed to *dynamic*). **2.** not moving, stationary. **3.** not changing. — **static** *n.* **1.** atmospherics. **2.** = **static electricity**, electricity present in a body and not flowing as current. —**statics** *n.* a branch of physics that deals with bodies at rest or forces in equilibrium.

station *n.* **1.** a place where a person or thing stands or is stationed. **2.** an establishment or building where a public service is based or which is equipped for certain activities, *the fire station*; *an agricultural research station.* **3.** a broadcasting establishment with its own frequency. **4.** a stopping-place on a railway with buildings for passengers or goods or both. **5.** position in

life, status, *she had ideas above her station.*
6. (*Austral.*) a large farming estate, a
sheep-run or its buildings. —*v.* to put at
or in a certain place for a purpose, *the
regiment was stationed in Germany.* □
station-master *n.* the official in charge of
a railway station. **Stations of the Cross,** a
series of 14 images or pictures representing
events in Christ's Passion before which
prayers are said in certain Churches.

stationary *adj.* **1.** not moving, not movable.
2. not changing in condition or quantity
etc.

stationer *n.* one who sells writing materials (paper, pens, ink, etc.).

stationery *n.* writing-paper, envelopes,
and other articles sold by a stationer.

statistician (stat-iss-**tish**-ăn) *n.* an expert
in statistics.

statistics (stă-**tist**-iks) *n.* the science of
collecting, classifying, and interpreting information based on the numbers of things.
statistic *n.* an item of information expressed in numbers. **statistical** *adj.*,
statistically *adv.*

statuary (**stat**-yoo-er-ĭ) *n.* statues.

statue *n.* a sculptured or cast or moulded
figure of a person or animal, usually of life
size or larger.

statuesque (stat-yoo-**esk**) *adj.* like a
statue in size or dignity or stillness.

statuette (stat-yoo-**et**) *n.* a small statue.

stature (**stat**-yer) *n.* **1.** the natural height
of the body. **2.** greatness gained by ability
or achievement.

status (**stay**-tŭs) *n.* (*pl.* statuses) **1.** a person's position or rank in relation to
others, a person's or thing's legal position.
2. high rank or prestige. □ **status symbol,**
a possesion or activity etc. regarded as
evidence of a person's high status.

status quo (stay-tŭs **kwoh**) the state of
affairs as it is or as it was before a recent
change, *restore the status quo.* (¶ Latin,
= the state in which.)

statute (**stat**-yoot) *n.* **1.** a law passed by
Parliament or a similar body. **2.** one of
the rules of an institution, *the University
Statutes.*

statutory (**stat**-yoo-ter-ĭ) *adj.* fixed or done
or required by statute.

staunch *adj.* firm in attitude or opinion or
loyalty. **staunchly** *adv.*

stave *n.* **1.** one of the curved strips of
wood forming the side of a cask or tub.
2. a staff in music (*see* staff sense 5). —*v.*
(stove *or* staved, staving) to dent or
break a hole, *stove* or *staved it in.* □
stave off, to ward off permanently or
temporarily, *we staved off disaster* (¶ not
stove in this sense).

stay¹ *n.* **1.** a rope or wire supporting or
bracing a mast, spar, pole, etc. **2.** any prop
or support, *he was the prop and stay of his
parents in their old age.*

stay² *v.* **1.** to continue to be in the same
place or state, *stay here*; *stay awake*; *stay
away from the meeting,* not go to it. **2.** to
remain or dwell temporarily, especially as
a guest or visitor. **3.** to satisfy temporarily,
we stayed our hunger with a sandwich. **4.** to
postpone, *stay judgement.* **5.** to pause in
movement or action or speech. **6.** to show
endurance, e.g. in a race or task; *stay the
course,* be able to reach the end of a race
etc. —**stay** *n.* **1.** a period of temporary
dwelling or visiting, *made a short stay in
Athens.* **2.** a postponement, e.g. of carrying
out a judgement, *was granted a stay of
execution.* □ **stay-at-home** *adj.* remaining at home habitually, (*n.*) a person who
does this. **staying-power** *n.* endurance.
stay-stitch *v.* to make a line of stitches
close to a curved or bias-cut edge to
prevent it from stretching when worked
on.

stayer *n.* a person with great staying-
power.

stays *pl. n.* (*old use*) a corset.

staysail *n.* a sail extended on a stay.

STD *abbrev.* subscriber trunk dialling.

stead (*pr.* sted) *n.* **In a person's** *or* **thing's
stead,** instead of him or it. **stand a person
in good stead,** to be of great advantage
or service to him.

steadfast (**sted**-fahst) *adj.* firm and not
changing or yielding, *a steadfast refusal.*
steadfastly *adv.*

steady *adj.* (steadier, steadiest) **1.** firmly
supported or balanced, not shaking or
rocking or tottering. **2.** done or operating
or happening in a uniform and regular
manner, *a steady pace.* **3.** behaving in a
serious and dependable manner, not frivolous or excitable. —*n.* (*Amer. informal*) a
regular boy-friend or girl-friend. —*adv.*
steadily. —*v.* (steadied, steadying) to
make or become steady. —**steadily** *adv.*,
steadiness *n.* □ **go steady,** (*informal*)
to go about regularly with a member of
the opposite sex though not yet engaged
to be married to him or her. **steady on!,**
slow! *or* stop!

steak *n.* **1.** a thick slice of meat (especially
beef) or fish, cut for grilling or frying etc.
2. beef from the front of an animal, cut
for stewing or braising. **steak-house** *n.* a
restaurant that specializes in serving
steaks.

steal *v.* (stole, stolen, stealing) **1.** to take
another person's property without right or
permission, to take dishonestly. **2.** to obtain

by surprise or a trick or surreptitiously, *stole a kiss*; *stole a look at her.* **3.** to move secretly or without being noticed, *stole out of the room.* —**steal** *n.* (*Amer. slang*) **1.** stealing, theft. **2.** an easy task, a good bargain. ☐ **steal a march on,** to gain an advantage over (a person) secretly or slyly or by acting in advance of him. **steal the show,** to outshine other performers unexpectedly.

stealth (*pr.* stelth) *n.* stealthiness.

stealthy (**stel**-thi) *adj.* (stealthier, stealthiest) acting or done in a quiet or secret way so as to avoid being noticed. **stealthily** *adv.*, **stealthiness** *n.*

steam *n.* **1.** invisible gas into which water is changed by boiling, used as motive power. **2.** the mist that forms when steam condenses in the air. **3.** energy or power; *run out of steam,* to become exhausted before something is finished. —**steam** *v.* **1.** to give out steam or vapour. **2.** to cook or treat by steam. **3.** to move by the power of steam, *the ship steamed down the river.* **4.** to cover or become covered with condensed steam, *the windows were steamed up.* ☐ **steamed up,** (*slang*) excited or angry. **steam-engine** *n.* an engine or locomotive driven by steam. **steam iron,** an electric iron that can emit jets of steam from its flat surface. **steam radio,** (*informal*) radio broadcasting regarded as antiquated by comparison with TV.

steamer *n.* **1.** a steam-driven ship. **2.** a container in which things are cooked or treated by steam.

steamroller *n.* a heavy slow-moving engine with a large roller, used in road-making. —*v.* to crush or defeat by weighty influence.

steamship *n.* a steam-driven ship.

steamy *adj.* (steamier, steamiest) like steam, full of steam. **steaminess** *n.*

steatite (**stee**-ă-tyt) *n.* a greyish talc that feels smooth and soapy.

steed *n.* (*poetical*) a horse.

steel *n.* **1.** a very strong alloy of iron and carbon much used for making vehicles, tools, weapons, etc.; *nerves of steel,* very strong nerves. **2.** a tapered usually roughened steel rod for sharpening knives. —*v.* to make hard or resolute, *steel oneself* or *steel one's heart.* ☐ **steel band,** a West Indian band of musicians with instruments usually made from oil-drums. **steel wool,** fine shavings of steel massed together for use as an abrasive. **worthy of his steel,** worthy as a fighter (¶ *steel* = sword).

steely *adj.* (steelier, steeliest) like steel in colour or hardness.

steep¹ *v.* **1.** to soak or be soaked in

liquid. **2.** to permeate thoroughly, *the story is steeped in mystery.*

steep² *adj.* **1.** sloping sharply not gradually. **2.** (*informal*, of a price) unreasonably high. **steeply** *adv.*, **steepness** *n.*

steepen *v.* to make or become steeper.

steeple *n.* a tall tower with a spire on top, rising above the roof of a church.

steeplechase *n.* **1.** a horse-race across country or on a course with hedges and ditches to jump. **2.** a cross-country race for runners. ☐ **steeplechaser** *n.* one who takes part in a steeplechase, a horse trained for this.

steeplejack *n.* a man who climbs tall chimneys or steeples to do repairs.

steer¹ *n.* a young male of domestic cattle, castrated and raised for beef.

steer² *v.* **1.** to direct the course of. **2.** to guide (a vehicle or boat etc.) by its mechanism. **3.** to be able to be steered, *the car steers well.* **steerer** *n.* ☐ **steer clear of,** to take care to avoid.

steerage *n.* **1.** steering. **2.** (*old use*) the cheapest section of accommodation for passengers in a ship, situated below decks.

steering *n.* the mechanism by which a vehicle or boat etc. is steered. **steering-wheel** *n.* a wheel for controlling this mechanism.

steersman *n.* (*pl.* steersmen) a person who steers a ship.

stellar *adj.* of a star or stars.

stem¹ *n.* **1.** the main central part (usually above the ground) of a tree or shrub or plant. **2.** a slender part supporting a fruit or flower or leaf. **3.** any slender upright part, e.g. that of a wineglass between bowl and foot. **4.** the main part of a noun or verb, from which other parts or words are made e.g. by altering the endings. **5.** the curved timber or metal piece at the fore end of a ship, a ship's bows. —*v.* (stemmed, stemming) to remove the stems from. ☐ **from stem to stern,** from end to end of a ship. **stem from,** to arise from, to have as its source.

stem² *v.* (stemmed, stemming) **1.** to restrain the flow of, to dam up. **2.** (in skiing) to slow one's movement by forcing the heel of one or both skis outwards. ☐ **stem-turn** *n.* a turn made by stemming with one ski.

stench *n.* a foul smell.

stencil *n.* **1.** a sheet of metal or card etc. with a design cut out, painted or inked over to produce a corresponding design on the surface below. **2.** a waxed sheet from which a stencil is made by a type-writer. **3.** the decoration or lettering etc.

produced by a stencil. —v. (stencilled, stencilling) to produce or ornament by means of a stencil.

stenographer (sten-og-ră-fer) n. a person who can write shorthand, one employed to do this.

stenography (sten-og-răfi) n. shorthand.

stentorian (sten tor-iăn) adj. (of a voice) extremely loud.

step v. (stepped, stepping) 1. to lift and set down the foot or alternate feet as in walking. 2. to move a short distance in this way, step aside; step into a job, to acquire it without effort. —step n. 1. a complete movement of one foot and leg in stepping. 2. the distance covered by this. 3. a short distance, it's only a step to the bus stop. 4. a series of steps forming a particular pattern in dancing. 5. the sound of a step, a manner of stepping as seen or heard, I recognized your step. 6. a rhythm of stepping, as in marching. 7. one of a series of things done in some process or course of action. 8. a level surface for placing the foot on in climbing up or down. 9. a stage in a scale of promotion or precedence. □ **in step**, stepping in time with other people in marching or dancing; conforming to what others are doing. **out of step**, not in step. **step by step**, one step at a time; proceeding steadily from one stage to the next. **step in**, to intervene. **step-in** adj. (of a garment) put on by being stepped into, without fastenings. **stepladder** n. a short ladder with flat steps (not rungs) and a framework that supports it. **step on it**, (slang) to hurry. **step out**, to walk briskly, to stride; to take part in lively social activities. **steps** pl. n. a step-ladder. **step up**, to increase, step up the voltage. **watch your step**, be careful.

step- prefix related by re-marriage of one parent. **stepchild** (pl. stepchildren), **stepdaughter**, **stepson** ns. the child of one's wife or husband, by an earlier marriage. **stepbrother**, **stepsister** ns. the child of one's stepfather or stepmother. **stepfather**, **stepmother** ns. the husband or wife of one's parent, by a later marriage.

stephanotis (stef-ăn-oh-tiss) n. a tropical climbing plant with fragrant white waxy flowers.

steppe (pr. step) n. a level grassy plain with few trees, especially in south-east Europe and Siberia.

stepping-stone n. 1. a raised stone providing a place to step on in crossing a stream etc. 2. a means or stage of progress towards achieving something.

stereo (ste-ri-oh or steer-i-oh) n. (pl. stereos) 1. stereophonic sound or recording.

2. a stereophonic record-player or radio set.

stereophonic (ste-ri-ŏ-**fon**-ik or steer-) adj. (of sound-reproduction) using two transmission channels in order to give the effect of naturally-distributed sound.

stereoscopic (ste-ri-ŏ-**skop**-ik or steer-) adj. giving a three-dimensional effect, e.g. in photographs.

stereotype (ste-ri-ŏ-typ or steer-) n. 1. a printing-plate cast from a mould of type. 2. an idea or character etc. that is standardized in a conventional form without individuality. **stereotyped** adj. standardized and hackneyed, stereotyped phrases such as 'it takes all sorts to make a world'.

sterile (ste-ryl) adj. 1. barren. 2. free from living micro-organisms. 3. unproductive, a sterile discussion. **sterility** (ster-il-iti) n.

sterilize (ste-ri-lyz) v. 1. to make sterile or free from micro-organisms. 2. to make unable to produce offspring, especially by removal or obstruction of reproductive organs. **sterilization** n.

sterling n. British money. —adj. 1. (of precious metal) genuine, of standard purity. 2. excellent, of solid worth, her sterling qualities.

stern [1] adj. strict and severe, not lenient or cheerful or kindly. **sternly** adv., **sternness** n.

stern [2] n. the rear end of a boat or ship. **stern sheets**, the space in a boat aft of the rowers' benches.

sternum n. the breastbone.

steroid (steer-oid) n. any of a group of organic compounds that includes certain hormones and other bodily secretions.

stertorous (ster-ter-ŭs) adj. making a snoring or rasping sound. **stertorously** adv.

stet v. (placed beside a word that has been crossed out by mistake) let it stand as written or printed. (¶ Latin, = let it stand.)

stethoscope (steth-ŏ-skohp) n. an instrument for listening to sounds within the body, e.g. breathing and heart-beats.

stetson n. a slouch hat with a very wide brim and a high crown.

stevedore (stee-vĕ-dor) n. a man employed in loading and unloading ships.

stew v. 1. to cook or be cooked by simmering for a long time in a closed vessel. 2. (slang) to study hard, stewing over his books. —n. a dish (especially of meat) made by stewing. □ **in a stew**, (informal) in a state of great anxiety or agitation. **stewed** adj. (of tea) strong and bitter from infusing for too long; (slang) drunk. **stew in one's own juice**, to be obliged to suffer the consequences of one's own actions.

steward *n.* **1.** a person employed to manage another's property, especially a great house or estate. **2.** one whose job is to arrange for the supply of food to a college or club etc. **3.** a passengers' attendant and waiter on a ship or aircraft or train. **4.** one of the officials managing a race-meeting or show etc.

stewardess *n.* a woman attendant and waitress on a ship or aircraft.

stick¹ *n.* **1.** a short relatively slender piece of wood for use as a support or weapon or as firewood; *only a few sticks of furniture,* items of furniture. **2.** a walking-stick. **3.** the implement used to propel the ball in hockey, polo, etc. **4.** punishment by caning or beating. **5.** a slender more or less cylindrical piece of a substance, e.g. sealing-wax, rhubarb, dynamite. **6.** a number of bombs released in succession to fall in a row. **7.** (*informal*) a stupid or uninteresting person. □ **stick-insect** *n.* an insect with a twig-like body.

stick² *v.* (stuck, sticking) **1.** to thrust (a thing or its point) into something, to stab. **2.** to fix by means of a pointed object. **3.** (*informal*) to put, *stick the parcel on the table.* **4.** to fix or be fixed by glue or suction etc. or as if by these. **5.** to fix or be fixed in one place and unable to move, *the boat stuck on a sandbank; I stuck on the last question,* found it too difficult to do. **6.** (*informal*) to remain in the same place, *they stuck indoors all day.* **7.** (*informal,* of an accusation) to be established as valid, *we couldn't make the charges stick.* **8.** (*slang*) to endure, to tolerate. **9.** (*informal*) to impose a difficult or unpleasant task upon, *we were stuck with the job of clearing up.* **10.** to provide (a plant) with a stick as a support. □ **stick at it,** (*informal*) to continue one's efforts. **stick in one's throat,** to be against one's principles. **stick-in-the-mud** *n.* a person who will not adopt new ideas etc. **stick it out,** to endure to the end in spite of difficulty or unpleasantness. **stick one's neck out,** to expose oneself deliberately to danger or argument. **stick out,** to stand above the surrounding surface; to be conspicuous; (*informal*) to persist in one's demands. **stick to,** to remain faithful to (a friend or promise etc.); to abide by and not alter, *he stuck to his story; stick to it,* = stick at it; *stick to one's guns,* hold one's position against attack or argument. **stick up,** (*slang*) to rob by threatening with a gun. **stick-up** *n.* (*slang*) a robbery of this kind. **stick up for,** (*informal*) = stand up for. **stick with,** to remain with or faithful to.

sticker *n.* **1.** an adhesive label or sign. **2.** a person who persists in his efforts.

sticking-plaster *n.* a strip of fabric with an adhesive on one side, used for covering small cuts.

sticking-point *n.* the point at which a thing stops and holds fast.

stickjaw *n.* (*informal*) hard toffee or a similar sweet.

stickleback *n.* a small fish with sharp spines on its back.

stickler *n.* a person who insists on something, *a stickler for punctuality.*

stickpin *n.* (*Amer.*) a tie-pin.

sticky *adj.* (stickier, stickiest) **1.** sticking or tending to stick to what is touched. **2.** (of weather) hot and humid, causing perspiration. **3.** (*informal*) making objections, *he was very sticky about giving me leave.* **4.** (*slang*) very unpleasant, *he'll come to a sticky end.* **stickily** *adv.,* **stickiness** *n.*

stiff *adj.* **1.** not bending or moving or changing its shape easily. **2.** not fluid, thick and hard to stir, *a stiff dough.* **3.** difficult, *a stiff examination.* **4.** formal in manner, not pleasantly sociable or friendly. **5.** (of a price or penalty) high, severe. **6.** (of a breeze) blowing briskly. **7.** (of a drink or dose) strong. **8.** (*informal*) to an extreme degree, *bored stiff.* —**stiff** *n.* (*slang*) **1.** a corpse. **2.** a hopeless person; *big stiff,* complete fool. —**stiffly** *adv.,* **stiffness** *n.* □ **stiff-necked** *adj.* obstinate; haughty. **stiff upper lip,** fortitude in enduring grief etc.

stiffen *v.* to make or become stiff. **stiffener** *n.*

stifle *v.* **1.** to suffocate, to feel or cause to feel unable to breathe for lack of air. **2.** to restrain or suppress, *stifled a yawn.* **stifling** *adj.*

stigma *n.* (*pl.* stigmas) **1.** a mark of shame, a stain on a person's good reputation. **2.** the part of a pistil that receives the pollen in pollination.

stigmata (stig-mă-tă) *pl. n.* marks corresponding to those left on Christ's body by the nails and spear at his Crucifixion.

stigmatize (stig-mă-tyz) *v.* to brand as something disgraceful, *he was stigmatized as a coward.*

stile *n.* an arrangement of steps or bars for people to climb in order to get over or through a fence etc. but preventing the passage of sheep or cattle.

stiletto *n.* (*pl.* stilettos) **1.** a dagger with a narrow blade. **2.** a pointed device for making eyelet-holes etc. □ **stiletto heel,** a high pointed heel on a shoe.

still¹ *adj.* **1.** without moving, without or almost without motion or sound. **2.** (of drinks) not sparkling or fizzy. —**still** *n.* **1.** silence and calm, *in the still of the night.*

2. a photograph as distinct from a motion picture, a single photograph taken from a cinema film. — *v.* to make or become still, *to still the waves.* —**still** *adv.* **1.** without or almost without moving. **2.** then or now or for the future as before, *the Pyramids are still standing.* **3.** nevertheless. **4.** in a greater amount or degree, *that would be still better* or *better still.* —**stillness** *n.* ☐ **still birth**, a birth in which the child is born dead. **still life**, a painting of lifeless things such as cut flowers or fruit.

still [2] *n.* a distilling apparatus, especially for making spirits. **still-room** *n.* a housekeeper's store-room in a large house.

stillborn *adj.* **1.** born dead. **2.** (of an idea or plan) not developing.

stilt *n.* **1.** one of a pair of poles with a rest for the foot some way up it, enabling the user to walk with feet at a distance above the ground. **2.** one of a set of piles or posts supporting a building etc. **3.** a long-legged marsh-bird.

stilted *adj.* stiffly or artificially formal, *written in stilted language.*

Stilton *n.* a rich blue-veined cheese.

stimulant *adj.* stimulating. —*n.* a stimulant drug or drink, a stimulating event etc.

stimulate *v.* **1.** to make more vigorous or active. **2.** to apply a stimulus to. **stimulation** *n.*, **stimulator** *n.*

stimulative (stim-yoo-lă-tiv) *adj.* stimulating.

stimulus *n.* (*pl.* stimuli, *pr.* **stim**-yool-I) something that rouses a person or thing to activity or energy or that produces a reaction in an organ or tissue of the body.

sting *n.* **1.** a sharp-pointed part or organ of an insect etc., used for wounding and often injecting poison. **2.** a stiff sharp-pointed hair on certain plants, causing inflammation if touched. **3.** infliction of a wound by a sting, the wound itself. **4.** any sharp bodily or mental pain, a wounding effect, *the sting of remorse.* —**sting** *v.* (stung, stinging) **1.** to wound or affect with a sting, to be able to do this. **2.** to feel or cause to feel sharp bodily or mental pain. **3.** to stimulate sharply as if by a sting, *was stung into answering rudely.* **4.** (*slang*) to cheat (a person) by overcharging, to extort money from. ☐ **stinging-nettle**, a nettle that stings. **sting-ray** *n.* a tropical fish with sharp spines that can cause severe wounds.

stingy (stin-ji) *adj.* (stingier, stingiest) spending or giving or given grudgingly or in small amounts. **stingily** *adv.*, **stinginess** *n.*

stink *n.* **1.** an offensive smell. **2.** (*informal*) an offensive fuss, *kicked up a stink about it.* —**stink** *v.* (stank *or* stunk, stinking) **1.** to give off an offensive smell. **2.** to seem very unpleasant or unsavoury or dishonest, *the whole business stinks.* ☐ **stink-horn** *n.* a fungus with an offensive smell. **stinking** *adj.* (*slang*) very bad, (*adv.*) extremely, *stinking rich.* **stink out**, to fill (a place) with an offensive smell; to drive out by a stink.

stinker *n.* **1.** a person or thing that stinks. **2.** (*slang*) something offensive or severe or difficult to do.

stint *v.* to restrict to a small allowance, to be niggardly, *don't stint them of food* or *stint on food.* —*n.* **1.** a limitation of supply or effort, *gave help without stint.* **2.** a fixed or allotted amount of work, *did her stint of filing.*

stipend (sty-pend) *n.* a salary, a clergyman's official income.

stipendiary (stip-**end**-i-er-i) *adj.* receiving a stipend. **stipendiary magistrate**, a paid professional magistrate.

stipple *v.* **1.** to paint or draw or engrave in small dots (not in lines or strokes). **2.** to roughen the surface of (cement etc.).

stipulate (stip-yoo-layt) *v.* to demand or insist upon as part of an agreement. **stipulation** *n.* stipulating; something stipulated.

stir *v.* (stirred, stirring) **1.** to move or cause to move, *not a leaf stirred; wind stirred the sand.* **2.** to mix or move (a substance) by moving a spoon etc. round and round in it. **3.** to arouse or excite or stimulate, *the story stirred their interest; stir up trouble.* — **stir** *n.* **1.** the act or process of stirring, *give the soup a stir.* **2.** a commotion or disturbance, excitement, *the news caused a stir.* ☐ **stir one's stumps**, (*humorous*) to begin moving, to hurry.

stirring *adj.* exciting, stimulating.

stirrup *n.* a metal or leather support for a rider's foot, hanging from the saddle. **stirrup-cup** *n.* a drink handed to a rider on horseback at a meet. **stirrup-pump** *n.* a small portable pump with a stirrup-shaped foot-rest, used for extinguishing small fires.

stitch *n.* **1.** a single movement of a threaded needle in and out of fabric in sewing or tissue in surgery. **2.** a single complete movement of a needle or hook in knitting or crochet. **3.** the loop of thread made in this way. **4.** a particular method of arranging the thread, *cross-stitch; purl stitch.* **5.** the least bit of clothing, *without a stitch on.* **6.** a sudden sharp pain in the muscles at the side of the body. —*v.* to sew, to join or close with stitches. ☐ **in**

stitches, (*informal*) laughing uncontrollably.

stitchwort *n.* a kind of chickweed.

stoat *n.* the ermine, especially when its fur is brown.

stock *n.* 1. an amount of something available for use, *has a stock of jokes.* 2. the total of goods kept by a trader or shopkeeper. 3. livestock. 4. a line of ancestry, *a woman of Irish stock.* 5. money lent to a government in return for fixed interest. 6. the capital of a business company, a portion of this held by an investor (differing from *shares* in that it is not issued in fixed amounts). 7. a person's standing in the opinion of others; *his stock is high,* he is well thought of. 8. liquid made by stewing bones or meat or fish or vegetables, used as a basis for making soup, sauce, etc. 9. a garden plant with fragrant single or double flowers. 10. the lower and thicker part of a tree trunk. 11. a growing plant into which a graft is inserted. 12. a part serving as the base, holder, or handle for the working parts of an implement or machine; *the stock of a rifle,* the wooden or metal part to which the barrel is attached. 13. a cravat worn as part of riding-kit. 14. a piece of black or purple fabric worn over the shirt front by a clergyman, hanging from a clerical collar. —**stock** *adj.* 1. kept in stock and regularly available, *one of our stock items.* 2. commonly used, *a stock argument.* —**stock** *v.* 1. to keep (goods) in stock. 2. to provide with goods or livestock or a supply of something, *stocked his farm with Jersey cows*; *a well-stocked library.* □ **in stock,** available in a shop etc. without needing to be obtained specially. **out of stock,** sold out. **stock-car** *n.* an ordinary car strengthened for use in racing where deliberate bumping is allowed. **Stock Exchange,** a place where stocks and shares are publicly bought and sold; an association of dealers conducting such business according to fixed rules. **stock-in-trade** *n.* all the stock and other requisites for carrying on a trade or business. **stock market,** the Stock Exchange or transactions there. **stock-pot** *n.* a cooking-pot in which stock is made and kept. **stock-room** *n.* a room where goods kept in stock are stored. **stocks** *pl. n.* a wooden framework with holes for the legs of a seated person, used like the pillory; a framework on which a ship rests during construction; *on the stocks,* being constructed or repaired. **stock size,** one of the standard sizes in which ready-made garments are made. **stock-still** *adj.* motionless. **stock-taking** *n.* making

an inventory of the stock in a shop etc.; review of one's position and resources. **stock up,** to assemble a stock of goods etc.

stockade *n.* a protective fence of upright stakes.

stockbreeder *n.* a farmer who raises livestock. **stockbreeding** *n.*

stockbroker *n.* a person who buys and sells stocks and shares (from stockjobbers) on behalf of customers.

stockdove *n.* a kind of wild pigeon.

stockholder *n.* a person who holds financial stock or shares.

Stockholm the capital of Sweden.

stockinet *n.* fine stretchable machine-knitted fabric used for underwear etc.

stocking *n.* a close-fitting covering for the foot and part or all of the leg. **in one's stockinged feet,** wearing stockings but not shoes. **stocking-stitch** *n.* alternate rows of plain and purl in knitting, giving a plain smooth surface on one side.

stockist *n.* a business firm that stocks certain goods for sale.

stockjobber *n.* a member of the Stock Exchange who buys and sells stocks and shares so as to profit by fluctuations in their prices, dealing with stockbrokers but not with the general public.

stockman *n.* (*pl.* stockmen) (*Austral.*) a man in charge of livestock.

stockpile *n.* an accumulated stock of goods or materials etc. kept in reserve. — *v.* to accumulate a stockpile of.

stockrider *n.* (*Austral.*) a herdsman on an unfenced station.

stocky *adj.* (stockier, stockiest) short and solidly built. **stockily** *adv.*, **stockiness** *n.*

stockyard *n.* an enclosure with pens etc. for the sorting or temporary keeping of livestock.

stodge *n.* (*informal*) stodgy food.

stodgy *adj.* (stodgier, stodgiest) 1. (of food) heavy and filling, indigestible. 2. (of a book etc.) written in a heavy uninteresting way. 3. (of a person) uninteresting, not lively. **stodgily** *adv.*, **stodginess** *n.*

stoep (*pr.* stoop) *n.* (in South Africa) a veranda at the front of a house.

stoic (stoh-ik) *n.* a stoical person.

stoical (stoh-ikăl) *adj.* calm and not excitable, bearing difficulties or discomfort without complaining. **stoically** *adv.*

stoicism (stoh-i-sizm) *n.* being stoical.

stoke *v.* to tend and put fuel on (a furnace or fire etc.). **stoke up,** to stoke and add fuel; (*informal*) to eat large quantities of food.

stoker *n.* 1. a person who stokes a furnace etc., especially on a ship. 2. a mechanical device for doing this.

stole[1] *n.* **1.** a clergyman's vestment consisting of a long strip of silk or other material worn round the neck with the ends hanging down in front. **2.** a woman's wide scarf-like garment worn round the shoulders.

stole[2], **stolen** *see* steal.

stolid *adj.* not feeling or showing emotion, not excitable. **stolidly** *adv.*, **stolidity** (stŏ-lid-iti) *n.*

stomach *n.* **1.** the internal organ in which the first part of digestion occurs. **2.** the abdomen. **3.** appetite for food. **4.** appetite or spirit for danger or an undertaking etc., *had no stomach for the fight.* —*v.* to endure or tolerate, *can't stomach all that violence.* □ **stomach-ache** *n.* pain in the belly or bowels. **stomach-pump** *n.* a syringe for emptying the stomach or forcing liquid into it.

stomp *v.* to tread heavily.

stone *n.* **1.** a piece of rock, usually detached from the earth's crust and of fairly small size. **2.** stones or rock as a substance or material, e.g. for building. **3.** a piece of stone shaped for a particular purpose, e.g. a tombstone or millstone. **4.** a precious stone (*see* precious). **5.** a small piece of hard substance formed in the bladder or kidney or gall-bladder. **6.** the hard case round the kernel of certain fruits, the seed of grapes. **7.** (*pl.* stone) a unit of weight, = 14 lb. —*adj.* made of stone, *stone floors.* —**stone** *v.* **1.** to pelt with stones. **2.** to remove the stones from (fruit). □ **leave no stone unturned**, to try every possible means. **Stone Age**, the very early period of civilization when weapons and tools were made of stone not metal. **stone-fruit** *n.* a fruit (e.g. plum, peach, cherry) containing a single stone. **stone's throw**, a short distance.

stone- *prefix* completely, *stone-cold, stone-deaf.*

stonechat *n.* a small black-and-white song-bird with a rattling cry.

stonecrop *n.* a kind of sedum with yellow flowers, growing on rocks and walls.

stoned *adj.* (*slang*) drunk.

stoneless *adj.* without stones.

stonemason *n.* a person who cuts and dresses stone or builds in stone.

stonewall *v.* to obstruct by stonewalling. **stonewalling** *n.* batting in cricket without attempting to score runs; obstructing a discussion etc. by non-committal replies.

stonework *n.* stone(s) forming a building or other structure.

stony *adj.* (stonier, stoniest) **1.** full of stones. **2.** hard as stone, unfeeling. **3.** not responsive, *a stony gaze.* **4.** (*slang*) = stony-broke. **stonily** *adv.* □ **stony-broke** *adj.* (*slang*) = broke.

stood *see* stand.

stooge *n.* (*slang*) **1.** a comedian's assistant, used as a target for jokes. **2.** a subordinate who does routine work. **3.** a person whose actions are entirely controlled by another. —**stooge** *v.* (*slang*) **1.** to act as a stooge. **2.** to wander about aimlessly.

stook *n.* an arrangement of sheaves of corn standing propped against each other.

stool *n.* **1.** a movable seat without arms or back. **2.** a footstool. **3.** the base of a plant from which new stems or foliage shoot up.

stool-pigeon *n.* a person acting as a decoy, especially to trap a criminal.

stools *pl. n.* faeces.

stoop *v.* **1.** to bend forwards and down. **2.** to condescend, to lower oneself morally, *he wouldn't stoop to cheating.* —*n.* a posture of the body with shoulders bent forwards, *he walks with a stoop.*

stop *v.* (stopped, stopping) **1.** to put an end to (movement or progress or operation etc.), to cause to halt or pause. **2.** to refrain from continuing, to cease motion or working. **3.** (*slang*) to receive on one's body, *stopped a bullet.* **4.** (*informal*) to stay, *we stopped to tea.* **5.** to keep back, to refuse to give or allow, *the cost will be stopped out of your wages*; *stop a cheque*, order the bank not to honour it when it is presented for payment. **6.** to close by plugging or obstructing, *stop the holes* or *stop them up.* **7.** to fill a cavity in (a tooth). **8.** to press down a string or block a hole in a musical instrument in order to obtain the desired pitch. —**stop** *n.* **1.** stopping, being stopped, a pause or check, *ran without a stop*; *put a stop to it*, cause it to cease. **2.** a place where a train or bus etc. stops regularly. **3.** a punctuation-mark, especially a full stop. **4.** an obstruction or device that stops or regulates movement or operation. **5.** a row of organ-pipes providing tones of one quality, the knob or lever controlling these; *pull out all the stops*, make all possible efforts. **6.** a key or lever regulating pitch in a wind-instrument. **7.** one of the standard sizes of aperture in an adjustable lens. □ **stop at nothing**, to be completely ruthless or unscrupulous. **stop down**, to reduce the aperture of a lens in photography. **stop-go** *n.* alternate stopping and progressing. **stop-light** *n.* a red light in traffic signals; one of a pair of red lights on the rear of a motor vehicle, showing when brakes are applied. **stop off** *or* **over**, to break one's journey. **stopover** *n.* a break in one's journey, especially for a night. **stopping-train** *n.* a train that stops at many stations between main stations. **stop-press** *n.* late news inserted in a newspaper after printing has begun. **stop-watch** *n.* a watch with mechanism for starting and stopping it at will, used in timing races etc.

stopcock *n.* a valve in a pipe to regulate the flow of liquid or gas, the handle etc. on the outside of the pipe by which it is adjusted.

stopgap *n.* a temporary substitute.

stoppage *n.* **1.** stopping, being stopped. **2.** an obstruction.

stopper *n.* a plug for closing a bottle etc. —*v.* to close with a stopper. □ **put a stopper on**, to cause to cease.

stopping *n.* a filling in a tooth.

storage *n.* **1.** storing of goods etc. or of information. **2.** space available for this. **3.** the charge for it. □ **storage heater**, an electric radiator accumulating heat in off-peak periods.

store *n.* **1.** a stock or supply of something available for use. **2.** a large shop selling goods of many kinds. **3.** a storehouse, a warehouse where things are stored. **4.** a device in a computer or calculator for storing and retrieving information. —**store** *v.* **1.** to collect and keep for future use. **2.** to put into a store. **3.** to put (furniture etc.) into a warehouse for temporary keeping. **4.** to stock with something useful, *a mind well stored with information.* □ **in store**, being stored; kept available for use; destined to happen, imminent, *there's a surprise in store for you.* **set store by**, to value greatly. **store-cattle** *n.* cattle kept for breeding or for future fattening. **store-room** *n.* a room used for storing things.

storehouse *n.* a building where things are stored; *a storehouse of information,* a book etc. containing much information.

storey *n.* (*pl.* storeys) one horizontal section of a building, all the rooms at the same level; *he's a bit weak in the top storey,* (*informal*) stupid or slightly insane. **storeyed** *adj.*

stork *n.* a large long-legged wading-bird with a long straight bill, sometimes nesting on buildings and humorously pretended to be the bringer of babies.

storm *n.* **1.** a violent disturbance of the atmosphere with strong winds and usually rain or snow or thunder etc. **2.** a violent shower of missiles or blows. **3.** a great outbreak of applause or anger or criticism etc. **4.** a violent military attack on a place. — **storm** *v.* **1.** (of wind or rain) to rage, to be violent. **2.** to move or behave violently

or very angrily, to rage, *stormed out of the room; stormed at us for being late.* **3.** to attack or capture by storm, *they stormed the citadel.* □ **storm-centre** *n.* the area at the centre of a storm; the centre of a disturbance or trouble. **storm in a teacup,** great agitation over a trivial matter. **storm-lantern** *n.* a hurricane lamp. **storm petrel,** a kind of petrel said to be active before storms. **storm-window** *n.* an additional window outside another for extra protection against storms. **take by storm,** to capture by a violent attack; to captivate rapidly.

stormy *adj.* (stormier, stormiest) **1.** full of storms, affected by storms, *a stormy night; stormy coasts.* **2.** (of wind etc.) violent as in a storm. **3.** full of violent anger or outbursts, *a stormy interview.* □ **stormy petrel,** a storm petrel (*see* storm); a person whose presence seems to foretell or attract trouble.

story[1] *n.* **1.** an account of an incident or of a series of incidents, either true or invented. **2.** the plot of a novel or play etc. **3.** a report of an item of news, material for this. **4.** (*informal*) a lie. □ **story-book** *n.* a book of fictional stories. **story-line** *n.* = sense 3 above. **story-teller** *n.* a person who narrates stories; (*informal*) a liar.

story[2] *n.* = storey.

stoup (*pr.* stoop) *n.* a stone basin for holy water, especially in the wall of a church.

stout *adj.* **1.** of considerable thickness or strength, *a stout stick.* **2.** (of a person) solidly built and rather fat. **3.** brave and resolute, *a stout heart.* —*n.* a strong dark beer brewed with roasted malt or barley. — **stoutly** *adv.,* **stoutness** *n.*

stove[1] *n.* **1.** an apparatus containing one or more ovens. **2.** a closed apparatus used for heating rooms etc. **3.** a hothouse. □ **stove-enamel** *n.* a heat-proof enamel produced by treating enamelled objects in a stove. **stove-enamelled** *adj.*

stove[2] *see* stave.

stow *v.* to place in a receptacle for storage. **stow away,** to put away in storage or in reserve; to conceal oneself as a stowaway.

stowage *n.* **1.** stowing, being stowed. **2.** space available for this. **3.** the charge for it.

stowaway *n.* a person who conceals himself on a ship or aircraft etc. so as to travel without charge or unseen.

strabismus (strā-**biz**-mǔs) *n.* a squint.

straddle *v.* **1.** to sit or stand across (a thing) with the legs or supports wide apart. **2.** to stand with the legs wide apart. **3.** to drop shots or bombs short of and beyond (a certain point).

strafe (*pr.* strahf *or* strayf) to bombard, to harass with gunfire. —*n.* a piece of strafing.

straggle *v.* **1.** to grow or spread in an irregular or untidy manner, not remaining compact. **2.** to go or wander separately not in a group, to drop behind others. **straggler** *n.*

straggly *adj.* straggling.

straight *adj.* (¶ Do not confuse with strait.) **1.** extending or moving continuously in one direction, not curved or bent. **2.** correctly arranged, in proper order, tidy. **3.** in unbroken succession, *ten straight wins.* **4.** candid, not evasive, honest. **5.** (*slang*) heterosexual. **6.** not modified or elaborate, without additions, (of alcoholic drinks) not diluted. —**straight** *adv.* **1.** in a straight line; *he shoots straight,* with good aim. **2.** direct, without delay, *went straight home.* **3.** straightforwardly, *told him straight.* — **straight** *n.* **1.** the straight part of something, e.g. the last section of a racecourse. **2.** (*slang*) a heterosexual person. **3.** a sequence of five cards in poker. —**straightness** *n.* □ **go straight,** to live an honest life after being a criminal. **straight away,** without delay. **straight-edge** *n.* a bar with one edge accurately straight, used for testing straightness. **straight face,** without a smile even though amused. **straight fight,** a contest between only two candidates. **straight off,** (*informal*) without hesitation or deliberation etc., *can't tell you straight off.*

straighten *v.* to make or become straight. ¶ Do not confuse *straightened* with straitened.

straightforward *adj.* **1.** honest, frank. **2.** (of a task etc.) without complications. **straightforwardly** *adv.,* **straightforwardness** *n.*

strain[1] *v.* **1.** to stretch tightly, to make taut. **2.** to injure or weaken by excessive stretching or by over-exertion, *strain one's heart.* **3.** to hold in a tight embrace. **4.** to make an intense effort; *strain one's ears,* try hard to hear. **5.** to apply (a meaning or rule etc.) beyond its true application. **6.** to pass through a sieve or similar device in order to separate solids from the liquid containing them, (of liquid) to filter. — **strain** *n.* **1.** straining, being strained, the force exerted. **2.** an injury caused by straining a muscle etc. **3.** a severe demand on one's mental or physical strength or on one's resources, exhaustion caused by this. **4.** a passage from a tune. **5.** the tone or style of something written or spoken, *continued in a more cheerful strain.* □ **strain**

at a gnat, to be excessively fussy about trivial things. **strain every nerve,** to make all possible efforts. **straining at the leash,** eager to begin.

strain[2] *n.* **1.** a line of descent of animals or plants or micro-organisms, a variety or breed of these, *a new strain of flu virus.* **2.** a slight or inherited tendency in a character, *there's a strain of insanity in the family.*

strained *adj.* (of behaviour or manner) produced by effort, not arising from genuine feeling; *strained relations,* unpleasant tension between people.

strainer *n.* **1.** a device for keeping something taut. **2.** a utensil for straining liquids.

strait *adj.* (*old use*) narrow, restricted. —*n.* a narrow stretch of water connecting two seas, the *Strait of Gibraltar.* □ **straits** *pl. n.* a strait; a difficult state of affairs, *in dire straits.* ¶ Do not confuse with straight.

straitened *adj.* made narrow, not spacious enough. **straitened circumstances,** barely sufficient money to live on. ¶ Do not confuse with straightened.

strait-jacket *n.* a strong jacket-like garment put round a violent person to restrain his arms. —*v.* **1.** to restrain by a strait-jacket. **2.** to restrict severely.

strait-laced *adj.* very prim and proper.

strake *n.* a continuous line of planking or metal plates from stem to stern of a ship.

strand[1] *n.* **1.** one of the threads or wires etc. twisted together to form a rope, yarn, or cable. **2.** a single thread or strip of fibre. **3.** a lock of hair.

strand[2] *n.* a shore. —*v.* to run or cause to run aground. □ **stranded** *adj.* left in difficulties, e.g. without funds or means of transport.

strange *adj.* **1.** not familiar or well known, not one's own, alien, *in a strange land.* **2.** unusual, surprising, *it's strange that you haven't heard.* **3.** fresh, unaccustomed, *she is strange to the work.* **strangely** *adv.,* **strangeness** *n.*

stranger *n.* **1.** a person in a place or company etc. that he does not belong to, a person one does not know. **2.** one who is unaccustomed to a certain feeling or experience or task, *a stranger to poverty.*

strangle *v.* **1.** to kill or be killed by squeezing the throat. **2.** to restrict or prevent the proper growth or operation or utterance of. **strangler** *n.*

stranglehold *n.* a strangling grip.

strangulate *v.* to compress (a vein or intestine etc.) so that nothing can pass through it.

strangulation *n.* **1.** strangling, being strangled. **2.** strangulating, being strangulated.

strap *n.* **1.** a strip of leather or other flexible material, often with a buckle, for holding things together or in place. **2.** a shoulder-strap. **3.** a loop for grasping to steady oneself in a moving vehicle. —**strap** *v.* (strapped, strapping) **1.** to secure with a strap or straps. **2.** to bind (an injury), *strap it up.* **3.** to beat with a strap.

strapless *adj.* without shoulder-straps.

strapped *adj.* (*slang*) short of something, *strapped for cash.*

strapping *adj.* tall and healthy-looking. —*n.* **1.** straps, material for making these. **2.** sticking-plaster etc. used for binding wounds or injuries.

strata *see* stratum.

stratagem (**strat**-ă-jĕm) *n.* a cunning method of achieving something, a piece of trickery.

strategic *or* **strategical** (stră-**tee**-jik-ăl) *adj.* **1.** of strategy. **2.** giving an advantage, *a strategic position.* ☐ **strategic materials**, those essential for war. **strategic weapons**, missiles etc. that can reach an enemy's home territory (as distinct from *tactical weapons* which are for use in a battle or at close quarters). **strategically** *adv.*

strategist (**strat**-i-jist) *n.* an expert in strategy.

strategy (**strat**-i-ji) *n.* **1.** the planning and directing of the whole operation of a campaign or war. **2.** a plan or policy of this kind or to achieve something, *our economic strategy.*

Strathclyde a region of Scotland.

strathspey (strath-**spay**) *n.* a kind of Scottish dance, music for this.

stratified *adj.* arranged in strata. **stratification** *n.*

stratosphere (**strat**-ŏ-sfeer) *n.* a layer of the earth's atmosphere between about 10 and 60 km above the earth's surface.

stratum (**strah**-tŭm *or* **stray**-tŭm) *n.* (*pl.* strata) **1.** one of a series of layers, especially of rock in the earth's crust. **2.** a social level or class, *the various strata of society.* ¶ The word *strata* is a plural; it is incorrect to speak of *a strata* or *this strata*, or of *stratas.*

straw *n.* **1.** dry cut stalks of grain used as material for bedding, thatching, fodder, etc. **2.** a single stalk or piece of this. **3.** a narrow straw-like tube of paper or plastic etc. for sucking up liquid in drinking. **4.** an insignificant amount, *don't care a straw.* ☐ **a straw in the wind**, a slight indication of how things may develop. **straw poll**, (*Amer.*) an unofficial poll as a test of general feeling.

strawberry *n.* a soft juicy edible red fruit with yellow seeds on the surface, the plant that bears it. **strawberry-mark** *n.* a reddish birthmark.

stray *v.* **1.** to leave one's group or proper place with no settled destination or purpose, to roam. **2.** to go aside from a direct course, to depart from a subject. —**stray** *adj.* **1.** having strayed. **2.** isolated, occurring here and there not as one of a group, *a stray taxi.* —*n.* person or domestic animal that has strayed, a stray thing.

streak *n.* **1.** a thin line or band of a different colour or substance from its surroundings; *a streak of lightning,* a flash. **2.** an element in a person's character, *has a jealous streak.* **3.** a spell or series, *had a long winning streak.* —**streak** *v.* **1.** to mark with streaks. **2.** to move very rapidly. **3.** to run naked through a public place as a humorous or defiant act. —**streaker** *n.*

streaky *adj.* full of streaks, (of bacon etc.) with alternate layers or streaks of fat and lean.

stream *n.* **1.** a body of water flowing in its bed, a brook or river. **2.** a flow of any liquid or of a mass of things or people. **3.** (in certain schools) a section into which children with the same level of ability are placed. **4.** the current or direction of something flowing or moving, *against the stream.* —**stream** *v.* **1.** to flow or move as a stream. **2.** to emit a stream of, to run with liquid, *the wound streamed blood; with streaming eyes.* **3.** to float or wave at full length. **4.** to arrange (schoolchildren) in streams. ☐ **on stream**, in active operation or production.

streamer *n.* **1.** a long narrow flag. **2.** a long narrow ribbon or strip of paper attached at one or both ends.

streamlet *n.* a small stream.

streamline *v.* **1.** to give a streamlined form to. **2.** to make more efficient by simplifying, removing superfluities, etc.

streamlined *adj.* having a smooth even shape that offers the least resistance to movement through air or water.

street *n.* a public road in a town or village with houses on one or both sides. **not in the same street with**, (*informal*) much inferior to. **on the streets**, living by prostitution. **streets ahead of**, (*informal*) much superior to. **street-walker** *n.* a prostitute seeking customers in the street. **up one's street**, (*informal*) within one's field of knowledge or interests.

streetcar *n.* (*Amer.*) a tram.

strength *n.* **1.** the quality of being strong, the intensity of this. **2.** a source of strength, the particular respect in which a person or thing is strong, *his strength is in his mathematical ability*. **3**. the number of people present or available, the full complement, *the department is below strength*. □ **in strength**, in large numbers, *supporters were present in strength*. **on the strength**, included as an official member of an organization. **on the strength of**, on the basis of, using (a fact etc.) as one's support.

strengthen *v*. to make or become stronger.

strenuous *adj*. **1**. energetic, making great efforts. **2**. requiring great effort, *a strenuous task*. **strenuously** *adv.*, **strenuousness** *n*.

streptococcus *n*. (*pl*. streptococci, *pr*. strep-tŏ-**kok**-I) any of a group of bacteria that cause serious infections. **streptococcal** *adj*.

streptomycin (streptŏ-**my**-sin) *n*. a kind of antibiotic drug.

stress *n*. **1**. a force acting on or within a thing and tending to distort it, e.g. by pressing or pulling or twisting it. **2**. difficult circumstances, mental or physical distress caused by these. **3**. = emphasis (*see* emphasis senses 1 and 3). —**stress** *v*. **1**. to lay emphasis on. **2**. to cause stress to.

stretch *v*. **1**. to pull out tightly or into a greater length or extent or size. **2**. to be able to be stretched without breaking, to tend to become stretched, *knitted fabrics stretch*. **3**. to be continuous from a point or between points, *the wall stretches right round the estate*. **4**. to thrust out one's limbs and tighten the muscles after being relaxed. **5**. to make great demands on the abilities of (a person). **6**. to strain to the utmost or beyond a reasonable limit; *stretch the truth*, to exaggerate or lie. — **stretch** *n*. **1**. stretching, being stretched. **2**. the ability to be stretched, *this elastic has lost its stretch*. **3**. a continuous expanse or tract, a continuous period of time. **4**. (*slang*) a period of service or imprisonment. —*adj*. able to be stretched, *stretch fabrics*. □ **at a stretch**, without interruption. **at full stretch** *or* **fully stretched**, working to the utmost of one's powers. **stretch a point**, to agree to something beyond the limit of what is normally allowed. **stretch one's legs**, to go walking as a relief from sitting or lying. **stretch out**, to extend (a hand or foot) by straightening the arm or leg.

stretcher *n*. **1**. a framework of poles, canvas, etc. for carrying a sick or injured person in a lying position. **2**. any of various devices for stretching things or holding things taut or braced. **3**. a board against which a rower braces his feet.

stretchy *adj*. (*informal*) able to be

stretched, liable to become stretched.

strew *v*. (strewed, strewn *or* strewed, strewing) to scatter over a surface, to cover with scattered things.

striation (stry-**ay**-shŏn) *n*. any of a series of ridges or furrows or linear marks. **striated** *adj*. marked with striations.

stricken *adj*. affected or overcome by an illness or shock or grief, *stricken with flu*; *grief-stricken*.

strict *adj*. **1**. precisely limited or defined, without exception or deviation. **2**. requiring or giving complete obedience or exact performance, not lenient or indulgent. **strictly** *adv.*, **strictness** *n*. □ **strictly speaking**, if one uses words in their exact sense.

stricture *n*. **1**. severe criticism or condemnation. **2**. abnormal constriction of a tube-like part of the body.

stride *v*. (strode, stridden, striding) **1**. to walk with long steps. **2**. to stand astride. — **stride** *n*. **1**. a single long step, the length of this. **2**. a person's manner of striding. **3**. progress, *has made great strides towards independence*. □ **get into one's stride**, to settle into a fast and steady pace of work. **take it in one's stride**, to do it without needing a special effort.

strident (**stry**-d'nt) *adj*. loud and harsh. **stridently** *adv.*, **stridency** *n*.

strife *n*. quarrelling, conflict.

strike *v*. (struck, striking) **1**. to bring or come into sudden hard contact with, to inflict (a blow), to knock with a blow or stroke. **2**. to attack suddenly, (of a disease) to afflict. **3**. (of lightning) to descend upon and blast. **4**. to produce (sparks or a sound etc.) by striking something, to produce (a musical note) by pressing a key, to make (a coin or medal) by stamping metal etc.; *strike a match*, ignite it by friction; *strike a bargain*, make one. **5**. to bring into a specified state by or as if by striking, *he was struck blind*. **6**. to indicate (the hour) or be indicated by a sound, *clock struck two*; *two o'clock struck*. **7**. (of plant-cuttings) to put down roots. **8**. to reach (gold or mineral oil etc.) by digging or drilling. **9**. to occur to the mind of, to produce a mental impression on, *an idea struck me*; *she strikes me as being efficient*. **10**. to lower or take down (a flag or tent etc.). **11**. to stop work in protest about a grievance. **12**. to penetrate or cause to penetrate, to fill with sudden fear etc. **13**. to proceed in a certain direction, *strike north-west through the forest*. **14**. to arrive at (an average or balance) by balancing or equalizing the items. **15**. to assume (an attitude) suddenly and dramatically. —**strike** *n*.

1. an act or instance of striking. **2.** an attack. **3.** a workers' refusal to work, in protest about a grievance. **4.** a sudden discovery of gold or oil etc. □ **on strike**, (of workers) striking. **strike-breaker** *n.* a person who works while fellow employees are on strike or who is employed in place of strikers. **strike-breaking** *n.* the action of a strike-breaker. **strike it rich**, to find a source of prosperity. **strike off**, to cross off; to remove (a person) from a professional register because of misconduct. **strike oil**, to find mineral oil by drilling etc.; to find a source of prosperity. **strike out**, to cross out. **strike pay**, an allowance made by a trade union to members on strike. **strike up**, to begin playing or singing; to start (a friendship etc.) rapidly or casually. **strike while the iron is hot**, to take action promptly at a good opportunity.

strikebound *adj.* immobilized by a workers' strike.

striker *n.* **1.** a person or thing that strikes. **2.** a worker who is on strike. **3.** a football player whose main function is to try to score goals.

striking *adj.* sure to be noticed, attractive and impressive. **strikingly** *adv.*

Strine *n.* Australian speech, especially of the more uneducated type. ¶ The alleged pronunciation of 'Australian' in Australian speech.

string *n.* **1.** narrow cord. **2.** a length of this or some other material used to fasten or lace or pull something, or interwoven in a frame to form the head of a racket. **3.** a piece of catgut or cord or wire stretched and caused to vibrate so as to produce tones in a musical instrument. **4.** a strip of tough fibre on a bean etc. **5.** a set of objects strung together or of people or events coming after one another. **6.** the racehorses trained at one stable. **7.** something ranked as one's first or second etc. resource; *have two strings to one's bow*, not be obliged to rely on only one resource. **8.** a condition that is insisted upon, *the offer has no strings attached*. —**string** *v.* (strung, stringing) **1.** to fit or fasten with string(s). **2.** to thread (beads etc.) on a string. **3.** to trim the tough fibre from (beans). □ **pull strings**, *see* pull. **string along**, (*informal*) to deceive. **string along with**, (*informal*) to accompany. **string bag**, a network shopping-bag. **string-course** *n.* a projecting horizontal line of bricks etc. round a building. **string out**, to spread out in a line; to cause to last a long time. **string quartet**, a quartet for stringed instruments. **strings** *pl. n.* stringed instruments; their

players. **string up**, to kill by hanging. **string vest**, a vest made of large mesh.

stringed *adj.* (of instruments) having strings that are played by touching or with a bow or plectrum.

stringent (strin-jĕnt) *adj.* **1.** (of a rule) strict. **2.** (of financial conditions) tight. **stringently** *adv.*, **stringency** *n.*

stringy *adj.* **1.** like string. **2.** (of beans etc.) having a strip of tough fibre.

strip[1] *v.* (stripped, stripping) **1.** to take off (clothes or coverings or parts etc.); *strip a machine down*, take it apart to inspect or adjust it. **2.** to undress oneself. **3.** to deprive, e.g. of property or titles. **4.** to tear away; *stripped the gearwheel*, tore off its cogs. □ **strip club**, a club at which strip-tease performances are given. **strip-tease** *n.* an entertainment in which a woman (or occasionally a man) gradually undresses before an audience.

strip[2] *n.* a long narrow piece or area. **strip cartoon**, = cartoon (sense 2). **strip lighting**, lighting by long tubular fluorescent lamps. **tear a person off a strip**, (*slang*) to rebuke him angrily.

stripe *n.* **1.** a long narrow band on a surface, differing in colour or texture from its surroundings. **2.** a chevron on a sleeve, indicating the wearer's rank. **striped** *adj.* marked with stripes.

stripling *n.* a youth.

stripper *n.* **1.** a person or thing that strips something. **2.** a device or solvent for removing paint etc. **3.** a strip-tease performer.

stripy *adj.* (*informal*) striped.

strive *v.* (strove, striven, striving) **1.** to make great efforts. **2.** to carry on a conflict.

strobe *n.* (*informal*) a stroboscope.

stroboscope (stroh-bŏ-skohp *or* strob-ŏ-skohp) *n.* an apparatus for producing a rapidly flashing bright light. **stroboscopic** (-skop-ik) *adj.*

strode *see* stride.

stroke[1] *n.* **1.** the act or process of striking something. **2.** a single movement or action or effort, a successful or skilful effort, *hasn't done a stroke of work*; *a stroke of genius*; *a stroke of luck*, a sudden fortunate occurrence. **3.** one of a series of repeated movements, a particular sequence of these (e.g. in swimming). **4.** one hit at the ball in various games, (in golf) this used as a unit of scoring. **5.** the oarsman nearest the stern of a racing boat, setting the time of the stroke. **6.** a mark made by a movement of a pen or paintbrush etc. **7.** the sound made by a clock striking; *on the stroke of ten*, exactly at ten o'clock. **8.** an attack of apoplexy or paralysis. —*v.* to act as stroke to (a boat or crew).

stroke[2] *v.* to pass the hand gently along the surface of. —*n.* an act or spell of stroking.

stroll *v.* to walk in a leisurely way. —*n.* a leisurely walk. —**stroller** *n.*

strong *adj.* **1.** having power of resistance to being broken or damaged or captured etc. **2.** capable of exerting great power, physically powerful, powerful through numbers or resources or quality; *a strong candidate*, one likely to win; *strong acids*, those with a powerful chemical effect. **3.** concentrated, having a large proportion of a flavouring or colouring element, (of a drink) containing much alcohol. **4.** having a considerable effect on one of the senses, *a strong smell*. **5.** having a certain number of members, *an army 5000 strong*. **6.** (of verbs) changing the vowel in the past tense (as *ring/rang, strike/struck*), not adding a suffix (as *float/floated*). —*adv.* strongly, vigorously, *going strong*. —**strongly** *adv.* □ **strong-arm tactics,** use of force or sheer strength. **strong-box** *n.* a strongly made small chest for valuables. **strong language,** forcible language, oaths or swearing. **strong-minded** *adj.* having a determined mind. **strong point,** a thing at which one excels. **strong-point** *n.* a specially fortified position in a system of defences. **strong-room** *n.* a room designed for storage and protection of valuables against fire or theft. **strong suit,** a suit (in a hand of cards) in which one can take tricks; a thing at which one excels.

stronghold *n.* **1.** a fortified place. **2.** a centre of support for a cause etc.

strontium (stron-ti-ŭm) *n.* a soft silver-white metal, having a radioactive isotope that concentrates in bones when taken into an animal's body.

strop *n.* a strip of leather on which a razor is sharpened, an implement or machine serving the same purpose. —*v.* (stropped, stropping) to sharpen on or with a strop.

stroppy *adj.* (*slang*) bad-tempered, awkward to deal with.

strove *see* strive.

struck *see* strike. □ **struck on,** (*slang*) impressed with, liking.

structural *adj.* **1.** of a structure or framework. **2.** used in construction of buildings etc., *structural steel*. **structurally** *adv.*

structure *n.* **1.** the way in which something is constructed or organized. **2.** a supporting framework or the essential parts of a thing. **3.** a constructed thing, a complex whole, a building.

struggle *v.* **1.** to move one's limbs or body

in a vigorous effort to get free. **2.** to make a vigorous effort under difficulties, to make one's way or a living etc. with difficulty. **3.** to try to overcome an opponent or problem etc. —*n.* a spell of struggling, a vigorous effort, a hard contest.

strum *v.* (strummed, strumming) to play unskilfully or monotonously on a musical instrument. —*n.* the sound made by strumming.

strung *see* string. □ **strung up,** mentally tense or excited.

strut *n.* **1.** a bar of wood or metal inserted into a framework to strengthen and brace it. **2.** a strutting walk. —*v.* (strutted, strutting) to walk in a pompous self-satisfied way.

'struth *int.* (*informal*) an exclamation of surprise. (¶ = God's truth.)

strychnine (strik-neen) *n.* a bitter highly poisonous substance, used in very small doses as a stimulant.

Stuart *n.* a member of the royal family of England from James I to Queen Anne. —*adj.* of the Stuarts.

stub *n.* **1.** a short stump. **2.** the counterfoil of a cheque or receipt or ticket etc. —*v.* (stubbed, stubbing) to strike against a hard object, *stub one's toe; stub out a cigarette*, extinguish it by pressing it against something hard.

stubble *n.* **1.** the lower ends of the stalks of cereal plants left in the ground after the harvest is cut. **2.** a short stiff growth of hair or beard, especially that growing after shaving. **stubbly** *adj.*

stubborn *adj.* obstinate, not docile, not easy to control or deal with. **stubbornly** *adv.*, **stubbornness** *n.*

stubby *adj.* (stubbier, stubbiest) short and thick.

stucco *n.* plaster or cement used for coating surfaces of walls or moulding to form architectural decorations. **stuccoed** *adj.*

stuck *see* stick[2]. —*adj.* **1.** unable to move or make progress, *I'm stuck!* **2.** (of an animal) that has been stabbed or had its throat cut. □ **get stuck into,** (*slang*) to begin working seriously at (a job etc.). **stuck on,** (*slang*) infatuated with (a person or thing). **stuck-up** *adj.* (*slang*) conceited, snobbish. **stuck with,** (*informal*) unable to get rid of.

stud[1] *n.* **1.** a short large-headed nail, a rivet, a small knob projecting from a surface. **2.** a device like a button on a shank, used e.g. to fasten a detachable shirt-collar. —*v.* (studded, studding) to decorate with studs or precious stones set into a surface, to strengthen with studs.

stud[2] *n.* **1.** a number of horses kept for

breeding. **2.** the place where these are kept. □ **at stud,** (of a male horse) available for breeding on payment of a fee.
stud-book *n.* a book containing the pedigrees of horses.
student *n.* a person who is engaged in studying something, a pupil at a university or other place of higher education or technical training, *medical students.*
studied *adj.* carefully and intentionally contrived, *answered with studied indifference.*
studio *n.* (*pl.* studios) **1.** the working-room of a painter, sculptor, photographer, etc. **2.** a room or premises where cinema films are made. **3.** a room from which radio or TV programmes are regularly broadcast or in which recordings are made. □ **studio couch,** a divan-like couch that can be converted into a bed. **studio flat,** a flat consisting of a bed-sittingroom with a kitchen and bathroom.
studious *adj.* **1.** involving study, habitually spending much time in studying. **2.** deliberate, painstaking, *studious politeness.* **studiously** *adv.*, **studiousness** *n.*
study *n.* **1.** the process of studying, the pursuit of some branch of knowledge. **2.** its subject, a thing that is investigated; *his face was a study,* he looked astounded. **3.** a work presenting the result of investigations into a particular subject, *the programme is a study of race relations in Britain.* **4.** a musical composition designed to develop a player's skill. **5.** a preliminary drawing, *a study of a head.* **6.** a room used by a person for work that involves studying. —**study** *v.* (studied, studying) **1.** to give one's attention to acquiring knowledge of (a subject). **2.** to examine attentively, *we studied the map.* **3.** to give care and consideration to, *she studies the convenience of others.*
stuff *n.* **1.** material. **2.** (*slang*) unnamed things, belongings, subject-matter, activities, etc., *leave your stuff in the hall; Westerns are kids' stuff; he knows his stuff,* is an expert in his subject or trade; *do your stuff,* your task or performance; *that's the stuff!,* that is good or what is required. **3.** (*slang*) valueless matter, trash, *stuff and nonsense!* —**stuff** *v.* **1.** to pack or cram, to fill tightly, to stop up. **2.** to fill the empty carcass of (a bird or animal) with material to restore its original shape, e.g. for exhibition in a museum. **3.** to fill with padding. **4.** to fill with savoury stuffing. **5.** to fill (a person or oneself) with food, to eat greedily. **6.** (*vulgar*) to copulate with (a woman). **7.** (*slang*) to dispose of as unwanted, *you can stuff the job, I don't want it.* □ **get**

stuffed!, (*slang*) go away, stop annoying me. **stuffed shirt,** (*informal*) a pompous person.
stuffing *n.* **1.** padding used to stuff cushions etc. **2.** a savoury mixture put as a filling into poultry, rolled meat, vegetables, etc. before cooking. □ **knock the stuffing out of,** (*informal*) to make feeble or weak, to defeat utterly.
stuffy *adj.* (stuffier, stuffiest) **1.** lacking fresh air or sufficient ventilation. **2.** dull, uninteresting. **3.** (of the nose) blocked with secretions so that breathing is difficult. **4.** (*informal*) old-fashioned and narrow-minded. **5.** (*informal*) showing annoyance. **stuffily** *adv.*, **stuffiness** *n.*
stultify *v.* (stultified, stultifying) to impair or make ineffective, *their uncooperative approach has stultified the discussions.* **stultification** *n.*
stum *n.* unfermented grape-juice, must.
stumble *v.* **1.** to strike one's foot on something and lose one's balance. **2.** to walk with frequent stumbles. **3.** to make a blunder or frequent blunders in speaking or playing music etc., *stumbled through the recitation.* —*n.* an act of stumbling. □ **stumble across** *or* **on,** to discover accidentally. **stumbling-block** *n.* an obstacle, something that causes difficulty or hesitation.
stump *n.* **1.** the base of a tree remaining in the ground when the rest has fallen or been cut down. **2.** a corresponding remnant of broken tooth or amputated limb or of something worn down. **3.** one of the three uprights of a wicket in cricket. —**stump** *v.* **1.** to walk stiffly or noisily. **2.** (of a wicket-keeper) to put out (a batsman) by dislodging his bails while he is out of his crease. **3.** (*informal*) to be too difficult for, to baffle, *the question stumped him.* □ **stump up,** (*slang*) to produce (an amount of money), to pay what is required.
stumpy *adj.* (stumpier, stumpiest) short and thick. **stumpiness** *n.*
stun *v.* (stunned, stunning) **1.** to knock senseless. **2.** to daze or shock by the impact of strong emotion.
stung *see* sting.
stunk *see* stink.
stunning *adj.* (*informal*) extremely attractive. **stunningly** *adv.*
stunt[1] *v.* to hinder the growth or development of.
stunt[2] *n.* (*informal*) something unusual or difficult done as a performance or to attract attention, *a publicity stunt.* **stunt flying,** aerobatics.
stupefy *v.* (stupefied, stupefying) **1.** to

dull the wits or senses of. **2.** to stun with astonishment. **stupefaction** *n.*

stupendous (stew-**pend**-ŭs) *adj.* amazing, exceedingly great, *they took stupendous risks.* **stupendously** *adv.*

stupid *adj.* **1.** not intelligent or clever, slow at learning or understanding things. **2.** in a state of stupor, *he was knocked stupid.* **stupidly** *adv.*, **stupidity** *n.*

stupor (**stew**-per) *n.* a dazed or almost unconscious condition brought on by shock, drugs, drink, etc.

sturdy *adj.* (sturdier, sturdiest) strongly built, hardy, vigorous. **sturdily** *adv.*, **sturdiness** *n.*

sturgeon *n.* (*pl.* sturgeon) a large shark-like fish with flesh that is valued as food and roe that is made into caviare.

stutter *v.* to stammer, especially by repeating the first consonants of words. —*n.* stuttering speech, a tendency to stutter.

sty *n.* a pigsty.

stye *n.* an inflamed swelling on the edge of the eyelid.

style *n.* **1.** the manner of writing or speaking or doing something (contrasted with the subject-matter or the thing done). **2.** shape or design, *a new style of coat.* **3.** elegance, distinction. **4.** a narrow extension of the ovary in a plant, supporting the stigma. *v.* to design or shape or arrange, especially in a fashionable style. □ **in style,** elegantly, luxuriously.

stylish *adj.* in fashionable style, elegant. **stylishly** *adv.*, **stylishness** *n.*

stylist *n.* **1.** a person who achieves or aims at a good style in what he does. **2.** a person who styles things.

stylistic *adj.* of literary or artistic style. **stylistically** *adv.*

stylized *adj.* made to conform to a conventional style.

stylus *n.* (*pl.* styluses) a needle-like device used to cut grooves in records or to follow such grooves in reproducing sound from records.

stymie (**sty**-mi) *n.* something that blocks or thwarts one's activities, *lay someone a stymie.* —*v.* (stymied, stymieing) to block or thwart the activities of.

styptic (**stip**-tik) *adj.* checking the flow of blood by causing blood-vessels to contract.

suasion (**sway**-zhŏn) *n.* persuasion. **moral suasion,** a strong recommendation that is not an order.

suave (*pr.* swahv) *adj.* smooth-mannered. **suavely** *adv.*, **suavity** *n.*

sub *n.* (*informal*) **1.** a submarine. **2.** a subscription. **3.** a substitute.

sub- *prefix* **1.** under. **2.** subordinate.

subaltern (**sub**-ăl-tern) *n.* a second lieutenant.

subaqua *adj.* (of sport etc.) taking place under water.

subarctic *adj.* of regions bordering on the Arctic Circle.

subatomic *adj.* (of a particle of matter) occurring in an atom, smaller than an atom.

subcommittee *n.* a committee formed for a special purpose from some members of the main committee.

subconscious *adj.* of our own mental activities of which we are not fully aware. —*n.* the part of the mind in which these activities take place. —**subconsciously** *adv.*

subcontinent *n.* a large land-mass that forms part of a continent.

subcontract (sub-kŏn-**trakt**) *v.* to give or accept a contract to carry out all or part of another contract. **subcontractor** *n.*

subculture *n.* a social culture within a larger culture.

subdivide *v.* to divide into smaller parts after a first division. **subdivision** *n.*

subdue *v.* **1.** to overcome, to bring under control. **2.** to make quieter or less intense; *subdued lighting,* not strong or intense.

sub-edit *v.* (sub-edited, sub-editing) to prepare (material) as a sub-editor.

sub-editor *n.* **1.** an assistant editor. **2.** a person who prepares material for printing in a book or newspaper etc. **sub-editorial** *adj.*

subheading *n.* a subordinate heading.

subhuman *adj.* less than human, not fully human.

subject[1] (**sub**-jikt) *adj.* **1.** not politically independent, *subject peoples.* **2.** owing obedience to, under the authority of, *we are all subject to the laws of the land.* — **subject** *n.* **1.** a person subject to a particular political rule, any member of a State except the supreme ruler, *British subjects.* **2.** the person or thing that is being discussed or described or represented or studied. **3.** the word or words in a sentence that name who or what does the action or undergoes what is stated by the verb, e.g. *the book'* in *the book fell off the table.* **4.** the theme or chief phrase in a sonata etc. □ **subject-matter** *n.* the matter treated in a book or speech etc. **subject to,** liable to, *trains are subject to delay during fog*; depending upon as a condition, *subject to your approval*; *subject to contract,* provided that a contract is made.

subject[2] (sub-**jekt**) *v.* **1.** to bring (a country) under one's control. **2.** to cause to undergo or experience, *subjecting the metal to severe tests*. **subjection** *n.*

subjective (sub-**jek**-tiv) *adj.* **1.** existing in a person's mind and not produced by things outside it, not objective. **2.** depending on personal taste or views etc. **subjectively** *adv.*

subjoin *v.* to add at the end.

sub judice (sub **joo**-dis-i) under judicial consideration, not yet decided (and, in the UK, for this reason not to be commented upon). ¶ Latin, = under a judge.

subjugate (**sub**-jŭ-gayt) *v.* to subdue or bring (a country etc.) into subjection. **subjugation** *n.*

subjunctive *adj.* of the form of a verb used in expressing what is imagined or wished or possible, e.g. *'were'* in *if I were you*. —*n.* a subjunctive form.

sublet *v.* (sublet, subletting) to let (accommodation etc. that one holds by lease) to a subtenant.

sublimate (**sub**-lim-ayt) *v.* to divert the energy of (an emotion or impulse arising from a primitive instinct) into a culturally higher activity. **sublimation** *n.*

sublime *adj.* **1.** of the most exalted or noble or impressive kind. **2.** extreme, lofty, like that of a person who does not fear the consequences, *with sublime indifference*. **sublimely** *adv.*, **sublimity** (sub-**lim**-iti) *n.*

subliminal (sub-**lim**-inăl) *adj.* below the threshold of consciousness; *subliminal advertising*, advertising presented by a very brief TV picture etc. that influences the viewer without his consciously perceiving it.

sub-machine-gun *n.* a lightweight machine-gun held in the hand for firing.

submarine *adj.* under the surface of the sea, *submarine cables.* —*n.* a ship that can operate under water.

submerge *v.* **1.** to place below water or other liquid, to flood. **2.** (of a submarine) to dive, to go below the surface. **submergence** *n.*, **submersion** *n.*

submersible *adj.* able to be submerged. —*n.* a ship or other craft that can operate under water.

submicroscopic *adj.* too small to be seen by an ordinary microscope.

subminiature *adj.* (of a camera) using extremely narrow film, especially 16 mm.

submission *n.* **1.** submitting, being submitted. **2.** something submitted, a theory etc. submitted by counsel to a judge or jury. **3.** being submissive, obedience.

submissive *adj.* submitting to power or authority, willing to obey. **submissively** *adv.*, **submissiveness** *n.*

submit *v.* (submitted, submitting) **1.** to yield (oneself) to the authority or control

of another, to surrender. **2.** to subject (a person or thing) to a process. **3.** to present for consideration or decision.

subnormal *adj.* **1.** less than normal. **2.** below the normal standard of intelligence.

subordinate¹ (sŭb-**or**-din-ăt) *adj.* **1.** of lesser importance or rank. **2.** working under the control or authority of another person. —*n.* a person in a subordinate position.

subordinate² (sŭb-**or**-din-ayt) *v.* to make subordinate, to treat as of lesser importance than something else. **subordination** *n.*

suborn (sŭb-**orn**) *v.* to induce (a person) by bribery or other means to commit perjury or some other unlawful act. **subornation** *n.*

subpoena (sub-**pee**-nă) *n.* a writ commanding a person to appear in a lawcourt. —*v.* (subpoenaed, subpoenaing) to summon with a subpoena.

sub rosa in confidence, in secrecy. (¶ Latin, = under the rose, which was an emblem of secrecy.)

subroutine *n.* a self-contained section of a computer program, for performing a specific task but not being a complete program.

subscribe *v.* **1.** to contribute (a sum of money); *subscribe to a periodical*, pay in advance for a series of issues. **2.** to sign, *subscribe one's name*; *subscribe a document*. **3.** to express one's agreement, *we cannot subscribe to this theory*.

subscriber *n.* **1.** a person who subscribes. **2.** one who rents a telephone. □ **subscriber trunk dialling**, a system of dialling numbers in trunk calls instead of asking an operator to obtain these.

subscription *n.* **1.** subscribing. **2.** money subscribed. **3.** a fee for membership of a society etc. □ **subscription concert**, one of a series of concerts arranged by a private organization, for which the costs are subscribed by sale of tickets in advance.

subsection *n.* a division of a section.

subsequent *adj.* following in time or order or succession, coming after. **subsequently** *adv.*

subservient *adj.* **1.** subordinate. **2.** servile, obsequious. **subservience** *n.*

subside *v.* **1.** to sink to a lower or to the normal level. **2.** (of land) to sink, e.g. because of mining operations underneath. **3.** to become less active or intense, *the excitement subsided*. **4.** (of a person) to sink into a chair etc. **subsidence** (sŭb-**sy**-děns or **sub**-sid-ěns) *n.*

subsidiary *adj.* **1.** of secondary importance.

2. (of a business company) controlled by another. —*n.* a subsidiary thing.

subsidize *v.* to pay a subsidy to or for, to support by subsidies.

subsidy *n.* a grant of money paid to an industry or other cause needing help, or to keep down the price at which commodities etc. are sold to the public.

subsist *v.* to exist or continue to exist, to keep oneself alive, *managed to subsist on a diet of vegetables.*

subsistence *n.* subsisting, a means of doing this. **subsistence level,** merely enough to supply the bare necessities of life.

subsoil *n.* soil lying immediately beneath the surface layer.

subsonic *adj.* (of speed) less than the speed of sound, (of aircraft) flying at subsonic speeds, not supersonic.

substance *n.* **1.** matter with more or less uniform properties, a particular kind of this. **2.** the essence of something spoken or written, *we agree with the substance of this argument.* **3.** reality, solidity. **4.** (*old use*) wealth and possessions, *waste one's substance.*

substandard *adj.* below the usual or required standard.

substantial *adj.* **1.** of solid material or structure. **2.** of considerable amount or intensity or validity, *a substantial fee; substantial reasons.* **3.** possessing much property or wealth, *substantial farmers.* **4.** in essentials, virtual, *we are in substantial agreement.* **substantially** *adv.*

substantiate (sŭb-**stan**-shi-ayt) *v.* to support (a statement or claim etc.) with evidence, to prove. **substantiation** *n.*

substantive[1] (sŭb-**stan**-tiv) *adj.* (of military rank) permanent, not temporary.

substantive[2] (sub-stăn-tiv) *n.* a noun.

substation *n.* a subordinate station, e.g. for the distribution of electric current.

substitute *n.* a person or thing that acts or serves in place of another. —*v.* **1.** to put or use as a substitute. **2.** (*informal*) to serve as a substitute. —**substitution** *n.*

substratum (sub-**strah**-tŭm *or* sub-**stray**-tŭm) *n.* (*pl.* substrata) an underlying layer or substance.

substructure *n.* an underlying or supporting structure.

subsume *v.* to bring or include under a particular rule or classification etc.

subtenant *n.* a person who rents accommodation etc. from one who holds it by lease not freehold. **subtenancy** *n.*

subterfuge (**sub**-ter-fewj) *n.* a trick or excuse used in order to avoid blame or defeat, trickery.

subterranean (subter-**ayn**-iăn) *adj.* underground.

subtitle *n.* **1.** a subordinate title. **2.** a caption on a cinema film, showing the dialogue etc. of a silent film or translating that of a foreign one. —*v.* to provide with a subtitle.

subtle (sut'l) *adj.* **1.** slight and difficult to detect or analyse. **2.** making or able to make fine distinctions, having acute perception, *a subtle mind.* **3.** ingenious, crafty. **subtly** *adv.,* **subtlety** (sut'l-ti) *n.*

subtopia (sub-**toh**-piă) *n.* unsightly suburbs, especially those spreading over the countryside. (¶ From 'suburban' and 'Utopia', which is used jokingly.)

subtotal *n.* the total of part of a group of figures.

subtract *v.* to deduct, to remove (a part or quantity or number) from a greater one. **subtraction** *n.*

subtropical *adj.* of regions bordering on the tropics.

suburb *n.* a residential district lying outside the central part of a town.

suburban (sŭb-**er**-băn) *adj.* **1.** of a suburb or suburbs. **2.** having only limited interests and narrow-minded views. □ **suburbanite** *n.* a person who lives in a suburb.

suburbia *n.* suburbs and their inhabitants.

subvention (sŭb-**ven**-shŏn) *n.* a subsidy.

subversion *n.* subverting.

subversive *adj.* tending to subvert.

subvert (sŭb-**vert**) *v.* to overthrow the authority of (a religion or government etc.) by weakening people's trust or belief.

subway *n.* **1.** an underground passage, e.g. for pedestrians to cross below a road. **2.** (*Amer.*) an underground railway.

subzero *adj.* (of temperatures) below zero.

succeed *v.* **1.** to be successful. **2.** to come next in time or order, to follow, to take the place previously filled by, *Edward the Seventh succeeded Queen Victoria* or *succeeded to the throne.*

success *n.* **1.** a favourable outcome, doing what was desired or attempted, the attainment of wealth or fame or position. **2.** a person or thing that is successful.

successful *adj.* having success. **successfully** *adv.*

succession *n.* **1.** following in order, a series of people or things following each other. **2.** succeeding to the throne or to an inheritance or position, the right of doing this, the sequence of people with this right. □ **in succession,** one after another.

successive *adj.* following one after another, in an unbroken series. **successively** *adv.*

successor *n.* a person or thing that succeeds another.

succinct (suk-**sinkt**) *adj.* concise, expressed briefly and clearly. **succinctly** *adv.*

succour (suk-er) *n.* help given in time of need. —*v.* to give such help.

succulent (suk-yoo-lĕnt) *adj.* **1.** juicy. **2.** (of plants) having thick fleshy leaves or stems. —*n.* a succulent plant.

succumb (sŭ-**kum**) *v.* to give way to something overpowering.

such *adj.* **1.** of the same kind or degree, *people such as these.* **2.** of the kind or degree described, *there's no such person.* **3.** so great or intense, *it gave her such a fright.* —*pronoun* that, the action or thing referred to, *such being the case, we can do nothing.* □ **as such**, as what has been specified, in itself, *interested in getting a good photograph, not in the castle as such.* **such-and-such** *adj.* particular but not now specified, *says he will arrive at such-and-such a time but it is always late.*

suchlike *adj.* (*informal*) of the same kind. **and suchlike**, and things of this kind.

suck *v.* **1.** to draw (liquid or air etc.) into the mouth by using the lip muscles, to draw liquid etc. from (a thing) in this way. **2.** to squeeze in the mouth by using the tongue, *sucking a toffee.* **3.** to draw in, *plants suck moisture from the soil; the canoe was sucked into the whirlpool.* —*n.* the act or process of sucking. □ **suck up to,** (*slang*) to toady to.

sucker *n.* **1.** a person or thing that sucks. **2.** an organ of certain animals, or a device of rubber etc., that can adhere to a surface by suction. **3.** a shoot coming up from the roots or underground stem of a tree or shrub. **4.** (*slang*) a person who is easily deceived. □ **be a sucker for,** (*slang*) to be always unable to resist the attractions of.

sucking-pig *n.* a pig that is not yet weaned.

suckle *v.* **1.** to feed (young) at the breast or udder. **2.** (of young) to take milk in this way. □ **suckling** *n.* a child or animal that is not yet weaned.

sucrose (sewk-rohz) *n.* sugar obtained from plants such as sugar-cane or sugar-beet.

suction *n.* **1.** sucking. **2.** production of a partial or complete vacuum so that external atmospheric pressure forces fluid or other substance into the vacant space or causes adhesion of surfaces, *vacuum cleaners work by suction.*

Sudan (sŭ-**dahn**) a country in north-east Africa. **Sudanese** (soo-dă-**neez**) *adj.* & *n.* (*pl.* Sudanese).

sudden *adj.* happening or done quickly or unexpectedly or without warning. **suddenly** *adv.*, **suddenness** *n.* □ **all of a sudden,** suddenly. **sudden death,** (*informal*) decision of a drawn or tied contest by the result of the next game or point.

suds *pl. n.* soapsuds.

sue *v.* (sued, suing) **1.** to begin legal proceedings against. **2.** to make an application, *sue for peace.*

suede (*pr.* swayd) *n.* leather with the flesh side rubbed so that it has a velvety nap. **suede-cloth** *n.* woven cloth imitating this.

suet *n.* hard fat from round the kidneys of cattle and sheep, used in cooking. **suet pudding,** a pudding made with flour and suet.

suety *adj.* like suet, (of the complexion) pallid.

suffer *v.* **1.** to undergo or be subjected to (pain, loss, grief, damage, etc.). **2.** to feel pain or grief, to be subjected to damage or a disadvantage. **3.** to permit. **4.** to tolerate; *she does not suffer fools gladly,* behaves intolerantly towards incompetent people. **suffering** *n.*

sufferance *n.* **on sufferance,** tolerated but only grudgingly or because there is no positive objection.

suffice (sŭ-**fys**) *v.* to be enough, to meet the needs of.

sufficient *adj.* enough. **sufficiently** *adv.*, **sufficiency** *n.*

suffix *n.* (*pl.* suffixes) a letter or combination of letters added at the end of a word to make another word (e.g. *y* added to *rust* to make *rusty*) or as an inflexion (e.g. *ing* added to *suck* to make *sucking*).

suffocate *v.* **1.** to kill by stopping the breathing. **2.** to cause discomfort to (a person) by making breathing difficult. **3.** to be suffocated. **suffocation** *n.*

Suffolk a county of England.

suffragan (suf-ră-găn) *n.* a **suffragan bishop,** a bishop consecrated to help the bishop of a diocese with administration; a bishop in relation to an archbishop.

suffrage (suf-rij) *n.* the right to vote in political elections.

suffragette (suf-ră-**jet**) *n.* a woman who, in the early 20th century, agitated for women to have the right to vote in political elections.

suffuse (sŭ-**fewz**) *v.* (of colour or moisture) to spread throughout or over. **suffusion** *n.*

sugar *n.* a sweet crystalline substance obtained from the juices of various plants. —*v.* to sweeten with sugar, to coat with sugar. □ **sugar-basin** *n.* a basin for holding sugar for use at meals. **sugar-beet** *n.* the kind of beet from which sugar is extracted. **sugar-bowl** *n.* a sugar-basin. **sugar-cane** *n.* a tropical grass with tall jointed stems from which sugar is obtained. **sugar-loaf** *n.* a solid cone-shaped mass of sugar, as sold in former times. **sugar soap**, an abrasive compound for cleaning or removing paint.

sugary *adj.* 1. containing or resembling sugar. 2. sweet, excessively sweet in style or manner. **sugariness** *n.*

suggest *v.* 1. to cause (an idea or possibility) to be present in the mind. 2. to propose (a plan or theory) for acceptance or rejection.

suggestible *adj.* 1. easily influenced by people's suggestions. 2. that may be suggested. **suggestibility** *n.*

suggestion *n.* 1. suggesting, being suggested. 2. something suggested. 3. a slight trace, *he speaks with a suggestion of a French accent.*

suggestive *adj.* 1. conveying a suggestion. 2. tending to convey an indecent or improper meaning. **suggestively** *adv.*

suicidal *adj.* 1. of suicide. 2. (of a person) liable to commit suicide. 3. destructive to one's own interests.

suicide *n.* 1. the intentional killing of oneself, an instance of this. 2. a person who commits suicide. 3. an act that is destructive to one's own interests; *political suicide*, ruination of one's own or one's party's political prospects. —*v.* to commit suicide. □ **commit suicide,** to kill oneself intentionally. **suicide pact,** an agreement between people to commit suicide together.

suit *n.* 1. a set of clothing to be worn together, especially a jacket and trousers or skirt. 2. clothing for use in a particular activity, *a space suit.* 3. a set of armour. 4. any of the four sets (spades, hearts, diamonds, clubs) into which a pack of cards is divided. 5. a lawsuit. 6. (*formal*) a request or appeal; *press one's suit*, to request persistently. —**suit** *v.* 1. to satisfy, to meet the demands or needs of. 2. to be convenient or right for. 3. to give a pleasing appearance or effect upon, *red doesn't suit her.* 4. to adapt, to make suitable, *suit your style to your audience; suit action to the word*, do at once the action just promised. □ **suit a person's book,** to be convenient for him. **suit yourself**, do as you please; find something that satisfies you.

suitable *adj.* right for the purpose or occasion. **suitably** *adv.*, **suitability** *n.*

suitcase *n.* a rectangular case for carrying

clothes, usually with a hinged lid and a handle.

suite *n.* 1. a set of rooms or furniture. 2. a set of attendants, a retinue. 3. a set of musical pieces or extracts.

suiting *n.* material for making suits.

suitor *n.* 1. a man who is courting a woman. 2. a person bringing a lawsuit.

sulk *v.* to be sulky. **sulks** *pl. n.* a fit of sulkiness.

sulky *adj.* (sulkier, sulkiest) sullen, silent or aloof because of resentment or bad temper. **sulkily** *adv.*, **sulkiness** *n.*

sullen *adj.* 1. gloomy and unresponsive from resentment or bad temper. 2. dark and dismal, *sullen skies.* **sullenly** *adv.*, **sullenness** *n.*

sully *v.* (sullied, sullying) to stain or blemish, to spoil the purity or splendour of, *sullied his reputation.*

sulpha *adj.* sulphonamide, *sulpha drugs.*

sulphate *n.* a salt of sulphuric acid.

sulphonamide (sul-**fon**-ă-myd) *n.* any of a group of chemical compounds with antibacterial properties.

sulphur *n.* a pale-yellow substance that burns with a blue flame and a stifling smell, used in industry and in medicine.

sulphuric (sul-**fewr**-ik) *adj.* containing a proportion of sulphur. **sulphuric acid**, a strong corrosive acid.

sulphurous (**sul**-fewr-ŭs) *adj.* 1. of or like sulphur. 2. containing a proportion of sulphur.

sultan *n.* the ruler of certain Muslim countries.

sultana *n.* 1. a seedless raisin; *sultana grape*, the small yellow grape from which it is produced. 2. the wife, mother, sister, or daughter of a sultan.

sultanate *n.* the territory of a sultan.

sultry *adj.* (sultrier, sultriest) 1. hot and humid. 2. (of a woman) of dark mysterious beauty. **sultriness** *n.*

sum *n.* 1. a total. 2. a particular amount of money, *for the sum of £5.* 3. a problem in arithmetic, *good at sums.* —*v.* (summed, summing) to find the sum of. □ **sum total,** a total. **sum up,** to give the total of; to summarize; (of a judge) to summarize the evidence or argument; to form an opinion of, *sum a person up.*

summarize *v.* to make or be a summary of.

summary *n.* a statement giving the main points of something briefly. —*adj.* 1. brief, giving the main points only, *a summary account.* 2. done or given without delay or attention to detail or formal procedure. — **summarily** *adv.*

summation (sum-**ay**-shŏn) *n.* finding of a total or sum, summing up.

summer *n.* the warmest season of the year, from June to August in the northern hemisphere. □ **summer-house** *n.* a light building in a garden or park, providing shade in summer. **summer pudding,** a pudding of soft fruit pressed in a bread or sponge-cake case. **summer school,** a course of lectures etc. held during the summer vacation. **summer-time** *n.* the season of summer. **summer time,** the time shown by clocks that are put forward in some countries in summer to give long light evenings during the summer months.

summery *adj.* like summer, suitable for summer.

summit *n.* **1.** the highest point of something, the top of a mountain. **2.** a **summit conference,** a meeting between heads of two or more governments.

summon *v.* **1.** to send for (a person), to order to appear in a lawcourt. **2.** to call together, to order to assemble, *summon a meeting.* **3.** to gather together (one's strength or courage) in order to do something. **4.** to call upon (a person etc.) to do something, *summon the fort to surrender.*

summons *n.* **1.** a command to do something or appear somewhere. **2.** an order to appear in a lawcourt, a document containing this. —*v.* to serve with a summons. (¶ It is equally correct to use *summon* as a verb with this meaning.)

sump *n.* **1.** an inner casing holding lubricating oil in a petrol engine. **2.** a hole or low area into which waste liquid drains.

sumptuous *adj.* splendid and costly-looking. **sumptuously** *adv.,* **sumptuousness** *n.*

sun *n.* **1.** the star round which the earth travels and from which it receives light and warmth. **2.** this light or warmth, *let the sun in.* **3.** any fixed star with or without planets. —*v.* (sunned, sunning) to expose to the sun; *sun oneself,* to bask in sunshine. □. **sun-blind** *n.* an awning over a window. **sun-dress** *n.* a dress allowing arms, shoulders, and back to be exposed to sun. **sun-glasses** *n.* spectacles with tinted lenses to protect the eyes from sunlight or glare. **sun-god** *n.* the sun worshipped as a god. **sun-hat, sun-helmet** *ns.* a hat or helmet worn to protect the head from sun. **sun-lamp** *n.* a lamp producing ultra-violet rays, with effects like those of the sun. **sun-ray pleats,** zigzag pleats radiating from the waist of a skirt. **sun-roof** *n.* a sliding panel in the roof of a saloon car, opened to admit sunlight. **sun-tan** *n.* tan produced by exposure to sun. **sun-tanned** *adj.* tanned by sun. **sun-trap** *n.* a sunny place, especially a sheltered one.

sun-up *n.* (*Amer.*) sunrise. **sun visor,** *see* visor.

sunbathe *v.* to expose one's body to the sun.

sunbeam *n.* a ray of sun.

sunburn *n.* tanning or inflammation of the skin caused by exposure to sun. **sunburnt** *adj.*

sundae (sun-day) *n.* a dish of ice cream and crushed fruit, nuts, syrup, etc.

Sunday *n.* **1.** the first day of the week, observed by Christians as a day of rest and worship. **2.** a newspaper published on Sundays. □ **Sunday best,** best clothes, kept for Sunday use. **Sunday painter,** an amateur painter, one who paints purely for pleasure. **Sunday school,** a school for religious instruction of children, held on Sundays.

sunder *v.* to break or tear apart, to sever.

sundew *n.* a small bog-plant with hairs secreting moisture that traps insects.

sundial *n.* a device that shows the time by means of the shadow of a rod or plate on a scaled dial.

sundown *n.* sunset.

sundry *adj.* various, several. **all and sundry,** everyone. **sundries** *pl. n.* various small items not named individually.

sunfish *n.* a large ocean fish with an almost spherical body.

sunflower *n.* a tall garden plant bearing large flowers with golden petals round a dark centre, producing seeds that yield an edible oil.

sung *see* sing.

sunk, sunken *see* sink. —*adjs.* lying below the level of the surrounding area. □ **sunk fence,** a ditch strengthened by a wall, forming a boundary without interrupting the view.

sunless *adj.* without sunshine.

sunlight *n.* light from the sun.

sunlit *adj.* lit by sunlight.

sunny *adj.* (sunnier, sunniest) **1.** bright with sunlight, full of sunshine. **2.** (of a person or mood) cheerful. **sunnily** *adv.* □ **the sunny side,** the more cheerful aspect of circumstances.

sunrise *n.* the rising of the sun, the time of this.

sunset *n.* **1.** the setting of the sun, the time of this. **2.** the western sky full of colour at sunset.

sunshade *n.* **1.** a parasol. **2.** an awning.

sunshine *n.* direct sunlight uninterrupted by cloud.

sunspot *n.* **1.** one of the dark patches sometimes observed on the sun's surface. **2.** (*informal*) a place with a sunny climate.

sunstroke *n.* illness caused by too much exposure to sun.

sup *v.* (supped, supping) **1.** to take (liquid) by sips or spoonfuls. **2.** to eat supper. —*n.* a mouthful of liquid, *neither bite nor sup.*

super *n.* (*informal*) **1.** a superintendent, especially in the police force. **2.** a supernumerary actor. —*adj.* (*slang*) excellent, superb.

super- *prefix* **1.** over, beyond. **2.** extremely.

superabundant *adj.* very abundant, more than enough. **superabundance** *n.*

superannuate *v.* **1.** to discharge (an employee) into retirement with a pension. **2.** to discard as too old for use.

superannuation *n.* **1.** superannuating. **2.** a pension granted to an employee on retirement, payment(s) contributed towards this during his employment.

superb *adj.* of the most impressive or splendid kind, excellent. **superbly** *adv.*

supercharge *v.* to increase the power of (an engine) by using a device that supplies air or fuel at above the normal pressure. **supercharger** *n.*

supercilious (soo-per-**sil**-iŭs) *adj.* with an air of superiority, haughty and scornful. **superciliously** *adv.*

superconductivity *n.* the property of certain metals, at temperatures near absolute zero, of having no electrical resistance, so that once a current is started it flows without a voltage to keep it going. **superconductive** *adj.,* **superconductor** *n.*

supercool *v.* to cool (a liquid) below its freezing-point without its becoming solid or crystalline.

super-ego (soo-per-**eg**-oh) *n.* a person's ideals for himself, acting like a conscience in directing his behaviour.

supererogation (soo-per-e-rŏ-**gay**-shŏn) *n.* the doing of more than is required by duty, *works of supererogation.*

superfatted *adj.* (of soap) containing extra fat.

superficial *adj.* **1.** of or on the surface, not deep or penetrating, *a superficial wound; superficial knowledge,* not thorough or penetrating. **2.** (of a person) having no depth of character or feeling. **superficially** *adv.,* **superficiality** (soo-per-fish-i-**al**-iti) *n.*

superfine *adj.* of extra-high quality.

superfluity (soo-per-**floo**-iti) *n.* a superfluous amount.

superfluous (soo-**per**-floo-ŭs) *adj.* more than is required. **superfluously** *adv.*

superheat *v.* to heat (liquid) above its boiling-point without allowing it to vaporize, to heat (vapour) above boiling-point.

superhuman *adj.* **1.** beyond ordinary human capacity or power. **2.** higher than humanity, divine.

superimpose *v.* to lay or place (a thing) on top of something else. **superimposition** *n.*

superintend *v.* to supervise. **superintendence** *n.*

superintendent *n.* **1.** a person who superintends. **2.** a police officer next above the rank of inspector.

superior *adj.* **1.** higher in position or rank. **2.** better or greater in some way, of high or higher quality. **3.** showing that one feels oneself to be better or wiser etc. than others, conceited, supercilious. **4.** not influenced by, not giving way to, *she is superior to flattery.* —**superior** *n.* **1.** a person or thing of higher rank or ability or quality. **2.** the head of a monastery or other religious community. —**superiority** *n.*

superlative (soo-**per**-lă-tiv) *adj.* **1.** of the highest degree or quality, *a man of superlative wisdom.* **2.** of a grammatical form that expresses the highest or a very high degree of a quality, e.g. *dearest, shyest, best.* —*n.* a superlative form of a word. —**superlatively** *adv.*

superman *n.* (*pl.* supermen) a man of superhuman powers.

supermarket *n.* a large self-service shop selling groceries and household goods.

supernatural *adj.* of or caused by power above the forces of nature. **supernaturally** *adv.*

supernumerary (soo-per-**new**-mer-er-i) *adj.* in excess of the normal number, extra. —*n.* a supernumerary person or thing.

superphosphate *n.* a fertilizer containing soluble phosphates.

superpower *n.* one of the most powerful nations of the world.

superscript *adj.* written or printed just above and to the right of a word or figure or symbol.

superscription *n.* a word or words written at the top or on the outside.

supersede (soo-per-**seed**) *v.* **1.** to take the place of, *cars have superseded horse-drawn carriages.* **2.** to put or use in place of (another person or thing).

supersonic *adj.* of or having a speed greater than that of sound.

superstar *n.* a great star in entertainment etc.

superstition *n.* **1.** belief that events can be influenced by certain acts or circumstances that have no demonstrable connection with them, an idea or practice based on this. **2.** a belief that is held by a number of people but without foundation.

superstitious *adj.* based on or influenced by superstition. **superstitiously** *adv.*

superstore *n.* a large supermarket, especially one with a sales area of at least 2500 sq. metres.

superstructure *n.* a structure that rests upon something else, a building as distinct from its foundations.

supertanker *n.* a very large tanker.

supervene (soo-per-**veen**) *v.* to occur as an interruption or a change from some condition or process. **supervention** (soo-per-**ven**-shŏn) *n.*

supervise *v.* to direct and inspect (work or workers or the operation of an organization). **supervision** *n.*, **supervisor** *n.*

supervisory (**soo**-per-vy-zer-i) *adj.* supervising, *supervisory duties.*

supine (**soo**-pyn) *adj.* **1.** lying face upwards (contrasted with *prone*). **2.** not inclined to take action, indolent. **supinely** *adv.*

supper *n.* an evening meal, the last meal of the day. **supperless** *adj.* without supper.

supplant *v.* to oust and take the place of.

supple *adj.* bending easily, flexible, not stiff. **supplely** *adv.*, **suppleness** *n.*

supplement[1] (**sup**-li-mĕnt) *n.* **1.** a thing added as an extra or to make up for a deficiency. **2.** a part added to a book etc. to give further information or to treat a particular subject, a set of special pages issued with a newspaper.

supplement[2] (**sup**-li-ment) *v.* to provide or be a supplement to.

supplementary *adj.* serving as a supplement.

suppliant (**sup**-li-ănt) *n.* a person asking humbly for something.

supplicate *v.* to ask humbly for, to beseech. **supplication** *n.*

supply *v.* (supplied, supplying) **1.** to give or provide with (something needed or useful), to make available for use. **2.** to make up for, to satisfy, *supply a need.* — **supply** *n.* **1.** providing of what is needed. **2.** a stock or store, an amount of something provided or available, *the water-supply; an inexhaustible supply of fish.* □ **on supply**, (of a schoolteacher) employed as one of a number of people available to work as substitutes for others in an emergency.

support *v.* **1.** to keep from falling or sinking, to hold in position, to bear the weight of. **2.** to give strength to, to enable to last or continue, *too little food to support life.* **3.** to supply with necessaries, *he has a family to support.* **4.** to assist by one's ap-

proval or presence or by subscription to funds, to be a fan of (a particular sports team); *support a resolution,* speak or vote in favour of it. **5.** to take a secondary part, *the play has a strong supporting cast.* **6.** to corroborate, to bring facts to confirm (a statement etc.). **7.** to endure or tolerate, *we cannot support such insolence.* —**support** *n.* **1.** supporting, being supported, *we need your support.* **2.** a person or thing that supports. — **supporter** *n.* □ **supporting price**, the minimum price guaranteed to farmers etc. and made up (if necessary) by government subsidy.

suppose *v.* **1.** to be inclined to think, to accept as true or probable, *I don't suppose they will come.* **2.** to assume as true for the purpose of argument, *suppose the world were flat.* **3.** to consider as a proposal, *suppose we try another.* **4.** to require as a condition, to presuppose, *that supposes a mechanism without flaws.* □ **be supposed to,** to be expected or intended to, to have as a duty. **supposed** *adj.* believed to exist or to have a certain character or identity, *his supposed brother.* **supposedly** (sŭ-**poh**-zidli) *adv.* according to supposition.

supposition *n.* supposing, what is supposed, *the article is based on supposition not on fact.*

suppositious (sup-ŏ-**zish**-ŭs) *adj.* hypothetical, based on supposition.

supposititious (sŭ-poz-i-**tish**-ŭs) *adj.* substituted for the real person or thing, spurious.

suppository (sŭ-**poz**-it-er-i) *n.* a solid piece of medicinal substance placed in the rectum or vagina or urethra and left to melt.

suppress *v.* **1.** to put an end to the activity or existence of, especially by force or authority, *suppress the rebellion.* **2.** to keep from being known or seen, *suppress the truth; suppress a newspaper,* prevent its publication. **suppression** *n.*

suppressible *adj.* able to be suppressed.

suppressor *n.* a person or thing that suppresses, a device to suppress electrical interference.

suppurate (**sup**-yoor-ayt) *v.* to form pus, to fester. **suppuration** *n.*

supra- *prefix* above, over.

supremacy (soo-**prem**-äsi) *n.* being supreme, the position of supreme authority or power.

supreme *adj.* **1.** highest in authority or rank, *the supreme commander.* **2.** highest in importance or intensity or quality, most outstanding, *supreme courage; the supreme sacrifice,* involving one's death (e.g. in war). **3.** (of food) served in a rich cream sauce, *chicken supreme.* **supremely** *adv.*

surcharge *n.* **1.** payment demanded in addition to the usual charge. **2.** an additional or excessive load. **3.** a mark printed over a postage stamp, changing its value. —**surcharge** *v.* **1.** to make a surcharge on, to charge extra. **2.** to overload. **3.** to print a surcharge on (a stamp).

surd *n.* a mathematical quantity (especially a root) that cannot be expressed in finite terms of whole numbers or quantities.

sure *adj.* **1.** having or seeming to have sufficient reason for one's beliefs, free from doubts; *be sure of a person,* able to rely on him. **2.** certain to do something or to happen, *the book is sure to be a success.* **3.** undoubtedly true, *one thing is sure.* **4.** reliable, secure, unfailing, *there's only one sure way*; *be sure to write,* do not fail to write. —*adv.* (*Amer. informal*) certainly, *it sure was cold.* —**sureness** *n.* □ **as sure as,** as certainly as. **for sure,** for certain. **make sure,** to act so as to be certain; to feel confident (perhaps mistakenly), *confound that man! I made sure he'd be here in time.* **sure enough,** certainly, in fact. **sure-fire** *adj.* (*Amer. slang*) certain to succeed. **sure-footed** *adj.* never slipping or stumbling. **to be sure,** it is admitted, certainly, *she's not perfect, to be sure.*

surely *adv.* **1.** in a sure manner, without doubt, securely. **2.** used for emphasis, *surely you won't desert us?* **3.** (as an answer) certainly, *'Will you help?' 'Surely.'*

surety (**shoor**-ti) *n.* **1.** a guarantee. **2.** a person who makes himself responsible for another person's payment of a debt or performance of an undertaking.

surf *n.* the white foam of waves breaking on a rock or shore. **surf-board** *n.* a long narrow board used in surf-riding. **surf-riding** *n.* the sport of balancing oneself on a board while being carried on waves to the shore.

surface *n.* **1.** the outside of an object. **2.** any of the sides of an object. **3.** the uppermost area, the top of a table or desk etc., *a working surface.* **4.** the top of a body of water. **5.** the outward appearance of something, the qualities etc. perceived by casual observation (as distinct from deeper or hidden ones). —*adj.* of or on the surface only, of the surface of the earth or sea (as distinct from in the air or underground, or under water). —**surface** *v.* **1.** to put a specified surface on. **2.** to come or bring to the surface. **3.** (*informal*) to wake after sleep or unconsciousness. □ **surface mail,** mail carried by sea not by air.

surfeit (**ser**-fit) *n.* too much of something (especially food and drink), a feeling of discomfort arising from this. —*v.* to cause to take too much of something, to satiate, to cloy.

surfer *n.* a person who goes surf-riding.

surfing *n.* surf-riding.

surge *v.* to move forward in or like waves, to increase in volume or intensity. —*n.* a wave, a surging movement or increase, an onrush.

surgeon *n.* a medical practitioner who performs surgical operations, a specialist in surgery.

surgery *n.* **1.** the treatment of injuries and disorders and disease by cutting or manipulation of the affected parts. **2.** the place where a doctor or dentist etc. gives advice and treatment to patients. **3.** (*informal*) the place where an MP etc. is regularly available for consultation. **4.** the hours during which a doctor etc. is available to patients at his surgery.

surgical *adj.* of surgery or surgeons, used in surgery. **surgically** *adv.* □ **surgical spirit,** methylated spirits used in surgery for cleansing etc.

Surinam (soor-i-**nam**) a country on the north coast of South America. **Surinamer** *n.,* **Surinamese** *adj.* & *n.* (*pl.* Surinamese)

surly *adj.* (surlier, surliest) bad-tempered and unfriendly. **surlily** *adv.,* **surliness** *n.*

surmise (ser-**myz**) *n.* a conjecture. —*v.* to conjecture.

surmount *v.* to overcome (a difficulty), to get over (an obstacle). **be surmounted by,** to have on or over the top, *the spire is surmounted by a weather-vane.*

surmountable *adj.* able to be overcome.

surname *n.* the name held by all members of a family. —*v.* to give as a surname.

surpass *v.* to do or be better than, to excel.

surpassing *adj.* greatly excelling or exceeding others. **surpassingly** *adv.*

surplice (**ser**-plis) *n.* a loose white vestment with full sleeves, worn over the cassock by clergy and choir at a religious service.

surplus (**ser**-plŭs) *n.* an amount left over after what is required has been used, especially an excess of public revenue over expenditure during a financial year.

surprise *n.* **1.** the emotion aroused by something sudden or unexpected. **2.** an event or thing that arouses this emotion. **3.** the process of catching a person etc. unprepared; *a surprise attack* or *visit,* one made unexpectedly. —**surprise** *v.* **1.** to cause to feel surprise. **2.** to come upon or

surrealism | sustain

attack suddenly and without warning, to capture in this way. **3.** to startle (a person) into action by catching him unprepared. **4.** to discover (a secret etc.) by unexpected action. □ **surprised** *adj.* experiencing surprise. **surprised at,** scandalized by, *we are surprised at your behaviour.* **surprising** *adj.* causing surprise. **surprisingly** *adv.*

surrealism (su-ree-ăl-izm) *n.* a 20th-century movement in art and literature that seeks to express what is in the subconscious mind by depicting objects and events as seen in dreams etc. **surrealist** *n.*, **surrealistic** *adj.*

surrender *v.* **1.** to hand over, to give into another person's power or control, especially on demand or under compulsion. **2.** to give oneself up, to accept an enemy's demand for submission; *surrender to one's bail,* to appear duly in a lawcourt after being released on bail. **3.** to give way to an emotion, *surrendered herself to grief.* **4.** to give up one's rights under (an insurance policy) in return for a smaller sum payable immediately. *—n.* surrendering, being surrendered.

surreptitious (su-rep-**tish**-ŭs) *adj.* acting or done stealthily. **surreptitiously** *adv.*

Surrey a county of England.

surrogate (**su**-rŏ-găt) *n.* a deputy.

surround *v.* **1.** to come or lie or be all round. **2.** to place all round, to encircle with enemy forces. *—n.* a border or edging, a floor-covering between carpet and walls. □ **be surrounded by** *or* **with,** to have on all sides. **surroundings** *pl. n.* the things or conditions around and liable to affect a person or place.

surveillance (ser-**vayl**-ăns) *n.* supervision or close observation, especially of a suspected person.

survey [1] (ser-**vay**) *v.* **1.** to look at and take a general view of. **2.** to make or present a survey of, *the report surveys progress made in the past year.* **3.** to examine the condition of (a building etc.). **4.** to measure and map out the size, shape, position, and elevation etc. of (an area of the earth's surface).

survey [2] (**ser**-vay) *n.* **1.** a general look at something. **2.** a general examination of a situation or subject, an account of this. **3.** the surveying of land etc., a map or plan produced by this.

surveyor *n.* a person whose job is to survey land or buildings.

survival *n.* **1.** surviving. **2.** something that has survived from an earlier time.

survive *v.* **1.** to continue to live or exist. **2.** to live or exist longer than, to remain alive or in existence after, *few flowers survived the frost.*

survivor *n.* one who survives, one who survives another.

sus *n.* (*slang*) **1.** a suspect. **2.** a suspicion. — *v.* (sussed, sussing) (*slang*) **sus out,** to investigate or reconnoitre.

susceptible (sŭ-**sep**-ti-bŭl) *adj.* **1.** liable to be affected by something; *susceptible to colds,* catching colds easily. **2.** impressionable, falling in love easily. **3.** able to undergo something; *susceptible of proof,* able to be proved. **susceptibility** *n.* □ **susceptibilities** *pl. n.* a person's feelings that may be hurt or offended.

susceptive (sŭ-**sep**-tiv) *adj.* susceptible.

suspect [1] (sŭ-**spekt**) *v.* **1.** to have an impression of the existence or presence of, *we suspected a trap.* **2.** to have suspicions or doubts about, to mistrust, *we suspect their motives.* **3.** to feel that (a person) is guilty but have little or no proof.

suspect [2] (**sus**-pekt) *n.* a person who is suspected of a crime etc. *—adj.* suspected, open to suspicion.

suspend *v.* **1.** to hang up. **2.** to keep from falling or sinking in air or liquid etc., *particles are suspended in the fluid.* **3.** to postpone, *suspend judgement.* **4.** to put a temporary stop to. **5.** to deprive temporarily of a position or a right. □ **suspended sentence,** sentence of imprisonment that is not enforced subject to good behaviour. **suspend payment,** (of a business company) to cease paying any of its debts when it recognizes that it is insolvent and unable to pay them all.

suspender *n.* an attachment to hold up a sock or stocking by its top. **suspender belt,** a woman's undergarment with suspenders for holding up stockings.

suspense *n.* a state or feeling of anxious uncertainty while awaiting news or an event etc.

suspension *n.* **1.** suspending, being suspended. **2.** the means by which a vehicle is supported on its axles. □ **suspension bridge,** a bridge suspended from cables that pass over supports at each end.

suspicion *n.* **1.** suspecting, being suspected. **2.** a partial or unconfirmed belief. **3.** a slight trace.

suspicious *adj.* feeling or causing suspicion. **suspiciously** *adv.*

suss *v.* = sus.

Sussex a former county of England, now divided into *East Sussex* and *West Sussex.*

sustain *v.* **1.** to support. **2.** to keep alive; *sustaining food,* food that keeps up one's strength. **2.** to keep (a sound or effort etc.) going continuously. **3.** to undergo, to suffer, *sustained a defeat.* **4.** to endure without giving way, *sustained the attack.* **5.** to confirm or uphold the validity of, *the objection was sustained.*

sustenance (**sus**-tin-ăns) *n.* **1.** the process of sustaining life by food. **2.** the food itself, nourishment.

suture (**soo**-cher) *n.* surgical stitching of a wound, a stitch or thread etc. used in this. —*v.* to stitch (a wound).

suzerain (**soo**-zer-ayn) *n.* **1.** a country or ruler that has some authority over another country which is self-governing in its internal affairs. **2.** an overlord in feudal times. **suzerainty** *n.*

svelte (*pr.* svelt) *adj.* (of a person) slender and graceful.

SW *abbrev.* south-west, south-western.

swab (*pr.* swob) *n.* **1.** a mop or absorbent pad for cleansing or drying or absorbing things. **2.** a specimen of a secretion taken with this. —*v.* (swabbed, swabbing) to cleanse or wipe with a swab.

swaddle *v.* to swathe in wraps or clothes or warm garments. **swaddling-clothes** *pl. n.* strips of cloth formerly wrapped round a new-born baby to restrain its movements.

swag *n.* **1.** loot. **2.** a carved ornamental festoon of flowers and fruit, hung by its ends. **3.** (*Austral.*) a bundle of personal belongings carried by a tramp etc.

swagger *v.* to walk or behave in a self-important manner, to strut. —*n.* a swaggering walk or way of behaving. —*adj.* **1.** (*informal*) smart, fashionable. **2.** (of a coat) shaped with a loose flare from the shoulders.

swagman *n.* (*pl.* swagmen) (*Austral.*) a tramp.

Swahili (swah-**hee**-li) *n.* a Bantu language widely used in East Africa.

swallow[1] *v.* **1.** to cause or allow (food etc.) to go down one's throat, to work the muscles of the throat as when doing this. **2.** to take in so as to engulf or absorb, *she was swallowed up in the crowd.* **3.** to accept; *swallow a story,* believe it too easily; *swallow an insult,* accept it meekly. **4.** to repress (a sound or emotion etc.), *swallowed a sob.* —*n.* the act of swallowing, the amount swallowed in one movement.

swallow[2] *n.* a small migratory insect-eating bird with a forked tail whose arrival in Britain is associated with the beginning of summer. □ **swallow-dive** *n.* a dive with arms outspread at the start. **swallow-tailed** *adj.* having a deeply forked tail.

swam *see* swim.

swamp *n.* a marsh. —*v.* **1.** to flood, to drench or submerge in water. **2.** to over-

whelm with a great mass or number of things. —**swampy** *adj.*

swan *n.* a large usually white water-bird with a long slender neck. —*v.* (swanned, swanning) (*slang*) to go in a leisurely majestic way like a swan, *swanning around.* □

swan-song *n.* a person's last performance or achievement or composition. (¶ From the old belief that a swan sang sweetly when about to die.) **swan-upping** *n.* the annual taking up and marking (by the appropriate authorities) of swans on the Thames.

swank *n.* (*informal*) **1.** boastful behaviour, ostentation. **2.** a person who behaves in this way. —*v.* (*informal*) to behave with swank. —**swanky** *adj.*

swansdown *n.* a swan's fine soft down, used for trimmings.

swap *v.* (swapping, swapped) (*informal*) to exchange. —*n.* (*informal*) **1.** an exchange. **2.** a thing suitable for swapping.

SWAPO *abbrev.* South West Africa People's Organization.

swarm[1] *n.* **1.** a large number of insects or birds or small animals or people flying or moving about in a cluster. **2.** a cluster of honey-bees leaving the hive with a queen bee to establish a new home. —**swarm** *v.* **1.** to move in a swarm, to come together in large numbers. **2.** (of bees) to cluster in a swarm. **3.** (of a place) to be crowded or overrun, *swarming with tourists.*

swarm[2] *v.* **swarm up,** to climb by gripping with arms and legs.

swarthy (**swor**-*th*i) *adj.* (swarthier, swarthiest) having a dark complexion.

swashbuckling *adj.* swaggering aggressively.

swastika (**swos**-tik-ă) *n.* a symbol formed by a cross with the ends bent at right angles, formerly used as a Nazi emblem.

swat *v.* (swatted, swatting) to hit hard with something flat, to crush (a fly etc.) in this way. **swatter** *n.*

swath (*pr.* swawth) *n.* (*pl.* swaths, *pr.* swaw*th*z) **1.** the space that a scythe or mowing-machine cuts in one sweep or passage. **2.** a line of grass or wheat etc. lying after being cut. **3.** a broad strip.

swathe (*pr.* sway*th*) *v.* to wrap in layers of bandage or wrappings or warm garments.

sway *v.* **1.** to swing or cause to swing gently, to lean from side to side or to one side. **2.** to influence the opinions or sympathy or actions of, *his speech swayed many voters.* **3.** to waver in one's opinion or attitude. —**sway** *n.* **1.** a swaying movement. **2.** influence, power, *hold sway.* □ **sway-backed** *adj.* having an abnormal inward curvature of the spine.

Swaziland (swah-zi-land) a country in south-east Africa. **Swazi** *adj. & n. (pl.* Swazis).

swear *v.* (swore, sworn, swearing) **1.** to state or promise on oath, *swear it* or *swear to it.* **2.** (*informal*) to state emphatically, *swore he hadn't touched it.* **3.** to cause to take an oath, *swore him to secrecy; the jury had been sworn.* **4.** to use curses or profane language in anger or surprise etc. — **swearer** *n.* □ **swear by,** (*informal*) to have great confidence in. **swear in,** to admit (a person) to office etc. by causing him to take an oath. **swear off,** to swear to abstain from. **swear-word** *n.* a profane word used in anger etc.

sweat *n.* **1.** moisture that is given off by the body through the pores of the skin. **2.** a state of sweating or being covered by sweat. **3.** (*informal*) a state of great anxiety. **4.** (*informal*) a laborious task. **5.** moisture forming in drops on a surface e.g. by condensation. —**sweat** *v.* **1.** to give out sweat, to cause to do this. **2.** to be in a state of great anxiety. **3.** to work long and hard. □ **old sweat,** (*informal*) a person with much experience. **sweat-band** *n.* a band of absorbent material for absorbing or wiping away sweat. **sweat blood,** to work very hard at something; to be in a state of great anxiety. **sweated labour,** labour of workers who have to endure long hours and low wages and poor conditions. **sweat it out,** (*informal*) to endure it to the end. **sweat off,** to get rid of by sweating. **sweat-shirt** *n.* a sleeved cotton sweater worn especially by athletes before or after exercise. **sweat-shop** *n.* a place where sweated labour is used.

sweater *n.* a jumper or pullover.

sweaty *adj.* damp with sweat.

swede *n.* a large yellow variety of turnip.

Swede *n.* a native of Sweden.

Sweden a country in northern Europe.

Swedish *adj.* of Sweden or its people or language. —*n.* the language of Sweden.

sweep *v.* (swept, sweeping) **1.** to clear away with or as if with a broom or brush. **2.** to clean or clear (a surface or area) by doing this. **3.** to move or remove by pushing, *the floods swept away fences.* **4.** to go smoothly and swiftly or majestically, *she swept out of the room.* **5.** to extend in a continuous line or slope, *the mountains sweep down to the sea.* **6.** to pass quickly over or along, *winds sweep the hillside; a new fashion is sweeping America.* **7.** to touch lightly. **8.** to make (a bow or curtsy) with a smooth movement. —**sweep** *n.* **1.** a sweeping movement. **2.** a sweeping line or slope. **3.** the act of sweeping with a broom etc., *give it a good sweep.* **4.** a chimney-sweep. **5.** a sweepstake. □ **make a clean sweep,** to get rid of everything or of all staff etc.; to win all the prizes. **sweep all before one,** to be very successful. **sweep hand** *or* **sweep-second hand,** an extra hand on a clock or watch, indicating seconds.

sweeper *n.* **1.** a person who sweeps a place. **2.** a thing that sweeps, a carpet-sweeper. **3.** a football player positioned just in front of the goalkeeper to tackle attacking players.

sweeping *adj.* **1.** of great scope, comprehensive, *sweeping changes.* **2.** (of a statement) making no exceptions or limitations, *sweeping generalizations.* □ **sweepings** *pl. n.* dust or scraps etc. collected by sweeping.

sweepstake *n.* **1.** a form of gambling on horse-races etc. in which the money staked is divided among those who have drawn numbered tickets for the winners. **2.** a race etc. with betting of this kind.

sweet *adj.* **1.** tasting as if containing sugar, not bitter. **2.** fragrant. **3.** melodious. **4.** fresh, (of food) not stale, (of water) not salt. **5.** pleasant, gratifying, (*informal*) pretty or charming. **6.** having a pleasant nature, lovable. —**sweet** *n.* **1.** a small shaped piece of sweet substance, usually made with sugar or chocolate and flavoured or with filling. **2.** a sweet dish forming one course of a meal. **3.** a beloved person. —**sweetly** *adv.*, **sweetness** *n.* □ **at one's own sweet will,** just as or when one pleases. **keep a person sweet,** to keep him well-disposed towards oneself. **sweet-and-sour** *adj.* cooked in sauce containing sugar and either vinegar or lemon. **sweet-brier** *n.* a small fragrant wild rose. **sweet cicely,** a fragrant wild plant with white flowers. **sweet corn,** a kind of maize with sweet grains. **sweet pea,** a climbing garden plant with fragrant flowers in many colours. **sweet potato,** a tropical climbing plant with sweet tuberous roots used for food. **sweet tooth,** a liking for sweet things. **sweet-william** *n.* a garden plant with clustered fragrant flowers.

sweetbread *n.* an animal's thymus gland or pancreas used as food.

sweeten *v.* to make or become sweet or sweeter. **sweetener, sweetening** *ns.* a substance used to sweeten food or drink.

sweetheart *n.* a person's beloved, one of a pair of people who are in love with each other.

sweetie *n.* (*informal*) **1.** a sweet. **2.** a sweetheart.

sweetish *adj.* rather sweet.

sweetmeal *adj.* (of biscuits) sweetened wholemeal.

sweetmeat *n.* a sweet, a very small fancy cake.

swell *v.* (swelled, swollen *or* swelled, swelling) **1.** to make or become larger because of pressure from within, to curve outwards. **2.** to make or become larger in amount or volume or numbers or intensity. —**swell** *n.* **1.** the act or state of swelling. **2.** the heaving of the sea with waves that do not break. **3.** a gradual increase of loudness in music, a mechanism in an organ for obtaining this. **4.** (*informal*) a person of high social position. —*adj.* (*informal*) smart, excellent. □ **swelled head,** (*slang*) conceit.

swelling *n.* an abnormally swollen place on the body.

swelter *v.* to be uncomfortably hot, to suffer from the heat.

swept *see* sweep. □ **swept-wing** *adj.* (of aircraft) with wings slanting backwards from the direction of flight.

swerve *v.* to turn or cause to turn aside from a straight course. —*n.* a swerving movement or direction.

swift *adj.* quick, rapid. —*n.* a swiftly-flying insect-eating bird with long narrow wings. —**swiftly** *adv.*, **swiftness** *n*

swig *v.* (swigged, swigging) (*informal*) to take a drink or drinks of, *swigging beer.* —*n.* (*informal*) a drink or swallow.

swill *v.* **1.** to pour water over or through, to wash or rinse. **2.** (of water) to pour. **3.** to drink in large quantities. —**swill** *n.* **1.** a rinse, *give it a swill.* **2.** a sloppy mixture of waste food fed to pigs.

swim *v.* (swam, swum, swimming) **1.** to propel the body through water by movements of the limbs or fins or tail etc. **2.** to cross by swimming, *swim the Channel.* **3.** to cause to swim, *swim your horse across the stream.* **4.** to float. **5.** to be covered or flooded with liquid, *eyes swimming in tears.* **6.** to seem to be whirling or waving, to have a dizzy sensation, *everything swam before her eyes; my head is swimming.* —**swim** *n.* **1.** a period of swimming. **2.** a deep pool frequented by fish in a river. □ **the main current of affairs.** — **swimmer** *n.* □ **in the swim,** active in or knowing what is going on. **swimming-bath** *n.* a swimming-pool. **swimming-pool** *n.* an artificial pool for swimming in. **swim-suit** *n.* a garment worn for swimming.

swimmingly *adv.* with easy unobstructed progress.

swindle *v.* to cheat (a person) in a busi-

ness transaction, to obtain by fraud. —*n.* a piece of swindling, a fraudulent person or thing. —**swindler** *n.*

swine *pl. n.* pigs. —*n.* (*pl.* swine) (*informal*) a hated person, a difficult or unpleasant thing. □ **swine-fever** *n.* a virus disease of pigs.

swineherd *n.* (*old use*) a person taking care of a number of pigs.

swing *v.* (swung, swinging) **1.** to move to and fro while hanging or supported, to cause to do this. **2.** to hang by its ends, *swung a hammock between the two trees.* **3.** to turn (a wheel etc.) smoothly, to turn to one side or in a curve, *the car swung into the drive.* **4.** to walk or run with an easy rhythmical movement. **5.** to lift with a swinging movement. **6.** to change from one opinion or mood etc. to another. **7.** to influence (voting etc.) decisively; *swing the deal,* (*Amer. informal*) to succeed in arranging it. **8.** (*slang*) to be executed by hanging. **9.** to play (music) with a swing rhythm. — **swing** *n.* **1.** a swinging movement or action or rhythm. **2.** a seat slung by ropes or chains for swinging in, a swing-boat, a spell of swinging in this. **3.** the extent to which a thing swings, the amount by which votes or opinions or points scored etc. change from one side to the other. **4.** a kind of jazz with the time of the melody varied while the accompaniment is in strict time. —**swinger** *n.* □ **in full swing,** with activity at its greatest. **swing-boat** *n.* a boat-shaped swing at fairs. **swing bridge,** a bridge that can be swung aside to allow ships to pass. **swing-door** *n.* a door that opens in either direction and closes itself when released. **swing the lead,** *see* lead². **swing-wing** *n.* an aircraft wing that can be moved to slant backwards.

swingeing (swinj-ing) *adj.* **1.** (of a blow) forcible. **2.** huge in amount or number or scope, *a swingeing increase in taxation.*

swinging *adj.* (*slang*) lively and up-to-date.

swinish *adj.* like a swine, beastly.

swipe *v.* (*informal*) **1.** to hit with a swinging blow. **2.** to steal, especially by snatching. —*n.* (*informal*) a swinging blow.

swirl *v.* to move or flow or carry along with a whirling movement. —*n.* a swirling movement.

swish *v.* to strike or move or cause to move with a hissing sound. —*n.* a swishing sound. —*adj.* (*informal*) smart, fashionable.

Swiss *adj.* of Switzerland or its people. —*n.* (*pl.* Swiss) a native of Switzerland. □ **Swiss roll,** a thin flat sponge-cake spread with jam etc. and rolled up.

switch *n.* **1.** a device that is operated to complete or break open an electric circuit. **2.** a device at the junction of railway tracks for diverting trains from one track to another. **3.** a flexible shoot cut from a tree, a tapering rod or whip resembling this. **4.** a tress of real or false hair tied at one end. **5.** a shift or change in opinion or methods or policy etc. —**switch** *v.* **1.** to turn (an electrical or other appliance) on or off by means of a switch. **2.** to transfer (a train) to another track. **3.** to divert (thoughts or talk) to another subject. **4.** to change or exchange (positions or methods or policy etc.). **5.** to whip with a switch. **6.** to swing round quickly, to snatch suddenly, *the cow switches her tail*; *switched it out of my hand.* □ **switched on,** (*slang*) alert to what is going on, up to date.

switchback *n.* **1.** a railway used for amusement at fairs etc. with a series of alternate steep descents and ascents. **2.** a road with alternate ascents and descents.

switchboard *n.* a panel with a set of switches for making telephone connections or operating electric circuits.

Switzerland a country in central Europe.

swivel *n.* a link or pivot between two parts enabling one of them to revolve without turning the other. —*v.* (swivelled, swivelling) to turn on or as if on a swivel. □ **swivel chair,** a chair with a seat that can turn horizontally on a pivot.

swizz *n.* (*slang*) a swindle, a disappointment.

swizzle *n.* **1.** (*informal*) a frothy mixed alcoholic drink. **2.** (*slang*) = swizz. □ **swizzle-stick** *n.* a stick used for stirring a drink to make it frothy or flat.

swollen *see* swell.

swoon *v.* to faint. —*n.* a faint.

swoop *v.* to come down with a rushing movement like a bird upon its prey, to make a sudden attack. —*n.* a swooping movement or attack. □ **at one fell swoop,** *see* fell².

swop *v.* (swopped, swopping) & *n.* = swap.

sword (*pr.* sord) *n.* a weapon with a long blade and a hilt. **sword-dance** *n.* a dance in which swords are brandished or a performer treads about swords placed on the ground. **sword-stick** *n.* a hollow walking-stick containing a blade that can be used as a sword.

swordfish *n.* a sea-fish with a long sword-like upper jaw.

swore, sworn *see* swear. —**sworn** *adj.* open and determined in devotion or enmity, *sworn friends*; *sworn foes.*

swot *v.* (swotted, swotting) (*school slang*) to study hard. —*n.* (*school slang*) **1.** hard study. **2.** a person who studies hard.

swum *see* swim.

swung *see* swing.

sybarite (sib-er-ryt) *n.* a person who is excessively fond of comfort and luxury. **sybaritic** (sib-er-it-ik) *adj.*

sycamore (sik-ă-mor) *n.* a large tree of the maple family.

sycophant (sik-ŏ-fant) *n.* a person who tries to win people's favour by flattering them. **sycophantic** (sik-ŏ-**fan**-tik) *adj.*, **sycophantically** *adv.*

syllabic (sil-**ab**-ik) *adj.* of or in syllables. **syllabically** *adv.*

syllable (sil-ă-bŭl) *n.* one of the units of sound into which a word can be divided, *there are two syllables in 'unit', three in 'divided', and one in 'can'.* **in words of one syllable,** expressed very simply or bluntly.

syllabub (sil-ă-bub) *n.* a dish made of sweetened whipped cream flavoured with wine etc.

syllabus (sil-ă-bŭs) *n.* (*pl.* syllabuses) an outline of the subjects that are included in a course of study.

syllogism (sil-ŏ-jizm) *n.* a form of reasoning in which a conclusion is reached from two statements, as in *'All men must die; I am a man; therefore I must die'.*

sylph (*pr.* silf) *n.* a slender girl or woman.

symbol *n.* **1.** a thing regarded as suggesting something or embodying certain characteristics, *the cross is the symbol of Christianity; the lion is the symbol of courage.* **2.** a mark or sign with a special meaning, such as mathematical signs (e.g. + and − for addition and subtraction), punctuation marks, written or printed forms of notes in music.

symbolic *or* **symbolical** *adj.* of or using or used as a symbol. **symbolically** *adv.*

symbolism *n.* use of symbols to express things.

symbolize *v.* **1.** to be a symbol of. **2.** to represent by means of a symbol.

symmetrical (sim-et-rik-ăl) *adj.* able to be divided into parts that are the same in size and shape and similar in position on either side of a dividing line or round a centre. **symmetrically** *adv.*

symmetry (sim-it-ri) *n.* **1.** being symmetrical. **2.** pleasing proportion between parts of a whole.

sympathetic *adj.* **1.** feeling or expressing or resulting from sympathy. **2.** likeable, *he's not a sympathetic character.* **3.** showing approval or support, *he is sympathetic to our plan.* **sympathetically** *adv.*

sympathize *v.* to feel or express sympathy. **sympathizer** *n.*

sympathy *n.* **1.** sharing or the ability to share another person's emotions or sensations. **2.** a feeling of pity or tenderness towards one suffering pain or grief or trouble. **3.** liking for each other produced in people who have similar opinions or tastes. □ **be in sympathy with**, to feel approval of (an opinion or desire).

symphony (**sim-fŏn-i**) *n.* a long elaborate musical composition (usually in several parts) for a full orchestra. **symphonic** (**sim-fon-ik**) *adj.* □ **symphony orchestra**, a large orchestra playing symphonies etc.

symposium (**sim-poh-ziŭm**) *n.* (*pl.* symposia) a meeting for discussion of a particular subject.

symptom *n.* a sign of the existence of a condition, especially a perceptible change from what is normal in the body or its functioning, indicating disease or injury.

symptomatic (**simp-tŏm-at-ik**) *adj.* serving as a symptom.

synagogue (**sin-ă-gog**) *n.* a building for public Jewish worship.

synchromesh (**sink-roh-mesh**) *n.* a device that makes parts of a gear revolve at the same speed while they are being brought into contact.

synchronize (**sink-rŏ-nyz**) *v.* **1.** to occur or exist at the same time. **2.** to operate at the same rate and simultaneously. **3.** to cause to occur or operate at the same time, to cause (clocks etc.) to show the same time. **synchronization** *n.*, **synchronizer** *n.*

synchronous (**sink-rŏn-ŭs**) *adj.* **1.** existing or occurring at the same time. **2.** operating at the same rate and simultaneously.

syncopate (**sink-ŏ-payt**) *v.* to change the beats or accents in (a passage of music) by putting a strong stress instead of a weak one (and vice versa). **syncopation** *n.*

syncope (**sink-ŏ-pi**) *n.* a faint, fainting.

syncretic (**sink-ret-ik**) *adj.* combining different beliefs or principles.

syndicate [1] (**sin-dik-ăt**) *n.* an association of people or firms combining to carry out a business or commercial undertaking.

syndicate [2] (**sin-dik-ayt**) *v.* **1.** to combine into a syndicate. **2.** to publish through an association that acquires stories, articles, cartoons, etc. for simultaneous publication in numerous newspapers and periodicals. **syndication** *n.*

syndrome (**sin-drohm**) *n.* **1.** a set of signs and symptoms that together indicate the presence of a disease or abnormal condition. **2.** a combination of opinions, behaviour, etc. that are characteristic of a particular condition.

synod (**sin-ŏd**) *n.* a council attended by senior clergy or church officials to discuss questions of policy, teaching, etc.

synonym (**sin-ŏ-nim**) *n.* a word or phrase with a meaning similar to that of another in the same language.

synonymous (**sin-on-im-ŭs**) *adj.* equivalent in meaning.

synopsis (**sin-op-sis**) *n.* (*pl.* synopses) a summary, a brief general survey.

synoptic (**sin-op-tik**) *adj.* **1.** of or forming a synopsis. **2.** of the **synoptic Gospels**, those of Matthew, Mark, and Luke which have many similarities (whereas that of John differs greatly).

syntax (**sin-taks**) *n.* the way in which words are arranged to form phrases and sentences. **syntactic** (**sin-tak-tik**) *adj.*, **syntactically** *adv.*

synthesis (**sin-thi-sis**) *n.* (*pl.* syntheses) **1.** the combining of separate parts or elements to form a complex whole. **2.** the combining of substances to form a compound, artificial production of a substance that occurs naturally in plants or animals.

synthesize (**sin-thi-syz**) *v.* to make by synthesis.

synthetic *adj.* **1.** made by synthesis, manufactured as opposed to produced naturally, *synthetic rubber*. **2.** (*informal*) artificial, affected, *decorated in synthetic Tudor style.* —*n.* a synthetic substance or fabric (e.g. nylon). —**synthetically** *adv.*

syphilis (**sif-i-lis**) *n.* a venereal disease transmitted by contact or contracted by an unborn child from its mother's blood.

syphon *n.* & *v.* = siphon.

Syria a country in the Middle East. **Syrian** *adj.* & *n.*

syringa (**si-ring-ă**) *n.* **1.** the mock orange (*see* mock). **2.** the botanical name for lilac.

syringe (**si-rinj**) *n.* **1.** a device for drawing in liquid and forcing it out again in a fine stream. **2.** a hypodermic syringe (*see* hypodermic). —*v.* to wash out or spray with a syringe.

syrinx (**si-rinks**) *n.* the part of a bird's throat where its song is produced.

syrup *n.* a thick sweet liquid, water in which sugar is dissolved. **syrupy** *adj.*

system *n.* **1.** a set of connected things or parts that form a whole or work together, *a railway system; the nervous system,* (*see* nervous); *the solar system,* (*see* solar). **2.** an animal body as a whole, *too much alcohol poisons the system.* **3.** a set of rules or principles or practices forming a particular philosophy or form of government etc.

4. a method of classification or notation or measurement etc., *the metric system.* **5.** orderliness, being systematic, *she works without system.* □ **get a thing out of one's system,** to be rid of its effects. **systems analysis,** analysis of an operation in order to decide how a computer may be used to perform it. **systems analyst,** an expert in systems analysis.

systematic *adj.* methodical, according to a plan and not casually or at random. **systematically** *adv.*

systematize (sis-těm-ă-tyz) *v.* to arrange according to a system. **systematization** *n.*

systemic (sis-**tem**-ik) *adj.* **1.** of or affecting the body as a whole. **2.** (of a fungicide etc.) entering a plant by way of the roots or shoots and passing into the tissues.

Tt

ta *int.* (*informal*) thank you.

tab *n.* a small projecting flap or strip, especially one by which something can be grasped or hung or fastened or identified. —*v.* (tabbed, tabbing) to provide with tabs. □ **keep a tab** *or* **tabs on,** (*informal*) to keep account of, to keep under observation. **pick up the tab,** (*Amer. informal*) to be the one who pays the bill.

TAB *abbrev.* typhoid-paratyphoid A and B vaccine.

tabard (**tab**-ard) *n.* **1.** a short tunic-like garment open at the sides, worn by a herald, emblazoned with the arms of the sovereign. **2.** a woman's garment shaped like this.

tabby *n.* a **tabby cat,** a cat with grey or brownish fur and dark stripes.

tabernacle *n.* **1.** (in the Bible) the portable shrine used by the Israelites during their wanderings in the wilderness. **2.** (in the RC Church) a receptacle containing consecrated elements of the Eucharist. **3.** a meeting-place for worship used by Nonconformists (e.g. Baptists) or Mormons. **4.** a socket or double post for a hinged mast that has to be lowered when passing under bridges.

table *n.* **1.** a piece of furniture consisting of a flat top supported on one or more legs. **2.** food provided at table; *she keeps a good table,* provides good meals. **3.** the flat part of a machine tool on which material is put to be worked. **4.** a list of facts or figures systematically arranged, especially in columns; *learn one's tables,* to learn the multiplication tables etc. in mathematics. —*v.* to submit (a motion or report in Par-

liament etc.) for discussion. □ **at table,** while taking a meal at a table. **on the table,** offered for consideration or discussion. **table-cloth** *n.* a cloth for covering a table, especially at meals. **table-cut** *adj.* (of a gem) cut with a large flat top. **table-linen** *n.* table-cloths, napkins, etc. **table manners,** ability to behave properly while eating at the table. **table-mat** *n.* a mat for protecting the surface of a table from hot dishes etc. **table salt,** salt powdered for use in a salt-cellar. **table tennis,** a game like lawn tennis played on a table with a net across it.

tableau (**tab**-loh) *n.* (*pl.* tableaux, *pr.* **tab**-lohz) **1.** a silent and motionless group of people etc. arranged to represent a scene. **2.** a dramatic or picturesque scene.

table d'hôte (tahbl **doht**) (of a restaurant meal) served at a fixed inclusive price.

tableland *n.* a plateau of land.

tablespoon *n.* **1.** a large spoon for serving food at the table. **2.** the amount held by this. **tablespoonful** *n.* (*pl.* tablespoonfuls)

tablet *n.* **1.** a slab or panel bearing an inscription or picture, especially one fixed to a wall as a memorial. **2.** a small flattish piece of a solid substance (e.g. soap). **3.** a small measured amount of a drug compressed into a solid form.

tabloid *n.* a newspaper (usually popular in style) with pages that are half the size of those of larger newspapers.

taboo *n.* a ban or prohibition on something that is regarded by religion or custom as not to be done or touched or used etc. —*adj.* prohibited by a taboo, *taboo words.* —*v.* to place under a taboo.

tabular (**tab**-yoo-ler) *adj.* arranged or displayed in a table or list.

tabulate (**tab**-yoo-layt) *v.* to arrange (facts or figures) in the form of a table or list. **tabulation** *n.*

tabulator *n.* **1.** a person or thing that tabulates facts or figures. **2.** a device on a typewriter for advancing to a series of set positions in tabular work.

tachograph (**tak**-ŏ-grahf) *n.* a device that automatically records the speed and travel-time of a motor vehicle in which it is fitted.

tacit (**tas**-it) *adj.* implied or understood without being put into words. **tacitly** *adv.*

taciturn (**tas**-i-tern) *adj.* habitually saying very little, uncommunicative. **taciturnity** (tas-i-**tern**-iti) *n.*

tack[1] *n.* **1.** a small nail with a broad head. **2.** a long stitch used to hold fabric in position lightly or temporarily, or (*tailor's tacks*) to mark the place for a tuck etc.

3. a rope for securing the corner of some sails, the corner to which this is fastened. **4.** the direction of a ship's course as determined by the position of its sails, a temporary oblique course to take advantage of a wind; *port tack,* with the wind on the port side. **5.** a course of action or policy, *he's on the wrong tack.* —**tack** *v.* **1.** to nail with a tack or tacks. **2.** to stitch with tacks. **3.** to add as an extra thing, *a service charge was tacked on to the bill.* **4.** to sail a zigzag course in order to take advantage of a wind, to make a tack or tacks.

tack² *n.* riding-harness, saddles, etc.

tackle *n.* **1.** a set of ropes and pulleys for lifting weights or working a ship's sails. **2.** equipment for a task or sport, *fishing-tackle.* **3.** the act of tackling in football. — **tackle** *v.* **1.** to grapple with, to try to deal with or overcome (an awkward thing or an opponent or problem); *tackle a person about something,* to initiate a discussion with him about an awkward matter. **2.** (in hockey, football, etc.) to intercept or seize and stop (an opponent running with the ball). —**tackler** *n.*

tacky *adj.* (tackier, tackiest) (of paint or varnish etc.) slightly sticky, not quite dry. **tackiness** *n.*

tact *n.* skill in avoiding giving offence or in winning goodwill by saying or doing the right thing.

tactful *adj.* having or showing tact. **tactfully** *adv.*

tactic *n.* a piece of tactics.

tactical *adj.* **1.** of tactics (distinguished from *strategic*). **2.** planning or planned skilfully. **tactically** *adv.* ☐ **tactical weapons,** *see* strategic weapons.

tactician (tak-**tish**-ăn) *n.* an expert in tactics.

tactics *n.* the art of placing or manœuvring forces skilfully in a battle (distinguished from *strategy*). —*pl. n.* manœuvring, procedure adopted in order to achieve something.

tactile (**tak**-tyl) *adj.* of or using the sense of touch, *tactile organs.*

tactless *adj.* lacking in tact. **tactlessly** *adv.,* **tactlessness** *n.*

tadpole *n.* the larva of a frog or toad etc. at the stage when it lives in water and has gills and a tail.

taffeta *n.* a shiny silk-like dress fabric.

taffrail (**taf**-rayl) *n.* a rail round the stern of a vessel.

tag¹ *n.* **1.** a metal or plastic point at the end of a shoelace etc. **2.** a label tied or stuck into something to identify it or show its price etc. **3.** any loose or ragged end or projection. **4.** a stock phrase or much-used quotation. —**tag** *v.* (tagged, tagging) **1.** to label with a tag. **2.** to attach, to add as an extra thing, *a postscript was tagged on to her letter.* **3.** (*informal*) to follow, to trail behind. ☐ **tag along,** (*informal*) to go along with another or others.

tag² *n.* a children's game in which one chases the rest until he touches another.

tagliatelle (tahl-yah-**tel**-i) *pl. n.* pasta in ribbon-shaped strips.

tail *n.* **1.** the hindmost part of an animal, especially when extending beyond the rest of the body; *with his tail between his legs,* (of an animal or person) looking defeated or dejected. **2.** something resembling this in its shape or position, the rear part, an inferior part, a part that hangs down or behind. **3.** the penis, the vulva. **4.** (*slang*) a person following or shadowing another. —**tail** *v.* **1.** to remove the stalks of, *top and tail gooseberries.* **2.** (*slang*) to follow closely, to shadow. ☐ **on a person's tail,** following him closely. **tail away,** = tail off (*see below*). **tail-back** *n.* a long line of traffic extending back from an obstruction. **tail-board** *n.* a downward-hinged or removable flap at the back of a cart or lorry. **tail-end** *n.* the hindmost or very last part. **tail-gate** *n.* a tail-board; a rear door in a motor vehicle. **tail-lamp, tail-light** *ns.* a light at the back of a vehicle or train or bicycle. **tail off,** to become fewer or smaller or slighter; to fall behind in a straggling line; (of remarks etc.) to end inconclusively. **tails** *pl. n.* a tailcoat, evening dress with this; the reverse of a coin, turned upwards after being tossed. **tail-spin** *n.* an aircraft's spiral dive with the tail making wider circles than the front. **tail wind,** a following wind.

tailcoat *n.* a man's coat with the skirt tapering and divided at the back, worn as part of formal evening dress or morning dress.

tailless *adj.* having no tail.

tailor *n.* a maker of men's clothes, especially to order. —*v.* **1.** to make (clothes) as a tailor, to make in a simple smoothly-fitting design. **2.** to make or adapt for a special purpose, *the new factory is tailored to our needs.* —**tailoress** *n.* ☐ **tailor-made** *adj.* made by a tailor; made in a simple smoothly-fitting design; perfectly suited for the purpose.

tailpiece *n.* a decoration printed in the blank space at the end of a chapter or book.

tailpipe *n.* the exhaust-pipe of a motor vehicle.

tailplane *n.* the horizontal surface of the tail of an aeroplane.

tailstock *n.* an adjustable part of a lathe, with a fixed spindle to support one end of the work-piece.

taint *n.* a trace of some bad quality or decay or infection. —*v.* to affect with a taint; *tainted meat*, slightly decayed.

Taiwan (ty-**wann**) an island off the southeast coast of China.

take *v.* (took, taken, taking) **1.** to get into one's hands by effort. **2.** to get possession of, to capture, to win, *took many prisoners*; *took first prize*. **3.** to be successful or effective, *the inoculation did not take*. **4.** to remove from its place, *someone has taken my bicycle*. **5.** to subtract. **6.** to make use of, to indulge in, *take this opportunity*; *take a holiday*; *take the first turning on the left*, go into it. **7.** to occupy (a position), especially as one's right; *take a chair*, sit down on one; *take the chair*, act as chairman. **8.** to obtain after fulfilling necessary conditions (*take a degree*), to obtain the use of by payment (*take lodgings*), to buy (a certain newspaper etc.) regularly. **9.** to use as a means of transport, *take the train*. **10.** to consume, *we'll take tea now*. **11.** to require, *it takes a strong man to lift that*; *these things take time*, require much time; *it takes some doing*, is hard to do; *do you take sugar?*, do you use it in tea etc. **12.** to cause to come or go with one, to carry or remove, *take the letters to the post*. **13.** to be affected by, to catch, *the sticks took fire*. **14.** to experience or exert (a feeling or effort), *took pity on him*; *take care*. **15.** to find out and record, *take his name*; *we'll take your measurements*. **16.** to interpret in a certain way, *we take it that you are satisfied*; *I take your point*, accept that it is valid. **17.** to adopt a specified attitude towards, *take things coolly*; *take it well*, not be upset or resentful. **18.** to accept, to endure, *take risks*; *he can't take a joke*, resents being laughed at. **19.** to perform, to deal with, to move round or over, *take a decision*; *took the corner too fast*; *take an examination*, sit for it; *take a subject at school*, to study or teach it. **20.** to make by photography, to photograph (a person or thing). —**take** *n.* **1.** the amount of game or fish etc. taken or caught. **2.** an instance of photographing a scene for a cinema film. □ **be taken by** *or* **with**, to find attractive. **be taken ill**, to become ill. **be taken short**, (*informal*) to be put at a disadvantage, especially by a sudden need to defecate or urinate. **take after**, to resemble (a parent etc.). **take against**, to develop a dislike of. **take away**, to remove or carry away; to subtract. **take-away** *adj.* (of food) bought at a restaurant

for eating elsewhere, (*n.*) a restaurant selling this. **take back**, to withdraw (a statement); to carry (a person) back in thought to a past time. **take down**, to write down (spoken words); to humiliate; to remove (a building or structure) by taking it to pieces. **take-home pay**, the amount remaining after tax etc. has been deducted from wages. **take in**, to accept into one's house etc.; to include; to make (a garment etc.) smaller; to understand; to deceive or cheat (a person); (*informal*) to visit (a place) en route. **take it into one's head**, to decide suddenly. **take it out of**, to exhaust the strength of. **take it out on**, to work off one's frustration by attacking or maltreating (a person etc.). **take it upon oneself**, to undertake, to assume a responsibility. **take life**, to kill. **take off**, to take (clothing etc.) from the body; to mimic humorously; to leave the ground and become airborne; *take oneself off*, depart; *I take off my hat to him*, applaud him as admirable. **take-off** *n.* a piece of humorous mimicry; the process of taking off in flying. **take on**, to acquire; to undertake (work or responsibility); to engage (an employee); to agree to play against (a person in a game); (*informal*) to show great emotion, to make a fuss. **take one's time**, to loiter, not to hurry in doing something. **take out**, to escort on an outing; to obtain or get (an insurance policy etc.) issued; (*Amer. slang*) to destroy, to kill; *take a person out of himself*, make him forget his troubles. **take over**, to take control of (a business etc.). **take-over** *n.* assumption of control (especially of a business). **take part**, to share in an activity. **take sides**, to support one side or another. **take stock**, to make an inventory of the stock in a shop etc., to examine one's position and resources. **take to**, to adopt as a habit or custom or course; to go to as a refuge; to develop a liking or ability for. **take to pieces**, to separate (a thing) into the pieces from which it was put together. **take up**, to take as a hobby or business; to make a protégé of (a person); to occupy (time or space); to begin (residence etc.); to resume at the point where something was left; to interrupt or correct or question (a speaker); to investigate (a matter) further; to shorten (a garment); to accept (an offer etc.); *take a person up on his offer*, accept it. **take-up spool**, the spool on to which film or tape etc. is wound after use. **take up with**, to begin to associate with.

taker *n.* a person who takes something (especially a bet), *there were no takers*.

taking *adj.* attractive, captivating. **takings** *pl. n.* money taken in business, receipts.

talc *n.* **1.** a soft smooth mineral that is powdered for use as a lubricant. **2.** talcum powder.

talcum *n.* = talc. **talcum powder,** talc powdered and usually perfumed, applied to the skin to make it feel smooth and dry.

tale *n.* **1.** a narrative or story. **2.** a report spread by gossip. □ **tale-bearer** *n.* a person who tells tales (*see* tell).

talent *n.* **1.** special or very great ability, people who have this. **2.** a unit of money used in certain ancient countries. □ **talent-scout** *n.* a person whose job is to find talented performers for the entertainment industry.

talented *adj.* having talent.

talisman (**tal**-iz-măn) *n.* (*pl.* talismans) an object supposed to bring good luck.

talk *v.* **1.** to convey or exchange ideas by spoken words. **2.** to have the power of speech, *child is learning to talk.* **3.** to express or utter or discuss in words, *you are talking nonsense; talk scandal.* **4.** to use (a particular language), *talk French.* **5.** to affect or influence by talking, *talked him into going to Spain.* **6.** to give away information, *we have ways of making you talk.* —talk *n.* **1.** talking, conversation, discussion. **2.** a style of speech, *baby-talk.* **3.** an informal lecture. **4.** rumour, gossip, its theme, *there is talk of a general election; it's the talk of the town.* **5.** talking or promises etc. without action or results. —**talker** *n.* □ **money talks,** it has influence. **now you're talking,** (*slang*) I welcome that offer or suggestion. **talk down,** to silence (a person) by talking loudly or persistently; to bring (a pilot or aircraft) to a landing by radio instructions from the ground. **talk down to,** to speak to in condescendingly simple language. **talk over,** to discuss. **talk through one's hat,** to talk nonsense. **talk to,** (*informal*) to reprove; *gave him a talking-to,* a reproof.

talkative *adj.* talking very much.

tall *n.* **1.** of more than average height. **2.** having a certain height, *six feet tall.* **tallness** *n.* □ **tall order,** (*informal*) a difficult task. **tall story,** (*informal*) one that is difficult to believe.

tallboy *n.* a tall chest of drawers.

tallish *adj.* rather tall.

tallow *n.* animal fat used to make candles, soap, lubricants, etc.

tally *n.* the reckoning of a debt or score. —*v.* (tallied, tallying) to correspond, *see that the goods tally with what we ordered; the two witnesses' stories tallied.*

tally-ho *int.* a huntsman's cry to the hounds on sighting the fox.

Talmud (**tal**-mŭd) *n.* a collection of ancient writings on Jewish civil and ceremonial law and tradition.

talon (**tal**-ŏn) *n.* a claw, especially of a bird of prey.

TAM *abbrev.* television audience measurement.

tamarind (**tam**-er-ind) *n.* **1.** a tropical tree bearing fruit with acid pulp. **2.** its fruit.

tamarisk (**tam**-er-isk) *n.* an evergreen shrub with feathery branches and spikes of pink or white flowers.

tambourine (tam-ber-**een**) *n.* a percussion instrument consisting of a small hoop with parchment stretched over one side, and jingling metal discs in slots round the hoop.

tame *adj.* **1.** (of animals) gentle and not afraid of human beings, not wild or fierce. **2.** docile. **3.** not exciting or interesting. —*v.* to make tame or manageable. —**tamely** *adv.,* **tameness** *n.* □ **tamer** *n.* a person who tames and trains wild animals, *lion-tamer.*

tameable *adj.* able to be tamed.

Tamil (**tam**-il) *n.* **1.** a member of a people of southern India and Sri Lanka. **2.** their language.

tam-o'-shanter *n.* a beret with a soft full top.

tamp *v.* to pack or ram down tightly.

tamper *v.* **tamper with,** to meddle or interfere with, to alter without authority, *he tampered with the switches;* to influence illegally, to bribe, *tamper with a jury.*

tampon *n.* a plug of absorbent material inserted into the body to stop bleeding or absorb natural secretions.

tan *v.* (tanned, tanning) **1.** to convert (animal hide) into leather by treating it with tannic acid or mineral salts etc. **2.** to make or become brown by exposure to sun. **3.** (*slang*) to thrash. —**tan** *n.* **1.** yellowish-brown. **2.** brown colour in skin exposed to sun. **3.** tree-bark used in tanning hides. —*adj.* yellowish-brown.

tandem *n.* **1.** a bicycle with seats and pedals for two or more people one behind another. **2.** an arrangement of people or things one behind another. —*adv.* one behind another. □ **in tandem,** arranged in this way.

tandoori *n.* food cooked over charcoal in a clay oven (*tandoor*).

tang *n.* **1.** a strong taste or flavour or smell. **2.** a projection on the blade of a knife or chisel etc. by which it is held firm in its handle.

tangent (**tan**-jĕnt) *n.* a straight line that

touches the outside of a curve but does not intersect it. **go off at a tangent,** to diverge suddenly from a line of thought etc. or from the matter in hand.

tangerine (tan-jer-**een**) *n.* **1.** a kind of small flattened orange from Tangier. **2.** its deep orange-yellow colour.

tangible (**tan**-ji-bǔl) *adj.* **1.** able to be perceived by touch. **2.** clear and definite, real, *tangible advantages.* **tangibly** *adv.,* **tangibility** *n.*

tangle *v.* **1.** to twist or become twisted into a confused mass. **2.** to entangle. **3.** to become involved in conflict with. —*n.* a tangled mass or condition.

tango¹ *n.* (*pl.* tangos) a ballroom dance with gliding steps, music for this. —*v.* to dance the tango.

tango² *n.* tangerine colour.

tangy (**tang**-i) *adj.* (tangier, tangiest) having a strong taste or flavour or smell.

tank *n.* **1.** a large container for holding liquid or gas. **2.** a heavily armoured fighting vehicle carrying guns and moving on Caterpillar tracks. —*v.* **tank up,** to fill the tank of a vehicle etc.; (*slang*) to drink heavily.

tankard *n.* a large one-handled drinking-vessel, usually of silver or pewter and often with a lid.

tanker *n.* a ship or aircraft or vehicle for carrying oil or other liquid in bulk.

tanner *n.* a person who tans hides into leather. **tannery** *n.* a place where hides are tanned into leather.

tannic *adj.* of tannin. **tannic acid,** tannin.

tannin *n.* any of several compounds obtained from oak-galls and various tree-barks (also found in tea), used chiefly in tanning and dyeing.

Tannoy *n.* (*trade mark*) a type of public-address system.

tansy *n.* a plant with yellow flowers in clusters and feathery leaves.

tantalize *v.* to tease or torment by the sight of something that is desired but kept out of reach or withheld. ¶ In Greek mythology, Tantalus was condemned to stand in Hades surrounded by water and fruit that receded when he tried to reach them.

tantalus *n.* a stand in which decanters of spirits are locked up but visible. ¶ From the name of *Tantalus* (see tantalize).

tantamount (**tant**-ǎ-mownt) *adj.* equivalent, *the Queen's request was tantamount to a command.*

tantrum *n.* an outburst of bad temper, especially in a child.

Tanzania (tan-ză-**nee**-ă) a country in East Africa. **Tanzanian** *adj. & n.*

tap¹ *n.* **1.** a device for drawing liquid from a cask or for allowing liquid or gas to come from a pipe in a controllable flow. **2.** a device for cutting a screw-thread inside a cavity. **3.** a connection for tapping a telephone. —**tap** *v.* (tapped, tapping) **1.** to fit a tap into (a cask) in order to draw out its contents. **2.** to draw off (liquid) by means of a tap or through an incision. **3.** to extract or obtain supplies or information from. **4.** to cut a screw-thread inside (a cavity). **5.** to make a connection in (a circuit etc.) so as to divert electricity or fit a listening-device for overhearing telephone communications. □ **on tap,** (of liquid or gas) ready to be drawn off by a tap; (*informal*) available. **tap-root** *n.* the chief root of a plant, growing straight downwards. **tap-water** *n.* water supplied through pipes to taps in a building.

tap² *v.* (tapped, tapping) **1.** to strike with a quick light blow, to knock gently on (a door etc.). **2.** to strike (an object) lightly against something. —*n.* a quick light blow, the sound of this. □ **tap-dance** *n.* a dance in which an elaborate rhythm is tapped with the feet. **tap-dancing** *n.*

tape *n.* **1.** a narrow strip of woven cotton etc. used for tying or fastening or labelling things, a piece of this stretched across a race-track at the finishing-line. **2.** a narrow continuous strip of paper or other flexible material (e.g. that on which a teleprinter prints a message), adhesive tape, insulating tape, magnetic tape. **3.** a tape-measure. **4.** a tape-recording. —**tape** *v.* **1.** to tie or fasten with tape. **2.** to record on magnetic tape. □ **have a person** *or* **thing taped,** (*slang*) to understand him or it fully, to have an organized method of dealing with it. **tape-measure** *n.* a strip of tape or flexible metal marked in inches or centimetres etc. for measuring length. **tape-record** *v.* to record on a tape-recorder. **tape recorder,** an apparatus for recording sounds on magnetic tape and playing back the recording. **tape recording,** a recording made on magnetic tape.

taper *n.* a slender candle, burnt to give a light or to light other candles etc. —*v.* to make or become gradually narrower. □ **taper off,** to become less in amount etc. or cease gradually.

tapestry (**tap**-i-stri) *n.* a piece of strong material with a pictorial or ornamental design woven into it or embroidered on it, used for hanging on walls or as an upholstery fabric.

tapeworm *n.* a tape-like worm that can

live as a parasite in the intestines of man and other animals.

tapioca (tap-i-**oh**-kă) *n.* a starchy substance in hard white grains obtained from cassava and used for making puddings.

tapir (**tay**-per) *n.* a small pig-like animal with a long flexible snout.

tappet *n.* a projection in a piece of machinery that causes a certain movement by tapping against something, used e.g. to open and close a valve.

taproom *n.* a room in a public house etc. where alcoholic drinks are on tap.

tar *n.* **1.** a thick dark inflammable liquid obtained by distilling wood or coal or peat etc. **2.** a similar substance formed by burning tobacco. —*v.* (tarred, tarring) to coat with tar. □ **be tarred with the same brush,** to have the same faults as someone else. **tar-seal** *v.* (*Austral.*) to surface (a road) with a mixture of tar and broken stone, (*n.*) a road surfaced in this way.

taradiddle *n.* (*informal*) a petty lie.

taramasalata (ta-ră-mă-să-**lah**-tă) *n.* paté made from the roe (*tarama*) of mullet or smoked cod.

tarantella (ta răn tel-ă) *n.* a rapid whirling South Italian dance.

tarantula (tă-**ran**-tew-lă) *n.* **1.** a large black spider of southern Europe **2.** a large hairy tropical spider.

tardy *adj.* (tardier, tardiest) **1.** slow to act or move or happen. **2.** behind time. **tardily** *adv.*, **tardiness** *n.*

tare[1] (*pr.* tair) *n.* a kind of vetch.

tare[2] (*pr.* tair) *n.* an allowance made to the purchaser for the weight of the container in which goods are packed, or for the vehicle transporting them, in instances where the goods are weighed together with their container or vehicle.

target *n.* **1.** the object or mark that a person tries to hit in shooting etc., a disc painted with concentric circles for this purpose in archery. **2.** a person or thing against which criticism or scorn etc. is directed. **3.** an objective, a minimum result aimed at, *export targets.*

tariff *n.* **1.** a list of fixed charges, especially for rooms and meals etc. at a hotel. **2.** duty to be paid on imports or exports.

Tarmac *n.* **1.** (*trade mark*) material for surfacing roads etc., consisting of broken stone or slag mixed with tar. **2.** *tarmac,* an area surfaced with this, especially on an airfield. —**tarmac** *v.* (tarmacked, tarmacking) to surface with Tarmac.

tarn *n.* a small mountain lake.

tarnish *v.* **1.** to lose or cause (metal) to lose its lustre by exposure to air or damp.

2. to stain or blemish (a reputation etc.). —*n.* loss of lustre, a stain or blemish.

tarot (**ta**-roh) *n.* a game played with a pack of 78 cards which are used also for fortune-telling.

tarpaulin (tar-**paw**-lin) *n.* **1.** canvas made waterproof, especially by being tarred. **2.** a sheet of this used as a covering.

tarragon (ta-ră-gŏn) *n.* a plant with leaves that are used for flavouring salads and in making a vinegar.

tarry[1] (**tar**-i) *adj.* of or like tar.

tarry[2] (**ta**-ri) *v.* (tarried, tarrying) (*old use*) to delay in coming or going.

tarsal *adj.* of the tarsus. —*n.* one of the tarsal bones.

tarsier (**tar**-si-er) *n.* a small monkey-like animal of the East Indies, with large eyes and a long tail.

tarsus *n.* the seven small bones that make up the ankle.

tart[1] *adj.* **1.** sharp-tasting, acid. **2.** sharp in manner, biting, *a tart reply.* **tartly** *adv.*, **tartness** *n.*

tart[2] *n.* **1.** a pie containing fruit or sweet filling. **2.** a piece of pastry with jam etc. on top. **3.** (*slang*) a girl or woman (especially of immoral character), a prostitute. —*v.* **tart up,** (*informal*) to dress or decorate gaudily or with cheap smartness; to smarten up.

tartan *n.* **1.** the distinctive pattern of a Highland clan, with coloured stripes crossing at right angles. **2.** a similar pattern. **3.** fabric woven in such a pattern.

tartar *n.* **1.** a hard chalky deposit that forms on the teeth. **2.** a reddish deposit that forms on the side of a cask in which wine is fermented. □ **cream of tartar,** *see* cream.

Tartar *n.* **1.** a member of a group of Central Asian peoples including Mongols and Turks. **2.** a person who is violent-tempered or difficult to deal with.

tartar sauce (**tar**-ter) a sauce of mayonnaise containing chopped gherkins etc.

tartaric (tar-**ta**-rik) *adj.* of or derived from tartar, *tartaric acid.*

tartlet *n.* a small pastry tart.

Tas. *abbrev.* Tasmania.

task *n.* a piece of work to be done. —*v.* to make great demands upon (a person's powers). □ **take a person to task,** to rebuke him. **task force,** a group and resources specially organized for a particular task.

taskmaster *n.* a person considered with regard to the way in which he imposes tasks, *a hard taskmaster.*

Tasmania (taz-**mayn**-iă) an island State

off the south-east coast of Australia. **Tasmanian** *adj.* & *n.*

Tass the telegraphic news-agency of the Soviet Union.

tassel *n.* **1.** a bunch of threads tied at one end and hanging loosely, used as an ornament. **2.** the tassel-like head of certain plants (e.g. maize). □ **tasselled** *adj.* ornamented with a tassel or tassels.

taste *n.* **1.** the sensation caused in the tongue by things placed upon it. **2.** the faculty of perceiving this sensation. **3.** a small quantity of food or drink taken as a sample, a slight experience of something, *a taste of fame.* **4.** a liking, *she has always had a taste for foreign travel*; *add sugar to taste*, in the amount that is liked. **5.** ability to perceive and enjoy what is beautiful or harmonious or to know what is fitting for an occasion etc., choice made according to this; *the remark was in bad taste*, was unsuitable or offensive. —**taste** *v.* **1.** to discover or test the flavour of (a thing) by taking it into the mouth. **2.** to be able to perceive flavours. **3.** to have a certain flavour, *it tastes sour.* **4.** to experience, *taste the joys of freedom.* —**taster** *n.* □ **taste-bud** *n.* one of the small projections on the tongue by which flavours are perceived.

tasteful *adj.* showing good taste. **tastefully** *adv.*, **tastefulness** *n.*

tasteless *adj.* **1.** having no flavour. **2.** showing poor taste, *tasteless decorations.* **tastelessly** *adv.*, **tastelessness** *n.*

tasty *adj.* (tastier, tastiest) having a strong flavour, appetizing. **tastily** *adv.*, **tastiness** *n.*

tat[1] *v.* (tatted, tatting) to do tatting, to make by tatting.

tat[2] *n.* tattiness, tawdry or fussily ornate things.

tat[3] *see* tit[2].

ta-ta *int.* (*informal*) goodbye.

tattered *adj.* ragged, torn into tatters.

tatters *pl. n.* rags, irregularly torn pieces.

tatting *n.* **1.** a kind of lace made by hand with a small shuttle. **2.** the process of making this.

tattle *v.* to chatter or gossip idly, to reveal information in this way. —*n.* idle chatter or gossip.

tattoo[1] *n.* **1.** an evening drum or bugle signal calling soldiers back to their quarters. **2.** an elaboration of this with music and marching, as an entertainment. **3.** a drumming or tapping sound.

tattoo[2] *v.* to mark (skin) with indelible patterns by puncturing it and inserting a dye, to make (a pattern) in this way. —*n.* a tattooed pattern.

tatty *adj.* (tattier, tattiest) **1.** ragged,

shabby and untidy. **2.** tawdry, fussily ornate. **tattily** *adv.*, **tattiness** *n.*

taught *see* teach.

taunt *v.* to jeer at, to try to provoke with scornful remarks or criticism. —*n.* a taunting remark.

Taurus (**tor**-ŭs) *n.* a sign of the zodiac, the Bull. **Taurean** *adj.* & *n.*

taut *adj.* stretched firmly, not slack. **tautly** *adv.*

tauten *v.* to make or become taut.

tautology (taw-**tol**-ŏji) *n.* saying of the same thing over again in different words, especially using a word or phrase of the same grammatical construction, as in 'free, gratis, and for nothing'. **tautological** (taw-tŏ-**loj**-ikăl) *adj.*, **tautologous** (taw-**tol**-ŏgŭs) *adj.*

tavern *n.* (*old use*) an inn or public house.

tawdry (**taw**-dri) *adj.* (tawdrier, tawdriest) showy or gaudy but without real value. **tawdrily** *adv.*, **tawdriness** *n.*

tawny *adj.* brownish-yellow, brownish-orange.

tawse (*pr.* tawz) *n.* (*Scottish*) a leather strap with a slit end, used for punishing children.

tax *n.* **1.** a sum of money to be paid by people or business firms to a government, to be used for public purposes. **2.** something that makes a heavy demand, *a tax on one's strength.* —**tax** *v.* **1.** to impose a tax on, to require (a person) to pay tax. **2.** to make heavy demands on. **3.** to pay the tax on, *the car is taxed until June.* **4.** to accuse in a challenging or reproving way, *taxed him with having left the door unlocked.* —**taxation** *n.* □ **tax-free** *adj.* exempt from taxes. **tax haven**, a country where income tax etc. is low.

taxable *adj.* able or liable to be taxed.

taxi *n.* (*pl.* taxis) a car that plies for hire, usually with a meter to record the fare payable. —*v.* (taxied, taxiing) **1.** to go or convey in a taxi. **2.** (of aircraft) to move along ground or water under its own power, especially before or after flying. □ **taxi-cab** *n.* a taxi.

taxidermy (**tak**-si-derm-i) *n.* the art of preparing and mounting the skins of animals in lifelike form. **taxidermist** *n.*

taxonomy (taks-**on**-ŏmi) *n.* the scientific process of classifying living things.

taxpayer *n.* a person who pays tax (especially income tax).

Tayside a region of Scotland.

TB *abbrev.* (*informal*) tuberculosis.

T-bone steak steak from the thin end of the loin, containing a T-shaped bone.

tea *n.* **1.** the dried leaves of the tea-plant.

2. the hot drink that is made by steeping these in boiling water. **3.** a meal at which tea is served, especially a light meal in the afternoon or evening. **4.** a drink made by steeping the leaves of other plants in water, *camomile tea; beef tea* (see beef). □ **tea-bag** *n.* a small porous bag holding about a teaspoonful of tea for infusion. **tea-break** *n.* an interruption of work allowed for drinking tea. **tea-chest** *n.* a light cubical chest lined with thin sheets of lead or tin, in which tea is exported. **tea-cloth** *n.* a cloth for a tea-table; a tea-towel. **tea-cosy** *n.* a cover placed over a teapot to keep the tea hot. **tea-leaf** *n.* a leaf of tea, especially after infusion. **tea-party** *n.* a party at which tea is served. **tea-plant** *n.* an evergreen shrub grown in China, India, etc. **tea-room** *n.* a tea-shop. **tea-rose** *n.* a kind of delicately-scented rose. **tea-set** *n.* a set of cups and plates etc. for serving tea. **tea-shop** *n.* a shop where tea is served to the public. **tea-towel** *n.* a towel for drying washed crockery etc.

teacake *n.* a kind of bun usually served toasted and buttered.

teach *v.* (taught, teaching) **1.** to impart information or skill to (a person) or about (a subject etc.). **2.** to do this for a living. **3.** to put forward as a fact or principle, *Christ taught forgiveness, taught that we must forgive our enemies.* **4.** to cause to adopt (a practice etc.) by example or experience, *(informal)* to deter by punishment etc., *that will teach you not to meddle.* □ **teach-in** *n.* a lecture and discussion on a subject of topical interest.

teachable *adj.* **1.** able to learn by being taught. **2.** (of a subject) able to be taught.

teacher *n.* a person who teaches others, especially in a school.

teaching *n.* what is taught, *the teachings of the Church.*

teacup *n.* a cup from which tea or other hot liquids are drunk.

teak *n.* **1.** the strong heavy wood of a tall evergreen Asian tree, used for making furniture and in shipbuilding. **2.** the tree itself.

teal *n.* (*pl.* teal) a small freshwater duck.

team *n.* **1.** a set of players forming one side in certain games and sports. **2.** a set of people working together. **3.** two or more animals harnessed together to draw a vehicle or farm implement. —*v.* to combine into a team or set or for a common purpose. □ **team spirit,** willingness to act for the good of one's group rather than oneself. **team-work** *n.* organized co-operation.

teapot *n.* a vessel with a lid and spout in which tea is made and from which it is poured.

tear¹ (*pr.* tair) *v.* (tore, torn, tearing) **1.** to pull forcibly apart or away or to pieces. **2.** to make (a hole or a split) in this way. **3.** to become torn, to be able to be torn, *paper tears easily.* **4.** to subject (a person etc.) to conflicting desires or demands, *torn between love and duty.* **5.** to run, walk, or travel hurriedly. —*n.* a hole or split caused by tearing. □ **tear one's hair,** to pull it in anger or perplexity or despair. **tear oneself away,** to leave in spite of a strong desire to stay. **that's torn it,** *(slang)* that has spoilt our plans or efforts.

tear² (*pr.* teer) *n.* a drop of the salty water that appears in or flows from the eye as the result of grief or other emotion, or irritation by fumes etc. **in tears,** shedding tears. **tear-drop** *n.* a single tear. **tear-gas** *n.* a gas that causes severe irritation of the eyes. **tear-jerker** *n.* (*informal*) a story etc. calculated to produce tears of sadness or sympathy. **without tears,** presented so as to be learnt or done easily, *French without tears.*

tearaway *n.* an impetuous hooligan.

tearful *adj.* shedding or ready to shed tears, sad. **tearfully** *adv.*

tearing (tair-ing) *adj.* violent, overwhelming, *in a tearing hurry.*

tease *v.* **1.** to try to provoke in a playful or unkind way by jokes or questions or petty annoyances. **2.** to pick (wool etc.) into separate strands. **3.** to brush up the nap on (cloth). —*n.* a person who is fond of teasing others.

teasel (tee-zĕl) *n.* **1.** a plant with bristly heads formerly used to brush up nap on cloth. **2.** a device used for this purpose.

teaser *n.* (*informal*) a problem that is difficult to solve.

teaspoon *n.* **1.** a small spoon for stirring tea. **2.** the amount held by this. **teaspoonful** *n.* (*pl.* teaspoonfuls)

teat *n.* **1.** a nipple on an animal's milk-secreting organ. **2.** a device of rubber etc. on a feeding-bottle, through which the contents are sucked.

Tech (*pr.* tek) *n.* (*informal*) a technical college or school.

technical *adj.* **1.** of the mechanical arts and applied sciences, *a technical education* or *school.* **2.** of a particular subject or craft etc. or its techniques, *the technical terms of chemistry; technical skill.* **3.** (of a book etc.) requiring specialized knowledge, using technical terms. **4.** in a strict legal sense, *technical assault.* **technically** *adv.*

technicality (tek-ni-kal-iti) *n.* **1.** being technical. **2.** a technical word or phrase or point, *was acquitted on a technicality.*

technician (tek-**nish**-ăn) *n.* **1.** an expert in the techniques of a particular subject or craft. **2.** a skilled mechanic.

Technicolor *n.* **1.** (*trade mark*) a process of producing cinema films in colour. **2.** vivid or artificially brilliant colour.

technique (tek-**neek**) *n.* the method of doing or performing something (especially in an art or science), skill in this.

technocracy (tek-**nok**-răsi) *n.* management by technocrats.

technocrat (**tek**-nŏ-krat) *n.* a technical expert who manages a country's resources.

technologist *n.* an expert in technology.

technology *n.* **1.** the scientific study of mechanical arts and applied sciences (e.g. engineering). **2.** these subjects, their practical application in industry etc. **technological** *adj.*, **technologically** *adv.*

tedder *n.* a machine for drying hay.

teddy-bear *n.* a soft furry toy bear.

Teddy boy (*informal*) a youth who affects Edwardian dress.

Te Deum (tee **dee**-ŭm) a Latin hymn beginning 'Te Deum laudamus' (= we praise thee O God).

tedious (**tee**-di-ŭs) *adj.* tiresome because of its length or slowness or dullness, boring. **tediously** *adv.*, **tediousness** *n.*

tedium (**tee**-di-ŭm) *n.* tediousness.

tee *n.* **1.** = T. **2.** the cleared space from which a player strikes the ball in golf at the beginning of play for each hole. **3.** a small pile of sand or piece of wood etc. on which the ball is placed for being struck. **4.** the mark aimed at in quoits, bowls, and curling. —*v.* (teed, teeing) to place (a ball) on a tee in golf. □ **tee off**, to play the ball from the tee.

teem[1] *v.* **1.** to be full of, *the river was teeming with fish.* **2.** to be present in large numbers, *fish teem in that river.*

teem[2] *v.* (of water or rain etc.) to pour.

teenage *adj.* of teenagers.

teenaged *adj.* in one's teens.

teenager *n.* a person in his or her teens.

teens *pl. n.* the years of a person's age from 13 to 19.

teeny *adj.* (teenier, teeniest) (*informal*) tiny.

tee-shirt *n.* = T-shirt.

teeter *v.* to stand or move unsteadily.

teeth *see* tooth.

teethe *v.* (of a baby) to have its first teeth beginning to grow through the gums. **teething troubles**, problems arising in the early stages of an enterprise.

teetotal *adj.* abstaining completely from alcoholic drinks. **teetotaller** *n.*

Tehran (tay-**rahn**) the capital of Iran.

telecommunications *pl. n.* the means of communication over long distances, as by cable, telegraph, telephone, radio, or TV.

telegram *n.* a message sent by telegraph.

telegraph *n.* a system or apparatus for sending messages to a distance, especially by transmission of electrical impulses along wires. —*v.* to send (a message) or communicate with (a person) by telegraph. □ **telegraph pole**, a pole supporting overhead wires for use in telegraphy.

telegraphist (til-**eg**-ră-fist) *n.* a person whose job is to send and receive messages by telegraph.

telegraphy (til-**eg**-ră-fi) *n.* the process of communication by telegraph. **telegraphic** (tel-i-**graf**-ik) *adj.* □ **telegraphic address**, an abbreviated or other registered address for use in telegrams.

telekinesis (tel-i-ky-**nee**-sis) *n.* the process of moving things without touching them and without using ordinary physical means.

telemetry til-**em**-it-ri) *n.* the process of recording the readings of an instrument at a distance, usually by means of radio.

telepath (**tel**-i-path) *n.* a telepathic person.

telepathic (tel-i-**path**-ik) *adj.* of or using telepathy, able to communicate by telepathy.

telepathy (til-**ep**-ă-thi) *n.* communication from one mind to another without the use of speech or writing or gestures etc. **telepathist** *n.* a telepath.

telephone *n.* **1.** a system of transmitting sound (especially speech) to a distance by wire or cord or radio. **2.** an instrument used in this, with a receiver and mouthpiece and a bell to indicate an incoming call. —*v.* to send (a message) or speak to (a person) by telephone. **telephonic** (teli-**fon**-ik) *adj.* □ **telephone directory**, a book listing the names and numbers of people who have a telephone. **telephone number**, a number assigned to a particular instrument and used in making connections to it.

telephonist (til-**ef**-ŏn-ist) *n.* an operator in a telephone exchange or at a switchboard.

telephony (til-**ef**-ŏni) *n.* the process of transmitting sound by telephone.

telephoto lens a lens producing a large image of a distant object that is photographed.

teleport (**tel**-i-port) *v.* to move by telekinesis.

teleprinter (**tel**-i-print-er) *n.* a device for typing and transmitting messages by telegraph, and for receiving and typing messages similarly.

telerecording *n.* recording of an item or programme to be transmitted by television.

telescope *n.* an optical instrument using lenses or mirrors or both to make distant objects appear larger when viewed through it. —*v.* 1. to make or become shorter by sliding overlapping sections one inside another. 2. to compress or become compressed forcibly. 3. to condense so as to occupy less space or time. □ **radio telescope**, an apparatus for collecting radio waves emitted by celestial objects and recording their intensity etc.

telescopic *adj.* 1. of a telescope, magnifying like a telescope. 2. visible only through a telescope, *telescopic stars*. 3. capable of being telescoped, *telescopic umbrella*. **telescopically** *adv.* □ **telescopic sight**, a telescope fitted to a rifle for magnifying the image of the target.

teletext *n.* a system in which information can be selected and produced on the screen of a suitably modified TV set (distinguished from *viewdata*).

televise *v.* to transmit by television.

television *n.* 1. a system for reproducing on a screen a view of scenes or events or plays etc. by radio transmission. 2. (also *television set*) an apparatus with a screen for receiving pictures transmitted in this way. 3. televised programmes, television as a medium of communication.

telex *n.* a system of telegraphy in which printed messages are transmitted and received by teleprinters installed in the senders' and receivers' offices, using public transmission lines. —*v.* to send (a message) or communicate with (a person) by telex.

tell *v.* (told, telling) 1. to make known, especially in spoken or written words. 2. to give information to. 3. to utter, *tell the truth*. 4. to reveal a secret, *promise you won't tell*. 5. to decide or determine, *how do you tell which button to press?* 6. to distinguish, *I can't tell him from his brother*. 7. to produce a noticeable effect, *the strain began to tell on him*. 8. to count; *tell one's beads*, to say prayers while counting beads on a rosary. 9. to direct or order, *tell them to wait*. □ **tell fortunes**, see fortune. **tell off**, (*informal*) to reprimand or scold; to count off or detach for duty, *six of us were told off to collect fuel*. **tell on**, (*informal*) to reveal the activities of (a person) by telling others. **tell tales**, to report what is meant to be secret. **tell the time**, to read the time from a clock. **you're telling me**, (*slang*) I am fully aware of that.

teller *n.* 1. a person who tells or gives an account of something. 2. a person appointed to count votes. 3. a bank cashier.

telling *adj.* having a noticeable effect, striking, *a telling argument*.

tell-tale *n.* 1. a person who tells tales. 2. a mechanical device that serves as an indicator. —*adj.* revealing or indicating something, *a tell-tale blush*.

telly *n.* (*slang*) television, a television set.

temerity (tim-e-riti) *n.* audacity, rashness.

temp *n.* (*informal*) a temporary employee.

temper *n.* 1. the state of the mind as regards calmness or anger, *in a good temper*. 2. a fit of anger, *in a temper*. 3. calmness under provocation, *keep* or *lose one's temper*. 4. a tendency to have fits of anger, *have a temper*. 5. the condition of a tempered metal as regards hardness and elasticity. —**temper** *v.* 1. to bring (metal) or be brought to the required degree of hardness and elasticity by heating and then cooling. 2. to bring (clay etc.) to the required consistency by moistening and mixing. 3. to moderate or soften the effects of; *temper justice with mercy*, be merciful in awarding punishment.

temperament *n.* a person's nature as it controls the way he behaves and feels and thinks, *a nervous temperament*.

temperamental *adj.* 1. of or in a person's temperament. 2. not having a calm temperament, having fits of excitable or moody behaviour. **temperamentally** *adv.*

temperance *n.* 1. self-restraint in one's behaviour or in eating and drinking. 2. total abstinence from alcoholic drinks.

temperate *adj.* 1. self-restrained in one's behaviour, moderate. 2. (of climate) having a mild temperature without extremes of heat and cold. **temperately** *adv.*

temperature *n.* 1. the intensity of heat or cold in a body or room or country etc. 2. a measure of this shown by a thermometer. 3. an abnormally high temperature of the body, *have a temperature*.

tempest *n.* a violent storm.

tempestuous (tem-**pest**-yoo-ŭs) *adj.* stormy, full of commotion.

Templar *n.* a member of a medieval religious and military order (*Knights Templars*) for protection of pilgrims to the Holy Land.

template *n.* 1. a pattern or gauge, usually of thin board or metal, used as a guide for cutting metal or stone or wood etc. or pieces of fabric, or for shaping plaster or concrete etc. 2. a timber or metal plate used to distribute weight in a wall or under a beam.

temple¹ *n.* a building dedicated to the presence or service of a god or gods. **Inner**

Temple, Middle Temple, two Inns of Court in London (*see* inn).

temple [2] *n.* the flat part at each side of the head between forehead and ear.

tempo *n.* (*pl.* tempos *or* tempi) **1.** the time or speed or rhythm of a piece of music, *in waltz tempo.* **2.** the pace of any movement or activity, *the tempo of the war is quickening.*

temporal (temp-er-ăl) *adj.* **1.** secular, of worldly affairs as opposed to spiritual; *lords temporal* (see lord). **2.** of or denoting time. **3.** of the temple(s) of the head, *the temporal artery.*

temporary *adj.* lasting or meant to last for a limited time only, not permanent. —*n.* a person employed temporarily. —**temporarily** (temp-er-er-ili) *adv.*

temporize *v.* to compromise temporarily, or avoid giving a definite answer or decision, in order to gain time. **temporization** *n.,* **temporizer** *n.*

tempt *v.* **1.** to persuade or try to persuade (especially into doing something wrong or unwise) by the prospect of pleasure or advantage. **2.** to arouse a desire in, to attract; *I'm tempted to question this,* feel inclined to do so. **3.** to risk provoking (fate or Providence) by deliberate rashness. **tempter** *n.,* **temptress** *n.*

temptation *n.* **1.** tempting, being tempted. **2.** something that tempts or attracts.

tempting *adj.* attractive, inviting, *a tempting offer.*

ten *adj.* & *n.* one more than nine (10, X).

tenable (ten-ăbŭl) *adj.* **1.** able to be defended against attack or objection, *a tenable position* or *theory.* **2.** (of an office) able to be held for a certain time or by a certain class of person etc. **tenability** *n.*

tenacious (tin-ay-shŭs) *adj.* **1.** holding or clinging firmly to something (e.g. rights or principles). **2.** (of memory) retentive. **3.** sticking firmly together or to an object or surface. **tenaciously** *adv.,* **tenacity** (tin-ass-iti) *n.*

tenancy *n.* **1.** the use of land or buildings as a tenant. **2.** the period of this.

tenant *n.* **1.** a person who rents land or buildings from a landlord. **2.** (in law) an occupant or owner of land or a building.

tenantry *n.* the tenants of land or buildings on one estate.

tench *n.* a freshwater fish of the carp family.

tend [1] *v.* to take care of or look after (a person or thing).

tend [2] *v.* **1.** to be likely to behave in a certain way or to have a certain characteristic. **2.** to have a certain influence, *recent laws tend to increase customers' rights.* **3.** to take

a certain direction, *the track tends upwards.*

tendency *n.* **1.** the way a person or thing tends to be or behave, *a tendency to fat* or *towards fatness; homicidal tendencies.* **2.** the direction in which something moves or changes, a trend, *an upward tendency.*

tendentious (ten-den-shŭs) *adj.* (of a speech or piece of writing etc.) aimed at helping a cause, not impartial.

tender [1] *adj.* **1.** not tough or hard, easy to chew, *tender meat.* **2.** easily damaged, delicate, *tender plants; of tender age,* young and vulnerable. **3.** sensitive, painful when touched. **4.** easily moved to pity or sympathy, *a tender heart.* **5.** loving, gentle. **tenderly** *adv.,* **tenderness** *n.*

tender [2] *v.* **1.** to offer formerly, *tender one's resignation.* **2.** to make a tender (for goods or work). —*n.* a formal offer to supply goods or carry out work at a stated price; *put work out to tender,* ask for such offers. □ **legal tender,** currency that must, by law, be accepted in payment.

tender [3] *n.* **1.** a person who tends or looks after something. **2.** a vessel or vehicle travelling to and from a larger one to convey stores or passengers etc. **3.** a truck attached to a steam locomotive, carrying fuel and water etc.

tenderfoot *n.* a newcomer who is unused to hardships, an inexperienced person.

tenderize *v.* to make more tender. **tenderizer** *n.*

tenderloin *n.* the middle part of pork loin.

tendon *n.* a strong band or cord of tissue connecting a muscle to some other part.

tendril *n.* **1.** a thread-like part by which a climbing plant clings to a support. **2.** a slender curl of hair etc.

tenement (ten-i-mĕnt) *n.* **1.** (in law) land or other permanent property held by a tenant, *lands and tenements.* **2.** a flat or room rented for living in. **3.** (in Scotland) a large house let in portions to a number of tenants.

tenet (ten-it) *n.* a firm belief or principle or doctrine of a person or group.

tenfold *adj.* & *adv.* ten times as much or as many.

Tenn. *abbrev.* Tennessee.

tenner *n.* (*informal*) £10, a ten-pound note.

Tennessee (ten-i-see) a State of the USA.

tennis *n.* either of two ball-games for 2 or 4 players, played with rackets over a net with a soft ball on an open court (*lawn tennis*) or with a hard ball in a walled court (*real tennis*).

tenon (ten-ŏn) *n.* a projection shaped to fit into a mortise.

tenor (ten-er) *n.* **1.** the general routine or course of something, *disrupting the even tenor of his life.* **2.** the general meaning or drift, *the tenor of his lecture.* **3.** the highest ordinary adult male singing-voice, a singer with this, a part written for it. **4.** a musical instrument with approximately the range of a tenor voice, *tenor saxophone.*

tenpin bowling a game similar to ninepins.

tense¹ *n.* any of the forms of a verb that indicate the time of action etc. as past or present or future, *'came' is the past tense of 'come'.*

tense² *adj.* **1.** stretched tightly. **2.** with muscles tight in attentiveness for what may happen. **3.** unable to relax, edgy. **4.** causing tenseness, *a tense moment.* —*v.* to make or become tense. **tensely** *adv.,* **tenseness** *n.*

tensile (ten-syl) *adj.* **1.** of tension; *tensile strength,* resistance to breaking under tension. **2.** capable of being stretched.

tension *n.* **1.** stretching, being stretched. **2.** tenseness, the condition when feelings are tense. **3.** the effect produced by forces pulling against each other. **4.** electromotive force, voltage, *high-tension cables.* **5.** (in knitting) the number of stitches and rows to a unit of measurement (e.g. 10 cm or 1 inch).

tent *n.* a portable shelter or dwelling made of canvas etc.

tentacle (tent-ă-kŭl) *n.* a slender flexible part extending from the body of certain animals (e.g. snails, octopuses), used for feeling or grasping things or moving.

tentative (tent-ă-tiv) *adj.* hesitant, not definite, done as a trial, *a tentative suggestion.* **tentatively** *adv.*

tenterhook *n.* each of the hooks that hold cloth stretched for drying during its manufacture. **on tenterhooks,** in a state of suspense or strain because of uncertainty.

tenth *adj. & n.* **1.** next after ninth. **2.** one of ten equal parts of a thing. **tenthly** *adv.*

tenuous (ten-yoo-ŭs) *adj.* **1.** very thin in form or consistency, *tenuous threads.* **2.** having little substance or validity, very slight, *tenuous distinctions.* **tenuously** *adv.,* **tenuousness** *n.,* **tenuity** (tin-yoo-iti) *n.*

tenure (ten-yer) *n.* the holding of office or of land or other permanent property or accommodation etc., the period or manner of this, *freehold tenure; she was granted security of tenure for six months.*

tepee (tee-pee) *n.* a wigwam.

tepid *adj.* slightly warm, lukewarm. **tepidity** (ti-pid-iti) *n.*

tercentenary (ter-sen-teen-er-i) *n.* a 300th anniversary.

term *n.* **1.** the time for which something lasts, a fixed or limited time, *during his term of office; a term of imprisonment.* **2.** completion of this, *a pregnancy approaching term.* **3.** one of the periods, each lasting for a number of weeks, during which instruction is given in a school, college, or university or in which a lawcourt holds sessions, alternating with holidays or vacations. **4.** each of the quantities or expressions in a mathematical series or ratio etc. **5.** a word or phrase considered as the name or symbol of something, *'the nick' is a slang term for 'prison'.* —*v.* to call by a certain term or expression, *this music is termed plainsong.* □ **come to terms,** to reach an agreement; to reconcile oneself to a difficulty etc., *came to terms with his handicap.* **terms** *pl. n.* language or the manner of its use, *protested in strong terms;* stipulations made, conditions offered or accepted, *peace terms;* payment offered or asked, *hire-purchase on easy terms;* a relation between people, *on friendly terms.* **terms of reference,** the scope of an inquiry or other activity.

termagant (ter-mă-gant) *n.* a shrewish bullying woman.

terminable *adj.* able to be terminated.

terminal *adj.* **1.** of or forming or situated at the end or boundary of something. **2.** forming or undergoing the last stage of a fatal disease, *terminal cancer.* **3.** of or done each term, *terminal examinations.* —**terminal** *n.* **1.** a terminating point or part. **2.** a terminus for railway trains or long-distance buses, a building (at an airport or in a town) where air passengers arrive and depart. **3.** a point of connection in an electric circuit or device. **4.** an apparatus for transmitting messages to and from a computer or communications system etc. —**terminally** *adv.*

terminate *v.* to end. **termination** *n.*

terminology *n.* **1.** the technical terms of a particular subject. **2.** proper use of words as names or symbols. **terminological** *adj.*

terminus *n.* (*pl.* termini, *pr.* ter-min-I) the end of something, the last station at the end of a railway or bus route.

termite *n.* a small insect that is very destructive to timber, especially in tropical areas (popularly called *white ant,* but not of the ant family).

tern *n.* a sea-bird with long pointed wings and a forked tail.

terrace *n.* **1.** a raised level place, one of a

series of these into which a hillside is shaped for cultivation. **2.** a flight of wide shallow steps, e.g. for spectators at a sports ground. **3.** a paved area beside a house. **4.** a row of houses joined to each other by party walls. —*v.* to form into a terrace or terraces. □ **terrace-house** *n.* a house forming one of a terrace.

terracotta *n.* **1.** a kind of brownish-red unglazed pottery. **2.** its colour.

terra firma dry land, the ground.

terrain (te-**rayn**) *n.* a stretch of land, with regard to its natural features.

terrapin (te-**ră**-pin) *n.* an edible North American freshwater tortoise.

terrestrial (tĕ-**rest**-riăl) *adj.* **1.** of the earth. **2.** of or living on land.

terrible *adj.* **1.** appalling, distressing. **2.** extreme, hard to bear, *the heat was terrible*. **3.** (*informal*) very bad, *I'm terrible at tennis*. **terribly** *adv.*

terrier *n.* a kind of small hardy active dog.

terrific *adj.* (*informal*) **1.** of great size or intensity, *a terrific storm*. **2.** excellent, *did a terrific job*. **terrifically** *adv.*

terrify *v.* (terrified, terrifying) to fill with terror. **terrified** *adj.* feeling terror.

terrine (tĕ-**reen**) *n.* **1.** pâté or a similar food. **2.** an earthenware dish holding this.

territorial *adj.* of a country's territory. — **Territorial** *n.* a member of the Territorial Army, a trained volunteer reserve force. □ **territorial waters**, the sea within a certain distance of a country's coast and subject to its control.

territory *n.* **1.** land under the control of a ruler or State or city etc. **2.** *Territory*, a country or area forming part of the USA or Australia or Canada but not ranking as a State or province. **3.** an area for which a person has responsibility or over which a salesman etc. operates. **4.** a sphere of action or thought, a province. **5.** an area claimed or dominated by one person or group or animal and defended against others.

terror *n.* **1.** extreme fear. **2.** a terrifying person or thing. **3.** (*informal*) a formidable person, a troublesome person or thing. **terror-stricken** *adj.* stricken with terror.

terrorism *n.* use of violence and intimidation, especially for political purposes. **terrorist** *n.*

terrorize *v.* to fill with terror, to coerce by terrorism. **terrorization** *n.*

terry *n.* a cotton fabric used for towels etc., with raised loops left uncut.

terse *adj.* concise, curt. **tersely** *adv.*, **terseness** *n.*

tertiary (**ter**-sher-i) *adj.* **1.** coming after secondary, of the third rank or stage etc. **2.** (of education) above secondary level.

Terylene *n.* (*trade mark*) a kind of synthetic textile fibre.

tessellated (**tess**-il-ayt-id) *adj.* (of a pavement) made from small flat pieces of stone in various colours arranged in a pattern.

test *n.* **1.** a critical examination or evaluation of the qualities or abilities etc. of a person or thing. **2.** a means or procedure for making this. **3.** an examination (especially in a school) on a limited subject. **4.** (*informal*) a test match. —*v.* to subject to a test. —**tester** *n.* □ **put to the test**, to cause to undergo a test. **stand the test**, to undergo it successfully. **test case**, a lawsuit providing a decision which is taken as applying to similar cases in the future. **test drive**, a drive taken in order to judge the performance of a car before buying it. **test-drive** *v.* to take a test drive in (a car). **test match**, a cricket or Rugby match between teams of certain countries, usually one of a series in a tour. **test pilot**, a pilot employed to fly new aircraft in order to test their performance. **test-tube** *n.* a tube of thin glass with one end closed, used in laboratories; *test-tube baby*, one conceived by artificial insemination, or developing elsewhere than in a mother's body.

testament *n.* **1.** a will. **2.** a written statement of one's beliefs. □ **Old Testament**, the books of the Bible telling of the history of the Jews and their beliefs. **New Testament**, the books of the Bible telling of the life and teaching of Christ and his earliest followers.

testamentary *adj.* of or given in a person's will.

testate (**tes**-tayt) *adj.* having left a valid will at death.

testator (tes-**tay**-ter) *n.* a person who has made a will. **testatrix** *n.* a woman testator.

testes *see* testis.

testicle *n.* a male reproductive organ in which sperm-bearing fluid is produced, (in man) each of the two enclosed in the scrotum.

testify *v.* (testified, testifying) **1.** to bear witness to (a fact etc.), to give evidence. **2.** to be evidence of.

testimonial *n.* **1.** a formal statement testifying to a person's character or abilities or qualifications. **2.** something given to a person to show appreciation of his services or achievements.

testimony *n.* **1.** a declaration or statement (especially one made under oath). **2.** evidence in support of something.

testis *n.* (*pl.* testes, *pr.* **tes**-teez) a testicle.

testy *adj.* easily annoyed, irritable. **testily** *adv.*, **testiness** *n.*

tetanus (tet-ăn-ŭs) *n.* a disease in which the muscles contract and stiffen (as in lockjaw), caused by bacteria that enter the body.

tetchy *adj.* peevish, irritable. **tetchily** *adv.*, **tetchiness** *n.*

tête-à-tête (tayt-ah-**tayt**) *n.* a private conversation, especially between two people. —*adv.* & *adj.* together in private.

tether *n.* a rope or chain by which an animal is fastened while grazing. —*v.* to fasten (an animal) with a tether. □ **at the end of one's tether**, having reached the limit of one's endurance.

tetrahedron (tet-ră-**hee**-drŏn) *n.* a solid with four sides, a pyramid with three triangular sides and a triangular base.

Teutonic (tew-**tonn**-ik) *adj.* **1.** of the Germanic peoples or their languages. **2.** German.

Tex. *abbrev.* Texas.

Texas a State of the USA. **Texan** *adj.* & *n.*

text *n.* **1.** the wording of something written or printed. **2.** the main body of a book or page etc. as distinct from illustrations or notes. **3.** a sentence from Scripture used as the subject of a sermon or discussion. **4.** a book or play etc. prescribed for study.

textbook *n.* a book of information for use in studying a subject.

textiles *pl. n.* woven or machine-knitted fabrics. **textile** *adj.* of textiles.

textual *adj.* of or in a text. **textually** *adv.*

texture *n.* the way a fabric or other substance feels to the touch, its thickness or firmness or solidity. **textured** *adj.* having a certain texture, *coarse-textured*; (of yarn or fabric) crimped or curled or looped.

Thailand (ty-land) a country in south-east Asia. **Thai** (*pr. as* tie) *adj.* & *n.*

thalidomide (thă-**lid**-ŏ-myd) *n.* a sedative drug found (in 1961) to have caused malformation of the limbs of babies whose mothers took it during pregnancy.

thallium (**thăl**-iŭm) *n.* a soft white poisonous metallic substance.

than *conj.* used to introduce the second element in a comparison, *his brother is taller than he is* or *taller than him*. ¶ These forms are preferred to *taller than he*. Note that *She likes you more than I do* does not mean the same as *She likes you more than me* (=more than she likes me).

thank *v.* to express gratitude to; *he has only himself to thank*, it is his own fault. **thank God** *or* **thank goodness**, an exclamation of relief. **thank-offering** *n.* an offering made as an act of thanks. **thanks** *pl. n.* expressions of gratitude; (*informal*) thank you. **thanks to**, on account of, as the result of. **thank you**, a polite expression of thanks. **thank-you** *n.* the expressing of thanks.

thankful *adj.* feeling or expressing gratitude. **thankfully** *adv.* in a thankful way; we are thankful, *thankfully, it has stopped raining*. (¶ This second use is similar to that of *hopefully* which many people regard as unacceptable.)

thankless *adj.* not likely to win thanks, *a thankless task*.

thanksgiving *n.* an expression of gratitude, especially to God. **Thanksgiving** *n.* (also *Thanksgiving Day*) a holiday for giving thanks to God, in the USA on the fourth Thursday in November, in Canada on the second Monday in October.

thankyou an incorrect way of writing *thank you*.

that *adj.* & *pronoun* (*pl.* those) the, the person or thing referred to or pointed to or understood, the further or less obvious one of two. —*adv.* so, to such an extent, *I'll go that far*. —**that** *relative pronoun* used to introduce a clause that is essential in order to define or identify something (¶ the word *which* or *who* or *whom* is often used instead), *the book that I sent you*; *the man that she married*. —*conj.* introducing a dependent clause, *we hope that all will go well*.

thatch *n.* **1.** a roof or roof-covering made of straw or reeds or palm-leaves. **2.** (*informal*) a thick growth of hair on the head. —*v.* to roof or cover with thatch, to make (a roof) of thatch. —**thatcher** *n.*

thaw *v.* **1.** to pass into a liquid or unfrozen state after being frozen. **2.** to become warm enough to melt ice etc. or to lose numbness. **3.** to become less cool or less formal in manner. **4.** to cause to thaw. —*n.* thawing, weather that thaws ice etc.

the *adj.* (called the *definite article*) **1.** applied to a noun standing for a specific person or thing (*the Queen; the man in grey*), or one or all of a kind (*diseases of the eye; the rich*), or an occupation or pursuit etc. (*too fond of the bottle*). **2.** (*pr. thee*) used to emphasize excellence or importance; *he's the Sir Lawrence*, the one who is so famous. **3.** (*informal*) my, our, your, etc., *the wife*. **4.** (of prices) per, *oysters at £5 the dozen*. —*adv.* in that degree, by that amount, *all the better; the more the merrier*.

theatre *n.* **1.** a building or outdoor structure for the performance of plays and similar entertainments. **2.** a room or hall for lectures etc. with seats in tiers. **3.** an operating-theatre. **4.** a scene of important events, *Belgium was the theatre of war.* **5.** the writing, acting, and producing of plays. □ **theatre weapons**, those that are of intermediate range, between tactical and strategic (*see* **strategic weapons**).

theatrical *adj.* **1.** of or for the theatre. **2.** (of behaviour) exaggerated and designed to make a showy effect. **theatrically** *adv.* □ **theatricals** *pl. n.* theatrical performances, *amateur theatricals*; theatrical behaviour.

thee *pronoun* the objective case of thou.

theft *n.* stealing.

their *adj.* of or belonging to them. **theirs** *possessive pronoun*, of or belonging to them, the thing(s) belonging to them. ¶ It is incorrect to write *their's* (see the note under its).

them *pronoun* **1.** the objective case of they, *we saw them.* **2.** (*informal*) = they, *it's them all right.*

theme (*pr.* theem) *n.* **1.** the subject about which a person speaks or writes or thinks. **2.** a melody which is repeated or on which variations are constructed.

themselves *pronoun* corresponding to *they* and *them*, used in the same ways as himself.

then *adv.* **1.** at that time. **2.** next, after that, and also. **3.** in that case, therefore, *if that's yours, then this must be mine.* —*adj.* of that time, *the then duke.* —*n.* that time, *from then on.*

thence *adv.* from that place or source.

thenceforth, thenceforward *advs.* from then on.

theodolite (thi-**od**-ŏ-lyt) *n.* a surveying-instrument with a rotating telescope used for measuring horizontal and vertical angles.

theologian (thi-ŏ-**loh**-jiǎn) *n.* an expert in theology.

theology (thi-**ol**-ŏji) *n.* the study of religion, a system of religion. **theological** *adj.*, **theologically** *adv.*

theorem *n.* **1.** a mathematical statement to be proved by a chain of reasoning. **2.** a rule in algebra etc., especially one expressed as a formula.

theoretical *adj.* based on theory not on practice or experience. **theoretically** *adv.*

theorist *n.* a person who theorizes.

theorize *v.* to form a theory or theories.

theory *n.* **1.** a set of ideas formulated (by reasoning from known facts) to explain something, *Darwin's theory of evolution.* **2.** an opinion or supposition. **3.** ideas or suppositions in general (contrasted with *practice*). **4.** a statement of the principles

on which a subject is based, *theory of music.*

theosophy (thi-**oss**-ŏfi) *n.* any of several systems of philosophy that aim at a direct knowledge of God by means of spiritual ecstasy and contemplation. **theosophical** *adj.*

therapeutic (th'e-ră-**pew**-tik) *adj.* of the healing of disease, curative. **therapeutically** *adv.* □ **therapeutics** *n.* medical treatment of disease.

therapist *n.* a specialist in a certain kind of therapy.

therapy *n.* **1.** any treatment designed to relieve or cure an illness or disability. **2.** physiotherapy, psychotherapy.

there *adv.* **1.** in or at or to that place. **2.** at that point in a process or series of events. **3.** in that matter, *I can't agree with you there.* **4.** used for emphasis in calling attention, *hey, you there!* **5.** used to introduce a sentence where the verb comes before its subject, *there was plenty to eat.* —*n.* that place, *we live near there.* —*int.* an exclamation of satisfaction or dismay (*there! what did I tell you!*) or used to soothe a child etc. (*there, there!*).

thereabouts *adv.* **1.** somewhere near there. **2.** somewhere near that number or quantity or time etc.

thereafter *adv.* after that.

thereby *adv.* by that means; *thereby hangs a tale,* there is something that could be told about that.

therefore *adv.* for that reason.

therein *adv.* (*formal*) in that place, in that respect.

thereof *adv.* (*formal*) of that, of it.

thereto *adv.* (*formal*) to that, to it.

thereupon *adv.* in consequence of that, immediately after that.

therm *n.* a unit of heat, used especially in measuring a gas supply (= 100,000 thermal units).

thermal *adj.* **1.** of heat, using or operated by heat. **2.** warm or hot, *thermal springs.* —*n.* a rising current of hot air. □ **thermal unit,** a unit for measuring heat.

thermidor (**therm**-i-dor) *n.* **lobster thermidor,** a mixture of lobster meat with mushrooms, cream, egg-yolks, and sherry, cooked in a lobster shell.

thermionic valve (thermi-**on**-ik) a vacuum tube in which a flow of electrons is emitted by heated electrodes, used in radio etc.

thermocouple *n.* a device for measuring temperatures by means of the thermo-electric voltage developing between two pieces of wire of different metals joined to each other at each end.

thermodynamics *n.* a branch of physics dealing with the relation between heat and other forms of energy.

thermoelectric *adj.* producing electricity by difference of temperature.

thermometer *n.* an instrument for measuring temperature, especially a graduated glass tube containing mercury or alcohol which expands when heated.

thermonuclear *adj.* of nuclear reactions that occur only at very high temperatures. **thermonuclear bomb,** a bomb that uses such reactions.

thermoplastic *adj.* becoming soft and plastic when heated and hardening when cooled. —*n.* a thermoplastic substance.

Thermos *n.* (*trade mark*) a kind of vacuum flask.

thermosetting *adj.* (of plastics) setting permanently when heated.

thermostat *n.* a device that automatically regulates temperature by cutting off and restoring the supply of heat to a piece of equipment or a room etc. **thermostatic** *adj.*, **thermostatically** *adv.*

thesaurus (thi-sor-ŭs) *n.* (*pl.* thesauri, *pr.* thi-**sor**-I) 1. a dictionary or encyclopaedia, *a thesaurus of slang.* 2. a book containing sets of words grouped according to their meanings.

these *see* this.

thesis (th'ee-sis) *n.* (*pl.* theses, *pr.* -seez) 1. a statement or theory put forward and supported by arguments. 2. a lengthy written essay submitted by a candidate for a university degree.

thews *pl. n.* muscles, muscular strength.

they *pronoun* 1. the people or things mentioned. 2. people in general, *they say the play is a success.* 3. those in authority, *they are putting a tax on margarine.* 4. used informally instead of 'he or she', *I am never angry with anyone unless they deserve it.*

they'd = they had, they would. **they'll** = they will. **they're** = they are. **they've** = they have.

thick *adj.* 1. of great or specified distance between opposite surfaces. 2. (of a line etc.) broad not fine. 3. made of thick material, *a thick coat.* 4. having units that are crowded or numerous, dense, *a thick forest; thick fog; thick darkness,* difficult to see through. 5. densely covered or filled, *her roses were thick with greenfly.* 6. (of a liquid or paste) relatively stiff in consistency, not flowing easily; *thick soup,* thickened. 7. (of the voice) not sounding clear. 8. (of an accent) very noticeable, *a thick brogue.* 9. stupid. 10. (*informal*) on terms of close association or friendliness, *her parents are very thick with mine.* —*adv.*

thickly, *blows came thick and fast* —*n.* the busiest part of a crowd or fight or activity, *in the thick of it.* —**thickly** *adv.* □ **a bit thick,** (*slang*) beyond what is reasonable or endurable. **thick ear,** (*slang*) an ear that is swollen as the result of a blow. **thick head,** stupidity; a feeling of muzziness. **thick-headed** *adj.* stupid. **thick-skinned** *adj.* not very sensitive to criticism or snubs. **thick-witted** *adj.* stupid. **through thick and thin,** in spite of all the difficulties.

thicken *v.* to make or become thicker or of a stiffer consistency; *the plot thickens,* becomes more complicated.

thicket *n.* a number of shrubs and small trees etc. growing close together.

thickish *adj.* rather thick.

thickness *n.* 1. the quality of being thick, the extent to which something is thick. 2. a layer, *use three thicknesses of cardboard.* 3. the part between opposite surfaces, *steps cut in the thickness of the wall.*

thickset *adj.* 1. with parts set or growing close together, *a thickset hedge.* 2. having a stocky or burly body.

thief *n.* (*pl.* thieves) one who steals, especially stealthily and without violence. **thievish** *adj.*, **thievery** *n.*

thieve *v.* to be a thief, to steal.

thigh *n.* the part of the human leg between hip and knee, the corresponding part in other animals.

thimble *n.* a small metal or plastic cap worn on the end of the finger to protect it and push the needle in sewing.

thimbleful *n.* (*pl.* thimblefuls) a very small quantity of liquid to drink.

thin *adj.* (thinner, thinnest) 1. of small thickness or diameter. 2. (of a line etc.) narrow, not broad. 3. made of thin material, *a thin dress.* 4. lean, not plump. 5. not dense or plentiful. 6. having units that are not crowded or numerous. 7. (of a liquid or paste) flowing easily, not thick. 8. lacking strength or substance or an important ingredient, feeble, *a thin excuse.* —*adv.* thinly, *cut the bread thin.* —*v.* (thinned, thinning) to make or become thinner. —**thinly** *adv.*, **thinness** *n.* □ **have a thin time,** (*slang*) to have an uncomfortable or wretched time. **thin end of the wedge,** a change that will open the way to further similar ones. **thin out,** to make or become fewer or less crowded; *thin out seedlings,* remove a few to improve the growth of the rest. **thin-skinned** *adj.* over-sensitive to criticism or snubs.

thine *adj. & possessive pronoun,* (*old use*) of or belonging to thee, the thing(s) belonging to thee.

thing *n.* 1. whatever is or may be an object

of perception or knowledge or thought.
2. an unnamed object or item, *there are 6 things on my list.* **3.** an inanimate object as distinct from a living creature. **4.** (in pity or contempt) a creature, *poor thing!* **5.** an act or fact or idea or task etc., *a difficult thing to do; she takes things too seriously.* **6.** a specimen or type of something, *the latest thing in hats.* □ **do one's own thing,** (*informal*) to follow one's own interests or urges. **have a thing about,** (*informal*) to have an obsession or prejudice about. **make a thing of it,** to get excited about it; to insist that it is important. **the thing,** what is conventionally proper or is fashionable; what is important or suitable, *that bowl is just the thing for roses.* **things** *pl. n.* personal belongings, clothing, *pack your things*; implements or utensils, *my painting things*; circumstances or conditions, *things began to improve.*

thingumajig, thingummy, thingumabob *ns.* (*informal*) what-d'you-call-it, what's-his-name.

think *v.* (thought, thinking) **1.** to exercise the mind in an active way, to form connected ideas. **2.** to have as an idea or opinion, *we think we shall win.* **3.** to form as an intention or plan, *can't think what to do next; she's thinking of emigrating; I couldn't think of doing that,* I regard that course as unacceptable. **4.** to take into consideration, *think how nice it would be.* **5.** to call to mind, to remember, *can't think where I put it.* **6.** to be of the opinion, to judge, *it is thought to be a fake.* —*n.* (*informal*) an act of thinking, *must have a think about that.* □ **put on one's thinking-cap,** (*informal*) to try to find a solution to a problem by thought. **think again,** to reconsider and change one's mind. **think aloud,** to utter one's thoughts as they occur. **think better of it,** to change one's mind after reconsideration. **think nothing of,** to consider unremarkable. **think out,** to analyse or produce by thought. **think over,** to reach a decision about by thinking. **think-tank** *n.* an organization providing advice and ideas on national and commercial problems. **think twice,** to consider very carefully before doing something. **think up,** (*informal*) to invent or produce by thought.

thinker *n.* a person who thinks deeply or in a specified way, *an original thinker.*

thinking *adj.* using thought or rational judgement about things, *all thinking men.*

thinner *n.* a substance for thinning paint.

thinnish *adj.* rather thin.

third *adj.* next after second. —*n.* **1.** something that is third. **2.** third-class honours

in a university degree. **3.** third gear. **4.** one of three equal parts of a thing. —**thirdly** *adv.* □ **third degree,** (*Amer.*) long and severe questioning by police to get information or a confession. **third party,** another person etc. besides the two principal ones involved. **third-party insurance,** that in which the insurer gives protection to the insured against liability for damage or injury to any other person. **third person,** *see* person. **third-rate** *adj.* very inferior in quality. **Third World,** the developing countries of Asia, Africa, and Latin America, considered as not politically aligned with Communist or Western nations.

thirst *n.* **1.** the feeling caused by a desire or need to drink. **2.** a strong desire, *a thirst for adventure.* —*v.* to feel a thirst.

thirsty *adj.* (thirstier, thirstiest) **1.** feeling thirst. **2.** (of land) in need of water. **3.** (*informal*) causing thirst, *thirsty work.* —**thirstily** *adv.*

thirteen *adj. & n.* one more than twelve (13, XIII). **thirteenth** *adj. & n.*

thirty *adj. & n.* three times ten (30, XXX). **thirtieth** *adj. & n.* □ **thirties** *pl. n.* the numbers or years or degrees of temperature from 30 to 39.

this *adj. & pronoun* (*pl.* these) **1.** the person or thing close at hand or touched or just mentioned or about to be mentioned, the nearer or more obvious one of two. **2.** the present day or time, *she ought to have been here by this.* —**this** *adv.* (*informal*) to such an extent, *we're surprised he got this far.* □ **this and that,** various things. **this world,** *see* world (sense 5).

thistle *n.* a prickly plant with purple, white, or yellow flowers.

thistledown *n.* the very light fluff on thistle seeds by which they are carried by the wind.

thither *adv.* (*old use*) to or towards that place.

thole *n.* (also *thole-pin*) a peg set in the gunwale of a boat to serve as a rowlock.

thong *n.* a narrow strip of hide or leather used as a fastening or lash etc.

thorax (**thor-**aks) *n.* the part of the body between head or neck and the abdomen. **thoracic** (thor-**ass**-ik) *adj.*

thorium (**thor-**iŭm) *n.* a radioactive metallic substance.

thorn *n.* **1.** a sharp pointed projection on a plant. **2.** a thorny tree or shrub. □ **a thorn in one's flesh,** a constant source of annoyance.

thornless *adj.* having no thorns.

thornproof *adj.* unable to be penetrated by thorns.

thorny *adj.* (thornier, thorniest) **1.** having many thorns. **2.** like a thorn. **3.** troublesome, difficult to deal with, *a thorny problem.*

thorough *adj.* complete in every way, not merely superficial, doing things or done with great attention to detail. **thoroughly** *adv.*, **thoroughness** *n.*

thoroughbred *adj.* (especially of a horse) bred of pure or pedigree stock. —*n.* a thoroughbred animal.

thoroughfare *n.* a public way open at both ends. **no thoroughfare,** (as a notice) this road is private or is obstructed.

thoroughgoing *adj.* thorough.

those *see* that.

thou *pronoun,* (*old use*) you.

though *conj.* in spite of the fact that, even supposing, *it's true, though hard to believe.* —*adv.* (*informal*) however, *she's right, though.*

thought¹ *see* think.

thought² *n.* **1.** the process or power of thinking. **2.** a way of thinking that is characteristic of a particular class or nation or period, *in modern thought.* **3.** meditation, *deep in thought.* **4.** an idea or chain of reasoning produced by thinking. **5.** an intention, *we had no thought of giving offence.* **6.** consideration, *after serious thought.* □ **a thought,** a little, somewhat, *cut it a thought thinner.* **thought-provoking** *adj.* giving rise to serious thought. **thought-reader** *n.* a person who perceives people's thoughts without these being spoken.

thoughtful *adj.* **1.** thinking deeply, often absorbed in thought. **2.** (of a book or writer or remark etc.) showing signs of careful thought. **3.** showing thought for the needs of others, considerate. **thoughtfully** *adv.*, **thoughtfulness** *n.*

thoughtless *adj.* **1.** not alert to possible effects or consequences. **2.** inconsiderate. **thoughtlessly** *adv.*, **thoughtlessness** *n.*

thousand *adj.* & *n.* ten hundred (1000, M), *a few thousand* (¶ not *a few thousands*). **thousandth** *adj.* & *n.*

thousandfold *adj.* & *adv.* one thousand times as much or as many.

thrall (*pr.* thrawl) *n.* **in thrall,** in bondage.

thrash *v.* **1.** to beat with a stick or whip. **2.** to defeat thoroughly in a contest. **3.** to thresh. **4.** to hit with repeated blows like a flail, to make violent movements. □ **thrash out,** to discuss thoroughly.

thread *n.* **1.** a thin length of any substance. **2.** a length of spun cotton or wool etc. used in making cloth or in sewing or knitting. **3.** something compared to this; *lose the thread of an argument,* lose the chain of thought connecting it; *pick up the*

threads, proceed with something after an interruption. **4.** the spiral ridge of a screw. —**thread** *v.* **1.** to pass a thread through the eye of (a needle). **2.** to pass (a strip of film etc.) through or round something into the proper position for use. **3.** to put (beads) on a thread. **4.** to cut a thread on (a screw). —**threader** *n.* □ **thread one's way,** to make one's way through a crowd or streets etc.

threadbare *adj.* **1.** (of cloth) with the nap worn off and threads visible. **2.** (of a person) wearing threadbare or shabby clothes.

threadworm *n.* a small thread-like worm, especially one sometimes found in the rectum of children.

threat *n.* **1.** an expression of one's intention to punish or hurt or harm a person or thing. **2.** an indication of something undesirable, *there's a threat of rain.* **3.** a person or thing regarded as liable to bring danger or catastrophe, *machinery was seen as a threat to people's jobs.*

threaten *v.* **1.** to make a threat or threats against (a person etc.), to try to influence by threats. **2.** to be a warning of, *the clouds threatened rain.* **3.** to seem likely to be or do something undesirable, *the scheme threatens to be expensive.* **4.** to be a threat to, *the dangers that threaten us.*

three *adj.* & *n.* one more than two (3, III). **three-cornered** *adj.* triangular; (of a contest) between three parties. **three-dimensional** *adj.* having three dimensions (length, breadth, depth). **three halfpence,** 1½p (formerly 1½d). **three-handed** *adj.* (of a card-game) played by three people. **three-lane** *adj.* marked out for three lanes of traffic. **three-legged** *adj.* having three legs; *three-legged race,* a race between pairs of runners with the right leg of one tied to the left leg of the other. **three-line whip,** *see* whip (sense 4). **three-piece suite,** a matching suite consisting of a settee and two easy chairs. **three-ply** *adj.* made of three strands or layers. **three-point turn,** a method of turning a vehicle in a narrow space by driving forwards, backwards, and forwards. **three-quarter** *adj.* consisting of three quarters of a whole, (*n.*) a player with a position just behind the half-backs in Rugby football. **three-quarters** *n.* three parts out of four, (*adv.*) to this extent. **the three Rs,** reading, (w)riting, and (a)rithmetic, as the basis of elementary education. **three-wheeler** *n.* a vehicle with three wheels.

threefold *adj.* & *adv.* **1.** three times as much or as many. **2.** consisting of three parts.

threepence (threp-ĕns) *n.* the sum of three pence. **threepenny** *adj.*

threescore *n.* (*old use*) sixty; *threescore years and ten,* the age of 70 as a normal limit of life.

threesome *n.* three people together, a trio.

thresh *v.* 1. to beat out or separate (grain) from husks of corn. 2. to make violent movements, *threshing about.*

threshold *n.* 1. a piece of wood or stone forming the bottom of a doorway. 2. the entrance of a house etc. 3. the point of entry or beginning of something, *on the threshold of a new era.* 4. the lowest limit at which a stimulus becomes perceptible. 5. the highest limit at which pain etc. is bearable.

threw *see* throw.

thrice *adv.* (*old use*) three times.

thrift *n.* 1. economical management of money or resources. 2. the sea-pink.

thrifty *adj.* (thriftier, thriftiest) practising thrift, economical. **thriftily** *adv.*

thrill *n.* a nervous tremor caused by emotion or sensation, a wave of feeling or excitement. —*v.* to feel or cause to feel a thrill.

thriller *n.* an exciting story or play or film, especially one involving crime.

thrips *n.* (*pl.* thrips) an insect that is harmful to plants. ¶ Note that *a thrips* is the correct singular form, not *a thrip.*

thrive *v.* (throve, thrived, thriving) 1. to grow or develop well and vigorously. 2. to prosper, to be successful, *a thriving industry.*

throat *n.* 1. the front of the neck. 2. the passage in the neck through which food passes to the oesophagus and air passes to the lungs. 3. a narrow passage or funnel.

throaty *adj.* 1. uttered deep in the throat. 2. hoarse. **throatily** *adv.*

throb *v.* (throbbed, throbbing) 1. (of the heart or pulse etc.) to beat with more than usual force or rapidity. 2. to vibrate or sound with a persistent rhythm; *a throbbing wound,* giving pain in a steady rhythm. —*n.* throbbing.

throes *pl. n.* severe pangs of pain. **in the throes of,** (*informal*) struggling with the task of, *in the throes of spring-cleaning.*

thrombosis (throm-**boh**-sis) *n.* formation of a clot of blood in a blood-vessel or organ of the body.

throne *n.* 1. the special chair or seat used by a king, queen, or bishop etc. on ceremonial occasions. 2. sovereign power, *came to the throne.*

throng *n.* a crowded mass of people. —*v.*

1. to come or go or press in a throng. 2. to fill (a place) with a throng.

throstle *n.* a thrush.

throttle *n.* a valve controlling the flow of fuel or steam etc. to an engine, the lever or pedal operating this. —*v.* to strangle. □ **throttle back** *or* **down,** to obstruct the flow of fuel or steam and reduce the speed of (an engine).

through *prep.* 1. from end to end or side to side of, entering at one side and coming out at the other. 2. between or among, *scuffling through fallen leaves.* 3. from beginning to end of, so as to have finished or completed; *he is through his exam,* has passed it. 4. (*Amer.*) up to and including, *Friday through Tuesday.* 5. by reason of, by the agency or means or fault of, *lost it through carelessness.* —**through** *adv.* 1. through something. 2. with a connection made to a desired telephone etc., *you're through.* 3. finished, *wait till I'm through with these papers.* 4. having no further dealings, *I'm through with that bastard!* —*adj.* going through something, (of traffic) passing through a place without stopping, (of travel or passengers etc.) going to the end of a journey without a change of line or vehicle etc. □ **through and through,** through again and again; thoroughly, completely.

throughout *prep. & adv.* right through, from beginning to end of (a place or course or period).

throughput *n.* the amount of material processed.

throve *see* thrive.

throw *v.* (threw, thrown, throwing) 1. to send with some force through the air or in a certain direction; *throw a shadow,* cause there to be one. 2. to use as a missile, *throw stones.* 3. to hurl to the ground, *the horse threw its rider.* 4. (*informal*) to disconcert, *the question threw me.* 5. to put (clothes etc.) on or off hastily or casually. 6. to cause (dice) to fall to the table, to obtain (a number) by this. 7. to shape (rounded pottery) on a potter's wheel. 8. to turn or direct or move (a part of the body) quickly, *threw his head back.* 9. to cause to be in a certain state, *they were thrown out of work; thrown into confusion.* 10. to cause to extend, *threw a bridge across the river.* 11. to move (a switch or lever) so as to operate it. 12. to have (a fit or tantrum). —**throw** *n.* 1. the act of throwing. 2. the distance something is or may be thrown. —**thrower** *n.* □ **throw a party,** (*slang*) to hold a party. **throw away,** to part with as useless or unwanted; to fail to make use of, *throw away an opportunity.*

throw-away *adj.* to be thrown away after one use. **throw-back** *n.* an animal etc. showing characteristics of an ancestor that is earlier than its parents. **throw cold water on,** *see* cold. **throw in,** to include (a thing) with what one is selling, without additional charge; to put in (a remark) casually or as an addition. **throw-in** *n.* the throwing in of a ball at football after it has gone out of play over the touch-line. **throw in the towel,** = throw up the sponge (*see* below). **throw off,** to manage to get rid of or become free from, *throw off a cold* or *one's pursuers*; to compose easily as if without effort, *threw off a few lines of verse*. **throw oneself into,** to engage vigorously in. **throw oneself on,** to entrust oneself entirely to (a person's mercy etc.). **throw out,** to throw away; to put out suddenly or forcibly; to expel (a troublemaker etc.); to build as a projecting part or thing; to reject (a proposed plan etc.); to confuse or distract (a person). **throw over,** to desert or abandon. **throw the book at,** (*informal*) to make all possible charges against (a person). **throw together,** to bring (people) casually into association. **throw up,** to raise quickly or suddenly; to bring to notice, *his researches threw up some interesting facts*; to resign from, *threw up one's job*; to vomit. **throw up the sponge,** to admit defeat or failure and abandon a contest or effort. (¶ From the practice of admitting defeat in a boxing-match by throwing into the air the sponge used between rounds.)

thrum *v.* (thrummed, thrumming) to strum, to sound monotonously. —*n.* a thrumming sound.

thrush[1] any of several song-birds, especially one with a brownish back and speckled breast.

thrush[2] *n.* 1. an infection in which a minute fungus produces white patches in the mouth and throat, especially in children. 2. a venereal infection caused by the same fungus.

thrust *v.* (thrust, thrusting) 1. to push forcibly. 2. to make a forward stroke with a sword etc. 3. to put forcibly into a position or condition, to force the acceptance of, *some have greatness thrust upon them.* — **thrust** *n.* 1. a thrusting movement or force. 2. a hostile remark aimed at a person. —**thruster** *n.*

thud *n.* a low dull sound like that of a blow or something that does not resound. —*v.* (thudded, thudding) to make a thud, to fall with a thud.

thug *n.* a vicious or brutal ruffian. **thuggery** *n.*

thumb *n.* 1. the short thick finger set apart from the other four. 2. the part of a glove covering this. —*v.* to wear or soil or turn pages etc. with the thumbs; *a well-thumbed book*, one that shows signs of much use. ☐ **be all thumbs,** to be very clumsy at handling things. **thumb a lift,** to obtain a lift by signalling with one's thumb, to hitch-hike. **thumb-index** *n.* a set of notches in the edges of a book's leaves, marked with letters etc. to enable the user to open the book directly at a particular section. **thumb-nail sketch,** a brief description of something. **thumb-nut** *n.* a nut shaped for the thumb to turn. **thumb one's nose,** to cock a snook (*see* snook). **thumb-pot** *n.* the smallest size of flower-pot. **thumbs down,** a gesture of rejection. **thumb-stall** *n.* a sheath to cover an injured thumb. **thumbs up,** a gesture or exclamation of satisfaction. **under a person's thumb,** completely under his influence.

thumbscrew *n.* 1. a former instrument of torture for squeezing the thumb. 2. a screw with a flattened head for the thumb to turn.

thump *v.* to beat or strike or knock heavily (especially with the fist), to thud. —*n.* a heavy blow, a dull sound made by this.

thumping *adj.* (*informal*) large, *a thumping lie.*

thunder *n.* 1. the loud noise accompanying lightning. 2. any similar noise, *thunders of applause.* —**thunder** *v.* 1. to sound with thunder, *it thundered.* 2. to make a noise like thunder, to sound loudly, *the train thundered past.* 3. to utter loudly, to make a forceful attack in words, *reformers thundered against gambling.* —**thundery** *adj.,* **thunderer** *n.* ☐ **steal a person's thunder,** to forestall him by using his ideas or words etc. before he can do so himself. (¶ From the remark of a dramatist when the stage thunder intended for his play was taken and used for another.)

thunderbolt *n.* 1. an imaginary destructive missile thought of as sent to earth with a lightning-flash. 2. a very startling and formidable event or statement.

thunderclap *n.* a clap of thunder.

thunderous *adj.* like thunder.

thunderstorm *n.* a storm accompanied by thunder.

thunderstruck *adj.* amazed.

Thursday *n.* the day of the week following Wednesday.

thus *adv.* 1. in this way, like this, *hold the wheel thus.* 2. as a result of this, *he was the eldest son and thus heir to the title.* 3. to this extent, *thus far.*

thwack *v.* to strike with a heavy blow. — *n.* a heavy blow, the sound of this.

thwart *v.* to prevent (a person) from

doing what he intends, to prevent (a plan etc.) from being accomplished. —*n.* an oarsman's bench across a boat.

thy *adj.* (*old use*) of or belonging to thee.

thyme (*pr. as* time) *n.* any of several herbs with fragrant leaves.

thymol *n.* a substance obtained from oil of thyme, used as an antiseptic.

thymus *n.* a gland near the base of the neck (in man, it becomes much smaller at the end of childhood).

thyroid *n.* the **thyroid gland**, a large ductless gland at the front of the neck, secreting a hormone which regulates the body's growth and development.

thyself *pronoun* corresponding to *thee* and *thou*, used in the same ways as himself.

tiara (ti-ar-ă) *n.* **1.** a woman's ornamental crescent-shaped head-dress, worn on ceremonial occasions. **2.** the pope's diadem, pointed at the top and surrounded by three crowns.

Tibet (tib-et) a former country north of India, now part of China. **Tibetan** *adj. & n.*

tibia *n.* the shin-bone.

tic *n.* an involuntary spasmodic twitching of the muscles, especially of the face.

tick¹ *n.* **1.** a regularly repeated clicking sound, especially that of a watch or clock. **2.** (*informal*) a moment. **3.** a mark (often √) placed against an item in a list etc. to show that it has been checked or is correct. —**tick** *v.* **1.** (of a clock etc.) to make a series of ticks. **2.** to put a tick beside (an item). □ **tick off**, to mark with a tick; (*slang*) to reprimand. **tick over**, (of an engine) to idle; (of activities) to continue in a routine way. **tick-tock** *n.* the ticking of a large clock. **what makes a person tick**, what makes him behave as he does.

tick² *n.* **1.** any of several blood-sucking mites or parasitic insects. **2.** (*slang*) an unpleasant or despised person.

tick³ *n.* the case of a mattress or pillow or bolster, holding the filling.

tick⁴ *n.* (*informal*) credit, *buying on tick.*

ticker *n.* (*informal*) **1.** a watch. **2.** a teleprinter. **3.** the heart. □ **ticker-tape** *n.* (*Amer.*) paper tape from a teleprinter etc., this or similar material thrown in long strips from windows to greet a celebrity.

ticket *n.* **1.** a written or printed piece of card or paper that entitles the holder to a certain right (e.g. to travel by train or bus etc. or to a seat in a cinema) or serves as a receipt. **2.** a certificate of qualification as a ship's master or pilot etc. **3.** a label attached to a thing and giving its price or other particulars. **4.** an official notification of a traffic offence, *parking ticket.* **5.** (*Amer.*) a list of the candidates put for-

ward by one party in an election. **6.** *the ticket*, (*slang*) the correct or desirable thing. —*v.* (ticketed, ticketing) to put a ticket on (an article for sale etc.).

ticking *n.* strong fabric for making ticks for mattresses or pillows etc.

tickle *v.* **1.** to touch or stroke lightly so as to cause a slight tingling sensation, usually with involuntary movement and laughter. **2.** to feel this sensation, *my foot tickles.* **3.** to amuse, to please (a person's vanity or sense of humour etc.). —*n.* the act or sensation of tickling. □ **tickled pink** *or* **to death**, (*informal*) extremely amused or pleased.

ticklish *adj.* **1.** sensitive to tickling. **2.** (of a problem) requiring careful handling. **ticklishness** *n.*

tick-tack *n.* a kind of semaphore signalling used by bookmakers on a racecourse.

tidal *adj.* of or affected by a tide or tides. **tidal wave**, a great ocean wave, e.g. one caused by an earthquake; a great wave of enthusiasm or indignation etc.

tidbit *n.* (*Amer.*) a titbit.

tiddler *n.* (*informal*) **1.** a stickleback or other small fish that children try to catch. **2.** an unusually small thing.

tiddly *adj.* (*slang*) slightly drunk.

tiddly-wink *n.* one of the small counters flicked into a cup in the game of **tiddly-winks**.

tide *n.* **1.** the regular rise and fall in the level of the sea, caused by the attraction of the moon and the sun. **2.** water as moved by this. **3.** a trend of opinion or fortune or events, *the rising tide of discontent.* **4.** (*old use*) a season, *yule-tide.* —*v.* to float with the tide. □ **tide a person over**, to help him through a difficult period by providing what he needs. **tide-mark** *n.* a mark made by the tide at high water; (*informal*) a line between washed and unwashed parts of a person's body, or on a bath showing the level of the water that has been used. **tide-table** *n.* a list of the times of high tide at a place.

tideless *adj.* without tides.

tideway *n.* the channel where a tide runs, the tidal part of a river.

tidings *pl. n.* news.

tidy *adj.* (tidier, tidiest) **1.** neat and orderly in arrangement or in one's ways. **2.** (*informal*) fairly large, considerable, *left a tidy fortune when he died.* —*n.* a receptacle for odds and ends. —*v.* (tidied, tidying) to make tidy. — **tidily** *adv.*, **tidiness** *n.*

tie *v.* (tied, tying) **1.** to attach or fasten or bind with a cord or something similar. **2.** to arrange (string or ribbon or a necktie etc.) to form a knot or bow, to form (a knot or bow) in this way. **3.** to unite (notes in music) with a tie. **4.** to make the same score as another competitor, *they tied for second place.* **6.** to restrict or limit to certain conditions or to an occupation or place etc. —**tie** *n.* **1.** a cord etc. used for fastening or by which something is tied. **2.** a necktie. **3.** something that unites things or people, a bond. **4.** something that restricts a person's freedom of action. **5.** a curved line (in a musical score) over two notes of the same pitch, indicating that the second is not sounded separately. **6.** equality of score between two or more competitors. **7.** a sports match between two of a set of competing teams or players. □ **fit to be tied,** (*slang*) very angry. **tie-beam** *n.* a horizontal beam connecting rafters. **tie-breaker** *n.* a means of deciding the winner when competitors have tied. **tie-clip** *n.* an ornamental clip for holding a necktie in place. **tie-dyeing** *n.* a method of producing dyed patterns by tying parts of a fabric so that they are protected from the dye. **tie in,** to link or (of information or facts) to agree or be connected with something else. **tie-pin** *n.* an ornamental pin for holding a necktie in place. **tie up,** to fasten with a cord etc.; to invest or reserve (capital etc.) so that it is not readily available for use; to make restrictive conditions about (a bequest etc.); to occupy (a person) so that he has no time for other things. **tie-up** *n.* a connection, a link.

tied *see* tie. —*adj.* **1.** (of a public house) bound to supply only a particular brewer's beer. **2.** (of a house) for occupation only by a person who works for its owner.

tier (*pr.* teer) *n.* any of a series of rows or ranks or units of a structure placed one above the other. **tiered** *adj.* arranged in tiers.

tiff *n.* a petty quarrel.

tiffin *n.* the midday meal in India etc.

tiger *n.* a large Asian animal of the cat family, with yellowish and black stripes. **tiger-cat** *n.* any of several animals resembling the tiger (e.g. the ocelot); the largest of the Australian marsupial cats. **tiger-lily** *n.* a tall garden lily with dark-spotted orange flowers. **tiger-moth** *n.* a moth with wings that are streaked like a tiger's skin.

tight *adj.* **1.** fixed or fastened or drawn together firmly and hard to move or undo. **2.** fitting closely, made so that a specified thing cannot penetrate, *a tight joint*; *watertight*; *tight controls,* strictly imposed. **3.** with things or people arranged closely together, *a tight little group*; *a tight schedule,* leaving no time to spare. **4.** tense,

stretched so as to leave no slack. **5.** (*informal*) drunk. **6.** (of money or materials) not easily obtainable, (of the money-market) in which money and credit are severely restricted. **7.** stingy, *tight with his money.* —*adv.* tightly, *hold tight.* —**tightly** *adv.*, **tightness** *n.* □ **in a tight corner** or **spot,** in a difficult situation. **tight-fisted** *adj.* stingy. **tight-lipped** *adj.* keeping the lips firmly together compressed to restrain one's emotion or comments; grim-looking.

tighten *v.* to make or become tighter. **tighten one's belt,** to content oneself with less food etc. when supplies are scarce.

tightrope *n.* a rope stretched tightly high above the ground, on which acrobats perform.

tights *pl. n.* **1.** a woman's garment worn in place of stockings, covering feet, legs, and lower part of the body. **2.** a close-fitting garment covering the legs and body, worn by acrobats, dancers, etc.

tightwad *n.* (*slang*) a stingy person.

tigress *n.* a female tiger.

tile *n.* **1.** a thin slab of baked clay or other material used in rows for covering roofs or walls or floors; *carpet tiles,* carpet made in small squares for laying in rows. **2.** one of the small flat pieces used in mah-jong. —*v.* to cover with tiles. □ **on the tiles,** (*slang*) on a drunken or immoral spree.

tiling *n.* a surface made of tiles.

till[1] *v.* to prepare and use (land) for growing crops. **tillage** *n.*

till[2] *prep. & conj.* up to (a specified time), up to the time when, *wait till evening*; *ring till someone answers.*

till[3] *n.* **1.** a cash-register. **2.** a receptacle for money behind the counter in a shop or bank etc.

tiller *n.* a horizontal bar by which the rudder of a small boat is turned in steering.

tilt *v.* **1.** to move or cause to move into a sloping position. **2.** to run or thrust with a lance in jousting. —*n.* tilting, a sloping position. □ **at full tilt,** at full speed, with full force. **tilt at windmills,** to battle with enemies who are only imaginary. (¶ From the story of Don Quixote who attacked windmills, thinking they were giants.)

timber *n.* **1.** wood prepared for use in building or carpentry. **2.** trees suitable for this. **3.** a piece of wood or a wooden beam used in constructing a house or ship. □ **timber-line** *n.* the level of land above which no trees grow. **timber-wolf** *n.* a large grey wolf of North America.

timbered *adj.* **1.** (of a building) constructed of timber or with a timber framework. **2.** (of land) wooded.

timbre (*pr.* tambr) *n.* the characteristic quality of the sound produced by a particular voice or instrument.

Timbuctoo *n.* a very remote place. ¶ From *Timbuktu* in West Africa.

time *n.* **1.** all the years of the past, present, and future. **2.** the passing of these taken as a whole, *time will show who is right.* **3.** a portion of time associated with certain events or conditions or experiences, *in Tudor times*; *in times of hardship*; *have a good time,* enjoy oneself. **4.** a portion of time between two points, the point or period allotted or available or suitable for something, *the time it takes to do this*; *now is the time to buy*; *lunch time.* **5.** the point of time when something must occur or end. **6.** an occasion or instance, *the first time we saw him*; *I told you three times*; *four times three,* three taken four times. **7.** a point of time stated in hours and minutes of the day, *the time is exactly two o'clock.* **8.** any of the standard systems by which time is reckoned, *Greenwich mean time.* **9.** measured time spent in work etc., *on short time*; *paid time and a half,* paid at that much more than the usual rate. **10.** tempo in music, rhythm depending on the number and accentuation of beats in a bar. —**time** *v.* **1.** to choose the time or moment for, to arrange the time of. **2.** to measure the time taken by (a race or runner or process etc.). □ **at the same time,** in spite of this, however. **at times,** sometimes. **do time,** (*informal*) to serve a prison sentence. **for the time being,** until some other arrangement is made. **from time to time,** at intervals. **half the time,** (*informal*) as often as not. **have a time,** to have a very bad (or very good) time. **have no time for,** to be unable or unwilling to spend time on, to despise. **in no time,** in an instant, very rapidly. **in one's time,** at a previous period in one's life. **in one's own time,** outside working hours; when one chooses to do something. **in time,** not late; eventually, sooner or later. **on time,** punctually. **time after time,** on many occasions, in many instances. **time and again** *or* **time and time again,** time after time. **time-and-motion** *adj.* concerned with measuring the efficiency of industrial or other operations. **time bomb,** a bomb that can be set to explode after a certain interval. **time-clock** *n.* a clock with a device for recording workmen's hours of work. **time-consuming** *adj.* occupying much time. **time exposure,** a photographic exposure in which the shutter is

left open for more than a second or two and not operated at an automatically-controlled speed. **time-honoured** *adj.* honoured because of long tradition or custom. **time-lag** *n.* an interval of time between two connected events. **time-limit** *n.* a limit of time within which something must be done. **the time of one's life,** a period of exceptional enjoyment. **times** *pl. n.* contemporary circumstances and customs, *times are bad; a sign of the times.* **time-sharing** *n.* operation of a computer by two or more users simultaneously. **time-sheet** *n.* a record of hours worked. **time-signal** *n.* an audible indication of the exact time of day. **time-switch** *n.* a switch that can be set to act automatically at a certain time. **time zone,** a region (between two parallels of longitude) where a common standard time is used.

timekeeper *n.* **1.** a person who times something, one who records workmen's hours of work. **2.** a person in respect of punctuality, a watch or clock in respect of its accuracy of operation, *a good timekeeper.*

timeless *adj.* **1.** not to be thought of as having duration. **2.** not affected by the passage of time.

timely *adj.* occuring at just the right time, *a timely warning.* **timeliness** *n.*

timepiece *n.* a clock or watch.

timer *n.* a person who times something, a timing device.

timetable *n.* a list showing the time at which certain events will take place, e.g. the series of lessons in school or the arrival and departure of public transport vehicles.

timid *adj.* easily alarmed, not bold, shy. **timidly** *adv.,* **timidity** (tim-**id**-iti) *n.*

timing *n.* the way something is timed.

timorous (**tim**-er-ŭs) *adj.* timid. **timorously** *adv.,* **timorousness** *n.*

timothy grass a kind of grass grown as fodder for cattle.

timpani (**timp**-ăn-ee) *pl. n.* kettledrums.

timpanist *n.* a person who plays the kettledrums in an orchestra.

tin *n.* **1.** a silvery-white metal. **2.** iron or steel sheets coated with tin. **3.** a box or other container made of tin plate, one in which food is sealed for preservation. — **tin** *v.* (tinned, tinning) **1.** to coat with tin. **2.** to seal in a tin for preservation. □ **tin can,** a tin for preserving food. **tin foil,** a thin sheet of tin or aluminium or tin alloy, used for wrapping and packing things. **tin god,** a person who is unjustifiably given great veneration. **tin hat,** (*Army slang*) a soldier's steel helmet. **tin-opener** *n.* a tool

for opening tins. **tin-pan alley,** the world
of the composers and publishers etc. of
popular music. **tin plate,** sheet iron or
sheet steel coated thinly with tin. **tin-plated** *adj.* coated with tin. **tin-tack** *n.* a
tin-coated iron tack.

tincture *n.* **1.** a solution consisting of a
medicinal substance dissolved in alcohol,
tincture of quinine. **2.** a slight tinge or trace
of some element or quality. —*v.* to tinge.

tinder *n.* any dry substance that catches
fire easily. **tinder-box** *n.* a metal box formerly used in kindling a fire, containing
dry material that caught fire from a spark
produced by flint and steel.

tine *n.* any of the points or prongs of a
fork or harrow or antler.

ting *n.* a sharp ringing sound. —*v.* to make
a ting.

tinge (*pr.* tinj) *v.* **1.** to colour slightly,
tinged with pink. **2.** to give a slight trace of
some element or quality to, *their admiration was tinged with envy.* —*n.* a slight
colouring or trace.

tingle *v.* to have a slight pricking or stinging sensation. —*n.* this sensation.

tinker *n.* **1.** a travelling mender of pots
and pans. **2.** a spell of tinkering, *have a
tinker at it.* —*v.* to work at something casually, trying to repair or improve it.

tinkle *n.* a series of short light ringing
sounds. —*v.* to make or cause to make a
tinkle.

tinny *adj.* **1.** of or like tin, (of metal
objects) not looking strong or solid. **2.**
having a metallic taste or a thin metallic
sound.

tinpot *adj.* (*contemptuous*) worthless.

tinsel *n.* a glittering metallic substance
used in strips or threads to give an inexpensive sparkling effect. **tinselled** *adj.*

tint *n.* **1.** a variety of a particular colour.
2. a slight trace of a different colour, *red
with a bluish tint.* —*v.* to apply or give a
tint to, to colour slightly.

tiny *adj.* (tinier, tiniest) very small.

tip[1] *n.* **1.** the very end of a thing, especially of something small or tapering. **2.** a
small part or piece fitted to the end of
something, *cigarettes with filter-tips.* —*v.*
(tipped, tipping) to provide with a tip,
filter-tipped. □ **on the tip of one's
tongue,** just about to be spoken or remembered. **tip of the iceberg,** *see* iceberg.

tip[2] *v.* (tipped, tipping) **1.** to tilt or topple,
to cause to do this. **2.** to discharge (contents of a truck or jug etc.) by doing this.
3. to strike or touch lightly. **4.** to name as a
likely winner of a contest etc. **5.** to make a
small present of money to (a person),

especially in acknowledgement of his services. —**tip** *n.* **1.** a small money present.
2. private or special information (e.g.
about horse-races or the stock-market)
likely to profit the receiver if he acts upon
it. **3.** a small but useful piece of advice on
how to do something. **4.** a slight tilt or push.
5. a place where rubbish etc. is tipped. —
tipper *n.* □ **tip-cart, tip-lorry** *n.* a
cart or lorry with the body pivoted for tipping out its contents. **tip off,** to give an
advance warning or hint or inside information to (a person). **tip-off** *n.* advance or
inside information etc. **tip a person the
wink,** to give him a private signal or information. **tip the balance** *or* **scale,** to be
just enough to cause one scale-pan to go
lower than the other; to be the deciding
factor for or against something. **tip-up** *adj.*
(of seats) able to be tipped up so as
to allow people to pass easily, e.g. in a
theatre.

tippet *n.* a small cape or collar of fur etc.
with ends hanging down in front.

tipple *v.* to drink (wine or spirits etc.), to
be in the habit of drinking. —*n.* (*informal*)
alcoholic or other drink.

tipstaff *n.* **1.** a sheriff's officer. **2.** the
metal-tipped staff that is his badge of office.

tipster *n.* a person who gives tips about
horse-races etc.

tiptoe *v.* (tiptoed, tiptoeing) to walk very
quietly or carefully, with heels not touching the ground. **on tiptoe,** walking or
standing in this way.

tiptop *adj.* (*informal*) excellent, very best,
tiptop quality.

tipsy *adj.* slightly drunk, showing or
caused by slight intoxication, *a tipsy lurch.*
tipsily *adv.,* **tipsiness** *n.* □ **tipsy-cake**
n. sponge-cake soaked in wine or spirits
and served with custard.

TIR *abbrev.* Transport International Routier. (¶ French, = international road transport.)

tirade (ty-**rayd**) *n.* a long angry or violent
piece of criticism or denunciation.

Tirana (ti-**rah**-nah) the capital of Albania.

tire[1] *v.* to make or become tired.

tire[2] *n.* (*Amer.*) a tyre.

tired *adj.* feeling that one would like to
sleep or rest. **tired of,** having had enough
of (a thing or activity) and feeling impatient or bored.

tireless *adj.* not tiring easily, having inexhaustible energy. **tirelessly** *adv.*

tiresome *adj.* annoying.

tiro (ty-roh) *n.* (*pl.* tiros) a beginner, a
novice.

'tis (*old use*) = it is.

tissue (**tiss**-yoo *or* **tish**-oo) *n.* **1.** the substance forming an animal or plant body, a particular kind of this, *muscular tissue.* **2.** tissue-paper. **3.** a disposable piece of soft absorbent paper used as a handkerchief etc. **4.** fine gauzy fabric. **5.** something thought of as an interwoven series, *a tissue of lies.* □ **tissue-paper** *n.* very thin soft paper used for wrapping and packing things.

tit ¹ *n.* any of several small birds, often with a dark top to the head.

tit ² *n.* **tit for tat**, an equivalent given in retaliation for an injury etc.

tit ³ *n.* (*vulgar*) **1.** a nipple or teat. **2.** either of a woman's breasts.

Titan (ty-tăn) *n.* a person of great size or strength or importance. ¶ The *Titans* were a race of giants in Greek mythology.

titanic (ty-tan-ik) *adj.* gigantic, immense.

titbit *n.* a choice bit of something, e.g. of food or gossip or information.

tithe (*pr.* tyth) *n.* one tenth of the annual produce of agriculture etc., formerly paid as tax to support clergy and church. **tithe-barn** *n.* a barn built to store tithes.

Titian (tish-ăn) *adj.* bright golden auburn as a colour of hair. ¶ Named after an Italian painter.

titillate (tit-i-layt) *v.* to excite or stimulate pleasantly. **titillation** *n.*

titivate (tit-i-vayt) *v.* (*informal*) to smarten up, to put the finishing touches to. **titivation** *n.*

title *n.* **1.** the name of a book or poem or picture etc. **2.** a word used to show a person's rank or office (e.g. *king, mayor, captain*) or used in speaking of or to him or her (e.g. *Lord, Mrs, Doctor*). **3.** the legal right to ownership of property, a document conferring this. **4.** a championship in sport, *the world heavyweight title.* —*v.* to give a title to (a book etc.). □ **credit titles,** see credit. **title-deed** *n.* a legal document proving a person's title to a property. **title-page** *n.* a page at the beginning of a book giving the title, author's name, and other particulars. **title-role** *n.* the part in a play etc. from which the title is taken, e.g. the part of Hamlet in the play of that name.

titled *adj.* having a title of nobility, *titled ladies.*

titter *n.* a high-pitched giggle. —*v.* to give a titter.

tittle-tattle *v.* to tattle. —*n.* tattle.

titular (tit-yoo-ler) *adj.* **1.** of or belonging to a title. **2.** having the title of ruler etc. ~ut without real authority, *the titular head* ~ *the State.*

~ *n.* (*slang*) a state of nervous agitation ~nfusion, *in a tizzy.*

~**tion** *n.* a junction where one road

or pipe etc. meets another but does not cross it, forming the shape of a T.

TNT *abbrev.* trinitrotoluene, a powerful explosive.

to *prep.* **1.** in the direction of, so as to approach or reach or be in (a place or position or state etc.), *walked to the station; rose to power; was sent to prison; back to back.* **2.** as far as, not falling short of, *patriotic to the core; from noon to 2 o'clock; goods to the value of £10; cooked to perfection.* **3.** as compared with, in respect of, *won by 3 goals to 2; made to measure; his remarks were not to the point.* **4.** for (a person or thing) to hold or possess or be affected etc. by, *give it to me; spoke to her; kind to animals; accustomed to it; drank a toast to the Queen.* —**to** (with a verb) **1.** forming an infinitive, or expressing purpose or consequence etc., *he wants to go; does it to annoy.* **2.** used alone when the verb is understood, *meant to call but forgot to.* —**to** *adv.* **1.** to or in the normal or required position, to a closed or almost closed position, *push the door to.* **2.** into a state of consciousness, *when she came to.* **3.** into a state of activity, *set to.* □ **to and fro,** backwards and forwards. **toing and froing,** going to and fro.

toad *n.* **1.** a frog-like animal living chiefly on land. **2.** a disliked person. □ **toad in the hole,** sausages baked in batter.

toadflax *n.* a wild plant with spurred yellow or purple flowers.

toadstool *n.* a fungus (especially a poisonous one) with a round top and a slender stalk.

toady *n.* a person who flatters and behaves obsequiously to another in the hope of gain or advantage for himself. —*v.* (toadied, toadying) to behave as a toady.

toast *n.* **1.** a slice of toasted bread. **2.** the person or thing in whose honour a company is requested to drink, the call to drink or an instance of drinking in this way. —**toast** *v.* **1.** to brown the surface of (bread etc.) by placing before a fire or other source of heat. **2.** to warm (one's feet etc.) in this way. **3.** to honour or pledge good wishes to by drinking. □ **have a person on toast,** (*slang*) to have him at one's mercy. **toast-master** *n.* a person who announces the toasts at a public dinner etc. **toast-rack** *n.* a rack for holding slices of toast at the table.

toaster *n.* an electrical device for toasting bread.

toasting-fork *n.* a long-handled fork for holding a slice of bread etc. before a fire to toast it.

tobacco *n.* **1.** a plant grown for its leaves which are used for smoking or for making snuff. **2.** its leaves, especially as prepared for smoking.

tobacconist *n.* a shopkeeper who sells cigarettes, cigars, and pipe-tobacco.

Tobago (tŏ-**bay**-goh) an island in the West Indies (*see* Trinidad). **Tobagan** *adj.* & *n.*

-to-be soon to become, *the bride-to-be.*

toboggan *n.* a long light narrow sledge curved upwards at the front, used for sliding downhill. **tobogganing** *n.* the sport of riding on a toboggan.

toby jug a mug or jug in the form of an old man with a three-cornered hat.

toccata (tŏ-**kah**-tă) *n.* a musical composition for a piano or organ etc.

tocsin *n.* **1.** a bell rung as an alarm-signal. **2.** a signal of disaster.

tod *n.* **on one's tod**, (*slang*) on one's own.

today *n.* this present day or age. —*adv.* **1.** on this present day. **2.** at the present time.

toddle *v.* **1.** (of a young child) to walk with short unsteady steps. **2.** (*informal*) to walk.

toddler *n.* a child who has only recently learnt to walk.

toddy *n.* a sweetened drink of spirits and hot water.

to-do *n.* a fuss or commotion.

toe *n.* **1.** one of the divisions (five in man) of the front part of the foot. **2.** the part of a shoe or stocking that covers the toes. **3.** the lower end or tip of a tool etc. — **toe** *v.* (toed, toeing) **1.** to touch or reach with the toes. **2.** to put a toe on or repair the toe of (a shoe or stocking). □ **be on one's toes**, to be alert or eager. **toe-cap** *n.* the outer covering of the toe of a boot or shoe. **toe-hold** *n.* a slight foothold. **toe in**, (of vehicle wheels) to be set so that the front part points slightly inwards; **toe out**, to be set so that the back part points slightly inwards. **toe the line**, to conform (especially under compulsion) to the requirements of one's group or party.

toff *n.* (*slang*) a distinguished or well-dressed person.

toffee *n.* **1.** a kind of sweet made with heated butter and sugar. **2.** a small piece of this. □ **can't do it for toffee**, (*slang*) is very bad at doing it. **toffee-apple** *n.* a toffee-coated apple on a stick. **toffee-nosed** *adj.* (*slang*) snobbish, pretentious.

tog [1] *v.* (togged, togging) (*slang*) **tog up** *or* **out**, to dress. □ **togs** *pl. n.* (*slang*) clothes.

tog [2] *n.* a unit used in measuring the power of clothing or bedding to keep the user warm by preventing body-heat etc. from escaping.

toga (**toh**-gă) *n.* a loose flowing outer garment worn by men in ancient Rome.

together *adv.* **1.** in or into company or conjunction, towards each other, so as to unite. **2.** one with another, *compare them together.* **3.** simultaneously, *both together exclaimed.* **4.** in an unbroken succession, *he is away for weeks together.* □ **together with**, as well as, and also.

toggle *n.* a fastening device consisting of a short piece of wood or metal etc. secured by its centre and passed through a loop or hole etc. **toggle-switch** *n.* a switch operated by a projecting lever.

Togo (**toh**-goh) a country in West Africa. **Togolese** *adj.* & *n.* (*pl.* Togolese)

toil *v.* **1.** to work long or laboriously. **2.** to move laboriously, *we toiled up the hill.* — *n.* hard or laborious work. —**toiler** *n.* □ **toil-worn** *adj.* worn by toil, showing marks of this.

toilet *n.* **1.** the process of dressing and grooming oneself. **2.** a lavatory, the room containing this. □ **toilet-paper** *n.* paper for use in a lavatory. **toilet-roll** *n.* a roll of toilet-paper. **toilet soap**, soap for washing oneself. **toilet-training** *n.* the process of training a child to control its urination and defecation and use a lavatory. **toilet water**, scented water for use on the skin.

toiletries *pl. n.* (in shops) articles or preparations used in washing and grooming oneself.

toilsome *adj.* involving toil.

token *n.* **1.** a sign or symbol or evidence of something, *a token of our esteem.* **2.** a keepsake or memorial of friendship etc. **3.** a voucher or coupon that can be exchanged for goods, *book token.* **4.** a device like a coin bought for use with machines etc. or for making certain payments, *milk tokens.* —*adj.* serving as a token or pledge but often on a small scale, *token resistance.* □ **by the same token**, similarly, moreover.

Tokyo (**toh**-ki-oh) the capital of Japan.

tolbooth (**tohl**-booth) *n.* (*Scottish, old use*) a town hall, a town prison.

told *see* tell. □ **all told**, counting everything or everyone, *we were 16 all told.*

tolerable *adj.* **1.** able to be tolerated, endurable. **2.** fairly good, passable. **tolerably** *adv.*

tolerance *n.* **1.** willingness or ability to tolerate a person or thing. **2.** the permitted variation in the measurement or weight etc. of an object.

tolerant *adj.* having or showing tolerance. **tolerantly** *adv.*

tolerate *v.* **1.** to permit without protest or interference. **2.** to bear (pain etc.), to be able to take (a medicine) or undergo (radiation etc.) without harm. **toleration** *n.*

toll¹ (*rhymes with* hole) *n.* **1.** a tax or duty paid for the use of a public road or harbour etc. or for service rendered. **2.** the loss or damage caused by a disaster or incurred in achieving something; *the death toll in the earthquake*, the number of deaths it caused. □ **take its toll**, to be accompanied by loss or injury etc. **toll-bridge** *n.* a bridge at which a toll is charged. **toll-gate** *n.* a gate across a road to prevent anyone passing until the toll has been paid. **toll-house** *n.* a house occupied by the collector of tolls on a road etc.

toll² (*rhymes with* hole) *v.* **1.** to ring (a bell) with slow strokes, especially for a death or funeral. **2.** (of a bell) to sound in this way, to indicate by tolling. —*n.* the stroke of a tolling bell.

Tom *n.* **Tom, Dick, and Harry,** (*usually contemptuous*) ordinary people, people taken at random.

tom *n.* a male animal, a tom-cat. **tom-cat** *n.* a male cat.

tomahawk *n.* **1.** a light axe used as a tool or weapon by North American Indians. **2.** (*Austral.*) a hatchet.

tomato *n.* (*pl.* tomatoes) a plant bearing a glossy red or yellow fruit eaten as a vegetable, the fruit itself.

tomb (*pr.* toom) *n.* **1.** a grave or other place of burial. **2.** a vault or stone monument in which one or more people are buried.

tomboy *n.* a girl who enjoys rough noisy recreations.

tombola (tom-**boh**-lă) *n.* a kind of lottery with prizes, resembling bingo.

tombstone *n.* a memorial stone set up over a grave.

tome (*rhymes with* home) *n.* a book or volume, especially a large heavy one.

tomfool *adj.* extremely foolish. —*n.* an extremely foolish person. —**tomfoolery** *n.*

tommy-gun *n.* a sub-machine-gun.

tommy-rot *n.* (*slang*) nonsense, an absurd statement or argument.

tomorrow *n.* **1.** the day after today. **2.** the near future. —*adv.* on the day after today, at some future date.

tom-tom *n.* **1.** an African or Asian drum beaten with the hands. **2.** a deep-toned drum used in jazz bands.

ton (*pr.* tun) *n.* **1.** a measure of weight, either 2240 lb (*long ton*) or 2000 lb (*short ton*). **2.** a measure of capacity for various materials, 40 cubic feet of timber. **3.** a unit of volume in shipping. **4.** (*informal*) a large amount, *tons of money*. **5.** (*slang*) a

speed of 100 m.p.h. □ **metric ton**, a tonne.

tonal (**toh**-năl) *adj.* **1.** of a tone or tones. **2.** of tonality. **tonally** *adv.*

tonality (tŏ-**nal**-iti) *n.* **1.** the character of a melody, depending on the scale or key in which it is composed. **2.** the colour scheme of a picture.

tone *n.* **1.** a musical or vocal sound, especially with reference to its pitch and quality and strength. **2.** the manner of expression in speaking or writing, *an apologetic tone.* **3.** any one of the five intervals between one note and the next which, together with two semitones, make up an octave. **4.** proper firmness of the organs and tissues of the body, *muscle tone.* **5.** a tint or shade of a colour, the general effect of colour or of light and shade in a picture. **6.** the general spirit or character prevailing, *set the tone with a dignified speech.* — **tone** *v.* **1.** to give a particular tone of sound or colour to. **2.** to harmonize in colour, *the curtains tone* or *tone in with the wallpaper.* **3.** to give proper firmness to (muscles or organs or skin etc.). —**toner** *n.* □ **tone-deaf** *adj.* unable to perceive accurately differences of musical pitch. **tone down**, to make or become softer in tone of sound or colour; to make (a statement) less strong or harsh. **tone-poem** *n.* an orchestral composition illustrating a poetic idea. **tone up**, to make or become brighter or more vigorous or intense.

toneless *adj.* without positive tone, not expressive. **tonelessly** *adv.*

Tonga a country consisting of a group of islands in the Pacific, also called the Friendly Islands. **Tongan** *adj.* & *n.*

tongs *pl. n.* an instrument with two arms joined at one end, used for grasping and holding things.

tongue *n.* **1.** the fleshy muscular organ in the mouth, used in tasting, licking, swallowing, and (in man) speaking. **2.** the tongue of an ox etc. as food. **3.** the ability to speak or manner of speaking, *a persuasive tongue*; *have lost one's tongue*, be too bashful or surprised to speak. **4.** a language, *his native tongue is German.* **5.** a projecting strip or flap. **6.** a tapering jet of flame. —*v.* to produce staccato or other effects in a wind instrument by use of the tongue. □ **tongue-lashing** *n.* a severe rebuke. **tongue-tied** *adj.* silent because of shyness or embarrassment; unable to speak normally because the ligament connecting the tongue to the base of the mouth is abnormally short. **tongue-twister** *n.* a sequence of words that is difficult to pronounce quickly and correctly, e.g. *she sells sea shells.* **with one's tongue hanging out,**

thirsty; eagerly expectant. **with one's tongue in one's cheek**, speaking with sly sarcasm.

tongued *adj*. **1**. having a tongue. **2**. having a specified manner of speaking, *sharp-tongued*.

tonic *n*. **1**. a medicine with an invigorating effect, taken after illness or weakness. **2**. anything that restores people's energy or good spirits. **3**. a keynote in music. **4**. tonic water. —*adj*. having the effect of a tonic, toning up the muscles etc. □ **tonic water**, mineral water, especially if slightly flavoured with quinine.

tonight *n*. **1**. the present evening or night. **2**. the evening or night of today. —*adv*. on the present evening or night or that of today.

tonnage (**tun**-ij) *n*. **1**. the carrying-capacity of a ship or ships, expressed in tons. **2**. the charge per ton for carrying cargo or freight.

tonne (*pr.* tun *or* **tun**-i) *n*. a metric ton, 1000 kg (35 lbs less than a long ton).

tonsil *n*. either of two small organs at the sides of the throat near the root of the tongue.

tonsillectomy *n*. surgical removal of tonsils.

tonsillitis *n*. inflammation of the tonsils.

tonsorial (ton-**sor**-iăl) *adj* (*humorous*) of a barber or his work.

tonsure (**ton**-sher) *n*. **1**. shaving the top or all of the head of a person entering certain priesthoods or monastic orders. **2**. the part of the head shaven in this way. **tonsured** *adj*.

too *adv*. **1**. to a greater extent than is desirable. **2**. (*informal*) very, *he's not too well today*. **3**. also, *take the others too*. □ **too bad**, (*informal*) regrettable, a pity. **too much for**, (*informal*) easily able to defeat (an opponent etc.); more than can be endured by (a person).

took *see* take.

tool *n*. **1**. a thing (usually something held in the hand) for working upon something. **2**. a simple machine, e.g. a lathe. **3**. anything used in an occupation or pursuit, *a dictionary is a useful tool*. **4**. a person used as a mere instrument by another. —**tool** *v*. **1**. to shape or ornament by using a tool. **2**. to provide oneself or equip (a factory etc.) with necessary tools, *tool up*. **3**. (*slang*) to drive or ride in a casual or leisurely way, *tooling along*.□ **tool-pusher** *n*. a worker directing drilling on an oil-rig.

toot *n*. a short sound produced by a horn or whistle etc. —*v*. to make or cause to make a toot.

tooth *n*. (*pl.* teeth) **1**. each of the hard white bony structures rooted in the gums, used for biting and chewing things. **2**. a similar structure in the mouth or alimentary canal of certain invertebrate animals. **3**. a tooth-like part or projection, e.g. on a gear, saw, comb, or rake. **4**. a liking for a particular type of food, *he has a tooth for crystallized fruit*. □ **fight tooth and nail**, to fight very fiercely. **in the teeth of**, in spite of; in opposition to; directly against (the wind). **put teeth into**, to make (a law or regulation) able to be applied effectively. **tooth-powder** *n*. a powder for cleaning the teeth.

toothache *n*. an ache in a tooth or teeth.

toothbrush *n*. a brush for cleaning the teeth; *toothbrush moustache*, a short straight bristly one.

toothcomb *n*. a comb with fine close-set teeth (¶ properly a *fine-tooth comb*, taken as a *fine toothcomb*).

toothed *adj*. **1**. having teeth. **2**. having teeth of a certain kind, *sharp-toothed*.

toothless *adj*. having no teeth.

toothpaste *n*. paste for cleaning the teeth.

toothpick *n*. a small pointed piece of wood etc. for removing bits of food from between the teeth.

toothy *adj*. having many or large teeth.

tootle *v*. **1**. to toot gently or repeatedly. **2**. (*informal*) to go in a casual or leisurely way, *tootle around*.

top¹ *n*. **1**. the highest point or part of something, the upper surface. **2**. the highest rank or degree, the highest or most honourable position, *he is at the top of his profession*. **3**. the utmost degree or intensity, *shouted at the top of his voice*. **4**. a thing forming the upper part of something, the creamy part of milk, a garment covering the upper part of the body. **5**. the covering or stopper of a bottle or tube. **6**. top gear. —*adj*. highest in position or rank or degree, *at top speed*; *top prices*. —**top** *v*. (topped, topping) **1**. to provide or be a top for. **2**. to reach the top of. **3**. to be higher than, to surpass; *top the list*, to be at the top of it. **4**. to add as a final thing or finishing touch. **5**. to remove the top of (a plant or fruit). **6**. (*slang*) to execute by hanging. **7**. (in golf) to strike (the ball) above its centre. □ **at the top of the tree**, in the highest rank in a profession etc. **on top**, above; in a superior position; in addition. **on top of**, in addition to; having mastered (a thing) thoroughly; *be on top of the world*, very happy. **top brass**, *see* brass, sense 7. **top coat**, an overcoat. **top dog**, (*slang*) the master or victor. **top**

drawer, the highest social position, *out of the top drawer*. **top-dress** *v*. to apply manure etc. on the top of soil without ploughing it in. **top-dressing** *n*. this process, the substance used. **top gear**, the highest gear, allowing parts to revolve fast. **top hat**, a man's tall stiff black or grey hat worn with formal dress. **top-heavy** *adj*. over-weighted at the top and therefore in danger of falling over. **top-notch** *adj*. (*informal*) first-rate. **top out**, to complete a building by adding the highest stone. **top-ranking** *adj*. of the highest rank. **top secret**, of the highest category of secrecy. **top up**, to fill up (a half-empty container).

top² *n*. a toy that spins on its point when set in motion by hand or by a string or spring etc. **sleep like a top**, to sleep soundly.

topaz (**toh**-paz) *n*. a semi-precious stone of various colours, especially yellow.

toper (**toh**-per) *n*. a habitual drunkard.

topi (**toh**-pi) *n*. a light pith sun-helmet.

topiary (**toh**-pi-er-i) *n*. the art of clipping shrubs etc. into ornamental shapes. —*adj*. of or involving this art.

topic *n*. the subject of a discussion or written work.

topical *adj*. having reference to current events. **topically** *adv*., **topicality** (top-i-**kal**-iti) *n*.

topknot *n*. a tuft or crest or knot of ribbon etc. on top of the head.

topless *adj*. **1.** (of a woman's garment) leaving the breasts bare. **2.** (of a woman) wearing such a garment.

topmost *adj*. highest.

topography (tŏ-**pog**-răfi) *n*. the features of a place or district, the position of its rivers, mountains, roads, buildings, etc. **topographical** (top-ŏ-**graf**-ikăl) *adj*.

topper *n*. (*informal*) a top hat.

topple *v*. **1.** to fall headlong or as if top-heavy, to totter and fall. **2.** to cause to do this. **3.** to overthrow, to cause to fall from authority, *the crisis toppled the government*.

topside *n*. **1.** a joint of beef cut from the upper part of the haunch. **2.** the side of a ship above the water-line.

topsoil *n*. the top layer of soil as distinct from the subsoil.

topsy-turvy *adv*. & *adj*. **1.** in or into a state of great disorder. **2.** upside-down.

toque (*rhymes with* coke) *n*. a woman's close-fitting brimless hat with a high crown.

tor *n*. a hill or rocky peak, especially in Devon and Cornwall.

torch *n*. **1.** a small hand-held electric lamp powered by a battery or electric power cell, contained in a case. **2.** a burning stick of resinous wood, or of combustible material fixed on a stick and ignited, used as a light for carrying in the hand. □ **carry a torch for**, to be filled with unreturned love for (a person).

torchlight *n*. the light of a torch or torches; *a torchlight procession*, one in which burning torches are used.

tore *see* tear¹.

toreador (torri-ă-dor) *n*. a bullfighter, especially on horseback.

torment¹ (**tor**-ment) *n*. **1.** severe physical or mental suffering. **2.** something causing this.

torment² (tor-**ment**) *v*. **1.** to subject to torment. **2.** to tease or try to provoke by annoyances etc. **tormentor** *n*.

torn *see* tear¹.

tornado (tor-**nay**-doh) *n*. (*pl*. tornadoes) **1.** a violent and destructive whirlwind advancing in a narrow path. **2.** a loud storm, *a tornado of applause*.

torpedo *n*. (*pl*. torpedoes) a cigar-shaped explosive underwater missile, launched against a ship from a submarine or surface ship or aircraft. —*v*. **1.** to destroy or attack with a torpedo. **2.** to ruin or wreck (a policy or conference etc.) suddenly.

torpid *adj*. sluggish and inactive. **torpidly** *adv*., **torpidity** (tor-**pid**-iti) *n*.

torpor (**tor**-per) *n*. a torpid condition.

torque (*pr*. tork) *n*. a force causing rotation in mechanism. **torque converter**, a device to transmit the correct torque from engine to axle in a motor vehicle.

torrent *n*. **1.** a rushing stream of water or lava. **2.** a downpour of rain. **3.** a violent flow, *a torrent of words*.

torrential (ter-**en**-shăl) *adj*. like a torrent.

torrid (*rhymes with* horrid) *adj*. **1.** (of climate or land) very hot and dry. **2.** intense, passionate, *torrid love-scenes*. □ **torrid zone**, the tropics.

torsion (tor-**shŏn**) *n*. **1.** twisting, especially of one end of a thing while the other is held fixed. **2.** the state of being spirally twisted.

torso (**tor**-soh) *n*. (*pl*. torsos) **1.** the trunk of the human body. **2.** a statue lacking head and limbs.

tort *n*. (in Law) any private or civil wrong (other than breach of contract) for which the wronged person may claim damages.

torte (**tor**-tĕ) *n*. a kind of rich round layer cake.

tortoise (**tor**-tŭs) *n*. a slow-moving four-footed reptile with its body enclosed in a hard shell, living on land or in fresh water.

tortoiseshell (**tor**-tŭ-shel) *n*. **1.** the semi-transparent mottled yellowish-brown shell of certain turtles, used for making combs etc. **2.** a cat or butterfly with mottled colouring resembling this. —*adj.* having such colouring.

tortuous (tor-tew-ŭs) *adj.* **1.** full of twists and turns. **2.** (of policy etc.) devious, not straightforward. **tortuously** *adv.*, **tortuosity** (tor-tew-**os**-iti) *n.*

torture *n.* **1.** the infliction of severe pain as a punishment or means of coercion. **2.** a method of torturing. **3.** severe physical or mental pain. —**torture** *v.* **1.** to inflict torture upon, to subject to great pain or anxiety. **2.** to force out of its natural position or shape. —**torturer** *n.*

Tory *n.* **1.** a member of the Conservative Party. **2.** a member of the political party in the 17th–19th centuries, opposed to the Whigs, which gave rise to the Conservative Party. —*adj.* Conservative.

tosh *n.* (*slang*) nonsense.

toss *v.* **1.** to throw lightly or carelessly or easily; *toss one's head,* to throw it back in contempt or impatience. **2.** to send (a coin) spinning in the air to decide something according to the way it lies after falling. **3.** to throw or roll about from side to side restlessly or with an uneven motion. **4.** to coat (food) gently shaking it in dressing etc. —**toss** *n.* **1.** a tossing action or movement. **2.** the result obtained by tossing a coin. □ **take a toss,** to be thrown from horseback. **toss off,** to drink off rapidly; to finish or compose rapidly or without much thought or effort; (*slang*) to masturbate. **toss up,** to toss a coin; to prepare (food) hastily. **toss-up** *n.* the tossing of a coin; an even chance.

tot[1] *n.* **1.** a small child. **2.** (*informal*) a small quantity of alcoholic drink, especially spirits.

tot[2] *v.* (totted, totting) **tot up,** (*informal*) to add up, *tot this up*; *it tots up to £20.* **totting-up** *n.* the adding of separate items, especially of convictions for driving offences to cause disqualification.

total *adj.* **1.** including everything or everyone, comprising the whole, *the total number of persons*; *a total eclipse,* in which the whole disc of the moon etc. is obscured. **2.** utter, complete, *in total darkness.* —*n.* the total number or amount, a count of all the items. —**total** *v.* (totalled, totalling) **1.** to reckon the total of. **2.** to amount to. —**totally** *adv.*

totalitarian (toh-tal-i-**tair**-iăn) *adj.* of a form of government in which no rival parties or loyalties are permitted, usually demanding total submission of the individual to the requirements of the State.

totality (toh-**tal**-iti) *n.* **1.** the quality of being total. **2.** a total number or amount.

totalizator *n.* a device automatically registering the number and amount of bets staked, with a view to dividing the total amount among those betting on the winner.

totalize *v.* to find the total of.

tote[1] *n.* (*slang*) a totalizator.

tote[2] *v.* (*Amer.*) to carry. **tote bag,** a large bag for carrying shopping or other items.

totem (toh-tĕm) *n.* **1.** a natural object, especially an animal, adopted among North American Indians as the emblem of a clan or family. **2.** an image of this. □ **totem-pole** *n.* a pole carved or painted with a series of totems.

t'other = the other.

totter *v.* **1.** to walk unsteadily. **2.** to rock or shake as if about to collapse. —*n.* an unsteady or shaky walk or movement. — **tottery** *adj.*

totting[1] *see* tot[2].

totting[2] *n.* collecting of items of value by dustmen from amongst refuse.

toucan (too-kan) *n.* a tropical American bird with an immense beak.

touch *v.* **1.** to be or come together so that there is no space between, to meet (another object) in this way. **2.** to put one's hand etc. on (a thing) lightly. **3.** to press or strike lightly. **4.** to draw or paint with light strokes, *touch the details in.* **5.** to move or meddle with, to harm, *leave your things here, no one will touch them.* **6.** to have to do with in the slightest degree, to attempt, *the firm doesn't touch business of that kind.* **7.** to eat or drink even a little of, *she hasn't touched her breakfast.* **8.** to reach, *the speedometer touched 120.* **9.** to equal in excellence, *no other cloth can touch it for quality.* **10.** to affect slightly. **11.** to rouse sympathy or other emotion in. **12.** (*slang*) to persuade to give money as a loan or gift, *touched him for a fiver.* —**touch** *n.* **1.** the act or fact of touching. **2.** the faculty of perceiving things or their qualities through touching them. **3.** small things done in producing a piece of work, *put the finishing touches.* **4.** a performer's way of touching the keys or strings of a musical instrument etc. **5.** a manner or style of workmanship, a person's special skill, *he hasn't lost his touch*; *the Nelson touch,* masterly handling of a situation. **6.** a relationship of communication or knowledge, *we've lost touch with her.* **7.** a slight trace, *there's a touch of frost in the air*; *a touch of flu.* **8.** the part of a football field outside the touch-lines. **9.** (*slang*) the act of obtaining money from a person; *a soft touch,* a person who readily gives money when asked. □ **in touch with**, in communication with; having interest in or information about. **out of touch**, no longer in touch with a person or subject etc. **touch-and-go** *adj.* uncertain as regards result. **touch bottom**, to reach the worst point of misfortune etc. **touch down**, (in Rugby football) to touch the ball on the ground behind either goal-line; (of an aircraft) to land. **touchdown** *n.* the act of touching down. **touch-judge** *n.* a linesman in Rugby football. **touch-line** *n.* the side limit of a football field. **touch off**, to cause to explode; to cause to start, *his arrest touched off a riot.* **touch on**, to deal with or mention (a subject) briefly. **touchpaper** *n.* paper impregnated with a substance that will make it burn slowly for igniting fireworks etc. **touch-typing** *n.* typewriting without looking at the keys. **touch up**, to improve (a thing) by making small alterations or additions. **touch wood**, to touch something made of wood in superstitious or humorous hope that this will avert ill luck.

touchable *adj.* able to be touched.

touché (too-shay) *int.* an acknowledgement that one's opponent has made a hit in fencing or a valid accusation or criticism in a discussion.

touched *adj.* **1.** caused to feel warm sympathy or gratitude. **2.** slightly mad.

toucher *n.* one who touches. **as near as a toucher**, (*informal*) very nearly.

touching *adj.* rousing kindly feelings or sympathy or pity. —*prep.* concerning. — **touchingly** *adv.*

touchstone *n.* a standard or criterion by which something is judged. ¶ Alloys of gold and silver were formerly tested by being rubbed against a fine-grained stone such as black jasper.

touchwood *n.* wood in a soft rotten state and easily inflammable, used as tinder.

touchy *adj.* (touchier, touchiest) easily offended. **touchiness** *n.*

tough *adj.* **1.** difficult to break or cut or chew. **2.** able to endure hardship, not easily hurt or damaged or injured. **3.** unyielding, stubborn, resolute; *get tough with a person*, to adopt a firm attitude in dealing with him. **4.** difficult, *a tough job.* **5.** (*informal*, of luck etc.) hard, unpleasant. **6.** (*Amer.*) vicious, rough and violent. —*n.* a rough and violent person, *young toughs.* — **toughly** *adv.*, **toughness** *n.* □ **tough-minded** *adj.* realistic and not sentimental.

toughen *v.* to make or become tough.

toupee (too-pay) *n.* a wig, an artificial patch of hair worn to cover a bald spot.

tour *n.* a journey through a country or town or building etc. visiting various places or things of interest, or giving performances. —*v.* to make a tour of. □ **on tour**, touring.

tour de force (toor dĕ **forss**) an outstandingly skilful performance or achievement.

tourism *n.* **1.** visiting places as a tourist. **2.** the business of providing accommodation and services etc. for tourists.

tourist *n.* a person who is travelling or visiting a place for recreation. **tourist class**, a class of passenger accommodation in a ship or aircraft etc., lower than first class. **tourist trap**, a place that exploits tourists. **Tourist Trophy**, an annual motor-cycle race held on the Isle of Man.

touristy *adj.* designed to attract tourists.

tourmaline (toor-mă-leen) *n.* a mineral of various colours, possessing unusual electric properties and used as a gem.

tournament (toor-nă-měnt) *n.* a contest of skill between a number of competitors, involving a series of matches.

tournedos (toor-nĕ-doh) *n.* (*pl.* tournedos) a small piece of fillet of beef cooked with a strip of fat wrapped round it.

tourniquet (toor-ni-kay) *n.* a device or a strip of material drawn tightly round a limb to stop the flow of blood from an artery by compressing it.

tousle (*rhymes with* **how**-zĕl) *v.* to make (hair etc.) untidy by ruffling it.

tout (*rhymes with* scout) *v.* **1.** to try busily to obtain orders for one's goods or services, *touting for custom.* **2.** to pester people to buy, *touting information.* —*n.* a person who touts things, a tipster touting information about racehorses etc.

tow[1] (*rhymes with* go) *n.* short coarse fibres of flax or hemp, used for making yarn etc. **tow-coloured** (of hair) very light in colour. **tow-headed** *adj.* having tow-coloured hair.

tow[2] (*rhymes with* go) *v.* to pull along behind one. —*n.* towing, being towed. □ **in tow**, being towed; (*informal*) following behind, under one's charge, *he arrived with his family in tow.* **on tow**, being towed. **tow-bar** *n.* a bar fitted to a car for towing a caravan etc. **towing-path** *or* **tow-path** *ns.* a path beside a canal or river for use when a horse is towing a barge etc.

towage *n.* the charge for being towed.

toward *prep.* = towards.

towards *prep.* **1.** in the direction of, *walked* or *faced towards the sea.* **2.** in relation to, regarding, *the way he behaved towards his children.* **3.** for the purpose of achieving or promoting, *efforts towards peace.* **4.** as a contribution to, *put the money* *towards a new bicycle.* **5.** near, approaching, *towards four o'clock.*

towel *n.* a piece of absorbent cloth or paper for drying oneself or wiping things dry. —*v.* (**towelled, towelling**) to wipe or dry with a towel.

towelling *n.* fabric for making towels.

tower *n.* a tall usually square or circular structure, either standing alone (e.g. as a fort) or forming part of a church or castle or other large building. —*v.* to be of great height, to be taller or more eminent than others, *he towered above everyone.* □ **the Tower,** the Tower of London, a former fortress and palace and State prison. **tower block,** a very tall block of flats or offices. **tower of strength,** a person who gives strong and reliable support.

towering *adj.* **1.** very tall, lofty. **2.** (of rage etc.) extreme, intense.

town *n.* **1.** a collection of dwellings and other buildings, larger than a village, especially one not created a city. **2.** its inhabitants. **3.** a town or city as distinct from country. **4.** the central business and shopping area of a neighbourhood. **5.** London, *went up to town from Leeds.* □ **go to town,** (*informal*) to do something lavishly or with great enthusiasm. **on the town,** on a spree in town. **town clerk,** an officer of the corporation of a town, in charge of records etc. **town crier,** an officer who formerly shouted public announcements in a town. **town hall,** a building containing local government offices and usually a hall for public events. **town house,** a residence in town as distinct from country; a terrace house or a house in a compact planned group in a town. **town planning,** preparation of plans for the regulated growth and improvement of towns.

townee *n.* (*contemptuous*) an inhabitant of a town.

townscape *n.* **1.** a picture of a town. **2.** the general appearance of a town.

townsfolk *n.* the people of a town.

township *n.* **1.** (*old use*) a small town or village that formed part of a large parish. **2.** (*Amer. & Canada*) a division of a county, a district six miles square. **3.** (*Austral. & N.Z.*) a small town.

townsman *n.* (*pl.* **townsmen**) a man who lives in a town.

townspeople *n.* the people of a town.

townswoman *n.* (*pl.* **townswomen**) a woman who lives in a town.

toxaemia (toks-**eem**-iă) *n.* **1.** blood-poisoning. **2.** a condition in pregnancy in which blood-pressure is abnormally high.

toxic *adj.* **1.** of or caused by poison. **2.** poisonous. **toxicity** (toks-**iss**-iti) *n.*

toxicology *n.* the scientific study of poisons. **toxicological** *adj.*, **toxicologist** *n.*

toxin *n.* a poisonous substance of animal or vegetable origin, especially one formed in the body by micro-organisms.

toxophily (toks-**off**-ili) *n.* archery.

toy *n.* **1.** a thing to play with, especially for a child. **2.** a thing intended for amusement rather than for serious use. —**toy** *adj.* **1.** serving as a toy. **2.** (of a dog) of a diminutive breed or variety, kept as a pet. —*v.* **toy with,** to handle or finger idly; to deal with or consider without seriousness, *toyed with the idea of going to Spain.*

toyshop *n.* a shop that sells toys.

trace¹ *n.* **1.** a track or mark left behind. **2.** a visible or other sign of what has existed or happened. **3.** a very small quantity, *contains traces of soda.* —**trace** *v.* **1.** to follow or discover by observing marks, tracks, pieces of evidence, etc. **2.** to mark out, to sketch the outline of, to form (letters etc.) laboriously, *traced his signature shakily; the policy he traced out was never followed.* **3.** to copy (a map or drawing etc.) on transparent paper placed over it or by using carbon paper below. □ **trace element,** a substance occurring or required, especially in soil, only in minute amounts.

trace² *n.* each of the two side-straps or chains or ropes by which a horse draws a vehicle. **kick over the traces,** (of a person) to become insubordinate or reckless.

traceable *adj.* able to be traced.

tracer *n.* **1.** a person or thing that traces. **2.** a bullet that leaves a trail of smoke etc. by which its course can be observed. **3.** a radioactive substance that can be traced in its course through the human body or a series of reactions etc. by the radiation it produces.

tracery *n.* **1.** an open-work pattern in stone (e.g. in a church window). **2.** a decorative pattern of lines resembling this.

trachea (trǎ-**kee**-ǎ *or* **tray**-kiǎ) *n.* the windpipe.

tracheotomy (tray-ki-**ot**-ŏmi) *n.* an opening made surgically into the trachea from the outside of the neck.

trachoma (trǎ-**koh**-mǎ) *n.* a contagious disease of the eye causing inflammation of the inner surface of the eyelids.

tracing *n.* a copy of a map or drawing etc. made by tracing it. **tracing-paper** *n.* transparent paper for making tracings.

track *n.* **1.** a mark or series of marks left by a moving person or animal or thing. **2.** a course taken. **3.** a course of action or procedure; *you're on the right track,* following the right line of procedure or inquiry etc. **4.** a path or rough road, especially one made by people or animals or carts etc. passing. **5.** a prepared course for racing etc. **6.** a section of a gramophone record with a recorded sequence, one channel of a recording tape. **7.** (in a computer etc.) the path along which information is recorded on a tape or disc or drum. **8.** a continuous line of railway; *single track*, only one pair of rails. **9.** the continuous band round the wheels of a tank or tractor etc. — **track** *v.* **1.** to follow the track of, to find or observe by doing this. **2.** (of wheels) to run so that the hinder wheel is exactly in the first wheel's track. **3.** (of a stylus) to follow a groove. **4.** (of a cine-camera) to move along a set path while taking a picture. **5.** (of electric current) to leak excessively between insulated points, e.g. in damp conditions. □ *in one's tracks*, (*slang*) where one stands, instantly. **keep** *or* **lose track of**, to keep or fail to keep oneself informed about. **make tracks**, (*slang*) to go away. **make tracks for**, (*slang*) to go to or towards. **track events**, (in sports) races as distinct from field events (*see* field). **track lighting**, room lighting using one or more electric lamps that can be slid along the metal track on which they are mounted. **track record**, a person's past achievements. **track suit**, a warm loose-fitting suit worn by an athlete etc. during practice.

tracker *n.* a person or thing that tracks. **tracker dog**, a police dog tracking by scent.

tract [1] *n.* **1.** a large stretch of land. **2.** a system of connected parts in an animal body along which something passes, *the digestive tract*.

tract [2] *n.* a pamphlet containing a short essay, especially on a religious subject.

tractable *adj.* easy to manage or deal with, docile. **tractability** *n.*

traction *n.* **1.** pulling or drawing a load along a surface. **2.** a continuous pull on a limb etc. in medical treatment. □ **traction-engine** *n.* a steam or diesel engine for drawing a heavy load along a road or across a field etc.

tractor *n.* **1.** a powerful motor vehicle for pulling farm machinery or other heavy equipment. **2.** a device supplying traction.

trad *n.* (*informal*) traditional jazz.

trade *n.* **1.** exchange of goods for money or other goods. **2.** business of a particular kind, *the tourist trade*. **3.** business carried on to earn one's living or for profit (distinguished from a *profession*), a skilled handicraft, *he's a butcher by trade*; *learn a trade*. **4.** the people engaged in a particular trade, *we sell cars to the trade, not to pri-*

vate buyers. **5.** a trade wind. —**trade** *v.* **1.** to engage in trade, to buy and sell. **2.** to exchange (goods etc.) in trading. —**trader** *n.* □ **trade in**, to give (a used article) as partial payment for another article. **trade-in** *n.* an article given in this way. **trade mark**, a manufacturer's or trader's registered emblem or name etc. used to identify his goods. **trade name**, a name given by a manufacturer to a proprietary article or material; the name by which a thing is known in the trade; the name under which a person or firm trades. **trade on**, to make great use of for one's own advantage, *trading on his brother's reputation*. **trade secret**, a technique used in the trade but kept from being generally known. **Trades Union Congress**, an association of representatives of British trade unions, meeting annually. **trade union**, (*pl.* trade unions) an organized association of employees engaged in a particular type of work, formed to protect and promote their common interests. **trade-unionist** *n.* a member of a trade union. **trade wind**, one of the winds blowing continually towards the equator over most of the tropics, from the north-east in the northern hemisphere and south-east in the southern hemisphere.

tradesman *n.* (*pl.* tradesmen) a person engaged in trade, especially a shopkeeper or roundsman.

trading *n.* buying and selling. **trading estate**, an area designed to be occupied by a group of industrial and commercial firms. **trading stamp**, a stamp given by a tradesman to a customer, quantities of which are exchangeable for various articles or for cash.

tradition *n.* **1.** the handing down of beliefs or customs from one generation to another, especially without writing. **2.** a belief or custom handed down in this way, a long-established custom or method of procedure. **traditional** *adj.*, **traditionally** *adv.*

traditionalist *n.* a person who follows or upholds traditional beliefs etc.

traduce (trǎ-**dewss**) *v.* to misrepresent in an unfavourable way. **traducement** *n.*

traffic *n.* **1.** vehicles or ships or aircraft moving along a route. **2.** trading, especially when illegal or morally wrong, *drug traffic*. —*v.* (trafficked, trafficking) to trade. —**trafficker** *n.* □ **traffic-lights** *pl. n.* an automatic signal controlling traffic at junctions etc. by means of coloured lights. **traffic warden**, an official who assists police in controlling the movement and parking of road vehicles.

tragedian (tră-**jeed**-iăn) *n*. **1**. a writer of tragedies. **2**. an actor in tragedy.

tragedy *n*. **1**. a serious play with unhappy events or a sad ending. **2**. the branch of drama that consists of such plays. **3**. an event that causes great sadness, a calamity.

tragic *adj*. **1**. of or in the style of tragedy, *he was a great tragic actor*. **2**. sorrowful. **3**. causing great sadness.

tragical *adj*. **1**. sorrowful. **2**. causing great sadness. **tragically** *adv*.

tragicomedy (traj-i-**kom**-idi) *n*. a play with both tragic and comic elements.

trail *v*. **1**. to drag or be dragged along behind, especially on the ground. **2**. to hang or float loosely, (of a plant) to grow lengthily downwards or along the ground. **3**. to move wearily, to lag or straggle. **4**. to be losing in a game or other contest. **5**. to diminish or become fainter, *her voice trailed away*. **6**. to follow the trail of, to track. —**trail** *n*. **1**. something that trails or hangs trailing. **2**. a line of people or things following behind something. **3**. a mark left where something has passed, *a trace, vandals left a trail of wreckage; a snail's slimy trail*. **4**. a track or scent followed in hunting. **5**. a beaten path, especially through a wild region.

trailer *n*. **1**. a truck or other container designed to be hauled by a vehicle. **2**. (*Amer.*) a caravan. **3**. a short extract from a film, shown in advance to advertise it. **4**. a person or thing that trails.

train *n*. **1**. a railway engine with a series of linked carriages or trucks. **2**. a number of people or animals moving in a line, *a camel train*. **3**. a body of followers, a retinue. **4**. a sequence of things, *a train of events; a train of thought; certain consequences followed in its train*, after it, as a result. **5**. a set of parts in machinery, actuating one another in a series. **6**. part of a long dress or robe that trails on the ground behind the wearer. **7**. a line of combustible material placed to lead fire to an explosive. —**train** *v*. **1**. to bring to a desired standard of efficiency or condition or behaviour etc. by instruction and practice. **2**. to undergo such a process, *she trained as a secretary*. **3**. to make or become physically fit for a sport by exercise and diet. **4**. to teach and accustom (a person or animal) to do something. **5**. to aim (a gun or camera etc.), *trained his gun on the doorway*. **6**. to cause (a plant) to grow in the required direction. □ **in train**, in preparation, *put matters in train for the election*. **in training**, undergoing training for a sport; physically fit as a result of this. **out of training**, not fit in

this way. **training shoes**, soft rubber-soled shoes of the type worn by athletes while exercising. **train-spotter** *n*. a collector of the identification-numbers of railway engines seen.

trainable *adj*. able to be trained.

trainee *n*. a person being trained for an occupation etc.

trainer *n*. **1**. a person who trains, one who trains racehorses or athletes etc. **2**. an aircraft or device simulating it used to train pilots.

trainsick *adj*. made sick or queasy by the motion of a train. **trainsickness** *n*.

traipse *v*. (*informal*) to trudge.

trait (*pr*. tray) *n*. a characteristic.

traitor *n*. a person who behaves disloyally, one who betrays his country. **traitorous** (**tray**-ter-ŭs) *adj*.

trajectory (**traj**-ik-ter-i) *n*. the path of a bullet or rocket etc. or of a body moving under certain forces.

tram *n*. a public passenger vehicle running on rails laid in the road. **tramcar** *n*. a tram. **tram-lines** *pl*. *n*. rails for a tram; (*informal*) the pair of parallel lines at each side of a doubles court in tennis etc.

trammel *n*. a kind of drag-net for catching fish. —*v*. (trammelled, trammelling) to hamper. □ **trammels** *pl*. *n*. things that hamper one's activities.

tramp *v*. **1**. to walk with heavy steps. **2**. to travel on foot across (an area), *tramping the hills*. **3**. to trample, *tramp it down*. — **tramp** *n*. **1**. the sound of heavy footsteps. **2**. a long walk, *went for a tramp*. **3**. a person who goes from place to place as a vagrant. **4**. (*slang*) a sexually immoral woman. **5**. a cargo boat that does not travel on a regular route.

trample *v*. to tread repeatedly with heavy or crushing steps, to crush or harm in this way.

trampoline (**tramp**-ŏ-leen) *n*. a sheet of strong canvas attached by springs to a horizontal frame, used for jumping on in acrobatic leaps.

trance *n*. **1**. a sleep-like state, e.g. that induced by hypnosis. **2**. a dreamy state in which a person is absorbed with his thoughts.

tranny *n*. (*slang*) a transistor radio.

tranquil *adj*. calm and undisturbed, not agitated. **tranquilly** *adv*., **tranquillity** *n*.

tranquillize *v*. to make tranquil, to calm.

tranquillizer *n*. a drug used to relieve anxiety and make a person feel calm.

transact *v*. to perform or carry out (business). **transactor** *n*.

transaction *n*. **1**. transacting. **2**. business transacted. □ **transactions** *pl*. *n*. a record of its proceedings published by a learned society.

transalpine *adj.* beyond the Alps (usually as viewed from Italy).

transatlantic *adj.* **1.** on or from the other side of the Atlantic. **2.** crossing the Atlantic, *a transatlantic flight.*

transceiver (tran-**seev**-er) *n.* a combined radio transmitter and receiver.

transcend (tran-**send**) *v.* **1.** to go or be beyond the range of (human experience or belief or powers of description etc.). **2.** to surpass.

transcendent (tran-**sen**-dĕnt) *adj.* going beyond the limits of ordinary experience, surpassing.

transcendental (tran-sen-**den**-t'l) *adj.* **1.** transcendent. **2.** abstract, obscure, visionary.

transcontinental *adj.* extending or travelling across a continent.

transcribe *v.* **1.** to copy in writing, to write out (shorthand etc.) in ordinary characters. **2.** to record (sound) for later reproduction or broadcasting. **3.** to arrange (music) for a different instrument etc. **transcriber** *n.,* **transcription** *n.*

transcript *n.* a written or recorded copy.

transducer *n.* a device that converts waves etc. from one system and conveys related waves to another (e.g. a radio receiver, which receives electromagnetic waves and sends out sound waves).

transept (**tran**-sept) *n.* the part that is at right angles to the nave in a cross-shaped church, either arm of this, *the north and south transepts.*

transfer¹ (trans-**fer**) *v.* (transferred, transferring) **1.** to convey or move or hand over (a thing) from one place or person or group etc. to another. **2.** to convey (a drawing or pattern etc.) from one surface to another. **3.** to change from one station or route or conveyance to another during a journey. **4.** to change to another group or occupation etc., *she has transferred to the sales department.*

transfer² (**trans**-fer) *n.* **1.** transferring, being transferred. **2.** a document that transfers property or a right from one person to another. **3.** a design that is or can be transferred from one surface to another, paper bearing such a design. □ **transfer fee,** a fee paid for transfer, especially of a professional footballer to another club. **transfer list,** a list of professional footballers available for transfer to other clubs.

transferable (trans-**fer**-ăbŭl) *adj.* able to be transferred.

transference (**trans**-fer-ĕns) *n.* transferring, being transferred.

transfigure *v.* to make a great change in the appearance of, especially to something nobler or more beautiful, *her face was transfigured by happiness.* **transfiguration** *n.* □ **the Transfiguration,** the Christian festival (6 August) commemorating Christ's transfiguration on the mountain.

transfix *v.* **1.** to pierce with or impale on something sharp-pointed. **2.** to make (a person) motionless with fear or astonishment etc.

transform *v.* **1.** to make a great change in the appearance or character of, *the caterpillar is transformed into a butterfly.* **2.** to change the voltage of (electric current). **3.** to become transformed. **transformation** *n.*

transformer *n.* an apparatus for reducing or increasing the voltage of alternating current.

transfuse *v.* to give a transfusion of (a fluid) or to (a person or animal).

transfusion *n.* an injection of blood or other fluid into a blood-vessel of a person or animal.

transgress *v.* **1.** to break (a rule or law etc.), to go beyond (a limitation). **2.** (*old use*) to sin. **transgression** *n.,* **transgressor** *n.*

transient (**tran**-zi-ĕnt) *adj.* passing away quickly, not lasting or permanent. — *n.* a temporary visitor or worker etc. —**transience** *n.*

transistor *n.* **1.** a semiconductor device with three electrodes, performing the same functions as a thermionic valve but smaller and using less power. **2.** a portable radio set equipped with transistors. □ **transistorized** *adj.* equipped with transistors rather than valves.

transit *n.* **1.** the process of going or conveying or being conveyed across or over or through, *the goods were delayed in transit.* **2.** the apparent passage of a heavenly body across the disc of the sun or a planet or across the meridian of a place, *to observe the transit of Venus.* —*v.* (transited, transiting) to make a transit across. □ **transit camp,** a camp for temporary accommodation of soldiers or refugees etc. **transit visa,** a visa allowing the holder to pass through a country but not to stay there.

transition (tran-**si**-zhŏn) *n.* the process of changing from one state or style etc. to another, *the transition from childhood to adult life.* **transitional** *adj.*

transitive *adj.* (of a verb) used with a direct object either expressed or understood, e.g. *pick peas* or *pick till you are tired* (but not in *he picked at the hole to make it bigger*). **transitively** *adv.*

transitory *adj.* existing for a time but not lasting.

translatable *adj.* able to be translated.

translate *v.* **1.** to express in another language or in simpler words, or in code for use in a computer. **2.** to be able to be translated, *the poems don't translate well.* **3.** to interpret, *we translated his silence as disapproval.* **4.** to move (a bishop) to another see, to move (a saint's relics etc.) to another place. **5.** (in the Bible) to convey to heaven without death. **translation** *n.*, **translator** *n.*

transliterate *v.* to represent (letters or words) in the letters of a different alphabet. **transliteration** *n.*

translucent (tranz-**loo**-sĕnt) *adj.* allowing light to pass through but not transparent. **translucence** *n.*

transmigration *n.* migration. **transmigration of the soul**, the passing of a person's soul into another body after his death.

transmissible *adj.* able to be transmitted.

transmission *n.* **1.** transmitting, being transmitted. **2.** a broadcast. **3.** the gear by which power is transmitted from engine to axle in a motor vehicle.

transmit *v.* (transmitted, transmitting) **1.** to send or pass on from one person or place or thing to another, *transmit the message*; *the disease is transmitted by mosquitoes.* **2.** to allow to pass through or along, to be a medium for, *iron transmits heat.* **3.** to send out (a signal or programme etc.) by telegraph wire or radio waves.

transmittable *adj.* able to be transmitted.

transmitter *n.* a person or thing that transmits, a device or equipment for transmitting electric or radio signals.

transmogrify *v.* (transmogrified, transmogrifying) (*humorous*) to transform, especially in a magical or surprising way. **transmogrification** *n.*

transmute *v.* to cause (a thing) to change in form or nature or substance. **transmutation** *n.*

transoceanic *adj.* **1.** on or from the other side of the ocean. **2.** crossing the ocean.

transom *n.* **1.** a horizontal bar of wood or stone across the top of a door or window. **2.** a window above the transom of a door or larger window. **3.** each of several beams fixed across the stern-post of a ship to give a flat stern.

transparency (trans-**pa**-rĕn-si) *n.* **1.** being transparent. **2.** a photographic slide, especially on film as distinct from glass.

transparent (trans-**pa**-rĕnt) *adj.* **1.** allowing light to pass through so that objects behind can be seen clearly. **2.** easily understood, (of an excuse or motive etc.) of such a kind that the truth behind it is easily perceived. **3.** clear and unmistakable, *a man of transparent honesty.* **transparently** *adv.*

transpire *v.* **1.** (of information etc.) to leak out, to become known, *no details of the contract were allowed to transpire.* **2.** (*informal*) to happen, *these events transpired a hundred years ago.* (¶ This use should be avoided if possible.) **3.** (of plants) to give off watery vapour from the surface of leaves etc. **transpiration** *n.*

transplant [1] (trans-**plahnt**) *v.* **1.** to remove and re-plant or establish elsewhere. **2.** to transfer (living tissue or an organ) from one part of the body or one person or animal to another. **3.** to be able to be transplanted. **transplantation** *n.*

transplant [2] (**trans**-plahnt) *n.* **1.** transplanting of tissue or an organ. **2.** something transplanted.

transport [1] (trans-**port**) *v.* **1.** to convey from one place to another. **2.** (*old use*) to deport (a criminal) to a penal settlement. **transportation** *n.*, **transporter** *n.* □ **transported** *adj.* carried away by strong emotion, *she was transported with joy.*

transport [2] (**trans**-port) *n.* **1.** the act or process of transporting something. **2.** means of conveyance, *have you got transport?* **3.** a ship or aircraft for carrying troops or supplies. **4.** the condition of being carried away by strong emotion, *in transports of rage.* □ **transport café**, a café catering chiefly for long-distance lorry drivers.

transportable *adj.* able to be transported.

transpose *v.* **1.** to cause (two or more things) to change places, to change the position of (a thing) in a series. **2.** to put (a piece of music) into a different key. **transposition** *n.*

transsexual *n.* a person who emotionally feels himself or herself to be a member of the opposite sex.

trans-ship *v.* (trans-shipped, trans-shipping) to transfer (cargo) from one ship or conveyance to another. **trans-shipment** *n.*

transubstantiation *n.* the doctrine that the bread and wine in the Eucharist are converted by consecration into the body and blood of Christ, though their appearance remains the same.

transuranic (trans-yoor-**an**-ik) *adj.* belonging to a group of radioactive elements whose atoms are heavier than those of uranium.

transverse *adj.* lying or acting in a cross-wise direction. **transversely** *adv.*

transvestism *n.* dressing in the clothing of the opposite sex, as a form of psychological abnormality. **transvestite** *n.* a person who does this.

trap *n.* **1.** a device for catching and holding animals. **2.** an arrangement for capturing or detecting a person unawares or making him betray himself, anything deceptive. **3.** a golf bunker. **4.** a device for sending something into the air to be shot at. **5.** a compartment from which a greyhound is released at the start of a race. **6.** a device for preventing the passage of water or steam or silt etc., a U-shaped or S-shaped section of a pipe that holds liquid and so prevents foul gases coming up from a drain. **7.** a two-wheeled carriage drawn by a horse. **8.** a trapdoor. **9.** (*slang*) the mouth, *shut your trap.* —*v.* (trapped, trapping) to catch or hold in a trap.

trapdoor *n.* a door in a floor or ceiling or roof.

trapeze *n.* a horizontal bar hung by ropes as a swing for acrobatics.

trapezium (tră-**pee**-ziŭm) *n.* **1.** a quadrilateral in which two opposite sides are parallel and the other two are not. **2.** (*Amer.*) a trapezoid.

trapezoid (**trap**-i-zoid) *n.* **1.** a quadrilateral in which no sides are parallel. **2.** (*Amer.*) a trapezium.

trapper *n.* a person who traps animals, especially for furs.

trappings *pl. n.* ornamental accessories or adjuncts, *he had all the trappings of high office but very little power.*

Trappist *n.* a member of a Cistercian order founded at La Trappe in France, noted for silence and other austerities.

traps [1] *pl. n.* percussion instruments in a jazz band.

traps [2] *pl. n.* (*informal*) personal belongings, baggage.

trash *n.* **1.** worthless stuff, rubbish. **2.** worthless people. **trashy** *adj.*

trauma (**traw**-mă) *n.* **1.** a wound or injury. **2.** emotional shock producing a lasting effect upon a person.

traumatic (traw-**mat**-ik) *adj.* **1.** of or causing trauma. **2.** (*informal*) of an experience) very unpleasant.

travel *v.* (travelled, travelling) **1.** to go from one place or point to another, to make a journey. **2.** to journey along or through, to cover (a distance) in travelling. **3.** to go from place to place as a salesman, *he travels in carpets.* **4.** (*informal*) to withstand a long journey, *some wines travel badly.* **5.** (*informal*) to move at high speed

along a road etc., *the car was certainly travelling.* —**travel** *n.* **1.** travelling, especially in foreign countries. **2.** the range or rate or method of movement of a machine part. □ **travel agency**, **travel agent**, one making arrangements for travellers. **travelled** *adj.* having travelled widely. **travelling clock**, a small clock in a case. **travelling crane**, a crane travelling along an overhead support. **travel-stained** *adj.* dirty from travel.

traveller *n.* **1.** a person who travels or is travelling. **2.** a travelling salesman. □ **traveller's cheque**, a cheque for a fixed amount, sold by a bank etc. and usually able to be cashed in various countries. **traveller's joy**, wild clematis.

travelogue (**trav**-ĕl-og) *n.* a film or illustrated lecture about travel.

traverse [1] (**trav**-ers) *n.* **1.** a thing (especially part of a structure) that lies across another. **2.** a zigzag course or road, each leg of this. **3.** a lateral movement across something. **4.** a steep slope that has to be crossed from side to side in mountaineering.

traverse [2] (tră-**vers**) *v.* to travel or lie or extend across. **traversal** *n.*

travesty (**trav**-iss-ti) *n.* an absurd or inferior imitation, *his trial was a travesty of justice.* —*v.* (travestied, travestying) to make or be a travesty of.

trawl *n.* a large wide-mouthed fishing-net dragged along the bottom of the sea etc. by a boat. —*v.* **1.** to fish with a trawl or seine. **2.** to catch by trawling.

trawler *n.* a boat used in trawling.

tray *n.* **1.** a flat utensil, usually with a raised edge, on which small articles are placed for display or carrying. **2.** a tray of food, *have a tray in one's room.* **3.** an open receptacle for holding a person's correspondence in an office. **4.** a tray-like (often removable) receptacle forming a compartment in a trunk or cabinet or other container.

treacherous *adj.* **1.** behaving with or showing treachery. **2.** not to be relied on, deceptive, not giving a firm support, *the roads were icy and treacherous.* **treacherously** *adv.*

treachery *n.* betrayal of a person or cause, an act of disloyalty.

treacle *n.* a thick sticky dark liquid produced when sugar is refined.

treacly *adj.* **1.** like treacle. **2.** excessively sweet or sentimental.

tread *v.* (trod, trodden, treading) **1.** to set one's foot down, to walk or step, (of a foot) to be set down. **2.** to walk on, to press or crush with the feet, to make (a path or trail or mark etc.) by walking. **3.** (of a male bird) to copulate with (a female bird). —**tread** *n.* **1.** the manner or sound of walking, *a heavy tread.* **2.** the top surface of a stair. **3.** the part of a wheel or tyre etc. that touches the ground. □ **tread on air,** to walk buoyantly because of happiness. **tread on a person's corns** *or* **toes,** (*informal*) to offend or vex him. **tread water,** to keep oneself upright in water by making treading movements with the legs.

treadle (**tred'**l) *n.* a lever worked by the foot to drive a wheel, e.g. in a lathe or sewing-machine. —*v.* to work a treadle.

treadmill *n.* **1.** a wide mill-wheel turned by the weight of people treading on steps fixed round its edge, formerly worked by prisoners as a punishment. **2.** tiring monotonous routine work.

treason *n.* treachery towards one's country or its ruler (e.g. by plotting the sovereign's death or engaging in war against him).

treasonable *adj.* involving the crime of treason.

treasure *n.* **1.** precious metals or gems, a hoard of these, *buried treasure.* **2.** a highly valued object, *art treasures.* **3.** a beloved or highly valued person. —*v.* to value highly, to keep or store as precious, *a treasured possession; treasure it up.* □ **treasure-house** *n.* a place in which treasure is stored or where things of great value or interest are to be found. **treasure-hunt** *n.* a search for treasure; a game in which players try to find a hidden object. **treasure trove,** gold or silver coins or plate or bullion found hidden and of unknown ownership; something very useful or desirable that a person finds.

treasurer *n.* a person in charge of the funds of an institution or club etc.

treasury *n.* **1.** a treasure-house, something regarded as containing things of great value or interest, *the book is a treasury of useful information.* **2.** *the Treasury,* the department managing the public revenue of a country. □ **treasury bill,** one of the bills of exchange issued by the government in return for sums of money lent by bankers, brokers, etc.

treat *v.* **1.** to act or behave towards or deal with (a person or thing) in a certain way, *treated him roughly; treat it as a joke.* **2.** to present or deal with (a subject), *recent events are treated in detail.* **3.** to give medical or surgical treatment to, *treated him for sunstroke; how would you treat a sprained ankle?* **4.** to subject (a substance or thing) to a chemical or other process.

5. to supply (a person) with food or entertainment etc. at one's own expense in order to give pleasure, to buy or give or allow to have as a treat, *treated myself to a taxi.* **6.** to negotiate terms, *treating with their enemies to secure a cease-fire.* — **treat** *n.* **1.** something that gives great pleasure, especially something not always available or that comes unexpectedly. **2.** an entertainment etc. designed to do this. **3.** the treating of others to something at one's own expense; *it's my treat,* I will pay.

treatise (**tree**-tiss) *n.* a written work dealing systematically with one subject.

treatment *n.* **1.** the process or manner of dealing with a person or thing. **2.** something done in order to relieve or cure an illness or abnormality etc.

treaty *n.* **1.** a formal agreement between two or more countries. **2.** a formal agreement between people, especially for the purchase of property at a price agreed between buyer and seller (not by auction).

treble *adj.* **1.** three times as much or as many. **2.** (of a voice etc.) high-pitched, soprano. —**treble** *n.* **1.** a treble quantity or thing. **2.** a hit in the narrow ring between the two middle circles of a dartboard, scoring treble. **3.** a bet where winnings and stakes from a race are restaked on a second and then a third race. **4.** a high-pitched or soprano voice etc., a person with this. — *v.* to make or become three times as much or as many, *costs had trebled.* —**trebly** *adv.* □ **treble chance,** a type of football pool in which matches are selected and points are awarded according to whether the result is a home win, an away win, or a draw.

tree *n.* **1.** a perennial plant with a single stem or trunk that is usually without branches for some distance above the ground. **2.** a Christmas tree. **3.** a framework of wood for various purposes; *shoe-tree,* see **shoe.** **4.** (*old use*) the cross on which Christ was crucified. **5.** a family tree (*see* **family**). —*v.* to force (a person or animal) to take refuge up a tree. □ **tree-creeper** *n.* a small bird that creeps on tree-trunks etc. **tree-fern** *n.* a large fern with an upright woody stem. **tree-house** *n.* a structure built in a tree, for children to play in. **tree surgeon,** a person who treats decayed trees in order to preserve them. **tree-top** *n.* the topmost branches of a tree. **up a tree,** (*slang*) in great difficulties.

treeless *adj.* without trees.

trefoil (**tref**-oil) *n.* **1.** a plant with three leaflets, e.g. clover. **2.** an ornament or design shaped like this.

trek *n.* a long arduous journey. —*v.* (trekked, trekking) to make a trek.

trellis *n.* a light framework of crossing wooden or metal bars, used to support climbing plants.

tremble *v.* **1.** to shake involuntarily from fear or cold etc., to quiver. **2.** to be in a state of great anxiety or agitation, *I tremble to think what has become of him.* —*n.* a trembling or quivering movement, a tremor.

trembler *n.* a spring that makes an electrical contact when shaken.

trembly *adj.* (*informal*) trembling.

tremendous *adj.* **1.** immense. **2.** (*informal*) excellent, *gave a tremendous performance.* **tremendously** *adv.*

tremolo (trem-ŏ-loh) *n.* (*pl.* tremolos) a trembling or vibrating effect in music or in singing.

tremor (trem-er) *n.* **1.** a slight shaking or trembling movement, a vibration; *an earth tremor,* a slight earthquake. **2.** a thrill of fear or other emotion.

tremulous (trem-yoo-lŭs) *adj.* **1.** trembling from nervousness or weakness. **2.** easily made to quiver. **tremulously** *adv.*

trench *n.* a deep ditch dug in the ground, e.g. for drainage or to give troops shelter from enemy fire. —*v.* to dig trenches in (ground). □ **trench coat,** a belted coat or raincoat with pockets and flaps like those of a military uniform coat.

trenchant (tren-chănt) *adj.* (of comments or policies etc.) penetrating, strong and effective, *made some trenchant criticisms or reforms.*

trencherman *n.* (*pl.* trenchermen) a person with regard to the amount he usually eats; *a good trencherman,* one who eats heartily.

trend *n.* the general direction that something takes, a continuing tendency, *the trend of prices is upwards.* **trend-setter** *n.* a person who leads the way in fashion etc.

trendy *adj.* (trendier, trendiest) (*informal*) up to date, following the latest trends of fashion. **trendily** *adv.*, **trendiness** *n.*

trepan (tri-pan) *n. & v.* (trepanned, trepanning) = trephine.

trephine (trif-een) *n.* a surgeon's cylindrical saw for removing a section of the skull. —*v.* to cut with a trephine.

trepidation (trep-i-day-shŏn) *n.* a state of fear and anxiety, nervous agitation.

trespass *v.* **1.** to enter a person's land or property unlawfully. **2.** to intrude or make use of unreasonably, *trespass on someone's time* or *hospitality.* **3.** (*old use*) to sin or do wrong, *as we forgive them that trespass against us.* —**trespass** *n.* **1.** the act of tres-

passing. **2.** (*old use*) sin, wrongdoing, *forgive us our trespasses.* —**trespasser** *n.*

tress *n.* a lock of hair. **tresses** *pl. n.* the hair of the head.

trestle *n.* **1.** one of a pair or set of supports on which a board is rested to form a table. **2.** an open braced framework for supporting a bridge. **trestle-table** *n.*

trews *pl. n.* close-fitting usually tartan trousers.

TRH *abbrev.* Their Royal Highnesses.

tri- *prefix* three, three times, triple.

triable *adj.* able to be tried.

triad (try-ad) *n.* **1.** a group or set of three. **2.** a Chinese secret organization.

trial *n.* **1.** an examination in a lawcourt by a judge in order to decide upon the guilt or innocence of an accused person. **2.** the process of testing qualities or performance by use and experience. **3.** a sports match to test the ability of players who may be selected for an important team. **4.** a test of individual ability on a motor cycle over rough ground or on a road. **5.** a person or thing that tries one's patience or endurance, a hardship. □ **on trial,** undergoing a trial; on approval. **trial and error,** the process of succeeding in an attempt by trying repeatedly and learning from one's failures.

triangle *n.* **1.** a geometric figure with three sides and three angles. **2.** something shaped like this, a percussion instrument consisting of a steel rod bent into this shape and struck with another steel rod.

triangular *adj.* **1.** shaped like a triangle. **2.** involving three people, *a triangular contest.*

triangulate *v.* **1.** to divide into triangles. **2.** to measure or map out (an area) in surveying by means of calculations based on a network of triangles measured from a base-line. **triangulation** *n.*

tribal *adj.* of a tribe or tribes.

tribe *n.* **1.** a racial group (especially in a primitive or nomadic culture) living as a community under one or more chiefs. **2.** a set or class of people, a flock, *he despises the whole tribe of politicians.*

tribesman *n.* (*pl.* tribesmen) a member of a racial tribe.

tribulation (trib-yoo-lay-shŏn) *n.* great affliction, a cause of this.

tribunal (try-bew-năl) *n.* a board of officials appointed to make a judgement or act as arbitrators on a particular problem or on problems of a certain kind.

Tribunite *n.* a member of the *Tribune Group* in the Labour Party, supporters of the extreme left-wing views put forward in the weekly journal 'Tribune'.

tributary *n.* a river or stream that flows

into a larger one or a lake. —*adj.* flowing in this way.

tribute *n.* **1.** something said or done or given as a mark of respect or admiration etc. **2.** an indication of the effectiveness of, *his recovery is a tribute to the doctors' skill.* **3.** payment that one country or ruler was formerly obliged to pay to a more powerful one. □ **pay tribute to,** to express respect or admiration for.

trice *n.* **in a trice,** in an instant.

triceps (**try**-seps) *n.* the large muscle at the back of the upper arm, which straightens the elbow.

trichology (trik-**ol**-ŏji) *n.* the scientific study of hair and its diseases. **trichologist** *n.* an expert in trichology.

trick *n.* **1.** something done in order to deceive or outwit someone. **2.** a deception or illusion, *a trick of the light.* **3.** a particular technique, the exact or best way of doing something. **4.** a feat of skill done for entertainment, *conjuring tricks.* **5.** a mannerism, *he has a trick of repeating himself.* **6.** a mischievous or foolish or discreditable act, a practical joke. **7.** the cards played in one round of a card-game, the round itself, a point gained as a result of this. **8.** a person's turn of duty at the helm of a ship, usually for two hours. —**trick** *v.* **1.** to deceive or persuade by a trick, to mislead. **2.** to deck or decorate, *trick it out* or *up.* □ **do the trick,** (*informal*) to achieve what is required. **how's tricks?,** (*slang*) how are things? **not miss a trick,** (*slang*) to be alert to everything. **trick or treat,** (*Amer.*) a phrase said by children who call at houses at Hallowe'en seeking to be given sweets etc. and threatening to do mischief if these are not provided.

trickery *n.* use of tricks, deception.

trickle *v.* **1.** to flow or cause to flow in a thin stream. **2.** to come or go slowly or gradually, *people trickled into the hall.* —*n.* a trickling flow, a small amount coming or going slowly, *a trickle of information.* □ **trickle-charger** *n.* a device for slow continuous charging of an accumulator.

trickster *n.* a person who tricks or cheats people.

tricky *adj.* (**trickier, trickiest**) **1.** crafty, deceitful. **2.** requiring skilful handling, *a tricky task.* **trickiness** *n.*

tricolour (**trik**-ŏl-er) *n.* a flag with three colours in stripes, especially that of France.

tricot (**trik**-oh) *n.* fine jersey fabric.

tricycle *n.* a three-wheeled pedal-driven vehicle. **invalid tricycle,** a three-wheeled motor vehicle for a disabled driver.

trident (**try**-d'nt) *n.* a three-pronged fish-

spear, carried by Neptune and Britannia as a symbol of power over the sea.

tried *see* try.

triennial (try-**en**-iăl) *adj.* **1.** lasting for three years. **2.** happening every third year. **triennially** *adv.*

triennium (try-**en**-iŭm) *n.* (*pl.* **trienniums**) a period of three years.

trier *n.* a person who tries hard, one who always does his best.

trifle *n.* **1.** something of only slight value or importance. **2.** a very small amount, especially of money, *it cost a mere trifle*; *he seems a trifle angry,* slightly angry. **3.** a sweet dish made of sponge-cake soaked in wine or jelly etc. and topped with custard and cream. —*v.* to behave or talk frivolously. —**trifler** *n.* □ **trifle with,** to toy with; to treat casually or without due seriousness.

trifling *adj.* trivial.

trigger *n.* a lever or catch for releasing a spring, especially so as to fire a gun. —*v.* to trigger off. □ **trigger-happy** *adj.* apt to shoot on slight provocation. **trigger off,** to set in action, to be the immediate cause of.

trigonometry (trig-ŏn-**om**-itri) *n.* the branch of mathematics dealing with the relationship of sides and angles of triangles etc.

trike *n.* (*informal*) a tricycle.

trilateral (try-**lat**-er-ăl) *adj.* having three sides or three participants.

trilby *n.* a man's soft felt hat with a lengthwise dent in the crown and a narrow brim.

trilingual (try-**ling**-wăl) *adj.* speaking or using three languages.

trill *n.* **1.** a vibrating sound made by the voice or in bird song. **2.** quick alternation of two notes in music that are a tone or semitone apart. —*v.* to sound or sing with a trill.

trillion *n.* **1.** a million million millions. **2.** (*Amer.*) a million millions.

trilogy (**tril**-ŏji) *n.* a group of three related literary or operatic works.

trim *adj.* (**trimmer, trimmest**) neat and orderly, having a smooth outline or compact structure. —*v.* (**trimmed, trimming**) **1.** to make neat or smooth by cutting away irregular parts. **2.** to remove or reduce by cutting. **3.** to ornament. **4.** to make (a boat or aircraft) evenly balanced by arranging the position of its cargo or passengers etc. **5.** to arrange (sails) to suit the wind. **6.** (*informal*) to cheat out of money, to get the better of (a person) in a bargain etc. **trim** *n.* **1.** condition as regards readiness or fitness, *in good trim.* **2.** trimming on a dress or furniture etc., the colour or type of upholstery and other fittings in a car. **3.** the trimming of hair etc. **4.** the balance or the even horizontal position of a boat in the water or an aircraft in the air. —**trimly** *adv.*, **trimness** *n.*, **trimmer** *n.*

trimaran (try-mǎ-ran) *n.* a vessel like a catamaran, with three hulls side by side.

trimming *n.* something added as an ornament or decoration on a dress or furniture etc. **trimmings** *pl. n.* pieces cut off when something is trimmed; the usual accompaniments of something, extras, *roast turkey and all the trimmings.*

trine *n.* (in astrology) the aspect of two heavenly bodies one-third of the zodiac (= 120°) apart, regarded as having a favourable influence. —*adj.* of or having this aspect.

Trinidad an island in the West Indies, forming part of the country of *Trinidad and Tobago.* **Trinidadian** (trin-i-**day**-diǎn) *adj.* & *n.*

trinity *n.* **1.** a group of three. **2.** *Trinity*, Trinity Sunday. □ **the Trinity**, the three persons of the Godhead (Father, Son, Holy Spirit) as constituting one God. **Trinity House**, the British institution that licenses ships' pilots and maintains lighthouses etc. **Trinity Sunday**, the Sunday after Whit Sunday, celebrated in honour of the Holy Trinity. **Trinity term**, the university and law term beginning after Easter.

trinket *n.* a small fancy article or piece of jewellery.

trio (**tree**-oh) *n.* (*pl.* trios) **1.** a group or set of three. **2.** a group of three singers or players, a musical composition for these.

triolet (**tree**-ŏ-let) *n.* a poem with eight lines and two rhymes, of which the first, fourth, and seventh lines are the same and the eighth line is the same as the second.

trip *v.* (tripped, tripping) **1.** to walk or run or dance with quick light steps, (of rhythm) to run lightly. **2.** to take a trip to a place. **3.** (*informal*) to have a long visionary experience caused by a drug. **4.** to stumble, to catch one's foot on something and fall, to cause to do this. **5.** to make a slip or blunder, to cause to do this. **6.** to release (a switch or catch) so as to operate a mechanism. —**trip** *n.* **1.** a journey or excursion, especially for pleasure. **2.** (*informal*) a long visionary experience caused by a drug. **3.** a stumble. **4.** a device for tripping a mechanism. □ **trip up**, to stumble or cause to stumble; to make a slip or blunder, to cause (a person) to do this so as to detect him in an error or inconsistency.

trip-wire *n.* a wire stretched close to the ground, actuating a trap or warning device etc. when tripped against.

tripartite (try-**par**-tyt) *adj.* consisting of three parts.

tripe *n.* **1.** the stomach of an ox etc. as food. **2.** (*slang*) nonsense, something worthless.

triple *adj.* **1.** consisting of three parts, involving three people or groups. **2.** three times as much or as many. —*v.* to make or become three times as much or as many. —**triply** *adv.* □ **triple crown**, the pope's tiara (*see* tiara); winning of all three of a group of important events in horse-racing, Rugby football, etc. **triple time**, (in music) rhythm with three beats to the bar.

triplet *n.* **1.** one of three children or animals born at one birth. **2.** a set of three things.

triplicate ¹ (**trip**-li-kǎt) *n.* one of three things that are exactly alike. —*adj.* threefold, being a triplicate. □ **in triplicate**, as three identical copies.

triplicate ² (**trip**-lik-ayt) *v.* to make or be three identical copies of. **triplication** *n.*

tripod (**try**-pod) *n.* a three-legged stand for a camera or surveying instrument etc.

Tripoli the capital of Libya.

tripos (**try**-poss) *n.* the final examination for the degree of BA at Cambridge University.

tripper *n.* a person who goes on a pleasure trip. **trippery** *adj.*

triptych (**trip**-tik) *n.* a picture or carving on three panels fixed or hinged side by side, especially as an altar-piece.

trisect (try-**sekt**) *v.* to divide into three equal parts. **trisection** *n.*

trite (*rhymes with* kite) *adj.* (of a phrase or opinion) commonplace, hackneyed.

triumph *n.* **1.** the fact of being successful or victorious, joy at this. **2.** a great success or achievement. —*v.* to be successful or victorious, to rejoice at one's success etc.; *triumph over difficulties*, overcome them.

triumphal *adj.* of or celebrating a triumph. **triumphal arch**, one built to commemorate a victory.

triumphant *adj.* **1.** victorious, successful. **2.** rejoicing at success etc. **triumphantly** *adv.*

triumvirate (try-**um**-ver-ǎt) *n.* a ruling group of three persons.

trivet (**triv**-it) *n.* an iron stand, especially a tripod, for a kettle or pot etc. placed over a fire. **as right as a trivet**, (*informal*) in good condition or health or circumstances.

trivia *pl. n.* trivial things.

trivial *adj.* of only small value or importance. **trivially** *adv.*, **triviality** (triv-i-**al**-iti) *n.*

trod, trodden *see* tread.

troglodyte (**trog**-lŏ-dyt) *n.* a cave-dweller in ancient times.

Trojan *adj.* of Troy (an ancient city in Asia Minor) or its people. —*n.* a native or inhabitant of Troy. □ **work like a Trojan**, to work with great energy and endurance.

troll[1] (*rhymes with* hole) *v.* **1.** to sing in a carefree jovial way. **2.** to fish by drawing bait along in the water.

troll[2] (*rhymes with* hole) *n.* a giant or a friendly but mischievous dwarf in Scandinavian mythology.

trolley *n.* (*pl.* **trolleys**) **1.** a platform on wheels for transporting goods, a small cart or truck. **2.** a small table on wheels or castors for transporting food or small articles.

trolley-bus *n.* a bus powered by electricity from an overhead wire to which it is linked by a pole and contact-wheel.

trollop *n.* a slatternly woman, a prostitute.

trombone *n.* a large brass wind instrument with a sliding tube.

troop *n.* **1.** a company of people or animals, especially when moving. **2.** a cavalry unit commanded by a captain, a unit of artillery. **3.** a unit of three or more Scout patrols. —*v.* to assemble or go as a troop or in great numbers. □ **trooping the colour**, the ceremony of carrying the regimental flag along ranks of soldiers. **troops** *pl. n.* soldiers, armed forces.

trooper *n.* **1.** a soldier in a cavalry or armoured unit. **2.** (*Amer.*) a member of a State police force. □ **swear like a trooper**, to swear forcibly.

¶ Do not confuse with trouper.

trophy *n.* **1.** something taken in war or hunting etc. as a souvenir of success. **2.** an object awarded as a prize or token of victory.

tropic *n.* a line of latitude 23°27′ north of the equator (*tropic of Cancer*) or the same latitude south of it (*tropic of Capricorn*). **tropics** *pl. n.* the region between these, with a hot climate.

tropical *adj.* of or found in or like the tropics.

troposphere (**trop**-ŏ-sfeer) *n.* the layer of atmospheric air extending about seven miles upwards from the earth's surface.

trot *n.* **1.** the running action of a horse etc. with legs moving as in a walk. **2.** a slowish run. —**trot** *v.* (**trotted, trotting**) **1.** to go or cause to go at a trot. **2.** (*informal*) to walk or go, *trot round to the chemist.* □ **on the trot**, (*informal*) continually busy, *kept him on the trot*; in succession, *for five weeks on the trot.* **trot out**, (*informal*) to produce, to bring out for inspection or approval etc., *trotted out the same old excuse.* **trotting-race** *n.* a horse-race in which the horses pull small vehicles.

Trot *n.* (*slang*) a Trotskyist.

Trotskyism *n.* the political or economic principles of Leon Trotsky (1879–1940), a Russian leader and revolutionary urging world-wide socialist revolution. **Trotskyist** *n.*, **Trotskyite** *n.*

trotter *n.* **1.** a horse of a special breed trained for trotting-races. **2.** an animal's foot as food, *pigs' trotters.*

troubadour (**troo**-băd-oor) *n.* a lyric poet in southern France etc. in the 11th–13th centuries, singing mainly of chivalry and courtly love.

trouble *n.* **1.** difficulty, inconvenience, distress, vexation, misfortune. **2.** a cause of any of these. **3.** conflict, public unrest. **4.** unpleasantness involving punishment or rebuke. **5.** faulty functioning of mechanism or of the body or mind, *engine trouble*; *stomach trouble.* —**trouble** *v.* **1.** to cause trouble or distress or pain or inconvenience to. **2.** to be disturbed or worried, to be subjected to inconvenience or unpleasant exertion, *don't trouble about it.* □ **be no trouble**, to cause no inconvenience or difficulty. **go to some trouble**, = take trouble. **in trouble**, involved in something liable to bring punishment or rebuke; (*informal*) pregnant while unmarried. **make trouble**, to stir up disagreement or disturbance or unpleasantness. **take trouble**, to use much care and effort in doing something; *take the trouble to do something*, exert oneself to do it. **trouble-maker** *n.* a person who habitually stirs up trouble. **trouble-shooter** *n.* a person employed to trace and correct faults in machinery etc. or to act as a mediator in disputes. **trouble-spot** *n.* a place where trouble frequently occurs.

troublesome *adj.* giving trouble, causing annoyance.

trough (*pr.* trof) *n.* **1.** a long narrow open receptacle, especially for holding water or food for animals. **2.** a channel for conveying liquid. **3.** a depression between two waves or ridges. **4.** an elongated region of low atmospheric pressure.

trounce *v.* **1.** to thrash. **2.** to defeat heavily.

troupe (*pr.* troop) *n.* a company of actors or acrobats etc.

trouper (**troop**-er) *n.* **1.** a member of a theatrical troupe. **2.** a staunch colleague, *a good trouper.*

¶ Do not confuse with trooper.

trousers *pl. n.* a two-legged outer garment reaching from the waist usually to the ankles. □ **trouser-suit** *n.* a woman's suit of jacket and trousers.

trousseau (**troo**-soh) *n.* a bride's collection of clothing etc. to begin married life.

trout *n.* (*pl.* trout) any of several chiefly freshwater fish valued as food and game. **old trout,** (*slang*) an objectionable woman.

trowel *n.* **1.** a small tool with a flat blade for spreading mortar etc. **2.** a small garden tool with a curved blade for lifting plants or scooping things.

troy weight a system of weights used for precious metals and gems, in which 1 pound = 12 ounces or 5760 grains.

truant *n.* **1.** a child who strays away from school without leave. **2.** a person who absents himself from work or duty. —*v.* to play truant. —**truancy** *n.* □ **play truant,** to stay away as a truant.

truce *n.* an agreement to cease hostilities temporarily.

truck¹ *n.* **1.** an open container on wheels for transporting loads, an open railway wagon, a hand-cart. **2.** a lorry.

truck² *n.* dealings. **have no truck with,** to have no dealings with.

truckle *v.* to submit obsequiously, *refusing to truckle to bullies.*

truckle-bed *n.* a low bed on wheels so that it can be pushed under another.

truculent (truk-yoo-lĕnt) *adj.* defiant and aggressive. **truculently** *adv.,* **truculence** *n.*

trudge *v.* to walk laboriously. —*n.* a trudging walk.

true *adj.* **1.** in accordance with fact. **2.** in accordance with correct principles or an accepted standard, rightly so called, genuine and not false, *he was the true heir*; *the true north,* according to the earth's axis, not the magnetic north. **3.** exact, accurate, (of the voice etc.) in good tune. **4.** accurately placed or balanced or shaped. **5.** loyal, faithful. —*adv.* truly, accurately. —**trueness** *n.* □ **true-blue** *adj.* completely true to one's principles, firmly loyal.

truffle *n.* **1.** a rich-flavoured fungus that grows underground and is valued as a delicacy. **2.** a soft sweet made of a chocolate mixture.

trug *n.* a shallow usually wooden basket used by gardeners.

truism (troo-izm) *n.* **1.** a statement that is obviously true, especially one that is hackneyed, e.g. *nothing lasts for ever.* **2.** a statement that merely repeats an idea already implied in one of its words, e.g. *there's no need to be unnecessarily careful.*

truly *adv.* **1.** truthfully. **2.** sincerely, genuinely, *we are truly grateful.* **3.** faithfully, loyally. □ **Yours truly,** see yours.

trump¹ *n.* (*old use*) the sound of a trumpet.

trump² *n.* **1.** a playing-card of a suit temporarily ranking above others. **2.** (*informal*) a person who behaves in a helpful or useful way. —*v.* to take (a card or trick) with a trump, to play a trump. □ **trump-card** *n.* a card of the trump suit; a valuable resource, a means of gaining what one wants. **trump up,** to invent (an excuse or accusation etc.) fraudulently. **turn up trumps,** (*informal*) to turn out successfully; to behave with great kindness or generosity.

trumpery *adj.* showy but worthless.

trumpet *n.* **1.** a metal wind instrument with a bright ringing tone, consisting of a narrow straight or curved tube flared at the end. **2.** something shaped like this. — **trumpet** *v.* (trumpeted, trumpeting) **1.** to blow a trumpet, to proclaim by or as if by the sound of a trumpet. **2.** (of an elephant) to make a loud resounding sound with its trunk.

trumpeter *n.* a person who plays or sounds a trumpet.

truncate (trunk-ayt) *v.* to shorten by cutting off the top or end. **truncation** *n.*

truncheon (trun-chŏn) *n.* a short thick stick carried as a weapon, especially by police.

trundle *v.* to roll along, to move along heavily on a wheel or wheels, *trundling a wheelbarrow; a bus trundled up.*

trunk *n.* **1.** the main stem of a tree. **2.** the body apart from head and limbs. **3.** a large box with a hinged lid for transporting or storing clothes etc. **4.** (*Amer.*) the boot of a car. **5.** the long flexible nose of an elephant. □ **trunk-call** *n.* a long-distance inland telephone call. **trunk-road** *n.* an important main road. **trunks** *pl. n.* shorts worn by men or boys for swimming, boxing, etc.; men's short underpants.

truss *n.* **1.** a bundle of hay or straw. **2.** a compact cluster of flowers or fruit. **3.** a framework of beams or bars supporting a roof or bridge etc. **4.** a padded belt or other device worn to support a hernia. — **truss** *v.* **1.** to tie or bind securely, *truss him up; truss a chicken,* fasten its legs and wings securely before cooking. **2.** to support (a roof or bridge etc.) with trusses.

trust *n.* **1.** firm belief in the reliability or truth or strength etc. of a person or thing. **2.** confident expectation. **3.** responsibility arising from trust placed in the person given authority, *a position of trust.* **4.** property legally entrusted to a person with instructions to use it for another's benefit or for a specified purpose. **5.** an organization founded to promote or preserve something, *Slimbridge Wildfowl Trust.* **6.** an association of business firms, formed to reduce or defeat competition; *anti-trust legislation*, laws to combat this. —**trust** *v.* **1.** to have or place trust in, to treat as reliable. **2.** to entrust. **3.** to hope earnestly, *I trust he is not hurt.* ☐ **in trust**, held as a trust (see sense 4). **on trust**, accepted without investigation, *don't take the statement on trust*; on credit, *they bought goods on trust*. **trust to**, to place reliance on, *trusting to luck*.

trustee *n.* **1.** a person who holds and administers property in trust for another. **2.** a member of a group of people managing the business affairs of an institution.

trustful *adj.* full of trust, not feeling or showing suspicion. **trustfully** *adv.*, **trustfulness** *n.*

trustworthy *adj.* worthy of trust, reliable. **trustworthiness** *n.*

trusty *adj.* (*old use*) trustworthy, *his trusty sword.* —*n.* a prisoner who is granted special privileges or given responsibilities because of continuous good behaviour.

truth *n.* **1.** the quality of being true. **2.** something that is true. ☐ **truth table**, a list indicating the truth or falsehood of various combinations of statements.

truthful *adj.* **1.** habitually telling the truth. **2.** true, *a truthful account of what happened.* **truthfully** *adv.*, **truthfulness** *n.*

try *v.* (tried, trying) **1.** to attempt, to make an effort to do something. **2.** to test, to use or do or test the possibilities of something in order to discover whether it is satisfactory or useful for a purpose, *try your strength*; *try soap and water*; *try Woolworths*; *try shaking it.* **3.** to try to open (a door or window) in order to discover whether it is locked. **4.** to be a strain on, *small print tries the eyes.* **5.** to examine and decide (a case or issue) in a lawcourt, to hold a trial of (a person), *he was tried for murder.* —**try** *n.* **1.** an attempt. **2.** a touchdown by a player in Rugby football, scoring points and entitling his side to a kick at goal. ☐ **try for**, to attempt to reach or attain or obtain, to compete for. **try it on**, (*informal*) to do something experimentally in order to discover whether it will be tolerated. **try-on** *n.* (*informal*) an experimental action of this kind. **try on**, to put (a garment etc.) on to see whether it fits and looks well. **try one's hand**, to attempt something for the first time. **try one's luck**, to attempt something to see if one can be successful. **try out**, to test by use. **try-out** *n.* a test of this kind.

trying *adj.* putting a strain on one's temper or patience, annoying.

tsar (*pr.* zar) *n.* the title of the former emperor of Russia.

tsetse fly (tset-si) a tropical African fly that carries and transmits disease (especially sleeping sickness) by its bite.

T-shirt *n.* a short-sleeved shirt having the shape of a T when spread out flat.

T-square *n.* a T-shaped instrument for measuring or obtaining right angles.

TT *abbrev.* **1.** tuberculin-tested. **2.** Tourist Trophy.

tub *n.* **1.** an open flat-bottomed usually round container used for washing or for holding liquids or soil for plants etc. **2.** (*informal*) a bath.

tuba (tew-bă) *n.* a large low-pitched brass wind instrument.

tubby *adj.* (tubbier, tubbiest) short and fat. **tubbiness** *n.*

tubal *adj.* of a tube or tubes, especially the bronchial or Fallopian tubes.

tube *n.* **1.** a long hollow cylinder, especially for holding or conveying liquids etc. **2.** anything shaped like this. **3.** a cylinder of flexible material with a screw cap, holding pastes etc. ready for use. **4.** (*informal*) the underground railway system in London.

tuber *n.* a short thick rounded root (e.g. of a dahlia) or underground stem (e.g. of a potato), producing buds from which new plants will grow.

tubercle (tew-ber-kŭl) *n.* a small rounded projection or swelling.

tubercular (tew-**ber**-kew-ler) *adj.* of or affected with tuberculosis.

tuberculin-tested (tew-**ber**-kew-lin) *adj.* (of milk) from cows tested for and free from tuberculosis.

tuberculosis (tew-ber kew-**loh**-sis) *n.* **1.** an infectious wasting disease affecting various parts of the body, in which tubercles appear on body tissue. **2.** tuberculosis of the lungs.

tuberose (tew-ber-ohz) *n.* a tropical plant with fragrant white funnel-shaped flowers.

tuberous *adj.* of or like a tuber, bearing tubers.

tubing *n.* tubes, a length of tube.

tubular *adj.* tube-shaped, (of furniture) made of tube-shaped pieces.

tubule (tew-bewl) *n.* a small tube or tube-shaped part.

TUC *abbrev.* Trades Union Congress.

tuck *n.* **1.** a flat fold stitched in a garment etc. to make it smaller or as an ornament. **2.** (*slang*) food, especially sweets and cakes and pastry etc. that children enjoy. —**tuck** *v.* **1.** to put a tuck or tucks in (a garment etc.). **2.** to turn (ends or edges etc.) or fold (a part) in or into or under something so as to be concealed or held in place.

3. to cover snugly and compactly, *tucked him up in bed.* **4.** to put away compactly, *tucked it in a drawer.* □ **tuck in,** (*slang*) to eat food heartily. **tuck-in** *n.* (*slang*) a large meal. **tuck into,** (*slang*) to eat (food) heartily. **tuck-shop** *n.* a shop selling tuck to schoolchildren.

tucker *n.* (*Austral. informal*) food.

Tudor *n.* a member of the royal family of England from Henry VII to Elizabeth I. —*adj.* of the Tudors, of or imitating the style of houses etc. of that period.

Tuesday *n.* the day of the week following Monday.

tuft *n.* a bunch of threads or grass or feathers or hair etc. held or growing together at the base. —*v.* to make depressions in (a mattress or cushion) by stitching tightly through it at a number of points, so as to hold the stuffing in place.

tufted *adj.* having a tuft or tufts, (of a bird) having a tuft of projecting feathers on its head.

tug *v.* (tugged, tugging) **1.** to pull vigorously or with great effort. **2.** to tow by means of a tug. —**tug** *n.* **1.** a vigorous pull. **2.** a small powerful boat for towing others. □ **tug of love,** (*informal*) a situation in which custody of a child is in dispute, e.g. between its parents who are separated. **tug of war,** a contest in which two teams hold a rope at opposite ends and pull until one hauls the other over a central point.

tuition (tew-ish-ŏn) *n.* the process of teaching, instruction.

tulip *n.* a garden plant growing from a bulb, with a large cup-shaped flower on a tall stem.

tulip-tree *n.* **1.** a kind of magnolia. **2.** a North American tree with large greenish tulip-like flowers.

tulle (*pr.* tewl) *n.* a kind of fine silky net used for veils and dresses.

tum *n.* (*humorous*) = tummy.

tumble *v.* **1.** to fall helplessly or headlong, to cause to do this (e.g. by pushing). **2.** to fall in value or amount. **3.** to roll over and over or in a disorderly way. **4.** to move or rush in a hasty careless way, *tumbled into bed.* **5.** (of a pigeon) to throw itself over backwards in flight. **6.** to throw or push carelessly in a confused mass. **7.** to rumple or disarrange. —**tumble** *n.* **1.** a tumbling fall. **2.** an untidy state, *things were all in a tumble.* □ **tumble-drier** *n.* a machine for drying washing in a heated drum that rotates. **tumble to,** (*informal*) to realize or grasp (the meaning of something).

tumbledown *adj.* falling or fallen into ruin, dilapidated.

tumbler *n.* **1.** a pigeon that tumbles in its flight. **2.** a drinking-glass with no handle or foot. **3.** a pivoted piece in a lock that holds the bolt until lifted by a key. **4.** any of several kinds of pivoted or swivelling parts in a mechanism. □ **tumbler-drier** *n.* a tumble-drier.

tumbrel *n.* (*old use*) an open cart, especially the kind used to carry condemned people to the guillotine during the French Revolution.

tummy *n.* (*informal*) the stomach.

tumour (tew-mer) *n.* an abnormal mass of new tissue growing on or in the body.

tumult (tew-mult) *n.* **1.** an uproar. **2.** a state of confusion and agitation, *her mind was in a tumult.*

tumultuous (tew-mul-tew-ŭs) *adj.* making a tumult, *tumultuous applause.*

tun *n.* **1.** a large cask for wine or beer etc. **2.** a measure of capacity (usually about 210 gallons).

tuna (tew-nă) *n.* (*pl.* tuna) **1.** tunny. **2.** (also *tuna-fish*) its flesh (usually tinned) as food.

tundra *n.* the vast level treeless Arctic regions where the subsoil is frozen.

tune *n.* a melody, especially a well-marked one. —*v.* **1.** to put (a musical instrument) in tune. **2.** to tune in (a radio receiver etc.). **3.** to adjust (an engine) to run smoothly. —**tuner** *n.* □ **in tune,** playing or singing at the correct musical pitch; *in tune with one's company,* in harmonious adjustment to it. **out of tune,** not in tune. **to the tune of,** to the considerable sum or amount of, *received compensation to the tune of £5000.* **tune in,** to set a radio receiver to the right wavelength to receive a certain transmitted signal. **tune up,** (of an orchestra) to bring instruments to the correct or uniform pitch.

tunable *adj.* able to be tuned.

tuneful *adj.* melodious, having a pleasing tune. **tunefully** *adv.,* **tunefulness** *n.*

tuneless *adj.* not melodious, without a tune. **tunelessly** *adv.*

tungsten (tung-stĕn) *n.* a heavy grey metallic substance used for the filaments of electric lamps and in making a kind of steel.

tunic *n.* **1.** a close-fitting jacket worn as part of a uniform. **2.** a woman's light hip-length garment worn over trousers or skirt. **3.** a loose garment reaching to the hips or knees.

tuning-fork *n.* a steel device like a two-pronged fork, which produces a note of fixed pitch (usually middle C) when struck.

Tunis (tew-nis) the capital of Tunisia.

Tunisia (tew-niz-iă) a country in North Africa. **Tunisian** *adj. & n.*

tunnel *n.* an underground passage, a passage for a road or railway through a hill or under a river etc., a passage made by a burrowing animal. —*v.* (tunnelled, tunnelling) to dig a tunnel, to make a tunnel through.

tunny *n.* a large sea-fish (also called *tuna*) used as food.

tup *n.* a male sheep, a ram.

tuppence *n.* = twopence.

tuppeny *adj.* = twopenny.

turban *n.* **1.** a man's head-dress of a scarf wound round a cap, worn especially by Muslims and Sikhs. **2.** a woman's hat resembling this.

turbid *adj.* **1.** (of liquids) muddy, not clear. **2.** confused, disordered, *a turbid imagination.* **turbidly** *adv.,* **turbidity** (ter-bid-iti) *n.*

turbine (ter-byn) *n.* a machine or motor driven by a wheel that is turned by a flow of water or gas, *gas turbine.*

turbo-jet *n.* **1.** a turbine engine that delivers its power in the form of a jet of hot gases. **2.** an aircraft driven by this instead of by propellers.

turbo-prop *n.* **1.** a jet engine in which a turbine is used as a turbo-jet and also to drive a propeller. **2.** an aircraft driven by this.

turbot *n.* a large flat sea-fish valued as food.

turbulent (ter-bew-lěnt) *adj.* **1.** in a state of commotion or unrest, (of air or water) moving violently and unevenly. **2.** unruly. **turbulently** *adv.,* **turbulence** *n.*

turd *n.* (*vulgar*) a ball or lump of excrement, *sheep turds.*

tureen (tewr-een) *n.* a deep covered dish from which soup is served at the table.

turf *n.* (*pl.* turfs *or* turves) **1.** short grass and the surface layer of earth bound together by its roots. **2.** a piece of this cut from the ground. **3.** a slab of peat for fuel. **4.** *the turf,* the racecourse, horse-racing. —*v.* to lay (ground) with turf. □ **turf accountant,** a bookmaker. **turf out,** (*slang*) to throw out.

turgid (ter-jid) *adj.* **1.** swollen or distended and not flexible. **2.** (of language or style) pompous, not flowing easily. **turgidly** *adv.,* **turgidity** (ter-jid-iti) *n.*

Turk *n.* a native or inhabitant of Turkey.

Turkey a country in Asia Minor and south-east Europe.

turkey *n.* (*pl.* turkeys) **1.** a large bird reared for its flesh. **2.** its flesh as food. □ **talk turkey,** (*Amer. informal*) to talk in a frank and business-like way.

turkeycock *n* a male turkey.

Turkish *adj.* of Turkey or its people or language. —*n.* the language of Turkey. □ **Turkish bath,** exposure of the whole body to hot air or steam to induce sweating, followed by washing. **Turkish coffee,** strong usually sweet black coffee made from very finely ground beans. **Turkish delight,** a sweet consisting of lumps of flavoured gelatine coated in powdered sugar. **Turkish towel,** a towel made in terry towelling.

turmeric (ter-mer-ik) *n.* **1.** a plant of the ginger family. **2.** its root powdered for use as a dye or stimulant or flavouring, especially in curry-powder.

turmoil (ter-moil) *n.* a state of great disturbance or confusion.

turn *v.* **1.** to move or cause to move round a point or axis; *turn somersaults,* perform them by turning one's body; *it would make him turn in his grave,* would disturb a dead person's eternal rest if he knew about it. **2.** to change or cause to change in position so that a different side becomes uppermost or nearest to a certain point. **3.** to give a new direction to, to take a new direction, to aim or become aimed in a certain way, *the river turns north at this point; turn the hose on them; our thoughts turned to Christmas presents.* **4.** to go or move or travel round, to go to the other side of; *turn the enemy's flank,* pass round it so as to attack him from the side or rear. **5.** to pass (a certain hour or age), *it's turned midnight.* **6.** to cause to go, to send or put, *turn the horse into the field.* **7.** to change or become changed in nature or form or appearance etc., *the caterpillar turned into a chrysalis; he turned Communist; the leaves turned or turned brown.* **8.** to make or become sour, *the milk has turned.* **9.** to make or become nauseated, *it turns my stomach.* **10.** to shape in a lathe. **11.** to give an elegant form to. —**turn** *n.* **1.** turning, being turned, a turning movement. **2.** a change of direction or condition etc., the point at which this occurs. **3.** an angle, a bend or corner in a road. **4.** character or tendency, *he's of a mechanical turn of mind.* **5.** service of a specified kind, *did me a good turn; it served its turn,* served a useful purpose. **6.** an opportunity or obligation etc. that comes to each of a number of people or things in succession, *wait your turn.* **7.** a short performance in an entertainment. **8.** (*informal*) an attack of illness, a momentary nervous shock. □ **at every turn,** in every place; continually. **in turn,** in succession; *in one's turn,* when one's turn comes. **not know which way to turn,** not know how to proceed or where to seek help. **not turn a hair,** to show no agitation. **out of turn**, before or after one's turn; *speak out of turn*, to speak in an indiscreet or presumptuous way. **to a turn**, so as to be cooked perfectly. **turn against**, to make or become hostile to. **turn away**, to send away, to reject. **turn down**, to fold down; to reduce the volume or flow of (sound or gas or heat etc.) by turning a knob or tap; to reject. **turn-down** *adj.* (of a collar) folding downwards. **turn in**, to hand in; to deliver as a score etc.; (*informal*) to go to bed; (*informal*) to abandon as a plan or work. **turn off**, to enter a side-road; to stop the flow or operation of by turning a tap or switch; (*informal*) to cause to lose interest. **turn of speed**, ability to go fast. **turn on**, to start the flow or operation of by turning a tap or switch; (*informal*) to excite (a person) sexually or with drugs etc.; (of events etc.) to depend on. **turn one's back on**, to abandon. **turn out**, to expel; to turn off (an electric light etc.); to equip or dress, *well turned out*; to produce by work; to empty and search or clean, *turn out the attic*; (*informal*) to come out; to call (a military guard) from the guard-room; to prove to be, to be eventually, *we'll see how things turn out*. **turn-out** *n.* the process of turning out a room etc.; the number of people who come to a public or social function; something arrayed, an outfit. **turn over**, to hand over; to transfer; to consider carefully, *turn it over in your mind*. **turn over a new leaf**, to abandon one's previous bad ways. **turn round**, to unload and reload (a ship etc.) so that it is ready to leave again. **turn-round** *n.* the time taken in this. **turn tail**, to run away. **turn the corner**, to pass a critical point safely, e.g. in an illness. **turn the tables**, to reverse a situation and put oneself in a superior position. **turn to**, to set about one's work. **turn turtle**, to capsize. **turn up**, to discover or reveal; to be found; to make one's appearance; to happen or present itself; to increase the volume or flow of (sound or gas or heat etc.) by turning a knob or tap; (*informal*) to sicken, to cause to vomit. **turn-up** *n.* a turned-up part, especially at the lower end of trouser legs; (*informal*) an unexpected event.

turncoat *n.* a person who changes his principles.

turner *n.* a person who works with a lathe. **turnery** *n.* this work or its products.

turning *n.* a place where one road meets another, forming a corner. **turning-point** *n.* a point at which a decisive change takes place.

turnip *n.* 1. a plant with a round white

root used as a vegetable and for feeding cattle etc. 2. its root.

turnover *n.* 1. turning over. 2. a small pasty in which a piece of pastry is folded over so as to enclose filling. 3. the amount of money turned over in a business. 4. the rate at which goods are sold. 5. the rate at which workers leave and are replaced, *a rapid turnover of staff*.

turnpike *n.* (*old use & Amer.*) a toll-gate, a road with toll-gates.

turnstile *n.* a device for admitting people to a building etc. one at a time, with barriers (often of horizontal bars) that revolve round a central post as each person passes through.

turntable *n.* a circular revolving platform or support, e.g. for the record in a record-player.

turpentine (ter-pĕn-tyn) *n.* an oil distilled from the resin of certain trees, used for thinning paint and as a solvent.

turpitude (ter-pi-tewd) *n.* wickedness.

turps *n.* (*informal*) turpentine.

turquoise (ter-kwoiz) *n.* 1. a sky-blue precious stone. 2. sky-blue or greenish-blue colour. —*adj.* of this colour.

turret *n.* 1. a small tower-like projection on a building or defensive wall. 2. a low usually revolving structure protecting a gun and gunners in a ship or aircraft or fort or tank. 3. a rotating holder for various dies and cutting-tools in a lathe or drill etc. **turreted** *adj.*

turtle *n.* 1. a sea-creature resembling a tortoise, with flippers used in swimming. 2. its flesh, used for making soup. □ **turtle-neck** *n.* a high round close-fitting neck on a knitted garment.

turtle-dove *n.* a wild dove noted for its soft cooing and for its affection towards its mate and young.

tusk *n.* one of the pair of long pointed teeth that project outside the mouth in the elephant, walrus, etc.

tusser *n.* a strong but coarse silk.

tussle *n.* a struggle, a conflict. —*v.* to take part in a tussle.

tussock *n.* a tuft or clump of grass.

tussore (tuss-or) *n.* = tusser.

tutelage (tew-til-ij) *n.* 1. guardianship. 2. instruction.

tutor *n.* 1. a private teacher. 2. a university teacher directing the studies of undergraduates. —*v.* to act as tutor to, to teach.

tutti-frutti (too-ti-**froo**-ti) *n.* ice-cream containing or flavoured with mixed fruits.

tutu (**too**-too) a ballet dancer's short skirt made of layers of stiffened frills.

tut-tut *int.* an exclamation of impatience or annoyance or rebuke.

Tuvalu (too-vah-loo) a country consisting of a group of islands in the western Pacific. **Tuvaluan** *adj. & n.*

tu-whit, tu-whoo an owl's cry.

tuxedo (tuks-ee-doh) *n.* (*pl.* tuxedos) (*Amer.*) a dinner-jacket, evening dress including this.

TV *abbrev.* television. **TV dinner**, a cooked meal for one person, packed and frozen in a foil tray ready for heating.

twaddle *n.* nonsense.

twain *adj. & n.* (*old use*) two.

twang *n.* **1.** a sharp ringing sound like that made by a tense wire when plucked. **2.** a nasal intonation in speech. —*v.* to make or cause to make a twang, to play (a guitar etc.) by plucking the strings.

'twas (*old use*) = it was.

tweak *v.* to pinch and twist sharply, to pull with a sharp jerk. —*n.* a sharp pinch or twist or pull.

twee *adj.* affectedly dainty or quaint.

tweed *n.* a twilled usually woollen material, often woven of mixed colours. **tweedy** *adj.* □ **tweeds** *pl. n.* clothes made of tweed.

tweet *n.* the chirp of a small bird. —*v.* to make a tweet.

tweeter *n.* a small loudspeaker for accurately reproducing high-frequency signals.

tweezers *pl. n.* small pincers for picking up or pulling very small things.

twelfth *adj. & n.* **1.** next after eleventh. **2.** one of twelve equal parts of a thing. **twelfthly** *adv.*

twelve *adj. & n.* one more than eleven (12, XII).

twenty *adj. & n.* twice ten (20, XX). **twentieth** *adj. & n.* □ **twenties** *pl. n.* the numbers or years or degrees of temperature from 20 to 29. **twenty-two** *n.* a line across the ground 22 metres from either goal in hockey and Rugby football, the space enclosed by this.

'twere (*old use*) = it were.

twerp *n.* (*slang*) a stupid or insignificant person.

twice *adv.* **1.** two times, on two occasions. **2.** in double amount or degree, *twice as strong.*

twiddle *v.* to twirl or handle aimlessly, to twist (a thing) quickly to and fro. —*n.* **1.** a slight twirl. **2.** a twirled mark or sign. —**twiddly** *adj.* □ **twiddle one's thumbs**, to twist them round each other idly for lack of occupation.

twig[1] *n.* a small shoot issuing from a branch or stem.

twig[2] *v.* (twigged, twigging) (*informal*)

to realize or grasp (the meaning of something).

twilight *n.* light from the sky when the sun is below the horizon (especially after sunset), the period of this.

twilit *adj.* dimly lit by twilight.

twill *n.* textile fabric woven so that parallel diagonal lines are produced. **twilled** *adj.* woven in this way.

'twill (*old use*) = it will.

twin *n.* **1.** one of two children or animals born at one birth. **2.** one of two people or things that are exactly alike. **3.** *the Twins*, a sign of the zodiac, Gemini. —*adj.* being a twin or twins, *twin sisters.* —*v.* (twinned, twinning) to combine as a pair. □ **twin beds**, a pair of single beds. **twin-engined** *adj.* having two engines. **twin set**, a woman's matching jumper and cardigan. **twin towns**, two towns (usually in different countries) that establish special cultural and social links.

twine *n.* strong thread or string made of two or more strands twisted together. —*v.* to twist, to wind or coil.

twinge (*pr.* twinj) *n.* a slight or brief pang.

twinkle *v.* **1.** to shine with a light that flickers rapidly, to sparkle. **2.** (of the eyes) to be bright or sparkling with amusement. **3.** (of the feet in dancing etc.) to move with short rapid movements. —*n.* a twinkling light or look or movement. □ **in the twinkling of an eye**, in an instant.

twirl *v.* to twist lightly or rapidly. —*n.* **1.** a twirling movement. **2.** a twirled mark or sign. —**twirly** *adj.*

twist *v.* **1.** to wind (strands etc.) round each other so as to form a single cord, to interweave. **2.** to make by doing this. **3.** to pass or coil round something. **4.** to give a spiral form to, e.g. by turning the ends in opposite directions. **5.** to take a spiral or winding form or course, to turn or bend round, *the road twisted and turned*; *he twisted round in his seat.* **6.** to rotate or revolve, to cause to do this. **7.** to wrench out of its normal shape; *a twisted mind*, one that works in a perverted way. **8.** to distort the meaning of, *tried to twist his words into an admission of guilt.* **9.** (*informal*) to swindle. —**twist** *n.* **1.** twisting, being twisted. **2.** something formed by twisting, a turn in a twisting course. **3.** a dance with vigorous twisting of the body. **4.** a peculiar tendency of mind or character. **5.** (*informal*) a swindle. —**twisty** *adj.* □ **round the twist**, (*slang*) crazy. **twist a person's arm**, (*informal*) to coerce him.

twister *n.* (*informal*) an untrustworthy person, a swindler.

twit[1] *v.* (twitted, twitting) to taunt.
twit[2] *n.* (*slang*) a foolish or insignificant person.
twitch *v.* **1.** to pull with a light jerk. **2.** to quiver or contract spasmodically. —*n.* a twitching movement.
twitcher *n.* (*informal*) a bird-watcher who eagerly seeks to have seen as many species as possible.
twitter *v.* **1.** to make a series of light chirping sounds. **2.** to talk rapidly in an anxious or nervous way. —*n.* twittering.
'twixt *prep.* = betwixt.
two *adj. & n.* one more than one (2, II). **be in two minds**, to be undecided. **be two a penny**, to be readily obtainable and so almost worthless. **two-dimensional** *adj.* having two dimensions (length, breadth). **two-edged** *adj.* having two cutting-edges; cutting both ways (*see* cut). **two-faced** *adj.* insincere, deceitful. **two-piece** *n.* a suit of clothes or a woman's swim-suit consisting of two separate parts. **two-ply** *adj.* made of two strands or layers. **two-time** *v.* (*slang*) to double-cross. **two-way** *adj.* involving two ways or participants; *two-way switch*, a switch that allows electric current to be turned on or off from either of two points; *two-way traffic*, lanes of traffic travelling in opposite directions.
twofold *adj. & adv.* **1.** twice as much or as many. **2.** consisting of two parts.
twopence (**tup**-ĕns) *n.* the sum of two pence; *don't care twopence,* care hardly at all.
twopenny (**tup**-ĕni) *adj.* costing or worth twopence. **twopenny-halfpenny** *adj.* insignificant, almost worthless.
twosome *n.* two people together, a couple or pair.
tycoon *n.* a wealthy and influential businessman or industrialist, a magnate.
tying *see* tie.
tyke *n.* an objectionable fellow.
Tyne and Wear (*pr.* weer) a metropolitan county of England.
Tynwald (**tin**-wolld) *n.* the governing assembly of the Isle of Man.
type *n.* **1.** a class of people or things that have characteristics in common, a kind. **2.** a typical example or instance. **3.** (*informal*) a person of specified character, *brainy types.* **4.** a small block with a raised letter or figure etc. used in printing, a set or supply or kind or size of these, *printed in large type.* —**type** *v.* **1.** to classify according to type. **2.** to write with a typewriter.
type-cast *v.* (type-cast, type-casting) to cast (an actor) in the kind of part which he has the reputation of playing successfully or which seems to fit his personality.
typescript *n.* a typewritten document.

typewriter *n.* a machine for producing characters similar to those of print by pressing keys which cause raised metal letters etc. to strike the paper, usually through inked ribbon.
typewritten *adj.* written with a typewriter.
typhoid fever a serious infectious feverish disease that attacks the intestines, caused by bacteria taken into the body in food or drink.
typhoon (ty-**foon**) *n.* a violent hurricane in the western Pacific.
typhus *n.* an infectious disease with fever, great weakness, and purple spots on the body.
typical *adj.* **1.** having the distinctive qualities of a particular type of person or thing, serving as a representative specimen, *a typical Scotsman.* **2.** characteristic, *he answered with typical curtness.* **typically** *adv.*
typify (**tip**-i-fy) *v.* (typified, typifying) to be a representative specimen of.
typist *n.* a person who types, especially one employed to do so.
typography (ty-**pog**-răfi) *n.* **1.** the art or practice of printing. **2.** the style or appearance of printed matter. **typographical** (ty-pŏ-**graf**-ikăl) *adj.*
tyrannical (ti-**ran**-ikăl) *adj.* as or like a tyrant, obtaining obedience from everyone by force or threats. **tyrannically** *adv.*
tyrannize (**ti**-ră-nyz) *v.* to rule as or like a tyrant.
tyrannosaur (ti-**ran**-ŏ-sor) *n.* a very large dinosaur (also called *Tyrannosaurus rex*) that walked on its hind legs.
tyrannous (**ti**-ră-nŭs) *adj.* tyrannical.
tyranny (**ti**-ră-ni) *n.* **1.** government by a tyrannical ruler. **2.** oppressive or tyrannical use of power.
tyrant (**ty**-rănt) *n.* a ruler or other person who uses his power in a harsh or oppressive way, one who insists on absolute obedience.
tyre *n.* a covering fitted round the rim of a wheel to absorb shocks, usually of reinforced rubber filled with air or covering a pneumatic inner tube.
tyro (**ty**-roh) *n.* (*pl.* tyros) = tiro.
Tyrol (ti-**rohl**) an Alpine district of Austria and Italy. **Tyrolean** (ti-rŏ-**lee**-ăn) *adj.*, **Tyrolese** (ti-rŏl-**eez**) *adj. & n.* (*pl.* Tyrolese)
Tyrone (ty-**rohn**) a county of Northern Ireland.

Uu

U (*pr.* yoo) *adj.* (*informal*) upper-class, supposedly characteristic of upper-class speech or behaviour.

ubiquitous (yoo-**bik**-wit-ŭs) *adj.* being everywhere at the same time. **ubiquity** *n.*

U-boat *n.* a German submarine, especially in the war of 1939–45.

udder *n.* a bag-like milk-secreting organ of a cow or ewe or female goat etc., with two or more teats.

UFO (**yoo**-foh) *abbrev.* unidentified flying object.

Uganda (yoo-**gan**-dă) a country in East Africa. **Ugandan** *adj.* & *n.*

ugh (*pr.* uh) *int.* an exclamation of disgust or horror.

ugli (**ug**-li) *n.* (*pl.* uglis) a citrus fruit that is a hybrid of grapefruit and tangerine.

ugly *adj.* (uglier, ugliest) **1.** unpleasant to look at or to hear. **2.** unpleasant in any way, hostile and threatening, *the crowd was in an ugly mood.* **ugliness** *n.* □ **ugly customer,** an unpleasantly formidable person. **ugly duckling,** a person who at first seems unpromising but later becomes much admired or very able (¶ like the cygnet in the brood of ducks in Hans Andersen's story).

UHF *abbrev.* ultra-high frequency.

UK *abbrev.* United Kingdom.

Ukrainian (yoo-**krayn**-iăn) *adj.* of the Ukraine, a region and republic of the USSR, north of the Black Sea.

ukulele (yoo-kŭ-**lay**-li) *n.* a small four-stringed guitar.

ulcer *n.* an open sore on the surface of the body or one of its organs. **ulcerous** *adj.*

ulcerate *v.* to cause an ulcer in or on, to become affected with an ulcer. **ulceration** *n.*

ulna (**ul**-nă) *n.* the thinner of the two long bones in the forearm, the corresponding bone in an animal. **ulnar** *adj.*

Ulster 1. a former province of Ireland comprising the present Northern Ireland and the counties of Cavan, Donegal, and Monaghan (which are now in the Republic of Ireland). **2.** (used loosely) = Northern Ireland.

ulterior *adj.* beyond what is obvious or admitted, *ulterior motives.*

ultimate *adj.* **1.** last, final; *the ultimate deterrent,* threatened use of nuclear weapons. **2.** basic, fundamental, *the ultimate cause.* **ultimately** *adv.*

ultimatum (ulti-**may**-tŭm) *n.* (*pl.* ultimatums) a final demand or statement of terms, rejection of which may lead to the ending of friendly relations or a declaration of war.

ultra- *prefix* beyond, extremely, excessively, *ultra-conservative, ultra-modern.*

ultra-high *adj.* (of frequency) in the range of 300 to 3000 megahertz.

ultramarine (ultră-mă-**reen**) *adj.* & *n.* bright deep blue.

ultramicroscopic *adj.* too small to be seen with an ordinary microscope.

ultrasonic (ultră-**sonn**-ik) *adj.* (of sound waves) with a pitch that is above the upper limit of normal human hearing.

ultraviolet *adj.* **1.** (of radiation) having a wavelength that is slightly shorter than that of visible light-rays at the violet end of the spectrum. **2.** of or using this radiation, *an ultraviolet lamp.*

umbel (**um**-běl) *n.* a flower-cluster like that of cow-parsley, in which the flowers are on stalks of nearly equal length springing from the same point on the main stem.

umber *n.* a natural colouring-matter like ochre but darker and browner. **burnt umber,** reddish-brown.

umbilical (um-**bil**-ikăl) *adj.* of the navel. **umbilical cord,** the flexible tubular structure of tissue connecting the placenta to the navel of the foetus and carrying nourishment to the foetus while it is in the womb.

umbra *n.* (*pl.* umbrae (*pr.* **um**-bree) *or* umbras) the dark central part of the shadow cast by the earth or the moon in an eclipse, or of a sunspot.

umbrage (**um**-brij) *n.* a feeling of being offended. **take umbrage,** to take offence.

umbrella *n.* **1.** a portable protection against rain, consisting of a circular piece of fabric mounted on a foldable frame of spokes attached to a central stick that serves as a handle. **2.** any kind of general protecting force or influence.

umpire *n.* a person appointed to see that the rules of a game or contest are observed and to settle disputes (e.g. in a game of cricket or baseball), or to give a decision on any disputed question. —*v.* to act as umpire in (a game).

umpteen *adj.* (*slang*) very many. **umpteenth** *adj.*

'un *pronoun* (*informal*) one, *a good 'un.*

---

un- *prefix* **1.** not, *uncertain, uncertainty.* **2.** reversing the action indicated by the simple verb (e.g. *unlock* = release from being locked).

¶ The number of words with this prefix is almost unlimited, and many of those whose meaning is obvious are not listed below.

UN *abbrev.* United Nations.

unable *adj.* not able.

unabridged *adj.* not abridged.

unaccompanied *adj.* 1. not accompanied. 2. without musical accompaniment.

unaccountable *adj.* 1. unable to be explained or accounted for. 2. not accountable for one's actions etc. **unaccountably** *adv.*

unaccustomed *adj.* not accustomed.

unadopted *adj.* (of a road) not taken over for maintenance by a local authority.

unadulterated *adj.* pure.

unalloyed (un-ă-**loid**) *adj.* not alloyed, pure, *unalloyed joy.*

un-American *adj.* 1. not in accordance with American characteristics. 2. contrary to the interests of the USA.

unanimous (yoo-**nan**-im-ŭs) *adj.* all agreeing in an opinion or decision, (of an opinion or decision etc.) held or given by everyone. **unanimously** *adv.*, **unanimity** (yoo-năn-**im**-iti) *n.*

unanswerable *adj.* unable to be answered or refuted by a good argument to the contrary.

unarmed *adj.* not armed, without weapons.

unasked *adj.* not asked, without being requested.

unassuming *adj.* not arrogant, unpretentious.

unattended *adj.* (of a vehicle) having no person in charge of it.

unavoidable *adj.* unable to be avoided. **unavoidably** *adv.*

unaware *adj.* not aware.

unawares *adv.* unexpectedly, without noticing.

unbacked *adj.* having no back or no backing, (in betting) having no backers.

unbalanced *adj.* 1. not balanced. 2. mentally unsound.

unbearable *adj.* not bearable, unable to be endured. **unbearably** *adv.*

unbeatable *adj.* impossible to defeat or surpass.

unbeaten *adj.* not defeated, (of a record etc.) not surpassed.

unbecoming *adj.* 1. not suited to the wearer, *an unbecoming hat.* 2. not suitable, *behaviour unbecoming to a gentleman.*

unbeknown *adj.* (*informal*) unknown, *they did it unbeknown to us,* without our being aware of it.

unbelievable *adj.* not believable. **unbelievably** *adv.*

unbeliever *n.* a person who does not believe, especially one not believing in Christianity or Islam.

unbend *v.* (unbent, unbending) 1. to change or become changed from a bent position. 2. to become relaxed or affable.

unbending *adj.* inflexible, refusing to alter one's demands.

unbiased *adj.* not biased.

unbidden *adj.* not commanded or invited.

unbirthday *adj.* **unbirthday present,** a present given on a day that is not the recipient's birthday.

unblock *v.* to remove an obstruction from.

unbolt *v.* to release (a door etc.) by drawing back the bolt(s).

unborn *adj.* not yet born.

unbosom *v.* **unbosom oneself,** to reveal one's thoughts or feelings.

unbounded *adj.* boundless, without limits.

unbreakable *adj.* not breakable.

unbridled *adj.* unrestrained, *unbridled insolence.*

unbroken *adj.* not broken, not interrupted.

unbusinesslike *adj.* not businesslike.

uncalled-for *adj.* offered or intruded impertinently or unjustifiably.

uncanny *adj.* 1. strange and rather frightening. 2. extraordinary, beyond what is normal, *they predicted the results with uncanny accuracy.* **uncannily** *adv.*

uncared-for *adj.* neglected.

unceasing *adj.* not ceasing. **unceasingly** *adv.*

unceremonious *adj.* without proper formality or dignity. **unceremoniously** *adv.*

uncertain *adj.* 1. not known certainly. 2. not knowing certainly. 3. not to be depended on, *his aim is uncertain.* 4. changeable, *an uncertain temper.* **uncertainly** *adv.*, **uncertainty** *n.* □ **in no uncertain terms,** clearly and forcefully.

unchristian *adj.* contrary to Christian principles, uncharitable.

uncial (**un**-si-ăl) *adj.* of or written in a script with rounded letters that are not joined together, found in manuscripts of the 4th–8th centuries, from which modern capital letters are largely derived. —*n.* an uncial letter or style or manuscript.

uncle *n.* 1. a brother or brother-in-law of one's father or mother. 2. (*children's informal*) prefixed to the Christian name of an unrelated man friend. □ **Uncle Sam,** (*informal*) the people of the USA. **Uncle Tom,** a Black who is subservient to whites (¶ named after the hero of *Uncle Tom's Cabin* by Mrs Stowe).

uncommon *adj.* not common, unusual.

uncommunicative *adj.* not inclined to give information or an opinion etc., silent.

uncompromising (un-**kom**-prŏ-my-zing) *adj.* not allowing or seeking compromise, inflexible.

unconcerned *adj.* not feeling or showing concern, free from anxiety.

unconditional *adj.* not subject to conditions or limitations, *unconditional surrender.* **unconditionally** *adv.*

unconscionable (un-kon-shŏn-ăbŭl) *adj.* 1. unscrupulous. 2. contrary to what one's conscience feels is right, outrageous.

unconscious *adj.* 1. not conscious, not aware. 2. done or spoken etc. without conscious intention, *unconscious humour.* —*n.* the unconscious mind, that part of the mind whose content is not normally accessible to consciousness but which is found to affect behaviour. **unconsciously** *adv.,* **unconsciousness** *n.*

uncooperative *adj.* not co-operative.

uncouple (un-**kup**-ŭl) *v.* to disconnect (railway carriages etc.) from being connected by a coupling.

uncouth (un-**kooth**) *adj.* awkward or clumsy in manner, boorish.

uncover *v.* 1. to remove the covering from. 2. to reveal or expose, *their deceit was uncovered.*

unction (**unk**-shŏn) *n.* 1. anointing with oil, especially as a religious rite. 2. pretended earnestness, excessive politeness.

unctuous (**unk**-tew-ŭs) *adj.* having an oily manner, smugly earnest or virtuous. **unctuously** *adv.,* **unctuousness** *n.*

uncut *adj.* not cut, (of a gem) not shaped by cutting, (of fabric) with the loops of the pile not cut.

undeceive *v.* to disillusion (a person).

undecided *adj.* 1. not yet settled or certain, *the point is still undecided.* 2. not yet having made up one's mind.

undeniable *adj.* impossible to deny, undoubtedly true. **undeniably** *adv.*

under *prep.* 1. in or to a position lower than, below. 2. less than, *it's under a mile from here.* 3. inferior to, of lower rank than, *no one under a bishop.* 4. governed or controlled by, *the country prospered under his rule.* 5. undergoing, *the road is under repair.* 6. subject to an obligation imposed by, *he is under contract to our firm.* 7. in accordance with, *it is permissible under our agreement.* 8. designated or indicated by, *writes under an assumed name.* 9. in the category of, *file it under 'Estimates'.* 10. (of land) planted with, *50 acres under wheat.* 11. propelled by, *under sail; under one's own steam,* moving without external aid. 12. attested by, *under my hand* (= signature) *and seal.* —**under** *adv.* 1. in or to a

lower position or subordinate condition. 2. in or into a state of unconsciousness. 3. below a certain quantity or rank or age etc., *children of five and under.* —*adj.* lower, situated underneath, *the under layers.* □ **under age,** not old enough, especially for some legal right; not yet of adult status. **under the sun,** anywhere in the world, existing. **under way,** moving on water; in progress. (¶ Sometimes incorrectly written as *under weigh* through confusion with *weigh anchor.*)

under- *prefix* 1. below, beneath, *underseal.* 2. lower, subordinate, *under-manager.* 3. insufficiently, incompletely, *undercooked.*

underachieve *v.* to do less well than was expected, especially in school-work.

underarm *adj.* & *adv.* 1. in the armpit. 2. (in cricket etc.) bowling or bowled with the hand brought forward and upwards and not raised above shoulder level. 3. (in tennis) with the racket moved similarly.

underbid *v.* (underbid, underbidding) 1. to make a lower bid than (another person). 2. to bid less than is justified in the game of bridge.

undercarriage *n.* an aircraft's landing-wheels and their supports.

undercharge *v.* to charge too low a price.

underclothes *pl. n.* underwear.

undercoat *n.* a layer of paint under a finishing coat, the paint used for this.

undercover *adj.* 1. doing things secretly, done secretly. 2. engaged in spying by working among those to be spied on, *undercover agents.*

undercurrent *n.* 1. a current that is below a surface or below another current. 2. an underlying feeling or influence or trend.

undercut *v.* (undercut, undercutting) 1. to cut away the part below. 2. to sell or work for a lower price than (another person).

underdeveloped *adj.* not fully developed, (of a film) not developed enough to give a satisfactory image, (of a country) not having reached its potential level in economic development.

underdog *n.* a person or country etc. in an inferior or subordinate position.

underdone *adj.* not thoroughly done, (of meat) not completely cooked throughout.

underestimate *v.* to make too low an estimate of. —*n.* an estimate that is too low. —**underestimation** *n.*

underexpose *v.* to expose for too short a time. **underexposure** *n.*

underfelt *n.* felt for laying under a carpet.

underfloor *adj.* situated beneath the floor.

underfoot *adv.* on the ground, under one's feet.

undergarment *n.* a piece of underwear.

undergo *v.* (underwent, undergone, undergoing) to experience, to endure, to be subjected to, *the new aircraft underwent intensive trials.*

undergraduate *n.* a member of a university who has not yet taken a degree.

underground[1] (un-der-**grownd**) *adv.* 1. under the surface of the ground. 2. in secret, into secrecy or hiding.

underground[2] (**un**-der-grownd) *adj.* 1. under the surface of the ground. 2. secret, of a secret political organization or one for resisting enemy forces controlling a country. —**underground** *n.* 1. an underground railway. 2. an underground organization.

undergrowth *n.* shrubs and bushes etc. growing closely, especially when beneath trees.

underhand[1] (**un**-der-hand) *adj.* 1. done or doing things in a sly or secret way. 2. (in cricket etc.) underarm.

underhand[2] (un-der-**hand**) *adv.* in an underhand manner. **underhanded** *adj.*

underlay[1] (un-der-**lay**) *v.* (underlaid, underlaying) to lay something under (a thing) as a support or in order to raise it.

underlay[2] (**un**-der-lay) *n.* a layer of material (e.g. felt, rubber, etc.) laid under another as a protection or support.

underlay[3] (un-der-**lay**) *see* underlie.

underlie *v.* (underlay, underlain, underlying) 1. to lie or exist beneath. 2. to be the basis of (a theory etc.), to be the facts that account for, *the underlying reasons for her behaviour.*

underline *v.* 1. to draw a line under. 2. to emphasize.

underling *n.* a subordinate.

undermanned *adj.* having too few people to operate it properly, understaffed.

undermentioned *adj.* mentioned below.

undermine *v.* 1. to make a mine or tunnel beneath, especially one causing weakness at the base. 2. to weaken gradually, *his health or confidence was undermined.*

underneath *prep.* beneath or below or on the inside of (a thing). —*adv.* at or in or to a position underneath something.

underpaid *adj.* paid too little.

underpants *pl. n.* a man's undergarment covering the lower part of the body and part of the legs.

under-part *n.* the part underneath.

underpass *n.* a road that passes under another, a crossing of this kind.

underpin *v.* (underpinned, underpinning) to support, to strengthen from beneath.

underprivileged *adj.* less privileged than others, not enjoying the normal standard of living or rights in a community.

underrate *v.* to underestimate.

underscore *v.* to underline.

undersea *adj.* below the surface of the sea.

underseal *v.* to coat the lower surface of (a motor vehicle etc.) with a protective sealing layer.

under-secretary *n.* a person who is directly subordinate to an official who has the title of 'secretary'.

undersell *v.* (undersold, underselling) to sell at a lower price than (another person).

under-sexed *adj.* having less than the normal degree of sexual desires.

undershoot *v.* (undershot, undershooting) (of an aircraft) to land short of, *the plane undershot the runway.*

undershot *adj.* (of a water-wheel) turned by water flowing under it.

under-side *adj.* the side or surface underneath.

undersigned *adj.* who has or have signed at the bottom of this document, *we, the undersigned.*

undersized *adj.* of less than the usual size.

underskirt *n.* a skirt for wearing beneath another, a petticoat.

underslung *adj.* 1. supported from above. 2. (of a vehicle chassis) hanging lower than the axles.

underspend *v.* (underspent, underspending) to spend too little.

understaffed *adj.* having less than the necessary number of staff.

understand *v.* (understood, understanding) 1. to perceive the meaning or importance or nature of; *we understand each other,* we know each other's views or are in agreement. 2. to know the ways or workings of, to know how to deal with, *he understands machinery.* 3. to know the explanation and not be offended, *we shall understand if you can't come.* 4. to become aware from information received, to draw as a conclusion, *I understand she is in Paris.* 5. to take for granted, *your expenses will be paid, that's understood.* 6. to supply (a word or words) mentally, *before 'coming?' the words 'are you' are understood.*

understandable *adj.* able to be understood. **understandably** *adv.*

understanding *adj.* having or showing insight or good judgement, or sympathy towards others' feelings and points of view. —*n.* 1. the power of thought, intelligence. 2. ability to understand. 3. ability to show insight or feel sympathy, kindly tolerance. **4.** harmony in opinion or feeling, *a better understanding between nations.* **5.** an informal or preliminary agreement, *reached an understanding.*

understate *v.* to state (a thing) in very restrained terms, to represent as being less than it really is. **understatement** *n.*

understeer *v.* (of a car etc.) to have a tendency to turn less sharply than was intended. —*n.* this tendency.

understudy *n.* a person who studies the part in a play or the duties etc. of another in order to be able to take his place at short notice if necessary. —*v.* (understudied, understudying) to act as understudy to, to learn (a part etc.) as understudy.

undertake *v.* (undertook, undertaken, undertaking) **1.** to agree or promise to do something, to make oneself responsible for, *undertook the cooking* or *to do the cooking.* **2.** to guarantee, *we cannot undertake that you will make a profit.*

undertaker *n.* one whose business is to prepare the dead for burial or cremation and make arrangements for funerals.

undertaking *n.* **1.** work etc. undertaken. **2.** a promise or guarantee. **3.** the business of an undertaker.

undertone *n.* **1.** a low or subdued tone; *they spoke in undertones,* spoke quietly. **2.** a colour that modifies another, *pink with mauve undertones.* **3.** an underlying quality or implication, an undercurrent of feeling, *a threatening undertone.*

undertow (**un**-der-toh) *n.* a current below the surface of the sea, moving in an opposite direction to the surface current.

undertrick *n.* a trick not taken and by which players fall short of a contract made in the game of bridge.

undervalue *v.* to put too low a value on.

underwater *adj.* situated or used or done beneath the surface of water. — *adv.* beneath the surface of water.

underwear *n.* garments worn under indoor clothing.

underweight *adj.* weighing less than is normal or required or permissible.

underwent *see* undergo.

underworld *n.* **1.** (in mythology) the abode of spirits of the dead, under the earth. **2.** the part of society habitually engaged in crime.

underwrite *v.* (underwrote, underwritten, underwriting) **1.** to sign and accept liability under (an insurance policy, especially for ships), thus guaranteeing payment in the event of loss or damage. **2.** to undertake to finance (an enterprise). **3.** to undertake to buy all the stock in (a company etc.) that is not bought by the public. **underwriter** *n.*

undeserved *adj.* not deserved as reward or punishment. **undeservedly** (un-di-**zerv**-idli) *adv.*

undesirable *adj.* not desirable, objectionable. —*n.* a person who is undesirable to a community.

undeveloped *adj.* not developed.

undies *pl. n.* (*informal*) women's underwear.

undignified *adj.* not dignified.

undo *v.* (undid, undone, undoing) **1.** to unfasten, to untie, to unwrap. **2.** to annul, to cancel the effect of, *cannot undo the past.*

undoing *n.* bringing or being brought to ruin, a cause of this, *drink was his undoing.*

undone *adj.* **1.** unfastened. **2.** not done, *left the work undone.* **3.** (*old use*) brought to ruin or destruction, *we are undone!*

undoubted *adj.* not regarded as doubtful, not disputed. **undoubtedly** *adv.*

undreamed-of, undreamt-of *adjs.* not imagined, not thought to be possible.

undress *v.* to take off one's clothes or the clothes of (another person). —*n.* the state of being not clothed or not fully clothed. **2.** clothes or a uniform for non-ceremonial occasions.

undue *adj.* excessive, disproportionate.

undulate (**un**-dew-layt) *v.* to have or cause to have a wavy movement or appearance. **undulation** *n.*

unduly *adj.* excessively, disproportionately.

undying *adj.* everlasting, never-ending, *undying fame.*

unearned *adj.* not earned; *unearned income,* income from interest on investments and similar sources, not wages or salary or fees.

unearth *v.* **1.** to uncover or obtain from the ground by digging. **2.** to bring to light, to find by searching.

unearthly *adj.* **1.** not earthly. **2.** supernatural, mysterious and frightening. **3.** (*informal*) absurdly early or inconvenient, *getting up at this unearthly hour.*

uneasy *adj.* **1.** not comfortable, *passed an uneasy night.* **2.** not confident, worried. **3.** worrying, *they had an uneasy suspicion that all was not well.* **uneasily** *adv.,* **uneasiness** *n.*

uneatable *adj.* not fit to be eaten (because of its condition).

uneconomic *adj.* not profitable, not likely to be profitable.

uneconomical *adj.* not economical.

uneducated *adj.* not educated, ignorant.

unemployable *adj.* unfitted for paid employment, e.g. because of character or lack of abilities.

unemployed *adj.* **1.** having no employment, temporarily without a paid job. **2.** not in use. **unemployment** *n.*

unending *adj.* endless.

unequal *adj.* **1.** not equal. **2.** (of work or achievements etc.) not of the same quality throughout. **3.** not with equal advantage to both sides, not well matched, *unequal bargain* or *contest*. **unequally** *adv.* □ **be unequal to,** (of a person) to be not strong enough or not clever enough etc. for, *was unequal to the task.*

unequalled *adj.* without an equal.

unequivocal (un-i-**kwiv**-ŏkăl) *adj.* clear and unmistakable, not ambiguous. **unequivocally** *adv.*

unerring *adj.* making no mistake, *with unerring accuracy.* **unerringly** *adv.*

UNESCO, Unesco (yoo-**ness**-koh) *abbrev.* United Nations Educational, Scientific, & Cultural Organization.

unethical *adj.* not ethical, unscrupulous in business or professional conduct. **unethically** *adv.*

uneven *adj.* **1.** not level or smooth. **2.** varying, not uniform. **3.** unequal, *an uneven contest.* **unevenly** *adv.*, **unevenness** *n.*

unexampled *adj.* having no precedent or nothing else that can be compared with it, *an unexampled opportunity.*

unexceptionable *adj.* with which no fault can be found. **unexceptionably** *adv.* ¶ Do not confuse with unexceptional.

unexceptional *adj.* not exceptional, quite ordinary. ¶ Do not confuse with unexceptionable.

unexpected *adj.* not expected. **unexpectedly** *adv.*

unfailing *adj.* never ending, constant, reliable, *his unfailing good humour.*

unfair *adj.* not impartial, not in accordance with justice. **unfairly** *adv.*, **unfairness** *n.*

unfaithful *adj.* **1.** not loyal, not keeping to one's promise. **2.** having committed adultery. **unfaithfully** *adv.*, **unfaithfulness** *n.*

unfamiliar *adj.* not familiar. **unfamiliarity** *n.*

unfasten *v.* to make loose, to open the fastening(s) of.

unfeeling *adj.* **1.** lacking the power of sensation or sensitivity. **2.** unsympathetic, not caring about others' feelings. **unfeelingly** *adv.*, **unfeelingness** *n.*

unfit *adj.* **1.** unsuitable. **2.** not in perfect health or physical condition. —*v.* (unfitted, unfitting) to make unsuitable.

unflappable *adj.* (*informal*) remaining calm in a crisis, not getting into a flap. **unflappability** *n.*

unfold *v.* **1.** to open, to spread (a thing) or become spread out. **2.** to become visible or known, *as the story unfolds.*

unforgettable *adj.* not able to be forgotten.

unfortunate *adj.* **1.** having bad luck. **2.** unsuitable, regrettable, *a most unfortunate choice of words.* —*n.* an unfortunate person. —**unfortunately** *adv.*

unfounded *adj.* with no foundation of fact(s).

unfreeze *v.* (unfroze, unfrozen, unfreezing) to thaw, to cause to thaw.

unfrock *v.* to deprive (a priest) of his priesthood.

unfurl *v.* to unroll, to spread out.

ungainly *adj.* awkward-looking, clumsy, ungraceful. **ungainliness** *n.*

unget-at-able *adj.* (*informal*) difficult or impossible to reach, inaccessible.

ungodly *adj.* **1.** not giving reverence to God, not religious, wicked. **2.** (*informal*) outrageous, very inconvenient, *phoning at this ungodly hour.*

ungovernable *adj.* uncontrollable, *an ungovernable temper.*

ungrateful *adj.* feeling no gratitude. **ungratefully** *adj.*

unguarded *adj.* **1.** not guarded. **2.** thoughtless, incautious, *in an unguarded moment.*

unguent (**ung**-wĕnt) *n.* an ointment or lubricant.

unhappy *adj.* (unhappier, unhappiest) **1.** not happy, sad. **2.** unfortunate. **3.** unsuitable. **unhappily** *adv.*, **unhappiness** *n.*

unhealthy *adj.* (unhealthier, unhealthiest) **1.** not having or not showing good health. **2.** harmful to health. **3.** (*informal*) unwise, dangerous.

unheard *adj.* not heard. **unheard-of** *adj.* not previously heard of or done.

unhinge *v.* to cause to become mentally unbalanced, *the shock unhinged his mind.*

unholy *adj.* (unholier, unholiest) **1.** wicked, irreverent. **2.** (*informal*) very great, outrageous, *making an unholy row.*

unhook *v.* **1.** to detach from a hook or hooks. **2.** to unfasten by releasing the hook(s).

unhoped-for *adj.* not hoped for or expected.

unhorse *v.* to throw or drag (a rider) from a horse.

unicorn *n.* a mythical animal resembling a horse with a single horn projecting from its forehead.

unidentified *adj.* not identified.

uniform *n.* distinctive clothing intended to identify the wearer as a member of a certain organization or group. —*adj.* always the same, not varying, *planks of uniform thickness.* —**uniformly** *adv.,* **uniformity** (yoo-ni-**form**-iti) *n.*

uniformed *adj.* wearing a uniform.

unify *v.* (unified, unifying) to form into a single unit, to unite. **unification** *n.*

unilateral (yoo-ni-**lat**-erăl) *adj.* one-sided, done by or affecting one person or group or country etc. and not another. **unilaterally** *adv.*

unimpeachable *adj.* completely trustworthy, not open to doubt or question, *unimpeachable honesty.* **unimpeachably** *adv.*

uninhabitable *adj.* not suitable for habitation.

uninhabited *adj.* not inhabited.

uninhibited *adj.* not inhibited, having no inhibitions.

uninspired *adj.* not inspired, (of speeches) commonplace, not outstanding.

unintelligible *adj.* not intelligible, impossible to understand. **unintelligibly** *adv.*

uninterested *adj.* not interested, showing or feeling no concern.

union *n.* **1.** uniting, being united. **2.** a whole formed by uniting parts, an association formed by the uniting of people or groups. **3.** a trade union. **4.** a coupling for pipes or rods. **5.** a fabric with mixed materials, e.g. cotton with linen or jute. □ **Union Jack.** the national flag of the United Kingdom. **Union of Soviet Socialist Republics,** a country (= Russia) extending from eastern Europe to the Pacific, consisting of 15 republics.

unionist *n.* **1.** a member of a trade union, a supporter of trade unions. **2.** one who favours union.

unionize *v.* to organize into or cause to join a trade union. **unionization** *n.*

unique (yoo-**neek**) *adj.* **1.** being the only one of its kind, *this vase is unique.* **2.** unusual, remarkable, *this makes it even more unique.* (¶ Many people regard the use in sense 2 as illogical and incorrect.) **uniquely** *adv.*

unisex (**yoo**-ni-seks) *n.* the tendency of the human sexes to become indistinguishable in dress etc. —*adj.* designed in a style suitable for people of either sex.

unison *n.* **in unison, 1.** sounding or singing together at the same pitch or a corresponding one. **2.** in agreement or concord, *all the firms acted in unison.*

unit *n.* **1.** an individual thing or person or group regarded for purposes of calculation etc. as single and complete, or as part of a complex whole, *the family as the unit of society.* **2.** a quantity chosen as a standard in terms of which other quantities

may be expressed, or for which a stated charge is made. **3.** a part or group with a specified function within a complex machine or organization. **4.** a piece of furniture for fitting with others like it or made of complementary parts. □ **unit pricing,** pricing of articles according to a standard unit (e.g. per kilogram or litre). **unit trust,** an investment company investing contributions from a number of people in various securities and paying them a dividend (calculated on the average return from these) in proportion to their holdings.

Unitarian (yoo-ni-**tair**-iăn) *n.* a member of a Christian religious sect maintaining that God is one person, not a Trinity.

unitary *adj.* of a unit or units.

unite *v.* **1.** to join together, to make or become one. **2.** to agree or combine or co-operate, *they all united in condemning the action.* □ **United Arab Emirates,** a group of countries on or near the Persian Gulf. **United Kingdom,** Great Britain and Northern Ireland. **United Nations,** an international peace-seeking organization of about 150 countries. **United Reformed Church,** that formed in 1972 from the English Presbyterian Church and the majority of the Congregational Church. **United States of America,** a country in North America consisting of 50 States and the District of Columbia.

unity *n.* **1.** the state of being one or a unit. **2.** a thing forming a complex whole. **3.** the number one in mathematics. **4.** harmony, agreement in feelings or ideas or aims etc., *dwell together in unity.*

universal *adj.* of or for or done by all. **universally** *adv.* □ **universal joint,** a joint that connects two shafts in such a way that they can be at any angle to each other.

universe *n.* all existing things, including the earth and its creatures and all the heavenly bodies.

university *n.* an educational institution that provides instruction and facilities for research in many branches of advanced learning, and awards degrees.

unjust *adj.* not just or fair. **unjustly** *adv.*

unkempt *adj.* looking untidy or neglected.

unkind *adj.* not kind, harsh. **unkindly** *adv.,* **unkindness** *n.*

unknown *adj.* not known, not identified. —*n.* an unknown person or thing. —*adv.* **unknown to,** without the knowledge of.

unladen *adj.* not laden; *unladen weight,* the weight of a vehicle etc. when not loaded with goods.

unlearn *v.* to cause (a thing) to be no longer in one's knowledge or memory.

unleash v. **1.** to set free from a leash or restraint. **2.** to set (a thing) free so that it can attack or pursue something.

unleavened (un-**lev**-ĕnd) adj. not leavened, (of bread) made without yeast or other raising agent.

unless conj. if . . . not, except when, we shall not move unless we are obliged to.

unlike adj. **1.** not like, different from. **2.** not characteristic of, such behaviour is quite unlike him. —prep. differently from, unlike her mother, she enjoys riding.

unlikely adj. **1.** not likely to happen or be true, an unlikely tale. **2.** not likely to be successful, the most unlikely candidate.

unlimited adj. not limited, very great in number or quantity.

unlined adj. **1.** without a lining. **2.** not marked with lines.

unlisted adj. not included in a list, not in a published list of telephone numbers or Stock Exchange prices.

unload v. **1.** to remove a load from (a ship etc.), to remove cargo. **2.** to get rid of. **3.** to remove the charge from (a gun etc.).

unlock v. **1.** to release the lock of (a door etc.). **2.** to release by or as if by unlocking.

unlooked-for adj. unexpected.

unlucky adj. not lucky, wretched, having or bringing bad luck. **unluckily** adv.

unman v. (unmanned, unmanning) to weaken the self-control or courage of (a man).

unmanned adj. operated without a crew, unmanned space flights.

unmarried adj. not married.

unmask v. **1.** to remove the mask from, to remove one's mask. **2.** to expose the true character of.

unmentionable adj. so bad or embarrassing or shocking that it may not be spoken of. **unmentionables** pl. n. unmentionable things or people.

unmistakable adj. clear and obvious, not able to be mistaken for another. **unmistakably** adv.

unmitigated (un-**mit**-i-gayt-id) adj. not modified, absolute, an unmitigated scoundrel.

unmoved adj. not moved, not changed in one's purpose, not affected by emotion.

unnatural adj. **1.** not natural or normal. **2.** lacking natural feelings of affection. **3.** artificial. **unnaturally** adv.

unnecessary adj. **1.** not necessary. **2.** more than is necessary, with unnecessary care. **unnecessarily** adv.

unnerve v. to cause to lose courage or determination.

unnumbered adj. **1.** not marked with a number. **2.** countless.

unobtrusive (un-ŏb-**troo**-siv) adj. not obtrusive, not making oneself or itself noticed. **unobtrusively** adv.

unoffending adj. not offending, harmless, innocent.

unofficial adj. not official; unofficial strike, one not formally approved by the strikers' trade union **unofficially** adv.

unpack v. to open and remove the contents of (luggage etc.), to take out from its packaging or from a suitcase etc.

unpaid adj. **1.** (of a debt) not yet paid. **2.** not receiving payment for work etc.

unparalleled adj. not paralleled, never yet equalled, unparalleled enthusiasm.

unparliamentary adj. contrary to parliamentary custom. **unparliamentary language,** oaths or abuse.

unperson n. a person whose name or existence is ignored or denied.

unpick v. to undo the stitching of.

unplaced adj. not placed as one of the first three in a race etc.

unpleasant adj. not pleasant. **unpleasantly** adv., **unpleasantness** n.

unpopular adj. not popular, not liked or enjoyed by people in general. **unpopularly** adv., **unpopularity** n.

unprecedented (un-**press**-i-dent-id) adj. for which there is no precedent, unparalleled.

unpredictable adj. impossible to predict.

unprejudiced adj. not prejudiced.

unpremeditated (un-pri-**med**-i-tayt-id) adj. not planned beforehand.

unprepared adj. not prepared beforehand, not ready or equipped to do something.

unprepossessing (un-pree-pŏ-**zess**-ing) adj. unattractive, not making a good impression.

unpretentious (un-pri-**ten**-shŭs) adj. not pretentious, not showy or pompous.

unprincipled adj. without good moral principles, unscrupulous.

unprintable adj. too rude or indecent to be printed.

unprofessional adj. **1.** not belonging to a profession. **2.** contrary to professional standards of behaviour.

unprofitable adj. **1.** not producing a profit. **2.** serving no useful purpose.

unqualified adj. **1.** (of a person) not legally or officially qualified to do something. **2.** not restricted or modified, gave it our unqualified approval.

unquestionable adj. not questionable, too clear to be doubted. **unquestionably** adv.

unquestioned adj. not disputed or doubted.

unquote v. (in dictation etc.) end the quotation, close the inverted commas, *Churchill said* (quote) *'We shall never surrender'* (*unquote*).

unravel v. (unravelled, unravelling) **1.** to disentangle. **2.** to undo (knitted fabric). **3.** to become unravelled.

unreadable *adj.* not readable.

unreal *adj.* not real, existing in the imagination only. **unreality** (un-ri-**al**-iti) *n.*

unreason *n.* lack of reasonable thought or action.

unreasonable *adj.* **1.** not reasonable in one's attitude etc. **2.** excessive, going beyond the limits of what is reasonable or just. **unreasonably** *adv.*

unreel v. to unwind from a reel.

unrelenting *adj.* not becoming less in intensity or severity.

unrelieved *adj.* not relieved, without anything to give variation, *unrelieved gloom; a plain black dress unrelieved by any touches of colour.*

unremitting (un-ri-**mit**-ing) *adj.* not relaxing or ceasing, persistent.

unrepeatable *adj.* **1.** that cannot be done or offered etc. again, *unrepeatable bargains.* **2.** too foul etc. to be said again.

unrequited (un-ri-**kwy**-tid) *adj.* (of love) not returned or rewarded.

unreservedly (un-ri-**zerv**-idli) *adv.* without reservation or restriction, completely.

unrest *n.* restlessness, agitation.

unrestrained *adj.* not restrained.

unrighteous *adj.* not righteous, wicked.

unripe *adj.* not yet ripe.

unrivalled (un-**ry**-văld) *adj.* having no equal, incomparable.

unroll v. to open or become opened after being rolled.

unruly (un-**roo** li) *adj.* not easy to control or discipline, disorderly. **unruliness** *n.*

unsaddle v. to remove the saddle from (a horse).

unsaid (un-**sed**) *see* **unsay.** —*adj.* not spoken or expressed, *many things were left unsaid.*

unsalted *adj.* not seasoned with salt.

unsavoury *adj.* **1.** disagreeable to the taste or smell. **2.** morally unpleasant or disgusting, *has an unsavoury reputation.*

unsay v. (unsaid, unsaying) to take back or retract, *what's said can't be unsaid.*

unscathed (un-**skay**th*d*) *adj.* without suffering any injury.

unscramble v. to sort out from a scrambled state, to make (a scrambled transmission) intelligible.

unscrew v. to loosen (a screw or nut etc.) by turning it, to unfasten by turning or removing screws, or by twisting.

unscripted *adj.* without a prepared script.

unscrupulous (un-**skroo**-pew-lŭs) *adj.* without moral scruples, not prevented from doing wrong by scruples of conscience. **unscrupulously** *adv.*

unseat v. **1.** to dislodge (a rider) from horseback or from a bicycle etc. **2.** to remove from a parliamentary seat, *was unseated at the last election.*

unseeded *adj.* (of a tennis-player etc.) not seeded (*see* seed v. sense 4).

unseemly *adj.* not seemly, improper.

unseen *adj.* **1.** not seen, invisible. **2.** (of translation) done without previous preparation. —*n.* a passage in a foreign language for unseen translation.

unselfish *adj.* not selfish, considering the needs of others before one's own. **unselfishly** *adv.*, **unselfishness** *n.*

unsettle v. to make uneasy, to disturb the settled calm or stability of. **unsettled** *adj.* not settled, liable to change.

unshakeable *adj.* not able to be shaken, firm.

unshockable *adj.* not able to be shocked.

unshrinkable *adj.* not liable to become shrunk.

unsightly *adj.* not pleasant to look at, ugly.

unsigned *adj.* not signed.

unskilled *adj.* not having or needing skill or special training.

unsociable *adj.* not sociable, withdrawing oneself from others.

unsocial *adj.* **1.** unsociable. **2.** not suitable for society. **3.** not conforming to standard social practices; *unsocial hours,* hours of work that involve working when most people are free.

unsolicited (un-sŏ-**liss**-it-id) *adj.* not asked for, given or done voluntarily.

unsophisticated *adj.* not sophisticated, simple and natural or naïve.

unsound *adj.* not sound or strong, not free from defects or mistakes. **of unsound mind,** insane.

unsparing (un-**spair**-ing) *adj.* giving freely and lavishly, *unsparing in one's efforts.*

unspeakable *adj.* too great or too bad to be described in words, very objectionable.

unspecified *adj.* not specified.

unstable *adj.* **1.** not stable, tending to change suddenly. **2.** mentally or emotionally unbalanced.

unsteady *adj.* not steady. **unsteadily** *adv.*, **unsteadiness** *n.*

unstinted *adj.* given freely and lavishly.

unstitch v. to undo the stitches of (something sewn).

unstuck *adj.* detached after being stuck on or together. **come unstuck,** (*informal*) to suffer disaster, to fail.

unstudied *adj.* natural in manner, not affected, *with unstudied elegance.*

unsubstantial *adj.* not substantial, flimsy, having little or no factual basis.

unsuitable *adj.* not suitable. **unsuitably** *adv.*

unsullied (un-**sul**-id) *adj.* not sullied, pure.

unsuspecting *adj.* feeling no suspicion.

unswerving *adj.* not turning aside, unchanging, *unswerving loyalty.*

untapped *adj.* not tapped, not yet made use of, *the country's untapped resources.*

untenable (un-**ten**-ăbŭl) *adj.* (of a theory) not tenable, not able to be held, because strong arguments can be produced against it.

unthinkable *adj.* incredible, too unlikely or undesirable to be considered.

unthinking *adj.* thoughtless, done or said etc. without consideration.

untidy *adj.* (untidier, untidiest) not tidy. **untidily** *adv.,* **untidiness** *n.*

untie *v.* (untied, untying) to unfasten, to release from being tied up.

until *prep. & conj.* = till², used especially when it stands first (e.g. *until last year we had never been abroad*), or in formal use.

untimely *adj.* 1. happening at an unsuitable time. 2. happening too soon or sooner than is normal, *his untimely death.*

unto *prep.* (*old use*) to.

untold *adj.* 1. not told. 2. not counted, too much or too many to be counted, *untold wealth* or *wealth untold.*

untouchable *adj.* not able to be touched, not allowed to be touched. —*n.* a member of the lowest Hindu caste in India, held to defile members of a higher caste on contact.

untoward (un-tŏ-**wor**'d) *adj.* inconvenient, awkward, *if nothing untoward happens.*

untraceable *adj.* unable to be traced.

untrammelled *adj.* not hampered.

untried *adj.* not yet tried or tested.

untrue *adj.* 1. not true, contrary to facts. 2. not faithful or loyal. **untruly** *adv.*

untruth *n.* 1. an untrue statement, a lie. 2. lack of truth. **untruthful** *adj.,* **untruthfully** *adv.*

unused *adj.* not yet used.

unusual *adj.* not usual, exceptional, remarkable. **unusually** *adv.*

unutterable *adj.* too great or too intense to be expressed in words, *unutterable joy.* **unutterably** *adv.*

unvarnished *adj.* 1. not varnished. 2. (of a statement etc.) plain and straightforward, *the unvarnished truth.*

unveil *v.* 1. to remove a veil from, to remove one's veil. 2. to remove concealing drapery from, as part of a ceremony, *unveiled the portrait.* 3. to disclose, to make publicly known.

unversed *adj.* not experienced in something, *he was unversed in court etiquette.*

unwanted *adj.* not wanted.

unwarrantable *adj.* unjustifiable.

unwarranted *adj.* unauthorized, unjustified.

unwary (un-**wair**-i) *adj.* not cautious.

unwell *adj.* not in good health.

unwholesome *adj.* 1. harmful to health or to moral well-being. 2. unhealthy-looking. **unwholesomeness** *n.*

unwieldy (un-**weel**-di) *adj.* awkward to move or control because of its size or shape or weight. **unwieldiness** *n.*

unwilling *adj.* not willing, reluctant, hesitating to do something. **unwillingly** *adv.*

unwind *v.* (unwound, unwinding) 1. to draw out or become drawn out from being wound. 2. (*informal*) to relax after a period of work or tension.

unwinking *adj.* 1. not winking, gazing or (of a light) shining steadily. 2. watchful.

unwisdom *n.* lack of wisdom.

unwise *adj.* not wise, foolish. **unwisely** *adv.*

unwitting *adj.* 1. unaware. 2. unintentional. **unwittingly** *adv.*

unwonted (un-**wohn**-tid) *adj.* not customary or usual, *spoke with unwonted rudeness.* **unwontedly** *adv.*

unworkable *adj.* not workable.

unworldly *adj.* not worldly, spiritually-minded. **unworldliness** *n.*

unworn *adj.* not yet worn.

unworthy *adj.* 1. not worthy, lacking worth or excellence. 2. not deserving, *he is unworthy of this honour.* 3. unsuitable to the character of a person or thing, *such conduct is unworthy of a king.*

unwrap *v.* (unwrapped, unwrapping) to open or become opened from being wrapped.

unwritten *adj.* not written; *an unwritten law,* one that rests on custom or tradition not on a statute.

unyielding *adj.* firm, not yielding to pressure or influence.

unzip *v.* (unzipped, unzipping) to open or become opened by the undoing of a zip-fastener.

up *adv.* 1. to an erect or vertical position, *stand up.* 2. to or in or at a higher place or level or value or condition, to a larger size, further north; *they are two goals up,* are winning by this amount; *I am £5 up on the transaction,* have gained this amount. 3. so as to be inflated, *pump up the tyres.* 4. at or towards a central place or a university. **5.** to the place or time or amount etc. in question, *up till now*; *can take up to four passengers*. **6.** out of bed, (of a stage curtain) raised at the start of a performance, (of a jockey) in the saddle. **7.** into a condition of activity or efficiency, *getting up steam*; *stirred up trouble*; *house is up for sale*; *the hunt is up*, is in progress. **8.** apart, into pieces, *tore it up*; *the road is up*, with surface broken or removed during repairs. **9.** into a compact state, securely, *pack it up*; *tie it up*. **10.** to be finished, *your time is up*. **11.** (*informal*) happening (especially of something unusual or undesirable), *something is up*. —**up** *prep*. **1.** upwards along or through or into, from bottom to top of. **2.** at a higher part of, *fix it further up the wall*. —**up** *adj*. **1.** directed upwards, *an up stroke*. **2.** travelling towards a central place, *an up train*; *the up platform*, for such a train. —**up** *v*. (upped, upping) (*informal*) **1.** to begin to do something suddenly or unexpectedly, *he upped and demanded an inquiry*. **2.** to raise, to pick up, *he upped with his fists*. **3.** to increase, *they promptly upped the price*. ☐ **on the up-and-up.** (*informal*) steadily improving; honest, honestly. **up against**, close to; in or into contact with; (*informal*) faced with, as an opponent or problem; *up against it*, in great difficulties. **up-and-coming** *adj*. (*informal*) enterprising and likely to be successful. **up and down**, to and fro. **up-and-over** *adj*. (of a door) opened by being raised and turned into a horizontal position. **up-country** *adv*. towards the interior of a country. **up front**, (*informal*) in front; in advance; straightforward, uninhibited. **up in**, (*informal*) knowledgeable about, *not very well up in mathematics*. **ups and downs**, alternate good and bad fortune. **up stage**, at or towards the back of a theatre stage. **up to**, occupied with, doing, *what is he up to?*; required as a duty or obligation from, *it's up to us to help her*; capable of, *don't feel up to a long walk*. **up to date**, in current fashion; in accordance with what is now known or required, *bring the files up to date*. **up-to-date** *adj*. in current fashion, in accordance with what is now known, *up-to-date clothes* or *information*.

upas-tree (yoo-păs) *n*. a Javanese tree yielding a poisonous sap.

upbeat *n*. an unaccented beat in music, when the conductor's baton moves upwards.

upbraid *v*. to reproach.

upbringing *n*. training and education during childhood.

update *v*. to bring up to date.

up-end *v*. to set or rise up on end.

upgrade *v*. to raise to a higher grade or rank.

upheaval *n*. **1.** a sudden heaving upwards. **2.** a violent change or disturbance.

upheave *v*. to lift forcibly.

uphill *adv*. in an upward direction, on an upward slope. —*adj*. **1.** going or sloping upwards. **2.** difficult, *it was uphill work*.

uphold *v*. (upheld, upholding) **1.** to support, to keep from falling. **2.** to support a decision or statement or belief.

upholster *v*. to put a fabric covering, padding, springs, etc. on (furniture). **upholsterer** *n*. ☐ **well-upholstered** *adj*. (*humorous*, of a person) fat.

upholstery *n*. **1.** the work of upholstering furniture. **2.** the material used for this.

upkeep *n*. keeping something in good condition and repair, the cost of this.

upland *n*. higher or inland parts of a country. —*adj*. of uplands.

uplift[1] (up-lift) *v*. to raise.

uplift[2] (up-lift) *n*. **1.** being raised. **2.** a mentally or morally elevating influence.

upon *prep*. on, *Stratford upon Avon*; *Christmas is almost upon us*. **once upon a time**, *see* once. **upon my word!**, an exclamation of shock or surprise.

upper *adj*. **1.** higher in place or position. **2.** situated on higher ground or to the north; *Upper Egypt*, the part furthest from the Nile delta. **3.** ranking above others; *the upper class*, people of the highest social class. —*n*. the part of a boot or shoe above the sole; *on one's uppers*, very short of money. ☐ **upper case**, capital letters for printing-type. **Upper Chamber** or **House**, the House of Lords as an assembly. **upper crust**, (*informal*) the aristocracy. **upper-cut** *n*. a blow in boxing, delivered upwards with the arm bent. **the upper hand**, mastery, dominance, *gained the upper hand*. **Upper Volta**, a country in West Africa.

uppermost *adj*. highest in place or rank. —*adv*. on or to the top or most prominent position.

uppish *adj*. pert, arrogant.

upright *adj*. **1.** in a vertical position. **2.** (of a piano) with the strings mounted vertically. **3.** strictly honest or honourable. —**upright** *n*. **1.** a post or rod placed upright, especially as a support. **2.** an upright piano. —**uprightness** *n*.

uprising *n*. a rebellion, a revolt against the authorities.

uproar *n*. an outburst of noise and excitement or anger.

uproarious *adj*. very noisy, with loud laughter. **uproariously** *adv*.

uproot v. 1. to pull out of the ground together with its roots. 2. to force to leave a native or established place, *we don't want to uproot ourselves and go to live abroad.*

upset¹ (up-**set**) v. (upset, upsetting) 1. to overturn, to become overturned. 2. to disrupt, *fog upset the timetable.* 3. to distress the mind or feelings of, to disturb the temper or digestion of. □ **upset the applecart**, to spoil a situation or someone's plans.

upset² (up-set) n. upsetting, being upset, *a stomach upset.*

upshot n. an outcome.

upside-down adv. & adj. 1. with the upper part underneath instead of on top. 2. in great disorder.

upstage adj. & adv. 1. nearer the back of a theatre stage. 2. snobbish, snobbishly. — **upstage** v. 1. to move upstage from (an actor) and make him face away from the audience. 2. to divert attention from or outshine (a person).

upstairs adv. up the stairs, to or on an upper floor. —adj. situated upstairs.

upstanding adj. well set up, strong and healthy.

upstart n. a person who has risen suddenly to a high position, especially one who behaves arrogantly.

upstream adj. & adv. in the direction from which a stream flows.

upsurge n. an upward surge, a rise.

uptake n. ability to understand what is meant, *quick in* or *on the uptake.*

uptight adj. (*informal*) 1. nervously tense. 2. annoyed.

upturn¹ (up-**tern**) v. to turn upwards, to turn upside down, to turn up (ground, in ploughing etc.).

upturn² (up-tern) n. 1. an upheaval. 2. an upward trend in business or fortune etc., an improvement.

upward adj. moving or leading or pointing towards what is higher or more important or earlier. **upwards** adv. towards what is higher etc.

upwind adj. & adv. in the direction from which the wind is blowing.

uranium (yoor-**ay**-niŭm) n. a heavy grey metal used as a source of nuclear energy.

urban adj. of or situated in a city or town. **urban guerrilla**, a terrorist operating in an urban area.

urbane (er-**bayn**) adj. having manners that are smooth and polite. **urbanely** adv., **urbanity** (er-**ban**-iti) n.

urbanize v. to change (a place) into a town-like area. **urbanization** n.

urchin n. 1. a mischievous or needy boy. 2. a sea-urchin.

Urdu (oor-doo) n. a language related to Hindi, one of the official languages of Pakistan.

ureter (yoor-ee-ter) n. either of the two ducts by which urine passes from the kidneys to the bladder.

urethra (yoor-ee-thră) n. the duct by which urine is discharged from the body.

urge v. 1. to drive onward, to encourage to proceed, *urging them on.* 2. to try hard or persistently to persuade, *urged him to accept the job.* 3. to recommend strongly with reasoning or entreaty, *urged on them the importance of keeping to the schedule.* —n. a feeling or desire that urges a person to do something.

urgent adj. 1. needing immediate attention or action or decision. 2. showing that something is urgent, *spoke in an urgent whisper.* **urgently** adv., **urgency** n.

urinal (yoor-in-ăl or yoor-I-năl) n. 1. a receptacle for urine, for use by a bedridden male person. 2. a structure to receive urine in a men's lavatory, a room or building containing this.

urinary (yoor-in-er-i) adj. of urine or its excretion, *urinary organs.*

urinate (yoor-in-ayt) v. to discharge urine from the body. **urination** n.

urine (yoor-in) n. waste liquid which collects in the bladder and is discharged from the body.

urn n. 1. a vase, usually with a stem and base, especially one used for holding the ashes of a cremated person. 2. a large metal container with a tap in which tea or coffee is made or from which it is served.

Uruguay (yoor-ŭ-gwy) a country in South America. **Uruguayan** adj. & n.

us pronoun 1. the objective case of we. 2. (*informal*) = we, *it's us.* 3. (*informal*) me, *give us your hand.*

US, USA abbrevs. United States of America.

usable adj. able to be used, fit for use.

usage (yoo-sij) n. 1. the manner of using or treating something, *it was damaged by rough usage.* 2. a habitual or customary practice, especially in the way words are used, *modern English usage.*

use¹ (pr. yooz) v. 1. to cause to act or serve for a purpose or as an instrument or as material for consumption. 2. to cause oneself to be known or addressed by (a name or title). 3. to treat in a specified way, to behave towards, *they used her shamefully.* 4. to exploit selfishly. **user** n. □ **use up**, to use the whole of (material etc.); to find a use for (remaining material or time); to exhaust or tire out.

use [2] (*pr.* yooss) *n.* **1.** using, being used. **2.** the right or power of using something, *lost the use of his arm.* **3.** the purpose for which something is used, work that a person or thing is able to do. □ **have no use for,** to have no purpose for which (a thing) can be used; to refuse to tolerate, to dislike. **make use of,** to use, to exploit.

used [1] (*pr.* yoozd) *adj.* (of clothes or vehicles) second-hand.

used [2] (*pr.* yoost) *v.* was or were accustomed in the past, *we used to go by train; they used not to do this.* —*adj.* having become familiar with (a thing) by practice or habit, *is used to getting up early.* □ **usedn't** (*pr.* yooz-nt) = used not.

useful *adj.* able to produce good results, able to be used for some practical purpose. **usefully** *adv.,* **usefulness** *n.* □ **make oneself useful,** to perform some practical or beneficial service.

useless *adj.* serving no useful purpose, not able to produce good results. **uselessly** *adv.,* **uselessness** *n*

usher *n.* **1.** a person who shows people to their seats in a public hall etc. or into someone's presence, or who walks before a person of rank. **2.** an official acting as doorkeeper in a lawcourt. —*v.* to lead in or out, to escort as usher.

usherette *n.* a woman who ushers people to their seats in a cinema or theatre.

usquebaugh (**us**-kwi-baw) *n.* whisky.

USSR *abbrev.* Union of Soviet Socialist Republics.

usual *adj.* such as happens or is done or used etc. in many or most instances; *the usual* or *my usual,* what I usually have, my usual drink etc. **usually** *adv.*

usurer (**yoo**-*zher*-er) *n.* a person who lends money at excessively high interest.

usurp (yoo-**zerp**) *v.* to take (power or a position or right) wrongfully or by force. **usurpation** *n.,* **usurper** *n.*

usury (**yoo**-*zher*-i) *n.* **1.** the lending of money at excessively high interest. **2.** an excessively high rate of interest.

Utah (**yoo**-tah) a State of the USA.

utensil (yoo-**ten**-sĭl) *n.* an instrument or container, especially for domestic use.

uterine (**yoo**-teryn) *adj.* of the uterus.

uterus (**yoo**-ter-ŭs) *n.* the womb.

utilitarian (yoo-tili-**tair**-iăn) *adj.* designed to be useful rather than decorative or luxurious, severely practical.

utility *n.* **1.** usefulness. **2.** a useful thing; *public utilities,* public services such as the supply of water or gas or electricity etc. —*adj.* severely practical. □ **utility room,** a room containing one or more large fixed domestic appliances (e.g. a washing-machine). **utility vehicle,** a vehicle serving various purposes.

utilize *v.* to use, to find a use for. **utilization** *n.*

utmost *adj.* furthest, greatest, extreme, *with the utmost care.* —*n.* the furthest point or degree etc. □ **do one's utmost,** to do as much as possible.

Utopia (yoo-**toh**-piă) *n.* an imaginary place or state of things where everything is perfect. **Utopian** *adj.* ¶ The title of a book by Sir Thomas More (1516), meaning 'Nowhere'.

utter [1] *adj.* complete, absolute, *utter bliss.* **utterly** *adv.*

utter [2] *v.* **1.** to make (a sound or words) with the mouth or voice, *uttered a sigh.* **2.** to speak, *he didn't utter.* **3.** to put (a forged banknote or coin etc.) into circulation. **utterance** *n.*

uttermost *adj.* & *n.* = utmost.

U-turn *n.* **1.** the driving of a vehicle in a U-shaped course so as to proceed in an opposite direction. **2.** a reversal of policy.

uvula (**yoov**-yoo-lă) *n.* the small fleshy projection hanging from the back of the roof of the mouth above the throat.

uxorious (uks-**or**-iŭs) *adj.* obsessively fond of one's wife.

Vv

V *abbrev.* volt(s).

Va. *abbrev.* Virginia.

vac *n.* (*informal*) **1.** a vacation. **2.** a vacuum cleaner.

vacancy *n.* **1.** the condition of being vacant, emptiness. **2.** an unoccupied position of employment, *we have a vacancy for a typist.* **3.** unoccupied accommodation, *this hotel has no vacancies.*

vacant *adj.* **1.** empty, not filled or occupied, *a vacant seat; applied for a vacant post.* **2.** showing no sign of thought or intelligence, having a blank expression. **vacantly** *adv.* □ **vacant possession,** (of a house etc.) the state of being empty of occupants and available for the purchaser to occupy immediately.

vacate (vă-**kayt**) *v.* to cease to occupy (a place or position).

vacation (vă-**kay**-shŏn) *n.* **1.** any of the intervals between terms in universities and lawcourts. **2.** (*Amer.*) a holiday. **3.** vacating, *immediate vacation of the house is essential.* —*v.* (*Amer.*) to spend a holiday.

vaccinate (**vak**-sin-ayt) *v.* to inoculate with a vaccine, especially against smallpox. **vaccination** *n.*

vaccine (vak-seen) *n.* **1.** a preparation of cowpox virus introduced into a person's bloodstream to immunize him against smallpox. **2.** any preparation used similarly to give immunity against an infection.

vacillate (vass-il-ayt) *v.* **1.** to waver, to keep changing one's mind. **2.** to swing or sway unsteadily. **vacillation** *n.*

vacuity (vă-kew-iti) *n.* **1.** emptiness. **2.** vacuousness.

vacuous (vak-yoo-ŭs) *adj.* empty-headed, inane, expressionless, *a vacuous stare*. **vacuously** *adv.,* **vacuousness** *n.*

vacuum *n.* (*pl.* vacuums *or, in science,* vacua) **1.** space completely empty of matter, space in a container from which the air has been pumped out. **2.** absence of normal or previous contents. **3.** (*informal*) a vacuum cleaner. —*v.* (*informal*) to clean with a vacuum cleaner. □ **vacuum cleaner,** an electrical appliance that takes up dust, dirt, etc. by suction. **vacuum flask,** a flask with a double wall that encloses a vacuum, used for keeping liquids hot or cold. **vacuum-packed** *adj.* sealed in a pack from which most of the air has been removed. **vacuum pump,** a pump for producing a vacuum. **vacuum tube,** a sealed tube with an almost perfect vacuum, allowing free passage of electric current.

vade-mecum (vah-di-may-kŭm) *n.* a handbook or other small useful work of reference.

Vaduz (va-doots) the capital of Liechtenstein.

vagabond *n.* a wanderer, a vagrant, especially an idle or dishonest one. —*adj.* of or like a vagabond.

vagary (vayg-er-i) *n.* a capricious act or idea or fluctuation, *vagaries of fashion*.

vagina (vă-jy-nă) *n.* the passage leading from the vulva to the womb in women and female animals. **vaginal** *adj.*

vagrant (vay-grant) *n.* a person without a settled home or regular work. **vagrancy** *n.*

vague *adj.* **1.** not clearly expressed or perceived or identified. **2.** not expressing one's thoughts clearly or precisely. **vaguely** *adv.,* **vagueness** *n.*

vain *adj.* **1.** conceited, especially about one's appearance. **2.** having no value or significance, *vain triumphs*. **3.** useless, futile, *in the vain hope of persuading him*. **vainly** *adv.* □ **in vain,** with no result, uselessly, *we tried, but in vain*. **take God's name in vain,** to use it irreverently.

vainglory *n.* extreme vanity, boastfulness. **vainglorious** (*adj*)

valance (val-ăns) *n.* a short curtain round the frame or canopy of a bedstead, or above a window or under a shelf.

vale *n.* a valley, *the Vale of Evesham*.

valediction (vali-dik-shŏn) *n.* saying farewell, the words used in this.

valedictory (vali-dik-ter-i) *adj.* saying farewell, *a valedictory speech*.

valence (vay-lĕns) *n.* the capacity of an atom to combine with another or others, as compared with that of the hydrogen atom, *carbon has a valence of four*.

valency (vay-lĕn-si) *n.* the unit of the combining-power of atoms, *carbon has 4 valencies*.

valentine *n.* **1.** a sweetheart chosen on St. Valentine's day (14 February, on which birds were supposed to pair). **2.** a card or picture etc. sent on this day (often anonymously) to one's valentine.

valerian (vă-leer-iăn) *n.* a strong-smelling herb with pink or white flowers.

valet (val-it *or* val-ay) *n.* **1.** a man's personal attendant who takes care of clothes etc. **2.** a hotel employee with similar duties. —*v.* (valeted, valeting) to act as valet to.

valetudinarian (vali-tew-din-air-iăn) *n.* a person who pays excessive attention to preserving his health.

Valhalla (val-hal-ă) *n.* (in Norse mythology) the hall in which the souls of slain heroes feasted.

valiant *adj.* brave, courageous. **valiantly** *adv.*

valid (val-id) *adj.* **1.** having legal force, legally acceptable or usable, *a valid passport*. **2.** (of reasoning etc.) sound and to the point, logical. **validity** (vă-lid-iti) *n.*

validate (val-id-ayt) *v.* to make valid, to confirm. **validation** *n.*

Valkyrie (val-ki-ri) *n.* (in Norse mythology) one of the war-maidens who selected heroes who were to die in battle.

Valletta (vă-let-ă) the capital of Malta.

valley *n.* (*pl.* valleys) **1.** a long low area between hills. **2.** a region drained by a river, *the Nile valley*.

valour (val-er) *n.* bravery, especially in fighting.

valse (*pr.* vahls) *n.* = waltz.

valuable *adj.* of great value or price or worth. **valuables** *pl. n.* valuable things, especially small personal possessions.

valuation *n.* estimation of a thing's value (especially by a professional valuer) or of a person's merit, the value decided upon.

value *n.* **1.** the amount of money or other commodity or service etc. considered to be equivalent to something else or for which a thing can be exchanged. **2.** desirability, usefulness, importance, *he learnt the value of regular exercise*. **3.** the ability of a thing to serve a purpose or cause an effect, *the food value of milk*; *news value*. **4.** the amount or quantity denoted by a figure etc., the duration of a musical sound indicated by a note, the relative importance of each playing-card etc. in a game; *tone values in a painting*, the relative lightness and darkness of its parts. — **value** *v.* **1.** to estimate the value of. **2.** to consider to be of great worth or importance. ☐ **value added tax**, tax on the amount by which the value of an article has been increased at each stage of its production. **values** *pl. n.* standards or principles considered valuable or important in life, *lack of moral values.*

valueless *adj.* having no value.

valuer *n.* a person who estimates values professionally.

valve *n.* **1.** a device for controlling the flow of gas or liquid through a pipe. **2.** a structure in the heart or in a blood-vessel allowing blood to flow in one direction only. **3.** a device for varying the length of the tube in a brass wind instrument. **4.** each half of the hinged shell of molluscs such as oysters. **5.** a thermionic valve (*see* thermionic).

valvular (**val**-vew-ler) *adj.* of the valves of the heart or blood-vessels.

vamoose *v.* (*slang*) to go away hurriedly.

vamp[1] *n.* the upper front part of a boot or shoe. — *v.* **1.** to make from odds and ends, *we'll vamp something up*. **2.** to improvise a musical accompaniment to a song or dance.

vamp[2] *n.* a seductive woman who uses her attraction to exploit men, an unscrupulous flirt. — *v.* to exploit or flirt with (a man) unscrupulously.

vampire *n.* **1.** a ghost or reanimated body supposed to leave a grave at night and suck the blood of living people. **2.** a person who preys on others. ☐ **vampire bat**, a tropical blood-sucking bat.

van[1] *n.* **1.** a covered vehicle for transporting goods or horses etc. or prisoners. **2.** a railway carriage for luggage or goods, or for the use of the guard.

van[2] *n.* the vanguard, the forefront.

van[3] *n.* (in tennis) vantage.

vandal *n.* a person who wilfully or maliciously damages public or private property or the beauties of nature. **vandalism** *n.* ¶ Named after the *Vandals*, a Germanic people who ravaged Gaul, Spain, North Africa, and Rome in the 4th–5th centuries, destroying many books and works of art.

vandalize *v.* to damage (property etc.) as a vandal.

vandyke beard a neat pointed beard like those in portraits by Van Dyck, a 17th-century portrait-painter.

vane *n.* **1.** a weather-vane. **2.** the blade of a propeller, sail of a windmill, or similar device acting on or moved by wind or water.

vanguard *n.* **1.** the foremost part of an army or fleet advancing or ready to do so. **2.** the leaders of a movement or fashion etc.

vanilla *n.* **1.** a flavouring obtained from the pods of a tropical climbing orchid, or made synthetically. **2.** this orchid.

vanish *v.* to disappear completely.

vanity *n.* **1.** conceit, especially about one's appearance. **2.** futility, worthlessness, something vain, *the pomps and vanity of this world*. ☐ **vanity bag** or **case**, a small bag or case used by a woman for carrying cosmetics etc.

vanquish *v.* to conquer.

vantage *n.* = advantage, especially as a score in tennis. **vantage-point** *n.* a place from which one has a good view of something.

Vanuatu (van-wah-too) an island country in the south-west Pacific.

vapid (**vap**-id) *adj.* insipid, uninteresting. **vapidity** (vă-**pid**-iti) *n.*

vaporize *v.* to convert or be converted into vapour. **vaporization** *n.*, **vaporizer** *n.*

vapour *n.* **1.** moisture or other substance diffused or suspended in air. **2.** the air-like substance into which certain liquid or solid substances can be converted by heating (*see* gas). **vaporous** *adj.*

variable *adj.* varying, changeable, (of a star) periodically varying in brightness. — *n.* something that varies or can vary, a variable quantity. **variability** *n.*

variance *n.* **at variance**, disagreeing, conflicting, (of people) in a state of discord or enmity.

variant *adj.* differing from something or from a standard, *'gipsy' is a variant spelling of 'gypsy'*. — *n.* a variant form or spelling etc.

variation *n.* **1.** varying, the extent to which something varies. **2.** a variant, a repetition of a melody in a different (usually more elaborate) form.

varicoloured (**vair**-i-kul-erd) *adj.* **1.** variegated in colour. **2.** of various or different colours.

varicose (**va**-ri-kohs) *adj.* (of a vein) permanently swollen or enlarged. **varicosity** (va-ri-**koss**-iti) *n.*

varied *see* vary. — *adj.* of different sorts, full of variety.

variegated (**vair**-i-gayt-id) *adj.* marked with irregular patches of different colours.

variety *n.* **1.** the quality of not being the same or of not being the same at all times. **2.** a quantity or range of different things, *for a variety of reasons.* **3.** a class of things that differ from others in the same general group, a member of such a class, *several varieties of spaniel.* **4.** an entertainment consisting of a series of short performances of different kinds (e.g. singing, dancing, acrobatics).

various *adj.* **1.** of several kinds, unlike one another. **2.** more than one, individual and separate, *we met various people.* **variously** *adv.*

varnish *n.* **1.** a liquid that dries to form a hard shiny transparent coating, used on wood or metal etc. **2.** nail varnish (*see* nail). —*v.* to coat with varnish.

vary *v.* (varied, varying) **1.** to make or become different, *you can vary the pressure*; *his temper varies from day to day.* **2.** to be different or of different kinds, *opinions vary on this point.*

vascular (**vas**-kew-ler) *adj.* consisting of vessels or ducts for conveying blood or sap within an organism, *vascular system.*

vase (*pr.* vahz) *n.* an open usually tall vessel of glass, pottery, etc. used for holding cut flowers or as an ornament.

vasectomy (vă-**sekt**-ŏmi) *n.* surgical removal of part of each of the ducts through which semen passes from the testicles, especially as a method of birth control.

Vaseline (**vas**-i-leen) *n.* (*trade mark*) petroleum jelly used as an ointment or lubricant.

vassal *n.* a humble servant or subordinate.

vast *adj.* **1.** immense, very great in area or size, *a vast expanse of water.* **2.** (*informal*) very great, *it makes a vast difference.* **vastly** *adv.*, **vastness** *n.*

vat *n.* a tank or other great vessel for holding liquids.

VAT *abbrev.* value added tax.

Vatican *n.* **1.** the pope's official residence in Rome. **2.** the papal government. ☐ **Vatican City**, an independent papal State in Rome, including the Vatican and St. Peter's.

vaudeville (**vaw**-dĕ-vil) *n.* variety entertainment.

vault [1] *n.* **1.** an arched roof. **2.** a vault-like covering; *the vault of heaven*, the sky. **3.** a cellar or underground room used as a place of storage. **4.** a burial chamber, *the family vault.* ☐ **vaulted** *adj.* covered with a vault, made in the form of a vault. **vaulting** *n.* the structure forming a vault.

vault [2] *v.* to jump or leap, especially while resting on the hand(s) or with the help of a pole, *vaulted the gate* or *over the gate.* —*n.* a leap performed in this way. ☐ **vaulting-horse** *n.* a padded structure for vaulting over in a gymnasium.

vaunt *v.* to boast. —*n.* a boast.

VC *abbrev.* Victoria Cross.

VD *abbrev.* venereal disease.

VDU *abbrev.* visual display unit (*see* visual).

've (*informal*, especially after pronouns) have, *they've finished.*

veal *n.* calf's flesh as food.

vector *n.* **1.** (in mathematics) a quantity that has both magnitude and direction (e.g. velocity, = speed in a given direction). **2.** the carrier of a disease or infection.

veer *v.* to change direction or course, (of wind) to change gradually in a clockwise direction.

vegan (**vee**-găn) *n.* a strict vegetarian who eats no animal products (e.g. eggs) at all.

vegetable *n.* **1.** a plant of which some part is used (raw or cooked) as food, especially as an accompaniment to meat. **2.** a person leading a dull monotonous life, one who is physically alive but mentally inert owing to injury or illness or abnormality. —*adj.* of or from or relating to plant life.

vegetarian *n.* a person who eats no meat.

vegetate (**vej**-i-tayt) *v.* to live an uneventful or monotonous life.

vegetation *n.* **1.** plants collectively. **2.** vegetating.

vehement (**vee**-i-měnt) *adj.* showing strong feeling, intense, *a vehement denial.* **vehemently** *adv.*, **vehemence** *n.*

vehicle (**vee**-i-kŭl) *n.* **1.** a conveyance for transporting passengers or goods on land or in space. **2.** a means by which something is expressed or displayed, *art can be a vehicle for propaganda*; *the play was an excellent vehicle for this actress's talents.*

vehicular (vi-**hik**-yoo-ler) *adj.* of vehicles, *vehicular traffic.*

veil *n.* a piece of fine net or other fabric worn as part of a head-dress or to protect or conceal the face. —*v.* to cover with or as if with a veil; *a veiled threat*, partially concealed. ☐ **beyond the veil**, in the unknown state of life after death. **draw a veil over**, to avoid discussing or calling attention to. **take the veil**, to become a nun.

veiling *n.* thin material for making veils.

vein *n.* **1.** one of the tubes carrying blood from all parts of the body to the heart. **2.** one of the thread-like structures forming the framework of a leaf or of an insect's wing. **3.** a narrow strip or streak of a different colour, e.g. in marble. **4.** a long continuous or branching deposit of mineral or ore, especially in a fissure. **5.** a mood or manner, *she spoke in a humorous vein.*

veined *adj.* filled or marked with veins.

veld (*pr.* velt) *n.* open grassland in South Africa.

veleta (vĕl-ee-tă) *n.* an old-fashioned ballroom dance in triple time.

vellum *n.* **1.** a kind of fine parchment. **2.** smooth writing-paper.

velocity *n.* speed, especially in a given direction.

velour (vil-**oor**) *n.* a plush-like fabric.

velvet *n.* **1.** a woven fabric (especially of silk or nylon) with thick short pile on one side. **2.** a furry skin covering a growing antler. **velvety** *adj.* ☐ **on velvet,** in an advantageous or prosperous position. **velvet glove,** outward gentleness of treatment.

velveteen *n.* cotton velvet.

venal (**veen**-ăl) *adj.* **1.** able to be bribed. **2.** (of conduct) influenced by bribery. **venality** (veen-**al**-iti) *n.*

vend *v.* to sell or offer for sale. **vending-machine** *n.* a slot-machine where small articles can be obtained.

vendetta (ven-**det**-ă) *n.* a feud.

vendor *n.* **1.** (especially in Law) a person who sells something. **2.** a vending-machine.

veneer *n.* **1.** a thin layer of finer wood covering the surface of cheaper wood in furniture etc. **2.** a superficial show of some good quality, *a veneer of politeness.* —*v.* to cover with a veneer.

venerable (**ven**-er-ăbŭl) *adj.* **1.** worthy of deep respect because of age or associations etc., *these venerable ruins.* **2.** the title of an archdeacon in the Church of England. **venerability** *n.*

venerate *v.* to regard with deep respect, to honour as hallowed or sacred. **veneration** *n.*, **venerator** *n.*

venereal (vin-**eer**-iăl) *adj.* (of disease or infection) contracted chiefly by sexual intercourse with a person who is already infected.

Venetian (vin-ee-shăn) *adj.* of Venice. **Venetian blind,** a window blind consisting of horizontal slats that can be adjusted to let in or exclude light.

Venezuela (ven-ez-**way**-lă) a country in South America. **Venezuelan** *adj. & n.*

vengeance *n.* retaliation for hurt or harm done to oneself or to a person etc. whom one supports. **take vengeance,** to inflict harm in retaliation. **with a vengeance,** in an extreme degree.

vengeful *adj.* seeking vengeance. **vengefully** *adv.*

venial (**veen**-iăl) *adj.* (of a sin or fault) pardonable, not serious.

venison (**ven**-i-sŏn) *n.* deer's flesh as food.

venom (**ven**-ŏm) *n.* **1.** poisonous fluid secreted by certain snakes, scorpions, etc. and injected into a victim by a bite or sting. **2.** strong bitter feeling or language, hatred.

venomous (**ven**-ŏm-ŭs) *adj.* **1.** secreting venom, *venomous snakes.* **2.** full of bitter feeling or hatred. **venomously** *adv.*

vent[1] *n.* a slit in a garment (especially a coat or jacket) at the bottom of a back or side seam.

vent[2] *n.* an opening allowing air or gas or liquid to pass out of or into a confined space, *a smoke vent.* —*v.* **1.** to make a vent in. **2.** to give vent to, *vented his anger on the office boy.* ☐ **give vent to,** to give an outlet to (feelings etc.), to express freely, *gave vent to his anger.*

ventilate *v.* **1.** to cause air to enter or circulate freely in (a room etc.). **2.** to express (an opinion etc.) publicly so that others may consider and discuss it. **ventilation** *n.*

ventilator *n.* a device for ventilating a room etc.

ventral *adj.* of or on the abdomen, *this fish has a ventral fin.* **ventrally** *adv.*

ventricle (**ven**-trik-ŭl) *n.* a cavity or chamber in an organ of the body, especially one of the two in the heart that pump blood into the arteries by contracting.

ventriloquist (ven-**tril**-ŏ-kwist) *n.* an entertainer who produces voice-sounds so that they seem to come from a source other than himself. **ventriloquism** *n.*

venture *n.* an undertaking that involves risk. —*v.* **1.** to dare, *did not venture to stop him.* **2.** to dare to go or do or utter, *did not venture forth; ventured an opinion.* ☐ **at a venture,** at random.

venturesome *adj.* ready to take risks, daring.

venue (**ven**-yoo) *n.* an appointed place of meeting, a place fixed for a sports match.

veracious (ver-**ay**-shŭs) *adj.* **1.** truthful. **2.** true. **veraciously** *adv.*, **veracity** (ver-**ass**-iti) *n.*

veranda *n.* a roofed terrace along the side of a house.

verb *n.* a word indicating action or occurrence or being, e.g. *bring, came, exist.*

verbal *adj.* **1.** of or in words, *verbal accuracy.* **2.** spoken, not written, *a verbal statement.* **3.** of a verb, *verbal inflexions.* —*n.* a verbal statement, especially one made to the police. —**verbally** *adv.* ☐ **verbal noun,** a noun (such as *singing, drinking*) derived from a verb.

verbalize *v.* to put into words.

verbatim (ver-**bay**-tim) *adv. & adj.* in exactly the same words, word for word, *copied it verbatim.*

verbena (ver-**been**-ă) *n.* the plant vervain or a cultivated variety of this. **lemon verbena,** a similar plant with lemon-scented leaves.

verbiage (**verb**-i-ij) *n.* an excessive number of words used to express an idea.

verbose (ver-**bohs**) *adj.* using more words than are needed. **verbosely** *adv.*, **verbosity** (ver-**boss**-iti) *n.*

verdant *adj.* (of grass or fields) green.

verdict *n.* **1.** the decision reached by a jury. **2.** a decision or opinion given after examining or testing or experiencing something.

verdigris (**verd**-i-grees) *n.* green rust on copper or brass.

verge *n.* **1.** the extreme edge or brink of something. **2.** the point beyond which something new begins or occurs, *on the verge of ruin.* **3.** the grass edging of a road or flower-bed etc. —*v.* **verge on,** to border on, to approach closely.

verger (**ver**-jer) *n.* **1.** a person who is care-taker and attendant in a church. **2.** an official who carries the mace etc. before a bishop or other dignitary.

veriest *adj.* (*old use*) most genuine, most truly so called, *the veriest simpleton knows that.*

verify *v.* (verified, verifying) to check the truth or correctness of, *please verify these figures.* **verification** *n.*, **verifier** *n.*

verily *adv.* (*old use*) in truth.

verisimilitude (ve-ri-sim-**il**-i-tewd) *n.* an appearance of being true.

veritable *adj.* real, rightly named, *a veritable villain.*

verity *n.* (*old use*) the truth of something.

vermicelli (verm-i-**sel**-i) *n.* pasta made in long slender threads; *chocolate vermicelli,* very small rod-shaped pieces of chocolate used for decorating cakes etc.

vermicide *n.* a medicinal drug that kills worms.

vermiform (**verm**-i-form) *adj.* worm-like in shape, *the vermiform appendix.*

vermilion *n. & adj.* bright red.

vermin *pl. n.* **1.** common animals and birds of an objectionable kind, especially those (such as foxes, rats, mice, owls) that injure crops or food or game. **2.** un-pleasant or parasitic insects (e.g. lice). **3.** people who are unpleasant or harmful to society.

verminous *adj.* infested with vermin.

Vermont (ver-**mont**) a State of the USA.

vermouth (**ver**-mŭth) *n.* white wine fla-voured with fragrant herbs.

vernacular (ver-**nak**-yoo-ler) *n.* **1.** the lan-guage of a country or district. **2.** homely speech.

vernal *adj.* of or occurring in the season of spring.

veronica *n.* a herb often with blue flowers, speedwell.

verruca (ver-**oo**-kă) *n.* a wart or wart-like swelling, especially on the foot.

versatile (ver-**să**-tyl) *adj.* able to do, or be used for, many different things. **versatility** (ver-să-**til**-iti) *n.*

verse *n.* **1.** a metrical form of composition, as distinct from prose. **2.** a metrical com-position. **3.** an author's metrical or poetical works. **4.** a group of lines forming a unit in a poem or hymn. **5.** each of the short num-bered divisions of a chapter of the Bible.

versed *adj.* **versed in,** experienced or skilled in, having a knowledge of.

versicle (**ver**-si-kŭl) *n.* each of the short sentences in the liturgy, said or sung by the clergyman and alternating with the responses' of the congregation.

version *n.* **1.** a particular person's account of a matter. **2.** a translation into another language, *the Revised Version of the Bible.* **3.** a special or variant form of a thing, *the de luxe version of this car.*

vers libre (*pr.* vair **leebr**) verse with no regular metrical pattern. (¶ French, = free verse.)

versus *prep.* against, *Arsenal versus Liver-pool.*

vertebra (**ver**-tib-ră) *n.* (*pl.* vertebrae, *pr.* **ver**-tib-ree) any of the individual bones or segments that form the backbone. **vertebral** *adj.*

vertebrate (**vert**-i-brăt) *n.* an animal that has a backbone.

vertex *n.* (*pl.* vertices, *pr.* **ver**-ti-seez) the highest point of a hill or structure, the apex of a cone or triangle.

vertical *adj.* **1.** perpendicular to the hori-zontal, moving or placed in this way, upright. **2.** in the direction from top to bottom of a picture etc. —*n.* a vertical line or part or position. —**vertically** *adv.*

vertigo (**vert**-i-goh) *n.* a sensation of diz-ziness and a feeling of losing one's bal-ance.

vervain (**ver**-vayn) *n.* a tall wild plant with hairy leaves and small flowers.

verve (*pr.* verv) *n.* enthusiasm, liveliness, vigour.

very *adv.* **1.** in a high degree, extremely, *very good.* **2.** in the fullest sense, *drink it to the very last drop.* **3.** exactly, *sat in the very same seat.* —**very** *adj.* **1.** itself or himself etc. and no other, actual, truly such, *it's the very thing we need!* **2.** extreme, utter, *at* *the very end.* □ **very well,** an expression of consent.

vesicle (vess-i-kŭl) *n.* **1.** a small hollow structure in a plant or animal body. **2.** a blister.

vespers *pl. n.* (in the RC Church) a church service held in the evening, evensong.

vessel *n.* **1.** a structure designed to travel on water and carry people or goods, a ship or boat. **2.** a hollow receptacle, especially for liquid. **3.** a tube-like structure in the body of an animal or plant, conveying or holding blood or other fluid.

vest[1] *n.* **1.** a knitted or woven undergarment covering the trunk of the body. **2.** (*Amer. & shop use*) a waistcoat. □ **vest pocket** *adj.* of a very small size, as if suitable for carrying in a waistcoat pocket.

vest[2] *v.* **1.** to confer as a firm or legal right, *the power of making laws is vested in Parliament*; *Parliament is vested with this power.* **2.** (*old use*) to clothe. □ **vested interest,** an advantageous right which is securely held by a person or group.

vestibule (vest-i-bewl) *n.* **1.** an entrance hall or lobby of a building. **2.** a church porch.

vestige *n.* **1.** a trace, a small remaining bit of what once existed, *not a vestige of the abbey remains.* **2.** a very small amount, *not a vestige of truth in it.*

vestigial (ves-tij-iăl) *adj.* remaining as a vestige of what once existed.

vestment *n.* a ceremonial robe or other garment, especially one worn by clergy or choir at a religious service.

vestry *n.* a room or building attached to a church, where vestments are kept and where clergy and choir robe themselves.

vet *n.* a veterinary surgeon. —*v.* (vetted, vetting) to examine carefully and critically for faults or errors etc.

vetch *n.* a plant of the pea family, used as fodder for cattle.

veteran *n.* a person with long experience, especially in the armed forces. **veteran car,** a car made before 1916, or before 1905.

veterinary (vet-rin-ri) *adj.* of or for the treatment of diseases and disorders of farm and domestic animals. **veterinary surgeon,** a person who is skilled in such treatment.

veto (veet-oh) *n.* (*pl.* vetoes) **1.** an authoritative rejection or prohibition of something that is proposed. **2.** the right to make such a rejection or prohibition. —*v.* (vetoed, vetoing) to reject or prohibit authoritatively.

vex *v.* to annoy, to irritate, to cause worry to (a person). **vexed question,** a problem that is difficult and much discussed.

vexation *n.* **1.** vexing, being vexed, a state of irritation or worry. **2.** something that causes this.

vexatious (veks-ay-shŭs) *adj.* causing vexation, annoying.

VHF *abbrev.* very high frequency.

via (vy-ă) *prep.* by way of, through, *from Exeter to York via London.*

viable (vy-ăbŭl) *adj.* **1.** (of a foetus) sufficiently developed to be able to survive after birth. **2.** (of plants) able to live or grow. **3.** practicable, able to exist successfully, *a viable plan*; *is the newly-created State viable?* **viability** *n.*

viaduct (vy-ă-dukt) *n.* a long bridge-like structure (usually with a series of arches) for carrying a road or railway over a valley or dip in the ground.

vial (vy-ăl) *n.* a small bottle, especially for liquid medicine.

viands (vy-ăndz) *pl. n.* articles of food.

vibes (*pr.* vybz) *pl. n.* (*informal*) **1.** a vibraphone. **2.** mental or emotional vibrations.

vibrant (vy-brănt) *adj.* vibrating, resonant, thrilling with energy or activity.

vibraphone (vy-bră-fohn) *n.* a percussion instrument like a xylophone but with electronic resonators underneath the bars, giving a vibrating effect.

vibrate *v.* **1.** to move rapidly and continuously to and fro. **2.** to resound, to sound with a rapid slight variation of pitch.

vibration *n.* a vibrating movement or sensation or sound. **vibrations** *pl. n.* mental stimuli thought to be given out by a person or place etc.; the emotional sensations these produce.

vibrato (vi-brah-toh) *n.* (*pl.* vibratos) a vibrating effect in music, with rapid slight variation of pitch.

vibrator (vy-bray-ter) *n.* a device that vibrates or causes vibration.

vibratory (vy-bră-ter-i) *adj.* causing vibration.

viburnum (vy-ber-nŭm) *n.* a kind of shrub, usually with white flowers.

Vic. *abbrev.* Victoria (Australia).

vicar *n.* (in the Church of England) a clergyman in charge of a parish where tithes formerly belonged to another person or an institution. **Vicar of Christ,** the pope.

vicarage *n.* the house of a vicar.

vicarious (vik-air-iŭs) *adj.* (of feelings or emotions) felt through sharing imaginatively in the feelings or activities etc. of another person, *vicarious pleasure.* **vicariously** *adv.*

vice[1] *n.* **1.** evil or grossly immoral conduct, great wickedness. **2.** a particular form of this, a fault or bad habit, *smoking isn't one of my vices*. 3. criminal and immoral practices such as prostitution.

vice² *n.* an instrument with two jaws that grip a thing securely so as to leave the hands free for working on it, used especially in carpentry and metal-working.

vice³ (vy-si) *prep.* in place of, *Mr Smith has been appointed as chief accountant vice Mr Brown, who has retired.*

vice- *prefix* 1. acting as substitute or deputy for, *vice-president.* 2. next in rank to, *vice-admiral.*

viceroy *n.* a person governing a colony or province etc. as the sovereign's representative.

vice versa (vy-si ver-să) the other way round, *we gossip about them and vice versa* (= and they gossip about us).

Vichy water (vee-shee) fizzy mineral water from Vichy in central France.

vicinity (vis-**in**-iti) *n.* the surrounding district; *there is no good school in the vicinity,* near by.

vicious (**vish**-ŭs) *adj.* 1. acting or done with evil intentions, brutal, strongly spiteful. 2. (of animals) savage and dangerous, bad-tempered. 3. severe, *a vicious wind.* **viciously** *adv.,* **viciousness** *n.* □ **vicious circle,** a state of affairs in which a cause produces an effect which itself produces or intensifies the original cause. **vicious spiral,** a similar continual interaction, e.g. causing a steady increase of both prices and wages.

vicissitude (viss-**iss**-i-tewd) *n.* a change of circumstances affecting one's life.

victim *n.* 1. a person who is injured or killed by another or as the result of an occurrence, *victims of the earthquake.* 2. a person who suffers because of a trick. 3. a living creature killed and offered as a religious sacrifice.

victimize *v.* to make a victim of, to single out (a person) to suffer ill treatment. **victimization** *n.*

victor *n.* the winner in a battle or contest.

victoria *n.* a victoria plum. **Victoria Cross,** a military decoration awarded for conspicuous bravery. **victoria plum,** a large red juicy variety of plum. **Victoria sandwich,** a kind of sponge-cake.

Victoria a State of Australia.

Victorian *adj.* belonging to or characteristic of the reign of Queen Victoria (1837–1901). —*n.* a person living at this time.

Victoriana (vik-tor-i-**ah**-nă) *pl. n.* objects from Victorian times.

victorious *adj.* having gained the victory.

victory *n.* success in a battle or contest or

game etc. achieved by gaining mastery over one's opponent(s) or achieving the highest score.

victualler (**vit**-ler) *n.* a person who supplies victuals. **licensed victualler,** the licensee of a public house.

victuals (**vit**-l'z) *pl. n.* food, provisions.

vicuña (vik-**yoo**-nă) *n.* 1. a South American animal related to the llama, with fine silky wool. 2. cloth made from its wool, an imitation of this.

video (**vid**-i-oh) *n.* recorded or broadcast pictures as distinct from sound. **video game,** any of the games in which points of light are moved on a TV screen by means of an electronic control.

videotape *n.* magnetic tape suitable for recording TV pictures and sound.

videotext *n.* 1. viewdata. 2. teletext.

vie *v.* (vied, vying) to carry on a rivalry, to compete, *vying with each other.*

Vienna the capital of Austria. **Viennese** *adj. & n.* (*pl.* Viennese)

Vietnam a country in south-east Asia. **Vietnamese** *adj. & n.* (*pl.* Vietnamese)

view *n.* 1. what can be seen from a specified point, fine natural scenery, *the view from the summit.* 2. range of vision, *the ship sailed into view.* 3. visual inspection of something, *we had a private view of the exhibition before it was opened.* 4. a mental survey of a subject etc. 5. a mental attitude, an opinion, *they have strong views about tax reform.* —**view** *v.* 1. to survey with the eyes or mind. 2. to inspect, to look over (a house etc.) with the idea of buying it. 3. to watch television. 4. to regard or consider, *we view the matter seriously.* □ **in view of,** having regard to, considering, *in view of the excellence of the work, we do not grudge the cost.* **on view,** displayed for inspection. **view halloo,** a huntsman's cry on seeing the fox break cover. **with a view to,** with the hope or intention of.

viewdata *n.* a system in which a TV set is connected to a central computer by means of a telephone link, so that information can be selected and produced on the TV screen (distinguished from *teletext*).

viewer *n.* 1. a person who views something. 2. a person watching a TV programme. 3. a device used in inspecting photographic slides etc.

viewfinder *n.* a device on a camera by which the user can see the area that will be photographed through the lens.

viewpoint *n.* a point of view, a standpoint.

vigil (**vij**-il) *n.* 1. staying awake to keep watch or to pray, a period of this, *keep* vigil; *a long vigil*. **2.** the eve of a religious festival.

vigilant (**vij**-i-lănt) *adj*. watchful, on the look-out for possible danger etc. **vigilantly** *adv*., **vigilance** *n*.

vigilante (vij-il-**an**-ti) *n*. a member of a self-appointed group of people who try to prevent crime and disorder in a community where law enforcement is imperfect or has broken down.

vignette (veen-**yet**) *n*. **1.** a photograph or portrait with the edges of the background gradually shaded off. **2.** a short description or character-sketch. —*v*. to shade off in the style of a vignette.

vigorous *adj*. full of vigour. **vigorously** *adv*., **vigorousness** *n*.

vigour *n*. **1.** active physical or mental strength, energy, flourishing physical condition. **2.** forcefulness of language or composition etc.

Viking (**vy**-king) *n*. a Scandinavian trader and pirate of the 8th–10th centuries.

vile *adj*. **1.** extremely disgusting, *a vile smell*. **2.** despicable on moral grounds. **3.** (*informal*) bad, *this vile weather*. **vilely** *adv*., **vileness** *n*.

vilify (**vil**-i-fy) *v*. (vilified, vilifying) to say evil things about. **vilification** *n*.

villa *n*. **1.** a detached or semi-detached house in a suburban or residential district. **2.** a country house, especially in Italy or southern France. **3.** a house for holiday-makers at the seaside etc.

village *n*. a collection of houses etc. in a country district, smaller than a town and usually having a church.

villager *n*. an inhabitant of a village.

villain (**vil**-ăn) *n*. **1.** a person who is guilty or capable of great wickedness, a wrongdoer. **2.** a character in a story or play whose evil actions or motives are important in the plot. **villainy** *n*.

villainous (**vil**-ăn-ŭs) *adj*. **1.** wicked, worthy of a villain. **2.** (*informal*) abominably bad, *villainous handwriting*. **villainously** *adv*.

vim *n*. (*informal*) vigour, energy.

vinaigrette (vin-i-**gret**) *n*. a small ornamental bottle for holding smelling-salts. **vinaigrette sauce**, salad dressing made of oil and vinegar.

vindicate (**vin**-dik-ayt) *v*. **1.** to clear of blame or suspicion. **2.** to justify by evidence or results, to prove (a thing) to be valid. **vindication** *n*., **vindicator** *n*.

vindictive (vin-**dik**-tiv) *adj*. having or showing a desire for revenge. **vindictively** *adv*., **vindictiveness** *n*.

vine *n*. a climbing or trailing woody-stemmed plant whose fruit is the grape.

vinegar *n*. a sour liquid made from wine, cider, malt, etc. by fermentation, used in flavouring food and for pickling.

vinegary *adj*. **1.** like vinegar. **2.** sour-tempered.

vinery (**vy**-ner-i) *n*. a greenhouse for a vine or vines.

vineyard (**vin**-yard) *n*. a plantation of vines producing grapes for wine-making.

vintage (**vint**-ij) *n*. **1.** the gathering of grapes for wine-making, the season of this. **2.** wine made from a particular season's grapes, the date of this as an indication of the wine's quality; *a vintage year*, one in which the wine is of high quality; *vintage wines*, from vintage years. **3.** the date or period when something was produced or existed. —*adj*. of high quality, especially from a past period. □ **vintage car**, a car made between 1917 and 1930.

vintner (**vint**-ner) *n*. a wine-merchant.

vinyl (**vy**-nil) *n*. a kind of plastic, especially polyvinyl chloride.

viol (**vy**-ŏl) *n*. a stringed musical instrument similar to a violin but held vertically.

viola[1] (vee-**oh**-lă) *n*. a stringed musical instrument slightly larger than a violin and of lower pitch.

viola[2] (vy-**ŏ**-lă) *n*. a plant of the genus to which pansies and violets belong, especially a hybrid cultivated variety.

violate *v*. **1.** to break or act contrary to (an oath or treaty etc.). **2.** to treat (a sacred place) with irreverence or disrespect. **3.** to disturb (a person's privacy). **4.** to rape. **violation** *n*., **violator** *n*.

violence *n*. being violent, violent acts or conduct etc. **do violence to**, to act contrary to, to be a breach of.

violent *adj*. **1.** involving great force or strength or intensity. **2.** involving the unlawful use of force, *violent crime*; *a violent death*, caused by physical violence, not natural. **violently** *adv*.

violet *n*. **1.** a small wild or garden plant, often with purple flowers. **2.** the colour at the opposite end of the spectrum from red, bluish-purple. —*adj*. bluish-purple.

violin *n*. a musical instrument with four strings of treble pitch, played with a bow.

violinist *n*. a person who plays the violin.

violoncello (vy-ŏ-lŏn-**chel**-oh) *n*. (*pl*. violoncellos) a cello.

VIP *abbrev*. very important person.

viper *n*. a small poisonous snake; *a viper in the bosom*, a person who betrays those who have helped him.

virago (vi-**rah**-goh) *n*. (*pl*. viragos) a shrewish bullying woman.

virgin *n.* **1.** a person (especially a woman) who has never had sexual intercourse. **2.** *the Virgin*, the Virgin Mary, mother of Christ. **3.** *the Virgin*, a sign of the zodiac, Virgo. —**virgin** *adj.* **1.** virginal. **2.** spotless, undefiled. **3.** untouched, in its original state, not yet used; *virgin soil*, not yet dug or used for crops; *virgin wool*, pure new wool. —**virginity** *n.* □ **virgin birth**, (in Christian teaching) the birth of Christ without a human father.

virginal *adj.* of or being or suitable for a virgin. **virginals** *pl. n.* a keyboard instrument of the 16th–17th centuries, the earliest form of harpsichord.

Virginia a State of the USA. **Virginia creeper**, an ornamental climbing plant with leaves that turn red in autumn.

Virgo (**ver**-goh) a sign of the zodiac, the Virgin. **Virgoan** (ver-goh-ăn) *adj. & n.*

virile (**vi**-ryl) *adj.* having masculine strength or vigour, having procreative power. **virility** (vi-**ril**-iti) *n.*

virology (vyr-**ol**-ŏji) *n.* the scientific study of viruses. **virological** *adj.*, **virologist** *n.*

virtual *adj.* being so in effect though not in name or according to strict definition, *he is the virtual head of the firm*; *gave what was a virtual promise*. **virtually** *adv.*

virtue *n.* **1.** moral excellence, goodness, a particular form of this, *patience is a virtue*. **2.** chastity, especially of a woman. **3.** a good quality, an advantage, *the seat has the virtue of being adjustable*. □ **by** *or* **in virtue of**, by reason of, because of, *he is entitled to a pension by virtue of his long service*. **make a virtue of necessity**, to do with a good grace what one must do anyway.

virtuoso (ver-tew-**oh**-soh) *n.* (*pl.* virtuosos *or* virtuosi) a person who excels in the technique of doing something, especially singing or playing music. **virtuosity** (ver-tew-**oss**-iti) *n.*

virtuous *adj.* having or showing moral virtue. **virtuously** *adv.*, **virtuousness** *n.*

virulent (**vi**-rew-lĕnt) *adj.* **1.** (of poison or disease) extremely strong or violent. **2.** strongly and bitterly hostile, *virulent abuse*. **virulence** *n.*

virus (**vy**-rŭs) *n.* (*pl.* viruses) a very simple organism (smaller than bacteria) capable of causing disease.

visa (**vee**-ză) *n.* an official stamp or mark put on a passport by officials of a foreign country to show that the holder may enter their country. **visaed** (**vee**-zăd) *adj.* marked with a visa.

visage (**viz**-ij) *n.* a person's face.

vis-à-vis (veez-ah-**vee**) *adv. & prep.* **1.** in a position facing one another, opposite to.

2. in relation to, as compared with.

viscera (**vis**-er-ă) *pl. n.* the internal organs of the body, especially the intestines.

viscid (**vis**-id) *adj.* (of liquid) thick and gluey. **viscidity** (vis-**id**-iti) *n.*

viscose (**vis**-kohz) *n.* **1.** cellulose in a viscous state, used in the manufacture of rayon etc. **2.** fabric made of this.

viscount (**vy**-kownt) *n.* **1.** a nobleman ranking between earl and baron, *Viscount Samuel*. **2.** the courtesy title of an earl's eldest son, *Viscount Linley*. **viscountess** *n.*

viscous (**vis**-kŭs) *adj.* thick and gluey, not pouring easily. **viscosity** (vis-**kos**-iti) *n.*

visibility *n.* **1.** being visible. **2.** the range or possibility of vision as determined by conditions of light and atmosphere, *the aircraft turned back because of poor visibility*.

visible *adj.* able to be seen or noticed. **visibly** *adv.* ¶ Do not confuse with visual.

vision *n.* **1.** the faculty of seeing, sight. **2.** something seen in the imagination or in a dream etc. **3.** imaginative insight into a subject or problem etc., foresight and wisdom in planning, *a statesman with vision*. **4.** a person or sight of unusual beauty.

visionary *adj.* **1.** existing only in the imagination, fanciful, not practical, *visionary schemes*. **2.** indulging in fanciful ideas or theories. —*n.* a person with visionary ideas.

visit *v.* **1.** to go or come to see (a person or place etc.) either socially or on business or for some other purpose. **2.** to stay temporarily with (a person) or at (a place). **3.** (in the Bible) to inflict punishment for, *visiting the sins of the fathers upon the children*. —*n.* an act of visiting, a temporary stay.

visitant *n.* **1.** a visitor, especially a supernatural one. **2.** a migratory bird that is a visitor to an area.

visitation *n.* **1.** an official visit, especially of inspection. **2.** trouble or disaster looked upon as punishment from God. **3.** *the Visitation*, a Christian festival on 2 July, commemorating the visit of the Virgin Mary to her kinswoman Elizabeth.

visitor *n.* **1.** one who visits a person or place. **2.** a migratory bird that lives in an area temporarily or at a certain season.

visor (**vy**-zer) *n.* **1.** the movable front part of a helmet, covering the face. **2.** the projecting front part of a cap. **3.** a **sun visor**, a fixed or movable shield at the top of a vehicle windscreen, protecting the eyes from bright sunshine etc.

vista *n.* **1.** a view, especially one seen through a long narrow opening such as an avenue of trees. **2.** a mental view of an extensive period or series of past or future events.

visual *adj.* of or used in seeing, received through sight; *a good visual memory*, ability to remember what one sees. ¶ Do not confuse with visible. **visually** *adv.* □ **visual aids**, pictures or film-strips etc. as an aid to teaching. **visual display unit**, a device resembling a TV screen, connected to a computer or similar apparatus, on which data can be displayed as they are received from the computer etc. or fed into it.

visualize *v.* to form a mental picture of. **visualization** *n.*

vital *adj.* **1.** connected with life, essential to life, *vital functions*. **2.** essential to the existence or success or operation of something, extremely important. **3.** full of vitality, *she's a very vital sort of person.* **vitally** *adv.* □ **vitals** *pl. n.* the vital parts of the body (e.g. heart, lungs, brain). **vital statistics**, statistics relating to population figures or births and deaths; (*informal*) the measurement of a woman's bust, waist, and hips.

vitality (vy-**tal**-iti) *n.* liveliness, vigour, persistent energy.

vitalize *v.* to put life or vitality into. **vitalization** *n.*

vitamin (**vit**-ă-min) *n.* any of a number of organic substances present in many foods and essential to the nutrition of man and other animals.

vitaminize *v.* to add vitamins to (a food).

vitiate (**vish**-i-ayt) *v.* **1.** to make imperfect, to spoil. **2.** to weaken the force of, to make ineffective, *this admission vitiates your claim.* **vitiation** *n.*

vitreous (**vit**-ri-us) *adj.* having a glass-like texture or finish, *vitreous enamel.*

vitrify (**vit**-ri-fy) *v.* (vitrified, vitrifying) to convert or be converted into glass or a glass-like substance, especially by heat. **vitrifaction** *n.*, **vitrification** *n.*

vitriol (**vit**-ri-ol) *n.* **1.** sulphuric acid or one of its salts. **2.** savagely hostile comments or criticism. **vitriolic** (vit-ri-**ol**-ik) *adj.*

vituperate (vi-**tew**-per-ayt) *v.* to use abusive language. **vituperation** *n.*

viva (**vy**-vă) *n.* a viva voce examination.

vivacious (viv-**ay**-shŭs) *adj.* lively, high-spirited. **vivaciously** *adv.*, **vivacity** (viv-**ass**-iti) *n.*

viva voce (vy-vă **voh**-chi) (of an examination in universities) oral, conducted orally, an oral examination.

vivid *adj.* **1.** (of light or colour) bright and strong, intense. **2.** producing strong and clear mental pictures, *a vivid description.* **3.** (of the imagination) creating ideas etc. in an active and lively way. **vividly** *adv.*, **vividness** *n.*

vivisection *n.* performance of surgical experiments on living animals.

vixen *n.* a female fox.

viz. *adv.* namely, *the case is made in three sizes, viz. large, medium, and small.* ¶ In reading aloud, the word 'namely' is usually spoken where 'viz.' (short for Latin *videlicet*) is written.

vizier (viz-**eer**) *n.* an official of high rank in certain Muslim countries.

V-neck *n.* a V-shaped neckline on a pull-over.

vocabulary *n.* **1.** a list of words with their meanings, especially one given in a reading-book etc. of a foreign language. **2.** the words known to a person or used in a particular book or subject etc.

vocal (**voh**-kăl) *adj.* **1.** of or for or uttered by the voice. **2.** expressing one's feelings freely in speech, *he was very vocal about his rights.* —*n.* a piece of sung music. —**vocally** *adv.*

vocalist (**voh**-kăl-ist) *n.* a singer, especially in a pop group.

vocalize (**voh**-kă-lyz) *v.* to utter.

vocation (vŏ-**kay**-shŏn) *n.* **1.** a feeling that one is called by God to a certain career or occupation. **2.** a natural liking for a certain type of work. **3.** a person's trade or profession. **vocational** *adj.* □ **vocational guidance**, advice about suitable careers.

vociferate (vŏ-**sif**-er-ayt) *v.* to say loudly or noisily, to shout. **vociferation** *n.*

vociferous (vŏ-**sif**-er-ŭs) *adj.* making a great outcry, expressing one's views forcibly and insistently. **vociferously** *adv.*

vodka *n.* alcoholic spirit distilled chiefly from rye, especially in Russia.

vogue *n.* **1.** current fashion, *large hats are the vogue.* **2.** popular favour or acceptance, *his novels had a great vogue ten years ago.* □ **in vogue**, in fashion.

voice *n.* **1.** sounds formed in the larynx and uttered by the mouth, especially human utterance in speaking, singing, etc. **2.** ability to produce such sounds, *she has a cold and has lost her voice; she is in good voice,* singing or speaking well. **3.** expression of one's opinion etc. in spoken or written words, the opinion itself, the right to express opinion, *gave voice to his indignation; I have no voice in the matter.* **4.** any of the sets of forms of a verb that show the relation of the subject to the action, *active voice; passive voice* (see the entries for *active* and *passive*). —*v.* to put into words, to express, *she voiced her opinion.* □ **voice-over** *n.* narration (e.g. in a film) by a voice not accompanied by a picture of the speaker.

void *adj.* **1.** empty, vacant. **2.** not legally valid. —*n.* empty space, emptiness. — **void** *v.* **1.** to make legally void, *the contract was voided by his death*. **2.** to excrete (urine or faeces).

voile (*pr.* voyl) *n.* a very thin light dress-material.

volatile (**vol**-ă-tyl) *adj.* **1.** (of a liquid) evaporating rapidly. **2.** (of a person) lively, changing quickly or easily from one mood or interest to another. **volatility** (vol-ă-**til**-iti) *n.*

vol-au-vent (**vol**-oh-vahn) *n.* a pie of puff pastry filled with a sauce containing meat or fish.

volcanic *adj.* of or from a volcano.

volcano *n.* (*pl.* volcanoes) a mountain or hill with openings through which lava, cinders, gases, etc. from below the earth's crust are or have been expelled.

vole (*rhymes with* hole) *n.* any of several small animals resembling rats or mice.

volition (vŏl-**ish**-ŏn) *n.* use of one's own will in choosing or making a decision etc.; *she did it of her own volition*, voluntarily.

volley *n.* (*pl.* volleys) **1.** simultaneous discharge of a number of missiles, the missiles themselves. **2.** a number of questions or curses etc. directed in quick succession at someone. **3.** return of the ball in tennis etc. before it touches the ground. — **volley** *v.* **1.** to discharge or fly or sound in a volley. **2.** to return (a ball) by a volley. □ **volley-ball** *n.* a game for two teams of players who volley a large ball by hand over a net.

volt (*rhymes with* bolt) *n.* a unit of electromotive force, force sufficient to carry one ampere of current against one ohm resistance.

voltage (**vohl**-tij) *n.* electromotive force expressed in volts.

volte-face (volt-**fahs**) *n.* a complete change of one's attitude towards something.

voluble (**vol**-yoo-bŭl) *adj.* talking very much, speaking or spoken with great fluency. **volubly** *adv.*, **volubility** (vol-yoo-**bil**-iti) *n.*

volume *n.* **1.** a book, especially one of a set. **2.** the amount of space (often expressed in cubic units) that a three-dimensional thing occupies or contains. **3.** the size or amount of something, a quantity, *the great volume of water pouring over the weir; the volume of business has increased*. **4.** the strength or power of sound, *the noise had doubled in volume*.

voluminous (vŏl-**yoo**-min-ŭs) *adj.* **1.** having great volume, bulky; *voluminous skirts*, large and full. **2.** (of writings) great in

quantity, (of a writer) producing many works, copious.

voluntary *adj.* **1.** acting or done or given etc. of one's own free will and not under compulsion. **2.** working or done without payment, *voluntary workers* or *work*. **3.** (of an organization) maintained by voluntary contributions or voluntary workers. **4.** (of bodily movements) controlled by the will. —*n.* an organ solo played before, during, or after a church service. —**voluntarily** *adv.*

volunteer *n.* **1.** a person who offers to do something. **2.** a person who enrols for military or other service voluntarily, not as a conscript. —*v.* to undertake or offer voluntarily, to be a volunteer.

voluptuous (vŏl-**up**-tew-ŭs) *adj.* **1.** fond of luxury or sumptuous living. **2.** giving a sensation of luxury and pleasure. **3.** (of a woman) having a full and attractive figure. **voluptuously** *adv.*, **voluptuousness** *n.*

vomit *v.* (vomited, vomiting) to eject (matter) from the stomach through the mouth, to be sick. —*n.* matter vomited from the stomach.

voodoo *n.* a form of religion based on belief in witchcraft and magical rites, practised by certain Blacks in the West Indies and America. **voodooism** *n.*

voracious (ver-**ay**-shŭs) *adj.* **1.** greedy in eating, ravenous. **2.** desiring much; *a voracious reader*, one who reads much and eagerly. **voraciously** *adv.*, **voracity** (vor-**ass**-iti) *n.*

vortex *n.* (*pl.* vortices (*pr.* **vor**-ti-seez) *or* vortexes) a whirling mass of water or air, a whirlpool or whirlwind.

vote *n.* **1.** a formal expression of one's opinion or choice on a matter under discussion, e.g. by ballot or show of hands. **2.** an opinion or choice expressed in this way, *the vote went against accepting the plan*. **3.** the total number of votes given by a certain group, *that policy will lose us the Labour vote*. **4.** the right to vote, *Swiss women now have the vote*. —**vote** *v.* **1.** to express an opinion or choice by a vote. **2.** to decide by a majority of votes. **3.** (*informal*) to declare by general consent, *the meal was voted excellent*. **4.** (*informal*) to suggest, *I vote that we avoid him in future*. —**voter** *n.* □ **vote down**, to reject (a proposal etc.) by votes.

votive (**voh**-tiv) *adj.* given in fulfilment of a vow, *votive offerings at the shrine*.

vouch *v.* **vouch for**, to guarantee the certainty or accuracy or reliability etc. of, *I will vouch for his honesty*.

voucher *n.* **1.** a document establishing that money has been paid or goods etc. delivered. **2.** a document (issued in token of payment made or promised) that can be exchanged for certain goods or services.

vouchsafe *v.* to give or grant in a gracious or condescending manner, *they did not vouchsafe a reply* or *to reply.*

vow *n.* a solemn promise or undertaking, especially in the form of an oath to God or a god or a saint. —*v.* to promise solemnly, *they vowed vengeance against their oppressor.*

vowel *n.* 1. a speech-sound made without audible stopping of the breath (opposed to a consonant). 2. a letter or letters representing such a sound, as a, e, i, o, u, ee.

voyage *n.* a journey by water or in space, especially a long one. —*v.* to make a voyage. —**voyager** *n.*

voyeur (vwah-**yer**) *n.* a person who obtains sexual gratification from looking at the sexual actions or organs of others.

V sign a gesture of victory or approval or vulgar derision, made by the raised hand with first and second fingers spread in the form of a V.

Vt. *abbrev.* Vermont.

vulcanize *v.* to treat (rubber or similar material) with sulphur etc. in order to increase its elasticity and strength. **vulcanization** *n.*

vulgar *adj.* 1. lacking in refinement or good taste, coarse. 2. commonly used and incorrect (but not coarse; *see* vulgarism, sense 1). **vulgarly** *adv.,* **vulgarity** *n.* □ **vulgar fraction,** a fraction represented by numbers above and below a line (e.g. $\frac{4}{5}$, $\frac{3}{8}$), not a decimal fraction.

vulgarism *n.* 1. a word or phrase used mainly by people who are ignorant of standard usage, *'he is learning her to drive' is a vulgar usage* or *is a vulgarism for 'he is teaching her'.* 2. a coarse word or phrase.

vulgarize *v.* 1. to cause (a person or his manners etc.) to become vulgar. 2. to reduce to the level of being usual or ordinary, to spoil by making ordinary or too well known. **vulgarization** *n.*

Vulgate (**vul**-gayt) *n.* the 4th-century Latin version of the Bible.

vulnerable (**vul**-ner-ăbŭl) *adj.* 1. able to be hurt or wounded or injured. 2. unprotected, exposed to danger or attack. **vulnerability** *n.*

vulture *n.* 1. a large bird of prey that lives on the flesh of dead animals. 2. a greedy person seeking to profit from the misfortunes of others.

vulva *n.* the external parts of the female genital organs.

vying *see* vie.

Ww

W. *abbrev.* 1. watt(s). 2. west.

WA *abbrev.* Western Australia.

wacky *adj.* (wackier, wackiest) (*slang*) crazy.

wad (*pr.* wod) *n.* 1. a lump or bundle of soft material used to keep things apart or in place, stop up a hole, etc. 2. a collection of documents or banknotes placed together. 3. (*slang*) a bun or sandwich etc., *tea and a wad.* —*v.* (wadded, wadding) to line or stuff or protect with wadding.

wadding *n.* soft fibrous material used for padding or packing or lining things.

waddle *v.* to walk with short steps and a swaying movement. —*n.* a waddling walk.

wade *v.* 1. to walk through water or mud or anything that prevents the feet from moving freely, to walk across (a stream etc.) in this way. 2. to make one's way slowly and with difficulty; *wade through a book,* read through it in spite of its dullness or difficulty or length etc. □ **wade in,** (*informal*) to intervene, to make a vigorous attack. **wade into,** (*informal*) to attack (a person or task) vigorously. **wading-bird** *n.* a long-legged water-bird that wades in shallow water.

wader *n.* a wading-bird.

waders *pl. n.* high waterproof boots worn in fishing etc.

wafer *n.* 1. a kind of thin light biscuit. 2. a thin disc of unleavended bread used in the Eucharist.

waffle[1] (**wof**-ĕl) *n.* (*informal*) vague wordy talk or write waffle.

waffle[2] (**wof**-ĕl) *n.* a small cake made of batter and eaten hot, cooked in a **waffle-iron** which has two metal pans, usually hinged together, marked with a projecting pattern that presses into the batter when they are closed upon it.

waft (*pr.* woft) *v.* to carry or travel lightly and easily through the air or over water.—*n.* a wafted odour.

wag[2] *n.* a person who is fond of making jokes or playing practical jokes.

wag[1] *v.* (wagged, wagging) to shake or move briskly to and fro; *tongues are wagging,* talk or gossip is going on.†*n.* a single wagging movement.

wage[1] *v.* to engage in, *wage war.*

wage[2] *n.,* wages *pl. n.* regular payment to an employee in return for his work or services, *he earns a good wage* or *good wages.*

wager (**way**-jer) *n.* a bet. —*v.* to bet.

waggish *adj.* of or like a wag, said or done in a joking way. **waggishly** *adv.*, **waggishness** *n.*

waggle *v.* to wag. —*n.* a waggling movement.

waggon *n.* = wagon.

waggoner *n.* = wagoner.

wagon *n.* **1.** a four-wheeled vehicle for carrying goods, pulled by horses or oxen. **2.** an open railway truck, e.g. for coal. **3.** a trolley for carrying food etc., *the tea-wagon.* □ **on the wagon** *or* **water-wagon**, (*slang*) abstaining from alcohol.

wagoner *n.* the driver of a wagon.

wagon-lit (vag-awn-**lee**) *n.* (*pl.* wagons-lits, *pr.* vag-awn-**lee**) a sleeping-car on a Continental railway.

wagtail *n.* any of several small birds with a long tail that moves up and down constantly when the bird is standing.

waif *n.* a homeless and helpless person, an unowned or abandoned child.

wail *v.* **1.** to utter a long sad cry, to lament or complain persistently. **2.** (of wind etc.) to make a sound like a person wailing. —*n.* a wailing cry or sound or utterance.

wain *n.* (*old use*) a farm wagon.

wainscot *n.* wooden panelling on the wall of a room. **wainscoting** *n.* wainscot, material for this.

waist *n.* **1.** the part of the human body below the ribs and above the bones of the pelvis, normally narrower than the rest of the body. **2.** the part of a garment covering this. **3.** a narrow part in the middle of a long object. **4.** (*Amer.*) a blouse or bodice. □ **waisted** *adj.* narrowed at the waist; having a waist of a certain kind, *thick-waisted.*

waistband *n.* a band (e.g. at the top of a skirt) that fits round the waist.

waistcoat *n.* **1.** a man's close-fitting waist-length sleeveless collarless garment buttoned down the front, worn over a shirt and under a jacket. **2.** a woman's similar garment.

waistline *n.* **1.** the circumference of the body at the waist. **2.** the narrowest part of a garment, fitting at or just above or below the waist.

wait *v.* **1.** to postpone an action or departure for a specified time or until some expected event occurs, *we waited until evening*; *wait your turn*, wait until it is your turn; *we'll wait dinner for you*, will postpone it until you are present. **2.** to be postponed, *this question will have to wait until our next meeting.* **3.** to wait on people at a meal. **4.** to stop a motor vehicle for a time at the side of a road, *No Waiting.* —*n.* an act or period of waiting, *we had a long wait*

for the train. □ **waiting game**, deliberate delay in taking action so as to act more effectively later. **waiting-list** *n.* a list of people waiting for a chance to obtain something when it becomes available. **waiting-room** *n.* a room provided for people to wait in, e.g. at a railway station or a doctor's or dentist's premises. **wait on**, to hand food and drink to (a person or persons) at a meal; to fetch and carry for (a person) as an attendant; (*formal*) to pay a respectful visit to (a person); (*incorrect use*) to wait for, *sorry we have no peas, we're waiting on them.*

waiter *n.* a man employed to serve food and drink to customers at tables in a hotel or restaurant. **waitress** *n.*

waive *v.* to refrain from using or insisting upon (one's right or claim or privilege etc.), to forgo or dispense with.
¶ Do not confuse with **wave**.

waiver *n.* the waiving of a legal right, a document recording this.
¶ Do not confuse with **waver**.

wake[1] *v.* (woke, woken, waking) **1.** = wake up (*see below*). **2.** to disturb with noise, to cause to re-echo, *the shout woke echoes in the valley.* □ **wake up**, to cease to sleep, to cause to cease sleeping; to become alert, to realize, *he woke up to the fact that she meant it*; to cease or cause to cease from inactivity or inattention etc., *he needs something to wake him up.*

wake[2] *n.* (*Irish*) a watch by a corpse before burial, lamentations and merry-making in connection with this. **wakes** *pl. n.* an annual holiday in industrial areas of northern England, *wakes week.*

wake[3] *n.* **1.** the track left on water's surface by a ship etc. **2.** air-currents left behind an aircraft etc. moving through air. □ **in the wake of**, behind; following after.

wakeful *adj.* **1.** (of a person) unable to sleep. **2.** (of a night etc.) with little sleep.

waken *v.* to wake.

waking *adj.* being awake, *in his waking hours.*

Wales the country forming the western part of Great Britain.

walk *v.* **1.** to progress by lifting and setting down each foot in turn so that one foot is on the ground while the other is being lifted, (of quadrupeds) to go with the slowest gait, always having at least two feet on the ground. **2.** to travel or go on foot, to take exercise in this way. **3.** to go over on foot, *walked the fields in search of wild flowers.* **4.** to cause to walk with one, to accompany in walking. **5.** to ride or lead (a horse or dog etc.) at a walking pace.

6. (of a ghost) to appear. —**walk** n. **1.** a journey on foot, especially for pleasure or exercise, *went for a walk.* **2.** the manner or style of walking, a walking pace. **3.** a place for walking, a route followed in walking. □ **walk away with,** (*informal*) to win easily. **walk off with,** (*informal*) to win easily, *walked off with the first prize;* to steal. **walk of life,** social rank, profession or occupation. **walk on air,** = tread on air (*see* tread). **walk out,** to go for walks with a person in courtship; to depart suddenly and angrily; to go on strike suddenly. **walk-out** n. a sudden angry departure, especially as a protest or strike. **walk out on,** to desert, to leave in the lurch. **walk-over** n. an easy victory or achievement. **walk tall,** to feel justifiable pride.

walkabout n. **1.** (*Austral.*) an Aboriginal's wandering in the bush. **2.** an informal stroll among a crowd by a visiting royal person etc.

walker n. **1.** a person who walks. **2.** a framework for a person (e.g. a baby or a crippled person) who is unable to walk without support.

walkie-talkie n. a small radio transmitter and receiver that a person can carry with him as he walks about.

walking-stick n. a stick carried or used as a support when walking.

walking-tour n. a tour made on foot.

walkway n. a passage for walking along (especially one connecting different sections of a building), a wide path in a garden etc.

wall n. **1.** a continuous upright structure forming one of the sides of a building or room, or serving to enclose or protect or divide an area. **2.** something thought of as resembling this in form or function, the outermost part of a hollow structure, tissue surrounding an organ of the body etc. —v. to surround or enclose with a wall, *a walled garden; wall up a fireplace,* block it with bricks etc. built as a wall. □ **drive** *or* **send a person up the wall,** (*informal*) to make him crazy or furious. **go to the wall,** to suffer defeat or failure or ruin, *the weakest goes to the wall.* **wall-painting** n. a painting applied directly to the surface of a wall. **wall-to-wall** adj. (of a carpet) covering the whole floor of a room.

wallaby (wol-ă-bi) n. a kind of small kangaroo.

wallet n. a small flat folding case for holding banknotes or small documents etc.

wall-eyed adj. having eyes that show an abnormal amount of white (e.g. as caused by a squint).

wallflower n. **1.** a garden-plant blooming in spring, with clusters of fragrant flowers. **2.** (*informal*) a woman sitting out dances for lack of partners.

wallop v. (walloped, walloping) (*slang*) to thrash, to hit hard, to beat. —n. (*slang*) **1.** a heavy resounding blow. **2.** beer or other drink.

walloping adj. (*slang*) big, thumping, *a walloping lie.* —n. (*slang*) a beating, a defeat.

wallow v. **1.** to roll about in water or mud or sand etc. **2.** to indulge oneself or take unrestrained pleasure in something, *wallowing in luxury.* —n. the act of wallowing.

wallpaper n. paper for pasting on the interior walls of rooms.

Wall Street the American money-market. ¶ The name of a street in New York City, in or near which the chief American financial institutions are concentrated.

walnut n. **1.** a nut containing an edible kernel with a wrinkled surface. **2.** the tree that bears it. **3.** the wood of this tree, used (especially as a veneer) in making furniture.

walrus n. a large amphibious animal of arctic regions, related to the seal and sea-lion and having a pair of long tusks. **walrus moustache,** a long thick moustache that hangs down at the sides.

waltz n. **1.** a ballroom dance for couples, with a graceful flowing melody in triple time. **2.** music for this. —**waltz** v. **1.** to dance a waltz. **2.** to move (a person) in or as if in a waltz. **3.** (*informal*) to move gaily or casually, *came waltzing in.* —**waltzer** n.

wan (*pr.* wonn) adj. (wanner, wannest) pallid, especially from illness or exhaustion; *a wan smile,* a faint smile from a person who is ill or tired or unhappy. **wanly** adv., **wanness** n.

wand n. **1.** a slender rod for carrying in the hand, especially one associated with the working of magic. **2.** a light pen (*see* light¹) for passing over a bar code.

wander v. **1.** to go from place to place without a settled route or destination or special purpose. **2.** (of a road or river) to wind, to meander. **3.** to leave the right path or direction, to stray from one's group or from a place. **4.** to digress from a subject; *his mind is wandering,* he is inattentive or speaking disconnectedly through illness or weakness. —n. an act of wandering. —**wanderer** n. □ **wandering Jew,** a legendary person said to have been condemned by Christ (as punishment for an insult) to wander the earth until Christ's second coming; a kind of trailing plant.

wanderlust n. strong desire to travel.

wane v. **1.** (of the moon) to show a gradually decreasing area of brightness after being full. **2.** to decrease in vigour or strength or importance, *his influence was waning.* □ **on the wane,** waning.

wangle v. (*slang*) to obtain or arrange by using trickery or improper influence or persuasion etc. —*n.* (*slang*) an act of wangling.

wank v. (*vulgar*) to masturbate. **wanker** n. (*vulgar*) an unpleasant or useless person.

want v. **1.** to desire, to wish for. **2.** to require or need, *your hair wants cutting*; *that wants some doing,* is hard to do; *you want to be more careful,* ought to be more careful. **3.** (*Amer. & Scottish informal*) to desire to come or go or get, *the cat wants out.* **4.** to lack, to have an insufficient supply of. **5.** to be without the necessaries of life, *waste not, want not*; *want for nothing,* not be needy. **6.** to fall short of, *it still wanted two hours till midnight.* —**want** n. **1.** a desire for something, a requirement, *a man of few wants.* **2.** lack or need of something, deficiency, *the plants died from want of water.* **3.** lack of the necessaries of life, *living in great want.* □ **want ad,** (*Amer.*) a newspaper advertisement by a person seeking something.

wanted adj. (of a suspected criminal) being sought by the police for questioning or arrest.

wanting adj. lacking, deficient, not equal to requirements.

wanton (**wonn**-tŏn) adj. irresponsible, lacking proper restraint or motives.

war n. **1.** strife (especially between countries) involving military or naval or air attacks. **2.** hostility between people. **3.** a strong effort to combat crime or disease or poverty etc. □ **at war,** engaged in a war. **have been in the wars,** (*humorous*) to show signs of injury or rough usage. **on the war-path,** seeking hostile confrontation or revenge. **war-cry** n. a word or cry shouted in attacking or in rallying one's side; the slogan of a political or other party. **war-dance** n. a dance performed by certain primitive peoples before battle or after a victory. **war-game** n. a game in which models representing troops etc. are moved about on maps; a training exercise in which sets of armed forces participate in mock opposition to each other. **war memorial,** a memorial erected to those who died in a war. **war of nerves,** an effort to wear down one's opponent by gradually destroying his morale. **war-paint** n. paint put on the body by certain primitive peoples before battle; (*informal*) ceremonial dress, make-up applied to the

skin etc. **war widow,** a woman whose husband has been killed in a war.

War. *abbrev.* Warwickshire.

warble v. to sing, especially with a gentle trilling note as certain birds do. —*n.* a warbling sound.

warble-fly n. a kind of fly whose larvae burrow under the skin of cattle etc.

warbler n. any of several small birds (not necessarily one noted for its song).

ward (*rhymes with* ford) n. **1.** a room with beds for a particular group of patients in a hospital. **2.** an area (e.g. of a city) electing a councillor to represent it. **3.** a person, especially a child, under the care of a guardian or the protection of a lawcourt. **4.** one of the notches and projections in a key (or the corresponding parts in a lock) designed to prevent the lock from being opened by a key other than the right one. —*v.* **ward off,** to keep at a distance (a person or thing that threatens danger), to fend off.

warden n. **1.** an official with supervisory duties. **2.** a churchwarden. **3.** the title of certain governors or presidents of colleges etc.

warder n. an official in charge of prisoners in a prison. **wardress** n.

wardrobe n. **1.** a large cupboard where clothes are stored, usually with pegs or rails etc. from which they hang. **2.** a stock of clothes. **3.** a theatrical company's stock of costumes.

wardroom n. the mess-room for commissioned officers in a warship.

ware [1] n. manufactured goods (especially pottery) of the kind specified, *delftware.* **wares** *pl. n.* articles offered for sale, *traders displayed their wares.*

ware [2] v. beware of, look out for, *ware hounds!*

warehouse n. a building for storing goods or for storing furniture on behalf of its owners.

warfare n. making war, fighting, a particular form of this, *guerrilla warfare.*

warhead n. the explosive head of a missile or torpedo or similar weapon.

warlike adj. **1.** fond of making war, aggressive, *a warlike people.* **2.** of or for war, *warlike preparations.*

warm adj. **1.** moderately hot, not cold or cool. **2.** (of clothes etc.) keeping the body warm. **3.** enthusiastic, hearty, *a warm supporter*; *the speaker got a warm reception,* a vigorous response (either favourable or unfavourable). **4.** kindly and affectionate, *she has a warm heart.* **5.** (of colours) suggesting warmth, containing reddish shades. **6.** (of the scent in hunting) still fairly fresh and strong. **7.** (of the seeker in children's games etc.) near the object sought, on the verge of finding it.—*v.* to make or become warm or warmer. **warmly** *adv.*, **warmness** *n.* □ **keep a place warm**, to occupy it temporarily so that it can be available for a certain person at a later date. **warm-blooded** *adj.* having blood that remains warm (ranging from 36–42°C) permanently. **warm-hearted** *adj.* having a kindly and affectionate disposition. **warming-pan** *n.* a covered metal pan with a long handle, formerly filled with hot coals and used for warming beds. **warm to**, to become cordial or well-disposed to (a person); to become more animated about (a task). **warm up**, to make or become warm; to reheat (food etc.); to prepare for athletic exercise by practice beforehand; to make or become more lively.

warmish *adj.* rather warm.

warmonger (**wor**-mung-er) *n.* a person who seeks to bring about war.

warmth *n.* warmness, the state of being warm.

warn *v.* to inform (a person) about a present or future danger or about something that must be reckoned with, to advise about action in such circumstances, *we warned them to take waterproof clothing.* □ **warn off**, to tell (a person) to keep away or to avoid (a thing); to prohibit from taking part in race-meetings.

warning *n.* something that serves to warn.

warp (*pr.* worp) *v.* **1.** to cause (timber etc.) to become bent by uneven shrinkage or expansion, to become bent in this way. **2.** to distort (a person's judgement or principles). —**warp** *n.* **1.** a warped condition. **2.** threads stretched lengthwise in a loom, to be crossed by the weft.

warrant (**wo**-rănt) *n.* **1.** written authorization to do something, *the police have a warrant for his arrest.* **2.** a voucher entitling the holder to receive certain goods or services, *a travel warrant.* **3.** a justification or authorization for an action etc., *he had no warrant for saying this.* **4.** a proof or guarantee. —**warrant** *v.* **1.** to serve as a warrant for, to justify, *nothing can warrant such rudeness.* **2.** to prove or guarantee; *he'll be back, I'll warrant you*, I assure you. □ **warrant-officer** *n.* a member of the armed services ranking between commissioned officers and NCOs.

warrantee (wo-răn-**tee**) *n.* a person to whom a warranty is made.

warrantor (**wo**-răn-ter) *n.* a person who makes a warranty.

warranty (**wo**-răn-ti) *n.* **1.** a guarantee, especially one given to the buyer of an article and involving a promise to repair defects that become apparent in it within a specified period. **2.** authority or justification for doing something.

warren *n.* **1.** a piece of ground in which there are many burrows in which rabbits live and breed. **2.** a building or district with many narrow winding passages.

warring *adj.* engaged in a war.

warrior *n.* a person who fights in battle, a member of any of the armed services.

Warsaw the capital of Poland.

warship *n.* a ship for use in war.

wart *n.* **1.** a small hard roundish abnormal growth on the skin, caused by a virus. **2.** a similar growth on a plant. **3.** (*informal*) an objectionable person. **warty** *adj.* □ **wart-hog** *n.* a kind of African pig with two large tusks and wart-like growths on its face. **warts and all**, without concealment of blemishes or defects or unattractive features.

wartime *n.* the period when a war is being waged.

Warwickshire (**wo**-rik-sher) a county of England.

wary (**wair**-i) *adj.* (**warier**, **wariest**) cautious, in the habit of looking out for possible danger or difficulty. **warily** *adv.*, **wariness** *n.*

was *see* be.

wash *v.* **1.** to cleanse with water or other liquid; *wash the stain away* or *out*, remove it by washing. **2.** to wash oneself, to wash clothes etc. **3.** to be washable. **4.** to flow past or against, to go splashing or flowing, *the sea washes the base of the cliffs*; *waves washed over the deck.* **5.** (of moving liquid) to carry in a specified direction, *a wave washed him overboard*; *the meal was washed down with beer*, beer was drunk with or after it. **6.** to sift (ore) by the action of water. **7.** to coat with a wash of paint or wall-colouring etc. **8.** (*informal*, of reasoning) to be valid, *that argument won't wash.* —**wash** *n.* **1.** washing, being washed, *give it a good wash.* **2.** *the wash*, the process of laundering. **3.** a quantity of clothes etc. that are being washed or to be washed or have just been washed. **4.** disturbed water or air behind a moving ship or aircraft etc. **5.** liquid food or swill for pigs etc. **6.** a thin coating of colour painted over a surface. □ **come out in the wash**, (of mistakes etc.) to be eliminated during the progress of work etc. **wash-basin** *n.* a basin (usually fixed to a wall) for washing one's hands in. **wash dirty linen in public**, to discuss one's family scandals or quarrels publicly. **washed-out** *adj.* faded by washing; faded-looking; pallid. **wash-house** *n.* an out-building where washing is done.

wash-leather n. chamois or similar leather; a piece of this. **wash one's hands of,** to refuse to take responsibility for. **wash out,** to wash (clothes etc.); to make (a game etc.) impossible by heavy rainfall; (*informal*) to cancel. **wash-out** n. (*slang*) a complete failure. **wash-room** n. (*Amer.*) a lavatory. **wash-stand** n. a piece of furniture to hold a basin and jug of water etc. for washing. **wash-tub** n. a tub for washing clothes. **wash up,** to wash (crockery etc.) after use; to cast up on the shore; (*Amer.*) to wash oneself; *be washed up,* (*slang*) to have failed, to be ruined.

Wash. *abbrev.* Washington.

washable *adj.* able to be washed without suffering damage.

washer n. 1. a machine for washing things. 2. a ring of rubber or metal etc. placed between two surfaces (e.g. under a nut) to give tightness or prevent leakage.

washerwoman n. (*pl.* washerwomen) a woman whose occupation is washing clothes etc.

washing n. clothes etc. that are being washed or to be washed or have just been washed. **washing-machine** n. a machine for washing clothes etc. **washing-powder** n. powder of soap or detergent for washing clothes etc. **washing-soda** n. sodium carbonate, used (dissolved in water) for washing and cleaning things. **washing-up** n. the process of washing dishes etc. after use, the dishes etc. for washing.

Washington 1. a State of the USA. 2. the administrative capital of the USA, covering the same area as the District of Columbia.

washy *adj.* 1. (of liquids) thin, watery. 2. (of colours) washed-out.

wasn't = was not.

wasp n. a stinging insect with a black and yellow striped body.

waspish *adj.* making sharp or irritable comments. **waspishly** *adv.,* **waspishness** n.

wassailing (woss-ăl-ing) n. (*old use*) making merry (especially at Christmas) with much drinking of spiced ale etc.

wast (*old use*) the past tense of be, used with *thou.*

wastage n. loss by waste; *natural wastage,* (of employees) leaving employment because of retirement or to take other jobs, not through being declared redundant.

waste v. 1. to use extravagantly or needlessly or without an adequate result; *he is wasted as a schoolmaster,* the job does not use his abilities fully; *advice is wasted on him,* has no effect when given. 2. to run to waste, *turn off that tap, the water is wasting.*

3. to fail to use (an opportunity). 4. to make or become gradually weaker, *wasting away for lack of food; a wasting disease.* —**waste** *adj.* 1. left over or thrown away because not wanted; *waste products,* useless by-products of manufacture or of a bodily process. 2. (of land) not used or cultivated or built on, unfit for use. —**waste** n. 1. an act of wasting or using something ineffectively, *a waste of time.* 2. waste material or food, waste products. 3. a stretch of waste land. □ **run to waste,** (of liquid) to flow away uselessly. **waste breath** *or* **words,** to talk uselessly. **waste paper,** paper regarded as spoilt or valueless and thrown away. **waste-paper basket,** an open container in which waste paper is placed for removal. **waste-pipe** n. a pipe that carries off water etc. that has been used or is not required.

wasteful *adj.* using more than is needed, showing waste. **wastefully** *adv.,* **wastefulness** n.

wasteland n. an expanse of waste land.

waster (wayst-er) n. 1. a wasteful person. 2. (*slang*) a wastrel.

wastrel (wayst-rěl) n. a good-for-nothing person.

watch v. 1. to look at, to keep one's eyes fixed on, to keep under observation. 2. to be on the alert, to take heed, *watch for an opportunity; watch your chance,* wait alertly for the right moment. 3. to be careful about. 4. to safeguard, to exercise protective care, *he employed a solicitor to watch his interests* or *watch over them.* —**watch** n. 1. the act of watching, especially to see that all is well, constant observation or attention, *keep watch.* 2. a period (usually 4 hours) for which a division of a ship's company remains on duty, a turn of duty, the part (usually half) of a ship's company on duty during a watch. 3. a small portable device indicating the time, usually worn on the wrist or carried in the pocket. —**watcher** n. □ **on the watch,** alert for something. **watch-dog** n. a dog kept to guard property etc.; a person who acts as guardian of people's rights etc. **watching brief,** the brief of a barrister who is present during a lawsuit in order to advise a client who is not directly concerned in it. **watch-night service,** a religious service on the last night of the year. **watch one's step,** to be careful not to stumble or fall or do something wrong. **watch out,** to be on one's guard. **watchtower** n. a tower from which observation can be kept.

watchful *adj.* watching or observing closely. **watchfully** *adv.,* **watchfulness** n.

watchmaker *n.* a person who makes or repairs watches.

watchman *n.* (*pl.* watchmen) a man employed to look after an empty building etc. at night.

watchword *n.* a word or phrase expressing briefly the principles of a party or group.

water *n.* **1.** a colourless odourless tasteless liquid that is a compound of oxygen and hydrogen. **2.** a sheet or body of water, e.g. a lake or sea. **3.** water as supplied for domestic use. **4.** a watery secretion (e.g. sweat or saliva), urine. **5.** a watery infusion or other preparation, *lavender water*; *soda water*. **6.** the level of the tide, *at high water*. **7.** the transparency and lustre of a gem; *a diamond of the first water*, of the finest quality. —**water** *v.* **1.** to sprinkle with water. **2.** to supply with water, to give drinking-water to (an animal). **3.** to dilute with water. **4.** (of a ship etc.) to take in a supply of water. **5.** to secrete tears or saliva; *make one's mouth water*, arouse desire. □ **by water**, (of travel) in a boat or ship or barge etc. **water-bed** *n.* a mattress filled with water. **water-bird** *n.* a bird that swims on or wades in water. **water-biscuit** *n.* an unsweetened biscuit made from flour and water. **water-bottle** *n.* a glass or metal container for holding drinking-water. **water buffalo**, the common domestic buffalo of India and Indonesia etc. **water bus**, a boat carrying passengers on a regular route on a lake or river. **water-butt** *n.* a barrel used to catch rainwater. **water-cannon** *n.* a device for shooting a powerful jet of water to disperse a crowd etc. **Water-carrier** *n.* a sign of the zodiac, Aquarius. **water-closet** *n.* a lavatory with a pan that is flushed by water. **water-colour** *n.* artists' paint in which the pigment is diluted with water (not oil); a picture painted with paints of this kind. **water down**, to dilute; to make less forceful or vivid. **water-glass** *n.* a thick liquid used for coating eggs in order to preserve them. **water-ice** *n.* an edible concoction of frozen flavoured water. **watering-can** *n.* a container with a long tubular spout, holding water for watering plants. **watering-place** *n.* a pool etc. where animals go to drink water; a spa or seaside resort. **water-jump** *n.* a place where a horse in a steeplechase etc. must jump over water. **water-level** *n.* the surface of water in a reservoir etc., the height of this; = water-table (*see below*). **water-lily** *n.* a plant that grows in water, with broad floating leaves and white, yellow, blue, or red flowers. **water-line** *n.* the line along which the surface of water touches a ship's side. **water-main** *n.* a main pipe in a water-supply system. **water-meadow** *n.* a meadow that is kept fertile by being flooded periodically by a stream. **watermelon** *n.* a melon with a smooth green skin, red pulp, and watery juice. **water-mill** *n.* a mill worked by a water-wheel. **water-pipe** *n.* a pipe conveying water. **water-pistol** *n.* a toy pistol that shoots a jet of water. **water polo**, a game played by teams of swimmers with a ball like a football. **water-power** *n.* power obtained from flowing or falling water, used to drive machinery or generate electric current. **water-rat** *n.* a rat-like animal that lives beside a lake or stream. **water-rate** *n.* the charge made for use of a public watersupply. **water-repellent** *adj.* not easily penetrated by water. **water-ski** *n.* (*pl.* water-skis) either of a pair of flat boards on which a person stands for waterskiing, the sport of skimming over the surface of water while holding a tow-line from a motor boat. **water-softener** *n.* a substance or apparatus for softening hard water. **water-splash** *n.* a section of a road where vehicles have to travel through a shallow stream or pool. **water-table** *n.* the level below which the ground is saturated with water. **water-tower** *n.* a tower that holds a water-tank at a height to secure pressure for distributing water. **water-way** *n.* a route for travel by water, a navigable channel. **water-weed** *n.* a weed growing in water. **water-wheel** *n.* a wheel turned by a flow of water, used to work machinery. **water-wings** *pl. n.* floats worn on the shoulders by a person learning to swim.

waterbrash *n.* watery fluid brought up into the mouth from the stomach in cases of heartburn.

watercourse *n.* a stream or brook or artificial waterway, its channel.

watercress *n.* a kind of cress that grows in streams or ponds, with strong-tasting leaves, used as salad.

watered *adj.* (of fabric, especially silk) having an irregular wavy marking.

waterfall *n.* a stream that falls from a height.

waterfowl *pl. n.* water-birds, especially game-birds that swim.

waterfront *n.* the part of a town that borders on a river or lake or sea.

waterless *adj.* without water.

waterlogged *adj.* **1.** (of timber or a ship) saturated or filled with water so that it will barely float. **2.** (of ground) so saturated with water that it is useless or unable to be worked.

Waterloo *n.* **meet one's Waterloo,** to lose a decisive contest. ¶ From the name of the village in Belgium where Napoleon was defeated in 1815.

waterman *n.* (*pl.* watermen) a boatman.

watermark *n.* **1.** a mark showing how high a river or tide rises or how low it falls. **2.** a manufacturer's design in some kinds of paper, visible when the paper is held against light.

waterproof *adj.* unable to be penetrated by water. —*n.* a waterproof coat or cape. —*v.* to make waterproof.

watershed *n.* **1.** a line of high land where streams on one side flow into one river or sea and streams on the other side flow into another. **2.** a turning-point in the course of events. **3.** a catchment area.

waterside *n.* the edge of a river or lake or sea.

waterspout *n.* a funnel-shaped column of water between sea and cloud, formed when a whirlwind draws up a whirling mass of water.

watertight *adj.* **1.** made or fastened so that water cannot get in or out. **2.** (of an excuse or alibi) impossible to set aside or disprove, (of an agreement) leaving no possibility of escape from its provisions.

waterworks *n.* an establishment with pumping machinery etc. for supplying water to a district.

watery *adj.* **1.** of or like water. **2.** made weak or thin by too much water. **3.** full of water or moisture, *watery eyes.* **4.** (of colours) pale; *a watery moon* or *sky,* looking as if rain will come. □ **watery grave,** death by drowning.

watt (*pr.* wot) *n.* a unit of electric power.

wattage (**wot**-ij) *n.* an amount of electric power, expressed in watts.

wattle¹ (**wot**'l) *n.* **1.** a structure of interwoven sticks and twigs used as material for fences, walls, etc. **2.** an Australian acacia with long flexible branches, bearing golden flowers adopted as the national emblem.

wattle² (**wot**'l) *n.* a red fleshy fold of skin hanging from the head or throat of certain birds, e.g. the turkey.

waul *v.* to caterwaul.

wave *n.* **1.** a ridge of water moving along the surface of the sea etc. or arching and breaking on the shore. **2.** something compared to this, e.g. an advancing group of attackers, a temporary increase of an influence or condition (*a wave of anger*), a spell of hot or cold weather (*a heat wave*). **3.** a wave-like curve or arrangement of curves, e.g. in a line or in hair. **4.** an act of waving. **5.** the wave-like motion by which

heat, light, sound, or electricity etc. is spread or carried, a single curve in the course of this. —**wave** *v.* **1.** to move loosely to and fro or up and down. **2.** to move (one's arm or hand or something held) to and fro as a signal or greeting. **3.** to signal or express in this way, *waved him away; waved goodbye.* **4.** to give a wavy course or appearance to. **5.** to be wavy. □ **wave aside,** to dismiss (an objection etc.) as unimportant or irrelevant. **wave down,** to signal (a vehicle or its driver) to stop, by waving one's hand.

¶ Do not confuse with waive.

waveband *n.* a range of wavelengths between certain limits.

wavelength *n.* the distance between corresponding points in a sound wave or an electromagnetic wave.

wavelet *n.* a small wave.

waver *v.* **1.** to be or become unsteady, to begin to give way, *the line of troops wavered and then broke; his courage wavered.* **2.** (of light) to flicker. **3.** to show hesitation or uncertainty, *he wavered between two opinions.* **waverer** *n.*

¶ Do not confuse with waiver.

wavy *adj.* (wavier, waviest) full of waves or wave-like curves.

wax¹ *n.* **1.** beeswax. **2.** any of various soft sticky substances that melt easily, (e.g. obtained from petroleum), used for various purposes such as making candles or polishes. **3.** a yellow wax-like substance secreted in the ears. **4.** (*informal*) a gramophone record, material for making this. — **wax** *v.* **1.** to coat or polish or treat with wax. **2.** (*informal*) to make a recording of.

wax² *v.* **1.** (of the moon) to show a bright area that is becoming gradually larger until it becomes full. **2.** to increase in vigour or strength or importance, *kingdoms waxed and waned.* **3.** (*old use*) to become, *they waxed fat.*

waxen *adj.* made of wax, like wax in its paleness or smoothness.

waxwing *n.* any of several small birds with small red tips (like sealing-wax) on some of its wing-feathers.

waxwork *n.* an object modelled in wax, especially a model of a person with the face etc. made in wax, clothed to look lifelike and to be exhibited.

waxy *adj.* like wax. **waxiness** *n.*

way *n.* **1.** a line of communication between places, e.g. a path or road. **2.** the best route, the route taken or intended, *asked the way to Norwich.* **3.** a method or style, a person's chosen or desired course of action, *do it my way; have one's way,* cause people to do as one wishes. **4.**

travelling-distance, *it's a long way to Tipperary*. **5.** the amount of difference between two states or conditions, *his work is a long way from being perfect*. **6.** space free of obstacles so that people can pass; *make way*, allow room for others to proceed. **7.** the route over which a person or thing is moving or would naturally move, *don't get in the way of the trucks*. **8.** a specified direction, *which way is she looking?* **9.** a manner, *she spoke in a kindly way*. **10.** a habitual manner or course of action or events, *you'll soon get into our ways*. **11.** a talent or skill, *she has a way with flowers*. **12.** advance in some direction, progress, *we made our way to the front*; *he started as office-boy and worked his way up*. **13.** a respect, a particular aspect of something, *it's a good plan in some ways*. **14.** a condition or state, *things are in a bad way*. — *adv.* (*informal*) far, *the shot was way off the target*. □ **by the way**, by the road-side during a journey; incidentally, as a more or less irrelevant comment. **by way of**, as a substitute for or a form of, *smiled by way of greeting*. **come one's way**, to fall to one's lot; to become available. **in a way**, to a limited extent; in some respects. **in no way**, not at all. **in the way**, forming an obstacle or hindrance. **look the other way**, deliberately ignore a person or thing. **on one's way**, in the process of travelling or approaching. **on the way**, on one's way; (of a baby) conceived but not yet born. **under way**, *see* under. **way back**, (*informal*) a long way back. **way-bill** *n.* a list of the passengers or goods carried by a vehicle. **way-leave** *n.* a right of way that is rented to a mine-owner, electricity company, etc. **way-out** *adj.* exaggeratedly unusual in style, exotic.

wayfarer *n.* a traveller, especially on foot.

wayfaring-tree *n.* a shrub that grows commonly along roadsides, with white flowers and with berries that turn red then black.

waylay *v.* (waylaid, waylaying) to lie in wait for, especially so as to talk to or rob.

wayside *n.* the side of a road or path, land bordering this.

wayward *adj.* childishly self-willed, not obedient or easily controlled. **waywardness** *n.*

WC *abbrev.* water-closet.

we *pronoun* **1.** used by a person referring to himself and another or others, or speaking on behalf of a nation or group or firm etc. **2.** used instead of 'I' by a royal person in formal proclamations and by the writer of an editorial article in a newspaper etc. **3.** (*humorous*) you, *and how are we today?*

w/e *abbrev.* week ending.

weak *adj.* **1.** lacking strength or power or number, easily broken or bent or defeated, *a weak barrier*; *a weak team*. **2.** lacking vigour, not acting strongly, *weak eyes*; *a weak stomach*, easily upset. **3.** not convincing or forceful, *the evidence is weak*. **4.** dilute, having little of a certain substance in proportion to the amount of water, *weak tea*; *a weak solution of salt and water*. **5.** (of verbs) forming the past tense etc. by adding a suffix (e.g. *walk/walked, waste/wasted*) not by changing the vowel (*see* strong, sense 6). □ **weak-kneed** *adj.* giving way weakly, especially when intimidated. **weak-minded** *adj.* lacking determination.

weaken *v.* to make or become weaker.

weakling *n.* a feeble person or animal.

weakly *adv.* in a weak manner. —*adj.* sickly, not robust.

weakness *n.* **1.** the state of being weak. **2.** a weak point, a defect or fault. **3.** inability to resist something, a particular fondness, *she has a weakness for coffee creams*.

weal[1] *n.* a ridge raised on the flesh by a stroke of a rod or whip.

weal[2] *n.* (*literary*) welfare, prosperity, *for the public weal*.

wealth *n.* **1.** riches, possession of these. **2.** a great quantity, *a book with a wealth of illustrations*. □ **wealth tax**, tax levied on a person's capital.

wealthy *adj.* (wealthier, wealthiest) having wealth, rich.

wean *v.* **1.** to accustom (a baby) to take food other than milk. **2.** to cause (a person) to give up a habit or interest etc. gradually.

weapon *n.* **1.** a thing designed or used as a means of inflicting bodily harm, e.g. a gun or bomb or hammer, or a horn or claw. **2.** an action or procedure used as a means of getting the better of someone in a conflict, *use the weapon of a general strike*.

weaponry *n.* weapons collectively.

wear[1] *v.* (wore, worn, wearing) **1.** to have on the body, e.g. as clothing or ornaments or make-up; *he wears his hair long*, keeps it that way. **2.** to have (a certain look) on one's face, *wearing a frown*. **3.** (*informal*) to accept or tolerate, *we suggested working shorter hours but the boss wouldn't wear it*. **4.** to injure the surface of or become injured by rubbing or stress or use, to make (a hole etc.) in this way. **5.** to exhaust or overcome by persistence, *wore down the opposition*. **6.** to endure continued use, *this fabric wears well*. **7.** (of time) to pass gradually, *the night wore on.* —**wear** *n.* **1.** wearing or being worn as clothing, *choose cotton for summer wear.* **2.** clothing, *men's wear is on the ground floor.* **3.** damage resulting from ordinary use. **4.** capacity to endure being used. *there's a lot of wear left in that coat.* —**wearer** *n.* □ **wear off,** to remove or be removed by wear; to become gradually less intense. **wear one's heart on one's sleeve,** to show one's affections quite openly. **wear out,** to use or be used until no longer usable. **wear the trousers,** (of a wife) to dominate her husband.

wear[2] *v.* (wore, wearing) to come or bring (a ship) about by turning its head away from the wind.

wearable *adj.* able to be worn.

wearisome *adj.* causing weariness.

weary *adj.* (wearier, weariest) **1.** very tired, especially from exertion or endurance. **2.** tired of something, *weary of war.* **3.** tiring, tedious. —*v.* (wearied, wearying) to make or become weary. —**wearily** *adv.*, **weariness** *n.*

weasel *n.* a small fierce animal with a slender body and reddish-brown fur, living on small animals, birds' eggs, etc.

weather *n.* the condition of the atmosphere at a certain place and time, with reference to the presence or absence of sunshine, rain, wind, etc. —*adj.* windward, *on the weather side.* —*v.* **1.** to dry or season by exposure to the action of the weather. **2.** to become dried or discoloured or worn etc. in this way. **3.** to sail to windward of, *the ship weathered the Cape.* **4.** to come safely through, *weathered the storm.* □ **keep a weather eye open,** to be watchful. **under the weather,** feeling unwell or depressed. **weather-beaten** *adj.* bronzed or damaged or worn by exposure to weather. **weather-vane** *n.* a weathercock.

weatherboard *n.* a sloping board for keeping out rain and wind, especially one attached at the bottom of a door.

weatherboarding *n.* a series of weatherboards with each overlapping the one below, fixed to the outside wall of light buildings.

weathercock *n.* a revolving pointer, often in the shape of a cockerel, mounted in a high place and turning easily in the wind to show from which direction the wind is blowing.

weatherman *n.* (*pl.* weathermen) a meteorologist, especially one who broadcasts a weather forecast.

weatherproof *adj.* unable to be penetrated by rain or wind.

weave[1] *v.* (wove, woven, weaving) **1.** to make (fabric etc.) by passing crosswise threads or strips under and over lengthwise ones. **2.** to form (thread etc.) into fabric in this way. **3.** to put together into a connected whole, to compose (a story etc.). —*n.* a style or pattern of weaving, *a loose weave.* —**weaver** *n.* □ **weaver-bird** *n.* a tropical bird that builds a nest of elaborately interwoven twigs etc.

weave[2] *v.* (weaved, weaving) to move from side to side in an intricate course, *weaved his way through the crowd.* **get weaving,** (*slang*) to begin action energetically.

web *n.* **1.** the network of fine strands made by a spider etc. **2.** a network, *a web of deceit.* **3.** skin filling the spaces between the toes of birds such as ducks and animals such as frogs. **webbed** *adj.* □ **web-footed** *adj.* having the toes joined by web. **web-offset printing,** printing by an offset process on a large roll of paper that unwinds.

webbing *n.* strong bands of woven fabric used in upholstery, belts, etc.

wed *v.* (wedded, wedding) **1.** to marry. **2.** to unite, *if we can wed efficiency to economy.* □ **wedded to,** devoted to and unable to abandon (an occupation or opinion etc.).

we'd = we had, we should.

wedding *n.* a marriage ceremony and festivities. **wedding-cake** *n.* a rich iced cake cut and eaten at a wedding. **wedding-ring** *n.* a ring placed on the bride's finger and usually worn permanently afterwards; one worn similarly by a married man.

wedge *n.* **1.** a piece of wood or metal etc. thick at one end and tapered to a thin edge at the other, thrust between things to force them apart or prevent free movement etc. **2.** a wedge-shaped thing, *a wedge of cake.* —**wedge** *v.* **1.** to force apart or fix firmly by using a wedge. **2.** to thrust or pack tightly between other things or people or in a limited space, to be immovable because of this.

Wedgwood *n.* (*trade mark*) a kind of fine pottery named after Josiah Wedgwood, its original 18th-century manufacturer. **Wedgewood blue,** the blue colour characteristic of this.

wedlock *n.* the married state; *born out of wedlock,* illegitimate.

Wednesday *n.* the day of the week following Tuesday.

wee[1] *adj.* **1.** (*Scottish*) little, *wee Georgie.* **2.** (*informal*) tiny, *it's a wee bit too long.*

wee[2] *n.* & *v.* (*slang*) = wee-wee.

weed *n.* **1.** a wild plant growing where it is not wanted. **2.** (*slang*) marijuana. **3.** a thin weak-looking person. —*v.* to

remove weeds from, to uproot weeds. □
weed-killer *n.* a substance used to destroy weeds. **weed out**, to remove as inferior or undesirable.

weeds *pl. n.* deep mourning formerly worn by widows.

weedy *adj.* **1.** full of weeds. **2.** thin and weak-looking.

week *n.* **1.** a period of seven successive days, especially one reckoned from midnight at the end of Saturday. **2.** the six days other than Sunday, the five days other than Saturday and Sunday, *never go there during the week*. **3.** the period for which one regularly works during a week, *a 40-hour week*.

weekday *n.* a day other than Sunday.

weekend *n.* Sunday and all or part of Saturday (or occasionally slightly longer), especially as a time for holiday or a visit. **weekending** *n.* making a week-end holiday or visit.

weekly *adj.* happening or published or payable etc. once a week. —*adv.* once a week. —*n.* a weekly newspaper or magazine.

weeny *adj.* (*informal*) tiny.

weep *v.* (wept, weeping) **1.** to shed tears **2.** to shed or ooze moisture in drops. —*n.* a spell of weeping.

weeping *adj.* (of a tree) having drooping branches, *weeping willow*.

weepy *adj.* (*informal*) inclined to weep, tearful.

weevil *n.* a kind of small beetle that feeds on grain, nuts, tree-bark, etc.

wee-wee *v.* (*children's use*) to urinate. —*n.* (*children's use*) urine, urination.

weft *n.* crosswise threads woven under and over the warp to make fabric.

weigh *v.* **1.** to measure the weight of, especially by means of scales or a similar instrument. **2.** to have a certain weight. **3.** to consider carefully the relative importance or value of, *weigh the pros and cons*. **4.** to have importance or influence, *this evidence weighed with the jury*. **5.** to be burdensome, *the responsibility weighed heavily upon him*. □ **under weigh**, (*incorrect use*) *see* under. **weigh anchor**, to raise the anchor and start a voyage. **weigh down**, to bring or keep down by its weight; to depress or make troubled, *weighed down with cares*. **weigh in**, to be weighed, (of a boxer) before a contest, (of a jockey) after a race. **weigh in with**, (*informal*) to contribute (a comment) to a discussion. **weigh one's words**, to select carefully those that convey exactly what one means. **weigh out**, to take a specified weight of (a substance) from a larger quantity. (of a jockey) to be weighed before a race. **weigh**

up, (*informal*) to assess, to form an estimate of.

weighbridge *n.* a weighing-machine with a plate set in a road etc. on to which vehicles can be driven to be weighed.

weight *n.* **1.** an object's mass numerically expressed according to a recognized scale of units. **2.** the property of heaviness. **3.** a unit or system of units by which weight is measured, *tables of weights and measures*; *troy weight*. **4.** a piece of metal of known weight used in scales for weighing things. **5.** a heavy object, especially one used to bring or keep something down, *the clock is worked by weights*. **6.** a load to be supported, *the pillars carry a great weight*. **7.** a heavy burden of responsibility or worry. **8.** importance, influence, a convincing effect, *the weight of the evidence is against you*. —**weight** *v.* **1.** to attach a weight to, to hold down with a weight or weights. **2.** to burden with a load. **3.** to bias or arrange the balance of, *the test was weighted in favour of candidates with scientific knowledge*. □ **carry weight**, to be influential. **throw one's weight about**, (*informal*) to use one's influence aggressively. **weight-lifter** *n.* a person who engages in **weight-lifting**, the athletic sport of lifting heavy weights.

weighting *n.* extra pay or allowances given in special cases, e.g. to allow for the higher cost of living in London.

weightless *adj.* having no weight, or with no weight relative to its surroundings (e.g. in a spacecraft moving under the action of gravity). **weightlessness** *n.*

weighty *adj.* (weightier, weightiest) **1.** having great weight, heavy. **2.** burdensome. **3.** showing or deserving earnest thought. **4.** important, influential. **weightily** *adv.*

weir (*pr.* weer) *n.* **1.** a small dam built across a river or canal so that water flows over it, serving to regulate the flow or to raise the level of water upstream. **2.** the water flowing over it in a waterfall.

weird *adj.* strange and uncanny or bizarre. **weirdly** *adv.*, **weirdness** *n.*

weirdie *n.* (*informal*) an eccentric person.

welcome *adj.* **1.** received with pleasure, *a welcome guest* or *gift*; *make a person welcome*, cause him to feel welcome. **2.** ungrudgingly permitted, *anyone is welcome to try it*; *you're welcome*, a polite phrase replying to thanks for something. —*int.* a greeting expressing pleasure at a person's coming. —**welcome** *v.* **1.** to greet with pleasure or ceremony. **2.** to be glad to receive, *we welcome this opportunity*. —*n.* a greeting or reception, especially a glad and kindly one.

weld *v*. **1**. to unite or fuse (pieces of metal) by hammering or pressure, usually after softening by heat. **2**. to make by welding. **3**. to be able to be welded. **4**. to unite into a whole. —*n*. a joint made by welding. — **welder** *n*.

welfare *n*. **1**. well-being. **2**. welfare work. □ **Welfare State**, a country seeking to ensure the welfare of all its citizens by means of social services operated by the State. **welfare work**, organized efforts to secure the welfare of a group of people (e.g. employees of a factory) or of the poor or disabled etc.

welkin *n*. (*poetical*) the sky, *cheered till the welkin rang*.

well¹ *n*. **1**. a shaft dug in the ground to obtain water or oil etc. from below the earth's surface. **2**. a spring serving as a source of water. **3**. an enclosed space resembling the shaft of a well, a deep enclosed space containing a staircase or lift in a building. **4**. a railed-off space for solicitors etc. in a lawcourt. —*v*. to rise or spring, *tears welled up in her eyes*.

well² *adv*. (better, best) **1**. in a good manner or style, satisfactorily, rightly. **2**. thoroughly, carefully, *polish it well*. **3**. by a considerable margin, *she is well over forty*. **4**. favourably, kindly, *they think well of him*. **5**. with good reason, easily, probably, *you may well ask*; *it may well be our last chance*. —**well** *adj*. **1**. in good health. **2**. in a satisfactory state or position, *all's well*. —*int*. expressing surprise or relief or resignation etc., or used to introduce a remark when one is hesitating. □ **as well, as well as**, *see* as. **be well away**, to have started and made considerable progress. **let well alone**, to leave things as they are and not meddle unnecessarily. **well-advised** *adj*. showing good sense. **well-being** *n*. good health, happiness, and prosperity. **well-born** *adj*. born of good family. **well-bred** *adj*. showing good breeding, well-mannered; (of a horse etc.) of good breed or stock. **well-connected** *adj*. related to good families. **well-disposed** *adj*. having kindly or favourable feelings (towards a person or plan etc.). **well-favoured** *adj*. good-looking. **well-groomed** *adj*. carefully tended, neat and clean in one's personal appearance. **well-heeled** *adj*. (*informal*) wealthy. **well-intentioned** *adj*. having or showing good intentions. **well-judged** *adj*. (of an action) showing good judgement or tact or aim. **well-knit** *adj*. having a compact body, not ungainly. **well-known** *adj*. known to many; known thoroughly. **well-mannered** *adj*. having

or showing good manners. **well-meaning, well-meant** *adjs*. acting or done with good intentions but not having a good effect. **well off**, in a satisfactory or good situation; fairly rich. **well oiled**, (*slang*) drunk. **well preserved**, (of an old person) showing little sign of age. **well-read** *adj*. having read much literature. **well-spoken** *adj*. speaking in a polite and correct way. **well-to-do** *adj*. fairly rich. **well-tried** *adj*. often tested with good result. **well-wisher** *n*. a person who wishes another well. **well-worn** *adj*. much worn by use; (of a phrase) much used, hackneyed.

we'll = we shall, we will.

wellnigh *adv*. almost.

wellies *pl. n*. (*informal*) wellingtons.

wellington *n*. a boot of rubber or similar waterproof material, usually reaching almost to the knee.

Wellington the capital of New Zealand.

Welsh *adj*. of Wales or its people or language. —*n*. **1**. the Welsh language. **2**. *the Welsh*, Welsh people. —**Welshman, Welshwoman** *ns*. □ **Welsh rabbit** or **rarebit**, melted or toasted cheese on toast. ¶ *Welsh rabbit* is the original name for this dish. The humorous use of *rabbit* was misunderstood and the word was altered to *rarebit* in an attempt to make it sound more understandable, but there is no independent evidence for the word *rarebit*.

welsh *v*. **1**. (of a bookmaker at a racecourse) to swindle by decamping without paying out winnings. **2**. to avoid paying one's just debts, to break an agreement, *they welshed on us* or *on the agreement*. **welsher** *n*.

welt *n*. **1**. a strip of leather etc. sewn round the edge of the upper of a boot or shoe for attaching it to the sole. **2**. a ribbed or strengthened border of a knitted garment, e.g. at the waist. **3**. a weal, the mark of a heavy blow.

welter *v*. (of a ship etc.) to be tossed to and fro on the waves. —*n*. a state of turmoil, a disorderly mixture.

welterweight *n*. a boxing weight (67 kg) between lightweight and middleweight.

wen *n*. a more or less permanent benign tumour on the skin, especially on the head.

wench *n*. (*old use*) a girl or young woman.

wend *v*. wend one's way, to go.

Wensleydale *n*. a kind of cheese made in Wensleydale in North Yorkshire.

went *see* go.

wept *see* weep.

were *see* be. **weren't** = were not.

werewolf (weer-wuulf) *n*. (*pl*. werewolves) (in myths) a person who at times turns into a wolf.

wert (*old use*) the past subjunctive of be, used with *thou*.

Wesleyan (**wez**-li-ăn) *adj*. of or based on the religious teachings of John Wesley (18th century; see also Methodist). —*n*. a follower of Wesley.

west *n*. **1.** the point of the horizon where the sun sets, opposite east. **2.** this direction. **3.** the western part of something. **4.** *the West*, Europe in contrast to Oriental countries; the non-Communist countries of Europe and America. —*adj*. & *adv*. towards or in the west; *a west wind*, blowing from the west. □ **go west**, (*slang*) to be destroyed or lost or killed. **West Country**, the south-western region of England. **West End**, the part of London near Piccadilly, containing famous theatres, restaurants, shops, etc. **West Germany**, the Federal Republic of Germany. **West Indian**, of or from the *West Indies*, islands off the coast of Central America; a person of West Indian birth or descent. **West Midlands**, a metropolitan county of England. **West Side**, (*Amer.*) the western part of Manhattan. **West Sussex**, a country of England. **West Virginia**, a State of the USA.

westering *adj*. (of the sun) moving towards the west.

westerly *adj*. in or towards the west; *a westerly wind*, blowing from the west (approximately). —*n*. a westerly wind.

western *adj*. of or in the west. —*n*. a film or story dealing with life in western North America during the wars with the Red Indians, or with cowboys etc. □ **Western Australia**, a State of Australia. **Western Church**, the Churches of western Christendom as distinct from the Eastern or Orthodox Church. **Western Isles**, an islands area of Scotland. **Western Samoa**, *see* Samoa.

westerner *n*. a native or inhabitant of the west.

westernize *v*. to make (an Oriental person or country) more like the West in ideas and institutions etc. **westernization** *n*.

westernmost *adj*. furthest west.

Westminster *n*. Parliament or the Houses of Parliament in London. ¶ From the name of the district of London where the Houses of Parliament (Palace of Westminster) are situated.

westward *adj*. & *adv*. in or towards the west. **westwards** *adv*.

wet *adj*. (wetter, wettest) **1.** soaked or covered or moistened with water or other liquid. **2.** rainy, *wet weather*. **3.** (of paint or ink etc.) recently applied and not yet dry. **4.** allowing the sale of alcohol. **5.** (*slang*, of a person) lacking good sense or mental vitality, dull. —**wet** *v*. (wetted, wetting) **1.** to make wet. **2.** to urinate. —**wet** *n*. **1.** moisture, liquid that wets something. **2.** wet weather. **3.** (*slang*) a drink. **4.** (*slang*) a dull person. —**wetly** *adv.*, **wetness** *n*. □ **wet behind the ears**, immature, inexperienced. **wet blanket**, a gloomy person who prevents others from enjoying themselves. **wet dock**, a dock in which a ship can float. **wet dream**, a sexual dream in which semen is emitted involuntarily. **wet-nurse** *n*. a woman employed to suckle another's child, (*v*.) to act as wet-nurse to, to look after or coddle as if helpless. **wet one's whistle**, (*informal*) to take a drink. **wet suit**, a porous garment worn by a skin-diver etc.

wether *n*. a castrated ram.

wettish *adj*. rather wet.

we've = we have.

whack *n*. **1.** a heavy resounding blow. **2.** (*informal*) an attempt, *have a whack at it*. **3.** (*slang*) a share, *do one's whack*. —*v*. to strike or beat vigorously; *whack out a solution to the problem*, produce one by vigorous thought.

whacked *adj*. (*informal*) tired out.

whacking *adj*. (*slang*) very large. —*adv*. (*slang*) very, *a whacking great house*.

whale *n*. any of several very large sea-animals some of which are hunted for their oil and flesh. —*v*. (*Amer. informal*) to beat or thrash. □ **a whale of a**, (*informal*) an exceedingly great or good, *had a whale of a time*.

whalebone *n*. a horny springy substance from the upper jaw of some kinds of whale, formerly used as stiffening.

whaler *n*. a person or ship engaged in hunting whales.

whaling *n*. hunting whales.

wham *int*. & *n*. the sound of a forcible impact.

whang *v*. to strike heavily and loudly. —*n*. a whanging sound or blow.

whangee *n*. **1.** a kind of bamboo grown in China and Japan. **2.** a cane made from this.

wharf (*pr*. worf) *n*. (*pl*. wharfs) a landing-stage where ships may moor for loading and unloading.

wharfinger (**wor**-fin-jer) *n*. the owner or supervisor of a wharf.

what *adj*. **1.** asking for a statement of amount or number or kind, *what stores have we got?* **2.** which, *what languages does he speak?* **3.** how great or strange or remarkable, *what a fool you are!* **4.** the or any that, *lend me what money you can spare.* —**what** *pronoun* **1.** what thing or things, *what did you say?*; *this is what I mean.* **2.** a request for something to be repeated because one has not heard or understood. —*adv.* to what extent or degree, *what does it matter?* —*int.* an exclamation of surprise. □ **what about,** what is the news about (a subject); what do you think of, how would you deal with; shall we do or have, *what about some tea?* **what-d'you-call it, what's-his** (*or* its)-**name,** substitutes for a name that one cannot remember. **what for?,** for what reason or purpose?; *give a person what for,* (*slang*) punish or scold him. **what have you,** other similar things. **what is more,** as an additional point, moreover. **what not,** other similar things. **whatnot** *n.* something trivial or indefinite; a stand with shelves for small objects. **what price?,** (*slang*) what is the chance of?; note the failure of. **what's what,** what things are useful or important etc., *she knows what's what.* **what with,** on account of (various causes), *what with overwork and undernourishment he fell ill.*

whatever *adj.* **1.** of any kind or number, *take whatever books you need.* **2.** of any kind at all, *there is no doubt whatever.* —*pronoun* anything or everything that, no matter what, *do whatever you like*; *keep calm, whatever happens.* □ **or whatever,** or anything similar.

whatsoever *adj.* & *pronoun* = whatever.

wheat *n.* grain from which flour is made, the plant that produces this.

wheatear *n.* a kind of small bird.

wheaten *adj.* made from wheat-flour.

wheatmeal *n.* wholemeal flour made from wheat.

wheedle *v.* to coax, to persuade or obtain by coaxing.

wheel *n.* **1.** a disc or circular frame arranged to revolve on a shaft that passes through its centre. **2.** something resembling this. **3.** a machine etc. of which a wheel is an essential part. **4.** motion like that of a wheel, or of a line of men that pivots on one end. —**wheel** *v.* **1.** to push or pull (a bicycle or cart etc. with wheels) along. **2.** to turn or cause to turn like a wheel, to change direction and face another way, *he wheeled round in astonishment.* **3.** to move in circles or curves. □ **at the wheel,** driving a vehicle or directing a ship's course; in control of affairs. **wheeling and dealing,** (*Amer.*) scheming so as to exert influence. **wheels** *pl. n.* (*slang*) a car. **wheels within wheels,** secret or indirect motives and influences interacting with one another.

wheelbarrow *n.* an open container for moving small loads, with a wheel or ball beneath one end, and two straight handles (by which it is pushed) and legs at the other.

wheelbase *n.* the distance between the front and rear axles of a vehicle.

wheelchair *n.* an invalid's chair on wheels.

wheelies *pl. n.* (*slang*) travelling a short distance with the front wheel(s) off the ground.

wheelwright *n.* a maker or repairer of wooden wheels.

wheeze *v.* to breathe with an audible hoarse whistling sound. —*n.* **1.** the sound of wheezing. **2.** (*slang*) a clever scheme or plan. —**wheezy** *adj.*

whelk *n.* any of several sea snails, especially one used as food.

whelp *n.* a young dog, a pup. —*v.* to give birth to (a whelp or whelps).

when *adv.* **1.** at what time? on what occasion? **2.** at which time, *there are times when joking is out of place.* —**when** *conj.* **1.** at the time that, on the occasion that, whenever, as soon as. **2.** although, considering that, since, *why risk it when you know it's dangerous?* —**when** *pronoun* what or which time, *from when does the agreement date?*

whence *adv.* & *conj.* from where, from what place or source, from which. ¶ In questions, *whence* is now replaced by *where . . . from.* The phrase *from whence* is found frequently in translations of the Bible and occurs also in Shakespeare and Dickens, but strictly the word *from* is unnecessary and should be omitted.

whenever *conj.* & *adv.* at whatever time, on whatever occasion, every time that.

where *adv.* & *conj.* **1.** at or in what or which place or position or circumstances. **2.** in what respect, from what place or source or origin. **3.** to what place. **4.** in or at or to the place in which, *leave it where it is.* —**where** *pronoun* what place, *where does she come from?*

whereabouts *adv.* in or near what place. —*n.* a person's or thing's approximate location, *his whereabouts is* or *are uncertain.*

whereas *conj.* **1.** since it is the fact that. **2.** but in contrast, *he is English, whereas his wife is French.*

whereby *adv.* by which.

wherefore *adv.* (*old use*) for what reason, for this reason.

wherein *adv.* in what, in which.

whereupon *adv.* after which, and then.

wherever *adv.* at or to whatever place.

wherewithal *n.* (*informal*) the things (especially money) needed for a purpose.

whet *v.* (whetted, whetting) **1.** to sharpen by rubbing against a stone etc. **2.** to stimulate, *whet one's appetite* or *interest*.

whether *conj.* introducing an alternative possibility, *we don't know whether she will come or not*.

whetstone *n.* a shaped stone used for sharpening tools.

whew *int.* an exclamation of astonishment or dismay or relief.

whey (*pr.* way) *n.* watery liquid left when milk forms curds, e.g. in cheese-making.

which *adj. & pronoun* **1.** what particular one or ones of a set of things or people, *which Bob do you mean?* **2.** and that, *we invited him to come, which he did very willingly.* —**which** *relative pronoun*, the thing or animal referred to, *the house, which is large, is left to his son.* (¶ Used especially of an incidental description rather than one which defines or identifies something.)

whichever *adj. & pronoun* any which, that or those which, *take whichever* or *whichever one you like*.

whiff *n.* a puff of air or smoke or odour.

Whig *n.* a member of the political party in the 17th–19th centuries opposed to the Tories, succeeded in the 19th century by the Liberal Party.

while *n.* a period of time, the time spent in doing something, *a long while ago*; *we've waited all this while*; *worth one's while* = worth while (*see* worth). —**while** *conj.* **1.** during the time that, as long as, *make hay while the sun shines.* **2.** although, *while I admit that he is sincere, I think he is mistaken.* **3.** on the other hand, *she is dark, while her sister is fair.* —*v.* **while away,** to pass (time) in a leisurely or interesting manner.

whilst *conj.* while.

whim *n.* a sudden fancy, a sudden unreasoning desire or impulse.

whimper *v.* to whine softly, to make feeble frightened or complaining sounds. —*n.* a whimpering sound.

whimsical (**wim**-zik-ǎl) *adj.* **1.** impulsive and playful. **2.** fanciful, quaint. **whimsically** *adv.*, **whimsicality** (wim-zi-**kal**-iti) *n.*

whimsy *n.* a whim.

whinchat *n.* a small brownish song-bird.

whine *v.* **1.** to make a long high complaining cry like that of a child or dog. **2.** to make a long high shrill sound resembling this. **3.** to complain in a petty or feeble way, to utter complainingly. —*n.* a whining cry or sound or complaint. —**whiner** *n.*, **whiny** *adj.*

whinge *v.* (whinged, whinging) (*dialect* or *Austral.*) to whine, to grumble persistently. —*n.* a whine or grumble.

whinny *n.* a gentle or joyful neigh. —*v.* (whinnied, whinnying) to utter a whinny.

whip *n.* **1.** a cord or strip of leather fastened to a handle, used for urging animals on or for striking a person or animal in punishment. **2.** a hunt official in charge of hounds. **3.** an official of a political party in parliament with authority to maintain discipline among members of his party, party discipline and instructions given by such officials, *asked for the Labour whip*. **4.** a written notice (underlined with a number of lines indicating the degree of urgency, e.g. *three-line whip*) issued by party whips, requesting members to attend on a particular occasion. **5.** a dessert made by whipping a mixture of cream etc. with fruit or flavouring. —**whip** *v.* (whipped, whipping) **1.** to strike or urge on with a whip. **2.** to beat (cream or eggs etc.) into a froth. **3.** to move or take suddenly, *whipped out a knife*. **4.** to overcast (an edge). □ **have the whip hand,** to be in a controlling position. **whip-round** *n.* an appeal for contributions from a group of people. **whip up,** to incite, to stir up, *whip up support for the proposal*.

whipcord *n.* **1.** cord made of tightly twisted strands. **2.** a kind of twilled fabric with prominent ridges.

whiplash *n.* the lash of a whip; *whiplash injury*, injury to the neck caused by a sudden jerk of the head (e.g. when travelling in a vehicle that collides with something).

whipper-in *n.* a person who is the whip of a pack of hounds.

whipper-snapper *n.* a young and insignificant person who behaves in a presumptuous way.

whippet *n.* a small dog resembling a greyhound, used for racing.

whipping-boy *n.* a person who is regularly made to bear the blame and punishment when someone is at fault. ¶ Formerly, a boy was educated with a young prince and whipped in his stead for the prince's faults.

whippy *adj.* flexible, springy.

whirl *v.* **1.** to swing or spin round and round, to cause to have this motion. **2.** to travel swiftly in a curved course. **3.** to convey or go rapidly in a vehicle, *the car whirled them away*. —**whirl** *n.* **1.** a whirling movement. **2.** a confused state, *her thoughts were in a whirl*. **3.** a bustling activity, *the social whirl*. **4.** (*Amer. slang*) a try, *give it a whirl*.

whirligig *n*. **1**. a spinning or whirling toy. **2**. a merry-go-round.

whirlpool *n*. a current of water whirling in a circle, often drawing floating objects towards its centre.

whirlwind *n*. a mass of air whirling rapidly about a central point; *a whirlwind courtship*, a very rapid one.

whirr *v*. to make a continuous buzzing or vibrating sound like that of a wheel etc. turning rapidly. —*n*. this sound.

whisk *v*. **1**. to move with a quick light sweeping movement. **2**. to convey or go rapidly, *he was whisked off to London*. **3**. to brush or sweep lightly from a surface, *whisked away the crumbs*. **4**. to beat (eggs etc.) into a froth. —**whisk** *n*. **1**. a whisking movement. **2**. an instrument for beating eggs etc. **3**. a bunch of strips of straw etc. tied to a handle, used for flicking flies away.

whisker *n*. **1**. one of the long hair-like bristles growing near the mouth of a cat and certain other animals. **2**. (*informal*) a very small distance, *within a whisker of it*. □ **whiskers** *pl. n*. hair growing on a man's face, especially on the cheek.

whiskery, whiskered *adjs*. having whiskers.

whiskey *n*. Irish whisky.

whisky *n*. **1**. spirit distilled from malted grain (especially barley). **2**. a drink of this.

whisper *v*. **1**. to speak or utter softly, using the breath but not the vocal cords. **2**. to converse privately or secretly, to plot or spread (a tale) as a rumour in this way. **3**. (of leaves or fabrics etc.) to rustle. —**whisper** *n*. **1**. a whispering sound or remark, whispering speech, *spoke in a whisper*. **2**. a rumour, *heard a whisper that the firm was closing down*. —**whisperer** *n*. □ **whispering gallery**, a gallery or dome in which the slightest sound made at a particular point can be heard at another far off.

whist *n*. a card-game usually for two pairs of players. **whist drive**, a series of games of whist in which a number of people take part, with certain players moving on to play against others after each round.

whistle *n*. **1**. a shrill sound made by forcing breath through the lips with these contracted to a narrow opening. **2**. a similar sound made by a bird or by something thrown, or produced by a pipe etc. **3**. an instrument that produces a shrill sound when air or steam is forced through it against a sharp edge or into a bell. —*v*. to make this sound, to summon or signal or produce a tune in this way. —**whistler** *n*. □ **whistle for**, (*informal*) to expect in vain, to wish for but have to go without.

whistle-stop *n*. (*Amer*.) a brief stop (during a tour made by a politician etc.) e.g. for purposes of electioneering.

whit *n*. the least possible amount, *not a whit better*.

Whit *adj*. of or including or close to **Whit Sunday**, the seventh Sunday after Easter, commemorating the descent of the Holy Spirit upon the Apostles at Pentecost.

white *adj*. **1**. of the very lightest colour, like snow or common salt. **2**. having a pale skin. **3**. pale in the face from illness or fear or other emotion. —**white** *n*. **1**. white colour. **2**. a white substance or material, white clothes. **3**. a white person. **4**. the white part of something (e.g. of the eyeball, round the iris). **5**. the transparent substance round the yolk of an egg, turning white when cooked. **6**. the white men in chess etc., the player using these. — **whitely** *adv*., **whiteness** *n*. □ **white admiral**, *see* admiral. **white ant**, a termite. **white Christmas**, one with snow. **white coffee**, coffee with milk or cream. **white-collar worker**, a worker who is not engaged in manual labour (e.g. an office worker). **white elephant**, a useless possession. **white feather**, a symbol of cowardice. **white flag**, a symbol of surrender. **White Friars**, Carmelites. **white frost**, frost causing a white deposit on exposed surfaces. **white heat**, the temperature at which heated metal looks white. **white hope**, a person who is expected to attain fame. **white horses**, white-crested waves on sea. **White House**, the official residence (in Washington) of the President of the USA. **white lie**, a harmless lie (e.g. one told for the sake of politeness). **White Paper**, a report issued by the government to give information on a subject. **White Russian**, Belorussian. **white sale**, a sale of household linen. **white slave**, a woman who is tricked and sent (usually abroad) into prostitution. **white slavery**, this practice or state. **white tie**, a man's white bow-tie worn with full evening dress. **white wine**, amber or golden or pale yellow wine, not red or rosé.

whitebait *n*. (*pl*. whitebait) a small silvery-white fish.

Whitehall *n*. the British Government. ¶ From the name of a London street where there are many Government offices.

whiten *v*. to make or become white or whiter.

whitewash *n*. **1**. a liquid containing quicklime or powdered chalk used for painting walls, ceilings, etc. **2**. a means of glossing over mistakes or faults so as to clear someone's reputation. —**whitewash**

v. **1.** to paint with whitewash. **2.** to clear the reputation of (a person etc.) by glossing over mistakes or faults.

Whitey *n.* (in Black use, *contemptuous*) a white person, white people collectively.

whither *adv.* (*old use*) to what place.

whiting *n.* (*pl.* whiting) a small sea-fish with white flesh, used as food.

whitish *adj.* rather white.

whitlow (**wit**-loh) *n.* a small abscess under or near a nail.

Whitsun *n.* Whit Sunday and the days close to it.

Whitsunday *n.* (in Scotland) a quarter-day, 15 May. ¶ Do not confuse with Whit Sunday.

whittle *v.* **1.** to trim or shape (wood) by cutting thin slices from the surface. **2.** to reduce by removing various amounts, *whittled down the cost by cutting out all but the essential items.*

whiz *v.* (whizzed, whizzing) **1.** to make a sound like that of something moving at great speed through air. **2.** to move very quickly. —*n.* a whizzing sound. □ **whiz-kid** *n.* (*informal*) an exceptionally brilliant or successful young person.

who *pronoun* **1.** what or which person or persons? **2.** the particular person or persons, *this is the man who wanted to see you.*

whoa *int.* a command to a horse etc. to stop or stand still.

who'd = who had, who would.

whodunit *n.* (*informal*) a detective or mystery story or play etc. (¶ Humorous representation of the incorrect phrase 'who done it?'.)

whoever *pronoun* any or every person who, no matter who.

whole *adj.* **1.** with no part removed or left out, *told them the whole story; whole wheat.* **2.** not injured or broken, *there's not a plate left whole.* —**whole** *n.* **1.** the full or complete amount, all the parts or members. **2.** a complete system made up of parts, *the universe is a whole and the earth is part of this.* □ **on the whole**, considering everything; in respect of the whole though some details form exceptions. **whole-hearted** *adj.* without doubts or reservations, *whole-hearted approval.* **whole holiday**, a single whole day taken as a holiday. **whole number**, a number consisting of one or more units with no fractions.

wholemeal *adj.* made from the whole grain of wheat etc.

wholesale *n.* the selling of goods in large quantities to be retailed by others. —*adj. & adv.* **1.** in the wholesale trade. **2.** on a large scale, *wholesale destruction.* —*v.* to

sell in the wholesale trade. —**wholesaler** *n.*

wholesome *adj.* good for physical or mental health or moral condition, showing a healthy condition. **wholesomeness** *n.*

who'll = who will.

wholly *adv.* entirely, with nothing excepted or removed.

whom *pronoun* the objective case of who.

whoop (*pr.* woop) *v.* to utter a loud cry of excitement. —*n.* this cry. □ **whoop it up**, (*slang*) to engage in noisy revelry.

whoopee *int.* an exclamation of exuberant joy. **make whoopee**, (*slang*) to engage in noisy revelry.

whooping-cough (**hoop**-ing) *n.* an infectious disease especially of children, with a cough that is followed by a long rasping indrawn breath.

whoops (*pr.* woops) *int.* (*informal*) an exclamation of surprise or apology.

whopper *n.* (*slang*) something very large.

whopping *adj.* (*slang*) very large or remarkable, *a whopping lie.*

whore (*pr.* hor) *n.* a prostitute, a sexually immoral woman.

whorl *n.* **1.** a coiled form, one turn of a spiral. **2.** a complete circle formed by ridges in a fingerprint. **3.** a ring of leaves or petals round a stem or central point.

who's = who is, who has. **Who's Who**, a reference book containing a list of notable people and facts concerning them.

¶ Do not confuse with whose.

whose *pronoun* of whom, of which, *the people whose house we admired; the house whose owner takes pride in it.*

¶ Do not confuse with who's.

why *adv.* **1.** for what reason or purpose? **2.** on account of which, *the reasons why it happened are not clear.* —*int.* an exclamation of surprised discovery or recognition. **whys and wherefores**, reasons.

wick *n.* a length of thread in the centre of a candle or oil-lamp or cigarette-lighter etc. by which the flame is kept supplied with melted grease or fuel. **get on a person's wick**, (*slang*) to annoy him.

wicked *adj.* **1.** morally bad, offending against what is right. **2.** very bad or formidable, severe. **3.** malicious, mischievous, *a wicked grin.* **wickedly** *adv.,* **wickedness** *n.*

wicker *n.* thin canes or osiers woven together as material for making furniture or baskets etc. **wickerwork** *n.*

wicket *n.* **1.** a wicket-door or wicket-gate. **2.** a set of three stumps and two bails used in cricket, defended by the batsman who is 'out' if the bails are knocked off by the ball. **3.** the part of a cricket ground between

or near the wickets. □ **wicket-door,
wicket-gate** *ns.* a small door or gate
usually beside or within a larger one for
use when this is not open. **wicket-
keeper** *n.* a fieldsman in cricket stationed
close behind the batsman's wicket.

wide *adj.* **1.** measuring much from side to
side, not narrow, *a wide river.* **2.** in width,
one metre wide. **3.** extending far, having
great range, *a wide knowledge of art.* **4.**
open to the full extent, *staring with wide
eyes.* **5.** at a considerable distance from the
point or mark aimed at; *his guess was wide
of the mark,* quite incorrect. —*adv.* widely,
to the full extent, far from the target. —*n.*
a bowled ball in cricket that passes the
wicket beyond the batsman's reach and
counts one point to his team. —**widely**
adv., **wideness** *n.* □ **give a wide berth to,**
see berth. **to the wide,** completely; *dead
to the wide,* unconscious or deeply asleep.
wide-angle *adj.* (of a lens) able to include a wider field of vision than a standard lens does. **wide awake,** completely
awake; (*informal*) fully alert. **wide boy,**
(*slang*) a man who is skilled in sharp practice. **wide-eyed** *adj.* with eyes opened
widely in amazement or innocent surprise. **wide open,** (of a place) exposed to
attack; (of a contest) with no contestant
who can be predicted as a certain winner.
wide-ranging *adj.* covering an extensive
range. **wide world,** the whole world,
great as it is.

widen *v.* to make or become wider.

widespread *adj.* found or distributed
over a wide area.

widgeon (**wij**-ŏn) *n.* any of several kinds
of wild duck.

widow *n.* a woman whose husband has
died and who has not married again.

widowed *adj.* made a widow or widower.

widower *n.* a man whose wife has died
and who has not married again.

width *n.* **1.** wideness. **2.** distance or measurement from side to side. **3.** a piece of
material of full width as woven, *use two
widths to make this curtain.*

wield (*pr.* weeld) *v.* **1.** to hold and use (a
weapon or tool etc.) with the hands. **2.** to
have and use (power).

wife *n.* (*pl.* wives) a married woman in
relation to her husband. **wifely** *adj.*

wig *n.* a covering made of real or artificial
hair, worn on the head.

wigging *n.* (*informal*) a lengthy rebuke, a
scolding.

wiggle *v.* to move or cause to move repeatedly from side to side, to wriggle. —*n.*
a wiggling movement.

Wight *see* Isle of Wight.

wigwam (**wig**-wam) *n.* a hut or tent made
by fastening skins or mats over a framework of poles, as formerly used by American Indians.

wilco *int.* = 'will comply', used in signalling etc. to indicate that directions received will be carried out.

wild *adj.* **1.** living or growing in its original
natural state, not domesticated or tame or
cultivated. **2.** not civilized, barbarous, *wild
tribes.* **3.** (of scenery) looking very
desolate, not cultivated. **4.** lacking restraint
or discipline or control, disorderly. **5.**
tempestuous, stormy, *a wild night.* **6.** full
of strong unrestrained feeling, very eager
or excited or enthusiastic or angry etc.
7. extremely foolish or unreasonable, *these
wild ideas.* **8.** random, *a wild guess.* —*adv.*
in a wild manner, *shooting wild.* —**wildly**
adv., **wildness** *n.* □ **run wild,** to grow
or live without being checked or dis-
ciplined or restrained. **sow one's wild
oats,** *see* oats. **the wilds,** districts far
from civilization. **wild-goose chase,** a
useless search, a hopeless quest. **wild silk,**
silk from wild silkworms, an imitation of
this. **Wild West,** the western States of the
USA during the period when they were
lawless frontier districts.

wildcat *adj.* **1.** reckless or impracticable
especially in business and finance, *wildcat
schemes.* **2.** (of strikes) unofficial and irresponsible.

wildebeest (**wil**-di-beest) *n.* a gnu.

wilderness *n.* a wild uncultivated area.

wildfire *n.* **spread like wildfire,** (of rumours etc.) to spread very fast.

wildfowl *n.* birds that are hunted as
game (e.g. ducks and geese, quail, phea-
sants.

wildlife *n.* wild animals collectively.

wile *n.* a piece of trickery intended to deceive or attract someone —*v.* **wile away,**
= while away (*see* while).

wilful *adj.* **1.** done with deliberate intention and not as an accident, *wilful murder.*
2. self-willed, obstinate, *a wilful child.*
wilfully *adv.,* **wilfulness** *n.*

will [1] *auxiliary verb* (wilt is used with
thou), *see* shall.

will [2] *n.* **1.** the mental faculty by which a
person decides upon and controls his own
actions or those of others. **2.** will-power.
3. determination; *they set to work with a
will,* in a determined and energetic way.
4. that which is desired or determined,
may God's will be done. **5.** a person's attitude in wishing good or bad to others;
good will (*see* good); *with the best will in
the world,* however good one's intentions
are. **6.** written directions made by a person

for the disposal of his property after his death. —**will** v. **1.** to exercise one's will-power, to influence or compel by doing this. **2.** to intend unconditionally, *God has willed it.* **3.** to bequeath by a will, *she willed her money to a hospital.* □ **at will,** whenever one pleases, *he comes and goes at will.* **have one's will,** to get what one desires. **will-power** n. control exercised by one's will, especially over one's own actions and impulses.

willies pl. n. **the willies,** (*slang*) nervous discomfort.

willing adj. **1.** doing readily what is required, having no objection. **2.** given or performed willingly, *we received willing help.* —n. willingness, *to show willing.* — **willingly** adv., **willingness** n.

will-o'-the-wisp n. a hope or aim that lures a person on but can never be fulfilled.

willow n. **1.** any of several trees or shrubs with very flexible branches, usually growing near water. **2.** its wood. □ **willow-herb** n. any of several wild flowers usually with pink petals. **willow-pattern** n. a conventional Chinese design including a willow-tree and a river, done in blue on a white background, especially on china.

willowy adj. **1.** full of willow trees. **2.** slender and supple.

willy-nilly adv. whether one desires it or not.

wilt¹ *see* will¹.

wilt² v. **1.** (of plants or flowers) to lose freshness and droop. **2.** to cause to do this. **3.** (of a person) to become limp from exhaustion. —n. a plant-disease that causes wilting.

Wilton n. a kind of carpet with loops cut into thick pile, first made at Wilton in Wiltshire.

Wilts. abbrev. Wiltshire.

Wiltshire a county of England.

wily (wy-li) adj. (wilier, wiliest) full of wiles, crafty, cunning. **wiliness** n.

wimple n. a medieval head-dress of linen or silk folded round the head and neck, covering all but the front of the face.

win v. (won, winning) **1.** to be victorious in (a battle or game or race etc.), to gain a victory. **2.** to obtain or achieve as the result of a battle or contest or bet etc. **3.** to obtain as a result of effort or perseverance, *he won their confidence.* **4.** to gain the favour or support of, *soon won his audience over.* —n. victory in a game or contest. □ **win through,** to achieve success eventually. **you can't win,** (*informal*) there is no way of achieving success or of pleasing people.

wince v. to make a slight involuntary movement from pain or distress or embarrassment etc. —n. a wincing movement.

winceyette n. a soft fabric woven of cotton and wool, used for nightclothes etc.

winch n. a machine for hoisting or pulling things by means of a cable which winds round a revolving drum or wheel. —v. to hoist or pull with a winch.

wind¹ (*rhymes with* tinned) n. **1.** a current of air either occurring naturally in the atmosphere or put in motion by the movement of something through the air or produced artificially by bellows etc. **2.** smell carried by the wind, *the deer we were stalking had got our wind.* **3.** gas forming in the stomach or intestines and causing discomfort. **4.** breath as needed in exertion or speech or for sounding a musical instrument. **5.** the wind instruments of an orchestra. **6.** useless or boastful talk. —**wind** v. **1.** to detect by the presence of a smell, *the hounds had winded the fox.* **2.** to cause to be out of breath, *we were quite winded by the climb.* □ **eye of the wind,** *see* eye. **get** *or* **have the wind up,** (*slang*) to feel frightened. **get wind of,** to hear a hint or rumour of. **in the wind,** happening or about to happen. **like the wind,** very swiftly. **put the wind up a person,** (*slang*) to make him feel frightened. **take the wind out of a person's sails,** to take away his advantage suddenly, to frustrate him by anticipating his arguments etc. **wind-break** n. a screen or row of trees etc. shielding something from the full force of the wind. **wind-cheater** n. a sports jacket of thin but windproof material fitting closely at the waist and cuffs. **wind instrument,** a musical instrument in which sound is produced by a current of air, especially by the player's breath (e.g. a trumpet or flute). **wind-jammer** n. a merchant sailing-ship. **wind's eye,** *see* eye. **wind-sock** n. a tube-shaped piece of canvas open at both ends, flown at an airfield to show the direction of the wind. **wind-swept** adj. exposed to strong winds.

wind² (*rhymes with* find) v. (wound (*rhymes with* found), winding) **1.** to go or cause to go in a curving or spiral or twisting course, *the road winds its way* or *winds through the hills.* **2.** to twist or wrap closely round and round upon itself so as to form a ball. **3.** to wrap, to encircle, *wound a bandage round his finger.* **4.** to haul or hoist or move by turning a handle or windlass etc., *wind the car window down.* **5.** to wind up (a clock etc.). —**wind** n. **1.** a bend or turn in a course. **2.** a single turn in winding a clock or string etc. —**winder** *n.* □ **winding-sheet** *n.* a sheet in which a corpse is wrapped for burial. **wind up**, to set or keep (a clock etc.) going by tightening its spring or adjusting its weights; to bring or come to an end; to settle and finally close the business and financial transactions of (a company going into liquidation); (*informal*) to come to a place, *he'll wind up in gaol.*

windbag *n.* (*informal*) a person who talks lengthily.

windfall *n.* **1.** an apple or pear etc. blown off a tree by the wind. **2.** a piece of unexpected good fortune, especially a sum of money acquired.

Windhoek (**vint**-huuk) the capital of Namibia.

windlass (**wind**-lăs) *n.* a device for pulling or hoisting things (e.g. a bucket of water from a well) by means of a rope or chain that winds round an axle.

windless *adj.* without wind.

windmill *n.* a mill worked by the action of wind on projecting parts (*sails*) that radiate from a central shaft.

window *n.* **1.** an opening in the wall or roof of a building or in a car etc. to admit light and often air, usually filled with glass in a fixed or hinged or sliding frame. **2.** this glass with or without its frame, *broke the window.* **3.** a space for the display of goods behind the window of a shop etc. **4.** an opening resembling a window. □ **window-box** *n.* a trough fixed outside a window, for growing plants and flowers. **window-dressing** *n.* the displaying of goods attractively in a shop window; presentation of facts so as to create a favourable impression. **window on the world**, a means of observing and learning about people of other countries. **window-seat** *n.* a seat fixed under a window that is in a recess or bay of a room. **window-shopping** *n.* looking at goods displayed in shop windows etc. without necessarily intending to buy.

windpipe *n.* the principal passage by which air reaches the lungs, leading from the throat to the bronchial tubes.

windscreen *n.* the glass in the window at the front of a motor vehicle.

windshield *n.* (*Amer.*) a windscreen.

windsurfing *n.* the sport of surfing on a board to which a sail is fixed (also called *sailboarding*). **windsurfer** *n.*

windward *adj.* situated in the direction from which the wind blows. —*n.* the windward side or region.

windy *adj.* (windier, windiest) **1.** with much wind, *a windy night.* **2.** exposed to high winds. **3.** wordy, full of useless talk, *a windy speaker.* **windiness** *n.*

wine *n.* **1.** fermented grape-juice as an alcoholic drink. **2.** a fermented drink made from other fruits or plants, *ginger wine.* **3.** dark purplish red. —*v.* to drink wine, to entertain with wine; *they wined and dined us,* entertained us to a meal with wine.

wineglass *n.* a glass for drinking wine from.

wing *n.* **1.** one of a pair of projecting parts by which a bird or bat or insect etc. is able to fly. **2.** a corresponding part in a non-flying bird or insect. **3.** one of the parts projecting widely from the sides of an aircraft and acting upon the air so that the aircraft is supported in flight. **4.** something resembling a wing in appearance or position (e.g. a thin projection on maple and sycamore seeds). **5.** a projecting part extending from one end of a building, *the north wing was added in the 17th century.* **6.** the part of the bodywork immediately above the wheel of a motor vehicle. **7.** either end of an army lined up for battle. **8.** either of the players (*left wing, right wing*) in football or hockey etc. whose place is at the extreme end of the forward line, the side part of the playing-area in these games. **9.** an air-force unit of several squadrons. **10.** a section of a political party or other group, with more extreme views than those of the majority. —**wing** *v.* **1.** to fly, to travel by means of wings, *a bird winging its way home.* **2.** to wound slightly in the wing or arm. □ **on the wing,** flying. **take wing,** to fly away. **under one's wing,** under one's protection. **wing-chair** *n.* an armchair with projecting side-pieces at the top of a high back. **wing commander,** an officer of the RAF, in charge of a wing (*see* sense 9). **wing-nut** *n.* a nut with projections so that it can be turned by thumb and finger on a screw. **wings** *pl. n.* the sides of a theatre stage out of sight of the audience; a pilot's badge in the RAF etc.; *waiting in the wings,* waiting in readiness.

wingding *n.* (*Amer. slang*) a wild party.

winged *adj.* having wings.

winger *n.* a wing forward in football etc.

wingless *adj.* without wings.

wink *v.* **1.** to close and open one eye deliberately, especially as a private signal to someone. **2.** (of a light or star etc.) to shine with a light that flashes quickly on and off or twinkles. —**wink** *n.* **1.** an act of winking. **2.** a brief period of sleep, *didn't sleep a wink.* □ **wink at,** to pretend not to notice something that should be stopped or condemned.

winker *n.* a small signal-light on a motor vehicle, flashing to indicate a change of direction of travel.

winkle *n.* an edible sea snail. —*v.* **winkle out,** to extract, to prise out. □ **winkle-pickers** *n.* shoes with long pointed toes.

winner *n.* 1. a person who wins. 2. something successful, *her latest novel is a winner.*

winning *see* win. —*adj.* charming, persuasive, *a winning smile.* □ **winning-post** *n.* a post marking the end of a race.

winnings *pl. n.* money won in betting or at cards etc.

winnow *v.* 1. to expose (grain) to a current of air by tossing or fanning it so that the loose dry outer part is blown away, to separate (chaff) in this way. 2. to sift or separate from worthless or inferior elements, *winnow out the truth from the falsehoods.*

wino (wy-noh) *n.* (*pl* winos) (*slang*) an alcoholic.

winsome *adj.* having an engagingly attractive appearance or manner.

winter *n.* the coldest season of the year, from December to February in the northern hemisphere. —*v.* to spend the winter, *decided to winter in Egypt.* □ **winter garden,** a garden or conservatory of plants kept flourishing in winter. **winter sports,** open-air sports on snow or ice (e.g. skiing, skating).

wintry *adj.* 1. of or like winter, cold, *wintry weather.* 2. (of a smile etc.) chilly, lacking warmth or vivacity.

winy *adj.* like wine, *a winy taste.*

wipe *v.* 1. to clean or dry the surface of by rubbing something over it. 2. to remove by wiping, *wipe your tears away.* 3. to spread (a substance) thinly over a surface. *n.* the act of wiping, *give this plate a wipe.* □ **wipe a person's eye,** (*slang*) to gain an advantage over him. **wipe out,** to cancel; to destroy completely, *the whole army was wiped out.*

wiper *n.* 1. something that wipes or is used for wiping. 2. a rubber strip mechanically moved to and fro across a windscreen to remove rain etc.

wire *n.* 1. a strand or slender usually flexible rod of metal. 2. a barrier or framework etc. made from this. 3. a piece of wire used to carry electric current. —**wire** *v.* 1. to provide or fasten or strengthen with wire(s). 2. to install wiring in (a house). □ **get one's wires crossed,** to become confused and misunderstand. **pull wires,** *see* pull. **wire-cutter** *n.* a tool for cutting wire. **wire-haired** *adj.* (of a dog) having stiff wiry hair. **wire-tapping** *n.* the tapping of telephone wires. **wire wheel,** a vehicle wheel with wire spokes. **wire wool,** a mass of fine wire used for cleaning kitchen utensils etc. **wire-worm** *n.* the destructive worm-like larva of a kind of beetle.

wireless *n.* 1. radio, radio communications. 2. a radio receiver or transmitter.

wiring *n.* a system of wires for conducting electricity in a building.

wiry *adj.* (wirier, wiriest) 1. like wire. 2. (of a person) lean but strong. **wiriness** *n.*

Wis. *abbrev.* Wisconsin.

Wisconsin (wis-kon-sin) a State of the USA.

wisdom *n.* 1. being wise, soundness of judgement. 2. wise sayings; *the Wisdom of Solomon,* a book of the Apocrypha. □ **wisdom tooth,** the third and hindmost molar tooth on each side of the upper and lower jaws, usually cut (if at all) after the age of 20.

wise[1] *adj.* 1. having or showing soundness of judgement. 2. having knowledge, *where ignorance is bliss, 'tis folly to be wise.* 3. (*Amer. slang*) aware, informed, *be* or *get wise to something; put him wise to it,* tell him about it. —*v.* (*Amer. slang*) to inform, *wise him up about it.* —**wisely** *adv.* □ **be none the wiser,** to know no more than before; to be unaware of what has happened. **wise guy,** (*informal*) a know-all. **wise man,** a wizard, one of the Magi. **wise woman,** a witch, a fortune-teller.

wise[2] *n.* (*old use*) way, manner, *in no wise.*

wiseacre (wy-zay-ker) *n.* a person who pretends to have great wisdom, a know-all.

wisecrack *n.* (*informal*) a witty or clever remark. —*v.* (*informal*) to make a wisecrack.

wish *n.* 1. a desire or mental aim. 2. an expression of desire about another person's welfare, *with best wishes.* —**wish** *v.* 1. to have or express as a wish. 2. to formulate a wish, *wish when you see a shooting star.* 3. to hope or express hope about another person's welfare, *wish me luck; wish someone well,* hope that he prospers; *wish him 'good day',* greet him in this way; *we wish you joy of it,* (used ironically) feel that you will have difficulty in enjoying it. 4. (*informal*) to foist, *the dog was wished on us while its owners were on holiday.* □ **wish for,** to desire to have, to express a wish that one may have (a thing).

wishbone *n.* a forked bone between the neck and breast of a bird (pulled in two between two persons, the one who gets the longer part having the supposed right to magic fulfilment of any wish).

wishful *adj.* desiring. **wishful thinking,** a belief that is founded on what one wishes to be true rather than on fact.

wishy-washy *adj.* weak or feeble in colour, character, etc., lacking strong or positive qualities.

wisp *n.* **1.** a small separate bunch or bundle of something, *wisps of hair.* **2.** a small streak of smoke or cloud etc. **3.** a small thin person. **wispy** *adj.*

wistaria (wis-**tair**-iă) *n.* a climbing plant with hanging clusters of blue, purple, or white flowers.

wistful *adj.* full of sad or vague longing. **wistfully** *adv.,* **wistfulness** *n.*

wit [1] *n.* **1.** the ability to combine words or ideas etc. ingeniously so as to produce a kind of clever humour that appeals to the intellect. **2.** a witty person. **3.** intelligence, understanding, *hadn't the wit to see what was needed; use your wits.* □ **at one's wits' end,** at the end of one's mental resources, not knowing what to do. **have** *or* **keep one's wits about one,** to be or remain mentally alert and intelligent or ready to act. **scared out of one's wits,** crazy with fear.

wit [2] *v.* (*old use*) **to wit,** that is to say, namely.

witch *n.* **1.** a person (especially a woman) who practises witchcraft. **2.** a bewitching woman; *old witch,* an ugly woman. □ **witch ball,** a coloured glass ball of the kind formerly hung up to keep witches away. **witch-doctor** *n.* the tribal magician of a primitive people. **witch-hazel** *n.* a North American shrub with yellow flowers; an astringent lotion prepared from its leaves and bark. **witch-hunt** *n.* a search to find and destroy or persecute people thought to be witches, or others suspected of holding unorthodox or unpopular views.

witchcraft *n.* the practice of magic.

witchery *n.* **1.** witchcraft. **2.** the bewitching power of something.

with *prep.* **1.** in the company of, among. **2.** having, characterized by, *a man with a sinister expression.* **3.** using as an instrument or means, *hit it with a hammer.* **4.** on the side of, of the same opinion as, *we're all with you on this matter.* **5.** in the care or charge of, *leave a message with the receptionist.* **6.** in the employment etc. of, *he is with Shell.* **7.** at the same time as, in the same way or direction or degree as, *rise with the sun; swimming with the tide; he became more tolerant with age.* **8.** because of, *shaking with laughter.* **9.** feeling or showing, *heard it with calmness.* **10.** under the conditions of, *sleeps with the window open; he won with ease,* easily; *with*

your permission, if you will allow it. **11.** by addition or possession of, *fill it with water; laden with baggage.* **12.** in regard to, towards, *lost my temper with him.* **13.** in opposition to, *he argued with me.* **14.** in spite of, *with all his roughness, he's very good-natured.* **15.** so as to be separated from, *we parted with our luggage reluctantly.* □ **be with child,** (*old use*) to be pregnant. **I'm not with you,** (*informal*) I cannot follow your meaning. **with it,** (*informal*) up-to-the-minute, capable of understanding and appreciating current fashions and ideas.

withdraw *v.* (withdrew, withdrawn, withdrawing) **1.** to take back or away, *withdrew troops from the frontier.* **2.** to remove (money deposited) from a bank etc. **3.** to cancel (a promise or statement etc.). **4.** to go away from company or from a place; *withdraw into oneself,* become unresponsive or unsociable.

withdrawal *n.* **1.** withdrawing. **2.** the process of ceasing to take drugs to which one is addicted, often with unpleasant reactions, *withdrawal symptoms.*

withdrawn *adj.* (of a person) unresponsive, unsociable.

wither *v.* **1.** to make or become shrivelled, to lose or cause to lose freshness and vitality. **2.** to subdue or overwhelm by scorn, *withered him with a glance.*

withers (**with**-erz) *pl. n.* the ridge between a horse's shoulder-blades.

withhold *v.* (withheld, withholding) **1.** to refuse to give or grant or allow, *withhold permission.* **2.** to hold back, to restrain, *we could not withhold our laughter.*

within *prep.* **1.** inside, enclosed by. **2.** not beyond the limit or scope of, *success was within our grasp; he acted within his rights.* **3.** in a time no longer than, *we shall finish within an hour.* —*adv.* inside, *seen from within.*

without *prep.* **1.** not having or feeling or showing, free from, *without food; they are without fear.* **2.** in the absence of, *no smoke without fire.* **3.** with no action of, *we can't leave without thanking them.* **4.** (*old use*) outside, *without a city wall.* —*adv.* outside, *the house as seen from without.* — *conj.* (*incorrect use*) unless, *they won't come without we pay their expenses.* □ **without prejudice,** *see* prejudice.

withstand *v.* (withstood, withstanding) to endure successfully.

withy (**with**-i) *n.* a tough flexible willow branch or osier etc. used for tying bundles etc.

witless *adj.* foolish, unintelligent.

witness *n.* **1.** a person who sees or hears something, *there were no witnesses to their quarrel.* **2.** a person who gives evidence in a lawcourt. **3.** a person who is present at an event in order to testify to the fact that it took place, one who confirms that a signature is genuine by adding his own signature. **4.** something that serves as evidence, *his tattered clothes were a witness to his poverty.* —*v.* to be a witness at or of, to sign (a document) as a witness. □ **bear witness,** see bear². **witness-box** *n.* an enclosure from which witnesses give evidence in a lawcourt. **witness-stand** *n.* (*Amer.*) a witness-box.

witted *adj.* having wits of a certain kind, *quick-witted.*

witter *v.* (*informal*) to speak at annoying length about trivial matters.

witticism (**wit**-i-sizm) *n.* a witty remark.

wittingly *adv.* knowing what one does, intentionally.

witty *adj.* (wittier, wittiest) full of wit. **wittily** *adv.*, **wittiness** *n.*

wizard *n.* **1.** a male witch, a magician. **2.** a person with amazing abilities, *a financial wizard.* —*adj.* (*slang*) wonderful, excellent. —**wizardry** *n.*

wizened (**wiz**-ĕnd) *adj.* full of wrinkles, shrivelled with age, *a wizened face.*

woad *n.* **1** a kind of blue dye formerly obtained from a plant of the mustard family. **2.** this plant.

wobble *v.* **1.** to stand or move unsteadily, to rock from side to side. **2.** (of the voice) to quiver. —*n.* a wobbling movement, a quiver. —**wobbly** *adj.*

wodge *n.* (*informal*) a chunk, a wedge.

woe *n.* **1.** sorrow, distress. **2.** trouble causing this, misfortune.

woebegone (**woh**-big-on) *adj.* looking unhappy.

woeful *adj.* **1.** full of woe, sad. **2.** deplorable, *woeful ignorance.* **woefully** *adv.*

wog *n.* (*slang, contemptuous*) a foreigner, especially one from the Middle East.

wok *n.* a Chinese cooking-vessel shaped like a large bowl

woke, woken *see* wake¹.

wold *n.* an area of open upland country.

wolf *n.* (*pl.* wolves) **1.** a fierce wild animal of the dog family, feeding on the flesh of other animals and often hunting in packs. **2.** a greedy or grasping person. **3.** (*slang*) a man who aggressively seeks to attract women for sexual purposes. —*v.* to eat (food) quickly and greedily. □ **cry wolf,** to raise false alarms (¶ like the shepherd-boy in the fable, so that eventually a genuine alarm is ignored). **keep the wolf from the door,** to ward off hunger or starvation. **wolf in sheep's clothing,** a person who appears friendly or harmless but is really an enemy. **wolf-whistle** *n.*

a whistle uttered by a man in admiration of a woman's appearance.

wolfhound *n.* any of several large dogs (e.g. a borzoi) of a kind originally used for hunting wolves.

wolverine (**wuul**-ver-een) *n.* a North American animal of the weasel family.

woman *n.* (*pl.* women) **1.** an adult female person. **2.** women in general. **3.** (*informal*) a charwoman. □ **woman of the streets,** a prostitute. **woman of the world,** see world. **Women's Lib,** a movement urging the liberation of women from domestic duties and from a subordinate role in society and business etc. **women's rights,** the right of women to have a position of legal and social equality with men.

womanhood *n.* the state of being a woman.

womanish *adj.* like a woman, suitable for women but not for men.

womanize *v.* (of a man) to seek the company of women for sexual purposes. **womanizer** *n.*

womanly *adj.* having or showing qualities that are characteristic of or suitable for a woman. **womanliness** *n.*

womb (*pr.* woom) *n.* the hollow organ (in woman and other female mammals) in which a child or the young is conceived and nourished while developing before birth, the uterus.

wombat *n.* an Australian animal resembling a small bear.

womenfolk *n.* women in general, the women of one's family.

won *see* win.

wonder *n.* **1.** a feeling of surprise mingled with admiration or curiosity or bewilderment. **2.** something that arouses this, a marvel, a remarkable thing or event. — **wonder** *v.* **1.** to feel wonder or surprise, *I wonder that he wasn't killed.* **2.** to feel curiosity about, to desire to know, to try to form an opinion or decision about, *we're still wondering what to do next.* □ **do or work wonders,** to produce remarkably successful results. **for a wonder,** as a welcome exception, *he was punctual, for a wonder.* **I shouldn't wonder,** (*informal*) I should not be surprised. **no wonder,** it is not surprising.

wonderful *adj.* marvellous, surprisingly fine or excellent. **wonderfully** *adv.*

wonderland *n.* a land or place full of marvels or wonderful things.

wonderment *n.* a feeling of wonder, surprise.

wondrous *adj.* (*old use*) wonderful. **wondrously** *adv.*

wonky *adj.* (*slang*) shaky, unsteady.

wont (*pr.* wohnt) *adj.* (*old use*) accustomed, *he was wont to go to bed early.* —*n.* a habit or custom, *went to bed early, as was his wont.*

won't = will not.

wonted (wohn-tid) *adj.* customary, *he listened with his wonted courtesy.*

woo *v.* (wooed, wooing) **1.** (*old use*) to court (a woman). **2.** to try to achieve or obtain, *woo fame or success.* **3.** to seek the favour of, to try to coax or persuade, *wooing customers into the shop.*

wood *n.* **1.** the tough fibrous substance of a tree and its branches, enclosed by the bark. **2.** this cut for use as timber or fuel etc. **3.** (also *woods*) trees growing fairly densely over an area of ground. **4.** a ball of wood or other material used in the game of bowls. **5.** a golf-club with a wooden head. □ **can't see the wood for the trees**, cannot get a clear view of the whole because of too many details. **out of the wood**, clear of danger or difficulty. **wood-pigeon** *n.* a kind of large pigeon. **woods** *pl. n.* (see sense 3).

woodbine *n.* wild honeysuckle.

woodcock *n.* a kind of game-bird related to the snipe.

woodcraft *n.* knowledge of woodland conditions, especially that used in hunting.

woodcut *n.* **1.** an engraving made on wood. **2.** a print made from this, especially as an illustration in a book.

wooded *adj.* covered with growing trees.

wooden *adj.* **1.** made of wood. **2.** stiff and unnatural in manner, showing no expression or animation. **woodenly** *adv.* □ **wooden spoon**, a spoon made of wood, used in cookery or given as a prize to the competitor with the lowest score.

woodland *n.* wooded country.

woodlouse *n.* (*pl.* **woodlice**) a small wingless creature with seven pairs of legs, living in decaying wood, damp soil, etc.

woodpecker *n.* a bird that clings to tree-trunks and taps them with its beak to discover insects.

woodwind *n.* **1.** any of the wind instruments of an orchestra that are (or were originally) made of wood, e.g. clarinet, oboe. **2.** these collectively.

woodwork *n.* **1.** the art or practice of making things from wood. **2.** things made from wood, especially the wooden fittings of a house.

woodworm *n.* the larva of a kind of beetle that bores into wooden furniture and fittings.

woody *adj.* **1.** like wood, consisting of wood, *the woody parts of a plant.* **2.** full of woods, *a woody area.*

woof *n.* the gruff bark of a dog. —*v.* to bark gruffly.

woofer (woo-fer) *n.* a loudspeaker for accurately reproducing low-frequency signals.

wool *n.* **1.** the fine soft hair that forms the fleece of sheep and goats etc. **2.** yarn made from this, fabric made from this yarn. **3.** something resembling sheep's wool in texture. **4.** a Black's short curly hair. □ **pull the wool over someone's eyes**, to deceive him. **wool-gathering** *n.* being in a dreamy or absent-minded state.

woollen *adj.* made of wool. **woollens** *pl. n.* woollen cloth or clothing.

woolly *adj.* (**woollier**, **woolliest**) **1.** covered with wool or wool-like hair. **2.** like wool, woollen, *a woolly hat.* **3.** not thinking clearly, not clearly expressed or thought out, vague. —*n.* (*informal*) a knitted woollen garment, a jumper or cardigan etc. —**woolliness** *n.* □ **woolly bear**, any of several furry larvae of insects; a large hairy caterpillar.

Woolsack *n.* the large wool-stuffed cushion on which the Lord Chancellor sits in the House of Lords.

woozy *adj.* (*Amer. informal*) dizzy, dazed.

Wop *n.* (*Amer. slang, contemptuous*) a person from southern Europe, especially an Italian.

Worcester (wuus-ter) *see* Hereford and Worcester.

word *n.* **1.** a sound or sounds expressing a meaning independently and forming one of the basic elements of speech. **2.** this represented by letters or symbols. **3.** something said, a remark or statement, *he didn't utter a word; too funny for words,* extremely funny. **4.** a message, information, *we sent word of our safe arrival.* **5.** a promise or assurance; *take my word for it,* accept my assurance that it is true. **6.** a command or spoken signal, *don't fire till I give you the word.* **7.** *the Word,* (in the Gospel of St. John) the Second Person of the Trinity. —*v.* to phrase, to select words to express, *word it tactfully.* □ **by word of mouth**, in spoken (not written) words. **have a word**, to converse briefly. **have words**, to quarrel. **a man of his word**, one who keeps his promises. **take someone at his word**, to act on the assumption that he means what he says. **word for word**, in exactly the same words; *translate it word for word,* literally. **the Word of God**, the Bible; = the Word (*see* sense 7). **word of honour**, a promise made upon one's honour (*see* honour). **word-perfect** *adj.* having memorized every word perfectly. **word processor**, a typewriter keyboard with a device that records typed words and displays them on a visual display unit (*see* visual) for editing and automatically printing in the chosen format.

wording *n.* the way something is worded.

wordless *adj.* without words, not expressed in words, *wordless sympathy.*

wordy *adj.* using too many words. **wordily** *adv.,* **wordiness** *n.*

wore *see* wear [1, 2].

work *n.* 1. use of bodily or mental power in order to do or make something, especially as contrasted with play or recreation. 2. something to be undertaken, the materials for this. 3. a thing done or produced by work, the result of action. 4. a piece of literary or musical composition, *one of Mozart's later works.* 5. what a person does to earn a living, employment. 6. doings or experiences of a certain kind, *nice work!* 7. ornamentation of a certain kind, articles having this, things or parts made of certain materials or with certain tools, *fine filigree work.* —**work** *v.* 1. to perform work, to be engaged in bodily or mental activity. 2. to make efforts, *work for peace.* 3. to be employed, to have a job, *she works in a bank.* 4. to operate, to do this effectively, *it works by electricity; a tin-opener that really works; that method won't work.* 5. to operate (a thing) so as to obtain material or benefit from it, *the mine is still being worked, my partner works the Liverpool area,* covers it in his work. 6. to purchase with one's labour, *work one's passage.* 7. to cause to work or function, *he works his staff very hard; can you work the lift?* 8. to bring about, to accomplish, *work miracles.* 9. to shape or knead or hammer etc. into a desired form or consistency, *work the mixture into a paste.* 10. to do or make by needlework or fretwork etc., *work your initials on it.* 11. to excite progressively, *worked them into a frenzy.* 12. to make (a way) or pass or cause to pass slowly or by effort, *the grub works its way into timber; work the stick into the hole.* 13. to become through repeated stress or pressure, *the screw had worked loose.* 14. to be in motion, *his face worked violently.* 15. to ferment, *the yeast began to work.* □ **at work,** working; at one's place of employment; operating, having an effect, *there are secret influences at work.* **give him the works,** (*slang*) give or tell him everything; give him cruel or drastic treatment. **work-basket** *n.* a basket holding sewing materials. **work-force** *n.* the total number of workers engaged or available. **work in,**

to find a place for, to insert. **work-in** *n.* a take-over by workers of a factory etc. threatened with closure. **work of art,** a fine picture or building or composition etc. **work off,** to get rid of by activity, *worked off his annoyance on his secretary.* **work on,** to use one's influence on (a person). **work out,** to find or solve by calculation; to be calculated, *it works out at £5 each;* to plan the details etc. of, *work out a plan;* to have a specified result, *it worked out very well.* **work-out** *n.* a practice or test, especially in boxing. **work over,** to examine thoroughly; to treat with violence. **works** *pl. n.* operations in building etc.; the operative parts of a machine; a place where industrial or manufacturing processes are carried on. **work-sheet** *n.* a paper on which work done is recorded. **work-shy** *adj.* disinclined to work. **work study,** study of people's work and methods, with a view to making them more efficient. **work to rule,** to follow the rules of one's occupation with excessive strictness in order to cause delay, as a form of industrial protest. **work-to-rule** *n.* this practice. **work up,** to bring gradually to a more developed state; to excite progressively; to advance gradually to a climax.

workable *adj.* able to be worked or used or acted upon successfully.

workaday *adj.* ordinary, everyday.

workaholic *n.* (*informal*) a person who is addicted to working.

worker *n.* 1. a person who works, one who works well or in a certain way, *a slow worker.* 2. a neuter or undeveloped female bee or ant etc. that does the work of the hive or colony but cannot reproduce. 3. a member of the working class.

workhouse *n.* a former public institution where people unable to support themselves were housed and (if able-bodied) made to work.

working *adj.* engaged in work, especially manual labour, working-class, *a working man.* —*n.* a mine or quarry etc., a part of this in which work is or has been carried on, *disused mine-workings.* □ **working capital,** capital used in the carrying on of business, not invested in its buildings and equipment etc. **working class,** the class of people who are employed for wages, especially in manual or industrial work. **working-class** *adj.* of the working class. **working day,** a day on which work is regularly done; the portion of the day spent in working. **working hours,** the hours regularly spent in work. **working knowledge,** knowledge adequate for dealing with something. **working order**, a condition in which a machine etc. works satisfactorily. **working party**, a group of people appointed to investigate and report or advise on something.

workman *n.* (*pl.* workmen) **1.** a man employed to do manual labour. **2.** a person who works in a certain way, *a conscientious workman.*

workmanlike *adj.* characteristic of a good workman, practical.

workmanship *n.* a person's skill in working, the quality of this as seen in something produced.

workpiece *n.* a thing for working on with a tool or machine.

worksheet *n.* a paper on which work done is recorded.

workshop *n.* a room or building in which manual work or manufacture is carried on.

world *n.* **1.** the universe, all that exists. **2.** the earth with all its countries and peoples. **3.** a heavenly body like it. **4.** a section of the earth, *the western world.* **5.** a time or state or scene of human existence; *this world,* this mortal life. **6.** the people or things belonging to a certain class or sphere of activity, *the sporting world; the insect world.* **7.** everything, all people, *felt that the world was against him.* **8.** material things and occupations (contrasted with spiritual), *renounced the world and became a nun.* **9.** a very great amount, *it will do him a world of good; she is worlds better today.* □ **for all the world like,** precisely like. **how** *or* **why in the world,** an emphatic form of *how, why,* etc. **man** *or* **woman of the world,** a person who is experienced in the ways of human society. **not for the world** *or* **for worlds,** not for anything no matter how great. **think the world of,** to have the highest possible opinion of. **world-beater** *n.* a person or thing surpassing all others. **World Cup,** an international competition in association football, held every fourth year. **world-famous** *adj.* famous throughout the world. **world power,** a country with influence in international politics. **world war,** a war involving many important countries; *First World War,* that of 1914–18; *Second World War,* 1939–45. **world-weary** *adj.* bored with human affairs. **world-wide** *adj.* extending through the whole world.

worldling *n.* a worldly person.

worldly *adj.* **1.** of or belonging to life on earth, not spiritual. **2.** devoted to the pursuit of pleasure or material gains or advantages. **worldliness** *n.* □ **worldly goods,** property. **worldly wisdom,**

wisdom and shrewdness in dealing with worldly affairs. **worldly-wise** *adj.*

worm *n.* **1.** any of several types of animal with a soft rounded or flattened body and no backbone or limbs. **2.** the worm-like larva of certain insects. **3.** an insignificant or contemptible person. **4.** the spiral part of a screw. —**worm** *v.* **1.** to move with a twisting movement like a worm; *worm one's way* or *oneself,* make one's way by wriggling or with slow or patient progress. **2.** to obtain by crafty persistence, *wormed the secret out of him.* **3.** to rid of parasitic worms. □ **worm-cast** *n.* a tubular pile of earth sent up by an earthworm on to the surface of the ground. **worm-eaten** *adj.* full of holes made by insect-larvae. **worm's-eye view,** (*humorous*) a view as seen from below or from a humble position.

wormwood *n.* **1.** a woody plant with a bitter flavour. **2.** bitter mortification.

wormy *adj.* full of worms, worm-eaten.

worn *see* wear¹. —*adj.* **1.** damaged by use or wear. **2.** looking tired and exhausted. —**worn-out** *adj.*

worried *adj.* feeling or showing worry.

worrisome *adj.* causing worry.

worry *v.* (worried, worrying) **1.** to be troublesome to, to disturb the peace of mind of. **2.** to give way to anxiety. **3.** to seize with the teeth and shake or pull about, *the dog was worrying a rat.* —**worry** *n.* **1.** a state of worrying, mental uneasiness. **2.** something that causes this. —**worrier** *n.* □ **worry beads,** a string of beads for fiddling with to occupy or calm oneself. **worry out,** to obtain (a solution to a problem etc.) by persistent effort.

worse *adj. & adv.* **1.** more bad, more badly, more evil or ill. **2.** less good, in or into less good health or condition or circumstances. —*n.* something worse, *there's worse to come.* □ **the worse for wear,** damaged by use; injured or exhausted. **worse luck!,** such is my bad fortune.

worsen *v.* to make or become worse.

worship *n.* **1.** reverence and respect paid to God or a god. **2.** acts or ceremonies displaying this. **3.** adoration of or devotion to a person or thing. **4.** a title of respect used to or of a mayor or certain magistrates, *his worship; your worship; their worships.* —**worship** *v.* (worshipped, worshipping) **1.** to honour as a deity, to pay worship to. **2.** to take part in an act of worship. **3.** to idolize, to treat with adoration. —**worshipper** *n.*

worshipful *adj.* (in certain titles of respect) honourable, *the Worshipful Company of Goldsmiths.*

worst *adj. & adv.* most bad, most badly, most evil or ill, least good. —*n.* the worst part or feature or state or event etc., *we are prepared for the worst.* —*v.* to get the better of, to defeat or outdo. □ **at worst**, in the worst possible case. **get the worst of**, to be defeated in. **if the worst comes to the worst**, if the worst happens.

worsted (**wuu**-stid) *n.* fine smooth yarn spun from long strands of wool, fabric made from this.

wort (*pr.* wert) *n.* (*old use* except in names of plants) plant, herb, *St. John's wort.*

worth *adj.* **1.** having a specified value, *a book worth £10.* **2.** giving or likely to give a satisfactory or rewarding return for, deserving, *the book is worth reading; the scheme is worth a trial.* **3.** possessing as wealth, having property to the value of, *he was worth a million pounds when he died.* —**worth** *n.* **1.** value, merit, usefulness, *people of great worth to the community.* **2.** the amount of something that a specified sum will buy, *give me a pound's worth of stamps.* □ **for all one is worth**, (*informal*) with all one's energy, making every effort. **for what it is worth**, without any guarantee or promise of its truth or usefulness etc. **worth while** *or* **worth one's while**, worth the time or effort needed, *the scheme isn't worth while.*

worthwhile *adj.* worth while, *a worthwhile undertaking.*

worthless *adj.* having no value or usefulness. **worthlessness** *n.*

worthy *adj.* (worthier, worthiest) **1.** having great merit, deserving respect or support, *a worthy cause; worthy citizens.* **2.** having sufficient worth or merit, *the cause is worthy of support.* —*n.* a worthy person. **worthily** *adv.*, **worthiness** *n.*

would *auxiliary verb* used **1.** in senses corresponding to will[1] in the past tense (*we said we would do it*), conditional statements (*you could do it if you would try*), questions (*would they like it?*) and polite requests (*would you come in please?*). ¶ With the verbs *like, prefer, be glad,* etc., 'I would' and 'we would' are often used informally, but 'I should' and 'we should' are required in formal written English. **2.** expressing something to be expected (*that's just what he would do!*) or something that happens from time to time (*occasionally the machine would go wrong*). **3.** expressing probability, *she would be about 60 when she died.* **4.** in an incorrect use with *I* and *we* (*see* should sense 4). □

would-be *adj.* desiring or pretending to be, *a would-be humorist.*

wouldn't = would not. □ **I wouldn't know**, (*informal*), I do not know and cannot be expected to know.

wound[1] (*pr.* woond) *n.* **1.** injury done to animal or vegetable tissue by a cut, stab, blow, or tear. **2.** injury to a person's reputation or feelings etc. —*v.* to inflict a wound or wounds upon.

wound[2] (*pr.* wownd) *see* wind[2].

woundwort (**woond**-wert) *n.* a wild plant with purplish flowers and hairy stems and leaves, formerly used to make ointments.

wove *see* weave[1]. —*adj.* (of paper) made on a frame of closely woven wire.

woven *see* weave.

wow *int.* an exclamation of astonishment or admiration. —*n.* (*slang*) a sensational success. —*v.* (*slang*) to impress or excite greatly.

w.p.m. *abbrev.* words per minute.

wrack *n.* seaweed thrown up on the shore or growing there, used for manure.

wraith (*pr.* rayth) *n.* a ghost, a spectral apparition of a living person supposed to be a sign that he will die soon.

wrangle *v.* to have a noisy angry argument or quarrel. —*n.* an argument or quarrel of this kind.

wrap *v.* (wrapped, wrapping) **1.** to enclose in soft or flexible material used as a covering. **2.** to arrange (a flexible covering or a garment etc.) round a person or thing, *wrap a scarf round your neck.* —*n.* a shawl or coat or cloak etc. worn for warmth. □ **under wraps**, in concealment or secrecy. **wrap over**, (of a garment) to overlap at the edges when worn. **wrapped up in**, with one's attention deeply occupied by, *she is completely wrapped up in her children*; deeply involved in, *the country's prosperity is wrapped up in its mineral trade.* **wrap up**, to enclose in wrappings; to put on warm clothing; (*slang*) to finish, to cease talking.

wrapper *n.* **1.** a cover of paper etc. wrapped round something. **2.** a loose dressing-gown.

wrapping *n.* material used to wrap something.

wrasse (*pr.* rass) *n.* a brightly-coloured sea-fish with thick lips and strong teeth.

wrath (*pr.* roth, *rhymes with* cloth) *n.* anger, indignation.

wrathful *adj.*, full of anger or indignation. **wrathfully** *adv.*

wreak (*pr.* reek) *v.* to inflict, to cause, *wreak vengeance on a person; fog wreaked havoc with the running of trains.*

wreath (*pr.* reeth) *n.* (*pl.* wreaths, *pr.* reethz) **1.** flowers or leaves etc. fastened into a ring and used as a decoration or placed on a grave etc. as a mark of respect. **2.** a curving line of mist or smoke.

wreathe (*pr.* reeth) *v.* **1.** to encircle or decorate with or as if with a wreath. **2.** to twist into a wreath; *their faces were wreathed in smiles,* wrinkled with smiling. **3.** to wind, *the snake wreathed itself round the branch.* **4.** to move in a curving line, *smoke wreathed upwards.*

wreck *n.* **1.** the disabling or destruction of something, especially of a ship by storms or accidental damage. **2.** a ship that has suffered wreck. **3.** the remains of a greatly damaged building or vehicle or thing. **4.** a person whose physical or mental health has been damaged or destroyed, *a nervous wreck.* —*v.* to cause the wreck of, to involve in shipwreck.

wreckage *n.* **1.** the remains of something wrecked. **2.** wrecking.

wrecker *n.* **1.** a person who wrecks something. **2.** a person employed in demolition work.

wren *n.* a very small usually brown songbird.

Wren *n.* a member of the WRNS (= Women's Royal Naval Service).

wrench *v.* to twist or pull violently round, to damage or pull by twisting, *wrenched it off.* —*n.* **1.** a violent twist or twisting pull. **2.** pain caused by parting, *leaving home was a great wrench.* **3.** an adjustable tool like a spanner for gripping and turning nuts, bolts, etc.

wrest (*pr.* rest) *v.* **1.** to wrench away, *wrested his sword from him.* **2.** to obtain by effort or with difficulty, *wrested a confession from him.* **3.** to twist or distort.

wrestle *v.* **1.** to fight (especially as a sport) by grappling with a person and trying to throw him to the ground. **2.** to fight with (a person) in this way, *police wrestled him to the ground.* **3.** to struggle to deal with or overcome, *wrestled with the problem.* —*n.* a wrestling-match, a hard struggle.

wretch *n.* **1.** a very unfortunate or miserable person. **2.** a despicable person. **3.** (in playful use) a rascal.

wretched (**rech**-id) *adj.* **1.** miserable, unhappy. **2.** of poor quality, unsatisfactory. **3.** causing discomfort or nuisance, confounded, *this wretched car won't start.* **wretchedly** *adv.,* **wretchedness** *n.*

wriggle *v.* to move with short twisting movements; *wriggle out of a difficulty,* escape from it cunningly. —*n.* a wriggling movement.

wring *v.* (wrung, wringing) **1.** to twist and squeeze in order to remove liquid. **2.** to remove (liquid) in this way. **3.** to squeeze

firmly or forcibly; *they wrung his hand,* squeezed it warmly or emotionally; *wring one's hands,* squeeze them together emotionally; *wring the bird's neck,* kill it by twisting its neck. **4.** to extract or obtain with effort or difficulty, *wrung a promise from him.* —*n.* a wringing movement, a squeeze or twist. □ **wringing wet,** so wet that moisture can be wrung from it.

wringer *n.* a device with a pair of rollers between which washed clothes etc. are passed so that water is squeezed out.

wrinkle *n.* **1.** a small crease, a small furrow or ridge in the skin (especially the kind produced by age). **2.** (*informal*) a useful hint about how to do something. —*v.* to make wrinkles in, to form wrinkles.

wrist *n.* **1.** the joint connecting hand and forearm. **2.** the part of a garment covering this. □ **wrist-watch** *n.* a watch worn on a strap or band etc. round the wrist.

wristlet *n.* a band or bracelet etc. worn round the wrist.

writ[1] (*pr.* rit) *n.* a formal written command issued by a lawcourt or ruling authority directing a person to act or refrain from acting in a certain way. **Holy Writ,** the Bible.

writ[2] *adj.* (*old use*) written. **writ large,** in an emphasized form, clearly recognizable.

write *v.* (wrote, written, writing) **1.** to make letters or other symbols on a surface, especially with a pen or pencil on paper. **2.** to form (letters or words or a message etc.) in this way; *write a cheque,* write the appropriate figures and words and signature etc. to make it valid. **3.** to compose in written form for publication, to be an author, *write books* or *music*; *he makes a living by writing.* **4.** to write and send a letter, *write to me often.* **5.** (*Amer.*) to write to, *I will write you soon.* **6.** to indicate clearly, *guilt was written all over her.* **7.** to enter (data) in or on any computer storage device or medium, to transfer from one storage device or medium to another, to output. □ **write down,** to put into writing. **write off,** to cancel; to recognize as lost. **write-off** *n.* something written off as lost, a vehicle too badly damaged to be worth repairing. **write out,** to write (a thing) in full or in a finished form. **write up,** to write an account of; to write entries in (a diary etc.); to praise in writing. **write-up** *n.* a published written account of something, a review.

writer *n.* **1.** a person who writes or has written something, one who writes in a certain way. **2.** a person who writes books etc., an author. □ **writer's cramp,** cramp in the muscles of the hand. **Writer to the**

Signet, a Scottish solicitor who conducts cases in the Court of Session.

writhe (*pr.* ry*th*) *v.* **1.** to twist one's body about, as in pain. **2.** to wriggle, *writhing snakes*. **3.** to suffer because of great shame or embarrassment, *writhing under the insult*.

writing *n.* **1.** handwriting. **2.** literary work, a piece of this, *in the writings of Charles Dickens*. □ **in writing**, in written form.

writing-case *n.* a case holding paper etc. for use in writing. **the writing on the wall**, an event signifying that something is doomed (¶ after the Biblical story of the writing that appeared on the wall of Belshazzar's palace, foretelling his doom).

writing-paper *n.* paper for writing on, especially for writing letters.

written *see* write.

wrong *adj.* **1.** (of conduct or actions) morally bad, contrary to justice or to what is right. **2.** incorrect, not true. **3.** not what is required or suitable or most desirable, *backed the wrong horse*; *get hold of the wrong end of the stick*, misunderstand a statement or situation; *wrong side*, (of fabric) the side that is not meant to show. **4.** not in a normal condition, not functioning normally, *there's something wrong with the gearbox*. —*adv.* in a wrong manner or direction, mistakenly, *you guessed wrong* —**wrong** *n.* **1.** what is morally wrong, a wrong action. **2.** injustice, an unjust action or treatment, *they did us a great wrong*. —**wrong** *v.* **1.** to do wrong to, to treat unjustly, *a wronged wife*. **2.** to attribute bad motives to (a person) mistakenly. —**wrongly** *adv.*, **wrongness** *n.* □ **get a person wrong**, to misunderstand him. **in the wrong**, not having justice or truth on one's side. **on the wrong side of**, in disfavour with or not liked by (a person); *on the wrong side of forty*, over 40 years old. **wrong-foot** *v.* to catch (a person) unprepared. **wrong-headed** *adj.* perverse and obstinate. **wrong 'un**, (*informal*) a person of bad character.

wrongdoer *n.* a person who acts contrary to law or to moral standards. **wrongdoing** *n.*

wrongful *adj.* contrary to what is fair or just or legal. **wrongfully** *adv.*

wrote *see* write.

wrought (*pr.* rawt) (*old use*) = worked. —*adj.* (of metals) beaten out or shaped by hammering. **wrought iron**, iron made by forging or rolling, not cast.

wrung *see* wring.

WRVS *abbrev.* Women's Royal Voluntary Service.

wry (*pr. as* rye) *adj.* (wryer, wryest) **1.**

twisted or bent out of shape. **2.** twisted into an expression of disgust or disappointment or mockery, *a wry face*. **3.** (of humour) dry and mocking. **wryly** *adv.*, **wryness** *n.*

wryneck *n.* a small bird related to the woodpecker, able to twist its head over its shoulder.

WS *abbrev.* Writer to the Signet.

wt. *abbrev.* weight.

W.Va. *abbrev.* West Virginia.

WW *abbrev.* World War.

WX *abbrev.* women's extra-large size.

wych-elm *n.* a kind of elm with broader leaves and more spreading branches than the common elm.

wynd (*rhymes with* mind) *n.* (*Scottish*) a narrow street, an alley.

Wyo. *abbrev.* Wyoming.

Wyoming (wy-**oh**-ming) a State of the USA.

Xx

xenophobia (zen-ŏ-**foh**-biä) *n.* strong dislike or distrust of foreigners.

Xerox (**zeer**-oks) *n.* (*trade mark*) **1.** a process for producing photocopies without the use of wet materials. **2.** a photocopy made in this way. —**xerox** *v.* to photocopy by a process of this kind.

Xmas *n.* = Christmas. ¶ The *X* represents the Greek letter chi (=ch), the first letter of *Christos* (the Greek word for *Christ*).

X-ray *n.* a photograph or examination made by means of a kind of electromagnetic radiation (*X-rays*) that can penetrate solids and make it possible to see into or through them —*v.* to photograph or examine or treat by this radiation.

xylophone (**zy**-lŏ-fohn) *n.* a musical instrument consisting of flat wooden bars, graduated in length, which produce different notes when struck with small hammers.

Yy

yacht (*pr.* yot) *n.* **1.** a light sailing-vessel for racing. **2.** a similar vessel for travel on sand or ice. **3.** a vessel used for private pleasure excursions. **yachtsman** *n.*

yachting *n.* racing or cruising in a yacht.

yack *v.* (*slang*) to chatter persistently.

yackety-yack *n.* (*slang*) persistent chatter.

yah *int.* an exclamation of scorn or defiance.

yak *n.* a long-haired ox of central Asia.
Yale *n.* (*trade mark*) a type of lock for doors etc.
yam *n.* **1.** the edible starchy tuber of a tropical climbing plant, the plant itself. **2.** the sweet potato (*see* sweet).
yank *v.* (*informal*) to pull with a sudden sharp tug. —*n.* (*informal*) a sudden sharp tug.
Yank *n.* (*informal*) = Yankee.
Yankee *n.* **1.** an American. **2.** (*Amer.*) an inhabitant of the northern States of the USA.
yap *n.* a shrill bark. —*v.* (yapped, yapping) **1.** to bark shrilly. **2.** (*informal*) to chatter.
yarborough (yar-ber-ŏ) *n.* a hand of cards in whist or bridge with no card above a 9. ¶ Named after the Earl of Yarborough (19th century) who is said to have betted against its occurrence.
yard¹ *n.* **1.** a measure of length, = 3 feet or 0·9144 metre. **2.** a long pole-like piece of wood stretched horizontally or crosswise from a mast to support a sail. □ **yard-arm** *n.* either end of a yard supporting a sail.
yard² *n.* **1.** a piece of enclosed ground, especially one attached to a building or surrounded by buildings or used for a particular kind of work etc., *a timber yard*. **2.** *the Yard*, (*informal*) Scotland Yard.
yardage *n.* a length measured in yards.
yardstick *n.* a standard of comparison.
yarn *n.* **1.** any spun thread, especially of the kinds prepared for knitting or weaving or rope-making. **2.** (*informal*) a tale, especially one that is exaggerated or invented. —*v.* (*informal*) to tell yarns.
yarrow (ya-roh) *n.* a plant with feathery leaves and strong-smelling white or pinkish flowers.
yashmak *n.* a veil concealing the face except for the eyes, worn in public by Muslim women in certain countries.
yaw *v.* (of a ship or aircraft etc.) to fail to hold a straight course, to turn from side to side. —*n.* a yawing movement or course.
yawl *n.* **1.** a kind of sailing-boat with two masts. **2.** a kind of fishing-boat.
yawn *v.* **1.** to open the mouth wide and draw in breath (often involuntarily), as when sleepy or bored. **2.** to have a wide opening, to form a chasm. —**yawn** *n.* **1.** the act of yawning. **2.** (*informal*) something boring.
yaws *n.* a tropical skin-disease causing raspberry-like swellings.
yd. *abbrev.* yard. **yds.** *abbrev.* yards.
ye¹ *pronoun*, (*old use*) you.

ye² *adj.* (*supposed old use*) the, *ye olde teashoppe*.
yea (*pr.* yay) *adv.* & *n.* (*old use*) yes.
yeah (*pr.* yair) *adv.* (*informal*) yes. **oh yeah?**, an expression of incredulity.
year *n.* **1.** the time taken by the earth to make one complete orbit of the sun, about 365¼ days. **2.** the period from 1 January to 31 December inclusive. **3.** any period of twelve consecutive months. □ **year-book** *n.* an annual publication containing current information about a particular subject.
years *pl. n.* age, time of life, *he looks younger than his years*; a very long time, *we've been waiting for years*.
yearling (yer-ling) *n.* an animal between 1 and 2 years old.
yearly *adj.* happening or published or payable etc. once a year, annual. —*adv.* annually.
yearn *v.* to be filled with great longing.
yeast *n.* a kind of fungus that causes alcohol and carbon dioxide to be produced while it is developing, used to cause fermentation in making beer and wines and as a raising agent in baking.
yeasty *adj.* frothy like yeast when it is developing. **yeastiness** *n.*
yell *v.* to give a loud cry, to shout. —*n.* a loud cry, a shout.
yellow *adj.* **1.** of the colour of buttercups and ripe lemons, or a colour approaching this. **2.** (*informal*) cowardly. —**yellow** *n.* **1.** yellow colour. **2.** a yellow substance or material, yellow clothes. —*v.* to make or become yellow. —**yellowness** *n.* □ **yellow fever**, a tropical disease with fever and jaundice. **yellow line(s)**, line(s) painted on the road beside a pavement to indicate that there are restrictions on the parking of vehicles. **yellow pages**, a section of a telephone directory printed on yellow pages and grouping entries for businesses under the type of goods or services that they offer. **yellow streak**, (*informal*) cowardice in a person's character.
yellowhammer *n.* a kind of bunting, the male of which has yellow head, neck, and breast.
yellowish *adj.* rather yellow.
yelp *n.* a sharp shrill cry or bark. —*v.* to utter a yelp.
Yemen (yem-ĕn) the name of two countries in the Arabian peninsula, *the Yemen Arab Republic* and *the People's Democratic Republic of Yemen*. **Yemeni** (yem-ĕni) *adj.* & *n.*, **Yemenite** (yem-ĕn-nyt) *adj.* & *n.*
yen¹ *n.* (*pl.* yen) the unit of money in Japan.
yen² *n.* (*Amer.*) a longing, a yearning.
yeoman (yoh-măn) *n.* (*pl.* yeomen) a man

who owns and farms a small estate.
yeoman of signals, a petty officer in the
Navy, concerned with signalling by flags
and other visual means. **Yeoman of the
Guard,** a member of the British sovereign's bodyguard, wearing Tudor dress as
uniform. **yeoman service,** long and useful
service.

yes *adv.* **1.** it is so, the statement is correct.
2. what you request or command will be
done. **3.** (as a question) what do you want?
4. (in answer to a summons etc.) I am
here. —*n.* the word or answer 'yes'. □
yes-man *n.* a man who always agrees
with his superior in a weak or sycophantic
way.

yesterday *n.* **1.** the day before today.
2. the recent past. —*adv.* on the day
before today, in the recent past.

yet *adv.* **1.** up to this or that time and continuing, still, *there's life in the old dog yet.*
2. by this or that time, so far, *it hasn't
happened yet.* **3.** besides, in addition, *heard
it yet again.* **4.** before the matter is done
with, eventually, *I'll be even with you yet.*
5. even, *she became yet more excited.* **6.**
nevertheless, *strange yet true.* —*conj.*
nevertheless, but in spite of that, *he
worked hard, yet he failed.*

yeti (yet-i) *n.* (*pl.* yetis) the native (Sherpa)
name for the 'Abominable Snowman' (*see*
abominable).

yew *n.* **1.** an evergreen tree with dark
green needle-like leaves and red berries.
2. its wood.

Yiddish *n.* a language used by Jews of cen-
tral and eastern Europe, based on a
German dialect and with words from
Hebrew and various modern languages.

yield *v.* **1.** to give or return as fruit or gain
or result, *the land yields good crops; the
investment yields 15.* **2.** to surrender, to
do what is requested or ordered, *the town
yielded; he yielded to persuasion.* **3.** to be
inferior or confess inferiority, *I yield to
none in appreciation of his merits.* **4.** (of
traffic) to allow other traffic to have right
of way. **5.** to be able to be forced out
of the natural or usual shape, e.g. under
pressure. —*n.* the amount yielded or produced, the quantity obtained.

yippee *int.* an exclamation of excitement.

YMCA *abbrev.* Young Men's Christian
Association.

yob *n.* (*slang*) a lout, a hooligan.

yobbo *n.* (*pl.* yobbos) (*slang*) = yob.

yodel (yoh-d'l) *v.* (yodelled, yodelling)
to sing, or utter a musical call, so that
the voice alternates continually between
falsetto and its normal pitch. —*n.* a
yodelling cry. —**yodeller** *n.*

yoga (yoh-gă) *n.* a Hindu system of meditation and self-control designed to produce mystical experience and spiritual
insight.

yoghurt (yog-ert) *n.* a food prepared from
milk that has been thickened by the action
of certain bacteria.

yoke *n.* **1.** a wooden cross-piece fastened
over the necks of two oxen or other animals pulling a cart or plough etc. **2.** a
piece of timber shaped to fit a person's
shoulders and to hold a pail or other load
slung from each end. **3.** a part of a garment fitting round the shoulders or hips
and from which the rest hangs. **4.** oppression, burdensome restraint, *throw off
the yoke of servitude.* —**yoke** *v.* **1.** to put a
yoke upon, to harness by means of a yoke,
yoke oxen to the plough. **2.** to unite, *yoked
to an unwilling partner.*

yokel (yoh-kĕl) *n.* a simple country fellow,
a country bumpkin.

yolk (*rhymes with* coke) *n.* the round
yellow internal part of an egg.

yomp *v.* (*slang*) to march across country
while humping one's heavy equipment and
weapons.

yon *adj.* & *adv.* (*dialect*) yonder.

yonder *adv.* over there. —*adj.* situated or
able to be seen over there.

yore *n.* **of yore,** of long ago.

yorker *n.* a ball bowled in cricket so that it
pitches just in front of the batsman.

Yorks. *abbrev.* Yorkshire.

Yorkshire a former county of England,
now divided among Humberside, North
Yorkshire, and the metropolitan counties
of South Yorkshire and West Yorkshire.
Yorkshire pudding, a baked batter pudding eaten with roast beef. **Yorkshire
terrier,** a small long-haired terrier.

you *pronoun* **1.** the person(s) addressed. **2.**
one, anyone, everyone, *you never can tell.*

you'd = you had, you would.

you'll = you will.

young *adj.* **1.** having lived or existed for
only a short time; *the young,* young
people; *the younger sons of earls,* those who
are not the eldest. **2.** not far advanced in
time, *the night is young.* **3.** youthful, having
little experience. **4.** used in speaking of or
to a young person, *young Smith.* —*n.* the
offspring of animals, before or soon after
birth.

youngish *adj.* fairly young.

youngster *n.* a young person, a child.

your *adj.* of or belonging to you.

you're = you are.

yours *possessive pronoun* **1.** belonging to
you, the thing(s) belonging to you. **2.** used
in phrases for ending letters, **Yours** or

Yours ever, used casually to friends. Yours faithfully, used for ending business or formal letters beginning 'Dear Sir' or 'Dear Madam'. Yours sincerely, used in letters to acquaintances and to friends (other than close friends), and often also in business letters addressing a person by name (e.g. beginning 'Dear Mr Brown'), where it is now more frequently used than *yours truly*. Yours truly, used to slight acquaintances and in business letters (less formal than *yours faithfully* but more formal than *yours sincerely*); (*informal*) = me, *the awkward jobs are always left for yours truly*. Yours very truly, a ceremonious form of *Yours truly* (now seldom used).

¶ It is incorrect to write *your's* (see the note under its).

yourself *pronoun* (*pl.* yourselves) corresponding to *you*, used in the same ways as himself.

youth *n.* (*pl.* youths, *pr.* yoo*thz*) 1. being young. 2. the period between childhood and maturity, the vigour or lack of experience etc. characteristic of this. 3. a young man, *a youth of 16*. 4. young people collectively, *the youth of the country*. □ **youth club,** a club where leisure activities are provided for young people. **youth hostel,** a hostel providing cheap accommodation where young people who are hiking or on holiday etc. may stay overnight. **youth hostelling,** staying in youth hostels.

youthful *adj.* 1. young, looking or seeming young. 2. characteristic of young people, *youthful impatience*. **youthfully** *adv.*, **youthfulness** *n.*

you've = you have.

yowl *n.* a loud wailing cry, a howl. —*v.* to utter a yowl.

Yo-yo *n.* (*pl.* Yo-yos) (*trade mark*) a toy consisting of two circular parts with a deep groove between, which can be made to rise and fall on a string (attached to it) when this is jerked by a finger.

YT *abbrev.* Yukon Territory.

yucca (**yuk**-ă) *n.* a tall plant with white bell-like flowers and stiff spiky leaves.

Yugoslavia (yoo-gŏ-**slah**-viă) a country in the Balkans, bordering on the Adriatic Sea. **Yugoslav** (**yoo**-gŏ-slahv), **Yugoslavian** *adjs.* & *ns.*

Yukon (**yoo**-kon) a Territory of north-west Canada.

yule (*pr.* yool) *n.* (*old use*) the Christmas festival, also called *yule-tide*. **yule log,** a large log traditionally burnt in the hearth on Christmas Eve.

YWCA *abbrev.* Young Women's Christian Association.

Zz

Zaïre (zah-**eer**) a country in Central Africa. **Zaïrean** *adj.* & *n.*

Zambia a country in Central Africa. **Zambian** *adj.* & *n.*

zany *n.* a comical or eccentric person. — *adj.* (zanier, zaniest) crazily funny.

zap *v.* (zapped, zapping) (*slang*) to hit, to attack, to knock out, to kill.

zeal (*pr.* zeel) *n.* enthusiasm, hearty and persistent effort.

zealot (**zel**-ŏt) *n.* a zealous person, a fanatic.

zealous (**zel**-ŭs) *adj.* full of zeal. **zealously** *adv.*

zebra (**zeb**-ră) *n.* an African animal of the horse family with a body entirely covered by black and white stripes. **zebra crossing,** a pedestrian crossing where the road is marked with broad white stripes.

zebu (**zee**-bew) *n.* a humped ox found in India, East Asia, and Africa.

Zen *n.* a form of Buddhism emphasizing the value of meditation and intuition.

zenith (**zen**-ith) *n.* 1. the part of the sky that is directly above an observer. 2. the highest point, *his power was at its zenith*.

zephyr (**zef**-er) *n.* a soft gentle wind.

zero *n.* (*pl.* zeros) 1. nought, the figure 0. 2. nothing, nil. 3. the point marked 0 on a graduated scale, especially on a thermometer. 4. the temperature corresponding to zero. —*v.* (zeroed, zeroing) to adjust (an instrument etc.) to zero. □ **zero hour,** the hour at which something is timed to begin. **zero in on,** to focus one's aim on, to go purposefully towards. **zero-rated** *adj.* (of goods or services) on which the purchaser pays no VAT and the seller can reclaim any VAT he has paid in connection with his work.

zest *n.* 1. keen enjoyment or interest. 2. a pleasantly stimulating quality, *the risk added zest to the adventure*. 3. the coloured part of the peel of an orange or lemon etc., used as flavouring. **zestful** *adj.*, **zestfully** *adv.*

zigzag *n.* a line or course that turns right and left alternately at sharp angles. —*adj.* & *adv.* forming or in a zigzag. —*v.* (zigzagged, zigzagging) to move in a zigzag course.

Zimbabwe (zim-**bahb**-wi) a country in central Africa. **Zimbabwean** *adj.* & *n.*

zinc *n.* a hard bluish-white metal.

zinnia (**zin**-iă) *n.* a daisy-like garden plant with brightly-coloured flowers.

Zion (**zy**-ŏn) *n.* 1. the holy hill of ancient Jerusalem, *Mount Zion*. 2. the Jewish religion. **3.** the Christian Church. **4.** the kingdom of heaven.

Zionism (zy-ŏn-izm) *n.* a movement founded in 1897 that has sought and achieved the founding of a Jewish homeland in Palestine. **Zionist** *n.*

zip *n.* **1.** a short sharp sound like that of a bullet going through the air. **2.** energy, vigour, liveliness. **3.** a zip-fastener. —**zip** *v.* (zipped, zipping) **1.** to open or close with a zip-fastener. **2.** to move with the sound of 'zip' or at high speed. □ **zip-bag** *n.* a travel-bag fastened by a zip-fastener. **zip-fastener** *n.* a fastening device consisting of two flexible strips of material with projections that interlock when brought together by a sliding tab.

zipper *n.* a zip-fastener.

zippy *adj.* (zippier, zippiest) lively and vigorous. **zippiness** *n.*

zircon (zer-kon) *n.* a bluish-white gem cut from a translucent mineral.

zither (zi*th*-er) *n.* a musical instrument with many strings stretched over a shallow box-like body, played by plucking with the fingers of both hands.

zodiac (zoh-di-ak) *n.* (in astrology) **1.** a band of the sky containing the paths of the sun, moon, and principal planets, divided into twelve equal parts (called *signs of the zodiac*) each named from a constellation that was formerly situated in it. **2.** a diagram of these signs. **zodiacal** (zŏ-**dy**-ăkăl) *adj.*

zombie *n.* **1.** (in voodoo) a corpse said to have been revived by witchcraft. **2.** (*informal*) a person thought to resemble this, one who seems to have no mind or will.

zone *n.* an area that has particular characteristics or a particular purpose or use. —*v.* **1.** to divide into zones. **2.** to arrange or distribute by zones, to assign to a particular area. —**zonal** *adj.*

zoo *n.* a place where wild animals are kept for exhibition and study.

zoology (zoh-**ol**-ŏji *or* zoo-ol-ŏji) *n.* the scientific study of animals. **zoological** *adj.* **zoologist** *n.* an expert in zoology. □ **zoological gardens,** a zoo.

zoom *v.* **1.** to move quickly, especially with a buzzing sound. **2.** to rise quickly, *prices had zoomed.* **3.** (in photography) to alter the size of the image by means of a zoom lens. □ **zoom lens,** a camera lens that can be adjusted from a long shot to a close-up (and vice versa), giving an effect of going steadily closer to (or further from) the subject.

Zoroastrian (zo-roh-**ast**-ri-ăn) *n.* a person who believes in **Zoroastrianism,** the ancient Persian religion based on the teachings of Zoroaster or Zarathustra (6th century BC) and his followers. —*adj.* of Zoroaster or Zoroastrianism.

zucchini (zuuk-ee-ni) *n.* (*pl.* zucchini *or* zucchinis) a courgette.

Zulu *n.* (*pl.* Zulus) **1.** a member of a Bantu people of South Africa. **2.** their language.